The Almanac
of American Politics
1976

*The Senators, the Representatives,
the Governors—their records,
states, and districts*

Michael Barone
Grant Ujifusa
Douglas Matthews

A Sunrise Book

E.P. Dutton & Co., Inc. New York

Respectfully dedicated to that vanishing species,
The American Voter.

ACKNOWLEDGMENTS

The authors gratefully acknowledge Joan Barone, without whom this book would probably never have been written; Christopher Buchanan, Betty Anne Clarke, Kim Hines, Tim Horan, Joe Iseman, Becca Lacy, Sheine Lacy, Keech Legrande, Kathy Ujifusa, Candy Verhulst, Nancy Greene Zanes, David Zimansky. Photo credits to Dev O'Neill.

Special thanks to Stewart Mott and Michael Ryan.

Published simultaneously in Canada by
Clarke, Irwin & Company Limited, Toronto and Vancouver

ISBN: 0-87690-187-9 (Cloth)
ISBN: 0-87690-188-7 (Paper)
Library of Congress Catalog Card Number: 72-96875

Dutton-Sunrise Inc., a subsidiary of E.P. Dutton & Co., Inc.

CONTENTS

ABBREVIATIONS

ABS	Absent *or* Abstain
ACA	Americans for Constitutional Action
ADA	Americans for Democratic Action
AEC	Atomic Energy Commission
AIP	American Independent party
CFA	Consumer Federation of America
CG	Coast Guard
CHOB	Cannon House Office Building
Co.	County, Company
Com.	committee
Const.	Constitutional party
COPE	Committee on Political Education
CSC	Civil Service Commission
D	Democrat
DFL	Democrat-Farmer-Labor party
DOC	Department of Commerce
DOD	Department of Defense
DOI	Department of the Interior
DOJ	Department of Justice
DOT	Department of Transportation
HEW	Department of Health, Education, and Welfare
HUD	Department of Housing and Urban Development
Ind.	Independent
Jt. Com.	Joint Committee
LCV	League of Conservation Voters
LHOB	Longworth House Office Building
Lib.	Liberal party
LWV	League of Women Voters
NAB	National Association of Businessmen
NASA	National Aeronautics and Space Agency
NE	Not [yet] Elected
NFU	National Farmers' Union
NSI	National Security Index of the American Security Council
NSOB	New Senate Office Building
OEO	Office of Economic Opportunity
OSOB	Old Senate Office Building
PF	Peace and Freedom party
P.O.	Post Office
R	Republican
Rank. Mbr.	Ranking Member
RHOB	Rayburn House Office Building
Sel. Com.	Select Committee
Sp. Com.	Special Committee
Sub.	Subcommittee
SW	Socialist Worker party
TD	Treasury Department
USAF	United States Air Force
USAFR	United States Air Force Reserve
USDA	United States Department of Agriculture
USMC	United States Marine Corps
USMCR	United States Marine Corps Reserve
VA	Veterans Administration

INTRODUCTION

The American political system is alive but ailing. In the last two years, the Congress, the courts and the press proved that even Presidents were subject to the rule of law, and the people saw the nation through the impeachment process with aplomb. But it was the same political system and the same people who had—not two years earlier—put Richard Nixon back into the White House by the largest popular vote margin in our history.

In the same period, and in large part because of the same scandal that toppled Nixon, the Congress finally got around to reforming our system of financing political campaigns. But even as the Congressmen were voting public subsidies for presidential candidates, they flatly refused to vote subsidies for congressional contests—which would have meant public money in the hands of their own opponents.

Less than a year after Nixon resigned, the war which had bedevilled his administration and Lyndon Johnson's before that finally ended, as the Khmer Rouge streamed into Phnom Penh and the Viet Cong renamed Saigon Ho Chi Minh City. Even though more than 50,000 Americans had died in what used to be called Indochina, the vast majority of Americans were quite willing, if not pleased, to let those places pass under the communist control.

Indeed, on all three of these issues—Watergate, campaign finance reform, Vietnam—public opinion had long been ahead of the politicians. The public became convinced of the President's guilt after the Saturday Night Massacre of October 1973, but the politicians paid little mind until anti-Nixon Democrats won five out of six special House elections (including Gerald Ford's seat in Grand Rapids) in the winter and spring of 1974. (See Michigan 5, 8, Pennsylvania 12, Ohio 1, California 5.) The public favored campaign finance reform long before Congress got around to doing anything about it. And the public response to the communist victories in Vietnam and Cambodia was not a bang, but a barely audible whimper—the public had fully expected it, and any anger the voters may have felt had long since vanished.

None of these things were understood early on by the politicians who occupy most of the top positions in Washington and the state capitals. Most of them—and all our Presidents from John Kennedy to Gerald Ford—grew to physical maturity in the years just before World War II, and into political maturity in the years just after. They absorbed, all too well, the lessons of the 1940s: the notion, in those days when the memory of Franklin Roosevelt was warm, that the public revered their President and resented any attack against him; the perception that the people would tolerate political hanky-panky if they liked the men at the top; the ironclad rule that no American President dare "lose" an Asian country to communists.

The elections of 1974 saw a transfer of power, in some minimal way, from this World War II generation which seems to have made such a botch of things to the generation which sooner or later must take over. The effects were most noticeable in the House of Representatives, where 75 new freshmen Democrats started a sort of revolution, and expelled three committee chairmen from power, and watched with detachment as Wilbur Mills's personal problems suddenly made him the *former* all-powerful Chairman of the House Ways and Means Committee. The freshmen had the courage to hold fast when President Ford and others of his generation called for increased American military aid to Vietnam and Cambodia—aid which would inevitably have led to American casualties and a step back into the quagmire of involvement. They understood, as Ford apparently did not, that the political axioms of the McCarthy era no longer applied. When it came to enacting their own legislative program, though, the freshmen and congressional Democrats had more trouble. At least at this writing, they were unable to overcome the inherent tendency of the legislative process toward delay and obstruction—or to summon up enough votes to override Ford's vetoes.

The people and the voters—and they are not quite the same, since fewer than half those eligible bothered to vote in 1974—are skeptical and sour; they doubt that government can accomplish much, and they don't believe much in politicians. The politicians who are willing to break away from the old rules—whether labelled left, right, or center, conservative or liberal in the old terminology—have not yet reached positions of power, or at least have not learned how to use the positions they have won. The result is a stalemate, and a tension. As David Broder of the Washington *Post* has pointed out, most of the major departures from the politics of the World War II generation are taking place in the states and, to an even greater extent, in local communities. These departures have yet to become decisive at the national level.

The Almanac of American Politics 1976 is a book primarily about that national level. We devote most of our attention to the Congress, although we do cover the political background of the Presidency and the various Governorships. For however much the institution may lag behind public opinion, and however low its standing in public opinion polls, it is the Congress that continues to affect most markedly the lives of Americans through its action—or inaction—in areas from energy policy to pension reform.

It is a feature of our system—and, we believe, a virtue—that officeholders of the greatest obscurity are sometimes called on to perform tasks of the greatest importance; an example is Peter Rodino, who, against the expectations of some, led the House Judiciary Committee carefully and fairly as it decided to impeach Richard Nixon. Another example, of course, is Gerald Ford, who, most people agree, has done a much more creditable job of being President than his critics had predicted.

One aim of the *Almanac* is to provide portraits of currently obscure figures in American politics who may play more important and visible roles in the years ahead—the Gerald Fords and Peter Rodinos of tomorrow. Another is to provide a picture of how the Congress works, and how members of Congress think and vote. But probably the most important aim is to provide a political portrait of the entire nation, state by state and congressional district by congressional district.

To list some important conditions, trends, and harbingers found within the states and districts:

Pennsylvania 7
New York 29
The kinds of seats the Democrats will have to hold if they want to maintain the bulge they now have in the House.

Ohio 23
The snarling apathy among working class Americans generally, and here the resentment of a Catholic incumbent Governor putting on a WASPy personal style.

New Jersey 1
Urban and suburban ethnics betrayed by the Nixon law and order rhetoric come back to the Democratic Party.

North Carolina
The Sam Ervin Revolution in Nixon Country.

Texas 13
Illinois 10
The unanticipated effects of Watergate—Republican candidates lose because Republican voters stay home.

Wisconsin 3
The gains made by Democrats in the Upper Midwest among morality-conscious outlanders.

Iowa 5
A congressional candidate shovels manure to get closer to the work-a-day world of ordinary citizens.

Colorado
Arizona
The transformation of a political culture by an influx of new arrivals.

Michigan 17
The crucial place of a new kind of liberal volunteer organization.

Massachusetts 9
The clout of the post-student generation in a busing-obsessed city.

Maine
The rise of the Independent politician, something that strikes fear in the hearts of party leaders everywhere.

California 23
The disintergration of the Reagan (anti-black, anti-hippie, anti-intellectual) constituency. See also New York and New York 1.

California
The trend-setter state elects a Governor espousing the politics of austerity and no bullshit.

Whether or not you are a political "buff," the social, ethnic, and economic factors which lead groups of Americans to believe one way or another are a fascinating study. Thus the *Almanac* is not only a field guide to the history and habits of the American political animal, but a portrait of the American people: what they believe, and why they believe what they do.

I. THE GOVERNOR—THE SENATOR—THE REPRESENTATIVE

A. Biographies and Career
This section lists the date each Governor, Senator, and Representative was first elected, when the Governors' and Senators' seats are up, their residence, and relevant facts about their personal background. Also listed is a brief outline of the politician's career, and his or her home and capitol offices—complete with telephone numbers.

B. Committees
Lawyers and pollsters know that the power to frame the question is often the power to determine the answer. In the Congress, as in most legislative bodies, the questions are usually framed by committees. Although bills may usually be amended on the floor, what comes out of committee remains the point of departure. Particularly in the House, committee decisions are so often ratified by the body as a whole that you might well think of your vote as electing a Representative to a committee rather than to the Congress as a whole.

Everyone who has read any of the literature about Congress knows about the power of committee chairmen. They can schedule meetings, nurse along or stifle legislation, and push bills through on the floor by main force. But all of these powers have been significantly curtailed in the last two years. In the House, committee meetings must be open to the public unless the committee votes, publicly, to close them; the more traditional Senate is moving slowly toward the same procedure. New, young members are no longer automatically following the lead of their chairmen. Most important, every chairman, at least in the House, knows that there are limits to how arbitrarily he can run his committee and how far he can deviate from the policies favored by a majority of his party—because chairmen can now be booted out. That is what the House Democratic Caucus did to Edward Hebert (Armed Services), Wright Patman (Banking), and Bob Poage (Agriculture). And every Chairman knows it could happen to him or her in the future.

Another significant change has come in the way committee assignments are made. It you are a newly elected Congressman from Iowa, you might very well want to sit on the Agriculture Committee. In the past you would have had to plead your case before your party's Committee on Committees, which was invariably dominated by senior members more conservative than the party as whole. That is still largely true of Republicans, but among Democrats there were big changes in 1974 and 1975. In the House, the committee assignment power was taken away from Wilbur Mills's Ways and Means Democrats and given to the more liberal Steering committee. And in the Senate, important assignments went to liberals rather than conservatives; thus James Abourezk of South Dakota rather than James Allen of Alabama won Sam Ervin's seat on the Senate Judiciary Committee.

The seniority system generally still holds sway, but it is no longer adhered to dogmatically. A member who got a seat on Ways and Means in 1958 still has seniority over a member who got his seat in 1965, but the senior member is no longer guaranteed automatic elevation to the Chairmanship when he becomes the most senior majority member on the committee.

In the committee section, we have listed each member's committee and subcommittee assignments and in parentheses his or her seniority on the committee and subcommittee. Seniority is calculated with reference only to other members of the same party. For Democrats, the first ranking member is the chairman, the second one is "2nd", and so on. (This is a slight variation from Congress's own method, which denominates the second person as "ranking member," but we believe our way is clearer for most readers.) For the Republicans, the most senior member is called the ranking member, the next one "2nd," and so on. In the appendix we have listed the full membership of all standing committees and subcommittees.

The following is a list of the committees of both branches, with a short description of the types of bills each considers. Jurisdictional boundaries are often fuzzy, so there will be some overlapping. More complete descriptions of important committees and subcommittees will be found in the Political Background sections of their chairmen.

Standing Committees of the Senate

Aeronautical and Space Sciences—aerospace activities and science (except military), NASA.
Agriculture and Forestry—agriculture, meat inspection, forestry, nutrition and antihunger programs, rural electrification.
Appropriations—all federal appropriations. Since the Appropriations Committee passes on federal spending for all departments and agencies, its subcommittees with jurisdiction over a given segment of the federal government are often as important in making policy as the standing committee with power over the same agency.
Armed Services—defense, naval petroleum reserves.
Banking, Housing, and Urban Affairs—banking and currency, public and private housing, controls or prices, of commodities, rents, and services, financial aid to industry except when under another committee's jurisdiction.
Budget—reconciliation of federal revenue and expenditure.
Commerce—interstate and foreign commerce, including transportation (railroads, buses, trucks, gas pipelines), communications (telephone, telegraph, radio, television), civil aeronautics, merchant marine and navigation, Coast Guard, fisheries and wildlife, Bureau of Standards.
District of Columbia—all lawmaking for the District of Columbia except appropriations.
Finance—taxation, including customs, tariffs, and import quotas, reciprocal trade agreements, social security, veterans' pensions and compensation.
Foreign Relations—foreign affairs, including consideration of all treaties.
Government Operations—structure of the federal government, including reorganizations, the budgetary process, and intergovernmental relations. The main function of the committee and its subcommittees is to investigate the efficiency of federal agencies; this has on occasion involved searing scrutiny of federal policies and operations in varied areas, as the decision surrounding the TFX, corruption in labor unions, and drug prices.
Interior and Insular Affairs—public lands and the minerals thereon, forest reserves and national parks, island possessions of the U.S., irrigation and reclamation, mining, oil conservation, Indians.
Judiciary—the federal judiciary and prison system, constitutional amendments and revision of statutes, antitrust, immigration and naturalization, bankruptcy, espionage, counterfeit, patent, copyright, and trademark law.
Labor and Public Welfare—education, labor, including the various antipoverty programs.
Post Office and Civil Service—civil service and post office, Census Bureau, National Archives.
Public Works—rivers and harbors, bridges and dams, navigation (on internal waterways) and flood control, water power, water pollution, federal buildings, highways.
Rules and Administration—credentials and election of Senators, corrupt practices, internal housekeeping matters.

Standing Committees of the House

Agriculture—agriculture, meat inspection, forestry, nutrition and antihunger programs, rural electrification.
Appropriations—all federal appropriations. Since the Appropriations Committee passes on federal spending for all departments and agencies, its subcommittees with jurisdiction over a given segment of the federal government are often as important in making policy as the standing committee with power over the same agency.
Armed Services—defense, naval petroleum reserves.
Banking and Currency—banking and currency, public and private housing, controls of prices and commodities, rents and services, and financial aid to industry except when under another committee's jurisdiction.
Budget—reconciliation of federal revenue and expenditure.
District of Columbia—all lawmaking for the District of Columbia except for appropriations.
Education and Labor—education, labor, welfare, including the various antipoverty programs.

International Relations—foreign affairs. The House Committee is generally considered less important than the Senate Committee on Foreign Relations because, *inter alia,* the Senate but not the House has the responsibility of approving or disapproving treaties and appointments to ambassadorships and other foreign-policy posts.

Government Operations—structure of the federal government, including reorganizations and the budgetary process, and intergovernmental relations. The main function of the committee and its subcommittees is to investigate the efficiency of federal agencies; this can involve close scrutiny of federal policies and operations in many areas. Until recently the House Committee (in contrast to its Senate counterpart) has been considered moribund.

House Administration—internal housekeeping matters.

Interior and Insular Affairs—public lands and the minerals thereon, forest reserves and national parks, island possessions of the U.S., irrigation and reclamation, mining, oil conservation, Indians.

Interstate and Foreign Commerce—interstate and foreign commerce, including transportation (railroads, buses, trucks, gas pipelines), communications (telephone, telegraph, radio, television), civil aeronautics, securities and power regulation, railroad labor and retirement, inland waterways, public health.

Judiciary—federal judiciary and prison system, constitutional amendments and revision of statutes, antitrust, immigration and naturalization, bankruptcy, espionage, counterfeit, patent, copyright, and trademark law.

Merchant Marine and Fisheries—merchant marine, navigation, water-borne common carriers except those under the jurisdiction of the Interstate Commerce Commission, Coast Guard, fisheries, and wildlife.

Post Office and Civil Service—civil service and Post Office, Census Bureau, National Archives.

Public Works—rivers and harbors, bridges and dams, navigation (on internal waterways) and flood control, water power, water pollution, federal buildings, highways.

Rules—conduct of House business. The Rules Committee is responsible for setting a "rule" for each bill that comes before the entire House. The "rule" sets the terms of debate and amendment; accordingly a Rules Committee hostile to a particular piece of legislation can often prevent its passage by granting an unfavorable "rule" or, on occasion, no "rule" at all. This power was used with great skill by ultraconservative Chairman Howard W. Smith of Virginia until his defeat in a Democratic primary in 1966.

Science and Astronautics—NASA, National Science Foundation, space research and development, and science scholarships.

Ways and Means—taxation, including customs, tariffs, and import quotas, reciprocal trade agreements, Social Security.

Joint Committees are made up of members from both houses, with the chairmanship rotating between senior House and Senate members of the majority party (since 1954, the Democrats). The Joint Committees on Congressional Operations, Defense Production, the Library, Navaho-Hopi Indian administration, Printing, and Reduction of Federal Expenditures handle their indicated subject matter without appreciable controversy. The Joint Committee on Internal Revenue Taxation is made up of members of the House Ways and Means and the Senate Finance committees: since these bodies do the actual legislating on tax matters, we also pass over this Joint Committee. That leaves two Joint Committees worthy of special attention.

Joint Committee on Atomic Energy—all matters relating to atomic energy and the Atomic Energy Commission. This committee by common consent has a very high degree of expertise in its field, and it is allowed access to internal (and often classified) information in a manner highly unusual for a congressional committee. It works very closely with the AEC.

Joint Economic Committee—set up under the Full Employment Act of 1946, it reviews the Economic Report of the President and makes recommendations and studies concerning the national economy.

C. Group Ratings

You can tell a lot about a person from knowing who his or her friends and enemies are. Legislators are no exception, which is why we have compiled this section. The "rating groups" abbreviated ADA, ACA, COPE, and so forth, are all political interest groups of one sort or another. Some base their judgments on general ideology, liberal or conservative; others focus on the economic and political interests of the particular group they represent, such as farmers or consumers; still others are concerned with a single issue, like defense spending. In most cases, the groups lobby members of Congress throughout the year on the issues in which they have their major interests.

What they all have in common is sufficient interest in how Congressmen and Senators vote on certain issues to "grade" them on their performances. These ratings as a collection constitute an extremely informative legislative report card on each person in Congress. For getting a fix on a particular legislator, a glance at this section, followed by a perusal of the "Key Votes" which follow, is a way of getting an idea of each member's stand on issues as we know them. To aid quick comprehension, we have arranged our various groups on a rough spectrum—"liberals" on the left and "conservatives" on the right, with single issue groups in the middle.

Each group rates legislators by singling out a number of votes it deems crucial. The legislator's "score" for the year is calculated simply by dividing the number of "correct" votes by the total number of votes chosen, ignoring absences. In some cases the groups themselves publish the ratings as a percentage and we have transcribed them directly; in others, only the "rights" and "wrongs" are indicated, in which case we have calculated the percentages ourselves with the permission of the group. Certain groups issue ratings only every two years, which accounts for dashes in the tables. Ratings are presented for 1972, 1973, and 1974; however legislators elected in 1974 were not rated by any of the groups in time for publication here.

To interpret these ratings, it is necessary to have a general idea of each groups, orientation, and the kinds of issues it bases its rating on. What follows is a brief description of each.

(1) ADA—Americans for Democratic Action, 1424 16th Street NW, Washington DC 20036; 202-265-5771. In its more than a quarter century of existance. ADA is known for a certain brand of liberalism at once too radical for conservatives and too conservative for radicals. Hubert Humphrey was an original member; Minnesota Congressman Donald Fraser is now National Chairman. ADA members push for economic legislation designed to reduce inequality, curtail rising defense spending and prevent encroachments on civil liberties. It rates members on a broad spectrum of issues.

(2) COPE—AFL-CIO Committee on Political Education, 815 16th Street NW, Washinton DC 20006; 202-637-5000. As the powerful and well-funded arm of the AFL-CIO, COPE keeps an alert eye on who is working for what it perceives to be the interests of the working man and woman. It is usually the most effective lobby on the Hill for the liberal side of issues. Its ratings cover a broad spectrum of issues, although it monitors few votes on foreign policy and defense spending.

(3) LWV—League of Women Voters, 1730 M Street NW, Washington DC 20036; 202-296-1770. The League of Women Voters has long been known as one of the most energetic, well-informed, and competent groups in the pursuit of good government. In 1971 the League began rating legislators for the first time, stressing issues as diverse as campaign finance reform, which it favors, and strip mining, which it opposes.

(4) Ripon—The Ripon Society, 1609 Connecticut Avenue NW, Washington DC 20009; 202-462-3277. Founded in 1962 by a group of young Republicans, the Ripon society has developed into an articulate and active progressive force in the Republican Party. Its basic policy thrust is libertarian: it is unfriendly not only to the big government inclinations of New Deal Democrats but to the overreaching powers of Nixon White House aides.

(5) NFU—National Farmers Union, 1012 14th Street NW, Washington DC 20005; 202-628-9774. NFU professes to represent the interests of small and middle-size farmers: it is inclined to favor policies producing higher farm supports. About half the votes on which its ratings are based are on farm issues; the other half are more general.

(6) LCV League of Conservation Voters, 324 C Street SE, Washington DC 20003; 202-547-7200. LCV is probably the most politically effective of the several groups which lobby for legislation and executive action to favor the environment and oppose those who despoil it. All the votes on which its ratings are based are on environmental issues.

(7) CFA—Consumer Federation of America, 1012 14th Street NW, Washington DC 20005; 202-737-3732. CFA is a group spawned in the mid-1960s as a pro-consumer counterweight to various business-oriented lobbies. The group presses for pro-consumer legislation and sometimes acts as a lobbying clearinghouse for consumer groups. Its ratings are based entirely on consumer issues.

(8) NAB—National Association of Businessmen, Inc., 1000 Connecticut Avenue NW, Washington DC 20036; 202-296-5773. NAB believes strongly in economy in government and each year presents its "Watchdog of the Treasury" award to members of Congress who, in its opinion, work most effectively toward that goal. Most of the votes on which its ratings are based are on spending issues.

(9) NSI—National Security Index of the American Security Council, 1101 17th Street NW, Washinton DC 20036; 202-296-4587. Founded in 1965, the Council feels that American security is best preserved by vigorous support for maintenance and development of large weapons systems. The Council enjoys support from a number of people prominent in business and the military.

(10) ACA—Americans for Constitutional Action, 955 L'Enfant Plaza SW, Suite 1000, Washinton DC 20024; 202-484-5525. ACA stands against "the current movement of our Nation into Socialism and a regimented society," and rates legislators accordingly. Its ratings cover a broad range of issues.

D. Key Votes

The question this section attempts to answer is which side of an important or revealing issue a legislator chose when presented with a clear choice for or against it.

It is, of course, a matter of considerable responsibility—and temerity—to condense the substance of a vote into a little headline squib and then to translate a "yea" or "nay" on the vote into a stance "for" or "against" what is sometimes a broader issue. Almost every vote on the floor of either branch reflects a complicated tug of war among some combination of interests trying to get something out of Congress. The process of condensing months of debate, amendment, pressure, persuasion, and compromise into a 15-letter description tends to obscure details, to say the least.

Nor are oversimplification and prejudice the only sources of possible distortion. How a Congressman or Senator votes on the floor is only one of the many components of his complex and endless job. Unfortunately, the others tend to be nonquantifiable or invisible. Indeed, a recorded vote may be positively misleading. Many are the stories of a legislator eviscerating some bill in the privacy (now disappearing) of committee chambers and then trumpeting support for the now hollow measure in public. A legislator might also promise some lobbyist his vote on an issue if the vote is close, abstain at the beginning of the roll call, and then vote the opposite way if the bill's fate does not hinge on a few votes.

Despite these imperfections, a legislator's voting record remains the best single objective indicator of his position on a specific issue and of his general ideological persuasion. We have striven to make the headlines in the Key Votes section straightforward, noninterpretive descriptions of the issues. You are either for or against the B-1 bomber, for or against public congressional election funds. On other issues, we believe a legislator's position on a broad issue can legitimately be inferred from his or her choice on a relatively narrow but carefully selected vote.

Three technical points: first, the FOR and AGN notation conveys the legislator's relationship to the basic concept of the bill. Depending on how the parliamentary question is framed, he can be for the concept and against the motion, or vice versa. Thus a "yea" vote in House vote #9 is a vote against (AGN) public transportation subsidies. Second, the notation NE means simply that the Senator or Congressman was not yet elected when the vote was taken. A third detail is our interpretation of paired votes. When a legislator wants to vote on a bill but finds in inconvenient or impossible to attend the session, he or she will sometimes call a colleague who takes an opposite position and ask him to refrain from voting. They form a "pair" on the record, with zero net result. The pairs are recorded, and we have taken a pair in favor to be the equivalent of a "yea," and a pair against as a "nay." When there is no such pair, and the member does not vote, we have noted ABS or absent.

Here are the vital statistics and a brief explanation of each of the 21 Senate and 15 House key votes:

SENATE

(1) No-Knock. S. 3355, 120 Cong. Rec. 103, July 11, 1974. This amendment sought repeal of the no-knock provisions of the 1970 Drug Abuse Prevention and Control Act and the 1970 District of Columbia Court Reform and Criminal Procedure Act. These no-knock provisions allowed police

to break into and enter dwellings without knocking and notifying the inhabitants of their identity. Passed 64–31. Yea = AGN No-Knock; Nay = FOR No-Knock.

(2) Busing. S. 1539, 120 Cong. Rec. 68, May 15, 1974. This vote came on a motion to table an amendment to the Elementary and Secondary Education Act Extension. The amendment would have banned busing for desegregation purposes to any but the school closest or next closest to a student's home, and allowed the reopening of school desegregation orders to so modify them. Passed 47–46. Yea = FOR Busing; Nay = AGN Busing.

(3) No-Fault. No-Fault Automobile Insurance, S. 354, 120 Cong. Rec. 60, May 1, 1974. A bill to mandate national conversion to the no-fault automobile insurance concept by establishing minimum no-fault insurance standards. States would have to enact these minimum standards or face federal imposition of stricter ones. No-fault insurance seeks to reduce insurance rates by eliminating the need to litigate for small accidents and passing on the savings to the buyer. Passed 53–42. Yea = FOR No fault; Nay = AGN No Fault.

(4) F-111. F-111 fighter/bomber aircraft, H.R. 3260, 121 Cong. Rec. 43, March 17, 1975. This amendment to the defense appropriations bill sought to rescind a previously appropriated $122.9 million for procurement of 12 of the F-111 aircraft. Passed 51–35. Yea = AGN F-111; Nay = FOR F-111.

(5) Death Pnlty. Death Penalty, S. 1401, 120 Cong. Rec. 33, March 13, 1974. In 1972, the Supreme Court struck down most then-existing death penalty statutes as unconstitutional in their application. This bill established new death penalty standards to make possible the reimposition of death penalties. Passed 54–33. Yea = FOR Death Pnlty; Nay = AGN Death Pnlty.

(6) Foreign Aid. S. 3394, 120 Cong. Rec. 168, December 4, 1974. This was the final vote on passage of the fiscal 1975 foreign aid authorization of $2.5 billion. Passed 46–45. Yea = FOR Foreign Aid; Nay = AGN Foreign Aid.

(7) Filibuster. Filibusters, S. Res. 4, 121 Cong. Rec. 37, March 7, 1975. Filibustering is a parliamentary device to delay or defeat a measure by marathon speechmaking. A vote to invoke cloture on the orator is then required before the entire legislative body can consider the measure. Under the Standing Rules of the Senate, 67 votes (two-thirds of the total) have been needed to invoke cloture. This was a resolution to amend those rules to reduce to 60 votes (three-fifths of the total) the number of votes needed to invoke cloture on a filibuster. Passed 56–27. Yea = AGN Filibuster; Nay = FOR Filibuster.

(8) Gov Abortn Aid. Government Abortion Assistance. The Supreme Court ruling establishing the right to an abortion under certain circumstances has not stilled the abortion controversy. S. 66, 121 Cong. Rec. 55, April 10, 1975. This motion killed an amendment which would have barred the use of Medicaid funds to encourage or facilitate abortions except to save the life of the mother. Passed 54–36. Yea = FOR Gov Abortn Aid; Nay = AGN Gov Abortn Aid.

(9) Cut Mil Brass. Reduce Officer Corps, H.R. 9286, 119 Cong. Rec. 139, September 22, 1973. An amendment to the Defense Department procurement bill, this bill would have required that the ranks of certain headquarters be reduced by at least 5,500 positions prior to July 1, 1974. Rejected 41–31. Yea = FOR Cut Mil Brass; Nay = AGN Cut Mil Brass.

(10) Gov Limousine. Government Limousines. H.R. 8825, 119 Cong. Rec. 129, September 7, 1973. This was an amendment to the Veterans Administration, Housing and Urban Development, and National Aeronautics and Space Agency funding bill to delete from the bill earlier amendments prohibiting the use of limousines by officials of agencies covered in the bill. Rejected 58–30. Yea = FOR Gov Limousine; Nay = AGN Gov Limousine.

(11) RR Featherbed. Railroad Featherbedding, H.R. 9142, 119 Cong. Rec. 194, December 11, 1973. This amendment to the Northeast Rail Service Act would have required that the old employee protection provisions of the bankrupt Penn Central be renegotiated by rail labor unions and railroads taking over operation of the lines. Rejected 59–37. Yea = AGN RR Featherbed; Nay = FOR RR Featherbed.

(12) Handgun License. Handgun Licensing and Registration, S. 1401, 120 Cong. Rec. 33, March 13, 1974. Despite persistent attempts, Congress has yet to pass rudimentary gun control legislation. This was a motion to table an amendment to the death penalty bill, which would have banned the sale of cheap handguns and required registration of all handguns and licensing of owners. Passed 68–21. Yea = AGN Handgun License: Nay = FOR Handgun License.

(13) Less Troops Abrd. Fewer U.S. Troops Stationed Abroad, S. 3000, 120 Cong. Rec. 81, June 6, 1974. An amendment to the defense budget to require the withdrawal of 76,000 U.S. military personnel stationed outside the borders of the U.S. Technically, it would have established ceilings on the maximum number of active duty military personnel and on the maximum number of such personnel that could be stationed abroad. Rejected 46–44. Yea = FOR Less Troops Abrd; Nay = AGN Less Troops Abrd.

(14) Resume Turk Aid. Resume Military Aid to Turkey, S 846, 121 Cong. Rec. 80, May 19, 1975. This bill permitted the President to resume conditionally the military aid to Turkey that was cut off after Turkey used U.S.-supplied weapons to invade Cyprus in 1974. The bill allowed resumption of aid if the President determined that this resumption would contribute to peace negotiations and Turkey observed the cease-fire and did not increase forces or weapons on Cyprus. Passed 41–40. Yea = FOR Resume Turk Aid; Nay = AGN Resume Turk Aid.

(15) Consumer Prot Agy. Consumer Protection Agency, S. 707, 120 Cong. Rec. 141, September 19, 1974. This was a motion to cut off a filibuster (invoke cloture) against a bill to establish an independent agency to represent consumers before other federal agencies and courts. Passage of the motion, which needed a two-thirds margin, would have cleared the way for a direct vote on the bill. Rejected 64–34. Yea = FOR Consumer Prot Agy; Nay = AGN Consumer Prot Agy.

(16) Forced Psych Tests. Forced Psychological Tests, S. 1539, 120 Cong. Rec. 67, May 14, 1974. An amendment to the Elementary and Secondary Education Act extension bill which would have provided that no student could be required to reveal information about his personal or family life or to undergo medical, psychological, or psychiatric examinations without parental consent. Rejected 43–40. Yea = AGN Forced Psych Tests; Nay = FOR Forced Psych Tests.

(17) Fed Campaign Subs. Federal Campaign Subsidies, S. 3044, 120 Cong. Rec. 53, April 11, 1974. Campaign reform, long a topic of legislative discussion, received an unexpected boost from public reaction to Watergate. This was the final passage of a bill to provide full public financing of federal general election campaigns and partial public financing of primary campaigns for federal offices, establish a ceiling on campaign contributions and spending, and impose criminal penalties for violations of the provisions of the act. Passed 53–32. Yea = FOR Fed Campaign Subs; Nay = AGN Fed Campaign Subs.

(18) Rhod Chrome Ban. Rhodesian Chrome Ban, S. 1868, 119 Cong. Rec. 199, December 18, 1973. This was the vote on passage of a bill to ban the importation of Rhodesian chrome ore as a sanction against Rhodesia's internal policies. Passed 54–37. Yea = FOR Rhod Chrome Ban; Nay = AGN Rhod Chrome Ban.

(19) Open Legis Meetings. Open Legislative Meetings, S. Res. 69, 119 Cong. Rec. 35, March 6, 1973. In recent years, considerable movement has been made toward limiting the powers of committees, especially in the House. This amendment to the Standing Rules of the Senate would have provided that a meeting of a Standing Committee of the Senate be closed to the public only by a vote taken in public by the members at the start of the meeting. Rejected 47–38. Yea = FOR Open Legis Meetings; Nay = AGN Open Legis Meetings.

(20) Strikers Food Stmps. Food Stamp Eligibility for Striking Workers, H.R. 16901, 120 Cong. Rec. 64, November 25, 1974. This was an amendment to the Agricultural, Environmental, and Consumer Protection Appropriations Act to prohibit the use of funds to make food stamps available to a household while its principle wage earner is on strike. Rejected 55–34. Yea = AGN Strikers Food Stmps; Nay = FOR Strikers Food Stmps.

(21) Gov Info Disclosr. Government Information Disclosure, S. 2543, 120 Cong. Rec. 76, May 30, 1974. Since the passage of the original Freedom of Information Act, various questions have

arisen in the litigation between citizens, including journalists, seeking to use it in the courts. This amendment was to resolve some of them in one vital area. It limited the grounds under which investigatory records compiled for law enforcement purposes could be withheld from the public and placed the legal burden of justifying non-disclosure of such records on the government. Passed 51–33. Yea = FOR Gov Info Disclosr; Nay = AGN Gov Info Disclosr.

HOUSE

(1) Foreign Aid. H.R. 4592, 121 Cong. Rec. 41, March 13, 1975. The fiscal 1975 foreign military and economic assistance bill incorporated the largest reduction ever in this increasingly criticized program. This was the final vote on the $3.5 billion aid package. Passed 212–201. Yea = FOR foreign aid; Nay = AGN foreign aid.

(2) Busing. H.R. 69, 120 Cong. Rec. 41, March 26, 1974. An amendment to ban busing for desegregation purposes to any except the school closest or next closest to a student's home and allow the reopening of school desegregation orders to bring about compliance with the provisions of the amendment. Passed 293–117. Yea = AGN busing; Nay = FOR busing.

(3) ABM. Safeguard Anti-Ballistic Missile, H.R. 16243, 120 Cong. Rec. 118, August 6, 1974. This amendment to the Defense Department appropriations bill would have curtailed further development of the controversial Safeguard ABM system by cutting maintenance, operations, research and development funds by some $82.5 million. Rejected 182–219. Yea = AGN ABM; Nay = FOR ABM.

(4) B-1 Bomber. H.R. 6674, May 19, 1975. This was an amendment to the military procurement bill to kill the B-1 Bomber weapons system, which was under attack as unneeded and vulnerable to attack. Rejected 164–227. Yea = AGN B-1 Bomber; Nay = FOR B-1 Bomber.

(5) Nerve Gas. H.R. 16243, 120 Cong. Rec. 118, August 6, 1974. An amendment to the military procurement bill to delete $5.8 million for the production of binary nerve gas. Passed 214–186. Yea = AGN Nerve Gas; Nay = FOR Nerve Gas.

(6) Gov Abortn Aid. Government Abortion Assistance, H.R. 1449, 120 Cong. Rec. 75, May 29, 1974. An amendment to the Community Services Act to bar community action programs from using family planning assistance funds for medical aid or supplies in abortion cases. Passed 209–91. Yea = AGN Gov Abortn Aid; Nay = FOR Gov Abortn Aid.

(7) Coed Phys Ed. Coeducational Physical Education, H.R. 5901, 121 Cong. Rec. 5, April 16, 1975. An amendment to the fiscal 1976 educational appropriations bill to prohibit the Department of Health Education and Welfare from issuing regulations to require integration by sex in physical education classes. Passed 253–145. Yea = AGN Coed Phys Ed; Nay = FOR Coed Phys Ed.

(8) Pov Lawyer Gag. Poverty Lawyer Gag, H.R. 7824, 119 Cong. Rec. 97, June 21, 1973. An amendment to the bill creating the Legal Services Corporation to provide legal services for the poor. The amendment was to extend restrictions on lobbying by lawyers in the legal services program to include efforts to influence administrative decisions by federal, state, and local government agencies. Passed 200–181. Yea = FOR Pov Lawyer Gag; Nay = AGN Pov Lawyer Gag.

(9) Pub Trans Sub. Mass Public Transportation Subsidy, H.R. 12859, 120 Cong. Rec. 125, August 15, 1974. This amendment to the transportation bill sought to prohibit operating (as opposed to construction) subsidies for public transit systems. Rejected 197–202. Yea = AGN Pub Trans Sub; Nay = FOR Pub Trans Sub.

(10) EZ Voter Regis. Easy Voter Registration, H.Res. 929, 120 Cong. Rec. 64, May 8, 1974. This resolution would have enabled the House to consider H.R. 8053, a bill establishing within the Bureau of the Census a Voter Registration Administration to create a nationwide postcard voter registration system. Rejected 197–204. Yea = FOR EZ Voter Regis; Nay = AGN EZ Voter Regis.

(11) Pub Cong Election $. Public Congressional Election Funds, H.R. 16090, 120 Cong. Rec. 74, August 8, 1974. This amendment to the Federal Elections Campaign Act would have provided for partial funding of congressional general election campaigns by providing for matching federal funds to be raised from the Presidential Campaign Fund dollar checkoff on tax returns. Rejected 187–228. Yea = FOR Pub Cong Election $; Nay = AGN Pub Cong Election $.

(12) Turkish Arms Cutoff. Cutoff of military aid to Turkey, H.J.R. 1163, 121 Cong. Rec. 157, October 16, 1974. This resolution to provide for a complete cutoff of military aid to Turkey if any United States equipment given to Turkey was shipped to Cyprus. Passed 194–144. Yea = FOR Turkish Arms Cutoff; Nay = AGN Turkish Arms Cutoff.

(13) Youth Camp Regs. Youth Camp Regulations, H.R. 46, 121 Cong. Rec. 59, April 17, 1975. A carrot-and-stick bill to provide federal assistance to states that developed and enforced federally approved safety standards for youth camps, and to provide for federal inspection and enforcement of national standards in states that did not develop their own. Passed 197–174. Yea = FOR Youth Camp Regs; Nay = AGN Youth Camp Regs.

(14) Strip Mine Veto, H.R. 25, June 10, 1975. The attempt to pass, over President Ford's May 20 veto, the bill establishing minimum federal standards for the regulation of surface mining and the reclamation of strip-mined land. Rejected 278–143, a two-thirds vote being necessary to override. Yea = AGN Strip Mine Veto; Nay = FOR Strip Mine Veto.

(15) Farm Bill Veto, H.R. 4296, May 13, 1975. This was an attempt to pass, over President Ford's May 1 veto, the bill to raise target prices and loan rates for 1975 crops of wheat, cotton, corn, and other feed grains, and to set dairy price supports at 80% of parity with quarterly adjustments. Rejected 245–182, a two-thirds vote being necessary to override. Yea = AGN Farm Bill Veto; Nay = FOR Farm Bill Veto.

E. Election Results.
A politician can do little without getting elected. This section of the Almanac tells you who got elected, and by how much—and gives you at least a hint as to why. We have included not only the results of the last two general elections which the officeholder won, but also the result of the most recent primary since, in many areas, the real decision is made in the primary contest.

Beyond this, the 1976 Almanac also provides the facts on how much money each candidate spent in the 1974 and 1972 general elections. The figures have been compiled by Common Cause, and are reprinted with their permission. For 1972 they cover only the period from April 7 to the end of the calendar year, unless the candidate voluntarily disclosed his spending over a longer period; for 1974, they cover spending from September 1, 1973 to December 31, 1974. Thus they will ordinarily include spending for primary as well as general elections. Sometimes the result will look a little odd, especially in the case of 1972 figures for candidates who had strenuous opposition in the primary, but little or none in the general election. But in most cases, the spending figures will indicate how seriously the seat was contested. For it is an unfortunate fact that, with only a few exceptions, you cannot win an election today without spending a lot of money.

The 1976 *Almanac* also presents, for the first time, election results for Gubernatorial races, and for the 1972 presidential primaries.

II. THE DISTRICT
This section presents the political, economic, and social demography of an officeholder's constituency.

A. Census Data
Along with voting figures, census returns are the hardest kind of data available for analysis of states and congressional districts. Fortunately, the 1970 census remains useful today because there has been relatively little population growth in the last half decade. We show not only total population, but the percentage of the population contained in government-designated standard metropolitan statistical areas (SMSAs) and central cities in 1970—a good indication of the urban-suburban-rural breakdown.

Every ten years the Census data requires a reapportionment of the nation's 435 House districts among the states, and during the 1960s the one-person-one-vote doctrine of the Supreme Court required frequent redistrictings. Now they are rare. Between 1972 and 1974 only California and Texas changed their congressional district lines; since the 1974 elections no state has (though there were attempts in Ohio and Illinois).

The census data section also shows the state's percentage of the total U.S. population—a useful figure for comparison with its share of the tax burden and federal expenditures. We show the state's median family income and the percentage of families making under $3,000 and over $15,000 per year; these are in 1970 dollars, but still give a good index of poverty and affluence. Finally, list the "median years education," which covers everyone over 25. The ranking of the states includes the 50 states only, and excludes the District of Columbia.

B. Federal outlays and tax burden

Politicians like to brag about how much federal money they have brought into their states or districts. We give you the actual figures. We also show how much of the federal tax burden each state bears; the figures are provided by the Tax Foundation, Inc., of New York, a nonprofit, nonpartisan agency whose credentials are beyond reproach. The data on how much money each state gets from Uncle Sam are from the fiscal year 1974 federal outlays published by the Office of Economic Opportunity. The reader should beware of reading too much into the data, since the lion's share of federal spending is fixed by automatic formulas (non-discretionary spending) which cannot be affected by the efforts of a single legislator, or indeed by an entire state delegation.

DOD	Department of Defense
AEC	Atomic Energy Commision
NASA	National Aeronautics and Space Administation
DOT	Department of Transportation
DOC	Department of Commerce
DOI	Department of the Interior
USDA	Department of Agriculture
HEW	Department of Health, Education, and Welfare
HUD	Department of Housing and Urban Development
VA	Veterans' Administration
EPA	Environmental Protection Agency
REVS	Revenue Sharing
Int.	Interest paid on government securities

For the 1976 *Almanac* we have decided not to calculate figures for federal outlays for each congressional district. OEO gives figures only for whole counties, but because the vast majority of congressional districts cut across county lines, the congressional district figures are difficult, if not impossible, to compute with any precision.

C. Economic base

Throughout the nineteenth century and into the twentieth, a major issue in American politics was the tariff, and an observer could predict how most members of Congress would vote by examining the economic bases of their constituencies. Today, it is still so; the tariff remains a major, if unreported, issue, and Congressmen from districts that produce textiles or steel or shoes have lately been working for various kinds of trade restrictions. But the economic base of a state illuminates much more than its Senators' position on trade restriction issues. It tells us something about the state's economic health, its prospects for growth, the jobs its citizens and voters hold, and the sources of wealth of its big money men. For that reason, we have listed each state's most important manufacturing, mining, finance, insurance, and real estate activities under the category of Economic Base. The classifications are derived from the Census Bureau's Standard Industrial Code. An effort has been made to be as specific as possible and to indicate by "especially" cases where one type of production is particularly important. Production activity is ranked in importance according to the number of people employed—the obvious classification in a book concerned with voters.

D. Political lineup

This is very simple—the Governor, the Senators, the House delegation, and the state legislatures, by party.

E. The Voters

You don't really know why candidates get elected until you know who votes—and why. We like to think of the American voter as a one person civics class, gravely weighing the issues and measuring the mettle of the competing candidates. But we know this is not so. Voters like to talk about being for the man, not the party; but there are still plenty who agree with the reasoning process ascribed to Harry Truman: "I vote for the better man. He is the Democratic nominee." And when people actually do "vote for the man," they often mean the only man in the race they've heard of, which in congressional races usually means the incumbent.

Political scientists have shown that, more often than not people inherit their political preferences, and that these preferences remain remarkably constant through the years. Accordingly, it makes some sense to analyze the electorate by blocs. One source of differentiation is economic status. We have provided an "employment profile" for each state and district, showing the percentage of employed persons working in white collar, blue collar, service (which are usually blue collar), and farm jobs. In addition, we have shown the "median family income" for each state and district. This gives you a quick picture of the economic and social nature of the constituency, but does not provide an automatic guide to voting behavior. The richest congressional district in terms of median family income, the 8th of Maryland, rejected the Republican candidacies of Richard Nixon twice and gave him a smaller than average majority the third time; the poorest, the 5th of Kentucky, is inevitably one of the most Republican districts in the nation. Thus conventional widsom that rich people vote Republican and poor people vote Democratic does not yield a very close understanding of American political preferences.

Another way to look at the electorate is along ethnic lines. We are past the time when Polish-Americans, say, will automatically vote for a Polish-American candidate; that kind of ethnic politics is more and more on the decline. But people who share an ethnic inheritance also tend to share a cultural background—and a political preference. So for every state and district, we have provided racial and ethnic percentages calculated from the 1970 census. The figures require some explanation to be useful. The racial category is obvious; and if blacks in central cities have been undercounted by the Census Bureau, as some have charged, then the kind of people who have avoided the census taker are also the kind least likely to participate in the political process. The Census also notes which of us were born in foreign countries or had parents who were; these two groups are lumped together as "foreign stock." Obviously, a foreign stock figure will understate the ethnicity of some areas (a lot of Boston Irish are descended from people who left the old country physically in the 1840s but whose hearts are still there) and will overstate the ethnicity of others (what reason is there to suppose that people born in the United Kingdom and living in Santa Barbara will vote any differently from the other people there?). The category "Spanish heritage" represents a variety of different groups: Mexican-Americans mainly in California, Texas, and Illinois; Puerto Ricans in New York and New Jersey; and the ancient Spanish-speaking community in New Mexico, which is older than Plymouth Rock. We have also included the category "French native tongue" in Maine, New Hampshire, Vermont, Massachusetts, Rhode Island, and upstate New York, to indicate people of French Canadian stock, and in Louisiana to indicate the so-called Cajuns; both groups have distinctive voting patterns. No group is shown unless it represents 1% or more of the state's or district's total population.

III. POLITICAL BACKGROUND
This is our interpretation of how things fit together. What kind of men and women are your Governors, Senators, and Representatives? What do they accomplish in office? How do they get elected, and what are their prospects for reelection—or defeat? What are the local issues, and local attitudes on national issues?

These are the questions the Political Background sections seek to answer. They form a kind of mosaic, we think, a picture of political leanings and trends throughout the nation and what they mean for the federal government and federal elections. Read them all, and we think you will get a pretty accurate picture of what is going on politically around the country and on Capitol Hill. But the *Almanac* is designed to be read and used piecemeal; you might want to begin with your home state, or with the member of a committee whose subject matter interests you, or with those members of Congress considered possible presidential prospects for 1976. We have tried to design the *Almanac* to make it easy to use, whatever your interest.

A. Statewide
American politics, for better or worse, is still the politics of the 50 states. There are signs that the national media have begun to homogenize our politics, to eliminate local peculiarities and to replicate conflicts along the same ideological lines throughout the nation. But even the most contemporary politics is the outgrowth of history, and for 180 years American politics has been a thing of unmatched diversity. Each state has been a little political arena all its own. The Electoral College system—whereby the winner takes all a state's electoral votes—has strengthened this

tendency, even in national contests; in most presidential elections, about half the states are not seriously contested by one candidate or the other. Most states have well-developed traditions of political conflict: New York City vs. upstate, Chicago vs. downstate Illinois, east Tennessee vs. middle Tennessee vs. west Tennessee. Some of these are changing; others remain rigidly fixed. We have tried to present them in their historical contexts and to explain what, if anything, these regional conflicts mean today.

Each state also has its own political flavor, an ambiance about its politicians and its voting behavior that is not found elsewhere. Connecticut, with its still strong tradition of straight tickets, lies right next to Massachusetts, where voters have been splitting their tickets on a massive scale for years. Illinois is a land of fabled political corruption and cronyism; Wisconsin just to the north, is as clean as a hound's tooth and has nothing resembling Richard J. Daley's machine. political patterns have grown up in response to local ground-rules, pressures, and personal initiatives; the voting public responds in various ways, and a political culture grows. We have attempted to impart the ambiance of the 50 political cultures which make up our Republic.

B. Congressional Districts

There has been a great deal of writing on the politics of the various states, but very little on the politics of individual congressional districts (CDs). One reason for the dearth of information about CDs is that they, unlike the states, usually do not have a political culture of their own. Each one is just a piece of a culture that exists on a statewide basis, and each is often made up of disparate elements of that culture. The trend toward heterogeneity has been increased by the Supreme Court's one-man-one-vote decision, *Wesberry v. Sanders*. Today, the districts are pretty much equal in population, at least according to the 1970 census; but the equal-population requirement makes for some odd political combinations. For example, the 200,000-population, old 4th Texas district, represented for nearly 50 years by Sam Rayburn, was a compact, homogeneous unit; so was the 900,000-population district that existed at the time of Rayburn's death, including all of Dallas County. Now Rayburn's successor has some of Dallas County in his district, and while that is clearly fairer, it makes a description of the current 4th district a more complicated affair. Nevertheless, we have tried to describe and analyze the politics of each district, and to indicate the impact its Congressman makes on Capitol Hill.

What were our sources? Just about everything: interviews with members of Congress and their aides, and with local politicians and political observers in Washington and around the country; newspapers, magazines, books; publicly available data, including the *Congressional Record*; and a lifelong collection of political and historical miscellany. We have paid particular attention to what we consider the hardest of data, the election returns; we taxpayers spend millions of dollars to obtain these figures, and political adversaries have the strongest incentives to make sure they are accurate. We have examined in detail returns going back at least to 1964, and we believe that, intelligently read, the election returns give as good an insight as can be had into what Americans think and believe about the issues of the day. They also provide clues for what we imagine must be one major interest of many of our readers: whether Senator X or Congressman Y can be beaten in the next election.

Anyone who spends considerable time and effort analyzing things as they are—particularly as they are in Congress—begins to think they must always remain so. We think the lesson of the last few years in American politics is that this is not so. The possibility for change is enormous; the voters are dissatisfied with the way the system works now, and are actively working for changes. Like most people who write about politics, we have some strong views as to what those changes should be, views which we hope to not unduly obtrude in this book. Our intention in compiling and writing the *Almanac* was to create something the American public would find useful in playing an informed role in the political process.

One final personal plea. Because nobody has made money writing or publishing this book, please try to keep from xeroxing any of its pages.

Michael Barone
Grant Ujifusa
Douglas Matthews

ALABAMA

Alabama is George Wallace country. Wallace has been a figure of national importance for more than a dozen years, since he stood in the schoolhouse door in 1963, but in Alabama he has been the dominant political figure since the 1958 gubernatorial primary—the election which he lost, and after which he vowed he would never again be "out-segged." He never has. Elected Governor in 1962, succeeded by his late wife Lurleen, reelected after a close primary win over interim Gov. Albert Brewer in 1970, Wallace had his easiest victory of all in 1974, when he was without significant opposition. (The Alabama Constitution had been changed to allow consecutive terms.) Other Southern politicians have enjoyed longtime dominance in their own bailiwicks—one thinks of Harry Byrd in Virginia or Orval Faubus in Arkansas. But only a very few, like Wallace and the legendary Huey Long of Louisiana, have had that special something which has allowed them to capture the imagination and harness the enthusiasm of voters nationally.

And Wallace has been around the national scene longer than the Kingfish ever was. Huey Long was murdered before he could run for President, but Wallace at this stage in our history has been seeking that office almost as long as Nelson Rockefeller or Hubert Humphrey. In 1964, when it was unheard of for a Southern segregationist politician to have a following elsewhere in the country, he ran close races against LBJ surrogates in Wisconsin, Indiana, and Maryland, demonstrating for the first time the potency of the white backlash in the North. In 1968, his third-party candidacy won 13.6% of the national vote—the strongest third-party effort since Bob LaFollette's Progressive Party in 1924—preventing Nixon and Humphrey from getting anything like a popular-vote majority. With rather small shifts in the returns, Wallace could easily have played a king-making role in the electoral college.

In 1972, Wallace decided to go back to the Democratic presidential primaries, and he did even better than 1964. Not only did he win in the Southern states like Florida, Tennessee, and North Caroline, but his "send 'em a message" campaign won Northern contests in Maryland and busing-obsessed Michigan. Wallace also finished a strong second in Wisconsin and Pennsylvania. Like his previous national campaigns, his 1972 effort was disorganized and lacked depth. The candidate made only a few appearances in each state—inevitably before friendly, cheering crowds—gave a set speech, and then retired to watch the votes pile up, as if by magic, on election night.

Then, just at the peak of his national career, the day before his smashing victories in the Michigan and Maryland primaries, George Wallace was shot. Paralyzed below the waist, forced to undergo numerous operations, Wallace has appeared sometimes to be depressed and withdrawn. But then he perks up, and his voice gains almost all of its old timbre. The question now is what he will do in 1976. No one doubts that he wants to run for President; it appears now that for all his primary runs and third party candidacies he has been seeking a way for a one-time vocal segregationist to make it to the White House. Wallace has managed to raise literally millions in small contributions through direct mail, and he has enough hard-core support—augmented, if anything by the respectability conferred by martyrdom—to run ahead of all other Democratic presidential possibilities in early 1975. But even more Democrats find Wallace totally unacceptable and would back anyone in the general election against him, even Gerald Ford; for all his talk of how he reflects the people's real views, Wallace is clearly the weakest candidate the Democrats could nominate. And of course they won't. In 1972, reporters speculated on how many delegates Wallace could win if he ran full slates in each state, and how many more votes he could win if he would put on a full-fledged campaign. The Wallace people now know how to win delegates commensurate with the Governor's level of popular support, but there is nothing to indicate that he can win more votes by intensive campaigning. Wallace is not an acquired taste: you either love him or hate him from the start, and you don't change your mind.

What is most ironic about the Alabamian's career is that this self-proclaimed champion of the little man actually backs some of the most conventional conservative economic programs; he may talk like a Southern factory worker, but he thinks like a Midwestern businessman. As labor politicos like to point out when Wallace threatens to make inroads in their constituencies, the Governor's Alabama actually has extremely low levels of minimum wages, unemployment compensation, and government spending on education.

But rightly or wrongly, people's opinions of George Wallace do not hinge on what he has done in workmen's compensation; they come from his record on race. Much was made in his 1974 race of the support he received from blacks; but when it is examined more closely, it became clear that black Wallace voters came mostly from isolated rural areas where local notables, eager for patronage or state aid, had endorsed the Governor. In Birmingham, and other big cities where most of Alabama's blacks live, Wallace received less than 10% of the vote. Nationwide and in Alabama, blacks and those who strongly supported civil rights legislation are Wallace's fiercest opponents. Those who opposed civil rights legislation or who believe that blacks have "gone too far" are Wallace's strongest supporters. Nobody is ever going to forget that Wallace is the man who in his first Alabama inaugural said that he was for segregation now and forever, and that he was the man who stood futilely in the schoolhouse door, defying a federal court integration order. The very segregationist record that first made Wallace a national figure also has made him unelectable as president. His only possible route to the White House—and undoubtedly the reason he remains a nominal Democrat—is if some candidate like Henry Jackson should opportunistically offer him the Vice Presidential nomination.

Wallace's verbal commitment to populism is not something he adopted solely to win votes nationally; it reflects something very deep in the Alabama political soil. It goes back at least to 1926, when the late Hugo Black was elected to the U.S. Senate over the opposition of the banks, railroad, and power companies. For 40 years—until Wallace came along—New Deal-style populists dominated the Alabama congressional delegation; its members took the obligatory stand against civil rights, but devoted most of their energy to housing, hospital, and highway programs.

Today only two of this breed, Senator John Sparkman and Congressman Bob Jones, remain in Congress. Most of the rest were beaten in the 1964 Goldwater landslide, when Republicans won five House seats and wiped out 87 years of Alabama seniority. Sparkman's populist credentials, in any case, are considerably less solid now than in 1952 when he was Adlai Stevenson's running mate. In Sparkman's 1972 reelection campaign, he reportedly received massive financial assistance from banking interests throughout the nation. The reason was simple: Sparkman was Chairman of the Senate Banking, Housing and Urban Affairs Committee, with jurisdiction over one of the most heavily regulated sectors of the economy. Two years later, the same bankers were pouring money into William Fulbright's reelection campaign in Arkansas—not because he had clout in the banking area, but because Sparkman was number two on Foreign Relations and could choose to take Fulbright's chairmanship. In which case, William Proxmire of Wisconsin, no friend of the big bankers, would chair the Banking Committee.

Which is exactly what happened: Sparkman, in effect, double-crossed the bankers whose aims he had usually supported and whose money he had gladly accepted. Now he is Chairman of Foreign Relations, the hawkish head of a dovish committee—in effect, keeping staff resources and scheduling out of the hands of anti-administration Democrats like next-in-line-to-be-Chairman Frank Church of Idaho. Sparkman's choice of Foreign Relations is just another sign that he considers this his last Senate term. Born 11 days before the turn of the century, he did not have much trouble beating his Republican opponent in 1972, the former Postmaster General Winton Blount, who managed to carry only one small county. But the primary, back in May, was very definitely a problem. Sparkman was hard-pressed by a field of challengers, especially state Auditor Melba Till Allen, who campaigned as a consumer advocate and charged that Sparkman was too close to the big bankers. Sparkman won a bare 50% of the votes, narrowly avoiding a runoff election; without a large majority in his old congressional district, along the Tennessee River in northern Alabama, he would have had a runoff and might well have lost. In any case, it appears this long career—Sparkman has been on Capitol Hill since 1936—will come to an end after the 1978 elections.

The state's other Senator is younger (64 in 1976), less senior (first elected in 1968), and not even close to being a committee chairman. Nevertheless, James B. Allen is making more headlines—and probably more impact on the national policy—than his senior colleague. Allen epitomizes an otherwise vanishing breed: the old-fashioned Southern Senator. He is a dull-looking man, with a thick accent, who has—more than just about anyone in the Senate—made himself a force to be reckoned with by mastering parliamentary procedure and working very hard. Allen will threaten a filibuster at just the moment when some liberal legislation is faltering, and he knows how to hold the floor and tie it up till its proponents make concessions. Allen has started these mini-filibusters so often that he quite often loses; and he is less adept at pushing through legislation, like anti-busing bills, that he wants. But when the fight came at the beginning of the 94th Congress to cut back on the Senate filibuster rule, it was Allen who was leading the forces on the traditional Southern side.

Allen has fewer troops to lead than did Richard Russell of Georgia in the old days—there are only half a dozen or so resolutely conservative Southern Democrats in the Senate any more. And he will never achieve the seniority required for real committee power, although the voters of Alabama reelected him in 1974 with scarcely a ripple of opposition either in the primary or the

general election. It did not hurt that Allen has always been a strong Wallace supporter, as his first Lieutenant Governor and then as state Senator, in a year when Wallace's opponents apparently decided not to surface.

The current Alabama House delegation is composed of four Democrats and three Republicans—indeed, the same seven men who have been serving since the 1968 election. All three Republicans were beneficiaries of the 1964 Goldwater landslide, and all have since strengthened their hold on office; the Democrats seem even more entrenched than the Republicans. Alabama's large black minority, which has managed to elect a record number of black officials (more than in any other state but Michigan), is carved up among the state's seven congressional districts. Thus though blacks have played important roles in some state legislative races, they have little leverage in House elections. The high point of black influence so far in statewide contests came in the 1972 Senate primary when most black voters went for Sparkman and helped him avoid a runoff. Further splintering black influence is the existence of the National Democratic Party of Alabama, which runs its own candidates; in some counties it has the allegiance of black voters, who do not participate in the often all-crucial Democratic primary.

Census Data Pop. 3,444,165; 1.70% of U.S. total, 21st largest; Central city, 26%; suburban, 27%. Median family income, $7,263; 48th highest; families above $15,000: 11%; families below $3,000: 19%. Median years education, 10.8.

1974 Share of Federal Tax Burden $3,213,783,000; 1.20% of U.S. total, 25th largest.

1974 Share of Federal Outlays $4,364,946,000; 1.62% of U.S. total, 20th largest. Per capita federal spending, $1268.

DOD	$1,167,603,000	20th (1.70%)	HEW	$1,511,901,000	21st (1.63%)
AEC	$64,000	45th (–)	HUD	$27,361,000	13th (2.81%)
NASA	$198,900,000	5th (6.70%)	VA	$270,641,000	19th (1.98%)
DOT	$191,666,000	16th (2.26%)	EPA	$18,736,000	29th (0.60%)
DOC	$25,573,000	10th (1.58%)	RevS	$103,569,000	21st (1.70%)
DOI	$15,559,000	35th (0.63%)	Int.	$88,594,000	28th (0.43%)
USDA	$226,058,000	24th (1.82%)	Other	$518,721,000	

Economic Base Agriculture, notably broilers, cattle, cotton lint and eggs; primary metal industries, especially blast furnaces and basic steel products, and iron and steel foundries; finance, insurance and real estate; apparel and other textile products, especially men's and boys' furnishings; textile mill products, especially cotton weaving mills; food and kindred products, especially meat products; lumber and wood products, especially sawmills and planing mills.

Political Line-up Governor, George C. Wallace (D). Senators, John J. Sparkman (D) and James B. Allen (D). Representatives, 7 (4 D and 3 R). State Senate (35 D); State House (105 D).

The Voters

Registration No party registration; no accurate total registration figures available.
Median voting age 42.
Employment profile White collar, 41%. Blue collar, 43%. Service, 13%. Farm, 3%.
Ethnic groups Black, 26%. Total foreign stock, 2%.

Presidential vote

1972	Nixon (R)	728,701	(74%)
	McGovern (D)	256,923	(26%)
1968	Nixon (R)	146,923	(14%)
	Humphrey (D)	196,579	(19%)
	Wallace (AI)	691,425	(67%)

Sen. John Sparkman (D) Elected 1946, seat up 1978; b. Dec. 20, 1899, Hartselle; home, Huntsville; U. of Ala., A.B., 1921, LL.B., 1923, A.M. 1924; Methodist.

Career Army, WWI; Practicing atty., 1923–36; U.S. House of Reps., 1937–46, Majority Whip; Dem. nominee for V.P., 1952.

Offices 3203 DSOB, 202-224-4124. Also Rm. 208, 1800 5th Ave., Birmingham 35102, 205-325-3883.

Committees

Foreign Relations (Chairman). Subcommittees: European Affairs (Chairman); Personnel (Chairman).

Banking, Housing and Urban Affairs (2d). Subcommittees: Financial Institutions; Housing and Urban Affairs (Chairman); Oversight; Small Business.

Joint Economic Committee (2d, Senate Side). Subcommittees: Inter-American Economic Relationships (Chairman); International Economics; Priorities and Economy in Government.

Group Ratings

	ADA	COPE	LWV	RIPON	NFU	LCV	CFA	NAB	NSI	ACA
1974	25	44	78	39	53	40	0	27	100	58
1973	12	70	38	46	71	–	30	–	–	46
1972	0	10	38	24	50	19	40	38	100	80

Key Votes

1) No-Knock	AGN	8) Gov Abortn Aid	AGN	15) Consumer Prot Agy	AGN
2) Busing	AGN	9) Cut Mil Brass	AGN	16) Forced Psych Tests	ABS
3) No Fault	AGN	10) Gov Limousine	FOR	17) Fed Campaign Subs	ABS
4) F-111	FOR	11) RR Featherbed	FOR	18) Rhod Chrome Ban	AGN
5) Death Penalty	ABS	12) Handgun License	AGN	19) Open Legis Meetings	AGN
6) Foreign Aid	FOR	13) Less Troop Abrd	ABS	20) Strikers Food Stmps	FOR
7) Filibuster	FOR	14) Resume Turk Aid	FOR	21) Gov Info Disclosure	ABS

Election Results

1972 general:	John Sparkman (D)	654,491	(63%)	($702,109)
	Winton M. Blount (R)	347,523	(34%)	($764,961)
	John L. LeFlore (NDPA)	31,421	(3%)	(NA)
1972 primary:	John Sparkman (D)	331,838	(50%)	
	Melba Till Allen (D)	194,690	(29%)	
	Lambert C. Mims (D)	87,461	(13%)	
	Four Others (D)	46,351	(7%)	
1966 general:	John Sparkman (D)	482,138	(61%)	
	John Grenier (R)	313,018	(39%)	

Sen. James B. Allen (D) Elected 1968, seat up 1980; b. Dec. 28, 1912, Gadsden; home, Gadsden; U. of Ala., U. of Ala. Law School.

Career Practicing atty., 1935–68; Ala. House of Reps., 1938–42; Navy, WWII; Ala. Senate, 1946–50; Lt. Gov. of Ala., 1951–55, 1963–67.

Offices 6205 DSOB, 202-224-5744. Also 5th Floor, Frank Nelson Bldg., Birmingham 35203, 205-325-3449; and P.O. Box 3294, Montgomery 36109, 205-265-9507.

Committees

Agriculture and Forestry (4th). Subcommittees: Agricultural Credit and Rural Electrification; Agricultural Research and General Legislation (Chairman); Environment,

Soil Conservation and Forestry; Rural Development.

Government Operations (6th). Subcommittees: Federal Spending Practices, Efficiency and Open Government; Oversight Procedures; Permanent Subcommittee on Investigations.

Rules and Administration (4th). Subcommittees: Printing; Restaurant (Chairman).

Group Ratings

	ADA	COPE	LWV	RIPON	NFU	LCV	CFA	NAB	NSI	ACA
1974	14	60	40	26	35	30	22	58	100	84
1973	5	36	10	29	50	–	8	–	–	70
1972	0	30	9	17	50	32	18	58	100	86

Key Votes

1) No-Knock	AGN	8) Gov Abortn Aid	AGN	15) Consumer Prot Agy	AGN
2) Busing	AGN	9) Cut Mil Brass	AGN	16) Forced Psych Tests	FOR
3) No Fault	AGN	10) Gov Limousine	AGN	17) Fed Campaign Subs	AGN
4) F-111	AGN	11) RR Featherbed	AGN	18) Rhod Chrome Ban	AGN
5) Death Penalty	FOR	12) Handgun License	AGN	19) Open Legis Meetings	AGN
6) Foreign Aid	AGN	13) Less Troop Abrd	AGN	20) Strikers Food Stmps	AGN
7) Filibuster	FOR	14) Resume Turk Aid	AGN	21) Gov Info Disclosure	AGN

Election Results

1974 general:	Jim Allen (D)	501,541	(96%)	($37,328)
	Alvin Abercrombie (Prohib.)	21,749	(4%)	($1,428)
1974 primary:	Jim Allen (D)	572,584	(83%)	
	John Taylor (D)	118,848	(17%)	
1968 general:	Jim Allen (D)	638,774	(70%)	
	Pery Hooper (R)	201,227	(22%)	
	Robert P. Schwenn (NDPA)	72,699	(8%)	

Gov. George C. Wallace (D) Elected 1970, term expires Jan. 1979; b. Aug. 25, 1919, Clio; U. of Ala., LL.B. 1942; Methodist.

Career Army Air Corps, WWII; Asst. Atty. Gen. of Ala., 1946; Ala. House of Reps., 1947–53; Judge, Ala. 3rd Judicial Circuit, 1953–62; Candidate for Dem. Nomination for Gov., 1958; Gov. of Ala., 1963–67; Amer. Ind. Party nominee for Pres., 1968.

Offices Executive Dept., Montgomery 36104, 205-832-3511.

Election Results

1974 general:	George C. Wallace (D)	497,574	(83%)
	Elvin McCary (R)	88,381	(15%)
	Jim Partain (Prohib.)	12,350	(2%)
1974 primary:	George C. Wallace (D)	536,235	(65%)
	Gene McLain (D)	249,695	(30%)
	Three Others (D)	42,381	(5%)
1970 general:	George C. Wallace (D)	637,046	(76%)
	John Logan Cashin (NDPA)	125,491	(15%)
	A. C. Shelton (Ind.)	75,679	(9%)

◆ ◆ ◆ ◆ ◆

FIRST DISTRICT

The Tombigbee and Alabama Rivers flow south from the Alabama Black Belt—named for the fertility of its black cotton-growing soil—to the port of Mobile and the Gulf of Mexico. Mobile (pop. 190,000) is Alabama's second largest city, and the largest port on the Gulf between New Orleans and Tampa. Dominated by usually sluggish industries—shipping, shipbuilding, and paper—the Mobile area has had no population growth since the 1950s.

Although 35% of its residents are black, Mobile is the most pro-Wallace of Alabama's large cities. It gave the Governor an overwhelming 68% in his 1968 presidential bid, and was the only metropolitan area to back him in the crucial 1970 gubernatorial primary. Not coincidentally, Mobile is the most blue-collar of Alabama's major cities; Wallace's support, here as in northern primaries, is greatest among blue collar workers among whom his frank and blunt image evoke the strongest reactions. The only discordant note here is the fact that Mobile's largest suburb, Prichard (pop. 41,000), elected a young black named Jay Cooper Mayor in 1972—even though the city is not majority black.

Alabama's 1st congressional district stretches from Mobile north to the Black Belt, and includes one black-majority county (Wilcox). But most of the people here live in and around Mobile, and Mobile County casts almost 80% of the district's votes. The 1st's feelings about national political figures can be gauged by the fact that Nixon in 1972, Wallace in 1968, and Goldwater in 1964 all received at least 70% of the district's votes.

The 1964 election also pretty well determined the outcome since of House races in the 1st. It was Barry Goldwater's strong showing a dozen years ago that probably more than anything else accounted for the victory of Republican W. Jack Edwards. Edwards had not previously held public office, but has since become thoroughly entrenched in the seat: he ran ahead of Richard Nixon in 1972.

In the House, Edwards has become one of the most well respected of Southern Republicans. He early won a seat on the Appropriations Committee, on which he is now the 8th ranking Republican. And in 1971, he narrowly (85–82) lost a bid to become Vice-Chairman of the House Republican Conference; today he is Secretary of the Conference, technically the highest ranking of the Southern Republicans. Edwards is regarded as a solid conservative, but a rather quiet-spoken one who takes care to understand other points of view. He seemed to know—unlike some of his Southern colleagues—how Richard Nixon could be in such trouble nationally in 1973 or 1974, when his Southern constituents (or at least the white ones) were still vociferously behind him.

Census Data Pop. 491,747. Central city, 39%; suburban, 38%. Median family income, $7,305; families above $15,000: 11%; families below $3,000: 18%. Median years education, 10.8.

The Voters

  Median voting age 42.
  Employment profile White collar, 41%. Blue collar, 42%. Service, 14%. Farm, 3%.
  Ethnic groups Black, 33%. Total foreign stock, 2%.

Presidential vote

1972	Nixon (R)	103,842	(76%)
	McGovern (D)	33,276	(24%)
1968	Nixon (R)	14,643	(10%)
	Humphrey (D)	27,878	(19%)
	Wallace (AI)	102,755	(71%)

Rep. Jack Edwards (R) Elected 1964; b. Sept. 20, 1928, Birmingham; home, Mobile; U. of Ala., B.S. 1952, LL.B. 1954; Presbyterian.

Career USMC, 1946–48, 1950–51; Instructor in Business Law, U. of Ala., 1954; Practicing atty., 1954–64.

Offices 2439 RHOB, 202-225-4931. Also 8011 Fed. Ofc. Bldg., 109 St. Joseph St., Mobile 36602, 205-690-2811.

Committees

Appropriations (8th). Subcommittees: Defense; Transportation.

Group Ratings

	ADA	COPE	LWV	RIPON	NFU	LCV	CFA	NAB	NSI	ACA
1974	10	0	27	54	25	31	17	67	78	71
1973	16	9	33	60	21	17	14	–	–	84
1972	0	10	11	54	50	18	50	88	100	78

Key Votes

1) Foreign Aid	AGN	6) Gov Abortn Aid	AGN	11) Pub Cong Election $	AGN
2) Busing	AGN	7) Coed Phys Ed	AGN	12) Turkish Arms Cutoff	ABS
3) ABM	FOR	8) Pov Lawyer Gag	FOR	13) Youth Camp Regs	AGN
4) B-1 Bomber	FOR	9) Pub Trans Sub	AGN	14) Strip Mine Veto	FOR
5) Nerve Gas	FOR	10) EZ Voter Regis	AGN	15) Farm Bill Veto	FOR

Election Results

1974 general	Jack Edwards (R)	60,710	(59%)	
	Augusta E. Wilson (D)	37,718	(37%)	($57,288)
	Mary B. McCarthy (D)	3,638	(4%)	(NA)
1974 primary:	Jack Edwards (R), unopposed			
1972 general:	Jack Edwards (R)	104,606	(77%)	($27,612)
	D. W. McCrory (D)	24,357	(18%)	($1,063)
	Thomas McAboy, Jr. (NDPA)	7,747	(6%)	(NA)

◆ ◆ ◆ ◆ ◆

SECOND DISTRICT

It was not until some years after Alabama was admitted to the Union that Southern planters, their soil in Virginia and the Carolinas growing tired, discovered the Black Belt of Alabama. The fertile black soil gave the region its name, and almost cried out for the crop that came to characterize the Confederacy: King Cotton. As every schoolchild knows, cotton was a crop that required cheap, abundant labor, and Alabama's Black Belt became slave territory; before the Civil War, slaves outnumbered whites as much as 10-1 in some counties. For years after the Civil War the majority of the Black Belt's citizens were the descendants of slaves. Only as black migration to the north went on and on did black percentages grow less, so that by the time the 1965 Voting Rights Act gave blacks the ballot, only a handful of small, predominantly rural counties were left with black majorities.

On a map, Alabama's congressional district lines look perfectly regular. Closer inspection, however, shows them to have been carefully crafted to divide the black majority counties among several districts, so as to prevent black voters from exerting a major influence in any congressional election. The 2d district, for example, contains only one black-majority county (Bullock), but just outside the district line there are three others (Macon, Lowndes, and Wilcox).

So the blacks in the 2d are heavily outnumbered by the white majority in Montgomery, the state's capital, and by those in the nearly all-white "piney woods" counties to the south of the Black Belt. The whites here are pleased to remind visitors that Montgomery was the Cradle of the Confederacy, the rebels' capital before Richmond. Local boosters are less likely to talk about the 1956 Montgomery bus boycott, which gave national prominence to a young black minister named Martin Luther King, Jr.

The 2d is basically an amalgam of the old 2d and 3d districts, a conjunction rendered necessary by the results of the 1970 census, which cost Alabama a congressional seat. Despite the death of the Democratic Congressman from the 3d, 28-year veteran George Andrews, the new 2d was still the most hotly-contested Alabama House race in 1972. The Democratic nominee carried the newly added portions of the district by 6,000 votes, but he was beaten as Republican incumbent William Dickinson carried Montgomery County by a sweeping 2-1 margin. As in many other parts of the South it was the urban areas which provided the Republican with his most commanding margins.

To the national press, Dickinson is perhaps best known for his charges in 1965 that the Selma marchers—who passed through part of the 2nd district—engaged in obscene conduct; though he promised to document the accusation, he never did. But through the vagaries of the seniority system, and because of the large numbers of retiring Republicans, Dickinson has risen to positions of at least theoretical influence: number one Republican on Wayne Hays' House Administration

Committee, number two, behind California's Bob Wilson, on Armed Services. But Dickinson's influence remains more theoretical than real. House Administration is definitely under Hays's thumb, and Dickinson, despite occasional contentiousness, differs so little from Armed Services' hawkish consensus that he makes little difference there—except, perhaps, to protect the interests of the district's two Air Force bases and giant Fort Rucker near Dothan.

Census Data Pop. 491,676. Central city, 27%; suburban, 7%. Median family income, $6,749; families above $15,000: 10%; families below $3,000: 21%. Median years education, 11.0.

The Voters

Median voting age 42.
Employment profile White collar, 42%. Blue collar, 39%. Service, 14%. Farm, 5%.
Ethnic groups Black, 30%. Total foreign stock, 2%.

Presidential vote

1972	Nixon (R)	107,702	(78%)
	McGovern (D)	31,190	(22%)
1968	Nixon (R)	12,337	(8%)
	Humphrey (D)	26,179	(18%)
	Wallace (AI)	109,223	(74%)

Rep. William L. Dickinson (R) Elected 1964; b. June 5, 1925, Opelika; home, Montgomery; U. of Ala., A.B. 1948, LL.B. 1950; Methodist.

Career Navy, WWII; Practicing atty., 1950–63; Judge, Opelika City Court, Lee Co. Court of Common Pleas and Juvenile Court, Fifth Judicial Circuit; Asst. V.P., Southern Railway System.

Offices 2436 RHOB, 202-225-2901. Also 401 P.O. Bldg., Montgomery 36104, 205-265-5611.

Committees

Armed Services (2d). Subcommittees: Investigations; Research and Development; Special Subcommittee on Intelligence.

House Administration (Ranking Member). Subcommittees: Parking.

Group Ratings

	ADA	COPE	LWV	RIPON	NFU	LCV	CFA	NAB	NSI	ACA
1974	5	0	25	40	17	13	0	80	90	92
1973	4	9	17	36	40	11	14	–	–	96
1972	0	0	20	46	40	2	0	92	100	95

Key Votes

1) Foreign Aid	AGN	6) Gov Abortn Aid	AGN	11) Pub Cong Election $	AGN
2) Busing	AGN	7) Coed Phys Ed	AGN	12) Turkish Arms Cutoff	AGN
3) ABM	FOR	8) Pov Lawyer Gag	FOR	13) Youth Camp Regs	AGN
4) B-1 Bomber	AGN	9) Pub Trans Sub	AGN	14) Strip Mine Veto	FOR
5) Nerve Gas	FOR	10) EZ Voter Regis	AGN	15) Farm Bill Veto	FOR

Election Results

1974 general:	William L. "Bill" Dickinson (R)	54,089	(66%)	($33,071)
	Clair Chisler (D)	27,729	(34%)	($6,134)
1974 primary:	William L. "Bill" Dickinson (R), unopposed			
1972 general:	William L. "Bill" Dickinson (R)	80,362	(55%)	($50,193)
	Ben C. Reeves (D)	60,769	(42%)	($122,067)
	Richar Boone (NDPA)	4,991	(3%)	(NA)

◆ ◆ ◆ ◆ ◆

THIRD DISTRICT

The 3d district of Alabama extends from the cotton-growing Black Belt in the southern part of the state to the red clay hills of the north. To the south is Tuskegee, a black-majority town in a black-majority county, and the home of Booker T. Washington's Tuskegee Institute; Tuskegee also has an ambitious young black Mayor, Johnny Ford, who made headlines by endorsing Richard Nixon and George Wallace. Also in the southern portion is Phenix City, a one-time Alabama "sin city" across the Chattahoochee River from Georgia's huge Fort Benning. A mid-1950s cleanup of Phenix City propelled a young prosecutor, John Patterson, into the Governor's chair; he beat George Wallace in the Democratic primary, and in fact was the last politician to beat Wallace in Alabama. In the northern part of the district is the small industrial city of Anniston (pop. 31,000), and, adjacent to the city, Fort McClellan. This area is one of the few in the state to show a significant population growth during the 1960s; like most of the areas in the Deep South, population growth here was heavily dependent on the military.

Outside of the Black Belt counties in the south, the 3d district is mostly white, and the whites living in the district's small towns and hilly farm country are George Wallace's kind of people. The current Congressman, Bill Nichols, was a Wallace floor leader in the Alabama Senate, and his House voting record is what one might expect from that history, keeping in mind the fact that the Wallace line on economic issues is considerably more business-oriented than the populistic tone of his rhetoric. In 1966, Nichols was the only Alabama Democrat who beat a Republican elected in the local Goldwater landslide two years before. Since then he has been sent back to Washington every two years with more than 75% of the votes. With a middle-level position on the House Armed Services Committee, Nichols has made little impression on Washington except to add another vote to the usually lopsided margins enjoyed by the committee's Southern Democrat-Republican majority.

Census Data Pop. 493,588. Central city, 0%; suburban, 16%. Median family income, $6,817; families above $15,000: 8%; families below $3,000: 19%. Median years education, 10.2.

The Voters

Median voting age 42.
Employment profile White collar, 34%. Blue collar, 50%. Service, 14%. Farm, 2%.
Ethnic groups Black, 31%. Total foreign stock, 1%.

Presidential vote

1972	Nixon (R)	....	98,640	(75%)
	McGovern (D)	....	33,480	(25%)
1968	Nixon (R)	....	14,611	(11%)
	Humphrey (D)	....	26,024	(19%)
	Wallace (AI)	....	98,246	(71%)

Rep. Bill Nichols (D) Elected 1966; b. Oct. 16, 1918, near Becker, Miss.; home, Sylacauga; Auburn U., B.S. 1939, M.S. 1941; Methodist.

Career Army, 1942–47; V.P. Parker Fertilizer Co., Pres., Parker Gin Co., 1947–66; Ala. Senate 1963–67.

Offices 2417 RHOB, 202-225-3261. Also Fed. Bldg., P.O. Box 2042, Anniston 36201, 205-236-5655.

Committees

Armed Services (12th). Subcommittees: Investigations; Military Compensation.

Group Ratings

	ADA	COPE	LWV	RIPON	NFU	LCV	CFA	NAB	NSI	ACA
1974	4	25	18	13	55	20	45	40	90	64
1973	8	36	42	20	80	12	57	–	–	74
1972	0	17	13	27	50	13	100	71	100	92

Key Votes

1) Foreign Aid	AGN	6) Gov Abortn Aid	AGN	11) Pub Cong Election $	AGN
2) Busing	AGN	7) Coed Phys Ed	AGN	12) Turkish Arms Cutoff	AGN
3) ABM	FOR	8) Pov Lawyer Gag	FOR	13) Youth Camp Regs	AGN
4) B-1 Bomber	FOR	9) Pub Trans Sub	AGN	14) Strip Mine Veto	FOR
5) Nerve Gas	FOR	10) EZ Voter Regis	AGN	15) Farm Bill Veto	AGN

Election Results

1974 general:	Bill Nichols (D)	63,582	(96%)	($2,538)
	James R. Connell (AI)	2,729	(4%)	(NA)
1974 primary:	Bill Nichols (D), unopposed			
1972 general:	Bill Nichols (D)	100,045	(77%)	($34,984)
	Robert M. Kerr (R)	27,253	(21%)	($6,718)
	John Ford (NDPA)	3,392	(3%)	(NA)

◆ ◆ ◆ ◆

FOURTH DISTRICT

Nowhere is the counterrevolution in Southern white politics—a movement sparked by the civil rights revolution of the 1960s—more clearly evident than in the 4th district of Alabama. As recently as a dozen years ago, this part of northern Alabama, situated between Birmingham on the south and the Tennessee River valley on the north, was a populist stronghold. The local Congressman, Carl Elliott, was considered reliable enough by the Kennedy Administration and the AFL-CIO to be a chosen one of the two members added to the Rules Committee when it was enlarged (or packed) in 1961. Unlike most of the rest of the South, organized labor was strong enough here to play some part in the district's politics. The workingmen from industrial towns like Gadsden, Jasper, and Cullman, and the leatherhanded farmers of the red clay hills, consistently supported economic liberals like Sens. Lister Hill and John Sparkman, and ex-Gov. "Kissin' Jim" Folsom against the more business-oriented candidates from the Black Belt.

In those days, race was not a big thing in the politics of the 4th. There were few blacks here, and it was assumed you were against civil rights bills, and that you'd support a filibuster if there was one. But that was not the main reason these men went to Washington, nor was it why most people in the 4th voted to send them there.

But as the national Democratic Party under Kennedy and Johnson became identified with the civil rights movement, attitudes in the 4th changed. In 1964, Goldwater Republicans swept the district; Carl Elliott was out, beaten by a Republican businessman named Jim Martin. Before 1964, the most important political fact about the voters of this district was that they were predominantly blue collar; from then on, the most important political fact has been that they are almost all white. Only 9% of the 4th's residents are black, the lowest percentage in Alabama. In the old days, that meant race wasn't important and the district was relatively liberal; now it means that there are few blacks to oppose the white consensus, and the district is overwhelmingly conservative.

Martin left the House after one term to run, quite unsuccessfully, against Lurleen Wallace in 1966, and he was replaced in Congress by Tom Bevill, a Wallace floor leader in the Alabama House. Bevill at first voted a very conservative line, and as a regional Democratic whip, he was more out of line with the majority of Congressmen of his party than anyone else holding a similar position. But more recently, as Republican administrations have been driving Democrats together, Bevill has been voting somewhat more often with other House Democrats, particularly on economic issues. He is about as invulnerable locally as any Congressman could be.

Census Data Pop. 492,196. Central city, 11%; suburban, 21%. Median family income, $6,350; families above $15,000: 7%; families below $3,000: 22%. Median years education, 9.9.

The Voters

Median voting age 44.
Employment profile White collar, 31%. Blue collar, 53%. Service, 11%. Farm, 5%.
Ethnic groups Black, 9%.

Presidential vote

1972	Nixon (R)	117,823	(78%)
	McGovern (D)	34,059	(22%)

1968	Nixon (R)	....	32,027	(19%)
	Humphrey (D)	....	15,710	(10%)
	Wallace (AI)	....	117,428	(71%)

Rep. Tom Bevill (D) Elected 1966; b. Mar. 27, 1921, Townley; home, Jasper; U. of Ala., B.S. 1943, LL.B. 1948; Baptist.

Career Army, WWII; Practicing atty., 1949–67; Ala. House of Reps., 1958–66.

Offices 1126 LHOB, 202-225-4876. Also 600 Broad St., Gadsden 35901, 205-546-0201.

Committees

Appropriations (27th). Subcommittees: Foreign Operations; Public Works.

Group Ratings

	ADA	COPE	LWV	RIPON	NFU	LCV	CFA	NAB	NSI	ACA
1974	14	56	9	20	30	35	63	42	89	64
1973	24	80	50	28	100	16	86	–	–	54
1972	19	82	9	17	50	5	100	46	100	65

Key Votes

1) Foreign Aid	AGN	6) Gov Abortn Aid	AGN	11) Pub Cong Election $	AGN
2) Busing	AGN	7) Coed Phys Ed	AGN	12) Turkish Arms Cutoff	AGN
3) ABM	FOR	8) Pov Lawyer Gag	FOR	13) Youth Camp Regs	AGN
4) B-1 Bomber	FOR	9) Pub Trans Sub	FOR	14) Strip Mine Veto	FOR
5) Nerve Gas	FOR	10) EZ Voter Regis	AGN	15) Farm Bill Veto	AGN

Election Results

1974 general:	Tom Bevill (D), unopposed			($5,174)
1974 primary:	Tom Bevill (D), unopposed			
1972 general:	Tom Bevill (D)	108,039	(70%)	($38,918)
	Ed Nelson (R)	46,551	(30%)	($12,550)

◆ ◆ ◆ ◆ ◆

FIFTH DISTRICT

The well-off northernmost part of Alabama owes most of its prosperity and recent growth to that behemoth George Wallace is always decrying: the federal government. Fifty years ago the Tennessee River coursed through the state's northern counties untamed, every spring flooding the farm country and small towns. Then the Tennessee Valley Authority, TVA, was created, and the alphabet agency damned the wild river for most of its length, produced cheap public power, and controlled the flooding. This part of Alabama was always populistic, and with the coming of TVA was pleased to send to Congress New Dealers like John J. Sparkman, who served in the House from what is now the 5th district from 1937 to 1946.

The federal government's largesse here was not limited to TVA. In 1950, Huntsville, one of the area's largest cities, was just a sleepy hill town of 14,000. Today its population is 137,000. The principal agent of change has been the Redstone Missile Arsenal, the home of hundreds of Army and NASA rocket engineers and technicians. In recent years the Pentagon and NASA have pumped into the seven counties that make up Alabama's 5th congressional district more than half a billion dollars a year, most of it going into Huntsville.

Although the Huntsville boom produced an influx of Yankees and Europeans (like Werner von Braun), most of the new migrants were from the South, and the politics of the area remained basically the same. The populist strain in Alabama politics, always strong here, was quieted in the

1960s, as it was elsewhere in the state, when racial issues became central in electoral politics. There are some signs the 5th is reverting, slowly, to its populist ways; there was, for example, a sharp rise in the Democratic percentage for President in 1972. The TVA city of Decatur, in the 5th, was the place where George Wallace saw fit to host Ted Kennedy on July 4, 1973; it was probably one of the few places in the state where both could have been received amicably.

In other elections, the 5th has been less Wallaceite than the rest of Alabama. Wallace ran worst here in the close 1970 gubernatorial primary than anywhere else in the state except Birmingham, and in 1972 this was John Sparkman's strongest territory. Even George McGovern got about 20% of the whites' votes here, far higher than one might have expected.

The career of Sparkman's successor in the House has been, up to now at least, something of a mirror of the changing attitudes in the district. For many years, northern Democrats could count on picking up the support of Robert E. Jones when they really needed it on economic issues. In 1961, for example, Jones was an important Southern backer of the Kennedy Administration's drive to "pack" the House Rules Committee. But with the rise of Wallace, Jones has voted less often—and less audibly—with the northerners. It was only when Nixon insisted on impounding some of his precious public works funds that Jones, like many other Southern Democrats, found himself making common cause with his northern brethren once again.

After 18 years in the House, Bob Jones finally achieved one of the goals held by so many congressmen: a committee chairmanship. Public Works, the committee Jones now heads, has long been known as the home of the pork barrel, where Congressmen cement personal alliances by voting each others' districts huge public works projects: dams, highways, post offices, etc. Traditionally, the Public Works Chairman has been a get-along-go-along guy, always ready to oblige a colleague with a project in return for help on something else. Bob Jones certainly fits this mold. The experience of his district and his own roots in the New Deal era, when good Democrats assumed heavy public works spending would work out for the public good, have conditioned Jones to discount entirely environmental objections to projects and economy-minded cavilling at the pork barrel. And he has never been the least bit sympathetic to those who argue that the gas tax trust fund should be used for total transportation needs, rather than just for highways. About half the Committee's Democrats and virtually all its Republicans share Jones's basic views, and so the likelihood is that—for all the talk of a new, freshman-oriented House—the Public Works Committee will retain an atmosphere and a record which would not much surprise someone suddenly propelled into 1976 from the 1940s.

Census Data Pop. 489,771. Central city, 28%; suburban, 18%. Median family income, $8,271; families above $15,000: 17%; families below $3,000: 15%. Median years education, 11.8.

The Voters

Median voting age 40.
Employment profile White collar, 47%. Blue collar, 38%. Service, 12%. Farm, 3%.
Ethnic groups Black, 13%. Total foreign stock, 2%.

Presidential vote

1972	Nixon (R)	98,504	(75%)
	McGovern (D)	33,603	(25%)
1968	Nixon (R)	23,576	(17%)
	Humphrey (D)	16,900	(13%)
	Wallace (AI)	94,659	(70%)

Rep. Robert E. Jones (D) Elected 1946; b. June 12, 1912, Scottsboro; home, Scottsboro; U. of Ala., LL.B. 1937; Methodist.

Career Practicing atty., 1937–40; Judge, Jackson Co. Court, 1940–43; Navy, WWII.

Offices 2426 RHOB, 202-225-4801. Also P.O. Bldg., Scottsboro 35768, 205-574-2618.

Committees

Public Works and Transportation (Chairman).

Group Ratings

	ADA	COPE	LWV	RIPON	NFU	LCV	CFA	NAB	NSI	ACA
1974	28	60	55	29	75	44	50	40	100	22
1973	33	90	45	50	100	20	86	–	–	33
1972	25	70	50	43	71	0	0	20	89	52

Key Votes

1) Foreign Aid	FOR	6) Gov Abortn Aid	AGN	11) Pub Cong Election $	AGN
2) Busing	AGN	7) Coed Phys Ed	AGN	12) Turkish Arms Cutoff	AGN
3) ABM	FOR	8) Pov Lawyer Gag	FOR	13) Youth Camp Regs	FOR
4) B-1 Bomber	FOR	9) Pub Trans Sub	FOR	14) Strip Mine Veto	AGN
5) Nerve Gas	FOR	10) EZ Voter Regis	AGN	15) Farm Bill Veto	AGN

Election Results

1974 general:	Robert E. Jones (D), unopposed			($1,262)
1974 primary:	Robert E. Jones (D), unopposed			
1972 general:	Robert E. Jones (D)	101,303	(75%)	($30,786)
	Dieter J. Schrader (R)	33,352	(25%)	($11,175)

◆ ◆ ◆ ◆ ◆

SIXTH DISTRICT

Birmingham was one of the few major Southern cities which was not on the map at the time of the Civil War. It was founded a few years later and named, in the hopes of a great industrial future, for the giant English manufacturing center. The hopes of the founders have been realized all too well. Birmingham is, and has been for many years, the major steel center in the South. But American steel has not been a super growth industry, and Birmingham, once just about the same size as Atlanta, has been left far behind its booming Georgian neighbor these last 20 years. While John Portman hotels were sprouting up in downtown Atlanta, the steel mills in Birmingham, set in valleys between high ridges, succeeded in so fouling the city's air that the federal government ordered them shut down for several days in 1972.

The city's reputation has not aided its economy. Most Americans, if not most Alabamians, still associate the city's name with the events of 1963, when the late Eugene "Bull" Connor, then police commissioner, set dogs and firehoses against peaceful civil rights demonstrators. Shortly thereafter, Connor seemed nonplussed when somebody set off a bomb in a black church and killed three young girls.

Birmingham, however, has long since repudiated Bull Connor, voting him out of office long before he died. And in the 1970 gubernatorial primary—the only time in the last dozen years George Wallace has faced a serious challenge—the city cast the heaviest anti-Wallace vote in the state. Commotion of any kind tends to deter investment, and as the 1960s went on, it became plain that neither Northern nor Southern money was finding its way to Birmingham. Businessmen could not deny the story told by the 1970 census: as metropolitan Atlanta's population rose 37% during the sixties, Birmingham's was up less than 3%.

Alabama's 6th congressional district takes in virtually all of the city of Birmingham and most of its suburbs, including comfortable Mountain Brook and Vestavia Hills, where most of the city's white establishment lives. Its Congressman is John H. Buchanan, Jr., a Republican who rode into office on the 1964 Goldwater wave and for the most part has managed to stay in with little difficulty since. Buchanan is a Baptist minister, and from his record in the House it seems fairly safe to say that he prefers fundamentalist preaching. At one point in his career, while serving on the old House Un-American Activities Committee, Buchanan surprised some observers by denouncing the Ku Klux Klan.

More recently, in 1974, Buchanan found himself in a more defensive posture. As the ranking Republican on Jack Brooks' Government Operations Subcommittee looking into White House expenditures, Buchanan felt obliged to attack Brooks' charges that Nixon was spending $14 million per year to operate San Clemente and Key Biscayne; fundamentalists usually find it unsettling to defend luxury. His strong pro-Nixon backing seems to be one reason Buchanan suddenly found himself in some political trouble in 1974, even in Birmingham. Another reason was of course the Democratic trend generally, and a third was his opponent, Birmingham Councilwoman Nina Miglionico. With an unlikely name for a Southern politician, Miglionico campaigned gamely and attacked Buchanan for his Nixon support. That she managed to make some inroads but still did not really come close enough to win shows that Buchanan's seat is probably safe; but at the same time, it shows that Deep South congressional politics has become a little more volatile than one might have thought.

Census Data Pop. 493,045. Central city, 61%; suburban, 39%. Median family income, $8,683; families above $15,000: 16%; families below $3,000: 13%. Median years education, 11.9.

The Voters

Median voting age 44.
Employment profile White collar, 52%. Blue collar, 34%. Service, 14%. Farm, –%.
Ethnic groups Black, 30%. Total foreign stock, 3%.

Presidential vote

1972	Nixon (R)	108,102	(72%)
	McGovern (D)	41,625	(28%)
1968	Nixon (R)	34,505	(23%)
	Humphrey (D)	40,290	(26%)
	Wallace (AI)	78,464	(51%)

Rep. John H. Buchanan (R) Elected 1964; b. Mar. 19, 1928, Paris, Tenn.; home, Birmingham; Samford U., B.A. 1949, U. of Va., Southern Theological Sem.; Baptist.

Career Navy WWII; Pastor of Baptist Churches, 1953–62; Finance Dir., Ala. Repub. Party, 1962–64.

Offices 2159 RHOB, 202-225-4921. Also Suite 105 Fed. Bldg., 1800 5th Ave. N., Birmingham 35203, 202-325-3861.

Committees

Education and Labor (9th). Subcommittees: Elementary, Secondary and Vocational Education; Equal Opportunities; Post-secondary Education.

International Relations (4th). Subcommittees: International Political and Military Affairs; International Operations.

Group Ratings

	ADA	COPE	LWV	RIPON	NFU	LCV	CFA	NAB	NSI	ACA
1974	29	0	70	67	36	33	0	50	100	71
1973	24	11	58	80	11	73	50	–	–	77
1972	6	18	42	69	57	54	50	73	100	73

Key Votes

1) Foreign Aid	FOR	6) Gov Abortn Aid	AGN	11) Pub Cong Election $	FOR
2) Busing	AGN	7) Coed Phys Ed	AGN	12) Turkish Arms Cutoff	FOR
3) ABM	FOR	8) Pov Lawyer Gag	FOR	13) Youth Camp Regs	FOR
4) B-1 Bomber	FOR	9) Pub Trans Sub	FOR	14) Strip Mine Veto	FOR
5) Nerve Gas	AGN	10) EZ Voter Regis	AGN	15) Farm Bill Veto	FOR

Election Results

1974 general:	John H. Buchanan, Jr. (R)	54,505	(58%)	($65,235)
	Nina Miglionico (D)	39,444	(42%)	($71,291)

1974 primary:	John H. Buchanan, Jr. (R), unopposed			
1972 general:	John H. Buchanan, Jr. (R)	91,499	(61%)	($33,976)
	Ben Erdreich (D)	54,497	(36%)	($18,947)
	Al Thomas (NDPA)	3,887	(3%)	(NA)

◆ ◆ ◆ ◆ ◆

SEVENTH DISTRICT

After the House Judiciary Committee finished its impeachment hearings in the summer of 1974, public opinion polls showed a perceptible rise in the estimation held by the American people toward their Congressmen, and one of the reasons was Walter Flowers of the 7th district of Alabama. Before the hearings, Flowers was not especially well known, even on the Hill. People who were for some reason interested could have discovered that he had first been elected as recently as 1968, that he was one of the few Southern Democrats on the Judiciary Committee, that he had risen in seniority on that body to the tenth position, that he had had significant primary opposition in 1972.

What such an inquirer would not have found out until the hearings began was that Flowers possessed one of the better minds on the committee, and the ability to express himself succinctly and sometimes poignantly. On the basis of his previous political record, observers thought him the most likely of the Committee's Democrats to vote against Nixon's impeachment. On substantive issues, Flowers had almost always taken the conservative side; he seemed to represent nicely the views of the small town bankers and businessmen he had undoubtedly had as legal clients back home in Tuscaloosa. And on most matters, he seemed to reflect the views of George Wallace—whose active opposition would likely end the career of any Alabama Congressman.

But impeachment turned out to be an issue that was decided, not on politics, but on the facts and the interpretations brought to them; and for Walter Flowers, that meant trouble. The easy course, as Nixon might have put it, was for the Congressman to support the President. Admittedly, his district gave Nixon his smallest Alabama percentage in 1972, but that was because it contained the largest percentage of blacks (38%); the whites were then, and so far as anyone could tell remained in 1974, solidly on Nixon's side. Moreover, the people who had worked for and supported Flowers in his tough 1972 primary against Alberta Murphy—a comparatively liberal white who got most of the black votes—were also the kind who tended to back Nixon most fervently.

So when Flowers decided that the facts compelled him to vote for impeachment, and when he and James Mann of South Carolina began meeting with like-minded Republicans led by Illinois' Tom Railsback, Flowers must have thought that his political career was coming to an end. Flowers himself played a significant role in the actual phrasing of the impeachment counts which passed, and his impassioned speech disclosing how he would vote constituted one of the most moving moments in the hearings. It also showed his political fears: he was careful to mention more than once that the Nixon people had poured money into Alabama to defeat George Wallace.

Perhaps it was that speech, or the tone of the hearings as a whole, or simply the facts of the case—but whatever it was, when Walter Flowers returned home to the 7th district, he found his constituents far less angry than he had anticipated. As it happened, Alabama's primary had already been held, and Flowers had opposition in November only from the National Democratic Party of Alabama (NDPA) candidate, who would win only a few votes, almost all from blacks. But his reception was such as to indicate that he has little reason to fear significant opposition based on his impeachment vote. Indeed, he may even find it easier to win the votes of his black constituents than he has in the past.

Census Data Pop. 492,142. Central city, 14%; suburban, 47%. Median family income, $6,806; families above $15,000: 10%; families below $3,000: 22%. Median years education, 10.4.

The Voters

Median voting age 43.
Employment profile White collar, 38%. Blue collar, 43%. Service, 15%. Farm, 4%.
Ethnic groups Black, 38%. Total foreign stock, 1%.

Presidential vote

1972	Nixon (R)		92,421	(66%)
	McGovern (D)		47,536	(34%)
1968	Nixon (R)		14,585	(10%)
	Humphrey (D)		43,408	(29%)
	Wallace (AI)		89,956	(61%)

Rep. Walter Flowers (D) Elected 1968; b. Apr. 12, 1933, Greenville; home, Tuscaloosa; U. of Ala., A.B. 1955, LL.B. 1957, U. of London 1957–58; Episcopalian.

Career Army, 1958–59; Practicing atty., 1959–69.

Offices 401 CHOB, 202-225-2665. Also, Fed. Bldg., Tuscaloosa 35401, 205-752-3578.

Committees

Judiciary (8th). Subcommittees: Administrative Law and Governmental Relations (Chairman); Monopolies and Commercial Law.

Science and Technology (6th). Subcommittees: Energy Research; Science, Research, and Technology; Space Science and Applications.

Group Ratings

	ADA	COPE	LWV	RIPON	NFU	LCV	CFA	NAB	NSI	ACA
1974	10	45	25	21	62	38	46	30	78	64
1973	16	55	45	31	89	17	63	–	–	60
1972	6	18	20	46	67	18	0	64	100	68

Key Votes

1) Foreign Aid	AGN	6) Gov Abortn Aid	AGN	11) Pub Cong Election $	AGN
2) Busing	AGN	7) Coed Phys Ed	AGN	12) Turkish Arms Cutoff	FOR
3) ABM	AGN	8) Pov Lawyer Gag	FOR	13) Youth Camp Regs	AGN
4) B-1 Bomber	FOR	9) Pub Trans Sub	AGN	14) Strip Mine Veto	FOR
5) Nerve Gas	FOR	10) EZ Voter Regis	AGN	15) Farm Bill Veto	AGN

Election Results

1974 general:	Walter Flowers (D)	73,203	(91%)	($26,604)
	Frank P. Walls (C)	5,175	(6%)	(NA)
	Lewis Black (NDPA)	2,085	(3%)	(NA)
1974 primary:	Walter Flowers (D)	73,190	(67%)	
	Alberta Murphy (D)	35,999	(33%)	
1972 general:	Walter Flowers (D)	95,060	(86%)	($16,303)
	Lewis Black (NDPA)	15,703	(14%)	(NA)

ALASKA

Alaska is the nation's largest state (586,000 square miles) and also its smallest (300,000 people). Alaskans live in the land of the midnight sun and of darkness at noon; of winter wind-chill factors that reach 100 below and of muggy, mosquito-filled summers; of the tallest mountains in North America and thousands of miles of rugged seacoast. It is a land where a penniless immigrant like Walter Hickel can make millions in the construction business, and where Eskimos and Aleuts live in grinding poverty. And perhaps most important these days, Alaska is the land of the great North Slope oil strike, of sudden boom coexisting with high unemployment.

It is hard for someone from the "lower 48" to grasp the size of Alaska. It is more than twice as large as Texas, and spans four different time zones. But for all its expanse, Alaska has only one railroad and few highways—the airplane is the only way one can really get around. Even the most isolated villages in the interior have an airstrip cleared on a frozen river or in the bush. A grim reminder of the state's unchartedness was the October 1972 plane crash that took the lives of the state's Congressman, Nick Begich, and House Majority Leader Hale Boggs.

Most of Alaska still belongs to the state of nature, the home of caribou and perhaps an occasional Eskimo hunter. Most of the population here is clustered in a few small urban areas, more than 40% in greater Anchorage alone. And though dreams of sudden riches still draw men to the Alaskan wilderness, the livelihood of most citizens here depends, directly or indirectly, on the federal government.

For years, Alaskans yearned for statehood, for control of their own affairs and release from the economic thrall of Washington and of Seattle. But Alaska is still an economic—and political—dependent. Decisions continue to be made in Washington, D.C., that will shape Alaska's future much as the Northwest Ordinance did Ohio's or the Homestead Act Nebraska's. For example, it was only in 1971, when Congress passed the Alaska Native Claims Act, that the most basic issue—the ownership of land—was settled. The natives—Eskimos, Aleuts, and Indians—had never surrendered title to the land to anyone, and the 1971 law gave them $962 million and 40 million acres—the money to be administered and the precise acreage chosen by 12 regional native corporations. The legislation also ended the freeze on federal lands imposed in 1966 by Interior Secretary Stewart Udall; this allowed the state to select the 103 million acres promised by the Statehood Act, and of course the state proceeded to choose the land with the greatest mineral potential.

Mineral potential in Alaska of course means oil—the huge oil strike on the remote North Slope. Total reserves are estimated at 10 billion barrels (east Texas, 5 billion; Kuwait, 62 billion), and the consortium of oil companies which bought the rights paid the state $900 million. Of course the big battle in recent years has been over the pipeline. The oil companies wanted it, the Interior Department wanted it, but environmentalists went to court and in 1973 got a ruling that the pipeline as planned was illegal because no statute allows Interior to lease as wide a right-of-away as it had leased to the oil companies. That made the demand for legislation irresistible. Joining the oil companies and the Nixon Administration was just about every Alaska politician in sight, for the oil companies had convinced the state's people that construction of the pipeline would provide thousands of jobs in a state that has chronic high unemployment. (They did not bother to mention that many of those jobs would be filled by skilled technicians from Texas and elsewhere.)

The boom psychology was accepted fully by Alaska's best known Senator, Mike Gravel. Up for reelection in 1974, Gravel was in serious trouble. He had been elected almost on a fluke in 1968, when his saturation TV documentary got him just enough votes to beat aging Sen. Ernest Gruening in the Democratic primary; he went on to win the general election against desultory opposition with less than a majority. Gravel ironically became as much a dove as Gruening, who had been one of the two Senators to vote against the Gulf of Tonkin resolution. In 1971, Gravel attempted to read into the Senate record massive excerpts from a copy of the then-banned Pentagon Papers. He was prevented by quick parliamentary footwork by Michigan's Robert Griffin, and so Gravel called a meeting of a subcommittee he chaired (Public Buildings and Grounds) and read from the papers until he collapsed in tears. That was scarcely Alaskan behavior, at least as Alaskans see it. Nor were they particularly pleased when Gravel made a quixotic run for Vice President at the 1972 Democratic National Convention. Alaska's representatives in Congress are supposed to get things for the state from the federal government, not monkey around for publicity's sake.

So in the summer of 1973 Mike Gravel needed very, very much to show that he still had clout in the Senate. The perfect vehicle was the pipeline bill, since the oil companies had persuaded Alaskans that the pipeline would solve all their problems. With Republican Sen. Ted Stevens, Gravel backed legislation drawn up by Henry Jackson to revise entirely federal land leasing law—a bill which would wipe out the court's decision, but still leave the question of the adequacy of Interior's Environmental Impact Statement unsettled. Then suddenly Gravel and Stevens pushed a bill which would dispense with the requirement of the Statement altogether, and allow the pipeline to go ahead immediately . Jackson was taken by surprise; he fought Gravel's measure because it might eviscerate the National Environmental Protection Act which he had authored and which required the Statement. But Gravel—with help from Stevens, and of course the oil companies—beat Jackson 50–49, and the pipeline went through.

It was the unusual case of one of the Senators with the least prestige in that body beating one of those with the most. It also mightily helped Gravel at home. He had been expecting strong opposition, perhaps from ex-Governor (1967–69) and Interior Secretary (1969–70) Walter Hickel; but Hickel, in a decision that would prove politically disastrous, decided to run for Governor again. The formidable primary opposition which had been expected also faded. As it turned out, Gravel had almost a free ride in the primary, and his opponent in the general election was a member of the national governing board of the John Birch Society, ex-state Sen. C. R. Lewis. With breaks like these Gravel got a second six years in the Senate. According to Jack Anderson, shortly after Gravel began his second term, one of his top aides sent him a memo suggesting he concentrate on becoming a "good Senator."

Gravel's colleague, Sen. Stevens, cuts a less tempestuous figure. A Republican with a somewhat independent voting record, he is not solidly aligned with either the liberal or the conservative wing of his party in the Senate. After a few years in the Alaska House and a short career as a prosperous Anchorage lawyer and in the Eisenhower Interior Department, Stevens was suddenly elevated to the Senate after the December 1968 death of Sen. Bob Bartlett—the man probably most responsible for Alaskan statehood. Stevens had to face the voters in 1970 for the remainder of Bartlett's unexpired term, and then again in 1972 for a full six years. He won both races handily, by margins approaching those Bartlett used to enjoy; he did so well (and had got so used to running campaigns) that Senate Republicans made him chairman of the Campaign Committee in 1975. Just past 50, and a member of the Appropriations Committee, Stevens appears to have a bright and influential, if rather quiet, future ahead of him in the Senate.

The state's single House seat has been held by as many men as both Senate seats taken together. The current incumbent, Don Young, was chosen in a March 1973 special election to replace Begich. That was at the height of the pipeline mania, when "Sierra Club" was the nastiest thing you could say in Alaska. Both Young, a riverboat captain and state legislator, and his opponent, Alaskan Native Federation president Emil Notti, were pipeline proponents. But Notti made the mistake of featuring Edward Kennedy, a pipeline foe, on his TV ads; the Republicans counterattacked fiercely. Aided by this and lingering resentment of the Native Claims Act, Young won narrowly; as an incumbent in 1974, he withstood the challenge of another native, Willie Hensley, much more easily. Young is the most conservative member of the current Alaska delegation, and the only one who serves on either house's Interior Committee, which has jurisdiction over so much legislation that is important to Alaska. (Both Gravel and Stevens left Senate Interior, apparently because it is totally dominated by Scoop Jackson.)

If boom mania dominated the Alaska body public in 1973 when the pipeline was being held up, it seemed to ebb noticeably by the time of the 1974 elections, after actual construction had begun. All those promised jobs were created, but Alaskans weren't getting many of them; the state's unemployment remained well above the 10% rate. The tiny port of Valdez, the southern terminus of the pipeline, was becoming prey to all the problems of mining boom towns. Before the pipeline, environmentalists seemed to most Alaskans to be ethereal types who muttered about fragile tundra, but were preventing them from making big profits from an upcoming boom. After construction began, it became obvious that the pipeline was mucking up the scenery, and that its benefits accrued to a rather small number of Alaskans—while others had to pay increased taxes for the higher level of services that the pipeline-inspired growth caused.

At least, this is what one must infer from the results of the 1974 Alaska gubernatorial race. The Democratic candidate was, as has always been the case, William Egan: one of the founders who had brought statehood to the frozen north, elected Governor in 1959, 1962, narrowly beaten by Hickel in 1966, elected again in 1970. Egan is a believer in growth and development; he is against those who would, in his view, lock up Alaska's resources in an icebox.

Egan's opponent was just the kind of man you would cast for an Alaska version of Mr. Smith Goes to Washington, Jay Hammond: a bearded bush pilot, a sometime poet, a man who wanted to preserve the great outdoor heritage of Alaska. Hammond was also the Mayor of Bristol Bay and a former state legislator; his opponents said that his concern was less for protecting nature than for a rigid laissez-faire philosophy which led him to oppose any government action. Whatever the accuracy of these characterizations, they stuck; the surprise was that Hammond was in the general election at all. To get there, he had to do what to outsiders anyway seemed the impossible, beat Wally Hickel, the one time cabinet secretary whose "listen to the kids" letter to Nixon at the time of the Cambodian invasion had led to his being fired. Hickel had impressed environmentalists during his brief tenure as Interior Secretary, but his background was that of a developer and an unabashed booster; and that, apparently, is how he appeared contrasted to Hammond.

At any rate, Hammond won, conclusively, and in the general election narrowly edged Egan; it was close only because of Egan's last minute charges that Hammond's running mate was a relative of an Interior Department Assistant Secretary who wanted to "lock Alaska up." There is no real consensus in this state yet as to what, precisely, should be done about growth and development. But the voters have, for the first time in their history, elected a Governor who is not hell bent for development, and it will be interesting to see just what kind of difference he will be able to make.

Census Data Pop. 302,173; 0.15% of U.S. total, 50th largest; Central city, 0%; suburban, 0%. Median family income, $12,441; 1st highest; families above $15,000: 38%; families below $3,000: 7%. Median years education, 12.5.

1974 Share of Federal Tax Burden $482,068,000; 0.18% of U.S. total, 49th largest.

1974 Share of Federal Outlays $1,135,875,000; 0.42% of U.S. total, 41st largest. Per capita federal spending, $3759.

DOD	$488,292,000	32d	(0.71%)	HEW	$139,304,000	49th	(0.15%)
AEC	$1,793,000	29th	(0.06%)	HUD	$1,292,000	49th	(0.13%)
NASA	$813,000	35th	(0.03%)	VA	$15,513,000	50th	(0.11%)
DOT	$237,014,000	11th	(2.80%)	EPA	$11,765,000	38th	(0.37%)
DOC	$18,319,000	15th	(1.16%)	RevS	$7,915,000	50th	(0.13%)
DOI	$89,822,000	7th	(3.65%)	Int.	$10,396,000	50th	(0.05%)
USDA	$22,396,000	45th	(0.18%)	Other	$91,241,000		

Economic Base Finance, insurance and real estate; food and kindred products, especially canned and cured sea foods; agriculture and fishing, notably fish, dairy products, eggs, potatoes and cattle; oil and gas field services, and other oil and gas extraction activity; paper pulp, and other paper and allied products.

Political Line-up Governor, Jay S. Hammond (R). Senators, Theodore F. Stevens (R) and Mike Gravel (D). Representatives, 1 R at large. State Senate (13 D and 7 R); State House (30 D, 9 R, 1 Ind.).

The Voters

Registration 170,511 Total. 49,518 D (29%); 26,570 R (16%); 91,533 Non-Partisan (54%); 2,890 Other (2%).
Median voting age 34.
Employment profile White collar, 55%. Blue collar, 30%. Service, 15%. Farm, 4%.
Ethnic groups Black, 3%. Indian, 16%. Total foreign stock, 11%.

Presidential vote

1972	Nixon (R)	55,349	(63%)
	McGovern (D)	32,967	(37%)
1968	Nixon (R)	37,600	(45%)
	Humphrey (D)	35,411	(43%)
	Wallace (AI)	10,024	(12%)

Sen. Ted Stevens (R) Appointed Dec 23, 1968, elected 1970, seat up 1978; b. Nov. 18, 1923, Indianapolis, Ind.; home, Anchorage; Oreg. St. U., Mont. St. U., UCLA, A.B. 1947, Harvard U. LL.B., 1950; Episcopalian.

Career Air Force, WWII; Practicing atty., 1950–53, 1961–68; U.S. Atty., 1953–56; U.S. Dept. of Interior, Legis. Council, 1956–58, Asst. to the Secy., 1958–60, Solicitor 1960–61; Alaska House of Reps., 1964–68.

Offices 411 RSOB, 202-224-3004. Also 215 Fed. Bldg., Anchorage 99501, 907-272-9561; and 200 Fed. Bldg., Fairbanks 99701, 907-452-5264.

Committees

Appropriations (7th). Subcommittees: Defense; Interior; Labor and HEW; Military Construction; State, Justice, Commerce, and The Judiciary; Transportation.

Commerce (3d). Subcommittees: Aviation; Communications; The Consumer; Foreign Commerce and Tourism; Merchant Marine; Oceans and Atmosphere; Subcommittee on Oil and Gas Production and Distribution.

Post Office and Civil Service (2d). Subcommittees: Compensation and Employment Benefits; Postal Operations.

Group Ratings

	ADA	COPE	LWV	RIPON	NFU	LCV	CFA	NAB	NSI	ACA
1974	75	83	88	44	80	58	67	14	0	33
1973	76	86	67	33	100	–	57	–	–	10
1972	75	100	100	71	100	53	100	11	20	0

Key Votes

1) No-Knock	ABS	8) Gov Abortn Aid	FOR	15) Consumer Prot Agy	FOR
2) Busing	ABS	9) Cut Mil Brass	FOR	16) Forced Psych Tests	ABS
3) No Fault	FOR	10) Gov Limousine	AGN	17) Fed Campaign Subs	FOR
4) F-111	AGN	11) RR Featherbed	ABS	18) Rhod Chrome Ban	ABS
5) Death Penalty	AGN	12) Handgun License	AGN	19) Open Legis Meetings	FOR
6) Foreign Aid	FOR	13) Less Troop Abrd	FOR	20) Strikers Food Stmps	FOR
7) Filibuster	FOR	14) Resume Turk Aid	AGN	21) Gov Info Disclosure	ABS

Election Results

1972 general:	Ted Stevens (R)	74,216	(77%)	($195,123)
	Gene Guess (D)	21,791	(23%)	($47,131)
1972 primary:	Ted Stevens (R), unopposed			
1970 general:	Ted Stevens (R)	47,908	(59%)	
	Wendell P. Kay (D)	32,636	(41%)	

Sen. Mike Gravel (D) Elected 1968, seat up 1980; b. May 13, 1930, Springfield, Mass.; home, Anchorage; Assumption Col., American Internatl. Col., Columbia U., B.S. 1956; Unitarian.

Career Army, 1951–54; Taxi driver 1956; Real estate developer 1956–68; Alaska House of Reps., 1962–66, Speaker 1965; Candidate for Dem. nomination for U.S. House of Reps., 1966.

Offices 4107 DSOB, 202-224-6665. Also 202 W. 4th Ave., Anchorage 99510, 907-274-9508, and P.O. Box 1480, Fairbanks 99701, 907-452-6227.

Committees

Finance (8th). Subcommittees: Energy (Chairman); Foundations; Health; International Finance and Resources.

Public Works (4th). Subcommittees: Environmental Pollution; Transportation; Buildings and Grounds.

Group Ratings

	ADA	COPE	LWV	RIPON	NFU	LCV	CFA	NAB	NSI	ACA
1974	52	91	100	55	82	25	55	17	90	21
1973	15	60	67	53	64	–	31	–	–	57
1972	35	86	82	68	67	32	73	36	80	38

Key Votes

1) No-Knock	AGN	8) Gov Abortn Aid	FOR	15) Consumer Prot Agy	FOR
2) Busing	FOR	9) Cut Mil Brass	AGN	16) Forced Psych Tests	FOR
3) No Fault	FOR	10) Gov Limousine	FOR	17) Fed Campaign Subs	FOR
4) F-111	FOR	11) RR Featherbed	FOR	18) Rhod Chrome Ban	FOR

5) Death Penalty	FOR	12) Handgun License	AGN	19) Open Legis Meetings	AGN
6) Foreign Aid	FOR	13) Less Troop Abrd	AGN	20) Strikers Food Stmps	FOR
7) Filibuster	AGN	14) Resume Turk Aid	ABS	21) Gov Info Disclosure	FOR

Election Results

1974 general:	Mike Gravel (D)	54,361	(58%)	($469,300)
	C. R. Lewis (R)	38,914	(42%)	($353,701)
1974 primary:	Mike Gravel (D)	22,834	(54%)	
	Gene Guess (D)	15,090	(36%)	
	Two Others (D)	4,123	(10%)	
1968 general:	Mike Gravel (D)	36,527	(45%)	
	Elmer Rasmuson (R)	30,286	(37%)	
	Ernest Gruening (write-in)	14,188	(18%)	

Gov. Jay Hammond (R) Elected 1974, term expires Dec. 1978; b. July 21, 1922, Troy, N.Y.; Penn. St. U., 1940–42, U. of Alaska, B.S. 1948.

Career Navy, WWII; Bush pilot, trapper, and guide, 1946–48; Pilot Agent, U.S. Fish and Wildlife Svc., 1948–56; Commercial fisherman and air taxi operator, 1956–74; Alaska House of Reps., 1959–65; Mgr., Bristol Bay Borough, 1965–67; Alaska Senate, 1967–72; Mayor, Bristol Borzough, 1972–74.

Offices Pouch A, State Capitol, Juneau 99811, 907-465-3500.

Election Results

1974 general:	Jay S. Hammond (R)	45,840	(48%)
	William A. Egan (D)	45,553	(47%)
	Joseph E. Vogler (AI)	4,770	(5%)
1974 primary:	Jay S. Hammond (R)	28,602	(46%)
	Walter J. Hickel (R)	20,728	(33%)
	Keith H. Miller (R)	10,864	(17%)
	Four Others (R)	2,427	(4%)

Rep. Don Young (R) Elected Mar. 6, 1973; b. June 9, 1933, Meridian, Cal.; home, Fort Yukon; Chico St. Col., B.A. 1956; Episcopalian.

Career Construction work, 1959; Teacher 1960–69; River boat Capt.; Fort Yukon City Cncl., Mayor; Alaska House of Reps., 1966–70; Alaska Senate 1970–73.

Offices 1210 LHOB, 202-225-5765. Also 115 Fed. Bldg., Anchorage 99501, 907-279-1587.

Committees

Interior and Insular Affairs (9th). Subcommittees: Indian Affairs; Public Lands.

Merchant Marine and Fisheries (9th). Subcommittees: Coast Guard and Navigation; Fisheries and Wildlife Conservation and the Environment; Merchant Marine.

Group Ratings

	ADA	COPE	LWV	RIPON	NFU	LCV	CFA	NAB	NSI	ACA
1974	11	30	20	38	50	33	8	60	100	75
1973	13	64	27	54	59	6	25	–	–	74

Key Votes

1) Foreign Aid	AGN	6) Gov Abortn Aid	AGN	11) Pub Cong Election $	AGN
2) Busing	AGN	7) Coed Phys Ed	AGN	12) Turkish Arms Cutoff	ABS
3) ABM	ABS	8) Pov Lawyer Gag	FOR	13) Youth Camp Regs	AGN
4) B-1 Bomber	ABS	9) Pub Trans Sub	AGN	14) Strip Mine Veto	FOR
5) Nerve Gas	ABS	10) EZ Voter Regis	FOR	15) Farm Bill Veto	FOR

Election Results

1974 general:	Donald E. Young (R)	51,641	(54%)	($140,729)
	William L. Hensley (D)	44,280	(46%)	($136,112)
1974 primary:	Donald E. Young (R), unopposed			
1973 special:	Donald E. Young (R)	35,123	(52%)	($107,824)
	Emil Notti (D)	33,044	(48%)	($102,998)

ARIZONA

To most Americans, Arizona brings to mind the Grand Canyon, Navajo hogans, Tombstone and Wyatt Earp, or maybe even London Bridge, which thanks to a developer, now sits proudly in a patch of Arizona desert. But in this state the attention of a political analyst is focused almost entirely on Phoenix and Tucson. Some 55% of the voters live in greater Phoenix, and another 21% in and around Tucson. In 1940, Arizona had a population of 550,000; by 1970, it reached 1,772,000, and according to Census estimates it grew to 2,153,000 in 1974—the fastest rate of growth of any state. A quite literal new majority, has completely transformed the politics of Arizona in the last 25 years.

The change here is best illustrated by the contrasting careers of the state's two best-known politicians: Congressman (1912–27) and Senator (1927–69) Carl Hayden, and Senator (1953–65, 1969–) Barry Goldwater. Hayden began his political career as a councilman in Tempe (formerly Hayden's Crossing) in 1902, when Phoenix was just a hot, sleepy depot-station on the Southern Pacific Railroad. Hayden was a Democrat, and a fairly conservative one—as was just about every successful Arizona politician until the 1950s. The state had a Democratic heritage that came out of the Southern origin of most of its early settlers, and the Mexican background of many of the rest. Although Arizona occasionally went Republican in national elections (it never supported a presidential loser until 1960), Hayden and his fellow Democrats rarely had any difficulty with the voters. The basic Hayden formula was to see that federal money—and water—was pumped into the state. He was especially interested in highways, but the last great legacy of his career was the Central Arizona Project, pushed through in 1968, when he was 91 years old. Interestingly, most of this water goes not to residential Phoenix, but to the agribusiness farms in the otherwise parched Gila River valley nearby.

The birth of Arizona's now dominant conservative Republicanism can be dated with some accuracy to the year 1949, when Barry Goldwater, then proprietor of his family's Phoenix department store, was elected to the Phoenix City Council. The next year Goldwater helped Republican Howard Pyle win the Governorship, and in 1952 Republicans swept the state: Eisenhower won its electoral votes, Pyle was reelected, and Goldwater went to the United States Senate. (The man he beat, Sen. Ernest MacFarland, was then Senate Majority Leader, and his political demise set the stage for Lyndon Johnson's ascent to the Senate Democratic leadership.) Goldwater won reelection by a large margin in 1958, again against MacFarland; the Republican directed the brunt of his rhetoric against national union leaders like the late Walter Reuther—targets with little electoral clout in Arizona.

The year 1958 was a bad one for conservative Republicans practically everywhere—except Arizona. So Goldwater's victory elevated him to national prominence. His frank, often blunt, and impolitic articulation of his beliefs brought him such devotion and volunteer support all over the country that he won the 1964 Republican presidential nomination despite his malapropisms and modesty.

Goldwater's resolute conservatism—he said he wanted to stop old federal programs, not start new ones—struck a chord in booming Arizona. The big influx of population here, as Neal Peirce points out in *The Mountain States of America*, consists of white-collar technicians from the South,

Midwest, and southern California—the kind of people who made all of metropolitan Phoenix more Republican in the 1972 presidential race than Orange County, California. The years since 1958 have been mostly Republican years in Arizona. This is the only state which has voted Republican in all four presidential elections since then; until 1974, Republicans had held the state governorship for 14 of 16 years; Goldwater's seat was held by ex-Gov. Paul Fannin in 1964 and 1970, and Goldwater himself returned to the Senate, forcing Hayden's retirement, in 1968.

In the course of all these successes, some of the young men who worked for Goldwater in the fifties have achieved high positions, most notably Supreme Court Justice William Rehnquist and House Minority Leader John Rhodes. Others have had similar rises—and then falls. Richard Kleindienst was Deputy Attorney General and Attorney General—but he plead guilty of not telling the truth before a Watergate grand jury. Robert Mardian was an Assistant Attorney General and close confidant of John Mitchell—and has been sentenced to 10 months in jail by Judge Sirica.

The fates of Kleindienst and Mardian symbolize what has been happening to Arizona's successful Republican Party these past few years. Just after the 1972 election, Goldwater and his friends seemed to be at the peak of success. Some thought that Goldwater himself might choose to retire in 1974; he would be able to return to his mountaintop home near Phoenix with the rare satisfaction that he accomplished most of what he had set out to do 25 years earlier. By supporting Richard Nixon loyally during the Reagan onslaught at the 1968 Republican convention, he had insured the nomination of a conservative candidate who could win; with the 1972 Nixon landslide the American people seemed to vindicate the positions Goldwater took in 1964.

But then came Watergate. Goldwater, one of the most principled and least ambitious politicans in Washington, turned out to have given his imprimatur to a man who was just the opposite. Occasionally, as the scandal unfolded, Goldwater would urge that Nixon just end it all by telling the whole truth—which showed, in retrospect, how little of the truth Goldwater knew, or suspected. Goldwater never really abandoned Nixon, and he saved the lash of his tongue for those who attacked him rather then the President and his men. But when it came time, after the release of the crucial tapes, Goldwater went with Hugh Scott to the White House and, without precisely saying so, let Nixon know he had lost all support on the Hill and must resign.

Perhaps because of Watergate, perhaps because he had intended to all along, Goldwater did run for another term at age 65. Against an unknown opponent, who waged a game but underfinanced campaign, Goldwater had a very solid 58% of the vote. In the Senate, he is slowly regaining the seniority he lost by giving up his seat in 1964 to run for President. The Arizonan, who was once a Brigadier General in the Air Force, retains his interest in military policy and holds a seat on Armed Services; he is also the ranking Republican on the Aeronautics and Space Sciences Committee. Ironically, this believer in low federal budgets works on the two areas where he favors heavy spending. Goldwater is not a legislator who pays close attention to details or strategy; he is a man who votes his convictions, wherever they may lead. For example, he was one of the Senate's leading opponents of the draft, on libertarian philosophical grounds, and he voted against the Nixon Administration's proposal to bail out Lockheed, in the belief that a commitment to free enterprise envisions the possibility of bankruptcy when a company is mismanaged.

In Goldwater and Paul Fannin, Arizona has about as conservative a Senate delegation as there is. After three two-year terms as Governor, Fannin won the seat Goldwater relinquished in 1964. He serves quietly on the Finance and Interior Committees, on the latter of which he is ranking Republican (but which is dominated by its Chairman, Henry Jackson of Washington). Fannin had an unexpectedly tough reelection race in 1970. Sam Grossman, the Democratic nominee, managed to fashion a lead in the polls until the Arizona *Republic*—part of the ultraconservative Pulliam chain—revealed that Grossman had claimed not long before, to be a resident of California. That cinched Fannin's second term, but he seems unlikely to win a third. In 1971, Fannin was arrested on a drunk driving charge in Phoenix; there were some indications that local officials had tried to cover it up and quash charges, and Jack Anderson played it heavily; finally, Fannin was cited for a traffic violation. That will not especially help his cause if he runs, nor will the fact that he will be 69; more likely, he will choose to retire.

A possible candidate, whether or not Fannin quits, is 2d district Congressman Morris Udall, a Democrat in this now Republican state who is also, however, running for President. (See Second District.) Indeed, Arizona has an unusually distinguished House delegation for a small state. Besides Udall, there is House Minority Leader John Rhodes, from the 1st district; and the 3d district's Sam Steiger is making a name for himself as perhaps the House's noisiest—and sometimes most effective—opponent of environmental measures.

In 1970 and 1972, Democrats in both state and congressional contests put up feisty battles, despite the seemingly overwhelming odds against them. In 1974, one of those Democrats was finally successful. Raul Castro (no relation to the Cuba Castros), born in Mexico, was a judge in Tucson in the fifties, Ambassador to Bolivia and El Salvador in the sixties, and Democratic nominee for Governor in 1970. He came surprisingly close to upsetting incumbent Jack Williams, a Republican who seemed unbeatable at the beginning of the campaign.

Castro's 1970 race was a considerable feat, and he was the clear favorite for the Democratic nomination in 1974. No strident liberal, Castro had pointedly refused to support a recall drive left by Cesar Chavez's United Farm Workers against Governor Williams in 1972; when the UFW got into trouble in California, it pulled totally out of Arizona, and the recall drive fizzled. It was, in other words, a good thing not to be associated with. Indeed, Castro's moderation was such that he could appeal to the so-called "pinto" Democrats, who still dominate the courthouses in the state's small counties and whose politics is reminiscent of Carl Hayden's.

But it was not the "pintos" who won for Castro in 1974, nor was it his fellow Mexican-Americans; only 19% of all Arizonans have Spanish-speaking backgrounds, and most of them do not register and vote. What won for Castro was home town support in Tucson and the good will his early lead built up for him among the mass of white, middle-class voters. In fact, Castro was lucky his early lead was so large, for the Republican nominee, Russell Williams (no relation to the incumbent), proved to be an attractive and aggressive candidate who nearly won.

Castro's victory symbolizes the end of an era, an era in which Arizona politics was dominated by Barry Goldwater and the men around him. Now the state is well into an era of political flux, when different kinds of candidates from different parties can all win elections. The Republicans still posses most of the advantages: plenty of money, unstinting support from the *Republic*, the fact that the Republican County Clerk in Phoenix does not exactly encourage blacks and chicanos to register and vote, the personal appeal of Barry Goldwater. The Democrats' advantages, in contrast, are few: a feistiness and willingness to work hard, and in some cases environmental issues.

Census Data   Pop. 1,772,482; 0.88% of U.S. total, 33rd largest; Central city, 27%; suburban, 48%. Median family income, $9,186; 24th highest; families above $15,000: 19%; families below $3,000: 11%.   Median years education, 12.3.

1974 Share of Federal Tax Burden $2,463,901,000; 0.92% of U.S. total, 31st largest.

1974 Share of Federal Outlays $3,002,385,000; 1.11% of U.S. total, 29th largest.   Per capita federal spending, $1963.

DOD	$1,028,853,000	23d (1.50%)	HEW	$864,262,000	34th (0.93%)
AEC	$291,000	35th (0.01%)	HUD	$7,908,000	32d (0.81%)
NASA	$5,877,000	23d (0.20%)	VA	$181,006,000	28th (1.32%)
DOT	$101,297,000	29th (1.20%)	EPA	$6,847,000	46th (0.22%)
DOC	$8,220,000	27th (0.51%)	RevS	$61,889,000	31st (1.02%)
DOI	$206,557,000	2d (8.39%)	Int.	$58,291,000	33d (0.28%)
USDA	$138,706,000	34th (1.11%)	Other	$332,381,000	

Economic Base   Finance, insurance and real estate; electrical equipment and supplies, especially electronic components and accessories; agriculture, notably cattle, cotton lint, lettuce and dairy products; metal mining, especially copper ores; machinery, especially office and computing machines; food and kindred products; tourism.

Political Line-up   Governor, Raul H. Castro (D). Senators, Paul J. Fannin (R) and Barry Goldwater (R). Representatives, 4 (3 R and 1 D). State Senate (18 D and 12 R); State House (33 R and 27 D).

The Voters

Registration   890,794 Total. 466,908 D (52%); 370,759 R (42%); 53,127 Other (6%).
Median voting age   42.
Employment profile   White collar, 51%. Blue collar, 32%. Service, 14%. Farm, 3%.
Ethnic groups   Black, 3%. Indian, 5%. Spanish, 19%. Total foreign stock, 17%. Canada, Germany, 1% each.

Presidential vote

1972	Nixon (R)	402,812	(67%)
	McGovern (D)	198,540	(33%)
1968	Nixon (R)	266,721	(55%)
	Humphrey (D)	170,514	(35%)
	Wallace (AI)	46,573	(10%)

Sen. Paul J. Fannin (R) Elected 1964, seat up 1976; b. Jan. 29, 1907, Ashland, Ky.; home, Phoenix; U. of Ariz., Stanford U. B.A. 1930; Methodist.

Career Partner, Fannin Bros., petroleum products distrib.; Gov. of Ariz., 1959–64.

Offices 3121 DSOB, 202-224-4521. Also 3417 Fed. Bldg., 230 N. 1st Ave., Phoenix 85025, 602-261-4486; and Rm. 8E Fed. Bldg., 301 W. Congress, Tucson 85701, 602-792-6336.

Committees

Interior and Insular Affairs (Ranking Member). Subcommittees: Energy Research and Water Resources; Indian Affairs; Minerals, Materials and Fuels; Special Subcommittee on Integrated Oil Operations.

Finance (2d). Subcommittees: Administration of the Internal Revenue Code; Energy; Health; International Trade; Supplemental Security Income.

Joint Economic Committee (4th, Senate Side). Subcommittees: Economic Progress; Fiscal Policy; Inter-American Economic Relationships.

Group Ratings

	ADA	COPE	LWV	RIPON	NFU	LCV	CFA	NAB	NSI	ACA
1974	0	9	33	50	6	13	0	82	100	100
1973	0	20	0	31	6	–	18	–	–	96
1972	5	0	20	41	22	4	0	91	100	95

Key Votes

1) No-Knock	FOR	8) Gov Abortn Aid	AGN	15) Consumer Prot Agy	AGN
2) Busing	AGN	9) Cut Mil Brass	AGN	16) Forced Psych Tests	AGN
3) No Fault	AGN	10) Gov Limousine	FOR	17) Fed Campaign Subs	AGN
4) F-111	FOR	11) RR Featherbed	AGN	18) Rhod Chrome Ban	AGN
5) Death Penalty	FOR	12) Handgun License	AGN	19) Open Legis Meetings	ABS
6) Foreign Aid	AGN	13) Less Troop Abrd	AGN	20) Strikers Food Stmps	AGN
7) Filibuster	ABS	14) Resume Turk Aid	FOR	21) Gov Info Disclosure	ABS

Election Results

1970 general:	Paul Fannin (R)	228,284	(56%)
	Sam Grossman (D)	179,512	(44%)
1970 primary:	Paul Fannin (R), unopposed		
1964 general:	Paul Fannin (R)	241,089	(51%)
	Roy Elson (D)	227,712	(49%)

Sen. Barry Goldwater (R) Elected 1968, seat up 1980; b. Jan. 1, 1909, Phoenix; home, Phoenix; U. of Ariz., 1928; Episcopalian.

Career Maj. Gen., USAFR, 1937–67; Phoenix City Cncl., 1949–51; U.S. Sen., 1952–64; Repub. nominee for Pres., 1964.

Offices 427 RSOB, 202-224-2235. Also 5001 Fed. Bldg., Phoenix 85025, 602-261-4086.

Committees

Aeronautical and Space Sciences (Ranking Member).

Armed Services (3d). Subcommittees: Intelligence; Military Construction Authorization; Preparedness Investigating; Research and Development; Tactical Air Power.

Select Committee on Intelligence Operations (3d).

Group Ratings

	ADA	COPE	LWV	RIPON	NFU	LCV	CFA	NAB	NSI	ACA
1974	6	10	33	39	12	25	0	78	100	100
1973	0	43	0	25	9	–	0	–	–	90
1972	5	0	0	36	20	0	0	100	90	87

Key Votes

1) No-Knock	FOR	8) Gov Abortn Aid	AGN	15) Consumer Prot Agy	AGN
2) Busing	ABS	9) Cut Mil Brass	AGN	16) Forced Psych Tests	ABS
3) No Fault	AGN	10) Gov Limousine	AGN	17) Fed Campaign Subs	ABS
4) F-111	FOR	11) RR Featherbed	AGN	18) Rhod Chrome Ban	AGN
5) Death Penalty	FOR	12) Handgun License	AGN	19) Open Legis Meetings	AGN
6) Foreign Aid	AGN	13) Less Troop Abrd	AGN	20) Strikers Food Stmps	AGN
7) Filibuster	ABS	14) Resume Turk Aid	FOR	21) Gov Info Disclosure	AGN

Election Results

1974 general:	Barry Goldwater (R)	320,396	(58%)	($394,042)
	Jonathan Marshall (D)	229,523	(42%)	($129,260)
1974 primary:	Barry Goldwater (R), unopposed			
1968 general:	Barry Goldwater (R)	274,607	(57%)	
	Roy Elson (D)	205,338	(43%)	

Gov. Raul H. Castro (D) Elected 1974, term expires Jan. 1979; b. June 12, 1916, Cananea, Sonora, Mexico; N. Ariz. U., B.A. 1939, U. of Ariz., J.D. 1949; Catholic.

Career U.S. Foreign Svc., Agua Prieta, Sonora, Mexico, 1941–46; Spanish Instr., U. of Ariz., 1946–49; Practicing atty., 1949–55, 1969–75; Pima Co. Atty., 1955–59; Judge, Pima Co. Superior Ct., 1959–64; U.S. Ambassador to El Salvedor, 1964–68; U.S. Ambassador to Bolivia, 1968–69.

Offices 1700 W. Washington, Phoenix 85007, 602-271-4331.

Election Results

1974 general:	Raul H. Castro (D)	278,375	(50%)
	Russ Williams (R)	273,674	(50%)
1974 primary:	Raul H. Castro (D)	115,268	(67%)
	Jack Ross (D)	31,250	(18%)
	Dave Moss (D)	19,143	(11%)
	Walter "Denver" Caudill (D)	5,843	(3%)

♦ ♦ ♦ ♦

FIRST DISTRICT

Phoenix is one of those instant cities that lie in what Kevin Phillips calls the Sun Belt. Such metropolises are almost totally the creation of the air-conditioned years after World War II. In 1940, Phoenix had 65,000 citizens; by 1970, just within the city limits, 581,000. Even in the years before the War, Phoenix was considered Arizona's Republican city, with Tucson—more Spanish, more Southern—the Democratic town. But if one were to judge just from the election returns, it seems that virtually every one of the hundreds of thousands of people who flocked to Phoenix in the postwar period were, or quickly became, Goldwater Republicans. No other major metropolitan area—and Phoenix certainly qualifies as one, with more than a million residents—has consistently voted as heavily Republican as the Arizona capital.

Why? Retirees, for one thing. Older people with enough money to afford living in a place like Del Webb's Sun City (nobody under 50, nobody with schoolchildren, and effectively no blacks) usually cast huge Republican majorities. But more important, most of the jobs that buttress the boom in Phoenix lie in the defense, electronic, and other technical industries. These are not people who, having moved west, miss the New York *Times*; they are quite content with Eugene Pulliam's militantly conservative Arizona *Republic*. Finally, there is the state's political culture. The Goldwater movement in the fifties and sixties, consisting mostly of clean-cut, talented, hardworking young men from Phoenix (often themselves immigrants from the Midwest) hit it off well with the influx of newcomers. The Democrats, most of them cigar-chewing oldtimers from dusty county seats, did not.

One of the crew-cut young men from the early days of the Goldwater movement—he finally let his hair grow out in the early seventies—is 1st district Congressman and House Minority Leader John Rhodes. In 1952, when Goldwater was first elected to the Senate, Rhodes became the first Republican Arizona ever sent to the U.S. House of Representatives. At that time, Rhodes's seat was all of Maricopa County, including Phoenix and all of its suburbs. But in the last ten years, the district has been pruned down by successive redistrictings, leaving Rhodes by 1972 with the bulk of the city's black and chicano populations, as well as with the 30,000 students at Arizona State University at Tempe (pronounced tem-PEE).

That has meant political trouble for Rhodes back home, even as he has been gaining power and prestige on Capitol Hill. In 1972, when he was Chairman of the House Republican Policy Committee and number two Republican on Appropriations, Rhodes beat an underfinanced opponent by only a 57–43 margin—far below the levels he was used to. Two years later, 33-year-old Patricia Fullinwider, a member of the Tempe school board, held Rhodes to 51%; some 7% of the vote was diverted, presumably from Rhodes, by a candidate on the "Pro-Life" (anti-abortion) line. In both years, Rhodes's opponents made a point of attacking his record on environmental issues—usually a strong point for Democrats in a western metropolitan area like this. It is hard, of course, to beat the House Minority Leader, but there are great psychic dividends if you can; we therefore can be reasonably sure that the Democrats will be trying hard again in 1976.

Rhodes is a Minority Leader in much the same mold as the man he succeeded, Jerry Ford. Like Ford, he is not a great orator, although his speaking style is smoother than the President's and his syntax is better. Nor, like Ford, is he an innovative thinker. He hews very closely to the solid conservative line, but less ideologically than pragmatically. He is also, it should not be forgotten, a bright man who knows how to tiptoe through political minefields without getting hurt.

Both men have perceived their job as organizing their minority of the House as solidly as they can, and both have done it well. Ford was the master of the little gesture, the constant keeping in touch with each House Republican which could net him some unlikely votes (like Pete McCloskey's) when he really needed them; Rhodes, though perhaps not quite so warm, works hard at the same task. Rhodes's problem in the 94th Congress is that there simply aren't very many Republicans, and fewer Democrats than ever who will vote steadily with the supposed opposition. Consequently, Rhodes will be working often, not to pass bills or even to stop them, but to provide the one-third-plus-one votes needed to uphold the President's veto. Beyond that, his job is to maintain the sort of protective cocoon around Republican House members, the kind of insularity that Ford always cultivated, and to avoid the contamination of fashionable liberal thinking (or the morning's Washington *Post*). House Republicans are not in demand much socially; they tend to talk mainly to themselves, or people very much like themselves—enough so that they could constantly overestimate the popular support Richard Nixon enjoyed during the Watergate affair. Rhodes is shrewd enough to know all this; his work now is to hunker down, hold his lines, and wait for that bright day in the future when he will have many more troops to lead.

Census Data Pop. 442,589. Central city, 52%; suburban, 48%. Median family income, $9,126; families above $15,000: 18%; families below $3,000: 10.1%. Median years education, 12.2.

The Voters

Median voting age 42.
Employment profile White collar, 52%. Blue collar, 32%. Service, 14%. Farm, 2%.
Ethnic groups Black, 6%. Indian, 1%. Spanish, 17%. Total foreign stock, 16%. Canada, Germany, 2% each.

Presidential vote

1972	Nixon (R)	98,436	(68%)
	McGovern (D)	46,573	(32%)
1968	Nixon (R)	67,853	(56%)
	Humphrey (D)	41,889	(35%)
	Wallace (AI)	11,012	(9%)

Rep. John J. Rhodes (R) Elected 1952; b. Sept. 18, 1916, Council Grove, Kans.; home, Mesa; Kans. St. U., B.S. 1938, Harvard U., LL.B. 1941; Methodist.

Career Air Force, WWII; Practicing atty., 1949–53; V.P., Farm & Home Like Ins. Co.

Offices 2310 RHOB, 202-225-2635. Also 6040 Fed. Bldg., Phoenix 85025, 602-261-3181.

Committees

Minority Leader.

Group Ratings

	ADA	COPE	LWV	RIPON	NFU	LCV	CFA	NAB	NSI	ACA
1974	6	10	67	45	42	25	8	67	83	62
1973	4	0	33	47	13	11	13	–	–	73
1972	6	30	27	54	50	25	0	89	100	67

Key Votes

1) Foreign Aid	FOR	6) Gov Abortn Aid	AGN	11) Pub Cong Election $	AGN
2) Busing	ABS	7) Coed Phys Ed	AGN	12) Turkish Arms Cutoff	AGN
3) ABM	FOR	8) Pov Lawyer Gag	FOR	13) Youth Camp Regs	AGN
4) B-1 Bomber	FOR	9) Pub Trans Sub	AGN	14) Strip Mine Veto	FOR
5) Nerve Gas	FOR	10) EZ Voter Regis	AGN	15) Farm Bill Veto	FOR

Election Results

1974 genral:	John J. Rhodes (R)	63,847	(51%)	($136,038)
	Patricia M. Fullinwider (D)	52,897	(42%)	($20,136)
	J. M. "Pro-Life" Sanders (LLJ)	8,199	(7%)	($2,632)
1974 primary	John J. Rhodes (R), unopposed			
1972 general:	John J. Rhodes (R)	80,453	(57%)	($48,315)
	Gerald A. Pollock (D)	59,900	(43%)	($28,646)

◆ ◆ ◆ ◆ ◆

SECOND DISTRICT

The last time a member of the House of Representatives went directly to the Presidency was when James A. Garfield did it in 1880. Few have tried since. The public, at least until the House Judiciary Committee's impeachment hearings, had opinions of Congressmen rather like Mark Twain's ("There is no distinctly native American criminal class except Congress"). But when Gerald Ford became President, the idea of a House-based candidate seemed less far-fetched to many, including some Congressmen. Two of the House's brighter liberals, Henry Reuss and David Obey of Wisconsin, were talking about it one day, and decided they'd start a House candidacy. After briefly reviewing some names, they came up with Mo Udall of Arizona's 2d district. Udall agreed to run if Reuss and Obey could get supporting signatures from one-tenth of all House Democrats. They did, and so the Udall candidacy was born.

It all sounds a little tongue in cheek, and at this writing there is no way of really telling whether it is. Udall has not yet raised anything like the amount of money a presidential candidate is thought to need, and of course his name recognition is about zero. But he does have certain advantages: most notably, after the withdrawals of Edward Kennedy and Walter Mondale, there is a dearth of candidates acceptable to the liberal wing which dominated the Democratic convention in 1972 and may well again in 1976. Udall is at least acceptable to that group.

Moreover, Udall has about as many political and legislative credentials as most of the Senators or Governors who are running. A member of the House since 1961 (he succeeded his brother, Stewart, who had become Secretary of the Interior), he has never had a leadership post. But he did challenge old John McCormack for the Speaker's post in 1969, and he ran a fairly strong second to the late Hale Boggs in the race for Majority Leader in 1971. In both cases, Udall's challenge of the established order of succession was premature: but at the same time it can be said that it showed the willingness to stand up for needed change even when it is unpopular (and, as it proved, in the short run unprofitable).

Udall also has a legislative record. He floor managed the strip mining bills of 1974 and 1975 through the House (they were finally vetoed by Jerry Ford) and was the chief House sponsor of the complex land use legislation that was scuttled by his fellow Arizonan, Sam Steiger, in 1974. Udall has steered through the current federal salary bill—always a touchy matter because Congressmen's own salaries are affected. And in 1973, he pushed through a reform of another touchy area, the congressional frank—the free mailing privilege which allows Congressmen to flood their districts with whatever the politicians want their constituents to read. And then there is the candidate's sense of humor. Udall keeps an indexed set of literally hundreds of jokes which he uses, with his light dry delivery, to liven up a speech. He is probably the funniest man now running, and the best at perceiving what is funny about himself. He is also the only candidate who used to play semi-pro basketball, the only one who is 6´5˝, the only one who has a glass eye (result of a childhood accident). Like George Romney, he is a Mormon, but far less pietistic.

Finally, Udall has a record of winning elections in what is, after all, a very Republican state. It helps that neither he nor Stewart is the first Udall in Arizona politics, and that there has usually been a Udall on the state Supreme Court. Nevertheless, this is a state which did not cotton much to the Kennedy and Johnson Administrations, and Udall barely won his first congressional election. Tucson (pop. 262,000), where more than half the people in the 2d district live, is still Arizona's Democratic city. But as Phoenix-type growth continues, the Spanish heritage is slowly being overcome by glass and steel and concrete, and the special flavor of the town—a flavor that always included a Democratic preference—is becoming homogenized. Running against this trend, Mo Udall has pretty consistently managed to increase his percentages to the point where he got a higher percent in the year of the Nixon landslide than did any of Arizona's three Republican Congressmen.

It is possible, of course, that Udall may eventually choose to run for Senator, or even for the House again; Arizona has a late filing date, and if his presidential candidacy falters, he will certainly be free to do so. In that case, the 2d district—Tucson and the desert country which is sprinkled with Indian reservations and old mining towns like Tombstone and Bisbee—will almost certainly go Democratic.

Census Data Pop. 443,117. Central city, 59%; suburban, 20%. Median family income, $8,832; families above $15,000: 17%; families below $3,000: 11%. Median years education, 12.3.

The Voters

Median voting age 42.
Employment profile White collar, 51%. Blue collar, 32%. Service, 15%. Farm, 2%.
Ethnic groups Black, 3%. Indian, 2%. Spanish, 27%. Total foreign stock, 23%. Canada, Germany, 2% each.

Presidential vote

1972	Nixon (R)	89,052	(57%)
	McGovern (D)	65,926	(43%)

1968	Nixon (R)	59,753	(50%)
	Humphrey (D)	49,567	(41%)
	Wallace (AI)	10,152	(8%)

Rep. Morris K. Udall (D) Elected May 2, 1961; b. June 15, 1922, St. Johns; home, Tucson; U. of Ariz., J.D. 1949; Church of Latter Day Saints.

Career Air Force, WWII; Pro basketball player, Denver Nuggets, 1948–49; Practicing atty., 1949–61; Pima Co. Atty., 1952–54.

Offices 1424 LHOB, 202-225-4066. Also 901 W. Congress, Tucson 85701, 602-792-6404.

Committees

Interior and Insular Affairs (4th). Subcommittees: Energy and the Environment (Chairman); Mines and Mining; Public Lands.

Post Office and Civil Service (2d).

Group Ratings

	ADA	COPE	LWV	RIPON	NFU	LCV	CFA	NAB	NSI	ACA
1974	83	100	100	57	100	88	82	10	38	8
1973	84	82	100	71	90	71	75	–	–	8
1972	100	100	100	77	86	80	100	0	0	0

Key Votes

1) Foreign Aid	FOR	6) Gov Abortn Aid	FOR	11) Pub Cong Election $	FOR
2) Busing	FOR	7) Coed Phys Ed	AGN	12) Turkish Arms Cutoff	ABS
3) ABM	AGN	8) Pov Lawyer Gag	AGN	13) Youth Camp Regs	FOR
4) B-1 Bomber	AGN	9) Pub Trans Sub	FOR	14) Strip Mine Veto	AGN
5) Nerve Gas	ABS	10) EZ Voter Regis	FOR	15) Farm Bill Veto	AGN

Election Results

1974 genral:	Morris K. Udall (D)	84,491	(62%)	($66,130)
	Keith Dolgaard (R)	51,886	(38%)	($100,581)
1974 primary:	Morris K. Udall (D), unopposed			
1972 general:	Morris K. Udall (D)	97,616	(63%)	($38,174)
	Gene Savoie (R)	56,188	(37%)	($31,694)

◆ ◆ ◆ ◆ ◆

THIRD DISTRICT

Arizona's 3d and 4th congressional districts are both hybrids: combinations of large parts of heavily Republican Phoenix and of the sparsely populated, traditionally Democratic northern counties of the state. Geographically, the 3d spans the desert expanse from Yuma (pop. 29,000), on the hot Colorado River just north of the Mexican border, past the town of Flagstaff (pop. 30,000)—known for Northern Arizona University and as one of the last places in the United States where one can be confident about finding clean air—up to Glen Canyon Dam and the Navajo and Hopi Reservations near the Utah state line.

Traditionally, this is "pinto" Democrat country—closer in spirit, say, to Arkansas than to Pennsylvania. Exceptions are the town of Prescott (pop. 23,000), long a Republican stronghold, where Barry Goldwater has begun all his Senate campaigns, and Movae County, where in 1972 newcomers ousted Democratic county officials for Republican ones.

But most of the votes in the 3d—61% of them in 1974 are cast in the heavily Republican Phoenix area. The district includes the west side of Phoenix, and just wings the city's small black and Mexican-American ghettoes. Phoenix is a new city; here on the west side the vacant lots between the small stucco houses and the gaudy roadside businesses easily grow back into small patches of Arizona desert. The 3d does not take in the richest parts of Phoenix; there is less grass here (it's expensive to water the stuff) and fewer palm trees. Yet there is little political difference between the people who live here and their richer neighbors in the northern and eastern parts of the city. Every white anglo section in Phoenix votes overwhelmingly Republican.

The Congressman from this hybrid district is something of a hybrid himself. Sam Steiger, a Jew from New York, lists his occupation as a Prescott rancher; in Washington, he lives on a farm in distant Fauquier County, Virginia, and so probably has the longest commute of anyone on the Hill. Steiger is not the most tactful man: early in his career, he allowed on a talk show as how many of his colleagues were drunks; as a result, this cost the district a project which otherwise would have gone through easily. And in 1972, he pointedly refused to endorse John Conlan, the Republican nominee for Congress in the adjacent 4th district. Conlan was elected anyway, leaving the Arizona delegation less than close-knit. The next year, a Steiger staffer admitted placing an illegal listening device in a San Diego hotel room during a Select Committee on Crime investigation.

For quite a while, shenanigans like these were about all there was to Steiger's House career. But in the 93d Congree he suddenly became a force to be reckoned with. In 1974, Arizona's Mo Udall was shepherding through the House the land-use bill, which would give the states certain aids and incentives to regulate land use in undeveloped and unzoned areas. It was fairly widely supported, and had little opposition. The Nixon Administration had declared its support. But the National Chamber of Commerce didn't like it, and neither did Sam Steiger. Operating from a fairly high position on the Interior Committee (4th ranking Republican then, 2d now) Steiger pushed forward a Chamber-written substitute, which would have little, if any effect on the practices Udall was aiming at. Moving quickly to a vote, before Udall could marshal his forces, Steiger got the House to amend Udall's bill by substituting his measure. Then, to show just how seriously he wanted any land use bill, Steiger dropped his own measure, and let it die. He had accomplished the fairly formidable task of killing a piece of legislation that appeared pretty certain of going through.

For this, and for virtually every other vote on environmental measures, Steiger was targeted on Environmental Action's Dirty Dozen list, and he drew an energetic opponent in Pat Bosch, director of the Phoenix United Fund. Cutting heavily into his Phoenix leads, and carrying many small towns, Bosch came within 3,000 votes of upsetting Steiger, who had not been considered in serious political trouble at all. Not too surprisingly, Steiger charged as the new year began that environmental groups were too powerful and had too much control over Congress; he can be pretty sure that they will be trying as hard as they can to beat him in 1976.

Census Data Pop. 443,201. Central city, 36%; suburban, 26%. Median family income, $8,964; families above $15,000: 16%; families below $3,000: 10%. Median years education, 12.2.

The Voters

Median voting age 41.
Employment profile White collar, 46%. Blue collar, 36%. Service, 13%. Farm, 5%.
Ethnic groups Black, 2%. Indian, 4%. Spanish, 19%. Total foreign stock, 15%. Canada, Germany, 1% each.

Presidential vote

1972	Nixon (R)	104,197	(72%)
	McGovern (D)	41,012	(28%)
1968	Nixon (R)	61,182	(55%)
	Humphrey (D)	37,291	(33%)
	Wallace (AI)	12,937	(12%)

Rep. Sam Steiger (R) Elected 1966; b. Mar. 10, 1929, New York, N.Y.; home, Prescott; Cornell U., 1946–48, Colo. A&M, B.S. 1950; Jewish.

Career Rancher; Army, Korea; Ariz. Senate, 1960–64; South Vietnam correspondent for Phoenix *Gazette* & Prescott *Courier*, 1965.

Offices 2432 RHOB, 202-225-4576. Also 5015 Fed. Bldg., Phoenix 85025, 602-261-4041.

Committees

Government Operations (7th). Subcommittees: Government Information and Individual Rights.

Interior and Insular Affairs (2d). Subcommittees: Energy and the Environment; Mines and Mining; Public Lands.

Group Ratings

	ADA	COPE	LWV	RIPON	NFU	LCV	CFA	NAB	NSI	ACA
1974	0	0	8	31	15	13	0	80	100	100
1973	0	11	13	20	32	5	14	–	–	100
1972	6	10	20	42	57	33	0	91	100	96

Key Votes

1) Foreign Aid	AGN	6) Gov Abortn Aid	AGN	11) Pub Cong Election $	AGN
2) Busing	AGN	7) Coed Phys Ed	AGN	12) Turkish Arms Cutoff	ABS
3) ABM	FOR	8) Pov Lawyer Gag	FOR	13) Youth Camp Regs	AGN
4) B-1 Bomber	FOR	9) Pub Trans Sub	AGN	14) Strip Mine Veto	FOR
5) Nerve Gas	FOR	10) EZ Voter Regis	AGN	15) Farm Bill Veto	FOR

Election Results

1974 general:	Sam Steiger (R)	71,497 (51%)	($203,899)
	Pat Bosch (D)	68,424 (49%)	($68,203)
1974 primary:	Sam Steiger (R), unopposed		
1972 general:	Sam Steiger (R)	90,710 (63%)	($37,691)
	Ted Wyckoff (D)	53,220 (37%)	($24,648)

◆ ◆ ◆ ◆ ◆

FOURTH DISTRICT

Every ten years, the United States Census Bureau reports shifts of population among and within the states. This requires the creation of perhaps one or two dozen new congressional districts, units with no previous separate existence and containing no incumbent Congressmen. Naturally, such districts are often the scenes of spirited contests, for the winner of the new seat and is an excellent bet to keep the job at least ten years, and more than likely for longer. They can go on to run for Senator, Governor, perhaps even President, while the losers usually return quietly to the obscurity of law practices, local businesses, and occasional political and charitable activity.

Of the dozen or so new districts created as a result of the 1970 census, the most fiercely contested race occurred in a rather unlikely spot: the 4th district of Arizona. The 4th's lines were drawn by the state's Republican legislature and approved by the then Republican Governor. Although they included some Democratic territory—notably old mining towns like Globe and Morenci and the Navajo Reservation in northeast Arizona—the new district without a doubt would be dominated by its share of Maricopa County (Phoenix), which would cast 67% of its total votes.

Moreover, this part of Maricopa included almost all of the most Republican areas of heavily Republican metropolitan Phoenix: the post suburbs of Scottsdale and Paradise Valley and the hilltop homes near the mountains that bisect the northern part of Phoenix itself. This is the part of Arizona where Barry Goldwater lives, an area that gave Richard Nixon a whopping 76% of the vote in 1972.

So it might be expected that a Republican in the Goldwater mold would win the House election here—which is what, after a bitter struggle, eventually happened. But the fact that there was such a struggle and that the winner's margins—both in his first race and in the 1974 election as well—were so much smaller than might have been expected is an index of the ferment in Arizona politics today.

First there were the 1972 primaries in which the candidates who seemed the favorites on the basis of past performance lost. Republican State Treasurer Ernest Garfield ran behind state Sen. John Conlan, son of onetime major league umpire Jocko Conlan; and 1970 Democratic Senate candidate Sam Grossman lost to millionaire laywer Jack Brown. Then, all the losing candidates refused to support the men who beat them. Brown quoted Republican Congressman San Steiger to the effect that Conlan was morally unfit for public office. Conlan countered with a list of Democrats-for-Conlan, and linked Brown with McGovern, amnesty, and the decriminalization of marijuana. It turned out to be the most expensive congressional race in the nation that year, with more than $500,000 spent by the two major party nominees, and more by primary losers like Garfield and Grossman. Conlan ran 18% behind Nixon, but managed to squeak out a 53–47 margin.

The 1974 race was somewhat calmer. Conlan had spent his time in office amassing an almost perfectly conservative voting record and using the frank and every other resource possible to make his name well-known and well-liked. His opponent this time was realtor Byron Brown (no relation to Jack), who spent fairly freely, but at nothing like 1972 levels. The tone of the campaign oratory was less vicious (though the Conlan-Steiger feud seemed to continue). It was, all in all, an easier victory for Conlan this time, even in a Democratic year, and an indication that that 1972 election probably did settle the representation for this district for a decade or more.

Census Data Pop. 443,575. Central city, 48%; suburban, 9%. Median family income, $9,886; families above $15,000: 23%; families below $3,000: 11%. Median years education, 12.3.

The Voters

Median voting age 42.
Employment profile White collar, 56%. Blue collar, 29%. Service, 12%. Farm, 3%.
Ethnic groups Black, 1%. Indian, 14%. Spanish, 13%. Total foreign stock, 13%. Canada, Germany, 1% each.

Presidential vote

1972	Nixon (R)	111,127	(71%)
	McGovern (D)	45,029	(29%)
1968	Nixon (R)	74,171	(59%)
	Humphrey (D)	40,592	(32%)
	Wallace (AI)	11,872	(9%)

Rep. John B. Conlan (R) Elected 1972; b. Sept. 17, 1930, Oak Park, Ill.; home, Phoenix; Northwestern U., B.S. 1951, Harvard U., LL.B. 1954, Fulbright Scholar at U. of Cologne, Acad. of Internatl. Law, The Hague.

Career Army, 1956–61; Practicing atty.; Instructor, U. of Md. and Ariz. St. U.; Ariz. Senate, 1965–72.

Offices 130 CHOB, 202-225-3361. Also 3449 Fed. Bldg., Phoenix 85025, 602-261-3071.

Committees

Banking, Currency and Housing (7th). Subcommittees: Domestic Monetary Policy; Housing and Community Development; International Trade, Investment and Monetary Policy.

Science and Technology (9th). Subcommittees: Aviation and Transportation R&D; Domestic and International Scientific Planning and Analysis; Energy Research, Development and Demonstration.

Group Ratings

	ADA	COPE	LWV	RIPON	NFU	LCV	CFA	NAB	NSI	ACA
1974	14	0	33	38	8	35	0	83	100	92
1973	8	18	17	20	22	11	0	–	–	100

Key Votes

1) Foreign Aid	AGN	6) Gov Abortn Aid	AGN	11) Pub Cong Election $	FOR
2) Busing	AGN	7) Coed Phys Ed	ABS	12) Turkish Arms Cutoff	ABS
3) ABM	FOR	8) Pov Lawyer Gag	FOR	13) Youth Camp Regs	AGN
4) B-1 Bomber	ABS	9) Pub Trans Sub	AGN	14) Strip Mine Veto	FOR
5) Nerve Gas	FOR	10) EZ Voter Regis	AGN	15) Farm Bill Veto	FOR

Election Results

1974 general:	John B. Conlan (R)	78,887	(55%)	($97,922)
	Byron T. Brown (D)	63,677	(45%)	($55,126)
1974 primary:	John B. Conlan (R), unopposed			
1972 general:	John B. Conlan (R)	82,511	(53%)	($156,662)
	Jack E. Brown (D)	73,309	(47%)	($318,254)

ARKANSAS

Fifteen years ago, the outlook for Arkansas was pretty bleak. The state had pretty well earned the Dogpatch reputation it held across the nation. Since the days of the Great Depression, the state had been losing population, and its young people continued to leave by the thousands, looking for jobs elsewhere. Arkansas' reputation as a relatively tolerant border state was shattered by the shenanigans of Gov. Orval Faubus, who blocked implementation of a federal court integration order, and forced President Eisenhower to send federal troops into Little Rock's Central High. (The Little Rock episode, however, guaranteed political success for Faubus, who was able to break the state's two-term tradition and remained Governor through 1966.)

Today, the picture has changed dramatically, and largely through the efforts of one man, former Governor (1966–70) Winthrop Rockfeller, who died in early 1973. Rockfeller had come to Arkansas after a notorious (and expensive) divorce, and Faubus had recruited him to help attract industry to the state. Once elected Governor, in 1966, Rockefeller worked even harder at it. Aided by a powerful congressional delegation, Rockefeller concentrated on getting small, nondefense industries whose plants could be located out in the country, near the people who needed jobs. Moreover, retirees and others seeking a life of greater tranquillity began to move in large numbers to the hills north and west of Little Rock. The 1970 census showed that northern Arkansas was one of the few non-metropolitan areas to score substantial population increases in the sixties, and in the seventies Arkansas has continued to grow faster than the nation as a whole, though not at a disastrously rapid rate.

Rockefeller also managed to effect a total change in the political atmosphere in the state. Unusual among modern Southern Republicans for his commitment to civil rights and his appointment of blacks to high government positions, Rockefeller managed to beat an outright segregationist in the 1966 gubernatorial race, and a Faubus protege in 1968. And when he was finally beaten himself in 1970, it was by a young, previously unknown Democrat named Dale Bumpers, who forthrightly declared that segregation is "immoral." Bumpers, for his part, was free to admit that a candidate like himself could not have won except for the example set by Rockefeller.

Having beaten one of the state's moderate and seemingly unbeatable officeholders in 1970, Bumpers went on in 1974 to whip another, Sen. J. William Fulbright. Bumpers had been, by all accounts, a successful and certainly an extremely popular Governor; he could easily have won a third term in '74. But the Governorship pays only $10,000 per year—the lowest salary in the nation for the post and a problem for a man like Bumpers who is not independently wealthy. And although he was beginning to attract attention as a possible presidential or vice-presidential candidate, Bumpers could not expect that national ticket–makers would bother to make the careful assessment of his record in Little Rock which they should before thrusting a man into position of such potential power.

So, not long before the 1974 filing date, Bumpers decided to oppose Fulbright. All of which struck the Senator as a little unfair. The two men's views on issues differed little, and over the years the usually urbane Fulbright had been able to beat the kind of segregationist candidates who were his only significant opponents. Fulbright's main interest, of course, was foreign policy. In the 1940s he had sponsored the scholarship program that bears his name, and in the 1950s he had become Chairman of the Senate Foreign Relations Committee. Under his leadership, the committee became the nation's leading forum for opposition to the Vietnam war and a reduction of American commitments abroad, including foreign aid. Fulbright, a former president of the University of Arkansas, is a contemplative man, who sometimes indulged in moody withdrawals from active politicking. But by 1974, he had seen American troops withdrawn from Vietnam, a detente policy established with Russia and China, and foreign aid drastically cut; he was also developing a good relationship with Secretary of State Kissinger. At 69, he wanted very much to remain in the Senate, and until Bumpers's last minute decision, it looked as if he could win a sixth term easily.

But Bumpers, the clean-cut young lawyer from tiny Charleston, was too popular. He avoided talking about specific issues, spent little money, declined to take out-of-state contributions (many strong backers of aid to Israel wanted to see Fulbright defeated)—and won easily. So Bumpers went on to the Senate, where he appears to be one of the brighter freshman—a politician who actually lives up to his press releases.

The senior Senator from there remains a man very much of the old guard, John L. McClellan, who turns 80 in 1976. and was first elected to Congress in 1934. A stern and austere conservative, McClellan has been in the Senate since 1942, and since 1972 has been chairman of the Appropriations Committee. McClellan won most national attention as Chairman of the Permanent Investigations Subcommittee, leading the televised inquiry into labor union corruption in the 1950s (the subcommittee's chief counsel was the young Robert F. Kennedy) and the TFX (F-111) contract hearings in the 1960s. He is a backer of hard-line anti-crime legislation, including revival of capital punishment, and usually votes with Chairman James Eastland on the Judiciary Committee. But McClellan's seat on Appropriations has meant more to Arkansas, for he has funneled large amounts of public works money into the state. His role is memorialized, even while he continues to serve in the Senate, in the naming of the recently opened McClellan-Kerr Arkansas River Navigation System—a hugely expensive project which has made Little Rock and Tulsa, Oklahoma seaports.

Such visible evidence of clout was undoubtedly an asset to McClellan in 1972 when he was challenged in the Democratic primary by 37-year-old Congressman David Pryor. Pryor was not the kind of politician you would expect to represent a Deep South district. He captured the seat in 1966, and quickly won a place on the vital Appropriations Committee, with a little help from his fellow Arkansan, Wilbur Mills. But instead of waiting for seniority to elevate him to power, Pryor began, quietly at first, to transgress the usual rules and customs by which young Southern Congressman order their conduct. Disturbed about the treatment of the elderly, Pryor worked anonymously for several weeks in a nursing home. Denied a subcommittee to investigate these institutions—which have been thriving on Medicare and Medicaid money—he rented three trailers and set up a volunteer staff of a vacant lot near Capitol Hill. At the same time, the Congressman began voting more and more with northern Democrats. Finally, as a member of the Credentials Committee at the 1968 Democratic national convention, he even voted against seating the regular all-white Mississippi delegation.

That such apostasy did not automatically bar him from a serious try at statewide office is evidence of the Rockefeller-inspired transformation of Arkansas politics. In 1972, Pryor hit hard on economic issues, and forced McClellan into a runoff. But in the next few weeks, McClellan responded with an active personal campaign and a well-financed attack on Pryor's liberalism and labor union contributors. Trotting out the usual conservative issues—busing and gun control and school prayer—McClellan managed to barely squeak out a win. It was, he promised, the last time he would run for office.

Pryor returned to Little Rock to practice law, and Bumpers' sudden decision to run for the Senate against Fulbright gave Pryor an opening to run for Governor. His opponent, as it turned out, was none other than Orval Faubus, trying for yet another comeback (Bumpers had beaten him in 1970). This time, Faubus concentrated heavily on the busing issue, and made some inroads, but Pryor won a solid victory. He is almost sure to win a second term in 1976, and in 1978 McClellan's seat will be up; it is risky to predict that far ahead, but Pryor certainly seems to be the favorite to win it.

Arkansas seems full of young, fairly liberal, personally attractive Democratic politicians these days—a type that simply was not around in the days before Winthrop Rockefeller (although, ironically, none is in Rockefeller's Republican Party). There are Bumpers and Pryor, of course, and state Attorney General Jim Guy Tucker and Congressman Ray Thornton and almost successful congressional candidate Bill Clinton. This is quite a contrast from the not-too-long-ago days when Arkansas' chief political asset was seniority. In 1966, the four-member Arkansas House delegation had a total of 104 years' seniority, and key committee posts on Rules, Commerce, Agriculture, and Ways and Means. In the years since, one of those congressmen has been defeated, two have voluntarily retired, and one, though he still hold office, has faded from the scene—Wilbur Mills.But in a day when talent and energy seem almost as important in advancing a state's interests on Capitol Hill as seniority, Arkansas appears almost as well served by its congressional delegation as in the past.

Census Data Pop. 1,923,295; 0.95% of U.S. total, 32nd largest; Central city, 17%; suburban, 14%. Median family income, $6,271; 49th highest; families above $15,000: 8%; families below $3,000: 22%. Median years education, 10.5.

1974 Share of Federal Tax Burden $1,767,581,000; 0.66% of U.S. total, 34th largest.

1974 Share of Federal Outlays $2,338,462,000; 0.87% of U.S. total, 33d largest. Per capita federal spending, $1215.

DOD	$358,537,000	35th (0.52%)	HEW	$913,323,000	33d (0.98%)
AEC	$106,000	39th (–)	HUD	$8,220,000	31st (0.84%)
NASA	$170,000	43d (0.01%)	VA	$194,290,000	25th (1.42%)
DOT	$65,332,000	39th (0.77%)	EPA	$13,022,000	37th (0.41%)
DOC	$7,225,000	30th (0.45%)	RevS	$62,838,000	30th (1.03%)
DOI	$7,095,000	45th (0.29%)	Int.	$87,785,000	29th (0.43%)
USDA	$366,252,000	10th (2.94%)	Other	$254,267,000	

Economic Base Agriculture, notably soybeans, broilers, cattle and cotton lint; food and kindred products, especially meat products; finance, insurance and real estate; lumber and wood products, especially sawmills and planing mills; electrical equipment and supplies, especially electrical industrial apparatus; apparel and other textile products, especially men's and boys' furnishings; furniture and fixtures, especially household furniture.

Political Line-up Governor, David H. Pryor (D). Senators, John L. McClellan (D) and Dale Bumpers (D). Representatives, 4 (3 D and 1 R). State Senate (33 D, 1 R, and 1 vac.); State House (97 D and 3 R).

The Voters

Registration 996,985 Total. No party registration.
Median voting age 45.
Employment profile White collar, 39%. Blue collar, 41%. Service, 13%. Farm, 7%.
Ethnic groups Black, 18%. Total foreign stock, 2%.

Presidential vote

1972	Nixon (R)	448,541	(69%)
	McGovern (D)	199,892	(31%)
1968	Nixon (R)	190,759	(31%)
	Humphrey (D)	188,228	(30%)
	Wallace (AI)	240,982	(39%)

Sen. John L. McClellan (D) Elected 1942, seat up 1978; b. Feb. 25, 1896, near Sheridan; home, Little Rock; studied law in father's office and admitted to Ark. bar in 1913; Baptist.

Career Practicing atty., 1913–17, 1919–35, 1939–42; Army, WWI; Malvern City Atty., 1920–26; Prosecuting Atty., Ark. 7th Jud. Dist., 1927–30; U.S. House of Reps., 1935–38.

Offices 3421 DSOB, 202-224-2353. Also 3030 Fed. Ofc. Bldg., Little Rock 72201, 501-378-6101.

Committees

Appropriations (Chairman). Subcommittees: Defense (Chairman); Interior; Legislative; State, Justice, Commerce, The Judiciary; Treasury, U.S. Postal Service and General Government.

Government Operations (2d). Subcommittees: Reports, Accounting and Management; Intergovernmental Relations; Permanent Subcommittee on Investigations.

The Judiciary (2d). Subcommittees: Antitrust and Monopoly Legislation; Criminal Laws and Procedures (Chairman); Constitutional Rights; Federal Charters, Holidays and Celebrations; Patents, Trademarks and Copyrights (Chairman).

Group Ratings

	ADA	COPE	LWV	RIPON	NFU	LCV	CFA	NAB	NSI	ACA
1974	10	18	20	25	41	15	22	42	80	89
1973	16	27	20	25	50	–	8	–	–	78
1972	10	0	44	25	75	0	18	60	90	69

Key Votes

1) No-Knock	FOR	8) Gov Abortn Aid	AGN	15) Consumer Prot Agy	AGN
2) Busing	AGN	9) Cut Mil Brass	AGN	16) Forced Psych Tests	AGN
3) No Fault	AGN	10) Gov Limousine	FOR	17) Fed Campaign Subs	AGN
4) F-111	FOR	11) RR Featherbed	FOR	18) Rhod Chrome Ban	AGN
5) Death Penalty	FOR	12) Handgun License	AGN	19) Open Legis Meetings	AGN
6) Foreign Aid	AGN	13) Less Troop Abrd	FOR	20) Strikers Food Stmps	AGN
7) Filibuster	ABS	14) Resume Turk Aid	FOR	21) Gov Info Disclosure	AGN

Election Results

1972 general:	John L. McClellan (D)	386,398	(61%)	($516,573)
	Wayne H. Babbitt (R)	248,238	(39%)	($72,643)
1972 runoff:	John L. McClellan (D)	242,983	(52%)	
	David Pryor (D)	224,262	(48%)	
1972 primary:	John L. McClellan (D)	220,588	(45%)	
	David Pryor (D)	204,058	(42%)	
	Ted Boswell (D)	62,496	(13%)	
	Foster Johnson (D)	6,358	(1%)	
1966 general:	John L. McClellan (D), unopposed			

Sen. Dale Bumpers (D) Elected 1974; b. Aug. 12, 1925, Charleston; home, Charleston; U. of Ark., Northwestern U., LL.B. 1951; Methodist.

Career USMC, WWII; Practicing atty., 1951–70; Charleston City Atty.; Gov. of Ark., 1970–74.

Offices 6313 DSOB, 202-224-4843. Also 2527 Fed. Bldg., 700 W. Capital, Little Rock 77201, 501-378-6286.

Committees

Aeronautical and Space Sciences (5th).

Interior and Insular Affairs (9th). Subcommittees: Energy Research and Water Resources; Environment and Land Resources; Minerals, Materials and Fuels; Parks and Recreation.

Group Ratings: Newly Elected

Key Votes

1) No-Knock	NE	8) Gov Abortn Aid	FOR	15) Consumer Prot Agy	NE
2) Busing	NE	9) Cut Mil Brass	NE	16) Forced Psych Tests	NE
3) No Fault	NE	10) Gov Limousine	NE	17) Fed Campaign Subs	NE
4) F-111	AGN	11) RR Featherbed	NE	18) Rhod Chrome Ban	NE
5) Death Penalty	NE	12) Handgun License	NE	19) Open Legis Meetings	NE
6) Foreign Aid	NE	13) Less Troop Abrd	NE	20) Strikers Food Stmps	NE
7) Filibuster	ABS	14) Resume Turk Aid	FOR	21) Gov Info Disclosure	NE

Election Results

1974 general:	Dale Bumpers (D)	461,056	(85%)	($335,874)
	John Harris Jones (R)	82,026	(15%)	($18,651)
1974 primary:	Dale Bumpers (D)	380,748	(65%)	
	J. William Fulbright (D)	204,630	(35%)	

Gov. David Pryor (D) Elected 1974, term expires Jan. 1977; b. 1934, Camden; U. of Ark., B.A. 1957, LL.B. 1964; Presbyterian.

Career Ed. and Publisher, *Ouachita Citizen*, Camden, 1957–61; Practicing atty., 1964–66; U.S. House of Reps., 1967–72; Candidate for Dem. nomination for U.S. Senate, 1972.

Offices State Capitol, Little Rock 72201, 501-371-2133.

Election Results

1974 general:	David Pryor (D)	358,018	(66%)
	Ken Coon (R)	187,872	(34%)
1974 primary:	David Pryor (D)	297,673	(51%)
	Orval E. Faubus (D)	193,105	(33%)
	Dr. Bob Riley (D)	92,612	(16%)

◆ ◆ ◆ ◆ ◆

FIRST DISTRICT

Eastern Arkansas—the flat, fertile, cotton-growing plains that line the west bank of the Mississippi River—is economically more tied to the state of Mississippi or Memphis, Tennessee, than to the hilly regions of central Arkansas or the Ozark Mountains. Like the Delta in Mississippi, eastern Arkansas is occupied by large farms and even plantations where, if one is enamored with the tradition of the Old South, the black folk do the cotton-picking and the white folk do the money-making—and the voting. This part of the state has never much supported any form of upcountry populism, though it does retain a nominal Democratic allegiance. And it has been the part of the state least appreciative of the progressive appeal of governors like Winthrop Rockefeller, Dale Bumpers, or David Pryor; it prefers the older, and more conservative politics of John McClellan and Orval Faubus.

Eastern Arkansas is the heart of the state's 1st congressional district. Although population-mandated redistricting has forced the inclusion of several hill counties, the flatlands along the unpredictable Mississippi still dominate the district's balloting. For 30 years, the 1st's Congressman was Ezekiel C. Gathings, who never won much national recognition, but rose diligently on the seniority ladder to become Chairman of Agriculture's Cotton Subcommittee. Gathings retired in 1968, and his successor, Bill Alexander, is a politician in much the same mold.

He early sought and received a seat on Agriculture; in 1975, he switched to the powerful Appropriations Committee. Alexander's voting record is not as conservative as his predecessor's but his main interests appear to be local: farm programs and river improvements.

Alexander's switch came in a year when seniority, suddenly, no longer conferred automatic power. For many years, Southerners have maintained more than proportional power in the House, because their constituents have elected 'em young and kept reelecting 'em every two years. But even before 1975, changes in Southern politics had reduced the number of one-party districts, and more Republicans and moderate Democrats were elected from the South. Alexander, then, as a young Southerner bent on accumulating seniority, is part of what seems to be a vanishing breed; and after 1975, he knows that no matter how senior he becomes, he cannot be unacceptable to the Northern-dominated Democratic caucus and hope to enjoy the power his seniority would in past days have entitled him to. It is true that he has little trouble winning reelection. In 1973, he had an altercation with a policeman at Washington National Airport, which some thought might cause him trouble in this Baptist district. But in 1974 he won easily, and no doubt will in the future.

Census Data Pop. 479,893. Central city, 0%; suburban, 10%. Median family income, $5,381; families above $15,000: 7%; families below $3,000: 29%. Median years education, 8.8.

The Voters

Median voting age 45.
Employment profile White collar, 34%. Blue collar, 40%. Service, 13%. Farm, 13%.
Ethnic groups Black, 23%. Total foreign stock, 1%.

Presidential vote

1972	Nixon (R)	98,979	(69%)
	McGovern (D)	45,355	(31%)
1968	Nixon (R)	39,137	(27%)
	Humphrey (D)	44,963	(31%)
	Wallace (AI)	60,971	(42%)

Rep. Bill Alexander (D) Elected 1968; b. Jan 16, 1934, Memphis, Tenn.; home, Osceola; U. of Ark., Southwestern at Memphis, B.A. 1957, Vanderbilt U., LL.B., 1960; Episcopalian.

Career Army, 1951–53; Practicing atty., 1960–69.

Offices 227 CHOB, 202-225-4076. Also 2313 Ark. Services Ctr., Jonesboro 72401, 501-972-4096.

Committees

Appropriations (30th). Subcommittees: District of Columbia; State, Justice, Commerce, and the Judiciary; Transportation.

Group Ratings

	ADA	COPE	LWV	RIPON	NFU	LCV	CFA	NAB	NSI	ACA
1974	22	60	44	20	67	39	64	55	67	57
1973	50	75	58	38	100	13	67	–	–	38
1972	19	40	60	42	86	24	0	22	80	44

Key Votes

1) Foreign Aid	AGN	6) Gov Abortn Aid	AGN	11) Pub Cong Election $	AGN
2) Busing	AGN	7) Coed Phys Ed	FOR	12) Turkish Arms Cutoff	FOR
3) ABM	FOR	8) Pov Lawyer Gag	AGN	13) Youth Camp Regs	FOR
4) B-1 Bomber	FOR	9) Pub Trans Sub	FOR	14) Strip Mine Veto	FOR
5) Nerve Gas	ABS	10) EZ Voter Regis	ABS	15) Farm Bill Veto	AGN

Election Results

1974 general:	Bill Alexander (D)	104,247	(91%)	($19,691)
	James Lawrence Dauer (R)	10,821	(9%)	($1,060)
1974 primary:	Bill Alexander (D), unopposed			
1972 general:	Bill Alexander (D), unopposed			($0)

◆ ◆ ◆ ◆ ◆

SECOND DISTRICT

In early 1973, Wilbur Mills was still on top of the game. Journalists, politicians, and businessmen constantly were asking his opinion on tax reform, curbs on foreign imports, wage and price controls. So often was Mills called the powerful-Chairman-of-the-powerful-Ways-and-Means-Committee that the cliche became a title in itself. His name was spoken in near sepulchral tones, and he was quoted at least twice a week by Evans and Novak, who praised him reverently. Predictably, Mills' presidential run in 1972 ended in total failure (he had got it into his head somehow that he was going to score big in the Massachusetts primary). But commentators never doubted that the Chairman had everything it took to be President; some condemned the system for keeping this unphotogenic Congressman out of the White House.

Two years later, Wilbur Mills was at best a tragic figure, at worst a laughingstock. In October 1974, park police found him, cut and bleeding, in the Washington Tidal Basin, trying to deter a stripper-friend (Fanne Fox, the Argentine firecracker) from throwing herself in. Then other stories began to come out: how Mills had frequented the Silver Slipper, a seedy night club where Fanne danced and where he one night bought $1400 worth of champagne. After his 1974 reelection, Mills, as if to confound his critics, appeared on stage with Fanne in Boston, saying that no one could topple him from power. He was wrong. A photograph of Chairman Mills with Fanne in Boston got top billing in the newspapers the next day, and his congressional career was over. The man who had been Chairman of the House Ways and Means Committee since 1958 entered Bethesda Hospital, announced from his bed he would relinquish the chairmanship, and, weeks later, issued a statement saying he was an alcoholic and would seek treatment.

Technically, Mills remains a Congressman and a member of the Ways and Means Committee. But no one expects to see him back active in the House. His troubles began during his presidential bid, in the course of which he collected a huge campaign treasury, most of it from businessmen with interests in legislation that had to see its way through Ways and Means. In 1973, Mills said he might retire because of a painful back condition, but surgery reportedly mended that. But all the while, he was apparently spending less time on business and more at the Silver Slipper. In other lines of work, Mills would have been allowed—and required—to retire quietly; in politics, he can nominally keep his job, but only under glare of national publicity.

It is worth looking back—if only to understand how the House works today, and how it is changing—at the basis of Mills's power, and how it was being eroded, slowly, even before his fall from grace. First, there was simply the jurisdiction of Ways and Means: it covered all tax, trade, Social Security, Medicare, and Medicaid legislation; moreover, its Democratic members made all committee assignments for members of their party. Second, there was Ways and Means' control over legislation once it left Committee: Mills invariably got a "closed rule" from the Rules Committee, which meant that a Ways and Means bill could not be amended on the floor; what the dozen or so members of Mills' unit had decided was the package the full House had to vote up or down. Third, Mills controlled all of Ways and Means' staff, so that other members could seldom prepare alternatives to the technical and complex legislation the Committee handled. Fourth, there were never any subcommittees whose existence would have given other members staff and leverage over legislation; all that was reserved for Mills. Fifth, Mills maintained close relations with the Committee's ranking Republicans, John Byrnes of Wisconsin up till 1972 and Herman Schneebeli of Pennsylvania thereafter. With Mills and the top Republican in agreement, other members of the House could do very little.

Add all of these levers to Mills' grasp of complex tax, trade, and Social Security matters, and you can understand why this one man often had more power to shape legislation that influenced the flow of billions of dollars than the rest of the 434 members of the House combined. Finally,

Mills was careful to bend with the prevailing wind when he found himself out of line with his colleagues. After the 1964 Johnson landslide, for example, the Congressman suddenly changed a long-held position and backed Medicare, which was certain to pass.

Al Ullman, the new Chairman of Ways and Means, has nothing like the power Mills once wielded. Just after the Boston stage incident, House Democrats voted to strip the power to make committee assignments from Ways and Means and gave it to the Democratic Steering Committee, chaired by the liberal Phil Burton of California. Mills's old turf has also lost some of its subject-matter jurisdiction. As early as 1973, House reformers obtained an "open rule" for legislation reported out of Ways and Means, one practical result of which was that in early 1975 the House overwhelmingly voted to amend a Ways and Means bill and repealed the oil depletion allowance. And just after the Tidal Basin incident, subcommittees of Ways and Means were created, which gave members of the Committee other than the Chairman leverage in drafting bills.

Most of these changes would have occurred even if Mills had not been found at the Tidal Basin. Although the Congressman had adjusted to the 1964 landslide well enough, he did not seem to understand the kind of freshmen elected ten years later. Well respected in the business community, Mills seemed to regard it as his constituency—not a popular position in the increasingly liberal Democratic caucus. Mills was also a bridge between Southern Democratic conservatives and Northern Democratic liberals; but he would have found his services less needed now that there are so few of the former and so many of the latter.

Before the Tidal basin debacle, Mills appeared totally immune to any political trouble. But as luck would have it, in 1974 he had a Republican opponent on the ballot for the first time ever. Thirty-year-old Judy Petty, of Reaganish bent, attacked Mills fiercely even as early as September for accepting illegal corporate contribution in his 1972 presidential campaign. She promised not to make an issue of Fanne Fox, but the stripper was of course much in the minds of the voters when Mills returned to the district, and, for the first time anyone could remember, he campaigned hard. He did manage to win, but only with an embarrassingly low 59% of the vote.

No one expects that the 2d district of Arkansas will elect Wilbur Mills again, and few expect Mrs. Petty to win either. The next Representative will almost certainly be chosen in the Democratic primary. The 2d includes parts of all of the topographical regions of Arkansas: some of the northern hill country, including Mills' home town of Kensett; some of the flat eastern Mississippi Delta land in Arkansas County; and Little Rock, the state capital. It is the last of these, Little Rock, that dominates the district's voting, casting with surrounding Pulaski County 53% of its ballots. Most likely the winner will be a Little Rock-based candidate, perhaps state Attorney General Jim Guy Tucker, a moderate-to-liberal Democrat in the Bumpers-Pryor tradition.

Little Rock is still internationally known for the intransigence of its whites in the 1957 school desegregation crisis when Eisenhower sent in federal troops. But today Little Rock is one of the most moderate, even liberal cities in the South—a transformation that Winthrop Rockefeller, Dale Bumpers, and, ironically, even Wilbur Mills can claim credit for.

Census Data Pop. 481,120. Central city, 40%; suburban, 27%. Median family income, $7,484; families above $15,000: 12%; families below $3,000: 16%. Median years education, 12.0.

The Voters

Median voting age 43.
Employment profile White collar, 46%. Blue collar, 37%. Service, 13%. Farm, 4%.
Ethnic groups Black, 16%. Total foreign stock, 3%.

Presidential vote

1972	Nixon (R)	100,761	(64%)
	McGovern (D)	56,514	(36%)
1968	Nixon (R)	43,451	(30%)
	Humphrey (D)	46,332	(32%)
	Wallace (AI)	54,248	(38%)

Rep. Wilbur D. Mills (D) Elected 1938; b. May 24, 1909, Kensett; home, Kensett; Hendrix Col., A.B. 1930, Harvard U., LL.B., 1933; Methodist.

Career County and Probate Judge, White Co., 1934–38.

Offices 1136 LHOB, 202-225-2506. Also 1527 Fed. Ofc. Bldg., Little Rock 72201, 501-378-5522.

Committees

Ways and Means (2d).

Group Ratings

	ADA	COPE	LWV	RIPON	NFU	LCV	CFA	NAB	NSI	ACA
1974	42	89	43	30	85	30	63	50	57	33
1973	50	75	25	38	67	33	0	–	–	29
1972	19	63	40	55	43	0	0	22	100	44

Key Votes

1) Foreign Aid	ABS	6) Gov Abortn Aid	AGN	11) Pub Cong Election $	FOR
2) Busing	AGN	7) Coed Phys Ed	ABS	12) Turkish Arms Cutoff	ABS
3) ABM	FOR	8) Pov Lawyer Gag	ABS	13) Youth Camp Regs	AGN
4) B-1 Bomber	ABS	9) Pub Trans Sub	AGN	14) Strip Mine Veto	FOR
5) Nerve Gas	FOR	10) EZ Voter Regis	FOR	15) Farm Bill Veto	AGN

Election Results

1974 general:	Wilbur D. Mills (D)	80,296	(59%)	($71,338)
	Judy Petty (R)	56,038	(41%)	($55,573)
1974 primary:	Wilbur D. Mills (D), unopposed			
1972 general:	Wilbur D. Mills (D), unopposed			($0)

◆ ◆ ◆ ◆ ◆

THIRD DISTRICT

The 3d district of Arkansas is the northwest quarter of the state. It is a region of green hills rising to mountains, of historic proverty, but recent prosperity. The new economic climate comes in large part from the retirees and younger people attracted by the area's mild climate, its scenic mountains and reservoirs, by jobs in its small industries, and by the low-keyed pace of life here. The cities of the 3d are medium-sized, the kind that most Americans say they prefer. Among them are such places as Fort Smith (pop. 62,000), on the Oklahoma border and Arkansas' second largest city; Fayetteville (pop. 30,000), site of the University of Arkansas and home of its former president, J. William Fulbright; and Hot Springs (pop. 35,000), the onetime gambling center and still a popular resort town. The district also contains the state's most reliably Republican territory, the mountain counties in the north which opposed the Confederacy and even in the depression of the thirties have remained faithful to the party of Union.

In this century—at least until Wilbur Mills got into trouble—this has been the only Arkansas district to be the site of real two-party political contests, and it is the only one today represented by a Republican Congressman. In 1966, the 3d surprised practically everyone when it ousted longtime Rep. James Trimble, then 72 and a member of the House Rules Committee, and elected in his place then state Republican Chairman John Paul Hammerschmidt. The new Congressman carried the Republican counties in the north by a large margin, and generally profited from Winthrop Rockefeller's strong win in the gubernatorial contest that year.

As a Congressman, Hammerschmidt has been a fairly reliable conservative, a member of the Public Works Committee who tends to support pork barrel projects and opposes things like diverting gasoline tax money to mass transit. Back in the district, he is known as a friendly Congressman who keeps in touch with his constituents constantly through newsletters and visits to the district, and that reputation was enough for him to win overwhelming victories against lackluster Democrats in 1968, 1970, and 1972.

But in 1974, he faced a different kind of opponent: 28-year-old Bill Clinton, a law professor at the University of Arkansas, and a veteran (though he didn't mention it much) organizer in the McGovern campaign. Clinton waged an energetic campaign, and his personality was at least as engaging as Hammerschmidt's. He also attacked the Congressman sharply on various issues, particularly in the economic area, and charged that he was working more for business interests than for ordinary people. It turned out to be a close race indeed, with Hammerschmidt squeaking to the narrowest victory of his career with only 52% of the vote. He was saved only by his strong showing in Fort Smith. It was, of course, a Democratic year in Arkansas like everywhere else, and it is not all apparent that Hammerschmidt will be beatable in 1976. Nevertheless, observers of the Arkansas political scene predict a long career ahead for Clinton, whether he runs for Congress again or for some other office.

Census Data Pop. 481,106. Central city, 13%; suburban, 9%. Median family income, $6,057; families above $15,000: 7%; families below $3,000: 20%. Median years education, 10.8.

The Voters

Median voting age 46.
Employment profile White collar, 38%. Blue collar, 42%. Service, 13%. Farm, 7%.
Ethnic groups Black, 3%. Total foreign stock, 3%.

Presidential vote

1972	Nixon (R)	138,541	(74%)
	McGovern (D)	47,922	(26%)
1968	Nixon (R)	73,001	(43%)
	Humphrey (D)	45,627	(27%)
	Wallace (AI)	51,343	(30%)

Rep. John Paul Hammerschmidt (R) Elected 1966; b. May 4, 1922, Harrison; home, Harrison; The Citadel, Okla. A&M Col., U. of Ark.; Presbyterian.

Career Army Air Corps, WWII; Bd. Chm., Hammerschmidt Lumber Co.; Chm., Ark. Repub. State Central Comm., 1964–.

Offices 2453 RHOB, 202-225-4301. Also Fed. Bldg., Fayetteville 72701, 501-443-2301.

Committees

Public Works and Transportation (5th). Subcommittees: Aviation; Economic Development; Water Resources.

Veterans' Affairs (Ranking Member). Subcommittees: Cemeteries and Burial Benefits; Compensation, Pension and Insurance; Hospitals.

Group Ratings

	ADA	COPE	LWV	RIPON	NFU	LCV	CFA	NAB	NSI	ACA
1974	10	18	25	53	50	6	0	70	88	79
1973	5	11	20	42	53	17	14	–	–	71
1972	6	9	25	38	71	26	0	67	100	74

Key Votes

1) Foreign Aid	AGN	6) Gov Abortn Aid	AGN	11) Pub Cong Election $	AGN
2) Busing	AGN	7) Coed Phys Ed	AGN	12) Turkish Arms Cutoff	ABS
3) ABM	FOR	8) Pov Lawyer Gag	ABS	13) Youth Camp Regs	AGN
4) B-1 Bomber	FOR	9) Pub Trans Sub	AGN	14) Strip Mine Veto	FOR
5) Nerve Gas	FOR	10) EZ Voter Regis	AGN	15) Farm Bill Veto	FOR

Election Results

1974 general:	John Paul Hammerschmidt (R)	89,324	(52%)	($101,709)
	Bill Clinton (D)	83,030	(48%)	($180,882)
	John Paul Hammerschmidt (R), unopposed			
1972 general:	John Paul Hammerschmidt (R)	144,571	(77%)	($27,588)
	Guy W. Hatfield (D)	42,481	(23%)	($4,243)

◆ ◆ ◆ ◆ ◆

FOURTH DISTRICT

Geographically the 4th congressional district of Arkansas takes in the southern third of the state. It stretches from the flat Delta lands along the Mississippi River, west across rolling hills to Texarkana, a town situated so squarely on the Arkansas-Texas border that the state line runs through City Hall. The principal towns in the district are quiet places like El Dorado (pop. 25,000), Camden (pop. 15,000), Arkadelphia (pop. 9,000), and Pine Bluff (pop. 57,000), the girlhood home of Martha Mitchell. The chief economic activity is raising chickens.

By many indices, the 4th is more like neighboring Mississippi or northern Louisiana than the rest of Arkansas. It has the largest black population in the state, 31%, and produced the state's largest vote for George Wallace in 1968, 46%. But the resemblance to the Deep South vanishes when one considers the kind of Congressmen the 4th has sent to Washington in the last decade.

The district's most recent ex-Representative, David Pryor (1966–73), achieved national distinction not for his opposition to civil rights legislation (he favored it), but for working incognito in a nursing home to learn more of conditions in such institutions, sponsoring remedial legislation, and setting up a volunteer subcommittee staff in a trailer when the House denied him funds for an investigation. In the 1972 Democratic primary, Pryor just missed unseating conservative Senator John McClellan; two years later, he handily captured the Governorship.

The present incumbent, former state Attorney General Ray Thornton, comes from a well-connected and influential Arkansas family. His uncle, W. R. Stephens, president of the Arkansas Louisiana Gas Company, was for many years considered a behind-the-throne kingmaker in the state. Thornton won the 1972 Democratic nomination in the four-candidate initial primary, barely avoiding a runoff with 50.8% of the vote. In the House, Thornton voted a moderate-to-liberal line, generally standing with the vast majority of House Democrats against the economic policies of the Nixon Administration. He made a few ripples by helping to found a Rural Caucus.

But his moments of greatest note came in the House Judiciary Committee hearings on impeachment. Speaking quietly and forcefully, Thornton helped to present the case against the President to the American people, and joined his northern colleagues in a unanimous Democratic bloc for Nixon's removal. He had mastered the facts, and his soft Southern accent gave his case even more credibility as he made it. It must not have been clear to Thornton how popular this position would be back home—where Nixon had received 69% of the votes in 1972—but it turned out to cause him no political problems. The voters of the 4th district have apparently got used to fairly liberal Congressmen, and are prepared to reelect them indefinitely.

Census Data Pop. 481,176. Central city, 16%; suburban, 8%. Median family income, $6,191; families above $15,000: 7%; families below $3,000: 23%. Median years education, 10.4.

The Voters

Median voting age 46.
Employment profile White collar, 36%. Blue collar, 44%. Service, 14%. Farm, 6%.
Ethnic groups Black, 31%. Total foreign stock, 1%.

Presidential vote

1972	Nixon (R)	107,470	(69%)
	McGovern (D)	49,108	(31%)
1968	Nixon (R)	35,170	(22%)
	Humphrey (D)	51,306	(32%)
	Wallace (AI)	74,420	(46%)

Rep. Ray Thornton (D) Elected 1972; b. July 16, 1928, Conway; home, Sheridan; St. Col. of Ark., U. of Ark., Yale U., B.A. 1950, U. of Tex., U. of Ark., J.D. 1956.

Career Navy, Korea; Practicing atty., 1957–70; Atty. Gen. of Ark., 1970–73.

Offices 1109 LHOB, 202-225-3772. Also 2520 Fed. Bldg., Pine Bluff 71601, 501-535-7750.

Committees

Judiciary (15th). Subcommittees: Crime; Criminal Justice.

Science and Technology (11th). Subcommittees: Domestic and International Scientific Planning and Analysis (Chairman); Energy Research, Development and Demonstration; Energy Research (Fossil Fuels).

Group Ratings

	ADA	COPE	LWV	RIPON	NFU	LCV	CFA	NAB	NSI	ACA
1974	39	55	33	47	79	38	23	58	75	53
1973	48	60	67	53	95	50	50	–	–	26

Key Votes

1) Foreign Aid	AGN	6) Gov Abortn Aid	AGN	11) Pub Cong Election $	AGN
2) Busing	AGN	7) Coed Phys Ed	AGN	12) Turkish Arms Cutoff	AGN
3) ABM	FOR	8) Pov Lawyer Gag	AGN	13) Youth Camp Regs	FOR
4) B-1 Bomber	FOR	9) Pub Trans Sub	FOR	14) Strip Mine Veto	FOR
5) Nerve Gas	FOR	10) EZ Voter Regis	FOR	15) Farm Bill Veto	AGN

Election Results

1974 general:	Ray Thornton (D), unopposed	($1,567)
1974 primary:	Ray Thornton (D), unopposed	
1972 general:	Ray Thornton (D), unopposed	($51,854)

CALIFORNIA

California, just a few years ago the most noticeably right wing major state, has now become a leftish state politically. The change was symbolized neatly by the change in the Governor's chair in early 1975: 63-year-old conservative Republican Ronald Reagan was out, 36-year-old liberal Democrat Jerry Brown was in. But this was not just the ordinary shifting between ins and outs that one sees after every election. It signalled the culmination of a major change in most Californians' political attitudes—not just their party preferences, but their feelings about what government can and should do. Ronald Reagan was the personification of a conservatism that believed in less government activity—but also implicitly promised that political leaders could accomplish things, like changing basic life styles, which were inherently beyond the competence of government. Jerry Brown, in contrast, seems to believe in a liberalism which means more government activity in some areas, but overall has a much more modest view of what government and politics can achieve.

If all this seems to run contrary to conventional political analysis, that is because it does. The standard picture of California politics for some Eastern observers is one of zaniness: as if, someone said, the country was tilted westward and all the loose nuts slid to the coast. California, to be sure, is a state of contradictions: one of the nation's most urbanized states, yet the home of vast agribusiness conglomerates; perhaps the most awe-inspiring scenic state, yet the most smoggy and pollution-ridden; the place where the peace movement first made an impact, yet a state still heavily dependent on money from giant defense firms and military bases.

Yet out of these contradictions, California has emerged as a national trend-setter—in suburbanization, in what a few years ago were considered bizarre life styles, and in politics. And perhaps the most noticeable trend in recent years has been this state's preference for candidates of the political "extremes", both the conservative right and the antiwar liberal left. Why? First of all, there are no political machines here to modulate such trends; the old bosses were wiped out by a series of reforms enacted by progressives in 1911. As a result, California is a state where the individual candidate's ideology—and personality—is of paramount importance. It is also a state where these things are communicated widely through the most sophisticated techniques of modern electioneering—sensitive polling, adept use of TV and other media, and pinpointed direct mail. California is, finally, a state where one of the most crucial factors in elections is the effort of people who are essentially volunteers, with no financial gain—or patronage jobs—at stake. Volunteers form not only the cadres of door-to-door campaigners, but also raise the vast amounts of money to pay for all that sophisticated electioneering. California is rapidly replacing New York as the political money center of the country—for candidates of both the right and the left.

Before one can understand the recent ascendancy of left-leaning politics in California, one must understand the earlier rise of the right. For this, it is necessary to go back to the early 1960s. Democrats were in control of things: in the White House, in the California Governor's mansion, and in the state legislature, where the legendary Jess Unruh had just begun his tenure as Speaker of the Assembly. Across the land, conventional wisdom had it that for Republicans to win elections they had to support many Democratic programs, to be seen as moderate or even liberal. A sizable number of California Republicans did not agree. They noted that Richard Nixon, through making concessions to such a strategy, lost the Presidency in 1960, and lost even more badly to Governor Pat Brown in 1962. These people believed very deeply that the nation was moving in the wrong direction under the Democrats. They were determined to do something about it, and they did—by electing Ronald Reagan Governor in 1966.

Reagan's victory, coming just two years after the smashing defeat of another right-winger, Barry Goldwater, shocked and surprised Eastern pundits. They would have been less surprised if they had been following California elections more closely over the preceding few years. In that time, the Republican right had scored a series of unexpected victories: Max Rafferty's election as Superintendent of Public Instruction in 1962, a couple of off year congressional races in 1963 (see Second and Thirty-Third Districts), George Murphy's election as U.S. Senator in 1964, and the repeal of the state's open housing law in a referendum that same year. Even Goldwater had done better than expected, with 46% of the vote in southern California, only a small drop from the 52% Nixon had received there four years earlier.

Behind all these victories was the new California homeowner's resentment of rapid and sometimes violent change. The Berkeley student uprising in 1964 and the Watts riot in 1965 evoked a hatred of those who were different, and Reagan, promising crackdowns on rioters and stern budget cuts, played on these hatreds skillfully. When he told the unpoor, unblack, and unrebellious that their basic impulses and fears were well-founded, that their way of life—whatever hippies and academics might think—was fundamentally *right*, the homeowners and taxpayers responded with millions of votes. Reagan was able to revolutionize California politics, successfully putting to the fore those issues where his positions commanded majority support. It was a masterful political achievement, and one which would be echoed nationally in the Nixon campaigns of 1968 and 1972.

But whatever the successes of the Reagan-Nixon politics nationally in that latter year, it reached its high point in California back in 1968. That year, the Republicans finally took control of the California legislature, after painstakingly picking off Democratic seats in each of the preceding three elections. The legislative victory was particularly dear to Reagan, for it promised that Republicans would redraw the state's congressional and legislative district lines and thus sew up political control of California for another ten years.

It was not to be. The Reagan Republicans were on the downslide of their success curve, their problems signalled even in their best year of 1968 by the victory of Democrat Alan Cranston over Rafferty in the Senate race. In 1970, Democrat John Tunney beat Senator Murphy by a solid 618,000 votes, and Reagan's victory margin was cut in half by the woefully underfinanced campaign of Jess Unruh. Part of the Reagan people's problem was bad selection of candidates; Rafferty, a Long Beach reporter found out, had sat out World War II with an alleged injury and then thrown away his crutches on VJ Day. (Rafferty was defeated for Superintendent in 1970 by a black educator, Wilson Riles, and today teaches at Troy State College in Alabama.) George

Murphy, the old song-and-dance man, turned out to be getting $20,000 a year and a Washington apartment from Technicolor, Inc., while serving in the Senate. Today he can sometimes be seen in Washington, a forlorn figure eking out a living as a lobbyist.

But such gaffes do not totally explain the right's problems. Reagan could point to some solid achievements in his years in office: he had pushed through an oft-copied welfare reform (with help from Democratic Speaker Bob Moretti) in 1971, and he had stablilized, if not the state budget, then at least the number of state employees. But Reagan's campaign style promised more than these governmental accomplishments, and his waning popularity was almost the inevitable price of his early success. If he had professed concern for ordinary middle class voters, it also became clear one of his major goals was reducing taxes on the rich. And if he had convinced Californians in 1966 that he would reassert and reestablish the values of the middle class against those who disdained them—hippies, blacks, and university professors—it became painfully apparent by the early seventies that he just couldn't do it. For every long-haired freak thumbing a ride on the Big Sur highway in 1966 there were a dozen by 1972; for every black who actually went looting in Watts in 1965, there were a dozen blacks in Afros sporting dashikis a few years later. Reagan could win at the polls, but California was changing anyway.

It would have been unthinkable back in 1966, for example, that a referendum to legalize marijuana would outpoll a referendum to clamp limits on obscene movies. Yet exactly that happened in California on 1972. In a performance that surely no other state but Massachusetts or Oregon could duplicate, some 33% of the California voters favored legalized pot; the proposition carried six of the state's 80 Assembly districts, and even got 187,000 votes in supposedly ultraconservative Orange County.

Demographic shifts—not so much in the population as a whole, but in the electrorate—are responsible for many of these changes. Much of the support for Reagan and Reaganites came from Midwestern and Southern migrants to California, people of the World War II generation (or earlier) whose kids were passing through the rebellious adolescent years just as Berkeley and Watts ignited. The older people wanted a return to the serenity and order they remembered, perhaps inaccurately, from their own younger days; they wanted their kids to honor them by trying to grow up to be like them. As time went on, the kids grew up and fashioned their own life-styles, which in turn seemed less threatening to their parents.

But one thing these new voters did remember was that politicians like Ronald Reagan and Richard Nixon had been winning votes by campaigning against them. Some 18% of California's potential voters in 1970 were under 25—a significantly larger percentage than in the nation as a whole—and nearly 10% of the potential electorate can be found in college or graduate school. The dormitories and communities around California's vast system of higher education produced huge majorities against candidates like Richard Nixon and Ronald Reagan following passage of the 18-year-old vote. And in the post-Vietnam years when the differences between the attitudes college and non-college youth have almost vanished—gas station attendants are as likely as Berkeley students to smoke pot these days, and Berkeley students as likely to drink beer—the huge California youth vote is overwhelming anti-Republican.

It should be no surprise that Democrats made major gains in the 1972 and 1974 elections here. Much like Barry Goldwater eight years before, George McGovern did not run so badly nor so far behind normal party levels in California as he did elsewhere; the supposedly "extremist" candidate was no more unacceptable to California voters than the "centrist" Hubert Humphrey. That same year, Democrats increased their margin in the state Assembly to nearly 2–1, and after the 1974 elections they held 55 of the 80 Assembly seats and 25 of the 40 Senate seats—an all-time high.

But the final humiliation for the Reagan people was that they didn't even have a candidate in the general election for Governor. Lieutenant Governor Ed Reinecke, hand-picked by Reagan for the job when Robert Finch became Nixon's HEW Secretary in 1969, turned out to be another bad choice; the obvious heir apparent was indicted for lying before the Watergate grand jury about the ITT affair, and was on trial as the primary was held in June. Despite all that, he received 30% of the vote—testimony of the continuing presence of undeterrable conservative voters in the Republican primary.

The winner of that election was Houston Flournoy, then state Controller and one of the luckiest people in California politics. A onetime college professor and moderate-to-liberal Assemblyman, Flournoy had decided to retire from politics when friends persuaded him, during the wee hours at a Sacramento night spot, to run for State Controller. The incumbent was Alan Cranston, who led the Democratic ticket in 1962; but so sweeping was the Reagan victory that Flournoy pulled an upset. He was reelected by a huge margin in 1970, but still the Governor's race looked like a long shot. But slowly other contenders dropped out—Robert Finch, former Defense Undersecretary David Packard, Attorney General Evelle Younger—leaving only Reinecke, who was promptly indicted.

Flournoy may also have been fortunate in the general election opponent he drew. Naturally, there had been a free-for-all for the Democratic nomination, as it became clear that the man who won it would be Governor, barring a major blunder. San Francisco Mayor Joseph Alioto was there, speaking out against crime (but embarrassed by his wife's temporary disappearance); Assembly Speaker Bob Moretti was buoyed by his success in stumping against Reagan's Proposition One in 1973 (a measure which would have put a lid on state taxes); Congressman Jerome Waldie made an extremely favorable impression on everyone during the impeachment hearings, which unfortunately for him were held a month after the primary; and millionaire businessman William Roth ran a quixotic campaign out of a trailer. Despite all this activity, the easy winner of the primary, with almost 40% of the vote, was the man who had led the polls from the beginning, Secretary of State Edmund G. (Jerry) Brown, Jr.

There are still those who believe that Jerry Brown's sole political asset is his father's name, and doubtless some people do vote for him thinking he is the Pat Brown, who beat Bill Knowland and Richard Nixon, and was Governor from 1959 to 1967. But Jerry Brown is quite a different sort of character. His father is (or was) gregarious; Jerry is quiet, almost sullen. His father was a "centrist" Democrat, ready to get along with anyone in the party; Jerry is a purist, a stickler for campaign finance reform, who pays little attention to the big contributors. There are those who see Brown as the psychological equivalent of Richard Nixon, a paranoid loner who won't level with anyone. The comparison is an unfair one; as befits a former seminarian, Brown is a devout believer in morality in politics. Indeed, he built his career as Secretary of State around enforcing hitherto ignored campaign financing laws, and pushing for new ones, including the sweeping Proposition Nine adopted by a 69–31 margin in the same June primary he won. Brown's endorsement of that Common Cause measure cost him the endorsement of the California AFL-CIO and the hatred of some old pols; but it also demonstrated his public appeal.

Brown's primary foes had campaigned on the assumption that he was so inexperienced and inarticulate that he would make a serious mistake and blow his lead. They underestimated their 36-year-old opponent; he kept his cool, and even developed a somewhat pleasant handshaking style. But in the general election, Jerry Brown did make a mistake: he coasted on his early lead. In late October and early November, Flournoy was closing hard. He played on voters' doubts about Jerry Brown's character—after all, it was Nixon's character, not his policies, the voters misjudged—and ran TV ads stressing Flournoy as a family man, and inferentially attacking Brown as a bachelor (and, some inaccurate whisperers said, a homosexual). Flournoy claimed that he had more expertise about state affairs, and that he would run the state government more rationally. But he was hurt by Gerald Ford's last minute trip to California—when the President quietly endorsed Flournoy and then proceeded to visit Richard Nixon in the hospital.

It was not Flournoy's positive campaign that made the final result so close as it was many voters' doubts about Jerry Brown. In the San Francisco Bay area, in particular, Brown ran poorly; liberally-inclined voters in the residential areas of the city and the San Mateo and Marin County suburbs, who had been trending Democratic during the Reagan years, found Flournoy an acceptable candidate and Brown a plastic one. It was Los Angeles County which saved Brown, giving him 53% of the vote. (This is an unusually high percentage: Brown ran just 2% ahead of the losing McGovern showing in the Bay area and 14% ahead in L.A. County.) Just as Reagan had been voted in, over Jerry Brown's father, by a sweep in right-trending votes from southern California, so Jerry Brown was voted in by a tide of left-trending votes in southern California.

The difference was that Reagan was swept in enthusiastically, Brown with mere acceptance. In the 1966 election Reagan won, turnout was at a record high. But in 1974, turnout was exceedingly low—lower even than in the 1958 election when Pat Brown had first been elected. That the trend of the electorate was definitely to the left in 1974 was shown by the results of the other races: all the Democratic statewide candidates but one ran well ahead of Brown, including state Senator Mervyn Dymally, a black who was elected Lieutenant Governor. Democrats ran far ahead of Brown—aggregating the statewide totals—for Congress, state Senate, and Assembly. But there was obviously little enthusiasm for anyone—especially the top-of-the-ticket candidates. Turnout was down as much in conservative Orange County as in radical Berkeley, down as much in the Bay Area as in Los Angeles County. It was as if the whole state was tired of politics.

This negative attitude could turn out to be a plus for Brown. If Reagan was brought down in part by the magnitude of the expectations he aroused, Brown scarcely faces the same problem. His initial acts as Governor were modest: he presented an economical state budget, initiated a few liberal changes he had long promised, and refused to attend a national Governors' conference in

Washington because he said he had better things to do in Sacramento. Brown talked during the campaign of a new society, and his ideas seem vaguely to include a kind of libertarian laissez faire with the old-fashioned Democratic notion that government should help people. He believes in decriminalizing marijuana, but he doesn't think he father was wrong to send troops in to quell the Berkeley demonstrators. He appointed a hip looking bunch of cabinet heads, half of whom were women; but they were not exactly sons and daughters of the Great Society: one was quoted as saying that sometimes the most radical thing to do is nothing. Brown made points with the public by spurning the luxuries of high office: he refused to move into the governor's mansion, sold the governor's plane, used a drab Plymouth instead of a limousine, flew tourist class on planes, etc. But in his first months in office he also had more than his share of solid substantive achievements. The most notable of them was settling the farm labor problem. For forty years no one had come up with a legislative solution which would allow farm labor unions their strongest weapon (the strike at harvest time) and at the same time provide for fair organization elections and basic fairness to the growers. Brown, with the help of some talented key legislators, did. That may not be enough to make him presidential timber. But just as Reagan demonstrated in his years in office that he was more than an actor with a good memory for his lines, so Brown has proved that he is more than his father's son and a purveyor of trendy phrases.

Governor Reagan had the option of running for the Senate in 1974, and one reason he passed it up was the popularity of the incumbent, Democrat Alan Cranston. Originally, Cranston had been an accidental Senator. After two terms as Controller and an upset loss to Flournoy in 1966, he sought the seat held by liberal Republican Thomas Kuchel in 1968. Kuchel would surely have won the general, but he was beaten in the primary by Max Rafferty, whom Cranston went on to defeat. The electoral strength of the right is shown by the fact that even with Rafferty as an opponent, Cranston took only 53 percent of the vote.

Cranston had begun his political career as a founder of the California Democratic Council (CDC), a volunteer group considered the liberal wing of the Democratic Party. Observers expected him to gravitate naturally to the articulate, but then pretty much powerless liberal wing of the Senate. Instead, he showed an unusual talent for maintaining good relations with conservatives and serving as a deal-maker when compromises could be struck. By 1974, when he was seeking his second term, Cranston had won the reputation in some quarters as the best liberal vote-counter in the Senate—a reputation he generally deserved, despite some gaffes early in his term. He shows the energy one might expect from a man who holds the world's 100 yard dash record for his age group.

Despite his talent at accommodation, Cranston can still usually be found on the liberal side of virtually every issue when it comes to a vote. One exception—when he literally swung the key vote that put through the $250 million bailout of Lockheed—was an understandable exception for a California Senator; Lockheed is one of the state's leading employers. In general, he has been willing to listen to, and often advance the causes of, the state's business interests. But overall, Cranston's voting record is almost unalloyedly liberal.

Perhaps it was the accommodating attitude, perhaps his hard work, that made Cranston such a strong candidate in 1974. Certainly one factor helped: the lack of significant opposition. Ronald Reagan only led the list of prominent California Republicans who declined to run in the year in which their California Republican President was ousted from office; others included men like Robert Finch, Evelle Younger, and David Packard. That gave the nomination, by default, to state Sen. H. L. "Bill" Richardson, a conservative who had dissented—from the right—to many of Reagan's programs. Richardson conducted what he called an educational campaign; it was woefully underfinanced, and the candidate himself admitted he had no chance to win. The result: the biggest win, a 63-37 romp, that any opposed Senate candidate of either party in California has won since Hiram Johnson of Progressive era fame.

The question for 1976 is whether the state's junior Senator, John V. Tunney, will get a similar kind of free ride. Like all of California's top officeholders, Tunney has been lucky. Son of the heavyweight boxer who whipped Jack Dempsey, law school roommate of Ted Kennedy, and alleged model for the movie *The Candidate*, Tunney moved to California as an Air Force lawyer, and ran for Congress the first election year after he got out of the military. That happened to be 1964, and he was elected, reelected in 1966, and again in 1968. Then he decided to try for the Senate against George Murphy, in a year when it was by no means clear that the right-wing tide which had brought him and his fellow former movie star Ronald Reagan to office was ebbing. It looked like a long shot for Tunney—who in fact had difficulty winning the Democratic nomination over leftish Rep. George Brown (see Thirty-Sixth district)—until Murphy's connection with Technicolor was disclosed. Then, Tunney won by a bigger margin than Ronald Reagan's that year.

Like Cranston, Tunney has a liberal voting record, with a definite pragmatic flavor to it. Probably his greatest impact on the Senate has come from his work on the Judiciary Committee. He was one of the leading inquisitors of Attorney General Richard Kleindienst, John Mitchell, and California Lieutenant Governor Ed Reinecke, in which the three were apparently covering up ITT's $200,000 gift to the Republican Party in return for the scheduling of the Republican national convention in San Diego. (This all happened in March and April of 1972, well before the Watergate—and in many ways, precursor of it.)

Tunney must run for reelection in 1976, and at this writing there seems no lack of opponents: Reagan, for one, is mentioned, as well as Finch, San Diego Mayor Pete Wilson, Younger, and others. No one is quite sure how strong a personal hold Tunney has over the electorate, but as a liberal Democrat he is well-positioned to benefit from the shift of the state's electorate to the left. If no strong opponent runs, he could be reelected as easily as Cranston was; if one does, he could conceivably lose. But then California Senate elections are usually uncertain: Cranston is the first incumbent Senator to win reelection since 1962.

California, as the largest state in population, also has the largest congressional delegation: 43 members, tipped heavily (28-15) in favor of the Democrats. Its Democratic members tend to be ideological liberals, its Republicans fierce conservatives, although there are a few exceptions in each case. For nearly ten years, a bipartisan group of California Congressmen, led by Phil Burton of San Francisco, managed to persuade the legislature that the state's congressional district lines should be drawn to protect incumbents. They succeeded in 1968 and 1972, but the state Supreme Court cried foul in the latter case, and ordered its own special masters to draw up a plan. That turned out to be more favorable to the Democrats than the one the usually partisan Burton had designed; that, and the strong Democratic trend in 1974, produced some surprising reversals, and the first big Democratic gains in the delegation since the Reagan-like conservatives began to pick off Democratic seats in 1963.

A word should be said about the California presidential primary. It used to a winner-take-all affair, which was especially important at the Democratic convention, where California had nearly 20% of the delegates. (You may remember Hubert Humphrey in 1972 attempting to overturn that rule despite a pre-primary commitment not to.) Now, the winner-take-all feature is technically gone, but candidates can still accomplish roughly the same thing running delegate candidates in each congressional district; within the districts, winner-take-all will often still prevail. There will still probably be a split in the Democratic primary, where results oscillate widely from area to area and from election to election; there is no correlation, for example, between voting patterns in the closely-contested 1968 and 1972 Democratic primaries.

As for the Republicans, conservatives have an overwhelming advantage in California, even more than in most states. The body of registered Republicans is a constricted constituency, far smaller than the number of people who regularly vote Republican for state and congressional office, and it has a heavy majority which prefers ideological conservative candidates. The only moderate or liberal to win a heavily contested race since Nixon beat Assemblyman Joseph Shell in 1962 was Flournoy in 1974. And even then, Reinecke, scarcely a strong candidate anyway, and under indictment, got nearly one-third of the Republican votes. California represents as good a chance as conservative Republicans have of upsetting Gerald Ford or whipping Nelson Rockefeller in the 1976 primaries; if there is a unity slate here (as was the case in 1972) it will be heavily tilted toward the conservatives who have provided most of the manpower and the money for the party since 1964.

One final note. The 1958 Democratic and 1966 Republican gubernatorial landslides in California preceded each party's presidential victories two years later. California's status as a national trend-setter is at stake in 1976.

Census Data Pop. 19,953,134; 9.86% of U.S. total, 1st largest; Central city, 36%; suburban, 56%. Median family income, $10,729; 9th highest; families above $15,000: 27%; families below $3,000: 8%. Median years education, 12.4.

1974 Share of Federal Tax Burden $28,924,051,000; 10.80% of U.S. total, 1st largest.

1974 Share of Federal Outlays $31,378,867,000; 11.62% of U.S. total, 2d largest. Per capita federal spending, $1573.

DOD	$11,940,242,000	1st (17.43%)	HEW	$9,582,066,000	2d (10.33%)
AEC	$333,655,000	3d (10.94%)	HUD	$73,585,000	1st (7.55%)
NASA	$1,125,857,000	1st (37.91%)	VA	$1,498,604,000	1st (10.95%)

DOT	$730,579,000	1st (8.63%)	EPA	$244,610,000	2d (7.78%)
DOC	$203,915,000	3d (12.64%)	RevS	$657,110,000	2d (10.81%)
DOI	$256,201,000	1st (10.41%)	Int.	$684,293,000	3d (3.33%)
USDA	$840,592,000	3d (6.75%)	Other	$3,208,558,000	

Economic Base Finance, insurance and real estate; agriculture, notably cattle, dairy products, grapes and hay; transportation equipment, especially aircraft and parts; electrical equipment and supplies, especially radio and television communication equipment; food and kindred products; machinery, especially office and computing machines; tourism; ordnance and accessories.

Political Line-up Governor, Edmund G. Brown, Jr. (D). Senators, Alan Cranston (D) and John V. Tunney (D). Representatives, 43 (28 D, 14 R, and 1 vac.). State Senate (24 D, 15 R, and 1 vac.); State Assembly (54 D, 25 R, and 1 vac.).

The Voters

Registration 6,411,253 Total. 3,616,589 D (56%); 2,464,569 R (38%); 282,137 Declined to state (4%); 21,768 AIP (–); 12,851 Peace and Freedom (–); 13,339 Miscellaneous (–).
Median voting age 41.
Employment profile White collar, 54%. Blue collar, 36%. Service, 13%. Farm, 2%.
Ethnic groups Black, 7%. Japanese, 1%. Spanish, 16%. Total foreign stock, 25%. Canada, UK, Germany, Italy, 2% each; USSR, 1%.

Presidential vote

1972	Nixon (R)	....	4,602,096	(57%)
	McGovern (D)	....	3,475,847	(43%)
1968	Nixon (R)	....	3,467,664	(48%)
	Humphrey (D)	....	3,244,318	(45%)
	Wallace (AI)	....	487,270	(7%)

1972 Democratic Presidential Primary

McGovern	1,550,652	(44%)
Humphery	1,375,064	(39%)
Wallace	268,551	(7%)
Chisholm	157,435	(4%)
others	212,816	(6%)

1972 Republican Presidential Primary

Nixon	2,058,825	(90%)
Ashbrook	224,922	(10%)

Sen. Alan Cranston (D) Elected 1968, seat up 1980; b. June 19, 1914, Palo Alto; home, Los Angeles; Pomona Col., 1932–33, U. of Mexico, 1935, Stanford U., B.A. 1936; Protestant.

Career Foreign Correspondent, Internatl. News. Svc., 1936–1938; Lobbyist, Common Cncl. for Amer. Unity, 1939; Army, WWII; Real estate business, 1947–67; Pres., United World Federalists, 1949–52; State Comptroller of Cal., 1958–66.

Offices 452 RSOB, 202-224-3553. Also 11000 Wilshire Blvd., Rm. 13220, Fed. Bldg., Los Angeles 90024, 213-824-7641, and 450 Golden Gate, Rm. 18051 Fed. Bldg., San Francisco 94102, 415-556-8440.

Committees

Banking, Housing and Urban Affairs (5th). Subcommittees: Housing and Urban Affairs; International Finance; Oversight; Production and Stabilization (Chairman); Securities.

Budget (6th).

Labor and Public Welfare (8th). Subcommittees: Aging; Alcoholism and Narcotics; Children and Youth; Education; Employment, Poverty, and Migratory Labor; The Handicapped; Health; Special Subcommittee on Human Resources (Chairman); Special Subcommittees on the National Science Foundation.

Veterans' Affairs (4th). Subcommittees: Health and Hospitals (Chairman); Housing and Insurance; Readjustment, Education and Employment.

Group Ratings

	ADA	COPE	LWV	RIPON	NFU	LCV	CFA	NAB	NSI	ACA
1974	100	91	100	70	100	93	77	40	11	0
1973	89	90	100	63	100	–	67	–	–	8
1972	90	100	100	67	90	92	100	8	0	5

Key Votes

1) No-Knock	AGN	8) Gov Abortn Aid	FOR	15) Consumer Prot Agy	FOR
2) Busing	FOR	9) Cut Mil Brass	FOR	16) Forced Psych Tests	FOR
3) No Fault	FOR	10) Gov Limousine	AGN	17) Fed Campaign Subs	FOR
4) F-111	AGN	11) RR Featherbed	FOR	18) Rhod Chrome Ban	FOR
5) Death Penalty	AGN	12) Handgun License	FOR	19) Open Legis Meetings	FOR
6) Foreign Aid	FOR	13) Less Troop Abrd	FOR	20) Strikers Food Stmps	FOR
7) Filibuster	AGN	14) Resume Turk Aid	AGN	21) Gov Info Disclosure	FOR

Election Results

1974 general:	Alan Cranston (D)	3,693,160	(63%)	($1,336,202)
	H. L. Richardson (R)	2,210,267	(37%)	($702,767)
1974 primary:	Alan Cranston (D)	2,262,574	(84%)	
	Howard L. Gifford (D)	318,080	(12%)	
	Frank Kacsinta (D)	127,149	(4%)	
1968 general:	Alan Cranston (D)	3,680,352	(53%)	
	Max Rafferty (R)	3,329,148	(47%)	

Sen. John V. Tunney (D) Elected 1970, seat up 1976; b. June 26, 1934, New York, N.Y.; home, Riverside; Yale U., B.A., 1956, Acad. of Internatl. Law, The Hague, Holland, 1957, U. of Va., LL.B. 1959; Catholic.

Career Practicing atty., 1959–60, 1963–64; Air Force, 1960–63; U.S. House of Reps., 1965–71.

Offices 1415 DSOB, 202-224-3841. Also 11000 Wilshire Blvd., Rm. 14223, Los Angeles 90024, 213-824-7344.

Committees

Commerce (10th). Subcommittees: Aviation; The Consumer; Environment; Merchant Marine; Oceans and Atmosphere; Special Subcommittee on Science, Technology, and Commerce (Chairman).

The Judiciary (8th). Subcommittees: Antitrust and Monopoly; Constitutional Rights (Chairman); Juvenile Delinquency.

Joint Committee on Atomic Energy (5th, Senate Side). Subcommittees: Agreements for Cooperation; ERDA, Environment and Safety; ERDA, Nuclear Energy; National Security.

Group Ratings

	ADA	COPE	LWV	RIPON	NFU	LCV	CFA	NAB	NSI	ACA
1974	95	89	100	74	94	83	88	42	20	0
1973	95	82	100	75	100	–	75	–	–	4
1972	90	100	100	75	90	90	100	25	10	5

Key Votes

1) No-Knock	AGN	8) Gov Abortn Aid	FOR	15) Consumer Prot Agy	FOR
2) Busing	FOR	9) Cut Mil Brass	AGN	16) Forced Psych Tests	FOR
3) No Fault	FOR	10) Gov Limousine	ABS	17) Fed Campaign Subs	FOR
4) F-111	AGN	11) RR Featherbed	FOR	18) Rhod Chrome Ban	FOR
5) Death Penalty	AGN	12) Handgun License	FOR	19) Open Legis Meetings	ABS
6) Foreign Aid	FOR	13) Less Troop Abrd	FOR	20) Strikers Food Stmps	FOR
7) Filibuster	AGN	14) Resume Turk Aid	AGN	21) Gov Info Disclosure	FOR

Election Results

1970 general:	John Tunney (D)	3,496,558	(55%)
	George Murphy (R)	2,877,617	(45%)
1970 primary:	John Tunney (D)	1,010,812	(42%)
	George Brown, Jr. (D)	812,463	(33%)
	Kenneth Hahn (D)	417,970	(17%)
	Four Others (D)	189,607	(8%)

Gov. Edmund G. Brown, Jr. (D) Elected 1974, term expires Jan. 1979; b. Apr. 7, 1938, San Francisco; U. of Cal., B.A. 1961, Yale U., J.D. 1964, U. of Santa Clara; Catholic.

Career Research atty., Cal. Supreme Ct.; Practicing atty.; Study for the Priesthood, Sacred Heart Novitiate, Los Gatos; Secy. of State of Cal., 1971–75.

Offices State Capitol, Sacramento 95814, 916-445-2841.

Election Results

1974 general:	Edmund G. Brown, Jr. (D)	3,131,648	(51%)
	Houston I. Flournoy (R)	2,952,954	(49%)
1974 primary:	Edmund G. Brown, Jr. (D)	1,085,752	(38%)
	Joseph L. Alioto (D)	544,007	(19%)
	Robert Moretti (D)	478,469	(17%)
	William M. Roth (D)	293,686	(10%)
	Jerome R. Waldie (D)	227,489	(8%)
	Baxter Ward (D)	79,745	(3%)
	Herbert Hafif (D)	77,505	(3%)
	Eleven Others (D)	88,110	(3%)

◆ ◆ ◆ ◆ ◆

FIRST DISTRICT

The 1st is physically the largest of California's 43 congressional districts. It extends from the Coast Range and the Oregon border to the Sierra Nevada south of Lake Tahoe. With 2% of the state's population, the district covers 22% of its terrain. Some of the county names here—Placer, Eldorado—recall the Gold Rush of 1849; many of the streams coursing down from the Sierra to the Central Valley probably look little different today from the days when the first prospectors began panning for gold in them more than 120 years ago.

But geography is an imprecise guide to political reality, and most of the voters in the 1st are concentrated, not in the Mother Lode country, but in two small, and totally separate parts of the district. Nearly 40% live in a series of towns and farms along the upper Sacramento River. The northern towns, Redding and Red Bluff, are traditionally Democratic; the southern ones, Chico and Oroville, traditionally Republican. (The presence of a state college in Chico, however, placed the town in the Democratic column in 1972 and 1974.) The other major concentration of people—about 20% of the district's total—is located in the northwest suburbs of Sacramento; like the capital's entire metropolitan area, this is usually a Democratic stronghold.

All of this adds up to a district that has been regarded over the years as safely Democratic. And correctly so: the 1st has not sent a Republican to Congress since 1942. (What is now the 1st district used to be known as the 2d, before the court-ordered 1973 redistricting.) The current Congressman, Harold T. (Bizz) Johnson, was first elected in 1958 when his predecessor, Clair Engle, went to the Senate. Since then, Johnson has been winning reelection by overwhelming margins; in 1972, he won 70% of the votes, while George McGovern could only manage 45% in the district. In 1974, Johnson did not even have a Republican opponent.

Johnson is one of those northern Democrats more comfortable with the traditional to-get-along-you-have-to-go-along philosophy of the House Democratic leadership than with the ideological thrust of the younger new majority of the House Democrats. Johnson, for example, is no adversary of high military spending, nor, as Chairman of various Interior subcommittees, has he admitted any doubt about the time-honored policy that building more dams and irrigating more land is an unalloyed good. At the same time, he has just about a perfect voting record as far as organized labor and Democratic-oriented farm groups are concerned. With his long legislative experience—he was a state Senator for ten years before his election to Congress—he has been effective in getting public works projects and federal money generally for his district. As the third-ranking Democrat on the Interior Committee, he has a good shot at being Chairman some day; only his advancing age (69 in 1976) would seem to be an obstacle.

Census Data Pop. 464,028. Central city, 0%; suburban, 19%. Median family income, $8,681; families above $15,000: 16%; families below $3,000: 11%. Median years education, 12.3.

The Voters

Median voting age 44.
Employment profile White collar, 45%. Blue collar, 33%. Service, 16%. Farm, 6%.
Ethnic groups Black, 2%. Indian, 1%. Spanish, 6%. Total foreign stock, 13%. Canada, 2%; UK, Germany, Italy, 1% each.

Presidential vote

1972	Nixon (R)	109,546,	(55%)
	McGovern (D)	87,914	(45%)
1968	Nixon (R)	82,631	(47%)
	Humphrey (D)	74,159	(43%)
	Wallace (AI)	17,075	(10%)

Rep. Harold T. Johnson (D) Elected 1958; b. Dec. 2, 1907, Yolo County; home, Roseville; U. of Nev.; Presbyterian.

Career Supervisor, Pacif. Fruit Express Co.; Dist. Chm., Brotherhood of Railway Clerks; City Cncl., Mayor of Roseville 1941–49, Cal. Senate, 1948–58.

Offices 2347 RHOB, 202-225-3076. Also P.O. Drawer 100, 320 Vernon St., Roseville 95678, 916-782-4411.

Committees

Interior and Insular Affairs (3d). Subcommittees: National Parks and Recreation; Public Lands; Water and Power Resources (Chairman).

Public Works and Transportation (3d). Subcommittees: Aviation; Economic Development; Surface Transportation; Water Resources.

Group Ratings

	ADA	COPE	LWV	RIPON	NFU	LCV	CFA	NAB	NSI	ACA
1974	45	91	58	44	79	53	85	9	88	13
1973	64	91	70	64	100	33	60	–	–	22
1972	44	82	58	50	100	13	0	17	90	30

Key Votes

1) Foreign Aid	FOR	6) Gov Abortn Aid	AGN	11) Pub Cong Election $	FOR
2) Busing	AGN	7) Coed Phys Ed	AGN	12) Turkish Arms Cutoff	FOR
3) ABM	FOR	8) Pov Lawyer Gag	AGN	13) Youth Camp Regs	FOR
4) B-1 Bomber	FOR	9) Pub Trans Sub	FOR	14) Strip Mine Veto	FOR
5) Nerve Gas	FOR	10) EZ Voter Regis	FOR	15) Farm Bill Veto	AGN

Election Results

1974 general:	Harold T. (Bizz) Johnson (D)	138,082	(86%)	($30,467)
	Dorothy D. Paradis (AI)	22,881	(14%)	($1,447)
1974 primary:	Harold T. (Bizz) Johnson (D)	63,354	(80%)	
	Marion W. Steele (D)	15,940	(20%)	
1972 general:	Harold T. (Bizz) Johnson (D)	149,590	(68%)	($37,981)
	Francis X. Callahan (R)	62,727	(29%)	($28,985)
	Dorothy D. Paradis (AI)	6,431	(3%)	(NA)

◆ ◆ ◆ ◆ ◆

SECOND DISTRICT

For 300 miles north out of San Francisco, the California coast extends in massive grandeur. Cut off by the Coast Range from the interior, this region is covered with Douglas firs and redwoods. The first white settlers here were Russians, down from Alaska, but little evidence remains of their activities here except for a number of place names. More enduring is the rocky, foggy coastline and redwoods; the new Redwoods National Park, a subject of controversy a few years back, attracts many tourists. This was lumbering country in the late nineteenth century, and the Victorian mansions in towns like Eureka and Mendocino testify to the richness of the harvest. But today it is not an area of great prosperity; the bulk of the recent population increase seems to be composed of veterans of the counterculture seeking a quiet, rural life in the hills of Mendocino and Sonoma Counties.

This "Redwood Empire" makes up most of the 2d congressional district of California, one that stretches from the Marin County line, just a few miles north of the Golden Gate, to the Oregon border. Metropolitan growth intrudes only in the southern part of Sonoma County, up to Santa Rosa, and in the southern edge of the wine-growing Napa valley. Politically, just about the whole area is marginal territory, generally voting for the winners of statewide races by something very close to the statewide percentage.

In congressional races, the 2d (renumbered in the 1973 redistricting) has followed the pattern of most California districts: regularly reelecting its Congressman, regardless of party. In 1958, on the retirement of a five-term Republican, the district sent Democrat Clement Miller to Washington. Miller, killed in a plane crash during the 1962 campaign, was the author of *Member of the House*, a collection of letters to friends which is probably the most sensitive account of the House in the late 1950s and early 1960s. Miller was reelected posthumously in 1962, but the winner of the special election to fill the vacancy in early 1963 was his 1962 opponent, Republican Don Clausen. With a voting record almost diametrically opposed to Miller's, Clausen has been winning just as solidly ever since. The two most recent elections show how well he has done: he ran 6% ahead of Richard Nixon in the district in 1972, and he withstood the 1974 Democratic sweep with little difficulty.

Clausen is third-ranking Republican on the Interior and Public Works Committees—both important assignments in this coastal district, where much of the land is still owned by the federal government. He maintains a low profile in Washington, voting most of the time with the well-disciplined Republican bloc. With seats on the two committees most closely concerned with ecological issues, Clausen tends to side with believers in more highways and dams rather than the new breed of environmentalists.

Census Data Pop. 464,028. Central city, 18%; suburban, 42%. Median family income, $9,474; families above $15,000: 19%; families below $3,000: 11%. Median years education, 12.3.

The Voters

Median voting age 45.
Employment profile White collar, 47%. Blue collar, 34%. Service, 15%. Farm, 4%.
Ethnic groups Indian, 2%. Spanish, 6%. Total foreign stock, 18%. Canada, UK, Germany, and Italy, 2% each.

Presidential vote

1972	Nixon (R)	119,136	(56%)
	McGovern (D)	92,863	(44%)
1968	Nixon (R)	80,612	(47%)
	Humphrey (D)	76,673	(45%)
	Wallace (AI)	14,481	(8%)

Rep. Don H. Clausen (R) Elected Jan. 22, 1963; b. Apr. 27, 1923, Humboldt County; home, Crescent City; San Jose St. Col., Cal. Poly., Weber Col., St. Mary's Col.; Lutheran.

Career Navy, WWII; Banking, insurance, professional aviation; Del Norte. Co. Supervisor.

Offices 2433 RHOB, 202-225-3311. Also 475 H St., Crescent City 95531, 707-464-3241.

Committees

Interior and Insular Affairs (3d). Sucommitttees: National Parks and Recreation; Public Lands; Territorial and Insular Affairs; Water and Power Resources.

Group Ratings

	ADA	COPE	LWV	RIPON	NFU	LCV	CFA	NAB	NSI	ACA
1974	14	0	42	44	57	35	25	55	100	64
1973	8	20	18	69	60	39	43	–	–	81
1972	0	27	40	44	83	27	0	73	100	75

Key Votes

1) Foreign Aid	AGN	6) Gov Abortn Aid	AGN	11) Pub Cong Election $	AGN
2) Busing	AGN	7) Coed Phys Ed	AGN	12) Turkish Arms Cutoff	FOR
3) ABM	FOR	8) Pov Lawyer Gag	FOR	13) Youth Camp Regs	ABS
4) B-1 Bomber	FOR	9) Pub Trans Sub	AGN	14) Strip Mine Veto	AGN
5) Nerve Gas	FOR	10) EZ Voter Regis	AGN	15) Farm Bill Veto	FOR

Election Results

1974 general:	Don H. Clausen (R)	95,929	(52%)	($75,641)
	Oscar "H." Klee (D)	77,232	(43%)	($53,942)
	Carole J. Glass (PF)	7,744	(4%)	($65)
1974 primary:	Don H. Clausen (R)	47,652	(83%)	
	Barbara A. Richter (R)	9,904	(17%)	
1972 general:	Don H. Clausen (R)	141,226	(62%)	($49,450)
	William A. Nighswonger (D)	77,610	(34%)	($6,601)
	Jonathan T. Ames (PF)	7,922	(3%)	(NA)

◆ ◆ ◆ ◆ ◆

THIRD DISTRICT

The 3d district of California consists of most of the city of Sacramento and some of its suburbs. The site of Sutter's Fort, Sacramento has been an important urban center since the Gold Rush of 1849; today it is the largest city in the Central Valley, the much-irrigated and incalculably rich farmland north along the Sacramento River and south along the San Joaquin. Ever since the Gold Rush, Sacramento has been a Democratic stronghold. These days the preference can be seen as a function of the large number of public employees—federal and local as well as state—who like most of their kind are not displeased with the idea of big government. In fact, the 3d district has a higher proportion of public employees than all but four others in the nation: three suburban Washington districts and the state of Alaska. Moreover, Sacramento is one of the few American cities with staunchly Democratic newspapers—part of the McClatchy chain that also dominates journalism in Modesto and Fresno farther south in the Valley. As a result, Sacramento's

Democratic voting habits are strong enough that this middle-class, middle-income district missed by just a hair going for George McGovern in 1972.

Naturally, the 3d sends a Democrat to Congress, and for the last 22 years he has been John E. Moss. Now past 60, Moss looks rather like the businessman he once was, and certainly nothing like a liberal young freshman. Yet for all those years he has been backing the causes and fighting the fights the new freshmen have just begun. That Moss was not an ordinary, moderate liberal Congressman became clear back in the late 1950s when he began sponsoring the Freedom of Information Act. Almost alone, Moss worked to force the government to give citizens access to the information their taxes pay for. There was no lobby battling for such legislation, no public demand or outcry—just John Moss. But finally, in the mid-sixties, FOIA passed. It has been somewhat disappointing to its backers, including Moss; the courts have tended to read the general rule allowing access far more narrowly than its exceptions. So far, the FOIA's chief beneficiary has been Ralph Nader and a few investigative reporters who have used it to ferret out information bureaucrats and political appointees would prefer being kept secret.

The independence and prickliness which kept Moss pressing for the FOIA when his own party was in control of the Executive Branch also prevented him from achieving any leadership position among House Democrats. But he has made his mark on the Commerce Committee. This body for years has been dominated by Congressmen sympathetic to the points of view of the businesses which their laws and the agencies they oversee are supposed to regulate. Not John Moss. As a subcommittee chairman in the 93d Congress, Moss took aim at what he considered abuses in the brokerage industry; he was also one of the leaders in the move to set up an independent Consumer Product Safety Commission, outside what he feels are industry-dominate regulatory agencies.

It is typical of Moss's bluntness that he was the first member of Congress to suggest, back in March 1973 as the Watergate mess was just breaking, that the House set up a procedure to pass on the impeachment of the President. Other, cooler heads said such talk was irresponsible; they were wrong and Moss was right. If the impeachment process had not been short-circuited by Nixon's resignation, television viewers would undoubtedly have been treated to Moss's loud, strident voice coming out of his stolid visage in denunciation of the man he had spotted long before as a criminal President.

With John Jarman of Oklahoma becoming a Republican early in 1975, Moss became the third-ranking Democrat on the Commerce Committee, but still, as the 94th Congress began, one with little real power. Freshmen votes changed that. Commerce was one of the committees with the largest infusion of new, liberal blood, and Moss ran against full committee Chairman Harley Staggers of West Virginia for the chairmanship of the Special Subcommittee on Investigations. This particular chair was a prize: the subcommittee had a budget 40% as large as all the other Commerce subcommittees put together. But Staggers, a pleasant, quiet man, had made little use of the staff resources and the subcommittee's jurisdiction over virtually every regulatory agency. Moss unseated Staggers comparatively easily, and can be expected to lead some searing probes of federal agencies during the 94th Congress. It was, after all, promises of lenient treatment of business that netted the Nixon people so much of the tainted money they used in Watergate and related misdeeds; Moss will be on the lookout for other, as yet undiscovered instances of favoritism.

Census Data Pop. 464,541. Central city, 44%; suburban, 56%. Median family income, $11,019; families above $15,000: 27%; families below $3,000: 7%. Median years education, 12.5.

The Voters

Median voting age 41.
Employment profile White collar, 62%. Blue collar, 25%. Service, 12%. Farm, 1%.
Ethnic groups Black, 5%. Japenese, 2%. Chinese, 2%. Spanish, 9%. Total foreign stock, 20%. Canada, UK, Germany, and Italy, 2% each.

Presidential vote

1972	Nixon (R)	103,642	(50%)
	McGovern (D)	101,927	(50%)
1968	Nixon (R)	71,328	(42%)
	Humphrey (D)	87,014	(52%)
	Wallace (AI)	10,602	(6%)

Rep. John E. Moss (D) Elected 1952; b. Apr. 13, 1915, Carbon County, Utah; home, Sacramento; Sacremento Col., 1931–33; Protestant.

Career Real Estate Broker; Retail merchant; Navy, WWII; Cal. Assembly, 1948–52.

Offices 2354 RHOB, 202-225-7136. Also 8058 Fed. Bldg., 650 Capitol Mall, Sacramento 95814, 916-449-3543.

Committees

Government Operations (3d). Subcommittees: Government Information and Individual Rights; Legislation and National Security.

.terstate and Foreign Commerce (3d). Subcommittees: Oversight and Investigations (Chairman).

Joint Committee on Atomic Energy (5th, House Side). Subcommittees: ERDA, Nuclear Energy; National Security.

Group Ratings

	ADA	COPE	LWV	RIPON	NFU	LCV	CFA	NAB	NSI	ACA
1974	70	100	73	40	85	86	90	10	0	8
1973	95	100	73	79	81	100	75	–	–	9
1972	94	100	92	78	50	86	0	20	0	6

Key Votes

1) Foreign Aid	AGN	6) Gov Abortn Aid	FOR	11) Pub Cong Election $	AGN
2) Busing,	FOR	7) Coed Phys Ed	FOR	12) Turkish Arms Cutoff	ABS
3) ABM	AGN	8) Pov Lawyer Gag	AGN	13) Youth Camp Regs	FOR
4) B-1 Bomber	AGN	9) Pub Trans Sub	FOR	14) Strip Mine Veto	AGN
5) Nerve Gas	AGN	10) EZ Voter Regis	FOR	15) Farm Bill Veto	AGN

Election Results

1974 general:	John E. Moss (D)	122,134	(72%)	($23,145)
	Ivaldo Lenci (R)	46,712	(28%)	($2,267)
1974 primary:	John E. Moss (D), unopposed			
1972 general:	John E. Moss (D)	151,706	(70%)	($39,314)
	John Rakus (R)	65,298	(30%)	($8,042)

◆ ◆ ◆ ◆ ◆

FOURTH DISTRICT

The low, flat delta lands where the Sacramento and San Joaquin Rivers empty into San Francisco Bay; the rich fruit-growing land of the lower Sacramento River valley; and some of the fast-growing suburbs of Sacramento itself make up California's 4th congressional district. The southern part of the 4th—Vallejo and surrounding Solano County—has long been industrial and Democratic. The same political inclination is shared by the Sacramento suburbs in Yolo and Sacramento Counties. Only the more sparsely populated northern counties—Colusa and Yuba—regularly turn in Republican majorities, and these are at the very least balanced by a new center of Democratic strength, the town of Davis, site of a medium-sized (15,000 students) branch of the University of California. Davis, not coincidentally, is the city with what is supposed to be the nation's most well-developed system of bicycle paths.

The 4th district was created by the California legislature after the 1960 census. It is not entirely by accident that its first and only Congressman has been a former state Assemblyman, Robert Leggett. Like many Congressmen, Leggett is a member of committees that are important to his district—Armed Services (the 4th contains three Air Force bases and a Naval shipyard) and Merchant Marine and Fisheries (Vallejo can accommodate ocean-going vessels).

Leggett, however, does not quite fit the usual mold. Not surprisingly, he lobbies hard for money for the giant Mare Island Naval Shipyard in Vallejo. But unlike most Congressmen who do such things, Leggett doesn't scratch the backs of his colleagues with similar problems. Instead, he is one of the maverick Democrats on Armed Services who opposed American involvement in Southeast Asia and wanted to cut the defense budget. The local defense facilities are apparently so well justified on military and technical grounds that they survive despite Leggett's stance. The late Armed Services Chairman Mendel Rivers once vowed vengeance on him, but never achieved it; the Pentagon's 1973 base cutbacks left the 4th district with 1,500 additional jobs.

Leggett's maverick stance and less than tactful personality have not especially helped him achieve power in the House; and the seniority system denied him a subcommittee chairmanship. When he finally got one, in 1973, it was the Panama Canal Subcommittee, not exactly a prize unless one is terribly interested in negotiations with Panama and Zonian affairs. Two years later, Leggett fared better when he fell heir to the Fisheries, Wildlife Conservation, and Environment Subcommittee—one of the more important handling ecological problems. Leggett is generally considered a friend of environmental activists.

Census Data Pop. 464,171. Central city, 25%; suburban, 63%. Median family income, $9,556; families above $15,000: 19%; families below $3,000: 9%. Median years education, 12.3.

The Voters

Median voting age 38.
Employment profile White collar, 51%. Blue collar, 30%. Service, 14%. Farm, 5%.
Ethnic groups Black, 6%. Spanish, 11%. Total foreign stock, 18%. Canada, Germany, 2% each; UK, Italy, 1% each.

Presidential vote

1972	Nixon (R)	88,410	(51%)
	McGovern (D)	83,334	(49%)
1968	Nixon (R)	56,297	(40%)
	Humphrey (D)	73,101	(51%)
	Wallace (AI)	13,015	(9%)

Rep. Robert L. Leggett (D) Elected 1962; b. July 26, 1926, Richmond; home, Vallejo; U. of Cal, B.A. 1947, J.D. 1950; Catholic.

Career Navy, WWII; Practicing atty., 1952–62; Cal. Assembly, 1960–62.

Offices 2263 RHOB, 202-225-5716. Also 1520 Tennessee St., Vallejo 94590, 707-552-0720.

Committees

Armed Services (9th). Subcommittees: Investigations; Research and Development.

Budget (8th).

Merchant Marine and Fisheries (8th). Subcommittees: Fisheries and Wildlife Conservation and the Environment (Chairman); Panama Canal.

Group Ratings

	ADA	COPE	LWV	RIPON	NFU	LCV	CFA	NAB	NSI	ACA
1974	91	100	92	53	100	69	100	30	20	8
1973	80	89	90	69	88	65	75	–	–	10
1972	88	70	100	67	80	40	0	0	11	10

Key Votes

1) Foreign Aid	FOR	6) Gov Abortn Aid	FOR	11) Pub Cong Election $	FOR
2) Busing	FOR	7) Coed Phys Ed	ABS	12) Turkish Arms Cutoff	FOR
3) ABM	AGN	8) Pov Lawyer Gag	ABS	13) Youth Camp Regs	ABS
4) B-1 Bomber	AGN	9) Pub Trans Sub	FOR	14) Strip Mine Veto	AGN
5) Nerve Gas	AGN	10) EZ Voter Regis	FOR	15) Farm Bill Veto	AGN

Election Results

1974 general:	Robert L. Leggett (D), unopposed		($11,977)
1974 primary:	Robert L. Leggett (D), unopposed		
1972 general:	Robert L. Leggett (D)	115,038 (67%)	($19,128)
	Benjamin Chang (R)	55,540 (33%)	($24,957)

◆ ◆ ◆ ◆ ◆

FIFTH DISTRICT

The 5th district of California takes in the northwest portion of San Francisco and all of Marin County, two of the more prosperous and scenic parts of the cosmopolitan San Francisco Bay area. The San Francisco portion includes the highest-income parts of the city: the expensive Pacific Heights, Marina, and Sea Cliff districts. But aside from the summits of the high hills and the land lying next to the Bay and the Ocean, this part of San Francisco is predominantly middle-class residential, the bedroom area of the city on the misty hills running to the sea. The tolerant ambiance of San Francisco is here, without all the outré accouterments which one finds in the neighboring 6th district. Many of the residents here are second- and third- generation Americans, not long removed from the poverty of their forebears. But the San Francisco tradition of sophistication and tolerance does seem to affect the voting habits of these middle-class people; unlike their cousins on the East Coast, they have never swung heavily over to the party of Richard Nixon.

The Marin portion of the 5th lies just across the Golden Gate Bridge. A series of suburbs nestled between rugged mountains and the Bay, this is the land of West Coast radical chic—the kind of suburbs where women wearing $80 sweaters go shopping in bare feet. Marin is one of the last places in California where there is a significant number of liberal registered Republicans, but the life style of these people—the marijuana referendum got 49% of the votes in 1972—has led them to vote increasingly Democratic. The only exception: when they have been turned off by the Democratic candidate, and the Republican alternative has a reputation as a moderate or liberal, as in the 1974 gubernatorial race.

For more than 20 years, from 1953 to 1974, the 5th district's Congressman was William S. Mailliard, a wealthy member of a WASPy patrician San Francisco family. For some years Mailliard had a fairly liberal voting record and little trouble winning reelection. With the rise of Ronald Reagan, he began to move to the right, and as ranking Republican on the Foreign Affairs Committee steadfastly supported the Vietnam policies of the Nixon Administration. Mailliard's only real remaining political asset was the support of the longshoremen's unions and the shipping industry, thanks to his support of maritime subsidies as a high-ranking member of the Merchant Marine and Fisheries Committee. In 1970 and 1972, Mailliard only managed 53% and 52% victories—way down from the 73% he won in 1968.

The final blow to Mailliard was the 1973 court-ordered redistricting. The boundaries of his district had been shaped for years by the bipartisan protect-the-incumbents plans put together by Congressman Phillip Burton of the next door 6th district. The new lines took out the middle-class Sunset area, and inserted the black Fillmore district into the 5th, and that was enough to insure the end of Mailliard's patrician Republicanism. The beneficiary, ironically, was the brother of the man who had kept the lines favorable to Mailliard, Assemblyman John Burton.

Six years younger than his brother Phil, Johnny Burton had succeeded to his brother's Assembly seat in 1964. At that time, he was considered a far-out liberal, sometimes a lone dissenter from the Assembly consensus. Both Burtons even then were opponents of American involvement in Vietnam; both spent much of their time working for the interests of their poorer constituents. By 1974, when he ran for Congress, Johnny Burton had become part of the California political establishment. A close ally of Speaker Bob Moretti, he was Chairman of the Assembly Rules Committee; an early McGovern backer, he was chairman of California's Democratic Party. (Another Burton friend was perhaps more familiar to televiewers: Willie L. Brown, then Chairman of the Assembly Ways and Means Committee and the speaker who made the impassioned plea for the McGovern position on the California delegation at the 1974 national convention. Brown was defeated for Assembly Speaker by yet another San Franciscan, Leo McCarthy, in 1974.) Some people may be inclined to ask just how the Burtons had sold out. But it was not the Burtons who had changed, but California politics; it had moved leftward to the positions the brothers held all along.

In early 1974, Mailliard resigned to become Ambassador to the Organization of American States—a graceful means of retirement. The leading candidate to succeed him was John Burton, and he received just barely over 50% against the field in the June 6 primary—which, under a peculiar California law, was enough to give him the seat. Burton appeared on national television, and casually mentioned that he was another vote for the impeachment of Richard Nixon. Five months later, with Nixon gone, Burton was reelected to a full term with a solid, but not dazzling, 60% of the vote; he will hold the seat without trouble. Most of his time, in any case, was spent helping his brother Phil win the chairmanship of the Democratic Steering Committee. As the brother of one of the leading—and most aggressive—liberal Democrats, Burton is sort of a power behind the throne; he also sits on the House Administration Committee, whose Chairman, Wayne Hays of Ohio, is often a key Burton ally.

Census Data Pop. 463,523. Central city, 54%; suburban, 46%. Median family income, $12,010; families above $15,000: 36%; families below $3,000: 7%. Median years education, 12.8.

The Voters

Median voting age 41.
Employment profile White collar, 69%. Blue collar, 17%. Service, 14%. Farm, –%.
Ethnic groups Black, 10%. Chinese, 5%. Japenese, 2%. Filipino, 2%. Spanish, 7%. Total foreign stock, 34%. UK, Germany, Italy, 3% each; Canada, USSR, Ireland, 2% each.

Presidential vote

1972	Nixon (R)	96,120	(46%)
	McGovern (D)	112,246	(54%)
1968	Nixon (R)	78,393	(42%)
	Humphrey (D)	99,705	(54%)
	Wallace (AI)	8,039	(4%)

Rep. John L. Burton (D) Elected June 4, 1974; b. Dec. 15, 1932; home, San Francisco; San Fran. St. Col., B.A. 1954, U. of San Fran., LL.B. 1960.

Career Army 1954–56; Deputy Atty. Gen. of Cal.; Cal. Assembly, 1965–74; Chm., Cal. Dem. Party, 1973–74.

Offices 1513 LHOB, 202-225-5161. Also 450 Golden Gate Ave., Box 36024, San Francisco 94102, 415-556-1333.

Committees

Government Operations (18th). Subcommittees: Conservation, Energy and Natural Resources; Intergovernmental Relations and Human Resources.

House Administration (17th). Subcommittees: Accounts; Elections; Electrical and Mechanical Office Equipment.

Group Ratings

	ADA	COPE	LWV	RIPON	NFU	LCV	CFA	NAB	NSI	ACA
1974	92	100	83	44	75	100	100	33	0	0

Key Votes

1) Foreign Aid	FOR	6) Gov Abortn Aid	NE	11) Pub Cong Election $	FOR
2) Busing	NE	7) Coed Phys Ed	FOR	12) Turkish Arms Cutoff	FOR
3) ABM	AGN	8) Pov Lawyer Gag	NE	13) Youth Camp Regs	FOR
4) B-1 Bomber	AGN	9) Pub Trans Sub	FOR	14) Strip Mine Veto	AGN
5) Nerve Gas	AGN	10) EZ Voter Regis	NE	15) Farm Bill Veto	AGN

Election Results

1974 general:	John Burton (D)	88,909	(60%)	($108,433)
	Thomas Caylor (R)	56,274	(38%)	($38,137)
	Raymond Broshears (PF)	4,033	(3%)	($650)

1974 primary:	John Burton (D)	50,567	(71%)
	Terrence McGuire (D)	9,508	(13%)
	Alan D. French (D)	6,329	(9%)
	Alan F. Reeves (D)	5,209	(7%)
1974 special:	John Burton (D)	73,114	(50%)
	Thomas Caylor (R)	30,908	(21%)
	Three others (D)	21,826	(15%)
	Three others (R)	20,299	(14%)

◆ ◆ ◆ ◆ ◆

SIXTH DISTRICT

Surveys show that San Francisco remains the city where Americans would most like to live and work. Each year hundreds of thousands of tourists come to San Francisco and are captivated by the foggy mornings and sunny afternoons, the vistas from the city's steep hills, the Union Square flower vendors, teeming Chinatown, and of course the cable cars. It is a place with a definite *esprit*: the first American city to rebel against freeways and proud of its newly operational rapid transit system, the BART. And San Francisco was also one of the first cities with a well-organized protest movement against the high-rises which have altered the traditional San Francisco view. But the tourist can still savor the San Francisco ambience in a host of famous restaurants or on one of the streets in North Beach; there is an almost Mediterranean atmosphere on these streets with their so resolutely American names.

Of the things that touch the tourist about San Francisco, the most notable for political analysts is the city's worldliness: its unselfconscious toleration of topless dancers, hippies, blacks, Mexicans, Chinese, and even homosexuals. Proud of its melange, the city also seems to remember its more radical past—not just the wild days of the Gold Rush, but the times in the early twentieth century when the radical Longshoremen's Union organized the docks and San Francisco became the most militant union town in the country. Today, the poor, the union members, the single, and the wealthy combine to produce a rare degree of toleration. This is certainly the only major city in the United States that could, as it did in 1972, vote to legalize marijuana. And it is the only city in the country where an elected Sheriff could conduct a voter registration drive among the inmates of the county jail.

What the tourist generally sees of San Francisco—and where its esprit is most pronounced —those parts are primarily within the bounds of the 6th congressional district. Places like Chinatown, Telegraph Hill and North Beach, Nob Hill and Union Square, are all here. And the district also reaches to the less distinctive middle-income Sunset neighborhood along the Ocean. But many, perhaps most, of its residents live in less picturesque, more depressing settings: the Mexican Mission district, the cut-off streets of the Hunters Point ghetto, the dreary treeless sameness of some of the subdivisions visible on the Bayshore Freeway. This is perhaps the most polyglot district in the nation: 12% black, 18% Spanish-speaking, 8% Chinese, 5% Italian, 4% Filipino, and even a few Samoans. Only about one-quarter of the district's residents are white, English-speaking, third-generation Americans.

In 1962, Richard Nixon, running for Governor of California, called on his opponent Pat Brown to repudiate the support of a maverick Assemblyman who had supported demonstrations to abolish the House Un-American Activities Committee. That Assemblyman was Phillip L. Burton, and that mention by Nixon was probably the first time Burton's name made the national wire services. Twelve years later, the tables were a little reversed. By December 1974, Richard Nixon had resigned the Presidency and had to be pardoned in order to avoid prosecution for criminal acts. And Phillip Burton had been elected Chairman of the House Democratic Caucus—and had unofficially become the most powerful Democrat in the new, freshman-filled 94th Congress.

That was the first time—for all Nixon's efforts in 1962—that Burton had become really known to the public; for years, he had been a man who was content to operate in the relative anonymity of legislative aisles and committee rooms. Burton's political career had begun, inauspiciously, when he ran for the Assembly in 1954: he was beaten by a dead man whose name remained on the ballot. Two years later, he won—the only Democrat to win a Republican Assembly seat in 1956—but he never became a power in the California Assembly as his brother John later did. (See Fifth District.) For Phil Burton's views were considered too far-out for him ever to be a legislative leader.

But they were not too radical for the eastern half of San Francisco, which elected him to Congress in early 1964, when incumbent Jack Shelley was elected Mayor. Burton got a seat on the Education and Labor Committee, and concentrated on welfare legislation, on which he became an expert. But he also kept championing apparently hopeless causes like stopping American involvement in Vietnam and abolishing Un-American Activities.

Through these years, Burton could not suppress his taste for legislative combat—and dealmaking. A sort of radical ward-heeler in spirit, he liked to put together unlikely coalitions—usually in order to achieve a favorite goal. One of his favorite vehicles was the bills introduced by liberal Republican Silvio Conte to limit the amount of money farmers could receive in subsidies. Burton would assemble a group of liberals who would oppose these laws, and at the same time extract votes from the Southerners who backed them most strongly for other, totally unrelated issues, like raising the minimum wage and providing miners compensation for black lung disease. Burton was also the man who assembled the whole California delegation, Republicans as well as Democrats, when redistricting time came around, to draw up a save-the-incumbents plan which all would back.

By 1971 and 1972, when Burton was head of the Democratic Study Group, he was recognized as the House's most politically savvy ultra-liberal. His style has more in common with the tough radicals who organized the San Francisco docks than with, say, professors at a Berkeley faculty meeting, and he made the DSG a real instrument of change. Under his leadership, the group rounded up votes on important issues, it assembled its own staff and prepared floor amendments which could pass, it raised campaign money and gave it to candidates who Phil Burton thought could win.

Burton's term as DSG head lasted only two years, but he continued to dominate the group thereafter, and in 1974 headed its campaign committee. Often operating in tandem with the gruff and not always so liberal Wayne Hays of the House Democratic Congressional Campaign Committee—the Democrats' official money-giving arm—Burton carefully meted out vitally needed campaign dollars to candidates he thought could win. Also, he provided them with help of a sophisticated kind that they might not be able to afford themselves, including polling. When 75 freshmen joined the Democratic caucus prior to swearing in, Phil Burton knew he had helped most of them, and they knew enough about him to know they wanted him in a leadership post. He easily beat fellow Californian Bernie Sisk, 162–111, for the Steering Committee post.

Burton is talked of as a future Speaker; more likely, he will run for Majority Leader if, as expected, Massachusetts's Tip O'Neill moves up to Speaker. At 50 (in 1976), Burton can afford to wait—though it's not his style. In any case, he is the first member of the leadership who has made it up on the basis of his own appeal rather than the blessing of the other leaders—breaking a chain of self-perpetuating House Speakers that goes back long before Sam Rayburn. Burton's main problem now is that he is not used to the spotlight. He is sometimes a trifle crude (he said he would "whack the asses" of some adversaries just after winning the House Democratic Caucus post), and his kind of wheeling-dealing is not designed for the television camera. But he has succeeded in making himself a major force in American politics, and without surrendering his basic principles. As good an example of that was something he did immediately after getting the Steering Committee chair, and typically, it was done behind the scenes. By simply persuading all its Democratic members but the Chairman to leave, Burton abolished the House Internal Security (formerly Un-American Activities) Committee. (See Missouri Eighth District). It was the committee which had first made Richard Nixon famous, and it was because Assemblyman Burton favored its abolition that Nixon called on Pat Brown to renounce him in 1962.

Census Data Pop. 463,521. Central city, 100%; suburban, 0%. Median family income, $10,606; families above $15,000: 27%; families below $3,000: 10%. Median years education, 12.3.

The Voters

Median voting age 45.
Employment profile White collar, 58%. Blue collar, 26%. Service, 16%. Farm, –%.
Ethnic groups Black, 12%. Chinese, 8%. Filipino, 4%. Spanish, 18%. Total foreign stock, 47%. Italy, 5%; Ireland, 3%; Canada, UK, 2% each; USSR,1%.

Presidential vote

1972	Nixon (R)	73,349	(43%)
	McGovern (D)	96,794	(57%)
1968	Nixon (R)	56,430	(32%)
	Humphrey (D)	105,703	(61%)
	Wallace (AI)	12,079	(67%)

Rep. Phillip Burton (D) Elected Feb. 18, 1964; b. June 1, 1926, Cincinnati, Ohio; home, San Francisco; USC, A.B. 1947; Golden Gate Law School, LL.B. 1952; Unitarian.

Career Army, WWII and Korea; Practicing atty.; Cal. Assembly, 1956–64.

Offices 2454 RHOB, 202-225-4965. Also Rm. 11104 Fed. Ofc. Bldg., 450 Golden Gate Ave., San Francisco 94102, 415-556-4862.

Committees

Education and Labor (11th). Subcommittees: Labor Standards; Manpower, Compensation, and Health and Safety.

Interior and Insular Affairs (5th). Subcommittees: Public Lands; Territorial and Insular Affairs (Chairman).

Group Ratings

	ADA	COPE	LWV	RIPON	NFU	LCV	CFA	NAB	NSI	ACA
1974	95	100	89	50	92	100	89	17	20	0
1973	100	100	92	57	100	94	100	–	–	8
1972	100	100	100	64	86	74	50	8	0	5

Key Votes

1) Foreign Aid	FOR	6) Gov Abortn Aid	ABS	11) Pub Cong Election $	FOR
2) Busing	FOR	7) Coed Phys Ed	FOR	12) Turkish Arms Cutoff	FOR
3) ABM	AGN	8) Pov Lawyer Gag	AGN	13) Youth Camp Regs	FOR
4) B-1 Bomber	AGN	9) Pub Trans Sub	FOR	14) Strip Mine Veto	AGN
5) Nerve Gas	AGN	10) EZ Voter Regis	FOR	15) Farm Bill Veto	AGN

Election Results

1974 general:	Phillip Burton (D)	85,712	(71%)	($32,038)
	Tom Spinosa (R)	26,260	(22%)	($10,749)
	Emily L. Siegel (PF)	4,814	(4%)	($20)
	Carl Richard Davis (AI)	3,430	(3%)	($0)
1974 primary:	Phillip Burton (D), unopposed			
1972 general:	Phillip Burton (D)	124,164	(82%)	($46,899)
	Edlo E. Powell (R)	27,474	(18%)	($18,715)

◆ ◆ ◆ ◆ ◆

SEVENTH DISTRICT

The 7th district of California, known before the 1973 redistricting as the 14th, is one of the more politically marginal in the San Francisco Bay area. Although of apparently regular, roughly rectangular shape, and lying wholly within Contra Costa County, the 7th is really a collection of heterogeneous industrial and suburban communities separated by high mountains. Richmond, a working-class city facing San Francisco Bay, is the anchor to the west; it supplies large Democratic margins in all elections, in part because of its large (36%) black population. Along the bay that leads to the Sacramento and San Joaquin River estuaries are the industrial towns of Martinez, Pittsburg, and Antioch—more Democratic bastions. Republican margins come from the more prosperous, faster-growing inland suburbs like Concord (now the 7th's largest city with 85,000 people) and Walnut Creek.

For nearly ten years, this varied suburban district was the political base of Jerome R. Waldie, a liberal Democrat who won it in a special election in 1965. A former majority leader of the California Assembly under Jess Unruh, Waldie came to Washington with considerable legislative skill and the desire to use it. But that was not considered the proper role of junior members in the somnolent House of the middle and late sixties—particularly when those junior members, like Waldie, took far-out positions like opposing American involvement in Vietnam. In 1969, disgusted with the slow pace of things, Waldie said the unsayable, that Speaker John McCormack ought to step down. Everyone knew that McCormack was a tired old man, and everyone clamored to say how wrong Waldie was. During most of the rest of his years in Washington, Waldie concentrated on mastering—and reforming—federal fringe benefits on the Post Office and Civil Service Committee, in the hope that changes in the way things like federal employees' health insurance worked would affect the entire health insurance system.

Some time well before 1974, Waldie had decided to give up his utterly safe seat in the House—he won 78% of the vote in 1972—and run for Governor of California. Ronald Reagan was retiring, it looked like a Democratic year, a crowded field of candidates promised that a relatively low percentage could win the primary, and Waldie was genuinely respected by people who knew him or were familiar with his record. But he had one problem: virtually none of the voters had ever heard of him. In late 1973, he walked from San Diego to Los Angeles, but his position in the polls increased only marginally. By early 1974, it was clear that he could not win, and he eventually finished a poor fifth, with 8% of the vote—but by that time, he had found a new preoccupation: impeachment.

Waldie was one of the first and most vocal members of the House Judiciary Committee to call for the impeachment of Richard Nixon, and he left no doubt that he thought the President had committed crimes in covering up the Watergate affair. During the impeachment hearings Waldie put on one of the most impressive performances on the majority side, at one point using his time and that yielded him by his colleagues to spin a narrative of all the complex things that were happening on each day as the break-in was planned, took place, and the coverup begun. It was an entirely extemporaneous performance, without notes or references; Waldie had learned the facts so well that he could recite them on demand, even adding humorous sarcastic touches. Today Waldie, for the first time in 20 years, is out of government, with no great prospects for elective office—a rather melancholy prospect for a man who, if he could have managed to win the gubernatorial primary, would surely have won the general election and would now be considered a prime presidential prospect.

Waldie's seat in Congress was taken by one of the youngest of the new freshmen, 29-year-old George Miller, Jr., son of a former state Senator. Two local legislative powers, Republican state Senator John Nejedly and Democratic Assemblyman John Knox, decided to retain their positions in Sacramento, and Miller faced tough competition only from 33-year-old Richmond Councilman Gary Fernandez, the Republican candidate. Miller had lost his late father's state Senate seat to Nejedly in a 1967 special election, but the name remained well enough known and Miller put on a good enough campaign to win comfortably in this Democratic year. He has received substantial publicity as a sort of typical Democratic freshman, and should have no trouble holding the district in future elections.

Census Data Pop. 464,283. Central city, 0%; suburban, 100%. Median family income, $11,826; families above $15,000: 31%; families below $3,000: 6%. Median years education, 12.4.

The Voters

Median voting age 41.
Employment profile White collar, 52%. Blue collar, 35%. Service, 12%. Farm, 1%.
Ethnic groups Black, 9%. Spanish, 10%. Total foreign stock, 19%. Canada, UK, Germany, Italy, 2% each. each.

Presidential vote

1972	Nixon (R)	100,894	(53%)
	McGovern (D)	89,056	(47%)
1968	Nixon (R)	66,818	(41%)
	Humphrey (D)	82,776	(50%)
	Wallace (AI)	15,598	(9%)

Rep. George Miller (D) Elected 1974; b. Richmond, May 17, 1945; home, Martinez; Diablo Valley Col., San Fran. St. Col., B.A. 1968, U. Cal. at Davis, J.D. 1972.

Career Legis. aide to Cal. Senate Majority Leader, 1969–74.

Offices 1532 LHOB, 202-225-5511. Also 367 Civic Dr., Pleasant Hill 94523, 415-687-3260.

Committees

Education and Labor (25th). Subcommittees: Elementary, Secondary and Vocational Education; Labor-Management Relations; Labor Standards; Select Subcommittee on Education.

Interior and Insular Affairs (27th). Subcommittees: Energy and the Environment; Territorial and Insular Affairs; Water and Power Resources.

Group Ratings: Newly Elected

Key Votes

1) Foreign Aid	FOR	6) Gov Abortn Aid	NE	11) Pub Cong Election $	NE
2) Busing	NE	7) Coed Phys Ed	FOR	12) Turkish Arms Cutoff	NE
3) ABM	NE	8) Pov Lawyer Gag	NE	13) Youth Camp Regs	FOR
4) B-1 Bomber	AGN	9) Pub Trans Sub	NE	14) Strip Mine Veto	AGN
5) Nerve Gas	NE	10) EZ Voter Regis	NE	15) Farm Bill Veto	AGN

Election Results

1974 general:	George Miller (D)	83,054	(56%)	($95,000)
	Gary Fernandez (R)	66,325	(44%)	($76,829)
1974 primary:	George Miller (D)	28,735	(38%)	
	Daniel C. Helix (D)	16,957	(22%)	
	Art Carter (D)	14,180	(19%)	
	Richard A. Besserra (D)	9,689	(13%)	
	Three others (D)	5,957	(8%)	

◆ ◆ ◆ ◆ ◆

EIGHTH DISTRICT

The most self-consciously radical congressional district in the nation is the 8th district of California. This is where the first of the great student rebellions of the sixties broke out, the Free Speech Movement of 1964 at the University of California's Berkeley campus. The 8th also includes most of the north Oakland black ghetto, the birthplace of the Black Panthers. It was the home lair of the Symbionese Liberation Army, which claimed credit for murdering the superintendent of the Oakland schools, who was a black, and the place where the SLA kidnapped Patricia Hearst. Also in the 8th a self-styled radical slate nearly took control of the Berkeley city government in 1971, and where Panther leader Bobby Seale was able to win 36% of the vote in the city's most recent mayoral election—testimony to the support a solid, grass-roots campaign can win for even a far-out candidate.

It is fitting, then, that the 8th district sends to Congress one of its few self-proclaimed radicals, Ronald Dellums. Dellums, a former social worker and Berkeley Councilman, defeated 12-year incumbent Jeffrey Cohelan 55–45 in the 1970 Democratic primary. The difference between the two was not so much over the issues that tend to arise in Congress—Cohelan had a solid liberal voting record—as it was over the tone and accents with which they approached the issues. The quiet spoken Cohelan had the support of organized labor and many oldtime liberals. The strident Dellum's main bases of supports were blacks (then 22%, now 18%, of the district's voting population) and students (now, with the 18-year-old vote, more than 15% of the total electorate). Dellums also did well among the district's high-income voters, many of them strongly antiwar, who live in the hills above Berkeley and Oakland.

Dellum's radical stance has infuriated California Republicans, who have poured considerable amounts of money into the race in this highly un-Republican district each of the three times

Dellums has run. Their efforts have been in vain. In 1972 and 1974, Dellums increased his percentages within the bounds of the original district, and in each case held his own in the Contra Costa suburbs (different ones each time) added by redistricting. Dellum's outspoken views do cost him some votes, but in this district he has enough to spare.

In the House, though not exactly a power, Dellums has done pretty well for a far-out junior member. In 1973 he became chairman of a District of Columbia subcommittee—thanks to the fact that Michigan's Charles Diggs succeeded South Carolina's John McMillan as chairman of the whole committee. And against the wishes of then Chairman Edward Hebert, Dellums won a seat on the Armed Services Committee that same year. In 1975 he became a member of the special committee investigating the CIA. The black Congressman, a Marine veteran, has held unofficial hearings on racism in the military and has visited bases and rapped with the enlisted men—sometimes to the distress of their officers. On the committee, Dellums is presently part of a minority that believes that the defense budget is bloated and ought to be cut—a minority that is increasing in numbers and clout.

Census Data Pop. 462,953. Central city, 50%; suburban, 50%. Median family income, $11,401; families above $15,000: 34%; families below $3,000: 9%. Median years education, 12.7.

The Voters

Median voting age 42.
Employment profile White collar, 66%. Blue collar, 22%. Service, 12%. Farm, –%.
Ethnic groups Black, 21%. Japanese, 1%. Chinese, 3%. Spanish, 7%. Total foreign stock, 27%. Canada, UK, Germany, Italy, 2% each.

Presidential vote

1972	Nixon (R)	85,741	(39%)
	McGovern (D)	136,330	(61%)
1968	Nixon (R)	78,753	(41%)
	Humphrey (D)	107,760	(55%)
	Wallace (AI)	8,285	(4%)

Rep. Ronald V. Dellums (D) Elected 1970; b. Nov. 24, 1935, Oakland; home, Berkeley; Oakland City Col., A.A. 1958, San Fran. St. Col., B.A. 1960; U. of Cal., M.S.W. 1962; Protestant.

Career USMC, 1954–56; Psychiatric Social Worker, Cal. Dept. of Mental Hygiene, 1962–64; Program Dir., Bayview Community Ctr., 1964–65; Dir., Hunter's Pt. Bayview Youth Opportunity Ctr., 1965–66; Assoc. Dir., San Fran. Econ. Opportunity Council's Concentrated Empl. Program, 1967–68; Berkely City Cncl., 1967–71.

Offices 1417 LHOB, 202-225-2661. Also 2490 Channing Way, Rm. 202, Berkely 94704, 415-548-7767.

Committees

Armed Services (19th). Subcommittees: Military Compensation; Military Personnel.

District of Columbia (4th). Subcommittees: Education, Labor and Social Services (Chairman); Fiscal Affairs.

Group Ratings

	ADA	COPE	LWV	RIPON	NFU	LCV	CFA	NAB	NSI	ACA
1974	96	90	92	56	85	100	100	20	10	7
1973	96	100	92	67	90	100	100	–	–	11
1972	88	100	91	77	71	93	100	8	0	9

Key Votes

1) Foreign Aid	FOR	6) Gov Abortn Aid	FOR	11) Pub Cong Election $	FOR
2) Busing	FOR	7) Coed Phys Ed	FOR	12) Turkish Arms Cutoff	FOR
3) ABM	AGN	8) Pov Lawyer Gag	AGN	13) Youth Camp Regs	FOR
4) B-1 Bomber	AGN	9) Pub Trans Sub	FOR	14) Strip Mine Veto	AGN
5) Nerve Gas	AGN	10) EZ Voter Regis	FOR	15) Farm Bill Veto	AGN

Election Results

1974 general:	Ronald V. Dellums (D)	95,041	(57%)	($78,339)
	Jack Redden (R)	66,386	(40%)	($19,878)
	John Holland (AI)	6,385	(4%)	($410)
1974 primary:	Ronald V. Dellums (D)	58,340	(68%)	
	Curtis C. Aller (D)	18,381	(21%)	
	Frederick H. Murphy (D)	9,139	(11%)	
1972 general:	Ronald V. Dellums (D)	126,913	(56%)	($100,853)
	Peter Hannaford (R)	86,587	(38%)	($100,286)
	Frank V. Cortese (AI)	13,550	(6%)	($48,980)

◆ ◆ ◆ ◆ ◆

NINTH DISTRICT

Not all of the East Bay across from San Francisco is a hotbed of political radicalism. The suburbs south of Oakland—places like San Leandro, San Lorenzo, Castro Valley—can sometimes seem like outposts of Middle America on San Francisco Bay. These are the places where the people who work at ordinary jobs in the East Bay's offices and factories live in comfortable, well-tended neighborhoods. These suburbs, together with the southern part of Oakland, about half black but mostly resolutely middle-class, and portions of eastern Alameda County suburbs over the range, form California's 9th congressional district.

More of the people who live here consider themselves Democrats than Republicans, and they usually contribute to Democratic margins. But, as is often the case where there is substantial racial change in neighborhoods (or where such change appears likely to occur soon), the white voters here are sometimes attracted to candidates of the Republican right. Another influence moving the middle-class parts of the East Bay in that direction is the Oakland *Tribune*, still owned by the conservative family of the late William F. Knowland, former Senator from the state and onetime (1953–55) Senate Majority Leader.

For 28 years the 9th district routinely sent Democrat George Miller to the House of Representatives. There he quietly accumulated seniority and became Chairman of the Science and Astronautics Committee. An unabashed booster of the space program, Miller had little in common with the new breed of Democrats who questioned large appropriations for space and the military. For years, he seemed to reflect the views of his district pretty accurately, and was reelected without difficulty.

But not in 1972. Miller was 81 when it came primary time in the district. His previous showings, it turned out, reflected more his opponents' weakness than his own strength. This time the main challenger was Fortney (Pete) Stark, a rather unusual banker and former board member of Common Cause. Stark, a strong opponent of the Vietnam war, attracted attention in the Bay Area some years earlier by erecting a large peace symbol atop the small bank he owned in suburban Walnut Creek. Many peace activists took the trouble to cross the mountains to open accounts there, and the bank—which Stark no longer owns—prospered.

Stark was already wealthy, and poured much of his own money into the campaign. He opened offices throughout the district, enlisted volunteers, and sent them out to canvass door to door; the candidate was busy speaking wherever he could find an audience. Meanwhile, Chairman Miller stayed in Washington; he was past the time that he could be an impressive candidate.

The result was an almost unprecedented rout. Stark won 56% of the votes, incumbent Miller only 22%. By comparison, the general election was expected to be anticlimactic; but it was 1972, McGovern was losing this ordinarily Democratic district, and Stark squeaked by with only 53% of the vote. He did far better in 1974, and will probably have little trouble in the future.

In his first term, Stark won assignment to the Banking and Currency Committee. He reversed the usual pattern: many members acquire banking interests and vote them once they get on the committee; Stark relinquished his bank stock and voted against many of the desires of the big financial institutions. In his second term, Stark moved to the Ways and Means Committee, where he can be counted on to support measures like ending the oil depletion allowance and making the tax structure more progressive. With the addition of Stark and several other young members, Ways and Means now almost has a liberal majority—for the first time in history.

Census Data Pop. 464,934. Central city, 28%; suburban, 72%. Median family income, $11,309; families above $15,000: 28%; families below $3,000: 7%. Median years education, 12.3.

The Voters

Median voting age 42.
Employment profile White collar, 52%. Blue collar, 35%. Service, 12%. Farm, 1%.
Ethnic groups Black, 14%. Spanish, 12%. Total foreign stock, 22%. Canada, UK, Germany, Italy, Portugal, 2% each.

Presidential vote

1972	Nixon (R)	92,267	(50%)
	McGovern (D)	91,030	(50%)
1968	Nixon (R)	64,529	(39%)
	Humphrey (D)	86,026	(52%)
	Wallace (AI)	14,037	(9%)

Rep. Fortney H. (Pete) **Stark** (D) Elected 1972; b. Nov. 11, 1931. Milwaukee, Wis.; home, Oakland; MIT, B.S. 1953, U. of Cal., M.B.A. 1959; Unitarian.

Career Air Force, 1955–57; Founder, Beacon Savings and Loan Assn., 1961; Founder and Pres., Security Natl. Bank, Walnut Creek, 1963–72.

Offices 1034 LHOB, 202-225-5065. Also 7 Eastmont Mall, Oakland 94605, 415-635-1092.

Committees

Ways and Means (20th). Subcommittees: Oversight; Public Assistance.

Group Ratings

	ADA	COPE	LWV	RIPON	NFU	LCV	CFA	NAB	NSI	ACA
1974	100	100	100	50	85	94	100	18	11	0
1973	96	100	82	60	100	94	100	–	–	16

Key Votes

1) Foreign Aid	FOR	6) Gov Abortn Aid	FOR	11) Pub Cong Election $	FOR
2) Busing	FOR	7) Coed Phys Ed	FOR	12) Turkish Arms Cutoff	FOR
3) ABM	AGN	8) Pov Lawyer Gag	AGN	13) Youth Camp Regs	FOR
4) B-1 Bomber	AGN	9) Pub Trans Sub	FOR	14) Strip Mine Veto	AGN
5) Nerve Gas	AGN	10) EZ Voter Regis	FOR	15) Farm Bill Veto	AGN

Election Results

1974 general:	Fortney H. (Pete) Stark, Jr. (D)	92,436	(71%)	($60,642)
	Edson Adams (R)	38,521	(29%)	($23,778)
1974 primary:	Fortney H. (Pete) Stark, Jr. (D)	50,761	(81%)	
	Manuel F. Alvarado (D)	11,722	(19%)	
1972 general:	Fortney H. (Pete) Stark, Jr. (D)	102,153	(53%)	($266,684)
	Lew M. Warden, Jr. (R)	90,970	(47%)	($44,499)

◆ ◆ ◆ ◆ ◆

TENTH DISTRICT

During the last decade or so, population growth in the San Francisco metropolitan area has been most rapid around the southern end of San Francisco Bay. The growth has centered around the old farm market town of San Jose—now indistinguishable from its suburban neighbors. Located in the area is much of northern California's defense business, notably the huge Lockheed plant in Sunnyvale. Many migrants to the area have come from the Southwest and points east, but most of them are natives of some other part of the Bay area. These are mainly white working-class people, many of whom grew up in neighborhoods which are now dominated by blacks in Oakland or hippies in San Francisco. Also here are the Mexican-Americans of San Jose, people who have moved up from farm labor camps to live in middle-class respectability.

The working class whites and the Mexican-Americans are the two groups which are electorally most important in the politics of California's 10th congressional district. Its terrain spans the southern edge of the Bay from Hayward in Alameda County, not far south of Oakland, to the edge of the Lockheed Sunnyvale plant, west of San Jose. The district lines in the San Jose area, though smoothed out in the 1973 redistricting, remain somewhat jagged and eccentric; for the 10th, they include virtually all the city's chicano population. The result is a congressional district which does not really constitute a community, but instead is a lumping together of people who for the most part vote the same way.

With a larger Mexican-American population than all but two other California districts, 26%, the 10th was intended to go Democratic, and it has. Since they were first drawn in 1962, the district lines have been shifted three times; but they have not substantially changed, and the district has continued to send Democrat Don Edwards, a wealthy title company owner, to the House.

Edwards is one of those relatively senior Congressmen now who is a prime beneficiary of the tidal wave of Democratic freshmen in the 94th Congress: he has the seniority and the experience to hold high committee positions, and at the same time reflects the views of the freshmen well enough that he can, for the first time, be sure of a large number of votes on the floor. Edwards has always been an outspoken liberal; he was an early opponent of the Vietnam war, and he was once chairman of Americans for Democratic Action. He is also the fourth ranking Democrat on the Judiciary and several years ago was floor manager for the Equal Rights Amendment, and a subcommittee chairman. During the impeachment hearings, Edwards was always reckoned as one of the sure anti-Nixon votes on the committee, and he was one of the senior members who voted against the criminal President on all five counts. More recently, it has been Edwards' subcommittee which has kept anti-abortion constitutional amendments from reaching the House floor. And he is also a member of the special committee investigating the CIA, though even two years ago it would have been unthinkable for a member as leftish as Edwards to be appointed to such a unit.

Edwards has had little trouble at the polls, although he did slip to 57% in 1968 at the height of Ronald Reagan's popularity. After that election, he reportedly considered retiring, but decided to stay on, and now wins by margins of nearly 3–1. A curious fact about this ultraliberal Congressman: he was once an FBI agent, but he seldom votes with the other ex-G-men on the Hill.

Census Data Pop. 463,419. Central city, 35%; suburban, 65%. Median family income, $11,095; families above $15,000: 24%; families below $3,000: 7%. Median years education, 12.2.

The Voters

Median voting age 38.
Employment profile White collar, 47%. Blue collar, 40%. Service, 12%. Farm, 1%.
Ethnic groups Black, 2%. Japanese, 1%. Spanish, 26%. Total foreign stock, 26%. Italy, 3%; Canada, Portugal, 2% each; UK, Germany, 1% each.

Presidential vote

1972	Nixon (R)	78,375	(47%)
	McGovern (D)	87,054	(53%)
1968	Nixon (R)	49,222	(37%)
	Humphrey (D)	72,256	(55%)
	Wallace (AI)	10,456	(8%)

Rep. Don Edwards (D) Elected 1962; b. Jan. 6, 1915, San Jose; home, San Jose; Stanford U., Stanford U. Law School; Unitarian.

Career FBI Agent, 1940–41; Navy, WWII; Pres., Valley Title Co., San Jose.

Offices 2240 RHOB, 202-225-3072. Also 40979 Fremont Blvd., Fremont 94538, 415-676-5337.

Committees

Judiciary (4th). Subcommittees: Civil and Constitutional Rights (Chairman).

Veterans' Affairs (4th). Subcommittees: Hospitals; Housing.

Group Ratings

	ADA	COPE	LWV	RIPON	NFU	LCV	CFA	NAB	NSI	ACA
1974	100	100	100	67	92	88	100	22	10	0
1973	100	100	82	64	100	88	100	–	–	12
1972	100	100	100	75	71	80	50	8	0	9

Key Votes

1) Foreign Aid	FOR	6) Gov Abortn Aid	FOR	11) Pub Cong Election $	FOR
2) Busing	FOR	7) Coed Phys Ed	FOR	12) Turkish Arms Cutoff	FOR
3) ABM	AGN	8) Pov Lawyer Gag	AGN	13) Youth Camp Regs	FOR
4) B-1 Bomber	AGN	9) Pub Trans Sub	FOR	14) Strip Mine Veto	AGN
5) Nerve Gas	AGN	10) EZ Voter Regis	FOR	15) Farm Bill Veto	AGN

Election Results

1974 general:	Don Edwards (D)	87,978	(77%)	($17,948)
	John M. Enright (R)	26,288	(23%)	($425)
1974 primary:	Don Edwards (D)	42,779	(78%)	
	Marian M. Banducci (D)	12,259	(22%)	
1972 general:	Don Edwards (D)	123,994	(72%)	($25,398)
	Herb Smith (R)	43,140	(25%)	($4,792)
	Edmond Kaiser (AI)	4,419	(3%)	(NA)

◆ ◆ ◆ ◆ ◆

ELEVENTH DISTRICT

The Peninsula is the bony finger of land south of San Francisco, connecting it with the rest of California. Almost down the Peninsula's middle runs the San Andreas Fault, which some experts believe will shift again within the next 20 years or so, to produce an earthquake like the one that devastated San Francisco in 1906. To the west of the Fault, the land is mountainous enough to discourage heavy settlement, except in the suburb of Pacifica which clings to the mountains above the Ocean. Most of the Peninsula's population is packed into neat little suburbs between the Fault and the salt flats and industrial areas being created by landfill dumped into San Francisco Bay.

The Peninsula suburbs, notably sunnier and warmer than the city, are occupied mainly by white collar people who commute to San Francisco or, more and more lately, work around San Jose or on the Peninsula itself. Politically, these towns behave more like Eastern upper-middle-income suburbs than like the arch-conservative towns around Los Angeles. Although the people here tend to register Republican to an extent greater than most Californians, they have often been repelled by the conservatism of some California Republican candidates, and vote for Democrats instead.

The 11th congressional district includes the bulk of the Peninsula suburbs—places like Daly City, South San Francisco, San Bruno, Millbrae, Burlingame, San Mateo, Belmont, San Carlos, and Redwood City. The redistricting situation here has been rather complicated: the current 11th includes four-fifths of San Mateo County, but Republican Pete McCloskey, who once represented all of San Mateo County, now represents the next-door 12th district.

Suffice it to say that the 11th, as it existed in 1972, was a district without an incumbent, and despite the fact that San Mateo had been represented by Republicans for more than 30 years, the new district fell rather easily into Democratic hands. The beneficiary was then Assemblyman Leo J. Ryan, who had been winning elections in the northern half of the Peninsula by huge margins. He was unchallenged in the primary, and won the general with the kind of margin—61%—that usually only congressional veterans enjoy. It is worth noting that California legislators, unlike those from any other state, have full-time staff and offices in their districts as well as in the capital; thus they have an opportunity to ingratiate themselves with their constituents year round, and are usually very hard to beat at election time.

Among the ultraliberal delegation from the Bay Area, Ryan is something of an anomaly: the only member who would feel more comfortable at a meeting of the cold war liberals of the Coalition for a Democratic Majority than at a session of the anti-Vietnam war liberals of the Americans for Democratic Action. He opposed the bombing of Cambodia in the 93d Congress, but supported aid to the same country and to Vietnam in the 94th. On domestic issues he ranks as a solid liberal Democrat.

Census Data Pop. 464,187. Central city, 0%; suburban, 100%. Median family income, $13,062; families above $15,000: 38%; families below $3,000: 4%. Median years education, 12.6.

The Voters

Median voting age 42.
Employment profile White collar, 59%. Blue collar, 29%. Service, 12%. Farm, –%.
Ethnic groups Black 2%. Japanese, 1%. Filipino, 1%. Spanish, 12%. Total foreign stock, 32%. Italy, 4%; Canada, UK, Germany, 3%; USSR, Ireland, 1% each.

Presidential vote

1972	Nixon (R)	105,286	(55%)
	McGovern (D)	85,842	(45%)
1968	Nixon (R)	73,049	(43%)
	Humphrey (D)	84,926	(50%)
	Wallace (AI)	12,608	(7%)

Rep. Leo J. Ryan (D) Elected 1972; b. May 5, 1925, Lincoln, Neb.; home, South San Francisco; Creighton U., B.S. 1949, M.S. 1951.

Career High school principal, superintendent, and teacher; So. San Fran. City Cncl, 1956–62, Mayor, 1962; Cal. Assembly, 1962–72.

Offices 119 CHOB, 202-225-3531. Also 181 2nd. Ave., Suite 400, San Mateo 94401, 415-348-1973.

Committees

Government Operations (16th). Subcommittees: Conservation, Energy and Natural Resources; Government Information and Individual Rights.

International Relations (16th). Subcommittees: International Operations; Oversight.

Group Ratings

	ADA	COPE	LWV	RIPON	NFU	LCV	CFA	NAB	NSI	ACA
1974	68	90	63	46	89	47	33	40	20	8
1973	73	90	82	78	72	58	67	–	–	27

Key Votes

1) Foreign Aid	FOR	6) Gov Abortn Aid	ABS	11) Pub Cong Election $	AGN
2) Busing	AGN	7) Coed Phys Ed	ABS	12) Turkish Arms Cutoff	ABS
3) ABM	AGN	8) Pov Lawyer Gag	AGN	13) Youth Camp Regs	ABS
4) B-1 Bomber	AGN	9) Pub Trans Sub	AGN	14) Strip Mine Veto	AGN
5) Nerve Gas	AGN	10) EZ Voter Regis	FOR	15) Farm Bill Veto	AGN

Election Results

1974 general:	Leo J. Ryan (D)	106,429	(76%)	($22,778)
	Brainard "Bee" G. Merdinger (R)	29,861	(21%)	($2,074)
	Nicholas W. Kudrovzeff (AI)	4,066	(3%)	($1,385)
1974 primary:	Leo J. Ryan (D)	55,945	(84%)	
	Lydia C. Merdinger (D)	10,860	(16%)	
1972 general:	Leo J. Ryan (D)	114,134	(61%)	($52,127)
	Charles E. Chase (R)	69,632	(37%)	($52,441)
	Nicholas Kudrovzeff (AI)	4,881	(3%)	(NA)

◆ ◆ ◆ ◆

TWELFTH DISTRICT

Pete McCloskey is an unusual Congressman. He is a Republican who challenged his party's President in the primaries in 1972, and was helped to victory by that President's hand-picked successor in 1974. He is a man who believes deeply in progressive Republicanism, and declined to leave the party like his friend Don Riegle of Michigan; yet after the election he did go to the trouble of changing his registration temporarily to "decline to state." He is a successful California politician who talks publicly about chucking it all and going back to law practice and whose House campaigns are among the most expensive in the nation. He is a man whose revulsion against the Vietnam war stemmed not only from his horror at the bombing, but also from his disgust at what the conflict was doing to the Marine Corps, in which he distinguished himself in combat during the Korean War. McCloskey is an ecology buff who—and there is more.

But it is better to start at the (political) beginning. For Paul N. (Pete) McCloskey, Jr., this was 1967. He was practicing law in Menlo Park, home of *The Whole Earth Catalog* and a comfortable suburb on the Peninsula south of San Francisco, when Congressman J. Arthur Younger, a conservative Republican, died. Though McCloskey had been active in community affairs and environmental causes, he had never been involved in politics. Nevertheless, he entered the race to succeed Younger. The candidate who got all the national publicity was Shirley Temple Black. But McCloskey had friends and supporters all over the district. As a liberal Republican, he appealed to the district's moderates—more numerous here than in most parts of California—who were dismayed by the recent takeover of Earl Warren's party by Ronald Reagan and his allies. Through good precinct work, McCloskey won the primary handily, the general election even more easily, and went to Capitol Hill.

At first, McCloskey was not so controversial. He stuck with the Republican leadership on many votes and compiled a middle-of-the-road record. His chief asset—ahead of his time nationally, but then appreciated in the district—was his strong belief in protecting the environment. But the conservatives back home would not forgive him for sinking the good ship Lollipop. McCloskey won only 53% of the vote in 1968 and 60% in 1970 against conservative primary opponents—low figures indeed for an incumbent congressman. General elections were easier. Republicans, having no place else to go, voted for him, and so did a great many Democrats attracted by his record and his personality.

McCloskey, however, was not content to take the safe political route, which means sending out tons of franked mail to deter opposition in the district. The Vietnam war rubbed his emotions raw. He sought out other Republicans, urging them to run against Nixon. None would, so he did. In New Hampshire, he nearly made the 20% mark he set for his candidacy, and toyed with the idea of staying in the race. But the money was running out, and he had a decision to make back home.

The filing date for the California primary was near, and McCloskey had to choose whether to run for reelection, and in which district to run. He had been representing all of San Mateo County, but redistricting had divided it up. Most had gone into a new district, what now is the 11th; the remainder had been joined to south of the communities to the south, going down into San Jose, to form what now is the 12th. McCloskey's residence was in what is now the 12th, and so he decided to run there, though most of the territory was unfamiliar. He faced even more fierce primary opposition than before, but fortunately for him, it was split. "Those two turkeys," as he called his opponents, got 31% and 25% of the vote; McCloskey won with 44%. In the general, a conservative Republican businessman named Gordon Knapp ran as a write-in, and won an astounding 10% of the votes—an indication that McCloskey continued to inspire diehard opposition.

That became even clearer in the 1974 primary. This time Knapp carried the conservative standard alone. The result was close, and McCloskey would surely have lost, but for two unrealted factors: (1) a change-your-registration drive at Stanford which had enrolled 2,000 student McCloskey voters as Republicans; and (2) a joint appearance before the primary with then Vice President Gerald Ford. McCloskey had been one of the very few Republicans to speak out on Watergate, even before the 1972 election; but of course that only infuriated Nixon loyalists, even though it would ultimately help him if—and when—he made the general election.

The irony of all this is that the 12th, as currently constituted, is really a Democratic district. George McGovern got 49% of the voters here in 1972, and Democratic candidates for other offices carried it easily in 1974. The 12th includes not only high-income, liberal-leaning Menlo Park and Palo Alto (the home of Stanford), and the woodsy suburbs of Portola Valley and Woodside; it also includes the middle-class and almost factory suburbs of Mountain View, Sunnyvale, and Santa Clara, and a bit of San Jose, in Santa Clara County. This is one of those areas where the pull of the ecology movement has been strongest; in the hilly affluent areas, and in the valley lands below, you cannot avoid seeing how fast the available land is being occupied; nor can you help noticing, as you drive on the Bayshore Freeway which links the communities of the 12th together, how the ugly industrial fill is gradually eating away at the expanse of San Francisco Bay. It is the kind of place where one constantly sees "Save the Bay" stickers, and where the Sierra Club does best in its membership drives.

Such environmental concerns have been moving voters here toward the Democrats, for the Reagan Republicans, in their view, inevitably tend to favor the short-term interests of business over the long-term needs of the environment. McCloskey, of course, is an exception to this rule—which is why he can win general elections so easily as a Republican. If he switched parties, he would undoubtedly win even more easily, since he could avoid the expensive and energy-consuming primaries he otherwise has to face every two years. But this is an obstinate man, who will not give up on even so impossible a goal as moving the California Republican Party toward the center. His 1974 campaign experience if anything will probably draw him closer to Republicans, for he is the kind of person who feels obliged if he can to make common cause with his party's President, and of course Jerry Ford helped him when he really needed it. So for Pete McCloskey and the 12th district, the political future looks obscure, as it has for some time.

Census Data Pop. 463,161. Central city, 3%; suburban, 97%. Median family income, $13,418; families above $15,000: 41%; families below $3,000: 5%. Median years education, 12.8.

The Voters

Median voting age 40.
Employment profile White collar, 65%. Blue collar, 24%. Service, 10%. Farm, 1%.
Ethnic groups Black, 4%. Japanese, 1%. Chinese, 1%. Spanish, 11%. Total foreign stock, 25%. Canada, UK, Germany, Italy, 2% each.

Presidential vote

1972	Nixon (R)	103,806	(53%)
	McGovern (D)	93,176	(47%)
1968	Nixon (R)	77,623	(47%)
	Humphrey (D)	79,731	(48%)
	Wallace (AI)	7,495	(5%)

Rep. Paul N. McCloskey, Jr. (R) Elected Dec. 12, 1967; b. Sept. 29, 1927, San Bernardino; home, Portola Valley; Occidental Col., Cal. Inst. of Tech., 1945–46, Stanford U., B.A. 1950, LL.B. 1953; Presbyterian.

Career Navy, 1945–47; USMC, Korea; Deputy Dist. Atty., Alameda Co., 1953–54; Practicing atty., 1955–67.

Offices 205 CHOB, 202-225-5411. Also 305 Grant Ave., Palo Alto 94306, 415-326-7383.

Committees

Government Operations (6th). Subcommittees: Conservation, Energy and Natural Resources; Government Information and Individual Rights.

Merchant Marine and Fisheries (3d). Subcommittees: Fisheries and Wildlife Conservation and the Environment; Merchant Marine.

Group Ratings

	ADA	COPE	LWV	RIPON	NFU	LCV	CFA	NAB	NSI	ACA
1974	81	91	100	100	92	73	46	55	20	15
1973	76	64	100	100	78	67	63	–	–	15
1972	50	72	100	100	67	85	100	50	11	8

Key Votes

1) Foreign Aid	FOR	6) Gov Abortn Aid	ABS	11) Pub Cong Election $	FOR
2) Busing	FOR	7) Coed Phys Ed	FOR	12) Turkish Arms Cutoff	AGN
3) ABM	AGN	8) Pov Lawyer Gag	AGN	13) Youth Camp Regs	FOR
4) B-1 Bomber	AGN	9) Pub Trans Sub	FOR	14) Strip Mine Veto	AGN
5) Nerve Gas	AGN	10) EZ Voter Regis	FOR	15) Farm Bill Veto	FOR

Election Results

1974 general:	Paul N. "Pete" McCloskey, Jr. (R)	103,692	(69%)	($166,441)
	Gary G. Gillmor (D)	46,383	(31%)	($37,128)
1974 primary:	Paul N. "Pete" McCloskey, Jr. (R)	29,727	(50%)	
	Gordon Knapp (R)	28,895	(48%)	
	John K. Fredrich (R)	1,096	(2%)	
1972 general:	Paul N. "Pete" McCloskey, Jr. (R)	110,988	(55%)	($321,558)
	James Stewart (D)	73,123	(36%)	($109,418)
	James Gordon Knapp (R, write-in)	19,377	(10%)	($75,970)

◆ ◆ ◆ ◆ ◆

THIRTEENTH DISTRICT

Twenty years ago, what is now the 13th congressional district of California was, for the most part, acres of vineyards and fruit orchards below the mountains of the Coast Range near San Jose. This was one of the richest agricultural areas in the country, but it was also directly in the path of some of the most explosive suburban growth the nation has ever seen. Santa Clara County, which includes San Jose and the 13th district, grew from 290,000 people in 1950 to 1,064,000 in 1970. In the 1960s alone, the 13th district just about doubled in population—a rate of growth exceeded by only four other districts in the United States.

Today, the vineyards are almost all gone, their owners having prudently recultivated the grapes in more remote places before selling the land to developers. There is still some agriculture in the southern part of the district, but the 13th is almost entirely suburban in character. The wealthier suburbs are, as usual in California, those higher up on the hills: here, Cupertino, Saratoga, Monte Sereno, and Los Gatos. But most of the district's population, nearly 60%, lives in San Jose. Technically a central city, San Jose, or at least this part of it, is about as suburban in aspect as one could want: a vast, prosperous area of shopping centers and stucco homes, virtually all of them new these last 20 or 25 years.

Ironically, the Congressman from this fast-growing suburban district is the former Mayor of San Jose who finally insisted that the process of growth had to take second place to the process of orderly planning. When Norman Mineta was elected Mayor in 1971, San Jose had grown from a small city of 95,000 in 1950 to a sprawling set of subdivisions of 445,000 in 1970. So rapid had been the growth that the city itself had difficulty maintaining, from day to day, a map which showed accurately all the streets which had been carved out by developers. Mineta said, in effect, "Enough," and pushed for zoning which would slow development to a pace that would allow the city to pay for the increased services it would require.

Mineta's policy was popular in San Jose, and in 1974, when Republican Congressman Charles Gubser decided to retire, Mineta was an obvious candidate. Gubser had been easily the most conservative member of the San Francisco Bay Area delegation, a Republican who enjoyed baiting Pete McCloskey for his apostasy, a member of the Armed Services Committee who believed, and advanced his beliefs with some acerbity, in a large defense budget and most of the policies the Pentagon pursued. At 58, after 22 years in the House, Gubser was tired; he probably could have been reelected, but he apparently did not look forward to the increasingly heated debate he faced both on the Hill and at home.

To succeed him, the Republicans chose former Assemblyman George Milias, considered a moderate, but with the unfortunate background, in a Watergate year, of having served in an executive position in the Nixon Administration. Both Mineta and Milias ran intelligent, expensive campaigns; both were well-known and well-liked. But Mineta, at least in this Democratic year, was stronger, and won a convincing victory. He probably will be able to hold on to this often Republican-leaning district in the future. He is, incidentally, the first American of Japanese descent to be elected to the Congress from any state outside Hawaii.

Census Data Pop. 466,988. Central city, 58%; suburban, 42%. Median family income, $12,972; families above $15,000: 37%; families below $3,000: 5%. Median years education, 12.7.

The Voters

Median voting age 38.
Employment profile White collar, 60%. Blue collar, 29%. Service, 10%. Farm, 1%.
Ethnic groups Black, 1%. Japanese, 1%. Spanish, 16%. Total foreign stock, 22%. Italy, 3%; Canada, UK, Germany, 2% each.

Presidential vote

1972	Nixon (R)	109,760	(58%)
	McGovern (D)	81,125	(42%)
1968	Nixon (R)	70,753	(49%)
	Humphrey (D)	66,852	(46%)
	Wallace (AI)	8,001	(5%)

Rep. Norman Y. Mineta (D) Elected 1974; b. Nov. 12, 1931, San Jose; home, San Jose; U. of Cal., B.S. 1953.

Career Army, 1953–56; Owner/Agent, Mineta Ins. Agency; San Jose City Cncl., 1967–71, Vice Mayor, 1968–71, Mayor, 1971–74.

Offices 510 CHOB, 202-225-2631. Also Golden Pacific Ctr., 1245 S. Winchester Blvd., Suite 310, San Jose 95128, 408-984-6045.

Committees

Post Office and Civil Service (17th). Subcommittees: Postal Service; Retirement and Employee Benefits.

Public Works and Transportation (17th). Subcommittees: Aviation; Investigations and Review; Public Buildings and Grounds; Surface Transportation.

Group Ratings: Newly Elected

Key Votes

1) Foreign Aid	FOR	6) Gov Abortn Aid	NE	11) Pub Cong Election $	NE
2) Busing	NE	7) Coed Phys Ed	FOR	12) Turkish Arms Cutoff	NE
3) ABM	NE	8) Pov Lawyer Gag	NE	13) Youth Camp Regs	FOR
4) B-1 Bomber	FOR	9) Pub Trans Sub	NE	14) Strip Mine Veto	AGN
5) Nerve Gas	NE	10) EZ Voter Regis	NE	15) Farm Bill Veto	AGN

Election Results

1974 general:	Norman Y. Mineta (D)	78,858	(53%)	($185,236)
	George W. Milias (R)	63,573	(42%)	($122,239)
	Elizabeth Cervantes Barron (PF)	3,866	(3%)	($612)
	Floyd S. Stancliffe (AI)	3,748	(2%)	($157)
1974 primary:	Norman Y. Mineta (D)	44,717	(78%)	
	Corinne Friedman (D)	7,465	(13%)	
	S. David Simpkins (D)	5,282	(9%)	

◆ ◆ ◆ ◆ ◆

FOURTEENTH DISTRICT

The 14th district of California occupies a portion of the state's Central Valley, probably the world's most productive farmland. Only 50 miles from San Francisco Bay, the 14th is cut off from that cosmopolitan influence by the peaks of the Coast Range and, politically at least, the district is almost part of another world. The prosperity of the cities here, the most notable of which is Stockton (pop. 107,000), is rooted firmly in agriculture. The farms of the area—the district goes as far north in the Valley as the suburbs of Sacramento and as far south as Stanislaus County around Modesto—are not as often in the hands of huge conglomerates as those in the southern reaches of the Valley. Many rather small, family-owned farms still exist in the 14th, as do a whole string of medium-sized cities along the Route 99 freeway. The district has a fair amount of industry, but agriculture is king.

Above the Valley, sometimes visible in the far distance, rises the Sierra, and the 14th, thanks to the 1973 redistricting, has its share of the Mother lode country and the mountains going as far as Yosemite and Lake Tahoe. But this area is underpopulated and of little significance politically; its importance is more tangential, for the mountains shed down numerous rivers much of the water the thirsty farms of the Valley need.

The political traditions of the Valley are Democratic—the result of the politics of its initial settlers, many from the South; of the Great Depression; and, to an unknown extent, of the Democratic politics of the McClatchy papers that dominate Valley journalism from Sacramento to Fresno. But there is little here of the new politics, as practiced by Democrats in the San Francisco suburbs. Social attitudes—measured with nice precision by the plethora of referenda on the California ballot—show the Valley to be decidely conservative on issues like capital punishment, coastal preservation, and marijuana.

The 14th district's Congressman, John J. McFall, is one of an older breed of Democrat, a man who surely feels more comfortable in a group of cigar-smoking party regulars or a union meeting than before a college audience. Organized labor can count on McFall's vote just about every time, but he is far less likely to support measures sought by environmentalists or opponents of high military spending. In Congress since 1957, McFall rose slowly and almost silently to the chairmanship of the Appropriations Transportation Subcommittee. It was in this capacity that he led the fight in the House for the Super Sonic Transport—a measure which passed the House, though most Democrats voted against it, but finally foundered in the Senate. McFall also serves on George Mahon's Defense Appropriations Subcommittee, a body usually generous with the Pentagon.

McFall is probably one of the greatest losers from the changes wrought by the House's Democratic freshmen of 1974. For before they came along, he seemed headed for the Speakership. His progression began in 1972, when Hale Boggs was killed in a plane crash. A few months later, House Majority Whip Tip O'Neill was elected Majority Leader, without substantial opposition. But when it came to the question of whether the new Whip—the number three man in the Democratic leadership—should be appointed by the Speaker and the Majority Leader or elected by the whole Democratic Caucus, there was a big fight. Speaker Albert and new Majority Leader O'Neill wanted to make the choice themselves; leaders of the Democratic Study Group, notably then outgoing chairman Phil Burton, wanted the caucus to decide.

Tradition was then still in the saddle, and Albert and O'Neil won—and promptly picked McFall as Whip. In the normal course of things, first O'Neill, and then McFall, would become Speaker: that is the path taken by Sam Rayburn (as long ago as 1940), John McCormack, and Carl Albert. In making their choice, Albert and O'Neill were catering to the tradition that any Speaker had to be acceptable to both wings of the Democratic Party, the generally liberal north and the more conservative South: with his solid labor and military records, McFall could appeal to both, and he was clearly no hell-raiser. But what Albert and the others had failed to see was that the two wings were becoming grossly unequal. The Southern conservatives were dying off, and being replaced by Republicans or by liberals and moderates. And the northern liberals were having their numbers augmented, usually by ideologically motivated young members who had promised their constituents that they would change the way business was done in the House.

The 1974 landslide produced a huge number of young Democrats—and spelled the end of the succession for John McFall. The key vote was the one by which San Francisco's Phil Burton was elected Chairman of the Democratic Steering Committee. Burton showed he had the votes and support of a clear majority in the caucus and he let it be known that, although he would not challenge O'Neill if Albert stepped down as Speaker, he would run for Majority Leader then. Barring massive defeats of 1974 freshmen in 1976—an unlikely prospect—Burton will have those votes in the future, which means that McFall will not.

Census Data   Pop. 464,656. Central city, 23%; suburban, 56%. Median family income, $9,348; families above $15,000: 18%; families below $3,000: 10%. Median years education, 12.1.

The Voters

Median voting age 44.
Employment profile White collar, 44%. Blue collar, 33%. Service, 14%. Farm, 9%.
Ethnic groups Black, 4%. Filipino, 2%. Spanish, 15%. Total foreign stock, 23%. Italy, 2%; Canada, UK, Germany, USSR, 1% each.

Presidential vote

1972	Nixon (R)	103,566	(58%)
	McGovern (D)	75,662	(42%)
1968	Nixon (R)	77,124	(48%)
	Humphrey (D)	69,015	(43%)
	Wallace (AI)	14,837	(69%)

Rep. John J. McFall (D) Elected 1956; b. Feb. 20, 1918, Buffalo, N.Y.; home, Manteca; Modesto Jr. Col, A.A., 1936, U. of Cal., A.B. 1938, LL.B. 1941; Episcopalian.

Career Army, WWII; Practicing atty., 1948–56; Mayor of Manteca, 1948–50; Cal. Assembly, 1951–56.

Offices 2346 RHOB, 202-225-2511. Also 146 N. Grant St., Manteca 95336, 209-823-1112.

Committees

Majority Whip

Appropriations (16th). Subcommittees: Defense; Legislative; Transportation (Chairman).

Group Ratings

	ADA	COPE	LWV	RIPON	NFU	LCV	CFA	NAB	NSI	ACA
1974	48	100	75	44	93	65	77	8	100	13
1973	48	82	83	71	100	44	88	–	–	15
1972	44	91	83	56	71	0	0	9	100	32

Key Votes

1) Foreign Aid	FOR	6) Gov Abortn Aid	FOR	11) Pub Cong Election $	AGN
2) Busing	FOR	7) Coed Phys Ed	AGN	12) Turkish Arms Cutoff	AGN
3) ABM	FOR	8) Pov Lawyer Gag	AGN	13) Youth Camp Regs	FOR
4) B-1 Bomber	FOR	9) Pub Trans Sub	FOR	14) Strip Mine Veto	AGN
5) Nerve Gas	FOR	10) EZ Voter Regis	FOR	15) Farm Bill Veto	AGN

Election Results

1974 general:	John J. McFall (D)	102,180	(71%)	($52,268)
	Charles M. Gibson (R)	34,775	(24%)	($4,154)
	Roger A. Blain (AI)	7,123	(5%)	($3,696)
1974 primary:	John J. McFall (D)	54,278	(81%)	
	John E. Rogers (D)	9,080	(13%)	
	William H. Romack (D)	4,060	(6%)	
1972 general:	John J. McFall (D), unopposed			

♦ ♦ ♦ ♦ ♦

FIFTEENTH DISTRICT

The 14th district of California is another Central Valley district, one of two dominated by the city of Fresno (pop. 165,000). Except for Sacramento, this is the part of the Valley that has maintained most steadily its Democratic leanings. One reason is its large (21%) Mexican-American population, the largest in the Valley except fot the next-door 17th district. The chicanos here are not only migrants who pass through; they are often middle-class citizens with roots in their communities—and they vote. Moreover, the Fresno area has a more heterogeneous population than many parts of the Valley. There are especially large numbers of Armenian-Americans, like novelist William Saroyan, who has moved back to Fresno. Another large group is made up of the descendants of the original Okies, the people who left the driedout fields of Oklahoma, Kansas, and Texas during the 1930s in search of the promised land of California. Here, as John Steinbeck chronicled in *The Grapes of Wrath,* these poor white people did backbreaking work in the steamy-hot fields for next to nothing and lived in miserable labor camps. Ironically, though perhaps not surprisingly, their sons and daughters are not particularly sympathetic—often even hostile—to the very similar plight of the Mexican-Americans in those same fields today.

The Congressman from the 15th district is himself a transplant from the Dust Bowl. B. F. (Bernie) Sisk grew up on the dusty plains of central Texas and moved to the Valley in 1937. Some 17 years later, he upset a Republican Congressman, and ever since his ingratiating personality has helped him to win reelection. He has also mirrored some of the changes in attitude of the people who have shared his odyssey. For his first ten years in the House, he was regarded as a typical northern liberal Democrat. But in the mid-sixties, as the Reagan tide began rolling in, Sisk became noticeably more conservative. In 1966 his vote in the House Rules Committee—to which he had been assigned to provide a liberal vote—killed home rule for the District of Columbia. (It finally passed in 1973.) He apparently shared the views of many Southerners that self-government would be too much of a burden for the black majority of the capital city, although he has since made great efforts to obtain a major league baseball team for Washington.

Sisk's conservative record—and, perhaps, his Texas twang—made him a favorite of some of the more conservative Southern Democrats. In 1970, he became a candidate for Majority Leader, reportedly at the behest of members like William Colmer of Mississippi, Omar Burleson of Texas, and Bob Sikes of Florida. For a while, Sisk's candidacy made inroads in the California and various Southern delegations, but it soon floundered on the hostility of organized labor.

Four years later, it was not so much labor as it was the changing balance between ideological liberals and get-along-go-along moderates and conservatives that undid Sisk's latest bid for power. Just after the 1974 election, he ran for Chairman of the House Democratic Caucus against San Francisco's Phillip Burton. In any previous year Burton, one of the powers in the Democratic Study Group, might have been considered too far to the left of the Democratic caucus to win; after the 1974 election, it was Sisk who was too far to the right. He lost 162–111. That will likely be his last bid for a leadership post, although he has always been reelected easily and his position on the Rules Committee (4th ranking Democrat) guarantee him leverage on some important issues in the future.

Fresno County, year after year, produces more dollars' worth of farm products than any other county in the nation, and Sisk's main legislative interest, according to the Nader Congress Project report, is agriculture. He has sponsored major water projects which would benefit, among others, J. G. Boswell, a cotton farmer in western Fresno County who has received more than $4 million in federal subsidy payments—the number one recipient of this form of corporate welfare in the nation. Sisk is less sympathetic to farm workers. He has sponsored a bill, opposed by Cesar Chavez's United Farm Workers, which would put such unions under the NLRB and thus deny them their strongest weapon, the boycott.

Census Data Pop. 465,631. Central city, 34%; suburban, 33%. Median family income, $7,930; families above $15,000: 14%; families below $3,000: 13%. Median years education, 11.8.

The Voters

Median voting age 43.
Employment profile White collar, 43%. Blue collar, 31%. Service, 14%. Farm, 12%.
Ethnic groups Black, 6%. Spanish, 21%. Total foreign stock, 21%. Germany, 2%; Canada, USSR, 1% each.

Presidential vote

1972	Nixon (R)	....	77,992	(51%)
	McGovern (D)	....	76,038	(49%)
1968	Nixon (R)	....	59,332	(41%)
	Humphrey (D)	....	73,063	(51%)
	Wallace (AI)	....	11,010	(8%)

Rep. B. F. Sisk (D) Elected 1954; b. Dec. 14, 1910, Montague, Tex.; home, Fresno; Abilene Christian Col., 1929–31; Church of Christ.

Career Day Laborer, refrigerator salesman, orchard and vineyard worker, 1937–45; tire sales business, 1946–54.

Offices 2217 RHOB, 202-225-6131. Also Rm. 2001, 1130 "O" St., Fresno 93721, 209-487-5004.

Committees

Rules (4th).

Group Ratings

	ADA	COPE	LWV	RIPON	NFU	LCV	CFA	NAB	NSI	ACA
1974	53	100	64	33	92	65	69	9	78	7
1973	58	82	75	54	89	44	50	–	–	17
1972	50	90	73	60	71	26	0	10	100	32

Key Votes

1) Foreign Aid	FOR	6) Gov Abortn Aid	FOR	11) Pub Cong Election $	AGN
2) Busing	AGN	7) Coed Phys Ed	AGN	12) Turkish Arms Cutoff	AGN
3) ABM	FOR	8) Pov Lawyer Gag	AGN	13) Youth Camp Regs	FOR
4) B-1 Bomber	FOR	9) Pub Trans Sub	FOR	14) Strip Mine Veto	AGN
5) Nerve Gas	FOR	10) EZ Voter Regis	ABS	15) Farm Bill Veto	AGN

Election Results

1974 General:	B. F. Sisk (D)	....	80,897	(72%)	($55,723)
	Carol O. Harner (R)	....	31,439	(28%)	($5,303)
1974 primary:	B. F. Sisk (D), unopposed			
1972 general:	B. F. Sisk (D)	....	134,132	(79%)	($54,890)
	Carol O. Harner (R)	....	35,385	(21%)	($19,219)

◆ ◆ ◆ ◆ ◆

SIXTEENTH DISTRICT

The 16th district of California boasts some of the most spectacular scenery in the nation, from the Monterey cypresses at Carmel's Pebble Beach, through the mountainous wild Big Sur coast, to William Randolph Hearst's San Simeon. Just to the east of this, the district also contains some of the nation's richest farmland: the lettuce fields of the Salinas Valley, the artichoke fields around Watsonville. This is John Steinbeck country; he grew up in Salinas, and the Cannery Row of Monterey he described still exists, if only as a tourist attraction.

The coastal counties have tended over the years to vote Republican. Landowners around Salinas and retirees in Santa Cruz and the Monterey peninsula tend to vote conservative; the district's Mexican-Americans and its sprinkling of artists and writers, liberal. But in the last few years, the 16th has moved slightly, though not yet decisively, to the left. Part of the reason is the impact of environmental issues, which have led many erstwhile upper- and middle-income Republicans to vote Democratic. But an even more important factor is the sudden addition in 1972 of a large new bloc in the electorate—students.

In this respect, the 16th is typical of many California districts. We tend to think that the student vote in the state is concentrated in Berkeley, but nothing like a majority of California students live there. More than 8% of the eligible voters here in the 16th are college students; most of them are enrolled either at California State Polytechnic in San Luis Obispo (middle of the road) or the University of California's unstructured branch at Santa Cruz (very liberal, 97% for McGovern in 1972).

What this has meant in congressional politics is that conservative Republican incumbent Burt Talcott, first elected in 1962 and reelected without difficulty in the sixties, has been the subject of fierce challenges in 1972 and 1974. Talcott is not the kind of person students would find simpatico. One of the most strait-laced members of Congress, he once chided his colleagues for wearing sport coats on the floor. A middle seniority member of the Appropriations Committee, Talcott makes little news, but almost always can be counted on to support conservative positions.

In the last two elections, his opponent has been Julian Camacho, a Mexican-American in a district where—in the farm towns especially—there is still substantial anti-Mexican prejudice. Nonetheless, with an underfinanced campaign, Camacho was able to hold Talcott down to 54% of the vote in 1972. Two years later, liberal and environmental groups targeted the district; Camacho had enough funds; but Talcott still won by the narrow margin of 2,100 votes. The question for 1976 is whether Camacho and the liberals will quit trying—or whether Talcott will face another tough fight, and possible defeat.

Census Data Pop. 465,345. Central city, 18%; suburban, 35%. Median family income, $9,384; families above $15,000: 20%; families below $3,000: 10%. Median years education, 12.4.

The Voters

Median voting age 40.
Employment profile White collar, 47%. Blue collar, 28%. Service, 16%. Farm, 9%.
Ethnic groups Black, 3%. Filipino, 2%. Spanish, 18%. Total foreign stock, 25%. Canada, UK, Germany, Italy, 2% each.

Presidential vote

1972	Nixon (R)	106,134	(56%)
	McGovern (D)	82,492	(44%)
1968	Nixon (R)	75,367	(51%)
	Humphrey (D)	62,408	(42%)
	Wallace (AI)	10,173	(7%)

Rep. Burt L. Talcott (R) Elected 1962; b. Feb. 22, 1920, Billings, Mont.; home, Salinas; Stanford U., B.A. 1942, LL.B. 1948; Methodist.

Career Army Air Corps, WWII; Commissioner of Athletics, Coast Counties Athletic League, 1954–58; Monterey Co. Supervisor, 1954–62.

Offices 1536 LHOB, 202-225-2861. Also P.O. Bldg., Salinas 93901, 408-424-2881.

Committees

Appropriations (7th). Subcommittees: HUD-Independent Agencies.

Group Ratings

	ADA	COPE	LWV	RIPON	NFU	LCV	CFA	NAB	NSI	ACA
1974	13	10	18	64	64	35	8	58	100	62
1973	0	10	50	50	28	10	17	–	–	82
1972	0	33	38	75	71	40	0	89	100	59

Key Votes

1) Foreign Aid	AGN	6) Gov Abortn Aid	AGN	11) Pub Cong Election $	AGN
2) Busing	AGN	7) Coed Phys Ed	AGN	12) Turkish Arms Cutoff	AGN
3) ABM	FOR	8) Pov Lawyer Gag	FOR	13) Youth Camp Regs	AGN
4) B-1 Bomber	FOR	9) Pub Trans Sub	AGN	14) Strip Mine Veto	AGN
5) Nerve Gas	FOR	10) EZ Voter Regis	AGN	15) Farm Bill Veto	FOR

Election Results

1974 general:	Burt L. Talcott (R)	76,356	(49%)	($152,455)
	Julian Camacho (D)	74,168	(48%)	($156,084)
	D. J. Mauro (AI)	4,589	(3%)	($1,665)
1974 primary:	Burt L. Talcott (R), unopposed			
1972 general:	Burt L. Talcott (R)	105,556	(54%)	($61,828)
	Julian Camacho (D)	84,174	(43%)	($57,865)
	Stanley K. Monteith (AI)	5,752	(3%)	(NA)

◆ ◆ ◆ ◆ ◆

SEVENTEENTH DISTRICT

As one moves farther south in California's Central Valley, one gradually moves from Democratic to Republican territory. The dividing line, insofar as there is one, seems to be somewhere between Fresno and Visalia, about halfway between Sacramento and the Tehachapi Mountains where the Valley abruptly ends. Precisely why that is the case no one is sure. It has something to do, no doubt, with the origins of the original settlers, the relative prosperity of the regions, etc. But there is definitely such a line, and the 17th congressional district of California sits astride it.

The 17th was a new district created by the California Supreme Court in its 1973 redistricting. Although it had no precise predecessor, its boundaries did include the home town of an incumbent Congressman, Republican Bob Mathias. Better known for winning the Olympic gold medal in the decathlon in 1948 and 1952, Mathias grew up in Tulare (pop. 16,000, one of the lines south and east—that is, on the Republican side—of our imaginary line. After a post-Olympic career in business, Mathias had been recruited to run for Congress in 1966, the same year Ronald Reagan was sweeping to a million-vote victory. The district was represented by Harlan Hagen, a 12-year veteran Democrat whose conservatism was closely tailored to the interest of the big growers in the region. But Mathias's local popularity—and the size of the Republican sweep—were so great that he overwhelmed the incumbent by an unusually large margin for a challenger.

Mathias made especially big gains among registered Democrats of Southern origin in nearby Kern County—which has since been removed from the district. Once in Congress, he won a seat on the Agriculture Committee, where even more than his predecessors he worked for the interests of the large agribusiness interests in the Valley. Not surprisingly, he was a strong opponent of efforts to unionize farm workers. Until 1974, Mathias seemed to have a safe seat.

Then, the redistricting pushed the district north above the imaginary line between Democratic and Republican territory. More than half the new 17th was in Fresno County—heavily Democratic, and never represented by Mathias before. Another 64,000 people were in Kings County—also heavily Democratic, and where Mathias had not had to campaign since his initial victory in 1966. Moreover, the Democrats had a strong candidate: John Krebs, member of the Fresno County Board of Supervisors, well-known throughout the county as a backer of planned growth. An immigrant from Germany with a Kissinger-like accent, Krebs was able to raise a substantial campaign treasury, and Mathias was clearly in trouble. In November, Krebs won a narrow victory, with big margins in Fresno and Kings Counties.

Census Data Pop. 465,492. Central city, 14%; suburban, 35%. Median family income, $8,672; families above $15,000: 17%; families below $3,000: 11%. Median years education, 12.1.

The Voters

Median voting age 41.
Employment profile White collar, 46%. Blue collar, 28%. Service, 12%. Farm, 14%.
Ethnic groups Black, 2%. Japanese, 1%. Spanish, 24%. Total foreign stock, 23%. USSR, 2%; Canada, 1%.

Presidential vote

1972	Nixon (R)	91,629	(58%)
	McGovern (D)	65,907	(42%)
1968	Nixon (R)	68,256	(49%)
	Humphrey (D)	61,100	(43%)
	Wallace (AI)	11,172	(8%)

Rep. John Krebs (D) Elected 1974; b. Dec. 17, 1926, Berlin, Germany; home, Fresno; U. of Cal., A.B. 1950, LL.B. 1957.

Career Army, 1952–54; Practicing atty., 1957–74; Fresno Co. Planning Comm., 1965–69; Fresno Co. Supervisor, 1970–74, Chm., Bd. of Supervisors, 1973–74.

Offices 435 CHOB, 202-225-3341. Also Rm. 4114, Fed. Bldg., 1130 "O" St., Fresno 93721, 209-487-5487.

Committees

Agriculture (19th). Subcommittees: Cotton; Dairy and Poultry; Forests.

Small Business (17th). Subcommittees: Energy and Environment; Government Procurement and International Trade.

Group Ratings: Newly Elected

Key Votes

1) Foreign Aid	FOR	6) Gov Abortn Aid	NE	11) Pub Cong Election $	NE
2) Busing	NE	7) Coed Phys Ed	FOR	12) Turkish Arms Cutoff	NE
3) ABM	NE	8) Pov Lawyer Gag	NE	13) Youth Camp Regs	FOR
4) B-1 Bomber	AGN	9) Pub Trans Sub	NE	14) Strip Mine Veto	AGN
5) Nerve Gas	NE	10) EZ Voter Regis	NE	15) Farm Bill Veto	AGN

Election Results

1974 general:	John Krebs (D)	66,675	(52%)	($130,565)
	Bob Mathias (R)	61,812	(48%)	($136,407)
1974 primary:	John Krebs (D)	34,477	(65%)	
	Vincent J. Lavery (D)	10,997	(21%)	
	Richard T. Morgan (D)	7,849	(15%)	

◆ ◆ ◆ ◆ ◆

EIGHTEENTH DISTRICT

The Central Valley of California stands out clearly on a relief map—a swatch of green down the central of the state, from up near Oregon to a point only 100 miles from Los Angeles, surrounded by the yellow and brown of the Coast Range and the Sierra Nevada. These flat, vast, heavily irrigated plains are probably the world's most productive agricultural land. The prosperity of the Central Valley has been built on the drive of agricultural entrepreneurs and the backs of migrant laborers. In the 1930s, the workers were the Okies forced off their land by swirling dust storms. Today, they are mainly Mexican-Americans (including some Mexicans who are brought across the border illegally). Both groups brought Democratic voting habits with them—to the extent that migrant workers vote. But underlying the common Democratic registration of the thirties migrants and the chicanos is a basic economic conflict: who is going to reap how much from the fruit of the land?

The descendants of the Okies, and others whose ancestors were more fortunate, believe that the demands of the farm workers, especially Cesar Chavez's United Farm Workers, will affect the Anglo's share of the pie. For everybody in the Valley partakes of the profits of big farming, and nobody in the Valley thinks that the big companies that dominate agribusiness will absorb any losses brought on by higher wages or better working conditions. So the politics in much of the Central Valley has come down to a conflict between the growers and the farm laborers, with the vast majority of the voters on the side of the growers. You could have seen the same thing in the thirties in towns dominated by the auto or steel industries: the only voters who supported the demands of the workers were the workers themselves; practically everybody else lined up against.

This conflict is especially intense in Kern County around Bakersfield, which forms the heart of California's 18th congressional district. This is the southern end of the Valley, and also the direct western terminus of the road from Oklahoma; it has an especially large number of descendants of the Dust Bowl migrants of the thirties, and more than an average number of Mexican-American farm workers. Chavez's headquarters for his first great strike and boycott, against table grape producers in 1965, was Delano, a dusty town some 25 miles north of Bakersfield. That was happening at just the same time Kern County was trending strongly toward the Republicans, despite Democratic traditions and heavily Democratic registration.

The Congressman from this area since that time has been a Republican more sympathetic to the growers than the farm workers, first Bob Mathias (see California 17), then after a number of redistrictings, William Ketchum. Ketchum was indeed rather lucky to inherit this district; he was originally an Assemblyman from Paso Robles, near the coast; he won the newly created, grotesquely shaped 36th district in 1972; following the 1973 redistricting, he found most of his territory in the new 18th, and moved his residence to Bakersfield. The 18th goes far above that, crossing the Sierras and including Death Valley, and also including northern Los Angeles County, north of the San Gabriel Mountains, an area of sparsely populated arid desert and of solid conservatism.

The bulk of the population, however, is in Kern County, and Ketchum, having survived two redistrictings and one Democratic landslide year, seems to be in very solid political shape. He is one of three California Republicans on the Interior Committee, which has jurisdiction over, among other things, the irrigation projects which are so vital to the Valley's economic health.

Census Data Pop. 463,813. Central city, 15%; suburban, 77%. Median family income, $9,300; families above $15,000: 19%; families below $3,000: 11%. Median years education, 12.1.

The Voters

Median voting age 42.
Employment profile White collar, 44%. Blue collar, 32%. Service, 14%. Farm, 10%.
Ethnic groups Black, 5%. Spanish, 15%. Total foreign stock, 15%. Canada, UK, 1% each.

Presidential vote

1972	Nixon (R)	....	106,941	(66%)
	McGovern (D)	....	55,207	(34%)
1968	Nixon (R)	....	78,261	(49%)
	Humphrey (D)	....	63,676	(40%)
	Wallace (AI)	....	17,647	(11%)

Rep. William M. Ketchum (R) Elected 1972; b. Sept. 2, 1921, Los Angeles; home, Bakersfield; Colo. School of Mines, USC; Episcopalian.

Career Rancher; Army, WWII; Cal. Assembly, 1966–72.

Offices 413 CHOB, 202-225-2915. Also 800 Truxtun Ave., #302, Bakersfield 93301, 805-323-8322.

Committees

Interior and Insular Affairs (8th). Subcommittees: Mines and Mining; Territorial and Insular Affairs; Water and Power Resources.

Ways and Means (12th). Subcommittees: Public Assistance; Unemployment Compensation.

Group Ratings

	ADA	COPE	LWV	RIPON	NFU	LCV	CFA	NAB	NSI	ACA
1974	5	0	18	36	25	24	0	75	100	93
1973	0	0	17	47	25	6	0	–	–	92

Key Votes

1) Foreign Aid	AGN	6) Gov Abortn Aid	ABS	11) Pub Cong Election $	AGN
2) Busing	AGN	7) Coed Phys Ed	AGN	12) Turkish Arms Cutoff	FOR
3) ABM	AGN	8) Pov Lawyer Gag	FOR	13) Youth Camp Regs	AGN
4) B-1 Bomber	FOR	9) Pub Trans Sub	AGN	14) Strip Mine Veto	FOR
5) Nerve Gas	FOR	10) EZ Voter Regis	AGN	15) Farm Bill Veto	FOR

Election Results

1974 general:	William M. Ketchum (R)	67,650	(53%)	($69,806)
	George A. Seielstad (D)	60,733	(47%)	($48,604)
1974 primary:	William M. Ketchum (R)	28,879	(71%)	
	Robert E. Nelson (R)	7,219	(18%)	
	Jim Miller (R)	4,560	(11%)	
1972 general:	William M. Ketchum (R)	88,071	(53%)	($106,576)
	Timothy Lemucchi (D)	72,623	(43%)	($58,066)
	William M. Armour (AI)	6,323	(4%)	($16,913)

◆ ◆ ◆ ◆ ◆

NINETEENTH DISTRICT

There are still parts of California where you can understand what brought so many people—retirees, young families, hoboes and millionaires—out here 30 or 40 years ago: the soft climate, the mountains falling into the sea, the peaceful small towns, and well -ordered smogless cities. One such area is the part of the state within the bounds of the 19th congressional district, which includes Santa Barbara County, much of Ventura County to the east, and a small part of San Luis Obispo County to the north. The Coast Range is as rugged, the Pacific as blue and warm, the towns—despite recent heavy growth—as pristine as any place along the coast.

This is also, for mystery fans, Ross Macdonald land. Macdonald lives here, in Santa Barbara, and most of his novels are set there or in other thinly-disguised towns along this coast. Indeed, in one of the most recent, *Sleeping Beauty*, he weaves the story around the famous Santa Barbara oil spill of 1969. The Interior Department had been allowing offshore oil drilling in the Santa Barbara Channel; something had gone wrong with the apparatus; and oil gushed out, covering the beaches, destroying the birds, fouling the very atmosphere. It was an incident which radicalized wealthy retirees and politicized young students—and, it can at least be argued, shoved the Santa Barbara community at least a couple of notches leftward.

Neither the oil spill, nor anything else, had that effect on the district's then Congressman, Republican Charles Teague. A member of the family that had started the Sunkist citrus combine, Teague was a senior member of the Agriculture and Veterans Committees, a genial older man who made few waves in the House. With the help of favorable redistricting—it retained the conservative area around Vandenberg Air Force Base, for example, but excluded the radical University of California Santa Barbara campus—Teague won reelection easily in 1972, but he died suddenly in 1973.

That meant that a special election was required early in 1974. It would come just after Democrats won two surprising victories in off year elections in Michigan and Ohio, and all the indicators seemed to be pointing toward a Democratic victory here too. But there was a difference. Under California law, anyone who wins 50% of the vote in a special election primary wins the seat automatically, and here in the 19th the Republicans were united around one candidate, while the Democrats were hopelessly divided. Moreover, the Democratic candidates were all unknown through the district, while the Republican, Robert J. Lagomarsino, had represented Ventura and Santa Barbara Counties in the state Senate since 1960. Lagomarsino made a careful and well-publicized point of saying that he would not necessarily support Richard Nixon, and indeed might even vote for impeachment, if elected. That was enough, apparently: within the bounds that Teague had won 74% in 1972, Lagomarsino took 53% in 1974—enough to win it all in the first primary. In the general that fall, he again had weak opposition and won 56% of the vote. It appears that he has mastered the process of holding on to this district, despite its leftward trend.

Census Data Pop. 465,095. Central city, 42%; suburban, 52%. Median family income, $10,241; families above $15,000: 24%; families below $3,000: 8%. Median years education, 12.5.

The Voters

Median voting age 40.
Employment profile White collar, 52%. Blue collar, 29%. Service, 14%. Farm, 5%.
Ethnic groups Black, 2%. Spanish, 20%. Total foreign stock, 24%. Canada, UK, Germany, 2% each.

Presidential vote

1972	Nixon (R)	....	110,267	(58%)
	McGovern (D)	....	79,671	(42%)
1968	Nixon (R)	....	77,900	(51%)
	Humphrey (D)	....	66,676	(43%)
	Wallace (AI)	....	9,111	(6%)

Rep. Robert J. Lagomarsino (R) Elected Mar. 5, 1974; b. Sept. 4, 1926, Ventura; home, Ventura; U. of Cal. at Santa Barbara, B.A. 1950, Santa Clara Law School LL.B. 1953.

Career Navy, WWII; Practicing atty., 1954–74; Ojia City Cncl., 1958, Mayor 1958–61; Calif. Senate, 1961–1974.

Offices 1319 LHOB, 202-225-3601. Also Studio 121, 814 State St., Santa Barbara 93102, 805-963-1708.

Committees

       Interior and Insular Affairs (13th). Subcommittees: National Parks and Recreation; Territorial and Insular Affairs.

International Relations (12th). Subcommittees: International Security and Scientific Affairs.

Group Ratings

	ADA	COPE	LWV	RIPON	NFU	LCV	CFA	NAB	NSI	ACA
1974	14	0	40	36	43	50	11	60	100	69

Key Votes

1) Foreign Aid	AGN	6) Gov Abortn Aid	AGN	11) Pub Cong Election $	AGN
2) Busing	AGN	7) Coed Phys Ed	AGN	12) Turkish Arms Cutoff	FOR
3) ABM	FOR	8) Pov Lawyer Gag	NE	13) Youth Camp Regs	AGN
4) B-1 Bomber	FOR	9) Pub Trans Sub	AGN	14) Strip Mine Veto	AGN
5) Nerve Gas	FOR	10) EZ Voter Regis	AGN	15) Farm Bill Veto	FOR

Election Results

1974 general:	Robert J. Lagomarsino (R)	84,249	(56%)	($74,832)
	James D. Loebl (D)	65,469	(44%)	($90,337)
1974 primary:	Robert J. Lagomarsino (R)	45,155	(91%)	
	Herbert A. Ford (R)	4,460	(9%)	
1974 special:	Robert J. Lagomarsino (R)	52,140	(54%)	
	James D. Loebl (D)	18,223	(19%)	
	James A. Browning, Jr. (D)	7,536	(8%)	
	Six others (5D, 1R)	19,311	(20%)	

◆ ◆ ◆ ◆ ◆

TWENTIETH DISTRICT

What is now the 20th congressional district of California is the lineal descendant of a seat which has been redistricted so many times since its initial creation in 1962 that it contains today virtually none of the territory it started with. As it is today, the 20th represents an attempt to gather together the people who have moved west, trying to leapfrog the suburban sprawl of Los Angeles. Thus it includes Malibu Beach and the rustic Topanga Canyon area, along the Ocean beyond the city limits; it includes the towns of Newhall and Saugus, above the mountains which are the northern boundary of the San Fernando Valley; and it includes fast-growing Ventura County suburbs like Simi Valley and Thousand Oaks (known to locals at T.O.), connected by freeway to Los Angeles, over the mountains to the east.

The 20th also contains—and about 40% of its residents live in—the western edge of Los Angeles' San Fernando Valley. All these varied areas have in common a political affection for the conservative right; this is the first, numerically, of those suburban Southern Californian districts which invariably provide large margins to conservative candidates. The 20th and its various predecessors have had a number of different kinds of Congressmen: a John Birch Society member; a Democratic Assembly veteran who ousted him and then, disgusted with the pace of Congress, retired; Ed Reinecke, who campaigned against obscenity, became Lieutenant Governor in 1969, and was convicted of perjury in 1974; and the present incumbent, son of Mr. Conservative, Barry Goldwater, Jr.

Young Goldwater won the district in a 1969 special election, largely because of his name, and for most of his early congressional career that was his only political asset. Once he was even caught dozing in the Senate gallery as his father was delivering a speech. But in recent years, Goldwater has grown more active. He lobbied hard to save the imperiled Lockheed loan legislation, and with Congressman Edward Koch of New York—a liberal Democrat and unlikely Goldwater crony—he has worked hard to protect the privacy of citizens from the computerized lists that proliferate in government (and private business) everywhere. It is a cause which, of course, is a perfectly respectable conservative one, no matter how much self-styled conservatives may have championed the power of the state over the individual in recent years; and it is a cause which, for once, Goldwater seems to have some passion for. There is talk that he may run for the Senate in 1976, but that would seem unmeet at a time when he is just beginning to find a place in the House, and at an age (38 in 1976) when his father was still running the family department store in Phoenix.

Census Data Pop. 466,149. Central city, 42%; suburban, 58%. Median family income, $13,583; families above $15,000: 42%; families below $3,000: 5%. Median years education, 12.7.

The Voters

Median voting age 39.
Employment profile White collar, 62%. Blue collar, 26%. Service, 10%. Farm, 2%.
Ethnic groups Spanish, 11%. Total foreign stock, 22%. Canada, 3%; UK, Germany, Italy, 2% each; USSR, 1%.

Presidential vote

1972	Nixon (R)	132,965	(68%)
	McGovern (D)	63,588	(32%)
1968	Nixon (R)	86,597	(58%)
	Humphrey (D)	53,907	(36%)
	Wallace (AI)	9,269	(6%)

Rep. Barry M. Goldwater, Jr. (R) Elected Apr. 29, 1969; b. July 15, 1938, Los Angeles; home, Woodland Hills; U. of Colo., 1957–60, Ariz. St. U., B.A. 1962; Episcopalian.

Career Stock broker, 1962–69.

Offices 1423 LHOB, 202-225-4461. Also 18751 Ventura Blvd., Tarzana 91356, 213-345-2345.

Committees

Public Works and Transportation (11th). Subcommittees: Aviation; Investigations and Review; Public Buildings and Grounds.

Science and Technology (7th). Subcommittees: Aviation and Transportation Research and Development; Energy Research, Development and Demonstration.

Group Ratings

	ADA	COPE	LWV	RIPON	NFU	LCV	CFA	NAB	NSI	ACA
1974	5	0	20	31	29	33	8	64	100	79
1973	4	9	25	50	11	19	13	–	–	96
1972	0	10	20	38	50	32	0	91	100	86

Key Votes

1) Foreign Aid	AGN	6) Gov Abortn Aid	ABS	11) Pub Cong Election $	AGN
2) Busing	AGN	7) Coed Phys Ed	AGN	12) Turkish Arms Cutoff	ABS
3) ABM	FOR	8) Pov Lawyer Gag	FOR	13) Youth Camp Regs	AGN
4) B-1 Bomber	FOR	9) Pub Trans Sub	AGN	14) Strip Mine Veto	FOR
5) Nerve Gas	FOR	10) EZ Voter Regis	AGN	15) Farm Bill Veto	FOR

Election Results

1974 general:	Barry Goldwater, Jr. (R)	98,410	(61%)	($80,385)
	Arline Mathews (D)	62,326	(39%)	($21,212)
1974 primary:	Barry Goldwater, Jr. (R)	50,877	(91%)	
	David L. G. Garner (R)	4,858	(9%)	
1972 general:	Barry Goldwater, Jr. (R)	119,475	(57%)	($134,263)
	Mark S. Novak (D)	88,548	(43%)	($42,840)

◆ ◆ ◆ ◆ ◆

TWENTY-FIRST DISTRICT

California's 21st congressional district is the heart of the San Fernando Valley. This vast expanse of land, surrounded on all sides by mountains, is almost entirely within the Los Angeles city limits. Annexed long ago, when it consisted of dusty fields and movie ranches—the movie *Chinatown* gives some of the details with fair accuracy—the Valley is now thoroughly filled up, but still suburban in character. The straight streets go on mile after mile, lined by neat stucco houses or by low-rise commercial clutter. At major intersections there are great shopping centers. Hanging overall is the Los Angeles smog, a little less dismal here than in downtown L.A., but still a depressing part of life for those who came here looking for the Golden West.

The Valley has seen southern California's boom industries rise and fall—first the movie business, now aerospace. With major cutbacks in government and airline orders, the giant aircraft factories here laid off thousands of workers in the early seventies, and they have not been hired back on. The earthquake of 1971, which did its greatest damage at the northern end of the Valley, occurred just as some big layoffs were announced. For once-secure San Fernando Valley residents, both were shocks: their jobs were at stake, and the Van Norman Dam—which nearly broke and whose reservoir would have destroyed tens of thousands of homes—meant that even their lives and possessions were endangered. Suddenly the big migration westward ended. People began moving back east from the Valley, while others sought to escape the smog by moving over the mountains west to Ventura County. The San Fernando boom had become a matter of history.

Some political observers like to use the San Fernando Valley as a kind of synonym for right-wing, quasi-racist suburbia. This is several degrees off the mark. Orange County is far more heavily Republican; the southeast factory suburbs of Los Angeles, next to the Watts ghetto, are far more plagued with racial fears. The valley politically is really middle of the road, for southern California. With the rise of right wing popularity in the early sixties, the Valley trended right—nearly defeating 21st district Congressman James Corman in 1964, for instance. But the Valley was also one of the first areas to move in the other direction, too. It gave George McGovern a significantly higher vote than his national percentage, and this virtually all-white area produced amazing numbers of votes for Mayor Thomas Bradley in 1973. Most of the state legislative seats here are held by Democrats; just after the Nixon landslide there was a special state Senate race in which both sides spent about $250,000, and the Democrat won handily. In 1974 the 21st district went solidly (57%) for Democratic gubernatorial candidate Jerry Brown.

The 21st district occupies the northeast corner of the Valley and spreads out almost to the Santa Monica Mountains in the south and to within four or five miles of the mountains to the west. It spreads, then, from Democratic North Hollywood, with its large Jewish population, through middle-class Van Nuys and Northridge to Pacoima, with the Valley's small black ghetto. The district is shaped not too much differently from the 22d district of the 1972 redistricting, which was designed for the express benefit of Democratic Congressman James Corman. First elected in 1960, Corman got into political trouble for taking a seat on Judiciary and working for civil rights legislation and, later, working against the amendment which would overturn the Supreme Court's decision outlawing compulsory prayers in public schools.

Following the 1968 election, Corman got a seat on the Ways and Means Committee. There he was one of the very few Congressmen who tried to buck Wilbur Mills. He introduced comprehensive tax reform legislation, and was a co-sponsor of the labor-backed comprehensive health care bill. With the great flood of freshmen in 1974—and the increase in the size of Ways and Means to accomodate them—Corman at least has the possibility of greater clout in the House. However, in early 1975, it was Bill Green of Pennsylvania, one notch below Corman in seniority, who was the sparkplug behind the move to attach the abolition of the oil depletion allowance to the presidentially-sought tax cut. Corman is now politically safe in his district, and with a changed House he has great leadership potential; the question is whether he will use it.

Census Data Pop. 464,934. Central city, 96%; suburban, 4%. Median family income, $11,440; families above $15,000: 29%; families below $3,000: 6%. Median years education, 12.4.

The Voters

Median voting age 41.
Employment profile White collar, 55%. Blue collar, 34%. Service, 11%. Farm, –%.
Ethnic groups Black, 4%. Spanish, 17%. Total foreign stock, 30%. Canada, Italy, 3% each; UK, Germany, Italy, 2% each; Poland, 1%.

Presidential vote

1972	Nixon (R)	....	98,207	(56%)
	McGovern (D)	....	76,271	(44%)
1968	Nixon (R)	....	76,740	(47%)
	Humphrey (D)	....	78,043	(48%)
	Wallace (AI)	....	8,997	(5%)

Rep. James C. Corman (D) Elected 1960; b. Oct. 20, 1920, Galena, Kans.; home, Van Nuys; UCLA, B.A. 1942, USC LL.B. 1948; Methodist.

Career USMC, WWII and Korea; Practicing atty., 1949–57; L. A. City Cncl., 1957–60; Natl. Advisory Comm. on Civil Disorders, 1967.

Offices 2252 RHOB, 202-225-5811. Also 14545 Friar St., Van Nuys 91401, 213-787-1776.

Committees

Small Business (5th). Subcommittees: Governmental Procurement and International Trade (Chairman); SBA and SBIC Legislation.

Ways and Means (9th). Subcommittees: Health; Public Assistance; Unemployment Compensation (Chairman).

Group Ratings

	ADA	COPE	LWV	RIPON	NFU	LCV	CFA	NAB	NSI	ACA
1974	86	100	75	57	86	71	83	18	20	8
1973	79	89	82	67	85	58	100	–	–	12
1972	94	100	90	73	71	47	50	8	14	12

Key Votes

1) Foreign Aid	FOR	6) Gov Abortn Aid	FOR	11) Pub Cong Election $	AGN
2) Busing	FOR	7) Coed Phys Ed	FOR	12) Turkish Arms Cutoff	FOR
3) ABM	AGN	8) Pov Lawyer Gag	AGN	13) Youth Camp Regs	FOR
4) B-1 Bomber	AGN	9) Pub Trans Sub	FOR	14) Strip Mine Veto	AGN
5) Nerve Gas	AGN	10) EZ Voter Regis	FOR	15) Farm Bill Veto	AGN

Election Results

1974 general:	James C. Corman (D)	....	88,915 (74%)	($77,204)
	Mel Nadell (R)	....	32,038 (26%)	($3,603)
1974 primary:	James C. Corman (D), unopposed			

1972 general:	James C. Corman (D)	123,863	(68%)	($58,544)
	Bruce P. Wolfe (R)	53,603	(29%)	($19,169)
	Ralph L. Shroyer (PF)	5,705	(3%)	(NA)

◆ ◆ ◆ ◆ ◆

TWENTY-SECOND DISTRICT

Pasadena (pop. 113,000) and Glendale (pop. 132,000) are two Los Angeles area towns with quite well-established images. From sources as diverse as the mid-sixties rock song "Little Old Lady from Pasadena" to Raymond Chandler's description of the massive houses of wealthy recluses, one gets a picture that is still substantially accurate. These are towns of large houses, of tree-shaded streets, of older, upper-income people whose basic instincts are profoundly conservative. All those adjectives certainly apply to California's 22d congressional district, which includes both Glendale and Pasadena, several adjacent suburbs, and the remote Tujunga part of Los Angeles.

There are a few discordant notes, however, mentioned neither by Jan and Dean nor Chandler. One is the large and growing black population in Pasadena. The city's school system has been under a federal court busing order, which an intransigent anti-busing school board has been trying to overturn. Much of the trouble stems from the discrepancy between the school population and the electorate. The students are 40% black and 12% chicano, while the voting population remains overwhelmingly Anglo white, weighted to the upper age and income brackets.

This age structure is typical of many older, well-to-do suburbs across the country, from Pasadena to Evanston to Scarsdale. As the older, deeply conservative people, who have dominated these communities for years, slowly die off, they are replaced by younger, more liberal residents. Sometimes these are young black families, or white faculty members (Pasadena is the home of Caltech), people who are notably more flexible in their political attitudes than their older neighbors. Twenty-five years ago, this kind of liberal (or at least the whites among them) would probably have moved to the tract houses at the farther edges of suburbia, like everyone else in their age group. Today these people seem to prefer the older, better-established suburbs, with their well-built, spacious houses and fully grown trees.

The political result of such preferences is that communities like Pasadena and Glendale have been moving slightly to the left. They still continue to give virtually every Republican candidate a huge majority, but, not, usually, as huge as in the past. McGovern, for example, did better than Humphrey here, despite the contrary trend in the rest of the nation; and though the changes seem marginal, obviously they can make all the difference in a close election.

Congressman H. Allen Smith, a 16-year Republican veteran, decided to retire in 1972. At age 63, this ranking Republican on the House Rules Committee apparently decided that he would never be Chairman. His successor was another staunch conservative, Assemblyman Carlos Moorhead. What was surprising about Moorhead was the low vote he won by in 1972 (57%) and 1974 (56%). Part of the reason was the leftward trend in the district we have already described, and the fact that Democrats, sensing the possibility of an upset, seem to have campaigned harder than usual. Surely part of the reason also was Moorhead's unprepossessing demeanor, familiar to television viewers from his performance in the House Judiciary Committee impeachment hearings. (There he followed fellow California Republican Charles Wiggins in defending Richard Nixon, but without Wiggins' brilliance.) Both factors would incline one toward predicting tough reelection fights for Moorhead in the future—but for the fact that this district starts off so heavily Republican that an upset is not really conceivable.

Census Data Pop. 464,760. Central city, 12%; suburban, 88%. Median family income, $11,741; families above $15,000: 33%; families below $3,000: 6%. Median years education, 12.6.

The Voters

Median voting age 46.
Employment profile White collar, 63%. Blue collar, 27%. Service, 11%. Farm, –%.
Ethnic groups Black, 6%. Spanish, 10%. Total foreign stock, 27%. Canada, UK, Germany, 3% each; Italy, 2%.

Presidential vote

	1972	Nixon (R)	134,792	(68%)
		McGovern (D)	62,080	(32%)

1968	Nixon (R)	125,454	(63%)
	Humphrey (D)	64,619	(32%)
	Wallace (AI)	10,497	(5%)

Rep. Carlos J. Moorhead (R) Elected 1972; b. May 6, 1922, Long Beach; home, Glendale; UCLA, B.A. 1943, USC, J.D. 1949; Presbyterian.

Career Army, WWII; Practicing atty., 1950–72; Cal. Assembly, 1966–72.

Offices 1208 LHOB, 202-225-4176. Also Rm. 404, 420 N. Brand Blvd., Glendale 91203, 213-247-8445.

Committees

Interstate and Foreign Commerce (13th). Subcommittees: Energy and Power.

Judiciary (8th). Subcommittees: Administrative Law and Governmental Relations; Claims and Governmental Relations.

Group Ratings

	ADA	COPE	LWV	RIPON	NFU	LCV	CFA	NAB	NSI	ACA
1974	9	0	17	47	29	29	0	83	100	87
1973	4	0	27	53	11	11	0	–	–	96

Key Votes

1) Foreign Aid	AGN	6) Gov Abortn Aid	AGN	11) Pub Cong Election $	AGN
2) Busing	AGN	7) Coed Phys Ed	AGN	12) Turkish Arms Cutoff	ABS
3) ABM	FOR	8) Pov Lawyer Gag	FOR	13) Youth Camp Regs	AGN
4) B-1 Bomber	FOR	9) Pub Trans Sub	AGN	14) Strip Mine Veto	AGN
5) Nerve Gas	FOR	10) EZ Voter Regis	AGN	15) Farm Bill Veto	FOR

Election Results

1974 general:	Carlos J. Moorhead (R)	81,641	(56%)	($51,841)
	Richard Hallin (D)	64,691	(44%)	($68,449)
1974 primary:	Carlos J. Moorhead (R)	54,540	(86%)	
	J. Dewitt Fox (R)	8,727	(14%)	
1972 general:	Carlos J. Moorhead (R)	122,309	(57%)	($97,617)
	John Binkley (D)	90,842	(43%)	($56,380)

◆ ◆ ◆ ◆ ◆

TWENTY-THIRD DISTRICT

The 23d congressional district of California is situated in one of the most prosperous—and famous—parts of Los Angeles, the west side. This includes middleclass West Los Angeles and well-to-do Westwood, around the UCLA campus, and over the mountains in the San Fernando Valley the communities of Reseda and Tarzana. Far better known, of course, is the separate city of Beverly Hills, one of the richest in the nation, still host every day to buses of tourists gawking at the homes of the stars. Nearby is glittering Century City, the giant office-and-apartment development built on the former Twentieth Century Fox backlot; above in the mountains, in Laurel and Coldwater Canyons, are the overpriced rustic cabins and tree-secluded mansions of the would-be and geniunely wealthy.

The 23d district is the most heavily Jewish congressional district in the nation outside New York City; and of course many of its residents were lured here from Manhattan by the entertainment business. It is also one of the most reliably Democratic high-income districts in the nation; Beverly Hills, with its large Jewish population, has the distinction of never having voted for Richard Nixon. Moreover, the district has additional national clout in that a very high—and recently rising-amount-of national campaign funds are raised within its bounds, most of the money for Democrats, but a lot for Republicans too.

Curiously, the 23d and its predecessor districts (numbered the 26th till 1974) has never elected a Jewish Congressman, though it has been represented by a string of famous people. One was James Roosevelt (1955-65), son of FDR; the younger Roosevelt's endorsement of Nixon in 1972 coincides with the legal troubles of Bernard Cornfield's Investors Overseas Service, of which he had been vice president. Another was Sam Yorty (1951-55), the three term Mayor of Los Angeles (1961-73), a hawkish Democrat (in the 1972 New Hampshire presidential primary) turned Republican (after his 1973 loss), with a left political past. And going back a few more years there was Helen Gahagan Douglas (1945-51), wife of actor Melvyn Douglas and once an actress herself; she was the target of Richard Nixon's famous 1950 Senate race, when he smeared her as the "Pink Lady."

All of these were Democrats, all considered liberals in their time. The district's current Congressman has similar political leanings, though so far he has had a more conventional, less theatrical political career. When he went to Congress after winning a 1965 special election, Rees was a ten-year veteran of the California legislature. Back in those days, before one-man-one-vote, he was the sole state Senator from Los Angeles County (pop. 7,032,000), representing more people than any other state legislator in American history. Rees has usually voted with the liberal Democratic bloc; though he has shown interest in mass transit legislation and congressional reform, he is probably better known for his puckish sense of humor.

Rees serves on the Banking and Currency Committee, where he has shared at least one attribute more in line with the older, conservative members than the younger liberal ones: owning bank stock. Former Chairman Wright Patman considered him a man who gave in to the views of the big banks, an opinion shared by some other liberals. Rees also serves on the House District of Columbia Committee, for which he volunteered back in 1972, when South Carolina's John McMillan still chaired it; now Rees has a subcommittee chairmanship, which of course is a less important position than it was before the home rule bill which Rees supported passed.

Census Data Pop. 464,026. Central city, 88%; suburban, 12%. Median family income, $14,141; families above $15,000: 46%; families below $3,000: 5%. Median years education, 12.9.

The Voters

Median voting age 44.
Employment profile White collar, 75%. Blue collar, 16%. Service, 9%. Farm, –%.
Ethnic groups Japanese, 1%. Spanish, 7%. Total foreign stock, 39%. USSR, 8%; Canada, 4%; UK, Germany, Poland, 3% each; Italy, Austria, 2% each; Hungary, 1%.

Presidential vote

1972	Nixon (R)	119,617	(50%)
	McGovern (D)	117,663	(50%)
1968	Nixon (R)	93,343	(43%)
	Humphrey (D)	116,397	(54%)
	Wallace (AI)	5,927	(3%)

Rep. Thomas M. Rees (D) Elected Dec. 15, 1965; b. Mar. 26, 1925, Los Angeles; home, Los Angeles; Occidental Col., B.A. 1950; Episcopalian.

Career Army, WWII; Attorney; Pres., Compania del Pacifico, Latin Amer. Export Co., 1952-70; Cal. Assembly, 1954-62; Cal. Senate, 1962-65.

Offices 1112 LHOB, 202-225-5911. Also 816 S. Robertson Blvd., Los Angeles 90035, 213-652-4000.

Committees

Banking, Currency and Housing (12th). Subcommittees: Economic Stabilization; Housing and Community Development; International Development Institutions and Finance; International Trade, Investment and Monetary Policy (Chairman).

District of Columbia (5th). Subcommittees: Fiscal Affairs; Judiciary.

Group Ratings

	ADA	COPE	LWV	RIPON	NFU	LCV	CFA	NAB	NSI	ACA
1974	85	100	82	60	80	93	67	17	11	17
1973	96	91	100	77	83	100	100	–	–	4
1972	88	73	100	64	71	79	100	9	11	4

Key Votes

1) Foreign Aid	FOR	6) Gov Abortn Aid	FOR	11) Pub Cong Election $	FOR
2) Busing	FOR	7) Coed Phys Ed	FOR	12) Turkish Arms Cutoff	AGN
3) ABM	AGN	8) Pov Lawyer Gag	AGN	13) Youth Camp Regs	FOR
4) B-1 Bomber	ABS	9) Pub Trans Sub	ABS	14) Strip Mine Veto	AGN
5) Nerve Gas	AGN	10) EZ Voter Regis	FOR	15) Farm Bill Veto	FOR

Election Results

1974 general:	Thomas M. Rees (D)	122,076	(71%)	($80,318)
	Jack E. Roberts (R)	48,826	(29%)	($5,520)
1974 primary:	Thomas M. Rees (D)	84,191	(93%)	
	Jack Yohanna (D)	6,157	(7%)	
1972 general:	Thomas M. Rees (D)	164,351	(69%)	($45,963)
	Philip Robert Rutta (R)	66,731	(28%)	($193)
	Mike Timko (PF)	8,313	(3%)	(NA)

◆ ◆ ◆ ◆ ◆

TWENTY-FOURTH DISTRICT

Hollywood, they told us a few years ago, was dead. The great movie studies were auctioning off old props, films were being shot in Spain or New Mexico where costs were lower, and the great moguls of the studios were gone, leaving their successors with only a fraction of their old power. True enough. But since then, Hollywood has come back, with hugely profitable movies like *The Godfather* and *The Sting*. Most of the studios are now booming, and if there is less work in movies in Los Angeles, there is more television—where California has long since supplanted New York. And if TV is a less than satisfying medium artistically, then the same complaint was made of the movies during their golden years in the thirties and forties.

Show Biz in California is still centered on the west side of Los Angeles, from the old Hollywood neighborhood itself (it is not a separate city), down to Beverly Hills and Westwood, and, over the mountains, in Universal City and downtown Burbank. Most of this territory, from Hollywood to the still gaudy Sunet Strip, is within the bounds of the 24th district of California. Here you will find Hollywood itself—with a rather disappointing Hollywood Boulevard and tawdry stucco side streets. To the north, their precipitous rise dominating the few smogless days, are the Santa Monica Mountains; among them are picturesque houses built along steep canyons or on flat-topped hills. North of the mountains, the 24th extends to Burbank and, in the other direction, toward comfortable Sherman Oaks. Here within the 24th (or just beyond, in the 23d district) are the old movie and new TV studios, almost all the agents and production companies.

Show Biz is in many ways a predominantly Jewish industry, and the 24th district, like the 23d, has a large Jewish population. Not everyone here lives on the well-manicured streets and spacious houses of nearby Beverly Hills or Hancock Park; there are also the near middle-class streets of the Fairfax district, an older Jewish neighborhood, and the somewhat newer, but otherwise similar precincts of North Hollywood on the other sides of the mountain. The district touches on the edge of the black ghetto at its southern edge, and also has a large Mexican-American population. But neither of these groups is especially likely to vote, and politically the ethnic flavor of the 24th is definitely Jewish.

This district was created quite anew by the Supreme Court-ordered redistricting of 1973; its territory had been divided up before between neighboring constituencies. What is odd is that it was not created earlier, in 1972, by the then California Assembly Reapportionment Committee Chairman, Henry Waxman, for he is the man who now represents it. That someone like Waxman should be a power in the Assembly says something about the fluidity and accessibility of power there (contrast the sluggishness and inaccessibility of power of the U.S. House, at least before 1975). Waxman was first elected to the Assembly only in 1968, when he was 29, but he chose the right side in the Speakership fight that year (Bob Moretti) and soon was an important chairman. Though Waxman has been accused of building his own little political machine on the west side of Los Angeles, it is certainly not a machine in the old sense, but rather a group of young politicos who can raise dollars and volunteers for each other. Thus in 1972, Waxman's friend Howard Berman was elected to the Assembly from a Hollywood Hills district which had never elected a Democrat before; the Waxman "machine' " had seen the lifestyle change there (from elderly WASP to hip young swingers) and ran their campaign accordingly. Berman, interestingly, is now Assembly Majority Leader, having switched in the 1974 Speakership contest from a Moretti ally (Willie Brown) to the winner (Leo McCarthy).

Anyway, once the 24th was unveiled in its present form, it became known as the Waxman district, and the young Assemblyman easily won the primary and general election. Waxman received the top freshman slots on both the Commerce and Science Committees—both of whose compositions have been so altered by new members as to be almost completely changed in character. With a safe seat and an almost Burtonesque flair for legislative politicking, Waxman could be an important member of the House for many years to come.

Census Data Pop. 465,475. Central city, 98%; suburban, 2%. Median family income, $10,137; families above $15,000: 28%; families below $3,000: 9%. Median years education, 12.5.

The Voters

Median voting age 47.
Employment profile White collar, 69%. Blue collar, 20%. Service, 11%. Farm, –%.
Ethnic groups Black, 5%. Japanese, 3%. Chinese, Filipino, 2% each. Spanish, 16%. Total foreign stock, 49%. USSR, 6%; Canada, UK, Germany, Poland, 3% each; Italy, 2%; Austria, Hungary, 1% each.

Presidential vote

1972	Nixon (R)	94,038	(49%)
	McGovern (D)	98,225	(51%)
1968	Nixon (R)	85,206	(43%)
	Humphrey (D)	105,462	(53%)
	Wallace (AI)	6,992	(4%)

Rep. Henry A. Waxman (D) Elected 1974; b. Sept. 12, 1939, Los Angeles; home, Los Angeles; UCLA, B.A. 1961, J.D. 1964; Jewish.

Career Practicing atty., 1965–68; Cal. Assembly, 1968–74.

Offices 1039 LHOB, 202-225-3976. Also Suite 600, 8455 W. Beverly Blvd., Los Angeles 90048, 312-651-1040.

Committees

Interstate and Foreign Commerce (20th). Subcommittees: Health and Environment; Oversight and Investigations.

Science and Technology (14th). Subcommittees: Domestic and International Scientific Planning and Analysis; Energy Research, Development and Demonstration; Energy Research (Fossil Fuels); Space Science and Applications.

Group Ratings: Newly Elected

Key Votes

1) Foreign Aid	FOR	6) Gov Abortn Aid	NE	11) Pub Cong Election $	NE
2) Busing	NE	7) Coed Phys Ed	FOR	12) Turkish Arms Cutoff	NE
3) ABM	NE	8) Pov Lawyer Gag	NE	13) Youth Camp Regs	FOR
4) B-1 Bomber	AGN	9) Pub Trans Sub	NE	14) Strip Mine Veto	AGN
5) Nerve Gas	NE	10) EZ Voter Regis	NE	15) Farm Bill Veto	AGN

Election Results

1974 general:	Henry A. Waxman (D)	87,521	(64%)	($95,151)
	Elliott Stone Graham (R)	45,128	(33%)	($22,411)
	David E. Davis (AI)	4,073	(3%)	($145)

1974 primary:	Henry A. Waxman (D)	53,228	(74%)
	Herb Selwyn (D)	10,455	(15%)
	Ross Hopkins (D)	8,115	(11%)

◆ ◆ ◆ ◆ ◆

TWENTY-FIFTH DISTRICT

The 1970 census tells us that almost 16% of all Californians are of "Spanish heritage." The vast majority of these people, of course, are Mexican-Americans, who constitute the largest and, in many respects, the most hidden ethnic group in the state. California blacks live in well-defined areas in a few cities, but Mexican-Americans can be found all over the state; no congressional district has less than 5% "Spanish heritage." Certainly there are some large Mexican-American areas, notably on the east side of Los Angeles and the adjacent suburb of East Los Angeles. But in general chicanos seem to blend in more easily with working or middle class whites than do blacks.

Politically, Mexican-Americans have long been the most under-represented group in the state. California sends three blacks to the House, but only one of its 43 Congressmen is of Spanish origin. There are only two Mexican-American state Senators and only four (out of 80) Assemblymen. Republicans have charged that Democrats slice up Mexican neighborhoods, to add Democratic votes to districts dominated by other groups; there is some truth in that, but Republican plans would result in the election of more Mexicans, but fewer Democrats, whom chicano voters almost always prefer. But it is a mistake to suppose Mexican-American votes are as solidly Democratic as blacks; their voting behavior is quite different. Conservative, race-baiting Mayor Sam Yorty, for example, always had a good vote in the east side of Los Angeles, where Richard Nixon also made some inroads in 1972.

In 1974, for the first time, the predominantly Mexican-American communities of eastern Los Angeles neighborhoods like Boyle Heights and Highland Park have been joined together with the suburb of East Los Angeles to form a single congressional district, the 25th. The district also includes downtown Los Angeles, MacArthur Park and Dodgers Stadium, and reaches west toward the seedy, once elegant Silver Lake district near Hollywood. Not surprisingly, the 25th is one of the poorest—and most Democratic—districts in California. Mexican-Americans, as they become better-off and more assimilated tend to move outward—generally to the east—to working and middle class suburbs. It is those who cannot get out who stay in the barrio.

For more than a decade, one or another downtown Los Angeles district has been electing and reelecting Congressman Edward Roybal. Though of Spanish descent, Roybal is hardly out of the barrio himself; he is from a well-to-do family from Albuquerque, New Mexico, where the Spanish-speaking community antedates Plymouth Rock. Immediately prior to this election to Congress in 1962, Roybal was serving as president pro tem of the Los Angeles City Council.

It has taken Roybal a while to find a comfortable niche in Congress. Assigned at first to Foreign Affairs, he found himself frustrated by the committee's leadership, inclined as it was to follow the Johnson and Nixon Administrations wherever they might lead. After building up some seniority, he switched in 1971 to Appropriations. There he has yet to rise to a subcommittee chairmanship; and barring something unusual, probably never will. He is known less for his committee work than for his faithful, very liberal voting record.

Census Data Pop. 464,972. Central city, 82%; suburban, 18%. Median family income, $7,804; families above $15,000: 13%; families below $3,000: 13%. Median years education, 10.3.

The Voters

Median voting age 41.
Employment profile White collar, 39%. Blue collar, 48%. Service, 13%. Farm, –%.
Ethnic groups Black, 5%. Japanese, Chinese, 2% each. Spanish, 60%. Total foreign stock, 55%. Canada, Germany, Italy, 1% each.

Presidential vote

1972	Nixon (R)	44,924	(43%)
	McGovern (D)	58,785	(57%)
1968	Nixon (R)	38,130	(34%)
	Humphrey (D)	67,627	(61%)
	Wallace (AI)	5,552	(5%)

Rep. Edward R. Roybal (D) Elected 1962; b. Feb. 10, 1916, Albuquerque, N.M.; home, Los Angeles; UCLA, Southwestern U.; Catholic.

Career Army, WWII; Dir. of Health Educ., L.A. Co. Tuberculosis & Health Assn., 1945–49; L.A. City Cncl., 1949–62, Pres. Pro Tempore, 1961–62.

Offices 2404 RHOB, 202-225-6234. Also Rm. 7110, New Fed. P.O. Bldg., 300 N. Los Angeles St., Los Angeles 90012, 213-688-4870.

Committees

Appropriations (23d). Subcommittees: Labor-HEW; Legislative; Treasury, Postal Service, and General Government.

Group Ratings

	ADA	COPE	LWV	RIPON	NFU	LCV	CFA	NAB	NSI	ACA
1974	100	100	100	56	100	88	85	22	10	0
1973	96	100	83	54	94	100	100	–	–	8
1972	100	100	100	56	83	79	100	9	0	10

Key Votes

1) Foreign Aid	FOR	6) Gov Abortn Aid	FOR	11) Pub Cong Election $	FOR
2) Busing	FOR	7) Coed Phys Ed	FOR	12) Turkish Arms Cutoff	FOR
3) ABM	AGN	8) Pov Lawyer Gag	AGN	13) Youth Camp Regs	FOR
4) B-1 Bomber	AGN	9) Pub Trans Sub	FOR	14) Strip Mine Veto	AGN
5) Nerve Gas	AGN	10) EZ Voter Regis	FOR	15) Farm Bill Veto	FOR

Election Results

1974 general:	Edward R. Roybal (D), unopposed			($24,630)
1974 primary:	Edward R. Roybal (D), unopposed			
1972 general:	Edward R. Roybal (D)	78,193	(68%)	($24,574)
	Bill Brophy (R)	32,717	(29%)	($31,143)
	Lewis McCammon (PF)	3,427	(3%)	(NA)

◆ ◆ ◆ ◆ ◆

TWENTY-SIXTH DISTRICT

The mountains that encircle the Los Angeles Basin are responsible for the area's mild climate; the desert to the north and east is usually 20 to 30 degrees hotter. But the mountains also bottle up the basin's air, allowing the sun to interact with automobile emissions to produce that peculiarly Los Angeles product known as photochemical smog. The same mountains provide a neat topographical barrier to dense settlement. North of the mountains, there are 133,000 people in Los Angeles County; in the smaller land area to the south nearly 7,000,000.

Partly because of the action of the smog, it is considered more pleasant to live at the slightly higher land up close against the mountains than in the flatter, hotter, smoggier valley below. That certainly is the case in the part of the Los Angeles Basin running east from the city toward San Bernardino, the area which just 30 years ago first elected Richard M. Nixon to Congress. Here the lower suburbs are mainly inhabited by people with blue-collar backgrounds and nominally Democratic allegiances to match, while the suburbs through which the aptly-named Foothill Boulevard passes—Sierra Madre, Arcadia, Monrovia, Bradbury, Duarte, Azusa, Glendora— are relatively high income and Republican. These communities form the ideological heart of California's 26th congressional district, which also includes below them the less distinguished suburbs of Temple City and San Gabriel and even working-class Baldwin Park. An exception to the rule we have just recited—it is not next to the mountains, but is still the most conservative of all—is the small community of San Marino, home of Los Angeles' wealthiest WASPs (like the Chandlers of the Los Angeles *Times*), which seldom delivers a Republican vote below 87%.

San Marino also happens to be home of the 26th district's Congressman, John H. Rousselot, who is not only a conservative Republican, but is also a proud member of that old liberal bugbear, the John Birch Society. His membership has given him some trouble in his political career. He was first elected to Congress in 1960, but was beaten in 1962, after the Democratic legislature went to great pains to draw him a district he couldn't win. (Too great pains, it turned out: another Republican captured the district a couple of elections later.) Rousselot then went back on the JBS payroll for a while, and in 1970, when Rep. Glenard P. Lipscomb died, Rousselot entered the primary and beat a moderate by 127 votes out of 87,000 cast. In the general election, he beat Myrlie Evers, widow of the slain Mississippi civil rights leader, by better than a 2-1 margin.

Some may visualize Rousselot as a hard-eyed fanatic. He is, to be sure, a man with a strong drive and energy which may derive, as in Theodore Roosevelt's case, from having been crippled in childhood. But he is also one of the more personable members of the House, with a ready sense of humor, prepared to trade quips with colleagues with whom he has nothing political in common. His Birch membership still gives him problems, and in 1975 he was defeated by the almost liberal Guy Vander Jagt of Michigan for the post of House Republican Campaign Committee Chairman. But in this heavily Republican district, he appears to have no political problems, and should be reelected indefinitely. Rousselot was, incidentally, a high school classmate of a very different California Republican, Pete McCloskey, and both were members of a sort of high school fraternity called the Amalgamated Federation of Virgins.

Census Data Pop. 464,122. Central city, 0%; suburban, 100%. Median family income, $11,668; families above $15,000: 31%; families below $3,000: 6%. Median years education, 12.5.

The Voters

Median voting age 44.
Employment profile White collar, 59%. Blue collar, 31%. Service, 10%. Farm, –%.
Ethnic groups Black, 1%. Spanish, 15%. Total foreign stock, 25%. Canada, 3%; UK, Germany, Italy, 2% each.

Presidential vote

1972	Nixon (R)	132,894	(70%)
	McGovern (D)	56,014	(30%)
1968	Nixon (R)	118,287	(62%)
	Humphrey (D)	61,046	(32%)
	Wallace (AI)	11,114	(6%)

Rep. John H. Rousselot (R) Elected June 30, 1970; b. Nov. 1, 1927, Los Angeles; home, San Marino; Principia Col., B.A. 1949; Christian Scientist.

Career Pres. and Owner, John H. Rousselot & Assoc., public relations consultants, 1954–58; Dir. of Public Info., Fed. Housing Admin., 1958–60; U.S. House of Reps., 1961–63; Management consultant, 1967–70.

Offices 1706 LHOB, 202-225-4206. Also 735 W. Duarte Rd., Arcadia 91006, 213-447-8125.

Committees

Banking, Currency and Housing (5th). Subcommittees: Financial Institutions Supervision, Regulation and Insurance; General Oversight and Renegotiation; Housing and Community Development.

Post Office and Civil Service (3d). Subcommittees: Census and Population; Employee Political Rights and Intergovernmental Programs.

Joint Economic Committees (4th, House Side). Subcommittees: Fiscal Policy; Inter-American Economic Relationships; International Economics; Priorities and Economy in Government; Urban Affairs.

Group Ratings

	ADA	COPE	LWV	RIPON	NFU	LCV	CFA	NAB	NSI	ACA
1974	5	0	0	29	0	31	0	91	100	93
1973	8	9	17	33	5	6	13	–	–	96
1972	0	38	17	20	40	18	50	100	86	94

Key Votes

1) Foreign Aid	AGN	6) Gov Abortn Aid	AGN	11) Pub Cong Election $	AGN
2) Busing	AGN	7) Coed Phys Ed	AGN	12) Turkish Arms Cutoff	ABS
3) ABM	FOR	8) Pov Lawyer Gag	FOR	13) Youth Camp Regs	AGN
4) B-1 Bomber	FOR	9) Pub Trans Sub	AGN	14) Strip Mine Veto	FOR
5) Nerve Gas	FOR	10) EZ Voter Regis	AGN	15) Farm Bill Veto	FOR

Election Results

1974 general:	John Rousselot (R)	82,735	(59%)	($66,043)
	Paul A. Conforti (D)	57,685	(41%)	($8,235)
1974 primary:	John Rousselot (R), unopposed			
1972 general:	John Rousselot (R)	144,057	(70%)	($61,473)
	Luther Mandell (D;	61,326	(30%)	($4,660)

◆ ◆ ◆ ◆ ◆

TWENTY-SEVENTH DISTRICT

The 27th district of California is a long, thin swath of land along the Pacific Ocean, from Pacific Palisades in the north to Palos Verdes in the south. Between these two hilly, high-income prominences overlooking the Ocean, there is a whole string of beach towns: sedate Santa Monica; seedy Venice (its 1920s canals now in ruins); flashy new Marina del Rey; Playa del Rey with Los Angeles International Airport right behind; El Segundo and its oil refineries; Manhattan and Hermosa and Redondo Beaches, with their close-packed little houses and narrow streets. For many years, the beach area has been heavily Republican, the voting habits of its towns dominated by the conservatism of elderly Midwestern migrants. But morality and mobility have produced a sharp leftward turn in recent years. The beach towns are now filling up with young people—singles, surfers, freaks, whatever—whose political instincts, if they get them to the polls at all, lead them to oppose the politics and social values of Ronald Reagan and Richard Nixon.

The 27th district is a district that went for Barry Goldwater in 1964, but in 1972 showed a swing toward the Democratic ticket despite its troubles elsewhere. This swing could cause problems for some politicians, but not for the district's Republican Congressman, Alphonzo Bell. Heir to an oil and aircraft fortune (his family name is memorialized in the working class suburbs of Bell and Bell Gardens), the Congressman has a reputation as a political moderate. It is not that he has a voting record like a Massachusetts Republican; it is just that, against the California setting, he contrasts so vividly with Reagan and his followers.

After a dozen years in the House, Bell enjoys high-ranking positions on both the Science and the Education and Labor Committees; on the latter he has sometimes combined with the 29th district Democrat Augustus Hawkins to fashion legislation. But he has also been interested, from time to time, in other political office. In 1969, he ran for Mayor of Los Angeles, making a respectable showing even while eliminated in the primary. He then enraged big Reagan backers like oilman Henry Salvatori by supporting black Councilman Thomas Bradley over incumbent Sam Yorty. (That time Bradley lost, but he came back to win in 1973.) In 1970, as a result of his support for Bradley, Bell faced well-financed conservative primary opposition, and managed to win only by a 56-44 margin. It is a measure of the leftward trend in California generally and in the beach towns in particular that Bell had no significant primary opposition in 1972 or 1974, while several Democrats each time took the trouble of seeking the nomination to oppose him. xxxxxx

That does not mean Bell is about to be defeated; although another Republican might have some trouble here, Bell is safe. But he is rumored, once again, to be interested in higher office—John Tunney's Senate seat in 1976.

Census Data Pop. 464,100. Central city, 25%; suburban, 75%. Median family income, $13,625; families above $15,000: 43%; families below $3,000: 5%. Median years education, 12.8.

The Voters

Median voting age 41.
Employment profile White collar, 67%. Blue collar, 23%. Service, 10%. Farm, –%.
Ethnic groups Black, 2%. Spanish, 9%. Total foreign stock, 27%. UK, 4%; Canada, 3%; Germany, USSR, 2% each. 1%.

Presidential vote

1972	Nixon (R)	....	138,282	(64%)
	McGovern (D)	....	78,853	(36%)
1968	Nixon (R)	....	109,925	(59%)
	Humphrey (D)	....	66,021	(35%)
	Wallace (AI)	....	10,491	(6%)

Rep. Alphonzo Bell (R) Elected 1960; b. Sept. 19, 1914, Los Angeles; home, Los Angeles; Occidental Col., B.A., 1938; Presbyterian.

Career Rancher; Pres., Bd. Chm., Bell Petroleum Co., 1938–60; Army Air Corps, WWII; Chm., Cal. Repub. Party, 1956–58.

Offices 3239 RHOB, 202-225-6451. Also Rm. 11000 Wilshire Blvd., Los Angeles 90024, 213-478-0111.

Committees

Education and Labor (3d). Subcommittees: Elementary, Secondary and Vocational Education; Labor Standards.

Science and Technology (2d). Subcommittees: Energy Research, Development and Demonstration; Energy Research (Fossil Fuels).

Group Ratings

	ADA	COPE	LWV	RIPON	NFU	LCV	CFA	NAB	NSI	ACA
1974	40	70	83	86	67	47	56	56	100	25
1973	50	67	83	100	57	64	40	–	–	29
1972	31	67	100	50	17	15	100	50	100	33

Key Votes

1) Foreign Aid	FOR	6) Gov Abortn Aid	AGN	11) Pub Cong Election $	AGN
2) Busing	FOR	7) Coed Phys Ed	AGN	12) Turkish Arms Cutoff	AGN
3) ABM	FOR	8) Pov Lawyer Gag	AGN	13) Youth Camp Regs	ABS
4) B-1 Bomber	FOR	9) Pub Trans Sub	ABS	14) Strip Mine Veto	AGN
5) Nerve Gas	FOR	10) EZ Voter Regis	AGN	15) Farm Bill Veto	FOR

Election Results

1974 general:	Alphonzo Bell (R)	102,663	(64%)	($32,270)
	John Dalessio (D)	52,236	(33%)	($29,025)
	Jerry Rubin (PF)	5,706	(4%)	($0)
1974 primary:	Alphonzo Bell (R)	46,082	(82%)	
	Alex T. Mlikotin (R)	10,348	(18%)	
1972 general:	Alphonzo Bell (R)	144,815	(62%)	($60,424)
	Michael Shapiro (D)	89,517	(38%)	($48,719)

◆ ◆ ◆ ◆ ◆

TWENTY-EIGHTH DISTRICT

In 1971, the California legislature decided to create a second black congressional district in Los Angeles County, and drew a peculiarly-shaped seat; two year later, the Supreme Court's redistricting plan smoothed out the district's sharp edges, but maintained essentially the same political complexion. The Los Angeles city limits wander through the 28th, as it is now numbered, enclosing the predominantly black area around the University of Southern California and the integrated Crenshaw neighborhood. (Crenshaw is a comfortable area named after a main street; it is a pocket of more or less stable and amiable integration, and the home of Los Angeles Mayor Thomas Bradley.) The suburban part black, part white city of Inglewood is also included, as is mostly white Culver City, and the well-to-do Palms district near West Los Angeles. The 28th overall is compact, residential (despite a few oil derricks in Ladera Heights), middle-class and middle-income—40% black, 12% Spanish, and 48% Anglo white.

The beneficiary of both redistricting plans was Yvonne Brathwaite Burke, who will be remembered by television viewers as the charming and competent vice-chairperson of the 1972 Democratic National Convention. Mrs. Burke, like so many other members of Congress from the state, is a product of the California Assembly, to which she was first elected as recently as 1966; in that body, which values seniority less and talent more than the U.S. House, she soon gained favorable attention. In 1972 she won her five-candidate Democratic primary with an absolute majority, and in this heavily Democratic district, she had no trouble winning the general election. Her articulate manner and rhetorical modesty—she prefers to be known as a liberal rather than a radical—has made her highly popular with white, as well as black, voters; and she had no difficulties when the 1973 redistricting reduced somewhat the percentage of blacks in the district.

After one term on Interior and Public Works, Burke won a seat on the Appropriations Committee; among its 55 members, she is the only woman (and one of only two blacks). She also made history in another way; married just after the 1972 primary, had a daughter, Autumn, in 1974—the first member of Congress ever to give birth.

Census Data Pop. 465,182. Central city, 70%; suburban, 30%. Median family income, $9,942; families above $15,000: 23%; families below $3,000: 9%. Median years education, 12.4.

The Voters

Median voting age 41.
Employment profile White collar, 54%. Blue collar, 31%. Service, 15%. Farm, –%.
Ethnic groups Black, 40%. Japanese, 4%. Chinese, 1%. Spanish, 12%. Total foreign stock, 26%. Canada, Germany, 2% each; UK, Italy, USSR, 1% each.

Presidential vote

1972	Nixon (R)	62,037	(37%)
	McGovern (D)	107,019	(63%)
1968	Nixon (R)	57,573	(33%)
	Humphrey (D)	109,210	(63%)
	Wallace (AI)	6,337	(4%)

Rep. Yvonne Brathwaite Burke (D) Elected 1972; b. Oct. 5, 1932, Los Angeles; home, Los Angeles; UCLA, A.A. 1951, B.A. 1953, USC, J.D. 1956; Methodist.

Career Practicing atty., 1956–66; Cal. Assembly, 1966–72; Vice Chm., Dem. Natl. Conv., 1972.

Offices 336 CHOB, 202-225-7084; Also Inglewood City Hall, 1 Manchester Blvd., Inglewood 90301, 213-678-5424.

Committees

Appropriations (32d). Subcommittees: HUD-Independent Agencies; State, Justice, Commerce, and the Judiciary.

Group Ratings

	ADA	COPE	LWV	RIPON	NFU	LCV	CFA	NAB	NSI	ACA
1974	95	100	92	67	92	93	100	22	14	0
1973	100	100	100	54	93	93	100	–	–	6

Key Votes

1) Foreign Aid	FOR	6) Gov Abortn Aid	FOR	11) Pub Cong Election $	FOR
2) Busing	FOR	7) Coed Phys Ed	FOR	12) Turkish Arms Cutoff	FOR
3) ABM	AGN	8) Pov Lawyer Gag	AGN	13) Youth Camp Regs	FOR
4) B-1 Bomber	FOR	9) Pub Trans Sub	FOR	14) Strip Mine Veto	AGN
5) Nerve Gas	AGN	10) EZ Voter Regis	FOR	15) Farm Bill Veto	AGN

Election Results

1974 general:	Yvonne Brathwaite Burke (D)	88,655	(80%)	($29,739)
	Tom Neddy (R)	21,957	(20%)	($0)
1974 primary:	Yvonne Brathwaite Burke (D)	67,336	(90%)	
	Leon E. Folton (D)	7,611	(10%)	
1972 general:	Yvonne W. Brathwaite (D)	123,468	(73%)	($138,024)
	Gregg Tria (R)	41,562	(25%)	($24,112)
	John Haag (PF)	3,612	(2%)	(N.A.)

♦ ♦ ♦ ♦ ♦

TWENTY-NINTH DISTRICT

Watts has been a familiar American place name since the 1965 riot there put it in the national headlines. Watts is the heart of the Los Angeles black community, directly south of the city's downtown. And, as official Los Angeles found out after 1965, despite its central location Watts is isolated from the mainstream of Los Angeles—off the principal bus lines, with no hospitals, few parks, little in the way of municipal facilities. The area's most distinctive feature is the Watts Tower, a weird sculpture of bits of broken glass and scrap metal, assembled over some 30 years by Italian immigrant Simon Rodia. New York journalists sent to Watts in the wake of the riot were quick to write that the place didn't look like a ghetto. Actually, more American blacks live in areas like Watts—small, frame, single- or double-family houses along quiet streets—than in areas like Harlem, with its five story, turn-of-the-century tenements.

Watts forms the heart of California's 29th congressional district, and it is the almost unanimously Democratic voting habits of the black areas which inevitably place the district in the Democratic column. But there is another side to the 29th worth noting, the almost impenetrable racial barrier of Alameda Street, just east of the Rodia Tower. Blacks are moving north, west, and south of Watts, but across Alameda the working class white suburbs—places like Huntington Park, Bell, and South Gate, which on first glance look not too much different—are determined to remain all white. This is California backlash country, where politicians like Ronald Reagan and Richard Nixon picked up vast number of erstwhile white Democratic votes following the Watts riot.

The 29th district also includes these areas, added to keep the black-majority district up to the one-man-one-vote population standard. Their inclusion has lowered the Democratic percentages here, but has had no impact whatever on election outcomes. Congressman Augustus Hawkins, first elected in 1962, has not had any trouble winning reelection.

Hawkins, now nearing 70, is probably the most experienced black legislator in the United States. For 28 years, from 1934 to 1962, he served in the California Assembly, and for most of that time was its only black member; in 1959, he was nearly elected Speaker. But California, which elected a black Lieutenant Governor in 1974, was not ready for that then, and so Hawkins had to settle for a seat in Congress. His experience has not been of the kind to produce verbal militance, and Hawkins is known as one of the quieter members of the Black Caucus. Nevertheless, he has proved able to work with the younger, more flamboyant black members.

Hawkins deserves some distinction for having been one of the two Congressmen who discovered the infamous tiger cage prisons in Vietnam in 1970, though in typical fashion he allowed a younger colleague (William Anderson of Tennessee) to get most of the publicity. After 10 years in the House, Hawkins achieved a chairmanship on an Education and Labor subcommittee; and he has helped to produce considerable education legislation. So after more than 40 years as a legislator, Hawkins has some considerable achievements to his credit; but like Satchel Paige, he has been denied by his race—or rather by white people's prejudice—from attaining all that he has been capable of.

Census Data Pop. 464,125. Central city, 57%; suburban, 43%. Median family income, $7,359; families above $15,000: 10%; families below $3,000: 17%. Median years education, 11.1.

The Voters

Median voting age 42.
Employment profile White collar, 36%. Blue collar, 46%. Service, 18%. Farm, –%.
Ethnic groups Black, 59%. Spanish, 15%. Total foreign stock, 15%.

Presidential vote

1972	Nixon (R)	33,571	(26%)
	McGovern (D)	96,415	(74%)
1968	Nixon (R)	29,315	(20%)
	Humphrey (D)	108,346	(75%)
	Wallace (AI)	6,665	(5%)

Rep. Augustus F. Hawkins (D) Elected 1962; b. Aug. 31, 1907, Shreveport, La.; home, Los Angeles; UCLA, A.B. 1931; USC Institute of Govt.; Methodist.

Career Real estate business; Cal. Assembly 1935–62.

Offices 2350 RHOB, 202-225-2201. Also 936 W. Manchester St., Los Angeles 90044, 213-750-0260.

Committees

Education and Labor (7th). Subcommittees: Equal Opportunities (Chairman); Manpower, Compensation, and Health and Safety; Post-secondary Education.

House Administration (6th). Subcommittees: Accounts; Electrical and Mechanical Office Equipment (Chairman); Personnel and Police.

Group Ratings

	ADA	COPE	LWV	RIPON	NFU	LCV	CFA	NAB	NSI	ACA
1974	100	100	88	82	91	91	90	25	10	0
1973	96	100	82	54	100	88	88	–	–	14
1972	81	90	100	63	71	63	0	10	0	6

Key Votes

1) Foreign Aid	FOR	6) Gov Abortn Aid	FOR	11) Pub Cong Election $	FOR
2) Busing	FOR	7) Coed Phys Ed	FOR	12) Turkish Arms Cutoff	ABS
3) ABM	AGN	8) Pov Lawyer Gag	AGN	13) Youth Camp Regs	FOR
4) B-1 Bomber	FOR	9) Pub Trans Sub	FOR	14) Strip Mine Veto	AGN
5) Nerve Gas	AGN	10) EZ Voter Regis	FOR	15) Farm Bill Veto	AGN

Election Results

1974 general:	Augustus F. (Gus) Hawkins (D) unopposed			($6,268)
1974 primary:	Augustus F. (Gus) Hawkins (D)	52,006	(87%)	
	Jim Young (D)	7,832	(13%)	
1972 general:	Augustus F. (Gus) Hawkins (D)	95,050	(83%)	($10,459)
	Rayfield Lundy (R)	19,569	(17%)	($325)

◆ ◆ ◆ ◆ ◆

THIRTIETH DISTRICT

The 30th congressional district of California is a string of suburbs in the San Gabriel Valley just east of Los Angeles. While the wealthy and comfortable suburban towns of the next-door 26th district hug the mountains, those of the 30th are in the lower part of the valley, below the San

Bernardino Freeway, where the smog fills the air from 7:30 AM on, and the Los Angeles and San Gabriel Rivers run (when there is any moisture in them at all) through open concrete conduits. What makes these suburbs at all interesting, however, is not the amount of particulate matter in the air, but rather the fact that they are becoming increasingly the home of the Los Angeles area's middle-income Mexican-American communities. Places like Monterey Park and Montebello, built up as comfortable Anglo suburbs in the forties and fifties, lie only a few miles from the East Los Angeles barrio, and it is here that people from the barrio, when they are able, are moving. The residential migration pattern here is not the kind of white flight and wholesale change in neighborhood complexion one sees when a white neighborhood becomes black; the process is slower, and somewhat more amiable.

But it has political consequences nonetheless. One of them is a reinforcement and magnification of the 30th district's traditional Democratic voting habits. The second is the increasing strength of candidates of Mexican-American descent. The first result helps the chances of political survival for Congressman George Danielson; the second tends to hurt them. Danielson has been a scrambler all his political life; from a neighborhood in Los Angeles' once proud, now seedy Silver Lake district he was elected to the California Assembly in 1962 and 1964, the state Senate in 1966 (against that political prankster Dick Tuck), and to Congress in 1970 and 1972. Danielson has always had many Mexican-American constituents, whom he has wooed in somewhat wooden Spanish. But he never seems to have established any close rapport with his district--as witness the ease with which he moved his legal residence from Silver Lake when the 1973 redistricting moved his territory entirely to the suburbs.

Danielson's initial problem here was that this new 30th district, which incorporated much of his old territory, also included the home of Congressman Chet Holifield, a House member since 1942 and dean of the state delegation. Holifield solved that problem by deciding, at age 71, to retire. That left as a second problem the fact that the district was 42% of Spanish heritage. So in 1974, Danielson did face strong primary opposition from Esteban Torres, former head of a local organization called Teluku. Here Danielson may well have been saved by his seat on the Judiciary Committee—and that body's investigation into the impeachment of Richard Nixon. This President certainly had no popularity left in the basically Democratic 30th, and Danielson was in a position to act against him. At any rate, Danielson won an absolute majority of the vote in the primary, just before the hearings were opened to the television cameras. Freed from reelection worries, he was able to proceed freely and rather aggressively against Nixon's defenders, and to make some telling points. His performance—a more impressive one than many of his constituents had expected—has probably put him in good shape to survive another chicano primary challenge in 1976; moreover, his former opponent Torres has been removed from the field by taking a job with Jerry Brown's administration in Sacramento.

Census Data Pop. 464,892. Central city, 0%; suburban, 100%. Median family income, $10,120; families above $15,000: 20%; families below $3,000: 8%. Median years education, 11.8.

The Voters

Median voting age 40.
Employment profile White collar, 42%. Blue collar, 48%. Service, 10%. Farm, –%.
Ethnic groups Japanese, 2%. Spanish, 42%. Total foreign stock, 34%. Canada, Italy, 2% each; UK, Germany, USSR, 1% each.

Presidential vote

1972	Nixon (R)	74,551	(54%)
	McGovern (D)	64,217	(46%)
1968	Nixon (R)	57,105	(40%)
	Humphrey (D)	74,645	(52%)
	Wallace (AI)	11,057	(8%)

Rep. George E. Danielson (D) Elected 1970; b. Feb. 20, 1915, Wausa, Neb.; home, Monterey Park; U. of Neb., B.A. 1937, J.D. 1939; Protestant.

Career Practicing atty.; FBI Agent, 1939–44; Navy, WWII; Asst. U.S. Atty., Southern Dist. of Cal., 1949–51; Cal. Assembly 1962–66; Cal. Senate, 1966–70.

Offices 312 CHOB, 202-225-5464. Also 879 S. Atlantic Blvd., Monterey Park 91754, 213-570-8216.

Committees

Judiciary (12th). Subcommittees: Administrative Law and Governmental Relations; Courts, Civil Liberties, and the Administration of Justice.

Veterans' Affairs (7th). Subcommittees: Cemeteries and Burial Benefits (Chairman); Hospitals.

Group Ratings

	ADA	COPE	LWV	RIPON	NFU	LCV	CFA	NAB	NSI	ACA
1974	77	100	73	53	92	69	73	29	22	0
1973	83	100	83	55	100	79	88	–	–	5
1972	75	91	64	75	83	82	50	8	40	29

Key Votes

1) Foreign Aid	FOR	6) Gov Abortn Aid	ABS	11) Pub Cong Election $	AGN
2) Busing	FOR	7) Coed Phys Ed	AGN	12) Turkish Arms Cutoff	FOR
3) ABM	AGN	8) Pov Lawyer Gag	ABS	13) Youth Camp Regs	FOR
4) B-1 Bomber	FOR	9) Pub Trans Sub	FOR	14) Strip Mine Veto	AGN
5) Nerve Gas	AGN	10) EZ Voter Regis	FOR	15) Farm Bill Veto	AGN

Election Results

1974 general:	George Danielson (D)	67,328	(74%)	($64,413)
	John J. Perez (R)	23,383	(26%)	($5,953)
1974 primary:	George Danielson (D)	31,201	(53%)	
	Esteban E. Torres (D)	21,589	(37%)	
	Anthony M. Sancher (D)	5,558	(10%)	
1972 general:	George Danielson (D)	92,856	(63%)	($30,832)
	Richard E. Ferraro (R)	49,590	(34%)	($14,526)
	John W. Blaine (PF)	5,552	(4%)	(N.A.)

◆ ◆ ◆ ◆ ◆

THIRTY-FIRST DISTRICT

The 31st district of California is a patch of fairly typical 1940s and 1950s Los Angeles County suburban territory, lying about 10 to 15 miles directly south of downtown Los Angeles and Beverly Hills. Most of it is made up of neat single-family pastel stucco houses, often with an above-ground backyard swimming pool and some slightly shabby lawn furniture. There are parcels of still-vacant land here and newly laid out subdivisions, and next to them the overgrown lots of factory workers' widows who are just barely getting by on Social Security. The 31st also contains sparkling sixties steel-and-glass shopping centers, and the fading pink stucco commercial strips of the forties. Undergirding the economy are the huge defense and auto assembly plants to the east and west—but lately they have been on short shifts, and workers have been laid off.

One thing about the 31st not quite typical—or at least not thought of as such—is the fact that 28 percent of its citizens are black. Not that it is integrated; quite the contrary. Blacks made up 71.5% of the population of Compton in 1970, and only .4% of Lynwood, which is right next door. What happens here is that the black ghetto running south of Watts extends right through the center of the district, dividing the white working-class suburbs of Lynwood and Paramount on the east from those of Hawthorne, Gardena, and Lennox on the west. Another fact of some demographic import: the western suburbs here, together with those in the adjacent 28th district, have the largest concentration of Japanese-Americans in California.

Some of these suburbs were part of the Assembly district which first sent Jess Unruh to Sacramento in 1954 and served as his ultimate electoral base during his terms as Speaker from 1961 to 1968. Among Unruh's Assembly friends and allies who have gone on to the House of Representatives is Congressman Charles H. Wilson of the 31st. His service in Washington has gone without much notice. An assignment to the Post Office and Civil Service Committee has produced few, if any, headlines, and the positions he has taken as a member of Armed Services have made it difficult to class him either with its pro-military majority or with its small group of cut-Pentagon-spending liberals. Wilson's chief problem at home has been to avoid primary competition. The black percentage in the district is likely to rise from the 1970 figure, leading to possible threats from black candidates, and he has been challenged by whites as well. Perhaps the greatest difficulty for such opponents is that the district, bifurcated by the ghetto as it is, has no life as a community on its own. Hence, Wilson's major electoral advantage—a familiar name that no one especially dislikes—may well be enough to carry him through another few primaries, if he chooses, having crossed 60 in 1977, to run again.

Census Data Pop. 463,470. Central city, 7%; suburban, 93%. Median family income, $10,042; families above $15,000: 20%; families below $3,000: 9%. Median years education, 12.1.

The Voters

Median voting age 39.
Employment profile White collar, 44%. Blue collar, 44%. Service, 12%. Farm, –%.
Ethnic groups Black, 28%. Japanese, 3%. Spanish, 15%. Total foreign stock, 20%. Canada, 2%; UK, Germany, Italy, 1% each.

Presidential vote

1972	Nixon (R)	64,074	(46%)
	McGovern (D)	73,874	(54%)
1968	Nixon (R)	52,964	(36%)
	Humphrey (D)	80,219	(55%)
	Wallace (AI)	12,326	(9%)

Rep. Charles H. Wilson (D) Elected 1962; b. Feb. 15, 1917, Magna, Utah; home, Hawthorne.

Career Army, WWII; Founder, Charles H. Wilson Insurance Co., 1945; Cal. Assembly 1954–62.

Offices 2335 RHOB, 202-225-5425. Also 15000 Aviation Blvd., Rm. 2W30, Lawndale 90261, 213-536-6680.

Committees

Armed Services (8th). Subcommittees: Military Installations and Facilities; Military Personnel.

Post Office and Civil Service (6th). Subcommittees: Employee Political Rights and Intergovernmental Programs; Postal Facilities, Mail, and Labor Management (Chairman).

Group Ratings

	ADA	COPE	LWV	RIPON	NFU	LCV	CFA	NAB	NSI	ACA
1974	44	100	67	46	83	85	80	33	78	23
1973	80	100	75	69	89	63	88	–	–	30
1972	38	90	55	60	50	26	50	11	75	44

Key Votes

1) Foreign Aid	AGN	6) Gov Abortn Aid	ABS	11) Pub Cong Election $	AGN
2) Busing	FOR	7) Coed Phys Ed	FOR	12) Turkish Arms Cutoff	AGN
3) ABM	FOR	8) Pov Lawyer Gag	AGN	13) Youth Camp Regs	FOR
4) B-1 Bomber	FOR	9) Pub Trans Sub	ABS	14) Strip Mine Veto	AGN
5) Nerve Gas	AGN	10) EZ Voter Regis	FOR	15) Farm Bill Veto	FOR

Election Results

1974 general:	Charles H. Wilson (D)	61,322	(70%)	($70,813)
	Norman A. Hodges (R)	23,359	(27%)	($38,954)
	William C. Taylor (PF)	2,377	(3%)	($577)
1974 primary:	Charles H. Wilson (D)	29,833	(56%)	
	Emily Card (D)	12,658	(24%)	
	Walter R. Tucker (D)	10,481	(20%)	
	Walter R. Tucker (D)	87,975	(52%)	($67,713)
	Ben Valentine (R)	71,395	(42%)	($62,875)
	Roberta Lynn Wood (PF)	8,788	(5%)	(N.A.)

◆ ◆ ◆ ◆ ◆

THIRTY-SECOND DISTRICT

The 32d is one of 16 congressional districts wholly or partially within Los Angeles County. The focus of the 32d is the busy port area of Los Angeles—San Pedro, Wilmington, and downtown Long Beach—and the nearby suburbs of Carson (blue collar) and Torrance (white collar). This is one of the most working-class districts in the Los Angeles area; people here tend to work on the docks, in one of the area's huge aircraft plants, or in the factories located in the industrial corridor to the northeast. There are—or were, when the 1970 census was taken—relatively few blacks, and most of them in Carson and Long Beach, but their numbers will doubtless increase as a result of population pressures from Compton and Watts to the north. The district also includes near the port a sizable Yugoslav-American community—proof that Los Angeles is not entirely without ethnic variety.

Most of the residents of the 32d are traditional Democrats, union members who supported the programs of Franklin D. Roosevelt (if they remember him) and John F. Kennedy, but who feel threatened by social trends not to their liking. On a few occasions, the district has even gone Republican—for Ronald Reagan in 1966 and Richard Nixon in 1972. In the latter case, this was the California district with just about the greatest defection from normal Democratic allegiance.

For many years this district—known before previous redistricting as the 35th and the 17th—routinely reelected Democratic Congressman Cecil King, co-sponsor of the original Medicare act. When King retired in 1968, a real battle developed between Democrat Glenn Anderson and Republican Joseph Blatchford. Anderson had been Lieutenant Governor for eight years under Pat Brown and was unlucky enough to have been acting chief executive when the Watts riot broke out. Afterwards some people accused Anderson of waiting too long before dispatching the National Guard; and in the 1966 election, he was beaten badly by Republican Robert Finch.

Two years later, Anderson just barely managed to squeak ahead of Blatchford—who later became head of the Peace Corps. In the House, Anderson, always strongly supported by labor, received the kind of mundane committee assignments that tend to accrue to representatives of port areas: Public Works and Merchant Marine and Fisheries. On both, the Californian has moved up rapidly in seniority, to the number seven position on Public Works, and, finally in 1975, to a subcommittee chairmanship (Aviation). Anderson's first moment in the congressional spotlight came, however, in 1973, when he was floor manager for the bill to bust the highway trust fund and allow states to use gasoline tax monies for mass transit. The move lost initially in the House, but the fund was partially—and effectively—busted through a conference committee compromise.

Anderson's district is a poignant example of the need for more and better mass transit. Today the 32d is girded by freeways, and those without cars must depend on an indifferent bus system. Some 40 years ago, however, this area had the most highly developed interurban rail system in the country; you could get from San Pedro or Long Beach to downtown L.A. in just about the same time it now takes on the clogged Harbor Freeway. And in those days there was no smog.

Census Data Pop. 466,639. Central city, 66%; suburban, 34%. Median family income, $9,873; families above $15,000: 22%; families below $3,000: 10%. Median years education, 12.2.

The Voters

Median voting age 40.
Employment profile White collar, 46%. Blue collar, 41%. Service, 13%. Farm, –%.
Ethnic groups Black, 8%. Japanese, 2%. Filipino, 2%. Spanish, 18%. Total foreign stock, 26%.
Canada, UK, Germany, Italy, 2% each; Yugoslavia, 1%.

Presidential vote

1972	Nixon (R)	82,921	(56%)
	McGovern (D)	65,507	(44%)
1968	Nixon (R)	63,126	(44%)
	Humphrey (D)	67,404	(48%)
	Wallace (AI)	11,734	(8%)

Rep. Glenn M. Anderson (D) Elected 1968; b. Feb. 21, 1913, Hawthorne; home, Harbor City; UCLA, B.A. 1936; Protestant.

Career Mayor of Hawthorne, 1940–43; Cal. Assembly, 1943, 1945–51; Army, WWII; Lt. Gov. of Cal., 1958–67.

Offices 1230 LHOB, 202-225-6676. Also 255 W. 5th. St., San Pedro 90731, 213-548-2551.

Committees

Merchant Marine and Fisheries (10th). Subcommittees: Fisheries and Wildlife Conservation and the Environment; Merchant Marine; Oceanography.

Public Works and Transportation (7th). Subcommittees: Aviation (Chairman); Surface Transportation; Water Resources.

Group Ratings

	ADA	COPE	LWV	RIPON	NFU	LCV	CFA	NAB	NSI	ACA
1974	76	100	64	40	83	76	83	40	22	7
1973	100	91	100	79	75	94	100	–	–	8
1972	75	91	75	69	57	68	100	8	10	10

Key Votes

1) Foreign Aid	AGN	6) Gov Abortn Aid	FOR	11) Pub Cong Election $	FOR
2) Busing	AGN	7) Coed Phys Ed	FOR	12) Turkish Arms Cutoff	FOR
3) ABM	AGN	8) Pov Lawyer Gag	AGN	13) Youth Camp Regs	FOR
4) B-1 Bomber	FOR	9) Pub Trans Sub	FOR	14) Strip Mine Veto	AGN
5) Nerve Gas	AGN	10) EZ Voter Regis	FOR	15) Farm Bill Veto	FOR

Election Results

1974 general:	Glenn M. Anderson (D)	84,428	(88%)	($44,232)
	Virgil V. Badalich (AI)	8,874	(9%)	($1,648)
	Frqnk H. Walker (PF)	2,963	(3%)	($0)
1974 primary:	Glenn M. Anderson (D), unopposed			
1972 general:	Glenn M. Anderson (D)	105,667	(75%)	($38,077)
	Vernon E. Brown (R)	35,614	(25%)	($3,079)

◆ ◆ ◆ ◆ ◆

THIRTY-THIRD DISTRICT

The 33d district of California is the end result of several redistrictings, centering on three southeast Los Angeles County suburbs: Norwalk (pop. 91,000), Downey (88,000), and Whittier (71,000). The last of course is the most famous: the boyhood home of Richard Nixon, the Quaker-founded town named after the New England poet, and the profoundly conservative little town in sunny California. The picture is not quite right any more, for Whittier has long since been swallowed up—and its own size swollen—by the advancing suburban tide of Los Angeles, and its special qualities have been diluted and even lost. The function which Whittier, together with the other suburbs of the 33d, serves is to house factory and lower- and middle-level white collar workers, people who in just about every way exemplify what we mean by middle class.

On paper, this makes a Democratic district, and in fact the 33d shows a healthy Democratic registration edge. But such figures prove far less than many political writers assume, and between 1958 and 1974 and 33d district was voting solidly Republican in every election—for Barry Goldwater as well as for Richard Nixon, for Ronald Reagan as well as Thomas Kuchel. Indeed, the right-wing Republicans seem to have had more strength here—certainly more enthusiasm and overt support—than the moderate Republicans who are supposed to be the party's own sure vote-winners.

To understand why, it is useful to go back to the early 1960s, when the smog was getting worse every year, taxes were rising as welfare costs went up, and students and blacks were rioting in Berkeley and Watts. With their values—and perhaps their savings—under attack, the middle class people of places like the 33d felt things were going sour, and it did not help that Watts itself was only a few miles away. It was against this background, after a conservative Democratic Congressman died, that conservative Republican Del Clawson won a special election in June 1963 in an area that includes much of what is now the 33d. That was the time President Kennedy was preparing his civil rights bill and Martin Luther King, Jr., was planning the march on Washington—a time of turmoil and uncertainty, and obviously a time when the people of the 33d wanted to go back to old certainties.

And that, after all, is what conservatives like Clawson, Goldwater, and, later, Ronald Reagan offered—not so much tax relief, as psychological reassurance, reassurance that their way of life was the right one and the things they had worked hard for were not to be scorned. Clawson, through shifting tides of redistricting, has been reelected easily ever since; he faced his toughest challenge in years in 1974 from the Mayor of Norwalk, and survived. He has apparently worked the constituency well, using the advantages that all incumbent members of Congress enjoy. He is now also a member of the House Rules Committee—not, to be sure, an articulate one, but one whose vote can reliably be counted on whatever the conservative side of an issue might be.

Census Data Pop. 464,494. Central city, 0%; suburban, 100%. Median family income, $12,340; families above $15,000: 33%; families below $3,000: 4%. Median years education, 12.4.

The Voters

Median voting age 40.
Employment profile White collar, 54%. Blue collar, 36%. Service, 10%. Farm, –%.
Ethnic groups Spanish, 18%. Total foreign stock, 22%. Canada, 3%; UK, Germany, Italy, 2% each.

Presidential vote

1972	Nixon (R)	126,430	(70%)
	McGovern (D)	55,330	(30%)
1968	Nixon (R)	91,466	(57%)
	Humphrey (D)	56,472	(35%)
	Wallace (AI)	12,003	(8%)

Rep. Del Clawson (R) Elected June 11, 1963; b. Jan. 11, 1914, Thatcher, Ariz.; home, Downey; Gila Col.; Church of Latter Day Saints.

Career Missionary, Church of Latter Day Saints, 1931–33; Salesman and bookkeeper, 1934–41; U.S. Employment Svc., Fed. Pub. Housing Auth., 1941–47; Mgr., Mutual Housing Assoc. of Compton, 1947–63; Compton City Cncl., 1953–57, Mayor, 1957–64.

Offices 2349 RHOB, 202-225-3576. Also 11600 S. Paramount Blvd., Suite D, Downey 90241, 213-923-9206.

Committees

Budget (5th).

Rules (4th).

Group Ratings

	ADA	COPE	LWV	RIPON	NFU	LCV	CFA	NAB	NSI	ACA
1974	0	0	0	33	0	7	0	82	100	100
1973	0	10	20	50	11	4	14	–	–	100
1972	0	13	11	23	29	0	50	100	100	100

Key Votes

1) Foreign Aid	AGN	6) Gov Abortn Aid	AGN	11) Pub Cong Election $	AGN
2) Busing	AGN	7) Coed Phys Ed	AGN	12) Turkish Arms Cutoff	AGN
3) ABM	FOR	8) Pov Lawyer Gag	ABS	13) Youth Camp Regs	AGN
4) B-1 Bomber	FOR	9) Pub Trans Sub	AGN	14) Strip Mine Veto	FOR
5) Nerve Gas	FOR	10) EZ Voter Regis	AGN	15) Farm Bill Veto	FOR

Election Results

1974 general:	Del Clawson (R)	72,471	(53%)	($76,246)
	Robert E. (Bob) White (D)	58,492	(43%)	($56,364)
	James C. (Jim) Griffin (AI)	4,725	(3%)	($2,348)
1974 primary:	Del Clawson (R), unopposed			
1972 general:	Del Clawson (R)	120,313	(61%)	($65,007)
	Conrad G. Touhey (D)	75,546	(39%)	($45,844)

♦ ♦ ♦ ♦ ♦

THIRTY-FOURTH DISTRICT

Long Beach (pop. 358,000) is one of the few Los Angeles area suburbs with an urban character of its own. Long Beach has long had a man-made harbor competitive with L.A.'s San Pedro next door; and endowed with a beach that gave the city its name, Long Beach drew thousands of Midwestern migrants during the 1920s and 1930s, and built its own downtown and boardwalk-cum-amusement park. Back in the thirties, the large number of retirees here contributed to California's zany political reputation, its attachment to welfare schemes like the Townsend Plan and the Ham 'n' Eggs movement (the latter of which helped to win the Governorship for Earl Warren in 1942). Oldtimers can still recall the Iowa picnics of the same period which drew more than 50,000 people to Long Beach.

Today, the atmosphere of Long Beach is different. Most of the town is filled with ordinary middle-class people with families. And retirees are just as likely to live in developments like the self-contained Rossmoor Leisure World, just across the line in Orange County, as in the stucco walk-up apartments a couple of blocks from the ocean. Suburbia has grown out to Long Beach and absorbed it.

This newer Long Beach is still the largest single part, despite several boundary changes, of the 34th congressional district of California. Under the current plan, the district extends into Orange County, including half of Huntington Beach (pop. 115,000) as well as Leisure World; in Los Angeles County, the district includes more than half of Long Beach—generally speaking, the city's more prosperous part—and the middle-income suburbs of Lakewood and Bellflower. As thus pieced together by California's Supreme Court, the 34th is basically a Republican district; it has supported Republican candidates in the vast majority of elections in recent years. But not so in 1974.

This was the year Republican Congressman Craig Hosmer chose to retire. A House member for 22 years, Hosmer used his high seniority position on Interior to fight attempts to curb strip mining of coal; he also got known for a certain little-old-lady-in-tennis-shoes zaniness by proposing, some years ago, that the Air Force drop the Vietnamese equivalent of voodoo dolls on the Viet Cong. But Hosmer's chief hobbyhorse was atomic energy; he would never have run for Congress but for a desire to serve on the Joint Committee on Atomic Energy, a body which had a very close relationship to the Atomic Energy Commission it was supposed to govern. At the time of his retirement, Hosmer was ranking Republican on the Joint Committee; ironically, the AEC was split up into two agencies during his last year in Congress.

Hosmer's successor in any other political year would probably have been a Republican, and in 1974 the party's nomination was won by Assemblyman Bill Bond of Long Beach. The Democratic nominee, Mark Hannaford, was reasonably well known as Mayor of Lakewood, and with the help of a big home town vote was able to win in November. Hannaford is one of three Democrats, all suburban Mayors, who were elected to fill seats Republicans might reasonably have expected to win. All are expected to vote somewhat more conservatively than most California Democratic Congressmen, who tend to come from safe districts and to depend for much of their support from ideologically motivated volunteers. All three of these districts, certainly the 34th, will be contested vigorously by Republicans in 1976.

Census Data Pop. 464,336. Central city, 42%; suburban, 58%. Median family income, $11,831; families above $15,000: 31%; families below $3,000: 5%. Median years education, 12.5.

The Voters

Median voting age 42.
Employment profile White collar, 57%. Blue collar, 32%. Service, 11%. Farm, –%.
Ethnic groups Spanish, 8%. Total foreign stock, 20%. Canada, 3%; UK, Germany, 2% each; Italy, Netherlands, 1% each.

Presidential vote

1972	Nixon (R)	135,141	(66%)
	McGovern (D)	70,071	(34%)
1968	Nixon (R)	105,492	(56%)
	Humphrey (D)	69,699	(37%)
	Wallace (AI)	12,707	(7%)

Rep. Mark W. Hannaford (D) Elected 1974; b. Feb. 7, 1925, Woodrow, Colo.; home, Lakewood; Ball St. U., B.A. 1950, M.A. 1956, John Jay Fellowship, Yale U., 1961–62.

Career Air Force, WWII; Assoc. Prof. of Poli. Sci., Long Beach City Col., 1966–74; Lakewood City Cncl., 1966–74, Mayor, 1968–70, 1972–74.

Offices 315 CHOB, 202-225-2415. Also 5175 E. Pacific Coast Hwy., Suite 405, Long Beach 90804, 213-498-3381.

Committees

Banking, Currency and Housing (29th). Subcommittees: Domestic Monetary Policy; Historic Preservation and Coinage; International Trade, Investment and Monetary Policy.

Veterans' Affairs (14th). Subcommittees: Cemeteries and Burial Benefits; Education and Training; Hopsitals.

Group Ratings: Newly Elected

Key Votes

1) Foreign Aid	AGN	6) Gov Abortn Aid	NE	11) Pub Cong Election $	NE
2) Busing	NE	7) Coed Phys Ed	FOR	12) Turkish Arms Cutoff	NE
3) ABM	NE	8) Pov Lawyer Gag	NE	13) Youth Camp Regs	FOR
4) B-1 Bomber	ABS	9) Pub Trans Sub	NE	14) Strip Mine Veto	AGN
5) Nerve Gas	NE	10) EZ Voter Regis	NE	15) Farm Bill Veto	AGN

Election Results

1974 general:	Mark W. Hannaford (D)	81,151	(51%)	($86,981)
	Bill Bond (R)	75,426	(47%)	($82,917)
	James Manis (AI)	3,279	(2%)	($1,321)
1974 primary:	Mark W. Hannaford (D)	15,131	(24%)	
	Dennis Murray (D)	12,888	(21%)	
	Nine others (D)	34,755	(55%)	

♦ ♦ ♦ ♦ ♦

THIRTY-FIFTH DISTRICT

It is hard to say just which suburban Los Angeles County congressional district is the lineal descendant of the one represented by Richard M. Nixon from 1947 to 1951. There have been five redistrictings since then, and the territory included in Nixon's 12th district, much more populous today than it was then, is divided among several seats now. The 26th has a reasonable claim to be the Nixon district, but so does the 33d which contains Whittier, Nixon's home town, and the 35th probably contains more of the acreage of Nixon's 12th—plus the home town of Jerry Voorhis, the liberal Democrat Nixon beat—than any of the others.

At any rate, the 35th includes the eastern Los Angeles County suburbs of West Covina (which is much larger than neighboring Covina), and Pomona and Claremont which between them contain several high-quality small colleges. Then, just across the San Bernardino County line, are several other highish income places: Ontario (with its own jet-size airport), Montclair, and Upland.

As districted by the California Supreme Court, the 35th had no incumbent Congressman and definite Republican complexion—two factors which made it attractive indeed to Victor Veysey. Veysey was the two-term Congressman from the old, pre-redistricting 43d district which, unfortunately for him, had been as totally partitioned and split between its neighbors as Poland had in the eighteenth century. There was no territory in common between the two districts, but that did not prevent Veysey from moving his residence from Brawley in the desert to the 33d.

The situation, however, may have prevented Veysey from winning the 1974 general election. Certainly his opponent, West Covina Mayor Jim Lloyd used the carpetbag issue. (Parenthetically, one must say that the occasional success of the carpetbag issue in congressional elections is perplexing, since the winner of any such election, by virtue of having won, does not continue to live in the district in any sense we understand "live" to mean.) Lloyd was helped also by the Democratic trend of the year, and perhaps by the fact that he was considered a somewhat conservative Democrat in this not very liberal district. A 21-year veteran of the Navy, Lloyd is not expected to fit in especially smoothly to the dovish California Democratic delegation, although there has been little trouble as yet. In any case, now that he has secured all the facilities an incumbent Congressman enjoys he has a solid chance of winning again in 1976, although surely the Republicans, if not the itinerant Veysey (who now is an Assistant Secretary of Defense in Washington), will contest the seat strongly.

Census Data Pop. 464,185. Central city, 14%; suburban, 86%. Median family income, $11,265; families above $15,000: 28%; families below $3,000: 6%. Median years education, 12.4.

The Voters

Median voting age 40.
Employment profile White collar, 52%. Blue collar, 34%. Service, 12%. Farm, 2%.
Ethnic groups Black, 3%. Spanish, 15%. Total foreign stock, 20%. Canada, 3%; UK, Germany, Italy, 2% each.

Presidential vote

1972	Nixon (R)	107,616	(66%)
	McGovern (D)	55,895	(34%)

1968	Nixon (R)	86,010	(57%)
	Humphrey (D)	55,442	(36%)
	Wallace (AI)	10,743	(7%)

Rep. Jim Lloyd (D) Elected 1974; b. Sept. 27, 1922, Helena, Mont.; home, West Covina; U. of Oreg., Tulane U., Stanford U., B.A. 1958, USC, M.A. 1966.

Career Navy, 1942–63; Public Relations Dir., Aerojet General Corp., 1963–65; Founder, Lloyd's Public Relations and Advertising, 1966; West Covina City Cncl., 1968–74, Mayor, 1973; Instructor, Mt. San Antonio Co., 1970–73.

Offices 222 CHOB, 202-225-2305. Also Suite 507, 100 S. Vincent St., West Covina 91790, 213-339-7356.

Committees

Armed Services (25th). Subcommittees: Research and Development; Seapower and Strategic and Critical Materials.

Science and Technology (17th). Subcommittees: Aviation and Transportation Research and Development; Science, Research, and Technology; Space Science and Applications.

Group Ratings: Newly Elected

Key Votes

1) Foreign Aid	FOR	6) Gov Abortn Aid	NE	11) Pub Cong Election $	NE
2) Busing	NE	7) Coed Phys Ed	FOR	12) Turkish Arms Cutoff	NE
3) ABM	NE	8) Pov Lawyer Gag	NE	13) Youth Camp Regs	AGN
4) B-1 Bomber	FOR	9) Pub Trans Sub	NE	14) Strip Mine Veto	AGN
5) Nerve Gas	NE	10) EZ Voter Regis	NE	15) Farm Bill Veto	FOR

Election Results

1974 general:	Jim Lloyd (D)	61,903	(50%)	($153,087)
	Victor V. Veysey (R)	61,168	(50%)	($147,861)
1974 primary:	Jim Lloyd (D)	11,333	(24%)	
	Bob Stafford (D)	7,637	(16%)	
	George A. Kasem (D)	6,604	(14%)	
	Mary Montes (D)	6,005	(12%)	
	Six others (D)	16,595	(34%)	

◆ ◆ ◆ ◆ ◆

THIRTY-SIXTH DISTRICT

Whatever the statistics may say about the decline of social mobility in our society, there are still plenty of Horatio Alger stories in the United States Congress. One of them belongs to Representative George E. Brown, Jr. In the early 1950s, Brown was an industrial physicist living in Monterey Park, a middle-class suburb east of Los Angeles. With his crew cut and slight paunch, Brown was scarcely distinguishable from tens of thousands of Los Angeles-area scientists and engineers—but for his Quaker upbringing, a strong belief in disarmament and peace, and nascent political yearnings. In 1954, he ran for and won a seat on the Monterey Park City Council. His interest in government whetted, he tried for the state Assembly and, in the very Democratic year of 1958, won. There he found himself on the committee in charge of drawing the state's congressional district lines and allotting the eight new districts California had gained in the 1960 census. One of those new seats came to be centered on Monterey Park, and so George Brown became a Congressman in 1962.

The story doesn't end there. In the House, Brown was one of the original peaceniks, even before the big escalation of the Vietnam war in 1965. Because many of his constituents considered his positions on issues far out, he had to fight hard each two years to win reelection. But he did win, and in 1970 he decided to make a try for the Senate. It looked like a dubious move at first. But Republican Sen. George Murphy got in serious trouble when it was revealed that Technicolor, Inc., was paying him $20,000 a year while he was serving in the Senate. Then, just a month before the primary, Richard Nixon invaded Cambodia, and a strong wave of antiwar feeling propelled Brown upward in the polls. Brown's underfinanced campaign nearly brought him even with the favorite, then-Congressman John Tunney, and a switch of 99,000 votes out of 2.4 million cast would have given the peacenik the nomination and—judging from the size of Tunney's subsequent victory—the Senate seat as well.

There is more. Relatively few ex-Congressmen make it back to Washington nowadays; it is just too wrenching to return without all that seniority you once had. (But see Illinois 10, Indiana 11.) Nevertheless Brown, motivated more by desire for peace than by hunger for power, decided to try anyway. Once again, redistricting gave him his chance. In 1971, the legislature created a new 38th district in the eastern end of the Los Angeles Basin, at the intersection of Los Angeles, San Bernardino, and Riverside Counties. The district included all the most Democratic parts of San Bernardino and Riverside—the Mexican-American barrio, the local University of California campus, and the working-class subdivisions around the giant Kaiser Steel plant in Fontana. Everyone assumed it would go Democratic in November. The primary field was crowded, with no less than eight Democrats and three Republicans.

Brown, having moved his residence to Colton in the district, was the favorite and managed to squeak out a win with 28% of the votes. He beat not only San Bernardino County Supervisor Reuben Ayala (himself the surprise winner in a 1974 special state Senate election) but also David Tunno, a former aide of now-Sen. Tunney. The Republicans, in the person of nominee Howard Snider, a local Mayor, hoped to capture the seat; they had Tunno's support and the benefit of a last-minute appearance by Richard Nixon. But Brown managed a convincing 56–44 win, even while Nixon carried the district.

Brown returned to serve on the Science Committee, as he had before, and also got a seat, as one of its few urban liberal members, on Agriculture. He made relatively few waves this time, his very liberal voting record not being as distinctive in the more liberal Democratic caucus as it had ten years before. In 1974, the district had been altered once again, theoretically making it more difficult for Brown to win. But he did not have significant opposition, and got the largest percentage he has ever won—another measure of the cresting trend in California politics. Thanks to the retirements or defeats of more senior (and more conservative) Democrats, Brown now has surprisingly seniority on Agriculture (10th of 29 Democrats) and Science (10th of 25 Democrats). In addition, he has the pleasure of seeing these panels, by the infusion of freshmen, rendered several degrees more liberal—a startling change from years past. Brown has foresworn any further Senate runs (and is on good terms with Tunney); he is in a position to look forward to long and—far more than might have been predicted for such a liberal—effective House service.

Census Data Pop. 463,898. Central city, 46%; suburban, 54%. Median family income, $9,407; families above $15,000: 18%; families below $3,000: 10%. Median years education, 12.2.

The Voters

Median voting age 40.
Employment profile White collar, 47%. Blue collar, 37%. Service, 14%. Farm, 2%.
Ethnic groups Black, 7%. Spanish, 18%. Total foreign stock, 19%. Canada, 2%; UK, Germany, 1% each.

Presidential vote

1972	Nixon (R)	80,137	(53%)
	McGovern (D)	69,883	(47%)
1968	Nixon (R)	64,868	(45%)
	Humphrey (D)	66,158	(46%)
	Wallace (AI)	12,566	(9%)

Rep. George E. Brown, Jr. (D) Elected 1972; b. Mar. 6, 1920, Holtville; home, Colton; UCLA, B.A. 1946.

Career Army, WWII; Monterey Park City Cncl., Mayor. 1954–58; Personnel, Engineering, and Management Consultant, City of Los Angeles, 1957–61; Cal. Assembly, 1959–62; U.S. House of Reps., 1963–71; Candidate for Dem. nomination for U. S. Senate, 1970.

Offices 2342 RHOB, 202-225-6161. Also 552 N. LaCadena St., Colton 92934, 714-825-2472.

Committees

Agriculture (10th). Subcommittees: Department Operations, Investigations, and Oversight; Domestic Marketing and Consumer Relations; Forests.

Science and Technology (9th). Subcommittees: Energy Research, Development and Demonstration; Environment and the Atmosphere (Chairman); Science, Research, and Technology.

Group Ratings

	ADA	COPE	LWV	RIPON	NFU	LCV	CFA	NAB	NSI	ACA
1974	100	100	82	47	100	87	100	25	20	0
1973	96	91	91	58	100	94	100	–	–	13

Key Votes

1) Foreign Aid	AGN	6) Gov Abortn Aid	FOR	11) Pub Cong Election $	FOR
2) Busing	FOR	7) Coed Phys Ed	FOR	12) Turkish Arms Cutoff	ABS
3) ABM	AGN	8) Pov Lawyer Gag	AGN	13) Youth Camp Regs	FOR
4) B-1 Bomber	AGN	9) Pub Trans Sub	FOR	14) Strip Mine Veto	AGN
5) Nerve Gas	AGN	10) EZ Voter Regis	FOR	15) Farm Bill Veto	AGN

Election Results

1974 general:	George E. Brown, Jr. (D)	69,766	(63%)	($43,635)
	Jim Osgood (R)	35,938	(32%)	($21,412)
	William Emery Pasley (AI)	5,711	(5%)	($1,450)
1974 primary:	George E. Brown, Jr. (D)	38,517	(76%)	
	Cloden Adkins (D)	6,746	(13%)	
	Fritz Mendoza (D)	5,585	(11%)	
1972 general:	George E. Brown, Jr. (D)	77,922	(56%)	($154,743)
	Howard J. Snider (R)	60,459	(44%)	($108,537)

◆ ◆ ◆ ◆ ◆

THIRTY-SEVENTH DISTRICT

At 20,000 square miles, San Bernardino County, California, is the largest county in the United States—about the size of West Virginia. Most of this expanse is uninhabitable desert, taking up four of the five hours of driving time on any overland trip from Los Angeles to Las Vegas. Geographically, the county makes a nice rectangular package, as does California's 37th congressional district, which includes most of the land area of San Bernardino and, in addition, most of the land area of Riverside County, itself a sizeable one, stretching almost from the Ocean to the Colorado River. About 80% of the population of these two counties, however, is tucked away in their western corners, in the farthest eastern reach of the Los Angeles Basin. Just beyond, the mountains, raised by thousands of years of earthquakes, stand and separate the heavily populated Basin from the dry, hot desert.

The 37th district boundary straddles these mountains; about 40% of its population is in the Basin, the other 60% to the west. The former area is dominated by upper-income parts of San Bernardino and its suburb of Redlands; the latter by Palm Springs and the other desert towns that have increasingly become the haven of wealthy Californians in search of clean air. These are more retirement than family communities, and overall the 37th district has one of the highest median ages of any part of California.

Until his death in a plane crash in February 1975, the Congressman from the 37th district was Republican Jerry Pettis. A self-made millionaire, former professor at Loma Linda University, and the only Seventh Day Adventist in Congress, Pettis was an interesting man; though by no means an outspoken maverick, he ventured often enough from the orthodoxy of his party to indicate the presence of an original mind. He had succeeded to a place on the House Ways and Means Committee, and had been running ahead of his party in this already heavily Republican district; but for the fearsome winds that brought his plane down in one of the mountain passes of his district, he could have pursued his congressional career for many years more.

The winner of the spring 1975 special election was the Congressman's widow, Shirley Pettis. She won more than 50% of the vote against a field of Democrats and Republicans (including another, unrelated Pettis), and under the peculiar California special election law was thus elected. There is no indication she will have difficulty holding the seat in 1976.

Census Data Pop. 462,640. Central city, 7%; suburban, 93%. Median family income, $8,794; families above $15,000: 19%; families below $3,000: 11%. Median years education, 12.3.

The Voters

Median voting age 46.
Employment profile White collar, 49%. Blue collar, 30%. Service, 16%. Farm, 5%.
Ethnic groups Black, 3%. Spanish, 15%. Total foreign stock, 20%. Canada, UK, Germany, 2% each.

Presidential vote

1972	Nixon (R)	107,237	(66%)
	McGovern (D)	54,835	(34%)
1968	Nixon (R)	81,898	(55%)
	Humphrey (D)	53,571	(36%)
	Wallace (AI)	13,733	(9%)

Rep. Shirley N. Pettis (R) Elected Apr. 19, 1975; b. July 12, 1924, Mountain View; home, Loma Linda; Andrews U., U. of Cal.; Seventh Day Adventist.

Career Co-Operator of Magnetic Tape Duplicators Co. and Audio Digest Foundation; Manager of family ranch.

Offices 1021 LHOB, 202-225-5861. Also 942 E. Highland Ave., San Bernardino 92404, 714-862-6030.

Committees NA

Group Ratings: Newly Elected

Key Votes

1) Foreign Aid	NE	6) Gov Abortn Aid	NE	11) Pub Cong Election $	NE
2) Busing	NE	7) Coed Phys Ed	NE	12) Turkish Arms Cutoff	NE
3) ABM	NE	8) Pov Lawyer Gag	NE	13) Youth Camp Regs	NE
4) B-1 Bomber	FOR	9) Pub Trans Sub	NE	14) Strip Mine Veto	AGN
5) Nerve Gas	NE	10) EZ Voter Regis	NE	15) Farm Bill Veto	FOR

Election Results

1975 special:	Shirley N. Pettis (R)	53,165	(60%)	(NA)
	Ron Pettis (D)	12,940	(15%)	(NA)
	James L. Mayfield (D)	11,140	(13%)	(NA)
	Ten others	10,637	(12%)	(NA)

◆ ◆ ◆ ◆ ◆

THIRTY-EIGHTH DISTRICT

"Orange County" are two words that have come to be a synonym for "conservative" in this country. Twenty years ago, Orange County, California, had all the notoriety that usually comes to a few thousand acres of citrus trees; its 1950 population was 216,000. By 1970 that figure had grown to 1,420,000. During this period of turbulent growth, Orange County has consistently turned in some of the highest Republican percentages in California (see also California 40), and, in some elections at least, in the whole country. Yet Orange County is not as monolithically conservative and Republican as is generally supposed. And one bit of evidence for that is the fact that it includes a congressional district, the 38th, which—through several redistrictings—has been held by Democrats since it was created in 1962.

Roughly speaking, the district includes the central portion of the heavily populated eastern half of Orange County, halfway between the Ocean and the hills which separate it from the San Gabriel valley of Los Angeles County. In its current borders, the 38th includes most of Santa Ana (including its predominantly Mexican-American community), virtually all of Garden Grove, and the bulk of the factory-worker suburbs of Buena Park, Stanton, and Westminster. These are places one could scarcely mistake for high-income areas, whether one is speeding by at 70 on the freeway, or driving down the little cul-de-sacs and curving streets favored by 1950s and 1960s developers for even the squarest tracts of land.

For 12 years the predecessor of the current 38th district, then numbered the 34th, was held by Richard T. Hanna, a genial, joke-telling, and, in his later years in Congress, bearded Democrat. Hanna had, as most Orange County Democrats must, several secrets for survival: careful redistricting (always done to incumbents' specifications, thanks to Phil Burton of San Francisco), a computerized list of 90,000 pro-Hanna voters, a good rapport (and a seat on Banking and Currency) with local savings and loans magnates, who of course had made huge fortunes off Orange County's growth. Still, Hanna was almost defeated in 1968, and in October 1972 he felt free (obliged?) to vote against Wright Patman's proposed investigation of the Watergate scandal. In his later years in Congress, Hanna had become an inveterate junketeer, with burgeoning business interests in places like Asia; in 1974, to pursue them, he retired from Congress at the youthful age of 60.

Naturally, with Hanna out of the way, the Republicans made a determined effort to capture the district, and it helped that the Supreme Court redistricting plan which settled the boundaries of the 38th district was not quite as favorable to the Democrats as previous districtings had been. The Republican candidate was a Vietnam war POW, Kenneth Rehmann; the Democrat, the Mayor of Santa Ana, Jerry Patterson. Around the land, there was a common assumption that voters would flock to the banners of POWs in 1974 just as they had elected discharged GIs of 1946 and 1948 (e.g., John Kennedy, Richard Nixon, Carl Albert, Gerald Ford, etc., etc.). But Vietnam was not WWII, and in 1974 not a single POW won a congressional election. Even in Orange County, the solidly conservative Rehmann was defeated by Patterson. The new Democratic Congressman will presumably have available to him at least some of the electioneering advantages which Hanna put to such successful use, and has probably a better than even chance of surviving in 1976. But unless all the air has gone out of the Republican Party by then—an unlikely prospect, despite repeated speculation—this will be one of the most spiritedly contested seats in California in that year.

Census Data Pop. 463,879. Central city, 56%; suburban, 44%. Median family income, $11,367; families above $15,000: 26%; families below $3,000: 5%. Median years education, 12.3.

The Voters

Median voting age 38.
Employment profile White collar, 48%. Blue collar, 39%. Service, 12%. Farm, 1%.
Ethnic groups Black, 2%. Spanish, 16%. Total foreign stock 20%. Canada, 3%; UK, 2%; Germany, Italy, 1% each.

Presidential vote

1972	Nixon (R)	107,451	(68%)
	McGovern (D)	50,126	(32%)
1968	Nixon (R)	75,642	(54%)
	Humphrey (D)	50,701	(37%)
	Wallace (AI)	12,649	(9%)

Rep. Jerry M. Patterson (D) Elected 1974; b. Oct. 25, 1934, El Paso, Tex.; home, Santa Ana; Long Beach St. U., B.A. 1960, UCLA, J.D. 1966; Congregationalist.

Career Coast Guard, 1953–57; Practicing atty., 1967–74; Santa Ana City Cncl., 1969–73, Mayor, 1973–74.

Offices 507 CHOB, 202-225-2965. Also 1200 N. Main St., Suite 214, Santa Ana 92701, 714-835-3811.

Committees

Banking, Currency and Housing (18th). Subcommittees: Economic Stabilization; Financial Institutions Supervision, Regulation and Insurance; Housing and Community Development.

Merchant Marine and Fisheries (25th). Subcommittees: Coastguard and Navigation; Fisheries and Wildlife Conservation and the Environment; Merchant Marine.

Group Ratings: Newly Elected

Key Votes

1) Foreign Aid	AGN	6) Gov Abortn Aid	NE	11) Pub Cong Election $	NE
2) Busing	NE	7) Coed Phys Ed	ABS	12) Turkish Arms Cutoff	NE
3) ABM	NE	8) Pov Lawyer Gag	NE	13) Youth Camp Regs	FOR
4) B-1 Bomber	FOR	9) Pub Trans Sub	NE	14) Strip Mine Veto	AGN
5) Nerve Gas	NE	10) EZ Voter Regis	NE	15) Farm Bill Veto	AGN

Election Results

1974 general:	Jerry M. Patterson (D)	68,335	(55%)	($165,696)
	David Rehmann (R)	52,207	(42%)	($120,744)
	Lee R. Rayburn (AI)	4,034	(3%)	($550)
1974 primary:	Jerry M. Patterson (D)	22,051	(47%)	
	Howard Adler (D)	17,134	(36%)	
	Leonard R. Holland (D)	5,850	(12%)	
	Albert E. Nasser (D)	2,358	(5%)	

◆ ◆ ◆ ◆ ◆

THIRTY-NINTH DISTRICT

One of the indisputable stars of the House Judiciary Committee hearings—and the only one on the side that history will record as wrong—was Congressman Charles Wiggins of the 39th district of California. On every point, over every disputed article, Wiggins was there to make the case for Richard Nixon, or at least the case that the case had not been made against Richard Nixon. He argued every point ably, often eloquently, in perfectly formed but at the same time easy, colloquial sentences, punctuated only occasionally—and even then their meaning was clear—with relevant legalisms. With his early 1960s style wavy gray hair, his mod suits, his air of assurance and concern, he looked like a competent, prosperous suburban trial lawyer—the kind of trial lawyer one would want on one's side if one ever got in trouble.

And that is precisely what Charles Wiggins was, ten years ago, before he was first elected to Congress in 1966—living proof of the proposition that there are talented people all over, out there in the boondocks, and on all sides of most questions. For Wiggins had not been affiliated with one of the big, prestigious Los Angeles law firms; he had practiced law out of his own small office in the suburbs east of Los Angeles, the same place where Richard Nixon first ran for Congress; and he had served, as Nixon never had, in local government, as Mayor and Councilman of his small suburb of El Monte.

It happens that El Monte is a Democratic suburb and was then in a district represented by a Democratic Congressman, but Wiggins' persuasiveness—and the fact that it was a good Republican year—won him the seat in 1966. He was immediately spotted as something of a Republican moderate, perhaps because many observers assume that intelligence is an indication of liberality; but of course he was a conservative, and often in the classic sense. Before impeachment, his most public moment came in the House when he led the floor fight against the Equal Rights Amendment—a fight he must have known he was going to lose, but thought should be made. It is typical of his prickly integrity that Wiggins also worked against the school-prayer amendment—a perennial electioneering subject for conservative Republicans—because he also believed that it was wrong.

And that, just about everyone had to concede was his motivation in leading the fight for Richard Nixon on the Judiciary Committee. More ably than any White House flack, Wiggins was making points for the President. He believed that impeachment was a dire remedy, to be resorted to in only the clearest of cases, and though he was, obviously, sincerely troubled by some of the things the Nixon White House and Nixon himself had done, he did not think impeachment was warranted. The facts, he felt, were consistent with other, innocent hypotheses, and he made that case as often, and as forcefully as he could. The moral authority he established while making it was nowise better evidenced by the fact that General Haig chose Wiggins to inspect, before anyone else in Congress, the June 23 tapes that so clearly incriminated Nixon. Wiggins' own sincerity is made plain by his response: he read them through three times, and told Haig that he could no longer defend Nixon; he made it clear that if these tapes were not published by the White House, he would make public their contents himself. That was the end, of course, for Richard Nixon, and for Charles Wiggins' great fight for him—a fight, it had already become clear, he would lose in the full House and lose in the Senate, but which would be fought well nonetheless.

Ironically, Wiggins was representing, at the time all this was happening, an eastern Los Angeles County district which included much of the territory that had elected Nixon to Congress in 1946 and 1948. The district lines have changed now and Wiggins now sits for an entirely Orange County district, which includes Nixon's birthplace. This 39th district is the northwest corner of Orange County, a solidly conservative Republican collection of well-to-do suburbs: Anaheim (home of Disneyland and Angels Stadium), Fullerton, Orange, La Habra, Brea. It is one of the two or three most solidly Republican districts in the state; Wiggins might have been in political trouble for opposing Nixon, but not here for supporting him. His 55% of the vote in 1974 was about as weak as possible. Wiggins has said that he is not wedded to the idea of a congressional career, and might like to retire sometime while he can still accumulate a good estate before retiring; if he does choose to do so, we can be sure that a conservative Republican, though probably not so articulate and perhaps not so principled a one, will represent this district.

Census Data Pop. 463,836. Central city, 33%; suburban, 67%. Median family income, $12,749; families above $15,000: 37%; families below $3,000: 5%. Median years education, 12.6.

The Voters

Median voting age 40.
Employment profile White collar, 60%. Blue collar, 28%. Service, 11%. Farm, 1%.
Ethnic groups Spanish, 11%. Total foreign stock, 19%. Canada, 3%; UK, Germany, 2% each; Italy, 1%.

Presidential vote

1972	Nixon (R)	142,003	(73%)
	McGovern (D)	53,220	(27%)
1968	Nixon (R)	107,183	(65%)
	Humphrey (D)	47,182	(29%)
	Wallace (AI)	10,097	(6%)

Rep. Charles E. Wiggins (R) Elected 1966; b. Dec. 3, 1927, El Monte; home, Fullerton; USC, B.S. 1953, LL.B. 1956; Methodist.

Career Army, WWII and Korea; Practicing atty., 1957–66; Chm., El Monte Planning Comm., 1954–60; El Monte City Cncl., Mayor, 1960–66.

Offices 2445 RHOB, 202-225-4111. Also 1400 N. Harbor Blvd., Fullerton 92635, 714-870-7266.

Committees

House Administration (4th). Subcommittees: Elections; Personnel and Police; Printing.

Judiciary (4th). Subcommittees: Courts, Civil Liberties; and the Administration of Justics; Criminal Justice.

Group Ratings

	ADA	COPE	LWV	RIPON	NFU	LCV	CFA	NAB	NSI	ACA
1974	23	9	33	88	23	25	0	80	89	73
1973	13	0	45	55	6	28	25	–	–	86
1972	6	13	56	60	29	40	50	100	100	63

Key Votes

1) Foreign Aid	FOR	6) Gov Abortn Aid	AGN	11) Pub Cong Election $	AGN
2) Busing	AGN	7) Coed Phys Ed	AGN	12) Turkish Arms Cutoff	AGN
3) ABM	FOR	8) Pov Lawyer Gag	FOR	13) Youth Camp Regs	AGN
4) B-1 Bomber	FOR	9) Pub Trans Sub	AGN	14) Strip Mine Veto	AGN
5) Nerve Gas	FOR	10) EZ Voter Regis	AGN	15) Farm Bill Veto	FOR

Election Results

1974 general:	Charles E. Wiggins (R)	89,220	(55%)	($53,292)
	William E. "Bill" Farris (D)	65,170	(40%)	($26,533)
	Pat P. Scalera (AI)	7,056	(4%)	($1,037)
1974 primary:	Charles E. Wiggins (R)	41,683	(74%)	
	Robert C. Ashley (R)	7,351	(13%)	
	Thurston A. Shinn (R)	7,024	(13%)	
1972 general:	Charles E. Wiggins (R)	118,631	(65%)	($34,643)
	Leslie W. Craven (D)	58,323	(32%)	($5,925)
	Alfred Ramirez (AI)	5,697	(3%)	(NA)

◆ ◆ ◆ ◆ ◆

FORTIETH DISTRICT

Only four congressional districts in the country more than doubled their populations during the 1960s. The one with by far the greatest growth—its population rose 130% in 10 years—was the 40th district of California, one of the three districts lying predominantly within the boundaries of Richard Nixon's birthplace and home turf, Orange County. Here one can find Nixon's forlorn estate at San Clemente, some miles up on the Pacific Coast Highway, the gleaming high rise on whose top floor Nixon's personal lawyer, Herbert Kalmbach, had his offices—and from which he went forth to collect the boodle. Watergate may be a building in Washington, but the scandal which brought Nixon down has just as many landmarks here in Orange County.

Long before Watergate, Orange County entered our political vocabulary as a synonym for conservative. The county's population grew at an astronomical rate—from 216,000 in 1950 to 703,000 in 1960 and 1,420,000 in 1970. Its Republican margins grew even faster. And the Republicans here were uniformly of the rightist variety. The Santa Ana *Register*, the paper with the largest circulation in the County, considered local boy Nixon a dangerous leftist; it was the *Register* which first printed articles about the unusual financing of San Clemente.

Why is Orange County so very conservative? There is a working assumption among political analysts that wealth produces conservatism. But that simple equation does not explain the situation here. The median income of the 40th district, to be sure, is high, but it is exceeded by that of eight other California districts, none of which produces Republican margins like the 40th (with one exception: the Orange County 39th district). There is wealth in Orange County, but most of the millionaires of greater Los Angeles live elsewhere, around Beverly Hills or San Marino. What is distinctive about the income levels in the 40th district is not how high they are, but how homogeneous: 69% of the families in 1970 had incomes between $7,000 and $24,000. These are similar kinds of subdivisions, all of which sprang up within a few years of each other.

Undergirding the economy of the 40th district is the defense industry. The middle class here is made up, more than is usual, of engineers, technicians, draftsmen—people who tend to be comfortable with techological precision and apprehensive about social change. Orange County has not provided them with a comfortable environment—contrary to their expectations. The fantastic growth that has made Orange County possible has also produced surroundings that convey little permanence; the 40th district is full of shopping centers and subdivions which did not exist ten years ago and which in another ten may be decaying.

Even more frightening to people who seek order and calm, Orange County has not been able to restore the old values of the left-behind Midwest or South, or to produce anything satisfactory to take their place. Orange Countians who sought a bucolic life are baffled by the habits of their own children, who prefer rock music to whatever their parents might like. The beleaguered residents of Orange County are the bedrock of southern California conservatism. They are men and women who have achieved modest success by most standards. When that success and their values were sneered at by outsiders and by their own children, they sought comfort in politics. And they found it, for a while at least, in the rhetoric of Ronald Reagan and Richard Nixon.

Now Reagan is gone from office, probably unelectable in California, and Nixon has resigned in disgrace. Only a few miles of vacant land remain between the subdivisions and the mountains, most of it part of the 80,000-acre Irvine Ranch, the most valuable piece of undeveloped property in the world. But in the wake of aircraft industry cutbacks, Orange County property is not always worth what it once was; the boom is over.

Even before Watergate, even in Orange County, the Reagan-Nixon politics was not working as before. Its rhetoric promised more than it could deliver. A politics based on economics can work; it can make the poor or the rich (or perhaps both) richer. But a politics based on the notion of reestablishing an imagined home-town moral order could not work in the long run. Reagan and Nixon could tell the people of Orange County that their basic impulses were right (even racial prejudice) and that there was nothing wrong with America and Orange County except their detractors. But neither Reagan nor Nixon could produce victory in a war most Americans believed was stupid, or make authentic popular heroes of the POW's. Nor could they stop the growth of the counterculture, or still the voices of angry blacks.

Watergate was the final irony. The very men who worked so hard to convince Americans that our government and our leaders were fundamentally decent and honest managed to demonstrate conclusively that just the opposite was true. Ronald Reagan could claim, as he did, that the people who planned and covered up the Watergate were not "criminals at heart"; but they were criminals according to the law, and in the settled judgment of the American people.

That consensus does not necessarily include everyone in Orange County or the 40th district, of course; and this remains the most Republican part of California. But the enthusiasm, the elan of the right here has vanished. As for the average conservative voter, turnout was down sharply in 1974. Which was no problem for Congressman Andrew Hinshaw, a conservative Republican, who first won the seat in 1972 when he beat ultra-conservative, John Birch Society member John Schmitz in the Republican primary. (Schmitz then became the American Independent Party candidate for President, winning few votes, but certainly qualifying as the contender with the best sense of humor.) But it was not long before Hinshaw was in trouble, too. Before his election to Congress, Hinshaw had been Orange County Assessor, and had been credited with doing a competent, honest job in an office which must have been full of temptations in those fast-growing years. But in the spring of 1975 he was indicted on bribery charges, and his political career put under a shadow. Unless he is cleared (there has been no trial at this writing), it seems almost certain he will be replaced by another conservative Republican (Schmitz?) in 1976.

Census Data   Pop. 464,254. Central city, 7%; suburban, 93%. Median family income, $12,093; families above $15,000: 35%; families below $3,000: 6%. Median years education, 12.8.

The Voters

Median voting age 37.
Employment profile White collar, 64%. Blue collar, 23%. Service, 12%. Farm, 1%.
Ethnic groups Black, 1%. Spanish, 8%. Total foreign stock, 19%. Canada, UK, 3% each; Germany, 2%; Italy, 1%.

Presidential vote

1972	Nixon (R)		157,926	(73%)
	McGovern (D)		59,110	(27%)
1968	Nixon (R)		98,841	(68%)
	Humphrey (D)		38,505	(27%)
	Wallace (AI)		7,604	(5%)

Rep. Andrew J. Hinshaw (R) Elected 1972; b. Aug. 4, 1923, Dexter, Mo.; home, Newport Beach; USC, B.S. 1950, USC School of Law, 1953–54.

Career Navy, WWII; Appraiser, L.A. Co. Assessor's Ofc., 1949-54; Sr. Appraiser, Cal. St. Board of Equalization, 1954–64; Orange Co. Assessor, 1965–72.

Offices 1128 LHOB, 202-225-5611. Also 811 N. Broadway, Santa Ana 92701, 714-836-2611.

Committees

Armed Services (12th). Subcommittees: Military Installations and Facilities; Research and Development.

Post Office and Civil Service (4th). Subcommittees: Census and Population; Postal Facilities, Mail, and Labor Management.

Joint Committee on Atomic Energy (4th, House Side). Subcommittees: National Security; ERDA, Nuclear Energy.

Group Ratings

	ADA	COPE	LWV	RIPON	NFU	LCV	CFA	NAB	NSI	ACA
1974	5	0	40	53	25	25	31	73	88	73
1973	4	9	22	83	10	28	13	–	–	92

Key Votes

1) Foreign Aid	AGN	6) Gov Abortn Aid	ABS	11) Pub Cong Election $	AGN
2) Busing	AGN	7) Coed Phys Ed	AGN	12) Turkish Arms Cutoff	AGN
3) ABM	FOR	8) Pov Lawyer Gag	ABS	13) Youth Camp Regs	AGN
4) B-1 Bomber	FOR	9) Pub Trans Sub	AGN	14) Strip Mine Veto	FOR
5) Nerve Gas	FOR	10) EZ Voter Regis	AGN	15) Farm Bill Veto	ABS

Election Results

1974 general:	Andrew Hinshaw (R)	116,449	(63%)	($72,022)
	Roderick J. "Rod" Wilson (D)	56,850	(31%)	($11,781)
	Grayson L. Watkins (AI)	10,498	(6%)	($1,241)
1974 primary:	Andrew Hinshaw (R)	52,929	(69%)	
	David C. Gubler (R)	13,150	(17%)	
	Roger G. Lamphear (R)	5,560	(7%)	
	Earl H. Carraway (R)	4,547	(6%)	
1972 general:	Andrew Hinshaw (R)	149,081	(66%)	($161,814)
	John W. Black (D)	77,817	(34%)	($10,515)

◆ ◆ ◆ ◆ ◆

FORTY-FIRST DISTRICT

San Diego is Navy country: Navy ships, Navy air stations, Navy training centers, Navy wives, Navy widows, Navy retirees, and Navy officers, at least when they are not at sea. San Diego is the home of the U.S. Navy's West Coast headquarters, and the Navy has literally made this city what it is today. Back before World War II, this was a small backward city with a pronounced Mexican flavor. Then the Navy came in, attracted by the superb natural harbor—and by the year-round sun, so much warmer than San Francisco. Now San Diego is a booming, WASPish, conservative city of 696,000 people, with almost that many again in its mostly comfortable suburbs.

Richard Nixon used to regard San Diego as his "lucky city", and at least till 1972 it was. San Diego could always be counted on to produce a large Republican margin on election day, and it was the San Diego *Union,* the flagship of the right-wing Copley chain, that harbored Nixon pressman Herb Klein between stints working for Nixon. Almost all the leading businessmen of San Diego, notably banker C. Arnholt Smith, were big Nixon campaign contributors, and Nixon always received a warm reception in the city. And so it was not so surprising that Richard Nixon chose San Diego, just a few miles down the sunny coast from San Clemente, to host the 1972 Republican national convention.

There were a few problems, however, as it came time to implement that decision in 1972. San Diego did not have much in the way of convention facilities or hotel rooms. California politicians like then Lieutenant Governor Ed Reinecke and San Diego Congressman Bob Wilson worked with campaign manager John Mitchell to smooth over some of the problems. And ITT—whose new San Diego hotels would receive needed publicity from the affair—agreed to guarantee the Republicans $400,000; perhaps, but probably not, coincidentally, a nasty antitrust case was settled on terms agreeable to ITT by John Mitchell's Justice Department. The story came out in the hearings on Richard Kleindienst's nomination to succeed Mitchell; Kleindienst and Reinecke have since both been adjudged guilty of lying in those hearings. The convention was rescheduled—purportedly because of the lack of hotel rooms, a problem that was known early on—to Miami Beach.

That is not all the bad luck to emanate from this episode, of course. Richard Nixon was forced out of the Presidency and had to be pardoned by his successor to avoid criminal prosecution. And C. Arnholt Smith, a close personal friend of Nixon's, saw his financial empire collapse and was named defendant in the largest income tax evasion case ever brought by the government.

In the course of all these events, the political environment of San Diego, and especially of that part of it contained within the 41st congressional district, has been changed. The district includes most of the city's more comfortable neighborhoods, like Mission Bay, and few of its black or Mexican-American slums; it is full of retired Navy personnel, who usually have strong right-wing views. But the 41st district also includes San Diego State College and the University of San Diego, and, increasingly, a younger population; the newer retirement subdivisions are being built in the hills of the city beyond the district, or in the suburbs. And, in the wake of ITT and Watergate, this part of the city has been showing increasingly liberal voting habits. The city's Mayor is a Republican moderate, Peter Wilson, who wants some limits on San Diego's hitherto rapid growth; and San Diego County is represented in the California Assembly by four Democrats and only one Republican.

Even the tenure of Bob Wilson (a friend of ITT's Harold Geneen and Dita Beard) was threatened in the election of 1974. Long the possessor of one of the safest of safe Republican seats, Wilson had not been accustomed to campaigning hard at home. Instead, he had served as chairman of the House Republican Congressional Campaign Committee, until he was unceremoniously dumped by the Nixon people in 1973. The next year his opponent was a 29-year-old teacher named Colleen O'Connor, a liberal Democrat who had won the nomination in a multi-candidate field and promised to take the ITT scandal and jam it down Wilson's throat. O'Connor attracted considerable attention by swimming several miles of ocean off San Diego's beaches; when asked whether she was scared of sharks, she replied, "If I can take care of the sharks in the Pacific Ocean, I can handle the jellyfish in Washington."

Wilson, of course, had all the support the local media and the big money in San Diego could give him, but what may have made the difference in the end was a critical mistake by O'Connor. She had limited her general election campaign spending to a single year's salary, $42,500–an attractive enough slogan, but one that makes little sense when one remembers that people run for Congress these days not for the money, but for power and what they can do with it. Unfortunately for her cause, that amount is simply not enough to win; few challengers have beaten an incumbent while spending so little in at least ten years. The upshot was a somewhat larger than expected, 54-53 Wilson victory.

Will Wilson face as vigorous a challenger in 1976? It seems not so likely: he won in what most people regard as the heaviest Democratic year likely to be seen for some time. But there does seem to be a ferment of liberal activity—and Democratic political successes—in San Diego, enough perhaps to cause him more electoral problems in the future than he ever had to face in that vanished past before 1974.

Census Data Pop. 464,046. Central city, 89%; suburban, 11%. Median family income, $11,118; families above $15,000: 29%; families below $3,000: 7%. Median years education, 12.6.

The Voters

Median voting age 39.
Employment profile White collar, 64%. Blue collar, 23%. Service, 13%. Farm, –%.
Ethnic groups Black, 1%. Spanish, 9%. Total foreign stock, 21%. Canada, 3%; UK, Germany, 2% each; Italy, 1%.

Presidential vote

1972	Nixon (R)	135,629	(63%)
	McGovern (D)	79,660	(37%)
1968	Nixon (R)	105,886	(60%)
	Humphrey (D)	61,498	(35%)
	Wallace (AI)	10,470	(6%)

Rep. Bob Wilson (R) Elected 1952; b. April 5, 1916, Calexico; home, San Diego; San Diego St. Col., 1933–35, Otis Art. Inst.; Presbyterian.

Career Advertising, public relations.

Offices 2307 RHOB, 202-225-3201. Also Suite E285, 123 Camino de la Reina, San Diego 92108, 714-299-2444.

Committees

Armed Services (Ranking Member). Subcommittees: Seapower and Strategic and Critical Materials; Special Subcommittee on Intelligence.

Group Ratings

	ADA	COPE	LWV	RIPON	NFU	LCV	CFA	NAB	NSI	ACA
1974	9	0	40	56	43	19	8	75	89	50
1973	0	30	40	67	17	25	14	–	–	80
1972	6	18	30	67	17	4	0	91	100	68

Key Votes

1) Foreign Aid	FOR	6) Gov Abortn Aid	AGN	11) Pub Cong Election $	AGN
2) Busing	AGN	7) Coed Phys Ed	AGN	12) Turkish Arms Cutoff	AGN
3) ABM	FOR	8) Pov Lawyer Gag	FOR	13) Youth Camp Regs	AGN
4) B-1 Bomber	FOR	9) Pub Trans Sub	AGN	14) Strip Mine Veto	FOR
5) Nerve Gas	FOR	10) EZ Voter Regis	AGN	15) Farm Bill Veto	FOR

Election Results

1974 general:	Bob Wilson (R)	94,709	(54%)	($149,467)
	Colleen Marie O'Connor (D)	74,823	(43%)	($51,980)
	Robert W. Franson (AI)	4,354	(3%)	($744)
1974 primary:	Bob Wilson (R), unopposed			
1972 general:	Bob Wilson (R)	155,269	(69%)	($32,066)
	Frank Caprio (D)	69,377	(31%)	($7,349)

◆ ◆ ◆ ◆ ◆

FORTY-SECOND DISTRICT

To many, San Diego evokes images of La Jolla, its shopping streets lined with boutiques and stockbrokers' offices, or Mission Bay, with its comfortable rambling homes of retired Naval officers, or perhaps just a picture of the magnificent Balboa Park Zoo. But there is another San Diego, just a few miles away, down by the docks and on the flat, dusty land going down to Tijuana. It is here where most of the city's blacks and Mexican-Americans reside, on the south side of San Diego and in the dockside suburbs of Chula Vista and National City. Together with a few suburbs and some middle-class neighborhoods, this poorer, blacker, browner part of San Diego makes up the 42d congressional district of California, the only San Diego district held by a Democrat.

This is, indeed, the only part of the San Diego area with traditional Democratic voting habits. When it came time, after the 1960 census, to create a second district in the area, the Democratic legislature made sure that all the heavily Democratic territory was contained in this seat, and it has been ever since. The first and, so far, only Congressman has been Democrat Lionel Van Deerlin, a former TV newscaster and editorialist. A generally liberal Democrat, Van Deerlin has by now achieved considerable seniority on the Commerce Committee and, finally in 1975, a subcommittee chairmanship. Van Deerlin generally votes with the pro-consumer bloc on the committee—a group which ordinarily lost most issues until the committee's membership was altered by the vast influx of liberal Democratic freshmen after the 1974 election.

But if one were to guess what history would remember, at least at this stage of his career, about Van Deerlin's career in Congress, it would be something that happened just after the most recent Republican landslide election, as Congress convened in 1967. Van Deerlin then was the first member to urge the ouster of then House Education and Labor Committee Chairman Adam Clayton Powell. Almost immediately a kind of hysteria swept the House. Members who would have grumbled only a bit, and then certainly privately, were complaining openly and bitterly about Powell's abuse of his powers—and the way he flaunted them. They reflected public opinion accurately: the American people were ready to put up with such shenanigans from white congressmen quietly; but when a black congressman was doing it, it had to stop immediately. Van Deerlin soon lost control of the anti-Powell movement, and so did everyone else. The House voted to oust Powell, and he vanished to Bimini, to be reelected again by his Harlem constituents but never again, in any meaningful sense, to serve. Two years later the Supreme Court, in Earl Warren's last major decision, would rule that the House acted unconstitutionally: it could have expelled Powell once he had been seated, but it could not prevent him from taking office, as it did, in the face of having obviously met the constitutional requirements. It was an ugly moment in our history, reflecting credit on just about no one; and Lionel Van Deerlin, for one, has not sought the national spotlight since.

Census Data   Pop. 464,208. Central city, 53%; suburban, 47%. Median family income, $8,960; families above $15,000: 16%; families below $3,000: 11%. Median years education, 12.2.

The Voters

Median voting age 35.
Employment profile White collar, 46%. Blue collar, 36%. Service, 17%. Farm, 1%.
Ethnic groups Black, 11%. Filipino, 2%. Spanish, 19%. Total foreign stock, 23%. Canada, 2%; UK, Germany, Italy, 1% each.

Presidential vote

1972	Nixon (R)	76,127	(57%)
	McGovern (D)	58,538	(43%)
1968	Nixon (R)	55,467	(45%)
	Humphrey (D)	57,228	(47%)
	Wallace (AI)	10,223	(8%)

Rep. Lionel Van Deerlin (D) Elected 1962; b. July 25, 1914, Los Angeles; home, San Diego; USC, B.A., 1937; Episcopalian.

Career Reporter and desk man, Minneapolis *Tribune*, Baltimore *Evening Sun*; City Ed., San Diego *Journal*; Army, WWII; News Director, San Diego TV Stations KFSD and XETV.

Offices 2427 RHOB, 202-225-5672. Also P.O. Box 729, San Diego 92112, 714-329-1708.

Committees

House Administration (12th). Subcommittees: Elections; Personnel and Police; Printing.

Interstate and Foreign Commerce (6th). Subcommittees: Consumer Protection and Finance (Chairman).

Group Ratings

	ADA	COPE	LWV	RIPON	NFU	LCV	CFA	NAB	NSI	ACA
1974	87	100	83	75	77	81	85	30	20	14
1973	83	91	92	71	84	81	100	–	–	8
1972	88	100	100	87	71	74	0	11	30	14

Key Votes

1) Foreign Aid	AGN	6) Gov Abortn Aid	FOR	11) Pub Cong Election $	FOR
2) Busing	FOR	7) Coed Phys Ed	AGN	12) Turkish Arms Cutoff	FOR
3) ABM	AGN	8) Pov Lawyer Gag	AGN	13) Youth Camp Regs	AGN
4) B-1 Bomber	FOR	9) Pub Trans Sub	FOR	14) Strip Mine Veto	AGN
5) Nerve Gas	AGN	10) EZ Voter Regis	FOR	15) Farm Bill Veto	FOR

Election Results

1974 general:	Lionel Van Deerlin (D)	70,579	(70%)	($38,462)
	Wes Marden (R)	30,435	(30%)	($10,555)
1974 primary:	Lionel Van Deerlin (D), unopposed			
1972 general:	Lionel Van Deerlin (D)	116,980	(74%)	($44,931)
	D. Richard Kau (R)	40,997	(26%)	($15,776)

◆ ◆ ◆ ◆ ◆

FORTY-THIRD DISTRICT

The 41st and 42d districts of California include most of the city of San Diego; the 43d includes almost all the rest of San Diego County, plus Imperial County and a small slice of Riverside County as well. This district has a somewhat complex history; suffice it to say that in its present form it includes most of the political base of Representative Clair Burgener (the San Diego suburbs), plus some territory that used to belong to Representative Victor Veysey. (The latter, knowing that Burgener would win any primary between them, moved to the newly created 35th district, but was beaten in the Democratic year of 1974 and is now an Assistant Secretary of the Army.) Most of the population of the new district is clustered around San Diego: the beach towns of Del Mar, Leucadia, and Carlsbad along the Ocean to the north; inland hill suburbs like Escondido; and the residential middle-class enclaves east of the city like El Cajon and Spring Valley. Farther inland one comes to the Indian reservations that dot the interior mountains. Across the mountains is the Imperial Valley, an incredibly rich agricultural area whose large landowners like to think of themselves as the last bastion of free enterprise but are actually the direct beneficiaries of millions of dollars the federal government has spent on irrigation projects.

Congressman Burgener, first elected in 1972, votes like a standard conservative Republican —which is surely in accord with the wishes of most of his constituents. A former state legislator, he was widely respected in Sacramento for his work on welfare legislation; in Washington, he has attracted little notice but won a seat on the Appropriations Committee in 1975. That Burgener is not just a run-of-the-mill legislator, however, is indicated by a proposal he has made, which cannot have pleased many of his senior colleagues: he believes no one should be allowed to serve in the Congress past age 70. In his early fifties himself, he probably has many years of service ahead.

Census Data Pop. 464,325. Central city, 9%; suburban, 75%. Median family income, $9,995; families above $15,000: 23%; families below $3,000: 9%. Median years education, 12.4.

The Voters

Median voting age 44.
Employment profile White collar, 52%. Blue collar, 30%. Service, 13%. Farm, 5%.
Ethnic groups Black, 1%. Spanish, 16%. Total foreign stock, 22%. Canada, UK, Germany, 2% each.

Presidential vote

1972	Nixon (R)	148,139	(68%)
	McGovern (D)	68,647	(32%)
1968	Nixon (R)	93,602	(60%)
	Humphrey (D)	50,642	(32%)
	Wallace (AI)	12,685	(8%)

Rep. Clair W. Burgener (R) Elected 1972; b. Dec. 5, 1921, Vernal, Utah; home, Rancho Sante Fe; San Diego St. U., A.B. 1950; Church of Latter Day Saints.

Career Army Air Corps, WWII; Pres. and Owner, Clair W. Burgener Co., Realtors, 1947–72; San Diego City Cncl., 1953–57, Vice-Mayor, 1955–56; Cal. Assembly, 1963–67; Cal. Senate, 1967–73.

Offices 316 CHOB, 202-225-3906. Also 7860 Mission Ctr. Ct., Suite 107, San Diego 92108, 714-299-4042.

Committees

Appropriations (18th). Subcommittees: District of Columbia; Public Works.

Group Ratings

	ADA	COPE	LWV	RIPON	NFU	LCV	CFA	NAB	NSI	ACA
1974	9	0	36	60	42	33	0	83	100	79
1973	4	10	33	53	5	11	13	–	–	92

Key Votes

1) Foreign Aid	AGN	6) Gov Abortn Aid	AGN	11) Pub Cong Election $	AGN
2) Busing	AGN	7) Coed Phys Ed	AGN	12) Turkish Arms Cutoff	AGN
3) ABM	FOR	8) Pov Lawyer Gag	FOR	13) Youth Camp Regs	ABS
4) B-1 Bomber	FOR	9) Pub Trans Sub	FOR	14) Strip Mine Veto	FOR
5) Nerve Gas	FOR	10) EZ Voter Regis	AGN	15) Farm Bill Veto	FOR

Election Results

1974 general:	Clair W. Burgener (R)	115,275	(60%)	($64,022)
	Bill Bandes (D)	75,629	(40%)	($22,055)
1974 primary:	Clair W. Burgener (R), unopposed			
1972 general:	Clair W. Burgener (R)	158,475	(68%)	($91,664)
	Bob Lowe (D)	68,381	(29%)	($4,917)
	Armin R. Moths (AI)	7,902	(3%)	(NA)

COLORADO

To outsiders, Colorado means backpacking in the Rockies, skiing at Aspen or Vail, or wandering through old mining towns like Central City. But the part of Colorado that matters most politically is the thin strip of land at the base of the Rockies' Eastern Slope, where the arid plateau of eastern Colorado yields suddenly to the mountains. Two-thirds of Colorado's voters live on this sliver of land running up and down the state, and the proportion is growing—Eastern Slope population rose 33% during the sixties, as compared with a modest 10% for the rest of the state. Attracted by the temperate climate, the proximity of winter and summer recreation, a local economy which was booming until just recently, newcomers continue to arrive, particularly in metropolitan Denver (which has 56% of the state population) and other Eastern Slope cities like Colorado Springs, Greeley, and Fort Collins.

In the days when the Eastern Slope did not so dominate Colorado, this rather homogeneous state had a politics of bipartisan conservatism. Republicans from the ranching and farming areas of the eastern plains vied against Democrats from the mountains of the Western Slope; but there were few differences on issues between them. But in the last dozen years, Colorado has been swept by two political movements, both notably more ideological than Colorado had been used to, and both given a major impetus by newcomers to the state. Both were rooted chiefly in the concerns of the people of the Eastern Slope; both relied heavily on volunteer activity by suburban housewives and, often, high school students; both reflected the changing concerns of Coloradans and both movements overturned the state's established political order: first the conservative Republicans, who established their hegemony in 1962; and then the new liberal Democrats, who swept the state in 1974.

First, the Republicans. In 1962 a group of young, personable, obscure Republicans got together and planned to unseat the state Democratic Governor and its senior Democratic Senator. Their candidates were John Love of Broadmoor (a suburb of Colorado Springs) for Governor and Peter Dominick of Englewood (a suburb of Denver) for Senator, and they both won handily. They were not the sort of moderate, middle-of-the-road Republicans, who were thought to be the key to the party's success; they (Dominick especially) were strong-minded conservatives, and they showed how much appeal their politics had in middle-class suburban neighborhoods. This was, remember, in the early Kennedy years—a time when the young, newly successful suburban migrants of Colorado were resenting the high level of federal taxes and were beginning to believe that what the country needed was far less government interference in their affairs. They were tired of steel-rimmed old time New Dealers who were spending their money to pay off union members and welfare recipients back in the wicked East; they were self-reliant Westerners, and they identified with the views and personalities of the well-groomed, well-to-do Love and Dominick. They formed the hard core that reelected Love in 1966 and 1970, Dominick in 1968, and Republican Senator Gordon Allott in 1966.

But as the years went on, these Colorado Republicans found themselves under attack by a new breed of Democrats. The source of their initial fervor and energy was opposition to the Vietnam war; by 1970, they were able to beat the more hawkish oldtime Democrats in statewide primaries. But as time went on, the issue they organized around was not so much the war as a strong insistence on reforming political procedures—and the environment.

In Colorado, as throughout the West, ecology-related issues became important as the sixties turned into the seventies. You only have to visit a place like Denver, not to mention Los Angeles, to see why. Everyday metropolitan concentrations have been changing the face of the land—and the quality of the air and water as well. In Eastern cities, suburbs shade gently into farmland; but beyond the last sidewalk of a Denver suburban development, you can see nothing but arid, virgin land and perhaps the side of a great mountain. Ecology issues almost inevitably involve a trade-off between somebody's economic gain and the general public's interest in environmental purity. Republicans in states like Colorado, with their belief in free enterprise and little government regulation, are inclined to sympathize with the affected business interests; the antiwar Democrats, by temperament, are inclined the other way—which, once the environment became an important issue, was by far the most popular.

The shift of opinion in Colorado became clear through the state's 1972 referendum on the Winter Olympics. A group of civic boosters had got together and sold the International Olympics

Committee on the idea of holding the winter games in Denver. Only after the promoters got the nod from the IOC did some problems come to light. For one thing, many of the events would have to be held more than 100 miles away, over mountains with no good highways; for another, the public would have to foot the bill for many new Olympic facilities, the primary beneficiaries of which would be hotel owners, real estate developers, and other believers in unrestrained growth. Republicans, like Gordon Allott, who was up for reelection that year, were strong Olympic boosters. Democrats, like Allott's little-known opponent, supported the referendum which would prohibit the state from spending any money on the Olympics—a referendum put on the ballot through the efforts of activists in the Denver area and various university towns.

Much to the chagrin of the people who have traditionally attempted—with much previous success—to promote and sell Colorado, the referendum to stop the Olympics won with a 61% margin. It would be inaccurate, however, to ascribe Haskell's victory solely to the Olympics issue. A former Republican state Representative from well-to-do Denver suburbs, Haskell has switched parties in 1970 out of opposition to the Nixon Administration's Vietnam policies. Haskell's campaign consisted primarily of a half-hour television ad, which tried to tell the voters who he was and concluded with film clips of statements made by Allott. They were devastating. A man who took delight in attacking the scared cows of liberals (conservative columnist George Will was then on his staff), Allott had come out acerbically for economic growth and against certain environmental protection policies. That was not the side to be on in Colorado in 1972.

But the politician who was the biggest winner of the Olympics referendum was state Representative Richard Lamm, a young law professor and Denver Democrat, who led the referendum campaign. He had already attracted controversy as the sponsor of Colorado's early liberalized abortion law; something of an outdoors buff, he exemplified the young newcomers to Colorado who didn't want the state "Californicated" in order to make profits for developers. Lamm had been considered a far-out politico as late as 1970; by 1974, he was running for Governor—and was considered the leading contender. Former Lieutenant Governor Mark Hogan, who had the misfortune to be in the real estate business though he favored limits on growth, was edged out of the race, unable to win much support; state Representative Thomas Farley, considered the candidate of the moderate wing of the party, decisively lost the primary.

In the general election, Lamm faced John Vanderhoof, a Republican who had moved up from the Lieutenant Governorship in 1973 when Love had gone to Washington for a brief stint as energy chief. Vanderhoof was not a sleek suburban conservative, but a rugged eastern plains politico: genial, moderately conservative, the kind of politician Colorado liked to elect in the 1940s and 1950s. He attacked Lamm as an outsider, as one who wanted to stop growth so suddenly that he would force thousands onto the unemployment lines. Lamm countered that he wanted controls on growth, and he was particularly insistent that he would work to prevent the federal government from allowing unchecked exploitation of surface coal and oil-bearing shale in Colorado. The voters had a clear choice, and on election day they came out for Lamm. It was an all the more meaningful result because Lamm, just before the September primary, had been forced to admit that he had omitted from his personal financial statement the fact that he owned certain mining stock. As Governor, Lamm moved quickly to head up a group of Rocky Mountain governors, all Democrats after the 1974 elections, to protect their resources from outside corporations—and federal interference. He was all for solving the energy crisis, said Lamm, but not at the cost of tearing up Colorado.

This was, obviously, a new kind of liberalism—not the kind of New Deal thinking that saw the federal government as the only champion of the common man. Like the conservatism of the Colorado Republicans, it owed some of its success to the desires of Coloradans—many of them newcomers—that certain things just be left alone. And like that earlier movement, it made its greatest gains over its party's previous showings in the politically volatile suburbs of Denver. Lamm even carried the suburbs, and so, incidentally, did the newly elected Democratic state Treasurer, Sam Browne—one of the organizers of the 1969 Moratorium movement. Together with others in the Moratorium, Browne had moved to Denver after its collapse, and had concentrated on grass roots politics there; one of the major planks in his campaign was that state moneys should be deposited in small banks throughout the state, to help the economies of the often dying small towns of the plains and mountains.

An even more unlikely result—as least from the perspective of 1972—occurred in Colorado's 1974 Senate race. This is a state, after all, which gave George McGovern only 36% of its votes in 1972, and which Senator Peter Dominick carried with 54% in 1962 and 59% in 1968. Yet in 1974 Gary Hart, McGovern's campaign manager, beat Dominick by an astounding margin of 59-41. How did this come to happen? First, Dominick, who suffered a heart attack several years ago, was not in the best of health; his voice was slightly slurred, and he had trouble campaigning effectively. Second, Hart in the Democratic Party positioned himself carefully between moderate

Martin Miller, a suburban Denver state legislator, and Herrick Roth, the former president of the state AFL-CIO who had lost that post for supporting McGovern in 1972. Third, Hart had early seized hold of the issues, long before the September primary, by accusing Dominick of "laundering" milk cooperative contributions to the 1972 Nixon campaign by channeling them through the Republican Senatorial Campaign Committee, which he then headed: these charges gave Hart the initiative among the Democrats and put Dominick on the defensive. Fifth, some foolish statements by Dominck (i.e., that Watergate was "insignificant"), and his ham-handed, last-minute campaign which stressed that Hart had not lived in the state very long. (Dominick himself is from the prep school East, and more than one quarter of the voters had moved into the state in the last five years.)

Finally, the changed political atmosphere of the state itself. For it was Dominick, with his reliably conservative record in the Senate, who was on the defensive, not Hart. Just as Republicans didn't have to be on the defensive for supporting Goldwater two years later in 1966, so Colorado Democrats did not need to be on the defensive about McGovern, even if they had run his campaign. Hart stressed that he was against many federal spending programs, and that he would work to protect Colorado's resources against exploitation by the federal government; he emphasized how he eschewed the oldtime Democratic liberalism, in favor of his own philosophy. With his cowboy boots and soft-spoken manner, he won an astonishing 59% of the votes, carrying even the most Republican of the Denver suburban counties.

Joseph Kraft among others has advanced the thesis that Colorado has become the political pace-setter among the states, and it may be so; we will have to wait on further elections, to see if the country will follow. But what it does show is the popularity of a new kind of liberalism, one that is wary of government involvement and values, if not the lessons of the past, and at least an appreciation for the gifts of nature. It is also a state which has shown—for conservative Republicans as well as liberal Democrats—the power of organized cadres of political volunteers, committed to candidates because of their stands on issues. For both these surges of what some might regard as the political extremes have been genuinely popular movements, with widespread, active support from larger numbers of people than we are accustomed to see involved in the American political process. What we will see now is how well these new Democrats who have captured the state govern.

Census Data Pop. 2,207,259; 1.09% of U.S. total, 30th largest; Central city, 34%; suburban, 38%. Median family income, $9,553; 21st highest; families above $15,000: 20%; families below $3,000: 9%. Median years education, 12.4.

1974 Share of Federal Tax Burden $3,079,876,000; 1.15% of U.S. total, 26th largest.

1974 Share of Federal Outlays $3,789,956,000; 1.40% of U.S. total, 25th largest. Per capita federal spending, $1717.

DOD	$1,164,124,000	21st (1.70%)	HEW	$924,232,000	31st (1.00%)
AEC	$114,424,000	12th (3.75%)	HUD	$10,957,000	25th (1.12%)
NASA	$193,423,000	6th (6.51%)	VA	$189,901,000	26th (1.39%)
DOT	$138,655,000	25th (1.64%)	EPA	$28,579,000	24th (0.91%)
DOC	$43,683,000	7th (2.71%)	RevS	$76,446,000	27th (1.26%)
DOI	$205,966,000	3d (8.37%)	Int.	$117,651,000	23d (0.57%)
USDA	$139,798,000	33d (1.12%)	Other	$442,117,000	

Economic Base Finance, insurance and real estate; agriculture, notably cattle, wheat, dairy products and corn; food and kindred products; machinery, especially electronic computing equipment; electrical equipment and supplies, especially electronic measuring instruments; printing and publishing, especially newspapers; tourism.

Political Line-up Governor, Richard D. Lamm (D). Senators Floyd K. Haskell (D) and Gary Hart (D). Representatives, 5 (3 D and 2 R). State Senate (19 D and 16 R); State House (39 D and 26 R).

The Voters

Registration 1,227,492 Total. 448,535 D (37%); 345,156 R (28%); 433,801 Unaffiliated (35%). *Median voting age* 40.
Employment profile White collar, 54%. Blue collar, 28%. Service, 14%. Farm, 4%.
Ethnic groups Black, 3%. Spanish, 13%. Total foreign stock, 13%. Germany, 2%, UK, USSR, 1% each.

Presidential vote

1972	Nixon (R)	....	597,189	(64%)
	McGovern (D)	....	329,980	(36%)
1968	Nixon (R)	....	409,345	(51%)
	Humphrey (D)	....	335,174	(42%)
	Wallace (AI)	....	60,813	(8%)

Sen. Floyd K. Haskell (D) Elected 1972, seat up 1978; b. Feb. 7, 1916, Morristown, N.J.; home, Littleton; Harvard U., A.B. 1937, LL.B., 1941.

Career Practicing atty., 1941, 1946–72; Army, WWII; Colo. Senate, elected as Repub., 1964–67; switched to Dem. party, Apr. 1970.

Offices 4101 DSOB, 202-224-5941. Also, Fed. Ofc. Bldg., 1961 Denver St., Denver 80202, 303-837-2411.

Committees

Finance (11th). Subcommittees: Administration of the Internal Revenue Code (Chairman); Health; Energy; International Trade.

Interior and Insular Affairs (6th). Subcommittees: Energy Research and Water Resources; Environment and Land Resources (Chairman); Indian Affairs; Parks and Recreation; Special Subcommittee on Integrated Oil Operations (Chairman).

Group Ratings

	ADA	COPE	LWV	RIPON	NFU	LCV	CFA	NAB	NSI	ACA
1974	81	60	100	57	100	80	100	40	0	17
1973	89	80	90	53	93	–	100	–	–	12

Key Votes

1) No-Knock	AGN	8) Gov Abortn Aid	FOR	15) Consumer Prot Agy	FOR
2) Busing	AGN	9) Cut Mil Brass	ABS	16) Forced Psych Tests	FOR
3) No Fault	FOR	10) Gov Limousine	FOR	17) Fed Campaign Subs	FOR
4) F-111	AGN	11) RR Featherbed	FOR	18) Rhod Chrome Ban	FOR
5) Death Penalty	FOR	12) Handgun License	AGN	19) Open Legis Meetings	FOR
6) Foreign Aid	ABS	13) Less Troop Abrd	FOR	20) Strikers Food Stmps	FOR
7) Filibuster	AGN	14) Resume Turk Aid	ABS	21) Gov Info Disclosure	FOR

Election Results

1972 general:	Floyd K. Haskell (D)	457,545	(51%)	($176,234)
	Gordon Allott (R)	447,957	(49%)	($308,305)
1972 primary:	Floyd K. Haskell (D)	77,574	(59%)	
	Anthony F. Vollack (D)	54,298	(41%)	

Sen. Gary Hart (D) Elected 1974, seat up 1980; b. Nov. 28, 1937, Ottawa, Kans.; home, Denver; Bethany Col., Yale U., LL.B. 1964.

Career Atty., U.S. Dept. of Justice; Special Asst. to U.S. Secy. of Interior; Practicing atty., 1967–74; Natl. Campaign Dir., McGovern for Pres., 1971–72.

Offices 4213 DSOB, 202-224-5852.

Committees

Armed Services (9th). Subcommittees: National Stockpile and Naval Petroleum Reserves; Tactical Air Power.

Public Works (9th). Subcommittees: Environmental Pollution, Panel on Environmental Science and Technology, Panel on Materials Policy (Chairman); Economic Development; Water Resources; Disaster Relief.

Select Committee on Intelligence Operations (3d).

Group Ratings: Newly Elected

Key Votes

1) No-Knock	NE	8) Gov Abortn Aid	FOR	15) Consumer Prot Agy	NE
2) Busing	NE	9) Cut Mil Brass	NE	16) Forced Psych Tests	NE
3) No Fault	NE	10) Gov Limousine	NE	17) Fed Campaign Subs	NE
4) F-111	AGN	11) RR Featherbed	NE	18) Rhod Chrome Ban	NE
5) Death Penalty	NE	12) Handgun License	NE	19) Open Legis Meetings	NE
6) Foreign Aid	NE	13) Less Troop Abrd	NE	20) Strikers Food Stmps	NE
7) Filibuster	AGN	14) Resume Turk Aid	AGN	21) Gov Info Disclosure	NE

Election Results

1974 general:	Gary W. Hart (D)	471,691	(59%)	($352,557)
	Peter H. Dominick (R)	325,508	(41%)	($502,343)
1974 primary:	Gary W. Hart (D)	81,161	(40%)	
	Herrick S. Roth (D)	66,819	(33%)	
	Marty Miller (D)	55,339	(27%)	

Gov. Richard D. Lamm (D) Elected 1974, term expires Jan. 1979; b. Aug. 3, 1935; U. of Wis., B.B.A. 1957, U. of Cal., LL.B. 1961.

Career CPA, 1961–62; Atty., Colo. Anti-Discrimination Comm., 1962–63; Practicing atty., 1963–75; Colo. House of Reps., 1966–75, Asst. Maj. Ldr., 1971–75; Assoc. Prof. of Law, U. of Denver, 1969–75.

Offices Rm. 136, State Capitol, Denver 80203, 303-892-2471.

Election Results

1974 general:	Dick Lamm (D)	441,199	(54%)
	John D. Vanderhoof (R)	378,907	(46%)
1974 primary	Dick Lamm (D)	120,452	(59%)
	Tom Farley (D)	84,796	(41%)

◆ ◆ ◆ ◆ ◆

FIRST DISTRICT

Within sight—except on days when smog obscures—of the Front Range of the Rockies lies the mile-high city of Denver, which got its start servicing the needs of local gold miners and cattle ranchers. Today it is the service and distribution center for the entire Rocky Mountain region, though its detractors like to call it just a salesman's town. Denver is now the largest metropolitan area in the Rocky Mountain states; in fact, the largest, except for Houston and Dallas, between the Missouri River and the West Coast. But even what the Census Bureau defines as the central city of Denver does not fit an Easterner's idea of what a city is. With no extensive manufacturing base, most of Denver looke like a suburb; the homes and lawns here, in needy as well as prosperous neighborhoods, have a resolute, well-tended order to them.

There are, of course, some less respectable, more rundown areas, for example on the west side where the chicanos live and on the north side where blacks tend to reside. In Denver, these two communities are of about equal size, but show little bond of common feeling; Denver is rare for a place in the West or Southwest in that it regards its blacks with more esteem than the Mexican-Americans.

Not that Denver is immune to the nation's urban ills. Back in 1970, the city's school board was swept out of office because it had transferred students among schools to eliminate segregation. An antibusing board was voted in, and then forced to continue the program by federal court order. And like many American cities, Denver is badly in need of an effective system of mass transit.

These two issues—busing and mass transit (it's funny how two words which are technically synonyms refer to entirely different political issues)—have been important factors in the two recent elections in which Denver's congressional district has changed hands. In 1970, when Colorado's 1st district included the entire city, veteran (1951–71) Rep. Byron Rogers was defeated by just 30 votes in the Democratic primary by a young lawyer named Craig Barnes, who was one of the lawyers who had got an injunction against the antibusing school board. In the general election, busing seemed to play a major role, as Barnes lost, 52–45 to Republican District Attorney Mike McKevitt.

Ordinarily when a Congressman is elected, he can use the advantages of his office, if not just his name recognition, to win by larger margins in later years. These advantages are increased when, as in the case of the 1st, a friendly legislature removes opposition territory from the district: in this case, some chicano precincts at the northern edge of the city. But McKevitt, unlike most of his colleagues, was clearly facing a tough race when he went home to compaign in 1972.

One reason was the rise of a young, liberal activist element within the local Democratic Party. Symbolic of this was the Democratic primary victory, by a 55–45 margin, of 32-year-old attorney Patricia Schroeder over an 18-year veteran of the state Senate. Schroeder drew much of her support from the same kind of people who were backing the ultimately successful referendum to ban the use of state money on the 1976 Winter Olympics, and from those who had supported Craig Barnes two years before. But she managed to project an image less far-out than Barnes's; among other things, she was opposed to busing, although she did not make it a major issue.

One issue the candidate did emphasize was mass transit. In Congress, McKevitt had voted against diverting money from the highway trust fund for mass transit; Schroeder took the opposite position. But most important to Schroeder was a large, well-organized, intensive volunteer effort—something that is seen increasingly more often in House contests, and which in considerable part was responsible for the dozens of Schroeder-type Democrats who won in 1974.

Schroeder broke several traditions when she came to the House, winning a seat on the House Armed Services Committee, and bringing her young children to the office with her. On Armed Services she was just one of several antiwar liberals, but she seemed even more than the others to irritate then Chairman Edward Hebert of Louisiana. She was, however, part of the House majority who voted to end the bombing of Cambodia during her first term, and managed to score points against existing military policy in committee. In 1974, Schroeder was rumored to be in trouble, partly because she refused to use all the incumbent's advantages she had; her opponent, state Representative Frank Southworth, was running hard on the busing issue. But as in most cities, busing had simmered down as an issue in Denver; a lot of parents still didn't like it, but it had ceased to be something you would base all your votes on. Southworth's candidacy fizzled, and Schroeder won fairly easily. She seems to be in a position now to win a long tenure, but for the fact that she reportedly is not all that enchanted with serving in Congress, and might just as soon get back to Denver one of these years. In that case, her place will probably be taken by someone else from the burgeoning liberal political culture of Colorado.

Census Data Pop. 441,881. Central city, 99%; suburban, 1%. Median family income, $9,977; families above $15,000: 24%; families below $3,000: 9%. Median years education, 12.5.

The Voters

Median voting age 42.
Employment profile White collar, 61%. Blue collar, 24%. Service, 15%. Farm, –%.
Ethnic groups Black, 10%. Spanish, 14%. Total foreign stock, 17%. Germany, USSR, UK, 2% each.

Presidential vote

1972	Nixon (R)	101,950	(55%)
	McGovern (D)	82,403	(45%)
1968	Nixon (R)	79,091	(45%)
	Humphrey (D)	86,119	(49%)
	Wallace (AI)	8,813	(5%)

Rep. Patricia Schroeder (D) Elected 1972; b. July 30, 1940, Portland, Oreg.; home, Denver; U. of Minn., B.S. 1961, Harvard U., J.D. 1964.

Career Field Atty., Natl. Labor Relations Bd., 1964–66; Practicing atty.; Lecturer and Law Instructor, Community Col. of Denver, 1969–70, U. of Denver, Denver Ctr., 1969, Regis Col., 1970–72; Hearing Officer, Colo. Dept. of Personnel, 1971–72; Legal Counsel, Colo. Planned Parenthood.

Offices 1131 LHOB, 202-225-4431. Also Denver Fed. Bldg., 1767 High St., Denver 80218, 303-837-2354.

Committees

Armed Services (21st). Subcommittees: Research and Development; Seapower and Strategic and Critical Materials.

Post Office and Civil Service (10th). Subcommittees: Census and Population (Chairman); Employee Political Rights and Intergovernmental Programs; Postal Facilities, Mail, and Labor Management.

Group Ratings

	ADA	COPE	LWV	RIPON	NFU	LCV	CFA	NAB	NSI	ACA
1974	100	91	100	62	86	100	77	27	10	7
1973	100	91	100	73	95	95	100	–	–	20

Key Votes

1) Foreign Aid	AGN	6) Gov Abortn Aid	FOR	11) Pub Cong Election $	FOR
2) Busing	FOR	7) Coed Phys Ed	FOR	12) Turkish Arms Cutoff	ABS
3) ABM	AGN	8) Pov Lawyer Gag	AGN	13) Youth Camp Regs	AGN
4) B-1 Bomber	AGN	9) Pub Trans Sub	FOR	14) Strip Mine Veto	AGN
5) Nerve Gas	AGN	10) EZ Voter Regis	FOR	15) Farm Bill Veto	AGN

Election Results

1974 general:	Patricia Schroeder (D)	94,583	(59%)	($104,126)
	Frank K. Southworth (R)	66,046	(41%)	($105,532)
1974 primary:	Patricia Schroeder (D), unopposed			
1972 general:	Patricia Schroeder (D)	101,832	(52%)	($80,508)
	James D. McKevitt (R)	93,733	(48%)	($78,436)

◆ ◆ ◆ ◆ ◆

SECOND DISTRICT

There is no district typical of those that produced the large 1974 crop of Democratic freshmen: some are suburban, some rural, some even urban; and they are scattered all over the land. But the 2d district of Colorado can be looked at as at least suggesting some of the trends which produced such a liberal Congress in a nation that increasingly likes to call itself conservative. And it produced a Congressman, Timothy Wirth, who has been called "the pick of the litter" of the freshmen, but in many ways personifies their common qualities.

The 2d is actually a fairly varied district, made up of three distinct parts. First, there is Jefferson County, just west of Denver and its fastest-growing suburban area, a place where young engineers and accountants and office clerks and assembly line workers and their families have been settling, within clear sight (on most days) of the Front Range. With an electronic industry base, this area has tended to vote conservative and Republican, as most such areas do. Second, there is Boulder County, with the University of Colorado dominating the neat town. In 1972 the 18-year-old vote produced a mini-revolution here, with a Democrat elected District Attorney; but two years later students were increasingly apathetic, and two councilmen who had voted for a gay right ordinance were recalled from office by the outraged townspeople. Third, there is a small Mexican-American neighborhood on the west side of Denver—which casts so few votes as to be almost negligible.

Jefferson and Boulder Counties had clearly been trending left in 1972, with ecology-related issues—like the Winter Olympics referendum—definitely favoring the Democrats. Clearly the area's traditional Republican majorities were threatened, and no one know it better than Congressman Donald Brotzman. Brotzman had been unseated once before, in the 1964 Democratic landslide, and he was determined it would not happen again. He stepped up his already heavy mailings and constituent service; he appeared in the district practically every weekend; he smiled and chatted even more genially, if that were possible, than before; and he even voted with the anti-Nixon Democrats on a fair number of issues—a clear departure from his rather conventional Republican voting record in the past.

But it was all not enough. Wirth, a 35-year-old former White House Fellow, was a classy candidate: handsome, knowledgeable, Ivy League-educated but from a poor family. For over a year he was working the district harder even than Brotzman, and emphasized particularly environmental issues. Like his ticket-mates Gary Hart and Dick Lamm, he approached issues not so much as an oldtime New Dealer than as a person who had serious doubts about government intrusions and at the same time wanted more progressive economic programs. It proved to be, by the narrowest of margins, a winning strategy.

Once elected, Wirth was the person who, rather than vacationing, put together the new Democratic freshmen as an organized group, setting up an office on Capitol Hill and hiring staff. In large part because of this initiative, the freshmen were able to assert themselves effectively in the first, pre-1975 meetings of House Democrats and to win a number of major battles—including much better committee assignments than freshmen had been accustomed to getting in the past. Wirth himself was one of 11 freshmen assigned to the Commerce Committee—who together changed its political complexion almost completely. If anyone can, he is expected to win reelection in 1976; but Brotzman has come back from a defeat once before, back in 1966, and he also is a formidable campaigner not to be underestimated.

Census Data   Pop. 439,399. Central city, 17%; suburban, 83%. Median family income, $11,201; families above $15,000: 26%; families below $3,000: 6%.   Median years education, 12.6.

The Voters

Median voting age 38.
Employment profile White collar, 60%. Blue collar, 28%. Service, 11%. Farm, 1%.
Ethnic groups Spanish, 10%. Total foreign stock, 12%. Germany, 2%; UK, USSR, 1% each.

Presidential vote

1972	Nixon (R)	142,326	(65%)
	McGovern (D)	76,789	(35%)
1968	Nixon (R)	86,156	(53%)
	Humphrey (D)	63,901	(40%)
	Wallace (AI)	11,277	(7%)

Rep. Timothy E. Wirth (D)   Elected 1974; b. Sept. 22, 1939, Santa Fe, N.M.; home, Denver; Harvard U., A.B. 1961, M.Ed. 1964, Stanford U., Ph.D. 1973.

Career   White House Fellow, Spec. Asst. to Secy. of HEW, 1967–68; Deputy Asst. Secy. of Educ., HEW, 1969–70; Businessman, Great Western United Corp.; Mgr., Rocky Mt. Ofc., Arthur D. Little, Inc., consultants.

Offices   516 CHOB, 202-225-2161. Also 9485 W. Colfax, Lakewood 80215, 303-234-5200.

Committees

Interstate and Foreign Commerce (22d). Subcommittees: Communications; Energy and Power; Health and Environment.

Science and Technology (25th). Subcommittees: Energy Research, Development and Demonstration; Energy Research (Fossil Fuels); Science, Research, and Technology.

Group Ratings: Newly Elected

Key Votes

1) Foreign Aid	FOR	6) Gov Abortn Aid	NE	11) Pub Cong Election $	NE
2) Busing	NE	7) Coed Phys Ed	FOR	12) Turkish Arms Cutoff	NE
3) ABM	NE	8) Pov Lawyer Gag	NE	13) Youth Camp Regs	AGN
4) B-1 Bomber	AGN	9) Pub Trans Sub	NE	14) Strip Mine Veto	AGN
5) Nerve Gas	NE	10) EZ Voter Regis	NE	15) Farm Bill Veto	AGN

Election Results

1974 general:	Timothy E. Wirth (D)	93,728	(52%)	($134,103)
	Donald G. Brotzman (R)	86,720	(48%)	($165,911)
1974 primary:	Timothy E. Wirth (D), unopposed			

◆ ◆ ◆ ◆ ◆

THIRD DISTRICT

Ordinarily, when the power over redistricting—control of the legislature and the governor's office—is in the hands of one party, the process goes smoothly. Not so in Colorado in 1972. Not until the last days of the legislative session was agreement reached on a major reshaping of the state's congressional district lines. One reason was that the state got a new district as a result of the 1970 census, which meant that various ambitious legislators had more than the usual interest in the way the lines were drawn. Another reason was Democratic Congressman Frank Evans.

One might suppose that a Republican legislature would try to make things as uncomfortable as possible for a Democratic Congressman. Not so in Evans's case. The legislature's aim was to draw him a district that would be as attractive as possible; that is, as Democratic as possible. The Republican legislators knew that Evans was unbeatable, whatever way they drew the lines. But they also knew that the more difficult they made it for him, the more likely he was to run for the Senate against three-term Republican incumbent Gordon Allott. The assumption at the time—it proved quite inaccurate, but was widely shared—was that Evans was the only Democrat who could give Allott trouble.

How does a Congressman get into a position so enviable that the opposition sweats to make things easy for him? Evans was one of the forty-odd Congressmen generally judged to have been carried into office by the Johnson landslide of 1964—to judge from the 1972 results, apparently the last presidential landslide in our history with significant coattail effects. In that year Evens beat an aging, veteran incumbent by a narrow margin, and by all the political lore then prevailing should have been eminently unseatable in 1966. The district, as it then stood, was the southeastern quarter of Colorado, which had two major urban centers, Colorado Springs (Republican) and Pueblo (Democratic). But the demography of the old district favored the Republicans, since Colorado Springs was growing rapidly while Pueblo, an old steel-mill town, was growing scarcely at all.

During his first term Evans, like many Democrats elected in 1964, made skillful use of the congressional frank (the free mailing privilege) and attended carefully to his constituents' problems. He compiled what was considered a middle-of-the-road record for a northern Democrat. In 1966 he won by a reasonably good—and therefore much better than expected—margin, which he kept increasing in subsequent elections. By 1970 he was even carrying staunchly Republican Colorado Springs. Meanwhile, he had won a seat on the Appropriations Committee.

This was the situation confronting the Republican redistricters in the spring of 1972. Their response was to take most of Colorado Springs out of the 3d district and place it into a new, heavily Republican 5th district. To make up for the loss of population, redistricters extended the 3d district across the Rockies, all the way to the Utah line to take in the southern half of the Western Slope. The new 3d would have been a tough district for many other Democrats, but everybody knew it would be easy for Evans, and it was. He was reelected even more easily in 1974, and has continued to advance upward on the Appropriations Committee.

Now the primary political threat to Evans comes not from Republicans but from the new breed of liberal Democrats who elected Governor Dick Lamm and Senator Gary Hart in 1974. They remember that Evans opposed their referendum against the Winter Olympics in 1972, and that he has not been particularly sympathetic to their views on other issues. One might suppose that in this rugged part of the state Evans would be safe in a primary, but even here candidates like Lamm and Hart have been able to win. So it could be that Evans will have to face opposition from a hitherto unexpected quarter in 1976.

Census Data Pop. 442,217. Central city, 28%; suburban, 17%. Median family income, $7,578; families above $15,000: 10%; families below $3,000: 13%. Median years education, 12.1.

The Voters

Median voting age 41.
Employment profile White collar, 43%. Blue collar, 33%. Service, 16%. Farm, 8%.
Ethnic groups Black, 2%. Spanish, 23%. Total foreign stock, 11%. Germany, 2%.

Presidential vote

1972	Nixon (R)	102,569	(64%)
	McGovern (D)	57,152	(36%)
1968	Nixon (R)	71,578	(46%)
	Humphrey (D)	71,673	(46%)
	Wallace (AI)	13,923	(9%)

Rep. Frank E. Evans (D) Elected 1964; b. Sept. 6, 1923, Pueblo; home, Pueblo; Pomona Col., 1941–43, U. of Denver, B.A. 1947, LL.B. 1949; Presbyterian.

Career Navy, WWII; Practicing atty., 1950–64; Colo. House of Reps., 1961–65, Dem. Floor Whip, 1963–65.

Offices 2443 RHOB, 202-225-4761. Also P.O. Box 5728, Pueblo 81002, 303-544-5277 ext. 313.

Committees

Appropriations (21st). Subcommittees: Agriculture and Related Agencies; Legislative.

Group Ratings

	ADA	COPE	LWV	RIPON	NFU	LCV	CFA	NAB	NSI	ACA
1974	90	100	91	53	100	67	85	33	20	14
1973	84	73	91	73	95	84	88	–	–	8
1972	75	82	89	67	86	40	100	33	22	10

Key Votes

1) Foreign Aid	AGN	6) Gov Abortn Aid	FOR	11) Pub Cong Election $	FOR
2) Busing	FOR	7) Coed Phys Ed	AGN	12) Turkish Arms Cutoff	ABS
3) ABM	AGN	8) Pov Lawyer Gag	AGN	13) Youth Camp Regs	AGN
4) B-1 Bomber	AGN	9) Pub Trans Sub	AGN	14) Strip Mine Veto	AGN
5) Nerve Gas	FOR	10) EZ Voter Regis	AGN		

Election Results

1974 general:	Frank E. Evans (D)	91,783	(68%)	($30,855)
	E. Keith Records (R)	43,298	(32%)	($5,120)
1974 primary:	Frank E. Evans (D)	29,385	(62%)	
	Harvey W. Phelps (D)	17,808	(38%)	
1972 general:	Frank E. Evans (D)	107,511	(66%)	($45,734)
	Chuck Brady (R)	54,556	(34%)	($9,435)

◆ ◆ ◆ ◆ ◆

FOURTH DISTRICT

It is in the nature of our political system that an obscure primary election in some far corner of the nation can have a substantial impact on the policy of the federal government. This is a corollary of the seniority system: what power years of service can confer, the voters can quickly revoke. A prime example was the 1972 primary race in the 4th district of Colorado, where Wayne N. Aspinall, Chairman of the House Interior Committee and *bête noir* of conservationists and environmentalists, was beaten. Back in 1948, Aspinall, then an attorney and sometime state Representative, was elected to the first of his twelve terms in the House. He was already 52 years old. The district from which he was elected consisted of all of the Western Slope counties of Colorado, an area of rugged mountains and very few people (less than 200,000 in 1970). Like many Western Congressmen, Aspinall wanted to get on the Interior Committee, which has jurisdiction over federal lands, reclamation, and water. He made it and, through good luck, became Chairman after the 1958 election.

From that position Aspinall could and did extract goodies for his district. More important, he mastered the committee's subject matter thoroughly, and also western water politics: when congressmen from Arizona or California or even Denver wanted to tap the plentiful supplies of water on the Western Slope, they had to give Aspinall what he wanted. And what he wanted, increasingly, was to promote the policies of maximum use of government lands and the resources on them.

These policies enraged environmentalists, and it is worth going over Aspinall's career if only to demonstrate the power they can exercise. Redistricting by 1970 had brought Aspinall several Eastern Slope counties—and his first primary opposition and close call in a general election. Further redistricting, in 1972, helped to finish him off; at that point, only 26% of his constituents lived in the old Western Slope counties he had so long represented. So in the primary that year Alan Merson, a young law professor with lots of help from environmental groups, whipped Aspinall. The most noteworthy result—one telling us a lot about the new Colorado—came in Aspen, where radical chic socialites mingle with street people and all try to spot the house of *Rolling Stone* National Affairs Editor Dr. Hunter Thompson. There the vote was 1,158 for the challenger and 99 for the incumbent Aspinall.

The district's Republican leanings, however, proved disastrous for Merson in the general election. The Republican candidate, James Johnson—considered a party moderate—campaigned as hard on environmental issues as Merson. But once in office, Johnson got rather low ratings from environmental groups, and in 1974 this hybrid Eastern Slope-Western Slope district was again the scene of a close battle, as Democrat John Carroll pressed the incumbent hard. It was not, of course, a Republican year, but the closeness of Johnson's margin—considering the fact that he had the advantages of incumbency for two years, as well as the district's basic Republican leanings—suggest that he is not terribly strong, and may face further difficult challenges in the future.

Census Data Pop. 442,024. Central city, 0%; suburban, 20%. Median family income, $8,992; families above $15,000: 15%; families below $3,000: 10%. Median years education, 12.4.

The Voters

Median voting age 40.
Employment profile White collar, 47%. Blue collar, 30%. Service, 14%. Farm, 9%.
Ethnic groups Spanish, 10%. Total foreign stock, 12%. USSR, 3%; Germany, 2%.

Presidential vote

1972	Nixon (R)	129,253	(67%)
	McGovern (D)	63,181	(33%)
1968	Nixon (R)	87,571	(55%)
	Humphrey (D)	57,216	(36%)
	Wallace (AI)	13,584	(9%)

Rep. James P. (Jim) **Johnson** (R) Elected 1972; b. June 2, 1930, Yankton, S.D.; home, Fort Collins; Northwestern U., B.A. 1952, U. of Colo., LL.B. 1959; Presbyterian.

Career USMC, 1952–56; Prosecuting Atty., 8th Jud. Dist. of Colo.; Municipal Judge, Ault and Ft. Collins, 1962–65.

Offices 514 CHOB, 202-225-4676. Also Fed. Bldg., Fort Collins 80521, 303-493-9132.

Committees

Agriculture (6th). Subcommittees: Forests; Livestock and Grains; Oilseeds and Rice.

Interior and Insular Affairs (12th). Subcommittees: Indian Affairs; Public Lands.

Group Ratings

	ADA	COPE	LWV	RIPON	NFU	LCV	CFA	NAB	NSI	ACA
1974	29	10	33	73	50	33	15	100	44	64
1973	52	27	42	71	83	18	50	–	–	67

Key Votes

1) Foreign Aid	AGN	6) Gov Abortn Aid	ABS	11) Pub Cong Election $	AGN
2) Busing	AGN	7) Coed Phys Ed	ABS	12) Turkish Arms Cutoff	ABS
3) ABM	AGN	8) Pov Lawyer Gag	FOR	13) Youth Camp Regs	ABS
4) B-1 Bomber	FOR	9) Pub Trans Sub	AGN	14) Strip Mine Veto	AGN
5) Nerve Gas	AGN	10) EZ Voter Regis	AGN	15) Farm Bill Veto	FOR

Election Results

1974 general:	James P. Johnson (R)	82,982	(52%)	($53,940)
	John S. Carroll (D)	76,452	(48%)	($62,704)
1974 primary:	James P. Johnson (R), unopposed			
1972 general:	James P. Johnson (R)	94,994	(51%)	($51,747)
	Alan Merson (D)	91,151	(49%)	($104,994)

◆ ◆ ◆ ◆ ◆

FIFTH DISTRICT

It is not often that a state as small as Colorado gains a congressional seat. Sixty years passed between the time Colorado got its fourth seat in 1910 and its fifth in 1970. Such a prize naturally proves tempting to politicians, and the Republican legislature haggled long and hard before drawing the current 5th district in 1972. (See Third District.) Like so many districts born of political in-fighting, the 5th looks fairly regular on the map; but when one looks more closely, it becomes clear that the district is centered on no cohesive community. The bulk of its people live in the Denver suburbs, north, east, and south of the city. As one proceeds clockwise in this manner, one goes from the more Democratic communities (Commerce City plus a chunk of Denver itself) to the middle-of-the road (Aurora) to the wealthy and heavily Republican (Englewood, Littleton).

To the south, after travelling Interstate 25 through some residential sprawl and then the arid, empty, mile-high plateau, lies Colorado Spring. This is a wealthy, fast-growing city, known for its military installations (the Air Force Academy, Fort Carson) and tourist attractions (Pike's Peak, the Garden of the Gods). Politically, Colorado Springs is a kind of Rocky Mountain San Diego, conservative and Republican—though it should be added that like the Denver suburbs the city has proved susceptible to Democrats like Dick Lamm who have stressed ecology issues.

The 5th also moves east to the Kansas border. It was out in this vast country that the first Colorado boomers, in the wake of the Gold Rush of 1858, set the cavalry on defenseless Cheyenne men, women, and children in the Sand Creek massacre. Today this part of Colorado has scarcely changed, a region of large cattle ranches, tumbleweed, and gas-station-stop towns along Interstate 70. It casts only 10% of the district's votes.

It should come as no surprise that the new Congressman from the 5th was a major power in the state legislature that drew the new district's boundaries. William Armstrong, the state Senate Majority Leader from 1969 to 1972, was so clearly in line for the seat that he faced no opposition in the Republican primary. His Democratic opponent Byron Johnson was a former Congressman (1959-61), but in a Republican district like this one he had no chance. The high point of the campaign was when Armstrong poo-pooed Johnson's charges that the Nixon Administration was corrupt. Armstrong is proof that not all the young members of Congress are ecology-minded liberals or veterans of the peace movement; he is quite a conservative Republican, and one who did not abandon his President until just about the last opportunity before his criminality was openly admitted. He might well have thought that 1974 could be a troublesome year for it; but in this already favorable district he still showed considerable talent for vote-winning by taking 58% of the ballots in 1974. The winner of a seat on the Appropriations Committee in 1975, he is likely to be around Capitol Hill for quite a long time.

Census Data Pop. 441,738. Central city, 26%; suburban, 68%. Median family income, $10,278; families above $15,000: 23%; families below $3,000: 7%. Median years education, 12.5.

The Voters

Median voting age 39.
Employment profile White collar, 55%. Blue collar, 29%. Service, 13%. Farm, 3%.
Ethnic groups Black, 2%. Spanish, 9%. Total foreign stock, 11%. Germany, 2%; UK, 1%.

Presidential vote

1972	Nixon (R)	121,492	(71%)
	McGovern (D)	50,546	(29%)
1968	Nixon (R)	72,124	(55%)
	Humphrey (D)	48,187	(37%)
	Wallace (AI)	11,676	(9%)

Rep. William L. Armstrong (R) Elected 1972; b. Mar. 16, 1937, Fremont, Neb.; home, Aurora; Tulane U., U. of Minn.; Lutheran.

Career Pres., Radio Stn. KOSI, Aurora; Colo. House of Reps., 1963–64; Colo. Senate, 1965–72, Majority Leader 1969–72.

Offices 223 CHOB, 202-225-4422. Also Suite 736, 1450 S. Havana St., Aurora 80012, 303-837-2655.

Committees

Appropriations (16th). Subcommittees: Legislative; Treasury, Postal Service; and General Government.

Group Ratings

	ADA	COPE	LWV	RIPON	NFU	LCV	CFA	NAB	NSI	ACA
1974	10	9	33	50	21	24	0	83	100	100
1973	8	0	33	69	20	21	0	–	–	92

Key Votes

1) Foreign Aid	AGN	6) Gov Abortn Aid	AGN	11) Pub Cong Election $	AGN
2) Busing	AGN	7) Coed Phys Ed	AGN	12) Turkish Arms Cutoff	FOR
3) ABM	FOR	8) Pov Lawyer Gag	FOR	13) Youth Camp Regs	AGN
4) B-1 Bomber	FOR	9) Pub Trans Sub	AGN	14) Strip Mine Veto	AGN
5) Nerve Gas	AGN	10) EZ Voter Regis	AGN	15) Farm Bill Veto	FOR

Election Results

1974 general:	William L. Armstrong (R)	85,326	(58%)	($108,701)
	Ben Galloway (D)	56,888	(38%)	($32,446)
	Stan Johnson (Inp.)	5,580	(4%)	($810)

1974 primary: William L. Armstrong (R), unopposed
1972 general: William L. Armstrong (R) 104,214 (63%) ($88,538)
               Bryron L. Johnson (D) 60,948 (37%) ($17,273)

CONNECTICUT

Connecticut is not, commonly considered, an especially innovative or adventuresome state. Our image of it is shaped by the "Connecticut Yankee" of Mark Twain's novel: a collection of small cities and little salt-box colonial house towns, of old WASPs with slightly dry New England accents, of whaling ships and low green mountains. The reality is perhaps even more prosaic. Connecticut is a state now predominantly made up of the descendants of more recent immigrants: Italian and Polish and Irish, 44% Catholic altogether, of small industrial cities and pleasant, occasionally wealthy suburbs. It is a state with a higher per capita income than any other but it seems to avoid, as New York certainly does not, the extremes of wealth and poverty. It is a state which is losing its identity because so much of it lies within the media markets of New York and Providence and Springfield, and it is a state which is overwhelmed numerically by its neighbors. Scarcely more people live in Connecticut than in the borough of Brooklyn.

Connecticut is but the first state ever to elect as Governor a woman campaigning in her own right. Other states have elected women: Wyoming elected Nellie Tayloe Ross in 1924, Texas elected Ma Ferguson in 1924 and 1932, and Alabama elected Lurleen Wallace in 1966. But Mrs. Ross was chosen to succeed her late husband, and Ferguson and Wallace were stand-ins for husbands barred from running. Not so with Ella Tambussi Grasso, Governor of Connecticut. She was elected on her own in 1974, after 20 years in public office, and with 59% of the vote against a strong opponent.

Governor Grasso's career in politics provides a good review of the changing nature of Connecticut politics, as well as the reasons for her own success. She was first elected to the General Assembly in 1952, two years before Abraham Ribicoff, then a not well-known former Congressman, was elected Governor. Ribicoff was the first non-WASP Governor; what probably made the difference in that election was an emotional speech (the American Dream speech it was called) he gave just before election day about his faith in opportunity for all Americans. Ribicoff was also helped by the efforts of the state Democratic organization. Connecticut at that time had probably the strongest political parties in the United States. The Republicans were controlled by a string of able leaders, the Democrats by the late John Bailey, state party chairman from 1946 to his death in 1975.

These men could deliver their party's delegations in the legislature and commanded huge majorities in the party conventions that chose nominees for Senator, Governor, and Congressman. Theoretically, candidates who lost on the convention floor could, if they had enough votes there, force a primary; in fact, no Democrat ever did until 1970, and no Republican ever has at all. Helping the bosses control things was the straight party lever. To activate the voting machine, you had to pull the straight party lever; then, if you wished, you could split your ticket, but few voters took the trouble to do so. The result was that all politicians had a stake in the success of the top of their tickets, and they came to trust the bosses' judgement on that. The power of the straight party lever can be gauged by the fact that in the 1956 Eisenhower landslide, the state elected six Republican Congressmen and no Democrats; two years later, when Abe Ribicoff was reelected Governor with a record margin, six Democrats and no Republicans were voted in.

If bosses like Bailey controlled things in Connecticut, one of the ways they held on to their power was to recognize rising political trends and attach themselves to them. Ella Grasso was known from the first as a sort of programmatic liberal, and in her second term in the legislature she became a floor leader; in effect, she was a contact between Bailey and the liberals. Moreover, in those days of ticket-balancing—the state's Congressman-at-Large, for example, was always of Polish descent—she had at least a double advantage: she was the daughter of Italian immigrants and also a Seven Sisters (Mount Holyoke) honors graduate. Also, she was a woman, which was not particularly important in those days; of more significance, she was a smart tactical politician, and she had earned the trust of both Bailey and the liberals who often mistrusted the boss. In 1958, Bailey's convention chose her to run for the office of Secretary of State, and in the Democratic landslide of that year she won easily. In the years that followed, she became well-known and popular throughout the state, and when the mandatory straight party lever was dropped she started to run farther and farther ahead of the state ticket.

For 16 years, Connecticut politics was dominated by Bailey and his Democrats, but that came to an abrupt end in 1970. Two years before, Bailey, as national Democratic chairman, had announced that no one but Lyndon Johnson would be nominated by the party in 1968; he was one of the Johnson loyalists whose ham-handed management of the convention helped insure Hubert Humphrey's defeat in November. But for the first time anyone could remember, that year the Democratic delegation was divided; for several McCarthy supporters, including actor Paul Newman, had forced elections for national delegate and won. It was symptomatic of the split that would sink the Democrats in 1970, between the programmatic, antiwar liberals on the one hand and the ethnic, machine-based party members on the other.

The party's candidate for Governor that year, Congressman Emilio Daddario of Hartford, seemed to be acceptable to both groups, but he turned out to be so bland and uninspiring to everyone that he was beaten, 54-46, by fiery, conservative Republican Congressman Thomas Meskill. In the Senate contest, Bailey wanted to dump Senator Thomas Dodd, who had been censured by his colleagues (Ribicoff and Russell Long dissenting) for misuse of campaign funds; and to placate both wings of the party Bailey proffered an otherwise unknown Stamford millionaire. That was a mistake: Bailey's choice was challenged in a primary—Connecticut's first statewide primary ever—by the Rev. Joseph Duffey, then national chairman of ADA, who amazingly beat Bailey's man. Then, in the general, Duffey faced opposition not only from Republican Congressman Lowell Weicker, but also from the ailing Senator Dodd, running now as an Independent. One suspects that Dodd's candidacy was inspired by Nixon Administration threats to prosecute him if he didn't run and split the Democratic vote, which is exactly what Dodd did. Lowell Weicker was the innocent beneficiary: he won the Senate seat with 42% of the vote, while Duffey had 34% and Dodd 24%, most of it from heavily Catholic industrial towns.

The difficult straits of the Democratic Party in 1970 can be shown by what happened to Ella Grasso. She was running for the 6th district congressional seat vacated by Meskill, and in this straight-ticket state she had to run 11% ahead of the top of the ticket to win, by a bare 4,063 votes.

Connecticut had no statewide contests in 1972, and by 1974 all segments of the Democratic Party were determined to avoid a replay of 1970. Abe Ribicoff was up for reelection, and he spent many weekends travelling around the state and talking to Democrats, trying to bring them together and, of course, getting them to work for his own cause. He had suffered a little from blue collar defections in 1968 because of his famous speech at the Chicago convention where, nominating George McGovern, he looked down at Mayor Daley and accused him of Gestapo-like tactics. In 1974, Ribicoff feared that his challenger would be 36-year-old Congressman Bob Steele, a Republican who had been reelected in the marginal 2d congressional district in 1972 with an impressive 66% of the vote. And Ribicoff knew, too, that the Democrats would have to come up with a gubernatorial candidate who could unite both sides of the party.

The obvious person was Grasso, reelected with 60% of the vote despite the Nixon landslide. But state Attorney General Robert Killian also wanted the nomination, and had some old-line support; he left the race only after Grasso forces won the state convention delegate race in his home town of Hartford, and ended up as the candidate for Lieutenant Governor on her ticket. Then, suddenly, Meskill decided not to run for reelection, seeking a prestigious federal judgeship instead. (His confirmation has been held up because of a poor Bar Association rating, and also because some believe his record in office shows lack of judicial temperament.) Steele, who had been considering the tough race against Ribicoff, decided to run for Governor instead. Despite some opposition from conservatives, he won the party's nomination, and the fight was on.

Grasso enjoyed wide popularity, but Steele took the initiative. He charged that the programs promised in the Democratic platform would require an increase in taxes, and started calling his opponent "Spender-Ella." The liberal Grasso felt forced to repeat over and over again that she would not allow an income tax in Connecticut. Steele also made points by putting a voluntary limit on contributions to his campaign; and despite the limit, he was still able to raise more money than Grasso.

Then the tide turned. Lowell Weicker, who inspite of similar politics was not close to Steele, accused him of making unfair attacks on his opponent. And Grasso helped herself by bringing a court action to block a utility rate increase. Electricity costs more in New England than in any other part of the nation, and utility rates are an especially important issue here. Grasso succeeded in obtaining an injunction; her campaign could now show voters concretely how she had worked for them—and got results. By election day, Grasso was far ahead and managed to carry traditionally Republican suburbs as well as of course the Democratic cities. Steele had run about as good a campaign and had been as tough an oppenent as possible, and Grasso still won with 59% of the vote. Like a number of Democratic Governors elected in 1974, she found the state's treasury in bad shape, and in her first year the sales tax was raised to a whopping 7%; yet she remains popular, and barring some fluke will be reelected.

That also seems the likely fate of Weicker, whose seat is up in 1976. He is one of those politicians who rises to high office with comparative ease, aided by feuds and squabbles among his opponents. An heir to the Squibb drug fortune, he was First Selectman (i.e., Mayor of Greenwich, as recently as 1968, when he was elected to the House; two years later, he was a minority winner in the Senate race. But from these precarious beginnings, he has won wide popularity, primarily as a result of his work on the Senate Watergate committee.

Weicker was one of the Senators who sought a seat on the committee, and the only one to run his own investigation with his personal staff. One of the Nixon henchmen once described him as "an excitable kid," and there was a certain truth to that description. He was constantly outraged by the testimony he heard, and often extemporaneously denounced the witnesses for what he considered dirty tricks; if his syntax failed occasionally, his indignation matched the public mood, particularly in Connecticut. He is not especially popular in Republican Party circles, both for his denunciations of Nixon and for his fairly frequent desertions of conservative orthodoxy; he has even toyed with the idea of leaving the party, although he surely won't do that. (An example of Weicker indignation, which hurt his cause: his spirited attack on Nixon loyalist Carl Curtis, who was running against—and of course easily beat—Jacob Javits of New York for a party leadership post.) There are a number of strong Democrats—notably Secretary of State Gloria Shaffer—who would like to challenge Weicker in 1976, but the incumbent seems to have considerable strength, and the betting would have to favor him.

Both the state's Senators, though in rather different ways, share the characterization of loner. If Weicker tends to dissent from his party rather noisily, and on widely publicized issues, Abraham Ribicoff does so in his firm, deliberate voice on matters not so well known. Ribicoff's political base is solid now: his career as a two-term Governor, an early backer of John F. Kennedy, HEW Secretary, and now three-term Senator has flowed with few hitches from his narrow victory in the 1954 election. As a senior member of the Senate Finance Committee, Ribicoff is not a vote one can automatically count on either side of an issue. He was largely responsible for keeping the Nixon Family Assistance Program alive, indeed long after the Nixon Administration had abandoned it. He also is a co-sponsor with Chairman Russell Long of a bill to insure people against catastrophic illness; it is opposed by organized labor and other groups which want a more comprehensive measure. Some years ago he joined Southerners in attaching to various bills amendments to desegregate not just the South, but the north as well—a brave gesture for a Senator from a predominantly suburban state, and one opposed by virtually all his northern Democratic colleagues. Ribicoff is a brave, serious man, just past 65, reelected comfortably in 1974. He is not the kind of Senator who builds coalitions or engenders mass support; he is one who must be dealt with, issue by issue, on the basis of his own personal beliefs and opinions.

Census Data Pop. 3,032,217; 1.50% of U.S. total, 24th largest; Central city, 35%; suburban, 47%. Median family income, $11,808; 2nd highest; families above $15,000: 31%; families below $3,000: 5%. Median years education, 12.2.

1974 Share of Federal Tax Burden $5,034,927,000; 1.88% of U.S. total, 18th largest.

1974 Share of Federal Outlays $5,568,808,000; 2.06% of U.S. total, 16th largest. Per capita federal spending, $1837.

DOD	$2,778,445,000	5th (4.06%)	HEW	$1,353,432,000	24th (1.46%)
AEC	$8,077,000	21th (0.27%)	HUD	$13,912,000	22d (1.43%)
NASA	$35,246,000	12th (1.19%)	VA	$165,005,000	31st (1.21%)
DOT	$129,580,000	26th (1.53%)	EPA	$86,173,000	10th (2.74%)
DOC	$6,066,000	35th (0.38%)	RevS	$76,446,000	27th (1.26%)
DOI	$8,057,000	43d (0.33%)	Int.	$523,306,000	6th (2.54%)
USDA	$43,742,000	41st (0.35%)	Other	$341,321,000	

Economic Base Transportation equipment, especially aircraft and parts; finance, insurance and real estate; machinery, especially general industrial machinery; fabricated metal products, especially cutlery, hand tools and hardware; electrical equipment and supplies; primary metal industries, especially nonferrous rolling and drawing; printing and publishing, especially newspapers and commercial publishing.

Political Line-up Governor, Ella T. Grasso (D). Senators, Abraham A. Ribicoff (D) Lowell P. Weicker, Jr. (R). Representatives, 6 (4 D and 2 R). State Senate (29 D and 7 R); State House (118 D and 33 R).

The Voters

Registration 1,562,171 Total. 574,238 D (37%); 420,821 R (27%); 566,531 Unaffiliated (36%); 581 Other (–).
Median voting age 43.
Employment profile White collar, 52%. Blue collar, 36%. Service, 11%. Farm, 1%.
Ethnic groups Black, 6%. Spanish, 2%. Total foreign stock, 32%. Italy, 8%, Canada, 4%, Poland, 3%, UK, Ireland, Germany, USSR, 2% each.

Presidential vote

1972	Nixon (R)	810,763	(59%)
	McGovern (D)	555,498	(41%)
1968	Nixon (R)	556,721	(44%)
	Humphrey (D)	621,561	(50%)
	Wallace (AI)	76,650	(6%)

Sen. Abraham Ribicoff (D) Elected 1962, seat up 1980; b. Apr. 9, 1910, New Britain; home, Hartford; New York U., U. of Chicago, LL.B. 1933; Jewish.

Career Conn. Gen. Assembly, 1939–42; Municipal Judge, Hartford, 1941–43; U.S. House of Reps., 1949–1953; Gov. of Conn., 1955–1961; Secy. of HEW, 1961–62.

Offices 321 RSOB, 202-224-2823. Also Suite 707, 450 Main St., Hartford 06103, 203-244-3545.

Committees

Government Operations (Chairman). Subcommittees: Federal Spending Practices, Efficiency and Open Government; Oversight Procedures.

Finance (4th). Subcommittees: Energy; Health; International Trade (Chairman); Social Security Financing.

Joint Economic Committee (4th, Senate Side). Subcommittees: Consumer Economics; Economic Growth; International Economics; Priorities and Economy in Government; Urban Affairs.

Group Ratings

	ADA	COPE	LWV	RIPON	NFU	LCV	CFA	NAB	NSI	ACA
1974	95	82	90	62	82	100	100	45	44	11
1973	90	91	100	78	82	–	92	–	–	14
1972	80	86	100	78	80	87	100	10	22	18

Key Votes

1) No-Knock	AGN	8) Gov Abortn Aid	FOR	15) Consumer Prot Agy	FOR
2) Busing	FOR	9) Cut Mil Brass	ABS	16) Forced Psych Tests	FOR
3) No Fault	FOR	10) Gov Limousine	AGN	17) Fed Campaign Subs	FOR
4) F-111	FOR	11) RR Featherbed	FOR	18) Rhod Chrome Ban	FOR
5) Death Penalty	FOR	12) Handgun License	FOR	19) Open Legis Meetings	FOR
6) Foreign Aid	FOR	13) Less Troop Abrd	FOR	20) Strikers Food Stmps	ABS
7) Filibuster	AGN	14) Resume Turk Aid	AGN	21) Gov Info Disclosure	FOR

Election Results

1974 general:	Abraham A. Ribicoff (D)	125,215	(68%)	($435,985)
	James H. Brannen III (R)	60,017	(32%)	($66,162)
1974 primary:	Abraham A. Ribicoff (D), nominated by convention			
1968 general:	Abraham A. Ribicoff (D)	655,043	(54%)	
	Edwin H. May, Jr. (R)	551,455	(46%)	

Sen. Lowell P. Weicker, Jr. (R) Elected 1970, seat up 1976; May 16, 1931, Paris, France; home, Greenwich; Yale U., B.A. 1953, U. of Va., LL.B. 1958; Episcopalian.

Career Army, 1953–55; Practicing atty.; Conn. Gen. Assembly, 1962–68; U.S. House of Reps., 1969–71.

Offices 324 RSOB, 202-224-4041. Also 102 U.S. Court House, 915 Lafayette Blvd., Bridgeport 06603, 203-325-3866.

Committees

Commerce (5th). Subcommittees: Communications; Environment; Oceans and Atmosphere; Surface Transportation; Special Subcommittee to Study Textile Industry; Special Subcommittee on Freight Car Shortage; Special Subcommittee on Oil and Gas Production and Distribution.

Government Operations (5th). Subcommittees: Federal Spending Practices, Efficiency and Open Government; Reports, Accounting and Management.

Group Ratings

	ADA	COPE	LWV	RIPON	NFU	LCV	CFA	NAB	NSI	ACA
1974	78	80	78	76	92	74	88	27	67	39
1973	55	50	80	82	47	–	42	–	–	50
1972	30	50	78	90	38	43	56	50	78	42

Key Votes

1) No-Knock	AGN	8) Gov Abortn Aid	FOR	15) Consumer Prot Agy	FOR
2) Busing	FOR	9) Cut Mil Brass	AGN	16) Forced Psych Tests	AGN
3) No Fault	FOR	10) Gov Limousine	AGN	17) Fed Campaign Subs	AGN
4) F-111	FOR	11) RR Featherbed	FOR	18) Rhod Chrome Ban	FOR
5) Death Penalty	AGN	12) Handgun License	AGN	19) Open Legis Meetings	FOR
6) Foreign Aid	AGN	13) Less Troop Abrd	ABS	20) Strikers Food Stmps	FOR
7) Filibuster	FOR	14) Resume Turk Aid	AGN	21) Gov Info Disclosure	FOR

Election Results

1970 general:	Lowell P. Weicker, Jr. (R)	443,008	(42%)
	Joseph P. Duffey (D)	360,094	(34%)
	Thomas J. Dodd (Ind.)	260,264	(24%)
1970 primary:	Lowell P. Weicker, Jr. (R)	77,057	(60%)
	John M. Lupton (R)	50,657	(40%)

Gov. Ella T. Grasso (D) Elected 1974, term expires Jan. 1979; b. May 10, 1919, Windsor Locks; Mt. Holyoke Col., B.A. 1940, M.A. 1942.

Career Asst. Research Dir., Conn. War Manpower Comm., WWII; Conn. House of Reps., 1953–59, Floor Leader, 1955; Secy. of State of Conn., 1959–71; U.S. House of Reps., 1971–75.

Offices State of Connecticut, Executive Chambers, Hartford 06115, 203-566-4840.

Election Results

1974 general:	Ella T. Grasso (D)	643,490	(59%)
	Robert H. Steele (R)	440,169	(41%)
1974 primary:	Ella T. Grasso (D)	nominated	by (convention)

◆ ◆ ◆ ◆ ◆

FIRST DISTRICT

Hartford is Connecticut's largest city, the state capital, and the headquarters of many of the nation's largest insurance companies. Hartford and its suburbs also contain much of Connecticut's defense industry—most notably United Aircraft's big airplane engine factories. As with most of Connecticut's larger cities, people have long since moved out from Hartford into a series of comfortable suburbs. They range from working class areas like East Hartford and Windsor on the Connecticut River to the high income WASP and Jewish precincts of West Hartford and Bloomfield. Hartford itself, with the bulk of the area's poor and black residents, has many of the typical urban problems. But here in this small city, with its gleaming new office buildings, its ornate state Capitol, and its high white collar employment, these problems do not seem as overwhelming as they do in New York or Philadelphia. And while the officeholders of those cities seem to be throwing in the towel, optimistic city fathers here have launched an ambitious and expensive regional development program—the Greater Hartford Process—for Hartford and its environs.

Hartford and the 1st congressional district, which includes the city and most of its suburbs, has long been the Democratic stronghold of Connecticut. This should be attributed in part to the efforts of the late John M. Bailey, longtime state (1946–75) and (1961–1968) national Democratic chairman; analysis of election returns shows that Bailey's machine traditionally turns out a higher number of low-income Democratic voters than in Connecticut's other cities. Given the traditional strength of the Democrats here, the present Congressman from the 1st, William Cotter, came to office in an unusual way. First, he beat the organization candidate in the primary, then he just barely won the general election. Cotter had several problems in the general, one of them being the poor showing of the 1970 Democratic gubernatorial candidate, his predecessor Emilio Daddario. Another was the independent candidacy of one Edward Coll. Connoisseurs of these things will remember Coll's performance as putative presidential candidate in the 1972 New Hampshire primary, when—with George McGovern and Edmund Muskie watching gravely—he announced he had a copy of the Manchester *Union Leader* in his hand and hoisted into full view a rubber rat.

Reelection has come rather easily for Cotter. He made headlines once as the first Congressman to endorse the 1973 meat boycott; but he is probably better known as a defendant, from the days when he was Connecticut's Insurance Commissioner, in a Ralph Nader suit to void the merger of ITT and the Hartford, one of the state's insurance giants. In 1975, Cotter won a seat on the expanded Ways and Means Committee.

Census Data Pop. 505,418. Central city, 35%; suburban, 47%. Median family income, $12,031; families above $15,000: 32%; families below $3,000: 6%. Median years education, 12.2.

The Voters

Median voting age 44.
Employment profile White collar, 58%. Blue collar, 31%. Service, 11%. Farm, –%.
Ethnic groups Black, 10%. Spanish, 3%. Total foreign stock, 34%. Italy, 7%; Canada, 6%; Poland, 4%; Ireland, 3%; USSR, UK, Germany, 2% each.

Presidential vote

1972	Nixon (R)	121,196	(51%)
	McGovern (D)	114,473	(49%)
1968	Nixon (R)	85,854	(39%)
	Humphrey (D)	125,090	(56%)
	Wallace (AI)	10,692	(5%)

Rep. William R. Cotter (D) Elected 1970; b. July 18, 1926, Hartford; home, Hartford; Trinity Col., Hartford, B.A., 1949; Catholic.

Career Member, Court of Common Council, Hartford, 1953; Aide to Gov. Abraham Ribicoff, 1955–57; Deputy Insurance Commissioner of Conn., 1957–64, Commissioner, 1964–70.

Offices 213 CHOB, 202-225-2265. Also 450 Main St., Hartford 06103, 203-244-2383.

Committees

Ways and Means (19th). Subcommittees: Health; Social Security.

Group Ratings

	ADA	COPE	LWV	RIPON	NFU	LCV	CFA	NAB	NSI	ACA
1974	62	100	75	50	83	75	82	33	50	21
1973	80	100	83	57	74	61	88	–	–	27
1972	63	91	75	71	71	51	100	17	25	18

Key Votes

1) Foreign Aid	FOR	6) Gov Abortn Aid	AGN	11) Pub Cong Election $	FOR
2) Busing	AGN	7) Coed Phys Ed	FOR	12) Turkish Arms Cutoff	FOR
3) ABM	AGN	8) Pov Lawyer Gag	AGN	13) Youth Camp Regs	FOR
4) B-1 Bomber	AGN	9) Pub Trans Sub	FOR	14) Strip Mine Veto	AGN
5) Nerve Gas	AGN	10) EZ Voter Regis	FOR	15) Farm Bill Veto	FOR

Election Results

1974 general:	William R. Cotter (D)	117,038	(64%)	($52,604)
	F. Mac Buckley (R)	67,080	(36%)	($28,045)
1974 primary:	William R. Cotter (D), unopposed			
1972 general:	William R. Cotter (D)	130,701	(58%)	($96,208)
	Richard M. Rittenband (R)	96,188	(42%)	($55,985)

◆ ◆ ◆ ◆ ◆

SECOND DISTRICT

The 2d district is the eastern half—geographically, at least—of Connecticut. The district has Yankee villages and high-income summer and retirement colonies with names like Old Saybrook and Old Lyme; it also has small and middle-sized mill towns like Norwich, Danielson, and Putnam. Traditional Yankee Republicanism still has some strength here, but the political balance lies in the hands of second- and third-generation ethnics in places like New London and Middletown. This mix makes the 2d a middle-of-the-road, bellwether district, at least when no incumbent is running. During the 1950s, when the straight party lever was still mandatory and few tickets were split, congressional elections were usually close in the 2d, with party control shifting a couple of times. More recent elections have shown a shift to the more common national trend: the election of a Congressman by close margin and his reelection by much larger margins as long as he keeps running.

So the 2d has had quite a number of Congressmen in the last 15 or 20 years, including such a heavyweight as Chester Bowles (1959–61), who was a prime candidate for Secretary of State while he served; a Republican with the marvellously WASPy name of Horace Seely-Brown, Jr.; and a Democrat of French Canadian origin named William St. Onge. Its most recent ex-Congressman is

Republican Bob Steele, elected by a small margin in 1970, reelected by a landslide (running well ahead of Nixon) in 1972. Steele was his party's gubernatorial candidate in 1974, and though he won only 41% of the vote against Ella Grasso, he showed considerable campaigning talent, and should be considered a very live political prospect for the future in Connecticut. Incidentally, he was once a CIA agent, as was his 1972 opponent, former Assistant Secretary of State for Far Eastern Affairs Roger Hilsman—the first recorded instance of two CIA veterans running against each other in a congressional race.

The seat is currently held by a 32-year-old Democrat, with the vaguely familiar name of Christopher J. Dodd. He is the son of former Congressman (1953–57) and Senator (1959–71) Thomas J. Dodd. The elder Dodd was not just another standard liberal Democrat; he was a vocal anti-Communist, and spent much of his congressional career trying to ferret out subversives. He also was a major force behind gun control, and Lyndon Johnson tantalized everyone by considering him for Vice President in 1964. Dodd's last years in the Senate were sad ones; he was attacked by Drew Pearson for misusing government and campaign funds, and never really answered the charges, and was finally censured by the Senate. The younger Dodd seems a somewhat more standard northern Democrat for his time. He serves on the Judiciary Committee, and the fact that he won with 60% of the vote in 1974, though it was a Democratic year, indicates that he is likely to keep winning the 2d for a considerable time to come—expect, perhaps, if Steele decides he would like to return to the House.

Census Data Pop. 505,493. Central city, 33%; suburban, 66%. Median family income, $10,885; families above $15,000: 24%; families below $3,000: 7%. Median years education, 12.1.

The Voters

Median voting age 40.
Employment profile White collar, 48%. Blue collar, 39%. Service, 12%. Farm, 1%.
Ethnic groups Black, 2%. Spanish, 1%. Total foreign stock, 26%. Canada, 6%; Italy, 4%; Poland, 3%; UK, Germany, 2% each; USSR, Ireland, 1% each.

Presidential vote

1972	Nixon (R)	127,923	(60%)
	McGovern (D)	85,382	(40%)
1968	Nixon (R)	82,739	(44%)
	Humphrey (D)	95,604	(51%)
	Wallace (AI)	10,025	(5%)

Rep. Christopher J. Dodd (D) Elected 1974; b. May 27, 1944, Willimantic; home, North Stonington; Providence Col., B.A. 1966, U. of Louisville, J.D. 1972.

Career Peace Corps, 1966–68; Army 1969–75.

Offices 429 CHOB, 202-225-2076. Also P.O. Bldg., New Haven 06510, 203-624-1308.

Committees

Judiciary (21st). Subcommittees: Civil and Constitutional Rights; Immigration, Citizenship, and International Law.

Science and Technology (19th). Subcommittees: Energy Research, Development, and Demonstration; Science, Research, and Technology.

Group Ratings: Newly Elected

Key Votes

1) Foreign Aid	FOR	6) Gov Abortn Aid	NE	11) Pub Cong Election $	NE
2) Busing	NE	7) Coed Phys Ed	FOR	12) Turkish Arms Cutoff	NE
3) ABM	NE	8) Pov Lawyer Gag	NE	13) Youth Camp Regs	FOR
4) B-1 Bomber	AGN	9) Pub Trans Sub	NE	14) Strip Mine Veto	AGN
5) Nerve Gas	NE	10) EZ Voter Regis	NE	15) Farm Bill Veto	AGN

Election Results

1974 general:	Christopher J. Dodd (D)	104,436	(60%)	($102,209)
	Samuel B. Hellier (R)	69,380	(40%)	($87,844)
1974 primary:	Christopher J. Dodd (D), unopposed			

◆ ◆ ◆ ◆ ◆

THIRD DISTRICT

The Italian-American has long been the forgotten man in American politics. He is too far up the ladder of economic security and social status to engage the sympathies of foundation executives and affluent academics; yet in ways that still hurt, he still suffers from the discrimination of the larger society, deprived of the advantages well-born WASPs take for granted. In the years of radical chic and the kind of electoral alliances symbolized by New York's John Lindsay (rich whites and poor blacks and browns), ethnics like the Italian-American were left out completely. Such people were condemned as Archie Bunkers, which of course some of them were; but the same people who did the condemning never seemed to have a harsh word for the misdeeds of some members of other groups.

There are more Italian-Americans, as the Census Bureau defines them, than any other ethnic group here and there are more of them in the 3d congressional district of Connecticut than in all but 13 of the nation's 435 districts. They settled here, mostly in the late nineteenth and early twentieth centuries, and found jobs in the factories of New Haven. There are still old, cohesive Italian-American communities in the city, but most of the descendents of the immigrants have since moved out to suburbs like West Haven, East Haven, and Hamden. Unlike most immigrant groups, the Italians of southern Connecticut gravitated politically to the Republican Party, because the Irish seemed to dominate the Democrats. To a surprising extent, the Italians maintained their Republican allegiance through the New Deal years; and today, probably a majority of the 3d district's Italian-Americans have a clear preference for the Republican Party—even though Connecticut's first Italian-American Governor, Ella Grasso, is a Democrat.

Most readers when thinking of the 3d district and New Haven think automatically of Yale, and perhaps of the famous urban renewal program of ex-Mayor Richard Lee. But Yale, which has fewer students (10,000) than Southern Connecticut State College, plays little part in the politics of the 3d, except perhaps to serve as a focus of resentment for the great majority. These are the people living in neat New England suburban houses, whose parents lived in what are now black ghettoes, and whose children will never go to Yale. Lee has not been Mayor since the long-ago year of 1969; his successor is an ally of Democratic Town Chairman Arthur Barbieri, a longtime antagonist of State Chairman John Bailey.

The Congressman from the 3d district, Robert Giaimo (pronounced JYE-moh), is a Barbieri ally and over the years has been very much a town rather than gown Democrat. A middle seniority member of Appropriations, Giaimo's thinking on issues is usually more in line with that of traditional big-city Democrats than with the liberals of the Democratic Study Group. But with all the assaults on congressional power made by the Nixon Administration, these two groups have tended to coalesce, and in recent years one could see Giaimo leading the fight—because of his committee position—against further American military action in or aid to Cambodia and Vietnam. Even more interesting, in 1975 Giaimo, as a member of the special House committee investigating the CIA, led the move to oust Chairman Lucien Nedzi, on the grounds that Nedzi had not been harsh enough on the Agency.

Oddly enough, Giaimo for many years had not been racking up huge majorities in this basically Democratic district; after 14 years in Congress, he received only 53% of the vote in 1972. Then, suddenly, his percentage shot up to 66% in the very Democratic year of 1974; he ran ahead of Ella Grasso and just barely behind Abraham Ribicoff in the district. This reflected in part a simple collapse of the Republican Party here, but it may also mean that Giaimo has finally managed to make his seat utterly secure.

Census Data Pop. 505,293. Central city, 27%; suburban, 62%. Median family income, $11,463; families above $15,000: 29%; families below $3,000: 6%. Median years education, 12.2.

The Voters

Median voting age 43.
Employment profile White collar, 53%. Blue collar, 35%. Service, 11%. Farm, 1%.

Ethnic groups Black, 9%. Spanish, 2%. Total foreign stock, 31%. Italy, 10%; Poland, Ireland, UK, Canada, USSR, Germany, 2% each.

Presidential vote

1972	Nixon (R)	142,569	(62%)
	McGovern (D)	87,766	(38%)
1968	Nixon (R)	96,553	(45%)
	Humphrey (D)	102,907	(48%)
	Wallace (AI)	16,308	(8%)

Rep. Robert N. Giaimo (D) Elected 1958; b. Oct. 15, 1919, New Haven; home, North Haven; Fordham Col., B.A., 1941, U. of Conn., LL.B. 1943; Catholic.

Career Army, WWII; Practicing atty., 1947–58; Chm., Personal Appeals Bd., North Haven, 1955–58.

Offices 2265 RHOB, 202-225-3661. Also 301 P.O.Bldg., New Haven 06510, 203-432-2043.

Committees

Appropriations (14th). Subcommittees: Defense; District of Columbia; Legislative.

Group Ratings

	ADA	COPE	LWV	RIPON	NFU	LCV	CFA	NAB	NSI	ACA
1974	68	80	55	53	79	69	92	42	50	21
1973	76	91	75	69	83	32	75	–	–	23
1972	31	70	45	69	57	47	0	40	20	45

Key Votes

1) Foreign Aid	AGN	6) Gov Abortn Aid	FOR	11) Pub Cong Election $	FOR
2) Busing	AGN	7) Coed Phys Ed	AGN	12) Turkish Arms Cutoff	FOR
3) ABM	AGN	8) Pov Lawyer Gag	FOR	13) Youth Camp Regs	FOR
4) B-1 Bomber	AGN	9) Pub Trans Sub	ABS	14) Strip Mine Veto	AGN
5) Nerve Gas	AGN	10) EZ Voter Regis	FOR	15) Farm Bill Veto	AGN

Election Results

1974 general:	Robert Giaimo :D)	114,316	(66%)	($40,079)
	James Altham, Jr. (R)	55,177	(32%)	($6,556)
	Peter Koltypin (GWP)	3,693	(2%)	($2,749)
1974 primary:	Robert Giaimo (D), unopposed			
1972 general:	Robert Giaimo (D)	121,217	(53%)	($79,608)
	Henry A. Povinelli (R)	106,313	(47%)	($33,591)

◆ ◆ ◆ ◆ ◆

FOURTH DISTRICT

If Hartford County has been the traditional home of Connecticut's Democrats, then Fairfield County has been the bedrock of the state's Republicans. Fairfield is one of the richest counties in the nation, a land of broad, well-manicured lawns sweeping down to Long Island Sound, of woodsy New Canaan and artsy-craftsy Westport, of commuters driving to the station to take the bedraggled New Haven Railroad into Manhattan. Unlike the rest of Connecticut, Fairfield County is in many ways an extension of New York City, economically and otherwise. People watch New York, not Connecticut television; they are Mets, not Red Soxs, fans; and their political attitudes more than in other parts of this small state, are shaped by what is happening in New York.

Most of the people of Fairfield County live in the 4th congressional district—a string of high-income, traditionally Republican towns along Long Island Sound: Greenwich, Stamford, Darien, Norwalk, Westport, Fairfield. But it would be inaccurate to infer that the harried advertising executive on an hour-and-a-quarter commute is the typical 4th district voter. For the 4th takes in the industrial city of Bridgeport—Connecticut's second largest—as well as the commuter towns; and even there, below the railroad station or around the old downtown, you can see the slightly shabby small houses where the district's poorer voters live. Some 10% of the 4th's residents are black, and it has a higher percentage of foreign stock residents than any other district in the state.

For analysis, you can divide the 4th into two convenient sections: the rich WASPy towns and Bridgeport. The richer residents, moved by the Vietnam war and, often, by the strange new habits of their children, have been edging to the left and toward the Democrats. Westport, for example, gave John Kennedy just 36% of its vote in 1960; it went 41% for George McGovern in 1972. By contrast, Bridgeport has been gyrating wildly in recent years. It went 61% for Kennedy in 1960, but by 1970—with the city's blue collar Catholics moving steadily to the right—it voted for Republican Thomas Meskill for Governor, and two years later gave Richard Nixon 55% of its votes. Watergate apparently disillusioned many of these members of the supposedly emerging Republican majority, and by 1974 Bridgeport was voting a whopping 71% for Ella Grasso for Governor.

That sudden switch meant trouble for Republican Congressman Stewart McKinney. A moderate-to-liberal Republican who had succeeded Lowell Weicker in this seat in 1970, McKinney had not had much trouble winning either that year or in 1972; in the latter year he even carried Bridgeport. But in 1974 he lost Bridgeport by more than 10,000 votes, and won the election with only 54% of the total vote. If he had not held his own (or in a couple of cases increased his percentage) in the richer towns, he might have lost; surely a stronger candidate could have beaten him.

Census Data Pop. 505,366. Central city, 68%; suburban, 32%. Median family income, $12,692; families above $15,000: 38%; families below $3,000: 5%. Median years education, 12.3.

The Voters

Median voting age 45.
Employment profile White collar, 56%. Blue collar, 33%. Service, 11%. Farm, –%.
Ethnic groups Black, 10%. Spanish, 5%. Total foreign stock, 35%. Italy, 8%; Poland, UK, 3% each; Canada, Ireland, Germany, USSR, 2% each.

Presidential vote

1972	Nixon (R)	138,496	(63%)
	McGovern (D)	81,802	(37%)
1968	Nixon (R)	105,455	(50%)
	Humphrey (D)	92,922	(44%)
	Wallace (AI)	13,159	(6%)

Rep. Stewart B. McKinney (R) Elected 1970; b. Jan. 30, 1931, Pittsburgh, Pa.; home, Fairfield; Princeton U., 1949–51, Yale U., B.A. 1958; Episcopalian.

Career Air Force, 1951–55; Pres., CMF Tires, Inc.; Real Estate Development; Conn. Gen. Assembly, 1967–70.

Offices 504 CHOB, 202-225-5541. Also Fed. Bldg., Lafayette Blvd., Bridgeport 06603, 203-384-2286.

Committees

Banking, Currency and Housing (6th). Subcommittees: Economic Stabilization; General Oversight and Renegotiation; Housing and Community Development.

District of Columbia (3d). Subcommittees: Commerce, Housing and Transportation; Education, Labor and Social Services; Fiscal Affairs.

Group Ratings

	ADA	COPE	LWV	RIPON	NFU	LCV	CFA	NAB	NSI	ACA
1974	70	64	92	88	71	65	67	36	56	21
1973	59	73	100	100	55	53	63	–	–	40
1972	63	60	75	75	50	73	100	67	25	28

Key Votes

1) Foreign Aid	FOR	6) Gov Abortn Aid	FOR
2) Busing	FOR	7) Coed Phys Ed	AGN
3) ABM	AGN	8) Pov Lawyer Gag	ABS
4) B-1 Bomber	AGN	9) Pub Trans Sub	FOR
5) Nerve Gas	AGN	10) EZ Voter Regis	AGN

11) Pub Cong Election $	FOR
12) Turkish Arms Cutoff	FOR
13) Youth Camp Regs	FOR
14) Strip Mine Veto	ABS
15) Farm Bill Veto	FOR

Election Results

1974 general:	Stewart B. McKinney (R)	83,630	(54%)	($94,365)
	James G. Kellis (D)	71,047	(46%)	($51,034)
1974 primary:	Stewart B. McKinney (R), unopposed			
1972 general:	Stewart B. McKinney (R)	135,883	(63%)	($112,669)
	James P. McLoughlin (D)	79,515	(37%)	($39,809)

◆ ◆ ◆ ◆ ◆

FIFTH DISTRICT

The 5th district is an amalgam of Connecticut's lesser known cities and towns which are spread out over the hills just north of Long Island Sound. The district includes the industrial city of Waterbury and the decaying mill towns of the Naugatuck valley; the relatively prosperous working class town of Meriden to the east; and Danbury, the onetime hat-manufacturing center, in the west. (Danbury is also known for its federal prison which has accommodated such varied political figures as the Berrigan brothers and G. Gordon Liddy, Jr.). The industrial cities and towns are all traditionally Democratic; found in between are the smaller, Yankee towns which are inevitably more Republican.

But the most important part of the 5th, politically, in the last two elections has been a small portion that was added in the redistricting following the 1970 census. With the Democrats then in control of the state legislature, a plan was passed and ultimately approved by the courts which added to the old, seemingly safe Democratic 5th the heavily Republican towns of New Canaan, Wilton, and Weston. The idea was to remove Republican votes from the adjacent 4th district and put that seat, on paper at least, within the reach of a Democratic challenger. But as often happens the redistricters miscalculated. They did not manage to make the 4th Democratic enough even for 1974, and the reconstituted 5th, as it has worked out, retired a veteran Democratic Congressman and has twice elected his Republican successor.

The Democratic incumbent was John Monagan, who had held the office since the Connecticut Democratic sweep of 1958. As a subcommittee chairman Monagan spent much of what turned out to be his last term investigating fraud and incompetence in the administration of the FHA; he also made the mistake of taking a government-paid trip to Europe in October 1972. In contrast, Republican Ronald Sarasin was campaigning up and down the district. The younger (45 vs 60) man must have made a particularly good impression on the district's new residents; while Monagan's style, redolent with old-fashioned Irish wit, did not seem to go over well—if they knew about him at all—with the WASP suburbanites of the new Republican towns. Monagan managed to carry that portion of the district which he had previously represented by 791 votes—a considerably smaller margin than he had enjoyed in the past. But he lost the new part of the 5th by 6,227.

It was much the same story in 1974. Sarasin had worked the district hard and compiled an often liberal voting record, but he still faced tough competition in the person of General Assembly Minority Leader and former Speaker William Ratchford. Ratchford was able to carry the old part of the district by 192 votes, but again Sarasin swept the new towns, this time with a 4,783-vote margin. The Connecticut Democrats had tried to win both the 4th and the 5th districts, and ended up losing both.

Census Data Pop. 505,316. Central city, 42%; suburban, 39%. Median family income, $12,200; families above $15,000: 33%; families below $3,000: 5%. Median years education, 12.2.

The Voters

Median voting age 44.
Employment profile White collar, 51%. Blue collar, 39%. Service, 10%. Farm, –%.
Ethnic groups Black, 4%. Spanish, 2%. Total foreign stock, 34%. Italy, 9%; Canada, 4%; Poland, 3%; UK, Ireland, Germany, 2% each; USSR, 1%.

Presidential vote

1972	Nixon (R)	144,149	(62%)
	McGovern (D)	87,747	(38%)
1968	Nixon (R)	96,604	(45%)
	Humphrey (D)	100,828	(47%)
	Wallace (AI)	15,503	(7%)

Rep. Ronald A. Sarasin (R) Elected 1972; b. Dec. 31, 1934, Fall River, Mass.; home, Beacon Falls; U. of Conn., B.S. 1960, J.D. 1963; Catholic.

Career Navy, 1952–56; Practicing atty.; Asst. Prof. of Law, New Haven Col., 1963–66; Conn. Gen. Assembly, 1968–72.

Offices 229 CHOB, 202-225-3822. Also 135 Grand St., Waterbury 06701, 203-573-1418.

Committees

Education and Labor (8th). Subcommittees: Agricultural Labor; Labor Standards; Manpower, Compensation, and Health and Safety.

Group Ratings

	ADA	COPE	LWV	RIPON	NFU	LCV	CFA	NAB	NSI	ACA
1974	65	91	75	75	86	53	77	67	70	33
1973	40	55	83	73	45	53	63	–	–	48

Key Votes

1) Foreign Aid	AGN	6) Gov Abortn Aid	AGN	11) Pub Cong Election $	FOR
2) Busing	AGN	7) Coed Phys Ed	AGN	12) Turkish Arms Cutoff	FOR
3) ABM	AGN	8) Pov Lawyer Gag	FOR	13) Youth Camp Regs	FOR
4) B-1 Bomber	AGN	9) Pub Trans Sub	FOR	14) Strip Mine Veto	AGN
5) Nerve Gas	AGN	10) EZ Voter Regis	FOR	15) Farm Bill Veto	FOR

Election Results

1974 general:	Ronald A. Sarasin (R)	94,998	(51%)	($134,440)
	William Ratchford (D)	90,407	(49%)	($86,808)
1974 primary:	Tonald A. Sarasin (R), unopposed			
1972 general:	Ronald A. Sarasin (R)	117,578	(51%)	($80,251)
	John S. Monagan (D)	112,142	49%)	($84,436)

◆ ◆ ◆ ◆ ◆

SIXTH DISTRICT

Some congressional districts seem to be made up of territory left over after everyone else has constructed his own constituency. Such a district is the 6th of Connecticut. Its population centers are widely dispersed, at just about the opposite ends of the district. Enfield and Windsor Locks, in the far northeast corner, are predominantly Italian-American and are part of the Hartford-to-Springfield (Massachusetts) industrial corridor. In the southeast corner of the 6th are Bristol and New Britain, the latter the city with the state's largest concentration of Polish-Americans. In the north central part of the district, amid the gentle mountains, are the mill towns of Torrington and Winsted, the latter of which is Ralph Nader's home town. In between these Democratic areas are the Yankee towns (like Sharon, home of the Buckley clan) and some posh Republican Hartford suburbs like Farmington, Avon, and Simsbury.

The 1964 legislature, which drew the district's lines (they have been altered only slightly since), expected the 6th to elect a Democrat, and generally it has; but overall the district must be classed as marginal. Indeed, in its relatively brief history, the 6th has had four different Representatives —practically a record in this day when Congressmen seek ever-longer seniority. The first, Bernard Grabowski, was the last beneficiary of the tradition that the state's Congressman-at-Large be of Polish descent; he was slated in 1962 when the incumbent rebelled against the leadership of Democratic State Chairman John Bailey. Grabowski did fine while riding the coattails of the state ticket in 1962 and 1964; left to his own devices in this rather disparate constituency in 1966, he lost. The winner was Thomas Meskill, the brash conservative Republican Mayor of New Britain, who went on to the Governorship in 1970. So too did Meskill's successor, Ella Grasso, after a narrow win here in 1970 and a solid reelection in 1972.

That left the district once again up for grabs in 1974. The winner was an unlikely one, at least from the perspective of traditional Connecticut politics: 30-year-old Toby Moffett, once a Nader's Raider and director of the Nader-inspired Connecticut Citizens' Action Group. Moffett's strong suit was constituency service—something 6th district residents were used to; Grasso has had a toll-free phone number she advertised as the "Ella-phone" to take complaints. Moffett used his campaign staff to solve constituent's problems all during the campaign and in the process demolished the Republican candidate, Patsy J. Piscopo, by almost a 2-1 margin. This was an even better showing than Grasso herself was making in the district, or had made two years before, and suggests that Moffett should have no trouble at all winning reelection—if he isn't already thinking about statewide office. After all, the 6th district has produced the last two Governors.

Census Data Pop. 505,331. Central city, 26%; suburban, 51%. Median family income, $11,898; families above $15,000: 30%; families below $3,000: 5%. Median years education, 12.2.

The Voters

Median voting age 43.
Employment profile White collar, 50%. Blue collar, 40%. Service, 9%. Farm, 1%.
Ethnic groups Black, 1%. Spanish, 1%. Total foreign stock, 32%. Italy, 6%; Canada, Poland, 5% each; Germany, UK, 2% each; Ireland, 1%.

Presidential vote

1972	Nixon (R)	136,430	(58%)
	McGovern (D)	98,328	(42%)
1968	Nixon (R)	89,516	(44%)
	Humphrey (D)	104,210	(51%)
	Wallace (AI)	10,963	(5%)

Rep. Anthony Toby Moffett (D) Elected 1974; b. Aug. 18, 1944, Holyoke, Mass.; home, Unionville; Syracuse U., A.B. 1966, Boston Col., M.A. 1968.

Career Dir., Ofc. of Students and Youth, Ofc. of the U.S. Commissioner of Educ., 1969–70; Staff aide to U.S. Sen. Walter Mondale of Minn., 1970–71; Dir., Conn. Citizens Action Group, 1971–74.

Offices 1008 LHOB, 202-225-4476. Also 245 Main St., Bristol 06010, 203-589-5750.

Committees

Government Operations (27th). Subcommittees: Commerce, Consumer and Monetary Affairs; Manpower and Housing.

Interstate and Foreign Commerce (27th). Subcommittees: Energy and Power; Oversight and Investigations.

Group Ratings: Newly Elected

Key Votes

1) Foreign Aid	AGN	6) Gov Abortn Aid	NE	11) Pub Cong Election $	NE
2) Busing	NE	7) Coed Phys Ed	FOR	12) Turkish Arms Cutoff	NE
3) ABM	NE	8) Pov Lawyer Gag	NE	13) Youth Camp Regs	FOR
4) B-1 Bomber	AGN	9) Pub Trans Sub	NE	14) Strip Mine Veto	AGN
5) Nerve Gas	NE	10) EZ Voter Regis	NE	15) Farm Bill Veto	AGN

Election Results

1974 general:	Anthony Toby Moffett (D)	122,785	(64%)	($144,806)
	Patsy J. Piscopo (R)	69–942	(36%)	($89,328)
1974 primary:	Anthony Toby Moffett (D)	19,448	(58%)	
	Stanley J. Pac (D)	14,070	(42%)	

DELAWARE

Delaware likes to boast that is was the "First State" because it ratified the Constitution before any other in 1787. But this tiny state's place in our national life depends less on that than on the fact that, because of its liberal incorporation laws and low taxes, it is the technical home of the most of the nation's large corporations and the fact that it is the real home of the Du Pont company. Du Pont, with annual revenues of more than $4 billion, clearly dominates this miniscule state, whose revenues are only about $300 million. And of course wealthy members of the Du Pont family—there are actually more than a thousand living Du Ponts—and corporate executives have a disproportionate say in what happens here. A few years ago, a group of Nader's Raiders wrote a book about Delaware called "The Company State"; while it stumbles over itself on occasion in its hurry to condemn the Du Ponts, its basic point—that the Du Ponts tend to run things—is not unsound.

The politics of Delaware (second smallest in area, fifth smallest in population) has infrequently engaged the attention of writers. Technically, it has as much clout in the U.S. Senate as California or New York; in fact, Delaware has seldom produced important Senators. Over the years, the state has wavered between Democrats and Republicans, with the Du Ponts (the company owns the Wilmington newspapers, though it says it is trying to sell them) entrenched in both parties. In the 1960s, the Republicans seemed to gain a decisive edge, in large part because of their dominance of fast-growing suburban New Castle County, which cast 61% of the state's vote in 1972. Another factor was the increasing attachment of the Du Pont establishment to the Republicans; many top officials, most of them Republicans, hold public office while on leave from jobs with the company.

This was the picture going into the 1972 elections, with a Republican Senate seat and the Republican-held Governorship up for grabs. Senator J. Caleb Boggs had held statewide office since 1946 without alienating any substantial segment of the electorate, and everyone expected he could win easily. Governor Russell Peterson had stirred more controversy. He was known best as the sponsor of a law to prevent industrial development—particularly oil refineries—on Delaware's coastline; also, and more disastrously, he had sponsored an increase in taxes after promising solemnly not to. Peterson faced substantial conservative primary opposition, and only won by a small margin. Republicans wanted to avoid any such turmoil in the Senate contest, and so persuaded a reluctant Boggs to seek, at 63, one more term—with help from Richard Nixon himself.

The outcome furnished proof, if any was needed, of the danger of imposing campaign strategies from Washington (or San Clemente). The Democratic Senate nomination went without contest to 29-year-old New Castle County Councilman Joseph Biden (who was forced to explain again and again that he would turn the constitutionally-required 30 before the beginning of the term). Biden campaigned actively everywhere, paying special attention to the two southern counties with their south-of-the-Mason-Dixon-line traditions. He assembled a large volunteer force to augment the efforts of his large family; his 27-year-old sister was his campaign manager. Biden bought no television time (Delaware has no VHF station) and to save mailing costs he had volunteers hand-deliver campaign literature to every house in the state. He did not attack his opponent ("He's really a nice guy"), but he stressed his opposition to the Vietnam war and his conviction that people had lost confidence in public institutions.

As the fall progressed, it became clear that Biden posed a genuine threat to his veteran rival; and on election night he won by a narrow 51–49 margin. Biden's youth, success, and large family pitching in reminded many people of the Kennedys. Then tragedy struck. Biden's wife and infant daughter were killed in an automobile accident shortly after the election. The new Senator mulled resigning; instead he commutes every day from Wilmington suburbs. He did find time to be one of the Democrats' most active stump campaigners across the country in 1974; and in the Senate with his sometimes brash articulateness he has attracted favorable notice.

As Biden was beating Caleb Boggs, Delaware was experiencing another of its close gubernatorial races. (No one has won the office with more than a 10,000-vote margin since World War II.) The winner, finally, was Sherman Tribbett, a conservatively inclined Democrat. Though he has not been counted as a friend of Peterson's coastal preservation law, it still has not been repealed-despite heavy pressure from oil companies and others.

Delaware's senior Senator, William V. Roth, had almost as quick a rise to prominence as Biden. In 1966, Roth won the state's single House seat; in 1970, he got the Republican nomination to succeed Sen. John Williams, who was so tenacious in the pursuit of wrongdoers like Bobby Baker that he became known as the "conscience of the Senate." Roth easily won the 1970 election. He may be categorized as conservative on substantive issues and a reformer in procedural matters. He has been particularly active in the attempts, finally successful in 1975, to open up Senate committee hearings to the public (unless the committee votes in public to make them secret). Roth's seat is up in 1976, and with Delaware's Democrats stronger now than they were six years ago, he may have a harder time holding it than he did winning it in the first place.

Certainly one politician who would someday like a Senate seat is Delaware's Congressman-at-Large Pierre S. Du Pont IV. Du Pont, who likes to be called Pete and has campaigned against corporate polluters (which in Delaware means just on thing) is a moderate, sometimes liberal Republican. He is also a rather voluble one, and on the Foreign Affairs Committee has made himself known as a leading opponent of Ford Administration policy on Cyprus and Cambodia. Personable, a good speaker, wealthy, young, Du Pont probably would have won the 1972 Senate race, if he could have got the nomination, but now he is almost foreclosed from seeking it. Roth he cannot challenge, and Biden will difficult indeed to beat in 1978.

Census Data Pop. 302,173; 0.15% of U.S. total, 46th largest; Central city, 15%; suburban, 56%. Median family income, $12,441; 14th highest; families above $15,000: 22%; families below $3,000: 8%. Median years education, 12.5.

1974 Share of Federal Tax Burden $910,572,000; 0.34% of U.S. total, 42d largest.

1974 Share of Federal Outlays $703,057,000; 0.26% of U.S. total, 48th largest. Per capita federal spending, $1283.

DOD	$140,564,000	45th (0.21%)		HEW	$213,926,000	47th (0.23%)
AEC	$–	– (–)		HUD	$4,552,000	38th (0.47%)
NASA	$1,956,000	30th (0.07%)		VA	$36,497,000	47th (0.03%)
DOT	$77,491,000	36th (0.92%)		EPA	$26,784,000	26th (0.85%)
DOC	$1,266,000	50th (0.08%)		RevS	$18,058,000	46th (0.30%)
DOI	$3,486,000	48th (0.14%)		Int.	$22,548,000	46th (0.11%)
USDA	$12,392,000	50th (0.10%)		Other	$143,537,000	

Economic Base Finance, insurance and real estate; chemicals and allied products, especially plastics materials and synthetics; food and kindred products, especially poultry dressing and canned fruits and vegetables; agriculture, notably broilers, corn, dairy products and soybeans; apparel and other textile products.

Political Line-up Governor, Sherman W. Tribbitt (D). Senators, William V. Roth, Jr. (R) and Joseph R. Biden, Jr. (D). Representatives, 1 D at large. State Senate (13 D and 8 R); State House (25 D and 16 R).

The Voters

Registration 278,525 Total. 117,963 D (42%); 95,543 R (34%); 64,636 Other (23%); 383 AIP (–).
Median voting age 41.
Employment profile White collar, 51%. Blue collar, 34%. Service, 13%. Farm, 2%.
Ethnic groups Black, 14%. Total foreign stock, 12%.

Presidential vote

1972	Nixon (R)	140,357	(60%)
	McGovern (D)	92,283	(40%)
1968	Nixon (R)	96,714	(45%)
	Humphrey (D)	89,194	(42%)
	Wallace (AI)	28,459	(13%)

Sen. William V. Roth, Jr. (R) Elected 1970, seat up 1976; b. July 22, 1921, Great Falls, Mont.; home, Wilmington; U. of Oreg., B.A. 1944, Harvard U., M.B.A. 1947, LL.B. 1947; Episcopalian.

Career Army, WWII; Practicing atty.; Chm., Del. Repub. State Comm., 1961–64; U.S. House of Reps., 1967–71.

Offices 4327 DSOB, 202-224-2441. Also 3021 Fed. Bldg., 844 King St., Wilmington 19801, 302-571-6291, and 200 U.S.P.O. Bldg., Georgetown 19947, 302-856-7690.

Committees

Finance (6th). Subcommittees: Foundations; International Finance and Resources; International Trade; Private Pension Plans.

Government Operations (3d). Subcommittees: Federal Spending Practices, Efficiency and Open Government; Intergovernmental Relations; Oversight Procedures; Reports, Accounting and Management; Permanent Subcommittee on Investigations.

Group Ratings

	ADA	COPE	LWV	RIPON	NFU	LCV	CFA	NAB	NSI	ACA
1974	38	18	60	55	35	71	63	100	80	74
1973	40	9	80	83	29	–	15	–	–	83
1972	25	10	36	68	30	54	64	100	80	73

Key Votes

1) No-Knock	AGN	8) Gov Abortn Aid	AGN	15) Consumer Prot Agy	FOR
2) Busing	AGN	9) Cut Mil Brass	FOR	16) Forced Psych Tests	AGN
3) No Fault	FOR	10) Gov Limousine	AGN	17) Fed Campaign Subs	AGN
4) F-111	AGN	11) RR Featherbed	AGN	18) Rhod Chrome Ban	FOR
5) Death Penalty	FOR	12) Handgun License	AGN	19) Open Legis Meetings	FOR
6) Foreign Aid	AGN	13) Less Troop Abrd	AGN	20) Strikers Food Stmps	AGN
7) Filibuster	FOR	14) Resume Turk Aid	AGN	21) Gov Info Disclosure	FOR

Election Results

1970 general:	William V. Roth (R)	96,021	(60%)
	Jacob W. Zimmerman (D)	64,835	(40%)
1970 primary:	William V. Roth (R), nominated by convention		

Sen. Joseph R. Biden, Jr. (D) Elected 1972, seat up 1978; b. Nov. 20, 1942, Scranton, Pa.; home, Wilmington; U. of Del., B.A. 1965, Syracuse U., J.D. 1968; Catholic.

Career Practicing atty., 1968–72; New Castle County Cncl., 1970–72.

Offices 440 RSOB, 202-224-5042. Also Rm. 6021 Fed. Bldg., Wilmington 19801, 302-571-6345.

Committees

Banking, Housing and Urban Affairs (7th). Subcommittees: Consumer Affairs (Chairman); Housing and Urban Affairs; International Finance; Oversight; Production and Stabilization.

Budget (9th).

Foreign Relations (10th). Subcommittees: African Affairs; Arms Control, International Organizations and Security Agreements; European Affairs; Oceans and International Environment.

Group Ratings

	ADA	COPE	LWV	RIPON	NFU	LCV	CFA	NAB	NSI	ACA
1974	85	64	90	50	94	89	100	45	11	5
1973	94	80	100	75	93	–	92	–	–	8

Key Votes

1) No-Knock	AGN	8) Gov Abortn Aid	AGN	15) Consumer Prot Agy	FOR
2) Busing	FOR	9) Cut Mil Brass	FOR	16) Forced Psych Tests	FOR
3) No Fault	FOR	10) Gov Limousine	AGN	17) Fed Campaign Subs	FOR
4) F-111	AGN	11) RR Featherbed	FOR	18) Rhod Chrome Ban	ABS
5) Death Penalty	AGN	12) Handgun License	AGN	19) Open Legis Meetings	FOR
6) Foreign Aid	AGN	13) Less Troop Abrd	FOR	20) Strikers Food Stmps	ABS
7) Filibuster	AGN	14) Resume Turk Aid	AGN	21) Gov Info Disclosure	FOR

Election Results

1972 general:	Joseph R. Biden, Jr. (D)	116,006	(51%)	($260,699)
	J. Caleb Boggs (R)	112,844	(49%)	($167,657)
1972 primary:	Joseph R. Biden, Jr. (D), nominated by			

Gov. Sherman W. Tribbitt (D) Elected 1972, term expires Jan. 1977; b. Nov. 9, 1922, Denton, Md.; Beacom Col., 1939–41.

Career Security Trust Co., Wilmington, 1941; Navy, WWII; Business partnership with father-in-law, 1945–; Del. House of Reps., 1957–65, 1971–73, Spkr., 1959–65, Minor Ldr., 1971–73; Lt. Gov. of Del., 1965–69.

Offices Legislative Hall, Dover 19001, 302-678-4626.

Election Results

1972 general:	Sherman W. Tribbitt (D)	117,274	(52%)
	Russell W. Peterson (R)	109,583	(48%)
1972 primary:	Sherman W. Tribbitt (D), nominated by convention		

Rep. Pierre S. du Pont IV (R) Elected 1970; b. Jan. 22, 1935, Wilmington; home, Rockland; Princeton U., B.S.E. 1956, Harvard U., LL.B. 1963; Episcopalian.

Career Navy, 1957–60; Business exec., Photo Products Div., E. I. du Pont Co., 1963–70; Del. House of Reps., 1968–70.

Offices 127 CHOB, 202-225-4165. Also 5021 Fed. Bldg., 844 King St., Wilmington 19801, 302-571-6181.

Committees

International Relations (6th). Subcommittees: International Resources, Food, and Energy; Investigations.

Merchant Marine and Fisheries (6th). Subcommittees: Coastguard and Navigation; Merchant Marine; Oceanography.

Group Ratings

	ADA	COPE	LWV	RIPON	NFU	LCV	CFA	NAB	NSI	ACA
1974	64	55	75	94	64	59	46	73	60	36
1973	52	36	75	93	45	89	63	–	–	48
1972	50	36	83	75	57	71	50	58	89	39

Key Votes

1) Foreign Aid	FOR	6) Gov Abortn Aid	AGN	11) Pub Cong Election $	FOR
2) Busing	AGN	7) Coed Phys Ed	FOR	12) Turkish Arms Cutoff	FOR
3) ABM	FOR	8) Pov Lawyer Gag	FOR	13) Youth Camp Regs	AGN
4) B-1 Bomber	FOR	9) Pub Trans Sub	FOR	14) Strip Mine Veto	AGN
5) Nerve Gas	AGN	10) EZ Voter Regis	AGN	15) Farm Bill Veto	FOR

Election Results

1974 general:	Pierre S. du Pont (R)	93,826	(60%)	($92,246)
	James R. Soles (D)	63,490	(40%)	($68,839)
1974 primary:	Pierre S. du Pont (R), unopposed			
1972 general:	Pierre S. du Pont (R)	141,237	(63%)	($82,333)
	Norma B. Handloff (D)	83,230	(37%)	($42,831)

DISTRICT OF COLUMBIA

In 1974, for the first time in 100 years, the residents of the capital of the United States of America were allowed to vote on who should head their local government. Back in 1874, Congress had taken away the District of Columbia's right to elect its local officials, in part because of the heavy spending of Governor Alexander Sheppard and in part because of fear of what was even then the city's large black electorate. Not until 1964 were residents of the District entitled to vote for President; not until 1968 could they elect their own school board; not until 1971 did Washington get a Delegate in the House of Representatives. During much of that period, the District's affairs were controlled by Chairman John McMillan and his fellow Dixiecrats on the House District of Columbia Committee—a body implacably hostile to the desires of the District's black majority until Southern domination of the Committee ended, with McMillan's defeat and the retirements of several others, in 1972. Within a year, home rule was law.

Why had it been so long coming? The basic reason was Congress's long standing fear of the city's black majority. Since before the Civil War, Washington has been a special city for blacks; the slave trade was abolished here as part of the Compromise of 1850, and it was a haven for free Negroes, who heavily outnumbered slaves here by the time Lincoln became President. Blacks formed more than one quarter of the electorate that gave power to Governor Sheppard's men; and blacks held high office under Sheppard's Republican government. At the northern edge of the South, Washington always had a larger percentage of blacks than most major cities; and when the capital's metropolitan population ballooned in the years of the New Deal and World War II and after, it was inevitable that, with the suburbs restricted to whites, the District would become majority black. That happened officially in the 1960 census; by 1970, the District was 71% black. Washington is now our only major city without a white working class; its whites live mostly in well-to-do areas west of Rock Creek Park or in redeveloped areas like Capitol Hill, and are well educated and wealthy. There are many well-to-do blacks in the District, too, although there is a middle class movement across the line into Prince Georges County (see Maryland 5).

One argument often advanced by opponents of home rule was that District residents were not much interested in local government anyway; and of course, with so little at stake, turnout in D.C. contests was often low. Indeed, this has continued to be the case in the only two elections here which have really decided something: the Democratic primary for District Delegate in 1971 and the Democratic contest for Mayor in 1974. And the results tend to prove that anything you may hear about the existence of political machines in the District is wrong. For the two candidates who won, Delegate (he likes to be called Congressman, but of course doesn't have a vote on the floor) Walter Fauntroy and Mayor Walter Washington, are sworn political enemies; yet both were elected by almost precisely the same constituency. And that is the group of older, more churchgoing, more conservative, poorer blacks. For all the commotion that is made about ghetto youths, the people who actually cast the votes in the increasingly deserted stretches of the central city are inclined to be middle aged and elderly women. They are the kind of people Richard Nixon never would have wanted to face in a jury: stout upholders of traditional morality, and at the same time hostile to those who had used antiblack rhetoric for political profit. They believed in Fauntroy, a youngish minister with a beautiful tenor, who had been an aide to Martin Luther King; and they believed in Walter Washington, the housing bureaucrat who made his way up the ladder and was appointed successively by Lyndon Johnson and Richard Nixon to head the city's government.

Washington won only by a hair, though; and it seemed that this city which has watched so many national campaigns contained no one with the ability to put together a local one. Washington could have pointed with pride to the job he had done with the police department (many more blacks than formerly, and much less crime); instead he hid from the electorate behind evasive press spokesmen and collected large contributions from the big retail interests. His opponent, Clifford Alexander, was striking a chord when he attacked the Mayor for the poor services the District's bloated bureaucracy renders; but he never could put together the organization necessary to get out the vote among alienated younger black voters. One factor about the election that must be encouraging to everyone: this was not a battle fought out on racial lines. The minority white voters split just as the blacks did: with the older and poorer going for Washington, the younger and more affluent for Alexander.

Walter Washington has already announced, though he is past 60, that he would like to be reelected Mayor again in 1978 and maybe again in 1982. It is not clear, though, that there is much demand for this. Most likely what we will see in District politics is a shift from the dominance of the elderly, poor voter toward the dominace of the younger, wealthier ones—more self-consciously liberal, but at the same time innocent of the visceral experience of being poor, or being caught up in the District bureaucracy. This is a politics and a government that doesn't work especially well, certainly not as well as those who have worked for racial equality here would like; but in a nation where well educated white electorates in states like Maryland and New Jersey elect one crook after another, in a nation where Richard Nixon is elected President by a record majority, who has standing to complain about the relatively minor shortcomings of the District of Columbia?

Rep. Walter E. Fauntroy (D) Elected Mar. 23, 1971; b. Feb. 6., 1933, Washington D.C.; Va. Union U., A.B. 1955, Yale U., B.D. 1958; Baptist.

Career Pastor, New Bethel Baptist Church, 1958–; Founder and former Dir., Model Inner City Community Org.; Dir., Washington Bureau, SCLC, 1961–71; Co-Ordinator, Selma to Montgomery March, 1965; Vice Chm., D.C. City Cncl., 1967–69; Natl. Co-Ordinator, Poor Peoples Campaign, 1969; Chm., Bd. of Dirs., Martin Luther King, Jr., Ctr. for Social Change, 1969–.

Offices 506 CHOB, 202-225-8050. Also 1121 Vermont Ave., NW, 20005, 202-254-6460.

Election Results

1974 general:	Walter E. Fauntroy (D)	66,337	(66%)
	James G. Banks (D)	21,874	(22%)
	William R. Phillips (R)	9,166	(9%)
	Anton V. Wood (D. C. State hood)	3,039	(3%)
1974 primary:	Walter E. Fauntroy (D), unopposed		
1972 general:	Walter E. Fauntroy (D)	95,300	(62%)
	William Chin-Lee (R)	39,487	(26%)
	Charles Cassell (Statehood)	18,730	(12%)

Election Results (Mayor)

1974 general:	Walter E. Washington (D)	84,676	(84%)
	Sam Harris (Ind.)	7,514	(7%)
	Jackson R. Champion (R)	3,703	(4%)
	Raymond V. Ellis (D.C. Statehood)	2,985	(3%)
	Nan Bailey (SW)	2,143	(2%)
1974 primary:	Walter E. Washington (D)	50,746	(54%)
	Clifford Alexander (D)	42,395	(46%)

FLORIDA

When V. O. Key published his definitive *Southern Politics* a quarter century ago, he described Florida politics as "every man for himself." The description is still apt, though just about everything else about Florida has changed. Back in 1950 the state had 2.5 million residents; now its population has swelled past 8 million, and by 1980 it will probably be our seventh largest state. This spectacular growth—more than 1.3 million just since 1970—has naturally complicated any description of Florida politics. The northern panhandle which used to dominate the state, remains a part of the Old South, much like the adjacent regions of Alabama and Georgia. The southern cities tend to reflect the northern origin of their inhabitants. Thus Miami Beach, full of Jewish ex-New Yorkers, votes like the Grand Concourse in the Bronx; while to take another example, Sarasota, occupied by well-to-do Midwestern WASPs, is Goldwaterish Republican like Chicago's suburban DuPage County. Blacks in various parts of the state are an important voting bloc, and so, increasingly, are the much more conservatively inclined Cuban-Americans of Miami.

The Florida climate, warm and wet, produces endless species of vegetation, and tends to rot paper and fabrics; the same climate also fosters various forms of human corruption. There was plenty of money to be made in a boom economy, and behind the proud high-rises that line the Atlantic from Miami to Palm Beach there are doubtless hundreds of stories of bribery and chicanery. Organized crime reportedly flourishes in Miami; the most recent Mayor there and a retiring U.S. Senator have been indicted, in separate cases; county sheriffs are almost routinely removed from office for various misdeeds. Since 1974 three state Supreme Court justices and three statewide elected Cabinet members have been forced to resign because of scandal.

Over all this lucrative dealing presides a man of a very different spirit, Governor Reubin Askew. Young (47 in 1976), a nonsmoker and nondrinker, Askew has the demeanor of a Sunday school teacher, which he is—and an unswerving, almost steely determination. Before 1970, he was an unknown state Senator from Pensacola, a small panhandle city 1,000 miles from Miami; he ran for Governor promising a corporate tax and other reforms. He upset the favorite in the primary and in the general election faced Republican incumbent Claude Kirk, a man whose flamboyance seemed to have degenerated into assininity. But Askew not only won the Governorship with a solid 57% of the vote; he also enacted his entire platform into law. He got the legislature and the voters to approve a corporate income tax structure. He pushed through to passage a statewide land-use bill. His only major defeat—his inability to persuade voters to reject an antibusing referendum in 1972—apparently only increased most Floridians' respect for him, much as they might disagree on that one issue.

So Askew went into the 1974 election with accomplishments virtually no other Governor in the nation could match. His main opponent in the primary was the Lieutenant Governor, an old-style north Florida politician who was badly defeated. His opponent in the general was the former state Senate president, a Democrat-turned-Republican who said that Askew was spending too much of the taxpayers' money. It didn't wash. Askew won easily. Since 1972, some have speculated that he would make an excellent vice-presidential (or even presidential) candidate; he has rebuffed all such suggestions, and even the most cynical of reporters seems willing now to take this austere man at his word.

Askew may be Florida's best known officeholder; his major competitor, at least through the end of 1974, was the state's then senior Senator Edward J. Gurney. Millions of Americans watched him on the Senate Watergate Committee, the closest thing there was to a Nixon defender on it. Within 18 months of his grueling cross-examination of John Dean, Gurney himself was in trouble; the first sitting Senator in 50 years to be indicted, for allegedly taking bribes from developers for interceding with the FHA. Gurney claimed that an aide had done whatever was wrong, without his knowledge; at this writing, the case has not come to trial. The investigation and indictment got Gurney out of the 1974 Senate race, but it is worth looking back over his career, which privides a succinct history of recent Florida politics.

A New Englander by birth, Gurney was practicing law in Orlando when the legislature in 1962 created a new congressional district in the Orlando-Cape Kennedy area; filled with Yankee immigrants and hard-line conservatives, it made Gurney the second Florida Republican elected to Congress since Reconstruction. (The first was William Cramer of St. Petersburg.) Six years later, when Senator George Smathers decided to retire in order to make lots more money as a Washington lobbyist, Gurney decided to run for the Senate. It was a good Republican year in Florida. Voters were fed up with the Johnson Administration, its expensive domestic programs, its civil rights laws, and its inflation; the Democratic nominee, former Governor LeRoy Collins, had the misfortune to have served under LBJ, and Gurney had no difficulty in attaching the dreaded "liberal" tag to him. Using the same tactic two years earlier, Gurney's fellow Republican Kirk had beaten Miami Mayor Robert King High for the Governship. Gurney likewise won easily.

But no sooner did Florida's Republicans believe that they had captured the state than they started fighting over the spoils. An elderly Democratic Senator was retiring in 1970, and Cramer was running—with Richard Nixon's blessing, he thought—for the seat. Suddenly, Kirk and Gurney got together in Gurney's house in Winter Haven and hatched the candidacy of one G. Harrold Carswell, just rejected by the Senate for a seat on the Supreme Court. Predictably, Cramer won the primary; registered Repulicans are few in north Florida where Carswell was most popular, and one-quarter of the Republican vote was in Cramer's own congressional district. The surprise, instead, was in the Democratic primary. Former Governor Farris Bryant, a conservative who had served in the Johnson Administration, was excepted to win the nomination; instead, he was beaten in the runoff by Polk County state Senator Lawton Chiles, who had walked the 1,003 miles from Pensacola to Miami.

The outcome showed the weakness of Florida's once unbeatable Republicans. They depended for their success on negative reaction to the Democratic administration in Washington, and were not able to adapt to the challenge of attractive, stay-at-home Floridians like Askew and Chiles. Chiles's walk—the first time it was tried by any politician—symbolized his willingness to listen to constituents in what has become an increasingly media-dominated state politically. Along the way, he was converted from Vietnam hawk to dove; once in office, he made it a practice to keep open office hours and even do a little more walking from time to time. In the Senate, Chiles has been a moderate-to-liberal Democrat, and has won seats on the Appropriations, Budget, and Government Operations Committees. Chiles's seat is up in 1976, and he will probably have a fairly strong Republican opponent; but odds are he will win.

Gurney's political fall happened so quickly that Republicans hardly had time for a full-fledged fight for the nomination; nonetheless there was a spirited primary between drugstore millionaire Jack Eckerd and state Public Utilities Commissioner Paula Hawkins, whom Eckerd narrowly beat. The Democrats, as usual, had a brawling primary and runoff; but as in 1970, it didn't seem to hurt too badly. The leading candidates were Congressman Bill Gunter, a young (40) Congressman from Orlando, a moderate in tune temperamentally with the state's less cosmopolitan areas, and Richard Stone, the resigned Secretary of State, who is Jewish, from Miami, and a Harvard graduate, but not all that much, he likes to remind folks, of a liberal. Stone took to playing the harmonica and spoons on campaign trips in north Florida, and managed an unlikely north-Miami alliance which put him into the runoff. Then he surprised everyone—most of all himself—by winning in the runoff. His big issue was dead chickens: Gunter had voted for a law, sponsored by Mississippi's James Eastland, to compensate owners of chickens which had died from a certain disease. Stone advanced the idea that the government ought not to pay for dead chickens, and at 46 won a Senate seat. It was a close race in the general against Eckerd, with John Grady, a Wallace-type candidate winning 16%of the vote. But Stone was able to amass large enough majorities in Miami and other Democratic centers to win convincingly.

Florida now has one of the nation's earliest presidential primaries, just a week after New Hampshire, but no one knows just how important it is. Back in 1972, when Jackson, Humphrey, Lindsay, and Muskie were all talking about making breakthroughs in Florida, commentators classed it as basically a northern state; when Wallace swept all but one of the state's congressional districts, they were quick to call it a Southern one. The truth is somewhere in between, but the fact remains that a Wallace can count on a larger vote here than in most northern states—in large part because Democratic registration is so much higher than the Democratic vote ever has been. The Republican primary, on the other hand, is a narrow group of voters, most of them originally from the north, and solidly conservative. Any "New South" Democrats in the 1976 race are probably going to have to go into Florida to show their strength, if any, against Wallace, if he runs; the resulting logjam could, once again, rob the Florida primary of much meaning.

Census Data   Pop. 6,789,443; 3.35% of U.S. total, 9th largest; Central city, 29%; suburban, 35%. Median family income, $8,261; 35th highest; families above $15,000: 17%; families below $3,000: 13%.   Median years education, 12.1.

1974 Share of Federal Tax Burden $10,230,544,000; 3.82% of U.S. total, 9th largest.

1974 Share of Federal Outlays $9,469,367,000; 3.51% of U.S. total, 8th largest.   Per capita federal spending, $1395.

DOD	$2,366,681,000	7th (3.46%)	HEW	$3,974,935,000	7th (4.28%)
AEC	$25,440,000	17th (0.83%)	HUD	$33,667,000	11th (3.45%)
NASA	$238,829,000	4th (8.04%)	VA	$608,434,000	5th (4.45%)
DOT	$306,560,000	7th (3.62%)	EPA	$150,532,000	4th (4.79%)
DOC	$23,546,000	11th (1.46%)	RevS	$175,593,000	10th (2.89%)
DOI	$17,360,000	33d (0.71%)	Int.	$174,634,000	16th (0.85%)
USDA	$266,425,000	19th (2.14%)	Other	$1,107,731,000	

Economic Base   Finance, insurance and real estate; agriculture, notably oranges, cattle, dairy products and grapefruit; food and kindred products, especially canned, cured and frozen foods; tourism; transportation equipment, especially aircraft and parts, and ship and boat building and repairing; electrical equipment and supplies, especially communication equipment.

Political Line-up   Governor, Reubin Askew (D). Senators, Lawton Chiles (D) and Richard Stone (D). Representatives, 15 (10 D and 5 R). State Senate (27 D, 12 R, and 1 Ind.); State House (86 D and 34 R).

The Voters

Registration   3,621,256 Total. 2,438,550 D (67%); 1,035,510 R (29%); 147,166 Other (4%). *Median voting age* 46.
Employment profile   White collar, 50%. Blue collar, 32%. Service, 15%. Farm, 3%.
Ethnic groups   Black, 15%. Spanish, 7%. Total foreign stock, 18%. Germany, UK, Canada, 2% each; Italy, USSR, 1% each.

Presidential vote

1972	Nixon (R)	1,857,759	(72%)
	McGovern (D)	718,117	(28%)
1968	Nixon (R)	886,804	(41%)
	Humphrey (D)	676,794	(31%)
	Wallace (AI)	624,207	(29%)

1972 Democratic Presidential Primary

Wallace	526,651	(42%)
Humphrey	234,658	(19%)
Jackson	170,156	(13%)
Muskie	112,523	(9%)
Lindsay	82,386	(6%)
McGovern	78,232	(6%)
others	59,948	(5%)

1972 Republican Presidential Primary

Nixon	360,278	(87%)
Ashbrook	36,617	(9%)
McCloskey	17,312	(4%)

Sen. Lawton Chiles (D) Elected 1970, seat up 1976; b. Apr. 3, 1930, Lakeland; home, Lakeland; U. of Fla., B.S. 1952, LL.B. 1955; Presbyterian.

Career Army, Korea; Practicing atty., 1955–71; Instructor, Fla. Southern Col., 1955–57; Fla. House of Reps., 1958–66; Fla. Senate 1966–70.

Offices 2107 DSOB, 202-224-5274. Also Fed. Bldg., Lakeland 33801, 813-688-6681.

Committees

Appropriations (14th). Subcommittees: Agriculture and Related Agencies; District of Columbia (Chairman); Foreign Operations; HUD and Independent Agencies; Interior; Labor and HEW.

Budget (7th).

Government Operations (7th). Subcommittees: Federal Spending Practices, Efficiency and Open Government (Chairman); Intergovernmental Relations; Oversight Procedures; Permanent Subcommittee on Investigations.

Group Ratings

	ADA	COPE	LWV	RIPON	NFU	LCV	CFA	NAB	NSI	ACA
1974	43	30	78	33	65	70	75	64	67	44
1973	75	73	80	47	88	–	54	–	–	35
1972	35	11	73	58	90	50	83	40	50	45

Key Votes

1) No-Knock	FOR	8) Gov Abortn Aid	FOR	15) Consumer Prot Agy	FOR
2) Busing	AGN	9) Cut Mil Brass	ABS	16) Forced Psych Tests	AGN
3) No Fault	AGN	10) Gov Limousine	AGN	17) Fed Campaign Subs	FOR
4) F-111	AGN	11) RR Featherbed	FOR	18) Rhod Chrome Ban	AGN
5) Death Penalty	FOR	12) Handgun License	AGN	19) Open Legis Meetings	FOR
6) Foreign Aid	AGN	13) Less Troop Abrd	AGN	20) Strikers Food Stmps	AGN
7) Filibuster	FOR	14) Resume Turk Aid	FOR	21) Gov Info Disclosure	FOR

Election Results

1970 general:	Lawton Chiles (D)	902,438	(54%)
	William C. Cramer (R)	772,817	(46%)
1970 run-off:	Lawton Chiles (D)	474,420	(66%)
	Farris Bryant (D)	247,211	(34%)
1970 primary:	Farris Bryant (D)	240,222	(33%)
	Lawton Chiles (D)	188,300	(26%)
	Fred Schultz (D)	175,745	(24%)
	Al Hastings (D)	91,948	(13%)
	Jeel T. Daves III (D)	33,939	(5%)

Sen. Richard (Dick) **Stone** (D) Elected 1974, seat up 1980; b. Sept. 22, 1928, New York, N.Y.; home, Tallahassee; Harvard U., A.B. 1949, Columbia U., LL.B. 1954; Jewish.

Career Practicing atty; Miami City Atty., 1966; Fla. Senate, 1967–1970; Fla. Secy. of State, 1970–74.

Offices 358 RSOB, 202-224-3041. Also 2639 N. Monroe, Suite 200-B, Talahassee 32303. 904-386-2120.

Committees

Agriculture and Forestry (8th). Subcommittees: Agricultural Credit and Rural Electrification; Agricultural Production, Marketing, and Stabilization of Prices; Foreign Agricultural Policy.

Interior and Insular Affairs (8th). Subcommittees: Energy Research and Water Resources; Minerals, Materials and Fuels; Parks and Recreation; Special Subcommittee on Integrated Oil Operations.

Veterans' Affairs (5th). Subcommittees: Compensation and Pension; Health and Hospitals; Housing and Insurance (Chairman).

Group Ratings: Newly Elected

Key Votes

1) No-Knock	NE	8) Gov Abortn Aid	AGN	15) Consumer Prot Agy	NE
2) Busing	NE	9) Cut Mil Brass	NE	16) Forced Psych Tests	NE
3) No Fault	NE	10) Gov Limousine	NE	17) Fed Campaign Subs	NE
4) F-111	AGN	11) RR Featherbed	NE	18) Rhod Chrome Ban	NE
5) Death Penalty	NE	12) Handgun License	NE	19) Open Legis Meetings	NE
6) Foreign Aid	NE	13) Less Troop Abrd	NE	20) Strikers Food Stmps	NE
7) Filibuster	AGN	14) Resume Turk Aid	AGN	21) Gov Info Disclosure	NE

Election Results

1974 general:	Richard Stone (D)	781,031	(43%)	($919,787)
	Jack Eckerd (R)	736,674	(41%)	($421,169)
	John Grady (AI)	282,659	(16%)	($148,495)
1974 run-off:	Richard Stone (D)	321,683	(51%)	
	Bill Gunter (D)	311,044	(49%)	
1974 primary:	Bill Gunter (D)	236,185	(30%)	
	Richard Stone (D)	157,301	(20%)	
	Richard Pettigrew (D)	146,728	(19%)	
	Mallory E. Horne (D)	90,684	(11%)	
	Seven others (D)	161,733	(20%)	

Gov. Reubin Askew (D) Elected 1970, term expires Jan. 1979; b. Sept. 11, 1928, Muskogee, Okla.; Fla. St. U., B.S., U. of Fla., LL.B. 1956; Presbyterian.

Career Army, Air Force; Asst. Escambia Co. Solicitor; Fla. House of Reps., 1959–63; Fla. Senate 1963–70, Pres. Pro Tempore.

Offices State Capitol, Tallahassee 32304, 904-488-4441.

Election Results

1974 general:	Reubin O'D, Askew (D)	1,118,954	(61%)
	Jerry Thomas (R)	709,438	(39%)

1974 primary:	Reubin O'D. Askew (D)	579,137	(69%)
	Ben Hill Griffin, Jr. (D)	137,008	(16%)
	Tom Adams (D)	85,557	(10%)
	Norman Bie (D)	39,758	(5%)
1970 general:	Reubin O'D. Askew (D)	984,305	(57%)
	Claude R. Kirk (R)	746,243	(43%)

◆ ◆ ◆ ◆ ◆

FIRST DISTRICT

One of the heaviest concentrations of military bases and installations in the nation can be found in the northern panhandle counties which make up Florida's 1st congressional district. There are many reasons for this concentration. Pensacola, the district's largest city, is an old Gulf of Mexico port, and there has been a naval station there just about as long as the United States has held the territory. There are more than 100 miles of coastline along the Gulf here, with a good port at Panama City as well as Pensacola. The climate is mild, the terrain inland flat and, where swampy, reclaimable. All of these factors have helped to bring to this area such huge facilities as Eglin Air Force Base, which spreads over the lion's share of three counties. And there is one more thing which has prompted the Defense Department to spend about $500 million here each year: the fact that Robert L. F. Sikes, Congressman from the 1st district, is Chairman of the House Appropriations Subcommittee on Military Construction.

Happily, Sikes's political philosophy and the interests of his district coincide. When he was first elected to the House in 1940, Sikes was one of many Southern Democrats who stood solidly with Franklin D. Roosevelt when he was pushing Lend-Lease and beginning the draft. Since then, the Congressman has remained convinced that the nation must be militarily strong, and that it is better to have spent too much on defense than to risk spending too little. To judge from recent election returns, these views are shared by the overwhelming majority of the voters of the 1st district. There are few blacks here on the coast or in the piney woods region inland, and the 1st has turned in some of the nation's largest majorities for George Wallace in 1968 and Richard Nixon in 1972.

The voters are even more enthusiastic in their support of Congressman Sikes, though he could have a little trouble in 1976 over charges he steered through a bill greatly enhancing the value of some land he owned. At 71, he is not especially elderly for a 36-year veteran of the House. He is the number three Democrat on the Appropriations Committee, behind 76-year-old Chairman George Mahon of Texas and 66-year-old Jamie Whitten of Mississippi, and in the way these things have been handled over his career, Sikes could expect to succeed to the chair when they are gone. But the liberals who now dominate the Democratic caucus may be a little wary of so promoting someone who differs so often with their views on just about every issue.

Census Data Pop. 452,562. Central city, 41%; suburban, 13%. Median family income, $7,621; families above $15,000: 12%; families below $3,000: 15%. Median years education, 12.1.

The Voters

Median voting age 38.
Employment profile White collar, 48%. Blue collar, 36%. Service, 15%. Farm, 1%.
Ethnic groups Black, 14%. Spanish, 2%. Total foreign stock, 5%.

Presidential vote

	1972	Nixon (R)	127,607	(84%)
		McGovern (D)	24,860	(16%)
	1968	Nixon (R)	30,438	(21%)
		Humphrey (D)	27,707	(19%)
		Wallace (AI)	87,844	(60%)

Rep. Robert L. F. Sikes (D) Elected 1940; b. June 3, 1906, Isabella, Ga.; home, Crestview; U. of Ga, B.S. 1927, U. of Fla., M.S. 1929; Methodist.

Career Fla. House of Reps., 1936–39.

Offices 2269 RHOB, 202-225-4136. Also Courthouse, Crestview 32536, 904-682-3132.

Committees

Appropriations (3d). Subcommittees: Defense; Military Construction (Chairman); Treasury, Postal Service, and General Government.

Group Ratings

	ADA	COPE	LWV	RIPON	NFU	LCV	CFA	NAB	NSI	ACA
1974	0	20	30	25	42	31	50	56	90	69
1973	4	36	27	21	79	11	43	–	–	73
1972	13	20	27	60	50	6	0	82	100	94

Key Votes

1) Foreign Aid	AGN	6) Gov Abortn Aid	AGN	11) Pub Cong Election $	AGN
2) Busing	ABS	7) Coed Phys Ed	AGN	12) Turkish Arms Cutoff	AGN
3) ABM	FOR	8) Pov Lawyer Gag	FOR	13) Youth Camp Regs	AGN
4) B-1 Bomber	FOR	9) Pub Trans Sub	AGN	14) Strip Mine Veto	FOR
5) Nerve Gas	FOR	10) EZ Voter Regis	AGN	15) Farm Bill Veto	AGN

Election Results

1974 general: Robert L. F. Sikes (D), unopposed
$5,740

Election Results

1974 primary: Robert L. F. Sikes (D), unopposed
1972 general: Robert L. F. Sikes (D), unopposed ....   ($36,651)

◆ ◆ ◆ ◆ ◆

SECOND DISTRICT

Like the 1st, the 2d district of Florida is part of Dixie in the northern part of the state—a region politically and sociologically not terribly different from neighboring south Georgia. For years this area's affection for racial segregation and the Democratic Party controlled its politics. In the days before the one-man-one-vote rule, rural legislators from this part of Florida—known as the Pork Chop Gang—dominated the state's politics. For some years, this part of Florida was overrepresented in the U.S. House of Representative; the current 2d is basically a consolidation of what were two separate districts before 1966.

There are, however, two significant differences between the 1st and 2d districts—differences that have not yet been decisive in congressional races, but still seem to have had a political effect. For one, the 2d is Florida's blackest district; some 28% of its residents and 20% of the registered voters are black. For the other, the 2d's two largest cities, Gainesville and Tallahassee, contain the state's two largest universities, the University of Florida and Florida State. Both of these schools draw most of their enrollment from south Florida, and these students, far more than those in most Southern universities, tend to support liberal candidates for public office. Altogether, some 13% of the 2d district's eligible voters are students, and although they have not yet turned out in proportionate numbers, their impact has been noticeable.

Thus the 2d district contains two sizeable voting blocs inclined to oppose the generally conservative politics of the district's Congressman, Democrat Don Fuqua. Since he was first elected to the House in 1962, Fuqua has usually voted with the dwindling number of conservative Southern Democrats on the Hill. With two exceptions, he has had little trouble at the polls. In 1966, he beat the more senior and slightly less conservative Rep. D. R. (Billy) Matthews when their seats were combined by redistricting.

The other exception was in 1972. In the Democratic primary that year, Fuqua got by an opponent who won most of his support from blacks and students without too much difficulty. But his voting record was affected: in 1973, for example, he voted against the bombing of Cambodia. Fuqua is now chairman of the Space Science and Applications Subcommittee and, like most Florida Congressman, a big booster of the space program and the proposals for a space shuttle—which would incidentally create hundreds of jobs in Florida's ailing space industry.

Census Data Pop. 452,633. Central city, 16%; suburban, 30%. Median family income, $7,071; families above $15,000: 13%; families below $3,000: 19%. Median years education, 11.3.

The Voters

  Median voting age 39.
  Employment profile White collar, 49%. Blue collar, 28%. Service, 16%. Farm, 7%.
  Ethnic groups Black, 28%. Spanish, 1%. Total foreign stock, 4%.

Presidential vote

1972	Nixon (R)	....	111,042	(69%)
	McGovern (D)	....	50,861	(31%)
1968	Nixon (R)	....	30,161	(21%)
	Humphrey (D)	....	39,071	(28%)
	Wallace (AI)	....	72,755	(51%)

Rep. Don Fuqua (D) Elected 1962; b. Aug. 20, 1933, Jacksonville; home, Alta; U. of Fla., B.S. 1957; Presbyterian.

Career Army, Korea; Fla. House of Reps., 1958–62.

Offices 2266 RHOB, 202-225-5235. Also 100 P.O. Bldg., Tallahassee 32302, 904-224-5710.

Committees

  Government Operations (12th). Subcommittees: Intergovernmental Relations and Human Resources; Legislation and National Security.

  Science and Technology (4th). Subcommittees: Energy Research, Development and Demonstration; Science, Research, and Technology; Space Science and Applications (Chairman).

Group Ratings

	ADA	COPE	LWV	RIPON	NFU	LCV	CFA	NAB	NSI	ACA
1974	18	30	42	36	67	50	67	30	88	64
1973	22	40	55	33	79	35	33	–	–	60
1972	13	22	36	50	57	40	0	36	100	68

Key Votes

1) Foreign Aid	AGN	6) Gov Abortn Aid	AGN	11) Pub Cong Election $	AGN
2) Busing	AGN	7) Coed Phys Ed	AGN	12) Turkish Arms Cutoff	AGN
3) ABM	FOR	8) Pov Lawyer Gag	FOR	13) Youth Camp Regs	ABS
4) B-1 Bomber	FOR	9) Pub Trans Sub	AGN	14) Strip Mine Veto	AGN
5) Nerve Gas	FOR	10) EZ Voter Regis	AGN	15) Farm Bill Veto	AGN

Election Results

1974 general:	Don Fuqua (D), unopposed			($32,316)
1974 primary:	Don Fuqua (D)	64,226	(86%)	
	Anthony P. (Tony) Wesolowski (D)	10,528	(14%)	
1972 general:	Don Fuqua (D), unopposed			($24,186)

◆ ◆ ◆ ◆ ◆

THIRD DISTRICT

Jacksonville is a border city—on the border between the Old South and the new boom lands of south Florida. It was long Florida's largest city and, on paper, it has regained that status by annexing most of surrounding Duval County; but in metropolitan population, Jacksonville has been eclipsed by Miami, Tampa, St. Petersburg, and even Fort Lauderdale. Jacksonville remains an important port, paper manufacturer, and banking and insurance center. Because of its coolish wintertime climate, Jacksonville has not attracted the retirees or northern migrants who flocked to Florida cities farther south. But it does have the largest black percentage of any major Florida city and also the largest percentage of people who voted for George Wallace in 1968—evidence, if any is needed, of the city's retained affinity to the Deep South.

The 3d congressional district of Florida includes almost all of Jacksonville and one small county to the north. Its Congressman since 1948, Democrat Charles Bennett, enjoys a reputation for probity and attention to duty which is second to none in the House. He was stricken by polio in the Army during World War II, and in his first campaign it was suggested that he was not physically up to representing the district. Perhaps to refute that, Bennett prided himself on attending every roll call and in the late sixties broke the record. After a while, it got to the point that roll calls were sometimes delayed to accommodate Bennett; finally he missed one. The Bennett record, as it stands, for 1951–72: 3,428 consecutive roll call votes.

Bennett is now a very senior member of the Armed Services Committee, just behind Chairman Mel Price and ousted Chairman Edward Hebert. In general, Bennett has supported existing levels of defense funding, and so most of the time has voted with the committee majority. However, he has on occasion dissented and opposed the bombing of Cambodia and Laos—a prime example of the shift from orthodoxy on the part of many Southern Democrats that was moving the House to the left on this issue even before the onslaught of freshmen in 1975.

Census Data Pop. 452,841. Central city, 0%; suburban, 95%. Median family income, $8,252; families above $15,000: 14%; families below $3,000: 14%. Median years education, 11.8.

The Voters

Median voting age 40.
Employment profile White collar, 50%. Blue collar, 34%. Service, 15%. Farm, 1%.
Ethnic groups Black, 26%. Spanish, 1%. Total foreign stock, 6%.

Presidential vote

1972	Nixon (R)	96,783	(70%)
	McGovern (D)	41,880	(30%)
1968	Nixon (R)	34,808	(26%)
	Humphrey (D)	47,330	(36%)
	Wallace (AI)	51,138	(38%)

Rep. Charles E. Bennett (D) Elected 1948; b. Dec. 2, 1910, Canton, N.Y.; home, Jacksonville; U. of Fla., B.A., J.D.; Deciples of Christ.

Career Practicing atty., 1934–42, 1947–48; Fla. House of Reps., 1941–42; Army, WWII.

Offices 2113 RHOB, 202-225-2501. Also Suite 352, Fed. Ofc. Bldg., 400 W. Bay St., Jacksonville 32202, 904-791-2587.

Committees

Armed Services (3d). Subcommittees: Military Installations and Facilities; Seapower and Strategic and Critical Materials (Chairman); Special Subcommittee on Intelligence.

Standards of Official Conduct (6th).

Group Ratings

	ADA	COPE	LWV	RIPON	NFU	LCV	CFA	NAB	NSI	ACA
1974	35	45	42	38	64	59	69	75	70	60
1973	36	45	50	40	60	58	88	–	–	70
1972	13	45	42	56	71	67	50	58	80	78

Key Votes

1) Foreign Aid	AGN	6) Gov Abortn Aid	AGN	11) Pub Cong Election $	AGN
2) Busing	AGN	7) Coed Phys Ed	AGN	12) Turkish Arms Cutoff	FOR
3) ABM	AGN	8) Pov Lawyer Gag	FOR	13) Youth Camp Regs	AGN
4) B-1 Bomber	FOR	9) Pub Trans Sub	AGN	14) Strip Mine Veto	AGN
5) Nerve Gas	AGN	10) EZ Voter Regis	FOR	15) Farm Bill Veto	FOR

Election Results

1974 general:	Charles E. Bennett (D), unopposed		($2,728)
1974 primary:	Charles E. Bennett (D)	34,924 (87%)	
	John F. Bowen (D)	5,361 (13%)	
1972 general:	Charles E. Bennett (D)	101,441 (82%)	($22,301)
	John F. Bowen (R)	22,219 (18%)	($2,439)

◆ ◆ ◆ ◆ ◆

FOURTH DISTRICT

The 4th congressional district is part of transitional Florida. Occupying territory south of Jacksonville and including some 96,000 residents of the city itself, the 4th sits at the divide of Old Dixie—northern Florida—and the boom land to the south. The terrain here lies just below the pale of wintertime frost—a fact of significance not just for the tourist trade, but for the district's big orange crop.

The 4th district also embodies transitional Florida politics. Its northern counties went for George Wallace in 1968, and will doubtless do so again if he becomes a third-party presidential candidate. The southern counties of Lake and Seminole (both partially within the district) near Orlando are solidly Republican. In the middle of the district, both geographically and politically, is Daytona Beach, famous for its rock-hard sand beach. Like much of Florida, this is a town of political contradictions: it can elect a black councilman and vote for George Wallace all in the same year.

The 4th's Congressman, Democrat William Chappell, may also be described as a transitional figure. Chappell was Speaker of the Florida House back in the early 1960s when the legislature was still dominated by Old South conservatives—the Pork Chop Gang—from the northern part of the state. In the House, he has been a member of the conservative Southern bloc, one of that now rarer breed of Democrats who vote more like Republicans. A man with such politics would seem to be well-positioned to win elections in this district, but Chappell's performance has not been especially impressive. He was first elected to the House in 1968 with 53% of the vote; he increased his margin to 58% in 1970, fell to 56% in 1972, and only in Democratic 1974 won with a solid 68%.

One problem that Chappell has is that some of his constituents have doubts about his honesty. In 1969, he was charged with diverting the salary of one of his employees to a third person—a criminal offense. In October 1972, Chappell was one of six Democrats on the House Banking and Currency Committee who voted against investigating the Watergate scandal; writer Marjorie Boyd has suggested that Chappell's vote on this sensitive matter was not unrelated to the fact that the federal government never prosecuted him. As yet, Chappell has not really faced formidable opposition; if he does, to judge from his previous performances, he might be in serious political trouble.

Chappell's current committee assignment is a lesson in the *plus ca change, plus c'est la meme chose* ways of the House. A junior member of Appropriations, he was picked over the various liberal Democrats who have joined the committee recently to serve on the Defense Subcommittee. That group is chaired by full Committee Chairman George Mahon of Texas, and five of its nine Democrats are conservative Southerners. Given its Republican members' conservatism, this means that the subcommittee is overwhelmingly favorable to high levels of military spending. To be sure, it has made some cuts in recent years; but it is by no means reflective of opinion in the House as a whole.

Census Data Pop. 452,076. Central city, 21%; suburban, 2%. Median family income, $7,719; families above $15,000: 15%; families below $3,000: 15%. Median years education, 12.1.

The Voters

Median voting age 47.
Employment profile White collar, 51%. Blue collar, 30%. Service, 15%. Farm, 4%.
Ethnic groups Black, 15%. Spanish, 1%. Total foreign stock, 11%. UK, Germany, Canada, 2% each.

Presidential vote

1972	Nixon (R)	135,945	(77%)
	McGovern (D)	41,660	(23%)
1968	Nixon (R)	60,666	(38%)
	Humphrey (D)	46,713	(29%)
	Wallace (AI)	53,340	(33%)

Rep. Bill Chappell, Jr. (D) Elected 1968; b. Feb. 3, 1922, Kendrick; home, Ocala; U. of Fla., B.A. 1947, LL.B. 1949; Methodist.

Career Navy, WWII; Marion Co. Prosecuting Atty., 1950–54; Fla. House of Reps., 1955–64, 1967–68, Spkr, 1961–63.

Offices 1124 LHOB, 202-225-4035. Also Rm. 258 Fed. Bldg., Ocala 32670, 904-629-0039.

Committees

Appropriations (28th). Subcommittees: Defense: District of Columbia; Foreign Operations.

Group Ratings

	ADA	COPE	LWV	RIPON	NFU	LCV	CFA	NAB	NSI	ACA
1974	9	30	25	13	55	24	42	67	89	57
1973	8	30	33	14	75	18	71	–	–	61
1972	0	10	18	43	57	0	50	75	100	95

Key Votes

1) Foreign Aid	FOR	6) Gov Abortn Aid	AGN	11) Pub Cong Election $	AGN
2) Busing	AGN	7) Coed Phys Ed	AGN	12) Turkish Arms Cutoff	AGN
3) ABM	FOR	8) Pov Lawyer Gag	FOR	13) Youth Camp Regs	AGN
4) B-1 Bomber	FOR	9) Pub Trans Sub	AGN	14) Strip Mine Veto	FOR
5) Nerve Gas	FOR	10) EZ Voter Regis	AGN	15) Farm Bill Veto	AGN

Election Results

1974 general:	Bibb Chappell, Jr. (D)	74,720	(68%)	($63,817)
	Warren Hauser (R)	34,867	(32%)	($17,116)
1974 primary:	Bill Chappell, Jr. (D), unopposed			
1972 general:	Bill Chappell, Jr. (D)	92,541	(56%)	($93,103)
	P. T. Fleuchaus (R)	72,960	(44%)	($38,840)

◆ ◆ ◆ ◆ ◆

FIFTH DISTRICT

The 5th congressional district of Florida, with its jigsaw puzzle like borders, is something of an anomaly: the only congressional district in the United States to elect a non-incumbent Democratic in the Republican landslide year of 1972 and then turn around and elect a Republican in the Democratic landslide year of 1974. It is a district which gathers together not a community or two, but some unrelated real estate connecting several thickly-populated parts of central

Florida. Its genesis was purely political; it was created by the Democratic Florida legislature for state Senator Bill Gunter of Orlando, and Gunter as expected won the congressional election here in 1972. Gunter then went on to almost win the Senate seat vacated by Edward Gurney in 1974, leaving behind the constituency that had been so carefully constructed.

This 5th district includes part of Orlando and part of Sanford in nearby Seminole County; it then sweeps across to the Gulf of Mexico and down the coast, including a part of the city of Clearwater, and terminates at a point near St. Petersburg. Interestingly, the 5th district includes 70% of the black residents of Orlando, Sanford, and Clearwater. Obviously, there was an attempt here to edge the district over into the Democratic column; ordinarily, virtually all the territory within its bounds has voted heavily Republican.

Gunter was able to overcome this usual Republican edge by piling up a big home town margin in Orlando and by carrying the black precincts by huge margins. Two years later, that formula failed to work for Democrat Jo Ann Saunders. The winner in a fairly close primary, she carried the Orlando area, but was unable to beat Republican Richard Kelly in the western counties of Pasco and Pinellas. Kelly's popularity was apparently unhurt even though, as a local judge, he had once been impeached, which, in the year of Richard Nixon's disgrace did not hurt him in the little clusters of glaring new condominums that make up an increasingly large part of his constituency. Kelly's reelection chances are probably good, barring a comeback effort by Gunter.

Census Data Pop. 452,965. Central city, 52%; suburban, 6%. Median family income, $6,910; families above $15,000: 12%; families below $3,000: 16%. Median years education, 11.7.

The Voters

Median voting age 50.
Employment profile White collar, 44%. Blue collar, 35%. Service, 14%. Farm, 7%.
Ethnic groups Black, 16%. Spanish, 1%. Total foreign stock, 12%. Germany, UK, Canada, 2% each.

Presidential vote

1972	Nixon (R)	143,766	(76%)
	McGovern (D)	44,600	(24%)
1968	Nixon (R)	57,450	(43%)
	Humphrey (D)	34,194	(26%)
	Wallace (AI)	42,394	(32%)

Rep. Richard Kelly (R) Elected 1974; b. July 31, 1924, Atlanta, Ga.; home, Zephyrhills; Colo. St. Col. of Ed., A.B. 1949, Vanderbilt Col. of Law, 1949, U. of Fla., J.D. 1952; Presbyterian.

Career USMC, WWII; Zephyrhills City Atty.; Sr. Asst., U.S. Dist. Atty., So. Dist. of Fla., 1956–59; Circuit Judge, 6th. Judicial Circuit of Fla., 1960–74.

Offices 1130 LHOB, 202-225-2176. Also 307 Elmco Bldg., 608 E. Semoran Blvd., Altamonte Springs 32701, 305-834-2662.

Committees

Agriculture (11th). Subcommittees: Conservation and Credit; Dairy and Poultry; Forests.

Banking, Currency and Housing (12th). Subcommittees: Economic Stabilization; Housing and Community Development; International Trade, Investment and Monetary Policy.

Group Ratings: Newly Elected

Key Votes

1) Foreign Aid	AGN	6) Gov Abortn Aid	NE	11) Pub Cong Election $	NE
2) Busing	NE	7) Coed Phys Ed	AGN	12) Turkish Arms Cutoff	NE
3) ABM	NE	8) Pov Lawyer Gag	NE	13) Youth Camp Regs	AGN
4) B-1 Bomber	FOR	9) Pub Trans Sub	NE	14) Strip Mine Veto	FOR
5) Nerve Gas	NE	10) EZ Voter Regis	NE	15) Farm Bill Veto	FOR

Election Results

1974 general:	Richard Kelly (R)	74,954	(53%)	($111,194)
	JoAnn Saunders (D)	63,610	(45%)	($62,119)
	Glenn W. Turner (Write-in)	3,518	(2%)	($32,957)
1974 primary:	Richard Kelly (R)	16,177	(52%)	
	Lew Earle (R)	15,043	(48%)	

◆ ◆ ◆ ◆ ◆

SIXTH DISTRICT

When somebody says St. Petersburg, almost everybody sees an image of elderly retirees sitting on park benches in the Florida sun. It would be misleading to imply that that image is the whole of St. Petersburg or Pinellas County. This large and growing city of 216,000 does have some light manufacturing and a large number of young families raising children. Nevertheless, the median age of Florida's 6th congressional district, which includes St. Petersburg and most of suburban Pinellas County, is the highest of any district in the nation. Some 50% of the 6th's eligible voters are over 58 years old, and fully 39% are 65 or older.

Most of these people were not, of course, born in St. Petersburg—or anywhere near Florida. They are immigrants from some other part of the South or, more likely, the north. The large Yankee concentration here produced the state's first center of Republican strength. Republicans first won big here in 1954, when William Cramer was elected to the U.S. House. Cramer, a tireless and effective partisan, built up Florida's Republican Party at home and rose to become ranking minority member of the pork-barreling Public Works Committee in Washington. In 1970, Cramer made a move for the Senate. Campaigning vigorously across the state, the Congressman stressed his support of Richard Nixon, of capital punishment, and his sponsorship of the "Rap Brown Law" that prohibits interstate travel to incite a riot.

But 1970 was not Bill Cramer's year. The founding father of Florida Republicanism still had to face former Judge G. Harrold Carswell in what became a bitter primary. Cramer disposed of Carswell neatly, but he could never catch up with the surprise winner of the Democratic nomination, "Walkin' Lawton" Chiles. The former Congressman now has a bustling law-and-lobbying practice in Washington and Florida; interestingly, one of his clients has been an association of directors of OEO community action programs—measures Cramer had opposed in the House. There is an old tradition in Washington of liberal politicians going into lobbying and selling out to conservative interests; Cramer is one of the first examples of a conservative ex-politician selling out to liberal monied interests.

Despite the general 1970 Republican debacle in Florida, state Sen. Bill Young had no trouble stepping into Cramer's House seat. Young is a usually reliable supporter of the House Republican leadership and sits on the Appropriations Committee. He has dissented from conservative orthodoxy occasionally; he, for example, opposed the cross-Florida barge canal. There is no indication that this elderly congressional district will do anything but continue to reelect its comparatively youthful (46 in 1976) Congressman in the years ahead.

Census Data Pop. 452,615. Central city, 52%; suburban, 48%. Median family income, $7,657; families above $15,000: 14%; families below $3,000: 12%. Median years education, 12.1.

The Voters

Median voting age 58.
Employment profile White collar, 55%. Blue collar, 28%. Service, 17%. Farm, –%.
Ethnic groups Black, 8%. Spanish, 1%. Total foreign stock, 22%. Germany, UK, 4% each; Canada, 3%; Italy, Ireland, Sweden, 1% each

Presidential vote

1972	Nixon (R)	154,765	(69%)
	McGovern (D)	68,214	(31%)
1968	Nixon (R)	87,839	(51%)
	Humphrey (D)	57,450	(33%)
	Wallace (AI)	26,711	(16%)

Rep. C. W. Bill Young (R) Elected 1970; b. Dec. 16, 1930, Harmarville, Pa.; home, Seminole; Methodist.

Career Aide to U.S. Rep. William C. Cramer of Fla., 1957-60; Fla. Senate, 1960-70, Minor. Ldr., 1966-70.

Offices 341 CHOB, 202-225-5961. Also 627 Fed. Bldg., 144 1st Ave. S., St. Petersburg 33701, 813-581-1980.

Committees

Appropriations (14th). Subcommittees: District of Columbia; HUD-independent Agencies.

Group Ratings

	ADA	COPE	LWV	RIPON	NFU	LCV	CFA	NAB	NSI	ACA
1974	5	0	50	47	36	59	8	83	89	86
1973	16	27	42	46	25	58	67	–	–	92
1972	13	18	45	69	14	43	100	100	100	87

Key Votes

1) Foreign Aid	AGN	6) Gov Abortn Aid	AGN	11) Pub Cong Election $	AGN
2) Busing	AGN	7) Coed Phys Ed	AGN	12) Turkish Arms Cutoff	AGN
3) ABM	FOR	8) Pov Lawyer Gag	FOR	13) Youth Camp Regs	AGN
4) B-1 Bomber	FOR	9) Pub Trans Sub	AGN	14) Strip Mine Veto	AGN
5) Nerve Gas	FOR	10) EZ Voter Regis	AGN	15) Farm Bill Veto	FOR

Election Results

1974 general:	C. W. Bill Young (R)	109,302	(76%)	($32,105)
	Mickey Monrose (D)	34,886	(24%)	($4,771)
1974 primary:	C. W. Bill Young (R), unopposed			
1972 general:	C. W. Bill Young (R)	156,150	(76%)	($31,686)
	Michael D. Plunkett (D)	49,399	(24%)	($2,925)

◆ ◆ ◆ ◆ ◆

SEVENTH DISTRICT

Tampa, population 277,000, dominates the 7th congressional district of Florida. This is a very different city from St. Petersburg, with which it is connected by a couple of bridges across Tampa Bay. If St. Petersburg is known for its many retirees, Tampa is almost as well known for its large and long-established Cuban-American community, and for being this nation's leading manufacturer of cigars. Tampa's Cuban community dates from long before Castro, and is much older—and not nearly so fast-growing—as Miami's; also, it is different politically. The anti-Castro Cubans of Miami tend toward Nixon Republicanism; the Cuban-Americans of Tampa are traditionally Democrats. Beyond the Cuban community in Ybor City, Tampa is as much a white working-class city as there is in Florida. The 1968 presidential election results here suggest the split in the electorate: 35% for Nixon (roughly corresponding to the number of northern migrants); 33% for Humphrey (Cubans, blacks, union members); 32% for Wallace (Southern-origin whites).

Until 1962, Tampa lay in the same congressional district as St. Petersburg. Then, following the 1960 census, a Tampa-centered district was created, and its Congressman since that time—the district has been numbered variously the 10th, 6th, and now the 7th—has been Democrat Sam Gibbons. Unlike most traditional Florida Democrats, Gibbons has supported civil rights legislation and voted more often than not with the bulk of northern Democrats. In his early career, he was one of a small, outnumbered group of liberal young Congressmen pushing for Congressional reform; in recent years, those causes he early championed have almost all come to pass.

After serving for several terms on Education and Labor, Gibbons won a seat on Ways and Means, where he espoused major tax reform and disagreed with some frequency with Chairman Wilbur Mills. After the 1972 election, he made an abortive run at the Majority Leadership vacated by the death of Hale Boggs. Gibbons was seldom successful in his fights with Mills, and had to withdraw from the leadership race; but with the influx of freshmen following the 1974 election, he is one of those middle-seniority members who suddenly has massive support for causes he used to lonesomely champion.

Census Data Pop. 452,820. Central city, 39%; suburban, 61%. Median family income, $8,256; families above $15,000: 14%; families below $3,000: 12%. Median years education, 12.

The Voters

Median voting age 43.
Employment profile White collar, 49%. Blue collar, 36%. Service, 13%. Farm, 2%.
Ethnic groups Black, 13%. Spanish, 12%. Total foreign stock, 14%. Italy, 2%; Germany, Canada, UK, 1% each.

Presidential vote

1972	Nixon (R)	99,739	(70%)
	McGovern (D)	43,347	(30%)
1968	Nixon (R)	43,565	(35%)
	Humphrey (D)	41,876	(34%)
	Wallace (AI)	39,555	(32%)

Rep. Sam Gibbons (D) Elected 1962; b. Jan. 20, 1920, Tampa; home, Tampa; U. of Fla., LL.B. 1947; Presbyterian.

Career Army, WWII; Practicing atty., 1947–62; Fla. House of Reps., 1952–58; Fla. Senate, 1958–62.

Offices 2161 RHOB, 202-225-3376. Also 510 Fed. Bldg., 500 Zack St., Tampa 33602, 813-228-2101.

Committees

Budget (12th).

Ways and Means (11th). Subcommittees: Oversight; Trade.

Group Ratings

	ADA	COPE	LWV	RIPON	NFU	LCV	CFA	NAB	NSI	ACA
1974	57	83	60	40	73	65	36	20	50	21
1973	59	73	89	79	85	78	71	–	–	27
1972	44	60	70	50	100	67	50	18	11	39

Key Votes

1) Foreign Aid	AGN	6) Gov Abortn Aid	ABS	11) Pub Cong Election $	AGN
2) Busing	AGN	7) Coed Phys Ed	ABS	12) Turkish Arms Cutoff	FOR
3) ABM	FOR	8) Pov Lawyer Gag	AGN	13) Youth Camp Regs	ABS
4) B-1 Bomber	AGN	9) Pub Trans Sub	AGN	14) Strip Mine Veto	AGN
5) Nerve Gas	AGN	10) EZ Voter Regis	FOR	15) Farm Bill Veto	AGN

Election Results

1974 general:	Sam Gibbons (D), unopposed	($6,228)
1974 primary:	Sam Gibbons (D), unopposed	

1972 general: Sam Gibbons (D)   91,931   (68%)   ($8,194)
                 Robert A. Carter (R)   43,343   (32%;   ($14,218)

◆ ◆ ◆ ◆ ◆

EIGHTH DISTRICT

Florida's 8th congressional district is made up of two areas. Somewhat less than half its population lives along the Gulf Coast in towns like Bradenton and Sarasota. These are relatively well-off, sun-baked communities with lots of migrants and retirees from the north; the voters here, in their golf courses and yacht basins and comfortable condominiums, are very conservative and very Republican. Separated from the Gulf Coast by miles of swampland is the citrus-growing country in and around Polk County. Here the towns are smaller and have fewer of the glittering new high rises that tower along the coast. The interior economy is geared more to agriculture than to winter tourists. Incongruously set amidst the boom cities of central Florida, Polk County remains a part of Old Dixie politically. In 1968, Polk preferred George Wallace to Richard Nixon, and in general the county will give local—but not national—Democratic candidates better vote totals than they get on the Gulf Coast. For 30 years, Polk County has been the home of one of the state's U.S. Senators; Bartow native Spessard Holland, long unbeatable, gave valuable help to Lakeland lawyer Lawton Chiles in his upset victory in 1970.

The 8th is one of those districts national Republican strategists have had their eye on for a long time—and never won. This territory has not gone for any Democratic presidential candidate since the 1940s; and even in congressional races, the strong Republican voting base in Sarasota and Bradenton should overcome any Democratic edge in Polk County. But up through 1974, at least, the 8th district has persisted in reelecting Democrat James A. Haley since 1952. Haley is a former owner, through marriage, of the Ringling Brothers Barnum and Bailey Circus, which is headquartered in Sarasota. His local connections, plus 22 years of service, are the principal reasons behind his continued victories. In some years, his margins have slipped—to as low as 53% in 1970.

Then, as a result of a 1972 Colorado primary, Haley succeeded the defeated Wayne Aspinall as Chairman of the House Interior Committee. Aspinall had been a dictatorial chairman, and one who aroused the wrath of environmental groups, which were largely responsible for beating him. Haley, less expert than Aspinall and more open to persuasion, has treated the environmentalists as just another pressure group, listening to them and sometimes acceding to their demands —although one would not suspect that this is where the conservative man's initial sympathies lie. The fair and loose way Haley has run the committee spared him any challenge in 1975, when several other committee chairmen were toppled; but it is possible that he will consider retirement. At 77 in 1976, he could again face a tough race in the district, and he will have had the satisfaction of having served as Interior Chairman for four years. If Haley does not run, Republicans will have at least a fair chance of capturing the district, providing they can come up with a creditable candidate.

Census Data Pop. 451,776. Central city, 0%; suburban, 8%. Median family income, $7,341; families above $15,000: 13%; families below $3,000: 16%. Median years education, 12.0.

The Voters

Median voting age 50.
Employment profile White collar, 43%. Blue collar, 35%. Service, 14%. Farm, 8%.
Ethnic groups Black, 14%. Spanish 2%. Total foreign stock 10%. Germany, Canada, 2% each; UK, 1%.

Presidential vote

1972	Nixon (R)	134,071	(79%)
	McGovern (D)	34,768	(21%)
1968	Nixon (R)	67,444	(44%)
	Humphrey (D)	33,031	(22%)
	Wallace (AI)	51,638	(34%)

Rep. James A. Haley (D) Elected 1952; b. Jan 4, 1899, Jacksonville, Ala.; home, Sarasota; U. of Ala., 1919–20; Methodist.

Career Army, WWI; CPA, 1925–1933; Gen. Mgr., John Ringling estate, 1933–43; V.P., Ringling Circus, 1943–45; Pres. and Dir., Ringling Bros. Barnum & Baily Circus, 1946–48; Fla. House of Reps., 1948–52.

Offices 1236 LHOB, 202-225-5015. Also P.O. Box 844, Bartow 33830, 813-533-2881.

Committees

Interior and Insular Affairs (Chairman).

Group Ratings

	ADA	COPE	LWV	RIPON	NFU	LCV	CFA	NAB	NSI	ACA
1974	19	18	36	14	50	50	33	92	89	67
1973	16	36	25	13	55	21	38	–	–	78
1972	0	9	10	23	43	20	50	100	100	100

Key Votes

1) Foreign Aid	AGN	6) Gov Abortn Aid	AGN	11) Pub Cong Election $	AGN
2) Busing	AGN	7) Coed Phys Ed	AGN	12) Turkish Arms Cutoff	FOR
3) ABM	FOR	8) Pov Lawyer Gag	FOR	13) Youth Camp Regs	AGN
4) B-1 Bomber	FOR	9) Pub Trans Sub	AGN	14) Strip Mine Veto	AGN
5) Nerve Gas	FOR	10) EZ Voter Regis	AGN	15) Farm Bill Veto	FOR

Election Results

1974 general:	James A. Haley (D)	111,523	(70%)	($15,879)
	Joe Z. Lovingwood (R)	48,240	(30%)	($45,650)
1974 primary:	James A. Haley (D)	31,439	(75%)	
	Larry P. Echols (D)	10,368	(25%)	
1972 general:	James A. Haley (D)	89,068	(58%)	($36,960)
	Roy Thompson (R)	64,920	(42%)	($38,587)

◆ ◆ ◆ ◆

NINTH DISTRICT

Everyone knows about Orange County, California, with its San Clemente estate, its Disneyland, and its fabled conservative politics. Less well known is Orange County, Florida, of which Orlando is the county seat. If you use the 1968 or 1972 presidential election returns as a benchmark, Orange County, Florida is at least a couple of shades more conservative than its California counterpart. The larger part of Orange County, plus Brevard County of Kennedy Space Center fame, make up Florida's 9th congressional district. In 1972, the 9th produced the sixth highest percentage for Richard Nixon among the 435 House districts across the nation.

This has been an explosive growth area, with plenty of Yankee migrants moving in and bringing their conservative Republicanism along. Historically, the economic base here was the orange crop, but as in the case of Orange County, California, oranges have been supplanted as the chief engine of growth by the Department of Defense and—until recently, anyway—the National Aeronautics and Space Administration. Orlando has the bulk of the area's defense plants, with more than $200 million in contracts, while the NASA money goes to Brevard County on the coast. A key local issue here is the space shuttle, which will supposedly create hundreds of space-related jobs in the area; without that, recent cuts in the space budget have left some fast-growing parts of Brevard almost empty again.

But if NASA is less generous, the 9th district got a boost from the same organization that sparked much of the growth in Orange County, California. The giant Disney World complex outside Orlando—eventually it will be a city in itself—has set attendance records, triggered a real estate boom, and created traffic jams of monumental proportions. Tourists coming to Florida used to ignore Orlando; now they flock here by the hundreds of thousands, staying as long as a week to catch both Disney World and the Space Center. It is fitting that the area's top attraction be one catering to children; for unlike so much of Florida, the Orlando area is not so much a retirees' haven as it is a place where young parents raise families.

The 9th district's Congressman is—no surprise—a conservative Republican. When the Orange-Brevard area first got its own congressional seat in 1962, the voters elected Edward Gurney to fill it; when he moved up to the Senate in 1968, his successor was his former law partner, Louis Frey, Jr. Like Gurney, Frey was originally from the northeast; like Gurney, he has compiled an almost solidly conservative voting record. For several years before the 1974 elections, rumors flew that Frey would run either for his old partner's Senate seat or against Governor Reubin Askew; he surprised everyone by doing neither, and instead was routinely reelected in the 9th district—as he doubtless will, barring statewide races—in the years ahead.

Census Data Pop. 452,923. Central city, 16%; suburban, 34%. Median family income, $10,267; families above $15,000: 24%; families below $3,000: 8%. Median years education, 12.5.

The Voters

Median voting age 41.
Employment profile White collar, 60%. Blue collar, 27%. Service, 12%. Farm, 1%.
Ethnic groups Black, 8%. Spanish, 2%. Total foreign stock, 11%. UK, Germany, Canada, 2% each.

Presidential vote

1972	Nixon (R)	132,323	(81%)
	McGovern (D)	32,041	(19%)
1968	Nixon (R)	71,359	(51%)
	Humphrey (D)	31,586	(23%)
	Wallace (AI)	37,097	(26%)

Rep. Louis Frey, Jr. (R) Elected 1968; b. Jan. 11, 1934, Rutherford, N. J.; home, Winter Park; Colgate U., B. A. 1955, U. of Mich., J. D. 1961; Lutheran.

Career Navy, 1955–58; Practicing atty., 1961–68.

Offices 214 CHOB, 202-225-3671. Also Rm. 222, 1041 Woodcock Rd., Orlando 32803, 305-894-3739.

Committees

Interstate and Foreign Commerce (8th). Subcommittees: Communications.

Science and Technology (6th). Subcommittees: Energy Research, Development and Demostration; Space Science and Applications.

Group Ratings

	ADA	COPE	LWV	RIPON	NFU	LCV	CFA	NAB	NSI	ACA
1974	9	0	50	50	50	50	33	83	100	75
1973	17	9	36	67	37	28	13	–	–	88
1972	13	9	45	57	43	53	0	92	100	91

Key Votes

1) Foreign Aid	AGN	6) Gov Abortn Aid	AGN	11) Pub Cong Election $	FOR
2) Busing	AGN	7) Coed Phys Ed	AGN	12) Turkish Arms Cutoff	AGN
3) ABM	FOR	8) Pov Lawyer Gag	FOR	13) Youth Camp Regs	AGN
4) B-1 Bomber	FOR	9) Pub Trans Sub	AGN	14) Strip Mine Veto	AGN
5) Nerve Gas	FOR	10) EZ Voter Regis	AGN	15) Farm Bill Veto	FOR

Election Results

1974 general:	Louis Frey, Jr. (R)	86,226	(77%)	($53,787)
	William D. Rowland (D)	26,255	(23%)	($5,044)
1974 primary:	Louis Frey, Jr. (R), unopposed			
1972 general:	Louis Frey, Jr. (R), unopposed			($2,255)

◆ ◆ ◆ ◆ ◆

TENTH DISTRICT

The 10th is one of three new congressional districts acquired by Florida in the 1970 census. It is also the only one of the three that the Democratic legislature conceded, without a struggle, to the opposition. The shape of the 10th makes little sense except as an agglomeration of all the Republican-leaning territory that south Florida's Democratic Congressmen didn't want. The district sweeps across the Florida peninsula, fronting on the Atlantic north of Palm Beach and on the Gulf of Mexico south from Sarasota to Naples. Accordingly, its population centers are widely dispersed. It goes as far north as the Disney World area near Orlando; it takes in some of the fast-growing suburban territory west of West Palm Beach; it includes the largest town on the Gulf Coast south of Sarasota, Fort Myers. In between, there is mostly the remarkable swamp that is the Everglades, the Sebring Grand Prix race course, and numerous orange groves.

The beneficiary of this handiwork, conceived by Democratic politicians, is Republican L.A. (Skip) Bafalis, Jr. For Bafalis, the creation of the 10th provided the opportunity for a political comeback: after six years in the Florida legislature, he had run for Governor in 1970 and, despite a campaign that attracted some attention, had won only 13% of the vote. In 1972, Bafalis had it much easier. He won the Republican nomination in the 10th without much fuss, and got a landslide 62% in the general election, despite a vigorous campaign by a young Democratic opponent.

In the House, Bafalis has been about as quiet as one expects traditional freshmen to be. He did join other Congressmen of Greek descent to lead the fight to cut off aid to Turkey in 1974. Now he has a seat on the Ways and Means Committee, where he is expected to generally take the conservative side on issues, but where his vote cannot be counted yet for sure on any side of an issue. He should be reelected without any difficulty.

Census Data Pop. 452,848. Central city, 0%; suburban, 6%. Median family income, $7,323; families above $15,000: 14%; families below $3,000: 15%. Median years education, 12.1.

The Voters

Median voting age 52.
Employment profile White collar, 43%. Blue collar, 33%. Service, 15%. Farm, 9%.
Ethnic groups Black, 14%. Spanish, 2%. Total foreign stock, 13%. Germany, UK, Canada, 2% each.

Presidential vote

1972	Nixon (R)	157,854	(79%)
	McGovern (D)	41,504	(21%)
1968	Nixon (R)	71,305	(47%)
	Humphrey (D)	37,224	(25%)
	Wallace (AI)	41,877	(28%)

Rep. L. A. (Skip) **Bafalis** (R) Elected 1972; b. Sept. 28, 1929, Boston, Mass.; home, Fort Myers Beach; St. Anselm's Col., A. B. 1952; Protestant.

Career Army, Korea; Banker; Fla. House of Reps., 1964–65; Fla. Senate, 1966–70, Minority Ldr., 1968; Cand. for Gov., 1970.

Offices 408 CHOB, 202-225-2536. Also Room 106 Fed. Bldg., Ft. Myers 33901, 813-334-4424.

Committees

Ways and Means (11th). Subcommittees: Oversight; Public Assistance.

Group Ratings

	ADA	COPE	LWV	RIPON	NFU	LCV	CFA	NAB	NSI	ACA
1974	9	10	45	31	50	47	33	80	100	79
1973	17	18	27	54	30	50	50	–	–	88

Key Votes

1) Foreign Aid	AGN	6) Gov Abortn Aid	AGN	11) Pub Cong Election $	AGN
2) Busing	AGN	7) Coed Phys Ed	AGN	12) Turkish Arms Cutoff	FOR
3) ABM	FOR	8) Pov Lawyer Gag	FOR	13) Youth Camp Regs	FOR
4) B-1 Bomber	FOR	9) Pub Trans Sub	AGN	14) Strip Mine Veto	AGN
5) Nerve Gas	FOR	10) EZ Voter Regis	AGN	15) Farm Bill Veto	FOR

Election Results

1974 general:	L. A. "Skip" Bafalis (R)	117,368	(74%)	($32,735)
	Evelyn Tucker (D)	41,925	(26%)	($4,360)
1974 primary:	L. A. "Skip" Bafalis (R), unopposed			
1972 general:	L. A. "Skip" Bafalis (R)	113,461	(62%)	($129,393)
	Bill Sikes (D)	69,502	(38%)	($55,035)

◆ ◆ ◆ ◆ ◆

ELEVENTH DISTRICT

Fifty years ago, Palm Beach was already a fashionable resort for the extremely wealthy. Across Lake Worth, West Palm Beach was a small town, a large percentage of whose residents devoted themselves to ministering to the needs of Palm Beach. Palm Beach has changed little since, but West Palm Beach, at the northern end of the "Gold Coast" that runs all the way to Miami, has been altered beyond recognition. High-rise apartment houses and condominiums practically form a wall that blocks off the mainland from the Atlantic. Jai alai frontons vie with gaudy bars for tourists' money, and the small motels of the forties have been replaced with giant motor inns.

The northern end of the Gold Coast—in rough terms from Pompano Beach in Broward County to West Palm Beach in Palm Beach County—is the 11th congressional district of Florida. Like Fort Lauderdale to the south, the 11th for many years has become ever more Republican as more and more people have moved here from the well-to-do suburbs of the Midwest and the Northeast. But these new voters have never been much of a problem for Democratic Congressman Paul Rogers. His margins have been holding up despite the vast changes that have occurred in the district he represents. The 11th and its predecessors (which only ten years ago included most of south Florida outside Miami) have more or less been the property of the Rogers family: the current Congressman was first elected in 1954 after the death of his father, who had represented the district since its creation in 1944.

During his first years in Congress, the younger Rogers had something of a playboy reputation. He settled down, however, after getting married in the early sixties. Soon after that, he took control of the Commerce Subcommittee on Public Health, first while the passive John Jarman of Oklahoma was its technical chairman, and then when he gained the chair in his own right. From that position, Rogers has become one of the major powers on health policy in the country. He assembled a solid staff, and personally mastered the subcommittee's subject matter. There are those who think Rogers has stretched his subcommittee's jurisdiction a little farther than it should go, but he is considered one of the more thoughtful and energetic subcommittee chairmen in the House. Rogers makes it a practice to obtain unanimity, or as close as he can to it, on his subcommittee, and he has become a master at selling a bill on the floor. It is a fact of life in the House that a member must specialize in order to have any impact; Rogers is one of the best examples of intelligent specialization.

Census Data Pop. 452,170. Central city, 13%; suburban, 87%. Median family income, $8,995; families above $15,000: 21%; families below $3,000: 11%. Median years education, 12.2.

The Voters

Median voting age 51.
Employment profile White collar, 49%. Blue collar, 31%. Service, 16%. Farm, 4%.
Ethnic groups Black, 18%. Spanish, 3%. Total foreign stock, 21%. Germany, UK, Canada, 3% each; Italy, 2%; Ireland, 1%.

Presidential vote

1972	Nixon (R)		146,024	(74%)
	McGovern (D)		50,733	(26%)
1968	Nixon (R)		74,707	(55%)
	Humphrey (D)		37,610	(28%)
	Wallace (AI)		24,016	(18%)

Rep. Paul G. Rogers (D) Elected Jan. 11, 1955; b. June 4, 1921, Ocilla, Ga.; home, West Palm Beach; U. of Fla., B. A. 1942, LL. B. 1948; Methodist.

Career Army, WWII; Practicing atty., 1948–54.

Offices 2407 RHOB, 202-225-3001. Also Rm. 321 Red. Bldg., West Palm Beach 33401, 305-832-6424.

Committees

Interstate and Foreign Commerce (5th). Subcommittees: Health and Environment (Chairman).

Merchant Marine and Fisheries (5th). Subcommittees: Coast Guard and Navigation; Fisheries and Wildlife Conservation and the Environment; Oceanography.

Group Ratings

	ADA	COPE	LWV	RIPON	NFU	LCV	CFA	NAB	NSI	ACA
1974	30	45	50	40	69	65	62	75	80	57
1973	48	36	58	50	50	42	63	–	–	67
1972	6	18	42	53	33	53	100	58	90	87

Key Votes

1) Foreign Aid	AGN	6) Gov Abortn Aid	AGN	11) Pub Cong Election $	AGN
2) Busing	AGN	7) Coed Phys Ed	AGN	12) Turkish Arms Cutoff	FOR
3) ABM	FOR	8) Pov Lawyer Gag	FOR	13) Youth Camp Regs	FOR
4) B-1 Bomber	FOR	9) Pub Trans Sub	AGN	14) Strip Mine Veto	AGN
5) Nerve Gas	FOR	10) EZ Voter Regis	FOR	15) Farm Bill Veto	FOR

Election Results

1974 general:	Paul G. Rogers (D), unopposed			($15,517)
1974 primary:	Paul G. Rogers (D)	32,956	(83%)	
	Robert D. (Bob) McBain (D)	6,648	(17%)	
1972 general:	Paul G. Rogers (D)	116,157	(60%)	($87,253)
	Joel Karl Gustafson (R)	76,739	(40%)	($59,108)

◆ ◆ ◆ ◆ ◆

TWELFTH DISTRICT

For some, Fort Lauderdale evokes memories of college sand-and-beer vacations in the spring, or maybe scenes from an Annette Funicello and Frankie Avalon movie. That is not, however, the impression the town fathers would like you to have; they have long since tried to discourage the influx of college spring vacationers who bring little money and scare away people who do. What they would prefer you to envision is a cosmopolitan, canalled tropical city, with miles of wide sand beach, lilting palm trees, and cultural attractions you would expect in a city many times its size. And there is some truth to that picture: this land dredged from swamp and muck is some of the most valuable real estate in the country. Fort Lauderdale's modest population of 172,000 conceals the fact that it is the center not only of Broward County (620,000), but of the whole Florida Gold Coast from Miami to Palm Beach (an area with a total population over two million).

The voting population of Fort Lauderdale and Broward County has moved here mostly from the upper-income suburbs of the East and Midwest. The new residents have tripled Broward's population in the last 20 years; back home, these people tended to be Republicans, and for many years they made this one of the leading Republican strongholds in the state. In those days it was convenient to think of Broward as Chicago suburb-Chicago *Tribune*-Protestant-Republican, in constrast to Miami and Dade County as New York City-New York *Times*-Jewish-Democratic. So it was fitting that the 12th congressional district, which includes most of Broward County and basically all of its two largest cities, Fort Lauderdale and Hollywood, should elect a Republican Congressman who was brought up in Chicago.

But all that may be changing, if the 1974 election returns are any indication. An increasing number of Jews and others who tend to be liberal Democratic voters have been moving into southern Broward--Hallandale and Hollywood--in recent years, and they appear to have made the county and the 12th district considerably less reliably Republican than in the past. Governor Askew and Senator Richard Stone both carried Broward easily in 1974, and Lawton Chiles probably will have little difficulty in doing so in 1976 (though he got only 43% here in 1970). Congressman J. Herbert Burke, with his conservative record, was very much in tune with the older, heavily Republican population mix one found here; he seems considerably more ill at ease with the newer, more marginal or even Democratic electorate he seems to face now. It may be that 1974 was simply such a heavily Democratic year as to push this otherwise irretrievably Republican district almost into the Democratic column; but the fact that the contest was close here indicates that Burke could well be in trouble in future years.

Census Data Pop. 453,053. Central city, 54%; suburban, 46%. Median family income, $9,717; families above $15,000: 22%; families below $3,000: 9%. Median years education, 12.2.

The Voters

Median voting age 48.
Employment profile White collar, 53%. Blue collar, 31%. Service, 15%. Farm, 1%.
Ethnic groups Black, 12%. Spanish, 3%. Total foreign stock, 25%. Italy, 4%; Germany, Canada, UK, 3% each; USSR, 2% Poland, Ireland, 1% each.

Presidential vote

1972	Nixon (R)	140,157	(72%)
	McGovern (D)	54,394	(28%)
1968	Nixon (R)	73,128	(53%)
	Humphrey (D)	41,686	(30%)
	Wallace (AI)	23,490	(17%)

Rep. J. Herbert Burke (R) Elected 1966; b. Jan. 14, 1913, Chicago, Ill.; home, Hollywwood; Chicago Central YMCA Col., A.A. 1936, Northwestern U. and Chicago Kent Col. of Law, LL. B. 1940; Catholic.

Career Practicing atty., 1940–42, 1945–66; Army, WWII.

Offices 2242 RHOB, 202-225-3026. Also 440 S. Andrews Ave., Ft. Lauderdale 33301, 303-522-3739.

Committees

House Administration (6th). Subcommittees: Accounts; Electrical and Mechnaical Office Equipment; Ad Hoc Restaurant.

International Relations (5th). Subcommittees: Future Foreign Policay Research and Development; International Operations.

Group Ratings

	ADA	COPE	LWV	RIPON	NFU	LCV	CFA	NAB	NSI	ACA
1974	10	10	45	43	18	43	23	83	80	87
1973	13	33	27	54	56	25	43	–	–	87
1972	13	20	36	45	17	41	50	92	100	100

Key Votes

1) Foreign Aid	AGN	6) Gov Abortn Aid	AGN	11) Pub Cong Election $	AGN
2) Busing	AGN	7) Coed Phys Ed	AGN	12) Turkish Arms Cutoff	ABS
3) ABM	FOR	8) Pov Lawyer Gag	FOR	13) Youth Camp Regs	AGN
4) B-1 Bomber	FOR	9) Pub Trans Sub	AGN	14) Strip Mine Veto	AGN
5) Nerve Gas	FOR	10) EZ Voter Regis	AGN	15) Farm Bill Veto	FOR

Election Results

1974 general:	J. Herbert Burke (R)	61,191	(51%)	($30,554)
	Charles (Charlie) Friedman (D)	58,899	(49%)	($32,038)
1974 primary:	J. Herbert Burke (R)	15,593	(75%)	
	Richard C. Burket (R)	5,285	(25%)	
1972 general:	J. Herbert Burke (R)	110,750	(63%)	($30,600)
	James T. Stephanis (D)	65,526	(37%)	($56,434)

◆ ◆ ◆ ◆ ◆

THIRTEENTH DISTRICT

Population growth required that a new congressional district be drawn in the Miami area following the 1970 census—primarily because more than 300,000 Cubans, refugees from Castro, had moved to greater Miami and Dade County during the 1960s. Ironically, the new district, the 13th, does not contain very many Cubans; most of them live in Claude Pepper's adjacent 14th district. Rather, the group which is politically dominant in the 13th district is its Jewish population. Some observers have noted a tendency to overestimate the clout of Jewish voters in Florida and certainly on the basis of raw numbers they are right. The 13th district, for example, is by no means majority Jewish; there are no precise figures available, but probably only two districts in the nation, both of them in Brooklyn, are. Indeed, only 4% of the residents of this district have Yiddish as their mother tongue, and there are plenty of other noticeable ethnic concentrations: WASPs in Miami Shores, blacks on the north side of Miami, white migrants from the Deep South in Hialeah. Altogether, probably only 15% of the residents of the 13th district are Jewish, and probably (because they are older and more likely to vote than average) about 25% of the voters. Nevertheless, all the leading candidates for Congress in the district's brief history have been Jewish; and in terms of vote in general elections, the district is as liberal as any (except perhaps the 14th) in Florida.

William Lehman, the 13th's Congressman, has had an interesting—and somewhat unusual —career. Lehman got his start in business as a used car dealer, known widely as "Alabama Bill." He reportedly developed the reputation, unusual in the trade, of being reliable and completely honest. Having mastered what the public usually rates as the least esteemed profession, Lehman decided to move up to what is usually considered the second least esteemed, politics. In the maelstrom of Dade County politics, Lehman got elected to the County School Board and, just before his run for Congress in 1972, became its Chairman.

Lehman demonstrated his political acumen by defeating two strong candidates in the Democratic primary and by winning, 62–38, over a hard-campaigning Republican in the general election. In 1974, he had another tough opponent, and was forced into a runoff, but again won fairly easily. At 63, Lehman is one of the older junior Congressmen, but he votes like a frisky freshman and—in political terms—can be counted as a liberal northerner.

Census Data Pop. 452,817. Central city, 9%; suburban, 91%. Median family income, $9,411; families above $15,000: 20%; families below $3,000: 9%. Median years education, 12.0.

The Voters

Median voting age 46.
Employment profile White collar, 49%. Blue collar, 34%. Service, 16%. Farm, 1%.
Ethnic groups Black, 18%. Spanish, 13%. Total foreign stock, 32%. USSR, 4%; Italy, 3%; Canada, Germany, Poland, UK, 2% each; Austria, 1%.

Presidential vote

1972	Nixon (R)	90,997	(56%)
	McGovern (D)	72,957	(44%)
1968	Nixon (R)	46,377	(35%)
	Humphrey (D)	64,160	(48%)
	Wallace (AI)	22,923	(17%)

Rep. William Lehman (D) Elected 1972; b. Oct. 5, 1931, Selma, Ala.; home, North Miami Beach; U. of Ala., B.S. 1934, U. of Miami, Teaching Certif., 1963, Additional Studies at Oxford U., Cambridge U., U. of Edinburgh, Harvard U., and Middlebury Col.; Jewish.

Career Auto dealer, 1936–42, 1946–72; Army Air Corps, WWII; Teacher, Pub. Schools, 1963, Miami Dade Jr. col., 1964–66; Dade Co. School Bd., 1964–70, Chm. 1971.

Offices 424 CHOB, 202-225-4211. Also 2020 N.E. 163rd St., Suite 108, N. Miami Beach 33162, 305-945-7518.

Committees

Education and Labor (17th). Subcommittees: Elementary, Secondary and Vocational Education; Manpower, Compensation, and Health and Safety; Select Subcommittee on Education.

Post Office and Civil Service (11th). Subcommittees: Census and Population; Postal Service.

Group Ratings

	ADA	COPE	LWV	RIPON	NFU	LCV	CFA	NAB	NSI	ACA
1974	86	91	90	57	92	94	73	18	25	7
1973	83	90	100	67	95	74	86	–	–	8

Key Votes

1) Foreign Aid	FOR	6) Gov Abortn Aid	FOR	11) Pub Cong Election $	FOR
2) Busing	FOR	7) Coed Phys Ed	FOR	12) Turkish Arms Cutoff	FOR
3) ABM	AGN	8) Pov Lawyer Gag	ABS	13) Youth Camp Regs	FOR
4) B-1 Bomber	AGN	9) Pub Trans Sub	FOR	14) Strip Mine Veto	AGN
5) Nerve Gas	AGN	10) EZ Voter Regis	FOR	15) Farm Bill Veto	AGN

Election Results

1974 general:	William Lehman (D), unopposed			($81,915)
1974 run-off	William Lehman (D)	32,677	(68%)	
	Mrs. Stanley (Joyce) Goldberg (D)	15,471	(32%)	
1974 primary:	William Lehman (D)	23,163	(45%)	
	Mrs. Stanley (Joyce) Goldberg (D)	15,663	(31%)	
	Three others (D)	12,085	(24%)	
1972 general:	William Lehman (D)	92,258	(62%)	($122,725)
	Paul D. Bethel (R)	57,418	(38%)	($31,660)

◆ ◆ ◆ ◆ ◆

FOURTEENTH DISTRICT

Claude Pepper is the grand old man of Florida politics. Back in 1936, he first went to Capitol Hill as a 36-year-old United States Senator. He was known even then for his old-fashioned Southern-style oratory, but once in the Senate he never became a member in good standing of the Southern establishment. When other Senators from Dixie began to sour on the New Deal, Pepper remained as loyal to FDR's domestic policies as he did to Roosevelt's conviction that the United States be fully prepared for another war in Europe. For these stands and for his devotion to civil liberties, the young Senator came to be called "Red Pepper." In 1950, during the era of Joe McCarthy, Pepper was defeated in a bitter Senate primary by Congressman George Smathers, and he retired to a lucrative Miami law practice.

Today, Smathers himself has retired (in 1968) to an extremely lucrative job as a Washington lobbyist, and Claude Pepper is back in Congress. After the 1960 census, when the Florida legislature was compelled to create a second Miami area House seat, Pepper was the logical choice to fill it. He won a solid majority in the 1962 Democratic primary and has since retained the seat without difficulty. The Congressman's oratorical style is still out of Dixie, but his record is such that he is a particular favorite of his black and Jewish constituents.

If Pepper had won the 1950 race against Smathers, he would have become Chairman of the Senate Foreign Relations Committee. As things are, Pepper cuts a lesser figure. But his years of experience on the Hill count for something—only one Senator (Randolph of West Virginia) and two Representatives (Patman and Mahon of Texas) preceded Pepper to Congress. He holds a seat on the often-crucial House Rules Committee, where he is expected to—and almost always does—advance the views of the House leadership and usually of House liberals. Pepper was also chairman of a Select Committee on Crime, which treated its controversial subject matter with more seriousness and less demagoguery than might have been expected until its term expired in 1973. Pepper also has plenty of time for Miami-based concerns. He has been a longtime advocate of increased trade and better relations with Latin America, as well as a rhetorical opponent of the Castro government. One of his major projects is Interama, an exposition park designed to promote U.S.-Latin American ties. The park, perhaps by a sentimental fillip of redistricting, is included in Pepper's 14th congressional district.

When Pepper was first elected to the House, his district's most important voting bloc was Jewish. Today, because of the Cuban influx into the Miami area and also because of redistricting, this is changing. More than 300,000 Cubans now live in and around Miami—and most reside in Pepper's district. Its boundaries, roughly speaking, include the northern half of Miami Beach, most of the city of Miami itself, and parts of the suburbs of Miami Springs and Hialeah. Between 30 and 40% of the district's residents are Cubans, and every day some of them are completing the requirements for naturalization—and registering to vote.

The Cubans are a diverse group politically, representing all types of opposition to the Castro regime: from right-wingers who would like a return to Batista-type dictatorship to mild socialists who oppose Castro's eradication of civil liberties. But overall, the political tendency of the Cubans is like that of their compatriots who invaded the Watergate under Howard ("Eduardo") Hunt—to the right. Coming largely out of Cuba's middle class, the migrants eagerly accepted menial jobs upon arrival in Miami and then rapidly worked themselves back up to an American version of middle-class status. And they tended to favor politicians like Richard Nixon who gave at least lip service to the anti-Castro cause. Overall, Miami's Cuban community favored the Vietnam war and produced big margins for Nixon in the 1972 elections. After Watergate the Cubans, like most Americans, have moved toward the Democrats; but for the future they are probably going to turn out to be considerably more conservative than most American ethnic groups. That does not mean much trouble for 76-year-old Claude Pepper, but it will affect the politics of Miami and the 14th district in the years to come.

Census Data Pop. 452,633. Central city, 58%; suburban, 42%. Median family income, $8,203; families above $15,000: 18%; families below $3,000: 13%. Median years education, 11.4.

The Voters

Median voting age 48.
Employment profile White collar, 46%. Blue collar, 37%. Service, 17%. Farm, –%.
Ethnic groups Black, 15%. Spanish, 41%. Total foreign stock, 56%. USSR, 4%; Poland, 2%; Germany, Canada, Italy, Austria, UK, 1% each.

Presidential vote

1972	Nixon (R)	70,005	(58%)
	McGovern (D)	50,458	(42%)
1968	Nixon (R)	37,739	(34%)
	Humphrey (D)	59,206	(53%)
	Wallace (AI)	13,831	(12%)

Rep. Claude Pepper (D) Elected 1962; b. Sept. 8, 1900, near Dudleyville, Ala.; home, Miami; U. of Ala, A.B. 1921, Harvard U., LL.B. 1924; Baptist.

Career Instructor in Law, U. of Ark., 1924–25; Practicing atty., 1925–36, 1951–62; Fla. House of Reps., 1929–30; Fla. Bd. of Pub. Welfare, 1931–32; Fla. Bd. of Law Examiners, 1933–34; U.S. Senate, 1937–51; Candidate for Dem. nomination for U.S. Senate, 1950, 1958.

Offices 2239 RHOB, 202-225-3931. Also 823 Fed. Bldg., 51 S.W. 1st Ave., Miami 33130, 305-350-5565.

Committees

Rules (6th).

Group Ratings

	ADA	COPE	LWV	RIPON	NFU	LCV	CFA	NAB	NSI	ACA
1974	50	100	73	43	93	64	80	0	67	15
1973	67	100	82	67	100	59	88	–	–	9
1972	50	89	90	64	100	26	100	0	60	30

Key Votes

1) Foreign Aid	FOR	6) Gov Abortn Aid	FOR	11) Pub Cong Election $	AGN
2) Busing	AGN	7) Coed Phys Ed	FOR	12) Turkish Arms Cutoff	FOR
3) ABM	FOR	8) Pov Lawyer Gag	ABS	13) Youth Camp Regs	ABS
4) B-1 Bomber	FOR	9) Pub Trans Sub	FOR	14) Strip Mine Veto	AGN
5) Nerve Gas	FOR	10) EZ Voter Regis	FOR	15) Farm Bill Veto	FOR

Election Results

1974 general:	Claude Pepper (D)	45,479	(69%)	($26,393)
	Mike Carricarte (R)	20,383	(31%)	($18,631)
1974 primary:	Claude Pepper (D), unopposed			
1972 general:	Claude Pepper (D)	75,131	(68%)	($95,864)
	Evelio S. Estrella (R)	35,935	(32%)	($34,921)

♦ ♦ ♦ ♦ ♦

FIFTEENTH DISTRICT

The suburbs of south Dade County are the fastest-growing part of the Miami metropolitan area. With relatively few Latins, or blacks, these places lack the special character of Miami, and the area's physical ambiance is not so different from that of Orange County, California. But while the people in California are bounded by ocean and mountains, the people here are hemmed in mainly by a giant swamp, the Everglades, from which their often valuable property was reclaimed. South Dade County is middle-class, middle- to upper-income territory that stretches out on both sides of U.S. 1 as it heads toward the Florida Keys.

The bulk of Florida's 15th congressional district lies in these southwest suburbs of Miami. Also in the district are the Keys (Monroe County), and some other territory which was obviously inserted for political reasons. The 15th, for example, includes the University of Miami in Coral Gables and the nearby Coconut Grove section of Miami, which is the closest thing in Florida to a student-street people community. The district also takes in a couple of blocks in downtown Miami, which connect the mainland 15th to its share of Miami Beach.

The part of Miami Beach in the district is the older, poorer, and almost entirely Jewish South Beach section, as well as the hall where both parties' 1972 national conventions were held. Those who think that the "Jewish vote" is not an important aspect of Miami politics should consider the role the South Beach plays in the 15th district. In 1972, Miami Beach (pop. 87,000) cast almost precisely half as many votes as the city of Miami (pop. 334,000). With only 7% of Dade County's population and 9% of its voters, Miami Beach cast 13% of its McGovern votes. This high-turnout, high-Democratic pattern is a typical one on the South Beach. The 15th's Congressman, Dante Fascell, did far better here than McGovern but was still in trouble because the southwest suburbs were going heavily for Nixon; Fascell also had an active, Jewish Republican opponent. That year, Fascell won only 57% of the vote; without the South Beach, he would have been close to 50%—a real squeaker.

That is not the experience Fascell has usually had, as the Democratic year of 1974 showed again, since he was first elected to Congress in 1954. Considered slightly less liberal than the 14th district's Claude Pepper, Fascell still votes more often with northern Democrats than with Southerners. He is rated by some observers as one of the House's leading legislative tacticians. One source of Fascell's local strength has been his long interest in Latin America and chairmanship of the Foreign Affairs subcommittee covering it.

Census Data Pop. 452,681. Central city, 8%; suburban, 81%. Median family income, $9,909; families above $15,000: 26%; families below $3,000: 11%. Median years education, 12.3.

The Voters

Median voting age 43.
Employment profile White collar, 60%. Blue collar, 24%. Service, 14%. Farm, 2%.
Ethnic groups Black, 11%. Spanish, 14%. Total foreign stock, 31%. USSR, 5%; Poland, UK, Germany, Canada, 2% each; Italy, Austria, 1% each.

Presidential vote

1972	Nixon (R)	104,864	(63%)
	McGovern (D)	60,483	(37%)
1968	Nixon (R)	52,286	(40%)
	Humphrey (D)	56,927	(44%)
	Wallace (AI)	20,469	(16%)

Rep. Dante B. Fascell (D) Elected 1954; b. Mar. 9, 1917, Bridge-hampton, L.I., N.Y.; home, Miami; U. of Miami, J.D. 1938; Protestant.

Career Practicing atty., 1938–42, 1946–54; Army, WWII; Legal Attache, Dade Co. St. Legislative Del., 1947–50; Fla. House of Reps., 1950–54; Mbr., U.S. Delegation to U.N., 1969.

Offices 2160 RHOB, 202-225-4506. Also 904 Fed. Bldg., 51 S.W. 1st Ave, Miami 33130, 305-350-5301.

Committees

Government Operations (4th). Subcommittees: Conservation, Energy and Natural Resources.

International Relations (5th). Subcommittees: International Organizations; International Political and Military Affairs (Chairman).

Group Ratings

	ADA	COPE	LWV	RIPON	NFU	LCV	CFA	NAB	NSI	ACA
1974	87	100	92	69	93	82	58	17	30	13
1973	88	91	100	73	85	79	88	–	–	7
1972	81	91	92	67	86	80	100	8	40	17

Key Votes

1) Foreign Aid	FOR	6) Gov Abortn Aid	FOR	11) Pub Cong Election $	FOR
2) Busing	AGN	7) Coed Phys Ed	FOR	12) Turkish Arms Cutoff	FOR
3) ABM	AGN	8) Pov Lawyer Gag	AGN	13) Youth Camp Regs	FOR
4) B-1 Bomber	AGN	9) Pub Trans Sub	FOR	14) Strip Mine Veto	AGN
5) Nerve Gas	AGN	10) EZ Voter Regis	FOR	15) Farm Bill Veto	FOR

Election Results

1974 general:	Dante B. Fascell (D)	68,064	(71%)	($41,957)
	S. Peter Capua (R)	28,444	(29%)	($47,775)
1974 primary:	Dante B. Fascell (D), unopposed			
1972 general:	Dante B. Fascell (D)	89,961	(57%)	($61,370)
	Ellis S. Rubin (R)	68,320	(43%)	($9,522)

GEORGIA

Since the days of the civil rights movement, we have been accustomed to thinking of Southern politics as a matter of black vs. white—with the whites almost invariably winning. In Georgia, it has been a little more complicated than that. The basic division here has been between the Atlanta metropolitan area and the rest of the state—mainly small cities and rural farm country. Atlanta—a bustling, sophisticated metropolis—likes to call itself "the world's next great city." It won its progressive reputation during the 1950s and 1960s under Mayors William Hartsfield and Ivan Allen. Backed by the late Ralph McGill's Atlanta *Constitution* and the city's business community, Hartsfield and Allen led white Atlanta in a plea for black equal rights and racial harmony. Among other things, Atlanta's position on race relations proved to be good economics; in the last 20 years Atlanta has become the number one business city in the South.

At the same time, it is possible to overstate the liberalism of metropolitan Atlanta. The central city itself, with its black majority, went for Democratic presidential candidates in 1968 and 1972, and in 1973 elected the first black Mayor of a major Southern city, 35-year-old Maynard Jackson. But all the post-1960 growth in booming Atlanta has been in the suburbs, and the voters there by no means share the political sympathies of the city's residents. Jackson would never have carried the suburbs, and the metropolitan area as a whole went for Richard Nixon in 1968 and gave him 70% of its vote in 1972. As for George Wallace, the fashionable Atlanta suburbanites have little use for the slicked-down-hair oratory of George Wallace; he ran a poor third in the metropolitan area in 1968, while carrying the state as a whole. But they are no more likely to be liberal than are the equally cosmopolitan and conservative suburbanites of Chicago and Los Angeles.

In the numbers battle between urbane and rustic Georgians, time is on the side of Atlanta: the fast-growing metropolitan area contained 30% of Georgia's residents in 1970 but was casting 35% of the state's vote by 1974. But it has taken greater Atlanta a long time to prevail, and 1974 was the first time the metropolis has won a political battle with the rest of the state in our time.

The central figure in this battle was the man whose image has dominated Georgia politics now for a decade, Lester Maddox. The word "image" is used advisedly, for even Maddox's strongest supporters cannot really tell you what he has accomplished; they only know what he stands for. And that, of course, though he doesn't quite say it this way any more, is segregation; this is the man who attacked blacks with axe-handles rather than integrate his restaurant in 1964. Maddox had run for office before that and, as a nuisance candidate, picked up a few votes; in 1966, he ran for Governor, and ran first in the Democratic primary. In the runoff, he was pitted against former Governor (1943-47) Ellis Arnall, a creature of that rare species, the genuine Southern liberal, who had the solid support of metropolitan Atlanta. Lester, peddling backward on his bicycle, won with huge majorities in the small counties. In the general, Maddox faced a sleeker, but just as conservative, Republican opponent, Howard Callaway; the latter got the most votes, but Arnall, running as a write-in, prevented either candidate from winning a majority and so the election went to the legislature, which promptly installed Maddox. (At the same time, it was busy barring from office a newly elected black state Representative named Julian Bond because he opposed the Vietnam war.)

Maddox was barred from seeking reelection in 1970, so he ran for Lieutenant Governor instead and won easily; he spent much of his spare time marketing Lester Maddox T-shirts in his Underground Atlanta shop. Naturally, he ran for Governor again in 1974, and of course was the man to beat. In the first Democratic primary, he had a wide lead, but fell considerably short of an absolute majority with 36% of the vote. A number of not very well known rivals jousted for second place, with state Representative George Busbee coming out slightly ahead. But that was a very significant margin, because it appeared that a statewide majority was—finally—sick of Lester Maddox, and Busbee, as the anti-Maddox candidate, was able to capture a solid 60% in the runoff. The Republican candidate was more an oddity than anything else: Ronnie Thompson, the Mayor of Macon, known as "Machine Gun" Thompson for ordering such weapons to be used in quelling riots. Thompson never captured the imagination of non-Atlanta Georgians, who though attracted by axehandles seem repelled by machine guns; he ran a pathetic 31%.

Maddox's initial victories convinced many canny politicians that, in order to win, they must paint themselves as aw-shucks country boys, a little wary of the Atlanta city slickers. Actually, these politicians—unlike Lester Maddox—are about as unsophisticated as that "barefoot boy from Wall Street", Wendell Willkie. An example of this trend was Governor Jimmy Carter, who was elected in 1970. During his campaign, in which he shook tens of thousands of hands, Carter liked to describe himself as a peanut farmer from Plains, Georgia. He placed somewhat less emphasis on the fact that he had served as a top aide to Admiral Hyman Rickover in the nuclear submarine program, and that his peanut farm was not a shack-and-40-acres affair but a well-managed, thriving business. Carter lost the Atlanta metropolitan area in both the primary and general election; but surprised some of his erstwhile supporters by coming out foresquare for integration. In his last year as Governor, he was pleased to appear with Mayor Jackson when the 'Atlanta Braves' Hank Aaron hit his 714th home run. He also applied some sophisticated management techniques, with considerable success, to the state budget and pushed for progressive tax reforms. Like Reubin Askew of Florida, he was highly popular going into the 1974 elections, and could easily have won a second term; unlike Askew, he was barred from running. Now he is running for President, vowing that he will go into all the primaries; barring a major upset of George Wallace, it looks like a uphill race.

Another sophisticated country boy who has made it big is U.S. Senator Sam Nunn. Early in 1972, the 34-year-old state Representative from Perry, Georgia, was unknown statewide; if anyone were to describe him then, it was probably as the grandnephew of former Representative (1914-65) Carl Vinson, the longtime Chairman of the House Armed Services Committee. The sitting Senator was David Gambrell, a Harvard-educated Atlanta lawyer, appointed by Carter to fill the vacancy caused by the death of the late Richard Russell. Gambrell's chief primary opponent was expected to be former Governor (1959-63) S. Ernest Vandiver, Russell's nephew by marriage.

Instead Nunn, featuring a media campaign based on the slogan "Get Tough in Washington" edged Vandiver out of second place in the primary and then whipped Gambrell in the runoff. Gambrell attributed his defeat to the voters' disenchantment with incumbents in a turbulent political year, but it would be better ascribed to the yoke of Atlanta hanging around his urban neck. Nunn was helped by last minute endorsements from such disparate figures as Maddox and Julian Bond. The latter was announced only in a mass mailing to blacks that arrived the morning of the election—in order to avoid antagonizing white voters in south Georgia. The general election contest between Nunn and Atlanta Republican Congressman Fletcher Thompson was more or less the same story. Rhetorically, they fought to see who could better denounce welfare cheaters and busing; Nunn apparently won. Thompson carried the Atlanta area; Nunn carried the rest of the state for a 54-46 victory.

Nunn was sworn in early to fill Russell's unexpired term, and promptly won Russell's seat on Armed Services—and the admiration of Russell's successor as Chairman, John Stennis of Mississippi. Stennis sent Nunn on a special mission to Europe, to come up with a recommendation for cutting back NATO force costs without reducing manpower substantially, and did so. On Armed Services, he generally sides with what must be called the hawks, who remain dominant on the committee; but he also brings to his work a new eye and an unwillingness to accept things simply because they've always been done that way. Nunn is 23 years younger than any more senior member of Armed Services; he appears unlikely to have any electoral problems in Georgia (smart enough for Atlanta, conservative enough for the rest of the state). Probably he will be Chairman one day.

Georgia's senior Senator already is a Chairman, and probably will remain one for some time. He is Herman Talmadge, who has been to all effects and purposes unopposed since he was first elected to the Senate in 1956. His political career began turbulently on the death of his father, Eugene Talmadge, a quasi-populist race-baiter and sometime Governor. Eugene died in 1946, just having been elected Governor for a fourth term; the legislature chose young (33) Herman to succeed him. Talmadge held the office for 67 days against the claims of the duly elected Lieutenant Governor, until the state Supreme Court declared the legislative election illegal. Herman then won the office on his own in 1948 and got a full four-year term in 1950. Two years after leaving the Governor's chair, Talmadge won election to the Senate, easing aside veteran (1923-57) Senator Walter George, the Chairman of the Foreign Relations Committee.

Talmadge's demeanor today shows no trace of the banana republic beginnings of his political career; he has gained a polish and respectability his father never knew. Chairman of the Senate Agriculture Committee, he often manages to weld an unusual group of liberals and conservatives behind a common policy; he is also second to Russell Long in seniority on the Senate Finance Committee. While impressing his colleagues on national issues, he has also managed to win the support of the Atlanta financial establishment and of the rural Georgians who always supported his father. Talmadge is reputed to be one of the brightest men in the Senate, but he usually remains closed-mouthed and uncommunicative in public. His incisive, to-the-heart-of-the-matter questioning as a member of the Watergate Committee gave the general public insight into how his mind works. He is, incidentally, an incredibly early riser; staffers are supposed to report to the office by 6 A.M.

There has been talk in the past that Talmadge was bored with his job, but he has shown no inclination yet to leave it, and the voters in turn have shown no inclination to see him go. His most interesting campaign was the 1968 primary when his opponent was a youthful black lawyer named Maynard Jackson, later to be Mayor of Atlanta; Talmadge reportedly built lines into the state's black communities after that. There was nothing interesting about the 1974 campaign; the Senator was reelected without contest and with scarcely any comment. He seems to have achieved much of the prestige of his former senior colleague, Richard Russell, but not his power; for there are far fewer conservative Southern Democrats, and they are less well placed, these days, to follow his lead. Talmadge would have to continue in office till the age of 81 to equal Russell's length of service in the Senate, which seems unlikely in this day of resistance to elderly candidates; but as yet there seems no obstacle ahead of him.

Census Data Pop. 4,589,575; 2.27% of U.S. total, 15th largest; Central city, 22%; suburban, 27%. Median family income, $8,165; 37th highest; families above $15,000: 15%; families below $3,000: 15%. Median years education, 10.8.

1974 Share of Federal Tax Burden $5,275,961,000; 1.97% of U.S. total, 17th largest.

1974 Share of Federal Outlays $5,579,266,000; 2.07% of U.S. total, 15th largest. Per capita federal spending, $1216.

DOD	$1,698,645,000	14th (2.48%)	HEW	$1,809,738,000	16th (1.95%)
AEC	$1,129,000	31st (0.04%)	HUD	$38,809,000	9th (3.98%)
NASA	$5,598,000	25th (0.19%)	VA	$331,301,000	13th (2.42%)
DOT	$210,186,000	13th (2.48%)	EPA	$63,184,000	14th (2.01%)
DOC	$13,178,000	22d (0.82%)	RevS	$126,240,000	15th (2.08%)
DOI	$18,938,000	29th (0.77%)	Int.	$118,042,000	21st (0.57%)
USDA	$396,250,000	8th (3.18%)	Other	$748,028,000	

Economic Base Textile mill products, especially cotton textile mills and floor covering mills; finance, insurance and real estate; agriculture, notably broilers, peanuts, eggs and cattle; apparel and other textile mill products, especially men's and boys' furnishings; food and kindred products; transportation equipment, especially motor vehicles and equipment.

Political Line-up Governor, George D. Busbee (D). Senators, Herman E. Talmadge (D) and Sam Nunn (D). Representatives, 10 (10 D). State Senate (51 D and 5 R); State House (157 D and 23 R).

The Voters

Registration 2,090,267 Total. No party registration.
Median voting age 40.
Employment profile White collar, 44%. Blue collar, 40%. Service, 13%. Farm, 3%.
Ethnic groups Black, 26%. Total foreign stock, 2%.

Presidential vote

1972	Nixon (R)	881,490	(75%)
	McGovern (D)	289,529	(25%)
1968	Nixon (R)	380,111	(30%)
	Humphrey (D)	334,439	(27%)
	Wallace (AI)	535,550	(43%)

Sen. Herman E. Talmadge (D) Elected 1956, seat up 1980; b. Aug. 9, 1913, near McRae; home, Lovejoy; U. of Ga., 1936, Northwestern U., LL.B. 1942; Baptist.

Career Navy, WWII; Practicing atty.; Gov. of Ga., 1949–55.

Offices 109 RSOB, 202-224-3643. Also 275 Peachtree St. N.E., Atlanta 30303, 404-681-3838.

Committees

Agriculture and Forestry (Chairman).

Finance (2d). Subcommittees: Administration of the Internal Revenue Code; Energy; Health (Chairman); International Trade.

Veterans' Affairs (2d). Subcommittees: Compensation and Pension (Chairman); Housing and Insurance; Readjustment, Education and Employment.

Group Ratings

	ADA	COPE	LWV	RIPON	NFU	LCV	CFA	NAB	NSI	ACA
1974	16	50	57	45	60	20	33	50	80	81
1973	17	45	20	13	56	–	31	–	–	70
1972	10	10	30	25	60	10	27	58	80	68

Key Votes

1) No-Knock	FOR	8) Gov Abortn Aid	FOR	15) Consumer Prot Agy	AGN
2) Busing	AGN	9) Cut Mil Brass	AGN	16) Forced Psych Tests	FOR
3) No Fault	AGN	10) Gov Limousine	AGN	17) Fed Campaign Subs	AGN
4) F-111	AGN	11) RR Featherbed	FOR	18) Rhod Chrome Ban	AGN
5) Death Penalty	FOR	12) Handgun License	AGN	19) Open Legis Meetings	AGN
6) Foreign Aid	ABS	13) Less Troop Abrd	FOR	20) Strikers Food Stmps	AGN
7) Filibuster	ABS	14) Resume Turk Aid	ABS	21) Gov Info Disclosure	AGN

Election Results

1974 general:	Herman E. Tallmadge (D)	627,376	(72%)	($65,207)
	Jerry Johnson (R)	246,866	(28%)	($12,856)
1974 primary:	Herman E. Tallmadge (D)	523,133	(81%)	
	Carlton Myers (D)	119,011	(19%)	
1968 general:	Herman E. Tallmadge (D)	885,093	(78%)	
	E. Earl Patton, Jr. (R)	256,793	(22%)	

Sen. Sam Nunn (D) Elected 1972, seat up 1978; b. Sept. 8, 1938, Perry; home, Perry; Emory U., A.B. 1960, LL.B. 1962; Methodist.

Career Coast Guard, 1959–60; Legal Counsel, U.S. House of Reps. Armed Services Comm., 1962–63; Farmer; Practicing atty., 1963–72; Ga. House of Reps., 1968–72.

Offices 110 RSOB, 202-224-3521. Also Rm. 430, 275 Peachtree St. N.E., Atlanta 30303, 404-526-4811.

Committees

Armed Services (7th). Subcommittees: General Legislation; Manpower and Personnel; National Stockpile and Naval Petroleum Reserves; Tactical Air Power.

Budget (10th).

Government Operations (8th). Subcommittees: Federal Spending Practices, Efficiency and Open Government; Oversight Procedures (Chairman); Reports, Accounting and Management; Permanent Subcommittee on Investigations.

Group Ratings

	ADA	COPE	LWV	RIPON	NFU	LCV	CFA	NAB	NSI	ACA
1974	14	36	44	43	38	43	33	67	90	78
1973	30	40	30	22	63	–	46	–	–	66

Key Votes

1) No-Knock	FOR	8) Gov Abortn Aid	FOR	15) Consumer Prot Agy	AGN
2) Busing	AGN	9) Cut Mil Brass	AGN	16) Forced Psych Tests	FOR
3) No Fault	AGN	10) Gov Limousine	AGN	17) Fed Campaign Subs	AGN
4) F-111	AGN	11) RR Featherbed	FOR	18) Rhod Chrome Ban	AGN
5) Death Penalty	FOR	12) Handgun License	AGN	19) Open Legis Meetings	AGN
6) Foreign Aid	AGN	13) Less Troop Abrd	AGN	20) Strikers Food Stmps	AGN
7) Filibuster	FOR	14) Resume Turk Aid	FOR	21) Gov Info Disclosure	AGN

Election Results

1972 general:	Sam Nunn (D)	635,970	(54%)	($567,968)
	Fletcher Thompson (R)	542,331	(46%)	($444,635)
1972 run-off:	San Nunn (D)	326,186	(52%)	
	David H. Gambrell (D)	299,919	(48%)	
1972 primary:	David Gambrell (D)	225,470	(31%)	
	Sam Nunn (D)	166,035	(23%)	
	S. Ernest Vandiver (D)	147,135	(21%)	
	Twelve others (D)	178,001	(25%)	

Gov. George Busbee (D) Elected 1974, term expires Jan., 1979; b. Aug. 7, 1927, Vienna; Abraham Baldwin Ag. Col., Duke U., U. of Ga., A.B. 1949, LL.B. 1952; Baptist.

Career Navy, WWII; Practicing atty., 1952–75; Ga. House of Reps., 1957–75, Asst. Admin. Floor Ldr., 1963–65, Admin. Floor Ldr., 1966, Maj. Ldr., 1967–75.

Offices State Capitol, Atlanta 30334, 404-656-1776.

Election Results

1974 general:	George Busbee (D)	646,777	(69%)
	Ronnie Thompson (R)	289,113	(31%)
1974 run-off:	George Busbee (D)	551,106	(60%)
	Lester Maddox (D)	369,608	(40%)
1974 primary:	Lester Maddox (D)	310,384	(36%)
	George Busbee (D)	177,997	(21%)
	Bert Lance (D)	147,026	(17%)
	David Gambrell (D)	66,000	(8%)
	Eight Others (D)	153,226	(18%)

◆ ◆ ◆ ◆ ◆

FIRST DISTRICT

It's like something out of *All the King's Men*. A young Southerner helps an older man win a seat in Congress after several unsuccessful tries. The young man goes to Washington and serves loyally for a couple of years as the Congressman's aide. Then the aide takes another job, and the Congressman finds himself in trouble back home. The big city in the district, with a large number of black voters, keeps supporting his opponents. His vote in the rural areas is not as strong as it should be. Then the former assistant decides to go home and run against his old boss—and wins.

The loser in this tale is G. Elliott Hagan, Congressman from the 1st district of Georgia from 1961 to 1973. The assistant, and now Congressman, is Ronald (Bo) Ginn, who worked in Hagan's first successful campaign and in his office for five years followed by a similar stint with Senator Herman Talmadge. The large city is Savannah (pop, 118,000) with its graceful antebellum tree-shaded streets and carefully laid-out series of parks. The rural territory is the cotton, peanut, and pine land of the southeastern corner of the state of Georgia.

The scenario should come as no surprise to readers of the 1972 edition of the *Almanac,* which analyzed Hagan's vulnerability. As the 1972 edition foresaw, redistricting played some role in the 1972 race. Three new counties, including the city of Brunswick and the posh resort of Sea Island, were added to the 1st. Here Ginn, the challenger, won better than 2-1 margins over the incumbent. And Hagan never did manage to carry Savannah, though he had represented it for 12 years. In the initial primary, Hagan lost the city to Tom Taggart, a young attorney who had strong support in the black community; in the runoff, he lost it to Ginn. Black voters shifted heavily from Taggart to Ginn in the runoff, and were as responsible as any identifiable group for the result, a 55-45 Ginn victory.

This was proof, among other things, that black voters in Georgia, even outside Atlanta, can make a difference in congressional elections. Ginn's record in the House suggests that they made the sensible choice. Though Ginn is by no means a northern-style liberal, he still casts quite a few votes with his fellow Democrats from the north. For black voters—and a fair number of whites, too—this is a decided improvement over the uniformly conservative voting record of Hagan.

Census Data Pop. 456,354. Central city, 26%; suburban, 15%. Median family income, $7,102; families above $15,000: 11%; families below $3,000: 19%. Median years education, 10.6.

The Voters

Median voting age 41.
Employment profile White collar, 39%. Blue collar, 40%. Service, 15%. Farm, 6%.
Ethnic groups Black, 34%. Total foreign stock, 3%.

Presidential vote

	1972	Nixon (R)	90,218	(75%)
		McGovern (D)	29,768	(25%)
	1968	Nixon (R)	35,520	(27%)
		Humphrey (D)	38,301	(29%)
		Wallace (AI)	58,480	(44%)

Rep. Bo Ginn (D) Elected 1972; b. May 31, 1934, Morgan; home, Millen; Abraham Baldwin Ag. Col., 1951–53, Ga. Southern Col., B.S. 1956; Baptist.

Career High school teacher; Asst. Mgr., Planters Electric Membership Corp., 1957–61; Admin. Asst. to U. S. Sen. Herman E. Talmadge, 1961–71; Cattle farmer and businessman, 1971–72.

Offices 508 CHOB, 202-225-5831. Also Rm. 304, Fed. Bldg., Brunswick 31520, 912-264-4040.

Committees

Merchant Marine and Fisheries (16th). Subcommittees: Fisheries and Wildlife Conservation and the Environment; Merchant Marine; Oceanography.

Public Works and Transportation (11th). Subcommittees: Aviation; Public Buildings and Grounds; Surface Transportation; Water Resources.

Group Ratings

	ADA	COPE	LWV	RIPON	NFU	LCV	CFA	NAB	NSI	ACA
1974	26	45	27	7	57	44	50	33	60	67
1973	40	64	50	33	95	21	50	–	–	56

Key Votes

1) Foreign Aid	AGN	6) Gov Abortn Aid	AGN	11) Pub Cong Election $	AGN
2) Busing	AGN	7) Coed Phys Ed	FOR	12) Turkish Arms Cutoff	FOR
3) ABM	AGN	8) Pov Lawyer Gag	FOR	13) Youth Camp Regs	AGN
4) B-1 Bomber	FOR	9) Pub Trans Sub	FOR	14) Strip Mine Veto	FOR
5) Nerve Gas	AGN	10) EZ Voter Regis	AGN	15) Farm Bill Veto	AGN

Election Results

1974 general:	Bo Ginn (D)	64,958	(86%)	($27,777)
	William L. (Bill) Gowan (R)	10,485	(14%)	($1,627)
1974 primary:	Bo Ginn (D), unopposed			
1972 general:	Bo Ginn (D), unopposed			($76,835)

◆ ◆ ◆ ◆ ◆

SECOND DISTRICT

The 2d congressional district is the southwest corner of Georgia. It is the most agricultural, the poorest and with the exception of Atlanta's 5th, the blackest congressional district in the state. The 2d is part of the still unreconstructed, economically underdeveloped Old South. The only areas of the district that experienced population growth in the sixties were those around its military installation; the rest of the district was slowly dying. Blacks still count for far less here than their numbers warrant—they don't vote much, apparently because of local pressures. This was one of George Wallace's banner congressional districts in 1968 and, despite Richard Nixon's strength here in 1972, it will undoubtedly be Wallace's once more should he run in either the primary or general election.

The young Congressman from the 2d, Democrat Dawson Mathis, is worthy of some note if only because of his previous occupation: he was a TV newscaster. There are dozens of former TV newsmen (even one TV weatherman, Dale Milford of Texas) in Congress today. Some of them, of course, took to the tube as a kind of moonlighting that would confer some political advantage. Others, like Mathis, earned their livelihood on the local airwaves. After six years as the nightly newsman on an Albany, Georgia, station that reaches most of the 2d district, Mathis, then still under 30, was probably better known than any of the district's politicians. This is the best explanation of how he won the 1970 Democratic primary and the general election when the 2d's aging incumbent retired.

Mathis embodies the traditional Southern Democrat's view of politics. When asked about his goals in Congress, he replied, "To represent the 2d district as long as I can." As a member of the Agriculture Committee, he has already jumped up to the number eight position among Democrats and a subcommittee chairmanship (Oilseeds and Rice)—a remarkable rise made possible by a spate of retirements, defeats, and deaths. But the very changes which have catapulted Mathis faster than he might have anticipated may also limit the heights to which he can reasonably aspire. With the House Democratic caucus in 1975 ousting a number of chairmen whose views were out of line with the liberal majority's, southerners like Mathias can no longer count on seniority to advance them to positions of great power. Mathis shows few signs of accommodating himself to this Democratic majority, but at the same time he seems assured of easy reelection as long as he runs; he may, then, be entered on a collision course, with the outcome uncertain.

Census Data Pop. 460,450. Central city, 16%; suburban, 4%. Median family income, $6,238; families above $15,000: 9%; families below $3,000: 23%. Median years education, 9.9.

The Voters

Median voting age 42.
Employment profile White collar, 36%. Blue collar, 38%. Service, 14%. Farm, 12%.
Ethnic groups Black, 37%. Total foreign stock, 1%.

Presidential vote

1972	Nixon (R)	80,769	(80%)
	McGovern (D)	20,745	(20%)
1968	Nixon (R)	23,508	(19%)
	Humphrey (D)	26,693	(21%)
	Wallace (AI)	74,740	(60%)

Rep. Dawson Mathis (D) Elected 1970; b. Nov. 30, 1940, Nashville; home, Albany; So. Ga. Col.; Baptist.

Career Radio stations WGNA, Nashville, and WCEH, Hawkinsville, 1959–64; News Dir., WALB-TV, Albany, 1964–70.

Offices 236 CHOB, 202-225-3631, Also City-County Govt. Bldg., 225 Pine Ave., Rm. 202, Albany 31705, 912-438-8607.

Committees

Agriculture (8th). Subcommittees: Forests; Oilseeds and Rice (Chairman); Tobacco.

House Administration (11th). Subcommittees: Elections; Personnel and Police; Printing; Ad Hoc Restaurant (Chairman).

Group Ratings

	ADA	COPE	LWV	RIPON	NFU	LCV	CFA	NAB	NSI	ACA
1974	9	10	18	0	54	33	17	70	100	86
1973	10	10	40	17	71	11	0	–	–	80
1972	0	27	25	25	71	12	50	46	100	91

Key Votes

1) Foreign Aid	AGN	6) Gov Abortn Aid	AGN	11) Pub Cong Election $	AGN
2) Busing	AGN	7) Coed Phys Ed	AGN	12) Turkish Arms Cutoff	AGN
3) ABM	AGN	8) Pov Lawyer Gag	ABS	13) Youth Camp Regs	AGN
4) B-1 Bomber	FOR	9) Pub Trans Sub	FOR	14) Strip Mine Veto	FOR
5) Nerve Gas	FOR	10) EZ Voter Regis	AGN	15) Farm Bill Veto	AGN

Election Results

1974 general:	Dawson Mathis (D), unopposed	($16,201)
1974 primary:	Dawson Mathis (D), unopposed	
1972 general:	Dawson Mathis (D), unopposed	($2,042)

◆ ◆ ◆ ◆ ◆

THIRD DISTRICT

The 3d district of Georgia is one of the state's several south Georgia districts. It has one good-sized city, Columbus (pop. 154,000), which in turn is dominated by one good-sized military installation, Fort Benning (pop. 27,000). Columbus is very much an Army town. Girls grow up here aspiring to marry young officers, and a local hero, Lieutenant William Calley was confined at Benning till released by court order in 1975. Fort Benning has a prouder history: it was here in the 1930s that Colonel George C. Marshall staged the manuevers that anticipated so much of the kind of fighting that occurred in World War II—showing a knack the Army has since lost of being ready to fight the next, rather than the last, war.

Benning is only one major military installation here; another is the Warner Robins Air Materiel Command in the eastern end of the 3d. Both, naturally, are of substantial economic importance to this otherwise rather depressed district. Benning may have been sited here first on the theory that the excruciatingly hot, humid Georgia climate would best condition soldiers for the rigors of combat. But students of relationships between the Pentagon and the congressional Armed Services Committees can think of other reasons.

For Georgia was represented by Senator Richard Russell, Chairman of the Senate Armed Services Committee for many years, and the 3d is just adjacent to the district represented by Carl Vinson, longtime Chairman of the House Armed Services Committee, for more than 50 years. The 3d also has the distinction, unique among non-Atlanta area Georgia districts, of having been represented by a Republican in recent years; he was Howard (Bo) Callaway, scion of a local textile family, elected in 1964 and defeated for Governor in 1966, Secratary of the Army under Nixon, and now head of Jerry Ford's reelection effort.

The current Congressman from the 3d, Democrat Jack Brinkley, was first elected in 1966. He is, not surprisingly, a member of the House Armed Services Committee, and very much on the side of its hawkish bipartisan majority. Brinkley is either exceedingly popular or else very lucky: from 1966 to 1974 he has had no primary or general election opposition since his first election a decade ago and in 1974 he won 88% of the vote against a Republican.

Census Data Pop. 460,749. Central city, 33%; suburban, 22%. Median family income, $7,550; families above $15,000: 12%; families below $3,000: 16%. Median years education, 10.9.

The Voters

Median voting age 38.
Employment profile White collar, 41%. Blue collar, 40%. Service, 15%. Farm, 4%.
Ethnic groups Black, 32%. Spanish, 1%. Total foreign stock, 4%.

Presidential vote

1972	Nixon (R)	81,300	(78%)
	McGovern (D)	23,534	(22%)
1968	Nixon (R)	27,837	(26%)
	Humphrey (D)	25,948	(24%)
	Wallace (AI)	52,278	(49%)

Rep. Jack Brinkley (D) Elected 1966; b. Dec. 22, 1930, Faceville; home, Columbus; Young Harris Col., B. A. 1949, U. of Ga., J.D. 1959; Baptist.

Career Public school teacher, 1949–51; Air Force, 1951–56; Practicing atty., 1959–67; Ga. House of Reps., 1965–66.

Offices 2412 RHOB, 202-225-5901. Also P.O. Box 349, Columbus 31902, 404-324-3091.

Committees

Armed Services (13th). Subcommittees: Military Compensation; Military Installations and Facilities.

Veterans' Affairs (9th). Subcommittees: Cemeteries and Burial Benefits; Compensation, Pension and Insurance; Hospitals; Housing, (Chairman).

Group Ratings

	ADA	COPE	LWV	RIPON	NFU	LCV	CFA	NAB	NSI	ACA
1974	9	36	33	14	43	31	23	64	90	87
1973	24	27	50	40	89	47	38	–	–	67
1972	19	18	33	31	43	20	0	42	100	77

Key Votes

1) Foreign Aid	AGN	6) Gov Abortn Aid	AGN	11) Pub Cong Election $	AGN
2) Busing	AGN	7) Coed Phys Ed	AGN	12) Turkish Arms Cutoff	FOR
3) ABM	AGN	8) Pov Lawyer Gag	FOR	13) Youth Camp Regs	FOR
4) B-1 Bomber	FOR	9) Pub Trans Sub	AGN	14) Strip Mine Veto	AGN
5) Nerve Gas	AGN	10) EZ Voter Regis	AGN	15) Farm Bill Veto	AGN

Election Results

1974 general:	Jack Brinkley (D)	67,438	(88%)	($26,824)
	Carl P. Savage, Jr. (R)	9,453	(12%)	($12,520)
1974 primary:	Jack Brinkley (D), unopposed			
1972 general:	Jack Brinkley (D), unopposed			($1,030)

◆　◆　◆　◆　◆

FOURTH DISTRICT

Stuck smack in the middle of the Old South is the booming metropolis of Atlanta—"the city," it liked to boast, "too busy to hate." The slogan grew out of Atlanta's reputation for racial tolerance and moderation, which it earned back in the 1950s and 1960s. But if Atlanta has practiced little overt segregation and possesses the sophistication of some northern cities, it has also developed some of their problems. Foremost among them, perhaps, is the white exodus from the central city, as metropolitan Atlanta has grown apace—up 91% between 1950 and 1970—whites have moved increasingly to the suburbs, while blacks have moved outward within Atlanta itself. The result: by 1970, the city of Atlanta was a majority black—the first such major city in the South—while the suburbs formed an almost all-white noose around its perimeter. Children growing up in metropolitan Atlanta, whether black or white, may well have less contact with members of the other race than they would have 20 years ago—or than they do in the now-integrated schools in the small towns and counties of south Georgia.

Just about half the residents of suburban Atlanta live in DeKalb County, just to the east of the city; together with a small part of the city and small, just-suburbanizing Rockdale County, DeKalb makes up the 4th congressional district of Georgia. This area is the home of the higher-income, better-educated Atlanta suburbanites; statistically, it is far closer to many such northern areas than to south Georgia. Politically, DeKalb and the 4th behave more like a northern constituency than like the non-Atlanta Georgia districts. When the district was first created in 1964, the result of a landmark Supreme Court case, it went for Lyndon Johnson and elected a liberal Democratic Congressman, while the rest of Georgia switched from its traditional

Democratic allegiance to the Republicanism of Barry Goldwater. In 1966, like many northern districts, the 4th elected a Republican Congressman and in the state elections gave a large majority to textile heir Bo Callaway over former chicken restauranteur Lester Maddox. In the years that followed, DeKalb generally preferred the Republicans smooth, neutral-accented candidates to the rural-oriented, Southern-accented candidates nominated by the Democrats. This is the only part of Georgia which has consistently elected a significant number of Republican state legislators.

But suddenly, in 1974, the 4th shifted—again in the same direction as the north. In the past three elections, Congressman Ben Blackburn, a quiet but staunch conservative, had been reelected with very little difficulty; he had 76% of the vote in 1972. But in 1974 he had strong opposition from another Atlanta attorney, Democrat Elliott Levitas. Blackburn had supported Richard Nixon to the very end; Levitas, a member of the Georgia legislature, was counted as a liberal. When the votes were in, Levitas had won in one of the biggest upsets in the South that year. Levitas will be working hard for reelection, but he can count on tough Republican opposition; the 4th may prove, once again, to be a good, if geographically unlikely, national barometer in 1976.

Census Data Pop. 459,335. Central city, 16%; suburban, 80%. Median family income, $11,750; families above $15,000: 31%; families below $3,000: 5%. Median years education, 12.4.

The Voters

Median voting age 38.
Employment profile White collar, 66%. Blue collar, 25%. Service, 9%. Farm, –%.
Ethnic groups Black, 15%. Spanish, 1%. Total foreign stock, 5%.

Presidential vote

1972	Nixon (R)	110,574	(77%)
	McGovern (D)	33,043	(23%)
1968	Nixon (R)	54,869	(48%)
	Humphrey (D)	31,233	(27%)
	Wallace (AI)	28,216	(25%)

Rep. Elliott H. Levitas (D) Elected 1974; b. Dec. 26, 1930, Atlant; home, Atlanta; Emory U., B.S., LL.B., Rhodes Scholar, Oxford U., M.A., U. of Mich.; Jewish.

Career Practicing atty., 1955–75; Air Force; Ga. House of Reps., 1965–75.

Offices 506 CHOB, 202-225-4272. Also 141 E. Trinity Pl., Decatur 30030, 404-377-1717.

Committees

Government Operations (25th). Subcommittees: Commerce, Consumer and Monetary Affairs; Intergovernmental Relations and Human Resources.

Public Works and Transportation (20th). Subcommittees: Aviation; Investigations and Review; Public Buildings and Grounds; Surface Transportation.

Group Ratings: Newly Elected

Key Votes

1) Foreign Aid	AGN	6) Gov Abortn Aid	NE	11) Pub Cong Election $	NE
2) Busing	NE	7) Coed Phys Ed	FOR	12) Turkish Arms Cutoff	NE
3) ABM	NE	8) Pov Lawyer Gag	NE	13) Youth Camp Regs	FOR
4) B-1 Bomber	FOR	9) Pub Trans Sub	NE	14) Strip Mine Veto	AGN
5) Nerve Gas	NE	10) EZ Voter Regis	NE	15) Farm Bill Veto	FOR

Election Results

1974 general:	Elliott H. Levitas (D)	61,211	(55%)	($121,724)
	Ben B. Blackburn (R)	49,922	(45%)	($160,151)
1974 primary:	Elliott H. Levitas (D)	36,137	(63%)	
	Bruce B. Gruber (D)	14,946	(26%)	
	Nick M. Belluso (D)	6,439	(11%)	

◆ ◆ ◆ ◆ ◆

FIFTH DISTRICT

In 1972 the 5th district of Georgia became the first Deep South congressional district since 1898 to elect a black man to Congress. Needless to say, the 5th is not a typical Deep South district: the bulk of it consists of the city of Atlanta, now a majority black, and a few sparsely-populated, affluent suburbs like Sandy Springs to the north. This territory has a long tradition of liberal politics. Atlanta has had moderate-to-liberal Mayors since the 1940s, and elected Maynard Jackson, a black, Vice-Mayor in 1969 and Mayor in 1973. The present 5th district was 44% black in 1970, and many of its whites were used to voting for blacks. Despite all these favorable circumstances, the election of Andrew Young, a minister and former executive director of Martin Luther King's Southern Christian Leadership Conference, was a formidable political achievement.

Only two years earlier, Young had been defeated soundly—57-43—by Republican Fletcher Thompson. That victory was due strictly to white votes. Thompson admitted that he had not met with a single black group for four years, and his campaign featured film clips which, Thompson claimed, showed that Young's election would produce the collapse of western civilization. Such hard-core tactics were particularly successful in the southern Fulton County suburbs, full of middle-income whites uneasy about the proximity of the black ghetto in next-door Atlanta.

But in 1972 a court-ordered redistricting plan removed south Fulton from the district, and Thompson decided to run for the Senate—unsuccessfully, as it turned out, though the race was close enough that he could have won with only a small share of blacks' votes. This time Young's Republican opponent was a relative moderate who ran a strong antibusing campaign, but avoided the shrillness of Thompson's approach. Young, with his black support solid, spent much time in the white community, opposing construction of a freeway there and also promising a clean-up of the Chattahoochee River. On election day, Young won 53% of the vote, including almost one-quarter of the white ballots.

In Washington and back home, Young is somewhat less strident than many black members of Congress; he is the only one, for example, who voted for the confirmation of Gerald Ford as Vice President. At the same time, he has been seen as a reasonable, dealable-with public official by the Atlanta establishment. In the House, Young won a seat on the Rules Committee in 1975, the first ever held by a black. He is sure to be a power in the years ahead.

Census Data   Pop. 460,589. Central city, 87%; suburban, 13%. Median family income, $9,050; families above $15,000: 24%; families below $3,000: 3%. Median years education, 12.1.

The Voters

Median voting age 40.
Employment profile White collar, 55%. Blue collar, 28%. Service, 17%. Farm, –%.
Ethnic groups Black, 44%. Spanish, 1%. Total foreign stock, 4%.

Presidential vote

1972	Nixon (R)	69,088	(52%)
	McGovern (D)	63,405	(48%)
1968	Nixon (R)	48,876	(35%)
	Humphrey (D)	66,131	(48%)
	Wallace (AI)	22,995	(17%)

Rep. Andrew Young (D) Elected 1972; b. Mar. 12, 1932, New Orleans, La.; home, Atlanta; Dillard U., Howard U., B.S. 1951, Hartford Theol. Sem., B.D. 1955; Congregationalist.

Career Pastor; Assoc. Dir., Dept. of Youth Work, Natl. Cncl. of Churches, 1957–61; So. Christ. Leadership Conf., Exec. Dir., 1964–67, Exec. V.P., 1967–70; Chm., Atlanta Community Relations Comm., 1970–72.

Offices 332 CHOB, 202-225-3801. Also 327 Old P.O. Bldg., Atlanta 30303, 404-688-8207.

Committees

Rules (11th).

Group Ratings

	ADA	COPE	LWV	RIPON	NFU	LCV	CFA	NAB	NSI	ACA
1974	95	89	100	67	91	93	100	17	10	0
1973	96	100	91	60	100	100	100	–	–	4

Key Votes

1) Foreign Aid	FOR	6) Gov Abortn Aid	FOR	11) Pub Cong Election $	FOR
2) Busing	FOR	7) Coed Phys Ed	FOR	12) Turkish Arms Cutoff	FOR
3) ABM	AGN	8) Pov Lawyer Gag	AGN	13) Youth Camp Regs	ABS
4) B-1 Bomber	AGN	9) Pub Trans Sub	ABS	14) Strip Mine Veto	AGN
5) Nerve Gas	AGN	10) EZ Voter Regis	FOR	15) Farm Bill Veto	AGN

Election Results

1974 general:	Andrew Young (D)	69,221	(72%)	($83,481)
	Wyman C. Lowe (R)	27,397	(28%)	($7,713)
1974 primary:	Andrew Young (D), unopposed			
1972 general:	Andrew Young (D)	72,289	(53%)	($159,431)
	Rodney M. Cook (R)	64,495	(47%)	($149,616)

◆ ◆ ◆ ◆ ◆

SIXTH DISTRICT

The 6th congressional district of Georgia presents a nice example of demographic change in the South. Ten years ago, the dominant city in the district was Macon (pop. 122,000); the Atlanta metropolitan area at the northern edge of the 6th had only 10% of the district's population. But in 1972 redistricting removed Macon and added several south Fulton County suburbs of Atlanta. Today, 48% of the 6th's population lives in metropolitan Atlanta. These suburbs—notably East Point, College Park, and Forest Park just to the south of the city—do not behave politically in the manner of the almost Yankee suburbs of the 4th district. South Fulton and Clayton Counties have generally given Republican candidates majorities, but they have also responded positively to the old-style Southern campaigns of George Wallace and Lester Maddox.

That should have been good news for Congressman John J. Flynt, Jr., a Democrat who in 1972 had held office with little opposition for nearly 20 years. A high-ranking member of the Appropriations Committee, Flynt is one of those powerful, usually silent Southern Democratic congressmen who for years have had influence beyond their numbers. A fiscal conservative, Flynt usually comes out on the side of trimming the federal budget; and although he came out against the Vietnam war in 1971, he has generally gone along with the Pentagon, or favored mild cuts, on military spending bills before the Defense Appropriations Subcommittee.

Flynt suddenly found himself in political trouble in 1974—but not for any of the things mentioned above. Instead, his problem was that he had rented out his farm to the Ford Motor Company for $12,500 a year, while back in Congress he supported the easing of auto emissions requirements. Flynt was unopposed in the primary, but in the general election he faced spirited opposition—centered on this issue—from 31-year-old Republican college professor Newt Gingrich. With support from environmental groups. Gingrich cut heavily into Flynt's usual margins and actually beat him in the Atlanta suburbs; only the rural vote in this Democratic year saved the incumbent. Interestingly, when he returned to Washington, Flynt was chosen Chairman of the Committee on Standards of Official Conduct.

Census Data Pop. 455,810. Central city, 5%; suburban, 43%. Median family income, $9,284; families above $15,000: 16%; families below $3,000: 10%. Median years education, 10.9.

The Voters

Median voting age 39.
Employment profile White collar, 44%. Blue collar, 44%. Service, 11%. Farm, 1%.
Ethnic groups Black, 19%. Total foreign stock, 2%.

Presidential vote

1972	Nixon (R)	96,213	(80%)
	McGovern (D)	24,717	(20%)
1968	Nixon (R)	38,996	(31%)
	Humphrey (D)	27,733	(22%)
	Wallace (AI)	58,042	(47%)

Rep. John J. Flynt, Jr. (D) Elected 1954; b. Nov. 8, 1914, Griffin; home, Griffin; U. of Ga., B.A. 1936, Emory U. Law School, 1937–38, Geo. Wash. U., LL.B. 1940; Methodist.

Career Asst. U.S. Atty., No. Dist. of Ga., 1940–41, 1945–46; Army, WWII; Ga. House of Reps., 1947–48; Solic. Gen., Griffin Judicial Circuit, 1949–54.

Offices 2110 RHOB, 202-225-4501. Also P.O. Box 103, Griffin 30223, 404-227-1621.

Committees

Standards of Official Conduct (Chairman).

Appropriations (12th). Subcommittees: Defense; State, Justice, Commerce and the Judiciary; Treasury, Postal Service, and General Government.

Group Ratings

	ADA	COPE	LWV	RIPON	NFU	LCV	CFA	NAB	NSI	ACA
1974	26	11	0	14	50	13	27	82	40	77
1973	9	0	36	8	61	6	29	–	–	88
1972	6	10	0	13	33	17	0	86	86	100

Key Votes

1) Foreign Aid	AGN	6) Gov Abortn Aid	AGN	11) Pub Cong Election $	AGN
2) Busing	AGN	7) Coed Phys Ed	AGN	12) Turkish Arms Cutoff	FOR
3) ABM	AGN	8) Pov Lawyer Gag	FOR	13) Youth Camp Regs	AGN
4) B-1 Bomber	FOR	9) Pub Trans Sub	AGN	14) Strip Mine Veto	FOR
5) Nerve Gas	AGN	10) EZ Voter Regis	FOR	15) Farm Bill Veto	AGN

Election Results

1974 general:	John J. Flynt, Jr. (D)	49,082	(51%)	($33,035)
	Newt Gingrich (R)	46,308	(49%)	($85,505)

1974 primary: John J. Flynt, Jr. (D), unopposed
1972 general: John J. Flynt, Jr. (D), unopposed ....   ($2,612)

◆ ◆ ◆ ◆ ◆

SEVENTH DISTRICT

The 7th congressional district of Georgia covers the northwest corner of the state. On the southeast, the district touches the Atlanta city limits; on the northwest, it reaches the bounds of Chattanooga, Tennessee. (There is some dispute here about the state line—some Georgians insist that the Lookout Mountain home of Tennessee Senator Bill Brock is actually in Georgia.) Most of the 7th's recent population growth has been around Marietta, in Cobb County near Atlanta, and in the Georgia suburbs of Chattanooga. Because there are few blacks in this part of north Georgia—no more than 5% of the electorate—racial issues have never played as big a role in politics here as in south Georgia. Nonetheless, George Wallace and Lester Maddox have had little trouble carrying the area. For many years, the economic mainstay of the district was textiles, but today its largest employer, and most significant politically, is the ailing Lockheed Corporation. Lockheed's huge plant at Marietta, in Cobb County some 30 miles from downtown Atlanta, is where the C-5As were built and the huge cost overruns incurred.

To understand just how important Lockheed is here, consider what happened to Henry Durham. Mr. Durham worked at Lockheed and knew something funny was going on, and so testified before Senator Proxmire's subcommittee which was looking into the overruns. After that Durham lost his job and found that no one in Marietta would speak to him or his family; finally, he had to leave town. In California a congressman like Pete McCloskey could vote against the Lockheed loan and still win reelection in a district with many Lockheed employees. Not so in Georgia; to oppose something a big corporate employer wanted would mean sure political death.

But that was not the reason for the defeat in 1974 of Congressman John W. Davis, who for 14 years represented the 7th district. As a senior member of the Science Committee, Davis had supported Lockheed and just about every other big defense contractor. Rather, his problem seems to have been alcohol; he told voters a few years ago that he had it licked, but apparently they didn't believe him—or didn't care. In any case, after only narrow victories in the 1972 primary and general elections, Davis was beaten in 1974. The winner, in the Democratic primary, was urologist Larry McDonald. As part of the huge 75-member class of Democratic freshmen, McDonald must feel a little out of place. Most of them are solid liberals; he is a member of the national council of the John Birch Society. Interestingly, McDonald was one of four freshmen to win a seat on the Armed Services Committee, and he and Jim Lloyd of California seem definitely attuned to the hawkish views of the committee's senior members. With the new freshman class, liberals had an excellent chance to increase their strength on this committee, but apparently were not able to take full advantage of the circumstances.

Census Data Pop. 460,095. Central city, 0%; suburban, 54%. Median family income, $9,223; families above $15,000: 16%; families below $3,000: 10%. Median years education, 10.6.

The Voters

Median voting age 40.
Employment profile White collar, 43%. Blue collar, 47%. Service, 9%. Farm, 1%.
Ethnic groups Black, 7%. Total foreign stock, 2%.

Presidential vote

1972	Nixon (R)	91,477	(83%)
	McGovern (D)	18,726	(17%)
1968	Nixon (R)	38,976	(33%)
	Humphrey (D)	23,143	(19%)
	Wallace (AI)	57,155	(48%)

Rep. Larry McDonald (D) Elected 1974; b. Apr. 1, 1935, Atlanta; home, Marietta; Davidson Dol., Emory U., M.D. 1957; Methodist.

Career U.S. Navy Physician and Overseas Flight Surgeon; Residency, Grady Mem. Hosp., Atlanta, and U. of Mich. Hosp., Ann Arbor, Mich.; Jr. Mbr., McDonald Urology Clinic , Atlanta.

Offices 1641 LHOB, 202-225-2931. Also 191 Lawrence St., Marietta 30060, 404-422-4480.

Committees

Armed Services (26th). Subcommittees: Research and Development; Seapower and Strategic and Critical Materials.

Group Ratings: Newly Elected

Key Votes

1) Foreign Aid	AGN	6) Gov Abortn Aid	NE	11) Pub Cong Election $	NE
2) Busing	NE	7) Coed Phys Ed	AGN	12) Turkish Arms Cutoff	NE
3) ABM	NE	8) Pov Lawyer Gag	NE	13) Youth Camp Regs	AGN
4) B-1 Bomber	FOR	9) Pub Trans Sub	NE	14) Strip Mine Veto	FOR
5) Nerve Gas	NE	10) EZ Voter Regis	NE	15) Farm Bill Veto	FOR

Election Results

1974 general:	Larry McDonald (D)	47,993	(50%)	($188,093)
	Quincy Collins (R)	47,450	(50%)	($66,827)
1974 primary:	Larry McDonald (D)	43,675	(52%)	
	John W. Davis (D)	41,052	(48%)	

◆ ◆ ◆ ◆ ◆

EIGHTH DISTRICT

The 8th congressional district is an elongated section of central and south Georgia. With the major exception of Macon (pop. 122,000), this is mostly a rural area that was once devoted to cotton, but now is mainly in peanuts, tobacco, and chickens. The once-fertile soil here has long since been worn down and for many years this was a part of the Deep South which people, both black and white, have been leaving. More than 30% of the district's residents are black, but black voters here seldom influence the outcome of elections. Black turnout is substantially lower here than in Atlanta, and in these rural counties there are few black political organizers.

With few blacks voting, the 8th district has delivered overwhelming majorities to candidates like Barry Goldwater, George Wallace, and Richard Nixon. In congressional elections, its political behavior has become just about as predictable. In 1966, a young businessman named Bill Stuckey beat the incumbent Congressman in the Democratic primary, and he has held on to the seat ever since. He was supposed to have been in trouble in 1972, when Macon was added to the district, but he easily won both the primary and the general (the latter against Macon Mayor "Machine Gun Ronnie" Thompson).

Stuckey is a member of the family that started the pecan candy and gift shops which can be seen at just about every Interstate highway interchange. He is also a member of the House Commerce Committee, which oversees most of the federal regulatory agencies. For many years, that committee has shown very little interest in stringent regulation and pro-consumer legislation; one of the reasons was the vote of Stuckey and other like-minded Democrats, who combined with the committee's Republicans to defeat such measures. But with the departure or retirement of seven Democrats in 1974, and the addition of a full dozen new freshman Democrats in 1975, the balance on the committee has tipped entirely. Now it is the members like Stuckey who will be on the defensive, at least until 1976.

Census Data Pop. 458,097. Central city, 27%; suburban, 5%. Median family income, $6,836; families above $15,000: 11%; families below $3,000: 20%. Median years education, 9.8.

The Voters

Median voting age 43.
Employment profile White collar, 37%. Blue collar, 42%. Service, 15%. Farm, 6%.
Ethnic groups Black, 31%.

Presidential vote

1972	Nixon (R)	91,338	(78%)
	McGovern (D)	26,033	(22%)
1968	Nixon (R)	33,603	(24%)
	Humphrey (D)	32,588	(23%)
	Wallace (AI)	75,777	(53%)

Rep. W. S. (Bill) **Stuckey, Jr.** (D) Elected 1966; b. May 25, Dodge County; home. Eastman; U. of Ga., B.B.A. 1956, LL.B. 1959; Episcopalian.

Career Exec. Vp., Stuckey's Inc., div. of Pet Milk Co.

Offices 2243 RHOB, 202-225-6531. Also Rm. 331 Fed. Bldg., College St., Macon 31201, 912-742-2161 ext. 2426.

Committees

District of Columbia (3d). Subcommittees: Commerce, Housing and Transportation (Chairman); Fiscal Affairs.

Interstate and Foreign Commerce (11th). Subcommittees: Consumer Protection and Finance; Oversight and Investigations.

Group Ratings

	ADA	COPE	LWV	RIPON	NFU	LCV	CFA	NAB	NSI	ACA
1974	26	60	33	36	62	33	67	50	56	54
1973	29	55	50	23	85	22	50	–	–	62
1972	0	30	25	38	67	5	0	44	88	90

Key Votes

1) Foreign Aid	AGN	6) Gov Abortn Aid	AGN	11) Pub Cong Election $	AGN
2) Busing	AGN	7) Coed Phys Ed	AGN	12) Turkish Arms Cutoff	FOR
3) ABM	AGN	8) Pov Lawyer Gag	FOR	13) Youth Camp Regs	AGN
4) B-1 Bomber	FOR	9) Pub Trans Sub	ABS	14) Strip Mine Veto	AGN
5) Nerve Gas	ABS	10) EZ Voter Regis	AGN	15) Farm Bill Veto	AGN

Election Results

1974 general:	W. S. (Bill) Stuckey, Jr. (D), unopposed .			($34,674)
1974 primary:	W. S. (Bill) Stuckey, Jr. (D)	52,814	(65%)	
	Harry Powell (D)	28,369	(35%)	
1972 general:	W. S. (Bill) Stuckey, Jr. (D)	71,283	(62%)	($103,254)
	Ronnie Thompson (R)	42,986	(38%)	($17,448)

◆ ◆ ◆ ◆ ◆

NINTH DISTRICT

The northeastern corner of Georgia is hundreds of miles from the cotton, peanut, and tobacco farmlands of Confederate south Georgia. Into this remote part of the state cuts the southernmost ridges of the Appalachians, and the culture here is more of the mountains than the Deep South. In some mountain counties a Republican tradition lives on from the days of the Civil War when this area opposed slavery and secession. And other mountain traditions survive: the red clay hills here are reputed to contain more moonshine stills than any other part of the United States.

This bit of Appalachia forms about half of the 9th congressional district of Georgia. The remainder includes, on the west, a few suburbs of Chattanooga, Tennessee, and to the south, some of the upland Piedmont counties adjoining Interstate 85. This highway might well be called the Textile Route; within a few miles of its interchanges, between Atlanta and Durham, North Carolina, lies perhaps half the textile manufacturing capacity in the United States. Moreover, metropolitan Atlanta is making its way inexorably north out Interstate 85 into the 9th's Gwinnett County, one of the fastest-growing in Georgia. The people moving out are not so much the urban sophisticates Atlanta likes to boast of as they are people who find in the hilly views from the new subdivisions or apartment complexes of Lilburn or Norcress a suggestion of the rural land they know so well.

Overall, the Dixie Democrats of the Piedmont and the foothills far outnumber the mountain Republicans in the 9th; Democrats lose this district only in national contests. In congressional elections they never have, and since 1952 the Congressman from the 9th has been Democrat Phil Landrum. Back in 1959 Landrum co-sponsored the House version of the Labor-Management Reporting and Disclosure Act, which generally prevailed over the Senate version; it is known now as the Landrum-Griffin Act, and is the only piece of labor legislation passed since the Taft-Hartley Act of 1947. For Landrum and Griffin, who is now a Senator from Michigan, this law represented something of a feat of legerdemain: their version was vehemently opposed by labor unions, and yet it passed through the heavily Democratic Congress elected in 1958. Since that time, Landrum has moved from Education and Labor to the Ways and Means Committee, on which he is probably the premier supporter of import restrictions on textiles. Landrum surprised some people when he switched from hawk to dove on Vietnam in 1971, but overall he maintains a strong conservative voting record. Now nearing 70, he seems unlikely to repeat his legislative feats of 1959 in the heavily Democratic Congress now sitting.

Census Data Pop. 457,247. Central city, 0%; suburban, 16%. Median family income, $7,657; families above $15,000: 10%; families below $3,000: 14%. Median years education, 9.6.

The Voters

Median voting age 41.
Employment profile White collar, 34%. Blue collar, 53%. Service, 9%. Farm, 4%.
Ethnic groups Black, 6%.

Presidential vote

1972	Nixon (R)	89,299	(82%)
	McGovern (D)	19,544	(18%)
1968	Nixon (R)	40,908	(32%)
	Humphrey (D)	25,000	(20%)
	Wallace (AI)	60,612	(48%)

Rep. Phil M. Landrum (D) Elected 1952; b. Sept. 10, 1909, Martin; home, Jasper; Mercer U., 1926–27, La. St. U., 1932, Piedmont Col., B.A. 1939, Atlanta Law School, LL.B. 1941; Baptist.

Career Supt. of Public Schools, Nelson, 1937–41; Army Air Corps, WWII; Asst. Atty. Gen. of Ga., 1946; Exec. Secy. to Gov. M.E. Thompson, 1947–48; Practicing atty., 1949–52.

Offices 2308 RHOB, 202-225-5211. Also P.O. Box 400, Jasper 30143, 404-692-2022.

Committees

Budget (11th).

Ways and Means (5th). Subcommittees: Public Assistance; Trade.

Group Ratings

	ADA	COPE	LWV	RIPON	NFU	LCV	CFA	NAB	NSI	ACA
1974	14	22	18	13	50	42	33	71	60	75
1973	19	20	30	20	72	14	43	–	–	73
1972	0	0	27	50	50	0	0	75	83	83

Key Votes

1) Foreign Aid	AGN	6) Gov Abortn Aid	AGN	11) Pub Cong Election $	AGN
2) Busing	AGN	7) Coed Phys Ed	ABS	12) Turkish Arms Cutoff	ABS
3) ABM	AGN	8) Pov Lawyer Gag	ABS	13) Youth Camp Regs	AGN
4) B-1 Bomber	FOR	9) Pub Trans Sub	ABS	14) Strip Mine Veto	FOR
5) Nerve Gas	ABS	10) EZ Voter Regis	AGN	15) Farm Bill Veto	FOR

Election Results

1974 general:	Phil M. Landrum (D)	64,096	(75%)	($17,710)
	Ronald D. Reeves, Sr. (R)	21,540	(25%)	($2,140)
1974 primary:	Phil M. Landrum (D)	56,611	(67%)	
	Herbert Jenkins, Jr. (D)	27,456	(33%)	
1972 general:	Phil M. Landrum (D;, unopposed			($1,378)

♦ ♦ ♦ ♦ ♦

TENTH DISTRICT

The 10th district of Georgia is a group of 21 counties in the northern part of the state. The district is anchored by the cities of Athens (pop. 44,000) in the northwest and Augusta (pop. 59,000) in the east. Athens, the site of the University of Georgia (and now home to Dean Rusk), and Augusta, home of the until recently all-white Masters golf tournament, both tend to vote almost like metropolitan Atlanta. In 1968, these two cities gave sizeable numbers of votes to Richard Nixon and Hubert Humphrey, and in statewide primaries and elections they have tended to support whoever is opposing Lester Maddox. Augusta has one of Georgia's best-organized black communities outside Atlanta, and moderate-to-liberal candidates can usually rely on a solid basis of support there.

The rest of the 10th district—primarily rural and small-town counties—has voting patterns that are entirely different. Out here Georgia Republicans get few votes indeed, and national Democrats get virtually all their support from black voters. There are a couple of counties with black majorities, and one with a black-controlled county government. But like most rural Southern areas where blacks are still in the majority, these counties are poor and their populations declining. The big new crop in these parts is catfish, the cotton fields having long since been exhausted.

The bulk of the 10th's votes are cast by Civil War Democrats, Southern conservatives who have been drawn away from their party's national ticket first by Goldwater, then by Wallace, and most recently by Richard Nixon. Since 1960, the local Congressman has been Democrat Robert G. Stephens, bearer of a proud antebellum name. For some years, Stephens has been one of the most powerful members of the House Banking and Currency Committee, swinging Dixiecrat votes for measures sought by the banking and real estate communities and opposed by former Chairman Wright Patman. Stephens was one of the leaders of the October 1972 move that squelched Patman's plans to investigate the Watergate scandal before Richard Nixon faced the voters.

In those days, conservative Democrats on the committee formed a crucial swing bloc of votes that could determine the outcome of just about every issue. Today, with the Democratic landslide of 1974, things are different. Banking and Currency now has 13 freshmen Democrats, virtually all of them liberals, and a pretty solid liberal majority. That leaves little room for Stephens to maneuver, though he is well respected for his legislative acumen and will do what he can. But Stephen's position under the new regime of Chairman Henry Reuss of Wisconsin is indicated by the fact that he is Chairman of the Historic Preservation and Coinage subcommittee, while four more important committees are chaired by less senior members.

Census Data Pop. 460,829. Central city, 13%; suburban, 22%. Median family income, $7,307; families above $15,000: 11%; families below $3,000: 17%. Median years education, 10.5.

The Voters

Median voting age 38.
Employment profile White collar, 39%. Blue collar, 43%. Service, 15%. Farm, 3%.
Ethnic groups Black, 33%. Total foreign stock, 3%.

Presidential vote

1972	Nixon (R)	81,220	(73%)
	McGovern (D)	30,014	(27%)
1968	Nixon (R)	36,243	(30%)
	Humphrey (D)	37,329	(31%)
	Wallace (AI)	46,908	(39%)

Rep. Robert G. Stephens, Jr. (D) Elected 1960; b. Aug. 14, 1913, Atlanta; home, Athens; U. of Ga., B.A. 1935, M.A. 1937, LL.B. 1941, U. of Hamburg, 1935–36; Presbyterian.

Career Army, WWII; Legal staff, Nuremberg trails, 1945; Practicing atty., 1946–61; Athens City Atty., 1947–50, Ga. Senate, 1951–53; Ga. House of Reps., 1953–59.

Offices 2410 RHOB, 202-225-4101' Also 304 E. Washington St., Athens 30601, 404-549-1421.

Committees

Banking, Currency and Housing (7th). Subcommittees: Historic Preservation and Coinage (Chairman); Housing and Community Development; International Development.

Interior and Insular Affairs (10th). Subcommittees: Indian Affairs; National Parks and Recreation; Territorial and Insular Affairs.

Group Ratings

	ADA	COPE	LWV	RIPON	NFU	LCV	CFA	NAB	NSI	ACA
1974	25	33	42	33	50	25	44	0	89	33
1973	20	20	60	36	79	31	50	–	–	57
1972	6	11	36	60	83	9	0	46	100	61

Key Votes

1) Foreign Aid	AGN	6) Gov Abortn Aid	AGN	11) Pub Cong Election $	AGN
2) Busing	AGN	7) Coed Phys Ed	ABS	12) Turkish Arms Cutoff	FOR
3) ABM	AGN	8) Pov Lawyer Gag	ABS	13) Youth Camp Regs	ABS
4) B-1 Bomber	ABS	9) Pub Trans Sub	FOR	14) Strip Mine Veto	FOR
5) Nerve Gas	FOR	10) EZ Voter Regis	AGN	15) Farm Bill Veto	AGN

Election Results

1974 general:	Robert G. Stephens, Jr. (D)	45,843	(68%)	($17,410)
	Gary Pleger (R)	21,214	(32%)	($18,788)
1974 primary:	Robert G. Stephens, Jr. (D), unopposed			
1972 general:	Robert G. Stephens, Jr. (D), unopposed .			($8,520)

HAWAII

Three thousand miles of Pacific Ocean separate Hawaii from the rest of the United States and, as one might expect, Hawaiian politics differs considerably from the mainland's. Part of the reason is the Islands' unusual ethnic and racial composition. The native Polynesians, the people Captain Cook found here in 1778 and whose royal family ruled Hawaii until 1898, are now a small minority, often intermixed with Asian and Caucasian stock. The Japanese-Americans, who first came to Hawaii to labor in the pineapple plantations, currently make up 28% of the state's population; there are also many Chinese and Filipino-Americans living here. Hawaii is the only state among the fifty where Caucasians—or haoles, as they are called—are a distinct minority.

For the first couple of years after statehood, Hawaii voted Republican; it had become a state during Eisenhower's second term, over the opposition of Southern Democrats. Soon, however, a remarkable Democratic organization took control of the state's politics. One of its leaders was John Burns, who was elected Governor in 1962 and remained in office till he retired, ill, in 1974. Another was Daniel Inuoye, the state's first Congressman-at-Large and Senator since 1962. Inuoye was a distinguished member of the group of Japanese-Americans who fought in the Nisei 442d Infantry Regimental Combat Team, the most decorated and most casualty-ridden American military unit in World War II. Returning to Hawaii after the war, Inuoye and other 442d veterans, like Congressman Spark Matsunaga, moved into the empty ranks of the territorial Democratic Party—and soon came to dominate it. The other major component of Hawaii's Democratic organization is the Internal Longshoremen's and Warehouseman's Union (ILWU). This is the largest union in ocean-commerce-dependent Hawaii, and an organization with a stormy radical past; its president is still Harry Bridges, who used to be denounced as a Communist and now deals amicably enough with big shipowners. The ILWU's clout at the polls in Hawaii is legendary; from 1960 until 1972, no major candidate endorsed by the ILWU lost an election.

The ILWU is probably the major reason why Hiram L. Fong—the only Republican Hawaii has ever elected to Congress—still sits in the United States Senate. A wealthy businessman of Chinese descent, Fong was considered a Republican liberal during the late 1950s and 1960s; but since Richard Nixon took office, he increasingly seemed to be doing the bidding of the conservative Republican administration. That, apparently, was unpopular with the voters, and in 1970 Fong would surely have been upset but for the support of the ILWU.

Despite the narrow margin of his reelection, Fong has operated as a kind of grandee in the Senate in recent years. He holds seats on the Appropriations and Judiciary Committees, and is ranking Republican on the Post Office and Civil Service Committee. It seemed to bother him not at all when his former administrative assistant, Robert Carson, was sent to jail; he is known for his assiduous fights for his choices for various patronage posts. Fong shows no sign of retiring when his term is up in 1976, but he does show signs of vulnerability and, at 69, he cannot be expected to be a heavy campaigner. The ILWU may be decisive again; if it decides to back a Democrat, Fong could conceivably retire. In any case, the seat is one that is definitely up for grabs.

That is certainly not the case with the seat held by the state's junior Senator, Daniel Inuoye; there is scarcely a safer seat in either house of Congress. In 1968, long before his service on the Watergate Committee made him a national figure, he received 83% of the vote in the general election; in 1974, opposed only by a candidate of the People's Party, he received the same percentage again. His dignified, well-prepared performance on the Watergate Committee gave him national popularity, the more so in the view of the provocation aimed at him by John J. Wilson's "the little Jap" remark. Since then, Inuoye has been mentioned with some frequency as a vice-presidential candidate, and would probably be a very popular choice. He would please many old-line elements in the party, who would remember how steadfastly he supported Lyndon Johnson—including his Vietnam war policy—in his days of travail; he also seems entirely acceptable to the McGovernish types. Also, Inuoye has been spoken of as a possible Majority Leader in the event Mike Mansfield steps down. He already holds as evidence of the high regard he has among the Senate leadership a seat on the Appropriations Committee, as well as on Commerce and D.C.

For nearly a dozen years after its first big victory in 1974, the Democratic machine built by Burns and Inuoye and the ILWU dominated the state's politics. That dominance almost came to an end in 1974, and is in serious future jeopardy. The issue which split the Democratic coalition was development. In 1970 Lieutenant Governor Thomas Gill had run against Burns on a platform of curbing development, particularly on Oahu, where 82% of the Islands' people live. Hawaii's population had been increasing rapidly—up 22% in the 1960s and another 10% from 1970 to 1974—and high rise hotels and apartments threatened to shut off Honolulu from its once pristine beaches. The Islands' tourist economy was dreadfully vulnerable to recession.

All these problems Burns and his Lieutenant Governor, George Ariyoshi, faced with the classic New Deal belief in growth; bring more money into Hawaii, and the problems would take care of themselves. Others disagreed. In the 1974 gubernatorial race, Ariyoshi—definitely the candidate of the Democratic establishment—faced challenges from Frank Fasi, the Mayor of Honolulu (recently enlarged to include all of Oahu), and Thomas Gill. Gill most strongly supported curbs on growth; Fasi, popular as Mayor, had been engaged in some bitter feuds with other Democrats and with Honolulu's newspapers. The three Democrats split the vote almost equally in all parts of the state. In Honolulu (as defined by its old city limits), which casts about half of Hawaii's votes, Gill had a paper-thin lead. Fasi carried the outer portion of Oahu, which casts another quarter of the votes; but the decisive edge was in the Neighbor Islands, as Hawaii, Maui, and Kauai are called. Here the Democratic organization was strongest among the heavily unionized agricultural workers and dockers who dominate the polls, and George Ariyoshi won nearly half the votes. That was enough to give him a 36-31-30 victory over Fasi and Gill.

The general election was just about as close. As candidate of the state's undisputed majority party, Ariyoshi could hardly have been expected to lose; moreover, his opponent, though a game campaigner, was 70 years old and a representative of the old haole families that still control so much of the Islands' private capital. But Ariyoshi was universally reckoned a dull candidate, and he won by only a 55-45 margin. He is the first Japanese-American elected Governor of a state.

Hawaii has two congressional districts: the 1st is all of the city of Honolulu, under its old limits; the 2d includes all the rest of Oahu and the Neighbor Islands. (The 2d has a considerably larger population, reflecting the large number of military personnel in Pearl Harbor and other bases; few vote here, and they are not counted for districting purposes.) Hawaii has never elected a Republican to the House, and the relatively good showings its candidates made in the Nixon landslide year are unlikely to be duplicated soon. Spark Matsunaga, the Congressman from the 1st district, has represented it since 1962; he received a lackluster 59% of the vote in 1974, but holds an important position in Washington as a member of the House Rules Committee. Patsy Takemoto Mink, the Representative from the 2d district, receives somewhat higher margins from her constituency, which in any case tends to be more Democratic in most elections. Unlike Inouye and Matsunaga, she was an early dove on Vietnam and was never as close to the congressional establishments as they have been.

Considering Hawaii's strong Democratic allegiance, it needs some explaining that the state went for Richard Nixon in 1972 by a thumping, more-than-national-average 63-37 margin. One reason is that the state's traditional progressive stance on domestic issues—Hawaii has statewide financing of public schools and one of the nation's most liberal abortion laws, for example—does not lead, as it often does on the mainland, to a dovish approach to foreign policy. The Japanese-Americans, in particular, can remember when their own loyalty as Americans was questioned, and this is the only state whose population center has been under direct attack from foreign bombers. It may make a difference, too, that Hawaii's economy would dry up if the military bases were removed from the state. Hawaii is one state which very much wants the United States to remain the only major military power in the Pacific.

Census Data   Pop. 769,913; 0.38% of U.S. total, 40th largest; Central city, 42%; suburban, 40%. Median family income, $11,552; 3rd highest; families above $15,000: 33%; families below $3,000: 7%. Median years education, 12.3.

1974 Share of Federal Tax Burden $1,516,057,000; 0.43% of U.S. total, 37th largest.

1974 Share of Federal Outlays $1,643,890,000; 0.61% of U.S. total, 37th largest.   Per capita federal spending, $2135.

DOD	$943,622,000	27th	(1.38%)	HEW	$285,049,000	44th	(0.31%)
AEC	$1,233,000	30th	(0.04%)	HUD	$6,110,000	36th	(0.63%)
NASA	$3,130,000	27th	(0.11%)	VA	$54,710,000	41st	(0.40%)
DOT	$92,061,000	32d	(1.09%)	EPA	$16,351,000	31st	(0.52%)
DOC	$5,863,000	37th	(0.36%)	RevS	$26,915,000	41st	(0.44%)
DOI	$7,865,000	44th	(0.32%)	Int.	$26,418,000	44th	(0.13%)
USDA	$33,784,000	42d	(0.27%)	Other	$140,779,000		

Economic Base   Finance, insurance and real estate; agriculture, notably sugarcane, pineapples, cattle and dairy products; food and kindred products; tourism; apparel and other textile products, especially women's and misses' outerwear; printing and publishing, especially newspapers; stone, clay and glass products, especially concrete, gypsum and plaster products.

Political Line-up   Governor, George R. Ariyoshi (D). Senators, Hiram L. Fong (R) and Daniel K. Inouye (D). Representatives, 2 D. State Senate (18 D and 7 R) and State House House (35 D and 16 R).

The Voters

Registration 343,404 Total. 190,270 D (55%); 47,815 R (14%); 105,319 Other (31%).
Median voting age 38.
Employment profile White collar, 50%. Blue collar, 31%. Service, 16%. Farm, 3%.
Ethnic groups Japanese, 28%. Chinese, 7%. Filipino, 12%. Total foreign stock, 33%.

Presidential vote

1972	Nixon (R)	168,865	(62%)
	McGovern (D)	101,409	(38%)
1968	Nixon (R)	91,425	(39%)
	Humphrey (D)	141,324	(60%)
	Wallace (AI)	3,469	(1%)

Sen. Hiram L. Fong (R) Elected July 28, 1959, seat up 1976; b. Oct. 1, 1907, Honolulu; home, Honolulu; U. of Hawaii, B.A. 1930, Harvard U., LL.B. 1935, Congregationalist.

Career Clerk, Pearl Harbor Supply Dept., 1924–27; Chf. Clerk, Honolulu Suburban Water System, 1930–32; Practicing atty.; Honolulu City and Co. Deputy Atty., 1935–38; Army Air Corps, WWII; Hawaii Territorial Legislature, 1938–54, Vice Spkr., 1944–48, Spkr., 1948–54; Farm operator; Founder and Bd. Chm. of several Insurance and Construction Corps.

Offices 2121 DSOB, 202-224-6361. Also 195 South St., Honolulu 96813, 808-538-7011.

Committees

Post Office and Civil Service (Ranking Member.)

Appropriations (4th). Subcommittees: Agriculture and Related Agencies; Defense; HUD and Independent Agencies; Labor and HEW; State, Justice, Commerce, The Judiciary.

The Judiciary (2d). Subcommittees: Antitruct and Monopoly; Constitutional Amendments; Constitutional Rights; Immigration and Naturalization; Juvenile Delinquency; Patents, Trademarks and Copyrights; Refugees and Escapees.

Group Ratings

	ADA	COPE	LWV	RIPON	NFU	LCV	CFA	NAB	NSI	ACA
1974	40	44	90	69	62	32	40	44	90	46
1973	16	36	78	56	56	–	27	–	–	58
1972	10	10	70	68	40	20	18	55	100	73

Key Votes

1) No-Knock	AGN	8) Gov Abortn Aid	FOR	15) Consumer Prot Agy	FOR
2) Busing	AGN	9) Cut Mil Brass	AGN	16) Forced Psych Tests	AGN
3) No Fault	ABS	10) Gov Limousine	ABS	17) Fed Campaign Subs	ABS
4) F-111	AGN	11) RR Featherbed	AGN	18) Rhod Chrome Ban	FOR
5) Death Penalty	ABS	12) Handgun License	ABS	19) Open Legis Meetings	AGN
6) Foreign Aid	FOR	13) Less Troop Abrd	AGN	20) Strikers Food Stmps	FOR
7) Filibuster	FOR	14) Resume Turk Aid	FOR	21) Gov Info Disclosure	FOR

Election Results

1970 general:	Hiram L. Fong (R)	124,163	(52%)
	Cecil Heftel (D)	116,597	(48%)
1970 primary:	Hiram L. Fong (R), unopposed		
1964 general:	Hiram L. Fong (R)	110,747	(53%)
	Thomas P. Gill (D)	96,789	(47%)

Sen. Daniel K. Inouye (D) Elected 1962, seat up 1980; b. Sept. 7, 1924, Honolulu; home, Honolulu; U. of Hawaii, B.A. 1950, Geo. Wash. U., J.D. 1952; Methodist.

Career Army, WWII; Honolulu Asst. Prosecuting Atty., 1953–54; Practicing atty., 1954–59; Hawaii Territorial House of Reps., 1954–58, Majority Ldr.; Hawaii Territorial Senate, 1958–59; U.S. House of Reps., 1959–63.

Offices 442 RSOB, 202-224-3934. Also 602 Capital Investment Bldg., 850 Richards St., Honolulu 96813, 808-538-3112.

Committees

Appropriations (10th). Subcommittees: Agriculture and Related Agencies; Defense; Foreign Operations (Chairman); Interior; Military Construction.

Commerce (9th). Subcommittees: Aviation; Communications; The Consumer; Foreign Commerce and Tourism (Chairman); Merchant Marine; Oceans and Atmosphere.

The District of Columbia (2d).

Group Ratings

	ADA	COPE	LWV	RIPON	NFU	LCV	CFA	NAB	NSI	ACA
1974	82	88	100	63	100	65	88	9	0	13
1973	78	91	80	50	93	–	82	–	–	15
1972	65	100	78	55	100	33	100	0	22	6

Key Votes

1) No-Knock	AGN	8) Gov Abortn Aid	FOR	15) Consumer Prot Agy	FOR
2) Busing	ABS	9) Cut Mil Brass	FOR	16) Forced Psych Tests	ABS
3) No Fault	FOR	10) Gov Limousine	AGN	17) Fed Campaign Subs	ABS
4) F-111	FOR	11) RR Featherbed	FOR	18) Rhod Chrome Ban	FOR
5) Death Penalty	AGN	12) Handgun License	FOR	19) Open Legis Meetings	AGN
6) Foreign Aid	FOR	13) Less Troop Abrd	ABS	20) Strikers Food Stmps	FOR
7) Filibuster	AGN	14) Resume Turk Aid	ABS	21) Gov Info Disclosure	ABS

Election Results

1974 general:	Daniel K. Inouye (D)	207,454 (83%)	($205,265)
	James D. Kimmel (People's Party)	42,767 (17%)	(NA)
1974 primary:	Daniel K. Inouye (D), unopposed		
1968 general:	Daniel K. Inouye (D)	189,248 (85%)	
	Wayne L. Thiessen (R)	34,008 (15%)	

Gov. George R. Ariyoshi (D) Elected 1974, after serving as Acting Gov. since Oct. 1973, term expires Dec. 1978; b. Mar. 12, 1926, Honolulu; U. of Hawaii, U. of Mich., B.A. 1949, J.D. 1952.

Career Army, WWII; Practicing atty., 1953–70; Hawaii Territorial House of Reps., 1954–58; Hawaii Territorial Senate, 1958–59, State Senate, 1959–70, Maj. Ldr., 1965–66, Maj. Floor Ldr., 1969–70; Lt. Gov. of Hawaii, 1970–74.

Offices Executive Chambers, State Capitol, Honolulu 96813, 808-548-5428.

Election Results

1974 general:	George Ariyoshi (D)	136,262	(55%)
	Randolph Crossley (R)	113,388	(45%)
1974 primary:	George Ariyoshi (D)	71,319	(36%)
	Frank F. Fasi (D)	62,023	(31%)
	Thomas P. Gill (D)	59,280	(30%)
	Two Others (D)	4,479	(2%)

◆ ◆ ◆ ◆ ◆

FIRST DISTRICT

Census Data Pop. 362,119. Central city, 90%; suburban, 10%. Median family income, $12,491; families above $15,000: 38%; families below $3,000: 6%. Median years education, 12.5.

The Voters

Median voting age 38.
Employment profile White collar, 55%. Blue collar, 29%. Service, 16%. Farm, –%.
Ethnic groups Japanese, 31%. Chinese, 10%. Filipino, 9%. Total foreign stock, 35%.

Presidential vote

	1972	Nixon (R)	82,729	(62%)
		McGovern (D)	49,994	(38%)
	1968	Nixon (R)	46,842	(40%)
		Humphrey (D)	69,715	(59%)
		Wallace (AI)	1,460	(1%)

Rep. Spark M. Matsunaga (D) Elected 1962; b. Oct. 8, 1916, Kukuiula; home, Honolulu; U. of Hawaii, B.Ed. 1941, Harvard U., J.D. 1951; Episcopalian.

Career Public school teacher, 1941; Army, WWII; Vets. Counsellor, Surplus Prop. Ofc., U.S. Dept. of Interior, 1945–47; Chf., Priority Claimants' Div., War Assets Admin., 1947–48; Honolulu Asst. Pub. Prosecutor, 1952–54; Practicing atty., 1954–63.

Offices 442 CHOB, 202-225-2726. Also Rm. 218, Fed. Bldg., Honolulu 96813, 808-531-6417.

Committees

Rules (7th).

Group Ratings

	ADA	COPE	LWV	RIPON	NFU	LCV	CFA	NAB	NSI	ACA
1974	87	100	91	43	100	71	83	17	22	0
1973	84	90	100	67	100	84	100	–	–	7
1972	75	82	90	84	100	67	0	0	30	9

Key Votes

1) Foreign Aid	FOR	6) Gov Abortn Aid	FOR	11) Pub Cong Election $	FOR
2) Busing	FOR	7) Coed Phys Ed	AGN	12) Turkish Arms Cutoff	FOR
3) ABM	FOR	8) Pov Lawyer Gag	AGN	13) Youth Camp Regs	FOR
4) B-1 Bomber	FOR	9) Pub Trans Sub	FOR	14) Strip Mine Veto	AGN
5) Nerve Gas	AGN	10) EZ Voter Regis	FOR	15) Farm Bill Veto	AGN

Election Results

1974 general:	Spark Matsunaga (D)	71,552	(59%)	($165,469)
	William B. Paul (R)	49,065	(41%)	($29,799)

1974 primary:	Spark Matsunaga (D), unopposed			
1972 general:	Spark Matsunaga (D)	73,826	(55%)	($127,753)
	Fred W. Rohlfing (R)	61,138	(45%)	($179,221)

◆ ◆ ◆ ◆ ◆

SECOND DISTRICT

Census Data Pop. 407,794. Central city, 0%; suburban, 66%. Median family income, $10,848; families above $15,000: 28%; families below $3,000: 7%. Median years education, 12.2.

The Voters

Median voting age 38.
Employment profile White collar, 44%. Blue collar, 35%. Service, 15%. Farm, 6%.
Ethnic groups Japanese, 25%. Chinese, 4%. Filipino, 16%. Total foreign stock, 32%.

Presidential vote

1972	Nixon (R)	86,136	(63%)
	McGovern (D)	51,415	(37%)
1968	Nixon (R)	42,770	(37%)
	Humphrey (D)	70,345	(61%)
	Wallace (AI)	1,648	(1%)

Rep. Patsy T. Mink (D) Elected 1964; b. Dec. 6, 1927, Paia; home, Waipahu; Wilson Col., 1946, U. of Neb., 1947, U. of Hawaii, B.A. 1948, U. of Chicago, J.D. 1951; Protestant.

Career Practicing atty., 1953–64; Business Law Prof., U. of Hawaii, 1953–56, 1959–62; Atty., Hawaii Territorial House of Reps., 1955; Hawaii Terr. House of Reps., 1956–58; Hawaii Terr. Senate, 1958–59; Hawaii State Senate, 1962–64.

Offices 2338 RHOB, 202-225-4906. Also 346 Fed. Bldg., Honolulu 96813, 808-531-4602.

Committees

Budget (13th).

Education and Labor (9th). Subcommittees: Elementary, Secondary and Vocational Education; Equal Opportunities; Select Subcommittee on Education.

Interior and Insular Affairs (7th). Subcommittees: Mines and Mining (Chairman); National Parks and Recreation; Territorial and Insular Affairs.

Group Ratings

	ADA	COPE	LWV	RIPON	NFU	LCV	CFA	NAB	NSI	ACA
1974	91	100	83	47	100	88	92	17	0	0
1973	96	91	100	71	95	95	100	–	–	11
1972	100	91	100	80	86	80	0	0	0	0

Key Votes

1) Foreign Aid	FOR	6) Gov Abortn Aid	FOR	11) Pub Cong Election $	AGN
2) Busing	FOR	7) Coed Phys Ed	FOR	12) Turkish Arms Cutoff	FOR
3) ABM	AGN	8) Pov Lawyer Gag	AGN	13) Youth Camp Regs	FOR
4) B-1 Bomber	AGN	9) Pub Trans Sub	FOR	14) Strip Mine Veto	AGN
5) Nerve Gas	AGN	10) EZ Voter Regis	FOR	15) Farm Bill Veto	AGN

Election Results

1974 general:	Patsy T. Mink (D)	86,916	(63%)	($97,104)
	Carla W. Coray (R)	51,894	(37%)	($34,089)
1974 primary:	Patsy T. Mink (D)	76,596	(79%)	
	George B. Carter (D)	19,998	(21%)	
1972 general:	Patsy T. Mink (D)	79,856	(57%)	($71,620)
	Diana Hansen (R)	60,043	(43%)	($39,836)

IDAHO

Back before the turn of the century, when William Jennings Bryan was urging Americans to abandon the gold standard for the unlimited coinage of silver, Idaho's silver interests dominated the state's politics. Although silver is still mined in places like Sunshine Mine near Kellogg, Idaho's principal economic concern today is agriculture. Potatoes, for which Idaho is famous, are grown in the rich farmlands of the panhandle region just east of Spokane, Washington, and along the Snake River valley in the southern part of the state. Because there is so much farmland here, Idaho's population is not concentrated in one or two large urban areas as in other Rocky Mountain and Pacific states. Idaho's largest city Boise (pop. 74,000)—like many Western cities, a conservative stronghold. The liberal voting base, if it can be called that, lies in the northern panhandle counties. But any liberalism, at least in terms of national politics, is vastly overmatched by the conservatism of the Snake River valley, and particularly of the large Mormon community there—the largest outside Utah.

In the recent past, Idaho politics seems to have travelled full circle—usually in just the opposite pattern of the nation as a whole. During the Eisenhower years, a public power vs. private power controversy over construction of Hell's Canyon Dam on the Snake River redounded to the benefit of the Democrats, who took the public power issue. During the late 1950s, Idaho Democrats won most of the state's Senate and House races. In 1960 John F. Kennedy, though a Catholic and an Easterner, got 46% of the state's votes—one of his better showings in the mountain states. But during the sixties, the people of Idaho seemed to become increasingly upset with what they saw as a Democratic administration dominated by an alien East Coast establishment.

In 1964, a strong conservative movement—it was especially strong in the southern Mormon counties—resulted in 49% of the state's vote going to Barry Goldwater. In that same year, the state's 2d congressional district ousted its Democratic Congressman for a conservative Republican—the only district outside the South to do so in the year of the LBJ landslide. By 1968, Hubert Humphrey got only 31% of the vote here, and George McGovern did even worse four years later. Meanwhile, 13% of Idaho voters supported George Wallace in 1968, his strongest showing west of Texas; and even John Schmitz, the hapless American Party candidate in 1972, got 9% of Idaho's votes—his best showing in the nation.

But if Idaho was shifting right in national politics in the middle sixties, it has been shifting notably to the left in local races in the early seventies. As Idahoans overwhelmingly rejected the candidacy of Hubert Humphrey, they reelected liberal Democratic Senator Frank Church with a resounding 60% of the vote. In 1972, when McGovern did worse here than in all but seven other states, Democrats came within 3% of electing another Senator. In 1974, Church was again reelected comfortably, and Democratic Governor Cecil Andrus, elected in an upset in 1970, was reelected with a landslide 71% of the vote.

Andrus's 1970 victory was one of the first signs of the burgeoning importance of environmental issues in Western electoral politics. His predecessor, crew-cut, ultraconservative Republican Don Samuelson, supported a mining company's proposal to extract molybdenum (a metal then in excess supply) from the White Clouds area, one of the scenic wonders of the Salmon River Mountains. Andrus attacked the proposal and won enough votes to carry the panhandle easily, hold even in Boise, and carry sometimes Democratic Pocatello in the southeast—and carry the state by 10,000 votes. After four years of Andrus's calm, conciliatory style, voters decided they wanted more, reelecting him almost unanimously, and incidentally electing Democrats to most of the statewide elective posts.

Andrus seems to have supplanted Church as the state's most popular Democrat; indeed, for a time in the late sixties, Church was just about the only elected Idaho Democrat. He was first elected to the Senate at the age of 32 in 1956, beating a Republican candidate with personal problems. Building up a friendship with Lyndon Johnson, Church soon won a seat on the Senate Foreign Relations Committee; when Johnson was President, he was one of the first Senators to take a stand against the Vietnam War. Doves who make scholarly speeches are not ordinarily very popular in Idaho. But Church has carefully catered to opinion at home. He has opposed federal gun control legislation, and he keeps a seat on the Senate Interior Committee (which most Senators relinquish, resenting Chairman Henry Jackson's dominance), and has kept careful watch over the state's water needs. (Much of Idaho's farmland would be worthless without irrigation.) Moreover, his continual attacks on the foreign aid program—he thinks it is so often misused to provide military aid to dictators, among other things, that we would be better off without it—endear him, for somewhat different reasons, to most Idaho voters.

As a final counter to criticism Church can invoke the memory of a famous Republican Senator from Idaho: William E. Borah. A progressive and isolationist, Borah served in the Senate from 1907 to 1940. Fiercely independent and scholarly, and an expert on foreign affairs, Borah is said to have enhanced Idaho's reputation as J. William Fulbright did Arkansas's; Church supporters argue that their man is in the same tradition.

At any rate, the 52-year-old Church is edging to the top of the seniority ladder on Foreign Relations, now ranking behind only John Sparkman, 77, and Mike Mansfield, 73. Since Sparkman surely won't run again in 1978, and Mansfield would have to step down from the Majority Leadership to be Chairman, Church has an excellent chance for the post soon. Already he was chosen in 1975 to be Chairman of the special panel to investigate the CIA; in years past, that position would probably have gone to a Southern conservative, but now Church is perceived—and accurately enough—as well within the Democratic mainstream and responsible enough for such a task. Indeed, as 1975 went on, Church was even being mentioned as a possible candidate for President; preoccupied with the CIA probe, he made no moves toward the nomination.

Church was probably in his deepest political trouble in Idaho when his seat came up in 1968, and he was saved, in large part, by his most bitter adversaries. More than a year before that election, right-wing groups started circulating recall petitions against Church. Their drive ultimately fizzled—it wasn't clear if a Senator *could* be recalled—and people tended to rally around Church. Then it was revealed that most of the money for the recall had come from California conservatives—which allowed Church partisans to rally against out-of-staters dabbling in Idaho politics. Finally, Church's opponent turned out to be Congressman George Hansen (on whom more below), an enthusiastic conservative but hardly an adept campaigner.

All of which resulted in a solid 60–40 Church victory, his biggest margin yet. For 1974, the betting was he would win by even more votes. His opponent was Bob Smith, an ordained minister and former aide to free-market enthusiast Congressman Steven Symms. But this time the conservatives did not tip their hand too early; Smith's campaign was quiet until October, when he started spending significant amounts of money. He cut noticeably into Church's lead, and by November the Senator was reelected by only a 57–43 margin. He had not been in real danger, but the outcome illustrated the fact that a liberal Democrat like Church is always going to be vulnerable in conservative Idaho.

The state's junior Senator, elected in 1972, is Republican James McClure. A three-term Congressman and member of his party's conservative wing, McClure won a hotly contested four-candidate Republican primary with 36% of the vote. Among the defeated candidates were former Governor (1955–71) Robert Smylie, beaten for renomination by Don Samuelson in 1970; and former (1965–69) and future (1975–) Congressman George Hansen. After the primary, Hansen reported that four big Idaho corporations had tried to talk him out of the race. That caused McClure some problems, and so did environmental issues; he is not one to interfere with businessmen's interference with the environment. McClure's Democratic opponent, Bud Davis, had the misfortune to have announced his support of the United Farm Workers' lettuce boycott. McClure charged that the UFW's next goal was the Idaho potato—a charge never given an ounce of substantiation—and insinuated that Davis was a potato-boycotter. Davis was forced to make the indisputable point that no Idaho politician would ever come out against the potato, but McClure's spurious charge may have made the difference in his 53-47 bid. In his first few years in the Senate, McClure has been quiet as freshman Senators historically have been; his vote can be counted just about invariably on the conservative side of issues.

When McClure went to the Senate, he left vacant the 1st congressional district, traditionally the more Democratic of Idaho's two seats. This includes the panhandle, which is connnected with the rest of Idaho by just one two-lane highway and no railroads; economically and sociologically this area is part of Spokane, Washington's "Inland Empire." With a large labor vote in Lewiston and

Coeur d'Alene, and the University of Idaho in Moscow, the panhandle often produces Democratic majorities.

But in 1st district politics these days, the panhandle is often outvoted by Boise and nearby Canyon County, both heavily conservative. These conservative votes were more than enough to produce 1972 and 1974 victories for Republican Steven Symms, a fruit rancher and businessman who was only 34 when he won his first term. His performance was impressive. In 1972, he beat the state Senate Majority Leader in the primary and did as well in the general as McClure had. In the Democratic year of 1974, he won with a convincing 58% of the vote; at the same time, his former aide Bob Smith was making a creditable showing against Frank Church. This is all the more remarkable in that Symms is that rarest of Congressmen these days, a free market ideologue; he likes to think of himself as a libertarian, and he doesn't hesitate to cast lone votes against legislation his principles oppose.

The state's 2d district is more of a geographic unit. Most of its people live within a dozen or so miles of the Snake River, in small cities or farmhouses near the irrigation ditches that bring water to the potato fields. The district includes Sun Valley, the Craters of the Moon National Monument, and Idaho's small slice of Yellowstone National Park. This is Mormon country and except for Pocatello (pop. 40,000) it is normally Republican. But even more significant, it is the home of Idaho's right-wing subculture. The John Birch Society is strong in the sparsely-populated farm counties and little mountain-locked towns, isolated from any center of urbanity. It is easy to see how a few enthusiastic, articulate right-wingers can come to dominate a town's school board and, by assiduous proselytizing change a small county's voting patterns. That is what appears to have been happening the last ten or fifteen years in southern Idaho; the results are all there to see in the election returns. They show up, for example, in the strong third-party finish of George Wallace in 1968, when in some Snake River counties he almost equalled Hubert Humphrey's totals—or in the fact that John Schmitz actually outran McGovern in four counties here in 1972.

Additional evidence comes from the 1974 congressional election, often referred to as the battle of the Hansens. The incumbent, Republican moderate Orval Hansen, had been first elected in 1968 when his predecessor, George Hansen stepped aside to run for the Senate. We have already seen how well George did in that contest; Orval, in contrast, won reelection easily in 1970 and 1972. His sometimes moderate or even liberal voting record helped him exceed even the usual high Republican percentages here. But many of the area's right-wingers were unhappy—from their point of view, quite sensibly—with Orval's record, and when George decided to challenge him in the 1974 primary they supported him enthusiastically. Orval carried Boise and Idaho Falls—the heaviest voting areas in the primary—but George carried almost all the smaller counties and cities like Pocatello and Twin Falls as well to beat his successor by a 52–48 margin.

That put George in the general election, this time against a Democrat named Max Hanson. Hoping to capitalize on moderates' resentment of George, Max campaigned vigorously making sure to mention that he was a conservative too. George had an additional problem: charges that he had utterly failed to report certain large campaign contributions. But that did not deter George's supporters and he went on to win a 56–44 victory; Max carried only Boise and Pocatello, and George won just about everything else. It was the second time he had captured the seat in a year of national Democratic landslide. Soon after being sworn in, George was formally charged with violating campaign disclosure laws, by filing inaccuate campaign finance reports weeks late and by accepting corporate contributions. Hansen was convicted in the spring of 1975; the judge at first sentenced him to jail, but then charged his mind. Theoretically, at least, the House could vote to expel him, although it is not expected to do so.

Census Data Pop. 713,008; 0.35% of U.S. total, 42nd largest; Central city, 11%; suburban, 5%. Median family income, $8,381; 34th highest; families above $15,000: 13%; families below $3,000: 11%. Median years education, 12.3.

1974 Share of Federal Tax Burden $776,664,000; 0.29% of U.S. total, 44th largest.

1974 Share of Federal Outlays $966,879,000; 0.36% of U.S. total, 44th largest. Per capita federal spending, $1356.

DOD	$125,345,000	46th (0.18%)	HEW	$308,181,000	42d (0.33%)
AEC	$106,190,000	15th (3.48%)	HUD	$2,134,000	44th (0.22%)
NASA	$16,000	49th (–)	VA	$54,710,000	41st (0.40%)
DOT	$43,549,000	44th (0.51%)	EPA	$7,926,000	44th (0.25%)
DOC	$3,553,000	43d (0.22%)	RevS	$25,326,000	43d (0.42%)

DOI	$51,973,000	15th (2.11%)	Int.	$24,446,000	45th (0.12%)
USDA	$112,076,000	37th (0.90%)	Other	$101,454,000	

Economic Base Agriculture, notably cattle, potatoes, dairy products and wheat; food and kindred products, especially canned, cured and frozen foods; lumber and wood products, especially general sawmills and planing mills; finance, insurance and real estate; chemicals and allied products, especially industrial chemicals; trailor coaches and other transportation equipment.

Political Line-up Governor, Cecil D. Andrus (D). Senators, Frank Church (D) and James A. McClure (R). Representatives, 2 R. State Senate (21 R and 14 D); State House (42 R and 28 D).

The Voters

Registration 440,114 Total. No party registration.
Median voting age 43.
Employment profile White collar, 43%. Blue collar, 33%. Service, 13%. Farm, 11%.
Ethnic groups Total foreign stock, 10%.

Presidential vote

1972	Nixon (R)	....	199,384	(71%)
	McGovern (D)	....	80,826	(29%)
1968	Nixon (R)	....	165,369	(57%)
	Humphrey (D)	....	89,273	(31%)
	Wallace (AI)	....	36,541	(13%)

Sen. Frank Church (D) Elected 1956, seat up 1980; b. July 25, 1924, Boise; home, Boise; Stanford U., B.A. 1947, LL.B. 1950; Presbyterian.

Career Army, WWII; Practicing atty., 1950–56; Keynote Spkr., Dem. Natl. Conv., 1960; Mbr., U.S. Delegation to U.N., 1966.

Offices 245 RSOB, 202-224-6142. Also 304 Fed. Ofc. Bldg., Boise 83702, 208-342-2711 ext. 363, and 204 Fed. Bldg., Pocatello 83201, 208-323-4650.

Committees

Foreign Relations (3d). Subcommittees: Foreign Assistance and Economic Policy; Multinational Corporations (Chairman).

Interior and Insular Affairs (2d). Subcommittees: Energy Research and Water Resources (Chairman); Environment and Land Resources; Parks and Recreation.

Select Committee on Intelligence Operations (Chairman).

Group Ratings

	ADA	COPE	LWV	RIPON	NFU	LCV	CFA	NAB	NSI	ACA
1974	83	56	90	33	88	86	77	45	0	23
1973	82	78	78	50	100	–	100	–	–	22
1972	70	80	90	72	88	78	90	33	0	17

Key Votes

1) No-Knock	AGN	8) Gov Abortn Aid	AGN	15) Consumer Prot Agy	FOR
2) Busing	FOR	9) Cut Mil Brass	FOR	16) Forced Psych Tests	AGN
3) No Fault	AGN	10) Gov Limousine	AGN	17) Fed Campaign Subs	FOR
4) F-111	ABS	11) RR Featherbed	FOR	18) Rhod Chrome Ban	ABS
5) Death Penalty	FOR	12) Handgun License	AGN	19) Open Legis Meetings	AGN
6) Foreign Aid	AGN	13) Less Troop Abrd	FOR	20) Strikers Food Stmps	ABS
7) Filibuster	FOR	14) Resume Turk Aid	AGN	21) Gov Info Disclosure	FOR

Election Results

1974 general:	Frank Church (D)	145,140	(57%)	($300,300)
	Robert L. Smith (R)	109,072	(43%)	($127,926)
1974 primary:	Frank Church (D)	53,659	(86%)	
	Leon Olson (D)	8,904	(14%)	
1968 general:	Frank Church (D)	173,482	(60%)	
	George V. Hansen (R)	114,394	(40%)	

Sen. James A. McClure (R) Elected 1972, seat up 1978; b. Dec. 27, 1924, Payette; home, Payette; U. of Idaho, J.D. 1950; Methodist.

Career Practicing atty., 1950–66; Payette Co. Atty., 1950–56; Payette City Atty., 1953–66; Idaho Senate 1960–66; U.S. House of Reps., 1967–73.

Offices 2106 DSOB, 202-224-2752. Also 304 N. 8th St., Rm. 434, Boise 83702, 208-343-1421.

Committees

Budget (5th).

Interior and Insular Affairs (4th). Subcommittees: Environment and Land Resources; Indian Affairs; Parks and Recreation; Special Subcommittee on Integrated Oil Operations.

Public Works (4th). Subcommittees: Environmental Pollution; Economic Development; Water Resources; Transportation; Buildings and Grounds.

Group Ratings

	ADA	COPE	LWV	RIPON	NFU	LCV	CFA	NAB	NSI	ACA
1974	0	18	22	36	18	33	11	75	100	100
1973	31	20	43	50	40	–	27	–	–	92
1972	0	20	17	40	0	0	–	86	100	94

Key Votes

1) No-Knock	FOR	8) Gov Abortn Aid	AGN	15) Consumer Prot Agy	AGN
2) Busing	AGN	9) Cut Mil Brass	AGN	16) Forced Psych Tests	AGN
3) No Fault	AGN	10) Gov Limousine	AGN	17) Fed Campaign Subs	AGN
4) F-111	FOR	11) RR Featherbed	AGN	18) Rhod Chrome Ban	AGN
5) Death Penalty	FOR	12) Handgun License	AGN	19) Open Legis Meetings	FOR
6) Foreign Aid	AGN	13) Less Troop Abrd	AGN	20) Strikers Food Stmps	AGN
7) Filibuster	FOR	14) Resume Turk Aid	FOR	21) Gov Info Disclosure	ABS

Election Results

1972 general:	James A. McClure (R)	161,804	(52%)
	William E. Davis (D)	140,913	(46%)
	Jean Stoddard (AI)	6,885	(2%)
1972 primary:	James A. McClure (R)	46,522	(36%)
	George Hansen (R)	35,412	(27%)
	Glen Wegner (R)	24,582	(19%)
	Robert E. Smylie (R)	22,497	(17%)

Gov. Cecil D. Andrus (D) Elected 1970, term expires Jan. 1979; b. Aug. 25, 1931, Hood River, Oreg.; Oregon St. U.

Career Navy, Korea; Dist. and St. Mgr., Paul Revere Life Ins. Co.; Idaho Senate.

Offices Statehouse, Boise 83720, 208-384-2100.

Election Results

1974 general:	Cecil D. Andrus (D)	184,182	(71%)
	Jack M. Murphy (R)	68,731	(26%)
	Nolan Victor (AI)	6,759	(3%)
1974 primary:	Cecil D. Andrus (D), unopposed		
1970 general:	Cecil D. Andrus (D)	128,004	(52%)
	Don Samuelson (R)	117,108	(48%)

◆ ◆ ◆ ◆ ◆

FIRST DISTRICT

Census Data Pop. 356,859. Central city, 15%; suburban, 10%. Median family income, $8,466; families above $15,000: 13%; families below $3,000: 11%. Median years education, 12.2.

The Voters

Median voting age 44.
Employment profile White collar, 43%. Blue collar, 34%. Service, 14%. Farm, 9%.
Ethnic groups Total foreign stock, 11%.

Presidential vote

1972	Nixon (R)	99,087	(69%)
	McGovern (D)	45,309	(31%)
1968	Nixon (R)	78,242	(54%)
	Humphrey (D)	49,194	(34%)
	Wallace (AI)	17,250	(12%)

Rep. Steven D. Symms (R) Elected 1972;b. Apr. 23, 1938, Nampa; home, Caldwell; U. of Idaho, B.S. 1960; Protestant.

Career USMC, 1960–63; Personnel and Production Mgr., V.P., Symms Fruit Ranch, Inc., 1963–72, Mbr., Bd. of Dirs., 1967–.

Offices 1410 LHOB, 202-225-6611. Also 304 N. 8th St., Rm. 134, Boise 83701, 208-336-1492.

Committees

Agriculture (5th). Subcommittees: Forests; Livestock and Grains.

Interior and Insular Affairs (11th). Subcommittees: Energy and the Environment; Water and Power Resources.

Group Ratings

	ADA	COPE	LWV	RIPON	NFU	LCV	CFA	NAB	NSI	ACA
1974	0	0	0	36	0	20	0	91	100	100
1973	9	9	17	33	15	5	0	–	–	96

Key Votes

1) Foreign Aid	AGN	6) Gov Abortn Aid	AGN	11) Pub Cong Election $	AGN
2) Busing	AGN	7) Coed Phys Ed	ABS	12) Turkish Arms Cutoff	ABS
3) ABM	FOR	8) Pov Lawyer Gag	FOR	13) Youth Camp Regs	AGN
4) B-1 Bomber	FOR	9) Pub Trans Sub	AGN	14) Strip Mine Veto	FOR
5) Nerve Gas	FOR	10) EZ Voter Regis	AGN	15) Farm Bill Veto	FOR

Election Results

1974 general:	Steven D. Symms (R)	75,404	(58%)	($125,268)
	J. Ray Cox (D)	54,001	(42%)	($43,784)
1974 primary:	Steven D. Symms (R), unopposed			
1972 general:	Steven D. Symms (R)	85,270	(56%)	($89,306)
	Edward V. Williams (D)	68,106	(44%)	($59,585)

◆ ◆ ◆ ◆ ◆

SECOND DISTRICT

Census Data Pop. 356,149. Central city, 6%; suburban, 1%. Median family income, $8,280; families above $15,000: 13%; families below $3,000: 11%. Median years education, 12.3.

The Voters

Median voting age 42.
Employment profile White collar, 43%. Blue collar, 31%. Service, 12%. Farm, 14%.
Ethnic groups Total foreign stock, 10%.

Presidential vote

1972	Nixon (R)	100,297	(74%)
	McGovern (D)	35,517	(26%)
1968	Nixon (R)	87,160	(59%)
	Humphrey (D)	40,079	(27%)
	Wallace (AI)	19,291	(13%)

Rep. George Hansen (R) Elected 1974; b. Sept. 14, 1930, Tetonia; home, Pocatello; Ricks Col., B.A. 1956, Idaho St. U.; Church of Latter Day Saints.

Career Air Force; High school teacher; Insurance and retailing business; Mayor of Alameda, 1961–62; Pocatello City Commissioner, 1962–65; U.S. House of Reps., 1965–69; Repub. nominee for U.S. Senate, 1968; Deputy Under Secy., U.S. Dept. of Agriculture, 1969–71.

Offices 1125 LHOB, 202-225-5531. Also 211 Fed. Bldg., Box 740, Idaho Falls 83401, 208-523-5341.

Committees

Banking, Currency and Housing (8th). Subcommittees: Domestic Monetary Policy; General Oversight and Renegotiation.

Veterans' Affairs (8th). Subcommittees: Cemeteries and Burial Benefits; Hospitals.

Group Ratings: Newly Elected

Key Votes

1) Foreign Aid	AGN	6) Gov Abortn Aid	NE	11) Pub Cong Election $	NE
2) Busing	NE	7) Coed Phys Ed	AGN	12) Turkish Arms Cutoff	NE
3) ABM	NE	8) Pov Lawyer Gag	NE	13) Youth Camp Regs	AGN
4) B-1 Bomber	FOR	9) Pub Trans Sub	NE	14) Strip Mine Veto	ABS
5) Nerve Gas	NE	10) EZ Voter Regis	NE	15) Farm Bill Veto	FOR

Election Results

1974 general:	George V. Hansen (R)	....	67,274	(56%)	($120,923)
	Max Hanson (D)	....	53,599	(44%)	($20,982)
1974 primary:	George V. Hansen (R)	....	22,114	(52%)	
	Orval Hansen (R)	....	20,109	(48%)	

ILLINOIS

As any reader of license plate slogans knows, Illinois is the "Land of Lincoln." More to the point, Illinois is also a land of tough, patronage-minded politicians, the home of Richard J. Daley's Democratic machine and the equally fearsome apparatus of the state's conservative Republicans. Not that this is the image one obtains from the roster of top statewide officeholders. Both parties have traditionally slated blue-ribbon candidates for the top slots, giving the nation such leaders as Abraham Lincoln and Stephen Douglas in 1858 and, more recently, Adlai Stevenson and Paul Douglas in 1858 and the state's current Senators, Republican Charles Percy and Democrat Adlai Stevenson III.

Such men are above any suspicion of dishonesty. But they are in that respect scarcely typical of Illinois politicians, or at least the public's view of them. Among most pols here, patronage is a way of life, and between elections the leaders of both parties can live together quite comfortably, sharing the spoils. Outright thievery exists, too: in the 1950s a Republican state Auditor stole $150,000, and in 1970 the Democratic Secretary of State died leaving $800,000 cash in shoeboxes in his dingy Springfield hotel room. The most widespread corruption exists probably in Chicago and Cook County. In the last few years, aggressive Republican prosecutors have won convictions against such major figures in the Daley machine as County Clerk Edward Barrett and City Council President Thomas Keane, and former Governor and Federal judge Otto Kerner. State's Attorney Edward Hanrahan, indicted for obstruction of justice in connection with the death of two Black Panther leaders, was acquitted but defeated by the voters in 1972, and his political career is over. (See Sixth District) Forty indictments for vote fraud in the March 1972 primary and intensive poll-watching have just about eliminated what Republicans claim was a pattern of massive vote fraud, especially in the West Side Chicago wards. But even Mayor Daley has been called on for explanations: he has admitted, for example, that he channeled hundreds of thousands of dollars insurance contracts to a firm that employs one of his sons.

In short, Mayor Daley's machine—the last major patronage-oriented, old-fashioned ward-based political organization in the country—is in bad shape. Daley himself, to be sure, was renominated for an unprecedented sixth term as Mayor in early 1975, but that victory show the weakness, not the strength, of the machine. Daley, after all, has the reputation of being one of the few Mayors who can actually make a city work, who can get big labor and big business to make peace, and can control the city budget and the city tax rate. And if Chicago's city services are not as good as that view suggests, they are at least the equal of those in large cities under supposedly more enlightened management. Certainly Alderman William Singer, the young maverick Alderman who was Daley's main competitor, could not claim similar expertise. Yet with all these advantages, the 73-year-old Daley received only 58% of the vote. It was a solid 2–1 win over Singer, but scarcely the kind of unanimous endorsement he must have wanted: more than four out of ten Chicago Democrats voted for someone else.

So it should not be so surprising, at least now in retrospect, that Daley's choice for Governor was beaten in the 1972 Democratic primary. There were a number of ironies here. The machine choice was then Lieutenant Governor Paul Simon, who had built his career as an authentic Downstate reformer; his strong backing from organized labor and favorable name recognition virtually forced the machine to endorse him. (See Twenty-fourth District) And Walker, though an out-and-out rebel who had written the report charging a "police riot" at the 1968 Democratic convention, was not the kind of programmatic liberal so many of his articulate supporters assumed. Once he got the nomination, the main theme of this former West Pointer and six-figure executive at Montgomery Ward was that the state budget must be cut. He attacked Republican incumbent Richard Ogilvie for supporting a new state income tax, and became a kind of populistic folk figure. He made only a mediocre showing in Chicago and its suburbs (outer Cook County and five surrounding counties), but actually carried usually Republican Downstate Illinois for a 51–49 statewide victory.

In office Walker has been engaged in a series of feuds with both parties in the legislature as well as with Mayor Daley. His adversaries consider him a grandstander, a man who poses as an economizer while fattening his own payroll with political appointees. He, apparently, considers himself a kind of tribune of the people, seeking to end the arrangements that have made it so comfortable to be a politician or a bureaucrat in Illinois, and not barred from using a wily politician's device to accomplish these ends. People around Walker have made it no secret that they consider their man fit to be a candidate for the Presidency in 1976; they have even had made thousands of copies of a record called "A Winner Walkin Home", which extols the Governor in a hillbilly twang. It seems unlikely at the moment that Walker can win any significant support within the professional political (or journalistic) community; if he has any desire to advance, it must be in the primaries. What about his chances if he decides to run for reelection in 1976? Probably good: he helped to elect a fair number of new state legislators in 1974. Possible opponents include state Attorney General William Scott, a conservative Republican, and Lieutenant Governor Neil Hartigan, a smooth youngish Daley Democrat. But Scott passed up the 1974 Senate race and Hartigan is the kind of politician who likes to wait for the sure things to come to him—which may well happen.

Governor and Mayor have always been the positions most Illinois pols care about; that's where the patronage and all the big contracts are. The two Senate seats are held, usually, by the blue-ribbon candidates both parties like to put up to attract independent voters. For more than 15 years they were held by Paul Douglas and Everett Dirksen, an odd couple if there ever was one, and as example of how the same state can continually reelect entirely different Senators. Douglas was an economics professor idealist, a liberal who battled against the filibuster and the oil depletion allowance in the days when the Senate, led by Lyndon Johnson, overwhelming supported them; he had the pleasure of seeing both seriously injured, if not killed, in 1975. Dirksen, the Senate Minority Leader when he died in 1969, was a natural deal-maker, a man who could shift stands on issues like civil rights adroitly enough to be hailed for statesmanship, a man who loved to orate floridly about the virtues of the marigold, but whose tiny Downstate law office at the same time was collecting fat fees from many of the nation's leading corporations.

Illinois' current Senators are more in the Douglas than the Dirksen mold: liberal on the issues, more pragmatic than the old professor but still not the leading movers and shakers in the Senate. Charles Percy was, in fact, a student of Douglas's at the University of Chicago before World War II. He rose quickly: president of Bell and Howell at 30, head of the Republican platform committee at 41, Senator at 47. With his blond hair and unwrinkled face, Percy is still described as young by some journalists, though he is nearing 60; he is still regarded by some as a sort of liberal Republican boy wonder, though he has not yet done what everyone has expected him to do for years—run for President. He was planning the groundwork for a serious, grueling campaign when Gerald Ford's accession to the Presidency seemed to sew up the Republican nomination for 1976; with the selection of Nelson Rockefeller as Vice President, the only wing of the party to which Percy appeals probably already has its candidate whenever Ford retires. In order to win, Percy would have had to effect a kind of revolution in the Republican Party; it would not have been enough to win primaries, but he would have had to oust conservative party officials all over the country and install people closer to his own views.

And those views, generally, are probably closer to those of most liberal Democratic Senators than to Republicans like the late Everett Dirksen. But all that can be overstated: though he was often an adversary of the Nixon Administration, he attempted in 1975 to come to the rescue of the Ford Administration's Cambodia policy by fashioning a compromise in the Senate Foreign Relations Committee. What is not in doubt about Percy is his ability to win general elections in Illinois. Running for a second term in 1972 he won with 62% of the vote—significantly ahead of

Richard Nixon. He had no difficulty capturing the traditional Republican vote, took a stunning 70% in the Chicago suburbs—which now cast 275,000 more votes than the city itself—and ran about even with his Democratic opponent in the South Side black ghetto.

Percy's percentage, a record, was topped in 1974 by his Democratic colleague, Adlai Stevenson III, when he won his first full term by a 63–37 margin. Stevenson had captured the seat four years before, after it was held for a matter of months by a conservative Republican appointed to fill the vacancy caused by Dirksen's death. Stevenson had been the target of a Nixon-Agnew brand law 'n' order campaign, complete with charges that the Democrat consorted with the likes of Yippie Jerry Rubin; Stevenson retaliated by hiring the prosecutor of the Chicago Seven as his campaign manager, wearing a flag pin in his lapel, and winning 58% of the vote. In 1974, several well-known Republicans, including Attorney General Scott and House Republican Conference Chairman John Anderson declined to run against him (actually they had to make their decisions in 1973, since Illinois's filing date is in December, the earliest in the nation.) With token opposition from an unknown and unfinanced Republican, Stevenson swept the state, winning 58% of the vote Downstate and 53% in the suburbs—to go with his 81-19 margin in the city of Chicago.

Stevenson is a quiet Senator who nonetheless takes strong positions on matters like ending military aid to Vietnam; he worked hard on issues like congressional and campaign reform. His speaking style, at first very hesitant, has improved during his political career, but he still lacks the homespun polish his father had. On the Banking and Commerce Committees, he is considered a reliable voice for consumer points of view, but not a major shaper of legislation.

In presidential elections, Illinois is one of our bellwether states: it has supported every winning candidate since Warren G. Harding in 1920. But the Illinois presidential primary has never been decisive in choosing either party's nominee. One reason is the early filing date, which scares off a lot of candidates, who want more time to make up their minds; another reason is the fact that the party machines have traditionally had the strength to elect the delegates they select. The preferential poll is just a beauty contest, imposing no obligation on delegates to support any candidate; in 1972, it was the scene of Edmund Muskie's only really solid victory, but no one much cared. For 1976, the delegates chosen on the Republican side are likely to be mainly conservative organization types (the Illinois delegation wouldn't back Percy on the question of delegate apportionment in 1972).

As for the Democrats, Richard Daley is likely to have less to say than might be expected. Even in 1972, Muskie and McGovern candidates carried most of the suburban congressional districts, and there is plenty of reason to believe organizational choices can be beaten Downstate. That leaves the seven Chicago districts, and two of these—the Lake front 9th and the South Side 1st—are sure to elect independents, leaving the Daley organization just five districts worth. It is unlikely that the Daley people will be thrown out again as they were in 1972, which was done only because they insisted on opposing the McGovern forces on the California challenge. But Daley will no longer control 100-plus delegate votes as he did in the 1968 convention.

Census Data Pop. 11,113,976; 5.49% of U.S. total, 5th largest; Central city, 37%; suburban, 43%. Median family income, $10,957; 7th highest; families above $15,000: 26%; families below $3,000: 8%. Median years education, 12.1.

1974 Share of Federal Tax Burden $17,113,397,000; 6.39% of U.S. total, 3rd largest.

1974 Share of Federal Outlays $12,094,107,000; 4.48% of U.S. total, 5th largest. Per capita federal spending, $1088.

DOD	$1,360,544,000	16th (1.99%)	HEW	$4,934,489,000	4th (5.32%)
AEC	$169,849,000	6th (5.57%)	HUD	$71,255,000	2d (7.31%)
NASA	$7,551,000	20th (0.25%)	VA	$590,557,000	7th (4.32%)
DOT	$308,118,000	6th (3.64%)	EPA	$114,903,000	6th (3.65%)
DOC	$17,375,000	16th (1.08%)	RevS	$310,504,000	4th (5.11%)
DOI	$25,947,000	23d (1.05%)	Int.	$676,427,000	4th (3.29%)
USDA	$560,191,000	4th (4.50%)	Other	$2,946,397,000	

Economic Base Finance, insurance and real estate; machinery, especially construction and related machinery; electrical equipment and supplies, especially communication equipment; fabricated metal products; agriculture, notably corn, soybeans, hogs and cattle; food and kindred products; printing and publishing, especially commercial printing; primary metal industries, especially blast furnaces and basic steel products.

Political Line-up Governor, Dan Walker (D). Senators, Charles H. Percy (R) and Adlai E. Stevenson (D). Representatives, 24 (12 D, 11 R, and 1 vac.) State Senate (33 D and 26 R); State House (101 D, 75 R and 1 vac.).

The Voters

Registration 5,905,633 Total. No Party Registration.
Median voting age 43.
Employment profile White collar, 49%. Blue collar, 37%. Service, 12%. Farm, 2%.
Ethnic groups Black, 13%. Spanish, 3%. Total foreign stock, 20%. Germany, Poland, 3% each; Italy, 2%; UK, 1%.

Presidential vote

1972	Nixon (R)	2,788,179	(59%)
	McGovern (D)	1,913,472	(41%)
1968	Nixon (R)	2,174,774	(47%)
	Humphrey (D)	2,039,814	(44%)
	Wallace (AI)	390,958	(8%)

1972 Democratic Presidential Primary

Muskie	766,914	(63%)
McCarthy	444,260	(36%)
others	13,970	(1%)
preference only		

1972 Republican Presidential Primary

Nixon	32,550	(97%)
others	1,019	(3%)
preference only		

Sen. Charles H. Percy (R) Elected 1966, seat up 1978; b. Sept. 27, 1919, Pensacola, Fla.; home, Wilmette; U. of Chi., B.A. 1941; Christian Scientist.

Career Corp. Exec., Bell & Howell, Co., Pres. and Chf. Exec. Officer, 1949–61, Bd. Chm., 1961–66; Navy, WWII; Rep. of Pres. Eisenhower to pres. inaugurations in Peru and Bolivia, 1956; Repub. nominee for Gov., 1964.

Offices 1200 DSOB, 202-224-2152. Also 219 S. Dearborn St., Suite 1860, Chicago 60604, 312-353-4952, and Old P.O. Bldg., Rm. 117, Springfield 62701, 217-525-4442.

Committees

Government Operations (Ranking Member). Subcommittees: Oversight Procedures; Reports, Accounting and Management; Permanent Subcommittees on Investigations.

Foreign Relations (5th). Subcommittees: Far Eastern Affairs; Multinational Corporations; Near Eastern and South Asian Affairs; Western Hemisphere Affairs.

Joint Economic Committee (2d, Senate Side). Subcommittees: Consumer Economics; Economic Growth; International Economics; Priorities and Economy in Government; Urban Affairs.

Group Ratings

	ADA	COPE	LWV	RIPON	NFU	LCV	CFA	NAB	NSI	ACA
1974	82	78	100	100	69	93	55	33	44	19
1973	67	75	100	100	69	–	58	–	–	17
1972	60	88	100	100	89	57	100	55	44	41

Key Votes

1) No-Knock	AGN	8) Gov Abortn Aid	FOR	15) Consumer Prot Agy	FOR
2) Busing	ABS	9) Cut Mil Brass	FOR	16) Forced Psych Tests	ABS
3) No Fault	FOR	10) Gov Limousine	FOR	17) Fed Campaign Subs	FOR
4) F-111	FOR	11) RR Featherbed	FOR	18) Rhod Chrome Ban	FOR
5) Death Penalty	AGN	12) Handgun License	FOR	19) Open Legis Meetings	FOR
6) Foreign Aid	FOR	13) Less Troop Abrd	AGN	20) Strikers Food Stmps	ABS
7) Filibuster	AGN	14) Resume Turk Aid	AGN	21) Gov Info Disclosure	FOR

Election Results

1972 general:	Charles H. Percy (R)	2,867,078	(62%)	($1,408,822)
	Roman Pucinski (D)	1,721,031	(38%)	($335,482)
1972 primary:	Charles H. Percy (R), unopposed			
1966 general:	Charles H. Percy (R)	2,100,449	(56%)	
	Paul H. Douglas (D)	1,678,147	(44%)	

Sen. Adlai E. Stevenson III (D) Elected 1970, seat up 1980; b. Oct. 10, 1930, Chicago; home, Chicago; Harvard U., A.B. 1952, LL.B. 1957; Unitarian.

Career USMC, Korea; Clerk to Ill. State Supreme Ct. Justice, 1957–58; Practicing atty.; Ill. House of Reps., 1965–67; State Treasurer of Ill., 1967–70.

Offices 456 RSOB, 202-224-2854. Also 230 S. Dearborn St., Chicago 60604, 312-353-5420, and Fed. Bldg., Rm. 108, 600 E. Monroe St., Springfield 62691, 217-525-4126.

Committees

Banking, Housing and Urban Affairs (6th). Subcommittees: Financial Institutions; International Finance (Chairman); Oversight; Production and Stabilization.

Commerce (11th). Subcommittees: Aviation; The Consumer; Environment; Foreign Commerce and Tourism; Surface Transportation; Special Subcommittee on Science, Technology, and Commerce; Special Subcommittee to Study Transportation on the Great Lakes-St. Lawrence Seaway; Special Subcommittee on Oil and Gas Production and Distribution (Chairman).

The District of Columbia (3d).

Group Ratings

	ADA	COPE	LWV	RIPON	NFU	LCV	CFA	NAB	NSI	ACA
1974	100	73	100	57	94	79	100	33	0	11
1973	89	82	100	65	100	–	85	–	–	7
1972	80	89	100	80	100	96	100	27	20	10

Key Votes

1) No-Knock	AGN	8) Gov Abortn Aid	FOR	15) Consumer Prot Agy	FOR
2) Busing	FOR	9) Cut Mil Brass	FOR	16) Forced Psych Tests	FOR
3) No Fault	FOR	10) Gov Limousine	AGN	17) Fed Campaign Subs	AGN
4) F-111	AGN	11) RR Featherbed	FOR	18) Rhod Chrome Ban	FOR
5) Death Penalty	AGN	12) Handgun License	FOR	19) Open Legis Meetings	FOR
6) Foreign Aid	FOR	13) Less Troop Abrd	FOR	20) Strikers Food Stmps	FOR
7) Filibuster	AGN	14) Resume Turk Aid	AGN	21) Gov Info Disclosure	FOR

Election Results

1974 general:	Adlai E. Stevenson III (D)	1,811,496	(63%)	($757,329)
	George M. Burditt (R)	1,084,884	(37%)	($488,556)
1974 primary:	Adlai E. Stevenson III (D)	822,248	(83%)	
	W. Dakin Williams (D)	169,662	(17%)	

| 1970 general: | Adlai E. Stevenson III (D) .... | 2,065,054 | (58%) |
| | Ralph Tyler Smith (R) .... | 1,519,718 | (42%) |

Gov. Dan Walker (D) Elected 1972, term expires Jan. 1977; b. Aug. 6, 1922, Washington, D.C.; U.S. Naval Acad., B.A. 1945, Northwestern U., LL.B. 1950; Methodist.

Career Navy, 1945–47, Korea; Law Clerk, U.S. Supreme Ct. Chf. Justice Fred Vinson, 1951; Admin. Aide to Gov. Adlaie E. Stevenson II, 1952; Practicing atty., 1953–66; Dir., Pioneer Trust & Savings Bank, and Montgomery Ward Life Ins. Co., 1966–71.

Offices Springfield 62706, 217-782-6830.

Election Results

1972 general:	Daniel Walker (D)	2,371,303	(51%)
	Richard B. Ogilvie (R)	2,293,809	(49%)
1972 primary:	Daniel Walker (D)	735,193	(51%)
	Paul Simon (D)	694,000	(49%)

◆ ◆ ◆ ◆ ◆

FIRST DISTRICT

In the spring of 1972, police beat up two black men on the South Side of Chicago. It was not the first time such a thing had happened without justification nor, assuredly, would it be the last. But this particular gratuitous act would turn out to be one with major consequences for Chicago politics, more profound perhaps than those which flowed from the police riot outside the Conrad Hilton in August 1968. For the two black men who were beaten happened to be well-to-do dentists, prominent in the community. Quite naturally, they complained to their old friend, Congressman Ralph Metcalfe of the 1st district of Illinois—the recent successor to William L. Dawson, and the undisputed leader of the black portion of Richard J. Daley's Democratic machine.

Metcalfe was appalled. He was by no means a maverick or a militant, not after 16 years of loyal service on the Chicago City Council and his selection as Dawson's successor. At 62, he was still best known from his days as an Olympics sprinter, when he finished just behind Jesse Owens in the 1936 games in Berlin. But these beatings were just too much for Metcalfe to stomach. The Congressman demanded a meeting with Mayor Daley—at his, Metcalfe's, office. The Mayor refused to come. And so began Metcalfe's break with the Daley machine.

Like any medieval monarch, Daley is not in the habit of responding to summonses to appear at other people's courts, but in Metcalfe's case he might have been wise to do so. For as the clear political leader of the South Side, Metcalfe held—and holds—a position of key importance to the Chicago machine. The South Side is the largest black ghetto in the United States, larger than Harlem or Bedford-Stuyvesant. And voters here come out and vote in much larger proportions. In the early sixties, when Daley faced a strong challenge from the Republicans and was losing most of the city's white wards, it was the solid vote from the South Side that kept him in office. And until 1972, the South Side had remained strongly with the machine. Metcalfe himself, challenged by a well-known insurgent black Alderman, had won 71% of the vote in his 1970 primary and 91% in the general election. And in the 1972 general election, as in 1968, the 1st district provided a higher Democratic percentage and majority than any other congressional district in the nation.

But even before the dentists were beaten up, the South Side—and Metcalfe—were growing restive with the machine. In 1972, Daley had first endorsed State's Attorney Edward Hanrahan for renomination. The black community hated Hanrahan for his role in a raid that left two Black Panther leaders dead. Metcalfe balked, and Daley—fearful of losing the South Side majorities for his other candidates—withdrew the Hanrahan endorsement. Hanrahan won the primary anyway; but in the general election, he lost most of the South Side wards to the winner, Republican Bernard Carey.

The same wards also went for Republican Senator Charles Percy over his challenger Roman Pucinski, whose campaign catered to the backlash, antibusing vote. During that campaign,

Metcalfe watched benignly as the Rev. Jesse Jackson led a massive ticket-splitting campaign, and the Congressman pointedly refused to endorse Hanrahan—a break with machine discipline which would have been unthinkable two years before. It was the first time the South Side had split its ticket to any appreciable extent—and there was more ticket-splitting here that year than anywhere else in Illinois.

But that was only the beginning of Metcalfe's rebellion. When Daley himself came up for renomination in 1975, Metcalfe endorsed rebel Alderman William Singer. One may gauge Daley's reaction by remembering that machine judges had for two years been trying to have Singer put in jail for having defied a court order and successfully challenged Daley and his machine delegates at the 1972 Democratic national convention. Jackson, Metcalfe's only rival as an independent black political leader in Chicago, endorsed a black candidate, who won less than 10% of the total vote; as between the two, it was clearly a victory for the Congressman.

About the only bar to Metcalfe's continued influence in Chicago politics is his age. He is past 65 now, and though a machine man like Dawson could maintain power when his health was gone, it is harder to do that as an insurgent. The fact that 42% of Chicago Democrats voted against Daley in 1975 indicates that the machine's days are numbered. Not too far in the future there will be a massive battle for control of the city government, and Congressman Ralph Metcalfe and the newly independent voters of the South Side will likely play a major role in determining the outcome.

Census Data   Pop. 462,434. Central city, 100%; suburban, 0%. Median family income, $8,373; families above $15,000: 17%; families below $3,000: 14%.   Median years education, 11.5.

The Voters

Median voting age 42.
Employment profile White collar, 46%. Blue collar, 35%. Service, 19%. Farm, –%.
Ethnic groups Black, 89%. Spanish, 1%. Total foreign stock, 5%.

Presidential vote

1972	Nixon (R)	16,998	(10%)
	McGovern (D)	145,003	(90%)
1968	Nixon (R)	16,308	(9%)
	Humphrey (D)	168,445	(90%)
	Wallace (AI)	3,249	(2%)

Rep. Ralph H. Metcalfe (D) Elected 1970; b. May 30, 1910, Atlanta Ga.; home, Chicago; Marquette U., Ph. B, 1936, U. of So. Cal., M. A. 1939; Catholic.

Career Coach and Instructor, Xavier U., 1936–42; Army, WWII; Dir. of Civil Rights for Chi. Comm. on Human Relations, 1945; Ill. St. Athletic Commissioner, 1949–52; Chi. City Cncl., 1955–70.

Offices 322CHOB, 202-225-4372. Also 454 E. 79th St., Chicago 60604, 312-651-4200.

Committees

Interstate and Foreign Commerce (16th). Subcommittees: Consumer Protection and Finance; Transportation and Commerce.

Merchant Marine and Fisheries (12th). Subcommittees: Merchant Marine; Panama Canal (Chairman).

Group Ratings

	ADA	COPE	LWV	RIPON	NFU	LCV	CFA	NAB	NSI	ACA
1974	95	90	92	50	100	88	92	20	14	0
1973	95	100	80	80	100	69	88	–	–	5
1972	31	100	90	60	86	52	–	10	0	7

Key Votes

1) Foreign Aid	FOR	6) Gov Abortn Aid	FOR	11) Pub Cong Election $	FOR
2) Busing	FOR	7) Coed Phys Ed	FOR	12) Turkish Arms Cutoff	FOR
3) ABM	AGN	8) Pov Lawyer Gag	ABS	13) Youth Camp Regs	ABS
4) B-1 Bomber	AGN	9) Pub Trans Sub	FOR	14) Strip Mine Veto	AGN
5) Nerve Gas	AGN	10) EZ Voter Regis	FOR	15) Farm Bill Veto	FOR

Election Results

1974 general:	Ralph H. Metcalfe (D)	75,206	(94%)	($37,900)
	Oscar H. Haynes (R)	4,399	(6%)	($833)
1974 primary:	Ralph H. Metcalfe (D), unopposed			
1972 general:	Ralph H. Metcalfe (D)	136,755	(91%)	($9,861)
	Louis H. Coggs (R)	12,877	(9%)	($1,235)

◆ ◆ ◆ ◆ ◆

SECOND DISTRICT

On the far South Side of Chicago, where the Calumet River has been deepened to accommodate the huge freighters of the Great Lakes, are the city's giant steel mills, ones that rival those of nearby Gary in size and stark grandeur. This part of Chicago is the heart of the city's heavy industry and has been since the Industrial Revolution first came to the Midwest. This same area was also the site of the Pullman strike of 1893, during which the laissez-faire President Cleveland sent in federal troops to uphold the rights of private capital. The Calumet steel mills neatly separate the 2d congressional district of Illinois into two distinct parts. To the east, along lakefront, are the large apartments and, behind them, comfortable houses in what used to be a predominantly Jewish neighborhood; to the north is the South Side black ghetto. West of the steel mills are middle-class neighborhoods, most of them inhabited by the members of various ethnic groups that have for so long contributed most of the labor that keeps the mills going.

Both parts of the 2d district have one thing in common: they have been the site of Chicago's—and probably the nation's—most rapid massive neighborhood racial change. In 1960, less than 20% of the residents of the current 2d district were black; in 1970, 40% were, and today blacks probably form a majority. Blockbusting techniques are a way of life here, and the first For Sale sign on a white block can still trigger a spasm of selling. Naturally, this change has affected the area's politics. Back in 1966 and 1968, Republican candidates, working on the fears of white voters, nearly captured the old 3d district, which included most of the territory now within the 2d. By 1970, however, enough blacks had moved in, and begun to vote, to push the Democratic percentage back up again. Thus McGovern won 66% of the vote in the same area where Humphrey could only take 56%.

The current Congressman from the 2d is Democrat Morgan Murphy, who won the old 3d district in 1970. Before his election, Murphy, son of the former head of Chicago's Commonwealth Edison, held a number of offices considered within the power of Mayor Daley's machine. As a machine loyalist, he beat a black candidate in the 1970 primary and then won the general election easily. In his first term in the House, Murphy attracted attention for exposing the wide extent of heroin addiction among American servicemen in Vietnam. In his second term, as a member of the Rules Committee, he worked more quietly; heeding the demands of building trades unionists, his vote helped to kill the federal land use bill in Rules.

The increasing black population in the 2d may represent a threat to Murphy's tenure, but so far he has only benefitted from the high Democratic percentages blacks help to produce. In 1974, he won 88% of the vote in the general election, and almost as much against a hapless primary opponent. In 1970, the machine was strong enough to win him half the black votes in the primary against a black candidate; whether this could happen again, if Murphy faced a creditable black challenger, is not clear.

Census Data Pop. 464,792. Central city, 100%; suburban, 0%. Median family income, $11,147; families above $15,000: 26%; families below $3,000: 7%. Median years education, 11.8.

The Voters

Median voting age 43.
Employment profile White collar, 48%. Blue collar, 39%. Service, 13%. Farm, –%.
Ethnic groups Black, 40%. Spanish, 5%. Total foreign stock, 25%. Poland, 4%; Italy, Ireland, Germany, 2% each; Yugoslavia, Sweden, 1% each.

Presidential vote

1972	Nixon (R)	60,220	(34%)
	McGovern (D)	116,534	(66%)
1968	Nixon (R)	66,747	(34%)
	Humphrey (D)	109,468	(56%)
	Wallace (AI)	20,658	(10%)

Rep. Morgan F. Murphy (D) Elected 1970; b. Apr. 16, 1932, Chicago; home, Chicago; Northwestern U., B.S. 1955, De Paul U., J.D. 1962; Catholic.

Career USMC, 1955–58; Admin. Asst. to Circuit Court Clerk, 1958–61; Practicing atty., 1962–70; Chm., Govt. Div., Crusade of Mercy, 1967–70.

Offices 137 CHOB, 202-225-3406. Also 1640 Dirksen Bldg., 219 S. Dearborn St., Chicago 60604, 312-353-5390

Committees

Rules (8th).

Group Ratings

	ADA	COPE	LWV	RIPON	NFU	LCV	CFA	NAB	NSI	ACA
1974	50	91	55	50	77	53	67	33	44	31
1973	82	100	92	67	100	74	86	–	–	4
1972	63	90	80	50	86	57	0	18	60	22

Key Votes

1) Foreign Aid	FOR	6) Gov Abortn Aid	AGN	11) Pub Cong Election $	AGN
2) Busing	AGN	7) Coed Phys Ed	AGN	12) Turkish Arms Cutoff	FOR
3) ABM	AGN	8) Pov Lawyer Gag	AGN	13) Youth Camp Regs	FOR
4) B-1 Bomber	AGN	9) Pub Trans Sub	FOR	14) Strip Mine Veto	AGN
5) Nerve Gas	FOR	10) EZ Voter Regis	FOR	15) Farm Bill Veto	AGN

Election Results

1974 general:	Morgan F. Murphy (D)	65,812	(88%)	($12,299)
	James J. Ginderske (R)	9,386	(12%)	($350)
1974 primary:	Morgan F. Murphy (D)	34,906	(79%)	
	Pery H. Hutchinson (D)	9,263	(21%)	
1972 general:	Morgan F. Murphy (D)	115,306	(75%)	($21,510)
	James E. Doyle (R)	38,391	(25%)	($3,044)

◆ ◆ ◆ ◆ ◆

THIRD DISTRICT

The 3d congressional district of Illinois, created by the state Supreme Court's redistricting plan in 1972, consists of the close-in southwest suburbs of the city plus about two wards' worth of Chicago itself. If one had to generalize about the area, one might say that this is the place where the whites from the older, ethnic neighborhoods of South Side Chicago have gone, either in flight as blacks move into their neighborhoods, or simply as they grow up and have to move some place to start their own families. There are small black ghettoes here in the towns of Markham and Harvey, but the overall ethnic tone is Irish-American, the group which always dominated the southwest Chicago wards until the blacks moved in. But not everyone is Irish; the area is an ethnic melting pot with Polish-, Italian-, Lithuanian-, German-, Dutch-, Swedish-, and Czech-Americans represented in significant numbers. The people here are much more likely to hold white-collar rather than blue-collar jobs, but one suspects the situation for their parents was just the reverse. So these are people whose hold on middle-class status is just a little precarious, their recent prosperity notwithstanding.

The 3d district is one of those areas that are crucial to the outcome of Cook County elections which, contrary to outsiders' preconceptions, are not automatically won by Mayor Daley's Democrats. Indeed, the Chicago suburbs taken as a whole, are more conservative and Republican than those of any other major city but Los Angeles. In numerous recent years Republicans, with huge suburban pluralities, have been able to beat Daley Democrats in races for patronge-rich offices for County Board President and Sheriff in 1966, for example, and State's Attorney in 1972. One Republican who won such a race is Robert P. Hanrahan (no relation to former State's Attorney Edward Hanrahan), who was elected County Superintendent of Schools. Then a young 32, Hanrahan had a good Irish name and good future prospects. He was beaten for reelection in the Democratic year of 1970, but two years later he ran for and won the new 3d district seat created by the Republican majority on the Supreme Court.

From there on in, it probably should have been easy for Hanrahan to hold that office, what with all the advantages congressional incumbents have these days. But perhaps he found the position a little too comfortable, driving around Washington in his Cadillac and maintaining his main home office in the faraway Chicago Loop rather than in the district. At any rate, Hanrahan found himself in trouble as Senator Adlai Stevenson was carrying this district. To just about everyone's surprise, 30-year-old Democrat Martin Russo beat Hanrahan by a 53-47 margin. Russo is a graduate of DePaul Law School (Daley's alma mater) and was an Assistant State's Attorney under Edward Hanrahan; he may be counted as a machine loyalist. Probably this will be a closely contested district in 1976.

Census Data   Pop. 461,180. Central city, 27%; suburban, 73%. Median family income, $12,762; families above $15,000: 34%; families below $3,000: 4%. Median years education, 12.2.

The Voters

Median voting age 44.
Employment profile White collar, 53%. Blue collar, 37%. Service, 10%. Farm, –%.
Ethnic groups Black, 5%. Spanish, 2%. Total foreign stock, 28%. Poland, 4%; Ireland, Germany, Italy, 3% each; Lithuania, UK, 2% each; Netherlands, Sweden, Czechoslovakia, 1% each.

Presidential vote

1972	Nixon (R)	155,092	(70%)
	McGovern (D)	65,226	(30%)
1968	Nixon (R)	105,041	(52%)
	Humphrey (D)	69,085	(34%)
	Wallace (AI)	28,019	(14%)

Rep. Martin A. Russo (D) Elected 1974; b. Jan. 23, 1944, Chicago; home, South Holland; De Paul U., B.S. 1965, J.D. 1967; Catholic.

Career Law Clerk for Ill. Appellate Ct. Judge John V. McCormack, 1967–68; Practicing atty.; Cook Co. Asst. States Atty., 1971–73.

Offices 128 CHOB, 202-225-5736. Also 468 Fed. Bldg., 219 S. Dearborn St. Chicago 60604, 213-353-8093.

Committees

Judiciary (23d). Subcommittees: Criminal Justice; Immigration, Citizenship and International Law.

Small Business (21st). Subcommittees: Activities of Regulatory Agencies; Energy and Environment.

Group Ratings: Newly Elected

Key Votes

1) Foreign Aid	FOR	6) Gov Abortn Aid	NE	11) Pub Cong Election $	NE
2) Busing	NE	7) Coed Phys Ed	AGN	12) Turkish Arms Cutoff	NE
3) ABM	NE	8) Pov Lawyer Gag	NE	13) Youth Camp Regs	FOR
4) B-1 Bomber	AGN	9) Pub Trans Sub	NE	14) Strip Mine Veto	AGN
5) Nerve Gas	NE	10) EZ Voter Regis	NE	15) Farm Bill Veto	FOR

Election Results

1974 general:	Martin A. Russo (D)	65,336	(53%)	($79,420)
	Robert P. Hanrahan (R)	58,891	(47%)	($40,912)
1974 primary:	Martin A. Russo (D), unopposed			

◆ ◆ ◆ ◆ ◆

FOURTH DISTRICT

The 4th congressional district of Illinois is the southwest corner of Cook County. The district includes the most Republican part of what is supposed to be one of the nation's prime Democratic counties. It really isn't, because the usually Republican suburbs now cast 43% of the County's total votes; as Chicago's population continues to fall, and the suburbs gain, that percentage is sure to rise even more in the next few elections. Chicago's suburbs radiate from the city like spokes on a wheel, and the 4th district contains two widely separated built-up areas, one of which extends almost due south of the city, the other directly west. Nevertheless, the 4th is an area of rather homogeneous political complexion. By most social and economic indicators, it resembles the neighboring 3d district; the 4th is a shade richer and a shade less ethnic. All of which surely means that the people here are sometimes just another generation removed from the ancestral immigrants who came to live in Chicago's slums.

The 4th is a very Republican district—one of about 65 of the current seats which went for Barry Goldwater in 1964. Its Congressman since 1958, Edward J. Derwinski, is a conservative proudly in the Goldwater mold. He is one of the last Congressmen on the Hill to retain a crew cut. Derwinski came to the House, back in 1958 when crew cuts were the style, as a very young man of 32. As a result of his seniority, he is now the ranking Republican on the House Post Office and Civil Service Committee. This is the body which set up the current federal-pay-raise legislation; it also passes on a seemingly endless number of questions about medical insurance and other fringe benefits. As a no-nonsense conservative, with few federal employees in his district, Derwinski can be expected to set himself against the 15-year trend of rapidly increasing federal salaries though not one suspects with much luck. Still only 50, Derwinski has the makings of an authentic congressional curmudgeon, perhaps along the lines of H. R. Gross of Iowa, whom he succeeded in the Post Office Committee slot.

Census Data Pop. 464,452. Central city, 0%; suburban, 100%. Median family income, $13,451; families above $15,000: 39%; families below $3,000: 3%. Median years education, 12.4.

The Voters

Median voting age 42.
Employment profile White collar, 56%. Blue collar, 35%. Service, 9%. Farm, –%.
Ethnic groups Black, 4%. Spanish, 2%. Total foreign stock, 23%. Poland, Germany, Italy, 3% each; Czechoslovakia, 2%; UK, Ireland, Canada, 1% each.

Presidential vote

1972	Nixon (R)	142,635	(71%)
	McGovern (D)	57,082	(29%)
1968	Nixon (R)	104,716	(56%)
	Humphrey (D)	59,200	(32%)
	Wallace (AI)	22,737	(12%)

Rep. Edward J. Derwinski (R) Elected 1958; b. Sept. 15, 1926, Chicago; home, Flossmoor; Loyola U., B.S. 1951; Catholic.

Career Ill. House of Reps., 1957–58; Mbr., U.S. Delegation to U.N., 1971.

Offices 1401 LHOB, 202-225-3961. Also 9838 S. Roberts Rd., Palos Hills 60465, 312-598-6700.

Committees

International Relations (2d). Subcommittees: International Organizations; Oversight.

Post Office and Civil Service Ranking Member. Subcommittees: Manpower and Civil Service.

Group Ratings

	ADA	COPE	LWV	RIPON	NFU	LCV	CFA	NAB	NSI	ACA
1974	11	0	45	50	40	40	17	78	100	69
1973	13	9	40	62	16	29	29	–	–	100
1972	6	27	33	64	33	0	0	100	100	80

Key Votes

1) Foreign Aid	AGN	6) Gov Abortn Aid	AGN	11) Pub Cong Election $	AGN
2) Busing	AGN	7) Coed Phys Ed	AGN	12) Turkish Arms Cutoff	FOR
3) ABM	FOR	8) Pov Lawyer Gag	FOR	13) Youth Camp Regs	FOR
4) B-1 Bomber	FOR	9) Pub Trans Sub	AGN	14) Strip Mine Veto	FOR
5) Nerve Gas	FOR	10) EZ Voter Regis	AGN	15) Farm Bill Veto	FOR

Election Results

1974 general:	Edward J. Derwinski (R)	68,428	(59%)	($41,646)
	Ronald A. Rodger (D)	47,096	(41%)	($18,301)
1974 primary:	Edward J. Derwinski (R), unopposed			
1972 general:	Edward J. Derwinski (R)	141,402	(71%)	($17,896)
	C. F. Dore (D)	59,057	(29%)	($11,342)

◆ ◆ ◆ ◆ ◆

FIFTH DISTRICT

In an unpretentious but reportedly comfortable house on the 3500 block of South Lowe Avenue in the 11th ward and the 5th congressional district in Chicago lives the most powerful ward committeeman in the United States. He is a man whose advice has been routinely sought by Presidents and Senators and Governors. For more than 20 years he has held other important offices, like Chairman of the Cook County Democratic Committee and Mayor of the City of Chicago. His name is Richard J. Daley, and no matter how he may be scorned or ridiculed or hated elsewhere, he is loved and admired in the 11th ward of Chicago.

Chicago is a city of neighborhoods, and Daley's neighborhood, Bridgeport, is typical both of the 11th ward and of the 5th district of which it is a part. More than 30% of the 5th's residents are black, but virtually all of them live at the fringes of the district, in the South Side or West Side ghettoes; the heart of the 5th, neighborhoods like Bridgeport, are definitely all white. The people here live, as Daley has all his life, in these neighborhoods with the dumpy looking frame houses and the sparkling clean sidewalks. On a nice day a visitor driving down South Lowe can see dozens of children with crisp Irish faces, playing noisily but always taking care not to injure the closely-tended manicured lawns. Blacks moving out from the center of the city have not found neighborhoods like Bridgeport hospitable (to say the least), and have avoided them. This choice urban property, not far from the Loop, thus remains the province of the tightly-knit white communities which, it seems, have always lived here. If there is something insular and anachronistic about these neighborhoods and something intolerant, there is also a vitality and rootedness unknown in the shopping center land of suburban America.

Very early in life, children in Bridgeport are taught their basic loyalties: the United States of America, the Roman Catholic Church, and the Democratic Party. But on occasion even some of these loyalties have been called into doubt. In the sixties, the people here lined the streets to watch the busloads of delegates be shepherded into the amphitheater where the Democratic national convention was being conducted. They did not, apparently, like what they saw: the national party appeared to them too sympathetic to demonstrators who did not properly respect the flag, and to blacks who would not respect established traditions. Hubert Humphrey got only 61% of the votes in this traditionally Democratic area, and George McGovern a rock-bottom 53%.

But with the revelations of Watergate and the depression/recession, the voters of the 5th district have returned to the Democratic Party with a vengeance; Senator Adlai Stevenson, never a particular favorite here in the past, received 86% of the district's vote in 1974. A similar percentage was amassed, one can be sure without much personal campaigning, by 78-year-old Congressman John Kluczynski, known as Johnny Klu to distinguish him from his brother Thomas C. "Tommy Klu" Kluczynski, Associate Justice of the Illinois Supreme Court. Johnny Klu had first been elected to Congress in 1950 and had risen to the chairmanship of the Roads Subcommittee. There he was a staunch ally of the highway lobby and opposed any effort to use gas tax money for mass transit. His position shifted, however, when the Chicago Transit Authority ran into trouble and needed an injection of cash; the Mayor presumably got on the phone and told him to stop voting like a Downstater. So Kluczynski had to abandon his highway builder friends; at about the same time, the power of his chairmanship of the Select Committee on the House Restaurant evaporated when Wayne Hays of Ohio decided to take over all its functions. It was, as it turned out, an unhappy end to a long career, for Johnny Klu, fresh from his largest victory percentage ever, died in February 1975.

The machine quickly chose the next Congressman, state Representative John Fary; the people ratified the choice in a 1975 special election. There is no more prospect for political change here in the 5th district than there is a chance that Bridgeport will somehow be transformed into some other kind of community. This is a kind of politics—and way of life—that has been vanishing in America these last 30 years, but it is still very much alive in this part of Chicago.

Census Data Pop. 465,990. Central city, 100%; suburban, 0%. Median family income, $9,881; families above $15,000: 20%; families below $3,000: 10%. Median years education, 10.2.

The Voters

Median voting age 44.
Employment profile White collar, 40%. Blue collar, 47%. Service, 13%. Farm, –%.
Ethnic groups Black, 31%. Spanish, 6%. Total foreign stock, 30%. Poland, 10%; Italy, Czechoslovakia, Lithuania, Germany, Ireland, 2% each; Yugoslavia, 1%.

Presidential vote

1972	Nixon (R)	86,644	(47%)
	McGovern (D)	96,012	(53%)
1968	Nixon (R)	55,992	(28%)
	Humphrey (D)	119,512	(61%)
	Wallace (AI)	21,366	(11%)

Group Ratings: Newly Elected

◆ ◆ ◆ ◆ ◆

SIXTH DISTRICT

The 6th congressional district is yet another suburban Chicago constituency. These are not the new suburbs, with their gleaming but pasteboardy houses stuck up on treeless lots one after another; it is, mostly, a series of older, established communities west and northwest of Chicago. Oak Park for one was the boyhood home of Ernest Hemingway; it is still a quiet middle-class community lying just across the city limits from part of the West Side Chicago ghetto. To the south, the very different town of Cicero has scarcely changed either since the thirties, when it was a Syndicate stronghold and bedroom community for Czechs and other Eastern European factory workers. In the mid-sixties, Cicero made headlines and TV footage when its citizens forcibly resisted the efforts of Martin Luther King to integrate the city. Cicero's politics is dominated by an anachronism from the 1920's: a working class, ethnic-based Republican machine. In just about every respect, Cicero resembles Chicago neighborhoods like Bridgeport (see Illinois 5), but for some reason—perhaps just because it is a suburb and Bridgeport is part of the city—the partisan political patterns here are just the opposite.

On the map, the remainder of the 6th district looks like a patchwork quilt of towns whose names are various combinations of "Park", "River," and "Forest," sometimes appended to more distinctive names. But most of these communities can claim some special quality. Maywood, for example, has a large black community, and Melrose Park is predominantly Italian-American. (Indeed, this is the most Italian of all of Illinois's districts; in the East, Italians have tended to stay in the central cities, but here they have long since moved out to the suburbs.) Then there is Rosemont, a tiny place 20 years ago situated near a dusty airfield named after someone called O'Hare. Since that time, primarily through the efforts of Richard J. Daley, O'Hare has become the busiest airport in the world, and little Rosemont has sprouted a couple of dozen high-rise motels and office buildings. It is perhaps the premier example of the kind of businessman's meeting place culture which has grown up around our major airports

From 1956 to 1974, the 6th's Congressman was Harold R. Collier, a classically conservative Cook County Republican. Collier was one of those Congressmen who surprised many observers by retiring in 1974. He was just 59, had already reached the second ranking Republican position on Ways and Means, and seemed to have a safe district. Apparently he was just tired of the job and the increasing pressure—increasing as bodies like Ways and Means were coming under closer and closer scrutiny. Plus he might have been scared by his prospective opponent for 1974, former Cook County State's Attorney Edward Hanrahan. Hanrahan was the man who had got into trouble by authorizing the raid that led to the death of two Black Panther leaders in 1971; he had been defeated in 1972 largely for that reason. But in that same election, he had done very well in the 6th; against a strong Republican candidate, he had about 48% of the vote.

At any rate, Collier retired, and most observers thought Hanrahan, a conservative Democrat in a conservative district and a Democratic year, had it locked. They reckoned without the hard work of Republican candidate Henry Hyde. Hyde was Majority Leader of the Illinois General Assembly, a conservative Republican and defender of the suburbs, and almost as well-known in the district as Hanrahan. Hanrahan's luck ran out, and Hyde won by a 53–47 margin. As one of the relatively few Republican freshmen, Hyde was able to get choice committee assignments on Banking and Currency and Judiciary; at 52, he is likely to be around for a long time provided he does not suddenly decide, as Collier did, to give it all up.

Census Data Pop. 461,360. Central city, 0%; suburban, 100%. Median family income, $12,700; families above $15,000: 35%; families below $3,000: 4%. Median years education, 12.2.

The Voters

Median voting age 45.
Employment profile White collar, 55%. Blue collar, 36%. Service, 9%. Farm, –%.
Ethnic groups Black, 3%. Spanish, 2%. Total foreign stock, 34%. Italy, 7%; Poland, Germany, Czechoslovakia, 4% each; Ireland, 2%; UK, Canada, Austria, 1% each.

Presidential vote

1972	Nixon (R)	147,633	(69%)
	McGovern (D)	66,815	(31%)
1968	Nixon (R)	119,634	(55%)
	Humphrey (D)	73,583	(34%)
	Wallace (AI)	23,249	(11%)

Rep. Henry J. Hyde (R) Elected 1974; b. Apr. 18, 1924, Chicago; home, Park Ridge; Georgetown U., B.S. 1947, Loyola U., J.D. 1949.

Career Navy, WWII; Practicing atty., 1950–75; Ill. House of Reps., 1967–74, Maj. Ldr., 1971–72.

Offices 1206 LHOB, 202-225-4561. Also Rm. 220, Oak Park P.O. Bldg., 901 Lake St., Oak Park 60301, 312-383-6881.

Committees

Banking, Currency and Housing (11th). Subcommittees: Financial Institutions Supervision, Regulation and Insurance; International Development Institutions and Finance; International Trade, Investment and Monetary Policy.

Judiciary (10th). Subcommittees: Criminal Justice.

Group Ratings: Newly Elected

Key Votes

1) Foreign Aid	FOR	6) Gov Abortn Aid	NE	11) Pub Cong Election $	NE
2) Busing	NE	7) Coed Phys Ed	AGN	12) Turkish Arms Cutoff	NE
3) ABM	NE	8) Pov Lawyer Gag	NE	13) Youth Camp Regs	AGN
4) B-1 Bomber	FOR	9) Pub Trans Sub	NE	14) Strip Mine Veto	FOR
5) Nerve Gas	NE	10) EZ Voter Regis	NE	15) Farm Bill Veto	FOR

Election Results

1974 general:	Henry J. Hyde (R)	66,027	(53%)	($175,087)
	Edward V. Hanrahan (D)	57,654	(47%)	($66,284)
1974 primary:	Henry J. Hyde (R)	15,192	(49%)	
	Roy C. Pechous (R)	7,484	(24%)	
	Four others (R)	8,526	(27%)	

◆ ◆ ◆ ◆ ◆

SEVENTH DISTRICT

The Loop is what one thinks of when one thinks of Chicago. Here, where high-rise construction was pioneered, stand the city's giant skyscrapers, including the new Sears and Roebuck Building—the world's tallest. Chicago also means the Near North Side, with its huge, well-designed high-rise apartment buildings along Lake Michigan and, behind them, alternately smart and raunchy shopping streets. This is all part of Illinois's 7th congressional district—the glamorous part, the part best known to the outside world. But beyond the Chicago River and the miles of railroad track—Chicago is still the nation's biggest rail center—lies the grim West Side ghetto. As one goes inland from the lakefront, the territory is at first a potpourri: the nation's largest skid row on West Madison, followed by odd settlements of American Indians and Appalachians. Then comes the West Side ghetto, which casts the bulk of the votes here in the 7th district.

The West Side is machine country. The black community here is more newly-arrived, less middle-class, and less well-organized than the blacks on the South Side (see Illinois 1). Some wards that are virtually 100% black still elect Jewish or Italian ward committeemen—the last vestige of their onetime ethnic composition. When the South Side wards broke party lines in 1972 and voted for Republicans Charles Percy for Senate and Bernard Carey for State's Attorney, the West Side stayed true to the machine, casting huge Democratic majorities for all offices.

Of all of Chicago's 50 wards, the 24th on the far West Side usually turns in the highest Democratic percentages—96% for George McGovern in 1972, for example. (Interestingly, the all-black 24th ward sits right next to all-white, heavily Republican Cicero.) In 1970, George W. Collins, then 24th ward Alderman, became Chicago's second black Congressman. In December 1972, Collins was killed in an airplane crash that also took the life of Dorothy Hunt, of Watergate fame. Collins' successor in Congress is his widow, Cardiss Collins, who won a special election in

June 1973. Her margin was so large and her opposition so negligible (her Republican opponent was Lar Daly, who likes to show up on TV talk shows wearing an Uncle Sam suit) that it appears that machine control on the West Side is undisputed. In the House, Collins can be counted as a solid vote for the Daley machine.

Census Data Pop. 464,283. Central city, 100%; suburban, 0%. Median family income, $7,536; families above $15,000: 13%; families below $3,000: 16%. Median years education, 9.7.

The Voters

Median voting age 39.
Employment profile White collar, 35%. Blue collar, 49%. Service, 16%. Farm, –%.
Ethnic groups Black, 55%. Spanish, 17%. Total foreign stock, 22%. Poland, 4%; Italy, 2%; USSR, 1%.

Presidential vote

1972	Nixon (R)	33,266	(26%)
	McGovern (D)	93,318	(74%)
1968	Nixon (R)	22,768	(15%)
	Humphrey (D)	126,222	(81%)
	Wallace (AI)	6,271	(4%)

Rep. Cardiss Collins (D) Elected June 5, 1973; b. Sept. 24, 1931, St. Louis, Mo.; home, Chicago; Northwestern U.; Baptist.

Career Stenographer, Ill. Dept. of Labor; Secy., accountant, and revenue auditor, Ill. Dept. of Revenue.

Offices 1123 LHOB, 202-225-5006. Also 219 S. Dearborn St., Suite 1632, Chicago 60604, 312-353-5754.

Committees

Government Operations (17th). Subcommittees: Commerce, Consumer, and Monetary Affairs; Government Activities and Transportation.

International Relations (19th). Subcommittees: International Organizations; International Resources, Food, and Energy.

Group Ratings

	ADA	COPE	LWV	RIPON	NFU	LCV	CFA	NAB	NSI	ACA
1974	89	90	83	50	77	81	92	18	20	7
1973	100	100	90	100	100	75	100	–	–	6

Key Votes

1) Foreign Aid	FOR	6) Gov Abortn Aid	FOR	11) Pub Cong Election $	FOR
2) Busing	FOR	7) Coed Phys Ed	FOR	12) Turkish Arms Cutoff	FOR
3) ABM	AGN	8) Pov Lawyer Gag	AGN	13) Youth Camp Regs	FOR
4) B-1 Bomber	AGN	9) Pub Trans Sub	FOR	14) Strip Mine Veto	AGN
5) Nerve Gas	AGN	10) EZ Voter Regis	FOR	15) Farm Bill Veto	FOR

Election Results

1974 general:	Cardiss Collins (D)	63,962	(88%)	($7,292)
	Donald L. Metzger (R)	8,800	(12%)	($18,822)
1974 primary:	Cardiss Collins (D), unopposed			
1973 special:	Cardiss Collins (D)	33,875	(93%)	(NA)
	Angel Moreno (Ind.)	1,429	(4%)	(NA)
	Lar Daly (R)	1,311	(4%)	(NA)

◆ ◆ ◆ ◆ ◆

EIGHTH DISTRICT

The 8th district of Illinois is part of the North and Northwest sides of Chicago. This is middle- and lower-middle-class country in decline, with strip commercial developments and neighborhoods of one- and two-family houses which probably ought to have been painted last year. Most of the district is resolutely all white, though it does include portions of the West Side ghetto. The atmosphere here is still decidedly ethnic, and the 8th is the heart of Chicago's North Side Polish community. (Altogether, it has the fourth highest concentration of Polish-Americans of any district in the nation.) Its residents, less prosperous than their cousins in the adjoining 11th district, are closer to the old country ways and more dependent on their ward organizations. This is the kind of urban area which many young middle-Americans, in their rush to the curved-street subdivisions and shopping centers of suburbia, are leaving behind. But it is still an area of considerable import in Chicago, and it is one which has not abandoned its ancestral allegiance to the Democratic Party, even in the Republican years of 1966, 1968, and 1972.

Of all of the Chicago Congressmen who belong to the Daley bloc in Congress, the clear and undoubted leader is Dan Rostenkowski, Representative from the 8th district. For many years Rostenkowski was the youngest member of the city's delegation, and though he has served since 1958 he is still under 50. In recognition of his status, House Democrats awarded him a seat on the Ways and Means Committee and, in 1968, elected him Democratic Caucus Chairman.

But somehow Rostenkowski has never achieved the leadership role he was obviously meant to fill. In 1970, a surprise offensive by Olin "Tiger" Teague of Texas ousted him from the Caucus Chairman post. Ways and Means lost much of its traditional clout in 1973 when House Democrats forced the Rules Committee to report out some of its bills with an open rule—that is, allowing amendment on the floor. And now Rostenkowski looks very much like a man whom time has passed by. The Caucus Chairman post he was once so chagrined to lose now belongs to left liberal Phillip Burton of San Francisco. Wilbur Mills, whom Rostenkowski admired, has been ousted from the chairmanship of Ways and Means. And though Rostenkowski himself is now fourth in seniority on that still powerful committee, that is no guarantee of the chairmanship some day, in light of House Democrats' increasing proclivity to throw out committee chairmen. Indeed, after Burton's elevation and the defeat of several committee chairmen in 1975, Rostenkowski could not hide his anger; as a man who has always sought dutifully to climb the ladders prescribed by his leaders, he was dismayed to find that the newcomers could just push them down. He still may be an important man in the House some day—but the chances are not as certain as they were just a few years ago.

Census Data   Pop. 459,902. Central city, 100%; suburban, 0%. Median family income, $9,867; families above $15,000: 20%; families below $3,000: 9%. Median years education, 10.1.

The Voters

Median voting age 42.
Employment profile White collar, 39%. Blue collar, 49%. Service, 12%. Farm, –%.
Ethnic groups Black, 18%. Spanish, 13%. Total foreign stock, 35%. Poland, 9%; Italy, 6%; Germany, 3%; Ireland, 2%; Greece, 1%.

Presidential vote

1972	Nixon (R)	71,343	(44%)
	McGovern (D)	90,093	(56%)
1968	Nixon (R)	65,086	(36%)
	Humphrey (D)	101,161	(55%)
	Wallace (AI)	16,056	(9%)

Rep. Dan Rostenkowski (D) Elected 1958; b. Jan. 2, 1928, Chicago; home, Chicago; Loyola U., 1948–51; Catholic.

Career Army, Korea; Ill. House of Reps., 1953–55; Ill. Senate, 1955–59.

Offices 2185 RHOB, 202-225-4061. Also 2148 N. Damen Ave., Chicago 60647, 312-276-6000.

Committees

Ways and Means (4th). Subcommittees: Health (Chairman): Trade.

Group Ratings

	ADA	COPE	LWV	RIPON	NFU	LCV	CFA	NAB	NSI	ACA
1974	50	90	60	60	83	67	67	17	44	36
1973	68	100	91	67	94	60	83	–	–	16
1972	38	90	60	62	86	56	–	0	78	18

Key Votes

1) Foreign Aid	FOR	6) Gov Abortn Aid	ABS	11) Pub Cong Election $	AGN
2) Busing	FOR	7) Coed Phys Ed	FOR	12) Turkish Arms Cutoff	FOR
3) ABM	AGN	8) Pov Lawyer Gag	AGN	13) Youth Camp Regs	FOR
4) B-1 Bomber	AGN	9) Pub Trans Sub	FOR	14) Strip Mine Veto	AGN
5) Nerve Gas	FOR	10) EZ Voter Regis	FOR	15) Farm Bill Veto	ABS

Election Results

1974 general:	Daniel D. Rostenkowski (D)	75,011	(87%)	($25,720)
	Salvatore E. Oddo (R)	11,664	(13%)	($0)
1974 primary:	Daniel D. Rostenkowski (D), unopposed			
1972 general:	Daniel D. Rostenkowski (D)	110,457	(74%)	($13,737)
	Edward Stepnowski (R)	38,758	(26%)	($225)

◆ ◆ ◆ ◆ ◆

NINTH DISTRICT

Along Chicago's Lake Shore Drive, overlooking Lake Michigan, are some of the nation's architecturally most distinguished high-rise apartment buildings. They stand, one hard on the heels of the next; there are more such classically modern buildings here, probably, than anywhere in the country. This is the face the nation's second city likes to show to the world: affluent, elegant, massive. Behind the apartment towers, however, lies another Chicago—an incredibly varied, sometimes funky, sometimes posh city. There are Appalachians, Italians, Mexicans, American Indians and blacks—all just a few blocks from the row of high rises. At the northern end of the lakefront, where the big buildings peter out to those of ten or even five stories, is Chicago's largest Jewish community, just south of the suburbs of Evanston and Skokie. The lakefront, and the territory just a mile or two behind it, forms Illinois's 9th congressional district, which stretches from the Near North Side to the northern city limits.

So constituted, the 9th includes that part of the city which—along with the Hyde Park area around the University of Chicago—has voted most dependably against the Daley machine. William Singer, won half as many votes as Daley did in the 1975 Mayoral primary, used to be an Alderman from this area; it has also produced the longest-tenured independent member of the city's congressional delegation, Congressman Sidney Yates.

Yates has represented the Lake Shore area in Congress since 1948—when Richard Daley had not even been elected Cook County Clerk—with the exception of two years spent in forced retirement following an unsuccessful, but impressive, attempt to unseat Senator Everett Dirksen in 1962. Despite President Kennedy's obvious eagerness to butter up Dirksen, Yates won 47% of the vote. With his solid base of support in the liberal community in Chicago, Yates had little trouble winning back his seat in 1964. One can think of the machine's sufferance of his independence as a kind of concession to what is, in their view at least, just another ethnic group in the city: the issue-oriented liberals.

Yates serves on the Appropriations Committee. But because of his run for the Senate, his seniority dates only from 1964; thus he is only the 19th ranked Democrat, rather than the 5th, on the Committee. He is, however, Chairman of the Interior Subcommittee—a body, like Yates himself, basically in sympathy with the goal of preserving the environment. As one of the senior liberals on Appropriations, Yates has also been one of the leaders in the various movements to cut American military activity in and aid to the dictator countries in Southeast Asia. There is no question but that he will be reelected as long as he likes.

Census Data Pop. 463,991. Central city, 100%; suburban, 0%. Median family income, $10,966; families above $15,000: 29%; families below $3,000: 8%. Median years education, 12.3.

The Voters

Median voting age 44.
Employment profile White collar, 64%. Blue collar, 25%. Service, 11%. Farm, –%.
Ethnic groups Black, 5%. Spanish, 9%. Total foreign stock, 41%. USSR, 6%; Germany, 5%; Poland, 3%; Ireland, Sweden, Italy, UK, 2% each; Austria, Canada, Yugoslavia, Greece, 1% each.

Presidential vote

1972	Nixon (R)	79,997	(42%)
	McGovern (D)	111,512	(58%)
1968	Nixon (R)	79,631	(38%)
	Humphrey (D)	118,287	(57%)
	Wallace (AI)	10,547	(5%)

Rep. Sidney R. Yates (D) Elected 1964; b. Aug. 27, 1909, Chicago; home, Chicago; U. of Chi., Ph.B. 1931, J.D. 1933; Jewish.

Career Practicing atty.; Asst. Atty. for Ill. St. Bank Receiver, 1935–37; Asst. Atty. Gen. attached to Ill. Commerce Comm., 1937–40; Navy, WWII; U.S. House of Reps., 1949–63; Dem. nominee for U.S. Senate, 1962.

Offices 2234 RHOB, 202-225-2111. Also 230 S. Dearborn St., Chicago 60604, 312-353-4596.

Committees

Appropriations (19th). Subcommittees: Interior (Chairman); Legislative; Transportation.

Group Ratings

	ADA	COPE	LWV	RIPON	NFU	LCV	CFA	NAB	NSI	ACA
1974	100	100	100	79	86	88	92	17	10	0
1973	96	100	83	73	75	95	100	–	–	12
1972	94	100	100	78	100	80	100	8	0	0

Key Votes

1) Foreign Aid	FOR	6) Gov Abortn Aid	FOR	11) Pub Cong Election $	FOR
2) Busing	FOR	7) Coed Phys Ed	FOR	12) Turkish Arms Cutoff	FOR
3) ABM	AGN	8) Pov Lawyer Gag	AGN	13) Youth Camp Regs	FOR
4) B-1 Bomber	AGN	9) Pub Trans Sub	FOR	14) Strip Mine Veto	AGN
5) Nerve Gas	AGN	10) EZ Voter Regis	FOR	15) Farm Bill Veto	FOR

Election Results

1974 general:	Sidney R. Yates (D), unopposed		($11,226)
1974 primary:	Sidney R. Yates (D;, unopposed		
1972 general:	Sidney R. Yates (D)	131,777 (68%)	($29,723)
	Clark W. Fetridge (R)	61,083 (32%)	($16,353)

◆ ◆ ◆ ◆ ◆

TENTH DISTRICT

The 10th district of Illinois is one of two new suburban Chicago congressional districts created by court order in 1971. The district is about as compact and contiguous as possible, and one of socio-economic homogeneity. Its sameness can be summed up in a single word: rich. According to the 1970 census, this was the second wealthiest congressional district in the United States, with a median family income over $16,000 (and which, with inflation, would be up toward the $25,000 level today). That figure was exceeded only in the 8th district of Maryland, a place where fast-rising federal salaries have inflated the income level. Incomes there depend in large part on taxes which the federal government will apply all its force, if necessary, to extract from its citizens; the people of the 10th district of Illinois, in contrast, tend to make their money producing goods and services other people pay for more or less voluntarily.

The 10th could easily be called the North Shore district. Its best known towns include Evanston, site of Northwestern University and for many years the home of the Women's Christian Temperance Union, along with Winnetka, Wilmette, and Glencoe, whose New Trier Township High School likes to consider itself (and could in fact be) the best public high school in the country. These suburbs along Lake Michigan were settled long ago, pioneered by commuters using Chicago's efficient railroad lines. The large houses and shady streets of the North Shore towns have a comfortable, lived-in look, and not a trace of shabbiness. West of the Lakefront are newer communities: the predominantly Jewish suburb of Skokie, which grew rapidly in the fifties; and farther inland, places like Niles, Des Plaines, Glenview, and Northbrook, situated on the northwest rail lines and freeways, right in the way of the great suburban expansion of the 1960s.

Conventional wisdom has long has it that the richer people are, the more Republican they vote. The 10th district nicely refutes this proposition. Though it is the richest of the suburban Chicago districts, it is the only one which refused to go for Barry Goldwater in 1964. Even in 1972, the 10th gave Richard Nixon no larger a percentage than he won in the nation as a whole. And in 1974, the 10th gave Senator Adlai Stevenson 57% of the vote—a better showing than he made in any other all-suburban district. There are several explanations for this voting behavior. First, there is the large Jewish community, centered in Skokie, which usually goes solidly Democratic: about two-thirds of metropolitan Chicago's large Jewish community live either here or in the 9th district, just to the south, in the city. Second, Evanston, once one of the state's premier Republican strongholds, has now gone Democratic as students at Northwestern got the vote and academics and professionals who used to live in Hyde Park, around the University of Chicago, have moved here. Finally, there is the general quiet move leftward among high-income WASPs, which makes itself felt in smaller and smaller Republican margins in the fashionable North Shore precincts. These are voters who were turned off by the Vietnam war and by the Nixon-Agnew administration's appeals to the prejudices of hard hats and Southern segregationists; they are people whose opposition to Democrats was long rooted in their notion that that party was rotten with corruption, and now find themselves opposing many Republicans for the same reason.

When created in 1971, the 10th district had no incumbent Congressman; since then, it has been the scene of two spirited contests between the same two candidates, whose results reflect the difference between the political years of 1972 and 1974. The Republican nominee, and winner in 1972, was Samuel H. Young, a conservatively inclined lawyer and sometime Republican officeholder. Young upset an organization choice in the 1972 primary, and was the recipient of large contributions from, among others, W. Clement Stone, the waxed-mustachioed insurance millionaire who also gave $2 million to Richard Nixon in 1972. Young represented the traditional Republican conservatism which until recently dominated the 10th district's suburbs, and continues to have considerable strength. In 1972, he campaigned in large part against George McGovern—who obviously was not going to carry this district—and in his two years as Congressman was almost invariably a supporter of Nixon Administration policies and, in the Watergate affair, Richard Nixon himself.

The Democratic candidate could hardly have been more different. Abner Mikva was a certified liberal: vice-chairman of Americans for Democratic Action, a labor and civil liberties lawyer, an advocate of tax reform. He was also, in 1972, a Congressman—from Chicago. Mikva had run for

Congress in the old 2d district which took in both Hyde Park and the Calumet steel mills in 1966 against the 84-year-old incumbent, Barratt O'Hara, the last member of Congress to be a veteran of the Spanish-American War. O'Hara had the support of the Daley organization, and Mikva lost that race; but he won an impressive 40% of the vote, and when he ran again in 1968, the machine capitulated to the inevitable and supported him. Then, in 1971, Mikva's old district was divided among its neighbors, and he decided to move to Evanston and run in the new 10th.

Mikva's campaigns in both 1972 and 1974 were based, to an even larger extent than Young's, on a massive volunteer organization. Once one gets beyond the Chicago city limits, one has passed the land of patronage politics; in the wealthy 10th district, a $6500 a year city job is not a suitable incentive to political activity. In 1972, this volunteer organization was not quite enough to prevent Mikva from losing by 7,000 votes. But it was the key ingredient—together with sophisticated polling of voters on issues—in his 3,000 vote victory in 1974. It helped, probably, that Stevenson was carrying the district while two years before Republican Senator Charles Percy had won it by a 76-24 margin. But this was one of the best-publicized congressional elections in the United States, and perhaps the one where the very different positions of the candidates were best known. Turnout was higher than in all but a handful of districts. The result was no accident of coattails; it was a reflection, as the 1972 outcome was, of the feelings of the people of this wealthy district.

Mikva's enforced absence from Congress in 1973 and 1974 prevented him from participating, as he otherwise would have, as a member of the Judiciary Committee in the hearings on the impeachment of Richard Nixon. Now, on his return, he has won a seat on Ways and Means. Will he win again in 1976? He has now the advantages of incumbency, which almost helped Young hang on despite his pro-Nixon stance, and the Congressman is also an effective and ebullient speaker. There will undoubtedly be another high-participation election here in the 10th district, but the odds now seem to favor Mikva.

Census Data Pop. 462,121. Central city, 0%; suburban, 100%. Median family income, $16,576; families above $15,000: 55%; families below $3,000: 3%. Median years education, 12.9.

The Voters

Median voting age 44.
Employment profile White collar, 74%. Blue collar, 18%. Service, 8%. Farm, –%.
Ethnic groups Black, 3%. Spanish, 1%. Total foreign stock, 31%. USSR, Germany, Poland, 4% each; Italy, UK, Sweden, Canada, 2% each; Austria, 1%.

Presidential vote

1972	Nixon (R)	147,305	(62%)
	McGovern (D)	89,630	(38%)
1968	Nixon (R)	123,878	(56%)
	Humphrey (D)	89,114	(41%)
	Wallace (AI)	6,786	(3%)

Rep. Abner J. Mikva (D) Elected 1974; b. Jan. 21, 1926, Milwaukee, Wis.; home, Evanston; U. of Chi., J.D. 1951.

Career Army Air Corps, WWII; Law Clerk for U.S. Supreme Ct. Justice Sherman Minton, 1951–52; Practicing atty., 1952–68; Ill. House of Reps., 1957–67; Candidate for Dem. nomination for U.S. House of Reps., 1966; U.S. House of Reps., 1969–73; Chm., Ill. Bd. of Ethics, 1973.

Offices 432 CHOB, 202-225-4835. Also 4016B Church St., Skokie 60076, 312-676-1350.

Committees

Ways and Means (23d). Subcommittees: Social Security; Trade.

Group Ratings: Newly Elected

Key Votes

1) Foreign Aid	FOR	6) Gov Abortn Aid	NE	11) Pub Cong Election $	NE
2) Busing	NE	7) Coed Phys Ed	FOR	12) Turkish Arms Cutoff	NE
3) ABM	NE	8) Pov Lawyer Gag	NE	13) Youth Camp Regs	FOR
4) B-1 Bomber	AGN	9) Pub Trans Sub	NE	14) Strip Mine Veto	AGN
5) Nerve Gas	NE	10) EZ Voter Regis	NE	15) Farm Bill Veto	FOR

Election Results

1974 general:	Abner J. Mikva (D)	83,457	(51%)	($286,225)
	Samuel H. Young (R)	80,597	(49%)	($251,249)
1974 primary:	Abner J. Mikva (D), unopposed			

♦ ♦ ♦ ♦ ♦

ELEVENTH DISTRICT

The 11th congressional district of Illinois is the northwest corner of the city of Chicago. Made up of comfortable middle-class neighborhoods, the 11th had the highest percentage of families with incomes over $15,000 in 1970. It is also the Chicago district with the lowest percentage of blacks and the highest proportion of people of foreign stock. When second- or third-generation ethnics can afford to leave their old neighborhoods, or when they feel they must because blacks are moving in, they tend to move here to the northwest side. Almost all of Chicago's ethnic groups are thus well represented in these middle-class wards, especially Poles, Germans, Italians, Jews, Irish, and Greeks.

These are not people who are particularly attracted by the WASP suburbs; indeed they seem to consider them cold and unhospitable—and Republican. For these are ancestral Democrats, people who grew up revering Franklin D. Roosevelt and think of the Daley machine, not as a group of crooks living off their tax dollars, but as friendly people who can help you out when you need something from the city or county. They also are—or were—the kind of Democrats who didn't especially like seeing their tax money spent on (black) welfare mothers and antipoverty programs.

These attitudes were reflected with almost pinpoint accuracy by the district's longtime (1955-73) Congressman, Roman C. Pucinski. In his early years he was a faithful supporter of Kennedy and Johnson Administration social programs, but after a near-defeat in 1966 he became something of a gadfly to antipoverty program administrators. In 1972, Pucinski brought these attitudes to his quixotic, underfinanced race against Senator Charles Percy. With machine support, but after having antagonized the black community, Pucinski managed to carry only the 11th, plus the 5th, 7th, and 8th congressional districts—the latter all machine strongholds.

Pucinski's replacement was one of two Chicago Democrats who were redistricted out of their seats. The other, maverick Abner Mikva, moved to the North Shore 10th, and eventually won in 1974. Frank Annunzio, the man who moved to the 11th, is a solid machine man. "Frank is on my list of ten congressmen most likely to get indicted in the next 15 years—not that I have any dirt on him," one source told *Rolling Stone*. "It's just that he's the *type* of guy who gets indicted at least once in his career. Big pal of Mayor Daley. Big pal of the retailers and catalog houses in Chicago." Indeed, no one has ever suggested that Annunzio has done anything criminal, though he did get enjoined from sending franked mail into the 11th in 1972 when he was, technically, representing an entirely separate constituency.

That also caused Annunzio some political problems. In the old district, which had a large black population, he had opposed antibusing amendments; once he moved into the almost all-white 11th, he unashamedly took just the opposite view. Alderman John Hoellen, who had got 49% of the vote against Pucinski in 1966, got 47% against Annunzio in 1972, but the Democrat had won and he appears likely to retain the seat for as long as he wants. The Republican Party, indeed, shows signs of imminent collapse here: Hoellen, after running so well so recently, was not only beaten as the Republican candidate against Mayor Daley in 1975; he was forced to leave the race because the machine men managed to defeat him as Alderman of the usually Republican 45th ward. In the House, Annunzio, a favorite of Chairman Wayne Hays on the House Administration

Committee, became in 1975 Chairman of the Consumer Affairs Subcommittee of Banking—a payoff, apparently, of his support for new Chairman Henry Reuss over his 78-year-old predecessor Wright Patman.

Census Data Pop. 461,079. Central city, 100%; suburban, 0%. Median family income, $12,005; families above $15,000: 31%; families below $3,000: 5%. Median years education, 11.5.

The Voters

Median voting age 48.
Employment profile White collar, 53%. Blue collar, 37%. Service, 10%. Farm, –%.
Ethnic groups Spanish, 2%. Total foreign stock, 47%. Poland, 10%; Germany, 7%; Italy, 5%; USSR, 3%; Ireland, Greece, Sweden, Austria, 2% each; UK, Yugoslavia, Czechoslovakia, Hungary, 1% each.

Presidential vote

1972	Nixon (R)	144,169	(63%)
	McGovern (D)	85,928	(37%)
1968	Nixon (R)	112,602	(47%)
	Humphrey (D)	105,630	(44%)
	Wallace (AI)	19,285	(8%)

Rep. Frank Annunzio (D) Elected 1964; b. Jan. 12, 1915, Chicago; home, Chicago; De Paul U., B.S. 1940; M.A. 1942; Catholic.

Career Public school teacher, 1935–43; Legis. and Ed. Dir., United Steelworkers of Amer., Chicago, Calumet Region Dist. 31, 1943–49; Dir., Ill. Dept. of Labor, 1949–52; Private businessman, 1952–64.

Offices 2303 RHOB, 202-225-6661. Also Suite 201, 4747 W. Peterson Ave., Chicago 60646, 312-736-0700.

Committees

Banking, Currency, and Housing (11th). Subcommittees: Consumer Affairs (Chairman); Financial Institutions Supervision, Regulation and Insurance; Historic Preservation and Coinage.

House Administration (7th). Accounts; Personnel and Police (Chairman); Ad Hoc Computer.

Group Ratings

	ADA	COPE	LWV	RIPON	NFU	LCV	CFA	NAB	NSI	ACA
1974	57	91	58	44	93	59	77	25	56	38
1973	72	100	75	53	100	74	88	–	–	15
1972	63	91	73	78	86	33	100	11	50	26

Key Votes

1) Foreign Aid	FOR	6) Gov Abortn Aid	AGN	11) Pub Cong Election $	AGN
2) Busing	AGN	7) Coed Phys Ed	AGN	12) Turkish Arms Cutoff	FOR
3) ABM	AGN	8) Pov Lawyer Gag	FOR	13) Youth Camp Regs	FOR
4) B-1 Bomber	FOR	9) Pub Trans Sub	FOR	14) Strip Mine Veto	AGN
5) Nerve Gas	AGN	10) EZ Voter Regis	FOR	15) Farm Bill Veto	AGN

Election Results

1974 general:	Frank Annunzio (D)	102,541	(72%)	($60,397)
	Mitchell G. Zadrozny (R)	39,182	(28%)	($33,362)
1974 primary:	Frank Annunzio (D)	69,698	(89%)	
	Aris F. Yanibas (D)	8,392	(11%)	
1972 general:	Frank Annunzio (D)	118,637	(53%)	($117,415)
	John J. Hoellen (R)	103,773	(47%)	($108,126)

♦ ♦ ♦ ♦ ♦

TWELFTH DISTRICT

Only four congressional districts in the nation more than doubled their population during the 1960s. Three were in California, and the other was the 12th district of Illinois. This is not a particularly neatly shaped district: it includes the six northwest townships of Cook County and, just to the north, the southern portion of Lake County. This territory includes the extremely wealthy North Shore suburbs of Highland Park and Lake Forest which in the 1972 election were at the same time the richest and least pro-Nixon parts of the district. But it is the suburbs farther west, just beyond booming O'Hare Airport, that have been growing the most rapidly. As one drives through, say, Schaumburg on the freeway, one sees the spectacle of one of the nation's largest Searses, surrounded by a giant shopping center—and right next to it a cornfield. The corn, one can predict, will not last for long: this is prime real estate, the place where young, affluent families from Chicago are naturally gravitating. There are fewer old people here, and more children, than in any other Illinois congressional district.

The 12th politically is more or less a descendant of the old 13th district, which also included all of what now is the 10th. For six years, until the Nixon Administration took office, that old district was represented by Donald Rumsfeld, now rescued from the ignominy of having served Nixon by a job as President Ford's top aide. As Congressman, Rumsfeld had a reputation in his district for being some kind of liberal Republican, though that seems to have been mainly because he was young and genial; his voting record was close to that of dour, aging Illinois conservatives.

Of the ideology of Rumsfeld's successor, Republican Philip Crane, there can be no doubt. A former professor at Peoria's Bradley University and an early supporter of Barry Goldwater in 1964, Crane is a conservative intellectual. His voting record is firmly based on his almost libertarian (tempered by anti-Communist) principles, and he often finds himself casting lone dissenting votes on liberal measures. Crane's militant conservatism weakened him in the old 13th district, particularly in the North Shore suburbs of Evanston, Winnetka, Wilmette, and Glencoe, and in predominantly Jewish Skokie. But all those suburbs are now in the 10th district, and in 1972 he won his first really solid majority in the newer 12th, which seems considerably less choosy about which ideological sort of Republicans it supports. Even against an opponent who campaigned hard in the Democratic year of 1974, Crane won a comfortable 61%, and should not have any difficulty winning again in the future.

Census Data Pop. 461,054. Central city, 0%; suburban, 100%. Median family income, $15,173; families above $15,000: 51%; families below $3,000: 2%. Median years education, 12.7.

The Voters

Median voting age 39.
Employment profile White collar, 67%. Blue collar, 25%. Service, 8%. Farm, –%.
Ethnic groups Spanish, 2%. Total foreign stock, 20%. Germany, 4%; Italy, Poland, 2% each; Canada, UK, Sweden, USSR, 1% each.

Presidential vote

1972	Nixon (R)	136,343	(71%)
	McGovern (D)	56,896	(29%)
1968	Nixon (R)	104,981	(65%)
	Humphrey (D)	48,572	(30%)
	Wallace (AI)	8,142	(5%)

Rep. Philip M. Crane (R) Elected Nov. 25, 1969; b. Nov. 3, 1930, Chicago; home, Mt. Prospect; De Paul U., Hillsdale Col., B.A., Ind. U., M.A., Ph.D., U. of Mich., U. of Vienna.

Career Instructor, Ind. U., 1960–63; Asst. Prof., Bradley U., 1963–67; Dir. of Schools, Westminster Acad., 1967–68.

Offices 1406 LHOB, 202-225-3711. Also Suite 101, 1450 S. New Wilke Rd., Arlington Heights 60005, 312-394-0790.

Committees

Ways and Means (8th). Subcommittees: Health; Social Security.

Group Ratings

	ADA	COPE	LWV	RIPON	NFU	LCV	CFA	NAB	NSI	ACA
1974	10	0	0	31	0	14	0	82	100	92
1973	9	9	9	42	5	6	0	–	–	100
1972	0	18	20	38	14	5	0	100	100	100

Key Votes

1) Foreign Aid	AGN	6) Gov Abortn Aid	AGN	11) Pub Cong Election $	AGN
2) Busing	AGN	7) Coed Phys Ed	AGN	12) Turkish Arms Cutoff	ABS
3) ABM	FOR	8) Pov Lawyer Gag	FOR	13) Youth Camp Regs	AGN
4) B-1 Bomber	FOR	9) Pub Trans Sub	AGN	14) Strip Mine Veto	FOR
5) Nerve Gas	FOR	10) EZ Voter Regis	AGN	15) Farm Bill Veto	FOR

Election Results

1974 general:	Philip M. Crane (R)	70,731	(61%)	($60,122)
	Betty C. Spence (D)	45,049	(39%)	($51,594)
1974 primary:	Philip M. Crane (R), unopposed			
1972 general:	Philip M. Crane (R)	152,938	(74%)	($52,661)
	E. L. Frank (D)	53,055	(26%)	($4,154)

◆ ◆ ◆ ◆ ◆

THIRTEENTH DISTRICT

The 13th congressional district of Illinois is a part of the Chicago metropolitan area far beyond the power of Mayor Daley's machine, but well within reach of the Chicago *Tribune*. The district forms a kind of cordon around the northern and western portions of the metropolitan area, as it stretches from the industrial town of Waukegan on Lake Michigan to a point below the German Catholic town of Aurora, due west of the Chicago Loop. This area is not quite as prosperous as the suburbs closer to Chicago; it contains pockets of urban poverty and rural shabbiness, as well as some working-class neighborhoods and middle-income towns. The suburban building boom invaded the district's cornfields with real force in the late sixties, but the growth here has not yet been as explosive—or disruptive—as in the neighboring 12th district.

In 1964, the 13th (then numbered the 12th) was among the group of Chicago suburbs and exurbs that went for Barry Goldwater. Extending around the city at a radius from 20 to 60 miles, they coincided roughly with the *Tribune*'s major circulation zone; these same suburbs went for Barry Goldwater in 1964, though similar suburbs of other Great Lakes metropolises—Detroit, Milwaukee, Cleveland, Buffalo—all went for Johnson. It may seem odd to make this connection between voting behavior and newspaper circulation, but only to those unfamiliar with the old *Tribune*. The paper today, while conservative editorially, is evenhanded in its choice of columnists and is usually reliable, even authoritative. But in the heyday of its founder, Colonel Robert McCormick, and for a decade or so afterward, the *Tribune* was the voice of Midwestern Republican conservatism and isolationism—a voice undisturbed by any discordant notes. Its news pages were as slanted as its editorials were opinionated, and it was taken as gospel by hundreds of thousands of suburban Chicago readers, as well as many more in the rural hinterland for miles around. The hard-nosed conservatism of the old *Tribune* still finds expression in Illinois politics and voter behavior today, and nowhere more than in the suburban belt around Chicago.

The 13th district's Congressman's tenure dates from 1962, when the *Tribune* was about to become more moderate, and the Congressman is noticeably more middle-of-the-road than the Republicans who represented Illinois when he was first elected. This is Robert McClory, familiar to most Americans from his role in the House Judiciary Committee impeachment proceedings. McClory was the second ranking Republican on the Committee—he lost the top spot by a flip of a coin a dozen years before, which gave Edward Hutchinson of Michigan greater seniority. A thin, nervous-seeming man, he was constantly commenting on the evidence, often with disapproval; he finally came out for impeaching Nixon for abuse of power, but not for his complicity in the cover-up, for which he felt the evidence was lacking. McClory was 66 at the time, but his political problems were somewhat less than they may have seemed. The Republican primary had long since passed in Illinois, and McClory had won handily; he faced strenuous opposition in the general election, but the district's *Tribune*-nourished Republicanism was enough to give him a 55-45 victory. (If he had stuck with Nixon all the way, however, he probably would have lost.) Presumably he can win again, although at his age there is always the possibility of retirement.

Census Data Pop. 463,096. Central city, 0%; suburban, 100%. Median family income, $11,994; families above $15,000: 31%; families below $3,000: 5%. Median years education, 12.2.

The Voters

Median voting age 39.
Employment profile White collar, 47%. Blue collar, 40%. Service, 12%. Farm, 1%.
Ethnic groups Black, 5%. Spanish, 3%. Total foreign stock, 18%. Germany, 4%; Poland, UK, Sweden, Canada, 1% each.

Presidential vote

1972	Nixon (R)	112,900	(70%)
	McGovern (D)	49,217	(30%)
1968	Nixon (R)	88,969	(61%)
	Humphrey (D)	46,166	(31%)
	Wallace (AI)	11,895	(8%)

Rep. Robert McClory (R) Elected 1962; b. Jan. 31, 1908, Riverside; home, Lake Bluff; Dartmouth Col., 1926–28, Chicago-Kent Col. of Law, LL.B. 1932.

Career Practicing atty.; Ill. House of Reps., 1951–53; Ill. Senate, 1953–63.

Offices 2452 RHOB, 202-225-5221. Also Kane County Municipal Bldg., 150 Dexter Ct., Elgin 60120, 312-697-5005.

Committees

Judiciary (2d). Subcommittees: Crime; Monopolies and Commercial Law.

Group Ratings

	ADA	COPE	LWV	RIPON	NFU	LCV	CFA	NAB	NSI	ACA
1974	24	9	75	79	50	24	23	67	70	40
1973	38	0	73	92	30	37	38	–	–	63
1972	38	18	73	69	43	25	0	73	78	45

Key Votes

1) Foreign Aid	FOR	6) Gov Abortn Aid	AGN	11) Pub Cong Election $	AGN
2) Busing	FOR	7) Coed Phys Ed	FOR	12) Turkish Arms Cutoff	AGN
3) ABM	FOR	8) Pov Lawyer Gag	AGN	13) Youth Camp Regs	AGN
4) B-1 Bomber	AGN	9) Pub Trans Sub	AGN	14) Strip Mine Veto	AGN
5) Nerve Gas	AGN	10) EZ Voter Regis	AGN	15) Farm Bill Veto	FOR

Election Results

1974 general:	Robert McClory (R)	51,405	(55%)	($38,921)
	Stanley W. Beetham (D)	42,903	(45%)	($39,642)
1974 primary:	Robert McClory (R)	29,368	(71%)	
	Edward M. Vass (R)	11,980	(29%)	
1972 general:	Robert McClory (R)	98,201	(61%)	($25,010)
	Stanley W. Beetham (D)	61,537	(39%)	($20,120)

♦ ♦ ♦ ♦ ♦

FOURTEENTH DISTRICT

If you take 1970 median family income as the standard, three of the nation's five richest congressional districts lie in the suburbs of Chicago. The 14th is one of them. And of all these rich districts, the 14th is indisputably the most heavily Republican and conservative. The district includes practically all of DuPage County, a fast-growing, wealthy group of suburbs directly west of Chicago, which regularly produces higher Republican percentages than Orange County, California. Appropriately, DuPage was also the site of the palatial estate of Colonel McCormick, the longtime owner of the Chicago *Tribune.* For almost fifty years, McCormick's paper was the house organ for his brand of conservative, isolationist Republicanism. And if DuPage County can no longer be counted as isolationist, then it certainly has remained conservative; the Colonel would not be displeased at how it has responded to the political choices put before it in the twenty years since his death. In 1964, for example, DuPage gave 60% of its votes to Barry Goldwater; in 1972, 75% for Richard Nixon. Indeed, the suburbs of Chicago, led by DuPage, have become the heartland of Illinois Republicanism, producing larger percentages and sometimes more votes for the party's candidates than historically Republican Downstate Illinois.

The Colonel might not be quite so pleased—at least not all the time—with the record of the 14th district's Congressman, John Erlenborn. He is, to be sure, one of the leading conservatives on the liberal-dominated Education and Labor Committee, as well as second-ranking Republican on Government Operations. But on occasion Erlenborn, if he has not exactly strayed from orthodoxy, has at least taken some positions which one might not have expected from a representative of his constituency. He has, for example, worked to break down Executive Branch secrecy, even at a time when that Branch was in the hands of his own party, and he voted for opening up the highway trust fund to spending for mass transit. Still under 50, he is one of the brighter conservative-to-moderate Republicans and, as might be expected, he has had little difficulty winning in this always Republican district.

Census Data Pop. 464,029. Central city, 0%; suburban, 100%. Median family income, $14,527; families above $15,000: 47%; families below $3,000: 2%. Median years education, 12.6.

The Voters

Median voting age 40.
Employment profile White collar, 65%. Blue collar, 27%. Service, 8%. Farm, –%.
Ethnic groups Spanish, 2%. Total foreign stock, 21%. Germany, 4%; Italy, Poland, UK, 2% each; Czechoslovakia, Canada, Sweden, 1% each.

Presidential vote

1972	Nixon (R)	163,652	(75%)
	McGovern (D)	53,631	(25%)
1968	Nixon (R)	118,955	(67%)
	Humphrey (D)	45,922	(26%)
	Wallace (AI)	13,082	(7%)

Rep. John N. Erlenborn (R) Elected 1964; b. Feb. 8, 1927, Chicago; home, Elmhurst; U. of Notre Dame, 1944, Ind. St. Teachers Col., 1944–45, U. of Ill., 1945–46, Loyola U., LL.B. 1949; Catholic.

Career Navy, WWII; Practicing atty., 1949–50, 1952–64; Asst. State's Atty., DuPage Co., 1950–52; Ill. House of Reps., 1957–65.

Offices 2236 RHOB, 202-225-3515. Also DuPage Co. Ctr., 421 N. County Farm Rd., Wheaton 60187, 312-668-1417.

Committees

Education and Labor (4th). Subcommittees: Labor Standards; Post-secondary Education.

Government Operations (2d). Subcommittees: Commerce, Consumer and Monetary Affairs; Legislation and National Security.

Group Ratings

	ADA	COPE	LWV	RIPON	NFU	LCV	CFA	NAB	NSI	ACA
1974	24	27	83	86	33	35	15	67	100	54
1973	25	0	63	100	22	33	17	–	–	60
1972	19	25	73	82	17	47	100	100	100	67

Key Votes

1) Foreign Aid	FOR	6) Gov Abortn Aid	AGN	11) Pub Cong Election $	AGN
2) Busing	ABS	7) Coed Phys Ed	AGN	12) Turkish Arms Cutoff	AGN
3) ABM	FOR	8) Pov Lawyer Gag	AGN	13) Youth Camp Regs	AGN
4) B-1 Bomber	FOR	9) Pub Trans Sub	AGN	14) Strip Mine Veto	FOR
5) Nerve Gas	AGN	10) EZ Voter Regis	AGN	15) Farm Bill Veto	FOR

Election Results

1974 general:	John N. Erlenborn (R)	77,718	(67%)	($34,214)
	Robert H. Renshaw (D)	38,981	(33%)	($3,474)
1974 primary:	John N. Erlenborn (R), unopposed			
1972 general:	John N. Erlenborn (R)	154,794	(73%)	($24,871)
	James M. Wall (D)	57,874	(27%)	($7,183)

◆ ◆ ◆ ◆ ◆

FIFTEENTH DISTRICT

The 15th congressional district of Illinois is part of the corn-growing prairie that stretches west from Chicago toward the Rocky Mountains more than a thousand miles away. This is some of the richest farmland in the nation, criss-crossed by railroads and highways radiating out from Chicago to gather in the products of its fields. Part of the 15th—the small, conservative city of Aurora—is only 30 miles from Chicago; from there one can proceed to DeKalb, site of Northern Illinois University, or south to small industrial towns like Ottawa and LaSalle and Streator which are on the way to Peoria. With its fertile soil and prosperous farmers, the 15th district has been, historically, one of the most solidly Republican constituencies in the nation; only LaSalle County ordinarily turns in a Democratic margin. Yet in the last five years, this area has had four different Congressmen—and one of them a Democrat.

Part of the reason for this was redistricting. The old districts represented by Republicans Charlotte Reid (former vocalist with Don McNeil's Breakfast Club) and Leslie Arends were combined; Reid resigned to take a place on the FCC, and her seat was won by Republican Clifford Carlson, who declined to face Arends in the 1972 general election. His reasoning was simple. Arends was one of the grand old men of the Republican Party, first elected to Congress in 1934, House Minority Whip since 1943 (except for the two occasions when Republicans had a majority, when he was Majority Leader). Arends, with his modishly long white hair curling up under his collar, remained a familiar figure in the House almost till he was 80, eagerly gladhanding his colleagues, joking with them and seeking their votes. A senior member of the hawkish Armed Services Committee, on issues he was Republican conservative orthodoxy personified. At home, he was considered invulnerable.

Yet in 1972, Arends received only 59% in the primary and 57% in the general in the 15th—far below what he had grown accustomed to. True, the change in district boundaries had forced him to run in unfamiliar territory, and he had never been one to send out tons of franked mail to impress his constituents. But at 77, Arends was just not much of a campaigner anymore, while his opponents, Aurora Mayor John Cunningham and Democrat Tim Hall, were able to make massive inroads. Arends made a nominal try for the Minority Leadership when Gerald Ford became Vice President, but House Republicans were not about to make a near-octogenarian their major spokesman. It was time for him to retire, and in 1974 he did—leaving the seat vacant in one of the most heavily Democratic years Illinois has lately seen.

The result was a wide-open battle. Hall, a 49-year-old teacher from the small town of Dwight, managed to beat Martin Dubin, a professor at NIU, for the Democratic nomination. There were five Republican candidates, and the winner, former Congressman Carlson, won with only 24% of the vote. In the Watergate-tinged general election, Hall was able to carry seven of the district's ten counties, and take the district by a 52-46 margin. This undoubtedly will be a fiercely contested race in 1976. Hall has now run here three times, as has Republican John Cunningham (who has yet to win his party's nominations); Republicans Carlson and William McConkey have both run twice. The 15th, which saw little political turbulence in the last 40 years, has been getting used to it in the past few.

Census Data Pop. 462,969. Central city, 0%; suburban, 33%. Median family income, $10,619; families above $15,000: 22%; families below $3,000: 6%. Median years education, 12.2.

The Voters

Median voting age 42.
Employment profile White collar, 41%. Blue collar, 42%. Service, 12%. Farm, 5%.
Ethnic groups Black, 2%, Spanish, 2%. Total foreign stock, 14%. Germany, 3%; Italy, UK, Sweden, 1% each.

Presidential vote

1972	Nixon (R)	133,061	(66%)
	McGovern (D)	68,288	(34%)
1968	Nixon (R)	110,036	(59%)
	Humphrey (D)	64,529	(35%)
	Wallace (AI)	11,832	(6%)

Rep. Tim L. Hall (D) Elected 1974; b. June 11, 1925, West Frankfort; home, Dwight; Ia. Wesleyan Col., B.A. 1951; So. Ill. U., M.S. 1956; Valpraiso U.; Methodist.

Career Coast Guard, WWII; High school teacher and principal; Training Co-ord., Wm. Fox Children's Ctr.

Offices 1221 LHOB, 202-225-2976. Also 107 Franklin St., Dwight 60420, 815-584-1084.

Committees

Education and Labor (27th). Subcommittees: Elementary, Secondary and Vocational Education; Post-secondary Education; Select Subcommittee on Education.

Science and Technology (21st). Subcommittees: Aviation and Transportation Research and Development; Science, Research, and Technology; Space Science and Applications.

Group Ratings: Newly Elected

Key Votes

1) Foreign Aid	FOR	6) Gov Abortn Aid	NE	11) Pub Cong Election $	NE
2) Busing	NE	7) Coed Phys Ed	FOR	12) Turkish Arms Cutoff	NE
3) ABM	NE	8) Pov Lawyer Gag	NE	13) Youth Camp Regs	FOR
4) B-1 Bomber	AGN	9) Pub Trans Sub	NE	14) Strip Mine Veto	AGN
5) Nerve Gas	NE	10) EZ Voter Regis	NE	15) Farm Bill Veto	AGN

Election Results

1974 general:	Tim L. Hall (D)	61,912	(52%)	($29,398)
	Cliffard D. Carlson (R)	54,278	(46%)	($110,540)
	K. Douglas Lassiter (Ind.)	2,817	(2%)	($1,256)
1974 primary:	Tim L. Hall (D)	8,986	(45%)	
	Martin D. Dubin (D)	6,783	(34%)	
	Emmett J. Slingsby (D)	4,275	(21%)	

◆ ◆ ◆ ◆ ◆

SIXTEENTH DISTRICT

The northwest corner of Illinois, which forms the state's 16th congressional district, is a little different politically, from the rest of the state. A little like Wisconsin or Iowa, this part of Illinois has a larger number of Scandinavian-Americans and a stronger good-government tradition than the patronage-ridden politics of Chicago and most of Downstate Illinois. The largest city here is Rockford, which is actually the state's second largest; but its metropolitan area population is only 272,00, which is pretty insignificant next to Chicago's nearly seven million. The rest of the 16th is primarily agricultural. Points of interest include Freeport, site of the most famous Lincoln-Douglas debate; and the home town of President U.S. Grant, Galena, once a thriving commercial center but now a Mississippi River backwater.

John B. Anderson has been the 16th's Congressman since the 1960 election. He began his House career in a fashion more or less indistinguishable from other Illinois Republicans, but as time went on he strayed more and more from their orthodoxy. At the same time, his parliamentary talents won him a seat on the House Rules Committee and, in 1969, the position of Chairman of the House Republican Conference.

Anderson's apostasy is not total, but it is frequent enough to irritate many conservative Republicans. For example, he opposed the bombing of Cambodia (even though he had previously voted against end-the-war legislation) and he fought against the Alaskan pipeline and for the route that would go through Canada to the oil-hungry Midwest. With Democrat Morris Udall of Arizona, Anderson sponsored a proposal to provide matching funds to candidates who raise certain amounts in small contributions; its basic principle has been embodied in the presidential financing statute passed in 1974. And even when Anderson has chosen to line up with the Republican Administration, he often seems to do so most enthusiastically on those measures with minimal, lukewarm White House support: for example, the family assistance plan and the move to allow local governments to tap the highway trust fund for mass transit.

Perhaps most irritating, for many House Republicans, was Anderson's stance on Watergate-related issues. He came out early and resoundingly against the Nixon Administration's broad view of executive privilege and its narrow view of what the people were entitled to know. Obviously skeptical of Nixon's protestations of innocence, Anderson was vigorously calling for explanations even before many Democrats. All of which led some Republicans to conclude that he was not really their man. Way back in 1971, Anderson had kept the Conference Chairman post against Samuel Devine of Ohio by a thin 89-81 margin; as the impeachment hearings opened, he might not have done so well among his fellow Republicans.

But the outcome of the Nixon mess vindicated Anderson's judgment, and the 1974 Democratic landslide sharply reduced the ranks of his critics. When he was challenged by Charles Wiggins at the beginning of 1975, the vote this time was a solid 85-52 margin.

The vote proved again, if any proof was needed, the conservative nature of the Republican House membership, for many had voted for Anderson despite, and not because of, his stands on issues. But it is also worth keeping in mind that Anderson is very definitely a Republican, and not a Democrat-in-disguise. He does believe that Republican economic policies are generally sounder and better for the nation, that the Pentagon budget should not be substantially tampered with, that the federal government is too big and should somehow be cut back. Indeed, throughout 1973 he was seriously considering making a run against Senator Adlai Stevenson, and not just out of vaulting ambition, but because he really differed with Stevenson on many issues. In the Watergate year, he decided wisely against making the race after a sophisticated poll showed him he would have a tough time in the primary with Nixon loyalists and in the general with Democrats and some Independents. The 16th district, on the other hand, with its tinge of good-government tradition, has suited Anderson just fine over the years. In 1974, however, a conservative independent got a surprising 16% of the vote—perhaps the hard-core Nixonites—which together with the Democrat's 29% held Anderson down to the unimpressive level of 55%. This is probably not a portent for future trouble—but it does illustrate the problems he would have had if he had run for the Senate.

Census Data Pop. 461,719. Central city, 32%; suburban, 36%. Median family income, $10,668; families above $15,000: 21%; families below $3,000: 7%. Median years education, 12.1.

The Voters

Median voting age 43.
Employment profile White collar, 41%. Blue collar, 43%. Service, 11%. Farm, 5%.
Ethnic groups Black, 4%. Spanish, 1%. Total foreign stock, 14%. Germany, Sweden, 3% each; Italy, 2%; UK, 1%.

Presidential vote

1972	Nixon (R)	120,432	(66%)
	McGovern (D)	62,339	(34%)
1968	Nixon (R)	102,066	(58%)
	Humphrey (D)	62,663	(36%)
	Wallace (AI)	11,524	(7%)

Rep. John B. Anderson (R) Elected 1960; b. Feb. 15, 1922, Rockford; home, Rockford; U. of Ill., B.A., J.D. 1946, Harvard U. LL.M. 1949; Evangelical Church.

Career Army, WWII; Practicing atty.; U.S. Foreign Svc., Germany, 1952–55; State's Atty., Winnebago Co., 1956–60.

Offices 1101 LHOB, 202-225-5676. Also 401 W. State St., Rockford 61101, 815-962-8807.

Committees

Rules (2d).

Joint Committee on Atomic Energy Ranking Member, House Side. Subcommittees: ERDA, Environment and Safety; ERDA, Nuclear Energy; Legislation; Licensing and Regulation; Military Applications.

Group Ratings

	ADA	COPE	LWV	RIPON	NFU	LCV	CFA	NAB	NSI	ACA
1974	50	45	91	100	64	58	18	56	90	33
1973	38	27	75	85	33	67	50	–	–	46
1972	44	36	91	100	50	6	0	89	89	43

Key Votes

1) Foreign Aid	FOR	6) Gov Abortn Aid	AGN	11) Pub Cong Election $	FOR
2) Busing	FOR	7) Coed Phys Ed	FOR	12) Turkish Arms Cutoff	AGN
3) ABM	AGN	8) Pov Lawyer Gag	AGN	13) Youth Camp Regs	AGN
4) B-1 Bomber	AGN	9) Pub Trans Sub	ABS	14) Strip Mine Veto	AGN
5) Nerve Gas	AGN	10) EZ Voter Regis	AGN	15) Farm Bill Veto	FOR

Election Results

1974 general:	John B. Anderson (R)	65,175	(55%)	($74,346)
	Marshall Hungness (D)	33,724	(29%)	($4,587)
	W. John Schade, Jr. (Ind.)	18,580	(16%)	($9,471)
1974 primary:	John B. Anderson (R), unopposed			
1972 general:	John B. Anderson (R)	129,640	(72%)	($33,544)
	John E. Devine, Jr. (D)	50,649	(28%)	($1,463)

◆ ◆ ◆ ◆

SEVENTEENTH DISTRICT

The 17th is one of Illinois's new congressional districts, the result of a federal court order issued in 1971. It combines the southern edge of the Chicago metropolitan area with the fertile farmland of the central Illinois prairie. The district's largest city is Joliet (pop. 78,000), an economically healthy manufacturing center 50 miles from Chicago; somewhat less prosperous is Kankakee (pop. 30,000), on the river and in the county of the same name, some 80 miles from Chicago and smack in the middle of the farmland. Taken together, this territory is politically marginal, normally running about 5% more Republican than the state as a whole. But taken unit by unit, it is widely varied. Agricultural Iroquois County is one of the most Republican in the state; Joliet inclines toward the Democrats; Chicago Heights and Park Forest are swing suburbs, likely to go with (and thus help determine) the winner of any statewide election.

The redistricting plan approved by the court had earlier passed the Illinois House, and the boundaries of the 17th were generally believed to have been sculpted especially for the incumbent House Speaker, W. Robert Blair. Considerable criticism ensued, and Blair never ran. Instead, the nomination went to Joliet State Representative George O'Brien, a veteran of Will County local government. O'Brien's 56-44 victory over Democrat John J. Houlihan followed roughly the established party preferences in the district. His squeak-through 51-49 margin in his 1974 rematch against Houlihan illustrates the effects of Watergate. Despite all the advantages of incumbency, O'Brien was not able to hold his own percentage against the same opponent. His percentages dropped most steeply in the Cook County portion of the district (Chicago Heights, etc.), which he carried in '72 but lost in '74, and in rock-ribbed Republican Iroquois County. Turnout was down sharply in Cook and Will Counties, indicating that traditional Republicans in these urban areas were simply not bothering to vote; while the decreasing O'Brien percentage in Iroquois clearly indicates a protest vote among morality-conscious Republicans. What will happen in November of 1976 is, of course, by no means clear; but with four years of incumbency now, even if the last two were thanks to a small margin, O'Brien should be the clear favorite.

Census Data   Pop. 462,943. Central city, 0%; suburban, 72%. Median family income, $11,286; families above $15,000: 26%; families below $3,000: 6%. Median years education, 12.0.

The Voters

Median voting age 41.
Employment profile White collar, 42%. Blue collar, 43%. Service, 12%. Farm, 3%.
Ethnic groups Black, 9%. Spanish, 3%. Total foreign stock, 16%. Germany, Italy, 2% each; Poland, 1%.

Presidential vote

1972	Nixon (R)	122,873	(66%)
	McGovern (D)	62,394	(34%)
1968	Nixon (R)	89,060	(52%)
	Humphrey (D)	61,674	(36%)
	Wallace (AI)	20,349	(12%)

Rep. George M. O'Brien (R) Elected 1972; b. June 17, 1917, Chicago; home, Joliet; Northwestern U., A.B. 1939, Yale U., J.D. 1947; Catholic.

Career Air Force, WWII; Practicing atty.; Will Co. Bd. of Supervisors, 1956–64; Ill. House of Reps., 1971–72.

Offices 422 CHOB, 202-225-3635. Also 57 N. Ottawa St., Joliet 60431, 815-727-4718.

Committees

Armed Services (6th). Subcommittees: Military Compensation; Military Personnel.

Veterans' Affairs (9th). Subcommittees: Cemeteries and Burial Benefits; Hospitals.

Group Ratings

	ADA	COPE	LWV	RIPON	NFU	LCV	CFA	NAB	NSI	ACA
1974	18	0	50	53	46	25	23	83	100	53
1973	17	27	73	71	35	19	29	–	–	68

Key Votes

1) Foreign Aid	ABS	6) Gov Abortn Aid	AGN	11) Pub Cong Election $	FOR
2) Busing	AGN	7) Coed Phys Ed	AGN	12) Turkish Arms Cutoff	AGN
3) ABM	FOR	8) Pov Lawyer Gag	AGN	13) Youth Camp Regs	ABS
4) B-1 Bomber	FOR	9) Pub Trans Sub	AGN	14) Strip Mine Veto	FOR
5) Nerve Gas	FOR	10) EZ Voter Regis	AGN	15) Farm Bill Veto	FOR

Election Results

1974 general:	George M. O'Brian (R)	59,984	(51%)	($80,053)
	John J. Houlihan (D)	56,541	(49%)	($24,863)
1974 primary:	George M. O'Brian (R), unopposed			
1972 general:	George M. O'Brian (R)	100,175	(56%)	($55,360)
	John J. Houlihan (D)	79,840	(44%)	($32,748)

◆ ◆ ◆ ◆ ◆

EIGHTEENTH DISTRICT

"Will it play in Peoria?" was a favorite question of former White House Advisor John Ehrlichman in the Nixon Administration, asked with the sneering implication that the questioner's way would and the critic's would not. After all, the expertise Nixon's men and Nixon himself brought to the White House—for none had ever occupied administrative positions in government—was not how to make policies work, but how to sell them. And for the Nixonites, that meant Peoria, a place in which coincidentally market researchers like to test commercial products, and one which had always, in the past, produced comfortable margins for Richard Nixon and his Republicans. Peoria (pop. 127,000), which is the heart of Illinois's 18th congressional district, has always epitomized Middle America—both its virtues and its failings. The Caterpillar tractor concern and other heavy industrial employers have kept the town humming; it is impervious to all but the most serious recessions, and provides a comfortable living to most of its inhabitants. It has produced some remarkable citizens, like Betty Friedan of women's liberation fame, and (technically his home was in Pekin, across the Illinois River) the late Everett McKinley Dirksen.

The Peoria that John Ehrlichman had in mind was one epitomized more by its Dirksens than its Friedans—an impression fortified by the list of men who have represented the 18th district in the House for the last 40 years. There was Everett Dirksen, who retired in 1948 when he thought he was going blind, recovered, and beat Senate Majority Leader Scott Lucas in the 1950 election. Dirksen, before all the fustian became a national legend, was a pillar of his party's Taft conservative wing. He was succeeded in the House by Harold H. Velde, who worked on the old House Un-American Activities Committee in its most un-American days. Velde was succeeded in 1956 by Robert Michel, then his administrative assistant, and now Minority Whip of the House of Representatives. Such steadfast Republican orthodoxy is hard to match.

But its steadfastness is not quite as great as appears, if one looks back at recent election returns. The 18th district was carried comfortably as long ago as 1970 by Senator Adlai Stevenson, running against an interim incumbent who conducted a Nixon-Agnew flag-pin-in-the-lapel, draft-dodgers-be-damned campaign. And then came Watergate which—the point cannot be made too strongly—did not play in Peoria at all. The ancestral Republicanism of the 18th district almost evaporated. Stevenson carried the district easily, and Congressman Michel was almost defeated. Against a little-known and underfinanced 29-year-old Democrat, Michel won only 53% of the vote in Peoria County and 55% in the district as a whole.

It would have been doubly embarrassing if Michel had lost. Not only does he have an historically safe Republican district, he was also at that time Chairman of the Republican Congressional Campaign Committee. He had long been a popular conservative (and star pitcher on the House Republican softball team) in the tight little world that conservative Republican congressmen live in, and had advanced nearly to the top of the seniority ladder on the House Appropriations Committee. When the Nixon people wanted to dump the HRCCC chairman in 1973, Michel ran against their choice, Clarence (Bud) Brown of Ohio, and easily beat him. It was a melancholy year to take the job: few promising Republican challengers would agree to run, many strong incumbents were retiring, and dozens of usually Republican seats were in danger.

Obviously, to judge from his election as Whip, none of the House Republicans blamed Michel, and none should. He can be expected to exert the same kind of leadership that Gerald Ford did in the past and John Rhodes does now. He will be solidly conservative on the issues, even occasionally disagreeing with the White House position. He will work tirelessly among the currently depleted ranks, winning every vote possible and staying on good terms even with those mavericks who usually go the other way. (It almost always pays off, sooner or later.) His job for 1976 will be mostly to uphold presidential vetoes; and his future may depend on whether Republicans are able to win back many of the seats they lost in 1974. It seems scarcely likely that Michel himself will have the kind of trouble that surprised him last time, but Peoria has at least made the point that it cannot be taken for granted.

Census Data Pop. 463,155. Central city, 27%; suburban, 40%. Median family income, $10,096; families above $15,000: 20%; families below $3,000: 7%. Median years education, 12.1.

The Voters

Median voting age 44.
Employment profile White collar, 44%. Blue collar, 38%. Service, 13%. Farm, 5%.
Ethnic groups Black, 4%. Total foreign stock, 9%. Germany, 2%; UK, 1%.

Presidential vote

1972	Nixon (R)	128,747	(66%)
	McGovern (D)	67,503	(34%)
1968	Nixon (R)	98,747	(51%)
	Humphrey (D)	77,938	(41%)
	Wallace (AI)	15,667	(8%)

Rep. Robert H. Michel (R) Elected 1956; b. Mar. 2, 1923, Peoria; home, Peoria; Bradley U., B.S. 1948; Apostolic Christian.

Career Army, WWII; Admin. Asst., U.S. Rep. Harold Velde, 1949–56.

Offices 2112 RHOB, 202-225-6201. Also 1007 1st Natl. Bank Bldg., Peoria 61602, 309-673-6358.

Committees

Minority Whip

Appropriations (2d). Subcommittees: Labor-HEW.

Group Ratings

	ADA	COPE	LWV	RIPON	NFU	LCV	CFA	NAB	NSI	ACA
1974	11	18	40	58	43	27	0	75	100	93
1973	0	0	9	33	15	6	14	–	–	88
1972	6	30	22	33	33	15	50	89	100	94

Key Votes

1) Foreign Aid	FOR	6) Gov Abortn Aid	ABS	11) Pub Cong Election $	AGN
2) Busing	AGN	7) Coed Phys Ed	AGN	12) Turkish Arms Cutoff	AGN
3) ABM	FOR	8) Pov Lawyer Gag	FOR	13) Youth Camp Regs	AGN
4) B-1 Bomber	FOR	9) Pub Trans Sub	AGN	14) Strip Mine Veto	FOR
5) Nerve Gas	FOR	10) EZ Voter Regis	AGN	15) Farm Bill Veto	FOR

Election Results

1974 general:	Robert H. Michel (R)	71,681	(55%)	($33,851)
	Stephen L. Nordvall (D)	59,225	(45%)	($10,776)
1974 primary:	Robert H. Michel (R), unopposed			
1972 general:	Robert H. Michel (R)	124,407	(65%)	($20,850)
	Stephen L. Nordvall (D)	67,514	(35%)	($2,901)

◆ ◆ ◆ ◆ ◆

NINETEENTH DISTRICT

Tom Railsback is one of forty-odd Republican Congressmen who were elected in Democratic districts in 1966—the best Republican congressional election year since Eisenhower won his second term. Railsback was then 34, an attorney from Rock Island, Illinois, who had been in practice for less than ten years, and a four-year veteran of the Illinois legislature. He was the kind of bright young man (John Anderson of the 16th district had been another, in 1960) whom the Republican elders of the area picked as their standard-bearer: a young lawyer who could stay in Congress many years and accumulate seniority and power one who was noticeably brighter and—this was important—more personable than the average Illinois small city Republican lawyer. Their hope, of course, was that he would prove to be a solid bulwark of conservative Republicanism, a faithful foot-soldier his first few years and then some day perhaps a leader in the House Republican caucus. And, in many respects, Tom Railsback has realized these hopes, but in some respects he must have severely disappointed the old timers who first blessed his candidacy.

For Railsback, as most literate Americans know, was part of the minority of the Republican minority on the House Judiciary Committee which was as responsible as anyone for convincing the American Congress and people that Richard Nixon ought to be removed from office. Indeed, he may have been the key figure on the Republican side. He became convinced early that he would have to vote for impeachment, and as the hearings went on he began meeting with like-minded Republicans and later, Southern Democrats to formulate strategy and draw up articles of impeachment they could agree on. In the process, Railsback gained an impressive mastery of the facts of the case—and a fervor that gave a certain eloquence to a speaking style that otherwise was anything but eloquent.

Something was made by commentators of Railsback's political predicament, caught between Nixon-loving Republicans and Nixon-hating Democrats and Independents. Actually, it never was as bad as he seemed to think. The Republican primary had taken place back in March, and Railsback had been unopposed. In the general, he had the support not only of the local Republican Party, which generally could be counted on to carry most of the rural counties at the northern and southern extreme of his district, but also of the local United Auto Workers, with their large membership at the agricultural machinery plants at Rock Island and Moline, in and around which almost half the people in his 19th district live. When he came out for impeachment, he destroyed the only issue which could possible have helped his Democratic opponent; the result, not surprisingly, was a solid 65–35 victory. Railsback has had a grueling tenth year in Congress; chances are he will have many more, perhaps less arduous.

Census Data Pop. 462,085. Central city, 27%; suburban, 40%. Median family income, $9,579; families above $15,000: 17%; families below $3,000: 9%. Median years education, 12.1.

The Voters

Median voting age 44.
Employment profile White collar, 39%. Blue collar, 39%. Service, 14%. Farm, 8%.
Ethnic groups Black, 2%. Spanish, 2%. Total foreign stock, 11%. Germany, Sweden, 2% each.

Presidential vote

1972	Nixon (R)	124,549	(62%)
	McGovern (D)	77,194	(38%)
1968	Nixon (R)	104,149	(53%)
	Humphrey (D)	80,058	(41%)
	Wallace (AI)	13,167	(7%)

Rep. Tom Railsback (R) Elected 1966; b. Jan. 22, 1932, Moline; home, Moline; Grinnell Col., B.A. 1954, Northwestern U., J.D. 1957; Congregationalist.

Career Army, 1957–59; Practicing atty., 1957–67; Ill. House of Reps., 1963–67.

Offices 2431 RHOB, 202-225-5905. Also Rm. 228, Fed. Bldg., 211 19th St., Rock Island 61201, 309-794-1681.

Committees

District of Columbia (5th). Subcommittees: Education, Labor, and Social Services; Judiciary.

Judiciary (3d). Subcommittees: Courts, Civil Liberties, and the Administration of Justice; Monopolies and Commercial Law.

Group Ratings

	ADA	COPE	LWV	RIPON	NFU	LCV	CFA	NAB	NSI	ACA
1974	35	45	75	88	64	31	15	36	89	46
1973	40	36	82	93	71	28	43	–	–	33
1972	44	22	100	100	67	42	0	60	89	47

Key Votes

1) Foreign Aid	FOR	6) Gov Abortn Aid	AGN	11) Pub Cong Election $	FOR
2) Busing	FOR	7) Coed Phys Ed	FOR	12) Turkish Arms Cutoff	AGN
3) ABM	AGN	8) Pov Lawyer Gag	AGN	13) Youth Camp Regs	AGN
4) B-1 Bomber	ABS	9) Pub Trans Sub	AGN	14) Strip Mine Veto	AGN
5) Nerve Gas	AGN	10) EZ Voter Regis	AGN	15) Farm Bill Veto	FOR

Election Results

1974 general:	Tom Railsback (R)	84,049	(65%)	($61,789)
	Jim Gende (D)	44,677	(35%)	($43,533)
1974 primary:	Tom Railsback (R), unopposed			
1972 general:	Tom Railsback (R;, unopposed			($25,610)

◆ ◆ ◆ ◆ ◆

TWENTIETH DISTRICT

The 20th district of Illinois is a descendant of the district that sent Abraham Lincoln, then a young Springfield lawyer and Whig politician, to the House of Representatives in 1846. The western part of the district, at least, sometimes seems to have changed little since the nineteenth century. It remains a land of fertile prairies, the bottomland of the Mississippi and Illinois Rivers, farm-marketing towns, and courthouse villages. The river port of Quincy on the Mississippi has not grown much since the turn of the century, nor has the little village of Nauvoo, from which the Mormons were expelled in the 1840s and led by Brigham Young to their promised land in Utah.

The largest city in the 20th district is Springfield (pop. 90,000). It must have been a bustling, perhaps even a gracious town in Abe Lincoln's and Mary Todd's time. Today it is a typical state capital: a middle-sized city with an old Capitol building, several not-so-elegant hotels, a small black ghetto, a little bit of industry, and a few shopping centers on the edge of town. Next to state government, the Lincoln tourist business seems to be the mainstay of the local economy.

On paper, the 20th is a politically marginal district. It sits right on the traditional boundary separating the Democratic counties to the south and the Republican ones to the north—a division that dates back to the days of Lincoln and Douglas. These same partisan preferences are still reflected in local elections, although in presidential contests the district has moved increasingly to the Republican side in recent years.

The 1960 census cost Illinois one congressional seat, and it came out of the rural areas in and near the current 20th. Two incumbents—Republican freshman Paul Findley and Democratic veteran Peter Mack—were forced to fight it out in the new 20th. Findley won that 1962 election and had precious little trouble winning for the next dozen years. A middle-ranking Republican on the Foreign Affairs Committee, Findley is considered a maverick not identified with any of the usual schools of thought. He has taken a particular interest in the affairs of NATO—an unusual preoccupation for a Congressman from an area that was traditionally known as isolationist. In the House generally, Findley is something of a loner, making his positions known in crisply articulated speeches but seldom gathering a bloc of votes around him. His rather diffident manner had proved popular with his constituents, but in 1974 he had a real contest. As in 1962, his opponent was Peter Mack, returning from his job at the Washington-based Southern Railway for a try in what presumably he perceived as a premier Democratic year. It was, and he reduced Findley's percentage from 69% to 55%—a formidable achievement but not, of course, one awarded with a seat in Congress. One may assume that Mack and others will draw the obvious lesson from this, to wit, that Findley cannot be beaten even in the most favorable of circumstances.

Census Data Pop. 464,551. Central city, 20%; suburban, 31%. Median family income, $9,269; families above $15,000: 17%; families below $3,000: 10%. Median years education, 12.0.

The Voters

Median voting age 46.
Employment profile White collar, 46%. Blue collar, 33%. Service, 14%. Farm, 7%.
Ethnic groups Black, 4%. Total foreign stock, 8%. Germany, 2%; Italy, UK, 1% each.

Presidential vote

1972	Nixon (R)	137,414	(64%)
	McGovern (D)	78,281	(36%)
1968	Nixon (R)	106,487	(50%)
	Humphrey (D)	87,504	(41%)
	Wallace (AI)	20,215	(9%)

Rep. Paul Findley (R) Elected 1960; b. June 23, 1921, Jacksonville; home, Pittsfield; Ill. Col., B.A. 1943; Congregationalist.

Career Navy, WWII; Pres., Pike Press, Inc., 1947–60.

Offices 2133 RHOB, 202-225-5271. Also 205 Fed. Bldg., Springfield 62701, 217,525-4231.

Committees

Agriculture (3d). Subcommittees: Domestic Marketing and Consumer Relations; Livestock and Grains; Oilseeds and Rice.

International Relations (3d). International Organizations; International Security and Scientific Affairs.

Group Ratings

	ADA	COPE	LWV	RIPON	NFU	LCV	CFA	NAB	NSI	ACA
1974	58	20	89	92	71	54	17	67	50	36
1973	64	27	75	93	44	58	63	–	–	58
1972	25	18	64	78	29	47	100	92	71	70

Key Votes

1) Foreign Aid	FOR	6) Gov Abortn Aid	ABS	11) Pub Cong Election $	AGN
2) Busing	FOR	7) Coed Phys Ed	ABS	12) Turkish Arms Cutoff	ABS
3) ABM	AGN	8) Pov Lawyer Gag	AGN	13) Youth Camp Regs	ABS
4) B-1 Bomber	AGN	9) Pub Trans Sub	AGN	14) Strip Mine Veto	AGN
5) Nerve Gas	AGN	10) EZ Voter Regis	AGN	15) Farm Bill Veto	FOR

Election Results

1974 general:	Paul Findley (R)	84,426	(55%)	($118,162)
	Peter F. Mack (D)	69,551	(45%)	($53,369)
1974 primary:	Paul Findley (R), unopposed			
1972 general:	Paul Findley (R)	148,419	(69%)	($71,187)
	Robert S. O'Shea (D)	67,445	(31%)	($15,671)

◆ ◆ ◆ ◆ ◆

TWENTY-FIRST DISTRICT

Downstate Illinois has always been regarded as overwhelmingly Republican. But that has never really been the case. The largest Republican margins in Illinois come out of the Chicago suburbs, and except for the fertile farmlands in the north central part of the state, Downstate might more accurately be described as marginally Republican. Take, for example, the 21st congressional district, located about halfway between Chicago and St. Louis. The 21st lies in flat prairie farm country, but most of its population is concentrated in three urban areas: Decatur (pop. 90,000), a factory town; Champaign-Urbana (total pop. 89,000), home of the University of Illinois; and Bloomington (pop. 66,000 with the suburb of Normal), an insurance town and ancestral home of the Stevenson family. These places are listed in the order of their traditional Democratic inclinations, but of late there have been changes, due primarily to the student vote. Some 15% of the eligible electorate here are college students—the largest proportion in Illinois, and obviously enough to tip a close election, if they get out and vote.

The sudden increase in student—and, presumably, Democratic—votes may have contributed to the 1972 retirement of 11-term incumbent William L. Springer. A knowledgeable conservative, Springer was ranking Republican and often the dominant voice on the House Commerce Committee; after retirement, he was nominated and, despite some opposition, confined to sit on the Federal Power Commission. Springer is the kind of Congressman one would expect to find in a Downstate Illinois district; his successor is a little different. He is, to be sure, a Republican, former state Representative Edward Madigan, from one of the smallest and most Republican counties in the district.

Apparently the 21st's voters expected him to vote much as Springer did; Madigan lost Champaign-Urbana and only carried Macon County (Decatur) by a hair in the 1972 election. But the then 36-year-old Congressman turned out to have more liberal proclivities than one might have thought. He was, for example, against the bombing of Cambodia, and for opening the highway trust fund to mass transit expenditures. He was also the only Illinois Republican to increase his percentage of the vote between the Republican year of 1972 and the Democratic year of 1974—from 55% to a very solid indeed 66%. Madigan turns 40 as 1976 begins, and he can be expected to remain in the House for many terms to come.

Census Data Pop. 464,693. Central city, 53%; suburban, 31%. Median family income, $10,043; families above $15,000: 21%; families below $3,000: 7%. Median years education, 12.3.

The Voters

Median voting age 38.
Employment profile White collar, 51%. Blue collar, 29%. Service, 15%. Farm, 5%.
Ethnic groups Black, 5%. Total foreign stock, 7%. Germany, 2%.

Presidential vote

1972	Nixon (R)	117,230	(62%)
	McGovern (D)	70,380	(38%)
1968	Nixon (R)	88,585	(53%)
	Humphrey (D)	65,529	(39%)
	Wallace (AI)	14,063	(8%)

Rep. Edward R. Madigan (R) Elected 1972; b. Jan. 13, 1936, Lincoln; home, Lincoln; Lincoln Col.; Catholic.

Career Owner, taxi and car leasing co.; Lincoln Bd. of Zoning Appeals; Ill. House of Reps., 1967–72.

Offices 1728 LHOB, 202-225-2371. Also 200 W. Church St., Champaign 61820, 217-356-8633.

Committees

Agriculture (7th). Subcommittees: Conservation and Credit; Tobacco.

Interstate and Foreign Commerce (12th). Subcommittees: Communications; Oversight and Investigations.

Group Ratings

	ADA	COPE	LWV	RIPON	NFU	LCV	CFA	NAB	NSI	ACA
1974	29	40	75	69	71	27	31	60	78	57
1973	17	27	82	87	42	16	38	–	–	73

Key Votes

1) Foreign Aid	AGN	6) Gov Abortn Aid	AGN	11) Pub Cong Election $	FOR
2) Busing	FOR	7) Coed Phys Ed	AGN	12) Turkish Arms Cutoff	AGN
3) ABM	FOR	8) Pov Lawyer Gag	FOR	13) Youth Camp Regs	AGN
4) B-1 Bomber	FOR	9) Pub Trans Sub	FOR	14) Strip Mine Veto	FOR
5) Nerve Gas	FOR	10) EZ Voter Regis	AGN	15) Farm Bill Veto	FOR

Election Results

1974 general:	Edward R. Madigan (R)	78,640	(66%)	($68,372)
	Richard N. Small (D)	40,896	(34%)	($21,431)
1974 primary:	Edward R. Madigan (R), unopposed			
1972 general:	Edward R. Madigan (R)	99,966	(55%)	($85,958)
	Lawrence E. Johnson (D)	82,523	(45%)	($29,802)

◆ ◆ ◆ ◆ ◆

TWENTY-SECOND DISTRICT

In years past, the assumption was that any Congressman who accumulated substantial seniority must hold a "safe" seat; else he would have been swept out of office in one of the periodic landslides won by the other party. That is decidedly not the case any more. And one good example of why not is Congressman George Shipley of the 22d district of Illinois. Still under 50, Shipley is already the tenth-ranking Democrat (out of 37) on the House Appropriations Committee, and the second-ranking member on its Agriculture and Legislative Subcommittees. Yet Shipley has held what must be counted as an exceedingly marginal district, and has been a top priority target for Republican campaigners in virtually every election since he first won the seat by 187 votes in the very Democratic year of 1958.

Why has Shipley continued to win? At first glance, the 22d does not look like promising Democratic territory. It is a collection of 20 predominantly rural Downstate Illinois counties; its largest cities are Danville (pop. 42,000) and Mattoon (pop. 19,000), neither known as bulwarks of Democratic strength. Few of these counties go Democratic in presidential or statewide races these days, although in landslides (Johnson 1964, Stevenson 1974) most do. But the people here are not the ancestral Republicans of northern Downstate Illinois. This area was settled largely by Southerners in the nineteenth century; people still have a noticeable drawl, and the whole area went for Douglas rather than Lincoln in 1858. Local elections are often won by Democrats, and so there was a partisan base for Shipley, himself a former county sheriff, to build on.

The other difference between Shipley and Congressmen from the forties and fifties who had lost, helplessly, when their party was in trouble, was the increasing advantages of incumbency —and the jet plane. Just as he was beginning his years in Congress, members from both parties were beginning to take advantage, in a major way, of the free congressional mailing privilege and the ability of Congressmen to handle constituents' problems with the federal and other governments to build a personal popularity base, in excess of party strength. Moreover, the early sixties was also the time when jet travel began, and a Congressman like Shipley could make it from his Capitol Hill office to Chicago or St. Louis, and thence on a smaller plane to his district, in two to three hours. So the voters of the 22d district could be exposed, just about every weekend rather than only on congressional recesses, to Shipley's genial, folksy personality and his assiduous campaigning.

Nevertheless, the apparent unpopularity of national Democratic policies in this area made Shipley a continued target. In 1970, he won only 54% of the vote against right-wing writer and activist Phyliss Schlafly, who since has become the nation's leading crusader against the Equal Rights Amendment. (Mrs. Schlafly believes that women's place is in the home; however, to allow her to keep up with her hectic schedule, she has a staff of servants.) Then, the 1972 redistricting plan badly hurt Shipley; a majority of the 22d district, as then drawn, was new to him. Nevertheless, he beat his active Republican opponent by a 53-47 margin in the new areas and clobbered him 64–36 in the old. In 1974, Shipley increased his margins slightly; he now seems to have transformed what was a prime marginal district into a safe seat.

That leaves him, presumably, more time to devote to his duties on the Appropriations Committee. He is not the most liberal of Democrats, and is basically more in sympathy with the oldtimers on the committee than with the new young liberals who control the party caucus. On the basis of strict seniority, Shipley is almost a sure bet to become Appropriations Chairman some day; he is 49, while each of the nine more senior members is at least 65.

Census Data Pop. 464,121. Central city, 0%; suburban, 1%. Median family income, $8,350; families above $15,000: 13%; families below $3,000: 12%. Median years education, 11.4.

The Voters

Median voting age 47.
Employment profile White collar, 37%. Blue collar, 40%. Service, 13%. Farm, 10%.
Ethnic groups Black, 1%. Total foreign stock, 4%. Germany, 1%.

Presidential vote

1972	Nixon (R)	141,820	(64%)
	McGovern (D)	80,804	(36%)
1968	Nixon (R)	117,778	(53%)
	Humphrey (D)	83,137	(37%)
	Wallace (AI)	22,977	(10%)

Rep. George E. Shipley (D) Elected 1958; b. Apr. 21, 1927, Olney; home, Olney; Baptist.

Career Richland Co. Deputy Sheriff, 1950–54, Sheriff 1954–58.

Offices 237 CHOB, 202-225-5001. Also 111 S. Boone St., Olney 62450, 618-395-2171.

Committees

Appropriations (10th). Subcommittees: Agriculture; HUD-Independent Agencies; Legislative.

Group Ratings

	ADA	COPE	LWV	RIPON	NFU	LCV	CFA	NAB	NSI	ACA
1974	36	44	33	17	85	69	18	78	80	50
1973	50	91	58	46	100	22	63	–	–	46
1972	25	67	27	31	83	25	100	30	67	57

Key Votes

1) Foreign Aid	AGN	6) Gov Abortn Aid	AGN	11) Pub Cong Election $	AGN
2) Busing	AGN	7) Coed Phys Ed	ABS	12) Turkish Arms Cutoff	FOR
3) ABM	AGN	8) Pov Lawyer Gag	FOR	13) Youth Camp Regs	FOR
4) B-1 Bomber	FOR	9) Pub Trans Sub	ABS	14) Strip Mine Veto	AGN
5) Nerve Gas	AGN	10) EZ Voter Regis	FOR	15) Farm Bill Veto	AGN

Election Results

1974 general:	George E. Shipley (D)	97,921	(60%)	($50,328)
	William A. Young (R)	65,731	(40%)	($91,781)
1974 primary:	George E. Shipley (D), unopposed			
1972 general:	George E. Shipley (D)	124,589	(57%)	($52,812)
	Robert B. Lamkin (R)	90,390	(41%)	($83,554)
	Cleo A. Duzan (Ind.)	5,389	(2%)	

◆ ◆ ◆ ◆ ◆

TWENTY-THIRD DISTRICT

The 23d congressional district of Illinois is the area around East St. Louis's Gateway Arch, where one can see East St. Louis, Belleville, and Granite City through the smog across the Mississippi River. These are not verdant St. Louis suburbs, but grimy industrial towns criss-crossed by miles of railroad track. They have all the problems usually associated with core-city areas: air pollution, inadequate housing, crime, and a declining tax base. East St. Louis became a majority black town in the sixties, but when the blacks took over city hall, they found the treasury virtually bare. The Illinois side of the St. Louis metropolitan area has a disproportionate share of its poor and low-income working-class residents; the rich stay very much on the Missouri side of the River.

The 23d is easily the most Democratic of all the Downstate Illinois congressional districts. But as in many working-class areas, the Democratic majority has disappeared in recent presidential elections: Humphrey won the district with only a plurality as George Wallace took 16% of the vote; McGovern lost the district altogether by a narrow margin. But in local elections, the 23d has remained as Democratic as it ever was. The last time a Republican was elected Congressman here was in 1942. He was defeated in 1944 by Democrat Mel Price, who has been reelected ever since—by margins of better than 2–1 since 1962 and with 80% of the vote in 1974.

In Congress, Price holds two key positions which, together, give him jurisdiction over a lion's share of the federal budget. He is a top member of the Joint Committee on Atomic Energy, serving on a rotating basis as Chairman during the 93d Congress. The Joint Committee has worked especially closely with the agency—now the agencies, since the old Atomic Energy Commission has been split in two—it oversees since it was created just after World War II. An original member of the Joint Committee, Price was a friend of longtime Chairman, former congressman Chet Holifield of California, and shared his belief in the basic purposes and practices of the AEC. Price is, for example, a backer of the controversial breeder reactor, and he was one of the authors of the Price-Anderson Act, which by providing federal insurance tends to set limits on the amount of private insurance operators of nuclear reactors must carry.

But even more important, Price is the new Chairman of the House Armed Services Committee. It is not a post he sought. Following the 1974 election, he was scheduled to be the second-ranking Democrat on the Committee, behind Chairman Edward Hebert of Louisiana. But the Democratic caucus, spurred by freshmen, dumped the autocratic Hebert, who could not hide his contempt for their different views, and installed Price. He is expected to be more even-handed than Hebert, but on basic policy questions he comes out the same way. Price, like so many members who served during World War II, believes in at least as large a defense budget as at present, and is not in particular sympathy with those who want to end U. S. military aid in Southeast Asia—although he has voted on occasion against the bombing of Cambodia. Indeed, some doves on the Committee have mixed feeling about Price's promotion; they believe he will be able to carry his bills on the floor more easily than Hebert would have.

Census Data Pop. 462,960. Central city, 0%; suburban, 100%. Median family income, $9,872; families above $15,000: 18%; families below $3,000: 10%. Median years education, 11.1.

The Voters

Median voting age 43.
Employment profile White collar, 45%. Blue collar, 41%. Service, 13%. Farm, 1%.
Ethnic groups Black, 15%. Spanish, 1%. Total foreign stock, 8%. Germany, 2%.

Presidential vote

1972	Nixon (R)	87,654	(53%)
	McGovern (D)	76,971	(47%)
1968	Nixon (R)	59,899	(35%)
	Humphrey (D)	83,886	(49%)
	Wallace (AI)	26,675	(16%)

Rep. Melvin Price (D) Elected 1944; b. Jan. 1, 1905, East St. Louis; home, East St. Louis; St. Louis U., 1923–25; Catholic

Career Newspaper correspondent, E. St. Louis *Journal*, St. Louis *Globe-Democrat*; Sports ed., E. St. Louis *News-Review*; St. Clair Co. Bd. of Supervisors, 1929–31; Secy. to U.S. Rep. Edwin M. Schaefer, 1933–43; Army, WWII.

Offices 2468 RHOB, 202-225-5661; Also Fed. Bldg., 650 Missouri Ave., East St. Louis 62201, 618-274-2200.

Committees

Armed Services (Chairman). Subcommittees: Military Compensation; Research and Development (Chairman); Special Subcommittee on Intelligence.

Standards of Official Conduct (2d).

Joint Committee on Atomic Energy (Vice Chairman).

Group Ratings

	ADA	COPE	LWV	RIPON	NFU	LCV	CFA	NAB	NSI	ACA
1974	43	100	83	38	93	59	83	0	80	13
1973	72	100	92	80	100	74	88	–	–	12
1972	69	91	92	76	71	47	100	9	90	17

Key Votes

1) Foreign Aid	FOR	6) Gov Abortn Aid	AGN	11) Pub Cong Election $	AGN
2) Busing	FOR	7) Coed Phys Ed	AGN	12) Turkish Arms Cutoff	FOR
3) ABM	FOR	8) Pov Lawyer Gag	AGN	13) Youth Camp Regs	FOR
4) B-1 Bomber	FOR	9) Pub Trans Sub	FOR	14) Strip Mine Veto	AGN
5) Nerve Gas	FOR	10) EZ Voter Regis	FOR	15) Farm Bill Veto	AGN

Election Results

1974 general:	Melvin Price (D)	78,347	(80%)	($27,847)
	Scott R. Randolph (R)	18,987	(20%)	($670)
1974 primary:	Melvin Price (D)	43,131	(90%)	
	William Ray Bordeaux (D)	4,659	(10%)	
1972 general:	Melvin Price (D)	121,682	(75%)	($17,134)
	Robert Mays (R)	40,428	(25%)	($2,734)

♦ ♦ ♦ ♦ ♦

TWENTY-FOURTH DISTRICT

Egypt is the name given the southernmost part of Illinois—the flat, fertile farmland where the Ohio River joins the Mississippi. This is low, alluvial land, subject to floods almost as often as ancient Egypt; it is protected today by giant levees, which rise above the fields and hide a view of the rivers. There is more than a touch of Dixie here: the southern tip of Illinois is closer to Jackson, Mississippi, than to Chicago. The unofficial capital of Egypt is Cairo (pronounced KAYroh), a declining town at the exact confluence of the two rivers. In recent years, Cairo has been the scene of a virtual war between its white majority and large black minority; it must surely be one of the grimmest small towns in America.

There are no official boundaries to Egypt, but it is safe to say that the 24th congressional district goes north considerably beyond them. The district takes in the coal-mining country around West Frankfort and Marion; this is one of the most heavily strip-mined areas in the United States. It extends almost to the suburbs of St. Louis, and includes Carbondale, site of troubled Southern Illinois University. (There was town-gown fighting here in the early sixties, and later the university president, a former Nixon pollster, fired many tenured faculty members.) Virtually all this territory is Democratic in most elections, whether from ancestral Southern allegiance, or because of coal miners' proclivities, or from the SIU students' preference for antiwar candidates. It has not been very supportive of national Democratic candidates, but in congressional races it has not veered from the Democrats for the last twenty years.

For most of that time, from 1954 to 1974, the Congressman from the district was Kenneth J. Gray, who deserves at least a footnote here. Besides being a politician, Gray also flew airplanes and helicopters, owned an airport, was the Congress's only licensed auctioneer, and an amateur magician. Once on the floor of the House, to demonstrate the effect a proposed public works project would have on his district, Gray produced a bouquet of red roses from his sleeve. As a senior member of Public Works, he was a devout pork-barreler, pushing projects for his district as if his political life depended on it—as it probably did in the fifties. He also was the major force behind the idea of remodeling Union Station in Washington to be a national visitors' center—a project that has resulted so far only in the evisceration of the station's lobby. During his career, Gray became chummy with who knows how many lobbyists, and when he retired in 1974 at the tender age of 50 he must have expected them to take care of him. To judge from subsequent news reports, they haven't, and Gray is apparently in trouble now for having allegedly used campaign funds to buy a helicopter and a white Cadillac limousine—and then having sold them and enjoyed the use of the money.

Gray's successor is quite another kind of politician: an almost austere liberal named Paul Simon. Formerly the editor of a small newspaper in the town of Troy, near East St. Louis, Simon was elected to the legislature as an independent Democrat and became known not only for his honesty, but also for his legislative skill. A strong liberal, he had backing from organized labor and independent elements and support from the Daley machine as well when he ran for Lieutenant Governor in 1968. Although a Republican won the top spot, Simon won too. He looked like a cinch for the gubernatorial nomination in 1972, as a man acceptable to all segments of the party, and would probably have beaten incumbent Richard Ogilvie, who had sponsored an income tax. But Simon refused to say that he would repeal the tax, while his opponent, the anti-Daley former Montgomery Ward executive Daniel Walker, hinted he would. Walker barely won the primary, with heavy support Downstate, and Simon retired to a professorship at SIU.

There he was, well within the bounds of the 24th district, when Kenny Gray announced he would retire. Simon was the obvious candidate, winning the primary with 68% of the vote and the general with 60%. At 48, with his old-fashioned horn-rimmed glasses, he does not fit the image of 1975's freshman Democrat, but he has supported all the reforms, and has the advantage of a safe district which will reelect him as long as he runs. However, if Dan Walker should, as he dearly wants to, run for President in 1976, Simon could well be a candidate for Governor—and at this early stage would seem the odds-on favorite to win.

Census Data Pop. 465,018. Central city, 0%; suburban, 0%. Median family income, $7,501; families above $15,000: 11%; families below $3,000: 17%. Median years education, 10.1.

The Voters

Median voting age 47.
Employment profile White collar, 38%. Blue collar, 40%. Service, 15%. Farm, 7%.
Ethnic groups Black, 4%. Total foreign stock, 5%. Germany, 1%.

Presidential vote

1972	Nixon (R)	138,435	(60%)
	McGovern (D)	92,910	(40%)
1968	Nixon (R)	112,667	(49%)
	Humphrey (D)	92.479	(41%)
	Wallace (AI)	23,147	(10%)

Rep. Paul Simon (D) Elected 1974; b. Nov. 29, 1928, Eugene, Oreg.; home, Carbondale; U. of Oreg., 1945–46, Dana Col., 1946–48; Lutheran.

Career Editor-Publisher, Troy *Tribune*, and newspaper weekly chain owner, 1948–66; Army, 1951–53; Ill. House of Reps., 1955–63; Ill. Senate 1963–69; Lt. Gov. of Ill, 1969–73; Candidate for Dem. nomination for Gov., 1972; Instructor, Sangamon St. U., 1973.

Offices 1724 LHOB, 202-225-5201. Also 107 Glenview Dr., Carbondale 62901, 618-457-4171.

Committees

Education and Labor (22d). Subcommittees: Elementary, Secondary and Vocational Education; Labor Standards; Post-secondary Education.

Post Office and Civil Service (16th). Subcommittees: Census and Population; Postal Facilities and Mail and Labor Management; Postal Service.

Group Ratings: Newly Elected

Key Votes

1) Foreign Aid	FOR	6) Gov Abortn Aid	NE	11) Pub Cong Election $	NE
2) Busing	NE	7) Coed Phys Ed	FOR	12) Turkish Arms Cutoff	NE
3) ABM	NE	8) Pov Lawyer Gag	NE	13) Youth Camp Regs	FOR
4) B-1 Bomber	AGN	9) Pub Trans Sub	NE	14) Strip Mine Veto	AGN
5) Nerve Gas	NE	10) EZ Voter Regis	NE	15) Farm Bill Veto	AGN

Election Results

1974 general:	Paul Simon (D)	108,417	(60%)	($223,163)
	Val Oshel (R)	73,634	(40%)	($50,566)
1974 primary:	Paul Simon (D)	47,727	(68%)	
	Joe R. Browning (D)	22,024	(32%)	

INDIANA

The most powerful political machines still functioning in this country are not to be found in the big cities of the East Coast, but rather in the heart of Middle America: in the city of Chicago, of course, and in the state of Indiana. Mayor Daley's machine is the more famous, but the Indiana machines, if less well known, are probably in better shape, as they hum away in Indianapolis, the state's other big cities, and practically all of Indiana's 92 county courthouses. Almost all public offices in Indiana, including judgeships and clerks of court, are partisan; and nearly every partisan official and each of the patronage employees he has installed must kick back 2% of his salary to the party coffers. In few other parts of the nation is this practice, redolent of the 1880s, so strenuously enforced. Because Indiana has about as many patronage jobs as any state in the country, and because both parties always retain control of certain lucrative city halls and county courthouses, these 2% "donations" keep both Democratic and Republican machines well financed.

Another factor contributes to the strength of the parties here. Candidates for statewide office are not chosen in primaries, but by party conventions. Primaries are used for nominees to the U.S. House and state legislatures, but even here local party organizations are seldom challenged. As a result, unorthodox candidates rarely surface in Indiana politics. The Democrats are moderates-to-liberals, acceptable to organized labor, which plays an important role in politics. The Republicans are almost always solid conservatives. Thus there is no Indiana equivalent of Illinois's Senator Charles Percy, nor has the Indiana Democratic Party ever found it useful to give a major nomination to such an unpolitical figure as Ohio's Senator John Glenn.

Since a lot is at stake in any Indiana election—not just in terms of what policies will be followed, but also in terms of cold hard cash—the Indiana party bosses try hard to slate candidates congenial to Hoosier mores. Elections in Indiana are therefore often very close. Senator Vance Hartke, for example, won his third term in 1970 by just over 4,000 votes out of 1,700,000 cast. And Senator Birch Bayh was first elected in 1962 by less than 11,000 votes. Also, because there are no great regional variations in political preference, the state's congressional districts change parties with unusual frequency. Democrats currently hold nine of the state's 11 seats, but that was a result of their winning only 54% of the total state congressional vote; in 1972, when they won 46%, they took only four of the 11. Though it seldom votes for any but a Republican presidential candidate (exception: it went 56% for Johnson in 1964), Indiana thus is a fairly good barometer of national opinion in state and congressional races. Like the nation, it has shown a marked preference for Republican Presidents and Democratic Senators for the past 15 years.

Indiana's machine politics has, on occasion, produced officeholders of large stature, and there is no better evidence for that than the candidates who faced each other in the 1968 Senate race here. Both Democrat Birch Bayh, who won the contest with 52% of the vote, and Republican William Ruckelshaus, who went on to a job in John Mitchell's Justice Department, have since become national figures, mentioned for a place on their party's national tickets. Ironically, Ruckelshaus, the loser, is if anything better known at this time. As Nixon's head of the Environmental Protection Agency, he had built up a reputation for integrity and even liberalness, which made him suddenly very attractive to the Nixon White House when they needed someone confirmable to appoint as head of the FBI in April 1973. There Ruckelshaus embarrassed his boss by revealing the illegal surveillance on Daniel Ellsberg which resulted in the dismissal of the government case against him. But that was as nothing to the embarrassment Ruckelshaus caused the President when, as Deputy Attorney General, he forced Nixon to fire him rather than having him fire Special Prosecutor Archibald Cox. The Saturday Night Massacre made Ruckelshaus, along with Attorney General Elliot Richardson, something of an unemployed national hero. But for some of the same reasons, it did not endear him to many high Indiana Republicans. Ruckelshaus would be a very strong candidate for statewide office, if he could get the Republican nomination—but at the moment that seems very unlikely.

Getting a state wide nomination (for Senator in 1962) was how Birch Bayh got his national start and stopping some key nominations (Clement Haynsworth and G. Harrold Carswell for Supreme Court) was how he became best known. Hard work has been the secret of Bayh's success. He took a hitherto unimportant subcommittee chairmanship, Constitutional Amendments, and steered three amendments to passage in the Congress—more than anyone since Madison shepherded through the Bill of Rights. They include the Equal Rights Amendment, still a subject of controversy in the state legislatures; the 26th Amendment, which establishes the 18-year-old vote in all elections; and perhaps the most important of all, the 25th Amendment on presidential succession. It was the 25th which provided a means of choosing a successor when Vice President Spiro Agnew was forced to resign—nomination by the President and confirmation by both Houses of Congress—and thus was the proximate cause of Gerald Ford, rather than Carl Albert, becoming President. It also provides, though few seem to have noticed it, a much more democratic way of choosing Vice Presidents than the traditional method of having a political convention go through the motions of ratifying the choice of one tired, usually poorly informed man.

Besides strengthening our organic law, Bayh has also been responsible for strengthening the body which interprets it, the Supreme Court. When civil rights and labor leaders were looking for a Senator to lead the seemingly hopeless fight against Judge Clement Haynsworth in 1969, Bayh volunteered—and managed to convince a majority of the Senate that the judge's ethical problems were too great to permit confirmation. Months later, the Senate was in the mood to confirm anyone Nixon put up, and Nixon responded by naming the previously unknown Judge Harrold Carswell. Once again, Bayh volunteered to lead the fight, and once again he succeeded, convincing a majority that Carswell was perhaps a racist and certainly a mediocrity. With all those achievements, Bayh launched a presidential campaign in 1971, assembling a talented staff and significant financing. But in a crowded field of candidates, progress was hard to discern, and when the Senator learned that Mrs. Bayh required breast surgery, he left the race.

Most Democratic Senators with such a record could have expected to win reelection easily in 1974. But Indiana's strong Republican Party was determined not to let the seat go by default and put up one of their strongest young officeholders, Indianapolis Mayor Richard Lugar. He had several issues he could work on, for Bayh had been bottling up in his subcommittee constitutional amendments to stop busing and to prohibit abortions; there was a busing case pending in Indianapolis, and older voters of all religious backgrounds reacted negatively to abortion. Bayh responded, again, with hard work and hustle. He campaigned all over the state, pitched horseshoes against all comers, talked and joked and chuckled in his arresting Hoosier accent. The wooden Lugar—long known as Richard Nixon's favorite Mayor—was no match. He also had problems of his own—a nasty little police scandal in Indianapolis. The ultimate result was a 52% Bayh victory; he managed to carry Indianapolis, and ran well in the industrial centers and the southern-accented part of the state below Indianapolis.

Despite the narrowness of his win, Bayh started considering again a run for the Presidency. He has the advantage of being acceptable to all wings of his national party—an advantage definitely not shared by apparent frontrunner Henry Jackson or former candidate George McGovern. He is not, however, particularly well-known, and as the race was beginning he had already lost some of his former backers to Jackson or other candidates.

Indiana's other Senator, Vance Hartke, has already run once for the Presidency, in 1972, and it is unlikely that he will do so again in 1976. The race in 1972 was financed, so far as can be determined (it occurred before the famous April 7 deadline, after which contributions had to be disclosed), by the railroads, railroad unions, and other interests favoring major legislation which Hartke has sponsored as a member of the Senate Commerce and Finance Committees. First elected in 1958, Hartke is well-positioned on such issues; as Chairman of the Surface Transportation Subcommittee, he has a lot to say about current and possible subsidies to railroads and trucking interests; as third ranking Democrat on the Finance Committee, he is in a good position to push, as he was in 1972, legislation to clamp limits on imports into the United States. Indeed, the course of Hartke's Senate career seems aimed at positioning him to become, some day, a major lobbyist on the lines of Florida's George Smathers—but at the moment, that does not seem to be his own ambition at all.

Rather, Hartke is determined to win a fourth term in 1976. Back in 1970, he only barely defeated Richard Roudebush, then an ultraconservative Congressman who, Hartke forces claimed, had never fully recovered from an earlier plane crash. It was one of the bitterest and many think—the dirtiest Senate races in recent years; ironically, Roudebush is now head of the Veterans' Administration and Hartke is Chairman of the Senate Veterans Affairs Committee. There is a widespread feeling, in Washington and in Indiana, that whatever popularity Hartke had then has largely evaporated, and that he enters the race as a pronounced underdog. If, indeed, he enters it at all, for it remains a possibility that the Democratic convention may dump him for someone like 9th district Congressman Lee Hamilton. The Republicans will undoubtedly put up a very conservative candidate—as they tend to do when they have a chance to win—and the resulting brouhaha may be as unedifying as the 1970 campaign, when Roudebush ran ads accusing Hartke of supplying rifles to the North Vietnamese and Hartke supporters whispered that Roudebush had been married four times.

The Governor of Indiana is a calmer sort of figure: Otis M. Bowen, M.D., as he signs his name, a Republican elected by a postwar-record margin in 1972 and the first Indiana Governor ever eligible for a second four-year term. Bowen, though he sponsored a major tax revision, appears to be widely popular, and his likely opponent, Secretary of State Larry Conrad, will have a difficult time beating him. That prognosis, plus the likelihood that Gerald Ford or whoever the Republican nominee is will carry this state, whatever nominee does elsewhere in the Midwest, makes the outlook for Hartke and most of the state's Democratic Congressmen a little pessimistic. Indiana, as much as any place in the country, still tends to be a straight-ticket state, and so 1976 looks like another series of pitched battles between the nation's roughest political machines.

Census Data Pop. 5,193,669; 2.57% of U.S. total, 11th largest; Central city, 34%; suburban, 27%. Median family income, $9,966; 19th highest; families above $15,000: 19%; families below $3,000: 8%. Median years education, 12.1.

1974 Share of Federal Tax Burden $6,668,601,000; 2.49% of U.S. total, 11th largest.

1974 Share of Federal Outlays $4,912,197,000; 1.82% of U.S. total, 18th largest. Per capita federal spending, $946.

DOD	$1,208,297,000	19th (1.76%)	HEW	$1,974,801,000	14th (2.13%)
AEC	$2,354,000	26th (0.08%)	HUD	$17,630,000	20th (1.81%)
NASA	$5,639,000	24th (0.19%)	VA	$254,806,000	20th (1.86%)
DOT	$114,018,000	27th (1.35%)	EPA	$60,223,000	16th (1.91%)
DOC	$16,658,000	17th (1.03%)	RevS	$129,578,000	14th (2.13%)
DOI	$16,441,000	34th (0.67%)	Int.	$314,243,000	10th (1.53%)
USDA	$208,978,000	25th (1.68%)	Other	$588,531,000	

Economic Base Primary metal industries, especially blast furnaces and steel mills; electrical equipment and supplies, radio and television receiving equipment; finance, insurance and real estate; transportation equipment, especially motor vehicles and equipment; agriculture, notably hogs, corn, soybeans and cattle; machinery, especially general industrial machinery; fabricated metal products, especially fabricated structural metal products.

Political Line-up Governor, Otis R. Brown (R). Senators, Vance Hartke (D) and Birch Bayh (D). Representatives, 11 (9 D and 2 R). State Senate (27 R and 23 D); State House (56 D and 44 R).

The Voters

Registration 2,937,114 Total. No Party Registration.
Median voting age 42.
Employment profile White collar, 42%. Blue collar, 43%. Service, 12%. Farm, 3%.
Ethnic groups Black, 7%. Spanish, 1%. Total foreign stock, 7%. Germany, 1%.

Presidential vote

1972	Nixon (R)	1,405,154	(66%)
	McGovern (D)	708,568	(34%)
1968	Nixon (R)	1,067,885	(50%)
	Humphrey (D)	806,659	(38%)
	Wallace (AI)	243,108	(11%)

1972 Democratic Presidential Primary

Humphrey	354,244	(47%)
Wallace	309,495	(41%)
Muskie	87,719	(12%)

1972 Republican Presidential Primary

Nixon	417,069	(100%)

Sen. Vance Hartke (D) Elected 1958, seat up 1976; b. May 31, 1919, Stendal; home, Evansville; Evansville Col., B.A. 1941, Ind. U., J.D. 1948; Lutheran.

Career Practicing atty., 1948–56; Deputy Prosecuting Atty., Vanderburgh Co., 1950–51; Mayor of Evansville, 1956–58.

Offices 313 RSOB, 202-224-4814. Also 447 Fed. Bldg., Indianapolis 46204, 317-269-7066, and 417 Fed. Bldg., 507 State St., Hammond 46320, 219-932-5500 ext. 281.

Committees

Veterans' Affairs (Chairman). Subcommittees: Readjustment, Education and Employment (Chairman).

Commerce (3d). Subcommittees: Aviation; Communications; The Consumer; Foreign Commerce and Tourism; Surface Transportation (Chairman); Special Subcommittee to Study Transportation on the Great Lakes-St. Lawrence Seaway; Special Subcommittee on Freight Car Shortage (Chairman).

Finance (3d). Subcommittees: Foundations (Chairman); Health; International Trade; Revenue Sharing.

Group Ratings

	ADA	COPE	LWV	RIPON	NFU	LCV	CFA	NAB	NSI	ACA
1974	85	82	71	53	92	53	83	22	0	19
1973	73	91	70	44	100	–	58	–	–	4
1972	65	100	83	65	100	72	100	33	0	6

Key Votes

1) No-Knock	AGN	8) Gov Abortn Aid	AGN	15) Consumer Prot Agy	FOR
2) Busing	FOR	9) Cut Mil Brass	FOR	16) Forced Psych Tests	FOR
3) No Fault	AGN	10) Gov Limousine	AGN	17) Fed Campaign Subs	FOR
4) F-111	ABS	11) RR Featherbed	FOR	18) Rhod Chrome Ban	FOR
5) Death Penalty	AGN	12) Handgun License	AGN	19) Open Legis Meetings	AGN
6) Foreign Aid	ABS	13) Less Troop Abrd	FOR	20) Strikers Food Stmps	FOR
7) Filibuster	AGN	14) Resume Turk Aid	AGN	21) Gov Info Disclosure	ABS

Election Results

1970 general:	R. Vance Hartke (D)	870,990	(50%)
	Richard L. Roudebush (R)	866,707	(50%)
1970 primary:	R. Vance Hartke (D), nominated at convention		
1964 general:	R. Vance Hartke (D)	1,128,505	(55%)
	D. Russell Bontrager (R)	941,519	(45%)

Sen. Birch Bayh (D) Elected 1962, seat up 1980; b. Jan. 22, 1928, Terre Haute; home, Terre Haute; Purdue U., B.S. 1951, Ind. St. Col., 1953–60, Ind. U., J.D. 1960; Lutheran.

Career Army, 1945–46; Farmer; Ind. House of Reps., 1955–63, Min. Ldr., 1957–58, 1961–62, Spkr., 1959–60.

Offices 363 RSOB, 202-224-5623. Also 416 Fed. Bldg., Indianapolis 46204, 317-269-6240.

Committees

Appropriations (12th). Subcommittees: Agriculture and Related Agencies; Housing, Urban Development and Independent Agencies; Labor and HEW; Transportation (Chairman); Treasury, U.S. Postal Service; and General Government.

The Judiciary (5th). Subcommittees: Antitrust and Monopoly; Constitutional Amendments (Chairman); Constitutional Rights; Juvenile Delinquency (Chairman).

Group Ratings

	ADA	COPE	LWV	RIPON	NFU	LCV	CFA	NAB	NSI	ACA
1974	87	100	80	41	100	92	88	44	0	6
1973	89	91	89	50	100	–	64	–	–	4
1972	80	88	89	81	100	52	100	10	10	6

Key Votes

1) No-Knock	AGN	8) Gov Abortn Aid	FOR	15) Consumer Prot Agy	FOR
2) Busing	FOR	9) Cut Mil Brass	FOR	16) Forced Psych Tests	FOR
3) No Fault	FOR	10) Gov Limousine	AGN	17) Fed Campaign Subs	FOR
4) F-111	ABS	11) RR Featherbed	FOR	18) Rhod Chrome Ban	FOR
5) Death Penalty	FOR	12) Handgun License	AGN	19) Open Legis Meetings	FOR
6) Foreign Aid	AGN	13) Less Troop Abrd	FOR	20) Strikers Food Stmps	FOR
7) Filibuster	AGN	14) Resume Turk Aid	AGN	21) Gov Info Disclosure	FOR

Election Results

1974 general:	Birch E. Bayh, Jr. (D)	889,269	(52%)	($1,024,486)
	Richard G. Lugar (R)	814,117	(48%)	($619,678)
1974 primary:	Birch E. Bayh, Jr. (D), nominated at convention			
1968 general:	Birch E. Bayh, Jr. (D)	1,060,456	(52%)	
	William D. Ruckelshaus (R)	988,571	(48%)	

Gov. Otis R. Bowen (R) Elected 1972, term expires 1977; b. Feb. 26, 1918, near Rochester; Ind. U., A.B. 1939, M.D. 1942; Lutheran.

Career Army Medical Corps, WWII; Physician; Marshall Co. Coroner; Ind. House of Reps., 1959–72, Spkr., 1967–72.

Offices Rm. 206 State House, Indianapolis 46204, 317-633-4567.

Election Results

1972 general:	Otis R. Bowen (R)	1,203,903	(57%)
	Matthew E. Welsh (D)	900,489	(43%)
1972 primary:	Otis R. Bowen (R), nominated by convention		

♦ ♦ ♦ ♦ ♦

FIRST DISTRICT

Anyone who has driven west on the Indiana Turnpike toward Chicago has seen it. Between the highway and the invisible shores of Lake Michigan is some of the most impressive and most polluted industrial landscape in the country. These are some of the nation's largest steel mills: from their chimneys and smoke stacks come sulphurous fumes by day and the flare of flame by night. This is the heart of the 1st congressional district of Indiana, the northwest corner of Hoosier America.

Without the giant steel mills, there would be no 1st district as we know it. The district's largest city, Gary, was founded in 1906 by J. Pierpont Morgan's colossal United States Steel Corporation and named for one of Morgan's partners, Chicago lawyer and U.S. Steel Chairman Elbert Gary. The site chosen was ideal. Iron ore from the Lake Superior ranges could be carried by Great Lakes freighters into the huge man-made port at the southern tip of Lake Michigan. And coal from southern Illinois or Kentucky or Pennsylvania could be transported to the mills on the great east-west rail lines, as they pass through Gary, Hammond, and East Chicago on their way to Chicago. Today no less than five of the great steel manufacturers have mills here, and the local economy is totally dominated by steel.

In the last 70 years, the steel mills have attracted thousands of immigrants to Gary and vicinity—Irish, Poles, Czechs, Ukrainians, and blacks from the American South. These groups, as even casual newspaper readers know, live in uneasy proximity. In 1967, Richard Hatcher, a black, won the Democratic nomination and was elected Mayor of Gary; in 1971, and 1975 he was reelected by solid margins. But his victories were due almost entirely to the fact that Gary had become a black-majority city; he had virtually no white support. Meanwhile, the Lake County Democratic machinery, as well as most of the county offices, have remained in the control of whites profoundly hostile to Hatcher. Lake County has for years been the scene of considerable political corruption, and sometimes of corrupt inertia; the Democrats in control here have always permitted the steel companies to determine the assessed valuation of their own mills for property tax purposes.

There have been some efforts here to unite the ethnics and the blacks around common problems and grievances, but the results have been disappointing. The foremost political fact of life—and it spreads far beyond Gary, to Hammond and East Chicago and the suburbs to the south—is the hostility between black and white. Inasmuch as blacks are overwhelmingly Democratic, that has had the effect of increasing the Republican vote among the whites. Much was made of George Wallace's carrying of this area in the 1964 and near-carry in the 1972 presidential primary. But perhaps even more significant was the fact that Richard Nixon carried Lake County and the 1st district in 1972, and that only in 1974 did a Democrat, Senator Birch Bayh, get a solid 61% of the vote here.

This is the district that sends to Washington the current Chairman of the House Rules Committee, Ray J. Madden, the oldest member of the United States Congress. For many years, Rules was controlled by a coalition of Southern Democrats and Republicans, led by Chairmen Howard Smith of Virginia and William Colmer of Mississippi. Even the so-called "packing" of the Committee, which Sam Rayburn got the House to approve by a 217–212 vote in 1961, did not make as much difference as some had hoped; it has only been since Colmer's retirement in 1972 that liberals have had a fairly dependable majority.

Even then, it is often not a workable majority. The theory behind the existence of the Rules Committee is that it should determine the order and procedures under which the full House can consider all bills. (In the Senate, this function is handled by the Majority Leader or Whip under the so-called consent procedure.) But of course the power to schedule legislation is the power not to schedule—and therefore to kill—it, and that is just what Rules majorities have done over the years. As late as 1974, a labor-conservative coalition on Rules pigeonholed and eventually killed the land use bill, for example.

Over all this Madden presides. For years labor, liberal, and civil rights groups have waited for him to become Chairman; by the time it happened, he seemed clearly beyond his best years. As Walter Taylor of the Washington Star told writer Britt Hume, "Madden is as senile as the day is long. He rambles on constantly about nongermane matters. The Rules Committee is a joke. It's run like a poker game. Everyone sits around this big table and they shout at each other."

But neither labor nor the bushy young freshmen who dominate the Democratic caucus want to get rid of Madden, fearing the conservative instincts of the next-in-line Democrat, James Delaney of New York. The same impulse governed when Madden faced a major challenge in the

1st district in 1972. His opponent was a 36-year-old state Senator named Adam Benjamin, who was genuinely popular. He easily outcampaigned Madden, whose stories of investigating the 1940 Katyn Forest massacre no longer fascinate his Polish-American audiences. But the Lake County Democratic machine, the Steelworkers, and Mayor Hatcher all formed an unlikely coalition behind Madden—and barely won. Madden was not challenged in 1974, but it scarcely seems likely he can hold on much longer. Perhaps a key figure will be 36-year-old Edward Sadlowski, elected in 1974 as head of the Steelworkers' giant District 13 here. Sadlowski ran as an insurgent against the union's current leadership, and his solid popularity could, if he decides to, tip the balance against Madden.

Census Data Pop. 471,761. Central city, 70%; suburban, 30%. Median family income, $10,706; families above $15,000: 22%; families below $3,000: 8%. Median years education, 11.6.

The Voters

Median voting age 42.
Employment profile White collar, 37%. Blue collar, 50%. Service, 13%. Farm, –%.
Ethnic groups Black, 24%. Spanish, 7%. Total foreign stock, 20%. Poland, 3%; Germany, 2%.

Presidential vote

1972	Nixon (R)	91,218	(53%)
	McGovern (D)	82,173	(47%)
1968	Nixon (R)	62,439	(34%)
	Humphrey (D)	92,640	(50%)
	Wallace (AI)	29,311	(16%)

Rep. Ray J. Madden (D) Elected 1942; b. Feb. 25, 1892, Waseca, Minn.; home, Gary; Creighton U., LL.B. 1913; Catholic.

Career Navy WWI; Practicing atty.; Municipal Judge, Omaha, Neb., 1916; Gary City Comptroller, 1935–38; Lake Co. Treasurer, 1938–42.

Offices 2409 RHOB, 202-225-2461. Also New P.O. Bldg., Hammond 46320, 219-931-8280.

Committees

Rules (Chairman).

Group Ratings

	ADA	COPE	LWV	RIPON	NFU	LCV	CFA	NAB	NSI	ACA
1974	58	100	83	62	77	76	77	20	50	0
1973	80	100	83	71	100	63	100	–	–	11
1972	81	91	100	62	86	61	100	0	22	9

Key Votes

1) Foreign Aid	AGN	6) Gov Abortn Aid	AGN	11) Pub Cong Election $	AGN
2) Busing	FOR	7) Coed Phys Ed	AGN	12) Turkish Arms Cutoff	FOR
3) ABM	AGN	8) Pov Lawyer Gag	AGN	13) Youth Camp Regs	FOR
4) B-1 Bomber	ABS	9) Pub Trans Sub	FOR	14) Strip Mine Veto	AGN
5) Nerve Gas	AGN	10) EZ Voter Regis	FOR	15) Farm Bill Veto	FOR

Election Results

1974 general:	Ray J. Madden (D)	71,759	(69%)	($20,416)
	Joseph Douglas Harkin (R)	32,793	(31%)	($10,369)
1974 primary:	Ray J. Madden (D)	44,348	(75%)	
	Charles G. Bannon (D)	7,966	(13%)	
	Three others (D)	7,062	(12%)	
1972 general:	Ray J. Madden (D)	95,873	(57%)	($72,655)
	Bruce R. Haller (R)	72,662	(43%)	($9,551)

◆ ◆ ◆ ◆ ◆

SECOND DISTRICT

"Don't confuse me with the facts. I've got a closed mind. I will not vote for impeachment. I'm going to stick with my President even if he and I have to be taken out of this building and shot." Those were the words of Congressman Earl Landgrebe, Republican, of the 2d district of Indiana, on August 7, 1974. The lurid Götterdamerung did not occur quite as Landgrebe foresaw. Instead, Richard Nixon resigned from office the next day, and the voters of the 2d district got rid of Congressman the way it is usually done in the United States by electing Landgrebe's opponent, Democrat Floyd Fithian, in November.

It was too bad, at least in the view of many aficionados of the absurd on Capitol Hill, for Landgrebe was one of the unintentionally funniest men ever to sit in Congress. He was not just a conservative Republican, although he certainly was that; he was a genuine small town zany, imported to Washington by political happenstance. The happenstance was his 22% victory in the ten-candidate 1968 Republican primary in this very Republican district. The 2d covers most of northwest Indiana, except for the industrial zone around Gary which forms the 1st district; this is fertile farmland, which has never spawned populists and has, for as long as anyone can remember, voted Republican. For 34 years, from 1934 to 1968, the 2d district was represented by none other than Charles A. Halleck, the tough conservative who as House Minority Leader from 1959 to 1965 used to appear with Everett Dirksen, his Senate counterpart, on what became known as the Ev 'n' Charlie show. Halleck was a hard-working leader, seldom losing key votes, and his ouster as Minority Leader—by a younger Michigan Congressman named Gerald Ford—came largely as a result of the depletion of Republican ranks in the Johnson landslide of 1964. At 68 and no longer a power, Halleck decided to retire, and that led to the election of Landgrebe, then a state Senator.

It took Landgrebe a little time to get known. Some unkind soul had placed him on the liberal Education and Labor Committee, with virtually all of whose members he had nothing in common. He also had a seat on the District of Columbia Committee, where he was the only member dead set against home rule for the nation's black-majority capital. And as time went on, people began to notice that he was doing things like being the only member to vote against the wildlife preservation bill.

In 1970, Landgrebe received only 50.4% of the vote in this very heavily Republican district; in 1972, he had primary opposition from a state Senator, supported by the local Republican organization. On that occasion, even Charlie Halleck came out against Landgrebe. (Halleck's son is a Washington judge who is likely to give police who abuse suspects' rights as much flak as his father used to give big spenders; the son may have moved his father a bit to the left.) That time, Landgrebe won with 54% of the vote; in the 1972 general election, while Richard Nixon was winning 74% in the 2d, Landgrebe squeaked by with 55%.

Landgrebe's 1972 opponent decided to try again in what seemed likely to be the more favorable year of 1974. He was Floyd Fithian, a professor at Purdue University in Lafayette, who could also say that he was a farmer. Fithian campaigned practically non-stop, but the outcome of the election—or, rather, the size of his margin—was the result of the incumbent's fervent defense of Richard Nixon. Landgrebe was the only Congressman to take the position that it was perfectly proper to burglarize the Watergate, and—as the statement quoted above indicates—he never abandoned his leader. The people of the 2d district, despite their longstanding Republicanism, had already done so; after all, one of the reasons they were Republicans was to oppose the kind of corruption you found under Democrats in Chicago and Gary. So Fithian got 61% of the vote, and Landgrebe was through. Can Fithian win in 1976? He has all the advantages of incumbency, plus a thorough familiarity with what is needed to run a winning campaign; he was also given a seat on the Agriculture Committee, which obviously is of interest to his constituents. But the Republicans are certain to put up a major challenge here, and they will have at least a good chance to win unless they should be so unwise as to nominate Landgrebe.

Census Data Pop. 472,460. Central city, 14%; suburban, 51%. Median family income, $10,377; families above $15,000: 21%; families below $3,000: 7%. Median years education, 12.2.

The Voters

Median voting age 40.
Employment profile White collar, 42%. Blue collar, 41%. Service, 12%. Farm, 5%.
Ethnic groups Spanish, 1%. Total foreign stock, 9%. Germany, 2%.

Presidential vote

1972	Nixon (R)	149,099	(74%)
	McGovern (D)	53,463	(26%)
1968	Nixon (R)	109,841	(58%)
	Humphrey (D)	58,461	(31%)
	Wallace (AI)	22,705	(12%)

Rep. Floyd J. Fithian (D) Elected 1974; b. Nov. 3, 1928, Vesta, Neb.; home, Lafayette; Peru St. Col., B.A. 1951, U. of Neb., M.A. 1955, Ph.D. 1964; Methodist.

Career Navy, 1951–54; Farmer; High School Teacher; Assoc. Prof. of History, Purdue U.

Offices 1205 LHOB, 202-225-5777. Also 5 N. Earl Ave., Lafayette 47905, 317-447-3181.

Committees

Agriculture (25th). Subcommittees: Domestic Marketing and Consumer Relations; Livestock and Grains; Oilseeds and Rice.

Group Ratings: Newly Elected

Key Votes

1) Foreign Aid	AGN	6) Gov Abortn Aid	NE	11) Pub Cong Election $	NE
2) Busing	NE	7) Coed Phys Ed	ABS	12) Turkish Arms Cutoff	NE
3) ABM	NE	8) Pov Lawyer Gag	NE	13) Youth Camp Regs	ABS
4) B-1 Bomber	AGN	9) Pub Trans Sub	NE	14) Strip Mine Veto	AGN
5) Nerve Gas	NE	10) EZ Voter Regis	NE	15) Farm Bill Veto	AGN

Election Results

1974 general:	Floyd J. Fithian (D)	101,856	(61%)	($155,580)
	Earl F. Landgrebe (R)	64,950	(39%)	($73,909)
1974 primary:	Floyd J. Fithian (D), unopposed			

◆ ◆ ◆ ◆ ◆

THIRD DISTRICT

"Supercongressman" was the way *Washington Monthly* writer Marjorie Boyd described John Brademas, Democratic Representative from the 3d district of Indiana. He is also a man of some contradictions. He is a Methodist of Greek descent whose district includes Notre Dame University; he is a bachelor in a Washington that has become for Congressmen a family town; and he is a Harvard graduate and Rhodes scholar who has succeeded in the rough-hewn field of Hoosier politics. Still under 50, he has been in the House for nearly 20 years, and has risen to the number five position among Democrats on the House Education and Labor Committee.

Brademas is probably the Congress's leading expert on the financing of higher education; he authored a major act on the subject in 1972, and now heads a subcommittee with jurisdiction over it and many other education programs. More recently, he has also assumed a major role in foreign policy. As leader of a group of half-a-dozen Congressmen of Greek ancestry, Brademas was the most vehement backer of a 1974 measure that would enforce a cutoff of military aid against Turkey. Under previous legislation, the cutoff should have gone into effect automatically when Turkey continued to invade Cyprus, but Secretary of State Kissinger—typically for an Executive Branch officer—simply refused to obey the law, claiming that he knew better. Kissinger lobbied heavily against Brademas's amendment, claiming that it would subvert negotiations between Greece and Turkey, but Brademas persisted, and finally it passed in November 1974.

Kissinger recognized Brademas as a heavy, a difficult adversary, and he is. He currently holds the title of Chief Deputy Whip, which technically means he sits on the leadership ladder below Speaker Albert, Majority Leader Tip O'Neill, and Majority Whip John McFall. In the past, this post would have led—directly, but very slowly—to the Speakership; now it is unlikely to do so, since Caucus Chairman Phillip Burton has his eyes set on that—and the votes to win it. But Brademas nonetheless remains important: conciliatory enough to deal with some of the older members, liberal enough to deal with the younger ones. He does, however, have one problem the other members of the leadership don't have to worry about: his district. Winning reelection in straight-ticket Indiana is not always easy, and St. Joseph, the industrial, Democratic heart of Brademas's 3d congressional district, has been leaning Republican of late. He had relatively close calls in the last two presidential years—52% in 1968 and 56% in 1972—and despite his much better showing in 1974 he cannot take the 3d for granted.

Census Data Pop. 471,849. Central city, 27%; suburban, 25%. Median family income, $10,606; families above $15,000: 22%; families below $3,000: 6%. Median years education, 12.1.

The Voters

Median voting age 43.
Employment profile White collar, 44%. Blue collar, 43%. Service, 12%. Farm, 1%.
Ethnic groups Black, 6%. Total foreign stock, 13%. Poland, 3%; Germany, 2%.

Presidential vote

1972	Nixon (R)	120,430	(64%)
	McGovern (D)	66,985	(36%)
1968	Nixon (R)	90,557	(48%)
	Humphrey (D)	76,833	(41%)
	Wallace (AI)	19,716	(11%)

Rep. John Brademas (D) Elected 1958; b. Mar. 2, 1927, Mishawaka; home, South Bend; Harvard U., B.A. 1949, Rhodes Scholar, Oxford U. Ph.D. 1954; Methodist.

Career Navy, 1945–46; Asst. Prof., St. Mary's Col., Notre Dame, Legis. Asst. to U.S. Sen. Pat McNamera of Mich., 1955; Admin. Asst. to U.S. Rep. Thomas Ludlow Ashley of Ohio, 1955; Exec. Asst. to Adlai E. Stevenson II, 1955–56.

Offices 2134 RHOB, 202-225-3915. Also Rm. 203, Fed. Bldg., South Bend 46601, 219-233-8203.

Committees

Education and Labor (5th). Subcommittees: Labor-Management Relations; Post-secondary Education; Select Subcommittee on Education (Chairman).

House Administration (5th). Subcommittees: Electrical and Mechanical Office Equipment; Library and Memorials; Printing (Chairman).

Group Ratings

	ADA	COPE	LWV	RIPON	NFU	LCV	CFA	NAB	NSI	ACA
1974	96	100	92	73	86	94	100	17	10	0
1973	96	100	92	67	95	89	88	–	–	7
1972	100	100	100	71	86	93	50	8	0	4

Key Votes

1) Foreign Aid	FOR	6) Gov Abortn Aid	FOR	11) Pub Cong Election $	FOR
2) Busing	FOR	7) Coed Phys Ed	FOR	12) Turkish Arms Cutoff	FOR
3) ABM	AGN	8) Pov Lawyer Gag	AGN	13) Youth Camp Regs	FOR
4) B-1 Bomber	AGN	9) Pub Trans Sub	FOR	14) Strip Mine Veto	AGN
5) Nerve Gas	AGN	10) EZ Voter Regis	FOR	15) Farm Bill Veto	AGN

Election Results

1974 general:	John Brademas (D)	89,306	(64%)	($145,733)
	Virginia R. Black (R)	50,116	(36%)	($16,184)
1974 primary:	John Brademas (D)	35,617	(79%)	
	Helen M. Calvin (D)	9,512	(21%)	
1972 general:	John Brademas (D)	103,949	(56%)	($133,634)
	Don M. Newman (R)	81,369	(44%)	($45,160)

◆ ◆ ◆ ◆ ◆

FOURTH DISTRICT

The 4th congressional district of Indiana centers on Fort Wayne, the state's second largest city (pop. 178,000). More than half the district's votes are cast here and in surrounding Allen County. Fort Wayne is a typical medium-sized Midwestern community, with a small black ghetto, nondescript frame houses that belong to the people who work in the factories, and a small neighborhood of imposing houses that belong to the people who own the factories.

The counties lying around Fort Wayne in the district are mostly agricultural flatland. Those to the south and west of the city have a Democratic tradition, while those to the north are heavily Republican. Any sophisticated public opinion survey of the two blocks of rural counties would probably disclose little difference on major issues; their political disagreements are largely a matter of upbringing and tradition, traceable ultimately to differences in attitudes toward the Civil War. Returns from the 1868 presidential election, for example, show configurations differing little from the closely contested 1962, 1968, 1970, and 1974 Indiana Senate races. Altogether, the 4th district is politically marginal, and as this district goes, so usually goes Indiana.

The 4th is one of those districts which was created for the benefit of one political party and wound up in the hands of the other. The 1968 race pitted two incumbents against each other: E. Ross Adair, then ranking Republican on the Foreign Affairs Committee, and Democrat J. Edward Roush, most of whose old constituency had been placed in the new 5th district. Adair won that time, but Roush gained revenge in 1970; high unemployment, much of it due to the General Motors strike, helped Roush, as did the settling of a decades-old feud in the Allen County Democratic organization.

The 1972 Almanac predicted a close race in the 4th, which had been redistricted once again by Republicans; and that proved to be one of the book's better predictions, as Roush won by a narrow 51–49 margin. For 1974, we predicted a slightly larger Roush margin—which is precisely what happened. Both times the 4th had been targetted by the Republicans, and the closeness of the 1976 race will depend on whether they make another major effort here. Our prediction is that they will have their hands full contesting other districts where Democrats won in 1974, and Roush will get, relatively speaking, an easy time of it.

Census Data Pop. 472,678. Central city, 38%; suburban, 22%. Median family income, $10,443; families above $15,000: 20%; families below $3,000: 7%. Median years education, 12.2.

The Voters

Median voting age 42.
Employment profile White collar, 44%. Blue collar, 42%. Service, 11%. Farm, 3%.
Ethnic groups Black, 4%. Total foreign stock, 6%. Germany, 2%.

Presidential vote

1972	Nixon (R)	130,321	(67%)
	McGovern (D)	63,938	(33%)
1968	Nixon (R)	103,502	(55%)
	Humphrey (D)	68,571	(37%)
	Wallace (AI)	15,511	(8%)

Rep. J. Edward Roush (D) Elected 1970; b. Sept. 12, 1920, Barnsdall, Okla.; home, Huntington; Huntington Col., B.A. 1938, Ind. U., J.D., 1949; United Brethren in Christ.

Career Army, WWII and Korea; Practicing atty.; Ind. House of Reps., 1949; Huntington Co. Prosecuting Atty., 1955–59.

Offices 2400 RHOB, 202-225-4436. Also 326 Fed Bldg., Ft. Wayne 46802, 219-742-6250.

Committees

Appropriations (25th). Subcommittees: Foreign Operations; HUD-Independent Agencies; Legislative.

Group Ratings

	ADA	COPE	LWV	RIPON	NFU	LCV	CFA	NAB	NSI	ACA
1974	74	82	67	63	92	71	69	58	40	33
1973	80	80	92	80	100	63	75	–	–	15
1972	50	91	67	69	100	64	100	17	40	30

Key Votes

1) Foreign Aid	AGN	6) Gov Abortn Aid	AGN	11) Pub Cong Election $	FOR
2) Busing	AGN	7) Coed Phys Ed	FOR	12) Turkish Arms Cutoff	FOR
3) ABM	AGN	8) Pov Lawyer Gag	AGN	13) Youth Camp Regs	FOR
4) B-1 Bomber	AGN	9) Pub Trans Sub	FOR	14) Strip Mine Veto	AGN
5) Nerve Gas	AGN	10) EZ Voter Regis	FOR	15) Farm Bill Veto	AGN

Election Results

1974 general:	J. Edward Roush (D)	83,604	(53%)	($57,615)
	Walter R. Helmke (R)	75,031	(47%)	($77,576)
1974 primary:	J. Edward Roush (D)	28,469	(90%)	
	Stephen G. Hope (D)	3,107	(10%)	
1972 general:	J. Edward Roush (D)	100,327	(51%)	($63,613)
	Allan Bloom (R)	94,492	(49%)	($165,984)

◆ ◆ ◆ ◆ ◆

FIFTH DISTRICT

The 5th congressional district lies smack in the middle of Indiana, which is to say in the middle of Middle America. The rich Hoosier farmland here is Farm Bureau country, and politically very conservative. There are also three medium-sized factory towns, Anderson, Kokomo, and Marion, as well as Peru, the boyhood home of Cole Porter. The district also dips down to include a small portion of the city of Indianapolis (an integrated, Democratic neighborhood, placed in this Republican district to render it politically harmless). Just to the north of the city are the political poles of the 5th: Hamilton County, which is high-income, exurban Indianapolis, and very heavily Republican; and Anderson, with its huge General Motors plant and thousands of UAW members, which is usually solidly Democratic.

That Anderson was included in this district by a Republican legislature is testimony to the 5th's heavy Republican margins and the confidence Republican leaders had in the political durability of Congressman Elwood Hillis. A relative newcomer to the House, Hillis was first elected in 1970, and reelected in 1972 with 64% of the vote. A conservative, he might be thought to have been in trouble in 1974. But though Democrats swept nine of Indiana's eleven districts, Hillis won with a solid 57%.

Why did Hillis win? First of all, at 48 he was able to campaign vigorously and as a newcomer he was well aware that he had to use the advantages of incumbency to the utmost. And secondly, the

Democrats did not target this district, as they did the 2d, 8th, 10th, and 11th—all of which they carried. Having survived what must be considered his toughest year, Hillis is likely to remain in the House for a long time.

Census Data Pop. 471,921. Central city, 25%; suburban, 17%. Median family income, $10,314; families above $15,000: 22%; families below $3,000: 7%. Median years education, 12.2.

The Voters

Median voting age 42.
Employment profile White collar, 41%. Blue collar, 44%. Service, 12%. Farm, 3%.
Ethnic groups Black, 6%. Total foreign stock, 4%.

Presidential vote

1972	Nixon (R)	135,915	(70%)
	McGovern (D)	58,893	(30%)
1968	Nixon (R)	102,153	(53%)
	Humphrey (D)	70,682	(37%)
	Wallace (AI)	19,443	(10%)

Rep. Elwood Hillis (R) Elected 1970; b. Mar. 6, 1926, Kokomo; home, Kokomo; Ind. U., B.S. 1949, J.D. 1952; Presbyterian.

Career Army, WWII; Practicing atty., 1952–71; Ind. House of Reps., 1967–71.

Offices 1721 LHOB, 202-225-5037. Also 504 Union Bank Bldg., Kokomo 46901, 317-457-4411.

Committees

Armed Services (11th). Subcommittees: Military Installatio; and Facilities; Military Personnel.

Veterans' Affairs (4th). Subcommittees: Cemeteries and Burial Benefits; Hospitals.

Group Ratings

	ADA	COPE	LWV	RIPON	NFU	LCV	CFA	NAB	NSI	ACA
1974	29	40	45	60	64	40	36	50	100	50
1973	18	50	45	83	60	44	67	–	–	72
1972	19	50	44	78	67	27	0	63	100	50

Key Votes

1) Foreign Aid	FOR	6) Gov Abortn Aid	AGN	11) Pub Cong Election $	FOR
2) Busing	AGN	7) Coed Phys Ed	FOR	12) Turkish Arms Cutoff	AGN
3) ABM	FOR	8) Pov Lawyer Gag	ABS	13) Youth Camp Regs	ABS
4) B-1 Bomber	FOR	9) Pub Trans Sub	AGN	14) Strip Mine Veto	FOR
5) Nerve Gas	FOR	10) EZ Voter Regis	AGN	15) Farm Bill Veto	AGN

Election Results

1974 general:	Elwood H. Hillis (R)	95,331	(57%)	($55,490)
	William T. Sebree (D)	73,239	(43%)	($18,758)
1974 primary:	Elwood H. Hillis (R), unopposed			
1972 general:	Elwood H. Hillis (R)	124,692	(64%)	($64,781)
	Kathleen Z. Williams (D)	69,746	(36%)	($9,026)

SIXTH DISTRICT

♦ ♦ ♦ ♦ ♦

The 6th district of Indiana was the scene in 1974 of one of the two biggest upsets in House races (the other was the 2d district of New York), when 28-year-old Democrat David Evans beat 24-year House veteran William Bray, the ranking Republican on the House Armed Services Committee. An unlikelier place for such a result could scarcely be imagined. The 6th takes in about a third of the recently expanded city of Indianapolis, four suburban counties, and a couple of townships in another county; and almost all the territory is usually solidly Republican. The exceptions are part of the Indianapolis black ghetto (put here to keep it out of the 11th district) and some working class neighborhoods around the Indianapolis Speedway; but in recent years, the latter had been trending to the Republicans, in apparent disgust with liberal Democratic programs.

At any rate metropolitan Indianapolis has always been one of our most Republican cities; it has never had the really large influxes of Eastern European immigrants who provide so many of the traditional Democratic votes in places like Chicago and Detroit and Cleveland, and its economic base is decidedly white collar, with banks, insurance companies, and state government all being major employers. Beyond that, there is an ethos here that is profoundly conservative, as one might expect in the city that is the headquarters of the American Legion and the home town of James Whitcomb Riley, Benjamin Harrison, and Tom Charles Huston. Indeed, the 6th district was the only one of Indiana's eleven as they exist today which went for Barry Goldwater in 1964, and so one might have thought that Congressman Bray would have no trouble, no matter how Democratic the year.

But party landslides produce a kind of Darwinian natural selection. Democrats in 1974 did not necessarily capture the seats where the Republicans were—on the basis of presidential or statewide votes—the weakest; rather, they tended to beat the Republicans who were the most complacent, who had not been working their district hard year in and year out. That appears to have been the case with Bray. Blessed with a supposedly solid Republican district, he had not bothered to return on weekends or to send out thousands of newsletters like his younger and technically more marginal colleagues Elwood Hillis and John Myers, both of whom survived the Democratic landslide. So Bray was ripe for being picked off. But even at that, Evans could scarcely have hoped to win without the straight ticket voting behavior which remains stronger here in Indiana than just about anywhere else in the country.

And that, of course, will be Evans's problem in 1976. No one supposes that the Democratic candidates for President or Governor or Senator Vance Hartke (assuming he gets the Democratic nomination) will carry the 6th district, so Evans knows he must make it on his own. Numerous ambitious young Indianapolis area Republicans undoubtedly see this as the district which could elect them to Congress for years (or until they are chosen to run for statewide office), and so Evans is assured of plenty of competition. It will be one of the toughest seats in the country for the Democrats to hold.

Census Data Pop. 471,595. Central city, 54%; suburban, 46%. Median family income, $10,497; families above $15,000: 20%; families below $3,000: 6%. Median years education, 12.0.

The Voters

Median voting age 41.
Employment profile White collar, 45%. Blue collar, 42%. Service, 11%. Farm, 2%.
Ethnic groups Black, 4%. Total foreign stock, 4%.

Presidential vote

1972	Nixon (R)	127,566	(74%)
	McGovern (D)	45,691	(26%)
1968	Nixon (R)	98,265	(54%)
	Humphrey (D)	55,664	(31%)
	Wallace (AI)	27,095	(15%)

Rep. David W. Evans (D) Elected 1974; b. Aug. 17, 1946, Lafayette; home, Indianapolis; Ind. U., B.A. 1967, 1967–70, Butler U. 1970–72.

Career Parochial school teacher and asst. principal, 1968–74; Dem. nominee for U.S. House of Reps., 1972.

Offices 513 CHOB, 202-225-2276. Also 4th Floor, Administration Bldg., Weir Cook Airport, Indianapolis 46241, 317-269-7364.

Committees

Banking, Currency and Housing (29th). Subcommittees: Economic Stabilization; International Development Institutions and Finance; General Oversight and Renegotiation.

Government Operations (26th). Subcommittees: Commerce, Consumer and Monetary Affairs; Government Activities and Transportation.

Group Ratings: Newly Elected

Key Votes

1) Foreign Aid	AGN	6) Gov Abortn Aid	NE	11) Pub Cong Election $	NE
2) Busing	NE	7) Coed Phys Ed	AGN	12) Turkish Arms Cutoff	NE
3) ABM	NE	8) Pov Lawyer Gag	NE	13) Youth Camp Regs	AGN
4) B-1 Bomber	AGN	9) Pub Trans Sub	NE	14) Strip Mine Veto	AGN
5) Nerve Gas	NE	10) EZ Voter Regis	NE	15) Farm Bill Veto	ABS

Election Results

1974 general:	David W. Evans (D)	78,414	(52%)	($15,846)
	William G. Bray (R)	71,134	(48%)	◄($45,740)
1974 primary:	David W. Evans (D)	10,407	(56%)	
	John Bardon (D)	5,528	(30%)	
	George F. Cooper (D)	2,526	(14%)	

◆ ◆ ◆ ◆ ◆

SEVENTH DISTRICT

Like the old Cannonball named after it, the Wabash River flows across the rolling farmland of western Indiana on its way to meet the Ohio and Mississippi. And in an almost straight line from Indianapolis to St. Louis runs the old National Road (now U.S. 40), paralleled closely by Interstate 70. The river and the road intersect in Terre Haute (pop. 70,000), the largest city in the 7th congressional district of Indiana. Terre Haute is a rough and rude town, once known for its gambling and vice; it has always had a strong Democratic machine, which more often than not has controlled the Vigo County Courthouse.

Apparently, the assumption was, when this district was created in basically its present form in 1965 by a Democratic legislature, that Vigo and some surrounding counties would put it in the Democratic column. They were wrong. 1966 was a good Republican year, and the winner was the young Republican candidate, John T. Myers. He has remained in the House ever since.

Indeed, Myers has never been seriously challenged, despite the fact that Indiana University at Bloomington has emerged as a potential base of Democratic strength as important, since 1972, as Terre Haute. For 1974, Myers's opponent was Eldon Tipton, the same man he had beaten in 1966. It was the elderly Tipton's fifth race for the House, all unsuccessful; Myers won 58% of the vote, and was one of only two Indiana Republicans who won reelection. He is now the tenth-ranked Republican on the House Appropriations Committee, and ranking member on its Public Works Subcommittee—a post from which he has an opportunity to perform that most traditional of congressional functions, steering pork barrel projects into his district.

Census Data Pop. 472,041. Central city, 15%; suburban, 29%. Median family income, $8,808; families above $15,000: 15%; families below $3,000: 10%. Median years education, 12.1.

The Voters

Median voting age 42.
Employment profile White collar, 42%. Blue collar, 39%. Service, 14%. Farm, 5%.
Ethnic groups Black, 2%. Total foreign stock, 4%.

Presidential vote

1972	Nixon (R)	135,270	(65%)
	McGovern (D)	72,718	(35%)
1968	Nixon (R)	98,751	(51%)
	Humphrey (D)	74,574	(38%)
	Wallace (AI)	21,677	(11%)

Rep. John T. Myers (R) Elected 1966; b. Feb. 8, 1927, Covington; home Covington; Ind. St. U., B.S. 1951; Episcopalian.

Career Army, WWII; Cashier and Trust Officer, Foundation Trust Co., 1954–66.

Offices 103 CHOB, 202-225-5805. Also Fed. Bldg., Terre Haute 47808, 812-238-1619.

Committees

Appropriations (10th). Subcommittees: Agriculture and Related Agencies; Public Works.

Group Ratings

	ADA	COPE	LWV	RIPON	NFU	LCV	CFA	NAB	NSI	ACA
1974	0	9	27	33	38	20	17	73	89	79
1973	4	10	17	43	47	2	14	–	–	79
1972	0	27	20	38	50	20	50	73	100	86

Key Votes

1) Foreign Aid	AGN	6) Gov Abortn Aid	AGN	11) Pub Cong Election $	AGN
2) Busing	AGN	7) Coed Phys Ed	AGN	12) Turkish Arms Cutoff	AGN
3) ABM	FOR	8) Pov Lawyer Gag	FOR	13) Youth Camp Regs	AGN
4) B-1 Bomber	FOR	9) Pub Trans Sub	AGN	14) Strip Mine Veto	FOR
5) Nerve Gas	FOR	10) EZ Voter Regis	AGN	15) Farm Bill Veto	AGN

Election Results

1974 general:	John T. Myers (R)	100,128	(58%)	($44,556)
	Elden C. Tipton (D)	73,802	(42%)	($13,916)
1974 primary:	John T. Myers (R), unopposed			
1972 general:	John T. Myers (R)	128,688	(62%)	($58,186)
	Warren Henegar (D)	80,145	(38%)	($40,000)

◆ ◆ ◆ ◆ ◆

EIGHTH DISTRICT

The 8th congressional district of Indiana is the southwest corner of the state. It contains the city of Evansville (pop. 138,000) on the Ohio River and several river counties so hilly that, by Midwestern standards, they might be considered mountainous. This part of Indiana was the first to be settled by white men. Vincennes, now a small town on the Wabash River, was once the metropolis of Indiana, and Robert Owen, the Scottish philanthropist, established the town of New Harmony downstream. (Owen's son was one of the first Congressmen from the area, elected in

1842 and 1844.) Today Evansville is a reasonably prosperous city (fourth largest in the state), but most of the rest of the district has suffered ever since the railroads took most of the freight business away from Ohio River steamboats.

Much of southwest Indiana was settled by German Catholics, who have traditionally voted Democratic. During the Civil War, most of the 8th was Copperhead country, friendly to the South and hostile to Mr. Lincoln's war. Today, though the issues have changed, the 8th remains generally Democratic—except in presidential contests when the Southern-accented Hoosiers here have not cottoned to the liberal candidates nominated by the national party. But Senators Bayh and Hartke both carry the district; indeed, Hartke is a native son, and was Mayor of Evansville just before he was elected Senator.

For many years, the 8th was represented by Winfield Denton, a middle-of-the-road Democrat. Apparently complacent after his big 1964 win, Denton was upset in 1966 by Evansville businessman Roger Zion. In 1970, Democrats targeted the district and cut Zion's margin, but were unable to dent his strength in Evansville, which casts about one-third of the district's votes. As a member of the Public Works Committee, Zion was disliked by ecology activists, and was placed on Environmental Action's Dirty Dozen list three times. The third time it—or other factors—proved fatal to his chances. Zion was opposed by Evansville state Senator Philip Hayes, a 34-year-old Democrat who used the Dirty Dozen designation and the fact that Zion had been mentioned unfavorably several times in Jack Anderson's column. Hayes' campaign was poorly financed, but apparently caught the voters' interest, and Zion was beaten by a surprisingly large 53-47 margin.

Hayes's political future probably depends on public reaction to the job freshmen Congressmen do and to whether the Indiana Republicans target this district. If they don't, he will probably win easily in 1976; if they do, he will have a tough race in a district that has proved over and over again its marginality.

Census Data Pop. 472,175. Central city, 29%; suburban, 12%. Median family income, $8,557; families above $15,000: 13%; families below $3,000: 11%. Median years education, 11.8.

The Voters

Median voting age 45.
Employment profile White collar, 38%. Blue collar, 44%. Service, 13%. Farm, 5%.
Ethnic groups Black, 3%. Total foreign stock, 2%. Germany, 1%.

Presidential vote

1972	Nixon (R)	138,545	(65%)
	McGovern (D)	73,835	(35%)
1968	Nixon (R)	108,377	(49%)
	Humphrey (D)	88,442	(40%)
	Wallace (AI)	22,330	(10%)

Rep. Philip H. Hayes (D) Elected 1974; b. Sept. 1, 1940, Battle Creek, Mich.; home, Evansville; Ind. U., B.A. 1963, J.D. 1967; Catholic.

Career Vanderburgh Co. Deputy Prosecuting Atty., 1967–68; Ind. Senate, 1971–74.

Offices 1132 LHOB, 202-225-4636. Also Fed. Bldg., Evansville 47708, 812-423-6871.

Committees

Banking, Currency and Housing (28th). Subcommittees: General Oversight and Renegotiation; Historic Preservation and Coinage; International Trade, Investment and Monetary Policy.

Science and Technology (15th). Subcommittees: Energy Research, Development and Demonstration; Energy Research (Fossil Fuels).

Group Ratings: Newly Elected

Key Votes

1) Foreign Aid	AGN	6) Gov Abortn Aid	NE	11) Pub Cong Election $	NE
2) Busing	NE	7) Coed Phys Ed	FOR	12) Turkish Arms Cutoff	NE
3) ABM	NE	8) Pov Lawyer Gag	NE	13) Youth Camp Regs	FOR
4) B-1 Bomber	AGN	9) Pub Trans Sub	NE	14) Strip Mine Veto	AGN
5) Nerve Gas	NE	10) EZ Voter Regis	NE	15) Farm Bill Veto	AGN

Election Results

1974 general:	Philip H. Hayes (D)	100,121	(53%)	($67,429)
	Roger H. Zion (R)	87,296	(47%)	($122,329)
1974 primary:	Philip H. Hayes (D)	25,472	(49%)	
	David Lance Cornwell (D)	18,588	(36%)	
	Two others (D)	8,203	(16%)	

◆ ◆ ◆ ◆ ◆

NINTH DISTRICT

What happens to Congressmen carried into office on the strength of a party landslide? Traditionally, they have been swept right back out again when there were no coattails to ride. But that has not necessarily been the case in recent years. Of course, we don't know yet what will happen to the 1974 Democrats, but of the Democratic Congressmen elected in 1964 in districts previously Republican, half survived the 1966 elections, and nearly half either still serve in the House or have retired voluntarily. One of the former is Lee Hamilton of Indiana's 9th district, and his case is instructive.

In 1964 Hamilton, then president of the Batholomew County Young Democrats, won a surprisingly big 12,000- vote victory over veteran Republican Congressman Earl Wilson. This was the year Lyndon Johnson became the first Democratic presidential candidate to carry the 9th—roughly, the southeast corner of Indiana. The district is basically Republican territory, from the hills along the Ohio River to the neat small city of Columbus, home of Cummins Engine and its scholarly president, J. Irwin Miller. (*Esquire* magazine once put liberal Republican Miller on its cover and suggested he should be president, an idea which, unfortunately, no one ever took up; instead Miller later found himself on Richard Nixon's enemies list.)

In his first term, Hamilton was especially successful in getting post office and public works projects for his district which, outside of Columbus, is far from prosperous; by 1966, his sharp campaigning and intelligent use of the advantages of incumbency helped him win reelection over a determined Republican opponent. By 1970, Hamilton was home free, running far ahead of his party's ticket, and in 1972 he took 63% of the vote—the best showing of any Indiana Democrat.

In the House, Hamilton generally has voted with the younger liberal Democrats, except when they moved away from supporting Lyndon Johnson's Vietnam war policies. It would not be quite accurate to call Hamilton a hawk, but he is no dove, either; he believes the United States should continue to have an activist foreign policy, and votes accordingly. This assumes importance because he is Chairman of the Foreign Affairs subcommittee which, among other things, handled the question of supplemental aid to Cambodia in 1975. When the question was posed between the open-ended commitment sought by the Ford Administration and the complete end of military aid favored by a majority of the House Democratic Caucus, Hamilton came out with the Democrats. But with Republican Pierre Du Pont, Hamilton worked to hammer out a compromise.

For Hamilton, 1976 could be a key political year: he may have to decide whether he wants the Senate seat held by fellow Democrat Vance Hartke, or whether he will continue in the House. There is no indication whatever that Hartke wants to retire, but his obvious political weakness and the fact that Indiana Senatorial nominees are chosen by convention, not primary, make it entirely possible that Hamilton could secure the nomination; in the general election, with his 9th district base, plus support from usually Democratic areas, he would be a strong candidate. If he chooses to remain in the House, on the other hand, he could count on climbing in seniority on Foreign Affairs, but he is unlikely to ever become Chairman because several more senior members are about his age.

Census Data Pop. 472,321. Central city, 0%; suburban, 34%. Median family income, $9,001; families above $15,000: 14%; families below $3,000: 9%. Median years education, 11.4.

The Voters

Median voting age 43.
Employment profile White collar, 37%. Blue collar, 47%. Service, 11%. Farm, 5%.
Ethnic groups Black, 2%. Total foreign stock, 2%.

Presidential vote

1972	Nixon (R)	123,569	(64%)
	McGovern (D)	70,613	(36%)
1968	Nixon (R)	94,673	(48%)
	Humphrey (D)	76,980	(39%)
	Wallace (AI)	26,178	(13%)

Rep. Lee H. Hamilton (D) Elected 1964; b. Apr. 20, 1931, Daytona Beach, Fla.; home, Columbus; DePauw U., B.A. 1952, Goethe U., Frankfort Germany, 1952–53, Ind. U., J.D. 1956; Methodist.

Career Practicing atty., 1956–64; Instructor, Amer. Banking Inst., 1960–61.

Offices 2344 RHOB, 202-225-5315. Also U.S.P.O., Columbus 47201, 812-372-2571.

Committees

International Relations (10th). Subcommittees: International Economic Policy; Investigations (Chairman).

Joint Economic Committee (5th, House Side). Subcommittees: Economic Progress; Fiscal Policy; Inter-American Economic Relationships; International Economics.

Group Ratings

	ADA	COPE	LWV	RIPON	NFU	LCV	CFA	NAB	NSI	ACA
1974	68	70	92	88	92	65	50	33	33	7
1973	80	73	83	73	100	68	75	–	–	4
1972	50	82	75	80	86	73	50	17	50	26

Key Votes

1) Foreign Aid	FOR	6) Gov Abortn Aid	AGN	11) Pub Cong Election $	FOR
2) Busing	AGN	7) Coed Phys Ed	AGN	12) Turkish Arms Cutoff	AGN
3) ABM	AGN	8) Pov Lawyer Gag	AGN	13) Youth Camp Regs	AGN
4) B-1 Bomber	FOR	9) Pub Trans Sub	AGN	14) Strip Mine Veto	AGN
5) Nerve Gas	AGN	10) EZ Voter Regis	FOR	15) Farm Bill Veto	AGN

Election Results

1974 general:	Lee H. Hamilton (D)	117,648	(71%)	($69,375)
	Delson Cox, Jr. (R)	47,881	(29%)	($7,553)
1974 primary:	Lee H. Hamilton (D), unopposed			
1972 general:	Lee H. Hamilton (D)	122,698	(63%)	($61,021)
	William A. Johnson (R)	72,325	(37%)	($6,389)

◆ ◆ ◆ ◆ ◆

TENTH DISTRICT

Before Robert and Helen Lynd published *Middletown* in the 1930s, most Americans imagined that small Midwestern cities were tightly knit, homogeneous communities. But the Lynds discovered in Middletown—which actually was Muncie, Indiana—a factory town divided sharply along class lines, with local affairs firmly controlled by a small business elite. Since the 1930s, the GM and other major plants have been unionized, blue-collar wages have risen greatly, and the power of the local elite has been slightly reduced. But the basic class divisions remain.

Nowhere are they so apparent as in politics. A New York *Times* article quoted a member of the Muncie elite as expressing the belief that everyone in the town was a Republican. All the members of the country club, perhaps, though one doubts even that; but overall, Muncie votes as often for Democrats as for Republicans. Life-and-death economic power remains in the hands of businessmen, which here means faraway GM executives in Detroit and New York and the Ball family in Muncie. And in late 1974 and early 1975, with the automobile business in depression, Muncie was, if anything, more class-conscious and class-divided than ever.

Muncie lies roughly in the middle of Indiana's 10th congressional district, and with 69,000 people is its largest city. The only other sizeable town, Richmond (pop. 44,000), is quite a different kind of place. It has a long standing of Quaker tradition and is the site of the Friends' Earlham College. But the Quakerism of this part of Indiana is closer to that of Richard Nixon's Whittier than to that of Philadelphia's American Friends Service Committee. Richmond has retained strong Republican voting habits from its antislavery days before the Civil War.

The 10th was the creation of the 1968 Republican redistricting, altered in 1972 to increase Republican chances. Yet today it is held by a Democrat, Philip Sharp, a former political science professor at Ball State University in Muncie. He is so typical of the 1974 House freshmen that the Washington *Post* chose him as a subject for a series of profiles through the life of the 94th Congress. But as yet, Sharp is less well-known, at least outside the 10th district, than the man he beat, Republican Congressman David Dennis. The two had faced each other twice before, in 1968, when Dennis barely won, 51–49, and in 1972, when he beat Sharp rather badly, 57–43. But in 1974, Sharp finally managed to win, by a solid 54–46 margin, and the main reason was something he didn't mention—he didn't have to—during his campaign: Dennis's performance on the House Judiciary Committee impeachment hearings.

Not that Dennis wasn't occasionally impressive and most of the time solidly competent in attacking and badgering those who sought to impeach the President. By demanding facts from the Democrats during the first day of televised hearings, he helped to make "specificity" a household word, and his peppery, cantankerous personality made a not unfavorable impression on millions of Americans as it had on hundreds of Richmond juries years before. Dennis's problem was that he came out on what was swiftly revealed to be the wrong side—defending our first criminal President.

That, plus former prosecutor Dennis's support of the Nixon pardon, might have been enough for a narrow Sharp victory. But Sharp had another issue: he and wife had long since made full revelations of their incomes and assets, and Dennis refused to do anything of the kind. In the last days of the campaign, Sharp hit hard on this issue and it undoubtedly helped to produce his surprisingly large victory. In the House, Sharp is one of the dozen freshmen whose presence has totally transformed the atmosphere and political proclivities of the House Commerce Committee; and after six years of campaigning, he should know as well as anyone how to use his official perquisites to advantage. Undoubtedly, Republicans will make a spirited effort to regain this seat in 1976, but Sharp has shown so much perseverance and hard work that is hard to see him losing.

Census Data Pop. 472,335. Central city, 15%; suburban, 27%. Median family income, $9,635; families above $15,000: 17%; families below $3,000: 8%. Median years education, 12.1.

The Voters

Median voting age 42.
Employment profile White collar, 37%. Blue collar, 47%. Service, 12%. Farm, 4%.
Ethnic groups Black, 3%. Total foreign stock, 3%.

Presidential vote

1972	Nixon (R)	129,455	(69%)
	McGovern (D)	57,073	(31%)
1968	Nixon (R)	99,345	(52%)
	Humphrey (D)	69,746	(36%)
	Wallace (AI)	22,440	(12%)

Rep. Philip R. Sharp (D) Elected 1974; b. July 15, 1942, Baltimore, Md.; home, Muncie; DePauw U., Georgetown U. School of Foreign Svc., B.S. 1964, Oxford U., 1966, Georgetown U., Ph.D. 1974; Methodist.

Career Legis. Aide to U.S. Sen. Vance Hartke, 1964–69; Asst. and Assoc. Prof. of Poli. Sci., Ball St. U., 1969–74; Dem. nominee for U.S. House of Reps., 1970, 1972.

Offices 1234 LHOB, 202-225-3023. Also Fed. Bldg., 401 S. High St., Muncie 47305, 317-289-7948.

Committees

District of Columbia (15th). Subcommittees: Commerce, Housing and Transportation; Bicentennial, the Environment, and the International Community.

Interstate and Foreign Commerce (23d). Subcommittees: Energy and Power; Oversight and Investigations.

Group Ratings: Newly Elected

Key Votes

1) Foreign Aid	AGN	6) Gov Abortn Aid	NE	11) Pub Cong Election $	NE
2) Busing	NE	7) Coed Phys Ed	AGN	12) Turkish Arms Cutoff	NE
3) ABM	NE	8) Pov Lawyer Gag	NE	13) Youth Camp Regs	AGN
4) B-1 Bomber	AGN	9) Pub Trans Sub	NE	14) Strip Mine Veto	AGN
5) Nerve Gas	NE	10) EZ Voter Regis	NE	15) Farm Bill Veto	AGN

Election Results

1974 general:	Philip R. Sharp (D)	85,418	(54%)	($74,199)
	David W. Dennis (R)	71,701	(46%)	($79,840)
1974 primary:	Philip R. Sharp (D)	24,307	(70%)	
	Four others (D)	10,611	(30%)	

◆ ◆ ◆ ◆ ◆

ELEVENTH DISTRICT

The 11th district of Indiana includes most of the city of Indianapolis, which a few years ago annexed almost all of its suburbs to preserve Republican control of City Hall. There are plenty of factories here, but overall Indianapolis is an office town, with major banks, insurance companies, and of course the state government. Like Columbus, the capital of Ohio, it never had the kind of migration of Eastern European ethnics which shaped the politics of Great Lakes cities to the north, and it remains today almost as resolutely Republican as it was in the 1920s.

As in all of Indiana, politics is a serious business here. Of the two major banks, for example, one is Republican and the other Democratic; naturally, both have an interest in which party wins the state Treasurer's office. Patronage is an integral part of politics, and civil service virtually unheard of; most state, county, and city employees must "contribute" 2% of their paychecks to the party which got them their jobs. The national headquarters of the American Legion stares down toward the federal building and the state Capitol; this is not, in any way, a city which you would associate with a sense of humor.

Yet Indianapolis sends to Congress one of the funniest members there, 11th district Congressman Andrew Jacobs. The proud owner of a Great Dane named C-5A, after the Lockheed transport which developed the giant cost overruns, Jacobs is a liberal Democrat who approaches politics with a carefree attitude. One day he handed out cigars when C-5A became a father; in fact, the dog trails around after him just about everywhere but on the House floor. Despite his ferocious appearance, C-5A is harmless—except to Missouri Congressman James Symington, whom he has bitten on two occasions.

Jacobs is not considered so harmless by Indianapolis Republicans; they have been trying to beat him since he first won the seat in an upset in the Johnson landslide of 1964. That year Jacobs, whose father had represented the district for two years following the surprise Truman victory in 1948, had the good fortune to be running against a non-incumbent in a district which then included all of Marion County. Two years later, he was the beneficiary of a Democratic redistricting, which pared away some of the suburbs, and he won again; he survived a Republican redistricting in 1968 and 1970. In that latter year, he won by his biggest margin, 58–42 against ultra-conservative state Senator Danny Burton.

But in 1972, the Republicans had had a chance to redistrict again, and this time they managed to take about half of Indianapolis's black precincts out of the 11th. In the primary, Burton was beaten by a mere 81 votes by the Rev. William Hudnut, who had the support of Mayor Richard Lugar's efficient—and extremely well-financed—machine. The more moderate Hudnut, basically a Nixon Republican, managed in that year of the Nixon landslide to beat Jacobs 51–49.

But then Hudnut had his problems. His Nixon loyalties a liability when the Watergate scandal unfolded, and locally his friend Mayor Lugar got into trouble with a police scandal, and ultimately he failed to carry the city in his 1974 race against Senator Birch Bayh. Jacobs was the Democratic candidate again, and although he ran what observers considered a relaxed campaign, he managed this time to win by a 52–48 margin. Returning to Washington he managed to garner a choice office and to win a seat on the Ways and Means Committee. But he was even luckier than that: on the way back to the capital after Thanksgiving 1974, he refused to pay an extra $17 for a first-class seat, the only kind available. That was the plane that crashed coming into Dulles Airport, killing all aboard. Good fortune seems to smile on Jacobs, and it is hard to believe that he will fail to win again in 1976, although the Republicans will surely by trying to beat him again.

Census Data Pop. 472,533. Central city, 93%; suburban, 7%. Median family income, $10,785; families above $15,000: 26%; families below $3,000: 7%. Median years education, 12.2.

The Voters

Median voting age 42.
Employment profile White collar, 53%. Blue collar, 34%. Service, 13%. Farm, –%.
Ethnic groups Black, 2%. Total foreign stock, 6%. Germany, 1%.

Presidential vote

1972	Nixon (R)	125,009	(66%)
	McGovern (D)	63,456	(34%)
1968	Nixon (R)	99,982	(52%)
	Humphrey (D)	74,066	(39%)
	Wallace (AI)	16,702	(9%)

Rep. Andrew Jacobs, Jr. (D) Elected 1974; b. Feb. 24, 1932, Indianapolis; home, Indianapolis; Ind. U., B.S. 1955, LL.B. 1958; Catholic.

Career USMC, Korea; Practicing atty., 1958–65, 1973–74; Ind. House of Reps. 1959–60; U.S. House of Reps., 1965–73.

Offices 1501 LHOB, 202-225-4011. Also 46 E. Ohio St., 441 A Fed. Bldg., Indianapolis 46204, 317-269-7331.

Committees

Ways and Means (22d). Subcommittees: Social Security; Unemployment Compensation.

Group Ratings: Newly Elected

Key Votes

1) Foreign Aid	AGN	6) Gov Abortn Aid	NE	11) Pub Cong Election $	NE
2) Busing	NE	7) Coed Phys Ed	FOR	12) Turkish Arms Cutoff	NE
3) ABM	NE	8) Pov Lawyer Gag	NE	13) Youth Camp Regs	FOR
4) B-1 Bomber	AGN	9) Pub Trans Sub	NE	14) Strip Mine Veto	AGN
5) Nerve Gas	NE	10) EZ Voter Regis	NE	15) Farm Bill Veto	FOR

Election Results

1974 general:	Andrew Jacobs, Jr. (D)	81,508	(52%)	($47,336)
	William H. Hudnut, III (R)	73,793	(48%)	($201,673)
1974 primary:	Andrew Jacobs, Jr. (D)	18,821	(86%)	
	Two others (D)	2,592	(14%)	

IOWA

Iowa brings to mind the America of the nineteenth century: Grant Wood's American Gothic; Main Street; county fair time; and acres upon acres of fields where the tall corn grows. Indeed, to this day, many aspects of life in Iowa have not been much affected by the twentieth century. Most Iowans, 99% of whom are white, still live on farms or in small towns, not in large cities or surrounding suburbs. The state has no military installations and very little defense industry. And Iowa politics has not been afflicted with the ills which seem to result from rapid urbanization; the state has no equivalent of the Chicago machine or of the right-wing movement once so important in southern California.

The economic base of Iowa remains pretty much as it was at the turn of the century. It is the largest state in which agriculture is still the major industry. Technology has changed the actual workings of the farms enormously, increasing their output and decreasing the number of actual farmers, but the livelihood of most Iowans still depends, directly or indirectly on the economics of corn, hogs, and beef cattle. Accordingly, Iowa remains a kind of economic colony, dependent on the price of commodities on the Chicago Board of Trade and upon decisions made by the Department of Agriculture in Washington and the congressional committees which, technically at least, set policy.

With its nineteenth century atmosphere, its dependence on farming, and its heavily white Anglo-Saxon Protestant population, Iowa is naturally considered a Republican state. And over the years it has been; Lyndon Johnson is the only Democratic presidential candidate it has supported in the last quarter-century. And yet Iowa seems on the verge of becoming an almost dependably Democratic state. Since 1954, it has had a Democratic Governor most of the time, and the current incumbent, Republican Robert Ray, owes much of his popularity to his liberal image. Both of the state's Senators are now Democrats, and so are five of the six Congressmen. The Democrats now control both houses of the state legislature.

Some may claim that this apparent Democratic dominance is just a fluke, the result of the 1974 anti-Nixon landslide. But it is the result actually of a longer leftward trend, one which is likely to continue. This is one of the four non-Southern states that gave George McGovern a higher percentage of its votes than it had given Hubert Humphrey in 1968; it was moving toward the Democrats while the rest of the country was moving toward Nixon. Traditional Republicanism here was based on frugality, honesty, and hostility toward the segregationist South. Nixon's Southern strategy, his continued high spending especially on defense (which benefits Iowa not at all), and, of course, his criminality has moved Iowa toward the Democrats. Perhaps even Nixon's preference, personally as well as politically, for the warm climes of San Clemente and Key Biscayne must have rasped against the grain of Iowans who had been taught that cold winters build character; and the fetid Caribbean aura of Watergate—the Cuban burglars, the Mexican laundry—could not have failed to repel them.

Perhaps typifying Iowans' reactions was that of Clark Mollenhoff, bureau chief of the Des Moines Register, which has statewide circulation here. A conservative Republican who had served briefly on Nixon's White House staff, Mollenhoff had been appalled there by the White House's insistence on covering up the Lockheed C-5A cost overruns and its determination to get rid of Ernest Fitzgerald, the Pentagon employee who had blown the whistle to Senator William Proxmire's committee. Later, by sheer force of will and the power of his vocal chords, Mollenhoff forced a reluctant federal hearing examiner to hear his testimony in the case. Probably no member of the Washington press corps was more visibly outraged by Watergate. And as that scandal went on, the *Register's* Washington bureau, under Mollenhoff's direction, ran a long series of investigative stories on the economics of the food business—revealing how laxly the Nixon government was regulating the big companies and how much they were getting away with.

Another figure who helped to lead Iowans away from Nixon's Republicans was former Senator Harold Hughes. A former truckdriver and cured alcoholic, Hughes had been elected Governor in an upset in 1962, and in that capacity built the state Democratic Party in his own image. A giant, deep-voiced, forceful man of unquestioned honesty, Hughes broke with Lyndon Johnson over the Vietnam war and gave the nominating speech for Eugene McCarthy at the 1968 Democratic convention. He also sponsored the resolution which resulted in the party reform commission which changed almost completely the means of selecting national convention delegates and, thus Presidents. Hughes was elected to the Senate in 1968, where be became just about the only dovish member of the Armed Services Committee; but no one ever dared to call him an effete snob. A deeply religious man, Hughes decided not to run for reelection—which he could easily have won—in 1974 in order to pursue a lay ministry.

Five years ago, John Culver was a Democratic Congressman from the 2d district of Iowa and Dick Clark, a former political science professor, was his administrative assistant. Today Clark and Culver—in that order—are the two U.S. Senators from Iowa. The way it came about, as well as the result, is rather unusual. In early 1972, Culver had been thinking about running against the state's Republican Senator, Jack Miller. A deep-dyed conservative, Miller had all the charisma one might expect from a former Sioux City tax lawyer; but he had won two elections, in 1960 and 1966, by good margins and was the kind of man Iowans had just about always sent to Washington. Culver did some scouting around, and finally decided the race would be too tough; instead, he sought another sure term in Congress. With no one else eager to run, Clark, who had put together Culver's grass roots organization in the 2d district, decided to make the race himself.

That was the year that dozens of candidates were walking through their states, and Clark, tall and husky like Hughes and in good physical condition, was one of the champion walkers. Dressed informally, he talked with Iowans across the state, and came over well. He became well-known while Miller worked on in Washington. Then, in October, Clark attacked Miller for voting, as a member of the Senate Finance Committee, for bills which would benefit certain large companies. Big corporations have often used conservative Senators from rural states to push measures which would help them, but Iowa voters apparently decided that they had had enough of this. Clark won an upset victory with 56% of the vote, carrying all six of the state's congressional districts.

In the Senate, Clark has been something of a tiger, unafraid of voting against the confirmation of Nixon appointees and raising questions about the way things have always been done. He has been most active as a member of the Agriculture Committee, and was the Senator who, as a member of the American delegation to the international food conference in Rome, organized other Senators against a policy espoused by Agriculture Secretary Earl Butz. Clark's popularity in Iowa seems, if anything, to be growing; he seems likely to be a major power in the Senate and a powerful political force in his home state as well.

After Clark's 1972 victory, just about no one downgraded Democratic chances to retain Hughes's seat in 1974. The candidate this time was a no longer reluctant John Culver. His Republican opponent was David Stanley, the youngish state legislator who had spent a major chunk of his family fortune in the 1968 campaign and came within 6,000 votes of upsetting Harold Hughes. Stanley was again spending, and attacking Culver on a variety of grounds; again he was close, but the Democrat won by a 52–48 margin. It was, perhaps the acid test for the proposition that Iowa had become a Democratic state, and it proved the case.

Culver has an unusual background for an Iowa politician. He was a college roommate of Senator Edward Kennedy and a slam-bang Harvard fullback in the early 1950s. He attended Harvard Law, served in administrative posts there, and then worked on Kennedy's staff. Sensing a Democratic year in 1964, he returned home to Cedar Rapids, campaigned hard, and upset a lackluster Republican with 51% of the vote. Culver was the only '64 Democrat in Iowa to survive the 1966 Republican sweep; he won easily again in 1968, 1970, and 1972. In the 93d Congress, he was head of the Democratic Study Group, the liberal organization which has increasingly dominated the party's caucus in the House. In the Senate, he was one of three freshmen assigned to the Armed Services Committee. Known for his short temper and iron will, Culver has since shouted down generals who he thought were not responsive to his questions—treatment they are certainly not used to.

Both Clark and Culver would appear to be in solid shape for reelection when their seats come up in 1978 and 1980—but for the presence on the scene of Governor Ray. Widely popular, Ray won his fourth term—and the first four-year term in Iowa's history—with 59% of the vote in the otherwise Democratic year of 1974; he is unlikely ever to be defeated for that office. He is the man who, when the Pentagon tried not to pay claims for houses damaged by military plane crashes, grounded National Guard planes in Iowa until the brass paid up. Ray has not been particularly interested in the Senate in the past, but he would have a serious chance of winning—and looks to be just about the only Iowa Republican in that position. Of course he has a long time to make his decision.

Census Data Pop. 2,825,041; 1.40% of U.S. total, 25th largest; Central city, 22%; suburban, 13%. Median family income, $9,017; 26th highest; families above $15,000: 16%; families below $3,000: 10%. Median years education, 12.2.

1974 Share of Federal Tax Burden $3,588,725,000; 1.34% of U.S. total, 22d largest.

1974 Share of Federal Outlays $2,847,925,000; 1.06% of U.S. total, 31st largest. Per capita federal spending, $1008.

DOD	$237,769,000	41st (0.35%)		HEW	$1,198,971,000	27th (1.29%)
AEC	$20,318,000	19th (0.67%)		HUD	$3,931,000	40th (0.40%)
NASA	$3,394,000	26th (0.11%)		VA	$184,488,000	27th (1.35%)
DOT	$81,624,000	34th (0.96%)		EPA	$55,979,000	18th (1.78%)
DOC	$2,339,000	47th (0.14%)		RevS	$86,287,000	25th (1.42%)
DOI	$9,129,000	41st (0.37%)		Int.	$178,137,000	15th (0.87%)
USDA	$450,685,000	5th (3.62%)		Other	$334,874,000	

Economic Base Agriculture, notably cattle, hogs, corn and soybeans; food and kindred products, especially meat products; finance, insurance and real estate; machinery, especially farm machinery; electrical equipment and supplies, especially household appliances; printing and publishing, especially newspapers; fabricated metal products, especially fabricated structural metal products.

Political Line-up Governor, Robert D. Ray (R). Senators, Dick Clark (D) and John C. Culver (D). Representatives, 6 (5 D and 1 R). State Senate (26 D and 24 R); State House (60 D and 40 R).

The Voters

Registration Statewide registration will be in effect for the first time by 1976, no figures yet available.
Median voting age 45.
Employment profile White collar, 43%. Blue collar, 31%. Service, 14%. Farm, 12%.
Ethnic groups Black, 1%. Total foreign stock, 11%. Germany, 4%.

Presidential vote

1972	Nixon (R)	....	706,207	(59%)
	McGovern (D)	....	496,206	(41%)
1968	Nixon (R)	....	619,106	(53%)
	Humphrey (D)	....	476,699	(41%)
	Wallace (AI)	....	66,422	(6%)

Sen. Dick Clark (D) Elected 1972, seat up 1978; b. Sept. 14, 1929, Paris, Ia.; home, Marion; U. of Md., Wiesbaden, Germany, 1950–52, U. of Frankfurt, Germany, 1950–52, Upper Ia. U., B.A. 1953, U. of Ia., M.A. 1956.

Career Army, 1950–52; Asst. Prof., Upper Ia. U., 1959–64; Admin. Asst. to U.S. Rep. John C. Culver, 1965–72.

Offices 404 RSOB, 202-224-3254. Also 733 Fed. Bldg., Des Moines 50309, 515-284-4721.

Committees

Agriculture and Forestry (7th). Subcommittees: Agricultural Production, Marketing, and Stabilization of Prices; Agricultural Research and General Legislation; Foreign Agricultural Policy; Rural Development (Chairman).

Foreign Relations (9th). Subcommittees: African Affairs (Chairman); Arms Control, International Organizations and Security Agreements; Multinational Corporations; Near Eastern and South Asian Affairs.

Group Ratings

	ADA	COPE	LWV	RIPON	NFU	LCV	CFA	NAB	NSI	ACA
1974	95	91	100	82	100	95	100	33	0	5
1973	94	82	100	44	100	–	100	–	–	4

Key Votes

1) No-Knock	AGN	8) Gov Abortn Aid	FOR	15) Consumer Prot Agy	FOR
2) Busing	FOR	9) Cut Mil Brass	FOR	16) Forced Psych Tests	FOR
3) No Fault	FOR	10) Gov Limousine	AGN	17) Fed Campaign Subs	FOR
4) F-111	AGN	11) RR Featherbed	FOR	18) Rhod Chrome Ban	FOR
5) Death Penalty	AGN	12) Handgun License	AGN	19) Open Legis Meetings	FOR
6) Foreign Aid	FOR	13) Less Troop Abrd	FOR	20) Strikers Food Stmps	FOR
7) Filibuster	AGN	14) Resume Turk Aid	ABS	21) Gov Info Disclosure	FOR

Election Results

1972 general:	Dick Clark (D)	662,637	(56%)	($241,803)
	Jack Miller (R)	530,525	(44%)	($328,263)
1972 primary:	Dick Clark (D), unopposed			

Sen. John C. Culver (D) Elected 1974; b. Aug. 8, 1932, Rochester, Minn.; home, Cedar Rapids; Harvard U., A.B. 1954, LL.B. 1962, Lionel de Jersey Harvard Scholar, Cambridge U., 1954–55; Presbyterian.

Career USMC 1955–58; Dean of Men, Harvard U., 1960; Legis. Asst. to U.S. Sen. Edward M. Kennedy, 1962–63; U.S. House of Reps., 1965–75.

Offices 1327 DSOB, 202-224-3744. Also Rm. 721 Fed. Bldg., Des Moines 50309, 515-284-4056.

Committees

Armed Services (8th). Subcommittees: Manpower and Personnel; Research and Development.

Public Works (7th). Subcommittees: Environmental Pollution, Panel on Environmental Science and Technology (Chairman); Water Resources (Chairman); Transportation; Buildings and Grounds.

Group Ratings

	ADA	COPE	LWV	RIPON	NFU	LCV	CFA	NAB	NSI	ACA
	100	91	100	87	100	77	82	33	10	8
1973	92	82	100	93	95	94	75	–	–	4
1972	88	82	91	77	100	83	100	10	0	0

Key Votes

1) No-Knock	NE	8) Gov Abortn Aid	FOR	15) Consumer Prot Agy	NE
2) Busing	NE	9) Cut Mil Brass	NE	16) Forced Psych Tests	NE
3) No Fault	NE	10) Gov Limousine	NE	17) Fed Campaign Subs	NE
4) F-111	AGN	11) RR Featherbed	NE	18) Rhod Chrome Ban	NE
5) Death Penalty	NE	12) Handgun License	NE	19) Open Legis Meetings	NE
6) Foreign Aid	NE	13) Less Troop Abrd	NE	20) Strikers Food Stmps	NE
7) Filibuster	AGN	14) Resume Turk Aid	AGN	21) Gov Info Disclosure	NE

Election Results

1974 general:	John C. Culver (D)	462,947	(52%)	($470,970)
	David M. Stanley (R)	420,546	(48%)	($336,067)
1974 primary:	John C. Culver (D), unopposed			

Gov. Robert D. Ray (R) Elected 1968, term expires Jan. 1979; b. Sept. 26, 1928, Des Moines; Drake U., B.A., LL.B.; Christian Church.

Career Practicing atty.; Law and Reading Clerk, Iowa Senate; Chm., Iowa Repub. St. Central Comm., 1965–68.

Offices State Capitol, Des Moines 50319, 515-281-5211.

Election Results

1974 general:	Robert Ray (R)	534,518	(59%)
	James F. Schaben (D)	377,553	(41%)
1974 primary:	Robert Ray (R), unopposed		
1972 general:	Robert Ray (R)	707,177	(59%)
	Paul Franzenburg (D)	487,282	(41%)

◆ ◆ ◆ ◆ ◆

FIRST DISTRICT

Of all the nation's 435 congressional districts, the one which has had the closest elections in the last dozen years, not just in November but also in primary contests, is the 1st district of Iowa. To visitors from New York or Los Angeles, this southeast corner of Iowa along the Mississippi River must look like rather an ordinary part of the Midwest, with a lot of farmland and some small manufacturing cities. But the 1st does have some distinctive features. The little city of Burlington (pop. 32,000) has given its name to a major railroad and has a Pulitzer Prize winning journalist, John McCormally of the *Hawkeye*. Davenport (pop. 98,000), the largest city in the district, is a marginally Republican town with a Democratic Mayor named Kathryn Kirschbaum; it is also the home of the Palmer School of Chiropractic. And Iowa City (pop. 47,000) is the site of the State University of Iowa, the largest institution of higher learning in the state, with 20,000 students.

But listing these features does not explain why this district has been one of the most marginal in the nation. The real explanation lies in personalities, particularly that of former Congressman Fred Schwengel. A sometimes liberal Republican with a wide range of interests, Schwengel is president of the National Capital Historical Society and a Lincoln buff. First elected to the House in 1954, he was something of a loner, and despite his liberal record lost the district to college professor John Schmidhauser in 1964. Schwengel won it back in 1966 and beat Schmidhauser again in 1968—all by narrow margins. In 1970, Schwengel faced former state Representative David Stanley in the Republican primary; Stanley, who had nearly beaten Senator Harold Hughes two years before, spent over $100,000 and got 44% of the vote. In the fall, Schwengel beat antiwar Democrat Edward Mezvinsky by only 765 votes.

From that time on, it looked like Mezvinsky's seat—and it was. He began by beating Schmidhauser by almost 2–1 in the Democratic primary. The general election was not so much a matter of positions on the issues as a contrast in attitudes and styles. Schwengel, the 65-year-old incumbent, was genial and often uncommittal on issues; Mezvinsky, the 35-year-old challenger, earnestly spoke out against the Nixon Administration's policies. That, hard work, and a good organization—plus strong majorities from students in Iowa City—gave Mezvinsky a comfortable 54–46 victory.

Mezvinsky was the most junior Democrat on the House Judiciary Committee which voted to impeach Richard Nixon. His speaking style was not considered as arresting as some others', and his advocacy of an article relating to Nixon's misuse of government funds on his person failed to carry. But if he did not completely shine, his earnestness and his position apparently did not hurt him with his constituents. He faced—appropriately, considering the district's history—the strongest challenge Republicans have made in any Iowa district recently; Mezvinsky won again by a 54–46 margin. Provided he does not face such well-financed opposition again, he can probably look forward to more comfortable victories in the future.

Census Data Pop. 471,260. Central city, 21%; suburban, 9%. Median family income, $9,594; families above $15,000: 18%; families below $3,000: 9%. Median years education, 12.3.

The Voters

Median voting age 42.
Employment profile White collar, 45%. Blue collar, 33%. Service, 14%. Farm, 8%.
Ethnic groups Black, 1%. Total foreign stock, 9%. Germany, 3%.

Presidential vote

1972	Nixon (R)	111,577	(56%)
	McGovern (D)	87,448	(44%)
1968	Nixon (R)	93,947	(50%)
	Humphrey (D)	81,468	(44%)
	Wallace (AI)	11,007	(6%)

Rep. Edward Mezvinsky (D) Elected 1972; b. Jan. 17, 1937, Ames; home, Iowa City; U. of Ia., B.A. 1960, U. of Cal., M.A., J.D.; Jewish.

Career Legis. Asst. to U.S. Rep. Neal Smith, 1965–67; Practicing atty., 1967–73; Ia. House of Reps., 1969–71; Dem. nominee for U.S. House of Reps., 1970.

Offices 1404 LHOB, 202-225-6576. Also 115 Fed. Bldg., Davenport 52801, 319-326-4088.

Committees

Government Operations (22d). Subcommittees: Commerce, Consumer and Monetary Affairs; Intergovernmental Relations and Human Resources.

Judiciary (17th). Subcommittees: Monopolies and Commercial Law.

Group Ratings

	ADA	COPE	LWV	RIPON	NFU	LCV	CFA	NAB	NSI	ACA
1974	96	100	100	69	100	76	92	33	10	0
1973	96	82	100	87	100	95	75	–	–	11

Key Votes

1) Foreign Aid	FOR	6) Gov Abortn Aid	FOR	11) Pub Cong Election $	FOR
2) Busing	FOR	7) Coed Phys Ed	FOR	12) Turkish Arms Cutoff	FOR
3) ABM	AGN	8) Pov Lawyer Gag	AGN	13) Youth Camp Regs	FOR
4) B-1 Bomber	AGN	9) Pub Trans Sub	FOR	14) Strip Mine Veto	AGN
5) Nerve Gas	AGN	10) EZ Voter Regis	FOR	15) Farm Bill Veto	AGN

Election Results

0974 general:	Edward Mezvinsky (D)	75,687	(54%)	($81,166)
	James A. S. Leach (R)	63,540	(46%)	($89,786)
1974 primary:	Edward Mezvinsky (D), unopposed			
1972 general:	Edward Mezvinsky (D)	107,099	(54%)	($113,546)
	Fred Schwengel (R)	91,609	(46%)	($69,615)

◆ ◆ ◆ ◆

SECOND DISTRICT

The 2d congressional district of Iowa is the northwest corner of the state. The district is dominated by Cedar Rapids (pop. 163,000), Iowa's second largest city, and by two aging Mississippi River towns about half that size, Dubuque and Clinton. Cedar Rapids has been politically marginal in recent years—a little more Democratic, usually, than the state as a whole. Clinton is heavily Republican; Dubuque, almost entirely populated by descendants of German Catholic immigrants, is heavily Democratic. The knobby hills that flank the Mississippi are less suitable for corn, hogs, and wheat than the rolling plains farther west.

Aside from the Des Moines-based 4th district, the 2d has been Iowa's most Democratic seat in the last several elections; it has not elected a Republican Congressman since 1962. Senator John Culver won the seat here in 1964, held on to it by a small margin in 1966—the only beneficiary of the Johnson landslide to do so in Iowa—and held it easily in the next three elections. With the aid of Dick Clark, then his administrative assistant and now the state's senior Senator, Culver built up a grass roots organization which, together with his general popularity, served him in good stead.

But for 1974, when Culver was running for the Senate, this was a close race indeed. The Democratic nomination was won by 28-year-old Michael Blouin, a Dubuque state Senator; since Dubuque casts as much as 40% of the votes in the district's Democratic primaries, Blouin had a home town advantage his opponents could not overcome. But in the general election, Dubuque does not bulk so large, and Blouin had difficulty against Republican nominee Tom Riley, a state Senator from Cedar Rapids. Riley had gotten 45% of the vote against Culver in 1968, and he put on a formidable campaign. Finally, in this Democratic year, Blouin pulled ahead; if he was the weakest of Iowa's six Democratic House candidates, he had one of the more Democratically inclined.

In the neighboring states of Minnesota and Wisconsin, Democrats have won just about every office there is, and for the most part Republicans have been totally unable to come up with serious candidates for Governor, Senator, or Congressman. This does not appear to be the case yet in Iowa. The Democrats here definitely have been winning, to the degree that Iowa must now be considered a Democratic state. But as the races in the 1st and 3d, as well as the 2d, districts show, the Republicans have not yet lain down and died. Consequently, we can expect to see a fairly hearty contest here in 1976, as Republicans hope that Blouin's 52–48 victory was just the result of a heavily Democratic year.

Census Data Pop. 471,933. Central city, 37%; suburban, 17%. Median family income, $9,511; families above $15,000: 17%; families below $3,000: 9%. Median years education, 12.2.

The Voters

Median voting age 43.
Employment profile White collar, 41%. Blue collar, 34%. Service, 13%. Farm, 12%.
Ethnic groups Total foreign stock, 10%. Germany, 4%.

Presidential vote

1972	Nixon (R)	108,517	(56%)
	McGovern (D)	86,714	(44%)

1968	Nixon (R)	96,936	(51%)
	Humphrey (D)	83,215	(44%)
	Wallace (AI)	9,684	(5%)

Rep. Michael T. Blouin (D) Elected 1974; b. Nov. 7, 1945, Jacksonville, Fla.; home, Dubuque; Loras Col., B.A. 1966; Catholic.

Career Elementary school teacher, 1967–69; Advertising consultant, 1970–74; Ia. House of Reps., 1968–72; Ia. Senate, 1973–75.

Offices 1118 LHOB, 202-225-2911. Also 222 Fed. Bldg., Dubuque 52011, 319-556-7575.

Committees

Education and Labor (19th). Subcommittees: Agricultural Labor; Elementary, Secondary and Vocational Education; Post-secondary Education.

Science and Technology (20th). Subcommittees: Energy Research (Fossil Fuels); Environment and the Atmosphere; Space Science and Applications.

Group Ratings: Newly Elected

Key Votes

1) Foreign Aid	AGN	6) Gov Abortn Aid	NE	11) Pub Cong Election $	NE
2) Busing	NE	7) Coed Phys Ed	FOR	12) Turkish Arms Cutoff	NE
3) ABM	NE	8) Pov Lawyer Gag	NE	13) Youth Camp Regs	FOR
4) B-1 Bomber	AGN	9) Pub Trans Sub	NE	14) Strip Mine Veto	AGN
5) Nerve Gas	NE	10) EZ Voter Regis	NE	15) Farm Bill Veto	AGN

Election Results

1974 general:	Michael T. Blouin (D)	73,416	(52%)	($137,750)
	Tom Riley (R)	69,088	(48%)	($107,884)
1974 primary:	Michael T. Blouin (D)	12,705	(45%)	
	Martin Jensen (D)	10,638	(38%)	
	Two others (D)	4,674	(17%)	

◆ ◆ ◆ ◆ ◆

THIRD DISTRICT

Iowa's 3d congressional district, in the north central part of the state, is almost perfectly square, with a few odd corners where counties were added or removed by redistricting. Its largest city, Waterloo (pop. 75,000), is a gritty factory town, with big meat packing and farm machinery plants and, next to Des Moines, Iowa's largest black population (6,500). Probably more typical of the district is Marshalltown (pop. 26,000), home town of Meredith Wilson (*The Music Man*) and Merle Miller (*Plain Speaking*)—a neat, pleasant Republican courthouse town in the middle of an agricultural county. The 3d is not all Republican; there are some heavily Catholic counties here which are historically Democratic; but until recently everyone thought of the area, and properly so, as quintessentially Republican.

Indeed, for 26 years, the 3d elected the quintessential Republican Congressman, H. R. Gross. Spending much of his time on the floor, decrying what he considered wasteful spending, objecting to unanimous consent requests, asking for quorum calls, Gross was the undisputed curmudgeon of the House. Many considered him a nit-picking pain in the neck, but the fact was that the fear of Gross made just about every bill manager with a request for federal funds study his bill a little more carefully—and sometimes modify it to eliminate something Gross might make trouble about. Gross had survived the 1964 Johnson landslide by the barest of margins, but in 1974, at the age of 75, he finally decided to retire.

It is a symptom of the leftward trend in Iowa politics that there was a spirited Democratic primary in the race to succeed Gross (even though the Democrats ultimately lost the district). The main contestants were Nicholas Johnson, a member of the Federal Communications Commission from 1966 to 1973, whose irreverence toward networks and station owners was legendary in Washington; and Steve Rapp, a 25-year-old state Representative, who just two years before had been a student at Harvard Law School and a McGovern volunteer in New Hampshire. The vote was so close that the outcome depended on a rerun in one precinct on an Indian reservation, where there had been no proper machine in the original primary. The two candidates campaigned door to door, often passing each other in the street, and Rapp won handily.

In the general election, Rapp was generally considered the favorite. But toward the end of October, H. R. Gross began campaigning heavily for the Republican, state Representative Charles Grassley. Something of an ultraconservative, Grassley ended up winning in this Democratic year by a narrow 51–49 margin. So despite the Democratic trend in Iowa generally—one in which the 3d district has participated in statewide elections—this district has not elected a Democratic Congressman since 1932; given that record, it is unlikely to do so in 1976.

Census Data Pop. 471,866. Central city, 16%; suburban, 12%. Median family income, $8,911; families above $15,000: 15%; families below $3,000: 10%. Median years education, 12.2.

The Voters

Median voting age 46.
Employment profile White collar, 40%. Blue collar, 32%. Service, 14%. Farm, 14%.
Ethnic groups Black, 2%. Total foreign stock, 12%. Germany, 5%.

Presidential vote

1972	Nixon (R)	119,372	(60%)
	McGovern (D)	78,687	(40%)
1968	Nixon (R)	108,995	(57%)
	Humphrey (D)	74,716	(39%)
	Wallace (AI)	9,169	(5%)

Rep. Charles E. Grassley (R) Elected 1974; b. Sept. 17, 1933, New Hartford; home, New Hartford; U. of No. Ia., B.A. 1955, M.A. 1956, U. of Ia., 1957–58; Baptist.

Career Farmer; Ia. House of Reps., 1959–74.

Offices 1213 LHOB, 202-225-3301. Also 900 Waterloo Bldg., Waterloo 50701, 319-232-6657.

Committees

Agriculture (12th). Subcommittees: Department Operations, Investigations and Oversight; Domestic Marketing and Consumer Relations; Family Farms and Rural Development.

Banking, Currency and Housing (13th). Subcommittees: Consumer Affairs; Housing Community Development; International Development Institutions and Finance.

Group Ratings: Newly Elected

Key Votes

1) Foreign Aid	AGN	6) Gov Abortn Aid	NE	11) Pub Cong Election $	NE
2) Busing	NE	7) Coed Phys Ed	AGN	12) Turkish Arms Cutoff	NE
3) ABM	NE	8) Pov Lawyer Gag	NE	13) Youth Camp Regs	AGN
4) B-1 Bomber	AGN	9) Pub Trans Sub	NE	14) Strip Mine Veto	FOR
5) Nerve Gas	NE	10) EZ Voter Regis	NE	15) Farm Bill Veto	AGN

Election Results

1974 general:				
	Charles E. Grassley (R)	77,468	(51%)	($107,102)
	Stephen J. Rapp (D)	74,895	(49%)	($100,007)

1974 primary:	Charles E. Grassley (R)	13,495	(42%)
	Robert E. Case (R)	9,044	(28%)
	Charlene Conklin (R)	6,043	(19%)
	Two others (R)	3,535	(11%)

◆ ◆ ◆ ◆ ◆

FOURTH DISTRICT

The 4th congressional district of Iowa is really a combination of two pre-1972 districts. More than half its votes are cast in Des Moines and Polk County, which is thus the dominant, though not the geographically central, part of the district. Des Moines, next to Dubuque, has traditionally been Iowa's most Democratic town; it is a major farm machinary manufacturing city, as well as a financial and commercial center for the surrounding farmland, and the state capital. Before 1972, Des Moines was the center of the 5th district, represented since 1958 by Democrat Neal Smith.

The other part of the current 4th is a portion of rural south central Iowa. This is WASP farm country, where the largest city is Ottumwa (pop. 29,000). In years past, this has generally been Republican territory; before 1972, it was represented by Republican John Kyl. It is a sign of how nonpartisan these things are in Iowa that a Republican legislature created the current 4th district, which gave Democrat Smith a decided advantage over Republican Kyl. Neither party in cut-throat politics states like Indiana or Illinois would have done this. Smith had previously represented 60% of the new 4th's residents, and he had run more strongly among them than Kyl had in his old area. As a result, Smith carried the new district with 60% of the vote, more indeed than Richard Nixon won here.

Smith is a man who seems to have been caught on the wrong side of a political generation gap. As a 16-year House veteran, he began to enjoy significant seniority just as seniority is being devalued by the incoming House freshmen. A moderate-to-liberal Democrat, he is a little too conservative for a majority of the 1975 Democratic caucus—after spending most of his political life to the left of most of his fellow Iowans. Once the most liberal member of the Iowa delegation, now he is probably the most conservative of its five Democrats.

Smith is the 13th-ranking Democrat on the House Appropriations Committee, but unlike several less senior members he has not yet become a subcommittee chairman. In early 1975, he launched a campaign for Chairman of the Budget Committee; instead, the caucus voted that post to the more liberal Brock Adams of Washington, with Smith ending up 6th in seniority. But next to these disappointments is the fact that the 1974 election, in which he won 64% of the vote, showed him to be in solid shape with all of the new 4th district.

Census Data Pop. 468,881. Central city, 43%; suburban, 18%. Median family income, $9,589; families above $15,000: 19%; families below $3,000: 9%. Median years education, 12.3.

The Voters

Median voting age 44.
Employment profile White collar, 51%. Blue collar, 30%. Service, 14%. Farm, 5%.
Ethnic groups Black, 3%. Total foreign stock, 9%. Germany, 1%.

Presidential vote

1972	Nixon (R)	117,283	(56%)
	McGovern (D)	92,752	(44%)
1968	Nixon (R)	92,788	(47%)
	Humphrey (D)	88,899	(45%)
	Wallace (AI)	14,467	(7%)

Rep. Neal Smith (D) Elected 1958; b. Mar. 23, 1920, Hendrick; home, Altoona; U. of Mo., 1945–46, Syracuse U., 1946–47, Drake U., LL.B. 1950; Methodist.

Career Farmer; Army Air Corps, WWII; Practicing atty., 1950–58; Chm., Polk Co. Bd. of Social Welfare; Asst. Polk Co. Atty., 1951.

Offices 2373 RHOB, 202-225-4426. Also 544 Insurance Exchange Bldg., Des Moines 50309, 515-284-4634.

Committees

Appropriations (13th). Subcommittees: Labor-HEW; State, Justice, Commerce, and the Judiciary.

Budget (6th).

Small Business (4th). Subcommittees: SBA and SBIC Legislation (Chairman).

Group Ratings

	ADA	COPE	LWV	RIPON	NFU	LCV	CFA	NAB	NSI	ACA
1974	76	100	91	47	100	82	69	36	33	7
1973	73	82	82	69	100	56	75	–	–	13
1972	50	90	75	82	100	27	50	17	44	22

Key Votes

1) Foreign Aid	FOR	6) Gov Abortn Aid	ABS	11) Pub Cong Election $	FOR
2) Busing	FOR	7) Coed Phys Ed	FOR	12) Turkish Arms Cutoff	FOR
3) ABM	AGN	8) Pov Lawyer Gag	AGN	13) Youth Camp Regs	FOR
4) B-1 Bomber	AGN	9) Pub Trans Sub	FOR	14) Strip Mine Veto	AGN
5) Nerve Gas	AGN	10) EZ Voter Regis	FOR	15) Farm Bill Veto	AGN

Election Results

1974 general:	Neal Smith (D)	96,755	(64%)	($0)
	Chuck Dick (R)	53,756	(36%)	($55,231)
1974 primary:	Neal Smith (D), unopposed			
1972 general:	Neal Smith (D)	125,431	(60%)	($56,370)
	John Kyl (R)	85,156	(40%)	($112,154)

◆ ◆ ◆ ◆ ◆

FIFTH DISTRICT

On paper, the southwestern corner of Iowa—the 5th congressional district—is the most Republican part of the state. That's not saying much, since Iowa is not the solidly Republican state it once was, and there is precious little regional variation here. But if there is a Republican section it is here, where the plains, as they roll to the Missouri River, are a little less verdant than they are farther east, and the fields more likely to be given over to grazing cattle than to corn or hogs. The district's largest city, Council Bluffs (pop. 61,000), lies just across the Missouri from Omaha, Nebraska; and it appears to lean more toward the conservatism of Omaha than to the increasingly Democratic politics of the rest of Iowa. Indeed, Council Bluffs was the one sizeable population center in the state which was not carried by Senator Dick Clark in 1972, and of all of Iowa's urban areas, it gave the largest percentage of its vote to Richard Nixon that year.

And until 1974, the 5th district had perhaps the most conservative Republican Congressman from Iowa, William J. Scherle. A big, bluff man, with no trace of subtlety, Scherle had a hair-trigger temper and a loud voice. Back in 1966, he unseated a '64 Democrat, and in the next two elections he won easily. But his hearty conservatism seemed to go over less well in 1972. One problem was the addition to the district that year of Ames (pop. 40,000, up 46% in the 1960s), home of Iowa State University and its 19,000 students.

For Ames was also the home of Tom Harkin, now the Democratic Congressman from the 5th. Harkin was not successful when he ran in 1972: he beat Scherle 55–45 in the new parts of the district, but Scherle carried the portions he had been representing by a solid 60–40 margin. But after losing, Harkin never stopped campaigning. Watergate probably did not help him too much, for Scherle, though he supported Nixon on most issues, was no defender of all the President's men; when Haldeman and Ehrlichman quit, he rose up on the floor and impulsively shouted, "Good riddance." What really won for Harkin in 1974 was his own hard work campaigning. And work it really was: he set aside one day a week in which he would actually work at some ordinary, often menial job in the district. The idea was to show voters that Harkin understood their daily lives, and the candidate at work provided some good footage for TV commercials, in one of which he was shown literally shovelling manure. In the end, Harkin won by a narrow 51–49 margin. For his 1976 campaign, when he undoubtedly will face a tough challenge, he will have the advantage of a record on the House Agriculture Committee.

In a year when POWs—who are for some reason considered the only certified heroes of the Vietnam war—were one and all defeated for congressional office, Harkin has a distinction that is scarcely noticed: he is the one of the first three Vietnam veterans elected to the Congress. It says something about the Vietnam war that this should be so, for in 1946 and 1948 literally dozens of World War II veterans were elected (including John F. Kennedy, Richard Nixon, Carl Albert, and Gerald Ford). It says something about the war also that Harkin, the only veteran yet elected, is one who believes that the war was a mistake and that the United States should extricate itself from any form of military involvement in Southeast Asia.

Census Data Pop. 470,214. Central city, 0%; suburban, 19%. Median family income, $8,338; families above $15,000: 14%; families below $3,000: 12%. Median years education, 12.2.

The Voters

Median voting age 46.
Employment profile White collar, 40%. Blue collar, 28%. Service, 14%. Farm, 18%.
Ethnic groups Total foreign stock, 9%. Germany, 3%.

Presidential vote

1972	Nixon (R)	125,720	(63%)
	McGovern (D)	74,495	(37%)
1968	Nixon (R)	110,002	(56%)
	Humphrey (D)	73,320	(37%)
	Wallace (AI)	12,741	(6%)

Rep. Tom Harkin (D) Elected 1974; b. Nov. 19, 1939, Cumming; home, Ames; Ia. St. U., B.S. 1962, Catholic U., J.D. 1972.

Career Navy, 1962–67; Staff aide to U.S. Rep. Neal Smith, 1969–70; Dem. nominee for U.S. House of Reps., 1972; Atty., Polk Co. Legal Aid Society, 1973–74.

Offices 514 CHOB, 202-225-3806. Also P.O. Box 264, 213 P.O. Bldg., Ames 50010, 515-232-6111.

Committees

Agriculture (20th). Subcommittees: Department Operations, Investigations and Oversight; Domestic Marketing and Consumer Relations; Livestock and Grains.

Science and Technology (16th). Subcommittees: Aviation and Transportation Research and Development; Energy Research, Development and Demonstration; Science, Research, and Technology.

Group Ratings: Newly Elected

Key Votes

1) Foreign Aid	FOR	6) Gov Abortn Aid	NE	11) Pub Cong Election $	NE
2) Busing	NE	7) Coed Phys Ed	FOR	12) Turkish Arms Cutoff	NE
3) ABM	NE	8) Pov Lawyer Gag	NE	13) Youth Camp Regs	AGN
4) B-1 Bomber	AGN	9) Pub Trans Sub	NE	14) Strip Mine Veto	AGN
5) Nerve Gas	NE	10) EZ Voter Regis	NE	15) Farm Bill Veto	AGN

Election Results

1974 general:	Tom Harkin (D)	81,146	(51%)	($120,544)
	Bill Scherle (R)	77,683	(49%)	($103,582)
1974 primary:	Tom Harkin (D), unopposed			

◆ ◆ ◆ ◆ ◆

SIXTH DISTRICT

The 6th congressional district of Iowa is the northwest corner of the state, where water and trees begin to get scarcer and the sky seems to get bigger. Except for Sioux City (pop. 85,000), the 6th is almost entirely rural, with small farm-market towns and towering grain elevators here and there in the landscape. The district has traditionally been Republican, like most of Iowa, but with some exceptions. Indeed, politically deviant counties dot the maps of all the Great Plains states. The deviance usually stems from their settlement by particular ethnic groups. A colony of German Catholics or Norwegians, to name one usually Democratic and one Republican group, would send encouraging letters back to the old country, and sometimes steamship passage and railroad fare so that relatives and friends could make their way to their new homes in Iowa or Kansas or the Dakotas. Thus one can make sense of the heavily Republican sentiments of Sioux County, Iowa in the 6th (settled by Dutch Protestants) or the Democratic leanings of Palo Alto County (German Catholics).

Palo Alto County is especially interesting for another reason. For as long as records go back, the county has voted for the winning presidential candidate. In the recent close elections of 1960 and 1968, Palo Alto maintained its record by going for John Kennedy and Richard Nixon respectively; and it barely kept its distinction by going 52–48 for Nixon over McGovern in 1972.

So it may have been of significance, then, that Palo Alto County did not go for Republican Congressman Wiley Mayne in either the 1970 or 1972 elections. Mayne, a mild-mannered lawyer from Sioux City, had won both those elections, but by margins which must have been disappointing to his supporters; indeed, his margins kept falling ever since Richard Nixon took office. And then, in 1974, Mayne lost not only Palo Alto, but the entire district.

The reason, of course, was Watergate, which brings up another cabalistic coincidence. The 1964 Democrat whom Mayne beat in 1966 to first take the district was Stanley Greigg, who was Deputy Chairman of the Democratic National Committee when its offices were burglarized and wiretapped by Nixon's men. (Greigg's office was just outside Larry O'Brien's.) And in the spring and summer of 1974, Wiley Mayne found himself sitting in judgment on the President as a member of the House Judiciary Committee. Viewers of the hearings who recall Mayne's performance would probably describe him as mousy and unconvincing; he followed the tack of Charles Wiggins and David Dennis in coming out against impeachment, but not with their competence or fervor. But while commentators were praising pro-impeachment congressmen like Republican Tom Railsback and Democrat Walter Flowers for their political courage (when it turned out their votes didn't hurt them politically), they might have given at least a little credit for courage to mousy Wiley Mayne. Although he came out on the wrong side, Mayne cast a vote that he must have known would hurt him in a political race that he must have known was the toughest he had ever faced.

For in 1972, in the year of Richard Nixon's great sweep, Wiley Mayne had been able to win only 52% of the vote against Democrat Berkley Bedell, and in 1974—with a lot of other issues besides Watergate helping the Democrats—Bedell was running again. Mayne may not have understood completely why Iowa was moving distinctly to the left, but he could hardly have helped knowing it was. Bedell, in any case, was an attractive candidate, wholly apart from national issues. As a boy in the little town of Spirit Lake, near the Minnesota border, he had been more interested in fishing than school; later, he never finished college, but started his own little company manufacturing fishing tackle. But it was not just ordinary fishing tackle; it was the monofilament fishing line, and Bedell became a millionaire. A deeply religious man, he also became a friend of Harold Hughes, and Hughes—himself from a small town in the 6th district—convinced him that he should enter politics. The result: his unsuccessful congressional race in 1972 and his election to the House by a solid 55–45 margin in 1974.

At 53, and with his strong religious background, Bedell seemed a little out of place with the new 75 Democratic freshmen. That impression was furthered when he nominated Gladys Spellman of Maryland for secretary of the freshman caucus; cries of MCP went in, and Bedell himself was given the post by acclamation. But on most issues Bedell has found himself in agreement with the freshmen, and his old-fashioned demeanor probably will help him back home when he seeks reelection in 1976. In any case, his strong showing in 1974 already makes him a decided favorite.

Census Data Pop. 470,867. Central city, 18%; suburban, 4%. Median family income, $8,314; families above $15,000: 14%; families below $3,000: 11%. Median years education, 12.2.

The Voters

Median voting age 47.
Employment profile White collar, 40%. Blue collar, 28%. Service, 14%. Farm, 18%.
Ethnic groups Total foreign stock, 16%. Germany, 5%.

Presidential vote

1972	Nixon (R)	123,738	(62%)
	McGovern (D)	76,110	(38%)
1968	Nixon (R)	116,438	(58%)
	Humphrey (D)	75,081	(37%)
	Wallace (AI)	9,354	(5%)

Rep. Berkley Bedell (D) Elected 1974; b. Mar. 5, 1921, Spirit Lake; home, Spirit Lake; Ia. St. U., 1940–42; Methodist.

Career Army Air Corps, WWII; Founder and Chm., Berkley & Co., fishing tackle manufacturers; Dem. nominee for U.S. House of Reps., 1972.

Offices 503 CHOB, 202-225-5476. Also 406 Fed. Bldg., Fort Dodge 50501, 515-573-7169.

Committees

Agriculture (22d). Subcommittees: Conservation and Credit; Family Farms and Rural Development; Livestock and Grains.

Small Business (18th). Subcommittees: Activities of Regulatory Agencies; Commodities and Services.

Group Ratings: Newly Elected

Key Votes

1) Foreign Aid	AGN	6) Gov Abortn Aid	NE	11) Pub Cong Election $	NE
2) Busing	NE	7) Coed Phys Ed	FOR	12) Turkish Arms Cutoff	NE
3) ABM	NE	8) Pov Lawyer Gag	NE	13) Youth Camp Regs	FOR
4) B-1 Bomber	AGN	9) Pub Trans Sub	NE	14) Strip Mine Veto	AGN
5) Nerve Gas	NE	10) EZ Voter Regis	NE	15) Farm Bill Veto	AGN

Election Results

1974 general:	Berkley Bedell (D)	86,315	(55%)	($130,742)
	Wiley Mayne (R)	71,695	(45%)	($96,085)
1974 primary:	Berkley Bedell (D), unopposed			

KANSAS

The political history of Kansas began with a rush in the 1850s, and the outcome of the struggle of that decade has pretty much shaped the state's politics since. The land here was virtually unsettled in 1850, and by the terms of the Kansas-Nebraska Act of 1854, the question whether Kansas would be a free or a slave state would be decided by the voters, ("squatter sovereignty." Everyone assumed Nebraska would be free soil, but Kansas—lying directly west of slaveholding Missouri—was in doubt. Almost immediately, proslavery Southerners and abolitionist New Englanders were financing like-minded settlers and moving them to Kansas; soon armed fighting broke out between Democratic "bushwhackers" and free soil "jayhawkers". Proslavery raiders from Missouri rode into the territory, and John Brown massacred anti-abolitionists at Pottawatomie Creek. This was "bleeding Kansas"—a major national issue and a proximate cause of the Civil War. When the South seceded in 1861, Kansas was admitted to the Union as a free state, with the Republican Party in solid control. There it has remained, with just a few exceptions, ever since.

The major exception to Republican hegemony was during the depression of the 1890s—the Populist revolt. During the previous decade, years of unusually high rainfall on the plains, Kansas had attracted hundreds of thousands of new settlers. Suddenly, the rain all but stopped; and that, together with a worldwide drop in wheat prices, showed that the Kansas plains could not support all those who had come to depend on them. The state's boom had gone bust; some Kansas counties have never again reached the population levels recorded in the 1890 census.

Suddenly Populists were beating Republicans in Kansas. They were politicians like Mary Ellen Lease ("What you farmers need to do is raise less corn and more hell") and "Sockless Jerry" Simpson, who served as a Congressman for a couple of terms. Lease, Simpson, and the simple farmers of the Populist Party became advocates of arcane doctrines of free silver and commodity credit programs. William Jennings Bryan, the lion of the prairies, was their man, and he swept Kansas in 1896.

The period of Populist dominance—colorful, revivalistic, desperate—was soon over. Around 1900 the nation began to enjoy a decade of agricultural prosperity so great that parity prices are still based on those years. With the small town Republicans back in control, Bryan failed to carry Kansas in 1900 or 1908. William Allen White, the progressive Republican editor of the Emporia *Gazette*, was the closest thing in the state to a radical.

But echoes of the farm revolt of the '90s can still be heard in Kansas politics. As in most Great Plains states, fewer and fewer Kansans make their livings as bona fide farmers, but the state's economy still depends heavily on agriculture. And agriculture, though we don't always think of it this way, is one of the most highly regulated and subsidized industries in the country. So naturally, when times are bad, farmers and others dependent on agriculture show a hair-trigger readiness to blame the federal government—and the administration in power.

Today, Kansas appears to be in Republican hands as much as ever. It has a Republican Governor, two Republican Senators, four Republican Congressmen out of five, an overwhelmingly Republican legislature. But that surface appearance is deceiving. In 1974 Democrat Robert Docking retired from his fourth two-year term as Governor, and that same year Democrats came within 13,000 votes of winning a Senate seat and missed retaining the Governorship by only 3,600. And if that represented something of a moral victory for the Democrats, it was even more testimony to the superior campaigning abilities of the Republicans.

Consider the plight of Robert Dole, just finishing up his first term in the Senate. When he was first elected, in 1968, Dole distinguished himself as a firm, unyielding supporter of the Nixon Administration. So often did he pop up and, without being asked, defend the President and his programs that Nixon himself made him Republican National Chairman in 1971. Dole continued in that position throughout 1972, saying what he was told to say (although he could not completely repress his sense of humor) and doing what the people at the Committee to Reelect the President told him to do. Among other things, this included deriding any criticism of the Watergate affair—quotes which Dole would regret later.

Democrats figured they had Dole in a perfect position: either he knew about Watergate and was lying (which no one really believed); or, from his high position in the campaign (as he had characterized it then) he should have known, and was negligent for not finding out. Moreover, Democrats had a strong candidate themselves: 2d district Congressman William Roy, one of 200 Americans who is both a physician and a lawyer. Roy had won an upset victory in 1970 and easily held his seat in 1972; he was especially strong around his home town of Topeka. In the House he had—unusually for such a junior member—pushed through to law a measure to provide health maintenance organizations for underserved areas.

At first, Dole countered with humor; when asked if he wanted Nixon to campaign for him, he said "I wouldn't mind if he flew over." But that wasn't enough, and at the end of the summer Dole fired most of his campaign staff and his ad agency, and went on the offensive. He ran a series of new TV spots, which showed a poster of him being splattered with mud and then, at the end, wiped clean. The message was that Roy and the Democrats, by bringing up Watergate, were unfairly smearing him and engaging in dirty politics-as-usual. It was probably the best single TV ad campaign of 1974. It turned the tide; Dole began moving up in the polls; Roy did not know how to respond. The final result was a 51–49 Dole victory. Roy had carried most of the state's urban areas, but Dole had virtually swept the small towns that have always been the bastions of Kansas Republicanism. He was especially strong (57% of the vote) in the 1st congressional district, the western geographical half of the state, which he had once represented.

The Democrats lost the Governorship in quite a different way. Docking, a conservative Democrat from the town of Arkansas City just above the Oklahoma border, had been a popular Governor, but toward the end of his term his brother became involved in a scandal; hence Docking's decision not to run for the Senate or for reelection. The clear favorite to replace him was Attorney General Vern Miller, if anything an even more conservative Democrat. Miller used to be Sedgwick County (Wichita) Sheriff, and he had always campaigned as a tough law-and-order man and a stern foe of student dissidents. Miller had carried every county in the state running for reelection in 1972, and he counted on his strength in the state's small towns and Wichita to give him a large majority in 1974.

But he reckoned without Robert Bennett, the president of the state Senate and the Republican gubernatorial nominee. Bennett's strength was in the well-to-do Kansas City suburbs in Johnson County, now the second largest county in the state, and he amassed a large majority there against the countrified Miller, lost by a smaller margin in Wichita, and managed to hold Miller even in the rest of the state, for a narrow victory. As much as Miller's law-and-order stance may have helped him in the small towns, it clearly hurt him in the universities. He lost Douglas County (the University of Kansas) by 6,400 votes and Riley County (Kansas State University) by 5,600; Bennett's statewide margin was only 3,600 votes. Bennett is one of two bearded Governors now (the other is Republican Jay Hammond of Alaska); but he is no radical. If he supported campaign finance reform, he is also a backer of the death penalty and tax reform to help corporations.

Next to the narrow victories of Dole and Bennett in 1974, Senator James Pearson's 72% of the vote in 1972 makes him seem unbelievably strong. Yet not too many months before he had won that margin, Pearson had been in serious political trouble. He had alienated many Kansas Republicans by voting against the Nixon Administration on issues like the ABM and a date-certain withdrawal from Vietnam, and there were rumors he would have conservative opposition in the Republican primary. But an early campaigning start by Pearson—and help from Bob Dole—put a stop to that, and then Pearson had another bit of luck: both then Governor Docking and then Attorney General Miller, at the height of their popularity, declined to make the race. Thus Pearson was virtually unopposed, and actually ran ahead of Nixon, as did other Republican liberals like Percy of Illinois, Brooke of Massachusetts, and Case of New Jersey. Pearson does not cut as liberal a figure in the Senate as these men; indeed, he is generally considered a not very voluble Senator. But he was co-leader, with Walter Mondale of Minnesota, of the successful move to get rid of the two-thirds filibuster rule in 1975, and he seems to have a few reasons to worry about future elections.

Census Data Pop. 2,249,071; 1.11% of U.S. total, 28th largest; Central city, 18%; suburban, 24%. Median family income, $8,690; 30th highest; families above $15,000: 16%; families below $3,000: 11%. Median years education, 12.3.

1974 Share of Federal Tax Burden $2,892,405,000; 1.08% of U.S. total, 27th largest.

1974 Share of Federal Outlays $2,856,772,000; 1.06% of U.S. total, 30th largest. Per capita federal spending, $1270.

DOD	$818,814,000	28th (1.20%)	HEW	$938,039,000	30th (1.01%)
AEC	$450,000	34th (0.01%)	HUD	$11,017,000	24th (1.13%)

NASA	$1,807,000	32d	(0.06%)	VA	$160,129,000	34th	(1.17%)
DOT	$96,858,000	31st	(1.44%)	EPA	$16,317,000	32d	(0.52%)
DOC	$6,739,000	34th	(0.42%)	RevS	$58,899,000	34th	(0.97%)
DOI	$12,382,000	38th	(0.50%)	Int.	$119,865,000	22d	(0.58%)
USDA	$291,219,000	16th	(2.33%)	Other	$324,237,000		

Economic Base Agriculture, especially cattle, wheat, hogs and sorghum grain; finance, insurance and real estate; transportation equipment, especially aircraft and parts; food and kindred products; machinery; printing and publishing, especially newspapers; oil and gas extraction, especially crude petroleum and natural gas.

Political Line-up Governor, Robert F. Bennett (R). Senators, James B. Pearson (R) and Bob Dole (R). Representatives, 5 (4 R and 1 D). State Senate (26 R and 14 D); State House (72 R and 53 D).

The Voters

Registration 1,032,823 Total. 219,365 D (21%); 352,767 R (34%); 459,691 Ind., Prohibitionist, and Conservative (45%).
Median voting age 44.
Employment profile White collar, 48%. Blue collar, 31%. Service, 13%. Farm, 8%.
Ethnic groups Black, 5%. Spanish, 2%. Total foreign stock, 8%. Germany, 2%.

Presidential vote

1972	Nixon (R)	619,812	(70%)
	McGovern (D)	270,287	(30%)
1968	Nixon (R)	478,674	(55%)
	Humphrey (D)	302,996	(35%)
	Wallace (AI)	88,921	(10%)

Sen. James B. Pearson (R) Appointed Jan. 31, 1962, elected Nov. 6, 1962, seat up 1978; b. May 7, 1920, Nashville, Tenn.; home, Prairie Village; Duke U., 1940–42, U. of Va., LL.B. 1950; Presbyterian.

Career Navy, WWII; Practicing atty.; Westwood, Fairway, and Lenexa City Atty., 1952–61; Asst. Johnson Co. Atty., 1952–54; Johnson Co. Probate Judge, 1954–56; Kans. Senate, 1956–60; Kans. St. Repub. Chm., 1960–61.

Offices 5313 DSOB, 202-224-4774. Also 600 Merchant's Natl. Bank Bldg., Topeka 66612, 913-357-4312.

Committees

Commerce (Ranking Member). Subcommittees: Aviation; Environment; Special Subcommittee on Freight Car Shortage.

Foreign Relations (4th). Subcommittees: African Affairs; European Affairs; Near Eastern and South Asian Affairs.

Joint Committee on Atomic Energy (3d, Senate Side). Subcommittees: Agreements for Cooperation; ERDA, Environment and Safety; Legislation.

Group Ratings

	ADA	COPE	LWV	RIPON	NFU	LCV	CFA	NAB	NSI	ACA
1974	65	64	100	71	88	70	66	27	57	21
1973	56	67	88	65	88	–	38	–	–	24
1972	45	40	80	88	70	26	100	58	78	35

Key Votes

1) No-Knock	AGN	8) Gov Abortn Aid	FOR	15) Consumer Prot Agy	FOR
2) Busing	FOR	9) Cut Mil Brass	ABS	16) Forced Psych Tests	AGN
3) No Fault	FOR	10) Gov Limousine	FOR	17) Fed Campaign Subs	FOR
4) F-111	FOR	11) RR Featherbed	AGN	18) Rhod Chrome Ban	FOR
5) Death Penalty	AGN	12) Handgun License	AGN	19) Open Legis Meetings	AGN
6) Foreign Aid	FOR	13) Less Troop Abrd	AGN	20) Strikers Food Stmps	FOR
7) Filibuster	AGN	14) Resume Turk Aid	FOR	21) Gov Info Disclosure	FOR

Election Results

1972 general:	James B. Pearson (R)	622,591	(72%)	($109,651)
	Arch O. Tetzlaff (D)	200,764	(23%)	($6,742)
	Gene F. Miller (Con.)	35,510	(4%)	(NA)
1972 primary:	James B. Pearson (R)	229,908	(82%)	
	Harlan Dale House (R)	49,825	(18%)	
1966 general:	James B. Pearson (R)	350,077	(54%)	
	J. Floyd Breeding (D)	303,223	(46%)	

Sen. Robert Dole (R) Elected 1968, seat up 1980; b. July 22, 1923, Russell; home, Russell; U. of Kans., 1941–43, Washburn Municipal U., B.A. and LL.B. 1952; Methodist.

Career Army, WWII; Kans. House of Reps., 1951–53; Russell Co. Atty., 1953–61; U.S. House of Reps., 1961–69; Chm., Repub. Natl. Comm., 1971–73.

Offices 2327 DSOB, 202-224-6521. Also Rm. 527, 2 Gateway Ctr., Kansas City 66101, 913-342-4525, and 701 Quincy St., Topeka 66603, 913-234-9946.

Committees

Agriculture and Forestry (3d). Subcommittees: Agricultural Credit and Rural Electrification; Agricultural Production, Marketing, and Stabilization of Prices; Agricultural Research and General Legislation; Foreign Agricultural Policy; Rural Development.

Budget (2d).

Finance (4th). Subcommittees: Administration of the Internal Revenue Code; Energy; Financial Markets; Health.

Post Office and Civil Service (4th). Subcommittees: Civil Service Policies and Practices; Postal Operations.

Group Ratings

	ADA	COPE	LWV	RIPON	NFU	LCV	CFA	NAB	NSI	ACA
1974	20	18	60	43	35	42	11	67	100	84
1973	10	27	60	56	56	–	17	–	–	82
1972	0	10	33	54	56	11	0	80	100	84

Key Votes

1) No-Knock	AGN	8) Gov Abortn Aid	AGN	15) Consumer Prot Agy	FOR
2) Busing	AGN	9) Cut Mil Brass	AGN	16) Forced Psych Tests	AGN
3) No Fault	AGN	10) Gov Limousine	FOR	17) Fed Campaign Subs	AGN
4) F-111	AGN	11) RR Featherbed	AGN	18) Rhod Chrome Ban	AGN
5) Death Penalty	FOR	12) Handgun License	AGN	19) Open Legis Meetings	FOR
6) Foreign Aid	AGN	13) Less Troop Abrd	AGN	20) Strikers Food Stmps	AGN
7) Filibuster	AGN	14) Resume Turk Aid	AGN	21) Gov Info Disclosure	AGN

Election Results

1974 general:	Bob Dole (R)	403,983	(51%)	($1,110,024)
	Bill Roy (D)	390,451	(49%)	($836,927)
1974 primary:	Bob Dole (R), unopposed			
1968 general:	Bob Dole (R)	490,911	(61%)	
	William I. Robinson (D)	315,911	(39%)	

Gov. Robert F. Bennett (R) Elected 1974, term expires Jan. 1979; b. May 23, 1927, Johnson County; U. of Kans., B.A. 1950, LL.B. 1952; Presbyterian.

Career USMC, WWII and Korea; Practicing atty., 1952–74; Mayor, Prairie Village; Kans. Senate, 1965–75, Sen. Pres., 1972–75.

Offices State Capitol, Topeka 66612, 913-296-3232.

Election Results

1974 general:	Robert F. Bennett (R)	387,792	(49%)
	Vern Miller (D)	384,115	(49%)
	Marshall Uncapher (Prohib.)	11,968	(2%)
1974 primary:	Robert F. Bennett (R)	67,346	(32%)
	Donald Concannon (R)	66,817	(32%)
	Forrest J. Robinson (R)	56,440	(27%)
	Bob Clack (R)	17,333	(8%)

◆ ◆ ◆ ◆ ◆

FIRST DISTRICT

The 1st congressional district of Kansas covers more than half the state's land area. It contains more counties (57) than any other congressional district in the country except the state of North Dakota which elects one Congressman-at-Large. This fact is not just a bit of trivia; it tells us a good deal about the expectations of the people who first settled this part of Kansas. Most of them came here in the 1880s from states like Illinois and Iowa and Missouri; when they organized counties, as they quickly did, they made them 36 miles square, just as they had been in the old Midwest. Deceived by a few years of unusually high rainfall, the settlers expected that the new counties would eventually contain as many people as the old ones back home; hence they were made geographically small. Not just the size of the units, but the grandiosity of the place names (Concordia, Minneapolis, Montezuma) testify to the settlers' hopes, dreams, and ambitions.

But they were never realized. Out here past the 98°, rainfall is normally half what it is in Illinois. In the early years of the nineteenth century, this part of the country had been considered part of the Great American Desert—a howling wilderness of aridity. The early settlers worked hard to disprove the image, but they never really succeeded. So the thousands more who were expected to come never arrived; today the average population of the 1st district's 57 counties is a scant 7,800.

Most are far less populous than that; the average is inflated by the district's "urban" concentrations. At 37,000, Salina is the district's largest city; Dodge City, terminus of the old cattle drives and once the home of Wyatt Earp, has just 14,000 people; Holcomb, made famous by Truman Capote's *In Cold Blood*, has less than 10,000. Hays, a German-Catholic town of 16,000, is one part of the district that generally goes Democratic—and often the only one. But the real 1st cannot be found in its towns. This is livestock and wheat country, one of the most agricultural districts in the nation. For miles on end, you can see nothing but rolling brown fields, sectioned off here and there by barbed wire fence, and in the distance perhaps a grain elevator towering over a tiny town.

The 1st is predominantly Republican, but subject to occasional fits of Democratic sentiment in periods of hard times. In 1956, 1958, and 1960, the western half of the present 1st district elected Democrat J. Floyd Breeding to the House. But his district was combined with Bob Dole's after the 1960 census, and Dole won the 1962 contest and has been carrying the 1st by wide margins ever since. When Dole moved up to the Senate in 1968, he was succeeded by a like-minded, but less articulate, Republican, Keith Sebelius. Sebelius is a Congressman who votes against the wishes of the Republican administration only with the greatest of reluctance and, as in the case of a sewer grant veto, because of the pressing needs of his district. His percentage of the vote wobbled a little unsteadily, but so far no one has been able to seriously challenge him.

Census Data   Pop. 447,787. Central city, 0%; suburban, 0%. Median family income, $7,820; families above $15,000: 12%; families below $3,000: 12%. Median years education, 12.2.

The Voters

    Median voting age 47.
    Employment profile White collar, 40%. Blue collar, 27%. Service, 14%. Farm, 19%.
    Ethnic groups Black, 1%. Spanish, 2%. Total foreign stock, 9%. Germany, 3%.

Presidential vote

1972	Nixon (R)	....	135,605	(72%)
	McGovern (D)	....	52,842	(28%)
1968	Nixon (R)	....	114,688	(60%)
	Humphrey (D)	....	60,939	(32%)
	Wallace (AI)	....	16,375	(9%)

Rep. Keith G. Sebelius (R) Elected 1968; b. Sept. 10, 1916, Almena; home, Norton; Fort Hays Kans. St. Col., A.B., Geo. Wash. U., J.D. 1939; Methodist

Career Practicing atty.; Army, WWII and Korea; Norton City Cncl., Mayor; Norton Co. Atty.; Kans. Senate, 1962–68.

Offices 1211 LHOB, 202-225-2725. Also P.O. Bldg., Dodge City 67801, 316-227-2244.

Committees

    Agriculture (2d). Subcommittees: Family Farms and Rural Development; Livestock and Grains.

Interior and Insular Affairs (6th). Subcommittees: Mines and Mining; National Parks and Recreastion.

Group Ratings

	ADA	COPE	LWV	RIPON	NFU	LCV	CFA	NAB	NSI	ACA
1974	17	0	17	40	58	18	0	83	80	57
1973	8	9	33	27	55	6	38	–	–	67
1972	0	18	18	44	43	20	0	83	88	95

Key Votes

1) Foreign Aid	AGN	6) Gov Abortn Aid	AGN	11) Pub Cong Election $	AGN
2) Busing	AGN	7) Coed Phys Ed	AGN	12) Turkish Arms Cutoff	AGN
3) ABM	AGN	8) Pov Lawyer Gag	FOR	13) Youth Camp Regs	AGN
4) B-1 Bomber	ABS	9) Pub Trans Sub	AGN	14) Strip Mine Veto	FOR
5) Nerve Gas	AGN	10) EZ Voter Regis	AGN	15) Farm Bill Veto	AGN

Election Results

1974 general:	Keith G. Sebelius (R)	101,565	(59%)	($60,893)
	Don Smith (D)	57,326	(33%)	($64,428)
	Thelma Morgan (AI)	13,009	(8%)	($13,642)
1974 primary:	Keith G. Sebelius (R), unopposed			
1972 general:	Keith G. Sebelius (R)	145,712	(78%)	($20,545)
	Morris Coover (D)	40,678	(22%)	($0)

◆ ◆ ◆ ◆ ◆

SECOND DISTRICT

The 2d congressional district of Kansas is the northeast corner of the state—and the only part of the state which has elected a Democratic Congressman since 1960. The 2d includes a small portion of Wyandotte County and Kansas City, which is practically the only part of the state that regularly votes against Republicans; but the portion is so small as to make little difference here. The real hub of the district is Topeka, the state capital and the 2d's largest city. Topeka is a clean-cut city of 125,000, pleasantly situated on the Kansas River; it is the home of the Menninger Clinic, of psychoanalytic fame, and of Alf M. Landon, the still vigorous and surprisingly progressive Republican who was beaten in the Roosevelt landslide of 1936.

Topeka casts about one-third of the 2d district's votes, and for years it has been almost as Republican as the surrounding countryside. But that has been changing recently, starting really in 1970, when the 2d district was the scene of one of the biggest election upsets in recent years. This was the defeat of Republican Congressman Chester Mize—a 68% winner two years before—by Democrat William Roy. It was the first time in 63 years the district had elected a Democrat. Roy, who is both a lawyer and a doctor, had managed to overcome the initial obstacle that beats most congressional challengers—anonymity—by spending over $100,000 and stressing his unique qualifications. Among them was the fact that he had delivered more than 5,000 babies in the Topeka area.

Roy was reelected easily in 1972, despite a concerted Republican effort to beat him, and he came within 13,000 votes of beating Senator Bob Dole in 1974—which would have made him the first Democratic Senator elected by Kansas voters since 1932. His successor in the House is another Democrat, Martha Keys. Her background is more than a bit unusual. She is the wife of a faculty member at Kansas State University in Manhattan and the sister of Lee Hart, wife of Colorado's Senator Gary Hart; she was state coordinator here for the ill-fated McGovern campaign in 1972. She also proved to be an effective campaigner. She beat her opponent, a 28-year-old state Representative from Topeka by a solid 57–42 margin in Topeka's Shawnee County, and carried all but four counties in the entire district. It was a comfortable victory and one which—taken together with the fact that she won a seat on the House Ways and Means Committee—seems to indicate that she will continue the Democratic tradition in this unlikely district.

Census Data Pop. 454,028. Central city, 28%; suburban, 14%. Median family income, $8,680; families above $15,000: 15%; families below $3,000: 11%. Median years education, 12.3.

The Voters

Median voting age 40.
Employment profile White collar, 49%. Blue collar, 30%. Service, 14%. Farm, 7%.
Ethnic groups Black, 6%. Spanish, 3%. Total foreign stock, 9%. Germany, 3%.

Presidential vote

1972	Nixon (R)	119,234	(70%)
	McGovern (D)	51,093	(30%)
1968	Nixon (R)	87,812	(54%)
	Humphrey (D)	55,430	(34%)
	Wallace (AI)	18,748	(12%)

Rep. Martha Keys (D) Elected 1974; b. Aug. 10, 1930, Hutchinson; home, Manhattan; Olivet Col. 1946–47, U. of Mo., B.A. 1951.

Career Kans. Coordinator, McGovern for Pres., 1972.

Offices 1207 LHOB, 202-225-6601. Also 909 Topeka Ave., Topeka 66612, 913-233-8951.

Committees

Ways and Means (24th). Subcommittees: Health; Unemployment Compensation.

Group Ratings: Newly Elected

Key Votes

1) Foreign Aid	AGN	6) Gov Abortn Aid	NE	11) Pub Cong Election $	NE
2) Busing	NE	7) Coed Phys Ed	FOR	12) Turkish Arms Cutoff	NE
3) ABM	NE	8) Pov Lawyer Gag	NE	13) Youth Camp Regs	FOR
4) B-1 Bomber	AGN	9) Pub Trans Sub	NE	14) Strip Mine Veto	AGN
5) Nerve Gas	NE	10) EZ Voter Regis	NE	15) Farm Bill Veto	AGN

Election Results

1974 general:	Martha Keys (D)	84,864	(56%)	($88,959)
	John C. Peterson (R)	67,650	(44%)	($114,214)
1974 primary:	Martha Keys (D)	12,789	(39%
	Jacob W. "Jake" Miller (D)	9,834	(30%)
	Three others (D)	9,859	(30%)

◆ ◆ ◆ ◆ ◆

THIRD DISTRICT

The 3d congressional district is a not very typical hunk of Kansas. It lies almost entirely within the Kansas City metropolitan area, and contains the state's most heavily Democratic and heavily Republican territory. More than 80% of the district's residents live in either heavily Democratic Wyandotte County (Kansas City, much smaller than its Missouri neighbor) or in heavily Republican Johnson County (prosperous Kansas City suburbs, including Overland Park, Prairie Village, and Shawnee Mission). On the Kansas side of the small street that separates Johnson County from Missouri live a disproportionate number of the metropolitan area's wealthiest and most conservative citizens—whose votes increase Kansas's already large Republican percentages. Just about the only issue Johnson and Wyandotte Counties can agree on is liquor-by-the-glass; both were strongly in favor in a recent referendum, though it lost statewide.

Also included in the 3d district is one small agricultural county and the city of Lawrence, home of the University of Kansas. A few years back, bearded and blue-jeaned students were involved in some police-student confrontations, and things were tense in River City, as the local counterculturists called it. Today, both town and gown are quieter, and more used to living with each other; the students have discovered the beer long quaffed by local residents; and gas station attendants have begun to discover, as students did a few years back, that the fields around Lawrence are a perfect place to grow marijuana.

If the 3d is not a typical Kansas district sociologically, it is not politically either. Democratic presidential candidates, and George Wallace too, have made stronger showings here than in any other Kansas seat. But they have come nowhere near to carrying the 3d, and in congressional politics this is about as safe a district for its Republican incumbent as any in the state. This represents a solid achievement for Congressman Larry Winn, first elected in 1966 and subject to a strong challenge as late as 1970. One thing which has helped the solidly conservative Winn is the fact that Johnson County has been growing so much faster than Wyandotte that it is increasingly dominating the district's politics. From 1966 to 1974, the total vote in Johnson has increased from 55,000 to 79,000, while that in Wyandotte County has barely increased, from 30,000 to 34,000.

Census Data Pop. 449,743. Central city, 0%; suburban, 83%. Median family income, $10,928; families above $15,000: 27%; families below $3,000: 7%. Median years education, 12.5.

The Voters

Median voting age 40.
Employment profile White collar, 58%. Blue collar, 29%. Service, 11%. Farm, 2%.
Ethnic groups Black, 8%. Spanish, 2%. Total foreign stock, 8%. Germany, 1%.

Presidential vote

1972	Nixon (R)	122,474	(67%)
	McGovern (D)	61,367	(33%)
1968	Nixon (R)	87,226	(52%)
	Humphrey (D)	63,698	(38%)
	Wallace (AI)	18,237	(11%)

Rep. Larry Winn, Jr. (R) Elected 1966; b. Aug. 22, 1919, Kansas City, Mo; home, Overland Park; U. of Kans., A.B. 1941; Protestant.

Career Radio announcer, WHB, Kandas City, Mo.; North American Aviation; Public Relations Dir., Amer. Red Cross, Kansas City, Mo.; Builder; V.P., Winn-Rau Corp., 1950–.

Offices 2430 RHOB, 202-225-2865. Also 204 Fed. Bldg., Kansas City 66101, 913-621-0832.

Committees

International Relations (9th). Subcommittees: International Political and Military Affairs; Investigations.

Science and Technology (5th). Subcommittees: Energy Research, Development and Demonstration; Environment and the Atmosphere; Space Science and Applications.

Group Ratings

	ADA	COPE	LWV	RIPON	NFU	LCV	CFA	NAB	NSI	ACA
1974	22	0	75	63	57	35	8	80	88	53
1973	24	27	60	67	55	35	50	–	–	68
1972	0	10	36	64	71	33	50	82	88	76

Key Votes

1) Foreign Aid	FOR	6) Gov Abortn Aid	AGN	11) Pub Cong Election $	FOR
2) Busing	AGN	7) Coed Phys Ed	AGN	12) Turkish Arms Cutoff	ABS
3) ABM	FOR	8) Pov Lawyer Gag	FOR	13) Youth Camp Regs	FOR
4) B-1 Bomber	FOR	9) Pub Trans Sub	AGN	14) Strip Mine Veto	FOR
5) Nerve Gas	AGN	10) EZ Voter Regis	AGN	15) Farm Bill Veto	AGN

Election Results

1974 general:	Larry Winn, Jr. (R)	89,694	(63%)	($77,681)
	Samuel J. Wells (D)	49,976	(35%)	($26,318)
	Ted E. Oakes (AI)	2,980	(2%)	(NA)
1974 primary:	Larry Winn, Jr. (R), unopposed			
1972 general:	Larry Winn, Jr. (R)	122,358	(71%)	($37,310)
	Charles Barsotti (D)	43,777	(25%)	($5,991)
	Warren E. Redding (C)	6,258	(4%)	

◆ ◆ ◆ ◆ ◆

FOURTH DISTRICT

Ever since the 1950 census, Wichita (pop. 277,000) officially has been the largest city in Kansas. Before World War II, Wichita, like most Kansas cities, was primarily a trading center for farm products, depending on the yields of the surrounding counties. But during the war and immediate postwar years, Wichita experienced a boom of sorts, sparked by the aviation industry. Boeing has a big plant here, as does Cessna, one of the nation's leading manufacturers of small planes. When the demand for military and civilian planes is high, Wichita does very well; when the 1960s boom tapered off, it does poorly. For several years in the early '60s Wichita was in sort of a local depression; the number of local jobs declined, and several thousand people simply moved away. Now the demand for small planes seems to be rising, and Wichita is still doing better. But its economy is tied inextricably to an unstable industry.

Because much of Wichita's work force came from the hills of Arkansas and Oklahoma, the city's voting habits have a tinge of the South in them. Though a heavily Republican city in presidential elections, Wichita has delivered large margins for Democratic candidates in state contests. Two beneficiaries of this pattern have been former Governor Robert Docking, who is from nearby Arkansas City (pronounced ar-KAN-sas here), and former Attorney General Vern

Miller, a law-and-order man who used to be Sheriff of Wichita's Sedgwick County and almost was elected Governor in 1974.

The 4th congressional district includes all of Wichita and most of its suburbs, plus some farming territory and the small city of Hutchinson to the north. In congressional elections, this part of Kansas has been voting Republican just about as long as anyone can remember. The 4th's current Congressman, first elected in 1960, is Garner E. Shriver (no relation to the Democrats' 1972 vice-presidential candidate). Shriver is a moderate-to-conservative Congressman not inclined to rock the boat; he goes along with the majority of his fellow Republicans except in the rare cases when he sees some compelling reason not to. Shriver has now reached the position of number four Republican on the House Appropriations Committee, and ranking Republican on the Foreign Operations Subcommittee. But he is a mild man, not the type to throw his weight around.

Before 1974, Shriver had always won reelection by wide margins. But in that year, he was challenged by Hutchinson state Senator Bert Chaney, and the veteran Republican ended up winning by only a 49–42 margin (an American Party candidate got the rest). When a veteran Congressman performs as weakly as that, it is usually a sign that he can be beaten—regardless of whether a given year is a landslide for his party or not. So the prospect for Shriver, now in his mid-60s, is for more tough races here in the 4th, should he choose to run.

Census Data Pop. 450,487. Central city, 61%; suburban, 8%. Median family income, $9,097; families above $15,000: 17%; families below $3,000: 9%. Median years education, 12.3.

The Voters

Median voting age 42.
Employment profile White collar, 51%. Blue collar, 32%. Service, 14%. Farm, 3%.
Ethnic groups Black, 7%. Spanish, 2%. Total foreign stock, 7%. Germany, 2%.

Presidential vote

1972	Nixon (R)	110,805	(68%)
	McGovern (D)	52,191	(32%)
1968	Nixon (R)	84,517	(54%)
	Humphrey (D)	58,290	(37%)
	Wallace (AI)	13,892	(9%)

Rep. Garner E. Shriver (R) Elected 1960; b. July 6, 1912, Towanda; home, Wichita; U. of Wichita, B.A. 1934, U. of So. Cal., 1936, Washburn Law School, J.D. 1940; Methodist.

Career Fox-Vilet Drug Co., 1934–36; High school teacher, 1936–37; Practicing atty., 1940–60; Navy, WWII; Kans. House of Reps., 1947–51; Kans. Senate, 1953–60.

Offices 2209 RHOB, 202-225-6216. Also P.O. Box 1974, 311 P.O. Bldg., 401 N. Market, Wichita, 316-265-4233.

Committees

Appropriations (4th). Subcommittees: Foreign Operations; Labor-HEW.

Budget (7th).

Group Ratings

	ADA	COPE	LWV	RIPON	NFU	LCV	CFA	NAB	NSI	ACA
1974	23	0	50	50	58	29	0	82	75	46
1973	8	18	33	67	50	24	50	–	–	68
1972	0	18	42	64	57	33	50	83	100	74

Key Votes

1) Foreign Aid	FOR	6) Gov Abortn Aid	AGN	11) Pub Cong Election $	FOR
2) Busing	AGN	7) Coed Phys Ed	ABS	12) Turkish Arms Cutoff	AGN
3) ABM	FOR	8) Pov Lawyer Gag	FOR	13) Youth Camp Regs	ABS
4) B-1 Bomber	ABS	9) Pub Trans Sub	AGN	14) Strip Mine Veto	FOR
5) Nerve Gas	AGN	10) EZ Voter Regis	AGN	15) Farm Bill Veto	AGN

Election Results

1974 general:	Garner E. Shriver (R)	70,401	(49%)	($67,446)
	Bert Chaney (D)	61,201	(42%)	($24,467)
	John S. Stevens (AI)	12,520	(9%)	($2,922)
1974 primary:	Garner E. Shriver (R), unopposed			
1972 general:	Garner E. Shriver (R)	120,120	(75%)	($34,954)
	John S. Stevens (D)	40,753	(25%)	($6,557)

◆ ◆ ◆ ◆ ◆

FIFTH DISTRICT

The southeast corner of Kansas has been nicknamed "the Balkans"—a reference to the Eastern European ancentry of some of the area's residents and to its low hill country, the outer fringe of the Ozarks. The hills here contain some coal, and the main town was named Pittsburg—another example of the unrealistic optimism of the people who settled the state. This part of Kansas never became a notable coal or manufacturing center and today, like much of rural America, it is in unmistakable decline. This southeast corner of Kansas is the heart of the state's 5th congressional district, which stretches north to a point near Kansas City and west toward the Wichita suburbs and beyond.

Emporia (pop. 23,000) is one of the larger towns that dot the district, and the home of William Allen White, the newspaper editor whose name was a household word a generation ago but which draws a blank today. White was the voice of progressive Kansas Republicanism. Horrified by the Populists in his youth, White was enchanted with Theodore Roosevelt, and came to understand the plight of those less fortunate than himself. Though a native of one of the nation's most isolationist regions, White was a leading spokesman for American aid to Britain during the ominous days before Pearl Harbor.

White has been dead now for 30 years, and in the years since his death his spirit has seldom been echoed in Kansas Republicanism. It is not particularly evident in the record of the current Congressman from the 5th district, Republican Joe Skubitz. First elected in 1962, Skubitz has quietly risen in seniority to the point that he is now ranking minority member of the House Interior Committee. His record is generally considered unfortunate by environmentalists, although he does not intransigently oppose all their causes. Over the years Skubitz has grown used to winning by large margins; and 1974 must have been a shock to him. State Senator Frank Gaines, his Democratic opponent, put on a serious campaign and won 45% of the vote, carrying the Wichita suburbs and coming close in the Balkans. Skubitz turns 70 before the 1976 election, and his relatively poor performance—even granting that it came in a heavily Democratic year—suggests that his congressional career may be coming to a close.

Census Data Pop. 447,026. Central city, 0%; suburban, 17%. Median family income, $7,450; families above $15,000: 10%; families below $3,000: 15%. Median years education, 12.1.

The Voters

Median voting age 48.
Employment profile White collar, 40%. Blue collar, 36%. Service, 14%. Farm, 10%.
Ethnic groups Black, 2%. Spanish, 1%. Total foreign stock, 6%. Germany, 1%.

Presidential vote

	1972	Nixon (R)	124,835	(71%)
		McGovern (D)	50,528	(29%)
	1968	Nixon (R)	100,825	(55%)
		Humphrey (D)	62,536	(34%)
		Wallace (AI)	20,869	(11%)

Rep. Joe Skubitz (R) Elected 1962; b. May 6, 1906, Frontenac; home, Pittsburg; Kans. St. Col., B.S. 1929, M.S. 1934, Washburn Law School, 1938, Geo. Wash. U., LL.B. 1944; Methodist.

Career High school teacher and principal, 1927–37; Practicing atty.; Admin. Asst., U.S. Sens. Clyde M. Reed and Andrew F. Schoeppel, 1952–62.

Offices 2211 RHOB, 202-225-3911. Also 1st and Locust St., Pittsburg 66762, 316-231-6200.

Committees

Interior and Insular Affairs (Ranking Member).

Interstate and Foreign Commerce (5th). Subcommittees: Transportation and Commerce.

Group Ratings

	ADA	COPE	LWV	RIPON	NFU	LCV	CFA	NAB	NSI	ACA
1974	17	18	33	38	50	24	23	82	70	64
1973	22	18	60	40	68	22	50	–	–	60
1972	6	30	36	43	71	16	50	91	100	82

Key Votes

1) Foreign Aid	AGN	6) Gov Abortn Aid	AGN	11) Pub Cong Election $	AGN
2) Busing	AGN	7) Coed Phys Ed	AGN	12) Turkish Arms Cutoff	AGN
3) ABM	AGN	8) Pov Lawyer Gag	FOR	13) Youth Camp Regs	AGN
4) B-1 Bomber	FOR	9) Pub Trans Sub	AGN	14) Strip Mine Veto	FOR
5) Nerve Gas	AGN	10) EZ Voter Regis	AGN	15) Farm Bill Veto	AGN

Election Results

1974 general:	Joe Skubitz (R)	88,646	(55%)	($64,968)
	Frank Gaines (D)	72,024	(45%)	($99,553)
1974 primary:	Joe Skubitz (R)	37,868	(87%)	
	Nat Leo (R)	5,772	(13%)	
1972 general:	Joe Skubitz (R)	128,639	(72%)	($21,765)
	Lloyd L. Kitch (D)	49,169	(28%)	($3,676)

KENTUCKY

In 1775 Daniel Boone made his way through the Cumberland Gap in the Appalachian Mountains and came upon what we know today as Kentucky—a fertile, virgin land of gently rolling hills. After the Revolutionary War, streams of people from Virginia traveled Boone's Wilderness Road and settled in the hills and countryside around Lexington. This exodus was the new nation's first frontier boom and, up to that time, one of the most extensive mass migrations in Western history. The census of 1790 recorded 73,000 Kentuckians; by 1820 there were 564,000, making this the sixth largest state in the nation. In those days, Kentucky was a frontier, its communities full of opportunity and unburdened by the hierarchies that structured the societies of coastal America. Henry Clay, to take the most famous example, came to Kentucky from Virginia as a penniless youth. By the time he was 30 he had done well enough in law and land speculation to build a mansion with silver doorknobs, and well enough in politics to become a United States Senator.

In some respects Kentucky hasn't changed much since Clay's time. The state is still largely rural: less than 25% of its residents live in greater Louisville and only 8% in the suburbs of Cincinnati, Ohio—the only major metropolitan areas in the state. During the past few decades, there has been continual migration out of the state; Kentuckians looking for jobs have moved out of the hills to the industrial towns of the Midwest, California, or Texas. As a result, the local landscape—the tobacco fields and thoroughbred horse country of the Blue Grass, the cotton farms near the Mississippi—has not changed much. Strip mining of coal, however, has left many of the green hillsides of the Appalachian ridges and the hills in the western part of the state barren and erose.

Politics, too, seems caught in a kind of time warp. As in many border state rural areas, political divisions in Kentucky are still based on the splits produced by the Civil War. In general the hill country was pro-Union and remains Republican; the major exceptions are the counties where the coal miners joined unions and now favor the Democrats. The Blue Grass region and the western part of the state, sometimes called the Pennyrile, were more likely to be slave-holding territory, and today they remain Democratic. Louisville, originally a German-influenced, antislavery river town, for years has supported a strong Republican organization.

Up through the 1950s, the Democratic counties always outvoted the Republican ones, and electoral decisions in Kentucky, as in most Southern states, were really made in the Democratic primary. The most famous figure to come out of this era was Alben W. Barkley, who was Congressman from Paducah (1913-27), U. S. Senator (1927-49), Senate Majority Leader (1937-47), Vice President under Harry Truman, and Senator again until his death in 1956. But time changed Kentucky's political patterns, marginally but enough to permit Republicans some victories. Democrats have lost the state in five of the last six presidential elections, and for one four-year period, 1967 to 1971, Republicans held the Governorship and both Senate seats. The first Republican victories were won by moderates from the traditional areas of Republican strength, the Cumberland Plateau and Louisville. In that category certainly fits Senator John Sherman Cooper, who between Senate terms (he kept winning elections to fill vacancies but for a long time lost the full terms) served as Ambassador to India; an opponent of American involvement in Southeast Asia, Cooper finally retired voluntarily, at the height of his popularity, in 1972. Another Republican moderate was Senator (1957-69) Thruston B. Morton, brother of Interior and Commerce Secretary Rogers Morton and one time (1960) Chairman of the Republican National Committee.

But after a while the states's political parties began to take stands more in line with the images projected by the national parties. Since the administration of Governor Bert Combs (1959-63), the Democrats have been notably more liberal than was traditional in Kentucky. And, as if in response, the Republicans became more conservative. The key figure here was Louie Nunn, who nearly won the Governorship in 1963, then did win it in 1967, and saw a protege—Kentucky does not allow its Governors to serve more than one term at a time and requires them to swear that they have never participated in a duel—come reasonably close to winning in 1971.

Now that era of a strong, conservative Republican Party is clearly over. Democrats hold the Governorship and both the state's Senate seats, and Republicans appear to be weaker in state elections than they were twenty years ago. The crucial election here was the gubernatorial contest of 1971. The candidates were Tom Emberton, Nunn's hand-picked choice, and Lieutenant Governor Wendell Ford, a Democrat whose economic policies gave him support from the teacher groups and organized labor, but whose Owensboro accent and conservative attitude on social issues made him acceptable to traditional rural Democrats who found their party's national candidates objectionable. Nunn had won his elections on social issues; Ford's major plank was repeal of the sales tax on food. He was elected by a comfortable 50–44 margin, and promptly made good on that promise.

Then Ford's Democrats went on to capture the state's two Senate seats in the next two elections. First up was Cooper's chair, vacated by his retirement. Louie Nunn made a last-minute decision to enter the race (reportedly at the prompting of Richard Nixon), which sparked a contentious Republican primary. On the Democratic side, all was harmony, with the nomination going virtually uncontested to state Senator (and Ford supporter) Walter "Dee" Huddleston. Nunn could apparently think of nothing but attempting to link Huddleston, a small town radio station owner, to George McGovern; the Democrat campaigned on his record in abolishing the sales tax on food. Huddleston virtually duplicated Ford's victory the year before, winning by a 52–48 margin with especially heavy support in rural and small town western Kentucky. Since that time, Huddleston has been one of the quieter voices in the Senate, maintaining a moderate profile and generally voting with most of his fellow Democrats. In 1975 he won a seat on the Appropriations Committee.

The 1974 election saw the completion of the Democratic sweep of major offices in Kentucky. The victim in this drama was Marlow Cook, the Republican incumbent elected in 1968 at the age of 42 after seven years as Jefferson County Judge (head of the government of the county that contains Louisville). Cook was the image of the youngish, efficiency-minded, moderate urban Republican; and for a while at least he was a rather unorthodox one. He voted against the Nixon Administration on measures like the ABM, for instance, and cast the crucial vote against the Supreme Court nomination of Judge Harrold Carswell.

But Cook was also an Administration man, and voted increasingly often on the Nixon side of things as time went on. The Democrats claimed he was out of touch with Kentucky and was enjoying too much the pleasures of Washington. With a head of prematurely white hair and a dignified bearing, he certainly looked like a Senator; but his air of authority sometimes seemed to slip into querulousness.

Cook's 1974 opponent was none other than Governor Wendell Ford, and the campaign turned out to be a bitter one. Cook had not taken much of an anti-Nixon position on Watergate; indeed, he was one of the almost solid Republican votes on the Judiciary Committee for the confirmation of appointees like Richard Kleindienst as Attorney General and L. Patrick Gray as head of the FBI. While Ford ran as the candidate who was closer to Kentuckians, Cook attacked the Governor for some minor scandals in his administration. But that was not enough for the Republican, and Ford won a solid 54–45 victory; indeed, Cook was the worst-beaten Republican Senate candidate in Kentucky since 1950.

As a governor, Ford was a supporter of Senator Edmund Muskie in the 1972 presidential race, and after the election was one of the Governors who strongly backed Robert Strauss for Democratic National Chairman. His seats on the Commerce and Science Committees do not afford him great opportunity for such a national role, but he will probably be heard from more often than Huddleston. Ford's election left the Governorship in the hands of Julian Carroll, another west Kentuckian who is not a political ally of Ford's.

The greatest obstacle to Carroll's election to a full term in 1975 fell when John Y. Brown, Jr., the Kentucky Fried Chicken millionaire who financed the Democratic National Committee telethons, announced he would not enter that race. Carroll faced relatively minor opposition in the primary from Jefferson County Judge Todd Hollenbach and in the general from a little known Republican. The 1975 election returns will give a good indication of whether the Democratic era which began in 1971 is, as seems likely, going to continue.

Census Data Pop. 3,219,311; 1.59% of U.S. total, 23rd largest; Central city, 17%; suburban, 23%. Median family income, $7,439; 46th highest; families above $15,000: 12%; families below $3,000: 18%. Median years education, 9.9.

1974 Share of Federal Tax Burden $3,240,565,000; 1.21% of U.S. total, 24th largest.

1974 Share of Federal Outlays $3,961,486,000; 1.46% of U.S. total, 23d largest. Per capita federal spending, $1230.

DOD	$988,809,000	25th (1.44%)	HEW	$1,455,791,000	22d (1.57%)
AEC	$129,080,000	10th (4.23%)	HUD	$15,944,000	21st (1.64%)
NASA	$482,000	38th (0.02%)	VA	$223,352,000	23d (1.63%)
DOT	$168,634,000	20th (1.99%)	EPA	$28,001,000	25th (0.89%)
DOC	$7,340,000	29th (0.45%)	RevS	$99,869,000	23rd (1.64%)
DOI	$15,248,000	36th (0.62%)	Int.	$140,396,000	17th (0.68%)
USDA	$202,555,000	27th (1.63%)	Other	$485,985,000	

Economic Base Agriculture, notably tobacco, cattle, dairy products, and hogs; finance, insurance and real estate; electrical equipment and supplies, especially household appliances; machinery; bituminous coal mining; apparel and other textile products, especially men's and boys' furnishings; food and kindred products, especially distilled liquor and other beverages.

Political Line-up Governor, Julian M. Carroll (D), acting. Senators, Walter Huddleston (D) and Wendell H. Ford (D). Representatives, 7 (5 D and 2 R). State Senate (28 D, 9 R, and 1 vac.); State House (77 D, 21 R, and 2 vac.).

The Voters

Registration 1,476,553 Total. 988,599 D (67%); 445,316 R (30%); 41,766 No Party (3%); 872 AIP (–).
Median voting age 43.
Employment profile White collar, 40%. Blue collar, 41%. Service, 13%. Farm, 6%.
Ethnic groups Black, 7%. Total foreign stock, 2%.

Presidential vote

1972	Nixon (R)	676,446	(65%)
	McGovern (D)	371,159	(35%)
1968	Nixon (R)	462,411	(44%)
	Humphrey (D)	397,541	(38%)
	Wallace (AI)	193,098	(18%)

Sen. Walter Huddleston (D) Elected 1972, seat up 1978; b. Apr. 15, 1926, Cumberland County; home, Elizabethtown; U. of Ky., B.A. 1949; Methodist.

Career Army, WWII; Sports and Program Dir., WKCT Radio, Bowling Green, 1949–52; Gen. Mgr., WIEL Radio, Elizabethtown, 1952–72; Partner and Dir., WLBN Radio, Lebanon, 1957–72; Ky. Senate, 1965–72, Maj. Floor Ldr., 1970, 1972.

Offices 3327 DSOB, 202-224-2542. Also Suite 136-C New Fed. Ofc. Bldg., 600 Federal Pl., Louisville 40202, 502-582-6304.

Committees

Agriculture and Forestry (6th). Subcommittees: Agricultural Credit and Rural Electrification; Agricultural Production, Marketing, and Stabilization of Prices (Chairman); Environment, Soil Conservation and Forestry.

Appropriations (16th). Subcommittees: District of Columbia; HUD and Independent Agencies; Legislative; Military Construction; Public Works; State, Justice, Commerce, and the Judiciary.

Select Committee on Intelligence Operations (5th).

Group Ratings

	ADA	COPE	LWV	RIPON	NFU	LCV	CFA	NAB	NSI	ACA
1974	55	70	83	33	82	35	77	10	22	26
1973	65	82	50	54	100	–	73	–	–	15

Key Votes

1) No-Knock	AGN	8) Gov Abortn Aid	FOR	15) Consumer Prot Agy	FOR
2) Busing	AGN	9) Cut Mil Brass	ABS	16) Forced Psych Tests	AGN
3) No Fault	AGN	10) Gov Limousine	AGN	17) Fed Campaign Subs	FOR
4) F-111	AGN	11) RR Featherbed	FOR	18) Rhod Chrome Ban	AGN
5) Death Penalty	FOR	12) Handgun License	AGN	19) Open Legis Meetings	AGN
6) Foreign Aid	FOR	13) Less Troop Abrd	AGN	20) Strikers Food Stmps	FOR
7) Filibuster	AGN	14) Resume Turk Aid	FOR	21) Gov Info Disclosure	AGN

Election Results

1972 general:	Walter "Dee" Huddleston (D)	528,550	(52%)	($658,590)
	Louie B. Nunn (R)	494,337	(48%)	($603,649)
1972 primary:	Walter "Dee" Huddleston (D)	106,144	(72%)	
	Four others (D)	42,109	(28%)	

Sen. Wendell H. Ford (D) Elected 1974, seat up 1980; b. Sept. 8, 1924, Daviess County; home, Owensboro; U. of Ky., Md. School of Insurance; Baptist.

Career Army, WWII; Family insurance business; Chf. Admin. Asst. to Gov. Bert Combs; Ky. Senate, 1965–67; Lt. Gov. of Ky., 1967–71; Gov. of Ky., 1971–74.

Offices 2106 DSOB, 202-224-4343. Also 172-C Fed. Bldg., 600 Federal Pl., Louisville 40202, 502-582-6251, and 108 Watts Fed. Bldg., Frankfort 40601, 502-223-2386.

Committees

Aeronautical and Space Sciences (5th.

Commerce (12th). Subcommittees: The Consumer; Foreign Commerce and Tourism; Surface Transportation.

Group Ratings: Newly Elected

Key Votes

1) No-Knock	NE	8) Gov Abortn Aid	FOR	15) Consumer Prot Agy	NE
2) Busing	NE	9) Cut Mil Brass	NE	16) Forced Psych Tests	NE
3) No Fault	NE	10) Gov Limousine	NE	17) Fed Campaign Subs	NE
4) F-111	AGN	11) RR Featherbed	NE	18) Rhod Chrome Ban	NE
5) Death Penalty	NE	12) Handgun License	NE	19) Open Legis Meetings	NE
6) Foreign Aid	NE	13) Less Troop Abrd	NE	20) Strikers Food Stmps	NE
7) Filibuster	AGN	14) Resume Turk Aid	FOR	21) Gov Info Disclosure	NE

Election Results

1974 general:	Wendell H. Ford (D)	399,406	(54%)	($1,006,670)
	Marlow W. Cook (R)	328,982	(44%)	($524,569)
	William E. Parker (A)	17,606	(2%)	($0)
1974 primary:	Wendell H. Ford (D)	136,458	(85%)	
	Harvey E. Brazen (D)	24,436	(15%)	

Gov. Julian Carroll (D) Succeeded Gov. Wendell H. Ford, who resigned to take U.S. Senate Seat, Dec. 28, 1974, term expires Dec. 1975; b. 1931, McCracken County; Paducah Jr. Col., U. of Ky., B.A. 1954, LL.B. 1956; Presbyterian.

Career Air Force; Practicing atty.; Ky. House of Reps., 1961–71, Spkr., 1968–71; Lt. Gov. of Ky., 1971–74.

Offices Frankfort 40601, 502-564-3450.

Election Results

1971 general:	Wendell H. Ford (D)	470,720	(53%)
	Thomas Emberton (R)	412,653	(47%)
1971 primary:	Wendell H. Ford (D)	237,815	(53%)
	Bert T. Combs (D)	195,678	(44%)
	Six Others (D)	15,174	(3%)

♦ ♦ ♦ ♦ ♦

FIRST DISTRICT

The western end of Kentucky is almost part of another state—not Tennessee, or Missouri across the river, but of Mississippi. This is low-lying land, protected from the great muddy river by high levees, and cut off from the rest of Kentucky by the dammed-up Tennessee and Cumberland Rivers. Economically, racially, politically, it resembles the Deep South: it raises cotton, has a large number of rural blacks, and was nearly carried by George Wallace in the 1968 presidential election. Just to the east is the region called the Pennyrile (named after pennyroyal, a prevalent variety of wild mint). This is a land of low hills and small farms, of little prosperity and little wealth. It is also the home of the west Kentucky coal fields—the site of much strip mining recently.

Both the western tip and the Pennyrile are ancestrally Democratic; and though they sometimes lean toward Deep South Democrats of the George Wallace stripe, they have been dependably Democratic in recent state elections.

It is in such obscure corners of the nation that electoral decisions are made which can affect policy in ways of which most citizens remain profoundly ignorant. That was surely the case here in the 1st district in 1974. For 16 years the district had been represented by Frank Stubblefield, a conservative, inarticulate Democrat who had risen to be come second-ranking member of the House Agriculture Committee. City folk tend to think of that body as solely the concern of farmers; but of course it is not. The Department of Agriculture is one of the largest of the federal bureaucracies, with jurisdiction over food marketing and inspection, food stamps, and the national forests, as well as over purely agricultural programs. Stubblefield, though Chairman of the Tobacco Subcommittee, had not been a leader in any of these areas, but he certainly would have been a force for conservative legislation in all of them if he had succeeded to the chairmanship. And, in early 1974, that looked fairly likely: Stubblefield was 67 and Chairman Bob Poage of Texas was 74.

Stubblefield had always won reelection easily, but that was not because of his own strength, but rather his opponents' weakness. In 1974 things were different. Stubblefield had the first substantial primary opposition he had faced since he first won the seat in 1958 in the person of state Senator Carroll Hubbard. A full 30 years younger than the incumbent, and well-known in his home area around Mayfield, Hubbard was able to win a 51–49 primary victory. And when the new Congressmen met in January, Hubbard was elected chairman of the Freshman Caucus and Thomas Foley of Washington, Chairman of the liberal Democratic Study Group, was number two on Agriculture. That last fact may have made the difference in the narrow unseating of Agriculture Chairman Poage; if the freshmen had not had Foley as the ready alternative, they might simply have decided to let the older man stay on.

As for Hubbard, he is probably more conservative than most of the freshmen Democrats —which is probably just what this conservative Democratic district wants. He seems well positioned to win reelection for years and years.

Census Data Pop. 460,754. Central city, 0%; suburban, 8%. Median family income, $6,788; families above $15,000: 8%; families below $3,000: 20%. Median years education, 9.9.

The Voters

Median voting age 45.
Employment profile White collar, 33%. Blue collar, 46%. Service, 13%. Farm, 8%.
Ethnic groups Black, 9%. Total foreign stock, 1%.

Presidential vote

1972	Nixon (R)	87,072	(63%)
	McGovern (D)	51,802	(37%)
1968	Nixon (R)	52,385	(33%)
	Humphrey (D)	61,978	(39%)
	Wallace (AI)	45,478	(28%)

Rep. Carroll Hubbard, Jr. (D) Elected 1974; b. July 7, 1937, Murray; home, Mayfield; Georgetown Col., Georgetown, Ky., B.A. 1959, U. of Louisville, J.D. 1962; Baptist.

Career Practicing atty., 1962–74; Ky. Senate, 1967–75.

Offices 423 CHOB, 202-225-3115. Also 145 E. Center St., McCoy Bldg., Madisonville 42431, 502-825-1371.

Committees

Banking, Currency and Housing (22d). Subcommittees: Economic Stabilization; Financial Institutions Supervision, Regulation and Insurance; International Development Institutions and Finance; International Trade, Investment and Monetary Policy.

Merchant Marine and Fisheries (21st). Subcommittees: Coast Guard and Navigation; Fisheries and Wildlife Conservation and the Environment; Panama Canal.

Group Ratings: Newly Elected

Key Votes

1) Foreign Aid	AGN	6) Gov Abortn Aid	NE	11) Pub Cong Election $	NE
2) Busing	NE	7) Coed Phys Ed	AGN	12) Turkish Arms Cutoff	NE
3) ABM	NE	8) Pov Lawyer Gag	NE	13) Youth Camp Regs	AGN
4) B-1 Bomber	FOR	9) Pub Trans Sub	NE	14) Strip Mine Veto	FOR
5) Nerve Gas	NE	10) EZ Voter Regis	NE	15) Farm Bill Veto	AGN

Election Results

1974 general:	Carroll Hubbard, Jr. (D)	70,723	(78%)	($64,599)
	Charles Thurman Banken, Jr. (R)	16,937	(19%)	($1,350)
	Dr. Robert W. Yoak (AI)	2,805	(3%)	($276)
1974 primary:	Carroll Hubbard, Jr. (D)	30,034	(51%)	
	Frank A. Stubblefield (D)	29,405	(49%)	

◆ ◆ ◆ ◆ ◆

SECOND DISTRICT

The 2d congressional district of Kentucky is a sprawling, largely rural area extending from the Blue Grass country not far from Lexington to the hilly Pennyrile area around Bowling Green. Its largest city is the prosperous manufacturing town of Owensboro (pop. 50,000) on the Ohio River. The best-known features of the district are Fort Knox, where the gold bullion is kept, and Bardstown, where one can find Stephen Foster's original "Old Kentucky Home." (Bardstown is also a town which suffered disproportionately from the Vietnam war. Sixteen of its sons died there, five of them within two weeks of each other.) Also here is the birthplace and boyhood home of Abraham Lincoln.

Kentucky was a slave state that was sharply split when the South seceded; for a while it said it was remaining neutral, but finally sided with the Union. Much of the current 2d was sympathetic to the South, and most of it still votes Democratic today. An exception to the pattern is a group of Republican counties in the center of this T-shaped district. Democratic presidential candidates have done very poorly here in recent years, but statewide candidates like Wendell Ford and Dee Huddleston, both 2d district residents, have carried it handily.

William H. Natcher, a conservative Democrat, has represented the 2d district since the election of 1952. He now enjoys the status of seventh-ranking Democrat on the House Appropriations Committee. In Washington, he is known mainly for serving as Chairman of the District of Columbia Subcommittee, in which capacity he has effectively controlled the D.C. budget for years. For most of that time, Natcher worked in tandem with the Southern Democrats who controlled the D.C.Committee—to the distress of most District residents. An example of Natcher's power was his insistence that an unwanted bridge and freeway be built before any money would be appropriated for the Washington Metro subway system. After years of controversy, Natcher's position was rejected on the House floor—perhaps because the proposed freeway would make incursions on wealthy neighborhoods familiar to most Congressmen as well as in the slums.

Natcher seldom loses one like that; he comes to his work well-prepared and may well know the D.C. budget better than some of the officials who administer it. Home rule has stripped Natcher of some of his power but—as might be expected—not all of it. Congress, which is to say Natcher, retains appropriation power, and the willingness to use it. Although Natcher is getting on in years, he has not faced tough opposition back home since he was first elected; no one can be sure, therefore, just how vulnerable he is.

Census Data Pop. 459,416. Central city, 11%; suburban, 6%. Median family income, $7,042; families above $15,000: 9%; families below $3,000: 18%. Median years education, 9.8.

The Voters

Median voting age 39.
Employment profile White collar, 35%. Blue collar, 42%. Service, 12%. Farm, 11%.
Ethnic groups Black, 6%. Total foreign stock, 2%.

Presidential vote

1972	Nixon (R)	88,384	(65%)
	McGovern (D)	46,922	(35%)
1968	Nixon (R)	59,449	(44%)
	Humphrey (D)	47,859	(35%)
	Wallace (AI)	28,221	(21%)

Rep. William H. Natcher (D) Elected Aug. 1, 1953; b. Sept. 11, 1909, Bowling Green; home, Bowling Green; West. Ky. St. Col., B.A. 1930, Ohio St. U., LL.B. 1933; Baptist.

Career Practicing atty., 1934–53; Fed. Conciliation Commissioner, West. Dist. of Ky., 1936–37; Warren Co. Atty., 1937–49; Navy, WWII; Commonwealth Atty., 8th Judicial Dist. of Ky., 1951–53.

Offices 2333 RHOB, 202-225-3501. Also 414 E. 10th St., Bowling Green 42101, 502-842-7376.

Committees

Appropriations (7th). Subcommittees: Agriculture and Related Agencies; District of Columbia (Chairman); Labor-HEW.

Group Ratings

	ADA	COPE	LWV	RIPON	NFU	LCV	CFA	NAB	NSI	ACA
1974	48	91	50	31	86	65	39	25	60	33
1973	52	82	58	40	95	42	88	–	–	26
1972	31	64	50	38	86	13	50	25	60	57

Key Votes

1) Foreign Aid	AGN	6) Gov Abortn Aid	AGN	11) Pub Cong Election $	AGN
2) Busing	AGN	7) Coed Phys Ed	AGN	12) Turkish Arms Cutoff	FOR
3) ABM	FOR	8) Pov Lawyer Gag	AGN	13) Youth Camp Regs	FOR
4) B-1 Bomber	AGN	9) Pub Trans Sub	FOR	14) Strip Mine Veto	AGN
5) Nerve Gas	FOR	10) EZ Voter Regis	FOR	15) Farm Bill Veto	AGN

Election Results

1974 general:	William H. Natcher (D)	56,502	(73%)	($14,505)
	Art Eddleman (R)	18,312	(24%)	($21)
	Leland Neville (AI)	2,586	(3%)	($782)

1974 primary:	William H. Natcher (D)	16,854	(75%)	
	Edward Drake (D)	5,635	(25%)	
1972 general:	William H. Natcher (D)	75,871	(62%)	($9,396)
	J. C. Carter (R)	47,436	(38%)	($7,327)

◆ ◆ ◆ ◆ ◆

THIRD DISTRICT

The 3d congressional district of Kentucky is made up of the city of Louisville and a few of its suburbs to the south and west. Despite the local pronunciation (LOO-uh-v'l), Louisville is not really a southern town; rather, it is an old river port, like Cincinnati or St. Louis. All three cities, and particularly their large German-American communities, were hostile to the Southern-leaning politics of their slaveholding rural neighbors at the time of the Civil War. Hence Louisville's persistent Republican tradition—which continued into the 1960s among the city's whites and blacks. Indeed, according to one estimate Richard Nixon got 30% of the black vote here in 1972—by a large margin his best such showing in the country.

The decade of the 1960's was a particularly good one for Louisville Republicans. They built a well-financed local organization and elected both a Mayor and a Jefferson County Judge (an administrative job) in 1961. Their candidates were talented, as judged from their later achievements: Mayor William Cowger was elected Congressman in 1966 and County Judge Marlow Cook became U.S. Senator in 1968. But, as sometimes happens, the Louisville Republicans soon found themselves in trouble. In 1969 the Democrats won back both major positions; and as the Nixon administration took office, Cowger and Cook found themselves feuding with Governor Louis Nunn and discovered their black support slipping away.

In 1970, the Democratic congressional candidate, state Senator Romano Mazzoli, waged an effective antiwar-oriented campaign. Incumbent Cowger, who was seriously ill, decided to wage an Agnewesque campaign that alienated many of his erstwhile black supporters while failing to attract many new white voters. The result was the closest 1970 congressional election, and Mazzoli won by 211 votes out of more than 100,000 cast. Mazzoli's subsequent showings are stunning examples of the strength a congressional incumbent can develop: the nation's most marginal winner, in a traditionally marginal district, was reelected with 63% of the vote in 1972 and 70% in 1974.

After two terms on the Education and Labor Committee, Mazzoli switched to Judiciary in 1975. But more likely his ambitions are at the statewide level. His problem now is that in Kentucky's current Democratic revival, there are precious few spots open. Democrats hold both Senate seats and the Governorship, and none of the incumbents shows any sign of retiring. And beyond that, there is plenty more talent, including Jefferson County Judge Todd Hollenbach and Louisville Mayor Harvey Sloane, both in their 30s. Sloane is particularly interesting: a well-to-do physician who moved to Louisville only in 1966 and ran a grass roots campaign in 1973, including a 250-mile walk through the city's neighborhoods.

Census Data Pop. 460,340. Central city, 79%; suburban, 21%. Median family income, $8,902; families above $15,000: 15%; families below $3,000: 11%. Median years education, 10.9.

The Voters

Median voting age 44.
Employment profile White collar, 44%. Blue collar, 42%. Service, 14%. Farm, –%.
Ethnic groups Black, 20%. Total foreign stock, 4%.

Presidential vote

	1972	Nixon (R)	78,143	(55%)
		McGovern (D)	63,796	(45%)
	1968	Nixon (R)	55,549	(38%)
		Humphrey (D)	66,483	(46%)
		Wallace (AI)	22,262	(15%)

Rep. Romano L. Mazzoli (D) Elected 1970; b. Nov. 2, 1932, Louisville; home, Louisville; Notre Dame U., B.S. 1954, U. of Louisville, J.D. 1960; Catholic.

Career Army, 1954–56; Law Dept., L & N Railroad Co., 1960–62; Practicing atty., 1962–70; Ky. Senate, 1967–71.

Offices 1212 LHOB, 202-225-5401. Also Fed. Bldg., 600 Federal Pl., Louisville 40202, 502-582-5129.

Committees

District of Columbia (9th). Subcommittees: Fiscal Affairs (Chairman): Judiciary.

Judiciary (19th). Subcommittees: Administrative Law and Governmental Relations; Monopolies and Commercial Law.

Group Ratings

	ADA	COPE	LWV	RIPON	NFU	LCV	CFA	NAB	NSI	ACA
1974	77	90	67	56	92	69	85	58	33	33
1973	80	64	83	87	65	95	100	–	–	26
1972	63	91	83	69	86	71	100	25	20	26

Key Votes

1) Foreign Aid	AGN	6) Gov Abortn Aid	AGN	11) Pub Cong Election $	FOR
2) Busing	AGN	7) Coed Phys Ed	FOR	12) Turkish Arms Cutoff	FOR
3) ABM	AGN	8) Pov Lawyer Gag	FOR	13) Youth Camp Regs	FOR
4) B-1 Bomber	AGN	9) Pub Trans Sub	FOR	14) Strip Mine Veto	AGN
5) Nerve Gas	AGN	10) EZ Voter Regis	FOR	15) Farm Bill Veto	FOR

Election Results

1974 general:	Romano L. Mazzoli (D)	75,571	(70%)	($28,353)
	Vincent N. Barclay (R)	28,812	(27%)	($2,446)
	William P. Chambers (AI)	3,383	(3%)	($117)
1974 primary:	Romano L. Mazzoli (D)	15,636	(91%)	
	Two others (D)	1,574	(9%)	
1972 general:	Romano L. Mazzoli (D)	86,810	(63%)	($58,410)
	Phil Kaelin, Jr. (R)	51,634	(37%)	($21,161)

◆ ◆ ◆ ◆ ◆

FOURTH DISTRICT

The 4th congressional district of Kentucky is a geographical oddity—the proximate result of the state's loss of a congressional district in the 1960 census and three subsequent redistrictings. The 4th today consists of two nearly equal-sized suburban areas connected by a thin strip of rural counties along the Ohio River. The first and larger of the suburban areas is Jefferson County, excluding the city of Louisville and the few adjacent suburbs which make up the 3d district. This part of the 4th is both prosperous and growing rapidly and, like most such places, tends to vote Republican. The other suburban part of the district lies across the Ohio River from Cincinnati. About half the voters here live in the old, decaying cities of Covington and Newport on the River. Like Cincinnati, these usually go Republican, although they have been known to swing the other way.

The connecting counties along the River are part of an older Kentucky. Bypassed by Interstate 71, the little tobacco towns retain nineteenth century Democratic voting habits, though the few ballots here get lost in the district-wide totals.

Since 1966, when the district took its present shape, the Congressman from the 4th has been Republican M.G. (Gene) Snyder; he also represented the old 3d district from 1962 to 1964, when he was swept out of office by the Johnson landslide. In his first election in the 4th, Snyder, whose political base was in Jefferson County, faced strong opposition in the primary from Campbell County (Newport) reform Sheriff George Ratterman, a onetime Cleveland Browns quarterback, and in the general from Congressman Frank Chelf, who had intended to retire but had gone back and run when the Democratic nominee died in November.

Snyder won that one, and did not have a serious challenge again until 1974. Then, suddenly, he became as controversial as his Goldwater leanings had made him in Louisville in 1964. He had recently been divorced, and now there were rumors his former wife wanted to run against him in the primary. And in the general election he was facing 32-year-old Kyle Hubbard, the brother of 1st district nominee (and now Congressman) Carroll Hubbard. Hubbard, helped by a strong local showing by Wendell Ford, carried the Cincinnati suburb part of the district, but Snyder was saved by his home area of Jefferson County. There he won an 8,000 vote majority, enough for a 52-48 win district-wide. Will Snyder be in trouble again in the future? His vulnerability in 1974 was as much personal as political, and so one will have to wait and see.

Census Data Pop. 458,896. Central city, 0%; suburban, 93%. Median family income, $10,359; families above $15,000: 21%; families below $3,000: 7%. Median years education, 12.0.

The Voters

Median voting age 41.
Employment profile White collar, 51%. Blue collar, 37%. Service, 10%. Farm, 2%.
Ethnic groups Black, 2%. Total foreign stock, 5%.

Presidential vote

1972	Nixon (R)	112,607	(70%)
	McGovern (D)	47,238	(30%)
1968	Nixon (R)	66,185	(47%)
	Humphrey (D)	48,000	(34%)
	Wallace (AI)	25,364	(18%)

Rep. Gene Snyder (R) Elected 1966; b. Jan. 26, 1928, Louisville; home, Jefferson County; Jefferson School of Law, LL.B. 1950; Protestant.

Career Practicing atty., 1950–67; Realtor and builder; Jeffersontown City Atty., 1954–58; Jefferson Co. 1st Dist. Magistrate, 1957–65.

Offices 2330 RHOB, 202-225-3465. Also 140 Chenoweth Ln., St. Matthews 40207, 502-895-6949.

Committees

Merchant Marine and Fisheries (4th). Subcommittees: Coast Guard and Navigation; Merchant Marine; Panama Canal.

Public Works and Transportation (4th) Subcommittees: Aviation; Investigations and Review; Water Resources.

Group Ratings

	ADA	COPE	LWV	RIPON	NFU	LCV	CFA	NAB	NSI	ACA
1974	20	9	9	14	36	13	42	100	56	80
1973	21	27	17	21	35	16	13	–	–	85
1972	6	27	18	43	57	40	100	91	56	91

Key Votes

1) Foreign Aid	AGN	6) Gov Abortn Aid	AGN	11) Pub Cong Election $	AGN
2) Busing	AGN	7) Coed Phys Ed	AGN	12) Turkish Arms Cutoff	ABS
3) ABM	FOR	8) Pov Lawyer Gag	FOR	13) Youth Camp Regs	AGN
4) B-1 Bomber	FOR	9) Pub Trans Sub	AGN	14) Strip Mine Veto	FOR
5) Nerve Gas	FOR	10) EZ Voter Regis	AGN	15) Farm Bill Veto	AGN

Election Results

1974 general:	Gene Snyder (R)	63,845	(52%)	($86,973)
	Kyle T. Hubbard (D)	59,539	(48%)	($82,150)
1974 primary:	Gene Snyder, unopposed			
1972 general:	Gene Snyder (R)	110,902	(74%)	($29,411)
	James W. Rogers (D)	39,332	(26%)	($375)

♦ ♦ ♦ ♦ ♦

FIFTH DISTRICT

If one wants proof that political preference in the United States is not simply a function of wealth—the rich voting Republican, the poor Democrat—consider some results from the close 1968 presidential race. Two the wealthiest suburbs in the United States—Beverly Hills, California and Scarsdale, New York—both went Democratic. At the same time, the 5th congressional district of Kentucky, with a median income several hundred dollars lower than any other in the nation, gave 59% of its vote to Richard Nixon. Only 20 of the nation's 435 congressional districts bettered the 5th's Republican percentage.

Nixon's performance here was, if anything, a little below the usual levels of Republican support. The hills and hollows of the Cumberland Plateau in south central Kentucky have consistently delivered some of the largest Republican majorities in the United States for more than a century. The small farmers here were hostile to the slave-holding South and to the uppity proslavery Blue Grass region to the north in the years around the Civil War. And living in one of the most isolated and provincial areas in the nation, the people here have remained staunchly Republican ever since.

Only in places where the United Mine Workers organized successfully in the 1930s have the mountain people switched to the Democrats. But there are far fewer mines and miners here than in the adjacent 7th district; about the only Democratic county here is "bloody Harlan", where in the 1930s the mine owners' men and UMW members shot and killed each other in pitched battles. But Harlan is less important than it was; as the mines petered out, its population declined from 64,000 in 1930 to 36,000 in 1970.

The Republican counties here have also been losing population, but not so rapidly. So in the 5th, winning the Republican primary is tantamount to winning the general election. When Congressman Eugene Siler retired in 1964, the Republican primary attracted no fewer than 15 entrants, as compared to only two in the Democratic. The Republican winner was Dr. Tim Lee Carter, who got a remarkable 45% of the total vote. One reason was that 13 of the 14 other candidates were from the eastern end of the district, while Carter shared the western counties with one weak rival. Goldwater's poor showing that year held Carter to a modest 53% victory in the 1964 general election, but he has won by solid margins ever since; in the otherwise Democratic year of 1974, he took 68% of the vote. A practicing physician for nearly 30 years, Carter is a member of the Health Subcommittee chaired and dominated by Paul Rogers of Florida.

Census Data Pop. 459,586. Central city, 0%; suburban, 0%. Median family income, $4,669; families above $15,000: 6%; families below $3,000: 33%. Median years education, 8.5.

The Voters

Median voting age 45.
Employment profile White collar, 33%. Blue collar, 43%. Service, 12%. Farm, 12%.
Ethnic groups Black, 3%.

Presidential vote

1972	Nixon (R)	117,821	(73%)
	McGovern (D)	44,287	(27%)
1968	Nixon (R)	95,407	(59%)
	Humphrey (D)	42,927	(26%)
	Wallace (AI)	23,681	(15%)

Rep. Tim Lee Carter (R) Elected 1964; b. Sept. 2, 1910, Tompkinsville; home, Tompkinsville; W. Ky. U., B.A. 1934, U. of Tenn., M.D. 1937; Baptist.

Career Internship, U.S. Marine Hosp. and Chicago Maternity Ctr.; Army, WWII; Practicing physician.

Offices 2441 RHOB, 202-225-4601. Also 203 S. Main St., Somerset 42501, 606-679-2544.

Committees

Interstate and Foreign Commerce (3d). Subcommittees: Health and Environment.

Small Business (6th). Subcommittees: SBA Oversight and Minority Enterprise.

Group Ratings

	ADA	COPE	LWV	RIPON	NFU	LCV	CFA	NAB	NSI	ACA
1974	9	10	50	60	43	31	17	58	63	54
1973	17	60	25	46	88	28	43	–	–	52
1972	6	10	50	50	50	17	50	56	100	69

Key Votes

1) Foreign Aid	AGN	6) Gov Abortn Aid	AGN	11) Pub Cong Election $	AGN
2) Busing	AGN	7) Coed Phys Ed	AGN	12) Turkish Arms Cutoff	AGN
3) ABM	FOR	8) Pov Lawyer Gag	FOR	13) Youth Camp Regs	AGN
4) B-1 Bomber	FOR	9) Pub Trans Sub	AGN	14) Strip Mine Veto	FOR
5) Nerve Gas	FOR	10) EZ Voter Regis	AGN	15) Farm Bill Veto	AGN

Election Results

1974 general:	Tim Lee Carter (R)	66,709	(68%)	($18,763)
	Lyle L. Willis (D)	28,706	(29%)	($228)
	Dr. Albert G. J. Cullum (AI)	2,467	(3%)	($2,557)
1974 primary:	Tim Lee Carter (R), unopposed			
1972 general:	Tim Lee Carter (R)	109,264	(74%)	($12,155)
	Lyle L. Willis (D)	39,301	(26%)	($216)

◆ ◆ ◆ ◆ ◆

SIXTH DISTRICT

Nobody, not Daniel Boone or Henry Clay, is a more famous Kentuckian these days than Colonel Harlan Sanders. If you really wanted to "visit the Colonel," you would have to travel all the way to Shelby County in the 6th congressional district of Kentucky. Not far from Lexington, the Colonel's home is a Blue Grass horse farm with a white wood fence and all the trimmings. If you were invited in you might see him sipping a mint julep and contemplating the pleasures of a fried chicken dinner to come. But the Colonel, now past 80, did not always live like this; till he was 65, he lived in the grimy little mountain town of Corbin, with scarcely an extra dime to spend. Then John Y. Brown, Jr., millionaire and sometimes Democratic politician, ate some fried chicken—and the rest is history.

Colonel Sanders, like most residents of the 6th district, is a Democrat. You may remember the image of him distributing boxes of chicken to hungry, usually McGovernite delegates at the 1972 Democratic national convention; you should remember, too, that he reserved his warmest greetings for Mrs. Cornelia Wallace. Many, if not most, of the Democrats of the 6th, would do the same; their party affiliation comes, ultimately, out of Civil War traditions and not from any sympathy with liberal programs. Indeed, Democratic strength in the 6th district has been on a long-term decline. The party's appeal is concentrated in the region's rural counties, which have been losing population. The political pivot of the district is Fayette County (Lexington)—the fastest-growing area in the state outside of the Louisville suburbs. Fayette County has become increasingly Republican in both national and statewide elections; it even went for Senator Marlow Cook in the 1974 contest. The 1972 redistricting also helped Republicans here by adding Republican parts of Kenton and Campbell Counties (Cincinnati suburbs).

All these demographic trends seemed to be moving the 6th into the Republican column, but before that could happen the Republican Party in Kentucky seemed virtually to collapse. Certainly Republicans have had enough good chances to take the district. Back in 1971, Congressman John C. Watts, then the second-ranking Democrat on the House Ways and Means Committee, dropped dead. Then, a year later, the young Democrat elected to succeed Watts decided he didn't want to raise his family in the Washington area, and so he declined to run in 1972.

But each time the Republicans failed to come up with a candidate and the resources needed to win. The current Congressman is John C. Breckinridge, a rather conservative Democrat who was Attorney General twice (1960–64, 1968–72). Breckinridge is the holder of one of the oldest and proudest names in the Commonwealth (Kentucky, like Virginia, Pennsylvania, and Massachusetts, is officially a commonwealth, not a state). He is the fifth Kentucky Breckinridge to serve in Congress; his namesake was Vice President under James Buchanan.

Breckinridge was 59 when first elected, making him the oldest freshman in the House that year. But he managed to do what most younger members accomplish: to win reelection by a smashing 72% of the vote.

Census Data Pop. 460,521. Central city, 24%; suburban, 27%. Median family income, $8,678; families above $15,000: 16%; families below $3,000: 12%. Median years education, 11.7.

The Voters

Median voting age 41.
Employment profile White collar, 46%. Blue collar, 34%. Service, 13%. Farm, 7%.
Ethnic groups Black, 9%. Total foreign stock, 2%.

Presidential vote

1972	Nixon (R)	101,147	(67%)
	McGovern (D)	50,777	(33%)
1968	Nixon (R)	61,072	(43%)
	Humphrey (D)	53,844	(38%)
	Wallace (AI)	28,328	(20%)

Rep. John Breckinridge (D) Elected 1972; b. Nov. 29, 1913, Washington, D.C.; home, Lexington; U. of Ky., A.B. 1937, LL.B. 1939; Presbyterian.

Career Practicing atty., 1940, 1946–72; Special Atty., Anti-Trust Div., U.S. Dept. of Justice, 1940–41; Army, WWII, Ky. House of Reps., 1956–60; Atty. Gen. of Ky., 1960–64, 1968–72.

Offices 125 CHOB, 202-225-4706. Also 305 Court Square Bldg., Lexington 40507, 606-253-1501.

Committees

Agriculture (14th). Subcommittees: Department Operations, Investigations and Oversight; Family Farms and Rural Development; Tobacco.

Small Business (15th). Subcommittees: SBA and SBIC Legislation; SBA Oversight and minority Enterprise.

Group Ratings

	ADA	COPE	LWV	RIPON	NFU	LCV	CFA	NAB	NSI	ACA
1974	50	82	100	67	79	63	77	17	100	27
1973	40	73	83	64	90	58	75	–	–	15

Key Votes

1) Foreign Aid	FOR	6) Gov Abortn Aid	AGN	11) Pub Cong Election $	FOR
2) Busing	FOR	7) Coed Phys Ed	FOR	12) Turkish Arms Cutoff	FOR
3) ABM	FOR	8) Pov Lawyer Gag	AGN	13) Youth Camp Regs	AGN
4) B-1 Bomber	FOR	9) Pub Trans Sub	AGN	14) Strip Mine Veto	AGN
5) Nerve Gas	FOR	10) EZ Voter Regis	FOR	15) Farm Bill Veto	AGN

Election Results

1974 general:	John B. Breckinridge (D)	63,010	(72%)	($20,932)
	Thomas F. Rogers III (R)	21,039	(24%)	($2,217)
	Fred Kerestesy (AI)	3,367	(4%)	($100)
1974 primary:	John B. Breckinridge (D)	21,202	(84%)	
	Robert K. Landrum (D)	4,023	(16%)	
1972 general:	John B. Breckinridge (D)	76,185	(53%)	($69,216)
	Laban P. Jackson (R)	68,012	(47%)	($82,152)

◆ ◆ ◆ ◆ ◆

SEVENTH DISTRICT

The 7th congressional district of Kentucky is part—some would say the heart—of Appalachia. Though the 5th district is officially the state's poorest, the 7th is still one of the most poverty-stricken in the entire country. The only city here of any size is Ashland (pop. 29,000) on the Ohio River near Huntington, West Virginia. The rural hills and hollows of the district, however, are some of the most densely populated rural land in the United States. Coal has been the region's economic mainstay. But since the economic collapse of the mines in the 1930s and 1940s, the 7th has been exporting its young men and women to the industrial cities of the north. Most of them continue to think of eastern Kentucky as "home." On holiday weekends Interstate 75 is jammed as thousands of people return from Detroit, Toledo, and Flint to see their families and the mountains where they grew up.

During the 1930s, the 7th was the scene of bitter struggles between the United Mine Workers and mine owners. Today the bitterness lingers and extends to other issues. One of them is strip mining. Some defend it, arguing that it produces jobs (though not nearly as many as deep mines used to). Other mountaineers strongly oppose the strippers because their giant machines cut ugly, often irreparable gouges in the gentle green hills. There is a boom here now—but here is considerable argument over how many really benefit from it.

The struggles of the '30s and the New Deal put an end to the Civil War allegiance to the Republican Party in most of the counties of the 7th district. Today the 7th as a whole is staunchly Democratic with only small pockets of Republican sentiment. Contrasting election results testify to the long isolation and insularity of the mountain counties. Knott County, for example, cast 65% of its votes for George McGovern in 1972, while Jackson County, 20 miles away and quite similar in outward appearance, went 92% for Richard Nixon.

The voters of the 7th have been especially fond of Democratic Congressman Carl Perkins, who has won recent elections by better than 2–1 margins and took 76% of the vote in 1974. First elected in 1948, Perkins has been, since the ouster of Adam Clayton Powell in 1967, Chairman of the House Education and Laobr Committee. At that time Perkins was a firm supporter of Lyndon Johnson's Great Society, and Education and Labor was a glamor committee, with jurisdiction over federal aid to education and the anti-poverty programs.

Of course, Education and Labor also has its more prosaic jurisdiction, including over our labor laws, which have not been changed in any major way since 1959. Perkins got to be Chairman just as organized labor was achieving a long-sought goal: putting so many liberal pro-labor congressmen on the Committee that there would never, ever (as there was in 1959) be reported out to the floor labor laws opposed by the AFL-CIO. The Committee is, if anything, even more liberal today; just as Pentagon boosters have packed Armed Services, labor supporters have packed Education and Labor.

This has produced other dividends, for there are now solid liberal majorities on Education and Labor on just about every issue. (The last remaining obstacle to that was senior Democrat Edith Green of Oregon; she left the Committee in 1973 and retired in 1974.) Perkins is not known as a particularly strong Chairman, but many of the junior members are talented, and the Kentuckian usually gets what he wants.

Census Data Pop. 459,798. Central city, 6%; suburban, 5%. Median family income, $5,528; families above $15,000: 6%; families below $3,000: 28%. Median years education, 8.7.

The Voters

Median voting age 44.
Employment profile White collar, 34%. Blue collar, 47%. Service, 12%. Farm, 7%.
Ethnic groups Black, 1%.

Presidential vote

1972	Nixon (R)	93,088	(58%)
	McGovern (D)	67,062	(42%)
1968	Nixon (R)	67,997	(42%)
	Humphrey (D)	74,283	(46%)
	Wallace (AI)	18,913	(12%)

Rep. Carl D. Perkins (D) Elected 1948; b. Oct. 15, 1912, Hindman; home, Hindman; Caney Jr. Col., Lees Jr. Col., U. of Louisville, Jefferson School of Law, LL.B. 1935; Baptist.

Career Practicing atty., 1935–48; Ky. House of Reps., 1940; Knott Co. Atty., 1941–48; Army, WWII.

Offices 2365 RHOB, 202-225-4935.

Committees

Education and Labor (Chairman). Subcommittees: Elementary, Secondary and Vocational Education (Chairman).

Group Ratings

	ADA	COPE	LWV	RIPON	NFU	LCV	CFA	NAB	NSI	ACA
1974	43	100	67	38	86	71	69	33	90	20
1973	60	100	58	60	100	47	75	–	–	15
1972	38	100	75	63	86	20	100	9	70	24

Key Votes

1) Foreign Aid	AGN	6) Gov Abortn Aid	AGN	11) Pub Cong Election $	AGN
2) Busing	FOR	7) Coed Phys Ed	FOR	12) Turkish Arms Cutoff	AGN
3) ABM	FOR	8) Pov Lawyer Gag	FOR	13) Youth Camp Regs	FOR
4) B-1 Bomber	FOR	9) Pub Trans Sub	FOR	14) Strip Mine Veto	AGN
5) Nerve Gas	AGN	10) EZ Voter Regis	FOR	15) Farm Bill Veto	AGN

Election Results

1973 general:	Carl D. Perkins (D)	71,221	(76%)	($2,100)
	Granville Thomas (R)	22,982	(24%)	($1)
1974 primary:	Carl D. Perkins (D), unopposed			
1972 general:	Carl D. Perkins (D)	94,840	(62%)	($5,766)
	Robert Holcomb (R)	58,286	(38%)	($48,035)

LOUISIANA

Forty years ago Huey P. Long was shot down and killed in the halls of the Capitol he built in Baton Rouge; but even today he remains an important influence in Louisiana politics. When he was murdered, Long had been a U.S. Senator for less than six years, and before that had served as Governor for less than a full four-year term. In that short span, however, Huey built monuments to himself and the people of Louisiana: the Capitol, Louisiana State University, a system of badly needed concrete roads, an old-age pension. Long dominated the politics of his state as no man had ever done in American history. He was a national force as well. His nebulous "Share the Wealth" program that would "Make Every Man a King" was popular enough that it moved FDR to back Social Security and the Wagner Act as he contemplated his reelection bid of 1936.

Huey Long was a brilliant man, and no one has ever taken his place. But his political allies and family members have been winning office in Louisiana since the 1930s. From 1937 till his death in 1972, Allen J. Ellender, Huey's Speaker of the Louisiana House, held the Kingfish's old seat in the Senate; and since 1948 the state's other Senate seat has been held by Huey's son, Russell Long, who was first elected when he reached the constitutional age of 30.

If Louisiana politics is remarkable for the influence of a man long dead, it is also remarkable for being conducted in French as well as English. New Orleans of course retains a French or, rather, Creole ambiance from its original settlers in the days before the Louisiana Purchase, and a kind of lazy tolerance of the unorthodox and the illicit. Surrounded by hundreds of miles of Baptist countryside, Catholic New Orleans is another world—an outpost, as A. J. Liebling once put it, of the Levant along the Gulf of Mexico.

An even more pronounced French influence can be found outside New Orleans in the bayou country south of Alexandria and west of the Mississippi River. This is Cajun country, the home of the descendants of the 4,000 Acadians expelled by the British from Nova Scotia in 1755; their fate has been known to thousands of schoolchildren thanks to Longfellow's "Evangeline." In present-day Cajun country, almost everyone is a Catholic, and a unique dialect of French is spoken.

Huey Long was one of the few Louisiana politicians able to run as well in the Baptist, prohibitionist north as in the joie de vivre Cajun south; and he did it without racial demogoguery. Long's program was strictly economic: fight the big money interests and spend lots of money on projects to help little people. Since Long's day, the northern parishes (the Louisiana word for county) have dominated the election returns, and racial issues and innuendoes have too often dominated political discourse. In 1964 and 1968, the northern parishes put the state in the Goldwater and Wallace columns, even though Johnson ran well among the Cajuns and Humphrey carried New Orleans. Only when the Cajun Catholics provided huge margins for Eisenhower and Kennedy in 1956 and 1960 did they prevail in presidential contests.

In state elections, the Governor has traditionally come out of the Protestant north; Long himself was from the scrubby hills of 88% Baptist Winn Parish. But that tradition was shattered in 1972. Congressman Edwin W. Edwards— a Cajun and proud of it despite his Welsh name—won the Governorship that year. With a somewhat liberal voting record in Washington and support from most blacks, Edwards would not have been electable a few years before; but he managed to just edge state Senator J. Bennett Johnston in the Democratic runoff and won easily in the general election. Edwards's inauguration provided an occasion for official recognition of the state's Cajun revival—an increased pride in the French language, Cajun traditions, and the justly praised bayou cuisine.

Ironically, just as Louisiana got its first Cajun Governor in decades, the southern, Catholic area lost its traditional hold on one of the state's Senate seats. Since 1936, Senator Ellender had been reelected virtually without opposition; he had become the Senate's most senior member, its President Pro Tem, and Chairman of the Appropriations Committee. Then, in 1972, at the age of 82, Ellender had substantial primary opposition from Johnston, fresh from his narrow loss in the Governor's race and just past 40. Suddenly, after the filing deadline but before primary day, Ellender died. Former Governor (1964-72) John McKeithen tried to get into the race, but failed, and Johnston won the primary and the general—McKeithen made a halfhearted race as an Independent—by default.

Edwards and Johnston have many of the same political assets. Both have that easy charm that so many Southern politicians seem to possess by inheritance; both are sharp dressers. But while Edwards has a reputation (though perhaps it's overblown) as a kind of liberal, Johnston is one of the most conservative Democrats in the Senate. Indeed, if one were looking for the young Senators who are likely to carry on the tradition established by Southern Democrats like Richard Russell, John Stennis, and John McClellan, the only names one can come up with are Johnston's and that of Sam Nunn of Georgia.

The state's other Senator, Russell Long, holds about as safe a seat as there is in Congress. At 58 he has 28 years of seniority and the prospect of being reelected for as long as he wants; he won with only token opposition in 1974. But Long's Senate career has had its ups and downs. One up was in 1965, when he was elected Majority Whip by an unusual coalition of Southerners and liberals. But after four stormy years—including a divorce and an apparent drinking problem—Long lost that post in a surprise upset to Edward Kennedy, who himself had some problems and lost the position to Robert Byrd in 1971.

Today Long's chief source of power is the chairmanship of the Senate Finance Committee, which he has held also since 1965. As Wilbur Mills did so many years on House Ways and Means, Long tries to dominate his committee by monolopozing staff resources, refusing to create subcommittees, and seeing that much of its business is conducted in secret sessions. Long is still fond of old-fashioned pork barrel joshing, but he is also becoming more adept at fashioning legislation which can command a solid majority in the Senate—which is, after all, what committees are supposed to do.

In some policy areas, the Chairman is very much the son of Huey Long. Thanks in large part to Russell Long, the Senate invariably votes for larger Social Security increases and, as in 1975, larger tax cuts than does the House; the conference committee usually settles for a figure in the middle. Back in the mid-'60s, at a time when few legislators were interested in campaign finance reform, Long pushed for a $1 checkoff on income tax forms to finance federal elections—a measure enacted in the Tax Reform Act of 1969. But unlike his father, Long is quite solicitous of the oil industry—one of Huey's favorite political targets. Russell, as he freely admits, has made hundreds of thousands of dollars investing in oil, and as a Senator from Louisiana, the nation's number two oil state, he sees nothing wrong with protecting the interests of the big oil companies. But Chairmen are not always all powerful these days, and Long was not able to prevent the repeal of the oil depletion allowance for the major companies in the 1975 tax cut bill.

In managing the 1975 tax cut bill on the floor of the Senate, Long lost control of the amending process, and a majority voted to use a clean bill put forward by Mike Mansfield as a substitute basis for debate. But that apparent legislative gaffe was as nothing compared to the performance of Long's Finance Committee on the Nixon Family Assistance Plan in 1970 and 1971. At that time Long had almost a mania for cracking down on welfare chiselers—an odd preoccupation, one would have thought, for Huey Long's son—and he so loaded the FAP bill with onerous crackdown provisions that virually all its liberal supporters disowned it. In the House, Wilbur Mills had long since pushed through a bill acceptable to a large majority; in the Senate, no bill ever reached the floor.

Over the years, Louisiana's House delegation, like those of most Southern states, specialized in the accumulation of seniority. But today, the state has practically none. House Majority Leader Hale Boggs was lost in a plane crash in 1972, and New Orleans's Edward Hebert was stripped of his Armed Services Chairmanship after the 1974 elections. Louisiana's main power in the House today is probably Joe Waggoner, a leader of the dwindling number of conservative Southern Democrats. There are currently two Republican Congressmen from the state, but both are the product of special circumstances; actually, the Republican Party is probably weaker here than in any other state of the union. Louisiana does not have a presidential primary; but its delegate selection process produced one of the yeastiest delegations to the 1972 Democratic national convention. Next to Governor Edwards sat black activists and young McGovern supporters; old line Democrats are not much used to electing delegates, and simply didn't show up.

Census Data Pop. 3,643,180; 1.80% of U.S. total, 20th largest; Central city, 31%; suburban, 23%. Median family income, $7,527; 43rd highest; families above $15,000: 13%; families below $3,000: 19%. Median years education, 10.8.

1974 Share of Federal Tax Burden $3,508,380,000; 1.31% of U.S. total, 23d largest.

1974 Share of Federal Outlays $3,907,822,000; 1.45% of U.S. total, 24th largest. Per capita federal spending, $1073.

DOD	$978,581,000	26th (1.43%)		HEW	$1,403,433,000	23d (1.51%)
AEC	$229,000	36th (0.01%)		HUD	$9,771,000	27th (1.00%)
NASA	$38,429,000	11th (1.29%)		VA	$244,082,000	21st (1.78%)
DOT	$163,988,000	22d (1.94%)		EPA	$13,580,000	36th (0.43%)
DOC	$66,439,000	5th (4.12%)		RevS	$140,069,000	13th (2.31%)
DOI	$12,464,000	37th (0.51%)		Int.	$96,326,000	26th (0.47%)
USDA	$326,122,000	12th (2.62%)		Other	$414,309,000	

Economic Base Finance, insurance and real estate; agriculture, notably cattle, soybeans, rice and dairy products; oil and gas extraction, especially oil and gas field services; food and kindred products; chemicals and allied products, especially industrial chemicals; transportation equipment, especially ship building and repairing.

Political Line-up Governor, Edwin W. Edwards (D). Senators, Russell B. Long (D) and J. Bennett Johnston, Jr. (D). Representatives, 8 (6 D and 2 R). State Senate (38 D and 1 vac.); State House (100 D, 4 R, and 1 vac.).

The Voters

Registration 1,723,518 Total. 1,332,479 D (96%); 47,432 R (3%); 23,469 Other (1%).
Median voting age 41.
Employment profile White collar, 45%. Blue collar, 36%. Service, 16%. Farm, 3%.
Ethnic groups Black, 30%. Spanish, 2%. Total foreign stock, 4%. French speaking, 16%.

Presidential vote

1972	Nixon (R)	686,852	(70%)
	McGovern (D)	298,142	(30%)
1968	Nixon (R)	257,535	(23%)
	Humphrey (D)	309,615	(28%)
	Wallace (AI)	530,300	(48%)

Sen. Russell B. Long (D) Elected 1948, seat up 1980; b. Nov. 3, 1918, Shreveport; home, Baton Rouge; La. St. U., B.A. 1941, LL.B. 1942; Methodist.

Career Navy, WWII; Practicing atty., 1945–47.

Offices 217 RSOB, 202-224-4623. Also 220 Fed. Bldg., 750 Fla. Ave., Baton Rouge 70801, 504-387-0181 ext. 445.

Committees

Finance (Chairman). Subcommittees: Supplemental Security Income (Chairman).

Commerce (6th). Subcommittees: Communications; Environment; Foreign Commerce and Tourism; Merchant Marine (Chairman); Oceans and Atmosphere; Surface Transportation; Special Subcommittee to Study Transportation on the Great Lakes-St. Lawrence Seaway.

Group Ratings

	ADA	COPE	LWV	RIPON	NFU	LCV	CFA	NAB	NSI	ACA
1974	15	38	60	19	73	21	0	30	71	67
1973	37	82	44	25	67	–	15	–	–	41
1972	15	43	50	27	44	5	45	46	89	45

Key Votes

1) No-Knock	ABS	8) Gov Abortn Aid	AGN	15) Consumer Prot Agy	AGN
2) Busing	AGN	9) Cut Mil Brass	FOR	16) Forced Psych Tests	FOR
3) No Fault	AGN	10) Gov Limousine	AGN	17) Fed Campaign Subs	ABS
4) F-111	AGN	11) RR Featherbed	FOR	18) Rhod Chrome Ban	FOR
5) Death Penalty	FOR	12) Handgun License	AGN	19) Open Legis Meetings	AGN
6) Foreign Aid	AGN	13) Less Troop Abrd	FOR	20) Strikers Food Stmps	AGN
7) Filibuster	AGN	14) Resume Turk Aid	ABS	21) Gov Info Disclosure	AGN

Election Results

1974 general:	Russell B. Long (D), unopposed			($498,774)
1974 primary:	Russell B. Long (D)	520,606	(75%)	
	Two others (D)	175,881	(25%)	
1968 general:	Russell B. Long (D), unopposed			

Sen. J. Bennett Johnston, Jr. (D) Elected 1972, seat up 1978; b. June 10, 1932, Shreveport; home, Shreveport; Wash. & Lee U., La. St. U., LL.B. 1956; Baptist.

Career Army, 1956–59; Practicing atty.; La. House of Reps., 1964–68, Floor Ldr.; La. Senate, 1968–72.

Offices 432 RSOB, 202-224-5824. Also 602 Fed. Bldg., 600 South St., New Orleans 70130, 504-589-2427, and 7A12 New Fed. Bldg. and Courthouse, 500 Fannin St., Shreveport 71102, 318-226-5085.

Committees

Appropriations (15th). Subcommittees: District of Columbia; Foreign Operations; HUD and Independent Agencies; Military Construction; Public Works; State, Justice, Commerce; The Judiciary.

Interior and Insular Affairs (4th). Subcommittees: Minerals, Materials and Fuels; Parks and Recreation (Chairman); Special Subcommittee on Integrated Oil Operations.

Group Ratings

	ADA	COPE	LWV	RIPON	NFU	LCV	CFA	NAB	NSI	ACA
1974	15	33	67	20	63	35	11	42	90	82
1973	37	50	70	44	75	–	31	–	–	54

Key Votes

1) No-Knock	ABS	8) Gov Abortn Aid	AGN	15) Consumer Prot Agy	AGN
2) Busing	AGN	9) Cut Mil Brass	AGN	16) Forced Psych Tests	AGN
3) No Fault	AGN	10) Gov Limousine	AGN	17) Fed Campaign Subs	AGN
4) F-111	FOR	11) RR Featherbed	ABS	18) Rhod Chrome Ban	FOR
5) Death Penalty	FOR	12) Handgun License	AGN	19) Open Legis Meetings	FOR
6) Foreign Aid	AGN	13) Less Troop Abrd	AGN	20) Strikers Food Stmps	AGN
7) Filibuster	AGN	14) Resume Turk Aid	FOR	21) Gov Info Disclosure	AGN

Election Results

1972 general:	J. Bennett Johnston, Jr. (D)	598,987	(55%)	($511,616)
	John J. McKeithen (Ind.)	250,161	(23%)	($394,510)
	Ben C. Toledano (R)	206,846	(19%)	($116,347)
	Hall M. Lyons (AI)	28,910	(3%)	
1972 primary:	J. Bennett Johnston, Jr. (D)	623,076	(79%)	
	Frank Tunney Allen (D)	88,198	(11%)	
	Allen J. Ellender (D)	73,088	(9%)	

 **Gov. Edwin W. Edwards (D)** Elected Feb. 1, 1972, term expires May, 1976; b. Aug. 7, 1927, Marksville; La. St. U., LL.B. 1949; Catholic.

Career Practicing atty.; Crowley City Cncl., 1954–62; La. Senate, 1964–65; U.S. House of Reps., 1965–72.

Offices State of La., Exec. Dept., Baton Rouge 70801, 504-389-5281.

Election Results

1972 general:	Edwin W. Edwards (D)	641,146	(57%)
	David C. Treen (R)	480,424	(43%)
1971 run-off:	Edwin W. Edwards (D)	584,262	(50%)
	J. Bennett Johnston (D)	579,774	(50%)
1971 primary:	Edwin W. Edwards (D)	276,397	(24%)
	J. Bennett Johnston (D)	208,830	(18%)
	Gillis W. Long (D)	164,276	(14%)
	Jimmie H. Davis (D)	138,756	(12%)
	Thirteen Others (D)	385,784	(33%)

◆ ◆ ◆ ◆

FIRST DISTRICT

Louisiana's 1st congressional district includes the northern and eastern parts of New Orleans and two parishes astride the lower Mississippi River. This is not the glamorous, tourist's part of New Orleans; the district boundary passes just north of the French Quarter, and includes an almost entirely residential part of the city. These are the basementless houses, built on oozy land below sea level, where the ordinary people of New Orleans live. Some, on streets stretching out toward Lake Pontchartrain, are modern 1950s vintage houses, the homes of the city's solid middle class; others are rickety frame homes for poor blacks or whites. (New Orleans has no black ghetto as such; there are blacks in most parts of the city.) Farther east, but still within the city limits, lies a swamp that stretches to the Mississippi border; it is just beginning to be reclaimed, and to be populated with giant apartment complexes and shopping centers.

A more famous part of the 1st district are the two small parishes, Plaquemines and St. Bernard. Here in the delta lands of the Mississippi River are insular communities of French-speaking river pilots and shrimp fishermen. Politics here is a serious business, controlled by men like the late Leander Perez of Plaquemines. Once a Huey Long supporter, Perez was such an ardent segregationist that he was excommunicated by the Catholic Church; but he could still deliver virtually all the votes in Plaquemines. Today his son continues machine control with only slightly reduced effectiveness; evidence appears in the 1972 Senate returns, as Plaquemines was one of only three parishes to go for former Governor John McKeithen over Senator Bennett Johnston.

The stakes in Plaquemines are not just segregation. This is rich oil country, with large offshore deposits; local landowners, among them very much the Perezes, are in a position to become very wealthy indeed. Obviously, it is convenient in such circumstances to have iron control of the local government. St. Bernard Parish used to have machine control almost as solid as Plaquemines; but there has been too much suburban expansion now, diluting the vote-power of the small communities which are the bulwark of machine support. Still, the vote here is solidly Wallace-conservative.

Congressional elections here have been won without fail since 1940 by Congressman F. Edward Hebert (pronounced ay-BEAR). It tells you something about how the seniority system operates that Hebert became Chairman of the House Armed Services Committee at the age of 70 after 30 years in Congress, and that when he was deposed as Chairman four years later by a Democratic majority clearly and totally opposed to his policy positions, many oldtimers thought it was an outrage. Hebert first came to Washington when the draft and Lend-Lease were subjects of heated controversy—and exceedingly close votes in the House. He was then, and is now, and more now, a man firmly convinced that military preparedness is an absolute necessity, and that it is better to spend too much on defense than to risk not having spent enough. He is also a believer in the notion, favored by his predecessors as Chairman, Carl Vinson of Georgia and Mendel Rivers of South Carolina, that the Pentagon ought to spend huge sums of money in the Chairman's home district. In the four years that Hebert was Chairman, the Pentagon pumped more than $100,000,000 into the New Orleans area—which previously had had relatively few defense installations for a port city.

Even his adversaries admitted that Hebert was a fairer Chairman than his predecessor Rivers, who for years combined arbitrariness with alcoholism. Hebert even went so far as to appoint one of the Committee's ranking doves, Lucien Nedzi of Michigan, to head the Intelligence Subcommittee, although he was careful also to see that all the other members were senior hawks—which may be one reason the Subcommittee never uncovered any of the CIA's shennanigans. Hebert also fought the assignment of even the few liberals, like Pat Schroeder and Ron Dellums, to what he persisted in seeing as his committee.

Hebert's downfall came after the 1974 elections, when the committee chairmen were asked to speak before the freshman caucus. With his usual New Orleans accent (which sounds something like Jersey City), Hebert was abrupt and unforthcoming; he obviously had contempt for the predominantly dovish freshmen, and he didn't mind letting them know it. What he apparently didn't realize was that they had the votes to finish him off. The Steering Committee had, by a narrow margin, recommended Hebert's retention, but the caucus disagreed by a 152–133 vote. Stung and surprised, Hebert said he would seek election on the floor, arguing that between Republicans and hawkish Democrats he had a majority in the full House. It was a lame argument; Democrats who would have voted for him had he won caucus approval would not touch him any more even if they agreed with his views, and the leadership of both parties let it be known that any one who voted for him risked losing their seniority.

Now Hebert sits rather forlornly as the number two Democrat on Armed Services, below his friend and new Chairman Mel Price of Illinois (who did not seek the job). He remains Chairman of the Investigations Subcommittee, and can still sometimes be heard bellowing like an old bull on the floor. But at 75, with no prospect of winning the Chair back, one wonders how long Hebert will want to remain in Congress.

Census Data Pop. 454,873. Central city, 69%; suburban, 25%. Median family income, $8,655; families above $15,000: 18%; families below $3,000: 14%. Median years education, 11.3.

The Voters

Median voting age 42.
Employment profile White collar, 52%. Blue collar, 34%. Service, 14%. Farm, –%.
Ethnic groups Black, 31%. Spanish, 4%. Total foreign stock, 7%. Italy, 2%; French-speaking, 8%.

Presidential vote

1972	Nixon (R)	91,347	(71%)
	McGovern (D)	37,676	(29%)
1968	Nixon (R)	36,495	(25%)
	Humphrey (D)	41,953	(29%)
	Wallace (AI)	66,056	(46%)

Rep. F. Edward Hebert (D) Elected 1940; b. Oct. 12, 1901, New Orleans; home, New Orleans; Tulane U., 1920–24; Catholic.

Career Asst. Sports Ed., New Orleans *Times-Picayune*; Promotion Dir., reporter, feature writer, columnist, and City Ed., New Orleans *States*.

Offices 2340 RHOB, 202-225-3015. Also 642 Fed. Bldg., 600 South St., New Orleans 70130, 504-589-2279.

Committees

Armed Services (2d). Subcommittees: Investigations (Chairman); Military Personnel; Special Subcommittee on Intelligence.

Group Ratings

	ADA	COPE	LWV	RIPON	NFU	LCV	CFA	NAB	NSI	ACA
1974	6	0	17	25	25	0	0	67	100	75
1973	6	30	44	40	63	29	50	–	–	60
1972	0	17	13	38	0	0	–	50	100	63

Key Votes

1) Foreign Aid	FOR	6) Gov Abortn Aid	AGN	11) Pub Cong Election $	AGN
2) Busing	AGN	7) Coed Phys Ed	AGN	12) Turkish Arms Cutoff	ABS
3) ABM	FOR	8) Pov Lawyer Gag	ABS	13) Youth Camp Regs	AGN
4) B-1 Bomber	FOR	9) Pub Trans Sub	ABS	14) Strip Mine Veto	FOR
5) Nerve Gas	FOR	10) EZ Voter Regis	AGN	15) Farm Bill Veto	FOR

Election Results

1974 general:	F. Edward Hebert (D), unopposed			($4,712)
1974 primary:	F. Edward Hebert (D)	65,443	(81%)	
	Two others (D)	15,782	(19%)	
1972 general:	F. Edward Hebert (D), unopposed			($500)

◆ ◆ ◆ ◆ ◆

SECOND DISTRICT

Since New Orleans fell into American hands with the Louisiana Purchase of 1803, it has been one of America's most cosmopolitan cities. The heritage of the city's French and Spanish past can still be seen in the French Quarter, where carefully preserved old houses with their iron balconies exist amid the swelter of tourist-packed bars and some of the nation's finest restaurants. New Orleans remains the nation's second busiest port, adding to its historic role as the outlet of the Mississippi Valley and entrepot of Latin American trade, the new function of shipping out much of Louisiana's oil in huge tankers.

It is the older, more distinctive part of New Orleans which makes up most of Louisiana's 2d congressional district. It begins at the French Quarter, its nineteenth century houses intact because the Americans built a new downtown to the west, to avoid the unfriendly, snobbish Creoles. Beyond that is the old slum known as the Irish Channel—New Orleans had more European immigration than any other part of the South—and the Garden District, with its antebellum houses covered with tangles of vines and Spanish moss. America's last trolley cars still run out to the Uptown section of large houses out near Tulane. The 2d includes most of New Orleans's richest citizens, but more than half the residents of this part of the city are black; and the blacks here, unlike those in rural Louisiana, have a long, steady tradition of voting on election day. They provide, for example, solid support to the city's surprisingly liberal Mayor, Moon Landrieu.

Besides New Orleans, the 2d district takes in part of suburban Jefferson Parish. The parish extends south through the swamps to Barataria Bay, where the pirate Jean Lafitte hung out before he ventured forth to help Andrew Jackson whip the British in 1815. The 2d's portion of Jefferson includes the old, small cities along the banks of the Mississippi which gave the parish, once upon a time, a reputation for vice and corruption; the district does not include the prosperous, fast-growing, conservative suburb of Metairie just south of Lake Pontchartrain.

From 1941 to 1943 and 1947 to 1972—28 years altogether—the 2d district was represented by Hale Boggs. He won his first race as a rebel against the local machine and after a spirited struggle in 1971 became House Majority Leader—just a step away from the Speaker's chair. Boggs's career ended suddenly in October 1972, when he was lost in a plane crash while campaigning with freshman Nick Begich of Alaska. Boggs was a mercurial man: a stirring oldtime orator, a gifted trader of votes, a Southerner who had a strong liberal record and had even dared to support the Civil Rights Acts of 1965 and 1968.

It is ironic that Boggs died just at the time when the Louisiana legislature had finally drawn an utterly safe seat for him. In 1964 and 1968, he had only barely survived strong challenges from Republican David Treen; in the latter year, his civil rights votes hurt him so much in the white wards of New Orleans and Jefferson Parish that he won by only a 51–49 margin. But in the current 2d, which is 40% black, he was easily reelected posthumously in 1972.

The Majority Leader's successor in the House is his widow, Lindy Boggs, who won a 1973 special election with 81% of the vote. Often when a congressman dies, his widow is elected as a temporary expedient; but this is not the case with Lindy Boggs. For many years she was rated as one of the most knowledgeable of congressional wives, and enjoyed wide respect in Washington. The worst anyone had to say about her was that she seemed sometimes just a little too nice to people. She has the manners of a girl raised on a plantation (which she was) and the political savvy of one who has been campaigning in New Orleans and living in Washington for 30 years (which she has). In the House, Mrs. Boggs has not been a particularly voluble member; she has voted a solid liberal line—which has meant declining the lead of New Orleans's other Congressman, the hawkish Edward Hebert.

Census Data Pop. 454,772. Central city, 61%; suburban, 39%. Median family income, $7,611; families above $15,000: 14%; families below $3,000: 18%. Median years education, 10.5.

The Voters

Median voting age 42.
Employment profile White collar, 47%. Blue collar, 35%. Service, 18%. Farm, –%.
Ethnic groups Black, 40%. Spanish, 4%. Total foreign stock, 8%. Italy, 1%; French-speaking, 11%.

Presidential vote

1972	Nixon (R)	65,036	(60%)
	McGovern (D)	43,702	(40%)
1968	Nixon (R)	31,993	(25%)
	Humphrey (D)	51,221	(40%)
	Wallace (AI)	45,894	(36%)

Rep. Lindy Boggs (D) Elected Mar. 20, 1973; b. Mar. 13, 1916, Brunswick Plantation; home, New Orleans; Sophie Newcomb Col. of Tulane U., B.A. 1935; Catholic.

Career Public school teacher; Gen. Mgr., campaigns of U.S. Rep. Hale Boggs; Co-Chm., Presidental Inaugural Balls, 1961, 1965.

Offices 1519 LHOB, 202-225-6636. Also Old. Fed. Bldg., 600 South St., New Orleans 70130, 504-589-2274.

Committees

Banking, Currency and Housing (16th). Subcommittees: Financial Institutions Supervision, Regulation and Insurance; Housing and Community Development; International Development Institutions and Finance.

House Administration (16th). Subcommittees: Elections; Library and Memorials; Ad Hoc Computer.

Group Ratings

	ADA	COPE	LWV	RIPON	NFU	LCV	CFA	NAB	NSI	ACA
1974	36	70	83	50	75	71	17	0	75	15
1973	73	91	91	67	100	74	75	–	–	10

Key Votes

1) Foreign Aid	FOR	6) Gov Abortn Aid	AGN	11) Pub Cong Election $	FOR
2) Busing	AGN	7) Coed Phys Ed	FOR	12) Turkish Arms Cutoff	FOR
3) ABM	FOR	8) Pov Lawyer Gag	AGN	13) Youth Camp Regs	FOR
4) B-1 Bomber	FOR	9) Pub Trans Sub	FOR	14) Strip Mine Veto	AGN
5) Nerve Gas	FOR	10) EZ Voter Regis	AGN	15) Farm Bill Veto	AGN

Election Results

1974 general:	Lindy (Mrs. Hale) Boggs (D)	53,802	(82%)	($49,846)
	Mrs. Diane Morphos (R)	9,632	(15%)	($7,192)
	Jules W. "Ted" Hillery (Ind.)	2,322	(4%)	($100)
1973 special:	Mrs. Hale "Lindy" Boggs (D)	43,255	(81%)	(NA)
1974 primary:	Lindy (Mrs. Hale) Boggs (D)	64,466	(87%)	
	Charles E. Clark (D)	6,840	(9%)	
	Rodney Fertel (D)	2,428	(3%)	
	Robert E. Lee (R)	10,315	(19%)	(NA)

◆ ◆ ◆ ◆ ◆

THIRD DISTRICT

Question: how does one go about becoming the first Republican member of Congress from Louisiana in the twentieth century? Answer: by trying, and trying, and trying again. That's how David Treen, now in his second term as Congressman from Louisiana's 3d district, did it. Back in 1964, when Barry Goldwater swept the state, Treen ran against Hale Boggs in the 2d district and got 45% of the vote. Four years later, he tried again and did even better with 49%. Both times, the big issue for Treen, a hard-line conservative, was civil rights.

Those two races occurred in the old 2d district, whose boundaries have since been redrawn considerably. After a 1971 gubernatorial race in which he got a respectable 43% of the vote, Treen decided to run for Congress again in 1972. This time he decided to run in the redistricted 3d. On first glance, this district looks like unlikely territory for a Republican. Most of the physical expanse of the 3d is Cajun country—miles of bayou and swamp giving way from time to time to little towns and crossroads where French remains the first language.

But 36% of the 3d's population (and more than 40% of its votes) are in suburban Jefferson Parish, just west of New Orleans. And most of that is the suburb of Metairie, Treen's political base. Here the lowlands between the Mississippi River levees and Lake Pontchartrain have been drained and subdivided, and filled with the kind of middle-income people who have little use for either the drawbacks or the charms of the city of New Orleans. The 3d's share of Metairie is 99% white (a small black ghetto is in the 2d district now), and pleased to remain that way; it votes extremely conservative. Treen had carried Metairie by solid margins before, and in 1972 it produced Richard Nixon's largest margins in Louisiana.

Treen had other things going for him. Incumbent Patrick Caffery, though only 40, had decided to retire from Congress. The winner of the Democratic primary was a man whose only real strength was in his remote home parish. Treen's hard campaigning won him 41% of the vote in the district outside Jefferson, and there he had a solid 73%—enough for a 54-46 margin. In 1974, Treen improved that percentage to 59%, despite the Democratic trend in the rest of the nation. In Washington he is a member, and thanks to recent defeats and retirements a high-ranking one, of the House Armed Services Committee, where he votes comfortably with the hawkish majority.

Census Data Pop. 455,575. Central city, 0%; suburban, 35%. Median family income, $9,146; families above $15,000: 16%; families below $3,000: 11%. Median years education, 11.3.

The Voters

Median voting age 38.
Employment profile White collar, 50%. Blue collar, 37%. Service, 11%. Farm, 2%.
Ethnic groups Black, 15%. Spanish, 2%. Total foreign stock, 5%. Italy, 1%; French-speaking, 29%.

Presidential vote

	1972	Nixon (R)	102,047	(76%)
		McGovern (D)	31,647	(24%)
	1968	Nixon (R)	40,392	(31%)
		Humphrey (D)	31,815	(24%)
		Wallace (AI)	58,934	(45%)

Rep. David C. Treen (R) Elected 1972; b. July 16, 1928, Baton Route; home, Metairie; Tulane U., B.A. 1948, LL.B. 1950; Methodist.

Career Practicing atty., 1950–51, 1957–72; Air Force, 1951–52; V.P. and Legal Counsel, Simplex Manufacturing Corp., 1952–57; Repub. nominee for U.S. House of Reps., 1962, 1964, 1968; Repub. nominee for Gov., 1972.

Offices 404 CHOB, 202-225-4031. Also Fed. Bldg., Suite 107, Houma 70360, 504-876-3033.

Committees

Armed Services (5th). Subcommittees: Military Compensation; Military Personnel.

Merchant Marine and Fisheries (7th). Subcommittees: Coast Guard and Navigation; Merchant Marine; Oceanography.

Group Ratings

	ADA	COPE	LWV	RIPON	NFU	LCV	CFA	NAB	NSI	ACA
1974	4	10	0	40	17	18	0	83	90	93
1973	0	10	17	33	16	11	0	–	–	100

Key Votes

1) Foreign Aid	AGN	6) Gov Abortn Aid	AGN	11) Pub Cong Election $	AGN
2) Busing	AGN	7) Coed Phys Ed	AGN	12) Turkish Arms Cutoff	FOR
3) ABM	FOR	8) Pov Lawyer Gag	FOR	13) Youth Camp Regs	AGN
4) B-1 Bomber	FOR	9) Pub Trans Sub	AGN	14) Strip Mine Veto	FOR
5) Nerve Gas	FOR	10) EZ Voter Regis	AGN	15) Farm Bill Veto	AGN

Election Results

1974 general:	David C. Treen (R)	55,574	(59%)	($190,135)
	Charles Grisbaum, Jr. (D)	39,412	(41%)	($173,627)
1974 primary:	David C. Treen (R), unopposed			
1972 general:	David C. Treen (R)	71.090	(54%)	($155,629)
	J. Louis Watkins (D)	60,521	(46%)	($229,767)

◆ ◆ ◆ ◆ ◆

FOURTH DISTRICT

Northern Louisiana is part of the Deep South, with none of the Creole ambiance of New Orleans or the French accents of the Cajun country. For 150 years, Baptist farmers have inhabited the upcountry hills around Shreveport, the commercial center and largest city (pop. 182,000) of the state's 4th congressional district. Shreveport itself is a town built by the descendants of the original Baptist settlers; with the discovery of oil some 30 years ago, the old farm-market town boomed. Only 15 miles from the Texas border, Shreveport is very close in spirit to the ultraconservative oil cities of east Texas.

The oldtime political tradition of the 4th is populist; it always supported Huey Long, who practiced law in Shreveport for a while. But more recently the district's political leanings can best be described as conservative—or at least that is the way the overwhelming majority of white voters here regard themselves. Solidly conservative is also the best description of the district's Congressman, Joe D. Waggoner, Jr., from the town of Plain Dealing. After winning a special election in 1961, Waggoner soon gained a reputation as a segregationist firebrand in the House of Representatives. Now with a seat on the Ways and Means Committee, he seems to have become one of the leading strategists of the conservative Southern Democrats.

Years ago, such an unofficial position would have made Waggoner the uncrowned king of the House. But today—and even before the crop of Democratic freshmen elected in 1974—Waggoner is not nearly so important a force. Twenty-five years ago, virtually everyone of the 100-odd

Southern House seats was held by a conservative Democrat; today, far less than half are. Moreover, with the caucus voting out conservative Southern committee chairmen, people like Waggoner can no longer count on seniority to give them automatic power. Indeed, the most poignant example of that is Waggoner's close friend, Wilbur Mills. If Mills had collapsed some years ago as he did in the fall of 1974, he might well have kept the Ways and Means chair; but with the new freshmen ready to vote him out, he had to resign it before they could take it away. The man who had to bring that melancholy news to Mills in Bethesda Hospital was Joe Waggoner; if one wants a tableau to illustrate the change in the ways of the House, the picture of the two Southerners conferring over a hospital bed would have to be it.

Census Data Pop. 455,272. Central city, 40%; suburban, 25%. Median family income, $7,336; families above $15,000: 11%; families below $3,000: 19%. Median years education, 11.5.

The Voters

Median voting age 41.
Employment profile White collar, 44%. Blue collar, 37%. Service, 17%. Farm, 2%.
Ethnic groups Black, 31%. Spanish, 1%. Total foreign stock, 3%.

Presidential vote

1972	Nixon (R)	89,754	(75%)
	McGovern (D)	29,203	(25%)
1968	Nixon (R)	32,635	(25%)
	Humphrey (D)	31,842	(24%)
	Wallace (AI)	66,398	(51%)

Rep. Joe D. Waggoner, Jr. (D) Elected Dec. 19, 1961; b. Sept. 7, 1918, near Plain Dealing; home, Plain Dealing; La. Polytechnic Inst., B.A. 1941; Methodist.

Career Army, WWII and Korea; Wholesale petroleum products distribution business, 1952–61; Bossier Parish School Bd., 1954–61, Pres., 1956–57; Mbr., La. St. Bd. of Educ., 1960–61.

Offices 221 CHOB, 202-225-2777. Also 500 Fannin St., Shreveport 71101, 318-226-5080.

Committees

Ways and Means (12th). Subcommittees: Health; Public Assistance; Social Security.

Group Ratings

	ADA	COPE	LWV	RIPON	NFU	LCV	CFA	NAB	NSI	ACA
1974	0	18	0	27	36	19	15	75	90	93
1973	0	20	17	13	65	0	13	–	–	78
1972	0	27	10	29	57	11	0	73	100	86

Key Votes

1) Foreign Aid	AGN	6) Gov Abortn Aid	ABS	11) Pub Cong Election $	AGN
2) Busing	AGN	7) Coed Phys Ed	AGN	12) Turkish Arms Cutoff	AGN
3) ABM	FOR	8) Pov Lawyer Gag	FOR	13) Youth Camp Regs	AGN
4) B-1 Bomber	FOR	9) Pub Trans Sub	AGN	14) Strip Mine Veto	FOR
5) Nerve Gas	FOR	10) EZ Voter Regis	AGN	15) Farm Bill Veto	AGN

Election Results

1974 general:	Joe D. Waggonner, Jr. (D), unopposed ..	($3,459)
1974 primary:	Joe D. Waggonner, Jr. (D), unopposed	
1972 general:	Joe D. Waggonner, Jr. (D), unopposed ..	($1,596)

◆ ◆ ◆ ◆ ◆

FIFTH DISTRICT

The upcountry 5th congressional district of Louisiana, the state's most rural, is part of the Deep South. Aside from the city of Monroe (pop. 56,000), the 5th has no urban center of any consequence. The agricultural establishments in this cotton and piney woods country range from large plantations along the Mississippi River to the small, poor hill farms in places like Winn Parish, the boyhood home of Huey P. Long. The 5th has the third highest black population (35% in 1970) of any of Louisiana's congressional districts; but here, unlike the 2d in New Orleans, blacks have little leverage. The usually monolithic white majority is firmly in control.

Since 1946, the 5th district has been represented by Otto E. Passman, a staunch conservative and stern critic of government spending. Passman is now the fourth-ranking Democrat on the House Appropriations Committee and Chairman of its Foreign Operations Subcommittee. Back in the 1950s and 1960s, Passman earned the reputation as the scourge of the foreign aid program, inevitably cutting its budget and subjecting many of its projects to ridicule. What Passman apparently found objectionable was the idea of giving money to funny-colored foreigners; the huge military aid projects currently under attack by liberals never seem to have bothered him at all.

Passman is an excitable man, one who twitches and jitters so much when he speaks that one colleague said he was the only man he knew who wears out his suits from the inside. For years, he grew accustomed to having no opposition in his district. But in 1972 a weak challenger held him to 61% of the vote—just 11% above the figure that would have forced him into a runoff. Passman is 76 now, and traditionally when an old officeholder is forced into a runoff, he is through politically. Probably somewhere in the 5th district there is an ambitious young politician —probably almost as conservative as Passman—who will take the old man on in the next election or so and beat him, if Passman doesn't retire first.

Census Data Pop. 455,205. Central city, 12%; suburban, 13%. Median family income, $5,762; families above $15,000: 8%; families below $3,000: 27%. Median years education, 10.1.

The Voters

Median voting age 44.
Employment profile White collar, 40%. Blue collar, 37%. Service, 16%. Farm, 7%.
Ethnic groups Black, 35%. Total foreign stock, 1%.

Presidential vote

1972	Nixon (R)	97,039	(73%)
	McGovern (D)	35,213	(27%)
1968	Nixon (R)	30,367	(21%)
	Humphrey (D)	33,068	(23%)
	Wallace (AI)	82,988	(57%)

Rep. Otto E. Passman (D) Elected 1946; b. June 27, 1900, near Franklinton; home, Monroe; Baptist.

Career Owner, Passman Investment Co.; Navy, WWII.

Offices 2108 RHOB, 202-225-2376. Also P.O. Box 6000, New P.O. Bldg., Monroe 71201, 318-387-1800.

Committees

Appropriations (4th). Subcommittees: Agriculture and Related Agencies; Foreign Operations.

Group Ratings

	ADA	COPE	LWV	RIPON	NFU	LCV	CFA	NAB	NSI	ACA
1974	5	40	11	29	50	25	0	50	90	75
1973	17	60	27	0	85	22	29	–	–	54
1972	6	43	17	38	40	7	0	86	100	80

Key Votes

1) Foreign Aid	FOR	6) Gov Abortn Aid	ABS	11) Pub Cong Election $	AGN
2) Busing	AGN	7) Coed Phys Ed	AGN	12) Turkish Arms Cutoff	AGN
3) ABM	FOR	8) Pov Lawyer Gag	AGN	13) Youth Camp Regs	AGN
4) B-1 Bomber	FOR	9) Pub Trans Sub	ABS	14) Strip Mine Veto	AGN
5) Nerve Gas	FOR	10) EZ Voter Regis	AGN	15) Farm Bill Veto	AGN

Election Results

1974 general:	Otto E. Passman (D), unopposed			($23,902)
1974 primary:	Otto E. Passman (D)	64,831	(75%)	
	Frank Tunney "Demp" Allen (D)	21,566	(25%)	
1972 general:	Otto E. Passman (D), unopposed			($37,545)

◆ ◆ ◆ ◆ ◆

SIXTH DISTRICT

When Governor-elect Huey P. Long moved to Baton Rouge in 1928, the Louisiana capital was a small, sleepy Southern town, with a population of 30,000. Today, Baton Rouge is a bustling, fast-growing city of 165,000—and the change is thanks both to the Kingfish and his bitterest political enemies. It was Long who built a major university in Baton Rouge (Louisiana State) as well as increasing vastly the size and scope of the state government. And it was his old enemies, the oil companies, who built the big refineries and petrochemical plants, the other basis of Baton Rouge's prosperity. Baton Rouge and its suburban fringe make up about half of Louisiana's 6th congressional district. The remainder is to the east, in farming and piney woods country; the most notable city here is Bogalusa (pop. 18,000), a lumber mill town on the Mississippi line and the scene over the years of Ku Klux Klan activity.

Petrochemicals and hooded robes have made a volatile political mix in the 6th district, which in recent years has experienced feverish congressional elections. So feverish were they that the district ended up electing a Republican Congressman in a special election in 1975. But the central figure in all these struggles is not the new Congressman but the old one, Representative John Rarick.

Aficionados of right-wing hate literature are going to miss Rarick, because he could be counted on to reprint in the *Congressional Record* just about any far right, anti-Semitic, or anti-black bilge that came across his desk. For eight years Rarick, originally a Yankee from Indiana, was the most rabidly right wing member of the House. Even other Southern conservatives had little use for him, and back home his strident, voluble rhetoric continually got him in trouble in his home town, Baton Rouge, a place not known for its liberalism.

Rarick's strength was in the rural parishes where memory of Klan activities has not died. That was where he won the votes necessary to beat 28-year House veteran Jimmy Morrison, a kind of Southern moderate, in the 1966 Democratic primary. It was the rural parishes that got him through again in 1968, when he got only 36% of the votes in Baton Rouge and was forced into a runoff; it was the rural parishes where he piled up enough votes to barely avoid runoffs in 1970 and 1972.

But in 1974 the rural parishes were not enough. Most Congressmen, once in office, quickly move into a position of political invulnerability; Rarick seemed to get more and more beatable. His main opponent in the 1974 primary was 29-year-old Baton Rouge sportscaster Jeff LaCaze, and when the counting was over LaCaze had won. But that was not the end of the story. There was—unusual for this district—a Republican candidate, 35-year-old Baton Rouge attorney W. Henson Moore, III, a staunch conservative. While LaCaze was receiving support from labor unions—eager to elect a friendly Congressman in this unlikely district—and blacks, Moore was attacking him for it—and inheriting Rarick's hard-core support. The November election was, literally, inconclusive. Moore had a 44-vote lead, but in one black Baton Rouge precinct where other Democrats had received several hundred votes, the voting maching lever next to Lacaze's name was stuck. He probably received more votes than his opponent, but we'll never know. The Louisiana Supreme Court ordered the race run again. This time, in early 1975, Moore hit Lacaze harder and harder, and with strong support from the rural parishes Rarick always carried won a solid victory. There are no signs yet that he will be as controversial a Congressman as Rarick was; given that, and the general propensity of voters to reelect incumbents, he may well have little difficulty winning again in 1976.

Census Data Pop. 456,178. Central city, 36%; suburban, 26%. Median family income, $8,230; families above $15,000: 16%; families below $3,000: 17%. Median years education, 12.0.

The Voters

Median voting age 39.
Employment profile White collar, 48%. Blue collar, 34%. Service, 15%. Farm, 3%.
Ethnic groups Black, 30%. Spanish, 1%. Total foreign stock, 3%. French-speaking 4%.

Presidential vote

1972	Nixon (R)	83,246	(70%)
	McGovern (D)	36,240	(30%)
1968	Nixon (R)	27,875	(21%)
	Humphrey (D)	33,967	(25%)
	Wallace (AI)	72,966	(54%)

Rep. W. Henson Moore (R) Elected Jan. 7, 1975; b. Oct. 4, 1939, Lake Charles; home, Baton Rouge; La. St. U., B.A. 1961, J.D. 1965, M.A. 1973; Episcopalian.

Career Army, 1965–67; Practicing atty., 1967–74.

Offices 427 CHOB, 202-225-3901. Also Rm. 236, Fed. Bldg., 750 Fla. Blvd., Baton Rouge 70801, 504-344-7679.

Committees

Agriculture (14th). Subcommittees: Cotton; Oilseeds and Rice; Tobacco.

House Administration (8th). Subcommittees: Elections; Electrical and Mechanical Office Equipment; Library and Memorials; Ad Hoc Computer.

Group Ratings: Newly Elected

Key Votes

1) Foreign Aid	AGN	6) Gov Abortn Aid	NE	11) Pub Cong Election $	NE
2) Busing	NE	7) Coed Phys Ed	AGN	12) Turkish Arms Cutoff	NE
3) ABM	NE	8) Pov Lawyer Gag	NE	13) Youth Camp Regs	AGN
4) B-1 Bomber	FOR	9) Pub Trans Sub	NE	14) Strip Mine Veto	FOR
5) Nerve Gas	NE	10) EZ Voter Regis	NE	15) Farm Bill Veto	AGN

Election Results

1975 Special:	W. Henson Moore (R)	74,802	(54%)	($158,971)
	Jeff La Caze (D)	63,366	(46%)	($229,335)
1974 primary:	W. Henson Moore (R), unopposed			

◆ ◆ ◆ ◆ ◆

SEVENTH DISTRICT

The 7th congressional district of Louisiana is one of the very few in the nation where nearly half the population grew up speaking a language other than English. Here the language is French, Cajun style, and it is the mother tongue of 44% of the 7th's residents. The district hugs the Gulf coast of Louisiana, as it moves east to west from the swamps of the Atchafalaya River through Lafayette (pop. 69,000) across to Lake Charles (pop. 78,000) and the Texas border.

Many rural backwaters like this are now depopulated and their traditions dying; not so the Cajun country in Louisiana. What has kept the people here is oil, in plenteous quantity under the swampy soil, with even more below the Gulf a few miles out to sea. Oil and attendant industries have provided jobs here while the rest of the country suffers through recession, and they have provided the money to keep all the Cajuns who wish to remain in their homeland. Beyond that, the Cajuns themselves increasingly are working to promote the use of French and to hold on to their regional traditions.

Naturally it was a source of great pride in these parts when 7th district Congressman Edwin W. Edwards—very much a Cajun, despite his name—was elected Governor in 1972. Edwards's successor in the House is a former member of his staff, John B. Breaux, also of French origin. His election in 1972, however, was by no means automatic. Breaux led a six-man Democratic primary, but his 42% of the vote was not enough to avoid a runoff. The second race was fundamentally a contest between Breaux's dominance in the eastern, more Cajun half of the district and his opponent's strength in his home area around Lake Charles. Breaux won with 55% of the vote, piling up bigger margins in the Cajun parishes than his opponent could in the west.

Breaux was the youngest member of the 93d Congress, and the vice-chairman of the freshman Democratic caucus. That body, however, was considerably less active than its counterpart in the 94th; there were far fewer freshman Democrats elected in 1972, and they were more split on the issues. Breaux, for example, did not turn out to have quite as liberal a voting record as his age had led some to expect. Now, at 32, Breaux is a comparatively senior young Democrat, with seats on the pork-barreling Public Works and Merchant Marine and Fisheries Committees. His lack of effective opposition in 1974 suggests that he will have little trouble winning reelection in future years.

Census Data Pop. 455,014. Central city, 32%; suburban, 24%. Median family income, $7,197; families above $15,000: 11%; families below $3,000: 19%. Median years education, 10.2.

The Voters

Median voting age 41.
Employment profile White collar, 42%. Blue collar, 38%. Service, 15%. Farm, 5%.
Ethnic groups Black, 21%. Total foreign stock, 2%. French-speaking, 44%.

Presidential vote

1972	Nixon (R)	85,502	(68%)
	McGovern (D)	41,032	(32%)
1968	Nixon (R)	32,953	(24%)
	Humphrey (D)	39,560	(28%)
	Wallace (AI)	67,241	(48%)

Rep. John B. Breaux (D) Elected Sept. 30, 1972; b. Mar. 1, 1944, Crowley; home, Crowley; U. of S.W. La., B.A. 1964, La. St. U., J.D. 1967; Catholic.

Career Practicing atty., 1967–68; Legis. Asst., Dist. Mgr. to U.S. Rep. Edwin W. Edwards, 1968–72.

Offices 204 CHOB, 202-225-2031. Also 2530 P.O. and Fed. Bldg., Lake Charles 70601, 318-433-1122.

Committees

Merchant Marine and Fisheries (13th). Subcommittees: Fisheries and Wildlife Conservation and the Environment; Merchant Marine; Oceanography.

Public Works and Transportation (13th). Subcommittees: Economic Development; Investigations and Review; Surface Transportation; Water Resources.

Group Ratings

	ADA	COPE	LWV	RIPON	NFU	LCV	CFA	NAB	NSI	ACA
1974	14	40	30	33	64	21	15	30	89	54
1973	35	90	44	36	90	13	38	–	–	41

Key Votes

1) Foreign Aid	FOR	6) Gov Abortn Aid	ABS	11) Pub Cong Election $	AGN
2) Busing	AGN	7) Coed Phys Ed	AGN	12) Turkish Arms Cutoff	ABS
3) ABM	FOR	8) Pov Lawyer Gag	ABS	13) Youth Camp Regs	AGN
4) B-1 Bomber	FOR	9) Pub Trans Sub	FOR	14) Strip Mine Veto	FOR
5) Nerve Gas	FOR	10) EZ Voter Regis	AGN	15) Farm Bill Veto	AGN

Election Results

1974 general:	John B. Breaux (D)	59,406	(89%)	($29,991)
	Jeremy J. Millett (Ind)	7,131	(11%)	($1,618)
1974 primary:	John B. Breaux (D)	71,848	(87%)	
	J. Vernon Hebert (D)	10,289	(13%)	
1972 general:	John B. Breaux (D), unopposed			($137,420)

◆ ◆ ◆ ◆ ◆

EIGHTH DISTRICT

After the lines for seven of Louisiana's eight congressional districts were drawn, the territory remaining became the steamshovel-shaped 8th district—or so, at least, it seems. This is a seat which has no real common sense of identity and which crosses the state's long-established regional borders; it contains one parish where 96% of the churchgoers are Catholic, and another where Catholics are heavily outnumbered by Baptists. Geographically, the 8th is bounded on the east by Lake Pontchartrain; then it moves up along the Mississippi and Red Rivers to a point within 30 miles of the Texas border. Politically, there are three factors which explain its rather unusual political behavior.

The first of these is its large black population—36%, the second highest in the state. In the days before the Civil War, the old sugar and cotton plantations along the Mississippi required hundreds of slaves to do the work today, blacks form the major voting bloc in West Feliciana and Pointe Coupee Parishes. Second, the district also has a high Cajun population; they are found particularly in the southern part of the district, especially in St. Landry and Evangeline Parishes. And third, there is the legacy of the Long family. A decade ago, the 8th still included the Longs' home parish of Winn; that is now in the 5th, but this is still very much Kingfish country.

All three of these factors combine to make the 8th a politically more liberal district than one might suspect for a chunk of basically small city and rural Louisiana. The 8th has been willing to elect a number of fairly liberal Democrats—at least if their name was Long. Indeed, an understanding of the congressional politics here requires a knowledge of the Long family tree; since 1952, only one Democratic primary has been won by someone outside the family. In 1952, 1954, and 1956, the district elected George S. Long, one of Huey's brothers, whose memories of the Kingfish doubtless came out fonder after his death than they would have before. George died in 1958, and his successor was one Harold B. McSween. But in 1960, Earl K. Long, another Kingfish brother, won the Democratic primary just after leaving the Governor's office in circumstances described brilliantly in A. J. Liebling's *The Earl of Louisiana*. But shortly after the primary, Earl dropped dead, giving McSween a chance to win one more term.

McSween was through in 1962, when he was beaten by Gillis W. Long, a cousin, who in turn lost two years later to another cousin, Speedy O. Long. Speedy was probably the most conservative of the 8th district Longs; he served happily on the Armed Services Committee until he decided to retire in 1972. The winner this time once again was Gillis.

Gillis Long's return to Congress marks a significant shift in Southern congressional politics. The year Gillis lost, 1964, was the year the civil rights revolution pushed most white Southern voters into the arms of arch-conservative candidates likes Barry Goldwater; district after district, including the 8th, repudiated one hundred years of history and went Republican for President. For some years thereafter, when a southern candidate got tagged as a liberal, that was it—he lost, as Gillis Long lost in 1964. By 1968, when Richard Nixon was first elected President, Southern politics seemed to be perfectly polarized: the majority whites all voting one way, the minority blacks all the other.

By 1972 it seemed that those days were gone, at least if the 8th district is any guide. Against four opponents, Gillis Long won his primary without a runoff. He took the general election with a solid 69% against both Republican and American Party candidates. Even George McGovern ran notably better than Hubert Humphrey had four years before. Of course, the 8th is not the average

Southern district; but the trend seems to be one of general application. Politicians who are known vaguely as liberals can once again win elections in the South.

How much of a liberal is Gillis Long? Well, he isn't a northern freshman type of firebrand, but he does generally support the House leadership, and seldom can be found allying himself with conservative Republicans. That is why the leadership saw that he was given a seat on the House Rules Committee after the 1972 election. Long is also considered one of the most capable and adept legislators in the House. Ten years ago, his political survival would have been—was—in doubt; today, as the 1974 election returns show, he appears to be unbeatable.

Census Data   Pop. 456,291. Central city, 0%; suburban, 0%. Median family income, $6,092; families above $15,000: 8%; families below $3,000: 26%. Median years education, 9.2.

The Voters

Median voting age 42.
Employment profile White collar, 36%. Blue collar, 39%. Service, 17%. Farm, 8%.
Ethnic groups Black, 36%. Total foreign stock, 2%. French-speaking, 28%.

Presidential vote

1972	Nixon (R)	73,297	(63%)
	McGovern (D)	43,429	(37%)
1968	Nixon (R)	25,451	(18%)
	Humphrey (D)	46,398	(33%)
	Wallace (AI)	70,218	(49%)

Rep. Gillis W. Long (D)   Elected 1972; b. May 4, 1923, Winnfield; home, Alexandria; La. St. U., B.A. 1949, J.D. 1951; Baptist.

Career   Army, WWII; Legal Counsel, U.S. Senate Comm. on Small Business, 1951; Chf. Counsel, U.S. House of Reps. Special Comm. on Campaign Expenditures; U.S. House of Reps., 1963–65; Asst. Dir., U.S. Ofc. of Econ. Opportunity, 1965–66; Legis. Counsel, Natl. Commission of Urban Growth Policy, 1968–69; Practicing atty., 1970–72.

Offices   215 CHOB, 202-225-4926. Also P.O. Box 410, Alexandria 71301, 318-487-4595.

Committees

Rules (9th).

Joint Economic Committee (6th, House Side). Subcommittees: Consumer Economics; Economic Progress; Fiscal Policy; Inter-American Economic Relationships; Priorities and Economy in Government; Urban Affairs.

Group Ratings

	ADA	COPE	LWV	RIPON	NFU	LCV	CFA	NAB	NSI	ACA
1974	59	80	83	47	92	59	33	25	50	23
1973	40	91	58	57	89	47	71	–	–	27

Key Votes

1) Foreign Aid	FOR	6) Gov Abortn Aid	AGN	11) Pub Cong Election $	FOR
2) Busing	AGN	7) Coed Phys Ed	AGN	12) Turkish Arms Cutoff	ABS
3) ABM	AGN	8) Pov Lawyer Gag	AGN	13) Youth Camp Regs	AGN
4) B-1 Bomber	FOR	9) Pub Trans Sub	FOR	14) Strip Mine Veto	AGN
5) Nerve Gas	FOR	10) EZ Voter Regis	FOR	15) Farm Bill Veto	AGN

Election Results

1974 general: Gillis W. Long (D), unopposed ....   ($36,325)

1974 primary:	Gillis W. Lond (D), unopposed			
1972 general:	Gillis W. Long (D)	72,607	(69%)	($107,919)
	S. R. Abramson (AI)	17,844	(17%)	($20,835)
	Roy C. Strikland (R)	15,517	(15%)	($5,612)

MAINE

We have known for some time that precisely the opposite of "As Maine goes, so goes the nation," is true—at least since James Farley changed the saying, after FDR's 1936 landslide, to "As Maine goes, so goes Vermont." Indeed, the saying got its start not because Maine was an accurate bellwether, but because up through the 1950s it held its general elections in September, on the sensible theory that they should not be conducted on a day likely to be snowy and when darkness would come before 5 PM. In any case, Maine's political behavior today is almost perfectly countercyclical. Maine's Democrats, for example, captured the Governorship and both the state's congressional seats in the generally Republican year of 1966. And in the Democratic year of 1974, Republicans won both House seats and the Democrats and the Republicans lost the Governorship to James Longley, running as the sole candidate of the Longley for Maine Party.

Thus the story of Maine politics today centers on the rise and apparent fall of the Democratic Party in this state known for its rock-ribbed Republicanism since the time of the Civil War. Among the reasons for the Democratic ascendancy were intelligent organization, attractive candidates, and the carelessness of Maine Republicans, who had enjoyed too much easy success. A key factor was Edmund Muskie. His plain and sincere manner, coupled with his clearly honest idealism, convinced many Yankee Republicans that Democrats were not all big city hacks, and that Muskie and his followers were decent men who could be trusted with government. And so Muskie won the Governorship in an upset in 1954, was reelected in 1956 with a solid 59%, and in 1960 beat an incumbent Senator by a 61–39 margin. In the years that followed, Democrats won the Governorship three times, eventually captured the congressional seats, and finally captured the other Senate seat. In fact, Maine was just one of several far northern states where a popular leader and competent followers built a strong Democratic Party in a state previously considered Republican; there was also the Minnesota of Hubert Humphrey, the Wisconsin of William Proxmire and Gaylord Nelson, the Michigan of G. Mennen Williams, and the South Dakota of George McGovern. During the 1960s and '70s, a half-dozen presidential candidates emerged from these movements—evidence of their quality.

Democrats in Maine benefitted from the state's changing demography. As young people left economically depressed Maine, the proportion of its traditionally Democratic ethnic voters increased—particularly those of French-Canadian descent. Though the standard image of a state of Mainer is a taciturn Yankee, fully one out of seven people here grew up speaking French. French Canadian and other Catholic voters in mill towns like Lewiston or the potato country of Aroostook County usually turn in lopsided margins for Democrats; Muskie, for example, won 88% of the vote in Lewiston in 1970. These same voters were largely responsible for Richard Nixon's easy 1972 Maine victory, as ethnic voters switched massively away from the McGovern ticket.

In August, 1968, Edmund Muskie was still largely unknown nationally. But he already had more than his share of legislative accomplishments. He had turned his seat on the lackluster Public Works Committee into an asset, by painstakingly putting together water pollution legislation long before environmental causes became fashionable. As a Senator from Maine, Muskie was already aware of possible conflicts between environmental concerns and the need for economic development. They are most visible in places like Machiasport, a depressed spot on the Maine coast where an oil refinery was proposed; the area desperately needed the jobs, but at the same time the danger to the beautiful coastline was obvious. Overall, Muskie has probably done more than any other Senator to reconcile such conflicting goals on both the national and local levels.

But it was his selection as the Democrats' 1968 vice-presidential candidate that made Muskie a national figure. His quiet Yankee style, his willingness to let opponents speak their piece, impressed voters all over the country in a year of political turbulence. Two years later, Muskie's low key performance on television just before the elections, especially in contrast to Nixon's frenzied speech shown just before, made Muskie the Democratic frontrunner for 1972. But in the spring of that year, Muskie's seemingly strong campaign fell to pieces. There were too many high-level advisers, too many prominent endorsements, not enough understanding of the new delegate-selection process, and not enough first-choice votes. Running as the candidate of a nonexistent "center" of his party, Muskie was probably the clear number two choice of most primary voters in states like Wisconsin, Pennsylvania, and Massachusetts. But he could not win as many first-choice votes as had been expected, and his candidacy collapsed.

Another reason for the Muskie collapse, it now appears, was systematic sabotage by Nixon campaign operatives. No one can say what would have happened in New Hampshire and the primaries that followed had there been no "Canuck" letter sent to the rabidly anti-Muskie Manchester *Union Leader*. That was apparently a White House dirty trick, and it led directly to the so-called crying incident in the snow, which in turn severely damaged voters' estimate of Muskie's character.

Now Muskie seems to have renounced national ambitions—though he says he will accept a draft if it comes—and is concentrating on the Senate and on Maine. In 1973, while the Watergate revelations were coming out, Muskie worked with Sam Ervin to draft the legislation that created the congressional budget committees. The idea was to set up a mechanism to coordinate congressional policy on spending and taxation. In 1974 Muskie decided to leave his seat on Foreign Relations to become the Chairman of the Budget Committee.

Muskie's other priority became seeking reelection to the Senate in 1976. That may not seem to be so difficult for a man who has not received less than 61% of the vote in Maine in the last twenty years. But the election in 1972 and 1974 of two young Republican Congressmen has certain parallels to the emergence of Muskie's own Democrats ten to twenty years before. And even more disturbing to the Senator was the election of James Longley as Governor in 1974.

Longley had campaigned as a non-politician and the candidate of a political party of his own making. Born poor, he became a wealthy businessman; a registered Democrat, he was commissioned by Governor Kenneth Curtis to recommend possible savings in state government. His report purported to show how the state could save $23.8 million a year. He proceeded to trumpet that figure all over the state in his race against Democrat George Mitchell, a Muskie protege, and Republican James Erwin, who had lost to Curtis by only 890 votes four years before. At first Longley's chances were counted as poor as independents' usually are; but by the first of November, his campaign was catching on. He was making inroads in mill towns like Lewiston but, even more important, he was cutting heavily into what was left of traditional Yankee Republican vote. There was a bigger than usual turnout on election day—in itself a deviation from the national trend—and when the votes were counted Longley had 40%, compared to 37% for Mitchell and 23% for the unfortunate Erwin.

Once in office, Longley's oft-voiced contempt for politicians got him into constant embroilments with the legislature; he seemed to delight in stern denunciations often in scatological terms of anyone who disagreed even mildly with him. When one examined his platform, it suddenly became not at all clear how the state was going to save the amount of money he had promised. But even if his methods were crude and unavailing, he had obviously hit upon something in the public mood, and his showing scared politicians not only in Maine, but across the country.

The Longley victory was not the only surprise result in recent Maine elections. Another was the defeat of Senator Margaret Chase Smith in 1972. Mrs. Smith had been a fixture in state politics since 1940, when she succeeded her husband in the House; in 1948, she had won an upset primary victory and went on to the Senate. But by 1972 she was politically vulnerable. At 74 she seldom travelled back to Maine and did not even maintain an office in the state. She spurned the constituency service work which has helped so many members of Congress to win easy reelection. She enjoyed a reputation for political independence, breaking away from the Nixon Administration on the ABM, SST, Carswell, and Haynsworth. But increasingly she was voting like an orthodox Republican. As always, she hired no campaign staff, bought no advertising, and refused to appear in the state except on weekends; her only campaign events were receptions where voters—most of them seemed to be elderly ladies—could shake her hand if they wanted.

That sort of reticence had worked in the past, and it was enough to produce a solid primary victory over businessman Robert Monks, who spent over $200,000 on his challenge. But in the general election, Mrs. Smith's support from older WASP voters was not enough. Her opponent, Congressman William Hathaway, had solid support in his own 2d district (the northern part of the state) and conducted an energetic campaign. While Mrs. Smith held her weekend receptions, Hathaway visited everyone of the state's 495 cities, towns, and plantations, and it paid off. He carried his 2d district 57–43, and split the 1st evenly. In the Senate, Hathaway has emerged as a talented, articulate member; he serves on the important Finance and Labor and Public Welfare Committees, and would appear to have a safe seat.

Maine's congressional district lines were designed in the 1960s by a Republican legislature, and were intended to split the Democratic strength in the state between the two districts. The 1st contains Portland and the mill towns of York County to the south; the 2d includes Bangor, Lewiston, and Aroostook County in the far north, all Democratic strongholds now. The Yankee Republican counties along the coast are also split between the two districts. The Republican strategy backfired, as Democrats won the 2d district in 1964 (Hathaway) and the 1st in 1966 (Peter Kyros). But now, once again, both seats are in Republican hands. The latest change occurred in 1974, when 26-year-old state Representative David Emery unseated Kyros in the 1st. Apparently Kyros' abrasive personality had irritated enough of his constituents to allow the energetic young Republican to win an upset victory in this Democratic year. As a member of the minority party in a House increasingly dominated by the Democratic caucus, Emery is not likely to play a particularly important legislative role, but his achievement in winning the seat at all suggests that he will be a strong candidate in future years.

Maine's other Republican Congressman is 36-year-old William Cohen of Bangor, elected in 1972 to Hathaway's 2d district seat, also in an upset victory. Cohen became exceedingly well-known nationally in 1974 as a member of the House Judiciary Committee; he was one of the Republicans who voted to impeach Richard Nixon. In his clear voice and with poetic idiom, he made some of the most telling points against the Republicans who were defending the President, and he seems to have a bright political future. In 1974 he was opposed by that electoral rarity, an antiwar Vietnam POW; but Cohen won with a landslide 71% of the vote. He is mentioned frequently as the Republicans' best hope for winning statewide office, and Muskie and other Democrats take his chances seriously indeed. At this writing, Cohen has not decided whether to run against Muskie in 1976, or to wait for some future chance; he can of course easily win reelection to the House, but to go to the Senate he must beat one of Maine's champion votegetters.

Census Data Pop. 993,663; 0.49% of U.S. total, 38th largest; Central city, 13%; suburban, 8%. Median family income, $8,205; 36th highest; families above $15,000: 11%; families below $3,000: 10%. Median years education, 12.1.

1974 Share of Federal Tax Burden $990,917,000; 0.37% of U.S. total, 41st largest.

1974 Share of Federal Outlays $1,157,121,000; 0.43% of U.S. total, 39th largest. Per capita federal spending, $1165.

DOD	$241,598,000	40th (0.35%)	HEW	$499,162,000	37th (0.54%)
AEC	$114,000	38th (–)	HUD	$3,287,000	41st (0.34%)
NASA	$69,000	47th (–)	VA	$82,535,000	37th (0.60%)
DOT	$36,169,000	50th (0.43%)	EPA	$24,741,000	27th (0.79%)
DOC	$4,973,000	38th (0.31%)	RevS	$37,841,000	37th (0.63%)
DOI	$5,908,000	46th (0.24%)	Int.	$37,770,000	37th (0.18%)
USDA	$25,146,000	44th (0.20%)	Other	$157,808,000	

Economic Base Leather footwear, and other leather and leather products; paper and allied products, especially paper mills other than building paper; agriculture, notably potatoes, eggs, broilers and dairy products; finance, insurance and real estate; food and kindred products; lumber and wood products.

Political Line-up Governor, James B. Longley (Ind.). Senators, Edmund S. Muskie (D) and William D. Hathaway (D). Representatives, 2 R. State Senate (19 R and 14 D); State House (91 D, 59 R, and 1 Ind.).

The Voters

Registration 613,227 Total. 212,175 D (35%); 237,828 R (39%); 163,224 Not Enrolled (27%).
Median voting age 44.
Employment profile White collar, 41%. Blue collar, 44%. Service, 12%. Farm, 3%.
Ethnic groups Total foreign stock, 19%. Canada, 14%.

Presidential vote

1972	Nixon (R)	256,458	(61%)
	McGovern (D)	160,584	(39%)
1968	Nixon (R)	169,254	(43%)
	Humphrey (D)	217,312	(55%)
	Wallace (AI)	6,370	(2%)

Sen. Edmund S. Muskie (D) Elected 1958, seat up 1976; b. Mar. 28, 1914, Rumford; home, Waterville; Bates Col., B.A. 1936, Cornell U., LL.B. 1939; Catholic.

Career Practicing atty.; Navy, WWII; Maine House of Reps., 1947–51, Minor. Ldr., 1949–51; Dir., Maine Ofc. of Price Stabilization, 1951–52; Gov. of Maine, 1955–59; Dem. nominee for V.P., 1968.

Offices 145 RSOB, 202-224-5344. Also 112 Main St., Waterville 04901, 207-873-3361, and New Fed. Bldg., 151 Forest Ave., Portland 04101, 207-775-3131 ext. 561 or 562.

Committees

Budget (Chairman).

Government Operations (4th). Subcommittees: Intergovernmental Relations (Chairman); Reports, Accounting and Management; Oversight Procedures.

Public Works (2d). Subcommittees: Environmental Pollution (Chairman); Economic Development; Transportation.

Group Ratings

	ADA	COPE	LWV	RIPON	NFU	LCV	CFA	NAB	NSI	ACA
1974	100	73	78	61	100	78	100	33	0	0
1973	95	82	100	75	100	–	91	–	–	0
1972	70	86	100	64	80	85	100	0	11	0

Key Votes

1) No-Knock	AGN	8) Gov Abortn Aid	FOR	15) Consumer Prot Agy	FOR
2) Busing	FOR	9) Cut Mil Brass	AGN	16) Forced Psych Tests	FOR
3) No Fault	FOR	10) Gov Limousine	AGN	17) Fed Campaign Subs	FOR
4) F-111	AGN	11) RR Featherbed	FOR	18) Rhod Chrome Ban	FOR
5) Death Penalty	AGN	12) Handgun License	FOR	19) Open Legis Meetings	FOR
6) Foreign Aid	FOR	13) Less Troop Abrd	FOR	20) Strikers Food Stmps	FOR
7) Filibuster	AGN	14) Resume Turk Aid	FOR	21) Gov Info Disclosure	FOR

Election Results

1970 general:	Edmund S. Muskie (D)	199,954	(62%)
	Neil S. Bishop (R)	123,906	(38%)
1970 primary:	Edmund S. Muskie (D), unopposed		
1964 general:	Edmund S. Muskie (D)	253,511	(67%)
	Clifford G. McIntire (R)	127,040	(33%)

Sen. William D. Hathaway (D) Elected 1972, seat up 1978; b. Feb. 21, 1924, Cambridge, Mass.; home, Auburn; Harvard U., A.B. 1949, LL.B. 1953; Episcopalian.

Career Army Air Corps, WWII; Practicing atty., 1953–64; Asst. Androscoggin Co. Atty., 1955–57; Hearing Examiner, State Liquor Comm., 1957–61; U.S. House of Reps., 1965–73.

Offices 248 RSOB, 202-224-2523. Also 202 Harlow St., New Fed. Ofc. Bldg., Bangor 04401, 207-942-8271 ext. 310, and 40 Pine St., Lewiston 04240, 207-783-2049.

Committees

Finance (10th). Subcommittees: Energy; Financial Markets; Health; Revenue Sharing (Chairman); Supplemental Security Income.

Labor and Public Welfare (9th). Subcommittees: Alcoholism and Narcotics (Chairman); Children and Youth; Education; Employment, Poverty, and Migratory Labor; The Handicapped; Health; Labor.

Group Ratings

	ADA	COPE	LWV	RIPON	NFU	LCV	CFA	NAB	NSI	ACA
1974	95	82	100	64	100	81	100	33	0	0
1973	95	73	100	50	100	–	92	–	–	4
1972	81	100	90	69	86	67	50	8	0	4

Key Votes

1) No-Knock	AGN	8) Gov Abortn Aid	FOR	15) Consumer Prot Agy	FOR
2) Busing	FOR	9) Cut Mil Brass	FOR	16) Forced Psych Tests	FOR
3) No Fault	FOR	10) Gov Limousine	AGN	17) Fed Campaign Subs	FOR
4) F-111	AGN	11) RR Featherbed	AGN	18) Rhod Chrome Ban	FOR
5) Death Penalty	AGN	12) Handgun License	FOR	19) Open Legis Meetings	FOR
6) Foreign Aid	FOR	13) Less Troop Abrd	FOR	20) Strikers Food Stmps	FOR
7) Filibuster	FOR	14) Resume Turk Aid	ABS	21) Gov Info Disclosure	FOR

Election Results

1972 general:	William D. Hathaway (D)	224,270	(53%)	($202,208)
	Margaret Chase Smith (R)	197,040	(47%)	($14,950)
1972 primary:	William D. Hathaway (D)	61,921	(91%)	
	Jack Louis Smith (D)	6,263	(9%)	

Gov. James B. Longley (I) Elected 1974, term expires Jan. 1979; b. Apr. 22, 1924; Bowdoin Col., B.A. 1947, Amer. Col. of Life Underwriters, C.L.U. 1954, U. of Maine, LL.B. 1957.

Career Practicing atty.; Gen. Agent, New Eng. Mutual Life Ins. Co.; Lecturer and Instr., Amer. Col. of Life Underwriters, 1957–65.

Offices Augusta 04880, 207-289-3531.

Election Results

1974 general:	James B. Longley (Ind.)	142,464	(40%)
	George J. Mitchell (D)	132,219	(37%)
	James S. Erwin (R)	84,176	(23%)
1974 primary:	James B. Longley (Ind.), unopposed		

♦ ♦ ♦ ♦ ♦

FIRST DISTRICT

Census Data Pop. 495,681. Central city, 13%; suburban, 15%. Median family income, $8,688; families above $15,000: 13%; families below $3,000: 9%. Median years education, 12.2.

The Voters

Median voting age 45.
Employment profile White collar, 44%. Blue collar, 42%. Service, 12%. Farm, 2%.
Ethnic groups Total foreign stock, 18%. Canada, 11%.

Presidential vote

1972	Nixon (R)	135,388	(61%)
	McGovern (D)	85,028	(39%)
1968	Nixon (R)	88,406	(43%)
	Humphrey (D)	112,843	(55%)
	Wallace (AI)	3,390	(2%)

Rep. David F. Emery (R) Elected 1974; b. Sept. 1, 1948, Rockland; home, Rockland; Worcester Polytechnic Inst., B.S. 1970.

Career Maine House of Reps., 1971–74.

Offices 425 CHOB, 202-225-6116. Also 46 Sewall St., Augusta 04330, 207-622-9328.

Committees

Merchant Marine and Fisheries (13th). Subcommittees: Coast Guard and Navigation; Fisheries and Wildlife Conservation and the Environment; Merchant Marine.

Science and Technology (12th). Subcommittees: Energy Research (Fossil Fuels); Science, Research, and Technology.

Group Ratings: Newly Elected

Key Votes

1) Foreign Aid	AGN	6) Gov Abortn Aid	NE	11) Pub Cong Election $	NE
2) Busing	NE	7) Coed Phys Ed	AGN	12) Turkish Arms Cutoff	NE
3) ABM	NE	8) Pov Lawyer Gag	NE	13) Youth Camp Regs	AGN
4) B-1 Bomber	AGN	9) Pub Trans Sub	NE	14) Strip Mine Veto	AGN
5) Nerve Gas	NE	10) EZ Voter Regis	NE	15) Farm Bill Veto	FOR

Election Results

1974 general:	David F. Emery (R)	94,203	(50%)	($68,040)
	Peter N. Kyros (D)	93,524	(50%)	($68,094)
1974 primary:	David F. Emery (R), unopposed			

♦ ♦ ♦ ♦ ♦

SECOND DISTRICT

Census Data Pop. 497,982. Central city, 13%; suburban, 1%. Median family income, $7,733; families above $15,000: 9%; families below $3,000: 11%. Median years education, 12.0.

The Voters

Median voting age 43.
Employment profile White collar, 37%. Blue collar, 47%. Service, 12%. Farm, 4%.
Ethnic groups Total foreign stock, 20%. Canada, 16%.

Presidential vote

1972	Nixon (R)	121,120	(62%)
	McGovern (D)	75,556	(38%)
1968	Nixon (R)	80,848	(43%)
	Humphrey (D)	104,469	(55%)
	Wallace (AI)	2,980	(2%)

Rep. William S. Cohen (R) Elected 1972; b. Aug. 28, 1940, Bangor; home, Bangor; Bowdoin Col., B.A. 1962, Boston U., LL.B. 1965; Unitarian.

Career Practicing atty., 1965–72; Asst. Penobscot Co. Atty., 1968; Instructor, Husson Col., 1968, U. of Maine, 1968–72; Bangor City Cncl., 1969–72, Mayor 1971–72.

Offices 412 CHOB, 202-225-6306. Also Fed. Bldg., Bangor 04401, 207-942-8271 ext. 417.

Committees

Judiciary (7th). Subcommittees: Immigration, Citizenship, and International Law; Monopolies and Commercial Law.

Small Business (9th). Subcommittees: Activities of Regulatory Agencies; Energy and Environment.

Group Ratings

	ADA	COPE	LWV	RIPON	NFU	LCV	CFA	NAB	NSI	ACA
1974	64	64	92	88	79	56	69	50	70	27
1973	52	64	83	87	55	58	88	–	–	27

Key Votes

1) Foreign Aid	FOR	6) Gov Abortn Aid	AGN	11) Pub Cong Election $	FOR
2) Busing	FOR	7) Coed Phys Ed	FOR	12) Turkish Arms Cutoff	AGN
3) ABM	AGN	8) Pov Lawyer Gag	AGN	13) Youth Camp Regs	AGN
4) B-1 Bomber	AGN	9) Pub Trans Sub	AGN	14) Strip Mine Veto	AGN
5) Nerve Gas	AGN	10) EZ Voter Regis	AGN	15) Farm Bill Veto	FOR

Election Results

1974 general:	William S. Cohen (R)	118,154	(71%)	($91,548)
	Markham L. Gartley (D)	47,399	(29%)	($30,412)
1974 primary:	William S. Cohen (R), unopposed			
1972 general:	William S. Cohen (R)	106,280	(54%)	($165,397)
	Elmer H. Violette (D)	89,135	(46%)	($94,696)

MARYLAND

Maryland's attenuated shape reflects the fact that it is one of our most diverse state; although it ranks only 42d in area, you can drive 350 miles wholly within its boundaries to get from one end to the other. In that distance you move from the south-of-the-Mason-Dixon-line Eastern Shore, through the booming suburbs of Washington and Baltimore, and up into the Appalachian mountains. Tiny Maryland has just about every kind of people; and in the last few presidential elections Maryland has been the best statistical mirror of the nation's total voting patterns. The nuts and bolts of Maryland politics, however, are anything but typical.

The original Mason-Dixon line was drawn to settle border disputes between Maryland and Pennsylvania, and Maryland retains even today a touch of the South. Up through World War II, conservative Democratic and Dixie-oriented Maryland, where one still finds an indigenous accent, dominated the state's politics; its only competition came from an old-fashioned machine in Baltimore. Today Baltimore—now almost half black but still controlled by remnants of the old machine—casts less than 20% of Maryland's votes. The rural areas cast only another 20%. The remaining 60% of the voters are split about equally between suburban Baltimore and the Maryland suburbs of Washington, D.C.

Just 40 miles apart, these two metropolitan areas could hardly be more different. A major port, Baltimore has big shipbuilding concerns and the nation's largest steel mill. The heavy industries attracted the kind of ethnic migration common to the big cities of the east coast, as well as a large black migration from the South. Of late, metropolitan Baltimore's growth has been a little sluggish; its politics—traditionally Democratic if one looks at party registration figures—swings often to the Republicans, at least in presidential and senatorial contests.

Washington, of course, is a one-company town, and the company is of course the federal government—perhaps the nation's most booming growth industry today. Accordingly, metropolitan Washington is in the midst of a major boom: of all the major urban agglomerations in the country, only Houston grew faster than Washington in the 1960s. And most of that growth took place in the Maryland suburbs, where the high-rise office buildings and apartment complexes stand in what was pasture land a few short years ago. The Maryland suburbs of Washington have none of the ethnic-industrial history of Baltimore, nor have they been part of the conservative Republican trend noticeable in the early '70s in the other east coast metropolitan areas. Montgomery County, northwest of Washington, is the nation's highest income major county; it is notably liberal in its politics; Montgomery County voters are especially fond of liberal Republican candidates like Senator Charles Mathias. Prince Georges, on the other side of Washington, is slightly more blue-collar and on occasion has given a large percentage of its votes to candidates like George Wallace. In 1972 and 1973 Prince Georges experienced an acrimonious controversy over a countywide school busing order, but the white backlash has been modulated by the large increase in the black population here. Middle-class blacks moving out of Washington have raised the county's black population from 31,000 in 1960 to 92,000 in 1970 and perhaps 110,000 today.

If Maryland is known for anything politically it is corruption. That may not be quite fair; but this is the state that gave the nation Spiro T. Agnew, the first criminal Vice President (if one excludes Aaron Burr) in our history. Another politician who has been accused—but at this writing not proven—to be corrupt is Agnew's successor as Governor, Marvin Mandel. Mandel was Speaker of the Maryland House of Delegates when Agnew became Vice President, and at the time the vacancy was filled by vote of the legislature. Mandel had—and has—the reputation as a legislative wizard, and so of course he became Governor. Once in office, he has proven to be unbeatable; he has run the state efficiently, without tax increases, and at the same time has pushed through many innovative programs. But many close observers have their doubts about the honesty of two of the Governor's closest friends and political associates, Harry Rodgers III and W. Dale Hess, and even of Mandel himself. In 1975, the usually precise Mandel has had to backtrack and contradict himself about the details of their relationship and it is at least clear that Rodgers and Hess have been making a great deal of money doing business with the state.

Ten years ago, Maryland had two Democratic Senators; today it has two Republicans. The man most responsible for the switch is not Agnew, who never did anything for Republican fortunes here, but the man who made Agnew's career possible. He is George Mahoney, a 72-year-old paving contractor who has run for Governor or Senator eight times and never won an election. In

1966 Mahoney decided to run for Governor on the platform of "Your home is your castle"—a thinly-disguised attack on open housing legislation. Mahoney won a narrow primary victory over liberal Congressman Carlton Sickles; in the general, blacks and liberals deserted the Democratic ticket by the thousands, and elected Agnew. If Sickles had gotten just 1,940 more votes, Agnew would almost certainly have remained a suburban Baltimore lawyer expounding on the need for stern parenthood and tough morality to clean up society while he figured out when he would collect his next payoff from government contractors. Instead, this man who never showed any great qualification for national or international leadership stood for five years just a heartbeat away from the Presidency.

Mahoney also played a part in the 1968 and 1970 Senate races. In 1968 he ran as an Independent and took 13% of the vote, enough to allow Congressman Charles Mathias to win easily with 48%. The incumbent, Daniel Brewster, had serious personal problems, and would ultimately be convicted on bribery charges (though the conviction would be reversed on appeal); Mathias probably would have won anyway, but as a liberal Republican he would have had a hard time taking the Eastern Shore and suburban Baltimore votes Mahoney siphoned away from the Democrat.

Mathias has now been reelected with a comfortable, though not overwhelming, 57% of the vote in 1974; it would have been higher but for the game campaigning of his opponent, Baltimore City Councilwoman Barbara Mikulski. With a generally liberal record, Mathias has managed to become one of the most respected Senators on either side of the aisle. He is perhaps best known for his role on the Judiciary Committee, where he declined to join other Republicans and was the deciding vote against the confirmation of FBI chief L. Patrick Gray, who had destroyed some of E. Howard Hunt's files. But Mathias has been active in other areas as well, helping to push through public financing of presidential campaigns, opening up executive branch files to legitimate inquiry, and with Frank Church of Idaho, comprehensively reviewing the vast state-of-emergency powers available to the President and sponsoring the law to put sensible limits on them. Mathias is obviously a man deeply concerned about the workings of the political process—and one whose career has done much to improve them. The Senator is not talky man; he tends to express his harshest judgments in brief similes. But in just a few years he has become one of those Senators whom others look to for the quality of his judgment.

Maryland's other Senator is less well known both nationally and in the state. Indeed, J. Glenn Beall, Jr., is probably sometimes confused with his father, who served in the Senate from 1953 to 1965, or his brother, George Beall, the steady-handed federal prosecutor who convicted Spiro Agnew, and several other Maryland politicians as well. Beall fidgets a bit under the label "conservative," but it is true that he has chosen to back the Nixon and Ford Administrations far more often than Mathias. Beall won his seat in 1970 against another Senator's son, Joseph Tydings. A big winner in 1964, Tydings had seemed unbeatable; but while Beall was campaigning quietly, Tydings became the number one target of the national gun lobby because of his support for gun control legislation. Then the Nixon White House got into the act. Charles Colson leaked to *Life* magazine charges that Tydings had used his influence to benefit a Florida company in which he was a large shareholder. Beall won the election by a 51–49 margin; a week later, John Mitchell's Justice Department cleared Tydings of any conflict of interest.

Thus Beall holds his seat, quite innocently on his own part, as a beneficiary of a Nixon dirty trick. There is a general feeling in Maryland that he is vulnerable in 1976, and Democrats have been lining up for the chance to oppose him. Governor Mandel has developed enough problems of his own since his 1974 reelection victory to almost surely keep him out of the race. But Barbara Mikulski, fresh from her strong showing against Mathias in 1974, is interested; so is Paul Sarbanes, the bright but reserved Congressman from Baltimore; so, reportedly, is Joseph Tydings himself.

Maryland has toyed with presidential primaries. It had one in 1964, which George Wallace won; didn't in 1968 when Wallace wouldn't have run anyway; had one again in 1972, which Wallace won—it was here, in a shopping center in suburban Laurel, that Wallace was campaigning when he was shot. As in so many other states, Maryland's primary is complicated by the fact that practically everybody—69% of the voters—registers Democratic, including a lot of people who never voted for Democrats in general elections. Thus the statewide results are heavily weighted by conservative suburbanites from Prince Georges, Baltimore, and Anne Arundel Counties, white ethnics in east Baltimore (the 3d congressional district), and Dixiecrats on the Eastern Shore.

Census Data Pop. 3,922,399; 1.94% of U.S. total, 18th largest; Central city, 23%; suburban, 61%. Median family income, $11,057; 5th highest; families above $15,000: 29%; families below $3,000: 7%. Median years education, 12.1.

1974 Share of Federal Tax Burden $5,945,499,000; 2.22% of U.S. total, 13th largest.

1974 Share of Federal Outlays $6,773,664,000; 2.51% of U.S. total, 13th largest. Per capita federal spending, $1727.

DOD	$2,045,155,000	11th (2.99%)	HEW	$2,213,649,000	11th (2.39%)
AEC	$144,178,000	9th (4.73%)	HUD	$18,896,000	18th (1.94%)
NASA	$268,873,000	3d (9.01%)	VA	$215,190,000	24th (1.57%)
DOT	$208,327,000	14th (2.46%)	EPA	$104,424,000	7th (3.32%)
DOC	$249,212,000	2d (15.45%)	RevS	$120,769,000	16th (1.99%)
DOI	$22,313,000	25th (0.91%)	Int.	$87,498,000	27th (0.43%)
USDA	$177,669,000	30th (1.43%)	Other	$897,511,000	

Economic Base Finance, insurance and real estate; primary metal industries, especially blast furnaces and steel mills; food and kindred products, agriculture, notably dairy products, broilers, cattle and corn; electrical equipment and supplies, especially communication equipment; transportation equipment, especially motor vehicles and equipment and ship building and repairing; apparel and other textile products.

Political Line-up Governor, Marvin Mandel (D). Senators, Charles McC. Mathias, Jr. (R) and J. Glenn Beall, Jr. (R). Representatives, 8 (5 D and 3 R). State Senate (39 D and 8 R); House of Delegates (126 D and 15 R).

The Voters

Registration 1,666,667 Total. 1,155,453 D (69%); 441,174 R (27%); 68,777 Declined to State (4%); 1,263 AIP (–).
Median voting age 41.
Employment profile White collar, 56%. Blue collar, 31%. Service, 12%. Farm, 1%.
Ethnic groups Black, 18%. Spanish, 1%. Total foreign stock, 12%, Germany, 2%, Italy, USSR, UK, Poland, 1% each.

Presidential vote

1972	Nixon (R)	829,305	(62%)
	McGovern (D)	505,781	(38%)
1968	Nixon (R)	517,995	(42%)
	Humphrey (D)	538,310	(44%)
	Wallace (AI)	178,734	(14%)

1972 Democratic Presidential Primary

Wallace	219,687	(39%)
Humphrey	151,981	(27%)
McGovern	126,978	(22%)
others	69,485	(12%)

1972 Republican Presidential Primary

Nixon	99,308	(86%)
McCloskey	9,223	(8%)
Ashbrook	6,718	(6%)

Sen. Charles McC. Mathias, Jr. (R) Elected 1968, seat up 1980; b. July 24, 1922, Frederick; home, Frederick; Haverford Col., B.A. 1944, U. of Md., LL.B. 1949; Episcopalian.

Career Navy, WWII; Asst. Atty. Gen. of Md., 1953–54; Frederick City Atty., 1954–59; Md. House of Delegates, 1959–60; U.S. House of Reps., 1961–69.

Offices 358 RSOB, 202-224-4654. Also 1616 Fed. Ofc. Bldg., 31 Hopkins Plaza, Baltimore 21201, 301-962.4850, and 202 P.O. Bldg., Hagerstown 21740, 301-733-2710.

Committees

The District of Columbia (Ranking Member).

Appropriations (8th). Subcommittees: District of Columbia; Foreign Operations; HUD and Independent Agencies; Legislative; Transportation.

Judiciary (5th). Subcommittees: Administrative Practices and Procedure; Antitrust and Monopoly; Constitutional Amendments; Juvenile Delinquency; Penitentiaries; Refugees and Escapees; Separation of Powers.

Select Committee on Intelligence Operations (4th).

Group Ratings

	ADA	COPE	LWV	RIPON	NFU	LCV	CFA	NAB	NSI	ACA
1974	90	80	100	73	94	89	86	33	11	0
1973	95	60	100	100	75	–	56	–	–	4
1972	60	80	100	87	67	57	82	60	38	32

Key Votes

1) No-Knock	AGN	8) Gov Abortn Aid	FOR	15) Consumer Prot Agy	FOR
2) Busing	FOR	9) Cut Mil Brass	ABS	16) Forced Psych Tests	FOR
3) No Fault	FOR	10) Gov Limousine	AGN	17) Fed Campaign Subs	FOR
4) F-111	AGN	11) RR Featherbed	AGN	18) Rhod Chrome Ban	FOR
5) Death Penalty	AGN	12) Handgun License	AGN	19) Open Legis Meetings	FOR
6) Foreign Aid	FOR	13) Less Troop Abrd	FOR	20) Strikers Food Stmps	ABS
7) Filibuster	AGN	14) Resume Turk Aid	FOR	21) Gov Info Disclosure	FOR

Election Results

1974 general:	Charles McC. Mathias, Jr. (R)	503,223	(57%)	($329,845)
	Barbara Mikulski (D(	374,563	(43%)	($74,311)
1974 primary:	Charles McC. Mathias, Jr. (R)	79,823	(76%)	
	Ross Z. Pierpont (R)	25,512	(24%)	
1968 general:	Charles McC. Mathias, Jr. (R)	541,893	(48%)	
	Daniel B. Brewster (D)	443,667	(39%)	
	George P. Mahoney (Ind.)	148,467	(13%)	

Sen. J. Glenn Beall, Jr. (R) Elected 1970, seat up 1976; b. June 19, 1927, Cumberland; home, Frostburg; Yale U., A.B. 1950; Episcopalian.

Career Navy, WWII; Family insurance business, 1952–69; Md. House of Delegates, 1963–69, Minor. Floor Ldr.; U.S. House of Reps., 1969–71.

Offices 362 RSOB, 202-224-4524. Also P.O., Cumberland 21501, 301-722-4535, and 1518 Fed. Bldg., Baltimore 21201, 301-962-3920.

Committees

Budget (3d).

Commerce (4th). Subcommittees: Aviation; Communications; The Consumer; Foreign Commerce and Tourism; Merchant Marine; Oceans and Atmosphere; Surface Transportation; Special Subcommittee on Science, Technology and Commerce; Special Subcommittee on Oil and Gas Production and Distribution.

Labor and Public Welfare (4th). Subcommittees: Aging; Alcoholism and Narcotics; Children and Youth; Education; Employment, Poverty, and Migratory Labor; The Handicapped; Health; Special Subcommittee on Human Resources.

Group Ratings

	ADA	COPE	LWV	RIPON	NFU	LCV	CFA	NAB	NSI	ACA
1974	38	55	100	73	59	60	44	42	80	39
1973	25	45	60	82	56	–	30	–	–	59
1972	20	50	73	58	50	20	36	58	100	65

Key Votes

1) No-Knock	FOR	8) Gov Abortn Aid	FOR	15) Consumer Prot Agy	FOR
2) Busing	AGN	9) Cut Mil Brass	AGN	16) Forced Psych Tests	AGN
3) No Fault	FOR	10) Gov Limousine	FOR	17) Fed Campaign Subs	FOR
4) F-111	FOR	11) RR Featherbed	AGN	18) Rhod Chrome Ban	AGN
5) Death Penalty	FOR	12) Handgun License	AGN	19) Open Legis Meetings	FOR
6) Foreign Aid	FOR	13) Less Troop Abrd	AGN	20) Strikers Food Stmps	FOR
7) Filibuster	AGN	14) Resume Turk Aid	AGN	21) Gov Info Disclosure	FOR

Election Results

1970 general:	J. Glenn Beall, Jr. (R)	484,960	(51%)
	Joseph D. Tydings (D)	460,422	(49%)
1970 primary:	J. Glenn Beall, Jr. (R)	99,687	(83%)
	Frederick Harry Lee Simms (R)	9,927	(8%)
	Wainwright Dawson, Jr. (R)	9,786	(8%)

Gov. Marvin Mandel (D) Elected by General Assembly, Jan. 7, 1969, term expires Jan. 1979; b. Apr. 19, 1920, Baltimore; U. of Md., LL.B. 1942.

Career Army, WWII; Md. House of Delegates, 1952–69, Spkr., 1963–69.

Offices State House, Annapolis 21404, 301-267-5591.

Election Results

1974 general:	Marvin Mandel (D)	602,648	(63%)
	Louise Gore (R)	346,449	(37%)
1974 primary:	Marvin Mandel (D)	254,509	(66%)
	Wilson K. Barnes (D)	96,902	(25%)
	Two Others (D)	36,023	(9%)
1970 general:	Marvin Mandel (D)	639,579	(67%)
	C. Stanley Blair (R)	314,336	(33%)

♦ ♦ ♦ ♦ ♦

FIRST DISTRICT

Until the completion of the Chesapeake Bay Bridge in 1952, the Eastern Shore of Maryland was virtually cut off from the rest of Maryland. The "Eastern" refers to the east shore of the Chesapeake; this is a part of Maryland that remains almost a world unto itself—a region of Southern drowsiness, chicken farms, and fishing villages. Before the Civil War, the Eastern Shore was very much slaveholding territory. Up through the 1960s, attachment to the mores of the South persisted; in fact, until 1964, Maryland had a public accommodations act which specifically excluded the Eastern Shore counties. Mostly rural, the economy of the area is buoyed by the dollars spent by tourists, summer people, and wealthy Easterners who have built estates here.

The Eastern Shore still bulks larger than its numbers in Maryland politics. It continues to produce important state legislators and figures like former Governor (1959-67) J. Millard Tawes. But because its population has not grown much—it only slightly more than doubled between 1790 and 1970—the Shore is less and less important electorally. The 1st congressional district is, by reputation, the Eastern Shore district; actually, only 53% of its residents live east of the Bay. The rest can be found in two entirely separate enclaves. The first is Harford County, a northern extension of the Baltimore metropolitan area; the second is Charles, St. Marys, and Calvert Counties, south of Annapolis. The latter are where Lord Baltimore's Catholics first settled Maryland, and there is a substantial rural Catholic population still; the area is also known for having had, till the 1960s, legalized slot machines.

The Eastern Shore and the two western shore parts of the 1st share the same basic political inclinations: high Democratic registration (68%) and equally high conservative voting habits (63% for Wallace in the 1972 primary and 72% for Nixon in the general). Fully 19% of the district's population is black—this is the farthest north you will find significant numbers of blacks in rural settings—but they have little leverage in elections here, since white opinion comes out close to unanimously against them.

Through a variety of circumstances, the 1st district has had five congressional elections in the last five years—more than any other district in the country. Rogers C.B. Morton, who won the seat in 1962 from an indicted Democratic incumbent, resigned after the 1970 election to become Secretary of the Interior (he is now Secretary of Commerce). Morton had been serving as Republican National Chairman; he is also the brother of former Kentucky Senator (1957-69) Thruston Morton and a close friend of President Gerald Ford. An imposing 6'7" aristocrat, Morton won reelection as Congressman easily and managed to pass the seat along to his administrative assistant, William O. Mills, a native Eastern Shoreman. But in the special 1971 election Mills won, Morton arranged a $25,000 loan for him from the Committee to Reelect the President. The loan was apparently never reported as required by Maryland law, and when the story appeared in the papers, just as the Watergate scandal was breaking in early 1973, Mills committed suicide.

The August 1973 special election was a contest between two conservative state Senators: 60-year-old Democrat Fred Malkus and 35-year-old Republican Robert Bauman. Malkus had apparently got his nomination through Governor Mandel in return for some legislative consideration; the Democrats could hardly have picked a weaker candidate. Vice President Agnew came and spoke in Bauman's behalf the Sunday before the election; it was his last campaign appearance. Nevertheless, Bauman won in what some said was a vindication of Republican fortunes, but turned out to be simply a reflection of the personal strength of two candidates.

Bauman turned out to be one of the more ideologically oriented conservatives in the House. Having won his special election, he must have expected his seat to remain relatively safe. But former state Insurance Commissioner Thomas Hatem, the Democrat slated to contest the seat in 1974, managed to make a race of it and win 47% of the vote. Only vestigial strength on the Eastern Shore preserved Bauman's seat. The question now is whether congressional politics is going to quiet down in the 1st, or whether it will be the scene again of close-fought battles.

Census Data   Pop. 489,455. Central city, 0%; suburban, 34%. Median family income, $8,925; families above $15,000: 17%; families below $3,000: 11%. Median years education, 11.1.

The Voters

Median voting age 41.
Employment profile White collar, 42%. Blue collar, 40%. Service, 13%. Farm, 5%.
Ethnic groups Black, 19%. Total foreign stock, 5%. Germany, 1%.

Presidential vote

1972	Nixon (R)	106,539	(72%)
	McGovern (D)	42,257	(28%)
1968	Nixon (R)	65,316	(46%)
	Humphrey (D)	44,979	(32%)
	Wallace (AI)	31,977	(22%)

Rep. Robert E. Bauman (R) Elected Aug. 21, 1973; b. Apr. 4, 1937, Easton; home, Easton; Georgetown U., B.S. 1959, J.D. 1964; Catholic.

Career Mbr., Minor. Staff, U.S. House of Reps. Comm. on The Judiciary, 1955–59; Founder and Natl. Chm., Young Americans for Freedom, 1962–65; Repub. Legislative Staff, U.S. House of Reps., 1965–68; Practicing atty., 1968–73; Md. Senate, 1971–73.

Offices 118 CHOB, 202-225-5311. Also Loyola Fed. Bldg., Goldsborough and Harrison Sts., Easton 21601, 301-822-4300.

Committees

Interior and Insular Affairs (10th). Subcommittees: Energy and the Environment; National Parks and Recreation.

Merchant Marine and Fisheries (10th). Subcommittees: Coast Guard and Navigation; Oceanography.

Group Ratings

	ADA	COPE	LWV	RIPON	NFU	LCV	CFA	NAB	NSI	ACA
1974	9	0	17	25	21	29	0	83	100	100
1973	0	33	25	50	43	14	20	–	–	86

Key Votes

1) Foreign Aid	AGN	6) Gov Abortn Aid	AGN	11) Pub Cong Election $	AGN
2) Busing	AGN	7) Coed Phys Ed	AGN	12) Turkish Arms Cutoff	FOR
3) ABM	FOR	8) Pov Lawyer Gag	NE	13) Youth Camp Regs	AGN
4) B-1 Bomber	FOR	9) Pub Trans Sub	AGN	14) Strip Mine Veto	FOR
5) Nerve Gas	FOR	10) EZ Voter Regis	AGN	15) Farm Bill Veto	FOR

Election Results

1974 general:	Robert E. Bauman (R)	59,570	(53%)	($137,046)
	Thomas J. Hatem (D)	52,853	(47%)	($48,043)
1974 primary:	Robert E. Bauman (R), unopposed			
1973 special:	Robert E. Bauman (R)	27,248	(51%)	($129,904)
	Frederick Malkus (D)	26,001	(49%)	($67,580)

◆ ◆ ◆ ◆ ◆

SECOND DISTRICT

Baltimore County is, as anyone who lives there will tell you, entirely separate from the city of Baltimore. It is, by definition of the Census Bureau, totally suburban; but it is far from homogeneous. In the north of the County lie verdant horse farms; just northwest of the city of Baltimore is the predominantly Jewish suburb of Pikesville; due north of Baltimore's downtown is WASPy, wealthy Towson; east of Baltimore are the working class suburbs of Dundalk and Sparrows Point. An exception to this diversity is race, for Baltimore County remains virtually all white.

This was the place that gave us Spiro Agnew. Like most of Maryland, Baltimore County registers and in local elections usually votes Democratic; over the years machine Democrats usually controlled the county courthouse. But in 1962, the Democrats had scandal problems and, much to everyone's surprise the Republican nominee for County Executive—former zoning board member Agnew—actually won. Doubtful of reelection four years later, Agnew got his party's nomination for Governor, which suddenly became worth something when the Democrats chose George Mahoney as their nominee. From County Executive to Governor to Vice President, Agnew gave mediocre performance and was rewarded with almost immediate advancement—and rewarded also, we know now, with a regular series of bribes and payoffs.

Agnew's Democratic successor, Dale Anderson, committed the same crimes; unfortunate enough never to have been Governor or Vice President, he has gone to jail. For years Anderson headed a Democratic machine which controlled Baltimore County goverment; after his conviction in 1974, his men were decisively defeated by a young and an apparently honest professor named Ted Venetoulis.

In Congress, Baltimore County has long been represented by a professor whose honesty is above reproach. In 1962, the Democrats in the 2d congressional district, which then included all of Baltimore County and two others besides, nominated Clarence D. Long, Ph.D., professor of economics at Johns Hopkins University. Apparently the idea was to put up a blue ribbon candidate to deflect scandal rumors; also, congressmen, unlike county executives, have little patronage to dispose of. In any case, Long won that election and, through a series of redistrictings, has been reelected ever since.

Currently the 2d includes most of Baltimore County, including Dundalk, Towson, and Pikesville, plus a small Jewish neighborhood in Baltimore City. The secret of Long's political success has been close attention to his territory. He returns from Washington every night to his home in the district, and throughout the year rides around in a trailer to meet constituents and handle the problems they bring to him.

In Washington many members of Congress regard Long—universally referred to as "Doc"—with the suspicion men of the world have traditionally reserved for professors. Nevertheless, he has won a seat on the Appropriations Committee. As one of the few members of Congress who had a son who served in the military in Vietnam, Long strongly supported the war policies of Johnson and Nixon for years. But he became a dove during the Cambodia invasion of 1970, and three years later was one of the main sponsors of the successful amendment cutting off American military spending there.

Census Data Pop. 491,331. Central city, 5%; suburban, 95%. Median family income, $12,140; families above $15,000: 33%; families below $3,000: 4%. Median years education, 12.1.

The Voters

Median voting age 42.
Employment profile White collar, 59%. Blue collar, 32%. Service, 8%. Farm, 1%.
Ethnic groups Black, 3%. Total foreign stock, 17%. USSR, 4%; Poland, Germany, Italy, 2% each; UK, 1%.

Presidential vote

1972	Nixon (R)	135,329	(68%)
	McGovern (D)	62,755	(32%)
1968	Nixon (R)	76,774	(45%)
	Humphrey (D)	72,706	(42%)
	Wallace (AI)	22,311	(13%)

Rep. Clarence D. Long (D) Elected 1962; b. Dec. 11, 1908, South Bend, Ind.; home, Ruxton; Wash. and Jeff. Col., B.A., Princeton U., M.A., Ph.D.; Presbyterian.

Career Navy, WWII; Prof. of Econ., Johns Hopkins U., 1946–64; Sr. Staff Mbr., Pres. Cncl. of Econ. Advisers, 1953–54, 1956–57; Acting Chm., Md. Dem. St. Central Comm., 1961–62.

Offices 2421 RHOB, 202-225-3061. Also Rm. 200, P.O. Bldg., Towson 21204, 301-828-6616.

Committees

Appropriations (18th). Subcommittees: Foreign Operations; Interior; Treasury, Postal Service, and General Government.

Group Ratings

	ADA	COPE	LWV	RIPON	NFU	LCV	CFA	NAB	NSI	ACA
1974	59	82	58	69	77	82	62	50	60	29
1973	67	70	64	67	80	68	63	–	–	33
1972	56	82	58	47	57	0	100	27	22	33

Key Votes

1) Foreign Aid	FOR	6) Gov Abortn Aid	AGN	11) Pub Cong Election $	AGN
2) Busing	AGN	7) Coed Phys Ed	FOR	12) Turkish Arms Cutoff	FOR
3) ABM	AGN	8) Pov Lawyer Gag	FOR	13) Youth Camp Regs	AGN
4) B-1 Bomber	FOR	9) Pub Trans Sub	AGN	14) Strip Mine Veto	AGN
5) Nerve Gas	AGN	10) EZ Voter Regis	FOR	15) Farm Bill Veto	FOR

Election Results

1974 general:	Clarence D. Long (D)	103,222	(77%)	($33,181)
	John M. Seney (R)	30,639	(23%)	($6,234)
1974 primary:	Clarence D. Long (D), unopposed			
1972 general:	Clarence D. Long (D)	123,346	(66%)	($66,425)
	John J. Bishop, Jr. (R)	64,119	(34%)	($75,606)

◆ ◆ ◆ ◆ ◆

THIRD DISTRICT

East Baltimore is a favorite of political sociologists. It is composed of white ethnic communities—Irish, Italian, German, Greek, and especially Polish—which seem to have changed little since the 1920s. The unique Baltimore row houses stand here as carefully maintained as ever, and the streets are spotless and teeming with children. But the politics of east Baltimore has been undergoing almost constant change. The old machine which once dominated these wards has now splintered into a dozen different factions. A newer breed of politician has begun to win elections here, by the old-fashioned political methods of door-to-door campaigning and close communication with neighborhood groups. One such politician is Barbara Mikulski, City Councilwoman, Democratic Senate candidate in 1974, and head of the national Democratic Party's committee on delegate selection. Another is 3d district Congressman Paul Sarbanes.

Sarbanes' district is centered on east Baltimore, and can best be described as containing the white-majority parts of Baltimore and some adjacent suburbs. The 3d proceeds west from east Baltimore to the city's revitalized downtown and the old neighborhoods near the harbor, including the one which contains Fort McHenry. Still farther west are the middle-class suburbs of Catonsville and Arbutus, where the row houses spread out to become detached homes. The 3d also proceeds north from east Baltimore, to take in the predominantly Catholic neighborhoods in the northeast quadrant of the city, Johns Hopkins University, and a small chunk of suburban Baltimore County.

The 3d district is a good place to examine the phenomenon—apparently arrested in 1974—of the switch of blue-collar ethnics from their traditional Democratic allegiance to the law 'n' order politics exemplified for a while by Richard Nixon and Spiro Agnew. This is an area that went for John F. Kennedy heavily in 1960, but cast only 41% of its votes to Hubert Humphrey in 1968, and a scant 33% to George McGovern in 1972. The switch seems to have reflected not so much an affection for Nixon and his policies as a feeling that the national Democrats were no longer concerned with the kind of problems people have here. Most residents of the 3d were well enough off that the economic programs of the oldline Democrats seemed irrelevant, yet they remained poor enough to resent the attention paid by fashionable liberals to blacks and other who were even worse off.

Now all that seems, at least for a while, to have disappeared. These newest converts to the politics of Richard Nixon seem to have been most affected by the disclosure that this man who paraded himself as the symbol of middle-class respectability was actually a crook. In 1974 Democratic percentages here was as high as they have ever been, and in the wake of Watergate and recession feeling toward most Republicans was at an all time low.

And no one ran better here than Congressman Paul Sarbanes, a man whose style has little in common with the Democratic ward-heelers who have traditionally represented their party here. A friend of Ralph Nader at Princeton, a Rhodes Scholar, a Harvard Law graduate, Sarbanes came up politically as the oldtimers used to: winning elections house by house, block by block in his home neighborhood. That is how he gained election to the Maryland House of Delegates, where he clashed bitterly with Marvin Mandel, and that is how he was elected to Congress in 1970. It helped that he had a solid legislative record in Annapolis, one that helped gain him the endorsements of the AFL-CIO, the UAW and the Teamsters when he ran against incumbent Congressman George Fallon, when Chairman of the House Public Works Committee. Sarbanes had national support from ecology groups, but it was his neighborhood backing that enabled him to beat Fallon by 2,000 votes.

Two years later, Mandel had seen that Sarbanes was placed in the same district with Congressman Edward Garmatz, then Chairman of the Merchant Marine and Fisheries Committee. But this time the older man decided to quit rather than fight, and Sarbanes easily won a second term. In 1974, virtually unopposed, he won 83% of the vote.

Sarbanes became something of a national figure as a member of the House Judiciary Committee and the manager of the first article of impeachment. It was in the latter capacity that he was the focus of Republican attacks purporting to seek greater specificity. Sarbanes' performance disappointed some of his admirers; he seemed not completely prepared for the Republicans' onslaught, and his pedestrian speaking style was anything but electrifying. But Sarbanes is not, and does not particularly pretend to be, a charismatic figure; indeed, he is an exceedingly cautious man—which often disappoints some of his liberal friends. He is also a very close-mouthed person when he wants to be; and though at this writing he may already have made up his mind whether he seeks Glenn Beall's Senate seat in 1976, he has not as yet told anyone.

Census Data Pop. 490,851. Central city, 80%; suburban, 20%. Median family income, $10,022; families above $15,000: 21%; families below $3,000: 9%. Median years education, 10.6.

The Voters

Median voting age 45.
Employment profile White collar, 54%. Blue collar, 35%. Service, 11%. Farm, –%.
Ethnic groups Black, 13%. Spanish, 1%. Total foreign stock, 15%. Germany, 3%; Italy, Poland, 2% each.

Presidential vote

1972	Nixon (R)	111,007	(67%)
	McGovern (D)	53,981	(33%)
1968	Nixon (R)	74,644	(44%)
	Humphrey (D)	69,694	(41%)
	Wallace (AI)	26,406	(15%)

Rep. Paul S. Sarbanes (D) Elected 1970; b. Feb. 3, 1933, Salisbury; home, Baltimore; Princeton U., A.B. 1954, Rhodes Scholar, Oxford U., B.A. 1957, Harvard U., LL.B. 1960; Greek Orthodox.

Career Law Clerk to Judge Morris A. Soper, U.S. 4th Circuit Ct. of Appeals, 1960–61; Practicing atty., 1961–62, 1965–71; Admin. Asst. to Chm. Walter W. Heller of the Pres. Cncl. of Econ. Advisers, 1962–63; Exec. Dir., Baltimore Charter Revision Comm., 1963–64; Md. House of Delegates, 1969–70.

Offices 317 CHOB, 202-225-4016. Also 1414 Fed. Ofc. Bldg., Baltimore 21201, 301-982-4436.

Committees

Judiciary (10th). Subcommittees: Immigration, Citizenship, and International Law; Monopolies and Commercial Law.

Merchant Marine and Fisheries (15th). Subcommittees: Coast Guard and Navigation; Merchant Marine.

Group Ratings

	ADA	COPE	LWV	RIPON	NFU	LCV	CFA	NAB	NSI	ACA
1974	91	91	92	57	86	94	100	17	10	0
1973	92	100	92	73	95	89	100	–	–	7
1972	88	91	82	67	86	93	100	8	0	9

Key Votes

1) Foreign Aid	FOR	6) Gov Abortn Aid	AGN	11) Pub Cong Election $	FOR
2) Busing	AGN	7) Coed Phys Ed	FOR	12) Turkish Arms Cutoff	FOR
3) ABM	AGN	8) Pov Lawyer Gag	AGN	13) Youth Camp Regs	FOR
4) B-1 Bomber	AGN	9) Pub Trans Sub	FOR	14) Strip Mine Veto	AGN
5) Nerve Gas	AGN	10) EZ Voter Regis	FOR	15) Farm Bill Veto	FOR

Election Results

1974 general:	Paul S. Sarbanes (D)	93,218	(84%)	($8,765)
	William H. Mathews (R)	17,967	(16%)	($193)
1974 primary	Paul S. Sarbanes (D), unopposed			
1972 general:	Paul S. Sarbanes (D)	93,093	(70%)	($61,272)
	Robert D. Morrow (R)	40,442	(30%)	($4,498)

◆ ◆ ◆ ◆ ◆

FOURTH DISTRICT

The 4th district contains all of Anne Arundel County (Annapolis and the Baltimore suburbs) and part of Prince Georges (near Washington). The creation of the district was greeted with cheers in Anne Arundel, which despite its population of nearly 300,000 had never had its own Congressman. With 60% of the district's voters Anne Arundel seemed likely to dominate the 4th's politics, and sure enough, when the 1972 results were in, the new Representative from the district was former Anne Arundel County Clerk Marjorie Holt.

Maryland's 4th congressional district, new for the 1972 election, runs from the Baltimore city limit to the District of Columbia line. In between it is mostly vacant land, waiting for the kind of rapid development that increased the district's population 66% in the 1960s. Lying in the middle of the district is Annapolis (pop. 29,000), the quaint eighteenth century town that contains Maryland's State House—the oldest capital in the nation still in use—and the United States Naval Academy. Moving inexorably over the low-lying hills and around the wide Chesapeake inlets toward Annapolis are the not-so-fashionable suburbs of Baltimore where most of the 4th district's residents live: Linthicum, Glen Burnie, Severna Park. On the other side of the district, near Washington, are the fast-growing communities of Oxon Hill, Suitland, and Camp Springs; nearer Annapolis, but stuck in the middle of the country, is the new townhouse and shopping center suburb of Crofton, where Spiro Agnew lives and works.

This is a district where two-thirds of the voters register Democratic, but less than one-third have voted for either of the last two Democratic presidential nominees. Mrs. Holt, a conservative Republican, had had a liberal Democratic opponent in the 1972 general, and beat him by a solid 59–41 margin. Some thought that her solid pro-Nixon voting record would make her weaker in 1974. But they reckoned without the slate-making prowess of Governor Marvin Mandel's Democrats. They named as their candidate Secretary of State Fred Wineland, a Mandel appointee and good-old-boy Prince Georges pol. Despite his conservatism on many issues, Wineland was able to win only 42% of the vote. Mrs. Holt is one of the first two women members of the House Armed Services Committee. But unlike Colorado's Pat Schroeder, the other, Mrs. Holt is anything but a scourge of the Pentagon; she routinely goes along with the Committee's still hawkish majority.

Census Data Pop. 495,249. Central city, 0%; suburban, 100%. Median family income, $11,892; families above $15,000: 32%; families below $3,000: 5%. Median years education, 12.3.

The Voters

Median voting age 37.
Employment profile White collar, 60%. Blue collar, 28%. Service, 11%. Farm, 1%.

Ethnic groups Black, 10%. Spanish, 2%. Total foreign stock, 10%. Germany, 2%; Italy, UK, 1% each.

Presidential vote

1972	Nixon (R)	107,379	(70%)
	McGovern (D)	44,937	(30%)
1968	Nixon (R)	55,177	(45%)
	Humphrey (D)	40,163	(33%)
	Wallace (AI)	26,609	(22%)

Rep. Marjorie S. Holt (R) Elected 1972; b. Sept. 17, 1920, Birmingham, Ala.; home, Severna Park; Jacksonville U., B.A. 1946, U. of Fla., J.D. 1949; Presbyterian.

Career Practicing atty., 1950–66; Anne Arundel Co. Supervisor of Elections, 1963–65; Anne Arundel Co. Clerk of the Circuit Ct., 1966–72.

Offices 1510 LHOB, 202-225-8090. Also 95 Aquahart Rd., Glen Burnie 21061, 301-768-8050.

Committees

Armed Services (9th). Subcommittees: Military Compensation; Military Personnel.

House Administration (7th). Subcommittees: Accounts; Electrical and Mechanical Office Equipment; Ad Hoc Computer

Group Ratings

	ADA	COPE	LWV	RIPON	NFU	LCV	CFA	NAB	NSI	ACA
1974	13	0	25	44	21	35	0	75	90	93
1973	4	27	17	40	30	5	13	–	–	93

Key Votes

1) Foreign Aid	AGN	6) Gov Abortn Aid	AGN	11) Pub Cong Election $	AGN
2) Busing	AGN	7) Coed Phys Ed	AGN	12) Turkish Arms Cutoff	FOR
3) ABM	FOR	8) Pov Lawyer Gag	FOR	13) Youth Camp Regs	AGN
4) B-1 Bomber	FOR	9) Pub Trans Sub	AGN	14) Strip Mine Veto	FOR
5) Nerve Gas	FOR	10) EZ Voter Regis	AGN	15) Farm Bill Veto	FOR

Election Results

1974 general:	Marjorie S. Holt (R)	61,208	(58%)	($99,717)
	Fred L. Wineland (D)	44,059	(42%)	($134,323)
1974 primary:	Marjorie S. Holt (R), unopposed	87,534	(59%)	($113,513)
	Werner Fornos (D)	59,877	(41%)	($145,973)

◆ ◆ ◆ ◆ ◆

FIFTH DISTRICT

The 5th congressional district of Maryland includes most of Prince Georges County, the largest suburban county in the state. Lying north and east of Washington, D.C., Prince Georges is a little less white-collar and less affluent than adjacent Montgomery County. Yet against national averages, Prince Georges appears wealthy indeed, and one reason is the relatively high wages paid by Uncle Sam. Fully 38% of the work force in the 5th is employed by the federal government, the highest such figure of any congressional district in the nation. The difference between Prince Georges and other Washington suburbs is not so much one of money as of status; rarely does anyone from P.G. towns like Hyattsville, College Park, or Bowie make the social chatter of Maxine Cheshire's column. The people living here are the bureaucrats who keep official Washington plugging along, day after day, come Johnson or Nixon or Ford, Vietnam or Cambodia or Watergate.

The 5th's population shot up 69% during the 1960s, making it one of the fastest-growing congressional district in the nation. The rapid growth here began in the 1950s, when metropolitan Washington's population burst outside the District line; the rush to the suburbs was accelerated, though it would have happened anyway, by the integration of the District schools in 1955. Today northeast and southeast Washington, the parts next to Prince Georges, are all black and so are adjacent sections of P.G. itself. Middle-class blacks today form the bulk of recent population increases in Prince Georges, as whites are moving out even beyond the County line; at the same time, the total pace of migration has slowed due to lack of sewer permits.

Back in the 1950s, Prince Georges was ruled by a Democratic machine of the kind one found in many small Maryland counties; it consisted of a few old men, one of them perhaps chewing tobacco, who liked to hang out in the dusty courthouse in tiny Upper Marlboro and talk about the old days. Needless to say, these old politicos didn't much care for the new suburbanites who quickly outnumbered their old friends, and the feeling was mutual. One of the leaders of an insurgent movement which took over the Democratic Party and the county government in the 1960s was Gladys Spellman, later a County Councilwoman and now Congresswoman from the 5th district.

Spellman proved to be expert at working with idealistic liberals and more practical-minded politicians who did not want to do away utterly with the patronage that is so much a part of Maryland politics. And she also proved adept at taking advantage of opportunities for herself. When Republican Congressman Lawrence Hogan decided to run for Governor rather than reelection in 1974, Spellman was ready, and she beat a couple of rivals in the primary and a Hogan protege in the general to become the first Democratic member of Congress elected from the area since 1966.

Once elected, Spellman was one of the organizers of the freshman caucus; nominated for secretary, the traditional woman's post, by Berkley Bedell of Iowa, she became vice chairman instead. Her experience taking over the reins of power from Prince Georges oldtimers may have been useful in plotting the ouster of aging and/or reactionary committee chairmen, in which Spellman played a major role. With the reams of publicity she has won as a leader of freshman causes, it seems hardly possible that she could lose in 1976, despite her rather close race in 1974. But she could have problems if Hogan tries to win his old seat back.

Hogan deserves at least a footnote here. A conservative Republican who picked up the seat from a lazy oldtime Democrat in 1968, Hogan was one of the unexpected stars of the Judiciary Committee impeachment hearings. He was the first Republican to announce publicly his support of impeachment, and though he did not work closely with other pro-impeachment Republicans he was one of the committee's most effective marshallers of facts. Hogan's career otherwise was frustrating: he was a strong backer of constitutional amendments to stop busing and abortions, and was unable to get either measure taken up for a vote. His campaign against Marvin Mandel in 1974 was, quite literally, abortive; against all the predictions, he managed to lose the Republican primary to conservative wheelhorse Louise Gore. Miss Gore had gone around the hustings to Republican women's groups, while Hogan had ignored the relatively few registered Republicans in his attempts to capitalize on people's suspicions about the honesty of Mandel and his administration. In fact, a good case remained to be made against Mandel, and if Hogan had gotten the nomination he might have been able to make it.

Census Data Pop. 482,721. Central city, 0%; suburban, 100%. Median family income, $12,286; families above $15,000: 33%; families below $3,000: 4%. Median years education, 12.5.

The Voters

Median voting age 34.
Employment profile White collar, 67%. Blue collar, 23%. Service, 10%. Farm, –%.
Ethnic groups Black, 16%. Spanish, 2%. Total foreign stock, 13%. Italy, 2%; Germany, UK, 1% each.

Presidential vote

1972	Nixon (R)	83,579	(57%)
	McGovern (D)	63,821	(43%)
1968	Nixon (R)	54,084	(41%)
	Humphrey (D)	55,619	(42%)
	Wallace (AI)	21,733	(17%)

Rep. Gladys Noon Spellman (D) Elected 1974; b. Mar. 2, 1918, New York, N.Y.; home, Laurel; Geo. Wash. U.

Career Public school teacher; Prince Georges Co. Bd. of Commissioners, 1962–74, Chm., Councilor-at-Large.

Offices 1117 LHOB, 202-225-4131. Also Suite 180, Presidential Bldg., 6525 Belcrest Rd., Hyattsville 20782, 301-436-8865.

Committees

Banking, Currency and Housing (24th). Subcommittees: Consumer Affairs; Economic Stabilization; Historic Preservation and Coinage.

Post Office and Civil Service (12th). Subcommittees: Census and Population; Employee Political Rights and Intergovernmental Programs; Retirement and Employee Benefits.

Group Ratings: Newly Elected

Key Votes

1) Foreign Aid	FOR	6) Gov Abortn Aid	NE	11) Pub Cong Election $	NE
2) Busing	NE	7) Coed Phys Ed	FOR	12) Turkish Arms Cutoff	NE
3) ABM	NE	8) Pov Lawyer Gag	NE	13) Youth Camp Regs	FOR
4) B-1 Bomber	AGN	9) Pub Trans Sub	NE	14) Strip Mine Veto	AGN
5) Nerve Gas	NE	10) EZ Voter Regis	NE	15) Farm Bill Veto	FOR

Election Results

1974 general:	Gladys Noon Spellman (D)	45,211	(53%)	($90,144)
	John B. Burcham, Jr. (R)	40,805	(47%)	($39,038)
1974 primary:	Gladys Noon Spellman (D)	21,470	(67%)	
	Karl H. Matthes (D)	10,446	(33%)	

◆ ◆ ◆ ◆ ◆

SIXTH DISTRICT

West of Baltimore and Washington a series of gentle Maryland hills rise to the low mountains of the Catoctins and the Appalachian ridges. Here is a land known for its fertile valleys and its antique cities, like Frederick (pop. 24,000), where Barbara Fritchie supposedly reared her old gray head. Also here are the small industrial cities of Hagerstown (pop. 36,000) and, high in the hills, Cumberland (pop. 30,000). The mountain folk and Pennsylvania Dutch who settled western Maryland left behind a Republican heritage, unusual in a state that is Democratic by tradition and custom. Nevertheless, a majority of the voters here, as in the rest of the state, are registered Democrats, simply because the Democratic primary is almost always where the action is. Come general election time, these same "Democrats" are ready to vote Republican once again.

The 6th congressional district includes all of western Maryland and a portion of suburban Baltimore County. The only part of the 6th which is markedly out of step with the conservative, rural mores of the district is the much-heralded "new town" of Columbia in Howard County. It is a planned, integrated development that had 8,000 people in 1970 and is supposed to house some 110,000 in 1982; Columbia is not as great a departure from other large suburban developments as it would like to think, but its new town rhetoric has had the politically significant effect of attracting a disproportionate amount of suburban liberals who would otherwise probably live in Baltimore County.

The dominant mores of the 6th have been fairly well reflected in the attitudes held by the district's last two Congressmen, Republican J. Glenn Beall, Jr., and Democrat Goodloe Byron. Beall served just two years after winning the seat in 1968, and then was elected U.S. Senator in 1970; Byron won a narrow victory in 1970 and resounding reelections in 1972 and 1974. Byron is about as conservative a congressional Democrat as there is from outside the South; he would seem to be considerably more vulnerable in his party's primary than in the general election.

Byron and Beall are examples of the dynastic lines that seem to dominate much of Maryland politics. Byron's father and mother served in the House from 1939 to 1943, when Beall's father succeeded to the seat. Beall, Sr., was reelected from the 6th until 1952, when he won election to the Senate. He retired involuntarily when he lost to Joseph Tydings, himself the son of a Senator. Young Tydings was beaten in turn by Beall, Jr., in 1970, and is at this writing thinking about challenging him in 1976. In a state with a politics of fabled corruption, apparently many voters find the assurance of character in a well-known pedigree.

Census Data   Pop. 491,839. Central city, 0%; suburban, 40%. Median family income, $9,749; families above $15,000: 20%; families below $3,000: 8%. Median years education, 11.6.

The Voters

Median voting age 42.
Employment profile White collar, 46%. Blue collar, 39%. Service, 11%. Farm, 4%.
Ethnic groups Black, 4%. Total foreign stock, 5%.

Presidential vote

1972	Nixon (R)	125,878	(71%)
	McGovern (D)	52,346	(29%)
1968	Nixon (R)	80,752	(51%)
	Humphrey (D)	51,456	(33%)
	Wallace (AI)	25,528	(16%)

Rep. Goodloe E. Byron (D) Elected 1970; b. June 22, 1929, Williamsport; home, Frederick; U. of Va., B.A. 1951, Geo. Wash. U., J.D. 1953; Episcopalian.

Career Army, 1955–58; Practicing atty.; Frederick Co. Atty., 1958; Md. House of Delegates, 1963–67; Md. Senate, 1967–71.

Offices 1730 LHOB, 202-225-2721. Also Frederick Shopping Ct., Frederick 21701, 301-662-8622.

Committees

Interior and Insular Affairs (20th). Subcommittees: Mines and Mining; National Parks and Recreation; Public Lands.

Interstate and Foreign Commerce (17th). Subcommittees, Communications.

Group Ratings

	ADA	COPE	LWV	RIPON	NFU	LCV	CFA	NAB	NSI	ACA
1974	13	18	17	31	36	29	23	67	90	71
1973	21	45	27	40	55	5	38	–	–	73
1972	6	18	17	27	67	43	100	50	100	83

Key Votes

1) Foreign Aid	AGN	6) Gov Abortn Aid	AGN	11) Pub Cong Election $	AGN
2) Busing	AGN	7) Coed Phys Ed	AGN	12) Turkish Arms Cutoff	FOR
3) ABM	FOR	8) Pov Lawyer Gag	ABS	13) Youth Camp Regs	AGN
4) B-1 Bomber	FOR	9) Pub Trans Sub	AGN	14) Strip Mine Veto	FOR
5) Nerve Gas	AGN	10) EZ Voter Regis	AGN	15) Farm Bill Veto	FOR

Election Results

1974 general:	Goodloe E. Byron (D)	90,882	(74%)	($31,308)
	Elton R. Wampler (R)	32,416	(26%)	($11,556)
1974 primary:	Goodloe E. Byron (D)	31,133	(75%)	
	Bruce L. Welch (D)	10,288	(25%)	
1972 general:	Goodloe E. Byron (D)	107,283	(65%)	($77,186)
	Edward J. Mason (R)	58,259	(35%)	($61,335)

SEVENTH DISTRICT

♦ ♦ ♦ ♦ ♦

Baltimore has always had a large black community. In 1960, 35% of its citizens were black; in 1970, 46% were; and today, surely the city has a black majority. Yet blacks have never really been a major electoral force in Baltimore as they have in such diverse cities as Chicago and Atlanta and Oakland; the current Mayor, Don Schaefer, elected in 1971 and reelected in 1975, is white and depends almost entirely on whites for his votes—and wins very nicely, thank you. White politicos still make the gut decisions about who will run—and who will win—in many virtually all-black parts of Baltimore, and the level of voter registration and participation in the ghetto is scandalously low. More, there are deep splits in Baltimore's black community, between the east side and west side ghettoes, and between the prominent Mitchell family and its enemies.

The one locus of political power for Baltimore's black community is Maryland's 7th congressional district. This seat includes almost all of Baltimore's west side and part of its east side; its boundaries were artfully enough drawn to include 86% of Baltimore's blacks and only 29% of its whites. The 7th was not always so constituted. Before the 1972 elections, the district was heavily Jewish, including the old Jewish neighborhoods on the west side (into which blacks were rapidly moving) and suburbs like Pikesville and Woodlawn. That provided a comfortable constituency for Congressman Samuel Friedel, an oldline Democrat who had accumulated enough seniority to have become Chairman of the House Administration Committee. But in 1970 Friedel got caught in a tough primary, with another Jewish candidate named Friedler, and Parren J. Mitchell, a professor at predominantly black Morgan State College. With the white vote split, Mitchell won by 38 votes. In the general election, Mitchell lost the white suburbs, but still managed a comfortable win.

Although technically a political novice, Mitchell was from anything but an unsophisticated political background. His older brother is Clarence Mitchell, the canny Washington lobbyist for the NAACP, and his nephew, Clarence Mitchell III, at the time was a Baltimore state Senator. But the Mitchells' prominence had made them political enemies as well as friends in the black community. In 1971, for example, Senator Mitchell had run for Mayor against Don Schaefer and George Russell, a black official with oldline black support. Russell's campaign was well-financed and might really have provided competition for Schaefer; Mitchell's was run on a shoestring, and almost explicitly for the purpose of diverting votes from Russell. Although Mitchell didn't divert enough to make any difference, Russell was furious and promptly ran against Parren Mitchell in the 1972 congressional primary. This election was held within the new boundaries, entirely within the city; Russell had a solid 46%, almost enough to beat Mitchell's 50%.

That was not exactly a reassuring result for the incumbent. Mitchell has the distinction of being the first black member of the House Banking and Currency Committee; but obviously his eyes are more on Baltimore than on congressional politics.

Census Data Pop. 487,832. Central city, 100%; suburban, 0%. Median family income, $7,841; families above $15,000: 13%; families below $3,000: 16%. Median years education, 9.8.

The Voters

Median voting age 42.
Employment profile White collar, 37%. Blue collar, 40%. Service, 23%. Farm, –%.
Ethnic groups Black, 74%. Total foreign stock, 5%.

Presidential vote

1972	Nixon (R)	32,369	(27%)
	McGovern (D)	89,041	(73%)
1968	Nixon (R)	22,429	(16%)
	Humphrey (D)	106,998	(77%)
	Wallace (AI)	9,066	(7%)

Rep. Parren J. Mitchell (D) Elected 1970; b. Apr. 29, 1922, Baltimore; home, Baltimore; Morgan St. Col., B.A. 1950, U. of Md., M.A. 1952, U. of Conn., 1960; Episcopalian.

Career Army, WWII; Prof. and Asst. Dir. of the Urban Studies Institute, Morgan St. Col.; Exec. Secy., Md. Comm. on Interracial Problems and Relations, 1963–65; Exec. Dir., Baltimore Community Action Agency, 1965–68.

Offices 414 CHOB, 202-225-4741. Also Rm. 1018, Geo. Fallon Fed. Ofc. Bldg., 31 Hopkins Plaza, Baltimore 21201, 301-962-3223.

Committees

Banking, Currency and Housing (14th). Subcommittees: General Oversight and Renegotiation; Housing and Community Development.

Budget (9th).

Small Business (10th). Subcommittees: SBA and SBIC Legislation; SBA Oversight and Minority Enterprise.

Group Ratings

	ADA	COPE	LWV	RIPON	NFU	LCV	CFA	NAB	NSI	ACA
1974	100	90	100	64	85	94	92	17	11	0
1973	100	100	92	73	95	95	100	–	–	4
1972	88	100	100	73	86	86	100	8	0	10

Key Votes

1) Foreign Aid	FOR	6) Gov Abortn Aid	FOR	11) Pub Cong Election $	FOR
2) Busing	ABS	7) Coed Phys Ed	FOR	12) Turkish Arms Cutoff	FOR
3) ABM	AGN	8) Pov Lawyer Gag	AGN	13) Youth Camp Regs	ABS
4) B-1 Bomber	AGN	9) Pub Trans Sub	FOR	14) Strip Mine Veto	AGN
5) Nerve Gas	AGN	10) EZ Voter Regis	FOR	15) Farm Bill Veto	AGN

Election Results

1974 general:	Parren J. Mitchell (D), unopposed			($22,376)
1974 primary:	Parren J. Mitchell (D), unopposed			
1972 general:	Parren J. Mitchell (D)	83,759	(80%)	($55,577)
	Verdell Adair (R)	20,876	(20%)	($592)

◆ ◆ ◆ ◆ ◆

EIGHTH DISTRICT

By virtually any measure one cares to use, the 8th congressional district of Maryland is the richest district in the country. It includes just about all of Maryland's Montgomery County—the hunk of ultra-valuable suburban and country real estate immediately northwest of Washington, D.C. Like Prince Georges to the east, Montgomery experienced a vast population increase during the 1950s and 1960s. The migrants here, however, were of a little different sort: they tended to have higher incomes, more education, and they were more likely to hold white-collar jobs. The typical resident of the 8th district is a high-ranking GS-15 civil servant or perhaps a lawyer in private practice; a person likely as not to have a graduate school degree, and one who professes vaguely liberal politics. Montgomery voters are usually willing tp plunk for the Democratic slate, but their favorite kind of candidate is a liberal Republican who cares deeply about the political process, like Senator Charles Mathias.

Thus radical chic is not the label one would use to describe the 8th district's politics; League of Women Voters liberal is closer. Both the local Democratic and Republican parties here are the most liberal in the state. Since 1966 the 8th's Congressman has been Gilbert Gude, an antiwar Republican with an ADA rating higher than those compiled by many Maryland Democrats. Gude had a tough fight in his first race when he won only 54% of the vote; but since then, he has been unbeatable, with 66% in the Democratic landslide year of 1974.

Like all Washington area Congressmen, Gude pays close attention to the complaints and gripes of his constituents, almost one-third of whom are government employees. Consequently, he is perhaps as much an ombudsman as a legislator. As a member of the District of Columbia Committee, Gude was always a strong supporter of home rule for the District. But like Mathias, he also insisted that the new D.C. government not have the power to tax the earning of suburbanites who work in the city—and there is a provision to that effect in the Home Rule Act that passed in 1973. The liberalism of the 8th district, after all, has its limits.

Census Data Pop. 493,121. Central city, 0%; suburban, 100%. Median family income, $17,102; families above $15,000: 58%; families below $3,000: 3%. Median years education, 13.2.

The Voters
Median voting age 41.
Employment profile White collar, 79%. Blue collar, 13%. Service, 7%. Farm, 1%.
Ethnic groups Black, 4%. Spanish, 3%. Total foreign stock, 21%. USSR, 3%; Germany, UK, 2% each; Canada, Poland, Italy, 1% each.

Presidential vote

1972	Nixon (R)	127,225	(57%)
	McGovern (D)	96,643	(43%)
1968	Nixon (R)	77,821	(44%)
	Humphrey (D)	85,063	(48%)
	Wallace (AI)	13,324	(8%)

Rep. Gilbert Gude (R) Elected 1966; b. Mar. 9, 1923, Washington, D.C.; home, Bethesda; U. of Md., 1941–43, Cornell U., B.S. 1948, Geo. Wash. U., M.A. 1958; Catholic.

Career Army, WWII; Md. House of Delegates, 1953–59; Md. Senate, 1963–67.

Offices 104 CHOB, 202-225-5341. Also 10400 Connecticut Ave., Suite 211, Kensington 20795, 301-443-6180.

Committees

District of Columbia (Ranking Member). Subcommittees: Commerce, Housing and Transportation; Government Operations; The Bicentennial, the Environment, and the International Community.

Government Operations (5th). Subcommittees: Conservation, Energy and Natural Resources.

Group Ratings

	ADA	COPE	LWV	RIPON	NFU	LCV	CFA	NAB	NSI	ACA
1974	78	90	83	93	77	100	85	25	20	20
1973	79	64	100	86	55	83	88	–	–	23
1972	81	73	92	100	86	93	100	25	10	18

Key Votes

1) Foreign Aid	FOR	6) Gov Abortn Aid	AGN	11) Pub Cong Election $	FOR
2) Busing	AGN	7) Coed Phys Ed	ABS	12) Turkish Arms Cutoff	FOR
3) ABM	AGN	8) Pov Lawyer Gag	AGN	13) Youth Camp Regs	ABS
4) B-1 Bomber	AGN	9) Pub Trans Sub	FOR	14) Strip Mine Veto	AGN
5) Nerve Gas	AGN	10) EZ Voter Regis	FOR	15) Farm Bill Veto	FOR

Election Results

1974 general:	Gilbert Gude (R)	104,675	(66%)	($48,063)
	Sidney Kramer (D)	54,112	(34%)	($43,889)
1974 primary:	Gilbert Gude (R)	19,737	(86%)	
	Sheldon Z. Kaplan (R)	3,271	(14%)	
1972 general:	Gilbert Gude (R)	137,287	(64%)	($61,904)
	Joseph G. Anastasi (D)	77,551	(36%)	($70,899)

MASSACHUSETTS

The bumper stickers started appearing shortly after the 1972 election: "Massachusetts—the one and only." In the cold, wet spring of 1973, as the full Watergate storm broke out, more came out. "Don't blame me—I'm from Massachusetts." And as Richard Nixon took his final presidential jetride back to San Clemente, Bay State cars were still sporting one which featured an outline of the state, with the words inside "We told you so." Before the 1972 election we called Massachusetts "the most liberal large state in the union"; to judge from the 1972 results, Massachusetts was the *only* liberal state. Now that just about everybody has seen through Richard Nixon, it is hard to remember just how aberrant Massachusetts's conduct seemed; in retrospect those Bay Staters were right who insisted that what really needs explanation is why the rest of the country went the other way.

For those with political memories that go back more than a decade, Massachusetts' status as the most liberal state is surprising. It has, to be sure, gone Democratic in every presidential election since 1928 except for the Eisenhower years. But this is also the land of flinty, conservative Yankees like the elder Henry Cabot Lodge who kept the U.S. out of the League of Nations or the bigoted Judge Webster Thayer who sent Sacco and Vanzetti to the gallows. It is a state which never gave Franklin Roosevelt much of a majority, and which enthusiastically supported Joe McCarthy's crusade against Communism in the early '50s. It is a state which banned the sale of birth control devices until the Supreme Court said it could no longer do so, and one whose local governments were reportedly riddled with corruption.

So how did Massachusetts come to be what it is, the premier liberal state? The first and easiest explanation is that this is a very heavily Democratic state, and that as the Democratic Party has moved left Massachusetts—unlike, say, New York—has moved with it. Indeed, it has become much *more* Democratic in recent years. When John F. Kennedy was elected President in 1960, Republicans had nearly half the state's congressional delegation, sizeable minorities in the state legislature, and they took 40% of the vote for Richard Nixon. Today Democrats hold ten of the twelve congressional seats, have better than 3–1 margins in the state legislature, and—to take just one figure—won 74% of the vote cast for state Senator in 1974. The Republican Party here, like so many of the elderly Yankees who were its most solid supporters, seems simply to have disappeared.

A second explanation was proffered by former Nixon aide and convicted felon Charles Colson, himself a Massachusetts native: that the state just has too many kooks. If Colson meant students, he had something; about 7% of the eligible voters here are students, a figure exceeded only in Utah, Colorado, and California. The student vote here went heavily for McGovern and against Nixon. But McGovern would still have carried Massachusetts, though by a narrow margin, even if not a single student had voted. The same can be said, incidentally, about the state's small (3%) black population.

For a sufficient explanation of Massachusetts' political behavior, we must go back further—to the origins of the state's political culture. The traumatic event that structured electoral politics here was not, as it was in so many states, the Civil War; instead, it was the Irish potato famine of the 1840s. The blight forced literally hundreds of thousands of Irish to immigrate to the United States, and nowhere did these new Americans make a greater impact than in Boston. In response, the established Yankees of the Commonwealth—still only a few years removed from a diehard allegiance to the Federalist Party—used to hang out "No Irish need apply" signs. But by the 1880s, the Irish were numerous enough to elect a Mayor of Boston, and since 1906 none but an Irish Catholic has held that job.

After the turn of the century, statewide elections became a sort of battleground between Yankee Protestant Republicans and Irish Catholic Democrats. The arrival of sizeable blocs of Italian, French Canadian, Portuguese, Jewish, and Polish voters complicated things; but in Massachusetts, as nowhere else in the country, the Irish remained *the* ethnic group. And even if issues, as we know them, were not always at stake, tribal loyalties were; and people rooted for candidates with the kind of fervor they reserve now for football teams. One classic Irish-Yankee confrontation was the 1916 Senate race between Republican Senator Henry Cabot Lodge and Democratic Mayor John F. (Honey Fitz) Fitzgerald. Lodge won that one, but 36 years later—and people still remembered—Honey Fitz's grandson, John F. Kennedy, evened the score by beating Lodge's grandson and namesake in the 1952 Senate race.

The Kennedy influence has played a crucial role in the formation of the state's current political attitudes. While retaining intense emotional support from the state's Irish and Catholic voters, the Harvard-educated, aristocratic, even Anglophilic Kennedys have also made Democrats respectable to the state's Yankees. They and most of the state's younger Democratic politicians are obviously far removed from the corruption and seamy dealmaking which used to characterize the lower levels of Massachusetts politics—something which cannot be said of Richard Nixon's Republicans.

Indeed, dislike of Nixon and his Southern strategy and, probably even more important, of the Vietnam war, has moved Massachusetts Yankees steadily to the left in the last dozen years. These are, after all, the descendants of those who stood against the expansionist wars against Mexico and Spain, who worked feverishly for the abolition of slavery, and generally have backed what were seen as hopelessly unrealistic causes until their goals were accomplished. It is worth noting that one of the first independent peace candidates in the country was Thomas Boylston Adams—one of *the* Adamses—in Massachusetts in 1966, and that as well-born and illustrious a Massachusetts Yankee as Samuel Eliot Morison never hid his distaste for Mr. Nixon and his war.

In New York, where the personification of upper-class liberalism was Mayor John Lindsay, a similar movement stirred an Archie Bunker counterrevolution among the ethnic masses. Not so in Massachusetts, where the central political figure is Edward M. Kennedy. If Kennedy's antiwar position helped to make him acceptable to WASP tastemakers, his revered position in the Catholic neighborhoods of Massachusetts—and this is a majority-Catholic state—made his antiwar position acceptable, indeed unexceptionable, there. (It was a state legislature full of local Irish and Italian pols that passed the Shea Act back in 1970, the law that sought to exempt Massachusetts men from military service in Vietnam.) It is, therefore, not so remarkable after all that Massachusetts alone among all our states voted not to reelect our first criminal President. Not just student-dominated Cambridge, but lower income Irish Somerville and uppercrust Yankee Lincoln all voted for McGovern over Nixon in 1972.

Things were not always so harmonious here. In 1962, Edward Kennedy, then 30 and an assistant District Attorney in Boston, ran for the Senate. Yankee voters resented his inexperience, and went heavily for Republican George Lodge; a leftish peace candidate received 2% of the vote. Once in the Senate, Kennedy impressed senior colleagues by his willingness to do the humdrum chores of a junior Senator and cultivated home voters by close attention to the problems of Massachusetts. After the death of President Kennedy, this youngest Kennedy began to involve himself in more substantive issues. He became the Senator best versed in the problems of Vietnamese refugees and, by the late sixties, the driving force behind legislation to provide federal financing for comprehensive medical care.

Kennedy also played a major role in the major revision of our immigration laws in 1965, and was the major strategist in the successful drive to eliminate the poll tax and, later, to enact the 18-year-old vote. By the late 1960s people no longer thought of Kennedy as a lightweight capitalizing on his family name; he had earned respect as a politician who studied hard, mastered issues, and steered complex legislation through the Senate. In early 1969, Kennedy mounted a surprise campaign and won the post of Majority Whip away from Russell Long of Louisiana.

Then, in July 1969, came Chappaquiddick. Kennedy, then the frontrunner for the 1972 Democratic presidential nomination, was no longer a candidate for national office. His standing in the Senate was also damaged: in 1971 he lost the Whip's post, much as he had won it, to a lightning-fast effort organized by the better-prepared Robert Byrd of West Virginia. Nevertheless, by early 1972 Kennedy again had emerged as an important legislator, especially in the field of health care; and in the eyes of the national press, at least, remained a presidential possibility. He turned down George McGovern's offer of the 1972 vice presidential nomination, as McGovern ought to have been but apparently was not expecting.

In the years that have followed 1972 almost everything Kennedy does continues to make big news. The courtroom was filled when he went to argue, successfully, his own case to establish Nixon's use of the pocket veto as illegal. A huge cadre of national reporters followed him to Decatur, Alabama, when he appeared with George Wallace on a Fourth of July platform in 1973. And there were big headlines in 1974 when he announced suddenly that he would not be a presidential candidate in 1976. That announcement followed by some weeks Robert Sherrill's devastating article on Chappaquiddick in the New York *Times* magazine; every time Kennedy opened himself up to questions, the subject of that five-year-old tragedy would predominate.

Kennedy thus comes up for reelection in Massachusetts in 1976, and as usual his prospects are good. Despite Chappaquiddick he won a solid 63% of the vote against a very competent liberal Republican in 1970; he will probably do somewhat better this time. Political commentators still cannot resist the idea of another Kennedy running for President, and they seem constantly to overestimate the general public's desire for a Kennedy revival in the White House. Few voters under 40 have much political memory of the years when John F. Kennedy was President; they are receding fast from the category of recent events into history. Kennedy, who tends to polarize the electorate, is not significantly stronger than other, far less well known potential Democratic candidates, and it is time that people simply took him at his word and let him run for reelection to the Senate.

Edward Brooke, Massachusetts's junior Senator, is the first black member of the upper house since Blanche K. Bruce was denied reelection by the Mississippi "home rule" legislature in 1880. A native of Washington, D.C., Brooke rose steadily in Massachusetts's liberal Republican Party from appointive positions to the Attorney General's office; on his way to that position, in the 1962 primary he beat one Elliot Richardson. In 1966 Brooke's election to succeed the retiring Leverett Saltonstall, the state's most durable Yankee Republican, surprised no one. Brooke combines liberal stands on most issues with a deep devotion to the Republican Party; after opposing the Nixon Administration on many crucial issues, he was still willing to second Nixon's renomination at Miami Beach.

Neither abrasive nor militant, Brooke has not regarded himself as a special representative of the black community, and he maintains not particularly close relations with the black members of the House. He has always won his elections in constituencies overwhelmingly white. Yet it should be noted that he reserved some of his most fervent criticism of the Nixon Administration for its nominations of Judges Haynsworth and Carswell to the Supreme Court.

For 12 of the 14 years between 1960 and 1974, Massachusetts was presided over by Republican Governors with liberal reputations: John Volpe, who became Secretary of Transportation in the first Nixon cabinet and is now Ambassador to Italy, and Francis Sargent. Sargent moved up from the Lieutenant governor post in 1969, and won a full term with an impressive margin over Boston Mayor Kevin White in 1970. But by 1974 Sargent was in trouble. He complained that being Governor was itself a handicap, he had had to make so many unpopular decisions; but his own tactlessness contributed to his problems. He even managed to get into a feud with other Massachusetts Republicans—a body of people so scarce you would think they'd stick together.

The Democratic nominee in 1974 was Michael Dukakis, former state legislator with a liberal reputation, former host on the public TV program The Advocates, unsuccessful candidate for Lieutenant Governor in 1970, and only the second non-Irish Democratic candidate for Governor in 50 years. Sargent's personality—and his decision to send troops into Boston to keep the peace during the busing crisis—dominated the campaign; but Dukakis easily won. Once in office he became a sort of East Coast Jerry Brown. He disappointed many of his old liberal supporters by supporting higher taxes and lower spending, and he delighted the public by doing things like riding the subway to work every day.

When Boston's John McCormack served as House Majority Leader and Speaker, the Massachusetts House delegation had a remarkable stability. Rumor had it that McCormack took great pains to insure the incumbency of the state's Congressmen of both parties. When McCormack retired in 1970, that pattern was already beginning to fade. Today, liberal Democrats hold 10 of the state's 12 House seats, and they could probably win the two others if the liberal Republicans who hold them now should retire.

Census Data Pop. 5,689,170; 2.81% of U.S. total, 10th largest; Central city, 30%; suburban, 54%. Median family income, $10,833; 8th highest; families above $15,000: 25%; families below $3,000: 6%. Median years education, 12.3.

1974 Share of Federal Tax Burden $8,007,768,000; 2.99% of U.S. total, 10th largest.

1974 Share of Federal Outlays $7,643,018,000; 2.83% of U.S. total, 11th largest. Per capita federal spending, $1344.

DOD	$2,270,367,000	8th	(3.32%)	HEW	$3,006,936,000	10th	(3.24%)
AEC	$14,436,000	20th	(0.47%)	HUD	$47,263,000	6th	(3.59%)
NASA	$46,018,000	10th	(1.55%)	VA	$434,149,000	9th	(3.17%)
DOT	$279,837,000	8th	(3.31%)	EPA	$70,160,000	13th	(2.23%)
DOC	$34,485,000	8th	(2.14%)	RevS	$193,783,000	8th	(3.19%)
DOI	$29,577,000	22d	(1.20%)	Int.	$216,181,000	13th	(1.05%)
USDA	$54,563,000	40th	(0.44%)	Other	$945,263,000		

Economic Base Finance, insurance and real estate; electrical equipment and supplies, especially communication equipment; machinery, especially special industry machinery; apparel and other textile products, especially women's and misses' outerwear; printing and publishing, especially newspapers and commercial printing; fabricated metal products; food and kindred products.

Political Line-up Governor, Michael S. Dukakis (D). Senators, Edward M. Kennedy (D) and Edward W. Brooke (R). Representatives, 12 (10 D and 2 R). State Senate (33 D and 7 R); State House (189 D, 46 R, and 3 Ind., and 1 vac.).

The Voters

Registration 2,828,309 Total. 1,226,824 D (43%); 476,491 R (17%); 1,124,994 Ind. (40%).
Median voting age 44.
Employment profile White collar, 53%. Blue collar, 34%. Service, 13%. Farm, 0%.
Ethnic groups Black, 3%. Spanish, 1%. Total foreign stock, 33%. Canada, 8%; Italy, 5%; Ireland, 4%; UK, 3%; Poland, USSR, 2% each; Portugal, 1%.

Presidential vote

1972	Nixon (R)	1,112,078	(45%)
	McGovern (D)	1,332,540	(55%)
1968	Nixon (R)	766,844	(33%)
	Humphrey (D)	1,469,218	(63%)
	Wallace (AI)	87,088	(4%)

1972 Democratic Presidential Primary

McGovern	325,673	(53%)
Muskie	131,709	(21%)
others	161,134	(26%)

1972 Republican Presidential Primary

Nixon	99,150	(81%)
McCloskey	16,435	(13%)
Ashbrook	4,864	(4%)
others	1,690	(1%)

Sen. Edward M. Kennedy (D) Elected 1962, seat up 1976; b. Feb. 22, 1932, Boston; home, Boston; Harvard U., A.B. 1956, Acad. of Internatl. Law, The Hague, Holland, 1958, U. of Va., LL.B. 1959; Catholic.

Career Army, 1951–53; Asst. Dist. Atty., Suffolk Co., 1961–62.

Offices 431 RSOB, 202-224-4543. Also Rm. 2400A JFK Fed. Bldg., Boston 02203, 617-223-2826.

Committees

The Judiciary (4th). Subcommittees: Administrative Practice and Procedure (Chairman); Antitrust and Monopoly Legislation; Constitutional Rights; Juvenile Delinquency; Refugees and Escapees (Chairman).

Labor and Public Welfare (4th). Subcommittees: Aging; Alcoholism and Narcotics; Children and Youth; Education; Employment, Poverty, and Migratory Labor; The Handicapped; Health (Chairman); Special Subcommittee on National Science Foundation (Chairman).

Joint Economic Committee (6th, Senate Side). Subcommittees: Consumer Economics; Economic Growth; Inter-American Economic Relationships; International Economics; Priorities and Economy in Government; Urban Affairs.

Group Ratings

	ADA	COPE	LWV	RIPON	NFU	LCV	CFA	NAB	NSI	ACA
1974	100	70	100	58	100	94	100	27	0	0
1973	95	91	100	67	100	–	100	–	–	4
1972	90	89	100	79	90	92	100	9	0	5

Key Votes

1) No-Knock	AGN	8) Gov Abortn Aid	FOR	15) Consumer Prot Agy	ABS
2) Busing	FOR	9) Cut Mil Brass	ABS	16) Forced Psych Tests	FOR
3) No Fault	FOR	10) Gov Limousine	AGN	17) Fed Campaign Subs	FOR
4) F-111	AGN	11) RR Featherbed	FOR	18) Rhod Chrome Ban	FOR
5) Death Penalty	AGN	12) Handgun License	FOR	19) Open Legis Meetings	FOR
6) Foreign Aid	FOR	13) Less Troop Abrd	FOR	20) Strikers Food Stmps	FOR
7) Filibuster	AGN	14) Resume Turk Aid	AGN	21) Gov Info Disclosure	FOR

Election Results

1970 general:	Edward M. Kennedy (D)	1,202,856	(63%)
	Josiah Spaulding (R)	715,978	(37%)
1970 primary:	Edward M. Kennedy (D), unopposed		
1964 general:	Edward M. Kennedy (D)	1,716,907	(75%)
	Howard Whitmore, Jr. (R)	587,663	(25%)

Sen. Edward W. Brooke (R) Elected 1966, seat up 1978; b. Oct. 26, 1919, Washington, D.C.; home, Newton Centre; Howard U., B.S. 1941, Boston U., LL.B. 1948, LL.M. 1950; Episcopalian.

Career Army, WWII; Chm., Boston Finance Comm., 1961–62; Atty. Gen. of Mass., 1963–66.

Offices 4121 DSOB, 202-224-2742. Also Rm. 2003F JFK Fed. Bldg., Boston 02203, 617-223-7240.

Committees

Appropriations (5th). Subcommittees: Foreign Operations; HUD and Independent Agencies; Labor and HEW; Military Construction; State, Justice, Commerce, The Judiciary.

Banking, Housing, and Urban Affairs (2d). Subcommittees: Consumer Affairs; Financial Institutions; Housing and Urban Affairs; Oversight; Securities.

Group Ratings

	ADA	COPE	LWV	RIPON	NFU	LCV	CFA	NAB	NSI	ACA
1974	76	82	100	91	88	90	100	20	30	5
1973	78	89	89	81	94	–	56	–	–	8
1972	80	90	100	96	80	77	100	33	33	19

Key Votes

1) No-Knock	AGN	8) Gov Abortn Aid	FOR	15) Consumer Prot Agy	FOR
2) Busing	FOR	9) Cut Mil Brass	AGN	16) Forced Psych Tests	FOR
3) No Fault	FOR	10) Gov Limousine	FOR	17) Fed Campaign Subs	FOR
4) F-111	AGN	11) RR Featherbed	FOR	18) Rhod Chrome Ban	FOR
5) Death Penalty	AGN	12) Handgun License	FOR	19) Open Legis Meetings	FOR
6) Foreign Aid	FOR	13) Less Troop Abrd	AGN	20) Strikers Food Stmps	FOR
7) Filibuster	AGN	14) Resume Turk Aid	AGN	21) Gov Info Disclosure	FOR

Election Results

1972 general:	Edward W. Brooke (R)	1,505,932	(65%)	($368,038)
	John J. Droney (D)	823,278	(35%)	($82,888)
1972 primary:	Edward W. Brooke (R), unopposed			
1966 general:	Edward W. Brooke (R)	1,213,472	(61%)	
	Endicott Peabody (D)	774,761	(39%)	

Gov. Michael S. Dukakis (D) Elected 1974, term expires 1979; b. 1933, Brookline; Swarthmore Col., B.A. 1955, Harvard U., LL.B. 1960.

Career Army, Korea; Practicing atty.; Mass. House of Reps., 1963–71; Dem. nominee for Lt. Gov., 1970; Moderator, "The Advocates", Natl. TV show.

Offices State House, Boston 02133, 617-727-2761.

Election Results

1974 general:	Michael S. Dukakis (D)	992,284	(56%)
	Francis W. Sargent (R)	784,353	(44%)
1974 primary:	Michael S. Dukakis (D)	444,590	(58%)
	Robert H. Quinn (D)	326,385	(42%)

◆ ◆ ◆ ◆ ◆

FIRST DISTRICT

The 1st congressional district of Massachusetts is the western end of the state: the Berkshire Mountains and most of Massachusetts's portion of the Connecticut River valley. The Berkshires are known as a summer resort area and for picturesque towns like Lenox, home of the Tanglewood music festival. More important politically are the old mill towns and manufacturing centers nestled in the mountains, like Pittsfield (pop. 57,000), the district's largest city, and North Adams (pop. 19,000). The second and third-generation immigrants packed into these tiny mill towns almost inevitably outvote the small town and farm Yankee Republicans by substantial margins.

The Connecticut valley is a similar place politically: small Republican towns more than offset by the occasional Democratic mill towns. In the middle of the valley are the college towns of Amherst (pop.18,000), with Amherst College and the University of Massachusetts, and Northampton (pop. 30,000), home of Smith College and Calvin Coolidge. Despite the presence of then-students Julie and David Eisenhower in 1968, none of these areas has ever voted for Richard Nixon. To the south are industrial and residential suburbs of Springfield: Holyoke (pop. 50,000), Westfield (pop. 31,000), and West Springfield (pop. 31,000).

In national elections, the 1st always votes Democratic; like 11 of the 12 Massachusetts congressional districts, it went for McGovern in 1972. But in congressional races, the 1st is still wedded to the Republicans which it once supported so steadily. Congressman Silvio Conte now has become so entrenched that he seldom has opposition and, when he does, he wins the 71% of the vote he took in the generally Democratic year of 1974. Conte's most notable challenge occurred in 1958, his first House race, from Williams College political scientist James MacGregor Burns. The professor got the national publicity but Conte—who had represented Berkshire County in the state Senate for eight years—got the local votes. So Burns went on to finish his Roosevelt biography, and Conte went down to Washington to become, in time, one of the few liberal Republicans on the House Appropriations Committee. Thanks to recent retirements and defeats, Conte is now the third-ranking minority member on that important body.

Conte has not been afraid to buck the Nixon and Ford Administrations on important issues. On the SST, for example, as the ranking Republican on the Transporation Appropriations Subcommittee, Conte was one of the project's leading opponents. A perennial Conte project is to place a ceiling on farm subsidy payments to any one farm owner. Though he has succeeded in getting a $20,000 limit imposed—and has helped to cut down the programs generally—Conte is more often frustrated by the power of the farm bloc and the willingness of labor-oriented liberals, often led by California's Phillip Burton, to barter away their votes on this issue for concessions from farm state and Southerners on matters that the liberals care more about.

Census Data Pop. 469,438. Central city, 23%; suburban, 38%. Median family income, $10,311; families above $15,000: 20%; families below $3,000: 7%. Median years education, 12.2.

The Voters

Median voting age 44.
Employment profile White collar, 49%. Blue collar, 36%. Service, 14%. Farm, 1%.
Ethnic groups Spanish, 1%. Total foreign stock, 27%. Canada, 7%; Poland, 5%; Italy, 3%; Ireland, UK, Germany, 2% each.

Presidential vote

1972	Nixon (R)	102,513	(49%)
	McGovern (D)	107,528	(51%)
1968	Nixon (R)	69,299	(37%)
	Humphrey (D)	111,303	(58%)
	Wallace (AI)	8,812	(5%)

Rep. Silvio O. Conte (R) Elected 1958; b. Nov. 9, 1921, Pittsfield; home, Pittsfield; Boston Col., Boston Col. Law School, LL.B. 1949; Catholic.

Career Served with the Seabees in the SW Pacific, WWII; Practicing atty., 1949–58; Mass. Senate, 1951–59.

Offices 239 CHOB, 202-225-5335. Also Suite 305, 100 North St., Pittsfield 01201, 413-442-0946.

Committees

Appropriations (3d). Subcommittees: Foreign Operations; Labor-HEW; Transportation.

Small Business (Ranking Member). Subcommittees: Energy and Environment.

Group Ratings

	ADA	COPE	LWV	RIPON	NFU	LCV	CFA	NAB	NSI	ACA
1974	87	82	100	94	71	80	75	58	33	8
1973	60	50	92	100	53	79	86	–	–	22
1972	60	100	93	50	93	100	33	44	22	

Key Votes

1) Foreign Aid	FOR	6) Gov Abortn Aid	AGN	11) Pub Cong Election $	FOR
2) Busing	FOR	7) Coed Phys Ed	FOR	12) Turkish Arms Cutoff	FOR
3) ABM	AGN	8) Pov Lawyer Gag	AGN	13) Youth Camp Regs	FOR
4) B-1 Bomber	FOR	9) Pub Trans Sub	AGN	14) Strip Mine Veto	AGN
5) Nerve Gas	AGN	10) EZ Voter Regis	FOR	15) Farm Bill Veto	FOR

Election Results

1974 general:	Silvio O. Conte (R)	107,285	(71%)	($47,736)
	Thomas R. Manning (D)	43,524	(29%)	($8,067)
1974 primary:	Silvio O. Conte (R), unopposed			
1972 general:	Silvio O. Conte (R), unopposed			($2,346)

◆ ◆ ◆ ◆ ◆

SECOND DISTRICT

The 2d congressional district of Massachusetts includes the city of Springfield, many of its suburbs, and a collection of rural and small industrial towns to the east. Springfield (pop. 163,000) and Chicopee (pop.66,000) are the Democratic bastions of the district, though most of the rest of the 2d usually produces Democratic margins as well. The image of the small New England town is of a clapboard housed village peopled by taciturn Yankees. But in fact so many of the WASPs have either died off or long since moved west, and in their places are people more likely to be of Irish, Italian, or Polish ancestral stock. The storefront here may have a New England Yankee facades, but hanging from them are signs with the Italian or Polish proprietors' names.

Springfield is the home town of several famous political pros: Lawrence O'Brien, the Democratic National Chairman whose telephone was the target of the Watergate buggers; the well-known (often through his own promotions) campaign consultant Joseph Napolitan; and Alaska Senator Mike Gravel. All grew up and learned their first political lessons in Springfield's wards and precincts; their own ethnic origins—Irish, Italian, French Canadian—suggest the variety of this small city.

Another Springfield political pro is 2d district Congressman Edward P. Boland, a Democrat who now has nearly 25 years' service in the House. For many years Boland was a bachelor and roomed with Tip O'Neill of Cambridge. Boland's marriage in 1973 ended that arrangement, but the Springfield congressman is still in close touch with his friend the Majority Leader. Like O'Neill, Boland is a politician who can bridge some of the gaps between the oldline big city Democrats and the younger, more ideological liberals who increasingly have come to dominate the Democratic caucus.

Boland is the sixth-ranking Democrat on the Appropriations Committee and Chairman of its HUD-Independent Agencies Subcommittee. At 65, he is comparatively youthful by committee standards, and has an outside chance of succeeding to the Chairmanship under the old seniority system. As the highest ranking northern Democrat, Boland also could conceivably be the beneficiary of a movement to dump Texas's George Mahon or the next man in line, Mississippi's Jamie Whitten. That, at the moment, is unlikely; Boland is not the type to encourage such a rebellion, and it is not clear whether there will be such a liberal predominance in the caucus in the 95th Congress as there has been in the 94th. In any case, Boland's reelection is not in doubt. There has been a Republican candidate against him only once in the last dozen years, and that one won only 26% of the vote.

Census Data Pop. 472,270. Central city, 49%; suburban, 28%. Median family income, $10,268; families above $15,000: 20%; families below $3,000: 7%. Median years education, 12.1.

The Voters

Median voting age 45.
Employment profile White collar, 45%. Blue collar, 42%. Service, 12%. Farm, 1%.
Ethnic groups Black, 5%. Spanish, 2%. Total foreign stock, 31%. Canada, 9%; Poland, 5%; Italy, 3%; Ireland, UK, 2% each; USSR, Germany, 1% each.

Presidential vote

1972	Nixon (R)	88,652	(48%)
	McGovern (D)	95,348	(52%)
1968	Nixon (R)	62,441	(34%)
	Humphrey (D)	114,197	(62%)
	Wallace (AI)	8,787	(5%)

Rep. Edward P. Boland (D) Elected 1952; b. Oct. 1, 1911, Springfield; home, Springfield; Boston Col. Law School; Catholic.

Career Mass. House of Reps, 1935–41; Hampton Co. Register of Deeds, 1941–42, 1946–49; Army, WWII; Military Aide to Gov. Paul A. Dever, 1949–52.

Offices 2111 RHOB, 202-225-5601. Also 1883 Main St., Springfield 01103, 413-733-4127.

Committees

Appropriations (6th). Subcommittees: HUD-Independent Agencies (Chairman); Public Works; Treasury, Postal Service, and General Government.

Group Ratings

	ADA	COPE	LWV	RIPON	NFU	LCV	CFA	NAB	NSI	ACA
1974	68	100	83	58	75	75	83	25	40	0
1973	80	100	83	73	83	67	88	–	–	8
1972	69	91	75	87	86	60	100	17	22	17

Key Votes

1) Foreign Aid	FOR	6) Gov Abortn Aid	AGN	11) Pub Cong Election $	FOR
2) Busing	AGN	7) Coed Phys Ed	AGN	12) Turkish Arms Cutoff	ABS
3) ABM	AGN	8) Pov Lawyer Gag	AGN	13) Youth Camp Regs	FOR
4) B-1 Bomber	ABS	9) Pub Trans Sub	FOR	14) Strip Mine Veto	AGN
5) Nerve Gas	AGN	10) EZ Voter Regis	FOR	15) Farm Bill Veto	FOR

Election Results

1974 general:	Edward P. Boland (D), unopposed	($56)
1974 primary:	Edward P. Boland (D), unopposed	
1972 general:	Edward P. Boland (D), unopposed	($1)

◆ ◆ ◆ ◆ ◆

THIRD DISTRICT

Worcester (pop.176,000), the second largest city in Massachusetts, is a manufacturing town that lies roughly in the geographical center of the state. Worcester is surrounded by an almost random assortment of comfortable suburbs and tiny mill towns. The thin New England soil only barely covers here and layers of rocks undergird everything. Though there are a number of colleges and universities about, they do not, as in the Boston area, have a major effect on the culture of the entire community. Nor is there quite as large or at least visible Yankee upperclass which has been moving to the left politically. This is nitty gritty New England, where the Democratic majorities result almost entirely from the all but genetically ingrained voting habits of middle and lower middle class voters of various ethnic backgrounds.

In congressional elections, the Worcester-based district (it used to be numbered the 4th, and now is the 3d), has been strongly Democratic for about as long as anyone can remember. From 1946 to 1972, it regularly elected and reelected Democratic Congressman Harold Donohue. Those who recall the less voluble members of the House Judiciary Committee impeachment hearings will perhaps remember Donohue, the 73-year-old, white-haired, Democrat who sat next to Chairman Peter Rodino. Thanks to seniority, Donohue was the committee's second-ranking Democrat; when Rodino vacated the chair, Donohue took over. His performance was not embarrassing, but he did seem to be performing by rote, and there was general agreement that it was a good thing he ranked behind Rodino, rather than ahead of him.

At that time Donohue had already announced his retirement, and he capped off his career by voting for the impeachment of the President he had worked next to in the Navy during World War II. Donohue had had a close call the last time a Republican ran against him, in 1970, and he missed his close friends John McCormack, the former Speaker who had retired in 1970, and Philip J. Philbin, the next-door Congressman who had been defeated by Father Drinan that same year.

Donohue's retirement set the stage for a compartively close election here. Favored was Democrat Joseph Early, a rather conservative veteran of the Massachusetts legislature—although one should keep in mind that around here "conservative" refers to the kind of politics practiced by people like Donohue, who had an 84 ADA record. Making an aggressive campaign of it was 31-year-old Republican David Lionett, also a state legislator, who was claiming to be more liberal than Early on some issues. Lionett made some inroads into the normal Democratic vote here, but could win only 38%; Early had 50% and an independent—an increasingly common phenomenon in Massachusetts—got 12%. Once in the House Early, presumably with the help of Majority Leader Tip O'Neill, got a seat on the Appropriations Committee; no one thinks the freshman will have trouble winning in the future.

Census Data Pop. 469,443. Central city, 38%; suburban, 36%. Median family income, $10,863; families above $15,000: 23%; families below $3,000: 6%. Median years education, 12.2.

The Voters

Median voting age 44.
Employment profile White collar, 49%. Blue collar, 38%. Service, 13%. Farm, –%.
Ethnic groups Total foreign stock, 32%. Canada, 8%; Italy, 5%; Ireland, 3%; UK, Poland, Sweden, 2% each; USSR, Lithuania, 1% each.

Presidential vote

1972	Nixon (R)	83,423	(46%)
	McGovern (D)	98,449	(54%)
1968	Nixon (R)	62,260	(32%)
	Humphrey (D)	125,551	(65%)
	Wallace (AI)	5,810	(3%)

Rep. Joseph D. Early (D) Elected 1974; b. Jan. 31, 1933, Worcester; home, Worcester; Col. of the Holy Cross, B.S. 1955; Catholic.

Career Navy, 1955–57; High school teacher and coach, 1959–63; Mass. House of Reps., 1963–74.

Offices 1032 LHOB, 202-225-6101. Also 34 Mechanic St., Rm. 203, Worcester 01608, 617-752-6718.

Committees

Appropriations (36th). Subcommittees: Foreign Operations; State, Justice, Commerce, and the Judiciary.

Group Ratings: Newly Elected

Key Votes

1) Foreign Aid	FOR	6) Gov Abortn Aid	NE	11) Pub Cong Election $	NE
2) Busing	NE	7) Coed Phys Ed	FOR	12) Turkish Arms Cutoff	NE
3) ABM	NE	8) Pov Lawyer Gag	NE	13) Youth Camp Regs	FOR
4) B-1 Bomber	AGN	9) Pub Trans Sub	NE	14) Strip Mine Veto	AGN
5) Nerve Gas	NE	10) EZ Voter Regis	NE	15) Farm Bill Veto	FOR

Election Results

1974 general:	Joseph D. Early (D)	78,244	(50%)	($120,584)
	David J. Lionett (R)	60,717	(38%)	($120,978)
	Douglas J. Rowe (IND.)	19,018	(12%)	($69,267)
1974 primary:	Joseph D. Early (D)	24,470	(32%)	
	Gerald D'Amico (D)	19047	(25%)	
	Paul V. Mullaney (D)	18,925	(25%)	
	Three Others (D)	14,670	(19%)	

◆ ◆ ◆ ◆ ◆

FOURTH DISTRICT

Dozens of Protestant clergymen have served in the House of Representatives, but until 1974 only one Roman Catholic priest had ever been elected Congressman: Father Robert F. Drinan of the 4th district of Massachusetts. From any perspective, he is an unusual political figure. With no political experience, Drinan beat an incumbent Congressman not once but twice in 1970, beat a tough Republican challenger two years later, was the first Congressman to introduce a resolution to impeach Richard Nixon, and voted as part of a large majority in the House Judiciary Committee to so impeach him.

The story begins in 1970, when Drinan was finishing 14 years as the highly respected Dean of the Boston College Law School. Living near the school, the priest was resident of what then was the 3d district—a geographic monstrosity stretching from suburban Newton, just outside Boston, some 100 miles out in a narrow corridor to the town of Fitchburg in central Massachusetts and beyond. For 28 years Congressman Philip J. Philbin had represented the 3d, combining a liberal record on domestic issues with a strong hawkish point of view as a member of the Armed Services Committee. In 1968, after redistricting had added Newton and several other Boston suburbs to the district, Philbin won only 49% of the vote in a four-candidate Democratic primary, and only 48% in the general election where an independent peace candidate finished second.

This was obviously a constituency waiting for a candidate. About half the district's population had not been represented by Philbin before 1968, and these people felt little rapport for this oldtime politician. The problem was to put together a majority composed of middle-class Newton, with its large Jewish population; Waltham, a Catholic working-class suburb; and the upper income, woodsy, WASPy towns of Weston, Lincoln, and Wayland—a majority large enough to overcome Philbin's predictable margins in the western end of the district. Drinan was chosen the candidate in a liberal caucus, and he became one of consultant John Marttila's first clients; a major grass-roots campaign beat Philbin in the primary. The old regular, refusing to accept defeat, ran in the general election as an Independent, and with a strong Republican candidate in the field, Drinan got just enough votes for a 38–36–26 victory.

Something similar happened in 1972. Republicans had been eyeing the district for a number of reasons. There was Drinan's low percentage in 1970; many Catholics oppose the idea of a priest in politics; and Drinan had lost the heavily Catholic, mill-town western end of the district. Redistricting complicated the picture, adding the prosperous Boston suburb of Brookline. Though the home of Brahmins like Elliot Richardson, Brookline is important politically for its large and elderly Jewish community. (In 1917 John F. Kennedy was born here in what was then and remains today a Jewish neighborhood.) The Republican candidate, state Representative Martin Linsky, was well-financed, and used the Israel issue even against the pro-Israel Drinan.

What saved Drinan in that election was his constituent service organization in the western part of the district—which he carried, in contrast to 1970. For Republican Linsky carried Brookline and cut into the Congressman's strength in Newton and other suburbs. In 1974, Brookline was again a trouble spot for Drinan, as it went for Independent candidate (and Democratic state Representative) Jon Rotenberg. Drinan has a solid record of supporting Israel and working for the rights of Soviet Jews; yet he keeps drawing opponents who try to imply, apparently on the basis of his even better known dovishness on Vietnam, that he is soft on Israel. The tactic seems not to be working, but so far it has prevented him from winning an absolute majority of the vote.

In his first term in the House Drinan, with his years of experience as a law school dean, was able to win a seat on the Judiciary Committee, which of course put him in the perfect position to act on his conviction that Richard Nixon had violated the Constitution and the laws of the land. Even here, however, Drinan was frustrated as the Committee majority declined to vote impeachment on the grounds that Nixon's bombing of Cambodia exceeded his legal powers, more it seemed out of a general weariness and relief at having voted impeachment on other grounds than out of any sustained examination of the case Drinan was presenting. Drinan also served on the House Internal Security Committee—until 1975, when Phil Burton of California persuaded all Democrats but the Chairman to leave it, and the committee, after more than 30 years of controversial existence, quietly went out of existence—which was Drinan's goal all along.

Census Data Pop. 476,130. Central city, 16%; suburban, 71%. Median family income, $12,409; families above $15,000: 36%; families below $3,000: 5%. Median years education, 12.5.

The Voters

Median voting age 42.
Employment profile White collar, 62%. Blue collar, 27%. Service, 11%. Farm, –%.
Ethnic groups Black, 1%. Spanish, 1%. Total foreign stock, 37%. Canada, 11%; Italy, USSR, 5% each; Ireland, 3%; UK, Poland, 2% each; Germany, 1%.

Presidential vote

1972	Nixon (R)	92,341	(44%)
	McGovern (D)	116,100	(56%)
1968	Nixon (R)	63,795	(33%)
	Humphrey (D)	124,055	(65%)
	Wallace (AI)	4,202	(2%)

Rep. Robert F. Drinan (D) Elected 1970; b. Nov. 15, 1920, Boston; home, Newton; Boston Col. A.B., 1942, M.A. 1947, Georgetown U., LL.B. 1949, LL.M. 1950, Gregorian U., Rome, Italy, 1954; Catholic.

Career Ordained Jesuit Priest, 1953–; Dean, Boston Col. Law School, 1956–70.

Offices 224 CHOB, 202-225-5931. Also 400 Totten Pond Rd., Bldg. 1, Waltham 02154, 617-890-9455.

Committees

Government Operations (21st). Subcommittees: Commerce, Consumer and Monetary Affairs; Intergovernmental Relations and Human Resources.

Judiciary (13th). Subcommittees: Civil and Constitutional Rights; Courts, Civil Liberties, and the Administration of Justice.

Group Ratings

	ADA	COPE	LWV	RIPON	NFU	LCV	CFA	NAB	NSI	ACA
1974	100	91	100	81	86	94	100	17	10	0
1973	100	91	92	73	75	100	100	–	–	7
1972	100	100	100	73	86	86	100	8	0	9

Key Votes

1) Foreign Aid	FOR	6) Gov Abortn Aid	FOR	11) Pub Cong Election $	FOR
2) Busing	FOR	7) Coed Phys Ed	FOR	12) Turkish Arms Cutoff	FOR
3) ABM	AGN	8) Pov Lawyer Gag	AGN	13) Youth Camp Regs	FOR
4) B-1 Bomber	AGN	9) Pub Trans Sub	FOR	14) Strip Mine Veto	AGN
5) Nerve Gas	AGN	10) EZ Voter Regis	FOR	15) Farm Bill Veto	FOR

Election Results

1974 general:	Robert F. Drinan (D)	77,286	(51%)	($178,871)
	Jon Rotenberg (Ind.)	52,785	(35%)	($76,576)
	Alvin Mandell (R)	21,922	(14%)	($14,322)
1974 primary:	Robert F. Drinan (D), unopposed			
1972 general:	Robert F. Drinan (D)	99,977	(49%)	($199,703)
	Martin A. Linsky (R)	93,927	(46%)	($148,285)
	John T. Collins (C)	11,141	(5%)	($22,579)

◆ ◆ ◆ ◆ ◆

FIFTH DISTRICT

The 5th congressional district of Massachusetts centers on two transportation arteries that have, at different times, been vital to the state's economic development. The first is the Merrimack River, whose falls provided the power for the great textile mills built by Boston Brahmins in the company towns they named for themselves, Lowell and Lawrence. Back in the mid-nineteenth century, the New England textile business was a boom industry that first employed local farm girls and then went on to hire hundreds of thousands of immigrants from Ireland and French Canada. Virtually all the New England textile firms have long since moved South and even abroad in search of lower wage levels; and with the mills of Lowell and Lawrence quiet, these cities suffered through a local depression that lasted something like 40 years.

Today both cities have perked up a bit, largely because of the peripheral influence of the area's other industrial artery, Route 128, a circumferential highway around greater Boston. Dozens of the nation's leading electronic and defense research firms, drawing brainpower from area universities, have located along both sides of the roadway. All have had their economic ups and downs; some of the latter came when Massachusetts absorbed nearly one-quarter of all Defense Department cutbacks in 1973—in apparent retaliation for its refusal to vote for Richard Nixon the previous year. But overall the economic effect has been positive, not only in the leafy suburbs at the southern end of the 5th district but even in Lowell and Lawrence.

Like all but one of Massachusetts's congressional districts, the 5th went for George McGovern in 1972. Yet for as long as anyone could remember, the district had been represented by a Republican Congressman. From 1924 to 1958, the 5th elected Edith Nourse Rogers, a genteel Republican who never had any trouble winning; her successor was F. Bradford Morse, a generally liberal Republican, who surprised a number of observers when he supported the Nixon candidacy before the 1968 Republican national convention. Presumably Morse had been persuaded to do so by another former member of Senator Leverett Saltonstall's staff, Charles Colson, who may also have had something to do with the way Morse left Congress. In 1972 Nixon nominated Morse to succeed Ralph Bunche as Undersecretary of the United Nations—a choice job which Morse, always interested in foreign policy, readily grabbed.

The resulting contest for the 5th district was one of the most expensive and acrimonious campaigns of 1972. It was also, as it turned out, one of the least conclusive—and one in which Colson's fine hand might conceivably have been found. The Democratic nominee was 28-year-old John Kerry, a Yale graduate who had made headlines as a leader of Vietnam Veterans Against the War. Kerry also made local headlines over switching his residence; when Morse had retired, he hurriedly moved to the 5th from the 3d district, where he had still earlier moved to run against incumbent Harold Donohue in the primary. Then, on the night before the primary, Kerry's brother was caught in the adjacent basement of a rival candidate's headquarters; he was, he said, searching for possible disruption of Kerry telephone banks. That story was played up big by the Lowell *Sun*, which also constantly harped on a book jacket photo of Kerry and other VVAW members carrying an upside-down American flag. An independent candidate spent all his time attacking Kerry, and then pulled out of the race before the general election—without letting anyone know where the money for his elaborate campaign came from.

All of this led some Kerry partisans to think that Colson, who had been known to have tried to discredit the antiwar veterans in just about anyway possible, was up to what turned out to be his usual dirty tricks. But even if that was true—no one can be sure yet—it almost certainly didn't matter. To be sure, the Republican candidate, former state Representative Paul Cronin, did win by a 53–47 margin. But in retrospect it seems to have been Kerry's weakness, the perception of him as an opportunist, which made the difference. This was one of the highest turnout elections in 1972, and Kerry was the only Democratic House candidate not running against an imcumbent who managed to lose a district McGovern was carrying.

In any case, the 1974 election seems to have demonstrated conclusively that it was Kerry's weakness, not Cronin's strength, which accounted for the 1972 result. Cronin was generally well liked, and did manage to make a flurry of news by pushing the construction of a refinery on the Merrimack during the height of the energy crisis. But for all that he was easily beaten by 33-year-old Middlesex County Commissioner Paul Tsongas. Tsongas is a liberal Democrat who fits in comfortably with the House Democratic freshmen; now that the district has finally elected a Democrat, it seems almost certain to continue routinely to do so in future years.

Census Data Pop. 473,154. Central city, 34%; suburban, 57%. Median family income, $11,532; families above $15,000: 29%; families below $3,000: 6%. Median years education, 12.3.

The Voters

Median voting age 43.
Employment profile White collar, 52%. Blue collar, 36%. Service, 11%. Farm, 1%.
Ethnic groups Spanish, 1%. Total foreign stock, 31%. Canada, 10%; Italy, 4%; UK, Ireland, 3% each; Poland, Greece, Germany, 1% each.

Presidential vote

1972	Nixon (R)	106,658	(47%)
	McGovern (D)	120,470	(53%)
1968	Nixon (R)	64,516	(34%)
	Humphrey (D)	118,447	(63%)
	Wallace (AI)	5,958	(3%)

Rep. Paul E. Tsongas (D) Elected 1974; b. Feb. 14, 1941, Lowell; home, Lowell; Dartmouth Col., B.A. 1962, Yale U., LL.B. 1967, Harvard U., 1973–.

Career Peace Corps, Volunteer, Ethiopia, 1962–64, Training Coord., West Indies, 1967–68; Mbr., Governor's Comm. on Law Enforcement, 1968–69; Mass. Deputy Asst. Atty. Gen., 1969–71; Practicing atty., 1971–74.

Offices 419 CHOB, 202-225-3411. Also Rm. 216, 50 Kearney Square, Lowell 01852, 617-459-0101.

Committees

Banking, Currency and Housing (26th). Subcommittees: Economic Stabilization; International Development Institutions and Finance; International Trade, Investment and Monetary Policy.

Interior and Insular Affairs (23d). Subcommittees: Energy and the Environment; National Parks and Recreation; Public Lands; Water and Power Resources.

Group Ratings: Newly Elected

Key Votes

1) Foreign Aid	FOR	6) Gov Abortn Aid	NE	11) Pub Cong Election $	NE
2) Busing	NE	7) Coed Phys Ed	FOR	12) Turkish Arms Cutoff	NE
3) ABM	NE	8) Pov Lawyer Gag	NE	13) Youth Camp Regs	FOR
4) B-1 Bomber	AGN	9) Pub Trans Sub	NE	14) Strip Mine Veto	AGN
5) Nerve Gas	NE	10) EZ Voter Regis	NE	15) Farm Bill Veto	AGN

Election Results

1974 general:	Paul E. Tsongas (D)	99,518	(61%)	($105,267)
	Paul W. Cronin (R)	64,596	(39%)	($124,049)
1974 primary:	Paul E. Tsongas (D)	45,655	(73%)	
	William Madden (D)	17,215	(27%)	

◆ ◆ ◆ ◆ ◆

SIXTH DISTRICT

The 6th congressional district of Massachusetts is the North Shore district. Along and just back of the rocky coast north of Boston are the estates of some of the Commonwealth's oldest families including—to name some still important politically—the Saltonstalls and the Lodges. Only a few miles away are the fishermen of Gloucester, suffering badly these days because the banks are being fished out by efficient Russian and Icelandic trawlers. Here also are the textile mill workers in Haverhill and Newburyport on the Merrimack River, and the artists and summer people of Rockport. To the south is Salem, where twenty witches were once hanged and pressed to death, and where Nathaniel Hawthorne's House of Seven Gables still stands in a neighborhood of neat nineteenth century homes. Also to the south of the district is the boating suburb of Marblehead, which Jews now share with WASPs, and Lynn, whose troubled shoe industry has been pressing hard for restriction against imports.

The 6th district is the site of the original gerrymander, named for the desire of its perpetrator, Elbridge Gerry, to push together all the area's Democrats in one misshapen seat. Since then, the North Shore's wealthy towns and Brahmin families have given the area a reputation for Republicanism it has sometimes since ceased to deserve. In recent years the 6th has even supported relatively unpopular Democrats like George McGovern. But for many years the district persisted in electing Republican Congressmen, at least if they were members of the Bates family: George J. Bates of Salem won from 1936 to 1950, and his son William up through 1968.

But Bates died suddenly in 1969, and in the special election to fill the vacancy, Democratic state Representative Michael Harrington waged a sophisticated and vigorous campaign to beat Republican state Senator William Saltonstall. The race tested the popularity of the Nixon

Administration's foreign policy and spending priorities: Harrington fervently opposed the Vietnam war and the ABM while Saltonstall, son of former Senator Leverett Saltonstall, supported Nixon on both issues. Harrington won that race with 52% of the vote; by 1970 he was able to win with 61% over Republican Howard Phillips, who would go on to brief national fame in early 1973 as the Nixon appointee who attempted illegally to dismantle the Office of Economic Opportunity.

Harrington has not always seemed happy with the pace of life in the House or with his position, for a time, as one of its more junior members. In the 92d Congress Harrington managed to win assignment to the Armed Services Committee, but this rather contentious dove had a number of run-ins with committee hawks that were so acrimonious that he moved to Foreign Affairs in 1973. (He had his revenge, however, since his Armed Services seat went to Ron Dellums of California.) The Congressman also created a furor while serving on the special committee investigating the CIA by accusing the Chairman, Lucien Nedzi, of not disclosing information he had received a year before on CIA involvement in assassinations. But the House decided not to condemn Nedzi, but rather to, in effect, condemn Harrington for allegedly making public information about CIA involvement in Chile.

With the assets of an Irish heritage and a Harvard education—not to mention a raft of cousins well connected in Massachusetts politics—Harrington could conceivably be a strong contender for statewide office; but with the Commonwealth's Senate seats held securely by Edward Kennedy and Edward Brooke, that avenue seems blocked now. In any case, with the influx of freshmen in to the 94th Congress, Harrington suddenly has dozens of new allies, and a chance to be part of the majority of the House most of the time. So it may be that he will decide that a long House career has its charms as well as its drawbacks.

Census Data Pop. 475,885. Central city, 10%; suburban, 72%. Median family income, $10,904; families above $15,000: 25%; families below $3,000: 6%. Median years education, 12.3.

The Voters

Median voting age 45.
Employment profile White collar, 52%. Blue collar, 36%. Service, 12%. Farm, –%.
Ethnic groups Total foreign stock, 31%. Canada, 10%; Italy, 4%; Ireland, UK, 3% each; USSR, Poland, Greece, 2% each.

Presidential vote

1972	Nixon (R)	104,027	(47%)
	McGovern (D)	116,157	(53%)
1968	Nixon (R)	76,125	(36%)
	Humphrey (D)	125,950	(60%)
	Wallace (AI)	6,588	(3%)

Rep. Michael Harrington (D) Elected Sept. 30, 1969; b. Sept. 2, 1936, Salem; home, Beverly; Harvard U., A.B. 1958, LL.B. 1961, 1962–63; Catholic.

Career Salem City Cncl., 1960–63; Practicing atty., 1962–; Mass. House of Reps., 1965–69.

Offices 405 CHOB, 202-225-8020. Also Salem P.O., Salem 01970, 617-745-5800.

Committees

Government Operations (20th). Subcommittees: Government Information and Individual Rights; Legislation and National Security.

International Relations (15th). Subcommittees: International Organizations; Investigations.

Group Ratings

	ADA	COPE	LWV	RIPON	NFU	LCV	CFA	NAB	NSI	ACA
1974	100	100	92	87	86	88	100	25	10	0
1973	100	91	100	71	90	93	86	–	–	4
1972	94	90	100	73	83	80	–	10	0	10

Key Votes

1) Foreign Aid	FOR	6) Gov Abortn Aid	FOR	11) Pub Cong Election $	FOR
2) Busing	FOR	7) Coed Phys Ed	FOR	12) Turkish Arms Cutoff	ABS
3) ABM	AGN	8) Pov Lawyer Gag	AGN	13) Youth Camp Regs	FOR
4) B-1 Bomber	AGN	9) Pub Trans Sub	FOR	14) Strip Mine Veto	AGN
5) Nerve Gas	AGN	10) EZ Voter Regis	FOR	15) Farm Bill Veto	FOR

Election Results

1974 general	Michael J. Harrington (D), unopposed ...			($29,810)
1974 primary:	Michael J. Harrington (D)	39,798	(71%)	
	Ronald E. Kowalski (D)	15,943	(29%)	
1972 general:	Michael Harrington (D)	139,697	(64%)	($114,317)
	James Brady Mosely (R)	78,381	(36%)	($93,400)

◆ ◆ ◆ ◆ ◆

SEVENTH DISTRICT

The 7th congressional district of Massachusetts is a collection of suburbs just north of Boston. Its sociological range extends from working class Chelsea, where Jewish immigrants first disembarked a half-century ago, to Melrose, a comfortable and still distinctly Yankee (and Republican) town. Most of the communities here lie somewhere in between the two extremes and contain many descendants of Irish and Italian immigrants who have reached some degree of financial security if not affluence. The political trend in the 7th illustrates the liberalization of Massachusetts politics in the last twenty years. In the 1950s, the 7th was considered a Republican district, and in 1960 John F. Kennedy was thought to have made an unusually strong showing here when he got 57% of the vote. But in 1968 Hubert Humphrey, though not of Boston Irish stock, got 66%, and four years later George McGovern got the same 57% native son Kennedy received.

Obviously, that trend represents a considerable shift of opinion; there are only a handful of districts in the nation where McGovern ran as well as Kennedy. It reflects also a growing belief here that voting for a Republican like Richard Nixon is somehow no longer respectable. To a considerable extent, the man responsible for this shift is Senator Edward Kennedy, whose positions on issues can hardly be attacked here, as they were in so much of the country by the likes of Spiro Agnew, as un-American. So these voters living north of Boston, many of whom supported Joe McCarthy in the 1950s, have for years now believed that American involvement in Southeast Asia was a mistake from the very start.

One of the beneficiaries of this liberal trend is Congressman Torbert Macdonald, a college roommate of John F. Kennedy. Macdonald was first elected in 1954, capturing the district from a Republican incumbent, and he has not had much trouble winning ever since. With his considerable seniority, Macdonald is now Chairman of the Commerce Subcommittee on Communications, on which he pushed for the media spending limits that were imposed in the 1972 campaign. He has also locked horns with the power companies—a popular stand back home, since utility rates in New England are the highest in the nation. But though Macdonald is the second-ranking Democrat on the full Commerce Committee, it seems unlikely at this writing that he will ever be Chairman. The likely successor is the number three Democrat, John Moss of California, who is considered more aggressive and hard-working, and who has already won the chairmanship of the Investigations Subcommittee away from full Committee Chairman Harley Staggers.

Census Data Pop. 476,565. Central city, 0%; suburban, 100%. Median family income, $11,406; families above $15,000: 28%; families below $3,000: 5%. Median years education, 12.3.

The Voters

Median voting age 45.
Employment profile White collar, 57%. Blue collar, 32%. Service, 11%. Farm, –%.
Ethnic groups Total foreign stock, 37%. Italy, 12%; Canada, 9%; Ireland, 4%; USSR, UK, 3% each; Poland, 1%.

Presidential vote

1972	Nixon (R)	91,607	(43%)
	McGovern (D)	122,026	(57%)
1968	Nixon (R)	64,760	(31%)
	Humphrey (D)	137,995	(65%)
	Wallace (AI)	7,053	(3%)

Rep. Torbert H. Macdonald (D) Elected 1954; b. June 6, 1917, Boston; home, Malden; home, Malden; Harvard U., A.B. 1940, LL.B. 1946; Catholic.

Career Navy, WWII; Practicing atty., 1946–54.

Offices 2470 RHOB, 202-225-2836. Also 2100A JFK Fed. Bldg., Boston 02203, 617-223-2781.

Committees

Government Operations (5th). Subcommittees: Conservation, Energy and Natural Resources; Government Information and Individual Rights.

Interstate and Foreign Commerce (2d). Subcommittees: Communications (Chairman).

Group Ratings

	ADA	COPE	LWV	RIPON	NFU	LCV	CFA	NAB	NSI	ACA
1974	71	100	64	64	83	69	91	33	25	10
1973	82	100	73	60	82	56	100	–	–	15
1972	56	89	70	71	86	74	100	22	14	11

Key Votes

1) Foreign Aid	FOR	6) Gov Abortn Aid	AGN	11) Pub Cong Election $	AGN
2) Busing	AGN	7) Coed Phys Ed	AGN	12) Turkish Arms Cutoff	FOR
3) ABM	AGN	8) Pov Lawyer Gag	AGN	13) Youth Camp Regs	FOR
4) B-1 Bomber	FOR	9) Pub Trans Sub	FOR	14) Strip Mine Veto	AGN
5) Nerve Gas	AGN	10) EZ Voter Regis	FOR	15) Farm Bill Veto	FOR

Election Results

1974 general:	Torbert H. Macdonald (D)	122,165 (80%)	($15,596)
	James J. Murphy (Ind.)	30,959 (20%)	($187)
1974 primary:	Torbert H. Macdonald (D), unopposed		
1972 general:	Torbert H. Macdonald (D)	135,193 (68%)	($19,918)
	Joan M. Aliberti (R)	64,357 (32%)	($25,213)

◆ ◆ ◆ ◆ ◆

EIGHTH DISTRICT

The 8th of Massachusetts is a congressional district with a number of distinctive feature. It is the home of no less than three major universities—Harvard, MIT, and Boston University—along with dozens of smaller colleges; in all, the 8th has the second highest proportion of college students—15% of the potential electorate—of any congressional district in the country. The 8th's distinctiveness—and its considerable variety—has also been evidenced by the representation it has had in the House over the years. From 1941 to 1943 its Congressman was Thomas H. Eliot, descendant of a Brahmin family and later the highly regarded President of Washington University. Eliot was succeeded for two terms by James Michael Curley, a roguish Irish politician and model for the hero of the novel *The Last Hurrah*. Curley was also Governor once (elected in 1936) and Mayor of Boston five times—elected, the last time, while serving a jail sentence.

The politician who succeeded Curley was a very different kind of Boston Irishman, a young Harvard graduate and former PT boat commander named John F. Kennedy. From all accounts, Kennedy knew little about politics when he first ran in 1946, and won largely because of his father's political acumen—and money. Nor was the young Kennedy a particularly enthusiastic junior member of the House, but he did go on to bigger things. Kennedy's successor was Thomas P. "Tip" O'Neill, Jr., who had already made his mark as the first Democrat in years to be Speaker of the Great and General Court of Massachusetts. Today, after more than 20 years in Congress, O'Neill is the Majority Leader of the House of Representatives, and quite likely the next Speaker.

O'Neill is a man of town, not gown, politics. Until the early 1970s, the university community in the 8th was not an especially important factor in congressional politics. The 8th has at least a dozen major neighborhood areas, each with its own political traditions and local alliances. These include the five wards in the city of Boston: East Boston, an Italian enclave separated from the rest of the city by the harbor; Charlestown, the insular (and now redeveloped) Irish community centered on Bunker Hill; the Back Bay, once the home of elderly Brahmin ladies, now largely given over to students; and Allston and Brighton, lower-middle-class communities with a significant Jewish population. Then there are the Irish and Italian communities in Cambridge and Somerville (plus some Portuguese-Americans in East Cambridge); the middle-class suburbs of Arlington and Watertown; and finally Belmont, the upper income suburban home of Harvard academics which is hardly a politically congenial place to its most famous resident, Robert Welch, head of the John Birch Society.

O'Neill has served as a bridge between various parts of his district and its large student and educated young community. But by temperament and background, O'Neill is most comfortable among experienced Irish pols. In the House he was a man who got along with the leadership (obtaining a seat on the Rules Committee) by going along. In 1967, however, he took the step—rare at the time—of coming out publicly against Johnson's policy in Vietnam. And he did it long before the student vote could have posed any threat to him in elections—and before anyone thought it ever could. More important, he said, were the arguments of his own children, who were strongly against the war; one of them, Thomas P. O'Neill III, is now Lieutenant Governor of the Commonwealth.

O'Neill was appointed Majority Whip in 1971, when he supported Hale Boggs's candidacy for Majority Leader and brought a number of Eastern votes along with him. Then, when Boggs was lost in a plane crash in 1972, this first dovish member of the Democratic leadership succeeded to his post, virtually without opposition. O'Neill's only plausible challenger for the Speakership whenever Carl Albert vacates it is California's Phillip Burton; and reporters have been finding considerable evidence of friction between them in the changes that have been occurring in the House since the 1974 Democratic landslide. Certainly O'Neill was not a strong backer of Burton for the position of Democratic Caucus Chairman, which he won with heavy support from freshmen. And there was considerable talk that O'Neill was behind the temporary dumping of House Administration Committee Chairman Wayne Hays, a Burton ally. But Burton has said he will not run for Speaker against O'Neill, as he would against anyone else; and that is evidence enough that O'Neill, for all his inherent cautiousness, still can win plenty of support from liberal freshmen Congressmen.

Perhaps O'Neill's finest hours came in the days before the Open House Judiciary Committee hearings on impeachment in 1974. Unlike some experienced leaders, O'Neill never seemed to doubt that serious consideration of impeachment—not avoidance of the issue—was the only responsible course to take.

Census Data Pop. 474,090. Central city, 35%; suburban, 65%. Median family income, $10,317; families above $15,000: 24%; families below $3,000: 7%. Median years education, 12.3.

The Voters

Median voting age 39.
Employment profile White collar, 63%. Blue collar, 24%. Service, 13%. Farm, –%.
Ethnic groups Black, 2%. Spanish, 1%. Total foreign stock, 41%. Italy, 10%; Canada, 8%; Ireland, 6%. UK, USSR, 2% each; Portugal, Greece, Germany, Poland, 1% each.

Presidential vote

1972	Nixon (R)	65,660	(34%)
	McGovern (D)	127,868	(66%)
1968	Nixon (R)	45,580	(24%)
	Humphrey (D)	136,775	(72%)
	Wallace (AI)	6,881	(4%)

Rep. Thomas P. O'Neill, Jr. (D) Elected 1952; b. Dec. 9, 1912, Cambridge; home, Cambridge; Boston Col., A.B. 1936; Catholic.

Career Insurance business; Mass. House of Reps., 1936–52, Minor. Ldr., 1947–48, Spkr., 1948–52; Cambridge School Comm., 1946–47.

Offices 2231 RHOB, 202-225-5111. Also 2200A JFK Fed. Bldg., Boston 02203, 617-223-2784.

Committees

Majority Leader

Budget (2d).

Group Ratings

	ADA	COPE	LWV	RIPON	NFU	LCV	CFA	NAB	NSI	ACA
1974	75	100	82	50	92	69	75	17	60	8
1973	76	91	100	60	100	53	100	–	–	16
1972	69	90	100	64	80	53	100	10	33	5

Key Votes

1) Foreign Aid	FOR	6) Gov Abortn Aid	ABS	11) Pub Cong Election $	AGN
2) Busing	FOR	7) Coed Phys Ed	AGN	12) Turkish Arms Cutoff	FOR
3) ABM	AGN	8) Pov Lawyer Gag	AGN	13) Youth Camp Regs	FOR
4) B-1 Bomber	FOR	9) Pub Trans Sub	FOR	14) Strip Mine Veto	AGN
5) Nerve Gas	AGN	10) EZ Voter Regis	FOR	15) Farm Bill Veto	AGN

Election Results

1974 general:	Thomas P. O'Neill, Jr. (D)	107,042	(88%)	($1,414)
	James H. Kiggen (U.S. Labor)	8,363	(7%)	($292)
	Laura Ross (Communist)	6,421	(5%)	($3,827)
1974 primary:	Thomas P. O'Neill, Jr. (D), unopposed			
1972 general:	Thomas P. O'Neill, Jr. (D)	142,470	(89%)	($35,901)
	John E. Power, Jr. (SW)	18,169	(11%)	($229)

◆ ◆ ◆ ◆ ◆

NINTH DISTRICT

Boston is the most politicized of cities. It was Boston whose malcontents did more than anyone else to start the American Revolution, and Boston that was the hotbed of the abolitionist movement which had so much to do with the start of the Civil War. Boston is also, and this is no coincidence, the nation's most Irish city, for the Irish seem to have some magical aptitude for politics. The proportion of Irish-Americans here does not really show up in the census figures, which show only the 7% who came themselves or whose parents came directly from Ireland; the fact is that there has been heavy Irish immigration here since 1840, and that the Boston Irish are remarkably unassimilated. In the old Irish neighborhoods of South Boston and Charlestown, people keep their ethnic identity though their ancestors may have stepped off the boat more than a century ago; this is not city where traditions are tossed aside lightly.

The Irish remain the most important ethnic group in Boston; they have held the Mayor's office without substantial interruption from 1906 to the present day. Much of the older Boston wealth, it is true, is still in WASPy hands, controlled by the kind of people who preserve Boston institutions like the Athenaeum and the Somerset Club and live in old houses on Louisburg Square in Beacon Hill. And much of the attention in Boston is given to the people who are, in a many ways, the spiritual (and sometimes lineal) descendants of Samuel Adams and his raucous friends: the leftish, recent-former-student, young, liberated people who make up an increasing percentage of the population here. For Boston is, in many ways, the nation's largest college town, not just with Harvard and MIT across the river in Cambridge, but with literally hundreds of other schools of all kinds and levels of repute. Boston is one of the few American cities where the local media, the big retailers, even the banks cater to this sort of constituency.

So we have this arresting paradox. Boston, which by some indications is solidly left wing (more than 60% for McGovern in 1972, for example), is also the site today of the nation's most virulent antibusing protest. The way to explain this seeming contradiction is to look at just who is upset, and at what. The antiwar movement, for example, had its major constituency in the post-student generation here; the Irish neighborhoods, after initial hostility, concurred. (It helped that Ted Kennedy took the antiwar position; the leading liberal politician here has been someone who is loved, not as in New York one who was hated, by the ethnic people of the middle class neighborhoods.) Busing is a problem that almost exclusively troubles the Irish ghettoes, like South Boston, where most of the violence has taken place.

Boston actually has a relatively small black population, and is one of the few major northern cities a majority of whose public school students are white; its schools could have been rather peaceably integrated, years ago, if there had been even an iota of cooperation from the School Committee led by the likes of Louise Day Hicks. But Hicks, the daughter of an old South Boston pol, and her colleagues have been fighting even the slightest concession for more than ten years—a strategy which has led proximately to the present drastic court orders. Hicks and allies have posed as the last defenders of the autonomy and safety of the white working class neighborhoods which truly are such an integral part of Boston; in fact, their actions seem simply to have brought things to a climax, from which they cannot escape or win.

Those who saw the pictures of Senator Edward Kennedy being spat on by antibusing protestors may have assumed that we will see in Boston the kind of political pattern we used to see in the Deep South (or saw in the Detroit suburbs in 1972): a massive shift of the vast majority of the electorate from the left to the right. This is not going to happen in Boston. For most of the community is not really involved in the busing controversy, one way or the other. For every antibusing white parent with children in the public schools, there is a black voter who is repelled by antibusing rhetoric. This is a Catholic city, where a public school education is by no means a tradition in many neighborhoods; and it is an old city, from which many young parents move to the suburbs to raise their families. The antibusing crusaders make a lot of noise and can win some elections. But it is by no means clear that they represent a majority, much less an overwhelming majority, of voter opinion in Boston.

Certainly the evidence of city and congressional elections is to the contrary. In 1967 and 1971 Boston elected Kevin White Mayor, both times over the opposition of Louise Day Hicks. White is widely regarded as a liberal; as an Irish Catholic, he has been able to run well in the ethnic neighborhoods, but he also has a strong post-student following as well. Hicks ran solely on the busing issue; White beat her soundly both times. In 1975, Hicks did not even bother to run—an indication that this shrewd politician had at last got the message of just how far the busing issue could carry her.

The major part of Boston forms the major part of Massachusetts's 9th congressional district, a constituency which was extended out to the suburbs for political reasons in the early seventies, but remains the most solidly Irish seat in the United States. For 45 years the 9th had the same Congressman, John W. McCormack, first elected in 1925 and returned to office every two years through 1968. By 1970, McCormack was old and out of touch, and when his aide Martin Sweig was caught using his office to solicit government favors for well paying clients, McCormack —though unblemished himself—decided to leave. In three elections, the turbulence of Boston politics gave the district three different Representatives; now, despite busing, the 9th seems to have settled down.

McCormack's immediate successor was none other than Louise Day Hicks, fresh from the School Committee and aiming for another shot at Mayor White. She won the primary with 39% of the vote—proof again that busing is not an issue that commands majority support here—and then won the general against split opposition. Mrs. Hicks made little impression in Washington; she remained interested in Boston politics, and the highlights of her single term was her race against White in 1971.

In 1972, Mrs. Hicks got her 38% of the vote in the primary, but this time she faced her toughest opposition in the general election. It came not from the Republican candidates (Republicans are scarce indeed here) but from a Democratic state Senator named Joseph Moakley who was running as an Independent. Moakley won 44% of the vote, Hicks 42%, and the Republican a hapless 14%. Hicks was hurt by the charge of office-hopping (she was elected to the City Council in 1973 and has stayed there since), while Moakley was the kind of liberal with roots in the Irish community that seems to be winning so many elections in Boston lately. Despite all the fuss about Judge Garrity's ruling, no antibusing candidate surfaced in the race for the 9th in 1974; indeed, there was scarcely a race at all, as Moakley won easily. For all the noise and tumult, he seems to have made of the 9th what a rather different Boston Irishman, John McCormack, had—a safe seat.

Census Data Pop. 473,680. Central city, 70%; suburban, 30%. Median family income, $10,144; families above $15,000: 25%; families below $3,000: 9%. Median years education, 12.2.

The Voters

Median voting age 43.
Employment profile White collar, 55%. Blue collar, 28%. Service, 17%. Farm, –%.
Ethnic groups Black, 20%. Spanish, 3%. Total foreign stock, 34%. Ireland, 7%; Italy, Canada, 5% each; UK, USSR, 2% each; Poland, Germany, 1% each.

Presidential vote

1972	Nixon (R)	68,748	(41%)
	McGovern (D)	100,720	(59%)
1968	Nixon (R)	46,437	(26%)
	Humphrey (D)	121,436	(69%)
	Wallace (AI)	8,478	(5%)

Rep. Joe Moakley (D) Elected 1972, as Independent, seated in Congress as Democrat, Jan. 3, 1973; b. Apr. 27, 1927, Boston; home, Boston; U. of Miami, B.A., Suffolk U., LL.B. 1956; Catholic.

Career Navy, WWII; Mass. House of Reps., 1953–65, Maj.Whip, 1957; Practicing atty., 1957–72; Mass. Senate, 1965–69; Boston City Cncl., 1971.

Offices 238 CHOB, 202-225-8273. Also 1900C JFK Fed. Bldg., Boston 02203, 617-223-5715.

Committees

Rules (10th).

Group Ratings

	ADA	COPE	LWV	RIPON	NFU	LCV	CFA	NAB	NSI	ACA
1974	77	100	83	50	93	92	85	17	10	7
1973	88	100	83	67	95	89	100	–	–	11

Key Votes

1) Foreign Aid	FOR	6) Gov Abortn Aid	AGN	11) Pub Cong Election $	FOR
2) Busing	AGN	7) Coed Phys Ed	AGN	12) Turkish Arms Cutoff	FOR
3) ABM	AGN	8) Pov Lawyer Gag	AGN	13) Youth Camp Regs	FOR
4) B-1 Bomber	AGN	9) Pub Trans Sub	FOR	14) Strip Mine Veto	AGN
5) Nerve Gas	AGN	10) EZ Voter Regis	FOR	15) Farm Bill Veto	AGN

Election Results

1974 general:	John Joseph Moakley (D)	94,804 (89%)	($74,237)
	Laurence R. Sherman (U.S. Labor)	11,344 (11%)	($42)
1974 primary:	John Joseph Moakley (D), unopposed		

1972 general:	John Joseph Moakley (Ind.)	70,571	(44%)	($157,560)
	Louise Day Hicks (D)	67,143	(42%)	($29,686)
	Howard M. Miller (R)	23,177	(14%)	($58,240)

◆ ◆ ◆ ◆ ◆

TENTH DISTRICT

The 10th congressional district of Massachusetts is one example of a grotesquely shaped monstrosity tailored to the political needs of one longtime incumbent, and now serving those of another in equally good fashion. The 10th is really two separate entities. In the north are the Boston suburbs: posh, WASPy Wellesley and somewhat less wealthy Natick next door. In the south is the city of Fall River (pop. 119,000 in 1910 and 96,000 in 1970), the district's largest; it is an aging mill town that never really recovered from the southward flight of its 101 cotton mills. The huge granite structures are now occupied, if at all, with marginal dress and curtain sweatshops which pay the French Canadian and Portuguese workers minimal wages. This end of the 10th is dominated politically by voters of Portuguese, French Canadian, and Italian descent, who ordinarily vote Democratic. The middle of the 10th, between the two ends of the district, is composed of sparsely populated towns spread out over the rolling hills between Boston and Providence. Among them are Foxboro, home of the resurgent New England Patriots, and North Attleboro, home of the 10th's longtime (1925–67) Congressman Joseph W. Martin, Jr.

For many years the district's boundaries were drawn to provide a safe seat for Martin, best known to historians of the New Deal as a member of FDR's famous Republican trio of Martin, Barton, and Fish. Beginning in 1939, Martin was the Republican leader in the House, serving twice (1947–49, 1953–55) as Speaker. As Martin aged, he became more and more congenial with Speaker Sam Rayburn and less able to perform his duties—both to the disgust of many Republican Congressmen. After the Democrats' big win in the 1958 elections, Martin was ousted from the Minority Leadership; he soon became a melancholy, forlorn old man. But he still was routinely returned to office by the voters of the 10th district for three more terms.

Then in 1966 Martin had an aggressive opponent in the Republican primary and, at 82, he was finally beaten. The winner was Margaret Heckler, a Wellesley attorney, who was then the only Republican member of the Massachusetts Governor's Council—an antique institution that survives from colonial days only in Massachusetts, New Hampshire, and Maine. The general election that followed was the toughest Mrs. Heckler has faced so far; although this is a liberal district—going for Humphrey in 1968 heavily and for McGovern in 1972—Heckler's record has been liberal enough to give her easy wins in subsequent years.

She might have had a harder time in 1974. As a member of the Banking and Currency Committee—a panel she has since left for a junior seat on Agriculture—she was part of the solid Republican bloc that voted against Wright Patman's proposed Watergate investigation in October 1972. With some Democratic votes, this killed any look into the seamy affairs of the Nixon Administration until after Nixon was reelected; and Mrs. Heckler's willingness to go along was noted on one of the White House tapes. However, there was not much of a Democratic campaign here in 1974, and Heckler had a free ride on that and other issues.

Census Data Pop. 477,054. Central city, 20%; suburban, 55%. Median family income, $10,747; families above $15,000: 24%; families below $3,000: 6%. Median years education, 12.1.

The Voters

Median voting age 44.
Employment profile White collar, 46%. Blue collar, 41%. Service, 12%. Farm, 1%.
Ethnic groups Total foreign stock, 32%. Canada, 8%; Portugal, 6%; UK, 3%; Italy, Ireland, Poland, 2% each; USSR, 1%.

Presidential vote

1972	Nixon (R)	100,844	(50%)
	McGovern (D)	102,368	(50%)
1968	Nixon (R)	70,773	(37%)
	Humphrey (D)	114,410	(60%)
	Wallace (AI)	6,842	(4%)

Rep. Margaret M. Heckler (R) Elected 1966; b. June 21, 1931, Flushing, N.Y.; home, Wellesley; Albertus Magnus Col., A.B. 1953, Boston Col., LL.B. 1956; Catholic.

Career Mbr., Mass. Governors Council, 1962–66.

Offices 343 CHOB, 202-225-4335. Also One Washington St., Wellesley Hills 92181, 617-235-3350.

Committees

Agriculture (9th). Subcommittees: Department Operations, Investigations and Oversight; Domestic Marketing and Consumer Relations.

Veterans Affairs (2d). Subcommittees: Education and Training; Hospitals.

Joint Economic Committee (3d, House Side). Subcommittees: Consumer Economics; Economic Growth; Economic Progress; Urban Affairs.

Group Ratings

	ADA	COPE	LWV	RIPON	NFU	LCV	CFA	NAB	NSI	ACA
1974	80	100	92	80	82	71	80	55	25	17
1973	72	91	83	92	56	84	88	–	–	22
1972	63	56	100	100	67	79	50	44	29	12

Key Votes

1) Foreign Aid	FOR	6) Gov Abortn Aid	AGN	11) Pub Cong Election $	FOR
2) Busing	AGN	7) Coed Phys Ed	FOR	12) Turkish Arms Cutoff	FOR
3) ABM	AGN	8) Pov Lawyer Gag	FOR	13) Youth Camp Regs	FOR
4) B-1 Bomber	AGN	9) Pub Trans Sub	FOR	14) Strip Mine Veto	AGN
5) Nerve Gas	AGN	10) EZ Voter Regis	FOR	15) Farm Bill Veto	FOR

Election Results

1974 general:	Margaret M. Heckler (R)	99,993	(64%)	($71,100)
	Barry F. Monahan (D)	55,871	(36%)	($34,012)
1974 primary:	Margaret M. Hecker (R), unopposed			
1972 general:	Margaret M. Heckler (R), unopposed			($10,518)

◆ ◆ ◆ ◆ ◆

ELEVENTH DISTRICT

The 11th congressional district of Massachusetts includes the southern third of Boston, most of the city's South Shore suburbs, and more suburban territory stretching south to include the shoe-manufacturing city of Brockton. With few exceptions, the 11th's Dorchester and Hyde Park wards of Boston and its suburban towns—like the older Quincy and Braintree, and the newer Canton, Stoughton, and Randolph, away from the Shore—are filled with the sons and daughters of Irish, Italian, and Jewish immigrants. Because most of these residents have remained loyal to their forebears' Democratic voting habits, the 11th has been heavily Democratic in recent years. Its Yankee minority, whose ancestors sent John Quincy Adams to the House for the last 16 years of his life (1831–48), has been steadily abandoning the Republican Party, thus adding to the Democratic majorities.

The succession of Congressmen from the district points up the changes that have occurred in the last generation of Massachusetts politics. For 30 years, from 1929 to 1959, the district's Congressman was a Brahmin Republican with the imposing name of Richard B. Wigglesworth. When he wisely chose to retire in 1958, his successor was James A. Burke, who has held the seat ever since. Before going to Congress, Burke had a leadership position in the Massachusetts legislature. Early in his career he won a seat on the House Ways and Means Committee, and today he is next in line for the Chairmanship behind the current chair, Al Ullman of Oregon, and his predecessor, Wilbur Mills. Burke is a man from the older, Irish tradition of Massachusetts politics, by temperament attuned to the traditional way of doing things in the House; he seemed happier when Mills was dominating Ways and Means than he is now that freshmen have a lot to say about what happens. Like most northern Democrats, Burke always has supported liberal domestic legislation; and as a Representative from Massachusetts he joined the opposition to American war policy in Southeast Asia when the Republicans took over the Presidency.

Burke seems to have had a sure understanding of the politics of the 1950s; he is a little more uncertain lately. He was a big booster of Wilbur Mills for the Presidency in 1972, and apparently it was his advice which convinced Mills that he could win an upset victory, or make a strong showing in the Massachusetts presidential primary. (Actually Mills got 3% of the vote.) Burke was also a name sponsor in the early '70s of the Burke-Hartke bill, a protectionist measure backed for awhile by the AFL-CIO. The idea was to protect industries like Brockton's shoe plants from foreign competition; but the day seems to be past when Congress can be stampeded into an orgy of protectionism by hard times. Burke holds his seat virtually unopposed—he has not had competition in either primary or general elections for years—and he will probably continue to do so for as long as he wants.

Census Data Pop. 475,789. Central city, 49%; suburban, 51%. Median family income, $11,052; families above $15,000: 25%; families below $3,000: 6%. Median years education, 12.3.

The Voters

Median voting age 45.
Employment profile White collar, 54%. Blue collar, 33%. Service, 13%. Farm, –%.
Ethnic groups Black, 2%. Total foreign stock, 35%. Ireland, Canada, 7% each; Italy, 6%; UK, USSR, 3% each; Poland, Lithuania, 1% each.

Presidential vote

1972	Nixon (R)	86,139	(43%)
	McGovern (D)	112,397	(57%)
1968	Nixon (R)	56,259	(28%)
	Humphrey (D)	132,497	(67%)
	Wallace (AI)	10,262	(5%)

Rep. James A. Burke (D) Elected 1958; b. Mar. 30, 1910, Boston; home, Milton; Suffolk U.; Catholic.

Career Boston City Registrar of Vital Statistics, 1938–41; Army, WWII; Mass. House of Reps., Asst. Maj. Ldr.; Vice Chm., Mass. Dem. Central Comm.

Offices 241 CHOB, 202-225-3215. Also Quincy P.O., 47 Washington St., Quincy 02169, 617-472-1314.

Committees

Ways and Means (3d). Subcommittees: Social Security (Chairman); Unemployment Compensation.

Group Ratings

	ADA	COPE	LWV	RIPON	NFU	LCV	CFA	NAB	NSI	ACA
1974	65	100	67	31	93	59	85	25	40	14
1973	80	100	83	80	90	63	100	–	–	11
1972	94	91	92	81	86	53	100	17	0	0

Key Votes

1) Foreign Aid	FOR	6) Gov Abortn Aid	AGN	11) Pub Cong Election $	AGN
2) Busing	AGN	7) Coed Phys Ed	AGN	12) Turkish Arms Cutoff	FOR
3) ABM	AGN	8) Pov Lawyer Gag	AGN	13) Youth Camp Regs	FOR
4) B-1 Bomber	FOR	9) Pub Trans Sub	FOR	14) Strip Mine Veto	AGN
5) Nerve Gas	AGN	10) EZ Voter Regis	FOR	15) Farm Bill Veto	AGN

Election Results

1974 general:	James A. Burke (D), unopposed		($39,707)
1974 primary:	James A. Burke (D)	60,921 (75%)	
	Joseph Tierney (D)	20,703 (25%)	
1972 general:	James A. Burke (D), unopposed		($15,971)

◆ ◆ ◆ ◆ ◆

TWELFTH DISTRICT

The 12th congressional district of Massachusetts is the closest thing to a Republican district, in national terms, in the overwhelmingly Democratic Commonwealth. It was the only Massachusetts district to deliver a majority, and then only a paper-thin one, to Richard Nixon; and for years it continued to elect a Republican Congressman. Like the 10th, the 12th was originally designed to elect a Republican. The heavily Democratic city of New Bedford (pop. 110,000), an old whaling port where the hard-pressed fishing industry is still important, was combined with traditionally Republican territory. This includes some of the more well-to-do South Shore suburbs of Boston (Weymouth, Hingham), most of Plymouth County, Cape Cod, and the two resort island of Martha's Vineyard and Nantucket. The last was the whaling port from which Herman Melville's Captain Ahab sailed in pursuit of Moby Dick and the ultimate Void; today, like the Vineyard, Nantucket is a place for summer people, where the quaint old New England houses are being restored with money from the S&H Green Stamp fortune.

The 12th has now broken with years of traditions, and elects, with quite a large margin last time, a Democratic Congressman, Gerry Studds. (His first name, a reminder that he is distantly descended from Elbridge Gerry of gerrymander fame, is pronounced with a hard "g".) How it came about is this. From 1958 through 1972, the 12th was represented by Hastings Keith, a Republican with a conservative record and a gray personality. Neither of these factors hurt him, however, until he was challenged both in the Republican primary, by right-leaning state Senator William Weeks, and in the general election by Studds. Keith barely survived both challenges, and wisely decided to retire in 1972. Thus the contest was between the well-financed Weeks and the well-manned campaign of Studds. With the credential of having worked in Eugene McCarthy's 1968 presidential campaign, and the rare asset of support from McCarthy himself, Studds was able to put together a formidable organization—and to raise a good amount of money.

But the thing which made the difference in 1972 was Studd's own hard work. After his 1970 loss, he went about learning Portuguese; and he boned up, as well, on the problems of the local fishing industry. Although the district went for Nixon at the same time, Studds managed to win by 1,118 votes.

Much of the initial fervor behind Studds's first two campaigns came from his opposition to the American war in Southeast Asia. But his committee assignments—Merchant Marine and Fisheries along with Public Works—suggest a close concern with the nitty-gritty economic problems of the district. His major legislative effort in his first term was sponsorship of a bill to redefine the limits of national waters—in order to prevent traditional New England fishing grounds from being fished clean by giant Russian and Icelandic trawlers. Studds's efforts were nicely rewarded in 1974. His Republican opponent was a conservative ideologue and veteran of the Young Americans for Freedom; and the Congressman received fully 75% of the vote. It looks as if this longtime Republican bastion has now become a safe Democratic seat.

Census Data Pop. 475,672. Central city, 21%; suburban, 47%. Median family income, $10,132; families above $15,000: 22%; families below $3,000: 8%. Median years education, 12.2.

The Voters

Median voting age 46.
Employment profile White collar, 48%. Blue collar, 38%. Service, 13%. Farm, 1%.
Ethnic groups Black, 2%. Total foreign stock, 31%. Canada, 7%; Portugal, 5%; UK, 4%; Italy, Ireland, 2% each; Poland, 1%.

Presidential vote

1972	Nixon (R)	121,406	(52%)
	McGovern (D)	113,109	(48%)

1968	Nixon (R)	84,470	(43%)
	Humphrey (D)	106,256	(54%)
	Wallace (AI)	7,406	(4%)

Rep. Gerry E. Studds (D) Elected 1972; b. May 12, 1937, Mineola, N.Y.; home, Cohasset; Yale U., B.A. 1959, M.A.T. 1961.

Career U.S. Foreign Service, 1961–63; Exec. Asst. to William R. Anderson, Pres. Consultant for a Domestic Peace Corps, 1963; Legis. Asst. to U.S. Sen. Harrison Williams of N.J., 1964; Prep. School Teacher, 1965–69.

Offices 1511 LHOB, 202-225-3111. Also 243 P.O. Bldg., New Bedford 02740, 617-999-1251.

Committees

Merchant Marine and Fisheries (17th). Subcommittees: Coast Guard and Navigation; Fisheries and Wildlife Conservation and the Environment; Oceanography.

Public Works and Transportation (14th). Subcommittees: Aviation; Public Buildings and Grounds; Surface Transportation.

Group Ratings

	ADA	COPE	LWV	RIPON	NFU	LCV	CFA	NAB	NSI	ACA
1974	100	100	92	69	86	82	77	17	10	7
1973	92	100	83	80	85	95	100	–	–	11

Key Votes

1) Foreign Aid	AGN	6) Gov Abortn Aid	FOR	11) Pub Cong Election $	FOR
2) Busing	FOR	7) Coed Phys Ed	FOR	12) Turkish Arms Cutoff	FOR
3) ABM	AGN	8) Pov Lawyer Gag	AGN	13) Youth Camp Regs	FOR
4) B-1 Bomber	AGN	9) Pub Trans Sub	FOR	14) Strip Mine Veto	AGN
5) Nerve Gas	AGN	10) EZ Voter Regis	FOR	15) Farm Bill Veto	FOR

Election Results

1974 general:	Gerry E. Studds (D)	138,779	(75%)	($103,350)
	J. Alan MacKay (R)	46,787	(25%)	($37,505)
1974 primary	Gerry E. Studds (D), unopposed			
1972 general	Gerry E. Studds (D)	117,710	(50%)	($195,758)
	William D. Weeks (R)	116,592	(50%)	($269,046)

MICHIGAN

To understand politics in Michigan, you should think of this as not one, but two states; divided, not between Upper and Lower Peninsulas (for the Upper Peninsula has only 315,000 people and the Lower 8.7 million), but between the Detroit metropolitan area and outstate Michigan. Not only politically but, to a greater extent than is generally appreciated, these are two quite different regions and not especially well-integrated economically. Metro Detroit—Wayne, Oakland, and Macomb Counties—was boom country in the 1910–30 era when the growth of the automobile business from small-bore luxury trade to the nation's biggest industry increased the area's population from 613,000 in 1910 to 2.2 million just before the Great Depression struck.

Today, metro Detroit is in another depression, thanks to the sagging fortunes of the auto industry on which it is still totally—perhaps fatally—dependent. Unemployment is well into the double digits, and since 1970 metro Detroit has actually lost population. The city of Detroit, as most television watchers know, has the highest murder rate of any major city in the country—the proximate result of the fact that practically every household in the city stocked up on guns after the 1967 riot. But people are leaving not only the city, but also its generally pleasant suburbs. Metro Detroit is not going to wither away, like some latter day gold mining town; there are four million people here still, and most will stay. But this is a city, and a metropolitan area, in deep trouble.

In contrast, outstate Michigan is doing rather nicely, thank you. There is a dependence on the auto industry here, too, with major plants in Flint, Lansing, Saginaw, Grand Rapids, and Kalamazoo—but it is not so total as in Detroit, at least if one takes outstate as a whole. Most of outstate Michigan never experienced the 1910–30 boom in the auto industry, and now for the most part it is not suffering too much in the bust. Population here has risen 3.9% since 1970, more than the national average; people seem especially eager to move to the quiet towns and evergreened hills of the sparsely-settled northern part of the Lower Peninsula. The medium-sized cities and small towns one finds dotting the state are the kind of places most Americans say they would like to live in; and for most people they provide a stable, safe way of life. Incomes, even of blue-collar workers, are high; crime is low; recreational facilities are close at hand; and so are virtually all of the state's major universities; which, together with state government, have provided a healthy growth industry for outstate. Outstate Michigan's recent growth means that it is starting to overshadow metro Detroit, not just statistically but politically; outstate's share of the statewide vote has grown from 51% in 1964 to 55% in 1972—and will almost certainly grow more by 1976.

Such changes have long-term political effects. Metro Detroit filled with auto workers from Poland and Alabama, southern Italy and eastern Kentucky and Ontario, has traditionally been heavily Democratic; outstate, peopled by offspring of the Yankee immigrants from the Upstate New York of the 1840s, has traditionally been Republican. But in recent years, metro Detroit, its white voters sometimes furiously opposed to threatened (but now stopped) metropolitan school busing and eager for state funds for Catholic schools, has been moving toward the Republicans. At the same time, outstate Michigan, in line with the same movement you can see in Wisconsin, Minnesota, and Iowa, has been trending toward the Democrats. The result is a volatile politics which requires in close statewide races considerable expertise and sensitivity to produce a winning percentage.

Overall, Michigan has to be classed as a heavily Democratic state; Humphrey carried it easily in 1968, and McGovern, despite the busing issue which was raging at the time, ran better here than in 42 of the 49 other states. But Republicans hold the Governorship and one Senate seat and have not totally unrealistic hopes for capturing the other Senate seat in 1976. All of which is testimony to their greater expertise at vote-winning, and the superiority of the team they put together in the 1960s over the one which has dominated the state's Democratic Party, at least at its top levels, since the 1950s. At the House level, in state legislative races, even in contests for local office, the Republicans seem almost to be vanishing from the political picture here. But in the big statewide races, where party preference is least likely to determine the result, the Republicans dominate; Michigan Democrats have not won a seriously contested race for Senator or Governor since 1960.

The Republicans' skill at campaigning can best be seen in the last two gubernatorial races, both of them contests between incumbent William Milliken and former state Senator Sander Levin. Milliken had inherited the Governorship when George Romney went to Washington to become HUD Secretary in 1969; Milliken went into the 1970 race not particularly well known but, importantly, not disliked. That, as much as anything else, is why he has been reelected. This seemingly pleasant, moderate-to-liberal Republican has never really threatened anyone's turf; even when he has taken stands on controversial issues, those on the other side don't seem much to mind. It is a measure of Milliken's electioneering skill that in both the last two elections he has taken what has turned out to be the less popular side of a referendum on the November ballot—he favored aid for parochial schools in 1970 and opposed a repeal of the sales tax on food in 1974—but both times he won the election anyway.

The biggest controversy Milliken has generated has been over his selection of a Lieutenant Governor candidate in 1974. His choice, a suburban Detroit state Representative, was known mainly as a vocal opponent of abortion, and his selection was seen, no doubt correctly, as a rather cynical attempt to endear the Governor with right-to-life voters. But then in late October it turned out that the running mate had made quite a lot of money in land deals in the same suburb where he had sat on the zoning board; Milliken had simply ignored warnings about this in selecting him. Too much ignoring, one would have thought, for Milliken's good image in this Watergate year; but somehow he and his image survived. The Detroit *Free Press*, whose reporters had made the revelations, flip-flopped shamelessly on the editorial page to save its Milliken endorsement, and the voters simply seemed unwilling to believe that Milliken had done anything shabby, however strong the evidence.

So the Republicans had won another close one, by a 52–48 margin. As he had in 1970, Milliken won a surprisingly strong 47% of the vote in the metro Detroit, primarily because of his assiduous cultivation of the Catholic vote (parochiaid, abortion). That same cultivation seems to have cost him some votes outstate, where he had only 56%—but weak as this is for a Republican, at least by historical standards, it was enough to win. Milliken's victories depended, technically, almost entirely on sophisticated polling, by Frederick Currier of Market Opinion Research, which was the chief CREEP pollster in 1972, and on topnotch television advertising. Even as George Romney and Milliken have been monopolizing the Governorship since 1962, the number of actual Republican Party workers seems to have dwindled.

If Milliken's version of a Republican Party resembles what was handed down to him from George Romney, the Democratic Party here is still very much the legacy of the G. Mennen Williams era. Back when Williams was first elected Governor in 1948, Michigan was still considered a Republican state (and with good reason: it voted for Dewey over Truman that year). Williams and his Democratic Party Chairman Neil Staebler (now a member of the Federal Elections Commission) changed that. Working closely with UAW politicos, they organized the votes of the vast number of migrants who had come to Detroit to work in the auto industry. Throughout the 1950s they were able to win overwhelming majorities from metro Detroit's blacks. Polish-Americans, Southern whites, and even immigrants from Canada—enough to overcome, although not by huge margins, the large majorities the Republicans continued to win outstate. Their campaign tactics were geared to the tastes of blue-collar voters, then considerably less sophisticated than now; and politics in Michigan almost resembled a form of class warfare. Williams' margin in one campaign, 1952, may have been supplied when his Republican opponent said you couldn't have a political meeting in February, because everyone's down in Florida then. Those were the days when auto workers didn't get paid vacations, and the icy Michigan winter intensified their resentment.

But class warfare politics has not been winning elections here since 1962, when George Romney put on a high-powered ad campaign in effect urging people to split their tickets for him. They did, and Michigan voters have been splitting their tickets ever since, to the great benefit of Romney and Milliken and Senator Robert Griffin.

Griffin is perhaps the most unlikely member of this trio, for he alone has not taken much trouble to classify himself as some kind of liberal. His name is on the Landrum-Griffin Act, the 1959 reform of the labor laws—and a piece of legislation definitely not favored by organized labor. Since 1969, Griffin has been the Republican Whip in the Senate, laboriously attending to housekeeping chores, but also fighting like a tiger for partisan causes. It was Griffin who, against all the odds, prevented Abe Fortas from becoming Chief Justice in 1968, by carrying on a sort of one-man filibuster; it was Griffin who with an adroit parliamentary manuever, prevented Alaska's Mike Gravel from reading the Pentagon papers on the floor of the Senate. Although he has dissented from Republican administrations occasionally—most notably on the Haynsworth nomination and the SST—overall he has one of the highest records of support for the Nixon and Ford Administrations. Indeed, he served with Ford in the House for almost ten years, and was one of the masterminds of the campaign that made him Minority Leader in 1965; Griffin is, needless to say, well-connected at the White House.

All of which makes one wonder just how Griffin gets elected in Michigan. In 1966, when he beat Mennen Williams by a thumping 56–44 margin, he ran as a fresh face against an oldtime politician; in 1972, he ran as the loudest shouter against busing. That was the year a federal court had ordered the two-thirds black schools of Detroit integrated with the more than 90% white schools of 56 suburban districts; the result was a sort of hysteria which had not been seen in the white South since the early 1960s. Griffin saw the busing issue coming, and seized it in 1971—in spite of a previous record of supporting civil rights measures. He was able to convince white suburban voters that he was more antibusing than his Democratic opponent, state Attorney General Frank Kelley, not so much because their positions differed as because Democrats, especially Michigan Democrats, have been closely identified with securing rights for blacks in the past. Kelley compounded the problem by stressing busing almost to the exclusion of other issues, on which the voters were far less likely to take Griffin's view of things.

One suspects that already Griffin is looking ahead, with foreboding, to 1978, when his seat is up. He has been mentioned as a possible choice of his old friend Gerald Ford for a seat on the Supreme Court, which would end his reelection problems. And it is possible, of course, that he will again face a weak opponent or that some issue like busing will again crop up. But it may be that

Griffin, for all his undoubted parliamentary skill, may be headed for a defeat in a state which only occasionally is fully on his side.

If Griffin seeks to camouflage or downplay many of his apparent disagreements with the state's voters, Michigan's other Senator, Philip Hart, follows quite the contrary course. Hart, for example, persisted in opposing antibusing amendments during the height of the 1972 controversy, because he felt that the legislation would attenuate civil rights—and despite outpourings of outraged mail. The busing crisis has all but disappeared now, since the Supreme Court's 1973 ruling overturning the cross-district busing decree; but at the time the Senator took his stand, it appeared likely to defeat the hitherto-unbeatable Hart should he choose to run again in 1976.

Now for reasons entirely unrelated Hart has chosen to retire. He will be leaving the Senate just when he has got to the point of being able to reach some of the goals he has long sought. For years, for example, Hart has been Chairman of the Antitrust and Monopoly Subcommittee, but has not been able to command a majority on it; in 1975 he can. The result could be sweeping new antitrust legislation, for Hart has proposed a law which would make illegal any firm having more than a specified share of the market. Hart has also been one of the most active pro-consumer members of the Senate Commerce Committee, and one of the Senate's leading backers of no fault auto insurance.

But perhaps Hart's greatest asset politically, more than his record, has been his character. He is an open, sometimes excruciatingly frank man, one who is always ready to recognize the good faith and beneficent intentions of adversaries. He sometimes seems to agonize over decisions, and is known to be frustrated in his work in the Senate. He has been called the conscience of the Senate, and yet he feels that he has done a poor job there—an opinion virtually no one shares. Now there is a host of ambitious Michigan politicians eager to run. Already 2d district Congressman Marvin Esch is considering a run for the Republican nomination, which might also attract former Lieutenant Governor James Brickley. Democratic contenders will certainly include 7th district Congressman Donald Riegle, like many outstate voters a former Republican; Attorney General Kelley; and possibly Secretary of State Richard Austin.

For six full years, from 1966 to 1972, there were no changes in the Michigan congressional delegation. Suddenly due to retirements, defeats, and one promotion—Gerald Ford's—there have been several. Republicans had a 12–7 edge in the state's congressional delegation as recently as 1973; now the margin is 11–8 for the Democrats. Michigan was the scene of two special elections in 1974, in Ford's 5th district in March and in the 8th district eight weeks later; Democrats captured both seats, incontestably demonstrating the American people's disgust with Richard Nixon.

Michigan had surprised the nation in quite another way in 1972, by casting 51% of the vote in its Democratic presidential primary for George Wallace. But there were a number of factors which suggest that that result is not replicable, and that the Alabamian would be more likely to win on the order of the 20% or so he has taken in Wisconsin and Pennsylvania. That primary came at the height of Michigan's mania over busing—an issue that cut for Wallace and won him as much as 85% of the vote in some Detroit suburbs. And secondly, that primary took place just the day after Wallace had been shot in Maryland. It is impossible to assess how much of a showing was a sympathy vote; but it surely influenced turnout in Wallace's favor, and it seemed to confer on him a kind of martyred respectability that probably enabled him to win many more votes than he would have otherwise.

Census Data Pop. 8,875,083; 4.38% of U.S. total, 7th largest; Central city, 28%; suburban, 49%. Median family income, $11,029; 6th highest; families above $15,000: 27%; families below $3,000: 7%. Median years education, 12.1.

1974 Share of Federal Tax Burden $12,614,100,000; 4.71% of U.S. total, 7th largest.

1974 Share of Federal Outlays $8,094,826,000; 3.00% of U.S. total, 9th largest. Per capita federal spending, $912.

DOD	$1,351,641,000	17th (1.97%)		HEW	$3,930,257,000	8th (4.24%)
AEC	$3,919,000	23d (0.13%)		HUD	$34,941,000	10th (3.59%)
NASA	$7,082,000	21st (0.24%)		VA	$462,790,000	8th (3.38%)
DOT	$216,661,000	12th (2.56%)		EPA	$79,478,000	12th (2.53%)
DOC	$14,811,000	19th (0.92%)		RevS	$258,088,000	6th (4.25%)
DOI	$21,085,000	27th (0.86%)		Int.	$556,445,000	5th (2.71%)
USDA	$204,534,000	26th (1.64%)		Other	$953,094,000	

Economic Base Motor vehicles and equipment, and other transportation equipment; machinery, especially metalworking machinery; finance, insurance and real estate; fabricated metal products, especially metal stampings; primary metal industries, especially iron and steel foundries; agriculture, notably dairy products, cattle, dry beans and corn; food and kindred products.

Political Line-up Governor, William G. Milliken (R). Senators, Philip A. Hart (D) and Robert P. Griffin (R). Representatives, 19 (12 D and 7 R). State Senate (24 D and 14 R); State House (66 D and 44 R).

The Voters

Registration 4,785,689 total. No party registration.
Median voting age 40.
Employment profile White collar, 45%. Blue collar, 41%. Service, 13%. Farm, 1%.
Ethnic groups Black, 11%. Spanish, 1%. Total foreign stock, 19%. Canada, 4%; Poland, Germany, UK, 2% each; Italy, 1%.

Presidential vote

1972	Nixon (R)	1,961,721	(57%)
	McGovern (D)	1,459,435	(43%)
1968	Nixon (R)	1,370,665	(42%)
	Humphrey (D)	1,593,082	(48%)
	Wallace (AI)	331,968	(10%)

1972 Democratic Presidential Primary

Wallace	809,239	(51%)
McGovern	425,694	(27%)
Humphrey	249,798	(16%)
others	103,342	(6%)

1972 Republican Presidential Primary

Nixon	321,652	(96%)
others	15,091	(4%)

Sen. Philip A. Hart (D) Elected 1958, seat up 1976; b. Dec. 10, 1912, Bryn Mawr, Pa.; home, Mackinac Island; Georgetown U., A.B. 1934, U. of Mich., J.D. 1937; Catholic.

Career Practicing Atty., 1938–41, 1946–48; Army, WWII; Mbr., Mich. Corporation and Securities Commission, 1949–50; Dir., Mich. Ofc. of Price Stabilization, 1951; U.S. Dist. Atty. for East. Mich., 1952; Lt. Gov. of Mich., 1955–59.

Offices 253 RSOB, 202-224-4825. Also 438 Fed. Bldg., Detroit 48226, 313-226-3188, and 580 Fed. Bldg., Grand Rapids 49502, 616-456-2218.

Committees

Commerce (4th). Subcommittees: Aviation; Communications; The Consumer (Vice Chairman); Environment (Chairman); Oceans and Atmosphere; Special Subcommittee to Study Transportation on the Great Lakes-St. Lawrence Seaway (Chairman); Special Subcommittee on Oil and Gas Production and Distribution.

The Judiciary (3d). Subcommittees: Antitrust and Monopoly (Chairman); Constitutional Rights; Juvenile Delinquency.

Select Committee on Intelligence Operations (2d).

Group Ratings

	ADA	COPE	LWV	RIPON	NFU	LCV	CFA	NAB	NSI	ACA
1974	100	73	90	67	100	100	88	18	0	0
1973	94	89	100	63	100	–	100	–	–	4
1972	95	100	100	74	90	84	100	0	0	5

Key Votes

1) No-Knock	AGN	8) Gov Abortn Aid	FOR	15) Consumer Prot Agy	FOR
2) Busing	FOR	9) Cut Mil Brass	ABS	16) Forced Psych Tests	FOR
3) No Fault	FOR	10) Gov Limousine	AGN	17) Fed Campaign Subs	FOR
4) F-111	ABS	11) RR Featherbed	FOR	18) Rhod Chrome Ban	FOR
5) Death Penalty	AGN	12) Handgun License	FOR	19) Open Legis Meetings	FOR
6) Foreign Aid	FOR	13) Less Troop Abrd	FOR	20) Strikers Food Stmps	FOR
7) Filibuster	AGN	14) Resume Turk Aid	FOR	21) Gov Info Disclosure	FOR

Election Results

1970 general:	Philip A. Hart (D)	1,744,672	(67%)
	Lenore Romney (R)	858,438	(33%)
1970 primary:	Philip A. Hart (D), unopposed		
1964 general:	Philip A. Hart (D)	1,996,912	(65%)
	Elly M. Peterson (R)	1,096,272	(35%)

Sen. Robert P. Griffin (R) Elected Appointed May 11, 1966, elected Nov. 8, 1966, seat up 1978; b. Nov. 6, 1923, Detroit; home, Traverse City; Central Mich. U., A.B., B.S. 1947, U. of Mich., J.D. 1950; United Church of Chirst.

Career Practicing atty., 1950–56; U.S. House of Reps., 1957–66.

Offices 353 RSOB, 202-224-6221. Also 1035 Fed. Bldg., Detroit 48226, 313-226-6020, and 780 Fed Bldg., Grand Rapids 49502, 616-456-2535.

Committees

Minority Whip

Commerce (2d). Subcommittees: Aviation; Communications; Foreign Commerce and Tourism; Merchant Marine; Oceans and International Environment; Special Subcommittee to Study Transportation on the Great Lakes-St. Lawrence Seaway.

Foreign Relations (6th). Subcommittees: African Affairs; Far Eastern Affairs; Oceans and International Environment.

Rules and Administration (3d). Subcommittees: Privileges and Elections; Standing Rules of the Senate.

Group Ratings

	ADA	COPE	LWV	RIPON	NFU	LCV	CFA	NAB	NSI	ACA
1974	19	27	75	64	44	42	55	40	80	67
1973	11	18	56	57	38	–	11	–	–	88
1972	15	10	60	74	63	59	67	70	88	74

Key Votes

1) No-Knock	FOR	8) Gov Abortn Aid	AGN	15) Consumer Prot Agy	AGN
2) Busing	AGN	9) Cut Mil Brass	AGN	16) Forced Psych Tests	AGN
3) No Fault	FOR	10) Gov Limousine	FOR	17) Fed Campaign Subs	AGN
4) F-111	FOR	11) RR Featherbed	AGN	18) Rhod Chrome Ban	FOR
5) Death Penalty	FOR	12) Handgun License	AGN	19) Open Legis Meetings	AGN
6) Foreign Aid	FOR	13) Less Troop Abrd	AGN	20) Strikers Food Stmps	AGN
7) Filibuster	AGN	14) Resume Turk Aid	FOR	21) Gov Info Disclosure	AGN

Election Results

1972 general:	Robert P. Griffin (R)	1,781,065	(53%)	($1,394,927)
	Frank J. Kelley (D)	1,577,178	(47%)	($547,819)

1972 primary: Robert P. Griffin (R), unopposed
1966 general: Robert P. Griffin (R) 1,363,808 (56%)
               G. Mennen Williams (D) 1,070,484 (44%)

Gov. William G. Milliken (R) Elected Appointed 1969, elected 1970, term expires Jan. 1979; b. Mar. 26, 1922; Yale U., B.A.

Career Army Air Corps, WWII; Pres., J.W. Milliken, Inc., Dept. Store Chain; Mich. Senate, 1961–65, Maj. Floor Ldr., 1963; Lt. Gov. of Mich., 1965–69.

Offices Executive Ofc., Lansing 48903, 517-373-3400.

Election Results

1974 general: William G. Milliken (R) 1,356,865 (52%)
               Sander M. Levin (D) 1,242,247 (48%)
1974 primary: William G. Milliken (R), unopposed
1970 general: William G. Milliken (R) 1,339,047 (51%)
               Sander M. Levin (D) 1,294,638 (49%)

◆ ◆ ◆ ◆ ◆

FIRST DISTRICT

The 1st congressional district of Michigan includes the north and near northwest sides of Detroit, plus the enclave-suburb of Highland Park. This territory presents a nice example of the pace of neighborhood change in twentieth century urban America. Sixty-odd years ago, the land here was given over completely to Michigan farms; at that time, Detroit's growth had not yet reached the southern boundary of the 1st, five miles north of the Detroit River. Then, in 1910, Henry Ford built his first big auto plant in Highland Park. At that time, as now, manufacturers located their factories at the edge of urban settlement, where a labor force is at hand, land prices are cheap, and room to expand is available. In the years that followed, mile after mile of closely spaced one- and two-family houses were built —the first subdivisions geared to the scale imposed by the automobile. Ethnic neighborhood patterns emerged: Polish in the eastern and southern parts of the current 1st; Jewish in the middle; and a rich WASP section just north of Highland Park. During the 1910-30 period, population growth was as explosive here as anywhere in the country, and even today most of the 1st's housing units were built in those two decades.

In the years following World War II, another kind of change took place here. In 1945, there were few black enclaves within the lines of the current 1st; even by 1950, less than 5% of the residents of the area were black. By 1970, that figure had risen to 70%. The first white exodus—rather, the first black movement in—occurred in the late 1940s and early 1950s. Thousands of blacks who had come to Detroit during the war left the small ghettoes in which they had been confined while whites fled to the outer limits of the city or the FHA-financed suburbs. Whole square miles of Detroit changed racial complexion within a year or two. Then in the wake of the 1967 riot, another particularly rapid racial transformation took place. What was previously Detroit's primary Jewish neighborhood along Seven Mile Road soon became heavily black. Around the same time, the city's most affluent area opened up to blacks; today parts of northwest Detroit contain elegant black or integrated neighborhoods.

There are still pockets of all-white territory in the 1st, particularly in the Polish neighborhoods which resist change of any sort. Generally speaking, the blacks in the 1st are more affluent and better educated than those in the next-door 13th district; most people here own their own homes. They are also far more likely to vote. Some analysts have speculated that blacks, as they grow more affluent, will, like members of so many other ethnic groups, grow more conservative and Republican. Maybe so, but the evidence in the 1st district is quite to the contrary; in the 1972 presidential race, this was the second most heavily Democratic congressional district in the country.

It therefore came as no surprise that the 1st district's Congressman, John Conyers, voted for the impeachment of Richard Nixon on the House Judiciary Committee. Indeed, Conyers had called for Nixon's impeachment even before 1972, for what the Congressman regarded as his illegal war-making activities. Conyers had always been outspoken; in 1964, when he was first elected to the House, there were only four other blacks there, and he was by far the most militant. He has the distinction of being one of the few Congressmen who has consistently and constantly opposed the Vietnam war. Conyers was also instrumental in setting up the Congressional Black Caucus, which now includes half a dozen members at least as voluble as he is. After ten years in Congress, Conyers has become a subcommittee chairman; but his power is held as a spokesman, not as a manueverer of the levers of legislative power.

Like most Congressmen, Conyers' first race was his toughest. In the 1964 Democratic primary he edged Richard Austin, his principal opponent, by 108 votes our of 60,000 cast. (In 1970, Austin became Michigan Secretary of State after a narrow defeat in the 1969 Detroit mayoralty election; both times Austin had Conyers' support.) Since his first election Conyers has won all elections in which he has had opposition, including primaries, by percentages ranging from 85% to 91%.

Census Data   Pop. 467,636. Central city, 92%; suburban, 8%. Median family income, $9,997; families above $15,000: 23%; families below $3,000: 10%. Median years education, 11.5.

The Voters

Median voting age 43.
Employment profile White collar, 41%. Blue collar, 42%. Service, 17%. Farm, –%.
Ethnic groups Black, 70%. Total foreign stock, 15%. Canada, Poland, 2% each; USSR, UK, Germany, 1% each.

Presidential vote

1972	Nixon (R)	22,815	(14%)
	McGovern (D)	137,732	(86%)
1968	Nixon (R)	25,093	(13%)
	Humphrey (D)	157,660	(83%)
	Wallace (AI)	8,241	(4%)

Rep. John Conyers, Jr. (D) Elected 1964; b. May 16, 1929, Detroit; home, Detroit; Wayne St. U., B.A. 1957, LL.B. 1958; Baptist.

Career Army, Korea; Legis. Asst. to U.S. Rep. John Dingell, 1958–61; Practicing atty., 1959–61; Referee, Mich. Workman's Comp. Dept., 1961–63.

Offices 2444 RHOB, 202-225-5126. Also 307 Fed. Bldg., 231 W. Lafayette St., Detroit 48226, 313-226-7022.

Committees

Government Operations (13th). Subcommittees: Government Information and Individual Rights; Manpower and Housing.

Judiciary (6th). Subcommittees: Crime (Chairman).

Group Ratings

	ADA	COPE	LWV	RIPON	NFU	LCV	CFA	NAB	NSI	ACA
1974	95	89	83	60	82	100	80	17	13	17
1973	95	100	89	73	83	93	100	–	–	11
1972	88	91	91	69	83	60	100	13	0	6

Key Votes

1) Foreign Aid	ABS	6) Gov Abortn Aid	FOR	11) Pub Cong Election $	FOR
2) Busing	FOR	7) Coed Phys Ed	FOR	12) Turkish Arms Cutoff	FOR
3) ABM	AGN	8) Pov Lawyer Gag	AGN	13) Youth Camp Regs	FOR
4) B-1 Bomber	AGN	9) Pub Trans Sub	FOR	14) Strip Mine Veto	AGN
5) Nerve Gas	AGN	10) EZ Voter Regis	FOR	15) Farm Bill Veto	FOR

Election Results

1974 general:	John Conyers, Jr. (D)	97,620	(91%)	($20,292)
	Walter F. Girardot (R)	9,358	(9%)	($85)
1974 primary:	John Conyers, Jr. (D), unopposed			
1972 general:	John Conyers, Jr. (D)	131,353	(89%)	($29,661)
	Walter F. Girardot (R)	16,096	(11%)	($978)

◆ ◆ ◆ ◆ ◆

SECOND DISTRICT

The 2d congressional district of Michigan is an odd amalgam: an admixture of university campuses, burgeoning suburbs, and aging factories. In rough terms, the district takes in the western and southern edges of the Detroit metropolitan area and lies entirely within the Detroit TV media market. But the 2d's most important city, Ann Arbor, thinks itself no part of what it considers a grimy and industrial Detroit. Ann Arbor (pop. 99,000) is the home of the University of Michigan (43,000 students), one of the nation's largest and most prestigious universities. This institution, along with Eastern Michigan University (18,000 students) in nearby Ypsilanti, gives the 2d the largest proportion of college students among elegible voters—15.2%—of any district in the nation. Indeed, the student vote here is so large that in Ann Arbor it spawned a third party which had some vitality until it became nothing more than a wreck-the-Democrats operation.

Ann Arbor is now solidly liberal, but until the late sixties and the coming of the student vote, this was a conservative Republican town. Its heritage stemmed from its large German-American population, many of whom are descended from immigrants fleeing from the failure of the revolutions of 1848. So until the coming of the student vote, the Democratic strength here lay in the working class wards of Ypsilanti, near the giant Willow Run plant, and in Monroe County to the south along Lake Erie. For the 1972 election the shape of the 2d was altered to include the Detroit suburb of Livonia (pop. 110,000), which despite the presence of a couple of GM plants is middle to upper middle income and, more often than not, Republican in politics. Livonia is a place that ballooned with instant subdivisions—its population in 1950 was just 17,000. But its demographic makeup, with large numbers of schoolchildren, means that it is outvoted by the less populous Ann Arbor in 2d district elections.

In the last two elections, the 2d district has been the scene of two reasonably close campaigns, both won by incumbent Republican Marvin Esch not so much on the basis of intrinsic strength as on adroit politicking—and hard work. As his rating by various groups indicate, Esch is a Congressman who has something in his record for everyone, and he is adroit at pointing out to different segments of his constituency those parts of this record which will appeal to them and at directing attention away from those parts which they will not.

Thus in 1972, when he faced state Representative Marvin Stempien of Livonia—who was largely responsible for that suburb's inclusion in the district—the major issue in the Detroit suburbs was busing; and Esch was prepared with a strong antibusing stance. At the same time, he could press the liberal aspects of his own record in Ann Arbor, and contrast them with his opponent's rather conservative views on some issues—all to his electoral benefit. Altogether, Esch had 56% of the vote—exactly the same percentage Richard Nixon was winning in the district.

Two years later Esch was the beneficiary of an unforeseeable set of circumstances. The August Democratic primary was so close a race beteen Edward Pierce, an Ann Arbor doctor who swept that city, and John Reuther, nephew of the late UAW President Walter Reuther, that there was a recount that stretched into September. Reuther finally came out ahead by 81 votes, but by that point hardly had time to put together a campaign. Even with these advantages Esch was able to win with only 54% of the vote—an indication that he was in deep trouble in this Democratic year.

It appears now that Esch has his sights set on Philip Hart's Senate seat, which is up and being vacated in 1976. The Congressman's great advantages will be his adroitness and middle of the road record; his greatest disadvantage the fact that he is scarcely known at all in most parts of the state. But that long shot of a race may be no more difficult than the task Esch has of winning in this multivarious district every two years, and the payoff much more. In the event Esch leaves the 2d, or even if he doesn't, there is likely to be a plethora of contenders here in 1976.

Census Data Pop. 466,852. Central city, 21%; suburban, 79%. Median family income, $12,908; families above $15,000: 37%; families below $3,000: 4%. Median years education, 12.4.

The Voters

Median voting age 36.
Employment profile White collar, 53%. Blue collar, 33%. Service, 13%. Farm, 1%.
Ethnic groups Black, 5%. Spanish, 1%. Total foreign stock, 17%. Canada, 4%; Germany, UK, 2% each; Poland, Italy, 1% each.

Presidential vote

1972	Nixon (R)		106,155	(56%)
	McGovern (D)		85,093	(44%)
1968	Nixon (R)		69,610	(45%)
	Humphrey (D)		70,528	(45%)
	Wallace (AI)		15,950	(10%)

Rep. Marvin L. Esch (R) Elected 1966; b. Aug. 4, 1927, Flinton; home, Ann Arbor; U. of Mich., A.B. 1950, M.A. 1951, Ph.D. 1957; Presbyterian.

Career Maritime Svc. and Army, WWII; Asst. Prof. of Speech, Wayne St. U., 1951–55; Lecturer, U. of Mich.-Wayne St. U. Inst. of Labor and Industrial Relations, 1955–64; Mich. House of Reps., 1965–66.

Offices 2353 RHOB, 202-225-4401. Also 200 E. Huron St., Ann Arbor 48108, 313-665-0618.

Committees

Education and Labor (5th). Subcommittees: Labor-Management Relations; Manpower, Compensation, and Health and Safety; Post-secondary Education.

Science and Technology (8th). Subcommittees: Energy Research, Development and Demonstration; Environment and the Atmosphere; Science, Research, and Technology.

Group Ratings

	ADA	COPE	LWV	RIPON	NFU	LCV	CFA	NAB	NSI	ACA
1974	57	56	82	69	92	57	36	56	60	31
1973	60	30	83	92	45	67	25	–	–	43
1972	56	30	75	84	100	63	50	44	60	39

Key Votes

1) Foreign Aid	FOR	6) Gov Abortn Aid	AGN	11) Pub Cong Election $	FOR
2) Busing	AGN	7) Coed Phys Ed	AGN	12) Turkish Arms Cutoff	FOR
3) ABM	AGN	8) Pov Lawyer Gag	AGN	13) Youth Camp Regs	FOR
4) B-1 Bomber	FOR	9) Pub Trans Sub	AGN	14) Strip Mine Veto	AGN
5) Nerve Gas	AGN	10) EZ Voter Regis	FOR	15) Farm Bill Veto	FOR

Election Results

1974 general:	Marvin L. Esch (R)	72,245	(54%)	($106,747)
	John S. Reuther (D)	62,755	(46%)	($112,860)
1974 primary:	Marvin L. Esch (R), unopposed			
1972 general:	Marvin L. Esch (R)	103,321	(56%)	($71,649)
	Marvin R. Stempien (D)	79,762	(44%)	($55,292)

♦ ♦ ♦ ♦ ♦

THIRD DISTRICT

The 3d congressional district of Michigan centers on the cities of Kalamazoo (pop. 86,000) and Battle Creek (pop. 39,000), and reaches north to include some of the suburbs of Lansing. This historically Republican territory enthusiastically attached itself to the Party as soon as it was created in 1854 and has seldom left it since. These are places where old fashioned virtues—honesty, thrift, reserve—are taken seriously, and where they are considered the heart of political morality. For years they were exemplified, at least for people here, by the Republican Party, but that seems to have changed with Richard Nixon. For even before the Watergate scandal broke, the 3d was moving left, giving George McGovern a higher percentage of its votes than Hubert Humphrey, and coming increasingly closer to going Democratic in state elections. Then came Watergate, and the 3d, like most of outstate Michigan, seemed ready for a shift to the left.

Indeed, just as 1974 began, the 3d seemed especially likely to show a direct Watergate impact. For the district's Congressman, Garry Brown, had got himself involved, innocently but involved, in part of the scandal. Brown, a feisty, hardworking Republican, is a member of the House Banking and Currency Committee, and could be counted on in the past to oppose just about anything the populist then Chairman, Wright Patman, wanted. One of the things Patman wanted, in the fall of 1972, was an investigation of Watergate. At the time, the scandal was generally ignored, except for the pages of the Washington *Post* —and among those inside the headquarters of CREEP and the White House who were plotting to cover it up. One of their most pliant tools, as it turned out, was Garry Brown. The CREEP people didn't want Patman's men subpoenaing them, and Brown was perfectly willing to cooperate. He helped line up every Republican on Banking and Currency against the Patman move; and either he or others got six of the Democrats to vote that way, too—enough for a majority.

Brown's activity in this was typical. He is just as aggressive and unyielding when arguing against the FDA on behalf of Upjohn, a Kalamazoo-based pharmaceutical manufacturer, or when pleading the interests of the company that builds Checker cabs, a big employer in the 3d. In those cases as in the Watergate, Brown does not seem to inquire into all the motives of his client; if he is convinced the cause is O.K., he just goes ahead and fights. In his defense, Brown says that he just did what any good partisan would do—to protect his party's interest in a general election.

Whether that is how a Congressman should view his duties was the issue in the race in the 3d in 1974—or, rather, should have been the issue. But though Brown was terribly vulnerable he had the luck to draw an opponent who declined to use the strongest issues. The Democrats had looked around for an ambitious young candidate; finding none of suitable quality, they settled on Paul Todd, a 53-year-old former Congressman who had won in the 1964 Democratic landslide and had been beaten by Brown two years later. Todd declined to use Watergate or the Patman investigation in any way during the campaign. And when Gerald Ford pardoned Richard Nixon, Todd came out in favor of Ford's action—allowing Brown to get into an anti-Nixon posture by displaying some dissatisfaction with the pardon.

Even at that, Brown only won by a 52-48 margin, by far his closest race since he first won the seat. Presumably he will not have as much trouble in 1976; the Watergate issue, and its peculiar relevance in the 3d, will have faded somewhat by then, and otherwise his constituents have relatively few complaints about him.

Census Data Pop. 467,546. Central city, 19%; suburban, 44%. Median family income, $10,913; families above $15,000: 25%; families below $3,000: 7%. Median years education, 12.2.

The Voters

Median voting age 40.
Employment profile White collar, 46%. Blue collar, 39%. Service, 13%. Farm, 2%.
Ethnic groups Black, 5%. Total foreign stock, 10%. Netherlands, Canada, 2% each; Germany, UK, 1% each.

Presidential vote

1972	Nixon (R)	118,023	(62%)
	McGovern (D)	71,608	(38%)
1968	Nixon (R)	91,974	(53%)
	Humphrey (D)	64,544	(37%)
	Wallace (AI)	17,857	(10%)

Rep. Garry Brown (R) Elected 1966; b. Aug. 12, 1923, Schoolcraft; home, Schoolcraft; Kalamazoo Col., B.A. 1951, Geo. Wash. U., LL.B. 1954; Presbyterian.

Career Army, 1946–47; Practicing atty., 1954–67; Commissioner of U.S. Dist. Ct., West. Dist. of Mich., 1957–62; Mich. Senate, 1962–66, Minor. Floor Ldr.

Offices 2446 RHOB, 202-225-5011. Also Rm. 2-1-36 Fed. Ctr., 74 N. Washington St., Battle Creek 49107, 616-962-1551.

Committees

Banking, Currency and Housing (3d). Subcommittees: Financial Institutions Supervision, Regulation and Insurance; Housing and Community Development; International Trade, Investment and Monetary Policy.

Government Operations (4th). Subcommittees: Commerce, Consumer and Monetary Affairs.

Joint Economic Committee (2d, House Side). Subcommittees: Consumer Economics; Economic Progress; International Economics; Priorities and Economy in Government; Urban Affairs.

Group Ratings

	ADA	COPE	LWV	RIPON	NFU	LCV	CFA	NAB	NSI	ACA
1974	38	27	75	64	71	38	27	67	78	33
1973	20	9	67	100	12	56	13	–	–	65
1972	13	9	60	88	50	56	0	100	100	64

Key Votes

1) Foreign Aid	FOR	6) Gov Abortn Aid	AGN	11) Pub Cong Election $	AGN
2) Busing	FOR	7) Coed Phys Ed	AGN	12) Turkish Arms Cutoff	AGN
3) ABM	FOR	8) Pov Lawyer Gag	FOR	13) Youth Camp Regs	AGN
4) B-1 Bomber	FOR	9) Pub Trans Sub	FOR	14) Strip Mine Veto	FOR
5) Nerve Gas	AGN	10) EZ Voter Regis	AGN	15) Farm Bill Veto	FOR

Election Results

1974 general:	Garry Brown (R)	70,157	(52%)	($52,305)
	Paul H. Todd, Jr. (D)	65,212	(48%)	($42,961)
1974 primary:	Garry Brown (R), unopposed			
1972 general:	Garry Brown (R)	110,082	(60%)	($23,116)
	James T. Brignall (D)	74,114	(40%)	($26,320)

◆ ◆ ◆ ◆ ◆

FOURTH DISTRICT

The 4th congressional district of Michigan is shaped like a very short L. It includes Michigan's southwest corner plus a string of counties along the state's border with Indiana and Ohio. The district's major urban concentration is the Benton Harbor-St. Joseph area on Lake Michigan. These two next door cities could hardly be less twinlike: Benton Harbor (pop. 16,000) is industrial, with a big RCA Whirlpool plant, and a majority of its citizens are black; while St. Joseph (pop. 11,000) is virtually all white and notably well-to-do. Besides Benton Harbor, there is also a black community of some size in and near Cassopolis and Dowagiac—descendants of slaves who found their way to these stations on the underground railway. For the most part, the 4th is agricultural and small town, with rolling hills, occasional lakes, and many dairy farms. The district has a relatively large number of German-Americans for Michigan; in ethnic composition it is more like northern Indiana or Ohio. The 4th is also disconnected from the rest of Michigan in another way: most of it is within the South Bend, Indiana, or Toledo, Ohio, media markets.

If you want to understand some of the political background of the 4th district, visit the county seat of Hillsdale. Here the courthouse and the local college were being built as the Republican Party was young, and the college, in particular, exemplified the things the Republicans then stood for. It believed in absolute honesty and was inclined toward temperance; it was one of the first American schools to admit women; and was strongly opposed to slavery.

Those were the principles which inspired the early idealistic Republicans of the nineteenth century; and Hillsdale and the 4th district invariably supported them. Now, when we are three-quarters through the twentieth, the political ambiance at Hillsdale is quite different (or perhaps it simply hasn't changed much): this was one of the few schools where there was virtually no protest against the Vietnam war; hair has always remained short here and skirts long; temperance is stll encouraged; but there is less emphasis on women's or black's rights than on a sort of libertarianism that must please some of the schools' big business benefactors.

That sort of Republicanism is typical of the 4th district as well, and of the two Congressmen who, between them, have represented the district for more than 40 years. From 1934 to 1962, the 4th elected Clare Hoffman, an irascible opponent of federal expenditures who made even H. R. Gross of Iowa look like a free-spending New Dealer. When Hoffman retired, there was a rather decorous Republican primary to replace him, and the winner of that contest, Edward Hutchinson, has represented the 4th ever since.

One scarcely needs to describe Hutchinson, although it is hard to resist noting that charisma cannot have been the key factor in that 1962 primary. He is familiar to most Americans now as the ranking Republican on the House Judiciary Committee—a plodding, often dull speaker who, with an earnestness that cannot be gainsaid, adheres to orthodox Republican conservatism. No one—until Nixon himself released the June 23 tape—could convince him Nixon was guilty of anything; and one wonders whether even that would have been enough had not other committee Republicans like Charles Wiggins made their stands known first.

When he first came to the House, Hutchinson and Robert McClory of Illinois, elected the same time and both assigned to the Judiciary Committee, had to flip a coin to see which would have seniority over the other. Hutchinson won, and when William McCulloch retired in 1972, he became the ranking minority member. At that point, Hutchinson had been known primarily for voting against civil rights legislation—an interesting deviation from the district's free soil traditions but perhaps not so out of line with Republican feeling here today. In any case, that flip of the coin gave us a pro-Nixon Republican instead of a wavering one as the titular spokesman for his party during the impeachment hearings; actually, it probably didn't matter much, since it is hard to see how Hutchinson had any impact on any vote but his own.

The length and strength of this district's Republican convictions have long led observers to suppose that Hutchinson can only be beaten in a primary. It turns out that that may have been wrong, at least in 1974, when he was held to 54% of the vote by an underfinanced Democrat; a really strong campaign might have beaten him. But that seems unlikely for the future. Hutchinson surely has only the primary to worry about. Only once has he been seriously challenged and then he won 61% to state Senator Charles Zollar's 34% But the Congressman's weak showing in 1974 must be construed as the district's comment on his impeachment hearings performance, and it is possible that future primary challenges could be more successful.

Census Data Pop. 467,140. Central city, 0%; suburban, 0%. Median family income, $9,693; families above $15,000: 18%; families below $3,000: 10%. Median years education, 12.1.

The Voters

Median voting age 43.
Employment profile White collar, 37%. Blue collar, 47%. Service, 12%. Farm, 4%.
Ethnic groups Black, 6%. Spanish, 1%. Total foreign stock, 10%. Germany, 3%; Canada, 1%.

Presidential vote

1972	Nixon (R)	116,712	(68%)
	McGovern (D)	55,846	(32%)
1968	Nixon (R)	91,836	(54%)
	Humphrey (D)	58,484	(34%)
	Wallace (AI)	20,275	(12%)

Rep. Edward Hutchinson (R) Elected 1962; b. Oct. 13, 1914, Fennville; home, St. Joseph; U. of Mich., A.B. 1936, J.D. 1938; Christian Scientist.

Career Practicing atty.; Army, WWII; Mich. House of Reps., 1947–51; Mich. Senate, 1951–60; Delegate and V.P., Mich. Constitutional Conv., 1961–62.

Offices 2336 RHOB, 202-225-3761. Also 201 Fed. Bldg., 175 W. Territorial Rd., Benton Harbor 49022, 616-925-7962.

Committees

Judiciary (Ranking Member). Subcommittees: Monopolies and Commercial Law.

Standards of Official Conduct (3d).

Group Ratings

	ADA	COPE	LWV	RIPON	NFU	LCV	CFA	NAB	NSI	ACA
1974	19	9	18	50	38	19	0	83	70	93
1973	4	9	17	47	25	6	29	–	–	93
1972	0	27	27	44	20	32	0	92	100	91

Key Votes

1) Foreign Aid	AGN	6) Gov Abortn Aid	ABS	11) Pub Cong Election $	AGN
2) Busing	AGN	7) Coed Phys Ed	AGN	12) Turkish Arms Cutoff	AGN
3) ABM	FOR	8) Pov Lawyer Gag	FOR	13) Youth Camp Regs	AGN
4) B-1 Bomber	FOR	9) Pub Trans Sub	AGN	14) Strip Mine Veto	FOR
5) Nerve Gas	FOR	10) EZ Voter Regis	AGN	15) Farm Bill Veto	FOR

Election Results

1974 general:	Edward Hutchinson (R)	64,731	(54%)	($8,254)
	Richard E. Daugherty (D)	55,469	(46%)	($7,606)
1974 primary:	Edward Hutchinson (R), unopposed			
1972 general:	Edward Hutchinson (R)	111,185	(67%)	($40,110)
	Charles W. Jameson (D)	54,141	(33%)	($12,300)

◆ ◆ ◆ ◆ ◆

FIFTH DISTRICT

The 5th congressional district of Michigan is a seat which has made history in two ways in the last two years: it gave the nation its 40th Vice President; and at the same time, by electing a member of the opposite party to replace him, it helped to make him the 38th President—and to get rid of the 37th. The Vice President and President of course is Gerald R. Ford, Jr., a man whose name was hardly a household word two years ago and now is known worldwide.

The 5th district and Grand Rapids, the city which dominates it, tell us a lot about Ford—both how he came to be what and where he is, and how he seems to be increasingly out of touch with the thinking of the American people. Indeed, Grand Rapids (pop. 197,000) is a city that almost cries out to characterize Middle America. Before Ford, it was best known for its furniture business which got a start here because of the then proximity of Michigan lumber. Today, Grand Rapids is more diversified—and doing quite well economically in these years of auto industry depression elsewhere in Michigan.

The nation's largest concentration of Dutch-Americans can be found living in and around Grand Rapids. Fully 7% of the 5th district's residents were either born in the Netherlands or had parents who were; and many more than 7% have Dutch names, as a glance at the city phone book's list of Vander....s will show. Visitors to present-day Amsterdam know that the European Dutch are highly tolerant of diverse life styles. But when these people emigrate it seems they become rigidly conservative. As evidence consider the Boers of South Africa and the Dutch of Grand Rapids. The still stern Michigan Calvinists of the Christian Reform Church—the dominant sect in Grand Rapids—frown on sinful activities like drinking, smoking, and dancing.

For many, many years these attitudes produced a strong allegiance to the Republican Party among the Dutch which, when combined with traditional Republican outstate Michigan leanings here, made this city and district a leading Republican bastion. The Grand Rapids Dutch produced Michigan's best known Senator, Arthur H. Vandenberg, who served from 1928 to his death in 1951. Born and bred an isolationist, Vandenberg went to his grave a deep-dyed, rather grandiloquent conservative. But after World War II he decided to change his mind, and cooperated with the Roosevelt and Truman Administrations on issues like the United Nations, the Marshall Plan, and the Truman Doctrine; when people (including Gerald Ford) speak of a "bipartisan foreign policy" today, they are usually referring to Vandenberg's role in those years.

When Vandenberg was serving as Chairman of the Senate Foreign Relations Committee, he was embarrassed by Grand Rapids's local Congressman, Bartel J. Jonkman—a man who in the years after World War II was fully as isolationist as he had been before Pearl Harbor. So in 1948 Vandenberg and other Republican internationalists supported the challenge of a young lawyer and former University of Michigan football captain in a primary campaign against Jonkman. The challenger was Gerald R. Ford, Jr., who won that race and won ever since—until he was chosen for the Vice Presidency and succeeded to the Presidency.

Ford obviously has not forgotten the issues of that first primary campaign. He succeeded then, in the face of conventional wisdom to the contrary, to prove that Grand Rapids Republicans would support a candidate who believed that the United States had a major role to play in the world; and today, he continues to believe that Southeast Asia is a kind of Munich, testing our wills, and that those who opposed his proposals for $1 billion to Vietnam, for example, are simply latter day Bartel Jonkmans.

This is not a particularly astute assessment of public opinion, but then Ford has not been in that business for a long time. His district was considered safe enough that he could marry his wife, a former dancer in Martha Graham's troupe, before the general election in 1948, although he had to delay the wedding till after the primary for fear that some Calvinist voters might be scandalized. Reelection wasn't a problem, but climbing in the House Republican hierarchy was. In 1965, Ford became Minority Leader by toppling Indiana's Charlie Halleck with the help of the likes of Melvin Laird, Charles Goodell, and Robert Griffin. In the years that followed, Ford's constituency was in the House: that often isolated group of men and women called the House Republicans, a group that speaks predominantly to itself, in pious tones, particularly when it discusses the policies of a Republican administration.

As Minority Leader, Jerry Ford almost never opposed the Nixon administration; one exception was that he opposed diverting money from the highway trust fund to pay for mass transit (and on that the vast majority of House Republicans went along with Ford, not Nixon). Ford built personal loyalties among many House Republicans by continuing to treat them kindly even when they voted with the other side; and he could appeal for, and sometimes win, their votes on crucial instances by maintaining such communication. Overall, House Republicans were better disciplined, both because they are more inclined to regimentation, and because Ford worked hard. He is not a brilliant man, but the statement that he played a football game once too often without a helmet overstates the case against him; and in any event, his chief asset in the House was hard work, not brilliance—which suited most House Republicans fine.

While tending his constituency of House Republicans, Ford did not exactly ignore his Grand Rapids constituency—but he seemed not to be paying much attention to it. In 1970 and 1972, he won only 61% of the vote here. That was enough in both cases for comfortable victories, but not nearly as much as most Congressmen with comparable seniority and prestige ordinarily get. Moreover, the Democratic presidential percentage went up here between 1968 and 1972 (as it did in outstate Michigan as a whole)—a tipoff that in this traditional bedrock of Republicanism, the Party was slowly losing ground during the Nixon years. That point was made again, with a noise that resounded across the nation, after Ford had been installed as Vice President, when it came time to pick his successor in the 5th district.

To be sure, there were some rather special circumstances in the February race. The Watergate scandal was as hot as ever, and in the wake of Agnew's sudden and almost entirely unlamented disappearance from high office people began to think that it would not be nearly as cataclysmic as commentators (especially pro-Nixon ones) thought it would be if Nixon went. Here in the 5th district the Republican nominee, state Senator Robert VanderLaan, was expected to win the special election. But the Democrat, attorney Richard VanderVeen (there was no confusion in

Grand Rapids, where people are used to Dutch names), was putting together a serious campaign. Suddenly, in the last weeks, he began attacking Nixon—and boosting Ford. "Gerald Ford should be President," read a big VanderVeen newspaper ad just a week before the election. One could feel the surge of enthusiasm as voters began to realize that they could actually do something to get rid of an unwanted President—and at the same time put in a man they had always liked. VanderVeen won with a solid 53% of the vote—the first time the district had been taken by a Democrat since 1910.

That this was not an accident was shown in November, when VanderVeen beat another well-financed Republican by an even more solid 55-45 margin. At the same time, Democrats were capturing one of the two state Senate seats in Grand Rapids's Kent County, and three of Kent's five seats in the state House of Representatives. Obviously Grand Rapids had been moving left even as it had been giving the nation a conservative President—and for reasons which he seems not to understand. It is not clear to him, apparently, why this area's traditional frugality should be applied to military aid to Vietnam as well as to other spending; why its penchant for honesty should be applied not only to crooks like Richard Nixon, but to officials who favor the interests of big corporations who are free with Republican contributions come election time. If Jerry Ford wants to understand today the Middle America he once represented so aptly, he ought to talk less to Republican congressional veterans and Metternich-obsessed national security advisors, and more to people like his own Democratic Congressman.

Census Data Pop. 467,543. Central city, 42%; suburban, 46%. Median family income, $10,550; families above $15,000: 22%; families below $3,000: 7%. Median years education, 12.1.

The Voters

Median voting age 42.
Employment profile White collar, 46%. Blue collar, 40%. Service, 12%. Farm, 2%.
Ethnic groups Black, 5%. Spanish, 1%. Total foreign stock, 17%. Netherlands, 7%; Poland, Canada, Germany, 2% each.

Presidential vote

1972	Nixon (R)	117,832	(61%)
	McGovern (D)	75,224	(39%)
1968	Nixon (R)	96,621	(54%)
	Humphrey (D)	69,234	(39%)
	Wallace (AI)	13,226	(7%)

Rep. Richard F. Vander Veen (D) Elected Feb. 18, 1974; b. Nov. 26, 1922, Grand Rapids; home, East Grand Rapids; U. of So. Carolina, A.B. 1946, Harvard U., LL.B. 1949; Presbyterian.

Career Navy, WWII and Korea; Practicing atty.; Mich. St. Mental Health Comm., 1958–64, Chm., 1964; Dem. nominee for U.S. House of Reps., 1958; Candidate for Dem. nomination for Lt. Gov., 1960; Mich. St. Highway Comm., 1964–69.

Offices 1232 LHOB, 202-225-3831. Also Rm. 166, Fed. Ofc. Bldg., Grand Rapids 49502, 616-451-2614.

Committees

Ways and Means (15th). Subcommittees: Oversight; Trade.

Group Ratings

	ADA	COPE	LWV	RIPON	NFU	LCV	CFA	NAB	NSI	ACA
1974	91	91	100	69	86	88	92	20	0	9

Key Votes

1) Foreign Aid	FOR	6) Gov Abortn Aid	FOR	11) Pub Cong Election $	FOR
2) Busing	FOR	7) Coed Phys Ed	FOR	12) Turkish Arms Cutoff	ABS
3) ABM	AGN	8) Pov Lawyer Gag	NE	13) Youth Camp Regs	FOR
4) B-1 Bomber	AGN	9) Pub Trans Sub	FOR	14) Strip Mine Veto	AGN
5) Nerve Gas	AGN	10) EZ Voter Regis	FOR	15) Farm Bill Veto	AGN

Election Results

1974 general:	Richard F. Vander Veen (D)	80,778	(55%)	($143,603)
	Paul G. Goebel, Jr. (R)	66,659	(45%)	($158,891)
1974 primary:	Richard F. Vander Veen (D), unopposed			
1974 special:	Richard F. Vander Veen (D)	53,083	(51%)	($63,444)
	Robert Vander Laan (R)	46,160	(44%)	($59,404)
	Lloyd Johnson (AIP)	4,544	(4%)	(NA)

◆ ◆ ◆ ◆ ◆

SIXTH DISTRICT

The 6th congressional district of Michigan is yet another Middle America chunk of outstate Michigan, and yet another district which switched from a Republican Congressman in 1972 to a Democrat in 1974. The largest city in the district, Lansing (pop. 130,000), is dominated by one growth industry, state government, and by another which seems in serious and quite possibly permanent decline, automobiles (the big Oldsmobile plant is here). Also in the 6th is Jackson, an older industrial city and site of the state prison, one of the nation's largest. The other notable presence here is East Lansing (pop. 47,000), until recently known politically as a high income, Republican suburb, but now more significant because it is the home of Michigan State University and its 41,000 students. Aside from these urban areas, the 6th is a collection of small towns and rural townships. Some, like Stockbridge and Mason, are old towns whose architecture is reminiscent of the Yankee migrants from upstate New York who first settled them; others, like Howell, are the scene of new subdivisions to which former residents of metropolitan Detroit, unhappy with the city's high crime and large black population, have been moving.

From 1956 to 1974, the incumbent Congressman here was a Republican and close follower of Gerald Ford, Charles Chamberlain. As a member of the House Ways and Means Committee, Chamberlain was clearly the auto industry's man on that body, pressing always for a repeal of the excise tax on cars and other measures wanted by GM, Ford, and Chrysler executives. But Chamberlain was perhaps better known in the district as a man with a hot temper, so hot that he had once driven his car at a Washington policeman who had tried to ticket him.

For whatever reasons, Chamberlain found himself in political trouble in 1972 even as Nixon was winning his landslide victory. The newly enfranchised students at Michigan State, as one might expect, wanted no part of this hawkish conservative; but neither, as it turned out, did many of the 6th's more conventional citizens when they were presented with a realistic alternative. That alternative was 29-year-old Democrat named Robert Carr, an assistant Attorney General with a Mark Spitz mustache, who ran the first serious campaign Democrats had put on in the district since 1958. Carr was able to raise money, to put creditable ads on the television, to get around the district and meet people, and to make himself well enough known to win 49% of the vote.

Immediately after the election, Carr decided to run again in 1974. Chamberlain, for his part, made the opposite decision; as early as March 1973 he announced his impending retirement—thus freeing himself from the irksome duties of attending to constituents' problems and answering their complaints on specific issues. For awhile, it looked as if Carr might win virtually unopposed. A conservative young Republican named Clifford Taylor won his party's nomination from a favored state Senator. But Taylor turned out to be as good a campaigner as Carr, and almost managed to turn things around. The final result was even closer than 1972: Carr won by only 647 votes, with just 50.2% of the vote.

In the House, Carr found himself very much in the mainstream of the Democratic caucus, dominated by the 75 freshmen most of them so much like himself. He won seats on the Armed Services and Interior Committees—both choice assignments which allow him to compile a record which would help him in 1976. But his most important action came outside the strict limits of his committee responsibilities. When Gerald Ford was pressing Congress hard for aid to Cambodia in March 1975, Carr demanded a Democratic caucus vote on the issue. The result, a 189–49 vote, effectively killed Ford's proposal. Many non-freshman Democratic Congressmen had an almost reflexive desire to achieve some kind of compromise. But the vote Carr forced demonstrated clearly that there was a majority in the House against any aid, including those 189 Democrats, others who had been absent from the caucus, and some Republicans to boot.

A word should be added here about the impact of Michigan State students on the district's politics. In a word, it has been less than expected. Electoral participation in 1974 was low, and Carr actually had a bigger majority in Jackson County than in Ingham, which includes Lansing and East Lansing. Moreover, minor party candidates, all with a leftist tinge, received 2,700 votes, with most of them going to the candidate of the Human Rights Party, which somehow conceives that its peacenik type objectives will best be achieved by diverting votes from Democrats and so helping to bring about the victory of conservative Republicans. The total irrationality of this kind of thinking has been demonstrated conclusively by Carr's brief congressional career.

Census Data Pop. 467,536. Central city, 38%; suburban, 54%. Median family income, $11,105; families above $15,000: 27%; families below $3,000: 6%. Median years education, 12.3.

The Voters

Median voting age 37.
Employment profile White collar, 50%. Blue collar, 34%. Service, 14%. Farm, 2%.
Ethnic groups Black, 5%. Spanish, 2%. Total foreign stock, 12%. Canada, Germany, 2% each; UK, Poland, 1% each.

Presidential vote

1972	Nixon (R)	115,810	(59%)
	McGovern (D)	80,875	(41%)
1968	Nixon (R)	86,772	(53%)
	Humphrey (D)	63,306	(38%)
	Wallace (AI)	14,901	(9%)

Rep. Bob Carr (D) Elected 1974; Mar. 27, 1943, Janesville, Wis.; home, East Lansing; U. of Wis., B.S. 1965, J.D. 1968, U. of Mich., 1968–69.

Career Staff Asst. to U.S. Sen. Gaylord Nelson of Wis., 1967; Staff Mbr., Mich. Senate Minor. Ldr.'s Ofc., 1968–69; Admin. Asst. to Atty. Gen. of Mich., 1969–70; Asst. Atty. Gen. of Mich., 1970–72; Counsel to Mich. Legislature Special Comm. on Legal Educ., 1972; Dem. nominee for U.S. House of Reps., 1972.

Offices 1608 LHOB, 202-225-4872. Also Rm. 245 Fed. Bldg., Lansing 48933, 517-489-6517.

Committees

Armed Services (24th). Subcommittees: Investigations; Seapower and Strategic and Critical Materials.

Interior and Insular Affairs (26th). Subcommittees: Energy and the Environment; Mines and Mining; National Parks and Recreation.

Group Ratings: Newly Elected

Key Votes

1) Foreign Aid	AGN	6) Gov Abortn Aid	NE	11) Pub Cong Election $	NE
2) Busing	NE	7) Coed Phys Ed	FOR	12) Turkish Arms Cutoff	NE
3) ABM	NE	8) Pov Lawyer Gag	NE	13) Youth Camp Regs	FOR
4) B-1 Bomber	AGN	9) Pub Trans Sub	NE	14) Strip Mine Veto	AGN
5) Nerve Gas	NE	10) EZ Voter Regis	NE	15) Farm Bill Veto	AGN

Election Results

1974 general:	Bob Carr (D)	73,956	(50%)	($157,478)
	Clifford W. Taylor (R)	73,309	(50%)	($119,329)
1974 primary:	Bob Carr (D)	20,576	(72%)	
	Charles P. Larrowe (D)	7,846	(28%)	

◆ ◆ ◆ ◆ ◆

SEVENTH DISTRICT

With five major General Motors plants, Flint (pop. 193,000) is probably the nation's largest company town. Some 60% of metropolitan Flint's wage earners are on the GM payroll, and although there is some GM white collar employment here, this is mainly the Chevrolet and Buick factory town. Flint has no five o'clock rush hour; its traffic jams come after three-thirty when the shifts break. Even those who have profited most handsomely from the auto industry have not taken themselves out of Flint: the plushest residential district here has a panoramic view of a Chevrolet plant. For years, civic life in Flint was dominated by Charles Stewart Mott, a member of the General Motors board of directors for 60 years and for most of that time the largest individual shareholder in the corporation; the old man ran his Mott Foundation, one of the nation's largest, out of Flint and concentrated on local projects until his recent death at age 97.

Flint owes its present existence to the boom years of the auto industry, the two decades between 1910 and 1930, supplemented by the war and postwar boom of the 1940s. During both periods, Flint attracted tens of thousands of immigrants from the rural South—whites from the hills of Kentucky and Tennessee and blacks from the cotton fields of Alabama and Mississippi. The politics of the migrants has usually been Democratic. Oldtimers here can still recall the sitdown strikes of the 1930s, led by three young unionists named Roy, Victor, and Walter Reuther; and of course the UAW remains a major political force here today. In more recent years Flint has seen racial friction split its working-class whites and blacks. In 1968 George Wallace had the support of many white UAW memmbers and a few local presidents; only a concerted union effort held him to 15% of the area's vote. But unlike Detroit, Flint had experienced no busing crisis; so in Flint, as in much of outstate Michigan, McGovern actually ran better in 1972 than Humphrey had four years before.

Flint is the nucleus of Michigan's 7th congressional district. The city's metropolitan area (and media market) coincides almost perfectly with the district lines of the 7th. Over the years, the district has usually gone Democratic in statewide contests—blue-collar Democrats tend to outnumber management Republicans. But the way in which the 7th came to have a Democratic Congressman is a little unusual. For the Congressman is Donald Riegle, who spent the first six years in the House as a Republican, each year growing increasingly uncomfortable in the party of Richard Nixon.

Indeed, Riegle's whole political career has been rather surprising, from its beginning in 1966. At that time, Flint was represented by a Democrat elected in the 1964 Johnson landslide, who was so sure of reelection that he spent most of his weekends puttering on his Virginia farm. Riegle, a Flint native, was then working on a doctorate at the Harvard Business School. Someone told him that the local Republicans were looking for a congressional candidate and, at 28, he returned and ran. With his management background, Riegle ran a professional campaign, hiring the then hot Spencer-Roberts consulting firm, and shaking hands vigorously all around. The result was a 54-46 upset—and an outspokenly ambitious young Congressman.

As Riegle notes in his book, *O Congress!*, he spoke quite openly then about running for President some day—a real taboo in the insular world of Republican Congressmen. Even more heinous, he found himself increasingly abandoning orthodox Republican positions. About the only senior Republican who remained friendly with him was Gerald Ford, who had got him a seat on the Appropriations Committee; Ford always tried to remain in contact with renegade Republicans, in the hope he might still get their votes on some issues.

Riegle's unusual conduct in Washington was matched at home. He paid close attention to the needs of his black constituents, and began to win some votes from the Democrats among them. As the years went on and his COPE record climbed towrd the 90s, he won first the neutrality and then, in 1970, the endorsement of the UAW—something previously unheard of for a Republican in class-conscious Flint.

But it was the war in Vietnam which produced Riegle's most emphatic dissent. Like John Lindsay and Ogden Reid of New York and Pete McCloskey of California, Riegle opposed the war policies of both Johnson and Nixon. In 1972 Riegle was the only Congressman to support McCloskey's primary challenge of Nixon; and by that time his rapport with his fellow Republican Congressmen had reached zero.

Unlike McCloskey, Riegle had never faced primary opposition at home; and general elections had been no problem either, with his support from usually Democratic groups. Nevertheless in early 1973—before the Watergate scandal broke and when Nixon still ran exceedingly high in the polls—Riegle left the Republican Party and became a Democrat. He thereby lost his seat on Appropriations, taking instead a junior slot on International Relations. Despite his loss of status, Riegle was immediately more comfortable in the Democratic caucus, and he seems to have anticipated nicely the spirit of the Democratic freshmen who so changed the ways of the House in 1975.

Curiously, Riegle's party switch in this Democratic district has cost him a few votes, though not enough to matter. In 1972, as a Republican, he won with 70%; in 1974, as a Democrat, with 66%. Apparently more Democrats were willing to cross over and vote for a like-minded congressman of the other party than Republicans are willing to vote for an apostate. In any case, Riegle has a safe seat. But even if he isn't saying so out loud any more, he has not renounced greater ambitions. Riegle will almost certainly be a candidate to succeed Senator Philip Hart in 1976, and if perchance he does not win that seat he will quite possibly challenge Senator Robert Griffin in 1978. His main problem, at least in the Democratic primary, is that he is not very well known in the Detroit metropolitan area, which casts more than half the primary vote. But he is an effective television campaigner, and has shown he knows how to win elections.

Census Data Pop. 466,287. Central city, 41%; suburban, 57%. Median family income, $11,207; families above $15,000: 27%; families below $3,000: 6%. Median years education, 12.1.

The Voters

Median voting age 40.
Employment profile White collar, 37%. Blue collar, 50%. Service, 12%. Farm, 1%.
Ethnic groups Black, 13%. Spanish, 1%. Total foreign stock, 12%. Canada, 3%; UK, 2%; Germany, 1%.

Presidential vote

1972	Nixon (R)	90,776	(54%)
	McGovern (D)	76,745	(46%)
1968	Nixon (R)	67,184	(39%)
	Humphrey (D)	77,858	(46%)
	Wallace (AI)	25,630	(15%)

Rep. Donald W. Riegle, Jr. (D) Elected 1966 as Republican, changed party affiliation to Democrat Feb. 27, 1973; b. Feb. 4, 1938, Flint; home, Flint; Flint Jr. Col., W. Mich. U., U. of Mich., B.A. 1960, Mich. St. U., M.B.A. 1961; Methodist.

Career Consultant, IBM Corp., 1961–64; Faculty Mbr., Mich. St. U., Boston U., Harvard U.

Offices 438 CHOB, 202-225-3611. Also 432 N. Saginaw St., Flint 48502, 313-239-5705.

Committees

International Relations (18th). Subcommittees: International Political and Military Affairs; International Security and Scientific Affairs.

Group Ratings

	ADA	COPE	LWV	RIPON	NFU	LCV	CFA	NAB	NSI	ACA
1974	100	91	100	62	92	93	91	25	14	7
1973	95	82	100	70	89	94	75	–	–	10
1972	94	90	100	84	83	83	100	20	0	5

Key Votes

1) Foreign Aid	AGN	6) Gov Abortn Aid	FOR	11) Pub Cong Election $	FOR
2) Busing	FOR	7) Coed Phys Ed	FOR	12) Turkish Arms Cutoff	FOR
3) ABM	ABS	8) Pov Lawyer Gag	ABS	13) Youth Camp Regs	FOR
4) B-1 Bomber	AGN	9) Pub Trans Sub	FOR	14) Strip Mine Veto	AGN
5) Nerve Gas	ABS	10) EZ Voter Regis	FOR	15) Farm Bill Veto	AGN

Election Results

1974 general:	Donald W. Riegle, Jr. (D)	81,014	(66%)	($46,731)
	Robert E. Eastman (R)	41,603	(34%)	($8,902)
1974 primary:	Donald W. Riegle, Jr. (D)	37,833	(81%)	
	Eugene L. Mattison (D)	8,874	(19%)	
1972 general:	Donald W. Riegle, Jr. (R)	114,656	(70%)	($23,892)
	Eugene L. Mattison (D)	48,883	(30%)	($1,200)

◆ ◆ ◆ ◆ ◆

EIGHTH DISTRICT

It was April 1974, and Richard Nixon was in trouble: the nation plainly did not believe his protestations of innocence in the Watergate scandal; there was no confidence in his ability to run the government; and people were blaming—not without reason, for they had nominated him for national office five times—the Republicans for the predicament they found themselves in. In February special elections, Democrats has already captured Gerald Ford's old congressional district in Grand Rapids, which had been safely Republican since 1910, and an almost equally solidly Republican district in Cincinnati. Now there was a special election in the 8th district of Michigan, called because Congressman James Harvey had resigned to become a federal judge. This was another district which had not gone Democratic for decades, and the Republicans were clearly in trouble. The national press, caught by surprise by the Democrats' upset victory in Grand Rapids, was now watching closely, probably more closely than they had watched any special election in history. For if the Republicans could not win here, it seemed they stood little prospect of winning anywhere.

Here was the 8th congressional district of Michigan, an area with little political impact on the nation since one of its Congressmen was the co-author of the Fordney-McCumber tariff. To understand the district's geography, you must know that Michigan's Lower Peninsula is shaped like a mittened hand; the 8th district includes most of the Thumb (as it is indeed called locally) and the bottom part of the index finger. The Thumb is almost entirely agricultural, tilled by descendants of the German and Canadian farmers who first settled the area more than a century ago. During all that time, the Thumb has been rock-solid Republican country, and it remained that way right up until 1975. Where the index finger emerges from the palm (this is not the local nomenclature) are Saginaw (pop. 92,000) and Bay City (pop. 49,000), which have been important towns here since the nineteenth century when they were both major lumber ports. Today they are sustained in large part by automobile plants, notably GM's Saginaw Steering, which makes more power steering equipment than any other plant in the world. Unlike most of th rest of outstate Michigan, the 8th district has few institutions of higher learning and relatively little economic growth.

The district owes its current shape to a Democratic redistricting, which placed Saginaw, with its large black population, and Bay City, with its many Polish-Americans, for the first time in the same district. These two groups are the basis of whatever Democratic strength there has been here in the past, but that was not enough in 1972 to beat Congressman Harvey, a low-key moderate who won over 60% of the vote.

Now in the 1974 special election, the candidates were James Sparling, Harvey's administrative assistant, who had won his primary easily, and J. Bob Traxler, a Democratic state legislator from Bay City. Sparling is a contentious man and, faced with the problem of Richard Nixon's unpopularity, and the fact that he had worked a couple of months himself on Nixon's White House staff, he attacked head on: by inviting Nixon into the district to campaign for him. It was not that he wanted to endorse everything Nixon did, he said, it was just that he wanted the President there. Nixon, eager to clutch at any chance of demonstrating his popularity, came and was paraded through small towns in the Thumb; he wisely avoided Saginaw and Bay City. Traxler's theme was simple: this was the voters' chance to show how much they disapproved of the Nixon Administration. It was, and they did. Traxler carried the Bay City area by a 2–1 margin, ran virtually even in Saginaw County, and lost the Thumb by only a 59–41 margin. (Harvey had won 70% of the vote there in 1972.) It was yet another in the string of upset Democratic victories in special elections that showed Congressmen—even Republicans—how devastatingly unpopular were Richard Nixon and his works.

By November, the national spotlight was gone, and so was Nixon. But Traxler had used the intervening months to great advantage, handling the usual constituency complaints in the way that has helped so many congressmen win reelection in theoretically hostile territory. Sparling again was running, but this time he did even worse. Traxler took 47% of the vote in the Thumb, 55% in Saginaw County, and 69% in the Bay City area, for a solid 56–44 victory. With the new Congress, he won a seat on the Appropriations Committee, and now this district appears to be settling down for a long period of Democratic incumbency.

Census Data Pop. 467,206. Central city, 30%; suburban, 45%. Median family income, $10,270; families above $15,000: 21%; families below $3,000: 9%. Median years education, 11.9.

The Voters

Median voting age 42.
Employment profile White collar, 38%. Blue collar, 45%. Service, 13%. Farm, 4%.
Ethnic groups Black, 6%. Spanish, 3%. Total foreign stock, 16%. Canada, 4%; Germany, 3%; Poland, 2%; UK, 1%.

Presidential vote

1972	Nixon (R)	106,524	(62%)
	McGovern (D)	65,422	(38%)
1968	Nixon (R)	87,500	(52%)
	Humphrey (D)	65,863	(39%)
	Wallace (AI)	14,012	(8%)

Rep. Bob Traxler (D) Elected April, 1974; b. July 21, 1931, Kawkawlin; home, Bay City; Mich. St. U., B.A. 1953, Detroit Col. of Law, LL.B. 1959.

Career Army, 1953–55; Asst. Bay Co. Prosecutor, 1960–62; Mich. House of Reps., 1963–74, Maj. Floor Ldr., 1965.

Offices 1526 LHOB, 202-225-2806. Also Rm. 102, Fed. Bldg., 500 Federal St., Saginaw 48602, 517-753-6444.

Committees

Appropriations (34th). Subcommittees: HUD-Independent Agencies; Military Construction.

Group Ratings

	ADA	COPE	LWV	RIPON	NFU	LCV	CFA	NAB	NSI	ACA
1974	68	100	80	50	100	63	80	67	25	18

Key Votes

1) Foreign Aid	FOR	6) Gov Abortn Aid	AGN	11) Pub Cong Election $	FOR
2) Busing	NE	7) Coed Phys Ed	AGN	12) Turkish Arms Cutoff	FOR
3) ABM	AGN	8) Pov Lawyer Gag	NE	13) Youth Camp Regs	FOR
4) B-1 Bomber	AGN	9) Pub Trans Sub	AGN	14) Strip Mine Veto	AGN
5) Nerve Gas	AGN	10) EZ Voter Regis	FOR	15) Farm Bill Veto	AGN

Election Results

1974 general:	Bob Traxler (D)	77,795	(56%)	($76,856)
	James M. Sparling (R)	61,578	(44%)	($82,879)
1974 primary:	Bob Traxler (D), unopposed			
1974 special:	Bob Traxler (D)	59,993	(51%)	($167,976)
	James Sparling, Jr. (R)	56,548	(49%)	($124,397)

◆ ◆ ◆ ◆ ◆

NINTH DISTRICT

From Gary, Indiana, up through Chicago and Milwaukee, north to towns like Sheboygan and Manitowoc, Wisconsin, the western shore of Lake Michigan is heavily industrial. Behind the giant sand dunes that line the eastern, Michigan side of the Lake, there are a few grimy industrial towns like Muskegon and old lumber ports like Ludington. But most of the Michigan side of Lake Michigan is given over to farming; despite the cold weather, fruits and vegetables do well here within a few miles of the shore.

Michigan's 9th congressional district contains most of this eastern shore of Lake Michigan. The 9th extends from Allegan County in the south to Leelenau in the north—the latter is the extended little finger of Michigan's mitten-shaped Lower Peninsula. Along with Grand Rapids, the southern portion of the district has the nation's largest concentration of Dutch-Americans; one of the cities here, Holland, holds a tulip festival every year, complete with people walking around in wooden shoes. The Dutch (see Fifth District) are probably the most conservative and Republican of all identifiable American ethnic groups; Ottawa County, which contains Holland and Zeeland, was one of only three Michigan counties to go for Barry Goldwater in 1964. To the north, the country is politically more varied. Muskegon returned to its ancestral Democratic ways, after a long period of Republican ascendancy, in 1974. The smaller counties are mostly Republican. An oddity here is tiny Lake County, a large number of whose residents are black and which always goes Democratic; it was one of five Michigan counties to go for George McGovern in 1972. Lake (which is actually not on Lake Michigan) contains one of the country's first black resort areas, formed at the turn of the century by members of Chicago's black bourgeoisie.

Though it no longer includes his home town of Traverse City, the 9th is Senator Robert Griffin's old congressional district which he relinquished for the risks of a Senate race in 1966. Griffin always won by big margins in the 9th; his closest call was in 1964, when he took 57% of the vote against a Democrat named Griffen. After the passage of the 1959 Landrum-Griffin Act, organized labor would dearly loved to have beaten Griffin, but the Republican always carried even Muskegon County, which has a large union membership. Griffin's successor, Guy VanderJagt, has done almost as well, winning all but one general election by at least 2–1 margins; in the Democratic year of 1974, he had a still comfortable 57%. VanderJagt's toughest test was the 1966 Republican primary, in which he managed to cover all the bases: he had represented the northern half of the district in the state Senate, while his Dutch name was an obvious and considerable asset in the southern half.

VanderJagt is one of an increasing number of former TV newscasters in Congress. He also has other talents, as witnessed by his law and bachelor of divinity degrees. As ranking minority member on the Government Operations Conservation and Natural Resources Subcommittee, he has shown considerable sympathy for environmental causes; he was largely responsible for the creation of the Sleeping Bear Dunes National Lakeshore in the northern part of the district—which Griffin had long blocked.

In the 94th Congress, VanderJagt moved to a position on the House Ways and Means Committee. He was also elected by his Republican colleagues as Chairman of the Republican Congressional Campaign Committee, beating ultraconservative John Rousselot of California. VanderJagt is regarded as a moderate, occasionally liberal Republican, with a high rating from the Ripon Society. He is not a loud dissenter from the party's conservative majority, but the fact that even such a mild maverick can win two such positions as he got shows that House Republicans—their ranks seriously depleted of conservatives in the 1974 election—are more open to heterodoxy than in the past.

Census Data Pop. 467,245. Central city, 13%; suburban, 48%. Median family income, $9,474; families above $15,000: 16%; families below $3,000: 9%. Median years education, 11.8.

The Voters

Median voting age 43.
Employment profile White collar, 37%. Blue collar, 46%. Service, 13%. Farm, 4%.
Ethnic groups Black, 4%. Spanish, 2%. Total foreign stock, 15%. Netherlands, 4%; Germany, Canada, 2% each; Poland, 1%.

Presidential vote

1972	Nixon (R)	....	130,463	(67%)
	McGovern (D)	....	64,561	(33%)
1968	Nixon (R)	....	102,528	(57%)
	Humphrey (D)	....	61,457	(34%)
	Wallace (AI)	....	15,814	(9%)

Rep. Guy Vander Jagt (R) Elected 1966; b. Aug. 26, 1931, Cadillac; home, Cadillac; Hope Col., B.A. 1953, Yale U., B.D., Rotary Fellow, Bonn U., Germany, 1956, U. of Mich., LL.B. 1960; Presbyterian.

Career Practicing atty., 1960–64; Mich. Senate, 1965–66.

Offices 1203 LHOB, 202-225-3511. Also 1611 Oak Ave., Muskegon 49442, 616-773-2870.

Committees

Ways and Means (6th). Subcommittees: Public Assistance; Trade.

Group Ratings

	ADA	COPE	LWV	RIPON	NFU	LCV	CFA	NAB	NSI	ACA
1974	23	20	60	67	69	33	15	73	67	38
1973	18	18	50	62	59	38	29	–	–	46
1972	25	27	70	87	67	73	0	100	100	64

Key Votes

1) Foreign Aid	FOR	6) Gov Abortn Aid	ABS	11) Pub Cong Election $	AGN
2) Busing	AGN	7) Coed Phys Ed	AGN	12) Turkish Arms Cutoff	AGN
3) ABM	FOR	8) Pov Lawyer Gag	FOR	13) Youth Camp Regs	AGN
4) B-1 Bomber	FOR	9) Pub Trans Sub	AGN	14) Strip Mine Veto	FOR
5) Nerve Gas	FOR	10) EZ Voter Regis	AGN	15) Farm Bill Veto	FOR

Election Results

1974 general:	Guy A. Vander Jagt (R)	....	87,551 (57%)	($51,196)
	Norm Halbower (D)	....	65,235 (43%)	($21,382)
1974 primary:	Guy A. Vander Jagt (R), unopposed			
1972 general:	Guy A. Vander Jagt (R)	....	132,268 (70%)	($23,887)
	Larry H. Olson (D)	....	56,236 (30%)	($4,636)

◆ ◆ ◆ ◆ ◆

TENTH DISTRICT

Draw a line on a map across Michigan's Lower Peninsula from Bay City to Muskegon. South of the line live 90% of the state's residents, almost half in the Detroit metropolitan area and the rest in and around the state's smaller industrial cities. North of the line, Michigan's land is covered with forests, and little of it has ever been farmed; the largest city in this part of the Lower

Peninsula has a population of only 18,000. The forests here were ravaged by the lumber barons at the turn of the century, and only now are growing back. For years, this area has depended economically on the tourist and recreation business. Every weekend during the summer, and during the hunting season in the fall, cars jam I-75, as city people flee to cottages on Michigan lakes or in the woods. The fishing here is excellent, as Ernest Hemingway learned as a boy during summer visits; it is even better now that the lakes have been stocked with huge coho salmon. As the sixties turned into the seventies, many people who had been coming up here for weekends and occasionally longer decided to move here altogether; wages are not as high as in the Detroit area, but the pace of life is slower and more pleasant. Today these north woods are in the midst of a minor population boom—something which they haven't experienced since the turn of the century.

The 10th congressional district spans the line across Lower Michigan. The district dips south to the Lansing city limits, and its lower counties are fairly thickly populated with small towns and farms. Up north, where the farms become woods, the biggest towns are Midland (pop. 35,000), the home of the Dow Chemical Company, whose production of napalm for Vietnam once made it controversial; Traverse City (pop. 18,000), which has produced both Governor William Milliken and Senator Robert Griffin; and Mount Pleasant (pop. 20,000), home of Central Michigan University (14,000 students).

The 10th was designed to be, and still remains, a Republican district—before 1972, it included Democratic Bay City, now transferred to the 8th. But like most outstate Michigan districts, the 10th has been trending Democratic. The movement has become apparent in presidential races (McGovern bested Humphrey's performance here), in statewide contests, and in 1974 in the race for the House.

This probably came as something of a surprise, and an unpleasant one, to Congressman Elford Cederberg. First elected in the Eisenhower year of 1952, Cederberg is one of five Republicans who can remember serving the last time their party controlled the House. (The others are Arizona's John Rhodes, California's Bob Wilson, Virginia's William Wampler, and Oklahoma's John Jarman, who was a Democrat until 1975.) Cederberg climbed the seniority ladder slowly, in the prescribed manner, and became ranking minority member of the House Appropriations Committee when two senior Republicans retired in 1972.

This position gives Cederberg opportunity to exercise his basically conservative instincts, and he does his best to trim federal spending according to the prescriptions of his old friend Jerry Ford. But that formula was not enough to give him his usual comfortable victory in 1974, when poorly financed Democrat Samuel Marble carried five of the district's counties, including the two biggest, and held Cederberg to 54% of the vote. Back even before 1972, the 7th district's Donald Riegle quoted Cederberg as saying, "It's just not as much fun here as it used to be." The Republican remembered, no doubt, the years when Congress did not meet year round, when most members—including many big city Democrats—were soundly conservative in their basic instincts, when Congressmen were not besieged by ecology activists, peace enthusiasts, and constituents not satisfied until a Congressman changed his mind. If, in addition to all that, Cederberg believes he will face a tough fight for reelection every two years, he might just choose to give it all up and retire, though he is not yet 60.

Census Data Pop. 467,547. Central city, 0%; suburban, 11%. Median family income, $9,299; families above $15,000: 17%; families below $3,000: 11%. Median years education, 12.1.

The Voters

Median voting age 41.
Employment profile White collar, 41%. Blue collar, 41%. Service, 14%. Farm, 4%.
Ethnic groups Spanish, 1%. Total foreign stock, 11%. Canada, 3%; Germany, 2%.

Presidential vote

1972	Nixon (R)	119,706	(64%)
	McGovern (D)	66,980	(36%)
1968	Nixon (R)	96,386	(58%)
	Humphrey (D)	55,600	(34%)
	Wallace (AI)	13,974	(8%)

Rep. Elford A. Cederberg (R) Elected 1952; b. Mar. 6, 1918, Bay City; home, Midland; Bay City Col.; Evangelical Church.

Career Army, WWII; Mgr., Nelson Mfg. Co.; Mayor of Bay City, 1949–53.

Offices 2306 RHOB, 202-225-3561. Also 624 E. Superior St., Alma 48801, 517-463-3010.

Committees

Appropriations (Ranking Member). Subcommittees: Legislative; State, Justice, Commerce, and the Judiciary.

Budget (2d).

Group Ratings

	ADA	COPE	LWV	RIPON	NFU	LCV	CFA	NAB	NSI	ACA
1974	10	0	64	40	64	33	0	70	100	50
1973	0	9	25	43	25	0	13	–	–	78
1972	0	18	27	57	29	20	0	92	100	68

Key Votes

1) Foreign Aid	FOR	6) Gov Abortn Aid	AGN	11) Pub Cong Election $	AGN
2) Busing	ABS	7) Coed Phys Ed	ABS	12) Turkish Arms Cutoff	AGN
3) ABM	FOR	8) Pov Lawyer Gag	FOR	13) Youth Camp Regs	AGN
4) B-1 Bomber	FOR	9) Pub Trans Sub	AGN	14) Strip Mine Veto	FOR
5) Nerve Gas	FOR	10) EZ Voter Regis	AGN	15) Farm Bill Veto	FOR

Election Results

1974 general:	Elford A. Cederberg (R)	78,897	(54%)	($38,876)
	Samuel D. Marble (D)	67,467	(46%)	($19,974)
1974 primary:	Elford A. Cederberg (R)	25,462	(77%)	
	Andrew J. Marks (R)	7,452	(23%)	
1972 general:	Elford A. Cederberg (R)	121,368	(67%)	($17,684)
	Bennie D. Graves (D)	56,149	(31%)	($4,666)
	Richard Friske (AI)	4,369	(2%)	(NA)

◆ ◆ ◆ ◆ ◆

ELEVENTH DISTRICT

Michigan's Upper Peninsula (or the U.P., as it is called) is a world unto itself. It is isolated most of the year from the rest of the state by the elements, and for years travel here was discouraged by the exorbitant tolls on the Mackinac (pronounced mackinaw) Straits Bridge. The U.P. was first settled around the turn of the century, when the iron and copper mines were booming, and the place had an air of the Wild West about it. The population influx here was polyglot: Irish, Italians, Swedes, Norwegians, and Finns, which remain the largest ethnic group here. While working in the mines, the immigrants picked up some radical social ideas and Democratic voting habits, the latter of which their descendants still retain. Some time ago, however, the mines petered out, leaving the U.P.'s suddenly stagnant economy dependent on summer tourists and fall hunters. (Farming has never been a big factor here; it has been known to snow in July.) After World War II, the young people of the Upper Peninsula began to move to Detroit, Chicago, and the West Coast; since the 1940 census, the U.P.'s population has hovered around 300,000 (it was 332,000 in 1920). In the seventies, as metropolitan areas became more unattractive and job opportunities scarcer there, the U.P. stopped losing so many people; still, the closest thing to a city here is Marquette (pop. 22,000).

The Upper Peninsula forms about two-thirds of Michigans's 11th congressional district. The 11th is altogether a vast expanse, with 40% of Michigan's land area, but only 5% of its population;

it is geographically the second largest congressional district east of the Mississippi River. From Tawas City, in the southern part of the 11th in the Lower Peninsula, to Ironwood, at the western tip of the Upper, is a distance of 477 miles. Obviously any serious congressional candidate here must have access to an airplane.

The Lower Peninsula portion of the 11th has neither the tradition of the mines nor the Democratic voting habits of the U.P. It is a more prosperous area, with a booming trade in tourists and, recently, heavy immigration. As a whole, the 11th is politically marginal, although oddly it has elected a Democrat to Congress only once since World War II. Before the 1964 redistricting, what is now the 11th contained two full districts and a part of a third—a vestige of the days when the Upper Peninsula had a far larger percentage of the state's inhabitants than it does now. In 1964, two incumbents, both of them Republicans, were prepared to square off in a primary when one of them died; the other lost in the fall to a Democrat. He, in turn, proved to be a poor campaigner, and lost the district to Republican Philip Ruppe in 1966.

Ruppe is the scion of a wealthy Upper Peninsula brewing family and, as befits a Republican from a marginal district, has compiled a moderate and sometimes even liberal voting record in the House. But even this was only barely enough to enable Ruppe to survive the 1974 Democratic landslide. Democrat Francis Brouillette's campaign was not particularly well financed, but he managed to carry the Upper Peninsula over Ruppe by a 51–49 margin. Indeed, the five counties added to the district in the Lower Peninsula in 1972 to bring it up to the statewide population average accounted for 2,426 of the Republican's 3,500-vote victory margin. This close call will undoubtedly move Ruppe to redouble his efforts to ingratiate himself with his constituents; but it may also inspire Democrats to make a serious effort to capture this district in 1976.

Census Data Pop. 467,547. Central city, 0%; suburban, 0%. Median family income, $7,884; families above $15,000: 10%; families below $3,000: 14%. Median years education, 12.0.

The Voters

Median voting age 45.
Employment profile White collar, 41%. Blue collar, 40%. Service, 16%. Farm, 3%.
Ethnic groups Total foreign stock, 23%. Canada, Finland, 5% each; Germany, Sweden, UK, 2% each; Italy, Poland, 1% each.

Presidential vote

1972	Nixon (R)	117,006	(57%)
	McGovern (D)	86,548	(43%)
1968	Nixon (R)	88,694	(48%)
	Humphrey (D)	85,510	(46%)
	Wallace (AI)	10,940	(6%)

Rep. Philip E. Ruppe (R) Elected 1966; b. Sept. 29, 1926, Laurium; home, Houghton; Central Mich. U., U. of Mich., Yale U., B.A. 1948; Catholic.

Career Navy, Korea; Bosch Brewing Co., Gen. Mgr., 1955–65, Pres., 1960–65.

Offices 203 CHOB, 202-225-4735. Also Rm. 32, Fed. Bldg., Marquette 49855, 906-228-8250.

Committees

Interior and Insular Affairs (4th). Subcommittees: Mines and Mining; National Parks and Recreation; Territorial and Insular Affairs.

Merchant Marine and Fisheries (Ranking Member).

Group Ratings

	ADA	COPE	LWV	RIPON	NFU	LCV	CFA	NAB	NSI	ACA
1974	30	38	73	100	58	53	18	70	56	42
1973	28	20	73	92	55	22	14	–	–	46
1972	44	40	82	78	80	54	0	80	63	29

Key Votes

1) Foreign Aid	FOR	6) Gov Abortn Aid	AGN	11) Pub Cong Election $	AGN
2) Busing	FOR	7) Coed Phys Ed	ABS	12) Turkish Arms Cutoff	ABS
3) ABM	AGN	8) Pov Lawyer Gag	AGN	13) Youth Camp Regs	ABS
4) B-1 Bomber	FOR	9) Pub Trans Sub	AGN	14) Strip Mine Veto	AGN
5) Nerve Gas	FOR	10) EZ Voter Regis	AGN	15) Farm Bill Veto	FOR

Election Results

1974 general:	Philip E. Ruppe (R)	83,293	(51%)	($45,240)
	Francis D. Brouillette (D)	79,793	(49%)	($62,656)
1974 primary:	Philip E. Ruppe (R), unopposed			
1972 general:	Philip E. Ruppe (R)	135,786	(70%)	($27,045)
	James E. McNamara (D)	58,334	(30%)	($526)

◆ ◆ ◆ ◆ ◆

TWELFTH DISTRICT

Macomb County, adjoining Detroit to the northeast, is an area of—till recently—fast-growing suburban sprawl of a type found in many of the nation's metropolitan areas. In 1950 Macomb had 184,000 people; by 1970 625,000—more than tripling in population in twenty years. The northern reaches of the county remain rural, but for twenty miles beyond Eight Mile Road, the Detroit city limit, Macomb is an agglomeration of neat suburbs, winding streets, thin-walled garden apartments, and gleaming new shopping centers. Unlike the new residents of similar places in California, the people here have roots, most of them in the east side of Detroit. The descendants of the Polish and Italian immigrants who came to man the east side auto plants have moved in just a generation to suburbs like Warren (pop. 179,000), East Detroit, Roseville, St. Clair Shores, and Sterling Heights.

Though filled with suburbs, Macomb remains blue collar territory, with most people here earning their livings in blue collar or service jobs. Thanks to high UAW wages, Macomb is also one of the most prosperous suburban counties in the nation, with a median family income over $12,000 in 1970. Yet the upward mobility has meant more in dollars and comfort than in status: even if you can buy a $55,000 house, it is still unpleasant to work on an assembly line.

Having absorbed a monumental population influx in the past twenty years, Macomb County has written its politics on a tabula rasa; its native aristocracy was too few in numbers to quiet and modulate changes in public opinion. This became most clear in 1972, when Macomb and other Detroit suburbs were facing a federal court order that would have required busing of students to and from the central city of Detroit to promote integration. Aside from a vestigial ghetto in the old county seat of Mount Clemens, Macomb has virtually no black residents; it is all white and quite happy to stay that way. Because of the sheer pressure of numbers, most of the population growth here was inevitable; but one motivating force behind many moves here was a desire to escape from Detroit, which was 42% black by 1970. So when it appeared that Macomb children might be bused below Eight Mile, the result was outrage—and a virtual political revolution. Nowhere in the Detroit area was antibusing fervor as intense as in Macomb County.

The busing furor resulted in a sharp—and apparently temporary—alteration of Macomb's traditional Democratic voting habits. For the migrants here had not originally switched parties on leaving the city; President Kennedy won 63% of Macomb's votes in 1960—his best showing in any all-suburban county in the nation. In 1968, George Wallace won 14% here, holding Hubert Humphrey to 55%; and in the 1972 Democratic primary, at the height of the busing controversy and the day after he was shot, Wallace took 67% of Macomb's votes. That fall, Richard Nixon won 64% of the vote, more than doubling his 1968 percentage. The switch from the national Democratic Party was almost as extensive here as it was in the Deep South following the civil rights revolution of the sixties.

But it was not just a shift of voting habits which happened in Macomb County in 1972. Rather, the enraged and seemingly desperate voters spawned a whole new civic culture. Antibusing organizations signed up thousands of members and practically every front door proudly wore a "This family will not be bused" sign. There was loud talk of civil disobedience, a revival of some of the ideas, if not the same accents, of the civil rights and peace movements of a few years before. As people do, people here turned to electoral politics as one way to achieve their goals, and many Macomb citizens saw the defeat of 12th district Congressman James O'Hara as one way to do that.

O'Hara, first elected in 1958, occupied what had always seemed to be a safe Democratic seat. He had been accustomed to winning as much as 75% of the vote, and had turned much of his attention to national matters. As Chairman of an Education and Labor subcommittee, he was one of the congressional favorites of organized labor, and an intelligent and shrewd legislative tactician. He had finished a humiliating last when he had run for House Majority Leader in 1971, mostly because he had always been a hawk on the Vietnam War and most of his natural reformer constituency was dovish. But he had been well enough thought of by all segments of the party to have been chosen as parliamentarian of the 1972 Democratic national convention, in which capacity he had made, under heavy pressure, the decisions which allowed George McGovern to retain the delegates he had won in the California primary. (Ironically, O'Hara was not a McGovern man at all; he undoubtedly would have preferred Humphrey to win the Democratic nomination.)

Suddenly in 1972 O'Hara found himself in trouble back home. The Congressman had already been taking a hard line antibusing position, backing a constitutional amendment to reverse court decisions for more than a year; indeed, he had been so dogged in his fight that he had antagonized many of his former liberal friends. But his reputation as a liberal and civil rights proponent and the very fact that he was a Democrat, and therefore a member of the party that virtually all blacks favored, worked heavily against him. Antibusing voters had greater confidence in the fervor of Republican candidate David Serotkin, who ran an aggressive, well-financed campaign that concentrated almost entirely on busing. The district lines had been altered before the election, removing part of traditionally Democratic Macomb and adding Republican St. Clair County (Port Huron) to the north. But in the end this benefitted O'Hara as much as Serotkin, for busing was not such a big issue there, and the incumbent was able to run far ahead of usual Democratic percentages outside Macomb. Overall, O'Hara was reelected with only 51% of the vote.

Then suddenly, even more rapidly than it had started, the antibusing furor was over. In July 1974 the Supreme Court overturned the metropolitan Detroit busing order. Eight Mile was a solid barrier against integration, and the antibusing movement disappeared. People who had been passing petitions and attending demostrations went back to their housework or their summer cottages; Macomb County reacted as negatively as any part of the nation to Richard Nixon's Watergate defense, but the reaction was a quiet, almost apathetic one. With a turnout lighter than in 1970, despite population growth, Jim O'Hara was reelected with 72% of the vote in 1974—as if the busing furor had never happened. Like many a religious revival, it produced much sound and fury while it was going on, but left virtually no trace that it had ever occurred. O'Hara was free to continue his House career as a senior liberal in, for the first time, an undisputedly liberal House; he will likely conclude, as certainly the Republicans already have, that he is once again unbeatable.

Census Data Pop. 467,543. Central city, 0%; suburban, 74%. Median family income, $12,003; families above $15,000: 31%; families below $3,000: 6%. Median years education, 12.1.

The Voters

Median voting age 40.
Employment profile White collar, 46%. Blue collar, 42%. Service, 11%. Farm, 1%.
Ethnic groups Black, 2%. Total foreign stock, 24%. Canada, 7%; Germany, Italy, 3% each; Poland, UK, 2% each.

Presidential vote

1972	Nixon (R)	112,291	(65%)
	McGovern (D)	61,288	(35%)
1968	Nixon (R)	61,859	(39%)
	Humphrey (D)	75,674	(48%)
	Wallace (AI)	20,093	(13%)

Rep. James G. O'Hara (D) Elected 1958; b. Nov. 8, 1925, Washington, D.C.; home, Utica; U. of Mich., B.A. 1954, LL.B. 1955; Catholic.

Career Army, WWII; Practicing atty., 1955–58.

Offices 2262 RHOB, 202-225-2106. Also 215 S. Gratiot St., Mt. Clemens 48043, 313-465-0911.

Committees

Budget (7th).

Education and Labor (6th). Subcommittees: Elementary, Secondary and Vocational Education; Manpower, Compensation, and Health and Safety; Post-secondary Education (Chairman).

Group Ratings

	ADA	COPE	LWV	RIPON	NFU	LCV	CFA	NAB	NSI	ACA
1974	65	100	64	38	93	69	100	18	30	13
1973	84	90	73	40	85	68	86	–	–	12
1972	75	100	83	62	100	60	100	0	11	10

Key Votes

1) Foreign Aid	FOR	6) Gov Abortn Aid	AGN	11) Pub Cong Election $	AGN
2) Busing	AGN	7) Coed Phys Ed	AGN	12) Turkish Arms Cutoff	ABS
3) ABM	FOR	8) Pov Lawyer Gag	AGN	13) Youth Camp Regs	FOR
4) B-1 Bomber	AGN	9) Pub Trans Sub	AGN	14) Strip Mine Veto	AGN
5) Nerve Gas	AGN	10) EZ Voter Regis	FOR	15) Farm Bill Veto	FOR

Election Results

1974 general:	James G. O'Hara (D)	89,822	(72%)	($22,289)
	Eugene J. Tyza (R)	34,293	(28%)	($997)
1974 primary:	James G. O'Hara (D), unopposed			
1972 general:	James G. O'Hara (D)	83,351	(51%)	($62,472)
	David M. Serotkin (R)	80,667	(49%)	($43,619)

◆ ◆ ◆ ◆ ◆

THIRTEENTH DISTRICT

The 13th congressional district of Michigan is Detroit's inner city, the only district completely contained within the Detroit city limits. Like the 1st, the 13th has a majority black population (66% in 1970, probably 75% today), but unlike the 1st it has only a smattering of middle class blacks. During the 1960s, the 13th suffered the largest population loss—19%—of any congressional district in the country, and this tells you about all you need to know about the quality of life for most people here. Many of the district's old buildings were bulldozed to make way for urban renewal projects and giant freeways, named for Motown auto magnates: Edsel B. Ford, Walter P. Chrysler, and the Fisher brothers of General Motors. An even more important factor in the district's population loss was the voluntary exodus of the black community itself. After the 1967 riot, many residents of this part of Detroit moved to the more middle class surroundings of the 1st district, leaving many neighborhoods utterly deserted and others pockmarked with vacant houses. The problem was compounded by the operations of the FHA here, which left 20,000 homes empty and huge profits for speculators—and shredded what were already only the tatters of reputation that former Governor and then HUD Secretary George Romney had left in his home town.

The Congressman from the 13th district is Charles C. Diggs, Jr., who in 1970—on the death of William Dawson and the defeat of Adam Clayton Powell—became at 48 the senior black member of the House. That in turn led to the creation of the Black Caucus, of which Diggs was the first Chairman; although not particularly militant himself, he was not the kind—Dawson and Powell were—to squelch the efforts of other blacks to organize and attack the powers that be. By trade Diggs is a mortician, like his late father who twenty years ago was the leading politician and one of the wealthiest men in Detroit's black community. Diggs Sr. masterminded his son's first congressional race in 1954; the old man had counted the votes and realized that there was a black majority in the 13th, and had his son whip the Irish incumbent in the primary. Ever since, Diggs has been unbeatable in his district. Though his record is solidly liberal and antiwar, Diggs is considered insufficiently militant by some black activists; and he really is a cautious man, less given to au courant rhetoric than some of his colleagues in the Black Caucus. Serious opposition, however, has never materialized in the 13th district and undoubtedly never will now that Diggs has more than 20 years of seniority and important committee and subcommittee chairmanships.

As recently as 1972, it seemed impossible that Diggs would be Chairman of the House District of Columbia Committee—or that the black-majority District would ever be given home rule. But that same year Chairman John McMillan of South Carolina, who had run District affairs in a quasi-dictatorial manner for more than twenty years, was defeated in his primary; and the two Southern Democrats just behind him in seniority had already announced their retirements. This left the chair to Diggs, who was of course committed to home rule. After considerable manuevering—and an agreement with William Natcher of Kentucky, Chairman of the District Appropriations Subcommittee—a home rule bill was passed, and Diggs relinquished with some reluctance much of the power he had so recently inherited.

Diggs's other chairmanship is also of special interest to many blacks: the International Affairs Committee's Subcommittee on Africa. Diggs travels to Africa frequently (some would say too frequently), and he is probably the House's leading expert on that often ignored continent. Naturally, he has been an opponent of South Africa's apartheid system and a backer of sanctions of Rhodesia; he has played some role in the efforts to stop the United States from importing Rhodesian chrome.

Census Data Pop. 465,076. Central city, 100%; suburban, 0%. Median family income, $7,770; families above $15,000: 13%; families below $3,000: 19%. Median years education, 10.0.

The Voters

Median voting age 44.
Employment profile White collar, 32%. Blue collar, 48%. Service, 20%. Farm, –%.
Ethnic groups Black, 66%. Spanish, 2%. Total foreign stock, 12%. Canada, Poland, 2% each; Germany, 1%.

Presidential vote

1972	Nixon (R)	20,561	(16%)
	McGovern (D)	104,556	(84%)
1968	Nixon (R)	18,192	(12%)
	Humphrey (D)	127,178	(82%)
	Wallace (AI)	9,780	(6%)

Rep. Charles C. Diggs, Jr. (D) Elected 1954; b. Dec. 2, 1922, Detroit; home, Detroit; U. of Mich., 1940–42, Fisk U., 1942–43, Wayne St. U., B.S. 1946, Detroit Col. of Law, 1950–51; Baptist.

Career Army Air Corps, WWII; Mortician, 1946–50; Mich. Senate, 1951–54.

Offices 2208 RHOB, 202-225-2261. Also 4825 Woodward Ave., Detroit 48201, 313-571-2100.

Committees

District of Columbia (Chairman).

International Relations (6th). Subcommittees: International Operations; International Resources, Food, and Energy.

Group Ratings

	ADA	COPE	LWV	RIPON	NFU	LCV	CFA	NAB	NSI	ACA
1974	92	100	91	60	83	100	90	14	33	0
1973	95	91	100	71	100	87	100	–	–	4
1972	88	89	100	67	86	70	100	14	14	5

Key Votes

1) Foreign Aid	FOR	6) Gov Abortn Aid	FOR	11) Pub Cong Election $	FOR
2) Busing	FOR	7) Coed Phys Ed	FOR	12) Turkish Arms Cutoff	FOR
3) ABM	ABS	8) Pov Lawyer Gag	AGN	13) Youth Camp Regs	ABS
4) B-1 Bomber	ABS	9) Pub Trans Sub	FOR	14) Strip Mine Veto	AGN
5) Nerve Gas	ABS	10) EZ Voter Regis	FOR	15) Farm Bill Veto	AGN

Election Results

1974 general:	Charles C. Diggs, Jr. (D)	63,246	(89%)	($400)
	George E. McCall (R)	8,036	(11%)	($194)
1974 primary:	Charles C. Diggs, Jr. (D), unopposed			
1972 general:	Charles C. Diggs, Jr. (D)	97,562	(87%)	($2,566)
	Leonard T. Edwards (R)	15,180	(13%)	($10)

◆ ◆ ◆ ◆ ◆

FOURTEENTH DISTRICT

The east side of Detroit is the heart of Michigan's 14th congressional district. It is composed of a series of residential neighborhoods of varying wealth which are nearly all white and all heavily Catholic. Suburban territory nicely brackets and defines the east side. To the east are the five Grosse Pointes: wealthy, conservative, and snobbish. But, it should be remembered, the Grosse Pointes include not only Detroit's leading families, like the Fords, but also upwardly mobile and well-to-do Irish and Italian Catholics, who politically are if anything even more conservative than their WASP neighbors.

In the district's southwest corner lies the enclave of of Hamtramck, a predominantly Polish-American city surrounded by Detroit. It was here that thousands of immigrants flocked to get jobs in the Dodge Main, Plymouth, and Packard automobile plant; in fact, during the 1910s, Hamtramck was the fastest-growing city in the country. In 1930, as many as 56,000 people lived here. Today, the population is down to 27,000, most of whom are old people. Hamtramck has been the butt of dozens of Polish jokes, but anybody who takes the trouble to visit the city will find freshly painted houses and carefully tended lawns—evidence of the pride of ownership found in so many Polish-American neighborhoods.

The people who were brought up in Hamtramck have moved by the thousands to the east side of Detroit and increasingly to the Macomb County suburbs, especially Warren. For the 1972 election, half of Warren and the suburb of East Detroit were added to the 14th for the first time. Their inclusion was appropriate, since most of the people there had moved from the confines of the old 14th; but it also created something of an upheaval in 14th district politics. In 1972 Warren and East Detroit were in the midst of a revivalistic furor over a federal court busing order which covered them as well as the city (see Twelfth District). Ironically, white parents on the east side had forced the entire issue; they did not want a busing order confined to the city alone, because it would mean that their children would have to attend schools that were two-thirds black. Such was the local scene confronting Congressman Lucien Nedzi when he sought reelection in 1972.

Nedzi had first captured the seat in a 1961 special election, and had won a tough primary against another incumbent after the 1964 redistricting. After that he had never had much trouble at the polls, though the Republican vote in the Grosse Pointes and a few east side precincts in Detroit had held his percentages slightly below those of other Detroit area Democrats. In recent years, he had not found it necessary to campaign hard, and instead had tended to his duties as a member—and often a dissenting one—of the House Armed Services Committee.

Now he was confronted with a lot of new territory and an issue that was getting many formerly apathetic voters out ringing doorbells against him. His chief opponent was Warren Councilman Howard Austin, who steadfastly refused to discuss any issue but busing, and did so with a singlemindedness that would have been considered old fashioned in the Deep South. The challenger carried the Macomb County part of the district by a wide margin and, in a four-man race, took 39% of the vote. Nedzi just squeaked by with 43%—and in the general election he did scarcely better, beating his Republican opponent 55–45.

That might have seemed an omen that Nedzi's congressional career was over, but the busing issue faded from the public consciousness more rapidly than it had come when the Supreme Court overturned the metropolitan Detroit court ruling. In 1974 Nedzi got 74% of the vote in a three-man primary, and 73% in the general election.

In the House Nedzi is known not so much for his position on busing (he is against it, and has supported such legislation) as he is for being the highest ranking dove on the Armed Services Committee. When he first began challenging high defense expenditures and was pushing the Nedzi-Whalen Amendment to end the war, Nedzi had virtually no allies on the committee and less than a majority on the House floor. Now Armed Services is leavened with more liberals, and the doves have something like an assured majority in the House as a whole. Nevertheless, Nedzi is not really a hero for them. One problem is that he has been Chairman for several years now of the Armed Services Subcommittee with jurisdiction over intelligence, but he did not come forward with any of the revelations about the CIA which have been filling the newspapers—even though the subcommittee heard about some of them. One reason is that Nedzi was hopelessly outvoted on his own subcommittee, the rest of whose members were the Armed Services Committee's senior hawks. In 1975 House Democrats set up another committee, this time packed with doves, to look into CIA domestic spying and involvement in assassinations. Nedzi was to be Chairman of this one too, but his fellow committee members insisted on dumping him when it became clear he had heard evidence of the assassination involvement more than a year before and had done nothing positive about it. The acrimony just might convince Nedzi to retire, prematurely, from the Congress.

Census Data Pop. 467,603. Central city, 47%; suburban, 53%. Median family income, $12,394; families above $15,000: 34%; families below $3,000: 5%. Median years education, 11.9.

The Voters

Median voting age 47.
Employment profile White collar, 50%. Blue collar, 39%. Service, 11%. Farm, –%.
Ethnic groups Black, 3%. Total foreign stock, 37%. Poland, 9%; Italy, Canada, 6% each; Germany, 4%; UK, 2%; Austria, Yugoslavia, 1% each.

Presidential vote

1972	Nixon (R)	85,618	(60%)
	McGovern (D)	57,045	(40%)
1968	Nixon (R)	69,970	(33%)
	Humphrey (D)	117,906	(55%)
	Wallace (AI)	27,116	(13%)

Rep. Lucien N. Nedzi (D) Elected Nov. 7, 1961; b. May 28, 1925, Hamtramck; home, Detroit; U. of Mich., B.A. 1948, J.D. 1951; Catholic.

Career Army, WWII and Korea; Practicing atty., 1952–61; Wayne Co. Public Administrator, 1955–61.

Offices 2418 RHOB, 202-225-6276. Also 20491 Van Dyke St., Detroit 48243, 313-892-4010.

Committees

Armed Services (6th). Subcommittees: Investigations; Military Personnel (Chairman); Special Subcommittee on Intelligence (Chairman).

House Administration (4th). Subcommittees: Electrical and Mechanical Office Equipment; Library and Memorials (Chairman).

Group Ratings

	ADA	COPE	LWV	RIPON	NFU	LCV	CFA	NAB	NSI	ACA
1974	79	100	73	50	92	87	85	33	22	14
1973	83	100	73	46	84	83	100	–	–	12
1972	75	91	82	69	100	67	100	8	0	9

Key Votes

1) Foreign Aid	FOR	6) Gov Abortn Aid	FOR	11) Pub Cong Election $	AGN
2) Busing	AGN	7) Coed Phys Ed	AGN	12) Turkish Arms Cutoff	FOR
3) ABM	ABS	8) Pov Lawyer Gag	AGN	13) Youth Camp Regs	FOR
4) B-1 Bomber	AGN	9) Pub Trans Sub	FOR	14) Strip Mine Veto	AGN
5) Nerve Gas	ABS	10) EZ Voter Regis	FOR	15) Farm Bill Veto	AGN

Election Results

1974 general:	Lucien N. Nedzi (D)	98,471	(73%)	($14,717)
	Herbert O. Steiger (R)	35,723	(27%)	($0)
1974 primary:	Lucien N. Nedzi (D)	38,438	(74%)	
	Two others (D)	13,613	(26%)	
1972 general:	Lucien N. Nedzi (D)	93,923	(55%)	($32,765)
	Robert V. McGrath (R)	77,273	(45%)	($16,568)

◆ ◆ ◆ ◆ ◆

FIFTEENTH DISTRICT

The 15th congressional district of Michigan is a collection of suburbs southwest of Detroit. No high income WASPy havens, these are bedroom communities occupied by the people who keep the paperwork and assembly lines of the auto companies moving. The various towns here have atmospheres reminiscent of their decades of greatest growth: Lincoln Park puts you back in the 1940s, Dearborn Heights recalls the 1950s, and Westland—a city named after a shopping center—embodies the 1960s. Most of these suburbs are predominantly blue collar, though only one of them, Inkster, has a significant number (44% in 1970) of blacks. Many of the citizens here grew up in the immigrant neighborhoods of southwest Detroit; many others, in the mountains of Kentucky and Tennessee.

The suburbs of most American cities, or so conventional wisdom has it, usually vote Republican. Not so here; most Detroit suburbs in most elections are solidly Democratic. Over the years the 15th district has more often than not turned in 2–1 Democratic margins in most elections. But that was decidedly not the case when a federal court entered a busing order that would merge Detroit and suburban schools; in the furor that resulted (see Twelfth District), there was a profound Republican surge here. The 15th, in any case, was somewhat disposed to a Southern strategy; 16% of the voters here in 1968 supported George Wallace—a higher percentage than in any other Michigan district. But is still surprised a lot of observers when in 1972 the 15th gave Richard Nixon 61% of its votes. Probably a lot of people in the district would rather forget that now; when the Supreme Court overturned the Detroit busing order, the furor it had caused disappeared like a summer storm.

The district's largest employer is the Ford Motor company and its Congressman, appropriately enough, is William D. Ford, a Democrat who is no relation to either Henry or Jerry. When the state legislature split the old 16th district in two in 1964, Ford, a young attorney active in the local politics of Taylor Township, jumped from the state Senate to the U.S. House. There he has remained, with little trouble since: he was fortunate in the busing year of 1972 to have faced only the most desultory of opposition. In Washington he serves rather quietly on the House Education and Labor Committee, where he is now eighth-ranking member; he has been particularly close to another Education and Labor veteran, James O'Hara of Michigan's 12th district. Like O'Hara, Ford is a favorite of organized labor, and usually has a close to 100 rating from COPE. With the busing issue gone, there is no reason to think he will not win reelection indefinitely.

Census Data Pop. 466,608. Central city, 0%; suburban, 100%. Median family income, $12,460; families above $15,000: 32%; families below $3,000: 4%. Median years education, 12.1.

The Voters

Median voting age 38.
Employment profile White collar, 42%. Blue collar, 47%. Service, 11%. Farm, –%.
Ethnic groups Black, 5%. Spanish, 1%. Total foreign stock, 19%. Canada, 5%; Poland, 3%; UK, Germany, Italy, 2% each.

Presidential vote

1972	Nixon (R)	94,812	(61%)
	McGovern (D)	61,803	(39%)
1968	Nixon (R)	41,959	(29%)
	Humphrey (D)	79,439	(55%)
	Wallace (AI)	23,973	(16%)

Rep. William D. Ford (D) Elected 1964; b. Aug. 6, 1927,Detroit; home, Taylor; Neb. Teachers Col., 1946, Wayne St. U., 1947–48, U. of Denver, B.S. 1949, J.D. 1951; United Church of Christ.

Career Practicing Atty., 1951–64; Taylor Twnshp. J.P., 1955–57; Melvindale City Atty., 1957–59; Mich Senate, 1963–65.

Offices 2238 RHOB, 202-225-6261. Also Wayne Fed. Bldg., Wayne 48184, 313-722-1411.

Committees

Education and Labor (8th). Subcommittees: Agricultural Labor (Chairman); Elementary, Secondary and Vocational Education; Labor-Management Relations.

Post Office and Civil Service (8th). Subcommittees: Manpower and Civil Service; Postal Service.

Group Ratings

	ADA	COPE	LWV	RIPON	NFU	LCV	CFA	NAB	NSI	ACA
1974	72	100	60	53	92	92	92	33	17	21
1973	87	100	75	57	94	89	88	–	–	19
1972	75	88	75	62	100	90	100	9	0	12

Key Votes

1) Foreign Aid	FOR	6) Gov Abortn Aid	FOR	11) Pub Cong Election $	AGN
2) Busing	AGN	7) Coed Phys Ed	AGN	12) Turkish Arms Cutoff	FOR
3) ABM	AGN	8) Pov Lawyer Gag	AGN	13) Youth Camp Regs	FOR
4) B-1 Bomber	AGN	9) Pub Trans Sub	ABS	14) Strip Mine Veto	AGN
5) Nerve Gas	AGN	10) EZ Voter Regis	FOR	15) Farm Bill Veto	ABS

Election Results

1974 general:	William D. Ford (D)	86,601	(79%)	($43,458)
	Jack A. Underwood (R)	23,028	(21%)	($79)
1974 primary:	William D. Ford (D), unopposed			
1972 general:	William D. Ford (D)	97,054	(67%)	($43,352)
	Ernest C. Fackler (R)	48,504	(33%)	($43)

◆ ◆ ◆ ◆ ◆

SIXTEENTH DISTRICT

Michigan's 16th congressional district is an industrial part of the Detroit metropolitan area made up of three distinct areas of roughly equal population: the Delray secion of Detroit, the Downriver suburbs, and the city of Dearborn. Delray, the southwest corner of Detroit, is an old ethnic neighborhood that looks much as it must have fifty years ago. The Downriver suburbs grow more prosperous and modern as one proceeds south along the Detroit River, though an insular quality remains in places like River Rouge and Ecorse, divided neatly into ethnic and black sections by the railroad tracks. Dearborn (pop. 104,000) is probably the district's most famous town; here the Ford Motor company has its headquarters and its giant Rouge plant.

Dearborn is also known for Orville Hubbard who, as every piece of city stationery tells you, has been Mayor since January 6, 1942. Hubbard has plastered the city with signs that say "Keep Dearborn clean", a slogan which some say is a euphemism for his primary (and successful) concern: keeping Dearborn white. Though Dearborn lies adjacent to part of the Detroit ghetto, and though thousands of blacks work in the Rouge, no blacks live in Dearborn and no one expects any to move in. Oddly enough, Hubbard was as vigorous an opponent of the Vietnam war as he is of suburban integration. He realized early on, from attending their funerals, that a disproportionate number of his working class constituents were being drafted—and killed—in the war. With his near dictatorial power over the city council, he got an antiwar referendum on the ballot and saw it approved as long ago as 1968.

The 16th is one of the nation's most heavily industrial districts. From the 1-75 bridge over the Rouge River, you can see the Ford Rouge plant and a couple of oil refineries on one side and the huge steel mills and chemical plants of the Downriver communities on the other. For the distinction of the premier industrial landscape of America, the scene here rivals the view of Gary from the Indiana Turnpike and the spectacle of northern New Jersey you see from the Pulaski Skyway. Almost flush up against the industrial plants and well within the range of their sulphurous odors are the neat, tightly-packed houses of the old ethnic neighborhood still mostly Polish, Hungarian, and Italian—but some now with considerable numbers of Mexican-Americans and Arabs. The 16th does contain a few high income WASP enclaves in the western part of Dearborn and on the island of Grosse Ile in the Detroit River; most of the district, however, is vintage Democratic country.

It is perhaps fitting that the Congressman from this pollution-ridden district is one of the leading conservationists in the House of Representatives. John D. Dingell, Jr., comes by this interest not from reading Sierra Club coffee table books, but from a lifelong love of hunting. As Chairman of the Fisheries and Wildlife Conservation Subcommittee for many years he has been responsible for many conservationist measures; he is also in large part responsible for the defeat in 1974 of the Bolling Committee reforms which would have abolished the parent Merchant Marine and Fisheries Committee, on which Dingell is the third-ranking Democrat. Dingell is now Chairman of the Commerce Subcommittee on Energy and Power and a fighter for the interests of consumer and against those of the big oil companies.

On other issues, Dingell is less likely to line up with the House's ideological liberals. From the same love of hunting that made him a conservationist, he is also an impassioned opponent of gun controls; and he was latecomer to the ranks of Vietnam doves. Alone of Detroit area Democrats with suburban constituents, Dingell did not face electoral trouble during the busing controversy of 1972; he had enough black constituents, and his antibusing stand seemed to voters genuine enough, that he did not face formidable opposition. Indeed, since he succeeded his father in a 1955 special election, Dingell has faced only one tough contest, when redistricting placed him in the same district with Congressman John Lesinski, Jr. Both were Democrats of Polish descent and both had succeeded their fathers, who had both first been elected to the House in 1932. But in those pre-busing days, Lesinski has voted against the Civil Rights Act of 1964—the only northern Democrat in the House to do so—while Dingell had voted for it; and Dingell had the vigorous support of organized labor in the primary. Though Lesinski had represented most of the new district, Dingell won handily and has not had electoral problems since.

Census Data Pop. 467,168. Central city, 29%; suburban, 71%. Median family income, $11,800; families above $15,000: 31%; families below $3,000: 6%. Median years education, 11.4.

The Voters

Median voting age 45.
Employment profile White collar, 43%. Blue collar, 45%. Service, 12%. Farm, –%.
Ethnic groups Black, 8%. Spanish, 3%. Total foreign stock, 31%. Poland, 7%; Canada, 5%; Italy, 3%; UK, Germany, Hungary, 2% each.

Presidential vote

1972	Nixon (R)	95,564	(54%)
	McGovern (D)	82,219	(46%)

	1968	Nixon (R)	49,774	(27%)
		Humphrey (D)	110,387	(60%)
		Wallace (AI)	23,555	(13%)

Rep. John D. Dingell (D) Elected Dec. 13, 1955; b. July 8, 1926, Colorado Springs, Colo.; home, Trenton; Georgetown U., B.S. 1949, J.D. 1952; Catholic.

Career Army, WWII; Practicing Atty., 1952–55; Research Asst. to U.S. Dist. Judge Theodore Levin, 1952–53; Wayne Co. Asst. Prosecuting Atty., 1953–55.

Offices 2210 RHOB, 202-225-4071. Also 4917 Schaefer Rd., Dearborn 48126, 313-846-1276.

Committees

Interstate and Foreign Commerce (4th). Subcommittees: Energy and Power (Chairman).

Merchant Marine and Fisheries (3d). Subcommittees: Fisheries and Wildlife Conservation and the Environment.

Small Business (3d). Subcommittees: Activities of Regulatory Agencies; Energy and Environment (Chairman).

Group Ratings

	ADA	COPE	LWV	RIPON	NFU	LCV	CFA	NAB	NSI	ACA
1974	60	100	67	33	92	94	80	18	50	23
1973	83	100	73	64	100	71	100	–	–	12
1972	63	89	83	73	100	90	100	20	30	15

Key Votes

1) Foreign Aid	FOR	6) Gov Abortn Aid	FOR	11) Pub Cong Election $	AGN
2) Busing	AGN	7) Coed Phys Ed	AGN	12) Turkish Arms Cutoff	FOR
3) ABM	AGN	8) Pov Lawyer Gag	AGN	13) Youth Camp Regs	FOR
4) B-1 Bomber	AGN	9) Pub Trans Sub	FOR	14) Strip Mine Veto	AGN
5) Nerve Gas	AGN	10) EZ Voter Regis	FOR	15) Farm Bill Veto	AGN

Election Results

1974 general:	John D. Dingell (D)	95,834	(79%)	($25,410)
	Wallace D. English	25,248	(21%)	($1,345)
1974 primary:	John D. Dingell (D), unopposed			
1972 general:	John D. Dingell (D)	110,715	(68%)	($26,593)
	William E. Rostron (R)	48,414	(30%)	($239)
	Peter P. Gayner (AI)	3,554	(2%)	(NA)

◆ ◆ ◆ ◆ ◆

SEVENTEENTH DISTRICT

Northwest Detroit is the most white middle class and most white collar part of the city. For mile after mile, the straight streets here are lined with single family homes, with the factories responsible, directly or indirectly, for their upkeep lying many miles away. For many years this part of Detroit has been the fulcrum of Michigan politics: as it goes, so goes the state. During the early 1950s, northwest Detroit was, as it had been for years, pretty solidly Republican. But in 1954, it delivered big margins for Governor G. Mennen Williams and retired several Republican legislators, including its Congressmen. Since then, northwest Detroit more often than not has voted Democratic, although it delivered majorities for Republicans like former Governor George Romney, current Governor William Milliken, Senator Robert Griffin, and President Richard Nixon.

Northwest Detroit is the heart of the 17th congressional district of Michigan; indeed, before the 1972 redistricting all of the 17th was within the Detroit city limits. Now, with population shifting outward to the suburbs, so has the district. It includes Redford Township, politically and sociologically just about indistinguishable from the northwest Detroit neighborhoods it adjoins; Southfield, with a large Jewish population, the fast-growing site of high-rise office buildings which are beginning to rival Detroit's downtown; and Farmington, west of Southfield, the only generally Republican part of the district.

For twenty years, from her first victory in 1954 to her retirement in 1974, the 17th district was represented by Congresswoman Martha Griffiths. After her initial victory, Griffiths became phenomenally popular in the district, winning as much as 80% of the vote in 1970. As a member of the Ways and Means Committee, she had played a major role in the repeal of the auto excise tax and had also been one of the name co-sponsors of the labor-supported, but still unpassed, bill to provide federal financing of comprehensive medical care. But what Griffiths will be most remembered for is the Equal Rights Amendment, regardless of its fate (currently uncertain) in the state legislatures. For years she had introduced this measure, only to see it bottled up in Emanuel Celler's Judiciary Committee. Finally, in 1971, Griffiths persuaded enough House members to sign a discharge petition and forced the measure out from under the hostile Celler, and pushed it to passage in the House. Her chief adversary on the floor, incidentally, was California's Charles Wiggins, who would later make a name for himself in the Nixon impeachment hearings—and the fact that she won over such an opponent testifies to her achievement.

Griffiths' retirement in 1974 was a surprise; she apparently was simply tired of commuting between her home in Detroit and the House in Washington. Since congressional seats don't open up very often these days, there was a flood of candidates in the Democratic primary which people supposed, correctly, would choose the next Congressman. The three major contenders were Joseph Levin, cousin of gubernatorial candidate Sander Levin, who didn't like Joseph's candidacy; Detroit school board member Patrick McDonald, who was trying to make a lifelong career out of his opposition to busing; and state Representative William Brodhead, whose base support was from a 17th district group called the Liberal Conference. This is a group worthy of some attention, not only because it ultimately prevailed in this race, because it resembles many groups of politically active people who have helped make the freshman class of the 94th Congress what it is. In the residential 17th there is no large base of clear liberal strength in elections, no major university or black ghetto where votes can easily be won by the hundreds. Yet the conference, formed in the late sixties to oppose the Vietnam war within the Democratic Party, through the efforts of its hundreds of volunteers, has been able to create a liberal vote base where none had previously existed. Organizing precinct by precinct, recruiting like-minded people through church and school organizations, tested in many campaigns, the Conference was a ready-made political organization when Brodhead entered the 17th district race—and one that had proven itself capable of winning those few extra votes per precinct that can make all the difference.

The endorsement that got the press play in this race was the UAW's. The Union, as it is called in Detroit, also settled on Brodhead, and it had its own cadres of workers, but it was a case of the Union ratifying the Conference's choice, and not vice versa. The other two major candidates, McDonald and Levin, had the advantages of well-known names, and in addition their campaigns were better financed than Brodhead's. But when the votes were counted,—and there were more cast here than in any other Michigan Democratic primary—Brodhead had finished ahead of McDonald by exactly 256 votes. The general election was anticlimatic; Brodhead had 70% of the vote. But it can be said that the result, in terms of the kind if not the party of the Congressman who was elected, would have been quite different were it not for this volunteer organization—the rough equivalents of which exist, often in the unlikeliest places, in Iowa and Colorado and Massachusetts and California.

In Washington, Brodhead won a seat on the Democratic Steering Committee and was one of those who played a major role in toppling several aging and/or conservative committee chairmen. He is one of those freshmen whose massive presence has altered the whole tone and character of the Commerce Committee. At 35, he appears to have a long congressional career ahead of him.

Census Data Pop. 467,544. Central city, 56%; suburban, 44%. Median family income, $13,449; families above $15,000: 41%; families below $3,000: 4%. Median years education, 12.3.

The Voters

Median voting age 45.
Employment profile White collar, 58%. Blue collar, 31%. Service, 11%. Farm, –%.
Ethnic groups Black, 2%. Spanish, 1%. Total foreign stock, 34%. Canada, 8%; Poland, UK, 4% each; Germany, USSR, 3% each; Italy, 2%.

Presidential vote

1972	Nixon (R)	118,347	(60%)
	McGovern (D)	77,659	(40%)
1968	Nixon (R)	79,749	(39%)
	Humphrey (D)	101,819	(50%)
	Wallace (AI)	21,458	(11%)

Rep. William M. Brodhead (D) Elected 1974; b. Sept. 12, 1941, Cleveland, Ohio; home, Detroit; John Carroll U., 1959–60, U. of Detroit, 1960–63, Wayne St. U., A.B. 1965, U. of Mich., J.D. 1967.

Career Practicing atty., 1968–71; Mich. House of Reps., 1971–75.

Offices 416 CHOB, 202-225-4961. Also 24261 Grand River Ave., Detroit 48219, 313-537-1400.

Committees

Interstate and Foreign Commerce (24th). Subcommittees: Communications; Consumer Protection and Finance; Energy and Power.

Post Office and Civil Service (15th). Subcommittees: Census and Population; Manpower and Civil Service; Postal Facilities, Mail, and Labor Management.

Group Ratings: Newly Elected

Key Votes

1) Foreign Aid	FOR	6) Gov Abortn Aid	NE	11) Pub Cong Election $	NE
2) Busing	NE	7) Coed Phys Ed	FOR	12) Turkish Arms Cutoff	NE
3) ABM	NE	8) Pov Lawyer Gag	NE	13) Youth Camp Regs	FOR
4) B-1 Bomber	AGN	9) Pub Trans Sub	NE	14) Strip Mine Veto	AGN
5) Nerve Gas	NE	10) EZ Voter Regis	NE	15) Farm Bill Veto	AGN

Election Results

1974 general:	William M. Brodhead (D)	94,242	(70%)	($55,180)
	Kenneth C. Gallagher (R)	39,856	(30%)	($97)
1974 primary:	William M. Brodhead (D)	17,314	(27%)	
	Patricia A. McDonald (D)	17,058	(27%)	
	Joseph Levin (D)	14,691	(23%)	
	Robert E. Fitzpatrick (D)	8,141	(13%)	
	Kathleen Straus (D)	5,213	(8%)	
	Dennis F. Shrewsbury (D)	563	(1%)	

♦ ♦ ♦ ♦ ♦

EIGHTEENTH DISTRICT

The 18th congressional district of Michigan—created in the 1972 redistricting—combines two areas that have little in common and that had never before joined together in the same constituency. In its brief history, the 18th has had two Congressmen: a Republican elected in 1972, the year of the busing furor in the Detroit suburbs, and a Democratic elected in his party's landslide year of 1974. One-third of the 18th's residents living in fast-growing Macomb County, in Sterling Heights and Warren, which in 1972 was the most vehemently antibusing part of the Detroit metropolitan area (see Twelfth District). Macomb had always been Democratic, but in that year Warren and Sterling Heights went for Republican candidates—not just Richard Nixon,

The other two-thirds of the 18th is the southeast corner of Oakland County—higher income, more white collar, and by tradition much more Republican than Macomb. This part of the district is about as diverse as suburban territory can be: it includes mostly Jewish Oak Park; Hazel Park and Madison Heights, where most residents are from the Kentucky and Tennessee hills; Royal Oak, solid middle class homeowners; and Troy, where the flat Michigan farmland has been converted to giant garden apartment complexes and shopping centers with stores like Saks Fifth Avenue.

In 1972, virtually all of this area was in a tizzy over busing—producing a vast new stream of political participants and a major alteration of normal voting patterns. In any other year, the winner would almost certainly have been Democrat Daniel Cooper, a state Senator who surprised some of his liberal friends by coming out against busing long before. But even the most vehement stand was not enough to convince many voters that Cooper was more solid on the issue than his Republican opponent, state Senator Robert Huber. For Huber had a history of constant, sometimes even flaky support of conservative causes: in 1970 he had foresaken a safe state Senate seat to run against Lenore Romney in the Republican Senate primary; when he had lost, by much less than expected, he organized his own Conservative Party. But when the busing issue heated up just as the new 18th district was created, Huber decided he would be a Republican again. He won the general election by a convincing, if not overwhelming, 53–47 margin, even carrying the traditionally Democratic Macomb County portion of the district.

By 1974 Huber's ultraconservative reputation had turned from an asset in a busing-mad district to a crushing liability in a constituency sick of Richard Nixon and all his kind. Huber was not only a solid right-winger in the House—with a reputation for zaniness that got him stuck on the hopelessly liberal Education and Labor Committee—he was also a constant and enthusiastic supporter of Nixon. As evidence accumulated in the Watergate case, Huber could only repeat how much he supported the President.

Not too surprisingly, there was a spirited contest for the Democratic nomination in 1974. Macomb County Treasurer Adam Nowakowski dominated the four-man race in his home area, taking 47% of the vote. But in Oakland, it was a two-candidate contest between former assistant Attorney General James Blanchard, who took 42% of the Oakland vote with big margins in Oak Park, and Hazel Park school superintendent Wilfred Webb, who with strong support in his home area took 37% in Oakland. Overall, Blanchard—the only candidate not so mesmerized by the district's history as to stress the busing issue—won, with 34% of the total vote.

By the time of the general election, it had been only four months since the Supreme Court had overturned the cross-district metropolitan Detroit busing decree, but the busing issue had vanished like a summer storm. With Nixon and the economy now the major issue the 18th—which had given the former only 35% of its vote in 1968—was turning heavily against the Republicans. Blanchard wound up beating Huber by a solid 59–41 margin; few incumbents, even in 1974, were more convincingly routed.

Blanchard is now one of the young liberals who have so transformed the ideological balance on the Banking and Science Committees since the Democratic freshmen came in. Barring the sudden emergence of another emotional issue like busing, he seems to be an easy bet for continued reelection in the years ahead.

Census Data Pop. 465,916. Central city, 0%; suburban, 100%. Median family income, $13,627; families above $15,000: 40%; families below $3,000: 3%. Median years education, 12.3.

The Voters

Median voting age 39.
Employment profile White collar, 57%. Blue collar, 34%. Service, 9%. Farm, –%.
Ethnic groups Total foreign stock, 29%. Canada, 7%; Poland, 4%; UK, 3%; Italy, Germany, USSR, 2%.

Presidential vote

1972	Nixon (R)	115,552	(63%)
	McGovern (D)	68,193	(37%)
1968	Nixon (R)	58,586	(35%)
	Humphrey (D)	89,485	(54%)
	Wallace (AI)	17,245	(10%)

Rep. James J. Blanchard (D) Elected 1974; b. Aug. 8, 1942, Detroit; home, Pleasant Ridge; Mich. St. U., B.A. 1964, M.B.A. 1965, U. of Minn., J.D. 1968.

Career Practicing atty., 1968–74; Legal Aide, Mich. St. Election Bureau, 1968–69; Admin. Asst. to Mich. Atty. Gen. Frank J. Kelley, 1970–71; Asst. Atty. Gen. of Mich.; Legal Advisor to Mich. Depts. of Licensing and Regulation, Commerce, and Agriculture.

Offices 515 CHOB, 202-225-2101. Also 310 W. 4th St., Royal Oak 48067, 313-543-1106.

Committees

Banking, Currency and Housing (19th). Domestic Monetary Policy; Economic Stabilization; International Trade, Investment and Monetary Policy.

Science and Technology (24th). Subcommittees: Domestic and International Scientific Planning and Analysis; Energy Research, Development and Demonstration; Environment and the Atmosphere.

Group Ratings: Newly Elected

Key Votes

1) Foreign Aid	FOR	6) Gov Abortn Aid	NE	11) Pub Cong Election $	NE
2) Busing	NE	7) Coed Phys Ed	AGN	12) Turkish Arms Cutoff	NE
3) ABM	NE	8) Pov Lawyer Gag	NE	13) Youth Camp Regs	FOR
4) B-1 Bomber	AGN	9) Pub Trans Sub	NE	14) Strip Mine Veto	AGN
5) Nerve Gas	NE	10) EZ Voter Regis	NE	15) Farm Bill Veto	FOR

Election Results

1974 general:	James J. Blanchard (D)	83,523	(59%)	($133,021)
	Robert J. Huber (R)	57,133	(41%)	($120,426)
1974 primary:	James J. Blanchard (D)	16,356	(34%)	
	Wilfred D. Webb (D)	14,885	(31%)	
	Adam E. Nowakowski (D)	11,714	(24%)	
	Michael F. O'Connor (D)	5,654	(12%)	

◆ ◆ ◆ ◆ ◆

NINETEENTH DISTRICT

Just under half of Oakland County, the second most populous county in Michigan, lies in the state's 19th congressional district, which also includes a small portion of Livingston County. Technically, almost all of the 19th is considered part of Detroit metropolitan area, but beyond the district's southern rim the influence of Detroit wanes. The northern part of Oakland County is still largely rural, with summer cottages lining the inland lakes and ski resourts resting on man-made hills. The 19th's largest city is Pontiac (pop. 85,000), for which the car is named and where—providing there's enough demand—it is still manufactured. Like Flint not far to the north, Pontiac is very much a General Motors town; and like Flint, most of its residents are natives of the Appalachian mountains or the Black Belts of the South. In 1971 Pontiac was the scene of one of the north's first and noisiest busing controversies; whites boycotted schools, private academies were established, and chesty, T-shirted Irene McCabe organized a Pontiac-to-Washington antibusing march. But within a year, Pontiac's busing order was working smoothly, and the city had less antibusing sentiment than the Detroit suburbs farther south, where residents lived in fearful anticipation of a busing order which had not yet been—and as it turned out never would be—implemented.

With whites moving out of its city limits, Pontiac does not cast very many votes any more, and the real political center of the 19th district are the suburbs of Birmingham and Bloomfield Hills, which together with similar adjacent communities had a 1970 population of 122,000. Along with the Grosse Pointes, these are Detroit's richest suburbs, with a large percentage of the top auto executives. But these Oakland County communities are somewhat more tolerant (Birmingham has an open housing ordinance, and the area has a large Jewish population) and artsy; they are Republican, but their Democrats are liberal enough that their voting habits were not altered perceptibly by the busing crisis which so shook the rest of the Detroit suburbs.

With Birmingham and Bloomfield heavily outvoting Pontiac, the 19th is a solidly Republican district. The only major electoral contest here came in 1972, when two incumbents faced off against each other in the Republican primary. William Broomfield, who had been in Congress since 1956 and had once represented all of Oakland County, had the advantage of having had his name attached to a temporarily successful (but ultimately unavailing) antibusing amendment. His opponent, Jack McDonald was unable to match Broomfield's recognition and was snowed under by Broomfield votes in the Birmingham-Bloomfield area.

Broomfield's political secret in the past has been assiduous cultivation of his constituents through the mail, and that has been enough to give him the seniority to be, for the first time in the 94th Congress, ranking Republican on the House International Affairs Committee. Scarcely an independent thinker, Broomfield can be counted on to speak out for whatever foreign policies the Ford Administration chooses. After all, as ranking Republican on the Asian and Pacific Subcommittee he gave his support, whenever it was asked, to what most Americans now firmly believe was this country's disastrous war policies in Southeast Asia.

Census Data Pop. 467,540. Central city, 0%; suburban, 95%. Median family income, $13,405; families above $15,000: 41%; families below $3,000: 5%. Median years education, 12.4.

The Voters

Median voting age 41.
Employment profile White collar, 53%. Blue collar, 35%. Service, 11%. Farm, 1%.
Ethnic groups Black, 5%. Spanish, 2%. Total foreign stock, 17%. Canada, 5%; UK, Germany, 2% each; Poland, 1%.

Presidential vote

1972	Nixon (R)	122,205	(68%)
	McGovern (D)	57,144	(32%)
1968	Nixon (R)	86,378	(52%)
	Humphrey (D)	61,150	(37%)
	Wallace (AI)	17,928	(11%)

Rep. William S. Broomfield (R) Elected 1956; b. Apr. 28, 1922, Royal Oak; home, Birmingham; Mich. St. U., B.A. 1951; Presbyterian.

Career Mich. House of Reps., 1949–55, Spkr. Pro Tem, 1953; Mich. Senate, 1955–57; Mbr. U.S. Delegation to U.N., 1967.

Offices 2435 RHOB, 202-225-6135. Also 430 N. Woodward St., Birmingham 48011, 313-642-3800.

Committees

International Relations (Ranking Member). Subcommittees: Oversight.

Small Business (5th). Subcommittees: Commodities and Services; Government Procurement and International Trade.

Group Ratings

	ADA	COPE	LWV	RIPON	NFU	LCV	CFA	NAB	NSI	ACA
1974	25	22	73	71	64	33	30	80	89	43
1973	23	9	40	92	25	38	63	–	–	71
1972	6	33	44	69	33	47	0	80	100	54

Key Votes

1) Foreign Aid	FOR	6) Gov Abortn Aid	AGN	11) Pub Cong Election $	FOR
2) Busing	AGN	7) Coed Phys Ed	AGN	12) Turkish Arms Cutoff	AGN
3) ABM	ABS	8) Pov Lawyer Gag	ABS	13) Youth Camp Regs	AGN
4) B-1 Bomber	ABS	9) Pub Trans Sub	AGN	14) Strip Mine Veto	FOR
5) Nerve Gas	ABS	10) EZ Voter Regis	AGN	15) Farm Bill Veto	FOR

Election Results

1974 general:	William S. Broomfield (R)	86,846	(63%)	($34,439)
	George F. Montgomery (D)	50,924	(37%)	($6,357)
1974 primary:	William S. Broomfield (R), unopposed			
1972 general:	William S. Broomfield (R)	123,697	(71%)	($41,708)
	George F. Montgomery (D)	50,355	(29%)	($9,566)

MINNESOTA

Over the years, Minnesota has been one of the major exporters of iron ore, wheat, flour, and political talent. In just the past two decades this relatively small state has given us Hubert Humphrey, Eugene McCarthy, Walter Mondale, Orville Freeman, Warren Burger (whose judicial career was preceded by a political one), and Harry Blackmun. And there are still plenty of people who remember when Minnesota in the 1930s was producing national figures like Harold Stassen (a very serious presidential contender until 1948) and Floyd B. Olson, the talented and promising Farmer-Labor Governor who died prematurely in 1936. No other state of this size—or any size—has produced so many presidential candidates in recent years, and few have maintained congressional delegations of similar distinction. Is it simply the work of the crisp northern air, or is there something unique about the politics of this state?

To go back to the beginning, Minnesota lay originally far to the north of the nation's great paths of east-west migration; Minneapolis and St. Paul share the same latitude as Portland, Maine or Vancouver, Washington. In the mid-nineteenth century, Yankee immigrants who swelled the populations of Iowa, Nebraska, and Kansas bypassed Minnesota and left it to the Norwegians, Swedes, and Germans, who were not deterred by its vast vacant plains and ferocious winters. The nation was knit together in those days by the great east-west railroads, and the twin cities of Minneapolis and St. Paul sprang up almost at once to become the center of a great agricultural empire stretching west from Minnesota through the Dakotas into Montana and beyond. The railroad magnates of St. Paul and the giant millers of Minneapolis absolutely governed the economic life of the vast Scandinavian-German province of America.

The various rebellions against this dominance have given the politics of Minnesota—and incidentally, of North Dakota—an almost Scandinavian ambiance. As in Wisconsin and North Dakota, a strong third party developed here in the years after the Populist era and that organization, the Farmer-Labor Party, dominated Minnesota politics during the 1930s. Its great leader was Olson, and it was beaten by Harold Stassen in 1938, but the party was still at least as important as the state's historically negligible Democrats when it joined with them—Hubert Humphrey was a leading author of this union—to form the Democratic-Farmer-Labor Party (DFL) in the forties. Idealistic, staffed with dozens of talented young men and women, the DFL, led by Humphrey, swept the elections of 1948—and has dominated the state's politics ever since. Other Democratic organizations that emerged in those years or later in northern states (e.g., Michigan, Maine) have since fallen on hard times; but today the DFL is flourishing as never before. It holds all of the state's top elective posts, both U.S. Senate seats, five of the eight House seats, including a 100–24 edge in the state House—and both houses of the state legislature with no real competition in sight. In an era when the public shows no particular allegiance to political parties as such, the DFL must be counted as the nation's leading state political party organization.

One might have thought that the DFL would have been hopelessly splintered by the competition between Humphreyites and labor on the one hand and McCarthyites and middle class antiwar liberals on the other in 1968. Instead, the party seemed determined to enlist the efforts of the best of both groups, and it came out of the 1970 and 1972 elections stronger than ever. In the latter year, the DFL—despite platform planks favoring amnesty and an end to discrimination on the basis of sexual preference—for the first time won control of both houses of the legislature (which the Republicans had held thanks to a nonpartisan system of election). And that same year Minnesota gave George McGovern 47% of its vote—his best showing in the nation outside Massachusetts and the District of Columbia.

How has Minnesota become so very liberal? One might point again to the unusual ethnic composition which produced its uncharacteristic political history. Ideas of government action, indeed of state ownership, hold little terror here; nor is there any history of corrupt Democratic machine politics—the Democrats never controlled anything—for Republicans to exploit on election day. Some of the rural parts of the state—the northern woods counties and the mining country of the Mesabi Range—actually produce higher Democratic percentages than do the Twin Cities. The Republicanism of the southern counties along the Iowa border has never been overwhelming, and in statewide contests is almost negligible; the same can be said of the Republican leanings of some of the wealthier Minneapolis suburbs. Even in the largest cities, there is no significant black populations whose demands could spark a white backlash.

But perhaps too much can be made of historical and sociological explanations, especially if one ignores one of the most fundamental reasons for the DFL's successes: top quality candidates. An example—and practically any DFL officeholder could be a good example—is Senator Walter Mondale. He came by his political offices by appointment, as state Attorney General in 1960, and to the U.S. Senate in 1964 (when Humphrey resigned to become Vice President). Mondale's selection proved to be an astute one; he has proved to be an adept legislative tactician and a highly successful votegetter.

Mondale is the kind of liberal who seems to have a strong gut feeling for the sufferings of the poor, the old, and the young, and the disadvantaged generally, and he has constantly been initiating legislation which he believes will help them. His most elaborate effort was the child care plan vetoed by President Nixon, and he has also—with a seat now on the Senate Finance Committee—been a leader in the cause of progressive tax reform. In 1975 Mondale was the leading strategist for the partially successful fight to prevent filibusters; as a result of his efforts, it now takes only 60 Senators, rather than two-thirds of those present and voting, to shut off debate. One of the most refreshing aspects of this Senator was his willingness, at the beginning of that fight, to admit that he had made a tactical error—and then work to rectify it.

For a time in 1974 Mondale was considered a very serious potential presidential candidate, and he toured the country in search of support. He found some, though his name identification among the general public did not rise much, and seemed to be on the way to a very possibly successful candidacy. Then Mondale surprised most of his supporters and staff by announcing that he would not run. His explanation—that he simply didn't want to sacrifice the time with his family that would be necessary—rang true, and for a least a year Minnesota was in the unusual position of not having a presidential contender.

For Hubert Humphrey, now the state's junior Senator, seemed adamant in his desire not to be a candidate for the Presidency in 1976 even after Mondale left the race. Humphrey knows the rigors of running better than anyone around. He entered the primaries in 1960, and lost to John Kennedy in Wisconsin and West Virginia. In 1964, he stood by as Lyndon Johnson teased him and others with the Vice Presidency, and then finally got it; but it turned out to be less than an useful prize, for Humphrey was tarred with the Vietnam war although he had virtually no part in setting the policies that produced it. His run for the Presidency in 1968 is probably fresh enough in most readers' memories not to need recapping here; after his narrow defeat, he went back to Minnesota and won the Senate seat Eugene McCarthy vacated in 1970. Then, in 1972, Humphrey plunged into the primaries again. With George McGovern, he eliminated the supposed frontrunner, Edmund Muskie, and then in California Humphrey slugged it out with the South Dakotan who was once his next door neighbor in suburban Maryland. That race inflicted wounds on both from which they have not yet recovered. When asked before the primary whether he would challenge its winner-take-all feature if he lost, Humphrey said no; then when he lost, narrowly, he turned around and did exactly that. He has no stomach for the primary route in 1976, but he will be available if the convention wants him—and stranger things have happened.

When Humphrey left the Senate to become Vice President in 1964, he was Majority Whip and the body's dominant figure. When he returned as a freshman in 1971, he had no leadership position and rather lackluster committee assignments. Nevertheless, Humphrey is still making news—and policy—today. He is now Chairman of the Joint Economic Committee and was a major advocate of the progressive tax cut in 1975; he is on Foreign Relations, and is one of those Senators Henry Kissinger consults when he wants to know what is saleable on the Hill; he is a member of the Agriculture Committee, and after all these years remains a staunch backer of the family farmer. But of course Humphrey in no way feels limited by the jurisdiction on his committee seats; he feels free, as always, to speak out on any issue that he feels strongly about—indeed, on any he is asked about.

Humphrey turns 65 in 1976 when, barring a convention draft, he will seek his fifth Senate term. He has been a figure of national note since 1948, when he delivered that memorable speech in the floor that turned the Democratic convention around and pushed through a liberal civil rights plank. No other political figure of such stature has proved so durable, not at least since Richard Nixon left for San Clemente, and few have proved as productive—or as ebullient. The years show on Humphrey a little now, and one senses a yearning for what might have been; but his career is far from over, and who knows where it might still lead him—or us.

Minnesota's Governor is another example of the DFL's facility for picking talented young candidates. In 1970 Wendell Anderson was an unknown state Senator, one of several candidates going across the state seeking the endorsement of the DFL state convention. Anderson got it and, in the seldom broken Minnesota tradition, was unopposed in the primary election. Elected by a 54–46 margin over the Republican Attorney General, Anderson compiled a popular record: no-fault auto insurance, a minimum wage law, a family farm act, campaign finance reform. But he also brought an easygoing style which was nicely epitomized by *Time* magazine's glowing cover story (1973) on him and Minnesota. Anderson was surly and uncommunicative with the press, but even that didn't seem to hurt him, and when 1974 came around no serious Republican candidate filed against him. The result was an unprecedented 65% of the vote for the incumbent, with every indication that he can win in similar fashion again and again. Anderson has sometimes been mentioned as a presidential candidate, but that seems a bit premature; he has not been as impressive as, say, Mondale in his national public appearances.

Minnesota's congressional delegation is as talented as its statewide officials. Minneapolis Congressman Donald Fraser has emerged as one of the leading liberal Democratic spokesmen on foreign affairs in the House, and the 7th district's Bob Bergland has significant impact on agricultural policy. There is even a Republican of note here, the 1st district's Albert Quie, who is a leading member of the House Education and Labor Committee.

Census Data   Pop. 3,805,069; 1.88% of U.S. total, 19th largest; Central city, 24%; suburban, 33%. Median family income, $9,928; 16th highest; families above $15,000: 20%; families below $3,000: 9%.   Median years education, 12.2.

1974 Share of Federal Tax Burden $4,820,675,000; 1.80% of U.S. total, 19th largest.

1974 Share of Federal Outlays $4,033,619,000; 1.49% of U.S. total, 22d largest.   Per capita federal spending, $1060.

DOD	$545,808,000	31st (0.80%)	HEW	$1,692,930,000	17th (1.36%)
AEC	$3,680,000	25th (0.12%)	HUD	$21,383,000	17th (2.19%)
NASA	$10,122,000	18th (0.34%)	VA	$279,590,000	16th (2.04%)
DOT	$143,441,000	24th (1.69%)	EPA	$40,875,000	22d (1.30%)
DOC	$14,039,000	20th (0.87%)	RevS	$119,575,000	18th (1.97%)
DOI	$31,616,000	22d (1.28%)	Int.	$198,378,000	14th (0.96%)
USDA	$430,049,000	6th (3.45%)	Other	$502,133,000	

Economic Base   Agriculture, notably cattle, dairy products, corn and hogs; finance, insurance and real estate; machinery, especially electronic computing equipment; food and kindred products, especially meat products; printing and publishing, especially commercial printing; electrical equipment and supplies; fabricated metal products, especially fabricated structural metal products.

Political Line-up   Governor, Wendell R. Anderson (DFL). Senators, Walter F. Mondale (DFL) and Hubert H. Humphrey (DFL). Representatives, 8 (5 DFL and 3 R). State Senate (38 DFL, 27 R, 1 Ind., and 1 vac.); State House (103 DFL and 31 R).

The Voters

Registration   1,922,462 Total. No party registration.
Median voting age 43.
Employment profile   White collar, 49%. Blue collar, 31%. Service, 13%. Farm, 7%.
Ethnic groups   Total foreign stock, 19%. Germany, 4%; Sweden, Norway, 3%; Canada, 2%.

Presidential vote

1972	Nixon (R)	....	898,269	(53%)
	McGovern (D)	....	802,346	(47%)
1968	Nixon (R)	....	658,643	(42%)
	Humphrey (D)	....	857,738	(54%)
	Wallace (AI)	....	68,931	(4%)

Sen. Walter F. Mondale (DFL) Appointed Dec. 30, 1964, elected 1966, seat up 1978; b. Jan. 5, 1928, Ceylon; home, Afton; Macalester Col., U. of Minn., B.A. 1951, LL.B. 1956.

Career Army, 1951–53; Practicing atty., 1956–60; Atty. Gen. of Minn., 1960–64.

Offices 443 RSOB, 202-224-5641. Also 172 Fed. Courts Bldg., 110 S. 4th St., Minneapolis 55401, 612-725-2041.

Committees

Budget (4th).

Finance (7th). Subcommittees: Foundations; Health; International Trade; Social Security Financing (Chairman).

Labor and Public Welfare (6th). Subcommittees: Alcoholism and Narcotics; Children and Youth (Chairman); Education; Employment, Poverty, and Migratory Labor; The Handicapped; Health; Labor; Special Subcommittee on Arts and Humanities; Special Subcommittee on National Science Foundation.

Select Committee on Intelligence Operations (4th).

Group Ratings

	ADA	COPE	LWV	RIPON	NFU	LCV	CFA	NAB	NSI	ACA
1974	100	82	100	65	100	88	88	40	0	0
1973	95	90	100	64	100	–	92	–	–	4
1972	95	90	100	76	100	92	100	0	0	0

Key Votes

1) No-Knock	AGN	8) Gov Abortn Aid	FOR	15) Consumer Prot Agy	FOR
2) Busing	FOR	9) Cut Mil Brass	FOR	16) Forced Psych Tests	FOR
3) No Fault	FOR	10) Gov Limousine	AGN	17) Fed Campaign Subs	FOR
4) F-111	ABS	11) RR Featherbed	FOR	18) Rhod Chrome Ban	FOR
5) Death Penalty	ABS	12) Handgun License	ABS	19) Open Legis Meetings	FOR
6) Foreign Aid	FOR	13) Less Troop Abrd	FOR	20) Strikers Food Stmps	FOR
7) Filibuster	AGN	14) Resume Turk Aid	ABS	21) Gov Info Disclosure	FOR

Election Results

1972 general:	Walter F. Mondale (DFL)	....	981,320	(57%)	($538,532)
	Phil Hansen (R)	....	742,121	(43%)	($304,750)
1972 primary:	Walter F. Mondale (DFL)	....	230,679	(90%)	
	Three others (DFL)	....	25,962	(10%)	

Sen. Hubert H. Humphrey (DFL) Elected 1970, seat up 1976; b. May 27, 1911, Wallace, S.D.; home, Waverly; Denver Col. of Pharmacy, 1932–33, U. of Minn., A.B. 1939, La. St. U., M.A. 1940, U. of Minn., 1940–41; Protestant.

Career Instructor, U. of Minn., 1940–41; Head of Minn. Branch of War Production Admin., 1941–42; Asst. Regional Dir., War Manpower Progress Comm., 1943; Prof., Army Air Force Training Program, Macalester Col., 1943–44; Mayor of Minneapolis, 1945–49; Co-Founder, Amers. for Dem. Action, 1947; U.S. Senate, 1949–64, Maj. Whip, 1961–64; Vice President of the United States, 1965–69; Prof., U. of Minn. and Macalester Col., 1969–70.

Offices 232 RSOB, 202-224-3244. Also 462 Fed. Courts Bldg., 110 S. 4th St., Minneapolis 55401, 612-725-2632.

Committees

Agriculture and Forestry (5th). Sucommittes: Agricultural Credit and Rural Electrification; Agriculture Production, Marketing, and Stabilization of Prices; Foreign Agricultural Policy (Chairman); Rural Development.

Foreign Relations (8th). Subcommittees: African Affairs; Arms Control, International Organizations and Security Agreements; Foreign Assistance and Economic Policy (Chairman); Near Eastern and South Asian Affairs; Western Hemisphere Affairs.

Joint Economic Committee (Chairman). Subcommittees: Consumer Economics (Chairman); Economic Growth; International Economics; Priorities and Economy in Government; Urban Affairs.

Group Ratings

	ADA	COPE	LWV	RIPON	NFU	LCV	CFA	NAB	NSI	ACA
1974	85	80	100	58	100	75	88	45	0	0
1973	85	90	90	60	100	–	82	–	–	0
1972	60	100	100	75	100	73	100	17	11	0

Key Votes

1) No-Knock	AGN	8) Gov Abortn Aid	FOR	15) Consumer Prot Agy	FOR
2) Busing	FOR	9) Cut Mil Brass	FOR	16) Forced Psych Tests	FOR
3) No Fault	FOR	10) Gov Limousine	AGN	17) Fed Campaign Subs	FOR
4) F-111	AGN	11) RR Featherbed	FOR	18) Rhod Chrome Ban	FOR
5) Death Penalty	AGN	12) Handgun License	FOR	19) Open Legis Meetings	FOR
6) Foreign Aid	FOR	13) Less Troop Abrd	FOR	20) Strikers Food Stmps	FOR
7) Filibuster	ABS	14) Resume Turk Aid	ABS	21) Gov Info Disclosure	FOR

Election Results

1970 general:	Hubert H. Humphrey (DFL)	788,256	(58%)
	Clark MacGregor (R)	568,025	(42%)
1970 primary:	Hubert H. Humphrey (DFL)	388,705	(81%)
	Earl D. Craig, Jr. (DFL)	88,709	(19%)

Gov. Wendell R. Anderson (DFL) Elected 1970, term expires Jan. 1979; b. Feb. 1, 1933, St. Paul; U. of Minn., B.A. 1954, LL.B. 1960.

Career Army, 1956–57; Minn. House of Reps., 1959–63; Minn. Senate, 1963–71; Practicing atty., 1960–70.

Offices State Capitol, St. Paul 55155, 612-296-3391.

Election Results

1974 general:	Wendell (Wendy) Anderson (DFL)	786,787	(65%)
	John W. Johnson (R)	367,722	(30%)
	James G. (Jim) Miles (Ind.)	60,150	(5%)
1974 primary:	Wendell (Wendy) Anderson (DFL)	254,671	(78%)
	Tom McDonald (DFL)	70,871	(22%)
1970 general:	Wendell (Wendy) Anderson (DFL)	737,921	(54%)
	Douglas M. Head (R)	621,780	(46%)

◆ ◆ ◆ ◆

FIRST DISTRICT

The 1st congressional district of Minnesota, the southeast corner of the state, is a region of farms, grain elevator towns, and small, pleasant cities. This is the Minnesota district with the most in common with the rest of the rural Midwest farther south; in its ethnic and political traditions, it is much like Iowa—that is, WASPier and at least until 1974, more Republican than Minnesota as a whole. The district's largest city, Rochester (pop. 53,000), is the home of the Mayo Clinic and until a few years ago of its onetime counsel and now Supreme Court Justice, Harry Blackmun. Rochester is a comparatively wealthy, idyllic, white-collar town; Olmsted County, of which it is a part, is the largest Minnesota county that failed to appear in the DFL column for either Hubert Humphrey in 1970 or Walter Mondale in 1972 (though like every county in the state it went for Governor Wendell Anderson in 1974).

The only discordant political notes in the 1st come from suburban Dakota County, across the Mississippi River from St. Paul, part of which was added to the district to meet the equal population standard. These are working-class suburbs, where newly laid out subdivisions thin out into Minnesota farmland. But the additional DFL votes here posed no political problem for Congressman Albert Quie, the most politically safe Republican in the entire state.

Quie came by that status by virtue of hard work—and by ignoring some of the standard political rules. First elected in a 1958 special election, he gave up early in his congressional career a seat on the Agriculture Committee—a plus, one would have thought, for any Congressman from this part of Minnesota. He moved instead to the Education and Labor Committee, on which he is now the ranking Republican member. On most educational and social issues Quie's position seems to lie somewhere between those of the committee's dominant liberal Democrats and its minority of Republican conservatives. During the spate of Great Society legislation coming out of the Johnson Administration, House Republicans under Gerald Ford promised a series of alternatives to Democratic proposals; but Quie and other Republicans on Education and Labor were the only ones who delivered many. In the years that followed, Quie was often able to form alliances with conservatively-inclined Democrats on the committee, and on some educational issues was able to put together a majority.

That is no longer possible, at least in the 94th Congress; there are too many liberal Democrats, enough to pass whatever they want. But Quie still can play an important legislative role by acting, as he has in the past, as an intermediary between a veto-bound Republican administration and a solidly liberal Democratic committee; he has on occasion put together compromises which produced solid legislative results. Undoubtedly, Quie's reputation for moderation, plus hard work on constituency matters, helps him win reelection easily. In the Democratic year of 1974, he still won with 63% of the vote.

Census Data Pop. 473,918. Central city, 11%; suburban, 43%. Median family income, $10,272; families above $15,000: 20%; families below $3,000: 8%. Median years education, 12.3.

The Voters

Median voting age 42.
Employment profile White collar, 46%. Blue collar, 30%. Service, 15%. Farm, 9%.
Ethnic groups Total foreign stock, 14%. Germany, 4%; Norway, 2%; Sweden, Canada, 1% each.

Presidential vote

1972	Nixon (R)	122,634	(60%)
	McGovern (D)	82,155	(40%)
1968	Nixon (R)	87,825	(47%)
	Humphrey (D)	91,41549	
	Wallace (AI)	7,645	(4%)

Rep. Albert H. Quie (R) Elected Feb. 18, 1958; b. Sept. 18, 1923, near Dennison; home, Dennison; St. Olaf Col., B.A. 1950; Lutheran.

Career Navy, WWII; Dairy Farmer; Minn. Senate, 1954–58.

Offices 2182 RHOB, 202-225-2271. Also 436 1st. Natl. Bank Bldg., Rochester 55901, 507-725-3680.

Committees

Education and Labor (Ranking Member). Subcommittees: Elementary, Secondary and Vocational Education.

Standards of Official Conduct (4th).

Group Ratings

	ADA	COPE	LWV	RIPON	NFU	LCV	CFA	NAB	NSI	ACA
1974	59	40	100	75	67	44	17	58	88	23
1973	25	0	42	60	55	53	25	–	–	54
1972	13	18	67	86	57	67	0	100	90	65

Key Votes

1) Foreign Aid	FOR	6) Gov Abortn Aid	AGN	11) Pub Cong Election $	FOR
2) Busing	FOR	7) Coed Phys Ed	AGN	12) Turkish Arms Cutoff	AGN
3) ABM	AGN	8) Pov Lawyer Gag	FOR	13) Youth Camp Regs	FOR
4) B-1 Bomber	AGN	9) Pub Trans Sub	AGN	14) Strip Mine Veto	AGN
5) Nerve Gas	AGN	10) EZ Voter Regis	AGN	15) Farm Bill Veto	AGN

Election Results

1974 general:				
	Albert H. Quie (R)	95,138	(63%)	($67,101)
	Ulric Scott (DFL)	56,868	(37%)	($54,539)
1974 primary:	Albert H. Quie (R), unopposed			
1972 general:	Albert H. Quie (R)	142,698	(71%)	($32,586)
	Charles S. Thompson (DFL)	59,106	(29%)	($438)

◆ ◆ ◆ ◆ ◆

SECOND DISTRICT

South central Minnesota, most of which is included in the state's 2d congressional district, is the most Republican part of this Democratic state. A majority of the people of the 2d live in the valley of the Minnesota River; the towns here—New Ulm and Mankato and St. Peter—are old and their political allegiances usually deeply-rooted and Republican. To the southeast, the district also takes in the small industrial and usually Democratic city of Austin, near the Iowa border; and the 2d also extends well into the Twin Cities metropolitan area to take in the heavily Republican high-income territory around Lake Minnetonka and a politically marginal section of Dakota County, south of St. Paul.

The Democratic tide of 1974 was the acid test of the strength of the 2d district's Republican tradition, and the tradition won. After 16 years in the House, much of it spent attending to the affairs of the District of Columbia, Republican Congressman Ancher Nelsen was retiring. He was 70 years old, and had won with a surprisingly low 57% of the vote in 1972. The Republican who won the 1974 nomination, 30-year-old Thomas Hagedorn, was one of the most conservative members of the Minnesota House, and the DFL Candidate, Robert Riggs, was hoping for an upset.

But it was not to be. Riggs made some gains over previous showings and carried some counties in the Minneapolis media market. But Hagedorn actually ran better than Nelsen had, not only in his home county of Watonwan, but also in Mankato and St. Peter. Still, some 45% of Hagedorn's margin was in the two small counties he had represented in the legislature, and his overall victory margin was 53–47. But given the Democratic sweep of the year—and given the seat on the Agriculture Committee Hagedorn won—it seems likely that this Minnesota Republican will be around for some time.

Census Data Pop. 476,647. Central city, 0%; suburban, 19%. Median family income, $9,703; families above $15,000: 19%; families below $3,000: 9%. Median years education, 12.2.

The Voters

Median voting age 43.
Employment profile White collar, 43%. Blue collar, 33%. Service, 12%. Farm, 12%.
Ethnic groups Total foreign stock, 14%. Germany, 5%; Norway, 2%; Sweden, 1%.

Presidential vote

1972	Nixon (R)	129,432	(59%)
	McGovern (D)	88,633	(41%)
1968	Nixon (R)	98,724	(50%)
	Humphrey (D)	90,522	(46%)
	Wallace (AI)	7,917	(4%)

Rep. Tom Hagedorn (R) Elected 1974; b. Nov. 27, 1943, Blue Earth; home, Truman; Lutheran.

Career Farmer; Minn. House of Reps., 1970–74.

Offices 325 CHOB, 202-225-2472.

Committees

Agriculture (13th). Subcommittees: Cotton; Dairy and Poultry; Livestock and Grains.

Public Works and Transportation (12th). Subcommittees: Public Buildings and Grounds; Surface Transportation; Water Resources.

Group Ratings: Newly Elected

Key Votes

1) Foreign Aid	AGN	6) Gov Abortn Aid	NE	11) Pub Cong Election $	NE
2) Busing	NE	7) Coed Phys Ed	AGN	12) Turkish Arms Cutoff	NE
3) ABM	NE	8) Pov Lawyer Gag	NE	13) Youth Camp Regs	AGN
4) B-1 Bomber	FOR	9) Pub Trans Sub	NE	14) Strip Mine Veto	FOR
5) Nerve Gas	NE	10) EZ Voter Regis	NE	15) Farm Bill Veto	AGN

Election Results

1974 general:	Tom Hagedorn (R)	88,071	(53%)	($148,833)
	Steve Babcock (DFL)	77,780	(47%)	($142,812)
1974 primary:	Tom Hagedorn (R)	22,577	(74%)	
	Lester Anderson (R)	7,807	(26%)	

◆ ◆ ◆ ◆ ◆

THIRD DISTRICT

The Minneapolis suburbs have for years been the fastest growing part of Minnesota. The gravity of metropolitan development seems to be pulling people west from the city, where the white collar suburbs have traditionally been located; and much of the force behind the development has come from the white collar industries of the area. Companies like Honeywell, 3M, General Mills, Control Data, and Investors Diversified Services are based in the Twin Cities, and have provided the largest share of the growth in jobs here in recent years. And the people who hold the jobs have been filling up what used to be the wheatfields and empty lakefronts west of Minneapolis.

Most of this suburban growth has occurred in a string of cities and townships west and southwest of Minneapolis; these, along with 18,000 residents of the city itself, make up Minnesota's 3d congressional district. Like most suburban districts, the 3d is not a sociological monolith. At the northern edge of the district, along the Mississippi as it flows into Minneapolis, are blue collar suburbs like Brooklyn Park (pop. 26,000) and Brooklyn Center (35,000). At the far southern end is aging, middle income Richfield (47,000) and Bloomington (82,000), the latter now the state's fourth largest city and the site of the stadium where the Twins and Vikings play. Lying in the middle of the district are high income WASP retreats like Plymouth, Golden Valley, and Minnetonka, along with Edina (44,000), perhaps the state's highest income and most Republican town. Just north of Edina is the predominantly Jewish suburb of St. Louis Park (49,000).

Despite the wealth of the district—it has by far the highest median income of any Minnesota seat—it is by no means heavily Republican; by most standards, in most states, it would be considered marginal. However, since 1960 it has elected only Republican Congressmen. For ten years the 3d elected Clark MacGregor, then one of the most competent Republicans in the House; in 1970, he was the sacrificial lamb candidate against Hubert Humphrey, for which he was rewarded with top Nixon Administration posts—first head lobbyist and then director of CREEP. MacGregor took the latter job only after he was given assurances that CREEP was not involved in the Watergate burglary. But he seems not to have investigated very thoroughly, and perhaps he suspected more than he let on; immediately after the election, he left the Nixon crowd to become a well-paid Washington lobbyist.

When MacGregor ran for the Senate in 1970, there was an exceedingly close race to succeed him. The winner, by a 51–49 margin, was state Representative Bill Frenzel, a moderate-to-liberal Republican, who has held the seat ever since. Frenzel is a voluble, sometimes outspoken man who has been most active in the area of campaign finance reform. He is impressive enough to have managed to win with a solid 60% in 1974 despite the fact that he admitted he had been more than a year late in filling his 1972 income tax return. There has been a little talk that Frenzel might decide to run against Hubert Humphrey in 1976. That would probably have the same effect as it did when his predecessor in the House did the same thing six years before: reelection for Humphrey, and a close race in the 3d district.

Census Data Pop. 472,662. Central city, 4%; suburban, 96%. Median family income, $13,248; families above $15,000: 38%; families below $3,000: 3%. Median years education, 12.7.

The Voters

Median voting age 39.
Employment profile White collar, 64%. Blue collar, 26%. Service, 10%. Farm, –%.
Ethnic groups Total foreign stock, 16%. Sweden, 3%; Norway, Germany, Canada, 2% each.

Presidential vote

1972	Nixon (R)	129,587	(59%)
	McGovern (D)	89,281	(41%)

1968	Nixon (R)	89,127	(46%)
	Humphrey (D)	98,643	(51%)
	Wallace (AI)	6,572	(3%)

Rep. Bill Frenzel (R) Elected 1970; b. July 31, 1928, St. Paul; home, Golden Valley; Dartmouth Col., B.A. 1950, M.B.A. 1951.

Career Navy, Korea; Pres., Minn. Terminal Warehouse Co., Minn. House of Reps., 1962–70.

Offices 1026 LHOB, 202-225-2871. Also 120 Fed. Bldg., 110 S. 4th St., Minneapolis 55401, 612-725-2173.

Committees

Ways and Means (9th). Subcommittees: Trade; Unemployment Compensation.

Group Ratings

	ADA	COPE	LWV	RIPON	NFU	LCV	CFA	NAB	NSI	ACA
1974	64	56	83	100	82	71	22	70	25	17
1973	54	9	73	100	47	84	50	–	–	44
1972	63	18	92	100	57	79	100	90	50	32

Key Votes

1) Foreign Aid	FOR	6) Gov Abortn Aid	AGN	11) Pub Cong Election $	AGN
2) Busing	FOR	7) Coed Phys Ed	FOR	12) Turkish Arms Cutoff	FOR
3) ABM	AGN	8) Pov Lawyer Gag	AGN	13) Youth Camp Regs	AGN
4) B-1 Bomber	AGN	9) Pub Trans Sub	AGN	14) Strip Mine Veto	AGN
5) Nerve Gas	AGN	10) EZ Voter Regis	FOR	15) Farm Bill Veto	FOR

Election Results

1974 general:	Bill Frenzel (R)	83,325	(60%)	($104,815)
	Bob Riggs (D)	54,630	(40%)	($33,486)
1974 primary:	Bill Frenzel (R), unopposed			
1972 general:	Bill Frenzel (R)	132,638	(63%)	($87,533)
	Jim Bell (DFL)	66,070	(31%)	($38,775)
	Donald Wright (Minnesota Taxpayers Party)	12,234	(6%)	(NA)

◆ ◆ ◆ ◆ ◆

FOURTH DISTRICT

St. Paul, the smaller of Minnesota's Twin Cities, is an old river town with a history something like that of St. Louis, hundreds of miles farther down on the Mississippi. Settled before Minneapolis, St. Paul was for some years the larger of the two as well as the state capital. While Minneapolis was attracting Swedes and WASPs, St. Paul got more Irish and German Catholics; while Minneapolis was becoming what it remains today, the nation's largest grain-milling center, St. Paul's economic role was as a transportation hub, a railroad center and river port. Long before the Democratic-Farmer-Labor Party was formed, St. Paul was one of the few places in Minnesota which usually voted Democratic; and through all the changes that have occurred since, the city and its suburbs have remained heavily Democratic (or DFL) to this day.

In these days when the one-person-one-vote rule requires intricately drawn congressional district borders, the 4th district of Minnesota is the closest thing in the nation to a district which is totally coincident with a single county: it includes all but the tiniest smidgin of St. Paul's Ramsey County. A solidly Democratic district, the 4th was represented for 10 years (1949–59) by Eugene McCarthy. In those days, McCarthy was not one to dabble in poetry; he was a team player, one of the founders of the liberal Democratic Study Group which dominates the House today, and also one who embraced rather than scorned all the often tiresome jobs politicians feel they must perform to survive.

McCarthy was happy with the pace of life in the House, attentive to his duties as a member of the Ways and Means Committee and adept at advancing liberal causes in what was then a profoundly conservative institution. But he ran for the Senate in 1958, perhaps with an eye to an eventual presidential candidacy, thus opening up the 4th district. His successor and the Congressman today is a rather different sort: Joseph Karth, a former union negotiator and state legislator. For many years Karth was a quiet, hard working member of the Science and Merchant Marine Committees; at the beginning of the 93d Congress, he joined Ways and Means, then still dominated by Wilbur Mills. Karth was one of the younger members who developed his own independent staff on Ways and Means matters, and he was less likely to follow Mills' counsel than that of organized labor. In 1966—the best year Republicans have had in Minnesota since the era of the other McCarthy—Karth was held to only 53% of the vote, but he wins now regularly with more than 70%, and should remain in the House, and on Ways and Means, for many more terms.

Census Data Pop. 473,902. Central city, 65%; suburban, 35%. Median family income, $11,306; families above $15,000: 26%; families below $3,000: 6%. Median years education, 12.4.

The Voters

Median voting age 41.
Employment profile White collar, 56%. Blue collar, 31%. Service, 13%. Farm, –%.
Ethnic groups Black, 2%. Total foreign stock, 19%. Germany, 3%; Sweden, Canada, 2% each; Norway, 1%.

Presidential vote

1972	Nixon (R)	95,201	(47%)
	McGovern (D)	107,924	(53%)
1968	Nixon (R)	63,721	(33%)
	Humphrey (D)	122,174	(63%)
	Wallace (AI)	8,517	(4%)

Rep. Joseph E. Karth (DFL) Elected 1958; b. Aug. 26, 1922, New Brighton; home, St. Paul; U. of Neb.; Presbyterian.

Career Army, WWII; 3M Corp.; Internatl. Rep., Oil, Chemical and Atomic Workers, AFL-CIO, 1947–58; Minn. House of Reps., 1950–58.

Offices 2408 RHOB, 202-225-6631. Also 544 Fed. Ofc. Bldg. and Courthouse, St. Paul 55101, 612-725-7869.

Committees

Ways and Means (13th). Subcommittees: Public Assistance; Social Security; Trade.

Group Ratings

	ADA	COPE	LWV	RIPON	NFU	LCV	CFA	NAB	NSI	ACA
1974	85	90	73	46	100	80	92	45	40	7
1973	78	91	100	73	94	94	100	–	–	4
1972	88	89	100	73	86	68	50	0	0	0

Key Votes

1) Foreign Aid	AGN	6) Gov Abortn Aid	ABS	11) Pub Cong Election $	FOR
2) Busing	FOR	7) Coed Phys Ed	FOR	12) Turkish Arms Cutoff	FOR
3) ABM	AGN	8) Pov Lawyer Gag	AGN	13) Youth Camp Regs	FOR
4) B-1 Bomber	AGN	9) Pub Trans Sub	FOR	14) Strip Mine Veto	AGN
5) Nerve Gas	AGN	10) EZ Voter Regis	FOR	15) Farm Bill Veto	AGN

Election Results

1974 general:	Joseph E. Karth (DFL)	95,437	(76%)	($58,551)
	Joseph A. Rheinberger (R)	30,083	(24%)	($5,740)
1974 primary:	Joseph E. Karth (DFL), unopposed			
1972 general:	Joseph E. Karth (DFL)	138,292	(72%)	($50,094)
	Steve Thompson (R)	52,786	(28%)	($3,926)

◆ ◆ ◆ ◆ ◆

FIFTH DISTRICT

The 5th congressional district of Minnesota is virtually all the city of Minneapolis and a couple of blue collar suburbs in Anoka County to the north. Minneapolis is known as the nation's leading grain milling center, and for its sophisticated white collar firms as well (see Third District). But the great business interests of Minneapolis do not account for the city's distinctive political tradition. This comes instead from the Swedish and other Scandinavian immigrants who first came here in the 1880s. They were probably attracted to Minnesota for two reasons: first, from the resemblance of the American north country, with its hilly countryside, thousands of glacier-carved lakes, and long cold winters, to the Scandinavia they had known; and second because there were opportunities here which native stock Americans, eager to head straight west out of Illinois and Missouri, failed to pursue. The Scandinavians have given Minneapolis a liberal political tradition, hospitable in their time to the Harold Stassens of the Republican Party as well as to the Hubert Humphreys of the DFL.

Against this tradition is the more recent reality: Minneapolis faces many of the problems of our central cities. Its older residents are dying out, their children having left for the suburbs; it has a disproportionate amount of poor residents, and a tax base which seems insufficient for supporting the level of services people become accustomed to in large cities. Despite the fact that there is a very small (4%) black population here, a law-and-order policeman named Charles Stenvig managed to get elected Mayor in 1969. Stenvig was finally beaten by the current DFL Mayor, Al Hofstede, in 1973, but the very fact that he was elected shows that there is a simmering discontent with life in the central city which one is unlikely to find in the more prosperous Twin Cities suburbs.

The Congressman from the 5th district is Donald Fraser, who first won in 1962 by beating incumbent Walter Judd, the 1960 Republican national convention keynoter and long the unofficial head of the China Lobby. Over the years, Fraser has devoted a lot of time to extracurricular activities. He was Chairman of the Democratic Study Group in the 91st Congress (1969–71). In 1971 and 1972, he led the Democratic Party's commission on reforming delegate selection; he was also a largely unsuccessful advocate of a formal party structure, with real power, on the European model. In 1973, he was elected head of Americans for Democratic Action.

But during all that time Fraser had been active legislatively, too. He was one of the original home rule backers on the District of Columbia Committee and saw that measure pass in 1973. And he is one of the leading dovish members of the sometimes hawkish International Affairs Committee. In that capacity, Fraser was lobbied heavily in 1975 when the Ford Administration wanted more military aid to Cambodia and South Vietnam; the Minnesotan surprised some of his friends by coming out for limited amounts of aid designed to produce a negotiated settlement. In just about any other state, Fraser would have long since been considered prime senatorial material; in talent-rich Minnesota, he has not received a call to higher office. His seat in the House is utterly safe.

Census Data Pop. 479,280. Central city, 87%; suburban, 13%. Median family income, $10,323; families above $15,000: 22%; families below $3,000: 8%. Median years education, 12.3.

The Voters

Median voting age 42.
Employment profile White collar, 55%. Blue collar, 30%. Service, 15%. Farm, –%.
Ethnic groups Black, 4%. Total foreign stock, 23%. Sweden, 5%; Norway, 4%; Germany, 3%; Canada, 2%; Poland, 1%.

Presidential vote

1972	Nixon (R)	92,951	(44%)
	McGovern (D)	116,090	(56%)
1968	Nixon (R)	75,684	(36%)
	Humphrey (D)	123,092	(59%)
	Wallace (AI)	9,161	(4%)

Rep. Donald M. Fraser (DFL) Elected 1962; b. Feb. 20, 1924, Minneapolis; home, Minneapolis; U. of Minn., B.A. 1944, LL.B. 1948.

Career Navy, WWII; Practicing atty., 1948–62; Minn. Senate, 1954-62; Chm., Natl. Dem. Party Comm. on Party Structure and Delegate Selection (McGovern Commission), 1971–72; Natl. Chm., Amers. for Dem. Action, 1973–74.

Offices 1111 LHOB, 202-225-4755. Also 180 Fed. Courts Bldg., 110 S. 4th St., Minneapolis 55401, 612-725-2081.

Committees

District of Columbia (2d). Subcommittees: Government Operations; The Bicentennial, the Environment, and the International Community.

International Relations (8th). Subcommittees: International Organizations (Chairman); International Trade and Commerce.

Group Ratings

	ADA	COPE	LWV	RIPON	NFU	LCV	CFA	NAB	NSI	ACA
1974	100	100	100	75	92	93	100	20	10	0
1973	100	90	100	93	95	89	100	–	–	4
1972	94	90	100	75	100	80	100	9	0	5

Key Votes

1) Foreign Aid	FOR	6) Gov Abortn Aid	FOR	11) Pub Cong Election $	FOR
2) Busing	FOR	7) Coed Phys Ed	ABS	12) Turkish Arms Cutoff	FOR
3) ABM	AGN	8) Pov Lawyer Gag	AGN	13) Youth Camp Regs	ABS
4) B-1 Bomber	AGN	9) Pub Trans Sub	FOR	14) Strip Mine Veto	AGN
5) Nerve Gas	AGN	10) EZ Voter Regis	FOR	15) Farm Bill Veto	AGN

Election Results

1974 general:	Donald M. Fraser (DFL)	90,012	(75%)	($63,397)
	Phil Ratté (R)	30,146	(25%)	($13,340)
1974 primary:	Donald M. Fraser (DFL), unopposed			
1972 general:	Donald M. Fraser (DFL)	135,108	(66%)	($93,628)
	Allan Davisson (R)	50,014	(24%)	($9,399)
	Norm Selby (Minnesota Taxpayers Party)	15,845	(8%)	(NA)
	William E. Peterson (SW)	4,233	(2%)	(NA)

◆ ◆ ◆ ◆

SIXTH DISTRICT

The 6th congressional district of Minnesota is farm country, the beginnings of the great wheat fields that sweep across Minnesota into the Dakotas and Montana. Long freight trains move through the landscape, on tracks first laid out by empire builders like James J. Hill of the Great Northern Railway. The groaning diesels pull cars west to the Pacific or east to St. Paul and Chicago; engines and cars whiz through dozens of little crossroads towns, each with its grain elevator and antique depot. The voting patterns of the 6th, the state's most marginal district, reflect the ethnic groups Hill and other railroad barons settled in this part of Minnesota: Republican Norwegians and WASPs, Democratic Swedes, and ticket-switching German Catholics.

The German population here is most heavily concentrated in Stearns County, which contains St. Cloud (pop. 39,000) and Sauk Centre (3,000), the boyhood home of Sinclair Lewis and the setting for his *Main Street.* Up until the outbreak of World War I, the Germans who settled here and elsewhere were regarded as the nation's "best" immigrants: thrifty and hardworking, just like the old Yankee stock. But on the outbreak of war with the Kaiser, these German-Americans found themselves at odds with the national mood. The teaching of their language was prohibited in many states; sauerkraut became liberty cabbage; and their entire heritage came to be regarded as subversive.

Not surprisingly, people here were very much against the idea of going to war with Germany in 1917, and twenty years later they again dreaded such a war. This was the part of Minnesota which sent the progressive, antiwar Charles A. Lindberg, Sr., to Congress during the First World War, and which produced his son, the aviator who became one of the popular leaders in the fight to keep the United States out of the Second. As Samuel Lubell has pointed out, Stearns County and places like it were the heart of isolationist sentiment in this country, switching wildly from one party to the other in an effort to prevent future wars with Germany or to avenge past ones.

Stearns County continues to play a pivotal role in the politics of the 6th district, although its German heritage is no longer so important. Contests here have been unusually close: no candidate in the past fifteen years has won more than 56% of the vote. For eight years, Republican John Zwach held the seat, but in 1972 Stearns County voted against him as the incumbent beat 28-year-old state legislator Richard Nolan by only a 51–49 margin; finishing out 40 years as a legislator, Zwach retired in 1974.

Nolan, who had decided to run again immediately after his 1972 loss, never stopped campaigning. His hard work deterred Eugene McCarthy, who grew up in the district, from making a run here; and his grueling schedule of canvassing in every town of any size in the district paid handsome dividends in 1974. His opponent that year was Jon Grunseth, a former aide to Zwach, who was even younger than Nolan; he proved to be an attractive candidate. But the DFL's hard work made the difference, and Nolan won by a 55–45 margin. In this marginal district, it is risky to make any predictions, but Nolan's margin seems large enough to indicate many future victories, and Minnesota Republicans may well be so dispirited as to fail to field any significant competition.

Census Data Pop. 476,748. Central city, 0%; suburban, 6%. Median family income, $7,984; families above $15,000: 12%; families below $3,000: 13%. Median years education, 11.5.

The Voters

Median voting age 46.
Employment profile White collar, 38%. Blue collar, 30%. Service, 13%. Farm, 19%.
Ethnic groups Total foreign stock, 18%. Germany, 6%; Norway, Sweden, 3% each.

Presidential vote

1972	Nixon (R)	114,196	(53%)
	McGovern (D)	102,231	(47%)
1968	Nixon (R)	90,969	(45%)
	Humphrey (D)	98,899	(49%)
	Wallace (AI)	10,101	(5%)

Rep. Richard Nolan (DFL) Elected 1974; b. Dec. 17, 1943, Brainerd; home, Waite Park; St. John's U., U. of Minn., B.A. 1962, U. of Md., 1967.

Career Laborer, United Parcel Svc., 1964–66; Staff Asst. to U.S. Sen. Walter F. Mondale, 1966–68; Educ. Dir. of Headstart in 3 Minn. Counties, 1968; Curriculum Coord., Adult Basic Educ., Little Falls School Dist., 1968; Teacher, 1968–69; Minn. House of Reps., 1968–72; Fed.-State Coord., Minn. House of Reps., 1973; Admin. Asst. to the Senior V.P. of Fingerhut Corp., 1973–74.

Offices 1019 LHOB, 202-225-2331.

Committees

Agriculture (16th). Subcommittees: Dairy and Poultry; Family Farms and Rural Development; Livestock and Grains.

Small Business (23d). Subcommittees: Commodities and Services; Government Procurement and International Trade.

Group Ratings: Newly Elected

Key Votes

1) Foreign Aid	AGN	6) Gov Abortn Aid	NE	11) Pub Cong Election $	NE
2) Busing	NE	7) Coed Phys Ed	FOR	12) Turkish Arms Cutoff	NE
3) ABM	NE	8) Pov Lawyer Gag	NE	13) Youth Camp Regs	FOR
4) B-1 Bomber	AGN	9) Pub Trans Sub	NE	14) Strip Mine Veto	AGN
5) Nerve Gas	NE	10) EZ Voter Regis	NE	15) Farm Bill Veto	AGN

Election Results

1974 general:	Richard Nolan (DFL)	96,465	(55%)	($139,342)
	Jon Grunseth (R)	77,797	(45%)	($121,048)
1974 primary:	Richard Nolan (DFL)	31,621	(71%)	
	Buford Johnson (DFL)	13,166	(29%)	

♦ ♦ ♦ ♦ ♦

SEVENTH DISTRICT

The 7th congressional district of Minnesota occupies the northwest quadrant of the state. This is the most sparsely populated part of Minnesota, with 39% of the state's land area but only 12% of its population. Along the Red River of the North just next to North Dakota are miles of wheat fields; to the east are acres of lakes, forests, and occasional resort communities. This is the country of the legendary Paul Bunyan and his blue ox Babe, whose statues stand together in Bemidji, a small town on the shores of one of Minnesota's 10,000 lakes. Not far away is Lake Itasca, the headwaters of the Mississippi River.

This district was settled by hardy Swedish and Norwegian lumberjacks and farmers. It has traditionally been politically marginal country. The Republican stronghold is heavily Norwegian Otter Tail County, near the southern end of the district; the strongest DFL territory is to the north, in counties which provided solid support to the old Farmer-Labor Party back in the 1930s.

The 7th has had a rather colorful recent political history, mostly due to the antics of one Andy Knutson. It seems that his wife, Coya, was the DFL Congresswoman from the district, and in 1958 he made newspapers all over the country in a plaintive statement urging her to come home. This was long before the term male chauvinism became popular, and Mrs. Knutson lost in the otherwise heavily Democratic year of 1958. For the next twelve years, the seat was held by Republican Odie Langen, an ultraconservative who was always targeted but never quite beaten by the DFL; the Knutsons, incidentally, were divorced in 1962. In 1968, after he had been in ten years, Langen came within 4,000 votes of losing to challenger Bob Bergland; in 1970, Bergland ran again, and finally won.

What has happened since is a good example of how a politically astute congressman can turn a marginal seat into a safe one. Bergland started off with good credentials: he had served in the Department of Agriculture and then returned to his farm in Roseau County on the Canadian border. (Of all the 535 members of Congress, only the three members of the Alaska delegation have residences farther north.) In 1970 and after, Bergland was an outspoken critic of Nixon Administration farm policies; the old incumbent Langen, perhaps unwisely, stuck up for his President. The year 1970 was the first one the DFL used computers as part of its get-out-the-vote drive, concentrating on the 7th district, and it paid off, as Bergland won a larger than expected 54–46 victory.

In the House, Bergland won a seat on the Agriculture Committee, and his actions there seem, in a district with one of the highest farm populations in the nation, to have pleased his constituents. In 1972, he climbed to a solid 59% of the vote; in 1974, against a 25-year-old Republican, he won an unprecedented 75%. Thanks to plentiful retirements among aging Southerners, Bergland is now the 9th ranking Democrat on the Agriculture Committee—and the holder of what now appears to be an utterly safe seat in the House.

Census Data   Pop. 472,753. Central city, 6%; suburban, 4%. Median family income, $7,089; families above $15,000: 10%; families below $3,000: 17%. Median years education, 10.9.

The Voters

Median voting age 48.
Employment profile White collar, 39%. Blue collar, 28%. Service, 15%. Farm, 18%.
Ethnic groups Total foreign stock, 21%. Norway, 7%; Germany, Sweden, 4% each; Canada, 2%.

Presidential vote

1972	Nixon (R)	118,727	(54%)
	McGovern (D)	100,410	(46%)
1968	Nixon (R)	94,790	(46%)
	Humphrey (D)	100,375	(49%)
	Wallace (AI)	10,253	(5%)

Rep. Bob Bergland (DFL) Elected 1970; b. July 22, 1928, Roseau; home, Roseau; U. of Minn., 1946–48; Lutheran.

Career Farmer; Midwest Area Dir., Ag. Stabilization and Conservation Svc., 1963–68.

Offices 1414 LHOB, 202-225-2165. Also Holiday Ofc. Bldg., 920 28th Ave. S., Moorhead 56560, 218-236-5050.

Committees

Agriculture (9th). Subcommittees: Conservation and Credit (Chairman); Dairy and Poultry; Livestock and Grains.

Small Business (11th). Subcommittees: Commodities and Services; SBA and SBIC Legislation.

Group Ratings

	ADA	COPE	LWV	RIPON	NFU	LCV	CFA	NAB	NSI	ACA
1974	86	100	100	56	100	76	75	17	10	0
1973	88	82	92	60	100	84	75	–	–	4
1972	75	82	91	81	100	50	0	0	10	0

Key Votes

1) Foreign Aid	FOR	6) Gov Abortn Aid	AGN	11) Pub Cong Election $	FOR
2) Busing	FOR	7) Coed Phys Ed	FOR	12) Turkish Arms Cutoff	FOR
3) ABM	AGN	8) Pov Lawyer Gag	AGN	13) Youth Camp Regs	ABS
4) B-1 Bomber	AGN	9) Pub Trans Sub	FOR	14) Strip Mine Veto	AGN
5) Nerve Gas	AGN	10) EZ Voter Regis	FOR	15) Farm Bill Veto	AGN

Election Results

1974 general:	Bob Bergland (DFL)	129,207	(75%)	($92,608)
	Dan Reber (R)	43,054	(25%)	($15,082)
1974 primary:	Bob Bergland (DFL), unopposed			

Election Results

1972 general:	Bob Bergland (DFL)	133,067	(59%)	($92,871)
	Jon Haaven (R)	92,283	(41%)	($90,524)

◆ ◆ ◆ ◆ ◆

EIGHTH DISTRICT

The 8th congressional district of Minnesota is the northeast corner of the state. Like the 7th, most of the acreage here is composed of lakes and forests. But the 8th has far fewer farmers, and most of its population is concentrated in a few urban areas. Because of redistricting, the 8th now reaches south to Anoka County—Democratic suburban territory which is part of the Minneapolis-St. Paul metropolitan area. But the focus of the district—and most of its population—is still in St. Louis County, in the Lake Superior port of Duluth (pop. 101,000) and the towns of the Mesabi Range. This part of Minnesota has long been the source of most of the nation's iron ore, which is scooped out of the low-lying hills of the Mesabi, transported by rail to Duluth, loaded on giant freighters, and shipped toward Chicago, Gary, Detroit, Cleveland, and Pittsburgh.

The entrepreneurs who first began these operations, more than sixty years ago, had little respect for the land, digging it up here and putting up a factory or loading dock there, and depositing the waste products of their works wherever they liked. The same sort of thing has continued not far from Duluth in Silver Bay, where an operation controlled by Armco Steel has been draining deadly mercury into Lake Superior for years; the company adamantly refuses to stop and if a federal court suit—still pending—forces them to do so, it promises to simply close down its operation.

Life has not been gentle here, with financial power in the hands of men like these and with the wintry climate that brings snow in as many as eleven months of the year. The men who came to work the Mesabi mines and the Duluth docks were mostly immigrants from Sweden, Finland, Norway, Italy, Poland, and Yugoslavia, and they brought with them few illusions. Their ethnic backgrounds and difficult economic lot disposed them early toward the Democratic-Farmer-Labor Party, and today the 8th is by far the most solidly DFL district in the state.

For nearly twenty years, the 8th elected John Blatnik to Congress. Generally regarded as a liberal Democrat, Blatnik had ambitions for the Senate seat to which Walter Mondale was appointed in 1964; instead, he finally in 1971 became Chairman of the House Public Works Committee. It was an example, and they are common under the seniority system, of a man coming to a position of power too late in his career. By that time Blatnik was 60 and in poor health. As Chairman, he proved to be a major disappointment to environmentalists; he inclined more to the pork-barrel philosophy of the Public Works staff than to a yearning to protect the environment. In 1974 he decided to retire.

In Minnesota politics, endorsement by a DFL nominating convention is so often tantamount to winning the party's nomination that few candidates will challenge an endorsed opponent in the primary. But that was not the case here when Blatnik retired; the 8th is the scene of often turbulent political infighting, and the opportunities to win this utterly safe DFL seat do not come along very often. So when Lieutenant Governor Rudy Perpich, member of a large political family in St. Louis County, won the convention vote, James Oberstar, Blatnik's administrative assistant, continued in the race undeterred. The well-financed Oberstar then pulled off a major upset, and of course went on to win the general election easily (although a candidate running under the Economic Justice banner won a surprising 10% of the vote). In the House, Oberstar promptly joined the Public Works Committee his boss had chaired, as well as Merchant Marine and Fisheries, which has some pork barrel business of its own and is obviously important to Duluth. He can be expected to continue in Blatnik's footsteps, and quite possibly for as long.

Census Data Pop. 479,159. Central city, 21%; suburban, 46%. Median family income, $9,393; families above $15,000: 14%; families below $3,000: 9%. Median years education, 12.1.

The Voters

Median voting age 44.
Employment profile White collar, 41%. Blue collar, 42%. Service, 14%. Farm, 3%.
Ethnic groups Total foreign stock, 24%. Sweden, 5%; Finland, 4%; Norway, 3%; Canada, Germany, 2% each.

Presidential vote

1972	Nixon (R)	....	95,536	(45%)
	McGovern (D)	....	115,622	(55%)

1968	Nixon (R)	57,803	(29%)
	Humphrey (D)	132,618	(67%)
	Wallace (AI)	8,765	(4%)

Rep. James L. Oberstar (DFL) Elected 1974; b. Sept. 10, 1934, Chisholm; home, Chisholm; Col. of St. Thomas, B.A. 1956, Col. of Europe, Bruges, Belgium, M.A. 1957.

Career Admin. Asst. to U.S. Rep. John A. Blatnik, 1965–74; Administrator, U.S. House of Reps. Comm. on Public Works, 1971–74.

Offices 323 CHOB, 202-225-6211. Also 515 W. 1st St., Duluth 55802, 218-727-7474.

Committees

Merchant Marine and Fisheries (27th). Subcommittees: Fisheries and Wildlife Conservation and the Environment; Merchant Marine; Oceanography.

Public Works and Transportation (21st). Subcommittees: Economic Development; Investigations and Review: Public Buildings and Grounds; Water Resources.

Group Ratings: Newly Elected

Key Votes

1) Foreign Aid	FOR	6) Gov Abortn Aid	NE	11) Pub Cong Election $	NE
2) Busing	NE	7) Coed Phys Ed	FOR	12) Turkish Arms Cutoff	NE
3) ABM	NE	8) Pov Lawyer Gag	NE	13) Youth Camp Regs	FOR
4) B-1 Bomber	AGN	9) Pub Trans Sub	NE	14) Strip Mine Veto	AGN
5) Nerve Gas	NE	10) EZ Voter Regis	NE	15) Farm Bill Veto	AGN

Election Results

1974 general:	James L. Oberstar (DFL)	104,740	(63%)	($106,186)
	Jerome (Jerry) Arnold (R)	44,298	(27%)	($38,435)
	William (Bill) Ojala (Economic Justice) .	16,932	(10%)	($3,833)
1974 primary:	James L. Oberstar (DFL)	50,493	(49%)	
	Rudy Perpich (DFL)	29,899	(29%)	
	Florian Chmielewski (DFL)	20,054	(20%)	
	Three others (DFL)	2,336	(2%)	

MISSISSIPPI

Mississippi, a land of gentle hills and fertile river bottoms, was once the booming frontier of the American South. In the late 1820s, land-hungry Jacksonian farmers poured in from Tennessee after the Choctaws and Chickasaws were driven out of the northern and central parts of the territory. The farmers and would-be planters eventually took political control of the state away from the already established Whig planters to the south, who had settled around Natchez just after the Louisiana Purchase. King Cotton brought all these people to Mississippi, and as fast as whites could move in they brought slaves—thousands and thousands of them—from Virginia and the Carolinas to work the cotton fields.

At the time of the Civil War, Mississippi had a larger proportion of blacks than any other state, and it still does. As recently as 1940, 49% of the people here were black; in 1970, the figure had dropped to a still high 37%. Naturally, the position and status of the black man early became the central issue of Mississippi politics, from the time the state elected Jefferson Davis to the Senate; and today, though there are signs of change, race is probably still the issue. From the 1890s through the 1960s, blacks were absolutely barred from any participation in the political life of Mississippi, and white politicians—and voters—supported this state of affairs with a unanimity seldom equalled in American politics.

But unanimity on other matters has not always characterized Mississippi politics. There is a continuing motif here of conflict between the wealthy planters of the Delta and the poor white farmers of the upcountry in the eastern part of the state. The latter came to power as long ago as 1912; their leaders are known not so much for their mild populism but for their race-baiting. Men like Senator (1934–47) Theodore Bilbo provided some of the most vicious racist demagoguery ever heard in American politics.

During the 1960s the basic premise of Mississippi politics—exclusion of blacks—was challenged for the first time since Yankee farm boys came south to fight the Civil War. Hundreds of civil rights activists descended upon the state and organized black voter registration drives. Local black leaders began to emerge: Charles Evers, Aaron Henry, Fannie Lou Hamer. By the time federal registrars were sent into the state under the Voting Rights Act of 1965 Mississippi blacks were ready to enter the voting stream. Even so, the classic sanctions against black political participation—economic reprisals and physical violence—continued to obtain in many parts of the state; and black voter participation is significantly lower here than in any other Southern state. It has been less than ten years that people here literally risked their lives to exercise this basic political right.

Sadly, the vote has not necessarily made much difference to many Mississippi blacks. For every victory of a Charles Evers—he is Mayor of tiny (pop. 1,725) Fayette—thousands of other blacks continued to be unrepresented. As long as whites vote monolithically—and in national elections, at least, they still very much do in Mississippi—blacks will remain a powerless minority. It has only been in a few congressional and state legislative races that the minority has been able to get enough leverage to influence the outcome—and of course you can't advertise such power here, or you risk getting whites to react against the candidates you support.

But having said all that, one must report that the tone of Mississippi politics has changed. In 1972 the Governorship passed from John Bell Williams, a former Congressman inclined to the old segregationist rhetoric, to William Waller, a Democrat who has attacked big business interests and called for racial harmony. And the frontrunner in the 1976 contest—held early in the year, not in November—is Lieutenant Governor William Winter, who might be called a conservative in most other states but is at least a moderate in Mississippi. And there is evidence that not just the rhetoric but the operations of government have actually changed.

Throughout its history, Mississippi has had little of the moderating influence that could have come from urban life or the economic interests of large business firms. Even today, Jackson, the state's capital and by far its largest city, has just 153,000 residents and no substantial suburbs. Economically, much of Mississippi remains a colony of the cotton exchanges and banks of Memphis and New Orleans; it should not be forgotten that this is still the poorest state in the nation. But if Mississippi's poverty and lack of a big business elite left it with little to lose by stubborn and even violent resistance to integration, it also leaves it free of the kind of domination by economic interests which is so much a factor in Southern states as diverse as Texas and the Carolinas.

Mississippi's two Senators reflect few, if any of the changes in the state's public life in the last decade; both have been serving since the 1940s. Both chair important committees, both are in their seventies, and neither has had any difficulty winning reelection. The senior Senator, James Eastland, has chaired the Judiciary Committee since the 1950s. The days are long gone when Eastland could bottle up civil rights legislation at will, and he no longer has a conservative majority on the committee on many issues. But he is still adept at using the leverage that a Chairman has to further what he believes is right. Eastland is not a voluble Senator; he prefers to gaze delphically, with a large cigar in his mouth and his shoulders stooped over; but no one gives him much trouble. For one thing, federal judgeship nominations all have to go through Eastland's committee, and he has been faithful in honoring any senator's veto over a nomination in his home state; not coincidentally, one of the federal judges in Mississippi, a man who once referred on the bench to blacks as monkeys and generally obstructed civil rights suits any way he could, was Eastland's law school roommate.

Eastland's record is almost solidly reactionary, and when he came up for reelection in 1972 the Nixon Administration owed him plenty of debts. As is his habit, he collected. Nixon was carrying the state over McGovern 80–20, and a Republican businessman was running against Eastland. The word soon came down from the White House that this was one Democratic Senator the President would like very much to see reelected, and he was, by a 59–39 margin. Without that intervention, Eastland might have had a close race. But apparently Eastland did not consider that he owed Nixon anything in return; when Watergate matters came before Judiciary, as during the confirmation hearings of various Attorneys General, Eastland chomped his cigar placidly, and let the committee's liberal majority work its will. The Chairman does not have to face the voters again until 1978, when he will be 74; and whether he intends to run then or not, he knew even in 1973 that Nixon would no longer be President five years later.

In January 1973, Mississippi's junior Senator, John Stennis, 71, was shot by a robber outside his Washington home. Gravely injured, Stennis recovered quite rapidly—testimony to his excellent physical condition and strong will. He has now long since returned to his place as Chairman of the Senate Armed Services Committee, and apparently expects to run for reelection in 1976.

As Armed Services Chairman, Stennis has been a pillar in what until fairly recently was our bipartisan foreign policy. He was, indeed, the Senate's major—and probably most influential—hawk, although he supported American war policy in Vietnam not so much out of enthusiasm for war as from a feeling that Congress must support the flag wherever the President seeks to plant it. Under Stennis, Armed Services has approved most Pentagon spending requests, and the CIA subcommittee which Stennis chairs has looked only cursorily into the affairs of the intelligence agency—a course Stennis explicitly defends. On domestic issues, Stennis is not nearly so influential or important; he tends to vote almost as conservatively as his colleague Eastland.

But what Stennis has been best known for is perhaps his reputation for fairness and probity—a reputation that got him embroiled in the Watergate mess in 1973. Confined to the hospital or his home, Stennis was obviously out of touch with opinion in the Senate (if not in Mississippi, where Nixon retained plenty of support to the end), and had made at least one stick-to-your-guns statement in public with Nixon. So when Nixon decided to get rid of Special Prosecutor Archibald Cox, Nixon tried to use Stennis, by proposing that the Senator authenticate the Watergate tapes, rather than the Special Prosecutor subpoena them. Cox refused to drop his subpoena, and was fired in the Saturday Night Massacre of October 1973. In retrospect, Nixon obviously was only using Stennis as part of a plan to get rid of Cox, for he surely did not want the Senator, no matter how inclined he was initially to support his President, to actually listen to what was on some of those tapes. In any case, Stennis's reputation was good enough that it was not significantly harmed by the episode.

Stennis's seat is up in 1976, and as noted he says he wants to run, although he turns 75 that year. Reportedly he would like to be succeeded, ultimately or perhaps then, by his son, John Stennis, Jr., currently a member of the Mississippi legislature. Whether such a succession can be arranged is unclear; Mississippi congressional politics has changed markedly in the last few years. Since the turn of the century, Mississippi had been inclined to select its Senators and Congressmen as young candidates in a Democratic primary, and then elect and reelect them so many times that they would pile up enough seniority to perhaps become committee chairmen. But in 1972, three of the state's five Congressmen, including House Rules Committee Chairman William Colmer, abruptly retired, and their seats were won by three young, talented politicians—two of them Republicans—who may have senatorial ambitions. Whether they will be satisfied, no one can say; but Mississippi seems to be in store for the kind of spirited contests for Senator that it usually has only for the Governorship.

Census Data Pop. 2,216,912; 1.10% of U.S. total, 29th largest; Central city, 11%; suburban, 7%. Median family income, $6,068; 50th highest; families above $15,000: 8%; families below $3,000: 25%. Median years education, 10.7.

1974 Share of Federal Tax Burden $1,821,144,000; 0.68% of U.S. total, 33d largest.

1974 Share of Federal Outlays $3,668,934,000; 1.36% of U.S. total, 26th largest. Per capita federal spending, $1655.

DOD	$1,348,353,000	18th (1.97%)	HEW	$1,265,530,000	25th (1.36%)
AEC	$95,000	40th (–)	HUD	$8,325,000	30th (0.85%)
NASA	$14,723,000	17th (0.50%)	VA	$164,972,000	32d (1.21%)
DOT	$64,377,000	40th (0.76%)	EPA	$10,550,000	39th (0.34%)
DOC	$21,126,000	13th (1.31%)	RevS	$100,956,000	22d (1.66%)
DOI	$17,759,000	31st (0.72%)	Int.	$75,542,000	31st (0.37%)
USDA	$322,879,000	13th (2.59%)	Other	$253,747,000	

Economic Base Agriculture, notably cattle, cotton lint, soybeans and broilers; apparel and other textile products, especially men's and boys' funrishings; finance, insurance and real estate; lumber and wood products, especially sawmills and planing mills; transportation equipment, especially motor vehicles and equipment and ship building and repairing; food and kindred products.

Political Line-up Governor, William L. Waller (D). Senators, James O. Eastland (D) and John C. Stennis (D). Representatives, 5 (3 D and 2 R). State Senate (50 D and 2 R); State House (119 D, 2 R, and 1 Ind.).

The Voters

Registration No accurate total registration figures available.
Median voting age 43.
Employment profile White collar, 39%. Blue collar, 41%. Service, 14%. Farm, 6%.
Ethnic groups Black, 37%. Total foreign stock, 1%.

Presidential vote

1972	Nixon (R)	505,125	(80%)
	McGovern (D)	126,782	(20%)
1968	Nixon (R)	88,516	(14%)
	Humphrey (D)	150,644	(23%)
	Wallace (AI)	415,349	(63%)

Sen. James O. Eastland (D) Elected 1942, seat up 1978; b. Nov. 28, 1904, Doddsville; home, Doddsville; U. of Miss., 1922–24, Vanderbilt U., 1925–26, U. of Ala., 1926–27; Methodist.

Career Practicing atty., 1927–41; Miss. House of Reps., 1928–32; U.S. Senate, 1941.

Offices 2241 DSOB, 202-224-5054. Also Rm. 532 P.O. Bldg., Jackson 39205, 601-352-6298, and Ruleville 38771, 601-756-4766.

Committees

President Pro Tempore of the Senate

The Judiciary (Chairman). Subcommittees: FBI Oversight (Chairman); Immigration and Naturalization (Chairman); Internal Security (Chairman).

Agriculture and Forestry (2d). Subcommittees: Agricultural Production, Marketing, and Stabilization of Prices; Environment, Soil Conservation and Forestry Chairman); Agricultural Research and General Legislation; Rural Development.

Group Ratings

	ADA	COPE	LWV	RIPON	NFU	LCV	CFA	NAB	NSI	ACA
1974	11	27	44	41	31	12	22	33	100	88
1973	6	38	20	18	50	–	11	–	–	70
1972	5	0	20	13	40	2	11	50	100	81

Key Votes

1) No-Knock	FOR	8) Gov Abortn Aid	AGN	15) Consumer Prot Agy	AGN
2) Busing	AGN	9) Cut Mil Brass	ABS	16) Forced Psych Tests	AGN
3) No Fault	AGN	10) Gov Limousine	FOR	17) Fed Campaign Subs	AGN
4) F-111	ABS	11) RR Featherbed	FOR	18) Rhod Chrome Ban	AGN
5) Death Penalty	ABS	12) Handgun License	AGN	19) Open Legis Meetings	AGN
6) Foreign Aid	AGN	13) Less Troop Abrd	AGN	20) Strikers Food Stmps	ABS
7) Filibuster	ABS	14) Resume Turk Aid	ABS	21) Gov Info Disclosure	AGN

Election Results

1972 general:	James O. Eastland (D)	375,102	(59%)	($410,221)
	Gil Carmichael (R)	249,779	(39%)	($154,913)
	Prentiss Walker (Ind.)	14,662	(2%)	
1972 primary:	James O. Eastland (D)	203,847	(70%)	
	Taylor Webb (D)	67,656	(23%)	
	Louis Fondren (D)	18,753	(6%)	
1966 general:	James O. Eastland (D)	258,248	(66%)	
	Prentiss Walker (R)	105,150	(27%)	
	Clifton R. Whitley (Ind.)	30,502	(8%)	

Sen. John C. Stennis (D) Elected Nov. 4, 1947, seat up 1976; b. Aug. 3, 1901, Kemper County; home, De Kalb; Miss. St. U., B.S. 1923, U. of Va., LL.B. 1928; Presbyterian.

Career Miss. House of Reps., 1928–32; Dist. Prosecuting Atty., 16th Judicial Dist., 1931–37; Circuit Judge, 1937–47.

Offices 205 RSOB, 202-224-6253. Also 303 P.O. Bldg., Jackson 39201, 601-353-5494.

Committees

Armed Services (Chairman). Subcommittees: Arms Control (Chairman); Intelligence; Preparedness Investigating (Chairman).

Aeronautical and Space Sciences (3d).

Appropriations (3d). Subcommittees: Agriculture and Related Agencies; Defense; HUD and Independent Agencies; Labor and HEW; Public Works (Chairman); Transportaion.

Group Ratings

	ADA	COPE	LWV	RIPON	NFU	LCV	CFA	NAB	NSI	ACA
1974	5	20	30	38	29	18	22	38	100	94
1973	0	25	0	40	71	–	0	–	–	100
1972	0	0	20	20	50	0	9	55	100	77

Key Votes

1) No-Knock	FOR	8) Gov Abortn Aid	AGN	15) Consumer Prot Agy	AGN
2) Busing	AGN	9) Cut Mil Brass	AGN	16) Forced Psych Tests	AGN
3) No Fault	AGN	10) Gov Limousine	FOR	17) Fed Campaign Subs	AGN
4) F-111	FOR	11) RR Featherbed	ABS	18) Rhod Chrome Ban	AGN
5) Death Penalty	FOR	12) Handgun License	AGN	19) Open Legis Meetings	AGN
6) Foreign Aid	AGN	13) Less Troop Abrd	AGN	20) Strikers Food Stmps	AGN
7) Filibuster	ABS	14) Resume Turk Aid	FOR	21) Gov Info Disclosure	AGN

Election Results

1970 general:	John C. Stennis (D)	286,622	(88%)
	William R. Thompson (Ind.)	37,593	(12%)
1970 primary:	NA		
1964 general:	John C. Stennis (D), unopposed		

Gov. William L. Waller (D) Elected 1971, term expires Jan. 1976; b. Oct. 21, 1926, Lafayette County; Memphis St. U., B.A., U. of Miss., LL.B.; Baptist.

Career Practicing atty.; Hinds Co. Dist. Atty., 1959–67.

Offices Miss. Exec. Dept., Jackson 39205, 601-354-7575.

Election Results

1971 general:	William L. Waller (D)	601,122	(78%)
	Charles Evers (Ind.)	172,762	(22%)
1971 run-off:	William L. Waller (D)	389,952	(54%)
	Charles L. Sullivan (D)	329,236	(46%)
1971 primary:	Charles L. Sullivan (D)	288,219	(38%)
	William L. Waller (D)	227,424	(30%)
	Jimmy Swan (D)	128,946	(17%)
	Four Others (D)	118,398	(16%)

◆ ◆ ◆ ◆ ◆

FIRST DISTRICT

The 1st congressional district of Mississippi occupies the northernmost section of the state. The 1st spans the gamut of Mississippi's geopolitical terrain, from the cotton-rich Delta along the Mississippi River to Tishomingo County on the Tennessee River in the state's northeast corner. The black majority in some of the Delta counties have been active—and occasionally successful—politically. As one moves east into the hill country, there are fewer and fewer blacks; instead, there are poor white farmers whose families have been working the hardscrabble land for more than a century without much luck. In the middle of the district lies Oxford, site of Ole Miss and of the racial disorders accompanying the enrollment of James Meredith in 1962, and also the lifelong home of William Faulkner.

The current Congressman from the 1st district was first chosen in a special election a month before Pearl Harbor; ever since, Jamie Whitten has been routinely reelected. The only possible threat to his incumbency could have come when blacks were enfranchised; his district then was entirely within the Delta, and was 59% black. The result was the creation on basically the current lines, which divide the Delta between four different districts.

In Washington, where he has more seniority than all but five other Congressmen, Whitten is Chairman of the Agriculture Subcommittee of the House Appropriations Committee. So ensconced, Whitten can do plenty for the rich Delta planters who have always supported him politically. Whitten takes the positions, popular in the big Delta mansions, of backing large government agricultural subsidies for owners of big cotton plantations, and opposing government programs to feed the poor. As a result, Senator James Eastland in next-door Sunflower County received more than $150,000 annually for years for not growing cotton on his plantation; not far away, children grow up crippled with malnutrition.

Because Whitten controls the purse strings of the Department of Agriculture—one of the largest government bureaucracies—he has been called the permanent Secretary of Agriculture. Policies he favors—like the crusade against the fire ant—are pursued avidly in the USDA; policies he doesn't like—like food stamps—often languish, whatever the rest of the Congress wants. Moreover, Whitten has friends not just in the Washington bureaucracy, but in state agriculture departments, which are politically important in many Southern states, and among county agricultural agents all over the nation. Whitten turns 66 in 1976—comparatively young for a congressional veteran, and despite the advent of all the new Democratic freshmen, his power over agriculture policy continues.

But the freshmen did lop off some of Whitten's subcommittee's jurisdiction. Just four years before, Appropriations Chairman George Mahon had given Whitten say over money for environmental programs, much to the horror of ecology activists. The results were predictable: Whitten had no sympathy whatever for environmental objectives, and he set about in his usual canny way to affect government policy his way. But one of the reforms passed through the caucus by the incoming freshmen after the 1974 election was to provide for caucus votes on the chairmanships of all Appropriations subcommittees. To forestall a move against Whitten, Chairman Mahon removed the environment from his subcommittee's jurisdiction, and the Mississippian survived with little opposition.

The next test of the freshmen's power may come when Mahon, who is 76, either retires or dies. Whitten is next in line to become Chairman, which is to say that in the ordinary course of the seniority system as it was before 1974, he would have become Chairman. Now it is at least possible that this not especially unpopular and certainly not senile, but definitely reactionary Democrat will not be advanced to that position by a caucus which is overwhelmingly of different views on practically every policy question.

Census Data Pop. 433,825. Central city, 0%; suburban, 0%. Median family income, $5,577; families above $15,000: 6%; families below $3,000: 28%. Median years education, 9.7.

The Voters

Median voting age 44.
Employment profile White collar, 34%. Blue collar, 45%. Service, 12%. Farm, 9%.
Ethnic groups Black, 35%.

Presidential vote

1972	Nixon (R)	92,680	(80%)
	McGovern (D)	23,058	(20%)
1968	Nixon (R)	17,832	(14%)
	Humphrey (D)	29,660	(23%)
	Wallace (AI)	82,062	(63%)

Rep. Jamie L. Whitten (D) Elected Nov. 4, 1941; b. Apr. 18, 1910, Cascilla; home, Charleston; U. of Miss.; Presbyterian.

Career Practicing atty.; School principal; Miss. House of Reps., 1931; Dist. Prosecuting Atty., 17th Judicial Dist., 1933–41.

Offices 2413 RHOB, 202-225-4306. Also P.O. Bldg., Charleston 38921, 601-647-2413.

Committees

Appropriations (2d). Subcommittees: Agriculture and Related Agencies (Chairman).

Group Ratings

	ADA	COPE	LWV	RIPON	NFU	LCV	CFA	NAB	NSI	ACA
1974	26	18	27	25	57	29	15	50	60	71
1973	13	30	25	8	80	5	43	–	–	74
1972	6	30	17	6	57	6	100	78	100	91

Key Votes

1) Foreign Aid	AGN	6) Gov Abortn Aid	AGN	11) Pub Cong Election $	AGN
2) Busing	AGN	7) Coed Phys Ed	AGN	12) Turkish Arms Cutoff	AGN
3) ABM	FOR	8) Pov Lawyer Gag	FOR	13) Youth Camp Regs	AGN
4) B-1 Bomber	FOR	9) Pub Trans Sub	FOR	14) Strip Mine Veto	AGN
5) Nerve Gas	FOR	10) EZ Voter Regis	AGN	15) Farm Bill Veto	AGN

Election Results

1974 general:	Jamie L. Whitten (D)	39,158 (88%)	($3,209)
	Jack Benney (Ind.)	5,250 (12%)	
1974 primary:	Jamie L. Whitten (D), unopposed		
1972 general:	Jamie L. Whitten (D), unopposed		($4,100)

◆ ◆ ◆ ◆ ◆

SECOND DISTRICT

The 2d congressional district of Mississippi, a belt of counties in the north central part of the state, stretches from the Mississippi River to the hill country along the Alabama border. The flat fertile land along the River is the Delta, an area not fully developed until after the Civil War. This was originally swampy land, divided by many rivers which run into the Mississippi and each other. In the late nineteenth century the land was drained, the great river lined with levees, and the Illinois Central track laid out of Memphis for New Orleans. It was discovered then that the topsoil here, accumulated over countless centuries of the Mississippi spring time floods, often reached depths of 25 feet. So the Delta wilderness of northern Mississippi, the destruction of which Faulkner lamented in stories like "The Bear," became the region of the state's largest and most productive cotton plantations.

That also meant that the Delta had Mississippi's largest concentration of blacks; though slavery had been abolished most blacks lived in terrible poverty at the turn of the century, and as sharecroppers or tenants would work for nearly nothing. That large black concentration is why Mississippi's congressional districts are drawn as they are, straight across the state combining black majority Delta counties with the almost all white hill country. Even at that, as recently as 1960, 51% of the population of the current 2d distict was black; in 1970, after another decade of black outmigration, that figure was down to a still high 46%. But only 39% of the population 18 and over was black, and until 1972 even this minority had no chance to flex any muscles in congressional elections. Then came the retirement of Congressman Thomas Abernethy, first elected in 1942.

Abernethy had served thirty years without attaining a committee chairmanship. As it happened, he would have if he had stayed on; South Carolina's John McMillan, Chairman of the House D.C Committee on which Abernethy was next in line, lost his primary that year. In any case, Abernethy's retirement triggered political fireworks back home: a nine-candidate Democratic primary and a strong Republican candidacy to boot. After all, it had been thirty years since the last time anyone got a seat in Congress, and it might well be another thirty years until the next.

The eventual outcome was something of a surprise. The new Congressman, David Bowen, a graduate of Harvard and Oxford, received only 15% of the vote in the first primary, edging former Congressman (1951-63) Frank Smith for second place—and a spot in the runoff. Smith had lost his seat when he had been placed in the same district with Jamie Whitten in 1962; he later wrote a book in which he lamented the hypocritical stance on civil rights he had felt obliged to take. Bowen is also a moderate by Mississippi standards; in the runoff he took majorities in some black areas, margins that may have produced his victory.

Bowen had a somewhat easier time of it in the general election, and in 1974 as well. His voting record in the House shows only the very slightest signs of liberalism. On the Agriculture Committee he has on occasion been part of the deals made between subsidy-hungry Southerners and food stamp-concerned northerners. Bowen is virtually certain of reelection to the House, but he may be aiming at a shot at one of Mississippi's Senate seats.

Census Data Pop. 440,689. Central city, 0%; suburban, 0%. Median family income, $5,446; families above $15,000: 7%; families below $3,000: 29%. Median years education, 9.9.

The Voters

Median voting age 43.
Employment profile White collar, 37%. Blue collar, 39%. Service, 15%. Farm, 9%.
Ethnic groups Black, 46%. Total foreign stock, 1%.

Presidential vote

1972	Nixon (R)	84,346	(77%)
	McGovern (D)	24,633	(23%)

1968	Nixon (R)	15,781	(13%)
	Humphrey (D)	30,303	(26%)
	Wallace (AI)	72,655	(61%)

Rep. David R. Bowen (D) Elected 1972; b. Oct. 21, 1932, Houston; home, Cleveland; Harvard U., A.B. 1954, Oxford U., M.A.; Protestant.

Career Asst. Prof., Miss. Col., 1958–59, Millsaps Col., 1959–64; U.S. Ofc. of Econ. Opportunity, 1966–67; U.S. Chamber of Commerce, 1967–68; Miss. Federal-State Coordinator, 1968–72.

Offices 116 CHOB, 202-225-5876. Also 101 S. Court St., Cleveland 38732, 601-846-1801.

Committees

Agriculture (11th). Subcommittees: Cotton (Chairman); Dairy and Poultry; Oilseeds and Rice.

Merchant Marine and Fisheries (18th). Subcommittees: Coast Guard and Navigation; Fisheries and Wildlife Conservation and the Environment; Panama Canal.

Group Ratings

	ADA	COPE	LWV	RIPON	NFU	LCV	CFA	NAB	NSI	ACA
1974	26	20	27	19	54	20	25	56	56	46
1973	25	27	36	46	79	11	50	–	–	56

Key Votes

1) Foreign Aid	AGN	6) Gov Abortn Aid	AGN	11) Pub Cong Election $	FOR
2) Busing	AGN	7) Coed Phys Ed	AGN	12) Turkish Arms Cutoff	AGN
3) ABM	FOR	8) Pov Lawyer Gag	FOR	13) Youth Camp Regs	AGN
4) B-1 Bomber	FOR	9) Pub Trans Sub	AGN	14) Strip Mine Veto	AGN
5) Nerve Gas	FOR	10) EZ Voter Regis	AGN	15) Farm Bill Veto	AGN

Election Results

1974 general:	David R. Bowen (D)	37,909	(66%)	($60,735)
	Ben F. Hilbun, Jr. (R)	15,876	(28%)	($27,000)
	H. B. Wells (Ind.)	3,573	(6%)	($3,824)
1974 primary:	David R. Bowen (D)	26,202	(82%)	
	Harry G. Robinson (D)	5,753	(18%)	
1972 general:	David R. Bowen (D)	69,892	(63%)	($142,522)
	Carl Butler (R)	39,117	(35%)	($80,449)
	Robert Coleman (Ind.)	2,801	(3%)	(NA)

◆ ◆ ◆ ◆ ◆

THIRD DISTRICT

The 3d is one of three Mississippi congressional districts that stretch from the heavily black Delta across the hills of central Mississippi to the Alabama border. Like the others, the 3d was constructed this way to prevent blacks from controlling or in any major way influencing the outcome of congressional elections here. Of all of Mississippi's districts, this is the most rural and agricultural. Its only city of any size is Meridian (pop. 45,000). More typical—and better known—is Philadelphia (pop. 6,000), near which three civil rights workers were found murdered in 1964.

The longtime (since 1942) Congressman from the 3d Philadelphia native W. Arthur Winstead, suffered a rude surprise in 1964: he was beaten by a Republican chicken farmer named Pretiss Walker. That year, as Barry Goldwater carried the state by a 7–1 margin, the unfortunate Winstead was the only incumbent with a Republican opponent; if there had been Republican candidates elsewhere, they too probably would have won, wiping out 95 years of Democratic seniority. Walker's later ventures in politics showed that his one victory was simply a function of

Goldwater coattails. He won just 27% of the vote against James Eastland in 1966, 39% in a 1968 congressional race, and a pathetic 2% as an independent candidate against Eastland in 1972.

When Walker ran for the Senate in 1966, the Democrats promptly recaptured the seat in the person of state Senator G.V. (Sonny) Montgomery, who has won since without trouble and usually without opposition. A veteran of both World War II and Korea, Montgomery serves on the Armed Services and Veterans Affairs Committees; he is an unabashed hawk and enthusiast for things military. But what may turn out to be Montgomery's moment in history came in 1974, when he was a frequent guest of a beleaguered Richard Nixon on the presidential yacht Sequoia. Montgomery stuck with his President all the way through the Watergate and impeachment crisis; and he urged Nixon to stick it out, assuring him that he had plenty of support left.

In retrospect, it is clear that Nixon and perhaps Montgomery were gravely misjudging the House. Back when Nixon was a member, in the late 1940s, there were almost one hundred Sonny Montgomerys, that is, conservative Southern Democrats who could be counted on to vote with Republicans on just about every important issue. By 1974, there were only twenty to thirty such Democrats who fit into the category. In the years between conservatives had retired by the dozen, and been replaced by Republicans or by considerably more moderate or even liberal Democrats. Nixon could not bring himself to believe that Montgomery was a vanishing breed; but he was, and is, which is one reason why Nixon would have been impeached even if he had not provided the Congress with what turned out to be a smoking pistol.

Census Data Pop. 445,713. Central city, 0%; suburban, 10%. Median family income, $5,320; families above $15,000: 6%; families below $3,000: 30%. Median years education, 10.2.

The Voters

Median voting age 45.
Employment profile White collar, 33%. Blue collar, 44%. Service, 13%. Farm, 10%.
Ethnic groups Black, 40%.

Presidential vote

1972	Nixon (R)	110,710	(79%)
	McGovern (D)	28,941	(21%)
1968	Nixon (R)	12,703	(9%)
	Humphrey (D)	32,431	(23%)
	Wallace (AI)	97,866	(68%)

Rep. G. V. (Sonny) **Montgomery** (D) Elected 1966; b. Meridian; home, Meridian; Miss St., U., B.S.; Episcopalian.

Career Army, WWII and Korea; Owner, Montgomery Insurance Agency; V.P., Greater Miss. Life Ins. Co.; Miss. Senate, 1956–66.

Offices 2367 RHOB, 202-225-5031. Also P.O. Box 5618, Meridian 39301, 601-693-6681.

Committees

Armed Services (16th). Subcommittees: Military Personnel; Seapower and Strategic and Critical Materials.

Veterans' Affairs (5th). Subcommittees: Compensation, Pension and Insurance (Chairman); Hospitals.

Group Ratings

	ADA	COPE	LWV	RIPON	NFU	LCV	CFA	NAB	NSI	ACA
1974	0	0	8	19	36	25	0	75	90	86
1973	4	18	17	21	60	0	25	–	–	85
1972	0	11	8	20	43	0	100	90	100	100

Key Votes

1) Foreign Aid	AGN	6) Gov Abortn Aid	AGN	11) Pub Cong Election $	AGN
2) Busing	AGN	7) Coed Phys Ed	AGN	12) Turkish Arms Cutoff	AGN
3) ABM	FOR	8) Pov Lawyer Gag	FOR	13) Youth Camp Regs	AGN
4) B-1 Bomber	FOR	9) Pub Trans Sub	AGN	14) Strip Mine Veto	FOR
5) Nerve Gas	FOR	10) EZ Voter Regis	AGN	15) Farm Bill Veto	AGN

Election Results

1974 general:	G. V. (Sonny) Montgomery (D), unpposed	($0)
1974 primary:	G. V. (Sonny) Montgomery (D), unpposed	
1972 general:	G. V. (Sonny) Montgomery (D), unpposed	($381)

◆ ◆ ◆ ◆ ◆

FOURTH DISTRICT

Mississippi's capital, Jackson (pop. 153,000), is the center of one of the state's two significant urban concentrations. It has experienced considerable growth in the last twenty years—aside from the Gulf Coast, just about the only part of Mississippi to have any. Much of Jackson's growth is accounted for by well-to-do whites; the city has its new subdivisions of pleasant, large houses inhabited by new Mississippi millionaries. Even the less well-to-do, people who were brought up on $3,000 incomes and now are making $16,000, more than they had ever expected, tend to think like nouveau riche. This comes out in a militant conservatism which is quite consistent with traditional white Mississippi politics, except for one thing—these new conservatives are just as inclined to vote for Republicans as for Democrats.

It is on the votes of such citizens—younger, better educated, upwardly mobile, urban and suburban—that the successes of the Republican Party in the South generally and in Mississippi in particular have been built. Thus the state's 4th congressional district, 48% of whose residents live in Jackson and surrounding Hinds County, has a Republican Congressman. It was bound to happen sooner or later; the seat here has changed hands several times in recent years. In 1965 Congressman John Bell Williams was stripped of his considerable seniority for openly supporting Barry Goldwater; he sulked on the back benches of Congress and was elected Governor in 1967. Williams was succeeded in Congress by his administrative assistant, Charles Griffin, who won a much publicized contest over Charles Evers, the black Mayor of tiny Fayette (pop. 1,725) in Jefferson County.

Indeed, although the wealthy subdivisions of Jackson are probably the most important part of the district politically, it is the other areas which inevitabley attract the most attention. Who is going to look at a 1967 tract house when you can gaze on an antebellum mansion of Natchez (pop. 20,000) or wander through the battlefield site at Vicksburg (pop. 26,000)? And what reporter is going to write a story on the upwardly mobile new reactionaries of Jackson when he can write about blacks winning, or at least seriously contesting, elections in the sparsely populated counties along the Mississippi River which were once the state's prime plantation country?

Thus it was vote-rich Jackson which really produced the electoral result when Congressman Griffin retired in 1972. The Democrats had had, as one might expect, a riproaring primary; the Republicans had quietly picked and financed very generously a bright young Jackson attorney named Thad Cochran. In the general election, Cochran took 57% of the vote in Hinds County, compared to the Democrat's 38%; and that was enough to give the Republican a 48–44 district-wide victory. A black independent candidate got 8% of the vote which, since it was denied to the Democrat, may also be said to have influenced the outcome—the first time blacks had had such leverage in a Mississippi congressional race. But without his bloc of votes from the affluent sections of Jackson, Cochran would never have been in contention.

In 1974, there was some fuss in the Democratic primary. In the first primary, the leader was James Meredith, the first black to enroll at Ole Miss; Meredith, an increasingly erratic and puzzling man, then said he would not enter the runoff because he didn't want to win, which leads one to wonder why he entered in the first place. The nomination to oppose Cochran went to an attorney named Kenneth Dean, who tried to unite poor whites and blacks. From the results it appears he succeeded only in attracting the latter, as Cochran won reelection with a solid 71% of the vote. So much for those who felt a Republican couldn't win in Mississippi without a popular presidential candidate at the top of the ticket. Cochran has proved that he is an attractive candidate and, still under 40, he might well be a statewide officeholder before another decade is out.

Census Data Pop. 444,704. Central city, 35%; suburban, 14%. Median family income, $6,802; families above $15,000: 12%; families below $3,000: 21%. Median years education, 11.8.

The Voters

Median voting age 43.
Employment profile White collar, 47%. Blue collar, 35%. Service, 15%. Farm, 3%.
Ethnic groups Black, 43%. Total foreign stock, 1%.

Presidential vote

1972	Nixon (R)	101,007	(76%)
	McGovern (D)	32,496	(24%)
1968	Nixon (R)	22,236	(16%)
	Humphrey (D)	41,696	(30%)
	Wallace (AI)	77,047	(55%)

Rep. Thad Cochran (R) Elected 1972; b. Dec. 7, 1937, Pontotoc; home, Jackson; U. of Miss., B.A. 1959, J.D. 1965, Rotary Fellow, Trinity Col., Dublin, Ireland, 1963–64; Baptist.

Career Navy, 1959–61; Practicing atty., 1965–72.

Offices 212 CHOB, 202-225-5865. Also 316 Fed. Bldg., Jackson 39205, 601-969-1352.

Committees

Public Works and Transportation (8th). Subcommittees: Aviation; Investigations and Review; Public Buildings and Grounds; Surface Transportation.

Standards of Official Conduct (6th).

Group Ratings

	ADA	COPE	LWV	RIPON	NFU	LCV	CFA	NAB	NSI	ACA
1974	18	11	25	47	42	13	8	73	90	85
1973	9	9	18	36	55	5	0	–	–	81

Key Votes

1) Foreign Aid	AGN	6) Gov Abortn Aid	AGN	11) Pub Cong Election $	FOR
2) Busing	AGN	7) Coed Phys Ed	AGN	12) Turkish Arms Cutoff	AGN
3) ABM	FOR	8) Pov Lawyer Gag	FOR	13) Youth Camp Regs	AGN
4) B-1 Bomber	FOR	9) Pub Trans Sub	AGN	14) Strip Mine Veto	FOR
5) Nerve Gas	FOR	10) EZ Voter Regis	AGN	15) Farm Bill Veto	AGN

Election Results

1974 general:	Thad Cochran (R)	62,634	(71%)	($83,884)
	Kenneth L. Dean (D)	25,699	(29%)	($11,360)
1974 primary:	Thad Cochran (R)	24,176	(99%)	
	Robert J. Coleman (R)	351	(1%)	
1972 general:	Thad Cochran (R)	67,655	(48%)	($100,634)
	Ellis B. Bodron (D)	62,148	(44%)	($100,128)
	Eddie L. McBride (Ind.)	11,571	(8%)	(NA)

◆ ◆ ◆ ◆ ◆

FIFTH DISTRICT

The 5th congressional district of Mississippi is the state's Gulf Coast district. About half its population lives in and around the Gulf cities of Biloxi, Gulfport, Pascagoula, and Moss

MISSISSIPPI

Point—the only significant urban concentration in Mississippi outside Jackson. The remainder live inland, in farm counties or in the middle-sized cities of Hattiesburg and Laurel. Much of this land is in piney woods, never containing many plantations. As a result there are relatively few blacks here—only 19% of the district's population, the lowest such figure in Mississippi. That figure has declined in recent years as whites move in from the surrounding countryside or even from the north; for this has been an area of considerable boom.

The vast majority of 5th district residents would surely be disgusted at the notion that they are the beneficiaries of a vast program of subsidization by the federal government. These often newly well-to-do people are fond of the illusion that they are the last individualists, people who have only themselves to thank for their comparative success; politically, this part of Mississippi is the part of the country perhaps most fiercely opposed to heavy government spending on the poor and disadvantaged. But hardly anybody here objects to the annual $500 million the Defense Department pours into the Litton Shipbuilding yards in Pascagoula. Litton is the California-based conglomerate whose former president, Roy Ash, served as Nixon's budget chief; Ash refused to disqualify himself on matters relating to contracts with Litton. Interestingly, though it had never built a ship, Litton got this contract over the more experienced Bath Iron Works in Maine. There are indications now that Litton simply bid it at a low figure on the assumption (generally justified in dealings with the Pentagon) that it could raise the price later and collect from Uncle Sam. In any case, Litton's performance has been shoddy: the project is poorly organized, qualified labor is not available, and completion dates have been missed. No one down here, however, dares to suggest the obvious: the government money wasted on the Litton contract is really a subsidy to that well-placed company and to the now prosperous Pascagoula area.

The Nixon Administration was certainly not displeased to be putting the money here in the state represented in the Senate by Armed Services Chairman John Stennis and Judiciary Chairman James Eastland and represented, then, in the House by 5th district Congressman and House Rules Committee Chairman William Colmer. The project's continuation was not hurt, either, by the fact that this was the congressional district that gave Richard Nixon his largest percentage of the vote in the 1972 general election—a near unanimous 87%.

That result was perfectly in accord with Colmer's representation of the district; though he was nominally a Democrat, the Nixon Administration had no more faithful supporter in the House. Colmer's successor might be called that, too; he is Trent Lott, who served for four years as Colmer's administrative assistant and then went on to carry the district as an out and out Republican. That party affiliation had its advantages: while ten Democrats carved each other up in a primary and runoff, Lott had only desultory competition for the Republican nomination, and could save most of his effort—and money—for the general election. In the latter contest, Lott won a solid 56% in 1972—which would have been higher but for the home county strength of the Democrat in Biloxi and Gulfport.

It came as no surprise to anyone that the Congressman from the number one Nixon district, as the most junior member of the House Judiciary Committee, was one of the staunchest defenders of the President in the impeachment hearings. A personable 32, Lott was able to make the point that he was the youngest member of the committee, supposed proof that young people were still with their President; and indeed, if the public opinion you followed most closely was that in the 5th district of Mississippi, you would have had a hard time understanding how hated Richard Nixon was in the rest of the nation in the summer of 1974. For here Nixon remained just about as strong as ever until his final resignation. Politics for these people is largely a matter of black vs. white, and Nixon had been the white man's candidate, which he would remain no matter how disgraceful his conduct.

Having supported Nixon to the end was no political liability for Lott; quite the contrary. Against a Democrat and a couple of independents, Lott received a huge 74% of the vote—solid proof he can retain this seat, if he wishes for life. Indeed, Lott entered Congress 11 years younger than Colmer was when he had; he could well have just as long a House career. In 1975, he switched from Judiciary to Rules, Colmer's old committee. But it is just as possible that he is contemplating (as Colmer once did) a Senate seat and, given his popularity in the 5th and his high recognition statewide from the Judiciary Committee hearings, he could well win.

Census Data   Pop. 451,981. Central city, 20%; suburban, 10%. Median family income, $7,053; families above $15,000: 9%; families below $3,000: 18%. Median years education, 11.9.

The Voters

Median voting age 40.
Employment profile White collar, 42%. Blue collar, 43%. Service, 13%. Farm, 2%.
Ethnic groups Black, 19%. Total foreign stock, 3%.

Presidential vote

1972	Nixon (R)	116,382	(87%)
	McGovern (D)	17,654	(13%)
1968	Nixon (R)	19,964	(16%)
	Humphrey (D)	16,554	(14%)
	Wallace (AI)	85,719	(70%)

Rep. Trent Lott (R) Elected 1972; b. Oct. 9, 1941, Grenada; home, Pascagoula; U. of Miss., B.A., 1963, J.D. 1967; Baptist.

Career Practicing atty., 1967–68; Admin. Asst. to U.S. Rep. William M. Colmer, 1968–72.

Offices 308 CHOB, 202-225-5772. Also P.O. Box 1557, Gulfport 39501, 601-864-7670.

Committees

Post Office and Civil Service (9th). Subcommittees: Manpower and Civil Service.

Rules (5th).

Group Ratings

	ADA	COPE	LWV	RIPON	NFU	LCV	CFA	NAB	NSI	ACA
1974	0	0	17	23	42	35	0	82	90	85
1973	5	10	9	27	58	11	0	–	–	84

Key Votes

1) Foreign Aid	AGN	6) Gov Abortn Aid	AGN	11) Pub Cong Election $	AGN
2) Busing	AGN	7) Coed Phys Ed	AGN	12) Turkish Arms Cutoff	AGN
3) ABM	FOR	8) Pov Lawyer Gag	FOR	13) Youth Camp Regs	AGN
4) B-1 Bomber	FOR	9) Pub Trans Sub	AGN	14) Strip Mine Veto	FOR
5) Nerve Gas	FOR	10) EZ Voter Regis	AGN	15) Farm Bill Veto	AGN

Election Results

1974 general:	Trent Lott (R)	52,489	(74%)	($31,464)
	W. W. Murphy (D)	10,333	(15%)	($2,163)
	Mrs. K. Mertz (Ind.)	6,404	(9%)	($3,180)
	G. Gilley (Ind.)	1,954	(3%)	($2,251)
1974 primary:	Trent Lott (R), unopposed			
1972 general:	Trent Lott (R)	77,826	(56%)	($119,190)
	Ben Stone (D)	62,101	(44%)	($163,976)

MISSOURI

Missouri is a border state, admitted to the Union in 1821 as part of the compromise that bears its name—a slave state whose borders jutted far north into free territory; a state which sent proslavery men over the border into Kansas in the 1850s to fight those sent in by abolitionists; a state which saw its own Civil War, one that was separated geographically but not spiritually from the conflict east of the Mississippi. Missouri was also a gateway to the west, an avenue for the great Yankee migrations west from Ohio, Indiana, and Illinois, and the eastern terminus of the Pony Express and the first Transcontinental Railroad.

Politically, Democrats have always dominated Missouri, but there has always been a Republican Party capable of winning at least some elections. The Democratic edge is the proximate result of Missouri's slave state background; Missouri's most famous Democrat, Harry S. Truman, had a grandfather who fought in the Rebel army, and his mother, who lived to see her son President, remained a Confederate sympathizer all her life. Truman's background—Southern rural and Kansas City urban—typified the tensions within the Missouri Democratic Party and also explains why Truman, who integrated the armed forces, could also react negatively to the lunch counter sit-ins of the early 1960s. Truman's combination of liberalism on economic issues, a mixed response on social questions, and an affection for old political friends still characterizes the state, if not the congressional, leaders of Missouri's Democrats.

Over the years this combination produced many election day victories—but not always by the large margins Truman won. Since 1948, presidential elections have been very close here; except for the landslides of 1964 and 1972, no presidential candidate has carried the state by more than 30,000 votes out of nearly two million cast. The big story here in state elections has been a Republican breakthrough after years of Democratic dominance. The first major GOP victory came in 1968 with the election of John Danforth as Attorney General. Danforth, a young heir to the Ralston Purina fortune, ran against Senator Stuart Symington two years later and took a surprisingly large 49% of the vote. As Danforth nearly pulled off that upset, another young Republican, Christopher (Kit) Bond, unseated the longtime state Auditor. In 1972, Bond ran for Governor and won by a solid 55–45 margin; the same year, Danforth was winning reelection with 63%, actually running ahead of Richard Nixon.

Both Bond and Danforth are young, 37 and 40 respectively; both are rich and went to Ivy League schools. Both have hired staffs with a range of expertise not ordinarily found in the sleepy capital of Jefferson City, and both have fashioned political careers out of attacks on the cronyism and old fashioned politicking of the once entrenched Missouri Democrats.

Danforth's near win in the 1970 Senate race surprised many of the nation's political pundits; it also surprised the man he nearly beat, Stuart Symington. Symington, then 69, had served three terms in the Senate after a successful career in business (Emerson Electric) and in the Truman Administration (Secretary of the Air Force). During the 1950s Symington became known as an advocate of greater military preparedness in general and of the big bomber in particular; he was considered formidable enough to have been a dark horse candidate for the Democratic presidential nomination in 1960.

Early in the course of the Vietnam war, this onetime Air Force oriented hawk became a committed dove, convinced that the war was futile and wrong. With seats on the Foreign Relations and Armed Services Committees—the only Senator then and now to sit on both—Symington was nicely placed to lobby for end-the-war legislation and against weapons systems like the ABM. He was part of an early dovish majority on Foreign Relations, and so he concentrated his efforts on the usually hawkish Armed Services panel, where he has had some successes. Second in seniority among the Committee's Democrats, he served as Acting Chairman when John Stennis of Mississippi was hospitalized after being shot in 1973.

During his heyday, Symington was quite a vote-getter in Missouri, actually running ahead of Lyndon Johnson in 1964. But his close call in 1970, and his age—he turns 75 when his seat is up in 1976—made it clear that this would be his last term in the Senate. He has announced his intention to retire, and the battle to succeed him should be a fierce one. On the Republican side, Danforth has cause to believe that his close race in 1970 entitles him to the nomination, and the earnest sort of oratory he showed in that campaign (if not the devotion to Richard Nixon he then professed) may very well make him the first Republican Senator elected in Missouri since 1946. For the Democrats, the most likely nominee is 2d district Congressman James Symington, well known in the St. Louis area and with at least name recognition in the rest of the state. Such a race would be an interesting contrast of styles—the affable Symington versus the intense Danforth—as well as a clash of rather different views. But Symington cannot count on winning the nomination without competition. Also interested are former Governor Warren Hearnes, his once bright reputation now tarnished by the goings on in Jefferson City, and ambitious 6th district Congressman Jerry Litton, who will likely campaign as the champion of the rural areas and small towns.

Missouri's other Senator, by his own admission, is a man whose name was not a household word—until July 1972 that is. When Thomas Eagleton was nominated for Vice President in Miami Beach, he was scarcely known outside Missouri. But at home his political career had been meteoric: circuit attorney in St. Louis at 27, state Attorney General at 31, Lieutenant Governor at 35, and U.S. Senator at 39. The race to become Senator was his toughest. In the primary, Eagleton had to beat incumbent Democrat Edward Long, who according to *Life* magazine had been receiving large retainers from one of Jimmy Hoffa's attorney, and had been running investigations of, inter alia, apparent government harassment of Hoffa. In the general election, Eagleton had to beat suburban St. Louis Congressman Thomas Curtis, a respected moderate. Eagleton did both, but by only narrow margins; and in early July 1972 he expected vigorous opposition from John Danforth in 1974.

What happened when George McGovern, at the last minute, picked Eagleton as his running mate everyone knows. Ten days later, Robert Boyd and Clark Hoyt of the Knight newspapers found out that Eagleton had twice been hospitalized and received electro-shock therapy for depression. The response to the news was mixed. Many felt compassion, while others did not want a man subject to such problems a heartbeat away from the Presidency. For his part Eagleton took his case to the public, and McGovern announced he was behind him 100%. A few days later, however, Eagleton was dropped from the ticket.

Public reaction to McGovern's decision was unmistakable. The episode cost McGovern whatever chance he had to get his campaign off the ground. Young voters in particular—the people McGovern absolutely needed—were turned off, apparently on the belief that jettisoning Eagleton, especially after promising not to, was a reversion to the old politics, evidence of an unenlightened fear of mental illness. But even if McGovern had taken the opposite course, he would have been in trouble, stuck with a lingering, damaging issue which would have dogged him, without any explicit mention from the Republicans, through the whole campaign. Eagleton's failure to tell the nominee about his problem, and the fact that it was later revealed, irretrievably wrecked the Democrats' chances in 1972.

But interestingly, neither Eagleton's omission nor the revelation seems to have harmed his political career at all, nor has his refusal to disclose his medical records. And, to be fair, his illnesses—the latest episode was in 1960—seem not to have affected his performance as a Senator, either. He has, in fact, been an active, successful Senator. In his first term he became Chairman of the Senate District of Columbia Committee, and had the satisfaction of helping the capital city to achieve home rule in 1973. An original sponsor of the war powers bill, he broke away when it was amended in a way that he believed gave the President too much discretion in deploying American military forces; his warnings here may well prove prophetic. He was the chief Senate sponsor of the successful 1973 move to stop the bombing in Cambodia.

After he was dropped from the national ticket in 1973, Eagleton was immensely popular, more than ever before, in Missouri. That was enough to deter Danforth from running against him, and instead Eagleton once again drew his 1968 opponent. Curtis had served—and resigned on principle—on Nixon's public television board; he had been out of the state and, at 63, was not the formidable candidate he had been six years before. The result was an Eagleton landslide of 60–40 proportions. Curtis is now back in Washington, as the head of the new Federal Elections Commission. It appears now that Eagleton has a lifetime safe Senate seat; one doubts, however, that he will ever appear on a national ticket again.

Despite the recent Republican resurgence in Missouri state politics, Missouri's House delegation remains Democratic by a 9–1 margin. Republicans have missed chances of picking up seats where aging Democrats retired (the 6th district in 1972) and have had difficulty holding onto the one seat they have (the 7th in 1974). Their best chance to pick up a seat in 1976 will come in the 2d district if Congressman James Symington decides to run for the Senate.

Census Data Pop. 4,677,399; 2.31% of U.S. total, 13th largest; Central city, 30%; suburban, 35%. Median family income, $8,908; 29th highest; families above $15,000: 17%; families below $3,000: 12%. Median years education, 11.8.

1974 Share of Federal Tax Burden $5,758,029,000; 2.15% of U.S. total, 14th largest.

1974 Share of Federal Outlays $6,798,031,000; 2.52% of U.S. total, 12th largest.   Per capita federal spending, $1454.

DOD	$2,111,761,000	9th (3.08%)		HEW	$2,176,385,000	12th (2.35%)
AEC	$109,136,000	14th (3.58%)		HUD	$23,778,000	14th (2.44%)
NASA	$31,598,000	14th (1.06%)		VA	$340,495,000	12th (2.49%)
DOT	$184,857,000	17th (2.18%)		EPA	$46,484,000	21st (1.48%)
DOC	$9,129,000	26th (0.57%)		RevS	$113,513,000	20th (1.87%)
DOI	$48,749,000	17th (1.98%)		Int.	$222,654,000	12th (1.08%)
USDA	$408,421,000	7th (3.28%)		Other	$971,071,000	

Economic Base Agriculture, notably cattle, hogs, soybeans and dairy products; finance, insurance and real estate; transportation equipment, especially motor vehicles and equipment; food and kindred products; printing and publishing; electrical equipment and supplies; apparel and other textile products, especially men's and boys' furnishings, and women's and misses' outerwear.

Political Line-up Governor, Christopher S. Bond (R). Senators, Stuart Symington (D) and Thomas F. Eagleton (D). Representatives, 10 (9 D and 1 R). State Senate (23 D and 11 R); State House (113 D and 50 R).

The Voters

Registration 2,165,407 Total. No party registration.
Median voting age 44.
Employment profile White collar, 47%. Blue collar, 36%. Service, 13%. Farm, 4%.
Ethnic groups Black, 10%. Total foreign stock, 7%, Germany, 2%.

Presidential vote

1972	Nixon (R)	1,153,852	(62%)
	McGovern (D)	697,147	(38%)
1968	Nixon (R)	811,932	(45%)
	Humphrey (D)	791,444	(44%)
	Wallace (AI)	206,126	(11%)

Sen. Stuart Symington (D) Elected 1952, seat up 1976; b. June 26, 1901, Amherst, Mass.; home, Clayton; Yale U., A.B. 1923; Episcopalian.

Career Army, WWI; Metal and electronic manufacturing business, 1923–27; Pres., Emerson Electric Mfg. Co., 1938–45; Chm., U.S. Surplus Property Bd., 1945; Asst. Secy. of War for Air, 1946–57; Secy. of the Air Force, 1947–50; Chm., Natl. Security Resources Bd., 1950–51; Administrator, Reconstruction Finance Corp., 1951–52.

Offices 229 RSOB, 202-224-6154. Also 7730 Carondelet St., St. Louis 63105, 314-425-3131, and 945 U.S. Court House, 811 Grand Ave., Kansas City 64106, 816-374-3068.

Committees

Aeronautical and Space Sciences (2d).

Armed Services (2d). Subcommittees: Arms Control; Intelligence; Military Construction Authorization (Chairman); National Stockpile and Naval Petroleum Reserves; Preparedness Investigating; Tactical Air Power.

Foreign Relations (4th). Subcommittees: Arms Control, International Organization and Security Agreements (Chairman); European Affairs; Multinational Corporations; Western Hemisphere Affairs.

Joint Committee on Atomic Energy (3d, Senate Side) Subcommittees: ERDA, Nuclear Energy; National Security (Chairman).

Group Ratings

	ADA	COPE	LWV	RIPON	NFU	LCV	CFA	NAB	NSI	ACA
1974	88	78	80	38	94	70	88	42	0	19
1973	88	75	78	31	94	–	62	–	–	12
1972	70	90	82	52	70	58	100	73	10	23

Key Votes

1) No-Knock	AGN	8) Gov Abortn Aid	FOR	15) Consumer Prot Agy	FOR
2) Busing	FOR	9) Cut Mil Brass	FOR	16) Forced Psych Tests	ABS
3) No Fault	FOR	10) Gov Limousine	AGN	17) Fed Campaign Subs	ABS
4) F-111	FOR	11) RR Featherbed	ABS	18) Rhod Chrome Ban	FOR
5) Death Penalty	FOR	12) Handgun License	FOR	19) Open Legis Meetings	AGN
6) Foreign Aid	AGN	13) Less Troop Abrd	FOR	20) Strikers Food Stmps	FOR
7) Filibuster	AGN	14) Resume Turk Aid	FOR	21) Gov Info Disclosure	FOR

Election Results

1970 general:	Stuart Symington (D)	....	654,831	(51%)
	John C. Danforth (R)	....	617,903	(49%)
1970 primary:	Stuart Symington (D)	....	392,670	(89%)
	Four others (D)	....	47,153	(11%)
1964 general:	Stuart Symington (D)	....	1,186,666	(67%)
	Jean Paul Bradshaw (R)	....	596,377	(33%)

Sen. Thomas F. Eagleton (D) Elected 1968, seat up 1980; b. Sept. 4, 1929, St. Louis; home, St. Louis; Amherst Col., B.A. 1950, Harvard U., LL.B. 1953; Catholic.

Career Navy, 1948–49; Practicing atty.; St. Louis Circuit Atty., 1956–60; Atty. Gen. of Mo., 1961–65; Lt. Gov. of Mo., 1965–69.

Offices 6235 DSOB, 202-224-5721. Also 213 Adams St., Rm. 206, Jefferson City 65101, 314-636-9811, and Rm. 911, Fed. Bldg., 811 Grand Ave., Kansas City 64106, 816-374-2747.

Committees

The District of Columbia (Chairman).

Appropriations (13th). Subcommittees: Agriculture and Related Agencies; Labor and HEW; State, Justice, Commerce, The Judiciary; Transportation; Treasury, U.S. Postal Service, and General Government.

Labor and Public Welfare (7th). Subcommittees: Aging (Chairman); Education; Health; Labor; Special Subcommittee on Arts and Humanities; Special Subcommittee on the National Science Foundation.

Group Ratings

	ADA	COPE	LWV	RIPON	NFU	LCV	CFA	NAB	NSI	ACA
1974	83	89	80	48	88	65	88	50	10	18
1973	100	80	89	33	94	–	80	–	–	8
1972	70	90	100	60	67	75	89	50	0	21

Key Votes

1) No-Knock	ABS	8) Gov Abortn Aid	AGN	15) Consumer Prot Agy	FOR
2) Busing	FOR	9) Cut Mil Brass	FOR	16) Forced Psych Tests	FOR
3) No Fault	AGN	10) Gov Limousine	ABS	17) Fed Campaign Subs	FOR
4) F-111	ABS	11) RR Featherbed	FOR	18) Rhod Chrome Ban	FOR
5) Death Penalty	AGN	12) Handgun License	AGN	19) Open Legis Meetings	FOR
6) Foreign Aid	AGN	13) Less Troop Abrd	FOR	20) Strikers Food Stmps	FOR
7) Filibuster	ABS	14) Resume Turk Aid	AGN	21) Gov Info Disclosure	FOR

Election Results

1974 general:	Thomas F. Eagleton (D)	735,433	(60%)	($647,143)
	Thomas B. Curtis (R)	480,900	(40%)	($362,804)
1974 primary:	Thomas F. Eagleton (D)	420,681	(87%)	
	Two others (D)	60,224	(13%)	
1968 general:	Thomas F. Eagleton (D)	880,113	(51%)	
	Thomas B. Curtis (R)	845,144	(49%)	

Gov. Christopher S. Bond (R) Elected 1972, term expires Jan. 1977; b. Mar. 6, 1939, St. Louis; Princeton U., A.B. 1960, U. of Va., LL.B. 1963; Presbyterian.

Career Clerk, U.S. Court of Appeals Chf. Judge Elbert P. Tuttle, 5th Circuit, Atlanta, Ga., 1963–64; Practicing atty., 1964–69; Asst. Atty. Gen. of Mo., 1969–70; State Auditor of Mo. 1971–73.

Offices Executive Ofc., State Capitol Bldg., Jefferson City 65101, 314-751-3222.

Election Results

1972 general:	Christopher Bond (R)	1,029,451	(55%)
	Edward L. Dowd (D)	832,751	(45%)
1972 primary:	Christopher Bond (R)	265,467	(75%)
	Gene McNary (R)	56,652	(16%)
	Three others (R)	31,179	(9%)

◆ ◆ ◆ ◆ ◆

FIRST DISTRICT

The 1st congressional district of Missouri is the northern half of the city of St. Louis and a slice of the separate, totally suburban St. Louis County to the west. Because of black migration and the transformation of neighborhood patterns within the city, the north side of St. Louis is predominantly black, and in 1968 the fourth Missouri redistricting of that decade made blacks a majority district-wide. Boundary adjustments in 1972 left a smaller black percentage in the 1st, although still a majority. The suburban part of the district hugs the western city limits of St. Louis, and is mostly white; there are, however significant and increasing numbers of blacks here in University City, Richmond Heights, and Webster Groves. The socio-economic makeup of the suburbs ranges from blue-collar in the north (Normandy, Bel-Ridge) to white collar in the south (Webster Groves, Brentwood). Lying in the middle is Clayton, the St. Louis County seat, which is developing into a center of large high-rise office buildings; it is also the home of Washington University and its adjacent liberal academic community.

The 1st is the most heavily Democratic congressional district in Missouri, the only one of the state's ten to give a majority to George McGovern, despite his having dumped 1st district resident Thomas Eagleton from his ticket. For years the 1st was represented in the House by Frank Karsten, a conventional liberal Democrat. But after the 1968 redistricting, Karsten retired and in effect ceded the seat to then Alderman and erstwhile civil rights activist William Clay. Clay had spurned the traditional, decaying political machines of St. Louis, and had built up a following of his own among blacks on the north side.

Clay was one of the first militant, outspoken blacks elected to Congress and one of those who made a voluble instrument of the Congressional Black Caucus. Back in 1963, he spent 105 days in jail for participating in a civil rights demonstration. With this kind of background, he has not run particularly well in the predominantly white suburbs; indeed, in 1972, he ran 9% behind McGovern in the St. Louis County portion of the 1st. Nevertheless, Clay is comfortably ensconced within the current borders of the 1st, which were drawn to his specifications after rival politicians in the Missouri legislature threatened to create a white majority 1st district. In Washington, Clay sits on the Education and Labor Committee, a body currently so packed with liberals that this Congressman's voice seldom rises above the din of the rest.

Census Data Pop. 468,056. Central city, 66%; suburban, 34%. Median family income, $8,485; families above $15,000: 17%; families below $3,000: 3%. Median years education, 10.7.

The Voters

Median voting age 45.
Employment profile White collar, 46%. Blue collar, 33%. Service, 21%. Farm, –%.
Ethnic groups Black, 54%. Total foreign stock, 8%. Germany, 2%.

Presidential vote

1972	Nixon (R)	45,765	(31%)
	McGovern (D)	101,307	(69%)
1968	Nixon (R)	41,869	(26%)
	Humphrey (D)	110,310	(68%)
	Wallace (AI)	9,671	(6%)

Rep. William (Bill) **Clay** (D) Elected 1968; b. Apr. 30, 1931, St. Louis; home, St. Louis; St. Louis U., B.S. 1953; Catholic.

Career Real estate broker; Life insurance business, 1959–61; St. Louis City Alderman, 1959–64; Business Rep., City Employees Union, 1961–64.

Offices 328 CHOB, 202-225-2406. Also 5980 Delmar Blvd., St. Louis 63112, 314-725-5770.

Committees

Education and Labor (13th). Subcommittees: Equal Opportunities; Labor-Management Relations; Labor Standards.

Post Office and Civil Service (9th). Subcommittees: Employee Political Rights and Intergovernmental Programs (Chairman); Postal Facilities, Mail, and Labor Management.

Group Ratings

	ADA	COPE	LWV	RIPON	NFU	LCV	CFA	NAB	NSI	ACA
1974	93	100	90	64	100	82	100	10	20	0
1973	100	100	91	69	95	100	100	–	–	8
1972	81	88	100	75	100	54	–	0	0	7

Key Votes

1) Foreign Aid	FOR	6) Gov Abortn Aid	FOR	11) Pub Cong Election $	FOR
2) Busing	FOR	7) Coed Phys Ed	FOR	12) Turkish Arms Cutoff	FOR
3) ABM	ABS	8) Pov Lawyer Gag	AGN	13) Youth Camp Regs	ABS
4) B-1 Bomber	AGN	9) Pub Trans Sub	ABS	14) Strip Mine Veto	AGN
5) Nerve Gas	ABS	10) EZ Voter Regis	FOR	15) Farm Bill Veto	AGN

Election Results

1974 general:	William (Bill) Clay (D)	61,933	(68%)	($43,810)
	Arthur O. Martin (R)	28,707	(32%)	($1,881)

1974 primary:	William (Bill) Clay (D)	39,141	(68%)	
	C. W. Gates (D)	18,150	(32%)	
1972 general:	William (Bill) Clay (D)	95,098	(64%)	($17,480)
	Richard O. Funsch (R)	53,596	(36%)	($59,672)

◆ ◆ ◆ ◆ ◆

SECOND DISTRICT

The 2d congressional district of Missouri is the heart of St. Louis County, a jurisdiction that lies adjacent to, but includes no part of, the city of St. Louis. The county originally set itself apart so that its predominantly rural affairs would not get lost in the business of the city; now St. Louis City is dwarfed in population and wealth by its suburban offspring. In the northern part of the 2d district, along Interstate 70, are blue collar communities like Jennings, Ferguson, Berkley, and Airport Township. Most of the people here grew up on the north side of St. Louis, which is now heavily black; many work in the giant McDonnell-Douglas aircraft plants located on the north side of St. Louis County. To the south of the district are WASPy, traditionally Republican suburbs like Kirkwood and Webster Groves, fully occupied in the 1950s and placid in their conservatism. To the west, the 2d has the bulk of the Jewish population of metropolitan St. Louis in University City and the towns lying north of the Daniel Boone Freeway. Here too is the ultraposh city of Ladue, home of most members of the St. Louis establishment (median family income in 1970: $32,000).

Altogether, the diverse makeup of the 2d district produces election results that are exceedingly close to those produced by the state as a whole and, indeed, by the nation as a whole. Thus in 1972, the 2d was carried comfortably by Richard Nixon, but at the same time it easily reelected its Democratic Congressman. Until 1968, the 2d was represented by a Republican well respected in the councils of his party, Thomas Curtis; he ran for the Senate that year and barely lost to Thomas Eagleton and now, after another loss, is the new Chairman of the new Federal Elections Commission.

Curtis's successor is James W. Symington, son of Senator Stuart Symington (and grandson of James Wadsworth, onetime Senator from New York). Like his father, Symington had held a number of important posts in a Democratic national administration; and like his father, he returned to Missouri when that administration's time seemed to be up and ran for office. Symington won easily in the 2d, and has been reelected without difficulty ever since. In the House, despite his wide range of administrative experience, he at first chose to play the role of the quiet, dutiful freshman. He is better known, at least in the Washington social circuit, as the Congressman who plays the guitar and sings songs of his own composition. Now Symington is preparing to run for his father's seat in the Senate, and he appears to have a good chance to win.

Census Data Pop. 468,808. Central city, 0%; suburban, 100%. Median family income, $12,597; families above $15,000: 35%; families below $3,000: 4%. Median years education, 12.4.

The Voters

Median voting age 42.
Employment profile White collar, 63%. Blue collar, 28%. Service, 9%. Farm, –%.
Ethnic groups Black, 4%. Total foreign stock, 12%. Germany, 2%; Italy, 1%.

Presidential vote

	1972	Nixon (R)	127,123	(63%)
		McGovern (D)	75,564	(37%)
	1968	Nixon (R)	85,185	(46%)
		Humphrey (D)	79,326	(43%)
		Wallace (AI)	18,994	(10%)

Rep. James W. Symington (D) Elected 1968; b. Sept. 28, 1927, Rochester, N.Y.; home, Clayton; Yale U., A.B. 1950, Columbia U., LL.B. 1954; Episcopalian.

Career USMC, 1945–46; Asst. St. Louis City Counselor, 1954–55; Practicing atty., 1955–58, 1960–61; U.S. Foreign Service, London, 1958–60; Deputy Dir., Food for Peace, 1961–62; Admin. Asst. to U.S. Atty. Gen. Robert F. Kennedy, 1962–63; Dir., Pres. Comm. on Juvenile Delinquency, 1965–66; Chf. of Protocol, U.S. Dept. of State, 1966–68.

Offices 307 CHOB, 202-225-2561. Also 10 S. Brentwood Blvd., Clayton 63105, 314-425-3096.

Committees

Interstate and Foreign Commerce (14th). Subcommittees: Health and Environment.

Science and Technology (5th). Subcommittees: Energy Research, Development and Demonstration; Science, Research, and Technology (Chairman); Space Science and Applications.

Group Ratings

	ADA	COPE	LWV	RIPON	NFU	LCV	CFA	NAB	NSI	ACA
1974	69	90	83	57	100	69	77	27	14	14
1973	83	90	92	80	100	88	83	–	–	8
1972	81	91	90	64	71	66	100	18	33	0

Key Votes

1) Foreign Aid	FOR	6) Gov Abortn Aid	ABS	11) Pub Cong Election $	FOR
2) Busing	AGN	7) Coed Phys Ed	FOR	12) Turkish Arms Cutoff	FOR
3) ABM	ABS	8) Pov Lawyer Gag	AGN	13) Youth Camp Regs	AGN
4) B-1 Bomber	AGN	9) Pub Trans Sub	ABS	14) Strip Mine Veto	AGN
5) Nerve Gas	ABS	10) EZ Voter Regis	ABS	15) Farm Bill Veto	AGN

Election Results

1974 general:	James W. Symington (D)	85,977	(61%)	($74,762)
	Howard C. Ohlendorf (R)	55,026	(39%)	($43,330)
1974 primary:	James W. Symington (D)	36,257	(72%)	
	John P. Doyle (D)	14,419	(28%)	
1972 general:	James W. Symington (D)	134,332	(64%)	($67,938)
	John W. Cooper, Jr. (R)	77,192	(36%)	($30,298)

◆ ◆ ◆ ◆ ◆

THIRD DISTRICT

Missouri's 3d congressional district consists of the south side of the city of St. Louis and an adjacent portion of suburban St. Louis County. The line drawn through the middle of St. Louis to separate the 1st from the 3d district also neatly separates the predominantly black part of the city from that part in the 3d district which remains overwhelmingly (92% in 1970, and not much lower today) white. Here on the south side there are still signs of the German immigrants who made St. Louis one of the nation's gemütlichkeit cities of the nineteenth century; today, as if in memory, an Altenheim (old people's home) still sits on the banks of the Mississippi. The most famous of the St. Louis Germans was Carl Schurz, a friend of Lincoln, a northern officer in the Civil War, a Secretary of the Interior, and U.S. Senator from Missouri.

Today in the ethnic and elderly neighborhoods of the south side of St. Louis (median voting age in this district is 50), people have stayed with a New Deal-bred Democratic preference or, in the slightly better off streets at the edge of the city, have remained Republican. The suburban portion of the district is a natural extension of the city. Most of the people now living here moved out along the radial avenues extending out of St. Louis. The suburban voters tend to be somewhat more conservative and Republican than their counterparts in the city, though their parents probably voted for Roosevelt and Truman.

Like many women elected to Congress, the Representative from the 3d district, Leonor K. Sullivan, won her seat following the death of her husband Congressman John B. Sullivan, who served intermittently during the 1940s and 1950s. A Republican captured the seat in a 1951 special election to fill Sullivan's vacancy, but Mrs. Sullivan beat him in 1952 and has won easily ever since.

Mrs. Sullivan is currently a high ranking member of the Banking and Currency Committee, although she was passed over for the more assertive Henry Reuss of Wisconsin when in 1975 longtime Chairman Wright Patman was successfully ousted. For many years, she had been Chairman of its Consumer Affairs Subcommittee, in which capacity she led the fight for the truth-in-lending law, her major congressional achievement; this was won over the strong opposition of the banking lobby and big retailers and amid general public apathy. Mrs. Sullivan lost that chair when Reuss took over the full committee, ostensibly because she has been a chairman of a full committee, Merchant Marine and Fisheries, since 1973; the more likely reason is that she supported Patman in the Patman-Reuss fight. Mrs. Sullivan is a traditionalist in many ways, despite her crusade for truth-in-lending; as head of Merchant Marine she has backed the continuation of heavy government subsidies to American shipping and shipbuilding industries and to members of the various maritime unions.

On the more personal level, Mrs. Sullivan is the woman member of Congress least sympathetic to the women's liberation movement and its ideas. She voted against the Equal Rights Amendment, the only Congresswoman to do so because she feared it would overthrow women's protective laws. She shuns terms like Ms., preferring to refer to herself as Mrs. John B. Sullivan; she insists on the coy woman's prerogative of keeping her age secret. The last is not a bad political move, since she is now somewhere over 70. In any case, it is a little sad to see this more than usually productive member of Congress so at odds with the trends and fads of the times; she is a woman who has missed out, but not by much, from a position of real legislative eminence.

Census Data Pop. 467,544. Central city, 67%; suburban, 33%. Median family income, $10,199; families above $15,000: 20%; families below $3,000: 8%. Median years education, 10.6.

The Voters

Median voting age 47.
Employment profile White collar, 52%. Blue collar, 36%. Service, 12%. Farm, –%.
Ethnic groups Black, 6%. Spanish, 1%. Total foreign stock, 15%. Germany, 4%; Italy, 2%.

Presidential vote

1972	Nixon (R)	102,959	(58%)
	McGovern (D)	73,362	(42%)
1968	Nixon (R)	70,887	(40%)
	Humphrey (D)	85,327	(48%)
	Wallace (AI)	21,754	(12%)

Rep. Leonor K. Sullivan (D) Elected 1952; b. St. Louis; home, St. Louis; Washington U.; Catholic.

Career Dir., St. Louis Comptometer School; Admin. Asst. to U.S. Rep. John B. Sullivan, 1941–51.

Offices 2221 RHOB, 202-225-2671. Also 2918 Fed. Bldg., 1520 Market St., St. Louis 63103, 314-425-4500.

Committees

Merchant Marine and Fisheries (Chairman).

Banking, Currency and Housing (4th). Subcommittees: Consumer Affairs; Economic Stabilization; Housing and Community Development.

Group Ratings

	ADA	COPE	LWV	RIPON	NFU	LCV	CFA	NAB	NSI	ACA
1974	59	100	45	21	83	71	75	25	67	9
1973	70	100	73	54	95	63	100	–	–	24
1972	38	100	80	40	86	67	100	22	56	25

Key Votes

1) Foreign Aid	AGN	6) Gov Abortn Aid	AGN	11) Pub Cong Election $	AGN
2) Busing	AGN	7) Coed Phys Ed	AGN	12) Turkish Arms Cutoff	FOR
3) ABM	AGN	8) Pov Lawyer Gag	FOR	13) Youth Camp Regs	FOR
4) B-1 Bomber	AGN	9) Pub Trans Sub	FOR	14) Strip Mine Veto	AGN
5) Nerve Gas	FOR	10) EZ Voter Regis	FOR	15) Farm Bill Veto	AGN

Election Results

1974 general:	Leonor K. (Mrs. John B.) Sullivan (D) ...	96,201	(75%)	($27,800)
	JoAnn P. Raisch (R)	31,489	(25%)	($2,254)
1974 primary:	Leonor K. (Mrs. John B.) Sullivan (D) ...	44,959	(90%)	
	Victoria Schmidt (D)	3,799	(8%)	
	Asen Dodov (D)	1,395	(3%)	
1972 general:	Leonor K. (Mrs. John B.) Sullivan (D) ...	124,365	(70%)	($29,225)
	Albert Holst (R)	54,523	(30%)	($5,151)

◆ ◆ ◆ ◆ ◆

FOURTH DISTRICT

The home district of the late Harry S. Truman was the 4th congressional district of Missouri. Truman's background—he never represented the district in the House, but served in the Senate from 1935 to 1945—tells us a lot about the district, even today. Truman was born in the town of Lamar, in the southern end of the 4th, near the Oklahoma and Arkansas borders. His family was Democratic, which means that in his mother's case at least it cherished a lifelong sympathy for the cause of the Confederacy. The largest city in the 4th district way at its other end, is Independence (pop. 111,000), an old courthouse town, where Truman lived on what is now Truman Road in a nineteenth century Victorian house belonging to his wife's family. Just a few blocks away is the Jackson County Courthouse where Truman was once County Judge (an administrative post) before his election to the Senate. In those days Independence was a small town, the incongruous seat of a county which included bustling Kansas City. Today, the suburban growth emanating from Kansas City has so ballooned the population of Independence that Truman's old Victorian town has almost entirely been engulfed.

The 4th district is a combination of rural Missouri counties, like the one Truman grew up in, and part of the Kansas City metropolitan area, where he began his political career. Its political history is almost totally Democratic. The rural counties, though to a lessened extent in recent years, clung to the party which had been the more sympathetic to slavery (or most unsympathetic to abolition). Kansas City has been Democratic since before the days of Tom Prendergast, the political boss who gave Truman his start and later ended up in jail. Truman himself had no part in Prendergast's graft but he was certainly a beneficiary of the fraudulently high number of votes the machine piled up; indeed, Jackson County has never again cast—or been reported to cast—so many votes as it did in the 1936 presidential election.

Like Truman, the current Congressman from the 4th district also served as Jackson County Judge, in William Randall's case, from 1946 to 1959. He won his seat in the House in a 1959 special election, and has since then been accumulating seniority on the Armed Servies and Government Operations Committees. Particularly on Armed Services, Randall has aligned himself with the Committee's more conservative Democrats; which is to say that when in doubt he supports the position taken by the military. On domestic issues, Randall is significantly more conservative than most northern Democrats.

Randall's approach looks like a formula tailor-made for the 4th district. But for a longtime incumbent, he has not done especially well at the polls. To be sure, he did received 68% of the vote in 1974, but that was a heavily Democratic year; two years before, he had got only 57%. But years rather than Republicans are more likely to retire him; he turns 67 in 1976.

Census Data Pop. 466,940. Central city, 2%; suburban, 47%. Median family income, $8,740; families above $15,000: 15%; families below $3,000: 12%. Median years education, 12.1.

The Voters

Median voting age 44.
Employment profile White collar, 42%. Blue collar, 38%. Service, 12%. Farm, 8%.
Ethnic groups Black, 2%. Total foreign stock, 4%. Germany, 1%.

Presidential vote

1972	Nixon (R)	131,874	(69%)
	McGovern (D)	60,472	(31%)
1968	Nixon (R)	85,872	(48%)
	Humphrey (D)	70,811	(40%)
	Wallace (AI)	22,118	(12%)

Rep. William J. Randall (D) Elected Mar. 3, 1959; b. July 16, 1909, Independence; home, Independence; U. of Mo., A.B. 1931, U. of Kansas City, LL.B. 1936; Methodist.

Career Practicing atty., 1936–43; Army, WWII; Judge of Jackson Co. Ct., 1946–58.

Offices 2469 RHOB, 202-225-2876. Also 219 Fed. Bldg., 301 W. Lexington St., Independence 64050, 816-252-7171.

Committees

Armed Services (7th). Subcommittees: Investigations; Military Installations and Facilities.

Government Operations (7th). Subcommittees: Government Activities and Transportation (Chairman); Manpower and Housing.

Group Ratings

	ADA	COPE	LWV	RIPON	NFU	LCV	CFA	NAB	NSI	ACA
1974	30	64	42	33	85	35	58	60	78	53
1973	38	80	33	38	95	53	63	–	–	44
1972	13	67	40	64	83	27	50	36	100	62

Key Votes

1) Foreign Aid	AGN	6) Gov Abortn Aid	AGN	11) Pub Cong Election $	AGN
2) Busing	AGN	7) Coed Phys Ed	AGN	12) Turkish Arms Cutoff	FOR
3) ABM	ABS	8) Pov Lawyer Gag	FOR	13) Youth Camp Regs	AGN
4) B-1 Bomber	FOR	9) Pub Trans Sub	AGN	14) Strip Mine Veto	FOR
5) Nerve Gas	ABS	10) EZ Voter Regis	FOR	15) Farm Bill Veto	AGN

Election Results

1974 general:	William J. Randall (D)	82,447	(68%)	($19,596)
	Claude Patterson (R)	39,055	(32%)	($12,771)
1974 primary:	William J. Randall (D)	40,578	(87%)	
	Forest Nave, Jr. (D)	6,303	(13%)	
1972 general:	William J. Randall (D)	108,131	(57%)	($24,531)
	Raymond E. Barrows (R)	80,228	(43%)	($5,922)

◆ ◆ ◆ ◆ ◆

FIFTH DISTRICT

The 5th congressional district of Missouri includes the heart of Kansas City—the central portion of the city, including its downtown and most of its industrial area, but not the vast expanse recently annexed north of the Missouri River. This is the heart of the Kansas City metropolitan area, an important manufacturing center and commercial hub for the farmlands of western Missouri and most of Kansas. The 5th includes the down town skyscrapers of Kansas City that sit up on the bluffs above the Missouri and the Kansas City stockyards; all of the city's large black ghetto and many of its white working class neighborhoods; and the upper income suburbs of the southwest portion of the city, just across the state line from the high income suburbs of Johnson County, Kansas.

In 1948 a 32-year-old World War II veteran who had only lived in Kansas City a couple of years, Richard Bolling, was elected Congressman from the 5th district. Democrat Bolling soon became one of Speaker Sam Rayburn's proteges, and the old Texan schooled him in the ways of the House. He won a seat on the Rules Committee, and after Rayburn's death in 1961, Bolling failed to get on track; John McCormack succeeded automatically to the Speakership, Carl Albert to the position of Majority Leader, and McCormack and Albert together picked as Whip and as the man they assumed would one day succeed them Hale Boggs of Louisiana. Whereupon Bolling seemed to renounce any leadership ambitions and turned instead to write two books denouncing the way things were done in the House. As his Rules Committee continued to be led by octogenarians, Bolling seemed to grow listless and apathetic; in 1970, he was accused of missing a key Rules vote when he refused to fly back from a Caribbean vacation to cast it (he denies the story).

That was probably the nadir of Bolling's congressional career; since then, he has shown a resurgence of interest—and power. When Carl Albert became Speaker in 1971, one of the members whose advice he came to rely on was Bolling's. On the Rules Committee, Bolling continues to languish in seniority behind 84-year-old Ray Madden of Indiana and 75-year-old James Delaney of New York, but he does manage sometimes to rescue order out of chaos.

Bolling's major effort in recent years, committee reform, turned out to be less than 100% successful, but it still has made some difference in the way the House works. Bolling chaired a special committee set up to reform the committee structure, which came out with a report that destroyed the power bases of too many people to pass. Such diverse congressmen opposed it as Phillip Burton of California (because it would split Education and Labor into two committees), Leonor Sullivan of Missouri (because it would have abolished the Merchant Marine and Fisheries Committee she chairs), John Dingell of Michigan (because it would have abolished his conservation subcommittee and would generally have weakened pro-environment forces), and Richard Ichord of Missouri (because it would have abolished Internal Security, which he then chaired). The Bolling Commission plan's fate was sealed when organized labor opposed it (they didn't want anyone messing with the liberal-packed Education and Labor), and another panel headed by retiring Julia Butler Hansen of Washington watered down its recommendations. Nevertheless, Bolling is at least partially responsible for the creation of the House Budget Committee, and for a reorganization of some chaotic subcommitee jurisdictions.

Interestingly, Bolling, who has been criticizing the House from what most people would regard as left-liberal is something of a cold warrior in foreign policy; in contrast Burton, who played a major role in beating down the Bolling Committee reforms, is a longtime dove. It seems unlikely now that Bolling will ever become Speaker, but a couple of timely retirements—or a decision by the Democratic Caucus that enough shenanigans are enough—will make him Rules Chairman. He has got to the age when men in business and the bureaucracy are at the peak of their powers; and it seems for once that the House is going to allow one of its most talented members to play a major role in what should be his most productive years—rather than wait, as so often happens, till the man is 75 and well past his prime.

Census Data Pop. 467,457. Central city, 93%; suburban, 7%. Median family income, $9,727; families above $15,000: 20%; families below $3,000: 9%. Median years education, 12.2.

The Voters

Median voting age 44.
Employment profile White collar, 53%. Blue collar, 32%. Service, 15%. Farm, –%.
Ethnic groups Black, 24%. Spanish, 3%. Total foreign stock, 9%. Germany, Italy, 1% each.

Presidential vote

1972	Nixon (R)	80,553	(53%)
	McGovern (D)	71,527	(47%)

1968	Nixon (R)	57,971	(37%)
	Humphrey (D)	83,098	(52%)
	Wallace (AI)	17,562	(11%)

Rep. Richard Bolling (D) Elected 1948; b. May 17, 1916, New York, N.Y.; home, Kansas City; U. of the South, B.A. 1937, M.A. 1939, Vanderbilt U., 1939–40; Episcopalian.

Career Army, WWII; Teacher and coach, Sewanee Military Acad.; Vets. Advisor and Dir. of Student Activities, U. of Kansas City.

Offices 2465 RHOB, 202-225-4535. Also 811 Grand Ave., Kansas City 64106, 816-842-4798.

Committees

Rules (3rd).

Joint Economic Committee (2d, House Side). Subcommittees: Consumer Economics; Fiscal Policy (Chairman); Urban Affairs.

Group Ratings

	ADA	COPE	LWV	RIPON	NFU	LCV	CFA	NAB	NSI	ACA
1974	84	100	92	67	100	63	82	22	57	0
1973	65	89	90	69	95	64	100	–	–	9
1972	75	90	90	73	86	66	100	0	44	17

Key Votes

1) Foreign Aid	FOR	6) Gov Abortn Aid	FOR	11) Pub Cong Election $	FOR
2) Busing	FOR	7) Coed Phys Ed	FOR	12) Turkish Arms Cutoff	ABS
3) ABM	FOR	8) Pov Lawyer Gag	AGN	13) Youth Camp Regs	FOR
4) B-1 Bomber	AGN	9) Pub Trans Sub	FOR	14) Strip Mine Veto	AGN
5) Nerve Gas	AGN	10) EZ Voter Regis	FOR	15) Farm Bill Veto	AGN

Election Results

1974 general:	Richard Bolling (D)	57,081	(70%)	($20,590)
	John J. McDonough (R)	24,699	(30%)	($9,247)
1974 primary:	Richard Bolling (D)	35,444	(83%)	
	Stella Sollars (D)	7,399	(17%)	
1972 general:	Richard Bolling (D)	93,812	(64%)	($25,054)
	Vernon E. Rice (R)	53,257	(36%)	($442)

◆ ◆ ◆ ◆ ◆

SIXTH DISTRICT

Northwest Missouri is most farmland, gentle hill country rolling down to the Missouri River and its tributaries. In many ways this is a place left behind by the twentieth century. The mechanization of the family farm has thinned out the population here, as young people seek better livings elsewhere. All the counties of northwest Missouri, except those in the Kansas City metropolitan area, had more people at the turn of the century than they do today. Perhaps the most melancholy story belongs to St. Joseph, once one of the leading ports of entry to the American West: it was here that Pony Express riders saddled up for the transcontinental sprint to Sacramento. As late as 1900, St. Joseph was still a solid commercial competitor of Kansas City, with a population of 102,000, compared to Kansas City's 163,000. Today metropolitan Kansas City has more than a million people, while St. Joseph's population has dwindled to 72,000 and is growing still smaller.

The 3th congressional district covers almost precisely the northwest corner of Missouri: the land north and east of the Missouri River, west of a line drawn north and south through the middle of the state. Though most of the expanse of the 6th is given over to agriculture, as it was at the turn of the century, most of its residents now live in metropolitan areas. Some are in St. Joseph, but by far the bulk of this population is in Clay and Platte Counties in metropolitan Kansas City. To give itself space to grow, Kansas City has systematically been annexing land in these two counties in the last fifteen years; much of it has been bulldozed for subdivisions or to accommodate Kansas City's giant new airport. The Census Bureau considers most of Clay and Platte Counties part of the central city, and technically they are; but their character, by any measure, is suburban.

For 18 years the 6th district was represented in the House by W. R. Hull, the kind of conservative Democrat rural Missourians have traditionally found congenial. But in his last few elections, Hull's margins started to slip, and he decided to retire in 1972. That left the Republicans with a good chance to win the district: they might well have carried the metro Kansas City counties, and the rural counties and St. Joseph had been trending Republican heavily in recent elections. Nevertheless, most of the action remained in the Democratic primary, a contest between suburban Kansas City state Representative Charles Broomfield and Livingston County farmer Jerry Litton. Litton won that with 36% of the vote, and the general proved almost anticlimactic: Litton won with a solid 55% as Republicans never really mounted serious campaign.

In his first term, Litton won the kind of publicity any freshman from such a district would crave. With a seat on the Agriculture Committee, and as a founder of a so far not very active Rural Caucus, Litton was able to portray himself as a vigorous battler for the family farm. More than that, he got into a fight with the Agriculture Department over whether the government should have access to farmers' tax returns. At this writing, however, he has not yet managed to ram through a bill which would prohibit the practice, nonetheless, when it came time for the 1974 election, Litton was not only unbeatable, he might as well have been unopposed. He won fully 79% of the vote, far more than his considerably more conservative predecessor had ever taken. He seems to be headed for a lifetime career in the House, if he wants it, but he is running for the Senate; seldom has Missouri been represented in the Senate by someone with as rural a background as Litton's though 46% of its votes are cast outside its two big metropolitan areas.

Census Data Pop. 469,642. Central city, 30%; suburban, 22%. Median family income, $8,507; families above $15,000: 14%; families below $3,000: 12%. Median years education, 12.1.

The Voters

Median voting age 45.
Employment profile White collar, 43%. Blue collar, 35%. Service, 12%. Farm, 10%.
Ethnic groups Black, 1%. Total foreign stock, 5%. Germany, 1%.

Presidential vote

1972	Nixon (R)	134,977	(67%)
	McGovern (D)	65,754	(33%)
1968	Nixon (R)	96,811	(49%)
	Humphrey (D)	82,503	(41%)
	Wallace (AI)	20,275	(10%)

Rep. Jerry Litton (D) Elected 1972; b. May 12, 1937, near Lock Springs; home, Chillicothe; U. of Mo., B.S. 1961; Protestant.

Career Rancher; Farm dir., The Columbia *Missourian* and KCHI Radio, 1955, KBIA Radio, 1960; Pres., Performance Registry Internatl., 1964.

Offices 1005 LHOB, 202-225-7041. Also Royal Inn, Rm. 102, 11828 Plaza Circle, Kansas City 64153, 816-243-5977.

Committees

Agriculture (13th). Subcommittees: Family Farms and Rural Development; Forests (Chairman); Livestock and Grains.

District of Columbia (12th). Subcommittees: Commerce, Housing and Transportation; Education, Labor and Social Services; Government Operations.

Group Ratings

	ADA	COPE	LWV	RIPON	NFU	LCV	CFA	NAB	NSI	ACA
1974	52	63	55	43	92	47	64	67	40	29
1973	54	73	50	43	95	33	57	–	–	32

Key Votes

1) Foreign Aid	AGN	6) Gov Abortn Aid	AGN	11) Pub Cong Election $	FOR
2) Busing	AGN	7) Coed Phys Ed	FOR	12) Turkish Arms Cutoff	ABS
3) ABM	AGN	8) Pov Lawyer Gag	FOR	13) Youth Camp Regs	AGN
4) B-1 Bomber	ABS	9) Pub Trans Sub	AGN	14) Strip Mine Veto	AGN
5) Nerve Gas	AGN	10) EZ Voter Regis	FOR	15) Farm Bill Veto	AGN

Election Results

1974 general:	Jerry Litton (D)	101,609	(79%)	($52,896)
	Grover H. Speers (R)	27,147	(21%)	($745)
1974 primary:	Jerry Litton (D), unopposed			
1972 general:	Jerry Litton (D)	110,047	(55%)	($188,642)
	Russell Sloan (R)	91,610	(45%)	($100,059)

◆ ◆ ◆ ◆ ◆

SEVENTH DISTRICT

Mention the Ozarks and you evoke an image of rural poverty: people with quaint accents living in hillside shacks, cut off from the currents of twentieth century America—a kind of Dogpatch. But for the Ozark Mountains of southwest Missouri, an area roughly coincident with the state's 7th congressional district, the Dogpatch image is far from accurate, and getting rapidly less so each year. Here you can find sizable and reasonably prosperous cities, like Springfield (pop. 120,000), the state's third largest, and Joplin (39,000). Outside the cities, there has been transformation of the landscape in recent years, as people from St. Louis or Kansas City build vacation homes or even year round residences in the pleasant green hills, with their relatively temperate climate, and along the large, often man-made lakes.

In many mountain areas—eastern Tennessee and central Kentucky spring to mind—political preferences have undergone little change in over a century; and this—despite the recent growth—has been the case in Missouri's Ozarks too. The people here did not share the slaveholding habits or the Confederate sympathies of many central Missourians, and during the Civil War period they became staunch Republicans, and have stayed that way. The Republican inclination has been strengthened by two factors: first, a distaste for the social programs pushed by the Democrats of the 1960s, and, second, the urban bred conservatism of many of the area's recent arrivals. (One thing many of them like about the Ozarks is that there are virtually no blacks here.) In the close statewide elections of 1968, 1970, and 1972, every county in the 7th district went for the Republican candidates; in the 1974 Eagleton landslide, this was the only district that the Democratic Senator failed to carry.

The 7th is also the only Missouri district to send a Republican to Congress. For 12 years, until his retirement in 1972, its Congressman was Dr. Durward G. Hall, who, often working in tandem with H.R. Gross of Iowa, was one of the sternest congressional watchdogs of the federal treasury. Like most conservatives, Hall was more generous with the military, in his case as a member of the Armed Services Committee.

With Hall retiring in what was shaping up as a big Republican year, the GOP nomination here was obviously going to be tantamount to election. The winner, by a 50–45 margin, was Sarcoxie auto dealer and Republican National Committeeman Gene Taylor; the loser, John Ashcroft, was appointed by Governor Bond to succeed himself as state Auditor and narrowly lost election to that post in 1974. Naturally, Taylor won the 1972 general election with ease. But in just two years he was facing trouble in the unlikely person of Richard Franks, a 31-year-old Springfield Democrat and former judge. Franks ran a fairly strong campaign and held Taylor to a surprisingly low 53% of the vote; a better financed effort might have changed the result entirely. Taylor, who has not yet developed a style to match Doc Hall's, still holds what must be classed as a safe seat—but not as safe as people thought a couple of years ago.

Census Data Pop. 466,699. Central city, 26%; suburban, 7%. Median family income, $6,832; families above $15,000: 9%; families below $3,000: 18%. Median years education, 11.7.

The Voters

Median voting age 47.
Employment profile White collar, 41%. Blue collar, 39%. Service, 13%. Farm, 7%.
Ethnic groups Total foreign stock, 3%.

Presidential vote

1972	Nixon (R)	153,239	(73%)
	McGovern (D)	57,616	(27%)
1968	Nixon (R)	112,012	(58%)
	Humphrey (D)	62,783	(32%)
	Wallace (AI)	19,718	(10%)

Rep. Gene Taylor (R) Elected 1972; b. Feb. 10, 1928, near Sarcoxie; home, Sarcoxie; S.W. Mo. St. Col.; Methodist.

Career Public school teacher; Pres., Gene Taylor Ford Sales, Inc.; Mayor of Sarcoxie, 1954–60.

Offices 1114 LHOB, 202-225-6536. Also 314A Wilhoit Bldg., Springfield 65806, 417-862-4317.

Committees

Post Office and Civil Service (6th). Subcommittees: Manpower and Civil Service; Retirement and Employee Benefits.

Public Works and Transportation (10th). Subcommittees: Aviation; Economic Development; Water Resources.

Group Ratings

	ADA	COPE	LWV	RIPON	NFU	LCV	CFA	NAB	NSI	ACA
1974	5	0	17	27	36	29	0	90	100	79
1973	5	18	9	50	37	12	17	–	–	87

Key Votes

1) Foreign Aid	AGN	6) Gov Abortn Aid	AGN	11) Pub Cong Election $	AGN
2) Busing	AGN	7) Coed Phys Ed	AGN	12) Turkish Arms Cutoff	ABS
3) ABM	FOR	8) Pov Lawyer Gag	FOR	13) Youth Camp Regs	AGN
4) B-1 Bomber	FOR	9) Pub Trans Sub	AGN	14) Strip Mine Veto	FOR
5) Nerve Gas	FOR	10) EZ Voter Regis	AGN	15) Farm Bill Veto	AGN

Election Results

1974 general:	Gene Taylor (R)	79,787	(52%)	($96,782)
	Richard L. Franks (D)	72,653	(48%)	($94,173)
1974 primary:	Gene Taylor (R)	40,997	(76%)	
	Alex Karmarkovic (R)	12,612	(24%)	
1972 general:	Gene Taylor (R)	132,780	(64%)	($97,127)
	William Thomas (D)	75,613	(36%)	($10,864)

◆ ◆ ◆ ◆ ◆

EIGHTH DISTRICT

After five redistrictings in less than fifteen years, the 8th congressional district of Missouri has at last got a fairly regular shape. Before the 1972 redistricting, we described it as a slingshot; today, it is a rather solid-based chocolate rooster. The comb includes Columbia, the district's largest city and the home of the University of Missouri; at just about where the ears would be if chickens had ears is Jefferson City, the sleepy little state capital; the tail feathers lie in the western end of suburban St. Louis County; and the feet or leg base is solidly in the Ozarks. These are areas of diverse political tendencies. Columbia, with a Dixie Democratic tradition, now is more liberal than ever with the 18-year-old vote. The St. Louis County suburbs are staunchly Republican. Probably the most interesting parts of the district are Jefferson City and the counties to the east, which have been strongly Republican since they were settled by antislavery German '48ers in the mid-nineteenth century. Though the Ozark counties are Republican, most of the rural counties in the 8th are traditional Missouri Democratic; the most notable features south of Jefferson City are Fort Leonard Wood, long one of the Army's centers for basic training, and the Lake of the Ozarks nearby.

Missouri legislatures and courts have five times redrawn the boundaries of this district, but elections here, at least since 1960, have always had precisely the same result: the election of Democratic Congressman Richard Ichord. For the most part Ichord's record is conservative, and he is entirely comfortable in his position as fifth ranking Democrat on the Armed Services Committee; he is seldom any less hawkish—occasionally more—than the committee's bipartisan majority or most of the military witnesses whose requests it respectfully hears, and almost always grants.

But Ichord is less likely to go down in history as a member of Armed Services than he is as the last Chairman of the House Internal Security Committee (HISC), formerly known as the House Un-American Activities Committee (HUAC). The Committee was long an anomaly. During its thirty years as a standing committee, it seldom reported out legislation; the only bill it ever really passed, the McCarran Act was for the most part ruled unconstitutional by the courts. Instead, HUAC specialized in hearings in which it would expose alleged Communists and subversives, not so much to reveal their leanings (which almost invariably were well known), but rather to cause them to lose their jobs and otherwise be injured for conduct the Committee deemed un-American, whatever that means.

The Committee can claim to have made the political career of at least one President, Richard Nixon, who first gained fame on HUAC as the interrogator of Alger Hiss, and of two politicians who had to leave office because of their criminal conduct, onetime Chairman J. Parnell Thomas (who met some of his old witnesses in prison) and of course Nixon himself. HUAC's clout in the House was maintained up through the 1960s by Francis Walter of Pennsylvania, who chaired not only the Committee but the Judiciary subcommittee which passed on private immigration bills; members who wanted to please their constituents by legalizing the importation of alien relatives (i.e., any big city Representative) needed to stay on Walter's good side, which is why there were only a handful of votes to abolish HUAC when California's James Roosevelt and the late William Fitts Ryan of New York raised the issue on the floor in the late fifties and early sixties.

For a long time, the abolish HUAC movement had only glacial success, getting up to around 40 supporters by the end of the 1960s. But public interest in the Committee's work was waning, and after Walter's death in 1963 it never had a Chairman with much influence in the House. Indeed, from that time on, the Chairmanship seemed to be a kind of jinx. Clyde Doyle of California, who succeeded Walter, died a few months later; and Joe Pool of Texas, who succeeded him, succumbed within a couple of years. Edwin Willis of Louisiana, the next Chairman, was unexpectedly beaten in his 1968 primary, and that left the chair to Richard Ichord.

Ichord claimed he wanted to tone down the circus atmosphere of so many of the Committee's past hearings, and he branched out to investigate the Ku Klux Klan as well as leftish organizations. But Ichord and his fellows still managed to convince themselves that the campus disorders of the late 1960s were organized by a national conspiracy; and they were still willing, despite a court order requiring them not to, to circulate a list of alleged subversives who spoke at various universities.

Such shenanigans didn't sit well with the new freshman Democrats elected to the House in 1974, and it is possible that HISC (the name change was another Ichord innovation) might have been abolished by majority vote on the floor. But instead it was killed in another way. California's Phillip Burton, the new Chairman of the Democratic Caucus, privately went about and got all the Committee's Democrats to resign except Ichord—Claude Pepper of Florida, Richardson Preyer of North Carolina, Father Robert Drinan of Massachusetts (who sought a seat on HISC solely and expressly to seek its abolition), and Mendel Davis of South Carolina. The only new Democrat who wanted to join was Larry McDonald, the Birch Society member from Georgia, but as a non lawyer he was ineligible under House rules. With virtually no Democratic members left on HISC, the Steering Committee just left it off the list of committee memberships to be approved—and it quietly died.

Interestingly, back in 1962, Richard Nixon had called on his gubernatorial opponent, Pat Brown, to renounce support from an Assemblyman named Phillip Burton because Burton favored abolition of HUAC (Brown declined). 1974 turned out to be a good year for Brown (whose son was elected Governor) and Burton (who achieved his long-sought objective), and a disastrous one for Nixon and the Committee which had done so much for him.

Census Data Pop. 467,532. Central city, 13%; suburban, 24%. Median family income, $7,743; families above $15,000: 14%; families below $3,000: 15%. Median years education, 11.2.

The Voters

Median voting age 40.
Employment profile White collar, 46%. Blue collar, 37%. Service, 12%. Farm, 5%.
Ethnic groups Black, 3%. Total foreign stock, 5%. Germany, 2%.

Presidential vote

1972	Nixon (R)	124,585	(68%)
	McGovern (D)	58,036	(32%)
1968	Nixon (R)	88,961	(54%)
	Humphrey (D)	59,344	(36%)
	Wallace (AI)	17,822	(11%)

Rep. Richard H. Ichord (D) Elected 1960; b. June 27, 1926, Licking; home, Houston; U. of Mo., B.S. 1949, J.D. 1952; Baptist.

Career Navy, WWII; Practicing atty.; Mo. House of Reps., 1952–60, Spkr. Pro-Tempore, 1957–58, Spkr., 1959–60.

Offices 2402 RHOB, 202-225-5155. Also P.O. Box 298, Jefferson City 65101, 314-634-3510.

Committees

Armed Services (5th). Subcommittees: Military Installations and Facilities (Chairman); Research and Development.

Group Ratings

	ADA	COPE	LWV	RIPON	NFU	LCV	CFA	NAB	NSI	ACA
1974	9	33	9	7	42	13	25	83	100	69
1973	8	45	27	36	70	2	50	–	–	79
1972	19	73	44	46	83	11	50	63	100	71

Key Votes

1) Foreign Aid	AGN	6) Gov Abortn Aid	AGN	11) Pub Cong Election $	AGN
2) Busing	AGN	7) Coed Phys Ed	ABS	12) Turkish Arms Cutoff	AGN
3) ABM	FOR	8) Pov Lawyer Gag	ABS	13) Youth Camp Regs	AGN
4) B-1 Bomber	FOR	9) Pub Trans Sub	AGN	14) Strip Mine Veto	FOR
5) Nerve Gas	FOR	10) EZ Voter Regis	AGN	15) Farm Bill Veto	AGN

Election Results

1974 general:	Richard H. Ichord (D)	86,595	(70%)	($50,156)
	James A. Noland, Jr. (R)	37,369	(30%)	($195)
1974 primary:	Richard H. Ichord (D)	36,055	(84%)	
	Sam C. Orr (D)	6,614	(16%	
1972 general:	Richard H. Ichord (D)	112,556	(62%)	($33,779)
	David R. Countie (R)	68,580	(38%)	($9,309)

◆ ◆ ◆ ◆ ◆

NINTH DISTRICT

The part of rural Missouri which most faithfully sustains a Southern Democratic tradition is not in the southern part of the state; rather, it is the Little Dixie region, north of the Missouri River and across the Mississippi from Illinois. The land here was settled early in the nineteenth century, mainly by migrants from Kentucky and Tennessee. During the Civil War some citizens of Little Dixie fought on the Confederate side, and at least one county declared itself independent of the unionist state of Missouri. Since then, not much urbanization has come to this part of Missouri—so little that Mark Twain would probably still recognize his native Hannibal, one of Little Dixie's largest towns, were it not for the tourist traps that use Twain himself for bait. Nor have voting habits changed much; this part of the state continues to be more Democratic than Missouri as a whole, and even George McGovern was able to carry a county here.

Little Dixie was once a congressional district unto itself. Now, because of the one-person-one-vote decision, the region has just a bare majority of the residents of Missouri's 9th congressional district. The rest of the 9th is the northern reaches of the St. Louis metropolitan area: fast-growing, conservative-trending St. Charles County and a northern chunk of St. Louis County, which is predominently blue-collar Democratic.

For some 40 years until his death in 1964 Clarence Cannon, Chairman of the House Appropriations Committee for more than two decades, was the Congressman from the 9th district. Cannon had been Parliamentarian of the House before he had been elected Congressman; he knew the arcane House rules as well as anyone, and indeed wrote the standard compilation of them. He was a crusty, fiercely independent conservative Democrat, who often refused to appropriate money for—and thereby killed—pet programs of the Kennedy and Johnson Administrations. During the Chairman's last year, he and his Senate counterpart, the late Carl Hayden, got into a monumental battle over which side of the Capitol a House-Senate conference committee meeting should take place. For several months there was a stalemate in this battle of octogenarians—and no federal budget.

Cannon's successor in the 9th district seat, William Hungate, is a Democrat who votes with his northern-accented colleagues on most issues. He has shown his integrity by resigning from a District of Columbia subcommittee when he felt the full committee chairman, John McMillan, was allowing it to be influenced by special interests; and he has shown his mastery of complex legal matters when as Chairman of a Judiciary subcommittee he presided over consideration of new federal court rules.

But Hungate is undoubtedly best known to the American public for his sense of humor. With his pronounced Missouri accent and his memory for hoary stories, Hungate was able to provide a number of humorous sidelights during the impeachment hearings. Fully a year before, he had recorded a ditty called "Down by the Old Watergate," which he could be heard singing by dialing a Democratic National Committee number. During the hearings itself, he was prone to make comments like—a propos of Nixon defenders' refusal to concede obvious inferences from the testimony—"There are some members here who, if an elephant walked into the room, might say, 'Wait. It might be a mouse with a glandular condition.'" Apparently some of Hungate's comments irritated some viewers, and he apologized for them as he announced he would vote for impeachment; but most, if not all, of them seem in retrospect to have been quite appropriate.

Hungate is one of those Congressmen who thinks he votes more liberal than many of his constituents might like, but the fact is that he has seldom had any difficulty winning reelection. The only time he had major trouble was in 1968, when Republican Christopher Bond, later state Auditor and now Governor, held him to 52% of the vote. (There is a move on in Missouri for Hungate to run against Bond in 1976.) More recently, Hungate has been winning by solid 2–1 margins; apparently little Dixie did not have as high a regard for Richard Nixon as did some parts of the Deep South.

Upon the retirement of the incumbent, Democrat Bill Burlison was elected Congressman from the 10th district in 1968; he was formerly prosecutor in Cape Girardeau, the district's largest urban concentration (pop. 31,000). Compiling a middle of the road voting record, Burlison has kept the low profile traditionally expected of junior House members. His committee choices have obviously been made with an eye to district matters. In 1973, he switched from Agriculture and Interior—two committees one might expect a junior Congressman from a rural, farming district to seek—to Appropriations, where his major subcommittee assignment is Agriculture.

Census Data Pop. 467,990. Central city, 0%; suburban, 49%. Median family income, $9,573; families above $15,000: 18%; families below $3,000: 11%. Median years education, 12.1.

The Voters

Median voting age 43.
Employment profile White collar, 45%. Blue collar, 36%. Service, 11%. Farm, 8%.
Ethnic groups Black, 3%. Total foreign stock, 5%. Germany, 2%.

Presidential vote

1972	Nixon (R)	129,159	(65%)
	McGovern (D)	69,218	(35%)
1968	Nixon (R)	81,840	(45%)
	Humphrey (D)	75,883	(42%)
	Wallace (AI)	23,189	(13%)

Rep. William L. Hungate (D) Elected 1964; b. Dec. 14, 1922, Benton, Ill.; home, Troy; Central Methodist Col., U. of Mich., U. of Mo., A.B. 1943, Harvard U., LL.B. 1948; First Christian Church.

Career Army, WWII; Practicing atty.; Lincoln Co. Prosecuting Atty., Special Asst. to the Atty. Gen. of Mo., 1958–64.

Offices 2437 RHOB, 202-225-2956. Also 219 W. College St., Troy 63379, 314-528-7533.

Committees

Judiciary (5th). Subcommittees: Criminal Justice (Chairman).

Small Business (7th). Subcommittees: Activities of Regulatory Agencies (Chairman); Governmental Procurement and International Trade.

Group Ratings

	ADA	COPE	LWV	RIPON	NFU	LCV	CFA	NAB	NSI	ACA
1974	68	91	55	27	93	44	62	50	10	27
1973	68	91	58	53	95	58	63	–	–	37
1972	50	82	44	64	100	40	50	20	30	18

Key Votes

1) Foreign Aid	AGN	6) Gov Abortn Aid	AGN	11) Pub Cong Election $	FOR
2) Busing	AGN	7) Coed Phys Ed	AGN	12) Turkish Arms Cutoff	FOR
3) ABM	AGN	8) Pov Lawyer Gag	FOR	13) Youth Camp Regs	AGN
4) B-1 Bomber	AGN	9) Pub Trans Sub	AGN	14) Strip Mine Veto	AGN
5) Nerve Gas	AGN	10) EZ Voter Regis	FOR	15) Farm Bill Veto	AGN

Election Results

1974 general:	William L. Hungate (D)	87,546	(66%)	($30,091)
	Milton Bischof, Jr. (R)	44,318	(34%)	($13,369)
1974 primary:	William L. Hungate (D), unopposed			
1972 general:	William L. Hungate (D)	132,150	(67%)	($26,147)
	Robert L. Prange (R)	66,528	(33%)	($7,719)

◆ ◆ ◆ ◆ ◆

TENTH DISTRICT

The 10th congressional district of Missouri is roughly congruent with the southeast corner of the state known as the Bootheel. This part of the country was first settled by Southerners coming up the Mississippi, looking for more fertile, moist, level land for growing cotton; they found it here, in the late nineteenth and early twentieth centuries, and since then the Bootheel has had more of a feel of the Deep South to it than any other part of Missouri. One gauge of this is the 19% of the vote won by George Wallace in the 10th district in 1968—a far better showing than the Alabamian made in any other Missouri congressional district.

Burlison is a good example of the kind of Congressman who pays close attention to his district and builds up a personal following far beyond the customary strength of his party—and one which is not especially affected by local sentiment toward his party's national leadership. Though Republicans have made a number of concerted attempts to beat him, Burlison continues to raise his margin each time out, winning with a huge 73% of the vote in 1974. He is now so well entrenched that former Governor Warren Hearnes, a Bootheel native, was reportedly deterrred from running against him when, in 1972, he was prohibited from running for a third term; and that same year, in the general election, George McGovern's weak showing here affected Burlison's performance not at all.

Census Data Pop. 466,731. Central city, 0%; suburban, 23%. Median family income, $7,048; families above $15,000: 9%; families below $3,000: 20%. Median years education, 9.4.

The Voters

Median voting age 45.
Employment profile White collar, 36%. Blue collar, 44%. Service, 13%. Farm, 7%.
Ethnic groups Black, 5%. Total foreign stock, 2%.

Presidential vote

1972	Nixon (R)	111,777	(66%)
	McGovern (D)	57,754	(34%)
1968	Nixon (R)	71,624	(42%)
	Humphrey (D)	66,638	(39%)
	Wallace (AI)	32,365	(19%)

Rep. Bill D. Burlison (D) Elected 1968; b. Mar. 15, 1935, Wardell; home, Cape Girardeau; S.E. Mo. St. Col., B.A. 1953, B.S. 1959, U. of Mo., LL.B. 1956, M.Ed. 1964; Baptist.

Career USMC, 1956–59; Practicing atty.; Business Law Instructor, S.E. Mo. St. Col.; Asst. Atty. Gen. of Mo., 1959–62; Cape Girardeau Co. Prosecuting Atty., 1962–68; Pres., Cape Girardeau Co. Bd. of Educ., 1966.

Offices 1338 LHOB, 202-225-4404. Also 246 New Fed. Bldg., Cape Girardeau 63701, 314-335-0101.

Committees

Appropriations (29th). Subcommittees: Agriculture and Related Agencies; Defense; District of Columbia.

Group Ratings

	ADA	COPE	LWV	RIPON	NFU	LCV	CFA	NAB	NSI	ACA
1974	45	73	42	38	77	41	62	73	22	40
1973	58	91	50	33	100	50	100	–	–	38
1972	44	73	55	40	86	27	50	18	60	48

Key Votes

1) Foreign Aid	AGN	6) Gov Abortn Aid	AGN	11) Pub Cong Election $	FOR
2) Busing	AGN	7) Coed Phys Ed	AGN	12) Turkish Arms Cutoff	AGN
3) ABM	ABS	8) Pov Lawyer Gag	AGN	13) Youth Camp Regs	AGN
4) B-1 Bomber	FOR	9) Pub Trans Sub	AGN	14) Strip Mine Veto	AGN
5) Nerve Gas	ABS	10) EZ Voter Regis	FOR	15) Farm Bill Veto	AGN

Election Results

1974 general:	Bill D. Burlison (D)	77,677	(73%)	($28,021)
	Truman Farrow (R)	29,050	(27%)	($2,063)

1974 primary:	Bill D. Burlison (D)	44,801	(80%)	
	Arthur T. Stephenson (D)	11,175	(20%)	
1972 general:	Bill D. Burlison (D)	106,301	(64%)	($14,730)
	M. Francis Svendrowski (R)	59,083	(36%)	($3,065)

MONTANA

Montana is the nation's 4th largest state in area, but only the 43d in population. To the west in the Big Sky Country are rugged mountains and to the east treeless plains; so vast and underpopulated is this state that you can often drive 40 miles down a road and not see another car. People here seem to like life under the Big Sky and prefer weekends of fishing, hunting, and boating to the headier attractions available in urban America. When massive forest fires hit, as in 1973, it was a big event and a cause for general unhappiness. By way of contrast, Montana's urban areas are scarcely big enough to impinge much on anyone's consciousness; the two largest, Billings and Great Falls, each has less than 90,000 people.

Montana's first white settlers were miners, some of whom found large deposits of gold, silver, and copper in the Rockies. Raucous mining towns sprang up, and the largest, Butte, which sat on "the richest hill on earth," was for many years the state's largest city. (Now most of the copper has been dug out, and Butte has been losing population.) Some time after the first miners arrived, cattlemen and dry land wheat farmers moved onto the plains and the river valleys of the state. Aside from mining, there has been little industrial development here, indeed little development of any kind. Even the tourist business has remained minor league, at least until the opening of the late Chet Huntley's Big Sky development.

For many years Montana politics has been a struggle between the mine owners, particularly Anaconda, power companies, and cattlemen on one side, all very much Republican, and the labor unions, miners, and some farmers on the other, all Democrats. Geographically, this has meant that the eastern plains generally go Republican and the western mountains Democratic. But geography is not the real split; this is almost class warfare politics, indeed perhaps the closest thing to it we have left in the United States.

Interestingly, the main national figure to come out of this politics of big stakes and big economic interests is a man we do not associate with that kind of thing at all: Senate Majority Leader Mike Mansfield. Nor does Mansfield have quite the kind of background one might expect in a Senator from this rugged outdoor state. He was born in Manhattan in 1903, and sent by his immigrant Irish parents (you can still hear a trace of their brogue) to live with relatives in Montana. After serving in the Navy (he enlisted at 14), the Army, and the Marines, and working in the mines, Mansfield went back to school and became a professor in—of all things—Far Eastern history at the University of Montana. In 1942, this young professor was elected to Congress, replacing Jeanette Rankin, the first woman to serve there. (In her two widely separated terms in the House, Rankin voted against American entry into both World War I and World War II; she survived to be a crusader against the Vietnam war and for women's rights in the 1970 and died in 1973 at 92.) Ten years later Mansfield was elected to the Senate; soon he was picked as Majority Whip by Lyndon Johnson, and he succeeded to the Majority Leadership when Johnson became Vice President—and has held that job longer than anyone else in history.

There is some irony in the last fact, for Mansfield has been criticized ever since he got the post for being too gentle and timid, and he himself prefers to be called a "coordinator" rather than a leader. Unlike Lyndon Johnson, he does not work feverishly to achieve compromises on major issues, nor is he particularly active in getting the numerous prima donnas on the Democratic side together on legislation. Perhaps the lesson is that there is not going to be an omnipotent Majority Leader in the Senate as long as the ideological and individualistic Democratic Senators don't want one—however Mansfield tried to operate.

With a seat on the Foreign Relations Committee, Mansfield maintains an interest in the subject he used to teach in college. He is one of the few Senators who was always skeptical about American involvement in Southeast Asia, and after trips to South Vietnam he advised Presidents Kennedy and Johnson to get American troops out—advice most of the American people today wish had been taken. Later Mansfield supported various end-the-war amendments and was a quiet force behind the successful congressional moves to limit further military involvement in Cambodia and South Vietnam. Another matter Mansfield has pushed for years, to date with little success, is reduction of American troop commitments in Europe.

Mansfield is generally admired as fair and open; he is usually ready to answer even embarrassing questions with a "yup" or "nope." But he is just as capable as any other Senator in standing up for the interests of his constituency: when Amtrak announced it would cut off rail passenger service in Montana, Mansfield moved quickly and made sure it did not. In Montana he has been unbeatable, so much so that he has felt free to support certain gun control legislation. But even Mansfield lost a few votes on that one in this state where many men shoot and hunt regularly; in 1970, a Missoula sporting goods dealer held Mansfield's share of the vote down to 61%.

Montana's other Senator, Lee Metcalf, has been anything but unbeatable, but as yet he has not been beaten. He was first elected in 1960, and reelected by narrow margins against undistinguished opponents in 1966 and 1972. Metcalf gets his most enthusiastic backing from organized labor, who appreciate not only his usual 100% COPE rating but also his crucial vote for the Lockheed loan. Metcalf has been particularly interested in power issues; he is a strong proponent of public power development and a vigorous critic of private utilities (which always have had plenty of clout in Montana).

Montana's two congressional districts roughly match the two halves of the state: the 1st, western, district includes most of the mountainous counties, and the cities of Butte, Missoula, and Helena, the state capital; the 2d eastern, district covers the broad expanse of plains leading up to the mountains.

For years the 1st district was held safely by Democrats, first by Mansfield (1943–1953), then Metcalf (1953–61, and then Arnold Olsen (1961–71). But Olsen never proved very popular; after winning five elections with less than 55% of the vote, Olsen lost to Dick Shoup, the Republican Mayor of Missoula, in 1970. Shoup beat Olsen again in 1972, but by 1974, when Olsen was beaten for the Democratic nomination, it became clear that these Republican victories were more the result of Olsen's weakness than of Shoup's strength. In his last term, Shoup had played a very constructive legislative role in fashioning a solution to the problems of the Northeast railroads (in cooperation with Brock Adams of Washington). But that issue had, as one might expect, little appeal in the 1st district of Montana, and Shoup was unseated by 32-year-old state Representative Max Baucus of Missoula by a solid 55–45 margin.

Montana's 2d district, though more Republican usually in statewide contests, has been held since a 1969 special election by Democrat John Melcher. This is a vast expanse—the fourth largest district in the nation in area—where cattle ranges stretch as far as the eye can see and towering buttes rise over the magnificently eroded high plains country. This is the agricultural part of the state, but still 40% of its votes are cast in Republican Billings and Democratic Great Falls. Melcher soon became something of a champion vote-getter in this rather unlikely territory; he got as much as 76% of the vote in the not very Democratic year of 1972. His criticisms of the Soviet grain deal and the big grain companies apparently added to his popularity then; his drop, to 63%, in 1974 seems to have been the result of a drunk driving arrest.

It seems likely that both of Montana's Senate seats will be open—or will at least change hands in the next few years. Mansfield has shown no inclination to retire in 1976, when his term is up; but he turns 73 then, and if he is reelected, it will doubtless be for his final term. Metcalf, though he will be a comparatively youthful 67 when his term is up, is generally considered likely to retire, and may well lose if he doesn't. The two most likely candidates at this writing, for either vacancy if it occurs, are the state's two Congressman, with Melcher, despite his 1974 problem, probably the stronger. Both will have the advantage of good committee assignments—Melcher is on Agriculture and Interior, Baucus on Agriculture Appropriations—and both will be favorably known to at least half the state's voters. In contrast, Republicans have few likely candidates at the moment.

One officeholder not likely to be a Senate candidate is Governor Thomas Judge, a liberal Democrat. Judge has been dogged by charges concerning a workmen's compensation scandal. At least in Montana, they seem to have overshadowed the record he has made as a strong critic of strip mining in the state (a booming growth industry of late) and as the organizer of the western governors' association, a group of Rocky Mountain Governors, all Democrats since the 1974 elections, who are determined to exert state control over the use of their lands and to stop the federal government from letting corporations—many of them staffed with big Republican contributors—from exploiting local resources. If there is to be a Senatorial candidate from the state level, it is more likely to be Democratic Lieutenant Governor Bill Christiansen, who was elected in 1972 with 57% of the vote, an even better showing than Judge's.

MONTANA

Census Data Pop. 694,409; 0.34% of U.S. total, 43rd largest; Central city, 18%; suburban, 7%. Median family income, $8,510; 32nd highest; families above $15,000: 14%; families below $3,000: 11%. Median years education, 12.3.

1974 Share of Federal Tax Burden $776,664,000; 0.29% of U.S. total, 45th largest.

1974 Share of Federal Outlays $1,044,544,000; 0.38% of U.S. total, 43d largest. Per capita federal spending, $1504.

DOD	$188,606,000	43d (0.27%)	HEW	$310,044,000	41st (0.33%)
AEC	$90,000	41st (−)	HUD	$3,085,000	42d (0.32%)
NASA	$45,000	48th (−)	VA	$49,607,000	43d (0.36%)
DOT	$68,491,000	38th (0.81%)	EPA	$10,130,000	40th (0.32%)
DOC	$3,589,000	42d (0.22%)	RevS	$23,823,000	44th (0.39%)
DOI	$69,520,000	11th (2.82%)	Int.	$36,182,000	40th (0.18%)
USDA	$166,292,000	32d (1.34%)	Other	$115,040,000	

Economic Base Agriculture, notably cattle, wheat, barley and dairy products; finance, insurance and real estate; lumber and wood products, especially sawmills and planing mills; primary nonferrous metals, and other primary metal industries; food and kindred products; metal mining.

Political Line-up Governor, Thomas L. Judge (D). Senators, Mike Mansfield (D) and Lee Metcalf (D). Representatives, 2 D. State Senate (30 D and 20 R); State House (67 D and 33 R).

The Voters

Registration 373,889 Total. No party registration.
Median voting age 43.
Employment profile White collar, 45%. Blue collar, 28%. Service, 15%. Farm, 12%.
Ethnic groups Indian, 4%. Total foreign stock, 17%.

Presidential vote

1972	Nixon (R)	183,976	(60%)
	McGovern (D)	120,197	(40%)
1968	Nixon (R)	138,835	(51%)
	Humphrey (D)	114,117	(42%)
	Wallace (AI)	20,015	(7%)

Sen. Mike Mansfield (D) Elected 1952, seat up 1976; b. Mar. 16, 1903, New York, N.Y.; home, Missoula; Mont. School of Mines, 1927–28; U. of Mont., B.A. 1933, M.A. 1934, U. of Cal., 1936–37; Catholic.

Career Navy, 1918–19; Army, 1919–20; USMC, 1920–22; Miner and mining engineer, 1922–30; Prof., U. of Mont. 1933–43; U.S. House of Reps., 1943–53; U.S. Senate Asst. Maj. Ldr., 1957–61, Maj. Ldr., 1961–.

Offices 133 RSOB, 202-222-2644.

Committees

Majority Leader

Appropriations (7th). Subcommittees: Defense; HUD and Independent Agencies; Interior; Military Construction (Chairman); State, Justice, Commerce, The Judiciary.

Foreign Relations (2d). Subcommittees: Far Eastern Affairs (Chairman); Personnel; Western Hemisphere Affairs.

Group Ratings

	ADA	COPE	LWV	RIPON	NFU	LCV	CFA	NAB	NSI	ACA
1974	89	70	67	41	94	63	88	33	0	6
1973	85	80	70	33	100	−	83	−	−	7
1972	80	88	70	57	100	63	100	0	10	5

Key Votes

1) No-Knock	FOR	8) Gov Abortn Aid	FOR	15) Consumer Prot Agy	FOR
2) Busing	FOR	9) Cut Mil Brass	FOR	16) Forced Psych Tests	AGN
3) No Fault	FOR	10) Gov Limousine	AGN	17) Fed Campaign Subs	FOR
4) F-111	ABS	11) RR Featherbed	FOR	18) Rhod Chrome Ban	FOR
5) Death Penalty	ABS	12) Handgun License	ABS	19) Open Legis Meetings	AGN
6) Foreign Aid	AGN	13) Less Troop Abrd	FOR	20) Strikers Food Stmps	FOR
7) Filibuster	AGN	14) Resume Turk Aid	FOR	21) Gov Info Disclosure	FOR

Election Results

1970 general:	Mike Mansfield (D)	150,060	(61%)
	Harold E. Wallace (R)	97,809	(39%)
1970 primary:	Mike Mansfield (D)	68,146	(77%)
	Two others (D)	20,117	(23%)
1964 general:	Mike Mansfield (D)	180,643	(65%)
	Alex Blewett (R)	99,367	(35%)

Sen. Lee Metcalf (D) Elected 1960, seat up 1978; b. Jan. 28, 1911, Stevensville; home, Helena; Stanford U., B.A., U. of Mont., LL.B. 1936; Methodist.

Career Practicing atty.; Mont. House of Reps., 1937; Asst. Atty. Gen. of Mont., 1937–41; Army, WWII; Assoc. Justice, Mont. Supreme Ct., 1946–52; U.S. House of Reps., 1953–61.

Offices 1121 DSOB, 202-224-2651. Also Diamond Block, Helena 59601, 406-442-4361, and Rm. 4435 Fed. Bldg., Billings 59101, 406-259-5966.

Committees

Government Operations (5th). Subcommittees: Intergovernmental Relations; Reports, Accounting and Management (Chairman).

Interior and Insular Affairs (3d). Subcommittees: Environment and Land Resources; Indian Affairs; Minerals, Materials and Fuels (Chairman).

Group Ratings

	ADA	COPE	LWV	RIPON	NFU	LCV	CFA	NAB	NSI	ACA
1974	95	70	90	70	88	83	100	9	14	18
1973	74	82	80	41	100	–	77	–	–	34
1972	40	100	100	76	100	57	100	10	0	6

Key Votes

1) No-Knock	AGN	8) Gov Abortn Aid	ABS	15) Consumer Prot Agy	FOR
2) Busing	FOR	9) Cut Mil Brass	FOR	16) Forced Psych Tests	AGN
3) No Fault	FOR	10) Gov Limousine	AGN	17) Fed Campaign Subs	FOR
4) F-111	AGN	11) RR Featherbed	FOR	18) Rhod Chrome Ban	FOR
5) Death Penalty	AGN	12) Handgun License	FOR	19) Open Legis Meetings	AGN
6) Foreign Aid	FOR	13) Less Troop Abrd	FOR	20) Strikers Food Stmps	FOR
7) Filibuster	AGN	14) Resume Turk Aid	ABS	21) Gov Info Disclosure	FOR

Election Results

1972 general:	Lee Metcalf (D)	163,609	(52%)	($136,551)
	Henry S. Hibbard (R)	151,316	(48%)	($286,748)
1972 primary:	Lee Metcalf (D)	106,491	(86%)	
	Jerome Peters (D)	16,729	(14%)	
1966 general:	Lee Metcalf (D)	138,166	(53%)	
	Tim Babcock (R)	121,697	(47%)	

Gov. Thomas L. Judge (D) Elected 1972, term expires Jan. 1977; b. Oct. 12, 1934, Helena; U. of Notre Dame, B.A., U. of Louisville.

Career Mont. House of Reps., 1961–67; Mont. Senate, 1967–69; Lt. Gov. of Mont., 1969–73.

Offices State Capitol, Helena 59601, 406-449-3111.

Election Results

1972 general:	Thomas L. Judge (D)	172,523	(54%)
	Ed Smith (R)	146,231	(46%)
1972 primary:	Thomas L. Judge (D)	75,917	(60%)
	Dick Dzivi (D)	38,639	(30%)
	Three Others (D)	12,238	(10%)

◆ ◆ ◆ ◆ ◆

FIRST DISTRICT

Census Data Pop. 347,447. Central city, 0%; suburban, 0%. Median family income, $8,576; families above $15,000: 13%; families below $3,000: 10%. Median years education, 12.3.

The Voters

Median voting age 43.
Employment profile White collar, 46%. Blue collar, 31%. Service, 15%. Farm, 8%.
Ethnic groups Indian, 3%. Total foreign stock, 16%.

Presidential vote

1972	Nixon (R)	92,166	(58%)
	McGovern (D)	65,384	(42%)
1968	Nixon (R)	65,689	(48%)
	Humphrey (D)	59,110	(43%)
	Wallace (AI)	11,227	(8%)

Rep. Max S. Baucus (D) Elected 1974; b. Dec. 11, 1941, Helena; home, Missoula; Stanford U., B.A. 1964, LL.B. 1967.

Career Staff Atty., Civil Aeronautics Bd., 1967–69; Legal Staff, Securities and Exchange Comm., 1969–71, Legal Asst. to the Chm., 1970–71; Practicing atty., 1971–75; Mont. House of Reps., 1973–75.

Offices 226 CHOB, 202-225-3211. Also Fed. Bldg., Box 1488, Missoula 59801, 406-728-2043.

Committees

Appropriations (37th). Subcommittees: Agriculture and Related Agencies; HUD-Independent Agencies.

Group Ratings: Newly Elected

Key Votes

1) Foreign Aid	FOR	6) Gov Abortn Aid	NE	11) Pub Cong Election $	NE
2) Busing	NE	7) Coed Phys Ed	FOR	12) Turkish Arms Cutoff	NE
3) ABM	NE	8) Pov Lawyer Gag	NE	13) Youth Camp Regs	AGN
4) B-1 Bomber	AGN	9) Pub Trans Sub	NE	14) Strip Mine Veto	AGN
5) Nerve Gas	NE	10) EZ Voter Regis	NE	15) Farm Bill Veto	AGN

Election Results

1974 general:	Max Baucus (D)	74,304	(55%)	($111,096)
	Richard G. Shoup (R)	61,309	(45%)	($101,118)
1974 primary:	Max Baucus (D)	29,762	(44%)	
	Pat Williams (D)	21,645	(32%)	
	Arnold Olsen (D)	16,929	(25%)	

◆ ◆ ◆ ◆ ◆

SECOND DISTRICT

Census Data Pop. 346,962. Central city, 35%; suburban, 14%. Median family income, $8,436; families above $15,000: 14%; families below $3,000: 11%. Median years education, 12.3.

The Voters

Median voting age 43.
Employment profile White collar, 45%. Blue collar, 25%. Service, 14%. Farm, 16%.
Ethnic groups Indian, 5%. Total foreign stock, 19%.

Presidential vote

	1972	Nixon (R)	91,810	(63%)
		McGovern (D)	54,813	(37%)
	1968	Nixon (R)	73,146	(53%)
		Humphrey (D)	55,007	(40%)
		Wallace (AI)	8,788	(6%)

Rep. John Melcher (D) Elected June 24, 1969; b. Sept. 6, 1924, Sioux City, Ia.; home, Forsyth; U. of Minn., 1942–43, Ia. St. U., D.V.M. 1950; Catholic.

Career Army, WWII; Veterinarian, 1950–69; Forsyth City Cncl., 1953–55, Mayor, 1955–61; Mont. House of Reps., 1961–63; Mont. Senate, 1963–67; Dem. nominee for U.S. House of Reps., 1966.

Offices 1224 LHOB, 202-225-1555. Also 1016 Fed. Bldg., Billings 59101, 406-248-7119.

Committees

Agriculture (7th). Subcommittees: Family Farms and Rural Development; Forests; Livestock and Grains.

Interior and Insular Affairs (12th). Subcommittees: Energy and the Environment; Indian Affairs; Mines and Mining; Public Lands (Chairman).

Group Ratings

	ADA	COPE	LWV	RIPON	NFU	LCV	CFA	NAB	NSI	ACA
1974	65	82	58	31	93	71	46	55	44	33
1973	76	73	67	57	100	61	86	–	–	19
1972	50	82	88	71	100	53	100	8	50	20

Key Votes

1) Foreign Aid	AGN	6) Gov Abortn Aid	AGN	11) Pub Cong Election $	FOR
2) Busing	FOR	7) Coed Phys Ed	AGN	12) Turkish Arms Cutoff	ABS
3) ABM	AGN	8) Pov Lawyer Gag	AGN	13) Youth Camp Regs	FOR
4) B-1 Bomber	FOR	9) Pub Trans Sub	FOR	14) Strip Mine Veto	AGN
5) Nerve Gas	AGN	10) EZ Voter Regis	FOR	15) Farm Bill Veto	AGN

Election Results

1974 general:	John Melcher (D)	74,860	(63%)	($57,016)
	John K. McDonald (R)	43,853	(37%)	($32,341)
1974 primary:	John Melcher (D), unopposed			
1972 general:	John Melcher (D)	114,524	(76%)	($49,092)
	Richard Forester (R)	36,063	(24%)	($10,475)

NEBRASKA

By just about any measurement—its preferences in presidential elections, its congressional delegation, its state politics—Nebraska has consistently been the nation's most Republican state. It came by that political allegiance in one cataclysmic decade which made Nebraska politically, economically, sociologically what it has remained ever since. This was the great land rush of the 1880s, when nearly half a million people, most of them from the Republican Midwest, surged into Nebraska. At the beginning of that ten year period, Nebraska had a population of 452,000; ten years later it reached 1,062,000—not far below the 1970 figure of 1,483,000.

Those were the boom years. As it happened, the 1880s were a time of plentiful rainfall on the high plains west of the Missouri River; the 1890s, sadly, were not. Indeed the '90s were a time of depression greater than any but the 1930s, and hard hit Nebraska produced the populist prairie radicalism of William Jennings Bryan, the "silver tongued orator of the Platte." Bryan's candidacy swept Nebraska in 1896 and came close to sweeping the nation, but in the next few years—years of prosperity on the farm—even Nebraska reverted to its Republican voting habits, favoring McKinley over Bryan in 1900. Since then, Nebraska's only notable lapse from conservative Republicanism was the career of George W. Norris, Congressman (1903–13) and Senator (1913–43). During the Progressive era, Norris led the House rebellion against Speaker Cannon in 1911; during the 1930s he pushed through the Norris-LaGuardia Anti-Injunction Act and the Tennessee Valley Authority.

Since 1900 most of Nebraska's growth has occurred in and around the state's two significant cities, Omaha (pop. 347,000) and Lincoln (pop. 150,000), which between them today contain about 40% of the state's people. Most of the immigrants to Omaha, a railroad, meatpacking, and manufacturing center, and Lincoln, the state capital and home of the University of Nebraska, come from the rural, Republican hinterland. There is also a sizable Eastern European, mainly Czech, community on the south side of Omaha which, like the city's small black ghetto, usually votes Democratic; so, too, do a few isolated German Catholic counties. But as a whole the Nebraska political picture is usually solidly Republican. In the presidential elections of 1960 and 1968, which were close in the rest of the nation, Richard Nixon carried both Omaha and Lincoln and lost only three or four small rural counties.

Yet if the state is overwhelmingly Republican in national and congressional elections, it has achieved a kind of equilibrium in state political contests. As in a number of plains states, Nebraska's minority Democrats have made especially strong efforts to win state offices—feeling free to outflank the Republicans on the right. Thus since 1960 Democrats have held the Governorship here for all but four years. In 1970, the Democratic gubernatorial candidate, J. J. Exon, won a 55% victory on a classically Republican platform—lower taxes and less government spending. In the next four years Exon was pretty largely faithful to his promises, and in 1974 he won 59% of the vote, as compared to the 36% won by his Republican opponent.

The junior Senator from Nebraska (junior by only a few weeks) is Carl Curtis, a veteran of 38 years on Capitol Hill, 16 in the House and 22 in the Senate, Chairman of the Senate Republican Conference, and ranking Republican on the Senate Finance Committee. From this impressive curriculum vitae one might conclude that Curtis is one of the most respected senior Senators; in fact, something uncomfortably close to the opposite is the case. He made a national spectacle of himself, after Richard Nixon released the damaging June 23 tape, scurrying around to one television studio after another asserting his continued belief in the President's innocence and fitness for office. Curtis is nothing if not faithful: he was always a solid conservative, a supporter down the line of Barry Goldwater and (when he was not too leftish) Richard Nixon, and he was not going to desert the latter—whatever the facts were. Such eminence as he has he owes to his steadiness.

His Senate Conference post came when he beat the personally unpopular Jacob Javits in 1975, apparently because Lowell Weicker, a Javits supporter, made an impassioned speech citing what he regarded as evidence of Curtis' unfitness; his conservative colleagues, whom he had always supported as steadfastly, if sometimes blindly as he had Nixon, could hardly desert him for his constancy. His position on the Finance Committee is a gift of the seniority system. And his continued reelection to public office has been the gift of the usually Republican voters of Nebraska—though even they nearly balked and ousted him in the otherwise Republican year of 1972.

Curtis's relatively close call—he won with 53% of the vote—was scarcely noticed on election night, since he did after all win as everyone expected; what makes it in retrospect remarkable is the identity of his opponent. For he was Terry Carpenter, one of the authentic zanies in American politics. Carpenter was then 72, and he had been around a long time. In 1932 he was elected to Congress as a Democrat in the Roosevelt landslide; in 1956 he surfaced as the delegate to the Republican National Convention who stood up and nominated a nonexistent Joe Smith for Vice President, as a protest against the renomination of Richard Nixon. In between, he ran for the Governorship three times and the U.S. Senate four, never coming closer to success than his 47% of the vote against Curtis. He also served in Nebraska's unique unicameral legislature from time to time, and between sessions operated—indeed, continues to operate—his gas station in Scottsbluff. In 1974, Carpenter nearly won election to the state Senate as a write-in candidate; he was beaten only when one of his opponents demanded a recount and apparently convinced the authorities that some of the Carpenter voters had mispelled his name.

As a matter of tradition, Nebraska has chosen one Senator from Omaha and one from the rural part of the state. For as long as Carl Curtis has been the latter, Roman Hruska, a fellow conservative Republican, has been the former. Hruska is somewhat more formidable, however. As ranking Republican on the Senate Judiciary Committee, he was a key defender of the Nixon Administration when its record was coming under fire, as during the Kleindienst nomination hearings and the proceedings which set up the office of special prosecutor. In every case, Hruska without apparently being told did just what the Nixon White House wanted him to.

But Hruska's moment in history undoubtedly came during the days when he was the chief Senate supporter of the nomination to the Supreme Court of Judge G. Harrold Carswell. In a radio interview Hruska's deep voice came across with the thought, "Even if he were mediocre, there are a lot of mediocre judges and people and lawyers. They are entitled to a little representation, aren't they, and a little chance? We can't have all Brandeises and Frankfurters and Cardozos and stuff like that there." This defense doomed Carswell's case; the absurdity of Hruska's proposition with its whiff of anti-Semitism, plus the obvious mediocrity of the nominee resulted in Carswell's rejection.

That comment may also have been part of the reason Hruska fared relatively poorly in the 1970 election, winning only 53% against former Governor Frank Morrison. Morrison had served as Governor from 1960 to 1966, had run against Hruska before in 1958 and against Curtis in 1966; in 1968 his wife had run for Congress, in 1972 he was chairman of the Nebraska McGovern delegation to the Democratic National Convention, and in 1974 he ran for state Attorney General. Morrison was, in other words, as strong a candidate as Democrats had here at the time. He had, also, the advantage of an unusual issue. It seemed that Hruska, who had dissented vigorously from the liberal conclusion of the President's commission on pornography, was part owner of a chain of drive-in theaters which showed movies like "The Blood Drinker," "Girl on a Chain Gang," and "Catch-22." The sight of Hruska pompously explaining his way out of that one would have been worth the price of admission.

Both of Nebraska's Senators were first elected in 1954, and both are getting on in years now: Hruska is 74 in 1976, Curtis 73. In light of his age and relatively poor performance last time, it was no surprise that Hruska has announced he will not run again in 1976; and one would not expect Curtis to run in 1978 either. In the ordinary course of events in this Republican state, that would mean that 2d district Congressman John McCollister of Omaha would succeed to Hruska's seat. Hruska has already endorsed him and probably 1st district Congressman Charles Thone to Curtis'. But that may not be quite what happens, for Governor Exon reportedly has senatorial ambitions too, and he should be at the very least a strong competitor for one of those seats. To judge from his record in Nebraska, Exon would be as conservative a Senator as any current non-Southern Democrat, but even that would represent a considerable change from Hruska or Curtis.

Census Data Pop. 1,483,791; 0.73% of U.S. total, 35th largest; Central city, 34%; suburban, 9%. Median family income, $8,562; 31st highest; families above $15,000: 15%; families below $3,000: 11%. Median years education, 12.3.

1974 Share of Federal Tax Burden $1,955,052,000; 0.73% of U.S. total, 32d largest.

1974 Share of Federal Outlays $1,736,274,000; 0.64% of U.S. total, 36th largest. Per capita federal spending, $1170.

DOD	$276,391,000	38th (0.40%)	HEW	$629,904,000	35th (0.68%)
AEC	$67,000	44th (–)	HUD	$6,559,000	33d (0.67%)
NASA	$424,000	39th (0.01%)	VA	$111,318,000	35th (0.81%)
DOT	$54,635,000	41st (0.65%)	EPA	$8,018,000	42d (0.25%)
DOC	$4,271,000	41st (0.26%)	RevS	$44,670,000	35th (0.73%)
DOI	$20,583,000	28th (0.84%)	Int.	$79,056,000	30th (0.38%)
USDA	$284,518,000	17th (2.28%)	Other	$215,860,000	

Economic Base Agriculture, notably cattle, corn, hogs and wheat; finance, insurance and real estate; food and kindred products, especially meat products; electrical equipment and supplies; machinery, especially farm machinery; printing and publishing, especially newspapers; fabricated metal products, especially fabricated structural metal products.

Political Line-up Governor, J. James Exon (D). Senators, Roman L. Hruska (R) and Carl T. Curtis (R). Representatives, 3 R. Unicameral legislature, 49 non-partisan members.

The Voters

Registration 787,850 Total. 363,227 D (46%); 387,388 R (49%); 37,235 Ind. (5%).
Median voting age 44.
Employment profile White collar, 45%. Blue collar, 28%. Service, 14%. Farm, 13%.
Ethnic groups Black, 3%. Total foreign stock, 14%. Germany, 4%.

Presidential vote

	1972	Nixon (R)	406,298	(71%)
		McGovern (D)	169,991	(29%)
	1968	Nixon (R)	321,163	(60%)
		Humphrey (D)	170,784	(32%)
		Wallace (AI)	44,904	(8%)

1972 Democratic Presidential Primary			*1972 Republican Presidential Primary*		
McGovern	79,309	(41%)	Nixon	179,464	(92%)
Humphrey	65,968	(34%)	McCloskey	9,011	(5%)
Wallace	23,912	(13%)	Ashbrook	4,996	(3%)
others	22,948	(12%)			

Sen. Roman L. Hruska (R) Elected 1954, seat up 1976; b. Aug. 16, 1904, David City; home, Omaha; U. of Omaha, 1923–25, U. of Chicago Law School, 1927–28, Creighton U., J.D. 1929: Unitarian.

Career Practicing atty., 1929–52; Mbr., Douglas Co. Bd. of Commissioners, 1944–52, Chm., 1945–52; U.S. House of Reps., 1953–54.

Offices 209 RSOB, 202-224-6651. Also P.O. Box 277, Omaha 68102, 402-221-4791.

Committees

The Judiciary (Ranking Member). Subcommittees: Antitrust and Monopoly; Constitutional Amendments; Constitutional Rights; Criminal Laws and Procedures; FBI Oversight; Improvement in Judicial Machinery; Juvenile Delinquency; Federal Charters, Holidays and Celebrations (Chairman).

Appropriations (2d). Subcommittees: Agriculture and Related Agencies; Defense; Interior; Public Works; State, Justice, Commerce, The Judiciary.

Group Ratings

	ADA	COPE	LWV	RIPON	NFU	LCV	CFA	NAB	NSI	ACA
1974	0	18	63	41	24	5	11	55	100	100
1973	0	18	20	38	24	–	0	–	–	93
1972	5	0	27	46	44	4	0	91	100	95

Key Votes

1) No-Knock	FOR	8) Gov Abortn Aid	AGN	15) Consumer Prot Agy	AGN
2) Busing	AGN	9) Cut Mil Brass	ABS	16) Forced Psych Tests	AGN
3) No Fault	AGN	10) Gov Limousine	FOR	17) Fed Campaign Subs	AGN
4) F-111	FOR	11) RR Featherbed	AGN	18) Rhod Chrome Ban	AGN
5) Death Penalty	FOR	12) Handgun License	AGN	19) Open Legis Meetings	AGN
6) Foreign Aid	ABS	13) Less Troop Abrd	AGN	20) Strikers Food Stmps	AGN
7) Filibuster	FOR	14) Resume Turk Aid	FOR	21) Gov Info Disclosure	AGN

Election Results

1970 general:	Roman L. Hruska (R)	240,894	(53%)
	Frank B. Morrison (D)	217,681	(47%)
1970 primary:	Roman L. Hruska (R)	159,059	(86%)
	Otis Glebe (R)	26,627	(14%)
1964 general:	Roman L. Hruska (R)	345,772	(61%)
	Raymond Arnt (D)	217,605	(39%)

Sen. Carl T. Curtis (R) Elected 1954, seat up 1978; b. Mar. 15, 1905, near Minden; home, Minden; Neb. Wesleyan U., Presbyterian.

Career Practicing atty., 1931–38; Kearney Co. Atty., 1931–35; U.S. House of Reps., 1939–55.

Offices 2213 DSOB, 202-224-4224. Also Masonic Bldg., Minden 68959, 308-832-2670.

Committees

Agriculture and Forestry (Ranking Member). Subcommittees: Agriculture Credit and Rural Electrification; Environment, Soil Conservation and Forestry; Rural Development.

Finance (Ranking Member). Subcommittees: Private Pension Plans; Social Security Financing; Supplemental Security Income.

Group Ratings

	ADA	COPE	LWV	RIPON	NFU	LCV	CFA	NAB	NSI	ACA
1974	0	18	30	39	24	5	0	75	100	100
1973	0	10	20	33	24	–	0	–	–	96
1972	0	0	18	46	30	0	18	90	100	100

Key Votes

1) No-Knock	FOR	8) Gov Abortn Aid	AGN	15) Consumer Prot Agy	AGN
2) Busing	AGN	9) Cut Mil Brass	AGN	16) Forced Psych Tests	ABS
3) No Fault	AGN	10) Gov Limousine	FOR	17) Fed Campaign Subs	AGN
4) F-111	FOR	11) RR Featherbed	AGN	18) Rhod Chrome Ban	AGN
5) Death Penalty	FOR	12) Handgun License	AGN	19) Open Legis Meetings	AGN
6) Foreign Aid	AGN	13) Less Troop Abrd	AGN	20) Strikers Food Stmps	AGN
7) Filibuster	FOR	14) Resume Turk Aid	FOR	21) Gov Info Disclosure	AGN

Election Results

1972 general:	Carl T. Curtis (R)	301,841	(53%)	($250,392)
	Terry Carpenter (D)	265,922	(47%)	($38,629)
1972 primary:	Carl T. Curtis (R)	141,213	(74%)	
	Three others (R)	49,222	(26%)	
1966 general:	Carl T. Curtis (R)	296,116	(61%)	
	Frank B. Morrison (D)	187,950	(39%)	

Gov. J. James Exon (D) Elected 1970, term expires Jan. 1979; b. Aug. 9, 1921, Geddes, S.D.; U. of Omaha; Episcopalian.

Career Army, WWII; Branch Mgr., Universal Finance Co., 1946–54; Pres., Exon's Inc., 1954–70; Vice Chm., Neb. St. Dem. Central Comm., 1964–68; Dem. Natl. Comm., 1968–69.

Offices State Capitol, Lincoln 68509, 402-471-2244.

Election Results

1974 general:	J. J. Exon (D)	267,012	(59%)
	Richard D. Marvel (R)	159,780	(35%)
	Ernest W. Chambers (Ind.)	24,320	(5%)
1974 primary:	J. J. Exon (D)	125,690	(88%)
	Richard D. Schmitz (D)	17,889	(12%)
1970 general:	J. J. Exon (D)	248,552	(55%)
	Norbert T. Tiemann (R)	201,994	(45%)

◆ ◆ ◆ ◆ ◆

FIRST DISTRICT

The 1st congressional district of Nebraska is a band of 27 counties in the eastern part of the state. Outside of Lincoln, the district's largest city (pop. 150,000), the economy of the 1st is based almost entirely on agriculture. The political inclination of the region is Republican, of course, but there are a couple of counties with large German Catholic communities in the middle of the district near the Platte River which are either Democratic or marginal. Lincoln, the state capital and the home of the University of Nebraska Cornhuskers, is traditionally Republican. But the city's large numbers of state employees have sometimes joined members of the university community to swing Lincoln into the Democratic column. But this vote can also work in the other direction, at least when anti-tax, anti-spending Governor J. J. Exon is running. In 1970, Exon carried most counties in the state but lost Lincoln, and in 1974 he ran worse than average here; state employees and academics are not especially found of politicians who slash the state budget.

For the past dozen years, the 1st has been closely contested an unusually large number of times. In 1964, it actually went Democratic, electing Clair Callan with 51% of the vote. In 1966 and 1968 Callan lost close elections to Robert Denney, who went on to become a federal judge; in 1970, when Denney was not running Callan ran as an independent, split the anti-Republican vote two ways, and helped elect Congressman Charles Thone, who in any case took 51% of the vote. Thone jumped to 64% in 1972, but fell back in 1974 to just 53% against Democrat Hess Dyas. Indeed, neither Thone nor any other Republican has carried Lancaster County, which contains Lincoln, since 1962, with the single exception of 1972. Thone is a former administrative assistant to Senator Hruska, and reportedly he would like to succeed Senator Curtis if he retires as expected in 1978. But Thone's rather shaky performance in his home district leaves his strength as a statewide candidate an open question.

Census Data Pop. 494,335. Central city, 30%; suburban, 6%. Median family income, $8,203; families above $15,000: 13%; families below $3,000: 12%. Median years education, 12.2.

The Voters

Median voting age 45.
Employment profile White collar, 43%. Blue collar, 27%. Service, 15%. Farm, 15%.
Ethnic groups Total foreign stock, 14%. Germany, 6%.

Presidential vote

1972	Nixon (R)	133,282	(67%)
	McGovern (D)	66,001	(33%)
1968	Nixon (R)	110,909	(60%)
	Humphrey (D)	61,274	(33%)
	Wallace (AI)	11,633	(6%)

Rep. Charles Thone (R) Elected 1970; b. Jan. 4, 1924, Hartington; home, Lincoln; U. of Neb., J.D. 1950; Presbyterian.

Career Army, WWII; Deputy Neb. Secy. of State, 1950–51; Asst. Atty. Gen. of Neb., 1951–52; Asst. U.S. Dist. Atty., Lincoln Ofc., 1952–54; Admin. Asst. to U.S. Sen. Roman Hruska, 1954–59; Practicing atty., 1959–71.

Offices 1524 LHOB, 202-225-4806. Also 120 Anderson Bldg., Lincoln 68508, 402-471-5175.

Committees

Agriculture (4th). Subcommittees: Department Operations, Investigations and Oversight; Livestock and Grains.

Government Operations (9th). Subcommittees: Government Activities and Transportation.

Group Ratings

	ADA	COPE	LWV	RIPON	NFU	LCV	CFA	NAB	NSI	ACA
1974	36	27	50	56	64	35	39	75	60	50
1973	40	9	42	67	70	68	50	–	–	63
1972	6	18	36	71	50	50	50	67	'89	59

Key Votes

1) Foreign Aid	AGN	6) Gov Abortn Aid	AGN	11) Pub Cong Election $	FOR
2) Busing	AGN	7) Coed Phys Ed	AGN	12) Turkish Arms Cutoff	ABS
3) ABM	AGN	8) Pov Lawyer Gag	FOR	13) Youth Camp Regs	AGN
4) B-1 Bomber	FOR	9) Pub Trans Sub	AGN	14) Strip Mine Veto	FOR
5) Nerve Gas	AGN	10) EZ Voter Regis	AGN	15) Farm Bill Veto	AGN

Election Results

1974 general:	Charles Thone (R)	82,353	(53%)	($98,307)
	Hess Dyas (D)	72,099	(47%)	($133,261)
1974 primary:	Charles Thone (R), unopposed			
1972 general:	Charles Thone (R)	126,789	(64%)	($90,130)
	Darrel E. Berg (D)	70,570	(36%)	($21,704)

◆ ◆ ◆ ◆ ◆

SECOND DISTRICT

The 2d congressional district is metropolitan Omaha and a couple of rural counties. The latter are politically negligible; metropolitan Omaha (Douglas and Sarpy Counties) cast three-quarters of the district's votes and invariably determines the winner of the House seat. Omaha has long been Nebraska's largest city; indeed, with Lincoln, it is the state's only large city. In recent years, Omaha has shown little growth; its major industries, meatpacking and railroading, have not been especially healthy. Still Omaha remains the commercial and industrial hub of much of the Great Plains—the largest city on the Union Pacific and Interstate 80 east-west routes between Chicago and Denver. Though Omaha contains significant numbers of Democratic Czechs and blacks, it tends to vote Republican and, at least in national elections by margins not much less than those turned in in rural Nebraska.

From 1956 to 1970, the 2d district was represented by Glenn Cunningham, who left his mark in Washington as the sponsor of the law requiring people who receive mail from Communist countries to register with the post office—a requirement which snares many more academics interested in Eastern European affairs and people with relatives in Iron Curtain countries than it does subversives. Cunningham was never especially popular with the voters of the 2d; he was nearly beaten in 1968 by Frank Morrison's wife, and in 1970 he was finally licked in the Republican primary. For some months Cunningham held a sinecure post in the Nixon Administration; more recently he was looking for work as an appliance salesman.

The Republican primary winner that year was John McCollister, then a Douglas County Commissioner. He was helped to a narrow victory in 1970 by his Democratic opponent's opposition to a measure which would have allowed public aid to parochial schools; he won again in 1972 comfortably and in 1974 by a 55–45 margin—the best for any of Nebraska's Republicans that year. There is little to report about McCollister's record in the House, except that he has been about as sympathetic to business on the floor and as a member of the Commerce Committee as one would expect from a conservative Nebraska Republican, and that his record has been moderate to conservative otherwise. It is entirely possible, however, that this not terribly important Congressman could become a United States Senator in 1976. He holds the Omaha seat, and thus is the heir to the so-called Omaha Senate seat now held by 74-year-old Roman Hruska. It is considered unlikely Hruska will run again and so McCollister—fresh from his reasonably good 1974 showing—would be the obvious Republican candidate. His major problem, provided he gets his party's nomination, would be whether he can beat Governor J. J. Exon, who may well be the Democratic candidate, and the strongest the Democrats have fielded in memory.

Census Data Pop. 495,095. Central city, 70%; suburban, 21%. Median family income, $10,163; families above $15,000: 21%; families below $3,000: 7%. Median years education, 12.4.

The Voters

Median voting age 40.
Employment profile White collar, 53%. Blue collar, 31%. Service, 14%. Farm, 2%.
Ethnic groups Black, 7%. Total foreign stock, 14%. Germany, 3%.

Presidential vote

1972	Nixon (R)		124,791	(69%)
	McGovern (D)		56,204	(31%)
1968	Nixon (R)		84,690	(52%)
	Humphrey (D)		59,078	(36%)
	Wallace (AI)		19,044	(12%)

Rep. John Y. McCollister (R) Elected 1970; b. June 10, 1921, Iowa City, Ia.; home, Omaha; U. of Ia., B.S. 1943; Presbyterian.

Career Navy, WWII; Pres. and Bd. Chm., McCollister & Co., lubricant manufacturers, 1953–70; Mbr., Douglas Co. Bd. of Commissioners, 1965–70.

Offices 217 CHOB, 202-225-4155. Also 215 N. 17th St., Omaha 68102, 402-221-3251.

Committees

Interstate and Foreign Commerce (9th). Subcommittees: Consumer Protection and Finance.

Small Business (4th). Subcommittees: Activities of Regulatory Agencies.

Group Ratings

	ADA	COPE	LWV	RIPON	NFU	LCV	CFA	NAB	NSI	ACA
1974	17	0	25	50	36	41	15	92	80	73
1973	4	0	25	60	45	16	13	–	–	74
1972	0	9	33	50	57	29	0	83	100	83

Key Votes

1) Foreign Aid	AGN	6) Gov Abortn Aid	AGN	11) Pub Cong Election $	AGN
2) Busing	AGN	7) Coed Phys Ed	AGN	12) Turkish Arms Cutoff	ABS
3) ABM	AGN	8) Pov Lawyer Gag	FOR	13) Youth Camp Regs	AGN
4) B-1 Bomber	ABS	9) Pub Trans Sub	AGN	14) Strip Mine Veto	FOR
5) Nerve Gas	FOR	10) EZ Voter Regis	AGN	15) Farm Bill Veto	AGN

Election Results

1974 general:	John Y. McCollister (R)	72,731	(55%)	($92,834)
	Daniel C. Lynch (D)	59,142	(45%)	($87,691)
1974 primary:	John Y. McCollister (R), unopposed			
1972 general:	John Y. McCollister (R)	114,669	(64%)	($74,569)
	Patrick L. Cooney (D)	64,696	(36%)	($22,050)

◆ ◆ ◆ ◆ ◆

THIRD DISTRICT

One-third of Nebraska's population is spread out over the western three-quarters of its land area—the state's 3d congressional district. As one drives west through this land, the rolling cornfields and wheatlands give way to sand hills and cattle country, much of it devoid of signs of human habitation for miles on end. This is the part of Nebraska to which settlers thronged during the unusually moist 1880s and which their descendants have been leaving often reluctantly, ever since. Today most of the people here live along the Platte River in and near towns like Grand Island (pop. 31,000), Hastings (23,000), Kearney (19,000), and Scottsbluff (14,000).

The 3d is conservative on most issues, and has been for years. But it stands ready to vote against whatever party occupies the White House whenever commodity or cattle prices drop. As recently as 1958, it elected a Democratic Congressman—two of them, in fact, since Nebraska at the time had four congressional districts. During the early 1960s, Congressman David Martin won by only small majorities. The reelection became easier for Martin, and he rose to become ranking Republican on the House Rules Committee when he retired from Congress in 1974.

The 3d district's taste for conventionally conservative Republicans was epitomized by Martin, who was a solid and dependable supporter of Minority Leaders Gerald Ford and John Rhodes. In selecting Martin's successor, the voters of the 3d were forced to pick a more unconventional Representative: either a Democrat or a woman. It was the closest contest the district had seen in years. The Democrat, farmer-businessman Wayne Ziebarth, had nearly won his party's Senate nomination two years before, and if he had won it, he might well have beaten Carl Curtis. As might be expected Ziebarth was conducting a well-financed campaign marred (or was it helped?) by an occasional male chauvinist remark.

His opponent, Republican Virginia Smith, was in any case no women's libber; to the contrary, she was the kind of person who would sign herself Mrs. Haven N. Smith, and her major national experience was not in some women's group, but on the board of the conservative American Farm Bureau Federation. Mrs. Smith won her primary narrowly over a 30-year-old male; and in the general election, she barely beat Ziebarth, by 737-vote margin. She currently sits on the Education and Labor and Interior Committees, here her conservative views are likely to be in the minority at least for the remainder of the 94th Congress. Her prospects for reelection—considering her narrow 1974 margins—appear good, if only because the really tough competition may very well gravitate to the races for U.S. Senate in 1976 and 1978.

Census Data Pop. 494,361. Central city, 0%; suburban, 0%. Median family income, $7,549; families above $15,000: 11%; families below $3,000: 13%. Median years education, 12.2.

The Voters

Median voting age 47.
Employment profile White collar, 38%. Blue collar, 27%. Service, 14%. Farm, 21%.
Ethnic groups Total foreign stock, 13%. Germany, 4%.

Presidential vote

1972	Nixon (R)	148,142	(76%)
	McGovern (D)	47,750	(24%)
1968	Nixon (R)	125,564	(66%)
	Humphrey (D)	50,432	(27%)
	Wallace (AI)	14,227	(7%)

Rep. Virginia Smith (R) Elected 1974; b. June 30, 1911, Randolph, Ia.; home, Chappell; U. of Neb., B.A. 1934; Methodist.

Career Natl. Chm., Amer. Farm Bureau Women, 1955–74; Chm., Pres. Task Force on Rural Development, 1971–72.

Offices 1005 LHOB, 202-225-6435.

Committees

Education and Labor (13th). Subcommittees: Manpower, Compensation, and Health and Safety; Post-secondary Education.

Interior and Insular Affairs (14th). Subcommittees: National Parks and Recreation; Water and Power Resources.

Group Ratings: Newly Elected

Key Votes

1) Foreign Aid	AGN	6) Gov Abortn Aid	NE	11) Pub Cong Election $	NE
2) Busing	NE	7) Coed Phys Ed	AGN	12) Turkish Arms Cutoff	NE
3) ABM	NE	8) Pov Lawyer Gag	NE	13) Youth Camp Regs	AGN
4) B-1 Bomber	FOR	9) Pub Trans Sub	NE	14) Strip Mine Veto	FOR
5) Nerve Gas	NE	10) EZ Voter Regis	NE	15) Farm Bill Veto	AGN

Election Results

1974 general:	Mrs. Haven Smith (R)	80,992	(50%)	($102,820)
	Wayne W. Ziebarth (D)	80,255	(50%)	($90,123)

1974 primary: Mrs. Haven Smith (R)   15,672   (21%)
                Don Blank (R)   15,531   (21%)
                Gerald A. Stromer (R)   13,942   (19%)
                J. James Waldron (R)   8,888   (12%)
                Four others (R)   19,489   (27%)

NEVADA

Nevada as an entity dates back to the discovery of the Comstock Lode in 1859—one of those huge mineral finds that triggered a rush of prospectors, speculators, and hangers on. Suddenly there was a large town here, Virginia City, and a territorial government in nearby Carson City; and when the Republicans desperately needed (or so they thought) electoral votes in 1864, they contrived to make these two towns, plus tens of thousands of square miles of the vacant, arid Great Basin to the north, west, and south, the state of Nevada. Statehood was achieved, and the electoral votes, cast in time, and Nevada thereby became our third western state.

But soon enough the veins of silver and gold petered out, and the prospector population scattered—to Lead, South Dakota; Bisbee, Arizona; and the Yukon River in Alaska. Nevada, with only about 100,000 residents, was left in economic doldrums for decades. During the depression of the 1930s, the state government was on the verge of complete collapse. So the legislature legalized gambling and liberalized its divorce laws at just about the same time as the federal government was finishing Hoover Dam near Las Vegas in 1936. These events brought Nevada tourists, six-week residents, water, and big—and often tainted—money.

Up through the end of World War II, Nevada's tiny population was still concentrated in the northwest end of the state, in and around Reno. But Reno's dominance was changed by a series of events which began when in 1947 Bugsy Siegel opened the Flamingo, the first big casino hotel on the Las Vegas Strip. At the same time, just outside Las Vegas, the Atomic Energy Commission established the Nevada Proving Grounds. Today, the big casinos and the AEC's successor agency are two of Las Vegas's—and Nevada's—three biggest employers; and the city itself has grown from a small desert gas station crossroads to a major urban center. Today Clark County, which includes Las Vegas, the Strip, and Hoover Dam, now has 56% of the state's population. Reno and surrounding Washoe County have 25%, leaving just 19% of the state's people in the so-called "cow counties."

That shift has had political as well as sociological consequences. Reno, surrounded by pine-clad, snow-capped mountains, remains as it always has been, for reasons not clear, a strongly Republican town. Las Vegas, in a dusty, bowl-like valley surrounded by bone-dry peaks, was Democratic in its early days, primarily from the Southern origin of many of its original settlers; and it remains Democratic today, for reasons again not entirely clear. But the state as a whole has, if anything, in recent years moved slightly toward the Republicans; what seems to be happening is that Nevada's traditionally conservative Democrats have been succeeded by more liberal ones, and while this has been a Democratic state, it has never been a particularly liberal one. Nevada Senators, for example, have always had a habit of voting against cutting off filibusters, on the theory that that tends to increase the power of the state's two Senate votes, which of course are all the political leverage the state has. And the state has a tradition of powerful, conservative Democratic Senators that goes back to Key Pittman, Chairman of the Foreign Relations Committee in the 1930s, and Pat McCarran, author of the antisubversive act which bears his name (and much of which has proved to be unconstitutional).

This tradition died slowly; it was continued, in modified form, by Senator Alan Bible, a protege of McCarran's who succeeded to his seat and eventually became Chairman of the Appropriations Interior Subcommittee before he decided to retire. Bible's decision was somewhat unexpected; he was only 65—young for a Senate veteran—and probably could have won another term easily. His seat would almost automatically have remained in Democratic hands if one of two things had happened: first, if Governor Mike O'Callaghan, overwhelmingly popular, had decided to run for it; or second, if former Governor (1967–70) Paul Laxalt had decided not to. But it worked out quite differently. O'Callaghan decided he wanted to stay in Carson City, and Laxalt, having settled his affairs as owner of a small casino, decided to have a go at it.

Laxalt is a conservative Republican with a record of strong vote-getting in Nevada. In 1964, he lost to Senator Howard Cannon by just 48 votes in that otherwise Democratic year; two years later, he beat two-term incumbent Governor Grant Sawyer. Laxalt's years as Governor coincided almost precisely with the time Howard Hughes resided in Las Vegas. Hughes' purchase of half the big casinos on the Strip, some of them reportedly previously owned by organized crime interests, was generally hailed as a good thing for Nevada, and by nobody less vigorously than Laxalt. Indeed, Laxalt is one of the few people who has talked to Hughes on the phone in the last twenty years. And when Laxalt decided to retire—for the sort of personal reasons which do not usually sway politicians—Hughes promptly decided to leave the state.

Laxalt probably could have won reelection easily in 1970; but when he entered the Senate race four years later he was the underdog. The favorite was Lieutenant Governor Harry Reid, a liberal Democrat from Las Vegas who seemed widely popular, especially in his home town. He had made a splash in the legislature advocating environmental, consumer protection, and anticrime bills; in high school he had been a student of his colleague, Governor O'Callaghan. But Reid had some problems in the primary from Maya Miller, a much older but just as attractive activist whose vibrant personality probably brought her as many votes as her liberal stands on issues. And in the general the 34-year-old Reid was hurt by his youthful appearance, in contrast to the graying good looks of the 52-year-old Laxalt.

The result was a photo finish. Reid carried Las Vegas easily but Laxalt had his previous strength in Reno and the cow counties, enough to lead by 624 votes. Recounts did not change the result much, and so Laxalt became the first Basque-American Senator—as well as the first Republican Senator elected in Nevada since 1952.

Laxalt's senior colleague is now the man he came so close to beating in 1964, Howard Cannon. Cannon is now fairly well known to most Americans as the Chairman of the Senate Rules Committee, an ordinarily unimportant body which passed on the nominations of Vice Presidents Ford and Rockefeller. Cannon deserves credit for asking astute questions such as grilling Ford in advance on whether a former President should be pardoned. "The American people wouldn't stand for it," Ford replied, quite correctly as it turned out. After the 1974 election, Cannon's Rules panel got another thorny problem, the question of who actually had won the Senate seat that year in New Hampshire. Cannon also sits on the Armed Services Committee, where he has voted both hawkish and dovish on different occasions; and on the Aeronautical and Space Sciences Committee. He is an airplane buff, a general in the Air Force Reserve who still pilots big jets; and generally a backer of the space program.

Cannon's major political strength lies in Clark County, where he was District Attorney for ten years before he was first elected Senator in 1958; even in his close call in 1964 he got more than 60% of the vote there, and he will probably get a large enough percentage there in 1976—particularly since there seems to be no well-known Republican opponent—to win a fourth term without too much trouble.

Nevada's only Congressman is also from Clark County; 39-year-old James Santini was a judge there before he was elected to Congress in 1974. Santini was blessed with a favorable political situation in the general. For years (1949–53, 1957–73), the state's at-large House seat had been held by Walter Baring, a self-described "states' rights Democrat," who was the most conservative Congressman of his party from outside the South. Baring won general elections easily, since most Republican supporters voted for him, but he was vulnerable in primaries, where his reactionary record hurt him. By 1972, he attracted significant opposition in James Bilbray, a wealthy Las Vegas businessman; with the help of environmentalists, who noticed Baring's climb toward the top of the Interior Committee, the old man was beaten. But the fallout from his primary fight, plus the strong Nixon showing here in 1972, allowed the victory in the general of David Towell, a conservative Republican from the tiny town of Gardnerville.

Towell's solid pro-Nixon voting record in a period when the President's popularity plummeted to nothing and the Congressman's lack of a significant electoral base made him extremely vulnerable in 1974. Santini, with his well-financed campaign, prevailed by a 56–36 margin—an unusually large one by which to knock off an incumbent. By all appearances, Santini is now well established in his seat.

But the most popular of all Nevada politicians at the moment is one who is not a part of the state's small congressional delegation; it is Governor Mike O'Callaghan. A veteran who lost a leg in Korea, O'Callaghan came to the Governorship by an odd route: a teacher near Las Vegas, he became active in party politics and was tapped for a series of appointive posts. His 1970 victory was by a small margin, but after four years in office he was unbeatable. His administration was generally conceded to have been honest and economy-minded, which is probably all most

Nevadans want from their state government; and he was elected by a near unanimous vote. Republicans made a little history here by giving their gubernatorial nomination to a woman; but Nevadans are still waiting for a woman to win a nomination worth having.

During the 1974 campaign, one legislative candidate in sparsely populated Nye, Mineral, and Esmeralda Counties was getting national attention. She was Beverly Harrell, proprietrix of the Cottontail Ranch, one of the legalized houses of prostitution which may be found in some of the cow counties. Ms. Harrell eventually lost the general election, despite the fun her candidacy provided for slogan-makers; but her candidacy does remind us why the law-and-order politics of the Nixon-Agnew era somehow never had much success here in anything goes Nevada.

Census Data   Pop. 488,738; 0.24% of U.S. total, 47th largest; Central city, 41%; suburban, 40%. Median family income, $10,687; 10th highest; families above $15,000: 25%; families below $3,000: 7%. Median years education, 12.4.

1974 Share of Federal Tax Burden $857,009,000; 0.32% of U.S. total, 43d largest.

1974 Share of Federal Outlays $764,010,000; 0.28% of U.S. total, 47th largest. Per capita federal spending, $1563.

DOD	$182,727,000	44th (0.27%)	HEW	$184,833,000	48th (0.20%)
AEC	$112,376,000	13th (3.69%)	HUD	$2,114,000	45th (0.22%)
NASA	$734,000	36th (0.02%)	VA	$37,501,000	46th (0.27%)
DOT	$54,406,000	42d (0.64%)	EPA	$17,766,000	30th (0.56%)
DOC	$2,171,000	48th (0.13%)	RevS	$13,472,000	48th (0.22%)
DOI	$38,096,000	19th (1.55%)	Int.	$16,766,000	49th (0.08%)
USDA	$14,660,000	49th (0.12%)	Other	$86,388,000	

Economic Base   Tourism; finance, insurance and real estate; agriculture, notably cattle, dairy products, hay and sheep; metal mining, especially copper ores; paper and allied products; primary metal industries, especially nonferrous rolling and drawing.

Political Line-up   Governor, Mike O'Callaghan (D). Senators, Howard W. Cannon (D) and Paul Laxalt (R). Representatives, 1 D at large. State Senate (17 D and 3 R); State Assembly (31 D and 9 R).

The Voters

Registration   222,132 Total. 129,820 D (58%); 75,773 R (34%); 16,079 Miscellaneous and Independent (7%); 460 AIP (–).
Median voting age   40.
Employment profile   White collar, 47%. Blue collar, 26%. Service, 25%. Farm, 2%.
Ethnic groups   Black, 6%. Spanish, 6%. Total foreign stock, 14%.

Presidential vote

1972	Nixon (R)	115,750	(64%)
	McGovern (D)	66,016	(36%)
1968	Nixon (R)	73,188	(47%)
	Humphrey (D)	60,598	(39%)
	Wallace (AI)	20,432	(13%)

Sen. Howard W. Cannon (D)   Elected 1958, seat up 1976; b. Jan. 26, 1912, St. George, Utah; home, Las Vegas; Dixie Jr. Col.; Ariz. St. Teachers Col., B.E. 1933, U. of Ariz., LL.B. 1937; Church of Latter Day Saints.

Career   Reference Atty., Utah Senate, 1938; Washington Co. Atty., 1940–41; Practicing atty., 1938–41, 1946–58; Army Air Corps, WWII; Las Vegas City Atty., 1949–58.

Offices   259 RSOB, 202-224-6244. Also 4-602 U.S. Fed. Bldg., Las Vegas Blvd. S., Las Vegas 89101, 702-385-6278, and Fed. Bldg., 300 Booth St., Reno 89503, 702-784-5544.

Committees

Rules and Administration (Chairman). Subcommittees: Computer Services (Chairman); Library (Chairman); Printing (Chairman); Standing Rules of the Senate.

Aeronautical and Space Sciences (4th).

Armed Services (4th). Subcommittees: Intelligence; Military Construction Authorization; National Stockpile and Naval Petroleum Reserves (Chairman); Preparedness Investigating; Tactical Air Power (Chairman).

Group Ratings

	ADA	COPE	LWV	RIPON	NFU	LCV	CFA	NAB	NSI	ACA
1974	37	40	70	45	76	38	50	22	90	32
1973	37	82	50	50	94	–	64	–	–	27
1972	25	44	45	48	70	11	88	50	75	45

Key Votes

1) No-Knock	FOR	8) Gov Abortn Aid	ABS	15) Consumer Prot Agy	FOR
2) Busing	AGN	9) Cut Mil Brass	AGN	16) Forced Psych Tests	FOR
3) No Fault	FOR	10) Gov Limousine	AGN	17) Fed Campaign Subs	FOR
4) F-111	FOR	11) RR Featherbed	FOR	18) Rhod Chrome Ban	AGN
5) Death Penalty	FOR	12) Handgun License	AGN	19) Open Legis Meetings	AGN
6) Foreign Aid	AGN	13) Less Troop Abrd	AGN	20) Strikers Food Stmps	FOR
7) Filibuster	AGN	14) Resume Turk Aid	FOR	21) Gov Info Disclosure	AGN

Election Results

1970 general:	Howard W. Cannon (D)	85,187	(58%)
	William J. Raggio (R)	60,838	(42%)
1970 primary:	Howard W. Cannon (D)	54,320	(89%)
	Two others (D)	6,510	(11%)
1964 general;	Howard W. Cannon (D)	67,336	(50%)
	Paul Laxalt (R)	67,288	(50%)

Sen. Paul Laxalt (R) Elected 1974, seat up 1980; b. Aug. 2, 1922, Reno; home, Carson City; Santa Clara U., 1940–43, U. of Denver, B.S., LL.B. 1949.

Career Army, WWII; Ormsby Co. Dist. Atty., 1951–54; Practicing atty., 1954–66, 1970–74; Lt. Gov. of Nev., 1963–66; Gov. of Nev., 1966–70.

Offices 145 RSOB, 202-224-3542. Also U.S. Fed. Bldg., Rm. 2016, 300 Booth St., Reno 89502, and U.S. Fed. Bldg., Rm. 4626, 300 Las Vegas Blvd. S., Las Vegas 89101.

Committees

Aeronautical and Space Sciences (3d).

Labor and Public Welfare (6th). Subcommittees: Alcoholism and Narcotics; Children and Youth; Special Subcommittee on National Science Foundation.

Group Ratings: Newly Elected

Key Votes

1) No-Knock	NE	8) Gov Abortn Aid	FOR	15) Consumer Prot Agy	NE
2) Busing	NE	9) Cut Mil Brass	NE	16) Forced Psych Tests	NE
3) No Fault	NE	10) Gov Limousine	NE	17) Fed Campaign Subs	NE
4) F-111	FOR	11) RR Featherbed	NE	18) Rhod Chrome Ban	NE
5) Death Penalty	NE	12) Handgun License	NE	19) Open Legis Meetings	NE
6) Foreign Aid	NE	13) Less Troop Abrd	NE	20) Strikers Food Stmps	NE
7) Filibuster	FOR	14) Resume Turk Aid	AGN	21) Gov Info Disclosure	NE

Election Results

1974 general;	Paul Laxalt (R)	79,605	(47%)	($385,861)
	Harry Reid (D)	78,981	(47%)	($400,553)
	Jack C. Doyle (Independent American)	10,887	(6%)	
1974 primary:	Paul Laxalt (R)	33,660	(81%)	
	Two others (R)	7,736	(19%)	

Gov. Mike O'Callaghan (D) Elected 1970, term expires Jan. 1979; b. Sept. 10, 1929, LaCrosse, Wis.; Gonzaga U., St. Martin's Col., Boise Jr. Col., A.A. 1950, U. of Idaho, B.S., M.A. 1956.

Career USMC, WWII; Air Force and Army, Korea; Public school teacher, 1956–61; Chf. Probate Officer and Dir. of Court Services, Clark Co., 1961–63; Dir., Nev. Dept. of Health and Welfare, 1963; Management Dir., Job Corps Conservation Ctrs.; Candidate for Dem. nomination for Lt. Gov., 1966; Dir., Western Region, U.S. Ofc. of Emergency Planning.

Offices Capitol Bldg., Carson City 89701, 702-885-5670.

Election Results

1974 general:	Mike O'Callaghan (D)	114,114	(67%)
	Shirley Crumpler (R)	28,959	(17%)
	James Ray Houston (Ind.)	26,285	(16%)
1974 primary:	Mike O'Callaghan (D)	69,089	(91%)
	Five others (D)	6,961	(9%)
1970 general:	Mike O'Callaghan (D)	70,697	(48%)
	Ed Fike (R)	64,400	(52%)
	Charles E. Springer (Ind.)	6,489	(4%)
	Daniel M. Hansen (IA)	5,415	(4%)

Rep. Jim Santini (D) Elected 1974; b. Aug. 13, 1937, Reno; home, Las Vegas; U. of Nev., B.S. 1959, Hastings Col. of Law, J.D. 1962.

Career Practicing atty.; Army, 1963–66; Clark Co. Deputy Dist. Atty., 1968–69; Public Defender, 1968–70; Justice of the Peace, 1970–72; Clark Co. Dist. Ct. Judge, 1972–74.

Offices 1408 LHOB, 202-225-5965. Also Suite 4-620 Fed. Bldg., 300 Las Vegas Blvd. S., Las Vegas 89101, 702-385-6575.

Committees

Interior and Insular Affairs (22d). Subcommittees: Mines and Mining; Public Lands; Water and Power Resources.

Interstate and Foreign Commerce (28th). Subcommittees: Oversight and Investigations; Transportation and Commerce.

Group Ratings: Newly Elected

Key Votes

1) Foreign Aid	FOR	6) Gov Abortn Aid	NE	11) Pub Cong Election $	NE
2) Busing	NE	7) Coed Phys Ed	FOR	12) Turkish Arms Cutoff	NE
3) ABM	NE	8) Pov Lawyer Gag	NE	13) Youth Camp Regs	FOR
4) B-1 Bomber	AGN	9) Pub Trans Sub	NE	14) Strip Mine Veto	AGN
5) Nerve Gas	NE	10) EZ Voter Regis	NE	15) Farm Bill Veto	FOR

Election Results

1974 general:	Jim Santini (D)	93,665	(56%)	($122,199)
	David Towell (R)	61,182	(36%)	($111,697)
	Joel Hansen (Ind.)	13,119	(8%)	(NA)

NEW HAMPSHIRE

Once every four years New Hampshire becomes the center of the nation's political attention. Presidential candidates trudge through the melting snow and gooey mud of the state's industrial cities and small New England towns, wooing the votes of less than 100,000 people. New Hampshire's presidential primary remains the first in the nation, (and the state is making every effort to assure it continues as such), and it continues to draw dozens of politicians, hundreds of journalists, and sometimes, thousands of idealistic volunteers to this out-of-the-way state. So deluged, the New Hampshire voters have a way of disproving the confident predictions of these outsiders. In 1964, for instance, when Barry Goldwater and Nelson Rockefeller both spent gobs of money here, New Hampshire Republicans surprised them both by producing a write-in victory for Henry Cabot Lodge, at the time the U.S. Ambassador in Saigon. Four years later, Eugene McCarthy's 42% of the vote against Lyndon Johnson destroyed the myth of an incumbent president's invulnerability. In 1972 George McGovern's surprisingly high 37% of the vote surprised everyone but his own canvassers—especially the strategists who had assumed that Edmund Muskie would sweep to victory without substantial primary opposition.

The secrets of all these unexpected successes seems to have been the power of good volunteer campaigns, supplemented—but never dominated—by good media. There are so few voters in New Hampshire, and the number of targets is further limited by the state's party registration system, that a candidate with a wide popular following can attract enough volunteers who will go door to door and talk with almost every potential voter. That kind of personal contact— and it is seldom as close after the presidential campaigns leave New Hampshire for larger states—seems to make all the difference; at this early state of the campaign, especially, many voters are willing to go for a candidate who has inspired some nice young (or old) person to come to their door and ask for their vote. So by early 1975 some of the more astute presidential hopefuls were already signing up New Hampshire political activists, people who can attract and deploy the volunteers that appear to be almost essential to victory.

As soon as the votes are counted, the politicians and their camp of followers leave, and by the second week of March New Hampshire, which casts only four electoral votes, often never sees a national candidate again. Politics in the state returns to normal, dominated as it is by fractious local politicians and by William Loeb, owner of the Manchester *Union Leader*. This newspaper reaches about one-quarter of the state's households with Loeb's ardent conservatism, his opposition to pornography, civil rights legislation, and taxes of all kinds. The *Union Leader* is outspoken about its political likes and dislikes, and those whom it dislikes claim that Loeb slants not just the paper's lengthy front page editorials, but also its news columns.

In many ways the *Union Leader*'s political clout has been overstated. There is no evidence it can make a major presidential contender out of a candidate with minimal volunteer support; Loeb tried that with Los Angeles Mayor Sam Yorty in the 1972 Democratic primary, and Yorty got only 6% of the vote. In statewide contests, Loeb has backed a string of losers: Mrs. Styles Bridges, the late Senator's widow (the 1962 Senate race); General Harrison Thyng (1966 Senate); and Democrats Emil Bussiere and Roger Crowley (1968 and 1970 Governor's races).

Loeb's influence is not so much positive as negative. It was Loeb's newspaper that published the letter, apparently written by White House staffer Ken Clawson, which accused Muskie of using the word "Canuck" derogatorily—a real problem in a state where 15% of the people are of French

Canadian background. Muskie denounced the *Union Leader*'s coverage in a snowbound scene outside the paper's offices; that was the time he appeared moved to tears by the *Union Leader*'s comments about his wife—an incident which probably destroyed his candidacy forever.

Loeb's vigorous opposition to sales and income taxes—New Hampshire is the only state left with neither—moved him to vigorously oppose governors like Democrat John King (1963–68) and moderate Republican Walter Peterson (1969–72). After his long losing streak in state elections, Loeb suddenly recouped his fortunes in 1972 when *Union Leader*-endorsed candidates won both the state's gubernatorial primaries. The winner in November, Meldrim Thomson, is a transplanted Southerner who stirred up a fuss by perusing confidential tax returns, and who emerged in 1974 as perhaps the most steadfastly pro-Nixon of all the nation's Governors (chief competition: Reagan of California and Godwin of Virginia). Thomson, reelected in 1974, seems rather zany to outsiders but is apparently taken quite seriously in New Hampshire; there is talk that he will run as a conservative opponent to President Gerald Ford in the 1976 presidential primary. That will not bar him from seeking another term as Governor; indeed, he could even win again.

One frustration for the *Union Leader* and Loeb has been the continued reelection of Senator Thomas McIntyre. His first victory, in a 1962 special election, was helped by feuding among Republicans following the death of Senator Styles Bridges. McIntyre's second victory, in 1966, seems all but inevitable in light of the fact that his Loeb-backed opponent was named Harrison Thyng. And in 1972, despite the strong Nixon showing here, McIntyre won a third term by a 57–43 margin over former Governor Wesley Powell, a man whose presidential preference every four years is carefully followed, for reasons which are wholly unclear.

McIntyre by instinct is a cautious, even conservative man. During the Johnson Administration, he was happy to support the President's domestic and foreign policy down the line; since that time he has often hesitated before bucking the Republicans. On the Armed Services Committee, McIntyre has been very much a swing vote. He has led almost successful moves to trim the costs of new weapons systems like the Trident missile, but he has also supported compromise proposals for continuation of military aid to South Vietnam. Thus though McIntyre is more of a liberal Democrat than anything else, he is not always comfortable in that category.

As for New Hampshire's other Senator—well, for some months, New Hampshire didn't have another Senator. On the morning after the 1974 election the outcome seemed clear, although surprisingly close: Republican Congressman Louis Wyman had beaten former state Insurance Commissioner John Durkin by 355 votes. But when the Secretary of State counted the votes again, he found Durkin the winner by the margin of exactly 10. Under New Hampshire law, these certified returns have to be signed by the Governor's Ballot Law Commission, usually a routine procedure; in this case Thomson's Commissioners investigated a couple hundred ballots and found that Wyman had won by 2 votes. Because of the confusion, the Senate declined to seat either candidate, and the problem was plopped into the hands of the Senate Rules Committee, for the Senate itself is the final judge of the qualifications of its members. But late July, 1975, Durkin fell in with Wyman, and agreed that the issue be returned to New Hampshire, where an election rematch is scheduled for September 15. Durkin, a liberal, hopes to get out his vote in the relatively liberal territory south of Concord; Wyman figures the voters' disgust with the Democratic Senate's inability to act will give him the seat.

Why had the election been so close in the first place? Wyman had been a solid vote-getter in New Hampshire since the 1950s, when he was state Attorney General and a minor league crusader against Communism. In 1962 he was elected to Congress in the 1st district; beaten in 1964, he came back in 1966, and by 1972 was winning easily. His kind of conservatism suits Loeb and the *Union Leader* fine, although Loeb like many others finds him personally unpleasant. Durkin entered the race unknown and underfinanced, scarcely a contender at all. But then it developed that Lou Wyman had helped Ruth Farkas get together with the men at CREEP, to whom Mrs. Farkas contributed $250,000 (after the election) and upon whose apparent recommendation she was appointed Ambassador to Luxembourg. (She is said to have complained, when offered Costa Rica, that $300,000 was an awful lot for a Central American country.) In stern New Hampshire, Wyman's Farkas connection did not go over well, despite his explanations that he had done nothing wrong; and that, along with Wyman's lackadaisical campaigning, was the reason the result had been so close.

With only the slightest changes, New Hampshire's two congressional districts have had the same boundaries since 1881. The lines neatly separate the cities of Manchester (pop. 87,000) and Nashua (pop. 55,000), both mill towns on the Merrimack River. Both Manchester and Nashua have large numbers of Irish, Italian, and especially French Canadian immigrants and their offspring, who form the major Democratic voting groups in this usually Republican state. The purpose of the 1881 redistricting was to put both districts permanently out of reach of the Democrats and to an amazing extent it has done just that.

The 1st district is dominated by Manchester, the state's largest city. There are also significant concentrations of people in the Portsmouth-Rochester area, near Maine, and along the Massachusetts border, where Boston area commuters, in search of life in the country and lower taxes, have been moving in great numbers. (Some commentators describe these Rockingham County voters as Massachusetts liberals; more likely, they are people who left Massachusetts in part because they didn't care much for the dominant liberalism and high taxes there.) When 1st district Congressman Louis Wyman ran for the Senate in 1974, there was a close race here, and the winner, in something of a surprise, was Democrat Norman D'Amours. A rather moderate Democrat, D'Amours has become a member of the Agriculture and Merchant Marine and Fisheries Committees; it will be interesting to see whether he survives politically the 1976 elections.

The 2d district is somewhat less urban than the 1st and, in recent statewide elections, slightly less conservative. But none of the statewide trends have had much influence on congressional elections here. The district has been represented in the House by Republican James Cleveland since 1962. Cleveland had a close race in 1964, but otherwise his mild mannered, moderate Republicanism seems to suit his constituents well. He is not a particularly assertive and ambitious man, and it says something about his character that although he had about as much reason as his colleague Wyman to suppose that he might win the 1974 senatorial race, he never entered it.

Census Data Pop. 737,681; 0.36% of U.S. total, 41st largest; Central city, 19%; suburban, 8%. Median family income, $9,682; 18th highest; families above $15,000: 17%; families below $3,000: 7%. Median years education, 12.2.

1974 Share of Federal Tax Burden $1,017,698,000; 0.38% of U.S. total, 40th largest.

1974 Share of Federal Outlays $896,014,000; 0.33% of U.S. total, 45th largest. Per capita federal spending, $1215.

DOD	$271,243,000	39th (0.40%)		HEW	$331,353,000	40th (0.36%)
AEC	$90,000	42d (–)		HUD	$4,263,000	39th (0.44%)
NASA	$727,000	37th (0.02%)		VA	$51,729,000	42d (0.38%)
DOT	$42,217,000	45th (0.50%)		EPA	$14,670,000	34th (0.47%)
DOC	$3,370,000	45th (0.21%)		RevS	$19,521,000	45th (0.32%)
DOI	$3,639,000	47th (0.15%)		Int.	$28,041,000	43d (0.14%)
USDA	$18,619,000	48th (0.15%)		Other	$106,532,000	

Economic Base Leather footwear, and other leather and leather products; tourism; electrical equipment and supplies; finance, insurance and real estate; machinery; textile mill products; rubber and plastics products not otherwise classified, especially miscellaneous plastics products.

Political Line-up Governor, Meldrim Thomson, Jr. (R). Senators, Thomas J. McIntyre (D) and John Durkin (D). Representatives, 2 (1 D and 1 R). State Senate (12 D and 12 R); State House (233 R and 167 D). ·

The Voters

Registration 280,260 Total. 115,797 D (41%); 164,463 R (59%).
Median voting age 43.
Employment profile White collar, 45%. Blue collar, 42%. Service, 12%. Farm, 1%.
Ethnic groups Total foreign stock, 23%. Canada, 13%.

Presidential vote

1972	Nixon (R)	....	213,724	(65%)
	McGovern (D)	....	116,435	(35%)
1968	Nixon (R)	....	154,903	(52%)
	Humphrey (D)	....	130,589	(44%)
	Wallace (AI)	....	11,173	(4%)

1972 Democratic Presidential Primary				1972 Republican Presidential Primary		
Muskie	41,235	(46%)		Nixon	79,239	(67%)
McGovern	33,007	(37%)		McCloskey	23,190	(20%)
others	14,612	(17%)		Ashbrook	11,362	(10%)
preference only				Others	3,417	(3%)

Sen. Thomas J. McIntyre (D) Elected 1962, seat up 1978; b. Feb. 20, 1915, Laconia; home, Laconia; Dartmouth Col., A.B. 1937, Boston U., LL.B. 1940; Catholic.

Career Practicing atty.; Army, WWII; Mayor of Laconia, 1949–51; Laconia City Solicitor, 1952–53; Dir., Laconia Industrial Development Corp., 1962.

Offices 125 RSOB, 202-224-2841. Also Fed. Bldg., Manchester 03105, 603-669-1232, and Fed. Bldg., Portsmouth 03801, 603-436-7720.

Committees

Armed Services (5th). Subcommittees: Arms Control; General Legislation; Intelligence; Preparedness Investigating; Research and Development (Chairman).

Banking, Housing and Urban Affairs (4th). Subcommittees: Financial Institutions (Chairman); Housing and Urban Affairs; International Finance; Oversight; Securities; Small Business.

Group Ratings

	ADA	COPE	LWV	RIPON	NFU	LCV	CFA	NAB	NSI	ACA
1974	80	80	90	57	88	82	88	50	40	0
1973	72	91	89	47	88	–	80	–	–	7
1972	35	88	100	80	78	76	100	50	78	33

Key Votes

1) No-Knock	AGN	8) Gov Abortn Aid	FOR	15) Consumer Prot Agy	FOR
2) Busing	FOR	9) Cut Mil Brass	AGN	16) Forced Psych Tests	FOR
3) No Fault	FOR	10) Gov Limousine	FOR	17) Fed Campaign Subs	FOR
4) F-111	ABS	11) RR Featherbed	FOR	18) Rhod Chrome Ban	FOR
5) Death Penalty	AGN	12) Handgun License	AGN	19) Open Legis Meetings	AGN
6) Foreign Aid	FOR	13) Less Troop Abrd	FOR	20) Strikers Food Stmps	FOR
7) Filibuster	AGN	14) Resume Turk Aid	AGN	21) Gov Info Disclosure	FOR

Election Results

1972 general;	Thomas J. McIntyre (D)	184,495	(57%)	($82,800)
	Wesley Powell (R)	139,852	(43%)	($104,779)
1972 primary:	Thomas J. McIntyre (D), unopposed			
1966 general:	Thomas J. McIntyre (D)	123,888	(54%)	
	Harrison R. Thyng (R)	105,241	(46%)	

Gov. Meldrim Thomson, Jr. (R) Elected 1972, term expires Jan. 1977; b. Mar. 8, 1912, Pittsburgh, Pa.; U. of Miami, Mercer U., U. of Ga., LL.B.; Protestant.

Career Instructor of Poli. Sci., U. of Ga.; Practicing atty.; Founder and Pres., Equity Publishing Co., Orford; Chm., Natl. Conservative Caucus.; Candidate for Repub. nomination for Gov., 1968, 1970.

Offices State Capitol, Concord 03301, 603-271-1110.

Election Results

1974 general:	Meldrim Thomson, Jr. (R)	115,933	(51%)
	Richard W. Leonard (D)	110,591	(49%)
1974 primary:	Meldrim Thomson, Jr. (R)	47,244	(55%)
	David L. Nixon (R)	37,286	(43%)
	Two Others (R)	1,523	(2%)
1972 general:	Meldrim Thomson, Jr. (R)	133,702	(52%)
	Roger J. Crowley (D)	126,107	(48%)

◆ ◆ ◆ ◆ ◆

FIRST DISTRICT

Census Data Pop. 367,075. Central city, 24%; suburban, 8%. Median family income, $9,631; families above $15,000: 17%; families below $3,000: 7%. Median years education, 12.2.

The Voters

Median voting age 43.
Employment profile White collar, 45%. Blue collar, 42%. Service, 12%. Farm, 1%.
Ethnic groups Total foreign stock, 23%. Canada, 13%.

Presidential vote

1972	Nixon (R)	111,167	(67%)
	McGovern (D)	54,375	(33%)
1968	Nixon (R)	78,662	(53%)
	Humphrey (D)	64,045	(43%)
	Wallace (AI)	6,347	(4%)

Rep. Norman E. D'Amours (D) Elected 1974; b. Oct. 14, 1937, Holyoke, Mass.; home, Manchester; Assumption Col., B.A. 1960, Boston U., LL.B. 1963.

Career Practicing atty.; Asst. Atty. Gen. of N.H., 1966–69; Criminal Law Instructor, St. Police Training School, 1967–69; Dir., Manchester Area School for Police Prosecutors, 1970; Manchester City Prosecutor, 1970–72; Instructor, St. Anselm's Col., 1972–73.

Offices 1330 LHOB, 202-225-5456. Also 50 Bridge St., Manchester 03101, 603-668-6800 and 669-7011 ext. 7707.

Committees

Agriculture (27th). Subcommittees: Department Operations, Investigations and Oversight; Domestic Marketing and Consumer Relations; Livestock and Grains.

Merchant Marine and Fisheries (24th). Subcommittees: Fisheries and Wildlife Conservation and the Environment; Merchant Marine; Oceanography.

Group Ratings: Newly Elected

Key Votes

1) Foreign Aid	AGN	6) Gov Abortn Aid	NE	11) Pub Cong Election $	NE
2) Busing	NE	7) Coed Phys Ed	AGN	12) Turkish Arms Cutoff	NE
3) ABM	NE	8) Pov Lawyer Gag	NE	13) Youth Camp Regs	FOR
4) B-1 Bomber	FOR	9) Pub Trans Sub	NE	14) Strip Mine Veto	AGN
5) Nerve Gas	NE	10) EZ Voter Regis	NE	15) Farm Bill Veto	AGN

Election Results

1974 general:	Norman E. D'Amours (D)	58,388	(52%)	($75,128)
	David A. Banks (R)	53,610	(48%)	($108,163)
1974 primary:	Norman E. D'Amours (D)	12,036	(50%)	
	Sylvia Chaplain (D)	7,998	(33%)	
	Joseph Cote (D)	4,140	(17%)	

◆ ◆ ◆ ◆ ◆

SECOND DISTRICT

Census Data Pop. 370,606. Central city, 15%; suburban, 8%. Median family income, $9,736; families above $15,000: 18%; families below $3,000: 7%. Median years education, 12.2.

The Voters

Median voting age 43.
Employment profile White collar, 45%. Blue collar, 42%. Service, 12%. Farm, 1%.
Ethnic groups Total foreign stock, 23%. Canada, 13%.

Presidential vote

1972	Nixon (R)	102,557	(62%)
	McGovern (D)	62,060	(38%)
1968	Nixon (R)	76,241	(52%)
	Humphrey (D)	66,544	(45%)
	Wallace (AI)	4,826	(3%)

Rep. James C. Cleveland (R) Elected 1962; b. June 13, 1920, Montclair, N.J.; home, New London; Colgate U., B.A. 1941, Yale U., LL.B. 1948; Protestant.

Career Army, WWII; Practicing atty., 1949–62; N.H. Senate, 1950–62, Maj. Floor Ldr., 1952–55.

Offices 2236 RHOB, 202-225-5206. Also 316 Fed. Bldg., Concord 03301, 603-224-4187.

Committees

House Administration (3d). Subcommittees: Accounts; Contracts; Paper Conservation; Printing.

Public Works and Transportation (2d). Subcommittees: Economic Development; Investigations and Review; Surface Transportation.

Group Ratings

	ADA	COPE	LWV	RIPON	NFU	LCV	CFA	NAB	NSI	ACA
1974	26	27	50	56	69	25	31	92	90	67
1973	20	36	33	73	45	32	57	–	–	63
1972	19	36	50	47	43	60	100	75	100	65

Key Votes

1) Foreign Aid	AGN	6) Gov Abortn Aid	AGN	11) Pub Cong Election $	FOR
2) Busing	AGN	7) Coed Phys Ed	AGN	12) Turkish Arms Cutoff	AGN
3) ABM	AGN	8) Pov Lawyer Gag	FOR	13) Youth Camp Regs	FOR
4) B-1 Bomber	FOR	9) Pub Trans Sub	AGN	14) Strip Mine Veto	FOR
5) Nerve Gas	AGN	10) EZ Voter Regis	AGN	15) Farm Bill Veto	FOR

Election Results

1974 general:	James C. Cleveland (R)	69,068	(64%)	($27,102)
	Helen L. Bliss (D)	38,463	(36%)	($15,835)
1974 primary:	James C. Cleveland (R)	35,682	(86%)	
	Lawrence Kamarck (R)	5,844	(14%)	
1972 general:	James C. Cleveland (R) $23,479	105,915	(68%)	
	Charles B. Officer (D) $37,030	50,066	(32%)	

NEW JERSEY

After years of obscurity, New Jersey in the early 1970s at last found a political identity: as the nation's most corrupt state. Though the eighth most populous state in the nation, New Jersey had long languished in national inattention. Sandwiched between New York and Philadelphia, some 78% of the state's residents live in one of those two metropolitan areas. People here read out of state newspapers, watch out of state TV stations, and follow out of state political contests; aside from Delaware, this is the only state without a VHF channel of its own. New Jersey residents are among the nation's best educated and most affluent voters, but they have been content over the years to leave politics to the local bosses. Even when they have responded to flagrant misdeeds by throwing the bums out, the candidates they vote in are usually the product of the same political system.

Thanks to several astute federal prosecutors, the list of New Jersey politicians convicted of crimes and, in most cases, sent to jail, reads like a Who's Who of Jersey Politics: former Newark Mayor (1963–71) and Congressman (1949–63) Hugh Addonizio; former Congressman (1959–73) Cornelius Gallagher; former New Jersey Secretaries of State Robert Burkhardt, a Democrat, and Paul Sherwin, a Republican; former Hudson County (Jersey City) Democratic boss John V. Kenny, and 1970 Republican Senate candidate Nelson Gross.

Why so much corruption in New Jersey, and why has it been exposed and prosecuted only in the last few years? The answer to the first question lies in the power of the county bosses of both political parties, and the answer to the second in a peculiar combination of political circumstances. The county machines have traditionally selected not only candidates for local office, but also for state legislature, Congress, and the Governorship. The last is of critical importance, for the Governor appoints the state Attorney General and all the county prosecutors. In making their prosecutorial appointments, Governors almost always defer to the county bosses who, after all, got them their jobs; and so the bosses of both parties have had effective control for years over law enforcement—or nonenforcement.

But the appointment of the federal prosecutor, the United States Attorney, is the prerogative of the senior U.S. Senator of the President's political party. Since Richard Nixon took office, that prerogative has belonged to Senator Clifford Case, a liberal Republican with few if any debts to local Republican organizations. The Senator's appointees, Frederick Lacey, Herbert Stern, and Jonathan Goldstein, have been responsible for virtually all the prosecutions of political figures here in the years since. Almost singlehandedly they have destroyed the old Hudson County Democratic machine and, without concern for partisan interests, have at least wounded just about every other county boss in the state.

This boom lowering has not made Case popular with old guard Republicans, but then he never has been. Case first won his Senate seat in 1954 by a narrow margin, after a career as a Wall Street lawyer, nine years in the House, and a stint with the Fund for the Republic. In the Senate he is ranking Republican on the Foreign Relations Committee, and was a leader in the fight to end American bombing of and military involvement in Cambodia. He is known more as a thoughtful and studious Senator than as a forceful and magnetic one; but he has had some success in quiet fights he has carried on over the years, like the one to get greater disclosure of Senator's personal and political finances.

Case's liberal record and craggy honesty have been rewarded generously over the years by the state's voters. In 1972, he won with 64% of the vote—a better performance than Richard Nixon's that year. Yet Case has always been at least theoretically vulnerable in the primary; Republicans, apparently believing he isn't one of them (which of course on most issues he isn't) gave an unknown conservative candidate 30% of the vote in the 1972 primary. Case will be 74 when his seat comes up again in 1978; presumably he will choose to retire then. But it is just possible, particularly considering his record in appointing U.S. Attorneys, that he will run and will win again.

Another term also seems the likely prospect for New Jersey's junior Senator, Democrat Harrison Williams. Back in 1969 and 1970, as Williams was completing his second term, he looked extremely vulnerable. As he later admitted, he was an alcoholic; he was censured by the state NAACP for showing up drunk at a breakfast meeting. His major legislative accomplishment at the time, a mass transit bill, had been passed in the middle sixties with little impact on the mostly suburban citizens of New Jersey. Republicans had had a series of winning political years, and New Jersey had been the one major Eastern state Richard Nixon had carried in 1968. Republican State Chairman Nelson Gross was preparing to run against Williams, complete with a large campaign chest and a taste for the low road, law 'n' order campaign that Spiro Agnew was patenting that year.

Gross made considerable headway, but in the end ran out of steam. In the spring of 1970, Williams—by then off the wagon and frank about his former drinking problem—had a stroke of luck: Senator Ralph Yarborough of Texas had been beaten in his primary, and that meant that Williams would succeed, if reelected, to the Chairmanship of the Senate Labor and Public Welfare Committee. Suddenly he became the number one recipient of labor political action funds and of other labor campaign assistance. To the extent that Gross's campaign was winning him votes in ethnic wards, Williams was making gains in white collar suburbs; the final result showed Williams with 56% of the vote, compared to Gross's 44%.

Williams now seems to be a more productive Senator than he was in the sixties; he has worked on the pension reform bill and also on reforming the securities industry. If he is not one of the Senate's heavyweights, he is still expected to win reelection fairly easily in 1976, barring some surprise candidacy.

Obviously, the big money and real corruption in New Jersey politics are in state and local, not congressional, politics. Though the names of the county bosses have changed, their power and in some cases their methods have not. Consider the way in which the last two Governors came to office. In 1969, Congressman William Cahill, a liberal Republican, was anointed by his party's major county leaders, and was elected in a landslide of discontent with the Democrats who had been ruling—and sometimes misruling—the state for the previous 16 years. Cahill's two top appointees, both cronies from south Jersey, got into serious trouble (both have since gone to jail) in his four year term, and he lost his nomination in 1973 to Congressman Charles Sandman. (See Second District.)

But 1973 was going to be a Democratic year. Till just before filing date it was unclear who their candidate would be. Then a group of Hudson and Middlesex County leaders initiated the candidacy of Brendan Byrne, an Essex County (Newark) judge who, as prosecutor, had been labelled unbuyable by a wire-tapped Mafia don. Byrne was just what New Jersey wanted: Irish and Ivy League, city wise and incorruptible. Yet even Byrne made at least one major appointment (Secretary of State Edward Crabiel, a Middlesex pol who supported him early) who turned out to have trouble with the law, though he was acquitted. And despite the heavy Democratic margins in the legislature swept in with Byrne, the new Governor was unable, as the two before him had been, of passing a much needed income tax. (New Jersey relies far too heavily on the often unfair and disparate property tax, and has a low level of state services.) Byrne reportedly began his term with visions of himself as a future Vice Presidential candidate; despite some substantial accomplishments, he still does not seem to have risen to national stature.

As a result of the 1974 Democratic sweep—the reader should consult the descriptions of the various districts—Democrats now have a 12–3 edge on the state's House delegation. It seems scarcely possible that that ratio could be retained after the 1976 elections. But of the Democrats swept in here in the 1964 landslide, all but two survived, and one of those was a victim of redistricting—which will not be a factor in New Jersey in 1976. Politicians here, as elsewhere, have mastered the art of using the advantages of congressional incumbency to insure continued reelection, and the apathetic, often poorly informed suburban voters here seem usually content to vote for a familiar name with no mark of indictment or support for an indictable President next to it.

Census Data   Pop. 7,168,164; 3.54% of U.S. total, 8th largest; Central city, 16%; suburban, 61%. Median family income, $11,403; 4th highest; families above $15,000: 30%; families below $3,000: 6%.   Median years education, 12.1.

1974 Share of Federal Tax Burden $11,623,183,000; 4.34% of U.S. total, 8th largest.

1974 Share of Federal Outlays $10,200,389,000; 3.77% of U.S. total, 6th largest. Per capita federal spending, $1423.

DOD	$11,111,111,000	1st (0.15%)		HEW	$3,078,769,000	9th (3.32%)
AEC	$21,049,000	18th (0.69%)		HUD	$41,532,000	8th (4.26%)
NASA	$32,646,000	13th (1.10%)		VA	$354,676,000	10th (2.59%)
DOT	$204,128,000	15th (2.41%)		EPA	$139,913,000	5th (4.45%)
DOC	$16,488,000	18th (1.02%)		RevS	$190,532,000	9th (3.13%)
DOI	$18,492,000	30th (0.75%)		Int.	$2,999,141,000	2d (14.58%)
USDA	$297,668,000	14th (2.39%)		Other	$1,053,032,000	

Economic Base Finance, insurance and real estate; chemicals and allied products, especially industrial chemicals and drugs; electrical equipment and supplies, especially communication equipment; apparel and other textile products, especially women's and misses' outerwear; machinery; fabricated metal products; food and kindred products.

Political Line-up Governor, Brendan T. Byrne (D). Senators, Clifford P. Case (R) and Harrison A. Williams, Jr. (D). Representatives, 15 (12 D and 3 R). State Senate (29 D, 10 R, and 1 Ind.); State General Assembly (66 D and 14 R).

The Voters

Registration 3,502,175 total. No party registration.
Median voting age 44.1
Employment profile White collar, 53%. Blue collar, 36%. Service, 11%. Farm, 0%.
Ethnic groups Black, 11%. Spanish, 2%. Total foreign stock, 30%. Italy, 7%; Germany, Poland, 3% each; UK, USSR, Ireland, 2% each; Austria, 1%.

Presidential vote

1972	Nixon (R)	....	1,845,502	(63%)
	McGovern (D)	....	1,102,211	(37%)
1968	Nixon (R)	....	1,325,467	(46%)
	Humphrey (D)	....	1,264,206	(44%)
	Wallace (AI)	....	262,187	(9%)

1972 Democratic Presidential Primary			*1972 Republican Presidential Primary*
Chisholm	51,433	(67%)	no candidates
others	25,401	(33%)	entered
(preference only)			

Sen. Clifford P. Case (R) Elected 1954, seat up 1978; b. Apr. 16, 1904, Franklin Park; home, Rahway; Rutgers U., A.B. 1925, Columbia U., LL.B. 1928; Presbyterian.

Career Practicing atty., 1928–53; Rahway Common Cncl., 1938–42; N.J. Gen. Assembly, 1943–44; U.S. House of Reps., 1945–53; Pres., Fund for the Republic, 1953–54.

Offices 315 RSOB, 202-224-3224. Also Rm. 837, Fed. Bldg., 970 Broad St., Newark 07102, 201-645-6040.

Committees

Appropriations (3d). Subcommittees: Defense; Agriculture and Related Agencies; Labor and HEW; Public Works; Transportation.

Foreign Relations (Ranking Member). Subcommittees: Arms Control, International Organizations and Security Agreements; European Affairs; Foreign Assistance and Economic Policy; Multinational Corporations; Personnel.

Joint Committee on Atomic Energy (2d, Senate Side). Subcommittees: Agreements for Cooperation; ERDA, Environment and Safety; ERDA, Nuclear Energy; National Security.

Group Ratings

	ADA	COPE	LWV	RIPON	NFU	LCV	CFA	NAB	NSI	ACA
1974	89	82	90	71	100	100	88	27	20	0
1973	85	82	100	82	75	–	92	–	–	3
1972	80	100	100	88	70	95	100	36	22	14

Key Votes

1) No-Knock	AGN	8) Gov Abortn Aid	FOR	15) Consumer Prot Agy	FOR
2) Busing	FOR	9) Cut Mil Brass	FOR	16) Forced Psych Tests	FOR
3) No Fault	FOR	10) Gov Limousine	AGN	17) Fed Campaign Subs	FOR
4) F-111	AGN	11) RR Featherbed	FOR	18) Rhod Chrome Ban	FOR
5) Death Penalty	AGN	12) Handgun License	FOR	19) Open Legis Meetings	FOR
6) Foreign Aid	FOR	13) Less Troop Abrd	AGN	20) Strikers Food Stmps	FOR
7) Filibuster	AGN	14) Resume Turk Aid	FOR	21) Gov Info Disclosure	FOR

Election Results

1972 general:	Clifford P. Case (R)	1,743,854	(64%)	($145,275)
	Paul J. Krebs (D)	963,573	(36%)	($46,160)
1972 primary:	Clifford P. Case (R)	187,268	(70%)	
	James Walter Ralph (R)	79,766	(30%)	
1966 general:	Clifford P. Case (R)	1,278,843	(60%)	
	Warren W. Wilentz (D)	788,021	(37%)	
	Robert Lee Schlachter (Con.)	53,606	(3%)	

Sen. Harrison A. Williams, Jr. (D) Elected 1958, seat up 1976; b. Dec. 10, 1919, Plainfield; home, Bedminster; Oberlin Col., B.A. 1941, Georgetown U. School of Foreign Service, Columbia U., LL.B. 1948; Presbyterian.

Career Navy, WWII; Practicing atty.; U.S. House of Reps., 1953–57.

Offices 352 RSOB, 202-224-4744. Also Rm. 939A Fed. Bldg., 970 Broad St., Newark 07102, 201-645-3030.

Committees

Labor and Public Welfare (Chairman). Subcommittees: Labor (Chairman).

Banking, Housing and Urban Affairs (3d). Subcommittees: Financial Institutions; Housing and Urban Affairs; International Finance; Oversight; Securities (Chairman).

Rules and Administration (5th). Subcommittees: Computer Services; Restaurant; Smithsonian Institution.

Group Ratings

	ADA	COPE	LWV	RIPON	NFU	LCV	CFA	NAB	NSI	ACA
1974	100	89	100	65	100	89	77	27	0	0
1973	89	91	100	53	94	–	88	–	–	0
1972	85	100	100	82	90	87	100	8	0	5

Key Votes

1) No-Knock	AGN	8) Gov Abortn Aid	FOR	15) Consumer Prot Agy	FOR
2) Busing	FOR	9) Cut Mil Brass	FOR	16) Forced Psych Tests	FOR
3) No Fault	FOR	10) Gov Limousine	AGN	17) Fed Campaign Subs	FOR
4) F-111	AGN	11) RR Featherbed	FOR	18) Rhod Chrome Ban	FOR
5) Death Penalty	AGN	12) Handgun License	FOR	19) Open Legis Meetings	ABS
6) Foreign Aid	FOR	13) Less Troop Abrd	FOR	20) Strikers Food Stmps	FOR
7) Filibuster	AGN	14) Resume Turk Aid	ABS	21) Gov Info Disclosure	FOR

Election Results

1970 general:	Harrison A. Williams, Jr. (D)	1,157,074	(56%)
	Nelson G. Gross (R)	903,026	(44%)
1970 primary:	Harrison A. Williams, Jr. (D)	190,692	(66%)
	Frank J. Guarini (D)	100,045	(34%)
1964 general:	Harrison A. Williams, Jr. (D)	1,677,515	(62%)
	Bernard M. Shanley (R)	1,011,280	(38%)

Gov. Brendan T. Byrne (D) Elected 1973, term expires Jan. 1978; b. Apr. 1, 1924, West Orange; Seton Hall U., Princeton U., A.B. 1949, Harvard U., LL.B. 1951.

Career Army Air Corps, WWII; Practicing atty.; Founder, Bd. Chm., Intercontinental Ins. Co.; Asst. Counsel, Exec. Secy. to Gov. Robert B. Meyner, 1955–58; Deputy Atty. Gen. in charge of Essex Co. Prosecutor's Ofc., 1958–59; Essex Co. Prosecutor, 1959–68; Pres., N.J. St. Bd. of Pub. Utilities, 1968–70; Superior Ct. Judge, 1970–72.

Offices Trenton 08625, 609-292-6000.

Election Results

1973 general:	Brendan T. Byrne (D)	1,414,613	(68%)
	Charles W. Sandman (R)	676,235	(32%)
1973 primary:	Brendan T. Byrne (D)	193,120	(45%)
	Ann Klein (D)	116,705	(27%)
	Ralph C. DeRose (D)	95,085	(22%)
	Two Others (D)	21,275	(5%)

◆ ◆ ◆ ◆

FIRST DISTRICT

The 1st congressional district of New Jersey is part of suburban Philadelphia, an area of the state more attuned to the city across the Delaware River than it is to Trenton or certainly to the suburbs around Newark. The 1st takes in a nice cross section of suburban America. Along the banks of the Delaware are the factories and oil tank farms of industrial cities like Camden (pop. 103,000), places that are declining in population and suffering from many of the same ills afflicting much larger central cities—except that here fewer people seem to care. To the east, on the flat plains of south Jersey, are the subdivisions of the 1940s, '50s, and '60s, that thin out into the truck farming vegetable and fruit country which they themselves once were. In general, the suburbs nearest the River vote Democratic; those farther inland tend to go Republican.

The 1st district is as good a place as any part of New Jersey to examine the fluctuations in the voting habits of the state's third and fourth generation ethnics, particularly Italian-Americans, who make up such a large part of the population here. (Perhaps one-third, no one knows precisely, of the state's and the 1st's residents are of Italian descent.) In the case of the 1st, most of these people have roots in one of the Italian neighborhoods of Philadelphia; they got somewhat better jobs than their parents, and moved across the River.

Crossing the Benjamin Franklin Bridge, they brought with them a preference for New Deal economic programs and for more conservative social policies, and so it was appropriate that for eight years this district was represented by William Cahill. Cahill was a liberal Republican in the sense that he backed some Democratic economic programs; indeed, his record was good enough that in 1969 he became Governor. Even before that he had moved, due to redistricting, to the 6th district, and the 1st, in 1966, was faced with a choice of a product of the Camden County Democratic machine or a conservative Republican. In a move that presaged the rightward trend of East Coast ethnics, the 1st picked the Republican, John Hunt, then Sheriff of Gloucester County.

Hunt was then a crew-cutted law enforcement official with a police background, nearing 60, with sternly conservative views on virtually all issues. He was a strong admirer of Richard Nixon and Frank Rizzo, and an outspoken hawk on the Armed Services Committee. When students roamed the House office buildings trying to lobby Congress against the 1970 invasion of Cambodia, Hunt was the only Congressman that literally chased them out of his office.

Right up through the 1972 elections, this kind of politics suited the erstwhile Democratic voters of the 1st district just fine. They were fed up with blacks, hippies, peace demonstrators, and ecology activists, and eager for a vigorous reassertion of the conservative values that governed their personal lives. Then came Watergate. Hunt's hero, Richard Nixon, was lying again and again and again—or so the people of the 1st thought. This President, who had stood up so valiantly against pornography and long hair and other signs of decaying Western civilization was proving himself to be a complete fraud. Disgusted, the voters here—and up and down the East Coast—quietly abandoned, seemingly tried to forget, their recent enthusiasm for Nixon; replacing it was the conviction that this President must be got rid of, as soon as possible.

John Hunt did not share this conviction. On the contrary, he was one of those Congressmen who stuck with Nixon to the bitter end, and whose initial impulse on the release of the damning June 23 tapes was to rally once again, as he had before through all the other accusations, to the cause of his President. Politically, it was not a wise move. Camden Assemblyman James Florio, who had lost to Hunt by a 53–47 margin in 1972, now trounced him by a 58–39 margin; his share of the vote in Camden County, the more ethnic part of the district, rose from 50% to 64%. Hunt's defeat signalled not only a change, and likely a permanent one, in the representation of the 1st district; this loss, together with other Republican defeats, signalled an end to the ethnic-based East Coast politics of conservatism that Richard Nixon and Spiro Agnew had done so much to foster. That kind of politics was as surely through as they were.

Census Data Pop. 478,002. Central city, 0%; suburban, 100%. Median family income, $10,314; families above $15,000: 20%; families below $3,000: 7%. Median years education, 11.3.

The Voters

Median voting age 43.
Employment profile White collar, 46%. Blue collar, 42%. Service, 11%. Farm, 1%.
Ethnic groups Black, 13%. Spanish, 2%. Total foreign stock, 18%. Italy, 5%; UK, Germany, Poland, 2% each; Ireland, 1%.

Presidential vote

1972	Nixon (R)	112,632	(60%)
	McGovern (D)	74,821	(40%)
1968	Nixon (R)	75,624	(40%)
	Humphrey (D)	87,392	(46%)
	Wallace (AI)	27,954	(15%)

Rep. James J. Florio (D) Elected 1974; b. Aug. 29, 1937, Brooklyn, N.Y.; home, Camden; Trenton St. Col., B.A. 1962, Columbia U., 1962–63, Rutgers U., J.D. 1967.

Career Practicing atty., 1967–74; N.J. Gen. Assembly, 1969–75.

Offices 1725 LHOB, 202-225-6501. Also 23 S. White Horse Pike, Somerdale 08083, 609-627-8222.

Committees

District of Columbia (16th). Subcommittees: Education, Labor and Social Services; Government Operations.

Interstate and Foreign Commerce (26th). Health and Environment; Transportation and Commerce.

Group Ratings: Newly Elected

Key Votes

1) Foreign Aid	FOR	6) Gov Abortn Aid	NE	11) Pub Cong Election $	NE
2) Busing	NE	7) Coed Phys Ed	FOR	12) Turkish Arms Cutoff	NE
3) ABM	NE	8) Pov Lawyer Gag	NE	13) Youth Camp Regs	FOR
4) B-1 Bomber	AGN	9) Pub Trans Sub	NE	14) Strip Mine Veto	AGN
5) Nerve Gas	NE	10) EZ Voter Regis	NE	15) Farm Bill Veto	AGN

Election Results

1974 general:	James J. Florio (D)	80,768	(58%)	($97,679)
	John E. Hunt (R)	54,069	(39%)	($57,787)
	James Perry (Independent Tax Watchers)	3,276	(2%)	($1,588)
1974 primary:	James J. Florio (D)	15,671	(83%)	
	Walter C. Gebelein, Jr. (D)	2,127	(11%)	
	Judith L. Holzer (D)	1,091	(6%)	

◆ ◆ ◆ ◆ ◆

SECOND DISTRICT

The 2d congressional district of New Jersey takes in Atlantic, Cape May, Cumberland, and Salem Counties, along with parts of Ocean and Burlington Counties; it is the largest and most sparsely populated district in the state. The flat, sometimes swampy lands of south Jersey are one of the premier vegetable farm areas in the country; and along the Ocean are the beach resorts of Atlantic City, Wildwood, and Cape May—some of the original beach towns in the United States. Cumberland and Salem Counties, like neighboring Delaware, have an almost Southern ambiance and an intermittent Democratic voting tradition that goes back to the nineteenth century. Cape May is a Republican bastion. Atlantic City, where most of the district's rather large black population lives, is a fast-decaying city known still for the Miss America pageant; until he was defeated in 1971, this was the home base of Republican boss Frank S. (Hap) Farley, who long dominated the state Senate and was a key figure in giving Richard Nixon vitally needed New Jersey votes at the 1968 Republican national convention. The fastest-growing part of the district is Ocean County, north of Atlantic City; here many of the 2d's residents are retirees from New York and Philadelphia in search of sandy beaches, clean air, and safe streets.

Until 1974, this district was the political property of Congressman Charles W. Sandman, Jr. In the middle sixties he was a prominent state Senator with an itch to run for Governor; defeated in the 1965 primary, he unseated an LBJ landslide Democrat in 1966 and became Congressman from the 2d. Sandman was known as an ultra-conservative, but he seems to have been less interested in national issues than in New Jersey problems, and he was the state's most consistent opponent of broad based taxes, especially the income tax. He ran for Governor again in 1969, and again lost the primary; but in 1973, with incumbent William Cahill's administration plagued with scandal, Sandman finally won and became the Republican nominee. It proved to be a worthless nomination; Democrat Brendan Byrne won by more than 2–1. The only part of the state where Charley Sandman ran at all well was in the 2d district, which he nearly carried.

But within a year Sandman's popularity in the 2d had evaporated. The reason, of course, was his performance in the House Judiciary Committee impeachment hearings. Speaking in a voice and with tones reminiscent of the late Senator Joseph McCarthy, Sandman did not try to hide his feeling that the televised hearings were a farce; in his view, the Democrats and some of the Republicans had already decided to vote against Nixon and would not be swayed by any arguments to the contrary. Like all the Committee's Nixon defenders, Sandman did not defend everything the President and his men had done; but he articulated a rather indulgent view of official wrongdoing, one which he had consistently held inasmuch as he had voted in 1967—and was one of the few conservative Republicans to do so—not to expel from the House the late Adam Clayton Powell.

What would have happened to Sandman electorally had the impeachment process gone ahead without a virtual confession from the President, no one knows; although one suspects it would not have been much different from what did happen. In any case, Sandman suffered one of the most precipitous declines in vote-getting ability in recent years. From 66% of the vote in his 1972 congressional race, to a near-carry in his disastrous 1973 gubernatorial run, Sandman's percentage in the 2d district fell to 42% in 1974. He failed to carry even his home county of Cape May. The voters' verdict was devastating and unequivocal; one must presume his political career is over.

The winner was William Hughes, a Democrat inclined to rather conservative rhetoric, who had run a strong race against Sandman in 1970 and then sat out 1972. He also won what was in effect Sandman's old seat on Judiciary, inasmuch as the Republicans lost committee posts in proportion to their losses in the Congress as a whole. Once installed in office, Hughes can probably count on the advantages that incumbents normally are able to parlay into continued reelection.

Census Data Pop. 478,126. Central city, 29%; suburban, 47%. Median family income, $9,039; families above $15,000: 17%; families below $3,000: 9%. Median years education, 11.1.

The Voters

Median voting age 48.
Employment profile White collar, 42%. Blue collar, 41%. Service, 15%. Farm, 2%.
Ethnic groups Black, 13%. Spanish, 2%. Total foreign stock, 20%. Italy, 5%; Germany, 3%; UK, USSR, 2% each; Poland, Ireland, 1% each.

Presidential vote

1972	Nixon (R)	138,957	(66%)
	McGovern (D)	73,018	(34%)
1968	Nixon (R)	91,726	(46%)
	Humphrey (D)	85,603	(43%)
	Wallace (AI)	23,194	(12%)

Rep. William J. Hughes (D) Elected 1974; b. Oct. 17, 1932, Salem; home, Ocean City; Rutgers U., A.B. 1955, J.D. 1958; Episcopalian.

Career Practicing atty., 1959–74; Cape May Co. Asst. Prosecutor, 1960–70; Ocean City Solicitor, 1970–74.

Offices 327 CHOB, 202-225-6572. Also 2920 Atlantic Ave., Atlantic City 08401, 609-345-4844.

Committees

Judiciary (22d). Subcommittees: Crime; Monopolies and Commercial Law.

Group Ratings: Newly Elected

Key Votes

1) Foreign Aid	AGN	6) Gov Abortn Aid	NE	11) Pub Cong Election $	NE
2) Busing	NE	7) Coed Phys Ed	AGN	12) Turkish Arms Cutoff	NE
3) ABM	NE	8) Pov Lawyer Gag	NE	13) Youth Camp Regs	FOR
4) B-1 Bomber	AGN	9) Pub Trans Sub	NE	14) Strip Mine Veto	AGN
5) Nerve Gas	NE	10) EZ Voter Regis	NE	15) Farm Bill Veto	AGN

Election Results

1974 general:	William J. Hughes (D)	109,763	(58%)	($115,365)
	Charles W. Sandman, Jr. (R)	79,064	(42%)	($98,734)
1974 primary:	William J. Hughes (D)	12,347	(55%)	
	Michael J. Matthews (D)	5,025	(22%)	
	Four others (D)	5,090	(23%)	

◆ ◆ ◆ ◆ ◆

THIRD DISTRICT

Monmouth County is a unit with a name made famous by a Revolutionary War battle and a twentieth century racetrack. Here, around the turn of the century, some of America's first beach resorts were created, to cater to the increasing number of people with the time and money for summer sojourns at the seashore. Beach manners have changed a lot since the days of full length swimsuits, but the Monmouth County shore still attracts hundreds of thousands of bathers every year. Its summer home areas, with houses ranging from shacks to mansions, have increasingly become year round communities, with many residents commuting to jobs in north Jersey and even Manhattan. The flatlands behind the beaches have been the area of greatest recent growth; here retirement villages and subdivisions attract people from the outer Jersey reaches of the New York metropolitan area.

Virtually all of Monmouth County, plus Lakewood Township and Point Pleasant in Ocean County just to the south, make up New Jersey's 3d congressional district. By tradition Monmouth is a Republican bastion but its voting patterns have become less predictable with recent growth. Nevertheless, the 3d district would almost certainly elect a Republican Congressman were it not for the presence of Democrat James Howard. Howard was lucky enough to have been a candidate in the LBJ landslide year of 1964, when the district's Republican Congressman, James Auchincloss, was retiring after 24 years in the House. Howard won with a scant 50.4% of the vote, and he has been working since to strengthen his position.

Over the years he seems to have succeeded, despite his generally liberal record on the issues. In 1970 and 1972 he was pressed hard by William Dowd, a former Nixon White House aide, who got 47% of the vote in the latter year. That was a sign that Howard might well be in trouble. Then came Watergate. Dowd's White House background—though he had been there long before—was now a liability, not an asset; and Dowd did not even bother to run. Suddenly Howard's percentage shot up from 53% to 70%. The 1976 election will tell us whether Howard is quite that firmly established here, but it seems unlikely that he could lose.

Census Data Pop. 475,599. Central city, 0%; suburban, 0%. Median family income, $11,291; families above $15,000: 30%; families below $3,000: 7%. Median years education, 12.3.

The Voters

Median voting age 43.
Employment profile White collar, 56%. Blue collar, 31%. Service, 12%. Farm, 1%.
Ethnic groups Black, 8%. Spanish, 1%. Total foreign stock, 25%. Italy, 5%; Germany, UK, 3% each; USSR, Poland, Ireland, 2% each.

Presidential vote

1972	Nixon (R)	133,272	(67%)
	McGovern (D)	65,028	(33%)
1968	Nixon (R)	90,913	(51%)
	Humphrey (D)	72,420	(41%)
	Wallace (AI)	13,260	(8%)

Rep. James J. Howard (D) Elected 1964; b. July 24, 1927, Irvington; home, Wall Township; St. Bonaventure U., B.A. 1952, Rutgers U., M.Ed. 1958; Catholic.

Career Navy, WWII; Teacher and Acting Principal, Wall Twnshp. School Dist., 1952–64.

Offices 2245 RHOB, 202-225-4671. Also P.O. Bldg., 801 Bangs Ave., Asbury Park 07712, 201-774-1600.

Committees

Public Works and Transportation (3d). Subcommittees: Investigations and Review; Surface Transportation (Chairman); Water Resources.

Group Ratings

	ADA	COPE	LWV	RIPON	NFU	LCV	CFA	NAB	NSI	ACA
1974	83	100	71	58	90	90	73	18	10	9
1973	92	100	75	64	95	94	100	–	–	4
1972	75	91	83	80	86	68	50	9	13	5

Key Votes

1) Foreign Aid	FOR	6) Gov Abortn Aid	ABS	11) Pub Cong Election $	AGN
2) Busing	AGN	7) Coed Phys Ed	FOR	12) Turkish Arms Cutoff	FOR
3) ABM	AGN	8) Pov Lawyer Gag	AGN	13) Youth Camp Regs	FOR
4) B-1 Bomber	AGN	9) Pub Trans Sub	FOR	14) Strip Mine Veto	AGN
5) Nerve Gas	AGN	10) EZ Voter Regis	FOR	15) Farm Bill Veto	AGN

Election Results

1974 general:	James J. Howard (D)	105,979	(70%)	($52,474)
	Kenneth W. Clark (R)	45,932	(30%)	($15,231)
1974 primary:	James J. Howard (D), unopposed			
1972 general:	James J. Howard (D)	103,893	(53%)	($62,773)
	William F. Dowd (R)	92,285	(47%)	($50,718)

◆ ◆ ◆ ◆ ◆

FOURTH DISTRICT

The 4th congressional district of New Jersey is one whose shape has undergone almost complete transformation not once but twice in the last decade. The one constant geographical feature of the district is the city of Trenton (pop. 104,000), the state capital, which, with surrounding Mercer County, is a Democratic stronghold. Under the current, court-imposed redistricting plan, the 4th extends south from Trenton into Burlington County, to a point almost directly across the Delaware River from Philadelphia. To the north and east, the 4th stretches across a narrow corridor toward Raritan Bay, which separates New Jersey from Staten Island. The district lines, of course, connect no cohesive community; rather, the 4th is a collection of older central cities, booming suburbs, and rolling farmlands. The closest thing these diverse areas have in common is a mild proclivity toward the Democratic Party.

During the transmogrifications of the 4th, the district sustained one other constant: the continued reelection of Congressman Frank Thompson. The Congressman is now the second-ranking Democrat on both the Education and Labor and the House Administration Committees, just below, respectively, Carl Perkins of Kentucky and Wayne Hays of Ohio. Several years younger than Perkins, Thompson has a good chance at someday chairing Education and Labor; and in 1974 it seemed for a while that he might succeed to the chair of House Administration. The Democratic Steering Committee voted to oust the cantankerous Hays for the good humored Thompson, apparently without Thompson's knowledge. Hays fought back hard, with the help of Caucus Chairman Phillip Burton (also an Education and Labor member); and Thompson did not have the votes in the full Democratic caucus to win.

But that was really just a sidelight to Thompson's major legislative preoccupation, which has been Education and Labor. Back in the 1950, that committee reported out legislation that ultimately became the Landrum-Griffin Act, several sections of which were vehemently opposed by organized labor. Such a bill is unlikely ever to come out of committee again. Today the Democratic members of Education and Labor are almost all northern liberals, and a number of Republicans on the body also fall into that category. One of the committee's most faithful friends of liberal causes in general and positions espoused by organized labor in particular is Frank Thompson. For years Thompson had a 100% COPE rating, while at the same time establishing a dovish record on foreign policy. Because both big labor and big management have learned to live with the country's basic labor legislation, there has been no push for major labor legislation in recent years—and Thompson has gotten his name on no big bills. But he is active legislatively: in 1973, for instance, Thompson was the driving force behind the act permitting labor unions to bargain for group legal services—a move that has the potential of vastly changing the structure of the legal profession.

Back in the 1950s, when he was still a junior member of the House, Thompson was one of the founders of the liberal Democratic Study Group. Today he is one of the few original leaders of this now dominant group left in the House; others have gone on to the Senate or, in the case of Eugene McCarthy, to quixotic presidential campaigns. In 1960 Thompson headed the voter registration drive in John Kennedy's presidential campaign, the last time the Democrats have conducted a really successful registration effort on a nationwide basis. Back home in the 4th district Thompson has won general elections routinely, whatever the boundaries set down for him. When the district's contours were changed, as in 1966 and 1972, Thompson did not run especially well in the areas added that were traditionally Republican; but in later elections he increased his percentages in such territory. The 1974 figures make it look as if he had substantial opposition in the primary; actually, it just came from the brother of an indicted Middlesex County Democratic leader, who got 61% of the vote in his home county and only 22% elsewhere. Overall, Thompson holds a safe seat.

Census Data Pop. 478,045. Central city, 22%; suburban, 45%. Median family income, $11,086; families above $15,000: 25%; families below $3,000: 6%. Median years education, 12.1.

The Voters

Median voting age 40.
Employment profile White collar, 49%. Blue collar, 38%. Service, 12%. Farm, 1%.
Ethnic groups Black, 13%. Spanish, 1%. Total foreign stock, 25%. Poland, 4%; Germany, 3%; UK, Hungary, USSR, 2% each; Ireland, Austria, 1% each.

Presidential vote

1972	Nixon (R)	102,645	(58%)
	McGovern (D)	74,902	(42%)
1968	Nixon (R)	64,841	(39%)
	Humphrey (D)	81,145	(48%)
	Wallace (AI)	22,228	(13%)

Rep. Frank Thompson, Jr. (D) Elected 1954, b. July 26, 1918, Trenton; home, Trenton; Wake Forest Col., Wake Forest Law School, LL.B.; Catholic.

Career Navy, WWII; Practicing atty., 1948–54; N.J. Gen. Assembly, 1949–53, Asst. Minor. Ldr., 1951, Minor. Ldr., 1953.

Offices 2109 RHOB, 202-225-3765. Also 10 Rutgers Pl., Trenton 08618, 609-599-1619.

Committees

Education and Labor (2d). Subcommittees: Labor-Management Relations (Chairman); Post-secondary Education.

House Administration (2d). Subcommittees: Accounts (Chairman); Library and Memorials; Paper Conservation.

Group Ratings

	ADA	COPE	LWV	RIPON	NFU	LCV	CFA	NAB	NSI	ACA
1974	84	100	78	58	92	79	100	25	0	0
1973	94	100	88	50	100	92	100	–	–	5
1972	75	88	91	60	100	76	100	11	0	6

Key Votes

1) Foreign Aid	FOR	6) Gov Abortn Aid	ABS	11) Pub Cong Election $	AGN
2) Busing	FOR	7) Coed Phys Ed	AGN	12) Turkish Arms Cutoff	FOR
3) ABM	AGN	8) Pov Lawyer Gag	ABS	13) Youth Camp Regs	FOR
4) B-1 Bomber	AGN	9) Pub Trans Sub	FOR	14) Strip Mine Veto	AGN
5) Nerve Gas	AGN	10) EZ Voter Regis	FOR	15) Farm Bill Veto	AGN

Election Results

1974 general:	Frank Thompson, Jr. (D)	82,195	(57%)	($44,542)
	Henry J. Keller (R)	40,797	(33%)	($11,891)
1974 primary:	Frank Thompson, Jr. (D)	11,317	(65%)	
	David B. Crabiel (D)	6,063	(35%)	
1972 general:	Frank Thompson, Jr. (D)	98,206	(58%)	($48,221)
	Peter P. Garibaldi (R)	71,030	(42%)	($7,983)

◆ ◆ ◆ ◆ ◆

FIFTH DISTRICT

Most people's image of New Jersey is the one you get on the drive from Newark Airport to Manhattan: factories belching smoke into the already smoggy air, swampland pocked with truck terminals and warehouses, grim lines of Jersey City rowhouses, and the docks on the Hudson River. But there is another New Jersey—one which begins 40 to 50 miles out of Manhattan, past the first ridge of mountains west of Newark. Such is the area that is New Jersey's 5th congressional district. Out here the high income suburbs fade into the elegant horse farm country around Morristown and Far Hills, Peapack and Bernardsville and Basking Ridge. The 5th also includes middle class suburbs, places like fast-growing Parsippany-Troy Hills, where subdivisions of tightly grouped houses sell for prices deemed moderate these days. But most of the 5th district, at least in area, from the horse country of Morris and Somerset Counties to the rich university town of Princeton, is high income territory; in fact, it ranks 11th in median family income of all the nation's 435 congressional districts.

It is appropriate, then, that the 5th has been represented by two of America's blueblooded-est members of Congress for the past twenty years. (And for nearly 30 years before, 1925–53, it was represented by a relative of industrialist Cyrus Eaton.) From 1953 to 1975, the district was represented by Peter H. B. Frelinghuysen, descendant of a fire-breathing eighteenth century Dutch-born preacher, and part of a family which has produced three United States Senators and a Secretary of State. A moderate Republican, Frelinghuysen lost a leadership post to Melvin Laird in 1965; in 1974, just before his retirement, he became ranking Republican on what was then called the House Foreign Affairs Committee. On that body he had steadfastly supported the Nixon and Ford Administrations' foreign policy; and that was one reason he was unusually hard pressed in his last election, in 1972, when he won an unusually low 62% of the vote.

Frelinghuysen's successor is another aristocrat, Millicent H. Fenwick of Bernardsville. She began her political career late, winning election to the New Jersey Assembly in 1969. She made a distinctive record in that rather undistinguished body, and was made head of the state Consumer Affairs Department.

As a congressional candidate in 1974, Fenwick was irresistible. Tall and thin, speaking with the kind of accent that is acquired only at the most fashionable girls' schools, she would at the end of some meetings take her pipe out of her purse and start puffing at it. In the fashion of the times, she made full disclosure of her net worth ($5 million) without seeming to provoke envy. In the Republican primary she beat former Assembly Speaker Thomas Kean, whom she describes as an old friend, by only 83 votes out of 25,000 cast. In the general election she faced competition from the same Democrat, 37-year-old Frederick Bohen, who had given Frelinghuysen unexpected trouble in 1972. But Fenwick won by the comfortable, though scarcely overwhelming, margin of 54–44.

As a junior member of the House, Fenwick can hardly have expected to become particularly prominent. But she was one of the members who visited South Vietnam in February 1975, and she returned troubled and torn. She wanted no more American military involvement in Southeast Asia, yet at the same time she wanted desperately to do something about the plight of the people she had seen there. This response typifies her rather unconventional, non-ideological approach to things, which undoubtedly irritates some of her colleagues; but it seems more than likely that she will be reelected for as long as she chooses to run.

Census Data Pop. 478,007. Central city, 0%; suburban, 54%. Median family income, $14,218; families above $15,000: 46%; families below $3,000: 3%. Median years education, 12.6.

The Voters

Median voting age 42.
Employment profile White collar, 65%. Blue collar, 26%. Service, 9%. Farm, –%.
Ethnic groups Black, 3%. Total foreign stock, 29%. Italy, 6%; Germany, UK, Poland, 3% each; USSR, Ireland, 2% each; Austria, Canada, Hungary, 1% each.

Presidential vote

1972	Nixon (R)	....	139,407	(66%)
	McGovern (D)	....	73,268	(34%)
1968	Nixon (R)	....	103,944	(53%)
	Humphrey (D)	....	77,217	(40%)
	Wallace (AI)	....	13,176	(7%)

Rep. Millicent Fenwick (R) Elected 1974; b. Feb. 25, 1910, New York, N.Y.; home, Bernardsville; Columbia U., 1933, New School for Social Research, 1942.

Career Assoc. Ed., Conde Nast Publications, 1938–52; Mbr., Bernardsville Borough Cncl., 1958–64; N.J. Gen. Assembly, 1969–72; Dir., N.J. Div. of Consumer Affairs, 1972–74.

Offices 1610 LHOB, 202-225-7300. Also 41 N. Bridge St., Somerville 08876, 201-722-8200.

Committees

Banking, Currency and Housing (14th). Subcommittees: Consumer Affairs; International Development Institutions and Finance; International Trade, Investment and Monetary Policy.

Small Business (10th). Subcommittees: Activities of Regulatory Agencies; SBA and SBIC Legislation.

Group Ratings: Newly Elected

Key Votes

1) Foreign Aid	FOR	6) Gov Abortn Aid	NE	11) Pub Cong Election $	NE
2) Busing	NE	7) Coed Phys Ed	FOR	12) Turkish Arms Cutoff	NE
3) ABM	NE	8) Pov Lawyer Gag	NE	13) Youth Camp Regs	AGN
4) B-1 Bomber	AGN	9) Pub Trans Sub	NE	14) Strip Mine Veto	AGN
5) Nerve Gas	NE	10) EZ Voter Regis	NE	15) Farm Bill Veto	FOR

Election Results

1974 general:	Millicent Fenwick (R)	....	81,498	(54%)	($131,861)
	Frederick M. Bohen (D)	....	66,380	(44%)	($117,033)
	John Giammarco (AI)	....	3,102	(2%)	($0)
1974 primary:	Millicent Fenwick (R)	....	12,509	(48%)	
	Thomas H. Kean (R)	....	12,426	(47%)	
	Charles E. Humiston (R)	....	1,248	(5%)	

◆ ◆ ◆ ◆ ◆

SIXTH DISTRICT

The 6th congressional district of New Jersey, like the 4th, is a weirdly shaped district, spanning the entire state from the Delaware River to the Atlantic Ocean. It brings into a single constituency people from sociologically diverse and geographically disparate communities. More than 60% of its residents live in the Philadelphia suburbs of Burlington and Camden Counties; important towns here include Cherry Hill (home of Muhammed Ali as well as many more conventional folks) and Willingboro (formerly Levittown), both of which more than doubled in population during the sixties. Another 20% of the 6th's residents live in another, even faster growing area on the Jersey Shore. Connecting these two regions—which have little in common except rapid growth rates and generally Republican political preferences—are the sparsely inhabited flatlands of south Jersey and the Army's Fort Dix.

The 6th was created in its present form by the 1966 redistricting, one that finally recognized that south Jersey was growing faster than the traditionally dominant northern part of the state. Its first Congressman was liberal Republican William Cahill, who had formerly represented the more marginal 1st district. Cahill was elected Governor in 1969, but has since fallen on sadder, scandal ridden times; up for reelection in 1973 with his two top appointees under either indictment or investigation, he was defeated in the Republican primary by Charles Sandman.

In 1970, the incumbentless 6th was the scene of a vigorous contest, as Democrat Charles Yates, a wealthy young businessman, tried to buck political odds. He managed to carry the Burlington County suburbs, but his margins here were not enough to beat Republican state Senator Edwin Forsythe, who won big majorities in Camden and Ocean Counties. Forsythe is a moderate Republican, which is to say that despite his generally conservative instincts he is not always to be found on the same side as the Republican leadership. He won reelection easily in 1972, but in 1974, facing Yates again, he was hard pressed. This time he edged the Democrat in all three counties, but not by much in any, for a 54–46 victory overall. Forsythe serves quietly on the Government Operations and Merchant Marine Committees; in 1975, he vacated his seat on the heavily liberal Education and Labor Committee.

Census Data Pop. 478,137. Central city, 0%; suburban, 78%. Median family income, $11,689; families above $15,000: 30%; families below $3,000: 5%. Median years education, 12.3.

The Voters

Median voting age 42.
Employment profile White collar, 59%. Blue collar, 31%. Service, 9%. Farm, 1%.
Ethnic groups Black, 5%. Total foreign stock, 21%. Italy, 5%; Germany, UK, 3% each; Poland, USSR, 2% each; Ireland 1%.

Presidential vote

1972	Nixon (R)	130,276	(66%)
	McGovern (D)	67,191	(34%)
1968	Nixon (R)	88,880	(50%)
	Humphrey (D)	70,760	(40%)
	Wallace (AI)	18,361	(10%)

Rep. Edwin B. Forsythe (R) Elected 1970; b. Jan. 17, 1916, Westtown, Pa.; home, Moorestown; Society of Friends.

Career Secy., Moorestown Bd. of Adjustment, 1948–52; Mayor of Moorestown, 1957–62; Chm., Moorestown Twnshp. Planning Bd., 1962–63; N.J. Senate 1963–69, Asst. Minor. Ldr., 1966, Minor. Ldr. 1967, Sen. Pres. and Acting Gov. of N.J., 1968, Pres. Pro Tempore, 1969.

Offices 331 CHOB, 202-225-4765. Also 301 Mill St., Moorestown 08057, 609-235-6622.

Committees

Government Operations (12th). Subcommittees: Conservation, Energy and Natural Resources; Government Activities and Transportation.

Merchant Marine and Fisheries (5th). Subcommittees: Fisheries and Wildlife Conservation and the Environment; Oceanography.

Group Ratings

	ADA	COPE	LWV	RIPON	NFU	LCV	CFA	NAB	NSI	ACA
1974	61	40	75	93	58	53	27	75	30	21
1973	44	55	67	93	40	47	75	–	–	37
1972	50	30	75	80	57	53	0	67	60	36

Key Votes

1) Foreign Aid	FOR	6) Gov Abortn Aid	AGN	11) Pub Cong Election $	FOR
2) Busing	AGN	7) Coed Phys Ed	AGN	12) Turkish Arms Cutoff	FOR
3) ABM	AGN	8) Pov Lawyer Gag	AGN	13) Youth Camp Regs	AGN
4) B-1 Bomber	AGN	9) Pub Trans Sub	FOR	14) Strip Mine Veto	AGN
5) Nerve Gas	AGN	10) EZ Voter Regis	AGN	15) Farm Bill Veto	FOR

Election Results

1974 general:	Edwin B. Forsythe (R)	81,190	(54%)	($46,521)
	Charles B. Yates (D)	70,353	(46%)	($66,501)
1974 primary:	Edwin B. Forsythe (R)	10,904	(90%)	
	Alexander Haak (R)	1,234	(10%)	
1972 general:	Edwin B. Forsythe (R)	123,610	(63%)	($38,604)
	Francis P. Brennan (D)	71,113	(37%)	($9,811)

◆ ◆ ◆ ◆ ◆

SEVENTH DISTRICT

Bergen County, the northeast corner of New Jersey, is one of the nation's most comfortable and wealthiest suburban areas. Just across the George Washington Bridge from New York, behind the Palisades that line the Hudson, are some of the state's wealthiest suburbs, sparsely settled (because of minimum acreage zoning), hilly, and tree shaded. Shopping centers, not skyscrapers, are the most prominent landmarks here, and although there are some out of gas industrial towns along the Passaic and Hackensack Rivers, the overall picture here is one of settled affluence and neat prosperity.

Bergen County is divided into two congressioanl districts; the 7th occupies roughly the western half of the county. Republicans drew the slightly irregular boundary lines to split the county's centers of Democratic strength evenly between the two districts; accordingly, the 7th bulges southward to take in industrial Hackensack and Jewish Teaneck, to go with the generally Republican suburbs to the north and west. But the redistricters' strategy, as so many do, went awry; and today both Bergen County districts, the 7th and the 9th, are represented by Democrats.

The 7th is the one which changed hands most recently, in 1974, with the defeat of Republican Congressman William Widnall, ranking minority member of the House Banking and Currency Committee. Widnall had been responsible for some provisions of the nations' housing laws over the years and had generally had a moderate to liberal record. Indeed, for many years, he seemed to suit this district perfectly, and was reelected with correspondingly large majorities. If he had won in 1974, he would have become the senior Republican in the House—but that was just the trouble. At 68 he was visibly past his prime, unable to campaign effectively and apparently unwilling to give his constituents the sort of services they have come to expect from their congressmen.

But Widnall still would have been reelected had he not faced spirited competition in the person of Democrat Andrew Maguire. A 35-year-old Ph-D. and former Ford Foundation official, Maguire soundly beat two well known Bergen County figures in the Democratic primary and went on to wage a textbook general election campaign. He enlisted volunteers, raised money, put out good media and door-to-door literature, and generally convinced the voters of the 7th district that he would represent them better and more actively than his opponent. He beat the previously unbeatable Widnall by a solid 50–44 margin.

In the House Maguire became part of the freshman contingent on the Commerce and Government Operations Committees which has changed so drastically their basic balance on major policy questions. He seems to show the kind of political astuteness and the stands on issues—he is an outspoken opponent of the big oil companies—that enable young Congressmen to turn a landslide year victory into a lifetime congressional career. Despite the Republican background of his district, it would be unwise to bet against Maguire in 1976.

Census Data Pop. 479,999. Central city, 0%; suburban, 100%. Median family income, $14,257; families above $15,000: 46%; families below $3,000: 3%. Median years education, 12.4.

The Voters

Median voting age 45.
Employment profile White collar, 65%. Blue collar, 27%. Service, 8%. Farm, –%.

Ethnic groups Black, 3%. Total foreign stock, 36%. Italy, 9%; Germany, 5%; Poland, UK, 3% each; USSR, Ireland, 2% each; Austria, Canada, Netherlands, 1% each.

Presidential vote

1972	Nixon (R)	....	150,619	(66%)
	McGovern (D)	....	76,583	(34%)
1968	Nixon (R)	....	121,037	(56%)
	Humphrey (D)	....	82,220	(38%)
	Wallace (AI)	....	11,103	(5%)

Rep. Andrew Maguire (D) Elected 1974; b. Mar. 11, 1939, Columbus, Ohio; home, Ridgewood; Oberlin Col., B.A. 1961, Woodrow Wilson and Danforth Fellow, U. of London, England, 1963, Harvard U., Ph.D. 1966.

Career U.N. Advisor on Political and Security Affairs, 1966–69; Dir., multi-development program, Jamaica, N.Y., 1969–72; Consultant, Natl. Affairs Div., Ford Foundation, 1972–74.

Offices 1313 LHOB, 202-225-4465. Also 115 W. Passaic St., Rochelle Park 07662, 201-843-0240.

Committees

Government Operations (28th). Subcommittees: Commerce, Consumer, and Monetary Affairs; Government Information and Individual Rights.

Interstate and Foreign Commerce (29th). Subcommittee: Energy and Power; Health and the Environment; Oversight and Investigations.

Group Ratings: Newly Elected

Key Votes

1) Foreign Aid	FOR	6) Gov Abortn Aid	NE	11) Pub Cong Election $	NE
2) Busing	NE	7) Coed Phys Ed	FOR	12) Turkish Arms Cutoff	NE
3) ABM	NE	8) Pov Lawyer Gag	NE	13) Youth Camp Regs	FOR
4) B-1 Bomber	AGN	9) Pub Trans Sub	NE	14) Strip Mine Veto	AGN
5) Nerve Gas	NE	10) EZ Voter Regis	NE	15) Farm Bill Veto	FOR

Election Results

1974 general:	Andrew Maguire (D)	79,808	(50%)	($137,280)
	William B. Widnall (R)	71,377	(44%)	($50,575)
	Milton Gralla (Ind. Citizens' Action)	9,520	(6%)	($25,000)
1974 primary:	Andrew Maguire (D)	11,274	(52%)	
	Ned J. Parsekian (D)	5,488	(25%)	
	Three others (D)	5,029	(23%)	

◆ ◆ ◆ ◆

EIGHTH DISTRICT

In the late eighteenth century Alexander Hamilton looked out across the Hudson River from Manhattan and predicted major industrial development around Paterson, New Jersey. Here, the great Federalist said, the falls of the Passaic River would provide the waterpower needed to drive the machines of the period. Hamilton died long before Paterson did in fact grow to become one of the largest industrial centers of New Jersey; indeed so great was the impact of industry that Hamilton's ideas play a part in Jerseyite William Carlos Williams' poem, *Paterson*. Today both Paterson and Passaic, just down the river, are industrial blue collar towns, with sizable black, Italian, Polish, and other ethnic communities. All of them traditionally vote Democratic. Clifton, which lies halfway between Paterson and Passaic, is more middle-class and Republican. West of

Paterson, before the first mountain ridges, is Wayne Township, a fast growing upper middle-class suburb and usually the source of Republican strength in the Paterson area.

Paterson, Passaic, Clifton, and Wayne make up the bulk of New Jersey's 8th congressional district, which includes most of surrounding Passaic County. Technically, this is a marginal district; it went for Nixon in 1968, Kennedy in 1960. But in congressional elections it has been pretty solidly Democratic, mostly because of the popularity of the last two congressmen. Charles Joelson, who represented the 8th from 1961 to 1969, was a liberal whose assiduous cultivation of his constituency brought him more than 60% of the vote in every election. Joelson retired from the House for the more placid life of a judge in 1969, a year New Jersey Democrats were in severe trouble. Republican legislative candidates had carried Passaic County in 1967, Nixon had won here in 1968, and William Cahill was about to win a landslide election as Governor. Despite all that, Democratic candidate Robert Roe was able to buck the tide and win by a paper thin margin of 960 votes.

Roe won subsequent elections much more easily, by 61%, 63%, and in 1974, 75% of the vote. As a former Mayor of Wayne Township, Roe has been able to carry his Republican home town by margins almost as large as those he wins in Paterson and Passaic. His reputation as an environmentalist is a help—he was state Conservation Commissioner before his election—even though he has been pushing, from his seat on the House Public Works Committee, a project which would severely disturb the ecological balance of the Passaic River basin.

Census Data Pop. 478,369. Central city, 59%; suburban, 41%. Median family income, $10,783; families above $15,000: 25%; families below $3,000: 7%. Median years education, 10.9.

The Voters

Median voting age 45.
Employment profile White collar, 46%. Blue collar, 44%. Service, 10%. Farm, –%.
Ethnic groups Black, 11%. Spanish, 4%. Total foreign stock, 38%. Italy, 10%; Poland, 5%; Germany, 3%; USSR, UK, Netherlands, Austria, Hungary, 2% each; Czechoslovakia, Ireland, 1% each.

Presidential vote

1972	Nixon (R)	111,671	(63%)
	McGovern (D)	65,125	(37%)
1968	Nixon (R)	82,011	(46%)
	Humphrey (D)	77,904	(44%)
	Wallace (AI)	17,639	(10%)

Rep. Robert A. Roe (D) Elected Nov. 4, 1969; b. Feb. 28, 1924, Wayne; home, Wayne; Oreg. St. U., Wash. St. U.; Catholic.

Career Army, WWII; Wayne Twnshp. Committeeman, 1955–56; Mayor, 1956–61; Passaic Co. Bd. of Freeholders, 1959–63, Dir., 1962–63; Commissioner, N.J. Dept. of Conservation and Econ. Development, 1963–69.

Offices 1007 LHOB, 202-225-5751. Also U.S.P.O., 194 Ward St., Paterson 07510, 201-523-5152.

Committees

Public Works and Transportation (8th). Subcommittees: Economic Development (Chairman); Surface Transportation; Water Resources.

Science and Technology (7th). Subcommittees: Aviation and Transportation Research and Development; Domestic and International Scientific Planning and Analysis; Space Science and Applications.

Group Ratings

	ADA	COPE	LWV	RIPON	NFU	LCV	CFA	NAB	NSI	ACA
1974	68	90	73	63	83	81	82	20	38	21
1973	77	100	73	53	75	82	86	–	–	22
1972	63	91	58	56	86	60	100	18	50	48

Key Votes

1) Foreign Aid	FOR	6) Gov Abortn Aid	AGN
2) Busing	AGN	7) Coed Phys Ed	AGN
3) ABM	FOR	8) Pov Lawyer Gag	AGN
4) B-1 Bomber	FOR	9) Pub Trans Sub	FOR
5) Nerve Gas	AGN	10) EZ Voter Regis	FOR

11) Pub Cong Election $	AGN
12) Turkish Arms Cutoff	FOR
13) Youth Camp Regs	FOR
14) Strip Mine Veto	AGN
15) Farm Bill Veto	FOR

Election Results

1974 general:	Robert A. Roe (D)	83,724	(75%)	($36,496)
	Herman Schmidt (R)	27,839	(25%)	($415)
1974 primary:	Robert A. Roe (D)	9,043	(92%)	
	Valerie Mazzeo (D)	753	(8%)	
1972 general:	Robert A. Roe (D)	104,381	(63%)	($66,706)
	Walter E. Johnson (R)	61,073	(37%)	($776)

◆ ◆ ◆ ◆ ◆

NINTH DISTRICT

In rough terms, the 9th congressional district of New Jersey is the eastern half of Bergen County and, to bring it up to the population standard, the northern end of Hudson County. North of the George Washington Bridge and west of the Palisades that rise above the Hudson are the wealthy, most heavily Republican parts of Bergen County: Tenafly, Dumont, Closter, Old Tappan. Near the Jersey end of the Bridge are several predominantly Jewish and politically liberal suburbs, the largest of which is Teaneck. Atop the Palisades, huge apartment towers overlook New York City, occupied by well-to-do people who wish to escape the city (and its taxes) but retain a view of Manhattan, and built, or so it appears from recent prosecutions in Fort Lee, by men ready to grease the palms of local officials in order to turn huge profits. South of the Bridge, toward and into Hudson County, are older, less affluent suburbs, where people guard their suburban gentility as if it were their lives and wear as a badge of their social distinction their Republican registration.

The Jersey Meadows separate the southern portion of the 9th district—a section with about one-fifth the district's population—from the rest. The Meadows are a swamp for which the state and private developers have great plans, including a stadium for the New York (Jersey?) football Giants. None of these plans has reached fruition yet, however, and today the Meadows are pocked with gas stations and their giant signs, oil tank farms, truck terminals, and eight lanes of Jersey Turnpike. The 9th's southern towns, lying right next to the Meadows, are dominated by Polish-American and Italian-American citizens who are traditional Democrats; this is the part of the district which produced the 9th's Congressman, Henry Helstoski.

From 1957 to 1964, Helstoski was the flamboyant Mayor of the town of East Rutherford (pop. 8,500). In 1964, for some reason, he decided to challenge the 9th's veteran (1939–43, 1951–65) Republican Congressman Frank Osmers; and in the Johnson landslide, the Democrat won by a 51–49 margin. As a Congressman, he was a liberal who opposed escalation of the Vietnam war as early as 1965, and was not expected to win reelection. But for 1966 the then Democratic legislature added the working class towns of Garfield, East Paterson, and Hackensack to the 9th—which were enough to save him. For 1968, the legislature, now turned Republican, redrew the district's lines for the benefit of Assembly Speaker Peter Moraites, who got 49% of the vote that year (and later went to jail for violating federal banking laws).

Since then, Helstoski has won fairly easily, even in 1974 when there were rumors that he was under investigation by federal prosecutors. More than anything else, his recent triumphs reflect his assiduous attention to his constituents. Like so many congressmen able to survive in seemingly hostile districts, Helstoski has taken full advantage of the franking (free mail) privilege—so full that his 1972 opponent obtained a court order against him. Barring serious difficulty with the law, he appears likely to keep winning—and to retain his seat on Ways and Means, obtained finally in 1975—for as long as he wants.

Census Data   Pop. 478,427. Central city, 0%; suburban, 100%. Median family income, $12,428; families above $15,000: 36%; families below $3,000: 5%. Median years education, 12.1.

The Voters

Median voting age 46.
Employment profile White collar, 58%. Blue collar, 34%. Service, 8%. Farm, –%.
Ethnic groups Black, 2%. Spanish, 1%. Total foreign stock, 44%. Italy, 12%; Germany, 5%; Ireland, Poland, 3% each; UK, USSR, 2% each; Austria, 1%.

Presidential vote

1972	Nixon (R)	146,286	(66%)
	McGovern (D)	74,851	(34%)
1968	Nixon (R)	112,279	(53%)
	Humphrey (D)	86,031	(41%)
	Wallace (AI)	13,160	(6%)

Rep. Henry Helstoski (D) Elected 1964; b. Mar. 21, 1925, Wallington; home, East Rutherford; Paterson St. Col., B.A. 1947, Montclair St. Col. M.A. 1949; Catholic.

Career Army Air Corps, WWII; Public school teacher, principal, and superintendent, 1949–62; East Rutherford Councilman, 1956, Mayor, 1957–64; Advertising management consultant, 1962–64.

Offices 2331 RHOB, 202-225-5061. Also 666 Paterson Ave., East Rutherford 07073, 201-939-9090.

Committees

Ways and Means (17th). Subcommittees: Oversight; Trade.

Group Ratings

	ADA	COPE	LWV	RIPON	NFU	LCV	CFA	NAB	NSI	ACA
1974	78	100	82	70	85	81	82	17	13	0
1973	92	100	92	73	85	89	100	–	–	11
1972	100	91	92	73	86	87	100	8	0	0

Key Votes

1) Foreign Aid	FOR	6) Gov Abortn Aid	ABS	11) Pub Cong Election $	AGN
2) Busing	AGN	7) Coed Phys Ed	AGN	12) Turkish Arms Cutoff	FOR
3) ABM	AGN	8) Pov Lawyer Gag	AGN	13) Youth Camp Regs	ABS
4) B-1 Bomber	AGN	9) Pub Trans Sub	FOR	14) Strip Mine Veto	AGN
5) Nerve Gas	AGN	10) EZ Voter Regis	ABS	15) Farm Bill Veto	FOR

Election Results

1974 general:	Henry Helstoski (D)	99,592	(65%)	($35,192)
	Harold A. Pareti (R)	50,859	(33%)	($23,813)
	Herb Shaw (Politicians Are Crooks)	3,460	(2%)	($104)
1974 primary:	Henry Helstoski (D)	21,985	(92%)	
	Arthur E. Lavis (D)	2,037	(8%)	
1972 general:	Henry Helstoski (D)	119,543	(56%)	($55,244)
	Alfred D. Schiaffo (R)	94,747	(44%)	($60,812)

◆ ◆ ◆ ◆ ◆

TENTH DISTRICT

Two years ago he was almost totally unknown outside his home town; today, he is a national figure and, to most Americans, something of a national hero. He is Peter W. Rodino, Jr.,

Congressman from the 10th district of New Jersey, Chairman of the House Judiciary Committee, and the man who presided over the hearings on the impeachment of Richard Nixon.

When it first became clear that Rodino would chair the hearings, some House observers were tremulous. He had only become Chairman of the full committee in 1973, following the defeat of New York's Emanuel Celler; and Celler, though 86 when he lost, was an assertive Chairman who let Rodino take little of the responsibilities of leadership. But the timorous observers were surprised, pleasantly. Relying on the Judiciary staff assembled largely by Celler as well as on the more publicized services of impeachment counsel John Doar, Rodino was able to master the factual and legal case against Nixon and to nail down any parliamentary difficulties as well. His chairing of the public and, by most reports, private hearings was even-tempered and fair; he was careful to give the minority every opportunity to get their views on the record. But there could be little doubt of where Rodino stood, in the face of massive evidence and, to be a bit cynical about it, in light of the overwhelming sentiments of his constituency; he came out solemnly on the side that Richard Nixon had to be removed from office.

One strength of the American political system is that it has produced people of extraordinary talent who have happened to find their way into crucial positions at critical times and who have performed far better than their records would have suggested. Such leaders sometimes come from the most unlikely places: a Lincoln from the then western hick town of Springfield, Illinois; a Franklin Roosevelt from the aristocratic patroon families of the Hudson valley. Within that tradition is Peter Rodino from Newark, New Jersey—a place that some, including its Mayor, have predicted will be the first American city to die.

A quarter century ago, when Peter Rodino was first elected to Congress, Newark was a fairly prosperous industrial city which also had a large white-collar employment base; it was the financial center of New Jersey, a city proud of its tree-shaded middle-class neighborhoods. Today, the downtown remains, although Prudential Insurance, the biggest employer here, is rapidly, though quietly, moving most of its operations to the suburbs. But much of the rest of Newark resembles Berlin after the war. With one notable exception, the middle class has left in search of nicer lawns and safer streets in the suburbs; most of the people remaining in Newark are here because they cannot get out. This is not just a matter of racial change, although Newark is by now almost two-thirds black; for black middle income people, just like whites, are abandoning the city for the more comfortable suburbs. Newark suffered through organized crime control of the local government during the 1960s, a major riot in 1967; now it is simply being abandoned.

The one exception to this pattern is the community Peter Rodino comes from, the Italian-Americans who remain in the North Ward. The Jews who once lived in Philip Roth's old Weequahic Park have long since gone to places like Maplewood and Short Hills; the Irish have vanished far beyond the city limits into Livingston or West Orange; the WASPs, to the extent there ever were any in Newark, are now far away in Morris and Somerset Counties. But many Italians remain, in the close knit neighborhoods where everybody knows everyone else, nobody steals or shoots anyone, and people speak Italian on the streets and in the shops.

The North Ward has steadily resisted black immigration, and after the 1967 riot it armed itself heavily, led by vigilante types like Anthony Imperiale, former Councilman, now Assemblyman, and on and off mayoral candidate. General anxiety and fear intensified when playwright and Newark political strategist Imamu Baraka spearheaded a drive to build a housing project mainly for blacks in the North Ward; the whites regarded it probably correctly, as a tactic to stampede the white minority out of the city limits.

For it is a white minority. Kenneth Gibson, a black engineer with little political background, beat former Congressman Hugh Addonizio, later convicted of bribery, for the Mayor's office in 1970; Gibson was easily reelected in 1974, and carried in a majority of black councilmen. The Newark school board has on occasion ordered the flying of the black liberation flag in the schools, making it fairly plain that whites are not welcome. The blacks are perhaps bitter because the city they finally inherited is virtually bankrupt; its tax base is badly eroded, and it must go begging to the state and federal governments every year for money for the most basic city services.

From all that, one might expect a turbulent congressional politics, and were it not for Peter Rodino that is probably what one would have. Indeed, even Rodino was challenged in 1972 by two black candidates, including Mayor William Hart of East Orange. Their argument, essentially, was not against Rodino's record, which was solidly pro-civil rights and indeed liberal on all issues, but rather that since the district had a black majority population, it ought to have a black Congressman. In a year in which several blacks were elected to Congress by majority white constituencies, a fairly large percentage of Newark and East Orange blacks rejected this reasoning, and Rodino won with 57% of the vote. In 1974, after helping to get rid of the President blacks have hated as no other, Rodino did not even have a black opponent. Nevertheless, he reportedly remains edgy and would like to see a change in the district lines, giving him a white-majority seat; but New Jersey Democrats, though in control of the Governorship and the legislature, are nervous about doing anything which would weaken the state's many freshmen Democrats. Most likely Rodino will continue to run—and to win—within the current boundaries of the 10th district, at least through the seventies.

Census Data Pop. 478,217. Central city, 80%; suburban, 20%. Median family income, $8,300; families above $15,000: 15%; families below $3,000: 13%. Median years education, 10.5.

The Voters

Median voting age 41.
Employment profile White collar, 39%. Blue collar, 46%. Service, 15%. Farm, –%.
Ethnic groups Black, 52%. Spanish, 6%. Total foreign stock, 23%. Italy, 7%; Poland, 2%; Ireland, USSR, Germany, UK, 1% each.

Presidential vote

1972	Nixon (R)	46,034	(37%)
	McGovern (D)	78,416	(63%)
1968	Nixon (R)	40,030	(28%)
	Humphrey (D)	91,975	(64%)
	Wallace (AI)	12,677	(9%)

Rep. Peter W. Rodino, Jr. (D) Elected 1948; b. June 7, 1909, Newark; home, Newark; Rutgers U., LL.B. 1937; Catholic.

Career Army, WWII; Practicing atty.

Offices 2462 RHOB, 202-225-3436. Also Suite 1435A, Fed. Bldg., 970 Broad St., Newark 07102, 201-645-3213.

Committees

Judiciary (Chairman). Subcommittees: Monopolies and Commercial Law (Chairman).

Group Ratings

	ADA	COPE	LWV	RIPON	NFU	LCV	CFA	NAB	NSI	ACA
1974	91	100	92	63	85	76	92	17	20	7
1973	96	100	92	73	90	83	88	–	–	8
1972	88	91	100	78	86	70	100	9	25	0

Key Votes

1) Foreign Aid	FOR	6) Gov Abortn Aid	AGN	11) Pub Cong Election $	FOR
2) Busing	FOR	7) Coed Phys Ed	FOR	12) Turkish Arms Cutoff	FOR
3) ABM	AGN	8) Pov Lawyer Gag	AGN	13) Youth Camp Regs	FOR
4) B-1 Bomber	ABS	9) Pub Trans Sub	FOR	14) Strip Mine Veto	AGN
5) Nerve Gas	AGN	10) EZ Voter Regis	FOR	15) Farm Bill Veto	FOR

Election Results

1974 general:	Peter W. Rodino, Jr. (D)	53,094	(81%)	($26,286)
	John R. Taliaferro (R)	9,936	(15%)	($0)
	Sandra Hill ("Unity Movement")	2,508	(4%)	($0)
1974 primary:	Peter W. Rodino, Jr. (D)	19,121	(89%)	
	Michael Giordano (D)	2,330	(11%)	
1972 general:	Peter W. Rodino, Jr. (D)	94,308	(80%)	($90,115)
	Kenneth C. Miller (R)	23,949	(20%)	($770)

◆ ◆ ◆ ◆

ELEVENTH DISTRICT

The 11th congressional district of New Jersey consists of most of suburban Essex County. This string of suburban towns around Newark is theoretically within commuting distance of New York, but as many people here work in downtown Newark itself or, more likely, in one of the New Jersey suburban office or factory developments. The district's ethnic concentrations tend to follow the radial avenues leading out of Newark. With a definite Italian-American flavor are the towns of Belleville, Bloomfield, and Nutley, all adjoining Newark's heavily Italian North Ward. There is a substantial Jewish population in South Orange and Maplewood, adjacent to what was once the Jewish part of Newark. An anomaly is Montclair, situated on a ridge overlooking the Manhattan skyline; part of it is high income WASP, part middle income black. Farther out are comfortable upper middle income places like Caldwell, Fairfield, and Essex Fells.

Before the 1972 redistricting, the 11th included the Central Ward of Newark and East Orange, both heavily black; as it stands today, the district is considerably less Democratic. But so far that fact has posed no problems for Congressman Joseph Minish. Back in 1962, Minish came out of the labor movement to replace Hugh Addonizio, who went on to become Mayor of Newark because, as Hugh told a friend at the time, you can make a million dollars there. Minish has seldom been seriously challenged, and has had no trouble winning. In the House he serves on the Banking and Currency Committee; according to the Nader Congress Project, his major legislative accomplishment is a bill setting up credit unions for servicemen living on bases overseas.

Census Data Pop. 475,297. Central city, 0%; suburban, 100%. Median family income, $12,508; families above $15,000: 36%; families below $3,000: 5%. Median years education, 12.2.

The Voters

Median voting age 47.
Employment profile White collar, 60%. Blue collar, 30%. Service, 10%. Farm, –%.
Ethnic groups Black, 7%. Total foreign stock, 38%. Italy, 11%; Poland, USSR, 4% each; Germany, UK, 3% each; Ireland, Austria, 2% each.

Presidential vote

1972	Nixon (R)	128,378	(60%)
	McGovern (D)	84,859	(40%)
1968	Nixon (R)	100,354	(46%)
	Humphrey (D)	100,188	(46%)
	Wallace (AI)	17,215	(8%)

Rep. Joseph G. Minish (D) Elected 1962; b. Sept. 1, 1916, Throop, Pa.; home, West Orange; Catholic.

Career Army, WWII; Political Action Dir., AFL-CIO Dist. 4, 1953–54; Exec. Secy., Essex W. Hudson Labor Cncl., 1954–61, Treas., 1961–62.

Offices 2162 RHOB, 202-225-5035. Also 308 Main St., Orange 07050, 201-645-6363.

Committees

Banking, Currency and Housing (10th). Subcommittees: Domestic Monetary Policy; General Oversight and Renegotiation (Chairman).

House Administration (13th). Subcommittees: Accounts; Electrical and Mechanical Office Equipment; Personnel and Police.

Group Ratings

	ADA	COPE	LWV	RIPON	NFU	LCV	CFA	NAB	NSI	ACA
1974	74	100	92	60	86	71	85	17	50	13
1973	84	100	92	60	72	84	86	–	–	22
1972	88	91	92	80	86	80	100	9	50	14

NEW JERSEY

535

Key Votes

1) Foreign Aid	FOR	6) Gov Abortn Aid	AGN	11) Pub Cong Election $	FOR
2) Busing	AGN	7) Coed Phys Ed	AGN	12) Turkish Arms Cutoff	FOR
3) ABM	AGN	8) Pov Lawyer Gag	AGN	13) Youth Camp Regs	FOR
4) B-1 Bomber	ABS	9) Pub Trans Sub	FOR	14) Strip Mine Veto	AGN
5) Nerve Gas	AGN	10) EZ Voter Regis	FOR	15) Farm Bill Veto	FOR

Election Results

1974 general:	Joseph G. Minish (D)	98,957	(70%)	($47,606)
	William B. Grant (R)	42,036	(30%)	($29,292)
1974 primary:	Joseph G. Minish (D), unopposed			
1972 general:	Joseph G. Minish (D)	120,277	(59%)	($68,709)
	Milton A. Waldor (R)	82,957	(41%)	($55,185)

◆ ◆ ◆ ◆ ◆

TWELFTH DISTRICT

The 12th congressional district of New Jersey contains all of Union County except for one small city and two townships. For the most part, the 12th is classic, if a little timeworn, suburban country. There are a few stereotypical WASP havens like Summit, but more typical of the district are places like Cranford, Westfield, and Union—places dominated by the sons and daughters of Italian, Polish, and German immigrants, whose claim on prosperity is now about a generation old but still psychologically at least precarious. Even the district's two most industrial cities, Elizabeth and Plainfield, are not afflicted with all the ills normally associated with central cities, though they have their poverty, crime, and riots. The district is bisected by perhaps the most garish strip highway in the East, U.S. 22; the frenetic neon signs that line the roadway are evidence of the energy contained in the leafy green, placid suburban streets just a block or two away in the darkness.

In Union County, political preferences tend to go down the middle of the road, with little enthusiasm for what may lie off center on either side. In the close national elections of 1960 and 1968, this New Jersey area came within a couple of percentage points of duplicating the national results for the major candidates. It is also a pretty accurate bellwether in state contests. Moreover, interestingly, both of New Jersey's current Senators spent time representing Union County in the House, Republican Clifford Case from 1945 to 1953 and Democrat Harrison Williams from 1953 to 1957. Congressman Williams was defeated for reelection in 1956 by the woman who represented the district for the next 16 years, Republican Florence P. Dwyer. Thanks to her liberal voting record and good constituency service, she won subsequent elections by record margins. When she retired in 1972, many observers expected to see the first closely contested congressional election here in years.

But it did not work out that way. State Senator Matthew Rinaldo, for five years a solid vote-getter in Union County, won the Republican primary and then easily defeated former state Senator Jerry English, a woman, in the general election. For a Republican, Rinaldo has compiled a generally liberal voting record, as his predecessor did. In 1974, he demonstrated for all who might have doubted his vote-getting ability when he won reelection in this Democratic year with 67% of the vote—far better than any other Jersey Republican. Rinaldo, who serves on the Commerce and Merchant Marine Committees, seems to have a long congressional future ahead of him.

Census Data Pop. 477,887. Central city, 0%; suburban, 100%. Median family income, $12,787; families above $15,000: 37%; families below $3,000: 5%. Median years education, 12.3.

The Voters

Median voting age 46.
Employment profile White collar, 56%. Blue collar, 34%. Service, 10%. Farm, –%.
Ethnic groups Black, 12%. Total foreign stock, 35%. Italy, 7%; Poland, Germany, 4% each; USSR, 3%; UK, Ireland, Austria, 2% each; Canada, 1%.

Presidential vote

1972	Nixon (R)	130,187	(63%)
	McGovern (D)	77,367	(37%)
1968	Nixon (R)	100,089	(48%)
	Humphrey (D)	93,199	(45%)
	Wallace (AI)	16,085	(8%)

Rep. Matthew J. Rinaldo (R) Elected 1972; b. Sept. 1, 1931, Elizabeth; home, Union; Rutgers U., B.S. 1953, Seton Hall U., M.B.A. 1959, NYU School of Public Admin., 1969.

Career Pres., Union Twnshp. Zoning Bd. of Adjustment, 1962–63; Union Co. Bd. of Freeholders, 1963–64; N.J. Senate, 1967–72.

Offices 314 CHOB, 202-225-5361. Also 1961 Morris Ave., Union 07083, 201-687-4235.

Committees

Interstate and Foreign Commerce (14th). Subcommittees: Consumer Protection and Finance.

Merchant Marine and Fisheries (12th). Subcommittees: Fisheries and Wildlife Conservation and the Environment; Panama Canal.

Group Ratings

	ADA	COPE	LWV	RIPON	NFU	LCV	CFA	NAB	NSI	ACA
1974	70	90	91	56	83	76	75	55	70	31
1973	48	91	67	80	47	89	88	–	–	44

Key Votes

1) Foreign Aid	FOR	6) Gov Abortn Aid	AGN	11) Pub Cong Election $	FOR
2) Busing	AGN	7) Coed Phys Ed	AGN	12) Turkish Arms Cutoff	FOR
3) ABM	AGN	8) Pov Lawyer Gag	FOR	13) Youth Camp Regs	FOR
4) B-1 Bomber	FOR	9) Pub Trans Sub	FOR	14) Strip Mine Veto	AGN
5) Nerve Gas	AGN	10) EZ Voter Regis	FOR	15) Farm Bill Veto	FOR

Election Results

1974 general:	Matthew J. Rinaldo (R)	92,829	(67%)	($127,890)
	Adam K. Levin (D)	46,246	(33%)	($143,895)
1974 primary:	Matthew J. Rinaldo (R)	10,427	(93%)	
	Lloyd J. Sherk (R)	777	(7%)	
1972 general:	Matthew J. Rinaldo (R)	127,690	(64%)	($131,790)
	Jerry F. English (D)	72,758	(36%)	($32,839)

◆ ◆ ◆ ◆

THIRTEENTH DISTRICT

The 13th congressional district of New Jersey is a new seat, first created in 1972, and in that brief time it has elected two different members of Congress—in two general elections that featured the same candidates. Geographically, it is the northwestern wedge of New Jersey, from Trenton to the Ramapo Mountains on the New York border. Twenty or thirty years ago, this area was almost entirely agricultural, with considerably more dairy cows than people. In the years since, nearby metropolitan areas have been invading the pastureland. In the southern part of the district, people have been pouring out of Trenton into suburban Mercer County, but the really substantial growth has been in Morris County. This is not posh horse farm country, like the part of Morris County in the 5th district; rather, the new settlement has been of people in the middle income class moving from New York or, more likely, the crowded older suburbs of north Jersey, into the townships around the small towns of Boonton and Dover and Netcong. They have brought with them generally conservative voting habits, even if they are often ancestral Democrats; part of the reason they have moved, in many cases at least, is a dislike of what they believe liberal policies have been doing to the communities they grew up in.

The boundaries of the 13th were drawn by a Republican legislature to elect a Republican Congressman—indeed, a rather specific Republican Congressman—and it worked at least the first time. Indeed, around the Jersey State House the 13th was known as the Maraziti district, after Joseph Maraziti, the state Senator most responsible for its creation and its first Congressman, elected in 1972.

Maraziti might have remained, in fact would certainly have remained, an obscure backbencher were it not for the fact that he sat on the Judiciary Committee which decided to impeach Richard Nixon. Maraziti, viewers of the hearings will remember, was the oldish junior Republican (he was 62 at the time), whose tongue-tied oratory always left him satisfied with the President's innocence. Named by *New Times* magazine as one of the ten dumbest members of Congress, Maraziti did precious little to dispel that reputation; and that alone may have been enough to finish him off in 1974. But he made another mistake: he had a woman on his congressional payroll who never showed up and whose relationship with the Congressman was apparently less professional than personal. Maraziti was not the person that you would cast as the proprietor of a government-subsidized love nest, but that apparently is what a lot of constituents concluded he was.

In any case, Maraziti went from being a 56–44 winner in 1972 to a 57–43 loser in 1974. His Democratic opponent in both elections, and the new Congresswoman, is Helen Stevenson Meyner, wife of a former (1954–62) New Jersey Governor and distant cousin of the Adlai Stevensons. Mrs. Meyner's extensive campaigning had won her far more votes than observers had thought likely in 1972, and in 1974 she concentrated on putting on a creditable, hardworking campaign while watching Maraziti's mistakes destroy him. Her toughest electoral test will probably come in 1976, when some Republican—almost certainly not Maraziti—will try to recapture the Maraziti district for his party. With the advantage of two years of incumbency, Meyner will likely be favored to win.

Census Data Pop. 478,164. Central city, 0%; suburban, 69%. Median family income, $11,731; families above $15,000: 30%; families below $3,000: 5%. Median years education, 12.3.

The Voters

Median voting age 42.
Employment profile White collar, 51%. Blue collar, 37%. Service, 10%. Farm, 2%.
Ethnic groups Black, 2%. Total foreign stock, 24%. Italy, Germany, 4% each; UK, 3%; Poland, 2%; Hungary, Ireland, USSR, Austria, 1% each.

Presidential vote

1972	Nixon (R)	141,609	(70%)
	McGovern (D)	61,509	(30%)
1968	Nixon (R)	103,051	(55%)
	Humphrey (D)	66,092	(36%)
	Wallace (AI)	16,548	(9%)

Rep. Helen S. Meyner (D) Elected 1974; b. Mar. 5, 1929, New York, N.Y.; home, Phillipsburg; Colo. Col., B.A. 1950.

Career Amer. Red Cross, Korea, 1950–52; Consumer Advisor, TWA; Newspaper columnist, 1962–69; Conductor of TV interview programs, 1965–68.

Offices 126 CHOB, 202-225-5801. Also 32 Bridge St., Lambertville 08530, 609-397-1830.

Committees

District of Columbia (13th). Subcommittees: Education, Labor and Social Services; The Bicentennial, the Environment, and the International Community.

International Relations (21st). Subcommittees: International Operations; Oversight.

Group Ratings: Newly Elected

Key Votes

1) Foreign Aid	FOR	6) Gov Abortn Aid	NE	11) Pub Cong Election $	NE
2) Busing	NE	7) Coed Phys Ed	FOR	12) Turkish Arms Cutoff	NE
3) ABM	NE	8) Pov Lawyer Gag	NE	13) Youth Camp Regs	FOR
4) B-1 Bomber	AGN	9) Pub Trans Sub	NE	14) Strip Mine Veto	AGN
5) Nerve Gas	NE	10) EZ Voter Regis	NE	15) Farm Bill Veto	AGN

Election Results

1974 general:	Helen S. Meyner (D)	86,043	(57%)	($121,940)
	Joseph J. Maraziti (R)	64,166	(43%)	($68,838)
1974 primary:	Helen S. Meyner (D)	8,259	(47%)	
	Joseph P. O'Doherty (D)	4,458	(26%)	
	Oscar W. Rittenhouse (D)	3,132	(18%)	
	Bernard Reiner (D)	1,595	(9%)	

◆ ◆ ◆ ◆ ◆

FOURTEENTH DISTRICT

"I am the law," Frank Hague used to say, and in Hudson County, New Jersey, he was. Back in the 1930s, when Hague was at the peak of his powers as boss of the Hudson County Democratic machine, he chose Governors and U.S. Senators, prosecutors and judges, and even had influence in the White House of Franklin D. Roosevelt. In Jersey City and other Hudson County towns—then and still the most densely populated part of the country outside Manhattan—Hague controlled almost every facet of life. He determined who could stay in business and who could not; he controlled tax assessments and the issuance of parking tickets; and he kept the CIO out of town for years (resulting in a major Supreme Court case). Hague's power was finally anchored in votes. Jersey City and Hudson County had huge payrolls, and every jobholder was expected to produce a certain number of votes on election day. Democratic candidates could expect a 100,000 vote margin in Hudson County, and since they often lost the rest of the state by less than that amount, they were indebted indeed. No wonder Democratic politicians from Roosevelt on down paid close attention to whatever Hague had to say—or wanted.

To the naked eye, Hudson County has changed little since Frank Hague's golden days. It still consists of the same series of towns on the Palisades ridge between New York harbor and the Jersey Meadows: in addition to Jersey City, places like Bayonne, Hoboken, Weehawken, and Union City. To exploit the view of the Manhattan skyline, some luxury high rise apartments have gone up in the northern end of the County; but most of Hudson County's residents still live in the same polluted Jersey air, the same fetid apartments and grimy two-family houses that were old when the nation fell into the Great Depression.

For many years now, Hudson County's population has been declining as virtually no one chooses to move in. Nearby Newark has shifted from white to black, but Hudson County's population and electorate remain predominantly Italian, Irish, and Polish, just as they have been from the turn of the century. There are some new Spanish speaking neighborhoods, but on the whole this remains one of the most insular places in the United States; people grow up here without ever crossing the River to New York, or ever meeting anyone from outside Hudson County. The tight knit neighborhoods, clustered around their parish churches and (at least till recently) their Democratic precinct captains are as isolated from the main currents of American life as a tiny community in an Appalachian hollow.

But in the last five years there has been a kind of political revolution in Hudson County. To oversimplify just a bit, what has happened is that all the people who had been running the machine Frank Hague left behind have been sent to jail. They include former County boss John V. Kenny, now in his 80s, former Jersey City Mayor Thomas Whelan, and former Congressman (1959–73) Cornelius Gallagher. Their convictions have been secured by the string of federal prosecutors appointed, in effect, by Senator Clifford Case; politically, they have been beaten by reformers led by Jersey City's new 34-year-old Mayor, Paul Jordan. Some people here are a little suspicious of the reformers, who have joined forces with some holdovers from the old machine days. But if they still play some political games—including securing the 1973 gubernatorial nomination for the then unknown Brendan Byrne—all the evidence indicates that the new bunch are unlike the old Hague and Kenny gangs in one very important respect: they are not stealing the public treasury blind.

In the old days, the Hague machine delivered huge margins to Democratic presidential candidates almost regardless of the tides of public opinion. But there has been relatively little ballot fraud in recent years, as evidenced by the fact that the conservatively inclined Catholic voters here were trending Republican heavily—until the Watergate. In the three-way 1968 race, Hubert Humphrey had only 52% of the vote here, and George McGovern could win only 39% of Hudson's votes in 1972. In the latter year even the Democratic percentage in Hudson County's 14th congressional district dropped notably.

But that year and every year Hudson County remains staunchly Democratic, and the machine imprimatur—now in the hands of Jordan's reformers—usually prevails on primary day. Certainly in the 14th district, which includes 78% of Hudson's residents, nomination in the Democratic primary continues to be tantamount to election. As it currently stands, the 14th is an amalgam of two districts once dominated by Hudson County; it now controls only one—a measure of population decline and the waning clout of the machine.

The 1972 amalgamation put two incumbent Democrats, the now-jailed Cornelius Gallagher and Dominick Daniels, together in the same district. The Jordan group thought that that might allow them to win the seat, in the person of West New York Mayor Anthony De Fino. But Daniels, who had represented most of the district for 14 years, took 50% of the primary vote, with a respectable 32% for De Fino and an embarrassing 15% for Gallagher. What helped Daniels, besides his Italian ancestry, was that he had never been implicated in any Hudson County corruption; nobody thinks he is crooked. In Washington he is a quiet Congressman, though he has high seniority seats on the Education and Labor and Post Office Committees. On all issues, he hews very close to the line set out by organized labor, which can count him a reliable vote for as long as his age (68 in 1976) permits him to run.

Census Data Pop. 477,939. Central city, 55%; suburban, 45%. Median family income, $9,607; families above $15,000: 19%; families below $3,000: 9%. Median years education, 10.3.

The Voters

Median voting age 45.
Employment profile White collar, 45%. Blue collar, 43%. Service, 12%. Farm, –%.
Ethnic groups Black, 13%. Spanish, 6%. Total foreign stock, 39%. Italy, 10%; Poland, 5%; Ireland, UK, 3% each; Germany, USSR, 2% each; Austria, 1%.

Presidential vote

1972	Nixon (R)	104,907	(60%)
	McGovern (D)	71,098	(40%)
1968	Nixon (R)	70,360	(37%)
	Humphrey (D)	102,257	(53%)
	Wallace (AI)	18,731	(10%)

Rep. Dominick V. Daniels (D) Elected 1958; b. Oct. 18, 1908, Jersey City; home, Jersey City; Fordham U., 1925–26, Rutgers U., LL.B. 1929; Catholic.

Career Practicing atty., 1930–58; Magistrait, Jersey City Municipal Ct., 1952–58.

Offices 2370 RHOB, 202-225-2765. Also 895 Bergen Ave., Jersey City 07306, 201-659-7700.

Committees

Education and Labor (4th). Subcommittees: Labor Standards; Manpower, Compensation; and Health and Safety.

Post Office and Civil Service (3d). Subcommittees: Retirement and Employee Benefits.

Group Ratings

	ADA	COPE	LWV	RIPON	NFU	LCV	CFA	NAB	NSI	ACA
1974	62	100	73	55	83	73	82	20	50	8
1973	83	100	75	60	90	65	100	–	–	19
1972	63	91	89	67	86	47	50	18	63	20

Key Votes

1) Foreign Aid	FOR	6) Gov Abortn Aid	AGN	11) Pub Cong Election $	AGN
2) Busing	AGN	7) Coed Phys Ed	AGN	12) Turkish Arms Cutoff	FOR
3) ABM	AGN	8) Pov Lawyer Gag	AGN	13) Youth Camp Regs	FOR
4) B-1 Bomber	ABS	9) Pub Trans Sub	FOR	14) Strip Mine Veto	AGN
5) Nerve Gas	AGN	10) EZ Voter Regis	FOR	15) Farm Bill Veto	FOR

Election Results

1974 general:	Dominick V. Daniels (D)	85,438	(80%)	($80,556)
	Claire J. Sheridan (R)	17,231	(16%)	
	John A. Alston (Good Neighbor)	4,266	(4%)	($3,821)
1974 primary:	Dominick V. Daniels (D)	30,408	(94%)	
	Thomas Caslander (D)	1,827	(6%)	
1972 general:	Dominick V. Daniels (D)	103,089	(62%)	($53,286)
	Richard T. Bozzone (R)	57,683	(35%)	($6320)
	Edward F. Zampella (Concerned and Capable)	5,188	(3%)	($7,923)

♦ ♦ ♦ ♦ ♦

FIFTEENTH DISTRICT

The 15th congressional district of New Jersey takes in most of Middlesex County, the state's fastest growing traditionally Democratic area. The 15th has the largest concentration of Hungarian-Americans of any congressional district in the nation, in and around New Brunswick; it also has sizeable number of Poles in Woodbridge and Italians in Perth Amboy. From the old ethnic neighborhoods in these small central cities, the children of hyphenated Americans have moved out into places like Edison Township, Piscataway Township, and Sayreville, where they live in what passes for pastoral splendor if you grew up in New Brunswick or Perth Amboy. These suburban voters have not totally forgotten their Democratic heritage, but they showed a tendency to ignore it, at least temporarily, when Richard Nixon and Spiro Agnew convinced them that liberal Democrats were trampling on the values their parents had imparted to them. Thus the comfortable Kennedy majority here in 1960 became a small Humphrey plurality in 1968 and a large (61–39) Nixon majority in 1972.

Middlesex County and the 15th district have long had a successful Democratic machine, run for many years by David Willentz, whose Perth Amboy law office somehow seemed to attract some of the state's largest businesses as clients. Middlesex acquired its own congressional district in 1962, and the Willentz machine picked Edward Patten as its candidate. Patten was then Secretary of State, an appointive position here in New Jersey, usually reserved for a political operator; he was elected to the House in 1962, and has remained there ever since.

On the campaign trail, Patten's greatest asset, along with the Willentz machine, is a garrulous sense of humor and that was his major resource when he turned aside a much publicized young peace candidate in the 1970 Democratic primary. In 1972, Patten, grown fat and getting close to 70, had trouble as Republican Fuller Brooks won 48% of the vote. Under more normal circumstances that might have been the signal for Patten to retire; the Republicans could have kept campaigning vigorously and might well have knocked Patten off in 1974. But any chance of that evaporated with Watergate. These ancestral Democrats forgot the social issues which were supposed to dominate the seventies when it became clear that the landslide President and Vice President were part of a gang of crooks. Patten had only token opposition and, at the age of 69, won with 72% of the vote. The 15th had become a solid Democratic district once again.

Census Data Pop. 477,949. Central city, 0%; suburban, 9%. Median family income, $11,793; families above $15,000: 29%; families below $3,000: 4%. Median years education, 12.1.

The Voters

Median voting age 41.
Employment profile White collar, 49%. Blue collar, 41%. Service, 10%. Farm, –%.
Ethnic groups Black, 6%. Spanish, 2%. Total foreign stock, 33%. Italy, Poland, 5% each;
Hungary, 4%; Germany, 3%; USSR, UK, Czechoslovakia, Austria, 2% each; Ireland, 1%.

Presidential vote

1972	Nixon (R)	118,439	(61%)
	McGovern (D)	74,752	(39%)
1968	Nixon (R)	76,756	(41%)
	Humphrey (D)	90,902	(48%)
	Wallace (AI)	20,591	(11%)

Rep. Edward J. Patten (D) Elected 1962; b. Aug. 22, 1905, Perth
Amboy; home, Perth Amboy; Newark St. Col., Rutgers U., LL.B. 1926,
B.S.Ed. 1928; Catholic.

Career Practicing atty., 1927–62; Public school teacher, 1927–34; Mayor
of Perth Amboy, 1934–40; Middlesex Co. Clerk, 1940–54; Secy. of State
of N.J., 1954–62.

Offices 2332 RHOB, 202-225-6301. Also Natl. Bank Bldg., Perth Amboy
08861, 201-826-4610.

Committees

Appropriations (17th). Subcommittees: Labor-HEW; Military Construction; Treasury, Postal
Service, and General Government.

Group Ratings

	ADA	COPE	LWV	RIPON	NFU	LCV	CFA	NAB	NSI	ACA
1974	70	100	83	63	86	65	67	8	60	7
1973	83	100	83	46	95	72	88	–	–	12
1972	81	82	83	67	86	47	100	25	56	22

Key Votes

1) Foreign Aid	FOR	6) Gov Abortn Aid	AGN	11) Pub Cong Election $	FOR
2) Busing	AGN	7) Coed Phys Ed	AGN	12) Turkish Arms Cutoff	FOR
3) ABM	AGN	8) Pov Lawyer Gag	AGN	13) Youth Camp Regs	FOR
4) B-1 Bomber	FOR	9) Pub Trans Sub	FOR	14) Strip Mine Veto	AGN
5) Nerve Gas	AGN	10) EZ Voter Regis	FOR	15) Farm Bill Veto	FOR

Election Results

1974 general:	Edward J. Patten (D)	92,593	(72%)	($38,113)
	Ernest J. Hammesfahr (R)	35,875	(28%)	($11,165)
1974 primary:	Edward J. Patten (D), unopposed			
1972 general:	Edward J. Patten (D)	98,155	(52%)	($27,605)
	Fuller H. Brooks (R)	89,400	(48%)	($51,081)

NEW MEXICO

It is a little known fact that New Mexico has voted for the winner in sixteen consecutive
presidential elections, ever since it was admitted to the Union in 1912—a record matched by no
other state. But this most reliable of bellwethers could hardly be more atypical. For one thing,

nearly one-third of its people in the ordinary course of things speak Spanish; and, it should be noted, few of them are recent migrants from Mexico or some other part of Latin America. Rather, most are the descendants of Spanish conquistadores and Pueblo Indians. An Hispanic civilization has existed in northern New Mexico around Santa Fe and Taos since 1610, and in the years before World War II the Hispanic community made up nearly half the state's population.

In vivid contrast to the Hispanic part of New Mexico is the area called Little Texas. With small cities, plenty of oil wells, vast cattle ranches, and desolate military bases, this region resembles, economically and politically, the adjacent high plains of west Texas. Oil is important here, but not as much as the military presence: a couple Air Force bases, and the Army's White Sands Missile Range, near Alamogordo, where the first atomic bomb was detonated.

In the middle of the state is Albuquerque which, with the coming of the air conditioner, grew from a small desert town into a booming Sun Belt City. Albuquerque is also heavily dependent on the military, and on the Energy Research and Development Administration (until recently, the Atomic Energy Commission). There are two bases within the city limits and its largest employer is the Bell System's Sandia Laboratories, an ERDA contractor. Metropolitan Albuquerque now has a little more than one-third the state's population—about the same proportion as the Hispanic areas and Little Texas and a couple of other Anglo strongholds, like uranium-rich Farmington, in the northwest corner of the state.

For many years New Mexico politics was a somnolent business. Local bosses—first Republican, then Democratic—controlled the large Hispanic vote, which meant that elections here were often only a ratification of the power brokers' decisions. The most interesting feature of this politics was the balanced ticket: New Mexico usually had one Spanish and one Anglo Senator, with the offices of Governor and Lieutenant Governor sometimes alternating between the two groups.

In the last couple of elections a new pattern has emerged. Hispanic and/or liberal Democrats have captured their party's nomination and piled up big majorities in the Hispanic areas, which generally have leaned Democratic since they went heavily for fellow Catholic John Kennedy in 1960. The Republicans, after some flirting with liberalism in the person of former Governor (1967–70) David Cargo, have pursued a conservative strategy, wooing away the voters of Little Texas from their traditional Democratic voting habits, hoping for fairly good margins in Albuquerque, and trying to avoid getting beaten too much in the Hispanic counties.

The results have been mixed: each party holds one Senate and one House seat, and the Governorship is Democratic by virtue of a 51–49 victory in 1974. The winner was state Senator Jerry Apodaca, a 40-year-old former Democratic state chairman, who became the first Hispanic Governor elected since 1918. Apodaca was strong in the Hispanic counties, where he got 62% of the vote. His oponent, Republican cattle rancher Joe Skeen, got 59% of the vote in the Little Texas counties, but it was not enough to win. Apodaca was something of a maverick in the state legislature, and he is the first New Mexico Governor to espouse the go-slow line on development which is suddenly so popular in the Rocky Mountain states.

This is the first time in New Mexico's history that the state has had simultaneously a Senator and a Governor of Hispanic origin. The Senator, of course, is Joseph Montoya, and apparently it was because of his Spanish heritage that he was tapped for service on the Senate Watergate Committee; reportedly Majority Leader Mike Mansfield feared the inquiry might focus in on the Cubans, and did not want the Senate to be considered anti-Spanish. Instead, Montoya—whose oratory comes across far better in Spanish than English—became one of the less acclaimed members of the Committee. During the course of the hearings, Montoya himself was accused of irregular reporting practices in his 1970 campaign, but was able to satisfy inquirers that he personally knew of no wrongdoing. More interesting, perhaps, is that he had been serving as Chairman of the Appropriations Subcommittee which had been so generous to the Nixon White House over the years.

Montoya is from an old Hispanic family in Sandoval County, and has held public office in New Mexico continuously, except for one two year period, since 1936, when he was elected to the state House of Representatives at the age of 21. Even so, when he was challenged in 1970 by conservative Little Texas rancher Anderson Carter (whose name is reminiscent of that of former Senator Clinton Anderson), Montoya received only a lackluster 53% of the vote. Now his seat is up in 1976, and it is hard to predict how he will do. No really formidable Republican opposition has arisen as yet, but what will really matter is the public's reaction to his performance on the Watergate Committee. In those weeks of hearings, New Mexico voters got a closer look at Montoya than they had in the previous 38 years of his political career; and how he impressed them will probably determine the result.

New Mexico's other Senator won in an election which at times seemed farcical. A disgruntled would-be candidate for the 1972 Senate seat vacated by Clinton Anderson filed a lawsuit and managed to have the state's $2,550 filing fee declared unconstitutional; whereupon a herd of political hopefuls—25 Democrats and seven Republicans—proceeded to file. The Democratic nomination was won (with 30% of the vote cast) by a former state Representative with the arresting name of Jack Daniels; the Republican candidate, as expected, was former Albuquerque Mayor, and nearly successful 1970 gubernatorial candidate Pete Domenici. This time Domenici won. He led 57–43 in his native Albuquerque, and had a small but sufficient edge in the Little Texas counties. But the key in his 54–46 statewide victory was his carrying the Hispanic counties. There have always been allegations of vote fraud here, and in 1972 Nixon was running stronger than usual, with Domenici, perhaps thanks to his vaguely Spanish sounding name, just behind.

In the Senate Domenici has been a rock solid conservative on just about every issue. In 1975 he was tapped, along with a number of other younger conservative Republicans, for a seat on the Senate Budget Committee. As for winning reelection, Domenici does not appear to be especially strong, but he did run stronger than Montoya last time.

Since the 1940 census, New Mexico has been entitled to two congressmen, but until 1968 both were elected at large. The switch to separate districts that year proved disastrous to the Democrats, who after winning the two seats routinely lost both of them to Republicans. The 1st district covers the northeastern and north central parts of the state, including Albuquerque and most of the Hispanic vote. Santa Fe, the small state capital and a city of old world charm, is here, as is Taos, which has attracted artists and hangers on since D. H. Lawrence came here to write in the 1920s.

The Democrats' problem in the 1st was mismatching candidate and district. In 1968 Anglo Congressman Thomas Morris was no match for Republican Manuel Lujan, Jr., son of a well known insurance man and political figure in Albuquerque. In 1972 Lujan became something of a national figure, as he seemed sometimes to get more TV exposure at the Republican national convention than Richard Nixon. As the only Republican major elected official of Spanish background, Lujan was given tube time by Republican strategists who were targetting Spanish-speaking voters, with considerable success in New Mexico and Texas as well. As a delegate, Lujan technically cast the lone convention vote for Pete McCloskey, but that was only because state law required the vote be cast, and Lujan was considered loyal enough to Nixon to be trusted to cast it.

The Nixon connection might be thought to have caused Lujan trouble in 1974, but it didn't. In fact, he actually increased his share of the vote from 56% in 1972 to 60% in 1974. One reason was the ineptitude of the compaign waged by his 1974 opponent, Lieutenant Governor Robert Mondragon; another was Lujan's own unstinting efforts. Of the four members of the New Mexico congressional delegation, he is probably the one with the most political savvy and drive.

New Mexico's 2d district includes most of Little Texas, the barren Rio Grande valley, the Navajo country around Gallup, and the Anglo mining town of Farmington in the state's northwest corner. Ancestrally, this is a Democratic district, but a conservative one—much like west Texas in its politics. One change of representation occurred in 1968, a year after the Pentagon closed down Walker Air Force Base near Roswell, then the largest city in the district (pop. 39,00). Within a year Roswell's population had dropped to 32,000, but not before the people there and elsewhere in the 2d had an opportunity to vote out Democratic Congressman E. S. Johnny Walker.

The winner of that election was conservative Republican Ed Foreman, who seems singlehandedly to be reviving a nineteenth century tradition of itinerant congressmen—if you lose a seat in one state, you move somewhere else and run again. In 1962 Foreman had captured the next door 16th district of Texas when the incumbent had been shown to have received a campaign contribution from Billie Sol Estes; two years later the conservative Republican was beaten. After his election in New Mexico, Foreman boasted that he was only the second person in this century to have won election from the House in two different states; in 1970, he gained the further distinction of being the only person in this century first elected and then defeated for reelection in two different states.

The man who beat him was Harold Runnels, a Democrat described as a "good old boy from Little Texas." That he is, and he serves as one of the hawkish members of the House Armed Services Committee. Runnels is not the most astute members of the House; indeed, he was named to *New Times's* list of the ten dumbest congressmen. In 1973 he announced that he had been purchasing documents from someone in the Pentagon because he could not obtain them through ordinary Committee channels—a bizarre little scandal that has never been resolved. It may, however, have had at least a tiny impact on the folks in the 2d district: in 1972 Runnels had won 72% of the vote, but in 1974—despite the general Democratic trend—he fell to a still robust 68%.

Census Data Pop. 1,016,000; 0.50% of U.S. total, 37th largest; Central city, 24%; suburban, 7%. Median family income, $7,845; 38th highest; families above $15,000: 15%; families below $3,000: 15%. Median years education, 12.2.

1974 Share of Federal Tax Burden $1,017,698,000; 0.38% of U.S. total, 39th largest.

1974 Share of Federal Outlays $2,031,613,000; 0.75% of U.S. total, 34th largest. Per capita federal spending, $2000.

DOD	$480,585,000	33d (0.70%)	HEW	$449,147,000	38th (0.48%)
AEC	$344,852,000	2d (11.32%)	HUD	$5,863,000	37th (0.60%)
NASA	$6,346,000	22d (0.21%)	VA	$92,991,000	38th (0.68%)
DOT	$87,075,000	33d (1.03%)	EPA	$6,531,000	47th (0.21%)
DOC	$7,005,000	32d (0.43%)	RevS	$38,820,000	36th (0.64%)
DOI	$167,012,000	6th (6.78%)	Int.	$44,491,000	35th (0.22%)
USDA	$128,307,000	35th (1.03%)	Other	$172,588,000	

Economic Base Agriculture, notably cattle, dairy products, hay and cotton lint; finance, insurance and real estate; oil and gas extraction, especially oil and gas field services; metal mining, especially uranium-radium-vanadium ores; food and kindred products; tourism.

Political Line-up Governor, Jerry Apodaca (D). Senators, Joseph M. Montoya (D) and Peter V. Domenici (R). Representatives, 2 (1 D and 1 R). State Senate (26 D, 13 R, and 3 vac.); State House (51 D and 19 R).

The Voters

Registration 504,197 Total. 324,975 D (64%); 147,773 R (29%); 29,329 Declined to state (6%); 2,120 Minor parties (–).
Median voting age 40.
Employment profile White collar, 51%. Blue collar, 30%. Service, 15%. Farm, 4%.
Ethnic groups Black, 2%. Indian, 7%. Spanish, 40%. Total foreign stock, 9%.

Presidential vote

1972	Nixon (R)	235,606	(63%)
	McGovern (D)	141,084	(37%)
1968	Nixon (R)	169,692	(52%)
	Humphrey (D)	130,081	(40%)
	Wallace (AI)	25,737	(8%)

1972 Democratic Presidential Primary

McGovern	51,011	(33%)
Wallace	44,843	(29%)
Humphrey	39,768	(26%)
others	17,671	(12%)

1972 Republican Presidential Primary

Nixon	49,067	(88%)
McCloskey	3,367	(6%)
others	3,035	(6%)

Sen. Joseph M. Montoya (D) Elected 1964, seat up 1976; b. Sept. 24, 1915, Pena Blanca; home, Santa Fe; Regis Col., 1931, 1933–34, Georgetown U., J.D. 1938; Catholic.

Career Practicing atty., 1939–64; N.M. House of Reps., 1936–40, Maj. Ldr., 1939–40; N.M. Senate, 1940–46, 1954–55, Maj. Whip, 1945–46; Lt. Gov. of N.M., 1947–51, 1955–57; U.S. House of Reps., 1957–65.

Offices 5229 DSOB, 202-224-5521. Also 9013 U.S. Courthouse, Albuquerque 87107, 505-766-2551.

Committees

Appropriations (9th). Subcommittees: Defense; Interior; Labor and HEW; Public Works; Treasury, U.S. Postal Service and General Government (Chairman).

Public Works (3d). Subcommittees: Environmental Pollution; Economic Development (Chairman); Transportation.

Joint Committee on Atomic Energy (4th, Senate Side). Subcommittees: Agreements for Cooperation; ERDA, Nuclear Energy; Legislation (Chairman); National Security.

Group Ratings

	ADA	COPE	LWV	RIPON	NFU	LCV	CFA	NAB	NSI	ACA
1974	65	60	67	33	76	50	44	25	20	22
1973	47	91	63	35	100	–	54	–	–	24
1972	45	90	70	35	88	42	90	40	60	24

Key Votes

1) No-Knock	AGN	8) Gov Abortn Aid	AGN	15) Consumer Prot Agy	FOR
2) Busing	ABS	9) Cut Mil Brass	FOR	16) Forced Psych Tests	AGN
3) No Fault	AGN	10) Gov Limousine	AGN	17) Fed Campaign Subs	FOR
4) F-111	AGN	11) RR Featherbed	FOR	18) Rhod Chrome Ban	ABS
5) Death Penalty	FOR	12) Handgun License	AGN	19) Open Legis Meetings	AGN
6) Foreign Aid	AGN	13) Less Troop Abrd	FOR	20) Strikers Food Stmps	FOR
7) Filibuster	ABS	14) Resume Turk Aid	AGN	21) Gov Info Disclosure	FOR

Election Results

1970 general:	Joseph M. Monotoya (D)	151,486	(53%)
	Anderson Carter (R)	135,004	(47%)
1970 primary:	Joseph M. Montoya (D)	85,285	(73%)
	Richard B. Edwards (D)	31,381	(27%)
1964 General	Joseph M. Montoya (D)	178,209	(55%)
	Edwin L. Mechem (R)	147,562	(45%)

Sen. Pete V. Domenici (R) Elected 1972, seat up 1978; b. May 7, 1932, Albuquerque; home, Albuquerque; U. of Albuquerque, 1950–52, U. of N.M., B.S. 1954, Denver U., LL.B. 1958; Catholic.

Career Practicing atty., 1958–72; Mbr., Albuquerque City Commission, 1966–68, Mayor Ex-Officio, 1967–68; Repub. nominee for Gov., 1970.

Offices 1251 DSOB, 202-224-6621. Also New Postal Bldg., Santa Fe 87501, 505-988-6511, and Fed. Bldg., & U.S. Courthouse, Rm. 10013, Albuquerque 87103, 505-766-3481.

Committees

Aeronautical and Space Sciences (2d).

Budget (6th).

Public Works (5th). Subcommittees: Environmental Pollution, Panel on Materials Policy; Economic Development; Water Resources; Transportation; Disaster Relief.

Group Ratings

	ADA	COPE	LWV	RIPON	NFU	LCV	CFA	NAB	NSI	ACA
1974	25	27	100	55	56	25	38	75	100	56
1973	10	18	40	60	38	–	8	–	–	89

Key Votes

1) No-Knock	AGN	8) Gov Abortn Aid	AGN	15) Consumer Prot Agy	FOR
2) Busing	AGN	9) Cut Mil Brass	AGN	16) Forced Psych Tests	AGN
3) No Fault	AGN	10) Gov Limousine	FOR	17) Fed Campaign Subs	FOR
4) F-111	AGN	11) RR Featherbed	AGN	18) Rhod Chrome Ban	AGN
5) Death Penalty	FOR	12) Handgun License	AGN	19) Open Legis Meetings	AGN
6) Foreign Aid		13) Less Troop Abrd	FOR	20) Strikers Food Stmps	AGN
7) Filibuster	AGN	14) Resume Turk Aid	FOR	21) Gov Info Disclosure	FOR

Election Results

1972 general:	Pete V. Domenici (R)	204,253	(54%)	($517,310)
	Jack Daniels (D)	173,815	(46%)	($496,980)
1972 primary:	Pete V. Domenici (R)	37,337	(64%)	
	David F. Cargo (R)	12,522	(21%)	
	Five others (R)	8,916	(15%)	

Gov. Jerry Apodaca (D) Elected 1974, term expires Jan. 1979; b. Oct. 3, 1934, Las Cruces; U. of N.M., B.S.E. 1957; Catholic.

Career High school teacher and coach; Insurance, real estate, and shoe retailing businesses; N.M. Senate, 1967–74.

Offices Executive-Legislative Bldg., State Capitol, Santa Fe 87501. 505-827-2221.

Election Results

1974 general	Jerry Apodaca (D)	164,177	(51%)
	Joseph R. Skeen (R)	160,430	(49%)
1974 primary:	Jerry Apodaca (D)	35,090	(24%)
	Odis Echols, Jr. (D)	25,760	(17%)
	Bobby M. Mayfield (D)	22,806	(15%)
	Two Others (D)	19,505	(13%)

◆ ◆ ◆ ◆ ◆

FIRST DISTRICT

Census Data Pop. 511,135. Central city, 48%; suburban, 14%. Median family income, $8,187; families above $15,000: 18%; families below $3,000: 15%. Median years education, 12.3.

The Voters

Median voting age 40.
Employment profile White collar, 57%. Blue collar, 26%. Service, 15%. Farm, 2%.
Ethnic groups Black, 1%. Indian, 3%. Spanish, 49%. Total foreign stock, 7%.

Presidential vote

	1972	Nixon (R)	125,326	(59%)
		McGovern (D)	85,996	(41%)
	1968	Nixon (R)	91,729	(52%)
		Humphrey (D)	75,328	(43%)
		Wallace (AI)	7,850	(5%)

Rep. Manuel Lujan, Jr. (R) Elected 1968; b. May 12, 1928, San Ildefonso; home, Albuquerque; St. Mary's Col., San Francisco, Cal., Col. of Santa Fe, B.S. 1950; Catholic.

Career Insurance agent; Vice Chm., N.M. Repub. Party.

Offices 1323 LHOB, 202-225-6316. Also Rm. 10001 Fed. Bldg., 500 Gold Ave., S.W., Albuquerque 87103, 505-766-2538.

Committees

Interior and Insular Affairs (5th). Subcommittees: Energy and the Environment; Water and Power Resources.

Joint Committee on Atomic Energy (2d, House Side). Subcommittees: Communities; ERDA, Nuclear Energy; National Security.

Group Ratings

	ADA	COPE	LWV	RIPON	NFU	LCV	CFA	NAB	NSI	ACA
1974	32	25	40	17	73	27	30	91	50	58
1973	23	30	22	44	47	31	29	–	–	76
1972	13	40	63	67	50	47	100	100	63	50

Key Votes

1) Foreign Aid	AGN	6) Gov Abortn Aid	AGN	11) Pub Cong Election $	AGN
2) Busing	AGN	7) Coed Phys Ed	AGN	12) Turkish Arms Cutoff	FOR
3) ABM	FOR	8) Pov Lawyer Gag	ABS	13) Youth Camp Regs	AGN
4) B-1 Bomber	ABS	9) Pub Trans Sub	AGN	14) Strip Mine Veto	ABS
5) Nerve Gas	AGN	10) EZ Voter Regis	ABS	15) Farm Bill Veto	FOR

Election Results

1974 general:	Manuel Lujan, Jr. (R)	106,268	(60%)	($150,825)
	R. A. Mondragon (D)	71,968	(40%)	($113,847)
1974 primary:	Manuel Lujan, Jr. (R), unopposed			
1972 general:	Manuel Lujan, Jr. (R)	118,403	(56%)	($212,093)
	Eugene Gallegos (D)	94,239	(44%)	($126,219)

◆ ◆ ◆ ◆ ◆

SECOND DISTRICT

Census Data Pop. 504,865. Central city, 0%; suburban, 0%. Median family income, $7,551; families above $15,000: 12%; families below $3,000: 16%. Median years education, 12.0.

The Voters

Median voting age 40.
Employment profile White collar, 45%. Blue collar, 35%. Service, 14%. Farm, 6%.
Ethnic groups Black, 2%. Indian, 11%. Spanish, 31%. Total foreign stock, 10%.

Presidential vote

1972	Nixon (R)	110,280	(67%)
	McGovern (D)	55,088	(33%)
1968	Nixon (R)	77,963	(52%)
	Humphrey (D)	54,753	(36%)
	Wallace (AI)	17,887	(12%)

Rep. Harold Runnels (D) Elected 1970; b. Mar. 17, 1924, Dallas, Tex.; home, Lovington; Cameron St. Agric. Col., B.S. 1943; Baptist.

Career Air Force, WWII; Employee of FBI; Mgr., Magnolia Amusement Co.; Partner, Southland Supply Co., 1952; Founder, Runnels Mud Co. and RunCo Acidizing and Fracturing Co.; N.M. Senate, 1960–70.

Offices 1535 LHOB, 202-225-2365. Also Suite A, McCrory Bldg., Lovington 88260, 505-396-2252.

Committees

Armed Services (17th). Subcommittees: Military Compensation; Research and Development.

Budget (15th).

Interior and Insular Affairs (16th). Subcommittees: Mines and Mining; Public Lands; Water and Power Resources.

Group Ratings

	ADA	COPE	LWV	RIPON	NFU	LCV	CFA	NAB	NSI	ACA
1974	17	33	9	20	54	13	0	73	67	64
1973	36	67	27	38	94	13	14	–	–	50
1972	25	55	27	14	71	37	0	88	100	91

Key Votes

1) Foreign Aid	AGN	6) Gov Abortn Aid	AGN	11) Pub Cong Election $	AGN
2) Busing	AGN	7) Coed Phys Ed	AGN	12) Turkish Arms Cutoff	FOR
3) ABM	FOR	8) Pov Lawyer Gag	FOR	13) Youth Camp Regs	AGN
4) B-1 Bomber	FOR	9) Pub Trans Sub	AGN	14) Strip Mine Veto	FOR
5) Nerve Gas	AGN	10) EZ Voter Regis	FOR	15) Farm Bill Veto	AGN

Election Results

1974 general:	Harold Runnels (D)	90,127	(68%)	($59,733)
	Donald W. Trubey (R)	43,045	(32%)	($22,131)
1974 primary:	Harold Runnels (D), unopposed			
1972 general:	Harold Runnels (D)	116,152	(72%)	($91,784)
	George E. Presson (R)	44,784	(28%)	($14,810)

NEW YORK

To understand New York politics and to understand the conventional wisdom about New York politics are two different things, and to comprehend the difference one must go back to the days when the latter was created. A good place to start is 1910, when the population of immigrant-swollen Manhattan was 2.3 million (as compared to 1.5 million today). Early to mid-twentieth century New York politics was shaped in almost every respect by the immigrants in a state where even today one-third of the people were either born abroad or had at least one foreign-born parent. It was the immigrant population that provided the real strength behind New York's political machines; Tammany Hall, the Manhattan machine, was led by Irish-Americans up through the 1940s and Italian-Americans thereafter, and the votes it and its counterparts in the Bronx and Brooklyn could deliver were mainly those of Irish and Italian immigrants. Jewish immigrants never liked Catholic dominated Tammany. In the 1910s they were electing Socialists to Congress; and in the 1930s and 1940s the American Labor and Liberal Parties were created so that Jewish immigrants who didn't read much English could vote for Roosevelt and LaGuardia on the same party lever.

New York City was then (and is now) about one quarter Jewish, and it was this leftish, anti-Tammany vote that became the fulcrum in state elections. In the twenties and thirties the progressive policies of Al Smith, Roosevelt, and Lehman helped win those Democrats the Governorship. (It is symptomatic of New York pundits' homage to the past that the New York *Times* continues to editorialize about the great tradition of these three Governors, none of whom has served in that office for more than thirty years.) In the forties and fifties, progressive policies—which is to say basic acceptance of the New Deal—helped to win enough Jewish votes for statewide victories for Governors Thomas E. Dewey and Nelson Rockefeller, as well as Senators Irving Ives (1947–59), Jacob Javits (1957–   ), and Kenneth Keating (1959–65). Indeed, such a strategy produced victories for Rockefeller as late as 1966 and Javits up through 1968.

From this basic perception of the New York electorate—machine Democrats and WASPy Upstate and wealthy Republicans balanced off evenly, with a decisive, leftish bloc of primarily Jewish immigrants making the choice—grew whole national political strategies. Apparently on the theory that all big states were like New York (although none of the rest have nearly so large a Jewish population), the idea became established that a Republican couldn't win the Presidency without appealing to such liberal independent blocs, and that they couldn't lose if they did so successfully. (Unfortunately for that notion, Dewey in 1948 and Nixon in 1960 ran such campaigns, and lost.) Liberal Democrats defended the Electoral College on the ground that it gives disproportionate leverage to minority groups in big states (i.e., Jews in New York).

Such is the conventional wisdom that developed about New York—and national—politics. It became fully articulated in the 1950s, just as the basic demographic conditions which had produced it were vanishing. For New York is no longer a state dominated by minorities as it was during the New Deal when a clear majority of its residents were either born in a foreign country or had a parent who was. (The figure now is down to about 30%.) Indeed, of the minorities that vote like left-leaning blocs these days, which is to say blacks and Spanish speaking people, New York has less than its share. New York City—all five boroughs, not just Manhattan—is one of our few major central cities which remains, for all its problems, a majority white Anglo middle class. By the same token, that middle class is subject to bouts of conservativism: remember that the liberal Mayor John Lindsay did not get a majority of the vote in New York City either time he ran, and that liberal Senator Jacob Javits has not received a statewide absolute majority since 1962. Chicago and even Los Angeles gave George McGovern higher percentages than New York City did in 1972, and New York state gave him no better a percentage than did that radical haven, the state of Iowa. The basic liberal Republican premise has been disproved: whatever else he did, Richard Nixon showed that a conservative Republican could win the Presidency, indeed could even win New York.

There was a time, as recently as twenty years ago, when there was a sizeable Irish machine vote left in parts of Manhattan, along Tenth Avenue on the West Side or Second Avenue on the East Side. That vote is gone, and the Catholic masses who once jammed Manhattan tenements have now—or their children and grandchildren have—long since moved to the farther reaches of Brooklyn, the Bronx, and Queens, and from there into the suburbs, even into counties (Orange, Dutchess) beyond the limits of the New York metropolitan area. Once these people all voted Democratic, for some coal at Christmas, or a job with the city; now they are a major conservative force, at least in most years.

What this has meant is the disappearance of the political machines as a significant electoral—which is to say vote-getting—force. There is still plenty of talk about which candidate the bosses are supporting, but it scarcely matters; the public makes its decision based on its own knowledge of the candidates, even if that comes mainly from television commercials, not because Meade Esposito or Pat Cunningham recommended some candidate. New York City's Democratic machines are now in another business entirely, the business of brokering judicial patronage. Due to rickety old laws, they still control Democratic judicial nominations, which are tantamount to election, and so they have a good deal to say about who gets appointed guardian, who gets the assessor's fee, who writes certain insurance contracts, etc. It is a tawdry little business which victimizes any innocent unfortunate enough to have dealings with the judicial system; but it has nothing to do with bosses jamming candidates and officeholders down the public's throat—something the current crop of bosses patently lack the ability to do. The classic work of political bosses is delivering votes from the ranks of the underprivileged who might otherwise not find their way to the polls. It is a measure of the vitality of the Democratic machines here that New York's blacks and Spanish speaking citizens have the lowest level of voter participation of any similar groups in the United States; they are less likely to vote than the blacks of the Mississippi Delta or the peons of the Lower Rio Grande valley of Texas.

If you want to find bosses in New York politics, the place to look is not in the Democratic City, but in Republican Nassau County and the Liberal Party. Nassau is run by a picturesque figure named Joseph Margiotta, who once reportedly told Bob Haldeman he would cancel a Nixon rally in Nassau unless he, Margiotta, and not some kid advance man, determined who would sit where on the dais. Margiotta runs an organization with a budget of more than $1 million a year, in comparison to the less than $100,000 figure spent by the fearsome Brooklyn Democratic machine. As for the Liberal Party, its whole *raison de'être* has long since vanished; the modern day equivalent of anti-Tammany, pro-Roosevelt voters are quite capable of splitting tickets themselves if they want to. The Liberal Party today is primarily in the business of finding patronage jobs and judgeships for the small coterie who run its affairs. Its proudest recent boast is that it provided a ballot line for John Lindsay when he lost the 1969 Republican primary, and so kept him in office; which is all very nice, except that Lindsay could have gotten on the ballot anyway, and probably would have got precisely the same number of votes whether or not he was the Liberal candidate.

The 1974 gubernatorial race nicely demolished some New York political myths—and demolished as well a basic strategy that had been working well for years for the Republicans. At the heart of the strategy was the convention system of nominating statewide candidates. Nelson Rockefeller several times vetoed state primary laws, partly because he suspected it might be difficult for him to win a primary, and partly because he wanted to saddle the Democrats with a convention. For any way you apportion the votes, the Democrats' state convention ends up with a majority or near majority controlled by the so-called bosses; and any candidate that they nominate could immediately be labelled by Republicans and disgruntled Democratic rivals—and there usually were some of them—as the bosses' candidate. Such was the script that had won for Rockefeller and Kenneth Keating in 1958; it was useful again in 1966.

By 1970, Rockefeller had finally given in to the advocates of a primary to the extent of allowing a loser at the convention to challenge the winner. This was even better for the Republicans: if the convention winner won the subsequent primary, he could be tarred as the creature of the bosses; if the convention loser won, he was the insurgent who had irrevocably split the Democratic primary. To make certain the Democrats wouldn't have time to recover from either charge, the Republicans pushed the primary date back to September in 1974.

By that time, Rockefeller had resigned the Governorship and had been replaced by Malcolm Wilson, the polysyllabic conservative who had seemed type cast for the office he held for 15 years, Lieutenant Governor. Wilson was the kind of man, philosophically and temperamentally, who dithered and finally refused to impose the alternate day gas system during the 1974 shortage because he disliked coercing people; New Yorkers, used to Governors who flaunted their achievements, were not amused.

Meanwhile, the Democratic nomination seemed sewed up by Howard Samuels. An unsuccessful candidate three times, Samuels had become a huge celebrity as the head of New York City's Off Track Betting System, and for the most part he seemed to be favorably regarded. With his initial strength in the polls, he got the support of the machine bosses and also of the New Democratic Coalition, the arm of the reform movement that has occasional minor effect on election outcomes. But while political reporters combed Upstate towns to find out how many Democratic county chairmen were backing Samuels, the real campaign was going on elsewhere—in the offices of a few campaign consultants and of a wealthy oil man named Edward Carey.

Carey's brother Hugh had been a Congressman from Brooklyn for 14 years, a generally liberal and thoroughly likeable Irishman who kept winning in a conservatively inclined, heavily Catholic district, and who had occasionally dabbled with the idea of running for higher office. This time it was for real. Edward Carey put up more than $1 million, and the Carey campaign hired media consultant David Garth. The result was a saturation TV ad campaign. It exploited the favorable aspects of Carey's personality, the fact that he looked like an Irish cop and voted like a Manhattan liberal, and by inference exploited the public's lack of enthusiasm for Samuels as a person. Samuels's support turned out to be as shallow as it was broad, and by primary day in September Carey won 61% of the vote—a result that so utterly confounded the experts as to prove, once and for all, their lack of expertise.

The usual Republican strategy at this point would be to label Carey, as McGovern had been labelled in 1972, as the candidate who was splitting the Democratic Party. The trouble was the label didn't fit—at all. On the contrary, Carey was just the kind of candidate Democrats in New York should have been looking for for years: a Catholic with 12 children, undisputably honest, with friendly ties to both regulars and reformers, and a good congressional record to boot. (He had been a big supporter of revenue sharing on the House Ways and Means Committee.) Malcolm Wilson, on the other hand, was burdened with the unpopularity of the Rockefeller record without the kind of resources—on the order of $10 million—Rockefeller had been accustomed to use every four years to change people's minds about the kind of job he had done. The result was the first Democratic gubernatorial victory here in twenty years, a Carey victory by a smashing 58–42 margin.

New York has a reputation, dating back from the 1920s and a bit shopworn these days, of progressive state government. But one is not especially surprised at people's cynicism here when one considers that Nelson Rockefeller, who might have been expected to be parsimonious, had doubled and redoubled state spending, and increased taxes; while Hugh Carey, who might have been expected to be a free spending Democrat, turns out to be a disciple of economy and fiscal discipline. Part of the problem is that some of Rockefeller's pet projects, like the ambitious Urban Development Corporation, have come crashing down in the year or two since he left Albany (the UDC defaulted on its bonds); while others, like the giant Albany Mall Rockefeller built, impose a heavy burden on state finances. In any case, there have been a rather large number of complaints about Carey since he has been in, coupled with continued comments that he would be as good a presidential candidate—and President—as the Democrats have got; the combination reflects an assessment of the difficulty of the job.

It could be worse. Abraham Beame, elected Mayor of New York by white middle-class civil servants who wanted a respite from the social activism—and incompetence—of John Lindsay, now finds it necessary to cut city spending so much that some of those civil servants (there are more than 300,000 of them) are losing their jobs. Reputed to be a fiscal wizard, Beame has presided over the bankruptcy of New York City; the city has enough cash to pay off its bond holders only because it has ceded to the state power to make many basic fiscal decisions.

The epitome of liberal New York Republicanism—indeed its last major political survivor today—is Senator Jacob Javits. In a poll of Senate aides conducted by Ralph Nader's Congress Watch, Javits was rated the brightest Senator and the second most influential. The influence derives not from any kind of popularity or capacity for camaraderie; Javits is considered personally rather unpleasant by most Senators. Nor is it due in any respect to leverage provided by party politics; in 1975 Javits was beaten for a party leadership position by the less than imposing Carl Curtis of Nebraska. Seniority helps, and Javits is now the ranking Republican on the Labor and Public Welfare Committee, and a senior member of Foreign Relations and Government Operations. But his real secrets are brains and hard work. He understands complex legislation like the pension reform bill he shepherded through in 1974, and can argue abstruse points almost mechanically on measures like the war powers act, which he sponsored in 1973. Hard work, solid preparation, analytical ability—these qualities, almost alone, have made Javits a power in the Senate.

He is not, however, as much of an electoral power among New York voters as generally thought. In his early career he was an amazing vote-getter, winning as a Republican a congressional seat in upper Manhattan, beating Franklin D. Roosevelt, Jr., for New York Attorney General in 1954, and beating Mayor Robert Wagner for the Senate in 1956. Since then, he has been winning by large margins basically because his opposition has been split between liberal Democrats and Conservative Party candidates. In 1968, Javits had slightly less than half the statewide vote; in 1974, only 46%—hardly showings of great strength.

In the latter race there was talk that he was in danger of being beaten by Ramsey Clark—the former Attorney General, butt of Nixon-Agnew oratory, and surprise winner of the Democratic primary (mainly because the other two candidates scarcely spent a dime on media). Clark came out of his primary with momentum and attention of the electrate, and impressed many by his refusal to take contributions over $100; he embarrassed Javits by calling on him to disqualify himself from voting on the Rockefeller vice presidential nomination because he had received a $5,000 contribution from Rockefeller. On more substantive issues, Clark argued that Javits hemmed and hawed too much, that during the Watergate scandal, for example, he was so hesitant to comment that he was taking no position on Nixon, while even his Conservative colleague, James Buckley, was calling for the President's resignation.

There is considerable truth to Clark's criticism. Javits is an inherently cautious man who seems to believe that, as a Jew from New York, it ill behooves him to get too far out in front on issues. If he has the solid support and gratitude from organized labor for his work on social legislation, he also is a favorite of the giants in the securities industry for the way he looks after Wall Street's interests. Throughout his public career, Clark if anything erred in the direction of too much candor, and the contest provided a nice contrast of styles as well as differences on at least a few issues.

The voters' verdict was an endorsement for neither. Clark won only 38% of the vote, the weakest showing of any Democratic senatorial candidate in 1974. But that put him within a few hundred thousand votes of beating Javits, who won only 46%. In none of New York's three basic regions, the City, the suburbs, or Upstate, did Javits have an absolute majority—a negative showing, one must conclude, for a man who has been running statewide races here for twenty years. The fact is that the kind of liberal Republicanism Javits has embodied has never had a particularly large vote base, and it is now smaller than ever. Javits probably never could have won a Republican primary (he has never had to face one since he ran for Congress), and few voters feel a strong commitment to him. He turns 72 in 1976, and though he seems to be in excellent health the political, if not the chronological facts, indicate that he is almost certainly serving his last Senate term.

If Javits's recent showings demonstrate the weakness of the liberal Republican strategy, the election of New York's other Senator, James Buckley, in 1970, shows how deeply this strategy was resented. Buckley was the Conservative candidate against Javits in 1968, winning 17% of the vote—more than anyone had expected and testimony to his appeal as a reasonable, affable candidate as well as a conservative ideologue. In 1970, the major party contest was between Charles Goodell, a Republican Congressman appointed to fill the vacancy caused by the death of Robert Kennedy, and Richard Ottinger, a Westchester County Congressman whose primary victory was due entirely to a saturation television ad campaign. Goodell was originally a conservative and one of those who had engineered the elevation of Gerald Ford to the Minority Leadership in 1965; but on his appointment to statewide office, he had taken liberal positions on many key issues, most notably the war in Vietnam, of which he soon became one of the most outspoken opponents. Ottinger's record was conventionally liberal, with a special emphasis on environmental issues.

Buckley's slogan capitalized on the fact that the major parties had, again as they just about always did, presented New York voters with a choice between two similarly liberal candidates: "Isn't it time *we* had a Senator?" The "we" included most of the 45% of the electorate that voted for Nixon in 1968, or the 47% who voted for him in 1960, or, for that matter, the 42% who would vote for Malcolm Wilson in 1974. With New York's Republicans refusing to allow primaries which might nominate such candidates, or to name one at a convention, this forty-odd percent had been unrepresented for years, and they were mad. It is important to remember also that Buckley's victory came just a year after the second minority election of Mayor John Lindsay. The Catholic middle classes of New York, convinced that this Manhattan Mayor saved all his sympathy for the black and poor and the WASPy and rich, hated Lindsay with the ferver green Irish used to hate orange; and Buckley's constituency was very much a Catholic one, based in New York City and especially in the suburbs. The Buckley candidacy picked up steam when Nixon and Rockefeller political operatives passed the word that it was all right to support the Conservative Buckley; and the signal was flashed for all to see when Vice President Agnew attended a Buckley dinner in New York and called Goodell the Christine Jorgensen of the Republican Party. That told conservative Republicans it was fine to vote for Buckley, and it gave Goodell a boost in support from liberal Democrats—a boost that robbed Ottinger of just enough votes to guarantee Buckley's 39% victory.

Buckley's seat is up in 1976. With New York's Republican Party having moved rapidly to the right since his victory, there is no doubt that he will be the Republican and Conservative nominee. As a Senator, he has been a quiet, principled conservative who is not considered a major mover of things legislatively. He professes an interest in conservation, but has far from a perfect record as far as environmentalists are concerned. But the most significant point of Buckley's record from an electoral perspective is that he simply has not been doing the kind of things a Senator can do to get himself reelected in a hostile constituency. He has not tended assiduously to casework, nor has he spent great amounts of time talking to voters around the state.

But the biggest problem for Buckley is not that, nor is it what the Democrats might do—there are a dozen Democrats who would like the nomination, and it is entirely unclear at this writing who will get it. (There is also a Republican, 23d district Congressman Peter Peyser, who wants to challenge him in a primary.) His greatest problem is that his core constituency has disappeared. The Catholic middle class in the late sixties and early seventies was deeply disenchanted with the liberal Democrats. These people felt that liberals favored blacks too much, that they were too sympathetic to bearded peace demonstrators and cared not at all for the needs and desires of middle class people like themselves. In New York, this feeling was probably more pronounced than anywhere, because of the personality and prominence of John Lindsay—a figure who totally polarized this electorate.

But the alienated voters for whom Lindsay and others represented liberals and liberalism have now been turned off even more by the Republicans. The Richard Nixon who assured them over and over again that their values, not those of the blacks or white liberals, were the right ones, proved to be an utter fraud; and these people are not about to forgive the party which nominated him five times for national office. The 1974 returns show a virtual disappearance of the conservative vote which was so important in New York in 1970 and 1972. Suffolk County, for example, a heavily Catholic, fast-growing suburban area on Long Island, delivered an absolute majority for Buckley in 1970, the only New York county to do so; in 1974 it went for Hugh Carey for Governor. Where Buckley, as the conservative candidate, got 40% of the vote in the New York metropolitan area in 1970, Malcolm Wilson, as the Republican-Conservative incumbent, got only 38% in 1974. Buckley's minority showing was enough to make him a Senator in a three-way race; but from the look of things it will be hard for him even to match it, and it appears very much as if he will have only one significant opponent.

The Conservative Party which nominated Buckley at that time was probably the most idealistic and vital political force in the state. Established as recently as 1962, it had taken it only eight years to elect a Senator of its own. But since that time the sort of cynicism which is the essence of the patronage-hungry Liberal Party seems to have affected the Conservatives also. In 1973, they nominated for Mayor Mario Biaggi, a Congressman and former policeman, and a Democrat. At first he led the polls in this crime-fearing city, but when it was revealed that he had lied about his testimony before a grand jury, Biaggi's campaign suddenly collapsed; the Conservatives, alas, were stuck with him on their ticket. Since then, the increasing conservatism of the Republican Party has made the Conservative organization a bit extraneous—just as the Democratic Party has indeed become more liberal than the Liberals (who were hawks on the Vietnam war just about all the way).

Census Data Pop. 18,241,266; 9.01% of U.S. total, 2nd largest; Central city, 51%; suburban, 35%. Median family income, $10,609; 11th highest; families above $15,000: 26%; families below $3,000: 8%. Median years education, 12.1.

1974 Share of Federal Tax Burden $26,647,621,000; 9.95% of U.S. total, 2d largest.

1974 Share of Federal Outlays $32,780,502,000; 12.14% of U.S. total, 1st largest. Per capita federal spending, $1802.

DOD	$3,610,529,000	3d (5.27%)	HEW	$10,228,564,000	1st (11.02%)
AEC	$174,256,000	5th (5.72%)	HUD	$64,330,000	4th (6.60%)
NASA	$67,865,000	9th (2.29%)	VA	$1,061,056,000	2d (7.75%)
DOT	$608,280,000	2d (7.18%)	EPA	$836,014,000	1st (26.58%)
DOC	$168,697,000	4th (10.46%)	RevS	$667,899,000	1st (11.15%)
DOI	$32,786,000	20th (1.33%)	Int.	$10,053,606,000	1st (48.89%)
USDA	$1,122,540,000	1st (9.01%)	Other	$4,084,080,000	

Economic Base Finance, insurance and real estate; apparel and other textile products, especially women's and misses' outerwear; electrical equipment and supplies, especially communication equipment; printing and publishing, especially commercial printing and newspapers; machinery, especially office and computing machines; food and kindred products, especially bakery products and beverages; agriculture, especially dairy products, cattle, eggs, and greenhouse products.

Political Line-up Governor, Hugh L. Carey (D). Senators, Jacob K. Javits (R) and James L. Buckley (C-R). Representatives, 39 (27 D and 12 R). State Senate (34 R and 26 D); State Assembly (87 D and 63 R).

The Voters

Registration 7,401,595 Total. 3,620,429 D (49%); 2,775,410 R (37%); 769,392 Blank, Missing, and Void (10%); 121,473 Conservative (2%); 114,891 Liberal (2%).
Median voting age 44.
Employment profile White collar, 55%. Blue collar, 31%. Service, 13%. Farm, 1%.
Ethnic groups Black, 12%. Spanish, 5%. Total foreign stock, 33%. Italy, 7%; USSR, Poland, Germany, 3% each; Ireland, UK, Canada, 2% each; Austria, 1%.

Presidential vote

1972	Nixon (R)	....	4,192,778	(59%)
	McGovern (D)	....	2,951,084	(41%)
1968	Nixon (R)	....	3,007,932	(45%)
	Humphrey (D)	....	3,378,470	(50%)
	Wallace (AI)	....	358,864	(5%)

Sen. Jacob K. Javits (R) Elected 1956, seat up 1980; b. May 18, 1904, New York City; home, New York City; Columbia U., NYU, LL.B. 1926; Jewish.

Career Practicing atty., 1927–41, 1945–46; Special Asst. to Chf. of U.S. Army Chemical Warfare Svc., 1941–42; Army, WWII; U.S. House of Reps., 1947–55; Atty. Gen. of N.Y. State, 1955–57.

Offices 321 RSOB, 202-224-6542. Also 110 E. 45th St., New York 10017, 212–867-7777, and 445 Broadway, Albany 12210, 518-472-6182.

Committees

Labor and Public Welfare (Ranking Member). Subcommittees: Alcoholism and Narcotics; Education; Employment, Poverty, and Migratory Labor; Health; Labor; Special Subcommittee on Arts and Humanities.

Foreign Relations (2d). Subcommittees: Arms Control, International Organizations and Security Agreements; European Affairs; Foreign Assistance and Economic Policy; Personnel; Western Hemisphere Affairs.

Government Operations (2d). Subcommittees: Oversight Procedures; Executive Reorganization and Government Research; Permanent Subcommittee on Investigations.

Joint Economic Committee (Ranking Member, Senate Side). Subcommittees: Consumer Economics; Economic Growth; Economic Progress; International Economics; Urban Affairs.

Group Ratings

	ADA	COPE	LWV	RIPON	NFU	LCV	CFA	NAB	NSI	ACA
1974	89	82	100	85	100	94	100	22	33	0
1973	79	78	90	82	94	–	80	–	–	8
1972	80	90	100	92	80	72	100	42	20	15

Key Votes

1) No-Knock	AGN	8) Gov Abortn Aid	FOR	15) Consumer Prot Agy	FOR
2) Busing	FOR	9) Cut Mil Brass	AGN	16) Forced Psych Tests	ABS
3) No Fault	FOR	10) Gov Limousine	FOR	17) Fed Campaign Subs	FOR
4) F-111	FOR	11) RR Featherbed	FOR	18) Rhod Chrome Ban	FOR
5) Death Penalty	AGN	12) Handgun License	FOR	19) Open Legis Meetings	AGN
6) Foreign Aid	FOR	13) Less Troop Abrd	AGN	20) Strikers Food Stmps	ABS
7) Filibuster	AGN	14) Resume Turk Aid	AGN	21) Gov Info Disclosure	FOR

Election Results

1974 general:	Jacob K. Javits (R-L)	....	2,340,188	(46%)	($1,090,437)
	Ramsey Clark (D)	....	1,973,781	(38%)	($855,576)
	Barbara A. Keating (C)	....	822,584	(16%)	($192,462)
1974 primary:	Jacob K. Javits (R-L), unopposed				
1968 general:	Jacob K. Javits (R-L)	....	3,269,772	(50%)	
	Paul O'Dwyer (D)	....	2,150,695	(33%)	
	James L. Buckley (C)	....	1,139,402	(17%)	

Sen. James L. Buckley (C-R) Elected 1970, seat up 1976; b. Mar. 9, 1923, New York City; home, New York City; Yale U., B.A. 1943, LL.B. 1949; Catholic.

Career Navy, WWII; Practicing atty., 1949–53; V.P. of Catawba Corp., 1953–70; Cons. Party nominee for U.S. Senate, 1968.

Offices 304 RSOB, 202-224-4451. Also 110 E. 45th St., Suite 400, New York 10017, 212-697-3000, and O'Brien Fed. Bldg., Pearl St. & Clinton Ave., Albany 12207, 518-449-1390.

Committees

Budget (4th).

Commerce (5th). Subcommittees: The Consumer; Environment; Foreign Commerce and Tourism; Oceans and Atmosphere; Surface Transportation; Special Subcommittee to Study Transportation on the Great Lakes-St. Lawrence Seaway.

Public Works (6th). Subcommittees: Environmental Pollution, Panel on Environmental Science and Technology; Water Resources; Transportation; Disaster Relief; Buildings and Grounds.

Joint Committee on Atomic Energy (4th, Senate Side). Subcommittees: Communities; Environment and Safety; National Security.

Group Ratings

	ADA	COPE	LWV	RIPON	NFU	LCV	CFA	NAB	NSI	ACA
1974	0	33	29	47	0	65	22	70	100	100
1973	15	11	50	73	20	–	20	–	–	96
1972	10	0	30	44	30	39	0	91	100	95

Key Votes

1) No-Knock	FOR	8) Gov Abortn Aid	AGN	15) Consumer Prot Agy	AGN
2) Busing	AGN	9) Cut Mil Brass	ABS	16) Forced Psych Tests	AGN
3) No Fault	AGN	10) Gov Limousine	FOR	17) Fed Campaign Subs	AGN
4) F-111	ABS	11) RR Featherbed	AGN	18) Rhod Chrome Ban	AGN
5) Death Penalty	FOR	12) Handgun License	AGN	19) Open Legis Meetings	AGN
6) Foreign Aid	ABS	13) Less Troop Abrd	AGN	20) Strikers Food Stmps	ABS
7) Filibuster	FOR	14) Resume Turk Aid	FOR	21) Gov Info Disclosure	ABS

Election Results

1970 general:	James L. Buckley (C)	2,288,190	(39%)
	Richard L. Ottinger (D)	2,171,232	(37%)
	Charles E. Goodell (R-L)	1,434,472	(24%)
1970 primary:	James L. Buckley (C), unopposed		

Gov. Hugh L. Carey (D) Elected 1974, term expires Jan. 1979; b. Apr. 11, 1919, Brooklyn; St. John's U., J.D. 1951; Catholic.

Career Army, WWII; Family petroleum distrib. business, 1947–51; Practicing atty., 1951–61; U.S. House of Reps., 1961–75.

Offices Executive Chamber, State Capitol, Albany 12224, 518-474-8390.

Election Results

1974 general:	Hugh L. Carey (D-L)	3,028,503	(58%)
	Malcolm Wilson (R-C)	2,219,667	(42%)
1974 primary:	Hugh L. Carey (D)	600,283	(61%)
	Howard J. Samuels (D)	387,369	(39%)

◆ ◆ ◆ ◆ ◆

FIRST DISTRICT

The 1st congressional district of New York includes the eastern end of Long Island, from 50 to 100 miles from Manhattan Island. The best known part of the district is the picturesque eastern tip which juts out into the Atlantic Ocean; here rich New Yorkers flock each summer to the fashionable beach resorts of the Hamptons and Montauk. The wealthy summer people pay little attention, however, to what happens here year round. Chic parties have been thrown in Southampton "cottages" to benefit migrant farmworkers in California, though the plight of those working in potato and vegetable farms is equally miserable.

Before World War II, virtually all of the current 1st district was agricultural, little changed from the days New Englanders moved across Long Island Sound during the seventeenth century. Today, metropolitan New York has moved in inexorably. The 1st district more than doubled in population during the sixties—by far the largest growth of any East Coast congressional district.

The mood out here is generally very conservative. A correlation seems to exist between conservative political attitudes and the desire to move this far away from New York City—a fear of crime, a dislike of blacks and Puerto Ricans, a desire to escape what is regarded as the chaos of the city for the simpler, less hectic pace of life on Long Island. There is also an ethnic basis for the 1st's conservatism. Jewish voters, who long provided the bulk of ideologically committed liberal votes in the New York area, simply have not moved to this area in great numbers; Suffolk County, which contains the 1st, is only 4% Jewish, while Nassau County, closer in and right next to the City, is 26% Jewish. Most of the new migrants to the 1st are Catholics of Italian, Irish, or German origin—people who grew up in the socially conservative atmosphere of old neighborhoods in New York's outer boroughs. Buttressing the area's political inclinations is the importance of defense industry to the local economy; among the biggest employers here are Grumman and Republic Aviation and the government's Brookhaven National Laboratory.

Thus in 1970 Suffolk was one of two New York counties carried by Conservative Senate candidate James Buckley, and there are parts of the 1st district where Conservative candidates in most years can outpoll Democrats. But 1974 showed a startling change in voting habits here. The Watergate and Richard Nixon's complicity in it seems to have wiped out half a generation's Republican voting habits and to have restored, perhaps temporarily, an often ancestral preference for the Democrats. Governor Hugh Carey, though a City Democrat, beat Catholic suburbanite Malcolm Wilson out here in a stunning reversal of form. It helped, of course, that Carey was also a Catholic, and not a man who seemed to harbor a visceral inclination toward Manhattan style radical chic.

The 1974 Democratic trend was good news for 1st district Congressman Otis Pike. This witty, nattily dressed Protestant first won the seat in 1960, when a Catholic led the Democratic ticket to a strong performance in this heavily Catholic district; and during the 1960s, Pike was carrying the district by a 2–1 margin. It helped him perhaps that he was a member of the House Armed Services Committee, though not always an orthodox one; it may have helped him also that he remained a genial skeptic about the efficacy of much domestic government spending. But with the rise of conservative strength in Suffolk County, Pike's margins began to drop; he was pressed hard by Rockefeller financed Republicans in 1970 and 1972.

Pike survived those tests (though he won the first by only a 52–48 margin), and was ready to win a much more comfortable 65% of the vote in 1974. After that election, he switched from Armed Services, on which he would have become the fifth-ranking Democrat, to Ways and Means. Apparently Pike doubted that he would ever be Armed Services Chairman—Upstate Democrat Sam Stratton, for one, stood in the way—and so decided to seek the more congenial environment of the post-Wilbur Mills Ways and Means Committee.

Census Data Pop. 467,742. Central city, 0%; suburban, 100%. Median family income, $11,643; families above $15,000: 30%; families below $3,000: 6%. Median years education, 12.3.

The Voters

Median voting age 41.
Employment profile White collar, 55%. Blue collar, 30%. Service, 14%. Farm, 1%.
Ethnic groups Black, 4%. Spanish, 1%. Total foreign stock, 28%. Italy, 7%; Germany, 4%; UK, Poland, Ireland, 2% each; USSR, 1%.

Presidential vote

1972	Nixon (R)	141,383	(70%)
	McGovern (D)	59,420	(30%)
1968	Nixon (R)	93,472	(59%)
	Humphrey (D)	50,908	(32%)
	Wallace (AI)	15,320	(10%)

Rep. Otis G. Pike (D) Elected 1960; b. Aug. 31, 1921, Riverhead; home, Riverhead; Princeton U., A.B. 1943, Columbia U., J.D. 1948; Congregationalist.

Career USMC, WWII; Practicing atty., 1953–60; J.P. of Riverhead, 1954–60; V.P., Long Island Home, Ltd.; Dir., Central Suffolk Hosp., Riverhead.

Offices 2428 RHOB, 202-225-3826. Also 209 W. Main St., Riverhead 11901, 516-727-2332.

Committees

Ways and Means (14th). Subcommittees: Health; Oversight; Trade.

Group Ratings

	ADA	COPE	LWV	RIPON	NFU	LCV	CFA	NAB	NSI	ACA
1974	74	82	75	69	86	94	92	42	30	20
1973	68	82	67	73	58	84	86	–	–	35
1972	63	82	83	47	43	87	100	33	50	39

Key Votes

1) Foreign Aid	AGN	6) Gov Abortn Aid	AGN	11) Pub Cong Election $	FOR
2) Busing	AGN	7) Coed Phys Ed	FOR	12) Turkish Arms Cutoff	FOR
3) ABM	AGN	8) Pov Lawyer Gag	FOR	13) Youth Camp Regs	AGN
4) B-1 Bomber	AGN	9) Pub Trans Sub	FOR	14) Strip Mine Veto	AGN
5) Nerve Gas	AGN	10) EZ Voter Regis	FOR	15) Farm Bill Veto	FOR

Election Results

1974 general:	Otis G. Pike (D)	101,130	(65%)	($26,907)
	Donald R. Sallah (R)	44,513	(29%)	($4,999)
	Seth C. Morgan (C)	10,038	(6%)	($4,114)
1974 primary:	Otis G. Pike (D), unopposed			
1972 general:	Otis G. Pike (D)	102,628	(53%)	($51,842)
	Joseph H. Boyd, Jr. (R)	72,133	(37%)	($90,302)
	Robert D. L. Gardiner (C)	18,627	(10%)	($37,877)

◆ ◆ ◆ ◆ ◆

SECOND DISTRICT

At the end of World War II, Suffolk County, which includes the eastern geographical half of Long Island, was largely given over to potato fields. It was also directly in the path of one of the major suburban migrations of our day. On the highways that Robert Moses had built to connect his parks to the middle class parts of New York City came tens of thousands of young veterans and their families, forsaking the rowhouse neighborhoods where they had grown up for the comparatively spacious lots and single family houses of Levittown and other Long Island subdivisions. The first wave of postwar migration was into Nassau County, and it was a pretty accurate cross section of all but the poorest New Yorkers: almost half Catholic, about one-quarter Jewish and one-quarter Protestant in background. Then, as Long Island developed an employment base of its own, the next wave of migration started, this time out as far as Suffolk County. But this second wave differed in character from the first: it was more Catholic and less Jewish, more blue collar (aircraft manufacturers were big Suffolk County employers) and less white collar, more Democratic perhaps in ancestral politics but fundamentally more conservative on most issues.

Such was the migration that made Suffolk County the fastest growing part of New York state in the sixties, as its population shot up 69%. That was, approximately, the rate of growth in that part of Suffolk County which makes up New York's 2d congressional district. Essentially this district covers the South Shore suburban communities of Suffolk, including all of the town of Islip and most of Babylon.

Using the 1972 election returns as a benchmark, the 2d is the second most conservative congressional district in New York state. But that did not prevent the district from favoring Democrat Hugh Carey over Republican Malcolm Wilson in the 1974 gubernatorial race, nor from electing a Democratic Congressman in the person of 25-year-old Thomas J. Downey. How a district that gave 72% of its vote for Richard Nixon and 66% for Republican Congressman James Grover two years before could switch so massively is a question worthy of a sophisticated piece of survey research. But a large part of the answer is undoubtedly the Watergate: the people here had relied on Richard Nixon as their champion against the forces of the new morality, and when Nixon turned out to have no morality at all they utterly abandoned him—and all who supported him.

That included Congressman Grover, who undoubtedly expected to be reelected comfortably as he had every two years since he had been first elected to Congress in 1962. He had risen in that time to become ranking Republican on the Merchant Marine and Fisheries Committee and second-ranking Republican on Public Works; from these comfortable positions he seems to have paid little attention to what was happening in the district. Downey, a law student and member of the Suffolk County legislature since 1971, hit hard on the Watergate issue, while the incumbent continued to profess his support of and admiration for his President. Moreover, Downey waged a more vigorous campaign than had been seen in these parts in many years, and so he was perfectly positioned to benefit from the surprisingly large Democratic trend. On the day following his victory, the New York *Times* ran a front page story on the race, complete with a picture of Downey playing basketball with his 11-year-old brother; the new Congressman-elect described the campaign with a run of basketball metaphors. He is now the most junior member of the House Armed Services Committee, as well as the youngest member of Congress; and it will be interesting to see how his political future goes.

Census Data Pop. 467,722. Central city, 0%; suburban, 100%. Median family income, $11,938; families above $15,000: 29%; families below $3,000: 4%. Median years education, 12.1.

The Voters

Median voting age 41.
Employment profile White collar, 49%. Blue collar, 37%. Service, 14%. Farm, –%.
Ethnic groups Black, 4%. Spanish, 2%. Total foreign stock, 28%. Italy, 9%; Germany, 3%; Ireland, UK, 2% each; Canada, Poland, 1% each.

Presidential vote

1972	Nixon (R)	123,030	(72%)
	McGovern (D)	46,695	(28%)
1968	Nixon (R)	84,034	(58%)
	Humphrey (D)	46,141	(32%)
	Wallace (AI)	14,650	(10%)

Rep. Thomas J. Downey (D) Elected 1974; b. Jan. 28, 1949, Ozone Park; home, West Islip; Cornell U., B.S. 1970, St. John's U. Law School, 1972–74.

Career Personnel management and labor relations, Macy's Dept. Store; Suffolk Co. Legislature, 1971–74.

Offices 1116 LHOB, 202-225-3335. Also 4 Updall Rd., West Islip 11759, 516-661-8777.

Committees

Armed Services (27th). Subcommittees: Military Compensation; Military Personnel.

Group Ratings: Newly Elected

Key Votes

1) Foreign Aid	FOR	6) Gov Abortn Aid	NE	11) Pub Cong Election $	NE
2) Busing	NE	7) Coed Phys Ed	AGN	12) Turkish Arms Cutoff	NE
3) ABM	NE	8) Pov Lawyer Gag	NE	13) Youth Camp Regs	FOR
4) B-1 Bomber	AGN	9) Pub Trans Sub	NE	14) Strip Mine Veto	AGN
5) Nerve Gas	NE	10) EZ Voter Regis	NE	15) Farm Bill Veto	FOR

Election Results

1974 general:	Thomas J. Downey (D)	58,289	(49%)	($44,423)
	James R. Grover, Jr. (R)	53,344	(45%)	($11,258)
	Neil Greene (C)	7,818	(7%)	($275)
1974 primary:	Thomas J. Downey (D), unopposed			

◆ ◆ ◆ ◆ ◆

THIRD DISTRICT

The 3d congressional district of New York is a new seat created following the 1970 census, which required that Long Island get an additional district. As in the case of all New York district lines drawn in the fifties, sixties, and seventies, this was carefully sculpted by Republican redistricters with the intent of maximizing Republican representation in the Congress. Somewhat more than half the 3d district's citizens live in Nassau County, in areas as diverse as fashionable and high income North Shore communities like Locust Point, somewhat less fashionable but nonetheless well to do Syosset in the middle of Long Island, and deeply conservative and middle income Massapequa on the South Shore. The remainder of the district is just to the east, in Suffolk County; that portion is dominated by the middle class town of Huntington, but also includes a small black ghetto of Wyandanch.

So far in its brief history the 3d district has been the scene of two close congressional races. Although the district was obviously intended to be Republican, a Democrat named Carter Bales made a game run for it in 1972, and managed a respectable showing. But the winner that year was Nassau County Controller Angelo Roncallo, a pillar of the smooth running Nassau Republican machine led by Assemblyman Joseph Margiotta. Once in office, Roncallo might have been expected to win easily. But instead he was indicted and tried on conspiracy and extortion charges.

Although he was acquitted, Roncallo sustained serious political injury. Perhaps people figured that someone so closely involved with the Nassau machine and accused of a crime must have done something shady, even if he got off on the specific charges. Certainly Roncallo was hurt because his troubles helped attract a strong Democratic opponent, Huntington Supervisor Jerome Ambro. Ambro had held office as a Democrat for six years in Republican Suffolk, and he had even been a candidate for Lieutenant Governor in 1970 (although he was beaten in the primary that year). He was benefitted, of course, by the vast shift toward the Democrats among Long Island voters, especially his fellow Catholics; he managed to hold Roncallo even in the Republican's home turf, Nassau; and to beat him decisively, by a 56–42 margin, in the Suffolk part of the district. Given the advantages of incumbency, and the unlikelihood of anything as cataclysmic as Watergate again vastly shifting Long Island political attitudes, Ambro has to be rated the favorite to win again here in 1976.

Census Data Pop. 467,894. Central city, 0%; suburban, 100%. Median family income, $14,396; families above $15,000: 47%; families below $3,000: 4%. Median years education, 12.5.

The Voters

Median voting age 42.
Employment profile White collar, 62%. Blue collar, 27%. Service, 11%. Farm, –%.
Ethnic groups Black, 5%. Total foreign stock, 32%. Italy, 9%; Germany, 4%; USSR, 3%; UK, Poland, Ireland, 2% each; Canada, Austria, 1% each.

Presidential vote

1972	Nixon (R)	137,271	(67%)
	McGovern (D)	68,617	(33%)
1968	Nixon (R)	103,012	(56%)
	Humphrey (D)	70,161	(38%)
	Wallace (AI)	11,195	(6%)

Rep. Jerome Ambro, Jr. (D) Elected 1974; b. June 27, 1928, Brooklyn; home, East Northport; NYU, B.A.; Catholic.

Career Army, Korea; Huntington Town Supervisor, 1968–74; Suffolk Co. Bd. of Supervisors, 1968–69.

Offices 1313 LHOB, 202-225-3865. Also 20 Crossways Park N., Woodbury 11797, 516-364-2177.

Committees

Public Works and Transportation (22d). Subcommittees: Investigations and Review; Water Resources.

Science and Technology (18th). Subcommittees: Domestic and International Scientific Planning and Analysis; Energy Research, Development and Demonstration; Environment and the Atmosphere.

Group Ratings: Newly Elected

Key Votes

1) Foreign Aid	FOR	6) Gov Abortn Aid	NE	11) Pub Cong Election $	NE
2) Busing	NE	7) Coed Phys Ed	AGN	12) Turkish Arms Cutoff	NE
3) ABM	NE	8) Pov Lawyer Gag	NE	13) Youth Camp Regs	FOR
4) B-1 Bomber	AGN	9) Pub Trans Sub	NE	14) Strip Mine Veto	AGN
5) Nerve Gas	NE	10) EZ Voter Regis	NE	15) Farm Bill Veto	FOR

Election Results

1974 general:	Jerome A. Ambro, Jr. (D)	76,383	(52%)	($77,140)
	Angelo D. Roncallo (R-C)	67,986	(46%)	($68,716)
	Arthur Hoffer (L)	3,191	(2%)	($2,847)
1974 primary:	Jerome A. Ambro, Jr. (D), unopposed			

◆ ◆ ◆ ◆ ◆

FOURTH DISTRICT

At the end of World War II, Nassau County on Long Island, just beyond the New York City limits, consisted mostly of potato fields. Here and there, in this flat country 30 or 40 miles east of Manhattan, a few subdivisions had been laid out before the war. On the North Shore and in places like Old Westbury sat the Gatsbyesque estates of some of New York's wealthiest families. But the vast center of Nassau County lay virtually undeveloped. It did not stay that way for long. Just after the war, a young builder named William Levitt built an entire townful of small tract houses and named it after himself, and soon Levittown came to symbolize Long Island's vast postwar growth. Young marrieds, after years of war and depression childhoods pent up in the city, flocked out to the Island and created a new life style.

So during the 1940s and 1950s Nassau County filled up, so much so that it has had very little growth since the 1960 census was taken. Twenty years ago, some observers opined that Nassau migrants switched from Democratic to Republican when they left New York City, but in retrospect this seems clearly wrong. It was not the county of residence that made the difference in voting habits (though it did make sense to register Republican in Nassau, since Republican primaries determined who would hold most local government positions). Rather, any rightward trend here was part of a national movement away from the New Deal and toward the politics of the Eisenhower era.

The 4th congressional district of New York is one of two seats which is entirely within Nassau County. The 4th includes many areas of the 1950s boom, including the original Levittown and next door Hicksville. Both these places have been losing population since 1960, as the original settlers aged and their children grew up and moved away. The district also includes posh Old Westbury and the black ghetto of New Cassel not far away. But the nucleus of the 4th, that part of it which connects the district with its predecessor seats, is a string of towns along the South Shore of Long Island. They include Oceanside, Freeport, and Merrick, where the large Jewish populations sustain marginal to Democratic voting habits. Also here are Bellmore, Wantagh, and Seaford, more heavily Catholic and usually much more Republican. Until 1972 these towns were all part of the old 5th district, which first elected the 4th's current Congressman, Republican Norman Lent.

Lent is the beneficiary of a couple of redistrictings. The first, which took effect in 1970, had as its sole intent the defeat of antiwar Democratic incumbent Allard Lowenstein. In 1967, Lowenstein, with his myriad contacts in universities and among liberal groups, helped to put together the antiwar campaign that ousted Lyndon Johnson from the Presidency. Lowenstein first tried to get Robert Kennedy into the race, and failed; he then enlisted Eugene McCarthy and supported him. Disenchanted with the conflict between McCarthy and Kennedy, Lowenstein left the national scene and, when Democratic Congressman Herbert Tenzer retired, Lowenstein, then a Manhattan resident, got into the 5th district race. With the help of student volunteers who canvassed practically the entire district, Lowenstein defeated the organization Democratic candidate in the primary, and then beat Conservative Mason Hampton, who had won the Republican nomination, in the general election.

Lowenstein's victory enraged New York Republicans. When it came time for them to redraw his district, Republican state legislators eliminated the Jewish, Democratic "Five Towns" (now in the current 5th district) and added heavily conservative though nominally Democratic Massapequa (now in the 3d). The new lines were enough to elect Lent, a state Senator who had made a name for himself as an opponent of busing.

The new boundaries drawn for 1972 proved even more helpful for Lent. Against weak opposition he won easily in that year, and in 1974, with the help of Joseph Margiotta's topflight Nassau County Republican organization, he beat a Democrat by a less than overwhelming, but still adequate 52–46 margin. As a member of the Commerce and Merchant Marine Committees, Lent has not been an important force legislatively; he can be expected to vote the conservative line reliably.

Census Data Pop. 467,610. Central city, 0%; suburban, 100%. Median family income, $14,376; families above $15,000: 46%; families below $3,000: 3%. Median years education, 12.4.

The Voters

Median voting age 43.
Employment profile White collar, 63%. Blue collar, 26%. Service, 11%. Farm, –%.
Ethnic groups Black, 3%. Total foreign stock, 33%. Italy, 7%; USSR, 5%; Germany, 4%; Poland, Ireland, 3% each; UK, Austria, 2% each; Canada, 1%.

Presidential vote

1972	Nixon (R)	138,983	(64%)
	McGovern (D)	78,124	(36%)
1968	Nixon (R)	105,061	(51%)
	Humphrey (D)	88,395	(43%)
	Wallace (AI)	11,378	(6%)

Rep. Norman F. Lent (R) Elected 1970; b. Mar. 23, 1931, Oceanside; home, East Rockaway; Hofstra Col., B.A. 1952, Cornell U., J.D. 1957; Methodist.

Career Navy, Korea; Practicing atty., 1957–70; Asst. East Rockaway Police Justice, 1960–62; N.Y. Senate, 1962–70.

Offices 428 CHOB, 202-225-7896. Also Rm. 300, 2280 Grand Ave., Baldwin 11510, 516-223-1616.

Committees

Interstate and Foreign Commerce (10th). Subcommittees: Oversight and Investigations.

Merchant Marine and Fisheries (11th). Subcommittees: Fisheries and Wildlife Conservation and the Environment; Oceanography.

Group Ratings

	ADA	COPE	LWV	RIPON	NFU	LCV	CFA	NAB	NSI	ACA
1974	30	27	67	56	46	59	54	58	100	67
1973	9	22	50	64	25	50	29	–	–	68
1972	13	44	50	80	17	64	100	70	100	53

Key Votes

1) Foreign Aid	FOR	6) Gov Abortn Aid	AGN	11) Pub Cong Election $	FOR
2) Busing	AGN	7) Coed Phys Ed	AGN	12) Turkish Arms Cutoff	FOR
3) ABM	FOR	8) Pov Lawyer Gag	ABS	13) Youth Camp Regs	FOR
4) B-1 Bomber	FOR	9) Pub Trans Sub	FOR	14) Strip Mine Veto	FOR
5) Nerve Gas	FOR	10) EZ Voter Regis	FOR	15) Farm Bill Veto	FOR

Election Results

1974 general:	Norman F. Lent (R-C)	85,382	(54%)	($53,568)
	Franklin H. Orenstein (D-L)	73,822	(46%)	($70,256)
1974 primary:	Norman F. Lent (R), unopposed			
1972 general:	Norman F. Lent (R)	125,422	(63%)	($45,306)
	Elaine B. Horowitz (D)	72,280	(37%)	($27,178)

◆ ◆ ◆ ◆ ◆

FIFTH DISTRICT

The 5th congressional district of New York, as it currently stands, includes most of the older suburban areas of Long Island. In the northern part of the district is Garden City, a WASPy suburb laid out in the 1920s; it is, as it has always been, heavily Republican. To the south are places like Hempstead, Rockville Centre, and Valley Stream, towns on radial highways leading into Queens. These places were developed somewhat later, and each of them has its own, slightly different character. Politically, these towns are a little more Democratic than average in Nassau County, and somewhat more Republican than New York state as a whole. At the southern end of the district, below Kennedy Airport and just north of the Atlantic, are Long Beach and the Five Towns—Lawrence, Inwood, Cedarhurst, Hewlett, and Woodmere—all developments that were begun in the 1920s, all heavily Jewish, and all solidly Democratic. All the towns so far mentioned together make for a marginal constituency; but the New York legislature, then solidly controlled by Republicans, was careful to add to them the heavily Republican suburbs of East Meadow and Uniondale, the latter the home of Nassau County Republican boss Joseph Margiotta.

Thus the 5th district, drawn as it was, represents a clear attempt to preserve the incumbency of a Republican Congressman. Its beneficiary is John Wydler, who first won his Nassau County seat in 1962 and for the next ten years won reelection without much difficulty. Wydler—part of the generation that came to maturity during World War II—was raised in Brooklyn and moved to Long Island, and found success in the Nassau County suburbs. He is a Congressman who generates little publicity, who has risen to high ranking positions on Government Operations and Science and Technology without any heralded legislative accomplishments, and who has become regional Republican whip without attracting notice as a future leadership type. Wydler has an almost entirely conventionally conservative voting record, and has shown an attention to the needs of his district which has in turn helped him win reelection by usually wide margins.

The one exception was 1974. For the first time, Wydler had really substantial opposition in the person of former Congressman (1969–71) Allard Lowenstein. (See Fourth District.) But Lowenstein, the now aging liberal who was as responsible as anyone for dumping Lyndon Johnson in 1968, had his problems. He had first run for Congress on Long Island in 1968, after moving from Manhattan; then, after losing in 1970, he had moved to Brooklyn to run against John Rooney in 1972 (see Fourteenth District); now, having lost there, he was back in Long Island. The district hopping issue may have been enough to make the difference; in any case, Wydler was the winner by a 54–46 margin.

Census Data Pop. 467,694. Central city, 0%; suburban, 100%. Median family income, $14,102; families above $15,000: 45%; families below $3,000: 5%. Median years education, 12.4.

The Voters

Median voting age 46.
Employment profile White collar, 65%. Blue collar, 24%. Service, 11%. Farm, –%.
Ethnic groups Black, 8%. Total foreign stock, 38%. Italy, 9%; USSR, 5%; Germany, 4%; Poland, Ireland, 3% each; UK, Austria, 2% each.

Presidential vote

1972	Nixon (R)	145,996	(63%)
	McGovern (D)	87,445	(37%)
1968	Nixon (R)	108,949	(50%)
	Humphrey (D)	98,158	(45%)
	Wallace (AI)	10,791	(5%)

Rep. John W. Wydler (R) Elected 1962; b. June 9, 1924, Brooklyn; home, Garden City; Brown U., 1941–42, 1945–47, Harvard U., LL.B. 1950; Episcopalian.

Career Air Force, WWII; Practicing atty., 1950–; U.S. Atty's Ofc., 1953–59; Mbr., State Investigation Comm. to probe New York City school construction irregularities.

Offices 2334 RHOB, 202-225-5516. Also 150 Old Country Rd., Mineola 11501, 516-248-7676.

Committees

Government Operations (9th). Subcommittees: Intergovernmental Relations and Human Resources.

Science and Technology (4th). Subcommittees: Aviation and Transportation Research and Development; Energy Research, Development and Demonstration; Space Science and Applications.

Group Ratings

	ADA	COPE	LWV	RIPON	NFU	LCV	CFA	NAB	NSI	ACA
1974	39	27	83	53	54	59	50	82	90	40
1973	17	36	58	80	33	50	67	–	–	58
1972	25	20	58	67	29	54	100	83	100	73

Key Votes

1) Foreign Aid	FOR	6) Gov Abortn Aid	AGN	11) Pub Cong Election $	FOR
2) Busing	AGN	7) Coed Phys Ed	AGN	12) Turkish Arms Cutoff	FOR
3) ABM	FOR	8) Pov Lawyer Gag	FOR	13) Youth Camp Regs	FOR
4) B-1 Bomber	FOR	9) Pub Trans Sub	FOR	14) Strip Mine Veto	FOR
5) Nerve Gas	AGN	10) EZ Voter Regis	AGN	15) Farm Bill Veto	FOR

Election Results

1974 general:	John W. Wydler (R-C)	91,677	(54%)	($68,115)
	Allard K. Lowenstein (D-L)	77,356	(46%)	($112,369)
1974 primary:	John W. Wydler (R), unopposed			
1972 general:	John W. Wydler (R)	133,332	(64%)	($44,644)
	Ferne M. Steckler (D)	67,709	(32%)	($25,333)
	Vincent A. Joy (C)	7,676	(4%)	(NA)

◆ ◆ ◆ ◆ ◆

SIXTH DISTRICT

New York's 6th congressional district consists of almost equal parts of the North Shore of Long Island in Nassau County and the Borough of Queens in New York City. The North Shore has long been famous as the home of rich and well born aristocrats like Theodore Roosevelt as well as nouveaux riches like Jay Gatsby who have tried to imitate the life style. Today huge WASPy estates still sit on peninsulas jutting out into Long Island Sound, as well as in towns like Sands Point and Port Washington. But politically more significant in the 6th district portion of the North Shore are wealthy, predominantly Jewish suburbs like Great Neck. Despite their wealth, Great Neck and surrounding towns invariably produce large Democratic majorities, even for McGovern in 1972; it is inland, to the south, in the less high income, more Protestant suburbs that one finds the greatest Republican strength in the North Shore area.

Another anomaly of the 6th district is that its suburban Nassau portion is more liberal and Democratic, at least in most years, than the part of it in Queens, which is technically, of course, part of the central city. The reason is that the district lines in Queens were drawn by a Republican legislature to include all possible neighborhoods of conservative homeowners and to exclude housing projects and high rise apartments inhabited mainly by Democrats. Indeed, the boundaries had a very specific purpose: to defeat Democratic Congressman Lester Wolff and to reelect Republican Seymour Halpern. Wolff had first been elected in the North Shore 3d district on the strength of the 1964 LBJ landslide; he had been reelected since with surprisingly large margins. Halpern had represented part of Queens since 1958, where his liberal record on economic issues had helped him win with large majorities.

On paper the odds favored Halpern. But there were other factors. Back in 1969, the *Wall Street Journal* had revealed that Halpern had received loans of $100,000 from various banks, without any collateral; they were apparently willing to make such unusual arrangements because the Congressman was a high ranking member of the House Banking and Currency Committee. Halpern resigned from the Committee and paid back the loans, and thanks to a deal between the Republican and Democratic organizations in Queens was spared any significant opposition in 1970. But in 1972 Wolff let it be known that he would use the loan issue, and Halpern retired precipitously.

The retirement gave the Republican nomination to conservative Queens Assemblyman John T. Gallagher, who actually carried the Queens portion of the district; it was only Wolff's large margin in Nassau that gave him a 52–48 victory. In 1974, however, it was another story. The criminality of Richard Nixon and Spiro Agnew seems to have deeply shaken the conservative New Yorkers, many of them ancestrally Democratic Catholics, who had supported their candidates and mouthed their catchwords; betrayed, they abandoned the Republican Party, producing a huge Democratic gain in erstwhile conservative (and Conservative) neighborhoods. As a result, Lester Wolff ran as well this time in Queens as in Nassau, and over all carried the district by a 67–33 margin. There is little to indicate that he will not be blessed with similarly large margins in the future.

Census Data Pop. 467,602. Central city, 54%; suburban, 46%. Median family income, $14,483; families above $15,000: 47%; families below $3,000: 4%. Median years education, 12.4.

The Voters

Median voting age 47.
Employment profile White collar, 68%. Blue collar, 22%. Service, 10%. Farm, –%.
Ethnic groups Black, 2%. Total foreign stock, 45%. Italy, 10%; USSR, Germany, 5% each; Poland, Ireland, 4% each; UK, 3%; Austria, 2%; Canada, Greece, 1% each.

Presidential vote

1972	Nixon (R)	140,072	(62%)
	McGovern (D)	84,480	(38%)
1968	Nixon (R)	108,298	(49%)
	Humphrey (D)	98,431	(45%)
	Wallace (AI)	12,106	(6%)

Rep. Lester L. Wolff (D) Elected 1964; b. Jan. 4, 1919, New York City; home, Great Neck; NYU, 1939; Jewish.

Career Lecturer, NYU, 1939–41; Army Air Corps, WWII; Head of Marketing Dept., Collegiate Institute, 1945–49; Bd. Chm., Coordinated Marketing Agency, 1945–64; Moderator and Producer, "Between the Lines", TV program, 1948–60; Mgr., U.S. Trade Missions, Philippines, 1962, Malaysia and Hong Kong, 1963.

Offices 2463 RHOB, 202-225-5956. Also 156A Main St., Port Washington 11050, 516-767-4343.

Committees

International Relations (11th). Subcommittees: Future Foreign Policy Research and Development (Chairman); International Operations.

Veterans' Affairs (8th). Subcommittees: Education and Training; Hospitals.

Group Ratings

	ADA	COPE	LWV	RIPON	NFU	LCV	CFA	NAB	NSI	ACA
1974	77	91	75	62	85	88	75	33	20	20
1973	80	91	92	64	60	84	100	–	–	22
1972	94	82	92	83	67	76	100	8	0	5

Key Votes

1) Foreign Aid	FOR	6) Gov Abortn Aid	FOR	11) Pub Cong Election $	FOR
2) Busing	AGN	7) Coed Phys Ed	FOR	12) Turkish Arms Cutoff	ABS
3) ABM	AGN	8) Pov Lawyer Gag	FOR	13) Youth Camp Regs	FOR
4) B-1 Bomber	ABS	9) Pub Trans Sub	FOR	14) Strip Mine Veto	AGN
5) Nerve Gas	AGN	10) EZ Voter Regis	FOR	15) Farm Bill Veto	FOR

Election Results

1974 general:	Lester L. Wolff (D-L)	101,237	(67%)	($54,012)
	Edythe Layne (R-C)	50,528	(33%)	($17,919)
1974 primary:	Lester L. Wolff (D), unopposed			
1972 general:	Lester L. Wolff (D-L)	109,620	(52%)	($64,069)
	John T. Gallegher (R-C)	103,038	(48%)	($45,449)

◆ ◆ ◆ ◆ ◆

SEVENTH DISTRICT

The 7th congressional district of New York in southern Queens takes in a series of middle class neighborhoods of varying ethnic composition. Just north of Kennedy Airport is the two family house neighborhood of Ozone Park, with a large Italian-American population. To the north, along Queens Boulevard, are the high rise apartments of Rego Park, which are predominantly Jewish, though the Forest Hills neighborhood in which they sit, with its old Tudor houses, was originally and discriminatorily WASPy. In addition, there are large black neighborhoods here, the slum area of South Jamaica and, overshadowing it, the larger middle class areas of Springfield Gardens and St. Albans. Altogether 37% of the district's residents are black, which makes them the 7th's largest ethnic group, but Italian-Americans are probably not far behind.

The 7th is a heavily Democratic district, largely because of the solidly Democratic allegiance of its black voters. But the 7th is also, on many issues, conservatively inclined, full of homeowners who feel oppressed by New York City's high taxes and high cost of living, and who nurtured an abiding hatred for what they felt was the scorn and neglect of the administration of Manhattan liberal WASP John Lindsay. In 1969, Lindsay failed to carry the 7th; contrariwise, the district produced a large vote for Senator James Buckley in 1970.

In congressional elections the 7th has backed moderate to liberal Democrat Joseph Addabbo since he first won in 1960. For some years Addabbo, in the tradition of most New York City Congressmen, was a quiet backbencher; he managed to win a seat on the conservatively inclined Appropriations Committee, and made few waves. But in 1970, he emerged from this obscurity as a vocal opponent of the supersonic transport (SST)—a position shared by many of his constituents who live directly under the flight paths to Kennedy Airport.

In the 93d and 94th Congress Addabbo bucked tradition even more strenuously. As the highest ranking member of the Defense Appropriations Subcommittee who had taken a position against American involvement in Indochina, Addabbo was the floor leader of the successful movement to stop the American bombing of Cambodia in 1973. He was not a particularly likely dove, but then an originally hawkish House was not eager to have its nose rubbed in what it had come to believe was its own mistakes by someone who had not shared in making them. The 51-year-old Addabbo is in an excellent position to move up to the Chairmanship of Defense Appropriations, which of course passes on the entire Pentagon budget; the three Democrats who currently outrank him there are all in their seventies.

Census Data Pop. 467,449. Central city, 100%; suburban, 0%. Median family income, $11,317; families above $15,000: 30%; families below $3,000: 7%. Median years education, 12.1.

The Voters

Median voting age 45.
Employment profile White collar, 59%. Blue collar, 27%. Service, 14%. Farm, –%.
Ethnic groups Black, 37%. Spanish, 2%. Total foreign stock, 41%. Italy, 7%; USSR, 5%; Poland, Germany, 4% each; Austria, Ireland, 2% each; UK, 1%.

Presidential vote

1972	Nixon (R)	66,305	(41%)
	McGovern (D)	93,806	(59%)
1968	Nixon (R)	46,602	(29%)
	Humphrey (D)	108,562	(67%)
	Wallace (AI)	7,658	(5%)

Rep. Joseph P. Addabbo (D) Elected 1960; b. Mar. 17, 1925, Queens; home, Ozone Park; CCNY, 1942–44, St. John's U., LL.B. 1946; Catholic.

Career Practicing atty., 1946–60.

Offices 2440 RHOB, 202-225-3461. Also 96–11 101st Ave., Ozone Park 11416, 212-845-3131.

Committees

Appropriations (15th). Subcommittees: Defense; Treasury, Postal Service, and General Government.

Small Business (6th). Subcommittees: Activities of Regulatory Agencies; Governmental Procurement and International Trade; SBA Oversight and Minority Enterprise (Chairman).

Group Ratings

	ADA	COPE	LWV	RIPON	NFU	LCV	CFA	NAB	NSI	ACA
1974	83	100	75	50	85	94	75	25	10	13
1973	83	100	75	73	94	65	100	–	–	20
1972	94	91	83	78	83	73	100	18	10	4

Key Votes

1) Foreign Aid	FOR	6) Gov Abortn Aid	FOR	11) Pub Cong Election $	FOR
2) Busing	AGN	7) Coed Phys Ed	AGN	12) Turkish Arms Cutoff	FOR
3) ABM	AGN	8) Pov Lawyer Gag	FOR	13) Youth Camp Regs	FOR
4) B-1 Bomber	AGN	9) Pub Trans Sub	FOR	14) Strip Mine Veto	AGN
5) Nerve Gas	AGN	10) EZ Voter Regis	FOR	15) Farm Bill Veto	FOR

Election Results

1974 general:	Joseph P. Addabbo (D-R-L), unopposed		($19,841)
1974 primary:	Joseph P. Addabbo (D), unopposed		
1972 general :	Joseph P. Addabbo (D-L)	104,110 (75%)	($22,487)
	John E. Hall (R)	28,296 (20%)	($1,540)
	Frank O. Wuertz (C)	6,053 (4%)	(NA)

◆ ◆ ◆ ◆

EIGHTH DISTRICT

Roughly speaking, the 8th congressional district of New York encompasses the central part of the borough of Queens. The district's tortuous boundaries were drawn to keep as many conservative and Republican voters as possible within the confines of the adjacent 6th and 9th districts; in effect, the 8th is a seat Republican redistricters conceded to the Democrats. The district radiates in three direction like spokes from the hub of a wheel. The hub is Flushing Meadow Park, site of the World's Fairs of 1939–40 and 1964–65, and today the home of Shea Stadium's Mets and Jets. One of the spokes passes through the middle class, predominantly Jewish neighborhood of Flushing on its way to Long Island Sound. Another proceeds east through Fresh Meadows and a neighborhood with the real estate promoter's name of Utopia, and on toward the Nassau County line. The third spoke moves west from Flushing Meadow to include the high rise complex of Lefrak City, a small black ghetto in Corona, and the two and four family house neighborhood of lower middle income whites called Jackson Heights.

These seemingly disparate areas all have certain things in common. All have large Jewish populations, as if the redistricters took care to gather together all the predominantly Jewish neighborhoods in Queens. And the district lines, as they writhe about manage to corral most of the borough's big high rise apartment complexes and many of its public housing projects. Before World War II, most of Queens was given over to neighborhoods of one and two family houses, inhabited by Irish, Italian, and German immigrants; it was a conservative suburban Republican stronghold that happened, technically, to be part of a Democratic central city. But after World War II, most of the growth here has come in the high rises, a large percentage of whose occupants are Jewish and liberal Democratic voters. So the 8th district may be said to be postwar Queens.

The liberal Democratic mood of the voters here is shaken occasionally. There were fierce neighborhood demonstrations when the Lindsay Administration wanted to built three 24-story high rises for lower and middle income residents in Forest Hills. Residents pointed out, correctly, that such an infusion of population would strain public facilities in the area; another reason, of course, for the strength, if not the existence, of the opposition was the fact that blacks and Puerto Ricans would be more common in the neighborhood. Perhaps it was only coincidence, but in 1972, just after this controversy began to boil, George McGovern only barely managed to carry the ordinarily heavily Democratic 8th district.

How much the district had gone back to normal by 1974 can be measured by comparing McGovern's 50% and Congressman Benjamin Rosenthal's 65% of the vote in 1972 with Rosenthal's 79% performance in 1974. Clearly Watergate had obliterated the salience of issues like Forest Hills, and Nixon's Republicans had replaced McGovern's and Lindsay's liberals as the pet hate of Queens homeowners and apartment dwellers.

Rosenthal has had an interesting congressional career, paralleling the metamorphosis of the New York City congressional delegation in recent years. He was first selected to run for the seat in 1962 by the Queens regular organization, at a time when young politicoes aspired more after judgeships than seats in Congress. He was a quiet freshman, but in his first few years found himself opposed to the Johnson Administration's policies in Vietnam, and increasingly voted with a small bloc of liberals who otherwise had never had the support of a Congressman from Queens.

By 1970, he was one of the leading advocates of consumer legislation in the House, and the major force behind the Consumer Protection Agency. His advocacy for this proposal got this rather stubborn young liberal in a feud with Chet Holifield, an oldtime liberal who had got more conservative on his way to becoming Chairman of the Government Operations Committee. Rosenthal also got into a bitter feud with fellow Queens Congressman James Delaney, whose vote on the Rules Committee once killed the CPA. But today those quarrels have been patched up. Rosenthal and Holifield managed to get together and co-sponsor the CPA bill before Holifield retired in 1974, and Rosenthal joined other liberals in electing the senior Delaney as chairman of their state Democratic delegation. Moreover, Rosenthal has also been active in his position as a member of the International Relations Committee; he was one of the leaders, for example, of the move to cut off military aid to Turkey in response to its treaty-breaking attack on Cyprus. The House—and its Holifields and Delaneys—seem to have grown into the sort of liberal idealism that Rosenthal has practiced for so long; and the Congressman himself seems to have learned, in this more hospitable environment, how to work with other legislators to accomplish desired ends.

Census Data Pop. 467,691. Central city, 100%; suburban, 0%. Median family income, $12,244; families above $15,000: 35%; families below $3,000: 5%. Median years education, 12.3.

The Voters

Median voting age 45.
Employment profile White collar, 68%. Blue collar, 23%. Service, 9%. Farm, –%.
Ethnic groups Black, 4%. Chinese, 1%. Spanish 2%. Total foreign stock, 59%. Italy, USSR, 8% each; Poland, 6%; Ireland, Germany, 4% each; Austria, 3%; UK, Greece, 2% each; Hungary, Rumania, 1% each.

Presidential vote

1972	Nixon (R)	94,222	(50%)
	McGovern (D)	95,212	(50%)
1968	Nixon (R)	61,484	(33%)
	Humphrey (D)	117,111	(63%)
	Wallace (AI)	8,709	(5%)

Rep. Benjamin S. Rosenthal (D) Elected Feb. 20, 1962; b. June 8, 1923, New York City; home, Elmhurst; Long Island U., CCNY, Brooklyn Law School, LL.B. 1949, LL.M. 1952; Jewish.

Career Army, WWII; Practicing atty.

Offices 2372 RHOB, 202-225-2601. Also U.S.P.O. 41–65 Main St., Flushing 11351, 212-939-8200.

Committees

Government Operations (8th). Subcommittees: Commerce, Consumer and Monetary Affairs (Chairman); Legislation and National Security.

International Relations (9th). Subcommittees: International Organizations; International Political and Military Affairs.

Group Ratings

	ADA	COPE	LWV	RIPON	NFU	LCV	CFA	NAB	NSI	ACA
1974	96	100	92	50	75	93	100	18	10	0
1973	100	100	92	69	85	100	100	–	–	12
1972	100	91	100	73	86	87	100	9	0	9

Key Votes

1) Foreign Aid	FOR	6) Gov Abortn Aid	FOR	11) Pub Cong Election $	FOR
2) Busing	FOR	7) Coed Phys Ed	ABS	12) Turkish Arms Cutoff	FOR
3) ABM	AGN	8) Pov Lawyer Gag	AGN	13) Youth Camp Regs	FOR
4) B-1 Bomber	AGN	9) Pub Trans Sub	FOR	14) Strip Mine Veto	AGN
5) Nerve Gas	AGN	10) EZ Voter Regis	FOR	15) Farm Bill Veto	FOR

Election Results

1974 general:	Benjamin S. Rosenthal (D-L)	90,200	(79%)	($14,100)
	Albert Lemishow (R-C)	23,980	(21%)	($880)
1974 primary:	Benjamin S. Rosenthal (D), unopposed			
1972 general:	Benjamin S. Rosenthal (D-L)	110,293	(65%)	($18,739)
	Frank A. LaPina (R-C)	60,166	(34%)	($6279)

◆ ◆ ◆ ◆ ◆

NINTH DISTRICT

It can be said with some certainty that Archie Bunker lives in the 9th congressional district of New York. The aerial shot taken by TV cameramen of Archie's neighborhood shows the kind of aging, though still neatly maintained, one and two family houses that line the streets of Jackson Heights, Long Island City, Ridgewood, or Glendale, Queens. Moreover, Archie's views are a fairly accurate, if exaggerated, portrayal of what appears from examination of the election returns to be the clear majority views in the 9th district. Geographically, the 9th is the Queens district closest to Manhattan's chic and liberal Upper East Side—but it is the farthest away in spirit. People here in Queens refer to Manhattan as "the City", as if it were some alien place; and in many ways, of course, it is.

The boundaries of the 9th district were carefully drawn to include the middle class, heavily Catholic Queens neighborhoods of conservative homeowners—people who live on salaries or wages that make middle class respectability hard to maintain in New York City. It is ironic—or at least a reversal of the conventional wisdom we inherit from the New Deal era—that the wealthy Upper East Side voted 58% for McGovern in 1972, while across the East River, the factory workers and doormen and waiters and clerks living in Long Island City and Sunnyside and Astoria went 73% for Richard Nixon; the rich voting for economic change, the relatively poor for the status quo. The 9th district total stems in part from the ethnic composition of this constituency: there are virtually no blacks or Puerto Ricans living here, and many of its present homeowners, living in neighborhoods near the Brooklyn line, fear that there soon will be. So the 9th, lying in the heart of New York City, produced the largest Nixon percentage of any congressional district in the state; in fact, Nixon's 73% here was exceeded in only two other congressional districts in the East, both of them in the heavily Republican, tradition-bound Pennsylvania Dutch country.

This part of Queens was not always so enthusiastically Republican, any more than it has remained so after 1972. The historic allegiance of at least a large minority of its residents was with the Democratic Party of Franklin D. Roosevelt and John F. Kennedy. But during the years the Democrats appeared more interested in ending the Vietnam war and advocating the interests of blacks and Puerto Ricans than they were in the welfare of people like Archie Bunker, the 9th shifted solidly to the Republicans. And in the years in which the district's new found political heroes, Richard Nixon and Spiro Agnew, were revealed irrefutably to have been nothing more than the criminals they leeringly loved to denounce, the 9th has shifted back toward the Democrats, at least temporarily.

Similar shifts can be discerned in the career of the 9th's Congressman, Democrat James J. Delaney. First elected in 1944, Delaney was defeated in the Republican sweep of 1946, then returned to the House in 1948, and reelected ever since. Early in his career he was considered a reliable enough supporter of Democratic programs to win a seat on the House Rules Committee, on which he now ranks just behind 84-year-old Chairman Ray Madden of Indiana. His most significant legislative achievement is the Delaney Amendment, which prohibits the sale of any drug known to produce cancer in animals; it has been attacked by the drug industry, but probably—for we do not know all the answers here—has saved quite a few lives.

But if Delaney has lined up with liberal Democrats on many issues, he has differed from them on others. Despite the continual personal pleas of President Kennedy, Delaney refused to vote a rule—that is, report to the floor—from the Rules Committee the administration's federal aid to education bill, because it did not include aid to parochial schools; Delaney's single vote killed federal aid to education for four years, until 1965. On other issues—like 8th district Congressman Ben Rosenthal's Consumer Protection Agency—Delaney more and more often found himself voting more with Republicans than Democrats as the sixties became the seventies. In 1970 he went so far as to publicly endorse Conservative Party candidate James Buckley for the Senate.

That may have marked the high water point of Delaney's conservative phase, for it enraged then Queens Democratic Chairman Matthew Troy, who ran a candidate against Delaney in the 1972 Democratic primary. Troy's candidate got 46% of the vote, and following Delaney's reelection that year he effected a reconciliation with the almost entirely liberal New York Democratic delegation, including Rosenthal, to whom he had long refused to speak. Delaney was accordingly elected chairman of delegation, and he started voting more often with Democrats and liberals on the Rules Committee. The 75-year-old Delaney would probably like to serve at least one more term—and he certainly could be reelected; Troy has been ousted and the Congressman gets three-party endorsement in the general. That would probably give him at least some time as Rules Chairman, and allow him a little more time to pave the way for the man who he certainly would like to see succeed him, his son Patrick. Indeed, without a Delaney in the race this is a district, perhaps the only one left in New York City, which could well go Republican.

Census Data Pop. 467,207. Central city, 100%; suburban, 0%. Median family income, $10,657; families above $15,000: 24%; families below $3,000: 7%. Median years education, 10.8.

The Voters

Median voting age 48.
Employment profile White collar, 53%. Blue collar, 34%. Service, 13%. Farm, –%.
Ethnic groups Black, 2%. Spanish, 2%. Total foreign stock, 55%. Italy, 14%; Germany, 8%; Poland, USSR, 3% each; Austria, Greece, UK, 2% each; Czechoslovakia, Hungary, 1% each.

Presidential vote

1972	Nixon (R)	128,699	(73%)
	McGovern (D)	46,700	(27%)
1968	Nixon (R)	98,641	(54%)
	Humphrey (D)	68,644	(37%)
	Wallace (AI)	16,997	(9%)

Rep. James J. Delaney (D) Elected 1948; b. Mar. 19, 1901, New York City; home, Long Island City; St. John's U., LL.B. 1932; Catholic.

Career Asst. Dist. Atty., Queens Co., 1936–44; U.S. House of Reps., 1945–47.

Offices 2267 RHOB, 202-225-3965. Also 100–35 Metropolitan Ave., Forest Hills 11375, 212-793-0729.

Committees

Rules (2d).

Group Ratings

	ADA	COPE	LWV	RIPON	NFU	LCV	CFA	NAB	NSI	ACA
1974	61	100	50	38	93	59	77	50	60	27
1973	48	100	67	40	89	50	100	–	–	38
1972	31	82	50	62	67	32	100	44	100	55

Key Votes

1) Foreign Aid	AGN	6) Gov Abortn Aid	AGN	11) Pub Cong Election $	AGN
2) Busing	AGN	7) Coed Phys Ed	AGN	12) Turkish Arms Cutoff	FOR
3) ABM	AGN	8) Pov Lawyer Gag	FOR	13) Youth Camp Regs	FOR
4) B-1 Bomber	FOR	9) Pub Trans Sub	FOR	14) Strip Mine Veto	AGN
5) Nerve Gas	AGN	10) EZ Voter Regis	FOR	15) Farm Bill Veto	FOR

Election Results

1974 general:	James J. Delaney (D-R-C)	92,231	(93%)	($29,698)
	Theodore E. Garrison (L)	6,924	(7%)	($1,846)
1974 primary:	James J. Delaney (D), unopposed			
1972 general:	James J. Delaney (D-R-C)	141,323	(93%)	($56,396)
	Loretta E. Gressey (L)	9,965	(7%)	(NA)

◆ ◆ ◆ ◆ ◆

TENTH DISTRICT

In early 1973, Mario Biaggi looked like the man most likely to become the next Mayor of New York. For eight years City Hall had been in the hands of John V. Lindsay, an Ivy League WASP who had been elected twice with less than an absolute majority of the vote and who each time had failed to carry the city outside Manhattan. Hostility to Lindsay was not simply a quaint practice of New York cab drivers; it was becoming a fundamental fact of middle class life, and New York, especially in its outer boroughs, remains a majority middle-class white city. Part of the discontent stemmed from the feeling that Lindsay was overly sympathetic to blacks and Puerto Ricans, and to a related fear of increasing crime. Part of it stemmed from a deterioration of city services, most notably in middle class areas at the edges of the city. Part of it stemmed from a basic cultural hostility to the kind of effete, snobbish Manhattanites who were perceived, correctly, as Lindsay's most enthusiastic backers.

For all of this, 10th district Congressman Mario Biaggi seemed like a campaign consultant's dream. On his retirement in 1968, Biaggi was the most decorated member of the New York Police force. He was elected Congressman three times from a heavily Italian middle–class district in the Bronx (to which a similar portion of Queens was added in 1972), with the endorsement of both the Democratic and the Conservative Parties; and the district he captured had formerly been represented by a Republican. The candidate himself still lived in a small apartment on Mosholu Boulevard in the Bronx, and he spoke the language of middle–class, Catholic New Yorkers in clear, unmistakable fashion.

The Italian-American mayoral aspirant was against crime and said he knew what to do about it. He was also, of course, for proper city services in middle class areas. But Biaggi was by no means a knee jerk conservative. He had worked to expose and improve conditions in hospitals for retarded children. As Congressman, he had taken action to assert the basic rights of servicemen. And he had voted for at least some measures to end the Vietnam war. Biaggi was, as the 1972 *Almanac* put it, a kind of urban populist with a law and order accent. Accordingly he represented pretty accurately the views of hundreds of thousands of New Yorkers, and in early 1973 it was plain that he was the only mayoral candidate who could evoke genuine enthusiasm and massive popular support.

But Biaggi was certainly not going to get any support from any of what John Lindsay had long before called the "power brokers." He did have the support of the Conservative Party, but he had obtained that only after making certain assurances about his past. And in fact there was widespread suspicion about Biaggi's basic honesty. Suddenly, in April 1973, the papers broke the story: Biaggi had lied when he said he had not taken the Fifth Amendment before a grand jury investigation. Brazenly Biaggi sued to get some, but not all, the grand jury records made public; the judge, not to be toyed with, revealed them all—and they confirmed that Biaggi had been lying. His constituency, which had rallied to him because they seemed to epitomize their concept of decency, now quickly evaporated; in the Democratic primary, he won only 21%, finishing third in a field of four.

Even in that rout, Biaggi retained a following, particularly in Italian-American neighborhoods like those that dominate the 10th district. But the spark had gone out. Biaggi had clearly been trying to compete in the big time with only minor league talent. A measure of the disenchantment here is not so much Biaggi's showing in the next general election as the fact that he managed to lose the Conservative primary to another candidate, leaving him, peculiarly, with the Democratic and Republican nominations, but not the Liberal and Conservative. For once it may have been significant how many votes a candidate got on each line. For running in a Democratic year, Biaggi the Democrat took only 54% of the vote—an indication that the Congressman, given a strong enough opponent, might be beatable in some future contest.

Census Data Pop. 474,745. Central city, 100%; suburban, 0%. Median family income, $9,988; families above $15,000: 22%; families below $3,000: 9%. Median years education, 10.7.

The Voters

Median voting age 45.
Employment profile White collar, 52%. Blue collar, 34%. Service, 14%. Farm, –%.
Ethnic groups Black, 13%. Spanish 9%. Total foreign stock, 47%. Italy, 17%; Ireland, 6%;
Germany, 3%; USSR, Poland, Greece, UK, 2% each; Austria, 1%.

Presidential vote

1972	Nixon (R)	103,372	(63%)
	McGovern (D)	60,343	(37%)
1968	Nixon (R)	77,684	(46%)
	Humphrey (D)	78,323	(46%)
	Wallace (AI)	13,830	(8%)

Rep. Mario Biaggi (D) Elected 1968; b. Oct. 26, 1917, New York City;
home, Bronx; N.Y. Law School, LL.B. 1963; Catholic.

Career Letter carrier, U.S.P.O., 1936–42; N.Y. City Police Dept.,
1942–65; Community Relations Specialist, N.Y. State Div. of Housing,
1961–63; Asst. to the N.Y. State Secy. of State, 1961–65; Practicing atty.,
1966–; Pres., Natl. Police Officers Assn., 1967.

Offices 211 CHOB, 202-225-2464. Also 2004 Williamsbridge Rd., Bronx
10461, 212-931-0100.

Committees

Education and Labor (15th). Subcommittees: Labor-Management Relations; Labor Standards;
Post-secondary Education.

Merchant Marine and Fisheries (9th). Subcommittees: Coast Guard and Navigation (Chairman);
Merchant Marine; Panama Canal.

Group Ratings

	ADA	COPE	LWV	RIPON	NFU	LCV	CFA	NAB	NSI	ACA
1974	32	82	58	25	75	53	75	36	100	62
1973	57	100	70	50	92	76	100	–	–	25
1972	56	91	75	50	71	40	100	25	50	27

Key Votes

1) Foreign Aid	FOR	6) Gov Abortn Aid	AGN	11) Pub Cong Election $	AGN
2) Busing	AGN	7) Coed Phys Ed	AGN	12) Turkish Arms Cutoff	FOR
3) ABM	ABS	8) Pov Lawyer Gag	FOR	13) Youth Camp Regs	FOR
4) B-1 Bomber	FOR	9) Pub Trans Sub	FOR	14) Strip Mine Veto	FOR
5) Nerve Gas	ABS	10) EZ Voter Regis	AGN	15) Farm Bill Veto	FOR

Election Results

1974 general:	Mario Biaggi (D-R)	75,375	(82%)	($16,524)
	Francis L. McHugh (C)	10,250	(11%)	($3,381)
	John P. Hagan (L)	5,797	(6%)	
1974 primary	Mario Biaggi (D), unopposed			
1972 general:	Mario Biaggi (D-R-C)	130,200	(94%)	($12,719)
	Michael S. Bank (L)	8,397	(6%)	(NA)

◆ ◆ ◆ ◆ ◆

ELEVENTH DISTRICT

The 11th congressional district of New York is the southeastern corner of Brooklyn, the extreme
southern and southeastern edges of Queens, and the Rockaway Peninsula. Separated from each

NEW YORK

other by marshy Jamaica Bay, and circling Kennedy Airport like a donut, these are geographically disparate areas and the neighborhoods contained within them are diverse. East New York in Brooklyn is an aging Italian community, hard by the black ghetto of Brownsville, which is in such miserable condition it is rapidly being abandoned. To the south, Canarsie and Flatlands are middle class Italian and Jewish communities. These two areas were developed on marshland sometime after the rest of Brooklyn; here, in 1970, the borough's first suburban style shopping center was opened. The Rockaway Peninsula, separating Jamaica Bay from the Ocean, is largely Jewish, with a black ghetto at one end. North of Kennedy Airport, entirely cut off from the rest of the district, is the middle–class black neighborhood of Springfield Gardens.

In the face of an increasing conservatism among its voters, the 11th remained heavily Democratic in local elections. Even as it went for Richard Nixon in 1972, the district provided its Democratic Congressman, Frank Brasco, a 2–1 reelection margin. But the next two years were not kind to either officeholder. Nixon, of course, was finally demonstrated to have criminally obstructed justice in the Watergate case. And Frank Brasco, first elected in 1966 at the age of 34 and seemingly destined for a long congressional career, was convicted in 1974 of taking bribes and sentenced to jail.

Brasco got his job through the Brooklyn Democratic machine, which had held the seat for thirty years for Eugene J. Keogh, and had never had any trouble protecting Brasco in the past. But the Congressman was convicted before the primary and he was not a candidate for reelection. Instead the Brooklyn organization supported Leonard Yoswein, a Beame administration official. But its support, even in the 11th which is the home district of supposed Brooklyn boss Meade Esposito, is worth considerably less than the amount of media attention devoted to it would suggest. The winner here was James Scheuer, a former Congressman from the faraway Bronx (1965-73), defeated in his primary in 1972 and now, technically, a Brooklyn resident. Actually, Scheuer's residence in all the districts he has represented has been largely fictitious; as a wealthy real estate promoter, he has had little desire to live in the east Bronx or Canarsie. But that is unlikely to affect his reelection chances which, for the moment at least, seem excellent. He is, incidentally, one of the "freshmen" whose presence in large numbers has so altered the composition and tone of the Commerce and Science Committees.

Census Data Pop. 469,790. Central city, 100%; suburban, 0%. Median family income, $10,834; families above $15,000: 26%; families below $3,000: 9%. Median years education, 11.7.

The Voters

Median voting age 43.
Employment profile White collar, 58%. Blue collar, 31%. Service, 11%. Farm, –%.
Ethnic groups Black, 17%. Spanish, 6%. Total foreign stock, 41%. Italy, 9%; USSR, 8%; Poland, 6%; Germany, Austria, Ireland, 2% each; UK, 1%.

Presidential vote

1972	Nixon (R)	80,662	(52%)
	McGovern (D)	75,129	(48%)
1968	Nixon (R)	52,709	(33%)
	Humphrey (D)	95,497	(61%)
	Wallace (AI)	9,281	(6%)

Rep. James H. Scheuer (D) Elected 1974; b. Feb. 6, 1920, New York City; home, Neponsit; Harvard Business School, 1943, Swarthmore Col., A.B. 1945, Columbia U., LL.B. 1948; Jewish.

Career Army Air Corps, WWII; Economist, U.S. Foreign Economic Admin., 1945–46; Mbr., Legal Staff, Ofc. of Price Stabilization, 1951–52; Pres., N.Y. City Citizens Housing and Planning Cncl.; U.S. House of Reps., 1965–73; Pres., Natl. Housing Conf., 1972–74.

Offices 2438 RHOB, 202-225-5471. Also 1943 Rockaway Parkway, Canarsie 11263, 202-251-2222.

Committees

Interstate and Foreign Commerce (18th). Subcommittees: Health and Environment; Oversight and Investigation.

Science and Technology (12th). Subcommittees: Aviation and Transportation Research and Development; Domestic and International Scientific Planning and Analysis; Environment and the Atmosphere; Science, Research, and Technology.

Group Ratings: Newly Elected

Key Votes

1) Foreign Aid	FOR	6) Gov Abortn Aid	NE	11) Pub Cong Election $	NE
2) Busing	NE	7) Coed Phys Ed	FOR	12) Turkish Arms Cutoff	NE
3) ABM	NE	8) Pov Lawyer Gag	NE	13) Youth Camp Regs	FOR
4) B-1 Bomber	AGN	9) Pub Trans Sub	NE	14) Strip Mine Veto	AGN
5) Nerve Gas	NE	10) EZ Voter Regis	NE	15) Farm Bill Veto	FOR

Election Results

1974 general:	James H. Scheuer (D)	62,388	(72%)	($301,135)
	Edward G. Desborough (R)	12,297	(14%)	($809)
	Christopher Acer (C)	7,181	(8%)	($865)
	Tibby Blum (L)	4,485	(5%)	(NA)
1974 primary:	James H. Scheuer (D)	19,028	(53%)	
	Leonard Yoswein (D)	16,587	(47%)	

◆ ◆ ◆ ◆ ◆

TWELFTH DISTRICT

One of the undeniable celebrities in the House of Representatives today is the member from the 12th congressional district of New York, Shirley Chisholm. Though she has been in the House since 1968—when she walloped former CORE Director (and later Nixon Administration official) James Farmer—Chisholm retains the image of the obstreperous freshman, rebelling against the powers that be, the image that she projected when she entitled her autobiography *Unbought and Unbossed*. The image is central to Chisholm's rise to fame, for it was her refusal to knuckle under to male political leaders in her home area of Bedford-Stuyvesant that helped her assemble the group of volunteers which, together with her own oratory, elected her to the New York Assembly in 1964 and four years later to Congress.

Today everyone remembers Chisholm as presidential candidate in 1972, the first black woman, as everyone must know, to run seriously for the office. She ran in most of the primaries—and joined the stop McGovern forces—clear through to the Democratic national convention in Miami Beach. Though she was unable to win as much as 10% of the vote in any state, she did manage to be treated on a par with other candidates when it came to television debates.

During the campaign, Ms. Chisholm often complained that people were not taking her seriously enough, and that she was as qualified for the office as the others. But around Capitol Hill many people sympathetic to her complained that she had done little legislative work, preferring the glamor of the lecture circuit to the hard work of the mark up session in the subcommittee room. There was considerable justice in this complaint; to call her one of the less active members of the Education and Labor Committee would be to put it mildly. In 1973, as if stung by some criticisms, she did become more involved, though quietly, in the legislative process. Her greatest achievement to date is the inclusion of domestic workers in the federal minimum wage law.

Chisholm talks from time to time about retiring; it sounds more like an effort to get people to pay more attention to her than a serious projection of what she is likely to do. When she was first elected, in 1968, her district included all of the Bedford-Stuyvesant section of Brooklyn; its lines had been drawn specifically to elect Brooklyn's first black member of Congress. For 1974, an ill-advised lawsuit forced the readjustment of the Brooklyn district lines, supposedly to produce two black-and-Puerto-Rican majority districts. In that respect the effort was entirely unsuccessful (see Fourteenth District), for minority voter participation is so low here—lower in New York City than anywhere else in the country—that blacks are easily outvoted by others. The drawers of the new district lines had hoped that Chisholm would run in the 46% black 14th district, but she wisely declined; no more than one-quarter of the actual voters there are black. Instead, she picked the new 12th, which includes the eastern half of Bedford-Stuyvesant, the huge Brooklyn ghetto; Bushwick, an old Italian neighborhood which is rapidly becoming a majority black; and Williamsburgh and Greenpoint, old ethnic Brooklyn neighborhoods whose aged residents are hostile to whatever they perceive as forces for change. The district was 54% black, 20% Puerto Rican, and 20% foreign stock in 1970; the figures have changed by now, but there is no base here for any candidate who could challenge Chisholm.

Census Data Pop. 467,726. Central city, 100%; suburban, 0%. Median family income, $6,432; families above $15,000: 7%; families below $3,000: 19%. Median years education, 9.6.

The Voters

Median voting age 38.
Employment profile White collar, 37%. Blue collar, 45%. Service, 18%. Farm, –%.
Ethnic groups Black, 54%. Spanish, 20%. Total foreign stock, 16%. Italy, 6%; Poland, 2%.

Presidential vote

1972	Nixon (R)	NA
	McGovern (D)	NA
1968	Nixon (R)	NA
	Humphrey (D)	NA
	Wallace (AI)	NA

Rep. Shirley Chisholm (D) Elected 1968; b. Nov. 30, 1924, Brooklyn; home, Brooklyn; Brooklyn Col., B.A. 1946, Columbia U., M.A. 1952, Methodist.

Career Nursery school teacher and dir., 1946–53; Dir., Hamilton Madison Child Care Ctr., 1954–59; Educ. Consultant, N.Y. City Div. of Day Care, 1959–64; N.Y. State Assembly, 1964–68.

Offices 123 CHOB, 202-225-6231. Also 1149 Eastern Ave., Brooklyn 11213, 212-596-3500.

Committees

Education and Labor (14th). Subcommittees: Elementary, Secondary and Vocational Education; Post-secondary Education; Select Subcommittee on Education.

Group Ratings

	ADA	COPE	LWV	RIPON	NFU	LCV	CFA	NAB	NSI	ACA
1974	100	100	82	80	78	80	100	18	13	10
1973	100	100	91	67	95	100	100	–	–	11
1972	69	100	100	64	83	83	100	9	0	7

Key Votes

1) Foreign Aid	FOR	6) Gov Abortn Aid	FOR	11) Pub Cong Election $	ABS
2) Busing	FOR	7) Coed Phys Ed	FOR	12) Turkish Arms Cutoff	FOR
3) ABM	ABS	8) Pov Lawyer Gag	AGN	13) Youth Camp Regs	FOR
4) B-1 Bomber	AGN	9) Pub Trans Sub	FOR	14) Strip Mine Veto	AGN
5) Nerve Gas	ABS	10) EZ Voter Regis	FOR	15) Farm Bill Veto	AGN

Election Results

1974 general:	Shirley Chisholm (D-L)	26,446	(81%)	($8,947)
	Francis J. Voyticky (R)	4,577	(14%)	($0)
	Martin Shephard, Jr. (C)	1,522	(5%)	(NA)
1974 primary:	Shirley Chisholm (D)	7,798	(67%)	
	Clarence A. Robertson (D)	3,872	(33%)	
1972 general:	Shirley Chisholm (D-L)	57,821	(90%)	($4,796)
	John M. Coleman (R)	6,373	(10%)	($0)

◆ ◆ ◆ ◆ ◆

THIRTEENTH DISTRICT

The 13th congressional district of New York, in south central Brooklyn, might be called the Ocean Parkway district: it takes in terrain from both sides of that thoroughfare as it makes its way from Prospect Park to Coney Island. There is a large Italian-American community in Bensonhurst, most of which was removed from the district by the 1974 redistricting; still the 13th, according at least to the census figures, is one of the most heavily Italian-American districts in the nation. But most of the neighborhoods here, from Midwood in the north, through the streets lined with low rise apartments along the Parkway, to Sheepshead Bay, Brighton Beach, and Coney Island in the south, are heavily Jewish. With Flatbush, most of which is in the 16th district, the 13th is the heart of Jewish Brooklyn. Though no reliable data exist, the 13th is probably the nation's most heavily Jewish district, and most likely the 13th and the 16th are the only Jewish majority districts in the nation. It is, of course, also overwhelmingly Democratic by tradition. So anyone who refuses to believe that George McGovern lost a large number of the normally Democratic ballots of elderly Jewish voters should take a look at the results here in the 13th, where Richard Nixon got 49% of the vote.

As well as being the heart of Jewish Brooklyn, the 13th district has always been one of the bastions of support for the Democratic machine here. With its patronage tentacles covering the Brooklyn courts and Borough Hall, the machine used to be able to man all the election districts here with faithful—and hungry—precinct workers who would tell their neighbors who it would be good to vote for; and generally they did. For these are not the wealthy, trendy, assimilated Jews of Manhattan's Upper East Side; these are people who own small stores or work for the city or as teachers, and who have been struggling to send their kids through school and to accumulate a decent retirement reserve for themselves. There has seldom been the time here, or the energy, for a reform politics; elections, like everything else, have been a business—and a tough one.

So for years the Congressman from the 13th has been a machine stalwart since the district was created in its current form in 1944: first Leo Rayfiel (1945–47), who became a federal judge; then Abraham Multer (1947–68), who finally got his state judgeship despite talk that he had been engaged in unsavory banking dealings in the Bahamas; and then Bertram Podell (1968–75), who sad to report ended up before the bench rather than on it. In 1973 Podell was indicted for taking $41,000 to get the Civil Aeronautics Board to award a Bahama route to a Florida airline; he claimed that this was just a plot by the Nixon Administration to discredit his attacks on Watergate, but after he lost his primary he pled guilty.

Podell's nomination in a 1968 special election had been a triumph for the Brooklyn machine in difficult times; he had been challenged by a peace candidate just after the Tet offensive, and was still associated with the Johnson Administration's prosecution of the Vietnam war. Podell's defeat in 1974 was a rebuke to the Brooklyn machine in a time of greater adversity, at least if one measures that by congressional elections; for this machine, which is supposed to be all powerful, originally supported only two of the six Brooklyn members of the House. The man who beat Podell, 36-year-old Stephen Solarz, was elected to the Assembly against a machine candidate in 1968, and fairly easily beat Podell in 1974. The general election, of course, was an anticlimax; Solarz won 82% of the vote. He is a member of the International Affairs and Post Office and Civil Service Committees, and there is no reason to believe this young liberal will not be around the Congress for many years to come.

Census Data Pop. 468,726. Central city, 100%; suburban, 0%. Median family income, $10,294; families above $15,000: 25%; families below $3,000: 9%. Median years education, 11.2.

The Voters

Median voting age 50.
Employment profile White collar, 64%. Blue collar, 28%. Service, 8%. Farm, –%.
Ethnic groups Black, 2%. Spanish, 2%. Total foreign stock, 61%. Italy, 16%; USSR, 14%; Poland, 9%; Austria, 4%; Germany, Hungary, Romania, 2% each; Ireland, UK, Czechoslovakia, 1% each.

Presidential vote

1972	Nixon (R)	NA
	McGovern (D)	NA
1968	Nixon (R)	NA
	Humphrey (D)	NA
	Wallace (AI)	NA

Rep. Stephen J. Solarz (D) Elected 1974; b. Sept. 12, 1940, New York City; home, Brooklyn; Brandeis U., A.B. 1962, Columbia U., M.A. 1967; Jewish.

Career N.Y. State Assembly, 1968–74.

Offices 1228 LHOB, 202-225-2361. Also 1628 Kings Hwy., Brooklyn 11229, 212-965-5100.

Committees

International Relations (20th). Subcommittees: International Economic Policy; International Resources, Food, and Energy.

Post Office and Civil Service (19th). Subcommittees: Employee Political Rights and Inter-governmental Programs; Manpower and Civil Service.

Group Ratings: Newly Elected

Key Votes

1) Foreign Aid	FOR	6) Gov Abortn Aid	NE	11) Pub Cong Election $	NE
2) Busing	NE	7) Coed Phys Ed	ABS	12) Turkish Arms Cutoff	NE
3) ABM	NE	8) Pov Lawyer Gag	NE	13) Youth Camp Regs	FOR
4) B-1 Bomber	AGN	9) Pub Trans Sub	NE	14) Strip Mine Veto	AGN
5) Nerve Gas	NE	10) EZ Voter Regis	NE	15) Farm Bill Veto	AGN

Election Results

1974 general:	Stephan J. Solarz (D-L)	91,008	(82%)	($65,334)
	Jack N. Dobosh (R-C)	20,229	(18%)	($623)
1974 primary:	Stephan J. Solarz (D)	22,533	(44%)	
	Bertram L. Podell (D)	17,339	(34%)	
	Robert Chira (D)	11,203	(22%)	

♦ ♦ ♦ ♦ ♦

FOURTEENTH DISTRICT

The 14th congressional district of New York, in Brooklyn, is about as polyglot an area as you can find in the United States. The district extends along the Brooklyn waterfront from the Italian neighborhood of Red Hook to the Queens border, past the renovated brownstones of Brooklyn Heights and Cobble Hill, with their affluent young (and politically liberal) residents. To the east is downtown Brooklyn, with a skyline that would be impressive anywhere but in New York; it is paled here by the vista from Brooklyn Heights of Lower Manhattan. Inland, the 14th extends far past the transitional Fort Greene area into Bedford-Stuyvesant. North are parts of Greenpoint and Williamsburgh, with large Orthodox and Hasidic Jewish and also Puerto Rican communities that live in uneasy proximity.

If you were to look at the census statistics about the 14th, you would be seriously mistaken about its political makeup—as were the people who brought the lawsuit to form its present boundaries. In 1970, some 46% of the district's residents were black, 18% were Puerto Ricans; but neither of these groups has much clout here, for the simple reason that they scarcely vote at all. Just consider the 1972 presidential election, when 76,000 people voted in what was then the heavily black 12th district; at the same time, in the 13th, which had the same total population, but which was a majority Jewish, 189,000 people voted. In the 14th as currently constituted, the voting blocs which really matter are the Italians in Red Hook in South Brooklyn, some of the old Hasidic Jews, and some few—far fewer than the population figures would suggest—middle–class blacks. These are the people who vote in Democratic primaries, and who therefore make whatever electoral decisions the 14th district is called upon to make.

In 1974, the 14th was called upon to elect a new Congressman. John Rooney, first chosen in a 1944 special election, seated in the House on D-Day, had finally decided to retire. For years Rooney was Chairman of the State, Justice, Commerce, and Judiciary Subcommittee of the House Appropriations Committee, in which capacity he terrorized diplomats who wanted larger expense allowances and always gave J. Edgar Hoover's FBI a larger appropriation than Hoover requested. Rooney's reactionary politics inspired primary challenges in 1968, 1970, and 1972, and none was ever successful, though at least one—Allard Lowenstein in 1972—seems to have been thwarted by vote-stealing tactics by Brooklyn machine hacks. In his last years in Congress Rooney sometimes, with visible reluctance, voted a liberal line on issues, to forestall the opposition; but even more often he simply failed to show up. Ill and tired, he finally faded away rather than died but the result, as far as the legislative process was concerned, was about the same.

Rooney's successor is the same man who poured $200,000 of his own money in an unsuccessful attempt to beat the old man in 1968. After exposure to the tactics of Rooney's minions, millionaire Fred Richmond apparently decided it was better to join than to try to beat them, and he did. He soon became a City Councilman (though there were rumors he continued to live in his posh Manhattan town house), and a foundation he controlled found itself pouring large amounts into projects which just happened to be situated within the borders of the 14th district.

In the 1974 Democratic primary Richmond was further blessed in that his main opponent was Donald Elliott, head of the city planning department under Mayor John Lindsay. Lindsay was never particularly popular outside Manhattan, and Richmond easily won that primary and the general election, in which Elliott was the Liberal nominee. Richmond now serves on the Agriculture Committee, which makes more sense for an urban representative than might at first seem to be the case; for that body has jurisdiction not only over food stamps but over a variety of policies which affect food prices and thus are of great interest to every city dweller.

Census Data Pop. 467,735. Central city, 100%; suburban, 0%. Median family income, $6,874; families above $15,000: 11%; families below $3,000: 17%. Median years education, 10.3.

The Voters

Median voting age 39.
Employment profile White collar, 47%. Blue collar, 37%. Service, 16%. Farm, –%.
Ethnic groups Black, 46%. Spanish, 18%. Total foreign stock, 28%. Italy, 5%; Poland, 2%; USSR, Hungary, 1% each.

Presidential vote

1972	Nixon (R)	NA
	McGovern (D)	NA
1968	Nixon (R)	NA
	Humphrey (D)	NA
	Wallace (AI)	NA

Rep. Frederick W. Richmond (D) Elected 1974; b. Nov. 15, 1923 Mattapan, Mass., home, Brooklyn; Harvard U., 1942–43, Boston U., B.A. 1945.

Career Navy, WWII; Pres., Greater N.Y. Urban League, 1959–64; Walco Natl. Corp., 1960–74; Bd. Chm., Carnegie Hall Corp., 1960–74; N.Y. City Human Rights Commissioner, 1964–70; Budget Dir., N.Y. State Cncl. on the Arts, 1965–74; N.Y. City Taxi and Limousine Commissioner, 1970–72; N.Y. City Cncl., 1973–74.

Offices 1533 LHOB, 202-225-5936. Also 1368 Fulton St., Brooklyn 11216, 212-522-7121.

Committees

Agriculture (15th). Subcommittees: Conservation and Credit; Department Operations, Investigations and Oversight: Domestic Marketing and Consumer Relations.

Small Business (19th). Commodities and Services; SBA Oversight and Minority Enterprise.

Group Ratings: Newly Elected

Key Votes

1) Foreign Aid	FOR	6) Gov Abortn Aid	NE	11) Pub Cong Election $	NE
2) Busing	NE	7) Coed Phys Ed	FOR	12) Turkish Arms Cutoff	NE
3) ABM	NE	8) Pov Lawyer Gag	NE	13) Youth Camp Regs	FOR
4) B-1 Bomber	AGN	9) Pub Trans Sub	NE	14) Strip Mine Veto	AGN
5) Nerve Gas	NE	10) EZ Voter Regis	NE	15) Farm Bill Veto	AGN

Election Results

1974 general:	Frederick W. Richmond (D)	33,195	(72%)	($245,533)
	Donald H. Elliott (L)	6,186	(13%)	($1,000)
	Michael Carbajal, Jr. (R)	5,360	(12%)	($84,180)
	Alexander W. Nojovits (C)	1,438	(3%)	($0)
1974 primary:	Frederick W. Richmond (D)	9,771	(42%)	
	Donald H. Elliott (D)	5,998	(26%)	
	Cesar A. Perales (D)	4,348	(19%)	
	David J. Billings (D)	3,052	(03%)	

◆ ◆ ◆ ◆ ◆

FIFTEENTH DISTRICT

To many who have never seen it, Brooklyn means nonstop slums, the tenement apartment of Ralph and Alice Kramden, and the fear of lurking crime. That is not an accurate, or at least a wholly accurate, picture. Brooklyn has all the diversity one might expect of a city of more than 2.5 million people. If Brooklyn has some of the nation's most fearsome slums—and it does in Brownsville and Bedford-Stuyvesant—New York's largest borough also has neighborhoods of $75,000 homes. And though the downtown streets are grimy, the parks of Brooklyn are green and its yacht harbors filled with wind blown sails and spinnakers. Nothing is dainty about Brooklyn, but in its pleasant middle class neighborhoods, the fear of crime is more academic than residents seem to want to admit. In short, a few trees do grow here.

A disproportionate share of Brooklyn's middle class neighborhoods lie within the boundaries of New York's 15th congressional district. The 15th begins amidst the newly renovated brownstones of Park Slope, a neighborhood just off Prospect Park—a one laid out by the architects of Central Park, and often considered their masterpiece. To the south is the Sunset Park neighborhood, which has the largest concentration of Norwegian-Americans between Bergen and Minneapolis. In the same area is Borough Park, a middle–class Irish and Italian area. And below that, where New York Harbor spills into the Atlantic and the Verrazano Bridge arches over to Staten Island, is Bay Ridge.

Except for restored Brooklyn Heights, Bay Ridge is probably Brooklyn's highest income neighborhood. But while Brooklyn Heights is home to the likes of Norman Mailer and WASPy Wall Streeters, Bay Ridge is a couple of steps upward on the ladder for middle–class Brooklynites of Irish or Italian ancestry; people here still take their political cues from the *Daily News*, not the *Times* or the *Wall Street Journal*. Bay Ridge residents are far more conservative than the really wealthy people of New York; indeed, this may be the city's most Republican and conservative, with both a capital and small c, neighborhood in New York. As the sixties turned into seventies, the rest of the 15th district also was becoming more conservative; by 1972 Republicans were representing most of the area in the state legislature.

Until 1960 what is now the 15th was a Republican stronghold in congressional elections. But in the year that John F. Kennedy was heading the ticket, a 41-year-old lawyer named Hugh Carey pulled a major upset in the district by beating the Republican incumbent. Despite Republican redistrictings and conservative trends, Carey continued to win here; he was one of the few New York politicians who could win Irish working class votes and at the same time maintain a voting record acceptable to ideological liberals. He switched from hawk to dove, for example, way back in 1966, reportedly from listening to the arguments of several of his twelve children.

Carey always had the ambition—and aptitude and talent, if he could get well known—for higher office. He actually ran for City Council President, a mostly honorific post which for some reason gives its holder great publicity, in 1969. In between bouts of City politics, he became something of a power in the House. In 1971 he led the Brooklyn delegation in supporting Hale Boggs for Majority Leader; as a reward for being on the winning side, he got a seat on Ways and Means. There he was a major pusher behind revenue sharing, and also urged, unsuccessfully, more tax breaks for parents with children in private schools.

Then in 1974 Carey decided to run for Governor—and won. That left his House seat up for grabs, and in another year, when the Republican President wasn't being driven from office for criminal conduct, the Republicans might have made a race of it. But in 1974, the only contest was in the Democratic primary, and the winner there was the machine choice, Leo Zeferetti. But Zeferetti had not come up through the usual Brooklyn clubhouse ladder; instead, like the Bronx's Mario Biaggi, he was a well known cop—in his case President of the Correction Officers Benevolent Association—and then moved quickly into electoral politics. With an Italian name, a police background, and roots in the district, Zeferetti was an unbeatable candidate, and he won with 58% of the vote—a notably better showing than Carey himself had made here in 1972. Now Zeferetti serves on the House Education and Labor Committee, a body so packed with liberals that any pertinent conservative impulses he may have will be unlikely to find an effective outlet; and on Merchant Marine and Fisheries, where he will surely vote to maintain the elaborate system of subsidies to business and labor which keeps everyone connected with the Brooklyn docks, among others, comfortably off despite possible lack of actual demand for their services.

Census Data Pop. 466,741. Central city, 100%; suburban, 0%. Median family income, $9,629; families above $15,000: 21%; families below $3,000: 10%. Median years education, 10.5.

The Voters

Median voting age 46.
Employment profile White collar, 54%. Blue collar, 34%. Service, 12%. Farm, –%.
Ethnic groups Black, 5%. Spanish, 9%. Total foreign stock, 50%. Italy, 21%; Ireland, 4%; Poland, 3%; USSR, UK, 2% each; Germany, Canada, Greece, 1% each.

Presidential vote

1972	Nixon (R)	NA
	McGovern (D)	NA
1968	Nixon (R)	NA
	Humphrey (D)	NA
	Wallace (AI)	NA

Rep. Leo C. Zeferetti (D) Elected 1974; b. July 15, 1927, Brooklyn; home, Brooklyn; NYU, CUNY.

Career Navy, WWII; Officer, N.Y. City Dept. of Correction, 1957–74; Pres., Correction Officers Benevolent Assn., 1969–74; Mbr., N.Y. State Crime Control Planning Bd., 1973.

Offices 1726 LHOB, 202-225-4105. Also 526 86th St., Brooklyn 11209, 212-680-1000.

Committees

Education and Labor (24th). Subcommittees: Elementary, Secondary and Vocational Education; Labor Standards; Select Subcommittee on Education.

Merchant Marine and Fisheries (26th). Subcommittees: Fisheries and Wildlife Conservation and the Environment; Merchant Marine; Oceanography.

Group Ratings: Newly Elected

Key Votes

1) Foreign Aid	FOR	6) Gov Abortn Aid	NE	11) Pub Cong Election $	NE
2) Busing	NE	7) Coed Phys Ed	AGN	12) Turkish Arms Cutoff	NE
3) ABM	NE	8) Pov Lawyer Gag	NE	13) Youth Camp Regs	FOR
4) B-1 Bomber	FOR	9) Pub Trans Sub	NE	14) Strip Mine Veto	AGN
5) Nerve Gas	NE	10) EZ Voter Regis	NE	15) Farm Bill Veto	FOR

Election Results

1974 general:	Leo C. Zeferetti (D-C)	53,733	(58%)	($53,775)
	Austin D. Canade (R)	34,814	(38%)	($39,133)
	Herbert M. Feinsod (L)	3,375	(4%)	(NA)
1974 primary:	Leo C. Zeferetti (D)	12,047	(50%)	
	Arthur J. Paone (D)	11,985	(50%)	

◆ ◆ ◆ ◆ ◆

SIXTEENTH DISTRICT

Flatbush is the heart of Brooklyn, square in the borough's geographical and psychological center. The name Flatbush, indeed, has become practically synonymous in the public mind with Brooklyn itself. Probably most of the people in Queens or Long Island have some roots in Brooklyn, or Flatbush; but a glance at the map shows how these places differ. Freeways crisscross the suburban terrain, and most of Queens as well; but Brooklyn has only one, running along its shore. Proposals for another, cutting across the borough, have been killed. Most of Flatbush and Brooklyn was laid out and occupied before the automobile became a necessity; and you can still live in these one and two family houses, walk to shop for things, take the subway to work, and get on quite as comfortably as most New Yorkers with cars.

During the 1910s and 1920s the then new neighborhoods of Flatbush and East Flatbush were attracting thousands of newly middle income Jews who had grown up on the Lower East Side or in some other Manhattan slum. Today Flatbush remains heavily Jewish, though more and more blacks have been moving in from Crown Heights and Bedford-Stuyvesant to the north. And as young people here grow up and move to Long Island, Westchester County, or the Upper East Side of Manhattan—or simply, as so many have done, leave the New York metropolitan area altogether—the average age of the people left in Flatbush has risen. Among the older people, there is a good deal of nervous talk about crime. Nevertheless, through all the years of law and order rhetoric from Richard Nixon and Spiro Agnew, Flatbush remained Democratic.

It is not too hard to sum up the succession of congressional representation here. In the 1920 Harding landslide the area that is now the 16th congressional district—including most of Flatbush and East Flatbush—elected a Republican Congressman. Two years later a 34-year-old Jewish lawyer won the Democratic nomination and unseated the incumbent by a small margin. For the next 24 elections the same man, slowly growing older, was elected again and again: Emanuel Celler, Chairman of the House Judiciary Committee, co-author of the Celler-Kefauver Amendments to the Clayton Antitrust Act, which effectively cut off the wave of corporate mergers in the late 1960s.

So in 1972, when 31-year-old Elizabeth Holtzman challenged Celler in the primary, no one paid much attention. Holtzman's only previous political experience was on Mayor Lindsay's staff (not a particularly good credential here) and election in 1970 as a Democratic district leader. She had a low campaign budget, and got little coverage in the press. But Holtzman made up for all that with intense personal campaigning, a vast volunteer program, and the kind of energy that promised that she would play close attention to the district and tend to its problems. Celler, in contrast, had long since tired of constituent matters; his "district office" was his law office in Manhattan. The challenger also attacked Celler for his opposition to the Equal Rights Amendment, which he had bottled up in committee for twenty years.

On primary day, Holtzman surprised virtually everyone by winning; if she had had just 611 fewer voters it would have been 88-year-old Manny Celler, rather than 65-year-old Peter Rodino, chairing the House Judiciary Committee hearings on the impeachment of Richard Nixon. As it happened, Elizabeth Holtzman was a junior member of the Committee, and her incisive, well prepared presentations were typical of the seriousness with which she approaches her congressional duties. In her first term she played an important role in formulating complex federal court rules, and also sued, with temporary success, to block the American bombing of Cambodia. In her second term, she won a seat on the House Budget Committee. Overall, Holtzman seems to have become something of a minor power in the House since she won her seat there: through brains and old fashioned hard work.

Census Data Pop. 466,756. Central city, 100%; suburban, 0%. Median family income, $10,504; families above $15,000: 26%; families below $3,000: 9%. Median years education, 12.0.

The Voters

Median voting age 46.
Employment profile White collar, 64%. Blue collar, 25%. Service, 11%. Farm, –%.
Ethnic groups Black, 22%. Spanish, 4%. Total foreign stock, 49%. USSR, 11%; Poland, 7%; Italy, 6%; Austria, Ireland, 3% each; Germany, UK, 2% each; Rumania, 1%.

Presidential vote

1972	Nixon (R)	74,403	(46%)
	McGovern (D)	86,597	(54%)
1968	Nixon (R)	50,182	(28%)
	Humphrey (D)	120,449	(68%)
	Wallace (AI)	6,730	(4%)

Rep. Elizabeth Holtzman (D) Elected 1972; b. Aug. 11, 1941, Brooklyn; home, Brooklyn; Radcliffe Col., B.A. 1962, Harvard U., J.D. 1965; Jewish.

Career Practicing atty., 1965–67, 1970–72; Asst. to the Mayor of N.Y. City, 1967–70.

Offices 1027 LHOB, 202-225-6616. Also 1452 Flatbush Ave., Brooklyn 11210, 212-859-9111.

Committees

Budget (16th).

Judiciary (16th). Subcommittees: Criminal Justice; Immigration, Citizenship, and International Law.

Group Ratings

	ADA	COPE	LWV	RIPON	NFU	LCV	CFA	NAB	NSI	ACA
1974	100	100	100	63	79	88	100	17	10	0
1973	100	100	92	73	95	94	100	–	–	11

Key Votes

1) Foreign Aid	FOR	6) Gov Abortn Aid	FOR	11) Pub Cong Election $	FOR
2) Busing	FOR	7) Coed Phys Ed	FOR	12) Turkish Arms Cutoff	FOR
3) ABM	AGN	8) Pov Lawyer Gag	AGN	13) Youth Camp Regs	FOR
4) B-1 Bomber	AGN	9) Pub Trans Sub	FOR	14) Strip Mine Veto	AGN
5) Nerve Gas	AGN	10) EZ Voter Regis	FOR	15) Farm Bill Veto	FOR

Election Results

1974 general:	Elizabeth Holtzman (D-L)	74,010	(79%)	($31,746)
	Joseph L. Gentile (R-C)	19,806	(21%)	($1,249)
1974 primary:	Elizabeth Holtzman (D), unopposed			
1972 general	Elizabeth Holtzman (D)	96,984	(66%)	($104,318)
	Nicholas R. Macchio, Jr. (R)	33,828	(23%)	
	Emanuel Celler (L)	10,337	(7%)	(NA)
	William Sampol (C)	6,743	(5%)	(NA)

◆ ◆ ◆ ◆ ◆

SEVENTEENTH DISTRICT

Staten Island is the smallest (pop. 312,000) and least densely populated of the five boroughs of New York City (5,000 people per square miles as against 31,000 for the rest of the City); it is also the most parochial, and atypical, part of New York. Parts of Staten Island retain a rural character, even in the wake of new development spurred by the opening of the Verrazano Narrows Bridge in 1965. Before that time, Staten Island was even more cut off: the only land route from the rest of New York City was through New Jersey.

And most Staten Islanders are quite happy with this isolation; they are in many ways more suburban than real suburbanites. A large proportion are middle income Italian and Irish Catholics, brought up often in Brooklyn and happy to leave the city behind. Politically, Staten Islanders are intensively conservative, with Conservative Party candidates sometimes outpolling Democrats here. Staten Island's most interesting political figure is state Senator John Marchi, an austere Thomistic conservative who was twice (1969, 1973) the Republican candidate for Mayor of New York. In the rest of the City, Marchi is considered too conservative; here on Staten Island, the local Conservative Party boycotted him as too liberal, because he supported a modified form of planned development for the Island.

Because its population has not merited a full congressional district, Staten Island over the years has been linked politically with various parts of Brooklyn or Manhattan. During the 1950s and '60s the Island was joined to several different parts of Brooklyn in what was then the 16th district. Today the number has changed to 17, and the borough to Manhattan. So now the conservative homeowners of Staten Island find themselves in the same constituency with elderly Jewish people living in housing projects and well to do Greenwich Village liberals. The Manhattan part of the district contains many other groups, but none casts enough votes to be of any great significance. The utter incompatibility of these two portions of the 17th is shown by the 1972 presidential returns: the Manhattan portion, with one-third of the district's votes, went 63% for McGovern, while Staten Island was 74% for Nixon.

Because the non-Staten Island part of the district has constantly been shifted beneath the feet of Democratic Congressman John Murphy, he has had to hustle to win reelection ever since he was first elected in 1962. Murphy had a particularly close call in 1970, when Republican Bay Ridge (see Fifteenth District), then in his district, gave his opponent a 7,000 vote margin and held the Democrat to 52% of the total vote.

Murphy is probably about the closest thing there could be to a Congressman acceptable to both parts of his district: a Democrat with a not especially liberal record, indeed a West Point graduate, with solid roots in Staten Island, and not totally unacceptable to Manhattan. Sometimes he must think he is running in two entirely different races. In 1974, for example, Murphy beat Republican Frank Biondolillo by a 57–30 margin on Staten Island, with the Conservative candidate winning 9% of the vote there. But on Manhattan, the main competition was Liberal candidate Jerome Kretchmer, a former Lindsay Administration Sanitation Commissioner who had run a brief and abortive campaign for Mayor in 1973; Kretchmer had run in the Democratic primary against Murphy, and in the general he got 23% of the vote in Manhattan, compared to the incumbent's 60%.

Census Data Pop. 467,656. Central city, 100%; suburban, 0%. Median family income, $10,632; families above $15,000: 26%; families below $3,000: 8%. Median years education, 11.8.

The Voters

Median voting age 41.
Employment profile White collar, 57%. Blue collar, 28%. Service, 15%. Farm, –%.
Ethnic groups Black, 6%. Chinese, 6%. Spanish, 7%. Total foreign stock, 40%. Italy, 12%; Poland, Ireland, USSR, Germany, UK, 2% each; Austria, 1%.

Presidential vote

1972	Nixon (R)	105,543	(62%)
	McGovern (D)	64,601	(38%)
1968	Nixon (R)	67,427	(46%)
	Humphrey (D)	67,720	(46%)
	Wallace (AI)	12,870	(9%)

Rep. John M. Murphy (D) Elected 1962; b. Aug. 3, 1926, Staten Island; home, Staten Island; Amherst Col., U.S. Military Acad., B.S. 1950; Catholic.

Career Army, WWII and Korea; Gen. Mgr. and Pres., Cleveland General Transportation Co.; Bd. of Dirs., Empire State Hwy. Transportation Assn., 1960–65.

Offices 2187 RHOB, 202-225-3371. Also Rm. 107, Gen. P.O., 550 Manor Rd., Staten Island 10314, 212-981-9800.

Committees

Interstate and Foreign Commerce (8th). Subcommittees: Communications; Energy and Power.

Merchant Marine and Fisheries (6th). Subcommittees: Coast Guard and Navigation; Merchant Marine; Oceanography (Chairman); Panama Canal.

Group Ratings

	ADA	COPE	LWV	RIPON	NFU	LCV	CFA	NAB	NSI	ACA
1974	50	100	75	25	80	86	90	0	78	23
1973	52	100	78	64	100	65	100	–	–	17
1972	38	89	80	80	86	41	100	13	100	30

Key Votes

1) Foreign Aid	FOR	6) Gov Abortn Aid	ABS	11) Pub Cong Election $	ABS
2) Busing	AGN	7) Coed Phys Ed	AGN	12) Turkish Arms Cutoff	FOR
3) ABM	FOR	8) Pov Lawyer Gag	ABS	13) Youth Camp Regs	FOR
4) B-1 Bomber	FOR	9) Pub Trans Sub	FOR	14) Strip Mine Veto	AGN
5) Nerve Gas	FOR	10) EZ Voter Regis	FOR	15) Farm Bill Veto	FOR

Election Results

1974 general:	John M. Murphy (D)	63,805	(58%)	($75,272)
	Frank Biondolillo (R)	28,269	(26%)	($6,760)
	Jerome Kretchmer (L)	10,622	(10%)	($50,964)
	Michael Ajello (C)	7,808	(7%)	($588)
1974 primary:	John M. Murphy (D)	18,544	(52%)	
	Jerome Kretchmer (D)	11,949	(34%)	
	Danielle M. Sandow (D)	3,006	(9%)	
	Peter J. Murray (D)	1,845	(5%)	
1972 general:	John M. Murphy (D)	92,252	(60%)	($105,581)
	Mario D. Belardino (R-C)	60,812	(40%)	($87,559)

◆ ◆ ◆ ◆ ◆

EIGHTEENTH DISTRICT

The 18th congressional district of New York is the silk stocking district. It is dominated by the chi chi Upper East Side of Manhattan which Theodore White, who himself lives in an East 64th Street townhouse, once called the "perfumed stockade." The 18th also includes the skyscrapers of midtown Manhattan and much of Greenwich Village, which in spite of its reputed Bohemianism contains many addresses as expensive and fashionable as any in New York City. By no means all the 18th is wealthy: the Stuyvesant Town housing development along the East River is middle class, and below that are the part ethnic, part street people slums of the Lower East Side (or the East Village, as it is often called now). But even with these areas, the 18th still is the most white collar of any American congressional district and has the fourth highest median income.

Moreover, the poor do not vote much in New York, so when we are talking about politics here, we are talking about the politics of the rich. And what is most noteworthy here is something a visitor from the 1930s—those days when Franklin Roosevelt was hated as a traitor to his class—would find unbelievable, the fact that the rich voters of the 18th district are among the most liberal, many would like to think radical, in the country. This is a district which even in 1972 gave George McGovern 58% of its vote—more than in all but six other New York districts (and twenty others in the rest of the country). Yet just ten years before, the silk stocking district—the boundaries and the district number have changed, but not significantly—was considered irrevocably Republican. Indeed it had supported Richard Nixon over John F. Kennedy in 1960.

There is no getting over the fact that the silk stocking district has shifted markedly to the left in the last decade or so—approximately since the demise of the literate and obdurately Republican New York *Herald Tribune*. A key transitional figure is John V. Lindsay, who served as the silk stocking Congressman from 1959 to 1965 and, of course, as Mayor of all New York City from 1966 to 1973; if Lindsay shifted most of the city sharply to the right—and he did—then he was partially responsible for, and partially reflective of, the shift to the left in the perfumed stockade. Lindsay first won the seat here as a liberal Republican, in notable contrast with his conservative predecessor; and in the House he often voted with the Kennedy Administration on important programs. But even more significant, he was a strong supporter of civil rights measures and one of the first congressional opponents of the Vietnam war. Lindsay early adopted the positions and priorities which would define the liberalism of the late sixties and early seventies.

But Lindsay was not simply a liberal Mayor; he was very much a Manhattan Mayor. In his 1969 reelection campaign, for example, Lindsay won only 42% of the vote citywide, but he took a near unanimous 80% on the Upper East Side. But the very things which attracted upper income liberals to Lindsay—his concern for blacks and Puerto Ricans, his civil libertarianism, his opposition to the Vietnam war—made him anathema to the white middle class which dominates New York City as a whole. The writers, painters, theater people, book editors, lawyers, and doctors of the 18th district loved him; the cab drivers, doormen, waiters, sanitation workers, policemen, office clerks, and janitors who live in the rest of the City hated him. They perceived, with some accuracy, the overarch element of "radical chic" that was definitely present in the Upper East Side's liberalism, the fact that silk stocking liberalism becomes more intense as the object of sympathy-the Black Panthers at Leonard Bernstein's famous party—grows more distant.

There was more than a touch of snobbery to the liberalism here, a feeling that since the working class people of Queens were white they must have had the same advantages that Upper East Siders take for granted, and therefore it was all right to look down on them for their low level of Big Apple achievement. The Lindsay electoral strategy of combining the top and the bottom of the New York electorate worked tactically (although it never produced a majority in the City); but as a formula for providing government in whose good faith people could have confidence, it was a disaster.

Lindsay is only the most prominent example of politicians on whom the silk stocking district and the rest of the City have had sharply different opinions. The 18th liked Adlai Stevenson better than John F. Kennedy in 1960, Eugene McCarthy over Robert Kennedy in 1968, and George McGovern over Richard Nixon in 1972. The wealthy precincts of Manhattan have also had a long affection for New York's Reform Democrats who—except for the successes of some individual candidates—have had minimal impact in the four outer boroughs. That so many, many words have been devoted to the reform movement is tied to the fact that Manhattan is overpopulated with writers, who tend to assume, like everyone else, that their own experience has instructive value for all. Actually, what the reform movement shows is that organization based on upper income, ideologically liberal volunteers can beat an organization based on judicial patronage, whose main electoral support comes from elderly ethnics who are either dying or moving out of the constituency because rents are rising. That is essentially how the so called reformers beat so called Tammany Hall in the early sixties; it was the natural result of the change in the sociological character and political style of the population of Manhattan Island.

Nevertheless, much is still made of some of these unremarkable victories, and it is symbolic that the 18th district's current Congressman, Edward Koch, is a man who first gained political fame as the man who beat then New York Democratic Chairman Carmine de Sapio in the race for district leader in Greenwich Village way back in 1963. That effectively ended de Sapio's political career (he later went to prison) and began Koch's: he became a City Councilman and, in 1968, Congressman. The liberal Republican the district had picked to succeed Lindsay was moving to his judgeship that year, and Koch, in beating blue-blood Republican Whitney North Seymour, Jr., became the first Democrat elected from the silk stocking district since 1934.

As a Congressman, Koch has avoided the contentiousness that characterizes some New York reform veterans; he even understands that there is a world beyond Manhattan, one that has legitimate claims on government. But like most Congressmen, he has concentrated on issues of particular interest to his district. In his case, that means mass transit, the tax law's discrimination against single people (56% of the adults in the 18th are not married), and the individual's right of privacy in the age of the computer. On the last, he has an interesting ally, California's Barry Goldwater, Jr.; this unlikely pair have been drafting thoughtful legislation on the subject together. Overall, Koch is gaining a reputation as one of New York City's most skillful legislative technicians, a man who can maintain his principles and at the same time accomplish something in a body which does not always share them.

Koch made moves to run for Mayor in 1973, and tried to tell non-Manhattan voters that he too cared about crime. But the field was glutted with Manhattan candidates in a city that was sick of its Manhattan Mayor, and Koch wisely left the race. His reelection percentages in the 18th district nicely chronicle its continuing leftward march: he won with 52% of the vote in 1968, 62% in 1970, 70% in 1972, and a near unanimous 77% in 1974. The Republican tradition in well-to-do Manhattan seems to be about as alive as the *Herald Tribune* that so long sustained it.

Census Data Pop. 467,533. Central city, 100%; suburban, 0%. Median family income, $14,853; families above $15,000: 50%; families below $3,000: 8%. Median years education, 13.0.

The Voters

Median voting age 44.
Employment profile White collar, 79%. Blue collar, 10%. Service, 11%. Farm, –%.
Ethnic groups Black, 4%. Chinese, 1%. Spanish, 7%. Total foreign stock, 44%. USSR, 7%; Germany, Poland, Italy, 4% each; Ireland, UK, Austria, 3% each; Hungary, 2%; Canada, France, Czechoslovakia, 1% each.

Presidential vote

1972	Nixon (R)	82,516	(42%)
	McGovern (D)	114,237	(58%)
1968	Nixon (R)	69,963	(35%)
	Humphrey (D)	121,186	(61%)
	Wallace (AI)	8,076	(4%)

Rep. Edward I. Koch (D) Elected 1968; b. Dec. 12, 1924, New York City; home, New York City; CCNY, NYU, LL.B. 1948; Jewish.

Career Army, WWII; Practicing atty., 1949–68; N.Y. City Cncl., 1967–68.

Offices 1134 LHOB, 202-225-2436. Also Rm. 3139, 26 Fed. Plaza, 10007, 212-264-1066.

Committees

Appropriations (31st). Subcommittees: District of Columbia; Foreign Operations; Transportation.

Group Ratings

	ADA	COPE	LWV	RIPON	NFU	LCV	CFA	NAB	NSI	ACA
1974	91	100	83	63	79	94	100	17	10	0
1973	96	91	100	85	82	100	100	–	–	13
1972	100	91	100	75	86	93	100	8	0	4

Key Votes

1) Foreign Aid	FOR	6) Gov Abortn Aid	FOR	11) Pub Cong Election $	FOR
2) Busing	FOR	7) Coed Phys Ed	FOR	12) Turkish Arms Cutoff	FOR
3) ABM	AGN	8) Pov Lawyer Gag	AGN	13) Youth Camp Regs	FOR
4) B-1 Bomber	AGN	9) Pub Trans Sub	FOR	14) Strip Mine Veto	AGN
5) Nerve Gas	AGN	10) EZ Voter Regis	FOR	15) Farm Bill Veto	FOR

Election Results

1974 general:	Edward I. Koch (D-L)	91,985	(77%)	($57,530)
	John Boogaerts, Jr. (R)	22,560	(19%)	($14,156)
	Gillian M. Drummond (C)	4,429	(4%)	($642)
1974 primary:	Edward I. Koch (D), unopposed			
1972 general:	Edward I. Koch (D-L)	125,117	(70%)	($69,295)
	Jane P. Langley (R-C)	52,379	(30%)	($120,351)

◆ ◆ ◆ ◆ ◆

NINETEENTH DISTRICT

In the years following World War I Harlem, whose tenements had been built just a couple of decades earlier for white working class people, became the center, and a relatively prosperous one, of black American culture. But the depression of the 1930s hit Harlem hard, and in many ways it has never recovered. A few middle class pockets are still left here, in apartment complexes built along the Harlem River or along the edge of Morningside Heights. But most of Harlem is very poor, and savaged with the problems of heroin and violent crime. For some years now, it has been the kind of place people will leave if they can; Harlem's population dropped fully 20% in the sixties, and perhaps by almost as much since then. The antipoverty programs of the Johnson Administration were supposed to help areas like Harlem, but they seem to have done more to employ skilled professionals than they have to raise poor people's incomes or their own abilities to do so.

For a quarter of a century, Harlem had one of the best known Congressmen in the entire nation, the late Adam Clayton Powell, Jr. His career peaked during the early sixties, when he was Chairman of the House Education and Labor Committee, which had jurisdiction over most of the social and antipoverty programs of the Kennedy and Johnson Administrations. Then in 1966, when he refused to pay a libel judgment to a plaintiff he had called a "bag woman," Powell's troubles with the New York courts became regular features of national TV newscasts. He got into even more trouble when it was learned that he had diverted staff salaries into his own ample bank account.

Harlem's voters ritually reelected him anyway, and after the Supreme Court case he returned to Capitol Hill in 1969. But he had to stay out of New York except on Sundays, to avoid process servers; and increasingly, he spent his time, by now a tired old man, at his luxurious home on Bimini.

When Powell was first elected in 1944, his district was just part of Harlem; under subsequent redistrictings, the district was enlargened to include all of Harlem and a part of the Manhattan's white liberal Upper West Side. Powell ignored this change, but it proved to be politically fatal to him when he was challenged by Assemblyman Charles Rangel in the 1970 Democratic primary. Rangel won by only 150 votes, and he carried the Upper West Side portion by much more; but the real story here was that Powell was no longer unbeatable in Harlem. Indeed, he stirred up so little enthusiasm that only 24,000 people voted in the primary at all, in a district with a population over 400,000.

Rangel's street-wise accent and geniality became nationally known in the course of the House Judiciary Committee's televised impeachment hearings. His political acumen is shown by the fact that he has since managed to get Hugh Carey's old seat on Ways and Means. Electorally, he has had no significant challenges. Since 1972, his district has been expanded to include a much more sizeable chunk of the Upper West Side, and now probably more than half its votes are cast outside Harlem.

Census Data Pop. 466,876. Central city, 100%; suburban, 0%. Median family income, $6,712; families above $15,000: 13%; families below $3,000: 18%. Median years education, 10.6.

The Voters

Median voting age 43.
Employment profile White collar, 49%. Blue collar, 27%. Service, 24%. Farm, –%.
Ethnic groups Black, 59%. Spanish, 17%. Total foreign stock, 18%. Italy, 2%; USSR, Germany, 1%.

Presidential vote

1972	Nixon (R)	24,302	(19%)
	McGovern (D)	106,164	(81%)
1968	Nixon (R)	16,073	(13%)
	Humphrey (D)	105,053	(84%)
	Wallace (AI)	3,924	(3%)

Rep. Charles B. Rangel (D) Elected 1970; b. June 11, 1930, New York City; home, New York City; NYU, B.S. 1957, St. John's U., LL.B. 1960; Catholic.

Career Army, 1948–52; Asst. U.S. Atty., So. Dist. of N.Y., 1961; Legal Counsel, N.Y. City Housing and Redevelopment Bd., Neighborhood Conservation Bureau; Gen. Counsel, Natl. Advisory Comm. on Selective Svc., 1966; N.Y. State Assembly, 1966–70.

Offices 107 CHOB, 202-225-4365. Also 144 W. 125th St., New York 10027, 212-866-8900.

Committees

Ways and Means (18th). Subcommittees: Oversight; Public Assistance.

Group Ratings

	ADA	COPE	LWV	RIPON	NFU	LCV	CFA	NAB	NSI	ACA
1974	95	100	91	71	86	88	91	17	10	0
1973	100	100	92	83	90	100	86	–	–	8
1972	94	90	100	60	86	89	100	9	0	4

Key Votes

1) Foreign Aid	FOR	6) Gov Abortn Aid	FOR	11) Pub Cong Election $	FOR
2) Busing	FOR	7) Coed Phys Ed	FOR	12) Turkish Arms Cutoff	FOR
3) ABM	AGN	8) Pov Lawyer Gag	ABS	13) Youth Camp Regs	FOR
4) B-1 Bomber	AGN	9) Pub Trans Sub	FOR	14) Strip Mine Veto	AGN
5) Nerve Gas	AGN	10) EZ Voter Regis	FOR	15) Farm Bill Veto	AGN

Election Results

1974 general:	Charles B. Rangel (D-L-R)	63,146	(97%)	($15,536)
	Charles G. Mills (C)	2,039	(3%)	($176)
1974 primary	Charles B. Rangel (D), unopposed			
1972 general:	Charles B. Rangel (D-L-R)	104,427	(98%)	($31,390)
	Marshall L. Dodge III (C)	2,517	(2%)	(NA)

◆ ◆ ◆ ◆ ◆

TWENTIETH DISTRICT

The West Side of Manhattan, the funkiest part of New York City, is a ployglot area so diverse that it defies accurate description. It's not a long way from Riverside Park and the Hudson River docks to the invisible line that separates the West Side from midtown or Harlem; but nearly every block in this short stretch seems to have its own peculiar character and so, it sometimes seems, does almost every building on every block. New York's 20th congressional district includes most of the West Side. It begins with a geographic salient into hip, expensive Greenwich Village, then moves up through renovated and raffish Chelsea, past apartment house complexes and the obscenity palaces of Times Square, north to the Upper West Side. Here the 20th includes the two blocks from Amsterdam Avenue to the Hudson, north all the way along the West Side Highway to the northern tip of Manhattan. Here well known writers and well paid professionals in West End Avenue apartments live in close and increasingly uneasy proximity to Puerto Ricans and welfare mothers in the side streets; students occupy cheap apartments around Columbia, and elderly ethnics live in even cheaper and definitely more dangerous surroundings in Washington Heights.

The 20th goes on to include the expensive apartment units and large single family homes of the Riverdale section of the Bronx. But because most of the district's votes are cast on the Upper West Side, its politics is worth some examination. For this is the heartland of much of Manhattan's reform Democratic politics. Back in the late fifties and early sixties upper income Stevenson enthusiasts broke the hold of Tammany up here; the aged ethnics whose votes propped up the machine were either dying or moving elsewhere in search of cheaper rents, and the machine people had no rapport with the growing constituency of reformers. The blacks and Puerto Ricans voted so seldom as to be electorally insignificant. By the middle sixties, the reformers had capured most of the local offices and, to the extent they had not already done so, they fell into fighting among themselves—the kind of bitter, acrimonious fighting of upper income professionals with nothing to lose but their egos.

The reform movement, for all its infatuation with itself, did produce one authentic hero, Congressman William Fitts Ryan. First elected in 1960, forced to beat another regular in the 1962 primary, he built up a solid constituency on the West Side, and pioneered many issues in the House. He was the first Congressman to condemn American involvement in Vietnam, and to vote against it; he led the biennial fight to abolish the House Un-American Activities Committee. He risked derision in the go-along House of the time, but he never stopped fighting, and eventually most of his causes seemed less extreme and more sensible to a majority of his colleagues.

Following Ryan's example, other reformers challanged other New York Congressmen, and one who won was attorney Bella Abzug, who beat Leonard Farbstein in the adjacent 19th district in 1970. By 1972, it became clear that Manhattan would have to lose a congressional seat, or most of one, so that it would have basically $3\frac{1}{2}$ districts; as recently as 1944, Manhattan had elected 13. The district that was eliminated was Abzug's; but in the new militant spirit of the women's movement she declined to accept the legislature's decision, and after some painful deliberation decided to run against Ryan. With the fearsome Abzug in the race, and the fractious West Siders forced to take sides, it was a bitter, bitter race; and the more so, as Ryan was gravely ill. The endorsements went heavily in Ryan's favor; people simply refused to forget what he had been doing for twelve years; and he won by better than a 2–1 margin. Then, three months after the primary, he died. The Democratic committee charged with selecting a new nominee picked Abzug, who was still serving out her term. The Liberal Party chose Ryan's widow; and the resulting contest was even more vitriolic than the primary. But this time Abzug won, with a comfortable 56% of the vote. By 1974, the West Side seemed finally to accept her; she had no primary opposition, and won the general election with 79% of the vote.

Bella Abzug is probably one of the best known members of the House of Representatives today. Her floppy hats, her raucous, New York accented voice, her rapid fire delivery are all familiar to millions of Americans. She is a favorite on the lecture circuit, and a leader of the National Women's Political Caucus. Tourists stare at her in the halls of the Capitol and ask for her autograph. She is the person you probably think of when you hear the phrase "militant Congresswoman."

Abzug's outspoken liberalism on issues and flamboyant personal style—she supposedly told former Doorkeeper Fishbait Miller to perform an impossible act when he told her to remove her hat—have led to a certain conventional wisdom about her performance as a legislator. She is too liberal, so it begins, and her raucous ways antagonize other members; any time she comes out in favor of something, this line goes on, it loses 20 or 30 votes. Something like that may have been true when Abzug first came into office, in 1971. But the House has changed a lot since then—and Abzug has changed a little, too. The greater shift has been the House's; it has moved far enough leftward to make most of Abzug's ideas not very distinctive any more. It has been some time since she found herself in a minority of three or some such number on what she considered an important issue. And in the meantime, Abzug has become a rather talented legislator. One of her secrets is hard work; she is known as one of the toughest tasksetters in the House, and her staff has an exceedingly high turnover rate, but when she comes into the subcommittee room she has usually done her homework.

It was such preparation, for example, which enabled her to make a point of order which forced a hostile Public Works Committee to delete provisions forcing through the construction of certain urban expressways. And when she confronted CIA Director William Colby with evidence that the CIA had spied on her, she had her facts—and the CIA—cold. So on both Public Works and Government Operations she has emerged as a major force, despite her lack of great seniority, and despite her refusal to be obsequious to older members. Her success goes against all the old unwritten rules that used to govern the House—and is part of the reason they don't apply any more.

Abzug is now talking about running for the Senate. Manhattan, of course, isn't all of New York City; indeed it only casts 6.6% of the statewide vote. But Abzug, like the many other Democrats who are interested, knows that Senator James Buckley is very vulnerable and that the winner of the Democratic primary need not have an absolute majority, but just a plurality. In a crowded field, more unlikely things than an Abzug victory might be possible. The state already has a woman as Lieutenant Governor—Mary Ann Krupsak, who won an upset victory in the 1974 primary—and perhaps New York is ready for a woman Senator as well.

Census Data Pop. 468,667. Central city, 100%; suburban, 0%. Median family income, $9,743; families above $15,000: 27%; families below $3,000: 9%. Median years education, 12.2.

The Voters

Median voting age 45.
Employment profile White collar, 64%. Blue collar, 22%. Service, 14%. Farm, –%.
Ethnic groups Black, 15% Chinese, 1%. Spanish, 9%. Total foreign stock, 52%. USSR, 6%; Germany, 5%; Ireland, 4%; Poland, 3%; Austria, Italy, UK, Greece, 2% each; Hungary, 1%.

Presidential vote

1972	Nixon (R)	57,319	(34%)
	McGovern (D)	109,341	(66%)
1968	Nixon (R)	40,319	(24%)
	Humphrey (D)	122,931	(72%)
	Wallace (AI)	8,273	(5%)

Rep. Bella S. Abzug (D) Elected 1970; b. July 24, 1920, New York City; home, New York City; Hunter Col., B.A. 1942, Columbia U., LL.B. 1945, Jewish Theological Seminary; Jewish.

Career Practicing atty., 1947–70; Organizer and Natl. Legis. Dir., Women's Strike for Peace, 1961; Co-Founder, New Democratic Coalition.

Offices 1507 LHOB, 202-225-5635. Also 252 7th Ave., New York 10001, 212-620-6701.

Committees

Governments Operations (14th). Subcommittees: Government Activities and Transportation; Government Information and Individual Rights (Chairperson).

Public Works and Transportation (12th). Subcommittees: Economic Development; Public Buildings and Grounds; Surface Transportation; Water Resources.

Group Ratings

	ADA	COPE	LWV	RIPON	NFU	LCV	CFA	NAB	NSI	ACA
1974	100	100	100	63	79	88	92	17	10	7
1973	100	100	92	80	90	100	100	–	–	7
1972	100	91	100	75	86	93	100	9	0	10

Key Votes

1) Foreign Aid	FOR	6) Gov Abortn Aid	FOR	11) Pub Cong Election $	FOR
2) Busing	FOR	7) Coed Phys Ed	FOR	12) Turkish Arms Cutoff	FOR
3) ABM	AGN	8) Pov Lawyer Gag	AGN	13) Youth Camp Regs	FOR
4) B-1 Bomber	AGN	9) Pub Trans Sub	FOR	14) Strip Mine Veto	AGN
5) Nerve Gas	AGN	10) EZ Voter Regis	FOR	15) Farm Bill Veto	FOR

Election Results

1974 general:	Bella S. Abzug (D-L)	76,074	(79%)	($12,655)
	Stephen Posner (R)	15,053	(16%)	($224)
	Timothy A. Mitchell (C)	4,687	(5%)	($4,376)
1974 primary:	Bella S. Abzug (D), unopposed			
1972 general:	Bella S. Abzug (D)	85,558	(56%)	($164,245)
	Priscilla M. Ryan (L)	43,045	(28%)	($51,412)
	Annette Flatto Levy (R)	18,024	(11%)	($2,360)
	Harvey J. Michelman (C)	6,253	(4%)	($5,261)

◆ ◆ ◆ ◆ ◆

TWENTY-FIRST DISTRICT

The 21st congressional district of New York is the South Bronx, geographically about a mile from Manhattan's posh Upper East Side, but a world apart in every other way. By any measure this is a slum and a picture of social disintegration. Most of its residents are minorities—44% Puerto Ricans, 43% black in the 1970 census—and unlike Harlem or even Bedford-Stuyvesant, there is no history to this community, no set of traditional institutions which might have some ability to handle its problems. As in most slum areas, a huge percentage of the residents are under 18 (here 43%), with many of them in large, often fatherless families. What is perhaps most dreadful is that this is a slum of relatively recent creation. Its last aged Jews and Italians are still fleeing to places farther out in the Bronx, and few of the people who live here now have any roots in the South Bronx.

Given all this, it is no surprise that people don't vote here much. But even so, the low level of political participation here is worthy of special attention. In 1972, only 28% of those eligible to vote did so; in 1974, only 11% did. In both cases this was the lowest voter turnout, on both a numerical and percentage basis, of any congressional district in the country. It bespeaks an overpowering cynicism—and an apathy on the part of political organizations who might be expected to do something about it. But here in the Bronx the regulars have their judgeship patronage, the reformers have a few offices here and there, and local Democratic candidates are confident of winning. Nobody cares about turnout in the South Bronx—or if people do, they are too frightened of the area to do anything about it.

The 21st district was set up within approximately its present lines with the expressed purpose of electing a Puerto Rican Congressman, and it has: Herman Badillo, former (1966–70) Borough President of the Bronx, and some day (he hopes) Mayor of New York. It is a measure of the low turnout in the Puerto Rican South Bronx that Badillo almost lost his first primary, in 1970, to an Italian candidate. In his first two terms, Badillo served on the Education and Labor Committee; now he has switched to Judiciary and Small Business.

But Herman Badillo is not a man who is especially interested in the Congress; he wants to be Mayor. Born in poverty in Puerto Rico, he moved to New York, worked his way through college, got a CPA certificate and a law degree, and then held an important post in the Wagner Administration. He was elected Borough President of the Bronx in 1965, and though he won by the barest of margins, he was a candidate for Mayor in 1969. He finished a creditable third in the Democratic primary, not far behind nominee Mario Procaccino and former Mayor Robert Wagner.

Badillo has been criticized for having steely hard ambition, but that is obviously what has gotten him this far—and may get him farther. When he ran for Mayor again in 1973, he was badly underfinanced and was running a shadow of a campaign; but he had become well enough known as a liberal and a member of a minority that he easily carried Puerto Rican and white liberal areas and did well among blacks—indeed, he even stimulated unusually good turnouts among blacks and Puerto Ricans. That was enough for 28% of the vote and second place and under a new law (designed to keep Lindsay from winning again) he faced a runoff with Controller Abraham Beame. This time Badillo was not so lucky: his presence seemed to stimulate a white flood—a huge turnout in conservative homeowner neighborhoods that gave Beame the nomination easily.

Badillo will almost certainly run again in 1977, and may do fairly well. Beame will be 71 then, and may well retire; even if he doesn't, the city may have gotten all the respite it so obviously needed after Lindsay's eight years and could be ready again for a new, younger leader. The hard working, middle class Badillo has as good a chance as any minority candidate to win mainland white votes in what is still a white middle class city; the more difficult question is why, with the

City virtually bankrupt and the only decisions left ones of retrenchment, a politician as bright as Badillo would want to be Mayor at all?

Census Data   Pop. 462,030. Central city, 100%; suburban, 0%. Median family income, $5,613; families above $15,000: 5%; families below $3,000: 23%. Median years education, 9.2.

The Voters

Median voting age 37.
Employment profile White collar, 37%. Blue collar, 42%. Service, 21%. Farm, –%.
Ethnic groups Black, 42%. Spanish, 44%. Total foreign stock, 14%. Italy, USSR, 1% each.

Presidential vote

1972	Nixon (R)	15,293	(20%)
	McGovern (D)	59,375	(80%)
1968	Nixon (R)	10,417	(14%)
	Humphrey (D)	59,363	(83%)
	Wallace (AI)	2,094	(3%)

Rep. Herman Badillo (D) Elected 1970; b. Aug. 21, 1929, Caguas, P.R.; home, Bronx; CCNY, B.A. 1951, Brooklyn Law School, LL.B. 1954; Protestant.

Career Practicing atty., 1955–70; CPA, 1956; Deputy Commissioner, N.Y. City Dept. of Real Estate, 1962; Commissioner, N.Y. City Dept. of Housing Relocation, 1962–65; Bronx Borough Pres., 1965–69; Adjunct Prof., Fordham U. Grad. School of Urban Educ., 1970–.

Offices 319 CHOB, 202-225-4361. Also 840 Grand Concourse, Bronx 10451, 212-860-6200.

Committees

Judiciary (18th). Subcommittees: Civil and Constitutional Rights; Courts, Civil Liberties, and the Administration of Justice.

Small Business (24th). Subcommittees: Commodities and Services; Energy and Environment.

Group Ratings

	ADA	COPE	LWV	RIPON	NFU	LCV	CFA	NAB	NSI	ACA
1974	100	100	100	63	86	94	91	25	10	0
1973	100	100	58	75	93	93	100	–	–	13
1972	100	91	100	73	83	86	–	8	0	4

Key Votes

1) Foreign Aid	FOR	6) Gov Abortn Aid	FOR	11) Pub Cong Election $	FOR
2) Busing	FOR	7) Coed Phys Ed	FOR	12) Turkish Arms Cutoff	FOR
3) ABM	AGN	8) Pov Lawyer Gag	ABS	13) Youth Camp Regs	FOR
4) B-1 Bomber	AGN	9) Pub Trans Sub	FOR	14) Strip Mine Veto	AGN
5) Nerve Gas	AGN	10) EZ Voter Regis	FOR	15) Farm Bill Veto	AGN

Election Results

1974 general:	Herman Badillo (D-L)	28,025	(97%)	($7,476)
	Mary C. Lynch (C)	959	(3%)	
1974 primary:	Herman Badillo (D), unopposed			
1972 general:	Herman Badillo (D-L)	48,441	(88%)	($52,558)
	Manuel A. Ramos (R)	6,366	(12%)	($26,950)

◆ ◆ ◆ ◆ ◆

TWENTY-SECOND DISTRICT

The 22 congressional district of New York runs from the Grand Concourse to Co-op City—the heart of the Bronx. Unlike Brooklyn, which has a history as a city on its own, the Bronx is wholly an offspring of Manhattan. It was largely vacant at the turn of the century, but within the decade the subways had been built which made it an easy commute to Manhattan. The Bronx quickly filled up: from 1900 to 1930 its population increased from 200,000 to 1,265,000—not far from the 1,449,000 of today. Initial settlement followed the subway and el lines, as Jews, Italians, and Irish left the teeming tenements of Manhattan for the comparatively spacious and comfortable apartments of the Bronx. There are several large parks and two major universities (NYU and Fordham) here, but few other amenities. The Bronx has never had much white collar employment, nor for that matter many factory jobs either; and it remains today basically a residential area.

The Grand Concourse was intended to be the showcase of the Bronx. Laid out as a broad boulevard, it was lined in the twenties with Art Deco apartment houses that were notably more elegant than those on nearby side streets; it was the place you moved to when you got that raise or your stock tip paid off. Lately the advancing slums of the South Bronx have shattered the tranquillity—and wrecked the real estate values—of the Concourse. Consequently, the elderly Jews who are the main residents of the Concourse's buildings have been moving out. One place they have headed, assuming they can get in, is Co-op City—a staggeringly vast complex of towering apartment buildings, financed mainly by an offshoot of the Amalgamated Clothing Workers Union. Co-op City is unspeakably ugly, situated on a flat swamp and overlooking a couple of expressways. Like so many buildings in New York—in the posh Upper East Side, as well as out here—it is totally, almost defiantly lacking in aesthetic merit; it is also miles past the nearest subway stop. But Co-op City does deliver clean, safe, relatively inexpensive housing, and that is the most hundreds of thousands of middle income New Yorkers can hope for.

Politics and population movements like the one from the Grand Concourse to Co-op City help to explain the convoluted boundaries of the 22d district. In tacit cooperation with the Bronx Democratic machine, the 1972 Republican legislature decided to place in one district the Bronx's two reform Democratic Congressmen. Eight years before Jonathan Bingham and James Scheuer had both won election to the House, both beating stalwarts of the Bronx machine; Bingham beat the boss himself, Charles A. Buckley, then Chairman of the House Public Works Committee. Neither Bingham nor Scheuer wanted to oppose the other, but both wanted to stay in Congress, and they fought it out; Bingham won, with 55% of the vote. Scheuer, incidentally, thanks to a timely indictment, found an incumbentless district elsewhere and is now Congressman from the 11th district in Brooklyn and Queens.

Bingham comes from a rather non-Bronx background. His father was a wealthy Republican Senator from Connecticut; he served as an aide to Governor Averell Harriman in the fifties and under Adlai Stevenson at the United Nations in the sixties. With such a background, he was well equipped to play a major legislative role when he came to the House in 1965; but the oldtimers who controlled committees then wanted to squelch his ambitions because he had had the effrontery to beat their old friend Buckley. It took Bingham a couple of terms to win assignment to the Foreign Affairs Committee, and even longer to get on Interior. But he finally has chalked up a major achievement. In December 1974 he was the man who moved in the Democratic Steering Committee that all committee chairmen be voted on separately; as a result, the committee voted to unseat two of them. It was a move toward greater responsiveness of chairmen to the caucus, which after all is elected by the people every two years; and away from the blind luck which determines success under the seniority system.

Census Data Pop. 466,931. Central city, 100%; suburban, 0%. Median family income, $8,850; families above $15,000: 18%; families below $3,000: 11%. Median years education, 11.1.

The Voters

Median voting age 47.
Employment profile White collar, 58%. Blue collar, 28%. Service, 14%. Farm, –%.
Ethnic groups Black, 18%. Spanish, 14%. Total foreign stock, 46%. USSR, 9%; Ireland, Poland, 6% each; Italy, 5%; Austria, 3%; Germany, UK, 2% each; Hungary, Rumania, 1% each.

Presidential vote

1972	Nixon (R)	67,371	(40%)
	McGovern (D)	101,683	(60%)
1968	Nixon (R)	45,102	(27%)
	Humphrey (D)	116,715	(69%)
	Wallace (AI)	8,077	(5%)

Rep. Jonathan B. Bingham (D) Elected 1964; b. Apr. 24, 1914, New Haven, Conn.; home, Bronx; Yale U., B.A. 1936, LL.B. 1939; United Church of Christ.

Career Correspondent, N.Y. *Herald Tribune*, 1935–38; Practicing atty., 1940–61; Army, WWII; Special Asst. to an Asst. Secy. of State, 1945–46; Asst. Dir., Ofc. of Internatl. Security Affairs, 1951; Secy. to Gov. Averell Harriman, 1955–58; Mbr., U.S. Delegation to U.N., 1961–63; U.S. Rep., U.N. Econ. and Social Cncl., and Chf. Advisor to Amb. Adlai E. Stevenson II, 1963–64.

Offices 2241 RHOB, 202-225-4411. Also Rm. 326 Wagner Bldg., 2488 Grand Concourse, Bronx 10458, 212-933-2310.

Committees

Interior and Insular Affairs (14th). Subcommittees: Energy and the Environment; Mines and Mining; National Parks and Recreation.

International Relations (12th). Subcommittees: International Security and Scientific Affairs; International Trade and Commerce (Chairman).

Group Ratings

	ADA	COPE	LWV	RIPON	NFU	LCV	CFA	NAB	NSI	ACA
1974	95	100	100	69	77	94	100	17	10	0
1973	100	91	100	73	100	95	100	–	–	0
1972	75	89	100	71	100	93	100	10	0	0

Key Votes

1) Foreign Aid	FOR	6) Gov Abortn Aid	FOR	11) Pub Cong Election $	FOR
2) Busing	FOR	7) Coed Phys Ed	FOR	12) Turkish Arms Cutoff	ABS
3) ABM	AGN	8) Pov Lawyer Gag	AGN	13) Youth Camp Regs	FOR
4) B-1 Bomber	AGN	9) Pub Trans Sub	FOR	14) Strip Mine Veto	AGN
5) Nerve Gas	AGN	10) EZ Voter Regis	FOR	15) Farm Bill Veto	AGN

Election Results

1974 general:	Jonathan B. Bingham (D-L)	77,157	(85%)	($6,545)
	Robert Black (R)	8,142	(9%)	
	John DiGiovanni (C)	5,333	(6%)	
1974 primary:	Jonathan B. Bingham (D), unopposed			
1972 general:	Jonathan B. Bingham (D-L)	107,448	(76%)	($126,138)
	Charles A. Avarello (R-C)	33,045	(24%)	($16,416)

◆　◆　◆　◆　◆

TWENTY-THIRD DISTRICT

The line that separates the Bronx from Westchester County marks the end of Democratic New York City and, traditionally, the beginning of the Republican suburbs and Upstate. Even in these days of ticket splitting there is still a major contrast here, and there is no better place to look at it than in the 23d congressional district of New York, one-third of which is in the northern Bronx and two-thirds in Westchester.

The Bronx portion of the district, a large middle class residential area, is totally cut off from the rest of the 23d by Van Cortlandt Park. Most of the people here are of Italian descent; as in all of New York City, they are more than normally likely to hold service or government jobs. The Democratic allegiance of this part of the Bronx springs from an immigrant heritage—the days when the Tammany block captain brought around enough coal for the rest of the winter in return for a couple of votes. Though the machine today provides little in the way of services, most voters here still believe that Democrats are more likely than Republicans to favor their interests as city dwellers.

The tradition in the Westchester portion of the 23d is quite different. This includes most of Yonkers, the towns of Greenburgh and Mount Pleasant, and the suburbs along the Hudson River where Washington Irving once lived. With a few exceptions, Republicans have been in control here for as long as anyone can remember; when Democrat Alfred Del Bello was elected County Executive in 1973, it was the first time in the nearly fifty years the office had existed that it had not been held by a Republican. People here may have ethnic and sociological backgrounds similar to those of people in middle class parts of the Bronx; but here they think of themselves as suburbanities, protecting their property from the taxing demands of the masses in the City. Their chosen instrument remains, as it always has been, the Republican Party.

The 23d district was established within its present boundaries for the 1972 election; for thirty years before that, no district had spanned the Bronx-Westchester line. Most of its territory had come from the old 25th district in Westchester. That seat had been lost in 1964 by Republican Robert Barry, who later went on to run for Congress in three different California districts, and was won that year by Democrat Richard Ottinger, who spent $250,000 of his family's money on the effort. Ottinger held the seat until his ill-fated 1970 race for the Senate, which cost his family even more money; then it was won, rather narrowly, by Republican Peter Peyser.

In 1972, there was a match between Peyser and Ottinger, trying for a comeback. Ottinger carried the Bronx portion of the district, but lost the Westchester he had once represented to its new Congressman; it was the closest race in New York that year and one of the closest in the nation. Ottinger was considering another run in 1974 when Ogden Reid, of the 24th district, announced his candidacy for Governor; Ottinger moved into that race, and won easily.

That gave Peyser a free—or at least easy—ride; he won by a solid 58–42 margin. For a man who began his career, as Mayor of Irvington, by urging parents to inform on their drug-using children, and who in his last two elections won the nomination of the Conservative Party, Peyser has a rather liberal record—although it is not the record of a Democrat in disguise. Having survived tough challengers and tough years, he looks to be in good shape for a long congressional career. But he has set higher sights, and says he intends to run against Senator James Buckley in 1976. Will he get enough votes at the convention to force a primary? It seems hardly likely, if the increasingly conservative New York Republicans are left to their own devices; nor does it seem much more likely that Nelson Rockefeller, in bad need of conservative delegate votes himself, will help.

Census Data   Pop. 467,778. Central city, 34%; suburban, 66%. Median family income, $12,693; families above $15,000: 39%; families below $3,000: 6%. Median years education, 12.3.

The Voters

Median voting age **46.**
Employment profile White collar, 62%. Blue collar, 26%. Service, 12%. Farm, –%.
Ethnic groups Black, 13%. Spanish, 2%. Total foreign stock, 42%. Italy, 13%; Ireland, 4%; USSR, Germany, Poland, 3% each; UK, Austria, 2% each; Canada, 1%.

Presidential vote

1972	Nixon (R)	120,690	(61%)
	McGovern (D)	76,152	(39%)
1968	Nixon (R)	99,301	(48%)
	Humphrey (D)	92,265	(45%)
	Wallace (AI)	13,532	(7%)

Rep. Peter A. Peyser (R) Elected 1970; b. Sept. 7, 1921, Cedarhurst; home, Irvington; Colgate U., B.A. 1943; Episcopalian.

Career Army, WWII; Life insurance agent; Mgr., Peter A. Peyser Agency, Mutual of N.Y., 1961–70; Mayor of Irvington, 1963–70.

Offices 1133 LHOB, 202-225-5536. Also Yonkers Gen. P.O., Rm. 209A, Yonkers 10701, 914-423-0990.

Committees

Agriculture (8th). Subcommittees: Cotton; Family Farms and Rural Development.

Education and Labor (7th). Subcommittees: Manpower, Compensation, and Health and Safety; Select Subcommittee on Education.

Group Ratings

	ADA	COPE	LWV	RIPON	NFU	LCV	CFA	NAB	NSI	ACA
1974	36	70	67	64	62	67	77	33	100	50
1973	45	82	92	71	55	56	71	–	–	35
1972	44	89	80	90	67	43	100	42	100	33

Key Votes

1) Foreign Aid	FOR	6) Gov Abortn Aid	AGN	11) Pub Cong Election $	FOR
2) Busing	AGN	7) Coed Phys Ed	FOR	12) Turkish Arms Cutoff	FOR
3) ABM	AGN	8) Pov Lawyer Gag	AGN	13) Youth Camp Regs	FOR
4) B-1 Bomber	FOR	9) Pub Trans Sub	FOR	14) Strip Mine Veto	AGN
5) Nerve Gas	AGN	10) EZ Voter Regis	AGN	15) Farm Bill Veto	FOR

Election Results

1974 general:	Peter A. Peyser (R-C)	80,361	(58%)	($73,506)
	William S. Greenawalt (D-L)	59,108	(42%)	($53,111)
1974 primary:	Peter A. Peyser (R)	8,181	(79%)	
	Anthony J. DeVito (R)	2,147	(21%)	
1972 general:	Peter A. Peyser (R-C)	99,777	(50%)	($154,567)
	Richard L. Ottinger (D-L)	98,335	(50%)	($195,784)

◆ ◆ ◆ ◆

TWENTY-FOURTH DISTRICT

In the conventional wisdom, New York's Westchester County is *the* suburb for the wealthy: not only the superrich like the Rockefellers of Pocantico Hills, but also the ordinary rich, the people who own those large, comfortable houses in Scarsdale and White Plains, with their gently sloping lawns shaded by towering trees; or the glassy contemporary houses in the woodsier hills of Pound Ridge, Armonk, and Briarcliff Manor. All of these places are in New York's 24th congressional district, the only seat entirely within Westchester County. But the conventional image of Westchester and the 24th is not entirely accurate. Plenty of rich people of course live here—the constituency ranks 18th in median income of the nation's 435 congressional districts. But taken as a whole, the 24th is not uniformly wealthy. More typical of Westchester than WASPy Bedford Village or Jewish Scarsdale are the predominantly Italian-American, middle income neighborhoods of Mount Vernon or Rye.

Westchester County and the 24th district are one of the ancestral homes of liberal establishment Republicanism. Upper income voters have set the tone, if they have not provided most of the votes, of Westchester Republican politics; and here you will find most of the major backers of candidates like Thomas E. Dewey, Dwight D. Eisenhower, and Nelson Rockefeller. In the Nixon years, upper income voters began moving to the left—Scarsdale, for example, went for Humphrey in 1968 and nearly for McGovern in 1972—but they were more than counterbalanced numerically by the middle income voters moving toward the Nixon version of the politics of law 'n' order.

The passage of the 24th district from a preserve of liberal Republicans to a battleground between liberal Democrats and conservative Republicans is nicely illustrated by the last few congressional elections here. From 1963 to 1975, the district was represented by Ogden Reid; as heir to the New York *Herald Tribune* fortune, as Eisenhower's Ambassador to Israel, and as a Nelson Rockefeller appointee, he was the personification of liberal Republican politics. Indeed, one of his grandfathers, Whitelaw Reid, had been among the founders of the Republican Party. In Congress, Reid's voting record was really more liberal than Republican; his main devotion to the party consisted of campaigning for Rockefeller any time he was running for President.

At general election time, Reid's brand of Republicanism made him unbeatable; but as time went on it caused him increasing troubles in primaries. In 1970, an unknown conservative challenger got 46% of the vote against him—evidence, if any was needed, that conservatively inclined Republican voters were tired of electing someone who stood opposite them on most major issues. As it happened, Reid was souring on Republicans, too; it didn't help that the party held most of the state's top elective posts, and that none of their holders was planning to retire. So in 1972 Ogden Reid became a Democrat, and survived a Republican challenge financed primarily by his old patron Nelson Rockefeller. Having won, Reid started running for Governor, as he had wanted to for years. But his candidacy never caught fire, and in 1974 he left the race—too late to run for Congress again, however.

The new Congressman from the 24th is a man with a very similar background, including a couple of terms in Congress and a yen for statewide office: Richard Ottinger, former (1965–71) Congressman from the other Westchester district, and Democratic nominee for U.S. Senate in 1970. Ottinger, too, is from a wealthy family with a Republican background (his uncle ran against, and nearly beat, Franklin D. Roosevelt in the 1928 gubernatorial race); but he has always run as a Democrat. Ottinger is probably one of the leading, certainly he was one of the earliest, environmentalists in the Congress. His record on issues of that sort, plus his celebrity status after so many well financed campaigns, gave him an easy 58–42 victory here in 1974. Reportedly Ottinger is considering the 1976 Senate race for the seat James Buckley edged him out of in 1970; if he does run, and vacate the 24th, will Reid run again?

Census Data Pop. 468,148. Central city, 0%; suburban, 100%. Median family income, $13,577; families above $15,000: 44%; families below $3,000: 5%. Median years education, 12.4.

The Voters

Median voting age 46.
Employment profile White collar, 63%. Blue collar, 24%. Service, 13%. Farm, –%.
Ethnic groups Black, 13%. Total foreign stock, 39%. Italy, 13%; USSR, Germany, Ireland, UK, 3% each: Poland, 2%; Austria, Canada, 1% each.

Presidential vote

1972	Nixon (R)	135,553	(61%)
	McGovern (D)	87,068	(39%)
1968	Nixon (R)	100,797	(48%)
	Humphrey (D)	95,508	(46%)
	Wallace (AI)	12,064	(6%)

Rep. Richard L. Ottinger (D) Elected 1974; b. Jan. 27, 1929; home, Pleasantville; Cornell U., B.A. 1950, Harvard U., LL.B. 1953, Internatl. Law Study, Georgetown U., 1960–61.

Career Practicing atty., 1955–60, 1972–74; International corp. contract mgr., 1960–61; Co-Founder, 2nd Staff Mbr. and Dir. of Programs for the West Coast of South America, Peace Corps, 1961–64; U.S. House of Reps., 1965–70; Dem. nominee for U.S. Senate, 1970; Organizer, Grassroots Action, Inc., non-profit consumer and environmental assistance org., 1971–72.

Offices 240 CHOB, 202-225-6506. Also 180 S. Broadway, White Plains 10605, 914-428-3040.

Committees

Interstate and Foreign Commerce (19th). Subcommittees: Energy and Power; Oversight and Investigations.

Science and Technology (13th). Subcommittees: Aviation and Transportation Research and Development; Energy Research, Development and Demonstration; Environment and the Atmosphere.

Group Ratings: Newly Elected

Key Votes

1) Foreign Aid	FOR	6) Gov Abortn Aid	NE	11) Pub Cong Election $	NE
2) Busing	NE	7) Coed Phys Ed	FOR	12) Turkish Arms Cutoff	NE
3) ABM	NE	8) Pov Lawyer Gag	NE	13) Youth Camp Regs	FOR
4) B-1 Bomber	AGN	9) Pub Trans Sub	NE	14) Strip Mine Veto	AGN
5) Nerve Gas	NE	10) EZ Voter Regis	NE	15) Farm Bill Veto	AGN

Election Results

1974 general:	Richard L. Ottinger (D)	82,542	(58%)	($120,896)
	Charles J. Stephens (R-C)	60,180	(42%)	($60,458)
1974 primary:	Richard L. Ottinger (D), unopposed			

◆ ◆ ◆ ◆ ◆

TWENTY-FIFTH DISTRICT

The 25th congressional district of New York occupies the heart of the Hudson River valley, extending from the Bear Mountain Bridge, some 30 miles north of Manhattan, to a point most of the way to Albany. Like most rivers in the country, the Hudson is hideously polluted, but its scenery retains much of the grandeur it had when it inspired the painters whose school bears its name in the early nineteenth century. In colonial days, and even after independence, this valley was a place that nurtured one of the few feudal social systems in the United States. The Dutch who originally colonized the Hudson had given huge land grants to the patroon families whose names are still well known: Schuyler, van Rensselaer, van Cortlandt, Roosevelt.

Since the mid-nineteenth century, the Hudson Valley has been predominantly Republican, and in the last few years that preference has been strengthened by the arrival of conservative minded, middle-class people from the New York area, who left the city and its close in suburbs in disgust and anger. Franklin Roosevelt won an upset victory in a state Senate race in the heavily Democratic year of 1910, but during the thirties and forties he was never able to carry his home area. Even more irritating to FDR, the Hudson valley persisted in reelecting as its Congressman Hamilton Fish, an isolationist Republican who hated Roosevelt bitterly—and was hated just as strongly back. The Fish family was as socially prominent as the Roosevelts, perhaps more so; Hamilton Fishes had been representing the area in Congress since 1842, and an earlier Hamilton Fish had been Secretary of State under Grant. Franklin Roosevelt had the pleasure of seeing the Hamilton Fish of his day finally defeated, in the 1944 election.

Subsequent Congressmen from the Hudson valley include a Republican named J. Ernest Wharton, who will probably best be remembered by history for having beaten Gore Vidal in the 1960 election; and Joseph Y. Resnick, a Democrat who beat Wharton four years later. Resnick was a self-made millionaire, a flamboyant domestic liberal, and a Vietnam hawk; he made an unsuccessful race for his party's Senate nomination in 1968, and died shortly thereafter.

That left the way for the Fish dynasty to retain control, in the person of 42-year-old Hamilton Fish, Jr. That year he had to get through a tough primary—one opponent was Dutchess County assistant D.A., G. Gordon Liddy, Jr.—and beat a vigorous and well financed Democratic opponent in the general election. Like his father, Fish is a Republican, but of a rather different sort. He has shown no particular inclination to repeal the New Deal, something his father, still alive at 88, would still like to see. He does share with his father a certain skepticism about American intervention abroad, and has voted against military involvement in Indochina.

But the Fishes, father and son, ended up disagreeing on the issue that has focused the most attention on the Congressman: the impeachment of Richard Nixon. As a member of the Judiciary Committee, Fish announced in his patrician tones, looking over his half glasses, that he would have to vote against Nixon. His father was a diehard Nixon defender, going so far as to authorize his signature on some back-the-President newspaper ads; apparently he was convinced that Congress was impeaching the wrong President, forty years too late.

In any case, it was the view of Congressman Fish which prevailed. He had relatively little trouble winning reelection; an energetic Democratic candidate was able only to hold his percentage down to 66%. That represented a small loss for Fish, but there can be no doubt that his decision on impeachment represented the will of the majority in this still heavily Republican district.

Census Data Pop. 467,859. Central city, 0%; suburban, 26%. Median family income, $11,885; families above $15,000: 32%; families below $3,000: 6%. Median years education, 12.3.

The Voters

Median voting age 42.
Employment profile White collar, 56%. Blue collar, 30%. Service, 13%. Farm, 1%.
Ethnic groups Black, 5%. Total foreign stock, 25%. Italy, 6%; Germany, 4%; UK, Ireland, 2% each; Canada, Poland, USSR, 1% each.

Presidential vote

1972	Nixon (R)	148,003	(70%)
	McGovern (D)	63,536	(30%)
1968	Nixon (R)	102,353	(55%)
	Humphrey (D)	68,225	(37%)
	Wallace (AI)	14,735	(8%)

Rep. Hamilton Fish, Jr. (R) Elected 1968; b. June 3, 1926, Washington, D.C.; home, Millbrook; Harvard U., A.B. 1949, NYU, LL.B. 1957; Episcopalian.

Career Navy, WWII; Practicing atty.; Vice Counsel, U.S. Foreign Svc., Ireland, 1951–53; Counsel, N.Y. State Assembly Judiciary Comm., 1961; Dutchess Co. Civil Defense Dir., 1967–68.

Offices 409 CHOB, 202-225-5441. Also 62 Market St., Poughkepsie 12601, 914-452-4220.

Committees

Judiciary (5th). Subcommittees: Administrative Law and Governmental Relations; Immigration, Citizenship, and International Law.

Small Business (7th). Subcommittees: Energy and Environment; SBA Oversight and Minority Enterprise.

Group Ratings

	ADA	COPE	LWV	RIPON	NFU	LCV	CFA	NAB	NSI	ACA
1974	38	50	91	80	67	81	54	50	89	50
1973	46	50	83	87	55	79	88	–	–	29
1972	38	55	89	100	57	80	0	58	100	29

Key Votes

1) Foreign Aid	FOR	6) Gov Abortn Aid	AGN	11) Pub Cong Election $	FOR
2) Busing	FOR	7) Coed Phys Ed	FOR	12) Turkish Arms Cutoff	FOR
3) ABM	ABS	8) Pov Lawyer Gag	AGN	13) Youth Camp Regs	ABS
4) B-1 Bomber	FOR	9) Pub Trans Sub	FOR	14) Strip Mine Veto	AGN
5) Nerve Gas	ABS	10) EZ Voter Regis	AGN	15) Farm Bill Veto	FOR

Election Results

1974 general:	Hamilton Fish, Jr. (R-C)	103,799	(66%)	($56,398)
	Nicholas B. Angell (D)	53,357	(34%)	($99,009)
1974 primary:	Hamilton Fish, Jr. (R), unopposed			
1974 general:	Hamilton Fish, Jr. (R-C)	144,386	(73%)	($23,208)
	John M. Burns III (D)	54,271	(27%)	($18,431)

◆ ◆ ◆ ◆ ◆

TWENTY-SIXTH DISTRICT

The 26th congressional district of New York lies just at the margin between the New York City suburbs and the vast expanse of Upstate New York. Fast-growing Rockland County, at the southern end of the district, is definitely within the City's orbit. Though it usually goes Republican, Rockland has a Democratic registration edge and a large (11%) Jewish population; many of the County's residents work in the City and commute across the George Washington or Tappan Zee bridges. North of Rockland and separated from it by a mountain ridge is Orange County, once a largely rural area, with one small stagnant city on the Hudson, Newburgh. In recent years, Orange County has been experiencing explosive growth, much of it resulting from the exodus of New York City policemen, firemen, and civil servants; they talk of wanting to protect their children from any contact with the horrors of the City even as they praise themselves implicitly for dealing with them.

By longstanding tradition, Orange County is Republican; and until 1974, at least, the new migrants seem to have made that preference as intense as in the county's California namesake. James Buckley was a big favorite here in 1970, and Richard Nixon in 1972. But as throughout the New York metropolitan area, the Watergate seems to have brought ancestral Democrats back to their party and to have caused them to forget their conservative leanings of recent years as if they had never existed. The long time Republican stronghold of Orange County gave Governor Hugh Carey 47% of its vote in 1974.

But in the elections immediately preceding, the 26th had been pretty solidly Republican—which was significant, because for a period of ten years this was a district which was closely and heatedly contested. It began in 1964, when conservative Republican incumbent Katharine St. George was upset by one of the unlikelier 1964 landslide Democrats, John G. Dow. Dow was then a 59-year-old business systems analyst and, even in 1965, an earnest peace advocate and dovish opponent of American military involvement in Indochina. He used to do things like vote for bills lifting the penalty for flag desecration and against measures that would increase penalties for drug use. Somehow Dow managed to win reelection in 1966, but he lost, as expected, in 1968 to Republican Martin McKneally, a former national commander of the American Legion.

A staunch law 'n' order man, McKneally looked like a cinch for reelection; if he was a little rough hewn for Rockland, he was just fine for Orange. But in the fall of 1970 it was revealed that he had not bothered to file federal income tax returns for several years. The Democratic nominee was, as usual, Dow, who won the election with 52% of the vote.

But 1972 was too much for this liberal Democrat. As in 1968, Richard Nixon carried a solid majority in the 26th, and Dow again lost in the presidential undertow. The victor this time was liberal Republican Assemblyman Benjamin Gilman, who won a minority victory, as the Conservative candidate took 13% of the vote. Two years later, though he still had Conservative opposition, Gilman did better, winning with 54%. The 69-year-old Dow was able to make it close only in Rockland, and lost Orange by nearly 2–1. A member of the Post Office and International Relations Committees, Gilman appears now to have won a safe seat.

Census Data Pop. 467,424. Central city, 0%; suburban, 49%. Median family income, $11,632; families above $15,000: 31%; families below $3,000: 6%. Median years education, 12.3.

The Voters

Median voting age 42.
Employment profile White collar, 53%. Blue collar, 32%. Service, 14%. Farm, 1%.
Ethnic groups Black, 6%. Spanish, 2%. Total foreign stock, 28%. Italy, 6%; Germany, USSR, Ireland, 3% each; Poland, UK, 2% each; Austria, Canada, 1% each.

Presidential vote

1972	Nixon (R)	133,873	(68%)
	McGovern (D)	63,450	(32%)
1968	Nixon (R)	89,655	(53%)
	Humphrey (D)	66,783	(39%)
	Wallace (AI)	13,301	(8%)

Rep. Benjamin A. Gilman (R) Elected 1972; b. Dec. 6, 1922, Poughkeepsie; home, Middletown; U. of Penn., B.S. 1946, N.Y. Law School, LL.B. 1950; Jewish.

Career Army Air Corps, WWII; Asst. Atty. Gen. of N.Y. State, 1953; Practicing atty., 1955–72; Atty., N.Y. State Temp. Comm. on the Courts, 1956–57; N.Y. State Assembly, 1967–72.

Offices 1226 LHOB, 202-225-3776. Also P.O. Bldg., 217 Liberty St., Newburgh 12550, 914-565-6400.

Committees

International Relations (10th). Subcommittees: International Resources, Food, and Energy.

Post Office and Civil Service (7th). Subcommittees: Postal Service.

Group Ratings

	ADA	COPE	LWV	RIPON	NFU	LCV	CFA	NAB	NSI	ACA
1974	27	73	75	63	77	88	69	55	100	40
1973	48	64	91	67	60	79	75	–	–	44

Key Votes

1) Foreign Aid	FOR	6) Gov Abortn Aid	AGN	11) Pub Cong Election $	FOR
2) Busing	AGN	7) Coed Phys Ed	FOR	12) Turkish Arms Cutoff	FOR
3) ABM	FOR	8) Pov Lawyer Gag	AGN	13) Youth Camp Regs	FOR
4) B-1 Bomber	FOR	9) Pub Trans Sub	FOR	14) Strip Mine Veto	AGN
5) Nerve Gas	FOR	10) EZ Voter Regis	AGN	15) Farm Bill Veto	FOR

Election Results

1974 general:	Benjamin A. Gilman (R)	81,562	(54%)	($91,812)
	John G. Dow (D-L)	58,161	(38%)	($43,097)
	Thomas Moore (C)	11,345	(8%)	($1,103)
1974 primary:	Benjamin A. Gilman (R), unopposed			
1972 general:	Benjamin A. Gilman (R)	90,922	(48%)	($112,729)
	John G. Dow (D)	74,906	(39%)	($52,197)
	Yale Rapkin (C-Ind.)	24,596	(13%)	($80,595)

◆ ◆ ◆ ◆ ◆

TWENTY-SEVENTH DISTRICT

New York's 27th congressional district extends along the state's southern border from the Catskills to the Southern Tier. The Catskills are famous for huge Borscht Belt hotels like Grossinger's and the Concord; for Dutch-descended Rip Van Winkle; and for the phenomenon of the Woodstock festival (which actually took place 50 miles from the little village of Woodstock). The low lying Catskills occupy most of the eastern half of the 27th; to the west the mountains subside into the Appalachian plateau. There begins the row of counties along New York's boundary with Pennsylvania known as the Southern Tier. Here is Binghamton, an old manufacturing city (with new IBM plants nearby) which is the largest in the district, and Ithaca, the home of Cornell University.

With the exception of Sullivan County in the Borscht Belt—one of three counties in the United States where Jews are the largest religious group—most of the 27th is ancestral Republican territory. It did not move as sharply to the right during the Nixon years, so that it became not much more Republican than the state as a whole. Then in 1974, it did not shift back to the Democrats as did ethnic middle class parts of the New York City metropolitan area. But it did come out of the Watergate years willing enough to vote Democratic to elect—for the first time since 1912—a Democratic Congressman.

That was one thing Congressman Howard Robison, who was retiring in 1974, had never expected: to be succeeded by a Democrat. When he was first elected to the House, in 1958, Upstate New York was still electing those oldtimers who had been some of the House's most powerful committee chairmen the last time the Republicans had a majority (1953–55); John Taber (Appropriations), Daniel Reed (Ways and Means), and the man Robison succeeded, Sterling Cole (Joint Committee on Atomic Energy). In this rather conservative company, Robison was a moderate; by the time he in turn retired, he was the senior Republican on the New York delegation, and all the old conservatives had long since gone.

Neither of the major contenders for Robison's seat were identified with his brand of moderate Republicanism. Former Binghamton Mayor Alfred Libous, the Republican, was known as a hard shell conservative; while the Democrat, former Tompkins County (Ithaca) D.A. Matthew McHugh, was considered a liberal. With a big vote in his home county (75%) and an even split in Binghamton, McHugh won, by a 53–43 margin. In the House he serves on the Agriculture Committee; in 1976 he will probably face a strong Republican challenge.

Census Data Pop. 467,980. Central city, 14%; suburban, 44%. Median family income, $9,904; families above $15,000: 20%; families below $3,000: 8%. Median years education, 12.3.

The Voters

Median voting age 42.
Employment profile White collar, 51%. Blue collar, 32%. Service, 14%. Farm, 3%.
Ethnic groups Black, 2%. Total foreign stock, 19%. Italy, 3%; Germany, UK, Poland, Czechoslovakia, 2% each; USSR, Austria, Canada, 1% each.

Presidential vote

1972	Nixon (R)	141,972	(64%)
	McGovern (D)	81,179	(36%)
1968	Nixon (R)	100,771	(54%)
	Humphrey (D)	73,629	(40%)
	Wallace (AI)	11,771	(6%)

Rep. Matthew F. McHugh (D) Elected 1974; b. Dec. 6, 1938, Philadelphia, Pa.; home, Ithaca; Mt. St. Mary's Col., Emmitsburg, Md., B.S. 1960, Villanova U., J.D. 1963; Immaculate Conception Church.

Career Practicing atty., 1964–74; Ithaca City Prosecutor, 1968; Tompkins Co. Dist. Atty., 1969–72.

Offices 1204 LHOB, 202-225-6335. Also 310 Fed. Bldg., Binghamton 13902, 607-723-4425.

Committees

Agriculture (23d). Subcommittees: Dairy and Poultry; Department Operations, Investigations and Oversight; Domestic Marketing and Consumer Relations.

Veterans' Affairs (19th). Subcommittees: Cemeteries and Burial Benefits; Hospitals.

Group Ratings: Newly Elected

Key Votes

1) Foreign Aid	FOR	6) Gov Abortn Aid	NE	11) Pub Cong Election $	NE
2) Busing	NE	7) Coed Phys Ed	AGN	12) Turkish Arms Cutoff	NE
3) ABM	NE	8) Pov Lawyer Gag	NE	13) Youth Camp Regs	FOR
4) B-1 Bomber	AGN	9) Pub Trans Sub	NE	14) Strip Mine Veto	AGN
5) Nerve Gas	NE	10) EZ Voter Regis	NE	15) Farm Bill Veto	AGN

Election Results

1974 general:	Matthew F. McHugh (D-L)	83,562	(53%)	($56,361)
	Alfred J. Libous (R)	68,273	(43%)	($62,196)
	Franklin B. Resseguie (C)	6,526	(4%)	($31,904)
1974 primary:	Matthew F.McHugh (D)	9,353	(46%)	
	Robert M. Kropp (D)	5,494	(27%)	
	William Schechter (D)	3,468	(17%)	
	Michael P. Sloan (D)	2,006	(10%)	

♦ ♦ ♦ ♦ ♦

TWENTY-EIGHTH DISTRICT

The 28th congressional district of New York is the Albany-Schenectady area, where the Mohawk River flows into the Hudson. The district contains virtually all of Albany and Schenectady Counties, plus the aging carpet mill town of Amsterdam in Montgomery County. Of these places, the most interesting and politically significant is Albany, where an old fashioned Democratic machine still holds sway over local politics. For fifty years this Albany machine has had the same boss, 89-year-old Daniel O'Connell, who has operated only from his house for years (John Kennedy went there to visit with him in 1960); since 1942, the city's mayor has been local aristocrat and machine stalwart Erastus Corning 2d. It remains the practice in Albany for all city employees to get clearance from their Democratic ward bosses, who themselves are often blessed with no-show jobs; and there is plenty of favoritism for well-connected contractors. And so the antique machine keeps control of the dwindling number of dollars generated by the sagging shopping areas and crumbling brownstone townhouses of Albany; people who can have been moving out of the city to its more spacious—and better governed—suburbs.

For years Albany has ground out the largest Democratic majorities between New York City and Buffalo, with some exceptions in recent years. These were partially due to the general rightward trend of ethnic voters in the Nixon years, but mostly the result of the clout of then Governor Nelson Rockefeller. For Albany is the state capital, and Rockefeller found it useful to get on well with Corning et al.—and vice versa. Thus Rockefeller poured $1 billion of bond money into the giant Albany Mall, which kept the construction industry here busy for years, and Albany gratefully responded by giving him and his friend Richard Nixon comfortable majorities in 1970 and 1972.

For a while Albany also had a Republican Congressman—evidence that the fabled machine was interested almost exclusively in preserving its hold on local government. When machine Democrat Leo O'Brien retired in 1966, the district was captured by liberal Republican Daniel Button. Button was reelected once easily, but in 1970 he was redistricted into the same seat as another incumbent, Democrat Samuel Stratton.

Stratton came out of Schenectady, an industrial town dominated economically by General Electric and more sympathetic than Albany to the Republican politics of GE's corporate hierarchy. Stratton was elected to the Schenectady Council in 1950, and became Mayor in 1956; in the 1958 Democratic sweep, he was elected Congressman. Twice the Republicans tried to redistrict him out of his seat, and twice failed; his assiduous personal campaigning was winning him 2–1 margins over serious opposition. And so by 1970, the legislature had in effect conceded him a safe seat; he reciprocated by beating Button 66–34.

That contest was one of the few that year that pitted a dovish Republican against a hawkish Democrat. Stratton had served on the Armed Services Committee since he entered Congress, and he had long been known as something of a maverick there. But that was not because he differed with the Committee majority's hawkish world view, but rather because of his pesky sniping at congressional sacred cows. (Stratton is, for example, the leading opponent of the move to increase office space and desecrate the Capitol by tearing down and redesigning its West Front.) Back in the days before Pearl Harbor, Stratton served as an aide to Congressman Thomas Eliot, who came from the Massachusetts district later represented by John F. Kennedy and Thomas "Tip" O'Neill;

Eliot was a supporter of FDR's military preparedness program, including the draft, and of aid to Britain.

That experience seems to have made a deep impression on Stratton, who today is one of the House's most steadfast hawks and opponents of what he considers appeasement. He continued to support the notion that this country ought to intervene militarily in Indochina until the bitter end. Undoubtedly he sees himself as an upholder of the ideals of Roosevelt and an opponent of today's Neville Chamberlains; most of his Democratic colleagues see him as a steadfastly wrongheaded zealot.

As the fourth-ranking Democrat on Armed Services Stratton, who is just turning 60, has a fair chance of some day becoming Chairman, unless his Democratic colleagues should decide his views are simply unacceptable. As for elections in the 28th district, his popularity is phenomenal and opposition insignificant. In 1972, he won 80% of the vote; in 1974, 81%.

Census Data Pop. 467,219. Central city, 13%; suburban, 47%. Median family income, $10,764; families above $15,000: 25%; families below $3,000: 6%. Median years education, 12.2.

The Voters

Median voting age 46.
Employment profile White collar, 58%. Blue collar, 29%. Service, 12%. Farm, 1%.
Ethnic groups Black, 4%. Total foreign stock, 27%. Italy, 7%; Poland, 4%; Germany, 3%; Canada, UK, Ireland, 2% each; USSR, 1%.

Presidential vote

1972	Nixon (R)	134,123	(57%)
	McGovern (D)	101,128	(43%)
1968	Nixon (R)	89,880	(41%)
	Humphrey (D)	121,389	(55%)
	Wallace (AI)	9,596	(4%)

Rep. Samuel S. Stratton (D) Elected 1958; b. Sept. 27, 1916, Yonkers; home, Amsterdam; U. of Rochester, B.A. 1937, Haverford Col., M.A. 1938, Harvard U., M.A. 1940; Presbyterian.

Career Secy. to U.S. Rep. Thomas H. Eliot of Mass., 1940–42; Navy, WWII and Korea; Deputy Secy. Gen., Far Eastern Comm., 1946–48; Radio and TV news commentator; College lecturer; Schenectady City Cncl., 1950–56, Mayor, 1956–59.

Offices 2302 RHOB, 202-225-5076. Also, U.S.P.O., Jay St., Schenectady 12305, 518-374-4547.

Committees

Armed Services (4th). Subcommittees: Investigation; Military Compensation (Chairman); Special Subcommittee on Intelligence.

Group Ratings

	ADA	COPE	LWV	RIPON	NFU	LCV	CFA	NAB	NSI	ACA
1974	35	100	64	31	79	63	75	18	100	36
1973	38	100	58	47	59	26	100	–	–	31
1972	38	82	73	78	71	47	50	18	100	22

Key Votes

1) Foreign Aid	FOR	6) Gov Abortn Aid	AGN	11) Pub Cong Election $	FOR
2) Busing	AGN	7) Coed Phys Ed	FOR	12) Turkish Arms Cutoff	AGN
3) ABM	FOR	8) Pov Lawyer Gag	FOR	13) Youth Camp Regs	AGN
4) B-1 Bomber	FOR	9) Pub Trans Sub	FOR	14) Strip Mine Veto	FOR
5) Nerve Gas	FOR	10) EZ Voter Regis	FOR	15) Farm Bill Veto	FOR

Election Results

1974 general:	Samuel S. Stratton (D)	156,439	(81%)	($26,618)
	Wayne E. Wagner (R)	33,493	(17%)	($11,069)
	Edward Breitenbach (C)	4,050	(2%)	($1,583)
1974 primary:	Samuel S. Stratton (D)	27,474	(90%)	
	Victor Caban (D)	3,118	(10%)	
1972 general	Samuel S. Stratton (D)	182,395	(80%)	($27,297)
	John F. Ryan, Jr. (R-C)	45,623	(20%)	($1,308)

◆ ◆ ◆ ◆ ◆

TWENTY-NINTH DISTRICT

The 29th congressional district of New York, once a basically rural area, is now on its way to being suburban. Although the district extends from the Dutchess County border in the south nearly to Lake Champlain in the north, more than half its residents live within twenty miles of Albany, the state capital, which is itself in the 28th District. Almost directly across the Hudson from Albany is Troy, now a dreary city of 63,000, but in the early nineteenth century a harbinger of the future as one of the first American cities with an economy based almost entirely on manufacturing. To the north is Saratoga County, site of the Revolutionary War battle and home of the famous race track, but politically most significant as the recipient of the population spillover from the Albany-Schenectady-Troy metropolitan area. This means an infusion of Catholic and at least ancestrally Democratic votes into a district that in its northern reaches is still dominated by Yankee Republicans and in its southern counties, one of which gave birth to Martin Van Buren, conservative minded Dutchmen.

It was the district's conservatives, basically, who were represented for 14 years by Republican Congressman Carleton J. King. King was out of the oldtime mold of Upstate Republicans: a conservative who had served as District Attorney of Saratoga County for more than ten years, and who then moved up to the apparently less demanding job of Congressman at the age of 56. On the floor and as a member of the Armed Services Committee, King never did anything remarkable. And if he was not as adept at servicing the needs of his constituents as were many of his younger colleagues, well, in this heavily Republican district he could be confident of reelection every two years anyway.

Or so he must have thought. Actually, King had solid warnings that he might be vulnerable. He won by only 1,109 votes in the 1964 LBJ landslide year. And he got a rather lackluster 57% of the vote in 1970, when his Democratic opponent was Rensselaer County (Troy) Clerk Edward Pattison. Pattison turned out to be a man with a nose for spotting years when Republicans like King might be in trouble, and he eagerly entered the 1974 race against him. King had been ill, and had uttered nary a word against Richard Nixon; Pattison campaigned actively. The result was a smashing 54–46 Pattison victory. Not only did the Democrat carry his home county with 62% of the vote and Saratoga with 55%; he just about broke even in the smaller counties that make up the rest of the district.

Pattison is one of those 1974 winners who will have to win again in 1976 if Democrats are to maintain the solid hold they now have on the House of Representatives. Despite the Republican background of the district, his chances look good. As incumbent, he has access to all the facilities and advantages the office provide, and at his age (38) he surely has the energy for the kind of nonstop communing with constituents which pays off on election day. The Republicans, of course, will try to win this district back. But barring the emergence of a major issue which is not as yet apparent, Pattison should definitely be the favorite to win.

Census Data Pop. 467,767. Central city, 13%; suburban, 47%. Median family income, $9,621; families above $15,000: 18%; families below $3,000: 8%. Median years education, 12.1.

The Voters

Median voting age 44.
Employment profile White collar, 47%. Blue collar, 38%. Service, 12%. Farm, 3%.
Ethnic groups Black, 2%. Total foreign stock, 18%. Italy, Canada, 3% each; Germany, UK, Ireland, 2% each; Poland, 1%.

Presidential vote

1972	Nixon (R)	156,842	(70%)
	McGovern (D)	67,570	(30%)
1968	Nixon (R)	112,265	(56%)
	Humphrey (D)	76,151	(38%)
	Wallace (AI)	11,412	(6%)

Rep. Edward W. Pattison (D) Elected 1974; b. Apr. 29, 1932, Troy; home, West Sand Lake; Cornell U., A.B. 1953, LL.B. 1957.

Career Army, 1954–56; Practicing atty., 1959–74; Rensselaer Co. Treas., 1969–74; Dem. nominee for U.S. House of Reps., 1970.

Offices 1127 LHOB, 202-225-5614. Also Rm. 206, Troy P.O., Troy 12181, 518-274-2958.

Committees

Judiciary (20th). Subcommittees: Administrative Law and Governmental Relations; Courts, Civil Liberties, and the Administration of Justice.

Group Ratings: Newly Elected

Key Votes

1) Foreign Aid	AGN	6) Gov Abortn Aid	NE	11) Pub Cong Election $	NE
2) Busing	NE	7) Coed Phys Ed	FOR	12) Turkish Arms Cutoff	NE
3) ABM	NE	8) Pov Lawyer Gag	NE	13) Youth Camp Regs	AGN
4) B-1 Bomber	AGN	9) Pub Trans Sub	NE	14) Strip Mine Veto	AGN
5) Nerve Gas	NE	10) EZ Voter Regis	NE	15) Farm Bill Veto	AGN

Election Results

1974 general	Edward W. Pattison (D-L)	100,324	(54%)	($36,227)
	Carleton J. King (R-C)	83,768	(46%)	($35,962)
1974 primary:	Edward W. Pattison (D)	5,437	(44%)	
	Joseph J. Marin (D)	3,172	(26%)	
	Edward J. Golden (D)	2,014	(16%)	
	William H. Colgan (D)	1,667	(14%)	

◆ ◆ ◆ ◆ ◆

THIRTIETH DISTRICT

The 30th congressional district of New York covers the northernmost reaches of New York state. In includes the counties across the St. Lawrence River from Canada and the ones at the eastern end of Lake Ontario. The large French Canadian population in Clinton and Franklin Counties, just 100 miles south of Montreal, forms the only Democratic voting bloc in the district; as one moves west and south, there are fewer French and more Yankees. Here in the farm country of the St. Lawrence and the Adirondacks, where it gets bitterly cold in the winter and not very warm in the summer, the voting preference is decidedly Republican—enough so to make the entire district Republican in most elections. Geographically, much of the 30th is taken up with the Adirondack Forest Preserve, a giant state park which the New York Constitution stipulates must remain "forever wild." North of the Preserve is Massena, on the St. Lawrence River, which has been blessed with the administrative headquarters of the St. Lawrence Seaway bureaucracy; but the Seaway itself has failed to live up to economic expectations—another blow to this chronically depressed area.

In 1964, the Congressman from the 30th district, conservative Republican Clarence Kilburn, having just turned 70, announced that he was retiring because of age. At the time that was an unusual move for a Congressman with considerable seniority and no reason to expect defeat. (It is considerably more common today, now that the congressional pension runs as high as $32,000 a year.) Kilburn's successor was Robert McEwen, a like minded Republican, who was a state

Senator from the area for ten years. In the House, McEwen turned out to be one of those quiet conservative Republicans who seldom says much and votes predictably. His orthodoxy helped win him a seat on the Appropriations Committee, on which he has been climbing slowly to a position of high seniority; in 1975, he became ranking minority member of the Military Construction Subcommittee.

McEwen had first won his seat in a Democratic year, and had little trouble holding it in the next several elections. But in 1974 he faced what turned out to be a much stronger than expected challenge from Democrat Roger Tubby. At 63, Tubby had had a long political past: he was press secretary to President Truman and a fixture at gatherings of out of office Truman liberals ever since. In most of the district, he managed to hold McEwen about even; were it not for the Republican's 66% in Oswego County, just north of conservative Syracuse, McEwen might have been in real trouble. It is not likely that this will recur, but it is proof, if any were needed, that 1974 was a Democratic year indeed.

Census Data Pop. 467,920. Central city, 0%; suburban, 20%. Median family income, $8,584; families above $15,000: 14%; families below $3,000: 10%. Median years education, 12.0.

The Voters

Median voting age 43.
Employment profile White collar, 41%. Blue collar, 37%. Service, 16%. Farm, 6%.
Ethnic groups Total foreign stock, 15%. Canada, 7%; Italy, 2%; UK, 1%.

Presidential vote

1972	Nixon (R)	122,127	(67%)
	McGovern (D)	60,180	(33%)
1968	Nixon (R)	93,004	(55%)
	Humphrey (D)	67,935	(40%)
	Wallace (AI)	7,306	(4%)

Rep. Robert C. McEwen (R) Elected 1964; b. Jan. 5, 1920, Ogdensburg; home, Ogdensburg; U. of Vt., U. of Penn., Albany Law School, LL.B. 1947; Presbyterian.

Career Army Air Corps, WWII; N.Y. State Senate, 1954–64.

Offices 2419 RHOB, 202-225-4611. Also 307 Fed. Bldg., Watertown 13601, 315-782-3150.

Committees

Appropriations (9th). Subcommittees: Military Construction; Treasury, Postal Service, and General Government.

Group Ratings

	ADA	COPE	LWV	RIPON	NFU	LCV	CFA	NAB	NSI	ACA
1974	16	20	50	40	50	27	9	67	90	77
1973	8	0	42	43	31	6	29	–	–	67
1972	0	22	44	69	33	27	0	89	100	67

Key Votes

1) Foreign Aid	FOR	6) Gov Abortn Aid	AGN	11) Pub Cong Election $	FOR
2) Busing	FOR	7) Coed Phys Ed	AGN	12) Turkish Arms Cutoff	AGN
3) ABM	ABS	8) Pov Lawyer Gag	FOR	13) Youth Camp Regs	AGN
4) B-1 Bomber	FOR	9) Pub Trans Sub	ABS	14) Strip Mine Veto	FOR
5) Nerve Gas	FOR	10) EZ Voter Regis	AGN	15) Farm Bill Veto	AGN

Election Results

1974 general:	Robert C. McEwen (R-C)	78,117	(55%)	($15,710)
	Roger W. Tubby (D-L)	63,893	(45%)	($25,944)
1974 primary:	Robert C. McEwen (R), unopposed			
1972 general:	Robert C. McEwen (R-C)	114,194	(66%)	($9,861)
	Ernest J. Labaff (D-L)	58,788	(34%)	($10,019)

◆ ◆ ◆ ◆ ◆

THIRTY-FIRST DISTRICT

The 31st congressional district of New York includes most of the Mohawk River Valley, much of the Adirondack Forest Preserve, and a couple of agricultural counties. These other areas add much to its scenic beauty, but most of the people here are concentrated within 30 miles of the Mohawk. During the Revolutionary War, this part of New York was the frontier, where American colonists fought the British and their Iroquois allies, both united in their desire to prevent American penetration of the continent. And this is where they failed, as chronicled in, *inter alia*, the movie *Drums Along the Mohawk*.

In the early years of the nineteenth century, the Mohawk valley became the major route west for migrating New England Yankees, some of whom stayed to settle the valley. When the Erie Canal, which runs parallel to the River, was opened in 1825, the nation had its first major, and for long its most important, path from the coast to the interior. The Canal was the cheapest way to get bulky agricultural products out of the old Northwest (Ohio, Indiana, etc.) and finished goods back into the interior. At first the Canal, and then the New York Central Railroad of the Vanderbilts, accounted for much of the phenomenal nineteenth century growth of New York and its port. Its competitors, Boston and Philadelphia, with no similar access inland, were left behind.

As migration slowed and trade increased, the Mohawk valley became one of the early industrial centers of the nation, and the little Oneida hamlets of Utica and Rome grew to become sizeable industrial centers. First settled by New England Yankees, these towns attracted a new wave of immigration from the Atlantic coast in the early twentieth century; today they are the most heavily Italian and Polish-American communities between Albany and Buffalo.

In most parts of the nation, a change in ethnic composition of such magnitude would have moved the area from Republican to Democratic politics. But not in Upstate New York, where suspicion of Democratic New York City has worked to the advantage of the Republican Party since it was founded. To be sure, Republicans here pay close attention to the pro-union, anti-abortion, and pro-aid to parochial schools sentiments of their blue collar Catholic constituents; theirs is a party which has long since broadened its base from the all but vanishing white Anglo-Saxon Protestants. And their adaptation has been successful. Only Democrats with the strongest emotional appeal to Catholic voters—like Robert Kennedy in 1964 or Hugh Carey in 1974—have carried Mohawk valley counties.

For 14 years, this district was represented by Alexander Pirnie, a Republican whose voting record and constituency services were well designed to win him maximum support at election time. As a member of the Armed Services Committee, Pirnie was a conservative on foreign and military policy; but he compiled a fairly liberal and pro labor record on domestic issues, enough so to win the Liberal Party line in his last three elections. In 1972, at age 69, Pirnie decided to retire.

As is usually the case here, it was the Republican primary which determined the Congressman's successor. In that contest, Herkimer County Assemblyman Donald Mitchell, who already had the Conservative nomination, defeated Oneida County Assemblyman John Buckley, who had the Liberal line. Mitchell was aided by the presence on the ballot of a number of minor candidates from Buckley's home county. The general election Mitchell won without much difficulty, and moved into Pirnie's old Armed Services seat—a good position to defend the interests of Rome's Griffis Air Force Base. Mitchell apparently spent his first term handling constituency matters well, for in the Democratic year of 1974, he won reelection with 60% of the vote—one of the best showings of any Upstate Republican.

Census Data Pop. 467,717. Central city, 30%; suburban, 44%. Median family income, $9,388; families above $15,000: 17%; families below $3,000: 8%. Median years education, 11.9.

The Voters

Median voting age 46.
Employment profile White collar, 44%. Blue collar, 39%. Service, 13%. Farm, 4%.
Ethnic groups Black, 2%, Total foreign stock, 22%. Italy, 6%; Poland, 3%; Germany, UK, Canada, 2% each.

Presidential vote

1972	Nixon (R)	140,433	(70%)
	McGovern (D)	61,141	(30%)
1968	Nixon (R)	100,614	(54%)
	Humphrey (D)	75,508	(40%)
	Wallace (AI)	10,833	(6%)

Rep. Donald J. Mitchell (R) Elected 1972; b. May 8, 1923, Ilion; home, Herkimer; Hobart Col., 1946–47, Columbia U., B.S. 1949, M.A. 1950; Methodist.

Career Navy, WWII; Optometrist, 1950–72; Herkimer Town Cncl., 1954–57, Mayor, 1957–61; Herkimer Town Zoning Bd. of Appeals, 1963; N.Y. State Assembly, 1965–72, Maj. Whip, 1969–72.

Offices 1527 LHOB, 202-225-3665. Also, 270 N. Main St., Herkimer 13350, 315-866-1051.

Committees

Armed Services (8th). Subcommittees: Investigations; Military Compensation.

Standards of Official Conduct (5th).

Group Ratings

	ADA	COPE	LWV	RIPON	NFU	LCV	CFA	NAB	NSI	ACA
1974	27	45	64	50	64	59	46	55	100	53
1973	12	36	55	50	61	36	86	–	–	75

Key Votes

1) Foreign Aid	FOR	6) Gov Abortn Aid	AGN	11) Pub Cong Election $	FOR
2) Busing	AGN	7) Coed Phys Ed	AGN	12) Turkish Arms Cutoff	AGN
3) ABM	FOR	8) Pov Lawyer Gag	FOR	13) Youth Camp Regs	AGN
4) B-1 Bomber	FOR	9) Pub Trans Sub	FOR	14) Strip Mine Veto	FOR
5) Nerve Gas	FOR	10) EZ Voter Regis	AGN	15) Farm Bill Veto	FOR

Election Results

1974 general:	Donald J. Mitchell (R-C)	94,319	(60%)	($71,642)
	Donald J. Reile (D)	59,639	(38%)	($30,820)
	Theodore L. Tolles (L)	4,281	(3%)	($46,099)
1974 primary:	Donald J. Mitchell (R), unopposed			
1972 general:	Donald J. Mitchell (R-C)	98,454	(51%)	($81,740)
	Robert Castle (D)	75,513	(39%)	($91,869)
	Frank A. Nichols (Action Party)	12,075	(6%)	($18,358)
	John T. Buckley (L)	7,179	(4%)	($39,643)

◆ ◆ ◆ ◆ ◆

THIRTY-SECOND DISTRICT

From the 1920s until 1974, Upstate and suburban Republicans controlled the New York legislature, with the only exceptions being after the Democratic landslides of 1936 and 1964. One of the way these Republicans—whose control in most of those years was firmly based on legislative malapportionment—extended their clout into national affairs was to draw with exceeding care the boundaries of New York's congressional districts so as to maximize the number of Republicans elected. Two Upstate New York cities—Buffalo and Rochester—were traditionally cut into two or three districts, each with plenty of suburban and rural territory to overpower any possible urban Democratic majority. During the 1960s, the legislators abandoned this ploy in Buffalo, where one city district became overwhelmingly Democratic, though they retained it in Rochester; and in 1970, they applied it to Syracuse.

Until then, it had scarcely been necessary. Syracuse and surrounding Onondaga County had been a single district for as long as anyone could remember, and they had the perfect population to continue in that status after the 1970 census. Moreover, Syracuse is in many ways Upstate New York's most militantly conservative and usually Republican city (although it voted against Nelson Rockefeller in 1966 because it considered him too much of a big spender). General Electric, as in much of Upstate New York, is the largest employer here, and it has propogated its conservative Republicanism as much as it is possible. But the real basis for the Syracuse area's conservatism—and it has been shared for years by the city's large blue collar Italian-American community, which elsewhere might be Democratic—is a fear and hostility toward Democratic New York City. There is a feeling that the City, if it ever got the chance, would tax honest, hardworking Upstaters to bankruptcy to support the kind of welfare cheaters and civil service loafers who, in this view, dominate New York City.

Indeed, Republicans carried Syracuse during the New Deal, and the only time Democrats have won here in memory was in 1964, when Lyndon Johnson and Robert Kennedy both carried Onondaga County by large margins. In the same year, the County dumped a longtime Republican Congressman in favor of Democrat James Hanley. The new Congressman was able to parlay the advantages of office and his own pleasant personality to victories in 1966 and 1968, and so in 1970 the legislature decided to do him in, by adding rural and small town Madison, Cortland, and Chenango Counties to his district, and removing half of Syracuse and Onondaga.

Well, it didn't work then, and it hasn't worked since. In the 1970 contest Hanley piled up large enough margins in Syracuse to exceed the Republican edges in the smaller counties. In 1972, the legislature modified the lines again, so that Onondaga cast only 58% of the new district's votes; nevertheless, Hanley's 68% in his home county was once again enough to win. And this time he had had two years of incumbency in the smaller counties, and won at least 40% in each of them. For 1974, it was much the same story. Hanley got 65% in Onondaga, and actually carried the smaller counties, taken together, with 53% of their vote. It undoubtedly helps him that his record in the House is only mildly liberal, but the real reasons for his continued victories are his personality and the impact of incumbency. There is no indication that any of this is going to change.

Census Data Pop. 467,826. Central city, 22%; suburban, 47%. Median family income, $10,416; families above $15,000: 22%; families below $3,000: 7%. Median years education, 12.3.

The Voters

Median voting age 41.
Employment profile White collar, 53%. Blue collar, 32%. Service, 12%. Farm, 3%.
Ethnic groups Black, 2%. Total foreign stock, 18%. Italy, 4%; Canada, Germany, UK, 2% each; Poland, 1%.

Presidential vote

1972	Nixon (R)	138,607	(70%)
	McGovern (D)	60,343	(30%)
1968	Nixon (R)	101,486	(55%)
	Humphrey (D)	72,172	(39%)
	Wallace (AI)	9,516	(5%)

Rep. James M. Hanley (D) Elected 1964; b. July 19, 1920, Syracuse; home, Syracuse; Catholic.

Career Army, WWII; Funeral home Dir.

Offices 106 CHOB, 202-225-3701. Also 370 Fed. Bldg., Syracuse 13202, 315-473-5657.

Committees

Banking, Currency and Housing (13th). Subcommittees: Financial Institutions Supervision, Regulation and Insurance; Housing and Community Development Institutions and Finance.

Post Office and Civil Service (5th). Subcommittees: Manpower and Civil Service; Postal Service (Chairman).

Small Business (13th). Subcommittees: SBA and SBIC Legislation; SBA Oversight and Minority Enterprise.

Group Ratings

	ADA	COPE	LWV	RIPON	NFU	LCV	CFA	NAB	NSI	ACA
1974	68	100	75	27	100	59	70	50	50	14
1973	63	90	92	67	84	56	86	–	–	17
1972	50	82	83	73	86	53	–	17	67	26

Key Votes

1) Foreign Aid	FOR	6) Gov Abortn Aid	AGN	11) Pub Cong Election $	FOR
2) Busing	AGN	7) Coed Phys Ed	AGN	12) Turkish Arms Cutoff	FOR
3) ABM	AGN	8) Pov Lawyer Gag	AGN	13) Youth Camp Regs	FOR
4) B-1 Bomber	FOR	9) Pub Trans Sub	FOR	14) Strip Mine Veto	AGN
5) Nerve Gas	AGN	10) EZ Voter Regis	FOR	15) Farm Bill Veto	AGN

Election Results

1974 general:	James M. Hanley (D)	88,660	(59%)	($70,820)
	William E. Bush (R-C)	61,379	(41%)	($24,942)
1974 primary:	James M. Hanley (D), unopposed			
1972 general:	James M. Hanley (D)	111,481	(57%)	($63,011)
	Leonard C. Koldin (R-C)	83,451	(43%)	($75,175)

♦ ♦ ♦ ♦ ♦

THIRTY-THIRD DISTRICT

The Finger Lakes of Upstate New York are long, narrow bodies of water, surrounded by the gentle hills; they lie within a triangle, the apexes of which are Syracuse, Rochester, and Elmira. The land above the Lakes is dotted with small towns to which some early nineteenth century Yankee, showing off his classical education, gave names: Ovid, Scipio, Romulus, Camillus, Pompey, and many others. The Finger Lakes region is pleasant vacation country, but it is best known for its increasingly respected vineyards and vintners. Just north of the Lakes is the line of the Erie Canal, now replaced by one with a less euphonious name: the New York State Barge Canal. Also here are the small industrial cities of Auburn, Geneva, and Canandaigua. The Finger Lakes countryside is Yankee and Republican; the towns heavily Catholic and conservative.

The Finger Lakes region accounts for about half of New York's 33d congressional district; the remainder is the west side of Syracuse and surrounding Onondaga County. (For a description of the districting, see Thirty-Second District.) In its short existence as a district, the 33d has elected two Republican Congressmen. John Terry, a former New York Assemblyman, was elected in 1970, but decided to retire in 1972, though only 48, because he didn't want to move his family to Washington. He was succeeded by former Syracuse Mayor William Walsh. Walsh had been succeeded in the mayor's office by a Democrat, Lee Alexander; but he remained very popular, and won 71% of the vote in 1972, and nearly as much two years later. Walsh has a somewhat unusual background for a Republican politician—he was a social worker for 15 years—but he has been for the most part conventionally conservative in his voting record and committee actions.

Census Data Pop. 467,610. Central city, 20%; suburban, 27%. Median family income, $9,851; families above $15,000: 19%; families below $3,000: 8%. Median years education, 12.1.

The Voters

Median voting age 44.
Employment profile White collar, 46%. Blue collar, 37%. Service, 14%. Farm, 3%.
Ethnic groups Black, 4%. Total foreign stock, 18%. Italy, 5%; Canada, UK, Germany, Poland, 2% each; Ireland, 1%.

Presidential vote

1972	Nixon (R)	135,504	(70%)
	McGovern (D)	59,196	(30%)
1968	Nixon (R)	97,648	(53%)
	Humphrey (D)	75,964	(41%)
	Wallace (AI)	10,566	(6%)

Rep. William F. Walsh (R) Elected 1972; b. July 11, 1912, Syracuse; home, Syracuse; St. Bonaventure Col., A.B. 1934, Catholic U. School of Social Work, 1941, U. of Buffalo, M.A. 1949, Syracuse U., 1950; Catholic.

Career Accountant, Remington Rand Corp., 1934; Sr. Caseworker, Onondaga Co. Welfare Dept., 1935–40; Army, Air Force, WWII; Asst. Area Supervisor, N.Y. State Dept. of Social Welfare, 1949; Area Dir., N.Y. State Comm. Against Discrimination, 1950–55; Onondaga Co. Dir. of Research and Development, 1958–59; Onondaga Co. Commissioner of Public Welfare, 1960–61; Mayor of Syracuse, 1952–69; N.Y. State Public Svc. Comm., 1970; V.P., Whitmorite, Inc., 1971–72.

Offices 206 CHOB, 202-225-3333. Also 303 Fed. Bldg., Syracuse 13202, 315-473-3333.

Committees

Public Works and Transportation (7th). Subcommittees: Public Buildings and Grounds; Surface Transportation; Water Resources.

Veterans' Affairs (6th). Subcommittees: Education and Training.; Housing.

Group Ratings

	ADA	COPE	LWV	RIPON	NFU	LCV	CFA	NAB	NSI	ACA
1974	26	64	55	50	62	31	54	45	100	46
1973	19	67	50	53	55	13	60	–	–	50

Key Votes

1) Foreign Aid	FOR	6) Gov Abortn Aid	AGN	11) Pub Cong Election $	FOR
2) Busing	AGN	7) Coed Phys Ed	AGN	12) Turkish Arms Cutoff	AGN
3) ABM	FOR	8) Pov Lawyer Gag	FOR	13) Youth Camp Regs	FOR
4) B-1 Bomber	FOR	9) Pub Trans Sub	FOR	14) Strip Mine Veto	FOR
5) Nerve Gas	FOR	10) EZ Voter Regis	AGN	15) Farm Bill Veto	FOR

Election Results

1974 general:	William F. Walsh (R)	97,380	(66%)	($39,085)
	Robert H. Bockman (D)	45,043	(31%)	($4857)
	Francis H. Aspinwall (C)	4,866	(3%)	($461)

1974 primary: William F. Walsh (R), unopposed
1972 general   William F. Walsh (R-C) 132,139   (71%)   ($34,795)
               Clarence Kadys (D) 53,039   (29%)   ($19,283)

◆ ◆ ◆ ◆ ◆

THIRTY-FOURTH DISTRICT

The 34th congressional district of New York lies along the southern shores of Lake Ontario, and includes the east side of the city of Rochester, eastern Monroe County, and Wayne County. Rochester's economy, to a greater extent than those of other Upstate New York cities, depends on white collar and highly skilled labor; major employers here are Eastman Kodak and Xerox. These high technology companies have given the Rochester area a healthier economy over the years than is found in Upstate cities which depend more on heavy industry.

The city of Rochester by itself is almost large enough to constitute a congressional district, and if it were one it would almost certainly elect Democrats. Knowing this, Republican legislators for years have split Rochester between two districts, adding plenty of heavily Republican suburban and rural territory to each. Consequently, both the 34th and 35th congressional districts are considered safely Republican. In the 34th, profoundly conservative Wayne County is a particular Republican stronghold and, incidentally, the birthplace of the Mormon church (see Utah).

Since 1963, the 34th's Congressman has been Frank Horton, on most issues Upstate New York's most liberal Republican. The political coloration has become traditional in the district; some years ago (1947–59) its Congressman was Kenneth Keating, later U.S. Senator, judge on New York's highest court, and Ambassador to India and Israel. Like Keating, Horton is more in tune with New Deal liberals on economic issues than in step with the dovish Democrats who today control their party's caucus in the House; he is really something of a liberal hawk, a sort of Republican Scoop Jackson. However you describe his politics, it is clear he is very popular in the 34th district. In 1972 he ran 10% ahead of Richard Nixon here, and in 1974, despite the Democratic trend and an opponent of substance, he got 68%. The only conceivable threat to his tenure is conservative primary opposition, which shows no signs of developing.

Census Data Pop. 467,461. Central city, 38%; suburban, 62%. Median family income, $12,082; families above $15,000: 34%; families below $3,000: 6%. Median years education, 12.2.

The Voters

Median voting age 44.
Employment profile White collar, 54%. Blue collar, 34%. Service, 11%. Farm, 1%.
Ethnic groups Black, 6%. Spanish, 1%. Total foreign stock, 27%. Italy, 7%; Germany, Canada, 3% each; UK, USSR, Poland, 2% each.

Presidential vote

1972	Nixon (R)	130,757	(63%)
	McGovern (D)	77,699	(37%)
1968	Nixon (R)	98,521	(51%)
	Humphrey (D)	88,744	(46%)
	Wallace (AI)	7,584	(4%)

Rep. Frank Horton (R) Elected 1962; b. Dec. 12, 1919, Cuero, Tex.; home, Rochester; La. St. U., B.A., 1941, Cornell U., LL.B. 1947; Presbyterian.

Career Army, WWII; Practicing atty., 1947–62; Rochester City Cncl., 1955–61.

Offices 2229 RHOB, 202-225-4916. Also 314 Fed. Bldg., Rochester 14614, 716-263-6270.

Committees

Government Operations (Ranking Member). Subcommittees: Legislation and National Security.

Joint Committee on Atomic Energy (3d, House Side). Subcommittees: Agreements for Cooperation; Legislation; National Security.

Group Ratings

	ADA	COPE	LWV	RIPON	NFU	LCV	CFA	NAB	NSI	ACA
1974	55	70	91	71	67	65	46	27	90	23
1973	44	64	92	93	55	53	50	–	–	36
1972	44	73	83	77	43	49	50	42	100	35

Key Votes

1) Foreign Aid	FOR	6) Gov Abortn Aid	FOR	11) Pub Cong Election $	FOR
2) Busing	FOR	7) Coed Phys Ed	FOR	12) Turkish Arms Cutoff	FOR
3) ABM	FOR	8) Pov Lawyer Gag	AGN	13) Youth Camp Regs	FOR
4) B-1 Bomber	FOR	9) Pub Trans Sub	FOR	14) Strip Mine Veto	AGN
5) Nerve Gas	AGN	10) EZ Voter Regis	AGN	15) Farm Bill Veto	FOR

Election Results

1974 general:	Frank Horton (R)	105,585	(68%)	($68,207)
	Irene Gossin (D)	45,408	(29%)	($26,379)
	J. Warren McGee (C)	4,309	(3%)	($230)
1974 primary:	Frank Horton (R), unopposed			
1972 general:	Frank Horton (R)	142,803	(73%)	($32,326)
	Jack Rubens (D)	46,509	(24%)	($5,411)
	Richard E. Lusink (C)	5,603	(3%)	(NA)

◆ ◆ ◆ ◆ ◆

THIRTY-FIFTH DISTRICT

The 35th congressional district of New York includes the western half of the city of Rochester, the western Monroe County suburbs, and the adjacent Upstate counties of Genesee, Wyoming, Livingston, and part of Ontario. This is fertile, rolling countryside, punctuated by small cities like Batavia, locale of novelist John Gardner's *Sunlight Dialogues*, and Attica, scene of the 1971 prison riot and tragedy. Some 400 miles from New York City, this part of New York has an almost Midwestern feeling about it; celebrity City politicians like Nelson Rockefeller, Jacob Javits, Robert Kennedy, and John Lindsay seemed as out of place campaigning here as they might have in southern Iowa. As in the case of the 34th district, the Republican voting habits of the smaller counties and the Rochester suburbs effectively overwhelm, at least in most elections, any Democratic margins that might come out of the city of Rochester.

This is the kind of district which, for the past century, has sent so many men to Washington to run our national affairs: conservative Republicans, most of them, small town lawyers with an aptitude for politics, with perhaps a small family fortune behind them, and a few years in the legislature. Typically, they have been elected young, returned to office more or less automatically, and wound up in important committee positions. They have written tariff laws, led the opposition to new federal programs, put together military budgets, and, remembering the issues that gave birth to their party, supported civil rights measures in a surprising number of cases. They were anonymous men, usually, with a WASPy name and rimless glasses; but they were often far brighter than sophisticated liberals gave them credit for. Through them, the small towns of Upstate New York and central Ohio and outstate Michigan and downstate Illinois have had a major effect on the way our government has been run.

Of late, the small town Republican districts do not seem to have been producing congressmen of much distinction or note; an exception is Barber Conable, of the 35th district. In his first few years, he caught the eye of the Republican leadership and was awarded a seat on the Ways and Means Committee; now he is the panel's second-ranking Republican, behind the hardly imposing Herman Schneebeli of Pennsylvania. Conable is not brilliant, but he is considered one of the brightest of the lackluster conservative Republicans. On most substantive issues, he stands with the conservative orthodoxy; on procedural issues, however, he was leading successful fights for reforms as early as 1970. Conable will not be a particular powerful person in the 94th Congress—there are too few Republican votes for that—but he will be a Congressman to watch for another decade or two.

Census Data Pop. 467,415. Central city, 26%; suburban, 51%. Median family income, $11,528; families above $15,000: 27%; families below $3,000: 5%. Median years education, 12.2.

The Voters

Median voting age 41.
Employment profile White collar, 46%. Blue collar, 40%. Service, 12%. Farm, 2%.
Ethnic groups Black, 6%. Total foreign stock, 20%. Italy, 6%; Canada, Germany, 3% each; UK, 2%; Poland, 1%.

Presidential vote

1972	Nixon (R)	134,216	(66%)
	McGovern (D)	70,126	(34%)
1968	Nixon (R)	94,124	(51%)
	Humphrey (D)	81,707	(44%)
	Wallace (AI)	8,853	(5%)

Rep. Barber B. Conable, Jr. (R) Elected 1964; b. Nov. 2, 1922, Warsaw; home, Alexander; Cornell U., B.A. 1942, LL.B. 1948; Methodist.

Career USMC, WWII and Korea; Practicing atty., 1949–64; N.Y. State Senate, 1963–64.

Offices 2228 RHOB, 202-225-3615. Also 311 Fed. Ofc. Bldg., 100 State St., Rochester 14614, 716-263-3125.

Committees

Budget (8th).

Ways and Means (2d). Subcommittees: Social Security; Trade.

Group Ratings

	ADA	COPE	LWV	RIPON	NFU	LCV	CFA	NAB	NSI	ACA
1974	41	20	82	80	42	40	0	91	80	50
1973	20	0	70	73	15	24	14	–	–	63
1972	6	20	50	81	17	48	100	91	100	65

Key Votes

1) Foreign Aid	FOR	6) Gov Abortn Aid	FOR	11) Pub Cong Election $	FOR
2) Busing	FOR	7) Coed Phys Ed	ABS	12) Turkish Arms Cutoff	ABS
3) ABM	FOR	8) Pov Lawyer Gag	AGN	13) Youth Camp Regs	FOR
4) B-1 Bomber	FOR	9) Pub Trans Sub	FOR	14) Strip Mine Veto	FOR
5) Nerve Gas	FOR	10) EZ Voter Regis	AGN	15) Farm Bill Veto	FOR

Election Results

1974 general:	Barber B. Conable Jr. (R)	90,269	(57%)	($75,157)
	Margaret Costanza (D)	63,012	(40%)	($79,560)
	Clarence E. Carman, Jr. (C)	4,667	(3%)	($1,743)

1974 primary:	Barber B. Conable, Jr. (R), unopposed			
1972 general:	Barber B. Conable, Jr. (R)	127,298	(69%)	($18,907)
	Terence J. Spencer (D)	53,321	(29%)	($6,753)
	Terence C. Brennan (C)	4,879	(3%)	(NA)

◆ ◆ ◆ ◆

THIRTY-SIXTH DISTRICT

The 36th congressional district of New York includes Niagara County, site of the Falls; part of suburban Erie County, just outside Buffalo; and the southern shore of Lake Ontario from the Niagara River to within a few miles of Rochester. From the Falls, power lines strung on gigantic pylons hum out to the urban Northeast, the Midwest, and eastern Canada. The city of Niagara Falls, despite its tourist business, is mostly industrial with many of its industries doing poorly of late; the city and its suburbs have both lost population since 1960. Though Niagara Falls has large Polish and Italian communities that lean Democratic, the rest of the county subscribes to Upstate New York Republicanism. The Erie County portion of the 36th includes the middle class and politically marginal suburbs of Tonawanda and Grand Island, as well as a few blocks of the city of Buffalo itself.

On paper, the 36th is politically marginal; yet till 1974 it was invariably captured by Republicans. Both its two most recent Congressmen will be familiar to television viewers. There is the frosty former judge, Henry Smith, who was a member of the House Judiciary Committee. A quiet conservative, Smith tantalized everybody by threatening to vote for impeachment because of the bombing of Cambodia; by deciding not to, he missed being a footnote in history. Smith served from the 1964 election until his voluntary retirement, at age 63, in 1974; his predecessor was none other than William E. Miller, one time (1961–64) Republican National Chairman, Barry Goldwater's running mate in 1964, and now known best as the holder of an American Express card. Both Miller and Smith were strong votegetters; Miller's heated partisan attacks probably appealed to his blue collar constituents, while Smith's visage of austere fairness surely helped him.

Smith's retirement opened up the district to what most people thought would be its closest race in years. The contenders were 42-year-old Russell Rourke, Smith's administrative assistant, and 35-year-old suburban Buffalo Assemblyman John LaFalce. But it turned out to be no contest. LaFalce won 64% of the vote in Erie County and 58% in Niagra, and only barely lost the remainder of the district, for a 60% victory district-wide. It was the first time since 1912 that a Democrat won the district, and from the size of LaFalce's majority it appears he will be the Congressman here for many years to come. He is now a member of the Banking and Currency Committee, and one of the reasons—along with 13 other freshman Democrats—the balance of opinion on that body has shifted from one favorable to the desires of the big banks to one more oriented to a consumer point of view.

Census Data Pop. 467,761. Central city, 7%; suburban, 93%. Median family income, $10,702; families above $15,000: 23%; families below $3,000: 6%. Median years education, 12.1.

The Voters

Median voting age 44.
Employment profile White collar, 47%. Blue collar, 40%. Service, 12%. Farm, 1%.
Ethnic groups Black, 3%. Total foreign stock, 27%. Canada, 7%; Italy, 5%; Poland, 4%; UK, Germany, 3% each.

Presidential vote

1972	Nixon (R)	119,213	(60%)
	McGovern (D)	78,931	(40%)
1968	Nixon (R)	84,839	(46%)
	Humphrey (D)	86,526	(47%)
	Wallace (AI)	13,219	(7%)

Rep. John J. LaFalce (D) Elected 1974; b. Oct. 6, 1939, Buffalo; home, Tonawanda; Canisius Col., B.S. 1961, Villanova U., J.D. 1964; Catholic.

Career Law Clerk, Ofc. of Gen. Counsel, U.S. Dept. of the Navy, 1963; Practicing atty.; Army, 1965–67; N.Y. State Senate, 1971–72; N.Y. State Assembly, 1973–74.

Offices 417 CHOB, 202-225-3231. Also Fed. Bldg., Buffalo 14202, 716-842-2880.

Committees

Banking, Currency and Housing (23d). Subcommittees: Economic Stabilization; Housing and Community Development; International Trade, Investment and Monetary Policy.

Small Business (16th). Subcommittees: Activities of Regulatory Agencies; Energy and Environment.

Group Ratings: Newly Elected

Key Votes

1) Foreign Aid	FOR	6) Gov Abortn Aid	NE	11) Pub Cong Election $	NE
2) Busing	NE	7) Coed Phys Ed	AGN	12) Turkish Arms Cutoff	NE
3) ABM	NE	8) Pov Lawyer Gag	NE	13) Youth Camp Regs	FOR
4) B-1 Bomber	AGN	9) Pub Trans Sub	NE	14) Strip Mine Veto	AGN
5) Nerve Gas	NE	10) EZ Voter Regis	NE	15) Farm Bill Veto	AGN

Election Results

1974 general:	John J. LaFalce (D-L)	90,498	(60%)	($65,761)
	Russell A. Rourke (R-C)	61,442	(40%)	($95,249)
1974 primary:	John J. LaFalce (D)	12,816	(65%)	
	Edward P. Jesella, Jr. (D)	3,588	(18%)	
	Glenn R. Nellis (D)	3,220	(16%)	

◆ ◆ ◆ ◆ ◆

THIRTY-SEVENTH DISTRICT

Buffalo is the second largest city in New York and one of the most important industrial centers on the Great Lakes. Huge steel mills line the shore of Lake Erie, as the principal east-west rail lines feed into downtown Buffalo and the industrial areas that circle it. This is the easternmost American port on the Great Lakes, and here giant freighters unload iron ore from the Mesabi Range and grain from the western prairies. Buffalo is one of the nation's leading steel producers and rivals Minneapolis as a miller of grain.

Both these basic industries, which form the basis of Buffalo's economy, do not usually ignite the interest of securities analysts. But at the turn of the century, they constituted the fastest growing, most dynamic sectors of the economy. Then there were flush times in Buffalo, as the city attracted tens of thousands of Polish and Italian immigrants, eager to work in its factories. Today, the city's steel mills, grain elevators, and docks, along with downtown and its radial avenues, still look like something out of the 1920s, only a little rundown and shabby. Idealistic hopes for something like a melting pot city have faded long since, as it became clear that Buffalo's ethnics and blacks would never much get along. In recent years the big money and the Buffalo branch of the State University of New York, have been moving to the suburbs, leaving the city and its problems behind.

Nearly all of Buffalo, together with the industrial city of Lackawanna to the south (home of Bethlehem's giant steel mill) and a few precincts in the suburban town of Cheektowaga, make up New York's 37th congressional district. This is, of course, a very heavily Democratic district—indeed the most solidly Democratic of any in Upstate New York. The 37th is also the home of a thriving organization, led by the party's recent state chairman, Joseph Crangle. Unlike its counterparts in New York City, this machine seems as interested in winning general elections for Congress and statewide office as it is in controlling patronage-rich judgeships.

This year the Crangle machine has elected two new Congressmen, both in their thirties. One was Assemblyman John LaFalce, who captured the formerly Republican 36th district; the other was Erie County Controller Henry Nowak, elected here in the 37th. Nowak succeeded Thaddeus J. Dulski, a 16-year veteran who finally became Chairman of the House Post Office and Civil Service Committee, but never left much of a legacy. Nowak's election was a cinch; he was easily nominated, with the imprimatur of the machine, and easily elected in this district which even George McGovern easily carried. Nowak serves on the Public Works Committee, and has at least some chance of someday becoming, as his predecessor did, Chairman.

Census Data Pop. 467,759. Central city, 92%; suburban, 8%. Median family income, $8,845; families above $15,000: 14%; families below $3,000: 11%. Median years education, 10.6.

The Voters

Median voting age 46.
Employment profile White collar, 43%. Blue collar, 43%. Service, 14%. Farm, –%.
Ethnic groups Black, 21%. Total foreign stock, 28%. Poland, 8%; Italy, 6%; Germany, Canada, 3% each; UK, Ireland, 1% each.

Presidential vote

1972	Nixon (R)	74,998	(43%)
	McGovern (D)	99,509	(57%)
1968	Nixon (R)	47,192	(25%)
	Humphrey (D)	123,678	(67%)
	Wallace (AI)	14,764	(8%)

Rep. Henry J. Nowak (D) Elected 1974; b. Feb. 21, 1935, Buffalo; home, Buffalo; Canisius Col., B.B.A. 1957, Buffalo Law School, J.D. 1961.

Career Army, 1957–58, 1961–62; Practicing atty.; Erie Co. Asst. Dist. Atty., 1964; Confidential Secy. to N.Y. State Supreme Ct. Justice Arthur J. Cosgrove, 1965; Erie Co. Comptroller, 1966–75.

Offices 1223 LHOB, 202-225-3306. Also U.S. Courthouse, Buffalo 14202, 716-853-4131.

Committees

District of Columbia (14th). Subcommittees: Commerce, Housing and Transportation; Judiciary.

Public Works and Transportation (23d). Subcommittees: Economic Development; Investigations and Review; Surface Transportation; Water Resources.

Group Ratings: Newly Elected

Key Votes

1) Foreign Aid	FOR	6) Gov Abortn Aid	NE	11) Pub Cong Election $	NE
2) Busing	NE	7) Coed Phys Ed	FOR	12) Turkish Arms Cutoff	NE
3) ABM	NE	8) Pov Lawyer Gag	NE	13) Youth Camp Regs	FOR
4) B-1 Bomber	AGN	9) Pub Trans Sub	NE	14) Strip Mine Veto	AGN
5) Nerve Gas	NE	10) EZ Voter Regis	NE	15) Farm Bill Veto	AGN

Election Results

1974 general:	Henry J. Nowak (D-L)	84,064	(75%)	($14,841)
	Joseph R. Bala (R-C)	27,531	(25%)	($20,717)
1974 primary:	Henry J. Nowak (D), unopposed			

◆ ◆ ◆ ◆ ◆

THIRTY-EIGHTH DISTRICT

The 38th congressional district of New York includes most of suburban Erie County, from the Buffalo city limits to the small state Indian Reservations at the northern and southern edges of the county. Altogether the district takes in the most prosperous part of the so-called Niagara Frontier, the heavily industrial Buffalo-Niagara Falls metropolitan area along the Canadian border. Buffalo and its suburbs are the Democratic bastion of Upstate New York; in fact, the region usually produces higher Democratic percentages, though of course not nearly so many votes, as metropolitan New York City. Buffalo is a place much more like Cleveland or Detroit than New York, and its residents—in large part, Polish, Italian, or black—are not as susceptible to either the City's fashionable liberalism or its Archie Bunker reaction as are people in the big city.

A totally suburban district, the 38th is the most Republican part of Erie County, with most of Buffalo's rather scant supply of wealthy suburban enclaves. Much of the district, however, is working class Democratic, particularly the suburbs closest to the Buffalo city limits, like the town of Cheektowaga (pop. 113,000). Here are the miles and miles of small tract houses to which people who grew up in the immigrant neighborhoods escaped. Overall, the 38th is probably as politically marginal as any district in New York state.

But in congressional races, this district—like so many others—is marginal only when no incumbent is running. Such was the case in 1970, when three-term incumbent Richard "Max" McCarthy stepped down to run unsuccessfully for the Senate. To succeed him, the Republicans had a hot candidate in Jack Kemp, public relations man for the biggest bank in Buffalo and former quarterback of the Buffalo Bills. Against him, the Democrats slated a little known lawyer, but after McCarthy lost the Senate primary, he tried to get the congressional nomination back. The attendant fracas may have been the main cause of Kemp's narrow 52–48 margin of victory.

A native of California, Kemp had a Ron Ziegleresque look back in those days when that was a political asset. After a big reelection win in 1972, there was talk that this strong backer of the Nixon Administration might run in the primary against liberal Senator Jacob Javits. The Watergate scandal put a quick stop to that; Kemp's record of almost unvarying support of Nixon was suddenly no longer so helpful. But it did not injure him at all in his race for reelection. The Democrats put up only a token candidate, and Kemp won 72% of the vote in 1974—the best showing that year of any Republican Congressman in New York. So there still may be some chance for statewide office for Kemp in the future.

Census Data Pop. 467,761. Central city, 0%; suburban, 100%. Median family income, $11,583; families above $15,000: 27%; families below $3,000: 4%. Median years education, 12.3.

The Voters

Median voting age 43.
Employment profile White collar, 52%. Blue collar, 36%. Service, 11%. Farm, 1%.
Ethnic groups Total foreign stock, 23%. Poland, 5%; Germany, 4%; Italy, Canada, 3% each; UK, 2%.

Presidential vote

	1972	Nixon (R)	132,331	(61%)
		McGovern (D)	85,221	(39%)
	1968	Nixon (R)	86,360	(45%)
		Humphrey (D)	88,720	(47%)
		Wallace (AI)	15,444	(8%)

Rep. Jack F. Kemp (R) Elected 1970; b. July 13, 1935, Los Angeles, Cal.; home, Hamburg; Occidental Col., B.A. 1957, Long Beach St. U., Cal. Western U.; Presbyterian.

Career Pro football quarterback, San Diego Chargers and Buffalo Bills, 1957–70, Co-Founder and Pres., AFL Players Assn., 1965–70, AFL Most Valuable Player, 1965; Army, 1958; TV and Radio Commentator; Special Asst. to Gov. Ronald Reagan of Cal., 1967, and to the Chm., Repub. Natl. Comm., 1969.

Offices 132 CHOB, 202-225-5265. Also 1101 Fed. Bldg., 111 W. Huron St., Buffalo 14202, 716-842-6876.

Committees

Appropriations (31st). Subcommittees: Defense; District of Columbia.

Group Ratings

	ADA	COPE	LWV	RIPON	NFU	LCV	CFA	NAB	NSI	ACA
1974	17	30	42	47	50	59	0	83	100	79
1973	13	33	50	67	17	28	13	–	–	80
1972	25	36	50	67	43	20	100	92	100	70

Key Votes

1) Foreign Aid	AGN	6) Gov Abortn Aid	AGN	11) Pub Cong Election $	FOR
2) Busing	AGN	7) Coed Phys Ed	AGN	12) Turkish Arms Cutoff	FOR
3) ABM	FOR	8) Pov Lawyer Gag	FOR	13) Youth Camp Regs	ABS
4) B-1 Bomber	FOR	9) Pub Trans Sub	FOR	14) Strip Mine Veto	FOR
5) Nerve Gas	FOR	10) EZ Voter Regis	FOR	15) Farm Bill Veto	FOR

Election Results

1974 general:	Jack F. Kemp (R-C)	026,687	(72%)	($11,609)
	Barbara C. Wicks (D-L)	48,929	(28%)	($11,038)
1974 primary:	Jack F. Kemp (R), unopposed			
1972 general:	Jack F. Kemp (R-C)	156,967	(73%)	($89,617)
	Anthony P. LoRusso (D-L)	57,585	(27%)	($20,342)

◆ ◆ ◆ ◆

THIRTY-NINTH DISTRICT

The 39th congressional district of New York is the western half of the Southern Tier—that is, the counties on the northern side of the boundary between New York and Pennsylvania. Extending from the small city of Elmira to Lake Erie, the district contains the Corning Glass Works in Steuben County, two state Indian reservations, and a point on the state's western boundary exactly 496 miles from New York City via the Thomas E. Dewey Thruway. The small cities scattered among the district's valleys—Jamestown, Olean, Hornell, Corning—and on the shore of Lake Erie—Dunkirk, Fredonia—tend to be Democratic or politically marginal, reflecting the preference of the Irish and Italian Catholics who came to this part of Upstate New York after it had first been settled by New England Yankees. Outside the towns the Yankee Republicans still predominate and, as in most of Upstate New York, control the district politically.

Before he was appointed to fill the late Robert Kennedy's Senate seat, Charles Goodell was Congressman from this district. In the House, Goodell was an innovative conservative, one of the leaders of the group—and it was a daring thing in those days—that rebelled against Charlie Halleck in 1965 and installed Gerald Ford as House Minority Leader. Once in the Senate, Goodell became the body's most outspoken dove, and also the target of a successful Nixon-Agnew purge effort in 1970. (The winner, of course, was Senator James Buckley.) Goodell, whom President Ford would later appoint head of his Clemency Board, was always popular in his home district, however. In the bad Republican year of 1964, he won with a margin larger than any other New York Republican's, and in 1970 he carried what is now the 39th district, even while running a poor third in most of the rest of the state.

The district's present Congressman, Republican James Hastings, is the kind of man for whom the term backbencher was invented. More conservative than Goodell, he is also less of a House leader. But, judging at least from the election returns, he is even more popular in the Southern Tier. In 1972, despite the addition of a substantial hunk of new territory, he won a huge 72% of the vote, 6% more than Nixon; and in 1974, when Hugh Carey was running even with Malcolm Wilson in this ordinarily Republican district, Hastings was winning with a reduced but still solid 60%. In the House he serves on two panels dominated by active legislators, and is not often heard from: Wayne Hays's House Administration Committee, and Paul Rogers' Health and the Environment Subcommittee.

Census Data Pop. 467,859. Central city, 0%; suburban, 1%. Median family income, $8,936; families above $15,000: 15%; families below $3,000: 9%. Median years education, 12.2.

The Voters

Median voting age 45.
Employment profile White collar, 43%. Blue collar, 39%. Service, 14%. Farm, 4%.
Ethnic groups Black, 1%. Total foreign stock, 14%. Italy, 3%; Sweden, Germany, Poland, 2% each; UK, Canada, 1% each.

Presidential vote

1972	Nixon (R)	101,792	(66%)
	McGovern (D)	51,963	(34%)
1968	Nixon (R)	99,328	(55%)
	Humphrey (D)	71,296	(39%)
	Wallace (AI)	11,290	(6%)

Rep. James F. Hastings (R) Elected 1968; b. Apr. 10, 1926, Olean; home, Rushford Lake; Methodist.

Career Navy, WWII; Mgr. and V.P., Radio WHDL, Olean, 1952–66; N.Y. State Assembly, 1962–65; Natl. Advertising Mgr., the Olean *Times–Herald*, 1964–66; N.Y. Senate, 1965–69; Real estate and insurance business, 1966–69.

Offices 113 CHOB, 202-225-3161. Also 122 P.O. Bldg., Jamestown 14701, 716-484-0252.

Committees

Budget (6th).

Interstate and Foreign Commerce (6th). Subcommittees: Health and Environment; Transportation and Commerce.

Group Ratings

	ADA	COPE	LWV	RIPON	NFU	LCV	CFA	NAB	NSI	ACA
1974	35	9	45	79	43	35	23	90	80	50
1973	16	27	27	71	41	33	14	–	–	59
1972	0	0	33	83	29	41	0	91	100	68

Key Votes

1) Foreign Aid	AGN	6) Gov Abortn Aid	AGN	11) Pub Cong Election $	FOR
2) Busing	AGN	7) Coed Phys Ed	AGN	12) Turkish Arms Cutoff	ABS
3) ABM	AGN	8) Pov Lawyer Gag	FOR	13) Youth Camp Regs	AGN
4) B-1 Bomber	FOR	9) Pub Trans Sub	AGN	14) Strip Mine Veto	AGN
5) Nerve Gas	AGN	10) EZ Voter Regis	AGN	15) Farm Bill Veto	FOR

Election Results

1974 general:	James F. Hastings (R)	87,321	(60%)	($39,974)
	William F. Parment (D-L)	53,866	(37%)	($7,857)
	Joseph V. Damiano (C)	3,832	(3%)	($1,194)
1974 primary:	James F. Hastings (R), unopposed			
1972 general:	James F. Hastings (R-C)	126,147	(72%)	($17,794)
	Wilbur White, Jr. (D)	49,253	(28%)	($1,663)

NORTH CAROLINA

For more than two centuries, differences between east and west have structured the politics of North Carolina. During the Revolutionary War the Tidewater towns and plantations in the east were Tory, while the Piedmont to the west was a hotbed of anti-British radicalism. Likewise during the Civil War, the east—where most of the state's slaveholders lived—was strongly pro-Confederate, while to the west, particularly in the mountains, there was considerable Union sentiment. Overall North Carolina was lukewarm enough about the Rebel cause to have declined to secede until Virginia did and so cut it off from the Union.

Each of North Carolina's regions has its traditional politics, developed largely from this Civil War heritage and from its industrial development. For North Carolina is a prosperous and, it would have you believe a progressive state, in large part because of the textile, furniture, and tobacco industries. In all three North Carolina ranks first in the nation; the industries have produced some millionaires here, and support a well to do white collar class. But what should not be forgotten, though it is not a fact North Carolina boosters dwell on, is that this is one of the most heavily blue collar states in the nation, and that blue collar wages here, especially in the dominant textile industry, are among the lowest in the nation—and so is the level of unionization. The progressive record of North Carolina government—its high spending on education and avoidance, for the most part, of racial demagoguery—rests very much on an unspoken, always adhered to policy of not disturbing or in any way discommoding the state's major economic interests.

Over the years, North Carolina has had a rather placid politics, marked not by major strife but by quiet accommodation. Republicans have always been a factor here, due to Republican strength in the western mountains and the western edge of the Piedmont, strength that goes back to Civil War days. Indeed, there were predictions of a GOP takeover since Republican Charles Jonas was elected to Congress in 1952. But it was a long time coming. Richard Nixon did manage to carry the state with 40% of the vote in 1968, but it was not until the year of his landslide reelection, 1972, that North Carolina finally went Republican in a major way, electing a Dixiecrat-turned-Republican Senator and, to everyone's surprise, a Republican Governor.

The Governor, James Holshouser, is more typical of traditional North Carolina Republicanism. He is from the western part of the state, a moderate on racial issues; one reason for his victory was the support he received from teachers in return for his backing of high state aid to education. Holshouser's victory also followed traditional regional patterns: he carried the mountains with 56% of the vote, and the big and small city studded Piedmont with 54%; he lost the east, traditionally the most Democratic and segregationist part of the state. Holshouser had difficulties, once in office, dealing with the heavily Democratic legislature, and was slow to make key appointments; though he is not much disliked, he seems unlikely to be remembered as one of the state's great Governors. Holshouser is ineligible for reelection, and in any case his party is being taken over by hard line conservatives, people out of the mold of Senator Jesse Helms.

Helms was the other big Republican winner here in 1972, and if he is the antithesis of the typical North Carolina Republican, he seems to be the kind of politician after which the party is molding its image. Before 1972 Helms was a Raleigh TV commentator, known for his right wing views; he attacked Richard Nixon for "appeasing Red China" when Nixon visited Peking. Through his hookup on the radio Tobacco Network, Helms was exceedingly well known in the small towns and farms of eastern Carolina; and as Democrat who had turned Republican because of his conservative views, he mirrored the political leanings of many voters there. The east was his real strength, not just in the Republican primary, which he won easily, but in the general election.

Helms knew he would have to face one of two opponents: 76-year-old Senator B. Everett Jordan, a textile millionaire appointed to the seat in 1958 in recognition of his services to the Democratic Party, or 4th district Congressman Nick Galifianakis, generally considered the most liberal member of the North Carolina delegation. As it happened, Galifianakis won (for North Carolinians who had trouble with his name, he said that it started with a gal and ended with a kiss); and he in turn was fairly easily beaten by Helms. Not only did this new Republican carry the Piedmont and the west; he also—unheard of for a Republican—carried the eastern counties, by a 53–47 margin.

Many Washington observers were inclined to lump Helms in with another conservative elected that same year, William Scott of Virginia, and to see both of them as boorish, demagogic rubes. It is true that Helms has certainly been one of the most conservative Senators, one of the few, for example, to oppose the nomination of Vice President Rockefeller from the right. But it would be wrong to consider Helms some kind of moron; on the contrary, he is a careful, intelligent spokesman for the things he believes in; a principled politician who managed to get himself elected in a year when his views seemed most congenial. He is not the sort to flinch from his principles when the going gets rough—which it has in North Carolina—and it is entirely possible that he will be a one-term Senator. But even if his brand of conservatism is out of fashion when his seat comes up in 1978, he has at least some personal followings, particularly in the east, and will be at the very least a formidable contender.

It is hard, when you look at election returns here for 1972 and 1974, to remember that they are from the same state, or in the same century. What happened—what utterly transformed opinion in North Carolina—was what changed it so much in all the country, the Watergate scandal and the revelation that the President the country had so gratefully reelected a year or two before was really a crook. But there was a special significance to all this in North Carolina. For this is a state which had just consummated its first wholehearted relationship with the party of Richard Nixon; and it is the state which gave the nation Sam Ervin.

As the Senate Watergate Committee began preparing its hearings, in the first months of 1973, Sam Ervin was 76 years old. He was known, already, as a constitutional scholar; and he had surprised some observers when he moved from opposing civil rights bills on constitutional grounds to opposing no-knock legislation because it violated the Fourth Amendment and defending the First Amendment rights of war protesters. What made Ervin special was that in these latter causes he was defending the rights of people whose views he did not at all share. For on most economic and foreign policy issues, he was a staunch conservative.

Ervin did not seem type cast as a leader of national opinion. As the hearings went on, he sometimes tired; he stammered, paused, stuttered—but when he got the question out or made the point, it usually went to the heart of the matter. He remained a master of the Constitution and the Bible and a North Carolina trial lawyer's lifetime collection of funny stories; and day by day, week by week, he visibly moved public opinion away from the President the voters had so recently reelected. There were many things you could criticize about Senator Sam's Watergate hearings, but overall they performed a magnificent national service, and none of the committee members more than Ervin.

After the hearings, at the height of his national fame—tourists in the Capitol halls would ignore Ted Kennedy and point to the surprisingly tall Ervin—Sam Ervin announced his retirement. Before that, North Carolinians had been speculating on the effect of his anti-Nixon stand. Initially, opinion was that he was in trouble; that North Carolina, like other Southern states, would stay with Nixon to the end. But there was a visible, audible shift in the fall of 1973, after the hearings had sunk in and Nixon had got rid of Archibald Cox. Suddenly it was apparent that Ervin was, indeed, a hero in his native state; that even at the age of 78 he would have been unbeatable; and that the Republican surge of 1972, the streaming of tens of thousands of longtime Democrats into the Republican column, had utterly vanished.

The Sam Ervin Revolution was overwhelming. The Republicans lost two apparently safe congressional districts here, their delegation in the state legislature was almost eliminated, and they were unable to recruit a candidate for the Senate of greater stature than a textile executive who happened to be a congressman's brother-in-law. The Democratic nomination was more fiercely contested. Henry Hall Wilson, a Kennedy appointee and former president of the Chicago Board of Trade, returned to his native state to run; and former Congressman Galifianakis, the Democratic nominee in 1972, decided at the last minute to make the race. But the strongest ndidate was Attorney General Robert Morgan, who combined liberal and conservative appeals. ck in 1960, he had been campaign manager for I. Beverly Lake, a law professor and regationist who nearly beat Terry Sanford for the Democratic nomination that year. As orney General, elected in 1968, he had left this political past behind and hired a number of ivist aides; in this state where big business has seldom encountered political opposition, he became known as an advocate of consumer's rights. It was perhaps his political past that helped him to the 59% of the vote in the eastern part of the state; he won in the decisive primary; but it was his more recent record which enabled him to win the creditable 44% in the rest of the state—enough to give him 50% overall, and avoid a runoff with Galifianakis.

The general election was anticlimactic. Morgan received a solid 63% of the vote, carrying all but seven of the state's 100 counties. Rufus Edmisten, the young Ervin protege and Watergate Committee aide who was the Democratic nominee for Attorney General, did almost as well, with 61%. That was, in fact, as good as Ervin's own performance six years before—a good measure of the force of the Ervin Revolution. Suddenly this was as Democratic a state as it had been in the 1940s. There is only one recent precedent for such a turnaround: the huge switch to the Democrats in the state of Texas and particularly in Dallas in 1964, almost as a sort of penance for the murder of President Kennedy.

Perhaps North Carolina's leading political figure now is a man who has not won an election here since 1960. He is Terry Sanford, the young, progressive Governor of the early 1960s, now president of Duke University and chairman of the national Democratic Party Charter Commission that, amid great controversy, set up rules for delegate selection in conventions after 1976. Sanford is now, s he was in 1972, a presidential candidate; but his chances rest on whether he can do better in his home state's presidential primary than he did in 1972. Then he lost to George Wallace, who got just over 50% of the vote; Sanford had a creditable, but still losing 37%. Whether Wallace can do so well in the Sam Ervin Revolution era—indeed, whether that apparent Revolution continues to shape political attitudes here—are the main questions facing North Carolina politics in 1976.

Census Data Pop. 5,082,059; 2.51% of U.S. total, 12th largest; Central city, 19%; suburban, 19%. Median family income, $7,770; 40th highest; families above $15,000: 12%; families below $3,000: 15%. Median years education, 10.6.

1974 Share of Federal Tax Burden $5,463,432,000; 2.04% of U.S. total, 15th largest.

1974 Share of Federal Outlays $5,259,678,000; 1.95% of U.S. total, 17th largest. Per capita federal spending, $1035.

DOD	$1,614,573,000	15th (2.36%)		HEW	$1,899,465,000	15th (2.05%)
AEC	$1,799,000	28th (0.06%)		HUD	$27,920,000	12th (2.87%)
NASA	$2,605,000	29th (0.09%)		VA	$343,210,000	11th (2.51%)
DOT	$156,116,000	23d (1.84%)		EPA	$102,237,000	8th (3.25%)
DOC	$21,573,000	12th (1.34%)		RevS	$156,171,000	11th (2.57%)
DOI	$21,806,000	26th (0.89%)		Int.	$113,394,000	20th (0.55%)
USDA	$291,802,000	15th (2.34%)		Other	$507,007,000	

Economic Base Textile mill products, especially knitting mills and yarn and thread mills; agriculture, notably tobacco, broilers, hogs and eggs; apparel and other textile products, especially men's and boys' furnishings; finance, insurance and real estate; household furniture, and other furniture and fixtures; food and kindred products, especially meat products; electrical equipment and supplies, especially communication equipment.

Political Line-up Governor, James E. Holshouser, Jr. (R). Senators, Jesse A. Helms (R) and Robert Morgan (D). Representatives, 11 (9 D and 2 R). State Senate (49 D and 1 R); State House (111 D and 9 R).

The Voters

Registration 2,279,646 Total. 1,654,304 D (73%); 537,568 R (24%); 87,744 Ind. or No Party (4%); 30 Labor (–).
Median voting age 40.
Employment profile White collar, 38%. Blue collar, 46%. Service, 11%. Farm, 5%.
Ethnic groups Black, 22%. Total foreign stock, 2%.

Presidential vote

1972	Nixon (R)	1,054,889	(71%)
	McGovern (D)	438,705	(29%)
1968	Nixon (R)	627,192	(40%)
	Humphrey (D)	464,113	(29%)
	Wallace (AI)	496,188	(31%)

1972 Democratic Presidential Primary

Wallace	413,518	(50%)
Sanford	306,014	(37%)
Chisholm	61,723	(8%)
others	40,155	(5%)

1972 Republican Presidential Primary

Nixon	159,167	(95%)
McCloskey	8,732	(5%)

Sen. Jesse A. Helms (R) Elected 1972, seat up 1978; b. Oct. 18, 1921, Monroe; home, Raleigh; Wingate Col., Wake Forest Col.; Baptist.

Career Navy, WWII; City Ed., The Raleigh *Times*; Admin. Asst. to U.S. Sens. Willis Smith, 1951–53, and Alton Lennon, 1953; Exec. Dir., N.C. Bankers Assn., 1953–60; Raleigh City Cncl., 1957–61; Exec. V.P., WRAL-TV and Tobacco Radio Network, 1960–72.

Offices 4104 DSOB, 202-224-6342. Also Fed. Bldg., Raleigh 27601, 919-755-4630, and Box 2944, Hickory 28601, 704-322-5170.

Committees

Agriculture and Forestry (5th). Subcommittees: Agricultural Credit and Rural Electrification; Agricultural Production, Marketing, and Stabilization of Prices; Environment, Soil Conservation and Forestry.

Banking, Housing and Urban Affairs (4th). Subcommittees: Financial Institutions; International Finance; Oversight; Production and Stabilization; Securities.

Group Ratings

	ADA	COPE	LWV	RIPON	NFU	LCV	CFA	NAB	NSI	ACA
1974	5	10	30	23	6	5	0	83	100	100
1973	0	18	0	33	12	–	8	–	–	100

Key Votes

1) No-Knock	FOR	8) Gov Abortn Aid	AGN	15) Consumer Prot Agy	AGN
2) Busing	AGN	9) Cut Mil Brass	AGN	16) Forced Psych Tests	AGN
3) No Fault	AGN	10) Gov Limousine	AGN	17) Fed Campaign Subs	AGN
4) F-111	AGN	11) RR Featherbed	AGN	18) Rhod Chrome Ban	AGN
5) Death Penalty	FOR	12) Handgun License	AGN	19) Open Legis Meetings	AGN
6) Foreign Aid	AGN	13) Less Troop Abrd	AGN	20) Strikers Food Stmps	AGN
7) Filibuster	FOR	14) Resume Turk Aid	FOR	21) Gov Info Disclosure	AGN

Election Results

1972 general:	Jesse A. Helms (R)	795,248	(54%)	($654,246)
	Nick Galifianakis (D)	677,293	(46%)	($470,093)
1972 primary:	Jesse A. Helms (R)	92,496	(60%)	
	James C. Johnson (R)	45,303	(29%)	
	William H. Booe (R)	16,032	(10%)	

Sen. Robert Morgan (D) Elected 1974, seat up 1980; b. Oct. 5, 1925, Lillington; home, Lillington; E. Carolina Col., 1942–44, U. of N.C., 1944–45, E. Carolina Col, B.S. 1947, Wake Forest U., LL.B. 1949; Baptist.

Career Practicing atty., 1950–69; Harnett Co. Clerk of Superior Ct., 1950–54; N.C. Gen. Assembly, 1955–57, 1959–61, 1963–68; Atty. Gen. of N.C., 1969–74.

Offices 1251 DSOB, 202-224-3154. Also 314 Century P.O., Raleigh 27602, 919-755-4236.

Committees

Banking, Housing and Urban Affairs (8th). Subcommittees: Consumer Affairs; Oversight; Securities; Small Business (Chairman).

Public Works (8th). Subcommittees: Environmental Pollution, Panel on Materials Policy; Economic Development; Water Resources; Disaster Relief; Buildings and Grounds (Chairman).

Select Committee on Intelligence Operations (6th).

Group Ratings: Newly Elected

Key Votes

1) No-Knock	NE	8) Gov Abortn Aid	ABS	15) Consumer Prot Agy	NE
2) Busing	NE	9) Cut Mil Brass	NE	16) Forced Psych Tests	NE
3) No Fault	NE	10) Gov Limousine	NE	17) Fed Campaign Subs	NE
4) F-111	AGN	11) RR Featherbed	NE	18) Rhod Chrome Ban	NE
5) Death Penalty	NE	12) Handgun License	NE	19) Open Legis Meetings	NE
6) Foreign Aid	NE	13) Less Troop Abrd	NE	20) Strikers Food Stmps	NE
7) Filibuster	ABS	14) Resume Turk Aid	ABS	21) Gov Info Disclosure	NE

Election Results

1974 general:	Robert Morgan (D)	633,775	(63%)	($781,201)
	William E. Stevens (R)	377,618	(37%)	($385,527)
1974 primary:	Robert Morgan (D)	294,986	(50%)	
	Nick Galifianakis (D)	189,815	(32%)	
	Henry H. Wilson (D)	67,247	(11%)	
	Seven others (D)	33,278	(6%)	

Gov. James E. Holshouser, Jr. (R) Elected 1972, term expires Jan. 1977; b. Oct. 8, 1934, Watauga County; Davidson Col., B.A., U. of N.C., LL.B.; Presbyterian.

Career N.C. House of Reps., 1963–67, 1969–73, Minor. Ldr., 1965; N.C. Repub. St. Chm., 1966–72.

Offices Administration Bldg., 116 W. Jones St., Raleigh 27611, 919-829-5811.

Election Results

1972 general:	James E. Holshouser (R)	767,470	(51%)
	Hargrove Bowles (D)	729,104	(49%)
1972 run-off:	James E. Holshouser (R)	69,916	(51%)
	James C. Gardner (R)	68,134	(49%)
1972 primary:	James C. Gardner (R)	84,906	(50%)
	James E. Holshouser (R)	83,637	(49%)
	Two Others (R)	2,040	(1%)

♦ ♦ ♦ ♦ ♦

FIRST DISTRICT

Since the end of the draft, eastern North Carolina has produced a larger percentage of volunteers for the Army and other military services than any other part of the country. Aggressive recruiting undoubtedly accounts for some the enlistments. But the total number signing up tells us a great deal about life on the rolling coastal plain east of Raleigh, a region that has no metropolitan area containing as many as 100,000 people. Plenty of people here still make their living on small tobacco farms, but more of them work in area textile mills, which are located in small towns and, to an increasing extent, simply along rural highways. The textile industry is largely nonunionized, the hours are long, the working conditions poor, and the wages low. Few young men (or women) from eastern North Carolina go to college; book-learning is not especially prized, and parents cannot afford the luxury of more schooling. So the choice comes down to the mills or the Army, and around here the Army often looks better.

North Carolina's 1st congressional district lies entirely within the state's eastern coastal zone. It includes the Outer Banks, the string of coastal islands beyond Pamlico and Albemarle Sounds where the Wright brothers first flew; also here is Cape Hatteras where countless ships have sunk. But nearly all the residents of the 1st live inland, in small cities like New Bern, Elizabeth City, and Greenville—at 29,000 the district's largest city. Even more live in the countryside, on small farms or in isolated houses or trailers. Some 36% of the residents of the 1st district are black, the second largest black population in North Carolina's 11 districts.

The white voters of the 1st district retain from their slaveholding days a Democratic preference. They steadfastly supported Democratic presidential candidates until 1968, when they went for Wallace. In 1972, this was the only North Carolina district to favor Democrat Nick Galifianakis over Republican Jesse Helms in the Senate race, and then only by the smallest majority. Two years later, after Watergate, the 1st reverted to its historical Democratic leanings, giving Democratic Senate candidate Robert Morgan fully 79% of its vote.

When Wallace was running in 1968, Congressman Walter Jones of the 1st district was one of several Southern Democrats who announced that, if the election went from the Electoral College to the House, he would vote for the candidate who carried his district-which of course turned out to be Wallace. Jones is one of the dwindling number of conservative Southern Democratic Congressman. He spent a dozen years in the state legislature before winning a 1966 special election to succeed Herbert Bonner, who had served in the House since 1940 and was Chairman of the Merchant Marine and Fisheries Committee at the time of his death. Today, Jones also serves on that panel and on the Agriculture Committee, where he is Chairman of the Tobacco Subcommittee. The last is a choice position for a Congressman with a tobacco growing district like the 1st; Jones has never had serious opposition, and seems destined to remain in the House as long as he wants.

Census Data Pop. 459,543. Central city, 0%; suburban, 0%. Median family income, $6,368; families above $15,000: 8%; families below $3,000: 22%. Median years education, 10.2.

The Voters

Median voting age 42.
Employment profile White collar, 36%. Blue collar, 40%. Service, 13%. Farm, 11%.
Ethnic groups Black, 36%. Total foreign stock, 1%.

Presidential vote

1972	Nixon (R)	83,557	(70%)
	McGovern (D)	35,333	(30%)
1968	Nixon (R)	31,143	(22%)
	Humphrey (D)	47,780	(34%)
	Wallace (AI)	62,324	(44%)

Rep. Walter B. Jones (D) Elected Feb. 5, 1966; b. Aug. 19, 1913, Fayetteville; home, Farmville; N.C. St. U., B.S. 1934; Baptist.

Career Office supply business, 1934–49; Mayor of Farmville, 1949–53; N.C. Gen. Assembly, 1955–59; N.C. Senate, 1965.

Offices 201 CHOB, 202-225-3101. Also P.O. Drawer 90, Farmville 27828, 919-753-3082.

Committees

Agriculture (5th). Subcommittees: Family Farms and Rural Development; Oilseeds and Rice; Tobacco (Chairman).

Merchant Marine and Fisheries (7th). Subcommittees: Coast Guard and Navigation; Merchant Marine; Oceanography.

Group Ratings

	ADA	COPE	LWV	RIPON	NFU	LCV	CFA	NAB	NSI	ACA
1974	14	36	22	13	57	46	46	60	67	71
1973	17	30	33	21	75	16	67	–	–	73
1972	19	18	25	31	43	2	0	50	89	83

Key Votes

1) Foreign Aid	AGN	6) Gov Abortn Aid	AGN	11) Pub Cong Election $	AGN
2) Busing	AGN	7) Coed Phys Ed	AGN	12) Turkish Arms Cutoff	AGN
3) ABM	FOR	8) Pov Lawyer Gag	FOR	13) Youth Camp Regs	AGN
4) B-1 Bomber	FOR	9) Pub Trans Sub	AGN	14) Strip Mine Veto	FOR
5) Nerve Gas	FOR	10) EZ Voter Regis	AGN	15) Farm Bill Veto	AGN

Election Results

1974 general:	Walter B. Jones (D)	55,323	(77%)	($14,958)
	Harry McMullan (R)	16,097	(23%)	($23,729)
1974 primary:	Walter B. Jones (D)	58,652	(90%)	
	Gene Leggett (D)	6,768	(10%)	
1972 general:	Walter B. Jones (D)	77,438	(69%)	($8,727)
	J. Jordan Bonner (R)	35,063	(31%)	($17,057)

◆ ◆ ◆ ◆ ◆

SECOND DISTRICT

North of Raleigh and south of the Virginia line, the 2d congressional district of North Carolina is situated on an inland portion of the coastal plain where it rises to become the Piedmont. This is a predominantly rural and small town district; its largest city, Rocky Mount, has only 34,000 people. And like much of North Carolina, the 2d's economy depends almost entirely on textiles and the tobacco crop. What makes the 2d distinctive politically is the size of its black population—some 40% of all its residents (though only 34% of those over 18) are black, the highest percentages in the state, and comparable with what you will find in the Deep South. To stem black outmigration—sometimes whole high school graduating classes get on the train and go north and to encourage black capitalism, former civil rights leader Floyd McKissick has been building a black new town—Soul City—in Warren County; after receiving some federal support, McKissick endorsed Richard Nixon in 1972. And indeed, black outmigration seems to have virtually stopped, but perhaps only because the job picture in northern cities is so discouraging.

The other distinctive thing about the 2d district is the presence here, since 1972, of Orange County. Most of the nation's Orange Counties, in California, Florida, and even New York, are profoundly conservative; this one, which contains the University of North Carolina and its beautiful little town of Chapel Hill, is the state's banner liberal county. It was one of two in the state which went for George McGovern in 1972 (the other was Northampton, a black majority area with a liberally inclined white boss, which is also in the 2d).

The addition of Orange County also made for the first seriously contested congressional race in the district since 1952, the year the 2d first elected Democratic Congressman L. H. Fountain. He is the kind of politician who wears white linen suits in the summertime and speaks with gentle Southern courtliness year round. During his 20 years in Congress, Fountain had compiled a solidly conservative voting record on both economic and racial issues. But as Chairman of the Intergovernmental Relations Subcommittee, he has been a crusader in one area: drug regulation. For more than a dozen years, Fountain has been holding hearings and arguing that the Food and Drug Administration has been all too liberal in allowing possibly dangerous drugs on the market; he has worked to penetrate the veil of secrecy which this bureaucracy—convinced that mere laymen cannot understand its workings—puts over its affairs. Fountain's subcommittee has jurisdiction over numerous other agencies; but he has, curiously, concentrated solely on the FDA and done, whatever one thinks about his views, a solid professional job of it.

The workings of the FDA, however, are not a big issue in the 2d district. The real issue, at least for most voters in the 1972 Democratic primary between Fountain and Chapel Hill Mayor Howard Lee, was race. Lee, a black elected by this liberal college town, conducted an energetic campaign, and claimed to have registered 18,000 black voters. He also sought white votes, and not just in Chapel Hill. Lee had fair success, but nevertheless Fountain still won with 59%.

The Lee effort remains one of the most successful black campaigns in Southern politics. Other blacks have won in technically white majority districts in the South, but only in cities like Atlanta, Houston, and Memphis. Campaigning in, say, Warren County is something else. Aside from McKissick's efforts, whites still control most of the money—and the jobs—here, and many blacks can recall not too many years ago when there was an active Ku Klux Klan organization in the 2d. Lee did not make another effort in 1974—the last election, though close, was decisive. Interestingly, this was the last Southern district to send a black to Congress in the era following Reconstruction; Republican George H. White, elected in 1898, was defeated in 1900—the beginning of a 28 year period in which no blacks served in Congress.

Census Data Pop. 457,601. Central city, 0%; suburban, 13%. Median family income, $6,550; families above $15,000: 9%; families below $3,000: 20%. Median years education, 9.8.

The Voters

Median voting age 42.
Employment profile White collar, 36%. Blue collar, 41%. Service, 13%. Farm, 10%.
Ethnic groups Black, 40%. Total foreign stock, 1%.

Presidential vote

1972	Nixon (R)	86,006	(64%)
	McGovern (D)	47,674	(36%)
1968	Nixon (R)	31,392	(22%)
	Humphrey (D)	48,483	(34%)
	Wallace (AI)	60,991	(43%)

Rep. L. H. Fountain (D) Elected 1952; b. Apr. 23, 1913, Leggett; home, Tarboro; U. of N.C., A.B. 1934, J.D. 1936; Presbyterian.

Career Practicing atty., 1936–42, 1946–52, Army, WWII; Reading Clerk, N.C. Senate, 1936–41; N.C. Senate, 1947–52.

Offices 2188 RHOB, 202-225-4531. Also P.O. Bldg., Tarboro 27886, 919-823-4200.

Committees

Government Operations (2d). Subcommittees: Conservation, Energy and Natural Resources; Intergovernmental Relations and Human Resources (Chairman).

International Relations (4th). Subcommittees: International Security and Scientific Affairs; Investigations.

Group Ratings

	ADA	COPE	LWV	RIPON	NFU	LCV	CFA	NAB	NSI	ACA
1974	13	27	17	27	57	41	39	83	90	67
1973	20	18	25	14	78	11	43	–	–	74
1972	6	27	25	40	57	20	50	90	100	91

Key Votes

1) Foreign Aid	AGN	6) Gov Abortn Aid	AGN	11) Pub Cong Election $	AGN
2) Busing	AGN	7) Coed Phys Ed	AGN	12) Turkish Arms Cutoff	AGN
3) ABM	FOR	8) Pov Lawyer Gag	FOR	13) Youth Camp Regs	AGN
4) B-1 Bomber	FOR	9) Pub Trans Sub	AGN	14) Strip Mine Veto	FOR
5) Nerve Gas	FOR	10) EZ Voter Regis	AGN	15) Farm Bill Veto	AGN

Election Results

1974 general:	L. H. Fountain (D), unopposed			
1974 primary	L. H. Fountain (D), unopposed			
1972 general:	L. H. Fountain (D)	88,798	(72%)	($40,630)
	Erick P. Little (R)	35,193	(28%)	($19,002)

◆ ◆ ◆ ◆

THIRD DISTRICT

The 3d district of North Carolina is one of small farms, small towns, and Atlantic shore seascapes. Lying in the middle of the state's coastal plain, the 3d runs from a point a few miles south of Raleigh and Durham to the Atlantic Ocean near Wilmington. The district's largest city is Goldsboro (pop. 26,000), but its largest concentration of people can be found in Camp Lejeune (pop. 34,000), the Marine Corps's giant base at the estuary of the New River. One of the Marines' most important installations, Camp Lejeune looms large in the economy of the district, though its voters have been disturbed by recent racial conflict at the base. Also in the 3d is an Air Force base near Goldsboro, with Fort Bragg just over the line in the 7th district.

The 3d's dependence on the military and its relatively low (27%) black percentage help to explain its very conservative political inclinations. In the 1972 presidential primary, the voters of the 3d gave George Wallace 59% of the vote—his best showing in any North Carolina congressional district. And in the general election of that year they left behind their traditional Democratic allegiances and gave a solid 60% to Republican Jesse Helms, whose ultraconservative commentaries on Raleigh's WRAL-TV had been beamed into much of the district for a dozen years. But two years later, the 3d district switched solidly back: native son Robert Morgan, a conservative Democrat, won a whopping 72% of the vote here in the 1974 Senate race.

In 1960, Congressman Graham Barden of the 3d, then Chairman of the House Education and Labor Committee, retired; he was succeeded in the chairmanship by Harlem's Adam Clayton Powell. (Barden was a stuffily and bigoted conservative; he refused even to call on Powell to speak.) Barden was succeeded in the 3d district by David Henderson, who had served briefly on the committee staff under Barden. But like most Southern Democrats, Henderson did not seek a seat on the increasingly liberal Education and Labor panel, and instead ended up on Post Office and Civil Service. Today, thanks to the 1974 retirement of Buffalo's Thaddeus Dulski, Henderson is a committee chairman himself; he must preside over such unpleasant tasks as determining civil service fringe benefits and staving off strikes by government workers. It is fair to say that the record of the Committee has not been exactly a boon to taxpayers over the last dozen or so years; federal salaries have gone up to levels that are comfortable indeed, and American postal service these days sometimes seems scarcely better than Italy's. Henderson is regarded, however, as more astute than his predecessor as Chairman.

Henderson has seldom had any trouble at the polls. In 1968, when a conservative Republican was running for Governor, his Republican opponent carried a couple of the larger counties in the district and 46%; but the same opponent declined to 40% in 1970, and Henderson has been unopposed in the last two general elections.

Census Data Pop. 458,000. Central city, 0%; suburban, 0%. Median family income, $6,193; families above $15,000: 6%; families below $3,000: 21%. Median years education, 10.4.

The Voters

Median voting age 37.
Employment profile White collar, 34%. Blue collar, 43%. Service, 12%. Farm, 11%.
Ethnic groups Black, 27%. Total foreign stock, 2%.

Presidential vote

1972	Nixon (R)	79,431	(74%)
	McGovern (D)	27,878	(26%)
1968	Nixon (R)	35,730	(30%)
	Humphrey (D)	32,586	(27%)
	Wallace (AI)	50,931	(43%)

Rep. David N. Henderson (D) Elected 1960; b. Apr. 16, 1921, near Hubert; home, Wallace; Davidson Col., B.S. 1942, U. of N.C., LL.B. 1949; Presbyterian.

Career Army Air Corps, WWII; Asst. Gen. Counsel, U.S. House of Reps. Comm. on Educ. and Labor, 1951–52; Practicing atty., 1952–60; Duplin Co. Solicitor of Gen. Ct., 1954–58, Judge, 1958–60.

Offices 235 CHOB, 202-225-3415. Also P.O. Box 591, Wallace 28466, 919-285-2102.

Committees

Post Office and Civil Service (Chairman). Subcommittees: Manpower and Civil Service.

Public Works and Transportation (4th). Subcommittees: Aviation; Economic Development; Public Buildings and Grounds.

Group Ratings

	ADA	COPE	LWV	RIPON	NFU	LCV	CFA	NAB	NSI	ACA
1974	13	40	33	13	50	41	36	73	90	57
1973	26	40	36	33	90	17	63	–	–	60
1972	13	27	18	33	57	4	50	50	100	73

Key Votes

1) Foreign Aid	AGN	6) Gov Abortn Aid	AGN	11) Pub Cong Election $	FOR
2) Busing	AGN	7) Coed Phys Ed	AGN	12) Turkish Arms Cutoff	AGN
3) ABM	FOR	8) Pov Lawyer Gag	FOR	13) Youth Camp Regs	AGN
4) B-1 Bomber	FOR	9) Pub Trans Sub	AGN	14) Strip Mine Veto	AGN
5) Nerve Gas	FOR	10) EZ Voter Regis	AGN	15) Farm Bill Veto	AGN

Election Results

1974 general:	David N. Henderson (D), unopposed	($560)
1974 primary:	David N. Henderson (D), unopposed	
1972 general:	David N. Henderson (D), unopposed	($4,258)

◆ ◆ ◆ ◆ ◆

FOURTH DISTRICT

The 4th congressional district of North Carolina consists of four counties in the middle of the state, where the state's coastal plain rises to meet the Piedmont. Raleigh (pop. 121,000) is the state capital and the district's largest city; it is also a tobacco center and the home of North Carolina State University. Durham (pop. 95,000), another tobacco center and the home of Duke University, has one of North Carolina's largest and politically most sophisticated black communities. The beginnings of a Boston Route 128 style electronics boom is evident in the Research Triangle area between Raleigh and Durham. The two other counties in the district are far smaller. Randolph, in the west, is traditionally Republican; and Chatham, closer to Raleigh and Durham, is traditionally Democratic.

The 4th's strong black and academic communities (before 1972, it also included the University of North Carolina at Chapel Hill) have made it one of the most liberal districts in North Carolina; in the 1972 presidential primary, for example, it was the only district which preferred former Governor Terry Sanford to George Wallace. Yet for three of the last four elections, this has been the most closely contested North Carolina district in House races. The reason is that the Democrats have run liberal to moderate candidates, and the Republicans have run very aggressive conservative campaigns; even if the 4th is liberal by North Carolina standards, it is pretty conservative when you put it in the national perspective. (Wallace, after all, in that 1972 primary had 43% of the vote here.)

The Congressman who had the most difficulty winning was Nick Galifianakis whose issue positions—including opposition to the Vietnam war—made him a prime Republican target in 1968 and 1970. In both years, he won just 52% of the votes against a Republican named Jack Hawke. In 1972—after Chapel Hill was taken from the district—Galifianakis apparently decided that trying to win here again would be no easier than running for the Senate, so he went into the latter race, beating Senator B. Everett Jordan in the primary, but losing to Raleigh TV commentator Jesse Helms in the general election.

Competition was vigorous to succeed Galifianakis. The eventual winner was state Representative Ike Andrews, from one of the smaller counties in the district. Andrews trailed Jyles Coggins 31% to 30% in the first primary, won the runoff 52–48, and won the general election by precisely 1,100 votes (50.4%). Andrews' narrow victory and his rather lackluster personality seemed to spell trouble for him in 1974. He attracted solid opponents in both the primary and general elections. But the electoral revolution wrought by Sam Ervin and the Watergate Committee in North Carolina apparently came to his rescue. In the primary, state Representative Robert Wynne pressed him in Raleigh's Wake County, but Andrews won overwhelmingly elsewhere, for a 64–36 margin. And in the general election Republican state Representative Ward Purrington could do no better than 35% of the vote. Andrews will have to do well in another, more normal election year before he convinces most observers he has a safe seat; but his performance in 1974, in light of the previous history of the district, shows just what a difference a couple of years have made in North Carolina's political behavior.

Census Data Pop. 467,046. Central city, 46%; suburban, 47%. Median family income, $8,999; families above $15,000: 16%; families below $3,000: 10%. Median years education, 11.5.

The Voters

Median voting age 39.
Employment profile White collar, 50%. Blue collar, 35%. Service, 12%. Farm, 3%.
Ethnic groups Black, 23%. Total foreign stock, 3%.

Presidential vote

1972	Nixon (R)	....	107,283	(69%)
	McGovern (D)	....	47,343	(31%)

1968	Nixon (R)	58,928	(40%)
	Humphrey (D)	46,425	(32%)
	Wallace (AI)	40,923	(28%)

Rep. Ike F. Andrews (D) Elected 1972; b. Sept. 2, 1925, Bonlee; home, Siler City; Mars Hill Col., U. of N.C., B.S. 1950, LL.B. 1952; Baptist.

Career Army, WWII; Practicing atty., 1952–72; N.C. Senate, 1959–61; N.C. Gen. Assembly, 1961–63, 1967–72, Maj. Ldr., Spkr. Pro Tempore.

Offices 228 CHOB, 202-225-1784. Also 220 Fed. Bldg., 310 New Bern Ave., Raleigh 27601, 919-755-4120.

Committees

Education and Labor (16th). Subcommittees: Elementary, Secondary and Vocational Education; Post-secondary Education.

Group Ratings

	ADA	COPE	LWV	RIPON	NFU	LCV	CFA	NAB	NSI	ACA
1974	33	44	40	14	78	40	55	75	67	42
1973	50	45	50	28	89	28	57	–	–	50

Key Votes

1) Foreign Aid	AGN	6) Gov Abortn Aid	AGN	11) Pub Cong Election $	FOR
2) Busing	AGN	7) Coed Phys Ed	AGN	12) Turkish Arms Cutoff	FOR
3) ABM	FOR	8) Pov Lawyer Gag	FOR	13) Youth Camp Regs	AGN
4) B-1 Bomber	FOR	9) Pub Trans Sub	AGN	14) Strip Mine Veto	FOR
5) Nerve Gas	FOR	10) EZ Voter Regis	ABS	15) Farm Bill Veto	AGN

Election Results

1974 general:	Ike F. Andrews (D)	62,6000	(65%)	($111,307)
	Ward Purrington (R)	33,521	(35%)	($93,916)
1974 primary:	Ike F. Andrews (D)	36,057	(64%)	
	Robert W. Wynne (D)	20,449	(36%)	
1972 general:	Ike F. Andrews (D)	73,072	(50%)	($110,947)
	R. Jack Hawke (R)	71,972	(50%)	($77,573)

◆ ◆ ◆ ◆ ◆

FIFTH DISTRICT

The 5th congressional district of North Carolina is part of the western Carolina hill country. While the tradition of the state's hot, swampy flatland is Democratic, that of the cool, green mountains has always been Republican. It is, however, a Republicanism more of an insurgent than a conservative kind—one that has grown out of a resistance to the domination of wealthy tobacco planters on the coast. If a respect for the "law 'n' order" exists in the mountain country, so also does a distrust of the federal government, whose image here is shaped by the revenuers going around smashing moonshine stills.

The largest city in the 5th district is one not far from the mountains, Winston-Salem (pop. 132,000). The name of the town suggests its dependence on the tobacco industry generally and the R. J. Reynolds Company in particular. West of Winston-Salem are the Republican mountain counties; to the south is Davidson County, a big furniture manufacturing center which like most of the Piedmont in the late sixties or early seventies was leaning Republican.

Winston-Salem itself more often than not goes Republican. But sometimes it shows a twinge of the ornery, populistic streak it shares with the mountain country, as in 1972 when it went for Democrat Nick Galifianakis over Republican Jesse Helms in the Senate race. That result presaged the reaction Winston-Salem, the 5th district, and all of North Carolina would have in 1974, after Sam Ervin's Watergate hearings had come to a close and Richard Nixon had been driven from office.

For this had been a safe Republican district since 1968, when Wilmer "Vinegar Bend" Mizell had beaten Democrat Smith Bagley in the congressional race. Bagley was an heir to the Reynolds tobacco fortune; Mizell, as baseball fans know, was a major league pitcher for several National League clubs in the 1950s and early 1960s. He had also been a local favorite playing for the Winston-Salem club in his minor league days; he was named "most popular player" and "Mr. Strikeout King," and when he retired from the majors he moved back to the area. Mizell was reelected with 58% and 60% of the vote, and in 1972 beat former Arkansas Congressman Brooks Hays, now a North Carolina resident, by a 65–35 margin.

That performance, plus his solid support of presumably popular Richard Nixon, made Mizell a senatorial hopeful for awhile in 1973 and 1974, but he was deterred from running by the popularity of Attorney General Robert Morgan, who ultimately won. Back in the 5th, he was facing what appeared to be weak opposition in the person of suburban newspaper publisher Stephen Neal. Neal's campaign was not especially well financed, and in early November he was reportedly prepared to lose. The major local issue—whether a dam should be built on the New River—was one on which the two candidates did not differ; indeed, Mizell had been leading the fight against the dam.

But when the votes came in, the result was an upset Neal victory. The Democrat had carried Winston-Salem's Forsyth County by a 55–45 margin, and he had carried every other county in the district except for mountain-surrounded Wilkes, long Republican stronghold. It was one of the most stunning House upsets in 1974. In Congress Neal serves on the Banking and Post Office Committees. Undoubtedly he will be pressed hard by the Republicans in 1976, but with the advantages of incumbency, and the post Watergate strength of the Democrats here, he looks to be a good bet for reelection.

Census Data   Pop. 462,401. Central city, 29%; suburban, 18%. Median family income, $8,191; families above $15,000: 12%; families below $3,000: 13%. Median years education, 10.3.

The Voters

Median voting age 41.
Employment profile White collar, 38%. Blue collar, 50%. Service, 9%. Farm, 3%.
Ethnic groups Black, 14%. Total foreign stock, 1%.

Presidential vote

1972	Nixon (R)	109,952	(71%)
	McGovern (D)	45,830	(29%)
1968	Nixon (R)	80,504	(49%)
	Humphrey (D)	44,362	(27%)
	Wallace (AI)	39,406	(24%)

Rep. Stephen L. Neal (D) Elected 1974; b. Nov. 7, 1934, Winston-Salem; home, Winston-Salem; U. of Cal. at Santa Barbara, U. of Hawaii, A.B. 1959; Episcopalian.

Career Mortgage banking business, 1959–66; Newspaper business, 1966–74, Pres., Community Press, Inc., Suburban Newspapers, Inc., King Publishing Co., Inc., and Yadkin Printing Co., Inc.

Offices 502 CHOB, 202-225-2071. Also 2217 Wachovia Bldg., Winston-Salem 27101, 919-723-9211.

Committees

Banking, Currency and Housing (17th). Subcommittees: Consumer Affairs; Domestic Monetary Policy; Financial Institutions Supervision, Regulation and Insurance; International Trade, Investment and Monetary Policy.

Post Office and Civil Service (13th). Subcommittees: Census and Population; Manpower and Civil Service.

Group Ratings: Newly Elected

Key Votes

1) Foreign Aid	ABS	6) Gov Abortn Aid	NE	11) Pub Cong Election $	NE
2) Busing	NE	7) Coed Phys Ed	FOR	12) Turkish Arms Cutoff	NE
3) ABM	NE	8) Pov Lawyer Gag	NE	13) Youth Camp Regs	AGN
4) B-1 Bomber	AGN	9) Pub Trans Sub	NE	14) Strip Mine Veto	AGN
5) Nerve Gas	NE	10) EZ Voter Regis	NE	15) Farm Bill Veto	AGN

Election Results

1974 general	Stephen L. Neal (D)	64,634	(52%)	($61,107)
	Wilmer (Vinegar Bend) Mizell (R)	59,182	(48%)	($62,930)
1974 primary:	Stephen L. Neal (D)	28,379	(85%)	
	Joe Felmet (D)	5,141	(15%)	

◆ ◆ ◆ ◆ ◆

SIXTH DISTRICT

The 6th congressional district of North Carolina takes in the cities of Greensboro (pop. 144,000), High Point (pop. 63,000), and Burlington (pop. 35,000)—all in the heart of the booming Piedmont region. One of the textile giants, Burlington Industries, has its Southern headquarters here, and most of the other big textile firms have mills. High Point is one of the major furniture manufacturing centers in the country, but the 6th has also moved beyond the traditional North Carolina industries of textiles, tobacco, and furniture: Western Electric, for example, is a big employer here now. The attendant influx of northern managerial and technical talent has been the standard explanation of Republican strength here, which generally has been growing since the 1950s; but actually most of the in-migrants are from the South, and their rightward political trend, up to 1974 anyway, represents a change in local electoral preference. Overall, voting habits are a little more conservative than in the next door 4th district, because the black and academic communities are much smaller here in the 6th.

In 1968, Congressman Horace Kornegay, a conservative Democrat, decided to retire, perhaps because he had barely won reelection two years before. In most Southern districts, the retirement of a veteran Congressman would have triggered a riproaring Democratic primary fight. But the 6th district of North Carolina had no primary: L. Richardson Preyer was nominated without opposition, as if by acclamation. The phenomenon is all the more remarkable because Preyer is something of a liberal by North Carolina standards. He does, however, have impeccable establishment credentials. He is an heir to the Richardson-Merrell drug fortune (Vicks Vaporub) and a graduate of Princeton and Harvard Law School. He became a local judge at 34, and was appointed to the federal bench in 1961. Preyer resigned from that judgeship, a lifetime appointment, to run for Governor in 1964.

Candidate Preyer conducted a campaign in the tradition, and with the blessing, of moderate Governor Terry Sanford. But with the conservative tide then sweeping the South in reaction to the Civil Rights revolution, Preyer lost the primary to conservative Dan Moore, and returned to legal and business circles in Greensboro.

In 1968 Preyer's local prominence made him the logical successor to Kornegay. And in spite of the strong Nixon-Wallace showing in the 6th district, he defeated a well known Republican in the general election. In 1970, he improved on his initial effort winning 66% of the vote in a three-candidate field. In 1972 he had no Republican opponent; in 1974, he won with 64%.

As a Congressman, Preyer has compiled a moderate to liberal voting record. He was one of two North Carolina members of the House to support antiwar legislation. At the same time, however, Preyer has backed military projects like the ABM, for which Western Electric, the prime contractor for the system, had more than $100 million in awards for work done in the district. A member of the Commerce Committee, Preyer spends much of his time working on tobacco legislation; he of course takes a position favorable to the interests of the North Carolina growers and manufacturers. The Congressman also serves on Paul Rogers' prolific Health and Environment Subcommittee.

As a former federal judge, Preyer introduced legislation written by the late Yale Law Professor Alexander Bickel designed to spur states into solving the problems for which federal courts have ordered busing schemes. Interestingly, Preyer was also a member of the House Internal Security Committee (formerly Un-American Activities); he was one of those persuaded to leave the

Committee by California's Phillip Burton—a move which led to HISC's demise. In apparent compensation he received a seat on Government Operations. Preyer's unsuccessful gubernatorial effort has apparently left him with little taste for statewide campaigns, and he is passing the age when he might be considered a prime senatorial contender; he will be 59 when Jesse Helms's term comes up in 1978.

Census Data Pop. 457,354. Central city, 45%; suburban, 18%. Median family income, $9,300; families above $15,000: 17%; families below $3,000: 9%. Median years education, 11.0.

The Voters

Median voting age 41.
Employment profile White collar, 43%. Blue collar, 45%. Service, 10%. Farm, 2%.
Ethnic groups Black, 21%. Total foreign stock, 2%.

Presidential vote

1972	Nixon (R)	97,946	(72%)
	McGovern (D)	38,163	(28%)
1968	Nixon (R)	59,401	(42%)
	Humphrey (D)	40,619	(29%)
	Wallace (AI)	42,214	(30%)

Rep. Richardson Preyer (D) Elected 1968; b. Jan. 11, 1919, Greensboro; home, Greensboro; Princeton U., A.B. 1941, Harvard U., LL.B. 1949; Presbyterian.

Career Navy, WWII; Practicing atty., 1950–56; Greensboro City Judge, 1953–54; Judge, N.C. Superior Ct., 1956–61; U.S. Dist. Judge, 1961–63; Candidate for Dem. nomination for Gov., 1964; Sr. V.P. and Trust Officer, N.C. Natl. Bank, 1964; City Exec., 1966.

Offices 403 CHOB, 202-225-3056. Also 249 Fed. Bldg., Greensboro 27401, 919-272-1161.

Committees

Government Operations (19th). Subcommittees: Conservation, Energy and Natural Resources; Government Activities and Transportation.

Interstate and Foreign Commerce (13th). Subcommittees: Health and Environment.

Group Ratings

	ADA	COPE	LWV	RIPON	NFU	LCV	CFA	NAB	NSI	ACA
1974	32	55	83	60	71	44	46	30	90	33
1973	52	55	75	62	90	61	86	–	–	37
1972	44	40	83	60	86	54	50	17	70	29

Key Votes

1) Foreign Aid	FOR	6) Gov Abortn Aid	AGN	11) Pub Cong Election $	FOR
2) Busing	AGN	7) Coed Phys Ed	FOR	12) Turkish Arms Cutoff	AGN
3) ABM	FOR	8) Pov Lawyer Gag	AGN	13) Youth Camp Regs	AGN
4) B-1 Bomber	FOR	9) Pub Trans Sub	AGN	14) Strip Mine Veto	AGN
5) Nerve Gas	FOR	10) EZ Voter Regis	AGN	15) Farm Bill Veto	AGN

Election Results

1974 general:	Richardson Preyer (D)	56,507	(64%)	($66,534)
	R. S. (Steve) Ritchie (R)	31,906	(36%)	($79,604)
1974 primary	Richardson Preyer (D), unopposed			
1972 general:	Richardson Preyer (D)	82,158	(94%)	($8,657)
	Lynwood Bullock (R)	5,331	(6%)	(NA)

◆ ◆ ◆ ◆ ◆

SEVENTH DISTRICT

The 7th congressional district of North Carolina is the southern portion of the state's coastal region, the part of North Carolina most like the Deep South. Wilmington (pop. 46,000) is an old Carolina coastal city that never became a major port—a would-be Charleston or Savannah. Fayetteville (pop. 53,000), the districts's other population center, lies across the rather sparsely settled coastal plain to the west. The city's population only slightly exceeds that of adjacent Fort Bragg, the huge Army base (pop. 47,000) to which Fayetteville owes much of its relative prosperity. Bragg is the home of the Army's 101st Airborne paratroopers, and nearby, along the garish strip highway with its X-rated drive in movies and topless night clubs, is the nation's largest concentration of Vietnamese restaurants.

The 7th has a fairly large number of blacks (26%), but its most notable minority consists of American Indians (7%). In fact, more Indians live here than in any other congressional district east of the Mississippi. Most of them are the Lumbees of Robeson County, and their place in the traditional caste system of the South has always been uncertain. From time to time, the Indians have had civil rights demonstrations, but they have also objected to having their children bused to go to school with blacks.

In 1968, the 7th showed a near even split in the presidential contest. Wallace finished first, but Nixon, who finished third, was only 6% behind the Alabamian. Four years later the district shifted in a big way to Nixon; McGovern apparently lost some Humphrey votes because of his stand on military spending, one that hardly sat well in places like Fayetteville or Fort Bragg. At the same time, however, the voters of the 7th elected a Democrat to the House by a solid margin. The new Congressman, Charles Rose III, is a liberal, at least by the standards of North Carolina. He is one of the young men tutored by former Governor (1961–65) Terry Sanford. Rose once worked for Sanford's law firm and supported him in his 1972 presidential bid; Sanford ran second in the North Carolina primary and remained a candidate at the Miami Beach convention.

After leaving Sanford's law firm, Rose, a Fayetteville native, became a prosecutor in his home town. In 1970 he quit to run for Congress. The incumbent was Alton Lennon, age 64 and a former U.S. Senator who was appointed in 1953 and defeated for a full term in 1954. In the Senate, Lennon had hired as an aide Jesse Helms, later an ultraconservative Senator himself; in the House, Lennon was a solid conservative and member of the Armed Services Committee. Apparently, however, he was a poor campaigner, as challenger Rose carried the counties around Fayetteville and wound up with 43% of the vote in the 1972 primary. So it was hardly a surprise when Lennon announced that he would retire in 1972.

Rose did not succeed to the seat without a contest, however. In the initial primary, he failed to win the 50% needed to avoid a runoff, and in that election he beat state Representative Hector McGeahy by a 55–45 margin. McGeahy tried again in 1974, and this time lost by a 61–29 margin. In the House, Rose serves on the Agriculture and House Administration Committees, and though he votes with most Democrats on most issues, he likes to describe himself as a conservative.

Census Data Pop. 467,476. Central city, 21%; suburban, 47%. Median family income, $6,875; families above $15,000: 9%; families below $3,000: 18%. Median years education, 11.2.

The Voters

Median voting age 35.
Employment profile White collar, 40%. Blue collar, 40%. Service, 13%. Farm, 7%.
Ethnic groups Black, 26%. Indian, 7%. Total foreign stock, 4%.

Presidential vote

1972	Nixon (R)	71,346	(70%)
	McGovern (D)	30,409	(30%)
1968	Nixon (R)	30,786	(30%)
	Humphrey (D)	35,336	(34%)
	Wallace (AI)	36,867	(36%)

Rep. Charles Rose (D) Elected 1972; b. Aug. 10, 1939, Fayetteville; home, Fayetteville; Davidson Col., A.B. 1961, U. of N.C., LL.B. 1964; Presbyterian.

Career Practicing atty., 1964–72; Chf. Dist. Ct. Prosecutor, 12th Judicial Dist., 1967–70.

Offices 218 CHOB, 202-225-2731. Also P.O. Box 1833, P.O. Bldg., Wilmington 28401, 919-763-3375.

Committees

Agriculture (12th). Subcommittees: Family Farms and Rural Development (Chairman); Oilseeds and Rice; Tobacco.

House Administration (15th). Subcommittees: Electrical and Mechanical Office Equipment; Ad Hoc Computer (Chairman).

Group Ratings

	ADA	COPE	LWV	RIPON	NFU	LCV	CFA	NAB	NSI	ACA
1974	36	56	22	20	67	50	22	45	67	58
1973	44	40	50	27	90	16	63	–	–	38

Key Votes

1) Foreign Aid	AGN	6) Gov Abortn Aid	FOR	11) Pub Cong Election $	AGN
2) Busing	AGN	7) Coed Phys Ed	FOR	12) Turkish Arms Cutoff	FOR
3) ABM	FOR	8) Pov Lawyer Gag	AGN	13) Youth Camp Regs	AGN
4) B-1 Bomber	FOR	9) Pub Trans Sub	FOR	14) Strip Mine Veto	FOR
5) Nerve Gas	FOR	10) EZ Voter Regis	FOR	15) Farm Bill Veto	AGN

Election Results

1974 general:	Charles Rose (D), unopposed			($39,315)
1974 primary	Charles Rose (D)	41,508	(61%)	
	Hector McGeahy (D)	19,774	(29%)	
	Peter R. Davis (D)	7,325	(11%)	
1972 general:	Charles Rose (D)	57,348	(61%)	($86,933)
	Jerry C. Scott (R)	36,726	(39%)	($12,402)

◆ ◆ ◆ ◆ ◆

EIGHTH DISTRICT

The 8th district of North Carolina consists of two areas: a hunk of the middle of the Piedmont textile country and the Sand Hills region of the state's coastal plain. The textile counties lie on both sides of Interstate 85 between Charlotte and Greensboro; along the way the roadway passes through the 8th district towns of Salisbury and Kannapolis (home of giant Cannon Mills). Here the textile magnates reign supreme. There is no nonsense about unions, or workers' rights—the boss calls the shots. He does in the mill anyway, and, it seems, in the voting booth as well. For this area, in election after election, is one of the most Republican and conservative in North Carolina.

The textile counties cast about two-thirds of the votes in the 8th district; the rest are from the more sparsely populated Sand Hills counties to the east. Here, even before 1974, you could find evidence of the traditional Democratic allegiance of the area, although it had been more likely to prefer George Wallace than the national Democrats of recent years.

For six years after its initial creation for the 1968 election, the 8th district elected a Republican Congressman—contrary to the expectations of the Democratic legislators who had drawn the district's lines. The winner, by a narrow margin in 1968 and much larger ones thereafter, was Earl Ruth, a conservative former Democrat and former basketball coach and athletic director at a small college in the area. By 1972 Ruth was even carrying the Sand Hills counties, and won the district as a whole with 60% of the vote.

Ruth was not only a conservative House member, he was one who—despite his seat on the liberal Education and Labor Committee—just couldn't seem to understand the views of those who disagreed with him. Opponents of the Vietnam war, journalists who suggested that Richard Nixon was guilty of improprieties in the Watergate—Ruth sputtered outrage at the notion that such people could be so substantially represented in the House. So it must have been incomprehensible, as well as galling, to him when he found himself in a close fight for reelection in 1974.

To be sure, his opponent, Bill Hefner, didn't sound like a left wing liberal himself. On the contrary, he was a country music disk jockey (and radio station owner) from conservative Kannapolis, and his campaign appearances featured very little anti-Nixon oratory and a great deal of country music. But the Sam Ervin Revolution that seems to have swept North Carolina in 1974 had its effect here. Hefner got 62% of the vote in the Sand Hill counties, as against the 49% the Democrat had got there two years before. And in the decisive Piedmont textile counties, Hefner raised the Democratic share from 34% to 54%, for a district-wide 57% victory. So Hefner—no relation to the *Playboy* king—went to Congress, and Ruth—of all unlikely things—became Governor of American Samoa. The prospects for 1976 are for another Hefner victory.

Census Data Pop. 454,275. Central city, 0%; suburban, 17%. Median family income, $7,872; families above $15,000: 9%; families below $3,000: 13%. Median years education, 10.0.

The Voters

Median voting age 43.
Employment profile White collar, 30%. Blue collar, 56%. Service, 10%. Farm, 4%.
Ethnic groups Black, 20%.

Presidential vote

1972	Nixon (R)	100,830	(73%)
	McGovern (D)	37,880	(27%)
1968	Nixon (R)	67,350	(44%)
	Humphrey (D)	39,820	(26%)
	Wallace (AI)	46,703	(30%)

Rep. W. G. (Bill) **Hefner** (D) Elected 1974; b. Apr. 11, 1930, Elora, Tenn.; home, Concord; Baptist.

Career Pres., WRKB Radio, Kannapolis; Mbr., Harvesters Quartet, with weekly TV show on WXII, Winston-Salem; Promoter, "Carolina Sings", gospel music entertainment.

Offices 1004 LHOB, 202-225-3715. Also 2202 S. Cannon Blvd., Kannapolis 28081, 704-933-1615.

Committees

Interstate and Foreign Commerce (25th). Subcommittees: Health and Environment; Transportation and Commerce.

Veterans' Affairs (13th). Subcommittees: Cemeteries and Burial Benefits; Compensation, Pension and Insurance; Hospitals.

Group Ratings: Newly Elected

Key Votes

1) Foreign Aid	AGN	6) Gov Abortn Aid	NE	11) Pub Cong Election $	NE
2) Busing	NE	7) Coed Phys Ed	ABS	12) Turkish Arms Cutoff	NE
3) ABM	NE	8) Pov Lawyer Gag	NE	13) Youth Camp Regs	ABS
4) B-1 Bomber	AGN	9) Pub Trans Sub	NE	14) Strip Mine Veto	FOR
5) Nerve Gas	NE	10) EZ Voter Regis	NE	15) Farm Bill Veto	AGN

Election Results

1974 general:	W. G. (Bill) Hefner (D)	61,591	(57%)	($71,793)
	Earl B. Ruth (R)	46,500	(43%)	($35,043)
1974 primary:	W. G. (Bill) Hefner (D), unopposed			

◆ ◆ ◆ ◆ ◆

NINTH DISTRICT

The name of Charlotte, North Carolina, will no doubt be linked in the minds of future American historians with the political and legal issue that we have come to know as "busing." For it was here that a federal judge not regarded as a liberal, ordered a plan for massive integration between Charlotte and surrounding Mecklenburg County. The district court's decision was reversed on appeal, but it was reinstated by a unanimous Supreme Court, led by Chief Justice Warren Burger. The Nixon-appointed jurist declared that transportation—that is, busing—could be ordered when it was necessary to achieve integration of the schools.

When the district court decision was announced, consternation followed in Charlotte. It was never, of course, a city known for its liberal social or political attitudes. In fact, quite the contrary is true. With 241,000 people, Charlotte is the largest city in North Carolina, but by no means a giant by national standards. It is a predominantly white collar city, having less manufacturing than other Piedmont centers. And that white collar population was for some time the factor behind the election and reelection of a Republican Congressman, Charles Jonas, and also behind the Republican majorities cast for presidential candidates like Dwight Eisenhower and Richard Nixon.

So it must have come as a shock to the citizens of Charlotte that an appointee of their choice for President ordered them to bus some of their children so that they could go to school with black children. Richard Nixon, after all, was a politician who had run as an enemy of the Warren Court. But what is interesting, politically, is that the shock and disappointment produced no electoral response among white people in Charlotte. One reason was that the busing plan, once implemented, worked smoothly. Another is that they had nowhere else to turn; Charlotte voted for those who called themselves anti-busing candidates, and busing came anyway.

So the reaction here after busing went into effect in 1971 was not what you found in so many southern cities in the sixties (or northern cities in the seventies) when integration orders came down entirely contrary to people's expectations. There was no particular surge to Nixon here in 1972; indeed, McGovern actually got a higher percentage of the vote than Humphrey had four years before (although that was not a very high percentage in the first place).

Nor did it have any particular effect in congressional elections. The 9th district of North Carolina, which includes Charlotte, Mecklenburg County, and two much smaller counties, had been electing Congressman Jonas for twenty years when he decided to retire in 1972. There was a spirited contest to succeed him between former Olympic distance runner Jim Beatty, a Democrat, and Davidson College chemistry professor and Mecklenburg County Commissioner James Martin, a Republican. With no disagreement on the busing issue, Martin won with a 59–41 margin—a pretty good indication of the general political balance here. Two years later, after the fall of Richard Nixon and the prominent role North Carolina's own Sam Ervin played in it had switched so many votes in the state, Martin had apparently worked his district well enough to survive comfortably, though not overwhelmingly, with 55% of the vote. After that victory, he won a seat on the House Ways and Means Committee—a signal that his Republican colleagues, at least, believed that his seat was basically safe and his views on issues conservatively sound. They are almost certainly correct on both counts.

Census Data Pop. 459,535. Central city, 52%; suburban, 25%. Median family income, $9,594; families above $15,000: 20%; families below $3,000: 9%. Median years education, 11.8.

The Voters

Median voting age 40.
Employment profile White collar, 51%. Blue collar, 37%. Service, 11%. Farm, 1%.
Ethnic groups Black, 22%. Total foreign stock, 3%.

Presidential vote

1972	Nixon (R)	102,879	(81%)
	McGovern (D)	23,918	(19%)
1968	Nixon (R)	73,070	(50%)
	Humphrey (D)	40,024	(28%)
	Wallace (AI)	32,252	(22%)

Rep. James G. Martin (R) Elected 1972; b. Dec. 11, 1935, Savannah, Ga.; home, Davidson; Davidson Col., B.S. 1957, Princeton U., Ph.D. 1960; Presbyterian.

Career Asst. Prof. of Chemistry, Davidson Col., 1960–64, Assoc. Prof., 1964–72; Mecklenburg Co. Bd. of Commissioners, 1966–72, Chm., 1967–68, 1970–71; Founder and First Chm., Centralina Regional Cncl. of Govts., 1966–69; V.P., Natl. Assoc. of Regional Cncls., 1970–72.

Offices 115 CHOB, 202-225-1976. Also 1215 American Bldg., Charlotte 28286, 704-376-7489.

Committees

Ways and Means (10th). Subcommittees: Health; Oversight.

Group Ratings

	ADA	COPE	LWV	RIPON	NFU	LCV	CFA	NAB	NSI	ACA
1974	17	9	40	50	50	40	8	83	100	80
1973	12	9	33	53	40	32	13	–	–	88

Key Votes

1) Foreign Aid	AGN	6) Gov Abortn Aid	FOR	11) Pub Cong Election $	AGN
2) Busing	AGN	7) Coed Phys Ed	AGN	12) Turkish Arms Cutoff	AGN
3) ABM	FOR	8) Pov Lawyer Gag	FOR	13) Youth Camp Regs	AGN
4) B-1 Bomber	ABS	9) Pub Trans Sub	AGN	14) Strip Mine Veto	FOR
5) Nerve Gas	AGN	10) EZ Voter Regis	AGN	15) Farm Bill Veto	FOR

Election Results

1974 general:	James G. Martin (R)	51,032	(55%)	($120,937)
	Milton Short (D)	41,387	(45%)	($54,071)
1974 primary:	James G. Martin (R), unopposed			
1972 general:	James G. Martin (R)	80,356	(59%)	($149,508)
	James Beatty (D)	56,171	(41%)	($63,107)

◆ ◆ ◆ ◆ ◆

TENTH DISTRICT

The 10th district of North Carolina is a collection of seven counties in the western Piedmont and the Appalachian mountains. The southern part of the district, on the South Carolina border, is dominated by the city of Gastonia (pop. 47,000), a textile mill town that traditionally votes Democratic. North of Gastonia, the hills rise to mountains around towns like Morganton, the home of former Senator Sam Ervin. This is furniture manufacturing country, and the farther one gets into the mountains, the more Republican the territory. The political preferences here reflect old Civil War allegiances, ones that have ceased to be of much importance in presidential politics. In local and congressional contests, however, they still matter.

The 10th took its shape in the 1968 redistricting, and has had only minor changes since. The 1968 contest featured two incumbents thrown into the same district to fight it out. Basil Whitener, a conservative Democrat, came into the fray with twelve years of seniority in the House, and during which time he had represented most of the counties in the new 10th. On the other hand, Republican James Broyhill had only six years of seniority. But the political trends in the district favored the Republican candidate—it was clear that Richard Nixon was going to carry the 10th easily in 1968.

The surprising thing was not that Broyhill won, but that his margin was so large. He lost the two counties around Gastonia by a total of 9,000 votes. But Broyhill carried the rest of the district—most of it Whitener's old territory—by 25,000 votes. In 1970, Whitener came back to try again and did worse; this time he lost even the Gastonia area. Against major party opposition in 1972, Broyhill won the biggest percentage of any opposed North Carolina Congressman, Democrat or Republican.

That victory made Broyhill an important figure in the North Carolina Republican Party. He was asked to be a candidate for the Senate in 1974, but declined; the nominee wound up being his brother-in-law, William Stevens. His 1974 reelection, with a less than expected 54% of the vote, elevated him to the number two Republican slot on the Commerce Committee, just behind Ohio's Sam Devine, who faces a tough fight in 1976. Broyhill's family owns a furniture manufacturing company, and on the Commerce Committee he accurately reflects Chamber of Commerce type views; he generally opposes government regulation of business, except in some cases when the regulators in effect help the businessmen set minimum prices. In 1975 he also won a seat on the House Budget Committee. In light of his political survival in 1974, he seems to be in good shape to continue his already long House career for many years.

Census Data Pop. 471,777. Central city, 0%; suburban, 0%. Median family income, $8,449; families above $15,000: 11%; families below $3,000: 10%. Median years education, 10.0.

The Voters

Median voting age 40.
Employment profile White collar, 30%. Blue collar, 59%. Service, 9%. Farm, 2%.
Ethnic groups Black, 11%.

Presidential vote

1972	Nixon (R)	105,093	(73%)
	McGovern (D)	38,202	(27%)
1968	Nixon (R)	75,393	(48%)
	Humphrey (D)	37,971	(24%)
	Wallace (AI)	45,157	(28%)

Rep. James T. Broyhill (R) Elected 1962; b. Aug. 19, 1927, Lenoir; home, Lenoir; U. of N.C., B.S. 1950; Baptist.

Career Broyhill Furniture Factories of Lenoir, 1945–62.

Offices 2227 RHOB, 202-225-2576. Also 116-D Pennton Ave., S.W., Lenoir 28645, 704-758-4247.

Committees

Budget (4th).

Interstate and Foreign Commerce (2d). Subcommittees: Energy and Power; Health and Environment.

Group Ratings

	ADA	COPE	LWV	RIPON	NFU	LCV	CFA	NAB	NSI	ACA
1974	19	0	27	44	50	53	31	100	90	79
1973	8	18	25	47	67	21	38	–	–	81
1972	0	9	27	63	29	58	100	100	89	82

Key Votes

1) Foreign Aid	AGN	6) Gov Abortn Aid	ABS	11) Pub Cong Election $	AGN
2) Busing	AGN	7) Coed Phys Ed	AGN	12) Turkish Arms Cutoff	AGN
3) ABM	AGN	8) Pov Lawyer Gag	FOR	13) Youth Camp Regs	AGN
4) B-1 Bomber	FOR	9) Pub Trans Sub	AGN	14) Strip Mine Veto	FOR
5) Nerve Gas	AGN	10) EZ Voter Regis	AGN	15) Farm Bill Veto	AGN

Election Results

1974 general:	James T. Broyhill (R)	63,382	(54%)	($78,850)
	Jack L. Rhyne (D)	53,131	(46%)	($19,607)
1974 primary:	James T. Broyhill (R), unopposed			
1972 general:	James T. Broyhill (R)	103,119	(73%)	($34,251)
	Paul L. Beck (D)	39,025	(27%)	($357)

◆ ◆ ◆ ◆ ◆

ELEVENTH DISTRICT

The 11th district of North Carolina occupies the western end of the state. Its main features include Asheville (pop. 57,000), the place to which Thomas Wolfe could not go home again, and the Great Smoky Mountains National Park. The park is the nation's most heavily visited: its roads have become so crowded that the Park Service was forced to install traffic lights—the first ever within a national park. During the summer it is 20 degrees cooler in the mountains than in the lowland towns not far away; the climatological endowment and the forested, green, fog-wisped mountains attract some seven million people to the Smokies each year. Over the years the same elements—the mountains, the cool climate—have made the western end of North Carolina a separate unit from the rest of the state. During the Civil War, it was the most reluctant part of North Carolina to secede. With few slaves (only 6% of the people here today are black), many of the small farmers in the hollows remained loyal to the Union.

So the ancestral political loyalty here is to the Republican Party, especially in the most isolated mountain counties. But western North Carolina is not as monolithically Republican as adjacent east Tennessee. People in the Carolina mountains have had the Republicans on the nearby Piedmont as well as the Democrats of the eastern coastal plain to react against. In any case, Jesse Helms, the ultraconservative TV commentator from faraway Raleigh, got only 53% of the vote in the 11th district on his way to becoming the first popularly elected Republican Senator in the history of North Carolina.

Moreover, the 11th has refused to elect Republican Congressmen, unlike the other western North Carolina districts. Instead, it has continued to reelect Democrat Roy Taylor by sizable, though not usually overwhelming, margins. First elected in a 1960 special election, Taylor is one of the relatively few Easterners on the House Interior Committee—of its 43 members, only 12 are from states east of the Mississippi River. After a dozen years of service and the defeat of several senior members opposed by environmentalists, Taylor has advanced to the number two position among Interior's Democrats. He is now directly in line to succeed 77-year-old James Haley of Florida, the Chairman of the Committee.

Taylor is considered a middle of the road man on most issues that come before Interior, willing to listen to the pleas of environmentalists as well as to those of people who seek more intensive use of public lands and resources. As Chairman of the National Parks and Recreation Subcommittee, the Congressman is an enthusiast for creating new parks. Since he became Chairman of that unit, some 1.5 million acres of parkland have been added to the national park system. On Interior, Taylor has also tried to improve the lot of the Cherokee Indians who live near the Smokies Park.

Census Data Pop. 467,051. Central city, 12%; suburban, 19%. Median family income, $6,857; families above $15,000: 8%; families below $3,000: 18%. Median years education, 10.5.

The Voters

Median voting age 44.
Employment profile White collar, 35%. Blue collar, 51%. Service, 11%. Farm, 3%.
Ethnic groups Black, 6%. Total foreign stock, 2%.

Presidential vote

1972	Nixon (R)	110,566	(71%)
	McGovern (D)	46,095	(29%)
1968	Nixon (R)	83,495	(48%)
	Humphrey (D)	50,707	(29%)
	Wallace (AI)	38,420	(22%)

Rep. Roy A. Taylor (D) Elected June 25, 1960; b. Jan. 31, 1910, Vader, Wash.; home, Black Mountain; Ashville-Biltmore Col., Maryville Col., B.A. 1931, Asheville U. Law School; Baptist.

Career Practicing atty.; Navy, WWII; N.C. Gen. Assembly, 1947–53.

Offices 2268 RHOB, 202-225-6402. Also P.O. Box 7216, Asheville 28807, 704-254-6526.

Committees

Interior and Insular Affairs (2d). Subcommittees: Indian Affairs; National Parks and Recreation (Chairman); Territorial and Insular Affairs.

International Relations (14th). Subcommittees: International Political and Military Affairs; International Trade.

Group Ratings

	ADA	COPE	LWV	RIPON	NFU	LCV	CFA	NAB	NSI	ACA
1974	18	27	50	25	64	53	39	82	100	67
1973	20	36	42	40	90	22	75	–	–	58
1972	19	36	50	50	71	40	0	50	90	70

Key Votes

1) Foreign Aid	AGN	6) Gov Abortn Aid	AGN	11) Pub Cong Election $	FOR
2) Busing	AGN	7) Coed Phys Ed	ABS	12) Turkish Arms Cutoff	AGN
3) ABM	FOR	8) Pov Lawyer Gag	FOR	13) Youth Camp Regs	AGN
4) B-1 Bomber	FOR	9) Pub Trans Sub	AGN	14) Strip Mine Veto	AGN
5) Nerve Gas	FOR	10) EZ Voter Regis	AGN	15) Farm Bill Veto	AGN

Election Results

1974 general:	Roy. A. Taylor (D)	89,163	(66%)	($18,796)
	Albert F. (Doc) Gilman (R)	45,983	(34%)	($4,999)
1974 primary	Roy A. Taylor (D), unopposed			
1972 general:	Roy A. Taylor (D)	94,465	(60%)	($21,721)
	Jesse I. Ledbetter (R)	64,062	(40%)	($12,066)

NORTH DAKOTA

North Dakota occupies the northern section of the Great Plains—one of the world's largest hunks of arable land. Most of North Dakota is wheat country, with the state producing some 17% of the nation's wheat crop; only Kansas grows more. As the North Dakota plains grow more arid toward the west, ranchers and the grazing of livestock predominate. Both varieties of agricultural experience here are demanding and discouraging. North Dakota is a hard, treeless land; its winters are cold with the plains open to Arctic blasts from Canada, and its summers are often too short and too dry. Some 50 years ago, the state had 632,000 people; by 1970, only 617,000. Moreover, for every 10 college graduates the state produces, seven choose to leave it. There are greener pastures elsewhere, as North Dakota now has a lower per capita income level than several states in the South.

About 25% of all North Dakotans still live on farms and ranches, the highest such percentage in any state. In some recent years, of course, the price of wheat and beef have been relatively high. But the more common lot of North Dakota farmers and ranchers has been a sad one. Because the economy of the state depends on the farmers who exert little control themselves over the fluctuations of commodity markets, North Dakota over the years has seen raging dissatisfaction with the farm programs of the federal government. By tradition, the most common topics of the state's political discourse are the minutiae of wheat and feed grain legislation. And agricultural discontent was the driving force behind the most interesting feature of the state's politics, its time of radicalism in the years around World War I.

Most of North Dakota's settlement occurred in the years between 1890 and 1901. A large portion of the settlers were of immigrant stock: Norwegians to the east, Canadians along the northern border, Volga Germans to the west, and native Germans throughout the state. (Volga Germans were people who migrated to Russia during the early 1800s, but who retained their German language and character. They are recorded in the U.S. Census figures as Russians.) All of the new North Dakotans lived on lonely, often marginal farms, cut off in many cases from the wider currents of American culture by the forbidding barrier of language. Their economic fate was at the mercy of the grain millers of Minneapolis, the railroads, the banks, and commodity traders.

These circumstances led A. C. Townley and William Lemke to organize the North Dakota Non-Partisan League (NPL) in 1915. Its program was frankly socialist—government ownership of the railroads and grain elevators—and, like many North Dakota ethnics, the League opposed going to war with Germany. The positions taken by the NPL won it many adherents in North Dakota, and the League spread into neighboring states. But North Dakota was its bastion; the NPL often determined the outcome of the usually decisive Republican primary, and sometimes swung its support to the otherwise hopelessly outnumbered Democrats. A particular favorite of the NPL was "Wild Bill" Langer, who served intermittently as Governor during the 1930s. He was elected Senator in 1940, but was allowed to take his seat only after a lengthy investigation of alleged campaign irregularities. His subsequent career was fully as controversial; Langer was the Senate's most unpredictable maverick until his death in 1959. (One of Langer's pet projects was to get a North Dakotan on the Supreme Court; he filibustered every nomination from 1954 till his death in an unsuccessful attempt to accomplish that end.)

Another NPL favorite was Congressman Usher Burdick, who served from 1935 to 1945 and then again from 1949 to 1959. Burdick, like Langer, was a nominal Republican, but usually voted with New Deal liberals on economic issues. Burdick's son, Quentin, a Democrat, was a member of the House when Langer died, and won a special election to fill the Senate seat after waging a campaign directed mainly at the allegedly iniquitous policies of Agriculture Secretary Ezra Taft Benson. The Non-Partisan League, of course, supported the younger Burdick. By the 1960s, however, its name had become misleading, since then as now it consistently supports Democratic candidates for office.

North Dakota is ordinarily a Republican state—only a few counties along the Canadian border or ones with a large Indian population regularly turn in Democratic majorities in presidential elections. But state elections are another matter, and in 1964 Quentin Burdick again demonstrated his appeal when he ran even with Lyndon Johnson's 58% in the state. In 1970, Burdick did even better, winning with 62% of the vote. The North Dakotan's victory illustrates some of the problems faced by Nixon strategists in their attempt to unseat liberal Democrats in 1970—or for that matter in 1972 and 1974. Congressman Thomas Kleppe, a millionaire (Gold Seal wax) who had run against Burdick in 1964, was again his opponent in 1970. Kleppe spent about $300,000—a huge sum in a state where $32.50 bought 30 seconds of prime time on the most powerful TV station. Kleppe bombarded North Dakota voters with TV spots that reminded them that Burdick had not voted in line with their presumed views on issues like school prayer, interstate travel to incite riots, and so on.

The feedback from the Kleppe media campaign was bad. North Dakota voters are accustomed to seeing their candidates in person, not hearing an ad man's message over the tube. Moreover, they simply could not believe that rough-hewn Quentin Burdick, Usher's son and their Senator for

10 years, was the awful man Kleppe said he was. Herschel Lashkowitz, the Mayor of Fargo, the state's largest city (pop. 53,000), summed it up: "people looked at those ads and then they thought of Quentin Burdick and they resented it."

Indeed, Burdick's record both on the Senate floor and in the Judiciary Committee was one of a quiet liberal. But he was on the right side of an issue much more important to North Dakotans than any of those issues of style and rhetoric that have won votes for Republicans in industrial cities. Interstate rioters may be bad, but worse was the Nixon Administration's wheat bill, which Burdick opposed. Kleppe on the other hand, had worked out the compromise measure as a member of the House Agriculture Committee. Farmers felt the legislation would produce a wheat surplus, the kind that clobbered the price for the commodity during the 1950s. Even the support of the state's senior Senator, Republican Milton Young, could not save Kleppe from the worst defeat ever suffered by a North Dakota Republican.

Burdick's seat is up in 1976, and he is expected to run again. His biggest problem, at least at the present time, appears to be his age; he turns 68 in 1976. But that will probably not cause him difficulty, for most of the candidates the Republicans might run are little known or respected—with one major exception. That is the state's Congressman-at-Large Mark Andrews. Andrews, a farmer, ran for Governor in 1962 when he was only 36, and ran the closest gubernatorial race of any Republican against Democratic Governor William Guy. The next year Andrews won a special election for a congressional seat, and has served in the House ever since. He is ranking minority member of the Agriculture Appropriations Subcommittee, and has not been hesitant about opposing Administration farm programs when they have been unpopular with North Dakota farmers. Andrews is a good speaker and campaigner, and could be a formidable candidate. The question is whether he wants to go now in 1976, or to wait until Senator Milton Young's seat is up in 1980, for Young has promised he will not run again.

Milton Young is not a name much known outside North Dakota; he is not even particularly well known in Washington political circles. Yet this quiet man has been a Senator from North Dakota since 1945, is the senior Republican in the Senate, indeed in the whole Congress, is ranking Republican on the Senate Appropriations Committee and an important voice on the Agriculture Committee. And in the Democratic year of 1974, when he was about to turn 77, Milton Young managed to win reelection, even if by only 177 votes, over Former Governor William Guy. Guy was a formidable opponent, a four-term Governor (1961–72) who enjoyed great popularity and, at 55, comparatively youthful. Guy ran a campaign which mentioned Young's age only inferentially, and as the challenger, he was expected to win. But he suffered from the independent candidacy of James Jungroth, a former Democrat who claimed that Guy had allowed too much development in the state (especially strip mining of coal) with too few environmental safeguards. The Jungroth candidacy took only 3% of the vote, but in this close a race that could well have been vital.

But probably the turning point of the campaign came when Young managed to neutralize the age issue. A karate practitioner, he ran TV ads showing him chopping a block of wood in two with his bare hand; he managed to campaign visibly and to remind North Dakotans that his halting speech was the result not of age but of a difficulty he always had. Young also benefitted from his role as the architect of the 1973 wheat bill, which had resulted in large increases in income for North Dakota farmers; and in what is now his last term in the Senate he will probably devote more attention to agriculture than to any other single issue.

Census Data   Pop. 617,761; 0.31% of U.S. total, 45th largest; Central city, 9%; suburban, 3%. Median family income, $7,836; 39th highest; families above $15,000: 13%; families below $3,000: 12%.   Median years education, 12.0.

1974 Share of Federal Tax Burden $723,101,000; 0.27% of U.S. total, 46th largest.

1974 Share of Federal Outlays $1,010,355,000; 0.37% of U.S. total, 43d largest.   Per capita federal spending, $1636.

DOD	$281,558,000	37th (0.41%)	HEW	$271,059,000	45th (0.29%)
AEC	$48,000	46th (–)	HUD	$1,406,000	48th (0.14%)
NASA	$–	– (–)	VA	$39,104,000	45th (0.29%)
DOT	$38,558,000	47th (0.46%)	EPA	$2,662,000	49th (0.08%)
DOC	$3,503,000	44th (0.22%)	RevS	$25,369,000	42d (0.42%)
DOI	$50,738,000	16th (2.06%)	Int.	$32,220,000	42d (0.16%)
USDA	$172,891,000	31st (1.39%)	Other	$91,239,000	

Economic Base Agriculture, notably wheat, cattle, barley and dairy products; finance, insurance and real estate; food and kindred products, especially dairy products; printing and publishing, especially newspapers; tourism; machinery, especially farm machinery.

Political Line-up Governor, Arthur A. Link (D). Senators, Milton R. Young (R) and Quentin N. Burdick (D). Representatives, 1 R at large. State Senate (34 R and 17 D); State House (62 R and 40 D).

The Voters

Registration No statewide registration.
Median voting age 44.
Employment profile White collar, 42%. Blue collar, 21%. Service, 16%. Farm, 21%.
Ethnic groups Total foreign stock, 24%. Norway, 6%; USSR, 5%.

Presidential vote

1972	Nixon (R)	174,109	(63%)
	McGovern (D)	100,384	(37%)
1968	Nixon (R)	138,669	(56%)
	Humphrey (D)	94,769	(38%)
	Wallace (AI)	14,244	(6%)

Sen. Milton R. Young (R) Appointed Mar. 12, 1945, elected June 25, 1946, seat up 1980; b. Dec. 6, 1897, Berlin; home, La Moure; N.D. St. Ag. Col., Graceland Col.; Church of Latter Day Saints.

Career Farmer; N.D. House of Reps., 1932–34; N.D. Senate, 1934–45, Pres. Pro Tempore, 1941–43, Maj. Floor Ldr., 1943.

Offices 5205 DSOB, 202-224-2043. Also Box 241, La Moure 58458, 701-883-5301, and Box 1036, Bismarck 58501, 701-223-3312.

Committees

Appropriations (Ranking Member). Subcommittees: Agriculture and Related Agencies; Defense; Interior; Public Works.

Agriculture and Forestry (2d). Subcommittees: Agricultural Production, Marketing, and Stabilization of Prices; Agricultural Research and General Legislation.

Group Ratings

	ADA	COPE	LWV	RIPON	NFU	LCV	CFA	NAB	NSI	ACA
1974	12	25	80	48	75	33	33	50	89	63
1973	5	45	11	35	53	–	17	–	–	52
1972	5	10	36	57	50	7	10	64	80	82

Key Votes

1) No-Knock	FOR	8) Gov Abortn Aid	AGN	15) Consumer Prot Agy	AGN
2) Busing	AGN	9) Cut Mil Brass	AGN	16) Forced Psych Tests	AGN
3) No Fault	AGN	10) Gov Limousine	FOR	17) Fed Campaign Subs	FOR
4) F-111	FOR	11) RR Featherbed	FOR	18) Rhod Chrome Ban	AGN
5) Death Penalty	FOR	12) Handgun License	AGN	19) Open Legis Meetings	AGN
6) Foreign Aid	AGN	13) Less Troop Abrd	ABS	20) Strikers Food Stmps	AGN
7) Filibuster	AGN	14) Resume Turk Aid	FOR	21) Gov Info Disclosure	FOR

Election Results

1974 general:	Milton R. Young (R)	114,852	(49%)	($300,121)
	William L. "Bill" Guy (D)	114,675	(49%)	($115,561)
	James R. Jungroth (Ind.)	6,679	(3%)	($13,187)

1974 primary: Milton R. Young (R), unopposed
1968 general: Milton R. Young (R) 154,968 (66%)
               Herschel Lasohkowitz (D) 80,815 (34%)

Sen. Quentin N. Burdick (D) Elected June 28, 1960, seat up 1976; b. June 19, 1908, Munich; home, Fargo; U. of Minn., B.A. 1931, LL.B. 1932; Congregationalist.

Career Practicing atty., 1932–58; Dem. nominee for Gov., 1946; U.S. House of Reps., 1959–60.

Offices 451 RSOB, 202-224-2551. Also Fed. Bldg., Fargo 58102, 701-237-4000, and Fed. Bldg., Bismarck 58501, 701-255-2553.

Committees

The Judiciary (5th). Subcommittees: Constitutional Rights; Improvements in Judicial Machinery (Chairman); Juvenile Delinquency; Penitentiaries (Chairman).

Post Office and Civil Service (3d). Subcommittees: Civil Service Policies and Practices; Compensation and Employment Benefits (Chairman).

Public Works (6th). Subcommittees: Economic Development; Water Resources; Transportation; Disaster Relief (Chairman).

Group Ratings

	ADA	COPE	LWV	RIPON	NFU	LCV	CFA	NAB	NSI	ACA
1974	81	91	80	59	100	55	88	42	0	11
1973	80	82	70	33	100	–	58	–	–	11
1972	75	90	73	56	100	58	100	55	0	14

Key Votes

1) No-Knock	AGN	8) Gov Abortn Aid	FOR	15) Consumer Prot Agy	FOR
2) Busing	FOR	9) Cut Mil Brass	ABS	16) Forced Psych Tests	FOR
3) No Fault	FOR	10) Gov Limousine	AGN	17) Fed Campaign Subs	FOR
4) F-111	AGN	11) RR Featherbed	FOR	18) Rhod Chrome Ban	FOR
5) Death Penalty	AGN	12) Handgun License	AGN	19) Open Legis Meetings	AGN
6) Foreign Aid	AGN	13) Less Troop Abrd	FOR	20) Strikers Food Stmps	FOR
7) Filibuster	AGN	14) Resume Turk Aid	AGN	21) Gov Info Disclosure	FOR

Election Results

1970 general: Quentin Burdick (D) 134,519 (62%)
               Thomas S. Kleppe (R) 82,996 (38%)
1970 primary: Quentin Burdick (D), unopposed
1964 general: Quentin Burdick (D) 149,264 (58%)
               Thomas S. Kleppe (R) 109,681 (42%)

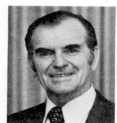

Gov. Arthur A. Link (D) Elected 1972, term expires Jan. 1977; b. May 24, 1914, McKenzie County; N.D. Agric. Col.; Lutheran.

Career Farmer; N.D. House of Reps., 1947–71, Minor. Floor Ldr., Spkr.; U.S. House of Reps., 1971–73.

Offices State Capitol Bldg., Bismarck 58505, 701-224-2200.

Election Results

1972 general:	Arthur A. Link (D)	143,899	(51%)
	Richard Larsen (R)	138,032	(49%)
1972 primary:	Arthur A. Link (D)	29,979	(93%)
	Edward P. Burns (D)	2,231	(7%)

Rep. Mark Andrews (R) Elected Oct. 22, 1963; b. May 19, 1926, Fargo; home, Mapleton; U.S. Military Acad., 1944–46, N.D. St. U., B.S. 1949; Episcopalian.

Career Farmer; Repub. nominee for Gov., 1962.

Offices 2411 RHOB, 202-225-2611. Also Fed. Bldg., Fargo 58102, 701-232-8030.

Committees

Appropriations (6th). Subcommittees: Agriculture and Related Agencies; State, Justice, Commerce, and the Judiciary.

Group Ratings

	ADA	COPE	LWV	RIPON	NFU	LCV	CFA	NAB	NSI	ACA
1974	27	55	58	27	93	53	54	50	56	47
1973	30	55	50	47	95	47	50	–	–	41
1972	6	36	36	67	71	47	50	67	88	57

Key Votes

1) Foreign Aid	AGN	6) Gov Abortn Aid	AGN	11) Pub Cong Election $	FOR
2) Busing	AGN	7) Coed Phys Ed	AGN	12) Turkish Arms Cutoff	ABS
3) ABM	FOR	8) Pov Lawyer Gag	FOR	13) Youth Camp Regs	FOR
4) B-1 Bomber	FOR	9) Pub Trans Sub	AGN	14) Strip Mine Veto	AGN
5) Nerve Gas	FOR	10) EZ Voter Regis	FOR	15) Farm Bill Veto	AGN

Election Results

1974 general:	Mark Andrews (R)	130,184	(56%)	($86,855)
	Byron L. Dorgan (D)	103,504	(44%)	($50,990)
1974 primary	Mark Andrews (R)	43,611	(78%)	
	L. L. "Pete" Naaden (R)	11,994	(22%)	
1972 general:	Mark Andrews (R)	195,368	(73%)	($58,196)
	Richard Ista (D)	72,850	(27%)	($18,935)

OHIO

Ohio is the epitome of Middle America: a land of carefully tended farms, God-fearing small towns, and sprawling industrial cities. In 1803, Ohio became the first state from the old Northwest Territory to be admitted to the Union, and within 25 years it was the fourth largest state in the nation. Its patterns of settlement were somewhat unusual. The first white people here moved up through Kentucky or down the Ohio River to the southwest corner of the state around Cincinnati. The old-stock Americans were then joined by Germans, who were fleeing the consequences of the failed European revolution of 1848. By the time of the Civil War, Cincinnati was a heavily German and pro-Union city and the fourth largest in the country. Meanwhile, the northeast corner of Ohio remained placid farmland, settled by Yankee migrants from New England and upstate New York. Not until the growth of the steel industry in the late nineteenth century did the huge industrial complexes of Cleveland, Akron, and Youngstown spring into being. By 1910, Cleveland was larger than Cincinnati and was itself the fourth largest city in the country.

In politics, Ohio has a reputation for being a profoundly Republican state, and though that is certainly an exaggeration, there is something to it. One factor which has helped the Republicans over the years is the decentralization of the state's urban population; Ohio has six metropolitan areas with more than half a million people. Consequently, no one city can provide a solid Democratic base, as Chicago has historically done in Illinois or Detroit in Michigan. Moreover, some Ohio cities—notably Cincinnati and Columbus—are themselves basically Republican. And Ohio has had a tradition of brilliant Republican politicians, like the nonideological technician Ray Bliss who served as his party's state chairman during most of the 1950s and 1960s.

But it would be more accurate to regard Ohio today as a marginal state politically—indeed, with its 25 key electoral votes, one of the prime marginal states in the country. In 1974, the Democrats scored a near sweep here, capturing a previously Republican Senate seat, and adding a U.S. House seat as well, winning all the minor statewide offices but Secretary of State, and taking solid margins in both houses of the state legislature. But their victory was not complete, for they lost the big one, the Governorship race, where incumbent John Gilligan was beaten by a mere 11,414 votes out of more than three million cast by former Governor (1963–71) James Rhodes.

It was not the result that people expected—even Rhodes went on television and conceded when he was behind in the early returns. Rhodes was 65, and if he had succeeded in keeping taxes low during his two terms, he had also provided exceedingly low levels of state services. Gilligan had raised taxes—and got the voters to approve the rise in a 1972 referendum—and had provided the kind of services most states do. Moreover, in the year of the Watergate, Rhodes steadfastly refused to reveal his sources of income or certain campaign contributions; and he has the additional shame of having presided over the National Guard and having defended its conduct in the Kent State massacre of 1970.

Gilligan, in contrast, was considered a national figure with legitimate presidential aspirations—if he won reelection by a solid margin. He had won four years before when Ohio went through a mini-Watergate of its own, with Republican officeholders and candidates implicated in a scandal involving a company called Crofters. It seems that Crofters made illegal contributions to the Republicans, and in return was given a couple of million dollars of illegal loans from the state treasury. Gilligan had been beaten for the Senate by William Saxbe in 1968; but he won with 56% of the vote in 1970, and with his programs winning basic public approval seemed on his way to reelection in 1974.

So what happened? It was probably, as Gilligan himself said, "a rejection of me personally." The Governor had a quick wit, and not always a kind one, and sometimes he even made jokes on himself which boomeranged. (At a county fair, when presented with a sheep, he said, "I don't shear sheep, I shear taxpayers.") The Rhodes campaign was aimed totally at exploiting this dislike of Gilligan, and its media was concentrated heavily in the ordinarily very Democratic Cleveland area. The returns from Cleveland's Cuyahoga County tell the story: Rhodes ran only 4,000 votes ahead of the weak 1970 Republican showing, but Gilligan received 110,000 fewer votes than he had four years before. Rhodes had banked on disenchantment among ordinary Democrats to keep them from the polls altogether, and he won, narrowly.

On election night what was happening in the Governor's race was very, very different from the results in the race for the U.S. Senate. For there the Democratic nominee, former astronaut and Columbus businessman John Glenn, was winning an overwhelming victory over Cleveland Mayor Ralph Perk. Glenn took 65% of the vote, more than twice Perk's 31% (two minor candidates split 4%); the Democrat carried every county in the state. But Perk, underfinanced, little known outside Cleveland and not particularly well liked there, was not in any sense a serious candidate; in supposedly Republican Ohio, the real battle for this originally Republican Senate seat had taken place in the Democratic primary in May. The seat had been won, by a 52–48 margin, by state Attorney General William Saxbe in 1968; and the garrulous, sometimes risque Saxbe had decided not to seek another term in 1974, more than a year before the election. Then in the wake of the Saturday night massacre, he was appointed Attorney General of the United States, less for his qualifications than because, as an incumbent Senator, he was virtually assured of Senate confirmation. Saxbe served less than a year in that post, backstopping Special Prosecutor Leon Jaworski against attacks from the Nixon White House, and then was graced with appointment as Ambassador to India.

The race for the Democratic nomination had heated up even before Saxbe announced his retirement from the Senate. The two chief contenders were the same men who had faced each other in the Senate primary four years before: Glenn and Cleveland businessman Howard Metzenbaum. In 1970, Metzenbaum had upset Glenn by pouring large amounts of his ample funds into a saturation TV advertising campaign and overtaking the complacent ex-astronaut;

and in the general election that year Metzenbaum had won 49% of the vote against Republican Robert Taft, Jr. When Saxbe resigned from the Senate, Gilligan appointed Metzenbaum to fill the vacancy, apparently on the theory that he was entitled to it by virtue of his 1970 showing; in any case, organized labor, which backed Gilligan strongly, were also in Metzenbaum's corner.

But something was different about the 1974 race—something that had not a little to do with the political atmosphere produced by Watergate. It happened that Metzenbaum had not paid $118,000 of income taxes the IRS claimed was due, and was suing for it; and that indeed he had not paid any taxes at all in some previous years. Glenn's campaign zeroed in on this, and attempted to contrast to it Glenn's full disclosure of his assets and income. The tactic apparently worked. Glenn won the primary with 54% of the vote; Metzenbaum carried only Cleveland, Cincinnati, Toledo, and two small counties, while Glenn won everything else. Although Metzenbaum might have had some trouble in the fall had he won the primary, once Glenn did the election was virtually over.

Ohio's other seat is currently held by the bearer of a proud Ohio name, Robert Taft, Jr. The son of the most prominent conservative Republican of his generation, the current Senator Taft is better described as a political moderate. While his father was anathema to organized labor, for example, Taft, Jr. is generally acceptable. One of the issues Taft has been most concerned about was amnesty, and he has pushed for a limited forgiveness beyond what President Ford has authorized. But in his single term on the minority side, he has not had any legislative accomplishments of the magnitude of the Taft-Hartley Act.

Taft's seat is up in 1976; he suffered a heart attack in 1974, and at this writing it is not clear whether he will be a candidate. The Republican Party machinery is in the hands of Governor Rhodes, who opposed and nearly beat Taft in the 1970 primary; the Senator can expect little help there. There is an assumption that a Taft is politically unbeatable in Ohio, but even the senior Taft won big only once (in 1950, when labor ran a heavy handed campaign against him that backfired), and Taft, Jr.'s own vote-winning record—a narrow defeat to Senator Stephen Young in 1964, a narrow victory in 1970—is not stellar.

In any case, there is no shortage of Democrats hungry for the seat, whether or not Taft runs. They include former Governor Gilligan, former Senator Metzenbaum, and 20th district Congressman James Stanton, Lieutenant Governor Richard Celeste, a Gilligan protege, and Attorney General William Brown. Brown, who won his office in 1970 at the age of 28 because of the familiarity of the Brown name and the Crofters problems of his opponent, might run for the Senate. But Celeste and Brown are more likely to square off for the gubernatorial nomination in 1978. Rhodes will then be 69, and it seems hard to believe that he will be the Republican candidate again—though he has in every year but one since 1958.

There was some question about Ohio's congressional district lines for 1976. After the 1974 elections, there was a week of overlap when Gilligan remained in office and the Democrats took over the legislature; the Democrats took that opportunity to remap the district lines, among other things. The outgoing Republican Lieutenant Governor, claiming that no legislation can pass without his signature (though the Ohio constitution clearly does not contemplate a lieutenant gubernatorial veto), refused to sign; and the issue is in the courts. If the Democrats' plan had prevailed, it would have had the effect of creating new, probably Democratic seats around the Dayton area (to replace the present 8th district), in central city Cincinnati and in central city Columbus (in both cases, parts of the city are now combined with parts of the suburbs to create Republican districts). But the courts ruled for the Republicans, and so the district lines will stay the same in this the only major state where Republicans have a majority (and a solid one, 15–8) in the House delegation.

Census Data Pop. 10,652,017; 5.26% of U.S. total, 6th largest; Central city, 32%; suburban, 45%. Median family income, $10,309; 13th highest; families above $15,000: 22%; families below $3,000: 8%. Median years education, 12.1.

1974 Share of Federal Tax Burden $13,819,269,000; 5.16% of U.S. total, 5th largest.

1974 Share of Federal Outlays $9,837,009,000; 3.64% of U.S. total, 7th largest. Per capita federal spending, $923.

DOD	$2,062,659,000	10th	(3.01%)	HEW	$4,170,375,000	6th	(4.49%)
AEC	$154,311,000	7th	(5.06%)	HUD	$41,836,000	7th	(4.29%)
NASA	$113,903,000	8th	(3.84%)	VA	$592,702,000	6th	(4.33%)
DOT	$257,853,000	9th	(3.05%)	EPA	$93,495,000	9th	(2.97%)
DOC	$10,272,000	23d	(0.64%)	RevS	$240,562,000	7th	(3.96%)
DOI	$24,581,000	24th	(1.00%)	Int.	$434,146,000	8th	(2.11%)
USDA	$347,841,000	11th	(2.79%)	Other	$1,292,473,000		

Economic Base Machinery, especially metalworking machinery; transportation equipment, especially motor vehicles and equipment; finance, insurance and real estate; primary metal industries, especially blast furnaces and basic steel products; fabricated metal products, especially metal stampings and fabricated structural metal products; electrical equipment and supplies, especially household appliances and electrical industrial apparatus; agriculture, especially dairy products, cattle, soybeans and corn.

Political Line-up Governor, James A. Rhodes (R). Senators, Robert Taft, Jr. (R) and John Glenn (D). Representatives, 23 (15 R and 8 D). State Senate (20 D, 12 R, and 1 vac.); State House (59 D and 40 R).

The Voters

Registration No statewide registration.
Median voting age 42.
Employment profile White collar, 45%. Blue collar, 41%. Service, 12%. Farm, 2%.
Ethnic groups Black, 9%. Total foreign stock, 12%. Germany, Italy, 2% each; Poland, UK, 1% each.

Presidential vote

1972	Nixon (R)	2,441,827	(61%)
	McGovern (D)	1,558,889	(39%)
1968	Nixon (R)	1,791,014	(45%)
	Humphrey (D)	1,700,586	(43%)
	Wallace (AI)	467,495	(12%)

1972 Democratic Presidential Primary

Humphrey	499,680	(41%)
McGovern	480,320	(40%)
Muskie	107,806	(9%)
Jackson	98,498	(8%)
McCarthy	26,026	(7%)

1972 Republican Presidential Primary

Nixon	692,828	(100%)

Sen. Robert Taft, Jr. (R) Elected 1970, seat up 1976; b. Feb. 26, 1917, Cincinnati; home, Cincinnati; Yale U., B.A. 1939, Harvard U., LL.B. 1942; Episcopalian.

Career Navy, WWII; Practicing atty., 1946–63, 1965–66; Ohio House of Reps., 1955–62, Maj. Floor Ldr., 1961–62; U.S. House of Reps., 1963–64, 1967–70; Repub. nominee for U.S. Senate, 1964.

Offices 405 RSOB, 202-224-2315. Also 754 U.S.P.O. and Court House, Cincinnati 45202, 513-684-3284, and 523 U.S. Customs and Court House, Cleveland 44114, 216-522-4850.

Committees

Armed Services (5th). Subcommittees: Arms Control; National Stockpile and Naval Petroleum Reserves; Preparedness Investigating; Research and Development.

Labor and Public Welfare (3d). Subcommittees: Aging; Children and Youth; Education; Employment, Poverty, and Migratory Labor; The Handicapped; Health; Labor; Railroad Retirement; Special Subcommittee on Arts and Humanities; Special Subcommittee on Human Resources.

Joint Economic Committee (3d, Senate Side). Subcommittees: Fiscal Policy; Inter-American Economic Relationships; International Economics; Priorities and Economy in Government.

Group Ratings

	ADA	COPE	LWV	RIPON	NFU	LCV	CFA	NAB	NSI	ACA
1974	38	64	100	87	47	57	22	80	67	42
1973	31	38	80	100	15	–	13	–	–	60
1972	25	20	70	86	33	26	33	78	100	70

Key Votes

1) No-Knock	AGN	8) Gov Abortn Aid	ABS	15) Consumer Prot Agy	AGN
2) Busing	FOR	9) Cut Mil Brass	ABS	16) Forced Psych Tests	AGN
3) No Fault	FOR	10) Gov Limousine	ABS	17) Fed Campaign Subs	AGN
4) F-111	ABS	11) RR Featherbed	AGN	18) Rhod Chrome Ban	AGN
5) Death Penalty	FOR	12) Handgun License	AGN	19) Open Legis Meetings	FOR
6) Foreign Aid	FOR	13) Less Troop Abrd	AGN	20) Strikers Food Stmps	FOR
7) Filibuster	AGN	14) Resume Turk Aid	FOR	21) Gov Info Disclosure	FOR

Election Results

1970 general:	Robert Taft, Jr. (R)	1,565,682	(51%)
	Howard M. Metzenbaum (D)	1,495,262	(49%)
1970 primary:	Robert Taft, Jr. (R)	472,202	(50%)
	James A. Rhodes (R)	466,932	(50%)

Sen. John Glenn (D) Elected 1974, seat up 1980; b. July 18, 1921, Cambridge; home, Columbus; Muskingum Col., B.S. 1939; Presbyterian.

Career USMC, 1942–65; NASA Astronaut, 1959–65, First American to orbit the Earth, 1962; Candidate for Dem. nomination for U.S. Senate, 1964, 1970; V.P., Royal Crown Cola Co., 1966–68, Pres., Royal Crown Internatl., 1967–69.

Offices 204 RSOB, 202-224-3353. Also 85 Marconi St., Columbus 43215, 614-469-6697.

Committees

The District of Columbia (4th).

Government Operations (9th). Subcommittees: Federal Spending Practices, Efficiency and Open Government; Reports, Accounting and Management. Permanent Subcommittee on Investigations.

Interior and Insular Affairs (7th). Subcommittees: Energy Research and Water Resources; Environment and Land Resources; Minerals, Materials and Fuels; Special Subcommittee on Integrated Oil Operations.

Group Ratings: Newly Elected

Key Votes

1) No-Knock	NE	8) Gov Abortn Aid	FOR	15) Consumer Prot Agy	NE
2) Busing	NE	9) Cut Mil Brass	NE	16) Forced Psych Tests	NE
3) No Fault	NE	10) Gov Limousine	NE	17) Fed Campaign Subs	NE
4) F-111	AGN	11) RR Featherbed	NE	18) Rhod Chrome Ban	NE
5) Death Penalty	NE	12) Handgun License	NE	19) Open Legis Meetings	NE
6) Foreign Aid	NE	13) Less Troop Abrd	NE	20) Strikers Food Stmps	NE
7) Filibuster	AGN	14) Resume Turk Aid	AGN	21) Gov Info Disclosure	NE

Election Results

1974 general:	John H. Glenn, Jr. (D)	1,930,670	(65%)	($1,149,130)
	Ralph J. Perk (R)	918,133	(31%)	($292,838)
	K. G. Harroff (Ind.)	76,882	(3%)	($7,978)
	Richard B. Kay (Ind.)	61,921	(2%)	($3,944)
1974 primary:	John H. Glenn, Jr. (D)	571,871	(54%)	
	Howard M. Metzenbaum (D)	480,123	(46%)	

Gov. James A. Rhodes (R) Elected 1974, term expires Jan. 1979; b. Sept. 13, 1909, Coalton; Ohio St. U.

Career Mayor of Columbus, 1943–53; Ohio St. Auditor, 1953–63; Gov. of Ohio, 1963–70; Writer and novelist; Chm., Natl. Council for Vocational Educ.

Offices Columbus 43215, 614-466-3526.

Election Results

1974 general:	James A. Rhodes (R)	1,493,679	(49%)
	John J. Gilligan (D)	1,482,191	(48%)
	Nancy Brown Lazar (Ind.)	95,625	(3%)
1974 primary:	James A. Rhodes (R)	385,669	(63%)
	Charles Fry (R)	183,899	(30%)
	Bert Dawson (R)	44,938	(7%)

◆ ◆ ◆ ◆ ◆

FIRST DISTRICT

The 1st district of Ohio is the eastern half of Cincinnati and suburban Hamilton County. This is, by and large, the more prosperous half of the old river city, which was the cultural and commercial capital of the Midwest even before the Tafts arrived. In some neighborhoods within Cincinnati and in the hills beyond the city limits are the fashionable estates of the city's elite. Probably the most prestigious is the suburb of Indian Hill, home of Senator Robert Taft, Jr. To the north, one finds a mix of shopping centers and high-income suburban terrain. Within the city itself are the formerly Jewish sections of Avondale and Walnut Hills, now predominantly black. Many neighborhoods, like Norwood, a suburban enclave surrounded by Cincinnati, are inhabited mainly by migrants from the hills of Kentucky and Tennessee. The 1st also has most of the city's Jewish population; from its early days as a heavily German river town, Cincinnati has had an important German Jewish community. Politically, it is more conservative and Republican than Jewish communities in other major cities. Over the years, many prominent Cincinnati Jews have supported the Tafts.

Cincinnati has a well-deserved reputation for being a Republican city. Of the nation's 25 largest metropolitan areas, only Dallas and San Diego turn in Republican margins with greater regularity. Such has been the case since before the Civil War, when Cincinnati was a German, pro-Union, and Republican island surrounded by a sea of Southern Democratic sentiment. Moreover, Cincinnati has never attracted large numbers of those ethnic groups which have traditionally voted for Democratic politicians. There are fewer blacks here than in Cleveland, Detroit, or Buffalo, and very few people of Eastern or Southern European origin. And many of the city's Appalachians come from solidly Republican mountain counties, bringing both their politics and religion to the big Ohio city.

Out of Cincinnati have come several prominent Republicans, including Chief Justice Salmon P. Chase, President and Chief Justice William Howard Taft, Speaker of the House Nicholas Longworth (whose nonagenatian widow, the former Alice Roosevelt, still reigns as one of Washington's social elite), and of course the late Senator Robert Taft. In more recent years the 1st district has produced a succession of congressmen of both parties who for one reason or another have achieved some national prominence. The string started in 1964, when John Gilligan, then a college professor and later Governor of Ohio, was elected Congressman in an upset; he was beaten here two years later by Robert Taft, Jr., later U. S. Senator. When Taft moved up to the Senate, he was succeeded by William Keating, a Republican whose Cincinnati lawyer brother is a national crusader against pornography, and who in 1974 succeeded Francis L. Dale, the original head of the Committee to Reelect the President, as president of Cincinnati *Enquirer*.

Keating is not particularly famous nationally—but he would have been if he had stayed in Congress, for he was a member of the House Judiciary Committee, and would have been forced to vote on the impeachment of Richard Nixon. (His place on the Committee was taken by the 5th district's Delbert Latta.)

Keating's resignation provided some guidance, however, for Judiciary Committee members who remained on, for it necessitated a special election—one of that series which showed the vast unpopularity of Richard Nixon. The contenders were two members of the Cincinnati Council: Democrat Thomas Luken and Republican Willis Gradison. And though there was some disagreement on other issues—Luken was against legalized abortion, Gradison wasn't—the main issue was Nixon, and Luken predictably won. As it turned out, this was the only special election whose result was overturned in November: then Gradison, better financed and a more savvy campaigner, won with 51% of the vote. That was still not an overwhelming endorsement, considering the Republican heritage of the district, but with the advantages of incumbency it seems likely enough that Gradison will be able to win in the future.

Census Data Pop. 462,725. Central city, 48%; suburban, 52%. Median family income, $10,535; families above $15,000: 26%; families below $3,000: 8%. Median years education, 12.1.

The Voters

Median voting age 43.
Employment profile White collar, 53%. Blue collar, 33%. Service, 14%. Farm, –%.
Ethnic groups Black, 20%. Total foreign stock, 9%. Germany, 2%.

Presidential vote

1972	Nixon (R)	111,925	(66%)
	McGovern (D)	57,516	(34%)
1968	Nixon (R)	88,124	(49%)
	Humphrey (D)	71,824	(40%)
	Wallace (AI)	20,838	(12%)

Rep. Willis D. Gradison, Jr. (R) Elected 1974; b. Dec. 28, 1928, Cincinnati; home, Cincinnati; Yale U., B.A. 1948, Harvard U., M.B.A. 1951, D.C.S. 1954.

Career Investment broker; Asst. to U.S. Under Secy. of the Treasury, 1953–55; Asst. to U.S. Secy. of HEW, 1955–57; Cincinnati City Cncl., 1961–74, Vice Mayor, 1967–71, Mayor, 1971.

Offices 1331 LHOB, 202-225-3164. Also 9407 Fed. Ofc. Bldg., 550 Main St., Cincinnati 45202, 513-684-2456.

Committees

Banking, Currency and Housing (10th). Subcommittees: Domestic Monetary Policy; Economic Stabilization; Financial Institutions Supervision, Regulation and Insurance.

Government Operations (14th). Subcommittees: Commerce, Consumer and Monetary Affairs; Government Activities and Transportation.

Group Ratings: Newly Elected

Key Votes

1) Foreign Aid	FOR	6) Gov Abortn Aid	NE	11) Pub Cong Election $	NE
2) Busing	NE	7) Coed Phys Ed	AGN	12) Turkish Arms Cutoff	NE
3) ABM	NE	8) Pov Lawyer Gag	NE	13) Youth Camp Regs	AGN
4) B-1 Bomber	FOR	9) Pub Trans Sub	NE	14) Strip Mine Veto	FOR
5) Nerve Gas	NE	10) EZ Voter Regis	NE	15) Farm Bill Veto	FOR

Election Results

1974 general	Willis D. Gradison, Jr. (R)	70,284	(51%)	($126,407)
	Thomas A. Luken (D)	67,685	(49%)	($79,500)
1974 primary:	Willis D. Gradison, Jr. (R)	16,437	(52%)	
	Willia, E. Flax (R)	14,148	(45%)	
	William H. McKinney (R)	849	(3%)	

◆ ◆ ◆ ◆ ◆

SECOND DISTRICT

The 2d congressional district of Ohio is the western half of Cincinnati and Hamilton County. On the whole, this is the less fashionable half of Cincinnati, though the 2d does have plenty of comfortable neighborhoods, mostly in the suburbs. For the most part, the district consists of middle and lower middle class neighborhoods spread out over Cincinnati's hills. The 2d also includes some of the older and poorer sections of the city, like the Appalacian Over the Rhine area (a name that recalls Cincinnati's German heritage). At the eastern end of the district winds Mill Creek, and next to it lies Cincinnati's industrial corridor. Here are the great Procter and Gamble soap factories and many of the city's machine tool makers; Cincinnati is a leader in both industries. Here also is the General Electric plant that was once ready to produce the engine for the Boeing's SST.

Like the 1st, the 2d overall is heavily Republican. In the case of both districts, the suburbs, not the population-losing city of Cincinnati, supply the lion's share of the Republican margin. The line between the districts splits the city's Democratic votes, but that line has now been redrawn by the new Democratic legislature in a plan currently under challenge in court. If it is upheld it would probably have the effect of creating a Democratic 1st district in the city and an extremely heavily Republican 2d consisting of most of the suburbs.

That would probably be to the liking of 2d district Congressman Donald Clancy. A former Cincinnati Councilman who was first elected to the House in 1960, Clancy is a conservative Republican who in most elections has not had much difficulty. But in years when the Republican Party has been hurt by scandals—by the Crofters affair in Ohio in 1970 or the Watergate nationally in 1974—Clancy has had problems; he was held to 56% of the vote in 1970 and 53% in 1974.

Clancy sat on the House Armed Services Committee until 1972, when he moved to Ways and Means, on which he is now the fourth ranking Republican. His past performances indicate he is not quite as safe as most Republicans with such posts, but he probably will have an easier time in 1976, whatever redistricting does to him.

Census Data Pop. 463,260. Central city, 49%; suburban, 51%. Median family income, $10,439; families above $15,000: 23%; families below $3,000: 8%. Median years education, 11.9.

The Voters

Median voting age 43.
Employment profile White collar, 53%. Blue collar, 34%. Service, 13%. Farm, –%.
Ethnic groups Black, 11%. Total foreign stock, 9%. Germany, 3%.

Presidential vote

1972	Nixon (R)	127,655	(67%)
	McGovern (D)	61,676	(33%)
1968	Nixon (R)	96,018	(52%)
	Humphrey (D)	63,535	(34%)
	Wallace (AI)	26,140	(14%)

Rep. Donald D. Clancy (R) Elected 1960; b. July 24, 1921, Cincinnati; home, Cincinnati; Xavier U., 1939–43, U. of Cinn., LL.B. 1948; Presbyterian.

Career Armed Forces, WWII; Practicing atty., 1948–60; Cincinnati City Cncl., 1951–57, Mayor, 1957–60.

Offices 2313 RHOB, 202-225-2216. Also 430 U.S.P.O. and Court House, Cincinnati 45202, 513-684-3738.

Committees

Ways and Means (4th). Subcommittees: Health; Oversight.

Group Ratings

	ADA	COPE	LWV	RIPON	NFU	LCV	CFA	NAB	NSI	ACA
1974	5	0	18	23	23	20	15	82	100	100
1973	0	9	17	40	15	6	13	–	–	96
1972	0	30	36	77	0	8	0	90	100	95

Key Votes

1) Foreign Aid	AGN	6) Gov Abortn Aid	AGN	11) Pub Cong Election $	AGN
2) Busing	AGN	7) Coed Phys Ed	AGN	12) Turkish Arms Cutoff	ABS
3) ABM	FOR	8) Pov Lawyer Gag	FOR	13) Youth Camp Regs	AGN
4) B-1 Bomber	FOR	9) Pub Trans Sub	AGN	14) Strip Mine Veto	ABS
5) Nerve Gas	FOR	10) EZ Voter Regis	AGN	15) Farm Bill Veto	FOR

Election Results

1974 general:	Donald D. Clancy (R)	71,512	(53%)	($33,369)
	Edward W. Wolterman (D)	62,530	(47%)	($13,089)
1974 primary:	Donald D. Clancy (R), unopposed			
1972 general:	Donald D. Clancy (R)	109,961	(63%)	($27,034)
	Penny Manes (D)	65,237	(37%)	($8,859)

◆ ◆ ◆ ◆ ◆

THIRD DISTRICT

In many ways Dayton, Ohio, is the typical American city. It sits on the old National Road that spans the middle of the Midwest; it is middle sized (metropolitan area pop. 850,000) and predominantly middle class. It has given birth to such American phenomena as the Wright brothers and the Phil Donahue Show. Like most central cities, Dayton itself is losing population; it is now about 30% black and even has a black Mayor. As in most metropolitan areas, the most substantial growth here lately has been in the suburbs, like middle class Kettering just south of the city. Dayton—or one of its suburbs—is the home of Richard Scammon and Ben Wattenberg's typical American voter: a housewife whose husband works in a factory and whose brother-in-law is a policeman. Usually a Democrat, she was, according to *The Real Majority*, worried about crime and inclined toward the law 'n' order politics of Richard Nixon.

That inclination turned out to be shorter lived than readers of Scammon and Wattenberg might have expected. Montgomery County, which includes Dayton, may have given Nixon 60% of its vote in 1972, but within two years it was voting 62–38 to reelect Democratic Governor John Gilligan. The *Real Majority* personification, nonetheless, is a reasonably accurate portrayal of the politics of the Dayton area, and of the major portion of it—all of Dayton and most of Montgomery County—which makes up Ohio's 3d congressional district.

Ohio Republicans have traditionally selected candidates suited to their various constituencies, and so after the 3d was won by a Democrat in 1964, they picked a comparatively liberal state Senator to run in 1966. That was Charles Whalen, and he won that year with 52% of the vote, and ever since has been the 3d's Congressman. Whalen's liberal record has attracted the support of many ordinarily Democratic voters. In the House, he labored for several years as the only dovish Republican on the Armed Services Committee; he was chief co-sponsor of the Nedzi-Whalen Act, the unsuccessful House vehicle for end-the-war legislation. In 1973, apparently unhappy with Armed Services, he transferred quietly to the International Relations Committee, on which he still is a fairly low ranking Republican. Whalen has had no difficulty winning reelection; in 1972 he had 76% of the vote, and in 1974 he was the only House Republican in the nation to run unopposed.

Census Data   Pop. 463,140. Central city, 53%; suburban, 47%. Median family income, $11,481; families above $15,000: 29%; families below $3,000: 7%. Median years education, 12.2.

The Voters

Median voting age 41.
Employment profile White collar, 51%. Blue collar, 37%. Service, 12%. Farm, –%.
Ethnic groups Black, 16%. Total foreign stock, 7%. Germany, 2%.

Presidential vote

1972	Nixon (R)	88,701	(58%)
	McGovern (D)	63,890	(42%)
1968	Nixon (R)	64,092	(40%)
	Humphrey (D)	76,285	(48%)
	Wallace (AI)	17,984	(11%)

Rep. Charles W. Whalen, Jr. (R) Elected 1966; b. July 31, 1920, Dayton; home, Dayton; U. of Dayton, B.S., 1942, Harvard U., M.B.A. 1946; Catholic.

Career Army, WWII; V.P., Dayton Dress Co., 1946–52; Ohio House of Reps., 1955–60; Ohio Senate, 1961–66; Prof. of Economics, U. of Dayton, 1962–66.

Offices 1035 LHOB, 202-225-6465. Also 315 Old P.O. Bldg., 118 W. 3rd St., Dayton 45402, 513-461-4830.

Committees

District of Columbia (7th). Subcommittees: Fiscal Affairs; Government Operations.

International Relations (7th). Subcommittees: International Economic Policy; International Trade and Commerce.

Group Ratings

	ADA	COPE	LWV	RIPON	NFU	LCV	CFA	NAB	NSI	ACA
1974	91	100	100	94	92	88	92	27	0	14
1973	84	100	100	100	60	95	88	–	–	11
1972	94	100	100	87	100	87	50	25	0	4

Key Votes

1) Foreign Aid	FOR	6) Gov Abortn Aid	AGN	11) Pub Cong Election $	FOR
2) Busing	FOR	7) Coed Phys Ed	FOR	12) Turkish Arms Cutoff	FOR
3) ABM	AGN	8) Pov Lawyer Gag	AGN	13) Youth Camp Regs	FOR
4) B-1 Bomber	AGN	9) Pub Trans Sub	FOR	14) Strip Mine Veto	AGN
5) Nerve Gas	AGN	10) EZ Voter Regis	FOR	15) Farm Bill Veto	FOR

Election Results

1974 general:	Charles W. Whalen, Jr. (R), unopposed .			($2,545)
1974 primary:	Charles W. Whalen, Jr. (R), unopposed			
1972 general:	Charles W. Whalen, Jr. (R)	111,253	(76%)	($17,973)
	John W. Lelak, Jr. (D)	34,819	(24%)	($3,930)

♦ ♦ ♦ ♦ ♦

FOURTH DISTRICT

The 4th congressional district of Ohio is a group of counties, mostly rural but usually with small cities, in the western part of the state. This is a deeply conservative part of the nation, a sort of Grant Woodish enclave set in industrial Middle America. It is somehow fitting that the town of Wapakoneta here in the 4th produced the first man to walk on the moon—the strait-laced and taciturn Neil Armstrong. The conservatism of the 4th runs so deep that it is often the most Republican district in Ohio, as it was in the 1972 presidential election. The district's urban centers, to the extent they can be called that, are as heavily Republican as the countryside, in some cases more so. Findlay (pop. 35,000) is an old Republican town, made newly prosperous as the headquarters of Marathon Oil. Allen County, which contains the district's largest city, Lima (pop. 53,000), was the largest county east of Chicago and north of Richmond, Virginia, to support the candidacy of Barry Goldwater in 1964. Then there are smaller Republican towns like Bucyrus, Piqua, and Upper Sandusky (which is nowhere near Sandusky).

For 25 years, Republican William McCulloch represented the 4th district. When he retired in 1972, McCulloch was dean of the Ohio delegation and the ranking Republican on the House Judiciary Committee, which has jurisdiction over civil rights legislation. Because McCulloch usually voted with other Midwestern conservatives, many of whom were leary about civil rights bills, but who trusted him, the Ohioan was able to swing many votes in favor of the Civil Rights Act of 1964. McCulloch was also a major backer of subsequent civil rights legislation, served on the Kerner Commission on Civil Disorders, and the presidential commission on violence chaired by Milton Eisenhower.

By 1972 McCulloch was 71 and seriously ill, and decided, after some hesitation, to retire. As it happened, his district had been combined with that of Jackson Betts, second-ranking Republican on Ways and Means, who at 68 decided to retire too. But there was no dogfight for the seat, as there surely would have been if this was Democratic territory; Republicans, at least Ohio Republicans, do not do things that way. The nominee and next Congressman was state Senator Tennyson Guyer, a former minister and public relations man for a tire company. Guyer is a deep-dyed conservative, apparently without the special interst in civil rights which animated Republicans from Charles Sumner and Thaddeus Stevens to William McCulloch. He quickly became a hawkish vote on the International Relations Committee and a member, until it was abolished in 1975, of the Internal Security Committee. Guyer was reelected easily with 62% of the vote in 1974; and he appears likely to win in the future.

Census Data Pop. 463,143. Central city, 12%; suburban, 31%. Median family income, $9,710; families above $15,000: 17%; families below $3,000: 8%. Median years education, 12.1.

The Voters

Median voting age 43.
Employment profile White collar, 38%. Blue collar, 46%. Service, 12%. Farm, 4%.
Ethnic groups Black, 3%. Total foreign stock, 4%. Germany, 1%.

Presidential vote

1972	Nixon (R)	120,089	(71%)
	McGovern (D)	49,780	(29%)
1968	Nixon (R)	99,879	(55%)
	Humphrey (D)	62,741	(35%)
	Wallace (AI)	18,848	(10%)

Rep. Tennyson Guyer (R) Elected 1972; b. Nov. 29, 1913, Findlay; home, Findlay; Findlay Col., B.S. 1934; Church of God.

Career Pastor, Celina Church of God; Mayor of Celina and Pres. of City Cncl., 1940–44; Dir. of Public Affairs, Cooper Tire & Rubber Co., 1950–72; Mbr., Exec. Comm., Ohio Repub. St. Comm., 1954–66; Ohio Senate, 1959–72.

Offices 114 CHOB, 202-225-2676. Also 658 W. Market St., Lima 45801, 419-223-0903.

Committees

International Relations (11th). Subcommittees: Future Foreign Policy Research and Development.

Veterans' Affairs (7th). Subcommittees: Cemeteries and Burial Benefits; Hospitals.

Group Ratings

	ADA	COPE	LWV	RIPON	NFU	LCV	CFA	NAB	NSI	ACA
1974	13	9	45	25	54	25	23	75	90	64
1973	13	10	42	62	53	21	50	–	–	72

Key Votes

1) Foreign Aid	FOR	6) Gov Abortn Aid	AGN	11) Pub Cong Election $	AGN
2) Busing	AGN	7) Coed Phys Ed	AGN	12) Turkish Arms Cutoff	AGN
3) ABM	FOR	8) Pov Lawyer Gag	FOR	13) Youth Camp Regs	AGN
4) B-1 Bomber	FOR	9) Pub Trans Sub	AGN	14) Strip Mine Veto	FOR
5) Nerve Gas	AGN	10) EZ Voter Regis	AGN	15) Farm Bill Veto	FOR

Election Results

1974 general:	Tennyson Guyer (R)	81,674	(62%)	($26,471)
	James L. Gehrlich (D)	51,065	(38%)	($8,704)
1974 primary:	Tennyson Guyer (R), unopposed			
1972 general:	Tennyson Guyer (R)	109,612	(63%)	($40,014)
	Dimitri Nicholas (D)	65,216	(37%)	($38,412)

◆ ◆ ◆ ◆

FIFTH DISTRICT

Some 150 years ago, New England Yankee farmers settled the flatlands in the northwest corner of Ohio; they were joined within a few years, by hardy German Protestants. The land here is more fertile and easier to work than the knobby hills of southern Ohio; its flatness and fertility must have amazed the early settlers. It is the beginning of the great corn and hog belt that stretches into Illinois and Iowa, and it is also one of the heartland areas of the Republican Party since it was founded in the 1850s.

Unlike so much of rural America, northwest Ohio has not been in economic or population decline. The fertility of its soil, the industry of its farmers, and, most important, its strategic location account for this happy state of affairs. For this area finds itself encircled by the giant industrial cities of the Midwest, and also lies on both sides of the nation's major east-west rail lines and Interstate highways. To take advantage of the proximity of markets and easy access to them, small factories have sprung up in the towns and countryside of northwest Ohio. These have provided marginal farmers with part-time employment, allowing them to remain on the land and still make a decent living.

The 5th congressional district covers most of northwest Ohio. Not included here is the city of Toledo and some of its suburbs which are in the 9th district. The 5th, as one might expect, is a solid Republican district which since 1958, has elected and reelected Congressman Delbert Latta. (The name, incidentally, is Welsh, not Italian.) Latta is one of those Congressmen who labored for years without public notice. As a member of the Rules Committee, he was often part, or even architect, of the coalition of conservative Republicans and Southern Democrats who would kill liberal legislation by refusing to schedule it for debate. Always a fierce partisan, Latta could be trusted to do the bidding of the Republican leadership; and in the leadership's councils he was always an advocate of hard line opposition to the schemes of the Democrats.

It was that well earned reputation which got Latta his seat on the Judiciary Committee in 1974, in time for the impeachment hearings. Congressman William Keating of the 1st district, a member of the Judiciary Committee, resigned at the beginning of the year and thus created a vacancy on the Republican side. The leadership, fearful that no one on the Committee would provide a spirited, no-holds-barred defense of Richard Nixon, tapped Latta. (This was before Charles Wiggins announced he was on Nixon's side.) Latta kept his seat on Rules, and was expected to (and did) stay on Judiciary only for the impeachment issue; although he was technically the junior member of the Committee, he was indeed the Administration's point man.

Although not indulging in quite the sarcasm of New Jersey's Charles Sandman, Latta did prove himself the master of the cheap shot. He returned again and again to how much the Judiciary hearings were costing, and he pilloried counsel Albert Jenner, himself a Republican but favoring impeachment, for having been a member of a committee which recommended the decriminalization of prostitution. But Latta's invoking of the causes of economy and prudery did not bring forth the kind of public support he may have remembered from his early days in politics in the 1950s. And overall his performance did far less to convince people of the correctness of his position than did those of Wiggins or even Indiana's David Dennis. That did not mean, however, that Latta faced substantial opposition at home. On the contrary, although Democrats like John Gilligan ran well in northwest Ohio, Latta had no problem winning with 63% of the vote; of all the Committee's anti-impeachment Republicans, only Mississippi's Trent Lott ran better in 1974.

Census Data Pop. 463,727. Central city, 0%; suburban, 37%. Median family income, $9,945; families above $15,000: 18%; families below $3,000: 8%. Median years education, 12.1.

The Voters

Median voting age 42.
Employment profile White collar, 37%. Blue collar, 46%. Service, 12%. Farm, 5%.
Ethnic groups Total foreign stock, 7%. Germany, 2%.

Presidential vote

1972	Nixon (R)	118,678	(66%)
	McGovern (D)	62,332	(34%)
1968	Nixon (R)	96,579	(55%)
	Humphrey (D)	61,852	(35%)
	Wallace (AI)	16,031	(9%)

Rep. Delbert L. Latta (R) Elected 1958; b. Mar. 5, 1920, Weston; home, Bowling Green; Ohio Northern U., A.B., LL.B.; Church of Christ.

Career Practicing atty.; Ohio Senate.

Offices 2309 RHOB, 202-225-4605. Also 305 Wood Co. Bank Bldg., Bowling Green 43402, 419-353-8871.

Committees

Budget (Ranking Member).

Ways and Means (5th). Subcommittees: Public Assistance; Trade.

Group Ratings

	ADA	COPE	LWV	RIPON	NFU	LCV	CFA	NAB	NSI	ACA
1974	10	0	25	21	50	18	23	67	100	86
1973	0	9	17	53	55	11	38	–	–	85
1972	0	0	42	60	43	27	100	92	100	91

Key Votes

1) Foreign Aid	AGN	6) Gov Abortn Aid	AGN	11) Pub Cong Election $	AGN
2) Busing	AGN	7) Coed Phys Ed	AGN	12) Turkish Arms Cutoff	AGN
3) ABM	FOR	8) Pov Lawyer Gag	FOR	13) Youth Camp Regs	AGN
4) B-1 Bomber	FOR	9) Pub Trans Sub	AGN	14) Strip Mine Veto	FOR
5) Nerve Gas	AGN	10) EZ Voter Regis	AGN	15) Farm Bill Veto	AGN

Election Results

1974 general:	Delbert L. Latta (R)	89,161	(63%)	($26,183)
	Bruce Edwards (D)	53,391	(37%)	($7,790)
1974 primary:	Delbert L. Latta (R), unopposed			
1972 general:	Delbert L. Latta (R)	132,032	(73%)	($24,016)
	Bruce Edwards (D)	49,465	(27%)	($3,645)

◆ ◆ ◆ ◆ ◆

SIXTH DISTRICT

The 6th district of Ohio is a rural district in the southern part of the state. Though the 6th touches the metropolitan areas of Cincinnati to the east and Columbus to the north, little in the 6th partakes of anything metropolitan. From the outer edges of urban Cincinnati and Columbus to the decaying industrial city of Portsmouth on the Ohio River, the district has a Southern-accented, small-town feeling. The rolling hill country of the valley of the Scioto River, which runs through Columbus, Chillicothe, and Portsmouth, was once Democratic terrain, reflecting the Southern origin of the valley's earliest settlers. Lately, like much of the South, this region of Ohio has become more conservative and far less Democratic; only tiny Pike County here delivers Democratic majorities with any reliability in statewide races. In the western part of the district, some Cincinnati exurban growth spilling into Clermont County, has contributed to the Republican trend in the 6th.

Until the late 1950s, the district, as a matter of tradition, sent a Democrat to the House. After the incumbent's death in 1959, the Republican organization of Ray Bliss carefully selected the party nominee, William Harsha, who won in 1960 and who has won reelection easily ever since. The former Scioto County (Portsmouth) prosecutor is a reliably conservative member of the reliably conservative Ohio Republican delegation.

During the last few Congresses, Harsha has been serving as the ranking minority member of the House Public Works Committee. Traditionally, the Committee has run a pork barrel operation, conferring federal projects and dollars upon the districts of deserving Congressmen. But in the last few years, Public Works has assumed a new importance—the place where the fate of much legislation concerning the environment is determined. Air and water pollution bills, for example, usually lie within the jurisdiction of Public Works.

In the 93d Congress, the most important piece of Public Works legislation affecting the environment was the highway bill. The big question was whether the highway trust fund, one financed by gasoline taxes, could be used on mass transit projects. It was a classic battle between the highwaymen and the trustbusters (as each side called the other), between basically rural interests and those of the big cities. Harsha stood solidly on the side of the highway boosters, and together with then House Minority Leader Gerald Ford rallied most House Republicans to his side—although the Nixon Administration took the opposite position. As it happened, some diversion was ultimately allowed, and there are moves afoot now to deflect a much larger share of the gas tax money away from interstate highways and toward other projects. Harsha, providing he doesn't decide to retire, can be counted on to resolutely oppose them. If he does retire, the Democratic Speaker of the Ohio House, Vernal Riffe, can be expected to give the Republican candidate a good run for his money.

Census Data Pop. 463,067. Central city, 0%; suburban, 37%. Median family income, $8,595; families above $15,000: 13%; families below $3,000: 13%. Median years education, 11.2.

The Voters

Median voting age 43.
Employment profile White collar, 37%. Blue collar, 46%. Service, 12%. Farm, 5%.
Ethnic groups Black, 2%. Total foreign stock, 2%.

Presidential vote

1972	Nixon (R)	118,484	(70%)
	McGovern (D)	49,892	(30%)
1968	Nixon (R)	86,824	(49%)
	Humphrey (D)	56,809	(32%)
	Wallace (AI)	32,180	(18%)

Rep. William H. Harsha (R) Elected 1960; b. Jan. 1, 1921, Portsmouth; home, Portsmouth; Kenyon Col., A.B. 1943, Western Reserve U., LL.B. 1947; Presbyterian.

Career USMC, WWII; Practicing atty., 1947–61; Portsmouth Asst. City Solicitor, 1947–51; Scioto Co. Prosecutor, 1951–55.

Offices 2457 RHOB, 202-225-5705. Also 285 Main St., Batavia 45103, 513-732-2247.

Committees

Public Works and Transportation (Ranking Member). Subcommittees: Transportation.

District of Columbia (2d). Subcommittees: Commerce, Housing and Transportation.

Group Ratings

	ADA	COPE	LWV	RIPON	NFU	LCV	CFA	NAB	NSI	ACA
1974	18	10	58	31	54	29	39	91	88	77
1973	17	0	33	57	63	37	38	–	–	71
1972	0	18	45	57	71	32	0	73	100	81

Key Votes

1) Foreign Aid	AGN	6) Gov Abortn Aid	AGN	11) Pub Cong Election $	FOR
2) Busing	AGN	7) Coed Phys Ed	AGN	12) Turkish Arms Cutoff	ABS
3) ABM	FOR	8) Pov Lawyer Gag	FOR	13) Youth Camp Regs	AGN
4) B-1 Bomber	FOR	9) Pub Trans Sub	AGN	14) Strip Mine Veto	FOR
5) Nerve Gas	FOR	10) EZ Voter Regis	ABS	15) Farm Bill Veto	FOR

Election Results

1974 general:	William H. Harsha (R)	93,400	(69%)	($14,306)
	Lloyd Allen Wood (D)	42,316	(31%)	($9,085)
1974 primary:	William H. Harsha (R), unopposed			
1972 general:	William H. Harsha (R), unopposed			($1,665)

◆ ◆ ◆ ◆ ◆

SEVENTH DISTRICT

Bellefontaine, Ohio, is the site of the first concrete street in the United States. And despite all the gouges and smotherings that concrete has wreaked upon the American landscape in the last 70 years, the first concrete street in Bellefontaine still lies there, with the old courthouse looming up on one side and a row of stores on the other. Bellefontaine is part of Ohio's 7th congressional district, most of which has enjoyed a similarly stable existence. It is true that the suburbs of Dayton have begun to encroach on the southwest corner of the district, where Wright-Patterson Air Force Base is located. But the industrial city of Springfield (pop. 81,000), the district's largest urban concentration, has grown little in the last 50 years. Neither has the city of Marion (pop. 39,000), where young Socialist-to-be Norman Thomas delivered newspapers edited by President-to-be Warren G. Harding.

From 1938 to 1965, the 7th was represented by Clarence J. Brown, a Republican newspaper editor. He was a man who himself seemed out of the era of Harding or McKinley. At the time of his death, Brown was the senior Republican on the House Rules Committee, where he often joined Chairman Howard Smith of Virginia to kill or postpone liberal legislation that they both heartily disdained. (But, in line with Republican tradition, Brown was always a strong backer of civil rights.) In a 1965 special election, the Congressman's son, Clarence J. (Bud) Brown, was chosen to succeed him. The younger Brown, however, did not become a member of Rules. Rather, he is now a high-ranking member of the Commerce and Government Operations Committees. His father would probably have disapproved of Brown's votes on a few issues. But for the most part he is a good soldier in the well disciplined bloc led, till 1973, by Gerald Ford and, since then, by Arizona's John Rhodes.

Brown has been considered for promotion several times, but never made it. In 1973, after the White House dumped California's Bob Wilson as Chairman of the Republican Congressional Campaign Committee, Brown sought the job. Unfortunately, word got out that he was the White House choice for the position which—because of Richard Nixon's fast declining popularity —effectively killed his candidacy. Robert Michel of Illinois won the post instead, and two years later moved up to the position of Minority Whip. Brown has also been mentioned as a possible candidate for statewide office in Ohio. But he declined to run for the Senate in 1974—though he could have had the nomination for the asking—and seems unlikely to run for it in 1976. Like many sons who inherit their father's political positions, he seems to lack that dollop of ambition that has made such a great difference and not always for the better, in so many political careers. Like his district, he seems content to let things be.

Census Data Pop. 463,217. Central city, 18%; suburban, 52%. Median family income, $10,132; families above $15,000: 20%; families below $3,000: 7%. Median years education, 12.1.

The Voters

Median voting age 41.
Employment profile White collar, 44%. Blue collar, 42%. Service, 11%. Farm, 3%.
Ethnic groups Black, 6%. Total foreign stock, 5%. Germany, 1%.

Presidential vote

1972	Nixon (R)	106,807	(67%)
	McGovern (D)	52,240	(33%)
1968	Nixon (R)	75,960	(48%)
	Humphrey (D)	61,715	(39%)
	Wallace (AI)	21,288	(13%)

Rep. Clarence J. Brown (R) Elected Nov. 2, 1965; b. June 18, 1927, Columbus; home, Urbana; Duke U., B.A. 1947, Harvard U., M.B.A. 1949; Presbyterian.

Career Navy, WWII and Korea; Ed., Blanchester *Star Republican*, 1948–53; Ed. and Co-Owner, Franklin *Cronicle*, 1953–57; Ed., Urbana *Daily Citizen*, 1957–62, Publisher, 1959–70; Founder and Mgr., Radio WCOM-FM; Pres., Brown Publishing Co., 1955-.

Offices 2242 RHOB, 202-225-4324; Also 220 P.O. Bldg., 150 N. Limestone St., Springfield 45501, 513-325-0474.

Committees

Government Operations (4th). Subcommittees: Government Information and Individual Rights; Intergovernmental Relations and Human Resources.

Interstate and Foreign Commerce (4th). Subcommittees: Energy and Power.

Joint Economic Committee (Ranking Member, House Side). Subcommittees: Economic Growth; Fiscal Policy; International Economics; Priorities and Economy in Government.

Group Ratings

	ADA	COPE	LWV	RIPON	NFU	LCV	CFA	NAB	NSI	ACA
1974	27	36	60	73	43	38	17	73	88	60
1973	9	0	36	87	22	33	25	–	–	71
1972	19	27	50	73	57	26	50	100	100	57

Key Votes

1) Foreign Aid	AGN	6) Gov Abortn Aid	AGN	11) Pub Cong Election $	AGN
2) Busing	FOR	7) Coed Phys Ed	AGN	12) Turkish Arms Cutoff	AGN
3) ABM	FOR	8) Pov Lawyer Gag	FOR	13) Youth Camp Regs	ABS
4) B-1 Bomber	FOR	9) Pub Trans Sub	AGN	14) Strip Mine Veto	FOR
5) Nerve Gas	FOR	10) EZ Voter Regis	AGN	15) Farm Bill Veto	FOR

Election Results

1974 general:	Clarence J. Brown (R)	73,503	(61%)	($85,485)
	Patrick L. Nelson (D)	34,828	(29%)	($27,676)
	Dorothy Franke (Ind.)	13,088	(11%)	($2,653)
1974 primary:	Clarence J. Brown (R), unopposed			
1972 general:	Clarence J. Brown (R)	112,350	(73%)	($31,534)
	Dorothy Franke (Ind.)	40,945	(27%)	($2,838)

◆ ◆ ◆ ◆ ◆

EIGHTH DISTRICT

Along the Indiana border, just north of Cincinnati and just west of Dayton, lies the 8th congressional district of Ohio. Though the suburban sprawl of both Cincinnati and Dayton spills into the 8th, the district is dominated by two aging cities in Butler County: Hamilton (pop. 67,000) and Middletown (pop. 48,000). In the 8th, the hilly Ohio River country slides into the flatter land of the northern part of the state. Over the years, the district has taken most of its settlers from around the Ohio River and farther south, a fact that shows up in the election returns. In most elections these days, the 8th is heavily Republican and conservative. But a Southern Democratic heritage does lie hidden here, one that surfaced in the hefty 18% of the vote cast for George Wallace in 1968. This was the highest percentage the Alabamian got in any Ohio district that year, and, outside Oklahoma, the best he did in any district in states that did not allow slavery at the time of the Civil War.

By just about any measure, this should be a safe Republican district. But though it has elected three Republican Congressmen in the relatively few years since it was created in 1964, none has had a particularly safe seat. Its first incumbent, a flamboyant young conservative named Buz Lukens, ran for Governor in 1970; a maverick in staid Ohio Republican circles, he retains statewide ambitions, if not viability. Lukens was succeeded by a crew cut young state Senator named Walter Powell. A rather stolid conservative, Powell never managed to get more than 52% of the vote; he decided that he didn't like the House and wanted to retire in 1974. He might well have been defeated had he run.

Powell's retirement produced a rather bizarre three corner race. The Democratic nominee, T. Edward Strinko, was a 30-year-old who had left the Foreign Service to make the race; the Republican, Thomas Kindness, was an Ohio state Representative and former Hamilton Mayor. But there was also a third candidate, Independent Donald Gingerich; he had been Powell's campaign manager and had also worked for the vice presidential candidacy of Curtis Lemay in 1968. Indeed, the final results seemed to parallel those from six years before. This was a district where Nixon got 48% of the vote, Humphrey 34%, and Wallace 18%. In 1974, the Republican, Kindness, was somewhat weaker at 42%. But the others were close on the mark: Strinko had 38% of the vote, Gingerich 20%. All of Kindness' margin and a little more came from his home of Butler County, which casts half the district's votes; outside Butler, the race was dead even (actually Strinko led by 218 votes).

In the House, Kindness has succeeded to the Judiciary Committee seat held, during the impeachment hearings, by Ohio's Delbert Latta. Incumbency will surely help him in 1976, but obviously a 42% winner has some work to do before he can be considered to hold a safe seat.

Census Data Pop. 462,915. Central city, 25%; suburban, 64%. Median family income, $10,455; families above $15,000: 21%; families below $3,000: 7%. Median years education, 11.8.

The Voters

Median voting age 40.
Employment profile White collar, 41%. Blue collar, 45%. Service, 11%. Farm, 3%.
Ethnic groups Black, 4%. Total foreign stock, 4%. Germany, 1%.

Presidential vote

1972	Nixon (R)	104,889	(69%)
	McGovern (D)	47,638	(31%)
1968	Nixon (R)	71,399	(48%)
	Humphrey (D)	50,913	(34%)
	Wallace (AI)	26,420	(18%)

Rep. Thomas N. Kindness (R) Elected 1974; b. Aug 26, 1929, Knoxville, Tenn.; home, Hamilton; U. of Md., A.B. 1951, Geo. Wash. U., LL.B. 1953; Presbyterian.

Career Practicing atty., 1954–57; Asst. Counsel, Legal Dept., Champion Internatl. Corp., 1957–73; Hamilton City Cncl., 1964–69, Mayor, 1964–67; Ohio House of Reps., 1971–74.

Offices 1440 RHOB, 202-225-6205. Also 202-225-6205. Also 801 High St., Hamilton 45011, 513-895-5656.

Committees

Judiciary (11th). Subcommittees: Commodities and Services; Government Procurement and International Trade.

Group Ratings: Newly Elected

Key Votes

1) Foreign Aid	AGN	6) Gov Abortn Aid	NE	11) Pub Cong Election $	NE
2) Busing	NE	7) Coed Phys Ed	AGN	12) Turkish Arms Cutoff	NE
3) ABM	NE	8) Pov Lawyer Gag	NE	13) Youth Camp Regs	AGN
4) B-1 Bomber	FOR	9) Pub Trans Sub	NE	14) Strip Mine Veto	FOR
5) Nerve Gas	NE	10) EZ Voter Regis	NE	15) Farm Bill Veto	FOR

Election Results

1974 general:	Thomas N. Kindness (R)	51,097	(42%)	($75,516)
	T. Edward Strinko (D)	45,701	(38%)	($73,951)
	Don Gingerich (Ind.)	23,616	(20%)	($36,039)
1974 primary:	Thomas N. Kindness (R)	7,715	(37%)	
	David S. Holcomb (R)	5,859	(28%)	
	Charles W. Patterson (R)	5,336	(26%)	
	John J. Wikle (R)	1,839	(9%)	

◆ ◆ ◆ ◆ ◆

NINTH DISTRICT

The city of Toledo rises incongruously from the flat plains of northwest Ohio; it is different from the surrounding countryside in just about every way. Situated in the middle of rich agricultural country, Toledo is heavily industrial; set among WASP farmers and small town residents, Toledo is heavily ethnic (mainly Polish-American); surrounded by one of the nation's traditionally staunchest Republican areas, Toledo is defiantly Democratic. Toledo, a Great Lakes port at the mouth of the Maumee River, handles more tonnage than Detroit, 60 miles away; and like Detroit, it experienced its period of most substantial growth between 1910 and 1930, during the initial expansion of the automobile industry. But although many of Toledo's big concerns remain heavily dependent on the car business, it is not a one industry town like Detroit, and so not in nearly as much economic trouble in recent years.

Lucas County, which contains Toledo, is one of two in Ohio that went for George McGovern in 1972. Except for a few suburban and rural townships, all of Lucas County makes up Ohio's 9th congressional district. The 9th, of course, is a Democratic stronghold; in fact, it is the only district in northwest Ohio that elects a Democratic Congressman. The current incumbent is Thomas Ludlow Ashley, first elected in 1954. He comes to the seat almost by inheritance. His great-grandfather, a radical Republican, was Toledo's Congressman during the Civil War years; and as Chairman of the Committee on Territories, he left his imprint on the nation by choosing the names for Montana and Wyoming and possibly others as well. The present Congressman Ashley serves on committees with jurisdiction more mundane: Merchant Marine and Fisheries and Banking and Currency. It is on the latter that he has had his greatest legislative impact, as something of an expert on housing and promoter of a national urban growth policy.

But in his most recent elections it has not been Ashley's legislative accomplishments or his voting record or even his services to constituents which have been the biggest issue. Rather, what apparently has been his biggest problem was a drunk driving arrest he suffered in Toledo in 1973, one for which Ashley eventually spent three days in jail. That is about the only thing that can account for his unusually poor performance in the very Democratic year of 1974, when he received only 53% of the vote against an underfinanced Republican named Charleton Finkbeiner. That represented a very substantial loss of popularity for Ashley—he had got 69% in 1972 as McGovern was barely carrying the district—and an indication that his 22-year congressional career may be coming to an end.

Census Data Pop. 463,286. Central city, 83%; suburban, 17%. Median family income, $10,786; families above $15,000: 24%; families below $3,000: 7%. Median years education, 12.1.

The Voters

Median voting age 44.
Employment profile White collar, 48%. Blue collar, 39%. Service, 13%. Farm, –%.
Ethnic groups Black, 12%. Spanish, 2%. Total foreign stock, 15%. Poland, Germany, 3% each; Canada, UK, 1% each.

Presidential vote

1972	Nixon (R)	83,768	(49%)
	McGovern (D)	87,151	(51%)
1968	Nixon (R)	66,329	(39%)
	Humphrey (D)	88,945	(52%)
	Wallace (AI)	16,371	(10%)

Rep. Thomas L. Ashley (D) Elected 1954; b. Jan. 11, 1923, Toledo; home, Maumee; Yale U., B.A. 1948, U. of Toledo Law School, Ohio St. U., LL.B. 1951; Episcopalian.

Career Army, WWII; Practicing atty., 1951–52; Co-Dir, Press Section, and Asst. Dir. of Special Projects, Radio Free Europe, 1952–54.

Offices 2406 RHOB, 202-225-4146. Also 234 Summit St., Fed. Ofc. Bldg., Toledo 43604, 419-248-5325.

Committees

Banking, Currency and Housing (5th). Subcommittees: Economic Stabilization (Chairman); Financial Institutions, Supervision, Regulation and Insurance; Housing and Community Development; International Trade, Investment and Monetary Policy.

Budget (4th).

Merchant Marine and Fisheries (2d). Subcommittees: Merchant Marine; Oceanography.

Group Ratings

	ADA	COPE	LWV	RIPON	NFU	LCV	CFA	NAB	NSI	ACA
1974	73	100	83	80	73	63	58	17	40	0
1973	96	70	100	78	89	89	83	–	–	9
1972	88	100	92	64	71	66	100	17	60	14

Key Votes

1) Foreign Aid	AGN	6) Gov Abortn Aid	FOR	11) Pub Cong Election $	AGN
2) Busing	FOR	7) Coed Phys Ed	ABS	12) Turkish Arms Cutoff	FOR
3) ABM	AGN	8) Pov Lawyer Gag	AGN	13) Youth Camp Regs	ABS
4) B-1 Bomber	FOR	9) Pub Trans Sub	FOR	14) Strip Mine Veto	AGN
5) Nerve Gas	AGN	10) EZ Voter Regis	FOR	15) Farm Bill Veto	AGN

Election Results

1974 general:	Thomas Ludlow Ashley (D)	64,831	(53%)	($24,409)
	Charleton S. Finkbeiner, Jr. (R)	57,892	(47%)	($33,472)
1974 primary:	Thomas Ludlow Ashley (D)	25,720	(79%)	
	Two others (D)	6,860	(21%)	
1972 general:	Thomas Ludlow Ashley (D)	110,450	(69%)	($17,416)
	Joseph C. Richards (R)	49,388	(31%)	($20,019)

◆ ◆ ◆ ◆ ◆

TENTH DISTRICT

The 10th district of Ohio is the state's southeast corner, a hilly, sparsely populated area. Though the district covers 14% of Ohio's land area, it contains only 4% of the state's residents. Marietta, on the Ohio River here, was the site of the first (1788) permanent American settlement in the Northwest Territory, ceded to the new nation by the British following the Revolutionary War. The town's Republican leanings are evidence still of the Yankee origin of its first settlers. Most of the 10th district, however, resembles West Virginia, across the Ohio River. The voters tend to think of themselves as Democrats and plunk for conservatives, which, these days, means almost exclusively for Republicans on the state and national levels. A glaring exception to the pattern is the town of Athens, where the enfranchisement of 18-year-olds at Ohio University has made for a complete turnaround in voting habits. Accordingly, Athens County, which contains Athens, was one of two Ohio counties that refused to give Richard Nixon a majority in 1972 (for the other, see Ninth District).

The 10th's Democratic-conservative tradition has produced rather frequent changes in the district's congressional representation—an unusual phenomenon in Ohio politics. In 1958, 1960, and 1964, conservative Democrat Walter Moeller was chosen to represent the 10th, when it had slightly different boundaries; in 1962, it elected Republican Homer Abele. But there has been no further change since 1966, when Republican Clarence Miller unseated Moeller by a 52–48 margin. Since then Miller has worked hard, in a long Ohio Republican tradition, to solidify his position in the district. His efforts have succeeded. He won 73% of the vote in 1972 and 70% in 1974—the latter the best showing for an opposed Ohio Republican in that heavily Democratic year.

Miller likes to boast that he has not missed a House roll call since he was first elected. As for committees, for his first six years in the House he advanced to reasonably high seniority positions on Agriculture and Public Works. But in 1973 he decided to switch to Appropriations, and is now ranking minority member on the Treasury-Postal Service General Government Subcommittee. Miller's positions on most issues are reliably conservative, and he has concentrated less on matters of major newsworthiness than on what will help make him more popular at home.

Census Data Pop. 463,353. Central city, 0%; suburban, 12%. Median family income, $7,894; families above $15,000: 10%; families below $3,000: 14%. Median years education, 11.8.

The Voters

Median voting age 43.
Employment profile White collar, 39%. Blue collar, 45%. Service, 13%. Farm, 3%.
Ethnic groups Black, 2%. Total foreign stock, 3%.

Presidential vote

1972	Nixon (R)	119,083	(67%)
	McGovern (D)	58,831	(33%)
1968	Nixon (R)	89,759	(52%)
	Humphrey (D)	67,417	(39%)
	Wallace (AI)	15,689	(9%)

Rep. Clarence E. Miller (R) Elected 1966; b. Nov. 1, 1917, Lancaster; home, Lancaster; Internatl. Correspondence School; Methodist.

Career Electrician; Lancaster City Cncl., 1957–63, Mayor 1964–66.

Offices 434 CHOB, 202-225-5131. Also 212 S. Broad St., Lancaster 43130, 614-654-5149.

Committees

Appropriations (12th). Subcommittees: State, Justice, Commerce, and the Judiciary; Treasury, Postal Service, and General Government.

Group Ratings

	ADA	COPE	LWV	RIPON	NFU	LCV	CFA	NAB	NSI	ACA
1974	35	0	41	44	54	24	15	100	60	80
1973	28	9	25	60	50	21	25	–	–	85
1972	6	0	33	56	43	60	50	100	90	87

Key Votes

1) Foreign Aid	AGN	6) Gov Abortn Aid	AGN	11) Pub Cong Election $	FOR
2) Busing	AGN	7) Coed Phys Ed	AGN	12) Turkish Arms Cutoff	FOR
3) ABM	FOR	8) Pov Lawyer Gag	FOR	13) Youth Camp Regs	AGN
4) B-1 Bomber	FOR	9) Pub Trans Sub	AGN	14) Strip Mine Veto	AGN
5) Nerve Gas	FOR	10) EZ Voter Regis	AGN	15) Farm Bill Veto	FOR

Election Results

1974 general:	Clarence E. Miller (R)	100,521	(70%)	($20,052)
	H. Kent Bumpass (D)	42,333	(30%)	($2,423)
1974 primary:	Clarence E. Miller (R), unopposed			
1972 general:	Clarence E. Miller (R)	129,683	(73%)	($26,983)
	Robert H. Whealey (D)	47,456	(27%)	($5,452)

◆ ◆ ◆ ◆ ◆

ELEVENTH DISTRICT

After putting in years of service on Capitol Hill, some Congressmen grow more grouchily conservative. They begin to feel comfortable in the company of their colleagues and resent the demands placed on them by outsiders. The veterans have metamorphosed from young crusaders to defenders of the establishment which they, after all, have become a part. The pattern is a common one, though perhaps not seen as often today as in the past. The opposite pattern also exists. Congressmen come to Washington as believers in political orthodoxy, convinced that whatever is, is probably for the best. Then, after a few years in Congress, they change. They begin to listen to argument and consider points of view not part of life back home; these politicians soon begin to vote and operate on committees in unorthodox fashion. Such is an increasingly common pattern in the House these days, and one exemplar is Congressman J. William Stanton of the 11th district of Ohio.

This is not what one would have predicted when Stanton first came to Congress. His first election, in 1964, was a considerable achievement. He ran in an 11th district that had rather different boundaries than at present. It included the steel-manufacturing city of Warren (pop. 63,000), no longer in the district, along with the Democratic-leaning Cleveland suburbs of Lake

County (Willowick, Wickliffe, and Willoughby), industrial Ashtabula County in the far northeast corner of the state, and Kent State University. The University was then less well-known than it is today, and of course it cast far fewer liberal votes. The old 11th was clearly a marginal district, having been won by a Democrat as recently as 1960. But Stanton, who campaigned as a conventional Ohio Republican conservative, managed to run almost 20% ahead of the Goldwater-Miller ticket and to capture the seat with 55% of the vote.

Stanton's vote-getting prowess has been further demonstrated by his landslide reelection victories in later elections—68% in 1970 and 1972, 61% in 1974. His success may be due in part to his liberal position on many issues. He has voted, for example, for end-the-war legislation and against the SST, and since his first election, his ADA and COPE ratings have risen substantially. A more typical wrench from tradition was his support for allowing states to divert some of their highway trust fund money for mass transit. Stanton voted for the move against the stern opposition of fellow Ohio Republican William Harsha, ranking Republican on the Public Works Committee.

Stanton's big majorities, however, are probably less a response to his voting record than an appreciation of the kind of constituency service that helps so many congressmen win easy reelection in technically marginal districts. Also, Stanton has been helped by successive redistrictings, which have made the 11th more Republican. It has long since lost Warren and by 1972 no longer included Kent or the easternmost (and most Democratic) suburbs in Lake County. The line-drawing was as much an accommodation of neighboring Democratic Congressmen as an attempt to aid Stanton, who doesn't need the help.

Stanton has been mentioned on a number of occasions as a candidate for statewide office, and he would be helped, in the Cleveland media market anyway, by his own popularity and that of 20th district Congressman James Stanton, a Democrat and no relation. But Stanton has not made the move to make the races and now, at 52, probably never will.

Census Data Pop. 462,701. Central city, 0%; suburban, 79%. Median family income, $11,142; families above $15,000: 25%; families below $3,000: 6%. Median years education, 12.2.

The Voters

Median voting age 41.
Employment profile White collar, 41%. Blue collar, 47%. Service, 10%. Farm, 2%.
Ethnic groups Black, 2%. Total foreign stock, 15%. Italy, UK, 2% each; Germany, Hungary, Czechoslovakia, 1% each.

Presidential vote

1972	Nixon (R)	104,236	(62%)
	McGovern (D)	63,864	(38%)
1968	Nixon (R)	71,395	(47%)
	Humphrey (D)	62,840	(41%)
	Wallace (AI)	17,970	(12%)

Rep. J. William Stanton (R) Elected 1964; b. Feb. 20, 1924, Painesville; home, Painesville; Georgetown U., B.S. 1949; Catholic.

Career Army, WWII; Lake Co. Commissioner, 1956–64.

Offices 2448 RHOB, 202-225-5306. Also 170 N. St. Clair St., Painesville 44077, 216-352-6167.

Committees

Banking, Currency and Housing (2d). Subcommittees: Economic Stabilization; Housing and Community Development; International Trade, Investment and Monetary Policy.

Small Business (2d). Subcommittees: SBA and SBIC Legislation.

Group Ratings

	ADA	COPE	LWV	RIPON	NFU	LCV	CFA	NAB	NSI	ACA
1974	30	36	67	69	64	47	36	33	90	40
1973	28	27	67	93	32	53	38	–	–	63
1972	19	30	70	80	43	52	50	91	100	52

Key Votes

1) Foreign Aid	FOR	6) Gov Abortn Aid	AGN	11) Pub Cong Election $	FOR
2) Busing	AGN	7) Coed Phys Ed	ABS	12) Turkish Arms Cutoff	AGN
3) ABM	FOR	8) Pov Lawyer Gag	FOR	13) Youth Camp Regs	ABS
4) B-1 Bomber	ABS	9) Pub Trans Sub	AGN	14) Strip Mine Veto	AGN
5) Nerve Gas	AGN	10) EZ Voter Regis	AGN	15) Farm Bill Veto	FOR

Election Results

1974 general:	J. William Stanton (R)	79,756	(61%)	($25,834)
	Michael D. Coffey (D)	52,017	(39%)	($35,009)
1974 primary:	J. William Stanton (R), unopposed			
1972 general:	J. William Stanton (R)	106,841	(68%)	($19,853)
	Dennis M. Callahan (D)	49,849	(32%)	($22,822)

◆ ◆ ◆ ◆ ◆

TWELFTH DISTRICT

In 1960, while campaigning in Columbus, Ohio, John F. Kennedy was greeted by a tumultuous crowd; he was moved to remark that Columbus was the city where he got the loudest cheers and the fewest votes. He was not far off the mark—at least about the votes. Columbus, like Cincinnati, is an urban Republican stronghold. Of all the urban counties in Ohio, Barry Goldwater made his best showing (46%) in Franklin County, which contains Columbus. The city's Republicanism can be explained by many of the factors that produce a similar political inclination in the rather similar city of Indianapolis, Indiana. Like Indianapolis, Columbus does have a significant black population (18%), but it has few residents of Eastern and Southern European ethnic stock. These are people who for years have provided the Democratic vote base in places like Gary in northwest Indiana, or in Cleveland and Youngstown in northeast Ohio. Like Indianapolis, the economy of Columbus is more white collar than most cities in the Great Lakes region. Major employers here include the state government (with patronage rolls dominated by Republicans and conservative Democrats), Ohio State University, and several big banks and insurance companies.

Columbus is divided into two congressional districts, the 12th and 15th, by a line that runs right through the middle of the city. It was carefully drawn by the Republican Ohio legislature to keep the city's students and blacks in the district (the 15th) where they can do the least harm. The 12th district takes in the east side of Columbus and its suburbs, along with two heavily Republican rural counties.

Yet despite the careful redistricting, and despite Columbus' overwhelmingly Republican heritage, 12th district Congressman Samuel Devine was almost defeated in 1974. And it was not as if Devine had not had warning that he might be in trouble. In 1970 and 1972, he was held to 58% and 56% of the vote, respectively, by public relations man James Goodrich, who was not considered the strongest possible opponent. Suddenly, in 1974, Devine was faced with more formidable opposition: Columbus Councilwoman Fran Ryan, whose opposition to Devine guaranteed her liberal support and whose rather cool conservative stand on some issues helped her win the endorsement of the usually Republican Wolfe newspapers, which have a monopoly here.

How did Devine come to be in such trouble? Part of the problem may have been that he came to be known as too conservative. In 1969 he started a group called the Republican Regulars, which stood in opposition to such Nixon Administration policies as the Family Assistance Plan. In 1971 he challenged Illinois' John Anderson for the chairmanship of the House Republican Conference, and just lost 88–82. Two years later he became ranking Republican on the House Commerce Committee, in which position he invariably opposed consumerist legislation and generally supported Chamber of Commerce type positions.

But it was not his conservatism which was too much for Columbus so much as it was his unsavory taste in political leaders. When Spiro Agnew was under attack for his alleged acceptance of bribes, Devine, along with Alabama's William Dickinson, appeared in Agnew's office with several dozen signatures of support they had solicited from their colleagues, many of whom are now ex-colleagues. And the day after Richard Nixon resigned the Presidency and flew back for the last time from the White House to San Clemente, one of the people he called on the phone was none other than Sam Devine. Fran Ryan didn't have to play up these associations very much; even Republican Columbus was disgusted with Agnew and Nixon, and the voters themselves could ask why this Congressman continued to believe in them after they had already been demonstrated to be criminals.

In any case, Ryan pressed Devine hard and nearly won. In fact, she carried Columbus and surrounding Franklin County; Devine's narrow 51–49 victory was due solely to majorities in the two small counties in the district. In most other districts, and with most other Congressmen, one could feel confident in saying that a Republican who had thus survived 1974 was probably a pretty good bet for reelection in 1976 and subsequent years. But not here. A man who has been so careless about opinion is his own constituency that he has lost most of his majority could very well be successfully challenged in a year which is not as favorable generally to the opposition as 1974.

Census Data Pop. 463,120. Central city, 55%; suburban, 41%. Median family income, $10,710; families above $15,000: 23%; families below $3,000: 6%. Median years education, 12.3.

The Voters

Median voting age 39.
Employment profile White collar, 54%. Blue collar, 34%. Service, 11%. Farm, 1%.
Ethnic groups Black, 10%. Total foreign stock, 7%. Germany, Italy, 1% each.

Presidential vote

1972	Nixon (R)	128,129	(68%)
	McGovern (D)	61,644	(32%)
1968	Nixon (R)	81,336	(51%)
	Humphrey (D)	54,511	(34%)
	Wallace (AI)	24,509	(15%)

Rep. Samuel L. Devine (R) Elected 1958; b. Dec. 21, 1915, South Bend, Ind., home, Columbus; Colgate U., 1933–34, Ohio St. U., 1934–37, U. of Notre Dame, J.D. 1940; Methodist.

Career FBI Agent, 1940–45; Practicing atty., 1945–55; Ohio House of Reps., 1951–55; Franklin Co. Prosecuting Atty., 1955–58.

Offices 2206 RHOB, 202-225-5355. Also 231 New Fed. Bldg., 85 Marconi Blvd., Columbus 43216, 614-221-3533.

Committees

House Administration (2d). Subcommittees: Accounts; Personnel and Police.

Interstate and Foreign Commerce (Ranking member).

Group Ratings

	ADA	COPE	LWV	RIPON	NFU	LCV	CFA	NAB	NSI	ACA
1974	4	0	9	44	8	20	9	78	90	100
1973	0	9	18	40	15	5	13	–	–	92
1972	0	20	18	45	0	8	–	100	100	100

Key Votes

1) Foreign Aid	AGN	6) Gov Abortn Aid	AGN	11) Pub Cong Election $	AGN
2) Busing	AGN	7) Coed Phys Ed	AGN	12) Turkish Arms Cutoff	AGN
3) ABM	FOR	8) Pov Lawyer Gag	FOR	13) Youth Camp Regs	AGN
4) B-1 Bomber	FOR	9) Pub Trans Sub	AGN	14) Strip Mine Veto	FOR
5) Nerve Gas	FOR	10) EZ Voter Regis	AGN	15) Farm Bill Veto	FOR

Election Results

1974 general:	Samuel L. Devine (R)	73,303	(51%)	($73,858)
	Fran Ryan (D)	70,818	(49%)	($94,243)
1974 primary:	Samuel L. Devine (R), unopposed			
1972 general:	Samuel L. Devine (R)	103,655	(56%)	($51,930)
	James W. Goodrich (D)	81,074	(44%)	($125,145)

◆ ◆ ◆ ◆ ◆

THIRTEENTH DISTRICT

The 13th congressional district of Ohio occupies the north central part of Ohio. It sits between the state's industrial, Democratic northeast and its rural, Republican northwest and central areas. The contours of the district have undergone marked changes in the course of redistrictings in 1964, 1968, and 1972. But throughout, the 13th has retained as a nucleus Lorain County, which contains about half the district's population. Most of the County's residents live in or near the industrial cities of Lorain and Elyria, the latter the only slightly disguised subject of Sherwood Anderson's *Winesburg, Ohio*. Lorain County also contains the little town of Oberlin, home of Oberlin College, founded by abolitionists and the first in the nation to admit both blacks and women, way back in 1833.

Before the 1964 redistricting, the 13th was a predominantly rural district that contained several Republican counties now in the 5th and 17th districts. Presently, the 13th has only one rural Republican county, Medina, and that is fast being transformed by migrants from the closer in suburbs of Cleveland and Akron. The rest of the district lies west of Lorain (industrial Sandusky in Erie County) or east of Medina (the Akron working class suburbs of Barberton and Norton).

As it now stands, the 13th often produces Democratic margins in statewide contests; it went, for example, for Governor John Gilligan in his losing race for reelection in 1974. But in congressional races it continues to reelect Republican incumbent Charles Mosher. With the possible exception of Dayton's Charles Whalen, Mosher is the most liberal Republican in the usually conservative Ohio delegation, indeed one of the most liberal Republicans in the House. As in the case of the 11th district's William Stanton, this is the result of a slow transformation of views; when he was first elected in 1960, Mosher generally went along with the conservative Republican House leadership. But his opposition to the Vietnam war—he was one of the first House Republicans to turn firmly against it—led him to change his mind on other issues in the late sixties and early seventies. He is now ranking minority member of the House Science and Technology Committee, and part of a liberal majority which tends to dominate that panel.

Fortunately for Mosher, his shift of opinion on issues has roughly coincided with similar shifts in his constituency wrought by redistricting. As the sixties passed into seventies, he was winning reelection easily. But in 1974, faced with the opposition of a Democrat whose major theme was the large number of children he had, Mosher received 58% of the vote—enough for a comfortable win but the lowest percentage he had received since 1964. That may be the result of the fact that it was, after all, a Democratic year; but it also may have been a response to Mosher's age. He turns 70 in 1976, and it is possible that he will choose to retire—or that some enterprising Democrat will use his comparative youth to try to beat this rather interesting and unconventional Congressman.

Census Data Pop. 464,056. Central city, 28%; suburban, 55%. Median family income, $10,795; families above $15,000: 22%; families below $3,000: 6%. Median years education, 12.1.

The Voters

Median voting age 41.
Employment profile White collar, 40%. Blue collar, 46%. Service, 12%. Farm, 2%.
Ethnic groups Black, 5%. Spanish, 2%. Total foreign stock, 15%. Germany, Hungary, 2% each; Poland, UK, Italy, Czechoslovakia, Yugoslavia, 1% each.

Presidential vote

1972	Nixon (R)	98,505	(59%)
	McGovern (D)	68,481	(41%)
1968	Nixon (R)	67,381	(43%)
	Humphrey (D)	71,992	(46%)
	Wallace (AI)	17,607	(11%)

Rep. Charles A. Mosher (R) Elected 1960; b. May 7, 1906, Sandwich, Ill.; home, Oberlin; Oberlin Col. A.B. 1928; United Church of Christ.

Career Ad. sales and copy, Aurora, Ill. *Daily Beacon-News*, 1929–38; Ad. Mgr., Janesville, Wis. *Daily Gazette*, 1938–40; Ed. and Pub., Oberlin *News-Tribune*, 1940–61; Pres. and Mgr., Oberlin Printing Co.; Vice Chm., Oberlin Village Cncl., 1945–51; Ohio Senate, 1951–61.

Offices 2368 RHOB, 202-225-3401. Also 517 E. 28th St., Lorain 44052, 216-244-1572.

Committees

Merchant Marine and Fisheries (2d). Subcommittees: Merchant Marine; Oceanography.

Science and Technology (Ranking Member).

Group Ratings

	ADA	COPE	LWV	RIPON	NFU	LCV	CFA	NAB	NSI	ACA
1974	83	60	92	100	75	56	50	45	20	21
1973	80	45	92	93	65	63	71	–	–	23
1972	56	50	83	75	67	73	100	44	17	21

Key Votes

1) Foreign Aid	FOR	6) Gov Abortn Aid	FOR	11) Pub Cong Election $	FOR
2) Busing	FOR	7) Coed Phys Ed	FOR	12) Turkish Arms Cutoff	FOR
3) ABM	AGN	8) Pov Lawyer Gag	AGN	13) Youth Camp Regs	FOR
4) B-1 Bomber	AGN	9) Pub Trans Sub	AGN	14) Strip Mine Veto	AGN
5) Nerve Gas	AGN	10) EZ Voter Regis	FOR	15) Farm Bill Veto	FOR

Election Results

1974 general:	Charles A. Mosher (R)	72,881	(58%)	($17,254)
	Fred M. Ritenauer (D)	53,766	(42%)	($14,889)
1974 primary:	Charles A. Mosher (R), unopposed			
1972 general:	Charles A. Mosher (R)	111,242	(68%)	($13,218)
	John Michael Ryan (D)	51,991	(32%)	($5,593)

◆ ◆ ◆ ◆ ◆

FOURTEENTH DISTRICT

Akron is the rubber capital of America, the city where most of our millions of automobile and truck tires are produced—and a city totally dependent on that one industry. It was an industry which developed relatively late: Cleveland was already one of the nation's biggest cities, and even nearby Canton, the home of President McKinley, was a bigger urban center at the turn of the century. Akron's growth came in the 1910–1930 period, when it attracted thousands of immigrants not so much from Eastern Europe as from West Virginia, giving the city a Southern-accented atmosphere it retains to this day. The newly booming city liked to cultivate its reputation as an all-American place by things like sponsoring the Soapbox Derby (a competition, it appears, for years marked by cheating). But the reality of life in Akron was that this was one of America's most class bound cities: a giant factory town where management lived as a privileged minority, quite out of contact—except possibly on the job—with the working class majority.

So it should not be surprising that Akron had a politics almost of class warfare from the late thirties, when the United Rubber Workers organized the plants, up into the late sixties. As a result, working class Akron and Summit County generally went Democratic in statewide contests. But in more local races, especially in the race for Ohio's 14th congressional district, which for years has contained all of Akron and most of Summit County, the management-oriented Republicans spent more money and showed more entrepreneurial skill. Akron was the home town of Ray Bliss, longtime Ohio Republican Chairman, and one of his first projects was to rescue the 14th district from the Democrats who had controlled it, with one exception, since the New Deal days. Bliss's candidate in 1950 was a garrulous plumber named William Ayres; he won that election and nine more, and by 1970 was ranking minority member of the House Education and Labor Committee.

But if Ayres's election and reelections had succeeded in moderating the class warfare tone of Akron politics, his occasional concessions to the basically Democratic politics of his district grew fewer and his personal campaigning more erratic. By 1970, Ayres was clearly in trouble; five Democrats were vying for the nomination to oppose him.

The choice of that candidate, and the nature of some of his support, tell us quite a lot about the declining importance of class politics in Akron and places like it. For the winner of the Democratic nomination was John Seiberling, a lawyer for Goodyear whose grandfather founded both the Seiberling and Goodyear tire companies. And Seiberling's credentials were not so much those of a supporter of the working class (though he had supported the 1970 United Rubber Workers strike, and refused to cross the picket line), as they were of an ecology buff (he had worked for some years to keep power lines and highways out of the Cuyahoga River valley). Ayres tried to make an issue out of a speech Seiberling made at the University of Akron just after the 1970 Kent State shootings (Kent was then in the 11th district, and now is in the 14th); the Democrat said that he tried to tell the students they should work within the system, and indeed Seiberling had the overwhelming bulk of student support. More than that: he also won the endorsement of the Akron *Beacon-Journal*, which had backed Ayres for 20 years. This is the flagship paper in the chain owned by John S. Knight, a conservative Republican on most issues, but a steady opponent of American involvement in Vietnam since the 1950s.

Seiberling won that election, by the surprisingly large margin of 56–44; his victory showed him winning not only the usual Democratic blue collar vote, but a crucial slice of the erstwhile Republican white collar vote as well. Since then, Seiberling has won the kind of overwhelming support Ayres never could: 74% in 1972, 75% in 1974. As a member of the Judiciary Committee, he was part of the majority that voted to impeach Richard Nixon, although he did surprise some observers (and some of his Kent State constituents, to whom he referred at this point) when he came out against impeachment for the bombing of Cambodia. Seiberling, as befits one long concerned with the environment, also serves on the Interior Committee. He is not a man especially enamored of the political life, but it appears he will continue to be living it for quite a few more years.

Census Data Pop. 464,578. Central city, 59%; suburban, 41%. Median family income, $10,876; families above $15,000: 24%; families below $3,000: 7%. Median years education, 12.2.

The Voters

Median voting age 42.
Employment profile White collar, 49%. Blue collar, 38%. Service, 13%. Farm, –%.
Ethnic groups Black, 11%. Total foreign stock, 14%. Italy, 2%; Germany, UK, Yugoslavia, Hungary, 1% each.

Presidential vote

1972	Nixon (R)	88,384	(48%)
	McGovern (D)	94,320	(52%)
1968	Nixon (R)	67,145	(39%)
	Humphrey (D)	85,837	(49%)
	Wallace (AI)	21,320	(12%)

Rep. John F. Seiberling (D) Elected 1970; b. Sept. 8, 1918, Akron; home, Akron; Harvard U., B.A. 1941, Columbia U., LL.B. 1949; Protestant.

Career Army, WWII; Practicing atty., 1949–53; Atty., Goodyear Tire and Rubber Co., 1954–70.

Offices 1225 LHOB, 202-225-5231. Also Fed. Bldg., 2 S. Main St., Akron 44308, 216-375-5710.

Committees

Interior and Insular Affairs (15th). Subcommittees: Energy and the Environment; Mines and Mining; National Parks and Recreation.

Judiciary (11th). Subcommittees: Civil and Constitutional Rights; Monopolies and Commercial Law.

Group Ratings

	ADA	COPE	LWV	RIPON	NFU	LCV	CFA	NAB	NSI	ACA
1974	96	91	92	53	93	100	92	17	10	0
1973	100	100	92	73	90	89	100	–	–	7
1972	100	100	100	84	83	86	100	0	0	5

Key Votes

1) Foreign Aid	FOR	6) Gov Abortn Aid	FOR	11) Pub Cong Election $	FOR
2) Busing	FOR	7) Coed Phys Ed	FOR	12) Turkish Arms Cutoff	FOR
3) ABM	AGN	8) Pov Lawyer Gag	AGN	13) Youth Camp Regs	FOR
4) B-1 Bomber	AGN	9) Pub Trans Sub	FOR	14) Strip Mine Veto	AGN
5) Nerve Gas	AGN	10) EZ Voter Regis	FOR	15) Farm Bill Veto	AGN

Election Results

1974 general:	John F. Seiberling (D)	93,931	(75%)	($16,666)
	Mark Figetakis (R)	30,603	(25%)	($13,840)
1974 primary:	John F. Seiberling (D), unopposed			
1972 general:	John F. Seiberling (D)	135,068	(74%)	($26,325)
	Norman W. Holt (R)	46,490	(26%)	($6,391)

◆ ◆ ◆ ◆ ◆

FIFTEENTH DISTRICT

The 15th congressional district of Ohio includes the west side of Columbus, its Franklin County suburbs, and Pickaway County to the south. Next to Cincinnati, Columbus is Ohio's most Republican metropolitan area; it is also the state's fastest growing major urban area (see Twelfth District). The 15th, as it was first created in the 1964 and 1968 redistrictings, was the more Republican of the two Columbus districts, in large part because of Upper Arlington. This suburb, just across the Olentangy River from the Ohio State campus, is the largest in the Columbus area (pop. 38,000) and one of the most Republican (78% for Nixon in 1968, 81% in 1972).

The first and only Congressman from the 15th has been Chalmers P. Wylie, a former state legislator and Columbus city attorney (an elective post). Wylie has compiled a solidly conservative record in Washington. He is best known among his colleagues for his work on the school prayer issue; Wylie perennially introduces and pushes an amendment to overturn the Supreme Court decision that prevents state-sponsored prayers in public schools.

Unlike Samuel Devine, who represents the other half of the Columbus area, Wylie has not attracted vigorous opposition in recent elections. Perhaps for that reason, the Republican redistricting of 1972, the legislature took some of the more troublesome areas out of Devine's 12th district and put them into Wylie's 15th. As a result, Wylie's portion of the city of Columbus actually goes Democratic in most elections; he has 17,000 more blacks and about that many more college students (mostly from the Ohio State campus) than he did before 1972. The two groups had already demonstrated their electoral clout when they voted solidly against conservative

Democratic Mayor Maynard E. Sensenbrenner and installed moderate Republican Tom Moody in 1971. Wylie is not their kind of Republican, and he slipped to 66% of the vote in 1972 and 62% in 1974. It is unlikely, however, that Wylie will be in much political danger in 1976.

Census Data Pop. 462,703. Central city, 52%; suburban, 32%. Median family income, $10,074; families above $15,000: 23%; families below $3,000: 9%. Median years education, 12.3.

The Voters

Median voting age 39.
Employment profile White collar, 57%. Blue collar, 29%. Service, 13%. Farm, 1%.
Ethnic groups Black, 13%. Total foreign stock, 7%. Germany, 1%.

Presidential vote

1972	Nixon (R)	....	119,846	(65%)
	McGovern (D)	....	65,381	(35%)
1968	Nixon (R)	....	87,406	(54%)
	Humphrey (D)	....	55,970	(35%)
	Wallace (AI)	....	18,578	(11%)

Rep. Chalmers P. Wylie (R) Elected 1966; b. Nov. 23, 1920, Norwich; home, Columbus; Otterbein Col., Ohio St. U., B.A., Harvard U., J.D.; Methodist.

Career Army, WWII; Asst Atty. Gen. of Ohio, 1948, 1951–54; Asst. Columbus City Atty., 1949–50, City Atty., 1953–56; Administrator, Ohio Bureau of Workmen's Comp., 1957; First Asst. to the Gov. of Ohio, 1957–58; Practicing atty., 1959–66; Ohio House of Reps., 1961–67.

Offices 2447 RHOB, 202-225-2015. Also Fed. Bldg., 85 Marconi Blvd., Columbus 43215, 614-469-5614.

Committees

Banking, Currency and Housing (4th). Subcommittees: Consumer Affairs; Financial Institutions Supervision, Regulation and Insurance; Housing and Community Development.

Vererans' Affairs (3d). Subcommittees: Compensation, Pension and Insurance; Education and Training.

Group Ratings

	ADA	COPE	LWV	RIPON	NFU	LCV	CFA	NAB	NSI	ACA
1974	26	0	42	56	40	41	8	82	71	58
1973	25	27	58	73	21	32	38	–	–	74
1972	6	18	45	58	43	40	100	100	100	83

Key Votes

1) Foreign Aid	AGN	6) Gov Abortn Aid	AGN	11) Pub Cong Election $	AGN
2) Busing	AGN	7) Coed Phys Ed	AGN	12) Turkish Arms Cutoff	FOR
3) ABM	FOR	8) Pov Lawyer Gag	FOR	13) Youth Camp Regs	ABS
4) B-1 Bomber	FOR	9) Pub Trans Sub	AGN	14) Strip Mine Veto	AGN
5) Nerve Gas	FOR	10) EZ Voter Regis	AGN	15) Farm Bill Veto	FOR

Election Results

1974 general:	Chalmers P. Wylie (R)	79,376	(62%)	($61,241)
	Manley "Mike" L. McGee (D)	49,683	(38%)	($21,960)
1974 primary:	Chalmers P. Wylie (R), unopposed			
1972 general:	Chalmers P. Wylie (R)	115,779	(66%)	($53,091)
	Manley "Mike" L. McGee (D)	55,314	(31%)	($23,398)
	Edward Price (AI)	4,820	(3%)	(NA)

◆ ◆ ◆ ◆ ◆

SIXTEENTH DISTRICT

Canton, Ohio is known, to the extent it is known at all today, as the home of the Pro Football Hall of Fame. But to American historians, Canton is most memorable as the home of President William McKinley. It was here that McKinley sat on his famous front porch in 1896 and received delegations of voters carefully selected by Republican organizations throughout the country. And it was also here that he received the news that he had been elected President over William Jennings Bryan. Some historians still cling to the notion that factory workers provided McKinley with the votes he needed to win only because their bosses threatened to fire them if they didn't. No more evidence of such coercion exists for this election than any other in our history; the fact, however unlikely it may seem in the political context of today, is that McKinley was the heavy choice of northern blue collar workers, and that they apparently believed that McKinley would provide the full dinner pail he promised.

Indeed, the case can be made that McKinley delivered admirably on that promise; in any case, a protracted period of prosperity and expansion followed his election. Much has happened since, and the loyalty of blue collar voters in most parts of the country has shifted away—though it returns from time to time—from Republicans. But in Canton, not so much has changed. This muscular city and the nearby towns of Massillon and Alliance, where some of our current National Football League teams got their start, still retains a basic preference for the Republican Party. And so does the 16th congressional district of Ohio, which includes Canton, Alliance, and Massillon in Stark County, plus Wayne County, a rural and small town area that includes John Dean's alma mater of Wooster College.

McKinley was elected to the House of Representatives six times from the rough equivalent of the 16th district. In those more volatile times, however, he lost the seat twice to Democrats —which didn't prevent him, in those days before the seniority system, from becoming Chairman of the House Ways and Means Committee. He is not the only House leader Canton has produced. More recently, 16th district Congressman Frank Bow, first elected in 1950, became ranking Republican on the House Appropriations Committee; he decided to retire in 1972 and died just weeks before his last term expired.

The current Congressman is Republican Ralph Regula, a former state Senator who, appropriately, is a graduate of the William McKinley School of Law. Regula is considered a political moderate and has solid popularity here: he won with 66% of the vote in 1974. In 1975 he joined the Appropriations Committee, where he serves on the rather liberal Interior Subcommittee and also on the panel which determines appropriations for Congress itself.

Census Data Pop. 463,699. Central city, 24%; suburban, 57%. Median family income, $10,197; families above $15,000: 19%; families below $3,000: 6%. Median years education, 12.1.

The Voters

Median voting age 43.
Employment profile White collar, 41%. Blue collar, 45%. Service, 12%. Farm, 2%.
Ethnic groups Black, 5%. Total foreign stock, 11%. Italy, 2%; Germany, UK, 1% each.

Presidential vote

1972	Nixon (R)	113,402	(65%)
	McGovern (D)	61,173	(35%)
1968	Nixon (R)	84,405	(50%)
	Humphrey (D)	66,946	(39%)
	Wallace (AI)	18,844	(11%)

Rep. Ralph S. Regula (R) Elected 1972; b. Dec. 3, 1924, Beach City; home, Navarre; Mt. Union Col., B.A. 1948, Wm. McKinley School of Law, LL.B. 1952.

Career Navy, WWII; Practicing atty., 1952–73; Ohio Bd. of Educ., 1960–64; Ohio House of Reps., 1965–66; Ohio Senate 1967–72.

Offices 1729 LHOB, 202-225-3876. Also 8787 Erie Ave. S.W., Box 1, Navarre 44662, 216-756-2635.

Committees

Appropriations (17th). Subcommittees: Interior; Legislative.

Group Ratings

	ADA	COPE	LWV	RIPON	NFU	LCV	CFA	NAB	NSI	ACA
1974	35	27	83	63	64	53	54	73	90	40
1973	39	18	64	77	30	53	29	–	–	68

Key Votes

1) Foreign Aid	FOR	6) Gov Abortn Aid	AGN	11) Pub Cong Election $	FOR
2) Busing	AGN	7) Coed Phys Ed	AGN	12) Turkish Arms Cutoff	FOR
3) ABM	FOR	8) Pov Lawyer Gag	AGN	13) Youth Camp Regs	AGN
4) B-1 Bomber	FOR	9) Pub Trans Sub	AGN	14) Strip Mine Veto	AGN
5) Nerve Gas	AGN	10) EZ Voter Regis	AGN	15) Farm Bill Veto	FOR

Election Results

1974 general:	Ralph S. Regula (R)	92,986	(66%)	($61,552)
	John G. Freedom (D)	48,754	(34%)	($15,985)
1974 primary:	Ralph S. Regula (R), unopposed			
1972 general:	Ralph S. Regula (R)	102,013	(57%)	($81,383)
	Virgil L. Musser (D)	75,929	(43%)	($23,328)

◆ ◆ ◆ ◆ ◆

SEVENTEENTH DISTRICT

If you were to try to determine who was— and remains—the least known of our candidates for the major party presidential nominations in 1972, you would almost have to come up, if you could remember it, with the name of John Ashbrook. He started the campaign unknown, and ended it that way; he fielded no significant campaign organization, and his personal appearances made virtually no impact; he raised little money and spent less. He got no more than 10% of the vote in any of the primaries he entered and he failed to win a single delegate vote at the Republican National Convention.

You would be hard put to find, in other words, a record of greater political futility. To be sure, this was not a race that Ashbrook expected to win, or even come close; his purpose, rather, was to make some points. But the points he finally made were just the opposite of what he wanted to establish.

To understand what Ashbrook wanted to do, you have to understand that he grew up believing what Richard Nixon, among others, was saying from the political stump. That was that we needed, in our policies at home, a shift from the welfare state of the New Deal and the Fair Deal back to reliance on the machanics of the free enterprise system; and that abroad, we needed to pursue an aggressive foreign policy and roll back the Iron Curtain, and to rid our government of those whose treasonous advice had resulted in our loss of China. These were the years, the early fifties, when Ashbrook graduated from Harvard and returned to Ohio to go to law school and run the family small town newspaper, that the China Lobby commanded genuine widespread support in the United States, when Chiang Kai–Shek ranked second only to Churchill as the foreigner we most admired. Ashbrook believed in what the major conservatives, including Nixon, were saying publicly in those days, and Ashbrook worked quietly to do something to achieve those ends starting in 1956 in the Ohio legislature and in 1960 moving to the Congress.

What sparked Ashbrook's candidacy in 1972 were two Nixon Administration policies: the adoption of wage and price controls and the opening to what Nixon suddenly was calling the People's Republic of China. Both violated Ashbrook's deepest feelings on domestic and foreign policy, and he was a politician of enough principle, in a year when many Republicans who believed as he did were fawning over Nixon, to have acted on them. Unfortunately for Ashbrook, they proved to be the two most popular policies of the Nixon Administration, the two primary reasons why Nixon was able to win more than 60% of the vote in 1972. Ashbrook had proved the contrary of what he had wanted: he proved that there was no longer, as there was in the 1950s, a significant constituency for the ideas in which he believed most strongly.

It was said when he was running that Ashbrook was taking no political risks with his own career, but that was not quite so. Aside from estranging himself utterly from the House Republican leadership, he also apparently jeopardized his hold on his district. On paper, it looks like solid Republican country: it is the 17th congressional district of Ohio, a collection of small towns and small farms in the north central part of the state. The largest city here is Mansfield (pop. 53,000), which almost never goes Democratic; neither, indeed, does any county here.

But after his 1972 presidential race, Ashbrook's percentage of the vote declined to 57% (ironically, an American Independent candidate took 4%); a not particularly strong Democrat in 1974 held him down to 53%. And in the House, Ashbrook must have been sorely disappointed when California's Phillip Burton engineered the abolition of the House Internal Security (formerly Un-American Activities) Committee, on which he had been serving as ranking minority member. Ashbrook now sits on the liberal dominated Education and Labor and Judiciary panels, where despite all his disappointments in recent years he still contributes constructively to debate and, occasionally, to legislation.

Census Data Pop. 462,846. Central city, 12%; suburban, 16%. Median family income, $9,460; families above $15,000: 16%; families below $3,000: 9%. Median years education, 12.1.

The Voters

Median voting age 42.
Employment profile White collar, 38%. Blue collar, 46%. Service, 12%. Farm, 4%.
Ethnic groups Black, 3%. Total foreign stock, 6%. Germany, 1%.

Presidential vote

1972	Nixon (R)	111,545	(69%)
	McGovern (D)	50,374	(31%)
1968	Nixon (R)	89,436	(54%)
	Humphrey (D)	58,551	(35%)
	Wallace (AI)	18,828	(11%)

Rep. John M. Ashbrook (R) Elected 1960; b. Sept. 21, 1928, Johnstown; home, Johnstown; Harvard U., A.B. 1952, Ohio St. U., J.D. 1955; Baptist.

Career Navy, 1946–48; Publisher, Johnstown *Independent*, 1953–60; Practicing atty., 1955–60; Ohio House of Reps., 1956–60.

Offices 1436 LHOB, 202-225-6431. Also 53 S. Main St., Johnstown 43031, 614-967-5941.

Committees

Education and Labor (2d). Subcommittees: Labor-Management Relations; Labor Standards.

Judiciary (9th). Subcommittees: Crime.

Group Ratings

	ADA	COPE	LWV	RIPON	NFU	LCV	CFA	NAB	NSI	ACA
1974	23	9	10	47	8	25	0	100	89	93
1973	14	20	11	55	16	7	13	–	–	95
1972	6	10	9	15	14	9	50	100	100	100

Key Votes

1) Foreign Aid	AGN	6) Gov Abortn Aid	FOR	11) Pub Cong Election $	AGN
2) Busing	AGN	7) Coed Phys Ed	AGN	12) Turkish Arms Cutoff	FOR
3) ABM	FOR	8) Pov Lawyer Gag	ABS	13) Youth Camp Regs	AGN
4) B-1 Bomber	FOR	9) Pub Trans Sub	AGN	14) Strip Mine Veto	FOR
5) Nerve Gas	AGN	10) EZ Voter Regis	AGN	15) Farm Bill Veto	FOR

Election Results

1974 general:	John M. Ashbrook (R)	70,708	(53%)	($90,357)
	David D. Noble (D)	63,342	(47%)	($57,646)
1974 primary:	John M. Ashbrook (R)	22,845	(71%)	
	David L. Martin (R)	9,458	(29%)	
1972 general:	John M. Ashbrook (R)	92,666	(57%)	($58,173)
	Raymond Beck (D)	62,512	(39%)	($13,062)
	Clifford J. Simpson (AI)	6,376	(4%)	(NA)

◆ ◆ ◆ ◆ ◆

EIGHTEENTH DISTRICT

Perhaps the most hated and the most feared member of the House of Representatives today is Congressman Wayne Hays of the 18th district of Ohio. In the last five years or so, Hays has become one of the most powerful members of Congress; in the last three years, he has become one of the most written about House members. Hays's power is all the more remarkable in that he holds several institutional positions which, until he held them, did not seem all that important; but he has made them great instruments of power. The Chairmanship of the House Administration Committee, for example, was considered so insignificant that Omar Burleson of Texas relinquished it in 1968 for a seat on Ways and Means. But Hays has used the housekeeping powers of the Committee to set up a computer information retrieval system, to bring the House into the twentieth century with an electronic voting system, to cut costs and raise prices in the House cafeteria, to take the operator's seats out of House elevators—all actions designed to give the taxpayer more value for his money. Nor did Hays stop there. He mercilessly slashed the staff of longtime House Doorkeeper Fishbait Miller, and was apparently responsible for the vote that ousted Miller altogether in 1975. On one occasion he refused to sign another congressman's aide's pay voucher, and he has been known to return to Ohio and leave dozens of them unsigned—and employees unpaid.

Wayne Hays, to put it bluntly, is a mean man, and he has not hesitated to use his meanness, and his reputation for it, to achieve his ends. After all, the House remains a place where even the most bitter disputes are cloaked in words of elaborate courtesy and where politicians, always hungry for approval, will blanch at even the hint of an insult. So when Hays is willing to stand up, and not just in the cloakroom but on the floor, and say that another member is senile, most Congressmen will be careful to stay out of his way. With his control over the housekeeping functions of the House almost total, Hays has even his potential enemies cowed; when he was voted, quite temporarily, out of his position as Chairman by the Democratic Steering Committee, it was only because it was a secret vote, and few reporters can get any member to say anything nasty about Hays on the record.

But Hays is not just a petty man who likes to get his way; he is also a legislator with substantial, if bitterly debated, accomplishments. House Administration has jurisdiction over campaign finance reform legislation, and Hays was the architect of the House's bill. He is an opponent of public financing of elections, and although that provision was eventually included in the legislation passed as a result of compromise with the Senate, there was certainly no nonsense about public financing of House elections—which would mean financing the campaigns of incumbents' opponents. On the contrary, there are many critics who say that Hays purposely set the limitations on spending in congressional races too low, so as to prevent challengers from putting together substantial campaign chests. And it is true that Hays's bill, by placing greater limitations on contributions from other groups, increased the power of the Democratic Congressional Campaign Committee, of which he happens to be Chairman.

When you talk about Hays as a power in the House these days, his name is almost always linked with that of Phillip Burton of California, Chairman of the Democratic Caucus. It is not an alliance which would have been indicated by their philosophies: Burton has been a Vietnam dove since 1964, for example, while Hays remained a hawk right through the final American evacuation in 1975. But what Hays and Burton had in common was that both were not particularly liked by the incumbent House leadership, and both are aggressive legislative manueverers—and crafters of laws—with an obvious admiration for each other's talents. Also, while Hays chaired the official campaign committee in 1974, Burton chaired the liberal Democratic Study Group's effort to elect new Democrats—which means between them that they provided often desperately needed funds and advice to most of the freshmen Democrats elected in 1974.

So when Hays was ousted by the Steering Committee from the House Administration chairmanship, Burton was his main ally in running the telephone blitz which resulted in Hays's

161–111 victory in the full Democratic caucus—a victory in which freshman votes were crucial. The Burton-Hays combine was also, so far as can be determined, utterly successful in the other chairmanship fights, in particular the elevation of Henry Reuss of Wisconsin over the aged Wright Patman of Texas on Banking and Currency.

The freshmen have been criticized for supporting Hays on the grounds that, considering his hawkish views and anti-public financing of campaigns stand, he is just not their kind of guy. But what Hays and Burton have done is nothing more than organizing the House as most sensible state legislatures are set up: to reflect the will of the majority of the majority party, and to reward those who assist in that effort and punish those who work against it. The same critics would doubtless have accused the freshmen of irresponsibility if they had dumped the indisputably intelligent Hays, or of inability to use the power they had if they had not dumped some other chairmen.

In any case Hays is not the sort of man whose views can be characterized by a simple word like "hawk." As much as he supported American military intervention in Indochina, he also opposed American support of the dictatorship in Greece—basically because he doesn't like dictators. Though he has sneering contempt for antiwar protestors, he is just as caustic toward the Pentagon brass. And if he doesn't like public financing of elections, he has also been a longtime supporter of restrictions on strip mining—he claims the coal companies beat him for reelection to the Ohio Senate in 1942 because of his stand on that issue.

Indeed, in the 18th district of Ohio, strip mining is liable to be a far more important issue than Greek dictators or campaign contribution limits. This is land, just across the Ohio River from West Virginia, of marginal farms and hills pockmarked by strip mines—a kind of rural industrial slum. There are no big cities here, just small towns like Steubenville (pop. 30,000), a place which has the distiction of having the dirtiest air in the United States. The people of the 18th are the kind of working class Americans who work hard, get little for it, and pay taxes with few complaints. They are ancestrally Democratic, and seldom—the 1972 presidential race was an exception—vote Republican. In the primary that year 61% of the Democrats here voted for Wayne Hays for President, and in the general election of 1974 66% of them voted for him for Congress. There is no likelihood that he will ever be defeated, nor that he will ever be (as he might like to be) Speaker; but he should remain for the next few years one of the most important and powerful members of the Congress.

Census Data Pop. 462,797. Central city, 7%; suburban, 32%. Median family income, $8,701; families above $15,000: 11%; families below $3,000: 11%. Median years education, 11.5.

The Voters

Median voting age 46.
Employment profile White collar, 34%. Blue collar, 51%. Service, 12%. Farm, 3%.
Ethnic groups Black, 2%. Total foreign stock, 12%. Italy, 3%; UK, 2%; Poland, Czechoslovakia, Germany, 1% each.

Presidential vote

1972	Nixon (R)	111,800	(61%)
	McGovern (D)	72,581	(39%)
1968	Nixon (R)	78,803	(41%)
	Humphrey (D)	95,894	(50%)
	Wallace (AI)	17,152	(9%)

Rep. Wayne L. Hays (D) Elected 1948; b. May 13, 1911, Bannock; home, Flushing; Ohio St. U., B.S. 1933, Duke U., 1935; Presbyterian.

Career Teacher, 1935–39; Mayor of Flushing, 1939–45; Ohio Senate, 1941–42; Army WWII; Belmont Co. Commissioner, 1945–49.

Offices 2264 RHOB, 202-225-6265. Also 150 W. Main St., St. Clairsville 43950, 614-695-4600.

Committees

House Administration (Chairman).

International Relations (3d). Subcommittees: International Operations (Chairman); Oversight.

Group Ratings

	ADA	COPE	LWV	RIPON	NFU	LCV	CFA	NAB	NSI	ACA
1974	32	100	40	25	83	71	70	36	89	38
1973	52	100	45	31	100	63	83	–	–	28
1972	38	100	75	40	80	32	100	18	88	41

Key Votes

1) Foreign Aid	FOR	6) Gov Abortn Aid	AGN	11) Pub Cong Election $	AGN
2) Busing	AGN	7) Coed Phys Ed	AGN	12) Turkish Arms Cutoff	FOR
3) ABM	FOR	8) Pov Lawyer Gag	FOR	13) Youth Camp Regs	FOR
4) B-1 Bomber	FOR	9) Pub Trans Sub	FOR	14) Strip Mine Veto	AGN
5) Nerve Gas	AGN	10) EZ Voter Regis	FOR	15) Farm Bill Veto	AGN

Election Results

1974 general:	Wayne L. Hays (D)	90,447	(66%)	($32,285)
	Ralph H. Romig (R)	47,385	(34%)	($2,347)
1974 primary:	Wayne L. Hays (D)	42,769	(80%)	
	Nick B. Karnick (D)	10,878	(20%)	
1972 general:	Wayne L. Hays (D)	128,663	(70%)	($20,009)
	Robert Stewart (R)	54,572	(30%)	($3,300)

◆ ◆ ◆ ◆ ◆

NINETEENTH DISTRICT

The 19th congressional district of Ohio is one of the most heavily industrial in the nation. Both Youngstown (pop. 140,000) and Warren (pop. 63,000), the district's two major cities, are important steel towns (Youngstown Sheet and Tube and Republic Steel). Situated about halfway between Cleveland and Pittsburgh, these two cities are also halfway between the docks that unload iron ore from the Great Lakes ranges and the coal fields of western Pennsylvania and West Virginia. Recently, they have been victims of the declining fortunes of the great steel firms. A few years ago, Youngstown simply closed down its school system for a couple of months—the first major city to go to this extreme because of lack of funds.

Even this somewhat depressed area has seen a flight to the suburbs—not just of people, but of industry. Some 15 miles east of Youngstown, for example, is the Lordstown GM assembly plant, probably the nation's most written-about factory in recent years. Designed as an ultramodern, capital-intensive facility, the operation was to turn out Vegas at the lowest possible cost; and it was located in a field next to the Ohio Turnpike, miles from anybody. The work force at the plant is young, a large percentage under 30. Not long after the factory went into production, the workers began to object to what they considered the inhuman pace of the assembly line. Management, they said, treated the workers like machines. There followed a full-scale strike over working conditions, which was settled finally after UAW officials came flying down from Detroit to find out what was going on.

Lordstown has come to represent a new industrial phenomenon, a revolt by young workers against the inhumanity of the work place. Older hands quite rightly point out that auto plants have never been pleasant places to work. But Lordstown surely does mark the beginning of something different in labor-management relations—and important contrast to the local heritage. For in the 1930s there were massive sit-down strikes in the steel mills of Youngstown and Warren, when the workers held the factories until management agreed to recognize their union. The participants in these sometimes bloody strikes had a specific cause, union recognition, and a general faith that once it was achieved life would be better for them. The Lordstown strikers, on the other hand, or so at least the flock of writers who went out to interview them found, had no cause, no faith, no sense of directed efforts, only a deep cynicism—to put in time, make money, and get out of the plant as soon as possible.

The same cynicism and indifference appears to have become a part of the politics of the 19th district. Back in the days of the New Deal and the bloody steel strikes, the majority of

Youngstown area voters—whether from West Virginia, Italy, or Czechoslovakia—had few doubts as to who was and who was not a political friend. The district went heavily for Franklin D. Roosevelt, Harry Truman, John F. Kennedy, and Lyndon Johnson. But lately that sentiment has shifted, or at least softened. In 1972, Richard Nixon actually carried the 19th district, though only by a small margin. And although John Gilligan swept the Youngstown and Warren areas with 63% of the vote in 1974, turnout there was down 5% from 1970 and down 8% from turnout in the last really big Democratic year in Ohio, 1958. It is not just a matter of confidence in the Democrats (or the Republicans) declining; there is a total lack of confidence in the political system itself. Young blue collar workers, in particular, seem to be quite ready to vote for a candidate like George Wallace—or just not vote at all.

The waning of the New Deal tradition in the 19th district was symbolized by the death in 1970 of its former Congressman, Michael J. Kirwan, at age 83. With a third-grade education and a canny political sense, Kirwan spent 34 years on Capitol Hill and became a power in the House. When he died, Kirwan was the number two Democrat on the Appropriations Committee and the shameless Chairman of its pork-barreling Public Works Subcommittee. He was also longtime Chairman of the Democratic Congressional Campaign Committee—a post that has devolved to Wayne Hays of the adjacent 18th district. Kirwan ruthlessly pushed his pet projects, including a $10 million aquarium for Washington, D.C., and a proposed Ohio River-Lake Erie Canal, known affectionately as "Mike's Ditch." After his death, both projects were abandoned.

Kirwan's successor, Democrat Charles Carney, is a 20-year veteran of the Ohio state Senate and a former staffer with the United Steel Workers and the United Rubber Workers. In 1970, Carney won a 13-candidate Democratic primary—the most crowded field in the country that year—and went on to beat Republican Margaret Dennison, whose husband had represented the neighboring 11th district during the 1950s. In 1972, the man who finished second in the primary again challenged Carney, and held him to 56% of the vote. Apparently Carney received the message—that he was not as popular as he might have thought—and began to use the resources of incumbency to build up his local popularity. In any case, in 1974 he attracted only two weak primary opponents and won 78% of the vote. As might be expected, this longtime labor man has a perfect voting record according to organized labor.

Census Data Pop. 463,625. Central city, 44%; suburban, 56%. Median family income, $10,311; families above $15,000: 21%; families below $3,000: 7%. Median years education, 12.1.

The Voters

Median voting age 44.
Employment profile White collar, 41%. Blue collar, 46%. Service, 12%. Farm, 1%.
Ethnic groups Black, 11%. Spanish, 1%. Total foreign stock, 23%. Italy, 6%; Czechoslovakia, 3%; UK, Poland, 2% each; Yugoslavia, Austria, Germany, Hungary, 1% each.

Presidential vote

1972	Nixon (R)	96,607	(52%)
	McGovern (D)	88,500	(48%)
1968	Nixon (R)	65,508	(36%)
	Humphrey (D)	98,277	(54%)
	Wallace (AI)	18,342	(10%)

Rep. Charles J. Carney (D) Elected 1970; b. Apr. 17, 1913, Youngstown; home, Youngstown; Youngstown St. U.; Catholic.

Career Pres., Dist. Cncl. no. 1, Utd. Rubber Workers, 1940–43, Staff Rep. and Dist. Dir., 1942–50; Staff Rep., Utd. Steelworkers of Amer., 1950–68; Ohio Senate, 1950–70, Minor Ldr., 1969–70.

Offices 1714 LHOB, 202-225-5261. Also 1108 Wick Bldg., Youngstown 44503, 216-746-8071.

Committees

Interstate and Foreign Commerce (15th). Subcommittees: Communications; Health and Environment.

Small Business (9th). Subcommittees: Commodities and Services (Chairman); Government Procurement and International Trade.

Veterans' Affairs (6th). Subcommittees: Hospitals.

Group Ratings

	ADA	COPE	LWV	RIPON	NFU	LCV	CFA	NAB	NSI	ACA
1974	73	100	67	47	86	76	90	30	20	23
1973	86	100	83	64	95	78	100	–	–	9
1972	75	100	91	46	83	53	100	11	22	11

Key Votes

1) Foreign Aid	FOR	6) Gov Abortn Aid	AGN	11) Pub Cong Election $	AGN
2) Busing	AGN	7) Coed Phys Ed	AGN	12) Turkish Arms Cutoff	ABS
3) ABM	AGN	8) Pov Lawyer Gag	AGN	13) Youth Camp Regs	FOR
4) B-1 Bomber	FOR	9) Pub Trans Sub	FOR	14) Strip Mine Veto	AGN
5) Nerve Gas	AGN	10) EZ Voter Regis	FOR	15) Farm Bill Veto	AGN

Election Results

1974 general:	Charles J. Carney (D)	97,709	(73%)		($15,133)
	James L. Ripple (R)	36,649	(27%)		($794)
1974 primary:	Charles J. Carney (D)	54,004	(78%)		
	Two others (D)	15,537	(22%)		
1972 general:	Charles J. Carney (D)	109,979	(64%)		($54,037)
	Norman M. Parr (R)	61,934	(36%)		($21,307)

◆ ◆ ◆ ◆ ◆

TWENTIETH DISTRICT

Down the center of Cleveland flows the Cuyahoga River, a waterway so polluted with industrial wastes that it once caught fire. On both sides of the Cuyahoga are Cleveland's giant steel mills and other factories—many of the same operations that made Cleveland the nation's fourth largest city in 1910. In the years that followed, Cleveland lost the auto industry to Detroit and otherwise failed to match the growth rate of big-city America; so the Cleveland metropolitan area is now only the twelfth largest in the nation. Moreover, the central city has more than its share of urban problems. These are symbolized by the Cuyahoga, and not just for its pollution: the river also divides the races in the city of Cleveland.

East of the Cuyahoga, most of Cleveland is black. Here and there are remnants of ethnic neighborhoods, called cosmo wards in Cleveland, which absorbed the Poles, Czechs, Hungarians, and Italians who came over on various grimy boats to work in the equally grimy steel mills along the Cuyahoga. But the vast majority of Clevelanders now living east of the river are black, and many of the black neighborhoods are so forbidding that Carl Stokes, the city's first and through 1975 anyway, only black Mayor (1967–71), lived in a Cleveland house that sat on the line separating the city from the posh suburb of Shaker Heights. By glaring contrast, Cleveland west of the Cuyahoga is just about 100% white. Here, in this largely working class area, are the city's remaining cosmo wards. The population in the wards is tipped toward the elderly end of the age scale, as younger people have moved out to suburbs like Parma (see Twenty-Third District).

Almost all of the west side of Cleveland, plus a couple of cosmo wards in the east, and a few suburbs to the South (Brook Park, Brooklyn, part of Parma, and Garfield Heights among them), make up the 20th congressional district of Ohio. A Democratic district by tradition, the people here have been upset for some time with the trends at work in the party of their ancestors. In 1967 and 1969, Carl Stokes's name on the Democratic line got him only around 20% of the votes in the area. The district went for Hubert Humphrey in 1968, but gave George Wallace a whopping 17% at the same time. In 1972, Richard Nixon carried the district.

For nearly 30 years, from 1943 to 1971, the 20th's Congressman was Michael Feighan, a rather conservative Democrat. As Chairman of the Judiciary Subcommittee on Immigration, Feighan managed to block liberalization of the nation'a immigration laws for many years. By doing so, Feighan insured that Congressmen who wanted to help constituents with immigration problems—and that meant big-city Democrats especially—were forced to deal with him on a case-by-case basis.

The laws were rewritten in 1965. Thereafter, Feighan seemed to lose his grip on the district. During the late 1960s, he encountered tough primary opposition. Then, in 1970, the 65-year-old Feighan was finally unseated by 38-year-old James Stanton, then President of the Cleveland City Council. In 1968, Stanton had been the Democratic nominee in the much more Republican 23d district, and had nearly won there. When he moved to the 20th for the 1970 election, Stanton proved so popular that he beat Feighan by 11,000 votes—in percentage terms, a 53–33 margin—with the rest going to a minor candidate. Stanton then won the general election with 81% of the votes, better than Feighan ever did.

Stanton has since increased his percentage to 82% in 1972 and a near unanimous 87% in 1974. In the House Stanton stands with other urban Democrats on most issues, though he tends to heed his constituency's instincts on matters of law 'n' order. Phenomenally popular in his home district and very well known in the state's largest media market, Stanton is considered a prospect for statewide office, and at this writing seems a likely candidate for the Senate in 1976.

Census Data Pop. 462,480. Central city, 65%; suburban, 35%. Median family income, $10,550; families above $15,000: 20%; families below $3,000: 7%. Median years education, 11.1.

The Voters

Median voting age 44.
Employment profile White collar, 41%. Blue collar, 47%. Service, 12%. Farm, –%.
Ethnic groups Black, 3%. Spanish, 2%. Total foreign stock, 32%. Poland, 6%; Czechoslovakia, Italy, 4% each; Germany, 3%; Hungary, Austria, Yugoslavia, 2% each; USSR, UK, Ireland, 1% each.

Presidential vote

1972	Nixon (R)	79,056	(52%)
	McGovern (D)	74,041	(48%)
1968	Nixon (R)	48,106	(29%)
	Humphrey (D)	89,863	(54%)
	Wallace (AI)	27,696	(17%)

Rep. James V. Stanton (D) Elected 1970; b. Feb. 27, 1932, Cleveland; home, Cleveland; U. of Dayton, A.B. 1958, Cleveland-Marshall Col. of Law, J.D. 1961; Catholic.

Career Air Force, Korea; Practicing atty.; Cleveland City Cncl., 1959–70, Pres., 1964–70.

Offices 1107 LHOB, 202-225-5871. Also Fed. Court House, 215 Superior Ave., Cleveland 44114, 216-522-4927.

Committees

Government Operations (15th). Subcommittees: Legislation and National Security; Manpower and Housing.

Public Works and Transportation (11th). Subcommittees: Aviation; Surface Transportation.

Group Ratings

	ADA	COPE	LWV	RIPON	NFU	LCV	CFA	NAB	NSI	ACA
1974	90	100	55	43	92	80	33	33	8	12
1973	74	100	83	64	95	75	86	–	–	–
1972	56	82	75	60	83	51	50	10	11	22

Key Votes

1) Foreign Aid	FOR	6) Gov Abortn Aid	ABS	11) Pub Cong Election $	AGN
2) Busing	AGN	7) Coed Phys Ed	FOR	12) Turkish Arms Cutoff	FOR
3) ABM	AGN	8) Pov Lawyer Gag	AGN	13) Youth Camp Regs	FOR
4) B-1 Bomber	FOR	9) Pub Trans Sub	FOR	14) Strip Mine Veto	AGN
5) Nerve Gas	AGN	10) EZ Voter Regis	FOR	15) Farm Bill Veto	AGN

Election Results

1974 general:	James V. Stanton (D)	86,405	(87%)	($26,109)
	Robert A. Frantz (R)	12,991	(13%)	($1,757)
1974 primary:	James V. Stanton (D)	40,665	(87%)	
	John T. Flanigan (D)	6,055	(13%)	
1972 general:	James V. Stanton (D)	100,678	(82%)	($44,272)
	Thomas E. Vilt (R)	16,624	(14%)	($8,157)
	Richard B. Kay (AI)	5,285	(4%)	(NA)

◆ ◆ ◆ ◆ ◆

TWENTY-FIRST DISTRICT

The 21st congressional district of Ohio is the east side of Cleveland (see Twentieth District), plus a couple of adjacent suburbs. This area was once a checkerboard of Polish, Czech, Hungarian, and Italian neighborhoods, but today it is heavily black (66% district-wide in 1970, more like 75% today). The central part of the 21st includes some of the poorest black ghettoes in the nation, while the black neighborhoods to the north and south are more middle-class. There are still a few ethnic ("cosmo" in Cleveland) enclaves left in the 21st, populated mainly by old people who cannot afford to move out of the city; this group has been the source of most of the district's rather pathetic minority of Republican votes in the past. The suburban cities in the district are either already a majority black (East Cleveland) or in the process of becoming so (Warrensville Heights). Ironically, some of Cleveland's wealthiest suburbs, like Shaker Heights and Cleveland Heights, are no more than a mile or two from some of the big city's most dilapidated slums.

Liberal Democrat Charles Vanik represented the 21st from 1955 until 1969. When the 1968 redistricting made it clear that the new 21st would have a solid black majority, Vanik left to run in the suburban 22d, where he ousted the Republican incumbent. His successor in the 21st was Louis Stokes, brother of then Cleveland Mayor (and now New York newscaster) Carl Stokes. Like his brother Congressman Stokes grew up in poverty, and was able to attend college and law school only after serving in the Army during World War II.

Stokes's election was a clear reflection of his brother's popularity on the east side. After the congressional victory of 1968, the two Stokes brothers put together their own political machine, known as the 21st District Caucus. It has suffered some defeats, as when black school board President Arnold Pinkney lost the Mayor's office to Republican Ralph Perk in 1971; and has since split into several groups. Mayor Stokes' departure from office and later from Cleveland obviously deprived it of patronage resources.

The Congressman is the older Stokes brother, and though he began his political career later, it has lasted far longer. When he first took office in 1968, Stokes, Bill Clay of St. Louis, and John Conyers of Detroit were the most militant voices in the what would soon become Congressional Black Caucus; they were soon joined, however, by other black Representatives who essentially shared their views. Stokes has served a term as Black Caucus Chairman, but for the long haul it is surely more significant that he was the first black member of the Appropriations Committee, and now ranks 24th on that body. His reelection has never been in doubt: he never has significant primary opposition, and in 1974 he got 82% of the vote.

Census Data Pop. 462,584. Central city, 87%; suburban, 13%. Median family income, $8,573; families above $15,000: 14%; families below $3,000: 16%. Median years education, 10.9.

The Voters

Median voting age 42.
Employment profile White collar, 37%. Blue collar, 44%. Service, 19%. Farm, –%.
Ethnic groups Black, 66%. Total foreign stock, 14%. Yugoslavia, Italy, Hungary, 2% each; Czechoslovakia, Poland, Germany, 1% each.

Presidential vote

1972	Nixon (R)	27,661	(21%)
	McGovern (D)	101,276	(79%)
1968	Nixon (R)	23,965	(15%)
	Humphrey (D)	123,971	(77%)
	Wallace (AI)	12,391	(8%)

Rep. Louis Stokes (D) Elected 1968; b. Feb. 23, 1925, Cleveland; home, Cleveland; Western Reserve U., 1946–48, Cleveland-Marshall Law School, J.D. 1953; Methodist.

Career Practicing atty., 1954–68.

Offices 303 CHOB, 202-225-7032. Also Rm. 2947, New Fed. Ofc. Bldg., 1240 E. 9th St., Cleveland 44199, 216-522-4900.

Committees

Appropriations (24th). Subcommittees: District of Columbia; HUD-Independent Agencies; Labor-HEW.

Budget (14th).

Group Ratings

	ADA	COPE	LWV	RIPON	NFU	LCV	CFA	NAB	NSI	ACA
1974	94	100	91	67	92	85	91	18	0	0
1973	100	100	91	73	93	100	100	–	–	10
1972	100	90	100	69	100	83	100	10	0	5

Key Votes

1) Foreign Aid	FOR	6) Gov Abortn Aid	FOR	11) Pub Cong Election $	FOR
2) Busing	FOR	7) Coed Phys Ed	FOR	12) Turkish Arms Cutoff	FOR
3) ABM	AGN	8) Pov Lawyer Gag	AGN	13) Youth Camp Regs	ABS
4) B-1 Bomber	AGN	9) Pub Trans Sub	FOR	14) Strip Mine Veto	AGN
5) Nerve Gas	AGN	10) EZ Voter Regis	ABS	15) Farm Bill Veto	AGN

Election Results

1974 general:	Louis Stokes (D)	58,969	(82%)	($42,214)
	Bill Mack (R)	12,986	(18%)	($0)
1974 primary:	Louis Stokes (D)	32,222	(71%)	
	Three others (D)	13,034	(29%)	
1972 general:	Louis Stokes (D)	99,190	(81%)	($17,718)
	James D. Johnson (R)	13,861	(11%)	($7,531)
	Joseph Pirincin (Socialist Labor)	5,779	(5%)	(NA)
	Cecil Lampkins (Ind.)	3,509	(3%)	(NA)

◆ ◆ ◆ ◆ ◆

TWENTY-SECOND DISTRICT

The 22d district of Ohio is the eastern half of the ring of suburbs around Cleveland, plus a very small part (12,000 residents) of the city itself. The various suburbs have been settled by people of varying ethnic stock, who have moved here following the radial avenues out of central-city Cleveland. There are suburbs that are predominantly Italian (Mayfield Heights), Serbian (Solon), Hungarian (Euclid), Jewish (University Heights, Beachwood), and high-income WASP (Gates Mills, Pepper Pike). The most well-known of the 22d's communities is also one of its most varied, Shaker Heights. This suburb, hard by the Cleveland city limits, contains the estate-like homes of some of Cleveland's wealthiest WASPs and Jews. Lying next to the Cleveland ghetto, Shaker Heights has been opened up in recent years to affluent blacks, as has Cleveland Heights, just to the north.

Before 1972, the 22d lay entirely within Cleveland's Cuyahoga county. With redistricting, it has now spread into adjacent Lake, Geauga, and Summit Counties. The move has made little difference in the sociological or political composition of the district. The appended territory is part of the Cleveland urban area, and new residents from it are moving out here daily.

On balance the 22d is a Democratic district, which has favored barely defeated candidates like Howard Metzenbaum (a Shaker Heights resident) in 1970 and John Gilligan in 1974. But for 30 years, the district always went Republican in House elections, thanks to the vote-getting prowess of Mrs. Frances P. Bolton. A member of the socially prominent Payne family, Mrs. Bolton succeeded her late husband in Congress in 1940, and was reelected enough times to become the ranking Republican on the House Foreign Affairs Committee. (One major Bolton contribution: she was disturbed that developers were going to put up a subdivision on the Potomac within sight of Mount Vernon, and so she bought the land herself to stop it.) But in 1968, her time was up. Democratic Congressman Charles Vanik, who had represented the 21st district in Cleveland for 14 years, moved into the 22d after his old seat had become a majority black. Vanik was almost 30 years younger than Mrs. Bolton, his Eastern European ancestry helped in many of the district's towns and his longtime support of Israel gave him a big edge in the Jewish suburbs.

After defeating Mrs. Bolton in 1968, Vanik has won reelection easily; in 1974, he announced that he would spend literally nothing on his campaign, did and won with 79% of the vote. Now the sixth-ranking Democrat on the House Ways and Means Committee, Vanik is in a position finally to see many of his liberal positions prevail. He was visibly chafing in the last years of Wilbur Mills' domination of the Committee, and was pushing for major progressive tax reforms. But even before Mills' fall from power, Vanik was able to outmaneuver him. He was the main House sponsor of the Jackson-Vanik Amendment, to deny the Soviet Union most favored nation treatment until they allowed free emigration of Jews and others; he rounded up a majority in the whole House in support, at which point Mills went along.

Census Data Pop. 462,271. Central city, 3%; suburban, 97%. Median family income, $13,427; families above $15,000: 41%; families below $3,000: 3%. Median years education, 12.5.

The Voters

Median voting age 45.
Employment profile White collar, 63%. Blue collar, 29%. Service, 8%. Farm, –%.
Ethnic groups Black, 2%. Total foreign stock, 32%. Italy, 5%. USSR, Poland, Germany, Yugoslavia, 3% each; Hungary, UK, Czechoslovakia, Austria, 2% each; Canada, 1%.

Presidential vote

1972	Nixon (R)	119,412	(57%)
	McGovern (D)	90,689	(43%)
1968	Nixon (R)	89,300	(44%)
	Humphrey (D)	96,883	(47%)
	Wallace (AI)	18,560	(9%)

Rep. Charles A. Vanik (D) Elected 1954; b. Apr. 7, 1913, Cleveland; home, Euclid; Western Reserve U., B.A. 1933, LL.B. 1936; Catholic.

Career Practicing atty.; Cleveland City Cncl., 1938–39; Ohio Senate, 1940–41; Cleveland Bd. of Educ., 1941–42; Navy, WWII; Cleveland Library Bd., 1946; Judge, Cleveland Municipal Ct., 1947–54.

Offices 2371 RHOB, 202-225-6331. Also 107 Old Fed. Bldg., Cleveland 44114, 216-522-4253.

Committees

Ways and Means (6th). Subcommittees: Health; Oversight (Chairman).

Group Ratings

	ADA	COPE	LWV	RIPON	NFU	LCV	CFA	NAB	NSI	ACA
1974	87	91	83	63	86	94	92	17	10	7
1973	92	100	92	73	75	95	88	–	–	11
1972	94	100	92	73	71	87	100	8	0	4

Key Votes

1) Foreign Aid	FOR	6) Gov Abortn Aid	AGN	11) Pub Cong Election $	FOR
2) Busing	AGN	7) Coed Phys Ed	FOR	12) Turkish Arms Cutoff	FOR
3) ABM	AGN	8) Pov Lawyer Gag	AGN	13) Youth Camp Regs	FOR
4) B-1 Bomber	AGN	9) Pub Trans Sub	FOR	14) Strip Mine Veto	AGN
5) Nerve Gas	AGN	10) EZ Voter Regis	FOR	15) Farm Bill Veto	FOR

Election Results

1974 general:	Charles A. Vanik (D)	112,671	(79%)	($649)
	William J. Franz (R)	30,585	(21%)	($4,190)
1974 primary:	Charles A. Vanik (D)	50,279	(88%)	
	William J. Kennick (D)	4,286	(8%)	
	Edward L. Viets (D)	2,566	(4%)	
1972 general:	Charles A. Vanik (D)	126,462	(66%)	($36,067)
	Donald W. Gropp (R)	64,577	(34%)	($128,430)

◆ ◆ ◆ ◆ ◆

TWENTY-THIRD DISTRICT

In rough terms, the 23d district of Ohio is the suburbs south and west of Cleveland. These can be divided, and considered, in two parts. The suburbs to the west are upper-middle-income WASPy towns like Lakewood, Rocky River, and Bay Village—all cast heavy Republican margins and front on Lake Erie. As one moves farther away from the Lake, Republican percentages tend to decline; and the suburbs to the south are basically Democratic. These were settled more recently, in the 1950s and 1960s, generally by people of Slavic and Hungarian descent who grew up in the smoggier, less spacious streets of the west side of Cleveland.

The largest and best known of these suburbs is Parma (pop. 100,000), most of which lies in the 23d. It is a diffuse town whose bowling alleys are closely monitored by national political reporters for signs of change in public opinion. Parma is heavily Polish, Ukrainian, and Slavic; it is ancestrally Democratic, but a place inclined to switch to Republican politicians in recent years. Parma went for Humphrey in 1968, but only by a plurality, as Wallace took 14% of its votes. Four years later, Nixon carried Parma, 59–41; but the town turned sharply against him as a result of the Watergate revelations. The dominant mood there now seems to be a sort of snarling apathy; in 1974, turnout was sharply down—a fact which resulted in the narrow defeat of Governor John Gilligan.

Gilligan's defeat tells us more than a little about the political attitudes of people here, and not just about their sour skepticism in 1974, but, retrospectively, how they came to be so inclined, before Watergate, to the politics of Richard Nixon and Spiro Agnew. For middle income Catholics of lower income background, as for most of us, politics is a form of cultural expression. And the politics these people have traditionally favored, which they grew up with, is Democratic ward politics, heavily ethnic in flavor, with candidates whose grammar is uncertain, whose machinations on occasion may be roguish; who support New Deal type economic programs but who are hostile to any challenges to the rigid social ethics of conservative Catholic priests of the 1930s. It is not hard to see why the Democratic politics of the 1960s—with its heavy emphasis on civil rights, social science jargon, and its sometimes sentimental attitude toward what it liked to call the disadvantaged—turned these people off. Some of that effect was inevitable from the policies such Democrats espoused, but the reaction in places like Parma was also a spurning of a style of political discourse which seemed to turn its back on and show scorn for the values these people had grown up with. They saw the same thing—though the policy issues were different—in Gilligan. Here was a man more or less from their own background, a Catholic and by no means an aristocrat like the Kennedys, whose self-deprecatory humor and irreverent attitudes made him seem more comfortable in the company of the WASP liberals, whom the people of Parma hate more than anyone. More than anything, they cannot forgive a man who rises from their own stratum of society and who seems happy to have done so. It is a strange thing, perhaps, to oust a Governor; but for these people, like so many others, the style of leadership is often more important than the substance.

The sour skepticism of the 23d district has produced a congressional politics here of unusual instability. For 20 years the district was represented by Republican William Minshall, a standard Ohio conservative who at the end of his service became ranking minority member of the Defense Appropriations Subcommittee. Minshall was closely challenged in 1968 by then Cleveland Council President James Stanton, who went on in the next election to become Congressman from the 20th district; in 1970, he turned back more easily a challenge from Ronald Mottl, a crew cut state Senator from Parma who made the mistake of divorcing his wife and marrying an 18-year-old beauty contest runner up just before beginning his campaign. In 1972, Minshall had his closest call beating by just a 49–47 margin 25-year-old Cleveland Councilman Dennis Kucinich.

That was enough for Minshall: he retired in 1974. Kucinich looked like the obvious favorite to win, but he is rather an odd sort of politician, a maverick who built up a public following and made many enemies by his sensational charges against many Cleveland area politicians. In 1974, Kucinich was feuding with local Democrats, and so he decided to run this time as an Independent. With a three-cornered race in the offing, the Republicans put up a strong candidate in the person of state Representative George Mastics. As for the Democrats, they had a fiercely contested primary, where James Celebreze, son of the former Cleveland Mayor and HEW Secretary, and Robert Sweeney, a perennial name candidate who managed to get elected Congressman-at-Large in 1964, were beaten by none other than Ronald Mottl. The general election was as close as could be: Kucinich had 30%, Mastics 31%, and Mottl 36%. Thus Mottle became the only crew-cut freshman Democrat, and the one with the lowest percentage of votes in his district. Somehow one assumes that however soured the voters of the 23d remain with politics, he should be reelected in 1976—but nothing, it seems, is for certain in this district.

Census Data Pop. 462,724. Central city, 9%; suburban, 91%. Median family income, $13,101; families above $15,000: 37%; families below $3,000: 3%. Median years education, 12.4.

The Voters

Median voting age 44.
Employment profile White collar, 61%. Blue collar, 30%. Service, 9%. Farm, –%.
Ethnic groups Total foreign stock, 28%. Czechoslovakia, 4%; Germany, Poland, Italy, 3% each; UK, Hungary, Austria, 2% each; Yugoslavia, Canada, Ireland, 1% each.

Presidential vote

1972	Nixon (R)	131,709	(65%)
	McGovern (D)	71,361	(35%)
1968	Nixon (R)	97,416	(51%)
	Humphrey (D)	74,119	(39%)
	Wallace (AI)	19,802	(10%)

Rep. Ronald M. Mottl (D) Elected 1974; b. Feb. 6, 1934, Cleveland; home, Parma; U. of Notre Dame, B.S., 1956, LL.B. 1957.

Career Army, 1957–58; Practicing atty., 1958–74; Cleveland Asst. Law Dir., 1958–60; Parma City Cncl., 1960–67, Pres., 1962–67; Ohio House of Reps., 1967–69; Ohio Senate, 1969–74.

Offices 1233 LHOB, 202-225-5731. Also 2951 Fed. Ofc. Bldg., 1240 E. 9th St., Cleveland 44199, 216-522-4382.

Committees

Education and Labor (26th). Subcommittees: Elementary, Secondary and Vocational Education; Post-secondary Education.

Veterans' Affairs (11th). Subcommittees: Cemeteries and Burial Benefits; Compensation, Pension and Insurance; Education and Training.

Group Ratings: Newly Elected

Key Votes

1) Foreign Aid	AGN	6) Gov Abortn Aid	NE	11) Pub Cong Election $	NE
2) Busing	NE	7) Coed Phys Ed	FOR	12) Turkish Arms Cutoff	NE
3) ABM	NE	8) Pov Lawyer Gag	NE	13) Youth Camp Regs	FOR
4) B-1 Bomber	FOR	9) Pub Trans Sub	NE	14) Strip Mine Veto	AGN
5) Nerve Gas	NE	10) EZ Voter Regis	NE	15) Farm Bill Veto	FOR

OKLAHOMA

Election Results

1974 general:	Ronald M. Mottl (D)	53,338	(36%)	($63,671)
	George E. Mastics (R)	46,810	(31%)	($78,348)
	Dennis J. Kucinich (Ind.)	45,186	(30%)	($18,195)
	Hugh J. Gallagher (Ind.)	3,461	(2%)	($4,841)
1974 primary:	Ronald M. Mottl (D)	21,533	(43%)	
	Robert E. Sweeney (D)	11,148	(22%)	
	James P. Celebreeze (D)	9,032	(18%)	
	Three others (D)	8,486	(17%)	

OKLAHOMA

Somebody said Oklahoma is a little cow, a little dirt, and a little oil. Ninety years ago, it was mostly dirt—impoverished Indian reservations onto which the Cherokees and the other Civilized Tribes had been herded from their ancestral lands in the South and Midwest. In 1889, the federal government decided to open up what is now Oklahoma to white settlement. On the morning of the great land rush, thousands of would-be homesteaders drove their wagons across the territorial line in a moment that numerous movies have captured.

The "Sooners," as they were called (for those who crossed the line sooner than they were supposed to), quickly came to out-number the Indians. Nonetheless, Oklahoma today has the largest Indian population of any state (97,000); the state, however, has no reservations, because the Indians are pretty well assimilated into the rest of the population. During its first years, Oklahoma held out great promise to the new white settlers, mainly from the South. But for many of them, the promise of Oklahoma turned as sour as it had for the transplanted Indians. The Depression and drought of the 1930s drove thousands of Okies, as they were called, to the greener fields of California. As it stands, the population of Oklahoma is about 2.5 million; at statehood in 1907, the figure was not all that much lower, at 1.5 million. Today 42 of the state's 77 counties contain fewer people than they did in 1907, and almost all of Oklahoma's recent growth has occurred in and around its two large cities, Oklahoma City and Tulsa.

The big political story of Oklahoma in the past quarter-century, at least through 1974, has been the steady rise of the Republican Party. Traditionally Oklahoma was a Democratic state, since most of its original settlers came from the South. But Oklahoma has always had a strong Republican minority, especially in the northwest and north central parts of the state, which were settled largely by people from Republican Kansas. But the fast-growing, oil-rich cities of Oklahoma City and Tulsa are now conservative Republican, urban strongholds, much like Dallas in Texas or Phoenix in Arizona. In the East and Midwest, the cities usually go Democratic and the countryside Republican; in Oklahoma and most of the southwest, the pattern is exactly the opposite. And here the urban share of the state's population—and votes—is growing. In 1964 both Oklahoma City and Tulsa went for Barry Goldwater, and together they cast 36% of the state's vote. In 1972, both cities went even more heavily for Richard Nixon than the rest of the state, and together they cast 40% of the state's vote.

The Republican trend has been most noticeable in presidential races. Since 1948, the state has gone Democratic only once, and that was Lyndon Johnson's narrow victory in 1964. In 1972, only one state, Mississippi, cast a higher percentage of its vote for Richard Nixon. In statewide races, however, it took Republicans some time to become competitive. The first breakthrough occurred in 1962, when Henry Bellmon was elected Governor. In 1966, the Republicans elected another Governor, and a Princeton-educated Catholic at that, Tulsa oil man Dewey Bartlett. In 1970 Democrat David Hall defeated Bartlett—the first Oklahoma Governor eligible for two consecutive terms—by 2,000 votes. Most of the Democrats' gains came in rural areas, where ancestral Democrats seemed less likely to associate the deep drawling Hall with national liberal Democrats than they had in previous years.

Today both the former Governors, Bellmon and Bartlett, sit in the United States Senate, and if they won by only narrow margins in their last races, both did manage to beat a determined and well-known Democrat, former Congressman Ed Edmondson. Bellmon had first been elected —after a brief period as Richard Nixon's first campaign chairman—in 1968, when he beat liberal

Democratic incumbent Mike Monroney. For 18 years, Monroney concentrated on things like bringing the Federal Aviation Administration's huge Aeronautical Center to Oklahoma City; but he had got out of touch with the state, and Bellmon swept the cities and made solid inroads in traditionally Democratic rural areas.

After that solid victory, Bellmon seemed sure to win in 1974. He spent most of his six years in the Senate as a strong Nixon supporter—a stance that didn't seem risky in a state which gave Nixon 75% of its votes in 1972. But Watergate destroyed Nixon's popularity here as elsewhere—and Bellmon seemed not to notice. As late as the spring of 1974, he said he would ask Nixon to come to Oklahoma to campaign for him, even if he were impeached—a request he never followed up on. Moreover, Bellmon, who was rumored to be considering retirement, did not have much in the line of legislative accomplishments to talk about. That was enough to give Edmondson an opening and he recovered much of the traditional Democratic strength in the smaller counties, particularly in his old 2d district. The final result showed the two candidates only 3,000 votes apart—but Bellmon had won another six years in the Senate. Indeed, he became something of a minor power as ranking minority member on the Budget Committee—one of a contingent of conservative Republicans on that body. Edmondson protested because of ballot irregularities in Tulsa county, which he lost heavily, but to no avail.

That was the second disappointment for Edmondson, a onetime liberal who had become increasingly conservative during the 1960s and early 1970s. Two years before he had run against Bartlett for the state's other seat which had been vacated by Fred Harris. Bartlett attempted to grasp firmly onto Nixon's coattails, while Edmondson spent much of his time stressing what should have been obvious, that his attitude toward McGovern was one of considerable distaste. But Edmondson only barely carried rural Oklahoma, and Bartlett took 59% of the vote in the two big city areas—enough for a 52–48 win. In the Senate Bartlett sits on the Armed Services and Interior Committees. Though he divested himself of all his personal holdings in oil, he remains one of the most faithful advocates of the positions taken by the oil companies. He has supported as faithfully the positions of the Nixon and Ford Administrations; he was the only member of the last congressional delegation to visit Vietnam and Cambodia in 1975 and return supporting wholeheartedly the Administration's policy there.

Obviously Oklahoma's Senate delegation is not as colorful as in the past. The state has been represented by the likes of Thomas P. Gore, who was blind and was read to by his grandson, Gore Vidal; and Robert Kerr, who was uncrowned king of the Senate when he died on New Year's Day 1963. Kerr unashamedly worked to increase his personal fortune and, as Chairman of the Senate Finance Committee and chief owner of the Kerr-McGee gas and oil combine, was well able to do so; he died worth $40 million. A permanent legacy of Kerr's clout is the McClellan-Kerr Navigation System on the Arkansas River, which has done the unlikely and made Tulsa a seaport. When Kerr died, the outgoing Governor, J. Howard Edmondson, had himself appointed to fill the vacancy; a talented young liberal, (and brother of Ed Edmondson), he was beaten in the 1964 primary by a state Senator named Fred Harris and, sadly, died a few years later.

Harris is a politician who has had at least one career that could be described as meteoric. As a young Oklahoma Senator, he had taken what were considered radical positions, serving on and endorsing the conclusions of the Kerner Commission that the black riots were a response to America's "white racism" and nearly succeeding in getting himself tapped as Hubert Humphrey's running mate in 1968. By 1971, Harris was in political trouble in Oklahoma; he announced as a presidential candidate, then left the race when his money ran out, and quietly vacated his Senate seat. In 1975, Harris started out again, calling himself a "new populist" and calling for a major restructuring of our economic system. Whether he would be able to put together the support needed to make him a serious candidate was unclear; his career had meteor-like flashed across the sky and crashed to ground, and he was trying to start flying again.

One reason Harris left the Senate was that his form of liberal Democratic politics was just not saleable in Oklahoma in 1972. The results of the 1974 gubernatorial elections indicate that at least some kind of anti-establishment politics is viable in the state now. For in that year Oklahomans elected a 33-year-old Democrat named David Boren, by a 64–36 margin—a bigger margin than those won by all but two other Governors in Oklahoma's history. Boren's symbol was the broom: he campaigned as someone who would clean up the mess left by the traditional politicians. And mess there was. Incumbent Governor Hall was under investigation almost from the time he took office for an alleged elaborate kickback scheme; he was indicted after he left office and convicted of bribery and extortion. In the Democratic primary, Hall was beaten both by Boren and Congressman Clem Rogers McSpadden, a rodeo organizer whose proudest boast was that he was Will Rogers's grandnephew. But the broom beat tradition in the runoff, and went on to his huge November victory.

Boren ran as an advocate of welfare and campaign spending reform and had helped defeat a highway bond issue which, he said, lacked safeguards against corruption. But Boren was not quite the stranger to politics he might have liked people to think, nor as much of a standard liberal as some of his stands suggested; his father served in Congress for ten years, and his father-in-law used to be Chairman of the Oklahoma American Party. Boren will be eligible to run for reelection in 1978; he will also be eligible, of course, to run against Senator Bartlett, whose seat us up then.

Census Data Pop. 2,559,253; 1.26% of U.S. total, 27th largest; Central city, 30%; suburban, 20%. Median family income, $7,720; 41st highest; families above $15,000: 13%; families below $3,000: 16%. Median years education, 12.1.

1974 Share of Federal Tax Burden $2,812,061,000; 1.05% of U.S. total, 28th largest.

1974 Share of Federal Outlays $3,587,165,000; 1.33% of U.S. total, 27th largest. Per capita federal spending, $1402.

DOD	$1,079,921,000	22d (1.58%)	HEW	$1,228,425,000	26th (1.32%)
AEC	$90,000	43d (–)	HUD	$8,593,000	29th (0.88%)
NASA	$1,226,000	33d (0.04%)	VA	$224,272,000	22d (1.64%)
DOT	$178,223,000	18th (2.10%)	EPA	$14,805,000	33d (0.47%)
DOC	$10,158,000	24th (0.63%)	RevS	$67,628,000	28th (1.11%)
DOI	$69,815,000	10th (2.84%)	Int.	$133,696,000	18th (0.65%)
USDA	$200,839,000	28th (1.61%)	Other	$369,474,000	

Economic Base Agriculture, notably cattle, wheat, dairy products and peanuts; finance, insurance and real estate; oil and gas extraction, especially oil and gas field services and crude petroleum and natural gas; machinery, especially construction and related machinery; fabricated metal products, especially fabricated structural metal products; food and kindred products; electrical equipment and supplies, especially communication equipment.

Political Line-up Governor, David L. Boren (D). Senators, Harry Bellmon (R) and Dewey F. Bartlett (R). Representatives, 6 (5 D and 1 R). State Senate (39 D and 9 R); State House (76 D and 25 R).

The Voters

Registration 1,047,135 Total. 802,619 D (77%); 233,003 R (22%); 11,513 Ind. (1%).
Median voting age 44.
Employment profile White collar, 48%. Blue collar, 33%. Service, 14%. Farm, 5%.
Ethnic groups Black, 7%. Indian, 4%. Spanish, 1%. Total foreign stock, 4%.

Presidential vote

1972	Nixon (R)	759,025	(75%)
	McGovern (D)	247,147	(25%)
1968	Nixon (R)	449,697	(48%)
	Humphrey (D)	301,658	(32%)
	Wallace (AI)	191,731	(20%)

Sen. Henry Bellmon (R) Elected 1968, seat up 1980; b. Sept. 3, 1921, Tonakawa; home, Billings; Okla. St. U., B.S. 1942; Presbyterian.

Career USMC, WWII; Wheat and cattle farmer; Okla. House of Reps., 1946–48; Okla. St. Repub. Chm., 1960–62; Gov. of Okla., 1963–67; Natl. Chm., Nixon-for-Pres. Comm., 1967–68.

Offices 125 RSOB, 202-224-5754. Also 820 Old P.O. Bldg., Oklahoma City 73102, 405-231-4941, and 3003 Fed. Bldg., Tulsa 74103, 918-581-7651.

Committees

Budget (Ranking Member).

Agriculture and Forestry (4th). Subcommittees: Agricultural Production, Marketing, and Stabilization of Prices; Agricultural Research and General Legislation; Foreign Agricultural Policy; Rural Development.

Appropriations (9th). Subcommittees: Agriculture and Related Agencies; HUD and Independent Agencies; Interior; Military Construction; Public Works; Treasury, U.S. Postal Service, and General Government.

Group Ratings

	ADA	COPE	LWV	RIPON	NFU	LCV	CFA	NAB	NSI	ACA
1974	25	13	50	60	20	29	0	50	80	75
1973	19	27	50	65	40	–	17	–	–	61
1972	10	22	57	56	70	19	9	38	100	65

Key Votes

1) No-Knock	ABS	8) Gov Abortn Aid	AGN	15) Consumer Prot Agy	AGN
2) Busing	FOR	9) Cut Mil Brass	ABS	16) Forced Psych Tests	AGN
3) No Fault	ABS	10) Gov Limousine	ABS	17) Fed Campaign Subs	AGN
4) F-111	AGN	11) RR Featherbed	AGN	18) Rhod Chrome Ban	AGN
5) Death Penalty	FOR	12) Handgun License	AGN	19) Open Legis Meetings	FOR
6) Foreign Aid	ABS	13) Less Troop Abrd	AGN	20) Strikers Food Stmps	AGN
7) Filibuster	FOR	14) Resume Turk Aid	FOR	21) Gov Info Disclosure	AGN

Election Results

1974 general:	Henry Bellmon (R)	390,997	(50%)	($622,480)
	Ed Edmondson (D)	387,162	(50%)	($195,429)
1974 primary:	Henry Bellmon (R)	132,888	(87%)	
	Warner M. Hornbeck (R)	19,733	(13%)	
1968 general:	Henry Bellmon (R)	470,120	(52%)	
	A. S. Mike Monroney (D)	419,658	(46%)	
	George Washington (AI)	19,341	(2%)	

Sen. Dewey F. Bartlett (R) Elected 1972, seat up 1978; b. Mar. 28, 1919, Marietta, Ohio; home, Tulsa; Princeton U., B.S. 1942; Catholic.

Career USMC, WWII; Farmer and rancher; Okla. Senate, 1963–67; Gov. of Okla., 1967–71.

Offices 140 RSOB, 202-224-4721. Also 820 Old 3rd St. P.O. Bldg., Oklahoma City 73102, 405-231-4941, and 333 W. 4th St., Rm. 3003, Tulsa 74103, 918-581-7191.

Committees

Armed Services (6th). Subcommittees: Arms Control; General Legislation; Manpower and Personnel; National Stockpile and Naval Petroleum Reserves.

The District of Columbia (2d).

Interior and Insular Affairs (5th). Subcommittees: Environment and Land Resources; Indian Affairs; Minerals, Materials and Fuels.

Group Ratings

	ADA	COPE	LWV	RIPON	NFU	LCV	CFA	NAB	NSI	ACA
1974	5	9	56	50	18	15	0	83	100	95
1973	15	9	40	67	25	–	0	–	–	96

Key Votes

1) No-Knock	FOR	8) Gov Abortn Aid	AGN	15) Consumer Prot Agy	AGN
2) Busing	AGN	9) Cut Mil Brass	ABS	16) Forced Psych Tests	AGN
3) No Fault	AGN	10) Gov Limousine	AGN	17) Fed Campaign Subs	AGN
4) F-111	AGN	11) RR Featherbed	AGN	18) Rhod Chrome Ban	AGN
5) Death Penalty	FOR	12) Handgun License	AGN	19) Open Legis Meetings	FOR
6) Foreign Aid	AGN	13) Less Troop Abrd	AGN	20) Strikers Food Stmps	AGN
7) Filibuster	FOR	14) Resume Turk Aid	FOR	21) Gov Info Disclosure	AGN

Election Results

1972 general:	Dewey F. Bartlett (R)	516,934	(53%)	($625,095)
	Ed Edmondson (D)	478,212	(48%)	($512,058)
1972 primary:	Dewey F. Bartlett (R)	94,935	(93%)	
	C. W. Wood (R)	7,029	(7%)	

Gov. David Boren (D) Elected 1974, term expires Jan. 1979; b. Apr. 21, 1941, Washington, D.C.; Yale U., B.A., Rhodes Scholar, Oxford U., M.A., U. of Okla., LL.B. 1968.

Career Okla. House of Reps., 1966–74; Practicing atty.

Offices Oklahoma City 73105, 405-521-2291.

Election Results

1974 general	David Lyle Boren (D)	514,389	(64%)
	Jim Inhofe (R)	290,459	(36%)
1974 run-off:	David Lyle Boren (D)	286,171	(54%)
	Clem Rogers McSpadden (D)	248,623	(46%)
1974 primary:	Clem Rogers McSpadden (D)	238,534	(38%)
	David Lyle Boren (D)	225,321	(36%)
	David Hall (D)	169,290	(27%)

◆ ◆ ◆ ◆ ◆

FIRST DISTRICT

Tulsa is a city built on oil—not, like Oklahoma City, because oil wells pump away in the middle of town, but because this is a major regional center of the oil industry, the place where the money comes rolling in. Even today, years after oil was first discovered in these parts, Tulsa is still growing rapidly. Like so many oil rich cities of the Southwest, Tulsa is very deeply conservative politically. More so, actually, than Dallas or Houston; the better comparison is to the smaller boom towns of Midland or Tyler, Texas. And it is not only the new rich that tilt Tulsa to the right; this is also the home of Oral Roberts University, and a center of genuine fundamentalist religious feeling. As a measure of its conservatism, consider the fact that greater Tulsa, cast a larger percentage of its vote (79%) for Richard Nixon in 1972 than any other substantial metropolitan area in the country outside the South.

Tulsa makes up the bulk of Oklahoma's 1st congressional district. The remainder consists of parts of neighboring counties, and much of that is suburban. The 1st also includes a part of the city of Bartlesville, another smaller, oil-boom town (headquarters of Phillips Petroleum). And because the boundaries were drawn by Democratic legislators, the 1st's portion of Bartlesville contains virtually all of the city's black population.

The legislators took some pains with the boundaries. The reason was that in 1972 for the first time in years there promised to be a real contest for the 1st. Page Belcher, a conservative Republican, had been the district's Congressman for 22 years. While in the House, he had succeeded to the position of ranking minority member of the Agriculture Committee—an assignment that was much more attractive and useful back in the early 1960s when the district included much of agricultural northwest Oklahoma. Belcher usually won reelection easily, but in

1970 he ran into a tough Democratic opponent, James Jones. Only 30 at the time, Jones was once an appointments secretary to President Johnson. The candidate, a native of Tulsa, conducted an aggressive campaign which brought him 44% of the votes.

With that, Belcher, at 73, decided to retire in 1972. But retirement did not leave the field clear for Jones, who was, of course, running again. His Republican opponent was J. M. Hewgley, former Mayor of Tulsa. Nevertheless, Jones captured the seat, getting 55% of the vote in Tulsa County and 55% district-wide. It was a formidable achievement; at the top of the ticket, George McGovern just barely got 20%. Having proved himself once, Jones was tested again in 1974. The problem was a memo he had written to the Associated Milk Producers, Inc., while in private law practice; Jones took credit for persuading Johnson to raise milk price supports, and got the milk men to give him an annual salary of $40,000 and law firm billings of $155,000. In the year of the Watergate—and the year Oklahoma Governor David Hall was beaten because of doubts about his ethics—this was not especially helpful; indeed, it sounded not all that different from the crime that John Connally then stood accused of (and on which he would later be acquitted).

But Jones dismissed the memo as a "tall story," leaving the implication that he had just been a clever lawyer getting a large fee out of some slick operators. And apparently people accepted his explanation. He got 81% of the vote in the Democratic primary and 68% in the general election. His opposition was weak, but he seems to have proved beyond all doubt that he is a champion vote-getter, and that he has made this once safe Republican seat into solid Democratic territory in congressional elections.

Census Data Pop. 425,620. Central city, 78%; suburban, 18%. Median family income, $7,720; families above $15,000: 13%; families below $3,000: 9%. Median years education, 12.1.

The Voters

Median voting age 42.
Employment profile White collar, 55%. Blue collar, 31%. Service, 13%. Farm, 1%.
Ethnic groups Black, 9%. Indian, 3%. Spanish, 1%. Total foreign stock, 4%.

Presidential vote

1972	Nixon (R)	133,381	(79%)
	McGovern (D)	35,199	(21%)
1968	Nixon (R)	86,106	(57%)
	Humphrey (D)	35,522	(23%)
	Wallace (AI)	30,440	(20%)

Rep. James R. Jones (D) Elected 1972; b. May 5, 1939, Muskogee; home, Tulsa; U. of Okla., A.B. 1961, Georgetown U., LL.B. 1964; Catholic.

Career Legis. Asst. to U.S. Rep. Ed Edmondson, 1961–64; Army, 1964–65; White House Staff Asst. to Pres. Lyndon B. Johnson, 1965–69; Practicing atty.

Offices 225 CHOB, 202-225-2211. Also 4536 Fed. Bldg., Tulsa 74103, 918-581-7111.

Committees

Ways and Means (21st). Subcommittees: Oversight; Social Security; Trade.

Group Ratings

	ADA	COPE	LWV	RIPON	NFU	LCV	CFA	NAB	NSI	ACA
1974	24	60	25	29	79	24	20	58	88	62
1973	29	55	58	33	65	26	43	–	–	54

Key Votes

1) Foreign Aid	AGN	6) Gov Abortn Aid	FOR	11) Pub Cong Election $	FOR
2) Busing	AGN	7) Coed Phys Ed	AGN	12) Turkish Arms Cutoff	AGN
3) ABM	FOR	8) Pov Lawyer Gag	AGN	13) Youth Camp Regs	AGN
4) B-1 Bomber	FOR	9) Pub Trans Sub	AGN	14) Strip Mine Veto	FOR
5) Nerve Gas	FOR	10) EZ Voter Regis	FOR	15) Farm Bill Veto	AGN

Election Results

1974 general:	James R. Jones (D)	88,159	(68%)	($60,686)
	George Alfred Mizer, Jr. (R)	41,697	(32%)	($17,878)
1974 primary:	James R. Jones (D)	52,806	(81%)	
	Lawrence E. Lane (D)	12,081	(19%)	
1972 general:	James R. Jones (D)	91,864	(55%)	($64,850)
	J. M. Hewgley, Jr. (R)	73,786	(45%)	($179,986)

◆ ◆ ◆ ◆ ◆

SECOND DISTRICT

The 2d congressional district of Oklahoma takes in all the northeast quadrant of the state, except for the Tulsa area that makes up the 1st district. The 2d is the place where most of Oklahoma's Indians, removed from their ancestral lands in the South and the Midwest, were forcibly relocated. Fully 8% of the population of the 2d is Indian, and probably a larger percentage can claim Indian blood. The county names echo the Civilized Tribes: Cherokee, Delaware, Ottawa, Osage, Creek. Beginning in 1889, white settlers from the Democratic Deep South and the Republican Ozarks moved in. As a result, the 2d district remains to this day something of a political borderland between Republican and Democratic territory. The Indians, unlike those in the northern plains or Rocky Mountain states, do not vote in any way markedly different from the rest of the population.

The district's largest city is Muskogee (pop. 37,000), a rather run-down Oklahoma rural center. Anyone who has heard Merle Haggard's classic "Okie from Muskogee" has a fair idea of the political leanings of the area; people here have little use for longhairs, peace demonstrators, or intellectuals of any sort. Will Rogers is remembered in these parts with favor; but Woody Guthrie, also a native Oklahoman, is not. Merle's daddy was from these parts, but the singer himself grew up an Okie in Bakersfield, California.

Until Democrat Ed Edmondson ran for the Senate in 1972, he represented the 2d district in the House for 20 years. His own changing views pretty well reflect the similarly changing views of his constituency. During the New Frontier, Edmondson was a fairly dependable supporter of the Kennedy Administration, which did not create too many problems for him at home. But during the Johnson and Nixon years, Edmondson grew steadily more conservative. By the time he ran for the Senate in 1972 and 1974, he embraced that label; and the reason he lost at least in his own estimation, was probably only because enough Oklahoma voters did not perceive him as conservative enough.

Edmondson left something behind him for his 20 years: as a member of the Interior and Public Works Committees, he had something to do with the building of the McClellan-Kerr Navigation System, which has made the Arkansas River navigable for ocean-going vessels all the way up to Tulsa. But Edmondson did not leave political stability behind him; on the contrary, in the few years he has been gone, the 2d district has had two Congressmen. The first was Clem Rogers McSpadden, a longtime state Senator, a grandnephew of Will Rogers, and the conductor of the National Finals Rodeo. McSpadden was very well known and won easily; but in 1974, with Governor David Hall reeling from charges of corruption, McSpadden decided to return home. He ran for Governor, led the first primary, but lost in the runoff to David Boren, the 33-year-old state Representative whose ubiquitous brooms caught the state's reform desire more than McSpadden's rodeo paraphernalia.

No one quite as popular as McSpadden ran to succeed him. The Democratic primary is still the place where the winner is picked here. In the initial contest, one Cecil Drummon was the leader, but in the runoff he was beaten by Tahlequah newspaper publisher Ted Risenhoover. In the general election, Risenhoover, a rather conservative Democrat, beat a full-blooded Creek who had the Republican nomination, by a 59–41 margin. He now serves on the Education and Labor and Interior Committees, and will likely win reelection without too much difficulty. The only major threat to his incumbency is that one of his two immediate predecessors, their hopes for statewide office thwarted in 1974 and incapable of satisfaction in 1976, will choose to run for the House again.

Census Data Pop. 426,778. Central city, 0%; suburban, 22%. Median family income, $9,527; families above $15,000: 19%; families below $3,000: 21%. Median years education, 12.3.

The Voters

Median voting age 47.
Employment profile White collar, 41%. Blue collar, 39%. Service, 15%. Farm, 5%.
Ethnic groups Black, 6%. Indian, 8%. Total foreign stock, 2%.

Presidential vote

1972	Nixon (R)	126,446	(73%)
	McGovern (D)	46,648	(27%)
1968	Nixon (R)	73,878	(45%)
	Humphrey (D)	55,776	(34%)
	Wallace (AI)	35,640	(22%)

Rep. Theodore M. Risenhoover (D) Elected 1974; b. Nov. 3, 1935, Stigler; home, Tahlequah; U. of Ala., 1960–61, Northeastern St. Col., B.S. 1965.

Career Air Force, 1955–63; Owner and Publisher, Tahlequah *Pictorial Press* and *Star Citizen*, 1965–; Pres., Web Offset Printers, Inc., 1965–; Okla. Crime Commission, 1970–74; Dem. nominee for Okla. State Senate, 1972.

Offices 1407 LHOB, 202-225-2701. Also P.O. Box 427, Muskogee 74401, 918-687-7509.

Committees

Education and Labor (21st). Subcommittees: Elementary, Secondary and Vocational Education; Labor Standards; Manpower, Compensation, and Health and Safety.

Interior and Insular Affairs (28th). Subcommittees: Indian Affairs; Public Lands; Water and Power Resources.

Group Ratings: Newly Elected

Key Votes

1) Foreign Aid	AGN	6) Gov Abortn Aid	NE	11) Pub Cong Election $	NE
2) Busing	NE	7) Coed Phys Ed	AGN	12) Turkish Arms Cutoff	NE
3) ABM	NE	8) Pov Lawyer Gag	NE	13) Youth Camp Regs	FOR
4) B-1 Bomber	FOR	9) Pub Trans Sub	NE	14) Strip Mine Veto	FOR
5) Nerve Gas	NE	10) EZ Voter Regis	NE	15) Farm Bill Veto	AGN

Election Results

1974 general:	Theodore M. (Ted) Risenhoover (D)	78,046	(59%)	($79,791)
	Ralph F. Keen (R)	54,110	(41%)	($19,395)
1974 Run-off	Theodore M. (Ted) Risenhoover (D)	54,684	(52%)	
	Cecil Drummond (D)	50,323	(48%)	
1974 primary:	Cecil Drummond (D)	29,111	(25%)	
	Theodore M. (Ted) Risenhoover (D)	22,876	(20%)	
	Bob Blackstock (D)	20,957	(18%)	
	L. V. Watkins (D)	18,064	(16%)	
	Two others (D)	25,067	(22%)	

◆ ◆ ◆ ◆ ◆

THIRD DISTRICT

In 1908, Carl Albert, now Speaker of the House, was born in the village of Bug Tussle, here in the 3d district of Oklahoma. His father was a coal miner in this poor country of red hills. The family never had much money, but young Carl was good at the books and won a scholarship to the University of Oklahoma. There he excelled in his studies, was on the debating team, and won a Rhodes Scholorship. After military service in World War II, "the little giant from Little Dixie" (he is 5´4˝) ran for Congress in 1946. Albert took the Democratic runoff primary by 330 votes out of 54,000 cast.

Republicans are scarce in the southern Oklahoma counties (Little Dixie) that make up the 3d congressional district. So Albert easily won the general election and went to Washington, where he quickly caught the eye of Sam Rayburn, whose Texas district lay just across the Red River from Albert's 3d. Albert became Majority Whip in 1955 and, on the elevation of John McCormack to the Speakership, Majority Leader in 1962.

It is a measure of how steeped in tradition—and remote from the public it is supposed to serve—that the House has long been, that it was taken utterly for granted, as a matter not worthy of comment much less criticism, that a decision made by two men, Rayburn and McCormack, twenty years before should ineluctably insure that, in 1975, Carl Albert is Speaker. But that is how things are in the House—or at least were until the influx of freshmen elected in 1974. Albert's selection as Speaker following McCormack's retirement in 1970 was automatic and unchallenged —despite the fact that many members were dissatisfied with his leadership. Albert was originally chosen for a top position in a Congress half of whose Democrats were conservative Southerners; Rayburn and McCormack were looking for a man who shared much of their background and had some sympathy, if not agreement with their views; they wanted, above all, a conciliator.

In all these respects Albert has pretty well met their expectations. But those are not the criteria any rational person would now apply to the job. The House Democrats today, aside from a couple of dozen conservative Southerners, are overwhelmingly of one inclination—call it liberal, or whatever—toward major policy positions. What they need is someone able to frame issues in a parliamentary setting so as to maximize their power, to galvanize their numbers into an effective legislative force. They need someone who will crack heads on occasion when it is necessary, and who relishes a fight when it is appropriate. And that, just about everyone would agree, is not a particularly good description of Carl Albert.

It would not be fair to Albert to suggest that he has not tried, and with some success to adapt his personality and style of leadership to the changing membership of the House and the Democratic caucus. With the retirement of Mississippi's William Colmer, in 1972, he seemed to take effective control of the Rules Committee and thus the flow of legislation, though on occasion it seemed to squirm away from him. He was ready to challenge aging committee chairmen like Hebert of Armed Services both on policy matters like the bombing of Cambodia and on that more personal matter of just who would sit on their committees (Albert got seats for California's Ron Dellums and Colorado's Pat Schroeder). After years of providing bipartisan imprimaturs to American military intervention in Indochina, Albert moved in the other direction in 1973. And on the personal level, Albert has shown himself able to get under control what had been a troublesome drinking problem. If much of the country had looked with as much trepidation as he did on the prospect—and it was quite possible before the confirmations of Vice Presidents Ford and Rockefeller—that he would become President, there is also every indication that he could have handled the job as competently as the man he recommended to Richard Nixon and who finally did assume it, Gerald Ford.

While Albert has had troubles in Washington he can do very little wrong back in the 3d district of Oklahoma. The 3d is the most Democratic district in the state, even though it delivered a solid majority to Richard Nixon in 1972. The banner Democratic counties are found along the Red River and in Albert's native coal mining counties just to the north. Farther north, the odd excrescence of the district was added to bring the population-losing 3d up to equal population standards. Albert's district is a hotbed of an old fashioned kind of populism. But it also has roots in the South, as shown by the 27% George Wallace took here in 1968; that percentage is the best he did in any congressional district outside the eleven states of the old Confederacy.

Albert's liberal voting record on economic issues and his hawkish record on foreign policy appeal to voters here, and they are willing to forgive him things like his strong support of civil rights. (When Albert was first elected, Oklahoma law required Negroes who ran for office to be labelled as such on the ballot.) Albert has said that he will retire from the Speakership, and presumably from the House, in 1978, when he turns 70; there is speculation that he may choose to do so sooner, in 1976. The House, in any case, has turned out to be a more turbulent place and the Speakership a more taxing job than Albert probably anticipated back in 1955, when he was, in effect, tapped for it. In any case, he will have no trouble winning reelection if he chooses to run; the main street in his old home town of McAlester has long since been renamed Carl Albert Parkway.

Census Data Pop. 426,596. Central city, 0%; suburban, 8%. Median family income, $6,567; families above $15,000: 9%; families below $3,000: 24%. Median years education, 10.9.

The Voters

Median voting age 49.
Employment profile White collar, 39%. Blue collar, 40%. Service, 15%. Farm, 6%.
Ethnic groups Black, 6%. Indian, 5%. Total foreign stock, 2%.

Presidential vote

1972	Nixon (R)	113,281	(70%)
	McGovern (D)	47,962	(30%)
1968	Nixon (R)	57,086	(35%)
	Humphrey (D)	63,021	(39%)
	Wallace (AI)	43,355	(27%)

Rep. Carl Albert (D) Elected 1946; b. May 10, 1908, McAlester; home, McAlester; U. of Okla, B.A. 1931, Rhodes Scholar, Oxford U., B.A. 1933, B.C.L. 1934; Methodist.

Career Legal Clerk, Fed. Housing Admin., 1934–37; Ohio Oil Co., 1937–40; Practicing atty., 1938–39, 1946; Army, WWII; U.S. House of Reps. Maj. Whip, 1955–62 Maj. Ldr., 1962–70, Spkr., 1971–.

Offices 2205 RHOB, 202-225-4565. Also Fed. Bldg., McAlester 74501, 918-423-7710.

Committees

The Speaker of the House.

Group Ratings: Newly Elected

Key Votes

1) Foreign Aid   AGN

Election Results

1974 general:	Carl Albert (D), unopposed			($18,034)
1974 primary:	Carl Albert (D)	122,144	(82%)	
	Two others (D)	26,340	(18%)	
1972 general:	Carl Albert (D)	101,732	(93%)	($7,275)
	Harold J. Marshall (Ind.)	7,242	(7%)	(NA)

◆ ◆ ◆ ◆ ◆

FOURTH DISTRICT

The 4th congressional district of Oklahoma includes most of southwestern Oklahoma and part of metropolitan Oklahoma City. The counties along the Red River, the state's southern border, resemble adjacent areas in Texas—cotton-growing Democratic strongholds. But as one moves north, the district becomes politically more marginal. The 4th's portion of Oklahoma City and its suburbs is definitely Republican, and so, more often than not, is Cleveland County, which contains Norman and the University of Oklahoma. The campus here is one where football, though tainted by scandal, remains more popular than Hesse, not to speak of leftish politics. The 1967 redistricting radically altered the 4th district, and the only county it now has in common with the pre-1967 district is Pottawatomie, the home of Congressman Tom Steed.

First elected in 1948 (when he beat the father of Oklahoma's Governor David Boren), Steed is a moderate to conservative Democrat. In the late sixties, he actually had some trouble at the polls. In 1966, a good Republican year in Oklahoma, Steed won reelection by a scant 364 votes. And in 1968, Steed was forced to run against another incumbent, Republican James Smith, whose home also lay in the redistricted 4th. The Steed-Smith Race possessed national significance that went unnoticed at the time. If Steed had lost, the Oklahoma delegation would have been deadlocked at three Democrats and three Republicans. Then if the presidential election had gone to the House—a real possibility, as George Wallace knew—Oklahoma would have had no vote in an election where each state, no matter how big, casts just one vote. The constitutional process could have resulted in a complete deadlock over the making of the President in 1968—which, as it turned out, might have been preferable to what happened.

The contingency, of course, never arose. And in any case, Steed won the election of 1968, improving on his showing the last time out. Still, the Republicans tried again in 1970. Their candidate this time was 28-year-old Jay Wilkinson, then a White House assistant and son of former University of Oklahoma football coach (and 1964 Republican Senate candidate) Bud Wilkinson. Wilkinson got large contributions from the Nixon White House and Nixon patrons like W. Clement Stone; but it was to no avail, as Steed won 64% of the vote.

The question about this campaign is why the White House got involved at all. Steed had pretty well demonstrated his strength; moreover, he was Chairman of the Appropriations Committee which must approve all White House funds. The Nixon people, as we know now, were busy bloating the White House budget—an enterprise to which Steed had never registered any objection. Why then did they try and rile him up? And why, once they did, did Steed simply continue to give the White House anything it wanted?

The answer, at least as Steed gave it once White House appropriations came under criticism, was that he did not want to do anything which could conceivably endanger the President's life—hence the extra shrubbery at San Clemente, the heater on the swimming pool, etc. And Steed's committee didn't want to obstruct the White House operations by pennypinching either. In any case, by 1974 Steed was having the experience—unusual, to say the least, for an Appropriations subcommittee chairman—of having his requests ridiculed and slashed on the House floor.

That cannot have been an especially pleasant time for this rather humorous veteran, but he weathered it and is back in business quietly again. As if to celebrate his 70th birthday, he was renominated and reelected totally without opposition in 1974. Will he run in 1976? No one is sure, but if he does he will probably win.

Census Data Pop. 426,330. Central city, 20%; suburban, 41%. Median family income, $5,846; families above $15,000: 7%; families below $3,000: 15%. Median years education, 10.2.

The Voters

Median voting age 38.
Employment profile White collar, 49%. Blue collar, 32%. Service, 14%. Farm, 5%.
Ethnic groups Black, 6%. Indian, 3%. Spanish, 3%. Total foreign stock, 5%.

Presidential vote

1972	Nixon (R)	107,548	(74%)
	McGovern (D)	37,542	(26%)
1968	Nixon (R)	60,270	(41%)
	Humphrey (D)	54,299	(37%)
	Wallace (AI)	31,065	(21%)

Rep. Tom Steed (D) Elected 1948; b. Mar. 2, 1904, near Rising Star, Tex.; home, Shawnee; Methodist.

Career Admin. Asst. to U.S. Reps. P.L. Gassaway, R.L. Hill, and Gomer Smith; Reporter, Bartlesville *Examiner,* McAlester *News Capital, Daily Oklahoman,* and Shawnee *News-Star*; Army, WWII; Ofc. of War Info., 1944–45; Automobile dealer, 1945–48.

Offices 2405 RHOB, 202-225-6165. Also 124 E. Main St., P.O. Box 1265, Norman 73069, 405-329-6500.

Committees

Appropriations (9th). Subcommittees: Transportation; Military Construction; Treasury, Postal Service and Gerneral Government (Chairman).

Small Business (2d). Subcommittees: Energy and Environment; government Procurement and International Trade.

Group Ratings

	ADA	COPE	LWV	RIPON	NFU	LCV	CFA	NAB	NSI	ACA
1974	9	55	42	31	71	31	25	50	100	67
1973	32	82	50	29	88	17	50	–	–	46
1972	19	73	44	44	86	11	0	40	100	62

Key Votes

1) Foreign Aid	AGN	6) Gov Abortn Aid	AGN	11) Pub Cong Election $	AGN
2) Busing	AGN	7) Coed Phys Ed	AGN	12) Turkish Arms Cutoff	AGN
3) ABM	FOR	8) Pov Lawyer Gag	AGN	13) Youth Camp Regs	AGN
4) B-1 Bomber	FOR	9) Pub Trans Sub	AGN	14) Strip Mine Veto	FOR
5) Nerve Gas	FOR	10) EZ Voter Regis	AGN	15) Farm Bill Veto	AGN

Election Results

1974 general:	Tom Steed (D), unopposed			($7,451)
1974 primary:	Tom Steed (D), unopposed			
1972 general:	Tom Steed (D)	85,578	(71%)	($6,609)
	William E. Crozier (R)	34,484	(29%)	($3,622)

◆ ◆ ◆ ◆ ◆

FIFTH DISTRICT

Oklahoma City is the capital of Oklahoma and its largest city (pop. 366,000). During the 1960s, the city fathers decided that they would not let the old city limits be a straitjacket, cutting off Oklahoma City from the prosperity and growth of the surrounding suburbs; and so they annexed so much territory that Oklahoma City now spills over into five counties and three congressional districts. Even ignoring the annexations, Oklahoma City is a sprawling and unplanned metropolis—towering above the dusty plains are a few skyscrapers, and right next to them are parking lots. As in the case of Tulsa, the wealth of Oklahoma City is based mainly on oil; on the grounds of the state Capitol there are still a few oil wells pumping away. Like most cities, especially oil cities, in the Southwest, Oklahoma City is basically conservative and Republican, but notably less so than Tulsa.

Sitting at just about midcontinent and far enough south to avoid the heaviest winter snows, Oklahoma City has become something of an aviation center, with an Air Force base and the FAA's Aeronautical Center both within the city limits. One suspects that their location was the work of the penultimate Congressman from the 5th district of Oklahoma, which includes most of Oklahoma City and surrounding Oklahoma County. That was Mike Monroney, a Democrat who served from 1939 to 1951. It is a measure of how little congressional politics changes in some Southwestern districts that there has only been one Congressman in the 5th since Monroney moved up to the Senate, Democrat-now-turned-Republican John Jarman.

Jarman was, for many years, a conservative Democrat with several political assets that guaranteed him easy reelection. He was a distinguished looking Oklahoman with an Ivy League education, his views did not upset any of the big local powers, and he had the solid support of the Oklahoma City newspapers, run by an old man named E. K. Gaylord. In the Congress, Jarman was a quiet member of the Commerce Committee. In the late sixties, he was Chairman of the Health Subcommittee, which he allowed the then second-ranking Democrat and now Chairman, Paul Rogers of Florida, to run; in 1971, he moved over to the Transportation and Aeronautics Subcommittee Chairmanship, where he was in a good position to protect some of Oklahoma City's interests. By that time he had also become the third-ranking Democrat on the full committee, behind Chairman Harley Staggers and Tobert Macdonald of Massachusetts.

But around then there came to be problems in Jarman's cozy political world. In Oklahoma City, E. K. Gaylord died in 1974 at 101, and the papers were no longer able to protect Jarman against aggressive Republican congressional candidates. He got only 65% of the vote in the 1972 primary—a poor score for a longtime incumbent—and 60% in the 1972 general election; by 1974, he was down to 61% in the primary, and in November of that year a young Republican named Mickey Edwards won 48% of the vote against him. When the House convened with all the new freshmen, the Commerce Committee ejected Staggers from his Investigations Subcommittee Chairmanship in favor of fourth-ranking Democrat John Moss—a sure sign that young, liberal Democrats would not allow the conservative, inactive Jarman to accede to the full committee chairmanship, and indeed might oust him from the post he held.

Facing a serious Republican challenge at home, and with his seniority as a Democrat worth less than it had been before, Jarman switched to the Republican Party in January 1975. His loss was not mourned much by Democrats; of course he lost his seat and seniority on Commerce. As for the Republicans, they gave him only their third spot on the Science and Technology Committee—an indication that they did not have to pay a particularly high price to get him. It seems especially sad, inasmuch as Jarman has served in the House longer than any other Republican; he was there two years before Minority Leader John Rhodes and ranking Appropriations member Elford Cederberg were first elected in 1952. Whether his switch will solve his political problems at home is not at all clear; he may indeed still face Republican opposition in the primary, and he surely will have an aggressive Democratic opponent in 1976.

Census Data   Pop. 426,484. Central city, 79%; suburban, 21%. Median family income, $7,569; families above $15,000: 12%; families below $3,000: 9%. Median years education, 12.1.

The Voters

Median voting age 42.
Employment profile White collar, 56%. Blue collar, 30%. Service, 13%. Farm, 1%.
Ethnic groups Black, 11%. Indian, 2%. Spanish, 2%. Total foreign stock, 4%.

Presidential vote

1972	Nixon (R)	126,859	(76%)
	McGovern (D)	39,955	(24%)
1968	Nixon (R)	67,193	(50%)
	Humphrey (D)	42,532	(32%)
	Wallace (AI)	24,428	(18%)

Rep. John Jarman (R) Elected 1950 as Democrat, changed party affiliation to Repub. Jan 24, 1975; 6. July 17, 1915, Sallisaw; home, Oklahoma City; Westminster Col., 1932-34, Yale U., B.A, 1937, Harvard U., LL.B. 1941; Presbyterian.

Career Army, WWII; Practicing atty.; Okla. House of Reps., 1947–48; Okla. Senate 1949–50.

Offices 2416 RHOB, 202-225-2132. Also 715 Fed. Bldg., Oklahoma City 73102, 405-231-4541.

Committees

Science and Technology (3d), Subcommittees: Domestic and International Scientific Planning and Analysis.

Group Ratings

	ADA	COPE	LWV	RIPON	NFU	LCV	CFA	NAB	NSI	ACA
1974	0	0	18	33	33	19	8	67	90	87
1973	4	18	18	36	21	31	0	–	–	76
1972	6	9	22	47	33	27	100	91	100	80

Key Votes

1) Foreign Aid	AGN	6) Gov Abortn Aid	AGN	11) Pub Cong Election $	AGN
2) Busing	AGN	7) Coed Phys Ed	AGN	12) Turkish Arms Cutoff	AGN
3) ABM	FOR	8) Pov Lawyer Gag	FOR	13) Youth Camp Regs	FOR
4) B-1 Bomber	FOR	9) Pub Trans Sub	AGN	14) Strip Mine Veto	FOR
5) Nerve Gas	FOR	10) EZ Voter Regis	AGN	15) Farm Bill Veto	FOR

Election Results

1974 general:	John Jarman (D)	52,107	(52%)	($46,295)
	M. H. Mickey Edwards (R)	48,705	(48%)	($31,255)
1974 primary:	John Jarman (D), unopposed			
1972 general:	John Jarman (D)	69,710	(60%)	($27,534)
	Llewellyn L. Keller, Jr. (R)	45,711	(40%)	($7,798)

♦ ♦ ♦ ♦ ♦

SIXTH DISTRICT

The 6th congressional district of Oklahoma occupies the northwest and north central part of the state. It includes the thin panhandle that goes west to touch the borders of Colorado and New Mexico. Aside from a small portion of Oklahoma City and its suburbs, the 6th is almost entirely small town and rural. Around the turn of the century, the plains west of Tulsa and Oklahoma City attracted thousands of migrants—probably a majority of them from nearby Kansas. Like so many settlers of the Great Plains, these people mistakenly assumed the land was more fertile and the rain fell more often than was really the case. The Dust Bowl of the 1930s hit already arid northwest Oklahoma hard, and in many ways it has yet to recover. In 1907, when Oklahoma was admitted to the Union, there were 401,000 people living in the counties now wholly contained in the 6th district. By 1970, that number was down to 390,000.

Due probably to the Kansas origin of its first settlers, the 6th has always been the most Republican part of Oklahoma. In the late sixties and early seventies, when the conservative trend in the state was shifting ancestral Democrats to the party of Nixon and Agnew, the 6th became one of the most Republican parts of the nation. In 1972, Richard Nixon won a larger share of the vote in the 6th district (79%) than in any other congressional district outside the Deep South.

But such trends can be short lived, and the Watergate scandal had its fallout here in Middle America as much as anywhere. Not only did the traditionally Democratic counties in the southern part of the district switch back to the Democrats in statewide races, so too, to a considerable extent, did the traditionally Republican counties of the north central region, around Enid and Ponca City. Republican Senator Henry Bellmon, a native of the 6th, did carry the district on his way to his narrow reelection victory, but Democrat David Boren carried all but one small county here on his way to the Governorship.

The 6th was also the scene of one of the nation's biggest upsets in House races in 1974. The incumbent was a 66-year-old Republican with the agreeable name of John N. Happy Camp, a solid conservative who had served 20 years in the state Senate and had first been elected to Congress in 1968. Reelected in 1972 with 73% of the vote, he did not seem to be in any conceivable political trouble. But Glenn English, the 33-year-old director of the state Democratic Party, ran a vigorous campaign which by its very nature contrasted his youth to Camp's age. English ended up carrying not only the traditionally Democratic counties near his home town in the southwest portion of the district, he even carried the only two counties in the state (Alfalfa and Major) which have Republican registration edges. English won by a solid 53–44 margin, and judging from the acumen that won the race for him, should be a solid favorite in 1976.

Census Data Pop. 427,445. Central city, 5%; suburban, 10%. Median family income, $9,305; families above $15,000: 19%; families below $3,000: 15%. Median years education, 12.3.

The Voters

Median voting age 45.
Employment profile White collar, 45%. Blue collar, 29%. Service, 15%. Farm, 11%.
Ethnic groups Black, 2%. Indian, 2%. Spanish, 1%. Total foreign stock, 5%.

Presidential vote

1972	Nixon (R)	150,998	(79%)
	McGovern (D)	39,712	(21%)
1968	Nixon (R)	101,498	(57%)
	Humphrey (D)	49,023	(28%)
	Wallace (AI)	26,737	(15%)

Rep. Glenn English (D) Elected 1974; b. Nov. 30, 1940, Cordell; home, Cordell; Southwestern St. Col., B.A. 1964.

Career Chf. Asst. to Majority Caucus, Cal. State Assembly; Exec. Dir., Okla. Dem. Party, 1969–73; Petroleum leasing business.

Offices 1108 LHOB, 202-225-5565. Also 800 W. Main St., Yukon 73099, 405-354-8638.

Committees

Agriculture (24th). Subcommittees: Conservation and Credit; Cotton; Livestock and Grains.

Government Operations (24th). Subcommittees: Government Activities and Transportation; Intergovernmental Relations and Human Resources.

Group Ratings: Newly Elected

Key Votes

1) Foreign Aid	AGN	6) Gov Abortn Aid	NE	11) Pub Cong Election $	NE
2) Busing	NE	7) Coed Phys Ed	AGN	12) Turkish Arms Cutoff	NE
3) ABM	NE	8) Pov Lawyer Gag	NE	13) Youth Camp Regs	AGN
4) B-1 Bomber	FOR	9) Pub Trans Sub	NE	14) Strip Mine Veto	FOR
5) Nerve Gas	NE	10) EZ Voter Regis	NE	15) Farm Bill Veto	AGN

Election Results

1974 general:	Glenn English (D)	76,392	(53%)	($78,411)
	John N. Happy Camp (R)	63,731	(44%)	($53,532)
	Bennett L. Basore (Ind.)	3,365	(2%)	($2,600)
1974 Run-off	Glenn English (D)	42,265	(56%)	
	David Hutchens (D)	32,830	(44%)	
1974 primary:	Glenn English (D)	32,720	(38%)	
	David Hutchens (D)	19,903	(23%)	
	Gary Green (D)	19,451	(23%)	
	Three others (D)	13,769	(16%)	

OREGON

Oregon these days seems to be some kind of progressive commonwealth, almost totally separated from the ills of the rest of the United States, out on the Pacific coast. It is a state which has decriminalized marijuana without any drastic repercussion, a state which has outlawed throwaway bottles and cans without hurting the glass and brewing industries. In a land which has always encouraged population influxes, it is a state whose most recent former Governor Tom McCall, urged people to come to visit, "But for heaven's sake don't come to live here!" Despite McCall's plea, Oregon's clean air and uncrowded spaces have been attracting people from the smog of California and the rigors of the East Coast. The state's population rose 18% during the sixties and another 8% from 1970 to 1974—both rates well above the national average. And for all its natural wonders, the state's people are still concentrated, more than 80% of them, in the Portland metropolitan area or the Willamette valley just to the south.

But because enough of the current cliche about Oregon is true, it is worth asking just how this state came to be what it is. A substantial part of the answer lies in the economic history of the West Coast in the years following World War II. Those were the days when California and, to a somewhat lesser extent, Washington were ballooning in population, its new residents attracted by the growing number of jobs in defense and aerospace industries. Oregon experienced little of this postwar boom; even in recent years the Defense Department spends less per capita here than in any other state except Iowa and West Virginia. The economy of Oregon has continued to depend on a much more old fashioned commodity—lumber. This does not provide the state with an entirely steady economy; when interest rates are high, money scarce, and housing starts down, the lumber industry suffers. But unlike a defense plant, it is never going to vanish utterly. There will always be Douglas firs in Oregon, and if Americans don't buy them perhaps the Japanese will.

If the economy of Oregon demonstrates a certain stability, so, too, does its politics. Unlike most states, no long-standing political divisions exist between various parts of the state. It is true that the coastal areas and the Columbia River valley are marginally more Democratic than the rest of the state; and that Salem, the state capital, is usually more Republican than Eugene, the site of the University of Oregon. Also, the low-lying, less affluent sections of Portland near the Columbia and Willamette Rivers are usually Democratic, while the city neighborhoods and suburbs in the surrounding hills are Republican. But there is not tradition here of regional rivalry—nothing like the difference between arch-conservative Orange County and liberal San Francisco in California.

It is therefore, no real surprise that Oregon tends to support candidates of the political center—but as center is defined here, not by East Coast political strategists. A prime example is McCall, elected Governor in 1966 and 1970. The national press called him a liberal Republican, in large part because of his stand on environmental issues; he was a strong backer, for example, of the no-throwaway law, and he strove to keep Oregon's growth within limits. But McCall was also simply an innovator; he is the man who came up, during the gas crisis of 1974, with the odd-even system for buying gas. And he was—and this makes little sense of the liberal category—a strong backer of American military involvement in Vietnam. McCall was elected with 55% of the vote in 1966 and 56% in 1970, both times beating Democrat Robert Straub. In 1974, McCall was ineligible to run, and Straub finally won.

Straub's victory was not only a result of his own efforts; it was also the result of a conservative swing among Oregon's dwindling number of registered Republicans. In the past, McCall and, before him, Mark Hatfield, had moved up from the Secretary of State's job to Governor, and the same was expected of Secretary of State Clay Myers in 1974. Myers had the reputation of being a liberal Republican, and had few enemies. But irregularities in his office's functions and the aggressive campaign of conservative state Senator Victor Atiyeh resulted in a massive upset; Atiyeh, a sort of Oregon version of Barry Goldwater, won with 61% of the primary vote. But in the general election the voters picked the candidate they thought would most closely continue McCall's policies: Robert Straub.

Another Oregon original was the late Wayne Morse. A University of Oregon law professor, Morse first won election to the Senate as a Republican in 1944. Later, from disgust at the Eisenhower Administration, Morse switched to Independent status, and then in 1956 and 1962 was reelected as a Democrat. Morse was one of the earliest and most vehement opponents of the Vietnam war; along with Alaska's Ernest Gruening, he was one of the only two Senators who voted against Lyndon Johnson's Gulf of Tonkin resolution in 1964. Morse was also an expert on labor negotiations, from his law school days, and so skilfull a mediator that Johnson called on him to perform despite his dovishness; by the middle sixties, Morse was Chairman of the Senate Labor and Public Welfare Committee.

Morse's strong views on the war—and his inclination to get into personal feuds as well—resulted in a disastrous split in the Democratic Party here in the sixties. In 1966, when his own candidate was beaten by hawkish Congressman Robert Duncan, Morse backed Republican Mark Hatfield for the state's other Senate seat. Hatfield won; two years later, Morse himself was challenged in the primary by Duncan, and then beaten in the general, by 3,000 votes, by state Representative Bob Packwood. Morse came back to run for the Senate—after another bitter primary with Duncan—against Hatfield in 1972, and in 1974 he was running, and winning, the Democratic nomination again at the age of 74. But Morse was also ill, and soon after winning the nomination died. He had had the satisfaction of 24 productive and prophetic years in the Senate and, near the end, the pleasure of leading the state's McGovern delegation at the 1972 Democratic national convention; but one imagines him still angry at some injustice—or some ingrate.

Packwood was a surprise winner in 1968, more a beneficiary of the controversies Morse aroused than of his own strong appeal. In the Senate, he has earned that ubiquitous label, liberal Republican, but it is important to realize on just which issues he did so. For Packwood has by no means been a dependable opponent of all the Nixon and Ford Administrations have done, and he has been on occasion a little hawkish on the issue Morse cared so much about, the war. Packwood is more the kind of Senator who is interested in reforming political processes than in redistributing income or wealth. But Packwood has been most known as an advocate of environmental causes. He is the Congress's leading proponent of zero population growth—a position not unpopular in heavily Protestant Oregon—and he has on occasion taken positions opposite those of the big lumber companies which are so important here.

These positions paid off politically for Packwood in 1974. After Morse died, the Democratic nomination was awarded by the appropriate committee to state Senator Betty Roberts, who had finished a close second in the gubernatorial primary. Roberts tried to stress economic issues, but her campaign was late getting off the ground, and never matched Packwood's in impact. Packwood's environmental record helped him to 55% of the vote statewide and 56% in the Portland metropolitan area—the latter a better showing than Richard Nixon had made there two years ago. Packwood was first elected to the Senate when he was 34, and while it is too early to say that he has a lifetime seat, he has clearly demonstrated considerable political staying power.

With Wayne Morse dead and Tom McCall at least temporarily retired, the grand old man of Oregon politics today is Senator Mark Hatfield, who is all of 54 years old. Hatfield was something of a prodigy: he went from being a political science professor at Willamette University to the stepping stone position of Secretary of State at age 34, and was elected Governor—in the Democratic year of 1958—at 36. A deeply religious man, Hatfield, like Morse, was an early Vietnam dove, and his 1966 Senate race presented the rather unusual spectacle of a dovish Republican versus a hawkish Democrat. In the Senate, Hatfield became best known for his position on the war; in 1970 and 1971 he was spending most of his efforts as co-sponsor of the McGovern-Hatfield Amendment to end the war. But Hatfield was not one who would think about leaving his party; he's regular Republican enough to have delivered Richard Nixon's nominating speech at the 1968 national convention, and he feels a continuing obligation to his party.

As Hatfield's first term was ending, and the 1972 election approaching, he appeared to be in political trouble. He had spent little time in the state, and there were rumors that candidates as diverse as Morse, McCall, and Portland Congresswoman Edith Green were planning to run against him. In 1971, the Senator went on a little publicized tour of Oregon, talking with voters informally. That seems to have made the difference: Hatfield was newly invigorated, was making points on issues other than the war, and was headed for his second Senate term. Republican opposition faded, Green decided against the race, Morse and Duncan bloodied each other again in the Democratic primary. In the general election, the candidates were two doves, Morse and Hatfield, the former of whom had endorsed the latter six years before. There were some differences between them: Morse had compiled a stronger labor record, Hatfield was more responsive to the state's lumber interests. But the real issue was the personalities—and ages—of the candidates, and Hatfield won 54–46.

Because the Oregon presidential primary takes place just a few weeks before the big contest in California, Oregon voters have often played a decisive role in national elections. In 1948, Oregon's voters eliminated Harold Stassen from any future serious consideration as a presidential candidate. In 1964, Oregon kept Nelson Rockefeller in the race against Barry Goldwater, whom the New Yorker almost beat in California. In 1968, Oregonians gave Eugene McCarthy a hefty boost when it chose him over Robert Kennedy—the only defeat any of the Kennedy brothers has ever suffered at the polls. Oregon's law, which is now being copied by an increasing number of states, requires that all candidates that are recognized as such by the news media to appear on the ballot. The law virtually guarantees an important test of the strength of all candidates.

A final word on presidential politics here. Oregon has gone Republican in five of the last six presidential elections, but seldom by large margins. During the same period, Democratic registration has risen substantially in Oregon. While the voters here seem to retain a narrow preference for liberal Republicans over liberal Democrats in statewide elections, they seem to be shifting to the left in presidential contests. Oregon is one of the four non-Southern states where George McGovern won a larger percentage of the votes in 1972 than Humbert Humphrey did in 1968. Consequently, though Oregon has plunked for Richard Nixon three times, it might very well find itself in the Democratic column in 1976.

Census Data Pop. 2,091,385; 1.03% of U.S. total, 31st largest; Central city, 25%; suburban, 36%. Median family income, $9,487; 22nd highest; families above $15,000: 18%; families below $3,000: 9%. Median years education, 12.3.

1974 Share of Federal Tax Burden $2,785,279,000; 1.04% of U.S. total, 29th largest.

1974 Share of Federal Outlays $3,587,165,000; 0.94% of U.S. total, 32d largest. Per capita federal spending, $1207.

DOD	$225,504,000	42d (0.33%)		HEW	$1,035,902,000	29th (1.12%)
AEC	$806,000	32d (0.03%)		HUD	$6,125,000	35th (0.63%)
NASA	$1,131,000	34th (0.04%)		VA	$166,473,000	30th (1.22%)
DOT	$108,542,000	28th (1.28%)		EPA	$54,840,000	17th (1.74%)
DOC	$13,265,000	21st (0.82%)		RevS	$59,664,000	32d (0.98%)
DOI	$167,170,000	5th (6.79%)		Int.	$71,687,000	32d (0.35%)
USDA	$266,646,000	18th (2.14%)		Other	$1,409,410,000	

Economic Base Lumber and wood products, especially millwork, plywood and related products, and sawmills and planing mills; agriculture, notably cattle, dairy products, wheat and greenhouse; finance, insurance and real estate; food and kindred products, especially canned, cured and frozen foods; machinery, especially construction and related machinery; paper and allied products, especially paper mills other than building paper; transportation equipment.

Political Line-up Governor, Robert W. Straub (D). Senators, Mark O. Hatfield (R) and Bob Packwood (R). Representatives, 4 D. State Senate (22 D, 7 R, and 1 Ind.); State House (38 D and 22 R).

The Voters

Registration 1,143,073 Total. 652,414 D (57%); 439,667 R (38%); 50,992 Other (4%). *Median voting age* 44.
Employment profile White collar, 48%. Blue collar, 34%. Service, 14%. Farm, 4%.
Ethnic groups Black, 1%. Spanish, 2%. Total foreign stock, 14%. Canada, 3%, Germany, 2%, UK, 1%.

Presidential vote

1972	Nixon (R)	486,686	(55%)
	McGovern (D)	392,760	(45%)
1968	Nixon (R)	408,433	(50%)
	Humphrey (D)	358,866	(44%)
	Wallace (AI)	49,683	(6%)

1972 Democratic Presidential Primary

McGovern	205,328	(50%)
Wallace	81,868	(20%)
Humphrey	51,163	(13%)
others	70,285	(17%)

1972 Republican Presidential Primary

Nixon	231,151	(82%)
McCloskey	29,365	(10%)
Ashbrook	16,696	(6%)
others	4,798	(2%)

Sen. Mark O. Hatfield (R) Elected 1966, seat up 1978; b. July 12, 1922, Dallas; home, Newport; Willamette U., B.A. 1943, Stanford U., A.M. 1948; Baptist.

Career Navy, WWII; Assoc. Prof. of Poli. Sci., Willamette U., 1949–56, Dean of Students, 1950–56; Oreg. House of Reps., 1950–54; Oreg. Senate, 1954–56; Secy. of State of Oreg., 1956–58; Gov. of Oreg., 1958–66.

Offices 463 RSOB, 202-224-3753. Also 475 Cottage St. N.E., Salem 97301, 503-363-1629, and 105 Pioneer Courthouse, Portland 97308, 503-221-3386.

Committees

Rules and Administration (Ranking Member). Subcommittees: Computer Services; Printing; Restaurant.

Appropriations (6th). Subcommittees: Agriculture and Related Agencies; Foreign Operations; Interior; State, Justice, Commerce, The Judiciary; Treasury, U.S. Postal Service, and General Government.

Interior and Insular Affairs (3d). Subcommittees: Energy Research and Water Resources; Environment and Land Resources; Parks and Recreation.

Group Ratings

	ADA	COPE	LWV	RIPON	NFU	LCV	CFA	NAB	NSI	ACA
1974	94	55	90	71	82	84	77	27	13	6
1973	89	33	90	82	76	–	58	–	–	30
1972	55	50	90	88	80	47	83	33	0	29

Key Votes

1) No-Knock	AGN	8) Gov Abortn Aid	AGN	15) Consumer Prot Agy	FOR
2) Busing	FOR	9) Cut Mil Brass	FOR	16) Forced Psych Tests	FOR
3) No Fault	FOR	10) Gov Limousine	ABS	17) Fed Campaign Subs	FOR
4) F-111	AGN	11) RR Featherbed	AGN	18) Rhod Chrome Ban	FOR
5) Death Penalty	ABS	12) Handgun License	ABS	19) Open Legis Meetings	FOR
6) Foreign Aid	AGN	13) Less Troop Abrd	FOR	20) Strikers Food Stmps	FOR
7) Filibuster	AGN	14) Resume Turk Aid	FOR	21) Gov Info Disclosure	FOR

Election Results

1972 general:	Mark O. Hatfield (R)	494,671	(54%)	($299,626)
	Wayne L. Morse (D)	425,036	(46%)	($251,904)
1972 primary:	Mark O. Hatfield (R)	171,594	(61%)	
	Lynn Engdahl (R)	63,859	(23%)	
	Two others (R)	44,217	(16%)	
1966 general:	Mark O. Hatfield (R)	354,391	(52%)	
	Robert B. Duncan (D)	330,374	(48%)	

Sen. Bob Packwood (R) Elected 1968, seat up 1980; b. Sept. 11, 1932, Portland; home, Portland; Willamette U., B.S. 1954, New York U. LL.B. 1957; Unitarian.

Career Practicing atty., 1958–68; Oreg. House of Reps., 1962–68.

Offices 1317 DSOB, 202-224-5244. Also P.O. Box 3621, Portland 97208, 503-233-4471.

Committees

Banking, Housing and Urban Affairs (3d). Subcommittees: Housing and Urban Affairs; International Finance; Oversight; Production and Stabilization; Small Business.

Finance (5th). Subcommittees: Energy; Health; International Trade; Revenue Sharing.

Group Ratings

	ADA	COPE	LWV	RIPON	NFU	LCV	CFA	NAB	NSI	ACA
1974	81	70	90	80	91	94	100	82	43	19
1973	63	20	100	88	56	–	40	–	–	36
1972	45	40	80	82	33	58	73	22	70	55

Key Votes

1) No-Knock	AGN	8) Gov Abortn Aid	FOR	15) Consumer Prot Agy	FOR
2) Busing	FOR	9) Cut Mil Brass	AGN	16) Forced Psych Tests	ABS
3) No Fault	FOR	10) Gov Limousine	FOR	17) Fed Campaign Subs	FOR
4) F-111	AGN	11) RR Featherbed	AGN	18) Rhod Chrome Ban	FOR
5) Death Penalty	ABS	12) Handgun License	ABS	19) Open Legis Meetings	FOR
6) Foreign Aid	AGN	13) Less Troop Abrd	ABS	20) Strikers Food Stmps	AGN
7) Filibuster	AGN	14) Resume Turk Aid	FOR	21) Gov Info Disclosure	FOR

Election Results

1974 general:	Robert W. Packwood (R)	420,984	(55%)	($333,004)
	Betty Roberts (D)	338,591	(45%)	($80,193)
1974 primary:	Robert W. Packwood (R), unopposed			
1968 general:	Robert W. Packwood (R)	408,825	(50%)	
	Wayne L. Morse (D)	405,380	(50%)	

Gov. Robert W. Straub (D) Elected 1974, term expires Jan. 1979; b. May 6, 1920, San Francisco, Cal.; Dartmouth Col., B.A., M.S.

Career Army, WWII; real estate and business; Oreg. Senate, 1959; State Treasurer of Oreg., 1965–72.

Offices Rm. 207, State Capitol, Salem 97301, 503-378-3111.

Election Results

1974 general:	Robert W. (Bob) Straub (D)	444,812	(58%)
	Victor Atiyeh (R)	324,751	(42%)
1974 primary:	Robert W. (Bob) Straub (D)	107,205	(34%)
	Betty Roberts (D)	98,654	(31%)
	Jim Redden (D)	88,795	(28%)
	Eight Others (D)	24,342	(8%)

◆ ◆ ◆ ◆

FIRST DISTRICT

The 1st district of Oregon occupies the northwest corner of the state. This is the area around the mouth of the Columbia River and the coastal counties of Clatsop, Tillamook, and Lincoln—all marginally Democratic. Most of the 1st residents, however, live in the Portland metropolitan area. The district includes that part of Portland west of the Willamette—hilly, high income neighborhoods that overlook the city's downtown and both the Williamette and Columbia Rivers. Here, as in most Western cities, more affluent people live in the hills, and poorer people in the flat parts of town. About a quarter of the district's votes are cast in Washington County, the fastest growing in the state; it is an affluent suburban area where the hills rise to meet the Coast Range west of Portland. The 1st also takes in the bulk of three Republican-leaning counties on the west bank of the Willamette. The Republican tendencies of these counties were somewhat lessened in 1972 by the enfranchisement of most of the 14,000 students at Oregon State University in Corvallis.

The 1st district was created in almost its present form in 1892, and for the first 80 years of its existence it never elected a Democratic Congressman. The Progressive era, the Depression, the Goldwater debacle of 1964—through every one of these this area, first settled by Yankee Republicans, stayed true to the party of its ancestors, at least in congressional contests.

But all that changed in 1974. The district had, in fact, been moving left for some time: it was 41% for Hubert Humphrey in 1968, about his national average; but 43% for George McGovern in 1972, several points better than he was doing nationally. Registration had long since shifted

Democratic here (as elsewhere in Oregon), and a preponderance of the state legislators from the area were Democratic. Moreover, in 1974, Republican Wendell Wyatt, who had represented the district since 1964, decided to retire.

The two main competitors for his seat were Republican Diarmuid O'Scannlain and Democrat Les AuCoin. O'Scannlain had been a McCall appointee in the environmental area, and thus was automatically awarded liberal credentials, despite his Young Americans for Freedom past; all in all, he seemed to be a rather conventional Republican, not much different from the men who had represented the district for years. AuCoin, at age 32, had already shown himself able to win election to the legislature from wealthy Washington County and, after one term, to become House Majority Leader. He easily beat a lackluster field of primary opponents, and in the general whipped O'Scannlain by a 56–44 margin. Indeed, he managed the considerable task of carrying every county in the district. AuCoin, who sits on the Banking and Merchant Marine Committees, has already shown enough political talent to win the next several congressional races here, and should win easily in 1976.

Census Data Pop. 523,428. Central city, 15%; suburban, 48%. Median family income, $10,430; families above $15,000: 24%; families below $3,000: 8%. Median years education, 12.5.

The Voters

Median voting age 43.
Employment profile White collar, 54%. Blue collar, 30%. Service, 13%. Farm, 3%.
Ethnic groups Spanish, 2%. Total foreign stock, 16%. Canada, 3%; Germany, UK, 2% each.

Presidential vote

1972	Nixon (R)	137,345	(57%)
	McGovern (D)	101,616	(43%)
1968	Nixon (R)	112,543	(54%)
	Humphrey (D)	85,679	(41%)
	Wallace (AI)	9,230	(4%)

Rep. Les AuCoin (D) Elected 1974; b. Oct. 21, 1942, Portland; home, Forest Grove; Pacific U., B.A. 1969.

Career Army, 1961–64; Newsman, Portland *Oregonian,* 1965–66; Dir, of Public Info. and Publications, Pacific U., 1966–73; Oreg. House of Reps., 1971–75, Maj. Ldr., 1973–75; Administrator, Skidmore, Owings, and Merrill, engineering firm, 1973–74.

Offices 329 CHOB, 202-225-0855. Also 1716 Fed. Bldg., 1220 SW 3rd Ave., Portland 97204, 503-221-2901.

Committees

Banking, Currency and Housing (25th). Subcommittees: Housing and Community Development; International Trade, Investment and Monetary Policy.

Merchant Marine and Fisheries (23d). Subcommittees: Coast Guard and Navigation; Fisheries and Wildlife Conservation and the Environment; Oceanography.

Group Ratings: Newly Elected

Key Votes

1) Foreign Aid	FOR	6) Gov Abortn Aid	NE	11) Pub Cong Election $	NE
2) Busing	NE	7) Coed Phys Ed	AGN	12) Turkish Arms Cutoff	NE
3) ABM	NE	8) Pov Lawyer Gag	NE	13) Youth Camp Regs	AGN
4) B-1 Bomber	AGN	9) Pub Trans Sub	NE	14) Strip Mine Veto	AGN
5) Nerve Gas	NE	10) EZ Voter Regis	NE	15) Farm Bill Veto	AGN

Election Results

1974 general:	Les AuCoin (D)	114,629	(56%)	($95,168)
	Diarmuid O'Scannlain (R)	89,848	(44%)	($83,659)
1974 primary:	Les AuCoin (D)	35,885	(49%)	
	Ralph Bunch (D)	16,156	(22%)	
	Three others (D)	21,649	(29%)	

◆ ◆ ◆ ◆ ◆

SECOND DISTRICT

The 2d congressional district of Oregon contains 25% of the state's population and 73% of its land area. Most of the land lies east of the Cascade Mountains: to the south, the terrain is desert-like; to the north, where rain falls in more generous amounts, one finds much of Oregon's vast forests and supplies of timber. Oregon east of the Cascades is a sparsely-populated region, with some 270,000 people in an area about the size of New England. Before 1965, the 2d district lay entirely east of the Cascades; it was therefore far out of line with the requirements of the one-person-one-vote ruling. So the redistricting of 1965 added the counties of Marion (Salem) and Linn (Albany) west of the mountains. The redistricting of 1971 modified the boundaries still further, moving the 2d into the Portland suburbs of Milwaukie and Oregon City.

All of this line-drawing failed to change the political complexion of the 2d very much. East Oregon is marginal political territory, where traditional Rocky Mountain populism on pocketbook issues—the area is especially keen on public power development—has been overmatched in recent years by the mountain country's dislike for what it considers effete liberalism or too solicitous concern for an environment that invites profitable exploitation.The 2d district portion west of the Cascades, which now comes close to outvoting East Oregon, is traditionally more Republican, but not by any great margin.

The name of the 2d district's Congressman, we wrote in 1974, was not much recognized then; it is, as we suggested, now. He is Al Ullman, a Democrat first elected in 1956, and, following the abdication of Wilbur Mills, Chairman of the House Ways and Means Committee. Ullman came to the Congress, like so many young men, as a fiery liberal; in recent years, he has sounded downright conservative. As a representative from a lumber district, he is suspicious of much of the environmental movement; as a Democrat loyal to the leadership, he was slow indeed to oppose American involvement in Southeast Asia; as a man who attained considerable seniority long before senility (he is still only 62), he bridles at attacks on the seniority system. And most important, as a witness before Mills's hearings, and a participant in discussions on the intricacies and subtleties of the Internal Revenue Code, he is not a noisy crusader for tax reform; and though he is willing, he is not especially eager, to disturb the status quo.

But when Ullman took over from Mills in late 1974, the question most observers were asking was not what Ullman's beliefs were, but simply whether he was up to the job. Washington had been convinced for a long time that Ways and Means handled such complicated stuff that only a wizard like Mills could understand it. In his first few months in the chair, Al Ullman disabused people of this notion. He steered the tax cut through the House; and if he lost on the oil depletion allowance (liberals wanted to attach it to the unvetoable tax cut; Ullman wanted to save it, so as to speed the tax cut along), he accepted his defeat in good grace and did not try to sabotage the will of the House in conference committee. He had more difficulty putting together an energy package—chiefly because he ignored the Democrats who said they would never vote for a gas tax, but his work here was again constructive and serious. In his personal appearances, he sometimes looked nervous, indeed seemed explicitly worried that he might be not up to the job; but his answers, whatever one might think of his views, showed that he was.

Ullman has, as one might expect, no political trouble at home; it would take something on the order of the Argentine firecracker to put him in political trouble. In 1972, he was altogether unopposed; in 1974, he took 81% of the vote in the primary and 78% in the general election, carrying every county each time. He is young enough that he can expect at least several more terms, but old enough (only five years younger than Mills) that he won't be Chairman forever as Mills once seemed destined to be.

Census Data Pop. 522,898. Central city, 12%; suburban, 29%. Median family income, $8,821; families above $15,000: 14%; families below $3,000: 11%. Median years education, 12.2.

The Voters

Median voting age 45.
Employment profile White collar, 43%. Blue collar, 34%. Service, 14%. Farm, 9%.
Ethnic groups Spanish, 2%. Total foreign stock, 12%. Canada, Germany, 2% each; UK, 1%.

Presidential vote

1972	Nixon (R)	....	123,857	(60%)
	McGovern (D)	....	81,195	(40%)
1968	Nixon (R)	....	104,600	(53%)
	Humphrey (D)	....	78,080	(40%)
	Wallace (AI)	....	13,099	(7%)

Rep. Al Ullman (D) Elected 1956; b. Mar. 9, 1914, Great Falls, Mont.; home, Baker; Whitman Col., A.B. 1935, Columbia U., M.A. 1939; Presbyterian.

Career Navy, WWII; Real estate broker and builder, 1945–56.

Offices 2207 RHOB, 202-225-5711. Also P.O. Box 247, Salem, 97308, 503-399-5724.

Committees

Ways and Means (Chairman).

Group Ratings

	ADA	COPE	LWV	RIPON	NFU	LCV	CFA	NAB	NSI	ACA
1974	62	82	73	36	100	56	46	42	50	21
1973	57	70	58	46	100	16	33	–	–	23
1972	38	60	89	73	100	26	50	30	20	18

Key Votes

1) Foreign Aid	FOR	6) Gov Abortn Aid	AGN	11) Pub Cong Election $	AGN
2) Busing	FOR	7) Coed Phys Ed	AGN	12) Turkish Arms Cutoff	AGN
3) ABM	FOR	8) Pov Lawyer Gag	FOR	13) Youth Camp Regs	FOR
4) B-1 Bomber	AGN	9) Pub Trans Sub	ABS	14) Strip Mine Veto	AGN
5) Nerve Gas	AGN	10) EZ Voter Regis	FOR	15) Farm Bill Veto	AGN

Election Results

1974 general:	Al Ullman (D)	....	140,963 (78%)	($49,496)
	Kenneth Alexander Brown (R)	....	39,441 (22%)	($629)
1974 primary:	Al Ullman (D)	....	56,225 (81%)	
	Steven Anderson (D)	....	13,041 (19%)	
1972 general:	Al Ullman (D), unopposed	....		($13,307)

◆ ◆ ◆ ◆ ◆

THIRD DISTRICT

Portland is Oregon's big city. Almost half the people of the state live within its metropolitan area, and far more than half within 60 miles of its downtown. The 3d congressional district of Oregon takes in most of Portland—the four-fifths of it that lies east of the Willamette River. The district also includes most of the Portland suburbs along the Willamette and Columbia Rivers. The 3d's eastern borders stretch to a point near the snow-covered peak of Mount Hood, which at 11,000 feet looks down on Portland, with its green, shady streets and its famous roses.

Portland has few of the problems usually associated with central cities. It has little crime, smog, or dilapidated housing. There is a movement to the suburbs, but the city itself retains a sound tax base. Portland is so idyllic that perhaps only its great distance from other urban centers has kept it from growing much faster than it has. One can understand why former Governor Tom McCall urged people not to move here—everyone's fear is that, somehow, this could become another Los Angeles.

For twenty years the 3d district was represented in the House by Democrat Edith Green, who came to the House with 12 years of classroom teaching experience and a reputation as a flaming liberal. That was in 1954, and the years changed her—or changed others so much that she seemed to change. By 1972, she was the second-ranking member of the liberal Education and Labor Committee, and one sorely at odds with the Committee's usually liberal majority. She stoutly resisted efforts to bypass local boards of education to stimulate innovation; she was suspicious of high funding; she persistently defended the educational establishment against liberal critics. On other issues, too, she was moving to the right. A supporter of Robert Kennedy in the 1968 Oregon primary, she voted against antiwar legislation thereafter and backed Washington's Scoop Jackson (to no perceptible effect) in 1972.

After that election, Mrs. Green moved off Education and Labor—despite her seniority—to a junior seat on HEW Appropriations. There theoretically she was in a position to sabotage her old adversaries' programs by not funding them; in fact, she seemed simply to be seeking a place to sulk. In 1974, she decided to retire, and sensibly so. She had rankled her colleagues so much that a year later, when her name was proposed for the board of the Legal Services Commission she had fought in Congress, no less than 60 Democratic Congressmen signed a petition opposing her.

Since this is, on paper at least, Oregon's most Democratic seat, the Democratic primary was expected to determine Mrs. Green's successor, and in a sense it did. But what was really crucial was the decision of Robert Duncan to file. Duncan has, by now, a long history in Oregon politics, and a fairly important one. He was elected to the House in 1962 and 1964 from the 4th district. A Navy veteran, he was a strong supporter of Lyndon Johnson's Vietnam war policy, and he ran as such for the Senate in 1966—nearly beating Mark Hatfield in the process, and beginning a long feud with Senator Wayne Morse, who had openly supported Hatfield. In 1968, Duncan had the satisfaction of seeing Morse defeated by Bob Packwood; in 1972, Duncan himself, by now a Portland lawyer, was beaten by Morse in Democratic primaries for the Senate nomination. By 1974, Duncan was as well and widely known as any Oregon politician; and with the war practically gone as an issue, his candidacy for Congress seemed unlikely to ignite the old feuds.

So Duncan passed up the chance for another Senate primary race against Morse, and filed instead for the 3d district. In the eight-man Democratic primary field, he received 34% of the vote, for an easy win; in the general election, he got 71% of the vote against Republican John Piacentini. Returning to the House after an eight year absence, Duncan had a slight seniority edge; he was ranked ahead of all other freshmen, and received a seat on the Appropriations Committee. With the last Americans now out of Ho Chi Minh City, it seems inconceivable that Duncan could lose this seat.

Census Data Pop. 522,258. Central city, 59%; suburban, 41%. Median family income, $10,001; families above $15,000: 19%; families below $3,000: 8%. Median years education, 12.3.

The Voters

Median voting age 45.
Employment profile White collar, 51%. Blue collar, 34%. Service, 14%. Farm, 1%.
Ethnic groups Black, 4%. Spanish, 2%. Total foreign stock, 18%. Canada, 3%; Germany, UK, 2% each.

Presidential vote

1972	Nixon (R)	106,955	(48%)
	McGovern (D)	115,283	(52%)
1968	Nixon (R)	93,641	(42%)
	Humphrey (D)	116,136	(53%)
	Wallace (AI)	10,757	(5%)

Rep. Robert Duncan (D) Elected 1974; b. Dec. 4, 1920, Normal, Ill.; home, Gresham; U. of Alaska, 1939–40, Ill. Wesleyan U., B.A. 1942; U. of Mich., LL.B. 1948; Methodist.

Career Navy Air Force, WWII; Practicing atty., 1948–63, 1967–74; Oreg. House of Reps., 1957–63; U.S. House of Reps., 1963–67.

Offices 330 CHOB, 202-225-4811. Also Rm. 706, U.S. Courthouse, Portland 97204, 503-221-2123.

Committees

Appropriations (35th). Subcommittees: Interior; Transportation.

Group Ratings: Newly Elected

Key Votes

1) Foreign Aid	FOR	6) Gov Abortn Aid	NE	11) Pub Cong Election $	NE
2) Busing	NE	7) Coed Phys Ed	AGN	12) Turkish Arms Cutoff	NE
3) ABM	NE	8) Pov Lawyer Gag	NE	13) Youth Camp Regs	AGN
4) B-1 Bomber	AGN	9) Pub Trans Sub	NE	14) Strip Mine Veto	AGN
5) Nerve Gas	NE	10) EZ Voter Regis	NE	15) Farm Bill Veto	AGN

Election Results

1974 general:	Robert B. Duncan (D)	129,290	(71%)	($84,124)
	John Piacentini (R)	54,080	(29%)	($54,285)
1974 primary:	Robert B. Duncan (D)	32,655	(34%)	
	Harl Haas (D)	18,115	(19%)	
	Vern Cook (D)	13,802	(15%)	
	Five others (D)	30,308	(32%)	

◆ ◆ ◆ ◆ ◆

FOURTH DISTRICT

The 4th district of Oregon occupies the southwest corner of the state. Though the district contains about half of Oregon's rocky and picturesque Pacific shoreline, most of its people are found inland, in the southern end of the Willamette River valley between the Coast Range and the Cascades. As in most of the West, few people actually live on farms, though the area produces much of Oregon's famed fruit crop. Instead, most of the people live in small, well-ordered cities like Medford, Grant's Pass, Roseburg, Coos Bay, and Springfield. The largest city here is Eugene (pop. 76,000), the home of the University of Oregon. The ballots of the university's peace-oriented students showed up clearly in the 1972 election returns.

As is the case throughout Oregon, the 4th district has no sharp extremes of political allegiance. As a result, party control of the district has changed six times in the last twenty years. In 1958, the 4th elected Democrat Charles O. Porter, considered a far-out peacenik both then and now; he was retired for a Republican named Edwin Durno in 1960, who was in turn beaten by Democrat Robert Duncan in 1962 (see Third District). Duncan ran for the Senate in 1966 and was succeeded by Republican John Dellenback, who was in turn beaten by Democrat James Weaver in 1974.

This was the biggest upset in Oregon in 1974. Dellenback had been known as a hard working, moderate Republican, who had risen to the number five minority seat on the Education and Labor Committee. With his bald forehead and crew cut, and his omnipresent bow ties, Dellenback scarcely presented a mod appearance, but he had a middle of the road voting record, more liberal on war and environmental than on straight economic issues. He seemed ideally suited to this district, with its Republican heritage and it slow, continual movement leftward.

But the Watergate seemed to move the 4th sharply left with a lurch—leaving Dellenback behind. His opponent was James Weaver, the same liberal Democrat he had beaten by a 58–42 margin in 1970. (Dellenback had been fortunate to draw former Congressman Porter as an opponent in 1972; he beat him 63–37.) The biggest difference between 1970 and 1974, at least in votes, was in Lane County and Eugene; the recently enfranchised students seemed to go heavily for Weaver. Now he serves as part of the liberal freshman caucus, and a member of the Agriculture and Interior Committees—good assignments for this district. But who can tell what will happen here in 1976? In an era when most Congressmen can use the advantages of incumbency to get themselves reelected, whatever the trends in public opinion, the 4th remains one of the nation's prime marginal districts, and it would be foolhardy to predict the result.

Census Data Pop. 522,801. Central city, 15%; suburban, 26%. Median family income, $8,854; families above $15,000: 14%; families below $3,000: 10%. Median years education, 12.2.

The Voters

Median voting age 43.
Employment profile White collar, 43%. Blue collar, 40%. Service, 13%. Farm, 4%.
Ethnic groups Spanish, 1%. Total foreign stock, 11%. Canada, Germany, 2% each; UK, 1%.

Presidential vote

1972	Nixon (R)	117,977	(56%)
	McGovern (D)	94,456	(44%)
1968	Nixon (R)	97,649	(51%)
	Humphrey (D)	78,971	(41%)
	Wallace (AI)	16,597	(9%)

Rep. James Weaver (D) Elected 1974; b. Aug. 8, 1927, Brookings, S.D.; home, Eugene; U. of Oreg., B.S. 1952.

Career Navy, WWII; Publisher's Rep., Prentice-Hall Co., 1954–58; Staff Dir., Oreg. Legislative Interim Comm. on Agriculture, 1959–60; Builder and apartment complex developer, 1960–75.

Offices 1723 LHOB, 202-225-6416. Also Fed. Bldg., 211 E. 7th Ave., Eugene 97401, 503-687-6732.

Committees

Agriculture (17th). Subcommittees: Department Operations, Investigations and Oversight; Forests; Livestock and Grains.

Interior and Insular Affairs (25th). Subcommittees: Energy and the Environment; Public Lands; Water and Power Resources.

Group Ratings: Newly Elected

Key Votes

1) Foreign Aid	AGN	6) Gov Abortn Aid	NE	11) Pub Cong Election $	NE
2) Busing	NE	7) Coed Phys Ed	FOR	12) Turkish Arms Cutoff	NE
3) ABM	NE	8) Pov Lawyer Gag	NE	13) Youth Camp Regs	AGN
4) B-1 Bomber	AGN	9) Pub Trans Sub	NE	14) Strip Mine Veto	AGN
5) Nerve Gas	NE	10) EZ Voter Regis	NE	15) Farm Bill Veto	AGN

Election Results

1974 general:	James Weaver (D)	97,580	(53%)	($42,271)
	John Dellenback (R)	86,950	(47%)	($52,614)
1974 primary:	James Weaver (D)	23,397	(35%)	
	Jack Ripper (D)	17,609	(27%)	
	Frank Barry (D)	17,599	(27%)	
	Two others (D)	7,515	(11%)	

PENNSYLVANIA

A look at the map will tell us how Pennsylvania got its nickname, the Keystone State. Pennsylvania connects New York state and New England with the rest of the country. For many years, the geography of Pennsylvania promised to make it the commercial and transportation hub of the nation, as indeed it was at the time the Constitution was ratified. But things failed to work out that way. The rugged mountains of central Pennsylvania stalled the early development of transportation arteries west. And it was New York City, rather than Philadelphia, that mushroomed thanks to the building of the Erie Canal and the first water-level railroad line west. In 1776, Philadelphia, the home of the remarkable Benjamin Franklin, was the nation's capital and largest city. Within 50 years, it was eclipsed by Washington in the affairs of government and New York City in commerce. And New Englanders will argue that Boston was never surpassed as the nation's center of culture and education.

During the late nineteenth century, however, Pennsylvania experienced a renaissance based on the then-booming industries of coal and steel. Immigrants poured in to work the mines of Scranton and the steel mills of Pittsburgh—flush towns in those days. The boom ended conclusively with the coming of the Great Depression of the 1930s, and good times have yet to return to much of Pennsylvania. The coal industry collapsed after World War II, and though doing better of late, employs far fewer people than it did in the 1920s. Pennsylvania steel, though also doing a bit better of late, has long since grown complacent. Because it chose to ignore technological advances following World War II, its ancient mills are today far less efficient than the modern steel plants constructed in bombed-out Germany and Japan. Indeed, the industry here appeared to have thrown in the towel in the early seventies, allying themselves with the United Steelworkers to back import quotas on steel, rather than striving for new ways to compete. A century ago, the steel producers made Pennsylvania the classic high tariff state, arguing that here must be protection for their "infant" industry; today, they appear to be conceding that American steel has become senile.

These economic developments have left Pennsylvania in rather sorry shape. People growing up here are as likely to leave the state as stay, while out-of-staters show little inclination to move in. In 1930, after its last decade of prosperity, Pennsylvania recorded 9.5 million residents; today, the number stands at 11.8 million—by far the smallest growth rate of the nation's ten biggest states. Once the nation's second largest state, by 1974 Pennsylvania had slipped to fourth, behind California, New York, and Texas. This sluggish growth has had political consequences. As recently as 1950, Pennsylvania had 32 seats in the House of Representatives; today it has only 25.

Traditionally, Pennsylvania was heavily Republican, the most Republican of all the big states; even in 1932, it stayed loyal and voted for Hoover over Roosevelt. For years Philadelphia was governed not by a Democratic, but by a Republican machine, which held on to the Mayor's office until reformer (and later Senator) Joseph Clark won it in 1951. The immigrant miners of northeast Pennsylvania and the steel workers of Pittsburgh were enrolled as Republicans as soon as their naturalization papers came through, and if they ended up supporting many candidates who were picked by their employers, there were also some noted progressive Republicans elected here.

What changed all this was, of course, the Depression and the New Deal; since then Pennsylvania has become a classic politically marginal state. But the central part of the state—the Welsh railroad workers in Altoona and the Pennsylvania Dutch farmers around Lancaster —remain the strongest Republican voting bloc in the east, and if greater Philadelphia has become Democratic in most elections, Republicans (especially Senator Richard Schweiker) remain competitive there. The great blue collar enclaves here—greater Pittsburgh and the whole western end of the state and the northeast region around Scranton, Wilkes-Barre, Allentown and Bethlehem, and Reading—are now Democratic bulwarks, although they are often attracted to candidates like George Wallace and the Richard Nixon of 1972. These are the places where organized labor, expecially the United Steelworkers, exert most of their electoral influence in the state.

Pennsylvania has always been a political machine state, and to some extent still is. A dozen years ago, the state government had 50,000 patronage employees, appointed for the most part on the recommendations of county political parties. That number was whittled down by Republican Governors William Scranton (1963-67) and Raymond Shafer (1967-71) and by their Democratic successor, Milton Shapp. A millionaire businessman, Shapp decided in the middle sixties that he would become Governor. He studied up on state problems, and in 1966 spent huge amounts of money on his media campaign and won the Democratic nomination—over a candidate endorsed by all the big machines. Shapp lost that election to Shafer, but he came back four years later, beat the same machine candidate in the primary, and then won the general election with 57% of the vote. He obviously was not the kind of officeholder interested in patronage—where would he find people interested in $8,500 a year jobs?—and so the machines have continued to decline.

By most accounts, Shapp has been an effective governor, though not quite so efficiency minded and divorced from politics as some expected. He won his most favorable publicity in his first term by hiring as Insurance Commissioner Herbert Denenberg, a professor at the University of Pennsylvania who has become nationally known as a crusader for consumers and the scourge of the big insurance companies. (Shapp and Denenberg had a falling out later, however.) Shapp also made national news, helping to settle the spontaneous truckers' strike in 1974, when the federal government seemed paralyzed in inaction. Shapp has attempted to be a national political mover, with less success; his ballyhooed support of Edmund Muskie in 1972 was followed by a fourth place Muskie finish in Pennsylvania's primary.

Shapp, the first Pennsylvania Governor eligible to run for reelection, was expected to win easily in 1974. His opponent was Drew Lewis, a young, wealthy suburban Philadelphia businessman. But in the last month of the campaign, a committee set up by majority Republicans in the legislature to embarrass Shapp began to find evidence of minor scandals in his administration. Shapp has never been especially popular with Catholic voters, and though he ran well in metropolitan Philadelphia, his percentages in western Pennsylvania sagged badly; he finally won with a solid, but scarcely overwhelming, 54% of the vote. Ineligible for a third term, past his sixtieth birthday, it is unlikely that Shapp will run another statewide race again; 1976 will probably be the last time he figures as a major force in Pennsylvania elections. In 1975 he claimed an interest in becoming a presidential candidate; local observers say it is his way of applying for a Cabinet post in a Democratic Adminstration.

Pennsylvania's senior Senator is Hugh Scott, the late Everett Dirksen's successor as Senate Minority Leader. Scott has won a number of elections in unlikely circumstances. From 1943 to 1959, he was a Congressman from Philadelphia, serving as Republican National Chairman during the Dewey campaign of 1948. Scott then chose the Democratic year of 1958 to run for the Senate, perhaps because he thought his seat would be wiped out by redistricting after 1960 (it was); he got enough voters to split tickets to win. In 1964, he talked as if the Goldwater candidacy were going to doom his career, but nonetheless managed to squeak through with 51% of the vote. In 1970, despite his national prominence, Scott was able to win only 52% of the vote against an obscure Democrat from the northeast corner of the state.

But Hugh Scott has long since moved from a preoccupation with vote getting to establishing his position as a leader of national influence. From his Dewey days, Scott had a reputation as a liberal; at the same time, he wanted to head the majority conservative group of Republican Senators. The key vote came after the sudden death of Minority Leader Everett Dirksen in 1969. Scott was fortunate that his opponent was Howard Baker of Tennessee, a bright conservative to be sure, and Dirksen's son-in-law, but then only a freshman; Scott beat him by a 24–19 vote, and repeated that victory as the new Congress convened in 1971.

In those days, Scott was busy alternating between buttressing his liberal reputation and placating the Nixon Administration and Senate colleagues. He opposed the Haynsworth nomination and Nixon's proposals for weakening the Voting Rights Act. But he supported Carswell, the ABM and SST, and strongly backed the Nixon Vietnam war policy. As it became clear that Nixon would be reelected easily in 1972, Scott seem to sign up on the Nixon-Agnew team without reservations. He applied the acid-amnesty-abortion label, rather inaccurately, to George McGovern; he had only scorn for those who disagreed with Administration policies. During the Watergate crisis, Scott, who had begun his career in Philadelphia as a supporter of civil rights and civil liberties, defended Nixon and his men constantly; at one point, he gave his personal assurance that there was nothing on the tapes which would incriminate Nixon. Scott was gulled, of course, as so many were; but he had contributed what was left of his reputation to the gulling. Scott will be 76 in 1976, just after the voters will have their chance to fill his seat; probably he would like to cap his career with a victory in this bicentennial year, but he seems unlikely to have enough political, if not physical, strength to win, The strongest potential contenders for the seat: Democratic Congressman William Green of Philadelphia, who has done more than any other member of Congress toward abolishing the oil depletion allowance; and Republican Congressman John Heinz of Pittsburgh, a liberal member of the 57 Varieties family. Other possible candidates include former Insurance Commissioner Denenberg and Secretary of State Robert Casey, both Democrats.

Pennsylvania's other Senator is a less known, more liberal Republican, Richard Schweiker of suburban Philadelphia. Schweiker won his seat almost unnoticed in 1968; he was a junior Congressman and he won more because of the weakness of his opponent, Senator Joseph Clark, than because of his own strength. Clark had antagonized gun owners by supporting gun control, and had somehow incurred the wrath of Italian-American groups; he failed to win the usual Democratic majorities in Catholic areas, and so Schweiker won. In the House, Schweiker had been a member of the Armed Services Committee, and he won a seat on the corresponding panel in the Senate—where he surprised many observers by blossoming forth as a dove. On domestic issues, he served on the Labor and Public Welfare Committee and earned a 100% COPE rating—an unusual distinction for a Pennsylvania Republican. By 1974, when he was up for reelection, Schweiker had emerged from under Scott's shadow, and when the votes were counted, Schweiker emerged as an electorally stronger politician than the man who had, for a while, been his mentor.

On Watergate, in particular, Schweiker declined to follow Scott's lead; instead, he early established his disagreement and dissatifaction with Nixon. He was wise to do so, for he attracted strong opposition. Denenberg resigned as Insurance Commissioner to run, and despite an inept campaign seemed to be enjoying a genuine public enthusiasm unusual indeed in 1974. But Denenberg was beaten in the primary by Pittsburgh Mayor Peter Flaherty, an unusual politician himself. Flaherty had beaten the Pittsburgh Democratic machine in 1969, and had since then cut spending, decreased the number of city employees, reduced services—and become immensely popular, not just in the population-losing city of Pittsburgh, but in the much larger media market which casts one-quarter of the state's vote. Flaherty won his primary solely because he had 64% of the vote in western Pennsylvania; he scarcely campaigned at all in the general election, and still won 59% of the vote in western Pennsylvania. Schweiker, on the other hand, worked hard and used every asset to full advantage—especially his endorsement from the AFL-CIO. And it paid off: he carried practically everything outside the range of Pittsburgh TV stations, losing only barely in the city of Philadelphia even as Shapp was winning 70% of the vote there.

Census Data Pop. 11,793,909; 5.83% of U.S. total, 3rd largest; Central city, 29%; suburban, 51%. Median family income, $9,554; 20th highest; families above $15,000: 18%; families below $3,000: 8%. Median years education, 12.0.

1974 Share of Federal Tax Burden $15,024,438,000; 5.61% of U.S. total, 4th largest.

1974 Share of Federal Outlays $13,089,453,000; 4.84% of U.S. total, 4th largest. Per capita federal spending, $1110.

DOD	$2,745,470,000	6th (4.01%)		HEW	$5,829,981,000	3d (6.28%)
AEC	$121,935,000	11th (4.00%)		HUD	$70,660,000	3d (7.25%)
NASA	$26,523,000	15th (0.89%)		VA	$708,818,000	4th (5.18%)
DOT	$453,806,000	3d (5.36%)		EPA	$154,493,000	3d (4.91%)
DOC	$20,385,000	14th (1.26%)		RevS	$317,650,000	3d (5.23%)
DOI	$76,911,000	9th (3.12%)		Int.	$483,821,000	7th (2.35%)
USDA	$255,390,000	20th (2.05%)		Other	$1,823,610,000	

Economic Base Primary metal industries, especially blast furnaces and steel mills; finance, insurance and real estate; apparel and other textile products, especially women's and misses' outerwear; machinery; electrical equipment and supplies, especially electronic components and accessories; fabricated metal products, especially fabricated structural metal products; food and kindred products, especially bakery products.

Political Line-up Governor, Milton J. Shapp (D). Senators, Hugh Scott (R) and Richard S. Schweiker (R). Representatives, 25 (14 D and 11 R). State Senate (30 D and 20 R); State House (113 D and 90 R).

The Voters

Registration 5,529,047 Total. 2,884,523 D (52%); 2,479,802 R (45%); 6,764 Constitutional (–); 157,958 AI (3%).
Median voting age 45.
Employment profile White collar, 45%. Blue collar, 42%. Service, 12%. Farm, 1%.
Ethnic groups Black, 9%. Total foreign stock, 18%. Italy, 4%, Poland, Germany, UK, 2% each; USSR, Austria, Czechoslovakia, Ireland, 1% each.

Presidential vote

1972	Nixon (R)	2,714,521	(60%)
	McGovern (D)	1,796,951	(40%)
1968	Nixon (R)	2,090,017	(44%)
	Humphrey (D)	2,259,405	(48%)
	Wallace (AI)	378,582	(8%)

1972 Democratic Presidential Primary

Humphrey	481,900	(35%)
Wallace	292,437	(21%)
McGovern	280,861	(21%)
Muskie	279,983	(20%)
others	39,658	(3%)

1972 Republican Presidential Primary

Nixon	4,953	(88%)
others	658	(12%)

Sen. Hugh Scott (R) Elected 1958, seat up 1976; b. 1900, Fredericksburg, Va.; home, Philadelphia; Randolph-Macon Col., A.B. 1919, U. of Va., LL.B. 1922; Episcopalian.

Career Practicing atty.; U.S. House of Reps., 1941–45, 1947–59; Navy, WWII and Korea; Natl. Chm., Repub. Party, 1948–49; Chm., Eisenhower Headquarters Comm., 1952; U.S. Senate Minor. Whip, 1969, Minor. Ldr., 1969–.

Offices 260 RSOB, 202-224-6324. Also 9456 Fed. Bldg., 600 Arch St., Philadelphia 19106, 215-597-0870, and 434 Fed. Bldg., 1000 Liberty Ave., Pittsburgh 15222, 412-261-3230.

Committees

Minority Leader

Foreign Relations (3d). Subcommittees: Far Eastern Affairs; Foreign Assistance and Economic Policy.

The Judiciary (3d). Subcommittees: Administrative Practice and Procedure; Constitutional Rights; Criminal Laws and Procedures; FBI Oversight; Improvement in Judicial Machinery; Patents, Trademarks and Copyrights; Penitentiaries; Separation of Powers.

Rules and Administration (2d). Subcommittees: Library; Smithsonian Institution.

Group Ratings

	ADA	COPE	LWV	RIPON	NFU	LCV	CFA	NAB	NSI	ACA
1974	45	70	100	68	67	52	50	50	78	41
1973	25	55	70	76	38	–	25	–	–	61
1972	35	60	80	75	44	26	63	56	89	55

Key Votes

1) No-Knock	FOR	8) Gov Abortn Aid	ABS	15) Consumer Prot Agy	FOR
2) Busing	FOR	9) Cut Mil Brass	AGN	16) Forced Psych Tests	AGN
3) No Fault	FOR	10) Gov Limousine	FOR	17) Fed Campaign Subs	FOR
4) F-111	AGN	11) RR Featherbed	AGN	18) Rhod Chrome Ban	FOR
5) Death Penalty	FOR	12) Handgun License	AGN	19) Open Legis Meetings	AGN
6) Foreign Aid	FOR	13) Less Troop Abrd	AGN	20) Strikers Food Stmps	FOR
7) Filibuster	AGN	14) Resume Turk Aid	FOR	21) Gov Info Disclosure	AGN

Election Results

1970 general:	Hugh Scott (R)	1,874,106	(52%)
	William Sesler (D)	1,653,774	(46%)
	Frank W. Gaydosh (Const.)	85,813	(2%)

1970 primary: Hugh Scott (R), unopposed
1964 general: Hugh Scott (R) 2,429,858 (51%)
               Genevieve Blatt (D) 2,359,223 (49%)

Sen. Richard S. Schweiker (R) Elected 1968, seat up 1980; b. June 1, 1926, Norristown; home, Worcester; Penn St. U., B.A. 1950; Central Schwenkfelder Church.

Career Navy, WWII; Business Exec., 1950–60; U.S. House of Reps., 1961–69.

Offices 347 RSOB, 202-224-4254. Also 2001 Fed. Bldg., Pittsburgh 15222, 412-644-3400, and 600 Arch St., Philadelphia 19106, 215-597-7200.

Committees

Appropriations (9th). Subcommittees: Defense; District of Columbia; Labor and HEW; Legislative; Public Works; Transportation.

Labor and Public Welfare (2d). Subcommittees: Aging; Alcoholism and Narcotics; Education; Employment, Poverty, and Migratory Labor; The Handicapped; Health; Labor; Special Subcommittee on National Science Foundation.

Select Committee on Intelligence Operations (5th).

Group Ratings

	ADA	COPE	LWV	RIPON	NFU	LCV	CFA	NAB	NSI	ACA
1974	85	91	80	61	88	76	88	33	33	16
1973	79	100	89	82	94	–	77	–	–	17
1972	60	100	100	88	70	79	100	42	70	27

Key Votes

1) No-Knock	AGN	8) Gov Abortn Aid	AGN	15) Consumer Prot Agy	FOR
2) Busing	AGN	9) Cut Mil Brass	AGN	16) Forced Psych Tests	FOR
3) No Fault	FOR	10) Gov Limousine	AGN	17) Fed Campaign Subs	FOR
4) F-111	AGN	11) RR Featherbed	FOR	18) Rhod Chrome Ban	FOR
5) Death Penalty	FOR	12) Handgun License	AGN	19) Open Legis Meetings	FOR
6) Foreign Aid	FOR	13) Less Troop Abrd	FOR	20) Strikers Food Stmps	FOR
7) Filibuster	ABS	14) Resume Turk Aid	AGN	21) Gov Info Disclosure	FOR

Election Results

1974 general: Richard S. Schweiker (R) 1,843,317 (54%) ($799,499)
                Pete Flaherty (D) 1,596,121 (46%) ($256,483)
1974 primary: Richard S. Schweiker (R), unopposed
1968 general: Richard S. Schweiker (R) 2,399,762 (52%)
                Joseph S. Clark (D) 2,117,662 (46%)
                Frank W. Gaydosh (Const.) 96,742 (2%)

Gov. Milton J. Shapp (D) Elected 1970, term expires Jan. 1979; b. June 25, 1912, Cleveland, Ohio; Case-Western U., B.S. 1933; Jewish.

Career Radiart Corp., 1933–40, production line, 1933–35, Eastern Sales Rep., 1935–38, Eastern Sales Mgr., 1938–40; Army, WWII; Founder, Jerrold Electronic Corp., inventors of cable TV, 1948; Organizer, Area Redevelopment Admin., U.S. Dept. of Commerce, 1961; Candidate for Dem. nomination for U.S. Senate, 1964; Dem. nominee for Gov., 1966.

Offices 255 Main Capitol, Harrisburg 17120, 717-787-2500.

Election Results

1974 general:	Milton Shapp (D)	1,878,252	(54%)
	Andrew L. Lewis (R)	1,578,917	(46%)
1974 primary:	Milton Shapp (D)	729,201	(70%)
	Martin P. Mullen (D)	199,613	(19%)
	Harvey F. Johnston (D)	106,474	(10%)
1970 general:	Milton Shapp (D)	2,043,029	(57%)
	Raymond Broderick (R)	1,542,854	(43%)

◆ ◆ ◆ ◆ ◆

FIRST DISTRICT

The 1st district of Pennsylvania is the southern end of the city of Philadelphia. The Schuylkill River divides the district into two just about equal parts. On the west bank is the University of Pennsylvania and, beyond the campus, the West Philadelphia black ghetto. On the east side of the river is the heavily Italian-American neighborhood of South Philadelphia. This is the stronghold of Mayor Frank Rizzo, who was renominated over an aristocratic state Senator by only a 50–43 margin in 1975.

Back during the Kennedy years of the early 1960s, both South and West Philadelphia voted overwhelmingly Democratic. But in recent years, as black areas have voted Democratic with near unanimity, South Philadelphia has shifted to the right. Rizzo is of course the favorite kind of candidate here—a nominal Democrat, a man who may rise enough in society to go to events in a dinner jacket, but who is still proud enough of his background as a tough patrolman to wear a billy club in his cummerbund. Rizzo was slated by Peter Camiel's Democratic machine in 1971, beat Congressman William Green in the primary and barely won over a black and liberal backed Republican, and then broke with Camiel over patronage. Camiel charged Rizzo with illegal dealmaking, whereupon the Philadelphia *Daily News* suggested that both men take a lie detector test. "If this machine says a man lied," said the Mayor, "he lied". But Camiel passed the test and Rizzo flunked it. Rizzo had been a solid Nixon supporter in 1972, but had seen Philadelphia go for McGovern anyway; now in this year of Watergate, when he was supporting Nixon strongly, his own integrity was smirched. For the people of South Philadelphia, who thought they had found a couple of genuine political heroes, were stuck with a couple of liars; and though they might try to deny it, they were sorely disenchanted.

The 1st district has been represented in the House since 1949 by Democrat William Barrett. He cuts an unobtrusive figure in Washington, though his name has been attached to some housing legislation. Barrett is now the third-ranking Democrat on the House Banking Committee—a position which represents a step down from 1974. For then Barrett ranked just behind Chairman Wright Patman, But after the 1974 elections Patman was ousted as Chairman, and replaced by formerly fourth-ranking Democrat Henry Reuss of Wisconsin. Reuss's victory was a victory, heretofore rare, of talent over seniority; he is generally considered one of the House's smarter members. Barrett, on the other hand, though he might not have deserved to make *New Times's* list of the ten dumbest Congressmen, is not regarded as a major intellect.

Barrett's continued incumbency is testimony of something, however, and that something is his real forte—tending his district. Representing a racially divided seat like the 1st, another congressman might have found himself in real political trouble. But Barrett has stayed away from divisive issues and instead concentrates on giving his constituents the kind of service they might expect from an old fashioned machine politician, which Barrett most assuredly is. Every night he flies home from Washington and holds office hours from 9 to1. Here, as he told one reporter, he tries to solve problems "on marital matters, child welfare, foreclosures, evictions—everything that affects the human person." There was a time when many political machines provided Barrett's kind of service; now so few do that when a young congressional candidate goes in heavily for constituency service, it is treated as a form of the new politics. Anyone interested in learning how the old politics works is advised to go up to Philadelphia some night and watch the seventy-plus Barrett while he is still in action.

Census Data Pop. 478,310. Central city, 100%; suburban, 0%. Median family income, $8,690; families above $15,000: 15%; families below $3,000: 12%. Median years education, 10.4.

The Voters

Median voting age **44.**
Employment profile White collar, 43%. Blue collar, 40%. Service, 17%. Farm, –%.
Ethnic groups Black, 39%. Total foreign stock, 23%. Italy, 13%; USSR, Ireland, 2% each; UK, 1%.

Presidential vote

1972	Nixon (R)	77,078	(42%)
	McGovern (D)	107,549	(58%)
1968	Nixon (R)	58,692	(29%)
	Humphrey (D)	128,387	(63%)
	Wallace (AI)	16,856	(8%)

Rep. William A. Barrett (D) Elected 1948; b. Aug. 14, c. 1900, Philadelphia; home, Philadelphia; St. Joseph's Col., Philadelphia; Catholic.

Career Real estate broker.

Offices 2304 RHOB, 202-225-4731. Also 2401 Wharton St., Philadelphia 19146, 215-389-2822.

Committees

Banking, Currency and Housing (3d). Subcommittees: Consumer Affairs; Domestic Monetary Policy; Financial Institutions Supervision, Regulation and Insurance; Housing and Community Development (Chairman).

Group Ratings

	ADA	COPE	LWV	RIPON	NFU	LCV	CFA	NAB	NSI	ACA
1974	71	100	78	46	93	60	83	17	50	13
1973	83	100	83	67	94	63	100	–	–	8
1972	81	100	92	64	86	8	100	8	0	5

Key Votes

1) Foreign Aid	AGN	6) Gov Abortn Aid	AGN	11) Pub Cong Election $	AGN
2) Busing	FOR	7) Coed Phys Ed	AGN	12) Turkish Arms Cutoff	FOR
3) ABM	AGN	8) Pov Lawyer Gag	AGN	13) Youth Camp Regs	FOR
4) B-1 Bomber	ABS	9) Pub Trans Sub	FOR	14) Strip Mine Veto	AGN
5) Nerve Gas	AGN	10) EZ Voter Regis	FOR	15) Farm Bill Veto	AGN

Election Results

1974 general:	William A. Barrett (D)	98,988	(77%)	($14,729)
	Russell M. Nigro (R)	29,772	(23%)	($7,841)
1974 primary:	William A. Barrett (D), unopposed			
1972 general:	William A. Barrett (D)	118,953	(67%)	($16,261)
	Gus A. Pedicone (R)	59,807	(33%)	($43,547)

◆ ◆ ◆ ◆ ◆

SECOND DISTRICT

The 2d district of Pennsylvania is an oddly shaped chunk of Philadelphia. Though the 2d was designed as the city's black district, it does not center on either one of the city's two large black ghettoes. Instead, the district takes in part of West Philadelphia and then moves across Fairmount Park and the Schuylkill River to encompass part of the North Philadelphia ghetto. The 2d proceeds north to include some of the more middle class black areas of Germantown, which at the time of the Revolution was a separate settlement from Philadelphia. The district then goes all the way out to the WASP upper income precincts of Chestnut Hill, where some of Philadelphia's richest and most prominent families have lived for generations. Chestnut Hill usually goes Republican, but its votes are swamped by the huge Democratic majorities coming out of the black neighborhoods to the south and east. Altogether, the 2d consistently reports the largest Democratic percentages in Pennsylvania.

Robert N.C. Nix has represented the 2d district since a special election held in 1958. He is the state's first, and so far only, black Congressman. In Washington, Nix is now the second most senior member of the Congressional Black Caucus, but he is scarcely the most active. He is a man who has the Philadelphia Democratic machine to thank for his political career, a politician who makes few waves of any kind. On the International Relations Committee, Nix has generally followed the lead of his fellow Pennsylvanian Chairman Thomas (Doc) Morgan, who for years supported the Vietnam policies of both Johnson and Nixon. Nix has had a subcommittee chairmanship now for some years but he has, to put it most charitably, been inactive.

Back home in the 2d district, Nix has shown a similar lassitude. He has shown neither a talent for rhetoric or much concern for his constituents' problems. In 1972, Nix won only 47% of the vote in his primary against three opponents, two of them white. Two years later, he faced a stronger challenge from 1971 mayoral candidate Hardy Williams; and although Nix won, 56–39, it was scarcely the sort of victory that demonstrated great strength, particularly in view of the fact that this Congressman has held office for nearly 20 years. Nix turns 71 not long after the 1976 primary; it will not be surprising if he is beaten there, or simply is not a candidate at all.

Census Data Pop. 470,267. Central city, 100%; suburban, 0%. Median family income, $8,670; families above $15,000: 19%; families below $3,000: 14%. Median years education, 11.4.

The Voters

Median voting age 45.
Employment profile White collar, 49%. Blue collar, 33%. Service, 18%. Farm, –%.
Ethnic groups Black, 65%. Total foreign stock, 15%. USSR, 4%; Italy, 2%; Ireland, UK, Germany, 1% each.

Presidential vote

1972	Nixon (R)	39,889	(25%)
	McGovern (D)	121,786	(75%)
1968	Nixon (R)	39,297	(21%)
	Humphrey (D)	146,658	(77%)
	Wallace (AI)	4,690	(2%)

Rep. Robert N. C. Nix (D) Elected May 30, 1958; b. Aug. 9, 1905, Orangeburg, S.C.; home, Philadelphia; Lincoln U., B.A. 1921, U. of Penn., LL.B. 1924; Baptist.

Career Practicing atty., 1925–28; Special Deputy Atty. Gen. of Penn., 1934–38.

Offices 2201 RHOB, 202-225-4001. Also 2139 N. 22nd St., Philadelphia 19121, 215-236-8341.

Committees

International Relations (7th). Subcommittees: International Economic Policy (Chairman); International Resources, Food, and Energy.

Post Office and Civil Service (4th). Subcommittees: Postal Facilities, Mail, and Labor Management; Postal Service.

Group Ratings

	ADA	COPE	LWV	RIPON	NFU	LCV	CFA	NAB	NSI	ACA
1974	75	100	73	46	93	81	92	17	43	8
1973	91	100	92	69	88	69	100	–	–	5
1972	88	100	92	53	100	47	100	8	20	17

Key Votes

1) Foreign Aid	FOR	6) Gov Abortn Aid	FOR	11) Pub Cong Election $	AGN
2) Busing	FOR	7) Coed Phys Ed	AGN	12) Turkish Arms Cutoff	FOR
3) ABM	AGN	8) Pov Lawyer Gag	AGN	13) Youth Camp Regs	FOR
4) B-1 Bomber	ABS	9) Pub Trans Sub	FOR	14) Strip Mine Veto	AGN
5) Nerve Gas	AGN	10) EZ Voter Regis	FOR	15) Farm Bill Veto	AGN

Election Results

1974 general:	Robert N. C. Nix (D)	75,033	(74%)	($12,122)
	Jesse W. Woods, Jr. (R)	26,353	(26%)	($15,833)
1974 primary:	Robert N. C. Nix (D)	27,195	(56%)	
	Hardy Williams (D)	19,126	(39%)	
	Robert Franklyn Stevenson (D)	2,175	(4%)	
1972 general:	Robert N. C. Nix (D)	107,509	(70%)	($4,073)
	Frederick D. Bryant (R)	45,753	(30%)	($4,936)

◆ ◆ ◆ ◆

THIRD DISTRICT

Whatever the opinion of W.C. Fields, Center City Philadelphia is one of the more amenable of American downtowns. The height of buildings here has been kept down to a reasonable 38 stories by an old ordinance that allows none to exceed the height of the spire on Philadelphia's ornate City Hall. Moreover, a large new urban renewal project, Penn Center, is going up on the site of the Penn Central tracks—the old "Chinese wall". Hard by the office buildings are the elegant Victorian neighborhoods around Rittenhouse Square and the restored eighteenth century town houses of Society Hill, near Independence Hall. But as one moves a few blocks north out of Center City, one comes to the nineteenth century suburbs now long since become slums. Much of the northern parts of the area described, along with some of Center City itself including Society Hill, lies in Pennsylvania's 3d congressional district.

At its western fringes, the 3d also takes in part of the black ghetto of North Philadelphia. But most of the district is made up of white neighborhoods where levels of income and education are little better than they are in the ghetto. An example is Kensington, north of Center City, which seems to have been transported intact straight out of the 1930s. Here, in the red brick Philadelphia rowhouses, live the Irish and Italians left behind after the postwar exodus to the suburbs. Most of these people own their own houses—Philadelphia is a city of homeowners, not renters. But the value of the real estate is pathetically low, since there is little demand for it. According to the Census Bureau, the median value of a homeowner's house here in 1970 was a meager $7,800—lower than in any other Philadelphia district. Kensington and neighborhoods like it are traditionally Democratic, but like other ethnic enclaves in Philadelphia, they have moved rightward in the Frank Rizzo years.

For the most part, the 3d is an amalgam of two previous congressional districts. Behind its formation is a tale of machine politics and insurgency, reward and punishment. The central figure in the tale is William J. Green III, son of a former Philadelphia Democratic boss and Congressman. Green himself was elected to the House at age 25 after his father's untimely death in 1964. The young man had accumulated all the rewards the machine could bestow: a safe House seat, the Philadelphia Democratic chairmanship, and a possible chance for future state or city wide office. But in 1968, Green split with then Mayor James H. J. Tate and the machine. The Congressman favored the candidacy of Robert Kennedy and wanted to open up the party to those previously excluded; Tate and the others preferred Hubert Humphrey's politics of joy and wanted to keep things as they were.

Then, in 1971, Green committed the ultimate apostasy. Mayor Tate and Peter Camiel, Democratic City Chairman, decided to run Police Commissioner Frank Rizzo for Mayor. Rizzo, of course, was a law and order hard liner and popular among the city's whites. Green didn't like Rizzo's ideas, and ran himself. The Congressman waged a well-financed, well-organized campaign, but lost the Democratic primary—partly because of the prowess of the machine, but more because of Rizzo's popularity in white, especially Italian, neighborhoods. Meanwhile, the men of the machine in the legislature presided over the evisceration of Green's old congressional district. He was dumped into the 3d, most of which had been represented by James (Digger) Byrne, a man once in the funeral directing business. Byrne had also served as 31st Ward Chairman for 38 years, as had his father for 42 years before that. The younger Byrne was definitely the organization's choice in 1972. The machine knew that within the boundaries of the new 3d, Green had lost to Rizzo by a margin exceeding 3–2.

But this time the result was different. Byrne did not command the impassioned loyalty Rizzo had, and he unwisely relied on his fellow ward chairmen to roll up votes for him. Green simply outcampaigned him; he rolled up huge margins in the district's black wards and won over hundreds of Rizzo voters in places like Kensington. Green took a solid 58% of the vote—and got a safe seat for as long as he wants to represent it.

Now Green turned his attention outward from the insular world of Philadelphia ward politics. He held a seat on the House Ways and Means Committee, which he hadn't done much with; now, suddenly, he took up the cause of repealing the oil depletion allowance. This was something Chairman Wilbur Mills definitely did not want to do; but in 1974, Green forced a vote on the floor of the House. In 1975, with a new Congress full of liberal freshmen, Green went even further. He forced a vote in the Democratic Caucus, which was heavily in favor of total repeal as an amendment to the unvetoable tax cut, over the opposition of new Ways and Means Chairman Al Ullman; he put enough pressure on Ullman to force him to stand up for repeal in conference. The result: the allowance was repealed altogether for the major oil companies, and phased out for the independents. Green who had been regarded before 1972 as a legislative lightweight, had succeeded in accomplishing what several generations of liberals had been unable to do.

With that credential, Green could likely be a strong candidate for Hugh Scott's Senate seat in 1976. The still young Congressman (38 in 1976) pointedly declined an offer by Peter Camiel of the machine's backing in a rematch in the 1975 primary against Rizzo, from whom Camiel had become estranged; apparently he saw little future in being Mayor of Philadelphia, and had ambitions elsewhere—either to continue as a major power in the House, or move onto the Senate.

Census Data Pop. 472,041. Central city, 100%; suburban, 0%. Median family income, $8,368; families above $15,000: 14%; families below $3,000: 13%. Median years education, 9.9.

The Voters

Median voting age 46.
Employment profile White collar, 40%. Blue collar, 45%. Service, 15%. Farm, –%.
Ethnic groups Black, 28%. Spanish, 5%. Total foreign stock, 22%. Poland, 4%; Italy, USSR, 3% each; Germany, UK, Ireland, 2% each.

Presidential vote

1972	Nixon (R)	74,829	(46%)
	McGovern (D)	86,379	(54%)
1968	Nixon (R)	57,238	(30%)
	Humphrey (D)	114,922	(60%)
	Wallace (AI)	18,395	(10%)

Rep. William J. Green (D) Elected Apr. 28, 1964; b. June 24, 1938, Philadelphia; home, Philadelphia; St. Joseph's Col., Philadelphia, B.A. 1960, Villanova U. Law School, 1961–63; Catholic.

Career Student until the death of his father, U.S. Rep. William J. Green, Jr., 1964; Candidate for Dem. nomination for Mayor of Philadelphia, 1971.

Offices 2434 RHOB, 202-225-6271. Also Fed. Ofc. Bldg., 600 Arch St., Philadelphia 19106, 215-923-9868.

Committees

Ways and Means (10th). Subcommittees: Social Security; Trade (Chairman).

Group Ratings

	ADA	COPE	LWV	RIPON	NFU	LCV	CFA	NAB	NSI	ACA
1974	83	100	92	56	92	88	92	17	10	0
1973	88	100	92	71	90	89	100	–	–	0
1972	100	89	100	80	86	74	100	9	0	5

Key Votes

1) Foreign Aid	FOR	6) Gov Abortn Aid	AGN	11) Pub Cong Election $	FOR
2) Busing	FOR	7) Coed Phys Ed	AGN	12) Turkish Arms Cutoff	FOR
3) ABM	AGN	8) Pov Lawyer Gag	AGN	13) Youth Camp Regs	FOR
4) B-1 Bomber	AGN	9) Pub Trans Sub	FOR	14) Strip Mine Veto	AGN
5) Nerve Gas	AGN	10) EZ Voter Regis	FOR	15) Farm Bill Veto	AGN

Election Results

1974 general:	William J. Green (D)	84,675	(75%)	($51,066)
	Richard P. Colbert (R)	27,692	(25%)	($3,082)
1974 primary:	William J. Green (D), unopposed			
1972 general:	William J. Green (D)	101,144	(64%)	($65,107)
	Alfred Marroletti (R)	57,787	(36%)	($16,938)

◆ ◆ ◆ ◆ ◆

FOURTH DISTRICT

The 4th congressional district of Pennsylvania is northeast Philadelphia, the most middle class, prosperous, and indeed a still growing part of Philadelphia. Geographically, most of the 4th is farther from Center City than the Main Line suburbs. Out here, some 10 to 20 miles from Independence Hall, middle income suburban tract housing was still going up during the 1960s. In fact, more than half the housing units in northeast Philadelphia were built after 1950; in the rest of the city, more than 80% went up before that. Most of the 4th's residents are migrants from more crowded areas closer to Center City. The district has a fair ethnic mixture, one representing the outward movement of various groups. Of these, the Jews are the most important politically; more than half the city's Jewish people live within this district.

The 4th is the least Democratic of Philadelphia's four districts, the only one to go for Richard Nixon in 1972. It is also the only district that the city's Republicans have contested seriously in the past several elections. In 1966, after a major redistricting, ailing Congressman Herman Toll retired, and Republican candidate Robert Cohen waged a vigorous campaign to capture the seat; he fell 7,000 votes short. And in 1972, Republican William Pfender ran an anti-welfare, antibusing campaign; his most important credential was that he, like Mayor Frank Rizzo, was a former policeman. For his efforts, he won 44% of the vote.

The winner in both cases was Democrat Joshua Eilberg, a veteran of the Philadelphia D.A.'s office and the Pennsylvania legislature, and a hard-fisted and loyal member of the Philadelphia Democratic organization. In Washington, Eilberg for years attracted little attention. His voting record was fairly liberal, as one would expect of a man with his background and a large Jewish constituency; his actions on the Judiciary Committee were predictable; he played little part in political intrigue, either in Washington or at home in Philadelphia. Apparently, too, he made little impression on his constituents; as late as May, 1974, an underfinanced primary opponent with the unethnic name of Chris Matthews was able to get 23% of the vote against him.

But only two months later, Eilberg was thrust in the national spotlight as a member of the Judiciary Committee considering the impeachment of Richard Nixon. As usual, Eilberg did nothing that was especially surprising. He wound up, as all the Committee's Democrats did, voting against Nixon; he made speeches decrying the President's conduct and that of his men. He did not shine or generate a national fan club, as some Judiciary members did; but by his general competence he strengthened the impression that so many people gained, that the House is composed of intelligent, decent men and women—far better in quality than the buffoons they are often imagined to be. In any case, Eilberg seems to have made a good impression on his constituents. This Congressman who had never received more than 60% of the vote suddenly got 71% in November 1974.

Census Data Pop. 474,684. Central city, 100%; suburban, 0%. Median family income, $11,069; families above $15,000: 24%; families below $3,000: 5%. Median years education, 11.9.

The Voters

Median voting age 45.
Employment profile White collar, 57%. Blue collar, 33%. Service, 10%. Farm, –%.
Ethnic groups Black, 5%. Total foreign stock, 32%. USSR, 8%; Italy, Germany, 4% each; Poland, Ireland, UK, 3% each; Austria, 1%.

Presidential vote

1972	Nixon (R)	131,066	(56%)
	McGovern (D)	100,940	(44%)
1968	Nixon (R)	87,115	(37%)
	Humphrey (D)	126,215	(54%)
	Wallace (AI)	20,977	(9%)

Rep. Joshua Eilberg (D) Elected 1966; b. Feb. 12, 1921, Philadelphia; home, Philadelphia; U. of Penn., B.S. 1941, Temple U., J.D. 1948; Jewish.

Career Navy, WWII; Practicing atty., 1948–66; Philadelphia Asst. Dist. Atty., 1952–54; Penn. House of Reps., 1955–67, Maj. Ldr., 1965–66.

Offices 1130 LHOB, 202-225-4661. Also 216 1st Fed. Bldg., Castor and Cottman Aves., Philadelphia 19111, 215-722-1717.

Committees

Judiciary (7th). Subcommittees: Immigration, Citizenship, and International Law (Chairman).

Merchant Marine and Fisheries (19th). Subcommittees: Energy Research (Fossil Fuels); Science, Research, and Technology.

Group Ratings

	ADA	COPE	LWV	RIPON	NFU	LCV	CFA	NAB	NSI	ACA
1974	73	100	83	53	93	69	92	25	20	8
1973	80	100	75	67	95	61	100	–	–	12
1972	81	91	73	67	86	43	100	8	0	13

Key Votes

1) Foreign Aid	FOR	6) Gov Abortn Aid	AGN	11) Pub Cong Election $	FOR
2) Busing	AGN	7) Coed Phys Ed	AGN	12) Turkish Arms Cutoff	FOR
3) ABM	AGN	8) Pov Lawyer Gag	AGN	13) Youth Camp Regs	FOR
4) B-1 Bomber	ABS	9) Pub Trans Sub	FOR	14) Strip Mine Veto	AGN
5) Nerve Gas	AGN	10) EZ Voter Regis	FOR	15) Farm Bill Veto	AGN

Election Results

1974 general:	Joshua Eilberg (D)	123,952	(71%)	($45,286)
	Isadore Einhorn (R)	50,688	(29%)	($4,059)
1974 primary:	Joshua Eilberg (D)	45,872	(77%)	
	Chris Matthews (D)	14,287	(23%)	
1972 general:	Joshua Eilberg (D)	129,105	(56%)	($61,471)
	William Pfender (R)	102,013	(44%)	($102,923)

♦ ♦ ♦ ♦ ♦

FIFTH DISTRICT

The 5th congressional district of Pennsylvania can be called an exurban Philadelphia district. It takes in the outer edges of suburban Delaware and Montgomery Counties, along with most of Chester County farther out. Though technically all within the Philadelphia metropolitan area, the

5th is really a kind of borderland where the influence of Philadelphia wanes and the Pennsylvania Dutch country begins. (see Sixteenth District) In other words, vintage John O'Hara country: grimy small industrial towns surrounded by large suburban estates, and the perfectly tended farms of the Brandywine, where the Wyeth family lives and paints. Not far away is the sleepy town of Oxford, home of Lincoln University, one of the nation's oldest black colleges—and a symbol of the area's Lincoln Republican heritage. The 5th also contains many of the famed Main Line suburbs of Philadelphia, so named because they lay on the main line of what was once the prosperous Pennsylvania Railroad, and what is now the bankrupt Penn Central. The 5th is a Republican district, very Republican. The only time it has been known to go Democratic was in the 1964 presidential election, and then by a very narrow margin.

The district has had bad luck with its recent Congressmen. G. Robert Watkins, a conservative Republican, died of a heart attack in the summer of 1970 after serving three terms. His successor, conservative Republican John Ware, served two more before he announced his retirement. In all likelihood, the 5th will be luckier with its current Congressman. Conservative Republican Richard Schulze, a veteran of three terms in the Pennsylvania House of Representatives, easily won his party's primary in 1974, despite the national publicity received by liberal Republican candidate Robin West. Though he was pressed somewhat more closely than he had expected in the general election, he still managed a comfortable 60% of the votes. But the big difference here is age. His predecessors Watkins and Ware died at 68 and left office at 66 respectively; Schulze, as he stands for reelection, is 47.

Census Data Pop. 474,435. Central city, 0%; suburban, 100%. Median family income, $12,148; families above $15,000: 33%; families below $3,000: 4%. Median years education, 12.4.

The Voters

Median voting age 42.
Employment profile White collar, 54%. Blue collar, 35%. Service, 9%. Farm, 2%.
Ethnic groups Black, 4%. Total foreign stock, 15%. Italy, 3%; UK, Germany, 2% each; Ireland, 1%.

Presidential vote

1972	Nixon (R)	131,393	(69%)
	McGovern (D)	58,454	(31%)
1968	Nixon (R)	104,074	(59%)
	Humphrey (D)	59,915	(34%)
	Wallace (AI)	13,703	(8%)

Rep. Richard T. Schulze (R) Elected 1974; b. Aug. 7, 1929, Philadelphia; home, Malvern; U. of Houston, 1949–50, Villanova U., 1952; Presbyterian.

Career Army, 1951-53; Proprietor, Home Appliance Ctr., Paoli; Chester Co. Register of Wills and Clerk of Orphans Ct., 1967–69; Penn. House of Reps., 1969–74.

Offices 1009 LHOB, 202-225-5761. Also 1106 N. Providence Rd., Media 19063, 215-566-0610.

Committees

Armed Services (13th). Subcommittees: Seapower and Strategic and Critical Materials.

Banking, Currency and Housing (9th). Subcommittees: Economic Stabilization; Historic Preservation and Coinage.

Group Ratings: Newly Elected

Key Votes

1) Foreign Aid	FOR	6) Gov Abortn Aid	NE	11) Pub Cong Election $	NE
2) Busing	NE	7) Coed Phys Ed	AGN	12) Turkish Arms Cutoff	NE
3) ABM	NE	8) Pov Lawyer Gag	NE	13) Youth Camp Regs	ABS
4) B-1 Bomber	FOR	9) Pub Trans Sub	NE	14) Strip Mine Veto	AGN
5) Nerve Gas	NE	10) EZ Voter Regis	NE	15) Farm Bill Veto	FOR

Election Results

1974 general:	Richard T. Schulze (R)	83,526	(60%)	($29,965)
	Leo D. McDermott (D)	56,626	(40%)	($39,922)
1974 primary:	Richard T. Schulze (R)	24,263	(45%)	
	John R. West (R)	15,666	(29%)	
	Three others (R)	13,563	(25%)	

◆ ◆ ◆ ◆ ◆

SIXTH DISTRICT

The 6th congressional district of Pennsylvania includes Berks and Schuylkill Counties and a small portion of Northumberland County. This is a region of both industry and agriculture, lying on the margin between the industrial northeast and the Pennsylvania Dutch country. Schuylkill County is anthracite country: a collection of small towns on rugged hills, originally set up to scrape the hard coal from under-ground, now scrambling for whatever industry they can attract. Reading, in Berks County, is a factory town (with an interesting recent history of lurid, open vice); Allentown and Bethlehem to the east are dominated economically by Bethlehem Steel's big operations here. The Dutch country obtrudes into Berks County, but politically the 6th district is more industrial than Dutch. The factory workers in Reading and the anthracite miners—or rather former miners—in Schuylkill County towns like Tamaqua and Mahanoy City vote Democratic in most elections; and this blue collar vote usually overcomes the Republican margins cast in the southern, agricultural area of the district. The hard pressed conditions of local industries have, if anything, intensified the 6th's Democratic leanings. Moreover, there are few blacks here, and accordingly little trace of the white backlash that has been so important in South Philadelphia.

For twenty years, from 1949 to 1969, the 6th was represented by George Rhodes. He was a stalwart Democrat, a labor leader, and one of the founders of the liberal Democratic Study Group which now dominates the House. He decided to retire in 1968 and was succeeded by Gus Yatron, a 12-year veteran of the state legislature and owner of a local ice cream business, who likes to consider himself a moderate. He serves on the House International Relations Committee, chaired by fellow Pennsylvanian Thomas (Doc) Morgan. Here Yatron has sometimes voted for antiwar measures, but usually sticks with the Committee's prevailing consensus. On one issue, however, he made a considerable fuss. He was part of the group of congressmen of Greek descent, led by Indiana's John Brademas, who protested Henry Kissinger's tilt toward Turkey in the Cyprus conflict—a tilt that became especially pronounced after the Greeks threw out the colonels and installed a democratic government. The Brademas group had strong and vocal support from thousands of Greek-Americans, including many like Yatron in the restaurant business; and they succeeded, finally, in cutting off American military aid to Turkey because of its obvious violations of international agreements.

Census Data Pop. 473,574. Central city, 19%; suburban, 44%. Median family income, $9,009; families above $15,000: 13%; families below $3,000: 8%. Median years education, 11.0.

The Voters

Median voting age 47.
Employment profile White collar, 35%. Blue collar, 53%. Service, 10%. Farm, 2%.
Ethnic groups Black, 1%. Total foreign stock, 14%. Poland, 3%; Italy, Germany, 2% each; Austria, Lithuania, 1% each.

Presidential vote

1972	Nixon (R)	114,537	(63%)
	McGovern (D)	66,807	(37%)

1968	Nixon (R)	90,818	(47%)
	Humphrey (D)	89,782	(46%)
	Wallace (AI)	12,956	(7%)

Rep. Gus Yatron (D) Elected 1968; b. Oct. 16, 1927, Reading; home, Reading; Kutztown St. Teachers Col., 1950; Greek Orthodox.

Career Pro. heavyweight boxer; Proprietor, Yatron's Ice Cream, 1950-69; Mbr., Reading School Bd., 1955-60; Penn. House of Reps., 1956-60; Penn. Senate, 1960-68.

Offices 313 CHOB, 202-225-5546. Also U.S.P.O. Bldg., 5th and Washington Sts., Reading 19603, 215-375-4573.

Committees

International Relations (13th). Subcommittees: International Resources, Food, and Energy; Investigations.

Small Business (14th). Subcommittees: Commodities and Services; SBA and SBIC Legislation.

Group Ratings

	ADA	COPE	LWV	RIPON	NFU	LCV	CFA	NAB	NSI	ACA
1974	52	90	50	43	92	73	75	27	50	20
1973	76	100	83	54	94	83	100	–	–	19
1972	44	100	50	33	83	63	50	30	22	40

Key Votes

1) Foreign Aid	FOR	6) Gov Abortn Aid	AGN	11) Pub Cong Election $	AGN
2) Busing	AGN	7) Coed Phys Ed	ABS	12) Turkish Arms Cutoff	FOR
3) ABM	AGN	8) Pov Lawyer Gag	AGN	13) Youth Camp Regs	FOR
4) B-1 Bomber	ABS	9) Pub Trans Sub	FOR	14) Strip Mine Veto	AGN
5) Nerve Gas	AGN	10) EZ Voter Regis	FOR	15) Farm Bill Veto	FOR

Election Results

1974 general:	Gus Yatron (D)	111,127	(76%)	($42,670)
	Stephen Postupack (R)	35,805	(24%)	($9,326)
1974 primary:	Gus Yatron (D), unopposed			
1972 general:	Gus Yatron (D)	119,557	(65%)	($56,237)
	Eugene W. Hubler (R)	64,076	(35%)	($16,623)

◆ ◆ ◆ ◆ ◆

SEVENTH DISTRICT

The 7th congressional district of Pennsylvania contains the larger part of Delaware County, a unit that for years has contained more people than the entire state of Delaware just to the south. This is, indeed since the turn of the century has been, a suburban area southwest of Philadelphia, but for the most part not an exclusive one. The towns here are strung out, not on the main line of the Pennsylvania Railroad, but along less fashionable tracks and radial roads. There are leafy, WASPy suburbs here, like Swarthmore, around the distinguished college of that name. But the more typical suburb here is a place like Upper Darby, where the grandchildren of immigrants who lived in South or West Philadelphia have moved out from the crowded slums to the relatively spacious and middle class streets of Delaware County.

The dominant political institution here for years has been the Delaware County War Board, a Republican machine which rivals in age the now dying Republican machine that for eighty years ruled Philadelphia. The War Board's initial strength, of course, was in the County's WASPs, but it adapted well to new tides of suburban immigration, and elicited strong allegiance from the Italian and Irish and Polish Americans who have moved here over the past forty or fifty years. Indeed, this allegiance was strengthened as late as 1972, when the Catholic citizens of Delaware County were even more likely than their Protestant neighbors to react negatively to the candidacy of George McGovern.

But 1974 was a year of real difficulty for the War Board. First, the organization decided, for reasons that have more to do with local politics than with what was happening in Washington, to dump the 7th district's reliably conservative Congressman Lawrence Williams. Most congressmen who had been in office, as Williams had, for eight years would have built up a loyalty among the district's voters that no machine could disturb; but not so in Delaware County. In the primary, County District Attorney Stephen McEwen, the War Board's choice, defeated Williams by a 49–46 margin. In most years that would have ended it, but not in 1974. The Democratic nominee, 31-year-old Methodist minister Robert Edgar, waged a stronger than usual campaign and ended up winning a 56% of the vote. Edgar has been a liberal member of the enlarged Democratic caucus, and his chances for reelection do not seem especially good; the big question here for 1976 is whether the War Board will be able to revive and support a strong candidacy against him in 1976.

Census Data Pop. 470,714. Central city, 0%; suburban, 100%. Median family income, $11,383; families above $15,000: 27%; families below $3,000: 5%. Median years education, 12.2.

The Voters

Median voting age 45.
Employment profile White collar, 57%. Blue collar, 33%. Service, 10%. Farm, –%.
Ethnic groups Black, 8%. Total foreign stock, 21%. Italy, 6%; Ireland, UK, 3% each; Germany, Poland, USSR, 1% each.

Presidential vote

1972	Nixon (R)	133,151	(64%)
	McGovern (D)	73,432	(36%)
1968	Nixon (R)	99,692	(48%)
	Humphrey (D)	85,858	(42%)
	Wallace (AI)	21,108	(10%)

Rep. Robert W. Edgar (D) Elected 1974; b. May 29, 1943, Philadelphia; home, Broomall; Lycoming Col., B.A. 1965, Drew U., M.Div. 1968; Methodist.

Career Minister; Utd. Protestant Chaplin, Drexel U., 1968–71; Co-Dir., People's Emergency Ctr., 1971–75.

Offices 117 CHOB, 202-225-2011. Also 242 Long Lane, Upper Darby 19082, 215-352-0790.

Committees

Public Works and Transportation (24th). Subcommittees: Investigations and Review; Surface Transportation; Water Resources.

Veterans' Affairs (17th). Subcommittees: Cemeteries and Burial Benefits; Education and Training.

Group Ratings: Newly Elected

Key Votes

1) Foreign Aid	FOR	6) Gov Abortn Aid	NE	11) Pub Cong Election $	NE
2) Busing	NE	7) Coed Phys Ed	FOR	12) Turkish Arms Cutoff	NE
3) ABM	NE	8) Pov Lawyer Gag	NE	13) Youth Camp Regs	FOR
4) B-1 Bomber	AGN	9) Pub Trans Sub	NE	14) Strip Mine Veto	AGN
5) Nerve Gas	NE	10) EZ Voter Regis	NE	15) Farm Bill Veto	AGN

Election Results

1974 general:	Robert W. Edgar (D)	89,680	(56%)	($38,819)
	Stephen J. McEwen, Jr. (R)	70,894	(44%)	($110,075)
1974 primary:	Robert W. Edgar (D)	10,511	(62%)	
	David Belitsky (D)	6,367	(38%)	

◆ ◆ ◆ ◆ ◆

EIGHTH DISTRICT

The 8th congressional district of Pennsylvania is one of four suburban Philadelphia districts. This one, aside from a few high income townships in Montgomery County, is entirely coextensive with Bucks County. The political complexion of Bucks County may have become familiar to some readers through the prose of best-selling author James Michener—one of the many writers and artists who live in Bucks' more bucolic reaches. Michener wrote a book about his efforts as Democratic County Chairman in behalf of John F. Kennedy in 1960. The author's work fell short; Kennedy lost the County, and the district, as most Democrats do.

But Kennedy's loss here does not mean that Bucks County has no pockets of Democratic strength. Admittedly, northern Bucks County is a pastoral place where writers and rentiers live in stone Quaker farmhouses set in rolling hills near villages like New Hope and Lumberville. But the lower end of the County, just beyond northeast Philadelphia, is predominantly industrial and blue collar. Here, near the site of U.S. Steel's huge Fairless works, is one of the original Levittowns. In the other suburban Philadelphia counties, most of the blue collar immigration took place long ago, when Philadelphia itself was solidly Republican and the suburban county machines were adept at enrolling new residents in their parties. But in Bucks, the blue collar migration came late, in the 1950s and even the 1960s, and there is a strong Democratic voting base here in Levittown and Bristol.

Nevertheless, the Congressman from the 8th district is a Republican, Edward (Pete) Biester, a member of Pennsylvania's current good sized bloc of liberal Republicans. First elected in 1966, Biester has won reelection easily; in what has been his toughest year to date, he got 56% of the vote in 1974. But Biester has, in various ways, missed out on the acclaim accorded some of the likeminded members of the Pennsylvania delegation, like suburban Pittsburgh's John Heinz. In 1973 he switched to what is now the International Relations Committee from Judiciary. That allowed him to participate in the decisions to help extricate the United States from involvement in Indochina, but at the same time he did not get the national exposure he would have gotten as a member of Judiciary during the hearings on the impeachment of Richard Nixon. Biester would probably have voted for impeachment, and could very well have made himself a formidable figure in Pennsylvania politics. As it is, he will probably settle for quite a few more years of service in the House.

Census Data Pop. 475,406. Central city, 0%; suburban, 100%. Median family income, $11,807; families above $15,000: 29%; families below $3,000: 4%. Median years education, 12.3.

The Voters

Median voting age 41.
Employment profile White collar, 52%. Blue collar, 38%. Service, 9%. Farm, 1%.
Ethnic groups Black, 2%. Total foreign stock, 18%. Germany, Italy, 3% each; UK, 2%; Poland, Ireland, USSR, 1% each.

Presidential vote

	1972	Nixon (R)	118,601	(65%)
		McGovern (D)	64,330	(35%)
	1968	Nixon (R)	84,293	(51%)
		Humphrey (D)	65,369	(39%)
		Wallace (AI)	17,107	(10%)

Rep. Edward G. Biester, Jr. (R) Elected 1966; b. Jan. 5, 1931, Trevose; home, Furlong; Wesleyan U., B.A. 1952, Temple U., LL.B. 1955; United Church of Christ.

Career Practicing atty., 1956–66; Bucks Co. Asst. Dist. Atty., 1958–64.

Offices 2351 RHOB, 202-225-4276. Also 68 E. Court St., Doylestown 18901, 215-348-4005.

Committees

District of Columbia (4th). Subcommittees: Education, Labor, and Social Services; Judiciary.

International Relations (8th). Subcommittees: International Economic Policy; International Trade and Commerce.

Group Ratings

	ADA	COPE	LWV	RIPON	NFU	LCV	CFA	NAB	NSI	ACA
1974	83	100	92	100	92	81	75	42	50	20
1973	64	80	92	93	60	88	88	–	–	19
1972	75	82	83	94	86	87	100	25	30	9

Key Votes

1) Foreign Aid	FOR	6) Gov Abortn Aid	AGN	11) Pub Cong Election $	FOR
2) Busing	AGN	7) Coed Phys Ed	AGN	12) Turkish Arms Cutoff	AGN
3) ABM	AGN	8) Pov Lawyer Gag	AGN	13) Youth Camp Regs	FOR
4) B-1 Bomber	AGN	9) Pub Trans Sub	FOR	14) Strip Mine Veto	AGN
5) Nerve Gas	AGN	10) EZ Voter Regis	FOR	15) Farm Bill Veto	AGN

Election Results

1974 general:	Edward G. Biester, Jr. (R)	75,313	(56%)	($9,660)
	William B. Moyer (D)	54,815	(41%)	($24,343)
	Robert D. McKenney (Constitutional) ...	3,763	(3%)	($0)
1974 primary:	Edward G. Biester, Jr. (R)	17,848	(67%)	
	William A. Duff (R)	8,943	(33%)	
1972 general:	Edward G. Biester, Jr. (R)	115,799	(64%)	($17,345)
	Alan Williams (D)	64,069	(36%)	($24,919)

◆ ◆ ◆ ◆ ◆

NINTH DISTRICT

The Appalachian Mountain chains run like a series of backbones through central Pennsylvania. Throughout the state's history, the mountains have constituted a formidable barrier, not so much because of their height, which is unimpressive, but because of their persistence: one rugged chain right after another for 50 to 100 miles. During the eighteenth century, the mountains provided eastern Pennsylvania with a kind of rampart against Indian attacks, but in the nineteenth century they proved less useful. The mountains prevented Pennsylvania from ever digging a satisfactory statewide canal system—the boom mode of transportation in the early nineteenth century. They also delayed, until other states had them, the building of an east-west railroad. Only the aggressive policy of the Pennsylvania Railroad, a relative latecomer to the business, saved the state from branch line status.

Before the 1972 redistricting, most of what is now the 9th district was part of the old 12th district. As it stands, the 9th is the only Pennsylvania district to lie wholly within the mountains. This part of the Alleghenies (as the Appalachians are often called in Pennsylvania) was first settled by poor Scottish and Ulster Irish farmers just after the Revolutionary War. They were a people of fierce independence and pride, as the Whiskey Rebellion demonstrated. Later, not much coal was found here in the southern half of the mountains. So what is now the 9th was spared the boom-then-bust cycle that the coal industry inflicted on places like Scranton and Wilkes-Barre.

However, the district's largest city, Altoona (pop. 62,000), has suffered from the decline of its major employer, the Pennsylvania Railroad. Altoona is located near the Horseshoe Curve, one of the engineering wonders of nineteenth century railroading, and the city has long been the home of many railroad employees. The city's declining population figures reflect the deterioration, and finally the bankruptcy, of what is now the Penn Central.

In 1972, a combination of redistricting and the journalistic efforts of Jack Anderson made for a change in the 9th's congressional representation. Somerset County, the home of former Congressman (1960-73) J. Irving Whalley, was removed from the district by the Democratic legislature. With the county gone, Whalley was faced with either running against fellow Republican John Saylor in the new 12th district or moving his residence to the 9th. Anderson effectively eliminated both options when he revealed that Whalley, a 72-year-old small town banker, had been demanding and receiving salary kickbacks from members of his staff. Whalley promptly decided not to run in 1972, and a year later pled guilty to federal criminal charges and was sentenced to jail.

Whalley's demise left the seat to be filled, in effect, in the Republican primary; this part of the mountains is as solidly Republican now as it was in the 1870s. The upset winner there was E.G. (Bud) Shuster, a 40-year-old entrepreneur who had made a fortune building up a business and then selling it to IBM. Shuster decided to settle in the southern Pennsylvania mountains, became interested in local affairs, decided to run for Congress, and beat favored state Senator D. Elmer Hawbaker. Two years later, after amassing a conservative record, and suffering the embarrassment of a suit from the stockholders in his former company, Shuster was able to win again, by the convincing if not overwhelming margin of 57–43.

Census Data Pop. 468,008. Central city, 13%; suburban, 26%. Median family income, $8,124; families above $15,000: 10%; families below $3,000: 10%. Median years education, 11.4.

The Voters

Median voting age 44.
Employment profile White collar, 34%. Blue collar, 50%. Service, 12%. Farm, 4%.
Ethnic groups Total foreign stock, 4%. Italy, 1%.

Presidential vote

1972	Nixon (R)	114,144	(74%)
	McGovern (D)	40,131	(26%)
1968	Nixon (R)	97,270	(59%)
	Humphrey (D)	51,959	(32%)
	Wallace (AI)	14,836	(9%)

Rep. Bud Shuster (R) Elected 1972; b. Jan. 23, 1932, Glassport; home, West Providence Township; U. of Pitt., B.S. 1954, Duquesne U., M.B.A., 1960, American U., Ph.D. 1967.

Career V.P., Radio Corp. of Amer.; Operator, Shuster Farms.

Offices 1110 LHOB, 202-225-2431. Also Suite M, Penn Alto Hotel, Altoona 16603, 814-946-1653.

Committees

Public Works and Transportation (6th). Subcommittees: Economic Development; Public Buildings and Grounds; Surface Transportation.

Group Ratings

	ADA	COPE	LWV	RIPON	NFU	LCV	CFA	NAB	NSI	ACA
1974	14	9	18	56	21	35	23	75	90	87
1973	4	9	17	53	40	5	13	–	–	85

Key Votes

1) Foreign Aid	AGN	6) Gov Abortn Aid	AGN	11) Pub Cong Election $	ABS
2) Busing	AGN	7) Coed Phys Ed	AGN	12) Turkish Arms Cutoff	AGN
3) ABM	FOR	8) Pov Lawyer Gag	FOR	13) Youth Camp Regs	AGN
4) B-1 Bomber	FOR	9) Pub Trans Sub	AGN	14) Strip Mine Veto	FOR
5) Nerve Gas	FOR	10) EZ Voter Regis	AGN	15) Farm Bill Veto	FOR

Election Results

1974 general:	E. G. Shuster (R)	73,881	(57%)	($60,691)
	Robert D. Ford (D)	56,844	(43%)	($32,281)
1974 primary:	E. G. Shuster (R), unopposed			
1972 general:	E. G. Schuster (R)	95,913	(62%)	($73,852)
	Earl P. Collins (D)	59,386	(38%)	($17,815)

♦ ♦ ♦ ♦ ♦

TENTH DISTRICT

Scranton is the anthracite town par excellence. Back around the turn of the century, hard coal was much in demand, as it was used to stoke the nation's home furnaces and pot-bellied stoves. Because the only major deposits of anthracite in the United States lay in the Scranton—Wilkes-Barre region of northeast Pennsylvania, these two cities happened upon flush times. Immigrants from Italy, Poland, Austria-Hungary, and Ireland poured in to join the Scots and Welsh already working the mines. Scranton became the third-largest city in Pennsylvania, its population peaking at 143,000 in 1930.

Soon thereafter, the demand for hard coal began to decline, as oil and gas furnaces grew more popular. Accordingly, since the 1930s, Scranton and the industrial Lackawanna area have experienced a kind of depression. Textile mills have arrived in some numbers, as the family of former Governor William Scranton—after whom the city was named—has made great efforts to attract new industry. But the city of Scranton, isolated in mountains, can no longer support the numbers it once could. In 1970, the city's population stood at 103,000, which was about the figure in 1900. And Scranton today continues to lose population.

A look at the edges of Scranton shows what happened to it. On one block stand some large houses, maintained with some care, but obviously built in the 1920s—the city's last boom decade. On the next block, one finds no new suburban tract housing or shopping centers, only trees and hills. In few parts of the country is such a sudden halt in urban development so apparent.

Scranton and the industrial towns around it make up about half of Pennsylvania's 10th congressional district. The 10th consists of a rather anomalous mix: the heavily ethnic city and surrounding Lackawanna county, combined with several Scots-Irish-Welsh counties in the Pocono Mountains (a favorite resort of many middle class New Yorkers), along with some counties out of the state's northern tier. As the number of votes in traditionally Democratic Scranton declines, the Republican leanings of the rest of the district have come to dominate the 10th more and more. Accordingly, statewide Republican candidates have done better and better here in recent elections.

The district has not elected a Democratic Congressman since the recession year of 1958. Two years after that, William Scranton was elected Congressman from the district—the start of a political career that saw him become Governor of Pennsylvania (1963-66) and the dark-horse presidential candidate of the Republican liberals in 1964. Scranton retired from office in 1966, and unlike so many other politicians, he has managed to make his decision to quit stick. He has emerged from his home near Scranton onto the national scene only briefly: to chair the presidential commission on the Kent State killings, whose results Nixon chose to ignore; and as one of those leading Republicans who planned Gerald Ford's transition into office.

Scranton's successor in the House is Joseph McDade, a liberal Republican in the Scranton mold. After close shaves in 1962 and 1964, McDade has gotten a firm hold on the district. In 1972, the Republican Congressman carried Lackawanna County by almost as much (70%) as the district as a whole; in 1974, despite the national Democratic trend, he still won a solid 65% of the vote—a performance exceeded by only one other Pennsylvania Republican. McDade is a member of the usually conservative Appropriations Committee and ranking minority member on its surprisingly liberal Interior Subcommittee.

Census Data Pop. 472,007. Central city, 22%; suburban, 36%. Median family income, $8,318; families above $15,000: 12%; families below $3,000: 10%. Median years education, 12.0.

The Voters

Median voting age 46.
Employment profile White collar, 38%. Blue collar, 47%. Service, 11%. Farm, 4%.
Ethnic groups Total foreign stock, 20%. Italy, Poland, 4% each; UK, Austria, Germany, 2% each; Ireland, 1%.

Presidential vote

1972	Nixon (R)	125,686	(64%)
	McGovern (D)	71,105	(36%)
1968	Nixon (R)	101,917	(49%)
	Humphrey (D)	94,627	(46%)
	Wallace (AI)	9,880	(5%)

Rep. Joseph M. McDade (R) Elected 1962; b. Sept. 29, 1931, Scranton; home, Scranton; U. of Notre Dame, B.A. 1953, U. of Penn, LL.B. 1956; Catholic.

Career Clerk to Chf. Fed. Judge John W. Murphy, 1956–57; Practicing atty., 1957–62; Scranton City Solicitor, 1962.

Offices 2202 RHOB, 202-225-3731. Also 1223 Northeastern Natl. Bank Bldg., Scranton 18503, 717-346-3834.

Committees

Appropriations (5th). Subcommittees: HUD-Independent Agencies; Interior.

Small Business (3d). Subcommittees: Government Procurement and International Trade.

Group Ratings

	ADA	COPE	LWV	RIPON	NFU	LCV	CFA	NAB	NSI	ACA
1974	43	64	75	81	71	65	58	58	70	40
1973	50	82	67	86	70	83	75	–	–	22
1972	38	56	75	80	50	32	0	42	100	42

Key Votes

1) Foreign Aid	FOR	6) Gov Abortn Aid	AGN	11) Pub Cong Election $	FOR
2) Busing	AGN	7) Coed Phys Ed	AGN	12) Turkish Arms Cutoff	FOR
3) ABM	AGN	8) Pov Lawyer Gag	AGN	13) Youth Camp Regs	FOR
4) B-1 Bomber	FOR	9) Pub Trans Sub	FOR	14) Strip Mine Veto	AGN
5) Nerve Gas	AGN	10) EZ Voter Regis	AGN	15) Farm Bill Veto	AGN

Election Results

1974 general:	Joseph M. McDade (R)	100,793	(65%)	($34,512)
	Thomas J. Hanlon (D)	54,401	(35%)	($11,146)
1974 primary:	Joseph M. McDade (R), unopposed			
1972 general:	Joseph M. McDade (R)	143,670	(74%)	($24,924)
	Stanley R. Coveleskie (D)	51,550	(26%)	($6,281)

◆ ◆ ◆ ◆ ◆

ELEVENTH DISTRICT

Nowhere did Hurricane Agnes, which inundated most of the Northeast in June 1972, do more damage than in the Wyoming valley around Wilkes-Barre, Pennsylvania. This was a city that **had** already had more than its share of natural and manmade disasters. As *Atlantic* editor Sanford Ungar, a native of the area, points out, the valley has long been vulnerable to such disaster; its cities lie in a narrow flood plain on both sides of the mighty Susquehanna River. The prosperity of Wilkes-Barre and the surrounding cities seemed at the turn of the century to be solidly anchored in the anthracite which underlay the whole region; but by 1930, the veins began to be worked out, and the demand for the hard coal declined so much (see Tenth District) that the Wyoming valley moved into what seemed a permanent depression. It was recovering fairly well by 1972, with infusions of government money and a thriving, if low wage, apparel industry, when Agnes struck. Suddenly, Wilkes-Barre was under water. At least 20% of the residents of Luzerne County were displaced from their homes, downtown Wilkes-Barre was submerged, many of the new plants were destroyed.

The savior of this community, as had been the case for at least twenty years, was the local Congressman, Daniel J. Flood. As a senior member of the Appropriations Committee and its Defense Subcommittee, Flood was in a position to do something; for example, when fires broke out in the top floors of flooded buildings downtown, with hydrants obviously unavailable, Flood picked up the phone and had a fireboat transported from Boston harbor to Wilkes-Barre in a C-5A transport. It was an act like this that earned Flood the title in a Harper's magazine article, of "the best Congressman."

"Best" may not be quite the right word, but "act" certainly is. For Flood comes to politics not so much as a lawyer (which he is), as from his background as a Shakespearean actor in the 1920s. His waxed mustache and eccentric costumes, his staccato delivery and oratorical flourishes make him one of the best shows on the floor of the House of Representatives; and he has been known to make appearances in his district—among crowds of rough-hewn coal miners—wearing a top hat and black cape and brandishing a cane.

Flood was first elected in 1944, then defeated in the Republican years of 1946 and 1952, when coattails still meant something, won again in 1954, and has been reelected ever since. In 1974 he got 75% of the vote, in 1972, 68%. As Chairman of the Labor-HEW Appropriations Subcommittee, he basically supports liberal economic programs; as Vice Chairman of the Defense Appropriations Subcommittee, he usually supports Pentagon requests, and has generally been a foreign policy hawk. Flood has also worked hard and shamelessly to benefit his economically hard pressed district, forcing the Army, for example, to buy products it otherwise would not touch because they are produced in Luzerne County.

Flood has passed his years of greatest influence in the House, although his act is definitely worth catching; visitors to Washington when he is floor managing a bill should definitely make a point of showing up in the House gallery to watch. But the crowd of liberal freshmen which now dominates the Democratic caucus and, often, the whole House is not particularly sympathetic to Flood's oft-repeated injunction to trust your Appropriations Committee, nor is his pattern of helping his own district one that many of the freshmen, most of them from fairly prosperous areas, are particularly eager to follow. Flood is now 73, and has licked a serious illness; it seems scarcely likely that he will retire, and inconceivable that his district would refuse to reelect him.

Census Data Pop. 470,457. Central city, 19%; suburban, 54%. Median family income, $8,161; families above $15,000: 10%; families below $3,000: 9%. Median years education, 11.6.

The Voters

Median voting age 47.
Employment profile White collar, 35%. Blue collar, 53%. Service, 11%. Farm, 1%.
Ethnic groups Total foreign stock, 25%. Poland, 6%; Italy, 4%; Austria, 3%; Czechoslovakia, UK, 2% each; Lithuania, Germany, 1% each.

Presidential vote

1972	Nixon (R)	113,556	(62%)
	McGovern (D)	68,764	(38%)
1968	Nixon (R)	84,118	(43%)
	Humphrey (D)	101,135	(52%)
	Wallace (AI)	10,244	(5%)

Rep. Daniel J. Flood (D) Elected 1954; b. Nov. 26, 1903, Hazleton; home, Wilkes-Barre; Syracuse U., B.A., M.A., Harvard Law School, 1925–26, Dickinson U., LL.B. 1929; Catholic.

Career Practicing atty., 1930–54; Atty., Home Owners' Loan Corp., 1934–35; Deputy Atty. Gen. of Penn. and Counsel for Penn. Liquor Control Bd., 1935–39; Dir., Penn. St. Treasury Bureau of Public Assistance Disbursements and Exec. Asst. to the St. Treasurer, 1941–44; U.S. House of Reps., 1945–47, 1949–53.

Offices 108 CHOB, 202-225-6511; Also Rm. 1015 Utd. Penn Bank Bldg., Wilkes-Barre 18701, 717-822-2194.

Committees

Appropriations (8th). Subcommittees: Defense; Labor-HEW (Chairman).

Group Ratings

	ADA	COPE	LWV	RIPON	NFU	LCV	CFA	NAB	NSI	ACA
1974	35	82	75	31	86	82	77	17	90	20
1973	56	100	83	57	100	63	75	–	–	15
1972	44	91	82	57	71	27	0	25	100	29

Key Votes

1) Foreign Aid	FOR	6) Gov Abortn Aid	AGN	11) Pub Cong Election $	AGN
2) Busing	AGN	7) Coed Phys Ed	AGN	12) Turkish Arms Cutoff	ABS
3) ABM	FOR	8) Pov Lawyer Gag	AGN	13) Youth Camp Regs	FOR
4) B-1 Bomber	FOR	9) Pub Trans Sub	FOR	14) Strip Mine Veto	AGN
5) Nerve Gas	FOR	10) EZ Voter Regis	FOR	15) Farm Bill Veto	AGN

Election Results

1974 general:	Daniel J. Flood (D)	111,572	(75%)	($40,699)
	Richard A. Muzyka (R)	38,106	(25%)	($3,369)
1974 primary:	Daniel J. Flood (D), unopposed			
1972 general:	Daniel J. Flood (D)	124,336	(68%)	($26,393)
	Donald B. Ayers (R)	57,809	(32%)	($10,113)

◆ ◆ ◆ ◆ ◆

TWELFTH DISTRICT

The hills of western Pennsylvania, eastern Ohio, and northern West Virginia that encircle the Pittsburgh metropolitan area are one of the few parts of the country that is predominantly industrial without a single major city. The easternmost part of these industrial mountains forms Pennsylvania's 12th congressional district: five counties and part of another, the largest city of which is Johnstown (pop. 42,000). More typical of the district are small towns like Kittanning and Punxsutawney, both with less than 10,000 residents. First settled by Scots Irish when it was still frontier in the 1790s, this region of the state became part of the bituminous coal belt in the late nineteenth century. Today coal is still important to the district's economy, but despite the recent improving fortunes of the fuel, the industry employs far fewer people than it did 30 years ago.

In statewide elections the 12th is as marginal as any district in Pennsylvania; it usually comes in a couple of points more Republican than the state as a whole, although Democrats have a small registration advantage. In congressional elections up through 1972, however, it was strongly Republican, thanks to the local popularity of Congressman John Saylor. First elected in 1950, Saylor was ranking Republican on the House Interior Committee and one of the chamber's foremost conservationists. Though he was accused of taking some environmental stands because of ties to the coal industry (e.g., his opposition to the atomic breeder reactor), Saylor showed a zeal for protecting the wilderness which was second to none, and generally strongly opposed proposals to give away mineral and timber rights on federal lands to private companies. His stands go back to the days when conservation was a term more common than ecology, and he did not speak in the accents of latter day environmentalists, but he had their solid support as long as he ran.

Saylor died in late 1973, and a special election was scheduled for early 1974 to replace him. In other times, it might have worked out to a referendum on Saylor's views, for the Republican candidate was his administrative assistant, Harry Fox, and the Democrat, a state Representative named John Murtha, had taken no particular stand on environmental issues. But this was the first of the 1974 special elections that, in effect, tested Richard Nixon's popularity and established, beyond doubt, that the country wanted to be rid of him. Murtha was reluctant indeed to use Watergate in any way, and tried to avoid the issue; but nonetheless he still won, if only by 242 votes, in a victory that could be interpreted as nothing else but a repudiation of Nixon.

Murtha is one of only three Vietnam veterans in the Congress (the others are Tom Harkin of Iowa and Larry Pressler of South Dakota); he served in the Marine Corps for seven years and won two Purple Hearts and a Bronze Star. It says something about national feeling toward the war that even in 1974, when it seemed American involvement had been ended successfully, this was not much of a political asset, and that the Congress in which Murtha serves contains nothing like the dozens of veterans (among them, John Kennedy, Lyndon Johnson, Richard Nixon, Gerald Ford) who were elected in the late 1940s. Murtha served quietly in the remainder of the 93d Congress to which he had been elected, spending apparently much time cultivating his district; it paid off in November 1974 when he beat the same opponent by a 58–42 margin. With that victory, and every indication that he now holds a safe seat, Murtha won a place on the Appropriations Committee.

Census Data Pop. 469,999. Central city, 9%; suburban, 47%. Median family income, $8,030; families above $15,000: 10%; families below $3,000: 11%. Median years education, 11.2.

The Voters

Median voting age 46.
Employment profile White collar, 35%. Blue collar, 50%. Service, 12%. Farm, 3%.
Ethnic groups Black, 1%. Total foreign stock, 15%. Italy, 3%; Czechoslovakia, Poland, Austria, 2% each; UK, Germany, 1% each.

Presidential vote

1972	Nixon (R)	112,694	(64%)
	McGovern (D)	64,049	(36%)
1968	Nixon (R)	91,394	(48%)
	Humphrey (D)	87,198	(46%)
	Wallace (AI)	12,186	(6%)

Rep. John P. Murtha (D) Elected Feb. 5, 1974; b. June 17, 1932, New Martinsville, W. Va; Home, Johnstown; U. of Pitt., B.A., Ind. U. of Penn.

Career USMC, Vietnam; Owner, Johnstown Minute Car Wash; Penn. House of Reps., 1969–74.

Offices 431 CHOB, 202-225-2065. Also 212 Fed. Bldg., Johnstown 15901, 814-535-3320.

Committees

Appropriations (33d). Subcommittees: Interior; Military Construction.

Group Ratings

	ADA	COPE	LWV	RIPON	NFU	LCV	CFA	NAB	NSI	ACA
1974	26	100	60	25	93	50	62	40	100	29

Key Votes

1) Foreign Aid	AGN	6) Gov Abortn Aid	AGN	11) Pub Cong Election $	AGN
2) Busing	AGN	7) Coed Phys Ed	AGN	12) Turkish Arms Cutoff	AGN
3) ABM	FOR	8) Pov Lawyer Gag	NE	13) Youth Camp Regs	FOR
4) B-1 Bomber	FOR	9) Pub Trans Sub	FOR	14) Strip Mine Veto	AGN
5) Nerve Gas	AGN	10) EZ Voter Regis	FOR	15) Farm Bill Veto	AGN

Election Results

1974 general:	John P. Murtha (D)	89,193	(58%)	($58,192)
	Harry M. Fox (R)	64,416	(42%)	($42,598)
1974 primary:	John P. Murtha (D)	37,293	(87%)	
	John Paul Paine (D)	5,705	(13%)	
1974 special:	John P. Murtha (D)	60,523	(50%)	($79,820)
	Harry M. Fox (R)	60,281	(50%)	($71,626)

◆ ◆ ◆ ◆ ◆

THIRTEENTH DISTRICT

The 13th congressional district of Pennsylvania, part of Montgomery County, is a fair cross section of the upper income Philadelphia suburbs. Along with the 5th district, the 13th contains the posh Main Line suburbs, places like Haverford, Bryn Mawr, and Ardmore—some of them with famous colleges and all with the patina of wealth and social standing and the dignity of age. The 13th also contains the 21st ward of Philadelphia, a well-to-do, Republican part of the city adjacent to the posh Chestnut Hill neighborhood. On the other side of Philadelphia are predominantly Jewish suburbs in places like Cheltenham Township, which are products mostly of the 1950s. As one moves away from the city limits, the land becomes hillier and more sparsely settled, with the exception of occasional old industrial towns like Norristown and Conshocken, hard by the banks of the Schuylkill River. Not far away is the growing area around King of Prussia and Valley Forge. Overall, the 13th is increasingly the residence of Pennsylvania's elite; it says something about the district that both major party candidates for governor and the Republican candidate for Senator in 1974 were all residents of this district.

The 13th is today, as it always has been, a solidly Republican district. It is not, however, as adamantly conservative as it was during the New Deal. It even went for Democratic Governor Milton Shapp, though not by much, in 1974, and its last two Congressmen have been liberal Republicans. Richard Schweiker represented the 13th for eight years before his election to the Senate in 1968. And the current Congressman, Lawrence Coughlin, has been something of a dove on Vietnam—reflecting, perhaps, the noticeable, though by no means majority, Quaker heritage of the area.

Until 1972, Coughlin was not as strong at the polls as his predecessor. But that year he was reelected with 67% of the vote. And as if to prove that that was no accident he won with 62% in 1974, despite the Democratic trend and a well known Democratic opponent. Like his colleague Pete Biester of the 8th district, Coughlin switched out of the Judiciary Committee in 1973—a move which deprived him of the national publicity and statewide exposure that could have made him a contender for Hugh Scott's Senate seat in 1976 or other statewide office. He has, instead, a seat on the Appropriations Committee, and the position as ranking Republican on its Legislative Subcommittee.

Census Data Pop. 473,179. Central city, 11%; suburban, 89%. Median family income, $13,251; families above $15,000: 41%; families below $3,000: 4%. Median years education, 12.4.

The Voters

Median voting age 45.
Employment profile White collar, 64%. Blue collar, 27%. Service, 9%. Farm, –%.
Ethnic groups Black, 4%. Total foreign stock, 25%. Italy, 6%; USSR, UK, Germany, 3% each; Poland, Ireland, 2% each.

Presidential vote

1972	Nixon (R)	135,464	(64%)
	McGovern (D)	77,715	(36%)
1968	Nixon (R)	110,987	(53%)
	Humphrey (D)	87,709	(42%)
	Wallace (AI)	12,316	(6%)

Rep. Lawrence Coughlin (R) Elected 1968; b. Apr. 11, 1929, Wilkes-Barre; home, Villanova; Yale U., B.A. 1950, Harvard U., M.B.A. 1954, Temple U., LL.B. 1958; Episcopalian.

Career USMC, Korea; Practicing atty., 1958–69; Penn. House of Reps., 1965–66; Penn. Senate, 1967–68.

Offices 336 CHOB, 202-225-6111. Also 607 Swede St., Norristown 19401, 215-277-4040.

Committees

Appropriations (13th). Subcommittees: Foreign Operations; Legislative.

Group Ratings

	ADA	COPE	LWV	RIPON	NFU	LCV	CFA	NAB	NSI	ACA
1974	75	60	92	93	77	88	62	73	56	20
1973	36	27	75	87	47	83	50	–	–	48
1972	38	36	83	87	71	86	100	67	75	35

Key Votes

1) Foreign Aid	FOR	6) Gov Abortn Aid	AGN	11) Pub Cong Election $	FOR
2) Busing	AGN	7) Coed Phys Ed	AGN	12) Turkish Arms Cutoff	ABS
3) ABM	AGN	8) Pov Lawyer Gag	AGN	13) Youth Camp Regs	ABS
4) B-1 Bomber	AGN	9) Pub Trans Sub	FOR	14) Strip Mine Veto	AGN
5) Nerve Gas	AGN	10) EZ Voter Regis	FOR	15) Farm Bill Veto	FOR

Election Results

1974 general:	Lawrence Coughlin (R)	98,985	(62%)	($62,677)
	Lawrence H. Curry (D)	59,433	(38%)	($22,039)
1974 primary:	Lawrence Coughlin (R), unopposed			
1972 general:	Lawrence Coughlin (R)	139,085	(67%)	($36,423)
	Katherine L. Camp (D)	69,728	(33%)	($34,263)

◆ ◆ ◆ ◆ ◆

FOURTEENTH DISTRICT

Pittsburgh, Pennsylvania's second largest city, was the first urban center of the American interior. Pittsburgh grew because of its propitious site; here the Allegheny and Monongahela Rivers join to form the Ohio. And where that happens—at the Golden Triangle—remains the city's focal point: it is now filled with high-rise buildings, products of a downtown renaissance. When most of the nation's commerce moved over water, Pittsburgh's location was ideal; and when the traffic switched to railroads, the city adapted nicely. By the turn of the century, Pittsburgh, with its large deposits of coal nearby, was the center of the steel industry, then the nation's largest and also one of the fastest growing segments of the economy. Today, Pittsburgh remains the headquarters of many of the nation's largest corporations: U.S. Steel and several other steel companies; Westinghouse; H.J. Heinz; and the giant concerns associated with the Mellon family, Alcoa, Gulf Oil, and Koppers.

But in spite of the city's recent progress—its program of downtown renewal and its relatively successful campaign against air pollution—Pittsburgh has been unable to keep pace with other major metropolitan areas. Its major industry, steel, has not shown much dynamism lately. As a result, the population of central city Pittsburgh has declined, and so also has the population of the entire Pittsburgh metropolitan area—the only major metropolitan area in the country to lose population during the 1960s.

The 14th congressional district of Pennsylvania includes most of the city of Pittsburgh, plus a few suburbs. The district takes in most of the city's landmarks: the Golden Triangle, the University of Pittsburgh and its skyscraper campus, and Carnegie Mellon University. Though few of the city's steel mills lie within the 14th, many of the steel workers do live here, mostly in ethnic neighborhoods nestled between the Pittsburgh hills. Only 21% of the people in the district are black—a far smaller figure than in most major industrial cities; employment opportunities in Pittsburgh peaked before the big waves of black migration from the South. Since the New Deal, the 14th has been solidly Democratic; in 1972, for example, it was one of only four districts in the state (the other three were in Philadelphia) which gave George McGovern a majority of its vote.

The district's Congressman is liberal Democrat William Moorhead. After nearly 20 years in the House, Moorhead is now a senior member of the Banking and Government Operations Committees. In the 93d Congress, he served as Chairman of the Foreign Operations and Government Information Subcommittee, in which capacity he tried to get some changes in our system of classifying documents. Now, in the 94th Congress, he is Chairman of the Conservation, Energy, and Natural Resources Subcommittee. Back home, Moorhead has never encountered a really serious challenge since he was first slated by Mayor (and later Governor) David Lawrence's organization in 1958. He has been criticized for having close ties to the Mellons, until 1971 he owned considerable stock in the Mellon bank, one of the nation's largest, while serving on Banking and Currency. He received only 59% of the vote in 1972, but bounced back to 77% in 1974.

Census Data Pop. 470,537. Central city, 83%; suburban, 17%. Median family income, $8,952; families above $15,000: 18%; families below $3,000: 11%. Median years education, 11.9.

The Voters

Median voting age 47.
Employment profile White collar, 53%. Blue collar, 29%. Service, 18%. Farm, –%.
Ethnic groups Black, 21%. Total foreign stock, 25%; Italy, 5%; Poland, Germany, 3% each; USSR, UK, Ireland, 2% each; Austria, 1%.

Presidential vote

1972	Nixon (R)	86,912	(48%)
	McGovern (D)	95,687	(52%)
1968	Nixon (R)	60,996	(30%)
	Humphrey (D)	122,887	(60%)
	Wallace (AI)	20,721	(10%)

Rep. William S. Moorhead (D) Elected 1958; b. Apr. 8, 1923, Pittsburgh; home, Pittsburgh; Yale U., B.A. 1944, Harvard U., J.D. 1949; Episcopalian.

Career Navy, WWII; Practicing atty., 1949–59; Pittsburgh Asst. City Solicitor, 1954–57; Mbr., Allegheny Co. Housing Auth., 1956–58; Mbr., Pittsburgh Art Commission, 1958.

Offices 2467 RHOB, 202-225-2301. Also 2007 Fed. Bldg., Pittsburgh 15222, 412-644-2870.

Committees

Banking, Currency and Housing (6th). Subcommittees: Financial Institutions Supervision, Regulation and Insurance; Housing and Community Development; International Trade, Investment and Monetary Policy.

Government Operations (6th). Subcommittees: Conservation, Energy and Natural Resources (Chairman); Legislation and National Security.

Joint Economic Committee (4th, House Side). Subcommittees: Consumer Economics; Economic Growth; Fiscal Policy; Inter-American Economic Relationships; International Economics; Urban Affairs (Chairman).

Group Ratings

	ADA	COPE	LWV	RIPON	NFU	LCV	CFA	NAB	NSI	ACA
1974	73	91	83	67	93	93	67	18	20	0
1973	84	100	92	69	100	78	100	–	–	0
1972	94	100	100	78	86	87	100	9	0	0

Key Votes

1) Foreign Aid	FOR	6) Gov Abortn Aid	AGN	11) Pub Cong Election $	FOR
2) Busing	FOR	7) Coed Phys Ed	FOR	12) Turkish Arms Cutoff	FOR
3) ABM	AGN	8) Pov Lawyer Gag	AGN	13) Youth Camp Regs	FOR
4) B-1 Bomber	AGN	9) Pub Trans Sub	FOR	14) Strip Mine Veto	AGN
5) Nerve Gas	AGN	10) EZ Voter Regis	FOR	15) Farm Bill Veto	AGN

Election Results

1974 general:	William S. Moorhead (D)	93,169	(77%)	($23,929)
	Zachary Taylor Davis (R)	27,116	(23%)	($1,129)
1974 primary:	William S. Moorhead (D), unopposed			
1972 general:	William S. Moorhead (D)	106,158	(59%)	($36,205)
	Roland S. Catarinella (R)	72,275	(41%)	($78,400)

◆ ◆ ◆ ◆ ◆

FIFTEENTH DISTRICT

The 15th congressional district of Pennsylvania is the industrial Lehigh Valley in the eastern part of the state. It is one of only two congressional districts in the country that is made up of two and only two whole counties (the other is the 4th of South Carolina). Here in Northampton and Lehigh Counties are the adjoining cities of Allentown and Bethlehem, the original home of Bethlehem Steel, the industry's number two producer. The 15th has some rural and Republican areas, especially along the southern edge of Lehigh County, where there is Pennsylvania Dutch influence. But most of the district's voters are members of families who work in steel or textile mills, and they vote Democratic in most elections. The first Pennsylvania Republican to carry this area in a long time was Senator Richard Schweiker in 1974—and it helped that he had the enthusiastic endorsement of organized labor.

From 1933 to 1963, Francis E. Walter represented this district in the House. Walter became a power on the Hill, chairing the House Un-American Activities Committee and the Judiciary Subcommittee on Immigration. Because of the nation's restrictive immigration laws—which Walter preserved from reform until his death—Congressmen with ethnic constituencies constantly found themselves seeking private bills for the relief of their constituents' relatives and friends. Thus many northerners who might have opposed HUAC had to be careful to stay on Walter's good side; and not until the early seventies was there any substantial number willing to vote to abolish the Committee. Walter will also go into history as the co-sponsor of the McCarran-Walter Act, a piece of antisubversive legislation, most of which has turned out to be unconstitutional.

Walter's successor, Fred Rooney, is a very different kind of congressman. Rather than worry about the enemy within, Rooney has devoted his legislative energies to matters that come before the House Interstate and Foreign Commerce Committee. Traditionally, that has been a business-oriented body, with Rooney one of its more consumer-minded members; today, after the 1974 elections, it has shifted far to the left. Rooney is Chairman of the Transportation and Commerce Subcommittee now, and number seven Democrat on the full Committee. He has no reelection problems: he won 61% of the vote in 1972, and was unopposed in 1974.

Census Data Pop. 469,672. Central city, 45%; suburban, 55%. Median family income, $10,171; families above $15,000: 19%; families below $3,000: 6%. Median years education, 11.7.

The Voters

Median voting age 45.
Employment profile White collar, 41%. Blue collar, 47%. Service, 11%. Farm, 1%.
Ethnic groups Black, 1%. Total foreign stock, 19%. Italy, Austria, 3% each; Hungary, Germany, Czechoslovakia, 2% each; Poland, UK, 1% each.

Presidential vote

1972	Nixon (R)	99,664	(60%)
	McGovern (D)	65,557	(40%)
1968	Nixon (R)	79,288	(46%)
	Humphrey (D)	86,587	(50%)
	Wallace (AI)	7,176	(4%)

Rep. Fred B. Rooney (D) Elected July 30, 1963; b. Nov. 6, 1925, Bethlehem; home, Bethlehem; U. of Ga., B.S. 1950; Catholic.

Career Army, WWII; Real estate and insurance broker; Penn. Senate, 1958–63.

Offices 2301 RHOB, 202-225-6411. Also 1 Bethlehem Plaza, Suite 1111, Bethlehem 18017, 215-866-0916.

Committees

Interstate and Foreign Commerce (7th). Subcommittees: Transportation and Commerce (Chairman).

Merchant Marine and Fisheries (14th). Subcommittees: Coast Guard and Navigation; Fisheries and Wildlife Conservation and the Environment; Merchant Marine.

Group Ratings

	ADA	COPE	LWV	RIPON	NFU	LCV	CFA	NAB	NSI	ACA
1974	48	91	82	47	86	75	82	18	67	13
1973	68	91	80	55	100	65	100	–	–	13
1972	56	89	73	60	100	68	50	27	50	15

Key Votes

1) Foreign Aid	FOR	6) Gov Abortn Aid	ABS	11) Pub Cong Election $	FOR
2) Busing	AGN	7) Coed Phys Ed	FOR	12) Turkish Arms Cutoff	FOR
3) ABM	AGN	8) Pov Lawyer Gag	ABS	13) Youth Camp Regs	FOR
4) B-1 Bomber	FOR	9) Pub Trans Sub	FOR	14) Strip Mine Veto	AGN
5) Nerve Gas	AGN	10) EZ Voter Regis	AGN	15) Farm Bill Veto	FOR

Election Results

1974 general:	Fred B. Rooney (D), unopposed			($12,261)
1974 primary:	Fred B. Rooney (D), unopposed			
1972 general:	Fred B. Rooney (D)	99,937	(61%)	($29,315)
	Wardell F. Steigerwalt (R)	64,560	(39%)	($2,170)

◆ ◆ ◆ ◆ ◆

SIXTEENTH DISTRICT

Millions of Americans know about Pennsylvania Dutch country: farms scrupulously tended and set out among rolling hills, barns decorated with hex signs, and Amish families clad in black, clattering along in horse-drawn carriages. Fewer Americans know that the Pennsylvania Dutch are actually German in origin ("Dutch" is a corruption of "Deutsch"). They are descended from members of Amish, Mennonite, and other pietistic sects who left the principalities of eighteenth century Germany for the religious freedom of William Penn's Quaker dominated colony of Pennsylvania. The Quakers were happy to welcome the Germans, but they were a little leery about living with them in Philadelphia. So they were sent to Germantown (now part of Philadelphia) until they could move out to what was then the frontier, the rolling green hills of Lancaster and York Counties. The land was naturally fertile, and careful cultivation by the Dutch vastly increased its productivity. Today, farms in Lancaster County continue to produce some of the highest per acre yields of any land on earth.

The Pennsylvania Dutch are perhaps the most conservative people in America. But unlike the residents of a conservative place like Orange County, California, the Dutch make no effort to restore an imagined paradise left behind. Instead, the people here believe that they live in a real and present paradise, and aside from unpleasant tourists, much evidence exists to support their belief. Of course, not all of the Pennsylvania Dutch have clung fast to the old traditions, but German names are exceedingly common here. Moreover, the farms managed with meticulous care and the factories without unions reflect some of the old Dutch heritage shared by most residents of the Lancaster area. During the early career of James Buchanan, who lived in Lancaster, the politics of the Pennsylvania Dutch country was Jeffersonian Democratic. But some years before the Civil War, the Dutch became Republican, a preference they have retained to this day. The heart of the Dutch country, Lancaster County, regularly returns Republican majorities on the order of 3–1—usually the highest of any area of similar size in the East.

The most Dutch of all the Pennsylvania congressional districts is the 16th, which includes all of Lancaster County and parts of Chester and Lebanan Counties. Of all the congressional districts in the East, the 16th cast the highest percentage of votes for Richard Nixon in 1968 (62%) and in 1972 (76%). The district's Congressman is Edwin Eshleman, a rather moderate Republican, given his constituency. Eshleman sits on the Education and Labor Committee, where he is somewhat more open to innovation than most Lancaster area Representatives have been, though he by no means has a liberal-labor voting record. He was first elected in 1966, and has had no problems in the Republican primary, the only election in which he could possibly lose his seat.

Census Data Pop. 467,811. Central city, 12%; suburban, 72%. Median family income, $9,905; families above $15,000: 18%; families below $3,000: 6%. Median years education, 11.4.

The Voters

Median voting age 43.
Employment profile White collar, 38%. Blue collar, 46%. Service, 12%. Farm, 4%.
Ethnic groups Black, 3%. Total foreign stock, 7%. Germany, Italy, 1% each.

Presidential vote

1972	Nixon (R)	115,651	(76%)
	McGovern (D)	37,223	(24%)
1968	Nixon (R)	97,356	(62%)
	Humphrey (D)	47,091	(30%)
	Wallace (AI)	13,307	(8%)

Rep. Edwin D. Eshleman (R) Elected 1966; b. Dec. 4, 1920, Lancaster County; home, Lancaster; Franklin and Marshall Col., B.S., Temple U.; Lutheran.

Career Coast Guard, WWII; Public school teacher, 1945–49; Dir. of Bureau of County Audits, Penn. Dept. of the Auditor Gen., 1949–53; Exec. Asst., Penn. Dept. of the Treasury, 1953–55; Penn. House of Reps., 1954–66.

Offices 2244 RHOB, 202-225-2411. Also 210 U.S.P.O., Lancaster 17604, 717-393-0666.

Committees

Education and Labor (6th). Subcommittees: Elementary, Secondary and Vocational Education; Post-secondary Education.

Group Ratings

	ADA	COPE	LWV	RIPON	NFU	LCV	CFA	NAB	NSI	ACA
1974	22	0	40	67	50	33	23	83	80	60
1973	17	18	42	73	39	5	38	–	–	62
1972	0	18	22	83	17	48	0	100	100	71

Key Votes

1) Foreign Aid	AGN	6) Gov Abortn Aid	AGN	11) Pub Cong Election $	FOR
2) Busing	AGN	7) Coed Phys Ed	AGN	12) Turkish Arms Cutoff	AGN
3) ABM	FOR	8) Pov Lawyer Gag	AGN	13) Youth Camp Regs	AGN
4) B-1 Bomber	FOR	9) Pub Trans Sub	AGN	14) Strip Mine Veto	FOR
5) Nerve Gas	AGN	10) EZ Voter Regis	AGN	15) Farm Bill Veto	FOR

Election Results

1974 general:	Edwin D. Eshleman (R)	73,130	(64%)	($6,996)
	Michael J. Minney (D)	40,273	(36%)	($4,507)
1974 primary:	Edwin D. Eshleman (R)	21,178	(84%)	
	Edward R. Mellinger, Jr. (R)	4,075	(16%)	
1972 general:	Edwin D. Eshleman (R)	112,292	(73%)	($14,041)
	Shirley S. Garrett (D)	40,534	(27%)	($2,242)

◆ ◆ ◆ ◆ ◆

SEVENTEENTH DISTRICT

The 17th congressional district of Pennsylvania lies at just about the center of the state, taking in a collection of counties along the Susquehanna River. The southern end of the district, around Harrisburg, contains nearly two-thirds of its population. The main industry here is, of course, state government. And while Harrisburg is historically Republican, that may have been due at least in part to the fact that Pennsylvania seldom elected Democratic Governors and was always a big patronage state; in any case, the usually Republican Harrisburg area went for incumbent Democratic Governor Milton Shapp in 1974.

Farther up the Susquehanna, there is some Democratic territory in Northumberland County, the waist, as it were, of the district. Here seams of anthracite once drew ethnics to towns like Sunbury and Shamokin. Right across the river are the Lewisburg and Allenwood federal prisons, where so many veterans of the Nixon Administration, as well as dignitaries like Jimmy Hoffa and Carmine DeSapio, did time. To the north is Williamsport, a small manufacturing town on the upper Susquehanna. Its All-American character makes it an appropriate host of the annual Little League World Series.

Despite Northumberland, the 17th is a heavily Republican district. In fact, it has not elected a Democratic Congressman in the twentieth century. The current incumbent, Herman Schneebeli, first won the seat in a 1960 special election, and has kept it ever since. For 10 years or so, Schneebeli labored in obscurity, little known to the press, and recognized by readers of the *Congressional Directory* as a middle-ranking Republican on the House Ways and Means Committee. Then, in the spring of 1972, the ranking Republican on the Committee, John Byrnes of Wisconsin, though only 59, decided to retire. So did Jackson Betts of Ohio, the number two Republican. Suddenly Herman Schneebeli found himself Wilbur Mills' Republican counterpart on Ways and Means, thanks to the wonder working seniority system.

Byrnes had worked with Mills, often as part of a team; when they agreed on things, they could usually get it down the throat of the rest of the House. But Schneebeli has never been regarded a heavyweight. And now with Mills gone from the chair, and new Chairman Al Ullman not enjoying his clout, there will likely be no Ullman-Schneebeli deals which the House will have to accept *faut de mieux*.

That leaves Schneebeli in a distinctively minority position, which is where he found himself in the 1974 and 1975 fights over the oil depletion allowance. Every step of the way Schneebeli has backed the positions of the big oil companies; most of the time—and it must be an unusual experience for a veteran of Ways and Means—he has lost. He has been little more successful supporting the fiscal and energy policies of the Ford Administration. It is possible that Schneebeli has great legislative talents, which he simply has not yet had an opportunity to display, given the heavy Democratic margins in the House and on the Committee. If so, it will come as a surprise to most close observers.

It will also be rather a contrast from Schneebeli's demonstrated weakness as a congressional candidate. Before 1970, he had encountered minimal Democratic opposition in this most Republican of districts; in 1970 and again in 1974, when Democrats did start waging genuine campaigns against him, he was able to raise well over $100,000 easily—such things are never difficult for men who have a major say over the nation's tax laws. Schneebeli should have realized that he was vulnerable on certain issues, and planned his campaign accordingly; his Democratic opponents have charged that he is solely the servant of big business interests, and that he has ignored the real interests of ordinary people in the district. And his record, viewed as a Democrat would view it, undoubtedly supports such charges. But there are replies Republicans can, and do, make; and other issues, on which their views are more popular, they raise; and there are always the little services an active Congressman can perform for his constituents, which can make so much difference at election time.

Apparently Schneebeli was not much good at any of these things. In 1970, he won a rather weak 58% of the vote; in 1974, a disastrously weak 52%—not the performance of a champion. 1976, one would think, will be a more Republican year, but Schneebeli will be 69, and may just have decided that he has had enough of fame, if not of power.

Census Data   Pop. 476,141. Central city, 14%; suburban, 33%. Median family income, $8,933; families above $15,000: 14%; families below $3,000: 8%. Median years education, 12.1.

The Voters

Median voting age 45.
Employment profile White collar, 44%. Blue collar, 42%. Service, 12%. Farm, 2%.
Ethnic groups Black, 6%. Total foreign stock, 8%. Italy, 1%.

Presidential vote

1972	Nixon (R)	119,178	(71%)
	McGovern (D)	48,205	(29%)
1968	Nixon (R)	104,128	(59%)
	Humphrey (D)	58,308	(33%)
	Wallace (AI)	13,613	(8%)

Rep. Herman T. Schneebeli (R) Elected Apr. 26, 1960; b. July 7, 1907, Lancaster; home, Williamsport; Dartmouth Col., B.A. 1930, M.C.S. 1931; Episcopalian.

Career Gulf Oil Corp., 1930–; Williamsport Distributor, 1939–; Army, WWII.

Offices 1336 LHOB, 202-225-4315. Also 1146 Fed. Bldg., Harrisburg 17108, 717-238-0395.

Committees

Ways and Means (Ranking Member).

Budget (3d).

Group Ratings

	ADA	COPE	LWV	RIPON	NFU	LCV	CFA	NAB	NSI	ACA
1974	26	0	36	56	33	29	0	92	60	57
1973	8	0	27	69	5	11	0	–	–	72
1972	0	20	33	60	0	40	0	100	80	79

Key Votes

1) Foreign Aid	FOR	6) Gov Abortn Aid	AGN	11) Pub Cong Election $	AGN
2) Busing	AGN	7) Coed Phys Ed	ABS	12) Turkish Arms Cutoff	AGN
3) ABM	AGN	8) Pov Lawyer Gag	FOR	13) Youth Camp Regs	AGN
4) B-1 Bomber	FOR	9) Pub Trans Sub	AGN	14) Strip Mine Veto	FOR
5) Nerve Gas	AGN	10) EZ Voter Regis	AGN	15) Farm Bill Veto	FOR

Election Results

1974 general:	Herman T. Schneebeli (R)	70,274	(52%)	($47,611)
	Peter C. Wambach (D)	64,576	(48%)	($38,899)

1974 primary: Herman T. Schneebeli (R), unopposed
1972 general: Herman T. Schneebeli (R)   120,214   (73%)   ($19,311)
                Donald J. Rippon (D)   44,202   (27%)   ($2,386)

◆ ◆ ◆ ◆

EIGHTEENTH DISTRICT

The 18th congressional district of Pennsylvania is the Pittsburgh suburban district. As is so often the case with suburban districts, the 18th is by no means a homogeneous area. The towns along the Allegheny and Ohio Rivers, which include some of the Pittsburgh area's smaller steel mills, are industrial, blue collar, and Democratic. They also are too numerous to list: at last count Allegheny County contained Pittsburgh and 128 cities, boroughs, and townships, almost half of them in the 18th district. In the hills that rise above both Rivers and all the smokestacks are the more comfortable, affluent, and Republican neighborhoods where management personnel live. Among these are places like Fox Chapel, middle-class Carnegie and Mount Lebanon, along with three Republican-leaning wards of Pittsburgh itself. All in all, the district is about as marginal as possible in statewide elections. In 1974, it appears to have been the only district to have gone for the losers in both major races, Republican gubernatorial candidate Drew Lewis and Pittsburgh Mayor Peter Flaherty, the Democratic nominee for Senator.

From the early 1940s to the early 1970s, there were two suburban Pittsburgh districts. Both were represented for almost all that time by Republicans who tended to vote the way labor wanted on economic issues—James Fulton and Robert Corbett. Both men died in 1971 and their districts were, in effect, combined into what is now the 18th. After a complicated series of special elections and primaries the new Congressman emerged in 1972, a young (then 34) liberal Republican named H. John Heinz III.

It is not an unfamiliar name, in Pittsburgh or for that matter around the country; the new Congressman is very definitely a member of the Heinz "57 Varieties" family, with all the wealth and privilege that entails. He is also a man of considerable charm and political skill. His strong liberal record has undoubtedly helped him, but these other qualities are certainly part of the reason for the vote-getting ability he has shown. In 1974, for example, not only did Heinz receive 72% of the vote in the general election—the best score for any Pennsylvania Republican and, indeed, one of the best in the country—he also received 25% of the vote in the Democratic primary, as a write-in candidate!

With this kind of popularity in Pittsburgh, and assured as he virtually is of the kind of warm reception the Pennsylvania media inevitably grants every rising Republican politician, Heinz is almost certain to try for statewide office in some future year. Certainly he would be the Republicans' strongest candidate to succeed Senator Hugh Scott if Scott should choose to retire in 1976; indeed, he would probably be stronger than Scott himself. He would also be a strong candidate for the Governorship in 1978, when incumbent Milton Shapp would no longer be eligible to run. In either case, Heinz can expect to face tough Democratic opposition. Philadelphia Congressman William Green may run for the Senate in 1976, Lieutenant Governor Ernest Kline would surely like to be Governor in 1978, and former Insurance Commissioner Herbert Denenberg could run for either office with some hope of winning. Pennsylvania, which for a long time has seemed to have a dearth of top notch politicians, now seems to have an overabundance of them.

Census Data   Pop. 472,074. Central city, 13%; suburban, 87%. Median family income, $10,770; families above $15,000: 25%; families below $3,000: 6%. Median years education, 12.2.

The Voters

Median voting age 46.
Employment profile White collar, 57%. Blue collar, 32%. Service, 11%. Farm, –%.
Ethnic groups Black, 2%. Total foreign stock, 24%. Italy, 5%; Germany, Poland, 3% each; UK, Austria, Czechoslovakia, 2% each; Yugoslavia, Ireland, 1% each.

Presidential vote

1972	Nixon (R)	125,938	(63%)
	McGovern (D)	74,949	(37%)
1968	Nixon (R)	92,077	(45%)
	Humphrey (D)	90,621	(44%)
	Wallace (AI)	21,508	(11%)

Rep. H. John Heinz III (R) Elected Nov. 2, 1971; b. Oct. 23, 1938, Pittsburgh; home, Pittsburgh; Yale U., B.A. 1960, Harvard U., M.B.A. 1963; Episcopalian.

Career Marketing, H. J. Heinz Co., Pittsburgh, 1965–70; Sales Rep., Internatl. Harvester, Australia; Special Asst. to U.S. Sen. Hugh Scott, 1964.

Offices 324 CHOB, 202-225-2035. Also 2031 Fed. Bldg., Pittsburgh 15222, 412-562-0533.

Committees

Interstate and Foreign Commerce (11th). Subcommittees: Energy and Power; Health and Environment.

Group Ratings

	ADA	COPE	LWV	RIPON	NFU	LCV	CFA	NAB	NSI	ACA
1974	59	82	92	80	86	63	69	58	38	14
1973	60	56	92	87	50	68	88	–	–	30
1972	63	55	83	93	86	83	100	57	14	9

Key Votes

1) Foreign Aid	FOR	6) Gov Abortn Aid	AGN	11) Pub Cong Election $	FOR
2) Busing	AGN	7) Coed Phys Ed	AGN	12) Turkish Arms Cutoff	FOR
3) ABM	AGN	8) Pov Lawyer Gag	AGN	13) Youth Camp Regs	FOR
4) B-1 Bomber	FOR	9) Pub Trans Sub	AGN	14) Strip Mine Veto	AGN
5) Nerve Gas	AGN	10) EZ Voter Regis	FOR	15) Farm Bill Veto	FOR

Election Results

1974 general:	H. John Heinz III (R)	107,723	(72%)	($89,449)
	Francis J. McArdle (D)	41,706	(28%)	($23,727)
1974 primary:	H. John Heinz III (R), unopposed			
1972 general:	H. John Heinz III (R)	144,521	(73%)	($103,542)
	Douglas Walgren (D)	53,929	(27%)	($3,123)

◆ ◆ ◆ ◆

NINETEENTH DISTRICT

The 19th congressional district of Pennsylvania—Adams and York Counties and most of Cumberland—sits at the western edge of the deeply conservative Pennsylvania Dutch country (see Sixteenth District). This is a land of rolling green farmland extending up to the base of the Appalachian ridges that begin to rise at the district's western boundary. The most famous part of the 19th is also the most sparsely populated, at least by permanent residents: Gettysburg, the tourist-thronged site of the Civil War's northernmost slaughter. Outside the town is the retirement home of the late President Eisenhower, who was of Pennsylvania Dutch stock himself; his father had migrated in the late nineteenth century with a group of Mennonite brethren out into Kansas and Texas.

The largest city in the district is York (pop. 50,000), which, from September of 1777 until June 1778, was the capital of a young nation. While the Continental Congress met at York, it passed the Articles of Confederation, received word from Ben Franklin in Paris that the French would help with money and ships, and issued the first proclamation calling for a national day of thanksgiving. Today, York is less Republican than other cities in the Pennsylvania Dutch area, perhaps because of the lingering influence of the old York *Gazette,* which until a recent change in ownership was one of the most liberal and antiwar newspapers in the United States.

The other large population center in the 19th is the fastest growing. This is Cumberland County around Camp Hill, Mechanicsburg, and Carlisle—just across the Susquehanna River from Harrisburg. During the last 20 years, Cumberland has absorbed most of the white exodus from the small state capital city. The county, already very Republican, is growing even more so.

The 19th is a Republican district that elected Democratic Congressmen in 1954, 1958 and 1964; with Milton Shapp carrying York County, it came close to going Democratic in the 1970 and 1974 gubernatorial races. That last year could also have been another year of party switch here. The incumbent was 78-year-old George Goodling, a farmer with the most conservative voting record in the Pennsylvania delegation. He had demonstrated no great vote-getting powers, beating unimpressive Democrats by unimpressive margins in the last two elections. Perhaps sensing his vulnerability, Goodling decided to retire.

Altogether, seven Republicans and seven Democrats ran to succeed him. The top Democrats turned out to be the party's 1970 and 1972 nominees; the top Republicans, John Eden, who had won 28% against the Congressman in the 1972 primary, and the Congressman's son William, a 47-year-old educator. It was the younger Goodling who had the most votes, with 40% in the primary to Eden's 33%, and 52% in the general election to Democrat Arthur Berger's 48%. That probably means that Goodling *fils* will win again, although it is always risky to say so in this seat. Footnote: one possible candidate who had been rumored interested in the seat, but never ran in the year of Watergate, was David Eisenhower, who votes from his grandmother's Gettysburg address.

Census Data Pop. 467,999. Central city, 11%; suburban, 89%. Median family income, $10,107; families above $15,000: 19%; families below $3,000: 6%. Median years education, 12.0.

The Voters

Median voting age 43.
Employment profile White collar, 44%. Blue collar, 43%. Service, 10%. Farm, –%.
Ethnic groups Black, 2%. Total foreign stock, 5%.

Presidential vote

1972	Nixon (R)	115,528	(72%)
	McGovern (D)	45,769	(28%)
1968	Nixon (R)	93,067	(58%)
	Humphrey (D)	53,049	(33%)
	Wallace (AI)	14,010	(9%)

Rep. William F. Goodling (R) Elected 1974; b. Dec. 5, 1927, Loganville; home, Jacobus; U. of Md., B.S. 1953, West. Md. Col., M.Ed. 1957, Penn St. U., 1958–62; Methodist.

Career Army, 1946–48; Public school teacher and administrator.

Offices 1713 LHOB, 202-225-5836. Also, Fed. Bldg., 200 S. George St., York 17403, 717-243-5432.

Committees

Education and Labor (12th). Subcommittees: Elementary, Secondary and Vocational Education; Labor Standards.

Small Business (12th). Subcommittees: SBA and SBIC Legislation; SBA Oversight and Minority Enterprise.

Group Ratings: Newly Elected

Key Votes

1) Foreign Aid	AGN	6) Gov Abortn Aid	NE	11) Pub Cong Election $	NE
2) Busing	NE	7) Coed Phys Ed	AGN	12) Turkish Arms Cutoff	NE
3) ABM	NE	8) Pov Lawyer Gag	NE	13) Youth Camp Regs	AGN
4) B-1 Bomber	FOR	9) Pub Trans Sub	NE	14) Strip Mine Veto	AGN
5) Nerve Gas	NE	10) EZ Voter Regis	NE	15) Farm Bill Veto	FOR

Election Results

1974 general:	William F. Goodling (R)	66,417	(52%)	($42,944)
	Arthur L. Berger (D)	61,414	(48%)	($67,162)
1974 primary:	William F. Goodling (R)	12,533	(40%)	
	John Eden (R)	10,457	(33%)	
	Five Others (R)	8,419	(27%)	

◆ ◆ ◆ ◆ ◆

TWENTIETH DISTRICT

The 20th congressional district of Pennsylvania could be called the Monongahela district. Most of its residents live in a string of industrial communities along the heavily polluted Monongahela River and a tributary, the Youghiogheny. "Monongahela," Walt Whitman once wrote, "it rolls off the tongue like venison." But during the last 100 years, area residents have sighted few deer and eaten little venison. What is more common here is steel. The 20th district probably makes as much steel as any congressional district in the nation. Here are the operations of Jones & Laughlin and no less than four mills of U.S. Steel. They are found along the banks of the Monongahela, which provide just about the only level land available in the Pittsburgh metropolitan area. Most of these mills are ancient and technologically backward; the best known of them is the Homestead Works, site of a great and bloody strike in 1892 when it was owned by Andrew Carnegie.

Not many blacks live in the district, only 7%, and these are not found in ghettoes, but live scattered through various Pittsburgh neighborhoods and the smaller towns like McKeesport, Clairton, and Duquesne. Most residents of the 20th are members of the white working class—the children and grandchildren of people who came from Slovakia, southern Italy, Poland, Wales, and the mountains of West Virginia and Pennsylvania to work in the steel mills. Many of them lived through the 1920s, when the prosperity of the great steel corporations failed to trickle down to its sweat-covered workers, through the privations of the 1930s and the exhilaration of the United Steel Workers' organizing the mills, and finally through the slow decline of the industry after World War II. Today, these steelworkers live in the same small frame houses found up and down the hills of Braddock, Swissvale, Homestead, and the Hazelwood and St. Clair neighborhoods of Pittsburgh. The populations of all these areas have declined; the children who grew up here have in many cases gotten better jobs and moved out, sometimes to outer suburbs, but in many cases away from the Pittsburgh area altogether. As a result, this is an old district, one where an unusual percentage of voters still remember the timbre of Franklin D. Roosevelt's voice.

The image of the American melting pot comes to us from the steel-making process. And in one respect, at least, communities of the 20th, though separated from each other by hills, have melted into a unit: their political preference, which is solidly Democratic. The one-person-one-vote ruling has forced the 20th to append some relatively affluent, Republican areas like Bethel Park and Monroeville. Overall, however, the district remains blue-collar and Democratic. Some of the voters here have become dissatisfied with the candidates nominated by the national Democratic Party. Pittsburgh people seem to prefer the earthier and socially more conservative candidates like the kind slated by the Allegheny County Democratic machine. In 1968, George Wallace got 13% of the 20th's votes—his best showing in any Pennsylvania district; and in 1972, the district recorded a 24% shift to Richard Nixon—again the largest such deflection among Pennsylvania districts.

But since the New Deal, the 20th has sent only Democrats to the House of Representatives, and it shows every sign of continuing to do so. The current Congressman is Joseph Gaydos, a former state Senator and attorney for United Mine Workers District 5. Gaydos had Democratic organization and union backing when he first won the seat in 1968; and in Washington, his record is what you might expect, solidly liberal on economic issues, more conservative on social matters. As a member of the Education and Labor Committee, Gaydos is considered a reliable labor vote. The safety of his seat seems in little doubt: in 1974 he received 82% of the vote—the best showing made by any opposed Pennsylvania Congressman.

Census Data Pop. 468,959. Central city, 14%; suburban, 86%. Median family income, $9,937; families above $15,000: 19%; families below $3,000: 7%. Median years education, 12.1.

The Voters

Median voting age 46.
Employment profile White collar, 50%. Blue collar, 38%. Service, 12%. Farm, –%.
Ethnic groups Black, 7%. Total foreign stock, 26%. Italy, Czechoslovakia, 4% each; Poland, UK, 3% each; Germany, Austria, Hungary, Yugoslavia, 2% each; Ireland, 1%.

Presidential vote

1972	Nixon (R)	108,506	(56%)
	McGovern (D)	83,576	(44%)
1968	Nixon (R)	66,107	(32%)
	Humphrey (D)	111,159	(54%)
	Wallace (AI)	27,052	(13%)

Rep. Joseph M. Gaydos (D) Elected 1968; b. July 3, 1926, Braddock; home, McKeesport; Duquesne U., U. of Notre Dame, LL.B. 1951; Catholic.

Career Navy, WWII; Deputy Atty. Gen. of Penn.; Asst. Allegheny Co. Solicitor; Gen. Counsel, Utd. Mine Workers of Amer., Dist. 5; Penn. Senate, 1967–68.

Offices 301 CHOB, 202-225-4631. Also Rm. 207, 224 5th Ave. Bldg., McKeesport 15132, 412-673-3756.

Committees

Education and Labor (12th). Subcommittees: Labor Standards; Manpower, Compensation, and Health and Safety.

House Administration (8th). Subcommittees: Contracts (Chairman); Elections; Electrical **and** Mechanical Office Equipment; Printing.

Group Ratings

	ADA	COPE	LWV	RIPON	NFU	LCV	CFA	NAB	NSI	ACA
1974	52	82	42	25	71	65	69	42	40	33
1973	80	100	75	43	85	79	100	–	–	26
1972	63	90	80	33	86	60	100	18	13	41

Key Votes

1) Foreign Aid	AGN	6) Gov Abortn Aid	AGN	11) Pub Cong Election $	AGN
2) Busing	AGN	7) Coed Phys Ed	AGN	12) Turkish Arms Cutoff	FOR
3) ABM	AGN	8) Pov Lawyer Gag	AGN	13) Youth Camp Regs	FOR
4) B-1 Bomber	AGN	9) Pub Trans Sub	FOR	14) Strip Mine Veto	AGN
5) Nerve Gas	AGN	10) EZ Voter Regis	FOR	15) Farm Bill Veto	AGN

Election Results

1974 general:	Joseph M. Gaydos (D)	112,237	(82%)	($24,778)
	Joseph J. Anderko (R)	25,129	(18%)	($101)
1974 primary:	Joseph M. Gaydos (D), unopposed			
1972 general:	Joseph M. Gaydos (D)	117,933	(62%)	($44,379)
	William R. Hunt (R)	73,817	(38%)	($63,843)

◆　◆　◆　◆　◆

TWENTY-FIRST DISTRICT

The 21st congressional district of Pennsylvania is Westmoreland County, just to the east of Pittsburgh, plus a small portion of suburban Allegheny County. It is a mixed area: there are a few wealthy enclaves here, like Ligonier, but most of Westmoreland is industrial—small factory towns that lie between the hills or along the Allegheny and Monongahela Rivers at the county's western edge. The district contains an especially large number of Italian-Americans, with other ethnic groups present in smaller numbers. The 21st is part of western Pennsylvania's "black country," so named for the region's bituminous coal deposits. Steel is the major industry here, as it is all over western Pennsylvania; the coal, of course, is a major reason why the steel industry grew here in the first place. Politically, western Pennsylvania in general and the 21st district in particular are heavily Democratic.

The Congressman from the 21st, Democrat John Dent, served for 19 years as one of his party's floor leaders in the Pennsylvania Senate before he was first elected to Congress in 1958. Like many members from safe districts, Dent has been quietly winning reelection by large margins and accumulating seniority. He is now the third-ranking Democrat on the House Education and Labor Committee, and Chairman of the Labor Standards Subcommittee. In that capacity, he is regularly the chief House sponsor of bills to raise the minimum wage.

Dent has always enjoyed the support of organized labor and, as it happens, pretty accurately reflects the views of the leadership of the AFL-CIO: liberal on economic issues, hawkish on foreign policy, and cautious on social issues—indeed, on the last named, Dent undoubtedly is more cautious than George Meany. Some of these attitudes may have been responsible for Dent's one excursion into statewide politics, when he ran against Senator Joseph Clark in the 1968 Democratic primary. Dent's candidacy served to highlight Clark's opposition to the Vietnam war and his support of gun control laws—both factors in his surprise loss in the general election that year; it also symbolized the estrangement of Dent's fellow Italian-Americans from the Senator. Dent himself also ran for reelection to the House that year, and shows every sign of continuing to do so, though he turns 68 in 1976.

Census Data Pop. 473,040. Central city, 0%; suburban, 100%. Median family income, $9,645; families above $15,000: 16%; families below $3,000: 7%. Median years education, 12.1.

The Voters

Median voting age 45.
Employment profile White collar, 45%. Blue collar, 43%. Service, 11%. Farm, 1%.
Ethnic groups Black, 2%. Total foreign stock, 21%. Italy, 6%; Poland, Czechoslovakia, Austria, UK, 2% each; Germany, Yugoslavia, 1% each.

Presidential vote

1972	Nixon (R)	99,366	(58%)
	McGovern (D)	73,049	(42%)
1968	Nixon (R)	69,023	(37%)
	Humphrey (D)	98,072	(53%)
	Wallace (AI)	19,543	(10%)

Rep. John H. Dent (D) Elected Jan. 21, 1958; b. Mar. 10, 1908, Johnetta; home, Ligonier; Catholic.

Career Mbr., Natl. Cncl., Utd. Rubber Workers of Amer., 1923–37; USMC, 1924–28; Jeannette City Cncl., 1932–34; Penn. House of Reps., 1934–36; Penn. Senate, 1936–58, Dem. Floor Ldr., 1939–58.

Offices 2104 RHOB, 202-225-5631. Also 35 W. Pittsburgh St., Greensburg 15601, 412-837-1026.

Committees

Education and Labor (3d). Subcommittees: Agricultural Labor; Labor Standards (Chairman); Manpower, Compensation, and Health and Safety.

House Administration (3d). Subcommittees: Accounts; Elections (Chairman); Parking.

Group Ratings

	ADA	COPE	LWV	RIPON	NFU	LCV	CFA	NAB	NSI	ACA
1974	62	100	50	36	100	69	83	36	50	29
1973	68	100	64	38	100	50	100	–	–	22
1972	56	78	73	43	80	47	50	25	100	42

Key Votes

1) Foreign Aid	AGN	6) Gov Abortn Aid	AGN	11) Pub Cong Election $	AGN
2) Busing	AGN	7) Coed Phys Ed	ABS	12) Turkish Arms Cutoff	FOR
3) ABM	AGN	8) Pov Lawyer Gag	AGN	13) Youth Camp Regs	FOR
4) B-1 Bomber	FOR	9) Pub Trans Sub	FOR	14) Strip Mine Veto	AGN
5) Nerve Gas	FOR	10) EZ Voter Regis	FOR	15) Farm Bill Veto	AGN

Election Results

1974 general:	John H. Dent (D)	88,701	(70%)	($26,636)
	Charles L. Sconing (R)	38,111	(30%)	($5,324)
1974 primary	John H. Dent (D), unopposed			
1972 general:	John H. Dent (D)	104,203	(62%)	($32,024)
	Thomas H. Young (R)	63,812	(38%)	($325)

◆ ◆ ◆ ◆ ◆

TWENTY-SECOND DISTRICT

The 22d congressional district of Pennsylvania is the northern tip of Appalachia—the southwest corner of the state between West Virginia and the Pittsburgh suburbs. The region is one of rugged hills and polluted rivers, lined with steel mills and blast furnaces. The operations here are smaller than those in the 20th district, which contain the really big mills; and the poverty endemic in West Virginia is also found here. Residents of Italian, Polish, and Czech descent have the same problems as the longer settled Scots Irish of the area. This is rough country: it was in a small town here—the district has no large city—that Joseph Yablonski, the insurgent candidate for president of the United Mine Workers, was found shot to death with his wife and daughter in 1969.

In 1972, for the first time since the New Deal, the 22d district plunked for a Republican presidential candidate. It remains, however, one of the state's safest Democratic districts in most elections. Since the election of 1944, the 22d has sent Democrat Thomas Morgan, a physician from tiny Fredericktown (pop. 1,067), to the House of Representatives. Through the inexorable workings of the seniority system, Doc Morgan has become Chairman of the International Relations Committee. The Chairman is not a scholar in the field; he is a bluff, gregarious man who seems most comfortable in the company of people from similar backgrounds (Wayne Hays, of the nearby 18th district of Ohio, is a member of the Committee, as are two other Pennsylvania Democrats). Morgan's Committee has been criticized over the years, and compared unfavorably to Senate Foreign Relations as J. William Fulbright ran it. Part of the difference was ideological: Fulbright opposed the Vietnam war, and conducted illuminating hearings on it; while Morgan supported the war well into the Nixon years, and Foreign Affairs (as the House committee used to be called) held no hearings of any kind on the war until 1971. Beyond that, the Senate committee has undoubtedly built up a more credentialed staff, with greater desire and capacity to probe behind Executive Branch statements. Morgan, on the other hand, seems to prefer operating in the atmosphere of bipartisan cooperation which characterized the beginning of his political career.

For many years, Morgan's basic predilections were reflected in the makeup of his Committee. But since the early seventies, the makeup of the Committee has changed; there are many more doves now, and members questioning the basic assumptions that have governed American foreign policy. Morgan found himself, in 1972, ordered by the Democratic caucus to report out an antiwar amendment; a year later, the balance on the Committee had changed and the Chairman supported the move to prohibit American bombing of Cambodia.

Over the years, Morgan has always been a solid vote-getter in the 22d district, with little to worry about in either general elections or primaries. That is still the case in general elections, but in the 1974 primary the Chairman had a rather nasty surprise. Six candidates ran against him, and though no one of them did particulary well, the Chairman ended up with only 48% of the vote. In the South, when that happens, there is a runoff—and the veteran forced into a runoff usually loses, if not in that election, then two years later. In Pennsylvania of course there is no runoff, but it would not be entirely surprising if more substantial opposition should surface and perhaps end Morgan's congressional career. Or, he may decide that, at 70, it is time to retire.

Census Data Pop. 469,778. Central city, 0%; suburban, 59%. Median family income, $8,396; families above $15,000: 13%; families below $3,000: 12%. Median years education, 11.7.

The Voters

Median voting age 46.
Employment profile White collar, 40%. Blue collar, 47%. Service, 12%. Farm, 1%.
Ethnic groups Black, 4%. Total foreign stock, 20%. Italy, 5%; Czechoslovakia, 3%; Poland, Austria, UK, 2% each; Germany, Yugoslavia, 1% each.

Presidential vote

1972	Nixon (R)	95,927	(57%)
	McGovern (D)	72,151	(43%)
1968	Nixon (R)	64,570	(35%)
	Humphrey (D)	101,381	(55%)
	Wallace (AI)	18,473	(10%)

Rep. Thomas E. Morgan (D) Elected 1944; b. Oct. 13, 1906, Ellsworth; home, Fredericktown; Waynesburg Col., B.S. 1930, Detroit Col. of Medicine and Surgery, M.B. 1933, Wayne U., M.D. 1934; Methodist.

Career Internship, Grace Hosp., Detroit, Mich., 1934; Practicing physician and surgeon, 1934–73.

Offices 2183 RHOB, 202-225-4665. Also 230-232 Washington Trust Bldg., Washington 15301, 412-228-2700.

Committees

International Relations (Chairman). Subcommittees: Oversight (Chairman).

Group Ratings

	ADA	COPE	LWV	RIPON	NFU	LCV	CFA	NAB	NSI	ACA
1974	47	80	75	38	93	65	83	18	57	15
1973	65	100	78	70	100	53	86	–	–	13
1972	69	91	91	67	67	33	100	0	100	17

Key Votes

1) Foreign Aid	FOR	6) Gov Abortn Aid	AGN	11) Pub Cong Election $	AGN
2) Busing	AGN	7) Coed Phys Ed	FOR	12) Turkish Arms Cutoff	FOR
3) ABM	FOR	8) Pov Lawyer Gag	AGN	13) Youth Camp Regs	FOR
4) B-1 Bomber	FOR	9) Pub Trans Sub	FOR	14) Strip Mine Veto	AGN
5) Nerve Gas	AGN	10) EZ Voter Regis	FOR	15) Farm Bill Veto	AGN

Election Results

1974 general:	Thomas E. Morgan (D)	83,654	(64%)	($64,572)
	James R. Montgomery (R)	41,706	(32%)	($173)
	John Bove (Constitutional)	6,226	(5%)	($4,131)
1974 primary:	Thomas E. Morgan (D)	33,570	(48%)	
	John W. Mc Ilvaine (D)	13,021	(19%)	
	Theodore J. Kozel (D)	8,016	(12%)	
	Emmett Nepa (D)	6,270	(9%)	
	Three Others (D)	8,657	(12%)	
1972 general:	Thomas E. Morgan (D)	100,918	(61%)	($32,157)
	James R. Montgomery (R)	65,005	(39%)	($807)

◆ ◆ ◆ ◆ ◆

TWENTY-THIRD DISTRICT

The 23d congressional district of Pennsylvania is the rural north central part of the state. The region is not only the most sparsely populated in Pennsylvania, but in the entire East. The district's terrain is mountainous, and its valleys have only a few small towns here and there. The only significant concentrations of people are found in the Nittany Valley to the south of the district, and around Oil City to the extreme west. The Nittany Valley is the home of Pennsylvania State University, commonly called Penn State, long known for its powerful football teams. Oil City is near the site of the nation's first oil well, sunk in 1859. Today, Pennsylvania crude—a relatively scarce but higher quality oil than that found in the Southwest—continues to occupy an important place in the region's economy.

The isolation of this part of Pennsylvania was ended by the recent opening of the Pennsylvania Shortway, a superhighway that has replaced the Pennsylvania Turnpike as the main road between New York and Chicago. Some people hoped that the Shortway would bring light industrial development to the area; all it seems to have attracted, however, are gas stations with 60-foot signs and Holiday Inns. So the 23d remains a rural and small town district, dominated by old-stock farmers. These people have lived apart from the movements of population and social change that have affected—and afflicted—their neighbors in other parts of the East and the Great Lakes region.

The area currently covered by the 23d has a long tradition of electing Republican Congressmen. The current Congressman, Albert Johnson, was first elected in 1963 and is now the ranking Republican on the House Banking and Currency committee. He is a solid conservative, a man with anything but a flamboyant personality, but has the sort of steady devotion to the cause of free enterprise that voters here have found so comforting over the years. From all that one might conclude that Johnson holds one of the House's safest seats.

Not so. In 1972, Johnson was held to 56% of the vote by a not very strong Democratic opponent. It was while that campaign was being waged that Johnson, together with all of Banking and Currency's Republicans, successfully joined several Democrats to block then Chairman Wright Patman from conducting an investigation of the Watergate. That was obviously not one of Johnson's strong points going into 1974, and Johnson suddenly found himself targeted. In the Republican primary, a challenger named Richard McCormack, who had gotten 39% of the vote, rose to 45% in 1974—still not enough to win a two-man race. And in the general election Nittany Valley attorney Yates Mast came within 6,981 of winning; it was a 53–47 election, but still a victory for Johnson.

Having survived this Democrat year, Johnson may appear to be home free. But he turns 70 in 1976; McCormack or some other Republican could challenge him again; and it is not totally out of the question that a Democrat might have a chance in a special election.

Census Data Pop. 469,717. Central city, 0%; suburban, 0%. Median family income, $8,272; families above $15,000: 11%; families below $3,000: 10%. Median years education, 12.1.

The Voters

Median voting age 42.
Employment profile White collar, 41%. Blue collar, 44%. Service, 13%. Farm, 2%.
Ethnic groups Total foreign stock, 10%. Italy, 2%; UK, Germany, 1% each.

Presidential vote

1972	Nixon (R)	105,463	(66%)
	McGovern (D)	54,138	(34%)
1968	Nixon (R)	88,223	(54%)
	Humphrey (D)	65,033	(40%)
	Wallace (AI)	9,321	(6%)

Rep. Albert W. Johnson (R) Elected Nov. 5, 1963; b. Apr. 17, 1906, Smethport; U. of Penn., 1926–27, Stetson U., LL.B. 1938.

Career Practicing atty.; Penn. House of Reps., 1946–63, Repub. Whip, 1951, 1955, Repub. Floor Ldr., 1953, 1957–63.

Offices 2233 RHOB, 202-225-5121. Also 205 Hamlin Bank Bldg., Smethport 16749, 814-887-2225.

Committees

Banking, Currency and Housing (Ranking Member). Subcommittees: Financial Institutions Supervision, Regulation and Insurance; Historic Preservation and Coinage; International Development Institutions and Finance.

Post Office and Civil Service (2d). Subcommittees: Postal Service.

Group Ratings

	ADA	COPE	LWV	RIPON	NFU	LCV	CFA	NAB	NSI	ACA
1974	10	9	58	54	57	35	8	64	100	42
1973	0	9	25	60	28	6	0	–	–	69
1972	0	82	42	57	43	17	0	100	100	70

Key Votes

1) Foreign Aid	FOR	6) Gov Abortn Aid	AGN	11) Pub Cong Election $	FOR
2) Busing	AGN	7) Coed Phys Ed	AGN	12) Turkish Arms Cutoff	AGN
3) ABM	FOR	8) Pov Lawyer Gag	FOR	13) Youth Camp Regs	FOR
4) B-1 Bomber	ABS	9) Pub Trans Sub	AGN	14) Strip Mine Veto	FOR
5) Nerve Gas	FOR	10) EZ Voter Regis	AGN	15) Farm Bill Veto	FOR

Election Results

1974 general:	Albert W. Johnson (R)	67,192	(53%)	($50,758)
	Yates Mast (D)	60,211	(47%)	($10,870)
1974 primary:	Albert W. Johnson (R)	21,540	(55%)	
	Richard McCormack (R)	17,603	(45%)	
1972 general:	Albert W. Johnson (R)	90,615	(56%)	($31,582)
	Ernest A. Kassab (D)	69,813	(44%)	($66,948)

◆ ◆ ◆ ◆ ◆

TWENTY-FOURTH DISTRICT

Situated in the northwest corner of the state, the 24th congressional district of Pennsylvania is part of the industrial Great Lakes region. It is a long way overland to the East Coast, and the district has none of metropolitan Philadelphia's seaboard ambiance. The city of Erie (pop. 129,000), the state's third largest, dominates the 24th. Like most industrial cities on the nation's polluted lake, Erie is a Democratic stronghold. As one goes inland, the territory becomes more Republican. An exception to the pattern is the steel town of Sharon, just a few miles from Youngstown, Ohio; like most towns dependent on steel mills, Sharon votes Democratic. All in all, the political balance in the 24th makes it one of the state's most marginal districts. In 1968, Humphrey edged Nixon here 49% to 46%, with 5% going to Wallace—a virtual mirror of the statewide results. It is also one of the few Pennsylvania districts to have changed partisan hands within memory.

The turnabout occurred in 1964, when Democrat Joseph Vigorito, an accountant and political unknown, unseated Republican Congressman James Weaver with 51% of the vote. Weaver was expected to come back and retake the seat in 1966, but instead Vigorito increased his share of the vote to 55%. In future elections, he rose to 69% by 1972.

Vigorito is one of the few northern Democrats on the House Agriculture Committee and one of the few Easterners on the Interior Committee. By now he has substantial seniority on both committees (4th on Agriculture), but by common consent is not a legislative powerhouse. Undoubtedly the low point in Vigorito's House career came when he was named one of the "ten dumbest Congressman" by *New Times* magazine. That label—and the nickname of "Jumping Joe" which the article used to describe him—not only seemed to hurt him on the Hill; they also seemed to erode some of the good will Vigorito had built up with twelve years of constituency services. In 1974, he was reduced to only 59% of the vote, despite the Democratic trend; and while the outlook is for him to win in the future, the seat is far more marginal now than before *New Times* spoke.

Census Data   Pop. 472,171. Central city, 27%; suburban, 28%. Median family income, $9,215; families above $15,000: 15%; families below $3,000: 8%. Median years education, 12.2.

The Voters

Median voting age 44.
Employment profile White collar, 42%. Blue collar, 45%. Service, 11%. Farm, 2%.
Ethnic groups Black, 3%. Total foreign stock, 16%. Italy, Poland, 3% each; Germany, 2%; UK, Czechoslovakia, 1%.

Presidential vote

1972	Nixon (R)	107,785	(61%)
	McGovern (D)	69,394	(39%)
1968	Nixon (R)	81,256	(46%)
	Humphrey (D)	85,763	(49%)
	Wallace (AI)	9,733	(6%)

Rep. Joseph P. Vigorito (D)   Elected 1964; b. Nov. 10, 1918, Niles, Ohio; home, Erie; U. of Penn., B.S. 1947, U. of Denver, M.B.A. 1949.

Career   Army, WWII; CPA; Asst. Prof., Penn. St. U., 1949–64.

Offices   440 CHOB, 202-225-5406. Also 107 U.S. Courthouse Bldg., Erie 16501, 814-455-1313.

Committees

Agriculture (4th). Subcommittees: Dairy and Poultry; Domestic Marketing and Consumer Relations (Chairman); Forests.

Interior and Insular Affairs (11th). Subcommittees: Energy and the Environment; Mines and Mining; Territorial and Insular Affairs.

Group Ratings

	ADA	COPE	LWV	RIPON	NFU	LCV	CFA	NAB	NSI	ACA
1974	67	100	55	53	100	71	85	42	30	7
1973	72	90	73	67	100	68	86	–	–	16
1972	44	100	70	50	86	33	50	10	40	23

Key Votes

1) Foreign Aid	AGN	6) Gov Abortn Aid	AGN	11) Pub Cong Election $	AGN
2) Busing	ABS	7) Coed Phys Ed	AGN	12) Turkish Arms Cutoff	ABS
3) ABM	FOR	8) Pov Lawyer Gag	FOR	13) Youth Camp Regs	FOR
4) B-1 Bomber	FOR	9) Pub Trans Sub	FOR	14) Strip Mine Veto	AGN
5) Nerve Gas	AGN	10) EZ Voter Regis	FOR	15) Farm Bill Veto	AGN

Election Results

1974 general:	Joseph P. Vigorito (D)	76,920	(59%)	($16,327)
	Clement R. Scalzitti (R)	54,277	(41%)	($3,619)
1974 primary:	Joseph P. Vigorito (D)	27,456	(69%)	
	Vincent N. De Luca (D)	10,076	(25%)	
	Lawrence G. Hamilla (D)	2,236	(6%)	
1972 general:	Joseph P. Vigorito (D)	122,092	(69%)	($13,504)
	Alvin W. Levenhagen (R)	55,406	(31%)	($10,479)

◆ ◆ ◆ ◆ ◆

TWENTY-FIFTH DISTRICT

The 25th congressional district is part of industrial western Pennsylvania. The district adjoins Ohio and the northern tip of the West Virginia panhandle. Almost half the people of the 25th live in Beaver County, where the steel mills sit in little grimy towns along the banks of the Ohio and Beaver Rivers; the best known of these towns is Beaver Falls, the boyhood home of former White House enemy Joe Namath. Like all of western Pennsylvania within 100 miles of Pittsburgh, Beaver County is rich in ethnic diversity, with especially large numbers of Italian-Americans. The County is ordinarily a Democratic bulwark. It has gone Republican only twice in recent elections—for Richard Schweiker over Joseph Clark in the 1968 Senate election, and for Richard Nixon over George McGovern in 1972.

The other two counties in the district are politically more marginal, Lawrence, dominated by the manufacturing city of New Castle, is Pennsylvania's bellwether county—or was until 1974, when it went for area favorite and Pittsburgh Mayor Peter Flaherty in his losing race against Senator Richard Schweiker. Butler County, a few miles distant from the industrial concentrations along the rivers, is less thickly settled and tends mildly toward Republicanism. The 25th also includes the northern tier of townships in Pittsburgh's Allegheny County, which usually go Republican.

Altogether, this is about as good an example of a district you would expect to be safe Democratic as you could find. And for twenty years it was held, seemingly safely, by Democrat Frank Clark. An economic policy liberal, a foreign policy hawk, and social conservative, Clark rose in seniority on the Merchant Marine and Fisheries and Public Works Committees. He was always a supporter of the coal interests, at least when labor and management agreed; for ten years, from 1964 to 1974, he led the successful battle to prevent construction of the Dickey-Lincoln hydroelectric project in Maine. In 1974, Clark was the leading sponsor in the House of a measure which would have required a certain percentage of oil imported into the United States to be in American registry ships—a requirement which would have the effect of seriously inflating the price of oil. Here as usual, Clark was supporting the positions held by the heavily subsidized American maritime industries and unions—one of the biggest spending lobbying groups in Washington.

It would seem that Clark had built a successful and secure career as a legislator. It was a long way from being police chief in the town of Bessemer—the position he held before his first election to Congress—and attending Nato conferences in Brussels and junketting through Europe; but he had made the jump, and seemed sure to stay on top. But it was not to be so. In 1972, he was challenged by a 35-year-old mechanical engineer named Gary Myers. As a Republican, he was not considered to have much chance. But he hacked away at Clark for supporting seniority, going on junkets, and opposing institutional reforms; and he held the incumbent to an unusually low 56% of the vote. There was a tendency to blame that result on the poor McGovern showing here, but obviously this was not the case: for other Pennsylvania Democrats had done just fine despite McGovern's dismal performances in their districts.

The real problem, and he himself would be the last to admit it, was Frank Clark. By 1974, he had given Myers, again his Republican opponent, more ammunition, and Myers was able to point out to the voters of the 25th that Clark's measure to require oil to be shipped in American bottoms would have cost them more money to benefit the maritime interests, which in turn were big contributors—indeed the main contributors—to Clark's campaign. So in this very Democratic year, in this solidly Democratic district, Democratic Congressman Frank Clark lost to Republican Gary Myers by a 54–46 margin. It was a tribute to the workings of the democratic process; all the benefits of incumbency and government-subsidized contributors were not enough to save Clark's seat.

It is too early now, probably, to say whether Myers has created a safe seat here for himself; he will probably face tough competition, unless it is from Clark, in 1976. But the fate of Clark is clearer, and sadder: in the waning hours of the 93d Congress he ran for the position of Doorkeeper of the House in the 94th and was ignominiously defeated winning only 34 votes from his 244 colleagues.

Census Data   Pop. 472,929. Central city, 0%; suburban, 50%. Median family income, $9,208; families above $15,000: 14%; families below $3,000: 8%. Median years education, 12.1.

The Voters

Median voting age 44.
Employment profile White collar, 39%. Blue collar, 48%. Service, 12%. Farm, 1%.
Ethnic groups Black, 3%. Total foreign stock, 19%. Italy, 5%; Poland, Yugoslavia, 2% each; UK, Germany, Czechoslovakia, Austria, 1% each.

Presidential vote

1972	Nixon (R)	103,715	(60%)
	McGovern (D)	67,926	(40%)
1968	Nixon (R)	73,104	(40%)
	Humphrey (D)	90,833	(50%)
	Wallace (AI)	16,987	(9%)

Rep. Gary A. Myers (R) Elected 1974; b. Aug. 16, 1937, Toronto, Ohio; home, Butler; U. of Cincinnati, B.S.M.E. 1960, U. of Pitt., M.B.A. 1964; Episcopalian.

Career   Mechanical engineer; Steel plant turn foreman.

Offices   1711 LHOB, 202-225-2565. Also 408 Beaver Valley Mall, Monaca 15061, 412-728-3500.

Committees

Public Works and Transportation (19th). Subcommittees: Economic Development; Investigations and Review; Surface Transportation.

Science and Technology (11th). Subcommittees: Domestic and International Scientific Planning and Analysis; Energy Research (Fossil Fuels); Environment and the Atmosphere.

Group Ratings: Newly Elected

Key Votes

1) Foreign Aid	FOR	6) Gov Abortn Aid	NE	11) Pub Cong Election $	NE
2) Busing	NE	7) Coed Phys Ed	AGN	12) Turkish Arms Cutoff	NE
3) ABM	NE	8) Pov Lawyer Gag	NE	13) Youth Camp Regs	AGN
4) B-1 Bomber	FOR	9) Pub Trans Sub	NE	14) Strip Mine Veto	AGN
5) Nerve Gas	NE	10) EZ Voter Regis	NE	15) Farm Bill Veto	FOR

Election Results

1974 general:	Gary A. Myers (R)	74,645	(54%)	($33,064)
	Frank M. Clark (D)	64,049	(46%)	($88,588)
1974 primary:	Gary A. Myers (R)	9,782	(31%)	
	Tim Shaffer (R)	7,557	(24%)	
	John J. Petrush (R)	5,899	(19%)	
	Three Others (R)	8,482	(27%)	

RHODE ISLAND

The state of Rhode Island and Providence Plantations—the full official name—owes its existence to a religious schism within the Massachusetts Bay Colony. Roger Williams, as most schoolchildren know, founded Providence in 1636 as a haven for dissident Calvinists fleeing the regime to the north. Williams had a profound—and for that day unusual—belief in religious and political freedom; he was the New World's first civil libertarian. Williams's colony soon attracted a motley gathering of Baptists, Antinomians, and even some Papists (Roman Catholics), along with a few American Indians. Williams, unlike many of his contemporaries and Americans to follow, was kindly disposed to the native Americans and became a scholar of their languages and customs.

Rhode Island's later history was almost as idiosyncratic. The descendants of Williams's colonists began to prosper and, as people do, grew more conservative. The "triangle trade" out of Newport—rum, sugar, and slaves—was especially lucrative. After the Revolutionary War, Rhode Island was the last of the 13 colonies to ratify the Constitution. It had declined to send delegates to the Convention for fear that any proposed Union could impose tariffs inimicable to the former colony's ocean-dependent trade. Only after the new nation threatened to sever commercial relations with Rhode Island did it agree to become the thirteenth state. As late as 1840, when most other states had granted the franchise to free white males, Rhode Island still allowed only large property holders to vote. The situation led to open revolt—the Dorr Rebellion; during the trouble, Rhode Island had two separate state governments, each claiming sovereignty.

In the state's economic history, the key event occurred in 1793, when Samuel Slater, a British emigre, built the nation's first water-powered cotton mill in Pawtucket and launched the nation's Industrial Revolution. During the nineteenth century, the textile industry in Rhode Island boomed, and the tiny state attracted immigrants eager to work the looms and toil on the cutting floor. They came from French Canada, Ireland, and especially from Italy. So by the turn of the century, this erstwhile colony of dissident Protestants had become the most heavily Roman Catholic state in the nation. Today, 64% of the citizens of Rhode Island are Catholic.

The Protestants and Catholics did not, of course, get along very well in politics. Long after they had become a minority, the Protestants, through the Republican Party, were able to maintain control of Rhode Island. The big switch came in 1928, when thousands of immigrants, especially women, who had never before voted, streamed to the polls and carried the state for Catholic Al Smith. Two years later in 1930, the Republicans were able to elect a Senator, but have never been able to elect one since. The last time any Republican has been sent to Congress from Rhode Island was in 1938. Since 1924, the state has gone Republican in presidential elections only three times, twice for Eisenhower and once for Nixon, and only once by anything like a substantial margin (1956).

The Republicans have done better in gubernatorial elections. They won in 1958, 1962, 1964, and 1966, and came close in the next three elections. But for most races the decisive battle, when there is one to be fought, is in the Democratic primary. And the outcome of that contest is almost always determined by the endorsement of the state Democratic machine. The endorsee, for one thing, gets the first line on the primary ballot, and apparently for most Rhode Island voters that is enough; since the Democrats took over in the thirties, only twice has an endorsed statewide candidate lost the primary.

The 1960 Senate race furnished one of these occasions, the winner being something of an anomaly in ethnic Rhode Island. For Claiborne deB. Pell is a blue blood WASP from Bellevue Avenue in Newport, where one finds the Vanderbilt and Auchincloss "cottages." Pell's father was a Congressman from New York for a term, a friend of Franklin D. Roosevelt, and Minister to Portugal and Hungary during the period just before and after 1939. With a background of this sort, Claiborne Pell served as a Foreign Service officer for several years. But such service hardly explains how he was able to beat former Governor (1951–59) Dennis J. Roberts and former Governor (1941–45), Senator (1947–49), and U.S. Attorney General (1949–52) J. Howard McGrath in the 1960 Democratic primary. (All of them were running for the seat first won by Theodore F. Green in 1936 when he was 69. An entire generation of Rhode Island politicians had made plans on the assumption that Green's seat would soon become available. Green, once Chairman of the Foreign Relations Committee, finally decided to retire when he reached 93.) Part of the reason for Pell's victory was the odor of scandal that attached itself to both of his rivals. But the win was also attributable to his quiet, aloof, but still vigorous style of compaigning.

That style was one reason why in 1972 Pell was challenged by Rhode Island's strongest Republican politician, former Governor (1963–69) John Chafee. During the first Nixon Administration, Chafee had served as Secretary of the Navy, a position which allowed him to return often to Rhode Island, to visit the Navy's major facilities in Newport and Quonset Point. Although he had been defeated for a fourth term for sponsoring an income tax, Chafee was still popular, and he believed that he could successfully attack some of Pell's preoccupations as esoteric (e.g., oceanography). But Chafee failed to account for the steel backbone which seems to lie beneath Pell's sometimes halting aristocratic demeanor. While Chafee was complaining about Pell's obscure interests, Pell was steering the higher education bill of 1972 through the Senate. And although Pell had gained more attention as an early dove on the Foreign Relations Committee, he gained more support, particularly from teachers, for his work on education. So although Chafee led in early polls, on election day Pell was the winner, by a 54–46 margin. It seems hardly likely that he will be so seriously challenged in the future.

That was not the only disappointment for Rhode Island Republicans that year. They had hoped that their candidate, former Attorney General Herbert de Simone, would beat the incumbent Governor, Frank Licht, who had violated one of his own promises and pushed through an income tax. But the Democrats were wise enough to get Licht to retire, and their new candidate, Warwick Mayor Philip Noel, beat De Simone by a 53–47 margin. Moreover, the Republican jubilation at carrying Rhode Island, albeit narrowly, for Richard Nixon quickly turned into a disbelieving and stony silence. For almost the first thing the new Nixon Administration did was to order massive naval base closings in Rhode Island. The state's entire Atlantic Fleet was transferred to more politically congenial locations like Norfolk, Charleston, and Mayport, Florida; the state lost 13,000 military personnel and nearly 5,000 civilian jobs, and absorbed more than half of the Navy's total cutbacks.

What made this especially embarrassing for Rhode Island Republicans is that just a few months before they had been running ads warning that precisely these dire consequences would ensue if the voters of the state were so foolish as to vote for George McGovern. So much for the credibility of the Republican Party here, and so much for its existence as a major political force in the state. The big story for 1973 and 1974 was the efforts of Governor Noel and the state government to compensate for the effects of the Navy cutbacks in a time of deepening recession; they were not wholly successful, but the voters obviously had a deep confidence in them. Noel was reelected in 1974 with a near-unanimous 78% of the vote. Noel carried every single precinct in the state. Even the last Attorney General Richard Israel, the last Republican statewide official and one popular for his role in fighting organized crime, was beaten in an upset by Democrat Julius Michaelson, who emphasized his determination to fight high utility rates.

Rhode Island's senior Senator, John Pastore, comes up for reelection in 1976. His is one of the authentic Horatio Alger stories of American politics. He grew up in a poor Italian neighborhood, and his father died young, but the future senator studied hard, went to college and law school, entered politics and was elected to the state legislature. At a time when Italian-Americans were becoming increasingly important in the state's politics, he was slated for Lieutenant Governor in 1944, and succeeded to the Governorship when McGrath resigned in 1945. Elected twice in his own right, he went on to the Senate in 1950. In his last election, in 1970, he received 68% of the vote; his opponent was John McLaughlin, who later achieved fame as the White House priest-in-residence who defended the morality of Richard Nixon in theological terms.

Pastore has now accumulated valuable seniority. As Chairman of the Commerce Committee's Communications Subcommittee, he is the most influential man on Capitol Hill on matters relating to television and other media. He was an author of the campaign media spending limit that took effect in 1972, and he has stood fast against attempts to alter the so-called fairness doctrine. Pastore also serves on the Appropriations Committee and alternates with Congressman Mel Price of Illinois as Chairman of the Joint Committee on Atomic Energy. This is a body which has maintained a close, even intimate, relationship with the body it regulates, formerly the Atomic Energy Commission, now split into two agencies, one to promote and the other to regulate nuclear energy. Over the years, Pastore was somewhat more sympathetic to the war policies and military programs of the Johnson and Nixon Administrations than was his colleague, Senator Pell; but on most major issues in the seventies, he came out on the side of the doves.

For more than 20 years, the Rhode Island congressional delegation kept the same kind of ethnic balance that one expects in a state where a party organization makes most of the political decisions. One Senator is an Italian-American, one a blue blood WASP. One Congressman, Fernand St Germain of the 1st district, is of French Canadian descent; the other, at least until

1974, always boasted an Irish name. Appropriately, the 1st is the more French Canadian of the districts; French is still spoken in the streets of Woonsocket and Central Falls, two textile mill towns in the district. The 1st also takes in the wealthier precincts of Providence, including Brown University, all of Pawtucket, and the east side of Narragansett Bay, including Newport. That old city, now hard hit by Navy cutbacks, sits on an island and votes Democratic; servants and their dependents outnumber the summertime patricians.

In the 1st, bread and butter issues are the staples of politics; the early seventies demand for textile import restrictions has been replaced, at least in intensity, by demands for action to counter the Navy cutbacks. Congressman St Germain, first elected in 1960, is less distinguished by his ideological fervor than by a close attention to district affairs. He is currently one of the higher ranking members of the Banking and Currency Committee; he uses his seniority not so much for shaping national housing policy or regulating Wall Street as for seeing that the 1st has, as it does, more federally funded senior citizen housing than any of the 434 other congressional districts. One of the more convivial members of Congress, St Germain combined an opposition to the Vietnam war with an opposition to the liberal conclusions of the presidential commission on obscenity. First elected when he was 32, and an easy winner since, St Germain could conceivably become Chairman of the full Committee sometime in the next dozen or so years.

The 2d district was the scene in 1974 of that most unusual event in Rhode Island politics, the defeat of an incumbent, organization-endorsed Democrat. The victim was Congressman Robert Tiernan, a House member since he narrowly won a special election in 1967. The district includes most of Rhode Island's faster growing suburbs, places like Cranston (pop. 73,000) and Warwick (pop. 83,000) filled with the relatively prosperous children of Italian immigrants. But the winner, in the 1974 Democratic primary, was a man who speaks very much in the accents of the working class, a housepainter and state Representative named Edward P. Beard. (One wonders if it helped or hurt him that his name, without the terminal "d", is the full name of A. A. Milne's Winnie the Pooh.) Beard campaigned as the champion of the little man in a state with more than its share of economic troubles; he boasted that he had never made more than $9,000 a year. Tiernan apparently had not been tending the home fences carefully enough; his old colleagues in the House took care of him in 1974 when Speaker Carl Albert named him to the new Federal Elections Commission.

Census Data Pop. 949,723; 0.47% of U.S. total, 39th largest; Central city, 36%; suburban, 49%. Median family income, $9,734; 17th highest; families above $15,000: 19%; families below $3,000: 9%. Median years education, 11.5.

1974 Share of Federal Tax Burden $1,205,169,000; 0.45% of U.S. total, 36th largest.

1974 Share of Federal Outlays $1,140,558,000; 0.42% of U.S. total, 40th largest. Per capita federal spending, $1200.

DOD	$291,674,000	36th (0.43%)		HEW	$478,670,000	37th (0.52%)
AEC	$592,000	33d (0.02%)		HUD	$8,735,000	28th (0.90%)
NASA	$354,000	40th (0.01%)		VA	$74,408,000	39th (0.54%)
DOT	$38,779,000	46th (0.46%)		EPA	$7,011,000	45th (0.22%)
DOC	$4,456,000	40th (0.28%)		RevS	$27,508,000	39th (0.45%)
DOI	$3,390,000	49th (0.14%)		Int.	$36,102,000	39th (0.18%)
USDA	$20,399,000	47th (0.16%)		Other	$148,480,000	

Economic Base Miscellaneous manufacturing industries, especially jewelry, silverware and plated ware; textile mill products, especially narrow fabric mills; finance, insurance and real estate; primary metal industries, especially nonferrous rolling and drawing; fabricated metal products; electrical equipment and supplies; machinery, especially metalworking machinery.

Political Line-up Governor, Philip W. Noel (D). Senators, John O. Pastore (D) and Claiborne Pell (D). Representatives, 2 D. State Senate (46 D and 4 R); State House (107 D and 17 R).

The Voters

Registration 514,334 Total. No party registration.
Median voting age 44.
Employment profile White collar, 45%. Blue collar, 42%. Service, 12%. Farm, 1%.
Ethnic groups Black, 3%. Total foreign stock, 33%. Italy, 8%, Canada, 7%, UK, 4%, Portugal, 3%.

Presidential vote

1972	Nixon (R)	220,383	(53%)
	McGovern (D)	194,645	(47%)
1968	Nixon (R)	122,359	(32%)
	Humphrey (D)	246,518	(64%)
	Wallace (AI)	15,678	(4%)

1972 Democratic Presidential Primary

McGovern	15,603	(41%)
Muskie	7,838	(21%)
Humphrey	7,701	(20%)
Wallace	5,802	(15%)
others	920	(3%)

1972 Republican Presidential Primary

Nixon	4,953	(88%)
others	658	(12%)

Sen. John O. Pastore (D) Elected 1950, seat up 1976; b. Mar. 17, 1907, Cranston; home, Cranston; Northeastern U., LL.B. 1931; Catholic.

Career R.I. House of Reps., 1935–38; Asst. Atty. Gen. of R.I., 1940–44; Lt. Gov. of R.I., 1944–45; Gov. of R.I., 1945–50.

Offices 3215, DSOB, 202-224-2921. Also 301 P.O. Annex, Providence 02903, 401-421-4583.

Committees

Appropriations (4th). Subcommittees: Defense; HUD and Independent Agencies; Public Works; State, Justice, Commerce, The Judiciary (Chairman); Transportation.

Commerce (2d). Communications (Chairman); The Consumer; Environment; Merchant Marine; Oceans and Atmosphere; Special Subcommittee to Study Textile Industry (Chairman); Special Subcommittee on Oil and Gas Production and Distribution.

Joint Committee on Atomic Energy (Chairman).

Group Ratings

	ADA	COPE	LWV	RIPON	NFU	LCV	CFA	NAB	NSI	ACA
1974	80	82	90	68	94	74	100	17	40	5
1973	79	100	90	63	94	–	82	–	–	15
1972	75	90	91	72	80	49	100	40	33	21

Key Votes

1) No-Knock	AGN	8) Gov Abortn Aid	AGN	15) Consumer Prot Agy	FOR
2) Busing	FOR	9) Cut Mil Brass	AGN	16) Forced Psych Tests	AGN
3) No Fault	FOR	10) Gov Limousine	AGN	17) Fed Campaign Subs	FOR
4) F-111	AGN	11) RR Featherbed	FOR	18) Rhod Chrome Ban	FOR
5) Death Penalty	AGN	12) Handgun License	FOR	19) Open Legis Meetings	AGN
6) Foreign Aid	AGN	13) Less Troop Abrd	FOR	20) Strikers Food Stmps	FOR
7) Filibuster	AGN	14) Resume Turk Aid	AGN	21) Gov Info Disclosure	ABS

Election Results

1970 general:	John O. Pastore (D)	230,469	(68%)
	John McLaughlin (R)	107,351	(32%)
1970 primary:	John O. Pastore (D)	54,090	(88%)
	John Quattrocchi, Jr. (D)	7,332	(12%)
1964 general:	John O. Pastore (D)	319,607	(83%)
	Ronald R. Langueux (R)	66,715	(17%)

Sen. Claiborne Pell (D) Elected 1960, seat up 1978; b. Nov. 22, 1918, New York, N.Y.; home, Newport; Princeton U., A.B. 1940, Columbia U., A.M., 1946; Episcopalian.

Career Coast Guard, WWII; U.S. Foreign Svc. and State Dept., Czechoslovakia and Italy, 1945–52; Exec. Asst. to R.I. Dem. St. Chm., 1952, 1954; Consultant, Dem. Natl. Comm., 1953–60; Dir., Internatl. Rescue Comm.; Mbr., U.S. Delegation to U.N., 1970.

Offices 325 RSOB, 202-224-4642. Also 418 Fed. Bldg., Providence 02903, 401-528-4547.

Committees

Foreign Relations (5th). Subcommittees: Arms Control, International Organizations and Security Agreements; European Affairs; Oceans and International Environment (Chairman); Western Hemisphere Affairs.

Labor and Public Welfare (3d). Subcommittees: Aging; Education (Chairman); The Handicapped; Health; Labor; Special Subcommittee on Arts and Humanities (Chairman); Special Subcommittee on National Science Foundation.

Rules and Administration (2d). Subcommittees: Library; Privileges and Elections (Chairman); Smithsonian Institution (Chairman).

Group Ratings

	ADA	COPE	LWV	RIPON	NFU	LCV	CFA	NAB	NSI	ACA
1974	100	80	90	68	94	89	100	30	10	6
1973	80	100	90	82	94	–	91	–	–	7
1972	75	88	100	77	86	72	100	38	30	16

Key Votes

1) No-Knock	AGN	8) Gov Abortn Aid	FOR	15) Consumer Prot Agy	FOR
2) Busing	FOR	9) Cut Mil Brass	FOR	16) Forced Psych Tests	FOR
3) No Fault	FOR	10) Gov Limousine	AGN	17) Fed Campaign Subs	FOR
4) F-111	AGN	11) RR Featherbed	FOR	18) Rhod Chrome Ban	FOR
5) Death Penalty	AGN	12) Handgun License	FOR	19) Open Legis Meetings	AGN
6) Foreign Aid	AGN	13) Less Troop Abrd	FOR	20) Strikers Food Stmps	FOR
7) Filibuster	AGN	14) Resume Turk Aid	AGN	21) Gov Info Disclosure	ABS

Election Results

1972 general:	Claiborne Pell (D)	221,942	(54%)	($528,347)
	John H. Chafee (R)	188,990	(46%)	($457,409)
1972 primary:	Claiborne Pell (D), unopposed			
1966 general:	Claiborne Pell (D)	219,331	(68%)	
	Harriet Briggs (R)	104,838	(32%)	

Gov. Philip W. Noel (D) Elected 1972, term expires Jan., 1977; b. June 6, 1931, Warwick; Brown U., B.A., Georgetown U., J.D.

Career Practicing atty.; Warwick City Cncl., 1960–66, Mayor, 1966–72.

Offices Executive Ofc., State House, Providence 02903, 401-277-2397.

Election Results

1974 general:	Philip W. Noel (D)	253,436	(78%)
	James W. Nugent (R)	69,224	(22%)
1974 primary:	Philip W. Noel (D), unopposed		
1972 general:	Philip W. Noel (D)	216,953	(53%)
	Herbert F. DeSimone (R)	194,315	(47%)

◆ ◆ ◆ ◆ ◆

FIRST DISTRICT

Census Data Pop. 475,441. Central city, 28%; suburban, 56%. Median family income, $9,713; families above $15,000: 19%; families below $3,000: 9%. Median years education, 11.4.

The Voters

Median voting age 43.
Employment profile White collar, 46%. Blue collar, 42%. Service, 12%. Farm, –%.
Ethnic groups Black, 3%. Total foreign stock, 35%. Canada, 9%; Portugal, Italy, 5% each; UK, 4%.

Presidential vote

1972	Nixon (R)	107,156	(52%)
	McGovern (D)	98,881	(48%)
1968	Nixon (R)	58,868	(31%)
	Humphrey (D)	126,226	(66%)
	Wallace (AI)	6,804	(4%)

Rep. Fernand J. St Germain (D) Elected 1960; b. Jan. 9, 1928, Blackstone, Mass; home, Woonsocket; Providence Col., Ph.B. 1948, Boston U., LL.B. 1955; Catholic.

Career Army, 1949–52; R.I. House of Reps., 1952–60; Practicing atty., 1956–.

Offices 2136 RHOB, 202-225-4911. Also 200 John E. Fogarty Bldg., Providence 02903, 401-528-4323.

Committees

Banking Currency and Housing (8th). Economic Stabilization; Financial Institutions Supervision, Regulation and Insurance (Chairman); General Oversight and Renegotiation; Housing and Community Development; International Trade, Investment and Monetary Policy.

Government Operations (10th). Subcommittees: Conservation, Energy and Natural Resources; Manpower and Housing.

Small Business (8th). Subcommittees: Energy and Environment; SBA Oversight and Minority Enterprise.

Group Ratings

	ADA	COPE	LWV	RIPON	NFU	LCV	CFA	NAB	NSI	ACA
1974	78	90	67	47	83	75	75	25	20	14
1973	91	100	91	64	80	78	86	–	–	8
1972	75	91	70	67	71	61	100	17	33	5

Key Votes

1) Foreign Aid	FOR	6) Gov Abortn Aid	AGN	11) Pub Cong Election $	FOR
2) Busing	AGN	7) Coed Phys Ed	FOR	12) Turkish Arms Cutoff	FOR
3) ABM	AGN	8) Pov Lawyer Gag	AGN	13) Youth Camp Regs	FOR
4) B-1 Bomber	AGN	9) Pub Trans Sub	FOR	14) Strip Mine Veto	AGN
5) Nerve Gas	AGN	10) EZ Voter Regis	FOR	15) Farm Bill Veto	FOR

Election Results

1974 general:	Fernand J. St. Germain (D)	105,288	(73%)	($59,244)
	Ernest Barone (R)	39,196	(27%)	($3,556)
1972 general:	Fernand J. St. Germain (D)	120,705	(62%)	($48,071)
	John M. Feeley (R)	67,125	(35%)	($21,371)
	Walter J. Miska (Ind.)	5,762	(3%)	(NA)
1974 primary:	Fernand J. St. Germain (D), unopposed			

◆ ◆ ◆ ◆ ◆

SECOND DISTRICT

Census Data Pop. 474,282. Central city, 44%; suburban, 42%. Median family income, $9,755; families above $15,000: 19%; families below $3,000: 9%. Median years education, 11.6.

The Voters

Median voting age 44.
Employment profile White collar, 45%. Blue collar, 42%. Service, 13%. Farm, –%.
Ethnic groups Black, 3%. Total foreign stock, 31%. Italy, 10%; Canada, 5%; UK, 3%; Portugal, 1%.

Presidential vote

1972	Nixon (R)	113,072	(54%)
	McGovern (D)	94,935	(46%)
1968	Nixon (R)	63,491	(33%)
	Humphrey (D)	120,292	(62%)
	Wallace (AI)	8,874	(5%)

Rep. Edward P. Beard (D) Elected 1974; b. Jan. 20, 1940, Providence; home, Cranston; Catholic.

Career Housepainter; R.I. Natl. Guard, 1960–66; R.I. House of Reps., 1973–75.

Offices 131 CHOB, 202-225-2735. Also 307 P.O. Annex, Providence 02903, 401-528-4861.

Committees

Education and Labor (23d). Subcommittees: Manpower, Compensation, and Health and Safety.

Veterans' Affairs (16th). Subcommittees: Hospitals; Housing.

Group Ratings: Newly Elected

Key Votes

1) Foreign Aid	FOR	6) Gov Abortn Aid	NE	11) Pub Cong Election $	NE
2) Busing	NE	7) Coed Phys Ed	FOR	12) Turkish Arms Cutoff	NE
3) ABM	NE	8) Pov Lawyer Gag	NE	13) Youth Camp Regs	ABS
4) B-1 Bomber	AGN	9) Pub Trans Sub	NE	14) Strip Mine Veto	AGN
5) Nerve Gas	NE	10) EZ Voter Regis	NE	15) Farm Bill Veto	AGN

Election Results

1974 general:	Edward P. Beard (D)	124,759	(78%)	($20,583)
	Vincent J. Rotondo (R)	34,728	(22%)	($41,113)
1974 primary:	Edward P. Beard (D)	24,045	(52%)	
	Robert O. Tiernan (D)	22,421	(48%)	

SOUTH CAROLINA

South Carolina has one of the most distinctive histories of any state, and to understand it one must go back to the very beginning. While the other Atlantic seaboard colonies were modelled on life in England, or on some religious ideal, the model which the first South Carolinians used was that of Barbados, a sugar-producing island in the West Indies. South Carolina was the only colony where blacks outnumbered whites massively in the colonial period, for the settlers here were almost all landholders who could grow their main crops—sugar, rice, indigo—only with the labor of vast numbers of slaves. So South Carolina produced a planter elite whose most memorable legacy were men like the Pinckneys and John C. Calhoun, and whose gravest fears were that their slaves would revolt, as they did in the Denmark Vesey uprising of 1822. It was South Carolina which was the proximate cause of the Civil War. This was the first state to secede, in 1860, even before Lincoln was inaugurated; it was the first state to engage in hostilities, when Charleston hotheads opened fire on the Union-held Fort Sumter in Charleston harbor in 1861.

So after the Civil War, it enraged the state's white minority to see blacks take political power. For a time during the 1870s, blacks controlled the South Carolina legislature and the state's congressional delegation. Such "outrages" of Reconstruction were soon ended, and the blacks—and most poor whites—were shorn of the franchise and all political rights. As the nineteenth century proceeded, the once booming port of Charleston settled into economic stagnation, as did the rest of the state. For most of the twentieth century, South Carolina has been among the lowest ranking states in per capita income, education levels, and health services. It has also had one of the lowest levels of electoral participation: as late as 1948, only 142,000 South Carolinians voted in the presidential election. Politics was still a matter that concerned only a small minority of the people of South Carolina.

Like the other Southern states, South Carolina has long since ceased to have a black majority, as blacks have migrated North and new whites have moved into the state. South Carolina has also long since ceased to be the nation's most Democratic state, which it was as recently as the presidential election of 1944. Since then, it has voted for the regular Democratic nominee only three times, and twice (1952 and 1960) by margins of less than 10,000. In 1964, Barry Goldwater carried the state easily, the first Republican to do so since Reconstruction. South Carolina again went Republican in 1968, but only after a massive shift in voting habits. The Voting Rights Act of 1965 enfranchised thousands of blacks, who voted almost to a person for Hubert Humphrey. The black votes, plus a few white ones (less than 10%) gave the Democrat 30% of the ballots statewide. George Wallace did significantly worse here than in the other states of the Deep South, finishing with 32% of the votes. Most of these came from whites who had carried the state for Kennedy in 1960—Democrats turned Dixiecrats. Richard Nixon captured the state's electoral votes with 38%—aside from Tennessee, his lowest winning percentage in any state.

The 1968 Nixon victory in South Carolina, as well as those in several other states, has been properly credited to one man: Strom Thurmond, who has remained a constant amidst the moiling changes in recent South Carolina politics. From 1947 to 1951, Thurmond served as Governor of the state, and in 1948 received 39 electoral votes for President on the States' Rights Democratic ticket. He was elected to the Senate in 1954 in a stunning victory as a write-in candidate. Then, pursuant to a 1954 campaign promise, Thurmond resigned and was returned to office in 1956. In 1964, Thurmond became a Republican out of enthusiasm for Barry Goldwater and a distaste for Lyndon Johnson and his policies. And in 1968, he lobbied effectively among Southern Republican convention delegations for Richard Nixon, preventing any Reagan breakthrough and getting Nixon his majority on the first ballot.

After the convention, Thurmond took to the stump in the South. He was persuasive because white Southerners knew that for 20 years Strom had stood for what they wanted—segregation and no civil rights nonsense. By 1968, to be sure, he professed to have modified his views, given the legislation that had already passed. But Southerners, black and white, believed that Thurmond would stand as hard as he could against any changes in what is called the Southern way of life. Thurmond is a man without guile, his beliefs are as sincere as his Southern accent is thick.

But Thurmond was not able to bask in glory too long. Back home, he stumped hard but unsuccessfully for Republican gubernatorial candidate Albert Watson in 1970. Watson did make an impression: before a crowd in the town of Lamar he urged people to stand up against a desegregation order; a few days later, a Lamar mob attacked and overturned three schoolbuses containing black childern. Watson lost that race to moderate Democrat John West, and in the months that followed there were complaints that Thurmond had not forced the Nixon Administration to deliver on some of his implied promises—especially halting school desegregation orders and getting firm import quotas on textiles (the state's biggest industry). Thurmond recovered gamely. He helped get some import quotas, made stern attacks on Nixon HEW policies, and, interestingly enough, hired black staff members and worked to provide solid constituency services—and federal aid dollars—for blacks. Even more important, the elderly Thurmond married a young beauty queen and for the first time became a father.

So by the time 1972 came around Thurmond was as strong as ever. Formidable Democrats—Governor West, former Governor Robert McNair—declined to run against him, and he won with 63% of the vote, just slightly more than he had gotten in 1966. He continues to serve on the Armed Services and Judiciary Committees, where he is a strong voice against, respectively, peaceniks and criminals. Will he run again in 1978, when he will be 76? No one is sure, but it is worth noting that his wife, Nancy, has proved to be popular with South Carolina voters, and is now beyond the constitutional age of 30. Other possible candidates include Republican Governor James Edwards, whose term expires then, and Charles "Pug" Ravenel, the young Democrat who won his party's gubernatorial primary in 1974—on whom more below.

South Carolina's junior Senator is Ernest F. Hollings, another former Governor with a rather different sort of career. Hollings won the Governorship as a moderate in 1958, and eight years later beat former Governor Donald Russell in the 1966 primary for the seat vacated by the death of Olin Johnston. That year was perhaps the crest of Republican sentiment here, although no one knew that at the time, and Hollings got only 51% of the vote against Marshall Parker. He has improved his showing substantially since: to 62% in 1968 and 71% in 1974, when he did not have significant opposition.

During his first years in the Senate, Hollings seemed to be gravitating to the right, to a sort of hawkish conservatism. Even now, his record is by no means liberal on all issues, but he has taken some dramatic stands on issues. His first big break from the past was on hunger. After visiting some desperately poor communities in the coastal counties of South Carolina, he was apparently genuinely shocked at what he saw: people who were scarcely part of the cash economy, suffering from severe malnutrition or even starvation. As a proper South Carolina booster, he had never really believed such things happened any more; but he dramatically announced his change of mind on the floor of the Senate and became one of the leading backers of legislation to end hunger in America.

In the 94th Congress, Hollings took the lead on another issue: the oil depletion allowance. The House, revolting against its leadership, had voted to get rid of it altogether; but in the Senate, no one wanted to stand up and advance such a position, which seemed likely to lose and surely to delay the tax cut bill. But Hollings did, and scored a singular success: the allowance was abolished for all but small producers. Overall, Hollings has become respected as a Senator of considerable legislative ability, and one who now clearly enjoys a safe seat; he has even been mentioned, from time to time, as a possible President or Vice President.

How did the Republicans come to win the Governorship in 1974? The answer lies not in their own campaigning, or in their candidate, James Edwards, a Charleston orthodontist who remained unknown virtually to the moment he won; it was all simply a result of what happened among the Democrats. Their race had been expected to be a contest between Lieutenant Governor Earl Morris and 3d district Congressman William Jennings Bryan Dorn, But a third candidate entered the field, 36-year-old Charles "Pug" Ravenel, a poor boy from Charleston who had been star quarterback of the Harvard football team, a businessman in New York who had returned to his native state. Ravenel had never run for office before, but he was able to raise enough money to make himself known around the state. The reaction was extremely favorable—especially in a year when voters were blase about most political candidates. Ravenel seemed to be putting together the classic, but seldom achieved, coalition of poor whites and blacks, plus young people. Turnout was extraordinarily high as he led his two major opponents in the first primary and then beat Dorn—visually the personification of the old politics—in the runoff. Ravenel promised to take South Carolina politics out of the hands of the people who had traditionally run things, and he was headed for a big victory in November.

Then disaster struck. A lawsuit challenged Ravenel's qualification to run under the state's five year residency requirement; and although the candidate had long since gotten a favorable court ruling, the state Supreme Court ruled against him. South Carolina legislators, whom Ravenel's campaign implicitly attacked, were unwilling to pass a constitutional amendment which would make him eligible; and so the Democrats had to choose another candidate. Not surprisingly, they picked the 58-year-old Dorn. From all his years in Washington, Dorn had a somewhat progressive record, but his old style appearance and oratory turned off many Ravenel voters. After some hesitation Ravenel did endorse him, but in a backhanded way; and given Ravenel's own campaign, he could not credibly have become a Dorn enthusiast anyway. In any case, this hubbub obviously helped the Republicans, and Edwards won by a 52–48 margin. His victory is anachronistic, like something out of the mid-sixties; Republicans ran strong campaigns here in 1966 and 1970 but, except for Thurmond and unless Edwards becomes surprisingly popular, they are not likely to do so again soon.

Census Data   Pop. 2,590,516; 1.28% of U.S. total, 26th largest; Central city, 9%; suburban, 30%. Median family income, $7,620; 42nd highest; families above $15,000: 11%; families below $3,000: 16%. Median years education, 10.5.

1974 Share of Federal Tax Burden $2,544,245,000; 0.95% of U.S. total, 30th largest.

1974 Share of Federal Outlays $3,011,082,000; 1.12% of U.S. total, 28th largest.   Per capita federal spending, $1162.

DOD	$1,005,487,000	24th (1.47%)	HEW	$918,517,000	32d (0.99%)
AEC	$146,168,000	8th (4.80%)	HUD	$10,308,000	26th (1.06%)
NASA	$297,000	41st (0.01%)	VA	$172,588,000	29th (1.26%)
DOT	$81,378,000	35th (0.96%)	EPA	$19,225,000	28th (0.61%)
DOC	$7,929,000	28th (0.49%)	RevS	$83,117,000	26th (1.37%)
DOI	$8,331,000	42d (0.34%)	Int.	$57,820,000	34th (0.28%)
USDA	$227,860,000	23d (1.83%)	Other	$272,057,000	

Economic Base   Textile mill products, especially cotton weaving mills; apparel and other textile products, especially women's and misses' outerwear; agriculture, notably tobacco, soybeans, cattle and cotton lint; finance, insurance and real estate; chemicals and allied products, especially plastics materials and synthetics; machinery, especially special industry machinery; food and kindred products.

Political Line-up   Governor, James B. Edwards (R). Senators, Strom Thurmond (R) and Ernest F. Hollings (D). Representatives, 6 (5 D and 1 R). State Senate (43 D, 2 R, and 1 vac.); State House (107 D and 17 R).

The Voters

   Registration   1,001,150 Total. No party Registration.
   Median voting age   40.
   Employment profile   White collar, 37%. Blue collar, 47%. Service, 12%. Farm, 4%.
   Ethnic groups   Black, 30%. Total foreign stock, 2%.

Presidential vote

1972	Nixon (R)	....	477,044	(72%)
	McGovern (D)	....	186,824	(28%)

1968	Nixon (R)	254,062	(38%)
	Humphrey (D)	197,486	(30%)
	Wallace (AI)	215,430	(32%)

Sen. Strom Thurmond (R) Elected 1956 as Democrat, changed party affiliation to Repub. Sept. 16, 1964, seat up 1978; b. Dec. 5, 1903, Edgefield; home, Aiken; Clemson Col., B.S. 1923, studied law at night; Baptist.

Career Teacher and coach, 1923–29; Edgefield Co. Supt. of Educ., 1929–33; Practicing atty., 1930–38, 1951–55; S.C. Senate, 1933–38; Circuit Judge, 1938–42; Army, WWII; Gov. of S.C., 1947–51; States Rights candidate for President of U.S., 1948; U.S. Senate, 1954–1956.

Offices 4241 DSOB, 202-224-5972. Also 1310 Lady St., Columbia 29201, 803-765-5496, and P.O. Drawer O, Charleston 19402, 803-772-3196.

Committees

Armed Services (Ranking Member). Subcommittees: Intelligence; Military Construction Authorization; Preparedness Investigating; Tactical Air Power.

The Judiciary (4th). Subcommittees: Administrative Practice and Procedure; Antitrust and Monopoly; Constitutional Amendments; Constitutional Rights; Criminal Laws and Procedures; FBI Oversight; Immigration and Naturalization; Internal Security.

Veterans' Affairs (2d). Subcommittees: Compensation and Pension; Health and Hospitals.

Group Ratings

	ADA	COPE	LWV	RIPON	NFU	LCV	CFA	NAB	NSI	ACA
1974	0	20	40	55	18	10	11	75	100	100
1973	0	18	10	38	35	–	0	–	–	89
1972	0	10	10	25	30	7	0	91	100	95

Key Votes

1) No-Knock	FOR	8) Gov Abortn Aid	AGN	15) Consumer Prot Agy	AGN
2) Busing	AGN	9) Cut Mil Brass	AGN	16) Forced Psych Tests	AGN
3) No Fault	AGN	10) Gov Limousine	FOR	17) Fed Campaign Subs	AGN
4) F-111	FOR	11) RR Featherbed	AGN	18) Rhod Chrome Ban	AGN
5) Death Penalty	FOR	12) Handgun License	AGN	19) Open Legis Meetings	AGN
6) Foreign Aid	FOR	13) Less Troop Abrd	AGN	20) Strikers Food Stmps	AGN
7) Filibuster	FOR	14) Resume Turk Aid	FOR	21) Gov Info Disclosure	ABS

Election Results

1972 general:	Strom Thurmond (R)	415,806	(63%)	($666,329)
	Eugene N. Zeigler (D)	241,056	(37%)	($167,755)
1972 primary:	Strom Thurmond, nominated at convention			
1966 general:	Strom Thurmond (R)	271,297	(62%)	
	Bradley Morrah, Jr. (D)	164,955	(38%)	

Sen. Ernest F. Hollings (D) Elected 1966, seat up 1980; b. Jan. 1, 1922, Charleston; home, Charleston; The Citadel, B.A. 1942, U. of So. Carolina, LL.B. 1947; Lutheran.

Career Practicing atty., 1947–58, 1963–66; S.C. House of Reps., 1949–55, Spkr. Pro Tem., 1951–55; Lt. Gov. of S.C., 1955–59; Gov. of S.C. 1959–63.

Offices 437 RSOB, 202-224-6121. Also 306 Fed. Bldg., Columbia 29201, 803-765-5731, and 103 Fed. Bldg., Spartanburg 29301, 803-585-3702.

Committees

Appropriations (11th). Subcommittees: Interior; Labor and HEW; Legislative (Chairman); Public Works; State, Justice, Commerce, The Judiciary.

Budget (5th).

Commerce (8th). Subcommittees: Aviation; Communications; Merchant Marine; Oceans and Atmosphere (Chairman); Surface Transportation; Special Subcommittee to Study Textile Industry; Special Subcommittee on Oil and Gas Production and Distribution (Vice Chairman).

Post Office and Civil Service (4th). Subcommittees: Compensation and Employment Benefits; Postal Operations (Chairman).

Group Ratings

	ADA	COPE	LWV	RIPON	NFU	LCV	CFA	NAB	NSI	ACA
1974	33	50	67	33	59	39	66	42	78	60
1973	50	60	56	44	88	–	50	–	–	44
1972	25	40	45	39	89	42	90	30	67	40

Key Votes

1) No-Knock	FOR	8) Gov Abortn Aid	FOR	15) Consumer Prot Agy	FOR
2) Busing	AGN	9) Cut Mil Brass	FOR	16) Forced Psych Tests	ABS
3) No Fault	AGN	10) Gov Limousine	AGN	17) Fed Campaign Subs	AGN
4) F-111	ABS	11) RR Featherbed	AGN	18) Rhod Chrome Ban	ABS
5) Death Penalty	ABS	12) Handgun License	ABS	19) Open Legis Meetings	FOR
6) Foreign Aid	AGN	13) Less Troop Abrd	ABS	20) Strikers Food Stmps	AGN
7) Filibuster	FOR	14) Resume Turk Aid	AGN	21) Gov Info Disclosure	ABS

Election Results

1974 general:	Ernest F. Hollings (D)	356,126 (71%)	($225,678)
	Gwen Bush (R)	146,645 (29%)	($6,754)
1974 primary:	Ernest F. Hollings (D), unopposed		
1968 general:	Ernest F. Hollings (D)	404,060 (62%)	
	Marshall Parker (R)	248,780 (38%)	

Gov. James B. Edwards (R) Elected 1974, term expires Jan. 1979; b. June 24, 1927, Hawthorne, Fla.; Col. of Charleston, B.S. 1950, U. of Louisville, D.M.D. 1955, U. of Penn., post-grad. medical school.

Career Navy, WWII and Korea; Deck Officer, Alcoa Steamship Co., 1950–51; Dentist, Internship and Residency, Henry Ford Hosp., Detroit, Mich., 1957–60; Repub. nominee for U.S. House of Reps., 1971; S.C. Senate, 1972–75.

Offices P.O. Box 11450, Columbia 29211, 803-758-3261.

Election Results

1974 general:	James B. Edwards (R)	266,109	(52%)
	William Jennings Bryan Dorn (D)	248,938	(48%)
1974 primary:	James B. Edwards (R), unopposed		

◆ ◆ ◆ ◆ ◆

FIRST DISTRICT

In the spring, the pastel row houses of Charleston are wreathed by the flowers of blossoming trees. There are few, if any, more beautiful urban scenes in America. Charleston, founded in 1670 and blessed with one of the finest harbors on the Atlantic, was one of the South's leading cities up to the time of the Civil War. Across its docks went cargoes of rice, indigo, and cotton—all crops cultivated by black slaves and designed to enrich the white planters amd merchants, who dominated the state's economy and political life. In the years following the Civil War, Charleston became an economic backwater. Today, the old part of the city, still beautifully preserved, houses fewer people than it did in 1860.

But in the mid-twentieth century, Charleston discovered a benefactor who restored some of its old majesty and much of its old power. His name was L. Mendel Rivers, Congressman from the 1st district of South Carolina for 30 years. He was also Chairman of the House Armed Services Committee from 1965 until his death in December 1970. Rivers was as proud of the Defense Department money he funneled into the Charleston area as he was of his super-patriotism (though he himself never served in the military). It was largely his doing that 35% of the payrolls in the 1st district come either from military installations or defense industries. The 1st district alone, which includes Charleston and several coastal, heavily black and rural counties, contains no less than 11 major naval installations.

With his long flowing white locks and his thick accent, Rivers looked and talked the part of a Southern Congressman. He was bellicose, self-righteous, and many said, too often drunk. According to all reports, however, he quit drinking completely during his last few years. Rivers, of course, compiled an unflinching pro-Pentagon, conservative record in the House. But the Congressman sometimes supported bread-and-butter economic legislation; he had begun life not as a Charleston aristocrat, but as a poor country boy. Invincible at the polls, Rivers won his last election in 1970 with no opposition in either the primary or general election.

On paper, the succession to Rivers looks pretty straightforward: he was succeeded by his godson, Mendel J. Davis, who has held the seat ever since. But it was not as simple as that, and the story tells us something about changes in recent South Carolina politics. In the 1971 special election Davis was faced with a Republican opponent, James Edwards—later to become Governor in 1974—who enlisted the aid of Vice President Agnew, Senator Buckley, and Governor Reagan; and there was an Independent black candidate as well. Davis won by only a 49–41 margin then, and in 1972 Republican J. Sidi Limehouse held him to just 54% of the vote.

Then things seemed to change, sharply. In 1973 Davis inherited his old mentor's seat, if not his seniority on the Armed Services Committee. Also in the 93d Congress, his liberal voting record on economic issues began winning him some friends who might have been considered unlikely a few years ago. By 1974, District of Columbia Delegate Walter Fauntroy was down in Charleston, campaigning for Davis. He had no primary opposition that year, and in the general election he won a whopping 74% of the vote—even as Republican Edwards was carrying the district 61–39 in the Governor's race. In 1975, Davis was one of the House Internal Security Committee Democrats persuaded to resign from that body—which resulted in its abolition. As a reward, he received a seat on Wayne Hays' House Administration Committee and, it seems, a safe seat in the House itself at last.

Census Data Pop. 442,646. Central city, 15%; suburban, 54%. Median family income, $7,355; families above $15,000: 12%; families below $3,000: 18%. Median years education, 11.4.

The Voters

Median voting age 36.
Employment profile White collar, 34%. Blue collar, 39%. Service, 15%. Farm, 2%.
Ethnic groups Black, 34%. Total foreign stock, 4%.

Presidential vote

1972	Nixon (R)	73,480	(69%)
	McGovern (D)	33,488	(31%)
1968	Nixon (R)	39,768	(38%)
	Humphrey (D)	37,187	(35%)
	Wallace (AI)	28,303	(27%)

Rep. Mendel J. Davis (D) Elected Apr. 27, 1971; b. Oct. 23, 1942, North Charleston; home, North Charleston; Col. of Charleston, B.S. 1966, U. of So. Carolina, J.D. 1970; Methodist.

Career Practicing atty., 1970–71.

Offices 230 CHOB, 202-225-3176. Also 640 Fed. Bldg., 334 Meeting St., Charleston 29403, 803-577-4171.

Committees

Armed Services (20th). Subcommittees: Military Installations and Facilities; Seapower and Strategic and Critical Materials.

House Administration (14th). Subcommittees: Accounts; Elections; Printing; Ad Hoc Restaurant.

Group Ratings

	ADA	COPE	LWV	RIPON	NFU	LCV	CFA	NAB	NSI	ACA
1974	30	55	18	38	64	35	46	27	100	50
1973	33	80	40	27	94	12	71	–	–	50
1972	13	75	38	50	100	1	0	30	100	53

Key Votes

1) Foreign Aid	AGN	6) Gov Abortn Aid	FOR	11) Pub Cong Election $	AGN
2) Busing	AGN	7) Coed Phys Ed	AGN	12) Turkish Arms Cutoff	FOR
3) ABM	FOR	8) Pov Lawyer Gag	ABS	13) Youth Camp Regs	FOR
4) B-1 Bomber	FOR	9) Pub Trans Sub	FOR	14) Strip Mine Veto	FOR
5) Nerve Gas	FOR	10) EZ Voter Regis	FOR	15) Farm Bill Veto	AGN

Election Results

1974 general:	Mendel J. Davis (D)	63,111	(74%)	($40,729)
	George B. Rast (R)	22,450	(26%)	($0)
1974 primary:	Mendel J. Davis (D), unopposed			
1972 general:	Mendel J. Davis (D)	61,625	(54%)	($84,377)
	J. Sidi Limehouse (R)	51,469	(46%)	($100,902)

◆ ◆ ◆ ◆ ◆

SECOND DISTRICT

Between the coastal swamps and the industrialized Piedmont of South Carolina, square in the middle of the state, lies the capital, Columbia. This is South Carolina's largest city (pop. 113,000) and its fastest growing. Like so many comparable cities in the South, during the sixties and early seventies Columbia was steadily trending more Republican. Some observers attributed this shift to an influx of Northerners, especially business executives; but that is surely wrong, for there are fewer people from out of state here than in just about any place in the nation. The Republican trend was something indigenous, the result of upwardly mobile people from the smaller towns and rural areas of the state moving here to take white collar jobs in state government, insurance, and banking. Uprooted from their traditionally Democratic rural environment, and thrust up several notches in social class, these migrants have found the state's Republicans younger, more modern, and hence more congenial than old style South Carolina Democrats. So Columbia and its all white suburbs, particularly those in Lexington County, had by the mid-seventies become a bastion of South Carolina Republicanism.

Columbia, with its suburbs in Richland and Lexington Counties, casts between 70% and 75% of the votes in the state's 2d congressional district. The remainder come from an older part of South Carolina: the black majority counties closer to the coast. The largest town here is Orangeburg (pop. 13,000), where white highway patrolmen massacred several black students at South Carolina State College in 1968. These lower counties usually go Democratic, but in most elections are heavily outvoted by Columbia and environs.

The election of 1974 saw a pronounced shift in the voting habits here, a noticeable shift away from the Republicans the district had preferred for more than a decade. From 1963 to 1971, the 2d district had been represented by Albert Watson, a flamboyant conservative who turned Republican when the Democratic caucus deprived him of his seniority for backing Barry Goldwater in 1964. Watson lost his seat when he ran for Governor in 1970—an ill-fated bid that saw him lose to moderate Democrat John West. He was succeeded by another Republican, Floyd Spence, who as a Democrat had lost to Watson in the 1962 primary. A genial man of the good old boy type, Spence won a seat on the Armed Services Committee—a good spot to tend to the needs of Columbia's Fort Jackson—and in 1972 won reelection unopposed in either primary or general election. He appeared to have a very safe seat indeed.

But 1974, at least through the October disqualification of Charles Ravenel, was not a good year for South Carolina Republicans. The top of the Democratic ticket—Ravenel and Hollings—were the sort of modern, well-spoken candidates who could win the support of many of Columbia's upwardly mobile whites and at the same time command near unanimous allegiance from the district's blacks. Once Ravenel was off the ballot, Republican gubernatorial candidate James Edwards did carry the 2d, but with only 55% of the vote; Hollings, at the same time, had 66% here. And even more surprisingly, the Democratic nominee made a real race of it, winning 43% of the vote—surprisingly because this candidate, Matthew Perry, was black. Perry carried the part of the district outside the Columbia metropolitan area and won enough white votes to carry the city of Columbia itself. He lost because Spence won an overwhelming percentage of the votes in the Columbia suburbs, 74% in Lexington County. That means that Spence can probably count on winning in the future—but he can also count on having to work for his victories. And aside from the question of who wins or loses, it also shows that a significant number of white voters in South Carolina—with the second highest black percentage of any state and a tradition of rigid segregation—are now willing to vote for someone who is black.

Census Data Pop. 446,267. Central city, 25%; suburban, 47%. Median family income, $7,900; families above $15,000: 14%; families below $3,000: 15%. Median years education, 11.4.

The Voters

Median voting age 37.
Employment profile White collar, 47%. Blue collar, 36%. Service, 14%. Farm, 3%.
Ethnic groups Black, 34%. Total foreign stock, 3%.

Presidential vote

1972	Nixon (R)	85,637	(69%)
	McGovern (D)	37,756	(31%)
1968	Nixon (R)	48,621	(42%)
	Humphrey (D)	37,542	(33%)
	Wallace (AI)	28,848	(25%)

Rep. Floyd Spence (R) Elected 1970; b. Apr. 9, 1928, Columbia; home, Lexington; U. of So. Carolina, B.A. 1952, LL.B. 1956; Lutheran.

Career Navy, Korea; Practicing atty.; S.C. House of Reps., 1956–62; S.C. Senate, 1966–70, Minor. Ldr.

Offices 120 CHOB, 202-225-2452. Also Rm. 104, 2001 Assembly St., Columbia 29201, 803-765-5871.

Committees

Armed Services (4th). Subcommittees: Research and Development; Seapower and Strategic and Critical Materials.

Standards of Official Conduct (Ranking Member).

Group Ratings

	ADA	COPE	LWV	RIPON	NFU	LCV	CFA	NAB	NSI	ACA
1974	9	0	0	31	36	31	0	75	100	93
1973	0	18	25	27	45	5	13	–	–	85
1972	0	11	25	38	40	7	50	90	100	95

Key Votes

1) Foreign Aid	AGN	6) Gov Abortn Aid	AGN	11) Pub Cong Election $	AGN
2) Busing	AGN	7) Coed Phys Ed	AGN	12) Turkish Arms Cutoff	FOR
3) ABM	FOR	8) Pov Lawyer Gag	FOR	13) Youth Camp Regs	AGN
4) B-1 Bomber	FOR	9) Pub Trans Sub	AGN	14) Strip Mine Veto	FOR
5) Nerve Gas	FOR	10) EZ Voter Regis	AGN	15) Farm Bill Veto	AGN

Election Results

1974 general:	Floyd D. Spence (R)	58,936	(57%)	($167,188)
	Matthew J. Perry (D)	45,205	(43%)	($92,813)
1974 primary	Floyd D. Spence (R), unopposed			
1972 general:	Floyd D. Spence (R), unopposed			($5,936)

◆ ◆ ◆ ◆ ◆

THIRD DISTRICT

As one moves inland from the South Carolina coast, one sees fewer and fewer black people. It is a matter of history and agricultural economics. The land along the coast is ideal for growing crops like rice and cotton, which require much labor; so the early planters kept thousands of slaves. Inland, the terrain is hilly, the rainfall less plentiful, and the soil less fertile; the tradition here is of one-family farms, few of which could have afforded to support slaves. And so, while many of the still rural counties along the coast are near-majority-black, the citizenry of the Piedmont country of the 3d congressional district is 77% white.

The 3d is an upcountry district, lying mostly along the Savannah River, the boundary with Georgia. The southern part of the district is Strom Thurmond territory: he grew up in Edgefield and maintains his residence in Aiken, a prosperous atomic energy city that lies halfway between Columbia and Augusta, Georgia. Like the Senator, Aiken and Edgefield moved into the Republican Party in the sixties, while the counties farther upriver remained traditionally Southern Democratic. George Wallace ran especially well here in 1968; Anderson, a heavily white textile town and the most populous city in the district (pop. 27,000), was the largest South Carolina city Wallace carried in 1968.

For a quarter of a century, the 3d district was represented in the House by William Jennings Bryan Dorn. He looked the part of a traditional Southern politician, with his white linen suits draped over his bit overweight person and his deep drawl; and he had the curriculum vitae of many a Southern pol—state legislator at 23, Congressman at 30, eventually Chairman of the House Veterans Affairs Committee. But Dorn was less successful at winning statewide office. In 1948, at 32, he was apparently too young to win the Democratic Senate nomination; in 1974, at 58, he lost the Democratic gubernatorial nomination to 36-year-old Charles Ravenel. Ravenel was eventually disqualified, and Dorn got the place he had lost in the runoff, but having gotten it that way, he ended up losing. There is a touch of tragedy here: Dorn was depicted as a sort of Senator Claghorn, yet he had a somewhat progressive record on many issues, and was by no means hostile to all new ideas.

Dorn had always carried the 3d easily; but it looked as if the seat could go Republican when he ran for Governor in 1974. Certainly it would have in, say, 1966, when Republican Marshall Parker nearly beat Senator Ernest Hollings and in the process won 52% of the vote in the 3d. In 1974, Parker was the congressional nominee here, but this time he not only lost to the Democrat, 38-year-old State Representative Butler Derrick, but lost big, by a 62–38 margin. It was evidence, if any more is needed, that the statewide Republican win in South Carolina in 1974 was a fluke, and that the state is instead trending strongly Democratic. Strom Thurmond's native Edgefield County, for example, which had given Parker 58% of its vote against Hollings in 1966, in 1974 voted only 13% for the Republican—which may not be unrelated to the fact that turnout rose 24%

between the two elections. Derrick, a moderate who managed to win a seat on the Budget Committee as well as on the Banking and Currency Committee, can be expected to win easily in future years.

Census Data Pop. 434,427. Central city, 0%; suburban, 35%. Median family income, $8,002; families above $15,000: 10%; families below $3,000: 13%. Median years education, 10.1.

The Voters

Median voting age 42.
Employment profile White collar, 32%. Blue collar, 56%. Service, 10%. Farm, 2%.
Ethnic groups Black, 23%. Total foreign stock, 1%.

Presidential vote

1972	Nixon (R)	84,401	(77%)
	McGovern (D)	24,723	(23%)
1968	Nixon (R)	41,678	(36%)
	Humphrey (D)	26,585	(23%)
	Wallace (AI)	47,223	(41%)

Rep. Butler Derrick (D) Elected 1974; b. Sept. 30, 1936, Johnston; home, Edgefield; U. of So. Carolina, B.A. 1958, U. of Ga., LL.B. 1965; Episcopalian.

Career Practicing atty., 1965–74; S.C. House of Reps., 1969–75.

Offices 415 CHOB, 202-225-5301. Also 315 S. McDuffie St., Anderson 29621, 803-224-7401.

Committees

Banking, Currency and Housing (27th). Subcommittees: Financial Institutions Supervision, Regulation and Insurance; General Oversight and Renegotiation; International Trade, Investment and Monetary Policy.

Budget (17th).

Group Ratings: Newly Elected

Key Votes

1) Foreign Aid	AGN	6) Gov Abortn Aid	NE	11) Pub Cong Election $	NE
2) Busing	NE	7) Coed Phys Ed	FOR	12) Turkish Arms Cutoff	NE
3) ABM	NE	8) Pov Lawyer Gag	NE	13) Youth Camp Regs	FOR
4) B-1 Bomber	FOR	9) Pub Trans Sub	NE	14) Strip Mine Veto	FOR
5) Nerve Gas	NE	10) EZ Voter Regis	NE	15) Farm Bill Veto	AGN

Election Results

1974 general	Butler Derrick (D)	55,120	(62%)	($176,022)
	Marshall Parker (R)	34,046	(38%)	($105,897)
1974 primary:	Butler Derrick (D)	36,501	(66%)	
	Jack F. McIntosh (D)	13,136	(23%)	
	George M. Jones (D)	6,138	(11%)	

◆ ◆ ◆ ◆ ◆

FOURTH DISTRICT

The major textile producing area in the United States is a strip of land lying along Interstate 85 in North and South Carolina. Two of the biggest textile centers here are Greenville and Spartanburg, South Carolina—the two cities, along with the counties that surround them, which make up the state's 4th congressional district. It will probably come as a surprise to many readers that this is one of the most industrialized, and most blue collar, parts of the nation; and it is surprising even for tourists who drive through the South Carolina Piedmont on their way south. For the mills are not concentrated in a few big factories, like giant steel plants, in the inner parts of the cities; they are all over, in small towns and suburbs, at interchanges on the Interstate as well as in Greenville and Spartanburg themselves. Few blacks reside here—only 18% districtwide, the lowest percentage in South Carolina. And there are even fewer union members: South Carolina has just about the least unionized work force of any state in the nation, and a major reason is the intransigent opposition of the mill owners to unionization. Wages are low, working conditions not especially good; but the people who run things here like it very much as it is.

Politically, Greenville and Spartanburg have different traditions. Greenville is the state's premier Republican city; there are lots of textile management types, and also a local establishment of considerable distinction, including federal Judge and former Supreme Court nominee Clement Haynsworth and former Governor (1963–66) and Senator (1966) Donald Russell, himself also now a federal judge. Spartanburg is a rougher, more blue collar town, traditionally Democratic. Its most famous citizen was the late Governor (1935–39, 1943–45) and Senator (1945–66) Olin Johnston, who was something of an oldtime Southern populist.

But the dominant fact of electoral politics here is that so few people vote. The turnout in 1972, for example, was lower in the 4th district than in just about any other in the nation (the exceptions: a couple of districts in the New York City slums). One can be sure that the well-off people here, the Deering-Milliken executives and bankers and insurance agents, vote; the people who do not obviously are the low wage textile workers. Many of them are from the country, working only temporarily (or so they hope); they may live in trailers or flimsy apartments, but they have not set down the roots that seem to be necessary for electoral participation. If there is a proletariat in the Marxian sense in the United States, it is here, and it is one which is largely excluded, even if self-excluded, from the political process.

No one can say how these non-voters would vote if they were to do so, but most likely they would be at least a little less Republican than those who do vote in the 4th district. In election after election this has been the most Republican district in the state, culminating in the 80% of the vote cast for Richard Nixon in 1972. The textile workers who do vote, it seems, have been less motivated by Democratic class consciousness (which would not make much sense in light of South Carolina's history anyway) than by a Middle American dislike of blacks and white liberals. But even here there was a noticeable shift toward the Democrats in 1974, accompanied by an increased turnout.

That did not make much difference, one way or the other, for the 4th district's Democratic Congressman, James Mann, who has never had much trouble winning elections anyway. Mann is very much a member of the Greenville establishment; a onetime state legislator and local prosecutor who succeeded Robert Ashmore in the seat in 1968 when Ashmore became a federal judge. On economic issues, Mann is a solid conservative; he has scored as low as zero on organized labor's rating. But he is known less for these views which reflect so accurately those in comfortable living rooms and country clubs near Greenville than for some of his views which probably didn't—and perhaps still do not. For Mann was a member of the House Judiciary Committee that voted to impeach Richard Nixon. And speaking in his slow, deliberate soft accents he delivered some of the most powerful speeches against the President. Mann had become convinced that Nixon had violated the Constitution, and he believed that he must —no matter whether 80% of his constituents had voted for Nixon—be "a watchman in the night."

Of all the pro-impeachment members of the Committee, Mann had the most reason to fear adverse constituency reaction, and apparently there was some. He won 66% of the vote in 1972, and only 62% in 1974—despite better showings by Democrats in most other South Carolina districts. He can probably be reelected as long as he wants to run, but he is a person who has tired of other jobs and may just decide not to go for it again some day. It would be quite fitting if, in such an event, he were to be offered what his predecessor was, a federal judgeship; for he clearly has demonstrated the sort of qualities which make an excellent judge.

Census Data Pop. 414,270. Central city, 15%; suburban, 43%. Median family income, $8,416; families above $15,000: 13%; families below $3,000: 11%. Median years education, 10.8.

The Voters

Median voting age 41.
Employment profile White collar, 39%. Blue collar, 49%. Service, 11%. Farm, 1%.
Ethnic groups Black, 18%. Total foreign stock, 2%.

Presidential vote

1972	Nixon (R)	77,547	(80%)
	McGovern (D)	19,702	(20%)
1968	Nixon (R)	49,835	(47%)
	Humphrey (D)	24,395	(23%)
	Wallace (AI)	32,587	(31%)

Rep. James R. Mann (D) Elected 1968; b. Apr. 27, 1920, Greenville; home, Greenville; The Citadel, B.A. 1941, of So. Carolina, LL.B. 1947; Baptist.

Career Practicing atty.; S.C. House of Reps., 1948–52; Solicitor, 13th Judicial Circuit of S.C., 1953–63.

Offices 1214 LHOB, 202-225-6030. Also P.O. Box 10011, Fed. Station, Greenville 29603, 803-232-1141.

Committees

District of Columbia (8th). Subcommittees: Judiciary (Chairman); The Bicentennial, the Environment, and the International Community.

Judiciary (9th). Subcommittees: Crime; Criminal Justice.

Group Ratings

	ADA	COPE	LWV	RIPON	NFU	LCV	CFA	NAB	NSI	ACA
1974	10	18	27	36	50	40	23	75	100	50
1973	24	0	67	43	63	28	38	–	–	67
1972	0	0	36	57	43	11	50	92	100	90

Key Votes

1) Foreign Aid	AGN	6) Gov Abortn Aid	AGN	11) Pub Cong Election $	AGN
2) Busing	AGN	7) Coed Phys Ed	AGN	12) Turkish Arms Cutoff	AGN
3) ABM	FOR	8) Pov Lawyer Gag	FOR	13) Youth Camp Regs	AGN
4) B-1 Bomber	FOR	9) Pub Trans Sub	AGN	14) Strip Mine Veto	FOR
5) Nerve Gas	FOR	10) EZ Voter Regis	AGN	15) Farm Bill Veto	AGN

Election Results

1974 general:	James R. Mann (D)	45,070	(63%)	($26,536)
	Robert L. Watkins (R)	26,185	(37%)	($13,994)
1974 primary:	James R. Mann (D), unopposed			
1972 general:	James R. Mann (D)	64,989	(66%)	($35,475)
	Wayne N. Whatley (R)	33,363	(34%)	($14,322)

◆ ◆ ◆ ◆ ◆

FIFTH DISTRICT

Stock car racing, one of the nation's most popular spectator sports, thrives best today in places like the 5th district of South Carolina. After World War II, New England textile mills fled to shiny new factories on the outskirts of small towns like Rock Hill and Gaffney in South Carolina. Here plenty of people were eager to work long hours for low wages under poor conditions, and few of them had any funny ideas about joining a union. In the textile towns and their outskirts, whites heavily outnumber blacks, though in some smaller, less developed counties, blacks still constitute a near majority of the population. But the political spirit that prevails in the 5th district is best symbolized by the fan at the stock car races—the yahooing, white Southerner whom W. J. Cash called a "hell of a fellow." The 5th is a traditionally Democratic district, but it was one of two South Carolina districts to go for George Wallace in 1968, and would again if he were to run.

The 5th is one of two South Carolina districts which saw their incumbent Congressmen retire in 1974. The 3d district's William Jennings Bryan Dorn nearly won the Governorship, while the 5th district's Thomas Gettys receded back into the political obscurity whence he had come. Gettys was perhaps the last Congressman to have served as a Postmaster—once the government's leading patronage post. In Washington, he was sometimes called the invisible man; in ten years of service, he made no particular impression.

That will probably not be the case with the district's new Congressman, Democrat Kenneth Holland. A former law partner of former Governor (1971–75) John West, Holland won his Democratic primary runoff narrowly and took 62% of the vote in the general election. He is now a member of the Public Works and Veterans Affairs Committees, and the kind of political moderate who may hold the balance of power in the House if too many of his fellow Democratic freshmen are defeated in 1976. There is little chance that will happen to Holland.

Census Data Pop. 441,907. Central city, 0%; suburban, 0%. Median family income, $7,623; families above $15,000: 9%; families below $3,000: 15%. Median years education, 9.8.

The Voters

   Median voting age 41.
   Employment profile White collar, 30%. Blue collar, 56%. Service, 12%. Farm, 2%.
   Ethnic groups Black, 32%. Total foreign stock, 1%.

Presidential vote

1972	Nixon (R)	78,994	(71%)
	McGovern (D)	32,044	(29%)
1968	Nixon (R)	39,722	(34%)
	Humphrey (D)	33,705	(29%)
	Wallace (AI)	43,635	(37%)

Rep. Kenneth L. Holland (D) Elected 1974; b. Nov. 24, 1934, Hickory, N.C.; home, Camden; U. of So. Carolina, A.B. 1960, LL.B. 1963; Methodist.

Career Employee, S.C. State Hwy. Comm., 1953–55; Instrumentman, Daniel Construction Co., 1956; Practicing atty., 1963–74; Legal Counsel, S.C. Dem. Party.

Offices 511 CHOB, 202-225-5501. Also 3 Lafayette Ct., Camden 29020, 803-432-4376.

Committees

Public Works and Transportation (18th). Subcommittees: Economic Development; Investigations and Review; Public Buildings and Grounds.

Veterans' Affairs (18th). Subcommittees: Education and Training; Hospitals.

Group Ratings: Newly Elected

Key Votes

1) Foreign Aid	AGN	6) Gov Abortn Aid	NE	11) Pub Cong Election $	NE
2) Busing	NE	7) Coed Phys Ed	ABS	12) Turkish Arms Cutoff	NE
3) ABM	NE	8) Pov Lawyer Gag	NE	13) Youth Camp Regs	ABS
4) B-1 Bomber	AGN	9) Pub Trans Sub	NE	14) Strip Mine Veto	FOR
5) Nerve Gas	NE	10) EZ Voter Regis	NE	15) Farm Bill Veto	AGN

Election Results

1974 general:	Kenneth L. Holland (D)	47,614	(62%)	($96,834)
	B. Len Phillips (R)	29,294	(38%)	($44,759)

1974 run-off:	Kenneth L. Holland (D)	32,549	(52%)
	Frank L. Roddey (D)	29,766	(48%)
1974 primary:	Kenneth L. Holland (D)	20,176	(32%)
	Frank L. Roddey (D)	17,051	(27%)
	John R. Justice (D)	11,406	(18%)
	Four others (D)	15,371	(24%)

◆ ◆ ◆ ◆ ◆

SIXTH DISTRICT

The 6th district of South Carolina takes in the northeastern corner of the state, where the Pee Dee and Santee Rivers flow. It is a region of tobacco farms, textile mills, and ocean beaches. Most of the 6th's residents and voters live in and around textile towns like Florence and Darlington, the latter the site of the Southern 500 stock car race. But the district is not nearly as white as the state's other textile districts. Some of the lowland counties here have black majority populations and near black majorities among its registered votes. Altogether, some 42% of the people of the 6th, and 36% of its over 18 population are black.

The fact that blacks now comprise, or can if they get out and vote, more than one-third of the electorate of the district has made for a revolution in the politics of the 6th. It is the only district in South Carolina—indeed, the only non-metropolitan district in the the entire South—to have gone for Hubert Humphrey in 1968, though by a narrow margin in a very close three-man contest; and in 1972, it cast a larger share of its vote for George McGovern than any other South Carolina district. But that share was only 32%—an example of what happens when virtually all blacks support and virtually all whites oppose a certain candidate. For an example of what happens when blacks and whites form an electoral coalition, we have to look at the 1972 and 1974 congressional races here.

For 34 years the Congressman from this district was John McMillan, Chairman since 1948 of the House District of Columbia Committee and—more important to the 6th—by 1972 the number two Democrat on the House Agriculture Committee. The Agriculture post gave him plenty to say about the district's most important crop, tobacco; the D.C. post made him for years the virtual dictator of the federal city. As one might guess, McMillan had little sympathy at all for the district's black majority; he regularly blocked home rule legislation; he conducted his committee meetings abitrarily and refused to recognize opponents; he infiltrated dozens of cronies into the District government. Some of the mismanagement and bloated payrolls of Washington's current home rule government are still directly traceable to McMillan.

McMillan apparently treated the 6th district about as peremptorily as he did the District of Columbia. He did little constituency work, and there were complaints he did not use his influence to obtain favorable tobacco allotments for the area. He even played games with history: for years he listed his birthdate as 1898, but in 1971 suddenly revealed it as 1902. McMillan was challenged seriously in the 1970 primary, and forced into the indignity of a runoff with a black candidate; again in the 1972 primary he was held below 50%, and this time in the runoff he lost to state Representative John Jenrette, a white with a reputation as a liberal.

It was undoubtedly that reputation which caused Jenrette's defeat in the general election that year; the winner was Edward Young, a Republican businessman and TV personality. With a seat on Agriculture (and the Tobacco Subcommittee), Young voted a solid conservative, pro-Nixon line; and most observers expected him to win again in 1972. But they figured without the Democratic surge that hit South Carolina that year. The Democratic nominee was again Jenrette, but this time he won, by a 52–48 margin. Jenrette won better than 60% of the vote in the low-lying black majority counties, made big gains in the stock car racing country around Darlington, and lost only one county (Florence, Young's home). Now he too serves on the Agriculture Committee and the Tobacco Subcommittee, and is the favorite to survive politically in 1976 against Young (who will be 56) or any other Republican.

Census Data Pop. 410,999. Central city, 0%; suburban, 0%. Median family income, $6,203; families above $15,000: 9%; families below $3,000: 23%. Median years education, 9.7.

The Voters

Median voting age 42.
Employment profile White collar, 33%. Blue collar, 43%. Service, 13%. Farm, 11%.
Ethnic groups Black, 42%. Total foreign stock, 1%.

Presidential vote

1972	Nixon (R)	76,985	(68%)
	McGovern (D)	36,846	(32%)
1968	Nixon (R)	34,438	(32%)
	Humphrey (D)	38,072	(35%)
	Wallace (AI)	34,834	(32%)

Rep. John W. Jenrette (D) Elected 1974; b. May 19, 1936, Conway; home, North Myrtle Beach; Wofford Col., B.A. 1958, U. of So. Carolina, LL.B. 1962; Methodist.

Career Army, 1958–59; Practicing atty., 1962–74; S.C. House of Reps., 1964–72.

Offices 1021 LHOB, 202-225-3315. Also P.O. Box 1347, Florence 29501, 803-665-0341.

Committees

Agriculture (26th). Subcommittees: Cotton; Oilseeds and Rice; Tobacco.

Post Office and Civil Service (18th). Subcommittees: Manpower and Civil Service; Retirement and Employee Benefits.

Group Ratings: Newly Elected

Key Votes

1) Foreign Aid	AGN	6) Gov Abortn Aid	NE	11) Pub Cong Election $	NE
2) Busing	NE	7) Coed Phys Ed	FOR	12) Turkish Arms Cutoff	NE
3) ABM	NE	8) Pov Lawyer Gag	NE	13) Youth Camp Regs	FOR
4) B-1 Bomber	FOR	9) Pub Trans Sub	NE	14) Strip Mine Veto	FOR
5) Nerve Gas	NE	10) EZ Voter Regis	NE	15) Farm Bill Veto	AGN

Election Results

1974 general:	John W. Jenrette, Jr. (D)	45,396	(52%)	($149,571)
	Ed. L. Young (R)	41,982	(48%)	($142,673)
1974 primary	John W. Jenrette, Jr. (D), unopposed			

SOUTH DAKOTA

South Dakota was once the heartland of the Sioux Indians, who roamed the plains hunting buffalo. Then the white man came and exterminated the buffalo and, in places like Wounded Knee, many of the Indians. Those who survived were herded onto reservations. Today, South Dakota has one of the highest Indian populations in the nation; one of twenty South Dakotans is an American Indian. As the Wounded Knee crisis of 1973 showed, proximity does not necessarily produce amity. There is as much anti-Indian feeling among whites in South Dakota as there is anywhere in the United States.

The Black Hills gold rush brought the first white settlers to the state. Men like Wild Bill Hickock, America's first dime novel hero, made legends in mining towns like Deadwood, Lead, and Spearfish, and then, as the rich viens petered out, moved on. They left behind the plains, which were slowly being peopled by homesteaders. Some of them were of Scandinavian stock, moving from Minnesota; but most were WASPs from Nebraska, Iowa, and points east. South Dakota experienced most of its population growth during two decades of agricultural prosperity—1880-90 and 1900-1910; the decade between the two, the 1890s, was a period of drought and depression. By 1910, the population of the state had reached seven-eighths of the current figure.

By 1910, the political character of South Dakota had also been set. During the 1890s, the state flirted briefly with Populism and William Jennings Bryan, but by the turn of the century, South Dakota had become almost as monolithically Republican as Nebraska. So later, South Dakotans never had much use for the radical, socialistic ideas of the Non-Partisan League, which enjoyed considerable success among the immigrant Scandinavians and Volga Germans of North Dakota.

As in other states of the Great Plains, voters in South Dakota have been chronically dissatisfied with the farm programs of national administrations, Republican and Democratic alike. But until very recently, that dissatisfaction seldom dented the state's commitment on Republican politics. Between 1936 and 1970, South Dakota sent only one Democrat—George McGovern—to Congress, and elected only one Democratic Governor, Ralph Herseth, who won a two year term in 1958.

Then, suddenly, in 1970, there was a startling shift in the state's voting patterns. Democrats were elected to the Governorship and both of South Dakota's two congressional districts. In 1972, McGovern failed to carry the state, but he got 46% of the vote here, better than almost everywhere else, and otherwise it was the best year ever for South Dakota Democrats. Congressman James Abourezk was elected to the Senate, Governor Richard Kneip was easily reelected, Democrats took majorities in both houses of the legislature, and won five of the seven statewide offices.

Now there has been at least a slight turnaround. While Democrats were gaining ground all over the country, they were losing a little in South Dakota. McGovern and Kneip were both reelected with significantly smaller majorities than the last times they had run. The Republicans had taken Abourezk's House seat in 1972, and now they upset the Democratic incumbent in the other district. Democrats lost control of the state House, though they kept the state Senate. Why this shift away from the Democrats, against the national trend? First, the Democrats had already made their big gains here, under the aegis of McGovern; indeed, they had proceeded to the stage where they felt they could afford the luxury of primary fights and political feuds. Second, the Republicans had recovered from their complaisance and, for once, had been fielding candidates attractive in their own right, not just because they bore the Republican label. Finally, the Indian uprising at Wounded Knee and the subsequent trial which kept the incident in the news all the way through the election seem to have created a kind of white backlash here.

The McGovern story is familiar by now: how the preacher's son drove his beat up car over back roads to set up Democratic county organizations, how he ran for Congress himself in 1956 and upset an overconfident incumbent, how he lost a Senate race in 1960, but—blessed with an opponent named Joe Bottum—won in 1962 by 597 votes. By 1968 McGovern was running for President at the Democratic convention as a sort of stand in for the late Robert Kennedy; by 1971, he was running again, this time very much alone. Indeed, it seemed like McGovern had no support at all until his higher than expected second place finish in New Hampshire and his victories in the Wisconsin and Massachusetts primaries.

McGovern's national success (success, that is, up to the 1972 Democratic convention) was grounded on his opposition to the Vietnam war. He was one of the first Senators to speak and vote against the war ("right from the start"), and was co-sponsor of the McGovern-Hatfield amendments to end the war in 1970 and 1971. But back home in South Dakota the underpinning of McGovern's success has always been the farm issue. He ran against Ezra Taft Benson back in 1950s, and he was back at it, running against Earl Butz, in 1974. In general, McGovern stands for high price supports and subsidies, if necessary, to farmers; and he remains a member, indeed the member next in line for the chairmanship, of the Senate Agriculture Committee.

After his first, brief run for the Presidency in 1968, McGovern had been grumbled at in South Dakota, but had rallied to beat a former Republican Governor named Archie Gubbrud by a 57–43 margin. But in 1974 McGovern had a tougher opponent: a former prisoner of war named Leo Thorsness. A personally engaging man, Thorsness was bitter about McGovern's antiwar stand, which he believed had prolonged the war; as the campaign went on, however, it became clear that the war was no longer much of an issue, and Thorsness had to talk about other things. This caused him some problems. His gut instincts favored untrammelled free enterprise, a position unpopular with South Dakota farmers at least on agricultural matters, and he simply didn't know much about the intricacies of price supports and stabilization programs.

It was by far the most lavishly financed campaign in South Dakota history. Thorsness was able to raise money from anti-McGovern enthusiasts all over the country (although he made the mistake of importing conservative consultant Lyn Nofziger, who had once held a Nixon appointment, and then abruptly firing him); McGovern spent something like $1 million, most of it, not on television, but on maintaining dozens of constituency service offices around the state. But what really matters in a small state like South Dakota is personal contact with the voters. McGovern renewed all the acquaintances he had made in twenty years of campaigning, and Thorsness, considering his naivete on the issues, did well in this regard too. Ultimately, McGovern won, but with only 53% of the vote, down 4% from 1968. His biggest losses were in the western part of the state: in the counties between the Missouri River and Rapid City, where most of the state's Indian reservations are, he ran more than 10% behind his 1968 showing. In the eastern part of the state, where one-third of the voters make their livings on farms, he ran just behind his performance six years before. Obviously the Wounded Knee and other Indian demonstrations —which McGovern had tried to mediate—had rebounded against the Democrats, who had always gotten the great bulk of the Indian vote. White voters switched to Republicans, and turnout among the Indians themselves was extremely low.

The same factor was basically responsible for the comparatively poor showing of Governor Richard Kneip. Beyond that Kneip, who enjoys a more conservative image than McGovern, had another problem: a primary challenge from Lieutenant Governor William Dougherty, a strong McGovern supporter. There was some legal question whether Kneip was eligible to run for another term; he declined from 60% of the vote in 1972 to 54% in 1974. His biggest losses were in the part of the state west of the Missouri, which he barely carried, again presumably because of the anti-Indian backlash. But Kneip's and McGovern's showings were not proof that the Democratic victories of 1970 and 1972 had been flukes; on the contrary, Democrats managed to increase their strength in the state Senate, and only barely (37–33) lost strength in the state House.

Perhaps the strongest Democrat in the state now is that surprising figure, Senator James Abourezk, the son of a Lebanese Indian trader. It has only been ten years since he graduated from law school, and eight years since he received only 44% of the vote in a race for state Attorney General. In 1970, Abourezk secured the Democratic nomination for the 2d district House seat over 28-year-old Donald Barnett, the Mayor of Rapid City during its disastrous 1972 flood. Normally the nomination would not have been a great prize, but the Republican incumbent was retiring, and the nomination to succeed him went not to the favorite, Lieutenant Governor James Abdnor, but to a man named Fred Brady, who proposed setting up compulsory youth camps to teach "decency and respect for the law." That was too much even for many South Dakota conservatives, and Abourezk got 52% of the vote and went to Congress.

Ordinarily, election by a skinny margin would have simply positioned Abourezk for a tough reelection struggle two years later. But ordinary was not a word that fit the South Dakota situation in 1972. George McGovern, of course, was busy running for President. Meanwhile, Senator Karl Mundt, a conservative Republican, had been incapacitated by a stroke; he failed to appear in the Senate from 1969 until his term expired after the 1972 elections. McGovern's campaigning and Mundt's condition gave Abourezk an opening. Soon the Congressman began to provide South Dakotans the kind of constituency service they had come to expect from their Senators. He made personal appearances all over the state. And through personal contact, which is so important in South Dakota politics, Abourezk's quick and often self-deprecating sense of humor overcame the qualms many voters had about the Congressman's solidly liberal record. As the 1972 Senate campaign began, Abourezk was far ahead in the polls. He easily won the Democratic nomination over a former state party chairman, and then almost as easily defeated the colorless Republican nominee, Robert Hirsch, former state Senate Majority Leader.

Abourezk's election transferred this South Dakota seat from one of the Senate's most conservative members (Mundt) to one of its most liberal. Always a vigorous opponent of the Nixon Administration and the Vietnam war, Abourezk is one of the Senators most ready to vote against administration nominees to various posts. He won a seat on the Interior Committee and the Chairmanship of its Indian Affairs Subcommittee and managed to champion Indian rights without seeming to alienate South Dakota whites. And, in 1975, his stands on issues did not prevent him from winning a seat on the Senate Budget Committee and, in direct competition with that master parliamentarian, James Allen of Alabama, a seat on the Senate Judiciary Committee. Abourezk still works hard at staying close to South Dakota; as he puts it, he is not afraid to get some manure on his boots. He is almost certain to face a strong challenge in 1978, when his seat is up, but he seems to be prepared to win. A sidelight: as the only Senator of Lebanese descent, Abourezk is one of the few Senators who is more sympathetic to Arab than to Israeli causes; and until limits were imposed on Senators' outside incomes, he was receiving substantial honoraria for speaking before Lebanese-American groups.

South Dakota still has two congressional districts; but because its population is basically stable, the state may well lose one of its seats after the 1980 census. The 1st district is the eastern edge of the state and includes its largest city, Sioux Falls (pop. 72,000); it is slightly more urban and more

Democratic than the 2d. The 2d includes the western half ot the state, including Rapid City (pop. 43,000), which is near the scenic Badlands, the Black Hills, and Mount Rushmore. It also includes most of the state's ranching territory, more sparsely settled and more Republican than the farm counties.

When Abourezk moved up to the Senate, the 2d district was captured by James Abdnor, the Republican who might well have beaten Abourezk in 1970 if he had won his party's nomination. A solid conservative, Abdnor if anything benefitted from the anti-Indian backlash in 1974; in any case, he won with a huge 68% of the vote. He seems to have achieved the kind of personal popularity which will make him unbeatable. Whether he will run for the Senate is unclear; he will be 55 when Abourezk's seat comes up.

Until the 1974 election, the 1st district seemed securely held by Democrat Frank Denholm, who had first won in 1970. Denholm had a considerably more conservative record and image than either McGovern and Abourezk; he had won in 1972 with 61% of the vote. But in 1974, he found himself under attack on an environmental issue: he supported the Oahe irrigation project, which would direct Missouri River water to irrigate 190,000 acres of land, while his Republican opponent, 32-year-old Larry Pressler, opposed it on environmental and economic grounds. A Rhodes Scholar and graduate of the Kennedy School at Harvard, Vietnam veteran, (one of three in Congress) and a veteran of the State Department as well, Pressler is one of those politicians with unabashed ambition and enthusiasm who seem sure they are destined to be President. Whatever his success at that, he has already proved himself a solid South Dakota personal campaigner, winning 55% of the vote against Denholm in 1974.

As a freshman Republican rather than Democrat, he is effectively shut off from most levers of power in the House; one can be reasonably sure that he will try for the Senate soon. That means he must run against either Abourezk (in 1978) or McGovern (in 1980), neither of whom it seems, at this writing, will be easy to beat. He has antagonized some people in Washington, and his main problem may well be the breadth of his ambitions. Eastern South Dakota has already produced more than its share of presidential candidates, in Humphrey (who was born and grew up here) and McGovern; the question is whether it wants any more.

Census Data Pop. 666,257; 0.33% of U.S. total, 44th largest; Central city, 11%; suburban, 3%. Median family income, $7,490; 44th highest; families above $15,000: 12%; families below $3,000: 15%. Median years education, 12.1.

1974 Share of Federal Tax Burden $642,757,000; 0.24% of U.S. total, 47th largest.

1974 Share of Federal Outlays $883,432,000; 0.33% of U.S. total, 46th largest. Per capita federal spending, $1326.

DOD	$124,212,000	47th (0.18%)	HEW	$307,855,000	43d (0.33%)
AEC	$25,000	47th (–)	HUD	$2,759,000	43d (0.28%)
NASA	$139,000	44th (–)	VA	$61,786,000	40th (0.45%)
DOT	$45,140,000	43d (0.53%)	EPA	$4,344,000	48th (0.14%)
DOC	$4,843,000	39th (0.30%)	RevS	$27,418,000	40th (0.45%)
DOI	$58,352,000	14th (2.37%)	Int.	$34,720,000	41st (0.17%)
USDA	$121,226,000	36th (0.97%)	Other	$90,613,000	

Economic Base Agriculture, notably cattle, hogs, wheat and dairy products; finance, insurance and real estate; food and kindred products, especially meat packing plants; printing and publishing, especially newspapers; metal mining, especially lode gold; tourism.

Political Line-up Governor, Richard F. Kneip (D). Senators, George S. McGovern (D) and James Abourezk (D). Representatives, 2 R. State Senate (19 D and 16 R); State House (37 R and 33 D).

The Voters

Registration 401,651 Total. 170,937 D (43%); 193,234 R (48%); 37,480 Other (9%).
Median voting age 45.
Employment profile White collar, 41%. Blue collar, 22%. Service, 15%. Farm, 22%.
Ethnic groups Indian, 5%. Total foreign stock, 16%. Germany, 4%.

Presidential vote

1972	Nixon (R)	166,476	(54%)
	McGovern (D)	139,945	(46%)
1968	Nixon (R)	149,841	(53%)
	Humphrey (D)	118,023	(42%)
	Wallace (AI)	13,400	(5%)

1972 Democratic Presidential Primary   *1972 Republican Presidential Primary*

McGovern .... 28,017 (100%)   Nixon 52,820 (100%)

Sen. George McGovern (D) Elected 1962, seat up 1980; b. July 19, 1922, Avon; home, Mitchell; Dakota Wesleyan U., B.A. 1945, Northwestern U., M.A. 1949, Ph.D. 1953; Methodist.

Career Army Air Corps, WWII; Prof. of History, Dakota Wesleyan U., 1949–53; Exec. Secy., S.D. Dem. Party, 1953–56; U.S. House of Reps., 1957–61; Dem. nominee for U.S. Senate, 1960; Special Asst. to Pres. John F. Kennedy and Dir. of Food for Peace, 1961–62; Chm., Dem. Comm. on Party Structure and Delegate Selection, 1969–70; Dem. nominee for President, 1972.

Offices 2313 DSOB, 202-224-2321. Also P.O. Box Z, Sioux Falls 57102, 605-339-2880.

Committees

Agriculture and Forestry (3d). Subcommittees: Agricultural Credit and Rural Electrification (Chairman); Agricultural Production, Marketing, and Stabilization of Prices; Agricultural Research and General Legislation; Foreign Agricultural Policy.

Foreign Relations (7th). Subcommittees: Arms Control, International Organizations and Security Agreements; Far Eastern Affairs; Foreign Assistance and Economic Policy; Near Eastern and South Asian Affairs (Chairman).

Group Ratings

	ADA	COPE	LWV	RIPON	NFU	LCV	CFA	NAB	NSI	ACA
1974	89	73	90	50	94	84	75	45	0	0
1973	94	80	100	50	100	–	100	–	–	4
1972	45	100	100	78	100	74	100	0	0	0

Key Votes

1) No-Knock	AGN	8) Gov Abortn Aid	FOR	15) Consumer Prot Agy	FOR
2) Busing	FOR	9) Cut Mil Brass	FOR	16) Forced Psych Tests	FOR
3) No Fault	AGN	10) Gov Limousine	AGN	17) Fed Campaign Subs	FOR
4) F-111	AGN	11) RR Featherbed	FOR	18) Rhod Chrome Ban	FOR
5) Death Penalty	AGN	12) Handgun License	AGN	19) Open Legis Meetings	FOR
6) Foreign Aid	AGN	13) Less Troop Abrd	FOR	20) Strikers Food Stmps	FOR
7) Filibuster	AGN	14) Resume Turk Aid	AGN	21) Gov Info Disclosure	ABS

Election Results

1974 general:	George McGovern (D)	147,929	(53%)	($1,172,831)
	Leo K. Thorsness (R)	130,955	(47%)	($528,817)
1974 primary:	George McGovern (D), unopposed			
1968 general:	George McGovern (D)	158,961	(57%)	
	Archie Gubbrud (R)	120,951	(43%)	

Sen. James Abourezk (D) Elected 1972, seat up 1978; b. Feb. 24, 1931, Wood; home, Rapid City; S.D. School of Mines, B.S. 1961, U. of S.D., J.D. 1966; Syrian Orthodox.

Career Navy, 1948–52; Practicing atty., 1966–70; U.S. House of Reps., 1971–73.

Offices 1105 DSOB, 202-224-5842. Also P.O. Box 1606, Sioux Falls 57101, 605-339-2880, and P.O. Box 850, Rapid City 57701, 605-343-6011.

Committees

Budget (8th).

Interior and Insular Affairs (5th). Subcommittees: Energy Research and Water Resources; Environment and Land Resources; Indian Affairs (Chairman).

Judiciary (9th). Subcommittees: Antitrust and Monopoly; Constitutional Amendments; Constitutional Rights; Separation of Powers (Chairman).

Group Ratings

	ADA	COPE	LWV	RIPON	NFU	LCV	CFA	NAB	NSI	ACA
1974	95	80	80	39	88	89	66	45	10	11
1973	95	89	90	33	94	–	100	–	–	0
1972	63	100	90	58	100	71	0	14	0	13

Key Votes

1) No-Knock	AGN	8) Gov Abortn Aid	FOR	15) Consumer Prot Agy	FOR
2) Busing	FOR	9) Cut Mil Brass	FOR	16) Forced Psych Tests	FOR
3) No Fault	FOR	10) Gov Limousine	ABS	17) Fed Campaign Subs	FOR
4) F-111	ABS	11) RR Featherbed	FOR	18) Rhod Chrome Ban	FOR
5) Death Penalty	AGN	12) Handgun License	AGN	19) Open Legis Meetings	FOR
6) Foreign Aid	AGN	13) Less Troop Abrd	FOR	20) Strikers Food Stmps	FOR
7) Filibuster	ABS	14) Resume Turk Aid	AGN	21) Gov Info Disclosure	FOR

Election Results

1972 general:	James Abourezk (D)	174,773	(57%)	($427,063)
	Robert Hirsch (R)	131,613	(43%)	($300,800)
1972 primary:	James Abourezk (D)	46,931	(79%)	
	George Blue (D)	12,163	(21%)	

Gov. Richard F. Kneip (D) Elected 1970, term expires Jan. 1979; b. Jan. 7, 1933, Elkton; S.D. St. U., St. John's U., Collegeville, Minn.; Catholic.

Career Air Force, 1951–55; Owner, Kneip Sales, wholesale milk equip. co.; S.D. Senate 1965–71.

Offices Executive Ofc., Pierre 57501, 605-224-3212.

Election Results

1974 general:	Richard F. Kneip (D)	149,151	(54%)
	John E. Olson (R)	129,077	(46%)
1974 primary:	Richard F. Kneip (D)	45,932	(66%)
	Bill Dougherty (D)	23,467	(34%)
1972 general:	Richard F. Kneip (D)	185,012	(60%)
	Carveth Thompson (R)	123,165	(40%)

FIRST DISTRICT

Census Data Pop. 333,107. Central city, 22%; suburban, 7%. Median family income, $7,695; families above $15,000: 12%; families below $3,000: 14%. Median years education, 12.1.

The Voters

Median voting age 45.
Employment profile White collar, 42%. Blue collar, 23%. Service, 16%. Farm, 19%.
Ethnic groups Indian, 1%. Total foreign stock, 18%. Germany, 4%.

Presidential vote

1972	Nixon (R)	80,576	(51%)
	McGovern (D)	76,932	(49%)
1968	Nixon (R)	75,400	(53%)
	Humphrey (D)	61,801	(43%)
	Wallace (AI)	5,513	(4%)

Rep. Larry Pressler (R) Elected 1974; b. Mar. 29, 1942, Humboldt; home, Humboldt; U. of S.D., B.A. 1964, Rhodes Scholar, Oxford U., 1966, Harvard U., M.A., J.D. 1971.

Career Army, Vietnam; Aide to U.S. Sen. Francis Case; Ofc. of Legal Advisor to U.S. Secy. of State, 1971–74.

Offices 1238 LHOB, 202-225-2801. Also 310 Fed. Bldg., Aberdeen 57401, 605-225-0250 ext. 471.

Committees

Education and Labor (11th). Subcommittees: Elementary, Secondary and Vocational Education; Select Subcommittee on Education.

Group Ratings: Newly Elected

Key Votes

1) Foreign Aid	AGN	6) Gov Abortn Aid	NE	11) Pub Cong Election $	NE
2) Busing	NE	7) Coed Phys Ed	AGN	12) Turkish Arms Cutoff	NE
3) ABM	NE	8) Pov Lawyer Gag	NE	13) Youth Camp Regs	FOR
4) B-1 Bomber	AGN	9) Pub Trans Sub	NE	14) Strip Mine Veto	AGN
5) Nerve Gas	NE	10) EZ Voter Regis	NE	15) Farm Bill Veto	AGN

Election Results

1974 general:	Larry Pressler (R)	78,266	(55%)	($58,106)
	Frank E. Denholm (D)	63,339	(45%)	($46,307)
1974 primary:	Larry Pressler (R)	22,724	(50%)	
	Ione Larsen (R)	13,940	(31%)	
	Cornelis Van Helden (R)	8,650	(19%)	

SECOND DISTRICT

Census Data Pop. 333,150. Central city, 0%; suburban, 0%. Median family income, $7,283; families above $15,000: 11%; families below $3,000: 16%. Median years education, 12.1.

The Voters

Median voting age 45.
Employment profile White collar, 40%. Blue collar, 21%. Service, 15%. Farm, 24%.
Ethnic groups Indian, 8%. Total foreign stock, 15%. Germany, 4%.

Presidential vote

1972	Nixon (R)	....	85,900	(58%)
	McGovern (D)	....	62,013	(42%)
1968	Nixon (R)	....	74,441	(54%)
	Humphrey (D)	....	56,222	(41%)
	Wallace (AI)	....	7,887	(6%)

Rep. James Abdnor (R) Elected 1972; b. Feb. 13, 1923, Kennebec; home, Kennebec; U. of Neb., B.S. 1945; Methodist.

Career Army, WWII; School teacher and coach; Farmer and rancher; S.D. Senate, 1956–68, Pres. Pro Tem, 1967–68; Lt. Gov. of S.D., 1969–71.

Offices 1230 LHOB, 202-225-5165. Also 439 Fed. Bldg., Pierre 57501, 605-224-2891.

Committees

Public Works and Transportaion (9th). Subcommittees: Aviation; Public Buildings and Grounds; Water Resources.

Veterans' Affairs (5th). Subcommittees: Education and Training; Hospitals; Insurance.

Group Ratings

	ADA	COPE	LWV	RIPON	NFU	LCV	CFA	NAB	NSI	ACA
1974	5	18	33	40	64	29	33	64	100	67
1973	4	11	18	36	75	11	14	–	–	76

Key Votes

1) Foreign Aid	AGN	6) Gov Abortn Aid	AGN	11) Pub Cong Election $	AGN
2) Busing	AGN	7) Coed Phys Ed	AGN	12) Turkish Arms Cutoff	ABS
3) ABM	FOR	8) Pov Lawyer Gag	FOR	13) Youth Camp Regs	AGN
4) B-1 Bomber	FOR	9) Pub Trans Sub	AGN	14) Strip Mine Veto	FOR
5) Nerve Gas	FOR	10) EZ Voter Regis	AGN	15) Farm Bill Veto	AGN

Election Results

1974 general:	James Abdnor (R)	....	88,746	(68%)	($66,250)
	Jack Weiland (D)	....	42,119	(32%)	($58,907)
1974 primary:	James Abdnor (R), unopposed				
1972 general:	James Abdnor (R)	....	79,546	(55%)	($96,252)
	Patrick McKeever (D)	....	65,415	(45%)	($62,235)

TENNESSEE

    To an amazing extent, ordinary Tennesseans are familiar with the political leanings of the various parts of their state, and so any study of Tennessee politics should begin with geography. The state is divisible into three distinct sections, each with its own history and political inclination. East Tennessee is part of the Appalachian chain, an area populated almost completely by white mountaineers. It was against secession and was the political base of Andrew Johnson, Lincoln's vice-presidential choice and successor; over the years, it has remained one of the most dependably Republican areas in the entire nation. The Republicanism of the mountaineers has usually been matched by the Democratic leanings of middle Tennessee. This is a region of hilly farmland which, in rough terms, lies between the lower Tennessee River and the mountains. Middle Tennessee was the home of Andrew Jackson, the first President to call himself a Democrat; and since Jackson's time, the area has remained Democratic in practically every election. West Tennessee, the flat cotton lands along the Mississippi River, was the part of the state with the largest slave-tended plantations. Like middle Tennessee, it is Democratic by tradition; but like the Deep South, in recent years it has been more willing than middle Tennessee to embrace candidates like Barry Goldwater, George Wallace, and Richard Nixon.

Urban-rural differences have not been nearly as important in Tennessee as elsewhere. The state's four large cities vote more like the rural territory around them than like each other. Recently, Memphis, with a large black vote, has been slightly less conservative than the rest of west Tennessee, while Chattanooga, on the Georgia border, is traditionally less Republican than east Tennessee. But the political behavior of Nashville and Knoxville is virtually indistinguishable from the rural counties around them. In general, the cities are gaining more political importance: in 1964, the four major urban counties cast 42% of the state's votes; in 1972, 46%.

So long as middle and west Tennessee remained strongly Democratic, the Republicans were unable to win an election, no matter how many votes the party of Lincoln piled up in east Tennessee. Between Reconstruction and the 1960s, the allegiances created by the Civil War were forsaken only twice: once in the 1920 Harding landslide, when a Republican Governor was elected, and again in 1928 when Protestant Tennessee rejected Catholic Al Smith for Herbert Hoover. Even the initial impact of the civil rights revolution failed to shake the old patterns of political preference. The state's two Senators during the 1950s and 1960s, Estes Kefauver and Albert Gore, had both come to office as reformers, beating aged veterans supported by the equally aged Crump machine in Memphis. And both Kefauver and Gore refused to sign the Southern Manifesto, a document circulated in the 1950s in opposition to the Supreme Court's first school desegregation decision. The key battle, or so it seemed, came in the 1960 primary, when Kefauver took a solid 65% of the vote against a hardline, well-financed segregationist opponent.

Kefauver had long since won national fame for his investigations of organized crime—the first nationally televised congressional hearings. Overnight, the Tennessee Senator became a major presidential contender, and won several presidential primaries in 1952. But he could not overcome the support Adlai Stevenson had among the power brokers of the Democratic Party. Trying again in 1956, Kefauver left the race and wound up as Stevenson's running mate, after edging out John F. Kennedy in a convention floor free-for-all. The last years of Kefauver's career were devoted to reform of the nation's drug laws. His tough bill, once gutted by lobbyists, was suddenly resurrected and passed in the wake of the publicity given the thalidomide tragedies.

Kefauver died in 1963. For his seat, there followed two spirited battles in the 1964 and 1966 Democratic primaries between Governor Frank Clement and Congressman Ross Bass. It seemed like the old days, when winning the Democratic primary was tantamount to victory. But times were changing. The civil rights issues had begun to make conservatives out of many of the state's traditional Democrats—people who used to be more concerned about the TVA and the price of farm commodities than about race. In 1964 Lyndon Johnson carried the state with just 55% of the vote, while Senator Albert Gore was reelected with a not very comfortable 54%. And in the other Senate race, for the rest of Kefauver's term, Congressman Bass came close to being upset by a young east Tennessee lawyer named Howard Baker, Jr.

Baker was then only 38, with a prosperous law practice and a fine political pedigree. Both his father (1951–63) and stepmother (1963–65) served as Republican Representatives from the 2d district; moreover, Baker's father-in-law was none other than Everett McKinley Dirksen. Earlier, Baker had passed up a chance to run in his parents' old district; instead, he assembled an able, young organization for the 1964 Senate bid. Baker's campaign used the latest sophisticated techniques. It was not the sort of affair, traditional in Tennessee, of coming around to a town and swapping stories with old courthouse regulars. Unlike so many Southern Republicans, however, Baker did not exploit the civil rights issue. He could easily have done so, because his opponent Bass was one of the few Southern Congressmen who voted for the Civil Rights Act of 1964.

Baker was well prepared for his next Senate campaign, in 1966. Longtime Governor (1953–58 and 1963–66) Frank Clement defeated Bass this time in the Democratic primary. Clement was a still young man who personified the old virtues—now liabilities—of traditional Tennessee Democrats. He was something of a liberal on issues, but it was not that so much that hurt him; it was his style. Those who can recall his keynote speech at the 1956 Democratic national convention remember his arm-waving, lectern-thumping, florid oratorical style. The speech was the kind that used to liven up a hot afternoon on the courthouse square, but in the age of television campaigning, it was obsolete. Long before the commentators began talking about the youth vote nationally, Howard Baker had sewed up the young vote in Tennessee—simply by exhibiting his calm, cool demeanor.

Baker won that election in 1966, and the same combination—a moderate conservatism on issues and a cool, reasonable personality—almost made him a major power in the Senate. From the time Nixon took office, Baker was an administration supporter on most issues; when his father-in-law died in 1969, he was considered capable enough to almost defeat (he lost 24–19) Pennsylvania's Hugh Scott for the post of Minority Leader. He departed on occasion from Republican orthodoxy: opposing repeal of the one-person-one-vote formula, for example, back in 1967, or in 1973 co-sponsoring the successful amendment to open up the highway trust fund for spending on mass transit projects.

But all this was of little importance to the millions who watched Baker at the Watergate hearings. As the Committee's ranking Republican, he strove not to lean too hard either way: he was not a Nixon loyalist like Ed Gurney, nor an obstreperous rebel like Lowell Weicker. If his philosophical inquiries at least got tiring, the clarity and precision of his language continued to be arresting. Baker did go off on a tangent himself, conducting a separate investigation of the CIA which failed to produce much fruit. But overall, he probably did convince the country that he was presidential material—or at least material for a mighty attractive presidential candidate. At the time, Baker was fresh from his victory over Democratic Congressman Ray Blanton in 1972.

Baker had won with 62% of the vote, carrying all eight of the state's congressional districts; Blanton had tried to blame Baker for some federal judges' busing decisions, but the attack never touched him. Now, Baker apparently is thinking of running for President—although he seems either deceptively hazy or naively ignorant of his plans. As the Republican who helped to bring a Republican President down, he still has some enemies in the Party, including conservatives who loathe Nixon but suspect the Senator of liberal deviation. At the same time, his generally conservative record on substantive issues makes him less attractive to the dwindling number of liberal Republicans than even, say, Vice President Nelson Rockefeller. What can be said with certainty about Baker's political future is that he should have no difficulty winning reelection as Senator from Tennessee.

This is something that cannot really be said about Tennessee's junior Republican Senator, Bill Brock. The millionaire heir to a candy fortune, Brock has had good luck so far. Back in 1962, he was elected Congressman in the 3d district in an upset, after a liberal Democrat beat the incumbent in the primary. He held onto his House seat, and in 1970 went after Senator Albert Gore. It was a classic confrontation between an old South progressive and a new South conservative, between the politics of Franklin Roosevelt and Harry Truman and the politics of Richard Nixon and Spiro Agnew. Brock was the handpicked candidate of the Nixon strategists, and they desperately wanted to beat Albert Gore.

Gore—"the old grey fox" one Tennessee Republican called him—had been around for a long time. First elected to the House in 1938, he moved up to the Senate in 1952. He was a dirt farmer's son who worked up through county politics and campaigned for Congress playing a fiddle in country towns. Later, as a member of the Senate Finance Committee, Gore was one of the chief advocates of the little man against the big interests; most notably, the Senator pushed for progressive tax reform and higher Social Security benefits.

But in 1970 Gore was vulnerable. During the mid-1960s he had become a critic of the Vietnam war—a stand not particularly popular in hell-of-a-fellow Tennessee. Moreover, the Senator had openly proclaimed his support for civil rights legislation, voted against the Haynsworth and Carswell nominations, and cast votes against the ABM and SST. Vice President Agnew thereupon called Gore the number one target of the Nixon Administration—a designation Gore acknowledged with pride. The Senator even welcomed Agnew to Tennessee when the Vice President arrived at the Memphis airport to denounce him. During the campaign, Republican orators were wont to follow Agnew's theme; they liked to call Gore the third Senator from Massachusetts—a reference perhaps to Edward Brooke, the black Senator from the New England state.

Brock had an excellent organization based on the Baker model, and plenty of money—the Nixon people stood ready to supply more whenever he needed it. His TV ads attacked Gore as a supporter of school busing, an opponent of school prayer, and in general a traitor to the South. The old grey fox fought back, citing the votes cast against Medicare and the Appalachia program by free market advocate Brock. The result proved closer than expected; Brock won only 52% of the vote. The results also showed that his victory could be credited almost entirely to his sophisticated attempts to play on Tennesseeans' racial fears and animosities; Gore's biggest losses came in-west Tennessee, the part of the state where racial issues cut deepest.

But however close his victory, it was enough to make Brock a Nixon Administration favorite. In 1972 he was Chairman of Young Americans for the President; in 1973, Chairman of the Senate Republican Campaign Committee. As the Watergate coverup started to unravel, Brock came out with a set of campaign reform proposals; he was being mentioned, as much as Baker then, as a possible presidential candidate. Then some unfavorable publicity surfaced in the spring of 1973—a protege was involved in a minor Nixon dirty trick, the Senator himself was financially interested in a land development scheme under attack for false advertising.

No one claimed Brock himself had done anything wrong, or indeed condoned any wrongdoing; but the presidential boomlet collapsed. It probably would have died soon anyway. There was no substance behind it, no support except from a few flaks and staffers. Brock is admired by some intellectual conservatives as a thoughtful man; and he does try to bring a fresh perspective to problems, a perspective grounded in an almost religious regard for the wonders of free market mechanisms. The question now is whether he has any particular political strength in Tennessee. He won in 1970, and then only barely, on an almost entirely negative campaign; the question is whether he has developed a more positive appeal. As for the opposition, who can say? There is likely to be a Democratic primary free-for-all, with perhaps half a dozen serious candidates; since there is no runoff in Tennessee, almost anyone could win.

That is more or less what happened in the 1974 gubernatorial race. For twenty years (1952–70) the Governorship was batted back and forth between Frank Clement and Buford Ellington; when the Democratic nomination finally went to another candidate, in 1970, the Republican nominee, a Memphis dentist named Winfield Dunn, won. In 1974, the Republicans had something of a fight for the nomination between a Dunn-Baker faction and a group purportedly loyal to Bill Brock; the former group, in the person of 34-year-old former Nixon White House aide Lamar Alexander, won. But this competition was as nothing compared to what happened among the Democrats: there were twelve candidates, at least eight of whom were counted as "serious". The eventual winner, former Congressman Ray Blanton had only 23% of the vote; he was the same man who had gotten a weak 38% of the vote against Howard Baker in 1972.

But 1974 was another story. Tennessee was the number one success story of the Nixon-Agnew Southern strategy, and with Nixon and Agnew both disgraced, those who had profited from that strategy were now suffering. Blanton ran a campaign with country, conservative tones, as befit a man who had represented conservative west Tennessee in Congress; there were occasional populist noises, but his victory in the primary was more due to his name familiarity than anything else. In the general election, he benefitted from simply being the Democratic candidate, which was suddenly an advantage in Tennessee; he ended up with a surprisingly easy 56% victory. Whether this will now be the norm in Tennessee politics, or is simply the fluke result of the Watergate year, we will have a better idea after the 1976 reelection campaign of Senator Brock.

Census Data   Pop. 3,924,164; 1.94% of U.S. total, 17th largest; Central city, 35%; suburban, 14%. Median family income, $7,447; 45th highest; families above $15,000: 12%; families below $3,000: 17%.   Median years education, 10.7.

1974 Share of Federal Tax Burden $4,204,700,000; 1.57% of U.S. total, 21st largest.

1974 Share of Federal Outlays $4,756,178,000; 1.76% of U.S. total, 19th largest.   Per capita federal spending, $1212.

DOD	$679,241,000	29th (0.99%)	HEW	$1,587,343,000	19th (1.71%)
AEC	$419,852,000	1st (13.78%)	HUD	$21,974,000	16th (2.25%)
NASA	$1,876,000	31st (0.06%)	VA	$304,090,000	15th (2.22%)
DOT	$164,158,000	21st (1.94%)	EPA	$49,419,000	20th (1.57%)
DOC	$9,885,000	25th (0.61%)	RevS	$113,974,000	19th (1.88%)
DOI	$11,733,000	40th (0.48%)	Int.	$124,731,000	19th (0.61%)
USDA	$392,056,000	9th (3.15%)	Other	$875,846,000	

Economic Base   Apparel and other textile products, especially men's and boys' furnishings; agriculture, notably cattle, dairy products, soybeans and tobacco; finance, insurance and real estate; chemicals and allied products, especially plastics materials and synthetics; electrical equipment and supplies, especially household appliances; food and kindred products; textile mill products, especially knitting mills.

Political Line-up Governor, Ray Blanton (D). Senators, Howard H. Baker, Jr. (R) and William E. Brock 3d (R). Representatives, 8 (5 D and 3 R). State Senate (20 D, 12 R, and 1 Ind.); State House (63 D, 34 R, 1 Ind., and 1 vac.).

The Voters

Registration 1,958,715 Total. No party registration.
Median voting age 42.
Employment profile White collar, 41%. Blue collar, 42%. Service, 13%. Farm, 4%.
Ethnic groups Black, 16%. Total foreign stock, 2%.

Presidential vote

1972	Nixon (R)	813,147	(69%)
	McGovern (D)	357,293	(31%)
1968	Nixon (R)	472,592	(38%)
	Humphrey (D)	351,233	(28%)
	Wallace (AI)	424,792	(34%)

1972 Democratic Presidential Primary				*1972 Republican Presidential Primary*		
Wallace	335,858	(68%)		Nixon	109,696	(96%)
Humphrey	78,350	(16%)		others	4,793	(4%)
McGovern	35,551	(7%)				
others	42,962	(9%)				

Sen. Howard H. Baker, Jr. (R) Elected 1966, Seat up 1978; b. Nov. 15, 1925, Huntsville; home, Huntsville; Tulane U., U. of the South, U. of Tenn., LL.B. 1949; Presbyterian.

Career Navy, WWII; Practicing atty., 1949–66.

Offices 4123 DSOB, 202-224-4944. Also 716 U.S. Courthouse, 801 Broadway, Nashville 37203, 615-749-5129, and 313 P.O. Bldg., Knoxville 37901, 615-546-5486.

Committees

Public Works (Ranking Member). Subcommittees: Environmental Pollution

Foreign Relations (7th). Subcommittees: African Affairs; Oceans and International Environment; Western Hemisphere Affairs.

Joint Committee on Atomic Energy (Ranking Member, Senate Side). Subcommittees: Communities; ERDA, Environment and Safety; ERDA, Nuclear Energy; National Security.

Select Committee on Intelligence Operations (2d).

Group Ratings

	ADA	COPE	LWV	RIPON	NFU	LCV	CFA	NAB	NSI	ACA
1974	16	30	88	68	64	47	29	38	100	72
1973	12	22	50	42	53	–	17	–	–	73
1972	0	13	50	40	40	0	0	40	100	71

Key Votes

1) No-Knock	AGN	8) Gov Abortn Aid	ABS	15) Consumer Prot Agy	AGN
2) Busing	AGN	9) Cut Mil Brass	AGN	16) Forced Psych Tests	AGN
3) No Fault	AGN	10) Gov Limousine	ABS	17) Fed Campaign Subs	AGN
4) F-111	FOR	11) RR Featherbed	AGN	18) Rhod Chrome Ban	AGN
5) Death Penalty	FOR	12) Handgun License	AGN	19) Open Legis Meetings	AGN
6) Foreign Aid	FOR	13) Less Troop Abrd	AGN	20) Strikers Food Stmps	AGN
7) Filibuster	FOR	14) Resume Turk Aid	ABS	21) Gov Info Disclosure	AGN

Election Results

1972 general:	Howard H. Baker, Jr. (R)	716,539	(62%)	($830,769)
	Ray Blanton (D)	440,599	(38%)	($244,653)
1972 primary:	Howard H. Baker, Jr. (R)	242,373	(97%)	
	Hubert Patty (R)	7,581	(3%)	
1966 general:	Howard H. Baker, Jr. (R)	483,063	(56%)	
	Frank G. Clement (D)	383,843	(44%)	

Sen. Bill Brock (R) Elected 1970, seat up 1976; b. Nov. 23, 1930, Chattanooga; home, Chattanooga; Washington and Lee U., B.S. 1953; Presbyterian.

Career Navy, 1953–56; Brock Candy Co., Field Rep., 1956–60, V.P. of Marketing, 1960–63; U.S. House of Reps., 1963–71.

Offices 254 RSOB, 202-224-3344. Also Rm. 319, Main P.O. Bldg., Knoxville 37901, 615-523-0992, and 204 Fed. Bldg., Chattanooga 37402, 615-756-4250.

Committees

Finance (6th). Subcommittees: Health; International Finance and Resources; Revenue Sharing; Financial Markets.

Government Operations (4th). Subcommittees: Federal Spending Practices, Efficiency and Open Government; Intergovernmental Relations; Reports, Accounting and Management; Permanent Subcommittee on Investigations.

Group Ratings

	ADA	COPE	LWV	RIPON	NFU	LCV	CFA	NAB	NSI	ACA
1974	14	18	70	55	24	26	0	70	100	94
1973	20	30	44	53	31	–	18	–	–	86
1972	0	0	14	47	17	11	0	88	100	88

Key Votes

1) No-Knock	AGN	8) Gov Abortn Aid	FOR	15) Consumer Prot Agy	AGN
2) Busing	AGN	9) Cut Mil Brass	ABS	16) Forced Psych Tests	AGN
3) No Fault	AGN	10) Gov Limousine	ABS	17) Fed Campaign Subs	AGN
4) F-111	FOR	11) RR Featherbed	AGN	18) Rhod Chrome Ban	AGN
5) Death Penalty	FOR	12) Handgun License	AGN	19) Open Legis Meetings	FOR
6) Foreign Aid	AGN	13) Less Troop Abrd	AGN	20) Strikers Food Stmps	AGN
7) Filibuster	FOR	14) Resume Turk Aid	FOR	21) Gov Info Disclosure	AGN

Election Results

1970 general:	William E. Brock III (R)	562,645	(52%)
	Albert Gore (D)	519,858	(48%)
1970 primary:	William E. Brock III (R)	176,703	(75%)
	Tex Ritter (R)	54,401	(23%)
	James Durelle Boles (R)	4,942	(2%)

Gov. Ray Blanton (D) Elected 1974, term expires Jan. 1979; b. Apr. 10, Hardin County; U. of Tenn., B.S.; Methodist.

Career Teacher; Co-Founder, B & B Construction Co.; Tenn. House of Reps., 1965–67; U.S. House of Reps., 1967–73; Dem. nominee for U.S. Senate, 1972.

Offices State Capitol, Nashville 37219, 615-741-2001.

Election Results

1974 general:	Ray Blanton (D)	575,205	(56%)
	Lamar Alexander (R)	457,095	(44%)
1974 primary:	Ray Blanton (D)	148,062	(23%)
	Jake Butcher (D)	131,412	(20%)
	Tom Wiseman (D)	89,061	(14%)
	Hudley Crockett (D)	86,852	(13%)
	Franklin Haney (D)	84,155	(13%)
	Seven Others (D)	111,768	(17%)

◆ ◆ ◆ ◆ ◆

FIRST DISTRICT

The 1st district of Tennessee is the far northeast corner of the state. Most of it is an extension of the Shenandoah Valley of Virginia and the Blue Ridge Mountains of the Appalachian chain. In fact, the district is closer to Richmond, Virginia, than to Memphis, Tennessee. Though the 1st is part of the Appalachian region, it is better off than most mountain areas of West Virginia and Kentucky. Because coal has never been very important here, the district has never been much affected by the ups or downs of that industry. In recent years, towns like Johnson City (pop. 33,000), Kingsport (pop. 31,000), and Bristol (pop. 20,000) have attracted new industry. The region has low taxes and its valleys provide reasonably level east-west transportation routes. Interstate 81, which is nearing completion, will also be an economic blessing.

The changing economy of the district has not, however, produced much shift in its political inclinations. For more than 100 years, the 1st has remained solidly Republican, as Republican as any district in Kansas or Nebraska. People up here in the mountains never had many slaves or much use for secession in 1861. They stayed loyal to the Union and to Mr. Lincoln throughout the Civil War. In fact, Lincoln picked a local boy, Andrew Johnson from Greeneville—one of the older small towns in the district—to be his Vice President in 1864. To this day, the voters of the 1st have continued to support the party of Union. Even in 1974, with the impact of Watergate, Republican gubernatorial candidate Lamar Alexander managed to carry the 1st, though with only 54% of the vote.

For 40 years, the congressional politics of the 1st was dominated by Republican B. Carroll Reece. He represented the district from 1921 to 1931, 1933 to 1947, and again from 1951 until his death in 1961. Reece also served as Republican National Chairman from 1946 to 1948; in 1948, perhaps thinking that another Republican decade like the 1920s was in the offing, he ran for the Senate in still solidly Democratic Tennessee and lost. Reece was succeeded in 1962 by Jimmy Quillen, a Republican conservative of similar bent. Quillen's seat on the House Rules Committee attests to the utter security of his tenure and the orthodoxy of his conservatism.

Census Data Pop. 490,518. Central city, 0%; suburban, 0%. Median family income, $6,820; families above $15,000: 8%; families below $3,000: 18%. Median years education, 9.8.

The Voters

Median voting age 42.
Employment profile White collar, 36%. Blue collar, 49%. Service, 10%. Farm, 5%.
Ethnic groups Black, 2%.

Presidential vote

1972	Nixon (R)	113,840	(78%)
	McGovern (D)	31,200	(22%)
1968	Nixon (R)	92,635	(60%)
	Humphrey (D)	30,418	(20%)
	Wallace (AI)	30,619	(20%)

Rep. James J. (Jimmy) **Quillen** (R) Elected 1962; b. Jan. 11, 1916, near Gate City, Va.; home, Kingsport; Methodist.

Career Founder and Publisher, Kingsport *Mirror*, 1936–39, Johnson City *Times*, 1939–44; Navy, WWII; Pres. and Bd. Chm., real estate and insurance businesses, 1946–; Dir., 1st Tenn. Bank, Kingsport; Tenn. House of Reps., 1955–62, Minor. Ldr., 1959–60.

Offices 102 CHOB, 202-225-6356. Also Rm. 157, 1st Floor, Fed. Bldg., Kingsport 37662, 615-247-8161.

Committees

Rules (Ranking Member).

Standards of Official Conduct (2d).

Group Ratings

	ADA	COPE	LWV	RIPON	NFU	LCV	CFA	NAB	NSI	ACA
1974	10	13	20	57	36	7	20	83	100	55
1973	0	0	18	38	37	6	17	–	–	75
1972	6	9	27	38	50	0	0	83	100	85

Key Votes

1) Foreign Aid	AGN	6) Gov Abortn Aid	AGN	11) Pub Cong Election $	AGN
2) Busing	AGN	7) Coed Phys Ed	AGN	12) Turkish Arms Cutoff	AGN
3) ABM	FOR	8) Pov Lawyer Gag	ABS	13) Youth Camp Regs	AGN
4) B-1 Bomber	FOR	9) Pub Trans Sub	AGN	14) Strip Mine Veto	FOR
5) Nerve Gas	FOR	10) EZ Voter Regis	AGN	15) Farm Bill Veto	FOR

Election Results

1974 general:	James H. Quillen (R)	76,394	(64%)	($10,683)
	Lloyd Blevins (D)	42,523	(36%)	($2,013)
1974 primary:	James H. Quillen(R), unopposed			
1972 general:	James H. Quillen (R)	110,868	(79%)	($3,799)
	Bernard Cantor (D)	28,736	(21%)	($5,807)

◆ ◆ ◆ ◆ ◆

SECOND DISTRICT

John Gunther called Knoxville, the largest city in east Tennessee (pop. 174,000), the "ugliest city I ever saw in America." It is, in fact, an undistinguished looking city, sitting in a hot valley flanked by nondescript hills that do not seem to anticipate the beautiful Smokies 40 miles away. A factory town like this one, one would think, is Democratic. Moreover, the thinking would continue, Knoxville is the headquarters of one of the most successful government projects in history, the Tennessee Valley Authority. The TVA has brought low cost power, recreational lakes, and plenty of jobs to Knoxville and the surrounding area. And the TVA, of course, is identified with the Democrats. But this is east Tennessee, and Knoxville, for all its factories and the TVA, has been one of the most heavily Republican cities in the country. Because the mountain allegiance to the party of Union dies hard, Knoxville, over the years, has seen its interests opposed by the traditional Democratic majority in the state.

Knoxville is the center of Tennessee's 2d congressional district, a safe Republican seat if there ever was one. It is also Senator Howard Baker's home base. Baker's father represented the district from 1951 till his death in 1963; he was succeeded for the remainder of the term by his widow. Baker, Jr., could have had the seat for the asking, but he decided to run for the Senate instead—with results that have made at least a little history.

So the Republican nomination went to then Knoxville Mayor John Duncan. He won by a comfortable margin in the Democratic year of 1964, and has been reelected easily ever since. Duncan does not make much noise around the Capitol, blending quietly into the conservative folds of the Republican caucus. But he does hold a position of potential power, as one of the middle ranking members of the House Ways and Means Committee. The Republican Committee on Committees—senior members from each state with Republican representation—has traditionally chosen anonymous, reliably conservative Congressmen like Duncan to serve on important committees like Ways and Means and Appropriations. Senior Republicans know that such men with safe seats are unlikely either to lose an election or spring unpleasant surprises on the leadership. The House Republican tradition has to account for the fact that the major committees are a couple of notches more conservative than the House as a whole.

Census Data Pop. 492,539. Central city, 35%; suburban, 34%. Median family income, $7,285; families above $15,000: 11%; families below $3,000: 17%. Median years education, 10.8.

The Voters

Median voting age 42.
Employment profile White collar, 43%. Blue collar, 42%. Service, 13%. Farm, 2%.
Ethnic groups Black, 6%. Total foreign stock, 1%.

Presidential vote

1972	Nixon (R)	112,505	(73%)
	McGovern (D)	40,799	(27%)
1968	Nixon (R)	86,588	(54%)
	Humphrey (D)	42,200	(26%)
	Wallace (AI)	31,762	(20%)

Rep. John J. Duncan (R) Elected 1964; b. Mar. 24, 1919, Scott County; home, Knoxville; Presbyterian.

Career Army, WWII; Asst. Atty. Gen. of Tenn., 1947–56; Knoxville Law Dir., 1956–59; Pres., Knoxville Pro Baseball Club, 1956–59; Mayor of Knoxville, 1959–64.

Offices 2458 RHOB, 202-225-5435. Also Rm. 314, P.O. Bldg., Knoxville 37902, 615-546-5686.

Committees

Ways and Means (3d). Subcommittees: Health; Oversight; Trade.

Group Ratings

	ADA	COPE	LWV	RIPON	NFU	LCV	CFA	NAB	NSI	ACA
1974	5	9	25	38	29	31	8	83	90	80
1973	12	18	25	27	55	16	38	–	–	85
1972	0	9	25	44	57	40	0	92	100	91

Key Votes

1) Foreign Aid	AGN	6) Gov Abortn Aid	AGN	11) Pub Cong Election $	AGN
2) Busing	AGN	7) Coed Phys Ed	AGN	12) Turkish Arms Cutoff	FOR
3) ABM	FOR	8) Pov Lawyer Gag	FOR	13) Youth Camp Regs	AGN
4) B-1 Bomber	FOR	9) Pub Trans Sub	AGN	14) Strip Mine Veto	FOR
5) Nerve Gas	FOR	10) EZ Voter Regis	AGN	15) Farm Bill Veto	FOR

Election Results

1974 general:	John Duncan (R)	87,419	(71%)	($28,825)
	Jesse Brown (D)	35,920	(29%)	($0)
1974 primary:	John Duncan (R)	38,284	(96%)	
	Boyce McCall (R)	1,553	(4%)	
1972 general	John Duncan (R), unopposed			($9,585)

◆ ◆ ◆ ◆ ◆

THIRD DISTRICT

The 3d congressional district of Tennessee is dominated by the city of Chattanooga (pop. 119,000). East of the city is the rugged hill country, solidly Republican since the Civil War except for Polk County, where the borders of Tennessee, North Carolina, and Georgia meet. This is a place with a political history as violent as any in America; three people were killed during the 1948 election. The 3d also includes the town of Dayton, the site of the Scopes trial of 1924, where William Jennings Bryan and Clarence Darrow debated whether the state of Tennessee could prohibit the teaching of Darwin's theory of evolution. Chattanooga itself was the focus of several Civil War battles (Lookout Mountain, Chickamauga), but it was only a village then; it is one of those Southern cities which, like Birmingham, grew as an industrial town in the New South years after the Civil War. Chattanooga therefore does not have a politics rooted as deeply in Civil War sentiments as most parts of Tennessee; traditionally, it has been Democratic, in contrast to the neighboring hill counties, but during the sixties and seventies it has been inclined to the Republicanism of Howard Baker and Bill Brock.

Indeed, Chattanooga and the 3d district have been the home base of two of the key figures in postwar Tennessee politics, Estes Kefauver and Bill Brock. Kefauver was first elected to Congress here in 1938, moving on to the Senate—and national fame—in 1948. Brock first won election in 1962. The conservative Democrat who succeeded Kefauver was beaten in the primary that year by a young liberal Democrat (by only 269 votes out of 70,000 cast). Brock, the Republican nominee who otherwise would surely have lost, campaigned hard against the Kennedys, socialism, and civil rights laws, and so began a major career. He was politically adept enough to be able to vote his convictions (e.g., against the Appalachia bill) and still survive here; and in 1970 he narrowly defeated Senator Albert Gore in a race that symbolized the end of Tennessee's liberal Democratic tradition and the ascendancy of its young, conservative Republicanism.

Brock's successor in the House, like Kefauver's, was considerably less famous, a Chattanooga state Senator named LaMar Baker (no relation to Howard). Baker won 53% of the vote in 1970 and 55% in 1972; in the House he was a member of the Agriculture and Public Works Committees, and became leader of a conservative bloc called Republican Steering Committee in 1974. As predicted, Baker faced tough competition that year. Three Democrats ran for the right to oppose him; the winner was Chattanooga TV personality Mort Lloyd. But Lloyd was killed in an August plane crash after the primary, and local Democrats gave their nomination to his widow, Marilyn. The Democratic tide was running strong, especially in the old Dixiecrat counties in the western part of the district, and Marilyn Lloyd ended up with 52% of the vote—a surprise victory and an unexpected addition to the ranks of women in the House. It seems unlikely that there will be a rematch of these two candidates in 1976—Baker will be 61 then, a little old to begin a House career again—but unless the Republican Party here has totally collapsed, it is likely that this district will once again be seriously contested.

Census Data Pop. 486,363. Central city, 25%; suburban, 40%. Median family income, $7,940; families above $15,000: 13%; families below $3,000: 15%. Median years education, 11.2.

The Voters

Median voting age 42.
Employment profile White collar, 42%. Blue collar, 45%. Service, 12%. Farm, 1%.
Ethnic groups Black, 11%. Total foreign stock, 2%.

Presidential vote

1972	Nixon (R)	108,187	(72%)
	McGovern (D)	41,430	(28%)
1968	Nixon (R)	63,359	(39%)
	Humphrey (D)	44,042	(27%)
	Wallace (AI)	53,448	(33%)

Rep. Marilyn Lloyd (D) Elected 1974; b. Jan. 3, 1929, Fort Smith, Ark.; home, Chattanooga; Shorter Col., 1967–70; Church of Christ.

Career Co-Owner and Mgr., WTTI Radio, Dalton, Ga.; Family agriculture flight service business.

Offices 1017 LHOB, 202-225-3271. Also 230 P.O. Bldg., Chattanooga 37401, 615-483-8611.

Committees

Public Works and Transportation (25th). Subcommittees: Aviation; Economic Development; Public Buildings and Grounds; Water Resources.

Science and Technology (23d). Subcommittees: Energy Research, Development and Demonstration; Energy Research (Fossil Fuels); Science, Research, and Technology.

Group Ratings: Newly Elected

Key Votes

1) Foreign Aid	AGN	6) Gov Abortn Aid	NE	11) Pub Cong Election $	NE
2) Busing	NE	7) Coed Phys Ed	AGN	12) Turkish Arms Cutoff	NE
3) ABM	NE	8) Pov Lawyer Gag	NE	13) Youth Camp Regs	AGN
4) B-1 Bomber	FOR	9) Pub Trans Sub	NE	14) Strip Mine Veto	AGN
5) Nerve Gas	NE	10) EZ Voter Regis	NE	15) Farm Bill Veto	AGN

Election Results

1974 general	Mrs. Mort Lloyd (D)	61,926	(52%)	($44,920)
	LaMar Baker (R)	55,580	(46%)	($96,717)
	Sarah Delaney (Ind.)	2,681	(2%)	($24,120)

♦ ♦ ♦ ♦ ♦

FOURTH DISTRICT

The Tennessee River crosses the state twice. The first time, the river heads south from its headwaters to Chattanooga; the second time, after turning around in Alabama and Mississippi, the river moves lazily north to its confluence with the Ohio River in Kentucky. Along most of its route, the Tennessee is made amenable to the needs of man by the presence of TVA dam sites. Between the two lengths of the river lies middle Tennessee, with most of its geographical expanse making up the state's 4th congressional district. To the east, the district is mountain country, but most of the 4th exists as part of the hilly farmlands of the Cumberland Plateau, which is known locally as the "dimple of the universe."

For 150 years, the Cumberland Plateau has been a region of small and medium-sized farms and small county seat towns; the 4th district's largest city is Murfreesboro (pop. 26,000). The first local hero in these parts was Andrew Jackson, victor at the Battle of New Orleans and seventh President of the United States. With the exception of a couple of mountain counties, the 4th district has remained loyal to Jackson's Democratic Party ever since. Indeed, it has produced a number of the party's national leaders, including Congressman (1907–21, 1923–31), Senator (1931–33), and Secretary of State (1933–44) Cordell Hull and Congressman (1939–53) and Senator (1953–71) Albert Gore.

The race issue in the 4th has seldom been the burning one that it has in other parts of the Deep South; this has always been a region of white small farmers, and only 6% of the district's current residents are black. Even in 1972, the district gave George McGovern 35% of its vote—a low figure, but indicating as high a level of support among whites as the Democratic nominee received anywhere in the South. At the same time, as Republican Senator Howard Baker was sweeping to an unprecedented statewide victory, he was receiving only 53% of the vote here. In just about every election, this is the most Democratic congressional district in Tennessee; in 1974, Governor Ray Blanton got 71% of the vote district-wide, and as much as 87% in some counties.

Gore's successor in the House is Joe L. Evins, a moderate to conservative Democrat. Winning reelection regularly with more than 70% of the vote (when he is opposed at all), Evins has quietly risen to a position of considerable leverage in the House. He is now the fifth-ranking member of the House Appropriations Committee, and Chairman of its Public Works Subcommittee. Evin's chairmanship, which he inherited from the late Mike Kirwan of Ohio, used to be one of the big plums in the House, for it amounted to the power of the purse over all the pork barrel projects that so many Congressmen considered crucial to their reelection. Now it is slightly less important: the new breed of liberal Democrats, elected from a suburban district in California or a rural part of Iowa, say, is not going to rise or fall because he did or did not obtain a new post office building. Evins still is able to use his leverage to his own advantage—his home town of Smithville (pop. 2,997) was one of the original Model Cities—but he is not the power he once might have been. Theoretically, he could remain around a long time; he is unbeatable at home, and he is only 66 while his predecessor Kirwan stayed around until he died at 83. But it is possible that he will choose some election year, perhaps but not likely 1976, to retire; life in the House recently has become considerably more hectic than men like Evins had got used to.

Census Data Pop. 492,124. Central city, 0%; suburban, 19%. Median family income, $6,451; families above $15,000: 8%; families below $3,000: 20%. Median years education, 9.2.

The Voters

Median voting age 43.
Employment profile White collar, 34%. Blue collar, 47%. Service, 11%. Farm, 8%.
Ethnic groups Black, 6%.

Presidential vote

1972	Nixon (R)	82,879	(65%)
	McGovern (D)	44,719	(35%)
1968	Nixon (R)	43,438	(29%)
	Humphrey (D)	42,847	(28%)
	Wallace (AI)	65,592	(43%)

Rep. Joe L. Evins (D) Elected 1946; b. Oct. 24, 1910, DeKalb County; home, Smithville; Vanderbilt U., A.B. 1933, Cumberland U., LL.B. 1934, Geo. Wash. U., 1938–40; Church of Christ.

Career Asst. Secy., Fed. Trade Comm., 1934–41; Army, WWII.

Offices 2300 RHOB, 202-225-4231. Also Fed. Bldg., Smithville 37166, 615-597-4099.

Committees

Small Business (Chairman).

Appropriations (5th). Subcommittees: HUD-Independent Agencies; Public Works (Chairman).

Group Ratings

	ADA	COPE	LWV	RIPON	NFU	LCV	CFA	NAB	NSI	ACA
1974	33	44	18	13	77	29	54	70	33	50
1973	50	78	63	17	94	31	100	–	–	19
1972	19	50	44	56	60	15	–	33	100	53

Key Votes

1) Foreign Aid	AGN	6) Gov Abortn Aid	AGN	11) Pub Cong Election $	AGN
2) Busing	AGN	7) Coed Phys Ed	AGN	12) Turkish Arms Cutoff	ABS
3) ABM	AGN	8) Pov Lawyer Gag	AGN	13) Youth Camp Regs	FOR
4) B-1 Bomber	AGN	9) Pub Trans Sub	AGN	14) Strip Mine Veto	FOR
5) Nerve Gas	AGN	10) EZ Voter Regis	FOR	15) Farm Bill Veto	AGN

Election Results

1974 general:	Joe L. Evins (D), unopposed			($4,776)
1974 primary:	Joe L. Evins (D), unopposed			
1972 general:	Joe L. Evins (D)	93,042	(81%)	($11,520)
	Billy Jo Finney (R)	21,689	(19%)	($1,738)

◆ ◆ ◆ ◆ ◆

FIFTH DISTRICT

Nashville is Tennessee's capital and second largest city; after its recent consolidation with surrounding Davidson County, it has the impressive population of 447,000. Because of its location in the center of the state, Nashville is in many ways more important to Tennessee than the larger Memphis. The two newspapers in Nashville neatly reflect the state's two party politics; the *Banner* is as firmly Republican as the *Tennesseean* is resolutely Democratic. The city is also a major center for printing and insurance. The activity for which Nashville is best known, however, is music. It has been the home of the Grand Ole Opry since the 1920s (Richard Nixon, in one of his last public appearances, came down here to dedicate the new building in 1974); and with several major recording studios, Nashville is the undisputed country and western music capital of the world, its fame is recorded in the Robert Altman film called simply, "Nashville."

Today country music millionaires live in suburban mansions that sit uncomfortably close to Nashville's older, established upper class. Country music personalities have even gotten into politics. The late Tex Ritter, for example, was an unsuccessful candidate for the Republican Senate nomination in 1970. And in the same year, Minnie Pearl indirectly contributed as much as anyone to the defeat of John J. Hooker, Jr., the Democratic gubernatorial candidate. Hooker promoted stock in the Minnie Pearl chicken franchise operation (later renamed Performance Systems). It was a bust, and Hooker lost many votes, particularly among disappointed Nashville investors.

Nashville lays claim to ornaments other than country music. The city contains several colleges, including Vanderbilt and Fisk Universities. Also here, not far from the old state Capitol, is the famous replica of the Parthenon. But Nashville's favorite shrine—and the one most significant politically—is the Hermitage, the home of Andrew Jackson, Old Hickory. Jackson moved to Nashville from the Carolinas when Tennessee was still very much the frontier. He made a small fortune, won election to the House while George Washington was still President, and was then elected to the Senate, where he served briefly just after he turned 30; for a few years after that, and as further proof that the early United States did not penalize youthful politicians, he served on the state Supreme Court. It was only after that youthful career, and after some financial setbacks, that Jackson made his national reputation as a merciless Indian fighter, the scourge of the British at New Orleans, and the common man's candidate for President. But he had already helped to set Nashville's political preferences. Jackson was a Democrat, and Nashville has remained, with only the most occasional exceptions, Democratic ever since.

The 5th congressional district includes Nashville and two small rural counties appended after the 1970 census. With the recent exceptions of the 1968 and 1972 presidential contests and the 1972 Senate election, the 5th always goes Democratic. In congressional elections, the Democratic margins here are almost invariably large. The district's current Congressman, Richard Fulton, has over the years been the most liberal member of the Tennessee delegation. He was first elected in 1962, when he ousted the conservative incumbent, a man named J. Carlton Loser. Fulton appeared to have lost that primary by 72 votes, but because of alleged vote fraud, neither candidate received the Democratic nomination; both ran as Independents in the general election, which Fulton won by a surprisingly large 17,000 vote margin. After one term in the House, Fulton caught the eye of the leadership, always on the lookout for fairly liberal Southern members, and won a seat on the House Ways and Means Committee.

In 1968, Fulton had an unexpected close call, barely winning reelection. Stung by that experience, he has rebounded and now wins easily; in 1974 he was unopposed. There have been rumors that he might be interested in statewide office, perhaps in opposing Senator Bill Brock in 1976, or in running for Mayor of Nashville. Whether or not he runs again in the 5th, it is a safe bet that a fairly liberal Democrat will again carry the district.

Census Data Pop. 490,178. Central city, 100%; suburban, 0%. Median family income, $9,231; families above $15,000: 18%; families below $3,000: 10%. Median years education, 11.9.

The Voters

Median voting age 41.
Employment profile White collar, 53%. Blue collar, 33%. Service, 13%. Farm, 1%.
Ethnic groups Black, 19%. Total foreign stock, 3%.

Presidential vote

1972	Nixon (R)	89,046	(63%)
	McGovern (D)	53,175	(37%)
1968	Nixon (R)	46,646	(31%)
	Humphrey (D)	47,636	(32%)
	Wallace (AI)	54,290	(37%)

Rep. Richard H. Fulton (D) Elected 1962; b. Jan. 27, 1927, Nashville; home, Nashville; U. of Tenn.; Methodist.

Career Navy, WWII; Real estate broker; Tenn. Senate, 1959–63.

Offices 2305 RHOB, 202-225-4311. Also 552 U.S. Courthouse, Nashville 615-749-5296.

Committees

Ways and Means (7th). Subcommittees: Health; Public Assistance (Chairman).

Group Ratings

	ADA	COPE	LWV	RIPON	NFU	LCV	CFA	NAB	NSI	ACA
1974	68	100	50	38	100	67	70	36	50	33
1973	63	91	58	60	95	61	86	–	–	28
1972	38	89	67	69	100	63	100	10	50	27

Key Votes

1) Foreign Aid	AGN	6) Gov Abortn Aid	AGN	11) Pub Cong Election $	AGN
2) Busing	AGN	7) Coed Phys Ed	AGN	12) Turkish Arms Cutoff	FOR
3) ABM	AGN	8) Pov Lawyer Gag	FOR	13) Youth Camp Regs	FOR
4) B-1 Bomber	ABS	9) Pub Trans Sub	FOR	14) Strip Mine Veto	AGN
5) Nerve Gas	ABS	10) EZ Voter Regis	FOR	15) Farm Bill Veto	AGN

Election Results

1974 general:	Richard Fulton (D)	88,206	(100%)	($34,502)
1974 primary:	Richard Fulton (D)	53,723	(76%)	
	Mary Anderson (D)	16,717	(24%)	
1972 general:	Richard Fulton (D)	93,555	(63%)	($83,697)
	Alfred Adams (R)	55,067	(37%)	($97,482)

♦ ♦ ♦ ♦ ♦

SIXTH DISTRICT

The 6th congressional district of Tennessee is a rather odd amalgam, stretching from the Nashville city limits in the heart of middle Tennessee to the city of Memphis on the Mississippi River in the west. Its shape is the result of the settlement of a redistricting problem which arose when Tennessee lost one of its nine congressional districts mandated by the 1970 census. The

Democratic legislature chose essentially to consolidate two districts: the middle Tennessee seat represented by William Anderson and the west Tennessee district represented by Ray Blanton. Both were Democrats, but Blanton was already running for the Senate at the time, and it was hoped that Anderson would prove to be strong enough to hold onto the new 6th.

In 1972, at least, both hopes were foiled. Blanton lost to Howard Baker by a record margin, failing even to carry this district. And Anderson, after eight years in Congress, was upset by Republican Robin Beard. Anderson had been a rather unusual Congressman for one representing part of rural Tennessee. The captain of the nuclear submarine Nautilus when it first sailed under the North Pole, he was anything but a hawkish conservative. He voted liberal on economic matters, spotlighted the tiger cage prison camps in Nguyen Van Thieu's South Vietnam, and attacked J. Edgar Hoover when the FBI chief accused the Berrigan brothers of plotting to kidnap Henry Kissinger. In Anderson's old constituency, most of it in solidly Democratic middle Tennessee, such behavior presented no political problems; and he had not had serious Republican opposition. But the west Tennessee counties he picked up in 1972 leaned more to the Democratic politics of George Wallace, and the part of Shelby County added to the district, a 99% white portion of Memphis and its suburbs (pop. 84,000), was anything but sympathetic.

A look at the percentages won by George McGovern in the three parts of the district measures the severity of Anderson's problems. In the five counties retained from the old 6th, McGovern took 36% of the votes—not bad at all compared to the rest of the South, and in these ticket-splitting days no problem at all for Anderson. In the 14 new rural counties, McGovern won 31%, not much worse. But in the Memphis-Shelby County portion of the new 6th, which cast 27% of the district's ballots, McGovern came away with a rock bottom 11%. This shows an almost monolithic white support for Nixon in these high income Memphis and suburban residential areas—one of which bears the appropriate name of Whitehaven.

The strength of Anderson's opposition compounded the incumbent's problems. The Republican nominee, Robin Beard, was typical of the young men that Senators Baker and Brock and Governor Dunn have attracted to careers in Tennessee politics. Beard was young (33), articulate, and solidly conservative. He was also experienced, having served two years as the head of the state personnel commission. Beard's identification with the district was tenuous—he was an east Tennessee native and lived in a Nashville suburb just over the Williamson County line. But the voters did not seem to mind.

The challenger cut Anderson's majorities sharply in both the rural portions of the district. In Anderson's old rural counties, Beard took 43% of the votes, and carried the 14 new rural counties with 52%. But Beard's attacks on busing and Anderson'a antiwar postions really scored in Memphis and Shelby County. Here the challenger clobbered Anderson by a 26,000 to 6,000 margin, which works out to 80% of the votes. The urban votes easily wiped out the 3,000 vote edge Anderson had accumulated in the rural areas.

The 1974 election might have been tougher for Beard. He had a vigorous opponent in Democrat Tim Schaeffer, and one who had not taken far out positions on issues like Anderson. Moreover, Beard himself had stayed solidly with Richard Nixon during the Watergate controversy, while voters at least in the rural part of the district were returning to the Democratic fold in droves. But Beard worked the district hard, concentrating on constituency services, and he attempted to submerge the Watergate issue in voters' minds by attacking people like Angela Davis and Daniel Ellsberg. The result was almost a carbon copy of the 1972 results. Aided by the suburban migration of parents eager to avoid busing in Nashville schools, Beard now carried the old 6th counties, as well as those that used to be in the 7th; once again, as if Watergate had never happened, he took 80% of the vote in Shelby County. With this victory in a difficult year, he seems to have made this a safe seat.

Census Data Pop. 472,341. Central city, 15%; suburban, 3%. Median family income, $7,151; families above $15,000: 12%; families below $3,000: 19%. Median years education, 10.3.

The Voters

Median voting age 42.
Employment profile White collar, 39%. Blue collar, 45%. Service, 11%. Farm, 5%.
Ethnic groups Black, 14%. Total foreign stock, 2%.

Presidential vote

1972	Nixon (R)	....	104,742	(72%)
	McGovern (D)	....	39,799	(28%)
1968	Nixon (R)	....	52,684	(33%)
	Humphrey (D)	....	36,380	(23%)
	Wallace (AI)	....	68,322	(43%)

Rep. Robin L. Beard (R) Elected 1972; b. Aug. 21, 1939, Knoxville; home, Franklin; Vanderbilt U., B.A. 1961; Methodist.

Career USMC, 1962–66; Assoc. Dir. of Alumni Development, Vanderbilt U., 1966–68; Tenn. State Personnel Commissioner, 1970–72.

Offices 124 CHOB, 202-225-2811. Also 710 N. Garden St., Columbia 38401, 615-388-2133.

Committees

Armed Services (7th). Subcommittees: Investigations; Military Installations and Facilities.

Post Office and Civil Services (8th). Subcommittees: Postal Facilities, Mail, and Labor Management; Retirement and Employee Benefits.

Group Ratings

	ADA	COPE	LWV	RIPON	NFU	LCV	CFA	NAB	NSI	ACA
1974	0	10	8	38	25	6	0	83	100	93
1973	0	10	17	33	50	6	17	–	–	89

Key Votes

1) Foreign Aid	AGN	6) Gov Abortn Aid	AGN	11) Pub Cong Election $	AGN
2) Busing	AGN	7) Coed Phys Ed	AGN	12) Turkish Arms Cutoff	AGN
3) ABM	FOR	8) Pov Lawyer Gag	FOR	13) Youth Camp Regs	AGN
4) B-1 Bomber	FOR	9) Pub Trans Sub	AGN	14) Strip Mine Veto	FOR
5) Nerve Gas	FOR	10) EZ Voter Regis	AGN	15) Farm Bill Veto	AGN

Election Results

1974 general:	Robin L. Beard (R)	76,928	(57%)	($189,216)
	Tim Schaeffer (D)	58,824	(43%)	($96,288)
1974 primary:	Robil L. Beard (R), unopposed			
1972 general:	Robin L. Beard (R)	77,263	(56%)	($151,605)
	William R. Anderson (D)	60,254	(44%)	($105,022)

♦ ♦ ♦ ♦ ♦

SEVENTH DISTRICT

The 7th congressional district of Tennessee is the northwest part of the state. The district extends from the TVA lakes of the Tennessee and Cumberland Rivers at the Kentucky state line to the city of Memphis. Physically and politically, the 7th resembles the Mississippi Delta or east Arkansas: flat cotton lands, occasional small towns, and a fairly large (19%), mostly rural black population. Outside of Memphis and Shelby County, the district's largest city is Jackson (pop. 39,000), whose political attitudes have much in common with its Mississippi namesake. Most of the counties here are traditionally Democratic, but only those around the Tennessee River have given statewide Democratic candidates majorities in recent years—except in 1974, when the whole area went solidly for Governor Ray Blanton. Indeed, this was the crucial part of the state for the victory of Senator Bill Brock in 1970, and it contributed as well to Senator Howard Baker's triumph in 1972. The Shelby County (Memphis) portion of the district, with 124,000 residents (26% of the district total), is 98% white, relatively high income, and heavily conservative—though not as devoted to the Republican Party as the 6th district's portion of Memphis.

Perhaps because of its long-standing Democratic tradition, Tennessee Republicans did not contest the seat in th 7th district for some time. From 1958 to 1969, the district was represented by conservative Democrat Bob Everett, who faced Republican opposition only once during his tenure. In 1969, Everett died, and a special election was called. George Wallace, who had carried nearly 50% of the vote within the district the year before, came in to campaign for American Party candidate William Davis, while Senator Howard Baker and other Republicans stumped for Republican Leonard Dunavant. The race got some attention in the national press as a test of the Wallace and Nixon strategies in the South.

The result made both look rather bad. Davis won 25% of the votes, Dunavant 24%, and the winner, conservative Democrat Ed Jones, took 51%. Jones, former state Commissioner of Agriculture, had not asked outsiders to come in and campaign for him; he wisely relied on the traditionally Democratic sentiments of the voters in his district. These people may plunk for Wallace in a presidential election, or go for a Republican like Nixon over a Democrat like McGovern, but most of them preferred to stay with a Tennessee Democrat in what is, after all, a local election. Then, too, against Wallace-backed and Nixon-backed candidates, Jones won the black vote with no effort at all.

In Congress, Jones received a seat on the House Agriculture Committee and its Cotton Subcommittee. With several surprise retirements and defeats, especially among Southern Democrats, Jones rose fast in seniority, and is now sixth-ranking Democrat on the full Committee and Chairman of the Dairy and Poultry Subcommittee. Back home, the voters are apparently content with his conservative record. He had no opposition in 1970, and won 70% of the vote against a Republican in 1972, including 54% in the Shelby County portion of the district. In 1974, he had only primary oposition, and won 72–28. At age 64, Jones seems to have an utterly safe district.

Census Data Pop. 487,097. Central city, 10%; suburban, 16%. Median family income, $7,030; families above $15,000: 10%; families below $3,000: 19%. Median years education, 10.2.

The Voters

Median voting age 43.
Employment profile White collar, 37%. Blue collar, 44%. Service, 12%. Farm, 7%.
Ethnic groups Black, 19%. Total foreign stock, 2%.

Presidential vote

1972	Nixon (R)	105,072	(75%)
	McGovern (D)	34,241	(25%)
1968	Nixon (R)	42,049	(28%)
	Humphrey (D)	35,390	(23%)
	Wallace (AI)	74,448	(49%)

Rep. Ed Jones (D) Elected Mar. 25, 1969; b. Apr. 20, 1912, Yorkville; home, Yorkville; U. of Tenn., B.S. 1934; Presbyterian.

Career Inspector, Tenn. Dept. of Agric., 1934–41; Supervisor, Tenn. Dairy Products Assn., 1941–43; Agric. Rep., Ill. Central R.R., 1943–48, 1952–69; Tenn. Commissioner of Agric., 1949–52.

Offices 1315 LHOB, 202-225-4714. Also P.O. Box 27190, 3179 N. Watkins St., Memphis 38127, 901-358-4094.

Committees

Agriculture (6th). Subcommittees: Cotton; Dairy and Poultry (Chairman); Oilseeds and Rice.

House Administration (9th). Subcommittees: Accounts; Contracts; Parking (Chairman); Ad Hoc Computer.

Group Ratings

	ADA	COPE	LWV	RIPON	NFU	LCV	CFA	NAB	NSI	ACA
1974	16	50	36	0	67	30	50	45	88	64
1973	27	67	42	29	89	11	67	–	–	48
1972	13	44	25	33	80	4	0	57	100	74

Key Votes

1) Foreign Aid	AGN	6) Gov Abortn Aid	AGN	11) Pub Cong Election $	AGN
2) Busing	AGN	7) Coed Phys Ed	AGN	12) Turkish Arms Cutoff	AGN
3) ABM	FOR	8) Pov Lawyer Gag	FOR	13) Youth Camp Regs	AGN
4) B-1 Bomber	FOR	9) Pub Trans Sub	ABS	14) Strip Mine Veto	ABS
5) Nerve Gas	AGN	10) EZ Voter Regis	FOR	15) Farm Bill Veto	AGN

Election Results

1974 general	Ed Jones (D), unopposed			($74,880)
1974 primary:	Ed Jones (D)	54,591	(72%)	
	Wayne Brown (D)	21,751	(28%)	
1972 general:	Ed Jones (D)	92,419	(70%)	($78,789)
	Stockton Adkins (R)	38,726	(30%)	($20,136)

◆ ◆ ◆ ◆ ◆

EIGHTH DISTRICT

Memphis, Tennessee's largest city (pop. 623,000), is set in the far southwest corner of the state. The city is the major financial and commercial center for much of the lower Mississippi Valley. As such, Memphis looks as much south to Mississippi and west to Arkansas as it does to the rest of Tennessee. In recent years, Memphis has grown rapidly, doubling its population since World War II. Most of the newcomers are from the Deep South, especially Mississippi. Blacks have found more economic opportunity here, and more political power; for some years now Memphis has elected black state legislators and even a black judge—Benjamin Hooks, now a member of the Federal Communications Commission.

Memphis is the home of many quintessentially American institutions. Beale Street here gave birth to jazz in the 1920s, and in the 1930s the first supermarket—a Piggly Wiggly—opened in Memphis. In the 1950s Memphis gave us Elvis Presley and the Holiday Inn (the first of which is no longer operated under that aegis, but sports a memorial plaque). Memphis, or at least the white majority here, likes to think of itself as a plain Middle American city, but the fact is that the prevailing community opinion, like the accent, remains Southern.

The city as a whole is dominated politically by its middle class whites. These are people, many from the small town South, who are now making more money than they ever imagined. They live comfortable lives in the vast suburban tracts that have sprung up inside and outside the expanding city limits in the last twenty years. Their political traditions are Democratic, but they now use their ballot to protect their new found prosperity—and the whiteness of their neighborhoods—by voting Republican. They are attracted particularly to youngish, lightly-accented candidates like Howard Baker and Bill Brock, whose sometimes cerebral conservatism and thoughtful, soft-spoken oratory symbolize the social distance they themselves have traversed.

There is one other fact that any political analyst should know about Memphis: this is one of the most segregated cities in the country. There is little of that phenomenon, once so common in Atlanta and still the case in New Orleans, of blacks and whites living in close proximity; the blacks are concentrated entirely in the central portions of the city, while the whites have long since moved to the newer subdivisions. Thirty years ago there were no differences between the voting habits of Memphis blacks and whites: they both went down the line for candidates endorsed by Boss Ed Crump's machine, which is to say Democrats. But long ago the white neighborhoods started moving toward the Republicans, while the blacks became more Democratic than ever. The result is voting patterns more racially polarized than in any other major American city. In 1972, for example, while more than 90% of Memphis's blacks were voting for George McGovern, Richard Nixon was receiving 89% of the vote in the 99% white portion of Memphis and Shelby County that is in the 6th congressional district.

Most of Memphis (and virtually none of the suburbs) is now in the Tennessee's 8th congressional district. For some years Tennessee legislators had drawn the lines to prevent a black majority district; but in 1972, to maximize the Democratic vote in the 8th, they made a district 47% of whose residents and 41% of whose eligible voters in 1970 were black. Those percentages have continued to rise slowly since then, as more blacks move here from rural areas and more whites move farther out in the city or the suburbs. And in major elections here the vote has seemed to parallel the racial percentages: the 8th district went 43% for McGovern in 1972, and 44% for Democratic congressional candidate J. O. Patterson the same year.

Now, after the 1974 elections, the 8th has a black Democratic Congressman, 31-year-old former state Representative Harold Ford. His was an upset victory, by a margin of only 744 votes he came out ahead of eight-year incumbent Dan Kuykendall. A Republican who had come surprisingly close to beating Senator Albert Gore in 1964, Kuykendall had won the seat in 1966 and had held it by paying close attention to his white constituents—and in effect convincing them of his allegiance by paying virtually no attention to its large black minority. Like all of Tennessee's Republican congressman (and unlike the canny Howard Baker) he was a bitter-end supporter of Richard Nixon; it was Kuykendall who received, and reported, a September 1974 call from Nixon himself, the one where the former President could not bring himself to pronounce the syllables of Leon Jaworski's name. The pardon may not have infuriated many white voters here—the majority probably remain Nixon fans to this day—but it affected just enough to give Democrat Ford the votes he needed to beat Kuykendall. The great mass of the votes were cast along racial lines—black Democrats for black Democrat Ford, white Republicans for white Republican Kuykendall. But just a small margin of whites switched to the Democrat, presumably because of Watergate and the pardon, and Ford was elected.

The new Congressman is part of a local political family; his older brother is a state legislator. In the House he sits on the Banking and Veterans Committees; he is expected to be a solid liberal vote. Once having won, he is probably indefinitely reelectable within the bounds of this district, if only by small margins; for the black percentage here continues to rise, and in racially polarized Memphis that means Democrats stand a better chance in the 8th every election.

Census Data Pop. 513,004. Central city, 99%; suburban, 1%. Median family income, $7,874; families above $15,000: 14%; families below $3,000: 15%. Median years education, 11.4.

The Voters

Median voting age 42.
Employment profile White collar, 47%. Blue collar, 36%. Service, 17%. Farm, –%.
Ethnic groups Black, 47%. Total foreign stock, 3%.

Presidential vote

1972	Nixon (R)	96,876	(57%)
	McGovern (D)	71,930	(43%)
1968	Nixon (R)	45,193	(28%)
	Humphrey (D)	72,320	(44%)
	Wallace (AI)	46,311	(28%)

Rep. Harold E. Ford (D) Elected 1974; b. May 20, 1945, Memphis; home, Memphis; Tenn. St. U., B.S. 1967, John Gupten Col., L.F.D., L.E.D. 1969; Baptist.

Career Mortician, 1969–75; Tenn. House of Reps., 1971–74.

Offices 1609 LHOB, 202-225-3265. Also 369 Fed. Bldg., Memphis 38103, 901-534-4131.

Committees

Banking, Currency and Housing (21st). Subcommittees: Domestic Monetary Policy; Housing and Community Development.

Veterans' Affairs (15th). Subcommittees: Cemeteries and Burial Benefits; Hospitals.

Group Ratings: Newly Elected

Key Votes

1) Foreign Aid	FOR	6) Gov Abortn Aid	NE	11) Pub Cong Election $	NE
2) Busing	NE	7) Coed Phys Ed	FOR	12) Turkish Arms Cutoff	NE
3) ABM	NE	8) Pov Lawyer Gag	NE	13) Youth Camp Regs	FOR
4) B-1 Bomber	AGN	9) Pub Trans Sub	NE	14) Strip Mine Veto	AGN
5) Nerve Gas	NE	10) EZ Voter Regis	NE	15) Farm Bill Veto	AGN

Election Results

1974 general:	Harold E. Ford (D)	67,925	(50%)	($146,940)
	Dan Kuykendall (R)	67,181	(50%)	($132,411)
1974 primary:	Harold E. Ford (D)	35,709	(63%)	
	Charles C. Burch (D)	8,173	(14%)	
	Mary Ann Guthrie (D)	7,551	(13%)	
	Three Others (D)	5,289	(9%)	

TEXAS

Everybody's image of Texas and the Texan is pretty much the same. It has something of John Wayne at the Alamo, cowboys and cattle on the Chisholm Trail, and happy new oil millionaires riding around in air-conditioned Cadillacs while their wives roll up bills at Neiman Marcus. The stereotype has some truth, but not much. Before the east Texas oil strike of the 1930s, the typical Texan was a poor dirt farmer, and even today the state has many more marginal farmers than oil millionaires. Moreover, the descendants of the white men who came to Texas with Sam Houston and defended the Alamo are greatly outnumbered by the 18% of all Texans who are of Mexican descent. And Neiman Marcus has far fewer people with charge accounts than the number of black Texans, who make up 12% of the state's population.

In one respect, however, the stereotypical picture of Texas is accurate: the state is a vast one. It is farther from El Paso to Texarkana—or from Amarillo to Brownsville—than it is from Chicago to New York. As one drives east to west across Texas, the scenery shifts from fertile lands that receive ample rain to flat, waterless desert. During the winter, blizzards sweep across the northern panhandle, while the Rio Grande basks in semitropical temperatures. Despite its size, Texas lost its status as the nation's biggest state when Alaska became one in 1959. Nevertheless, during the 1960s, Texas passed both Illinois and Ohio to become the fourth largest in population, and by 1980, Texas will outrank Pennsylvania to occupy the number three position.

"In no other state," writes Neal Peirce, an expert on all 50 of them, "has the control (of a single moneyed establishment) been so direct, so unambiguous, so commonly accepted." Of course, the biggest money here is in oil. But Texas millionaires are also big in petrochemicals, construction (Brown & Root, an LBJ favorite), insurance, and computers. Ross Perot, an old IBM salesman, made millions when he set up his own company and designed programs for Medicaid adminstrators; Perot thus became the first welfare millionaire. Almost without exception, the big money men are conservative and, bowing to local traditions, they have chosen—at least until very recently—to exert control through the Democratic Party. Big money put pressure on congressional powers like Speaker Sam Rayburn and Senate Majority Leader Lyndon Johnson, neither of whom brooked any tampering with the oil depletion allowance. But the rich have devoted most of their efforts to statewide politics. Their heroes are Tory Democrats like ex-Governor (1963-68) John B. Connally. As Governor, Connally permitted some progressive legislation to be enacted, but never anything that would really hurt the state's moneyed establishment. To note just one fact, Connally's home state is the only one of the seven largest with no income tax.

It should not be surprising, then, that some of the state's most important political figures have been caught in scandals; as the history of the Nixon Administration shows, politicians who are inclined even altruistically to benefit the rich often wind up caught with sticky fingers. Connally himself, of course, has been acquitted of accepting bribes to promote the cause of the milk lobby before President Nixon; but the fact remains that he was an intermediary, though not a criminal one, in a scheme to benefit a major economic pressure group in return for campaign contributions in the hundreds of thousands of dollars. Indeed, Watergate itself was foreshadowed here in Texas by a scandal—or series of scandals—revolving around a promoter named Frank Sharp, which hit with full force during the 1972 campaign. In the process a Speaker of the Texas House, Gus Mutscher was convicted and spent 5 years on probation; and Lieutenant Governor Ben Barnes, the talented young politico who had been expected to win the Governorship easily that year, and whom Lyndon Johnson at least predicted would some day be President, finished a humiliating third in the Democratic gubernatorial primary—a political has-been at 33. And Barnes was not accused of doing anything illegal; his offense was that a wealthy friend has loaned him a lot of money without collateral, and enabled Barnes to get wealthy himself through some sure fire investments.

The 1972 primary was probably the high point of revulsion against scandal in Texas politics. Not only did Barnes finish third, the incumbent Governor, Preston Smith, was fourth, with only 8% of the vote; he had been peripherally involved with Sharp. Even more surprising was the candidate who finished second in that race: state Representative Frances Farenthold, a woman, a Catholic, a critic of the Texas Rangers, and the only state legislator to vote against a resolution honoring President Johnson when he returned home.

But things returned to normal in the runoff that year, and have remained there ever since. Farenthold managed to win 45% of the vote against Dolph Briscoe, the noncommital conservative she referred to as "a bowl of pabulum." But that, of course, was not enough. Briscoe was pressed again in the general election that year. The candidate of La Raza Unida Party (which may well have been financed by Republicans to drain Mexican-American votes away from Democrats) got 200,000 votes, and Briscoe managed only a minority victory over the ultraconservative Republican nominee, state Senator Henry Grover; but again, it was enough. Reportedly the biggest landowner in Texas, Briscoe has run a conservative, colorless administration. People figure, apparently correctly, that he is too rich to steal, and he has not allowed any issues to arise that would rile up any group of voters. Indeed, the highlight of his administration so far is the persistent rumor—one he came out of virtual seclusion in 1975 to deny—that he is mentally ill. In 1974 Farenthold ran again in the primary; but while the rest of the country was exercised by Watergate, Texas had quite forgotten Sharpstown, and she managed to carry only two of the state's 254 counties. In the general election, Briscoe again won easily, and was thereby elected to the state's first four year gubernatorial term. Indeed, he could even run again in 1978, and bring a whole decade of somnolent conservatism to Texas's once turbulent state politics.

Briscoe's triumphs were all the more impressive in that they ran against the flow of demographic change in Texas. His greatest strength, and that of all the Tory Democrats before him, had been in rural and small town Texas, a part of the state which is losing population—and votes. In 1960 the 221 Texas counties with fewer than 50,000 people cast 33% of the state's votes; in 1972, they cast only 26%. The big cities, Houston, Dallas, Fort Worth, and San Antonio, where politics is increasingly a struggle between ideologically motivated conservative Republicans and liberal Democrats, have been increasing their theoretical clout; in 1960, they cast 36% of the state's vote, in 1972, 43%.

Another election which ran against these trends was the victory of Senator Lloyd Bentsen in 1970. The genesis of his candidacy was the feud which brought John Kennedy to Dallas that terrible day in November 1963, the ideological and personal struggle between liberal Democratic Senator Ralph Yarborough and John Connally. Yarborough had first won with a minority of the vote in a 1957 special election, and had been reelected in 1958 and 1964 primarily because Lyndon Johnson squelched Tory opposition. But in 1970 Connally and others had their candidate in Lloyd Bentsen, a former Congressman (1947–55), who as a young man had urged nuclear bombing of North Korea.

Bentsen came from a wealthy family in the lower Rio Grande Valley, an almost feudal region where the Mexican-American majority has always allowed wealthy Anglos to run things. He was a county judge at 25 and a Congressman at 27; he quit politics at 33 to become a millionaire in his own right. Bentsen was scarcely at all known at the beginning of 1970, but he ran a campaign which was, to say the least, well financed. He ran clips of the police riot outside the 1968 Democratic national convention and implied that somehow Yarborough was responsible for it—a preview, in short, of the kind of campaign Nixon and Agnew would run for various Republicans that fall. Bentsen's fluent Spanish, perhaps, helped him to cut into Yarborough's usual Mexican-American majorities; and the old (66) Senator's flaming oratory failed to win him the rural votes he had once got. The result was a 54% Bentsen victory in the primary.

For the general election, Bentsen switched strategies as abruptly as a soap executive changes the pitch of a commercial when he moves into a different market. He knew that previous Tory candidates had lost to Senator John Tower because of liberal defections, and he knew that the Republicans had, in Congressman George Bush, a strong candidate with possible appeal to liberals. So Bentsen courted and won over important figures like state Senator (and now Congresswoman) Barbara Jordan, Congressman Henry Gonzalez, and the leaders of the state AFL-CIO. At the same time, his primary campaign assured him of the support of traditional rural Democrats, who came out in major force in an unsuccessful attempt to defeat a liquor-by-the-glass referendum. The Republican media wizards who had considered Bush their most telegenic candidate that year had not figured out how to sell a product of Eastern prep schools, which Bush was, to Texas dirt farmers.

It might not be worth going into such detail on Bentsen's initial race but for the light it sheds on his subsequent career—and his race for the Presidency in 1976. For it shows that without ever really changing his principles, Bentsen is capable of vastly altering his public image. Just after he won, Spiro Agnew claimed his election was an ideological victory for the Nixon Administration, and Bentsen replied sharply that it was not—and he was right. Even his enemies now admit that he has a brilliant, supple mind, and that he uses it. On major issues, Bentsen has usually lined up with other Democrats on roll calls, even on issues like the bombing of Cambodia (he was against) and on the oil depletion allowance. On the latter, in 1975 he demonstrated his talents as a legislator—and a politician. He voted for eliminating the allowance for the major oil producers, but at the same time introduced a successful amendment to retain it, although scaled down, for minor producers. This had the effect of placing him in opposition to what had been a longtime major Texas interest group in the public eye, while at the same time retaining the support of the small producers, many of whom are Texas multimillionaires in the habit of making large campaign contributions.

Bentsen also showed considerable skill in the successful pension reform bill in 1974; with the drafting skill of a corporate lawyer and the eye for essentials of a successful businessman, he helped sculpt a bill which was technically sound and which also received the blessing of organized labor. His admirers point to examples like these when asked why Bentsen should be President; if the issue is competence, they say, he has shown he has it. The country, in this view, more than anything else needs a man who can make its major institutions work, and Bentsen, they believe, is such a man. The case against him is the other side of the coin: his detractors argue that he is a man of no fixed beliefs, a technician who does not really care about people and who cannot be counted on to maintain his principles when the going gets rough.

By early 1975 Bentsen had proved his managerial acumen once again by putting together a talented presidential campaign staff and using his position as Democratic Senatorial Campaign Committee Chairman in 1974 to get around the country and visit with party functionaries of all kinds. The question is, where is he going to get his first line votes? It is all very well to say that no candidate will enter the convention with a majority, and that delegates will be casting around for someone acceptable to everyone, a category Bentsen presumably fills. It is another thing to see how Bentsen is going to avoid winning a humiliatingly low percentage of the votes in the initial primaries and having his campaign collapse around him.

Back in Texas, Tory Democratic operatives have been doing something to assure Bentsen of a solid delegate base. The system of choosing delegates there, together with the old unit rule, resulted in delegations almost unanimously behind the Democratic establishment, like the one John Connally led at Chicago in 1968. But with the unit rule outlawed, liberals and Wallaceites, independent blacks and chicanos have been elected. The 1975 legislature has passed a law which would substitute a primary, with the winner in effect taking all the delegates for each given congressional district; the anticipated effect is that Bentsen would control the whole delegation, or almost all of it. As for the 1976 Senate race, Bentsen remains eligible to run under the old law passed to allow Lyndon Johnson to run for the Senate and the Vice Presidency simultaneously in 1960, and he intends to run for both. Few doubt that he can win reelection to the Senate easily.

Bentsen's senior colleague, John Tower, is something of an accidental Senator—a beneficiary of good luck and hard work; he is now, after some years of obscurity, one of the more important Republicans in the Senate. In 1959, Tower was an unknown professor at Midwestern University in Wichita Falls, financially well off but politically nowhere, an ideological conservative Republican in a pragmatically Democratic state. In 1960 he waged a quixotic campaign against Lyndon Johnson, and partly because of resentment over Johnson's double candidacy that year—and remember that the Kennedy-Johnson ticket won just 51% of the vote in Texas—won a surprisingly good 41% of the vote. In the 1961 special election to fill Johnson's seat, he ran again, and this time beat the ultra-conservative Democrat appointed to fill the vacancy. Five years later Tower won with his largest margin to date—57%—against Attorney General Waggoner Carr, a Tory Democrat in preference to whom many liberals voted for Tower (in the probably mistaken belief that he would be easier to dislodge some day).

Only in 1972 did Tower really win a solid victory that can be described without footnotes, beating a mildly liberal Democrat named Barefoot Sanders by a 55–45 margin. Even here, Tower was helped by an unanticipated trend. As late as 1968, the rural areas of Texas had remained solidly Democratic, providing key votes in Hubert Humphrey's 41–40 victory over Richard Nixon in the state. But in 1972, the rural areas went for Nixon by better than a 2–1 margin, and they also went, for the first time, solidly for a state Republican candidate, Tower. So this Senator, whose political base had previously been very much in Texas's big cities, seemed to carve out a new and larger constituency for himself.

Tower now is the ranking Republican on the Banking, Housing, and Urban Affairs Committee, and number two Republican on Armed Services. He is also the ranking Republican on the special committee investigating the CIA, in which capacity he has worked well with the ideologically very different Chairman, Frank Church of Idaho. As a solid conservative, Tower generally opposes high federal spending on domestic programs and supports generous outlays for military and space spending; it helps him politically (although he is the kind of man who would take the same stand if it didn't) that Texas receives a disproportionately large 8% of the federal defense outlays and 10% of the spending on the space program. In his first years in the Senate, Tower behaved like an accidental Senator who would soon be gone, enjoying the prerequisites of office and attending to his duties dilettantishly. But he has long since become a harder worker, and has become known as one of the stronger intellects on his side of the aisle.

The Texas House delegation has always been powerful, but today is probably weaker than ever before. Back in the days of Speaker Sam Rayburn (who died in 1961), the state's delegation consisted almost exclusively of conservative-leaning Democrats from rural and small town districts. Many had been county judges before they took office; unlike, say, their New York counterparts, they considered a congressional seat, not a judgeship, the pinnacle of their careers, and they stayed in Washington a long time and amassed great seniority. Since then, the one-person-one-vote decisions have required the elimination of some of the old rural districts, and the new members elected from the big cities have usually been liberal Democrats or conservative Republicans. Moreover, the newly assertive Democratic caucus has not been kind to some of the Texans blessed with power over the years by the seniority system. For the 94th Congress, two Texas Chairmen were dethroned, Wright Patman of Banking because of his age (81) and Bob Poage of Agriculture both because of his age and his conservative leanings. If most of the 1974 liberal freshmen are reelected, that will be bad news for another still powerful Texas Chairman, 76-year-old George Mahon of Appropriations; his problem is that his basic philosophic leanings are those far more common among congressional Republicans these days than among Democrats.

Census Data Pop. 11,196,730; 5.53% of U.S. total, 4th largest; Central city, 48%; suburban, 25%. Median family income, $8,486; 33rd highest; families above $15,000: 17%; families below $3,000: 13%. Median years education, 11.7.

1974 Share of Federal Tax Burden $13,658,580,000; 5.10% of U.S. total, 6th largest.

1974 Share of Federal Outlays $14,337,329,000; 5.31% of U.S. total, 3d largest. Per capita federal spending, $1280.

DOD	$5,140,718,000	2d (7.51%)	HEW	$4,235,647,000	5th (4.57%)
AEC	$33,056,000	16th (1.08%)	HUD	$63,762,000	5th (6.54%)
NASA	$294,448,000	2d (9.92%)	VA	$832,446,000	3d (6.09%)
DOT	$410,319,000	4th (4.85%)	EPA	$61,629,000	15th (1.96%)
DOC	$30,340,000	9th (1.88%)	RevS	$288,685,000	5th (4.75%)
DOI	$59,593,000	12th (2.42%)	Int.	$322,338,000	9th (1.57%)
USDA	$992,254,000	2d (7.97%)	Other	$1,572,094,000	

Economic Base Finance, insurance and real estate; agriculture, notably cattle, sorghum grain, cotton lint and dairy products; transportation equipment, especially aircraft; food and kindred products, especially meat products; oil and gas extraction, especially oil and gas field services; boys' furnishings; machinery, especially construction and related machinery.

Political Line-up Governor, Dolph Briscoe (D). Senators, John G. Tower (R) and Lloyd M. Bentsen (D). Representatives, 24 (21 D and 3 R). State Senate (28 D and 3 R); State House (135 D and 15 R).

The Voters

Registration 5,376,537 Total. No party registration.
Median voting age 41.
Employment profile White collar, 49%. Blue collar, 34%. Service, 13%. Farm, 4%.
Ethnic groups Black, 12%. Spanish, 18%. Total foreign stock, 11%.

Presidential vote

1972	Nixon (R)	2,298,896	(67%)
	McGovern (D)	1,154,289	(33%)
1968	Nixon (R)	1,227,844	(40%)
	Humphrey (D)	1,266,804	(41%)
	Wallace (AI)	584,269	(19%)

Sen. John Tower (R) Elected May 27, 1961, seat up 1978; b. Sept. 29, 1925, Houston; home, Wichita Falls; Southwestern U., B.A. 1948, U. of London, 1952, SMU, M.A., 1953; Methodist.

Career Navy, WWII; Prof. of Government, Midwestern U., 1951–61.

Offices 142 RSOB, 202-224-2934. Also 961 Fed. Ofc. Bldg., 300 E. 8th St., Austin 78701, 512-397-5933, and 1714 Fed. Bldg., 1114 Commerce St., Dallas 75202, 214-749-7525.

Committees

Banking, Housing and Urban Affairs (Ranking Member). Subcommittees: Financial Institutions; Housing and Urban Affairs; International Finance; Oversight; Securities.

Armed Services (2d). Subcommittees: Arms Control; General Legislation; Military Construction Authorization; Preparedness Investigating; Tactical Air Power.

Select Committee on Intelligence Operations (Vice Chairman).

Group Ratings

	ADA	COPE	LWV	RIPON	NFU	LCV	CFA	NAB	NSI	ACA
1974	5	18	60	45	19	10	14	80	100	88
1973	0	18	20	38	29	–	27	–	–	92
1972	0	0	18	38	40	0	0	80	100	94

Key Votes

1) No-Knock	FOR	8) Gov Abortn Aid	FOR	15) Consumer Prot Agy	AGN
2) Busing	AGN	9) Cut Mil Brass	AGN	16) Forced Psych Tests	AGN
3) No Fault	AGN	10) Gov Limousine	FOR	17) Fed Campaign Subs	AGN
4) F-111	FOR	11) RR Featherbed	AGN	18) Rhod Chrome Ban	AGN
5) Death Penalty	FOR	12) Handgun License	AGN	19) Open Legis Meetings	AGN
6) Foreign Aid	FOR	13) Less Troop Abrd	AGN	20) Strikers Food Stmps	AGN
7) Filibuster	FOR	14) Resume Turk Aid	FOR	21) Gov Info Disclosure	AGN

Election Results

1972 general:	John G. Tower (R)	1,822,877	(55%)	($2,301,870)
	Barefoot Sanders (D)	1,511,985	(45%)	($629,008)
1972 primary:	John G. Tower (R), unopposed			
1966 general:	John G. Tower (R)	841,501	(57%)	
	Waggoner Carr (D)	643,855	(43%)	

Sen. Lloyd Bentsen (D) Elected 1970, seat up 1976; b. Feb. 11, 1921, Mission; home, Houston; U. of Tex., LL.B. 1942; Presbyterian.

Career Army Air Corps, WWII; Judge, Hidalgo Co., 1946; U.S. House of Reps., 1949–55; Pres., Lincoln Consolidated, financial holding co.

Offices 240 RSOB, 202-224-5922. Also Fed. Bldg., 9th Floor, Austin 78701, 512-397-5834.

Committees

Finance (9th). Subcommittees: Financial Markets (Chairman); International Finance and Resources; Private Pension Plans; Social Security Financeing.

Public Works (5th). Subcommittees: Environmental Pollution, Panel on Environmental Science and Technology, Panel on Materials Policy; Water Resources; Transportation (Chairman).

Joint Economic Committee (5th, Senate Side). Subcommittees: Economic Growth (Chairman); Economic Progress; Fiscal Policy; Inter-American Economic Relationships; International Economics; Urban Affairs.

Group Ratings

	ADA	COPE	LWV	RIPON	NFU	LCV	CFA	NAB	NSI	ACA
1974	40	45	86	24	59	39	33	58	75	41
1973	58	64	67	39	71	–	27	–	–	41
1972	35	30	50	48	67	26	91	60	70	45

Key Votes

1) No-Knock	AGN	8) Gov Abortn Aid	FOR	15) Consumer Prot Agy	FOR
2) Busing	AGN	9) Cut Mil Brass	ABS	16) Forced Psych Tests	ABS
3) No Fault	AGN	10) Gov Limousine	AGN	17) Fed Campaign Subs	FOR
4) F-111	FOR	11) RR Featherbed	FOR	18) Rhod Chrome Ban	FOR
5) Death Penalty	FOR	12) Handgun License	AGN	19) Open Legis Meetings	FOR
6) Foreign Aid	FOR	13) Less Troop Abrd	AGN	20) Strikers Food Stmps	AGN
7) Filibuster	AGN	14) Resume Turk Aid	AGN	21) Gov Info Disclosure	AGN

Election Results

1970 general:	Lloyd Bentsen (D)	1,226,568	(53%)
	George Bush (R)	1,071,234	(47%)
1970 primary:	Lloyd Bentsen (D)	841,316	(54%)
	Ralph W. Yarborough (D)	726,477	(46%)

Gov. Dolph Briscoe, Jr. (D) Elected 1972, term expires Jan. 1979; b. April 23, 1923, Uvalde; U. of Tex., B.A. 1943.

Career Cattle rancher; Armed Forces, WWII; Tex. House of Reps., 1949–57.

Offices State Capitol, Austin 78711, 512-475-4101.

Election Results

1974 general:	Dolph Briscoe (D)	1,016,334	(63%)
	Jim Granberry (R)	514,725	(32%)
	Ramsey Muniz (La Raza Unida)	93,295	(6%)
1974 primary:	Dolph Briscoe (D)	1,025,632	(70%)
	Frances Farenthold (D)	437,287	(30%)

1972 general:	Dolph Briscoe (D)	1,633,970	(48%)
	Henry C. Grover (R)	1,534,060	(45%)
	Ramsey Muniz (La Raza Unida)	214,194	(6%)

◆ ◆ ◆ ◆ ◆

FIRST DISTRICT

The 1st district of Texas is the northeast corner of the state. Its largest cities are Marshall (pop. 22,000), Paris (pop. 23,000), and the Texas half of Texarkana (pop. 30,000). The character of the district has remained agricultural; in fact this part of Texas is that rarity, a part of the South where an old populist tradition retains at least a little vitality. Like Jim Hogg, the populist Governor of Texas in the 1890s, the farmers and townspeople of the 1st are suspicious of bankers, insurance companies, oil men, and Republicans. Neither are they especially fond of race-mixers; in 1968, George Wallace almost carried the 1st, running a close second to Hubert Humphrey.

It is therefore fitting that Wright Patman represents the district in Congress. Born in 1893, Patman first went to Washington in 1929. These two years are the dates of the greatest financial crashes in American history, and Patman has not forgotten them. He brought to Congress the attitudes of a farmer who lost his savings in a failing bank and a shrewd country lawyer's understanding of the workings of American financial institutions. In most Congressmen, such traits would deserve only passing comment; but for twelve years Wright Patman was Chairman of the House Banking and Currency Committee.

In his second term in Congress Patman made some history by submitting a resolution for the impeachment of Treasury Secretary Andrew Mellon; the beleaguered Hoover Administration, rather than face the charge, packed off the millionaire to London as Ambassador to Britain. The Congressman from Texas never let up on the big financiers. Patman was long known for his zealous attacks on the big New York banks and the Federal Reserve Board, and he never hesitated to take on the longtime (1951–69) Fed Chairman William McChesney Martin, who was otherwise a sacred cow on Capitol Hill and Wall Street. Patman has also decried the abuses of the big foundations, and helped to frame the recent laws restricting their operations. And Patman was the man who blew the whistle on the Nixon Administration's plan to bail out the Penn Central Railroad.

But for all that Patman was never a powerful Committee Chairman, and he finally lost his chair—ironically, as a result of liberal gains in the Democratic caucus—in 1975. Housing legislation went through the committee fairly amicably, but it was not really Patman's specialty; and on banking issues, he usually failed to come up with a committee majority. He tried to rule, then, by using the powers of the chair; but that became increasingly difficult as he grew older. In October 1972 Patman wanted to conduct an investigation of the Watergate, but he was stymied by an alliance of Nixon-loyal Republicans and conservative Democrats led by Garry Brown of Michigan and Robert Stephens of Georgia. It was typical of Patman's stewardship: noble intentions, vindicated thoroughly by history—but not the ability to carry them out.

And that was why Patman was dumped by the Democrats at the beginning of the 94th Congress, that and the fact that, at 81, he was just too old. When he appeared before a freshman caucus, Patman seemed to have trouble following the questions. The freshmen, many of them from shaky seats, did not want this man explaining Democratic policy on national TV to their constituents. So most of the freshmen and a majority of the caucus ended up voting—after some complicated parliamentary doings—for the fourth-ranking Democrat on the Committee, Henry Reuss of Wisconsin. A considerably more sophisticated man, or at least so most members believe, Reuss is also nearly 20 years younger and a far more effective speaker and advocate. Patman retains the chair of a subcommittee, and seems resigned to his ouster, although one cannot help thinking that he must wonder why these young populists decided to go after the most senior populist (indeed, the most senior Congressman) of all.

Patman has also had more troubles in his district in the last two elections than he had had since 1928. In 1972, challenger Fred Hudson got 43% of the vote in the Democratic primary; in 1974, Hudson and another challenger held Patman to 54%. Republicans are no threat here, but with his Chairmanship gone Patman may well choose to retire, and if he does not, it is by no means impossible that he will lose. Somehow this genial populist seems to deserve a kinder fate, but the days are gone when a Congressman could remain in office and gain a position of high power simply through seniority.

Census Data Pop. 466,545. Central city, 7%; suburban, 8%. Median family income, $6,543; families above $15,000: 8%; families below $3,000: 21%. Median years education, 10.6.

The Voters

Median voting age 49.
Employment profile White collar, 37%. Blue collar, 44%. Service, 13%. Farm, 6%.
Ethnic groups Black, 22%. Spanish, 1%. Total foreign stock, 1%.

Presidential vote

1972	Nixon (R)	100,495	(70%)
	McGovern (D)	42,139	(30%)
1968	Nixon (R)	40,125	(27%)
	Humphrey (D)	56,764	(38%)
	Wallace (AI)	52,979	(35%)

Rep. Wright Patman (D) Elected 1928; b. Aug. 6, 1893, Patman's Switch; home, Texarkana; Cumberland U., LL.B. 1916; Baptist.

Career Army, WWI; Cotton farmer; Tex. House of Reps., 1921–24; Dist. Atty., 5th Judicial Dist., 1924–29.

Offices 2328 RHOB, 202-225-3035. Also P.O. Box 1868, Texarkana 75501, 214-793-2471.

Committees

Banking, Currency and Housing (2d). Subcommittees: Domestic Monetary Policy (Chairman); Financial Institutions Supervision, Regulation and Insurance.

Interior and Insular Affairs (29th). Subcommittees: Public Lands.

Joint Economic Committee (Vice Chairman). Subcommittees: Economic Progress (Chairman); Priorities and Economy.

Group Ratings

	ADA	COPE	LWV	RIPON	NFU	LCV	CFA	NAB	NSI	ACA
1974	38	78	67	30	78	46	45	0	71	29
1973	46	88	56	25	100	38	100	–	–	21
1972	13	72	33	33	86	19	100	29	100	50

Key Votes

1) Foreign Aid	FOR	6) Gov Abortn Aid	FOR	11) Pub Cong Election $	AGN
2) Busing	ABS	7) Coed Phys Ed	AGN	12) Turkish Arms Cutoff	ABS
3) ABM	ABS	8) Pov Lawyer Gag	ABS	13) Youth Camp Regs	AGN
4) B-1 Bomber	ABS	9) Pub Trans Sub	FOR	14) Strip Mine Veto	FOR
5) Nerve Gas	FOR	10) EZ Voter Regis	ABS	15) Farm Bill Veto	AGN

Election Results

1974 general:	Wright Patman (D)	49,426	(69%)	($141,936)
	James W. Farris (R)	22,619	(31%)	($111,902)
1974 primary:	Wright Patman (D)	57,609	(54%)	
	Fred Hudson (D)	28,106	(27%)	
	Glen Jones (D)	20,167	(19%)	
1972 general:	Wright Patman (D), unopposed			($26,423)

◆ ◆ ◆ ◆ ◆

SECOND DISTRICT

The 2d congressional district of Texas is an almost entirely rural and small town part of east Texas; the largest cities here are Orange (pop. 24,000) and Lufkin (pop. 23,000). More than any other Texas district, the 2d is an extension of the Deep South. Farmers from that region first settled this none too fertile land; their lot was a hard one, and to this day residents of this part of east Texas retain a streak of populism. During the 1930s, it was here in the 2d district that the first really big Texas oil strikes were made. But for the most part, the money went elsewhere—to Houston and Dallas, and to smaller towns like Tyler and Longview.

For 20 years, the 2d district was represented by a man who fit in easily with the older, more conservative Southern Democrats on Capitol Hill. For most of his career, Congressman John Dowdy worked anonymously; he became a high seniority member of the Judiciary Committee and one of the quiet anti-home rule powers of the House District of Columbia Committee. As often as not, he was unopposed in primaries and general elections.

This pleasant existence came to an end when Dowdy was indicted on federal bribery charges in 1970. He was unopposed on the ballot, but 25% of the voters in the district took the trouble to write someone in; it was obvious that Dowdy was through. In 1972, Dowdy was convicted, and thus ineligible to run again anyway; so instead he ran his wife, who was also collecting a comfortable salary as a member of his staff. But for all of Dowdy's fulminations against the Eastern liberals and homosexuals who had supposedly caused all his troubles, Mrs. Dowdy received only a pathetic 18% of the vote in the Democratic primary.

The winner of that election, and the Congressman from the 2d today, was state Senator Charles Wilson. In Austin, he had earned the "liberal" tag because of his support of progressive taxation and his opposition to the kind of Tory cronyism which has bred so much corruption. But at the same time Wilson retained the hell of a fellow style that is almost de rigueur in east Texas campaigning. Wilson has been criticized by some conservationists for not supporting a larger preserve in the Great Thicket area in the 2d district. But overall, he seems to be representing his constituents to their liking; at least, he had no opposition at all in 1974.

Census Data Pop. 466,565. Central city, 5%; suburban, 28%. Median family income, $7,259; families above $15,000: 10%; families below $3,000: 19%. Median years education, 10.5.

The Voters

Median voting age 44.
Employment profile White collar, 38%. Blue collar, 44%. Service, 14%. Farm, 4%.
Ethnic groups Black, 20%. Spanish 3%. Total foreign stock, 2%.

Presidential vote

1972	Nixon (R)	96,398	(68%)
	McGovern (D)	46,325	(32%)
1968	Nixon (R)	37,398	(27%)
	Humphrey (D)	48,651	(36%)
	Wallace (AI)	50,002	(37%)

Rep. Charles Wilson (D) Elected 1972; b. June 1, 1933, Trinity; home, Lufkin; Sam Houston St. U., U.S. Naval Acad., B.S. 1956; Methodist.

Career Navy, 1956–60; Mgr., retail lumber store; Tex. House of Reps., 1961–66; Tex. Senate, 1967–72.

Offices 1504 LHOB, 202-225-2401. Also Fed. Bldg., Lufkin 75901, 713-632-2434.

Committees

International Relations (17th). Subcommittees: International Security and Scientific Affairs.

Veterans' Affairs (10th). Subcommittees: Education and Training; Hospitals; Housing.

Group Ratings

	ADA	COPE	LWV	RIPON	NFU	LCV	CFA	NAB	NSI	ACA
1974	45	82	60	53	85	63	55	50	90	40
1973	48	91	58	36	94	44	63	–	–	32

Key Votes

1) Foreign Aid	FOR	6) Gov Abortn Aid	ABS	11) Pub Cong Election $	FOR
2) Busing	AGN	7) Coed Phys Ed	AGN	12) Turkish Arms Cutoff	AGN
3) ABM	FOR	8) Pov Lawyer Gag	AGN	13) Youth Camp Regs	AGN
4) B-1 Bomber	FOR	9) Pub Trans Sub	FOR	14) Strip Mine Veto	ABS
5) Nerve Gas	FOR	10) EZ Voter Regis	FOR	15) Farm Bill Veto	AGN

Election Results

1974 general:	Charles Wilson (D), unopposed			($18,405)
1974 primary	Charles Wilson (D), unopposed			
1972 general:	Charles Wilson (D)	100,345	(74%)	($93,579)
	Charles D. Brightwell (R)	35,600	(26%)	($2,784)

◆ ◆ ◆ ◆ ◆

THIRD DISTRICT

The rich Texan in all the rich Texan jokes probably lives on the north side of Dallas. This is where the late right wing oilman H. L. Hunt lived in his oversized replica of Mount Vernon, and where Jimmy Ling built his huge mansion before he was driven out of the conglomerate he had put together. The north side is also the fastest growing part of the Dallas-Fort Worth metropolitan area; affluence has pushed the boundaries of development northward, past the Dallas city limits through suburbs like Irving, Farmers Branch, and Richardson, and on into the southern edges of Collin and Denton Counties. Along with most of north Dallas, these suburban areas form the 3d congressional district of Texas.

Dallas is the older and more conservative of the state's two great cities. The wealth in Houston is based on oil and chemicals; in Dallas, more on oil and high finance and, lately, computers. Until recently Dallas, though smaller than Houston had larger bank deposits, and Dallas still ranks as the Southwest's leading financial, banking, and insurance center. Though the big oil companies prefer Houston to Dallas as their headquarters, Dallas can still boast firms like Texas Instruments. All in all, Dallas is more white collar and more Republican. In fact, Dallas was the first part of the state to send a Republican to Congress since Reconstruction—Bruce Alger in 1952. Today, Dallas and suburbs send two Republicans to the House—the only Southern metropolitan area to do so.

The 3d district, because it is the richest part of Dallas, is also the most conservative and the most Republican. In fact, the 3d's current boundaries were drawn precisely to corral most of the Republican parts of Dallas into a single congressional district. The 3d was first created in 1965, when the one-person-one-vote ruling forced the Texas legislature to eliminate a rural district and cede it to Dallas. The district's first Congressman was the picturesque sort of Southern Democrat now increasingly uncommon—a rotund, garrulous, bibulous man named Joe Pool. He was elected Congressman-at-Large from the state in 1962 and 1964; after that seat was eliminated, he ran in the 3d and won in 1966. Following a brief term as Chairman of the House Un-American Activities Committee, he died in 1967.

Pool was succeeded by Republican James Collins. Like all the Republicans who represented Texas in Congress during the 1960s, Collins lost a race—to Pool in 1966—before winning his seat. And like most Texas Congressmen, Collins is a wealthy man (insurance and other ventures). In Congress he has, of course, voted a solid conservative line. What is unusual about Collins is a touch of scandal. His former administrative assistant was convicted and sent to federal prison for exacting kickbacks from members of Collin's staff. Collins himself was accused of involvement in the scheme by Jack Anderson, but after some investigation John Mitchell's Justice Department decided not to seek an indictment. That scandal got Collins a primary opponent in 1972, but he won by a solid 2-1 margin, and has not had any trouble holding the seat since.

Census Data Pop. 466,266. Central city, 54%; suburban, 46%. Median family income, $13,395; families above $15,000: 41%; families below $3,000: 4%. Median years education, 12.9.

The Voters

Median voting age 39.
Employment profile White collar, 74%. Blue collar, 19%. Service, 7%. Farm, –%.
Ethnic groups Black, 1%. Spanish, 5%. Total foreign stock, 8%. Germany, 1%.

Presidential vote

1972	Nixon (R)	174,319	(80%)
	McGovern (D)	43,972	(20%)
1968	Nixon (R)	109,721	(63%)
	Humphrey (D)	43,546	(25%)
	Wallace (AI)	20,158	(12%)

Rep. James M. Collins (R) Elected Aug. 24, 1968; b. Apr. 29, 1916, Hallsville; home, Dallas; SMU, B.S.C., 1937, Northwestern U., M.B.A. 1938, American Col., C.L.U., 1940, Harvard U., M.B.A. 1943; Baptist.

Career Army, WWII; Pres., Consolidated Industries, Inc., and Internatl. Industries, Inc.; Pres., Fidelity Union Life Ins. Co., 1954–65.

Offices 2419 RHOB, 202-225-4201. Also 1100 Commerce St., Rm. 5C48, Dallas 75202, 214-749-2453.

Committees

Interstate and Foreign Commerce (7th). Subcommittees: Oversight and Investigations.

Post Office and Civil Service (5th). Subcommittees: Employee Political Rights and Intergovernmental Programs.

Group Ratings

	ADA	COPE	LWV	RIPON	NFU	LCV	CFA	NAB	NSI	ACA
1974	9	0	0	44	0	13	8	83	100	93
1973	0	9	17	33	0	11	0	–	–	100
1972	6	9	18	21	14	24	50	92	89	91

Key Votes

1) Foreign Aid	AGN	6) Gov Abortn Aid	AGN	11) Pub Cong Election $	AGN
2) Busing	AGN	7) Coed Phys Ed	AGN	12) Turkish Arms Cutoff	ABS
3) ABM	FOR	8) Pov Lawyer Gag	FOR	13) Youth Camp Regs	AGN
4) B-1 Bomber	FOR	9) Pub Trans Sub	AGN	14) Strip Mine Veto	FOR
5) Nerve Gas	FOR	10) EZ Voter Regis	AGN	15) Farm Bill Veto	FOR

Election Results

1974 general:	James M. Collins (R)	63,489	(65%)	($192,058)
	Harold Collum (D)	34,623	(35%)	($79,372)
1974 primary:	James M. Collins (R)	11,89	(82%)	
	Jim White (R)	2,596	(18%)	
1972 general:	James M. Collins (R)	122,984	(73%)	($147,487)
	George A. Hughes, Jr. (D)	44,708	(27%)	($2,775)

◆ ◆ ◆ ◆

FOURTH DISTRICT

The 4th congressional district of Texas is part of the Red River Valley. From the time it was first settled by white men more than a century ago until the 1972 elections, the valley has been staunchly Democratic. This is a part of Texas where the Deep South becomes the Southwest. As one moves west, there are fewer and fewer blacks: only 15% here in the 4th compared to 22% in the 1st district to the east. The 4th, moreover, has virtually no Mexican-Americans. From the early days, the valley has been peopled mostly by poor white farmers and the residents of the small towns where the farm families come to market every Saturday.

Though never rich or cosmopolitan, the Red River Valley can claim a number of famous sons. Dwight Eisenhower was born in Texas just a few miles south of the river, and Carl Albert comes from Bug Tussle, Oklahoma, just to the north. But the valley's most fabled son is Mister Sam, Speaker Sam Rayburn, who represented the 4th district in Congress from 1913 to 1961. Rayburn's career spans almost all of our modern political history. When the young Texan was first elected, Henry Adams still lived in Lafayette Park across from the White House. Rayburn saw Washington grow from the provincial outpost disdained by the Boston Brahmin into the most powerful city in the world.

Rayburn entered the House just after it had freed itself from the iron rule of Speaker Joe Cannon. In 1961, Rayburn went home to die just a few months after he had led, and won, a struggle to increase the membership of the Rules Committee—an attempt to restore power to the Speaker and to take it away from a reactionary committee chairman. During Rayburn's first term in the House, President Wilson, working with Speaker Champ Clark and Majority Leader Oscar Underwood, enacted the entire Democratic legislative program with automatic votes from the Democratic caucus. A half century later, the Rules Committee fight exposed all the cracks and fissures that had developed within the caucus since Wilson's time.

"To get along, you have to go along," Mister Sam often said, and in saying, he admitted that the Democratic Party, split by civil rights and other issues, could no longer operate as a cohesive unit. Members of the party would simply have to take account of the differences among them. Aside from the four years the Republicans controlled the House, Rayburn held the Speakership from 1940 to 1961—for 17 years, longer than anyone else has ever occupied the post. Critics said that he did not exert his power often enough or forcefully enough; Rayburn replied that a heavy hand would only lead to the dissolution of the Democratic Party.

Sam Rayburn also witnessed nearly all the modern political history of Texas. Back in 1912, when he was first elected the big oil strikes lay in the future and big oil money was not yet a factor in Texas politics. Fifty years later, oil dominated the state in just about every conceivable way. Rayburn, as much as anyone, built the politics of oil into the congressional establishment. He made certain, for example, that any Congressman who wanted to cut the oil depletion allowance never got a seat on the tax-writing Ways and Means Committee; and the allowance was not really abolished till 1975, 14 years after Rayburn's death. Rayburn was also largely responsible for the cohesiveness of the Texas delegation, whether the issue was oil, cotton, or military installations. The result: Texas almost always got what it wanted.

Oil changed Sam Rayburn's Texas, and so did shifts in population. In 1912, towns like Rayburn's Bonham (1970 pop. 7,698) were typical of the state—small, dusty agricultural market centers. By 1961, Dallas and Houston had begun to dominate Texas politics, and the state had just elected its first Republican Senator since Reconstruction. Today, Bonham is no longer part of Rayburn's 4th; the town was moved into Wright Patman's 1st district to satisfy the equal population requirement. As it stands now, two-thirds of the 4th is classified as metropolitan, most of it part of the Dallas Standard Metropolitan Statistical Area. Since Rayburn's death, the 4th has also come to include the archconservative, heavily Republican oil towns of Tyler and Longview. These are here mainly because populistic Wright Patman wanted no part of them, and his son chaired the redistricting committee in the Texas Senate.

Rayburn's successor in the 4th district is Ray Roberts, who was born some three weeks after Mister Sam was first sworn in. When first elected in 1962, Roberts was a state Senator and, before that, a staff assistant to the Speaker. He is a man out of the Rayburn mold. When Lyndon Johnson was President, the White House could usually count on Roberts to deliver a liberal vote when needed. But lately, the Congressman's record has grown conservative, reflecting the changing attitudes of his constituency. In 1960, Kennedy carried the 4th, but eight years later Humphrey lost to Nixon within the district's current boundaries. In 1972, McGovern lost the 4th district by better than 2–1.

Since the last couple of redistrictings, Roberts has never really been tested in the district. He beat former Congressman (1939–53, 1957–67) Lindley Beckworth in the 1966 primary when Beckworth's district was eliminated; that was his last tough fight. The Republicans have run candidates against him the last two times, but have failed to win more than 30% of the vote.

Census Data Pop. 466,234. Central city, 24%; suburban, 44%. Median family income, $8,032; families above $15,000: 13%; families below $3,000: 14%. Median years education, 11.6.

The Voters

Median voting age 43.
Employment profile White collar, 44%. Blue collar, 38%. Service, 14%. Farm, 4%.
Ethnic groups Black, 15%. Spanish, 3%. Total foreign stock, 3%.

Presidential vote

1972	Nixon (R)	....	105,236	(72%)
	McGovern (D)	....	41,471	(28%)
1968	Nixon (R)	....	50,332	(37%)
	Humphrey (D)	....	48,436	(36%)
	Wallace (AI)	....	36,088	(27%)

Rep. Ray Roberts (D) Elected Jan. 30, 1962; b. Mar. 28, 1913, Collin County; home, McKinney; Tex. A&M, N. Tex. St., U. of Tex.; Methodist.

Career Dir., Natl. Youth Admin., 1935–40; Staff of U.S. House of Reps. Spkr. Sam Rayburn, 1940–42; Navy, WWII and Korea; Tex. Senate, 1955–62.

Offices 2455 RHOB, 202-225-6673. Also P.O. Box 388, McKinney 75069, 214-542-2617.

Committees

Veterans' Affairs (Chairman). Subcommittees: Cemeteries and Burial Benefits; Compensation, Pension and Insurance.

Public Works and Transportation (5th). Subcommittees: Economic Development; Public Buildings and Grounds; Water Resources (Chairman).

Group Ratings

	ADA	COPE	LWV	RIPON	NFU	LCV	CFA	NAB	NSI	ACA
1974	0	20	18	7	43	17	11	45	89	71
1973	12	33	25	14	68	18	0	–	–	67
1972	6	27	18	20	50	11	0	64	100	87

Key Votes

1) Foreign Aid	AGN	6) Gov Abortn Aid	AGN	11) Pub Cong Election $	AGN
2) Busing	AGN	7) Coed Phys Ed	AGN	12) Turkish Arms Cutoff	AGN
3) ABM	FOR	8) Pov Lawyer Gag	FOR	13) Youth Camp Regs	AGN
4) B-1 Bomber	FOR	9) Pub Trans Sub	AGN	14) Strip Mine Veto	FOR
5) Nerve Gas	FOR	10) EZ Voter Regis	AGN	15) Farm Bill Veto	AGN

Election Results

1974 general:	Ray Roberts (D)	....	48,209	(75%)	($16,337)
	Dick Le Tourneau (R)	....	16,113	(25%)	($28,765)
1974 primary:	Ray Roberts (D), unopposed	....			
	1972 general:	....			
	Ray Roberts (D)	....	95,674	(70%)	($6,383)
	James Russell (R)	....	40,548	(30%)	($685)

◆ ◆ ◆ ◆ ◆

FIFTH DISTRICT

The political history of the 5th congressional district of Texas has been shaped in a special way by the event that is perhaps central to the political history of the 1960s: the assassination in Dallas of President Kennedy in November 1963. For the ten years preceding the murder, Dallas was personified in the minds of many by its Congressman, Bruce Alger, a Republican. Alger was a raucous and fiery ideological right winger, who had won the seat (which then included all of Dallas County) in 1952. In Washington he did little, critics said, except to rant incessantly at liberals. Alger's moment in American history came in 1960, when he took part in a pushing-and-shoving demonstration against Lyndon and Lady Bird Johnson in a Dallas hotel lobby.

The Kennedy assassination seemed to create a politics of remorse among Texans generally and among Dallas residents in particular. In 1964, LBJ captured his home state by a huge majority, and even carried Dallas County in the process. The Dallas establishment was in a mood to atone for what seemed to be the city's violent predilections, as memories of the assassination lingered. As for Bruce Alger, he symbolized what the Dallas establishment wanted to forget. Though he had won previous elections easily, Alger managed only 43% of the vote in 1964—less than Barry Goldwater got in the district.

The winner was Earle Cabell, a former Dallas Mayor and, accordingly, a member in good standing of the city's business and financial elite. That elite had its own political instrument, the Citizens' Charter Commission (CCA), which had dominated city politics for the preceding 20 years. During the Johnson years, Cabell compiled a moderate-to-conservative record in Washington. Thereafter, he was mostly conservative—notably as a high ranking member of the House District of Columbia Committee. Cabell and his friends in the CCA seemed to have adjusted successfully to post-assassination politics, and they were as much in the saddle in Dallas as ever as the sixties turned into seventies.

Suddenly, the Dallas political establishment found itself the victim of one shocking defeat after another. In 1971, the CCA's candidate for Mayor was defeated by an upstart named Wes Wise—who proved to be so popular that he has won ever since. In 1972, the Democratic Tory establishment candidate for Governor, 35-year-old Lieutenant Governor Ben Barnes, was beaten as a result of the Frank Sharp scandal—thus ending a career that was supposed to eventually send Barnes to the White House. And that fall there followed the defeat of Congressman Earle Cabell.

It was partly Cabell's own fault. Two years before he had been challenged in the primary by liberal state Senator Mike McKool, and having survived that Cabell persuaded the legislature to remove significant numbers of black voters from the district. It turned out he needed them in 1972. His Republican opponent, 30-year-old Alan Steelman, ran an energetic campaign. He had the advantage, then, of having been a Nixon Administration appointee, and at the same time of opposing the Dallas establishment on a major issue. The question was whether the Trinity River Canal should be built, a $1.3 billion program to make the river navigable from the Gulf of Mexico to downtown Dallas. Businessmen and local boosters were enthusiastic about the idea of Dallas becoming a seaport; Steelman questioned the cost and the whole idea. Endless, uncontrolled growth, he argued, was not necessarily a good thing, even for Dallas; moreover, the benefits would accrue to a well-placed minority, while the majority would bear most of the costs.

When the votes were counted, Steelman had fashioned a major upset, winning with 56% of the total. A few months later his stance on the canal was vindicated when voters in a 17-county area including Dallas rejected a proposition which would have levied a tax needed to finance the project. In Congress, Steelman has taken a liberal stand on environmental issues—he was one of only three Texas members to vote to open up the highway trust fund for mass transit projects. But on most issues he is inclined to vote with the Republican administration.

Steelman was the main target of a successful redistricting suit in 1974. The plaintiffs requested only minor adjustments in Texas's other districts, but they refashioned the boundaries of the Dallas area districts substantially. Steelman lost wealthy precincts in north Dallas to the 3d district, and gained some black and white working class areas which usually supported liberal Democrats. His general election opponent was the omnipresent McKool—who had run in the next door 24th district in 1972—and the outcome was close: in a low turnout, Steelman took 52% of the vote. That would seem, although nothing is so sure in Dallas these days, that he has won a solid hold on this district.

Census Data Pop. 466,620. Central city, 63%; suburban, 37%. Median family income, $9,480; families above $15,000: 17%; families below $3,000: 9%. Median years education, 11.6.

The Voters

Median voting age 38.
Employment profile White collar, 48%. Blue collar, 38%. Service, 14%. Farm, –%.
Ethnic groups Black, 20%. Spanish, 7%. Total foreign stock, 5%.

824   TEXAS

Presidential vote

1972	Nixon (R)	78,522	(64%)
	McGovern (D)	43,354	(36%)
1968	Nixon (R)	43,716	(40%)
	Humphrey (D)	45,325	(41%)
	Wallace (AI)	21,329	(19%)

Rep. Alan Steelman (R) Elected 1972; b. Mar. 15, 1942, Little Rock, Ark.; home, Mesquite; Baylor U., B.A. 1964, SMU, M.L.A. 1971; Baptist.

Career Exec. Dir., Sam Wyly Foundation of Dallas, 1969; Exec. Dir., Pres. Advisory Cncl. on Minority Business Enterprise, 1969-72.

Offices 437 CHOB, 202-225-2231. Also Suite 9C60, 1100 Commerce St., Dallas 75202, 214-749-7277.

Committees

Government Operations (10th). Subcommittees: Manpower and Housing

Interior and Insular Affairs (7th). Subcommittees: Energy and the Environment; Mines and Mining; National Parks and Recreation.

Group Ratings

	ADA	COPE	LWV	RIPON	NFU	LCV	CFA	NAB	NSI	ACA
1974	36	27	58	75	50	75	31	91	90	53
1973	32	10	42	73	22	67	13	–	–	72

Key Votes

1) Foreign Aid	ABS	6) Gov Abortn Aid	FOR	11) Pub Cong Election $	AGN
2) Busing	AGN	7) Coed Phys Ed	AGN	12) Turkish Arms Cutoff	ABS
3) ABM	FOR –	8) Pov Lawyer Gag	AGN	13) Youth Camp Regs	AGN
4) B-1 Bomber	FOR	9) Pub Trans Sub	AGN	14) Strip Mine Veto	AGN
5) Nerve Gas	AGN	10) EZ Voter Regis	AGN	15) Farm Bill Veto	FOR

Election Results

1974 general:	Alan Steelman (R)	28,446	(52%)	($168,457)
	Mike McKool (D)	26,190	(48%)	($122,086)
1974 primary:	Alan Steelman (R), unopposed			
1972 general:	Alan Steelman (R)	74,932	(56%)	($69,581)
	Earle Cabell (D)	59,601	(44%)	($67,800)

◆ ◆ ◆ ◆ ◆

SIXTH DISTRICT

On the map, the 6th district of Texas looks like a predominantly rural and small town district. As it stretches south out of Dallas and Fort Worth to a point near Houston, the district moves through Waxahachie and Hillsboro to Bryan and College Station, home of Texas A&M. Some blacks live in the rural counties here (10% district-wide), as do a few Mexican-Americans (5%). But overall, poor white farmers and their children who have moved to town dominate this part of the 6th. Raised as staunch Democrats, the farmers and their offspring still vote Democratic from Congressman on down. In recent statewide and national elections, however, they have switched in vast numbers to Republicans like Richard Nixon and John Tower; in fact, this shift is as extensive here as any place in the country.

The map, however, is misleading. For the majority of the 6th district's population lives in metropolitan areas, and almost precisely half live in either Dallas or Tarrant (Fort Worth) Counties. The shape of the 6th represents the typical response of the Texas legislature to the one-person-one-vote doctrine; rather than eliminate an underpopulated rural district, tack on enough metropolitan territory to preserve the seat for the incumbent.

The incumbent in this case is Olin E. (Tiger) Teague, one of the more senior and more personally popular members of the House. Teague first won his seat in a 1946 special election, while still a colonel in the Army; he was a much-decorated and severely wounded combat veteran of World War II. He was one of the first World War veterans elected to Congress, elected just before the rush that brought in John Kennedy, Richard Nixon, Carl Albert, and Gerald Ford. Teague sought and obtained a seat on the Veterans' Affairs Committee, and for years that was his chief source of power. He served as Chairman of that body from 1963 to 1973, a period when its proper subject matter, though not necessarily its attention, shifted from the problems of World War II and Korean veterans (of whom there are dozens in Congress) to the rather different problems of the veterans of the Vietnam war (none of whom reached the House till 1974). During most of his tenure, Congressmen generally were pleased with the way Teague balanced the claims of the veterans with fiscal constraints. But during his later years in the chair, as both costs and expectations rose, veterans' programs came under attack from Vietnam vets who pointed out that the GI bill didn't cover the cost of college like it used to.

In 1973, Teague moved from the chair of Veterans, where he remains the second-ranking Democrat, to the chair of Science and Aeronautics, a committee he has served on since its formation. Teague has always enthusiastically supported manned space flights and high levels of military spending; and it does not hurt that a disproportionate amount of such expenditures come to Texas.

Back in 1971, Teague won the Chairmanship of the House Democratic Caucus. It was the result of a lightning coup, in which he ousted the napping Dan Rostenkowski of Illinois; Teague's Southern connection, hard work on his behalf (he says he supported Rostenkowski), and friendships from the paddle ball court made the difference. He gave up the post, as per the Caucus rule, four years later, at which point it was won by the quite different Phillip Burton of California. There was a rumor afloat for awhile that Richard Nixon wanted to appoint Teague head of the Veterans' Administration, but that never happened, and perhaps was only an attempt by Nixon to curry favor with Teague and his friends as impeachment was coming up.

Census Data Pop. 466,285. Central city, 44%; suburban, 36%. Median family income, $9,417; families above $15,000: 20%; families below $3,000: 12%. Median years education, 12.0.

The Voters

Median voting age 42.
Employment profile White collar, 53%. Blue collar, 32%. Service, 11%. Farm, 4%.
Ethnic groups Black, 10%. Spanish, 5%. Total foreign stock, 5%.

Presidential vote

1972	Nixon (R)	114,865	(72%)
	McGovern (D)	43,610	(28%)
1968	Nixon (R)	56,848	(42%)
	Humphrey (D)	52,934	(39%)
	Wallace (AI)	26,002	(19%)

Rep. Olin E. Teague (D) Elected Aug. 22, 1946; b. Apr. 6, 1910, Woodward, Okla.; home, College Station; Tex. A&M, 1928–32; Baptist.

Career Supt., College Station Post Ofc., 1932–40; Army, WWII.

Offices 2311 RHOB, 202-225-2002. Also U.S. P.O. Bldg., Bryan 77801.

Committees

Science and Technology (Chairman).

Standards of Official Conduct (3d).

Veterans' Affairs (2d). Subcommittees: Compensation, Pension and Insurance; Education and Training (Chairman).

Group Ratings

	ADA	COPE	LWV	RIPON	NFU	LCV	CFA	NAB	NSI	ACA
1974	8	10	14	25	27	33	0	67	83	89
1973	33	33	60	22	71	8	0	–	–	61
1972	6	33	27	29	40	0	50	82	100	90

Key Votes

1) Foreign Aid	AGN	6) Gov Abortn Aid	AGN	11) Pub Cong Election $	ABS
2) Busing	ABS	7) Coed Phys Ed	ABS	12) Turkish Arms Cutoff	ABS
3) ABM	FOR	8) Pov Lawyer Gag	AGN	13) Youth Camp Regs	AGN
4) B-1 Bomber	FOR	9) Pub Trans Sub	ABS	14) Strip Mine Veto	FOR
5) Nerve Gas	FOR	10) EZ Voter Regis	AGN	15) Farm Bill Veto	AGN

Election Results

1974 general:	Olin E. Teague (D)	53,345	(83%)	($7,249)
	Carl A. Nigliazzo (R)	10,908	(17%)	($1,203)
1974 primary	Olin E. Teague (D), unopposed			
1972 general	Olin E. Teague (D)	100,917	(73%)	($3,668)
	Carl A. Nigliazzo (R)	38,086	(27%)	($2,287)

◆ ◆ ◆ ◆ ◆

SEVENTH DISTRICT

Houston is the biggest boom city in Texas. In fact, it is the fastest growing major metropolitan area in the entire nation. New skyscrapers, hotels, apartment buildings, and suburban homes spring up constantly. One after another, the big oil companies are moving their centers of operations to Houston, as are many big petrochemical and electronics firms. Houston today is enjoying—or suffering—the kind of boom growth that Los Angeles experienced in the 1950s, or Chicago in the 1880s.

The biggest boom in Houston has occurred on the west side. Though it has few of the big office buildings, those who occupy the most luxurious executive suites during the day come home in the evening to the west side. The 7th congressional district of Texas takes in virtually all of this posh west side of Houston. It starts off with the rapidly expanding suburbs of the north, near the airport; moves through the ultraexpensive River Oaks section, where many of the state's richest and most powerful people live (John Connally, for one); and on to the new neighborhood named after the Sharpstown shopping center. It is characteristic of boom towns in general and Houston in particular that the namesake and developer of that center, Frank Sharp, was the central figure in the state's juiciest political scandal in years.

Fewer blacks (2%) and Mexican-Americans (6%) live in the 7th than any other Texas district—this richest part of Houston is for Anglo whites only. The district's statistics are spectacular. Its population more than doubled during the 1960s—the third fastest rate of any of the nation's 435 congressional districts: only California's 40th in Orange County and New York's 1st at the eastern end of Long Island grew faster. Some 77% of the employed residents of the 7th hold white collar jobs—again the third highest percentage of any congressional district, behind Maryland's 8th in suburban Washington and the 18th of New York on Manhattan's Upper East Side. In terms of median family income, the 7th ranks not quite so high—17th in the nation—but it is still far ahead of any other Texas district and indeed of any in the South outside the Washington suburbs of Virginia.

The 7th is superlative in still another respect: its preference for Republican politics. Of all current congressional districts, only three gave Richard Nixon a higher percentage of their votes in 1968; four years later, only four Deep South districts recorded larger Nixon percentages. So it is no surprise that the 7th, ever since its creation in something like its present form in 1965, has elected nothing but Republican Congressmen. Its first Representative was George Bush, an oil millionaire with a background unusual for a Texas politician. Bush's father, a partner in Brown Brothers Harriman, was a Connecticut Senator from 1953 to 1963, and the younger Bush attended only the most proper schools back East. Then he moved to Texas, made his own fortune in oil, and entered politics.

Richard Nixon and his political strategists, for reasons that are obscure to many others, always considered Bush a highly merchandisable candidate. The fact is that he has lost twice in races for the Senate, in 1964 and 1970, despite impressive campaign treasuries and potential; that he was scarcely more successful as Republican National Chairman during the disastrous year of 1974. Bush was also, by Nixon's appointment, U.S. Ambassador to the United Nations, and now serves as the American representative in Peking. But the only elective office he has ever held is one he scarcely could have lost, as Congressman from the 7th district, elected in 1966 and 1968, between his two Senate bids. Though he liked to appear as some sort of moderate, he voted basically the orthodox conservative Republican line.

The current Congressman, Bill Archer, comes from a more conventional Texas background. A successful businessman, he was elected to the Texas legislature as a Democrat, then became a Republican. With a safe seat in Congress and a pleasant manner, Archer appears destined to rise in the Republican Caucus. During his first term, he was elected to the Chowder and Marching Society, an unofficial group from whose ranks spring most of the Republican leadership (including one Gerald Ford). After two years on the Banking and Currency Committee, he was elevated to Ways and Means in 1973. His main mission there, of course, was to have been the preservation of the oil depletion allowance—a mostly lost cause now, though Archer can be counted on to continue to vote the wishes of the big oil companies. In his official biography, Archer noted that he received the highest percentage—83%—of any opposed Republican House candidate in 1972. He slipped in 1974, but only to 79%.

Census Data   Pop. 466,336. Central city, 77%; suburban, 23%. Median family income, $13,561; families above $15,000: 41%; families below $3,000: 3%. Median years education, 13.0.

The Voters

Median voting age 38.
Employment profile White collar, 77%. Blue collar, 16%. Service, 6%. Farm, 1%.
Ethnic groups Black, 2%. Spanish, 6%. Total foreign stock, 10%. Germany, UK, 1% each.

Presidential vote

1972	Nixon (R)	161,078	(81%)
	McGovern (D)	37,172	(19%)
1968	Nixon (R)	88,438	(65%)
	Humphrey (D)	29,218	(21%)
	Wallace (AI)	19,089	(14%)

Rep. Bill Archer (R) Elected 1970; b. Mar. 22, 1928, Houston; home, Houston; Rice U., 1946–46, U. of Tex., B.B.A., LL.B. 1951; Catholic.

Career Air Force, Korea; Pres., Uncle Johnny Mills, Inc., 1953–61; Hunters Creek Village Cncl. and Mayor Pro Tem, 1955–62; Tex. House of Reps., 1966–70; Dir., Heights State Bank, Houston, 1967–70; Practicing atty., 1968–71.

Offices 1024 LHOB, 202-225-2571. Also Suite 5607 Fed. Bldg., 515 Rusk St., Houston 77002, 713-226-4941.

Committees

Ways and Means (5th). Subcommittees: Social Security; Trade.

Group Ratings

	ADA	COPE	LWV	RIPON	NFU	LCV	CFA	NAB	NSI	ACA
1974	0	0	0	44	0	24	0	83	100	100
1973	8	9	17	60	5	5	0	–	–	96
1972	6	9	18	38	14	21	100	92	100	100

Key Votes

1) Foreign Aid	AGN	6) Gov Abortn Aid	AGN	11) Pub Cong Election $	AGN
2) Busing	AGN	7) Coed Phys Ed	AGN	12) Turkish Arms Cutoff	AGN
3) ABM	FOR	8) Pov Lawyer Gag	FOR	13) Youth Camp Regs	AGN
4) B-1 Bomber	FOR	9) Pub Trans Sub	AGN	14) Strip Mine Veto	FOR
5) Nerve Gas	FOR	10) EZ Voter Regis	AGN	15) Farm Bill Veto	FOR

Election Results

1974 general:	Bill Archer (R)	70,363	(79%)	($80,941)
	Jim Brady (D)	18,524	(21%)	($10,827)
1974 primary:	Bill Archer (R), unopposed			
1972 general:	Bill Archer (R)	171,127	(82%)	($72,173)
	Jim Brady (D)	36,899	(18%)	($18,500)

◆ ◆ ◆ ◆ ◆

EIGHTH DISTRICT

When visitors come to Houston, the home folks like to show the out-of-towners the sights of the city: the gleaming new skyscrapers downtown; the River Oaks mansions of Ima Hogg (daughter of 1890s populist Governor Jim Hogg); Rice University and the expanse of the Texas Medical Center; and, of course, the Astrodome. The drive takes the visitor southwest from downtown; seldom is an outsider escorted to the east and northeast parts of Houston. Here are the industrial and working class sections of the city that make up Texas's 8th congressional district. The tremendous growth of Houston's petrochemical and oil industries has produced some of the nations's worst air pollution. From a downtown high-rise, one can look out across the flat Texas plains, but the view of east Houston is obscured by a smoggy haze. Below the smog flows the sluggish Houston Ship Channel, a marvel of engineering that made this inland city a major American port. Unfortunately, the waterway is so full of sludge and effluent from the chemical plants and refineries that the Ship Channel is something of a fire hazard.

The 8th is mostly white working class, though some 19% of its residents are black. This part of Houston has not experienced the kind of growth that has hit the west side of town. And the homes here are less likely to enjoy the benefits of air conditioning; they are often within sight (or smell) of chemical plants and refineries. Most people in the 8th are natives of the Texas countryside, or some other place in the rural South. Their politics combines populism and racial fears, as was demonstrated in the 1968 presidential election: 46% for Humphrey, 28% for Wallace, and only 26% for Nixon.

Fifteen years ago, the 8th district included all of Harris County, which in 1970 had a population of 1,741,000. Obviously, that arrangement could not survive the one-person-one-vote doctrine. So the 8th was pared down over time to its present boundaries. Meanwhile, however, the district continued to reelect Albert Thomas, a get-along-go-along Democrat, to the House. Thomas climbed to high rank on and chaired its committee with jurisdiction over the space program the Appropriations Committee; more than anyone else he was responsible for bringing the NASA Manned Space Craft Center to the Houston area (though it is in the 22d district, not the 8th). After Thomas died in 1965, he was succeeded for the remainder of his term, in time honored fashion, by his widow.

Thomas' eventual successor, Bob Eckhardt, who was first elected in 1966, is a man of far different politics. Eckhardt is one of that hardy breed, the Texas liberal. Before coming to Washington, he spent eight years in the Texas legislature, where he fought valiantly, though usually without success, for what he believed. He continues to do so in Congress. Liberals from other parts of the country may get discouraged during a losing streak, and even drop out of politics; Texas liberals, who never really expect to win anything anyway, fight on—and keep their sense of humor, too. Eckhardt is that kind of man—and the most outspoken and scholarly member of the Texas delegation as well. Traditionally, Texas Congressmen have preferred to work in the cloakrooms, whispering quietly to each other. Eckhardt, sporting a bow tie and a brightly colored shirt, does most of his work in committee sessions and on the floor. He is a longtime trial lawyer, and the possessor of one of the rare eloquences in the House; he has the gift, too, of being able to explain abstruse legal matters lucidly and persuasively.

Eckhardt is a middle level member of the Commerce Committee, and one of its most reliably pro-consumer members. But, more important, he is also Chairman of the Democratic Study Group. He won that position in a rare contest with William Ford of Michigan, and by a narrow margin; the DSG, in this freshman-loaded Congress, is apparently finally seen as something worthwhile to head.

Census Data Pop. 466,704. Central city, 48%; suburban, 52%. Median family income, $9,555; families above $15,000: 15%; families below $3,000: 9%. Median years education, 10.9.

The Voters

Median voting age 39.
Employment profile White collar, 40%. Blue collar, 47%. Service, 13%. Farm, –%.
Ethnic groups Black, 19%. Spanish, 10%. Total foreign stock, 7%.

Presidential vote

1972	Nixon (R)	66,870	(55%)
	McGovern (D)	54,313	(45%)
1968	Nixon (R)	27,293	(26%)
	Humphrey (D)	48,559	(46%)
	Wallace (AI)	28,873	(28%)

Rep. Bob Eckhardt (D) Elected 1966; b. July 16, 1913, Austin; home, Harris County; U. of Tex., B.A. 1935, LL.B. 1939; Presbyterian.

Career Practicing atty., 1939–42, 1944–67; Army Air Corps, WWII; Tex. House of Reps., 1958–66.

Offices 1741 LHOB, 202-225-4901. Also 8632 Fed. Bldg., 515 Rusk St., Houston 77002, 713-226-4931.

Committees

Interior and Insular Affairs (19th). Subcommittees: Energy and the Environment; Mines and Mining; National Parks and Recreation.

Interstate and Foreign Commerce (12th). Subcommittees: Consumer Protection and Finance; Energy and Power.

Group Ratings

	ADA	COPE	LWV	RIPON	NFU	LCV	CFA	NAB	NSI	ACA
1974	95	100	92	53	93	94	85	17	11	8
1973	96	100	92	57	89	95	100	–	–	8
1972	94	90	100	71	100	90	50	0	0	5

Key Votes

1) Foreign Aid	FOR	6) Gov Abortn Aid	FOR	11) Pub Cong Election $	FOR
2) Busing	FOR	7) Coed Phys Ed	FOR	12) Turkish Arms Cutoff	FOR
3) ABM	AGN	8) Pov Lawyer Gag	AGN	13) Youth Camp Regs	FOR
4) B-1 Bomber	AGN	9) Pub Trans Sub	FOR	14) Strip Mine Veto	AGN
5) Nerve Gas	AGN	10) EZ Voter Regis	FOR	15) Farm Bill Veto	AGN

Election Results

1974 general:	Bob Eckhardt (D)	30,158	(72%)	($12,841)
	Donald D. Whitefield (R)	11,605	(28%)	($10,008)
1974 primary:	Bob Eckhardt (D)	19,671	(77%)	
	David Shall (D)	5,929	(23%)	
1972 general:	Bob Eckhardt (D)	73,909	(65%)	($15,463)
	Lewis Emerich (R)	39,636	(35%)	($9,392)

◆ ◆ ◆ ◆

NINTH DISTRICT

The 9th congressional district of Texas is the eastern segment of the state's Gulf Coast—an area of big refineries, petrochemical plants, and other factories. It is, in other words, an area dominated by heavy industry, and it has one of the highest concentrations of blue collar workers in Texas. It is dominated by two urban centers of roughly equal size. On Galveston Bay, which leads into the Houston Ship Channel, are the cities of Galveston (pop. 61,000) and Texas City (pop. 38,000). Galveston, one of the oldest cities in Texas, is situated on a sand bar where the Bay empties into the Gulf of Mexico. It was the state's first port, but now handles far less tonnage than Houston or Texas City. The other major population center in the 9th lies around Beaumont (pop. 115,000) and Port Arthur (pop. 57,000). Like Galveston and Texas City, these are industrial towns dominated by the oil and petrochemical industries. The 9th also includes a small portion of Harris County and Houston.

Most of the residents of the district are migrants from the rural South. Some 22% of them are black; another 6% are Cajuns from nearby southern Louisiana. To a surprising extent the people here have retained populistic, Democratic voting habits. These political attitudes are fostered by the Texas labor movement, which is stronger in the 9th than in just about any other part of the state. Though plenty of votes were cast here for George Wallace in 1968 (26%), Hubert Humphrey still carried the district. In 1972, George McGovern ran only 2% behind Humphrey's 1968 showing—the closest the South Dakotan came to matching the Minnesotan in any Texas congressional district. Also in 1972, the 9th was one of the few Texas districts to go for Democrat Barefoot Sanders over Republican Senator John Tower.

Before the 1965 redistricting, Galveston-Texas City and Beaumont-Port Arthur were in two separate districts. Congressman Clark Thompson, who served from 1933 to 1935 and from 1947 to 1967, represented the former and was a member of the Ways and Means Committee. As the elder of two incumbents thrown together by redistricting, Thompson decided to retire. His decision left the seat to Jack Brooks, who continues to occupy it. Brooks is a Texas Congressman in the Sam Rayburn tradition. He often, though not always, takes liberal positions on issues and stays close to the House leadership. His rather liberal voting record, especially his vote for the Civil Rights Act of 1964, was noteworthy in the early 1960s, when his district included some east Texas rural counties akin to the Deep South.

As the third-ranking member of the Judiciary Committee, Brooks was an important part of the impeachment proceedings of 1974. There was little doubt where he stood. As Chairman of a Government Operations Subcommittee which had looked into the financing of the Nixon homes in San Clemente and Key Biscayne, he had sharply criticized the White House, to the discomfiture of many Republicans; and he is by nature a partisan, aggressive man. In any case, Brooks voted for all five resolutions of impeachment, and was one of the main supporters of the unsuccessful move to impeach Nixon for misappropriation of government funds.

Only 30 when he was first elected to Congress in 1952, Brooks has finally moved into the positions of power he has long sought. He is now the number two member of Judiciary, in line for the chair if Peter Rodino should leave, and the Chairman of Government Operations. In that latter position, he is expected to lead aggressive investigations into what has been going on in the Executive Branch; if he does not share all the policy positions of the new Democratic freshmen, he is at least as aggressive as any of them.

Census Data Pop. 466,678. Central city, 60%; suburban, 38%. Median family income, $9,344; families above $15,000: 17%; families below $3,000: 11%. Median years education, 11.5.

The Voters

Median voting age 42.
Employment profile White collar, 45%. Blue collar, 40%. Service, 14%. Farm, 1%.
Ethnic groups Black, 22%. Spanish, 7%. Total foreign stock, 7%.

Presidential vote

1972	Nixon (R)	86,079	(60%)
	McGovern (D)	58,117	(40%)
1968	Nixon (R)	46,166	(32%)
	Humphrey (D)	61,422	(42%)
	Wallace (AI)	37,740	(26%)

Rep. Jack Brooks (D) Elected 1952; b. Dec. 18, 1922, Crowley, La; home, Beaumont; Lamar Jr. Col., 1939–41, U. of Tex., B.J. 1943, J.D. 1949; Methodist.

Career USMC, WWII; Tex. House of Reps., 1946–50; Practicing atty., 1949–52.

Offices 2449 RHOB, 202-225-6565. Also 230 Fed. Bldg., Beaumont 77701, 713-838-0271.

Committees

Government Operations (Chairman). Subcommittees: Communications; Consumer Protection and Finance; Energy and Power.

Judiciary (2d). Subcommittees: Monopolies and Commercial Law.

Group Ratings

	ADA	COPE	LWV	RIPON	NFU	LCV	CFA	NAB	NSI	ACA
1974	45	80	42	40	83	47	36	42	80	38
1973	48	100	50	27	100	17	83	–	–	25
1972	25	90	64	40	86	25	100	9	100	35

Key Votes

1) Foreign Aid	FOR	6) Gov Abortn Aid	AGN	11) Pub Cong Election $	AGN
2) Busing	AGN	7) Coed Phys Ed	AGN	12) Turkish Arms Cutoff	ABS
3) ABM	FOR	8) Pov Lawyer Gag	AGN	13) Youth Camp Regs	AGN
4) B-1 Bomber	FOR	9) Pub Trans Sub	AGN	14) Strip Mine Veto	AGN
5) Nerve Gas	FOR	10) EZ Voter Regis	FOR	15) Farm Bill Veto	AGN

Election Results

1974 general	Jack Brooks (D)	37,275	(62%)	($79,023)
	Coleman R. Ferguson (R)	22,935	(38%)	($12,805)
1974 primary:	Jack Brooks (D), unopposed			
1972 general:	Jack Brooks (D)	89,113	(66%)	($33,565)
	Randolph Reed (R)	45,462	(34%)	($6,527)

◆ ◆ ◆ ◆ ◆

TENTH DISTRICT

The 10th congressional district of Texas is the LBJ congressional district. Here in central Texas the towns are farther apart and trees less common than in east Texas; the land is less fertile, and there is much less rain. Lyndon Johnson was born and raised and began his political career amid the rolling hills of central Texas, which yield a living only to those who work hard. The 10th district left its mark on Johnson. The comparative poverty of its people—especially back in the 1930s, when Johnson was a young man—helped to shape his populistic impulses. And the comparatively good relations here between the Anglo majority and the black (presently 14%) and the Mexican-American (also 14%) minorities helped shape the Johnson who would push Congress into passing the Civil Rights Acts of 1964 and 1965.

Johnson, in turn, has certainly left his imprint on the 10th district. Though its boundaries have changed, the district still includes the town of Johnson City and the LBJ Ranch in Blanco County; Southwest Texas State Teachers College in San Marcos, where Johnson got his degree; and Austin, the state capital and site of the Lyndon B. Johnson Library. Also in Austin is television station KTBC (renamed, since Johnson's death, KLBJ)—the cornerstone of the Johnson family fortune.

Austin (pop. 251,000) has grown substantially since Johnson represented the 10th; and today the city contains half the district's residents. Unlike most Texas cities, Austin is not an oil town, or an idustrial town, or even a farm-market town. Instead, it is dominated by growth industries like state government and higher education (the University of Texas). Accordingly, Austin has more than its proportionate share of liberal intellectuals. The city contains not just the headquarters of

LBJ's operations, but also of Texas liberalism. That hardy creed is maintained, in the face of all manner of adversity, by the *Texas Observer*, an irreverent periodical devoted to the shenanigans of Texas politicians.

Austin and surrounding Travis County usually turn in Democratic majorities. But when the Democratic nominee in a major statewide race is a conservative, Austin will sometimes go Republican. That is what happened, for example, when the Democrats nominated a conservative to oppose Senator John Tower in 1966; Tower took an unlikely 62% of the Travis vote. And in 1972, Democratic gubernatorial nominee Dolph Briscoe got only a plurality in Travis as liberals voted for the ultraconservative Republican or the candidate of La Raza Unida.

Despite the prominence of the local liberal vote—and despite the number of new liberal votes coming out of the University of Texas campus here (39,000 students)—the liberals have remained a negligible force in 10th district congressional races. When Johnson ran for the Senate in 1948, he was succeeded in the House by Homer Thornberry, a moderate-to-liberal Democrat who was appointed to the federal bench in 1963. Judge Thornberry was Johnson's nominee to fill the Supreme Court vacancy which would have been created had Abe Fortas been confirmed as Chief Justice. No one took exception to Thornberry's performance as a judge, but the nomination did smack of cronyism, and certainly contributed to Fortas' rejection in the Senate.

Thornberry's successor in the House is a member in good standing of the state's Tory Democratic establishment. Congressman J. J. (Jake) Pickle over the years seems to have shifted from a liberal line to conservative and back, at least partways, to liberal. He is generally sympathetic to the economic interests of Texans, whether they happen to be rich or poor, and perhaps like LBJ fails to see why there need be any conflict between the two. Locally, he has never been close to the liberals; but in Washington, he has shown the same visceral dislike of Richard Nixon, that one sees in the 9th district Congressman Jack Brooks—and used to see in Lyndon Johnson.

Census Data Pop. 466,313. Central city, 54%; suburban, 9%. Median family income, $7,825; families above $15,000: 16%; families below $3,000: 16%. Median years education, 11.8.

The Voters

Median voting age 39.
Employment profile White collar, 53%. Blue collar, 26%. Service, 16%. Farm, 5%.
Ethnic groups Black, 14%. Spanish, 14%. Total foreign stock, 10%. Germany, 2%; Czech, 1%.

Presidential vote

1972	Nixon (R)	104,400	(59%)
	McGovern (D)	71,161	(41%)
1968	Nixon (R)	52,125	(40%)
	Humphrey (D)	60,205	(46%)
	Wallace (AI)	17,474	(14%)

Rep. J. J. Pickle (D) Elected Dec. 17, 1963; b. Oct. 11, 1913, Big Spring; home, Austin; U. of Tex., B.A. 1938; Methodist.

Career Area Dir., Natl. Youth Admin., 1938–41; Navy, WWII; Co-Organizer, KVET radio, Austin; Advertising and public relations business; Dir., Texas State Dem. Exec. Comm., 1957–60; Mbr., Texas Employment Commission, 1961–63.

Offices 231 CHOB, 202-225-4865. Also 763 Fed. Bldg., Austin 78701. 512-397-5921.

Committees

Ways and Means (16th). Subcommittees: Oversight; Social Security; Unemployment Compensation.

Group Ratings

	ADA	COPE	LWV	RIPON	NFU	LCV	CFA	NAB	NSI	ACA
1974	22	63	45	57	73	53	43	44	75	38
1973	50	45	45	42	85	37	38	–	–	42
1972	13	36	50	31	67	26	50	27	100	65

Key Votes

1) Foreign Aid	AGN	6) Gov Abortn Aid	AGN	11) Pub Cong Election $	AGN
2) Busing	AGN	7) Coed Phys Ed	AGN	12) Turkish Arms Cutoff	FOR
3) ABM	FOR	8) Pov Lawyer Gag	FOR	13) Youth Camp Regs	AGN
4) B-1 Bomber	FOR	9) Pub Trans Sub	FOR	14) Strip Mine Veto	AGN
5) Nerve Gas	FOR	10) EZ Voter Regis	ABS	15) Farm Bill Veto	AGN

Election Results

1974 general:	J. J. (Jake) Pickle (D)	76,240	(80%)	($180,294)
	Paul A. Weiss (R)	18,560	(20%)	($500)
1974 primary:	J. J. (Jake) Pickle (D)	67,794	(67%)	
	Larry Bales (D)	29,034	(29%)	
	E. H. Meadows (D)	3,938	(4%)	
1972 general:	J. J. (Jake) Pickle (D)	130,973	(91%)	($0)
	Melissa Singler (SW)	12,682	(9%)	(NA)

◆ ◆ ◆ ◆ ◆

ELEVENTH DISTRICT

The 11th congressional district lies deep in the heart of Texas. Made up of all or part of 19 counties, the district sits slightly off the geographical center of the state, but just about at its center of population. The 11th includes two good-sized cities, Waco (pop. 95,000) and Temple (pop. 33,000), and a huge Army base, Fort Hood (pop. 33,000). The rest of the district is classic Texas agricultural country, given over to cotton, livestock, and occasional small towns. People here are descended from settlers who came from the Deep South in the nineteenth century. And for the most part they have remained solidly Democratic ever since. They have supported conservative Democrats—this was the only district to go for Senator John Tower's opponent in 1966—and for liberals—Hubert Humphrey got over 50% of the vote here in 1968. Only in 1972 did this part of central Texas bridle at the Democratic ticket, giving 70% of its vote to Richard Nixon and 55% to Tower. But that behavior has not yet been repeated, nor has it been replicated in contests farther down the ballot, like the one for Congressman from the 11th district.

"Contest" is hardly the right word, for the 11th district's Congressman, W. R. Poage, has usually been reelected without opposition since he first won the seat in 1936. Poage had a Republican opponent in 1964, and got a 81% of the vote; another Republican ran ten years later, at which time an older Poage won 83%. Poage could conceivably have more trouble in primaries. An undistinguished state Senator won 40% of the vote against him in 1972, though a completely unknown opponent took only 19% two years later. But so far really formidable opposition has failed to materialize.

How much longer this can go on is unclear. Poage was born three days before the turn of the century, has been in Congress now for 40 years, in House seniority is outranked only by fellow Texans Wright Patman and George Mahon. He was also, until the freshmen swept him out in the 1974 elections swept him out, Chairman of the House Agriculture Committee. Why did he lose? Not so much because people disliked him; he is usually genial, and if he ran committee meetings a little peremptorily, he never got involved in any feuds. Nor was there an ambitious aspirant seeking the post; the number two Democrat, Thomas Foley of Washington, supported Poage. No, the problem simply was that, at 74, Poage was getting a bit too old and not very presentable in front of TV cameras; in the 93d Congress, he had suffered the embarrassment of having to take a major farm bill he was managing off the floor and back to committee. And on most major issues, Poage was simply too far to the right of most Democrats; he votes, more often than not, like a conservative Republican.

And so this pleasant man, one of the prime beneficiaries of the seniority system, became one of the first casualties of its demise. Columnists Evans and Novak and other defenders of what used to be the status quo lamented that the ouster of Poage as Chairman was capricious; but it was scarcely more so than the process by which he had got the chair in the first place. Poage himself took his defeat smiling, and seemed genuinely pleased to be able to savor the pleasures of being a senior Congressman (and Chairman still of an important subcommittee) in official Washington without doing much work. Whether he will retire in 1976, or continue to enjoy congressional life, is not clear.

Census Data Pop. 466,258. Central city, 20%; suburban, 11%. Median family income, $6,755; families above $15,000: 10%; families below $3,000: 18%. Median years education, 11.2.

The Voters

Median voting age 43.
Employment profile White collar, 44%. Blue collar, 33%. Service, 15%. Farm, 8%.
Ethnic groups Black, 12%. Spanish, 9%. Total foreign stock, 8%. Germany, 2%.

Presidential vote

1972	Nixon (R)	91,162	(70%)
	McGovern (D)	39,753	(30%)
1968	Nixon (R)	37,267	(31%)
	Humphrey (D)	59,505	(50%)
	Wallace (AI)	21,925	(19%)

Rep. W. R. Poage (D) Elected 1936; b. Dec. 28, 1899, Waco; home, Waco; U. of Tex., U. of Colo., Baylor U., A.B. 1921, LL.B. 1924; Universalist.

Career Practicing atty., 1924–36; Tex. House of Reps., 1925–29; Tex. Senate 1931–37.

Offices 2107 RHOB, 202-225-6105. Also 205 Fed. Bldg., Waco 76701, 817-752-7272.

Committees

Agriculture (2d). Subcommittees: Conservation and Credit; Cotton; Livestock and Grains (Chairman).

Group Ratings

	ADA	COPE	LWV	RIPON	NFU	LCV	CFA	NAB	NSI	ACA
1974	0	25	17	38	55	18	0	58	88	83
1973	21	36	33	27	70	16	0	–	–	58
1972	6	33	18	33	43	0	50	67	100	81

Key Votes

1) Foreign Aid	AGN	6) Gov Abortn Aid	ABS	11) Pub Cong Election $	AGN
2) Busing	AGN	7) Coed Phys Ed	AGN	12) Turkish Arms Cutoff	AGN
3) ABM	FOR	8) Pov Lawyer Gag	FOR	13) Youth Camp Regs	ABS
4) B-1 Bomber	FOR	9) Pub Trans Sub	AGN	14) Strip Mine Veto	FOR
5) Nerve Gas	FOR	10) EZ Voter Regis	ABS	15) Farm Bill Veto	AGN

Election Results

1974 general:	W. R. Poage (D)	46,828	(83%)	($8,606)
	Don Clements (R)	9,883	(17%)	($190)
1974 primary:	W. R. Poage (D)	50,692	(81%)	
	Connie Lawson (D)	12,053	(19%)	
1972 general:	W. R. Poage (D), unopposed			($76,358)

◆ ◆ ◆ ◆ ◆

TWELFTH DISTRICT

"Cowtown" is what Dallasites are inclined to call Fort Worth. Though the two are often considered twin cities, Dallas (pop. 844,000) long ago eclipsed Fort Worth (pop. 393,000) in size and wealth. Other differences also exist. According to the cliche, Dallas is the end of the East and Fort Worth the beginning of the West. There is some geographical truth to this: the Balcones Escarpment, which separates dry west Texas from humid east Texas, runs between the two cities, somewhere around Freeway Stadium and Six Flags Over Texas in Arlington. Economically the idea makes sense too. Fort Worth did in fact get its start as a cowtown, a place where cowboys drove longhorns to the railhead and later to local stockyards. In the years when Dallas was becoming the leading banking and insurance center of the Southwest, Fort Worth was growing as a meat-packing, blue collar factory town.

Even the kinds of defense contracts awarded to the two cities illustrate how they differ. Dallas produces radar systems, infrared detecting devices, and special communications equipment—all spinoffs of its high technology, high value-added electronics and computer industries. Fort Worth, meanwhile, is one of the nation's leading recipients of Defense Department funds, because the General Dynamics plant here produces the F-111—as the result of a contract award made during the Kennedy Administration after some Texas string-pulling.

Given these differences, Fort Worth is, as one would expect, less Republican and generally less conservative than Dallas. The 12th congressional district, which includes most of Fort Worth and the Tarrant County suburbs to the north, is therefore one of the state's more liberally inclined seats. Since the elections of 1954, the 12th has sent Congressman Jim Wright to Washington. During his first years of service, Wright was the foremost liberal in the Texas delegation. He remains one of its enthusiastic backers of liberal positions on economic issues. But on other issues, he has found that his views diverge from those held by most House Democrats. For one thing, Wright has always supported American military intervention in Southeast Asia; in 1969, he was chief sponsor of a resolution which, in the face of the Moratorium demonstrations, was meant to be an endorsement of Nixon's Vietnam war policy. For another, Wright does not share the enthusiasm seen in many younger, less senior Democrats—and some Republicans—for environmental causes.

Indeed, Wright's major role in Congress these days seems to be as an adversary to such causes. He is a senior member of the Public Works Committee, a body whose leadership has always been more sympathetic to the idea of building dams and roads than to the notion that you ought to care about the rivers and earth you are building them on. In 1973, Wright was the main opponent of the move to prevent opening the highway trust fund to expenditures for mass transit; he was successful in the House, with the help of the highway lobby of course and of Gerald Ford, but he lost out in conference committee.

But if Wright is the friend of one big lobby, he is certainly not a favorite of the oil lobby which is so important in Texas politics. In 1974, he was head of a Democratic panel which was supposed to draw up an energy policy; though nothing came of his plan (House Ways and Means Chairman Al Ullman, among others, didn't like it), it was not what the oil companies wanted either. In any case, the big oil money certainly did not flow to Wright when he ran for the Senate. In 1961, in the special election to fill Lyndon Johnson's seat, he ran a close third behind William Blakeley, the ultra-conservative Democrat who had been appointed *ad interim*, and John Tower, the Republican who upset Blakeley in the runoff. In 1966, he wanted another shot at Tower's seat. But the Tory establishment and Governor John Connally decided that state Attorney General Waggoner Carr was to be the party's candidate. Unable to raise the big money, Wright went on TV and asked for $10 contributions. He received a lot of them, but not enough for a Senate race in Texas.

Wright might very well have won the Senate seat had he been able to get into either general election. Both time Tower was helped by liberal voters who refused to support the Democratic nominee—and would certainly have voted for Wright. By now Wright has given up hopes of statewide office; at 54, he is comfortable in his senior position in the House. In the 12th district, he wins routine reelection, usually without opposition.

Census Data Pop. 466,930. Central city, 61%; suburban, 39%. Median family income, $9,441; families above $15,000: 18%; families below $3,000: 9%. Median years education, 11.6.

The Voters

Median voting age 41.
Employment profile White collar, 47%. Blue collar, 39%. Service, 13%. Farm, 1%.
Ethnic groups Black, 16%. Spanish, 7%. Total foreign stock, 6%.

Presidential vote

1972	Nixon (R)	75,156	(62%)
	McGovern (D)	45,508	(38%)
1968	Nixon (R)	39,826	(37%)
	Humphrey (D)	51,584	(48%)
	Wallace (AI)	16,613	(15%)

Rep. Jim Wright (D) Elected 1954; b. Dec. 22, 1922, Fort Worth; home, Fort Worth; Weatherford Col., U. of Tex.; Presbyterian.

Career Army Air Corps, WWII; Partner, trade extension and advertising firm; Tex. House of Reps.; Mayor of Weatherford; Pres., Tex. League of Municipalities, 1953.

Offices 2459 RHOB, 202-225-5071. Also 9A10 Fed. Bldg., 819 Taylor St., Fort Worth 76102, 817-334-3212.

Committees

Budget (3d).

Government Operations (9th). Subcommittees: Government Information and Individual Rights; Legislation and National Security.

Public Works and Transportation (2d). Subcommittees: Aviation; Investigations and Review (Chairman); Surface Transportation.

Group Ratings

	ADA	COPE	LWV	RIPON	NFU	LCV	CFA	NAB	NSI	ACA
1974	33	70	50	23	86	44	39	9	100	31
1973	42	80	70	43	94	53	57	–	–	24
1972	19	80	55	58	83	25	20	50	0	100

Key Votes

1) Foreign Aid	FOR	6) Gov Abortn Aid	AGN	11) Pub Cong Election $	AGN
2) Busing	AGN	7) Coed Phys Ed	AGN	12) Turkish Arms Cutoff	FOR
3) ABM	FOR	8) Pov Lawyer Gag	AGN	13) Youth Camp Regs	AGN
4) B-1 Bomber	FOR	9) Pub Trans Sub	FOR	14) Strip Mine Veto	AGN
5) Nerve Gas	FOR	10) EZ Voter Regis	FOR	15) Farm Bill Veto	AGN

Election Results

1974 general:	Jim Wright (D)	42,632	(79%)	($118,839)
	James S. Garvey (R)	11,543	(21%)	($65,161)
1974 primary:	Jim Wright (D), unopposed			
1972 general:	Jim Wright (D), unopposed			($2,765)

♦ ♦ ♦ ♦ ♦

THIRTEENTH DISTRICT

The 13th congressional district of Texas is an entity which is totally the creation of politics, an amalgam of two old congressional districts which, because of the one-person-one-vote doctrine, had to be combined, but which had always been separate and rather different regions. The old 13th district, which forms the eastern part of the current seat, is part of the agricultural land of the

Red River Valley; like all of that valley, it is traditionally heavily Democratic. (See Fourth District.) Typical of the rural territory here is Archer County, where *The Last Picture Show* was filmed. It is dusty land, with empty skylines; it only grudgingly yields a good living. Virtually all the people here are white Anglos. After the movie appeared, one reader of the New York *Times* wrote in to ask where the blacks and chicanos were; the fact is that there are virtually none in Archer City. Indeed, that is almost as true of Wichita Falls (pop. 97,000), the largest city in this part of the district, the home of Midwestern University where John Tower used to teach before he was elected Senator.

The other half of the 13th district is the old 18th, situated on the High Plains of the Texas panhandle, drier and less fertile land than the Red River Valley. West of the 100th meridian, the land is full of dry gullies that swell to floods when it rains. But it seldom does; instead, the wind blows as hard and as unremittingly as anywhere in the United States. Over the years, most of the panhandle farmers and ranchers seem to have moved into Amarillo (pop. 127,000) and smaller places like Pampa and Borger. First settled by people from neighboring northwest Oklahoma and western Kansas, the panhandle has always been one of the most Republican areas of Texas. In recent years, the heavily conservative leanings of Amarillo—known, locally at least, as the helium capital of the world—have strengthened the region's traditional Republicanism.

The combining of the old 13th and 18th districts must have inspired feelings of nausea in Graham Purcell, the moderate Democrat who had represented the 13th, and Bob Price, the conservative Republican rancher who represented the 18th. Each knew that the 1972 contest between them would be hard fought and decided, probably, by a narrow margin; and each knew that he could well lose his seat. As it happened, in the course of the next two elections both did.

The first to lose was Purcell. He had hoped to make an issue of farm policy—both he and Price served on Agriculture—and the Russian wheat deal; Price in turn probably wanted to tie the Democrat to McGovern. But what really happened is that each of the old districts simply stayed loyal to its Congressman. In 1968—the last time Price and Purcell had both had general election opposition—the combined Republican-Democratic vote within the confines of the new 13th district gave the Republican a 54–46 edge. The result in 1972: 55% for Price, 45% for Purcell.

The vista ahead looked good for Price. But something—we must assume it was Watergate—sharply changed the political patterns here. Price drew strong opposition in 1974, in the person of state Senator Jack Hightower; and he lost, with only 42% of the vote. It was not so much a change in sentiment of the voters. Hightower increased Purcell's percentage in the old 13th portion of the district from 66% to 75%, but in the old 18th part improved only from 34% to 37%. No, the real change was in who the voters were. The traditionally Republican old 18th had cast 63% of the district's total vote in 1972; two years later, the voters here, dispirited by Watergate, cast only 48% of the district votes. If turnout in the old 18th portion had declined by the same proportion as in the old 13th, Price would have gotten something like 49% of the vote—perhaps enough to win. He may have been one of the true, and quite unanticipated, political casualties of Watergate.

Hightower has the reputation of a moderate Democrat. With seats on the Agriculture and Small Business Committees, and the advantages of incumbency, he should be hard to beat in 1976 although predictions like that in this district sometimes prove to be incorrect.

Census Data Pop. 466,663. Central city, 48%; suburban, 10%. Median family income, $8,182; families above $15,000: 14%; families below $3,000: 11%. Median years education, 12.1.

The Voters

Median voting age 43.
Employment profile White collar, 46%. Blue collar, 32%. Service, 14%. Farm, 8%.
Ethnic groups Black, 5%. Spanish, 6%. Total foreign stock, 4%.

Presidential vote

1972	Nixon (R)	115,660	(76%)
	McGovern (D)	36,339	(24%)
1968	Nixon (R)	71,606	(46%)
	Humphrey (D)	53,248	(34%)
	Wallace (AI)	32,017	(20%)

Rep. Jack Hightower (D) Elected 1974; b. Sept. 6 1926, Memphis; home, Vernon; Baylor U., B.A. 1949, LL.B. 1951; Baptist.

Career Navy, WWII; Practicing atty., 1951–74; Tex. House of Reps., 1953–54; Dist. Atty., 1955–61; Tex. Senate, 1965–74.

Offices 1315 LHOB, 202-225-3706. Also 310 P.O. Bldg., Amarillo 79105, 806-376-2381.

Committees

Agriculture (21st). Subcommittees: Conservation and Credit; Cotton; Livestock and Grains.

Small Business (25th). Subcommittees: Activities of Regulatory Agencies; Government Procurement and International Trade.

Group Ratings: Newly Elected

Key Votes

1) Foreign Aid	AGN	6) Gov Abortn Aid	NE	11) Pub Cong Election $	NE
2) Busing	NE	7) Coed Phys Ed	ABS	12) Turkish Arms Cutoff	NE
3) ABM	NE	8) Pov Lawyer Gag	NE	13) Youth Camp Regs	ABS
4) B-1 Bomber	FOR	9) Pub Trans Sub	NE	14) Strip Mine Veto	FOR
5) Nerve Gas	NE	10) EZ Voter Regis	NE	15) Farm Bill Veto	AGN

Election Results

1974 general:	Jack Hightower (D)	34,375	(58%)	($124,132)
	Robert Price (R)	25,153	(42%)	($157,697)
1974 primary:	Jack Hightower (D)	45,378	(65%)	
	Ray Ruffin (D)	14,627	(21%)	
	Louis Finney (D)	9,598	(14%)	

◆ ◆ ◆ ◆ ◆

FOURTEENTH DISTRICT

The 14th congressional district of Texas moves along the state's steamy Gulf Coast from the Brazosport area just south of Houston to Padre Island, the National Seashore below Corpus Christi. Behind the sand bars that protect the harbors from the Gulf are some of the largest oil refineries and chemical plants in Texas, in places like Brazosport, Port Lavaca, Victoria, and Corpus Christi (pop. 204,000), the district's largest city. There are plans to build an offshore "superport" in Brazosport to accommodate giant oil tankers.

The 14th is sweaty, heavy industry country. It is one of the few parts of Texas where the state's labor unions have much influence. Few blacks live this far south and west in Texas, and they make up only 7% of the district's population. But the 14th does have a large Mexican-American minority (37%). On economic issues, this district is one of the more liberal in the state. In statewide primaries, it has supported liberal candidates like former Senator Ralph Yarborough and Frances Farenthold, who once represented Corpus Christi in the state legislature.

The 14th's current Congressman, John Young, has held the office since he knocked off an incumbent in the 1956 primary. Young's votes in the House were part of the majorities fashioned by Speakers Sam Rayburn and John McCormack for the passage of liberal legislation in the sixties; indeed, he was an important part of their plans, as a member of the key Rules Committee. Lately, he has voted with House liberals with far less frequency, generally only on issues that unite all Democrats against virtually all the Republicans. Part of the reason is undoubtedly the Vietnam war. Like others in the dwindling band of economic liberals who backed the war, Young seems to have got out of touch with the main bloc of liberals, and increasingly out of sympathy with them.

Nevertheless, he remains at least somewhat responsive to the House leadership, and his vote on Rules is usually cast to allow liberal legislation to reach the floor. At home, Young's record in the House sets pretty well. Anyway, since 1964 he has run into only one opponent in either the primary or the general election. Yancy White, who ran against him in the 1972 primary, tried to win labor, Mexican-American, and youth support, and ended up winning 34% of the vote—an amount suggesting a certain weakness in the incumbent, but not enough at least yet to make the difference. But no one ran against him in 1974 and, at this writing, no major opposition has emerged in 1976. Though Young is only 60, he has had problems with his eyesight, and could conceivably retire; for the moment, that seems to be the only way the seat will change hands.

Census Data Pop. 466,437. Central city, 44%; suburban, 17%. Median family income, $7,683; families above $15,000: 13%; families below $3,000: 16%. Median years education, 11.1.

The Voters

Median voting age 42.
Employment profile White collar, 44%. Blue collar, 36%. Service, 15%. Farm, 5%.
Ethnic groups Black, 7%. Spanish, 37%. Total foreign stock, 13%. Germany, 1%.

Presidential vote

1972	Nixon (R)	84,574	(61%)
	McGovern (D)	54,815	(39%)
1968	Nixon (R)	45,033	(34%)
	Humphrey (D)	68,864	(52%)
	Wallace (AI)	19,433	(14%)

Rep. John Young (D) Elected 1956; b. Nov. 10, 1916, Corpus Christi; home, Corpus Christi; St. Edwards U., B.A. 1937, U. of Tex. Law School, 1937–40; Catholic.

Career Practicing atty., 1940–56; Asst. Nueces Co. Atty., 1947–50, Co. Atty., 1951–52, Judge, 1953–56.

Offices 2204 RHOB, 202-225-2831. Also U.S. Courthouse, 521 Starr St., Corpus Christi 78401, 512-888-3141.

Committees

Rules (5th).

Joint Committee on Atomic Energy (2d, House Side). Subcommittees: Communities (Chairman); ERDA, Nuclear Energy; National Security.

Group Ratings

	ADA	COPE	LWV	RIPON	NFU	LCV	CFA	NAB	NSI	ACA
1974	26	64	17	31	79	25	23	25	100	33
1973	28	80	58	33	85	28	57	–	–	41
1972	19	73	50	38	86	13	0	27	100	55

Key Votes

1) Foreign Aid	FOR	6) Gov Abortn Aid	AGN	11) Pub Cong Election $	AGN
2) Busing	AGN	7) Coed Phys Ed	AGN	12) Turkish Arms Cutoff	AGN
3) ABM	FOR	8) Pov Lawyer Gag	AGN	13) Youth Camp Regs	AGN
4) B-1 Bomber	FOR	9) Pub Trans Sub	FOR	14) Strip Mine Veto	FOR
5) Nerve Gas	FOR	10) EZ Voter Regis	FOR	15) Farm Bill Veto	AGN

Election Results

1974 general:	John Young (D), unopposed	($2,361)
1974 primary:	John Young (D), unopposed	
1972 general:	John Young (D), unopposed	($17,706)

◆ ◆ ◆ ◆ ◆

FIFTEENTH DISTRICT

South Texas lives closer to the feudal ages than any region in the United States. Here are the fabled Texas ranches: the King Ranch covers more acreage than Rhode Island, and produces an annual income of $25 million—mostly from oil, not cattle. Just down the road (which is to say, in the next county) is a spread, not too much smaller, which belongs to former White House Counselor Anne Armstrong and her husband. Farther south is the Lower Rio Grande Valley. Here, thanks to irrigation water and the semitropical climate, are fields of cotton, fruits, and vegetables tended by Mexican farm hands. Cesar Chavez tried to do some organizing among the laborers, but without much success.

This is the land of Texas's 15th congressional district. It includes not only the Lower Rio Grande, but also some of the interior counties between Corpus Christi and Laredo, though it contains neither of those two cities. Though 75% of the residents of the district are of Mexican stock, virtually all the important decisions here are made by Anglo ranchers, bankers, lawyers, and farmers. Evidence of Anglo power is rife in the election returns, too. Thus Richard Kleberg, owner of the King Ranch, represented this part of Texas in the House from 1931 to 1945; a young poor boy from the hills around Austin named Lyndon Johnson got his first government job in Kleberg's office.

Another Lower Rio Grande Congressman was Lloyd Bentsen. His father had made a fortune in land in the Valley (and was accused of selling parcels to Northern retirees which lacked water and sewers); young Lloyd was elected County Judge at 25 and Congressman at 27, in 1946. Bentsen retired from the House in 1954 to make a fortune of his own in Houston; his successor was Joe M. Kilgore, a pillar of the Connally Tory Democratic establishment. Kilgore wanted badly to run against Ralph Yarborough in the 1964 Senate primary; LBJ persuaded him not to, and six years later Yarborough was beaten by Bentsen.

In the smaller counties of the district, the voters are easy to manipulate. Almost all of them are cast by Mexican-American field hands whose jobs depend on a single landowner. The evidence is plain from the election returns: Jim Hogg County, for example, went 82% for Humphrey in 1968 and 47% for Nixon in 1972. Most interesting is the voting history of Duval County, long the fiefdom of the Parr family. Its most famous performance came in the 1948 Senate runoff primary. After some delay, Duval reported 4,622 votes for Lyndon Johnson and 40 for his opponent. Inasmuch as the county had gone just the other way a few weeks before, people were suspicious of the result; but it was certified, and "Landslide Lyndon" carried the state by 87 votes. Now the reign of the Parrs seems to be over. George Parr, the latest "Duke of Duval" was sentenced to jail on an income tax charge and killed himself in 1974. But probably the same kind of power will be exerted by a Mexican-American family which used to be allied with the Parrs.

When Kilgore retired from the House, in 1964, someone apparently decided that it was time the 15th had a Mexican-American Congressman, and accordingly Eligio de la Garza was elected. He had shown his reliability through twelve years as a state Representative; he is by no means a favorite of the militant young chicanos, and generally votes like other conservative Texas Democrats. The seniority system has been especially kind to de la Garza. Mainly because of the retirement of aging Southern Democrats, he is now the third-ranking Democrat on the Agriculture Committee and Chairman of its Department Operations Subcommittee. Of the two senior Democrats, Chairman Thomas Foley may run for the Senate in the next few years, and former Chairman Bob Poage is 76; thus de la Garza has an excellent chance of becoming Chairman soon. The few times he has had opponents in the 15th he has won easily.

Census Data Pop. 466,359. Central city, 37%; suburban, 32%. Median family income, $5,059; families above $15,000: 8%; families below $3,000: 29%. Median years education, 8.3.

The Voters

Median voting age 41.
Employment profile White collar, 40%. Blue collar, 34%. Service, 13%. Farm, 13%.
Ethnic groups Spanish, 75%. Total foreign stock, 36%.

Presidential vote

1972	Nixon (R)	65,696	(55%)
	McGovern (D)	53,967	(45%)

Rep. E de la Garza (D) Elected 1964; b. Sept. 22, 1927, Mercedes; home, Mission; Edinburg Jr. Col., St. Mary's U., San Antonio, LL.B. 1952; Catholic.

Career Navy, WWII; Army, Korea; Practicing atty., 1952–64; Tex. House of Reps., 1952–64.

Offices 1434 LHOB, 202-225-2531. Also 801 Quince St., McAllen 78501, 512-682-5545.

Committees

Agriculture (3d). Subcommittees: Conservation and Credit; Cotton; Department Operations, Investigations and Oversight (Chairman).

Merchant Marine and Fisheries (11th). Subcommittees: Coast Guard and Navigation; Fisheries and Wildlife Conservation and the Environment; Oceanography.

Group Ratings

	ADA	COPE	LWV	RIPON	NFU	LCV	CFA	NAB	NSI	ACA
1974	18	40	33	18	79	8	10	42	78	67
1973	26	60	50	23	84	11	25	–	–	54
1972	13	60	56	54	86	18	50	27	100	55

Key Votes

1) Foreign Aid	AGN	6) Gov Abortn Aid	ABS	11) Pub Cong Election $	AGN
2) Busing	AGN	7) Coed Phys Ed	AGN	12) Turkish Arms Cutoff	AGN
3) ABM	FOR	8) Pov Lawyer Gag	FOR	13) Youth Camp Regs	AGN
4) B-1 Bomber	FOR	9) Pub Trans Sub	ABS	14) Strip Mine Veto	FOR
5) Nerve Gas	FOR	10) EZ Voter Regis	FOR	15) Farm Bill Veto	AGN

Election Results

1974 general:	E. (Kika) De La Garza (D), unopposed ..	($1,562)
1974 primary:	E. (Kika) De La Garza (D), unopposed	
1972 general:	E. (Kika) De La Garza (D), unopposed ..	($4,456)

♦ ♦ ♦ ♦ ♦

SIXTEENTH DISTRICT

"West of the Pecos" is a phrase associated with the frontier justice of Judge Roy Bean, but it is also a pretty fair description of the location of the 16th congressional district of Texas. When Bean held court in his barroom in the town of Langtry, there was precious little of anything except uninhabited desert west of the Pecos. Today, there is not much more—except for the city of El Paso. With 359,000 residents, El Paso dominates the 16th district. Aside from the little town of Pecos (pop. 12,000) and the district's portion (pop. 49,000) of the oil rich, conservative city of Odessa, El Paso is the only significant population center in the 16th. Typical of the landscape beyond is the harsh desert of Loving County, which in 1970 had a population of 164 people—the lowest population of any county in the nation.

El Paso is a Sun Belt city that mushroomed after World War II. Its economy was fueled by the nearby presence of giant military installations like Fort Bliss and the White Sands Proving Grounds. Across the Rio Grande, whose flow is only a trickle most of the year, lies Ciudad Juarez, Mexico, which has an even larger population. A majority of El Paso's residents are Mexican in origin, though no one can say just how many live here. This part of Texas gave us the word "wetback", and many Mexican nationals still cross the border, legally and illegally, every day looking for higher paying jobs in the United States.

Power in El Paso rests firmly in the hands of Anglos, as Mexican-Americans do not cast anything like their proportionate share of votes. The hottest issue in the city a few years back was the strike at the Farah plant. Non-unionized El Paso has become the western center of the garment industry, with so much cheap labor around. The National Labor Relations Board finally ordered an election at Farah, but the basic problem—this is a low wage industry even when unions are voted in—remains.

The 16th is one of the few Texas districts to change partisan hands within recent memory. The Billie Sol Estes scandal of 1962 accounts for the shift. Estes, a businessman from Pecos, was caught defrauding the Department of Agriculture and was eventually sent to prison. Because he had contributed to campaigns of several prominent Texas Democrats, area Republicans smelled a potential issue. One of the recipients of Estes's generosity was the 16th's then Congressman, J. T. (Slick) Rutherford, a moderate Democrat first elected in 1954. Rutherford will be perhaps best remembered in American history for having once employed Larry L. King, now a famous journalist. During the campaign, Republican candidate Ed Foreman trumpeted the Estes-Rutherford connection up and down the district, and the Goldwaterite won the seat here in 1962.

Foreman's tenure was short-lived. In 1964, he was beaten by Democrat Richard White, the current incumbent. Foreman later moved to New Mexico, got elected to Congress again in 1968 and lost again in 1970—setting a record for himself in the process. White is a Texas moderate who has compiled a liberal record on several issues, including civil rights, which pleases the district's Mexican-American voting minority. At the same time, White's record shows a kind of innate conservatism, attuned with the desires of the Anglo voting majority. The Congressman is not an especially forceful campaigner, and the inclusion of part of Republican Odessa in the district in 1972 might well have inspired spirited opposition. But it didn't, and White appears to have a safe seat.

Census Data Pop. 466,663. Central city, 81%; suburban, 9%. Median family income, $7,936; families above $15,000: 14%; families below $3,000: 12%. Median years education, 12.0.

The Voters

Median voting age 38.
Employment profile White collar, 49%. Blue collar, 36%. Service, 13%. Farm, 2%.
Ethnic groups Black, 3%. Spanish, 50%. Total foreign stock, 34%. Germany, 2%.

Presidential vote

1972	Nixon (R)	69,211	(64%)
	McGovern (D)	39,749	(36%)
1968	Nixon (R)	40,900	(43%)
	Humphrey (D)	40,510	(43%)
	Wallace (AI)	13,164	(14%)

Rep. Richard C. White (D) Elected 1964; b. Apr. 29, 1923, El Paso; home, El Paso; U. of Tex. at El Paso, U. of Tex., B.A. 1946, LL.B. 1949; Episcopalian.

Career USMC, WWII; Practicing atty., 1949–64; Tex. House of Reps., 1955–58.

Offices 2423 RHOB, 202-225-4831. Also Rm. 146 U.S. Courthouse, El Paso 79901, 915-543-7650.

Committees

Armed Services (11th). Subcommittees: Military Installations and Facilities; Research and Development.

Post Office and Civil Service (7th). Subcommittees: Retirement and Employee Benefits.

Group Ratings

	ADA	COPE	LWV	RIPON	NFU	LCV	CFA	NAB	NSI	ACA
1974	9	18	36	14	50	27	8	42	80	67
1973	28	36	42	36	85	22	25	–	–	52
1972	13	45	42	38	71	27	50	33	100	57

Key Votes

1) Foreign Aid	AGN	6) Gov Abortn Aid	AGN	11) Pub Cong Election $	AGN
2) Busing	AGN	7) Coed Phys Ed	AGN	12) Turkish Arms Cutoff	AGN
3) ABM	FOR	8) Pov Lawyer Gag	FOR	13) Youth Camp Regs	AGN
4) B-1 Bomber	FOR	9) Pub Trans Sub	AGN	14) Strip Mine Veto	FOR
5) Nerve Gas	AGN	10) EZ Voter Regis	AGN	15) Farm Bill Veto	AGN

Election Results

1974 general: Richard C. White (D), unopposed .... ($11,373)
1974 primary: Richard C. White (D), unopposed
1972 general   Richard C. White (D), unopposed .... ($2,009)

◆ ◆ ◆ ◆

SEVENTEENTH DISTRICT

Why has the Texas delegation always been so powerful in the House, and the much larger New York delegation so impotent? The answer lies in the seniority system, and the difference between Texas and New York politics. It can be summed up this way: in Texas judges become Congressmen, and in New York Congressmen become judges. New York judgeships pay something like $40,000 a year; the hours are short, and the working conditions excellent: besides, most New Yorkers consider Washington scarcely more civilized than Albany. So it is no surprise that in the last 20 years, nine New York City Congressmen have resigned to become judges.

In Texas, the story is just the opposite. Small county judgeships pay only a pittance, and bright young men run for them as a first step on the political ladder. So it should be no surprise that seven of the current members of the Texas delegation, including Senator Lloyd Bentsen, once served as either county judge or district attorney. Moreover, only one Texas Congressman has resigned in recent years to become a judge: Homer Thornberry, who was proferred a seat on the U.S. Court of Appeals by his predecessor in the House, Lyndon Johnson. When Texas Congressmen do quit, they quit like former Congressman Frank Ikard, himself an ex-judge: Ikard left to become head of the American Petroleum Institute at $200,000 a year.

One of the former county judges who is now a Congressman is Omar Burleson of the 17th district. His career illustrates the value of seniority in Texas politics. Burleson was one of the many World War II veterans elected to the House in 1946, and one of the half dozen who remain there. For a decade or two, he rose on the seniority ladder, finally achieving the pinnacle of many a congressman's dreams: a committee chairmanship. To be sure, it was only House Administration, then considered a musty housekeeping body, but its potential for power has since been demonstrated by Ohio's Wayne Hays. But that chairmanship was not what Burleson or the powers that be in Texas wanted. In 1966, Congressman Clark Thompson of the state's 9th district decided to retire. Thompson held the Texas seat on the Ways and Means Committee, where he could protect the 27½% oil depletion allowance. Big oil wanted that seat to stay in Texas hands. The industry candidate was Burleson, who was perfectly willing to surrender his chairmanship for it.

But House liberals had other ideas. They supported Congressman Jacob Gilbert of the Bronx, a machine liberal who might not take so kindly to the politics of oil. After a heated struggle, Gilbert won the seat by one vote in the Democratic caucus. The liberals would have lost, but for the unavoidable absence of the Mississippi delegation, which had returned to Jackson to watch former colleague John Bell Williams sworn in as Governor. So Burleson had to bide another two years chairing his committee. He finally won the seat on Ways and Means after the 1968 election. Ironically, it was only after the Texas seat was reoccupied that Congress began to cut the oil depletion allowance in the Tax Reform Act of 1969. But Burleson, the ex-Chairman, remains content today as the eighth-ranking Democrat on Ways and Means. At 70, he is too old to succeed to a chairmanship ever again.

Burleson represents a district that is the geographical heart of Texas: acres and acres of arid farming and grazing land west of Dallas and Fort Worth and north of San Antonio and Austin. This 17th district has only two urban centers of any size, Abilene (pop. 89,000) and Big Spring (pop. 28,000)—both profoundly conservative towns. This is traditionally Texas Democratic country, though it shifted, apparently temporarily, to the Republicans in 1972. Burleson has not had an opponent in either primary or general election since 1964 when the Republicans, apparently anticipating a Goldwater landslide in Texas, ran candidates in every one of the state's congressional districts (every one of them lost). It appears that local politicians now assume Burleson is unbeatable; at any rate, he has got a free ride longer than any other member of Congress. He also has one of the Congress's most conservative voting records. A possible replacement if Burleson should retire would be former Lieutenant Governor Ben Barnes. He was widely touted as presidential material until he ran a disastrous third in the 1972 Democratic gubernatorial primary. Barnes was only 33 then, and comes from Brown County in the 17th; he may be ready for a political comeback.

Census Data Pop. 466,432. Central city, 19%; suburban, 5%. Median family income, $7,144; families above $15,000: 11%; families below $3,000: 16%. Median years education, 11.2.

The Voters

Median voting age 46.
Employment profile White collar, 40%. Blue collar, 34%. Service, 15%. Farm, 11%.
Ethnic groups Black, 4%. Spanish, 9%. Total foreign stock, 4%.

Presidential vote

1972	Nixon (R)	97,197	(73%)
	McGovern (D)	36,122	(27%)
1968	Nixon (R)	50,810	(37%)
	Humphrey (D)	60,904	(44%)
	Wallace (AI)	26,085	(19%)

Rep. Omar Burleson (D) Elected 1946; b. Mar. 19, 1906, Anson; home, Anson; Abilene Christian Col., 1924–26, Hardin Simmons U., 1926–27; Cumberland U. Law School, 1927–29; Church of Christ.

Career Jones Co. Atty., 1931–35, Judge, 1935–40; FBI Agent, 1940–41; Secy. to U.S. Rep. Sam Russell, 1941–42; Gen. Counsel, Natl. Capital Housing Auth., 1942; Navy, WWII.

Offices 2369 RHOB, 202-225-6605. Also New Fed. Bldg., Rm. 2101, 3rd and N. Pine Sts., Abilene 79601, 915-673-7221.

Committees

Budget (10th).

Ways and Means (8th). Subcommittees: Health; Unemployment Compensation.

Group Ratings

	ADA	COPE	LWV	RIPON	NFU	LCV	CFA	NAB	NSI	ACA
1974	0	0	0	25	36	18	0	67	90	80
1973	0	0	8	13	58	0	0	–	–	80
1972	0	9	0	31	43	13	50	91	100	90

Key Votes

1) Foreign Aid	AGN	6) Gov Abortn Aid	AGN	11) Pub Cong Election $	AGN
2) Busing	AGN	7) Coed Phys Ed	AGN	12) Turkish Arms Cutoff	AGN
3) ABM	FOR	8) Pov Lawyer Gag	FOR	13) Youth Camp Regs	AGN
4) B-1 Bomber	FOR	9) Pub Trans Sub	AGN	14) Strip Mine Veto	FOR
5) Nerve Gas	FOR	10) EZ Voter Regis	AGN	15) Farm Bill Veto	AGN

Election Results

1974 general	Omar Burleson (D), unopposed	($9,200)
1974 primary:	Omar Burleson (D), unopposed	
1972 general	Omar Burleson (D), unopposed	($5,341)

◆ ◆ ◆ ◆ ◆

EIGHTEENTH DISTRICT

Texas politics in general and Houston politics in particular are full of anomalies. For example, the liberal candidate for Mayor of Houston in 1973 (and the winner) was Fred Hofheinz, son of the flamboyant judge who built and runs the Astrodome. The conservative candidate was a Councilman named Dick Gottlieb. Consider another oddity. In this muscular, macho city, the two leading party strategists are women. There is Nancy Palm, until recently leader of Houston's Republicans, considered an ultraconservative in conflict with the party's conservative Dallas wing. Palm has had some notable near-successes, particularly in 1972, when her candidate for Governor, state Senator Hank Grover, came within 100,000 votes of beating conservative Democrat Dolph Briscoe. Far to the left of Palm is Billie Carr, leader of a liberal organization which wins primaries and gets the vote out in general elections with as telling effect as Palm's Republicans. It was Carr's people who were in large part responsible for Hofheinz's victory, and the election of a liberal school board in Houston; they see that Houston votes for the liberal statewide candidates in the Democratic primary, and maximize the number of liberal votes here in general elections.

One reason behind the relative success of the liberals is the political sophistication of Houston's black community. According to the Joint Center on Political Studies, Houston blacks vote Democratic in greater proportion than blacks just about anywhere else in the United States; what is more important, blacks turn out here in fairly high numbers. By contrast, Houston's Mexican-Americans, scattered throughout the city, are fractious and inclined to conservatism. The most sophisticated and politically savvy product of Houston black politics is Congresswoman Barbara Jordan.

Barbara Jordan is one of those people with a long string of firsts: along with Andrew Young, the first black elected to Congress from the South in the twentieth century; the first black woman elected to Congress from the South; the first black member of the Texas state Senate; etc.

But her career is even more remarkable than any list of firsts can convey. It was just eight years ago (1967) that she was elected, at age 31, to the Texas Senate—a body with only 31 members, 30 of them men and white, most of them from rural areas and responsive to the wishes of conservative lobbyists. Nevertheless, within four years, Jordan was president pro tempore of the Senate; in that capacity she served as acting Governor (another first) whenever Governor Preston Smith and Lieutenant Governor Ben Barnes were out of the state. How did she achieve such success in a forum like the Texas Senate? First, by hard work and thorough knowledge of the issues; few of her colleagues dared debate her. Second, by political horse-trading as shrewd as had been seen in Austin in some time. That is how she got the lines of the 18th congressional district drawn where they are, for example. The men she dealt with met political disaster—Smith and Barnes were defeated in the 1972 primary, the House Speaker then went to jail. But Barbara Jordan got a district which was 42% black and 19% Mexican-American. And she beat a state Representative who was fond of militant rhetoric with 81% of the vote in the Democratic primary.

Now Barbara Jordan is a national figure. Not many who heard her opening speech at the Judiciary Committee hearings will forget the deep voice or the poignancy of her description of how the Constitution was not originally intended for people like her—but how it now served, and governed, all of us. She proved again and again that she was not one to be crossed lightly. She knew the law and the facts, and presented them in discourses which could only be labelled as authoritative.

Jordan has her share of detractors, mostly liberals who feel she sold out by, for example, supporting Lloyd Bentsen staunchly in the 1970 Senate race after his right wing campaign had beaten Ralph Yarborough in the primary. Her reply, in effect, is that she has never sold out her constituents on legislative issues (and her record is one of most liberal in the House) and that there is nothing wrong with dealing with those who are powerful if you get enough in return. She is also accused of ambition, and does not really deny the charge. Washington observers are inclined to doubt that she could be elected Senator from Texas, but this is a state that gave another woman, Frances Farenthold, 44% in the 1972 gubernatorial runoff primary, and as a result of the Judiciary Committee hearings Jordan now is favorably recognized all over the state. There is not much reason to suppose that Texas is any less ready these days to elect a black Senator than, say, Illinois or Pennsylvania; it could easily happen one of these elections.

One thing no one accuses Barbara Jordan of is laziness. She is unmarried, spends all her time on politics and legislation; she is never caught unprepared or negligent of her duties. She could not have thought (or did she?) as she was growing up in the Houston ghetto, going to college and law school in the fifties, that she would become a national leader. But she is, and there seem to be no limits on how far she can go.

Census Data Pop. 466,520. Central city, 100%; suburban, 0%. Median family income, $7,288; families above $15,000: 10%; families below $3,000: 15%. Median years education, 10.4.

The Voters

Median voting age 39.
Employment profile White collar, 40%. Blue collar, 40%. Service, 20%. Farm, –%.
Ethnic groups Black, 44%. Spanish, 19%. Total foreign stock, 12%.

Presidential vote

1972	Nixon (R)	34,355	(31%)
	McGovern (D)	75,243	(69%)
1968	Nixon (R)	24,533	(24%)
	Humphrey (D)	62,464	(62%)
	Wallace (AI)	13,644	(14%)

Rep. Barbara Jordan (D) Elected 1972; b. Feb. 21, 1936, Houston; home, Houston; Tex. Southern U., B.A. 1956, Boston U., LL.B. 1959; Baptist.

Career Admin. Asst. to Judge of Harris Co., 1959–66; Tex. Senate, 1966–72, Pres. Pro Tempore, 1972; Vice Chm., Tex. Dem. Party.

Offices 1534 LHOB, 202-225-3816. Also Fed. Bldg., 515 Rusk St., Houston 77002, 713-226-5724.

Committees

Government Operations (23d). Subcommittees: Intergovernmental Relations and Human Resources; Manpower and Housing.

Judiciary (14th). Subcommittees: Administrative Law and Governmental Relations; Monopolies and Commercial Law.

Group Ratings

	ADA	COPE	LWV	RIPON	NFU	LCV	CFA	NAB	NSI	ACA
1974	91	91	92	56	100	75	69	27	20	7
1973	100	100	91	53	95	79	88	–	–	4

Key Votes

1) Foreign Aid	FOR	6) Gov Abortn Aid	FOR	11) Pub Cong Election $	FOR
2) Busing	FOR	7) Coed Phys Ed	FOR	12) Turkish Arms Cutoff	FOR
3) ABM	AGN	8) Pov Lawyer Gag	AGN	13) Youth Camp Regs	FOR
4) B-1 Bomber	AGN	9) Pub Trans Sub	FOR	14) Strip Mine Veto	AGN
5) Nerve Gas	AGN	10) EZ Voter Regis	FOR	15) Farm Bill Veto	AGN

Election Results

1974 general	Barbara Jordan (D)	36,597	(86%)	($31,587)
	Robbins Mitchell (R)	6,053	(14%)	($504)
1974 primary:	Barbara Jordan (D), unopposed			
1972 general	Barbara Jordan (D)	85,672	(82%)	($57,065)
	Paul Merritt (R)	19,355	(18%)	($3,257)

◆ ◆ ◆ ◆ ◆

NINETEENTH DISTRICT

The 19th congressional district of Texas takes in part of the flat, dusty plains and the distant, treeless skyline of west Texas. The small towns and ranching communities of the district, which never had many people, are now in general economic and population decline. Two oil cities, Lubbock (pop. 149,000) and Midland (pop. 59,000), plus the smaller portion (pop. 29,000) of another oil city, Odessa, dominate the 19th. Lubbock owes most of its present size and prosperity to expansion in the decade following World War II. Midland and Odessa are creatures of the Permian Basin oil boom of the 1950s. One of the beneficiaries of that era was George Bush, formerly Congressman from Houston and twice defeated Senate candidate, later Republican National Chairman (during the Watergate years of 1973 and 1974) and now U.S. representative in Peking. Recently, the aura of boom has worn thin, and the cities have grown only a little or not at all. In 1971, a tornado hit downtown Lubbock, as if the elements wanted to reclaim the land from the confident men who had so recently built their hopes upon it.

The voters of the 19th district have the privilege of sending to the House of Representatives one of its most senior and powerful members, George Mahon. A county district attorney when he was first elected in 1934, Mahon has been the Chairman of the House Appropriations Committee since the death of Clarence Cannon 30 years later; for some years before that, and to this day, Mahon has also chaired the Defense Appropriations Subcommittee. The two positions give him as much influence as anybody in Congress over the size and scope of the federal budget, for by tradition all appropriation bills originate in the House. Moreover when, as usually happens, the Senate sets different figures, the discrepancies are resolved in Conference committees; there the House conferees, including Mahon, are usually more knowledgeable, better prepared, and more stubborn—and more often than not get their way.

Mahon, a tall, slender man whose dark hair belies his age (76), is considered a generally fair-minded chairman; but his leanings on policy are very much more conservative than those of the overwhelming majority of his fellow Democrats. In recent years, he has found himself in the uncomfortable position of losing some fights on the floor of the House, and of having his power pruned back by his fellow Democrats. One reason is his support over the years of high military budgets; like most senior Congressmen whose memories go back to the isolationist days before World War II, he likes to say that he would rather err by giving the Pentagon too much than too little. That is not an attitude that is totally shared in the House any more, nor was Mahon's total support of Nixon and Ford Administration war policies in Southeast Asia; he was beaten on that as long ago as 1971.

Over the years Mahon's Appropriations Committee has been a force for conservative limits on government spending. The Chairman has tried to see that few ideological liberals get on his committee, and even after the 1974 Democratic landslide was able to avoid a solid liberal contingent from being added. Appropriations and its important subcommittees like to meet in quiet, secret sessions; when the House voted to require all committee hearings to be held in public unless the committee publicly voted to close them, Mahon announced that he expected Appropriations and its subcommittees to do just that on every occasion. The creation of the House Budget Committee in 1974 must also be considered as something of an infringement on Mahon's turf; the idea was that Budget would set spending and tax limits—which is to say that the House felt Appropriations was not setting an articulated policy on spending.

Another, more minor rebuke was administered to Mahon by the Democratic caucus: in 1973 he had given jurisdiction over environmental programs to the subcommittee headed by Jamie Whitten of Mississippi, no friend of the ecologists. After the 1974 elections, the caucus voted to give itself the right to approve or disapprove Appropriations subcommittee chairmen, a move clearly aimed at Whitten; to save Whitten's chair, Mahon agreed to transfer the environmental area to another subcommittee.

Back home, the Congressman has, of course, had little trouble winning reelection. The last time the Republicans fielded a candidate against him was in 1964, and Mahon took 78% of the vote. But the brute facts of demography have forced Texas redistricters to make the 19th more Republican, at least on paper—which could make a difference if Mahon is not a candidate.

Census Data Pop. 466,649. Central city, 50%; suburban, 9%. Median family income, $8315; families above $15,000: 16%; families below $3,000: 12%. Median years education, 12.1.

The Voters

Median voting age 40.
Employment profile White collar, 47%. Blue collar, 29%. Service, 13%. Farm, 11%.
Ethnic groups Black, 6%. Spanish, 19%. Total foreign stock, 7%.

Presidential vote

1972	Nixon (R)	108,282	(76%)
	McGovern (D)	33,494	(24%)
1968	Nixon (R)	66,070	(48%)
	Humphrey (D)	40,901	(29%)
	Wallace (AI)	31,371	(23%)

Rep. George H. Mahon (D) Elected 1934; b. Sept. 22, 1900, near Haynesville, La.; home, Lubbock; Simmons U., B.A. 1924, U. of Tex. LL.B. 1925, U. of Minn., 1925; Methodist.

Career Practicing atty., 1925–34; Mitchell Co. Atty., 1926; Dist. Atty., 32nd Judicial Dist., 1927–34.

Offices 2314 RHOB, 202-225-4005. Also Fed. Bldg., Lubbock 79401, 806-763-1161.

Committees

Appropriations (Chairman). Subcommittees: Defense (Chairman).

Group Ratings

	ADA	COPE	LWV	RIPON	NFU	LCV	CFA	NAB	NSI	ACA
1974	9	40	25	44	69	12	8	50	90	71
1973	9	10	50	33	68	16	0	–	–	61
1972	6	30	8	25	43	7	50	80	100	77

Key Votes

1) Foreign Aid	FOR	6) Gov Abortn Aid	AGN	11) Pub Cong Election $	AGN
2) Busing	AGN	7) Coed Phys Ed	AGN	12) Turkish Arms Cutoff	AGN
3) ABM	FOR	8) Pov Lawyer Gag	FOR	13) Youth Camp Regs	AGN
4) B-1 Bomber	FOR	9) Pub Trans Sub	AGN	14) Strip Mine Veto	FOR
5) Nerve Gas	FOR	10) EZ Voter Regis	FOR	15) Farm Bill Veto	AGN

Election Results

1974 general:	George Mahon (D), unopposed	($2,044)
1974 primary:	George Mahon (D), unopposed	
1972 general:	George Mahon (D), unopposed	($4,358)

◆ ◆ ◆ ◆ ◆

TWENTIETH DISTRICT

San Antonio was the most important town in Texas when the state was part of Mexico. It was here, of course, that Santa Ana and his troops wiped out Davie Crockett, Jim Bowie, and 184 others at the Alamo. (Crockett was a Tennessee Congressman in 1827–31 and 1833–35; if he had not lost the 1834 election, he would never have left Tennessee.) Today, San Antonio is Texas's third largest city (pop. 654,00). Because it has never been a center of the Texas boom industries of oil, electronics, or high finance, San Antonio has not grown as fast as Houston, Dallas, or even Fort Worth. This is not a withering city, though, and it has retained an Hispanic ambiance along the San Antonio River that winds its way through the tree-shaded center of town. The Alamo is nearby, overrun by tourists—a monument to John Wayne patriotism, though it represents a defeat unparalleled in our history till Vietnam.

Only 130 miles from the Mexican border, San Antonio is 50% Mexican-American, which makes this the most Mexican-American of any major city in the country. That is the basic demographic fact underlying one of the brands of politics that is important here. The other is symbolized by the presence of several large military installations. There is Fort Sam Houston, with 10,000 men; the Brooks Aero Medical Center, the major medical facility of the Air Force; and no less than three Air Force bases either within the city limits or just outside them. San Antonio politics, then, has always been a struggle between liberals, who count on the Mexican-Americans for most of their votes, and conservatives, whose constituency is the well-to-do middle class which is so often dependent, in one way or another, on the military establishment.

Control has oscillated between the two groups. In the 1930s, San Antonio elected as its Congressman a witty liberal named Maury Maverick. But he was beaten in the 1938 Democratic primary by Paul J. Kilday, who headed a conservative political machine that dominated politics here for the next 20 years or so; it didn't hurt that Kilday was a member of the House Armed Services Committee, and carefully watched out for San Antonio's interests. The machine's domination ended by 1961, when Kilday resigned to become a judge on the U.S. Court of Military Appeals. He was succeeded by a young Mexican-American lawyer and state Senator, Henry B. Gonzalez, then 35. Gonzalez was the first Mexican-American Congressman from the district. He campaigned as an outspoken liberal and, with the help of some Anglo as well as many Mexican-American votes, he in effect reversed the result of the 1938 primary.

Gonzalez is now a high ranking member of the Banking and Currency Committee and Chairman of its Subcommittee on International Development Institutions and Finance. Over the years, most members of Banking have been known for their solicitude toward the troubles of big bankers. But Gonzalez anticipated by more than a decade the attitudes of the freshmen elected in 1974, who now cast a decisive bloc on votes on the committee. He is a man of stubborn rectitude; unlike so many of his colleagues, he has declined offers of lucrative bank stock and directorships. Gonzalez's integrity has also cost him the enthusiasm, if not the support, of many liberals—he was once their favorite Texas politician. Long after it was fashionable among liberals, Gonzalez continued to back Lyndon Johnson's conduct of the Vietnam war. And the Congressman has little but scorn for the younger generation of chicano militants who preach a kind of political separatism. Gonzalez is convinced that for Mexican-Americans to achieve the social and economic goals they seek they must work with others with similar interests. These days, the Congressman finds himself reasonably comfortable at meetings of the Texas delegation, where he was once not altogether welcomed.

But some of them must wonder about one of his latest projects. He is a sponsor of a resolution to provide for further investigation of the assassinations of the Kennedys and Martin Luther King, Jr. It is a sign of how well Gonzalez is now respected in all quarters that his sponsorship is taken as evidence that serious-minded people are concerned about this issue—rather than as evidence that he has turned into some kind of nut.

When Gonzalez was first elected, all of San Antonio and surrounding Bexar County made up the 20th congressional district. The one-person-one-vote doctrine and shifts of population have pared down the territory. It now includes only the central portion of San Antonio, along with Fort Sam Houston and a little suburban land around Kelly Air Force Base. The Anglo areas of Alamo Heights and Castle Hills and the northern part of the city lie in the 21st district, leaving most of San Antonio's Mexican-American population and virtually all of its small black community in the 20th. The arrangement gives the district a solid 60% Mexican-American majority; accordingly, the 20th is often the most liberal in Texas. Henry B., as he is often called, has not had trouble in recent elections and expects none in the future, even though some of the young militants grumble about his performance.

Census Data Pop. 466,514. Central city, 92%; suburban, 8%. Median family income, $6,566; families above $15,000: 7%; families below $3,000: 18%. Median years education, 9.4.

The Voters

Median voting age 40.
Employment profile White collar, 42%. Blue collar, 40%. Service, 18%. Farm, –%.
Ethnic groups Black, 11%. Spanish, 60%. Total foreign stock, 25%. Germany, 1%.

Presidential vote

1972	Nixon (R)	37,021	(40%)
	McGovern (D)	56,470	(60%)
1968	Nixon (R)	22,233	(25%)
	Humphrey (D)	61,572	(69%)
	Wallace (AI)	5,648	(6%)

Rep. Henry B. Gonzalez (D) Elected Nov. 4, 1961; b. May 3, 1916, San Antonio; home, San Antonio; San Antonio Col., U. of Tex., St. Mary's U., San Antonio, LL.B.; Catholic.

Career Army, WWII; Bexar Co. Chf. Probation Officer, 1946; Work with bilingual publications; Teacher, San Antonio Night School Program; San Antonio City Cncl., 1953–56, Mayor Pro Tem., 1955–56; Tex. Senate, 1956–61.

Offices 2312 RHOB, 202-225-3236. Also 203 Fed. Bldg., San Antonio 78205, 512-223-8851.

Committees

Banking, Currency and Housing (9th). Subcommittees: Consumer Affairs; General Oversight and Renegotiation; Housing and Community Development; International Development Institutions and Finance (Chairman).

Small Business (12th). Subcommittees: SBA and SBIC Legislation; SBA Oversight and Minority Enterprise.

Group Ratings

	ADA	COPE	LWV	RIPON	NFU	LCV	CFA	NAB	NSI	ACA
1974	45	90	75	31	92	59	42	9	70	43
1973	65	91	70	42	95	28	50	–	–	19
1972	56	100	83	44	86	40	50	0	67	26

Key Votes

1) Foreign Aid	AGN	6) Gov Abortn Aid	AGN	11) Pub Cong Election $	AGN
2) Busing	FOR	7) Coed Phys Ed	AGN	12) Turkish Arms Cutoff	AGN
3) ABM	FOR	8) Pov Lawyer Gag	ABS	13) Youth Camp Regs	AGN
4) B-1 Bomber	FOR	9) Pub Trans Sub	FOR	14) Strip Mine Veto	ABS
5) Nerve Gas	FOR	10) EZ Voter Regis	FOR	15) Farm Bill Veto	AGN

Election Results

1974 general:	Henry B. Gonzalez (D), unopposed			($1,012)
1974 primary:	Henry G. Gonzalez (D), unopposed			
1972 general:	Henry B. Gonzalez (D)	81,443	(97%)	($1,012)
	Steven Wattenmaker (SW)	2,596	(3%)	(NA)

◆　◆　◆　◆　◆

TWENTY-FIRST DISTRICT

Most of the physical expanse of the 21st congressional district of Texas is unpopulated—a vast near-desert given over to the raising of cattle and cotton, the pumping of oil, and the extraction of natural gas. But this mostly vacant land is not what is important politically; it merely serves to place in one district two disparate urban areas, one of which is so large that it casts more than two-thirds of the votes in the district. That is Bexar County, which is to say the north side of San Antonio and its northern suburbs—the heavily Anglo, conservative, and Republican portion of this predominantly Mexican-American city. The district's other urban center is San Angelo (pop. 65,000). Before the 1965 redistricting, which brought part of Bexar County and San Antonio into the 21st, San Angelo was the largest city in an underpopulated district, and it shares the conservative Democratic inclination of the surrounding rural counties.

Also noteworthy are the Texas German areas around San Antonio, which lie in both the 21st and 23d districts. Towns like New Braunfels and Fredericksburg (where Lyndon Johnson used to go to church) were founded by '48ers—liberal Germans who left Europe after the failure of the revolutions of 1848 and settled on the frontier of southern Texas. Because the Germans considered slaveholding barbarous, they soon became attracted to the then radical Republican Party, and their opposition to secession solidified their allegiance to the party of Lincoln. To this day, the counties in which the descendants of the '48ers are still a majority—Comal, Kendall, Gillespie, Kerr—cast huge Republican majorities in almost every election.

All in all, the composition of the district has made the 21st pretty solidly Republican in most recent statewide elections. But it has remained Democratic in congressional contests. After all, the 21st is the lineal descendant, though one vastly altered, from the district that elected John Nance Garner to the House from 1902 to 1932; Garner was Speaker from 1931 to 1933, and Vice President under Franklin D. Roosevelt for eight years. Not long after Garner returned to Uvalde, in 1942, the 21st district elected O. C. Fisher as Congressman; he rose to the number three spot on the Armed Services Committee, compiled an unblemished conservative record, and retired in 1974 when he became entitled to the maximum congressional pension.

That left the seat open for the first time in a generation, and resulted in the most hotly contested congressional race in recent Texas history, complete with primary, runoff, and close general election. The ultimate winner was about as far removed from the stereotype of a Texas politician as one could imagine. He was Robert Krueger, a 39-year-old member of an old Texas German family, a graduate of Oxford University, a Shakespeare scholar and dean at Duke, who had returned to New Braunfels to run the family hosiery mill.

How did Krueger win? First of all, he spent money—indeed, more money, over $300,000, than any other successful congressional candidate in the nation in 1974 (although relatively few had to finance three closely contested elections). The money undoubtedly helped him to get taken seriously as a candidate, but he also demonstrated the ability to beat better known candidates. Thus in the first primary he ran behind San Antonio state Senator Nelson Wolff; but in the runoff, with plenty of support from the Texas German areas and the other small rural counties, he upset Wolff. In the general, Krueger faced Doug Harlan, a young, moderate Republican who had won 43% of the vote against Fisher two years before. But Krueger almost managed to duplicate Fisher's showing in the rural areas, and actually did better in Bexar County; Fisher, the old San Angelo-based incumbent, had lost it by 10,000 votes, while the younger, more modern Krueger lost by only 2,000. What did not play much of a part in the Kruger 52–48 victory was ideology. Both Krueger and Wolff maintained that they were basically conservatives, and so did Harlan.

The 21st was the Republican's best chance to pick up a Texas district in many years, and they were unable to manage it—which tells us more about the state of the Texas Republican Party than whatever fantasies of high office may still be entertained by John Connally and his friends. Krueger has shown he knows how to win a close election, and with the advantages of incumbency, he could probably stay in Congress as long as Fisher did—though he may decide he wants to try yet another career.

Census Data Pop. 466,753. Central city, 42%; suburban, 17%. Median family income, $8,789; families above $15,000: 20%; families below $3,000: 11%. Median years education, 12.2.

The Voters

Median voting age 43.
Employment profile White collar, 57%. Blue collar, 26%. Service, 11%. Farm, 6%.
Ethnic groups Black, 2%. Spanish, 24%. Total foreign stock, 14%. Germany, 2%.

Presidential vote

1972	Nixon (R)	120,737	(76%)
	McGovern (D)	38,623	(24%)
1968	Nixon (R)	71,002	(52%)
	Humphrey (D)	46,713	(34%)
	Wallace (AI)	18,488	(14%)

Rep. Robert (Bob) **Krueger** (D) Elected 1974; b. Sept. 19, 1935, New Braunfels; home, New Braunfels; SMU, B.A. 1957, Duke U., M.A. 1958, Oxford U., B.Litt., 1961, Ph.D. 1964.

Career Assoc. Prof. of English, Duke U., 1961–73, Vice Provost and Dean of the Col. of Arts and Sciences; Bd. Chm., Comal Hosiery Mills; Partner, Krueger Brangus Ranch.

Offices 512 CHOB, 202-225-4236. Also P.O. Box 1355, Del Rio 78840, 512-775-4351.

Committees

Interstate and Foreign Commerce (21st). Subcommittees: Energy and Power; Oversight and Investigations.

Science and Technology (22d). Subcommittees: Energy Research, Development and Demonstration; Energy Research (Fossil Fuels); Science, Research, and Technology.

Group Ratings: Newly Elected

Key Votes

1) Foreign Aid	FOR	6) Gov Abortn Aid	NE	11) Pub Cong Election $	NE
2) Busing	NE	7) Coed Phys Ed	AGN	12) Turkish Arms Cutoff	NE
3) ABM	NE	8) Pov Lawyer Gag	NE	13) Youth Camp Regs	AGN
4) B-1 Bomber	FOR	9) Pub Trans Sub	NE	14) Strip Mine Veto	AGN
5) Nerve Gas	NE	10) EZ Voter Regis	NE	15) Farm Bill Veto	AGN

Election Results

1974 general:	Robert Krueger (D)	53,543	(53%)	($358,645)
	Doug Harlan (R)	45,959	(45%)	($164,675)
	Ed Gallion (AI)	2,254	(2%)	($9,260)
1974 run-off:	Robert Krueger (D)	29,332	(52%)	
	Nelson Wolff (D)	27,515	(48%)	
1974 primary:	Nelson Wolff (D)	32,877	(40%)	
	Robert Krueger (D)	26,361	(32%)	
	John H. Poerner (D)	14,742	(18%)	
	Three Others (D)	8,024	(10%)	

◆ ◆ ◆ ◆ ◆

TWENTY-SECOND DISTRICT

The 22d district of Texas moves from the south side of Houston across the coastal plain to the Brazosport area on the Gulf of Mexico. This territory was almost vacant 25 years ago. Like so many other Sun Belt boom areas, its subsequent development would not have occurred but for the air conditioner. Life here goes on inside: in air conditioned houses, air conditioned shopping malls, and in the air conditioned Houston Astrodome. Outside is the shimmering heat and an almost eerie silence.

The 22d takes in the prosperous, middle class, and rapidly growing suburban tracts of south Houston, including the Astrodome and Rice University. Though most of the area's blacks were placed in Barbara Jordan's 18th district, some 13% of the Houston residents of the 22d are black. The 22d also includes a substantial population in southeastern Harris County—the middle income suburb of Pasadena and down around the burgeoning NASA Manned Spacecraft Center between the Gulf Freeway and Galveston Bay. Houston Congressman (1937–65) Albert Thomas, a Democrat, brought the NASA complex to the city, but the technicians and astronauts who live near the facility cast heavy Republican margins.

The 22d also includes exurban Fort Bend and Brazoria Counties, which have just begun to experience the phenomenal growth that has hit the south and west sides of Houston. But 70% of the district's voters live in Houston and Harris County; accordingly, this part of the 22d is the political focus of the constituency.

The 22d district was first created in 1957, when the Texas legislature eliminated the state's at-large seat and gave rapidly growing Harris County a second Congressman. The district's first and only Representative has been Democrat Bob Casey. After nearly 20 years in the House, Casey occupies a middle seniority position on the Appropriations Committee. On the death of Alabama's George Andrews in 1971, Casey succeeded to the chairmanship of the Legislative Subcommittee. This unit accounts for only a small portion of the federal budget, but it is an important one on Capitol Hill—the Congress's own money. That gives Casey a lot of potential influence among, say, Congressmen who want more staff for their subcommittee, but so far at least he has not used this position the way Chairman Wayne Hays of the House Administration Committee has his.

On most issues, Casey is a vocal conservative. He is especially fond of portraying himself as a hardline opponent of crime. Nevertheless, Casey has been unable to create a safe seat in the 22d. As a Democrat, he is a potential target of Houston's archconservative Republicans, who have otherwise carried the district in presidential, gubernatorial, and senatorial races. And as a conservative, Casey is no favorite of Houston's liberal Democrats. But so far no really significant opposition has emerged. The 1972 redistricting removed some blacks from the district, which helped Casey in primaries; and Republicans have not done well here since 1972, which helps him in general elections. Though he remains potentially vulnerable, it is more likely that retirement (he is 61) rather than defeat will remove him from the Congress.

Census Data Pop. 466,707. Central city, 38%; suburban, 61%. Median family income, $11,022; families above $15,000: 25%; families below $3,000: 6%. Median years education, 12.3.

The Voters

Median voting age 38.
Employment profile White collar, 54%. Blue collar, 34%. Service, 11%. Farm, 1%.
Ethnic groups Black, 13%. Spanish, 10%. Total foreign stock, 9%.

Presidential vote

1972	Nixon (R)	100,489	(65%)
	McGovern (D)	53,818	(35%)
1968	Nixon (R)	54,339	(43%)
	Humphrey (D)	46,320	(37%)
	Wallace (AI)	25,980	(20%)

Rep. Bob Casey (D) Elected 1958; b. July 27, 1915, Joplin, Mo.; home, Houston; U. of Houston, S. Tex. School of Law. 1934–40; First Christian Church.

Career Practicing atty., 1940–43, 1947–51; Alvin City Atty., 1940–43; Asst. Dist. Atty., Houston, 1943–47; Tex. House of Reps., 1949–50; Harris Co. Judge, 1950–58.

Offices 2256 RHOB, 202-225-5951. Also Rm. 12102, 515 Rusk St., Houston 77002, 713-226-4486.

Committees

Appropriations (20th). Subcommittees: Agriculture and Related Agencies; Labor-HEW; Legislative (Chairman).

Group Ratings

	ADA	COPE	LWV	RIPON	NFU	LCV	CFA	NAB	NSI	ACA
1974	4	27	17	19	57	24	8	58	100	80
1973	12	36	25	20	80	16	13	–	–	62
1972	6	27	25	27	43	7	100	60	100	73

Key Votes

1) Foreign Aid	AGN	6) Gov Abortn Aid	AGN	11) Pub Cong Election $	AGN
2) Busing	AGN	7) Coed Phys Ed	AGN	12) Turkish Arms Cutoff	AGN
3) ABM	FOR	8) Pov Lawyer Gag	FOR	13) Youth Camp Regs	AGN
4) B-1 Bomber	FOR	9) Pub Trans Sub	AGN	14) Strip Mine Veto	FOR
5) Nerve Gas	FOR	10) EZ Voter Regis	AGN	15) Farm Bill Veto	AGN

Election Results

1974 general:	Bob Casey (D)	47,783	(71%)	($118,186)
	Ron Paul (R)	19,483	(29%)	($16,206)
1974 primary:	Bob Casey (D)	32,524	(66%)	
	J. Kent Hackleman (D)	16,411	(34%)	
1972 general:	Bob Casey (D)	101,786	(71%)	($93,322)
	James Griffin (R)	42,194	(29%)	($3.108)

◆ ◆ ◆ ◆ ◆

TWENTY-THIRD DISTRICT

From San Antonio south, Texas is majority Mexican-American. Much of the territory can be called feudal: desert-like rural counties where big landowners effectively run the lives of their Mexican field hands. Seeds of protest against the old order have sprouted in little towns like Crystal City, Carrizo Springs, and Cotulla. Here, because of "brown power" movements, the Mexican-American majorities have for the first time elected chicanos, often young militants, to local office. The stakes are sometimes high, for local office can confer the power to tax the Anglo landowners. This is also the part of the state where La Raza Unida Party is strongest. In 1972, its candidate for Governor got 6% of the statewide vote and as much as 52% in small counties here. LRU professes a complete disenchantment with the major parties (although there is talk it accepted Republican money in 1972, when it refused to endorse McGovern). But it is hard to see how such a movement can make much headway statewide in a Texas that remains 70% white Anglo.

The ferment of chicano political separatism is as powerful in the 23d congressional district as anywhere in Texas. Some 51% of the district's residents are of Spanish origin. But "brown power" is still nothing like a major political force. It has had its greatest success in the little towns between San Antonio and Laredo, but in Laredo itself—a heavily Mexican-American town on the Rio Grande—politics goes on much as it always has. The 23d also includes 92,000 people living on the south and east sides of San Antonio, many of them Mexican-Americans. But this part of the district is middle class country, where voters have retained traditional Democratic allegiances or have moved quietly to the Republicans. The rest of the district is a group of counties east and southeast of San Antonio. The area contains some Texas Germans (see Twenty-first District) and a fairly large Mexican-American minority; nevertheless, the politics of Texas Tory Democrats is what usually finds favor in these parts. John Connally himself, once the state's dominant Democrat and now a Republican, comes from Wilson County in the 23d.

The 1965 redistricting created the 23d in something like its present form. From the large Mexican-American population, it was clear that the 23d would be one of the state's more liberal congressional districts. And since 1966, it has elected one of the state's more liberal Congressmen, Democrat Abraham (Chick) Kazen. Of Lebanese descent, Kazen spent 20 years in the Texas legislature before winning his House seat. In Washington, the Congressman has compiled the record of an LBJ liberal: pretty close to the AFL-CIO line on domestic issues, combined with support of the Vietnam war and high levels of military spending. Back home, Kazen has had little trouble winning reelection. And despite the activities of young chicano militants and the LA Raza Unida Party, the Congressman is unlikely to encounter any in the near future.

Census Data Pop. 466,424. Central city, 35%; suburban, 22%. Median family income, $6,512; families above $15,000: 9%; families below $3,000: 20%. Median years education, 9.8.

The Voters

Median voting age 41.
Employment profile White collar, 43%. Blue collar, 35%. Service, 13%. Farm, 9%.
Ethnic groups Black, 3%. Spanish, 49%. Total foreign stock, 23%. Germany, 2%.

Presidential vote

1972	Nixon (R)	72,629	(62%)
	McGovern (D)	44,843	(38%)
1968	Nixon (R)	33,947	(35%)
	Humphrey (D)	49,709	(52%)
	Wallace (AI)	12,307	(13%)

Rep. Abraham Kazan, Jr. (D) Elected 1966; b. Jan. 17, 1919, Laredo; home, Laredo; U. of Tex., 1937–40, Cumberland U. Law School, 1941; Catholic.

Career Air Force, WWII; Practicing atty., 1945–66; Tex. House of Reps., 1947–53; Tex. Senate, 1953–66, Pres. Pro Tempore, 1959.

Offices 1514 LHOB, 202-225-4511. Also Rm. 201 Fed. Bldg., Laredo 78040, 512-723-4336.

Committees

Armed Services (22d). Subcommittees: Military Installations and Facilities; Military Personnel.

Interior and Insular Affairs (9th). Subcommittees: Mines and Mining; National Parks and Recreation; Water and Power Resources.

Group Ratings

	ADA	COPE	LWV	RIPON	NFU	LCV	CFA	NAB	NSI	ACA
1974	16	56	36	31	83	20	13	33	88	46
1973	30	64	60	25	85	17	25	–	–	44
1972	13	64	44	50	86	13	0	9	100	45

Key Votes

1) Foreign Aid	AGN	6) Gov Abortn Aid	AGN	11) Pub Cong Election $	AGN
2) Busing	AGN	7) Coed Phys Ed	AGN	12) Turkish Arms Cutoff	FOR
3) ABM	FOR	8) Pov Lawyer Gag	ABS	13) Youth Camp Regs	AGN
4) B-1 Bomber	FOR	9) Pub Trans Sub	AGN	14) Strip Mine Veto	FOR
5) Nerve Gas	FOR	10) EZ Voter Regis	FOR	15) Farm Bill Veto	AGN

Election Results

1974 general	Abraham Kazen, Jr. (D), unopposed			($43,515)
1974 primary:	Abraham Kazen, Jr. (D)	44,070	(71%)	
	Jon Roland (D)	10,376	(17%)	
	Jake Johnson (D)	7,669	(12%)	
1972 general:	Abraham Kazen, Jr. (D), unopposed			($8,354)

◆ ◆ ◆ ◆ ◆

TWENTY-FOURTH DISTRICT

The 24th congressional district of Texas is known as the Mid-Cities district. It sits between Dallas and Fort Worth and contains parts of both. It was first created in the 1972 redistricting, under which it had one of the most grotesque shapes of any district in the nation. Now the district has been smoothed out considerably as a result of a 1973 federal court redistricting decree, but it remains an amalgam of quite disparate parts of the Dallas-Fort Worth metropolitan area, with no sense of a single community about it.

Geographically the district appears to consist of two tentacles emanating from the Dallas-Fort Worth Regional Airport—a Texas-sized monstrosity where everything (pay toilets, a transit system that doesn't work well) costs a quarter and where the dollar changing machines give you 95 cents in coins. One tentacle reaches into Dallas, which contains precisely half the district's population. This is not the wealthy, ultraconservative part of Dallas you have read about, however; that is in the 3d district to the north. It is rather a part of the city south of downtown, centered on a neighborhood called Oak Cliff. This area once boasted some of Dallas's largest mansions, which sat on a bluff overlooking the Trinity River; today few of the mansions remain, and Oak Cliff is a black ghetto. Altogether, 49% of the 24th's Dallas population is black—and of course a major liberal voting force in the district.

The Dallas tentacle also contains the middle class, considerably more conservative suburbs of Irving and Grand Prairie. This merges, really, into the second, Fort Worth tentacle, which moves south and west from the Airport. It includes the western edge of Fort Worth, and the suburbs of Euless and Arlington; the last of these is the more interesting, or at least the most flamboyant. Thanks in large part to the promotional activities of its mayor, Arlington has grown from a town of 7,000 in 1950 to a suburb of 44,000 in 1960 and a city of 90,000 in 1970. Situated along the Dallas-Fort Worth Turnpike, Arlington attracts thousands each year to the Six Flags Over Texas amusement park. It is also the smallest city with a major league baseball franchise, the Texas Rangers, who play the game in an aptly-named place called Turnpike Stadium.

The Mid-Cities district has been the scene of two hotly-contested Democratic primaries since it was created. In 1972, when the district contained more suburbs and fewer blacks, there were three main competitors: liberal Dallas state Senator Mike McKool, conservative Dallas Councilman Jesse Price, and WFAA-TV weathercaster Dale Milford. Price's law 'n' order campaign resulted in a poor third finish; McKool lost narrowly, as he had two years before and would two years later in the nearby 5th district. In the general election, the Mid-Cities district elected the first TV weatherman in Congress.

Milford likes to emphasize the fact that he was not simply an announcer who read the weather report over the air; he was a professional meteorologist who ran a successful weather forecasting business on the side. Temperamentally, he seems inclined to the conservative politics of the Texas Tory Democratic establishment; but in the 93d Congress at least, when so many issues involved confrontations between the executive and legislative branches, he voted with some frequency with the liberal majority of Democrats. Nevertheless, in 1974 Milford was again faced with a tough primary; the competition was a young attorney, Martin Frost, who was also a newcaster on educational station KERA-TV in Dallas. Frost could count on support in black precincts in Dallas and ran an effective door-to-door campaign. But it was not enough to beat the incumbent (though he was named as one of Environmental Action's Dirty Dozen), who won by a 58–42 margin. The 24th is the most liberal district in the Dallas-Fort Worth metropolitan areas; it voted 40% for George McGovern in 1972, above the national average. The question for future years is whether Milford's voting record will satisfy his constituents as much as his weather forecasts used to.

Census Data Pop. 466,875. Central city, 54%; suburban, 46%. Median family income, $9,583; families above $15,000: 18%; families below $3,000: 9%. Median years education, 11.9.

The Voters

Median voting age 37.
Employment profile White collar, 48%. Blue collar, 38%. Service, 14%. Farm, –%.
Ethnic groups Black, 26%. Spanish, 7%. Total foreign stock, 5%.

Presidential vote

1972	Nixon (R)	70,819	(60%)
	McGovern (D)	47,374	(40%)
1968	Nixon (R)	37,138	(38%)
	Humphrey (D)	44,635	(45%)
	Wallace (AI)	16,963	(17%)

Rep. Dale Milford (D) Elected 1972; b. Feb. 18, 1926, Bug Tussle; home, Grand Prairie; Baylor U., B.A. 1957; Lutheran.

Career Weather Observer, Civil Aeronautics Bd., 1942–44; Army Air Corps, 1944–53; Weatherman, WFAA-TV, 1953–71, Aerospace Ed., 1968–71; Aircraft dealer, 1957–59; Meteorological consultant, 1959–72.

Offices 427 CHOB, 202-225-3605. Also 221 W. Main St., Suite 106, P.O. Box 1450, Grand Prairie 75050, 214-263-4526.

Committees

Public Works and Transportation (16th). Subcommittees: Aviation; Investigations and Review; Public Buildings and Grounds; Transportation.

Science and Technology (10th). Subcommittees: Aviation and Transportation Research and Development (Chairman); Domestic and International Scientific Planning and Analysis; Environment and the Atmosphere.

Group Ratings

	ADA	COPE	LWV	RIPON	NFU	LCV	CFA	NAB	NSI	ACA
1974	16	11	10	33	18	27	0	70	57	75
1973	21	36	30	47	50	24	14	–	–	67

Key Votes

1) Foreign Aid	AGN	6) Gov Abortn Aid	FOR	11) Pub Cong Election $	ABS
2) Busing	AGN	7) Coed Phys Ed	AGN	12) Turkish Arms Cutoff	AGN
3) ABM	FOR	8) Pov Lawyer Gag	FOR	13) Youth Camp Regs	ABS
4) B-1 Bomber	FOR	9) Pub Trans Sub	AGN	14) Strip Mine Veto	FOR
5) Nerve Gas	FOR	10) EZ Voter Regis	AGN	15) Farm Bill Veto	FOR

Election Results

1974 general:	Dale Milford ()	36,058	(76%)	($62,603)
	Joseph Beaman, Jr. (R)	9,698	(20%)	($1,285)
	Earl W. Armstrong (AI)	1,653	(3%)	($2,706)
1974 primary:	Dale Milford (D)	20,643	(58%)	
	Martin Frost (D)	14,989	(42%)	
1972 general:	Dale Milford (D)	91,054	(65%)	($92,963)
	Courtney Roberts (R)	48,853	(35%)	($33,247)

UTAH

In 1827, Joseph Smith, a young Palmyra, New York farmer, experienced a vision in which the Angel Moroni appeared to him. Moroni was a prophet of the lost tribe of Israel (the American Indians) which had presumably found its way to the New World some six hundred years before the birth of Christ. Moroni told Smith where to unearth several golden tablets inscribed with hieroglyphical writings. With the help of some magic spectacles, Smith translated the tablets and published them as the Book of Mormon in 1830. He then declared himself a prophet and founded a religious group he called the Church of Jesus Christ of Latter Day Saints.

The group was just one wave in a wash of religious revivalism, prophecy, and utopianism that swept across upstate New York—Palmyra lies just east of Rochester—during the 1820s and 1830s; the region was so alive with religious enthusiasm that it was known as the "burned-over district." Very quickly, the prophet's new sect attracted hundreds of converts. Persecuted for their beliefs, these Mormons, as they were called, moved west to Ohio, Missouri, and then Illinois. In 1844, the Mormon colony at Nauvoo, Illinois contained some 15,000 members, all living under the strict theocratic auspices of Joseph Smith. In secular Illinois politics, Nauvoo—which was then the largest city in the state—often swung the balance of power between the contending Democrats and Whigs. It was also here that Smith received a revelation to begin the practice of polygamy, which led to his death at the hands of a mob in 1844.

After the murder, the new president of the church, the remarkable Brigham Young, decided to move the faithful, "the saints," farther west into territory that was still part of Mexico and far beyond the pale of white settlement. Young led a migration across the Great Plains and into the Rocky Mountains. In 1847, the prophet and his followers stopped along the western slope of the Wasatch Range, and as Brigham Young viewed the valley of the Great Salt Lake spread out below, he uttered the now famous words, "This is the place."

The place was Utah. It is the only state that continues to live by the teachings of the church responsible for its founding. Throughout the nineteenth century, "Zion" attracted thousands of converts from the Midwest, the north of England, and Scandinavia. The object of religious fear, prejudice, and perhaps some envy, Utah was not granted statehood until 1896, when the church renounced polygamy. The state now has more than a million people, with 88% of them living within 60 miles of the Great Salt Lake; they reside hundreds of miles from other significant concentrations of people. Presently, more than 70% of all Utahans are members of the Church of Jesus Christ of Latter Day Saints (LDS).

The distinctive features of the LDS faith dominate Utah politics. Leaders of the church have always exerted great political influence. For one thing, Utah has sent very few Gentiles (non-Mormons) to Congress during nearly 80 years of statehood. Currently, the church owns one of the two leading Salt Lake City newspapers and an influential television station. It also has holdings in an insurance company, various banks, and real estate, and runs the largest department store in Salt Lake City. The Mormon hierarchy confidently takes stands on secular matters, economic and political. It strongly supports, for example, Utah's right-to-work law.

One church doctrine in particular has embarrassed many Mormons—the faith denies blacks, having been cursed in the Bible, the "priesthood," i.e., full-fledged membership in the church. All Mormons are lay people, as the church does not employ a professional clergy; but laymen may be called to service, and seldom refuse. (That is what happened, for example, to former Congressman Wayne Owens, who lost the 1974 Senate race; he was sent by the church to eastern Canada in 1975, and thus effectively removed from the 1976 gubernatorial race.) Revision of church doctrine, if it is to come, awaits a revelation to the LDS President, an office held by the most senior of the church's twelve Apostles. They are invariably old men, beyond the age even Congressmen continue to exercise power; when President David McKay, former Agriculture Secretary, died in 1970 at age 96, he was succeeded by Joseph Fielding Smith, who was 93 at the time. Smith died, and was succeeded by his counsellor Harold B. Lee, who in turn died suddenly. Spenser Kimball then became President, but he has had an operation for throat cancer. And it now appears that Ezra Taft Benson, who can't seem to keep politics and religion apart at all, is in line.

In general the LDS doctrine carries the virtues of nineteenth century upstate New York Protestantism to their logical end. Even today, Mormons are forbidden to consume alcohol, tobacco, coffee, or tea, though dancing at church social events has always been encouraged. (Perhaps as a corollary, incidence of some cancers is significantly lower among Mormons than among the general population.) Many so-called "Jack Mormons", however, violate doctrine without overly stern reprimand from the community; but a visitor to some corners of Utah still risks a disapproving look if he asks to buy a pack of cigarettes. Many young Mormons still give two years of their lives to "missions" both at home and overseas, in which they attempt to win new converts to the faith; and members are required to pledge a tithe of 10% of their income to the church.

That income is often substantial, as Mormons possess a deserved reputation for hard work and tend to do well in business and the professions. Indeed, that may be one reason why Utahans reacted so negatively to the trend of politics and public policy in the 1960s; not only was the federal administration pushing civil rights laws, but it was also rewarding (or seeming to) people who shirked their obligation to work hard. Utah had been a Democratic state during the New Deal period; and John Kennedy, though he lost, ran well here in 1960 (perhaps because he was seen as fellow object of religious discrimination). But in 1964, Barry Goldwater won 45% of the vote here, and eight years later Richard Nixon was carrying the state with a record 72%. Even Utah's young people, at least those who stay close to the church, are part of the trend. At Brigham

Young University—a Mormon institution known for its conservatism—Nixon took 79%, Schmitz 15%, and McGovern only 6% in 1972.

But this Republican surge in national elections has not produced straight ticket Republican victories in Utah contests. On the contrary, Utah Democrats now hold the Governor's chair, one of the two Senate seats (and they came close to winning the other in 1974), and both the U. S. House seats. The reason for these victories cannot be summarized as a single trend; rather it is the result of a different set of factors in each case, which have allowed these Democrats to reach office, where they have become so popular they have not (or at least not yet) lost.

Take Governor Calvin Rampton, for example. He was the Democratic nominee in 1964, a good Democratic year, after Republicans had held the Governorship throughout the postwar period. It was time for a change, and Rampton won with 57% of the vote. His conservative policies have not antagonized any large number of voters in this conservative state, and so in these split ticket times he was reelected with 69% of the vote in 1968 and 70% in 1972. In that last election, he ran a full 42% ahead of George McGovern—a good measure of his popularity. Rampton will surely win if he runs in 1976; but he is reported to be ready to retire, and there will surely be a spirited scramble, among both Republicans and Democrats, for the post.

Or consider the case of the state's senior Senator, Democrat Frank Moss. he was first elected in 1958, because of a split in the Republican Party between incumbent Senator Arthur Watkins, chairman of the committee that recommended the censure of Joe McCarthy, and J. Bracken Lee, former Governor and later Mayor of Salt Lake City. Lee jumped into the Senate race as an Independent and allowed Moss to capture the seat with just 39% of the vote. Moss was blessed with having to run for reelection in the Democratic year of 1964, when he beat the ultraconservative president of Brigham Young University, Ernest Wilkinson, with 57% of the vote.

Moss was supposed to encounter a tougher race in 1970. The Republican candidate, Congressman Laurence Burton of the 1st district, waged a campaign typical of Nixon-backed challengers that year. He called Moss a radical for opposing the Vietnam war and Nixon's appointments to the Supreme Court. Burton's effort was well financed. Moreover, both Nixon and Agnew—presumed to be popular in Utah—flew in to help out. But Moss led in the polls all the way, and wound up winning by a margin close to the one he got in 1964.

Moss possessed several assets in the campaign that Burton could not match. Utah, like all small states, tends to value the seniority of its congressional delegation. Moss had 12 years of seniority and the chair of the Interior Committee's Subcommittee on Minerals, Materials, and Fuels—an important post for a Senator from one of the leading copper-producing states. And as Chairman of the Commerce Committee's Consumer Subcommittee, Moss had long been one of the Senate's most active advocates of consumer legislation. But even more important in Utah was the fact that Moss was the sponsor and the driving force behind the law that banned cigarette advertising from television. To Mormons, smoking is a sin. And Moss's victory over the tobacco lobby probably impressed the voters of Utah more than the Senator's ability to defend the state's interest in national parks, Hill Air Force Base, and so on.

Since that last victory, Moss has been especially vigorous on the consumer front. As one of the leading sponsors of the Consumer Product Safety Commission, Moss has worked to insure that the law actually works and that, as required, the agency is insulated completely from the executive branch. He is also one of the leading sponsors of the Consumer Protection Agency, and of national no-fault automobile insurance. Moss's seat comes up in 1976; at this writing, his most likely opponent appears to be State Attorney General Vernon Romney (a cousin of George). Romney is well liked, and it looks like this will be a seriously contested seat. But keep in mind that with the single exception of Moss's first victory, no incumbent Utah Senator has been beaten since 1950.

That record must be a source of encouragement to Utah's new Senator, Jake Garn, who was elected by a small margin in 1974. The seat that he won had been occupied for 24 years by Wallace Bennett, a conservative Republican and former president of the National Association of Manufacturers, whose voting record on most issues was the complete opposite of Moss's. Bennett's retirement was prudent: he was 76; he had won only 54% of the vote the last time out; and his son Robert had been the proprietor of the CIA-run public relations agency which had been the apparent employer of Howard Hunt at the time he was doing dirty tricks for the White House. In Garn, Bennett has a successor whose record will probably please him—a solidly conservative Republican. And the fact that his victory was by no means assured from the start tells us something about the volatile nature of Utah politics.

Indeed, the favorite at the outset of the race was 2d district Democratic Congressman Wayne Owens. Just two years before, Owens had beaten Republican Congressman Sherman Lloyd. A big element in that race was the 35-year-old Owen's 689-mile hike the length of the state; the youthful and fit candidate emphasized his stands on environmental issues. His devout Mormonism erased any doubts conservative Utahans may have had about his service on the staffs of Robert and Edward Kennedy.

But that had not been forgotten by Governor Rampton, who remembered that Owens, working for Robert Kennedy in 1968, had won some delegate posts away from the Governor himself, who had remained a big fan of Lyndon Johnson. Six years later, Rampton was still mad, and against Owens he promoted the candidacy of his friend Donald Holbrook, who was unknown publicly and appeared to have no other support. In Utah a candidate who wins 70% of the vote at a party's state convention cannot be challenged in a primary, and against Rampton's strongest efforts Owens got the 70% by the smallest possible margin. But the bitterness remained. Even more damaging to Owens was his performance as a member of the House Judiciary Committee during the hearings on the impeachment of Richard Nixon. It was not so much his pro-impeachment vote that hurt as his demeanor; he appeared tired, sometimes seemed to mumble when he was speaking, and overall his showing seemed to be eclipsed by other committee members on both sides of the issue.

After that, Garn started moving up in the polls. Owens made some gains in October, but the final result was a 50% Garn victory.

Utah has two congressional districts, and though they both stretch far from the Wasatch Front along the Great Salt Lake, their populations are both concentrated there: 88% of the state's voters are in the Salt Lake City media market. The 1st district covers the eastern half of the state, but its main population concentrations are just north of Salt Lake City, in the well to do suburbs of David County and around the working class town of Ogden, and just to the south of the capital, around the heavily conservative, very Mormon cities of Provo and Orem. Politically, this is the more conservative and Republican of the two districts, and the Democrat it has elected since 1970 reflects that leaning. He is K. Gunn McKay, nephew of the late LDS President David McKay, former aide to Governor Rampton, and one of the most conservative northern Democrats in Congress. Elected by a narrow margin in 1970, McKay won easily in 1972 and 1974; it is possible that he might go for Governor in 1976.

The 2d district includes several of the state's western counties, but for all practical purposes it is the Salt Lake City district; 86% of the vote is cast in Salt Lake County. It has elected three Congressmen now in the last three elections, all by narrow margins; the current incumbent is a Democrat named Allan Howe, a former aide to Moss and Rampton.

Census Data Pop. 1,059,273; 0.52% of U.S. total, 36th largest; Central city, 31%; suburban, 47%. Median family income, $9,320; 23rd highest; families above $15,000: 17%; families below $3,000: 9%. Median years education, 12.5.

1974 Share of Federal Tax Burden $1,248,242,000; 0.42% of U.S. total, 38th largest.

1974 Share of Federal Outlays $1,613,669,000; 0.60% of U.S. total, 38th largest. Per capita federal spending, $1513.

DOD	$632,302,000	30th (0.12%)	HEW	$401,742,000	39th (0.43%)
AEC	$1,949,000	27th (0.06%)	HUD	$2,039,000	47th (0.21%)
NASA	$9,260,000	19th (0.31%)	VA	$78,505,000	38th (0.57%)
DOT	$68,580,000	37th (0.81%)	EPA	$7,954,000	43d (0.25%)
DOC	$7,201,000	31st (0.45%)	RevS	$36,394,000	38th (0.60%)
DOI	$47,820,000	18th (1.94%)	Int.	$36,319,000	38th (0.18%)
USDA	$60,709,000	39th (0.49%)	Other	$222,895,000	

Economic Base Finance, insurance and real estate; agriculture, notably cattle, dairy products, turkeys and sheep; primary metal industries; metal mining; food and kindred products; transportation equipment, especially aircraft and parts; apparel and other textile products, especially women's and misses' outerwear.

Political Line-up Governor, Calvin L. Rampton (D). Senators, Frank E. Moss (D) and Jake Garn (R). Representatives, 2 D. State Senate (15 D and 14 R); State House (40 D and 35 R).

The Voters

Registration 618,873 Total. No party registration.
Median voting age 39.
Employment profile White collar, 52%. Blue collar, 32%. Service, 13%. Farm, 3%.
Ethnic groups Spanish, 4%. Total foreign stock, 12%. UK, 3%.

Presidential vote

1972	Nixon (R)	323,643	(72%)
	McGovern (D)	126,284	(28%)
1968	Nixon (R)	238,728	(57%)
	Humphrey (D)	156,665	(37%)
	Wallace (AI)	26,906	(6%)

Sen. Frank E. Moss (D) Elected 1958, seat up 1976; b. Sept. 23, 1911, Holladay; home, Salt Lake City; U. of Utah, B.A. 1933, Geo. Wash. U., J.D. 1937; Church of Latter Day Saints.

Career Law Clerk, Utah Supreme Ct.; Practicing atty.; Atty. for U.S. Securities and Exchange Comm., 1934–39; Army Air Corps, WWII; Salt Lake City Judge, 1941–50; Salt Lake Co. Atty., 1951–58.

Offices 115 RSOB, 202-224-5251. Also 5430 New Fed. Bldg., Salt Lake City 84138, 801-524-5934.

Committees

Aeronautical and Space Sciences (Chairman).

Budget (3d;.

Commerce (7th). Subcommittees: Aviation; Communications; The Consumer (Chairman); Environment (Vice Chairman); Foreign . Commerce and Tourism; Oceans and Atmosphere; Special Subcommittee on Freight Car Shortage; Special Subcommittee on Oil and Gas Production and Distribution.

Post Office and Civil Service (5th). Subcommittees: Civil Service Policies and Practices; Compensation and Employment Benefits; Postal Operations.

Group Ratings

	ADA	COPE	LWV	RIPON	NFU	LCV	CFA	NAB	NSI	ACA
1974	82	73	100	62	100	63	88	40	13	6
1973	89	91	100	63	100	–	91	–	–	14
1972	70	90	100	60	100	42	100	10	0	15

Key Votes

1) No-Knock	AGN	8) Gov Abortn Aid	FOR	15) Consumer Prot Agy	FOR
2) Busing	FOR	9) Cut Mil Brass	ABS	16) Forced Psych Tests	ABS
3) No Fault	FOR	10) Gov Limousine	ABS	17) Fed Campaign Subs	FOR
4) F-111	AGN	11) RR Featherbed	FOR	18) Rhod Chrome Ban	FOR
5) Death Penalty	FOR	12) Handgun License	AGN	19) Open Legis Meetings	FOR
6) Foreign Aid	FOR	13) Less Troop Abrd	ABS	20) Strikers Food Stmps	FOR
7) Filibuster	AGN	14) Resume Turk Aid	AGN	21) Gov Info Disclosure	FOR

Election Results

1970 general:	Frank Moss (D)	210,207	(57%)
	Laurence J. Burton (R)	159,004	(43%)
1970 primary:	Frank Moss (D), unopposed		
1964 general:	Frank Moss (D)	227,822	(57%)
	Ernest L. Wilkinson (R)	169,562	(43%)

Sen. Jake Garn (R) Elected 1974, seat up 1980; b. Oct. 12, 1932, Richfield; home, Salt Lake City; U. of Utah, B.S. 1955; Church of Latter Day Saints.

Career Navy, 1956–60; Asst. Mgr., Salt Lake Ofc., Home Life Insurance Co. of New York, 1961–66; Salt Lake City Commission, 1967–71; Mayor of Salt Lake City, 1971–74.

Offices 4203 DSOB, 202-224-5444. Also 4227 Fed. Bldg., Salt Lake City 84111, 801-524-5938.

Committees

Aeronautical and Space Sciences (4th).

Banking, Housing and Urban Affairs (5th). Subcommittees: Consumer Affairs; Housing and Urban Affairs; International Finance; Oversight; Small Business.

The District of Columbia (3d).

Group Ratings: Newly Elected

Key Votes

1) No-Knock	NE	8) Gov Abortn Aid	AGN	15) Consumer Prot Agy	NE
2) Busing	NE	9) Cut Mil Brass	NE	16) Forced Psych Tests	NE
3) No Fault	NE	10) Gov Limousine	NE	17) Fed Campaign Subs	NE
4) F-111	FOR	11) RR Featherbed	NE	18) Rhod Chrome Ban	NE
5) Death Penalty	NE	12) Handgun License	NE	19) Open Legis Meetings	NE
6) Foreign Aid	NE	13) Less Troop Abrd	NE	20) Strikers Food Stmps	NE
7) Filibuster	AGN	14) Resume Turk Aid	FOR	21) Gov Info Disclosure	NE

Election Results

1974 general:	Jake Garn (R)	210,299	(50%)	($363,162)
	Wayne Owens (D)	185,377	(44%)	($445,500)
	Bruce Bangerter (A)	24,966	(6%)	($1,488)
1974 primary:	Jake Garn (R), unopposed			

Gov. Calvin L. Rampton (D) Elected 1964, term expires Jan. 1977; b. Nov. 6, 1913, Bountiful; U. of Utah, B.S. 1936, J.D. 1940, also Geo. Wash. U. Law School.

Career Admin. Asst., U.S. Rep. J. W. Robinson, 1936–38; Davis. Co. Atty, 1939–40; Utah Asst. Atty. Gen., 1941–42, 1946–48; Army, WWII; Chf., U.S. Army Sr. Claims Comm., Paris, 1945; Practicing atty., 1946–64.

Offices Rm. 210 State Capitol, Salt Lake City 84114, 801-328-5231.

Election Results

1972 general:	Calvin L. Rampton (D)	331,998	(70%)
	Nicholas L. Strike (R)	144,449	(30%)
1972 primary:	Calvin L. Rampton (D), unopposed		
1968 general:	Calvin L. Rampton (D)	289,283	(69%)
	Carl W. Buehner (R)	131,729	(31%)

FIRST DISTRICT

◆ ◆ ◆ ◆ ◆

Census Data Pop. 529,688. Central city, 28%; suburban, 41%. Median family income, $9,080; families above $15,000: 16%; families below $3,000: 9%. Median years education, 12.5.

The Voters

Median voting age 38.
Employment profile White collar, 50%. Blue collar, 33%. Service, 13%. Farm, 4%.
Ethnic groups Spanish, 4%. Total foreign stock, 10%. UK, 2%.

Presidential vote

1972	Nixon (R)	166,517	(77%)
	McGovern (D)	50,225	(23%)
1968	Nixon (R)	119,524	(59%)
	Humphrey (D)	69,487	(34%)
	Wallace (AI)	14,758	(7%)

Rep. K. Gunn McKay (D) Elected 1970; b. Feb. 23, 1925, Ogden; home, Huntsville; Weber St. Col., 1958–60, Utah St. U., B.S. 1962; Church of Latter Day Saints.

Career Coast Guard, WWII; small business and teaching; Utah House of Reps., 1962–66; Admin. Asst. to Gov. Calvin L. Rampton, 1967–70.

Offices 1427 LHOB, 202-225-0453. Also Suite 213, 1st Security Bank, 92 N. University Ave., Provo 84601, 801-373-4150.

Committees

Appropriations (26th). Subcommittees: District of Columbia; Interior; Military Construction.

Group Ratings

	ADA	COPE	LWV	RIPON	NFU	LCV	CFA	NAB	NSI	ACA
1974	58	75	58	36	100	44	33	42	50	15
1973	48	70	67	43	94	17	80	–	–	20
1972	31	89	44	46	100	21	0	30	80	30

Key Votes

1) Foreign Aid	ABS	6) Gov Abortn Aid	AGN	11) Pub Cong Election $	FOR
2) Busing	AGN	7) Coed Phys Ed	AGN	12) Turkish Arms Cutoff	FOR
3) ABM	ABS	8) Pov Lawyer Gag	AGN	13) Youth Camp Regs	ABS
4) B-1 Bomber	FOR	9) Pub Trans Sub	AGN	14) Strip Mine Veto	AGN
5) Nerve Gas	AGN	10) EZ Voter Regis	FOR	15) Farm Bill Veto	AGN

Election Results

1974 general:	Gunn McKay (D)	124,793	(63%)	($25,611)
	Ron Inkley (R)	62,807	(32%)	($10,938)
	L. S. Brown (AI)	11,664	(6%)	($1,945)
1974 primary:	Gunn McKay (D), unopposed			
1972 general:	Gunn McKay (D)	127,027	(55%)	($52,320)
	Robert K. Wolthuis (R)	96,296	(42%)	($62,472)
	L. S. Brown (AI)	6,043	(3%)	(NA)

◆ ◆ ◆ ◆ ◆

SECOND DISTRICT

Census Data Pop. 529,585. Central city, 33%; suburban, 53%. Median family income, $9,537; families above $15,000: 18%; families below $3,000: 8%. Median years education, 12.5.

The Voters

Median voting age 40.
Employment profile White collar, 53%. Blue collar, 32%. Service, 13%. Farm, 2%.
Ethnic groups Spanish, 5%. Total foreign stock, 14%. UK, 3%.

Presidential vote

1972	Nixon (R)	157,126	(67%)
	McGovern (D)	76,059	(33%)
1968	Nixon (R)	119,204	(55%)
	Humphrey (D)	87,178	(40%)
	Wallace (AI)	12,148	(6%)

Rep. Allan T. Howe (D) Elected 1974; b. Sept. 6, 1927, South Cottonwood; home, Salt Lake City; U. of Utah, B.S. 1952, LL.B. 1954; Church of Latter Day Saints.

Career Coast Guard, 1946–47; Practicing atty, 1955–74; South Salt Lake City Atty., 1956–59; Admin. Asst. to U.S. Sen. Frank E. Moss, 1959–64; Legal Counsel and Admin. Asst. to Gov. Calvin L. Rampton, 1965–68; Exec. Dir., Four Corners Regional Development Comm., 1968–72.

Offices 1525 LHOB, 202-225-3011. Also 2311 Fed. Bldg., 125 S. State St., Salt Lake City 84111, 801-524-5583.

Committees

Interior and Insular Affairs (24th). Subcommittees: Mines and Mining; National Parks and Recreation; Water and Power Resources.

Public Works and Transportation (19th). Subcommittees: Aviation; Economic Development; Investigations and Review; Water Resources.

Group Ratings: Newly Elected

Key Votes

1) Foreign Aid	AGN	6) Gov Abortn Aid	NE	11) Pub Cong Election $	NE
2) Busing	NE	7) Coed Phys Ed	AGN	12) Turkish Arms Cutoff	NE
3) ABM	NE	8) Pov Lawyer Gag	NE	13) Youth Camp Regs	AGN
4) B-1 Bomber	AGN	9) Pub Trans Sub	NE	14) Strip Mine Veto	AGN
5) Nerve Gas	NE	10) EZ Voter Regis	NE	15) Farm Bill Veto	AGN

Election Results

1974 general:	Allan T. Howe (D)	105,739	(50%)	($95,540)
	Stephen M. Harmsen (R)	100,259	(47%)	($103,717)
	Roben J. Schafer (AI)	6,482	(3%)	($1,103)
1974 primary:	Allan T. Howe (D)	18,890	(56%)	
	Daryl J. McCarty (D)	15,039	(44%)	

VERMONT

In many ways, Vermont still seems to be in the nineteenth century. The classic New England town squares still stand here; the cows still graze on the hillsides; the taciturn Yankee farmers still tap the sugar maple trees in the early spring; the autumn foliage remains perhaps the most magnificent in the world. Vermont remains, by the census definition, the most rural state, with two-thirds of its population outside urban areas. But even so, the 1960s and 1970s have been bringing change here. There are now large IBM and GE complexes around Burlington, the state's largest city (pop. 38,000). The ski resort and summer home industries have boomed so much that the price of rural land has skyrocketed, forcing many farmers to sell. From 1850 to 1960, Vermont's population hovered between 300,000 and 400,000; only in 1963 were there finally more people than cows in the state. But in 1970, there were 444,000 people in Vermont, and today there are more than 470,000.

There have also been massive political changes here—massive enough that this state, long the most Republican in the nation, today has a Democratic Governor and a Democratic United States Senator. Before 1960, the only areas of Democratic strength in the state were the small Irish and French Canadian communities in Burlington and other towns near the Canadian border. But in 1962 a Burlington lawyer named Philip Hoff managed to win enough Yankee votes to add to that traditional Catholic base to win election as Vermont's first Democratic Governor in 109 years. Hoff was a popular Governor; he was reelected in 1964 and 1966. But his personal problems (including, he admitted, alcoholism) eventually caught up with him when he ran for the Senate in 1970. Not only did he lose the Yankee support he previously had enjoyed, he also lost in the traditionally Democratic parts of the state to the colorless incumbent, Republican Winston Prouty. A year later, Prouty died. Republican Governor Deane Davis appointed the state's Congressman-at-Large, Robert Stafford, to fill the vacancy. Stafford, who had the reputation of a moderate, even liberal Republican (though the timing of his appointment was engineered by the Nixon White House, which needed his vote in the Senate on a particular issue), was elected easily with 64% of the vote. It seemed the state's brief Democratic era was over.

But then came the surprise Democratic victory in the gubernatorial election of 1972. The issue was growth, and the state's response to it. Both Hoff and Davis had pushed environmental controls, but the Republican candidate, Luther Hackett, wanted to ease them. His opponent, an unknown Democrat named Thomas Salmon, took vigorous exception; the top priority, he said, was preserving the basic character of Vermont. It was a theme that evoked a positive response both in the traditionally Democratic Catholic neighborhoods and in those pristine Yankee villages where people valued their Republicanism less than their Vermont heritage. Despite some controversy—he was attacked for appointing one of the "Chicago Seven" to a state position—Salmon was reelected easily in 1974 with 60% of the vote.

That election really showed Salmon's commitment to state government, for he certainly could have run for and almost certainly would have won the Senate seat vacated, after 34 years, by George Aiken. Over the years Aiken had become a kind of state monument—a Vermonter of Robert Frostian image, a progressive Governor in the '30s who had campaigned for years against high power rates, a skeptical observer as ranking member of the Senate Foreign Relations Committee of this country's involvement in the Vietnam quagmire. Aiken had been reelected in 1968 with no opposition; he almost certainly could have won in 1974. But at 82 he decided finally to retire to his farm in Putney; the delights of the capital remained resistible to this man who had once written a book called *Pioneering with Fruits and Berries*.

Aiken had his own candidate to succeed himself, Charles Ross, whose appointement to the Federal Power Commission the Senator had brought about during the Kennedy Administration. But the old man was not able to pass on the mantle: Ross was not particularly well known in Vermont, and Congressman-at-Large Richard Mallary got 59% of the vote in the Republican primary. But Mallary had a strong Democratic opponent in Chittenden County (Burlington) State's Attorney Patrick Leahy. Though only 34, Leahy had already made a name for himself by trying all major felony cases personally and by attacking the big oil companies during the gasoline crisis.

At first it was an almost friendly campaign; the two candidates agreed on spending limits, with the incumbent Mallary voluntarily accepting a lower figure. Mallary had the advantage of statewide recognition; Leahy of strong loyalties in his home area. The result was close, but Leahy managed to win with 49% of the vote; he got more than 60% of the vote in the Burlington area, and at the same time had worked the southern part of the state hard enough to get respectable totals there. It was the first time a Democrat had ever been elected to the Senate in Vermont. Leahy now sits on the Agriculture and Armed Services Committee; he is not one of the Senate's most outspoken liberals, but he is less hawkish than veterans of Armed Services might expect.

While Salmon and Leahy were both winning, the Republicans still managed to retain the state's single at-large congressional seat. With Mallary running for the Senate, the Republican nominee was James Jeffords, a former state Attorney General who promised to be a more or less liberal Republican in the tradition of Stafford and Mallary. The Democrat, former Burlington Mayor Francis Cain, could call on the sympathies of traditional Democrats here, but he failed to make much headway among the Yankees, and lost 53–40.

The big race for 1976 will be the contest for Stafford's seat. The incumbent will probably win easily unless he is opposed by Governor Salmon; it then could be quite a battle. Those who can remember when James Farley said, "As goes Maine, so goes Vermont," can scarcely believe that this state could elect two Democratic Senators; and it seems highly unlikely. Yet Stafford has never really been tested by a strong opponent, and it is not clear how deep his support is.

Census Data   Pop. 444,732; 0.22% of U.S. total, 48th largest; Central city, 0%; suburban, 0%. Median family income, $8,928; 28th highest; families above $15,000: 16%; families below $3,000: 9%.   Median years education, 12.2.

1974 Share of Federal Tax Burden $482,068,000; 0.18% of U.S. total, 48th largest.

1974 Share of Federal Outlays $530,988,000; 0.20% of U.S. total, 49th largest.   Per capita federal spending, $1194.

DOD	$81,350,000	50th (0.12%)	HEW	$232,375,000	46th (0.25%)
AEC	$19,000	48th (–)	HUD	$2,078,000	46th (0.21%)
NASA	$89,000	46th (–)	VA	$33,668,000	49th (0.25%)
DOT	$36,184,000	49th (0.43%)	EPA	$8,227,000	41th (0.26%)
DOC	$1,412,000	49th (0.09%)	RevS	$36,394,000	38th (0.60%)
DOI	$47,820,000	18th (1.94%)	Int.	$16,908,000	48th (0.08%)
USDA	$21,921,000	46th (0.18%)	Other	$12,543,000	

Economic Base   Agriculture, notably dairy products, cattle, eggs and forest products; finance, insurance and real estate; electrical equipment and supplies, especially electronic components and accessories; machinery, especially metal working machinery; printing and publishing, especially book printing; lumber and wood products; cut stone and stone products, and other stone, clay and glass products.

Political Line-up   Governor, Thomas P. Salmon (D). Senators, Robert T. Stafford (R) and Patrick J. Leahy (D). Representatives, 1 R at large. State Senate (18 R and 12 D); State House (77 R and 73 D).

The Voters

Registration   266,649 Total. No party registration.
Median voting age 42.
Employment profile   White collar, 46%. Blue collar, 35%. Service, 14%. Farm, 5%.
Ethnic groups   Total foreign stock, 18%. Canada, 10%.

Presidential vote

1972	Nixon (R)	117,149	(63%)
	McGovern (D)	68,174	(37%)
1968	Nixon (R)	85,142	(53%)
	Humphrey (D)	70,255	(44%)
	Wallace (AI)	5,104	(3%)

Sen. Robert T. Stafford (R) Appointed Sept. 16, 1971, elected Jan. 7, 1972, seat up 1976; b. Aug. 8, 1913, Rutland; home. Rutland; Middlebury Col., B.S. 1935, U. of Mich., Boston U., LL.B. 1938; Congregationalist.

Career Rutland City Prosecuting Atty., 1938–42; Navy, WWII and Korea; Rutland Co. State's Atty., 1947–51; Deputy Atty. Gen. of Vt., 1953–55, Atty. Gen. of Vt., 1955–57; Lt. Gov. of Vt., 1957–59; Gov. of Vt., 1959–61; U.S. House of Reps., 1961–1971.

Offices 5219 DSOB, 202-224-5141. Also P.O. Box 161, Burlington 05401, 802-775-5446, and 27 S. Main St., Rutland 05701, 802-864-7814.

Committees

Labor and Public Welfare (5th). Subcommittees: Aging; Children and Youth; Education; The Handicapped; Health; Labor; Special Subcommittee on Arts and Humanities; Special Subcommittee on Human Resources; Special Subcommittee on National Science Foundation.

Public Works (3d). Subcommittees: Environmental Pollution, Panel on Environmental Science and Technology, Panel on Materials Policy; Economic Development; Water Resources; Transportation.

Veterans' Affairs (3d). Subcommittees: Housing and Insurance; Readjustment, Education and Employment.

Group Ratings

	ADA	COPE	LWV	RIPON	NFU	LCV	CFA	NAB	NSI	ACA
1974	68	73	100	83	100	70	88	55	44	11
1973	63	73	100	83	67	–	69	–	–	19
1972	45	70	90	76	33	50	75	25	50	33

Key Votes

1) No-Knock	AGN	8) Gov Abortn Aid	FOR	15) Consumer Prot Agy	FOR
2) Busing	FOR	9) Cut Mil Brass	AGN	16) Forced Psych Tests	FOR
3) No Fault	FOR	10) Gov Limousine	FOR	17) Fed Campaign Subs	FOR
4) F-111	FOR	11) RR Featherbed	FOR	18) Rhod Chrome Ban	FOR
5) Death Penalty	FOR	12) Handgun License	AGN	19) Open Legis Meetings	FOR
6) Foreign Aid	FOR	13) Less Troop Abrd	AGN	20) Strikers Food Stmps	FOR
7) Filibuster	AGN	14) Resume Turk Aid	FOR	21) Gov Info Disclosure	FOR

Election Results

1972 special:	Robert T. Stafford (R)	45,888	(64%)	(NA)
	Randolph T. Major (D)	23,842	(33%)	(NA)
	Bernard Sanders (Liberty Union)	1,571	(2%)	(NA)
1972 primary:	Robert T. Stafford (R), unopposed			

Sen. Patrick J. Leahy (D) Elected 1974, seat up 1980; b. Mar. 31, 1940, Montpelier; home, Burlington; St. Michael's Col., Winooski, B.A. 1961, Georgetown U., J.D. 1964; Catholic.

Career Practicing atty., 1964–74; Chittenden Co. State's Atty., 1966–74.

Offices 1203 DSOB, 202-224-4242. Also 135 Church St., Burlington 05401, 802-863-2525.

Committees

Agriculture and Forestry (9th). Subcommittees: Environment, Soil Conservation, and Forestry; Agricultural Research and General Legislation; Rural Development.

Armed Services (10th). Subcommittees: General Legislation; Military Construction Authorization; Research and Development.

Group Ratings: Newly Elected

Key Votes

1) No-Knock	NE	8) Gov Abortn Aid	FOR	15) Consumer Prot Agy	NE
2) Busing	NE	9) Cut Mil Brass	NE	16) Forced Psych Tests	NE
3) No Fault	NE	10) Gov Limousine	NE	17) Fed Campaign Subs	NE
4) F-111	AGN	11) RR Featherbed	NE	18) Rhod Chrome Ban	NE
5) Death Penalty	NE	12) Handgun License	NE	19) Open Legis Meetings	NE
6) Foreign Aid	NE	13) Less Troop Abrd	NE	20) Strikers Food Stmps	NE
7) Filibuster	AGN	14) Resume Turk Aid	ABS	21) Gov Info Disclosure	NE

Election Results

1974 general:	Patrick J. Leahy (D)	70,629	(49%)	($152,817)
	Richard W. Mallary (R)	66,223	(46%)	($90,617)
	Bernard Sanders (Liberty Union)	5,901	(4%)	(NA)
1974 primary:	Patrick J. Leahy (D)	19,801	(84%)	
	Nathaniel Frothingham (D)	3,703	(16%)	

Gov. Thomas P. Salmon (D) Elected 1972, term expires Jan. 1977; Boston Col., B.A. 1954, LL.B. 1957, New York U., LL.M.

Career Practicing atty.; Rockingham Town Cncl., 1960–62; Judge, Bellows Falls Municipal Ct., 1962–65; Vt. House of Reps., 1965–70, Minor. Ldr., 1969–70.

Offices Pavilion Ofc. Bldg., Montpelier 05602, 802-828-3333.

Election Results

1974 general:	Thomas P. Salmon (D)	79,584	(56%)
	Walter L. "Peanut" Kennedy (R)	53,677	(38%)
	Martha Abbott (Liberty Union)	7,629	(5%)
1974 primary:	Thomas P. Salmon (D)	18,498	(84%)
	John F. "Buzzy" Reilly (D)	3,537	(16%)
1972 general:	Thomas P. Salmon (D)	104,533	(56%)
	Luther F. Hackett (R)	82,491	(44%)

Rep. James M. Jeffords (R) Elected 1974; b. May 11, 1934, Rutland; home, Montpelier; Yale U., B.S. 1956, Harvard U., LL.B. 1962.

Career Navy, 1956–59; Law Clerk to U.S. Dist. Ct. Judge Ernest W. Gibson, 1962; Practicing atty., 1963–75; Chm., Rutland Co. Bd. of Property Tax Appeals, 1964–66; Vt. Senate, 1967–68; Atty. Gen. of Vt., 1969–73.

Offices 501 CHOB, 202-225-4115. Also P.O. Box 676, Fed. Bldg., Montpelier 05602, 802-223-5274.

Committees

Agriculture (10th). Subcommittees: Conservation and Credit; Dairy and Poultry.

Education and Labor (10th). Subcommittees: Elementary, Secondary and Vocational Education; Select Subcommittee on Education.

Group Ratings: Newly Elected

Key Votes

1) Foreign Aid	FOR	6) Gov Abortn Aid	NE	11) Pub Cong Election $	NE
2) Busing	NE	7) Coed Phys Ed	FOR	12) Turkish Arms Cutoff	NE
3) ABM	NE	8) Pov Lawyer Gag	NE	13) Youth Camp Regs	FOR
4) B-1 Bomber	AGN	9) Pub Trans Sub	NE	14) Strip Mine Veto	AGN
5) Nerve Gas	NE	10) EZ Voter Regis	NE	15) Farm Bill Veto	AGN

Election Results

1974 general:	James M. Jeffords (R)	74,561	(53%)	($5,883)
	Francis J. Cain (D)	56,342	(40%)	($47,037)
	Michael Parenti (Liberty Union)	9,961	(7%)	(NA)
1974 primary:	James M. Jeffords (R)	18,573	(40%)	
	Madeline B. Harwood (R)	16,345	(35%)	
	John S. Burgess (R)	11,453	(25%)	

VIRGINIA

Fifteen years ago, any analysis of Virginia politics started and ended with a description of the Byrd machine. This was a unique organization that enjoyed complete domination of the state's politics from 1925—the year Harry Flood Byrd was elected Governor—until 1964. Political machines of the common variety are operated by men who can make what they regard as a good living only in politics, and do so by manipulating large blocs of votes in big cities. In contrast, the men of the Byrd machine were usually bankers, established lawyers, wealthy businessmen, and gentleman farmers—people who dominated life in the small towns of the Shenandoah Valley, Byrd's home bailiwick, or in Southside Virginia, an area that is really part of the Deep South. The key to the machine's success was a small electorate. The state's voting laws, especially the poll tax, kept turnout low and effectively excluded blacks and most poor whites from the ballot box. So the succession of Byrd machine Governors included personal friends and social equals of those who ran the Virginia Electric and Power Company (VEPCO), the state's largest banks, and the University of Virginia. All were rich, elderly, respected, reserved, and, of course, conservative.

The same set of adjectives certainly applied to Harry Byrd himself. Though he served only one term as Governor, Byrd easily controlled the machine and thus the politics of Virginia from the United States Senate for more than 30 years. Ironically, Byrd's path to the Senate was smoothed by Franklin D. Roosevelt, but the Virginian soon turned against FDR, and Byrd's name came to represent an opposition to government spending and budget deficits. As Chairman of the Senate Finance Committee and founder and Chairman of the Joint Committee on Reduction of Federal Expenditures, Byrd possessed two forums from which to promulgate his views. The chairmanship of the Finance Committee, of course, was what made the Senator powerful, since the unit must approve all federal taxation; the Joint Committee never did much to reduce expenditures. Despite Byrd's best efforts, the federal budget continued to grow inexorably over the years; in 1965, Byrd resigned from the Senate just as Congress had finished enacting most of Lyndon Johnson's Great Society programs.

During the mid-1950s, the Byrd machine made its only appeal to the mass of public opinion. This was Massive Resistance Program: for several years, Virginia schools under federal court orders to integrate were shut down by the state, as attempts were made to subsidize private, all-white academies. (The state did nothing, however, for the black children out of school.) But the program of defiance collapsed, and the Byrd Governor then in office capitulated and agreed to comply with the law. The style of Massive Resistance was typical of the Byrd machine: its oratory was closer in spirit to John C. Calhoun's stringent interpretation of the Constitution than the standing-in-the-school-house-door bombast of Orval Faubus and George Wallace. But for once the Byrd machine had opened the door for mass participation in the electoral process, and while it had found the formula for at least some conservative victories—appeal to racial fears and animosities—it had also accelerated the trends which have destroyed the machine as it had always existed.

Indeed, as Byrd was leaving the Senate, his machine was visibly collapsing. A large part of the reason was simple demography. The Washington suburbs, where the small town lawyers and bankers of the Byrd machine were never much in evidence, grew from 5% of the state's population in 1940 to 21% in 1975. The industrial Tidewater area around Norfolk and Newport News, with its large Navy bases, grew from 13% to 22% in the same period. The western mountain part of the state continued, as always, to be an anti-Byrd stronghold; while the Voting Rights Act of 1965 enfranchised many blacks in Southside Virginia, long a Byrd stronghold. Altogether, that left the heart of Harry Byrd's Virginia—Richmond, Southside, the Piedmont, the Shenendoah Valley—as a minority of the state.

Since that time Virginia's politics has been as volatile as that of any state. More often than not, conservatives in the Byrd mold (some of them very much Byrd men) have won elections; but they have had real competition, and their victories have not been the product of an articulated organization, but more often of a crude, racially based media campaign strategy.

Such was certainly the case in the elections of both Senator William L. Scott and Governor Mills Godwin. Both were elected as Republicans, but their real roots—especially in the case of Godwin, who had been elected Governor before, in 1965—were in the Byrd organization. Scott has the distinction of having been named the dumbest member of Congress by *New Times* magazine, in response to which he called a press conference to rebut the charge, not wholly with success. Scott is the closest thing we have to an accidental Senator today. A government employee for 27 years, who managed to save enough to buy a comfortable house in the Virginia suburbs, Scott had the good fortune to be the Republican nominee in the 8th congressional district in 1966. That was the year House Rules Committee Chairman Howard Smith, a conservative power, was defeated in the Democratic primary; the liberal who beat him was unable, by a hair, to beat Scott in the general.

After three undistinguished terms in the House, Scott ran for the Senate in 1966—a year when no one else wanted the Republican nomination. The incumbent was William Spong, a moderate, perhaps even liberal Democrat, and a former state Senator from the Tidewater area who had been elected with 59% of the vote in 1966. A scholarly, quiet man, Spong had expected to be reelected easily, and through October of 1972 that appeared to be what was going to happen. But suddenly Scott received an infusion of money on the order of $250,000 from a little known millionaire; a series of backlash-provoking TV commercials followed; and Scott won with 51% of the vote.

His chances of duplicating that triumph when his seat comes up in 1978 seem to be minimal. Though he may be little known in the nation at large, his naming as the dumbest member of Congress only confirmed what many Virginians had come to believe. Scott's hard line conservatism continues to appeal to many voters here, but some of them have been embarrassed by his maladroitness. In his 1972 race, for example, he ran just about even in the northern Virginia suburbs of Washington; now those same areas are represented in the House by two liberal Democrats, and it is hard to believe that they will go for Scott again. Naturally, any number of Democrats are looking forward to running in 1978.

Virginia's other Senator is the holder of a more familiar name, Harry Byrd, Jr. For years he waited in the Virginia state Senate to succeed his father, also tending to the family's Shenandoah Valley newspaper chain and apple orchards (the Byrds are among the largest apple growers in the nation). In 1965 he was appointed to the Senate; in 1966, he was elected to the remainder of his father's term with only 54% of the vote. He was hurt by increasing Republican strength and an Independent candidacy in the traditional—and growing—anti-Byrd parts of the state. In the Senate, too, Byrd did not enjoy the power his father had. The conservative Southern bloc the elder Byrd had often led had been diminished in size and seniority by retirements, Republican victories, and the election of some moderate or even liberal Democrats.

In 1970, Byrd correctly perceived that he would have difficulty winning the Democratic primary back home, and so he ran as an Independent. It was a way of keeping his options open in the Senate. If, as Nixon strategists hoped, the Republicans had gained control of the Senate, Byrd would have been free to switch parties—and perhaps to lead an exodus of Southern conservatives to the GOP. But when the Democrats won, Byrd was able, by the simple expedient of voting with them to organize the Senate, to maintain his seniority on the Armed Services and Finance Committees. Byrd won that election, again, with only 54% of the vote, but this time his victory was by a much more comfortable margin: for both the Democrats and Republicans had insisted on running candidates of their own, and hopelessly split the anti-Byrd vote.

Byrd is up again in 1976, and at 61 there is no indication he will not run. The question is, under whose aegis. At this writing it seems very possible he will campaign as a Democrat again. That will insure his seniority, and the liberal Democrats who secured control of their party in 1970 when the remnants of the Byrd machine walked out have suffered since a series of defeats that makes a Byrd candidacy considerably more palatable to them. In any case, Byrd will be a favorite for reelection; if he does not have any major legislative accomplishments, he does not possess the temperament or ideology that seeks them, and Virginians may be satisfied with his efforts to have citizenship posthumously restored to Robert E. Lee.

Virginia's Governor today, Mills Godwin, is perhaps the least active chief executive in the nation. It is generally agreed now that he came out of retirement in 1973 for one purpose and one purpose only: to defeat Henry Howell. One of the real originals in American politics, Howell built up a reputation as a state Senator from Norfolk as an opponent of the Byrd machine, of VEPCO and the big banks, and as a supporter of racial equality. In a 1971 special election he won the post of Lieutenant Governor with a minority of the vote, and in 1973 he seemed to be, finally, a majority winner, running on the slogan of "Keep the big boys honest." Howell is a garrulous campaigner, who likes to play country music and gab with ordinary Virginians in his thick accent, but his campaign suffered from a lack of direction. When Godwin began attacking Howell hard for his alleged support of school busing, Howell switched from the issue that favored him—repeal of the sales tax on food—to a defensive stance on the issue Godwin was raising. The result was a narrow 51% Godwin victory, followed by Godwin's do nothing term in office.

Godwin's nomination by the Republicans signalled the ascendancy in that party of the hardline conservatives, and the defeat of the party's traditional, more moderate leadership, centered in the mountains in the western part of the state. This traditional Republicanism had its genesis in an opposition to the slaveholding, Democratic sentiments of Southside Virginia; the Godwin nomination was an embrace of that old Democratic tradition. Godwin's predecessor, Linwood Holton, was an exemplar of the older Republicanism, a generally successful Governor who was estranged from the Nixon Administration he generally supported because he refused to deplore or decry federal court busings decisions. Holton left office a minority in his own party; but he may have a sympathetic successor in Lieutenant Governor John Dalton, another mountain Republican, who will almost surely run for Governor in 1977. Another likely candidate is Attorney General Andrew Miller, the son (like Dalton) of a longtime Byrd foe, who passed up the 1973 race; but he may well have to win a primary against none other than Henry Howell, who is inclined now to run as a Democrat. So if Virginia politics remains predominantly conservative, it is still extremely volatile, and anything could happen.

Census Data Pop. 4,648,494; 2.30% of U.S. total, 14th largest; Central city, 24%; suburban, 37%. Median family income, $9,045; 25th highest; families above $15,000: 20%; families below $3,000: 11%. Median years education, 11.7.

1974 Share of Federal Tax Burden $5,972,281,000; 2.23% of U.S. total, 12th largest.

1974 Share of Federal Outlays $8,021,191,000; 2.97% of U.S. total, 10th largest. Per capita federal spending, $1726.

DOD	$3,597,171,000	4th (5.25%)	HEW	$1,640,218,000	18th (1.77%)
AEC	$6,511,000	22d (0.21%)	HUD	$18,136,000	19th (1.86%)
NASA	$140,295,000	7th (4.73%)	VA	$323,812,000	14th (2.37%)
DOT	$367,537,000	5th (4.34%)	EPA	$52,178,000	19th (1.66%)
DOC	$360,925,000	1st (22.37%)	RevS	$120,096,000	17th (1.98%)
DOI	$80,033,000	8th (3.25%)	Int.	$103,773,000	25th (0.50%)
USDA	$199,688,000	29th (1.60%)	Other	$1,010,818,000	

Economic Base Finance, insurance and real estate; agriculture, notably dairy products, tobacco, cattle and broilers; textile mills products, especially cotton weaving mills; apparel and other textile products, especially men's and boy's furnishings, and women's and misses outwear; chemicals synthetics; food and kindred products; electrical equipment and supplies.

Political Line-up Governor, Mills E. Godwin, Jr. (R). Senators, Harry F. Byrd, Jr. (Ind.) and William Lloyd Scott (R). Representatives, 10 (5 D and 5 R). State Senate (35 D and 5 R); House of Delegates (66 D, 19 R, and 15 Ind.).

The Voters

Registration 2,050,809 Total. No party registration.
Median voting age 40.
Employment profile White collar, 49%. Blue collar, 36%. Service, 12%. Farm, 3%.
Ethnic groups Black, 19%. Spanish, 1%. Total foreign stock, 5%.

Presidential vote

1972	Nixon (R)	988,493	(69%)
	McGovern (D)	438,887	(31%)
1968	Nixon (R)	590,319	(44%)
	Humphrey (D)	442,387	(33%)
	Wallace (AI)	321,833	(24%)

Sen. Harry F. Byrd, Jr. (I) Appointed Nov. 12, 1965, elected 1966 as Democrat, re-elected 1970 as Independent, seat up 1976; b. Dec. 20, 1914, Winchester; home, Winchester; Va. Military Inst., 1931–33, U. of Va., 1933–35; Episcopalian.

Career Newspaper editor; Orchardist; Navy, WWII; Va. Senate, 1948–65.

Offices 417 RSOB, 202-224-4024. Also Winchester 22601, 703-662-7745.

Committees

Armed Services (6th). Subcommittees: Arms Control; General Legislation (Chairman); Manpower and Personnel; Military Construction Authorization; Preparedness Investigating.

Finance (5th). Subcommittees: Administration of the Internal Revenue Code; Energy; Financial Markets; International Finance and Resources (Chairman); Private Pension Plans.

Group Ratings

	ADA	COPE	LWV	RIPON	NFU	LCV	CFA	NAB	NSI	ACA
1974	10	27	33	35	29	14	22	83	90	100
1973	15	0	0	33	29	–	8	–	–	86
1972	20	10	18	28	30	26	9	100	80	91

Key Votes

1) No-Knock	AGN	8) Gov Abortn Aid	AGN	15) Consumer Prot Agy	AGN
2) Busing	AGN	9) Cut Mil Brass	AGN	16) Forced Psych Tests	AGN
3) No Fault	AGN	10) Gov Limousine	AGN	17) Fed Campaign Subs	AGN
4) F-111	AGN	11) RR Featherbed	AGN	18) Rhod Chrome Ban	AGN
5) Death Penalty	FOR	12) Handgun License	AGN	19) Open Legis Meetings	AGN
6) Foreign Aid	AGN	13) Less Troop Abrd	AGN	20) Strikers Food Stmps	AGN
7) Filibuster	FOR	14) Resume Turk Aid	AGN	21) Gov Info Disclosure	AGN

Election Results

1970 general:	Harry F. Byrd, Jr. (Ind.)	506,327	(54%)
	George C. Rawlings, Jr. (D)	294,582	(31%)
	Ray Garland (R)	144,765	(15%)
1970 primary:	Harry F. Byrd, Jr. (Ind.), unopposed		
1966 special:	Harry F. Byrd, Jr. (D)	389,028	(54%)
	Lawrence M. Taylor (R)	272,804	(38%)
	John W. Carter (Ind.)	57,692	(8%)

Sen. William Lloyd Scott (R) Elected 1972, seat up 1978; b. July 1, 1915, Williamsburg; home, Fairfax; Geo. Wash. U., J.D. 1938; Methodist.

Career Trial Atty., U.S. Dept. to Justice, and other fed. govt. positions, 1934–61; Practicing atty., 1961–66; U.S. House of Reps., 1967–73.

Offices 3109 DSOB, 202-224-2023. Also 400 N. 8th St., Suite 8000, Richmond 23240, 803-649-0049.

Committees

Armed Services (4th). Subcommittees: General Legislation; Manpower and Personnel; National Stockpile and Naval Petroleum Reserves; Preparedness Investigating.

The Judiciary (6th). Subcommittees: Constitutional Amendments; Criminal Laws and Procedures; FBI Oversight; Immigration and Naturalization; Improvement in Judicial Machinery; Internal Security; Penitentiaries.

Veterans' Affairs (4th). Subcommittees: Housing and Insurance; Readjustment, Education and Employment.

Group Ratings

	ADA	COPE	LWV	RIPON	NFU	LCV	CFA	NAB	NSI	ACA
1974	16	20	22	14	19	5	0	70	89	100
1973	12	22	0	50	13	–	0	–	–	96
1972	0	9	11	25	43	20	50	56	100	100

Key Votes

1) No-Knock	FOR	8) Gov Abortn Aid	FOR	15) Consumer Prot Agy	AGN
2) Busing	AGN	9) Cut Mil Brass	AGN	16) Forced Psych Tests	AGN
3) No Fault	AGN	10) Gov Limousine	AGN	17) Fed Campaign Subs	ABS
4) F-111	FOR	11) RR Featherbed	AGN	18) Rhod Chrome Ban	ABS
5) Death Penalty	FOR	12) Handgun License	AGN	19) Open Legis Meetings	AGN
6) Foreign Aid	AGN	13) Less Troop Abrd	FOR	20) Strikers Food Stmps	AGN
7) Filibuster	FOR	14) Resume Turk Aid	AGN	21) Gov Info Disclosure	AGN

Election Results

1972 general:	William Lloyd Scott (R)	718,337	(51%)	($619,908)
	William B. Spong, Jr. (D)	643,963	(46%)	($380,921)
	Horace Henderson (Ind.)	33,912	(2%)	(NA)
1972 primary:	William Lloyd Scott (R), unopposed			

Gov. Mills E. Godwin (R) Elected 1973, term expires Jan. 1968; b. Nov. 19, 1914, Chuckatuck; Col. of William & Mary, U. of Va., LL.B. 1938; Protestant.

Career FBI Agent; Practicing atty.; Va. House of Delegates, 1948–52; Va. Senate, 1952–60; Lt. Gov. of Va., 1962–66; Gov. of Va., 1966–70.

Offices State Capitol, Richmond 23219, 804-770-2211.

Election Results

1973 general:	Mills E. Godwin, Jr. (R)	525,075	(51%)
	Henry Howell (Ind.)	510,103	(49%)
1973 primary:	Mills E. Godwin, Jr. (R), nominated by convention		

◆ ◆ ◆ ◆ ◆

FIRST DISTRICT

The 1st congressional district is part of Tidewater Virginia, the lowlands by the wide tidal inlets of the Atlantic Ocean and Chesapeake Bay. The district includes the southern tip of the Delmarva Peninsula, where there is an annual roundup of wild Chincoteague ponies, and the rural Northern Neck counties that have changed little since George Washington's time—when they produced such worthies as Washington himself and the various Lees. But the district's population is concentrated in the Hampton Roads area, where 62% of the district's residents live, mostly in Newport News (pop. 138,000) and Hampton (pop. 120,000).

This is a fast growing, industrialized area, which owes much of its great prosperity to the federal government. Hampton Roads—the strait that separates Newport News and Hampton on the north from Norfolk and Portsmouth on the south—is one of the best natural harbors on the Atlantic seaboard, and is now the headquarters of the Atlantic Fleet. Most of the naval bases are on the south side of the Roads, but here in the 1st is the Newport News Shipbuilding and Dry Dock Company, one of the nation's biggest shipbuilders, with about half a billion dollars a year in Navy orders alone. Altogether, the Defense Department spends nearly one billion dollars yearly in this district—obviously the basis of its current prosperity.

Newport News also prospers from the massive subsides the government pays the shipbuilding and shipping industries, and it does the 1st district no harm that its Congressman, Democrat Thomas Downing, serves on the Merchant Marine and Science Committees. For many Congressmen, these would be humdrum assignments; for Downing, they are politically invaluable. As Chairman now of the Merchant Marine Subcommittee, he can be sure that the Newport News firm will not be slighted; as Chairman till 1975 of the NASA Oversight Subcommittee, he was—and remains—in a position to defend the interests of the big NASA facilities in Hampton.

So it should be no surprise that the 1st is one of the few Virginia congressional districts that has not had a major contest in recent years. It is also one in which the state's Republicans have failed to come even close. Downing has been unopposed in three of the last five general elections, and received well above 70% of the vote in the other two. Without Downing in the race, the district would be a far more marginal one, although Newport News and Hampton—both with large black and white working class neighborhoods—usually go for liberal Democrats in Virginia state elections.

Census Data Pop. 465,981. Central city, 56%; suburban, 7%. Median family income, $8,490; families above $15,000: 16%; families below $3,000: 13%. Median years education, 11.5.

The Voters

Median voting age 40.
Employment profile White collar, 45%. Blue collar, 38%. Service, 14%. Farm, 3%.
Ethnic groups Black, 30%. Spanish, 1%. Total foreign stock, 5%.

Presidential vote

1972	Nixon (R)	95,400	(69%)
	McGovern (D)	43,069	(31%)
1968	Nixon (R)	47,210	(35%)
	Humphrey (D)	45,273	(34%)
	Wallace (AI)	40,601	(31%)

Rep. Thomas N. Downing (D) Elected 1958; b. Feb. 1, 1919, Newport News; home, Newport News; Va. Military Ist., B.S. 1940, U. of Va., LL.B. 1947; Episcopalian.

Career Army, WWII; Practicing atty., 1947–58.

Offices 1116 LHOB, 202-225-4261. Also 1 Court St., Hampton 23369, 804-722-2886.

Committees

Merchant Marine and Fisheries (4th). Subcommittees: Merchant Marine (Chairman); Oceanography; Panama Canal.

Science and Technology (3d). Subcommittees: Energy Research (Fossil Fuels); Space Science and Applications.

Group Ratings

	ADA	COPE	LWV	RIPON	NFU	LCV	CFA	NAB	NSI	ACA
1974	10	18	17	27	54	25	15	73	100	86
1973	9	22	25	23	79	11	29	–	–	76
1972	0	18	27	38	29	13	0	92	88	95

Key Votes

1) Foreign Aid	AGN	6) Gov Abortn Aid	AGN	11) Pub Cong Election $	AGN
2) Busing	AGN	7) Coed Phys Ed	AGN	12) Turkish Arms Cutoff	AGN
3) ABM	ABS	8) Pov Lawyer Gag	FOR	13) Youth Camp Regs	AGN
4) B-1 Bomber	FOR	9) Pub Trans Sub	AGN	14) Strip Mine Veto	FOR
5) Nerve Gas	ABS	10) EZ Voter Regis	AGN	15) Farm Bill Veto	FOR

Election Results

1974 general:	Thomas N. Downing (D), unopposed			($2,897)
1974 primary:	Thomas N. Downing (D), unopposed			
1972 general:	Thomas N. Downing (D)	100,901	(78%)	($48,469)
	Kenneth D. Wells (R)	28,310	(22%)	($35,264)

◆ ◆ ◆ ◆ ◆

SECOND DISTRICT

Norfolk, Virginia is the headquarters of the Navy's Atlantic Fleet. Within its city limits is one of the world's largest naval bases and more than a half dozen other naval installations, not to mention the dozen or so military facilities in nearby Portsmouth, Virginia Beach, or in Hampton and Newport News across Hampton Roads. The naval buildup here during and after World War II is what has made Norfolk what it is today. Before World War II, it was a city of 144,000 with perhaps another 100,000 in adjacent areas; today, Norfolk is the center of an urban agglomeration of nearly a million people. Suburban homes have sprouted in the low-lying land near the wide inlets off the bay, and shopping centers put up at freeway interchanges. During the 1960s, the area of fastest growth shifted east, to the high income suburb of Virginia Beach.

Politically, Norfolk is a working class town. For the most part, Navy personnel do not vote here, and their absence from the electorate shows up in low turnout figures. The Norfolk voter is more likely to be a blue collar worker, who moved here from a small town in Southside Virginia or eastern North Carolina looking for a job. It is a heavily segregated city, and the large black minority is solidly Democratic in all elections; the whites, in recent presidential contests, have gone almost to a person for Richard Nixon and George Wallace. But among the working class whites there is still an attraction to populist-sounding bread and butter liberal economic programs. This is the home turf of former Lieutenant Governor Henry Howell, who nearly was elected Governor as an Independent in 1973 and will probably try again as a Democrat in 1977; Howell has forged a black-white coalition in Norfolk and throughout the Hampton Roads area by stressing his opposition to the big banks and utilities which have always gotten their way in Virginia politics.

But Howell's kind of politics has had little effect on elections in the 2d congressional district, which include Norfolk and virtually all of high income and 91% white Virginia Beach. For 22 years, the district sent a relatively conservative Democrat, Porter Hardy, to the House, and watched him rise to a high seniority position on the House Armed Services Committee. Hardy retired in 1968, and the resulting contest was a close one. Because a Howell-type Democrat was hurt by intraparty feuding, the Republican nominee, G. William Whitehurst, came away with a 54–46 victory. It probably did not hurt that Whitehurst, a professor at Old Dominion College, was also a local TV commentator.

Since his first election, Whitehurst has won reelection easily. He is one of those Congressmen who return to the district every weekend, and who takes care to speak before and attend to the needs of even those constituents who one would think are not ideologically disposed to support him. His diligence has paid off at the polls, as it usually does for most such incumbents. It also helps that Whitehurst, like his predecessor, is a member of the House Armed Service Committee—a crucial position when your district, as the 2d does, receives something like $400 million of Pentagon money every year. Whitehurst was caught up in some minor controversy in 1974, and with the anti-Republican trend running in Virginia as elsewhere, seemed to be in slightly more trouble than before; but he still won with 60% of the vote.

Census Data Pop. 464,692. Central city, 66%; suburban, 34%. Median family income, $8,733; families above $15,000: 18%; families below $3,000: 12%. Median years education, 12.1.

The Voters

  Median voting age 34.
  Employment profile White collar, 55%. Blue collar, 30%. Service, 15%. Farm, –%.
  Ethnic groups Black, 22%. Spanish, 2%. Total foreign stock, 8%. UK, 1%.

Presidential vote

1972	Nixon (R)	73,728	(68%)
	McGovern (D)	35,107	(32%)
1968	Nixon (R)	37,700	(38%)
	Humphrey (D)	37,647	(38%)
	Wallace (AI)	25,038	(25%)

Rep. G. William Whitehurst (R) Elected 1968; b. Mar. 12, 1925, Norfolk; home, Virginia Beach; Washington & Lee U., B.A. 1950, U. of Va., M.A. 1951, W.Va. U., Ph.D. 1962; Methodist.

Career Navy, WWII; Prof. of History, Old Dominion Col., 1950–68, Dean of Students, 1963–68; News analyst, WTAR-TV, Norfolk, 1962–68.

Offices 424 CHOB, 202-225-4215. Also Rm. 201 Fed. Bldg., Norfolk 23510, 804-441-6763.

Committees

Armed Services (3d). Subcommittees: Military Installations and Facilities; Research and Development.

Group Ratings

	ADA	COPE	LWV	RIPON	NFU	LCV	CFA	NAB	NSI	ACA
1974	5	0	50	62	46	21	8	73	100	93
1973	0	18	20	67	25	17	25	–	–	88
1972	6	0	27	60	29	26	0	78	100	86

Key Votes

1) Foreign Aid	AGN	6) Gov Abortn Aid	AGN	11) Pub Cong Election $	FOR
2) Busing	AGN	7) Coed Phys Ed	AGN	12) Turkish Arms Cutoff	ABS
3) ABM	FOR	8) Pov Lawyer Gag	ABS	13) Youth Camp Regs	AGN
4) B-1 Bomber	FOR	9) Pub Trans Sub	AGN	14) Strip Mine Veto	FOR
5) Nerve Gas	FOR	10) EZ Voter Regis	AGN	15) Farm Bill Veto	FOR

Election Results

1974 general:	G. William Whithurst (R)	49,369	(60%)	($83,545)
	Robert R. Richards (D)	32,923	(40%)	($44,418)
1974 primary:	G. William Whitehurst (R), unopposed			
1972 general:	G. William Whitehurst (R)	79,672	(73%)	($45,864)
	L. Charles Burlage (D)	28,803	(27%)	($42,790)

◆ ◆ ◆ ◆ ◆

THIRD DISTRICT

Richmond, once the capital of the Confederacy, remains the capital of Virginia and a major tobacco producing center. In many ways, Richmond is also still the state's most important city, although it is now eclipsed in size by the Washington suburbs and the Tidewater area around Norfolk. But Richmond still is not only the governmental center of Virginia, it is also the headquarters of the big economic interests which remain so important here. The state government remains securely in the hands of conservative Democrat turned conservative Republican, Mills Godwin; the Virgina Electric and Power Company and the big banks remain securely in the hands of the likeminded men, many of them personal friends of Godwin, who have carefully seen to it that their corporate interests are always helped and never hampered by the state. The dominant newspapers, the Richmond *Times-Leader* and *News-Dispatch*, are just as conservative. During the 1950s, they provided the most intellectually phrased defense of segregation in the nation, the product of then editor James Jackson Kilpatrick; today, they continue to be one of the major journalistic conservative voices around.

Virginia's 3d congressional district consists of Richmond and virtually all of its two principal suburban counties, Henrico and Chesterfield. This is the area covered by the Richmond school case, in which a federal district judge ordered busing from Richmond, where blacks have a heavy majority in the public schools, to virtually all white Henrico and Chesterfield. The decision was reversed ultimately by an evenly divided court, but from the time the decision was announced Richmond area whites—already heavily conservative—trended sharply to the right. The city itself, with its large minority of well-organized black voters, sometimes goes for liberal candidates (like Henry Howell in 1973), but the Henrico and Chesterfield cast lopsided margins for conservatives (86% for Richard Nixon in 1972).

The 3d district's Congressman, David Satterfield III, came to the seat more or less by inheritance. It had been held by his father from 1937 to 1945, then by a Byrd Democrat who retired in 1964, and ever since by Satterfield *fils*. But the succession was not automatic. In 1964 Satterfield had strong opposition from both a liberal Independent and a conservative Republican (Richard Obenshain, now Vice Chairman of the Republican National Committee); the Democrat won with only 35% of the vote, running second to Obenshain in the suburban counties and to the Independent in Richmond. The last substantial challenge came in 1970, when a moderate Republican, a protege of Governor Linwood Holton, tried to put together the votes of black Richmond residents and well-to-do suburbanites. The latter would have none of it, and Satterfield won with an impressive 67% of the vote. In the Congress, he is a member of the Veterans and Commerce Committees, and of the Health subcommittee chaired by Florida's Paul Rogers.

Census Data Pop. 465,289. Central city, 54%; suburban, 46%. Median family income, $9,945; families above $15,000: 21%; families below $3,000: 8%. Median years education, 11.7.

The Voters

Median voting age 42.
Employment profile White collar, 55%. Blue collar, 32%. Service, 13%. Farm, –%.
Ethnic groups Black, 26%. Total foreign stock, 5%.

Presidential vote

1972	Nixon (R)	117,472	(72%)
	McGovern (D)	44,566	(28%)
1968	Nixon (R)	78,797	(51%)
	Humphrey (D)	46,336	(30%)
	Wallace (AI)	29,265	(19%)

Rep. David E. Satterfield III (D) Elected 1964; b. Dec. 2, 1920, Richmond; home, Richmond; U. of Richmond, U. of Va.; Episcopalian.

Career Navy, WWII; Practicing atty., 1948–50, 1953–65; Asst. U.S. Atty., 1950–53; Richmond City Cncl., 1954–56; Va. House of Delegates, 1960–64.

Offices 2348 RHOB, 202-225-2815. Also Fed. Ofc. Bldg., Richmond 23240, 804-782-2519.

Committees

Interstate and Foreign Commerce (9th). Subcommittees: Health and Environment.

Veterans' Affairs (3d). Subcommittees: Hospitals (Chairman); Housing.

Group Ratings

	ADA	COPE	LWV	RIPON	NFU	LCV	CFA	NAB	NSI	ACA
1974	0	0	0	19	21	24	15	83	100	87
1973	0	18	18	27	26	11	25	–	–	92
1972	0	9	18	19	29	13	50	91	100	100

Key Votes

1) Foreign Aid	AGN	6) Gov Abortn Aid	AGN	11) Pub Cong Election $	AGN
2) Busing	AGN	7) Coed Phys Ed	AGN	12) Turkish Arms Cutoff	FOR
3) ABM	FOR	8) Pov Lawyer Gag	FOR	13) Youth Camp Regs	AGN
4) B-1 Bomber	FOR	9) Pub Trans Sub	AGN	14) Strip Mine Veto	FOR
5) Nerve Gas	FOR	10) EZ Voter Regis	AGN	15) Farm Bill Veto	FOR

Election Results

1974 general:	David E. Satterfield III (D)	64,627	(90%)	($4,406)
	Alan Robert Ogden (Ind.)	7,574	(10%)	($0)
1974 primary:	David G. Satterfield III (D), unopposed			
1972 general:	David E. Satterfield III (D), unopposed .			($0)

◆ ◆ ◆ ◆ ◆

FOURTH DISTRICT

The 4th district of Virginia presents a good example of the changes wrought in congressional districting by the one-person-one-vote rulings. In the past ten years, the 4th has shifted from an almost entirely rural, small county-district to a predominantly urban one. Before the 1965 redistricting, the 4th took in most of Southside Virginia, tobacco growing country south of Richmond, with small courthouse towns and the continuing dominance of a large black population by white landowners. Today, the district's boundaries have been moved sharply to the east, and more than two-thirds of its population is in the Tidewater area: the industrial, 40% black city of Portsmouth (pop. 110,000), blue collar suburban Chesapeake (pop. 89,000, 23% black), and the smaller cities of Nansemond and Suffolk. It also includes the old city of Petersburg, a major center when it was the focus of several Civil War battles and not much bigger now, and the virtually all white conservative suburbs of Colonial Heights and Hopewell.

The 1972 redistricting eliminated from the 4th Appomattox Court House, the place where Lee surrendered to Grant, but more significant politically as the home of then Congressman Watkins

Abbitt, an old style Byrd Democrat. Abbitt retired in 1972 and free finally to express himself openly supported Richard Nixon for reelection. Abbitt's retirement left the 4th the scene of a major conflict; there were no fewer than three Independent candidates (one a write-in who got 5% of the vote) as well as the Republican and Democratic. The winner, with 47% of the vote, was Republican Robert Daniel, a former CIA agent and local farmer and businessman.

Despite Watergate, and all the changes wrought thereby, Daniel was able to use the advantages of incumbency well enough to win again in 1974, but again with only 47% of the vote. The opposition was split again, as it had been in 1972, this time between Portsmouth Delegate Lester Schlitz, a liberal Democrat, and a black candidate who was running as an Independent. The latter cut heavily into what otherwise would have been Schlitz's vote in the Southside counties and the Petersburg area, leaving the Democrat with only 36%. But indications are that a single candidate against Daniel would have a good chance winning. In any case, Daniel (no relation to Dan Daniel of the 5th district) remains a conservative member of the Armed Services Committee.

Census Data Pop. 465,738. Central city, 35%; suburban, 39%. Median family income, $8,294; families above $15,000: 13%; families below $3,000: 12%. Median years education, 10.4.

The Voters

Median voting age 41.
Employment profile White collar, 39%. Blue collar, 43%. Service, 15%. Farm, 3%.
Ethnic groups Black, 37%. Total foreign stock, 3%.

Presidential vote

1972	Nixon (R)	85,780	(65%)
	McGovern (D)	45,346	(35%)
1968	Nixon (R)	38,500	(28%)
	Humphrey (D)	48,549	(36%)
	Wallace (AI)	49,568	(36%)

Rep. Robert W. Daniel, Jr. (R) Elected 1972; b. Mar. 17, 1936, Richmond; home, Spring Grove; U. of Va., B.A. 1958, Columbia U., M.B.A. 1961; Episcopalian.

Career Practicing financial analyst, 1961–62; Instructor of Economics, U. of Richmond Business School, 1963; CIA, 1964–68; Owner and operator, Brandon agricultural enterprise.

Offices 1331 LHOB, 202-225-6365. Also 209 P.O. Bldg., Petersburg 23803, 804-732-2544.

Committees

Armed Services (10th). Subcommittees: Investigations; Seapower and Strategic and Critical Materials.

District of Columbia (6th). Subcommittees: Fiscal Affairs; Bicentennial, the Environment, and the International Community.

Group Ratings

	ADA	COPE	LWV	RIPON	NFU	LCV	CFA	NAB	NSI	ACA
1974	0	0	8	44	33	25	0	83	100	92
1973	0	18	17	29	30	11	13	–	–	85

Key Votes

1) Foreign Aid	AGN	6) Gov Abortn Aid	AGN	11) Pub Cong Election $	AGN
2) Busing	AGN	7) Coed Phys Ed	ABS	12) Turkish Arms Cutoff	ABS
3) ABM	FOR	8) Pov Lawyer Gag	FOR	13) Youth Camp Regs	AGN
4) B-1 Bomber	FOR	9) Pub Trans Sub	AGN	14) Strip Mine Veto	FOR
5) Nerve Gas	FOR	10) EZ Voter Regis	AGN	15) Farm Bill Veto	FOR

Election Results

1974 general:	Robert W. "Bob" Daniel, Jr. (R)	48.032	(47%)	($79,134)
	Lester E. Schlitz (D)	36,489	(36%)	($79,837)
	Curtis W. Harris (Ind.)	17,224	(17%)	($17,329)
1974 primary:	Robert W. "Bob" Daniel, Jr. (R) unopposed			
1972 general:	Robert W. "Bob" Daniel, Jr. (R)	57,520	(47%)	($59,140)
	Robert E. Gibson (D)	45,796	(37%)	($40,546)
	Robert R. Hardy (Ind.)	8,668	(7%)	(NA)
	William E. Ward (Write-in)	6,172	(5%)	(NA)
	John G. Vonetes (Ind.)	4,003	(3%)	(NA)

◆ ◆ ◆ ◆ ◆

FIFTH DISTRICT

The 5th district of Virginia covers most of Southside Virginia, from the Richmond city limits out to the Blue Ridge near Roanoke. The eastern counties are flat and humid, and the most heavily black part of the district. Slowly, as the land gets hillier, it rises into the Piedmont, and moves past textile and furniture manufacturing cities like Danville (pop. 46,000) and Martinsville (pop. 19,000). As one goes west, there is more livestock and less tobacco, more whites with mountain accents and fewer blacks. Altogether, the 5th is only 29% black—significantly less than the figure for blacks in the 4th district, which takes in Southside counties just to the east.

Southside Virginia was always a stronghold for Byrd Democrats, with its politics firmly in the hands of prosperous bankers and planters who still remember the Civil War. More recently, Southside has fallen into the racially polarized voting patterns that characterize the Deep South. This is one of the two Virginia districts (the other is the 4th) that went for George Wallace in 1968, and the one where the Alabamian got his highest percentage. And despite Southside's Democratic heritage, the 5th was Republican challenger William Scott's best district in his 1972 race against moderate Democrat Sen. William Spong.

For 15 years, until his retirement in 1968, Congressman William Tuck represented the 5th in the House. A former Governor (1946–50) and Byrd machine stalwart, Tuck was an ardent segregationist and an equally ardent opponent of the one-person-one-vote doctrine (which, as it happens, has significantly changed the political balance in Virginia). The current incumbent is a more up-to-date conservative Democrat, W. C. (Dan) Daniel, a former executive at Danville's Dan River Mills and a former national commander of the American Legion. In his first election, Daniel got spirited competition from both Republican and Independent candidates, who held his share of the vote down to 55%. In 1970, the incumbent Congressman rolled up a margin more typical in Southside Virginia, 70%; in 1972 and 1974 he was unopposed. Daniel is one of three Virginia members of the House Armed Services Committee, where he is a determined and unswerving supporter of the panel's pro-Pentagon majority.

Census Data Pop. 462,807. Central city, 0%; suburban, 13%. Median family income, $7,471; families above $15,000: 10%; families below $3,000: 15%. Median years education, 9.4.

The Voters

Median voting age 43.
Employment profile White collar, 32%. Blue collar, 52%. Service, 10%. Farm, 6%.
Ethnic groups Black, 29%. Total foreign stock 1%.

Presidential vote

1972	Nixon (R)	101,546	(72%)
	McGovern (D)	39,194	(28%)
1968	Nixon (R)	54,213	(35%)
	Humphrey (D)	40,770	(26%)
	Wallace (AI)	59,451	(38%)

Rep. Dan Daniel (D) Elected 1968; b. May 12, 1914, Chatham; home, Danville; Baptist.

Career Asst. to Bd. Chm., Dan River Mills, Inc., and various other business positions, 1939–68; Va. House of Delegates, 1959–68.

Offices 1705 LHOB, 202-225-4711. Also 202 P.O. Bldg., Danville 24541, 703-792-1280.

Committees

Armed Services (5th). Subcommittees: Military Personnel.

District of Columbia (11th). Subcommittees: Commerce, Housing, and Transportation; Education, Labor, and Social Services; Fiscal Affairs.

Group Ratings

	ADA	COPE	LWV	RIPON	NFU	LCV	CFA	NAB	NSI	ACA
1974	0	0	0	13	36	18	8	75	100	80
1973	4	18	17	27	55	11	25	–	–	85
1972	0	10	17	31	33	20	0	90	100	100

Key Votes

1) Foreign Aid	AGN	6) Gov Abortn Aid	AGN	11) Pub Cong Election $	AGN
2) Busing	AGN	7) Coed Phys Ed	AGN	12) Turkish Arms Cutoff	FOR
3) ABM	FOR	8) Pov Lawyer Gag	FOR	13) Youth Camp Regs	AGN
4) B-1 Bomber	FOR	9) Pub Trans Sub	AGN	14) Strip Mine Veto	FOR
5) Nerve Gas	FOR	10) EZ Voter Regis	AGN	15) Farm Bill Veto	FOR

Election Results

1974 general:	W. C. (Dan) Daniel (D), unopposed		($1,165)
1974 primary:	W. C. (Dan) Daniel (D), unopposed		
1972 general:	W. C. (Dan) Daniel (D), unopposed		($3,429)

◆ ◆ ◆ ◆ ◆

SIXTH DISTRICT

The most Republican part of Virginia is the great valley west of the Blue Ridge around Roanoke (pop. 92,000). Because this fertile land was never given over to slave-tended antebellum plantations, the hardy farmers here were not especially sympathetic to the cause of the Confederacy. In the hundred years following the Civil War, the Roanoke area was usually the most Republican—or least Democratic—region of the state; it was always suspicious of the Byrd machine, and to some extent, of its close alliance with Virginia's largest and most powerful economic interests. Though the boundaries have shifted many times in the last two decades, the 6th congressional district has always centered on Roanoke. Also in the district are much of the valley and the mountains to the north, and the more Democratic Southside city of Lynchburg (pop. 54,000). Ordinarily, the 6th is the state's most Republican district. It was the only one in Virginia to give Richard Nixon an absolute majority in 1968, and in 1972 gave him a higher percentage than any other district in the state.

Moreover, the 6th is the only Virginia district not to have elected a Democratic Congressman since 1950. In 1952, out of distaste for the national Democratic ticket, Harry Byrd's organization quietly passed the word that it was all right to vote for Eisenhower. Byrd's "golden silence" carried the Commonwealth for the Republican, and indeed it has gone Republican in every presidential election since except 1964. At the same time—and this was a result that Byrd must have liked far less—aggressive young Republican candidates won in three of Virginia's ten congressional districts.

One of them was Richard Poff, a 29-year-old lawyer who unseated the complacent 66-year-old incumbent Democrat in the 6th in 1952. In the years that followed, Poff began to win reelection by large margins; so the Byrd machine, pleased with his conservative record, abandoned any serious attempt to defeat him. By 1971, before he was 50, Poff was the second ranking Republican on the House Judiciary Committee, a solid conservative respected for his intelligence and integrity. After the defeats of the Haynsworth and Carswell nominations, the story came out that Nixon was seriously considering appointing Poff to the Supreme Court; some controversy arose, and Poff withdrew his name from consideration. Apparently unhappy with that episode, Poff surprised observers even more by announcing he would retire from the House in 1972; he did, and was quickly appointed to the Virginia Court of Appeals by Governor Linwood Holton.

Poff's decision to leave Congress left the 6th district seat to M. Caldwell Butler, former Republican leader in the Virginia House of Delegates and, before that, a law partner of Holton's. Elected by a 55–39 margin (there was an Independent candidate), Butler seemed to follow the Nixon Administration on most issues in the House; he also followed his predecessor, Poff, on the Judiciary Committee. It was that assignment which gave him national fame. For if Butler was in most respects a loyal Republican, he was even more loyal to his duty as a lawyer and a judge. He studied the evidence carefully, reportedly aided by his wife, who read _All the President's Men_ to him in the evenings; and he came to the conclusion that Richard Nixon was guilty and should be impeached. Butler joined with other Republicans and conservative Southern Democrats to draw up articles of impeachment they could agree on, and in the public hearings his rapid fire delivery in his peppery voice, his occasional sense of humor, and his lawyer's instinct for the main issue helped to cinch the case against the President.

From a political point of view, Butler was probably the least likely pro-impeachment vote; he was a Republican from a Republican district in the South, where Nixon's popularity suffered least (though it suffered grievously even there) of any region in the country. Faced again with an Independent as well as a Democratic opponent, Butler's share of the vote fell from 55% in 1972 to 46% in 1974. In the part of the district west of the Blue Ridge, in Southside Virginia, where Nixon presumably remained most popular, Butler's percentage fell 20%; around Roanoke and in the mountain counties, it fell scarcely at all even though, his opponent was the Roanoke Sheriff. It seems hardly likely that he will be politically vulnerable in some future year, but of all the pro-impeachment members of the Judiciary Committee, Butler seems to have suffered the most politically for his decision.

Census Data Pop. 464,356. Central city, 31%; suburban, 25%. Median family income, $8,594; families above $15,000: 14%; families below $3,000: 10%. Median years education, 11.3.

The Voters

Median voting age 43.
Employment profile White collar, 43%. Blue collar, 42%. Service, 13%. Farm, 2%.
Ethnic groups Black, 12%. Total foreign stock, 2%.

Presidential vote

1972	Nixon (R)	104,443	(75%)
	McGovern (D)	35,356	(25%)
1968	Nixon (R)	74,741	(53%)
	Humphrey (D)	34,679	(24%)
	Wallace (AI)	32,625	(23%)

Rep. M. Caldwell Butler (R) Elected 1972; b. June 22, 1925, Roanoke; home, Roanoke; U. of Richmond, A.B. 1948, U. of Va., LL.B. 1950; Episcopalian.

Career Practicing atty., 1950–72; Va. House of Delegates, 1962–71, Minor. Ldr., 1966–71.

Offices 109 CHOB, 202-225-5431. Also 313 U.S.P.O. and Courthouse Bldg., 900 Church St., Lynchburg 24505, 804-845-1378.

Committees

Judiciary (6th). Subcommittees: Civil and Constitutional Rights.

Small Business (8th). Subcommittees: Commodities and Services; Energy and Environment.

Group Ratings

	ADA	COPE	LWV	RIPON	NFU	LCV	CFA	NAB	NSI	ACA
1974	9	9	25	60	50	12	9	75	89	87
1973	0	0	17	53	30	5	25	–	–	78

Key Votes

1) Foreign Aid	AGN	6) Gov Abortn Aid	AGN	11) Pub Cong Election $	AGN
2) Busing	AGN	7) Coed Phys Ed	AGN	12) Turkish Arms Cutoff	AGN
3) ABM	FOR	8) Pov Lawyer Gag	FOR	13) Youth Camp Regs	AGN
4) B-1 Bomber	FOR	9) Pub Trans Sub	AGN	14) Strip Mine Veto	FOR
5) Nerve Gas	FOR	10) EZ Voter Regis	AGN	15) Farm Bill Veto	FOR

Election Results

1974 general:	M. Caldwell Butler (R)	45,805	(46%)	($63,622)
	Paul Puckett (D)	27,350	(27%)	($25,933)
	Warren D. Saunders (Ind.)	26,466	(27%)	($57,819)
1974 primary:	M. Caldwell Butler (R), unopposed			
1972 general:	M. Caldwell Butler (R)	75,189	(55%)	($116,363)
	Willis M. Anderson (D)	53,928	(39%)	($49,078)
	Roy R. White (Ind.)	8,531	(6%)	(NA)

◆ ◆ ◆ ◆ ◆

SEVENTH DISTRICT

East and west of the Blue Ridge Mountains in northern Virginia is some of the most beautiful countryside in the United States. Away from the tidal flatlands, the climate is cool and salubrious; the flowering bushes and trees in the spring provide an even greater riot of color than the turning leaves in the fall; the mountains protect against icy blasts. The Piedmont, or eastern side of the Blue Ridge was once part of giant landownings, like those of Lord Fairfax, Washington's patron; much of the land here is now the property of some of the nation's wealthiest families, who spend their winters riding in the hunt. West of the mountains is the Shenandoah Valley, once the granary of the Confederacy and still marvelously fertile land, though now more often given over to orchards. The region's major cities—Winchester (pop. 14,000) and Harrisonburg (pop. 14,000) in the Valley and Charlottesville (pop. 38,000) and Fredericksburg (pop. 14,000) in the Piedmont—still retain an old-fashioned ambiance, at least in the narrow streets of their downtowns, though a McDonald's culture has begun to develop on the bypass roads on the outskirts.

This is the land of the 7th congressional district of Virginia—the northern part of the state beyond the Washington metropolitan area. It was the home of three Presidents (Jefferson, Madison, and Monroe) and the scene of more carnage and killing in the Civil War than any other area of comparable size in the nation. The district is also the home turf of the twentieth century Byrd dynasty. The late Senator Harry Byrd, Sr., developed one of the world's largest and most productive apple farms in the Shenandoah Valley, and also acquired newspapers in Winchester and Harrisonburg; his son, the current Senator, retains these interests. The 7th today continues to be solid Byrd country in most elections—which means that it has often switched from its traditional Democratic preference to Nixon Republicanism.

Nowhere has that trend been better illustrated than in the 7th district's congressional representation. From 1962 to 1971 the Congressman here was John O. Marsh, a nominal Democrat and now a top White House official in the Ford Administration. Marsh may have wanted renomination in 1970, but that was the year the local Democratic Party organization was taken over by anti-Byrd liberals; Marsh hesitated and finally decided not to run. The Byrd imprimatur—unofficially, but without any doubt—went not to the Democrat, a liberal former ambassador, but to the Republican, state Senator J. Kenneth Robinson. Back in 1962 he had nearly beaten Marsh; later, he had been elected to the state legislative vacancy caused by the elevation of Harry Byrd, Jr., to the United States Senate. The Byrd machine, driven out of the Democratic Party, seems to have reappeared in Republican guise.

A solid conservative, Robinson was elected easily in 1970 and 1972. But in 1974 Democratic candidate George Gilliam waged a sort of populist campaign and held Robinson to 53% of the vote; Gilliam made his greatest inroads among traditional Democratic voters, who were apparently unhappy with Robinson's and Richard Nixon's Republicans. Robinson, now climbing in seniority on the Appropriations Committee, will probably have it easier in future elections.

Census Data Pop. 465,342. Central city, 0%; suburban, 8%. Median family income, $7,952; families above $15,000: 13%; families below $3,000: 12%. Median years education, 10.5.

The Voters

Median voting age 42.
Employment profile White collar, 40%. Blue collar, 42%. Service, 13%. Farm, 5%.
Ethnic groups Black, 15%. Total foreign stock, 3%.

Presidential vote

1972	Nixon (R)	104,720	(73%)
	McGovern (D)	39,691	(27%)
1968	Nixon (R)	66,452	(50%)
	Humphrey (D)	37,190	(28%)
	Wallace (AI)	29,949	(22%)

Rep. J. Kenneth Robinson (R) Elected 1970; b. May 14, 1916, Winchester; home, Winchester; Va. Polytechnic Inst., B.S. 1937; Society of Friends.

Career Family fruit growing and packing business, 1937–42; Army, WWII; Dir., Winchester Cold Storage, R & T Packing Corp., Inc., Winchester Apple Growers Assn., and Green Chemical Co.; Va. Senate, 1965–70.

Offices 418 CHOB, 202-225-6561. Also 112 N. Cameron St., P.O. Box 136, Winchester 22601, 703-667-0990.

Committees

Appropriations (11th). Subcommittees: Agriculture and Related Agencies; Defense.

Group Ratings

	ADA	COPE	LWV	RIPON	NFU	LCV	CFA	NAB	NSI	ACA
1974	0	0	9	40	36	13	0	83	100	93
1973	0	9	17	33	25	0	13	–	–	85
1972	0	9	17	31	29	7	0	92	100	100

Key Votes

1) Foreign Aid	AGN	6) Gov Abortn Aid	AGN	11) Pub Cong Election $	AGN
2) Busing	AGN	7) Coed Phys Ed	AGN	12) Turkish Arms Cutoff	AGN
3) ABM	FOR	8) Pov Lawyer Gag	FOR	13) Youth Camp Regs	AGN
4) B-1 Bomber	FOR	9) Pub Trans Sub	AGN	14) Strip Mine Veto	FOR
5) Nerve Gas	FOR	10) EZ Voter Regis	AGN	15) Farm Bill Veto	FOR

Election Results

1974 general:	J. Kenneth Robinson (R)	54,267	(53%)	($96,443)
	George H. Gilliam (D)	48,611	(47%)	($62,839)
1974 primary:	J. Kenneth Robinson (R), unopposed			
1972 general:	J. Kenneth Robinson (R)	89,120	(66%)	($73,777)
	Murat Willis Williams (D)	45,513	(34%)	($44,972)

◆ ◆ ◆ ◆ ◆

EIGHTH DISTRICT

The 8th is the fastest growing congressional district in Virginia. Indeed, only 11 other districts in the country experienced faster population growth during the 1960s, and despite the slow growth philosophy of some local officials, this has continued to be one of the fastest growing districts in the East during the 1970s. Basically, the 8th covers the southern portion of the northern Virginia suburbs of Washington, D.C. Just across the Potomac from Washington is Alexandria (pop. 110,000); it is a city whose old town section recalls the Potomac tobacco port George Washington once frequented. Today, it is more significant politically that Alexandria has a fairly sizeable black population (14%) and an even higher proportion (over two-thirds) of families who live in rented houses or, more and more often, high rise apartments. South of Alexandria are the Mount Vernon, Annandale, and Springfield sections of Fairfax County—still sprouting with new, high-priced subdivisions despite the negative attitude of the Fairfax County Board of Supervisors. Then follows Prince William County, which more than doubled in population in the 1960s; with less strict zoning than Fairfax, it has been filling up with lower salaried federal and blue collar workers. The 8th also contains a small portion of rural Stafford County, south of Prince William.

The primary engine of growth here has been that growth industry, the federal government. Federal paychecks have more than doubled since 1960, and here in the 8th, 29% of all wage-earners cash their government checks every two weeks.

The boundary changes the 8th has undergone show some of the changes wreaked in Virginia politics generally over the last decade or so. Back in the 1960s, the 8th spread far out into the Piedmont countryside, and included relatively little of the Fairfax County suburbs. But even this small infusion of a different world into the conservative courthouse and banker cliques that had dominated Virginia politics was enough to make a revolution, and revolution it was when Congressman Howard Smith was defeated in the 1966 Democratic primary. For Smith, an unbending conservative and canny legislative operator, had been Chairman of the House Rules Committee since 1955, and in that capacity had been able to throttle dozens of liberal bills. At 83, he was just not able to cope with the politics of the Washington suburbs, of a Virginia suddenly without a poll tax or its restrictive registration laws.

The liberal who beat Smith did not win that year; instead, the seat went by a narrow margin to the Republican candidate, William Scott, now a U.S. Senator (and voted the "dumbest man in Congress" by *New Times* magazine). Scott, a Fairfax County suburbanite with the gut conservatism and distaste for the city and its black majority that characterizes many of his fellows, won reelection in 1968 and 1970; he might have been in trouble later, but for his inspired decision to run for the Senate in 1972. He was succeeded by a man of like mind, Delegate Stanford Parris, a lawyer and Chrysler-Plymouth dealer, who won with only 44% of the vote (there were two Independents in the race).

Parris was expected to win in 1974, too, by just about everyone, including Gerald Ford, until recently a resident of Alexandria, who went out and campaigned for him. But it was to no avail. The Democratic tide was sweeping strongly in the Washington suburbs and Democratic candidate Herbert Harris won easily, with 58% of the vote. Harris was already well known as a member of the slow-growth Fairfax County Board of Supervisors; he campaigned hard as an opponent of the big utilities. In the House he now sits on the District of Columbia and Post Office and Civil Service Committees—two bodies on which he can represent the interests of his constituents as suburbanites and federal employees. He should be a solid favorite for reelection in 1976.

Census Data Pop. 464,038. Central city, 0%; suburban, 98%. Median family income, $13,146; families above $15,000: 40%; families below $3,000: 4%. Median years education, 12.7.

The Voters

Median voting age 36.
Employment profile White collar, 68%. Blue collar, 21%. Service, 10%. Farm, 1%.
Ethnic groups Black, 7%. Spanish, 2%. Total foreign stock, 11%. Germany, UK, 1% each.

Presidential vote

1972	Nixon (R)	94,715	(67%)
	McGovern (D)	46,870	(33%)
1968	Nixon (R)	47,505	(45%)
	Humphrey (D)	39,796	(38%)
	Wallace (AI)	17,375	(17%)

Rep. Herbert E. Harris II (D) Elected 1974; b. Apr. 14, 1926, Kansas City, Mo.; home, Mount Vernon; Mo. Valley Col., U. of Notre Dame, Rockhurst Col., B.A., Georgetown U., J.D.; Catholic.

Career Navy, WWII; Internatl. trade atty.; Fairfax Co. Bd. of Supervisors, 1968–74, Vice Chm., 1971–74, Chm., 1974; Commissioner, No. Va. Transportation Comm., 1968–74; Vice Chm., Washington Metropolitan Area Transit Auth., 1971–74.

Offices 1229 LHOB, 202-225-4376. Also 9256 Mosby Street, Manassas 22110, 703-368-1331.

Committees

District of Columbia (10th). Subcommittees: Commerce, Housing and Transportation; The Bicentennial, the Environment, and the International Community (Chairman).

Post Office and Civil Service (14th). Subcommittees: Employee Political Rights and Intergovernmental Programs; Retirement and Employee Benefits.

Group Ratings: Newly Elected

Key Votes

1) Foreign Aid	FOR	6) Gov Abortn Aid	NE	11) Pub Cong Election $	NE
2) Busing	NE	7) Coed Phys Ed	FOR	12) Turkish Arms Cutoff	NE
3) ABM	NE	8) Pov Lawyer Gag	NE	13) Youth Camp Regs	FOR
4) B-1 Bomber	AGN	9) Pub Trans Sub	NE	14) Strip Mine Veto	AGN
5) Nerve Gas	NE	10) EZ Voter Regis	NE	15) Farm Bill Veto	FOR

Election Results

1974 general:	Herbert E. Harris II (D)	53,074	(58%)	($80,932)
	Stanford E. Parris (R)	38,997	(42%)	($149,450)
1974 primary:	Herbert E. Harris II (D)	7,578	(53%)	
	Frank E. Mann (D)	3,815	(26%)	
	Richard L. Faflaw (D)	3,023	(21%)	

◆ ◆ ◆ ◆ ◆

NINTH DISTRICT

The southwest corner of Virginia is perhaps the only part of the nation known in ordinary discourse by the number of its congressional district: the Fighting Ninth. Part of the Appalachian mountain country, the 9th probably has more in common with neighboring eastern Kentucky and Tennessee than with the rest of Virginia. It is not, however, one of the poorer regions of Appalachia. The area has never been as dependent on coal as southern West Virginia; moreover, it has recently benefitted from some economic development in the valley that reaches from the Shenendoah to Knoxville, Tennessee, along Interstate 81. The mountain area of southwest Virginia is a place with its own cultural traditions, where the federal government still means the hated revenuers. And every August it hosts the Galax Old Time Fiddlers' Convention, where fiddlers and guitar, banjo, and mandolin pickers from several states around make some of the most exhilarating music ever produced by the minds—and hands—of man.

The Fighting Ninth never did cotton much to the Byrd organization. In fact, its Republican tradition goes back to the days of the Civil War, when the virtually all white mountaineers had little use for slavery and the Confederacy. Moreover, the local breed of Democrats date mostly from the New Deal days, and their devotion to Franklin D. Roosevelt is, quite sensibly, mutually exclusive with a liking for the Harry Byrds, Sr. and Jr. In 1970, for example, this was the only part of the state Byrd, Jr., could not carry in his Independent candidacy for the Senate. The Fighting Ninth has a taste for raucous, noisy politics: it went for the loud conservatism of Senator William Scott in 1972 and for the yahooing populism of Independent gubernatorial candidate Henry Howell in 1973.

The current Congressman from the Fighting Ninth is Republican William Wampler. First elected in 1952, when he was only 26, Wampler was defeated in 1954 and 1956 by liberal

Democrat Pat Jennings. For a while he returned to his furniture and carpet business, but by 1966 he apparently sensed the public's disenchantment with the Great Society (and Vietnam war) of Lyndon Johnson. He ran once again, and this time defeated Jennings; the latter has made no effort to run again, but rather has carved out a comfortable niche for himself as Clerk of the House.

Wampler is one of only four Republicans who can remember serving in a House in which his party had the majority; he is also ranking minority member on the Agriculture Committee and, incidentally, the brother-in-law of Tennessee Senator Howard Baker. But none of these credentials prevented him from having a difficult time of it in the 1974 election. Though he was reelected with 73% of the vote in 1972, he had tough competition from local businessman, and populistic Democrat, Charles Horne. Utilizing much of the organization that had carried the Fighting Ninth for Henry Howell the year before, and benefitting from the anti-Republican Watergate tide, Horne was able to win 49% of the vote. It was not, of course, enough; and Wampler, given another two years of the advantages of incumbency, will probably win again in 1976. But nothing is for sure in the Fighting Ninth.

Census Data Pop. 465,136. Central city, 0%; suburban, 0%. Median family income, $6,608; families above $15,000: 7%; families below $3,000: 19%. Median years education, 8.8.

The Voters

Median voting age 42.
Employment profile White collar, 32%. Blue collar, 52%. Service, 11%. Farm, 5%.
Ethnic groups Black, 2%. Total foreign stock, 1%.

Presidential vote

1972	Nixon (R)	95,065	(68%)
	McGovern (D)	44,540	(32%)
1968	Nixon (R)	75,781	(49%)
	Humphrey (D)	53,436	(35%)
	Wallace (AI)	25,105	(16%)

Rep. William C. Wampler (R) Elected 1966; b. Apr. 21, 1926, Pennington Gap; home, Bristol; Va. Polytechnic Inst., B.S. 1948, U. of Va. Law School, 1949–50; Presbyterian.

Career Navy, WWII; Newspaperman, Bristol *Herald Courier* and *Virginia-Tennessean;* U.S. House of Reps., 1953–55; Repub. nominee for U.S. House of Reps., 1954, 1956; Special Asst. to the Gen. Mgr., Atomic Energy Comm., 1955; Furniture and carpet business, 1955–66; Bristol Utilities Bd. and Redevelopment and Housing Auth., 1965–66.

Offices 2422 RHOB, 202-225-3861. Also 524 Cumberland St., Bristol 24201, 703-669-9451.

Committees

Agriculture (Ranking Member). Subcommittees: Tobacco.

Group Ratings

	ADA	COPE	LWV	RIPON	NFU	LCV	CFA	NAB	NSI	ACA
1974	13	18	42	44	57	41	39	67	100	67
1973	4	18	17	47	65	11	38	–	–	78
1972	6	40	27	31	67	40	0	83	100	85

Key Votes

1) Foreign Aid	AGN	6) Gov Abortn Aid	AGN	11) Pub Cong Election $	AGN
2) Busing	AGN	7) Coed Phys Ed	AGN	12) Turkish Arms Cutoff	AGN
3) ABM	FOR	8) Pov Lawyer Gag	FOR	13) Youth Camp Regs	AGN
4) B-1 Bomber	FOR	9) Pub Trans Sub	AGN	14) Strip Mine Veto	FOR
5) Nerve Gas	FOR	10) EZ Voter Regis	AGN	15) Farm Bill Veto	AGN

Election Results

1974 general:	William C. Wampler (R)	68,183	(51%)	($116,944)
	Charles J. Horne (D)	65,783	(49%)	($232,341)
1974 primary:	William C. Wampler (R), unopposed			
1972 general:	William C. Wampler (R)	98,178	(73%)	($23,937)
	Zane Dale Christian (D)	36,000	(27%)	($29,534)

◆ ◆ ◆ ◆ ◆

TENTH DISTRICT

It finally happened. After a generation—22 years—the 10th congressional district of Virginia decided not to reelect its controversial Congressman, Republican Joel T. Broyhill. A man of undoubted competence and a Congressman who worked hard to solve the problems many of his constituents had with the federal government, Broyhill was almost always out front on issues, with a truculent conservatism which, for that generation, reflected the mood of the people here in the affluent northern Virginia suburbs of Washington, D.C. But with the Democratic tide of 1974, and with an equally important generational change, Broyhill found out that he no longer represented a majority. It is worth looking at this change, not just because it had important consequences for congressional politics, but because it tells us something of more general application about the mood of affluent America.

Broyhill first won the seat back in 1952, on the coattails of Dwight D. Eisenhower, in a new district which for the first time gave the Virginia suburbs of Washington their own Congressman. It was an affluent district; with the rise of federal salaries in the 1960s, it had the seventh highest median family income of any district in the nation by 1970. The federal employees were important: in that same year, 31% of all the wage and salary earners here worked for the federal government, the highest such percentage in any district in the country. And—this was important—it was virtually all white even in 1970, when some suburban neighborhoods allowed blacks to move in, 95% of the people in the 10th were white.

Broyhill was in the real estate business himself, and that was appropriate. For when he was first elected, the suburb of Arlington (technically a county) and Fairfax County beyond it were the scene of massive suburban outmigration. Young, well-to-do white people, the World War II generation who were beginning families, were moving out here from the District of Columbia—partly to escape the blacks (particularly when the District schools were integrated in 1954), but also simply because there was no more room left in District. In their elegant houses, over their well-tended lawns, they built the life style that characterized the Eisenhower era. Though they were its beneficiaries, they were skeptical of the trend toward a larger federal government that had begun with Franklin Roosevelt's New Deal; they were more concerned now about property taxes (lower in Virginia than in the District or Maryland) and about the schools (it is generally agreed that their quality here was good, certainly better than the District). They wanted little to do with the District, and crossed the bridges over the Potomac as seldom as possible; but they were also ready to bristle if they were treated unfairly by the government bureaucracies they very often worked for.

Joel Broyhill suited these new suburbanites perfectly. He voted a conservative line on the House floor, to keep their income taxes low. As a member of the House District of Columbia Committee, he worked hard to see that the black majority District would not have self-government, and would not be able in any way to tax the suburbanites. And he was one of the first Congressmen to fully grasp the notion that the best way to get reelected is to go to bat for your constituents when they have problems with the government, federal, state, or local. In his 22 years in Congress, Broyhill resolved the complaints of more than 100,000 constituents; there were few offices that took care of constituents' needs and complaints with more efficiency.

For most Congressmen that would have been the end of the matter; running such an efficient office, and simply avoiding riling any significant number of constituents would have guaranteed easy reelection for years. But Broyhill should be credited with having voted his conscience and having advanced his views so strongly that few constituents doubted where he stood—even though many were unhappy with his stand. His opposition to D.C. home rule, for example, was shared by a solid majority of Virginia suburbanites in 1960; but by the early seventies, according to Washington *Post* surveys, opinion had turned around. But not Broyhill's: he opposed home rule to the end. Nor was he willing to truckle to the increasing sentiment for mass transit over highways in northern Virginia in the seventies. Instead, he continued his support of building Interstate 66 through many pleasant Arlington neighborhoods which didn't want it. By 1974 Broyhill was perhaps the Congressman in the nation best known by his constituents; they knew not only who he was but also what he stood for. And that is what ultimately did him in.

For change had been coming slowly to the Virginia suburbs. The children who had jammed the schools of Arlington in the fifties had grown up, gone to college, and moved away—if not physically, they had at least rejected the attitudes their parents had had in the fifties. Now Arlington classrooms are uncrowded, and some schools are closed; and one of the fastest growing parts of Fairfax County is Reston, the "new town" which seems to attract primarily McGovern voters. With fewer children and a more secure affluence, these new suburbanites are significantly more liberal in their political attitudes. Many of them came to political maturity as opponents of the Vietnam war and supporters of racial integration; and they accurately came to see Joel Broyhill as the personification of all the political ideas they detested.

Broyhill was always controversial enough that he never received more than 60% of the vote—the minimum most Congressmen who conducted efficient offices come to expect. He was nearly defeated in the Democratic year of 1964, and in 1972, when Richard Nixon was carrying the district, he got only 56% of the vote. In 1974 Democrats apparently sensed that he was vulnerable. There was a hotly contested primary, and the winner was Arlington County Supervisor Joseph Fisher. At 60, he was a professional economist and part of the liberal group who had taken total control of Arlington government away from conservative Republicans, reflecting the changes in political attitudes here that would decide the 1974 contest. With a solid precinct organization in Arlington, plenty of money, and solid credentials, Fisher was able to wage a strong campaign, and he ended up winning 54% of the vote. The Eisenhower years in northern Virginia were officially over.

In the past few freshmen, even those as well connected as Fisher, could expect to play much role in shaping legislation. But Fisher is the kind of determined man who, at his age, was not about to wait 20 years to influence policy, and with the infusion of freshmen into the Congress, he had real clout. He won a seat on the House Ways and Means Committee (on which Broyhill had also sat) and became one of Chairman Al Ullman's chief advisors on energy policy. Of course he is running hard already for 1976, and he has learned from Broyhill's career that efficient constituency service is a must for political survival here. Barring some massive reversion to the fifties, Fisher should be reelected in 1976.

Census Data Pop. 465,115. Central city, 0%; suburban, 100%. Median family income, $14,457; families above $15,000: 47%; families below $3,000: 4%. Median years education, 12.9.

The Voters

Median voting age 40.
Employment profile White collar, 75%. Blue collar, 15%. Service, 9%. Farm, 1%.
Ethnic groups Black, 5%. Spanish, 3%. Total foreign stock, 15%. UK, Germany, 2% each.

Presidential vote

1972	Nixon (R)	115,664	(64%)
	McGovern (D)	65,148	(36%)
1968	Nixon (R)	69,600	(48%)
	Humphrey (D)	58,661	(40%)
	Wallace (AI)	18,247	(12%)

Rep. Joseph L. Fisher (D) Elected 1974; b. Jan. 11, 1914, Pawtucket R.I.; home, Arlington; Bowdoin Col., B.S. 1935, Harvard U., Ph.D. 1947, Geo. Wash. U., M.A. 1951; Unitarian.

Career Planner, Natl. Resources Planning Bd., 1939–42; Economist, U.S. State Dept., 1942–43; Army, WWII; Exec. Officer and Sr. Economist, Cncl. of Econ. Advisors, 1947–53; Assoc. Dir., Resources for the Future, Inc., private research foundation, 1953–59, Pres., 1959–74.

Offices 318 CHOB, 202-225-5136. Also 809 W. Broad St., Falls Church 22046, 703-534-2888.

Committees

Ways and Means (25th). Subcommittees: Trade; Unemployment Compensation.

Group Ratings: Newly Elected

Key Votes

1) Foreign Aid	FOR	6) Gov Abortn Aid	NE	11) Pub Cong Election $	NE
2) Busing	NE	7) Coed Phys Ed	FOR	12) Turkish Arms Cutoff	NE
3) ABM	NE	8) Pov Lawyer Gag	NE	13) Youth Camp Regs	FOR
4) B-1 Bomber	AGN	9) Pub Trans Sub	NE	14) Strip Mine Veto	AGN
5) Nerve Gas	NE	10) EZ Voter Regis	NE	15) Farm Bill Veto	AGN

Election Results

1974 general:	Joseph L. Fisher (D)	67,184	(54%)	($144,751)
	Joel T. Broyhill (R)	56,649	(46%)	($248,709)
1974 primary:	Joseph L. Fisher (D)	10,788	(42%)	
	Ruffus Phillips (D)	7,764	(30%)	
	Martha V. Pennino (D)	5,648	(22%)	
	Dennis Gregg (D)	1,391	(5%)	

WASHINGTON

In the far northwest corner of the continental United States lies the state of Washington. The massive Cascade Range separates the state into two topographical regions. To the east is the so-called Inland Empire. Here the Columbia River winds its way through plateau country; along the route its waters are backed up into giant reservoirs, the largest of which is Roosevelt Lake behind the Grand Coulee Dam. Except for the cities of Spokane and Yakima, and the urban complex around ERDA's Hanford Works, the Inland Empire is predominantly rural. Wheat is the biggest crop here, though apples and hops are also raised—Washington is the West's largest beer producer. Like most of rural America, this part of Washington experienced little population growth in the 1960s. The more populous region of the state is the urban complex west of the Cascades around Puget Sound. The hilly land around the island-studded Sound accounts for 65% of the state's residents; thanks to the Olympic Mountains to the west, the area enjoys a mild, though rainy, climate. Today, there is a strip of continuous urban development for more than 50 miles along the Sound, from Everett south through Seattle and beyond Tacoma.

Scandinavian immigrants from Minnesota, Wisconsin, and the Dakotas bulked large among Washington's first settlers. They rode the Great Northern and Northern Pacific west, and soon gave the territory a radical political cast. In the years before World War I, the IWW, also known as the "Wobblies," had its largest following in Washington; even today the state ranks third (after West Virginia and Michigan) in the percentage of its wage-earners who are union members. The

Scandinavians also helped to nurture a political atmosphere hospitable to public power and the development of cooperatives. During the New Deal, the Puget Sound area gave Franklin D. Roosevelt some of his largest majorities anywhere. In recent years, Washington has lost some of its cultural and political distinctiveness, as management personnel from various parts of the country have moved in. What brought many of them here and what still shapes the politics of the state is the aircraft industry, notably the Boeing concern.

Building airplanes is anything but a stable business enterprise. In the late 1960s it became clear that Boeing, and the state of Washington with it, was in trouble. Though it had, and still has, a reputation as one of the nation's most dependable and honest defense contractors, Boeing lost out on a couple of major awards: the TFX (F-111) went to General Dynamics of Lyndon Johnson's Texas, and the NASA Apollo project went to California's North American Aviation. Moreover, the anticipated demand for the fuel-guzzling jumbo jet 747 peaked and declined early. In 1969, Boeing employed 101,000 people in Washington a figure that represented 8% of the state's total work force; by the end of 1970, Boeing's Washington payroll had shrunk to 38,000. Boom became depression, and thousands of white collar executives and engineers, as well as production workers, found themselves living on unemployment checks. Boeing payrolls have now somewhat recovered to about 50,000 but 55,000 people left the state between 1970 and 1973, and the total population here—which rocketed in the 1950s and 1960s—has been basically stable since 1970.

The two Senators from Washington, Warren Magnuson and Henry Jackson, have often (and unfairly) been called "the Senators from Boeing." And in 1970 and 1971, the two Democrats allied themselves with the Nixon Administration to obtain government support for Boeing's supersonic transport (SST). The move was ultimately unsuccessful, an unusual experience for Magnuson and Jackson; for few other states—none outside the South—could have called on a pair of Senators with comparable seniority and clout. Magnuson was first elected to the Senate in 1944, after spending eight years in the House; and Jackson, after spending twelve years in the House, was elected to the Senate in 1952. The two have now accumulated 76 years of seniority on Capitol Hill, and they know their way around. Both have been committee chairmen for many years now, Magnuson of Commerce and Jackson of Interior; both are highly regarded experts in their fields, and in others as well. And both have proved beyond doubt their popularity in the state of Washington.

The state's senior Senator, Warren Magnuson, is less well known nationally than Jackson, but he retains at least as much clout in the Senate. Though he has long worked with Jackson on most issues, they parted company some time ago on foreign policy; to oversimplify it a bit, Magnuson is basically a dove, while Jackson remains basically a hawk. Magnuson is anything but an accomplished orator, and at 71 he is less adept at getting around than he used to be. But he still knows how to use the levers of legislative power. With his seniority and experience, he has the operating style of one of those Southern committee chairmen of yore, but he uses it to far different purposes. Long before Ralph Nader was heard of, Magnuson was fighting for proconsumer legislation, and he continues to do so with great effectiveness. He is also a senior member of the Appropriations Committee, and Chairman of its HEW and Labor Subcommittee. As such, he has a major voice in just about every area of domestic policy when he chooses to raise it; when he talks, bureaucrats—and Cabinet Secretaries—listen.

Magnuson has seldom been in political trouble at home, though he did have a close call back in 1962. But in 1968 and 1974 he was reelected with 65% and 63% of the vote. He will probably not run again, but he has at least four more years ahead as a major power in the Senate.

Whether Senator Jackson will run for reelection when his term is up in 1976 is unclear; for he has now become a very serious presidential candidate indeed. He tried once before in 1972, but his campaign never got off the ground. George Wallace attracted the antibusing voters he was aiming at in Florida, and he got no more than 13% in any of the primaries. But everyone expects he will do much better this time—at this writing he is probably the leading candidate for the nomination. The impetus for the Jackson candidacy comes from those Democrats who are liberal on domestic policies and basically hawkish (though Jackson dislikes the word) on foreign policy. And his backers believe that Jackson has shown by his work in the Senate that he has mastered more subjects a President must understand than any other American legislator.

There is at least a strong case to be made for that belief. As Chairman of the Interior Committee, Jackson demonstrated a keen interest in ecological concerns long before they became a matter of public interest. He is regarded as the father of the Environmental Protection Act, which set up the Environmental Protection Agency and required the filing of environmental impact statements before most government projects can proceed. He is the Senator who pushed through the 1973 law which enabled the building of the Alaskan oil pipeline and at the same time insisted on many environmental safeguards which the oil companies had originally been unwilling to provide. But Jackson does not want to be regarded as an all out ecology freak or an exponent of zero population growth. He appeals to businessmen as a politician who insists on the importance of economic growth as well as environmental safeguards.

Jackson is also a leading member of the Armed Services Committee and, by general acclaim, an expert on weapons systems. In the 1950s he believed, with John Kennedy and Lyndon Johnson, that the Eisenhower Administration was spending too little on defense; and Jackson has supported big defense budgets ever since. Indeed, his stance on such issues was so congenial to Richard Nixon's that Nixon offered him the post of Secretary of Defense. Jackson has always been a strong opponent of Communism (though he was an early opponent of Joe McCarthy, too), and he is skeptical about Henry Kissinger's detente; he insists that the United States is making too many concessions to the Russians and not getting enough for them. He always supported the Johnson and Nixon Vietnam war policies, and strongly opposed end-the-war amendments; to this day, he continues to believe that the American effort in Vietnam (though not all its details) was strategically and morally right. He has also been known as a strong, perhaps the strongest, backer of American aid to Israel; and it was his amendment to the trade bill, requiring free emigration for Jews and others before the Soviet Union would be granted most favored nation treatment, which ultimately scuttled Kissinger's trade agreement with Russia.

On domestic issues, Jackson has shown slightly less interest; he generally backs the liberal Democratic line, though in 1972 he made a point of his opposition to federal court busing decisions. In 1973 and 1974, his major interests coincided happily with the nation's. As Chairman of the Government Operations Permanent Investigations Subcommittee, he lambasted the oil companies for rising prices in 1973, for example; and with American involvement in Vietnam out of the way, he gained stature as a foreign policy expert, and frequent adversary of Henry Kissinger.

Jackson has two major problems as a presidential candidate: he is still not terribly well known, and he faces the implacable hostility of the portion of the Democratic Party that nominated George McGovern in 1972. At this writing, he is not known by almost half the American electorate; this will probably change in the course of the primaries, unless he runs unexpectedly poorly in the early contests. He certainly has the financial support necessary. He has already collected large sums, much of it from ardent supporters of Israel who appreciate his long record on Middle Eastern policy, much of it from businessmen who see him as a more congenial kind of politician than most liberal Democrats. The antiwar left is another matter. There are literally thousands of Democrats, including now some members of Congress, who got into politics primarily because of their opposition to the Vietnam war; why should they now support a man who was one of its major proponents? Jackson is making moves to mollify them, not so much to get their support before the convention (which would be impossible), but to insure they will not bolt to some third party candidate like Eugene McCarthy if he should win the nomination. But he is, in any case, running against the tide of change in the Democratic Party.

If he loses the nomination at the Democratic convention in July 1976, Jackson has the option of filing for another term in the Senate in the last week of July. And to win that he scarcely has to campaign; he won 84% of the vote in 1970. If he doesn't run, the leading candidate to succeed him will be 7th district Congressman Brock Adams, a liberal more in the Magnuson than the Jackson mold, who is now Chairman of the House Budget Committee (but can only serve two terms as such); Adams is already well known to most of the state's voters because he is from the Seattle area. Another possible contender is 5th district Congressman Thomas Foley, but to run he would have to give up his position as House Agriculture Committee Chairman, and his Spokane base does not leave him particularly well known in the Puget Sound area. On most issues, Foley would probably line up as Jackson would.

Both Adams and Foley are Democrats; the state has a Governor, Daniel Evans, who is a liberal Republican, who is well thought of far beyond Olympia, and who might be a strong candidate for the Senate. Evans has served three terms now, but has never run against a really strong Democrat; he declined to make the race against the then 69-year-old Magnuson in 1974, and so may have lost his chance. In any case, Washington has not elected a Republican Senator since 1946, and the state now has only one Republican Congressman; even an Evans as the Republican candidate would have to be considered the underdog.

Census Data   Pop. 3,409,169; 1.68% of U.S. total, 22nd largest; Central city, 27%; suburban, 39%. Median family income, $10,404; 12th highest; families above $15,000: 23%; families below $3,000: 8%.   Median years education, 12.4.

1974 Share of Federal Tax Burden $4,418,952,000; 1.65% of U.S. total, 20th largest.

1974 Share of Federal Outlays $5,637,398,000; 2.09% of U.S. total, 14th largest. Per capita federal spending, $1654.

DOD	$1,852,469,000	12th (2.71%)	HEW	$1,584,147,000	20th (1.71%)
AEC	$313,386,000	4th (10.28%)	HUD	$23,584,000	15th (2.42%)
NASA	$19,092,000	16th (0.64%)	VA	$273,386,000	18th (2.00%)
DOT	$238,293,000	10th (2.81%)	EPA	$35,912,000	23d (1.14%)
DOC	$49,037,000	6th (3.04%)	RevS	$88,257,000	24th (1.45%)
DOI	$183,705,000	4th (7.45%)	Int.	$116,884,000	24th (0.57%)
USDA	$246,458,000	21st (1.98%)	Other	$612,788,000	

Economic Base Finance, insurance and real estate; transportation equipment, especially aircraft and parts; agriculture, notably wheat, dairy products, cattle and apples; lumber and wood products, especially sawmills and planing mills; food and kindred products, especially canned, cured and frozen foods; paper and allied products; primary metal industries, especially primary nonferrous metals.

Political Line-up Governor, Daniel J. Evans (R). Senators, Warren G. Magnuson (D) and Henry M. Jackson (D). Representatives, 7 (6 D and 1 R). State Senate (30 D and 19 R); State House (62 D and 36 R).

The Voters

Registration 1,896,214 Total. No party registration.
Median voting age 42.
Employment profile White collar, 51%. Blue collar, 33%. Service, 13%. Farm, 3%.
Ethnic groups Black, 2%. Spanish, 2%. Total foreign stock, 19%. Canada, 4%, Germany, UK, Norway, 2% each; Sweden, 1%.

Presidential vote

1972	Nixon (R)	837,135	(60%)
	McGovern (D)	568,334	(40%)
1968	Nixon (R)	588,510	(45%)
	Humphrey (D)	616,037	(47%)
	Wallace (AI)	96,990	(7%)

Sen. Warren G. Magnuson (D) Elected 1944, seat up 1980; b. Apr. 12, 1905, Moorhead, Minn.; home, Seattle; U. of N.D., 1923, N.D. St. U., 1924, U. of Wash., J.D. 1929; Lutheran.

Career Practicing atty.; Wash. House of Reps. 1933–34, Asst. U.S. Dist. Atty., West Dist. of Wash., 1934; King Co. Prosecuting Atty., 1934–36; U.S. House of Reps., 1937–44.

Offices 127 RSOB, 202-224-2621. Also 1010 5th Ave., Rm. 900, Seattle 98104, 206-442-5545, and W. 290 Riverside Ave., Rm. 576, Spokane 99201, 509-456-4654.

Committees

Commerce (Chairman). Subcommittees: Aviation; Special Subcommittee on Freight Car Shortage; Special Subcommittee on Oil and Gas Production and Distribution.

Appropriations (2d). Subcommittees: Defense; Labor and HEW (Chairman); Public Works; State, Justice, Commerce, The Judiciary; Transportation.

Budget (2d).

Group Ratings

	ADA	COPE	LWV	RIPON	NFU	LCV	CFA	NAB	NSI	ACA
1974	81	80	100	36	100	71	88	9	60	11
1973	76	100	80	40	100	–	100	–	–	13
1972	60	100	91	56	100	42	100	40	50	19

Key Votes

1) No-Knock	AGN	8) Gov Abortn Aid	ABS	15) Consumer Prot Agy	FOR
2) Busing	FOR	9) Cut Mil Brass	AGN	16) Forced Psych Tests	FOR
3) No Fault	FOR	10) Gov Limousine	AGN	17) Fed Campaign Subs	FOR
4) F-111	FOR	11) RR Featherbed	FOR	18) Rhod Chrome Ban	FOR
5) Death Penalty	FOR	12) Handgun License	AGN	19) Open Legis Meetings	AGN
6) Foreign Aid	ABS	13) Less Troop Abrd	FOR	20) Strikers Food Stmps	FOR
7) Filibuster	AGN	14) Resume Turk Aid	AGN	21) Gov Info Disclosure	FOR

Election Results

1974 general:	Warren G. Magnuson (D)	611,811	(63%)	($463,116)
	Jack Metcalf (R)	363,626	(37%)	($63,153)
1974 primary:	Warren G. Magnuson (D)	228,038	(91%)	
	John (Hugo Frye) Patric (D)	23,438	(9%)	
1968 general:	Warren G. Magnuson (D)	796,183	(65%)	
	Jack Metcalf (R)	435,894	(35%)	

Sen. Henry M. Jackson (D) Elected 1952, seat up 1976; b. May 31, 1912, Everett; home, Everett; U. of Wash., LL.B. 1935; Presbyterian.

Career Practicing atty., 1936–38; Snohomish Co. Prosecuting Atty., 1938–40; U.S. House of Reps., 1941–53.

Offices 137 RSOB, 202-224-3441. Also 802 U.S. Courthouse, Seattle 98104, 206-442-7476.

Committees

Interior and Insular Affairs (Chairman). Subcommittees: Energy Research and Water Resources; Environment and Land Resources; Indian Affairs; Minerals, Materials and Fuels; Parks and Recreation.

Armed Services (3d). Subcommittees: Arms Control (Chairman); Military Construction Authorization; Preparedness Investigating; Tactical Air Power.

Government Operations (3d). Subcommittees: Oversight Procedures; Permanent Subcommittee on Investigations (Chairman).

Joint Committee on Atomic Energy (2d, Senate Side). Subcommittees: Communities; ERDA, Nuclear Energy (Chairman); Legislation; National Security.

Group Ratings

	ADA	COPE	LWV	RIPON	NFU	LCV	CFA	NAB	NSI	ACA
1974	62	82	90	43	100	71	88	17	90	11
1973	55	100	90	56	100	–	85	–	–	21
1972	40	100	91	56	90	40	100	11	80	38

Key Votes

1) No-Knock	AGN	8) Gov Abortn Aid	FOR	15) Consumer Prot Agy	FOR
2) Busing	FOR	9) Cut Mil Brass	AGN	16) Forced Psych Tests	FOR
3) No Fault	FOR	10) Gov Limousine	AGN	17) Fed Campaign Subs	FOR
4) F-111	FOR	11) RR Featherbed	FOR	18) Rhod Chrome Ban	FOR
5) Death Penalty	FOR	12) Handgun License	AGN	19) Open Legis Meetings	AGN
6) Foreign Aid	FOR	13) Less Troop Abrd	AGN	20) Strikers Food Stmps	FOR
7) Filibuster	AGN	14) Resume Turk Aid	AGN	21) Gov Info Disclosure	FOR

Election Results

1970 general:	Henry M. Jackson (D)	879,385	(84%)
	Charles W. Elicker (R)	170,790	(16%)
1970 primary:	Henry M. Jackson (D)	497,309	(84%)
	Carl Maxey (D)	79,201	(13%)
	Two others (D)	13,507	(2%)
1964 general:	Henry M. Jackson (D)	875,950	(72%)
	Lloyd J. Andrews (R)	337,138	(28%)

Gov. Daniel J. Evans (R) Elected 1964, term expires Jan. 1977; b. Oct. 16, 1925, Seattle; U. of Wash., B.S. 1948, M.S. 1949; Congregationalist.

Career Navy, WWII and Korea; Engineer; Wash. House of Reps., 1956–65, Repub. Floor Ldr., 1961–65; Keynote Spkr., Repub. Natl. Conv., 1968.

Offices State Capitol, Olympia 98504, 206-753-6780.

Election Results

1972 general:	Daniel J. Evans (R)	747,825	(51%)
	Albert D. Rosellini (D)	630,613	(43%)
	Vick Gould (Taxpayer $ to stop taxe$) ...	86,843	(6%)
1972 primary:	Daniel J. Evans (R)	224,953	(68%)
	Perry B. Woodall (R)	100,372	(30%)
	Two Others (R)	5,910	(2%)
1968 general:	Daniel J. Evans (R)	747,825	(54%)
	Albert D. Rossellini (D)	630,613	(46%)

◆ ◆ ◆ ◆ ◆

FIRST DISTRICT

Every major American city is divided into distinct neighborhoods. There is always a part of town where the wealthier, more white collar, better-educated people tend to live. In Seattle, this has been on the north side, in the hills between Puget Sound and Lake Washington. Accordingly, the pleasant neighborhoods around the lake and the University of Washington have always been the more Republican part of Seattle, even though many of the younger affluent people have moved out to the suburbs. The north side contains the heart of Washington's 1st congressional district—the only part of the state to send a Republican to Congress.

Before the 1972 redistricting, the 1st district was more Republican than it is now. A redistricting plan concocted by a geography professor sheared off several high income, heavily Republican areas, and added some Democratic territory—notably Mountlakes Terrace, a blue collar community just across the line in Snohomish County. But despite the addition and the presence of the university, the north side of the city remains a Republican district; it also retains most of Seattle's largest suburb of Bellevue (pop. 61,000), a Republican area east of Lake Washington. In the old district, the big race, when one took place, occurred in the Republican primary; in the new district, there were real contests in both the primary and the general election.

For the 18 years before 1972 the 1st district saw little political turbulence at all. Things were quiet from 1952, when Republican Thomas Pelly was first elected, until 1970, when state Senator Joel Pritchard challenged Pelly in the Republican primary. Pelly was then ranking Republican on the House Merchant Marine and Fisheries Committee, but he was also 68; he refused to fly in airplanes, and so only visited the district when he could afford the time to take the train. Pritchard, a liberal in the mold of Governor Daniels Evans, was well known in the district and won 47% of the vote, and Pelly decided to retire in 1972.

But it was not quite smooth sailing for Pritchard. Senator Henry Jackson, after his humiliating showing in the presidential primaries, was ready to flex his political muscles in Washington, and he was strongly backing the candidacy of 30-year-old Democrat John Hempelmann, a former Jackson staffer. Jackson was Hempelmann's main resource, and on the Senator's strength the Democrat nearly won; Pritchard had a far lower than expected 51% of the vote. Once in office, however, the Republican was able to use the advantages of incumbency to the point that he had little difficulty in the Democratic year of 1974. He serves on the Government Operations and Merchant Marine Committees, and is on record to the effect that no member of Congress should serve more than 12 years: that means he will probably retire in 1984.

Census Data Pop. 465,810. Central city, 68%; suburban, 32%. Median family income, $12,084; families above $15,000: 33%; families below $3,000: 5%. Median years education, 12.7.

The Voters

Median voting age 42.
Employment profile White collar, 65%. Blue collar, 23%. Service, 12%. Farm, –%.
Ethnic groups Spanish, 2%. Total foreign stock, 25%. Canada, 6%; Norway, UK, 3% each; Germany, Sweden, 2% each.

Presidential vote

1972	Nixon (R)	137,563	(58%)
	McGovern (D)	97,967	(42%)
1968	Nixon (R)	NA	
	Humphrey (D)	NA	
	Wallace (AI)	NA	

Rep. Joel Pritchard (R) Elected 1972; b. May 5, 1925, Seattle; home, Seattle; Marietta Col., 1946–48; Presbyterian.

Career Army, WWII; Griffin Envelope Co., 1948–72, Pres., 1970–72; Wash. House of Reps., 1958–66; Wash. Senate, 1966–70.

Offices 133 CHOB, 202-225-6311. Also 2888 Fed. Bldg., 915 2nd Ave., Seattle 98174, 206-442-4220.

Committees

Government Operations (11th). Subcommittees: Legislation and National Security; Manpower and Housing.

Merchant Marine and Fisheries (8th). Subcommittees: Fisheries and Wildlife Conservation and the Environment; Merchant Marine.

Group Ratings

	ADA	COPE	LWV	RIPON	NFU	LCV	CFA	NAB	NSI	ACA
1974	76	73	73	77	71	79	42	42	30	13
1973	68	45	92	73	42	61	75	–	–	33

Key Votes

1) Foreign Aid	AGN	6) Gov Abortn Aid	FOR	11) Pub Cong Election $	FOR
2) Busing	AGN	7) Coed Phys Ed	AGN	12) Turkish Arms Cutoff	FOR
3) ABM	AGN	8) Pov Lawyer Gag	AGN	13) Youth Camp Regs	AGN
4) B-1 Bomber	AGN	9) Pub Trans Sub	AGN	14) Strip Mine Veto	AGN
5) Nerve Gas	AGN	10) EZ Voter Regis	FOR	15) Farm Bill Veto	FOR

Election Results

1974 general:	Joel Pritchard (R)	108,391	(71%)	($84,093)
	W. R. (Walkin' Will) Knedlik (D)	44,655	(29%)	($7,108)
1974 primary:	Joel Pritchard (R), unopposed			
1972 general:	Joel Pritchard (R)	107,581	(51%)	($112,933)
	John Hempelmann (D)	104,959	(49%)	($84,136)

◆ ◆ ◆ ◆ ◆

SECOND DISTRICT

The 2d congressional district of Washington is the far northwest corner of the continental United States. This is a region of towering mountains, of heavily wooded inlets, and of gentle rain and fog. The 2d takes in the sparsely populated island in Puget Sound and the Straits of Juan de Fuca, along with the counties just east of the Sound from Seattle to the Canadian border. Most of the population of the district is concentrated in a narrow strip of land between the Sound and the Cascade Mountains, in or near cities like Bellingham, Everett, and several suburbs of Seattle. Politically, the district is marginal, usually leaning slightly Democratic in national elections.

The 2d perhaps best illustrates the Washington tradition in congressional politics: it elects a young Congressman in a good year for his party, continues to reelect him, and turns him out only if he gets overconfident in a bad year for his party. From 1941 to 1953, the 2d was represented by Scoop Jackson. Perhaps anticipating the Eisenhower landslide of 1952, Jackson decided on a Senate try rather than risk a House contest that might have been riskier than usual. His successor in the House was Republican Jack Westland, who won routine reelection until 1964 when the Goldwater debacle apparently caught him napping.

The winner that year was Democrat Lloyd Meeds, who, like Jackson 24 years earlier, ran for Congress while serving as Snohomish County (Everett) Prosecutor. Ever since, Meeds has been reelected with near automatic regularity; in 1972, he was anything but napping, as he ran 22% ahead of George McGovern is his district. As a member of the Education and Labor and Interior Committees, Meeds usually votes with the liberals. The Congressman's political coloration combines a Jacksonish attitude toward issues with a more dovish strain of liberalism.

Census Data Pop. 472,289. Central city, 11%; suburban, 54%. Median family income, $10,563; families above $15,000: 22%; families below $3,000: 8%. Median years education, 12.4.

The Voters

Median voting age 41.
Employment profile White collar, 48%. Blue collar, 37%. Service, 12%. Farm, 3%.
Ethnic groups Spanish, 1%. Total foreign stock, 20%. Canada, 5%; Norway, UK, Germany, Sweden, 2% each.

Presidential vote

	1972	Nixon (R)	121,349	(62%)
		McGovern (D)	75,728	(38%)
	1968	Nixon (R)	NA	
		Humphrey (D)	NA	
		Wallace (AI)	NA	

Rep. Lloyd Meeds (D) Elected 1964; b. Dec. 11, 1927, Dillon, Mont.; home, Everett; Everett Community Col., Gonzaga U., LL.B. 1958; Episcopalian.

Career Navy, 1946–47; Service station owner and operator, 1950–54; Spokane Co. Deputy Prosecuting Atty., 1958; Snohomish Co. Deputy Prosecuting Atty., 1959–60, Prosecuting Atty., 1962–64; Practicing atty., 1961–62.

Offices 2352 RHOB, 202-225-2605. Also 201 Fed. Bldg., Everett 98201, 106-252-3188.

Committees

Education and Labor (10th). Subcommittees: Agricultural Labor; Elementary, Secondary and Vocational Education; Manpower, Compensation, and Health and Safety; Select Subcommittee on Education.

Interior and Insular Affairs (8th). Subcommittees: Indian Affairs (Chairman); National Parks and Recreation; Territorial and Insular Affairs; Water and Power Resources.

Group Ratings

	ADA	COPE	LWV	RIPON	NFU	LCV	CFA	NAB	NSI	ACA
1974	86	100	100	67	93	88	92	17	22	0
1973	92	82	92	60	100	68	88	–	–	4
1972	75	100	91	64	100	57	50	0	30	13

Key Votes

1) Foreign Aid	FOR	6) Gov Abortn Aid	FOR	11) Pub Cong Election $	FOR
2) Busing	FOR	7) Coed Phys Ed	FOR	12) Turkish Arms Cutoff	FOR
3) ABM	AGN	8) Pov Lawyer Gag	AGN	13) Youth Camp Regs	FOR
4) B-1 Bomber	AGN	9) Pub Trans Sub	FOR	14) Strip Mine Veto	AGN
5) Nerve Gas	AGN	10) EZ Voter Regis	FOR	15) Farm Bill Veto	AGN

Election Results

1974 general:	Lloyd Meeds (D)	81,565	(61%)	($65,954)
	Ronald C. Reed (R)	53,157	(39%)	($14,317)
1974 primary:	Lloyd Meeds (D), unopposed			
1972 general:	Lloyd Meeds (D)	114,900	(60%)	($42,062)
	Bill Reams (R)	75,181	(40%)	($54,717)

◆ ◆ ◆ ◆ ◆

THIRD DISTRICT

Lumber is one of Washington's more important industries. And nowhere in the state is lumber a more important part of the economy than in the damp, mountainous region along the Pacific coast and the lower Columbia River. This is the state's 3d congressional district, which encircles the Seattle and Tacoma metropolitan areas, and just fails to include the industrial town of Vancouver, right across the Columbia from Portland, Oregon. The district is predominantly rural; its biggest cities include Longview (pop. 28,000) and Olympia (pop. 23,000). But the 3d's largest center of population is the Army's Fort Lewis (pop. 38,000), which sits at the district's edge, near Tacoma. The political atmosphere in the 3d has not really changed too much since the turn of the century, when the lumberjacks first attacked the firs and the sawmill towns grew up on the bays off the Pacific and Puget Sound. It is an atmosphere that retains a kind of rough hewn populist, Democratic aura reminiscent of the days when the IWW was trying to organize the lumbercamps.

This is a district where the politics of lumber is important; indeed, one can even argue that it played a decisive role in deciding the congressional election of 1974. It was expected to be a close contest. Democratic incumbent Julia Butler Hansen was retiring after 14 years of service; she was Chairwoman of the Appropriations Interior Subcommittee, with power over, among other things, lumber on federal lands. But she was past 60 and tired of the responsibilities of a House member; she announced tartly that she was going to go back home, take her phone off the hook, and tell people to go to hell when she felt like it.

Ordinarily one would expect a Democrat to win here, but in 1974 the Republicans were running a strong candidate, Washington Secretary of State Ludlow Kramer. One of the young, moderate Republicans brought into government and elective office by Governor Daniel Evans, Kramer was originally from Seattle, but had settled in the state capital of Olympia; and before the primary he became even better known in a rather unusual fashion. For Kramer was the man Randolph Hearst asked to come to San Francisco to duplicate the success of a program in Washington in distributing free food to the poor. Kramer's success in the Bay area was at best spotty, but he at least had shown good intentions—and had gotten publicity most congressional candidates would give their whole campaign treasury for.

Moreover, the man Kramer was running against, Clark County Auditor Don Bonker, was a Democrat he had beaten once before, in their 1972 race for Secretary of State. And not only had Kramer won, he had also got 53% of the vote in the confines of the district. But Bonker had a strong issue of his own: lumber exports. Washington and Oregon recently have been exporting thousands of yards of lumber to Japan—lumber which many observers claim should be left standing in American forests. Kramer favored unlimited exports to the Japanese, on the theory the local economy would benefit. Bonker favored some limitations of exports, on the theory that otherwise the forests would be destroyed.

Whether is was the Hearst incident or the lumber exports, or whether it was just a matter of 1974, Bonker won—and won big, with a whopping 62% of the vote. In the House, he sits on the International Relations and Merchant Marine Committees. He appears to be infinitely reelectable here in the 3d district, and he has some time even to cultivate statewide ambitions, such as a desire to run for Senator Warren Magnuson's seat when it is up in 1980.

Census Data Pop. 506,840. Central city, 0%; suburban, 36%. Median family income, $9,736; families above $15,000: 18%; families below $3,000: 9%. Median years education, 12.2.

The Voters

Median voting age 40.
Employment profile White collar, 42%. Blue collar, 42%. Service, 13%. Farm, 3%.
Ethnic groups Black, 1%. Spanish, 2%. Total foreign stock, 15%. Canada, 3%; Germany, 2%; UK, Norway, Sweden, 1% each.

Presidential vote

1972	Nixon (R)	112,130	(58%)
	McGovern (D)	82,747	(42%)
1968	Nixon (R)	NA	
	Humphrey (D)	NA	
	Wallace (AI)	NA	

Rep. Don Bonker (D) Elected 1974; b. Mar. 7, 1937, Denver, Colo.; home, Olympia; Clark Col., Vancouver, Wash., A.A. 1962, Lewis & Clark Col., B.A. 1964, American U., 1964–66.

Career Coast Guard, 1955–59; Research asst. to U.S. Sen. Maurine B. Neuberger of Oreg., 1964–66; Clark Co. Auditor, 1966–74; Candidate for Secy. of State of Wash., 1972.

Offices 1531 LHOB, 202-225-2536. Also, 209 Federal Bldg., Olympia 98501, 206-753-9528.

Committees

International Relations (22d). Subcommittees: International Trade and Commerce; Investigations.

Merchant Marine and Fisheries (22d). Subcommittees: Coast Guard and Navigation; Fisheries and Wildlife Conservation and the Environment; Merchant Marine.

Group Ratings: Newly Elected

Key Votes

1) Foreign Aid	FOR	6) Gov Abortn Aid	NE	11) Pub Cong Election $	NE
2) Busing	NE	7) Coed Phys Ed	AGN	12) Turkish Arms Cutoff	NE
3) ABM	NE	8) Pov Lawyer Gag	NE	13) Youth Camp Regs	AGN
4) B-1 Bomber	AGN	9) Pub Trans Sub	NE	14) Strip Mine Veto	AGN
5) Nerve Gas	NE	10) EZ Voter Regis	NE	15) Farm Bill Veto	AGN

Election Results

1974 general:	Don Bonker (D)	93,980	(62%)	($81,853)
	A. Ludlow Kramer (R)	58,774	(38%)	($136,810)
1974 primary:	Don Bonker (D)	24,234	(36%)	
	Robert C. (Bob) Bailey (D)	22,028	(33%)	
	Robert Corcoran (D)	11,171	(17%)	
	Three others (D)	9,795	(15%)	

◆ ◆ ◆ ◆ ◆

FOURTH DISTRICT

For most of its length in Washington, the Columbia River flows either within or along the borders of the 4th congressional district. To the west, the district expands to the city of Vancouver (pop. 42,000), across the Columbia from Portland, Oregon. Upriver, the 4th cuts through the Cascade Mountains at Bonneville Dam, past McNary Dam to the town of Richland near ERDA's Hanford Works, and still farther upriver past Wenatchee to the Grand Coulee Dam. In area, the 4th is the state's largest congressional district, and most of the area encompassed is taken up by the Cascades and its ridges, blessed with picturesque names like Horse Heaven Hills. The district's largest center of population does not lie along the Columbia, but instead in the fertile Yakima valley, which contains the district's largest city of Yakima (pop. 45,000). The valley produces a great share of the state's agricultural crops; not just wheat, but also apples, hops, and other vegetables and fruits.

The 1972 redistricting changed the 4th substantially. Its lines were drawn by an academic geographer, not a group of politicians. The old district was the southeast quarter of the state; the redistricting cost its seven southeastern counties and extended its territory all the way up to the Canadian border. The new shape was thought to threaten the seat of freshman Congressman Mike McCormack, inasmuch as it excluded the city of Pasco, where the Democratic challenger had won a large majority in his 1970 upset of Republican incumbent Catherine May.

It is fairly unusual these days for a challenger to unseat an incumbent Congressman. It is even more unusual in Washington, where, aside from 1964 when four Republican incumbents lost, only one other incumbent House member besides Mrs. May has been defeated in the last 20 years. Several factors account for McCormack's victory in 1970. As a 14-year veteran of the state legislature, he was well known and well liked in the Richland-Pasco area. Mrs. May, on the other hand, had recently been divorced and remarried; more important, she had not returned to the district very often (today, as Catherine May Bedell, she is Chairman of the U.S. Tariff Commission). There was also discontent among the district's farmers; in some farm counties, McCormack equalled Lyndon Johnson's 1964 showings.

But most important was the support of Senator Henry Jackson, who was up for reelection in 1970 and finished with 84% of the state's votes. Jackson did not confine his efforts for McCormack to a few stump speeches. The Senator raised money (especially through organized labor), appeared constantly on McCormack TV ads, and in general tried to define the race as a referendum on Jackson, rather than Mrs. May. The strategy worked, and McCormack won with 53% of the votes.

Reelection in 1972 was supposed to be tougher for McCormack. Neither Jackson nor Senator Warren Magnuson was on the ticket, but Richard Nixon and Governor Daniel Evans, both Republicans who had carried the 4th easily, were. Nevertheless, McCormack capitalized on the traditional Democratic leanings of Vancouver to carry the new counties in the district by a bare margin, and took 60% in the counties in the old district, thanks to work courting the constituency. In 1974, a Democratic year and after another term, McCormack won even more easily. A seat on Public Works obviously confers benefits on a Congressman representing a district on the

Columbia River and all its dams; and membership on the Joint Committee on Atomic Energy has some value for a district that receives more than $200 million annually from ERDA.

Census Data Pop. 467,171. Central city, 0%; suburban, 25%. Median family income, $9,206; families above $15,000: 17%; families below $3,000: 11%. Median years education, 12.2.

The Voters

Median voting age 44.
Employment profile White collar, 44%. Blue collar, 34%. Service, 12%. Farm, 10%.
Ethnic groups Spanish, 4%. Total foreign stock, 14%. Canada, 3%; Germany, 2%. UK, 1%.

Presidential vote

1972	Nixon (R)	112,728	(59%)
	McGovern (D)	77,042	(41%)
1968	Nixon (R)	NA	
	Humphrey (D)	NA	
	Wallace (AI)	NA	

Rep. Mike McCormack (D) Elected 1970; b. Dec. 14, 1921, Basil, Ohio; home, Richland; U. of Toledo, 1949–43, Wash. St. U., B.S. 1948, M.S. 1949, Gonzaga U. Law School.

Career Army, WWII; Research scientist, Atomic Energy Comm. Hanford Project, 1950–70; Wash. House of Reps., 1956–60; Wash. Senate 1960–70.

Offices 1503 LHOB, 202-225-5816. Also Fed. Bldg., Richland 99352, 509-942-7273.

Committees

Public Works and Transportation (10th). Subcommittees: Economic Development; Surface Transportation; Water Resources.

Science and Technology (8th). Subcommittees: Energy Research, Development and Demonstration (Chairman); Energy Research (Fossil Fuels); Environment and the Atmosphere; Science, Research, and Technology.

Joint Committee on Atomic Energy (4th, House Side). Subcommittees: ERDA, Environment and Safety (Chairman); ERDA, Nuclear Energy; Legislation.

Group Ratings

	ADA	COPE	LWV	RIPON	NFU	LCV	CFA	NAB	NSI	ACA
1974	86	100	67	53	100	44	75	36	22	7
1973	82	89	73	85	100	39	86	–	–	21
1972	63	90	80	50	100	57	0	9	22	18

Key Votes

1) Foreign Aid	AGN	6) Gov Abortn Aid	FOR	11) Pub Cong Election $	FOR
2) Busing	FOR	7) Coed Phys Ed	FOR	12) Turkish Arms Cutoff	FOR
3) ABM	AGN	8) Pov Lawyer Gag	AGN	13) Youth Camp Regs	FOR
4) B-1 Bomber	AGN	9) Pub Trans Sub	FOR	14) Strip Mine Veto	AGN
5) Nerve Gas	AGN	10) EZ Voter Regis	FOR	15) Farm Bill Veto	AGN

Election Results

1974 general:	Mike McCormack (D)	84,949	(59%)	($52,217)
	Floyd Paxton (R)	59,249	(41%)	($106,726)

1974 primary:	Mike McCormack (D)	34,388	(74%)	
	Jim Martin (D)	12,335	(26%)	
1972 general:	Mike McCormack (D)	97,593	(52%)	($66,130)
	Stewart Bledsoe (R)	89,812	(48%)	($141,560)

◆ ◆ ◆ ◆ ◆

FIFTH DISTRICT

The 5th district is the western part of Washington state. It is the heart of the Inland Empire, and centers on Spokane (pop. 170,000), the state's second largest city. Lying between the Cascades and the Rockies, the land here was originally arid plateau; but with the help of irrigation, it has become one of the major wheat growing regions in the United States. Much of the water is provided by the Grand Coulee Dam, that engineering marvel of the New Deal; the reclamation project also furnishes cheap public hydroelectric power. So enjoying the lowest electric power rates in the country, Washington has always been a big backer of public power development.

In the intermountain West, Spokane is the largest city north of Salt Lake City. Spokane County, which contains the city and its suburbs, has nearly 60% of the 5th district's people and voters. Because Spokane is somewhat more conservative than the cities on Puget Sound, the 5th district is inclined toward the Republican column in statewide races. The inclination is strengthened by the conservative Republican preference of Walla Walla and other towns in the southern portion of the district.

For the past 32 years, the 5th district has had only two Congressmen: conservative Republican Walt Horan, who served from 1943 to 1965, and Democrat Thomas Foley, who, after beating Horan in 1964, has won easily ever since. Though Foley has a fairly solid liberal voting record on most issues, he has backed military spending projects like the ABM. Considered a Jackson man, Foley served as a Jackson staffer on the Senate Interior Committee before running for Congress. In the election of 1964, he received a lot of help from Jackson, whose seat was up the same year.

Foley has been a lucky player at the seniority game. As a freshman, he was assigned to the Agriculture and Interior Committees, both choice spots for a Congressman from this district. By 1974 he had risen to the 6th ranking position among Interior's Democrats—a good climb for less than 10 years of service. But his rise on Agriculture was even more rapid. Over the years, most of the Democrats on the Agriculture Committee have come from the South; relatively few Northern Democrats come from farming districts, and those who do often have shaky holds on their seats. By 1970 Foley ranked 8th among Agriculture's 20 Democrats. But in 1972 three senior Democrats retired and two more were defeated; in the 1974 primary season, second ranking Frank Stubblefield of Kentucky was beaten in his Democratic primary, leaving Foley just behind 77-year-old Bob Poage in seniority.

That was a good place to be as the 75 Democratic freshmen elected in 1974 proceeded to change all the old rules. One of their targets, as it turned out, was Poage. He was old (though not senile) and he ran the Committee a bit highhandedly (but better than many chairmen); but his real offense was that he was a bleak reactionary on virtually every issue. The new Democrats, quite logically, did not see why they should elevate to power a man who shared virtually none of their views when the ready alternative, Foley, shared practically all of them. Foley himself did not seek the chair; he backed Poage—which just made things easier when he won. The old man was genial and Foley's pleasant personality helped to heal any wounds in the Committee.

When he was elected Chairman, Foley was finishing out a term as head of the liberal Democratic Study Group. On the Agriculture Committee, he seems committed to the traditional Democratic policy of high price supports to farmers, and he has a good enough rapport with other powerful Democrats (e.g., Phillip Burton of California) to weld together a coalition of Southern rural and Northern urban Democrats on this kind of issue. At 47, Foley could, if he wants, remain Chairman for 20 years or more. But he also has ambitions for the Senate. He might be interested in running in 1976, if Scoop Jackson wins his party's presidential nomination and leaves his Senate seat; or he might go after the seat Senator Warren Magnuson is expected to vacate in 1980. His main difficulty is that as Congressman from Spokane, he is scarcely known in the Seattle media market, where more than two-thirds of the state's voters live; but he certainly would be a formidable candidate. It is an interesting dilemma, one that many politicians would like to be in a position to ponder.

Census Data Pop. 471,144. Central city, 35%; suburban, 24%. Median family income, $9,164; families above $15,000: 17%; families below $3,000: 10%. Median years education, 12.4.

The Voters

Median voting age 43.
Employment profile White collar, 49%. Blue collar, 28%. Service, 16%. Farm, 7%.
Ethnic groups Black, 1%. Spanish, 2%. Total foreign stock, 16%. Canada, 4%; Germany, 2%; UK, Norway, Sweden, 1% each.

Presidential vote

1972	Nixon (R)	126,627	(63%)
	McGovern (D)	72,966	(37%)
1968	Nixon (R)	NA	
	Humphrey (D)	NA	
	Wallace (AI)	NA	

Rep. Thomas S. Foley (D) Elected 1964; b. Mar. 6, 1929, Spokane; home, Spokane; U. of Wash., B.A. 1951, LL.B. 1957; Catholic.

Career Practicing atty.; Spokane Co. Deputy Prosecuting Atty., 1958–60; Instructor, Gonzaga U. Law School, 1958–60; Asst. Atty. Gen. of Wash., 1960–61; Asst. Chf. Clerk and Special Counsel, U.S. Senate Comm. on Interior and Insular Affairs, 1961–63.

Offices 1201 LHOB, 202-225-2006; Also 574 U.S. Courthouse, Spokane 99201, 509-456-4680.

Committees

Agriculture (Chairman).

Standards of Official Conduct (5th).

Group Ratings

	ADA	COPE	LWV	RIPON	NFU	LCV	CFA	NAB	NSI	ACA
1974	86	100	90	50	100	71	92	33	25	0
1973	84	91	92	78	95	76	100	–	–	19
1972	69	82	100	81	83	60	50	9	50	9

Key Votes

1) Foreign Aid	FOR	6) Gov Abortn Aid	ABS	11) Pub Cong Election $	FOR
2) Busing	ABS	7) Coed Phys Ed	ABS	12) Turkish Arms Cutoff	ABS
3) ABM	AGN	8) Pov Lawyer Gag	AGN	13) Youth Camp Regs	AGN
4) B-1 Bomber	AGN	9) Pub Trans Sub	AGN	14) Strip Mine Veto	AGN
5) Nerve Gas	AGN	10) EZ Voter Regis	FOR	15) Farm Bill Veto	AGN

Election Results

1974 general:	Thomas S. Foley (D)	87,959	(64%)	($48,059)
	Gary G. Gage (R)	48,739	(36%)	($12,228)
1974 primary:	Thomas S. Foley (D)	42,428	(85%)	
	Gene Kraft (D)	4,453	(9%)	
	Clarice Privette (D)	2,777	(6%)	
1972 general:	Thomas S. Foley (D)	150,580	(81%)	($27,476)
	Clarice Privette (R)	34,742	(19%)	($500)

◆ ◆ ◆ ◆ ◆

SIXTH DISTRICT

Tacoma (pop. 154,000), the second largest city on Puget Sound, has always lived in the shadow of its larger neighbor, Seattle. Back in 1900, just before the state's most explosive decade of growth, Tacoma was still a creditable rival—it had 37,000 people to Seattle's 80,000. But in the years that followed, Seattle's growth took off, while Tacoma got itself embroiled in an unsuccessful attempt to rewrite history and change the name of Mount Rainier (which lies in Pierce County like the city) to Mount Tacoma. Subsequently, Seattle grew, diversified, became too dependent on the aircraft industry, and floundered in the early 1970s; but it remains the largest urban area in the Pacific Northwest, one with the amenities (and few of the problems) one associates with that status. Tacoma, meanwhile, remained mostly a lumber town (Weyerhaeuser), with only about one-quarter the population of its larger neighbor. Tacoma never experienced the white collar influx that descended upon Seattle; it stayed a blue collar town, and usually the most Democratic part of Washington.

Tacoma is the heart of the state's 6th congressional district, which includes the city and virtually all of its suburbs. The 6th also crosses the Puget Sound Narrows (where the Tacoma Straits Bridge collapsed in 1940) to include Kitsap County, which lies directly across the Sound from Seattle. Despite Tacoma's Democratic leanings, a Republican Congressman represented the district for 20 years, from 1945 to 1965, a politician with the asset here of an unmistakably Scandinavian name, Thor Tollefson. In the Johnson landslide of 1964, Tollefson was upset by Democrat Floyd Hicks, who resigned a local judgeship to make the race. Hicks has won reelection easily ever since. In Washington, he serves on the Armed Services Committee, where he has on occasion sided with the dovish minority—but not often, nor with any particular fervor. Anyway, Hicks has local interests to protect: there are several big Navy facilities in and around Bremerton in Kitsap County, and giant (pop. 38,000) Fort Lewis lies just outside the district boundary near Tacoma. Hicks has said he is tired of being in Congress and would rather be a judge, but so far he has made little progress toward this goal.

Census Data Pop. 454,793. Central city, 32%; suburban, 47%. Median family income, $10,481; families above $15,000: 22%; families below $3,000: 8%. Median years education, 12.3.

The Voters

Median voting age 42.
Employment profile White collar, 50%. Blue collar, 36%. Service, 13%. Farm, 1%.
Ethnic groups Black, 3%. Spanish, 1%. Total foreign stock, 19%. Canada, Germany, 3% each; Norway, UK, 2% each; Sweden, 1%.

Presidential vote

1972	Nixon (R)	115,377	(60%)
	McGovern (D)	75,698	(40%)
1968	Nixon (R)	NA	
	Humphrey (D)	NA	
	Wallace (AI)	NA	

Rep. Floyd V. Hicks (D) Elected 1964; b. May 29, 1915, Prosser; home, Tacoma; Cen. Wash. St. Col., B.Ed. 1938, Wash. St. U., U. of Wash., LL.B. 1948.

Career School teacher and coach, 1935–42; Army Air Corps, WWII; Practicing atty., 1949–60, 1963–64; Judge, Pierce Co. Superior Ct., 1961–63.

Offices 1202 LHOB, 202-225-5926. Also 210 Broadway, Tacoma 98402, 206-593-6536.

Committees

Armed Services (10th). Subcommittees: Research and Development; Seapower and Strategic and Critical Materials.

Government Operations (11th). Subcommittees: Government Activities and Transportation; Manpower and Housing (Chairman).

Group Ratings

	ADA	COPE	LWV	RIPON	NFU	LCV	CFA	NAB	NSI	ACA
1974	74	100	75	56	93	65	77	25	60	14
1973	64	91	67	60	95	58	75	–	–	30
1972	69	91	92	63	86	33	50	17	56	13

Key Votes

1) Foreign Aid	AGN	6) Gov Abortn Aid	FOR	11) Pub Cong Election $	FOR
2) Busing	FOR	7) Coed Phys Ed	AGN	12) Turkish Arms Cutoff	FOR
3) ABM	AGN	8) Pov Lawyer Gag	AGN	13) Youth Camp Regs	AGN
4) B-1 Bomber	AGN	9) Pub Trans Sub	FOR	14) Strip Mine Veto	AGN
5) Nerve Gas	AGN	10) EZ Voter Regis	FOR	15) Farm Bill Veto	AGN

Election Results

1974 general:	Floyd V. Hicks (D)	95,354	(72%)	($10,357)
	George M. Nalley (R)	37,400	(28%)	($8,185)
1974 primary:	Floyd V. Hicks (D)	40,433	(72%)	
	Byron Brady (D)	12,629	(23%)	
	C. E. (Buck) Stevens (D)	2,811	(5%)	
1972 general:	Floyd V. Hicks (D)	126,349	(72%)	($7,770)
	Thomas C. Lowry (R)	48,914	(28%)	($23,888)

◆ ◆ ◆ ◆ ◆

SEVENTH DISTRICT

The 7th district of Washington is the south side of Seattle and its suburbs. Seattle has fewer urban ills than most major cities. The crime rate is relatively low, and the city neighborhoods on the steep hills overlooking Puget Sound or Lake Washington retain a comfortable and forever green look, thanks to the almost constant rain. But as in other major metropolitan areas, the population here has been shifting to the suburbs. Seattle's downtown, which is part of the 7th district, is doing well commercially, but few people live in it anymore. To the south is the city's not-so-large black ghetto; nearly half of the state's blacks live in the 7th, but only 7% of the district's residents are black. Though the 7th also contains smaller Mexican-American and Asian communities, most of south side Seattle remains working class white.

The real heart of the district, however, are the suburbs south of the city. Here the major Boeing plants are located, along with the people who work—or used to work—in them. Though a few wealthy, heavily Republican suburbs—a part of Bellevue and Mercer Island—were added to the district after the 1970 census, most of the subdivisions are places like Renton and Kent, which are occupied by blue collar and white collar clerical workers. Up through the 1950s and 1960s, this area of rapid growth exuded the kind of prosperity built on the boom in the aircraft industry and attendant high union wages. But as the 1960s ended, the fortunes of the Boeing company—then the district's major employer—turned sour, and the 7th, along with the entire Seattle area, was thrown into a kind of depression. White collar workers found themselves in unemployment lines, and real estate values plummeted as people moved south or east to find work. The affluence of the 7th was based on brittle foundations: the inherently unstable aircraft industry. Like the 1930s, people who had prided themselves on what they had achieved found themselves helpless to preserve it in the face of economic forces beyond their control.

Nevertheless, the Boeing depression did not have much of an effect on the political behavior of the 7th district. Specifically, the voters here did not seem inclined to blame liberal Democrats—most of whom, nationally, had opposed Boeing's SST—for their plight. True, Richard Nixon won 56% of the vote here; but that was considerably less than his national average. And in congressional and senatorial elections, the 7th has been going even more heavily Democratic than ever, particularly for Congressman Brock Adams.

Like all members of the Washington delegation, Adams was a strong proponent of Boeing's SST, but on most military and defense spending matters he has been more inclined to vote with mildly dovish Senator Warren Magnuson than with hawkish Senator Henry Jackson. But that has not been Adams's area of specialization—of which there are actually several. He spent most of 1973 fashioning a bill to provide home rule for the District of Columbia, which finally passed that year; it is probably a matter of no moment to most of his constituents, but it was something that had to be done, and Adams proved himself a good legislative craftsman. In 1974, as a member of the Commerce Subcommittee on Transportation and Aeronautics, he concentrated on drafting a plan to provide a sound financial base for the nation's northeastern railroads; he worked closely with Montana's Congressman Dick Shoup, a Republican defeated in 1974, in an effort that transcended party and business-labor lines—and finally won the approval of all groups. Then in 1974, Adams concentrated on becoming the Chairman of the new Budget Committee and, once he won by beating Iowa's Neal Smith, performing his duties as such. The idea of the Committee (there is also one in the Senate, chaired by Edmund Muskie) is to provide fixed figures for taxes and expenditures which Congress must tailor its other programs to; it is a recognition that the kind of macroeconomic planning necessary today was not really possible under the old haphazard congressional procedures. So far Adams seems to be leading the Committee responsibly, if a little more cautiously than some of his liberal friends might like.

Adams will be eligible to serve only four years as Budget Chairman and he may not last as long as that; he is known to want to run for the Henry Jackson's Senate seat if Jackson is nominated for the Presidency in 1976. As a candidate, Adams can show a broad range of experience and accomplishment in national legislation; he can also boast of having been chosen one of the ten brightest Congressmen by *New Times* magazine. As a Congressman from the Seattle area—and one who has won reelection with as much as 85% of the vote—he is well known already to most of the state's voters and would be a formidable candidate indeed.

Census Data Pop. 420,058. Central city, 43%; suburban, 57%. Median family income, $11,706; families above $15,000: 30%; families below $3,000: 6%. Median years education, 12.4.

The Voters

Median voting age 41.
Employment profile White collar, 54%. Blue collar, 33%. Service, 13%. Farm, –%.
Ethnic groups Black, 7%. Spanish, 2%. Total foreign stock, 22%. Canada, 4%; UK, Germany, Norway, 2% each; Sweden, 1%.

Presidential vote

1972	Nixon (R)	111,127	(56%)
	McGovern (D)	85,891	(44%)
1968	Nixon (R)	NA	
	Humphrey (D)	NA	
	Wallace (AI)	NA	

Rep. Brock Adams (D) Elected 1964; b. Jan. 13, 1927, Atlanta, Ga.; home, Seattle; U. of Wash., B.A. 1949, Harvard U., LL.B. 1952; Episcopalian.

Career Navy, WWII; Practicing atty., 1952–61; U.S. Dist. Atty., West Dist. of Wash., 1961–64.

Offices 2235 RHOB, 202-225-3106. Also 2990 Fed. Ofc. Bldg., 915 2nd Ave., Seattle 98174, 206-442-7478.

Committees

Budget (Chairman).

Interstate and Foreign Commerce (10th). Subcommittees: Transportation and Commerce.

Group Ratings

	ADA	COPE	LWV	RIPON	NFU	LCV	CFA	NAB	NSI	ACA
1974	91	100	91	75	79	93	100	25	20	0
1973	96	100	73	73	79	72	88	–	–	21
1972	94	100	100	62	100	48	100	9	22	9

Key Votes

1) Foreign Aid	AGN	6) Gov Abortn Aid	FOR	11) Pub Cong Election $	FOR
2) Busing	FOR	7) Coed Phys Ed	AGN	12) Turkish Arms Cutoff	FOR
3) ABM	AGN	8) Pov Lawyer Gag	AGN	13) Youth Camp Regs	FOR
4) B-1 Bomber	AGN	9) Pub Trans Sub	FOR	14) Strip Mine Veto	AGN
5) Nerve Gas	AGN	10) EZ Voter Regis	FOR	15) Farm Bill Veto	ABS

Election Results

1974 general:	Brock Adams (D)	85,593	(71%)	($46,122)
	Raymond Pritchard (R)	34,847	(29%)	($2,309)
1974 primary:	Brock Adams (D), unopposed			
1972 general:	Brock Adams (D)	140,307	(85%)	($36,058)
	J. J. Freeman (R)	19,889	(12%)	($512)
	Thomas Forsythe (Write-in)	4,128	(3%)	(NA)

WEST VIRGINIA

West Virginia is in the middle of the Appalachian chain that separates the East Coast from the vast Mississippi Valley of mid-America. This is a state with scarcely a mile of level ground, and it has been said that if the mountains were ironed out, West Virginia would fill the whole nation. Perhaps; in any case, the mountains and the narrow twisting roads that wind through them give West Virginia an isolation and a sense of distance from the rest of the country. This is not a state that thinks of itself as part of the East or the Midwest or even the South; the term Appalachia is used more often lately (with a hard "ch"), but people here really think of themselves as West Virginians.

It is an identity hard won. Until 1863, these mountain counties were part, a misfit part, of Virginia. There were few slaves here; in the late 1820s, legislators from the mountain counties teamed up with Jeffersonian aristocrats and nearly abolished slavery in the Commonwealth. But the spectre of slave rebellions and the increasing profitability of breeding slaves for sale in the cotton belts of the Deep South strengthened the peculiar institution in the rest of Virginia, and the mountain counties went their own way. They opposed secession, they stayed part of the Union and continued to send Congressmen to Washington; and in 1863, after a dispute over the name (it was nearly Kanawha), West Virginia was admitted to the Union as a separate state.

The new state contained about one-quarter the residents of old Virginia. But in the years that followed the Civil War, West Virginia grew much faster than its parent. The reason was simple: coal. Under virtually all the mountains here, and often near the surface, are rich veins of bituminous coal, the essential fuel for industry and home heating in the late nineteenth and early twentieth century. West Virginia was a kind of frontier then: men from all over the Appalachian region and even some immigrants from Southern and Eastern Europe came to work the booming mines.

The working conditions in the mines were never very good; indeed, they were often deadly. Lovers of country music know something of life in coal company towns and the credit practices of company stores, where workers and their families were required to buy all their goods. During the 1930s, bloody strikes were common, as John L. Lewis' United Mine Workers established itself as the bargaining agent for the miners—so successfully that West Virginia is now the most unionized state in the nation. But just as unionization was completed, the coal industry entered a decades-long decline. The railroads switched from the coal-powered steam engine to the oil-powered Diesel. Homes switched from messy coal to clean oil or gas. After World War II, Lewis worked with the companies to encourage mechanization of the industry and reduce the work force. Their program was a vast success—but something of a disaster for West Virginia. In 1950, the state's population exceeded two million; by 1970, as thousands left to look for work elsewhere, the figure was down to 1,744,000.

Recently the coal industry has come on better times. As other fuels—notably oil—become more expensive, coal becomes more attractive. And there is plenty of it: West Virginia alone has enough coal to supply the nation for hundreds of years. But this new prosperity has brought new problems. Strip mining is now common in West Virginia; and despite company claims about reclamation, it leaves ugly, irreparable scars on the once green hlls. And despite company claims that stripping is a boon to ordinary West Virginians, the technique actually employs far fewer miners than underground mining. The Buffalo Creek disaster of 1972—where a company-constructed dam burst and the flood waters destroyed a small town—showed once again how casual the cost-conscious companies are about safety and how poorly and sometimes corruptly the state and federal regulatory authorities operate. The companies are also careless about their wastes, and hundreds of the narrow valleys and hollows of West Virginia suffer from serious air and water pollution.

In all this, the companies for a long time enjoyed the support and connivance of the United Mine Workers. Lewis' successor, Tony Boyle, continued the cozy relationship with the companies his predecessor had pioneered, and carried Lewis' one man dictatorship over the union to criminal lengths. In 1968 union Vice President Jock Yablonski ran against Boyle. He was defeated because of massive ballot irregularities—which the Nixon Labor Department for many months refused to do anything about—and after the election Yablonski, his wife and daughter were murdered by thugs hired by Boyle. The Labor Department finally ordered and supervised a new election, in which the Miners for Democracy candidate, Arnold Miller, defeated Boyle in 1972; and Boyle has now been convicted of murder.

The new leadership has completely changed the way the UMW is run. The close relations with the companies—they lobbied together against antipollution legislation, for example, under Boyle—are over, and the union now actively promotes safety in the mines. Miller has gone so far as to indicate at least an open mind about whether strip mining should be banned altogether—a move supported by only a few West Virginia politicians, including Congressman Ken Hechler and former Secretary of State Jay Rockefeller. But old Boyle cronies retain power in some West Virginia UMW locals, particularly in the isolated, though densely populated, southern counties.

Politics in West Virginia is a rough—and often corrupt—business. Many state jobs are still filled by patronage, and bribery is not uncommon. One recent former Governor W. W. Barron (1961–64) has gone to jail, and the current Governor, Republican Arch Moore, was once under investigation by the Internal Revenue Service—until the Nixon Administration put a stop to it. Vote fraud is so much a matter of course that the returns from Mingo County, to take the most notorious example, are interpreted as indicating who the county leaders were paid off by, rather than which candidate the local voters actually preferred. As in underdeveloped nations, so in this impoverished state, idealism and altruism are scarce commodities in politics. In a state where most of the executive positions are held by outsiders in companies headquartered elsewhere, the best avenues to riches are through political and union office.

The most surprising election result in recent years in West Virginia was the reelection of Governor Moore over Democratic challenger Rockefeller in 1972. A former Congressman from the 1st district, Moore parlayed his folksy manner and scandals among the Democrats into a narrow gubernatorial win in 1968. Two years later, he secured passage of a state constitutional amendment which made him eligible for a second term. His 1972 slogan summed up the case for him tersely: "Reelect a good Governor." And at least by comparison with some recent predecessors, he had conducted an honest and efficient administration; he had built some badly needed roads, and had presided over the state when the upturn in the coal industry had at last stopped the outmigration of people the state had experienced since the 1940s.

Moore was able to portray himself as a booster of the good things in West Virginia, and to depict Rockefeller as a carper—and a carpetbagger. And Rockefeller was, certainly, an outsider: he had first moved to West Virginia in 1964 to work in the antipoverty program. He decided to stay in the state and enter politics, easily winning election to the legislature (1966) and as Secretary of State (1968). He risked positions very unpopular in some quarters—like opposing strip mining—and unlike Moore he stressed the state's ills, not its strengths. The oldline Democratic politicians had little use for him, and their hostility showed up in the fact that the convivial Moore carried many usually heavy Democratic counties. Perhaps only in defeat was Rockefeller able to convince West Virginians of his commitment to the state. Instead of returning to the comfortable life he could have in New York, be came President of West Virginia Wesleyan College in Buckhannon in 1973; and he appears now to be running for Governor once again. Moore will not be eleigible in 1976, and at this writing Rockefeller seems to be the favorite to win—though he will probably have competition in both the primary and the general election.

The other major race on the 1972 ballot was not much of a contest. Senator Jennings Randolph was easily reelected with 66% of the vote. Randolph is one of the most experienced war horses on Capitol Hill. He first came to Washington in 1932, as a 30-year-old freshman New Deal Congressman. Defeated in the Republican year of 1946, he became a Hill lobbyist, but he kept a hand in West Virginia politics. In 1958 he won election to the Senate, and he has had little trouble staying there ever since.

Randolph is now Chairman of the Senate Public Works Committee, the keeper of the traditional pork barrel. He remains a kind of old fashioned New Dealer, willing and even eager to issue job creating projects to his Senate colleagues. But Public Works is probably more important now as the committee which passes on the bulk of air and water pollution legislation. Here the legislative workload has usually been hefted by Maine's Edmund Muskie. A cautious man, Muskie has been able to clear his work with Randolph, who in turn of course attends to the interests of West Virginia—which means coal. On one major issue they differed: whether the states could use highway trust fund money for mass transit projects. Muskie favored the proposals; Randolph who sees the highway program as a way to create jobs and tie isolated communities together, opposed it. Muskie won that one, and with a fairly good margin in the Senate; it is an illustration that the days when committee chairmen always prevailed on major issues are long over. Randolph will probably retire when his seat comes up in 1978; he will be 76 then. A possible successor is young (33) state Supreme Court Justice Richard Neely, grandson of longtime Senator and Governor Matthew Neely, who held statewide office intermittently from 1923 to 1958.

West Virginia's junior Senator is a man who cuts an increasingly important national figure—Senate Majority Whip Robert Byrd. No relation to the Virginia Byrds, Robert Byrd comes from a background of extreme poverty. Though his power comes from the leadership position he holds by vote of the increasingly liberal Democratic Caucus, his instincts are basically conservative. He quit the Ku Klux Klan as late as 1945, a year before he was elected to the West Virginia House of Delegates. In Congress, he has voted against civil rights legislation and conducted what some considered a vindictive campaign against alleged welfare abuses in the District of Columbia. Byrd moved from the state legislature to the U.S. House in 1952, and on to the Senate in 1958. His success owes nothing to gladhanding or charm or even patrongage. His secret, rather, was the same one that got him the Whip's job and now makes him the very possible successor to Majority Leader Mike Mansfield: hard work.

For Byrd is a charmless, dour, deadly serious man. He courts Senators with the same assiduity that prompts him to keep card files on thousands of West Virginians, so he can write and telephone them constantly, asking their opinons on issues. In 1969 and 1970, when Edward Kennedy was Whip, Byrd was Secretary of the Senate Democratic Conference. In that position, he paid meticulous attention to the petty details that make the lives of Senators easier: keeping them informed of the pace of floor debate and the schedule of upcoming votes, helping them to get amendments before the Senate, arranging pairs, and so forth. He showed his colleagues elaborate courtesy, writing them thank you notes on the slightest pretext. It all paid off in 1971, when Byrd suddenly challenged Kennedy for the Whip post. The West Virginian did not announce his candidacy until he was absolutely sure of a majority, which he got by securing Richard Russell's deathbed proxy.

As Whip, Byrd has continued to attend to the smallest details. Other Senators' legislative assistants who call Byrd's office to learn the order of debate often find the phone answered by the Senator himself—who helpfully and courteously answers all their questions. But such diligence alone did not move him into contention for the Majority Leadership; beyond that, his record no longer is the epitome of Southern conservatism it once was. Fortunately for Byrd, the kind of issues which came before the Senate, especially between Nixon's landslide reelection and his resignation, tended to take the form of conflict between the executive and legislative branches; and Byrd had little problem backing the legislative branch every time.

Here, too, the Senator's penchant for hard work has paid off. While L. Patrick Gray testified before the Judiciary Committee during his hearings for confirmation as head of the FBI, Byrd made a close study of the record. Byrd's scrutiny enabled him to put the question that forced Gray to admit that then White House Counsel John Dean "probably lied" to him—an admission that contributed mightily to the unravelling of the Watergate coverup. Later, Byrd was ready with proposals to promote the independence of the FBI, and also made a solid case against the Nixon position on executive privilege.

Byrd has moved toward the center of his party on other issues. He does not talk much about welfare chiselers these days; rather, he does things like urge that the United States resume normal diplomatic relations with Cuba. And he has come forward with dozens of solid proposals on other matters, though his name has been attached to no major piece of legislation. If Mansfield does not allow himself to be chosen Majority Leader again in 1977, Byrd will likely be the favored candidate for the post, despite his past; at the moment, his major competion appears to be Senator Alan Cranston of California.

Byrd's rise in West Virginia politics is also attributable to hard work. He was never part of the clubby, good old boy atmosphere of West Virginia's Democratic politics, nor was he an important participant in the patronage system. In 1952, cut off from funds by the party for his past membership in the Klan, Byrd financed his own House campaign with contributions of fifty cents and a dollar. Now he is of course invulnerable in West Virginia. In 1970, he whipped a liberal primary challenger with 89% of the vote, and in the general election became the first candidate in history to carry all of the state's 55 counties, some of them rock-ribbed Republican since the Civil War. He can obviously win reelection easily in 1976. He apparently nurtures some ambitions for the Presidency; but he has no real constituency in the party outside the Senate, and while he might like a draft, it is highly unlikely to come.

Census Data Pop. 1,744,237; 0.86% of U.S. total, 34th largest; Central city, 13%; suburban, 19%. Median family income, $7,414; 47th highest; families above $15,000: 10%; families below $3,000: 17%. Median years education, 10.6.

1974 Share of Federal Tax Burden $1,714,018,000; 0.64% of U.S. total, 35th largest.

1974 Share of Federal Outlays $1,967,096,000; 0.73% of U.S. total, 35th largest. Per capita federal spending, $1127.

DOD	$115,666,000	48th (0.17%)	HEW	$1,028,058,000	29th (1.11%)
AEC		– (–)	HUD	$6,553,000	34th (0.67%)
NASA	$138,000	45th (–)	VA	$147,236,000	36th (1.08%)
DOT	$177,570,000	19th (2.10%)	EPA	$14,668,000	35th (0.47%)
DOC	$4,980,000	37th (0.31%)	RevS	$59,651,000	33d (0.98%)
DOI	$17,563,000	32d (0.71%)	Int.	$42,662,000	36th (0.21%)
USDA	$78,238,000	38th (0.63%)	Other	$274,113,000	

Economic Base Bituminous coal mining; chemicals and allied products, especially industrial chemicals; primary metal industries, especially blast furnaces and basic steel products; stone, clay and glass products, especially glassware, pressed or blown; finance, insurance and real estate; agriculture, especially cattle, dairy products, apples and eggs.

Political Line-up Governor, Arch A. Moore, Jr. (R). Senators, Jennings Randolph (D) and Robert C. Byrd (D). Representatives, 4 D. State Senate (26 D and 8 R); House of Delegates (86 D and 14 R).

The Voters

Registration 1,024,688 Total. 664,915 D (65%); 341,068 R (33%); 18,705 Other (2%).
Median voting age 45.
Employment profile White collar, 40%. Blue collar, 45%. Service, 13%. Farm, 2%.
Ethnic groups Black, 4%. Total foreign stock, 4%.

Presidential vote

1972	Nixon (R)	484,964	(64%)
	McGovern (D)	277,435	(36%)
1968	Nixon (R)	307,555	(41%)
	Humphrey (D)	374,091	(50%)
	Wallace (AI)	72,560	(10%)

1972 Democratic Presidential Primary

Humphrey	246,596	(67%)
Wallace	121,888	(33%)

1972 Republican Presidential Primary

no candidates
entered

Sen. Jennings Randolph (D) Elected 1958, seat up 1978; b. Mar. 8, 1902, Salem; home, Elkins; Salem Col., B.A. 1924; Baptist.

Career Ed. Staff, Clarksburg *Daily Telegram*, 1924–25; Assoc. Ed., W. Va. *Review*, 1925–26; Prof. and Athletic Dir., Davis & Elkins Col., 1926–32; Instructor and Business Col. Dean, Southeastern U.; U.S. House of Reps., 1933–47; Asst. to the Pres. and Dir. of Public Rel., Capital Airlines, 1947–58.

Offices 5121 DSOB, 202-224-6472. Also 315-16 P.O. & Court House, 400 Davis Ave., Elkins 26241, 304-636-5100.

Committees

Public Works (Chairman). Subcommittees: Environmental Pollution.

Labor and Public Welfare (2d). Subcommittees: Aging; Alcoholism and Narcotics; Children and Youth; Education; Employment, Poverty, and Migratory Labor; The Handicapped (Chairman); Labor; Special Subcommittee on Human Resources.

Post Office and Civil Service (2d). Subcommittees: Civil Service Policies and Practices (Chairman); Postal Operations.

Veterans' Affairs (3d). Subcommittees: Compensation and Pension; Health and Hospitals.

Group Ratings

	ADA	COPE	LWV	RIPON	NFU	LCV	CFA	NAB	NSI	ACA
1974	74	70	80	41	82	43	66	25	40	13
1973	60	90	50	33	100	–	38	–	–	29
1972	40	70	64	46	80	20	91	50	40	28

Key Votes

1) No-Knock	AGN	8) Gov Abortn Aid	AGN	15) Consumer Prot Agy	FOR
2) Busing	FOR	9) Cut Mil Brass	FOR	16) Forced Psych Tests	ABS
3) No Fault	AGN	10) Gov Limousine	AGN	17) Fed Campaign Subs	FOR
4) F-111	FOR	11) RR Featherbed	FOR	18) Rhod Chrome Ban	AGN
5) Death Penalty	FOR	12) Handgun License	AGN	19) Open Legis Meetings	AGN
6) Foreign Aid	AGN	13) Less Troop Abrd	FOR	20) Strikers Food Stmps	FOR
7) Filibuster	AGN	14) Resume Turk Aid	ABS	21) Gov Info Disclosure	AGN

Election Results

1972 general:	Jennings Randolph (D)	486,310	(66%)	($133,670)
	Louise Leonard (R)	245,531	(34%)	($45,513)
1972 primary:	Jennings Randolph (D), unopposed			
1966 general:	Jennings Randolph (D)	292,325	(60%)	
	Francis J. Love (R)	198,891	(40%)	

Sen. Robert C. Byrd (D) Elected 1958, seat up 1976; b. Jan. 15, 1918, North Wilkesboro, N.C.; home, Sophia; Beckley Col., Concord Col., Morris Harvey Col., Marshall Col.; Baptist.

Career W. Va. House of Reps., 1946–50; W. Va. Senate, 1950–52; U.S. House of Reps., 1953–59; U.S. Senate Majority Whip, 1971–.

Offices 105 RSOB, 202-224-3954.

Committees

Majority Whip

Appropriations (5th). Subcommittees: Agriculture and Related Agencies;

Interior (Chairman); Labor and HEW; Public Works; Transportation.

The Judiciary (7th). Subcommittees: Constitutional Rights.

Rules and Administration (3d). Subcommittees: Privileges and Elections; Standing Rules of the Senate (Chairman).

Group Ratings

	ADA	COPE	LWV	RIPON	NFU	LCV	CFA	NAB	NSI	ACA
1974	52	82	60	26	76	43	66	25	40	47
1973	60	91	40	24	94	–	54	–	–	38
1972	35	70	45	32	90	20	90	46	70	50

Key Votes

1) No-Knock	FOR	8) Gov Abortn Aid	FOR	15) Consumer Prot Agy	FOR
2) Busing	AGN	9) Cut Mil Brass	FOR	16) Forced Psych Tests	AGN
3) No Fault	FOR	10) Gov Limousine	AGN	17) Fed Campaign Subs	AGN
4) F-111	FOR	11) RR Featherbed	FOR	18) Rhod Chrome Ban	AGN
5) Death Penalty	FOR	12) Handgun License	AGN	19) Open Legis Meetings	AGN
6) Foreign Aid	AGN	13) Less Troop Abrd	FOR	20) Strikers Food Stmps	FOR
7) Filibuster	AGN	14) Resume Turk Aid	FOR	21) Gov Info Disclosure	AGN

Election Results

1970 general:	Robert C. Byrd (D)	345,965	(78%)
	Elmer H. Dodson (R)	99,663	(22%)
1970 primary:	Robert C. Byrd (D)	195,725	(89%)
	John J. McOwen (D)	24,286	(11%)
1964 general:	Robert C. Byrd (D)	515,015	(68%)
	Cooper P. Benedict (R)	246,072	(32%)

Gov. Arch A. Moore, Jr. (R) Elected 1968, term expires Jan. 1977; b. Apr. 16, 1923, Moundsville; Lafayette Col., W. Va. U., A.B. 1948, LL.B. 1951; Methodist.

Career Army, WWII; Practicing atty.; W. Va. House of Delegates, 1953–57; U.S. House of Reps., 1957–69.

Offices Charleston 25305, 304-348-2000.

Election Results

1972 general:	Arch A. Moore (R)	423,817	(55%)
	John D. Rockefeller IV (D)	350,462	(45%)
1972 primary:	Arch A. Moore (R), unopposed		
1968 general:	Arch A. Moore (R)	378,315	(51%)
	James M. Sprouse (D)	365,530	(49%)

◆ ◆ ◆ ◆ ◆

FIRST DISTRICT

West Virginia's northern panhandle is the least isolated part of the state—the terrain here is just hilly, not mountainous. The panhandle is steel country that sits along the Ohio River just west of Pittsburgh and south of Youngstown, Ohio. Along the River are the giant blast furnaces in Wheeling (pop. 48,000), the home town of Walter Reuther, and Weirton (pop. 27,000). With the Pittsburgh area, the panhandle is also one of the leading glassmaking areas of the country. Not surprisingly, industrial pollution here is a major problem; the Ohio River valley around Wheeling has the worst air in the United States, and the Ohio itself is filthy. Another problem is the sagging economy: steel is not the healthy industry it once was.

The towns of Clarksburg (pop. 24,000) and Fairmont (pop. 25,000), the panhandle, and the Ohio River counties as far south as Parkersburg (pop. 44,000) make up West Virginia's 1st congressional district. Aside from a few rural counties and Parkersburg, which tend to go Republican, the 1st district is Democratic territory in most elections. But such has not always been the case in congressional elections, thanks to the vote-getting prowess of Arch Moore, former 1st district Congressman and now Governor. Moore was first elected to the House in 1956, when Eisenhower swept the state and the Republicans won a Senate seat and the Governorship. Though the years to come proved less happy for the GOP, Moore, an enthusiastic campaigner and unabashed booster of West Virginia, won reelection by larger and larger margins. He faced his toughest contest in 1962, when he was thrown into the same district with Democratic incumbent Cleveland Railey. Moore won a solid 61% of the vote against the 76-year-old Democrat; two years later, despite Barry Goldwater's disastrous showing here, Moore won with 71%.

Electoral achievements of that magnitude are enough to make a man think of bigger things, so Moore decided to run for Governor in 1968. The experts figured his chances were slim; but relying on home district strength, the Republican defeated former Governor (1957–60) Cecil Underwood in the primary and edged Democratic State Chairman James Sprouse by 12,000 votes in the general—with the help of a 36,000 vote margin within the boundaries of what then was the 1st district.

Moore's successor in the House, Robert Mollohan, is the Democrat Moore beat back in 1956. A veteran of the West Virginia political wars, Mollohan now serves on the House Armed Services Committee. Here he usually finds himself agreeing with the unit's hawkish majority; in 1973, for example, he was the only member of the West Virginia delegation to vote to continue the bombing of Cambodia. Mollohan's prospects for reelection appear good. In 1970 he beat Sam Huff, former New York Giants linebacker, in the Democratic primary, and then took 62% of the vote in the general election. The addition of Republican Parkersburg to the district in 1972 did nothing to prevent him from winning by even greater margins in that year and 1974.

Census Data Pop. 436,337. Central city, 17%; suburban, 22%. Median family income, $8,457; families above $15,000: 12%; families below $3,000: 12%. Median years education, 11.6.

The Voters

Median voting age 45.
Employment profile White collar, 39%. Blue collar, 47%. Service, 13%. Farm, 1%.
Ethnic groups Black, 2%. Total foreign stock, 9%.

Presidential vote

1972	Nixon (R)	126,902	(64%)
	McGovern (D)	70,735	(36%)
1968	Nixon (R)	83,951	(42%)
	Humphrey (D)	99,294	(50%)
	Wallace (AI)	16,366	(8%)

Rep. Robert H. Mollohan (D) Elected 1968; b. Sept. 18, 1909, Gransville; home, Fairmont; Glenville Co., Shepherd Col.; Baptist.

Career W. Va. Chf., Misc. Tax Div., and cashier, IRS, 1933–36; Dist. Mgr. and State Personnel Dir., Works Projects Admin., 1937–40; State Dir., U.S. Census, 1940; Supt., W. Va. Industrial School for Boys, 1945–49; U.S. Marshall, North. Dist. of W. Va., 1949–51; Clerk, U.S. Senate Comm. on the Dist. of Columbia.

Offices 339 CHOB, 202-225-4172. Also Rm. 603, Deveny Bldg., Fairmont 26554, 304-363-3356.

Committees

Armed Services (14th). Subcommittees: Investigations; Seapower and Strategic and Critical Materials.

House Administration (10th). Subcommittees: Accounts; Library and Memorials; Paper Conservation (Chairman).

Group Ratings

	ADA	COPE	LWV	RIPON	NFU	LCV	CFA	NAB	NSI	ACA
1974	47	100	30	43	90	47	75	30	100	33
1973	40	100	55	38	94	47	100	–	–	24
1972	19	90	33	46	100	33	50	10	100	26

Key Votes

1) Foreign Aid	AGN	6) Gov Abortn Aid	AGN	11) Pub Cong Election $	ABS
2) Busing	AGN	7) Coed Phys Ed	AGN	12) Turkish Arms Cutoff	ABS
3) ABM	FOR	8) Pov Lawyer Gag	AGN	13) Youth Camp Regs	FOR
4) B-1 Bomber	ABS	9) Pub Trans Sub	AGN	14) Strip Mine Veto	ABS
5) Nerve Gas	FOR	10) EZ Voter Regis	FOR	15) Farm Bill Veto	ABS

Election Results

1974 general:	Robert H. Mollohan (D)	72,457	(60%)	($62,952)
	Joe Laurita, Jr. (R)	48,966	(40%)	($105,927)
1974 primary:	Robert H. Mollohan (D)	45,175	(87%)	
	Howard L. Shackelford (D)	6,661	(13%)	
1972 general:	Robert H. Mollohan (D)	130,062	(69%)	($29,619)
	George E. Kapnicky (R)	57,274	(31%)	($2,392)

◆ ◆ ◆ ◆ ◆

SECOND DISTRICT

The 2d district of West Virginia occupies the eastern part of the state, and contains the most mountainous and sparsely populated counties of West Virginia. The district extends from Harper's Ferry, not far from Washington, D.C., where John Brown's raiders seized the arsenal in 1859, south and west to Fayette County, near the state capital of Charleston, and to Monroe County, not far from the Kentucky line. In the northwest part of the district, not far from Pittsburgh, is the 2d's only significant city, Morgantown (pop. 29,000)—part of the industrial Monongahela River valley and home of West Virginia University.

The problems of the 2d are typical of the entire Appalachian region. For one thing, there are virtually no four-lane highways in the district, and the existing roads, twisting around the mountains, effectively make the rural coal towns here more remote from the East Coast than the geographically more distant cities of the Great Lakes. For another thing, the beauty of the West Virginia hills is often despoiled by emissions from coal mines and paper mills, and by the ugly scars left by strip miners. And what is even worse for the people who want to stay here, many of the industries have been gradually leaving.

The political map of the 2d district is an odd looking patchwork of Democratic industrial and mining areas and Republican mountain strongholds. In most statewide elections, the district is marginal but in congressional elections, it is solidly Democratic. Congressman Harley Staggers has represented the 2d in the House since the 1948 election; recently, he has grown accustomed to winning percentages approaching 70%. For the past nine years, Staggers has served as Chairman of the House Interstate and Foreign Commerce Committee. This unit has jurisdiction over most of the federal regulatory agencies, and passes on most consumer legislation.

Staggers is a pleasant man with good intentions, but it must be said that he is one of the less effective committee chairmen in the House. The most overt demonstration of that came in 1971, when Staggers sought a contempt citation against CBS for refusing to provide the committee with outtakes—unedited pieces of film—from the controversial documentary "The Selling of the Pentagon." The Commerce Committee dutifully voted for contempt, but the full House, under pressure from liberals and the usually conservative broadcasting lobby, voted Staggers down—the first time in recent memory that a chairman has been so repudiated. Like other chairmen, Staggers attempted to gather the committee's power into his own hands. He saw, for example, that the Subcommittee on Investigations that he chaired received the lion's share of all subcommittee appropriations and staff, much to the chagrin of active subcommittee chairmen like Paul Rogers of Florida and John Moss of California. Yet at the same time, the Investigations Subcommittee was almost totally inactive.

The election of 1974 put an end to that state of affairs. Suddenly there were 75 new Democratic freshmen in the House—and 12 freshmen out of 29 Democrats on the Commerce Committee. John Moss, who had become the full Committee's third-ranking Democrat, ran against Staggers for the chair of the Investigations Subcommittee, and won. It was a humiliating defeat for Staggers; it meant that he had lost control of his own committee, and that Moss was a kind of de facto chairman in his stead. It is possible, if enough freshmen are reelected, that Moss could successfully challenge Staggers for the Chairmanship in 1977; another possibility is that Staggers will choose to retire in 1976, when he turns 69 and will have served 28 years in the House. If he does quit, it is almost a certainty that a Democrat will be elected to succeed him; except for Governor Arch Moore, no Republican has been elected to Congress from West Virginia since 1956.

Census Data Pop. 436,140. Central city, 0%; suburban, 0%. Median family income, $6,437; families above $15,000: 7%; families below $3,000: 20%. Median years education, 9.9.

The Voters

Median voting age 45.
Employment profile White collar, 37%. Blue collar, 45%. Service, 14%. Farm, 4%.
Ethnic groups Black, 4%. Total foreign stock, 3%.

Presidential vote

1972	Nixon (R)	124,917	(65%)
	McGovern (D)	66,597	(35%)
1968	Nixon (R)	80,122	(43%)
	Humphrey (D)	86,730	(47%)
	Wallace (AI)	17,904	(10%)

Rep. Harley O. Staggers (D) Elected 1948; b. Aug. 3, 1907, Keyser; home, Keyser; Emory & Henry Col., A.B. 1931; Methodist.

Career High school teacher and coach; Head Coach, Potomac St. Col.; Mineral Co. Sheriff, 1937–41; Right-of-Way Agent, W. Va. Road Comm., 1941–42; Dir., W. Va. Ofc. of Govt. Reports, 1942; Navy, WWII.

Offices 2366 RHOB, 202-225-4331. Also 116 N. Court St., Lewisburg 24901, 304-645-1278.

Committees

Interstate and Foreign Commerce (Chairman).

Group Ratings

	ADA	COPE	LWV	RIPON	NFU	LCV	CFA	NAB	NSI	ACA
1974	45	82	58	31	86	71	83	10	80	31
1973	64	100	64	25	94	65	100	–	–	19
1972	31	90	55	62	86	16	50	18	89	33

Key Votes

1) Foreign Aid	AGN	6) Gov Abortn Aid	AGN	11) Pub Cong Election $	AGN
2) Busing	FOR	7) Coed Phys Ed	AGN	12) Turkish Arms Cutoff	FOR
3) ABM	FOR	8) Pov Lawyer Gag	AGN	13) Youth Camp Regs	FOR
4) B-1 Bomber	FOR	9) Pub Trans Sub	FOR	14) Strip Mine Veto	AGN
5) Nerve Gas	FOR	10) EZ Voter Regis	FOR	15) Farm Bill Veto	AGN

Election Results

1974 general:	Harley O. Staggers (D)	73,683	(64%)	($15,484)
	William H. Loy (R)	40,779	(36%)	($30,995)
1974 primary:	Harley O. Staggers (D), unopposed			
1972 general:	Harley O. Staggers (D)	128,286	(70%)	($29,520)
	David Dix (R)	54,949	(30%)	($3,897)

◆ ◆ ◆ ◆ ◆

THIRD DISTRICT

Charleston is West Virginia's capital, the center of its largest metropolitan area, and, until the 1970 census, the state's largest city (that title now belongs to Huntington). Along the banks of the Kanawha River (pronounced kan-AW) stands the Capitol building, one of the largest and most beautiful in the country; but a little more typical of Charleston are the large Union Carbide plants a little farther downriver. Like most West Virginia cities, Charleston is situated in a narrow river valley, hemmed in by mountains; so situated, the city is victim to a smog which sometimes rivals that of Los Angeles. Though there are a few skyscraper buildings here, the country atmosphere still prevails; this is where irate fundamentalist parents literally started riots over the allegedly liberal and pornographic contents of school textbooks in 1974.

Charleston and surrounding Kanawha County form the population center and political pivot of West Virginia's 3d congressional district. Upriver in the mountains is coal mining country, the kind of destitute hollows where Jay Rockefeller lived when he first came to the state as an antipoverty worker. The territory below Charleston, down to the Ohio River, is less mountainous and also less densely populated. The coal counties are usually heavily Democratic; the Ohio River counties, however, seem to retain a Republicanism that goes back to the days when West Virginia first became a state during the Civil War. Charleston itself, perhaps surprisingly for an industrial city, leans a little more to the Republicans than to the Democrats. One factor behind this may be the large number of patronage jobs in the capital, all of which lie firmly in the hands of Republican Governor Arch Moore.

Just as Jay Rockefeller is typical of the younger, more idealistic West Virginia politicians—a breed that has met with mixed results lately—the 3d district's Congressman, John Slack, is typical of the older, more patronage oriented, go-along-to-get-along breed of West Virginia Democrats. Slack, a former real estate man, made his way to Congress via the Kanawha County Assessor's office, and is one of two former assessors in Congress. (The other is Andrew Hinshaw of California's Orange County, who is currently under indictment.) Slack's politics are fairly conservative; he votes liberal often enough to please organized labor, but not often enough to satisfy other liberal groups. His presence and that of other, similarly inclined Democrats from non-Southern states is one of the reasons why the House Appropriations Committee is much more conservative on most issues that the House as a whole—even after the 1974 crop of freshmen came in.

For the first time in years, Slack had a significant primary challenge in 1974. It came from Paul Kaufman, an antipoverty lawyer and 1968 gubernatorial candidate who represents a considerably more liberal brand of Democratic politics; Kaufman was able to mount a strong campaign, but he was bedevilled by the presence of a third candidate and fell far short winning. Slack's victory, plus the retirement of New York's John Rooney, gave Slack the Chairmanship of the State, Justice, Commerce, and Judiciary Subcommittee—a position which Rooney once parleyed to great power, but which Slack so far has not used so aggressively.

Census Data Pop. 434,165. Central city, 16%; suburban, 36%. Median family income, $7,574; families above $15,000: 11%; families below $3,000: 18%. Median years education, 10.8.

The Voters

Median voting age 44.
Employment profile White collar, 44%. Blue collar, 43%. Service, 12%. Farm, 1%.
Ethnic groups Black, 3%. Total foreign stock, 2%.

Presidential vote

1972	Nixon (R)	122,907	(62%)
	McGovern (D)	74,219	(38%)

1968	Nixon (R)	82,591	(43%)
	Humphrey (D)	88,493	(47%)
	Wallace (AI)	19,110	(10%)

Rep. John M. Slack (D) Elected 1958; b. Mar. 18, 1915, Charleston; home, Charleston; Va. Military Inst.; Presbyterian.

Career Armed Forces, WWII; Mbr., Kanawha Co. Court, 1948–52; Kahawa Co. Assessor, 1952–58.

Offices 2230 RHOB, 202-225-2711. Also New Fed. Ofc. Bldg., 500 Quarrier St., Charleston 25301, 304-343-8923.

Committees

Appropriations (11th). Subcommittees: Public Works; State, Justice, Commerce and the Judiciary (Chairman).

Group Ratings

	ADA	COPE	LWV	RIPON	NFU	LCV	CFA	NAB	NSI	ACA
1974	30	100	42	36	86	47	39	33	90	43
1973	44	100	42	33	95	26	88	–	–	33
1972	25	70	42	29	83	11	50	27	100	62

Key Votes

1) Foreign Aid	AGN	6) Gov Abortn Aid	AGN	11) Pub Cong Election $	AGN
2) Busing	AGN	7) Coed Phys Ed	AGN	12) Turkish Arms Cutoff	AGN
3) ABM	FOR	8) Pov Lawyer Gag	FOR	13) Youth Camp Regs	AGN
4) B-1 Bomber	FOR	9) Pub Trans Sub	FOR	14) Strip Mine Veto	FOR
5) Nerve Gas	FOR	10) EZ Voter Regis	FOR	15) Farm Bill Veto	AGN

Election Results

1974 general:	John M. Slack (D)	77,586	(69%)	($54,008)
	William L. Larcamp (R)	35,623	(31%)	($8,123)
1974 primary:	John M. Slack (D)	36,986	(61%)	
	Paul J. Kaufman (D)	14,196	(23%)	
	Darrell V. McGraw, Jr. (D)	9,786	(16%)	
1972 general:	John M. Slack (D)	118,346	(64%)	($12,019)
	T. David Higgins (R)	67,441	(36%)	($4,358)

◆ ◆ ◆ ◆ ◆

FOURTH DISTRICT

The 4th district of West Virginia is the southern part of the state—most of it coal country. In fact, the eight counties of the 4th have probably produced more bituminous coal over the years than any other single congressional district in the United States. Not all the district is coal country, however; it also contains the state's largest city, Huntington (pop. 74,000), a manufacturing and railroad junction town on the Ohio River. But from the banks of the Ohio, the mountains rise steeply, and the heart of the 4th lies in the small coal towns sitting between the mountainsides. In the 1950s and 1960s, the coal counties were hit hard by the decline of employment in the mines; the population of the counties now in the 4th declined from 579,000 in 1950 to 437,000 in 1970. Recently, the area has bounded back, as demand for coal has increased and economic conditions in the places which West Virginians used to move to look relatively forbidding; by the middle 1970s, the Census Bureau estimates, the 4th's population has turned around and risen to over 450,000.

The politics of this poverty stricken area has not developed along the altruistic lines liberal reformers would like to believe. In a place like southern West Virginia, there is no way for a bright young man to make money except by owning a coal company, or by winning public or union office. The latter are often more lucrative than their official salaries suggest; corruption is common, and there are counties here where one is still supposed to be able to buy votes. In such surroundings, there is little room for concern about things like unsafe mine conditions, black lung disease, or air and water pollution. People are inclined to get what they can, and not to worry about the problems of others.

But that is not the only kind of politics you can find here, as the results of the 1972 congressional election show. This was that rare event in these parts, a real contest, at least in the Democratic primary. (Republicans rarely win anything in the 4th, although Richard Nixon and Governor Arch Moore carried the district in 1972.) West Virginia had lost a congressional seat in the 1970 census, and two Congressmen were thrown together in the 4th, Ken Hechler of Huntington and James Kee of Bluefield.

There could not have been a greater contrast between the two. Kee was the scion of a local political dynasty: his father had won the seat in 1932, his mother had captured it on the father's death in 1951, and the son had won it when his mother retired in 1964. The younger Kee was not a man to make waves. He had one of the highest absenteeism rates in the House, and no significant legislative accomplishments; he had succeeded in enlisting the support of the Boyle leadership in the United Mine Workers and that of the major coal companies as well by regularly voting their interests when he did show up.

Hechler, in contrast, was a highly active and controversial politician. His background was unusual for West Virginia: he was a professor, an assistant in the Truman White House, a speechwriter for Adlai Stevenson. After the 1956 campaign, he got a job at Marshall University in Huntington and became a commentator on local TV. And in 1958, he challenged the incumbent Congressman, an 83-year-old Republican.

Hechler won that year, and he has been running and winning ever since. He has shown himself to be an untiring and resourceful campaigner, with a taste for the kind of highjinks that many of his former academic colleagues find distasteful. But Hechler does more than campaign hard and provide good constituency service. He took on the coal companies and the Boyle leadership of the UMW over black lung legislation, and won. He was the first major political figure in West Virginia—or anywhere—to propose an absolute ban on strip mining. And in 1969 and 1971, he campaigned hard for UMW insurgent candidates Joseph Yablonski and Arnold Miller.

These things take political—and physical—courage. Many West Virginia politicians felt that opposition to strip mining would produce little but political suicide, even if fewer men are actually employed in strip operations than coal company propaganda suggests. And in light of what happened to Yablonski, it took raw guts for Hechler to campaign in the coal counties for Miller. But Hechler's courage paid off. In the 1972 primary, he finished first among 64 candidates to become West Virginia's Delegate-at-Large to the Democratic national convention. And on the same day, he won his primary against Kee and a third candidate (who happened to be Congressman Harley Staggers' son-in-law) with a solid 52% of the vote. Hechler won a whopping 77% of the vote in the three counties that were in his old district, and in the five coal counties formerly represented by Kee, Hechler ran just 1,500 votes behind his complacent opponent.

In 1972, Jay Rockefeller, whose positions on the issues were similar to those of Hechler, ran for Governor and lost to incumbent Republican Arch Moore. Why did Hechler triumph and other candidates like him lose? For one thing, Hechler had been at it longer. For another, his commitment to West Virginia and to the poor people of the hollows is clear; in an age of distrust of politicians, Hechler has established real credibility. He has taken real risks in behalf of what he believes are the interests of ordinary West Virginians. That is rare enough anywhere, and against the cynical backdrop of West Virginia politics, people seem to appreciate it.

Census Data Pop. 437,595. Central city, 17%; suburban, 16%. Median family income, $7,039; families above $15,000: 9%; families below $3,000: 19%. Median years education, 10.1.

The Voters

Median voting age 45.
Employment profile White collar, 42%. Blue collar, 46%. Service, 12%. Farm, –%.
Ethnic groups Black, 7%. Total foreign stock, 2%.

Presidential vote

1972	Nixon (R)	110,238	(63%)
	McGovern (D)	65,884	(37%)

1968	Nixon (R)	60,891	(34%)
	Humphrey (D)	99,574	(55%)
	Wallace (AI)	19,180	(11%)

Rep. Ken Hechler (D) Elected 1958; b. Sept. 20, 1914, near Roslyn, L.I., N.Y.; home, Huntington; Swarthmore Col., A.B. 1935, Columbia U., M.A. 1936, Ph.D. 1940; Episcopalian.

Career Section Chf., Census, 1940; Personnel Officer, Ofc. of Emergency Mgmt., 1941; Analyst, Bureau of the Budget, 1941–42, 1946–67; Army, WWII; Asst. Prof. of Poli. Sci., Princeton U., 1947–49; Special Asst. to Pres. Harry S. Truman, 1949–53; Assoc. Dir., Amer. Poli. Sci. Assoc., 1953–56; Research Dir., Stevenson-Kefauver Campaign, 1956; Assoc. Prof., Marshall U., 1957; Admin. Asst. to U.S. Sen. John A. Carroll of Colo., 1957; Commentator, WHTN-TV, Huntington, 1957–58.

Offices 242 CHOB, 202-225-3452. Also Rm. 219, P.O. Bldg., Huntington 25712, 304-697-7343.

Committees

Science and Technolgy (2d). Subcommittees: Energy Research, Development and Demonstration; Energy Research (Fossil Fuels) (Chairman); Environment and the Atmosphere.

Group Ratings

	ADA	COPE	LWV	RIPON	NFU	LCV	CFA	NAB	NSI	ACA
1974	87	91	75	63	86	88	77	42	0	47
1973	88	100	67	73	85	89	100	–	–	22
1972	100	100	92	81	86	93	100	17	0	13

Key Votes

1) Foreign Aid	AGN	6) Gov Abortn Aid	AGN	11) Pub Cong Election $	AGN
2) Busing	FOR	7) Coed Phys Ed	AGN	12) Turkish Arms Cutoff	FOR
3) ABM	AGN	8) Pov Lawyer Gag	AGN	13) Youth Camp Regs	AGN
4) B-1 Bomber	AGN	9) Pub Trans Sub	FOR	14) Strip Mine Veto	FOR
5) Nerve Gas	AGN	10) EZ Voter Regis	FOR	15) Farm Bill Veto	FOR

Election Results

1974 general:	Ken Hechler (D), unopposed			($449)
1974 primary:	Ken Hechler (D), unopposed			
1972 general:	Ken Hechler (D)	100,600	(61%)	($20,249)
	Joe Neal (R)	64,242	(39%)	($36,362)

WISCONSIN

Wisconsin is a state of political anomalies. It spawned Bob LaFollette and the Progressive movement, and Joe McCarthy and his campaign against Communists in high places. Richard Nixon has carried Wisconsin, the state where the Republican Party was founded, three times, and yet the same state appears now to have become one of the nation's most Democratic at all levels. Wisconsin is heavily industrial, though it is also the nation's leading producer of dairy products; a heavily urban state, yet filled with lakes and forests.

Wisconsin probably owes its unusual politics to the German and Scandinavian immigrants who first settled it. Here, as in Minnesota and the Dakotas, the immigrants left a distinctive kind of political stamp. In all three states there developed—against the background of an overwhelming dominance by the Republican Party—a politics of almost radical economic reform and an isolationist foreign policy. The term "progressive" was coined in Wisconsin, and it was personified by Robert "Fighting Bob" LaFollette. Elected Governor in 1900, he completely revamped the state government before going on to the Senate in 1906. There LaFollette supported other insurgent reformers and voted against American entry into World War I. In 1924, he ran for President under the banner of the Progressive Party, and won 18% of the nation's votes—the best third-party showing in the last 60 years. La Follette's sons sustained the tradition of Wisconsin progressivism. Robert LaFollette, Jr., served in the Senate from 1925 to 1947, and Philip LaFollette was Governor of the state from 1935 to 1942. During the 1930s, the LaFollettes ran on the Progressive Party line in Wisconsin and dreamed of forming a national third party. But the onset of World War II destroyed the plans of the isolationist reformers. And in 1946, Senator LaFollette, busy with the congressional reorganization act in Washington, was upset in the 1946 Republican primary by one Joseph R. McCarthy.

How did the state produce politicians as different as LaFollette and McCarthy at roughly the same time? Part of the answer lies in the leanings of Wisconsin's ethnic groups, especially those of the largest—the German-Americans. These people supported both LaFollette isolationism and McCarthy anticommunism. As Samuel Lubell pointed out, much of the impetus behind postwar hard-line anticommunism came from those who never believed we should have fought World War II—a conflict which the United States, allied with Communists, waged against Germany. In any case, McCarthy was far less typical of Wisconsin than were the LaFollettes. "Tail-gunner Joe" won his first primary in an upset; moreover, his two victories in the general elections of 1946 and 1952 occurred in heavily Republican years, and only the first did he win by a large margin. If McCarthy had not died a broken man in 1957, after his censure by the Senate in 1954, he would probably have been defeated in the 1958 elections.

During the McCarthy years, conservative Republicans dominated Wisconsin elections more or less by default. The party's Progressive faction was dormant, and the Democrats had never been a factor in state politics. But in the early 1950s, a group of liberal Democrats—none of whom had even held public office—assumed control over the hulk of the party, and they laid plans to make it a majority force. A simple recitation of their names gives evidence of their success: Senator William Proxmire, Senator Gaylord Nelson, Governor Patrick Lucey, Congressmen Henry Reuss and Robert Kastenmeier. The group's first victory occurred in the 1957 special election to fill McCarthy's Senate vacancy. The Republican nominee was former Governor (1951–56) Walter Kohler; the Democratic choice was Proxmire, fresh from three electoral defeats in three consecutive gubernatorial campaigns. But in 1957, the booming economy of the mid-Eisenhower years had begun to turn sour: factories were laying off workers and the farm belt, burdened by surpluses, was beginning to revolt. Proxmire's previous campaigning finally paid off; he beat Kohler by a whopping 56–41 margin. Since then, the Democrats have won every Wisconsin Senate election, and they seem almost certain to continue to do so for at least the next ten years.

Proxmire was an unorthodox Senator from the start. He is the only Senator who runs four miles from his home to Capitol Hill every morning, the only one to stand, not sit, at his desk, and the first to have hair transplants (he was later joined by South Carolina's Strom Thurmond, who seldom votes with Proxmire, but is also a physical fitness fanatic). Almost as soon as he walked into the Senate chamber, he managed to irritate then all-powerful Senate Majority Leader Lyndon Johnson; sage insiders quickly wrote off Proxmire as an unreliable maverick and a political accident. During the 1960s, the Senator seemed to specialize in hopeless causes; in 1964, for example, he began an attack on Boeing supersonic transport (SST). But in the years that followed the Senate was undergoing more change than aficionados of its once arcane ways noticed. By 1971, Proxmire had finished off the SST once and for all.

But Proxmire did not stop with the SST. He has also proved nettlesome to big defense contractors, the Pentagon, and their assorted friends in other ways. Proxmire was the Senator who brought A. Ernest Fitzgerald to a congressional hearing, where the later-fired Pentagon analyst revealed the huge cost overruns run up by Lockheed in its production of the C-5A. It is not only the big issues that fascinate Proxmire; he has also led moves to cut down on the number of government limousines, and the number of enlisted men working as servants for generals and admirals. And the military are not his only targets; he has also taken to issuing press releases denouncing as a waste of the government's money federally financed studies of things like romantic love.

Even as Proxmire was thus irritating higher ups in the Senate and the executive branch, he was climbing in seniority. He is now the eighth-ranking Democrat on the Senate Appropriations Committee, and Chairman of its subcommittee with jurisdiction over HUD, space, science, and veterans programs. And in 1975, after the defeat of Arkansas's J. William Fulbright and the decision of Alabama's John Sparkman to succeed him as Chairman of the Foreign Relations Committee, Proxmire got Sparkman's old job as Chairman of the rather grandiosely titled Banking, Housing, and Urban Affairs Committee. That was a day long dreaded by the nation's banking and housing industries. Despite his long ago populist past, Sparkman had been more than sympathetic to the problems faced by the big moneyed interests in these areas; Proxmire, on the other hand, seems not to care at all how he gets along with the people his committee deals with. But if Proxmire is uninterested in continuing cozy relationships, he is also by no means the unrelenting foe of the big banks that former House Banking Chairman Wright Patman was. Proxmire is, after all, a graduate of the Harvard Business School.

In 1964, Proxmire won reelection by a margin smaller than expected; he had apparently been taking Wisconsin voters for granted. But by 1970, Proxmire had conclusively demonstrated his popularity. His opponent, a former general manager of the Milwaukee Bucks basketball team, attacked Proxmire for attacking the Pentagon. This was not especially good strategy in Wisconsin, which ranks 46th in per capita Defense Department outlays, with only Michigan, Oregon, Iowa, and West Virginia behind. Proxmire won 71% of the vote that year, and carried all 72 of the state's counties. His seat comes up in 1976, and he can be counted on to do just as well again, if indeed the weak Wisconsin Republican Party can find anyone to run against him at all.

Proxmire would like to be President, and probably he could win the primary in Wisconsin if he entered it—his last minute endorsement of George McGovern was a big factor in McGovern's win here in 1972. But he is not known all that well outside Wisconsin, and few professional politicians like or trust him, at least not enough to support him for the Presidency.

Before Proxmire's 1970 victory, the state's top Democratic vote getter was Senator Gaylord Nelson. When Nelson first became Governor of Wisconsin in 1959, he launched an attack against industrial polluters and sponsored programs to protect the environment. He thus anticipated by at least a decade the politics of ecology, back in the days when such programs were more appreciated by hunters and fishermen than by university students. Nelson was reelected Governor in 1960, and two years later unseated four term, 78-year-old Senator Alexander Wiley.

Nelson has not attracted quite as much publicity in the Senate as Proxmire, nor has he emerged as a maverick quite so often. Nevertheless, Nelson was one of the very first Senators to speak and vote against the Vietnam war, after Wayne Morse and Ernest Gruening voted against the Gulf of Tonkin Resolution. He has led a fight to cut drug prices and require use of generic, rather than trade names; he has battled against high postal rates that threaten to put heterodox magazines, of both right and left, out of business. As a member of the Labor and Public Welfare committee, he has a near perfect COPE record; as a member of the Finance Committee he has always supported liberal causes such as eliminating the oil depletion allowance.

Nelson is undoubtedly a talented man, but does not have the ambition that is so apparent in so many of his colleagues. He does not seek national publicity, and in 1972 when George McGovern was ready to name him his Vice Presidential candidate, he insisted he didn't want it. At home, Nelson's political position is entirely secure. He won reelection with 62% of the vote in 1968 and 62% in 1974.

Wisconsin, for the first time in its history, has Democrats occupying all the main statewide offices: Secretary of State, Treasurer, Attorney General, and of course Governor and Lieutenant Governor. The Governor is Patrick Lucey, part of the Madison-based liberals that took over the Democratic Party in the 1950s, elected Lieutenant Governor in 1962 and 1964, unsuccessful gubernatorial candidate in 1966, a winner in 1970 with 55% of the vote, and reelected with 54% in 1974. Lucey has been a fairly innovative Governor, pushing property tax reform (always a hot issue in Wisconsin, where property taxes are among the highest in the nation) and campaign finance reform. He was perhaps, a little disappointed in the size of his margin, particularly since it was won against a weak and virtually unknown Republican, former Madison Mayor William Dyke. But he did succeed in getting huge Democratic majorities in both houses of the legislature. Indeed, the Republican Party, once so dominant here, seems to be vanishing from existence. Its sole signs of life are young, moderate candidates like 6th district Congressman William Steiger and state Senator Thomas Petri, who made a favorable impression while losing overwhelmingly to Gaylord Nelson in 1974. But somehow this group seems to lack the depth of support and the feel for changes in public opinion which Proxmire, Nelson, Lucey, et al. had in the fifties.

As an index of Democratic dominance here now, consider the state's congressional delegation. In 1968, when Richard Nixon was elected President, the most noteworthy members of the Wisconsin delegation were Republicans: the wily Melvin Laird and John Byrnes, ranking minority member of Ways and Means. Republicans won seven of Wisconsin's ten House seats that year; today they hold only two of nine. The new Congressmen are liberal Democrats whose positions on issues are similar to those of Nelson and Proxmire (and George McGovern); these were not victories won by catering to the "center", but represented a major shift in the state's political ·attitudes.

Wisconsin has one of the nation's earliest—and sometimes its most important—presidential primaries, in late March. John Kennedy's win here over Hubert Humphrey was an indispensable step on his way to the 1960 nomination, and George McGovern's victory here in a crowded field in 1972—with 30% of the vote, when he was getting 3% in the national polls—showed that he was a serious candidate indeed. (Curiously, Humphrey, though he is from next door Minnesota, has shown disappointing strength here.) Wisconsin gave George Wallace surprisingly large support in 1964 and 1972, on both of which occasions the Alabamian zeroed in on the property tax issue. But it is worth remembering that Wallace's showing in 1972 was only 22% of the vote, though he was perhaps the best known of the candidates.

There is always some to-do (usually from losing candidates) about the fact that Wisconsin has no party registration, and so allows supposed Republicans to vote in Democratic primaries, and vice versa. But there is precious little evidence of mischievous crossovers, and the increasing proportion of voters who choose to participate in the Democratic rather than the Republican primary reflects only the fact that Republicans have seldom had a significant contest here and that an increasing percentage of people are voting Democratic in general elections. While Wisconsin's Democrats are inclined to favor candidates of the antiwar left (McCarthy in 1968, McGovern in 1972), its Republicans show no strain of the progressivism that once made the LaFollettes the dominant force; they voted happily for Richard Nixon. Indeed, the LaFollettes themselves now are solid Democrats; Douglas is now Secretary of State and Bronson, Attorney General, and both may eventually face off against Lieutenant Governor Martin Schreiber to see who will succeed Governor Lucey.

Census Data Pop. 4,417,933; 2.18% of U.S. total, 16th largest; Central city, 27%; suburban, 30%. Median family income, $10,065; 15th highest; families above $15,000: 20%; families below $3,000: 8%. Median years education, 12.1.

1974 Share of Federal Tax Burden $5,436,650,000; 2.03% of U.S. total, 16th largest.

1974 Share of Federal Outlays $4,047,285,000; 1.50% of U.S. total, 21st largest. Per capita federal spending, $916.

DOD	$381,776,000	34th (0.56%)		HEW	$2,021,442,000	13th (2.18%)
AEC	$3,859,000	24th (0.13%)		HUD	$13,445,000	23d (1.38%)
NASA	$3,073,000	28th (1.03%)		VA	$276,753,000	17th (2.02%)
DOT	$98,920,000	30th (1.17%)		EPA	$84,596,000	11th (2.69%)
DOC	$6.962,000	33d (0.43%)		RevS	$153,140,000	12th (2.52%)
DOI	$11,746,000	39th (0.48%)		Int.	$271,931,000	11th (1.32%)
USDA	$233,058,000	22d (1.87%)		Other	$486,584,000	

Economic Base Agriculture, notably dairy products, cattle, hogs and corn; machinery, especially engines and turbines; finance, insurance and real estate; food and kindred products, especially dairy products, and beverages; electrical equipment and supplies, especially electrical industrial apparatus; fabricated metal products; paper and allied products, especially paper mills, other than building paper.

Political Line-up Governor, Patrick J. Lucey (D). Senators, William Proxmire (D) and Gaylord Nelson (D). Representatives, 9 (7 D and 2 R). State Senate (18 D, 13 R and 2 vac.); State Assembly (63 D and 36 R).

The Voters

Registration No statewide registration.
Median voting age 43.
Employment profile White collar, 43%. Blue collar, 37%. Service, 14%. Farm, 6%.
Ethnic groups Black, 3%. Total foreign stock, 17%. Germany, 5%; Poland, 2%; Norway, 1%.

Presidential vote

1972	Nixon (R)	....	989,430	(55%)
	McGovern (D)	....	810,174	(45%)

1968	Nixon (R)	809,997	(48%)
	Humphrey (D)	748,804	(44%)
	Wallace (AI)	127,835	(8%)

1972 Democratic Presidential Primary

McGovern	333,528	(30%)
Wallace	248,676	(22%)
Humphrey	233,748	(21%)
Muskie	115,811	(10%)
Jackson	88,068	(8%)
Lindsay	75,579	(7%)
others	33,174	(2%)

1972 Republican Presidential Primary

Nixon	277,601	(97%)
others	8,843	(3%)

Sen. William Proxmire (D) Elected Aug. 1957, seat up 1976; b. Nov. 11, 1915, Lake Forest, Ill.; home, Madison; Yale U., B.A. 1938, Harvard U., M.B.A. 1940, M.P.A. 1948; Episcopalian.

Career Wis. House of Reps., 1951; Dem. nominee for Gov., 1952, 1954, 1956; Pres., Artcraft Press, 1953–57.

Offices 5241 DSOB, 202-224-5653. Also Rm. 612, 30 W. Mifflin St., Madison 53703, 608-252-5338, and Rm. 344, Fed. Bldg., Milwaukee 53202, 414-272-0388.

Committees

Banking, Housing and Urban Affairs (Chairman). Subcommittees: Financial Institutions; Housing and Urban Affairs; International Finance; Oversight (Chairman); Securities.

Appropriations (8th). Subcommittees: Agriculture and Related Agencies; Defense; Foreign Operations; HUD and Independent Agencies (Chairman).

Joint Economic Committee (3d, Senate Side). Subcommittees: Consumer Economics; Economic Growth; Economic Progress; Fiscal Policy; Priorities and Economy in Government (Chairman).

Group Ratings

	ADA	COPE	LWV	RIPON	NFU	LCV	CFA	NAB	NSI	ACA
1974	81	82	80	70	88	86	100	75	10	26
1973	85	82	80	44	82	–	85	–	–	28
1972	75	70	82	72	80	90	100	67	0	18

Key Votes

1) No-Knock	AGN	8) Gov Abortn Aid	AGN	15) Consumer Prot Agy	FOR
2) Busing	AGN	9) Cut Mil Brass	FOR	16) Forced Psych Tests	AGN
3) No Fault	FOR	10) Gov Limousine	AGN	17) Fed Campaign Subs	FOR
4) F-111	AGN	11) RR Featherbed	FOR	18) Rhod Chrome Ban	FOR
5) Death Penalty	AGN	12) Handgun License	AGN	19) Open Legis Meetings	FOR
6) Foreign Aid	AGN	13) Less Troop Abrd	FOR	20) Strikers Food Stmps	FOR
7) Filibuster	AGN	14) Resume Turk Aid	AGN	21) Gov Info Disclosure	FOR

Election Results

1970 general:	William Proxmire (D)	948,445	(71%)
	John E. Erickson (R)	381,297	(29%)
1970 primary:	William Proxmire (D), unopposed		
1964 general:	William Proxmire (D)	892,013	(53%)
	Wilbur N. Renk (R)	780,116	(47%)

Sen. Gaylord Nelson (D) Elected 1962, seat up 1980; b. June 4, 1916, Clear Lake; home, Madison; San Jose St. Col., B.A. 1939, U. of Wis., LL.B. 1942; Methodist.

Career Army, WWII; Practicing atty., 1946–58; Wis. Senate, 1948–58; Gov. of Wis., 1958–62.

Offices 221 RSOB, 202-224-5323. Also 517 E. Wisconsin Ave., Rm. 570, Milwaukee 53202, 414-224-3965.

Committees

Finance (6th). Subcommittees: International Trade; Private Pension Plans (Chairman); Revenue Sharing; Supplemental Security Income.

Labor and Public Welfare (5th). Subcommittees: Aging; Alcoholism and Narcotics; Children and Youth; Employment, Poverty, and Migratory Labor (Chairman); Health; Labor; Special Subcommittee on Arts and Humanities; Special Subcommittee on Human Resources.

Group Ratings

	ADA	COPE	LWV	RIPON	NFU	LCV	CFA	NAB	NSI	ACA
1974	100	82	88	45	100	79	100	50	0	6
1973	95	82	100	60	100	–	100	–	–	4
1972	95	90	100	72	90	100	100	18	0	9

Key Votes

1) No-Knock	AGN	8) Gov Abortn Aid	FOR	15) Consumer Prot Agy	FOR
2) Busing	FOR	9) Cut Mil Brass	FOR	16) Forced Psych Tests	AGN
3) No Fault	FOR	10) Gov Limousine	AGN	17) Fed Campaign Subs	FOR
4) F-111	AGN	11) RR Featherbed	FOR	18) Rhod Chrome Ban	FOR
5) Death Penalty	ABS	12) Handgun License	ABS	19) Open Legis Meetings	FOR
6) Foreign Aid	AGN	13) Less Troop Abrd	FOR	20) Strikers Food Stmps	FOR
7) Filibuster	ABS	14) Resume Turk Aid	AGN	21) Gov Info Disclosure	FOR

Election Results

1974 general:	Gaylord A. Nelson (D)	740,700	(62%)	($247,555)
	Thomas E. Petri (R)	429,327	(36%)	($80,590)
	Gerald L. McFarren (AI)	24,003	(2%)	(NA)
1974 primary:	Gaylord A. Nelson (D), unopposed			
1968 general:	Gaylord A. Nelson (D)	1,020,931	(62%)	
	Jerris Leonard (R)	633,910	(38%)	

Gov. Patrick J. Lucey (D) Elected 1970, term expires Jan. 1979; b. Mar. 21, 1918, LaCrosse; St. Thomas Col., U. of Wis., B.A.

Career Army, WWII; Dairy farm mgr.; Wis. House of Reps., 1949–51; Candidate for U.S. House of Reps., 1950; Campaign Mgr., Thomas Fairchild for U.S. Senate, 1952, James Doyle for Gov., 1954, William Proxmire for U.S. Senate, 1957; Chm., Wis. Dem. Party, 1957–63; Lt. Gov. of Wis., 1965–67; Dem. nominee for Gov., 1966.

Offices 115 East, State Capitol, Madison 53702, 608-266-1212.

Election Results

1974 general:	Patrick J. Lucey (D)	628,639	(54%)
	William D. Dyke (R)	497,195	(43%)
	William H. Upham (AI)	33,528	(3%)

1974 primary:	Patrick J. Lucey (D)	259,001	(78%)
	Edmond Hou-Seye (D)	72,113	(22%)
1970 general:	Patrick J. Lucey (D)	728,403	(55%)
	Jack B. Olson (R)	602,617	(45%)

◆ ◆ ◆ ◆ ◆

FIRST DISTRICT

Until the impeachment crisis made celebrities of many previously obscure congressmen, there was little question which member of the House was consistently churning out the most headlines and solid news stories. He was not Speaker Carl Albert or Minority Leader John Rhodes, or even Chairman Wayne Hays of the House Administration Committee; it was a 36-year-old third-term Democrat from the 1st district of Wisconsin named Les Aspin. He is not chairman of any committee or subcommittee, far from it; nor can he command a majority on the committee on which he serves, Armed Services. But press releases from his office keep coming out day after day, and they get printed—if not on the front page, at least on inside pages—because Aspin generates solid copy. Most of his revelations concern the Pentagon; how desk-bound Air Force generals get flight pay, how a well connected big contractor gets bailed out by friends in uniform, how cost overruns are piled up and readily approved by the brass.

Aspin has done more than generate news; on some occasions, at least, he has got results. On the flight pay issue, Aspin and New York's Otis Pike defeated then Chairman Edward Hebert on the floor of the House, and over Hebert's opposition Aspin was able in 1973 to get the House to vote to cut $950 million out of the Pentagon budget. And Aspin does not confine himself totally to military issues. He was a critic of the Alaska pipeline and a leader of House efforts to promote the construction of a pipeline through Canada to the Midwest. He has also spoken out on school bus safety, industrial polluters, and food and drug contamination.

But it is on defense that he has made his biggest name, and indeed he has been so successful that he may actually have hurt his own cause. His stinging triumphs over Herbert on the floor may have convinced a crucial number of Representatives to vote against the Louisianan for Chairman in 1975—with the result that Illinois's Mel Price now heads Armed Services. Price differs little from Hebert on substance, but he is better liked and more trusted by House Democrats (in part because he is a solid liberal on domestic issues) and in 1975 he was able to make enough cuts in the Pentagon budget requests that the demands by Aspin and others for further cuts fell flat. (Some of Price's budget slashes were purely cosmetic, e.g., deletion of money for military aid to South Vietnam after Saigon had been renamed Ho Chi Minh City.) But Aspin's presence on the Committee and his continuing, dogged criticism of the Pentagon does make a difference, and he is now clearly a man to be reckoned with.

How does Aspin do it? For one thing, he knows his technical stuff. Before he turned 30, Aspin had served as a staff aide to Chairman Walter Heller of the Council of Economic Advisors and to Defense Secretary Robert McNamara. He is better equipped than most Pentagon critics to ferret out examples of waste and mismanagement, and he has built a small staff which does little else. Politically, Aspin is also something of a wunderkind. While he was in his twenties he served as an aide to Senator William Proxmire and in 1968, while employed at the Pentagon, he worked on the Wisconsin primary campaign of Lyndon Johnson. Aspin reportedly told the Administration that the situation was hopeless—an analysis that was probably as unwelcome as it was accurate.

Aspin's constituency is Wisconsin's 1st district, the southeast corner of the state. The district contains a fairly good microcosm of Wisconsin as a whole. In the eastern part of the 1st, along Lake Michigan, are the industrial cities of Racine and Kenosha, both prone to high unemployment in times of recession. Farther inland is the Republican stronghold of Walworth County, an area of small farms around the posh resort of Lake Geneva. To the west are the cities of Janesville and Beloit; like Racine and Kenosha, these are predominantly industrial, but they are smaller and have much less pronounced ethnic ties. Here the blue collar workers are usually Yankees or German-Americans from the farm counties of southern Wisconsin; these towns ordinarily produce Republican majorities.

When Aspin first ran in 1970, the 1st was the state's most marginal congressional district. During the 1960s, no one won an election here with more than 53% of the vote. For most of that decade, aside from the two years after 1964, the district was represented by Republican Henry Schadeberg, a Congregationalist minister of conservative bent. Schadeberg voted against measures like the Civil Rights Act of 1968, higher minimum wages, and the Peace Corps. In 1970, with rising unemployment, Schadeberg attracted formidable opposition; in the Democratic primary Aspin won by only 20 votes over Douglas LaFollette (now Wisconsin Secretary of State).

The general election was another story. Aspin attacked Schadeberg's record on the Vietnam war and pollution issues. But the challenger spent the most time talking about his academic speciality: economics, with heavy emphasis on unemployment. Schadeberg's response was weak: "I haven't noticed many people out of work." But the statistics and the unemployment lines belied the Congressman's assessment. Aspin won with an astounding 61% of the vote—a figure that made Schadeberg the most soundly defeated House incumbent in recent years.

Aspin was a Republican target in 1972, when his opponent charged that his support of emission control standards for automobiles was endangering people's jobs at the American Motors assembly plant in Kenosha. But Aspin won with 65% of the vote that year and with 71% in 1974. His political future in the 1st seems secure, and but for the stranglehold that William Proxmire and Gaylord Nelson have on Wisconsin's two Senate seats, he might well be a strong Senate candidate. There is another possible avenue, however, which may have crossed his mind; there is already a precedent for choosing a well-informed and canny Wisconsin Congressman as Secretary of Defense.

Census Data Pop. 490,817. Central city, 35%; suburban, 23%. Median family income, $10,478; families above $15,000: 20%; families below $3,000: 6%. Median years education, 12.1.

The Voters

Median voting age 42.
Employment profile White collar, 41%. Blue collar, 42%. Service, 14%. Farm, 3%.
Ethnic groups Black, 3%. Spanish, 2%. Total foreign stock, 18%. Germany, 4%; Italy, 2%; Poland, 1%.

Presidential vote

1972	Nixon (R)	111,281	(59%)
	McGovern (D)	77,321	(41%)
1968	Nixon (R)	86,577	(48%)
	Humphrey (D)	77,191	(43%)
	Wallace (AI)	16,550	(9%)

Rep. Les Aspin (D) Elected 1970; b. July 21, 1938, Milwaukee; home, Racine; Yale U., B.A. 1960, Oxford U., M.A. 1962, MIT, Ph.D., 1965; United Church of Christ.

Career Staff Asst. to U.S. Sen. William Proxmire, 1960; Staff Asst. to Chm. Walter Heller, Pres. Cncl. of Econ. Advisers, 1963; Army, 1966–68; Asst. Prof. of Economics, Marquette U., 1969–70.

Offices 439 CHOB, 202-225-3031. Also Rm. 200, 603 Main St., Racine 52403, 414-632-8194.

Committees

Armed Services (18th). Subcommittees: Military Compensation; Military Personnel.

Government Operations (29th). Subcommittees: Government Activities and Transportation; Manpower and Housing.

Group Ratings

	ADA	COPE	LWV	RIPON	NFU	LCV	CFA	NAB	NSI	ACA
1974	96	100	100	80	86	79	92	20	0	7
1973	92	90	92	79	100	94	100	–	–	12
1972	94	82	100	80	86	86	50	8	0	0

Key Votes

1) Foreign Aid	AGN	6) Gov Abortn Aid	AGN	11) Pub Cong Election $	FOR
2) Busing	FOR	7) Coed Phys Ed	AGN	12) Turkish Arms Cutoff	ABS
3) ABM	AGN	8) Pov Lawyer Gag	AGN	13) Youth Camp Regs	FOR
4) B-1 Bomber	AGN	9) Pub Trans Sub	FOR	14) Strip Mine Veto	AGN
5) Nerve Gas	AGN	10) EZ Voter Regis	FOR	15) Farm Bill Veto	AGN

Election Results

1974 general:	Les Aspin (D)	81,902	(70%)	($30,443)
	Leonard W. Smith (R)	34,288	(30%)	($7,629)
1974 primary:	Les Aspin (D), unopposed			
1972 general:	Les Aspin (D)	122,973	(65%)	($70,326)
	Merrill E. Stalbaum (R)	66,665	(35%)	($12,062)

♦ ♦ ♦ ♦ ♦

SECOND DISTRICT

Madison (pop. 173,000) is Wisconsin's second largest city and the state capital. Of more significance politically, Madison is one of the nation's most important university communities —home of the University of Wisconsin and its 30,000 students. The University was a factor in Wisconsin politics long before the current interest in student votes. Back in 1900, Robert LaFollette, a Madison native, was elected Governor; once in office, he called on professors from the University to set up the Wisconsin Tax Commission and to draft a state workmen's compensation law—both first in the nation. Wisconsin's progressive movement, including the *Progressive* magazine, which is published in Madison, has always relied heavily on the University community. Consequently, Madison has always been the major center of Wisconsin liberalism.

But by the 1950s, after Joe McCarthy had defeated Senator Robert LaFollette, Jr., the original Progressive movement had petered out almost completely. Though Madison stayed with the LaFollettes' odyssey into the Progressive Party and back again into Republican ranks, the Wisconsin GOP by the 1950s was firmly in the hands of conservatives. So Madison became the center of the rising liberal movement that resuscitated the Democratic Party. Today, the city remains the home base of Senators William Proxmire and Gaylord Nelson and Governor Patrick Lucey. And in the spring of 1973, Madison elected as Mayor 28-year-old Paul Soglin, who called himself a "mellowed radical." Finally, the Madison *Capital Times,* one of two local newspapers, is one of the most liberal in the country.

Madison is the center of Wisconsin's 2d congressional district, with Madison and surrounding Dane County casting 62% of the district's votes. The history of Madison's representation in the House runs a rough parallel to the politics of the state as a whole. During the 1950s, its Congressman was Glenn Davis, at that time a strong supporter of Joe McCarthy and later Congressman from the 9th district until his defeat. The Republicans failed to hold the seat in 1958 when a Democratic tide saw Senator William Proxmire elected to a full term and Gaylord Nelson win his first gubernatorial race. In the same year, liberal Democrat Robert Kastenmeier captured the House seat by a narrow margin. In Washington, Kastenmeier did not behave like a typical freshman willing to pay any price for reelection. Instead, he quickly established himself as one of the most liberal members of the House. His original staff included such people as Marcus Raskin—later an aide to President Kennedy, head of the leftish Institute for Policy Studies, and a co-defendant in the Spock-Coffin trial.

In 1960 and 1962, Kastenmeier won reelection with only thin majorities. He was unable to carry the Milwaukee suburbs of Waukesha County, then in the district, and the dairy country around Madison was always less progressive than the capital city. But the 1963 redistricting removed Waukesha from the district, and Kastenmeier won his first big majority in the 1964 Johnson landslide. Since then, he has been reelected easily. In 1970 and 1972, he won 68% of the vote; in 1974, 65%.

The student vote here has of course helped Kastenmeier who was one of the very first congressional opponents of the Vietnam war. But another factor in the Congressman's growing strength is the slow leftward trend in both Madison and the surrounding agricultural countryside—a movement that is perceptible in the entire Upper Midwest. In 1972, George McGovern carried the 2d district in both the primary and the general election; in fact, he took a larger percentage of the votes here than Hubert Humphrey did in 1968.

Until 1974, Kastenmeier was a Congressman little known outside his district, climbing slowly to a high seniority position on the House Judiciary Committee. Suddenly, the impeachment hearings focused national attention on the Committee and its members. Kastenmeier, as fourth-ranking Democrat, was considered the most senior absolutely sure vote for impeachment, back in those days when it was not clear that the Congress, like the country, was desperately eager to get rid of what it had become convinced was our first criminal President. Kastenmeier's rather languid speaking style may have bothered some of those most strongly partial to his position; but he did uphold the pro-impeachment cause at every stage of the battle. And if he did not seem as militant as some of his constituents would have liked, he was the member who insisted that each article of impeachment be voted on separately, after evidence pertaining to it was discussed. Some of the Republicans and conservative Democrats favoring impeachment had wanted to wait and hold all the roll calls at the end, as if somehow people wouldn't notice; Kastenmeier's firm stance insured an orderly and sensible procedure which tied together members' interpretation of the facts and their action on them.

Census Data Pop. 490,941. Central city, 35%; suburban, 24%. Median family income, $10,397; families above $15,000: 23%; families below $3,000: 7%. Median years education, 12.4.

The Voters

Median voting age 40.
Employment profile White collar, 49%. Blue collar, 28%. Service, 14%. Farm, 9%.
Ethnic groups Total foreign stock, 13%. Germany, 4%; Norway, 2%.

Presidential vote

1972	Nixon (R)	108,506	(49%)
	McGovern (D)	111,508	(51%)
1968	Nixon (R)	84,220	(46%)
	Humphrey (D)	89,620	(49%)
	Wallace (AI)	9,170	(5%)

Rep. Robert W. Kastenmeier (D) Elected 1958; b. Jan. 24, 1924, Beaver Dam; home, Sun Prairie; U. of Wis., LL.B. 1952.

Career Practicing atty., 1952–58.

Offices 2232 RHOB, 202-225-2906. Also 119 Monona Ave., Madison 53703, 608-252-5206.

Committees

Interior and Insular Affairs (6th). Subcommittees: National Parks and Recreation; Territorial and Insular Affairs.

Judiciary (3d). Subcommittees: Courts, Civil Liberties, and the Administration of Justice (Chairman).

Group Ratings

	ADA	COPE	LWV	RIPON	NFU	LCV	CFA	NAB	NSI	ACA
1974	95	89	92	63	92	94	85	20	0	0
1973	100	82	92	73	100	100	100	–	–	20
1972	100	91	92	75	86	93	50	8	0	9

Key Votes

1) Foreign Aid	AGN	6) Gov Abortn Aid	AGN	11) Pub Cong Election $	FOR
2) Busing	FOR	7) Coed Phys Ed	FOR	12) Turkish Arms Cutoff	FOR
3) ABM	AGN	8) Pov Lawyer Gag	AGN	13) Youth Camp Regs	FOR
4) B-1 Bomber	AGN	9) Pub Trans Sub	FOR	14) Strip Mine Veto	AGN
5) Nerve Gas	AGN	10) EZ Voter Regis	ABS	15) Farm Bill Veto	AGN

Election Results

1974 general:	Robert W. Kastenmeier (D)	93,561	(65%)	($17,663)
	Elizabeth T. Miller (R)	50,890	(35%)	($16,658)
1974 primary:	Robert W. Kastenmeier (D), unopposed			
1972 general:	Robert W. Kastenmeier (D)	148,136	(68%)	($24,997)
	J. Michael Kelly (R)	68,167	(32%)	($23,080)

◆ ◆ ◆ ◆ ◆

THIRD DISTRICT

The 3d district of Wisconsin occupies the western and southwestern parts of the state. This is rolling farmland, stretching some 200 miles along the Mississippi and St. Croix Rivers. The countryside here probably looks little different from when it first attracted white settlers in the 1840s and 1850s—in the south is gentle, hilly dairy land; in the north, more forests. The district has only two significant urban centers, LaCrosse (pop. 51,000) and Eau Claire (pop. 44,000), both with names that recall the French chevaliers who came paddling down the Mississippi and St. Croix in the seventeenth century. The 3d of Wisconsin is one of the nation's premier dairy districts; its Congressman inevitably finds himself concerned with the arcane details of milk marketing regulations and import restrictions on Dutch and Swiss cheese.

The 3d is one of those Upper Midwest districts that trended Democratic even in the 1972 presidential election, and then ousted a longtime Republican Congressman in 1974. The incumbent was Vernon Thomson, 69 years old, a conservative Republican elected Governor in 1956, defeated by Gaylord Nelson in 1958, and elected to Congress in 1960. Thomson seemed to have a safe Republican seat sewed up, and his voting record proceeded accordingly: a steady adherence to the conservative orthodoxy of Republican leaders like Charles Halleck, Gerald Ford, and John Rhodes.

But as the sixties turned to seventies, something unexpected began happening in the 3d district. Unemployment became a serious problem, especially in traditionally Republican La Crosse. On the four campuses of the Wisconsin State University system in the district, there were 23,000 students, a full 8% of the district's eligible voters in 1972 when they were enfranchised; they were upset by the Vietnam war and generally unsympathetic to the party of Richard Nixon. Little did the Republican legislators who located the campuses in the Wisconsin boondocks dream that in so doing thousands of Democratic votes were being planted in the fertile political soil of the Upper Midwest. And while the Nixon Administration, supported by votes from Thomson, poured money into Sun Belt defense contractors like Lockheed and Litton, this area received little from the federal treasury. Moreover, Wisconsin voters, accustomed to clean government, were especially upset about Watergate—particularly, one might guess, with the fetid Caribbean aura, with its Cuban burglars and laundered Mexican money.

So after years of easy reelection, Thomson was held to 55% of the vote in 1970 and 1972. Several Democrats scrapped for the nomination to oppose him in the 1974 election. The winner was Assistant House Majority Leader Al Baldus, the more liberal of the major contenders. Baldus was a colorless campaigner, but carried all the counties in the northern part of the district and LaCrosse as well for a 52–48 victory. After his defeat, Thomson was named a member of the new Federal Election Commission by Minority Leader Rhodes; Baldus sits on the Agriculture and Small Business Committees. Odds favor the reelection of the Democrat in 1976.

Census Data Pop. 491,034. Central city, 10%; suburban, 6%. Median family income, $8,485; families above $15,000: 14%; families below $3,000: 12%. Median years education, 12.1.

The Voters

Median voting age 45.
Employment profile White collar, 37%. Blue collar, 33%. Service, 15%. Farm, 15%.
Ethnic groups Total foreign stock, 13%. Norway, Germany, 4% each; Sweden, 1%.

Presidential vote

1972	Nixon (R)	122,445	(59%)
	McGovern (D)	85,348	(41%)
1968	Nixon (R)	102,105	(53%)
	Humphrey (D)	77,099	(40%)
	Wallace (AI)	12,656	(7%)

Rep. Alvin Baldus (D) Elected 1974; b. Apr. 27, 1927, Hancock County, Ia.; home, Menomonie; Austin Jr. Col., A.A. 1958.

Career Merchant Marine, WWII; Army, Korea; Farm machinery salesman, 1953–63; Investment broker, Investors Diversified Services, 1963–74; Wis. House of Reps., 1966–74, Asst. Maj. Floor Ldr., 1972.

Offices 509 CHOB, 202-225-5506. Also 510 S. Barstow St., Fed. Bldg., Rm. 16, Eau Claire 54701, 715-835-4671.

Committees

Agriculture (18th). Subcommittees: Conservation and Credit; Dairy and Poultry; Family Farms and Rural Development.

Small Business (22d). Subcommittees: Activities of Regulatory Agencies; SBA Oversight and Minority Enterprise.

Group Ratings: Newly Elected

Key Votes

1) Foreign Aid	AGN	6) Gov Abortn Aid	NE	11) Pub Cong Election $	NE
2) Busing	NE	7) Coed Phys Ed	FOR	12) Turkish Arms Cutoff	NE
3) ABM	NE	8) Pov Lawyer Gag	NE	13) Youth Camp Regs	FOR
4) B-1 Bomber	AGN	9) Pub Trans Sub	NE	14) Strip Mine Veto	AGN
5) Nerve Gas	NE	10) EZ Voter Regis	NE	15) Farm Bill Veto	AGN

Election Results

1974 general:	Alvin Baldus (D)	76,668	(52%)	($72,958)
	Vernon W. Thomson (R)	71,171	(48%)	($87,902)
1974 primary:	Alvin Baldus (D)	14,826	(40%)	
	Theodore Fetting (D)	13,370	(36%)	
	Two others (D)	8,856	(24%)	

◆ ◆ ◆ ◆

FOURTH DISTRICT

The 4th district of Wisconsin is the south side of Milwaukee and the Milwaukee County suburbs to the south and west. The Milwaukee River splits the city into two distinct sections. Traditionally, the north side has been German; today, it includes practically all of Milwaukee's medium-sized black community. Like all of Wisconsin, the south side has large numbers of German-Americans, but since the days of industrial growth at the turn of the century, south side Milwaukee has been the Polish part of town. Today, the south remains all white and heavily Polish, while the suburbs to the south are filled mainly with the newly prosperous blue and white collar descendants of the original Polish immigrants. The western suburbs, Wauwatosa and West Allis, are more German and more white collar.

Numerous magazine articles have characterized the south side as the home of the white backlash and a stronghold of George Wallace. It is true that Wallace nearly carried the district in the 1964 presidential primary, but the Alabamian's showing was as much a revolt against the unpopular tax program of the Democratic Governor, President Johnson's stand-in, as anything else. In 1968, the 4th district actually cast just under 10% of its votes for Wallace—far less than he got in many other northern districts or the nation as a whole. In the 1972 presidential primary, Wallace failed to carry the 4th; instead, George McGovern surprised virtually everybody and won here. Much of the credit for the triumph goes to 27-year-old Carl Wagner, described by writer Hunter Thompson as "one of the best field organizers in the business." McGovern's performance in the 4th marked a critical point in the primary. The South Dakotan demonstrated that he could carry even solid blue collar areas; meanwhile, the fact that Edmund Muskie lost one of the nation's most heavily Polish-American districts pretty well finished his campaign.

The south side had a Democratic tradition long before the rest of Wisconsin developed one. In fact, its current Congressman, Clement Zablocki, was first elected nearly 30 years ago, in 1948. Most of Zablocki's attitudes seem closer to those held by machine Democrats from cities like

Chicago and Philadelphia than to those belonging to the ideological liberals in the rest of the Wisconsin delegation. For example, he is the only Wisconsin Democrat to have supported the Vietnam policies of the Johnson and Nixon Administrations. And his approach to social programs, one that he presumably shares with his constituency, has been considerably more conservative.

Thanks to his abundant seniority, Zablocki is the number two Democrat on the House International Relations Committee. He first joined that unit when many of his Polish-American constituents felt convinced, understandably but unrealistically, that the United States should liberate Poland and the other countries of Eastern Europe from Soviet domination. Zablocki, not surprisingly, has a rather hawkish and hardline anti-communist record. But he also showed considerable flexibility and legislative skill in handling the war powers legislation, in which he successfully pushed through the House a bill with tough limitations on presidential warmaking powers. Zablocki is not a particularly talented speaker, but he does seem to be a competent legislative work horse. It is possible, if International Relations Chairman Thomas (Doc) Morgan of Pennsylvania has as much trouble as the 1974 primary results suggest, that Zablocki will become Chairman of International Relations soon.

Census Data Pop. 490,690. Central city, 46%; suburban, 54%. Median family income, $11,285; families above $15,000: 24%; families below $3,000: 5%. Median years education, 12.1.

The Voters

Median voting age 44.
Employment profile White collar, 47%. Blue collar, 40%. Service, 13%. Farm, –%.
Ethnic groups Spanish, 2%. Total foreign stock, 24%. Germany, Poland, 6% each; Austria, 1%.

Presidential vote

1972	Nixon (R)	96,755	(49%)
	McGovern (D)	99,537	(51%)
1968	Nixon (R)	74,783	(39%)
	Humphrey (D)	100,446	(52%)
	Wallace (AI)	18,968	(10%)

Rep. Clement J. Zablocki (D) Elected 1948; b. Nov. 18, 1912, Milwaukee; home, Milwaukee; Marquette U., Ph.B. 1936; Catholic.

Career Organist and choir dir., 1932–48; High school teacher, 1938–40; Wis. Senate, 1942–48.

Offices 2184 RHOB, 202-225-4572. Also 1401 W. Lincoln Ave., Milwaukee 53215, 414-383-4000.

Committees

International Relations (2d). Subcommittees: International Security and Scientific Affairs (Chairman); Oversight.

Group Ratings

	ADA	COPE	LWV	RIPON	NFU	LCV	CFA	NAB	NSI	ACA
1974	50	91	91	15	93	69	83	17	60	13
1973	56	82	75	60	100	47	88	–	–	22
1972	44	91	75	63	83	33	50	17	100	26

Key Votes

1) Foreign Aid	FOR	6) Gov Abortn Aid	AGN	11) Pub Cong Election $	FOR
2) Busing	AGN	7) Coed Phys Ed	AGN	12) Turkish Arms Cutoff	AGN
3) ABM	AGN	8) Pov Lawyer Gag	AGN	13) Youth Camp Regs	FOR
4) B-1 Bomber	FOR	9) Pub Trans Sub	FOR	14) Strip Mine Veto	AGN
5) Nerve Gas	AGN	10) EZ Voter Regis	FOR	15) Farm Bill Veto	AGN

Election Results

1974 general:	Clement J. Zablocki (D)	84,768	(72%)	($9,852)
	Lewis D. Collison (R)	27,818	(24%)	($5,986)
	Herbert O. Jahnke (AI)	4,404	(4%)	($184)
1974 primary:	Clement J. Zablocki (D), unopposed			
1972 general:	Clement J. Zablocki (D)	149,078	(77%)	($15,871)
	Phillip D. Mrozinski (R)	45,003	(23%)	($375)

◆ ◆ ◆ ◆ ◆

FIFTH DISTRICT

The 5th congressional district of Wisconsin is made up of the north side of Milwaukee, from the center of town north to the city limits. The north side is the traditionally German half of Milwaukee, with the gemütlichkeit atmosphere of old Milwaukee now, thanks to beer ads, part of the nation's heritage. For years Milwaukee has been famous for its beer, and today, as the ads remind us, it is the home of Schlitz, Miller's, Pabst, Blatz, and others. Not as well known is that for years Milwaukee supported its own unique kind of politics, which had roots deep in the German tradition. During the years when Robert LaFollette and his progressive Republicans were ruling the rest of Wisconsin, Milwaukee was electing a series of Socialist Party Mayors and Congressmen. The most notable among them was Victor Berger, who served in the House from 1911 to 1913 and again from 1923 to 1929.

After the 1918 and 1920 elections, Berger was denied his seat because of his opposition to American entry into World War I. For those who think that prosecution of antiwar dissenters is only a recent phenomenon in the United States, it should be remembered that in 1919 Berger was sentenced to 20 years in prison for having written antiwar articles. The prosecution was brought under the Wilson Administration and, after the conviction was reversed by the Supreme Court, all charges were dropped by the "return to normalcy" Harding Administration. It is a measure of the strength of German Milwaukee's opposition to World War I that Berger was reelected to Congress while his case was on appeal and after he had been denied his seat.

Today, many descendants of the first German immigrants have left the north side for the suburbs, and some of them have been replaced by blacks from the rural South. In 1970, some 21% of the 5th's population was black, which may not seem an especially high figure, but still represents 82% of the black population of the entire state. In the middle sixties, Milwaukee was the scene of some racial turbulence, as blacks led by Father James Groppi and others protested the City Council's refusal to enact an open housing ordinance. But the militants never prevailed over the opposition of Mayor Henry Maier; and Milwaukee probably has a better racial situation than most American cities.

Since the 1954 election, the 5th has been represented in the House by Henry Reuss, member of an aristocratic Milwaukee German family. Reuss is one of the most senior and intellectually most distinguished liberals in the House, and is now Chairman of the House Banking and Currency Committee.

That was not a position that Reuss was expected to have as the 1974 election returns came in. His seniority had already given him some high positions; he had been, for example, Chairman of the International Finances Subcommittee, in which capacity he was probably the leading congressional expert on such mysterious matters as the balance of payments, the gold market, and the ups and downs of the various European and Asian currencies and the American dollar.

Then in the 93d Congress, Reuss had been Chairman of the Government Operations Subcommittee on Conservation and Natural Resources. Here Reuss occupied an excellent position to monitor government environmental programs, and his record in the field was one that made him one of the congressional heroes of the ecology movement. It was Reuss, for example, who unearthed the 1899 Refuse Act, which baldly prohibits the dumping of pollutants in interstate waterways. The ancient statute had been completely forgotten, but Reuss persuaded the government to revive it, and the law is now a major weapon against industrial polluters.

But all these achievements would not have made Reuss Banking Chairman in the ordinary way these things have worked in Congress the last 60 years—when seniority, not talent, has been the sole criterion for advancement. In 1974, Reuss was only the fourth-ranking Democrat on the Banking Committee, behind 81-year-old Wright Patman of Texas and septuagenarians William Barrett of Pennsylvania and Leonor Sullivan of Missouri. But the 75 new freshmen elected in 1974 were ready for a change. Patman, they discovered when he spoke before their freshman caucus, had passed his prime, and seemed to have difficulty following a line of thought. Barrett was considered, to put it bluntly, not very bright, and Sullivan, while serving quite adequately as Chairman of the Merchant Marine and Fisheries Committee, was so disinclined to challenge the seniority rule that it seemed to make no sense to promote her.

Reuss, on the other hand, was eager for the Chairmanship; he only held out against announcing for it until he was sure he had enough votes to win. In December 1974, the Democratic Steering committee voted to oust Patman and install Reuss, and the full Democratic Caucus—after some machinations we need not consider in detail—concurred. Some critics of the freshmen (and of Reuss) have argued that the whole exercises was in vain, or even wrongheaded. Wasn't Patman, they said, the populist Chairman, the opponent of the big banks whose sentiments the freshmen generally shared? Perhaps, though not entirely. Patman had the kind of distrust of banks of an old farmer who stows his money under the mattress; Reuss, while he believes in stringent regulation and has no illusions that bankers have eleemosynary motives, thinks banks are an integral and useful part of the economy. For most freshmen, the one view was old fashioned and silly, the other sophisticated and attractive. Moreover, the freshmen simply did not want the public to be treated to the vision of Patman as the main House spokesman on such important matters as wage and price controls or housing—over which Banking and Currency has jurisdiction. And they were disturbed by reports that Patman had run his committee arbitrarily—though at the same time not very well, since he often could not get a majority of committee members behind his policies.

Reuss does not seem likely to have that problem. Thirteen of the Committee's 29 Democrats are freshmen, and most of the others (including Patman, who is still a subcommittee chairman) are inclined to follow his lead on major issues. He is now recognized as one of the leading congressional authorities on the economy, with the clout as well as the expertise needed to speak definitively on the subject. And his selection as Chairman means that the House has begun, after so many years, to begin to behave like a sensible legislative body, reposing power not by virtue of seniority, but rather in people whose policies and competence the majority has confidence in.

Census Data Pop. 490,708. Central city, 100%; suburban, 0%. Median family income, $10,067; families above $15,000: 19%; families below $3,000: 9%. Median years education, 12.0.

The Voters

Median voting age 42.
Employment profile White collar, 47%. Blue collar, 38%. Service, 15%. Farm, –%.
Ethnic groups Black, 21%. Spanish, 2%. Total foreign stock, 21%. Germany, 7%; Poland, 2%; Italy, Austria, 1% each.

Presidential vote

1972	Nixon (R)	71,196	(42%)
	McGovern (D)	97,596	(58%)
1968	Nixon (R)	63,698	(37%)
	Humphrey (D)	92,352	(54%)
	Wallace (AI)	14,581	(9%)

Rep. Henry S. Reuss (D) Elected 1954; b. Feb. 22, 1912, Milwaukee; home, Milwaukee; Cornell U., A.B. 1933, Harvard U., LL.B. 1936; Episcopalian.

Career Practicing atty.; Asst. Corp. Counsel, Milwaukee Co., 1939–40; Asst. Gen. Counsel, OPA, 1941–42; Army, WWII; Chf., Price Control Branch, Ofc. of Military Govt. for Germany, 1945; Deputy Gen. Counsel, Marshall Plan, 1949; Milwaukee Co. Grand Jury Special Prosecutor, 1950.

Offices 2186 RHOB, 202-225-3571. Also Rm. 400, 517 E. Wisconsin Ave., Milwaukee 53202, 414-272-1226.

Committees

Banking, Currency and Housing (Chairman).

Joint Economic Committee (3d, House Side). Subcommittees: Economic Progress; International Economics (Chairman).

Group Ratings

	ADA	COPE	LWV	RIPON	NFU	LCV	CFA	NAB	NSI	ACA
1974	96	100	91	88	83	88	92	17	10	0
1973	88	91	100	71	100	95	100	–	–	8
1972	100	82	100	81	71	83	100	8	0	4

Key Votes

1) Foreign Aid	FOR	6) Gov Abortn Aid	AGN	11) Pub Cong Election $	FOR
2) Busing	FOR	7) Coed Phys Ed	FOR	12) Turkish Arms Cutoff	FOR
3) ABM	AGN	8) Pov Lawyer Gag	AGN	13) Youth Camp Regs	FOR
4) B-1 Bomber	AGN	9) Pub Trans Sub	FOR	14) Strip Mine Veto	AGN
5) Nerve Gas	AGN	10) EZ Voter Regis	FOR	15) Farm Bill Veto	AGN

Election Results

1974 general:	Henry S. Reuss (D)	65,060	(80%)	($2,073)
	Mildred A. Morries (R)	16,293	(20%)	($459)
1974 primary:	Henry S. Reuss (D), unopposed			
1972 general:	Henry S. Reuss (D)	127,273	(79%)	($12,613)
	Frederick Van Hecke (R)	33,627	(21%)	($4,743)

◆ ◆ ◆ ◆ ◆

SIXTH DISTRICT

The 6th district of Wisconsin is an almost perfectly rectangular slice of central Wisconsin, which extends from Lake Michigan to a point near the Mississippi River. On the Lake are the cities of Manitowoc (pop. 33,000) and Sheboygan (pop. 48,000), both of which lean Democratic. During the 1950s, Sheboygan was the scene of a bitter, eight-year-long UAW strike against the Kohler Company. To the west are the quiet, more Republican cities of Oshkosh (pop. 53,000) and Fond du Lac (pop. 35,000); both of them lie along Lake Winnebago, the state's largest inland lake. The rest of the district is rural dairy country, with small paper mill towns here and there.

The 6th district also includes the small town of Ripon (pop. 7,053), where the Republican Party is said to have been founded in 1854. (Jackson, Michigan, also claims the distinction.) It is therefore appropriate that the 6th sends to Congress one of the Republican Congressmen favored by the Ripon Society, Republican William Steiger. When first elected in 1966, Steiger was the youngest member of Congress, at 28; so youthful was his appearance that he was sometimes mistaken for a page. But he had already spent six years in the Wisconsin legislature, and won a seat in the House after scoring a relatively easy upset of a Democrat elected in the LBJ landslide.

Steiger's record on substantive matters is really not as liberal as the Ripon group would like. In the Education and Labor Committee and on the floor, Steiger has often supported the positions of the Nixon and Ford Administration on both domestic and foreign policy issues. But he has saved his major initiatives for issues where Administration and Ripon goals coincide. For example, he was one of the important congressional backers of the abolition of the draft, though not as a member of the Armed Services Committee; and today he is ready, at the slightest provocation, to spring to the defense of the all-volunteer Army.

Steiger also has a major political assignment outside the halls of the Capitol. He heads the Republican Party's national Rule 29 Committee, which was mandated by the 1972 national convention to come up with a set of delegate selection rules to, in the oft used phrase, broaden the base of the party. Southerners and conservatives attacked his appointment, since Steiger was part of the unsuccessful move at the 1972 Convention to increase the share of delegates allotted to the most populous states. As head of the committee, Steiger has proceeded in typically cautious style; but he is moving in a minefield, and any step off the main path could set off an explosion.

Reelection is no problem for Steiger. His speaking skills long since overcame whatever detriment his youthful appearance might have been. Moreover, like so many other Congressmen, Steiger augments his reelection chances by providing capable ombudsman-like services to his constituents. Despite the recent Democratic surge in Wisconsin, Steiger was reelected with 66% of the vote in 1972 (9% ahead of Nixon) and 59% in 1974 (when an Anerican Party candidate with a local base took 5%). He is the only Wisconsin congressional Republican Democrats made no attempts to beat the latter year. Nonetheless, Steiger does not seem to have the ambition to do what just about no other Wisconsin Republican plausibly can: run for statewide office. He seems happy with the career he has carved out in the House and the Republican Party, and unwilling to take the risks any statewide race would entail.

Census Data Pop. 490,934. Central city, 12%; suburban, 21%. Median family income, $9,727; families above $15,000: 17%; families below $3,000: 8%. Median years education, 12.1.

The Voters

Median voting age 44.
Employment profile White collar, 38%. Blue collar, 41%. Service, 13%. Farm, 8%.
Ethnic groups Total foreign stock, 14%. Germany, 6%.

Presidential vote

1972	Nixon (R)	114,461	(57%)
	McGovern (D)	85,778	(43%)
1968	Nixon (R)	97,980	(52%)
	Humphrey (D)	79,801	(42%)
	Wallace (AI)	11,810	(6%)

Rep. William A. Steiger (R) Elected 1966; b. May 15, 1938, Oshkosh; home, Oshkosh; U. of Wis., B.S. 1960; Episcopalian.

Career Natl. Chm., College Young Repubs., 1959–61; Wis. House of Reps., 1961–66; Pres., Steiger-Rathke Development Co.

Offices 1025 LHOB, 202-225-2476. Also 219 Washington Ave., Oshkosh 54901, 414-231-6333.

Committees

Ways and Means (7th). Subcommittees: Social Security; Unemployment Compensation.

Group Ratings

	ADA	COPE	LWV	RIPON	NFU	LCV	CFA	NAB	NSI	ACA
1974	48	27	100	88	50	47	17	55	89	33
1973	32	9	67	93	35	58	43	–	–	60
1972	25	22	82	75	43	63	0	91	100	48

Key Votes

1) Foreign Aid	FOR	6) Gov Abortn Aid	AGN	11) Pub Cong Election $	FOR
2) Busing	FOR	7) Coed Phys Ed	FOR	12) Turkish Arms Cutoff	AGN
3) ABM	FOR	8) Pov Lawyer Gag	AGN	13) Youth Camp Regs	FOR
4) B-1 Bomber	FOR	9) Pub Trans Sub	AGN	14) Strip Mine Veto	FOR
5) Nerve Gas	AGN	10) EZ Voter Regis	AGN	15) Farm Bill Veto	AGN

Election Results

1974 general:	William A. Steiger (R)	86,652	(59%)	($51,495)
	Nancy J. Simenz (D)	51,571	(35%)	($6,128)
	Harvey C. LeRoy (AI)	7,432	(5%)	($2,449)
1974 primary:	William A. Steiger (R), unopposed			
1972 general:	William A. Steiger (R)	130,701	(66%)	($33,599)
	James A. Adams (D)	63,643	(32%)	($6,528)
	Valeria M. Sitter (AI)	4,260	(2%)	(NA)

◆ ◆ ◆ ◆ ◆

SEVENTH DISTRICT

Northern Wisconsin is a land of forests and lakes and mines. Two natural resources dominate here, the dairy cow and the tree; without them, there would be virtually no people here at all. This is the land of Wisconsin's 7th congressional district, which stretches from near Green Bay in the south up to the edge of Duluth, Minnesota. Superior, the Wisconsin town directly next to Duluth, is like its neighbor an iron ore port, with scarcely any other reason to exist there on the icy fastness of Lake Superior. In contrast, most of the employment in towns like Wausau, Stevens Point, and Wisconsin Rapids, in the southern part of the district, depends on the lumber and paper mills. All these places were off the beaten track of east-west migration; they attracted their own unusual ethnic groups, like the Finns of Superior and the Poles of Stevens Point. The politics of northern Wisconsin and the 7th district has always had a rough hewn quality about it, a certain populistic edge, though as is the case throughout Wisconsin the ancestral political preference is Republican.

The current boundaries of the 7th district are the result of the redistricting of 1972, which combined the old 7th with the old 10th—a seat Wisconsin lost because of sluggish population growth in the 1960s. The two Congressmen who were thrown together presented quite a contrast. The 10th had been represented for 30 years by Alvin O'Konski, a Republican who often voted liberal on economic programs and who, on foreign and military affairs, was isolationist in the 1940s and hawkish in the 1960s. O'Konski had been a solid votegetter for years, but he stumbled badly in 1970, when he got 51% of the votes; he had pleaded congressional business as the cause of his total absence from the district, but a local reporter had found out he was spending weekends in Bethesda Naval Hospital. O'Konski was the second-ranking Republican on the House Armed Services Committee at this time, and trying, in the old manner, to do something for his district. The something was Project Sanguine, a Navy program to plant electronic sensors in thousands of northern Wisconsin acres to act as a giant antenna to receive low frequency communications from submarines. But when the first sensors were planted, local TV reception was disturbed and electric appliances jammed. By 1972, O'Konski's strenuous backing of Sanguine was no longer an asset.

O'Konski's 1972 opponent was a veteran of just three years in Congress, and of six years before that in the Wisconsin legislature, 34-year-old Democrat David Obey. He had represented the southern part of the new 7th district, which technically was the less Democratic section. Indeed, the fact that Obey was a congressman at all was a major upset; in 1969, he had won the seat vacated by Secretary of Defense Melvin Laird. Obey had won that race by working hard and picking his issues carefully; he campaigned then vigorously against the Republican Governor's sales tax. In 1972, Obey steered clear of most controversy (though he made it clear he was against Sanguine) and let his good record of constituency service and O'Konski's age work for him.

Obey won that election with a very solid 63% of the vote; he appears to have a lifetime safe seat. Incidentally, after the election, Laird in one of his last acts as Defense Secretary, cancelled Sanguine; he had not yet given up all hope of running for office in Wisconsin again. In his first full term in Congress, Obey had won a seat on the Appropriations Committee; now, after easy reelection in 1974, he ranks 23d of the Committee's 37 Democrats—far ahead of any other Democrat in his thirties. Obey is not oratorically inclined, but he works hard, knows his issues, and is not caught unprepared; he seems to have created the kind of political career he wanted for himself, and is enjoying its pursuit. Like many of the younger Democrats with very liberal voting records, Obey does not talk like a bleeding heart crusader; that is not his style. Instead, he gets things done.

A footnote on Obey: he may turn out to be the instigator of a successful presidential candidacy. One day in 1974 he was talking with Henry Reuss of the 5th district about the way House members were not considered serious candidates for President—though they may know more and have demonstrated more leadership than some of their better known Senate counterparts. Reuss and Obey decided to ask Arizona's Morris Udall if he would run; Udall said he would if they could round up the signatures of one-tenth the Democratic members of the House in support of his candidacy; they did, and he ran. This genesis gave Udall the added benefit of some assured support in Wisconsin, with its sometimes crucial early primary.

Census Data Pop. 491,030. Central city, 7%; suburban, 3%. Median family income, $8,424; families above $15,000: 12%; families below $3,000: 12%. Median years education, 11.8.

The Voters

Median voting age 46.
Employment profile White collar, 38%. Blue collar, 38%. Service, 14%. Farm, 10%.
Ethnic groups Total foreign stock, 19%; Germany, 6%; Poland, Sweden, Norway, 2% each; Canada, 1%.

Presidential vote

1972	Nixon (R)	110,826	(53%)
	McGovern (D)	98,230	(47%)
1968	Nixon (R)	86,217	(44%)
	Humphrey (D)	95,168	(48%)
	Wallace (AI)	15,369	(8%)

Rep. David R. Obey (D) Elected Apr. 1, 1969; b. Oct. 3, 1938, Okmulgee, Okla.; home, Wausau; U. of Wis., Marathon, U. of Wis., Madison, M.A. 1960.

Career Wis. House of Reps., 1962–68.

Offices 208 CHOB, 202-225-3365. Also Fed. Bldg., Wausau 54401, 715-842-5606.

Committees

Appropriations (22d). Subcommittees: Foreign Operations; Labor-HEW.

Group Ratings

	ADA	COPE	LWV	RIPON	NFU	LCV	CFA	NAB	NSI	ACA
1974	87	91	92	67	93	88	85	25	10	7
1973	96	70	83	77	100	100	86	–	–	19
1972	100	100	92	67	86	91	100	0	0	0

Key Votes

1) Foreign Aid	AGN	6) Gov Abortn Aid	AGN	11) Pub Cong Election $	FOR
2) Busing	FOR	7) Coed Phys Ed	AGN	12) Turkish Arms Cutoff	AGN
3) ABM	AGN	8) Pov Lawyer Gag	AGN	13) Youth Camp Regs	FOR
4) B-1 Bomber	AGN	9) Pub Trans Sub	FOR	14) Strip Mine Veto	AGN
5) Nerve Gas	AGN	10) EZ Voter Regis	FOR	15) Farm Bill Veto	AGN

Election Results

1974 general:	David R. Obey (D)	104,468	(71%)	($25,807)
	Josef Burger (R)	43,558	(29%)	($12,683)
1974 primary:	David R. Obey (D), unopposed			
1972 general:	David R. Obey (D)	135,385	(63%)	($64,054)
	Alvin E. O'Konski (R)	80,207	(37%)	($42,772)

◆　◆　◆　◆　◆

EIGHTH DISTRICT

The 8th of Wisconsin might be called the Packers' district. Centered on the Midwest metropolis of Green Bay (pop. 87,000), it is the home of the Green Bay Pakers and the smallest city with any kind of bigtime professional athletic franchise. The team here is a remnant of the early days of pro football, when the National Football League included such teams as Jim Thorpe's Canton Bulldogs. During the 1960s "the Pack" under Vince Lombardi was a stringently disciplined unit that dominated the NFL and the fantasy life of millions of American males. The Packers are the aspect of the 8th district best known to the outside world, though this 13-county district in northeast Wisconsin has other features of note. It includes the city of Appleton (pop. 57,000), Joe

McCarthy's home town. Nathan Pusey, later president of Harvard, served in the same office in Lawrence College in Appleton in the early 1950s and was defying McCarthy's pronunciamentos even then. Also, the 8th district contains the only recently formed county in the United States, Menominee, which was created when the Menominee Indian Reservation was liquidated in accordance with the termination policy of the Eisenhower Administration.

Though the 8th is generally considered a solid Republican district, that is not quite right. Green Bay, which usually goes Republican, is a German Catholic town that gave a majority of its votes to John Kennedy in 1960 and even gave George McGovern a fair percentage in 1972. There are some heavily Republican counties here (Shawano, Waupaca), but also some that usually go Democratic (Florence, Forest). The balance, and more than half the votes, are cast in Brown and Outgamie Counties which contain Green Bay and Appleton respectively.

From 1945 to 1973, the 8th district was represented by John Byrnes, a man who shared some of the views, but little of the temperament, of the late Senator from Appleton. When Byrnes announced his surprise decision to retire in 1972, he was the third most senior Republican in the House and ranking minority member of the House Ways and Means Committee. Byrnes used to work closely with Wilbur Mills. Usually the two of them could get a bill safely through the Committee, then shepherd it easily through the floor of the House (where the Rules Committee would usually not allow any amendments), and then defend it successfully in conference committee. The result was a concentration of legislative power in the hands of two men unequalled just about anywhere else in the legislative process. Fans of Mills and Byrnes argued that this was justified by the responsible results; others felt, particularly as the years went on, that the results however good were not worth the distortion of the legislative process.

One thing that may have prompted Byrnes to retire was the uncomfortably close margin, 55–45, by which he beat Jesuit priest Robert Cornell in the 1970 election. In 1972, Cornell tried again. This time his Republican opponent was Harold Froehlich, Minority Leader of the Wisconsin Assembly, and the outcome was even closer; Cornell got 49%. But Froehlich was elected, and went on to serve on the Judiciary Committee, where he was the most visibly reluctant of the anti-Nixon voters on either side of the aisle. Indeed, on most substantive issues, Froehlich had spent most of his time steadfastly supporting the President.

Was his impeachment vote, or his obvious reluctance to cast it, the reason for Froehlich's defeat in 1974? Probably not. Cornell was the candidate again, and before the hearings he assured Froehlich he would not make an issue of impeachment one way or the other. Probably it didn't matter—or simply strengthened the Democratic trend that had been visible in the area for some time. The heavily Catholic 8th, after going for Kennedy in 1960, had turned sour on Lyndon Johnson's Democrats, but started switching again when they left the White House. Thus Humphrey's 35% of the vote in 1968 turned into McGovern's 39% in 1972, in sharp contrast to the national trend. In that context, it was perfectly natural that Father Cornell should incrase from 45% in 1970 to 49% in 1972 and a winning 54% in 1974.

Cornell is now the second priest elected to the House, and if he is not as outspoken as his colleague Robert Drinan of Massachusetts, he is still a solidly liberal Democrat. Will he be reelected in 1976? No one seems to know, but the trend in this heavily Catholic district seems to favor him.

Census Data Pop. 490,974. Central city, 29%; suburban, 27%. Median family income, $9,190; families above $15,000: 15%; families below $3,000: 9%. Median years education, 12.1.

The Voters

   Median voting age 45.
   Employment profile White collar, 39%. Blue collar, 40%. Service, 13%. Farm, 8%.
   Ethnic groups Total foreign stock, 14%. Germany, 5%; Poland, Canada, 1% each.

Presidential vote

1972	Nixon (R)	122,672	(61%)
	McGovern (D)	76,912	(39%)
1968	Nixon (R)	106,148	(57%)
	Humphrey (D)	66,437	(35%)
	Wallace (AI)	15,145	(8%)

Rep. Robert J. Cornell (D) Elected 1974; b. Dec. 16, 1919, Gladstone, Mich.; home, DePere; St. Norbert Col., B.A. 1941, Catholic U., M.A. 1947, Ph.D. 1957; Catholic.

Career Catholic high school teacher, 1941–47; Ordained Catholic Priest, 1944; Assoc. Prof. of History and Poli. Sci., St. Norbert Col., 1947–74, Dean of Men, 1953–56.

Offices 1512 LHOB, 202-225-5665. Also Rm. 207, Fed. Bldg., 325 E. Walnut St., Green Bay 54301, 414-465-3931.

Committees

Education and Labor (20th). Subcommittees: Labor Standards; Select Subcommittee on Education.

Veterans' Affairs (12th). Subcommittees: Cemeteries and Burial Benefits; Education and Training; Housing.

Group Ratings: Newly Elected

Key Votes

1) Foreign Aid	FOR	6) Gov Abortn Aid	NE	11) Pub Cong Election $	NE
2) Busing	NE	7) Coed Phys Ed	AGN	12) Turkish Arms Cutoff	NE
3) ABM	NE	8) Pov Lawyer Gag	NE	13) Youth Camp Regs	FOR
4) B-1 Bomber	AGN	9) Pub Trans Sub	NE	14) Strip Mine Veto	AGN
5) Nerve Gas	NE	10) EZ Voter Regis	NE	15) Farm Bill Veto	AGN

Election Results

1974 general:	Robert J. Cornell (D)	79,923	(54%)	($60,736)
	Harold V. Froehlich (R)	66,889	(46%)	($93,272)
1974 primary:	Robert J. Cornell (D)	21,458	(56%)	
	Donald R. Zuidmulder (D)	16,957	(44%)	

♦ ♦ ♦ ♦ ♦

NINTH DISTRICT

The 9th is Wisconsin's only predominantly suburban congressional district and also its fastest growing. It was first created in 1963 when population changes and the Supreme Court's one-person-one-vote decision required the elimination of a rural district and the full recognition of the growth of Milwaukee's suburbs. Today—the district was redrawn in 1971—the 9th forms something of an arc north and west of Milwaukee. The district includes the wealthy, long established suburbs like Shorewood and Whitefish Bay, just north of downtown Milwaukee on Lake Michigan, and a ring of suburbs around Milwaukee in Ozaukee, Washington, and Waukesha Counties: Mequon, Germantown, Menomonee Falls, Brookfield, and New Berlin. The territory combines country clubs, tree-shaded streets, shopping centers, and starkly new suburban housing. Though the 9th also includes some of the rural dairy country between Milwaukee and Madison, most of its residents live in Waukesha County, which grew from 158,000 in 1960 to 231,000 in 1970.

The district was originally designed to remove Republican voters from Robert Kastenmeier's 2d and Henry Reuss's 5th districts. The job was done so well that the 9th is the state's most heavily Republican district. Its creation also set the stage for the political comeback of Glenn Davis, who had represented the old 2d district, including Madison, from 1947 to 1957. A strong supporter of Joseph McCarthy and Richard Nixon, Davis relinquished the seat to make an unsuccessful primary bid against moderate Senator Alexander Wiley in 1956, and he ran unsuccessfully again for the vacancy caused by McCarthy's death a year later. But in 1964, despite the LBJ landslide, Davis was returned to Congress from the 9th district, and by a margin large enough that he must have expected automatic reelection and greater seniority on the House Appropriations Committee.

But just as Davis's first House career had collapsed as his friend McCarthy was dying, so his second career collapsed as his other friend Richard Nixon was forced from office. Davis knew he would have trouble in 1974: he had only won 48% of the vote in 1970, and though he was reelected easily in 1972, 1974 looked very much like a Democratic year in Wisconsin, even in the 9th. Moreover, he had primary opposition from a young, wealthy, conservative state Senator named Robert Kasten. Tossed about by such winds, Davis looked for a safe port; and for awhile thought he had found one in a vacant federal judgeship in Milwaukee. Nixon was prepared to appoint him; and Senator William Proxmire declined to veto the appointment. But then the Bar Association came out stoutly against him, and Senator Gaylord Nelson decided that Davis simply should not get a lifetime judgeship. Within three weeks, Davis lost the judgeship and his primary—his career was over a second and apparently final time.

The Democratic nominee, Lynn Adelman, might have been able to beat Davis in the general, with all the wounds the 60-year-old veteran had sustained; he was not able to get more than 45% of the vote against the 32-year-old Kasten. That makes Kasten easily the most conservative member of the Wisconsin delegation, and probably as safe politically as any of the state's liberal Democrats, though it is too early yet to tell for sure.

Census Data Pop. 490,805. Central city, 0%; suburban, 86%. Median family income, $12,479; families above $15,000: 34%; families below $3,000: 4%. Median years education, 12.4.

The Voters

Median voting age 42.
Employment profile White collar, 51%. Blue collar, 35%. Service, 11%. Farm, 3%.
Ethnic groups Spanish, 1%. Total foreign stock, 16%. Germany, 6%.

Presidential vote

1972	Nixon (R)	131,288	(63%)
	McGovern (D)	77,944	(37%)
1968	Nixon (R)	108,269	(56%)
	Humphrey (D)	70,741	(37%)
	Wallace (AI)	13,602	(7%)

Rep. Robert W. Kasten, Jr. (R) Elected 1974; b. June 19, 1942, Milwaukee; home, Thiensville; U. of Ariz., B.A. 1964, Columbia U., M.B.A. 1966.

Career Air Force, 1967–72; V.P. and Dir., Gilbert Shoe Co.; Wis. Senate, 1972–74.

Offices 1113 LHOB, 202-225-5101. Also 333 Bishop's Way, Brookfield 53005, 404-784-1111.

Committees

Government Operations (13th). Subcommittees: Intergovernmental Relations and Human Resources; Manpower and Housing.

Group Ratings: Newly Elected

Key Votes

1) Foreign Aid	AGN	6) Gov Abortn Aid	NE	11) Pub Cong Election $	NE
2) Busing	NE	7) Coed Phys Ed	AGN	12) Turkish Arms Cutoff	NE
3) ABM	NE	8) Pov Lawyer Gag	NE	13) Youth Camp Regs	AGN
4) B-1 Bomber	FOR	9) Pub Trans Sub	NE	14) Strip Mine Veto	AGN
5) Nerve Gas	NE	10) EZ Voter Regis	NE	15) Farm Bill Veto	AGN

Election Results

1974 general:	Robert W. Kasten (R)	77,733	(53%)	($91,770)
	Lynn S. Adelman (D)	66,071	(45%)	($104,934)
	William D. Quirk (AI)	3,037	(2%)	($0)
1974 primary:	Robert W. Kasten (R)	22,749	(57%)	
	Glenn R. Davis (R)	17,054	(43%)	

WYOMING

Wyoming is the closest thing we have left to the old Wild West. It is one of the few states where ranchers, through the Wyoming Stock Growers' Association, and a railroad, the Union Pacific, remain major political powers. The ranchers were of course the first white settlers here; the railroad's powers come from the land grants it received for building the transcontinental railroad through the southern part of the state more than 100 years ago. Politically, the ranchers, the small businessmen, and the farmers who work the irrigated land in the north have usually voted heavily Republican. The people who came to build and maintain the UP, along the state's southern edge, have usually been staunch Democrats. This is the basic political split in the state. There are no big urban concentrations, and only five "cities" with populations over 10,000, the largest of which is Cheyenne (pop. 41,000). More common are places like Ten Sleep (pop. 320) or Medicine Bow (pop. 455). Between the Wyoming settlements, for stretches of 50 and 100 miles, lies the high, desolate, and serene plateau of the Rocky Mountains to the east and the south, and the mountains themselves to the west and north.

But Wyoming's serenity has been disturbed mightily of late. The culprit—though by no means all Wyomingites look at it this way—is a boom in mining and minerals, just in time for the nation's energy crisis. The mineral boom first struck in Campbell County, in the northern part of the state; it has spread through Casper—always an oil town, and not far from the original Teapot Dome—to the area around Rock Springs. New oil wells have been drilled, new natural gas deposits discovered, and in addition to that, there is coal. Wyoming is one of those western and plains states that sits on huge seams of low sulphur coal near the surface of the land. Once this coal was considered low grade, too far from any market, and not worth developing; now, with the price of coal very high and with new stripping technique available, it is well worth exploiting.

The mineral boom has provided Wyoming, a state until 1970 of stagnant growth and a sagging local economy, with sudden injections of money—and of people, who in turn demand government services. Wyoming has by no means turned strongly against further growth and development, as has neighboring Colorado. There is simply too much vacant land here, and it seems hard to believe that the basic character of Wyoming life will be altered. Nevertheless, there is an uneasiness. The state's highly popular Governor from 1967 to 1974, Republican Stanley Hathaway, generally came out on the side of growth, rather than controls—as was revealed, despite some attempts to portray him as more evenhanded, in the hearings on his confirmation as Secretary of the Interior.

But in the 1974 gubernatorial race, one of the major issues was whether to build a slurry pipeline—a device to mix coal with water and pipe it out of state to market. Hathaway favored the plan, as did the conservative Republican nominee, state Senator Dick Jones, winner of a virtually even four-man race. But the Democrat, Ed Herschler, was opposed; he claimed that the slurry pipeline would tend to deplete Wyoming's water resources. Apparently the voters agreed. Herschler carried the traditionally Democratic southern counties of the state by huge margins, and ran about even in the usually Republican north as some farmers and ranchers figured coal companies would bid up the cost of water. He was weak only in Casper, because he opposed the extension of the local junior college into a four year school. Wyoming is still small enough that such issues can make a difference in statewide races.

In senatorial and congressional races, Wyoming is a state caught up in a love-hate relationship with the federal government. Out here on the frontier, people—especially well to do people—like to think of themselves as self-sufficient pioneers. The dominant political rhetoric is a Goldwaterish opposition to the federal government and its activities. Yet sparsely populated Wyoming, even with its mineral boom, would be even more vacant and economically shaky without the feds. The federal contributions are many: the oil depletion allowance, still a boon to small producers; national parks, forests, and other lands (some of which are leased to sheep and cattle interests at bargain rates); the Bureau of Reclamation, which provides cheap water; federal subsidies to feeder airlines, to agriculture, to highway construction. Over the years, Wyoming has received about $4 for each $3 it sends to Washington in taxes.

One politician who seems to have mastered Wyoming's love-hate relationship with Washington is the state's senior Senator, Gale McGee. He has an unlikely background for a western Senator: he was a history professor at the University of Wyoming before he first won the seat in 1958. In his first years in the Senate he was rather obscure, lost in the crowd of Democrats elected in 1958;

and as the 1964 election approached, he seemed to be in trouble. Wyoming had been trending sharply to the right in intervening years, and McGee, with his pro-labor, liberal record, seemed especially vulnerable in that Goldwater year. But the Arizonan did not carry Wyoming, and neither did McGee's Republican opponent, state chairman John Wold. Since that time, McGee has been more of a standout. He is the Chairman now of the Post Office and Civil Service Committee, in which capacity he has proved his legislative abilities. His most notable achievement was the passage through the Senate (it is not law yet) of postcard registration, a pet measure of Democrats and organized labor; McGee had to break a filibuster led by Alabama's James Allen to push it through. McGee is also known as one of the Senate's more hawkish Democrats; he tends toward the same impulses as Henry Jackson—never flinching from support of the Vietnam war, always a strong supporter of Israel. McGee is also one of the Senate's premier orators; his main competitor is another mountain state Democrat of more dovish disposition, Frank Church of Idaho.

Over the years McGee's politics has gone over well in Wyoming. When the 1970 election rolled around, the Senator had something to please everyone: a liberal domestic record for organized labor, a hawkish stand on the war for admirers of Richard Nixon, and 12 years of seniority to boot. He brushed aside a challenge from a peace candidate in the primary, talked (with the help of George McGovern) a liberal antiwar Casper lawyer from running as an independent, and then beat the same Republican who had opposed him in 1964. This time McGee won 56% of the vote. How will he do in 1976? Nothing can be taken for granted. But Wyoming was as hospitable to Democrats in 1974 as it has been ever since the year McGee first won, and he still continues the strenuous rounds of personal campaigning which remain so important in such a lightly populated state. At this point it does not appear that the Republicans have great hopes of beating McGee.

The state's junior Senator, Clifford Hansen, is more in line with what we think of as traditional Wyoming. He is a conservative Republican, a Teton County cattle rancher who served as Governor from 1963 to 1966; he was well positioned when aging Republican Senator Milward Simpson decided to retire in 1966, and he ran for and won the seat. Hansen is not invariably an orthodox conservative—back in 1964 he dabbled with the idea of supporting Rockefeller over Goldwater, and years later he opposed the Nixon supersonic transport. But as a member of the Senate Finance Committee, Hansen can usually be counted on to see things as the large corporate lobbyists and the oil companies would like. Hansen had a rough race winning the seat the first time, against Congressman Teno Roncalio; but in 1972, the genial and affable Republican was reelected with 71% of the vote, and can probably spend the rest of his life, if he wants, in the Senate.

Roncalio is Wyoming's one and only Congressman. He is an Episcopalian Democrat whose father was an Italian immigrant and Union Pacific worker in Rock Springs. First elected to the House in the Johnson landslide of 1964, Roncalio lost the Senate race to Hansen in 1966. He sat out the 1968 elections, supporting Robert Kennedy for President, and in 1970 won his House seat back again. Roncalio got 51% of the vote that year, 52% in 1972, and a comparative landslide of 55% in 1974. His political secret—indeed the secret of all successful Wyoming politicians—is personal campaigning; anyone who wants to run for office here had better be prepared to explain his stands on the issues, eye-to-eye. It is a exhausting process, driving in a car or riding in a light airplane for miles on end between Wyoming's small settlements.

The fact that Roncalio did not run for the Senate in 1972, and has promised not to do so in the future, is a break with Wyoming tradition; the Congressman-at-large seat here has been bandied back and forth between the two parties these last thirty years largely because incumbents keep insisting on running for the Senate. The most noteworthy Wyoming Congressman-at-large of recent years was William Henry Harrison, a conservative Republican and a descendant of the two Presidents Harrison, who served four separated terms (1953–55, 1961–65, 1967–69) punctuated by Senate bids. The idea is that since you have to run statewide anyway, you might as well go for the six year term and the national exposure. This reasoning has proven persuasive to Congressmen Frank Barrett in 1952, Harrison in 1954, Keith Thomson in 1960, Roncalio in 1966, and John Wold in 1970. Only Barrett and Thomson won, and Thomson died of a heart attack a month after the election.

Census Data   Pop. 332,416; 0.16% of U.S. total, 49th largest; Central city, 0%; suburban, 0%. Median family income, $8,944; 27th highest; families above $15,000: 16%; families below $3,000: 9%.   Median years education, 12.4.

1974 Share of Federal Tax Burden $428,504,000; 0.16% of U.S. total, 50th largest.

1974 Share of Federal Outlays $491,644,000; 0.18% of U.S. total, 50th largest.   Per capita federal spending, $1479.

DOD	$109,376,000	49th (0.16%)		HEW	$125,244,000	50th	(0.13%)
AEC	$118,000	37th (–)		HUD	$887,000	50th	(0.09%)
NASA	$284,000	42d (0.01%)		VA	$34,998,000	48th	(0.26%)
DOT	$37,996,000	48th (0.45%)		EPA	$1,201,000	50th	(0.04%)
DOC	$2,690,000	46th (0.17%)		RevS	$11,584,000	49th	(0.19%)
DOI	$58,358,000	13th (2.37%)		Int.	$17,691,000	47th	(0.09%)
USDA	$29,286,000	43d (0.24%)		Other	$61,931,000		

Economic Base   Agriculture, notably cattle, sheep, sugar beets and dairy products; oil and gas extraction, especially oil and gas field services; finance, insurance and real estate; metal mining, especially uranium-radium-vanadium ores; petroleum refining and other petroleum and coal products; food and kindred products.

Political Line-up   Governor, Ed Herschler (D). Senators, Gale W. McGee (D) and Clifford P. Hansen (R). Representatives, 1 D at large. State Senate (15 D and 15 R); State House (32 R, 29 D, and 1 Ind.).

The Voters

Registration   185,000 Total. 69,651 D (38%); 85,711 R (46%); 29,638 Unclassified (16%). *Median voting age* 42.
Employment profile   White collar, 47%. Blue collar, 30%. Service, 14%. Farm, 9%.
Ethnic groups   Total foreign stock, 11%.

Presidential vote

	1972	Nixon (R)	100,464	(69%)
		McGovern (D)	44,358	(31%)
	1968	Nixon (R)	70,927	(56%)
		Humphrey (D)	45,173	(36%)
		Wallace (AI)	11,105	(9%)

Sen. Gale W. McGee (D) Elected 1958, seat up 1976; b. Mar. 17, 1915, Lincoln, Neb.; home, Laramie; Neb. St. Teachers Col., A.B. 1936, U. of Colo., M.A. 1939, U. of Chicago, Ph.D. 1947; Presbyterian.

Career   High school teacher, 1937–40; Prof. of Amer. History, Neb. Wesleyan U., 1940–43, Ia. St. U. 1943–44, U. of Notre Dame, 1944–45, U. of Chicago, 1945–46, U. of Wyo., 1946–58; Legis. Asst. to U.S. Sen Joseph O'Mahoney, 1955–56.

Offices   244 RSOB, 202-224-6441. Also Rm. 2003, Casper Fed. Bldg., Casper 82601, 307-265-550, and O'Mahoney Fed. Ctr., 2121 Capitol Ave., Cheyenne 82001, 307-778-2220.

Committees

Post Office and Civil Service (Chairman).

Appropriations (6th). Subcommittees: Agriculture and Related Agencies (Chairman); Defense; Foreign Operations; Interior; Public Works.

Foreign Relations (6th). Subcommittees: African Affairs; Arms Control, International Organizations and Security Agreements; Foreign Assistance and Economic Policy; Near Eastern and South Asian Affairs; Western Hemisphere Affairs (Chairman).

Group Ratings

	ADA	COPE	LWV	RIPON	NFU	LCV	CFA	NAB	NSI	ACA
1974	59	78	100	58	81	47	75	11	86	21
1973	33	89	67	31	100	–	63	–	–	15
1972	35	83	100	50	89	24	100	14	80	40

Key Votes

1) No-Knock	AGN	8) Gov Abortn Aid	AGN	15) Consumer Prot Agy	FOR
2) Busing	FOR	9) Cut Mil Brass	AGN	16) Forced Psych Tests	FOR
3) No Fault	FOR	10) Gov Limousine	FOR	17) Fed Campaign Subs	ABS
4) F-111	FOR	11) RR Featherbed	FOR	18) Rhod Chrome Ban	FOR
5) Death Penalty	FOR	12) Handgun License	AGN	19) Open Legis Meetings	AGN
6) Foreign Aid	FOR	13) Less Troop Abrd	AGN	20) Strikers Food Stmps	FOR
7) Filibuster	FOR	14) Resume Turk Aid	FOR	21) Gov Info Disclosure	FOR

Election Results

1970 general:	Gale W. McGee (D)	67,207	(56%)
	John S. Wold (R)	53,279	(44%)
1970 primary:	Gale W. McGee (D)	32,956	(80%)
	D. P. Svilar (D)	8,448	(20%)
1964 general:	Gale W. McGee (D)	76,485	(54%)
	John S. Wold (R)	65,185	(46%)

Sen. Clifford P. Hansen (R) Elected 1966, seat up 1978; b. Oct 16, 1912, Zenith; home, Jackson; U. of Wyo., B.S. 1934; Episcopalian.

Career Cattle rancher; Teton Co. Commissioner, 1943–51; Gov. of Wyo., 1963–67.

Offices 3229 DSOB, 202-224-3424. Also Rm. 2021 Fed. Bldg., Cheyenne 82001, 307-778-2220 ext. 2478, and 3201 Fed. Bldg., 100 E. "B" St., Casper 82601, 307-234-7664.

Committees

Veterans' Affairs (Ranking Member;. Subcommittees: Compensation and Pension; Health and Hospitals.

Finance (3d). Subcommittees: Energy; Foundations; International Trade; Social Security Financing.

Interior and Insular Affairs (2d). Subcommittees: Energy Research and Water Resources; Environment and Land Resources; Minerals, Materials and Fuels; Parks and Recreation.

Group Ratings

	ADA	COPE	LWV	RIPON	NFU	LCV	CFA	NAB	NSI	ACA
1974	0	9	44	45	12	10	0	83	100	100
1973	0	18	0	33	7	–	8	–	–	96
1972	0	0	20	25	33	8	0	91	100	95

Key Votes

1) No-Knock	FOR	8) Gov Abortn Aid	AGN	15) Consumer Prot Agy	AGN
2) Busing	AGN	9) Cut Mil Brass	AGN	16) Forced Psych Tests	AGN
3) No Fault	AGN	10) Gov Limousine	FOR	17) Fed Campaign Subs	AGN
4) F-111	FOR	11) RR Featherbed	AGN	18) Rhod Chrome Ban	AGN
5) Death Penalty	FOR	12) Handgun License	AGN	19) Open Legis Meetings	AGN
6) Foreign Aid	AGN	13) Less Troop Abrd	AGN	20) Strikers Food Stmps	AGN
7) Filibuster	FOR	14) Resume Turk Aid	FOR	21) Gov Info Disclosure	AGN

Election Results

1972 general:	Clifford P. Hansen (R)	101,314	(71%)	($169,878)
	Mike M. Vinich (D)	40,753	(29%)	($10,411)
1972 primary:	Clifford P. Hansen (R), unopposed			
1966 general:	Clifford P. Hansen (R)	63,548	(52%)	
	Teno Roncalio (D)	59,141	(48%)	

Gov. Ed Herschler (D) Elected 1974, term expires Jan. 1979; b. Oct. 27, 1918, Lincoln County; U. of Colo., B.A., U. of Wyo., LL.B. 1949; Episcopalian.

Career USMC, WWII; Practicing atty., 1949–74; Kemmerer Town Atty., 1949–74; Lincoln Co. Prosecuting Atty.; Wyo. House of Reps., 1960–69.

Offices Capitol Bldg., Cheyenne 82002, 307-777-7434.

Election Results

1974 general:	Ed Herschler (D)	71,741	(56%)
	Dick Jones (R)	56,645	(44%)
1974 primary:	Ed Herschler (D)	19,997	(47%)
	Harry E. Leimback (D)	15,255	(36%)
	John J. Rooney (D)	7,674	(18%)

Rep. Teno Roncalio (D) Elected 1970; b. Mar. 23, 1916, Rock Springs; home, Cheyenne; U. of Wyo., LL.B. 1947.

Career Asst. to U.S. Sen. Joseph O'Mahoney, 1941; Army, WWII; Practicing atty., 1949–64; Founder and Bd. Chm., Cheyenne Natl. Bank, 1960–68; Founder and Pres., 1st Natl. Bank, Gillette, 1962–65; U.S. House of Reps., 1965–67; Dem. nominee for U.S. Senate, 1966.

Offices 1314 LHOB, 202-225-2311.

Committees

Interior and Insular Affairs (13th). Subcommittees: Energy and the Environment; National Parks and Recreation; Water and Power Resources.

Public Works and Transportation (9th). Subcommittees: Aviation; Investigations and Review; Public Buildings and Grounds (Chairman).

Joint Committee on Atomic Energy (3d, House Side). Subcommittees: Agreements for Cooperation (Chairman); ERDA, Nuclear Energy; National Security.

Group Ratings

	ADA	COPE	LWV	RIPON	NFU	LCV	CFA	NAB	NSI	ACA
1974	67	82	67	50	100	75	62	56	63	21
1973	75	100	64	54	95	63	100	–	–	27
1972	50	55	60	54	100	79	100	97	25	36

Key Votes

1) Foreign Aid	AGN	6) Gov Abortn Aid	FOR	11) Pub Cong Election $	FOR
2) Busing	FOR	7) Coed Phys Ed	AGN	12) Turkish Arms Cutoff	ABS
3) ABM	FOR	8) Pov Lawyer Gag	AGN	13) Youth Camp Regs	FOR
4) B-1 Bomber	AGN	9) Pub Trans Sub	FOR	14) Strip Mine Veto	AGN
5) Nerve Gas	AGN	10) EZ Voter Regis	FOR	15) Farm Bill Veto	AGN

Election Results

1974 general:	Teno Roncalio (D)	69,434	(55%)	($52,860)
	Tom Stroock (R)	57,499	(45%)	($98,581)
1974 primary:	Teno Roncalio (D), unopposed			
1972 general:	Teno Roncalio (D)	75,632	(52%)	($50,548)
	Bill Kidd (R)	70,667	(48%)	($122,580)

SENATE COMMITTEES

Committee on Aeronautical and Space Sciences

Frank E. Moss (Utah), Chairman

Democratic Majority (6 D). Moss, Symington (Mo.), Stennis (Miss.), Cannon (Nev.), Ford (Ky.), Bumpers (Ark.).
Republican Minority (4 R). Goldwater (Ariz.), Dominici (N.M.), Laxalt (Nev.), Garn (Utah).

(No Subcommitees)

Committee on Agriculture and Forestry

Herman E. Talmadge (Ga.), Chairman

Democratic Majority (9 D). Talmadge, Eastland (Miss.), McGovern (S.D.), Allen (Ala.), Humphrey (Minn.), Huddleston (Ky.), Clark (Iowa), Stone (Fla.), Leahy (Vt.).
Republican Minority (5 R). Curtis (Nev.), Young (N.D.), Dole (Kan.), Bellmon (Okla.), Helms (N.C.).

Subcommittees

(The Chairman and ranking minority member are ex officio members of all subcommittees.)

AGRICULTURAL CREDIT AND RURAL ELECTRIFICATION

George McGovern, Chairman

Majority (5 D). McGovern, Allen, Humphrey, Huddleston, Stone.
Minority (3 R). Curtis, Dole, Helms.

AGRICULTURAL PRODUCTION, MARKETING AND STABILIZATION OF PRICES

Walter D. Huddleston, Chairman

Majority (6 D). Huddleston, McGovern, Eastland, Humphrey, Clark, Stone.
Minority (4 R). Young, Bellmon, Dole, Helms.

AGRICULTURAL RESEARCH AND GENERAL LEGISLATION

James B. Allen, Chairman

Majority (5 D). Allen, Eastland, Clark, McGovern, Leahy.
Minority (3 R). Dole, Young, Bellmon.

ENVIRONMENT, SOIL CONSERVATION AND FORESTRY

James O. Eastland, Chairman

Majority (4 D). Eastland, Allen, Huddleston, Leahy.
Minority (2 R). Helms, Curtis.

FOREIGN AGRICULTURAL POLICY

Hubert Humphrey, Chairman

Majority (5 D). Humphrey, McGovern, Huddleston, Clark, Stone.
Minority (3 R). Bellmon, Helms, Dole.

RURAL DEVELOPMENT

Dick Clark, Chairman

Majority (5 D). Clark, Humphrey, Eastland, Allen, Leahy.
Minority (3 R). Curtis, Dole, Bellmon.

Committee on Appropriations

John L. McClellan (Ark.), Chairman

Democratic Majority (16 D). McClellan, Magnuson (Wash.), Stennis (Miss.), Pastore (R.I.), Byrd (W.Va.), McGee (Wyo.), Mansfield (Mont.), Proxmire (Wis.), Montoya (N.M.), Inouye (Hawaii), Hollings (S.C.), Bayh (Ind.), Eagleton (Mo.), Chiles (Fla.), Johnston (La.), Huddleston (Ky.).
Republican Minority (10 R). Young (N.D.), Hruska (Neb.), Case (N.J.), Fong (Hawaii), Brooke (Mass.), Hatfield (Oreg.), Stevens (Alaska), Mathias (Md.), Schweiker (Penn.), Bellmon (Okla.).

Subcommittees

(The Chairman and ranking minority member are ex officio members of all subcommittees.)
AGRICULTURE AND RELATED AGENCIES
Gale W. McGee, Chairman

Majority (8 D). McGee, Stennis, Proxmire, Byrd, Inouye, Bayh, Eagleton, Chiles.
Minority (4 R). Fong, Hruska, Young, Hatfield.
Ex Officio: Talmadge, Eastland, Dole.
DEFENSE
John L. McClellan, Chairman

Majority (9 D). McClellan, Stennis, Pastore, Magnuson, Mansfield, McGee, Proxmire, Montoya, Inouye.
Minority (6 R). Young, Hruska, Case, Fong, Stevens, Schweiker.
Ex Officio: Symington, Jackson, Thurmond.
Intelligence Operations: McClellan, Stennis, Pastore, Young, Hruska.
DISTRICT OF COLUMBIA
Lawton Chiles, Chairman

Majority (3 D). Chiles, Johnston, Huddleston.
Minority (2 R). Mathias, Schweiker.
Ex Officio: Eagleton, Inouye, Bartlett.
FOREIGN OPERATIONS
Daniel K. Inouye, Chairman

Majority (5 D). Inouye, Proxmire, McGee, Chiles, Johnston.
Minority (3 R). Brooke, Hatfield, Mathias.
HOUSING AND URBAN DEVELOPMENT, AND INDEPENDENT AGENCIES
William Proxmire, Chairman

Majority (8 D). Proxmire, Pastore, Stennis, Mansfield, Bayh, Chiles, Johnston, Huddleston.
Minority (5 R). Mathias, Case, Fong, Brooke, Bellmon.
Aeronautical and Space Activities: Moss, Symington, Goldwater.
INTERIOR
Robert C. Byrd, Chairman

Majority (7 D). Byrd, McClellan, McGee, Montoya, Inouye, Mansfield, Hollings.
Minority (5 R). Stevens, Young, Hruska, Hatfield, Bellmon.
LABOR & HEALTH, EDUCATION AND WELFARE
Warren G. Magnuson, Chairman

Majority (9 D). Magnuson, Stennis, Byrd, Proxmire, Montoya, Hollings, Eagleton, Bayh, Chiles.
Minority (5 R). Stevens, Young, Hruska, Hatfield, Bellmon.
LEGISLATIVE
Ernest F. Hollings, Chairman

Majority (3 D). Hollings, McClellan, Huddleston.
Minority (2 R). Schweiker, Mathias.
MILITARY CONSTRUCTION
Mike Mansfield, Chairman

Majority (4 D). Mansfield, Inouye, Johnston, Huddleston.
Minority (3 R). Stevens, Bellmon, Brooke.
PUBLIC WORKS
John C. Stennis, Chairman

Majority (9 D). Stennis, Magnuson, Byrd, Pastore, McGee, Montoya, Hollings, Johnston, Huddleston.
Minority (6 R). Hatfield, Young, Hruska, Case, Schweiker, Bellmon.
STATE, JUSTICE, COMMERCE, THE JUDICIARY
John O. Pastore, Chairman

Majority (8 D). Pastore, McClellan, Mansfield, Hollings, Magnuson, Eagleton, Johnston, Huddleston.
Minority (5 R). Hruska, Fong, Brooke, Hatfield, Stevens.

TRANSPORTATION
Birch Bayh, Chairman

Majority (6 D). Bayh, Byrd, Stennis, Magnuson, Pastore, Eagleton.
Minority (4 R). Case, Stevens, Mathias, Schweiker.

TREASURY, U.S. POSTAL SERVICE, GENERAL GOVERNMENT
Joseph M. Montoya, Chairman

Majority (4 D). Montoya, Bayh, Eagleton, McClellan.
Minority (2 R). Bellmon, Hatfield.
Postal Service Items: McGee, Randolph, Fong.

Committee on Armed Services
John C. Stennis (Miss.), Chairman

Democratic Majority (10 D). Stennis, Symington (Mo.), Jackson (Wash.), Cannon (Nev.), McIntyre (N.H.), Byrd (Va.), Nunn (Ga.), Culver (Iowa), Hart (Colo.), Leahy (Vt.).
Republican Minority (6 R). Thurmond (S.C.), Tower (Tex.), Goldwater (Ariz.), Scott (Va.), Taft (Ohio), Bartlett (Okla.).

Subcommittees

ARMS CONTROL
Henry M. Jackson, Chairman

Majority (5 D). Jackson, Stennis, Symington, McIntyre, Byrd.
Minority (3 R). Tower, Taft, Bartlett.

INTELLIGENCE
John C. Stennis, Chairman

Majority (4 D). Stennis, Symington, Cannon, McIntrye.
Minority (2 R). Goldwater, Thurmond.

MANPOWER AND PERSONNEL
Sam Nunn, Chairman

Majority (3 D). Nunn, Byrd, Culver.
Minority (2 R). Scott, Bartlett.

MILITARY CONSTRUCTION AUTHORIZATION
Stuart Symington, Chairman

Majority (5 D). Symington, Jackson, Cannon, Byrd, Leahy.
Minority (3 R). Tower, Thurmond, Goldwater.

NATIONAL STOCKPILE & NAVAL PETROLEUM RESERVES
Howard W. Cannon, Chairman

Majority (4 D). Cannon, Symington, Nunn, Hart.
Minority (3 R). Scott, Taft, Bartlett.

PREPAREDNESS INVESTIGATING
John C. Stennis, Chairman

Majority (6 D). Stennis, Symington, Jackson, Cannon, McIntyre, Byrd.
Minority (5 R). Thurmond, Tower, Goldwater, Scott, Taft.

RESEARCH AND DEVELOPMENT
Thomas J. McIntyre, Chairman

Majority (3 D). McIntyre, Culver, Leahy.
Minority (2 R). Taft, Goldwater.

TACTICAL AIR POWER
Howard W. Cannon, Chairman

Majority (5 D). Cannon, Symington, Jackson, Nunn, Hart.
Minority (3 R). Goldwater, Tower, Thurmond.

Committee on Banking, Housing and Urban Affairs

William Proxmire (Wis.), Chairman

Democratic Majority (8 D). Proxmire, Sparkman (Ala.), Williams (N.J.), McIntyre (N.H.), Cranston (Cal.), Stevenson (Ill.), Biden (Del.), Morgan (N.C.).
Republican Minority (5 R). Tower (Tex.), Brooke (Mass.), Packwood (Oreg.), Helms (N.C.), Garn (Utah).

Subcommittees

CONSUMER AFFAIRS
Joseph R. Biden, Jr., Chairman

Majority (3 D). Biden, Proxmire, Morgan.
Minority (2 R). Garn, Brooke.

FINANCIAL INSTITUTIONS
Thomas J. McIntyre, Chairman

Majority (5 D). McIntyre, Proxmire, Sparkman, Williams, Stevenson.
Minority (3 R). Tower, Brooke, Helms.

HOUSING AND URBAN AFFAIRS
John Sparkman, Chairman

Majority (6 D). Sparkman, Proxmire, Williams, McIntyre, Cranston, Biden.
Minority (4 R). Brooke, Tower, Packwood, Garn.

INTERNATIONAL FINANCE
Adlai E. Stevenson III, Chairman

Majority (6 D). Stevenson, Proxmire, Williams, McIntyre, Cranston, Biden.
Minority (4 R). Packwood, Tower, Helms, Garn.

OVERSIGHT
William Proxmire, Chairman

Majority (8 D). Proxmire, Sparkman, Williams, McIntyre, Cranston, Stevenson, Biden, Morgan.
Minority (5 R). Tower, Brooke, Packwood, Helms, Garn.

PRODUCTION AND STABILIZATION
Alan Cranston, Chairman

Majority (3 D). Cranston, Stevenson, Biden.
Minority (2 R). Helms, Packwood.

SECURITIES
Majority (5 D). Williams, McIntyre, Cranston, Stevenson, Morgan.
Minority (3 R). Brooke, Tower, Helms.

SMALL BUSINESS
Robert Morgan, Chairman

Majority (3 D). Morgan, Sparkman, McIntyre.
Minority (2 R). Garn, Packwood.

Committee on Budget

Edmund S. Muskie (Maine), Chairman

Democratic Majority (10 D). Muskie, Magnuson (Wash.), Moss (Utah), Mondale (Minn.), Hollings (S.C.), Cranston (Cal.), Chiles (Fla.), Abourezk (S.D.), Biden (Del.), Nunn (Ga.).
Republican Minority (6 R). Bellmon (Okla.), Dole (Kan.), Beall (Md.), Buckley (N.Y.), McClure (Idaho), Domenici (N.M.).

(No Subcommittees)

Committee on Commerce

Warren G. Magnuson (Wash.), Chairman

Democratic Majority (12 D). Magnuson, Pastore (R.I.), Hartke (Ind.), Hart (Mich.), Cannon (Nev.), Long (La.), Moss (Utah), Hollings (S.C.), Inouye (Hawaii), Tunney (Cal.), Stevenson (Ill.), Ford (Ky.).
Republican Minority (6 R). Pearson (Kan.), Griffin (Mich.), Stevens (Alaska), Beall (Md.), Weicker (Conn.), Buckley (N.Y.).

Subcommittees

AVIATION
Howard W. Cannon, Chairman

Majority (9 D). Cannon, Magnuson, Hart, Hartke, Hollings, Inouye, Moss, Tunney, Stevenson.
Minority (4 R). Pearson, Stevens, Griffin, Beall.

COMMUNICATIONS
John O. Pastore, Chairman

Majority (8 D). Pastore, Hartke, Hart, Long, Moss, Cannon, Hollings, Inouye.
Minority (4 R). Griffin, Stevens, Beall, Weicker.

CONSUMER
Frank E. Moss, Chairman

Majority (9 D). Moss, Hart, Pastore, Hartke, Inouye, Cannon, Tunney, Stevenson, Ford.
Minority (3 R). Buckley, Beall, Weicker.

ENVIRONMENT
Philip A. Hart, Chairman

Majority (6 D). Hart, Moss, Pastore, Long, Tunney, Stevenson.
Minority (3 R). Weicker, Buckley, Pearson.

FOREIGN COMMERCE AND TOURISM
Daniel K. Inouye, Chairman

Majority (7 D). Inouye, Hartke, Cannon, Long, Moss, Stevenson, Ford.
Minority (4 R). Buckley, Stevens, Griffin, Beall.

MERCHANT MARINE
Russell B. Long, Chairman

Majority (5 D). Long, Pastore, Hollings, Inouye, Tunney.
Minority (3 R). Beall, Griffin, Stevens.

OCEANS AND ATMOSPHERE
Ernest F. Hollings, Chairman

Majority (7 D). Hollings, Pastore, Hart, Long, Inouye, Moss, Tunney.
Minority (4 R). Stevens, Beall, Buckley, Weicker.

SURFACE TRANSPORTATION
Vance Hartke, Chairman

Majority (6 D). Hartke, Cannon, Hollings, Long, Stevenson, Ford.
Minority (3 R). Weicker, Beall, Buckley.

OCEAN POLICY STUDY
Warren G. Magnuson, Chairman

Majority (12 D). Magnuson, Hollings, Pastore, Hartke, Hart, Cannon, Long, Moss, Inouye, Tunney, Stevenson, Ford.
Minority (6 R). Pearson, Griffin, Stevens, Beall, Weicker, Buckley.

SPECIAL SUBCOMMITTEE ON SCIENCE, TECHNOLOGY AND COMMERCE
John V. Tunney, Chairman

Majority (2 D). Tunney, Stevenson.
Minority (1 R). Beall.

SPECIAL SUBCOMMITTEE ON OIL AND NATURAL GAS PRODUCTION AND DISTRIBUTION
Adlai E. Stevenson III, Chairman

Majority (6 D). Stevenson, Hollings, Magnuson, Pastore, Hart, Moss.
Minority (3 R). Stevens, Beall, Weicker.

SPECIAL SUBCOMMITTEE TO STUDY TEXTILE INDUSTRY
John O. Pastore, Chairman

Majority (2 D). Pastore, Hollings.
Minority (1 R). Weicker.

SPECIAL SUBCOMMITTEE TO STUDY TRANSPORTATION ON THE GREAT LAKES-ST. LAWRENCE SEAWAY
Philip A. Hart, Chairman

Majority (4 D). Hart, Hartke, Long, Stevenson.
Minority (2 R). Griffin, Buckley.

SPECIAL SUBCOMMITTEE ON FREIGHT CAR SHORTAGE
Vance Hartke, Chairman

Majority (4 D). Hartke, Cannon, Moss, Magnuson.
Minority (2 R). Pearson, Weicker.

Committee on the District of Columbia

Thomas F. Eagleton (Mo.), Chairman

Democratic Majority (4 D). Eagleton, Inouye (Hawaii), Stevenson (Ill.), Glenn (Ohio).
Republican Minority (3 R). Mathias (Md.), Bartlett (Okla.), Garn (Utah).

(No Subcommittees)

COMMITTEE OF FINANCE
Russell B. Long (La.), Chairman

Democratic Majority (11 D). Long, Talmadge (Ga.), Hartke (Ind.), Ribicoff (Conn.), Byrd (Va.), Nelson (Wis.), Mondale (Minn.), Gravel (Alaska), Bentsen (Tex.), Hathaway (Maine), Haskell (Colo.).
Republican Minority (7 R). Curtis (Neb.), Fannin (Ariz.), Hansen (Wyo.), Dole (Kan.), Packwood (Oreg.), Roth (Del.), Brock (Tenn.).

Subcommittees

ADMINISTRATION OF THE INTERNAL REVENUE CODE
Floyd K. Haskell, Chairman

Majority (3 D). Haskell, Talmadge, Byrd.
Minority (2 R). Dole, Fannin.

ENERGY
Mike Gravel, Chairman

Majority (6 D). Gravel, Talmadge, Ribicoff, Byrd, Hathaway, Haskell.
Minority (4 R). Hansen, Fannin, Dole, Packwood.

FOUNDATIONS
Vance Hartke, Chairman

Majority (3 D). Hartke, Mondale, Gravel.
Minority (2 R). Hansen, Roth.

HEALTH
Herman E. Talmadge, Chairman

Majority (7 D). Talmadge, Hartke, Ribicoff, Mondale, Gravel, Hathaway, Haskell.
Minority (4 R). Dole, Fannin, Packwood, Brock.

INTERNATIONAL FINANCE AND RESOURCES
Harry F. Byrd, Chairman

Majority (3 D). Byrd, Gravel, Bentsen.
Minority (2 R). Roth, Brock.

REVENUE SHARING
William D. Hathaway, Chairman

Majority (3 D). Hathaway, Hartke, Nelson.
Minority (2 R). Packwood, Brock.

SOCIAL SECURITY FINANCING
Walter F. Mondale, Chairman

Majority (3 D). Mondale, Ribicoff, Bentsen.
Minority (2 R). Hansen, Curtis.

SUPPLEMENTAL SECURITY INCOME
Russell B. Long, Chairman

Majority (3 D). Long, Nelson, and Hathaway.
Minority (2 R). Fannin, Curtis.

Committee on Foreign Relations

John Sparkman (Ala.), Chairman

Democratic Majority (10 D). Sparkman (Ala.), Mansfield (Mont.), Church (Idaho), Symington (Mo.), Pell (R.I.), McGee (Wyo.), McGovern (S.D.), Humphrey (Minn.), Clark (Iowa), Biden (Del.).
Republican Minority (7 R). Case (N.J.), Javits (N.Y.), Scott (Penn.), Pearson (Kan.), Percy (Ill.), Griffin (Mich.), Baker (Tenn.).

Subcommittees

AFRICAN AFFAIRS
Dick Clark, Chairman

Majority (4 D). Clark, McGee, Humphrey, Biden.
Minority (3 R). Pearson, Griffin, Baker.

ARMS CONTROL, INTERNATIONAL ORGANIZATIONS AND SECURITY AGREEMENTS
Stuart Symington, Chairman

Majority (7 D). Symington, Pell, McGee, McGovern, Humphrey, Clark, Biden.
Minority (2 R). Javits, Case.

EUROPEAN AFFAIRS
John Sparkman, Chairman

Majority (4 D). Sparkman, Symington, Pell, Biden.
Minority (3 R). Case, Javits, Pearson.

FAR EASTERN AFFAIRS
Mike Mansfield, Chairman

Majority (2 D). Mansfield, McGovern.
Minority (3 R). Scott, Percy, Griffin.

FOREIGN ASSISTANCE AND ECONOMIC POLICY
Hubert Humphrey, Chairman

Majority (4 D). Humphrey, Church, McGee, McGovern.
Minority (3 R). Case, Javits, Scott.

MULTINATIONAL CORPORATIONS
Frank Church, Chairman

Majority (3 D). Church, Symington, Clark.
Minority (2 R). Case, Percy.

NEAR EASTERN AND SOUTH ASIAN AFFAIRS
George McGovern, Chairman

Majority (4 D). McGovern, McGee, Humphrey, Clark.
Minority (2 R). Percy, Pearson.

OCEANS AND INTERNATIONAL ENVIRONMENT
Claiborne Pell, Chairman

Majority (2 D). Pell, Biden.
Minority (2 R). Griffin, Baker.

PERSONNEL
John Sparkman, Chairman

Majority (2 D). Sparkman, Mansfield
Minority (2 R). Case, Javits.

WESTERN HEMISPHERE AFFAIRS
Gale W. McGee, Chairman

Majority (5 D). McGee, Mansfield, Symington, Pell, Humphrey.
Minority (3 R). Baker, Javits, Percy.

Committee on Government Operations

Abraham Ribicoff (Conn.), Chairman

Democratic Majority (9 D). Ribicoff, McClellan (Ark.), Jackson (Wash.), Muskie (Maine), Metcalf (Mont.), Allen (Ala.), Chiles (Fla.), Nunn (Ga.), Glenn (Ohio).
Republican Minority (5 R). Percy (Ill.), Javits (N.Y.), Roth (Del.), Brock (Tenn.), Weicker (Conn.).

Subcommittees

PERMANENT SUBCOMMITTEE ON INVESTIGATIONS
Henry M. Jackson, Chairman

Majority (6 D). Jackson, McClellan, Allen, Nunn, Chiles, Glenn.
Minority (4 R). Percy, Javits, Roth, Brock.

FEDERAL SPENDING PRACTICES, EFFICIENCY AND OPEN GOVERNMENT
Lawton M. Chiles, Chairman

Majority (5 D). Chiles, Nunn, Metcalf, Allen, Glenn.
Minority (3 R). Weicker, Roth, Brock.

OVERSIGHT PROCEDURES
Sam Nunn, Chairman

Majority (5 D). Nunn, Jackson, Muskie, Allen, Chiles.
Minority (3 R). Javits, Percy, Roth.

REPORTS, ACCOUNTING AND MANAGEMENT
Lee Metcalf, Chairman

Majority (5 D). Metcalf, McClellan, Muskie, Nunn, Glenn.
Minority (4 R). Brock, Percy, Roth, Weicker.

Committee on Interior and Insular Affairs

Henry M. Jackson (Wash.), Chairman

Democratic Majority (9 D). Jackson, Church (Idaho), Metcalf (Mont.), Johnston (La.), Abourezk (S.D.), Haskell (Colo.), Glenn (Ohio), Stone (Fla.), Bumpers (Ark.).
Republican Minority (5 R). Fannin (Ariz.), Hansen (Wyo.), Hatfield (Oreg.), McClure (Idaho), Bartlett (Okla.).

Subcommittees

(The Chairman and ranking minority member are ex officio members of all subcommittees.)

ENERGY RESEARCH AND WATER RESOURCES
Frank Church, Chairman

Majority (7 D). Church, Jackson, Abourezj, Haskell, Glenn, Stone, Bumpers.
Minority (3 R). Hatfield, Hansen, Fannin.

ENVIRONMENT AND LAND RESOURCES
Floyd K. Haskell, Chairman

Majority (7 D). Haskell, Jackson, Church, Metcalf, Abourezk, Glenn, Bumpers.
Minority (4 R). McClure, Hatfield, Hansen, Bartlett.

INDIAN AFFAIRS
James Abourezk, Chairman

Majority (4 D). Abourezk, Jackson, Metcalf, Haskell.
Minority (3 R). Bartlett, McClure, Fannin.

MINERALS, MATERIALS AND FUELS
Lee Metcalf, Chairman

Majority (6 D). Metcalf, Jackson, Johnston, Glenn, Stone, Bumpers.
Minority (3 R). Fannin, Hansen, Bartlett.

PARKS AND RECREATION
J. Bennett Johnston, Jr., Chairman

Majority (6 D). Johnston, Jackson, Church, Haskell, Stone, Bumpers.
Minority (3 R). Hansen, Hatfield, McClure.

INTEGRATED OIL OPERATIONS
Floyd K. Haskell, Chairman

Majority (4 D). Haskell, Johnston, Glenn, Stone.
Minority (3 R). Bartlett, McClure, Fannin.

Committee on the Judiciary

James O. Eastland (Miss.), Chairman

Democratic Majority (9 D). Eastland, McClellan (Ark.), Hart (Mich.), Kennedy (Mass.), Bayh (Ind.), Burdick (N.D.), Byrd (W.Va.), Tunney (Cal.), Abourezk (S.D.).
Republican Minority (6 R). Hruska (Neb.), Fong (Hawaii), Scott (Penn.), Thurmond (S.C.), Mathias (Md.), Scott (Va.).

Subcommittees

ADMINISTRATIVE PRACTICE AND PROCEDURE
Edward M. Kennedy, Chairman

Majority (5 D). Kennedy, Hart, Byrd, Burdick, Tunney.
Minority (3 R). Thurmond, Mathias, Scott (Penn.).

ANTITRUST AND MONOPOLY
Philip A. Hart, Chairman

Majority (6 D). Hart, McClellan, Kennedy, Tunney, Bayh, Abourezk.
Minority (4 R). Hruska, Fong, Thurmond, Mathias.

CONSTITUTIONAL AMENDMENTS
Birch Bayh, Chairman

Majority (5 D). Bayh, Eastland, Burdick, Abourezk, Hart.
Minority (5 R). Fong, Hruska, Thurmond, Mathias, Scott (Va.).

CONSTITUTIONAL RIGHTS
John V. Tunney, Chairman

Majority (6 D). Tunney, McClellan, Kennedy, Bayh, Hart, Abourezk.
Minority (3 R). Hruska, Fong, Thurmond.

CRIMINAL LAWS AND PROCEDURES
John L. McClellan, Chairman

Majority (5 D). McClellan, Hart, Eastland, Kennedy, Byrd.
Minority (4 R). Hruska, Scott (Penn.), Thurmond, Scott (Va.)

F.B.I. OVERSIGHT
James O. Eastland, Chairman

Majority (5 D). Eastland, McClellan, Hart, Byrd, Bayh.
Minority (3 R). Hruska, Scott (Penn.), Thurmond.

FEDERAL CHARTERS, HOLIDAYS AND CELEBRATIONS
Roman L. Hruska, Chairman

Majority (1 D). McClellan.
Minority (1 R). Hruska.
IMMIGRATION AND NATURALIZATION
James O. Eastland, Chairman

Majority (4 D). Eastland, McClellan, Kennedy, Hart.
Minority (2 R). Fong, Thurmond.
IMPROVEMENT IN JUDICIAL MACHINERY
Quentin N. Burdick, Chairman

Majority (4 D). Burdick, McClellan, Hart, Abourezk.
Minority (3 R.). Hruska, Scott (Penn.), Scott (Va.).
INTERNAL SECURITY
James O. Eastland, Chairman

Majority (3 D). Eastland, McClellan, Chairman
Minority (2 R). Thurmond, Scott (Va.).
JUVENILE DELINQUENCY
Birch Bayh, Chairman

Majority (5 D). Bayh, Hart, Burdick, Kennedy, Tunney.
Minority (3 R). Hruska, Fong, Mathias.
PATENTS, TRADEMARKS AND COPYRIGHTS
John L. McClellan, Chairman

Majority (3 D). McClellan, Hart, Burdick.
Minority (2 R). Scott (Penn.), Fong.
PENETENTIARIES
Quentin N. Burdick, Chairman

Majority (3 D). Burdick, Hart, Bayh.
Minority (2 R). Mathias, Scott (Va.).
REFUGEES AND ESCAPEES
Edward M. Kennedy, Chairman

Majority (3 D). Kennedy, McClellan, Hart.
Minority (2 R). Fong, Mathias.
SEPARATION OF POWERS
James Abourezk, Chairman

Majority (4 D). Abourezk, McClellan, Burdick, Byrd.
Minority (2 R). Mathias, Scott (Penn.).
Committee on Labor and Public Welfare

Harrison A. Williams (N.J.), Chairman

Democratic Majority (9 D). Williams, Randolph (W.Va.), Pell (R.I.), Kennedy (Mass.), Nelson (Wis.), Mondale (Minn.), Eagleton (Mo.), Cranston (Cal.), Hathaway (Maine).
Republican Minority (6 R). Javits (N.Y.), Schweiker (Penn.), Taft (Ohio), Beall (Md.), Stafford (Vt.), Laxalt (Nev.).

Subcommittees

AGING
Thomas F. Eagleton, Chairman

Majority (7 D). Eagleton, Cranston, Kennedy, Randolph, Williams, Pell, Nelson.
Minority (4 R). Beall, Schweiker, Taft, Stafford.
ALCOHOLISM AND NARCOTICS
William D. Hathaway, Chairman

Majority (7 D). Hathaway, Randolph, Williams, Kennedy, Mondale, Cranston, Nelson.
Minority (4 R). Schweiker, Javits, Beall, Laxalt.

CHILDREN AND YOUTH
Walter F. Mondale, Chairman

Majority (7 D). Mondale, Williams, Randolph, Kennedy, Nelson, Cranston, Hathaway.
Minority (4 R). Stafford, Taft, Beall, Laxalt.

EDUCATION
Claiborne Pell, Chairman

Majority (8 D). Pell, Randolph, Williams, Kennedy, Mondale, Eagleton, Cranston, Hathaway.
Minority (5 R). Beall, Javits, Schweiker, Stafford, Taft.

EMPLOYMENT– POVERTY AND MIGRATORY LABOR
Gaylord Nelson, Chairman

Majority (7 D). Nelson, Kennedy, Mondale, Cranston, Randolph, Hathaway, Williams.
Minority (4 R). Taft, Javits, Schweiker, Beall.

HANDICAPPED
Jennings Randolph, Chairman

Majority (7 D). Randolph, Cranston, Williams, Pell, Kennedy, Mondale, Hathaway.
Minority (4 R). Stafford, Taft, Schweiker, Beall.

HEALTH
Edward M. Kennedy, Chairman

Majority (8 D). Kennedy, Williams, Nelson, Eagleton, Cranston, Pell, Mondale, Hathaway.
Minority (5 R). Schweiker, Javits, Beall, Taft, Stafford.

LABOR
Harrison A. Williams, Chairman

Majority (7 D). Williams, Randolph, Pell, Nelson, Eagleton, Hathaway, Mondale.
Minority (4 R). Javits, Schweiker, Taft, Stafford.

SPECIAL SUBCOMMITTEE ON ARTS AND HUMANITIES
Claiborne Pell, Chairman

Majority (5 D). Pell, Nelson, Eagleton, Mondale, Williams.
Minority (3 R). Javits, Taft, Stafford.

SPECIAL SUBCOMMITTEE ON HUMAN RESOURCES
Alan Cranston, Chairman

Majority (4 D). Cranston, Randolph, Nelson, Williams.
Minority (3 R). Beall, Stafford, Taft.

SPECIAL SUBCOMMITTEE ON NATIONAL SCIENCE FOUNDATION
Edward M. Kennedy, Chairman

Majority (6 D). Kennedy, Pell, Eagleton, Cranston, Mondale, Williams.
Minority (3 R). Laxalt, Stafford, Schweiker.

Committee on Post Office and Civil Service

Gale W. McGee (Wyo.), Chairman

Democratic Majority (5 D). McGee, Randolph (W.Va.), Burdick (N.D.), Hollings (S.C.), Moss (Utah).
Republican Minority (4 R). Fong (Hawaii), Stevens (Alaska), Bellmon (Okla.), Dole (Kan.).

Subcommittees

(The Chairman is ex officio member of all subcommittees.)
CIVIL SERVICE POLICIES AND PRACTICES
Jennings Randolph, Chairman

Majority (3 D). Randolph, Burdick, Moss.
Minority (2 R). Bellmon, Dole.

COMPENSATION AND EMPLOYMENT BENEFITS
Quentin N. Burdick, Chairman

Majority (3 D). Burdick, Hollings, Moss.
Minority (2 R). Stevens, Bellmon.

POSTAL OPERATIONS
Ernest F. Hollings, Chairman

Majority (3 D). Hollings, Moss, Randolph.
Minority (2 R). Dole, Stevens.

Committee on Public Works

Jennings Randolph (W.Va.), Chairman

Democratic Majority (9 D). Randolph, Muskie (Maine), Montoya (N.M.), Gravel (Alaska), Bentsen (Tex.), Burdick (N.D.), Culver (Iowa), Morgan (N.C.), Hart (Colo.).
Republican Minority (5 R). Baker (Tenn.), Buckley (N.Y.), Stafford (Vt.). McClure (Idaho), Domenici (N.M.).

Subcommittees

BUILDINGS AND GROUNDS
Robert Morgan, Chairman

Majority (3 D). Morgan, Gravel, Culver.
Minority (2 R). Buckley, McClure

DISASTER RELIEF
Quentin N. Burdick, Chairman

Majority (3 D). Burdick, Morgan, Hart.
Minority (2 R). Domenici, Buckley.

ECONOMIC DEVELOPMENT
Joseph M. Montoya, Chairman

Majority (5 D). Montoya, Muskie, Burdick, Morgan, Hart.
Minority (3 R). McClure, Stafford, Domenici.

ENVIRONMENTAL POLLUTION
Edmund S. Muskie, Chairman

Majority (7 D). Muskie, Montoya, Bentsen, Gravel, Culver, Morgan, Hart.
Minority (4 R). Buckley, Stafford, McClure, Domenici.

PANEL ON ENVIRONMENTAL SCIENCE AND TECHNOLOGY
John C. Culver, Chairman

Majority (3 D). Culver, Bentsen, Hart.
Minority (2 R). Buckley, Stafford.

PANEL ON MATERIALS POLICY
Gary Hart, Chairman

Majority (3 D). Hart, Bentsen, Morgan.
Minority (2 R). Stafford, Domenici.

TRANSPORTATION
Lloyd Bentsen, Chairman

Majority (6 D). Bentsen, Montoya, Gravel, Muskie, Burdick, Culver.
Minority (4 R). Stafford, Buckley, Domenici, McClure.

WATER RESOURCES
Mike Gravel, Chairman

Majority (6 D). Gravel, Bentsen, Burdick, Culver, Morgan, Hart.
Minority (4 R). Domenici, Buckley, Stafford, McClure.

Committee on Rules and Administration

Howard W. Cannon (Nev.), Chairman

Democratic Majority (5 D). Cannon, Pell (R.I.), Byrd (W.Va.), Allen (Ala.), Williams (N.J.).
Republican Minority (3 R). Hatfield (Oreg.), Scott (Penn.), Griffin (Mich.).

Subcommittees

COMPUTER SERVICES
Howard W. Cannon, Chairman

Majority (2 D). Cannon, Williams.
Minority (1 R). Hatfield.

LIBRARY
Howard W. Cannon, Chairman

Majority (2 D). Cannon, Pell.
Minority (1 R). Scott.

PRINTING
Howard W. Cannon, Chairman

Majority (2 D). Cannon, Allen.
Minority (1 R). Hatfield.

PRIVILEGES AND ELECTIONS
Claiborne Pell, Chairman

Majority (2 D). Pell, Byrd.
Minority (1 R). Griffin.

RESTAURANT
James B. Allen, Chairman

Majority (2 D). Allen, Williams.
Minority (1 R). Hatfield.

SMITHSONIAN INSTITUTION
Claiborne Pell, Chairman

Majority (2 D). Pell, Williams.
Minority (1 R). Scott.

STANDING RULES ON THE SENATE
Robert C. Byrd, Chairman

Majority (2 D). Byrd, Cannon.
Minority (1 R). Griffin.

Committee on Veterans' Affairs

Vance Hartke (Ind.), Chairman

Democratic Majority (5 D). Hartke, Talmadge (Ga.), Randolf (W.Va.), Cranston (Cal.), Stone (Fla.).
Republican Minority (4 R). Hansen (Wyo.), Thurmond (S.C.), Stafford (Vt.). Scott (Va.).

Subcommittees

COMPENSATION AND PENSION
Herman E. Talmadge, Chairman

Majority (3 D). Talmadge, Randolph, Stone.
Minority (2 R). Hansen, Thurmond.

HEALTH AND HOSPITALS
Alan Cranston, Chairman

Majority (3 D). Cranston, Randolph, Stone.
Minority (2 R). Thurmond, Hansen.

HOUSING AND INSURANCE
Richard (Dick) Stone, Chairman

Majority (3 D). Stone, Talmadge, Cranston.
Minority (2 R). Scott, Stafford.

READJUSTMENT, EDUCAITON AND EMPLOYMENT
Vance Hartke, Chairman

Majority (3 D). Hartke, Talmadge, Cranston.
Minority (2 R). Stafford, Scott.

Select Committee to Study Govermental Operations with Respect to Intelligence Activities
Frank Church (Idaho), Chairman

Democratic Majority (6 D). Church, Hart (Mich.), Hart (Colo.), Mondale (Minn.), Huddleston (Ky.), Morgan (N.C.).
Republican Minority (5 R). Tower (Tex.), Baker (Tenn.), Goldwater (Ariz.), Mathias (Md.), Schweiker (Penn.).

(No Subcommittees)

Select Committee on Nutrition and Human Needs
George McGovern (S.D.), Chairman

Democratic Majority (8 D). McGovern, Talmadge (Ga.), Hart (Mich.), Mondale (Minn.), Kennedy (Minn.), Nelson (Wis.), Cranston (Cal.), Humphrey (Minn.).
Republican Minority (5 R). Percy (Ill.), Dole (Kan.), Bellmon (Okla.), Schweiker (Penn.), Taft (Ohio).

(No Subcommittees)

Select Committee on Small Business
Gaylord Nelson (Wis.), Chairman

Democratic Majority (10 D). Nelson, Sparkman (Ala.), McIntyre (N. H.), Nunn (Ga.), Johnston (La.), Hathaway (Maine), Abourezk (S.D.), Haskell (Colo.), Clark (Iowa), Mondale (Minn.).
Republican Minority (7 R). Javits (N.Y.), Beall (Md.), Brock (Tenn.), Weicker (Conn.), Barlett (Okla.), Laxalt (Nev.), 1 vacancy.

Subcommittees

ENVIRONMENTAL, RURAL AND URBAN ECOMONIC DEVELOPMENT
Sam Nunn, Chairman

Majority (5 D). Nunn, Abourezk, Johnston, Haskell, Nelson.
Minority (4 R). Brock, Beall, Weicker, Javits.

FINANCING AND INVESTMENT
John Sparkman, Chairman

Majority (5 D). Sparkman, Hathaway, Haskell, McIntyre, Nelson.
Minority (4 R). Brock, Laxalt, Javits, 1 vacancy.

GOVERNMENT PROCUREMENT
William D. Hathaway, Chairman

Majority (5 D). Hathaway, Johnston, Sparkman, Mondale, Nelson.
Minority (4 R). Weicker, Bartlett, Laxalt, Javits.

GOVERNMENT REGULATION
Thomas J. McIntyre, Chairman

Majority (5 D). McIntyre, Nunn, Clark, Mondale, Nelson.
Minority (4 R). Beall, Weicker, Brock, Javits.

MONOPOLY
Gaylord Nelson, Chairman

Majority (5 D). Nelson, McIntyre, Hathaway, Abourezk, Haskell.
Minority (4 R). Bartlett, Beall, Javits, 1 vacancy.

RETAILING, DISTRIBUTION, AND MARKETING PRACTICES
J. Bennett Johnston, Jr., Chairman

Majority (5 D). Johnston, Abourezk, Clark, Nunn, Nelson.
Minority (4 R). Laxalt, Bartlett, Javits, 1 vacancy.

Select Committee on Standards and Conduct

Howard H. Cannon (Nev.), Chairman

Democratic Majority (3 D). Cannon, Stennis (Miss.), Talmadge (Ga.).
Republican Minority (3 R). Young (N.D.), Curtis (Neb.), Brooke (Mass.).

Special Committee on Aging

Frank Church (Idaho), Chairman

Democratic Majority (13 D). Church, Williams (N.J.), Randolph (W.Va.), Muskie (Maine), Moss (Utah), Kennedy (Mass.), Mondale (Minn.), Hartke (Ind.), Pell (R.I.), Eagleton (Mo.), Tunney (Cal.), Chiles (Fla.), Clark (Iowa).
Republican Minority (9 R). Fong (Hawaii), Hansen (Wyo.), Brooke (Mass.), Percy (Ill.), Stafford (Vt.), Beall (Md.), Domenici (N.M.), Brock (Tenn.), Bartlett (Okla.).

CONSUMER INTEREST OF THE ELDERLY

Frank Church, Chairman

Majority (11 D). Church, Williams, Muskie, Kennedy, Mondale, Hartke, Eagleton, Chiles, Moss, Tunney, Clark.
Minority (7 R). Brooke, Fong, Hansen, Percy, Stafford, Domenici, Brock.

EMPLOYMENT AND RETIREMENT INCOMES

Jennings Randolph, Chairman

Majority (9 D). Randolph, Church, Moss, Mondale, Hartke, Kennedy, Tunney, Chiles, Clark.
Minority (6 R). Brock, Fong, Hansen, Percy, Stafford, Beall.

FEDERAL, STATE AND COMMUNITY SERVICES

Edward M. Kennedy, Chairman

Majority (6 D). Kennedy, Hartke, Pell, Eagleton, Tunney, Clark.
Minority (4 R). Beall, Brooke, Percy, Bartlett.

HEALTH OF THE ELDERLY

Edmund S. Muskie, Chairman

Majority (11 D). Muskie, Moss, Williams, Kennedy, Mondale, Hartke, Pell, Eagleton, Tunney, Chiles, Clark.
Minority (7 R). Domenici, Hansen, Brooke, Percy, Stafford, Beall, Bartlett.

HOUSING FOR THE ELDERLY

Harrison A. Williams, Chairman

Majority (11 D). Williams, Church, Muskie, Kennedy, Mondale, Pell, Tunney, Chiles, Moss, Hartke, Clark.
Minority (7 R). Hansen, Fong, Brooke, Stafford, Domenici, Brock, Bartlett.

LONG TERM CARE

Frank E. Moss, Chairman

Majority (11 D). Moss, Williams, Church, Muskie, Kennedy, Pell, Eagleton, Tunney, Mondale, Chiles, Clark.
Minority (7 R). Percy, Fong, Brooke, Beall, Domenici, Brock, Bartlett.

RETIREMENT AND THE INDIVIDUAL

Walter F. Mondale, Chairman

Majority (8 D). Mondale, Kennedy, Hartke, Pell, Eagleton, Chiles, Williams, Muskie.
Minority (5 R). Stafford, Hansen, Percy, Beall, Domenici.

Special Committee on National Emergencies and Delegated Emergency Powers

Frank Church (Idaho) and Charles Mathias (Md.), Co-Chairmen

Majority (4 D). Church, Hart (Mich.), Pell (R.I.), Stevenson (Ill.).
Minority (4 R). Mathias, Case (N.J.), Pearson (Kan.), Hansen (Wyo.).

HOUSE COMMITTEES

Committee on Agriculture
Thomas S. Foley (Wash.), Chairman

Democratic Majority (29 D). Foley, Poage (Tex.), de la Garza (Tex.), Vigorito (Penn.), Jones (N.C.), Jones (Tenn.), Melcher (Mont.), Mathis (Ga.), Bergland (Minn.), Brown (Cal.), Bowen (Miss.), Rose (N.C.), Litton (Mo.), Breckenridge (Ky.), Richmond (N.Y.), Nolan (Minn.), Weaver (Oreg.), Baldus (Wis.), Krebs (Cal.), Harkin (Iowa), Hightower (Tex.), Bedell (Iowa), McHugh (N.Y.), English (Okla.), Fithian (Ind.), Jenrette (S.C.), D'Amours (N.H.), 2 vacancies.
Republican Minority (14 R). Wampler (Va.), Sebelius (Kans.), Findley (Ill.), Thone (Neb.), Symms (Idaho), Johnson (Colo.), Madigan (Ill.), Peyser (N.Y.), Heckler (Mass.), Jeffords (Vt.), Kelly (Fla.), Grassley (Iowa), Hagedorn (Minn.), Moore (La.).

Subcommittees

(The chairman and ranking minority member are ex officio members of all subcommittees.)
CONSERVATION AND CREDIT
Bob Bergland, Chairman

Majority (8 D). Bergland, Poage, de la Garza, Baldus, English, Richmond, Hightower, Bedell.
Minority (3 R). Madigan, Jeffords, Kelly.
COTTON
David R. Bowen, Chairman

Majority (8 D). Bowen, Jones (Tenn.), Krebs, Hightower, Poage, de la Garza, English, Jenrette.
Minority (3 R). Moore, Peyser, Hagedorn.
DAIRY AND POULTRY
Ed Jones (Tenn.), Chairman

Majority (8 D). Jones (Tenn.), Vigorito, Bowen, Nolan, Baldus, Krebs, McHugh, Bergland.
Minority (3 R). Jeffords, Kelley, Hagedorn.
DEPARTMENT OPERATIONS, INVESTIGATIONS AND OVERSIGHT
E de la Garza, Chairman

Majority (8 D). de la Garza, Brown, Richmond, Harkin, McHugh, D'Amours, Breckenridge, Weaver.
Minority (3 R). Thone, Heckler, Grassley.
DOMESTIC MARKETING AND CONSUMER RELATIONS
Joseph P. Vigorito, Chairman

Majority (8 D). Vigorito, Brown, D'Amours, Richmond, Fithian, Harkin, McHugh, 1 vacancy.
Minority (3 R). Findley, Heckler, Grassley.
FAMILY FARMS AND RURAL DEVELOPMENT
Charles Rose, Chairman

Majority (8 D). Rose, Breckinridge, Bedell, Jones (N.C.), Melcher, Litton, Nolan, Baldus.
Minority (3 R). Peyser, Sebelius, Grassley.
FORESTS
Jerry Litton, Chairman

Majority (8 D). Litton, Melcher, Weaver, Vigorito, Krebs, Brown, Mathis, 1 vacancy.
Minority (3 R). Symms, Johnson, Kelly.
LIVESTOCK AND GRAINS
W. R. Poage, Chairman

Majority (12 D). Poage, Melcher, Bergland, Litton, Weaver, Harkin, Hightower, Bedell, English, Fithian, Nolan, D'Amours.
Minority (6 R). Sebelius, Findley, Thone, Symms, Johnson, Hagedorn.
OILSEEDS AND RICE
Dawson Mathis, Chairman

Majority (8 D). Mathis, Jones (N.C.), Jenrette, Jones (Tenn.), Bowen, Rose, Fithian, 1 vacancy.
Minority (3 R). Johnson, Findley, Moore.

TOBACCO
Walter B. Jones (N.C.), Chairman

Majority (8 D). Jones, Mathis, Rose, Breckinridge, Jenrette, 3 vacancies.
Minority (3 R). Wampler, Madigan, Moore.

Committee on Appropriations

George H. Mahon (Tex.), Chairman

Democratic Majority (37 D). Mahon, Whitten (Miss.), Sikes (Fla.), Passman (La.), Evins (Tenn.), Boland (Mass.), Natcher (Ky.), Flood (Penn.), Steed (Okla.), Shipley (Ill.), Slack (W.Va.), Flynt (Ga.), Smith (Iowa), Giaino (Conn.), Addabbo (N.Y.), McFall (Cal.), Patten (N.J.), Long (Md.), Yates (Ill.), Casey (Tex.), Evans (Colo.), Obey (Wis.), Roybal (Cal.), Stokes (Ohio), Roush (Ind.), McKay (Utah), Bevill (Ala.), Chappell (Fla.), Burlison (Mo.), Alexander (Ark.), Koch (N.Y.), Burke (Cal.), Murtha (Penn.), Traxler (Mich.), Duncan (Oreg.), Early (Mass.), Baucus (Mont.)
Republican Minority (18 R). Cederberg (Mich.), Michel (Ill.), Conte (Mass.), Shriver (Kans.), McDade (Penn.), Andrews (N.D.), Talcott (Cal.), Edwards (Ala.), McEwan (N.Y.), Myers (Ind.), Robinson (Va.), Miller (Ohio), Coughlin (Penn.), Young (Fla.), Kemp (N.Y.), Armstrong (Colo.), Regula (Ohio), Burgener (Cal.).

Subcommittees

AGRICULTURE AND RELATED AGENCIES
Jamie L. Whitten, Chairman

Majority (8 D). Whitten, Shipley, Evans, Burlison, Baucus, Passman, Natcher, Casey.
Minority (3 R). Andrews, Robinson, Myers.

DEFENSE
George H. Mahon, Chairman

Majority (9 D). Mahon, Sikes, Flood, Addabbo, McFall, Flynt, Giaimo, Chappell, Burlison.
Minority (3 R). Edwards, Robinson, Kemp.

DISTRICT OF COLUMBIA
William H. Natcher, Chairman

Majority (8 D). Natcher, Giaimo, Stokes, McKay, Chappell, Burlison, Alexander, Koch.
Minority (3 R). Young, Kemp, Burgener.

FOREIGN OPERATIONS
Otto E. Passman, Chairman

Majority (8 D). Passman, Long, Roush, Obey, Bevill, Chappell, Koch, Early.
Minority (3 R). Shriver, Conte, Coughlin.

HUD—INDEPENDENT AGENCIES
Edward P. Boland, Chairman

Majority (8 D). Boland, Evins, Shipley, Roush, Traxler, Baucus, Stokes, Burke.
Minority (3 R). Talcott, McDade, Young.

INTERIOR
Sidney R. Yates, Chairman

Majority (5 D). Yates, McKay, Long, Murtha, Duncan.
Minority (2 R). McDade, Regula.

LABOR—HEALTH, EDUCATION, AND WELFARE
Daniel J. Flood, Chairman

Majority (8 D). Flood, Natcher, Smith, Casey, Patten, Obey, Roybal, Stokes.
Minority (3 R). Michel, Shriver, Conte.

LEGISLATIVE
Bob Casey, Chairman

Majority (8 D). Casey, Shipley, Giaimo, McFall, Yates, Evans, Roybal, Roush.
Minority (4 R). Coughlin, Cederberg, Armstrong, Regula.

MILITARY CONSTRUCTION
Robert L. F. Sikes, Chairman

Majority (6 D). Sikes, Patten, McKay, Murtha, Traxler, Steed.
Minority (2 R). Myers, Burgener.

PUBLIC WORKS
Joe L. Evins, Chairman

Majority (6 D). Evins, Boland, Whitten, Slack, Passman, Bevill.
Minority (2 R). Myers, Burgener.

STATE, JUSTICE, COMMERCE, AND JUDICIARY
John M. Slack, Chairman

Majority (6 D). Slack, Smith, Flynt, Alexander, Burke, Early.
Minority (3 R). Cederberg, Andrews, Miller.

TRANSPORTATION
John J. McFall, Chairman

Majority (6 D). McFall, Yates, Steed, Koch, Alexander, Duncan.
Minority (2 R). Conte, Edwards.

TREASURY—POSTAL SERVICE—GENERAL GOVERNMENT
Tom Steed, Chairman

Majority (8 D). Steed, Addabbo, Roybal, Sikes, Boland, Flynt, Patten, Long.
Minority (3 R). Miller, McEwan, Armstrong.

Committee on Armed Services

Melvin Price (Ill.), Chairman

Democratic Majority (27 D). Price, Hebert (La.), Bennett (Fla.), Stratton (N.Y.), Ichord (Mo.), Nedzi (Mich.), Randall (Mo.), Charles H. Wilson (Cal.), Leggett (Cal.), Hicks (Wash.), White (Tex.), Nichols (Ala.), Brinkley (Ga.), Mollohan (W.Va.), Dan Daniel (Va.), Montgomery (Miss.), Runnels (N.M.), Aspin (Wis.), Dellums (Cal.), Davis (S.C.), Schroeder (Colo.), Kazen (Tex.), Won Pat (Guam), Carr (Mich.), Lloyd (Cal.), McDonald (Ga.), Downey (N.Y.).
Republican Minority (13 R). Bob Wilson (Cal.), Dickinson (Ala.), Whitehurst (Va.), Spence (S.C.), Treen (La.), O'Brien (Ill.), Beard (Tenn.), Mitchell (N.Y.), Holt (Md.), Robert W. Daniel (Va.), Hillis (Ind.), Hinshaw (Cal.), Schulze (Penn.)

Subcommittees

(The chairman and ranking minority member are ex officio members of all subcommittees.)
INVESTIGATIONS
F. Edward Hebert, Chairman

Majority (9 D). Hebert, Randall, Leggett, Nichols, Mollohan, Dan Daniel, Carr, Stratton, Nedzi.
Minority (4 R). Beard, Mitchell, Dickinson, Robert W. Daniel.

MILITARY COMPENSATION
Samuel S. Stratton, Chairman

Majority (9 D). Stratton, Nichols, Brinkley, Runnels, Aspin, Dellums, Won Pat, Downey, Price.
Minority (4 R). O'Brien, Mitchell, Holt, Treen.

MILITARY INSTALLATIONS AND FACILITIES
Richard H. Ichord, Chairman

Majority (9 D). Ichord, Randall, Charles H. Wilson, White, Brinkley, Davis, Kazen, Won Pat, Bennett.
Minority (4 R). Whitehurst, Beard, Hillis, Hinshaw.

MILITARY PERSONNEL
Lucien N. Nedzi, Chairman

Majority (9 D). Nedzi, Charles H. Wilson, Daniel, Montgomery, Aspin, Dellums, Kazen, Downey, Hebert.
Minority (4 R). Treen, Holt, Hillis, O'Brien.

RESEARCH AND DEVELOPMENT
Melvin Price, Chairman

Majority (9 D). Price, Leggett, Hicks, White, Runnels, Schroeder, Lloyd, McDonald, Ichord.
Minority (4 R). Dickinson, Spence, Hinshaw, Whitehurst.

SEAPOWER AND STRATEGIC AND CRITICAL MATERIALS
Charles E. Bennett, Chairman

Majority (9 D). Bennett, Hicks, Mollohan, Montgomery, Davis, Schroeder, Carr, Lloyd, McDonald.
Minority (4 R). Spence, Robert W. Daniel, Schulze, Bob Wilson.

SPECIAL SUBCOMMITTEE ON INVESTIGATIONS
Lucien N. Nedzi, Chairman

Majority (5 D). Nedzi, Price, Hebert, Bennett, Stratton.
Minority (2 R). Bob Wilson, Dickinson.

Committee on Banking, Currency, and Housing

Henry S. Reuss (Wis.), Chairman

Democratic Majority (29 D). Reuss, Patman (Tex.), Barrett (Penn.), Sullivan (Mo.), Ashley (Ohio), Moorhead (Penn.), Stephens (Ga.), St Germain (R.I.), Gonzalez (Tex.), Minish (N.J.), Annunzio (Ill.), Rees (Cal.), Hanley (N.Y.), Mitchell (Md.), Fauntroy (D.C.), Boggs (La.), Neal (N.C.), Patterson (Cal.), Blanchard (Mich.), Maguire (N.J.), Ford (Tenn.), Hubbard (Ky.), LaFalce (N.Y.), Spellman (Md.), AuCoin (Oreg.), Tsongas (Mass.), Derrick (S.C.), Hayes (Ind.), Hannaford (Cal.).
Republican Minority (14 R). Johnson (Penn.), J. William Stanton (Ohio), Brown (Mich.), Wylie (Ohio), Rousselot (Cal.), McKinney (Conn.), Conlan (Ariz.), Hansen (Idaho), Schulze (Penn.), Gradison (Ohio), Hyde (Ill.), Kelly (Fla.), Grassley (Iowa), Fenwick (N.J.).

Subcommittees

CONSUMER AFFAIRS
Frank Annunzio, Chairman

Majority (7 D). Annunzio, Sullivan, Spellman, Barrett, Gonzales, Fauntroy, Neal.
Minority (3 R). Wylie, Fenwick, Grassley.

DOMESTIC MONETARY POLICY
Wright Patman, Chairman

Majority (7 D). Patman, Minish, Ford, Hannaford, Neal, Blanchard, Barrett.
Minority (3 R). Conlan, Hansen, Gradison.

ECONOMIC STABILIZATION
Thomas L. Ashley, Chairman

Majority (11 D). Ashley, Blanchard, Hubbard, LaFalce, Sullivan, Rees, Patterson, Maguire, Spellman, Tsongas, St Germain.
Minority (5 R). McKinney, Stanton, Schulze, Gradison, Kelly.

FINANCIAL INSTITUTIONS SUPERVISION, REGULATION AND INSURANCE
Fernand J. St Germain, Chairman

Majority (13 D). St. Germain, Annunzio, Barrett, Hanley, Moorhead, Hubbard, Patman, Neal, Patterson, Derrick, Ashley, Fauntroy, Boggs.
Minority (6 R). Rousselot, Johnson, Wylie, Brown, Gradison, Hyde.

GENERAL OVERSIGHT AND RENEGOTIATION
Joseph G. Minish, Chairman

Majority (7 D). Minish, Mitchell, Derrick, Hayes, Gonzalez, St Germain, Boggs.
Minority (3 R). Hansen, Rousselot, McKinney.

HISTORIC PRESERVATION AND COINAGE
Robert G. Stephens, Jr., Chairman

Majority (5 D). Stephens, Spellman, Annunzio, Hayes, Hannaford.
Minority (2 R). Schulze, Johnson.

HOUSING AND COMMUNITY DEVELOPMENT
William A. Barrett, Chairman

Majority (17 D). Barrett, Sullivan, Ashley, Moorhead, Stephens, St Germain, Gonzalez, Mitchell, Hanley, Fauntroy, Boggs, Patterson, Maguire, Ford, LaFalce, AuCoin, Rees.
Minority (8 R). Brown, Stanton, Rousselot, Wylie, McKinney, Conlan, Kelly, Grassley.

INTERNATIONAL DEVELOPMENT INSTITUTIONS AND FINANCE
Henry B. Gonzalez, Chairman

Majority (9 D). Gonzalez, Tsongas, Boggs, Stephens, Hanley, Rees, Fauntroy, Spellman, Hubbard.
Minority (4 R). Johnson, Hyde, Grassley, Fenwick.

INTERNATIONAL TRADE, INVESTMENT AND MONETARY POLICY
Thomas M. Rees, Chairman

Majority (13 D). Rees, Neal, Hayes, Hannaford, Blanchard, Maguire, AuCoin, Tsongas, Moorhead, St Germain, Hubbard, LaFalce, Ashley.
Minority (6 R). Stanton, Brown, Conlan, Hyde, Kelly, Fenwick.

Committee on Budget

Brock Adams (Wash.), Chairman

Democratic Majority (17 D). Adams, O'Neill (Mass.), Wright (Tex.), Ashley (Ohio), Giaimo (Conn.), Smith (Iowa), O'Hara (Mich.), Leggett (Cal.), Mitchell (Md.), Burleson (Tex.), Landrum (Ga.), Gibbons (Fla.), Mink (Hawaii), Stokes (Ohio), Runnels (N.M.), Holtzman (N.Y.), Derrick (S.C.).
Republican Minority (8 R). Latta (Ohio), Cederberg (Mich.), Schneebeli (Penn.), Broyhill (N.C.), Clawson (Cal.), Hastings (N.Y.), Shriver (Kans.), Conable (N.Y.).

(No subcommittees)

Committee on the District of Columbia

Charles C. Diggs, Jr. (Mich.), Chairman

Democratic Majority (17 D). Diggs, Fraser (Minn.), Stuckey (Ga.), Dellums (Cal.), Rees (Cal.), Fauntroy (D.C.), Howard (N.J.), Mann (S.C.), Mazzoli (Ky.), Harris (Va.), Dan Daniel (Va.), Litton (Mo.), Meyner (N.J.), Nowak (N.Y.), Sharp (Ind.), Florio (N.J.), 1 vacancy.
Republican Minority (8 R). Gude (Md.), Harsha (Ohio), McKinney (Conn.), Biester (Penn.), Railsback (Ill.), Robert W. Daniel (Va.), Whalen (Ohio), 1 vacancy.

Subcommittees

COMMERCE, HOUSING, AND TRANSPORTATION
W. S. (Bill) Stuckey, Jr., Chairman

Majority (6 D). Stuckey, Nowak, Litton, Harris, Dan Daniel, Sharp.
Minority (3 R). Gude, Harsha, McKinney.

EDUCATION, LABOR, AND SOCIAL SERVICES
Ronald V. Dellums, Chairman

Majority (6 D). Dellums, Florio, Dan Daniel, Meyner, Litton, 1 vacancy.
Minority (3 R). Biester, McKinney, Railsback.

FISCAL AFFAIRS
Romano L. Mazzoli, Chairman

Majority (6 D). Mazzoli, Rees, Dellums, Fauntroy, Stuckey, Dan Daniel.
Minority (3 R). McKinney, Robert W. Daniel, Whalen.

GOVERNMENT OPERATIONS
Walter E. Fauntroy, Chairman

Majority (6 D). Fauntroy, Fraser, Litton, Florio, 2 vacancies.
Minority (3 R). Whalen, Gude, 1 vacancy.

JUDICIARY
James R. Mann, Chairman

Majority (6 D). Mann, Rees, Nowak, Fauntroy, Mazzoli, 1 vacancy.
Minority (3 R). Railsback, Harsha, Biester.

THE BICENTENNIAL, THE ENVIRONMENT, AND THE INTERNATIONAL COMMUNITY
Herbert E. Harris II, Chairman

Majority (5 D). Harris, Fraser, Meyner, Sharp, Mann.
Minority (3 R). Robert W. Daniel, Gude, 1 vacancy.

Committee on Education and Labor

Carl D. Perkins (Ky.), Chairman

Democratic Majority (27 D). Perkins, Thompson (N.J.), Dent (Penn.), Daniels (N.J.), Brademas (Ind.), O'Hara (Mich.), Hawkins (Cal.), Ford (Mich.), Mink (Hawaii), Meeds (Wash.), Philip Burton (Cal.), Gaydos (Penn.), Clay (Mo.), Chisholm (N.Y.), Biaggi (N.Y.), Andrews (N.C.), Lehman (Fla.), Benitez (P.R.), Blouin (Iowa), Cornell (Wis.), Risenhoover (Okla.), Simon (Ill.), Beard (R.I.), Zeferetti (N.Y.), Miller (Cal.), Mottl (Ohio), Hall (Ill.).
Republican Minority (13 R). Quie (Minn.), Ashbrook (Ohio), Bell (Cal.), Erlenborn (Ill.), Esch (Mich.), Eshleman (Penn.), Peyser (N.Y.), Sarasin (Conn.), Buchanan (Ala.), Jeffords (Vt.), Pressler (S.D.), Goodling (Penn.), Smith (Neb.).

Subcommittees

(The chairman and ranking minority member are ex officio members, with vote, of all subcommittees.)

AGRICULTURAL LABOR
William D. Ford, Chairman

Majority (4 D). Ford, Blouin, Meeds, Dent.
Minority (1 R). Sarasin.

ELEMENTARY, SECONDARY AND VOCATIONAL EDUCATION
Carl D. Perkins, Chairman

Majority (15 D). Perkins, Ford, Mink, Meeds, Chisholm, Andrews, Lehman, Risenhoover, Simon, Mottl, Hall, Blouin, O'Hara, Zeferetti, Miller.
Minority (7 R). Quie, Bell, Eshleman, Buchanan, Pressler, Goodling, Jeffords.

EQUAL OPPORTUNITIES
Augustus F. Hawkins, Chairman

Majority (4 D). Hawkins, Clay, Benitez, Mink.
Minority (1 R). Buchanan.

LABOR-MANAGEMENT RELATIONS
Frank Thompson, Jr., Chairman

Majority (6 D). Thompson, Brademas, Ford, Clay, Biaggi, Miller.
Minority (2 R). Ashbrook, Esch.

LABOR STANDARDS
John H. Dent, Chairman

Majority (12 D). Dent, Daniels, Burton, Gaydos, Clay, Biaggi, Benitez, Zeferetti, Miller, Cornell, Risenhoover, Simon.
Minority (5 R). Erlenborn, Sarasin, Ashbrook, Bell, Goodling.

MANPOWER, COMPENSATION, AND HEALTH AND SAFETY
Dominick V. Daniels, Chairman

Majority (10 D). Daniels, Dent, O'Hara, Burton, Gaydos, Beard, Hawkins, Lehman, Meeds, Risenhoover.
Minority (4 R). Esch, Peyser, Sarasin, Smith.

POSTSECONDARY EDUCATION
James G. O'Hara, Chairman

Majority (12 D). O'Hara, Brademas, Biaggi, Andrews, Blouin, Thompson, Mottl, Hawkins, Chisholm, Benitez, Simon, Hall.
Minority (5 R). Eshleman, Erlenborn, Esch, Buchanan, Smith.

SELECT EDUCATION
John Brademas, Chairman

Majority (10 D). Brademas, Mink, Meeds, Chisholm, Lehman, Cornell, Beard, Zeferetti, Miller, Hall.
Minority (4 R). Bell, Peyser, Jefford, Pressler.

Committee on International Relations

Thomas E. Morgan (Penn.), Chairman

Democratic Majority (25 D). Morgan, Zablocki (Wis.), Hays (Ohio), Fountain (N.C.), Fascell (Fla.), Diggs (Mich.), Nix (Penn.), Fraser (Minn.), Rosenthal (N.Y.), Hamilton (Ind.), Wolff (N.Y.), Bingham (N.Y.), Taylor (Penn.), Harrington (Mass.), Ryan (Cal.), Wilson (Tex.), Riegle (Mich.), Collins (Ill.), Solarz (N.Y.), Meyner (N.J.), Bonker (Wash.), 3 vacancies.
Republican Minority (12 R). Broomfield (Mich.), Derwinski (Ill.), Findley (Ill.), Buchanan (Ala.), Burke (Fla.), du Pont (Del.), Whalen (Ohio), Biester (Penn.), Winn (Kans.), Gilman (N.Y.), Guyer (Ohio), Lagomarsino (Cal.).

Subcommittees

(The chairman and ranking minority member are ex officio members of all standing subcommittees.)

FUTURE FOREIGN POLICY RESEARCH AND DEVELOPMENT
Lester L. Wolff, Chairman

Majority (5 D). Wolff, Morgan, Zablocki, Hays, Yatron.
Minority (2 R). Burke, Guyer.

INTERNATIONAL ECONOMIC POLICY
Robert N.C. Nix, Chairman

Majority (5 D). Nix, Hamilton, Solarz, 2 vacancies.
Minority (2 R). Whalen, Biester.

INTERNATIONAL OPERATIONS
Wayne L. Hays, Chairman

Majority (5 D). Hays, Diggs, Wolff, Ryan, Meyner.
Minority (2 R). Buchanan, Burke.

INTERNATIONAL ORGANIZATIONS
Donald M. Fraser, Chairman

Majority (5 D). Fraser, Fascell, Rosenthal, Harrington, Collins.
Minority (2 R). Derwinski, Findley.

INTERNATIONAL POLITICAL AND MILITARY AFFAIRS
Dante B. Fascell, Chairman

Majority (5 D). Fascell, Rosenthal, Taylor, Wilson, Riegle.
Minority (2 R). Winn, Buchanan.

INTERNATIONAL RESOURCES, FOOD, AND ENERGY
Charles C. Diggs, Jr., Chairman

Majority (5 D). Diggs, Nix, Collins, Solarz, 1 vacancy.
Minority (2 R). Gilman, du Pont.

INTERNATIONAL SECURITY AND SCIENTIFIC AFFAIRS
Clement J. Zablocki, Chairman

Majority (5 D). Zablocki, Fountain, Bingham, Wilson, Riegle.
Minority (2 R). Findley, Lagomarsino.

INTERNATIONAL TRADE AND COMMERCE
Jonathan B. Bingham, Chairman

Majority (5 D). Bingham, Fraser, Taylor, Bonker, 1 vacancy.
Minority (2 R). Biester, Whalen.

INVESTIGATIONS
Lee H. Hamilton, Chairman

Majority (5 D). Hamilton, Fountain, Yatron, Harrington, Bonker.
Minority (2 R). du Pont, Winn.

OVERSIGHT
Thomas E. Morgan, Chairman

Majority (5 D). Morgan, Zablocki, Hays, Ryan, Meyner.
Minority (2 R). Broomfield, Derwinski.

Committee on Government Operations

Jack Brooks (Tex.), Chairman

Democratic Majority (29 D). Brooks, Fountain (N.C.), Moss (Cal.), Fascell (Fla.), Macdonald (Mass.), Moorhead (Penn.), Randall (Mo.), Rosenthal (N.Y.), Wright (Tex.), St Germain (R.I.), Hicks (Wash.), Fuqua (Fla.), Conyers (Mich.), Abzug (N.Y.), James V. Stanton (Ohio), Ryan (Cal.), Collins (Ill.), John L. Burton (Cal.), Preyer (N.C.), Harrington (Mass.), Drinan (Mass.), Mezvinsky (Iowa), Jordan (Tex.), English (Okla.), Levitas (Ga.), Evans (Ind.), Moffett (Conn.), Maguire (N.J.), Aspin (Wis.).
Republican Minority (14 R). Horton (N.Y.), Erlenborn (Ill.), Wydler (N.Y.), Brown (Ohio), Gude (Md.), McCloskey (Cal.), Steiger (Ariz.), Brown (Mich.), Thone (Neb.), Steelman (Tex.), Pritchard (Wash.), Forsythe (N.J.), Kasten (Wis.), Gradison (Ohio).

Subcommittees

(The chairman and ranking minority member are ex officio members of all subcommittees on which they do not hold a regular assignment.)

COMMERCE, CONSUMER, AND MONETARY AFFAIRS
Benjamin S. Rosenthal, Chairman

Majority (8 D). Rosenthal, Collins, Drinan, Levitas, Evans, Moffett, Maguire, Mezvinsky.
Minority (3 R). Brown, Gradison, Erlenborn.

CONSERVATION, ENERGY, AND NATURAL RESOURCES
William S. Moorhead, Chairman

Majority (8 D). Moorhead, Fascell, Ryan, Fountain, Burton, Macdonald, St Germain, Preyer.
Minority (3 R). Gude, McCloskey, Forsythe.

GOVERNMENT ACTIVITIES AND TRANSPORTATION
William J. Randall, Chairman

Majority (8 D). Randall, Collins, English, Abzug, Preyer, Evans, 2 vacancies.
Minority (3 R). Thone, Forsythe, Gradison.

GOVERNMENT INFORMATION AND INDIVIDUAL RIGHTS
Bella S. Abzug, Chairman

Majority (8 D). Abzug, Wright, Ryan, Conyers, Macdonald, Moss, Harrington, Maguire.
Minority (3 R). Steiger, Brown, McCloskey.

INTERGOVERNMENTAL RELATIONS AND HUMAN RESOURCES
L. H. Fountain, Chairman

Majority (8 D). Fountain, Fuqua, Mezvinsky, Jordan, Burton, Drinan, English, Levitas.
Minority (3 R). Wydler, Brown, Kasten.

LEGISLATION AND NATIONAL SECURITY
Jack Brooks, Chairman

Majority (8 D). Brooks, Moss, Rosenthal, Wright, Fuqua, Moorhead, Stanton, Harrington.
Minority (3 R). Horton, Erlenborn, Pritchard.

MANPOWER AND HOUSING
Floyd V. Hicks, Chairman

Majority (7 D). Hicks, Randall, St Germain, Conyers, Stanton, Jordan, Moffett.
Minority (3 R). Steelman, Pritchard, Kasten.

Committee on House Administration

Wayne L. Hays (Ohio), Chairman

Democratic Majority (17 D). Hays, Thompson (N.J.), Dent (Pa.), Nedzi (Mich.), Brademas (Ind.), Hawkins (Cal.), Annunzio (Ill.), Gaydos (Penn.), Jones (Tenn.), Mollohan (W.Va.), Mathis (Ga.), Van Deerlin (Cal.), Minish (N.J.), Davis (S.C.), Rose (N.C.), Boggs (La.), John L. Burton (Cal.).
Republican Minority (8 R). Dickinson (Ala.), Devine (Ohio), Cleveland (N.H.), Wiggins (Cal.), Butler (Va.), Burke (Fla.), Holt (Md.), Moore (La.).

Subcommittees

ACCOUNTS
Frank Thompson, Jr., Chairman

Majority (9 D). Thompson, Dent, Hawkins, Annunzio, Jones, Mollohan, Minish, Davis, Burton.
Minority (4 R). Devine, Cleveland, Burke, Holt.

CONTRACTS
Joseph M. Gaydos, Chairman

Majority (2 D). Gaydos, Jones.
Minority (1 R). Cleveland.

ELECTIONS
John H. Dent, Chairman

Majority (7 D). Dent, Mathis, Van Deerlin, Davis, Boggs, Burton, Gaydos.
Minority (3 R). Butler, Wiggins, Moore.

ELECTRICAL AND MECHANICAL OFFICE EQUIPMENT
Augustus F. Hawkins, Chairman

Majority (7 D). Hawkins, Nedzi, Rose, Brademas, Burton, Gaydos, Minish.
Minority (3 R). Burke, Holt, Moore.

LIBRARY AND MEMORIALS
Lucien N. Nedzi, Chairman

Majority (5 D). Nedzi, Brademas, Thompson, Boggs, Mollohan.
Minority (2 R). Butler, Moore.

PAPER CONSERVATION
Robert H. Mollohan, Chairman

Majority (2 D). Mollohan, Thompson.
Minority (1 R). Cleveland.

PARKING
Ed Jones, Chairman

Majority (2 D). Jones, Dent.
Minority (1 R). Dickinson.

PERSONNEL AND POLICE
Frank Annunzio, Chairman

Majority (5 D). Annunzio, Mathis, Van Deerlin, Minish, Hawkins.
Minority (2 R). Devine, Wiggins.

HOUSE COMMITTEES

PRINTING
John Brademas, Chairman

Majority (5 D). Brademas, Gaydos, Van Deerlin, Mathis, Davis.
Minority (2 R). Cleveland, Wiggins.

COMPUTER (AD HOC)
Charles Rose, Chairman

Majority (5 D). Rose, Jones, Burton, Boggs, Annunzio.
Minority (2 R). Holt, Moore

RESTAURANT (AD HOC)
Dawson Mathis, Chairman

Majority (2 D). Mathis, Davis
Minority (R). Burke.

Committee on Interior and Insular Affairs

James A. Haley (Fla.), Chairman

Democratic Majority (29 D). Haley, Taylor (N.C.), Johnson (Cal.), Udall (Ariz.), Phillip Burton (Cal.), Kastenmeier (Wis.), Mink (Hawaii), Meeds (Wash.), Kazen (Tex.), Stephens (Ga.), Vigorito (Penn.), Melcher (Mont.), Roncalio (Wyo.), Bingham (N.Y.), Seiberling (Ohio), Runnels (N.M.), Won Pat (Guam), de Lugo (V.I.), Eckhardt (Tex.), Byron (Md.), Benitez (P.R.), Santini (Nev.), Tsongas (Mass.), Howe (Utah), Weaver (Oreg.), Carr (Mich.), Miller (Cal.), Risenhoover (Okla.), Patman (Tex.).
Republican Minority (14 R). Skubitz (Kans.), Steiger (Ariz.), Clausen (Cal.), Ruppe (Mich.), Lujan (N.M.), Sebelius (Kans.), Steiger (Ariz.), Clausen (Cal.), Young (Alaska), Bauman (Md.), Symms (Idaho), Johnson (Colo.), Lagomarsino (Cal.), Smith (Neb.).

Subcommittees

(The chairman and ranking minority member are ex officio members of all subcommittees.)
ENERGY AND THE ENVIRONMENT
Morris K. Udall, Chairman

Majority (13 D). Udall, Vigorito, Roncalio, Bingham, Seiberling, de Lugo, Eckhardt, Benitez, Tsongas, Weaver, Carr, Miller, Melcher.
Minority (6 R). Steelman, Skubitz, Steiger, Lujan, Bauman, Symms.

INDIAN AFFAIRS
Lloyd Meeds, Chairman

Majority (5 D). Meeds, Stephens, Risenhoover, Taylor, Melcher.
Minority (2 R). Young, Johnson.

MINES AND MINING
Patsy T. Mink, Chairman

Majority (13 D). Mink, Kazen, Vigorito, Melcher, Bingham, Seiberling, Runnels, Eckhardt, Bryon, Santini, Howe, Carr, Udall.
Minority (6 R). Ruppe, Skubitz, Steiger, Sebelius, Steelman, Ketchum.

NATIONAL PARKS AND RECREATION
Roy A. Taylor, Chairman

Majority (17 D). Taylor, Johnson, Kastenmeier, Kazen, Stephens, Roncalio, Bingham, Seiberling, Won Pat, de Lugo, Eckhardt, Byron, Tsongas, Howe, Carr, Mink, Meeds.
Minority (8 R). Sebelius, Skubitz, Clausen, Ruppe, Steelman, Bauman, Lagomarsino, Smith.

PUBLIC LANDS
John Melcher, Chairman

Majority (11 D). Melcher, Udall, Runnels, Byron, Santini, Tsongas, Weaver, Risenhoover, Patman, Johnson, Burton.
Minority (5 R). Steiger, Skubitz, Clausen, Young, Johnson.

TERRITORIAL AND INSULAR AFFAIRS
Phillip Burton, Chairman

Majority (11 D). Burton, Taylor, Kastenmeier, Mink, Stephens, Vigorito, Won Pat, de Lugo, Benitez, Miller, Meeds.
Minority (5 R). Ketchum, Skubitz, Clausen, Ruppe, Lagomarsino.

WATER AND POWER RESOURCES
Harold T. Johnson, Chairman

Majority (13 D). Johnson, Meeds, Kazen, Roncalio, Runnels, Won Pat, Benitez, Santini, Tsongas, Howe, Weaver, Miller, Reisenhoover.
Minority (6 R). Lujan, Skubitz, Clausen, Ketchum, Symms, Smith.

Committee on Interstate and Foreign Commerce

Harley O. Staggers (W.Va.), Chairman

Democratic Majority (29 D). Staggers, Macdonald (Mass.), Moss, (Cal.), Dingell (Mich.), Rogers (Fla.), Van Deerlin (Cal.), Rooney (Penn.), Murphy (N.Y.), Satterfield (Va.), Adams (Wash.), Stuckey (Ga.), Eckhardt (Tex.), Preyer (N.C.), Symington (Mo.), Carney (Ohio), Metcalfe (Ill.), Byron (Md.), Scheuer (N.Y.), Ottinger (N.Y.), Waxman (Cal.), Krueger (Tex.), Wirth (Colo.), Sharp (Ind.), Brodhead (Mich.), Hefner (N.C.), Florio (N.J.), Moffett (Conn.), Santini (Nev.), Maquire (N.J.).
Republican Minority (14 R). Devine (Ohio), Broyhill (N.C.), Carter (Ky.), Brown (Ohio), Skubitz (Kans.), Hastings (N.Y.), Collins (Tex.), Frey (Fla.), McCollister (Neb.), Lent (N.Y.), Heinz (Penn.), Madigan (Ill.), Moorhead (Cal.), Rinaldo (N.J.).

Subcommittees

The chairman and ranking minority member are ex officio members, with vote, of all subcommittees.

COMMUNICATIONS
Torbert H. Macdonald, Chairman

Majority (6 D). Macdonald, Murphy, Carney, Byron, Wirth, Brodhead.
Minority (2 R). Frey, Madigan.

CONSUMER PROTECTION AND FINANCE
Lionel Van Deerlin, Chairman

Majority (6 D). Van Deerlin, Stuckey, Eckhardt, Metcalfe, Brodhead, Scheuer.
Minority (2 R). McCollister, Rinaldo.

ENERGY AND POWER
John D. Dingell, Chairman

Majority (10 D). Dingell, Wirth, Sharp, Brodhead, Murphy, Eckhardt, Ottinger, Krueger, Moffett, Maguire.
Minority (4 R). Brown, Moorhead, Broyhill, Heinz.

HEALTH AND THE ENVIRONMENT
Paul G. Rogers, Chairman

Majority (11 D). Rogers, Satterfield, Preyer, Symington, Scheuer, Waxman, Hefner, Florio, Carney,'Wirth, Maguire.
Minority (4 R). Carter, Broyhill, Hastings, Heinz.

OVERSIGHT AND INVESTIGATIONS
John E. Moss, Chairman

Majority (10 D). Moss, Ottinger, Krueger, Moffett, Santini, Stuckey, Scheuer, Waxman, Sharp, Maguire.
Minority (4 R). Collins, Lent, Madigan, Rinaldo.

TRANSPORTATION AND COMMERCE
Fred B. Rooney, Chairman

Majority (6 D). Rooney, Adams, Metcalfe, Hefner, Santini, Florio.
Minority (2 R). Skubitz, Hastings.

Committee on the Judiciary
Peter W. Rodino, Jr. (N.J.), Chairman

Democratic Majority (23 D). Rodino, Brooks (Tex.), Kastenmeier (Wis.), Edwards (Cal.), Hungate (Mo.), Conyers (Mich.), Eilberg (Penn.), Flowers (Ala.), Mann (S.C.), Sarbanes (Md.), Seiberling (Ohio), Danielson (Cal.), Drinan (Mass.), Jordan (Tex.), Thornton (Ark.), Holtzman (N.Y.), Mezvinsky (Iowa), Badillo (N.Y.), Mazzoli (Ky.), Pattison (N.Y.), Dodd (Conn.), Hughes (N.J.), Russo (Ill.).

Republican Minority (11 R). Hutchinson (Mich.), McClory (Ill.), Railsback (Ill.), Wiggins (Cal.), Fish (N.Y.), Butler (Va.), Cohen (Maine), Moorhead (Cal.), Ashbrook (Ohio), Hyde (Ill.), Kindness (Ohio).

Subcommittees

ADMINISTRATIVE LAW AND GOVERNMENTAL RELATIONS
Walter Flowers, Chairman

Majority (5 D). Flowers, Danielson, Jordan, Mazzoli, Pattison.
Minority (2 R). Moorhead, Fish.

CIVIL AND CONSTITUTIONAL RIGHTS
Don Edwards, Chairman

Majority (5 D). Edwards, Seiberling, Drinan, Badillo, Dodd.
Minority (2 R). Butler, Kindness.

COURTS, CIVIL LIBERTIES, AND THE ADMINISTRATION OF JUSTICE
Robert W. Kastenmeier, Chairman

Majority (5 D). Kastenmeier, Danielson, Drinan, Badillo, Pattison.
Minority (2 R). Railsback, Wiggins.

CRIME
John Conyers, Jr., Chairman

Majority (5 D). Conyers, Mann, Danielson, Thornton, Hughes.
Minority (2 R). McClory, Ashbrook.

CRIMINAL JUSTICE
William L. Hungate, Chairman

Majority (5 D). Hungate, Mann, Thornton, Holtzman, Russo.
Minority (2 R). Wiggins, Hyde.

IMMIGRATION, CITIZENSHIP, AND INTERNATIONAL LAW
Joshua Eilberg, Chairman

Majority (5 D). Eilberg, Sarbanes, Holtzman, Dodd, Russo.
Minority (2 R). Fish, Cohen.

MONOPOLIES AND COMMERCIAL LAW
Peter W. Rodino, Jr., Chairman

Majority (9 D). Rodino, Brooks, Flowers, Sarbanes, Seiberling, Jordan, Mezvinsky, Mazzoli, Hughes.
Minority (4 R). Hutchinson, McClory, Railsback, Cohen.

Committee on Merchant Marine and Fisheries
Leonor K. Sullivan (Mo.), Chairman

Democratic Majority (27 D). Sullivan, Ashley (Ohio), Dingell (Mich.), Downing (Va.), Rogers (Fla.), Murphy (N.Y.), Jones (N.C.), Leggett (Cal.), Biaggi (N.Y.), Anderson (Cal.), de la Garza (Tex.), Metcalfe (Ill.), Breaux (La.), Rooney (Penn.), Sarbanes (Md.), Ginn (Ga.), Studds (Mass.), Bowen (Miss.), Eilberg (Penn.), de Lugo (V.I.), Hubbard (Ky.), Bonker (Wash.), AuCoin (Oreg.), D'Amours (N.H.), Patterson (Cal.), Zeferetti (N.Y.), Oberstar (Minn.).

Republican Minority (13 R). Ruppe (Mich,), Mosher (Ohio), McCloskey (Cal.), Snyder (Ky.), Forsythe (N.J.), du Pont (Del.), Treen (La.), Pritchard (Wash.), Young (Alaska), Bauman (Md.), Lent (N.Y.), Rinaldo (N.J.), Emery (Maine).

Subcommittees

The chairman and ranking minority member are ex officio members of all subcommittees.
COAST GUARD AND NAVIGATION
Mario Biaggi, Chairman

Majority (15 D). Biaggi, Murphy, Jones, de la Garza, Sarbanes, Studds, Bowen, de Lugo, Hubbard, Eilberg, Rogers, Rooney, Bonker, AuCoin, Patterson.
Minority (6 R). du Pont, Snyder, Treen, Young, Bauman, Emery.
FISHERIES AND WILDLIFE CONSERVATION AND THE ENVIRONMENT
Robert L. Leggett, Chairman

Majority (18 D). Leggett, Dingell, Rogers, Anderson, de la Garza, Breaux, Rooney, Studds, Bowen, Bonker, AuCoin, D'Amours, Ginn, Hubbard, Patterson, Zeferetti, Oberstar, de Lugo.
Minority (8 R). Forsythe, McClosky, Pritchard, Young, Bauman, Lent, Rinaldo, Emery.
MERCHANT MARINE
Thomas N. Downing, Chairman

Majority (19 D). Downing, Ashley, Dingell, Anderson, Rooney, Sarbanes, Ginn, Eilberg, Patterson, Zeferetti, Oberstar, Biaggi, de Lugo, Bonker, D'Amours, Jones, Breaux, Metcalfe, Murphy.
Minority (8 R). McCloskey, Mosher, du Pont, Snyder, Treen, Pritchard, Young, Emery.
OCEANOGRAPHY
John M. Murphy, Chairman

Majority (15 D). Murphy, Ashley, Downing, Rogers, Jones, Metcalfe, Breauz, AuCoin, Anderson, de la Garza, Ginn, Studds, D'Amours, Zeferetti, Oberstar.
Minority (6 R). Mosher, Forsythe, de Pont, Treen, Bauman, Lent.
PANAMA CANAL
Ralph H. Metcalfe, Chairman

Majority (7 D). Metcalfe, Leggett, Downing, Murphy, Biaggi, Bowen, Hubbard.
Minority (2 R). Snyder, Rinaldo.
Committee on Post Office and Civil Service

David N. Henderson (N.C.), Chairman

Democratic Majority (19 D). Henderson, Udall (Ariz.), Daniels (N.J.), Nix (Penn.), Hanley (N.Y.), Charles H. Wilson (Cal.), White (Tex.), Ford (Mich.), Clay (Mo.), Schroeder (Colo.), Lehman (Fla.), Spellman (Md.), Neal (N.C.), Harris (Va.), Brodhead (Mich.), Simon (Ill.), Mineta (Cal.), Jenrette (S.C.), Solarz (N.Y.).
Republican Minority (9 R). Derwinski (Ill.), Johnson (Penn.), Rousselot (Cal.), Hinshaw (Cal.), Collings (Tex.), Taylor (Mo.), Gilman (N.Y.), Beard (Tenn.), Lott (Miss.).

Subcommittees

(The chairman and ranking minority member are ex officio voting members of all subcommittees on which they do not hold a regular assignment.)
CENSUS AND POPULATION
Patricia Schroeder, Chairman

Majority (6 D). Schroeder, Lehman, Neal, Spellman, Brodhead, Simon.
Minority (2 R). Rousselot, Hinshaw.
EMPLOYEE POLITICAL RIGHTS AND INTERGOVERNMENTAL PROGRAMS
William (Bill) Clay, Chairman

Majority (6 D). Clay, Spellman, Solarz, Wilson, Harris, Schroeder.
Minority (2 R). Collins, Rousselot.
MANPOWER AND CIVIL SERVICE
David N. Henderson, Chairman

Majority (7 D). Henderson, Ford, Neal, Brodhead, Jenrette, Solarz, Hanley.
Minority (3 R). Derwinski, Lott, Taylor.

POSTAL FACILITIES– MAIL– AND LABOR MANAGEMENT
Charles H. Wilson, Chairman

Majority (6 D). Wilson, Nix, Clay, Schroeder, Brodhead, Simon.
Minority (2 R). Hinshaw, Beard.

POSTAL SERVICE
James M. Hanley, Chairman

Majority (6 D). Hanley, Nix, Ford, Lehman, Simon, Mineta.
Minority (2 R). Johnson, Gilman.

RETIREMENT AND EMPLOYEE BENEFITS
Richard C. White, Chairman

Majority (6 D). White, Daniels, Harris, Spellman, Mineta, Jenrette.
Minority (2 R). Taylor, Beard.

Committee on Public Works and Transportation

Robert E. Jones (Ala.), Chairman

Democratic Majority (27 D). Jones, Wright (Tex.), Johnson (Cal.), Henderson (N.C.), Roberts (Tex.), Howard (N.J.), Anderson (Cal.), Roe (N.J.), Roncalio (Wyo.), McCormack (Wash.), James V. Stanton (Ohio), Abzug (N.Y.), Breaux (La.), Studds (Mass.), Ginn (Ga.), Milford (Tex.), Mineta (Cal.), Holland (S.C.), Howe (Utah), Levitas (Ga.), Oberstar (Minn.), Ambro (N.Y.), Nowak (N.Y.), Edgar (Penn.), Lloyd (Tenn.), 2 vacancies.
Republican Minority (13 R). Harsha (Ohio), Cleveland (N.H.), Clausen (Cal.), Snyder (Ky.), Hammerschmidt (Ark.), Shuster (Penn.), Walsh (N.Y.), Cochran (Miss.), Abdnor (S.D.), Taylor (Mo.), Goldwater (Cal.), Hagedorn (Minn.). Myers (Penn.),

Subcommittees

(The chairman and the ranking minority member of the committee are ex officio members of all subcommittees.)

AVIATION
Glenn M. Anderson, Chairman

Majority (14 D). Anderson, Henderson, Roncalio, Stanton, Studds, Milford, Mineta, Howe, Levitas, Wright, Johnson, Ginn, Lloyd, 1 vacancy.
Minority (6 R). Snyder, Hammerschmidt, Cochran, Abdnor, Taylor, Goldwater.

ECONOMIC DEVELOPMENT
Robert A. Roe, Chairman

Majority (14 D). Roe, Abzug, Henderson, Roberts, Holland, Howe, Oberstar, Nowak, Lloyd, McCormack, Breaux, Studds, Johnson, 1 vacancy.
Minority (6 R). Hammerschmidt, Cleveland, Clausen, Shuster, Taylor, Myers.

INVESTIGATIONS AND REVIEW
Jim Wright, Chairman

Majority (14 D). Wright, Milford, Holland, Howard, Roncalio, Mineta, Levitas, Ambro, Oberstar, Breaux, Howe, Nowak, Edgar, 1 vacancy.
Minority (6 R). Cleveland, Clausen, Snyder, Cochran, Goldwater, Myers.

PUBLIC BUILDINGS AND GROUNDS
Teno Roncalio, Chairman

Majority (14 D). Roncalio, Roberts, Henderson, Abzug, Studds, Ginn, Milford, Mineta, Holland, Levitas, Oberstar, Lloyd, 2 vacancies.
Minority (6 R). Walsh, Shuster, Cochran, Abdnor, Goldwater, Hagedorn.

SURFACE TRANSPORTATION
James J, Howard, Chairman

Majority (16 D). Howard, Wright, Johnson, Anderson, Roe, McCormack, Stanton, Abzug, Breaux, Studds, Ginn, Mineta, Levitas, Ambro, Nowak, Edgar.
Minority (7 R). Shuster, Cleveland, Clausen, Walsh, Cochran, Hagedorn, Myers.

WATER RESOURCES
Ray Roberts, Chairman

Majority (16 D). Roberts, Johnson, Howard, Roe, McCormack, Breaux, Ginn, Oberstar, Ambro, Edgar, Lloyd, Anderson, Abzug, Howe, Nowak, 1 vacancy.
Minority (7 R). Clausen, Snyder, Hammerschmidt, Walsh, Abdnor, Taylor, Hagedorn.

Committee on Rules

Ray J. Madden (Ind.), Chairman

Democratic Majority (11 D). Madden, Delaney (N.Y.), Bolling (Mo.), Sisk (Cal.), Young (Tex.), Pepper (Fla.), Matsunaga (Hawaii), Murphy (Ill.), Long (La.), Moakley (Mass.), Young (Ga.).
Republican Minority (5 R). Quillen (Tenn.), Anderson (Ill.), Latta (Ohio), Clawson (Cal.), Lott (Miss.).

(No subcommittees)

Committee on Science and Technology

Olin E. Teague (Tex.), Chairman

Democratic Majority (25 D). Teague, Hechler (W.Va.), Downing (Va.), Fuqua (Fla.), Symington (Mo.), Flowers (Ala.), Roe (N.J.), McCormack (Wash.), Brown (Cal.), Milford (Tex.), Thornton (Ark.), Scheuer (N.Y.), Ottinger (N.Y.), Waxman (Cal.), Hayes (Ind.), Harkin (Iowa), Lloyd (Cal.), Ambro (N.Y.), Dodd (Conn.), Blouin (Iowa), Hall (Ill.), Krueger (Tex.), Lloyd (Tenn.), Blanchard (Mich.), Wirth (Colo.).
Republican Minority (12 R). Mosher (Ohio), Bell (Cal.), Jamran (Okla.), Wydler (N.Y.), Winn (Kans.), Frey (Fla.), Goldwater (Cal.), Esch (Mich.), Conlan (Ariz.), Ketchum (Cal.), Myers (Penn.), Emery (Maine).

Subcommittees

(The chairman and ranking minority member are ex officio members, with vote, of all subcommittees.)

AVIATION AND TRANSPORTATION RESEARCH AND DEVELOPMENT
Dale Milford, Chairman

Majority (7 D). Milford, Roe, Scheuer, Harkin, Lloyd, Hall, Ottinger.
Minority (3 R). Wydler, Goldwater, Conlan.

DOMESTIC AND INTERNATIONAL SCIENTIFIC PLANNING AND ANALYSIS
Robert A. Roe, Chairman

Majority (6 D). Roe, Milford, Scheuer, Waxman, Ambro, Blanchard.
Minority (2 R). Conlan, Myers.

ENERGY RESEARCH, DEVELOPMENT AND DEMONSTRATION
Mike McCormack, Chairman

Majority (16 D). McCormack, Hechler, Fuqua, Symington, Brown, Thornton, Ottinger, Waxman, Hayes, Harkin, Ambro, Dodd, Krueger, Lloyd, Blanchard, Wirth.
Minority (7 R). Goldwater, Bell, Wydler, Winn, Frey, Esch, Conlan.

ENERGY RESEARCH, DEVELOPMENT AND DEMONSTRATION (FOSSIL FUELS)
Ken Hechler, Chairman

Majority (11 D). Hechler, Downing, Flowers, McCormack, Thornton, Waxman, Hayes, Blouin, Krueger, Lloyd, Wirth.
Minority (4 R). Bell, Ketchum, Myers, Emery.

ENVIRONMENT AND THE ATMOSPHERE
George E. Brown, Jr., Chairman

Majority (10 D). Brown, Hechler, McCormack, Milford, Ottinger, Hayes, Ambro, Blouin, Blanchard, Scheuer.
Minority (4 R). Esch, Winn, Myers, Emery.

SCIENCE, RESEARCH AND TECHNOLOGY
James W. Symington, Chairman

Majority (14 D). Symington, Fugua, Flowers, McCormack, Brown, Thornton, Scheuer, Harkin, Lloyd, Dodd, Hall, Krueger, Lloyd, Wirth.
Minority (4 R). Mosher, Esch, Ketchum, Emery.

SPACE SCIENCE AND APPLICATIONS
Don Fuqua, Chairman

Majority (9 D). Fuqua, Downing, Symington, Flowers, Roe, Lloyd, Hall, Waxman, Blouin.
Minority (4 R). Winn, Wydler, Frey, Ketchum.

Committee on Small Business

Joe L. Evins (Tenn.), Chairman

Democratic Majority (25 D). Evins, Steed (Okla.), Dingell (Mich.), Smith (Iowa), Corman (Cal.), Addabbo (N.Y.), Hungate (Mo.), St Germain (R.I.), Carney (Ohio), Mitchell (Md.), Bergland (Minn.), Gonzalez (Tex.), Hanley (N.Y.), Yatron (Penn.), Breckinridge (Ky.), LaFalce, (N.Y.), Krebs (Cal.), Bedell (Iowa), Richmond (N.Y.), Evans (Ind.), Russo (Ill.), Baldus (Wis.), Nolan (Minn.), Badillo (N.Y.), Hightower (Tex.).
Republican Minority (12 R). Conte (Mass.), J. William Stanton (Ohio), McDade (Penn.), McCollister (Neb.), Broomfield (Mich.), Carter (Ky.), Fish (N.Y.), Butler (Va.), Cohen (Maine), Fenwick (N.J.), Kindness (Ohio), Goodling (Penn.).

Subcommittees

(The chairman and ranking minority member are ex officio members, with vote, of all subcommittees.)

ACTIVITIES OF REGULATORY AGENCIES
William L. Hungate, Chairman

Majority (8 D). Hungate, Bedell, LaFalce, Russo, Baldus, Hightower, Addabbo, Dingall.
Minority (3 R). McCollister, Cohen, Fenwick.

COMMODITIES AND SERVICES
Charles J. Carney, Chairman

Majority (8 D). Carney, Bergland, Yatron, Bedell, Richmond, Evans, Nolan, Badillo.
Minority (3 R). Broomfield, Butler, Kindness.

ENERGY AND ENVIRONMENT
John D. Dingell, Chairman

Majority (8 D). Dingell, Steed, St Germain, LaFalce, Krebs, Evans, Russo, Badillo.
Minority (4 R). Conte, Fish, Cohen, Butler.

GOVERNMENT PROCUREMENT AND INTERNATIONAL TRADE
James C. Corman, Chairman

Majority (8 D). Corman, Steed, Addabbo, Carney, Nolan, Krebs, Hightower, Hungate.
Minority (3 R). McDade, Kindness, Broomfield.

SBA AND SBIC LEGISLATION
Neal Smith, Chairman

Majority (8 D). Smith, Bergland, Gonzalez, Corman, Mitchell, Hanley, Yatron, Breckinridge.
Minority (3 R). Stanton, Fenwick, Goodling.

SEA OVERSIGHT AND MINORITY ENTERPRISE
Joseph P. Addabbo, Chairman

Majority (8 D). Addabbo, Mitchell, Hanley, St Germain, Gonzalez, Richmond, Baldus, Breckinridge.
Minority (3 R). Carter, Goodling, Fish.

Committee on Standards of Official Conduct

John J. Flynt (Ga.), Chairman

Democrats (6). Flynt, Price (Ill.), Teague (Tex.), Hebert (La.), Foley (Wash.), Bennett (Fla.).
Republicans (6). Spence (S.C.), Quillen (Tenn.), Hutchinson (Mich.), Quie (Minn.), Mitchell (N.Y.), Cochran (Miss.).

Committee on Ways and Means
Al Ullman (Oreg.), Chairman

Democratic Majority (25 D). Ullman, Mills (Ark.), Burke (Mass.), Rostenkowski (Ill.), Landrum (Ga.), Vanik (Ohio), Fulton (Tenn.), Burleson (Tex.), Corman (Cal.), Green (Penn.), Gibbons (Fla.), Waggonner (La.), Karth (Minn.), Pike (N.Y.), Vander Veen (Mich.), Pickle (Tex.), Halstoski (N.J.), Rangel (N.Y.), Cotter (Conn.), Stark (Cal.), Jones (Okla.), Jacobs (Ind.), Mikva (Ill.), Keys (Kans.), Fisher (Va.).
Republican Minority (12 R). Schneebell (Penn.), Conable (N.Y.), Duncan (Tenn.), Clancy (Ohio), Archer (Tex.), Vander Jagt (Mich.), Steiger (Wis.), Crane (Ill.), Frenzel (Minn.), Martin (N.C.), Bafalis (Fla.), Ketchum (Cal.).

Subcommittees
HEALTH
Dan Rostenkowski, Chairman

Majority (9 D). Rostenkowski, Corman, Pike, Vanik, Fulton, Burleson, Waggonner, Cotter, Keys.
Minority (4 R). Duncan, Crane, Martin, Clancy.

OVERSIGHT
Charles A. Vanik, Chairman

Majority (9 D). Vanik, Gibbons, Pike, Vander Veen, Pickle, Helstoski, Rangel, Stark, Jones.
Minority (4 R). Clancy, Bafalis, Martin, Duncan.

PUBLIC ASSISTANCE
Richard H. Fulton, Chairman

Majority (7 D). Fulton, Corman, Rangel, Stark, Landrum, Waggonner, Karth.
Minority (3 R). Vander Jagt, Bafalis, Ketchum.

SOCIAL SECURITY
James A. Burke, Chairman

Majority (9 D). Burke, Waggonner, Green, Jacobs, Pickle, Cotter, Jones, Mikva, Karth.
Minority (4 R). Archer, Conable, Steiger, Crane.

TRADE
William J. Green, Chairman

Majority (11 D). Green, Landrum, Gibbons, Karth, Vander Veen, Rostenkowski, Jones, Mikva, Fisher, Pike, Helstoski.
Minority (5 R). Conable, Archer, Vander Jagt, Frenzel, Duncan.

UNEMPLOYMENT COMPENSATION
James C. Corman, Chairman

Majority (7 D). Corman, Burleson, Burke, Keys, Fisher, Pickle, Jacobs.
Minority (3 R). Steiger, Frenzel, Ketchum.

Committee on Veterans' Affairs

Ray Roberts (Tex.), Chairman

Democratic Majority (19 D). Roberts, Teague (Tex.), Satterfield (Va.), Edwards (Cal.), Montgomery (Miss.), Carney (Ohio), Danielson (Cal.), Wolff (N.Y.), Brinkley (Ga.), Wilson (Tex.), Mottl (Ohio), Cornell (Wis.), Hefner (N.C.), Hannaford (Cal.), Ford (Tenn.), Beard (R.I.), Edgar (Penn.), Holland (S.C.), McHugh (N.Y.).
Republican Minority (9 R). Hammerschmidt (Ark.), Heckler (Mass.), Wylie (Ohio), Hillis (Ind.), Abdnor (S.D.), Walsh (N.Y.), Guyer (Ohio), Hansen (Idaho), O'Brien (Ill.).

Subcommittees

CEMETERIES AND BURIAL BENEFITS
George Danielson, Chairman

Majority (9 D). Danielson, Roberts, Edgar, McHugh, Cornell, Hefner, Hannaford, Ford, Beard.
Minority (4 R). Hillis, Hammerschmidt, Hansen, O'Brien.

COMPENSATION, PENSION AND INSURANCE
G. V. (Sonny) Montgomery, Chairman

Majority (7 D). Montgomery, Teague, Roberts, Brinkley, Wilson, Hefner, Mottle.
Minority (3 R). Wylie, Hammerschmidt, Guyer.

EDUCATION AND TRAINING
Olin E. Teague, Chairman

Majority (8 D). Teague, Wolff, Mottl, Cornell, Hannaford, Edgar, Holland, Ford.
Minority (3 R). Heckler, Wylie, Walsh.

HOSPITALS
David E. Satterfield, Chairman

Majority (14 D). Satterfield, Edwards, Montgomery, Carney, Danielson, Wolff, Wilson, Ford, Beard, Hefner, Hannaford, Holland, McHugh, Mottl.
Minority (7 R). Hammerschmidt, Heckler, Hillis, Abdnor, Guyer, Hansen, O'Brien.

HOUSING
Jack Brinkley, Chairman

Majority (6 D). Brinkley, Carney, Satterfield, Edwards, Cornell, Beard.
Minority (2 R). Abdnor, Walsh.

Select Committee on Intelligence

Lucien N. Nedzi (Mich.), Chairman

Democratic Majority (7 D). Nedzi, Giaimo (Conn.), Edwards (Cal.), Stanton (Ohio), Harrington (Mass.), Dellums (Cal.), Murphy (Ill.).
Republican Minority (3 R). McClory (Ill.), Treen (La.), Kasten (Wis.).

JOINT COMMITTEES

Joint Committee on Atomic Energy

Sen. John O. Pastore (R.I.), Chairman

Rep. Melvin Price (Ill.), Vice Chairman.

Senate Members

Democratic Majority (5 D). Pastore, Jackson (Wash.), Symington (Mo.), Montoya (N.M.), Tunney (Cal.).
Republican Minority (4 R). Baker (Tenn.), Case (N.J.), Pearson (Kans.), Buckley (N.Y.).

House Members

Democratic Majority (5 D). Price, Young (Tex.), Roncalio (Wyo.), McCormack (Wash.), Moss (Cal.).
Republican Minority (4 R). Anderson (Ill.), Lujan (N.M.), Horton (N.Y.), Hinshaw (Cal.).

Subcommittees

AGREEMENTS FOR COOPERATION
Rep. Teno Roncalio, Chairman

Majority (3 D). Rep. Roncalio; Sens. Montoya, Tunney.
Minority (4 R). Sens. Case, Pearson; Reps. Anderson, Horton.

COMMUNITIES
Rep. John Young, Chairman

Majority (2 D). Rep. Young; Sen. Jackson.
Minority (3 R). Sens. Baker, Buckley; Rep. Lujan.

ERDA, ENVIRONMENT AND SAFETY
Rep. Mike McCormack, Chairman

Majority (2 D). Rep. McCormack; Sen. Tunney.
Minority (4 R). Sens. Baker, Case, Buckley; Rep. Anderson.

ERDA, NUCLEAR ENERGY
Sen. Henry M. Jackson, Chairman

Majority (8 D). Sens. Jackson, Symington, Montoya, Tunney; Reps. Young, Roncalio, McCormack, Moss.
Minority (6 R). Sens. Baker, Case, Pearson; Reps. Anderson, Lujan, Hinshaw.

LEGISLATION
Sen. Joseph M. Montoya, Chairman

Majority (3 D). Sens. Montoya, Jackson; Rep. McCormack.
Minority (3 R). Sen. Pearson; Reps. Anderson, Horton.

NATIONAL SECURITY
Sen. Stuart Symington, Chairman

Majority (7 D). Sens. Symington, Jackson, Montoya, Tunney; Reps. Young, Roncalio, Moss.
Minority (6 R). Sens. Baker, Case, Buckley; Reps. Lujan, Horton, Hinshaw.

Joint Economic Commitee

Sen. Hubert H. Humphrey (Minn.), Chairman

Rep. Wright Patman (Tex.), Vice Chairman

Senate Members

Democratic Majority (6 D). Humphrey, Sparkman (Ala.), Proxmire (Wis.), Ribicoff (Conn.), Bentsen (Tex.), Kennedy (Mass.).
Republican Minority (4 R). Javits (N.Y.), Percy (Ill.), Taft (Ohio), Fannin (Ariz.).

House Members

Democratic Majority (6 D). Patman, Bolling (Mo.), Reuss (Wis.), Moorhead (Penn.), Hamilton (Ind.), Long (La.).
Republican Minority (4 R). Brown (Ohio), Brown (Mich.), Heckler (Mass.), Rousselot (Cal.).

Subcommittees

CONSUMER ECONOMICS
Sen. Hubert H. Humphrey, Chairman

Majority (7 D). Sens. Humphrey, Proxmire, Kennedy; Reps. Bolling, Moorhead, Long.
Minority (4 R). Sens. Javits, Percy; Reps. Brown (Mich.), Heckler.

ECONOMIC GROWTH
Sen. Lloyd M. Bentsen, Jr., Chairman

Majority (6 D). Sens. Bentsen, Proxmire, Ribicoff, Humphrey, Kennedy; Rep. Moorhead.
Minority (4 R). Sens. Javits, Percy; Reps. Brown (Mich.), Heckler.

ECONOMIC PROGRESS
Rep. Wright Patman, Chairman

Majority (6 D). Reps. Patman, Reuss, Hamilton, Long; Sens. Proxmire, Bentsen.
Minority (4 R). Reps. Brown (Mich.), Beckler; Sens. Fannin, Javits.

FISCAL POLICY
Rep. Richard Bolling, Chairman

Majority (6 D). Reps. Bolling, Moorhead, Long, Hamilton; Sens. Proxmire, Bentsen.
Minority (4 R). Reps. Brown (Ohio), Rousselot; Sens. Taft, Fannin.

INTER-AMERICAN ECONOMIC RELATIONSHIPS
Sen. John Sparkman, Chairman

Majority (6 D). Sens. Sparkman, Bentsen, Kennedy; Reps. Moorhead, Long, Hamilton.
Minority (4 R). Sens. Taft, Fannin; Reps. Heckler, Rousselot.

INTERNATIONAL ECONOMICS
Rep. Henry S. Reuss, Chairman

Majority (8 D). Reps. Reuss, Moorhead, Hamilton; Sens. Sparkman, Ribicoff, Humphrey, Bentsen, Kennedy.

Minority (6 R). Reps. Brown (Ohio), Brown (Mich.), Rousselot; Sens. Javits, Percy, Taft.

PRIORITIES AND ECONOMY IN GOVERNMENT
Sen. William Proxmire, Chairman

Majority (8 D). Sens. Proxmire, Sparkman, Ribicoff, Humphrey, Kennedy; Reps. Patman, Hamilton, Long.

Minority (5 R). Sens Percy, Taft; Reps. Rousselot, Brown (Ohio), Brown (Mich.).

URBAN AFFAIRS
Rep. William S. Moorhead, Chairman

Majority (7 D). Reps. Moorhead, Bolling, Long; Sens. Ribicoff, Humphrey, Bentsen, Kennedy.

Minority (5 R). Reps. Brown (Mich.), Heckler, Rousellot; Sens. Percy, Javits.

ALABAMA

(7 districts)

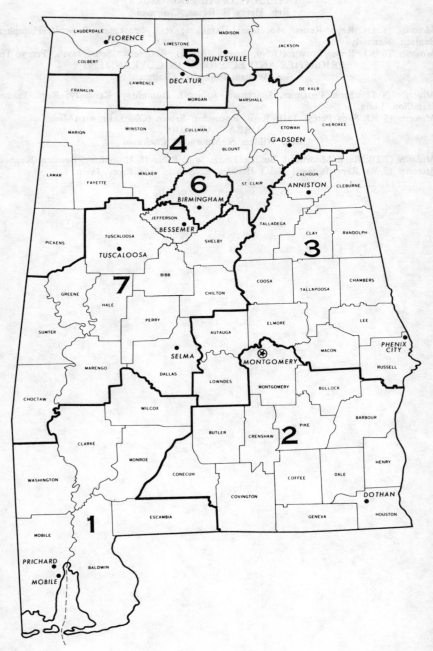

ALASKA

(1 at large)

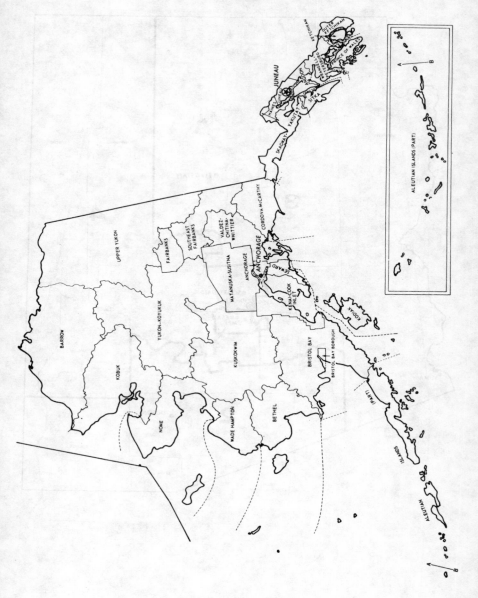

ARIZONA

(4 districts)

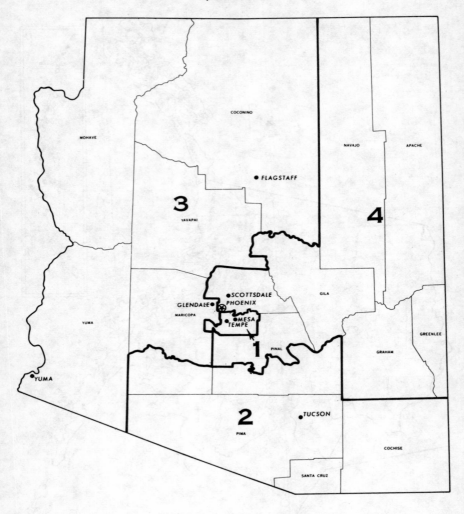

ARKANSAS

(4 districts)

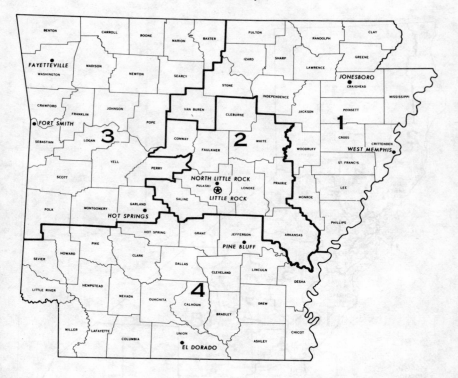

BENTON CARROLL BOONE MARION BAXTER FULTON RANDOLPH CLAY

FAYETTEVILLE MADISON NEWTON SEARCY IZARD SHARP GREENE

WASHINGTON *JONESBORO*
CRAIGHEAD

STONE LAWRENCE

CRAWFORD JOHNSON VAN BUREN CLEBURNE INDEPENDENCE JACKSON POINSETT MISSISSIPPI

FRANKLIN POPE

FORT SMITH **1** CROSS CRITTENDEN

SEBASTIAN LOGAN CONWAY WHITE WOODRUFF *WEST MEMPHIS*

3 FAULKNER **2**

YELL PERRY ST. FRANCIS

SCOTT NORTH LITTLE ROCK PRAIRIE LEE
PULASKI
LONOKE
LITTLE ROCK

POLK MONTGOMERY GARLAND SALINE MONROE

HOT SPRINGS PHILLIPS

PIKE HOT SPRING GRANT JEFFERSON ARKANSAS

SEVIER HOWARD CLARK *PINE BLUFF*

DALLAS CLEVELAND LINCOLN DESHA

LITTLE RIVER HEMPSTEAD **4**

NEVADA OUACHITA CALHOUN BRADLEY DREW

MILLER LAFAYETTE UNION CHICOT

COLUMBIA *EL DORADO* ASHLEY

CALIFORNIA

(43 districts)

1 CONCORD
2 STOCKTON
3 OAKLAND
4 SAN MATEO
5 MODESTO
6 SAN JOSE
7 SIMI VALLEY
8 OXNARD
9 LOS ANGELES
10 ONTARIO
11 ANAHEIM
12 SANTA ANA
13 EL CAJON
14 CHULA VISTA

LOS ANGELES COUNTY

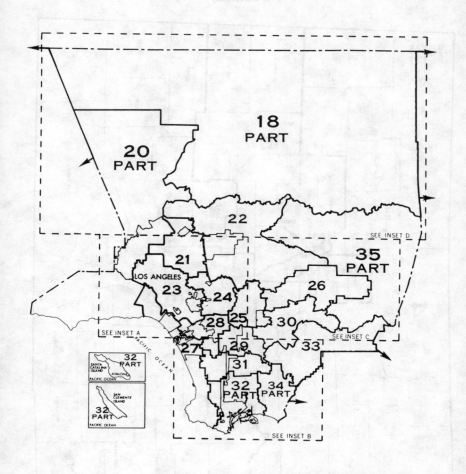

Districts established November 28, 1973

COLORADO

(5 districts)

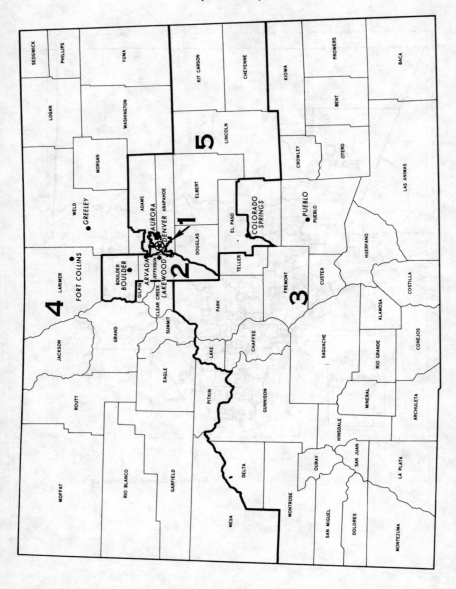

CONNECTICUT

(6 districts)

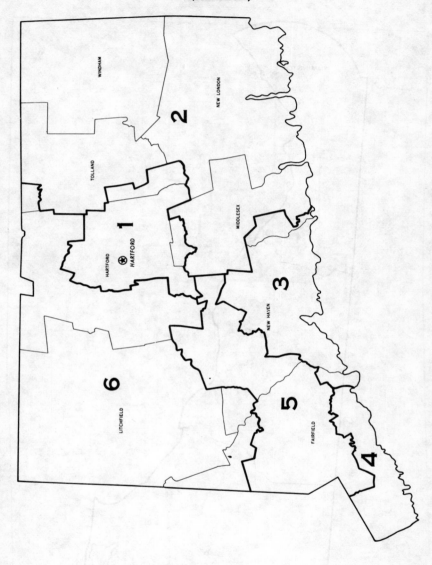

DELAWARE

(1 at large)

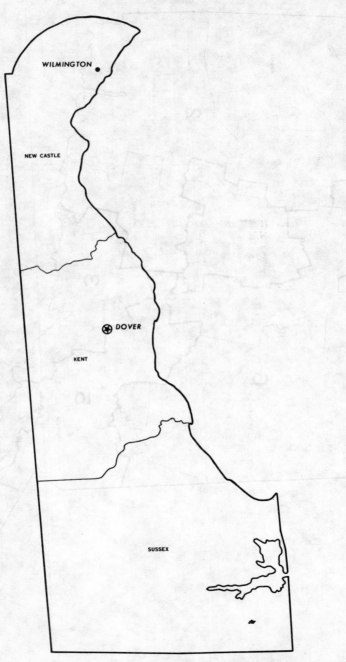

WILMINGTON •

NEW CASTLE

⊗ DOVER

KENT

SUSSEX

FLORIDA

(15 districts)

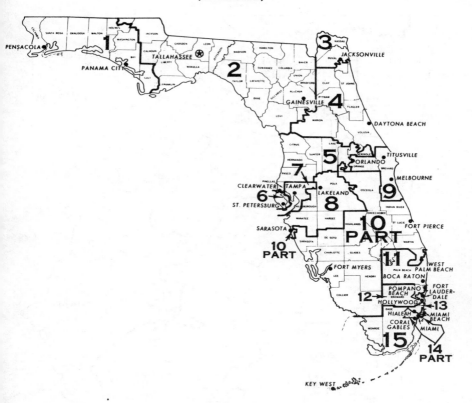

GEORGIA

(10 districts)

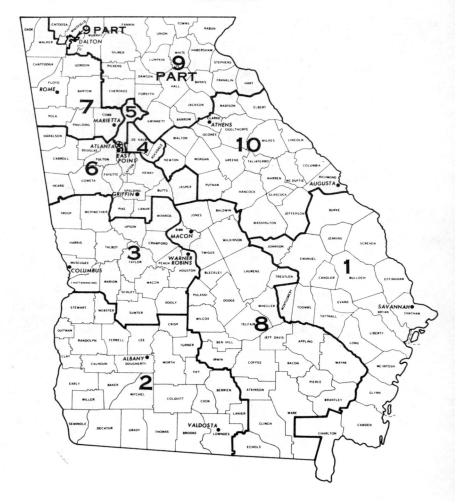

HAWAII

(2 districts)

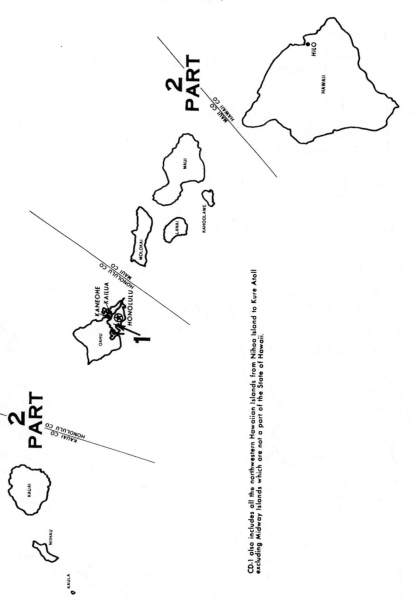

PART 2

KAUAI CO
HONOLULU CO

KAUAI

NIIHAU

KAULA

PART 2

MAUI CO
HAWAII CO

HILO

HAWAII

MAUI

MOLOKAI

LANAI

KAHOOLAWE

HONOLULU CO
MAUI CO

KANEOHE
KAILUA
HONOLULU
OAHU

1

CD 1 also includes all the northwestern Hawaiian Islands from Nihoa Island to Kure Atoll excluding Midway Islands which are not a part of the State of Hawaii.

IDAHO

(2 districts)

ILLINOIS

(24 districts)

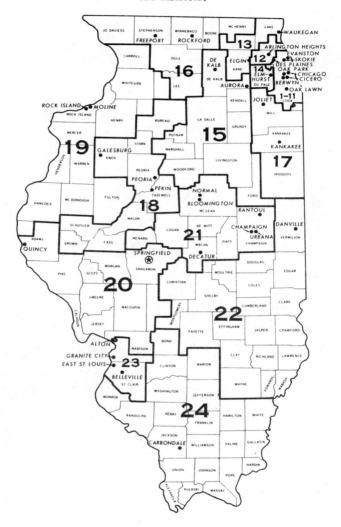

JO DAVIESS | STEPHENSON | WINNEBAGO | BOONE | MCHENRY | LAKE | WAUKEGAN
FREEPORT | ROCKFORD | **13** | ARLINGTON HEIGHTS | EVANSTON | SKOKIE
CARROLL | OGLE | DE KALB | ELGIN | **12** | DES PLAINES | OAK PARK | CHICAGO
16 | KANE | **14** | ELM- HURST | CICERO | BERWYN
WHITESIDE | DE KALB | AURORA | DU PAGE | OAK LAWN
LEE | KENDALL | JOLIET | **1-11** COOK
ROCK ISLAND | MOLINE | HENRY | BUREAU | LA SALLE | GRUNDY | WILL
ROCK ISLAND | PUTNAM | KANKAKEE
MERCER | STARK | MARSHALL | KANKAKEE
19 | GALESBURG | KNOX | **15** | LIVINGSTON | **17**
HENDERSON | WARREN | PEORIA | WOODFORD | IROQUOIS
PEORIA | PEKIN | TAZEWELL | NORMAL BLOOMINGTON | FORD
HANCOCK | MCDONOUGH | FULTON | MASON | **18** | MC LEAN | RANTOUL
SCHUYLER | MENARD | LOGAN | DE WITT | **21** | CHAMPAIGN URBANA | DANVILLE
ADAMS | BROWN | CASS | PIATT | CHAMPAIGN | VERMILION
QUINCY | MORGAN | SPRINGFIELD ⭐ | MACON | DECATUR | DOUGLAS | EDGAR
PIKE | SCOTT | SANGAMON | CHRISTIAN | MOULTRIE | COLES
GREENE | MACOUPIN | SHELBY | CLARK
20 | MONTGOMERY | CUMBERLAND
JERSEY | FAYETTE | EFFINGHAM | JASPER | CRAWFORD
CALHOUN | ALTON | BOND | **22**
GRANITE CITY | MADISON | CLAY | RICHLAND | LAWRENCE
EAST ST LOUIS | **23** | CLINTON | MARION | WAYNE | EDWARDS | WABASH
BELLEVILLE | ST CLAIR | WASHINGTON | JEFFERSON
MONROE | PERRY | **24** | HAMILTON | WHITE
RANDOLPH | FRANKLIN | SALINE | GALLATIN
JACKSON | CARBONDALE | WILLIAMSON | HARDIN
UNION | JOHNSON | POPE
ALEXANDER | PULASKI | MASSAC

COOK AND DU PAGE COUNTIES

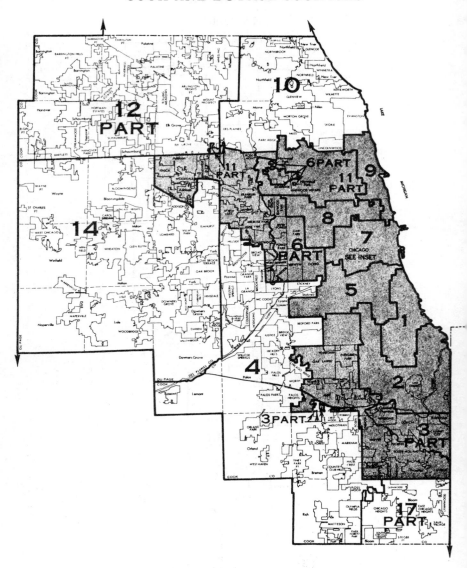

INDIANA

(11 districts)

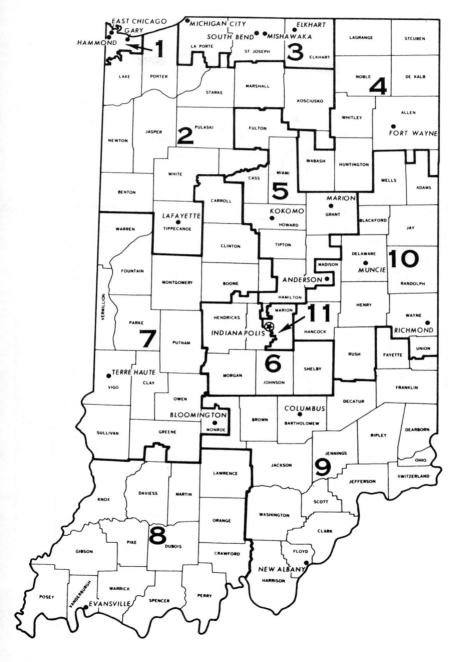

IOWA

(6 districts)

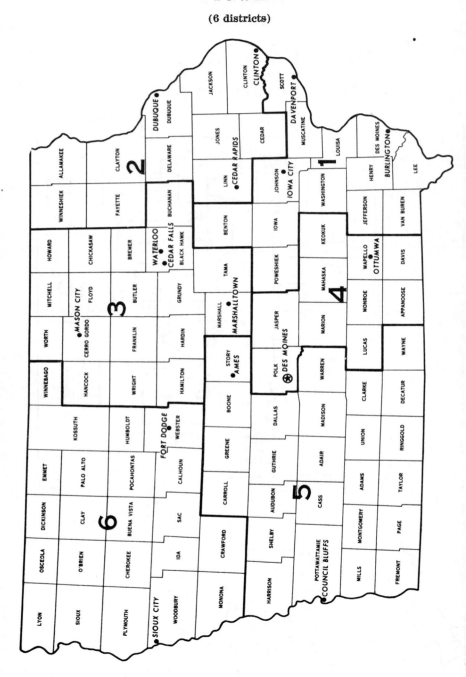

KANSAS

(5 districts)

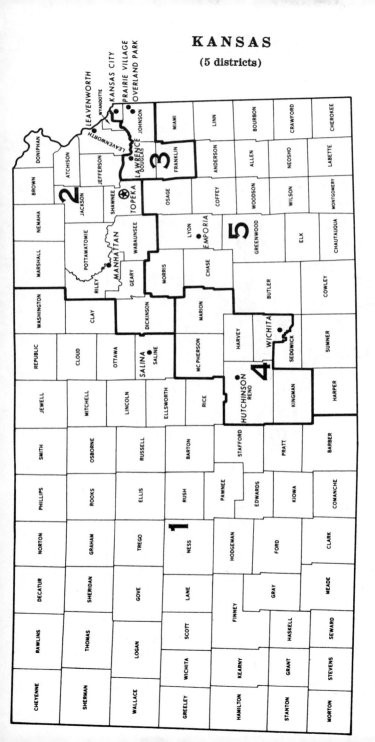

KENTUCKY

(7 districts)

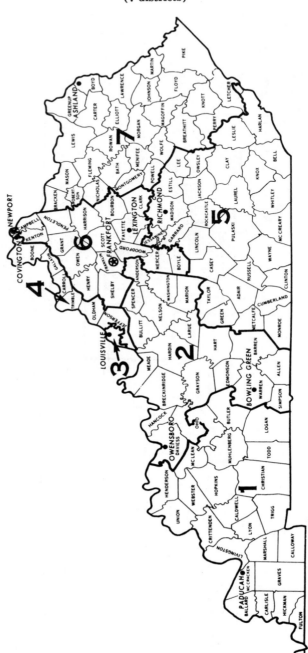

LOUISIANA

(8 districts)

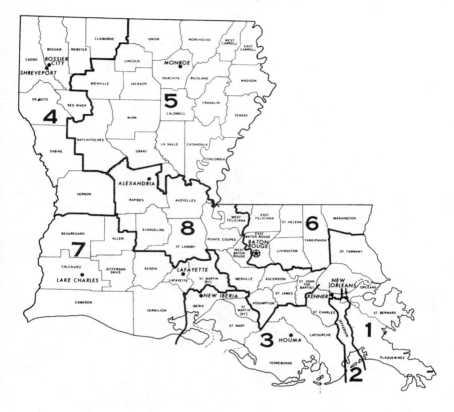

MAINE

(2 districts)

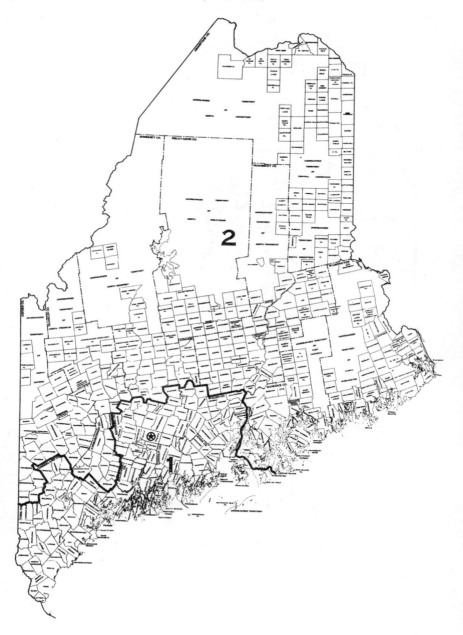

MARYLAND

(8 districts)

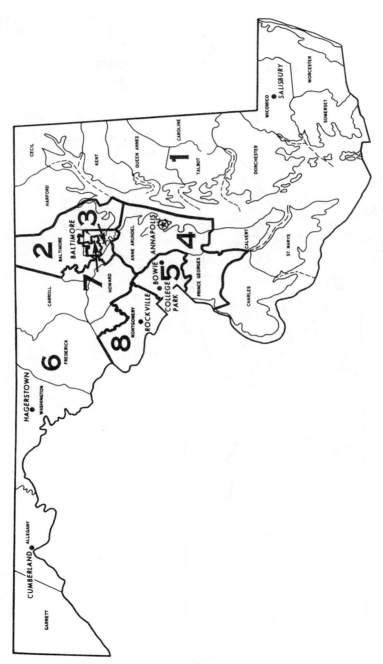

MASSACHUSETTS

(12 districts)

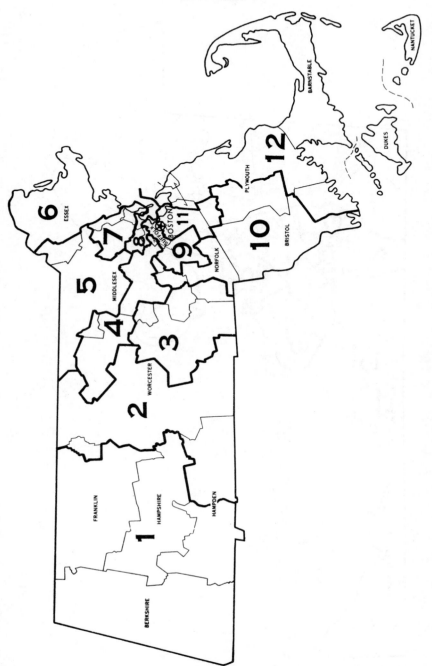

MICHIGAN

(19 districts)

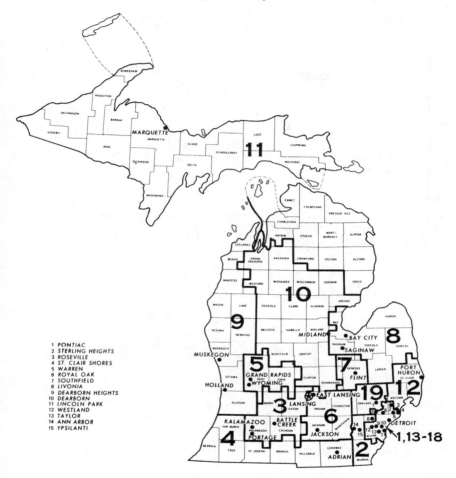

1 PONTIAC
2 STERLING HEIGHTS
3 ROSEVILLE
4 ST. CLAIR SHORES
5 WARREN
6 ROYAL OAK
7 SOUTHFIELD
8 LIVONIA
9 DEARBORN HEIGHTS
10 DEARBORN
11 LINCOLN PARK
12 WESTLAND
13 TAYLOR
14 ANN ARBOR
15 YPSILANTI

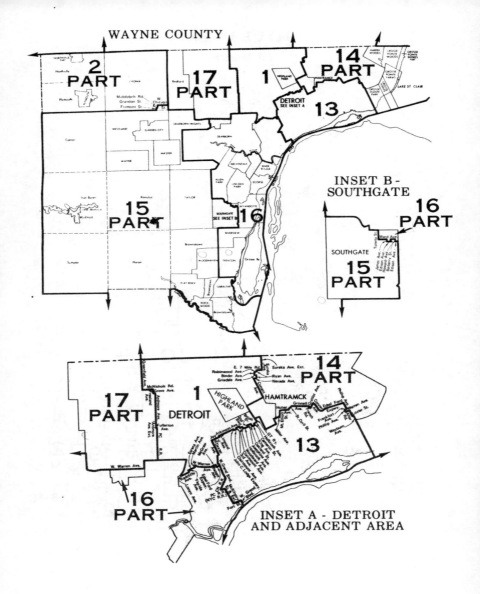

WAYNE COUNTY

2 PART

17 PART

1

14 PART

DETROIT
SEE INSET A

13

INSET B –
SOUTHGATE

15 PART

16

16 PART

SOUTHGATE

15 PART

17 PART

1
DETROIT

HIGHLAND PARK

HAMTRAMCK

14 PART

13

16 PART

INSET A – DETROIT
AND ADJACENT AREA

MINNESOTA

(8 districts)

MISSISSIPPI

(5 districts)

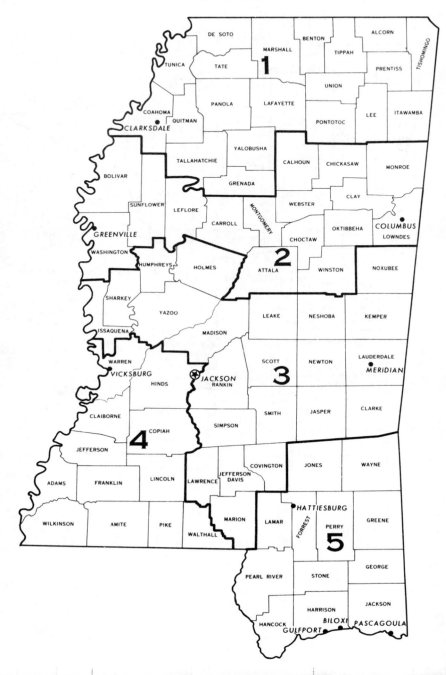

MISSOURI

(10 districts)

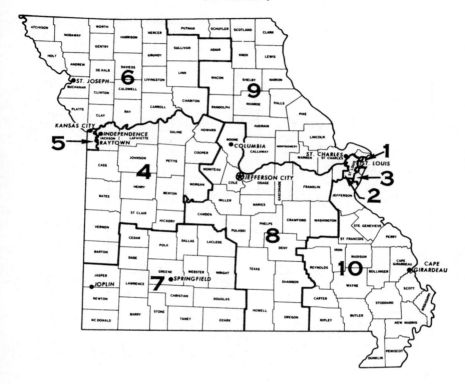

MONTANA

(2 districts)

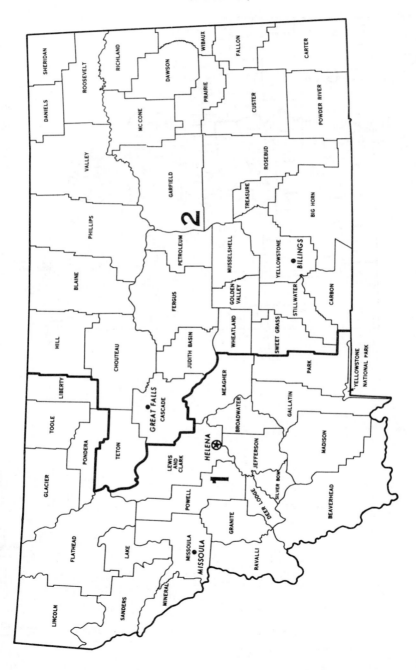

NEBRASKA

(3 districts)

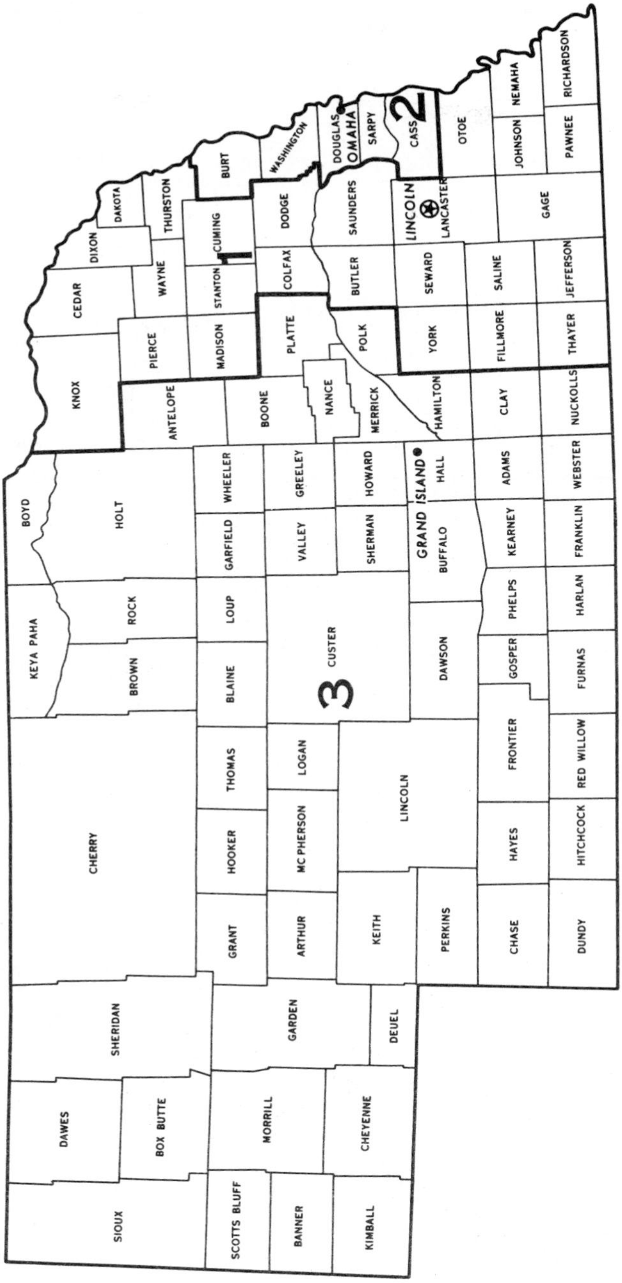

SIOUX
DAWES
BOX BUTTE
SHERIDAN
SCOTTS BLUFF
BANNER
MORRILL
KIMBALL
CHEYENNE
GARDEN
DEUEL
CHERRY
GRANT
ARTHUR
KEITH
PERKINS
CHASE
DUNDY
HOOKER
MC PHERSON
LINCOLN
HAYES
HITCHCOCK
THOMAS
LOGAN
FRONTIER
RED WILLOW
KEYA PAHA
ROCK
BROWN
BLAINE
LOUP
CUSTER
DAWSON
GOSPER
PHELPS
FURNAS
HARLAN
BOYD
HOLT
GARFIELD
WHEELER
VALLEY
GREELEY
SHERMAN
HOWARD
BUFFALO
HALL
GRAND ISLAND
KEARNEY
FRANKLIN
WEBSTER
ADAMS
KNOX
ANTELOPE
BOONE
NANCE
MERRICK
HAMILTON
CLAY
NUCKOLLS
CEDAR
PIERCE
MADISON
PLATTE
POLK
YORK
FILLMORE
THAYER
DIXON
WAYNE
STANTON
COLFAX
BUTLER
SEWARD
SALINE
JEFFERSON
DAKOTA
THURSTON
CUMING
DODGE
SAUNDERS
LINCOLN
LANCASTER
GAGE
BURT
WASHINGTON
DOUGLAS
OMAHA
SARPY
CASS
OTOE
JOHNSON
PAWNEE
NEMAHA
RICHARDSON

NEVADA

(1 at large)

NEW HAMPSHIRE

(2 districts)

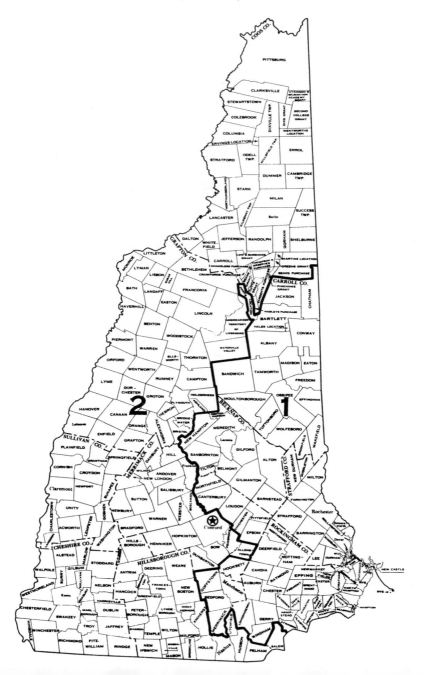

NEW JERSEY

(15 districts)

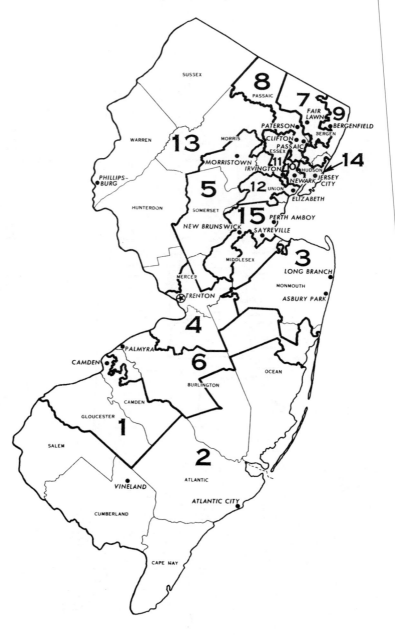

BERGEN, ESSEX, HUDSON, MORRIS, PASSAIC, AND UNION COUNTIES

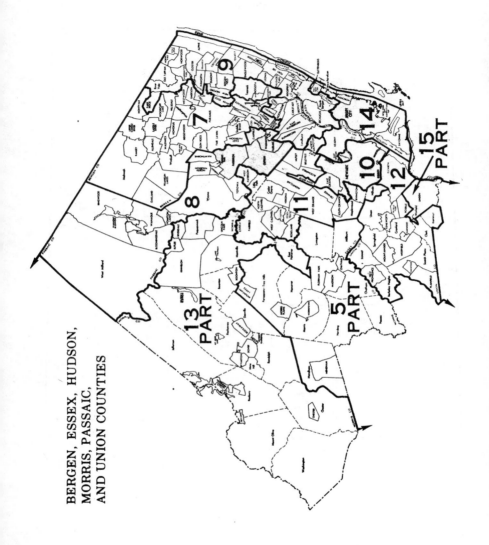

NEW MEXICO

(2 districts)

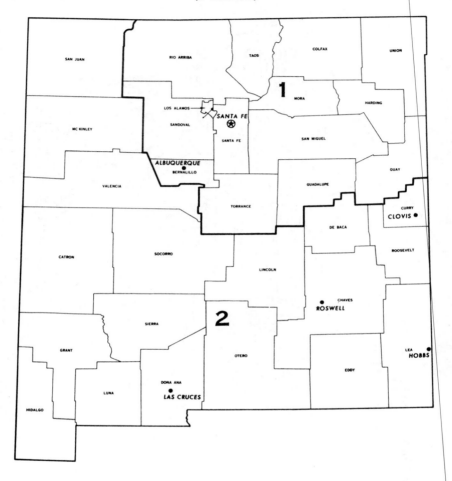

NEW YORK

(39 districts)

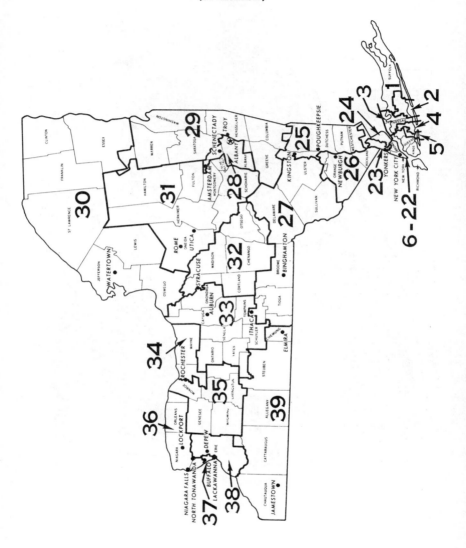

Districts 6-11 and 16-23 established March 28, 1972.
Districts 12-15 established May 30, 1974.
Preliminary map, subject to correction

INSET A - BRONX AND NEW YORK
(MANHATTAN) COUNTIES

NEW YORK CITY

NORTH CAROLINA

(11 districts)

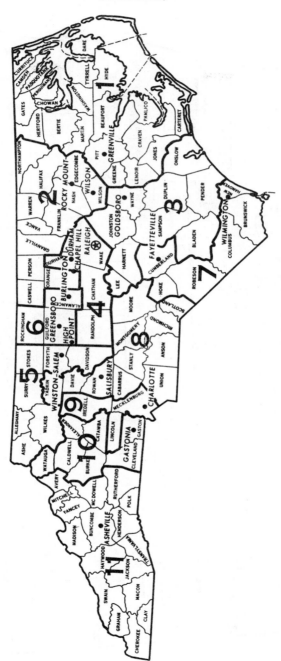

NORTH DAKOTA

(1 at large)

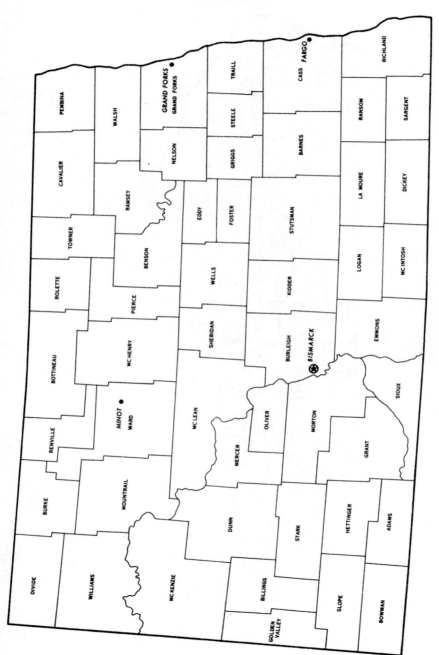

OHIO

(23 districts)

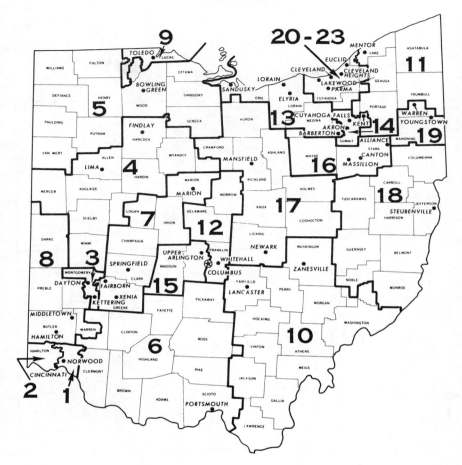

CUYAHOGA, MEDINA, AND SUMMIT COUNTIES

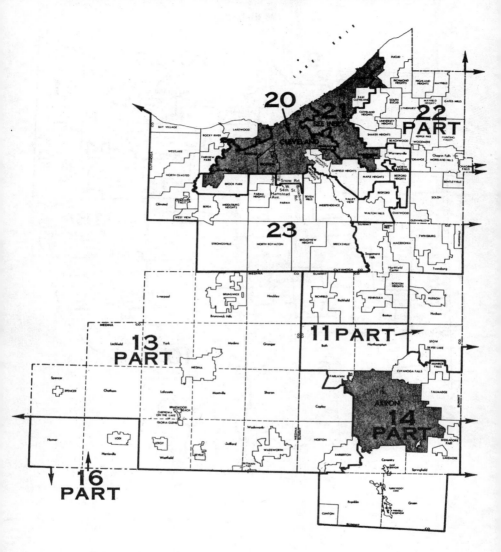

OKLAHOMA

(6 districts)

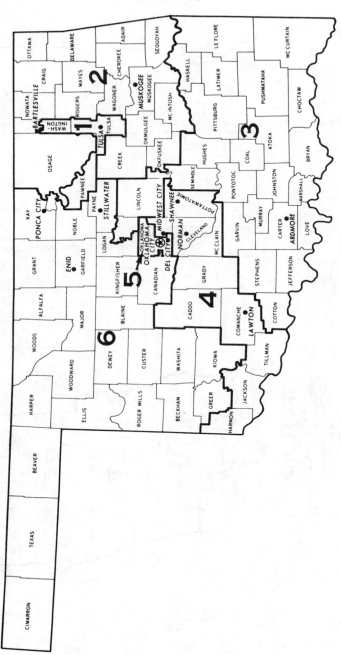

OREGON

(4 districts)

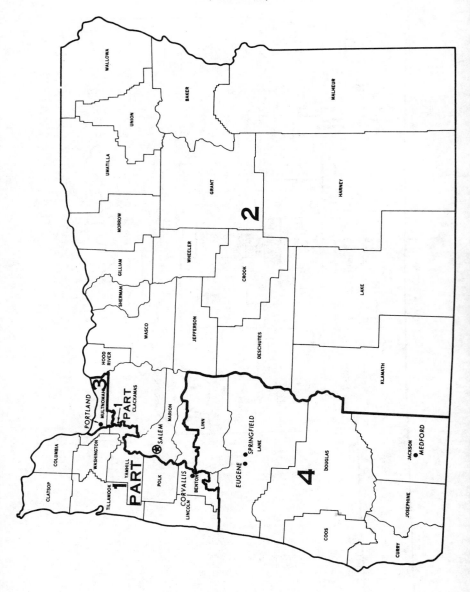

PENNSYLVANIA

(25 districts)

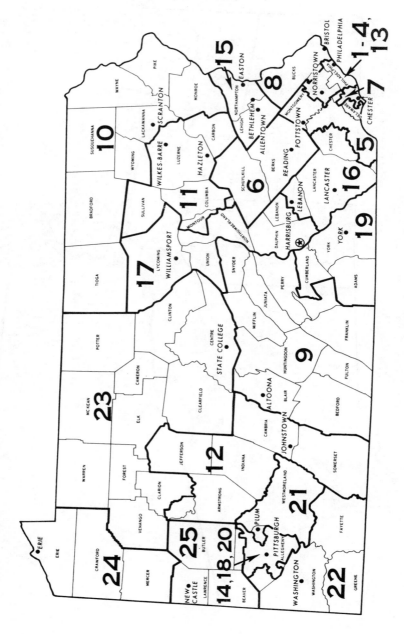

RHODE ISLAND

(2 districts)

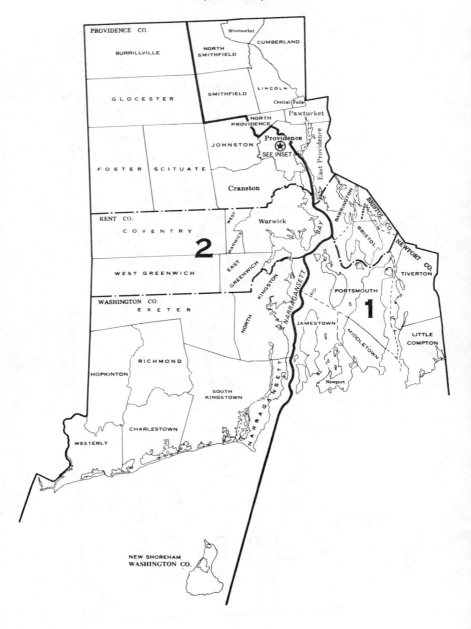

SOUTH CAROLINA

(6 districts)

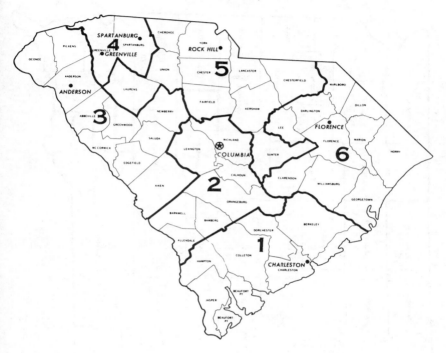

SOUTH DAKOTA

(2 districts)

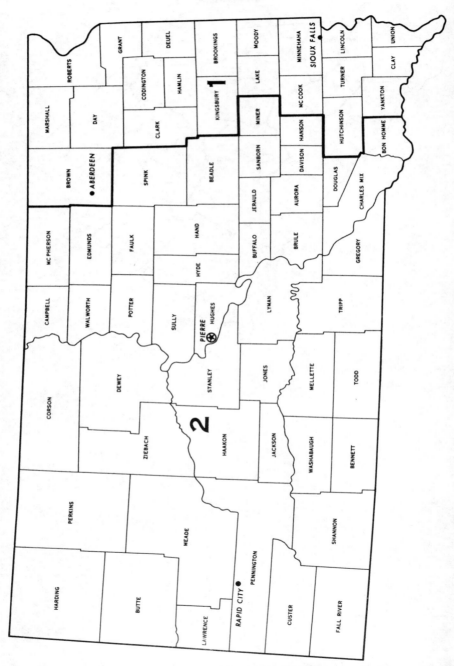

TENNESSEE

(8 districts)

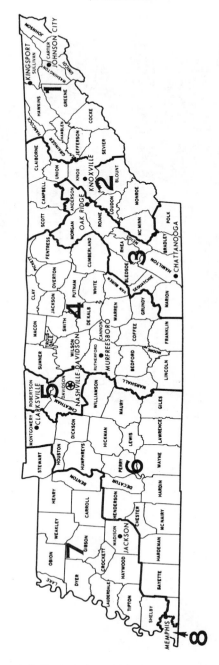

TEXAS

(24 districts)

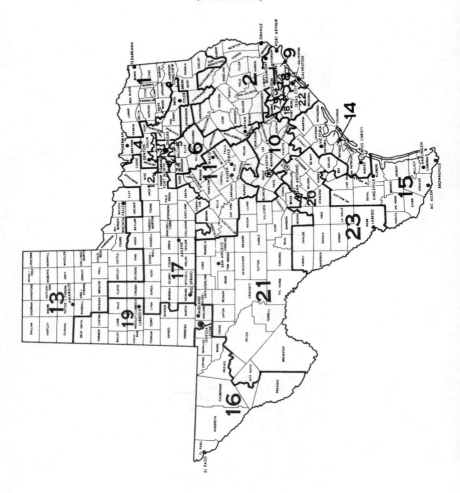

UTAH

(2 districts)

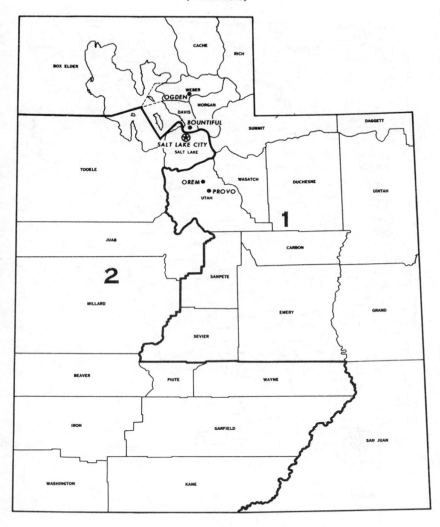

VERMONT

(1 at large)

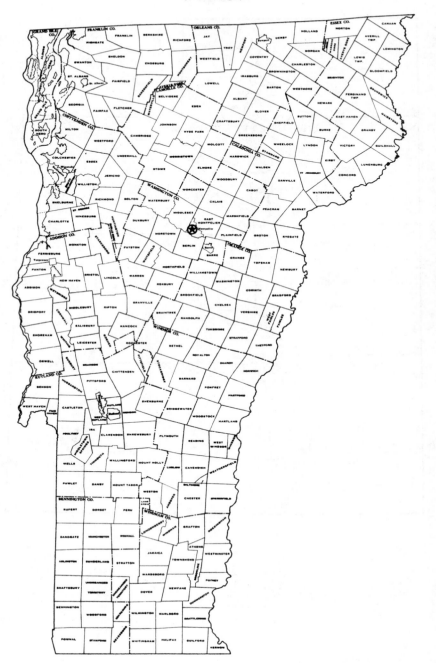

VIRGINIA

(10 districts)

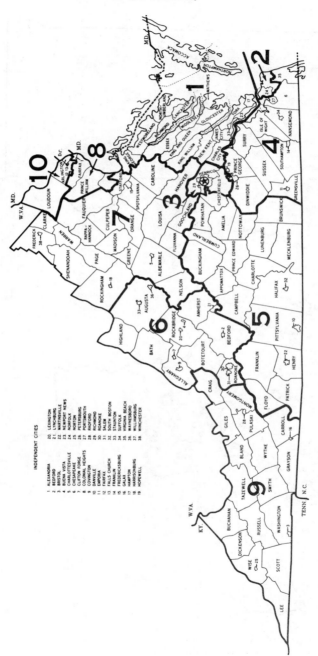

INDEPENDENT CITIES

1 ALEXANDRIA
2 BEDFORD
3 BRISTOL
4 BUENA VISTA
5 CHARLOTTESVILLE
6 CHESAPEAKE
7 CLIFTON FORGE
8 COLONIAL HEIGHTS
9 COVINGTON
10 DANVILLE
11 EMPORIA
12 FAIRFAX
13 FALLS CHURCH
14 FRANKLIN
15 FREDERICKSBURG
16 GALAX
17 HAMPTON
18 HARRISONBURG
19 HOPEWELL

20 LEXINGTON
21 LYNCHBURG
22 MARTINSVILLE
23 NEWPORT NEWS
24 NORFOLK
25 NORTON
26 PETERSBURG
27 PORTSMOUTH
28 RADFORD
29 RICHMOND
30 ROANOKE
31 SALEM
32 SOUTH BOSTON
33 STAUNTON
34 SUFFOLK
35 VIRGINIA BEACH
36 WAYNESBORO
37 WILLIAMSBURG
38 WINCHESTER

WASHINGTON

(7 districts)

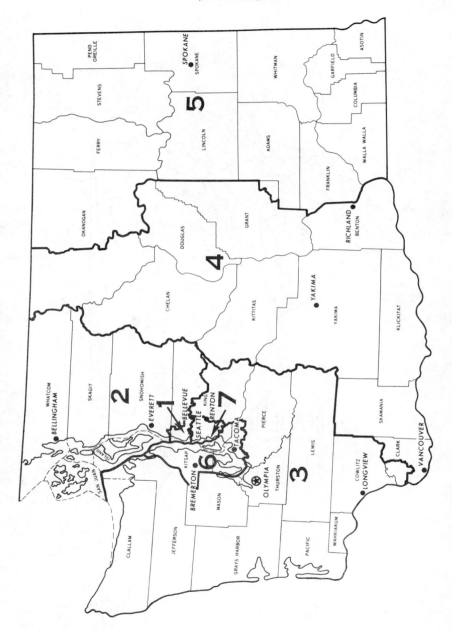

WEST VIRGINIA

(4 districts)

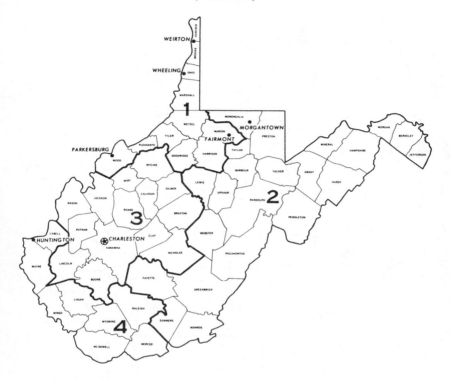

WISCONSIN

(9 districts)

WYOMING

(1 at large)

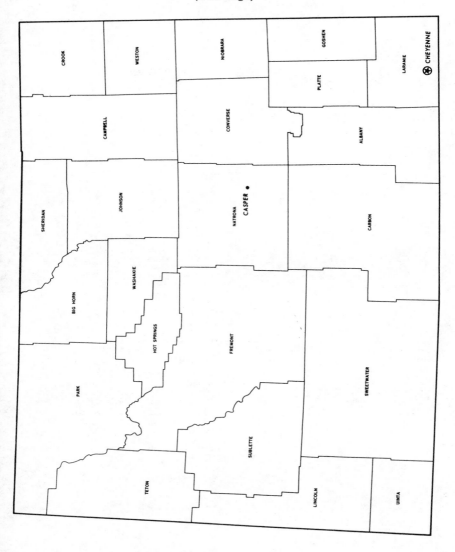

INDEX